# McKinney's®
# New York
# Rules of Court:
# KeyRules

## Volume IIB - Federal
## District Courts

## 2017 Edition

THOMSON REUTERS®

Mat #41778434

**ISBN:** 978-0-314-68145-4

# PREFACE

McKinney's® New York Rules of Court: KeyRules provides the practitioner with a comprehensive "single source" procedural guide for civil practice in the United States District Courts for the Southern, Eastern, Northern and Western Districts of New York, combining applicable provisions of the Federal Rules of Civil Procedure, United States Code, local rules of practice, and analytical materials.

This book consists of outlines of the applicable rules of practice, timing requirements, filing and service requirements, hearing requirements, checklists, and other pertinent documents related to pleadings, motions, and discovery requests in United States District Courts.

Please note that the ordering of jurisdictions in this book has been changed from previous volumes to more closely match the companion Court Rules volume.

THE PUBLISHER

October 2016

# CONTACT US

For additional information or research assistance call our reference attorneys at 1-800-REF-ATTY (1-800-733-2889). Contact our U.S. legal editorial department directly with your questions and suggestions by email at editors.us-legal@tr.com.

# ADDITIONAL KEYRULES COVERAGE ON WESTLAW

Additional KeyRules documents for McKinney's® New York Rules of Court: KeyRules are available on Thomson Reuters Westlaw under Secondary Sources>KeyRules>District Courts>New York. Included on Thomson Reuters Westlaw are all the documents in this book, plus the following:

## Motions, Oppositions and Replies
- Motion to Dismiss for Improper Venue
- Motion for Sanctions
- Motion for Protective Order
- Motion for More Definite Statement
- Motion for Post-Trial Relief

## Requests, Notices and Applications
- Response to Interrogatories
- Response to Request for Production of Documents
- Response to Request for Admissions

# Courts Covered

# Table of Contents

## SOUTHERN DISTRICT OF NEW YORK

## EASTERN DISTRICT OF NEW YORK

TABLE OF CONTENTS

# UNITED STATES DISTRICT COURT

# SOUTHERN DISTRICT OF NEW YORK

## Pleadings
## Complaint

### Document Last Updated September 2016

**A. Checklist**

(I)  ❑ Matters to be considered by plaintiff

   (a)  ❑ Required documents

      (1)  ❑ Civil cover sheet

      (2)  ❑ Complaint

      (3)  ❑ Summons

      (4)  ❑ Electronic case filing rules and instructions (NY R USDCTSD CM/ECF, S.D.)

      (5)  ❑ Judge's individual practices

      (6)  ❑ Notice, consent, and reference of a civil action to a magistrate judge

      (7)  ❑ Filing fee

      (8)  ❑ Affidavit proving service

   (b)  ❑ Supplemental documents

      (1)  ❑ Notice and request for waiver of service

      (2)  ❑ Notice of constitutional question

      (3)  ❑ Notice of issue concerning foreign law

      (4)  ❑ Nongovernmental corporate disclosure statement

      (5)  ❑ Related case statement

      (6)  ❑ Statement explaining untimely electronic filing

      (7)  ❑ Courtesy copies

   (c)  ❑ Timing

      (1)  ❑ A civil action is commenced by filing a complaint with the court

      (2)  ❑ If a defendant is not served within ninety (90) days after the complaint is filed, the court—on motion or on its own after notice to the plaintiff—must dismiss the action without prejudice against that defendant or order that service be made within a specified time

(II)  ❑ Matters to be considered by defendant

   (a)  ❑ Required documents

      (1)  ❑ Answer

      (2)  ❑ Certificate of service

   (b)  ❑ Supplemental documents

      (1)  ❑ Waiver of the service of summons

      (2)  ❑ Notice of constitutional question

      (3)  ❑ Notice of issue concerning foreign law

    (4) ❑ Nongovernmental corporate disclosure statement

    (5) ❑ Statement explaining untimely electronic filing

    (6) ❑ Courtesy copies

  (c) ❑ Timing

    (1) ❑ A defendant must serve an answer:

      (i) ❑ Within twenty-one (21) days after being served with the summons and complaint; or

      (ii) ❑ If it has timely waived service under FRCP 4(d), within sixty (60) days after the request for a waiver was sent, or within ninety (90) days after it was sent to the defendant outside any judicial district of the United States

    (2) ❑ The United States, a United States agency, or a United States officer or employee sued only in an official capacity must serve an answer to a complaint, counterclaim, or crossclaim within sixty (60) days after service on the United States attorney

    (3) ❑ A United States officer or employee sued in an individual capacity for an act or omission occurring in connection with duties performed on the United States' behalf must serve an answer to a complaint, counterclaim, or crossclaim within sixty (60) days after service on the officer or employee or service on the United States attorney, whichever is later

    (4) ❑ Unless the court sets a different time, serving a motion under FRCP 12 alters these periods as follows:

      (i) ❑ If the court denies the motion or postpones its disposition until trial, the responsive pleading must be served within fourteen (14) days after notice of the court's action; or

      (ii) ❑ If the court grants a motion for a more definite statement, the responsive pleading must be served within fourteen (14) days after the more definite statement is served

    (5) ❑ Defendant is given a reasonable time of at least thirty (30) days after a waiver of service request is sent—or at least sixty (60) days if sent to defendant outside any judicial district of the United States—to return the waiver

## B. Timing

1. *Commencing an action.* A civil action is commenced by filing a complaint with the court. FRCP 3.

  a. *Statute of limitations.* An action will be barred if it is not commenced within the period set forth in the applicable statute of limitations. Under the Federal Rules of Civil Procedure (FRCP), an action is commenced by filing a complaint with the court. Thus, in a suit on a right created by federal law, filing a complaint suffices to satisfy the statute of limitations. FEDPROF § 61:2.

    i. *Federal question cases.* Absent a specific statutory provision for tolling the statute of limitations, in federal question cases, the filing of the complaint will toll the statute, even if not all filing fees have been paid, although some courts have added the requirement of reasonable diligence in effecting service. FEDPROF § 61:2.

    ii. *Diversity cases.* In diversity actions the matter is less clear. In the landmark Ragan case, the Supreme Court held in construing FRCP 3 that if, under local law, an action is not commenced until the defendant has been served, the statute is not tolled until service has been accomplished. FEDPROF § 61:2; Ragan v. Merchants Transfer & Warehouse Co., 337 U.S. 530, 69 S.Ct. 1233, 93 L.Ed. 1520 (1949). However, in a subsequent case, the Supreme Court distinguished Ragan in holding that the provision of FRCP 4 governing methods of service prevails over a conflicting state rule requiring personal service. FEDPROF § 61:2; Hanna v. Plumer, 380 U.S. 460, 85 S.Ct. 1136, 14 L.Ed.2d 8 (1965). The court reaffirmed Ragan and held that (1) a state law mandating actual service of a summons to toll the statute of limitations must be followed in a diversity case, and (2) FRCP 3 only governs other timing requirements in the federal rules. FEDPROF § 61:2; Walker v. Armco Steel Corp., 446 U.S. 740, 100 S.Ct. 1978, 64 L.Ed.2d 659 (1980).

2. *Service of summons and complaint.* If a defendant is not served within ninety (90) days after the complaint is filed, the court—on motion or on its own after notice to the plaintiff—must dismiss the action without

prejudice against that defendant or order that service be made within a specified time. But if the plaintiff shows good cause for the failure, the court must extend the time for service for an appropriate period. FRCP 4(m) does not apply to service in a foreign country under FRCP 4(f) or FRCP 4(j)(1) or to service of a notice under FRCP 71.1(d)(3)(A). FRCP 4(m).

3. *Computation of time*

    a.  *Computing time.* FRCP 6 applies in computing any time period specified in the Federal Rules of Civil Procedure, in any local rule or court order, or in any statute that does not specify a method of computing time. FRCP 6(a). In computing any period of time prescribed or allowed by the Local Civil Rules of the United States District Courts for the Southern and Eastern Districts of New York or the Local Admiralty and Maritime Rules, the provisions of FRCP 6 shall apply unless otherwise stated. NY R USDCTS&ED Civ Rule 6.4.

        i.  *Period stated in days or a longer unit.* When the period is stated in days or a longer unit of time:

- Exclude the day of the event that triggers the period;

- Count every day, including intermediate Saturdays, Sundays, and legal holidays; and

- Include the last day of the period, but if the last day is a Saturday, Sunday, or legal holiday, the period continues to run until the end of the next day that is not a Saturday, Sunday, or legal holiday. FRCP 6(a)(1). In the Local Civil Rules of the United States District Courts for the Southern and Eastern Districts of New York, as in the Federal Rules of Civil Procedure as amended effective December 1, 2009, Saturdays, Sundays, and legal holidays are no longer excluded in computing periods of time. If the last day of the period is a Saturday, Sunday, or legal holiday, the period continues to run until the end of the next day that is not a Saturday, Sunday, or legal holiday. NY R USDCTS&ED Civ Rule 6.4.

       ii.  *Period stated in hours.* When the period is stated in hours:

- Begin counting immediately on the occurrence of the event that triggers the period;

- Count every hour, including hours during intermediate Saturdays, Sundays, and legal holidays; and

- If the period would end on a Saturday, Sunday, or legal holiday, the period continues to run until the same time on the next day that is not a Saturday, Sunday, or legal holiday. FRCP 6(a)(2). In the Local Civil Rules of the United States District Courts for the Southern and Eastern Districts of New York, as in the Federal Rules of Civil Procedure as amended effective December 1, 2009, Saturdays, Sundays, and legal holidays are no longer excluded in computing periods of time. If the last day of the period is a Saturday, Sunday, or legal holiday, the period continues to run until the end of the next day that is not a Saturday, Sunday, or legal holiday. NY R USDCTS&ED Civ Rule 6.4.

      iii.  *Inaccessibility of the clerk's office.* Unless the court orders otherwise, if the clerk's office is inaccessible:

- On the last day for filing under FRCP 6(a)(1), then the time for filing is extended to the first accessible day that is not a Saturday, Sunday, or legal holiday; or

- During the last hour for filing under FRCP 6(a)(2), then the time for filing is extended to the same time on the first accessible day that is not a Saturday, Sunday, or legal holiday. FRCP 6(a)(3).

      iv.  *"Last day" defined.* Unless a different time is set by a statute, local rule, or court order, the last day ends:

- For electronic filing, at midnight in the court's time zone; and

- For filing by other means, when the clerk's office is scheduled to close. FRCP 6(a)(4).

      v.  *"Next day" defined.* The "next day" is determined by continuing to count forward when the period is measured after an event and backward when measured before an event. FRCP 6(a)(5).

      vi.  *"Legal holiday" defined.* "Legal holiday" means:

- The day set aside by statute for observing New Year's Day, Martin Luther King Jr.'s

> Birthday, Washington's Birthday, Memorial Day, Independence Day, Labor Day, Columbus Day, Veterans' Day, Thanksgiving Day, or Christmas Day;
>
> - Any day declared a holiday by the President or Congress; and
> - For periods that are measured after an event, any other day declared a holiday by the state where the district court is located. FRCP 6(a)(6).

    b. *Computation of electronic filing deadlines.* You can file electronically twenty-four (24) hours a day, seven (7) days a week, three hundred sixty-five (365) days a year. NY R USDCTSD CM/ECF, S.D.(II)(13)(13.10). Electronic filing must be completed before midnight local time where the Court is located in order to be considered timely filed that day. NY R USDCTSD CM/ECF, S.D.(I)(3)(3.3); NY R USDCTSD CM/ECF, S.D.(II)(13)(13.10); NY R USDCTSD CM/ECF, S.D.(II)(19)(19.4). An electronically filed document is deemed filed on the "filed on" date indicated on the Notice of Electronic Filing (NEF). NY R USDCTSD CM/ECF, S.D.(II)(13)(13.11).

       i. *Technical failures.* A Filing User whose filing is made untimely as the result of a technical failure may seek appropriate relief from the Court. NY R USDCTSD CM/ECF, S.D.(I)(11). If you missed a filing deadline when the ECF system was out of order, attach a statement to your filing explaining how the interruption in service prevented you from filing in a timely fashion. NY R USDCTSD CM/ECF, S.D.(II)(23)(23.5).

    c. *Extending time*

       i. *In general.* When an act may or must be done within a specified time, the court may, for good cause, extend the time:

> - With or without motion or notice if the court acts, or if a request is made, before the original time or its extension expires; or
> - On motion made after the time has expired if the party failed to act because of excusable neglect. FRCP 6(b)(1).

       ii. *Exceptions.* A court must not extend the time to act under FRCP 50(b), FRCP 50(d), FRCP 52(b), FRCP 59(b), FRCP 59(d), FRCP 59(e), and FRCP 60(b). FRCP 6(b)(2).

       iii. Refer to the United States District Court for the Southern District of New York KeyRules Motion for Continuance/Extension of Time document for more information on extending time.

4. *Individual judge practices.* Refer to the Miscellaneous section of this document for information on individual judge practices on timing of documents.

## C. General Requirements

1. *Pleading, generally*

    a. *Pleadings allowed.* Only these pleadings are allowed: (1) a complaint; (2) an answer to a complaint; (3) an answer to a counterclaim designated as a counterclaim; (4) an answer to a crossclaim; (5) a third-party complaint; (6) an answer to a third-party complaint; and (7) if the court orders one, a reply to an answer. FRCP 7(a).

    b. *Pleading to be concise and direct.* Each allegation must be simple, concise, and direct. No technical form is required. FRCP 8(d)(1).

    c. *Alternative statements of a claim or defense.* A party may set out two or more statements of a claim or defense alternatively or hypothetically, either in a single count or defense or in separate ones. If a party makes alternative statements, the pleading is sufficient if any one of them is sufficient. FRCP 8(d)(2).

    d. *Inconsistent claims or defenses.* A party may state as many separate claims or defenses as it has, regardless of consistency. FRCP 8(d)(3).

    e. *Construing pleadings.* Pleadings must be construed so as to do justice. FRCP 8(e).

2. *Pleading special matters*

   a. *Capacity or authority to sue; Legal existence*

      i. *In general.* Except when required to show that the court has jurisdiction, a pleading need not allege:

         • A party's capacity to sue or be sued;

         • A party's authority to sue or be sued in a representative capacity; or

         • The legal existence of an organized association of persons that is made a party. FRCP 9(a)(1).

      ii. *Raising those issues.* To raise any of those issues, a party must do so by a specific denial, which must state any supporting facts that are peculiarly within the party's knowledge. FRCP 9(a)(2).

   b. *Fraud or mistake; Conditions of mind.* In alleging fraud or mistake, a party must state with particularity the circumstances constituting fraud or mistake. Malice, intent, knowledge, and other conditions of a person's mind may be alleged generally. FRCP 9(b).

   c. *Conditions precedent.* In pleading conditions precedent, it suffices to allege generally that all conditions precedent have occurred or been performed. But when denying that a condition precedent has occurred or been performed, a party must do so with particularity. FRCP 9(c).

   d. *Official document or act.* In pleading an official document or official act, it suffices to allege that the document was legally issued or the act legally done. FRCP 9(d).

   e. *Judgment.* In pleading a judgment or decision of a domestic or foreign court, a judicial or quasi-judicial tribunal, or a board or officer, it suffices to plead the judgment or decision without showing jurisdiction to render it. FRCP 9(e).

   f. *Time and place.* An allegation of time or place is material when testing the sufficiency of a pleading. FRCP 9(f).

   g. *Special damages.* If an item of special damage is claimed, it must be specifically stated. FRCP 9(g).

   h. *Admiralty or maritime claim*

      i. *How designated.* If a claim for relief is within the admiralty or maritime jurisdiction and also within the court's subject-matter jurisdiction on some other ground, the pleading may designate the claim as an admiralty or maritime claim for purposes of FRCP 14(c), FRCP 38(e), and FRCP 82 and the Supplemental Rules for Admiralty or Maritime Claims and Asset Forfeiture Actions. A claim cognizable only in the admiralty or maritime jurisdiction is an admiralty or maritime claim for those purposes, whether or not so designated. FRCP 9(h)(1).

      ii. *Designation for appeal.* A case that includes an admiralty or maritime claim within FRCP 9(h) is an admiralty case within 28 U.S.C.A. § 1292(a)(3). FRCP 9(h)(2).

3. *Complaint.* A pleading that states a claim for relief must contain: (1) a short and plain statement of the grounds for the court's jurisdiction, unless the court already has jurisdiction and the claim needs no new jurisdictional support; (2) a short and plain statement of the claim showing that the pleader is entitled to relief; and (3) a demand for the relief sought, which may include relief in the alternative or different types of relief. FRCP 8(a).

   a. *Statement of jurisdiction.* Federal courts are courts of limited jurisdiction, and it is presumed that they are without jurisdiction unless the contrary affirmatively appears. FEDPROC § 62:38; Kirkland Masonry, Inc. v. C.I.R., 614 F.2d 532 (5th Cir. 1980). Therefore, in order for a complaint to comply with the requirement that it contain a short and plain statement of the grounds upon which the court's jurisdiction depends, the jurisdictional basis must be alleged affirmatively and distinctly on the face of the complaint. FEDPROC § 62:38; Spain v. U.S. Through Atomic Nuclear Regulatory Commission Through U.S. Atomic Safety and Licensing Bd., 397 F.Supp. 15 (M.D.La. 1975).

      i. Although it has been said that the jurisdictional statement requirement contemplates reference to a federal statute, a sufficient jurisdictional statement is not made by simply citing a federal statute without alleging facts which bring the plaintiff within the purview of the statute. FEDPROC § 62:38; Atkins v. School Bd. of Halifax County, 379 F.Supp. 1060 (W.D.Va. 1974); Sims v. Mercy Hospital of Monroe, 451 F.2d 171 (6th Cir. 1971).

    ii.   Improper venue is an affirmative defense, and a complaint need not include allegations showing venue to be proper. FEDPROC § 62:38; Ripperger v. A.C. Allyn & Co., 113 F.2d 332 (2d Cir. 1940).

  b.  *Statement of claim*

    i.   *Notice pleading.* Because the only function left exclusively to the pleadings by the Federal Rules of Civil Procedure is that of giving notice, federal courts frequently have said that the Federal Rules of Civil Procedure have adopted a system of "notice pleading." FPP § 1202; Swierkiewicz v. Sorema N.A., 534 U.S. 506, 122 S.Ct. 992, 152 L.Ed.2d 1 (2002). To comply with the requirement that a complaint contain a short and plain statement of the claim, a pleading must give the opposing party fair notice of the nature of a claim and of the basis or grounds for it, so that the defendant will at least be notified as to which of its actions gave rise to the claim upon which the complaint is based. FEDPROC § 62:45.

      •  *Plausibility standard.* Bell Atlantic Corporation v. Twombly and Ashcroft v. Iqbal have paved the way for a heightened "plausibility" pleading standard that requires plaintiffs to provide greater factual development in their complaints in order to survive a FRCP 12(b)(6) motion to dismiss. FPP § 1202; Bell Atlantic Corp. v. Twombly, 550 U.S. 544, 127 S.Ct. 1955, 167 L.Ed.2d 929, 68 Fed.R.Serv.3d 661 (2007); Ashcroft v. Iqbal, 556 U.S. 662, 129 S.Ct. 1937, 173 L.Ed.2d 868 (2009). In discussing what appears to be the new plausibility standard, the Court [in Bell Atlantic Corp. v. Twombly] stated: "While a complaint attacked by a FRCP 12(b)(6) motion to dismiss does not need detailed factual allegations. . .a plaintiff's obligation to provide the 'grounds' of his 'entitle[ment] to relief' requires more than labels and conclusions, and a formulaic recitation of the elements of a cause of action will not do. . .Factual allegations must be enough to raise a right to relief above the speculative level." FPP § 1216; Bell Atlantic Corp. v. Twombly, 550 U.S. 544, 127 S.Ct. 1955, 167 L.Ed.2d 929, 68 Fed.R.Serv.3d 661 (2007).

    ii.  *Facts and evidence.* The complaint need only state enough facts to raise a reasonable expectation that discovery will reveal evidence of the necessary elements. FEDPROC § 62:52; Phillips v. County of Allegheny, 515 F.3d 224 (3d Cir. 2008). A complaint is not intended to formulate issues or fully summarize the facts involved. FEDPROC § 62:52; Hill v. MCI WorldCom Communications, Inc., 141 F.Supp.2d 1205 (S.D.Iowa 2001). Under notice pleading, the full development of the facts and the narrowing of contested issues are accomplished through discovery and other pretrial procedures. FEDPROC § 62:52.

    iii.  *Particularity.* The claim should be particularized sufficiently for the defendant to prepare an adequate defense, file a responsive pleading, determine whether the defense of res judicata is appropriate, and commence discovery, and should insure that the court is sufficiently informed to determine the issue presented and to decide whether the complaint states a claim upon which relief can be had. FEDPROC § 62:45; Kelly v. Schmidberger, 806 F.2d 44, 6 Fed.R.Serv.3d 798 (2d Cir. 1986); Frank v. Mracek, 58 F.R.D. 365 (M.D.Ala. 1973); Barlow v. Pep Boys, Inc., 625 F.Supp. 130 (E.D.Pa. 1985); Philadelphia Dressed Beef Co. v. Wilson & Co., 19 F.R.D. 198 (E.D.Pa. 1956); Luckett v. Cohen, 145 F.Supp. 155 (S.D.N.Y. 1956).

  c.  *Demand for relief sought.* FRCP 8(a)(3) does not require a party to frame the demand for judgment according to a prescribed form or set of particular words; any concise statement identifying the remedies and the parties against whom relief is sought will be sufficient. FPP § 1255; Chandler v. McKee Foods Corp., 2009 WL 210858 (W.D.Va. 2009). Moreover, the pleader need only make one demand for relief regardless of the number of claims that are asserted. FPP § 1255; Liberty Mut. Ins. Co. v. Wetzel, 424 U.S. 737, 96 S.Ct. 1202, 47 L.Ed.2d 435 (1976).

    i.   Relief must be requested as to each defendant. FEDPROC § 62:58; RKO-Stanley Warner Theatres, Inc. v. Mellon Nat. Bank & Trust Co., 436 F.2d 1297 (3d Cir. 1970).

4.  *Joinder*

  a.  *Joinder of claims.* A party asserting a claim, counterclaim, crossclaim, or third-party claim may join, as independent or alternative claims, as many claims as it has against an opposing party. FRCP 18(a).

    i.   *Joinder of contingent claims.* A party may join two claims even though one of them is contingent on the disposition of the other; but the court may grant relief only in accordance with the parties' relative substantive rights. In particular, a plaintiff may state a claim for money and a claim to set aside a conveyance that is fraudulent as to that plaintiff, without first obtaining a judgment for the money. FRCP 18(b).

b. *Joinder of parties; Required*

    i. *Persons required to be joined if feasible; Required party.* A person who is subject to service of process and whose joinder will not deprive the court of subject-matter jurisdiction must be joined as a party if:

- In that person's absence, the court cannot accord complete relief among existing parties; or

- That person claims an interest relating to the subject of the action and is so situated that disposing of the action in the person's absence may: (1) as a practical matter impair or impede the person's ability to protect the interest; or (2) leave an existing party subject to a substantial risk of incurring double, multiple, or otherwise inconsistent obligations because of the interest. FRCP 19(a)(1).

    ii. *Joinder of parties by court order.* If a person has not been joined as required, the court must order that the person be made a party. A person who refuses to join as a plaintiff may be made either a defendant or, in a proper case, an involuntary plaintiff. FRCP 19(a)(2).

    iii. *Venue.* If a joined party objects to venue and the joinder would make venue improper, the court must dismiss that party. FRCP 19(a)(3).

    iv. *When joinder of parties is not feasible.* If a person who is required to be joined if feasible cannot be joined, the court must determine whether, in equity and good conscience, the action should proceed among the existing parties or should be dismissed. FRCP 19(b). For a list of the factors for the court to consider in determining whether joinder of parties is feasible, refer to FRCP 19(b)(1) through FRCP 19(b)(4).

    v. *Pleading the reasons for nonjoinder.* When asserting a claim for relief, a party must state:

- The name, if known, of any person who is required to be joined if feasible but is not joined; and

- The reasons for not joining that person. FRCP 19(c).

    vi. *Exception for class actions.* FRCP 19 is subject to FRCP 23. FRCP 19(d). For information on class actions, refer to FRCP 23.

c. *Joinder of parties; Permissible*

    i. *Persons who may join or be joined*

- *Plaintiffs.* Persons may join in one action as plaintiffs if: (1) they assert any right to relief jointly, severally, or in the alternative with respect to or arising out of the same transaction, occurrence, or series of transactions or occurrences; and (2) any question of law or fact common to all plaintiffs will arise in the action. FRCP 20(a)(1).

- *Defendants.* Persons—as well as a vessel, cargo, or other property subject to admiralty process in rem—may be joined in one action as defendants if: (1) any right to relief is asserted against them jointly, severally, or in the alternative with respect to or arising out of the same transaction, occurrence, or series of transactions or occurrences; and (2) any question of law or fact common to all defendants will arise in the action. FRCP 20(a)(2).

- *Extent of relief.* Neither a plaintiff nor a defendant need be interested in obtaining or defending against all the relief demanded. The court may grant judgment to one or more plaintiffs according to their rights, and against one or more defendants according to their liabilities. FRCP 20(a)(3).

    ii. *Protective measures.* The court may issue orders—including an order for separate trials—to protect a party against embarrassment, delay, expense, or other prejudice that arises from including a person against whom the party asserts no claim and who asserts no claim against the party. FRCP 20(b).

    d.   *Misjoinder and nonjoinder of parties.* Misjoinder of parties is not a ground for dismissing an action. On motion or on its own, the court may at any time, on just terms, add or drop a party. The court may also sever any claim against a party. FRCP 21.

5.   *Right to a jury trial; Demand*

    a.   *Right preserved.* The right of trial by jury as declared by U.S.C.A. Const. Amend. VII, or as provided by a federal statute, is preserved to the parties inviolate. FRCP 38(a).

    b.   *Demand.* On any issue triable of right by a jury, a party may demand a jury trial by:

        i.   Serving the other parties with a written demand—which may be included in a pleading—no later than fourteen (14) days after the last pleading directed to the issue is served; and

        ii.   Filing the demand in accordance with FRCP 5(d). FRCP 38(b).

    c.   *Specifying issues.* In its demand, a party may specify the issues that it wishes to have tried by a jury; otherwise, it is considered to have demanded a jury trial on all the issues so triable. If the party has demanded a jury trial on only some issues, any other party may—within fourteen (14) days after being served with the demand or within a shorter time ordered by the court—serve a demand for a jury trial on any other or all factual issues triable by jury. FRCP 38(c).

    d.   *Waiver; Withdrawal.* A party waives a jury trial unless its demand is properly served and filed. A proper demand may be withdrawn only if the parties consent. FRCP 38(d).

    e.   *Admiralty and maritime claims.* The rules in FRCP 38 do not create a right to a jury trial on issues in a claim that is an admiralty or maritime claim under FRCP 9(h). FRCP 38(e).

6.   *Complex civil cases.* For information on procedures for complex civil cases, refer to NY R USDCTSD Order 11 Misc 00388.

7.   *Related cases.* It shall be the continuing duty of each attorney appearing in any civil or criminal case to bring promptly to the attention of the Court all facts which said attorney believes are relevant to a determination that said case and one or more pending civil or criminal cases should be heard by the same Judge, in order to avoid unnecessary duplication of judicial effort. As soon as the attorney becomes aware of such relationship, said attorney shall notify the Judges to whom the cases have been assigned. NY R USDCTS&ED Civ Rule 1.6(a). If counsel fails to comply with NY R USDCTS&ED Civ Rule 1.6(a), the Court may assess reasonable costs directly against counsel whose action has obstructed the effective administration of the Court's business. NY R USDCTS&ED Civ Rule 1.6(b).

    a.   *Determination of relatedness.* Subject to the limitations set forth in NY R USDCTSD Div. Bus., Rule 13(a)(2), a civil case, bankruptcy appeal, or motion to withdraw the bankruptcy reference will be deemed related to one or more civil cases, appeals or motions when the interests of justice and efficiency will be served. In determining relatedness, a judge will consider whether (A) the actions concern the same or substantially similar parties, property, transactions or events; (B) there is substantial factual overlap; (C) the parties could be subjected to conflicting orders; and (D) whether absent a determination of relatedness there would be a substantial duplication of effort and expense, delay, or undue burden on the Court, parties or witnesses. NY R USDCTSD Div. Bus., Rule 13(a)(1). Nothing in this NY R USDCTSD Div. Bus., Rule 13 is intended to preclude parties from moving for consolidated proceedings under FRCP 42. NY R USDCTSD Div. Bus., Rule 13(a)(1). Notwithstanding NY R USDCTSD Div. Bus., Rule 13(a)(1):

        i.   Civil cases shall not be deemed related merely because they involve common legal issues or the same parties. NY R USDCTSD Div. Bus., Rule 13(a)(2)(A).

        ii.   Other than cases subject to NY R USDCTSD Div. Bus., Rule 4(b) and actions seeking the enforcement of a judgment or settlement in or of an earlier case, civil cases presumptively shall not be deemed related unless both cases are pending before the Court (or the earlier case is on appeal). NY R USDCTSD Div. Bus., Rule 13(a)(2)(B).

    b.   *Procedure in regard to cases said to be related*

        i.   *Disclosure of contention of relatedness.* When a civil case is filed or removed or a bankruptcy appeal or motion to withdraw the reference of an adversary proceeding from the bankruptcy court is filed, the person filing or removing shall disclose on form JSC44C any contention of relatedness and shall file a Related Case Statement stating clearly and succinctly the basis for the contention. A copy of the civil cover sheet and Related Case Statement shall be served with the complaint, notice of removal, notice of appeal, or motion. Any party may contest a claim of relatedness by any other in writing addressed to the judge having the case with the lowest docket number of all cases claimed to be related. However, the foregoing shall not delay the assignment process or the operation of NY R USDCTSD Div. Bus., Rule 13. NY R USDCTSD Div. Bus., Rule 13(b)(1). [Editor's note: the reference to form JSC44C is likely meant to be form JS44C-SDNY: Civil Court Cover Sheet].

    ii. *Claims of relatedness by other parties.* A party other than the one filing a case, bankruptcy appeal or motion to withdraw the reference that contends its case is related to another may so advise in writing the judge assigned in its case and request a transfer of its case to the judge that the party contends has the related case with the lowest docket number. If the assigned judge believes the case is related under NY R USDCTSD Div. Bus., Rule 13(a), he or she shall refer the question to the judge having the case with the lowest docket number. In the event the latter judge agrees, the case shall be transferred to that judge unless the Assignment Committee disagrees. NY R USDCTSD Div. Bus., Rule 13(b)(3).

  c. For more information on related cases, refer to NY R USDCTSD Div. Bus., Rule 13.

8. *Alternative dispute resolution (ADR).* The U.S. District Court for the Southern District of New York provides litigants with opportunities to discuss settlement through judicial settlement conferences and mediation. NY R USDCTS&ED Civ Rule 83.9(a).

  a. *Consideration of alternative dispute resolution.* In all civil cases, including those eligible for mediation pursuant to NY R USDCTS&ED Civ Rule 83.9(e), each party shall consider the use of mediation or a judicial settlement conference and shall report to the assigned Judge at the initial FRCP 16(b) case management conference, or subsequently, whether the party believes mediation or a judicial settlement conference may facilitate the resolution of the lawsuit. Judges are encouraged to note the availability of the mediation program and/or a judicial settlement conference before, at, or after the initial FRCP 16(b) case management conference. NY R USDCTS&ED Civ Rule 83.9(d).

  b. *Mediation.* In mediation, parties and counsel meet, sometimes collectively and sometimes individually, with a neutral third party (the mediator) who has been trained to facilitate confidential settlement discussions. The parties articulate their respective positions and interests and generate options for a mutually agreeable resolution to the dispute. The mediator assists the parties in reaching their own negotiated settlement by defining the issues, probing and assessing the strengths and weaknesses of each party's legal positions, and identifying areas of agreement and disagreement. The main benefits of mediation are that it can result in an expeditious and less costly resolution of the litigation, and can produce creative solutions to complex disputes often unavailable in traditional litigation. NY R USDCTS&ED Civ Rule 83.9(b).

    i. *Mediation program eligibility.* All civil cases other than Social Security, habeas corpus, and tax cases are eligible for mediation, whether assigned to Manhattan or White Plains. NY R USDCTS&ED Civ Rule 83.9(e)(1).

      • The Board of Judges may, by Administrative Order, direct that certain specified categories of cases shall automatically be submitted to the mediation program. The assigned District Judge or Magistrate Judge may issue a written order exempting a particular case with or without the request of the parties. NY R USDCTS&ED Civ Rule 83.9(e)(2).

      • For all other cases, the assigned District Judge or Magistrate Judge may determine that a case is appropriate for mediation and may order that case to mediation, with or without the consent of the parties, before, at, or after the initial FRCP 16(b) case management conference. Alternatively, the parties should notify the assigned Judge at any time of their desire to mediate. NY R USDCTS&ED Civ Rule 83.9(e)(3).

  c. *Judicial settlement conferences.* Judicial settlement conferences may be ordered by District Judges or Magistrate Judges with or without the request or consent of the parties. NY R USDCTS&ED Civ Rule 83.9(f).

  d. For more information on alternative dispute resolution (ADR), refer to NY R USDCTS&ED Civ Rule 83.9.

9. *Individual judge practices.* Refer to the Miscellaneous section of this document for information on individual judge practices on general requirements for documents.

## D. Documents

1. *Required documents*

   a. *Civil cover sheet.* A civil cover sheet is submitted with each civil complaint filed in the district court. Copies of the cover sheet may be obtained from the Clerk of Court. 2 FEDFORMS § 3:29(Comment). When a complaint or the first document is filed in a civil action or proceeding, counsel shall accurately complete and file form JS44C-SDNY: Civil Court Cover Sheet, in triplicate, consistent with NY R USDCTSD Div. Bus., Rule 18. NY R USDCTSD Div. Bus., Rule 4(a).

      i. *Related cases.* When a civil case is filed or removed or a bankruptcy appeal or motion to withdraw the reference of an adversary proceeding from the bankruptcy court is filed, the person filing or removing shall disclose on form JSC44C any contention of relatedness. A copy of the civil cover sheet and Related Case Statement shall be served with the complaint, notice of removal, notice of appeal, or motion. NY R USDCTSD Div. Bus., Rule 13(b)(1). [Editor's note: the reference to form JSC44C is likely meant to be form JS44C-SDNY: Civil Court Cover Sheet]. Refer to the General Requirements section of this document for more information.

      ii. *Designation of White Plains cases.* At the time of filing, the plaintiff's attorney shall designate on the civil cover sheet whether the case should be assigned to White Plains or Manhattan in accordance with NY R USDCTSD Div. Bus., Rule 18. NY R USDCTSD Div. Bus., Rule 18(a).

         • A civil case shall be designated for assignment to White Plains if: (i) the claim arose in whole or in major part in the Counties of Dutchess, Orange, Putnam, Rockland, Sullivan and Westchester (the "Northern Counties") and at least one of the parties resides in the Northern Counties; or (ii) the claim arose in whole or in major part in the Northern Counties and none of the parties resides in this District. NY R USDCTSD Div. Bus., Rule 18(a). A civil case may also be designated for assignment to White Plains if: (iii) the claim arose outside this district and at least some of the parties reside in the Northern Counties; or (iv) at least half of the parties reside in the Northern Counties. NY R USDCTSD Div. Bus., Rule 18(a).

         • All civil cases other than those specified in the NY R USDCTSD Div. Bus., Rule 18(a)(i), NY R USDCTSD Div. Bus., Rule 18(a)(ii), NY R USDCTSD Div. Bus., Rule 18(a)(iii), and NY R USDCTSD Div. Bus., Rule 18(a)(iv) and Social Security and habeas corpus petitions brought under 28 U.S.C.A. § 2241 which are assigned on a district-wide basis shall be designated for assignment to Manhattan. NY R USDCTSD Div. Bus., Rule 18(a).

   b. *Complaint.* Refer to the General Requirements section of this document for the form and contents of the complaint.

   c. *Summons.* A summons must be served with a copy of the complaint. FRCP 4(c)(1). A summons must:

      i. Name the court and the parties;

      ii. Be directed to the defendant;

      iii. State the name and address of the plaintiff's attorney or—if unrepresented—of the plaintiff;

      iv. State the time within which the defendant must appear and defend;

      v. Notify the defendant that a failure to appear and defend will result in a default judgment against the defendant for the relief demanded in the complaint;

      vi. Be signed by the clerk; and

      vii. Bear the court's seal. FRCP 4(a)(1).

   d. *Electronic case filing rules and instructions (NY R USDCTSD CM/ECF, S.D.).* In order to alert an adversary to the requirements of Electronic Case Filing and the assigned Judge's Individual Practices you are required to send to all parties the following documents (available on the court's website), either as a pdf attachment to an e-mail or in paper form: Electronic Case Filing Rules & Instructions (this document (NY R USDCTSD CM/ECF, S.D.)). NY R USDCTSD CM/ECF,

S.D.(II)(14)(14.8)(a). Pro se litigants who are not Filing Users are exempt from NY R USDCTSD CM/ECF, S.D.(II)(14)(14.8). NY R USDCTSD CM/ECF, S.D.(II)(14)(14.8).

e.  *Judge's individual practices.* In order to alert an adversary to the requirements of Electronic Case Filing and the assigned Judge's Individual Practices you are required to send to all parties the following documents (available on the court's website), either as a pdf attachment to an e-mail or in paper form: the Individual Practices of the assigned Judge. Pro se litigants who are not Filing Users are exempt from NY R USDCTSD CM/ECF, S.D.(II)(14)(14.8). NY R USDCTSD CM/ECF, S.D.(II)(14)(14.8)(b). Pro se litigants who are not Filing Users are exempt from this Rule. NY R USDCTSD CM/ECF, S.D.(II)(14)(14.8).

f.  *Notice, consent, and reference of a civil action to a magistrate judge.* When a civil action is filed with the Clerk, the Clerk shall give the filing party notice of the Magistrate Judge's consent jurisdiction in a form approved by the Court, with sufficient copies to be served with the complaint on adversary parties. A copy of such notice shall be attached to any third-party complaint served by a defendant. NY R USDCTS&ED Civ Rule 73.1(a). For more information on consent jurisdiction procedure, refer to NY R USDCTS&ED Civ Rule 73.1.

g.  *Filing fee.* The clerk of each district court shall require the parties instituting any civil action, suit or proceeding in such court, whether by original process, removal or otherwise, to pay a filing fee. 28 U.S.C.A. § 1914(a). Each district court by rule or standing order may require advance payment of fees. 28 U.S.C.A. § 1914(c). The Clerk shall not be required to render any service for which a fee is prescribed by statute or by the Judicial Conference of the United States unless the fee for the particular service is paid to the Clerk in advance or the Court orders otherwise. NY R USDCTS&ED Civ Rule 1.7(a). For information on filing fees and the District Court Miscellaneous Fee Schedule, refer to 28 U.S.C.A. § 1914 and NY R USDCTSD Fee Schedules, S.D.

h.  *Affidavit proving service.* Unless service is waived, proof of service must be made to the court. Except for service by a United States marshal or deputy marshal, proof must be by the server's affidavit. FRCP 4(l)(1). Electronically file the proof of service for the initiating document on the ECF system (do not e-mail); and deliver the original paper proof of service, with summons attached, to the Clerk's Office. Include a copy of the ECF Notice of Electronic Filing (NEF or filing receipt). NY R USDCTSD CM/ECF, S.D.(II)(14)(14.9); NY R USDCTSD CM/ECF, S.D.(I)(19)(19.3)(a). Pro se litigants who have been granted in forma pauperis (IFP) status are exempt from NY R USDCTSD CM/ECF, S.D.(II)(14)(14.9). Pro se litigants who have not been granted IFP status shall deliver the original paper proof of service with summons attached to the Clerk's Office. NY R USDCTSD CM/ECF, S.D.(II)(14)(14.9); NY R USDCTSD CM/ECF, S.D.(I)(19)(19.3). Refer to the Filing and Service Requirements section of this document for more information.

2.  *Supplemental documents*

a.  *Notice and request for waiver of service.* An individual, corporation, or association that is subject to service under FRCP 4(e), FRCP 4(f), or FRCP 4(h) has a duty to avoid unnecessary expenses of serving the summons. The plaintiff may notify such a defendant that an action has been commenced and request that the defendant waive service of a summons. The notice and request must:

  i.   Be in writing and be addressed:

  - To the individual defendant; or

  - For a defendant subject to service under FRCP 4(h), to an officer, a managing or general agent, or any other agent authorized by appointment or by law to receive service of process;

  ii.  Name the court where the complaint was filed;

  iii. Be accompanied by a copy of the complaint, two (2) copies of a waiver form appended to FRCP 4, and a prepaid means for returning the form;

  iv.  Inform the defendant, using the form appended to FRCP 4, of the consequences of waiving and not waiving service;

  v.   State the date when the request is sent;

vi.   Give the defendant a reasonable time of at least thirty (30) days after the request was sent—or at least sixty (60) days if sent to the defendant outside any judicial district of the United States—to return the waiver; and

vii.  Be sent by first-class mail or other reliable means. FRCP 4(d)(1).

b.  *Notice of constitutional question.* A party that files a pleading, written motion, or other paper drawing into question the constitutionality of a federal or state statute must promptly:

   i.   *File notice.* File a notice of constitutional question stating the question and identifying the paper that raises it, if:

   - A federal statute is questioned and the parties do not include the United States, one of its agencies, or one of its officers or employees in an official capacity; or

   - A state statute is questioned and the parties do not include the state, one of its agencies, or one of its officers or employees in an official capacity; and

   ii.  *Serve notice.* Serve the notice and paper on the Attorney General of the United States if a federal statute is questioned—or on the state attorney general if a state statute is questioned—either by certified or registered mail or by sending it to an electronic address designated by the attorney general for this purpose. FRCP 5.1(a).

   iii. *No forfeiture.* A party's failure to file and serve the notice, or the court's failure to certify, does not forfeit a constitutional claim or defense that is otherwise timely asserted. FRCP 5.1(d).

c.  *Notice of issue concerning foreign law.* A party who intends to raise an issue about a foreign country's law must give notice by a pleading or other writing. In determining foreign law, the court may consider any relevant material or source, including testimony, whether or not submitted by a party or admissible under the Federal Rules of Evidence. The court's determination must be treated as a ruling on a question of law. FRCP 44.1.

d.  *Nongovernmental corporate disclosure statement*

   i.   *Contents.* A nongovernmental corporate party must file two (2) copies of a disclosure statement that:

   - Identifies any parent corporation and any publicly held corporation owning ten percent (10%) or more of its stock; or

   - States that there is no such corporation. FRCP 7.1(a).

   ii.  *Time to file; Supplemental filing.* A party must:

   - File the disclosure statement with its first appearance, pleading, petition, motion, response, or other request addressed to the court; and

   - Promptly file a supplemental statement if any required information changes. FRCP 7.1(b). For purposes of FRCP 7.1(b)(2), "promptly" shall mean "within fourteen days," that is, parties are required to file a supplemental disclosure statement within fourteen (14) days of the time there is any change in the information required in a disclosure statement filed pursuant to those rules. NY R USDCTS&ED Civ Rule 7.1.1.

e.  *Related case statement.* When a civil case is filed or removed or a bankruptcy appeal or motion to withdraw the reference of an adversary proceeding from the bankruptcy court is filed, the person filing or removing. . .shall file a Related Case Statement stating clearly and succinctly the basis for the contention. A copy of the civil cover sheet and Related Case Statement shall be served with the complaint, notice of removal, notice of appeal, or motion. NY R USDCTSD Div. Bus., Rule 13(b)(1). Refer to the General Requirements section of this document for more information.

f.  *Statement explaining untimely electronic filing.* If you missed a filing deadline when the ECF system was out of order, attach a statement to your filing explaining how the interruption in service prevented you from filing in a timely fashion. NY R USDCTSD CM/ECF, S.D.(II)(23)(23.5).

g.  *Courtesy copies.* Read the judge's Individual Practices to determine if a courtesy copy of the case initiating documents should be submitted to chambers. NY R USDCTSD CM/ECF, S.D.(II)(14)(14.4); NY R USDCTSD CM/ECF, S.D.(II)(13)(13.17). Judges' Individual Practices should continue to be followed with respect to delivery of courtesy copies. NY R USDCTSD CM/ECF, S.D.(I)(3)(3.4).

3. *Individual judge practices.* Refer to the Miscellaneous section of this document for information on individual judge practices on required documents.

## E. Format

1. *Form of documents*

   a. *Paper.* Every pleading, written motion, and other paper must: be plainly written, typed, printed, or copied without erasures or interlineations which materially deface it. NY R USDCTS&ED Civ Rule 11.1(a)(1).

   b. *Typeface, margin, and spacing.* The typeface, margins, and spacing of all documents presented for filing must meet the following requirements:

      i. All text must be twelve (12) point type or larger, except for text in footnotes which may be ten (10) point type;

      ii. All documents must have at least one (1) inch margins on all sides;

      iii. All text must be double-spaced, except for headings, text in footnotes, or block quotations, which may be single-spaced. NY R USDCTS&ED Civ Rule 11.1(b).

   c. *Caption; Names of parties.* Every pleading must have a caption with the court's name, a title, a file number, and a FRCP 7(a) designation. The title of the complaint must name all the parties; the title of other pleadings, after naming the first party on each side, may refer generally to other parties. FRCP 10(a). Every pleading, written motion, and other paper must: bear the docket number and the initials of the District Judge and any Magistrate Judge before whom the action or proceeding is pending, NY R USDCTS&ED Civ Rule 11.1(a)(2).

   d. *Paragraphs; Separate statements.* A party must state its claims or defenses in numbered paragraphs, each limited as far as practicable to a single set of circumstances. A later pleading may refer by number to a paragraph in an earlier pleading. If doing so would promote clarity, each claim founded on a separate transaction or occurrence—and each defense other than a denial—must be stated in a separate count or defense. FRCP 10(b).

   e. *Adoption by reference; Exhibits.* A statement in a pleading may be adopted by reference elsewhere in the same pleading or in any other pleading or motion. A copy of a written instrument that is an exhibit to a pleading is a part of the pleading for all purposes. FRCP 10(c).

   f. *Acceptance by the clerk.* The clerk must not refuse to file a paper solely because it is not in the form prescribed by the Federal Rules of Civil Procedure or by a local rule or practice. FRCP 5(d)(4).

2. *Form of electronic documents*

   a. *PDF-A.* All documents electronically filed on the ECF system must be in PDF-A format (portable document format). A PDF-A file is created using PDF writer software such as Adobe Acrobat (go to the Adobe website for details). PDF-A files cannot be altered, providing security to the filer and the Court. NY R USDCTSD CM/ECF, S.D.(II)(23)(23.2).

   b. *Size limitation.* No single PDF file may be larger than four megabytes (4 MB). If the filing is too large, the ECF system will not allow it to be filed, and you will not see a Notice of Electronic Filing (NEF or filing receipt) screen. To determine the size of an Adobe Acrobat PDF file click on File, Document Properties, Summary. NY R USDCTSD CM/ECF, S.D.(II)(23)(23.3).

      i. Converting documents directly from a word processor to PDF-A format creates the smallest possible file in terms of computer memory. If that is not possible, scan your document at low resolution. Within the Adobe Acrobat program, on the "Scan Manager" screen, adjust the settings for black and white and 200 dpi (dots per inch). This allows more pages to fit into a single PDF-A file. If that does not work, separate an oversized file into 2 or more parts. Simply label each file 1a, 1b, 1c, etc. Only relevant excerpts of exhibits should be electronically filed. NY R USDCTSD CM/ECF, S.D.(II)(23)(23.4).

   c. *Attachments and exhibits.* Filing Users must submit in electronic form all documents referenced as exhibits or attachments, unless the Court permits paper filing. NY R USDCTSD CM/ECF, S.D.(I)(5)(5.1).

    i.  A Filing User must submit as exhibits or attachments only those excerpts of the referenced documents that are relevant to the matter under consideration by the Court. Excerpted material must be clearly and prominently identified as such. Filing Users who file excerpts of documents as exhibits or attachments under this procedure do so without prejudice to their right to file timely additional excerpts or the complete document. Responding parties may file timely additional excerpts that they believe are relevant or the complete document. A party may move before the Court for permission to serve and file in hard copy documents that cannot be reasonably scanned. NY R USDCTSD CM/ECF, S.D.(I)(5)(5.2).

    ii.  Exhibits must be filed only as attachments to a document, such as a motion or an affidavit. Do not use the ECF Filing Event for "Motion" to file exhibits separately. Exhibits are the only items that should be attached to electronically filed documents. You are limited to electronically filing only relevant excerpts of exhibits. Excerpts must be clearly identified as such. If the exhibit is too large to be scanned and electronically filed you may contact the ECF Help Desk. NY R USDCTSD CM/ECF, S.D.(II)(15)(15.6).

  d.  *Letters.* Parties should consult the assigned judge's Individual Practices to determine if the judge accepts letters at all and, if he or she does, whether the judge has any page limitations on letters and/or requires courtesy copies of letters filed on ECF (and, if so, by what means of delivery). All letters addressed to the Court must include a subject line with the case name and docket number (e.g., "Re: Doe v. Smith, 13 Civ. 1234 (ABC)"). NY R USDCTSD CM/ECF, S.D.(II)(13)(13.1).

  e.  *Proposed orders, proposed judgments, stipulations and consents.* Any document that requires the signature of a judge should not be electronically filed except as an exhibit to another document. Proposed orders, judgments, stipulations and consents should not be submitted through the ECF system. Instead they should be sent by e-mail to the Clerk. Proposed orders should be submitted in word processing format (WordPerfect or Word) rather than as a PDF document. Stipulations should be submitted in PDF-A format. Stipulations must contain ink signatures not s/. Faxed or emailed signatures are acceptable. Please note that Stipulations of Voluntary Dismissal pursuant to FRCP 41(a)(1)(A)(ii) do not require the signature of a judge and must be electronically filed on the ECF system. Questions may be directed to the Orders and Judgments Clerk at the phone numbers listed in NY R USDCTSD CM/ECF, S.D.(II)(18)(18.3). NY R USDCTSD CM/ECF, S.D.(II)(18)(18.3).

    i.  Email the proposed order, judgment or stipulation to the email addresses listed in NY R USDCTSD CM/ECF, S.D.(II)(18)(18.3). NY R USDCTSD CM/ECF, S.D.(II)(18)(18.3).

    ii.  Pro se litigants who are not Filing Users are exempt from that portion of NY R USDCTSD CM/ECF, S.D.(II)(18)(18.3) that requires litigants to email proposed orders, judgments, stipulations and consents, and shall deliver such documents to the Clerk's Office in paper form. NY R USDCTSD CM/ECF, S.D.(II)(18)(18.3).

3.  *Signing of pleadings, motions and other papers*

  a.  *Signature.* Every pleading, written motion, and other paper must be signed by at least one attorney of record in the attorney's name—or by a party personally if the party is unrepresented. The paper must state the signer's address, e-mail address, and telephone number. FRCP 11(a). Every pleading, written motion, and other paper must: have the name of each person signing it clearly printed or typed directly below the signature. NY R USDCTS&ED Civ Rule 11.1(a)(3).

    i.  *Electronic signatures.* The user log-in and password required to submit documents to the ECF system serve as the Filing User's signature on all electronic documents filed with the Court. NY R USDCTSD CM/ECF, S.D.(I)(8)(8.1); NY R USDCTSD CM/ECF, S.D.(II)(13)(13.14). They also serve as a signature for purposes of the Federal Rules of Civil Procedure, including FRCP 11, the Local Civil Rules of the United States District Courts for the Southern and Eastern Districts of New York, and any other purpose for which a signature is required in connection with proceedings before the Court. NY R USDCTSD CM/ECF, S.D.(I)(8)(8.1).

    •  *Signature block.* Electronically filed documents must include a signature block and must set forth the name, address, telephone number and e-mail address all in compliance with the Federal Rules of Civil Procedure and NY R USDCTS&ED Civ Rule 11.1. In the absence of a scanned signature image, the name of the Filing User under whose log-in and password the document is submitted must be preceded by an "s/" typed in the space where the signature would otherwise appear. NY R USDCTSD CM/ECF, S.D.(I)(8)(8.2); NY R USDCTSD CM/ECF, S.D.(II)(13)(13.14).

- *Documents requiring the signature of a party or witness.* A document requiring the signature of a party or witness shall be electronically filed in a scanned format that contains an image of the actual signature. NY R USDCTSD CM/ECF, S.D.(I)(8)(8.4); NY R USDCTSD CM/ECF, S.D.(II)(13)(13.14).

- *Documents requiring the signature of a judge.* A Filing User submitting a document electronically that requires a judge's signature must promptly deliver the document in such other form, if any, as the Court requires. NY R USDCTSD CM/ECF, S.D.(I)(4)(4.2).

- *Documents requiring multiple signatures.* Documents requiring signatures of more than one party must be electronically filed either by: (a) submitting a scanned document containing all necessary signatures; (b) representing the consent of the other parties on the document; (c) identifying on the document the parties whose signatures are required and by the submission of a notice of endorsement by the other parties no later than three business days after filing; or (d) in any other manner approved by the Court. NY R USDCTSD CM/ECF, S.D.(I)(8)(8.5).

   ii. *No verification or accompanying affidavit required for pleadings.* Unless a rule or statute specifically states otherwise, a pleading need not be verified or accompanied by an affidavit. FRCP 11(a).

   iii. *Unsigned papers.* The court must strike an unsigned paper unless the omission is promptly corrected after being called to the attorney's or party's attention. FRCP 11(a).

b. *Representations to the court.* By presenting to the court a pleading, written motion, or other paper—whether by signing, filing, submitting, or later advocating it—an attorney or unrepresented party certifies that to the best of the person's knowledge, information, and belief, formed after an inquiry reasonable under the circumstances:

   i. It is not being presented for any improper purpose, such as to harass, cause unnecessary delay, or needlessly increase the cost of litigation;

   ii. The claims, defenses, and other legal contentions are warranted by existing law or by a nonfrivolous argument for extending, modifying, or reversing existing law or for establishing new law;

   iii. The factual contentions have evidentiary support or, if specifically so identified, will likely have evidentiary support after a reasonable opportunity for further investigation or discovery; and

   iv. The denials of factual contentions are warranted on the evidence or, if specifically so identified, are reasonably based on belief or a lack of information. FRCP 11(b).

c. *Sanctions.* If, after notice and a reasonable opportunity to respond, the court determines that FRCP 11(b) has been violated, the court may impose an appropriate sanction on any attorney, law firm, or party that violated FRCP 11(b) or is responsible for the violation. FRCP 11(c)(1). Refer to the United States District Court for the Southern District of New York KeyRules Motion for Sanctions document for more information.

4. *Privacy protection for filings made with the court*

a. *Redacted filings.* Unless the court orders otherwise, in an electronic or paper filing with the court that contains an individual's Social Security number, taxpayer-identification number, or birth date, the name of an individual known to be a minor, or a financial-account number, a party or nonparty making the filing may include only:

   i. The last four (4) digits of the Social Security number and taxpayer-identification number;

   ii. The year of the individual's birth;

   iii.  The minor's initials; and

   iv.  The last four (4) digits of the financial-account number. FRCP 5.2(a); NY R USDCTSD CM/ECF, S.D.(II)(21)(21.3).

   v.  Caution should be exercised when filing documents that contain the following:

- Personal identifying numbers (PIN #'s), such as a driver's license number;
- Medical records, treatment and diagnosis;
- Employment history;
- Individual financial information;
- Proprietary or trade secret information;
- Information regarding an individual's cooperation with the government. NY R US-DCTSD CM/ECF, S.D.(II)(21)(21.4).

b.  *Exemptions from the redaction requirement.* The redaction requirement does not apply to the following:

   i.  A financial-account number that identifies the property allegedly subject to forfeiture in a forfeiture proceeding;

   ii.  The record of an administrative or agency proceeding;

   iii.  The official record of a state-court proceeding;

   iv.  The record of a court or tribunal, if that record was not subject to the redaction requirement when originally filed;

   v.  A filing covered by FRCP 5.2(c) or FRCP 5.2(d); and

   vi.  A pro se filing in an action brought under 28 U.S.C.A. § 2241, 28 U.S.C.A. § 2254, or 28 U.S.C.A. § 2255. FRCP 5.2(b).

c.  *Limitations on remote access to electronic files; Social Security appeals and immigration cases.* Unless the court orders otherwise, in an action for benefits under the Social Security Act, and in an action or proceeding relating to an order of removal, to relief from removal, or to immigration benefits or detention, access to an electronic file is authorized as follows:

   i.  The parties and their attorneys may have remote electronic access to any part of the case file, including the administrative record;

   ii.  Any other person may have electronic access to the full record at the courthouse, but may have remote electronic access only to:

- The docket maintained by the court; and
- An opinion, order, judgment, or other disposition of the court, but not any other part of the case file or the administrative record. FRCP 5.2(c).

d.  *Filings made under seal.* The court may order that a filing be made under seal without redaction. The court may later unseal the filing or order the person who made the filing to file a redacted version for the public record. FRCP 5.2(d). For more information on sealing documents, refer to NY R USDCTSD CM/ECF, S.D.(I)(6).

e.  *Protective orders.* For good cause, the court may by order in a case:

   i.  Require redaction of additional information; or

   ii.  Limit or prohibit a nonparty's remote electronic access to a document filed with the court. FRCP 5.2(e).

f.  *Option for additional unredacted filing under seal.* A person making a redacted filing may also file an unredacted copy under seal. The court must retain the unredacted copy as part of the record. FRCP 5.2(f); NY R USDCTSD CM/ECF, S.D.(II)(21)(21.5).

g.  *Option for filing a reference list.* A filing that contains redacted information may be filed together with a reference list that identifies each item of redacted information and specifies an appropriate

identifier that uniquely corresponds to each item listed. The list must be filed under seal and may be amended as of right. Any reference in the case to a listed identifier will be construed to refer to the corresponding item of information. FRCP 5.2(g); NY R USDCTSD CM/ECF, S.D.(II)(21)(21.5).

    h.  *Responsibility for redaction.* It is the sole responsibility of counsel and the parties to be sure that all documents comply with the rules of this Court requiring redaction of personal identifiers. Neither the judge nor the Clerk of Court will review documents for compliance with these rules. NY R USDCTSD CM/ECF, S.D.(II)(21)(21.2).

    i.  *Waiver of protection of identifiers.* A person waives the protection of FRCP 5.2(a) as to the person's own information by filing it without redaction and not under seal. FRCP 5.2(h).

    j.  For more information on privacy and public access to ECF cases, refer to NY R USDCTSD CM/ECF, S.D.(II)(21).

  5.  *Individual judge practices.* Refer to the Miscellaneous section of this document for information on individual judge practices on formatting documents.

## F. Filing and Service Requirements

  1.  *Filing requirements.* A civil action is commenced by filing a complaint with the court. FRCP 3. The first step in a civil action in a United States district court is the filing of the complaint with the clerk or the judge. FPP § 1052. Filing a complaint requires nothing more than delivery of the document to a court officer authorized to receive it. FPP § 1052; Central States, Southeast & Southwest Areas Pension Fund v. Paramount Liquor Co., 34 F.Supp.2d 1092 (N.D.Ill. 1999). Complaints and all subsequent papers are accepted at either courthouse, regardless of the place for which the case is designated. NY R USDCTSD Div. Bus., Rule 22.

    a.  *Opening a civil case.* Attorneys seeking to commence a new civil case are required to electronically file the new case on the Court's ECF system. NY R USDCTSD CM/ECF, S.D.(II)(14)(14.1). In civil cases the filing of the initial papers, including complaints, notices, petitions, etc., the payment of any applicable fees and the request for and issuance of summonses will be accomplished electronically. NY R USDCTSD CM/ECF, S.D.(I)(1)(1.2); NY R USDCTSD CM/ECF, S.D.(What's New).

      i.  With certain exceptions listed in NY R USDCTSD CM/ECF, S.D, new civil cases are no longer filed in hard copy form with the Clerk's Office. NY R USDCTSD CM/ECF, S.D.(What's New); NY R USDCTSD CM/ECF, S.D.(II)(14)(14.1). The following cases must not be electronically filed and must be filed in the traditional manner, on paper:

- Civil cases that include an Order to Show Cause, Temporary Restraining Order, or other documents sought to be filed under seal;
- Civil cases commenced by a pro se party;
- Habeas Corpus cases filed pursuant to 28 U.S.C.A. § 2255 (prisoner in Federal custody);
- False Claims Act cases (Qui Tam or "whistleblower" cases) filed pursuant to 31 U.S.C.A. § 3729 et seq. NY R USDCTSD CM/ECF, S.D.(II)(14)(14.2).

      ii.  Any party unable to electronically file must seek permission of the court to file in the traditional manner, on paper. Any such request made after business hours may be submitted through the night depository box maintained pursuant to NY R USDCTS&ED Civ Rule 1.1. NY R USDCTSD CM/ECF, S.D.(II)(14)(14.1).

      iii.  For more information on opening a civil action, refer to NY R USDCTSD CM/ECF, S.D.(II)(14).

    b.  *Pro se incarcerated litigants.* Individuals who are incarcerated and are filing their legal documents pro se may benefit from a special "mailbox rule," which fixes the time of commencement of an action at the point when the complaint enters the prison mail system, rather than when it reaches the court clerk. FPP § 1052; Houston v. Lack, 487 U.S. 266, 276, 108 S.Ct. 2379, 2385, 101 L.Ed.2d 245 (1988).

    c.  *Night depository.* A night depository with an automatic date stamp shall be maintained by the Clerk of the Southern District in the Pearl Street Courthouse. After regular business hours, papers for the

District Court only may be deposited in the night depository. Such papers will be considered as having been filed in the District Court as of the date stamped thereon, which shall be deemed presumptively correct. NY R USDCTS&ED Civ Rule 1.2.

d. *Electronic filing*

　　i. *Authorization of electronic filing program.* A court may, by local rule, allow papers to be filed, signed, or verified by electronic means that are consistent with any technical standards established by the Judicial Conference of the United States. A local rule may require electronic filing only if reasonable exceptions are allowed. A paper filed electronically in compliance with a local rule is a written paper for purposes of the Federal Rules of Civil Procedure. FRCP 5(d)(3).

- The Court will accept for filing documents submitted, signed or verified by electronic means, that comply with the rules in NY R USDCTSD CM/ECF, S.D. NY R USDCTSD CM/ECF, S.D.(I). The information in NY R USDCTSD CM/ECF, S.D. applies only to cases assigned to the ECF system. NY R USDCTSD CM/ECF, S.D.(Introduction).

- Parties serving and filing papers shall follow the instructions regarding Electronic Case Filing (ECF) published on the website of each respective Court. A paper served and filed by electronic means in accordance with such instructions is, for purposes of FRCP 5, served and filed in compliance with the Local Civil Rules of the Southern and Eastern Districts of New York. NY R USDCTS&ED Civ Rule 5.2(a). Parties have an obligation to review the Court's actual order, decree, or judgment (on ECF), which controls, and should not rely on the description on the docket or in the ECF Notice of Electronic Filing (NEF). NY R USDCTS&ED Civ Rule 5.2(c).

- The following should be observed when filing electronically: (1) the Federal Rules of Civil Procedure, (2) the Local Civil Rules of the United States District Courts for the Southern and Eastern Districts of New York, (3) the assigned judge's Individual Practices, and (4) the Court's Electronic Case Filing Rules & Instructions (NY R USDCTSD CM/ECF, S.D.). NY R USDCTSD CM/ECF, S.D.(Introduction).

　　ii. *Scope of electronic filing.* Except as expressly provided and in exceptional circumstances preventing a party from filing electronically, all documents required to be filed with the Court must be filed electronically. Any party unable to comply with this requirement must seek permission of the Court to file in the traditional manner, on paper. Any such application made after regular business hours may be submitted through the night depository box maintained pursuant to NY R USDCTS&ED Civ Rule 1.2. NY R USDCTSD CM/ECF, S.D.(I)(1)(1.1).

- *Documents filed by pro se litigants.* Unless otherwise ordered by the Court, documents filed by pro se litigants must be filed in the traditional manner, on paper, and will be scanned and docketed by the Clerk's Office into the ECF system. NY R USDCTSD CM/ECF, S.D.(I)(1)(1.1). Pro se litigants must file pleadings and documents in the traditional manner on paper unless the assigned judge has granted permission to electronically file on the ECF system. NY R USDCTSD CM/ECF, S.D.(Introduction).

- *Letters.* Except for letters to be filed under seal, letters addressed to judges who accept letters may be filed electronically. Parties should consult the assigned judge's Individual Practices to determine if the judge accepts letters at all and, if he or she does, whether the judge has any page limitations on letters and/or requires courtesy copies of letters filed on ECF (and, if so, by what means of delivery). NY R USDCTSD CM/ECF, S.D.(II)(13)(13.1). Letters solely between parties or their counsel or otherwise not addressed to the Court may not be filed electronically on ECF (except as exhibits to an otherwise properly filed document). NY R USDCTSD CM/ECF, S.D.(II)(13)(13.1). For more information on filing letters, refer to NY R USDCTSD CM/ECF, S.D.(II)(13)(13.1).

- *Proposed orders, judgments and decrees.* Proposed orders, judgments and decrees shall be presented as directed by the ECF rules published on the website of each respective Court. NY R USDCTS&ED Civ Rule 77.1. For more information, refer to NY R USDCTS&ED Civ Rule 77.1.

iii. *Exceptions to electronic filing.* In an ECF case, the documents that should not be electronically filed include:

- Miscellaneous Case initiating documents, NY R USDCTSD CM/ECF, S.D.(II)(18)(18.2);

- Proposed orders; proposed judgments, stipulations; consents, NY R USDCTSD CM/ECF, S.D.(II)(18)(18.3);

- Orders to show cause / temporary restraining orders, NY R USDCTSD CM/ECF, S.D.(II)(18)(18.4);

- Sealed documents, NY R USDCTSD CM/ECF, S.D.(II)(18)(18.5); and

- Surety bonds, NY R USDCTSD CM/ECF, S.D.(II)(18)(18.6).

- In cases where the record of an administrative or other prior proceeding must be filed with the Court, such record may be served and filed in hard copy without prior motion and order of the Court. NY R USDCTSD CM/ECF, S.D.(I)(5)(5.3).

- For more documents excepted from electronic filing, and for more information on such documents, refer to NY R USDCTSD CM/ECF, S.D.(II)(18).

iv. *Consequences of electronic filing.* Except as otherwise provided in NY R USDCTSD CM/ECF, S.D.(I)(4), electronic filing of a document in the ECF system consistent with these procedures, together with the transmission of a Notice of Electronic Filing (NEF) from the Court, constitutes filing of the document for all purposes of the Federal Rules of Civil Procedure and the Local Civil Rules of the United States District Courts for the Southern and Eastern Districts of New York and constitutes entry of the document on the docket kept by the Clerk under FRCP 58 and FRCP 79. NY R USDCTSD CM/ECF, S.D.(I)(3)(3.1).

v. For more information on electronic filing, refer to NY R USDCTSD CM/ECF, S.D.

2. *Issuance of summons.* On or after filing the complaint, the plaintiff may present a summons to the clerk for signature and seal. If the summons is properly completed, the clerk must sign, seal, and issue it to the plaintiff for service on the defendant. A summons—or a copy of a summons that is addressed to multiple defendants—must be issued for each defendant to be served. FRCP 4(b).

a. *Electronic request and issuance.* Summonses will be requested and issued electronically on the ECF system. NY R USDCTSD CM/ECF, S.D.(What's New); NY R USDCTSD CM/ECF, S.D.(I)(1)(1.2). After electronically filing a new case, a party must electronically file a REQUEST FOR ISSUANCE OF SUMMONSES and attach proposed summonses in PDF format to the filing. The Clerk's Office will review the REQUEST and use the ECF system to issue summonses suitable for printing. NY R USDCTSD CM/ECF, S.D.(II)(14)(14.6).

b. *Amendments.* The court may permit a summons to be amended. FRCP 4(a)(2).

3. *Service requirements.* A summons must be served with a copy of the complaint. The plaintiff is responsible for having the summons and complaint served within the time allowed by FRCP 4(m) and must furnish the necessary copies to the person who makes service. FRCP 4(c)(1). Although new civil cases must be commenced with the court through electronic filing, the method of serving a summons and complaint remains the same pursuant to FRCP 4. NY R USDCTSD CM/ECF, S.D.(II)(14)(14.7).

a. *By whom served.* Any person who is at least 18 years old and not a party may serve a summons and complaint. FRCP 4(c)(2).

i. *By a marshal or someone specially appointed.* At the plaintiff's request, the court may order that service be made by a United States marshal or deputy marshal or by a person specially appointed by the court. The court must so order if the plaintiff is authorized to proceed in forma pauperis under 28 U.S.C.A. § 1915 or as a seaman under 28 U.S.C.A. § 1916. FRCP 4(c)(3).

b. *Serving an individual within a judicial district of the United States.* Unless federal law provides otherwise, an individual—other than a minor, an incompetent person, or a person whose waiver has been filed—may be served in a judicial district of the United States by:

i. Following state law for serving a summons in an action brought in courts of general jurisdiction in the state where the district court is located or where service is made; or

   ii.  Doing any of the following:

- Delivering a copy of the summons and of the complaint to the individual personally;

- Leaving a copy of each at the individual's dwelling or usual place of abode with someone of suitable age and discretion who resides there; or

- Delivering a copy of each to an agent authorized by appointment or by law to receive service of process. FRCP 4(e).

c.  *Serving an individual in a foreign country.* Unless federal law provides otherwise, an individual— other than a minor, an incompetent person, or a person whose waiver has been filed—may be served at a place not within any judicial district of the United States:

   i.  By any internationally agreed means of service that is reasonably calculated to give notice, such as those authorized by the Hague Convention on the Service Abroad of Judicial and Extrajudicial Documents;

   ii.  If there is no internationally agreed means, or if an international agreement allows but does not specify other means, by a method that is reasonably calculated to give notice:

- As prescribed by the foreign country's law for service in that country in an action in its courts of general jurisdiction;

- As the foreign authority directs in response to a letter rogatory or letter of request; or

- Unless prohibited by the foreign country's law, by: (1) delivering a copy of the summons and of the complaint to the individual personally; or (2) using any form of mail that the clerk addresses and sends to the individual and that requires a signed receipt; or

- By other means not prohibited by international agreement, as the court orders. FRCP 4(f).

d.  *Serving a minor or an incompetent person.* A minor or an incompetent person in a judicial district of the United States must be served by following state law for serving a summons or like process on such a defendant in an action brought in the courts of general jurisdiction of the state where service is made. A minor or an incompetent person who is not within any judicial district of the United States must be served in the manner prescribed by FRCP 4(f)(2)(A), FRCP 4(f)(2)(B), or FRCP 4(f)(3). FRCP 4(g).

e.  *Serving a corporation, partnership, or association.* Unless federal law provides otherwise or the defendant's waiver has been filed, a domestic or foreign corporation, or a partnership or other unincorporated association that is subject to suit under a common name, must be served:

   i.  In a judicial district of the United States:

- In the manner prescribed by FRCP 4(e)(1) for serving an individual; or

- By delivering a copy of the summons and of the complaint to an officer, a managing or general agent, or any other agent authorized by appointment or by law to receive service of process and—if the agent is one authorized by statute and the statute so requires—by also mailing a copy of each to the defendant; or

   ii.  At a place not within any judicial district of the United States, in any manner prescribed by FRCP 4(f) for serving an individual, except personal delivery under FRCP 4(f)(2)(C)(i). FRCP 4(h).

f.  *Serving the United States and its agencies, corporations, officers, or employees*

   i.  *United States.* To serve the United States, a party must:

- Deliver a copy of the summons and of the complaint to the United States attorney for the district where the action is brought—or to an assistant United States attorney or clerical employee whom the United States attorney designates in a writing filed with the court clerk—or send a copy of each by registered or certified mail to the civil-process clerk at the United States attorney's office;

- Send a copy of each by registered or certified mail to the Attorney General of the United States at Washington, D.C.; and

- If the action challenges an order of a nonparty agency or officer of the United States, send a copy of each by registered or certified mail to the agency or officer. FRCP 4(i)(1).

ii. *Agency; Corporation; Officer or employee sued in an official capacity.* To serve a United States agency or corporation, or a United States officer or employee sued only in an official capacity, a party must serve the United States and also send a copy of the summons and of the complaint by registered or certified mail to the agency, corporation, officer, or employee. FRCP 4(i)(2).

iii. *Officer or employee sued individually.* To serve a United States officer or employee sued in an individual capacity for an act or omission occurring in connection with duties performed on the United States' behalf (whether or not the officer or employee is also sued in an official capacity), a party must serve the United States and also serve the officer or employee under FRCP 4(e), FRCP 4(f), or FRCP 4(g). FRCP 4(i)(3).

iv. *Extending time.* The court must allow a party a reasonable time to cure its failure to:

- Serve a person required to be served under FRCP 4(i)(2), if the party has served either the United States attorney or the Attorney General of the United States; or
- Serve the United States under FRCP 4(i)(3), if the party has served the United States officer or employee. FRCP 4(i)(4).

g. *Serving a foreign, state, or local government*

i. *Foreign state.* A foreign state or its political subdivision, agency, or instrumentality must be served in accordance with 28 U.S.C.A. § 1608. FRCP 4(j)(1).

ii. *State or local government.* A state, a municipal corporation, or any other state-created governmental organization that is subject to suit must be served by:

- Delivering a copy of the summons and of the complaint to its chief executive officer; or
- Serving a copy of each in the manner prescribed by that state's law for serving a summons or like process on such a defendant. FRCP 4(j)(2).

h. *Territorial limits of effective service*

i. *In general.* Serving a summons or filing a waiver of service establishes personal jurisdiction over a defendant:

- Who is subject to the jurisdiction of a court of general jurisdiction in the state where the district court is located;
- Who is a party joined under FRCP 14 or FRCP 19 and is served within a judicial district of the United States and not more than one hundred (100) miles from where the summons was issued; or
- When authorized by a federal statute. FRCP 4(k)(1).

ii. *Federal claim outside state-court jurisdiction.* For a claim that arises under federal law, serving a summons or filing a waiver of service establishes personal jurisdiction over a defendant if:

- The defendant is not subject to jurisdiction in any state's courts of general jurisdiction; and
- Exercising jurisdiction is consistent with the United States Constitution and laws. FRCP 4(k)(2).

i. *Asserting jurisdiction over property or assets*

i. *Federal law.* The court may assert jurisdiction over property if authorized by a federal statute. Notice to claimants of the property must be given as provided in the statute or by serving a summons under FRCP 4. FRCP 4(n)(1).

ii. *State law.* On a showing that personal jurisdiction over a defendant cannot be obtained in the district where the action is brought by reasonable efforts to serve a summons under FRCP 4, the court may assert jurisdiction over the defendant's assets found in the district. Jurisdiction is acquired by seizing the assets under the circumstances and in the manner provided by state law in that district. FRCP 4(n)(2).

    j.  *Proving service*

        i.  *Affidavit required.* Unless service is waived, proof of service must be made to the court. Except for service by a United States marshal or deputy marshal, proof must be by the server's affidavit. FRCP 4(l)(1).

       ii.  *Service outside the United States.* Service not within any judicial district of the United States must be proved as follows:

- If made under FRCP 4(f)(1), as provided in the applicable treaty or convention; or

- If made under FRCP 4(f)(2) or FRCP 4(f)(3), by a receipt signed by the addressee, or by other evidence satisfying the court that the summons and complaint were delivered to the addressee. FRCP 4(l)(2).

      iii.  *Validity of service; Amending proof.* Failure to prove service does not affect the validity of service. The court may permit proof of service to be amended. FRCP 4(l)(3).

      iv.  *Results of filing a waiver of service.* When the plaintiff files a waiver, proof of service is not required and FRCP 4 applies as if a summons and complaint had been served at the time of filing the waiver. FRCP 4(d)(4).

    k.  *Service of other process.* For information on service of other process, refer to FRCP 4.1.

4.  *Individual judge practices.* Refer to the Miscellaneous section of this document for information on individual judge practices on filing and serving documents.

## G. Hearings

1.  There is no hearing contemplated in the federal statutes or rules for the complaint and summons.

## H. Forms

### 1. Official Federal Complaint and Summons Forms

    a.  Rule 4 notice of a lawsuit and request to waive service of summons. FRCP 4.

### 2. Federal Complaint and Summons Forms

    a.  Summons. 2 FEDFORMS § 3:23.

    b.  Summons; With proof of service. 2 FEDFORMS § 3:24.

    c.  Summons; Suit against officers of the United States. 2 FEDFORMS § 3:26.

    d.  Request for summons. 2 FEDFORMS § 3:27.

    e.  Civil cover sheet. 2 FEDFORMS § 3:29.

    f.  Motion for appointment of person to serve process. 2 FEDFORMS § 3:30.

    g.  Motion for appointment of United States marshal to serve process. 2 FEDFORMS § 3:34.

    h.  Notice of lawsuit and request for waiver of service of summons and waiver of summons. 2 FEDFORMS § 3:36.

    i.  Motion for payment of costs of personal service. 2 FEDFORMS § 3:37.

    j.  Affidavit of personal service; Delivery to individual. 2 FEDFORMS § 3:54.

    k.  Declaration of service; Delivery to individual. 2 FEDFORMS § 3:55.

    l.  Declaration of service; Delivery at usual place of abode or residence. 2 FEDFORMS § 3:56.

    m.  Declaration of service; Service on corporation; Delivery to officer. 2 FEDFORMS § 3:57.

    n.  Declaration of service; Service on United States. 2 FEDFORMS § 3:69.

    o.  Declaration of service; Service on officer of United States. 2 FEDFORMS § 3:71.

    p.  Complaint. 2 FEDFORMS § 7:14.

    q.  Introductory clause; Single claim stated. 2 FEDFORMS § 7:16.

    r.  Introductory clause; Several claims stated in separate counts. 2 FEDFORMS § 7:18.

s.   Allegations on information and belief. 2 FEDFORMS § 7:19.

t.   General prayer for relief. 2 FEDFORMS § 7:21.

u.   Disparate treatment; Sex discrimination; Sexual harassment and constructive discharge. 2A FED-FORMS § 7:143.

v.   Against manufacturer for negligent design and manufacture. 2B FEDFORMS § 7:426.

w.   Complaint; Single count. FEDPROF § 1:68.

x.   Complaint; Multiple counts; With same jurisdictional basis. FEDPROF § 1:69.

y.   Complaint; Multiple counts; With different jurisdictional basis for each. FEDPROF § 1:70.

z.   Civil cover sheet; General form. FEDPROF § 1:144.

## I.  Applicable Rules

1.  *Federal rules*

   a.   District court; Filing and miscellaneous fees; Rules of court. 28 U.S.C.A. § 1914.

   b.   Commencing an action. FRCP 3.

   c.   Summons. FRCP 4.

   d.   Serving and filing pleadings and other papers. FRCP 5.

   e.   Constitutional challenge to a statute; Notice, certification, and intervention. FRCP 5.1.

   f.   Privacy protection for filings made with the court. FRCP 5.2.

   g.   Computing and extending time; Time for motion papers. FRCP 6.

   h.   Pleadings allowed; Form of motions and other papers. FRCP 7.

   i.   Disclosure statement. FRCP 7.1.

   j.   General rules of pleading. FRCP 8.

   k.   Pleading special matters. FRCP 9.

   l.   Form of pleadings. FRCP 10.

   m.   Signing pleadings, motions, and other papers; Representations to the court; Sanctions. FRCP 11.

   n.   Joinder of claims. FRCP 18.

   o.   Required joinder of parties. FRCP 19.

   p.   Permissive joinder of parties. FRCP 20.

   q.   Misjoinder and nonjoinder of parties. FRCP 21.

   r.   Right to a jury trial; Demand. FRCP 38.

   s.   Determining foreign law. FRCP 44.1.

2.  *Local rules*

   a.   Night depository. NY R USDCTS&ED Civ Rule 1.2.

   b.   Duty of attorneys in related cases. NY R USDCTS&ED Civ Rule 1.6.

   c.   Fees of court clerks and reporters. NY R USDCTS&ED Civ Rule 1.7.

   d.   Electronic service and filing of documents. NY R USDCTS&ED Civ Rule 5.2.

   e.   Computation of time. NY R USDCTS&ED Civ Rule 6.4.

   f.   Disclosure statement. NY R USDCTS&ED Civ Rule 7.1.1.

   g.   Form of pleadings, motions, and other papers. NY R USDCTS&ED Civ Rule 11.1.

   h.   Submission of orders, judgments and decrees. NY R USDCTS&ED Civ Rule 77.1.

   i.   Alternative dispute resolution (Southern District only). NY R USDCTS&ED Civ Rule 83.9.

   j.   Electronic case filing rules and instructions. NY R USDCTSD CM/ECF, S.D.

    k.    Civil actions or proceedings (filing and assignment). NY R USDCTSD Div. Bus., Rule 4.

    l.    Related cases. NY R USDCTSD Div. Bus., Rule 13.

    m.    Designation of White Plains cases. NY R USDCTSD Div. Bus., Rule 18.

    n.    Filing at either courthouse. NY R USDCTSD Div. Bus., Rule 22.

## J.  Miscellaneous

**NOTE: Individual judges' rules may apply. For available judge-level information, refer to:**

DISTRICT JUDGE RONNIE ABRAMS: NY R USDCTSD Abrams-Civ Prac; NY R USDCTSD Abrams-Crim Prac; NY R USDCTSD Abrams-Pro Se; NY R USDCTSD Abrams-Case Mgt; NY R USDCTSD Abrams-Jury.

DISTRICT JUDGE DEBORAH A. BATTS: NY R USDCTSD Batts-Practices.

DISTRICT JUDGE RICHARD M. BERMAN: NY R USDCTSD Berman-Practices; NY R USDCTSD Berman-Default; NY R USDCTSD Berman-Sentencing; NY R USDCTSD Berman-Media.

DISTRICT JUDGE VINCENT L. BRICCETTI: NY R USDCTSD Briccetti-Practices; NY R USDCTSD Briccetti-Plan; NY R USDCTSD Briccetti-Notice.

DISTRICT JUDGE VERNON S. BRODERICK: NY R USDCTSD Broderick-Civil; NY R USDCTSD Broderick-Crim; NY R USDCTSD Broderick-Case Mgt; NY R USDCTSD Broderick-Jury.

DISTRICT JUDGE NAOMI REICE BUCHWALD: NY R USDCTSD Buchwald-Practices.

DISTRICT JUDGE VALERIE E. CAPRONI: NY R USDCTSD Caproni-Prac; NY R USDCTSD Caproni--Pro Se; NY R USDCTSD Caproni-Case Mgt; NY R USDCTSD Caproni-Crim Prac.

DISTRICT JUDGE ANDREW L. CARTER JR.: NY R USDCTSD Carter-Practices.

DISTRICT JUDGE KEVIN P. CASTEL: NY R USDCTSD Castel-Practices; NY R USDCTSD Castel-Default; NY R USDCTSD Castel-Scheduling; NY R USDCTSD Castel-Complex; NY R USDCTSD Castel-Trials; NY R USDCTSD Castel-Sentencing.

DISTRICT JUDGE DENISE L. COTE: NY R USDCTSD Cote-Civil Practices; NY R USDCTSD Cote-Pro Se; NY R USDCTSD Cote-Maritime Ord; NY R USDCTSD Cote-Crim Practices; NY R USDCTSD Cote-Crim Trials; NY R USDCTSD Cote-Sentencing.

DISTRICT JUDGE PAUL A. CROTTY: NY R USDCTSD Crotty-Practices; NY R USDCTSD Crotty-Sentencing; NY R USDCTSD Crotty-Calls; NY R USDCTSD Crotty-Scheduling.

DISTRICT JUDGE GEORGE B. DANIELS: NY R USDCTSD Daniels-Practices.

DISTRICT JUDGE KEVIN T. DUFFY: NY R USDCTSD Duffy-Practices.

DISTRICT JUDGE PAUL A. ENGELMAYER: NY R USDCTSD Engelmayer-Practices; NY R USDCTSD Engelmayer-Scheduling; NY R USDCTSD Engelmayer-Sentencing; NY R USDCTSD Engelmayer-Pro Se; NY R USDCTSD Engelmayer-Crim.

DISTRICT JUDGE KATHERINE POLK FAILLA: NY R USDCTSD Failla-Civ Prac; NY R USDCTSD Failla-Crim Prac; NY R USDCTSD Failla-Case Mgt.

DISTRICT JUDGE KATHERINE B. FORREST: NY R USDCTSD Forrest-Civil Prac; NY R USDCTSD Forrest-Crim Prac; NY R USDCTSD Forrest-Crim Pretrial; NY R USDCTSD Forrest-Scheduling; NY R US-DCTSD Forrest-Patent Scheduling; NY R USDCTSD Forrest-Sentencing; NY R USDCTSD Forrest-Order 1; NY R USDCTSD Forrest-Order 2.

DISTRICT JUDGE JESSE M. FURMAN: NY R USDCTSD Furman-Civil Prac; NY R USDCTSD Furman-Crim Prac; NY R USDCTSD Furman-Pro Se Prac; NY R USDCTSD Furman-Trials; NY R USDCTSD Furman-Scheduling; NY R USDCTSD Furman-Rights.

DISTRICT JUDGE PAUL G. GARDEPHE: NY R USDCTSD Gardephe-Civ Prac; NY R USDCTSD Gardephe-Pretrial; NY R USDCTSD Gardephe-Prot Ord; NY R USDCTSD Gardephe-Maritime; NY R USDCTSD Gardephe-Crim Prac; NY R USDCTSD Gardephe-Trial.

DISTRICT JUDGE THOMAS P. GRIESA: NY R USDCTSD Griesa-Practices.

DISTRICT JUDGE CHARLES S. HAIGHT: NY R USDCTSD Haight-Practices.

DISTRICT JUDGE ALVIN K. HELLERSTEIN: NY R USDCTSD Hellerstein-Practices; NY R USDCTSD Hellerstein--Sept 11.

DISTRICT JUDGE LEWIS A. KAPLAN: NY R USDCTSD Kaplan-Practices; NY R USDCTSD Kaplan-Sentencing.

DISTRICT JUDGE KENNETH M. KARAS: NY R USDCTSD Karas-Practices; NY R USDCTSD Karas-Case Mgt; NY R USDCTSD Karas-Default; NY R USDCTSD Karas-Sentencing; NY R USDCTSD Karas-Rights.

DISTRICT JUDGE JOHN F. KEENAN: NY R USDCTSD Keenan-Practices.

DISTRICT JUDGE JOHN G. KOELTL: NY R USDCTSD Koeltl-Practices.

DISTRICT JUDGE VICTOR MARRERO: NY R USDCTSD Marrero-Practices; NY R USDCTSD Marrero-Scheduling; NY R USDCTSD Marrero-Default; NY R USDCTSD Marrero-Trial Proc.

DISTRICT JUDGE COLLEEN McMAHON: NY R USDCTSD McMahon-Practices; NY R USDCTSD McMahon-RICO; NY R USDCTSD McMahon-Copies; NY R USDCTSD McMahon-Scheduling; NY R USDCTSD McMahon-Elec Disc; NY R USDCTSD McMahon-Sentencing.

DISTRICT JUDGE ALISON J. NATHAN: NY R USDCTSD Nathan-Civ Prac; NY R USDCTSD Nathan-Crim Prac; NY R USDCTSD Nathan-Pro Se; NY R USDCTSD Nathan-Scheduling.

DISTRICT JUDGE J. PAUL OETKEN: NY R USDCTSD Oetken-Civ Prac; NY R USDCTSD Oetken-Case Mgt; NY R USDCTSD Oetken-Crim Prac; NY R USDCTSD Oetken-Pro Se.

DISTRICT JUDGE WILLIAM H. PAULEY, III: NY R USDCTSD Pauley-Crim Cases; NY R USDCTSD Pauley-Practices.

DISTRICT JUDGE LORETTA A. PRESKA: NY R USDCTSD Preska-Practices.

DISTRICT JUDGE JED S. RAKOFF: NY R USDCTSD Rakoff-Practices; NY R USDCTSD Rakoff-Scheduling; NY R USDCTSD Rakoff-Prot Ord; NY R USDCTSD Rakoff-Maritime Ord.

DISTRICT JUDGE EDGARDO RAMOS: NY R USDCTSD Ramos--Practices; NY R USDCTSD Ramos-Case Mgt.

DISTRICT JUDGE NELSON S. ROMAN: NY R USDCTSD Roman-Civ Prac; NY R USDCTSD Roman-Pro Se; NY R USDCTSD Roman-Crim Prac; NY R USDCTSD Roman-Case Mgt.

DISTRICT JUDGE LEONARD B. SAND: NY R USDCTSD Sand-Practices.

DISTRICT JUDGE LORNA G. SCHOFIELD: NY R USDCTSD Schofield-Civ Prac; NY R USDCTSD Schofield-Crim Prac; NY R USDCTSD Schofield-Sched; NY R USDCTSD Schofield-Pro Se; NY R USDCTSD Schofield-Advice.

DISTRICT JUDGE CATHY SEIBEL: NY R USDCTSD Seibel-Practices.

DISTRICT JUDGE LOUIS L. STANTON: NY R USDCTSD Stanton-Practices; NY R USDCTSD Stanton-Pretrial.

DISTRICT JUDGE SIDNEY H. STEIN: NY R USDCTSD Stein-Practices.

DISTRICT JUDGE RICHARD J. SULLIVAN: NY R USDCTSD Sullivan-Practices; NY R USDCTSD Sullivan-Scheduling; NY R USDCTSD Sullivan-Sentencing; NY R USDCTSD Sullivan-Juries; NY R USDCTSD Sullivan-Trial; NY R USDCTSD Sullivan-Default.

DISTRICT JUDGE LAURA TAYLOR SWAIN: NY R USDCTSD Swain-Practices; NY R USDCTSD Swain-Trial; NY R USDCTSD Swain-Crim Trial; NY R USDCTSD Swain-Juries; NY R USDCTSD Swain-Sentencing; NY R USDCTSD Swain-Rights.

DISTRICT JUDGE ROBERT W. SWEET: NY R USDCTSD Sweet-Practices.

DISTRICT JUDGE ANALISA TORRES: NY R USDCTSD Torres-Civ Prac; NY R USDCTSD Torres-Pro Se; NY R USDCTSD Torres-Scheduling.

DISTRICT JUDGE KIMBA M. WOOD: NY R USDCTSD Wood-Practices; NY R USDCTSD Wood-Scheduling; NY R USDCTSD Wood-Discovery; NY R USDCTSD Wood-RICO; NY R USDCTSD Wood-Juries; NY R USDCTSD Wood-Trial; NY R USDCTSD Wood-Media.

DISTRICT JUDGE GREGORY H. WOODS: NY R USDCTSD Woods-Civ Prac; NY R USDCTSD Woods-Pro

Se; NY R USDCTSD Woods-Sched; NY R USDCTSD Woods-Crim Prac; NY R USDCTSD Woods-Protect Order; NY R USDCTSD Woods-Speedy Trial.

MAGISTRATE JUDGE JAMES L. COTT: NY R USDCTSD Cott-Practices; NY R USDCTSD Cott-Settlement.

MAGISTRATE JUDGE PAUL E. DAVISON: NY R USDCTSD Davison-Practices.

MAGISTRATE JUDGE RONALD L. ELLIS: NY R USDCTSD Ellis-Practices.

MAGISTRATE JUDGE KEVIN N. FOX: NY R USDCTSD Fox-Practices; NY R USDCTSD Fox-Settlement.

MAGISTRATE JUDGE JAMES C. FRANCIS: NY R USDCTSD Francis-Practices.

MAGISTRATE JUDGE DEBRA FREEMAN: NY R USDCTSD Freeman-Practices; NY R USDCTSD Freeman-Settlement.

MAGISTRATE JUDGE GABRIEL W. GORENSTEIN: NY R USDCTSD Gorenstein-Practices; NY R USDCTSD Gorenstein-Ackn.

MAGISTRATE JUDGE FRANK MAAS: NY R USDCTSD Maas-Practices; NY R USDCTSD Maas-Discontinuance; NY R USDCTSD Maas-Conf; NY R USDCTSD Maas-Settlement.

MAGISTRATE JUDGE JUDITH C. McCARTHY: NY R USDCTSD McCarthy-Practices; NY R USDCTSD McCarthy-Conduct.

MAGISTRATE JUDGE BARBARA MOSES: NY R USDCTSD Moses-Practices.

MAGISTRATE JUDGE SARAH NETBURN: NY R USDCTSD Netburn-Civil; NY R USDCTSD Netburn-Settlement; NY R USDCTSD Netburn-Case Mgt; NY R USDCTSD Netburn--Pro Se.

MAGISTRATE JUDGE ANDREW J. PECK: NY R USDCTSD Peck-Practices; NY R USDCTSD Peck-Order; NY R USDCTSD Peck-Rule 502(d).

MAGISTRATE JUDGE HENRY PITMAN: NY R USDCTSD Pitman-Practices.

MAGISTRATE JUDGE LISA MARGARET SMITH: NY R USDCTSD Smith-Practices; NY R USDCTSD Smith-Trials.

# Pleadings
## Answer

**Document Last Updated September 2016**

A. **Checklist**

(I) ❑ Matters to be considered by plaintiff

    (a) ❑ Required documents

        (1) ❑ Civil cover sheet

        (2) ❑ Complaint

        (3) ❑ Summons

        (4) ❑ Electronic case filing rules and instructions (NY R USDCTSD CM/ECF, S.D.)

        (5) ❑ Judge's individual practices

        (6) ❑ Notice, consent, and reference of a civil action to a magistrate judge

        (7) ❑ Filing fee

        (8) ❑ Affidavit proving service

    (b) ❑ Supplemental documents

        (1) ❑ Notice and request for waiver of service

        (2) ❑ Notice of constitutional question

        (3) ❑ Notice of issue concerning foreign law

    (4) ❑ Nongovernmental corporate disclosure statement

    (5) ❑ Related case statement

    (6) ❑ Statement explaining untimely electronic filing

    (7) ❑ Courtesy copies

(c) ❑ Timing

    (1) ❑ A civil action is commenced by filing a complaint with the court

    (2) ❑ If a defendant is not served within ninety (90) days after the complaint is filed, the court—on motion or on its own after notice to the plaintiff—must dismiss the action without prejudice against that defendant or order that service be made within a specified time

(II) ❑ Matters to be considered by defendant

  (a) ❑ Required documents

    (1) ❑ Answer

    (2) ❑ Certificate of service

  (b) ❑ Supplemental documents

    (1) ❑ Waiver of the service of summons

    (2) ❑ Notice of constitutional question

    (3) ❑ Notice of issue concerning foreign law

    (4) ❑ Nongovernmental corporate disclosure statement

    (5) ❑ Statement explaining untimely electronic filing

    (6) ❑ Courtesy copies

  (c) ❑ Timing

    (1) ❑ A defendant must serve an answer:

      (i) ❑ Within twenty-one (21) days after being served with the summons and complaint; or

      (ii) ❑ If it has timely waived service under FRCP 4(d), within sixty (60) days after the request for a waiver was sent, or within ninety (90) days after it was sent to the defendant outside any judicial district of the United States

    (2) ❑ The United States, a United States agency, or a United States officer or employee sued only in an official capacity must serve an answer to a complaint, counterclaim, or crossclaim within sixty (60) days after service on the United States attorney

    (3) ❑ A United States officer or employee sued in an individual capacity for an act or omission occurring in connection with duties performed on the United States' behalf must serve an answer to a complaint, counterclaim, or crossclaim within sixty (60) days after service on the officer or employee or service on the United States attorney, whichever is later

    (4) ❑ Unless the court sets a different time, serving a motion under FRCP 12 alters these periods as follows:

      (i) ❑ If the court denies the motion or postpones its disposition until trial, the responsive pleading must be served within fourteen (14) days after notice of the court's action; or

      (ii) ❑ If the court grants a motion for a more definite statement, the responsive pleading must be served within fourteen (14) days after the more definite statement is served

    (5) ❑ Defendant is given a reasonable time of at least thirty (30) days after a waiver of service request is sent—or at least sixty (60) days if sent to defendant outside any judicial district of the United States—to return the waiver

## B. Timing

1. *Answer.* Unless another time is specified by FRCP 12 or a federal statute. . .a defendant must serve an answer: (1) within twenty-one (21) days after being served with the summons and complaint; or (2) if it

has timely waived service under FRCP 4(d), within sixty (60) days after the request for a waiver was sent, or within ninety (90) days after it was sent to the defendant outside any judicial district of the United States. FRCP 12(a)(1)(A).

   a. *Time to serve other responsive pleadings.* Unless another time is specified by FRCP 12 or a federal statute, the time for serving a responsive pleading is as follows:

      i. *Answer to counterclaim or crossclaim.* A party must serve an answer to a counterclaim or crossclaim within twenty-one (21) days after being served with the pleading that states the counterclaim or crossclaim. FRCP 12(a)(1)(B).

      ii. *Reply to an answer.* A party must serve a reply to an answer within twenty-one (21) days after being served with an order to reply, unless the order specifies a different time. FRCP 12(a)(1)(C).

   b. *United States and its agencies, officers, or employees sued in an official capacity.* The United States, a United States agency, or a United States officer or employee sued only in an official capacity must serve an answer to a complaint, counterclaim, or crossclaim within sixty (60) days after service on the United States attorney. FRCP 12(a)(2).

   c. *United States officers or employees sued in an individual capacity.* A United States officer or employee sued in an individual capacity for an act or omission occurring in connection with duties performed on the United States' behalf must serve an answer to a complaint, counterclaim, or crossclaim within sixty (60) days after service on the officer or employee or service on the United States attorney, whichever is later. FRCP 12(a)(3).

   d. *Effect of a FRCP 12 motion on the time to serve a responsive pleading.* Unless the court sets a different time, serving a motion under FRCP 12 alters the periods in FRCP 12(a) as follows:

      i. If the court denies the motion or postpones its disposition until trial, the responsive pleading must be served within fourteen (14) days after notice of the court's action; or

      ii. If the court grants a motion for a more definite statement, the responsive pleading must be served within fourteen (14) days after the more definite statement is served. FRCP 12(a)(4).

2. *Waiver of service.* The notice and request for waiver must give the defendant a reasonable time of at least thirty (30) days after the request was sent—or at least sixty (60) days if sent to defendant outside any judicial district of the United States—to return the waiver. FRCP 4(d)(1)(F).

   a. *Time to answer after a waiver.* A defendant who, before being served with process, timely returns a waiver need not serve an answer to the complaint until sixty (60) days after the request was sent—or until ninety (90) days after it was sent to the defendant outside any judicial district of the United States. FRCP 4(d)(3).

3. *Computation of time*

   a. *Computing time.* FRCP 6 applies in computing any time period specified in the Federal Rules of Civil Procedure, in any local rule or court order, or in any statute that does not specify a method of computing time. FRCP 6(a). In computing any period of time prescribed or allowed by the Local Civil Rules of the United States District Courts for the Southern and Eastern Districts of New York or the Local Admiralty and Maritime Rules, the provisions of FRCP 6 shall apply unless otherwise stated. NY R USDCTS&ED Civ Rule 6.4.

      i. *Period stated in days or a longer unit.* When the period is stated in days or a longer unit of time:

- Exclude the day of the event that triggers the period;

- Count every day, including intermediate Saturdays, Sundays, and legal holidays; and

- Include the last day of the period, but if the last day is a Saturday, Sunday, or legal holiday, the period continues to run until the end of the next day that is not a Saturday, Sunday, or legal holiday. FRCP 6(a)(1). In the Local Civil Rules of the United States District Courts for the Southern and Eastern Districts of New York, as in the Federal Rules of Civil Procedure as amended effective December 1, 2009, Saturdays, Sundays, and legal holidays are no longer excluded in computing periods of time. If the last day of the period is a Saturday, Sunday, or legal holiday, the period continues to run until the end of the next day that is not a Saturday, Sunday, or legal holiday. NY R USDCTS&ED Civ Rule 6.4.

ii. *Period stated in hours.* When the period is stated in hours:

- Begin counting immediately on the occurrence of the event that triggers the period;

- Count every hour, including hours during intermediate Saturdays, Sundays, and legal holidays; and

- If the period would end on a Saturday, Sunday, or legal holiday, the period continues to run until the same time on the next day that is not a Saturday, Sunday, or legal holiday. FRCP 6(a)(2). In the Local Civil Rules of the United States District Courts for the Southern and Eastern Districts of New York, as in the Federal Rules of Civil Procedure as amended effective December 1, 2009, Saturdays, Sundays, and legal holidays are no longer excluded in computing periods of time. If the last day of the period is a Saturday, Sunday, or legal holiday, the period continues to run until the end of the next day that is not a Saturday, Sunday, or legal holiday. NY R USDCTS&ED Civ Rule 6.4.

iii. *Inaccessibility of the clerk's office.* Unless the court orders otherwise, if the clerk's office is inaccessible:

- On the last day for filing under FRCP 6(a)(1), then the time for filing is extended to the first accessible day that is not a Saturday, Sunday, or legal holiday; or

- During the last hour for filing under FRCP 6(a)(2), then the time for filing is extended to the same time on the first accessible day that is not a Saturday, Sunday, or legal holiday. FRCP 6(a)(3).

iv. *"Last day" defined.* Unless a different time is set by a statute, local rule, or court order, the last day ends:

- For electronic filing, at midnight in the court's time zone; and

- For filing by other means, when the clerk's office is scheduled to close. FRCP 6(a)(4).

v. *"Next day" defined.* The "next day" is determined by continuing to count forward when the period is measured after an event and backward when measured before an event. FRCP 6(a)(5).

vi. *"Legal holiday" defined.* "Legal holiday" means:

- The day set aside by statute for observing New Year's Day, Martin Luther King Jr.'s Birthday, Washington's Birthday, Memorial Day, Independence Day, Labor Day, Columbus Day, Veterans' Day, Thanksgiving Day, or Christmas Day;

- Any day declared a holiday by the President or Congress; and

- For periods that are measured after an event, any other day declared a holiday by the state where the district court is located. FRCP 6(a)(6).

b. *Computation of electronic filing deadlines.* You can file electronically twenty-four (24) hours a day, seven (7) days a week, three hundred sixty-five (365) days a year. NY R USDCTSD CM/ECF, S.D.(II)(13)(13.10). Electronic filing must be completed before midnight local time where the Court is located in order to be considered timely filed that day. NY R USDCTSD CM/ECF, S.D.(I)(3)(3.3); NY R USDCTSD CM/ECF, S.D.(II)(13)(13.10); NY R USDCTSD CM/ECF, S.D.(II)(19)(19.4). An electronically filed document is deemed filed on the "filed on" date indicated on the Notice of Electronic Filing (NEF). NY R USDCTSD CM/ECF, S.D.(II)(13)(13.11).

i. *Technical failures.* A Filing User whose filing is made untimely as the result of a technical failure may seek appropriate relief from the Court. NY R USDCTSD CM/ECF, S.D.(I)(11). If you missed a filing deadline when the ECF system was out of order, attach a statement to your filing explaining how the interruption in service prevented you from filing in a timely fashion. NY R USDCTSD CM/ECF, S.D.(II)(23)(23.5).

c. *Extending time*

   i. *In general.* When an act may or must be done within a specified time, the court may, for good cause, extend the time:

   - With or without motion or notice if the court acts, or if a request is made, before the original time or its extension expires; or

   - On motion made after the time has expired if the party failed to act because of excusable neglect. FRCP 6(b)(1).

   ii. *Exceptions.* A court must not extend the time to act under FRCP 50(b), FRCP 50(d), FRCP 52(b), FRCP 59(b), FRCP 59(d), FRCP 59(e), and FRCP 60(b). FRCP 6(b)(2).

   iii. Refer to the United States District Court for the Southern District of New York KeyRules Motion for Continuance/Extension of Time document for more information on extending time.

d. *Additional time after certain kinds of service.* When a party may or must act within a specified time after service and service is made under FRCP 5(b)(2)(C), FRCP 5(b)(2)(D), FRCP 5(b)(2)(E), or FRCP 5(b)(2)(F), three (3) days are added after the period would otherwise expire under FRCP 6(a). FRCP 6(d). Overnight delivery service shall be deemed service by mail for purposes of FRCP 5 and FRCP 6. NY R USDCTS&ED Civ Rule 5.3.

4. *Individual judge practices.* Refer to the Miscellaneous section of this document for information on individual judge practices on timing of documents.

## C. General Requirements

1. *Pleading, generally*

a. *Pleadings allowed.* Only these pleadings are allowed: (1) a complaint; (2) an answer to a complaint; (3) an answer to a counterclaim designated as a counterclaim; (4) an answer to a crossclaim; (5) a third-party complaint; (6) an answer to a third-party complaint; and (7) if the court orders one, a reply to an answer. FRCP 7(a).

b. *Pleading to be concise and direct.* Each allegation must be simple, concise, and direct. No technical form is required. FRCP 8(d)(1).

c. *Alternative statements of a claim or defense.* A party may set out two or more statements of a claim or defense alternatively or hypothetically, either in a single count or defense or in separate ones. If a party makes alternative statements, the pleading is sufficient if any one of them is sufficient. FRCP 8(d)(2).

d. *Inconsistent claims or defenses.* A party may state as many separate claims or defenses as it has, regardless of consistency. FRCP 8(d)(3).

e. *Construing pleadings.* Pleadings must be construed so as to do justice. FRCP 8(e).

2. *Pleading special matters*

a. *Capacity or authority to sue; Legal existence*

   i. *In general.* Except when required to show that the court has jurisdiction, a pleading need not allege:

   - A party's capacity to sue or be sued;

   - A party's authority to sue or be sued in a representative capacity; or

   - The legal existence of an organized association of persons that is made a party. FRCP 9(a)(1).

   ii. *Raising those issues.* To raise any of those issues, a party must do so by a specific denial, which must state any supporting facts that are peculiarly within the party's knowledge. FRCP 9(a)(2).

b. *Fraud or mistake; Conditions of mind.* In alleging fraud or mistake, a party must state with particularity the circumstances constituting fraud or mistake. Malice, intent, knowledge, and other conditions of a person's mind may be alleged generally. FRCP 9(b).

c. *Conditions precedent.* In pleading conditions precedent, it suffices to allege generally that all conditions precedent have occurred or been performed. But when denying that a condition precedent has occurred or been performed, a party must do so with particularity. FRCP 9(c).

d. *Official document or act.* In pleading an official document or official act, it suffices to allege that the document was legally issued or the act legally done. FRCP 9(d).

e. *Judgment.* In pleading a judgment or decision of a domestic or foreign court, a judicial or quasi-judicial tribunal, or a board or officer, it suffices to plead the judgment or decision without showing jurisdiction to render it. FRCP 9(e).

f. *Time and place.* An allegation of time or place is material when testing the sufficiency of a pleading. FRCP 9(f).

g. *Special damages.* If an item of special damage is claimed, it must be specifically stated. FRCP 9(g).

h. *Admiralty or maritime claim*

   i. *How designated.* If a claim for relief is within the admiralty or maritime jurisdiction and also within the court's subject-matter jurisdiction on some other ground, the pleading may designate the claim as an admiralty or maritime claim for purposes of FRCP 14(c), FRCP 38(e), and FRCP 82 and the Supplemental Rules for Admiralty or Maritime Claims and Asset Forfeiture Actions. A claim cognizable only in the admiralty or maritime jurisdiction is an admiralty or maritime claim for those purposes, whether or not so designated. FRCP 9(h)(1).

   ii. *Designation for appeal.* A case that includes an admiralty or maritime claim within FRCP 9(h) is an admiralty case within 28 U.S.C.A. § 1292(a)(3). FRCP 9(h)(2).

3. *Answer*

   a. *Defenses; Admissions and denials*

      i. *In general.* In responding to a pleading, a party must: (1) state in short and plain terms its defenses to each claim asserted against it; and (2) admit or deny the allegations asserted against it by an opposing party. FRCP 8(b)(1).

         • The purpose of an answer is to formulate issues by means of defenses addressed to the allegations of the complaint, and to give the plaintiff notice of the defenses he or she will be called upon to meet. FEDPROC § 62:70; Lopez v. U.S. Fidelity & Guaranty Co., 15 Alaska 633, 18 F.R.D. 59 (1955); Moriarty v. Curran, 18 F.R.D. 461 (S.D.N.Y. 1956).

         • An answer is adequate where it accomplishes these purposes, even if it contains general and specific denials and at the same time asserts additional facts by way of justification or explanation, and even if it sets forth conclusions of law. FEDPROC § 62:70; Johnston v. Jones, 178 F.2d 481 (3d Cir. 1949); Burke v. Mesta Mach. Co., 5 F.R.D. 134 (W.D.Pa. 1946).

      ii. *Denials; Responding to the substance.* A denial must fairly respond to the substance of the allegation. FRCP 8(b)(2).

      iii. *General and specific denials.* A party that intends in good faith to deny all the allegations of a pleading—including the jurisdictional grounds—may do so by a general denial. A party that does not intend to deny all the allegations must either specifically deny designated allegations or generally deny all except those specifically admitted. FRCP 8(b)(3).

      iv. *Denying part of an allegation.* A party that intends in good faith to deny only part of an allegation must admit the part that is true and deny the rest. FRCP 8(b)(4).

      v. *Lacking knowledge or information.* A party that lacks knowledge or information sufficient to form a belief about the truth of an allegation must so state, and the statement has the effect of a denial. FRCP 8(b)(5).

         • An answer merely stating that the defendant lacks knowledge to form a belief as to the plaintiff's allegations, and making no statement as to his or her lack of information, has been held to be insufficient, the court suggesting that the phrase might be used in an attempt to mask the defendant's inability to make a good-faith denial of the allegations. FEDPROC § 62:73; Gilbert v. Johnston, 127 F.R.D. 145 (N.D.Ill. 1989).

vi. *Effect of failing to deny.* An allegation—other than one relating to the amount of damages—is admitted if a responsive pleading is required and the allegation is not denied. If a responsive pleading is not required, an allegation is considered denied or avoided. FRCP 8(b)(6).

b. *Affirmative defenses.* In responding to a pleading, a party must affirmatively state any avoidance or affirmative defense, including: (1) accord and satisfaction; (2) arbitration and award; (3) assumption of risk; (4) contributory negligence; (5) duress; (6) estoppel; (7) failure of consideration; (8) fraud; (9) illegality; (10) injury by fellow servant; (11) laches; (12) license; (13) payment; (14) release; (15) res judicata; (16) statute of frauds; (17) statute of limitations; and (18) waiver. FRCP 8(c)(1).

   i. *Mistaken designation.* If a party mistakenly designates a defense as a counterclaim, or a counterclaim as a defense, the court must, if justice requires, treat the pleading as though it were correctly designated, and may impose terms for doing so. FRCP 8(c)(2).

c. *How to present defenses.* Every defense to a claim for relief in any pleading must be asserted in the responsive pleading if one is required. But a party may assert the following defenses by motion: (1) lack of subject-matter jurisdiction; (2) lack of personal jurisdiction; (3) improper venue; (4) insufficient process; (5) insufficient service of process; (6) failure to state a claim upon which relief can be granted; and (7) failure to join a party under FRCP 19. FRCP 12(b).

   i. A motion asserting any of these defenses must be made before pleading if a responsive pleading is allowed. If a pleading sets out a claim for relief that does not require a responsive pleading, an opposing party may assert at trial any defense to that claim. FRCP 12(b).

   ii. Refer to the United States District Court for the Southern District of New York KeyRules Motion to Dismiss for Lack of Subject Matter Jurisdiction, Motion to Dismiss for Lack of Personal Jurisdiction, Motion to Dismiss for Improper Venue, and Motion to Dismiss for Failure to State a Claim documents for more information on motions under FRCP 12(b)(1), FRCP 12(b)(2), FRCP 12(b)(3), and FRCP 12(b)(6).

d. *Waiving and preserving certain defenses.* No defense or objection is waived by joining it with one or more other defenses or objections in a responsive pleading or in a motion. FRCP 12(b).

   i. *When some are waived.* A party waives any defense listed in FRCP 12(b)(2) through FRCP 12(b)(5) by:

   - Omitting it from a motion in the circumstances described in FRCP 12(g)(2); or
   - Failing to either: (1) make it by motion under FRCP 12; or (2) include it in a responsive pleading or in an amendment allowed by FRCP 15(a)(1) as a matter of course. FRCP 12(h)(1).

   ii. *When to raise others.* Failure to state a claim upon which relief can be granted, to join a person required by FRCP 19(b), or to state a legal defense to a claim may be raised:

   - In any pleading allowed or ordered under FRCP 7(a);
   - By a motion under FRCP 12(c); or
   - At trial. FRCP 12(h)(2).

   iii. *Lack of subject matter jurisdiction.* If the court determines at any time that it lacks subject-matter jurisdiction, the court must dismiss the action. FRCP 12(h)(3).

4. *Counterclaim and crossclaim*

a. *Compulsory counterclaim*

   i. *In general.* A pleading must state as a counterclaim any claim that—at the time of its service—the pleader has against an opposing party if the claim:

   - Arises out of the transaction or occurrence that is the subject matter of the opposing party's claim; and
   - Does not require adding another party over whom the court cannot acquire jurisdiction. FRCP 13(a)(1).

   ii. *Exceptions.* The pleader need not state the claim if:

   - When the action was commenced, the claim was the subject of another pending action; or

- The opposing party sued on its claim by attachment or other process that did not establish personal jurisdiction over the pleader on that claim, and the pleader does not assert any counterclaim under FRCP 13. FRCP 13(a)(2).

b. *Permissive counterclaim.* A pleading may state as a counterclaim against an opposing party any claim that is not compulsory. FRCP 13(b).

c. *Relief sought in a counterclaim.* A counterclaim need not diminish or defeat the recovery sought by the opposing party. It may request relief that exceeds in amount or differs in kind from the relief sought by the opposing party. FRCP 13(c).

d. *Counterclaim against the United States.* The Federal Rules of Civil Procedure do not expand the right to assert a counterclaim—or to claim a credit—against the United States or a United States officer or agency. FRCP 13(d).

e. *Counterclaim maturing or acquired after pleading.* The court may permit a party to file a supplemental pleading asserting a counterclaim that matured or was acquired by the party after serving an earlier pleading. FRCP 13(e).

f. *Crossclaim against a coparty.* A pleading may state as a crossclaim any claim by one party against a coparty if the claim arises out of the transaction or occurrence that is the subject matter of the original action or of a counterclaim, or if the claim relates to any property that is the subject matter of the original action. The crossclaim may include a claim that the coparty is or may be liable to the cross-claimant for all or part of a claim asserted in the action against the cross-claimant. FRCP 13(g).

g. *Joining additional parties.* FRCP 19 and FRCP 20 govern the addition of a person as a party to a counterclaim or crossclaim. FRCP 13(h).

h. *Separate trials; Separate judgments.* If the court orders separate trials under FRCP 42(b), it may enter judgment on a counterclaim or crossclaim under FRCP 54(b) when it has jurisdiction to do so, even if the opposing party's claims have been dismissed or otherwise resolved. FRCP 13(i).

5. *Third-party practice*

   a. *Timing of the summons and complaint.* A defending party may, as third-party plaintiff, serve a summons and complaint on a nonparty who is or may be liable to it for all or part of the claim against it. But the third-party plaintiff must, by motion, obtain the court's leave if it files the third-party complaint more than fourteen (14) days after serving its original answer. FRCP 14(a)(1).

   b. *Third-party defendant's claims and defenses.* The person served with the summons and third-party complaint—the "third-party defendant":

      i. Must assert any defense against the third-party plaintiff's claim under FRCP 12;

      ii. Must assert any counterclaim against the third-party plaintiff under FRCP 13(a), and may assert any counterclaim against the third-party plaintiff under FRCP 13(b) or any crossclaim against another third-party defendant under FRCP 13(g);

      iii. May assert against the plaintiff any defense that the third-party plaintiff has to the plaintiff's claim; and

      iv. May also assert against the plaintiff any claim arising out of the transaction or occurrence that is the subject matter of the plaintiff's claim against the third-party plaintiff. FRCP 14(a)(2).

   c. For more information on third-party practice, refer to FRCP 14.

6. *Right to a jury trial; Demand*

   a. *Right preserved.* The right of trial by jury as declared by U.S.C.A. Const. Amend. VII, or as provided by a federal statute, is preserved to the parties inviolate. FRCP 38(a).

   b. *Demand.* On any issue triable of right by a jury, a party may demand a jury trial by:

      i. Serving the other parties with a written demand—which may be included in a pleading—no later than fourteen (14) days after the last pleading directed to the issue is served; and

      ii. Filing the demand in accordance with FRCP 5(d). FRCP 38(b).

   c. *Specifying issues.* In its demand, a party may specify the issues that it wishes to have tried by a jury;

otherwise, it is considered to have demanded a jury trial on all the issues so triable. If the party has demanded a jury trial on only some issues, any other party may—within fourteen (14) days after being served with the demand or within a shorter time ordered by the court—serve a demand for a jury trial on any other or all factual issues triable by jury. FRCP 38(c).

d. *Waiver; Withdrawal.* A party waives a jury trial unless its demand is properly served and filed. A proper demand may be withdrawn only if the parties consent. FRCP 38(d).

e. *Admiralty and maritime claims.* The rules in FRCP 38 do not create a right to a jury trial on issues in a claim that is an admiralty or maritime claim under FRCP 9(h). FRCP 38(e).

7. *Complex civil cases.* For information on procedures for complex civil cases, refer to NY R USDCTSD Order 11 Misc 00388.

8. *Related cases.* It shall be the continuing duty of each attorney appearing in any civil or criminal case to bring promptly to the attention of the Court all facts which said attorney believes are relevant to a determination that said case and one or more pending civil or criminal cases should be heard by the same Judge, in order to avoid unnecessary duplication of judicial effort. As soon as the attorney becomes aware of such relationship, said attorney shall notify the Judges to whom the cases have been assigned. NY R USDCTS&ED Civ Rule 1.6(a). If counsel fails to comply with NY R USDCTS&ED Civ Rule 1.6(a), the Court may assess reasonable costs directly against counsel whose action has obstructed the effective administration of the Court's business. NY R USDCTS&ED Civ Rule 1.6(b).

a. *Determination of relatedness.* Subject to the limitations set forth in NY R USDCTSD Div. Bus., Rule 13(a)(2), a civil case, bankruptcy appeal, or motion to withdraw the bankruptcy reference will be deemed related to one or more civil cases, appeals or motions when the interests of justice and efficiency will be served. In determining relatedness, a judge will consider whether (A) the actions concern the same or substantially similar parties, property, transactions or events; (B) there is substantial factual overlap; (C) the parties could be subjected to conflicting orders; and (D) whether absent a determination of relatedness there would be a substantial duplication of effort and expense, delay, or undue burden on the Court, parties or witnesses. NY R USDCTSD Div. Bus., Rule 13(a)(1). Nothing in this NY R USDCTSD Div. Bus., Rule 13 is intended to preclude parties from moving for consolidated proceedings under FRCP 42. NY R USDCTSD Div. Bus., Rule 13(a)(1). Notwithstanding NY R USDCTSD Div. Bus., Rule 13(a)(1):

    i. Civil cases shall not be deemed related merely because they involve common legal issues or the same parties. NY R USDCTSD Div. Bus., Rule 13(a)(2)(A).

    ii. Other than cases subject to NY R USDCTSD Div. Bus., Rule 4(b) and actions seeking the enforcement of a judgment or settlement in or of an earlier case, civil cases presumptively shall not be deemed related unless both cases are pending before the Court (or the earlier case is on appeal). NY R USDCTSD Div. Bus., Rule 13(a)(2)(B).

b. *Procedure in regard to cases said to be related*

    i. *Disclosure of contention of relatedness.* When a civil case is filed or removed or a bankruptcy appeal or motion to withdraw the reference of an adversary proceeding from the bankruptcy court is filed, the person filing or removing shall disclose on form JSC44C any contention of relatedness and shall file a Related Case Statement stating clearly and succinctly the basis for the contention. A copy of the civil cover sheet and Related Case Statement shall be served with the complaint, notice of removal, notice of appeal, or motion. Any party may contest a claim of relatedness by any other in writing addressed to the judge having the case with the lowest docket number of all cases claimed to be related. However, the foregoing shall not delay the assignment process or the operation of NY R USDCTSD Div. Bus., Rule 13. NY R USDCTSD Div. Bus., Rule 13(b)(1). [Editor's note: the reference to form JSC44C is likely meant to be form JS44C-SDNY: Civil Court Cover Sheet].

    ii. *Claims of relatedness by other parties.* A party other than the one filing a case, bankruptcy appeal or motion to withdraw the reference that contends its case is related to another may so advise in writing the judge assigned in its case and request a transfer of its case to the judge that the party contends has the related case with the lowest docket number. If the assigned judge believes the case is related under NY R USDCTSD Div. Bus., Rule 13(a), he or she shall refer the question to the judge having the case with the lowest docket number. In the event the latter judge agrees, the case shall be transferred to that judge unless the Assignment Committee disagrees. NY R USDCTSD Div. Bus., Rule 13(b)(3).

   c. For more information on related cases, refer to NY R USDCTSD Div. Bus., Rule 13.

9. *Alternative dispute resolution (ADR).* The U.S. District Court for the Southern District of New York provides litigants with opportunities to discuss settlement through judicial settlement conferences and mediation. NY R USDCTS&ED Civ Rule 83.9(a).

   a. *Consideration of alternative dispute resolution.* In all civil cases, including those eligible for mediation pursuant to NY R USDCTS&ED Civ Rule 83.9(e), each party shall consider the use of mediation or a judicial settlement conference and shall report to the assigned Judge at the initial FRCP 16(b) case management conference, or subsequently, whether the party believes mediation or a judicial settlement conference may facilitate the resolution of the lawsuit. Judges are encouraged to note the availability of the mediation program and/or a judicial settlement conference before, at, or after the initial FRCP 16(b) case management conference. NY R USDCTS&ED Civ Rule 83.9(d).

   b. *Mediation.* In mediation, parties and counsel meet, sometimes collectively and sometimes individually, with a neutral third party (the mediator) who has been trained to facilitate confidential settlement discussions. The parties articulate their respective positions and interests and generate options for a mutually agreeable resolution to the dispute. The mediator assists the parties in reaching their own negotiated settlement by defining the issues, probing and assessing the strengths and weaknesses of each party's legal positions, and identifying areas of agreement and disagreement. The main benefits of mediation are that it can result in an expeditious and less costly resolution of the litigation, and can produce creative solutions to complex disputes often unavailable in traditional litigation. NY R USDCTS&ED Civ Rule 83.9(b).

      i. *Mediation program eligibility.* All civil cases other than Social Security, habeas corpus, and tax cases are eligible for mediation, whether assigned to Manhattan or White Plains. NY R USDCTS&ED Civ Rule 83.9(e)(1).

- The Board of Judges may, by Administrative Order, direct that certain specified categories of cases shall automatically be submitted to the mediation program. The assigned District Judge or Magistrate Judge may issue a written order exempting a particular case with or without the request of the parties. NY R USDCTS&ED Civ Rule 83.9(e)(2).

- For all other cases, the assigned District Judge or Magistrate Judge may determine that a case is appropriate for mediation and may order that case to mediation, with or without the consent of the parties, before, at, or after the initial FRCP 16(b) case management conference. Alternatively, the parties should notify the assigned Judge at any time of their desire to mediate. NY R USDCTS&ED Civ Rule 83.9(e)(3).

   c. *Judicial settlement conferences.* Judicial settlement conferences may be ordered by District Judges or Magistrate Judges with or without the request or consent of the parties. NY R USDCTS&ED Civ Rule 83.9(f).

   d. For more information on alternative dispute resolution (ADR), refer to NY R USDCTS&ED Civ Rule 83.9.

10. *Individual judge practices.* Refer to the Miscellaneous section of this document for information on individual judge practices on general requirements for documents.

## D. Documents

1. *Required documents*

   a. *Answer.* Refer to the General Requirements section of this document for information on the form and contents of the answer.

   b. *Certificate of service.* FRCP 5(d) requires that the person making service under FRCP 5 certify that service has been effected. FRCP 5(Advisory Committee Notes). Having such information on file may be useful for many purposes, including proof of service if an issue arises concerning the effectiveness of the service. FRCP 5(Advisory Committee Notes).

    i.   Such paper service [on attorneys and pro se parties who are not Filing or Receiving Users] must be documented by electronically filing proof of service. NY R USDCTSD CM/ECF, S.D.(I)(9)(9.2); NY R USDCTSD CM/ECF, S.D.(I)(19)(19.3)(b). Pro se parties who are not Filing Users are exempt from that portion of NY R USDCTSD CM/ECF, S.D.(I)(19)(19.3) requiring proof of service to be filed electronically. NY R USDCTSD CM/ECF, S.D.(I)(19)(19.3).

2.  *Supplemental documents*

    a.  *Waiver of the service of summons.* An individual, corporation, or association that is subject to service under FRCP 4(e), FRCP 4(f), or FRCP 4(h) has a duty to avoid unnecessary expenses of serving the summons. FRCP 4(d)(1). Waiving service of a summons does not waive any objection to personal jurisdiction or to venue. FRCP 4(d)(5). If a defendant located within the United States fails, without good cause, to sign and return a waiver requested by a plaintiff located within the United States, the court must impose on the defendant:

        i.   The expenses later incurred in making service; and

        ii.  The reasonable expenses, including attorney's fees, of any motion required to collect those service expenses. FRCP 4(d)(2).

    b.  *Notice of constitutional question.* A party that files a pleading, written motion, or other paper drawing into question the constitutionality of a federal or state statute must promptly:

        i.   *File notice.* File a notice of constitutional question stating the question and identifying the paper that raises it, if:

- A federal statute is questioned and the parties do not include the United States, one of its agencies, or one of its officers or employees in an official capacity; or

- A state statute is questioned and the parties do not include the state, one of its agencies, or one of its officers or employees in an official capacity; and

        ii.  *Serve notice.* Serve the notice and paper on the Attorney General of the United States if a federal statute is questioned—or on the state attorney general if a state statute is questioned—either by certified or registered mail or by sending it to an electronic address designated by the attorney general for this purpose. FRCP 5.1(a).

        iii.  *No forfeiture.* A party's failure to file and serve the notice, or the court's failure to certify, does not forfeit a constitutional claim or defense that is otherwise timely asserted. FRCP 5.1(d).

    c.  *Notice of issue concerning foreign law.* A party who intends to raise an issue about a foreign country's law must give notice by a pleading or other writing. In determining foreign law, the court may consider any relevant material or source, including testimony, whether or not submitted by a party or admissible under the Federal Rules of Evidence. The court's determination must be treated as a ruling on a question of law. FRCP 44.1.

    d.  *Nongovernmental corporate disclosure statement*

        i.   *Contents.* A nongovernmental corporate party must file two (2) copies of a disclosure statement that:

- Identifies any parent corporation and any publicly held corporation owning ten percent (10%) or more of its stock; or

- States that there is no such corporation. FRCP 7.1(a).

        ii.  *Time to file; Supplemental filing.* A party must:

- File the disclosure statement with its first appearance, pleading, petition, motion, response, or other request addressed to the court; and

- Promptly file a supplemental statement if any required information changes. FRCP 7.1(b). For purposes of FRCP 7.1(b)(2), "promptly" shall mean "within fourteen days," that is, parties are required to file a supplemental disclosure statement within fourteen (14) days of the time there is any change in the information required in a disclosure statement filed pursuant to those rules. NY R USDCTS&ED Civ Rule 7.1.1.

e. *Statement explaining untimely electronic filing.* If you missed a filing deadline when the ECF system was out of order, attach a statement to your filing explaining how the interruption in service prevented you from filing in a timely fashion. NY R USDCTSD CM/ECF, S.D.(II)(23)(23.5).

f. *Courtesy copies.* Read the judge's Individual Practices to learn if courtesy copies are required. NY R USDCTSD CM/ECF, S.D.(II)(13)(13.17). Judges' Individual Practices should continue to be followed with respect to delivery of courtesy copies. NY R USDCTSD CM/ECF, S.D.(I)(3)(3.4).

3. *Individual judge practices.* Refer to the Miscellaneous section of this document for information on individual judge practices on required documents.

## E. Format

1. *Form of documents*

   a. *Paper.* Every pleading, written motion, and other paper must: be plainly written, typed, printed, or copied without erasures or interlineations which materially deface it. NY R USDCTS&ED Civ Rule 11.1(a)(1).

   b. *Typeface, margin, and spacing.* The typeface, margins, and spacing of all documents presented for filing must meet the following requirements:

      i. All text must be twelve (12) point type or larger, except for text in footnotes which may be ten (10) point type;

      ii. All documents must have at least one (1) inch margins on all sides;

      iii. All text must be double-spaced, except for headings, text in footnotes, or block quotations, which may be single-spaced. NY R USDCTS&ED Civ Rule 11.1(b).

   c. *Caption; Names of parties.* Every pleading must have a caption with the court's name, a title, a file number, and a FRCP 7(a) designation. The title of the complaint must name all the parties; the title of other pleadings, after naming the first party on each side, may refer generally to other parties. FRCP 10(a). Every pleading, written motion, and other paper must: bear the docket number and the initials of the District Judge and any Magistrate Judge before whom the action or proceeding is pending, NY R USDCTS&ED Civ Rule 11.1(a)(2).

   d. *Paragraphs; Separate statements.* A party must state its claims or defenses in numbered paragraphs, each limited as far as practicable to a single set of circumstances. A later pleading may refer by number to a paragraph in an earlier pleading. If doing so would promote clarity, each claim founded on a separate transaction or occurrence—and each defense other than a denial—must be stated in a separate count or defense. FRCP 10(b).

   e. *Adoption by reference; Exhibits.* A statement in a pleading may be adopted by reference elsewhere in the same pleading or in any other pleading or motion. A copy of a written instrument that is an exhibit to a pleading is a part of the pleading for all purposes. FRCP 10(c).

   f. *Acceptance by the clerk.* The clerk must not refuse to file a paper solely because it is not in the form prescribed by the Federal Rules of Civil Procedure or by a local rule or practice. FRCP 5(d)(4).

2. *Form of electronic documents*

   a. *PDF-A.* All documents electronically filed on the ECF system must be in PDF-A format (portable document format). A PDF-A file is created using PDF writer software such as Adobe Acrobat (go to the Adobe website for details). PDF-A files cannot be altered, providing security to the filer and the Court. NY R USDCTSD CM/ECF, S.D.(II)(23)(23.2).

   b. *Size limitation.* No single PDF file may be larger than four megabytes (4 MB). If the filing is too large, the ECF system will not allow it to be filed, and you will not see a Notice of Electronic Filing (NEF or filing receipt) screen. To determine the size of an Adobe Acrobat PDF file click on File, Document Properties, Summary. NY R USDCTSD CM/ECF, S.D.(II)(23)(23.3).

      i. Converting documents directly from a word processor to PDF-A format creates the smallest possible file in terms of computer memory. If that is not possible, scan your document at low resolution. Within the Adobe Acrobat program, on the "Scan Manager" screen, adjust the settings for black and white and 200 dpi (dots per inch). This allows more pages to fit into a single PDF-A file. If that does not work, separate an oversized file into 2 or more parts. Simply label each file 1a, 1b, 1c, etc. Only relevant excerpts of exhibits should be electronically filed. NY R USDCTSD CM/ECF, S.D.(II)(23)(23.4).

c. *Attachments and exhibits.* Filing Users must submit in electronic form all documents referenced as exhibits or attachments, unless the Court permits paper filing. NY R USDCTSD CM/ECF, S.D.(I)(5)(5.1).

   i. A Filing User must submit as exhibits or attachments only those excerpts of the referenced documents that are relevant to the matter under consideration by the Court. Excerpted material must be clearly and prominently identified as such. Filing Users who file excerpts of documents as exhibits or attachments under this procedure do so without prejudice to their right to file timely additional excerpts or the complete document. Responding parties may file timely additional excerpts that they believe are relevant or the complete document. A party may move before the Court for permission to serve and file in hard copy documents that cannot be reasonably scanned. NY R USDCTSD CM/ECF, S.D.(I)(5)(5.2).

   ii. Exhibits must be filed only as attachments to a document, such as a motion or an affidavit. Do not use the ECF Filing Event for "Motion" to file exhibits separately. Exhibits are the only items that should be attached to electronically filed documents. You are limited to electronically filing only relevant excerpts of exhibits. Excerpts must be clearly identified as such. If the exhibit is too large to be scanned and electronically filed you may contact the ECF Help Desk. NY R USDCTSD CM/ECF, S.D.(II)(15)(15.6).

d. *Letters.* Parties should consult the assigned judge's Individual Practices to determine if the judge accepts letters at all and, if he or she does, whether the judge has any page limitations on letters and/or requires courtesy copies of letters filed on ECF (and, if so, by what means of delivery). All letters addressed to the Court must include a subject line with the case name and docket number (e.g., "Re: Doe v. Smith, 13 Civ. 1234 (ABC)"). NY R USDCTSD CM/ECF, S.D.(II)(13)(13.1).

e. *Proposed orders, proposed judgments, stipulations and consents.* Any document that requires the signature of a judge should not be electronically filed except as an exhibit to another document. Proposed orders, judgments, stipulations and consents should not be submitted through the ECF system. Instead they should be sent by e-mail to the Clerk. Proposed orders should be submitted in word processing format (WordPerfect or Word) rather than as a PDF document. Stipulations should be submitted in PDF-A format. Stipulations must contain ink signatures not s/. Faxed or emailed signatures are acceptable. Please note that Stipulations of Voluntary Dismissal pursuant to FRCP 41(a)(1)(A)(ii) do not require the signature of a judge and must be electronically filed on the ECF system. Questions may be directed to the Orders and Judgments Clerk at the phone numbers listed in NY R USDCTSD CM/ECF, S.D.(II)(18)(18.3). NY R USDCTSD CM/ECF, S.D.(II)(18)(18.3).

   i. Email the proposed order, judgment or stipulation to the email addresses listed in NY R USDCTSD CM/ECF, S.D.(II)(18)(18.3). NY R USDCTSD CM/ECF, S.D.(II)(18)(18.3).

   ii. Pro se litigants who are not Filing Users are exempt from that portion of NY R USDCTSD CM/ECF, S.D.(II)(18)(18.3) that requires litigants to email proposed orders, judgments, stipulations and consents, and shall deliver such documents to the Clerk's Office in paper form. NY R USDCTSD CM/ECF, S.D.(II)(18)(18.3).

3. *Signing of pleadings, motions and other papers*

   a. *Signature.* Every pleading, written motion, and other paper must be signed by at least one attorney of record in the attorney's name—or by a party personally if the party is unrepresented. The paper must state the signer's address, e-mail address, and telephone number. FRCP 11(a). Every pleading, written motion, and other paper must: have the name of each person signing it clearly printed or typed directly below the signature. NY R USDCTS&ED Civ Rule 11.1(a)(3).

      i. *Electronic signatures.* The user log-in and password required to submit documents to the ECF

system serve as the Filing User's signature on all electronic documents filed with the Court. NY R USDCTSD CM/ECF, S.D.(I)(8)(8.1); NY R USDCTSD CM/ECF, S.D.(II)(13)(13.14). They also serve as a signature for purposes of the Federal Rules of Civil Procedure, including FRCP 11, the Local Civil Rules of the United States District Courts for the Southern and Eastern Districts of New York, and any other purpose for which a signature is required in connection with proceedings before the Court. NY R USDCTSD CM/ECF, S.D.(I)(8)(8.1).

- *Signature block.* Electronically filed documents must include a signature block and must set forth the name, address, telephone number and e-mail address all in compliance with the Federal Rules of Civil Procedure and NY R USDCTS&ED Civ Rule 11.1. In the absence of a scanned signature image, the name of the Filing User under whose log-in and password the document is submitted must be preceded by an "s/" typed in the space where the signature would otherwise appear. NY R USDCTSD CM/ECF, S.D.(I)(8)(8.2); NY R USDCTSD CM/ECF, S.D.(II)(13)(13.14).

- *Documents requiring the signature of a party or witness.* A document requiring the signature of a party or witness shall be electronically filed in a scanned format that contains an image of the actual signature. NY R USDCTSD CM/ECF, S.D.(I)(8)(8.4); NY R USDCTSD CM/ECF, S.D.(II)(13)(13.14).

- *Documents requiring the signature of a judge.* A Filing User submitting a document electronically that requires a judge's signature must promptly deliver the document in such other form, if any, as the Court requires. NY R USDCTSD CM/ECF, S.D.(I)(4)(4.2).

- *Documents requiring multiple signatures.* Documents requiring signatures of more than one party must be electronically filed either by: (a) submitting a scanned document containing all necessary signatures; (b) representing the consent of the other parties on the document; (c) identifying on the document the parties whose signatures are required and by the submission of a notice of endorsement by the other parties no later than three business days after filing; or (d) in any other manner approved by the Court. NY R USDCTSD CM/ECF, S.D.(I)(8)(8.5).

ii. *No verification or accompanying affidavit required for pleadings.* Unless a rule or statute specifically states otherwise, a pleading need not be verified or accompanied by an affidavit. FRCP 11(a).

iii. *Unsigned papers.* The court must strike an unsigned paper unless the omission is promptly corrected after being called to the attorney's or party's attention. FRCP 11(a).

b. *Representations to the court.* By presenting to the court a pleading, written motion, or other paper—whether by signing, filing, submitting, or later advocating it—an attorney or unrepresented party certifies that to the best of the person's knowledge, information, and belief, formed after an inquiry reasonable under the circumstances:

i. It is not being presented for any improper purpose, such as to harass, cause unnecessary delay, or needlessly increase the cost of litigation;

ii. The claims, defenses, and other legal contentions are warranted by existing law or by a nonfrivolous argument for extending, modifying, or reversing existing law or for establishing new law;

iii. The factual contentions have evidentiary support or, if specifically so identified, will likely have evidentiary support after a reasonable opportunity for further investigation or discovery; and

iv. The denials of factual contentions are warranted on the evidence or, if specifically so identified, are reasonably based on belief or a lack of information. FRCP 11(b).

c. *Sanctions.* If, after notice and a reasonable opportunity to respond, the court determines that FRCP 11(b) has been violated, the court may impose an appropriate sanction on any attorney, law firm, or party that violated FRCP 11(b) or is responsible for the violation. FRCP 11(c)(1). Refer to the United States District Court for the Southern District of New York KeyRules Motion for Sanctions document for more information.

4. *Privacy protection for filings made with the court*

a. *Redacted filings.* Unless the court orders otherwise, in an electronic or paper filing with the court that contains an individual's Social Security number, taxpayer-identification number, or birth date, the name of an individual known to be a minor, or a financial-account number, a party or nonparty making the filing may include only:

    i. The last four (4) digits of the Social Security number and taxpayer-identification number;

    ii. The year of the individual's birth;

    iii. The minor's initials; and

    iv. The last four (4) digits of the financial-account number. FRCP 5.2(a); NY R USDCTSD CM/ECF, S.D.(II)(21)(21.3).

    v. Caution should be exercised when filing documents that contain the following:

       • Personal identifying numbers (PIN #'s), such as a driver's license number;

       • Medical records, treatment and diagnosis;

       • Employment history;

       • Individual financial information;

       • Proprietary or trade secret information;

       • Information regarding an individual's cooperation with the government. NY R USDCTSD CM/ECF, S.D.(II)(21)(21.4).

b. *Exemptions from the redaction requirement.* The redaction requirement does not apply to the following:

    i. A financial-account number that identifies the property allegedly subject to forfeiture in a forfeiture proceeding;

    ii. The record of an administrative or agency proceeding;

    iii. The official record of a state-court proceeding;

    iv. The record of a court or tribunal, if that record was not subject to the redaction requirement when originally filed;

    v. A filing covered by FRCP 5.2(c) or FRCP 5.2(d); and

    vi. A pro se filing in an action brought under 28 U.S.C.A. § 2241, 28 U.S.C.A. § 2254, or 28 U.S.C.A. § 2255. FRCP 5.2(b).

c. *Limitations on remote access to electronic files; Social Security appeals and immigration cases.* Unless the court orders otherwise, in an action for benefits under the Social Security Act, and in an action or proceeding relating to an order of removal, to relief from removal, or to immigration benefits or detention, access to an electronic file is authorized as follows:

    i. The parties and their attorneys may have remote electronic access to any part of the case file, including the administrative record;

    ii. Any other person may have electronic access to the full record at the courthouse, but may have remote electronic access only to:

       • The docket maintained by the court; and

       • An opinion, order, judgment, or other disposition of the court, but not any other part of the case file or the administrative record. FRCP 5.2(c).

d. *Filings made under seal.* The court may order that a filing be made under seal without redaction. The court may later unseal the filing or order the person who made the filing to file a redacted version for the public record. FRCP 5.2(d). For more information on sealing documents, refer to NY R USDCTSD CM/ECF, S.D.(I)(6).

e. *Protective orders.* For good cause, the court may by order in a case:

    i. Require redaction of additional information; or

ii. Limit or prohibit a nonparty's remote electronic access to a document filed with the court. FRCP 5.2(e).

f. *Option for additional unredacted filing under seal.* A person making a redacted filing may also file an unredacted copy under seal. The court must retain the unredacted copy as part of the record. FRCP 5.2(f); NY R USDCTSD CM/ECF, S.D.(II)(21)(21.5).

g. *Option for filing a reference list.* A filing that contains redacted information may be filed together with a reference list that identifies each item of redacted information and specifies an appropriate identifier that uniquely corresponds to each item listed. The list must be filed under seal and may be amended as of right. Any reference in the case to a listed identifier will be construed to refer to the corresponding item of information. FRCP 5.2(g); NY R USDCTSD CM/ECF, S.D.(II)(21)(21.5).

h. *Responsibility for redaction.* It is the sole responsibility of counsel and the parties to be sure that all documents comply with the rules of this Court requiring redaction of personal identifiers. Neither the judge nor the Clerk of Court will review documents for compliance with these rules. NY R USDCTSD CM/ECF, S.D.(II)(21)(21.2).

i. *Waiver of protection of identifiers.* A person waives the protection of FRCP 5.2(a) as to the person's own information by filing it without redaction and not under seal. FRCP 5.2(h).

j. For more information on privacy and public access to ECF cases, refer to NY R USDCTSD CM/ECF, S.D.(II)(21).

5. *Individual judge practices.* Refer to the Miscellaneous section of this document for information on individual judge practices on formatting documents.

## F. Filing and Service Requirements

1. *Filing requirements.* Any paper after the complaint that is required to be served—together with a certificate of service—must be filed within a reasonable time after service. FRCP 5(d)(1). Complaints and all subsequent papers are accepted at either courthouse, regardless of the place for which the case is designated. NY R USDCTSD Div. Bus., Rule 22.

a. *How filing is made; In general.* A paper is filed by delivering it:

i. To the clerk; or

ii. To a judge who agrees to accept it for filing, and who must then note the filing date on the paper and promptly send it to the clerk. FRCP 5(d)(2).

b. *Night depository.* A night depository with an automatic date stamp shall be maintained by the Clerk of the Southern District in the Pearl Street Courthouse. After regular business hours, papers for the District Court only may be deposited in the night depository. Such papers will be considered as having been filed in the District Court as of the date stamped thereon, which shall be deemed presumptively correct. NY R USDCTS&ED Civ Rule 1.2.

c. *Electronic filing*

i. *Authorization of electronic filing program.* A court may, by local rule, allow papers to be filed, signed, or verified by electronic means that are consistent with any technical standards established by the Judicial Conference of the United States. A local rule may require electronic filing only if reasonable exceptions are allowed. A paper filed electronically in compliance with a local rule is a written paper for purposes of the Federal Rules of Civil Procedure. FRCP 5(d)(3).

- The Court will accept for filing documents submitted, signed or verified by electronic means, that comply with the rules in NY R USDCTSD CM/ECF, S.D. NY R USDCTSD CM/ECF, S.D.(I). The information in NY R USDCTSD CM/ECF, S.D. applies only to cases assigned to the ECF system. NY R USDCTSD CM/ECF, S.D.(Introduction).

- Parties serving and filing papers shall follow the instructions regarding Electronic Case Filing (ECF) published on the website of each respective Court. A paper served and filed by electronic means in accordance with such instructions is, for purposes of FRCP 5, served and filed in compliance with the Local Civil Rules of the Southern and Eastern

Districts of New York. NY R USDCTS&ED Civ Rule 5.2(a). Parties have an obligation to review the Court's actual order, decree, or judgment (on ECF), which controls, and should not rely on the description on the docket or in the ECF Notice of Electronic Filing (NEF). NY R USDCTS&ED Civ Rule 5.2(c).

- The following should be observed when filing electronically: (1) the Federal Rules of Civil Procedure, (2) the Local Civil Rules of the United States District Courts for the Southern and Eastern Districts of New York, (3) the assigned judge's Individual Practices, and (4) the Court's Electronic Case Filing Rules & Instructions (NY R USDCTSD CM/ECF, S.D.). NY R USDCTSD CM/ECF, S.D.(Introduction).

ii.  *Scope of electronic filing.* Except as expressly provided and in exceptional circumstances preventing a party from filing electronically, all documents required to be filed with the Court must be filed electronically. Any party unable to comply with this requirement must seek permission of the Court to file in the traditional manner, on paper. Any such application made after regular business hours may be submitted through the night depository box maintained pursuant to NY R USDCTS&ED Civ Rule 1.2. NY R USDCTSD CM/ECF, S.D.(I)(1)(1.1).

- *Documents filed by pro se litigants.* Unless otherwise ordered by the Court, documents filed by pro se litigants must be filed in the traditional manner, on paper, and will be scanned and docketed by the Clerk's Office into the ECF system. NY R USDCTSD CM/ECF, S.D.(I)(1)(1.1). Pro se litigants must file pleadings and documents in the traditional manner on paper unless the assigned judge has granted permission to electronically file on the ECF system. NY R USDCTSD CM/ECF, S.D.(Introduction).

- *Letters.* Except for letters to be filed under seal, letters addressed to judges who accept letters may be filed electronically. Parties should consult the assigned judge's Individual Practices to determine if the judge accepts letters at all and, if he or she does, whether the judge has any page limitations on letters and/or requires courtesy copies of letters filed on ECF (and, if so, by what means of delivery). NY R USDCTSD CM/ECF, S.D.(II)(13)(13.1). Letters solely between parties or their counsel or otherwise not addressed to the Court may not be filed electronically on ECF (except as exhibits to an otherwise properly filed document). NY R USDCTSD CM/ECF, S.D.(II)(13)(13.1). For more information on filing letters, refer to NY R USDCTSD CM/ECF, S.D.(II)(13)(13.1).

- *Proposed orders, judgments and decrees.* Proposed orders, judgments and decrees shall be presented as directed by the ECF rules published on the website of each respective Court. NY R USDCTS&ED Civ Rule 77.1. For more information, refer to NY R USDCTS&ED Civ Rule 77.1.

iii.  *Exceptions to electronic filing.* In an ECF case, the documents that should not be electronically filed include:

- Miscellaneous Case initiating documents, NY R USDCTSD CM/ECF, S.D.(II)(18)(18.2);
- Proposed orders; proposed judgments, stipulations; consents, NY R USDCTSD CM/ECF, S.D.(II)(18)(18.3);
- Orders to show cause / temporary restraining orders, NY R USDCTSD CM/ECF, S.D.(II)(18)(18.4);
- Sealed documents, NY R USDCTSD CM/ECF, S.D.(II)(18)(18.5); and
- Surety bonds, NY R USDCTSD CM/ECF, S.D.(II)(18)(18.6).
- In cases where the record of an administrative or other prior proceeding must be filed with the Court, such record may be served and filed in hard copy without prior motion and order of the Court. NY R USDCTSD CM/ECF, S.D.(I)(5)(5.3).
- For more documents excepted from electronic filing, and for more information on such documents, refer to NY R USDCTSD CM/ECF, S.D.(II)(18).

iv.  *Consequences of electronic filing.* Except as otherwise provided in NY R USDCTSD CM/ECF, S.D.(I)(4), electronic filing of a document in the ECF system consistent with these procedures, together with the transmission of a Notice of Electronic Filing (NEF) from the Court, constitutes filing of the document for all purposes of the Federal Rules of Civil Procedure and the Local Civil Rules of the United States District Courts for the Southern and Eastern Districts of New York and constitutes entry of the document on the docket kept by the Clerk under FRCP 58 and FRCP 79. NY R USDCTSD CM/ECF, S.D.(I)(3)(3.1).

    v. For more information on electronic filing, refer to NY R USDCTSD CM/ECF, S.D.

2. *Service requirements*

  a. *Service; When required*

    i. *In general.* Unless the Federal Rules of Civil Procedure provide otherwise, each of the following papers must be served on every party:

- An order stating that service is required;
- A pleading filed after the original complaint, unless the court orders otherwise under FRCP 5(c) because there are numerous defendants;
- A discovery paper required to be served on a party, unless the court orders otherwise;
- A written motion, except one that may be heard ex parte; and
- A written notice, appearance, demand, or offer of judgment, or any similar paper. FRCP 5(a)(1).

    ii. *If a party fails to appear.* No service is required on a party who is in default for failing to appear. But a pleading that asserts a new claim for relief against such a party must be served on that party under FRCP 4. FRCP 5(a)(2).

    iii. *Seizing property.* If an action is begun by seizing property and no person is or need be named as a defendant, any service required before the filing of an appearance, answer, or claim must be made on the person who had custody or possession of the property when it was seized. FRCP 5(a)(3).

  b. *Service; How made*

    i. *Serving an attorney.* If a party is represented by an attorney, service under FRCP 5 must be made on the attorney unless the court orders service on the party. FRCP 5(b)(1).

    ii. *Service in general.* A paper is served under FRCP 5 by:

- Handing it to the person;
- Leaving it: (1) at the person's office with a clerk or other person in charge or, if no one is in charge, in a conspicuous place in the office; or (2) if the person has no office or the office is closed, at the person's dwelling or usual place of abode with someone of suitable age and discretion who resides there;
- Mailing it to the person's last known address—in which event service is complete upon mailing;
- Leaving it with the court clerk if the person has no known address;
- Sending it by electronic means if the person consented in writing—in which event service is complete upon transmission, but is not effective if the serving party learns that it did not reach the person to be served; or
- Delivering it by any other means that the person consented to in writing—in which event service is complete when the person making service delivers it to the agency designated to make delivery. FRCP 5(b)(2).

    iii. *Service by overnight delivery.* Service upon an attorney may be made by overnight delivery service. "Overnight delivery service" means any delivery service which regularly accepts items for overnight delivery. Overnight delivery service shall be deemed service by mail for purposes of FRCP 5 and FRCP 6. NY R USDCTS&ED Civ Rule 5.3.

    iv. *Service by electronic means.* Parties serving and filing papers shall follow the instructions regarding Electronic Case Filing (ECF) published on the website of each respective Court. A paper served and filed by electronic means in accordance with such instructions is, for purposes of FRCP 5, served and filed in compliance with the Local Civil Rules of the United States District Courts for the Southern and Eastern Districts of New York. NY R USDCTS&ED Civ Rule 5.2(a). Parties have an obligation to review the Court's actual order, decree, or judgment (on ECF), which controls, and should not rely on the description on the docket or in the ECF Notice of Electronic Filing (NEF). NY R USDCTS&ED Civ Rule 5.2(c).

- *Notice of electronic filing (NEF).* In cases assigned to the ECF system, service is complete provided all parties receive a Notice of Electronic Filing (NEF), which is sent automatically by email from the Court (see the NEF for a list of who did/did not receive notice electronically). Transmission of the NEF constitutes service upon all Filing and Receiving Users who are listed as recipients of notice by electronic mail. NY R USDCTSD CM/ECF, S.D.(I)(9)(9.1). In cases assigned to the ECF system, if all parties receive a NEF, service is complete upon transmission of the NEF by the Court, and you are not required to serve a paper copy. NY R USDCTSD CM/ECF, S.D.(II)(19)(19.2). It remains the duty of Filing and Receiving Users to maintain current contact information with the court and to regularly review the docket sheet of the case. NY R USDCTSD CM/ECF, S.D.(I)(9)(9.1).

- *Mailing of court-initiated documents.* The Clerk's Office will no longer mail paper copies of court-initiated documents to Filing and Receiving Users. The Clerk's Office will mail copies of all court-initiated documents to pro se parties who have not registered as Filing or Receiving Users. NY R USDCTSD CM/ECF, S.D.(II)(19)(19.1).

- *No receipt of a NEF.* If any party does not receive a NEF, you are required to accomplish service on that party in the traditional manner, in paper form. NY R USDCTSD CM/ECF, S.D.(II)(19)(19.2). The NEF receipt will inform you who will receive notice of the filing "electronically" (by e-mail from the Court) and who will receive notice "by other means" (traditional service in paper form). NY R USDCTSD CM/ECF, S.D.(II)(19)(19.2).

- *Service on non-filing or non-receiving users.* Attorneys and pro se parties who are not Filing or Receiving Users must be served with a paper copy of any electronically filed pleading or other document. Service of such paper copy must be made according to the Federal Rules of Civil Procedure and the Local Civil Rules of the United States District Courts for the Southern and Eastern Districts of New York. NY R USDCTSD CM/ECF, S.D.(I)(9)(9.2). Such paper service must be documented by electronically filing proof of service. NY R USDCTSD CM/ECF, S.D.(I)(9)(9.2); NY R USDCTSD CM/ECF, S.D.(II)(19)(19.2). Where the Clerk scans and electronically files pleadings and documents on behalf of a pro se party, the associated NEF constitutes service. NY R USDCTSD CM/ECF, S.D.(I)(9)(9.2).

- For more information on service by electronic means, refer to NY R USDCTSD CM/ECF, S.D.(II)(19).

    v. *Using court facilities.* If a local rule so authorizes, a party may use the court's transmission facilities to make service under FRCP 5(b)(2)(E). FRCP 5(b)(3).

  c. *Serving numerous defendants*

    i. *In general.* If an action involves an unusually large number of defendants, the court may, on motion or on its own, order that:

- Defendants' pleadings and replies to them need not be served on other defendants;

- Any crossclaim, counterclaim, avoidance, or affirmative defense in those pleadings and replies to them will be treated as denied or avoided by all other parties; and

- Filing any such pleading and serving it on the plaintiff constitutes notice of the pleading to all parties. FRCP 5(c)(1).

    ii. *Notifying parties.* A copy of every such order must be served on the parties as the court directs. FRCP 5(c)(2).

3. *Individual judge practices.* Refer to the Miscellaneous section of this document for information on individual judge practices on filing and serving documents.

ANSWER

## G. Hearings

1. *Hearing on FRCP 12 defenses before trial.* If a party so moves, any defense listed in FRCP 12(b)(1) through FRCP 12(b)(7)—whether made in a pleading or by motion—and a motion under FRCP 12(c) must be heard and decided before trial unless the court orders a deferral until trial. FRCP 12(i).

2. *Individual judge practices.* Refer to the Miscellaneous section of this document for information on individual judge practices on hearings.

## H. Forms

### 1. Official Federal Answer Forms

   a. Rule 4 waiver of the service of summons. FRCP 4.

### 2. Federal Answer Forms

   a. Generally. 2B FEDFORMS § 8:10.

   b. Introduction to separate defenses. 2B FEDFORMS § 8:11.

   c. Presenting defenses. 2B FEDFORMS § 8:12.

   d. With counterclaim for interpleader. 2B FEDFORMS § 8:13.

   e. Denials and admissions. 2B FEDFORMS § 8:14.

   f. Denials, admissions and affirmative defenses. 2B FEDFORMS § 8:15.

   g. Separate answer of two defendants; Duty of fair representation. 2B FEDFORMS § 8:16.

   h. Separate answer of third defendant. 2B FEDFORMS § 8:17.

   i. Reciting paragraphs and subparagraphs of complaint; Account malpractice. 2B FEDFORMS § 8:18.

   j. One of multiple defendants. 2B FEDFORMS § 8:21.

   k. Answer to complaint for employment discrimination. 2B FEDFORMS § 8:22.

   l. Denial of particular averment. 2B FEDFORMS § 8:24.

   m. Admission of particular averment. 2B FEDFORMS § 8:25.

   n. Denial of all averments of paragraph. 2B FEDFORMS § 8:26.

   o. Admission of all averments of paragraph. 2B FEDFORMS § 8:27.

   p. Denial in part and admission in part of paragraph. 2B FEDFORMS § 8:28.

   q. General denial. 2B FEDFORMS § 8:29.

   r. Qualified general denial. 2B FEDFORMS § 8:30.

   s. Denial of knowledge or information sufficient to form a belief. 2B FEDFORMS § 8:31.

   t. Denial of jurisdictional allegations; Jurisdictional amount. 2B FEDFORMS § 8:32.

   u. Denial of jurisdictional allegations; Federal question. 2B FEDFORMS § 8:34.

   v. Denial of jurisdictional allegations; Diversity of citizenship. 2B FEDFORMS § 8:37.

   w. Contributory negligence. 2B FEDFORMS § 8:58.

   x. Fraud. 2B FEDFORMS § 8:74.

   y. Mistake. 2B FEDFORMS § 8:85.

   z. Statute of limitations. 2B FEDFORMS § 8:103.

## I. Applicable Rules

1. *Federal rules*

   a. Summons. FRCP 4.

   b. Serving and filing pleadings and other papers. FRCP 5.

   c. Constitutional challenge to a statute; Notice, certification, and intervention. FRCP 5.1.

   d. Privacy protection for filings made with the court. FRCP 5.2.

    e.   Computing and extending time; Time for motion papers. FRCP 6.

    f.   Pleadings allowed; Form of motions and other papers. FRCP 7.

    g.   Disclosure statement. FRCP 7.1.

    h.   General rules of pleading. FRCP 8.

    i.   Pleading special matters. FRCP 9.

    j.   Form of pleadings. FRCP 10.

    k.   Signing pleadings, motions, and other papers; Representations to the court; Sanctions. FRCP 11.

    l.   Defenses and objections; When and how presented; Motion for judgment on the pleadings; Consolidating motions; Waiving defenses; Pretrial hearing. FRCP 12.

    m.   Counterclaim and crossclaim. FRCP 13.

    n.   Third-party practice. FRCP 14.

    o.   Right to a jury trial; Demand. FRCP 38.

    p.   Determining foreign law. FRCP 44.1.

2.  *Local rules*

    a.   Night depository. NY R USDCTS&ED Civ Rule 1.2.

    b.   Duty of attorneys in related cases. NY R USDCTS&ED Civ Rule 1.6.

    c.   Electronic service and filing of documents. NY R USDCTS&ED Civ Rule 5.2.

    d.   Service by overnight delivery. NY R USDCTS&ED Civ Rule 5.3.

    e.   Computation of time. NY R USDCTS&ED Civ Rule 6.4.

    f.   Disclosure statement. NY R USDCTS&ED Civ Rule 7.1.1.

    g.   Form of pleadings, motions, and other papers. NY R USDCTS&ED Civ Rule 11.1.

    h.   Submission of orders, judgments and decrees. NY R USDCTS&ED Civ Rule 77.1.

    i.   Alternative dispute resolution (Southern District only). NY R USDCTS&ED Civ Rule 83.9.

    j.   Electronic case filing rules and instructions. NY R USDCTSD CM/ECF, S.D.

    k.   Related cases. NY R USDCTSD Div. Bus., Rule 13.

    l.   Filing at either courthouse. NY R USDCTSD Div. Bus., Rule 22.

## J. Miscellaneous

**NOTE: Individual judges' rules may apply. For available judge-level information, refer to:**

DISTRICT JUDGE RONNIE ABRAMS: NY R USDCTSD Abrams-Civ Prac; NY R USDCTSD Abrams-Crim Prac; NY R USDCTSD Abrams-Pro Se; NY R USDCTSD Abrams-Case Mgt; NY R USDCTSD Abrams-Jury.

DISTRICT JUDGE DEBORAH A. BATTS: NY R USDCTSD Batts-Practices.

DISTRICT JUDGE RICHARD M. BERMAN: NY R USDCTSD Berman-Practices; NY R USDCTSD Berman-Default; NY R USDCTSD Berman-Sentencing; NY R USDCTSD Berman-Media.

DISTRICT JUDGE VINCENT L. BRICCETTI: NY R USDCTSD Briccetti-Practices; NY R USDCTSD Briccetti-Plan; NY R USDCTSD Briccetti-Notice.

DISTRICT JUDGE VERNON S. BRODERICK: NY R USDCTSD Broderick-Civil; NY R USDCTSD Broderick-Crim; NY R USDCTSD Broderick-Case Mgt; NY R USDCTSD Broderick-Jury.

DISTRICT JUDGE NAOMI REICE BUCHWALD: NY R USDCTSD Buchwald-Practices.

DISTRICT JUDGE VALERIE E. CAPRONI: NY R USDCTSD Caproni-Prac; NY R USDCTSD Caproni--Pro Se; NY R USDCTSD Caproni-Case Mgt; NY R USDCTSD Caproni-Crim Prac.

DISTRICT JUDGE ANDREW L. CARTER JR.: NY R USDCTSD Carter-Practices.

DISTRICT JUDGE KEVIN P. CASTEL: NY R USDCTSD Castel-Practices; NY R USDCTSD Castel-Default;

NY R USDCTSD Castel-Scheduling; NY R USDCTSD Castel-Complex; NY R USDCTSD Castel-Trials; NY R USDCTSD Castel-Sentencing.

DISTRICT JUDGE DENISE L. COTE: NY R USDCTSD Cote-Civil Practices; NY R USDCTSD Cote-Pro Se; NY R USDCTSD Cote-Maritime Ord; NY R USDCTSD Cote-Crim Practices; NY R USDCTSD Cote-Crim Trials; NY R USDCTSD Cote-Sentencing.

DISTRICT JUDGE PAUL A. CROTTY: NY R USDCTSD Crotty-Practices; NY R USDCTSD Crotty-Sentencing; NY R USDCTSD Crotty-Calls; NY R USDCTSD Crotty-Scheduling.

DISTRICT JUDGE GEORGE B. DANIELS: NY R USDCTSD Daniels-Practices.

DISTRICT JUDGE KEVIN T. DUFFY: NY R USDCTSD Duffy-Practices.

DISTRICT JUDGE PAUL A. ENGELMAYER: NY R USDCTSD Engelmayer-Practices; NY R USDCTSD Engelmayer-Scheduling; NY R USDCTSD Engelmayer-Sentencing; NY R USDCTSD Engelmayer-Pro Se; NY R USDCTSD Engelmayer-Crim.

DISTRICT JUDGE KATHERINE POLK FAILLA: NY R USDCTSD Failla-Civ Prac; NY R USDCTSD Failla-Crim Prac; NY R USDCTSD Failla-Case Mgt.

DISTRICT JUDGE KATHERINE B. FORREST: NY R USDCTSD Forrest-Civil Prac; NY R USDCTSD Forrest-Crim Prac; NY R USDCTSD Forrest-Crim Pretrial; NY R USDCTSD Forrest-Scheduling; NY R USDCTSD Forrest-Patent Scheduling; NY R USDCTSD Forrest-Sentencing; NY R USDCTSD Forrest-Order 1; NY R USDCTSD Forrest-Order 2.

DISTRICT JUDGE JESSE M. FURMAN: NY R USDCTSD Furman-Civil Prac; NY R USDCTSD Furman-Crim Prac; NY R USDCTSD Furman-Pro Se Prac; NY R USDCTSD Furman-Trials; NY R USDCTSD Furman-Scheduling; NY R USDCTSD Furman-Rights.

DISTRICT JUDGE PAUL G. GARDEPHE: NY R USDCTSD Gardephe-Civ Prac; NY R USDCTSD Gardephe-Pretrial; NY R USDCTSD Gardephe-Prot Ord; NY R USDCTSD Gardephe-Maritime; NY R USDCTSD Gardephe-Crim Prac; NY R USDCTSD Gardephe-Trial.

DISTRICT JUDGE THOMAS P. GRIESA: NY R USDCTSD Griesa-Practices.

DISTRICT JUDGE CHARLES S. HAIGHT: NY R USDCTSD Haight-Practices.

DISTRICT JUDGE ALVIN K. HELLERSTEIN: NY R USDCTSD Hellerstein-Practices; NY R USDCTSD Hellerstein--Sept 11.

DISTRICT JUDGE LEWIS A. KAPLAN: NY R USDCTSD Kaplan-Practices; NY R USDCTSD Kaplan-Sentencing.

DISTRICT JUDGE KENNETH M. KARAS: NY R USDCTSD Karas-Practices; NY R USDCTSD Karas-Case Mgt; NY R USDCTSD Karas-Default; NY R USDCTSD Karas-Sentencing; NY R USDCTSD Karas-Rights.

DISTRICT JUDGE JOHN F. KEENAN: NY R USDCTSD Keenan-Practices.

DISTRICT JUDGE JOHN G. KOELTL: NY R USDCTSD Koeltl-Practices.

DISTRICT JUDGE VICTOR MARRERO: NY R USDCTSD Marrero-Practices; NY R USDCTSD Marrero-Scheduling; NY R USDCTSD Marrero-Default; NY R USDCTSD Marrero-Trial Proc.

DISTRICT JUDGE COLLEEN McMAHON: NY R USDCTSD McMahon-Practices; NY R USDCTSD McMahon-RICO; NY R USDCTSD McMahon-Copies; NY R USDCTSD McMahon-Scheduling; NY R USDCTSD McMahon-Elec Disc; NY R USDCTSD McMahon-Sentencing.

DISTRICT JUDGE ALISON J. NATHAN: NY R USDCTSD Nathan-Civ Prac; NY R USDCTSD Nathan-Crim Prac; NY R USDCTSD Nathan-Pro Se; NY R USDCTSD Nathan-Scheduling.

DISTRICT JUDGE J. PAUL OETKEN: NY R USDCTSD Oetken-Civ Prac; NY R USDCTSD Oetken-Case Mgt; NY R USDCTSD Oetken-Crim Prac; NY R USDCTSD Oetken-Pro Se.

DISTRICT JUDGE WILLIAM H. PAULEY, III: NY R USDCTSD Pauley-Crim Cases; NY R USDCTSD Pauley-Practices.

DISTRICT JUDGE LORETTA A. PRESKA: NY R USDCTSD Preska-Practices.

DISTRICT JUDGE JED S. RAKOFF: NY R USDCTSD Rakoff-Practices; NY R USDCTSD Rakoff-Scheduling; NY R USDCTSD Rakoff-Prot Ord; NY R USDCTSD Rakoff-Maritime Ord.

DISTRICT JUDGE EDGARDO RAMOS: NY R USDCTSD Ramos--Practices; NY R USDCTSD Ramos-Case Mgt.

DISTRICT JUDGE NELSON S. ROMAN: NY R USDCTSD Roman-Civ Prac; NY R USDCTSD Roman-Pro Se; NY R USDCTSD Roman-Crim Prac; NY R USDCTSD Roman-Case Mgt.

DISTRICT JUDGE LEONARD B. SAND: NY R USDCTSD Sand-Practices.

DISTRICT JUDGE LORNA G. SCHOFIELD: NY R USDCTSD Schofield-Civ Prac; NY R USDCTSD Schofield-Crim Prac; NY R USDCTSD Schofield-Sched; NY R USDCTSD Schofield-Pro Se; NY R USDCTSD Schofield-Advice.

DISTRICT JUDGE CATHY SEIBEL: NY R USDCTSD Seibel-Practices.

DISTRICT JUDGE LOUIS L. STANTON: NY R USDCTSD Stanton-Practices; NY R USDCTSD Stanton-Pretrial.

DISTRICT JUDGE SIDNEY H. STEIN: NY R USDCTSD Stein-Practices.

DISTRICT JUDGE RICHARD J. SULLIVAN: NY R USDCTSD Sullivan-Practices; NY R USDCTSD Sullivan-Scheduling; NY R USDCTSD Sullivan-Sentencing; NY R USDCTSD Sullivan-Juries; NY R USDCTSD Sullivan-Trial; NY R USDCTSD Sullivan-Default.

DISTRICT JUDGE LAURA TAYLOR SWAIN: NY R USDCTSD Swain-Practices; NY R USDCTSD Swain-Trial; NY R USDCTSD Swain-Crim Trial; NY R USDCTSD Swain-Juries; NY R USDCTSD Swain-Sentencing; NY R USDCTSD Swain-Rights.

DISTRICT JUDGE ROBERT W. SWEET: NY R USDCTSD Sweet-Practices.

DISTRICT JUDGE ANALISA TORRES: NY R USDCTSD Torres-Civ Prac; NY R USDCTSD Torres-Pro Se; NY R USDCTSD Torres-Scheduling.

DISTRICT JUDGE KIMBA M. WOOD: NY R USDCTSD Wood-Practices; NY R USDCTSD Wood-Scheduling; NY R USDCTSD Wood-Discovery; NY R USDCTSD Wood-RICO; NY R USDCTSD Wood-Juries; NY R USDCTSD Wood-Trial; NY R USDCTSD Wood-Media.

DISTRICT JUDGE GREGORY H. WOODS: NY R USDCTSD Woods-Civ Prac; NY R USDCTSD Woods-Pro Se; NY R USDCTSD Woods-Sched; NY R USDCTSD Woods-Crim Prac; NY R USDCTSD Woods-Protect Order; NY R USDCTSD Woods-Speedy Trial.

MAGISTRATE JUDGE JAMES L. COTT: NY R USDCTSD Cott-Practices; NY R USDCTSD Cott-Settlement.

MAGISTRATE JUDGE PAUL E. DAVISON: NY R USDCTSD Davison-Practices.

MAGISTRATE JUDGE RONALD L. ELLIS: NY R USDCTSD Ellis-Practices.

MAGISTRATE JUDGE KEVIN N. FOX: NY R USDCTSD Fox-Practices; NY R USDCTSD Fox-Settlement.

MAGISTRATE JUDGE JAMES C. FRANCIS: NY R USDCTSD Francis-Practices.

MAGISTRATE JUDGE DEBRA FREEMAN: NY R USDCTSD Freeman-Practices; NY R USDCTSD Freeman-Settlement.

MAGISTRATE JUDGE GABRIEL W. GORENSTEIN: NY R USDCTSD Gorenstein-Practices; NY R US-DCTSD Gorenstein-Ackn.

MAGISTRATE JUDGE FRANK MAAS: NY R USDCTSD Maas-Practices; NY R USDCTSD Maas-Discontinuance; NY R USDCTSD Maas-Conf; NY R USDCTSD Maas-Settlement.

MAGISTRATE JUDGE JUDITH C. McCARTHY: NY R USDCTSD McCarthy-Practices; NY R USDCTSD McCarthy-Conduct.

MAGISTRATE JUDGE BARBARA MOSES: NY R USDCTSD Moses-Practices.

MAGISTRATE JUDGE SARAH NETBURN: NY R USDCTSD Netburn-Civil; NY R USDCTSD Netburn-Settlement; NY R USDCTSD Netburn-Case Mgt; NY R USDCTSD Netburn--Pro Se.

MAGISTRATE JUDGE ANDREW J. PECK: NY R USDCTSD Peck-Practices; NY R USDCTSD Peck-Order; NY R USDCTSD Peck-Rule 502(d).

MAGISTRATE JUDGE HENRY PITMAN: NY R USDCTSD Pitman-Practices.

MAGISTRATE JUDGE LISA MARGARET SMITH: NY R USDCTSD Smith-Practices; NY R USDCTSD Smith-Trials.

# Pleadings
# Amended Pleading

**Document Last Updated September 2016**

## A. Checklist

(I) ❑ Matters to be considered by plaintiff or defendant

    (a) ❑ Required documents

        (1) ❑ Amended pleading

        (2) ❑ Certificate of service

    (b) ❑ Supplemental documents

        (1) ❑ Notice of constitutional question

        (2) ❑ Notice of issue concerning foreign law

        (3) ❑ Statement explaining untimely electronic filing

        (4) ❑ Courtesy copies

    (c) ❑ Timing

        (1) ❑ A party may amend its pleading once as a matter of course within:

            (i) ❑ Twenty-one (21) days after serving it, or

            (ii) ❑ If the pleading is one to which a responsive pleading is required, twenty-one (21) days after service of a responsive pleading or twenty-one (21) days after service of a motion under FRCP 12(b), FRCP 12(e), or FRCP 12(f), whichever is earlier

## B. Timing

1. *Amended pleading*

    a. *Amending as a matter of course.* A party may amend its pleading once as a matter of course within:

       i.  Twenty-one (21) days after serving it, or

      ii.  If the pleading is one to which a responsive pleading is required, twenty-one (21) days after service of a responsive pleading or twenty-one (21) days after service of a motion under FRCP 12(b), FRCP 12(e), or FRCP 12(f), whichever is earlier. FRCP 15(a)(1).

    b. *Extension of time.* If the time for serving the responsive pleading is extended by a motion for enlargement of time under FRCP 6(b), or by a stipulation, the period for amending as of right also may be enlarged. FPP § 1480.

    c. *Other amendments.* In all other cases, a party may amend its pleading only with the opposing party's written consent or the court's leave. The court should freely give leave when justice so requires. FRCP 15(a)(2). Refer to the United States District Court for the Southern District of New York KeyRules Motion for Leave to Amend document for more information.

2. *Time to respond to an amended pleading.* Unless the court orders otherwise, any required response to an amended pleading must be made within the time remaining to respond to the original pleading or within fourteen (14) days after service of the amended pleading, whichever is later. FRCP 15(a)(3).

3. *Computation of time*

    a. *Computing time.* FRCP 6 applies in computing any time period specified in the Federal Rules of Civil Procedure, in any local rule or court order, or in any statute that does not specify a method of computing time. FRCP 6(a). In computing any period of time prescribed or allowed by the Local Civil Rules of the United States District Courts for the Southern and Eastern Districts of New York or the Local Admiralty and Maritime Rules, the provisions of FRCP 6 shall apply unless otherwise stated. NY R USDCTS&ED Civ Rule 6.4.

i. *Period stated in days or a longer unit.* When the period is stated in days or a longer unit of time:

- Exclude the day of the event that triggers the period;

- Count every day, including intermediate Saturdays, Sundays, and legal holidays; and

- Include the last day of the period, but if the last day is a Saturday, Sunday, or legal holiday, the period continues to run until the end of the next day that is not a Saturday, Sunday, or legal holiday. FRCP 6(a)(1). In the Local Civil Rules of the United States District Courts for the Southern and Eastern Districts of New York, as in the Federal Rules of Civil Procedure as amended effective December 1, 2009, Saturdays, Sundays, and legal holidays are no longer excluded in computing periods of time. If the last day of the period is a Saturday, Sunday, or legal holiday, the period continues to run until the end of the next day that is not a Saturday, Sunday, or legal holiday. NY R USDCTS&ED Civ Rule 6.4.

ii. *Period stated in hours.* When the period is stated in hours:

- Begin counting immediately on the occurrence of the event that triggers the period;

- Count every hour, including hours during intermediate Saturdays, Sundays, and legal holidays; and

- If the period would end on a Saturday, Sunday, or legal holiday, the period continues to run until the same time on the next day that is not a Saturday, Sunday, or legal holiday. FRCP 6(a)(2). In the Local Civil Rules of the United States District Courts for the Southern and Eastern Districts of New York, as in the Federal Rules of Civil Procedure as amended effective December 1, 2009, Saturdays, Sundays, and legal holidays are no longer excluded in computing periods of time. If the last day of the period is a Saturday, Sunday, or legal holiday, the period continues to run until the end of the next day that is not a Saturday, Sunday, or legal holiday. NY R USDCTS&ED Civ Rule 6.4.

iii. *Inaccessibility of the clerk's office.* Unless the court orders otherwise, if the clerk's office is inaccessible:

- On the last day for filing under FRCP 6(a)(1), then the time for filing is extended to the first accessible day that is not a Saturday, Sunday, or legal holiday; or

- During the last hour for filing under FRCP 6(a)(2), then the time for filing is extended to the same time on the first accessible day that is not a Saturday, Sunday, or legal holiday. FRCP 6(a)(3).

iv. *"Last day" defined.* Unless a different time is set by a statute, local rule, or court order, the last day ends:

- For electronic filing, at midnight in the court's time zone; and

- For filing by other means, when the clerk's office is scheduled to close. FRCP 6(a)(4).

v. *"Next day" defined.* The "next day" is determined by continuing to count forward when the period is measured after an event and backward when measured before an event. FRCP 6(a)(5).

vi. *"Legal holiday" defined.* "Legal holiday" means:

- The day set aside by statute for observing New Year's Day, Martin Luther King Jr.'s Birthday, Washington's Birthday, Memorial Day, Independence Day, Labor Day, Columbus Day, Veterans' Day, Thanksgiving Day, or Christmas Day;

- Any day declared a holiday by the President or Congress; and

- For periods that are measured after an event, any other day declared a holiday by the state where the district court is located. FRCP 6(a)(6).

b. *Computation of electronic filing deadlines.* You can file electronically twenty-four (24) hours a day, seven (7) days a week, three hundred sixty-five (365) days a year. NY R USDCTSD CM/ECF, S.D.(II)(13)(13.10). Electronic filing must be completed before midnight local time where the Court is located in order to be considered timely filed that day. NY R USDCTSD CM/ECF, S.D.(I)(3)(3.3); NY R USDCTSD CM/ECF, S.D.(II)(13)(13.10); NY R USDCTSD CM/ECF, S.D.(II)(19)(19.4). An electronically filed document is deemed filed on the "filed on" date indicated on the Notice of Electronic Filing (NEF). NY R USDCTSD CM/ECF, S.D.(II)(13)(13.11).

    i. *Technical failures.* A Filing User whose filing is made untimely as the result of a technical failure may seek appropriate relief from the Court. NY R USDCTSD CM/ECF, S.D.(I)(11). If you missed a filing deadline when the ECF system was out of order, attach a statement to your filing explaining how the interruption in service prevented you from filing in a timely fashion. NY R USDCTSD CM/ECF, S.D.(II)(23)(23.5).

  c. *Extending time*

    i. *In general.* When an act may or must be done within a specified time, the court may, for good cause, extend the time:

- With or without motion or notice if the court acts, or if a request is made, before the original time or its extension expires; or

- On motion made after the time has expired if the party failed to act because of excusable neglect. FRCP 6(b)(1).

    ii. *Exceptions.* A court must not extend the time to act under FRCP 50(b), FRCP 50(d), FRCP 52(b), FRCP 59(b), FRCP 59(d), FRCP 59(e), and FRCP 60(b). FRCP 6(b)(2).

    iii. Refer to the United States District Court for the Southern District of New York KeyRules Motion for Continuance/Extension of Time document for more information on extending time.

  d. *Additional time after certain kinds of service.* When a party may or must act within a specified time after service and service is made under FRCP 5(b)(2)(C), FRCP 5(b)(2)(D), FRCP 5(b)(2)(E), or FRCP 5(b)(2)(F), three (3) days are added after the period would otherwise expire under FRCP 6(a). FRCP 6(d). Overnight delivery service shall be deemed service by mail for purposes of FRCP 5 and FRCP 6. NY R USDCTS&ED Civ Rule 5.3.

4. *Individual judge practices.* Refer to the Miscellaneous section of this document for information on individual judge practices on timing of documents.

## C. General Requirements

1. *Pleading, generally*

  a. *Pleadings allowed.* Only these pleadings are allowed: (1) a complaint; (2) an answer to a complaint; (3) an answer to a counterclaim designated as a counterclaim; (4) an answer to a crossclaim; (5) a third-party complaint; (6) an answer to a third-party complaint; and (7) if the court orders one, a reply to an answer. FRCP 7(a).

  b. *Pleading to be concise and direct.* Each allegation must be simple, concise, and direct. No technical form is required. FRCP 8(d)(1).

  c. *Alternative statements of a claim or defense.* A party may set out two or more statements of a claim or defense alternatively or hypothetically, either in a single count or defense or in separate ones. If a party makes alternative statements, the pleading is sufficient if any one of them is sufficient. FRCP 8(d)(2).

  d. *Inconsistent claims or defenses.* A party may state as many separate claims or defenses as it has, regardless of consistency. FRCP 8(d)(3).

  e. *Construing pleadings.* Pleadings must be construed so as to do justice. FRCP 8(e).

2. *Pleading special matters*

  a. *Capacity or authority to sue; Legal existence*

    i. *In general.* Except when required to show that the court has jurisdiction, a pleading need not allege:

- A party's capacity to sue or be sued;

- A party's authority to sue or be sued in a representative capacity; or

- The legal existence of an organized association of persons that is made a party. FRCP 9(a)(1).

    ii.  *Raising those issues.* To raise any of those issues, a party must do so by a specific denial, which must state any supporting facts that are peculiarly within the party's knowledge. FRCP 9(a)(2).

  b.  *Fraud or mistake; Conditions of mind.* In alleging fraud or mistake, a party must state with particularity the circumstances constituting fraud or mistake. Malice, intent, knowledge, and other conditions of a person's mind may be alleged generally. FRCP 9(b).

  c.  *Conditions precedent.* In pleading conditions precedent, it suffices to allege generally that all conditions precedent have occurred or been performed. But when denying that a condition precedent has occurred or been performed, a party must do so with particularity. FRCP 9(c).

  d.  *Official document or act.* In pleading an official document or official act, it suffices to allege that the document was legally issued or the act legally done. FRCP 9(d).

  e.  *Judgment.* In pleading a judgment or decision of a domestic or foreign court, a judicial or quasi-judicial tribunal, or a board or officer, it suffices to plead the judgment or decision without showing jurisdiction to render it. FRCP 9(e).

  f.  *Time and place.* An allegation of time or place is material when testing the sufficiency of a pleading. FRCP 9(f).

  g.  *Special damages.* If an item of special damage is claimed, it must be specifically stated. FRCP 9(g).

  h.  *Admiralty or maritime claim*

    i.  *How designated.* If a claim for relief is within the admiralty or maritime jurisdiction and also within the court's subject-matter jurisdiction on some other ground, the pleading may designate the claim as an admiralty or maritime claim for purposes of FRCP 14(c), FRCP 38(e), and FRCP 82 and the Supplemental Rules for Admiralty or Maritime Claims and Asset Forfeiture Actions. A claim cognizable only in the admiralty or maritime jurisdiction is an admiralty or maritime claim for those purposes, whether or not so designated. FRCP 9(h)(1).

    ii.  *Designation for appeal.* A case that includes an admiralty or maritime claim within FRCP 9(h) is an admiralty case within 28 U.S.C.A. § 1292(a)(3). FRCP 9(h)(2).

3.  *Amended pleading*

  a.  *Amendments before trial.* The function of FRCP 15(a), which provides generally for the amendment of pleadings, is to enable a party to assert matters that were overlooked or were unknown at the time the party interposed the original complaint or answer. FPP § 1473; Smiga v. Dean Witter Reynolds, Inc., 766 F.2d 698, 703 (2d Cir. 1985).

    i.  *Matters contained in amended pleading under FRCP 15(a).* Although FRCP 15(a) does not expressly state that an amendment must contain only matters that occurred within a particular time period, FRCP 15(d) provides that any "transaction, occurrence, or event that happened after the date of the pleading" should be set forth in a supplemental pleading. FPP § 1473. Thus, impliedly, an amended pleading, whether prepared with or without leave of court, only should relate to matters that have taken place prior to the date of the earlier pleading. FPP § 1473; Ford Motor Co. v. U.S., 19 C.I.T. 946, 896 F.Supp. 1224, 1230 (1995).

    ii.  *Amending as a matter of course.* The right to amend as of course is not restricted to any particular litigant or pleading. FPP § 1480. It is a right conferred on all of the parties to an action and thus extends to persons who were not original parties to the litigation, but are brought into the action by way of counterclaim, crossclaim, third-party claim, or defensive interpleader. FPP § 1480; Johnson v. Walsh, 65 F.Supp. 157 (W.D.Mo. 1946).

      - *Amending a complaint with multiple defendants.* When a number of defendants are involved in an action, some of whom have answered and some of whom have filed no responsive pleading, the plaintiff can amend as a matter of course as to those defendants who have not answered. FEDPROC § 62:267; Pallant v. Sinatra, 7 F.R.D. 293 (S.D.N.Y. 1945). A plaintiff may not file an amended complaint as of right against those defendants who have not yet answered, if he or she has amended the complaint once already as a matter of course. FEDPROC § 62:267; Glaros v. Perse, 628 F.2d 679 (1st Cir. 1980).

iii. *Amending with leave of court.* Refer to the United States District Court for the Southern District of New York KeyRules Motion for Leave to Amend document for information on amending the pleadings with leave of court.

iv. *Types of amendments permitted under FRCP 15(a)*

- *Cure a defective pleading.* Perhaps the most common use of FRCP 15(a) is by a party seeking to amend in order to cure a defective pleading. FPP § 1474.

- *Correct insufficiently stated claims or defenses.* A more common use of FRCP 15(a) amendments is to correct insufficiently stated claims or defenses. Typically, amendments of this character involve either adding a necessary allegation in order to state a claim for relief or correcting a misnomer of a party to the action. FPP § 1474.

- *Change nature or theory of claim or capacity of party.* Courts also have allowed a party to amend in order to change the nature or theory of the party's claim or the capacity in which the party is bringing the action. FPP § 1474.

- *State additional claims or defenses or drop claims or defenses.* Plaintiffs and defendants also have been permitted to amend their pleadings to state additional claims, to assert additional defenses, or to drop claims or defenses. FPP § 1474; Weinberger v. Retail Credit Co., 498 F.2d 552, 554, n.4 (4th Cir. 1974).

- *Increase amount of damages or elect a different remedy.* A FRCP 15(a) amendment also is appropriate for increasing the amount of damages sought, or for electing a different remedy than the one originally requested. FPP § 1474; McFadden v. Sanchez, 710 F.2d 907 (2d Cir. 1983).

- *Add, substitute, or drop parties.* Finally, a party may make a FRCP 15(a) amendment to add, substitute, or drop parties to the action. FPP § 1474.

b. *Amendments during and after trial*

i. *Based on an objection at trial.* If, at trial, a party objects that evidence is not within the issues raised in the pleadings, the court may permit the pleadings to be amended. The court should freely permit an amendment when doing so will aid in presenting the merits and the objecting party fails to satisfy the court that the evidence would prejudice that party's action or defense on the merits. The court may grant a continuance to enable the objecting party to meet the evidence. FRCP 15(b)(1).

ii. *For issues tried by consent.* When an issue not raised by the pleadings is tried by the parties' express or implied consent, it must be treated in all respects as if raised in the pleadings. A party may move—at any time, even after judgment—to amend the pleadings to conform them to the evidence and to raise an unpleaded issue. But failure to amend does not affect the result of the trial of that issue. FRCP 15(b)(2).

iii. Refer to the United States District Court for the Southern District of New York KeyRules Motion for Leave to Amend document for more information on moving to amend the pleadings.

c. *Relation back of amendments*

i. *When an amendment relates back.* An amendment to a pleading relates back to the date of the original pleading when:

- The law that provides the applicable statute of limitations allows relation back;

- The amendment asserts a claim or defense that arose out of the conduct, transaction, or occurrence set out—or attempted to be set out—in the original pleading; or

- The amendment changes the party or the naming of the party against whom a claim is asserted, if FRCP 15(c)(1)(B) is satisfied and if, within the period provided by FRCP 4(m) for serving the summons and complaint, the party to be brought in by amendment: (1) received such notice of the action that it will not be prejudiced in defending on the merits; and (2) knew or should have known that the action would have been brought against it, but for a mistake concerning the proper party's identity. FRCP 15(c)(1).

ii.   *Notice to the United States.* When the United States or a United States officer or agency is added as a defendant by amendment, the notice requirements of FRCP 15(c)(1)(C)(i) and FRCP 15(c)(1)(C)(ii) are satisfied if, during the stated period, process was delivered or mailed to the United States attorney or the United States attorney's designee, to the Attorney General of the United States, or to the officer or agency. FRCP 15(c)(2).

d.   *Effect of an amended pleading.* A pleading that has been amended under FRCP 15(a) supersedes the pleading it modifies and remains in effect throughout the action unless it subsequently is modified. FPP § 1476. Once an amended pleading is interposed, the original pleading no longer performs any function in the case and any subsequent motion made by an opposing party should be directed at the amended pleading. FPP § 1476; Ferdik v. Bonzelet, 963 F.2d 1258, 1262 (9th Cir. 1992); Davis v. TXO Production Corp., 929 F.2d 1515, 1517 (10th Cir. 1991).

4.   *Amended complaint.* Refer to the United States District Court for the Southern District of New York KeyRules Complaint document for the requirements specific to the amended complaint.

5.   *Amended answer.* Refer to the United States District Court for the Southern District of New York KeyRules Answer document for the requirements specific to the amended answer.

6.   *Right to a jury trial; Demand*

a.   *Right preserved.* The right of trial by jury as declared by U.S.C.A. Const. Amend. VII, or as provided by a federal statute, is preserved to the parties inviolate. FRCP 38(a).

b.   *Demand.* On any issue triable of right by a jury, a party may demand a jury trial by:

i.   Serving the other parties with a written demand—which may be included in a pleading—no later than fourteen (14) days after the last pleading directed to the issue is served; and

ii.   Filing the demand in accordance with FRCP 5(d). FRCP 38(b).

c.   *Specifying issues.* In its demand, a party may specify the issues that it wishes to have tried by a jury; otherwise, it is considered to have demanded a jury trial on all the issues so triable. If the party has demanded a jury trial on only some issues, any other party may—within fourteen (14) days after being served with the demand or within a shorter time ordered by the court—serve a demand for a jury trial on any other or all factual issues triable by jury. FRCP 38(c).

d.   *Waiver; Withdrawal.* A party waives a jury trial unless its demand is properly served and filed. A proper demand may be withdrawn only if the parties consent. FRCP 38(d).

e.   *Admiralty and maritime claims.* The rules in FRCP 38 do not create a right to a jury trial on issues in a claim that is an admiralty or maritime claim under FRCP 9(h). FRCP 38(e).

7.   *Complex civil cases.* For information on procedures for complex civil cases, refer to NY R USDCTSD Order 11 Misc 00388.

8.   *Related cases.* It shall be the continuing duty of each attorney appearing in any civil or criminal case to bring promptly to the attention of the Court all facts which said attorney believes are relevant to a determination that said case and one or more pending civil or criminal cases should be heard by the same Judge, in order to avoid unnecessary duplication of judicial effort. As soon as the attorney becomes aware of such relationship, said attorney shall notify the Judges to whom the cases have been assigned. NY R USDCTS&ED Civ Rule 1.6(a). If counsel fails to comply with NY R USDCTS&ED Civ Rule 1.6(a), the Court may assess reasonable costs directly against counsel whose action has obstructed the effective administration of the Court's business. NY R USDCTS&ED Civ Rule 1.6(b).

a.   *Determination of relatedness.* Subject to the limitations set forth in NY R USDCTSD Div. Bus., Rule 13(a)(2), a civil case, bankruptcy appeal, or motion to withdraw the bankruptcy reference will be deemed related to one or more civil cases, appeals or motions when the interests of justice and efficiency will be served. In determining relatedness, a judge will consider whether (A) the actions concern the same or substantially similar parties, property, transactions or events; (B) there is substantial factual overlap; (C) the parties could be subjected to conflicting orders; and (D) whether absent a determination of relatedness there would be a substantial duplication of effort and expense, delay, or undue burden on the Court, parties or witnesses. NY R USDCTSD Div. Bus., Rule 13(a)(1). Nothing in this NY R USDCTSD Div. Bus., Rule 13 is intended to preclude parties from moving for consolidated proceedings under FRCP 42. NY R USDCTSD Div. Bus., Rule 13(a)(1). Notwith-standing NY R USDCTSD Div. Bus., Rule 13(a)(1):

    i.   Civil cases shall not be deemed related merely because they involve common legal issues or the same parties. NY R USDCTSD Div. Bus., Rule 13(a)(2)(A).

    ii.   Other than cases subject to NY R USDCTSD Div. Bus., Rule 4(b) and actions seeking the enforcement of a judgment or settlement in or of an earlier case, civil cases presumptively shall not be deemed related unless both cases are pending before the Court (or the earlier case is on appeal). NY R USDCTSD Div. Bus., Rule 13(a)(2)(B).

b.  *Procedure in regard to cases said to be related*

    i.   *Disclosure of contention of relatedness.* When a civil case is filed or removed or a bankruptcy appeal or motion to withdraw the reference of an adversary proceeding from the bankruptcy court is filed, the person filing or removing shall disclose on form JSC44C any contention of relatedness and shall file a Related Case Statement stating clearly and succinctly the basis for the contention. A copy of the civil cover sheet and Related Case Statement shall be served with the complaint, notice of removal, notice of appeal, or motion. Any party may contest a claim of relatedness by any other in writing addressed to the judge having the case with the lowest docket number of all cases claimed to be related. However, the foregoing shall not delay the assignment process or the operation of NY R USDCTSD Div. Bus., Rule 13. NY R USDCTSD Div. Bus., Rule 13(b)(1). [Editor's note: the reference to form JSC44C is likely meant to be form JS44C-SDNY: Civil Court Cover Sheet].

    ii.   *Claims of relatedness by other parties.* A party other than the one filing a case, bankruptcy appeal or motion to withdraw the reference that contends its case is related to another may so advise in writing the judge assigned in its case and request a transfer of its case to the judge that the party contends has the related case with the lowest docket number. If the assigned judge believes the case is related under NY R USDCTSD Div. Bus., Rule 13(a), he or she shall refer the question to the judge having the case with the lowest docket number. In the event the latter judge agrees, the case shall be transferred to that judge unless the Assignment Committee disagrees. NY R USDCTSD Div. Bus., Rule 13(b)(3).

c.  For more information on related cases, refer to NY R USDCTSD Div. Bus., Rule 13.

9.  *Alternative dispute resolution (ADR).* The U.S. District Court for the Southern District of New York provides litigants with opportunities to discuss settlement through judicial settlement conferences and mediation. NY R USDCTS&ED Civ Rule 83.9(a).

a.  *Consideration of alternative dispute resolution.* In all civil cases, including those eligible for mediation pursuant to NY R USDCTS&ED Civ Rule 83.9(e), each party shall consider the use of mediation or a judicial settlement conference and shall report to the assigned Judge at the initial FRCP 16(b) case management conference, or subsequently, whether the party believes mediation or a judicial settlement conference may facilitate the resolution of the lawsuit. Judges are encouraged to note the availability of the mediation program and/or a judicial settlement conference before, at, or after the initial FRCP 16(b) case management conference. NY R USDCTS&ED Civ Rule 83.9(d).

b.  *Mediation.* In mediation, parties and counsel meet, sometimes collectively and sometimes individually, with a neutral third party (the mediator) who has been trained to facilitate confidential settlement discussions. The parties articulate their respective positions and interests and generate options for a mutually agreeable resolution to the dispute. The mediator assists the parties in reaching their own negotiated settlement by defining the issues, probing and assessing the strengths and weaknesses of each party's legal positions, and identifying areas of agreement and disagreement. The main benefits of mediation are that it can result in an expeditious and less costly resolution of the litigation, and can produce creative solutions to complex disputes often unavailable in traditional litigation. NY R USDCTS&ED Civ Rule 83.9(b).

    i.   *Mediation program eligibility.* All civil cases other than Social Security, habeas corpus, and tax cases are eligible for mediation, whether assigned to Manhattan or White Plains. NY R USDCTS&ED Civ Rule 83.9(e)(1).

    •  The Board of Judges may, by Administrative Order, direct that certain specified categories of cases shall automatically be submitted to the mediation program. The assigned District Judge or Magistrate Judge may issue a written order exempting a particular case with or without the request of the parties. NY R USDCTS&ED Civ Rule 83.9(e)(2).

- For all other cases, the assigned District Judge or Magistrate Judge may determine that a case is appropriate for mediation and may order that case to mediation, with or without the consent of the parties, before, at, or after the initial FRCP 16(b) case management conference. Alternatively, the parties should notify the assigned Judge at any time of their desire to mediate. NY R USDCTS&ED Civ Rule 83.9(e)(3).

c. *Judicial settlement conferences.* Judicial settlement conferences may be ordered by District Judges or Magistrate Judges with or without the request or consent of the parties. NY R USDCTS&ED Civ Rule 83.9(f).

d. For more information on alternative dispute resolution (ADR), refer to NY R USDCTS&ED Civ Rule 83.9.

10. *Individual judge practices.* Refer to the Miscellaneous section of this document for information on individual judge practices on general requirements for documents.

## D. Documents

1. *Required documents*

   a. *Amended pleading.* Refer to the General Requirements section of this document for the form and contents of the amended pleading.

   b. *Certificate of service.* FRCP 5(d) requires that the person making service under FRCP 5 certify that service has been effected. FRCP 5(Advisory Committee Notes). Having such information on file may be useful for many purposes, including proof of service if an issue arises concerning the effectiveness of the service. FRCP 5(Advisory Committee Notes).

      i. Such paper service [on attorneys and pro se parties who are not Filing or Receiving Users] must be documented by electronically filing proof of service. NY R USDCTSD CM/ECF, S.D.(I)(9)(9.2); NY R USDCTSD CM/ECF, S.D.(I)(19)(19.3)(b). Pro se parties who are not Filing Users are exempt from that portion of NY R USDCTSD CM/ECF, S.D.(I)(19)(19.3) requiring proof of service to be filed electronically. NY R USDCTSD CM/ECF, S.D.(I)(19)(19.3).

2. *Supplemental documents*

   a. *Notice of constitutional question.* A party that files a pleading, written motion, or other paper drawing into question the constitutionality of a federal or state statute must promptly:

      i. *File notice.* File a notice of constitutional question stating the question and identifying the paper that raises it, if:

         - A federal statute is questioned and the parties do not include the United States, one of its agencies, or one of its officers or employees in an official capacity; or

         - A state statute is questioned and the parties do not include the state, one of its agencies, or one of its officers or employees in an official capacity; and

      ii. *Serve notice.* Serve the notice and paper on the Attorney General of the United States if a federal statute is questioned—or on the state attorney general if a state statute is questioned—either by certified or registered mail or by sending it to an electronic address designated by the attorney general for this purpose. FRCP 5.1(a).

      iii. *No forfeiture.* A party's failure to file and serve the notice, or the court's failure to certify, does not forfeit a constitutional claim or defense that is otherwise timely asserted. FRCP 5.1(d).

   b. *Notice of issue concerning foreign law.* A party who intends to raise an issue about a foreign country's law must give notice by a pleading or other writing. In determining foreign law, the court may consider any relevant material or source, including testimony, whether or not submitted by a party or admissible under the Federal Rules of Evidence. The court's determination must be treated as a ruling on a question of law. FRCP 44.1.

    c. *Statement explaining untimely electronic filing.* If you missed a filing deadline when the ECF system was out of order, attach a statement to your filing explaining how the interruption in service prevented you from filing in a timely fashion. NY R USDCTSD CM/ECF, S.D.(II)(23)(23.5).

    d. *Courtesy copies.* Filers should review the judge's Individual Practices to determine if courtesy copies are necessary. NY R USDCTSD CM/ECF, S.D.(II)(15)(15.1); NY R USDCTSD CM/ECF, S.D.(II)(13)(13.17). Judges' Individual Practices should continue to be followed with respect to delivery of courtesy copies. NY R USDCTSD CM/ECF, S.D.(I)(3)(3.4).

3. *Documents required for an amended complaint adding a new claim for relief or new party.* Refer to the United States District Court for the Southern District of New York KeyRules Complaint document for the documents for an amended complaint adding a new claim for relief or being filed and served against a new party.

4. *Individual judge practices.* Refer to the Miscellaneous section of this document for information on individual judge practices on required documents.

## E. Format

1. *Form of documents*

    a. *Paper.* Every pleading, written motion, and other paper must: be plainly written, typed, printed, or copied without erasures or interlineations which materially deface it. NY R USDCTS&ED Civ Rule 11.1(a)(1).

    b. *Typeface, margin, and spacing.* The typeface, margins, and spacing of all documents presented for filing must meet the following requirements:

        i. All text must be twelve (12) point type or larger, except for text in footnotes which may be ten (10) point type;

        ii. All documents must have at least one (1) inch margins on all sides;

        iii. All text must be double-spaced, except for headings, text in footnotes, or block quotations, which may be single-spaced. NY R USDCTS&ED Civ Rule 11.1(b).

    c. *Caption; Names of parties.* Every pleading must have a caption with the court's name, a title, a file number, and a FRCP 7(a) designation. The title of the complaint must name all the parties; the title of other pleadings, after naming the first party on each side, may refer generally to other parties. FRCP 10(a). Every pleading, written motion, and other paper must: bear the docket number and the initials of the District Judge and any Magistrate Judge before whom the action or proceeding is pending, NY R USDCTS&ED Civ Rule 11.1(a)(2).

    d. *Paragraphs; Separate statements.* A party must state its claims or defenses in numbered paragraphs, each limited as far as practicable to a single set of circumstances. A later pleading may refer by number to a paragraph in an earlier pleading. If doing so would promote clarity, each claim founded on a separate transaction or occurrence—and each defense other than a denial—must be stated in a separate count or defense. FRCP 10(b).

    e. *Adoption by reference; Exhibits.* A statement in a pleading may be adopted by reference elsewhere in the same pleading or in any other pleading or motion. A copy of a written instrument that is an exhibit to a pleading is a part of the pleading for all purposes. FRCP 10(c).

    f. *Acceptance by the clerk.* The clerk must not refuse to file a paper solely because it is not in the form prescribed by the Federal Rules of Civil Procedure or by a local rule or practice. FRCP 5(d)(4).

2. *Form of electronic documents*

    a. *PDF-A.* All documents electronically filed on the ECF system must be in PDF-A format (portable document format). A PDF-A file is created using PDF writer software such as Adobe Acrobat (go to the Adobe website for details). PDF-A files cannot be altered, providing security to the filer and the Court. NY R USDCTSD CM/ECF, S.D.(II)(23)(23.2).

    b. *Size limitation.* No single PDF file may be larger than four megabytes (4 MB). If the filing is too large, the ECF system will not allow it to be filed, and you will not see a Notice of Electronic Filing

(NEF or filing receipt) screen. To determine the size of an Adobe Acrobat PDF file click on File, Document Properties, Summary. NY R USDCTSD CM/ECF, S.D.(II)(23)(23.3).

    i. Converting documents directly from a word processor to PDF-A format creates the smallest possible file in terms of computer memory. If that is not possible, scan your document at low resolution. Within the Adobe Acrobat program, on the "Scan Manager" screen, adjust the settings for black and white and 200 dpi (dots per inch). This allows more pages to fit into a single PDF-A file. If that does not work, separate an oversized file into 2 or more parts. Simply label each file 1a, 1b, 1c, etc. Only relevant excerpts of exhibits should be electronically filed. NY R USDCTSD CM/ECF, S.D.(II)(23)(23.4).

c. *Attachments and exhibits.* Filing Users must submit in electronic form all documents referenced as exhibits or attachments, unless the Court permits paper filing. NY R USDCTSD CM/ECF, S.D.(I)(5)(5.1).

    i. A Filing User must submit as exhibits or attachments only those excerpts of the referenced documents that are relevant to the matter under consideration by the Court. Excerpted material must be clearly and prominently identified as such. Filing Users who file excerpts of documents as exhibits or attachments under this procedure do so without prejudice to their right to file timely additional excerpts or the complete document. Responding parties may file timely additional excerpts that they believe are relevant or the complete document. A party may move before the Court for permission to serve and file in hard copy documents that cannot be reasonably scanned. NY R USDCTSD CM/ECF, S.D.(I)(5)(5.2).

    ii. Exhibits must be filed only as attachments to a document, such as a motion or an affidavit. Do not use the ECF Filing Event for "Motion" to file exhibits separately. Exhibits are the only items that should be attached to electronically filed documents. You are limited to electronically filing only relevant excerpts of exhibits. Excerpts must be clearly identified as such. If the exhibit is too large to be scanned and electronically filed you may contact the ECF Help Desk. NY R USDCTSD CM/ECF, S.D.(II)(15)(15.6).

d. *Letters.* Parties should consult the assigned judge's Individual Practices to determine if the judge accepts letters at all and, if he or she does, whether the judge has any page limitations on letters and/or requires courtesy copies of letters filed on ECF (and, if so, by what means of delivery). All letters addressed to the Court must include a subject line with the case name and docket number (e.g., "Re: Doe v. Smith, 13 Civ. 1234 (ABC)"). NY R USDCTSD CM/ECF, S.D.(II)(13)(13.1).

e. *Proposed orders, proposed judgments, stipulations and consents.* Any document that requires the signature of a judge should not be electronically filed except as an exhibit to another document. Proposed orders, judgments, stipulations and consents should not be submitted through the ECF system. Instead they should be sent by e-mail to the Clerk. Proposed orders should be submitted in word processing format (WordPerfect or Word) rather than as a PDF document. Stipulations should be submitted in PDF-A format. Stipulations must contain ink signatures not s/. Faxed or emailed signatures are acceptable. Please note that Stipulations of Voluntary Dismissal pursuant to FRCP 41(a)(1)(A)(ii) do not require the signature of a judge and must be electronically filed on the ECF system. Questions may be directed to the Orders and Judgments Clerk at the phone numbers listed in NY R USDCTSD CM/ECF, S.D.(II)(18)(18.3). NY R USDCTSD CM/ECF, S.D.(II)(18)(18.3).

    i. Email the proposed order, judgment or stipulation to the email addresses listed in NY R USDCTSD CM/ECF, S.D.(II)(18)(18.3). NY R USDCTSD CM/ECF, S.D.(II)(18)(18.3).

    ii. Pro se litigants who are not Filing Users are exempt from that portion of NY R USDCTSD CM/ECF, S.D.(II)(18)(18.3) that requires litigants to email proposed orders, judgments, stipulations and consents, and shall deliver such documents to the Clerk's Office in paper form. NY R USDCTSD CM/ECF, S.D.(II)(18)(18.3).

3. *Signing of pleadings, motions and other papers*

a. *Signature.* Every pleading, written motion, and other paper must be signed by at least one attorney of record in the attorney's name—or by a party personally if the party is unrepresented. The paper must state the signer's address, e-mail address, and telephone number. FRCP 11(a). Every pleading,

written motion, and other paper must: have the name of each person signing it clearly printed or typed directly below the signature. NY R USDCTS&ED Civ Rule 11.1(a)(3).

  i.  *Electronic signatures.* The user log-in and password required to submit documents to the ECF system serve as the Filing User's signature on all electronic documents filed with the Court. NY R USDCTSD CM/ECF, S.D.(I)(8)(8.1); NY R USDCTSD CM/ECF, S.D.(II)(13)(13.14). They also serve as a signature for purposes of the Federal Rules of Civil Procedure, including FRCP 11, the Local Civil Rules of the United States District Courts for the Southern and Eastern Districts of New York, and any other purpose for which a signature is required in connection with proceedings before the Court. NY R USDCTSD CM/ECF, S.D.(I)(8)(8.1).

  - *Signature block.* Electronically filed documents must include a signature block and must set forth the name, address, telephone number and e-mail address all in compliance with the Federal Rules of Civil Procedure and NY R USDCTS&ED Civ Rule 11.1. In the absence of a scanned signature image, the name of the Filing User under whose log-in and password the document is submitted must be preceded by an "s/" typed in the space where the signature would otherwise appear. NY R USDCTSD CM/ECF, S.D.(I)(8)(8.2); NY R USDCTSD CM/ECF, S.D.(II)(13)(13.14).

  - *Documents requiring the signature of a party or witness.* A document requiring the signature of a party or witness shall be electronically filed in a scanned format that contains an image of the actual signature. NY R USDCTSD CM/ECF, S.D.(I)(8)(8.4); NY R USDCTSD CM/ECF, S.D.(II)(13)(13.14).

  - *Documents requiring the signature of a judge.* A Filing User submitting a document electronically that requires a judge's signature must promptly deliver the document in such other form, if any, as the Court requires. NY R USDCTSD CM/ECF, S.D.(I)(4)(4.2).

  - *Documents requiring multiple signatures.* Documents requiring signatures of more than one party must be electronically filed either by: (a) submitting a scanned document containing all necessary signatures; (b) representing the consent of the other parties on the document; (c) identifying on the document the parties whose signatures are required and by the submission of a notice of endorsement by the other parties no later than three business days after filing; or (d) in any other manner approved by the Court. NY R USDCTSD CM/ECF, S.D.(I)(8)(8.5).

  ii.  *No verification or accompanying affidavit required for pleadings.* Unless a rule or statute specifically states otherwise, a pleading need not be verified or accompanied by an affidavit. FRCP 11(a).

  iii.  *Unsigned papers.* The court must strike an unsigned paper unless the omission is promptly corrected after being called to the attorney's or party's attention. FRCP 11(a).

b. *Representations to the court.* By presenting to the court a pleading, written motion, or other paper—whether by signing, filing, submitting, or later advocating it—an attorney or unrepresented party certifies that to the best of the person's knowledge, information, and belief, formed after an inquiry reasonable under the circumstances:

  i.  It is not being presented for any improper purpose, such as to harass, cause unnecessary delay, or needlessly increase the cost of litigation;

  ii.  The claims, defenses, and other legal contentions are warranted by existing law or by a nonfrivolous argument for extending, modifying, or reversing existing law or for establishing new law;

  iii.  The factual contentions have evidentiary support or, if specifically so identified, will likely have evidentiary support after a reasonable opportunity for further investigation or discovery; and

  iv.  The denials of factual contentions are warranted on the evidence or, if specifically so identified, are reasonably based on belief or a lack of information. FRCP 11(b).

c. *Sanctions.* If, after notice and a reasonable opportunity to respond, the court determines that FRCP 11(b) has been violated, the court may impose an appropriate sanction on any attorney, law firm, or

party that violated FRCP 11(b) or is responsible for the violation. FRCP 11(c)(1). Refer to the United States District Court for the Southern District of New York KeyRules Motion for Sanctions document for more information.

4. *Privacy protection for filings made with the court*

    a. *Redacted filings.* Unless the court orders otherwise, in an electronic or paper filing with the court that contains an individual's Social Security number, taxpayer-identification number, or birth date, the name of an individual known to be a minor, or a financial-account number, a party or nonparty making the filing may include only:

        i. The last four (4) digits of the Social Security number and taxpayer-identification number;

        ii. The year of the individual's birth;

        iii. The minor's initials; and

        iv. The last four (4) digits of the financial-account number. FRCP 5.2(a); NY R USDCTSD CM/ECF, S.D.(II)(21)(21.3).

        v. Caution should be exercised when filing documents that contain the following:

- Personal identifying numbers (PIN #'s), such as a driver's license number;
- Medical records, treatment and diagnosis;
- Employment history;
- Individual financial information;
- Proprietary or trade secret information;
- Information regarding an individual's cooperation with the government. NY R US-DCTSD CM/ECF, S.D.(II)(21)(21.4).

    b. *Exemptions from the redaction requirement.* The redaction requirement does not apply to the following:

        i. A financial-account number that identifies the property allegedly subject to forfeiture in a forfeiture proceeding;

        ii. The record of an administrative or agency proceeding;

        iii. The official record of a state-court proceeding;

        iv. The record of a court or tribunal, if that record was not subject to the redaction requirement when originally filed;

        v. A filing covered by FRCP 5.2(c) or FRCP 5.2(d); and

        vi. A pro se filing in an action brought under 28 U.S.C.A. § 2241, 28 U.S.C.A. § 2254, or 28 U.S.C.A. § 2255. FRCP 5.2(b).

    c. *Limitations on remote access to electronic files; Social Security appeals and immigration cases.* Unless the court orders otherwise, in an action for benefits under the Social Security Act, and in an action or proceeding relating to an order of removal, to relief from removal, or to immigration benefits or detention, access to an electronic file is authorized as follows:

        i. The parties and their attorneys may have remote electronic access to any part of the case file, including the administrative record;

        ii. Any other person may have electronic access to the full record at the courthouse, but may have remote electronic access only to:

- The docket maintained by the court; and
- An opinion, order, judgment, or other disposition of the court, but not any other part of the case file or the administrative record. FRCP 5.2(c).

    d. *Filings made under seal.* The court may order that a filing be made under seal without redaction. The court may later unseal the filing or order the person who made the filing to file a redacted version for the public record. FRCP 5.2(d). For more information on sealing documents, refer to NY R USDCTSD CM/ECF, S.D.(I)(6).

e. *Protective orders.* For good cause, the court may by order in a case:

   i. Require redaction of additional information; or

   ii. Limit or prohibit a nonparty's remote electronic access to a document filed with the court. FRCP 5.2(e).

f. *Option for additional unredacted filing under seal.* A person making a redacted filing may also file an unredacted copy under seal. The court must retain the unredacted copy as part of the record. FRCP 5.2(f); NY R USDCTSD CM/ECF, S.D.(II)(21)(21.5).

g. *Option for filing a reference list.* A filing that contains redacted information may be filed together with a reference list that identifies each item of redacted information and specifies an appropriate identifier that uniquely corresponds to each item listed. The list must be filed under seal and may be amended as of right. Any reference in the case to a listed identifier will be construed to refer to the corresponding item of information. FRCP 5.2(g); NY R USDCTSD CM/ECF, S.D.(II)(21)(21.5).

h. *Responsibility for redaction.* It is the sole responsibility of counsel and the parties to be sure that all documents comply with the rules of this Court requiring redaction of personal identifiers. Neither the judge nor the Clerk of Court will review documents for compliance with these rules. NY R USDCTSD CM/ECF, S.D.(II)(21)(21.2).

i. *Waiver of protection of identifiers.* A person waives the protection of FRCP 5.2(a) as to the person's own information by filing it without redaction and not under seal. FRCP 5.2(h).

j. For more information on privacy and public access to ECF cases, refer to NY R USDCTSD CM/ECF, S.D.(II)(21).

5. *Individual judge practices.* Refer to the Miscellaneous section of this document for information on individual judge practices on formatting documents.

## F. Filing and Service Requirements

1. *Filing requirements.* Any paper after the complaint that is required to be served—together with a certificate of service—must be filed within a reasonable time after service. FRCP 5(d)(1). Complaints and all subsequent papers are accepted at either courthouse, regardless of the place for which the case is designated. NY R USDCTSD Div. Bus., Rule 22. After a case is opened in accordance with NY R USDCTSD CM/ECF, S.D.(II)(14), all subsequent amended complaints, intervenor complaints, third party complaints, etc. must be filed electronically on the ECF system. When filing, select only those parties the amended pleading is filed against. Do not select "all plaintiffs" or "all defendants" unless it is appropriate. NY R USDCTSD CM/ECF, S.D.(II)(15)(15.1). For more information on filing amended pleadings, refer to NY R USDCTSD CM/ECF, S.D.(II)(15).

   a. *How filing is made; In general.* A paper is filed by delivering it:

      i. To the clerk; or

      ii. To a judge who agrees to accept it for filing, and who must then note the filing date on the paper and promptly send it to the clerk. FRCP 5(d)(2).

   b. *Night depository.* A night depository with an automatic date stamp shall be maintained by the Clerk of the Southern District in the Pearl Street Courthouse. After regular business hours, papers for the District Court only may be deposited in the night depository. Such papers will be considered as having been filed in the District Court as of the date stamped thereon, which shall be deemed presumptively correct. NY R USDCTS&ED Civ Rule 1.2.

   c. *Electronic filing*

      i. *Authorization of electronic filing program.* A court may, by local rule, allow papers to be filed, signed, or verified by electronic means that are consistent with any technical standards established by the Judicial Conference of the United States. A local rule may require electronic filing only if reasonable exceptions are allowed. A paper filed electronically in compliance with a local rule is a written paper for purposes of the Federal Rules of Civil Procedure. FRCP 5(d)(3).

         • The Court will accept for filing documents submitted, signed or verified by electronic means, that comply with the rules in NY R USDCTSD CM/ECF, S.D. NY R USDCTSD CM/ECF, S.D.(I). The information in NY R USDCTSD CM/ECF, S.D. applies only to cases assigned to the ECF system. NY R USDCTSD CM/ECF, S.D.(Introduction).

- Parties serving and filing papers shall follow the instructions regarding Electronic Case Filing (ECF) published on the website of each respective Court. A paper served and filed by electronic means in accordance with such instructions is, for purposes of FRCP 5, served and filed in compliance with the Local Civil Rules of the Southern and Eastern Districts of New York. NY R USDCTS&ED Civ Rule 5.2(a). Parties have an obligation to review the Court's actual order, decree, or judgment (on ECF), which controls, and should not rely on the description on the docket or in the ECF Notice of Electronic Filing (NEF). NY R USDCTS&ED Civ Rule 5.2(c).

- The following should be observed when filing electronically: (1) the Federal Rules of Civil Procedure, (2) the Local Civil Rules of the United States District Courts for the Southern and Eastern Districts of New York, (3) the assigned judge's Individual Practices, and (4) the Court's Electronic Case Filing Rules & Instructions (NY R USDCTSD CM/ECF, S.D.). NY R USDCTSD CM/ECF, S.D.(Introduction).

ii. *Scope of electronic filing.* Except as expressly provided and in exceptional circumstances preventing a party from filing electronically, all documents required to be filed with the Court must be filed electronically. Any party unable to comply with this requirement must seek permission of the Court to file in the traditional manner, on paper. Any such application made after regular business hours may be submitted through the night depository box maintained pursuant to NY R USDCTS&ED Civ Rule 1.2. NY R USDCTSD CM/ECF, S.D.(I)(1)(1.1).

- *Documents filed by pro se litigants.* Unless otherwise ordered by the Court, documents filed by pro se litigants must be filed in the traditional manner, on paper, and will be scanned and docketed by the Clerk's Office into the ECF system. NY R USDCTSD CM/ECF, S.D.(I)(1)(1.1). Pro se litigants must file pleadings and documents in the traditional manner on paper unless the assigned judge has granted permission to electronically file on the ECF system. NY R USDCTSD CM/ECF, S.D.(Introduction).

- *Letters.* Except for letters to be filed under seal, letters addressed to judges who accept letters may be filed electronically. Parties should consult the assigned judge's Individual Practices to determine if the judge accepts letters at all and, if he or she does, whether the judge has any page limitations on letters and/or requires courtesy copies of letters filed on ECF (and, if so, by what means of delivery). NY R USDCTSD CM/ECF, S.D.(II)(13)(13.1). Letters solely between parties or their counsel or otherwise not addressed to the Court may not be filed electronically on ECF (except as exhibits to an otherwise properly filed document). NY R USDCTSD CM/ECF, S.D.(II)(13)(13.1). For more information on filing letters, refer to NY R USDCTSD CM/ECF, S.D.(II)(13)(13.1).

- *Proposed orders, judgments and decrees.* Proposed orders, judgments and decrees shall be presented as directed by the ECF rules published on the website of each respective Court. NY R USDCTS&ED Civ Rule 77.1. For more information, refer to NY R USDCTS&ED Civ Rule 77.1.

iii. *Exceptions to electronic filing.* In an ECF case, the documents that should not be electronically filed include:

- Miscellaneous Case initiating documents, NY R USDCTSD CM/ECF, S.D.(II)(18)(18.2);

- Proposed orders; proposed judgments, stipulations; consents, NY R USDCTSD CM/ECF, S.D.(II)(18)(18.3);

- Orders to show cause / temporary restraining orders, NY R USDCTSD CM/ECF, S.D.(II)(18)(18.4);

- Sealed documents, NY R USDCTSD CM/ECF, S.D.(II)(18)(18.5); and

- Surety bonds, NY R USDCTSD CM/ECF, S.D.(II)(18)(18.6).

- In cases where the record of an administrative or other prior proceeding must be filed with the Court, such record may be served and filed in hard copy without prior motion and order of the Court. NY R USDCTSD CM/ECF, S.D.(I)(5)(5.3).

- For more documents excepted from electronic filing, and for more information on such documents, refer to NY R USDCTSD CM/ECF, S.D.(II)(18).

iv. *Consequences of electronic filing.* Except as otherwise provided in NY R USDCTSD CM/ECF, S.D.(I)(4), electronic filing of a document in the ECF system consistent with these procedures, together with the transmission of a Notice of Electronic Filing (NEF) from the Court, constitutes filing of the document for all purposes of the Federal Rules of Civil Procedure and the Local Civil Rules of the United States District Courts for the Southern and Eastern Districts of New York and constitutes entry of the document on the docket kept by the Clerk under FRCP 58 and FRCP 79. NY R USDCTSD CM/ECF, S.D.(I)(3)(3.1).

v. For more information on electronic filing, refer to NY R USDCTSD CM/ECF, S.D.

2. *Service requirements*

   a. *Service; When required*

      i. *In general.* Unless the Federal Rules of Civil Procedure provide otherwise, each of the following papers must be served on every party:

         - An order stating that service is required;
         - A pleading filed after the original complaint, unless the court orders otherwise under FRCP 5(c) because there are numerous defendants;
         - A discovery paper required to be served on a party, unless the court orders otherwise;
         - A written motion, except one that may be heard ex parte; and
         - A written notice, appearance, demand, or offer of judgment, or any similar paper. FRCP 5(a)(1).

      ii. *If a party fails to appear.* No service is required on a party who is in default for failing to appear. But a pleading that asserts a new claim for relief against such a party must be served on that party under FRCP 4. FRCP 5(a)(2).

      iii. *Seizing property.* If an action is begun by seizing property and no person is or need be named as a defendant, any service required before the filing of an appearance, answer, or claim must be made on the person who had custody or possession of the property when it was seized. FRCP 5(a)(3).

   b. *Service; How made*

      i. *Serving an attorney.* If a party is represented by an attorney, service under FRCP 5 must be made on the attorney unless the court orders service on the party. FRCP 5(b)(1).

      ii. *Service in general.* A paper is served under FRCP 5 by:

         - Handing it to the person;
         - Leaving it: (1) at the person's office with a clerk or other person in charge or, if no one is in charge, in a conspicuous place in the office; or (2) if the person has no office or the office is closed, at the person's dwelling or usual place of abode with someone of suitable age and discretion who resides there;
         - Mailing it to the person's last known address—in which event service is complete upon mailing;
         - Leaving it with the court clerk if the person has no known address;
         - Sending it by electronic means if the person consented in writing—in which event service is complete upon transmission, but is not effective if the serving party learns that it did not reach the person to be served; or
         - Delivering it by any other means that the person consented to in writing—in which event service is complete when the person making service delivers it to the agency designated to make delivery. FRCP 5(b)(2).

iii. *Service by overnight delivery.* Service upon an attorney may be made by overnight delivery service. "Overnight delivery service" means any delivery service which regularly accepts items for overnight delivery. Overnight delivery service shall be deemed service by mail for purposes of FRCP 5 and FRCP 6. NY R USDCTS&ED Civ Rule 5.3.

iv. *Service by electronic means.* Parties serving and filing papers shall follow the instructions regarding Electronic Case Filing (ECF) published on the website of each respective Court. A paper served and filed by electronic means in accordance with such instructions is, for purposes of FRCP 5, served and filed in compliance with the Local Civil Rules of the United States District Courts for the Southern and Eastern Districts of New York. NY R USDCTS&ED Civ Rule 5.2(a). Parties have an obligation to review the Court's actual order, decree, or judgment (on ECF), which controls, and should not rely on the description on the docket or in the ECF Notice of Electronic Filing (NEF). NY R USDCTS&ED Civ Rule 5.2(c).

- *Notice of electronic filing (NEF).* In cases assigned to the ECF system, service is complete provided all parties receive a Notice of Electronic Filing (NEF), which is sent automatically by email from the Court (see the NEF for a list of who did/did not receive notice electronically). Transmission of the NEF constitutes service upon all Filing and Receiving Users who are listed as recipients of notice by electronic mail. NY R USDCTSD CM/ECF, S.D.(I)(9)(9.1). In cases assigned to the ECF system, if all parties receive a NEF, service is complete upon transmission of the NEF by the Court, and you are not required to serve a paper copy. NY R USDCTSD CM/ECF, S.D.(II)(19)(19.2). It remains the duty of Filing and Receiving Users to maintain current contact information with the court and to regularly review the docket sheet of the case. NY R USDCTSD CM/ECF, S.D.(I)(9)(9.1).

- *Mailing of court-initiated documents.* The Clerk's Office will no longer mail paper copies of court-initiated documents to Filing and Receiving Users. The Clerk's Office will mail copies of all court-initiated documents to pro se parties who have not registered as Filing or Receiving Users. NY R USDCTSD CM/ECF, S.D.(II)(19)(19.1).

- *No receipt of a NEF.* If any party does not receive a NEF, you are required to accomplish service on that party in the traditional manner, in paper form. NY R USDCTSD CM/ECF, S.D.(II)(19)(19.2). The NEF receipt will inform you who will receive notice of the filing "electronically" (by e-mail from the Court) and who will receive notice "by other means" (traditional service in paper form). NY R USDCTSD CM/ECF, S.D.(II)(19)(19.2).

- *Service on non-filing or non-receiving users.* Attorneys and pro se parties who are not Filing or Receiving Users must be served with a paper copy of any electronically filed pleading or other document. Service of such paper copy must be made according to the Federal Rules of Civil Procedure and the Local Civil Rules of the United States District Courts for the Southern and Eastern Districts of New York. NY R USDCTSD CM/ECF, S.D.(I)(9)(9.2). Such paper service must be documented by electronically filing proof of service. NY R USDCTSD CM/ECF, S.D.(I)(9)(9.2); NY R USDCTSD CM/ECF, S.D.(II)(19)(19.2). Where the Clerk scans and electronically files pleadings and documents on behalf of a pro se party, the associated NEF constitutes service. NY R USDCTSD CM/ECF, S.D.(I)(9)(9.2).

- For more information on service by electronic means, refer to NY R USDCTSD CM/ECF, S.D.(II)(19).

v. *Using court facilities.* If a local rule so authorizes, a party may use the court's transmission facilities to make service under FRCP 5(b)(2)(E). FRCP 5(b)(3).

c. *Serving numerous defendants*

i. *In general.* If an action involves an unusually large number of defendants, the court may, on motion or on its own, order that:

- Defendants' pleadings and replies to them need not be served on other defendants;

- Any crossclaim, counterclaim, avoidance, or affirmative defense in those pleadings and replies to them will be treated as denied or avoided by all other parties; and

- Filing any such pleading and serving it on the plaintiff constitutes notice of the pleading to all parties. FRCP 5(c)(1).

  ii. *Notifying parties.* A copy of every such order must be served on the parties as the court directs. FRCP 5(c)(2).

3. *Service requirements of an amended complaint asserting new or additional claims for relief.* The service of amended pleadings is generally governed by FRCP 5. Thus, except for an amended pleading against a defaulting party that does not assert new or additional claims for relief, an amended pleading must be served in accordance with FRCP 5. FEDPROC § 62:263; International Controls Corp. v. Vesco, 556 F.2d 665, 23 Fed.R.Serv.2d 923 (2d Cir. 1977). However, while FRCP 5 permits service of an amended complaint on counsel, where the amended complaint contains an entirely different cause of action that could not have been properly served originally by the method used in serving the original complaint, the amended complaint must be served in accordance with the terms of FRCP 4. FEDPROC § 62:263; Lasch v. Antkies, 161 F.Supp. 851 (E.D.Pa. 1958). If a party is added when electronically filing an amended pleading, a summons should be requested by electronically filing a REQUEST FOR ISSUANCE OF SUMMONS and attaching a proposed summons in PDF/A format. Where multiple parties are added, a rider may be attached to a single summons listing all new parties. In response, the Clerk's Office will electronically file a SUMMONS ISSUED event containing a summons with an electronic seal suitable for printing. Summons forms are available on the court's website. A summons is not necessary when no party is added to a case. NY R USDCTSD CM/ECF, S.D.(II)(15)(15.2). Refer to the United States District Court for the Southern District of New York KeyRules Complaint document for more information on serving the amended complaint in accordance with FRCP 4.

4. *Individual judge practices.* Refer to the Miscellaneous section of this document for information on individual judge practices on filing and serving documents.

## G. Hearings

1. *Hearings, generally.* Generally, there is no hearing contemplated in the federal statutes or rules for the amended pleading.

  a. *Amended answer; Hearing on FRCP 12 defenses before trial.* If a party so moves, any defense listed in FRCP 12(b)(1) through FRCP 12(b)(7)—whether made in a pleading or by motion—and a motion under FRCP 12(c) must be heard and decided before trial unless the court orders a deferral until trial. FRCP 12(i).

2. *Individual judge practices.* Refer to the Miscellaneous section of this document for information on individual judge practices on hearings.

## H. Forms

### 1. Federal Amended Pleading Forms

  a. Notice; Of filing amended pleading as of course. AMJUR PP FEDPRAC § 153.

  b. Amendment; Of pleading as of course. AMJUR PP FEDPRAC § 154.

  c. Civil cover sheet. 2 FEDFORMS § 3:29.

  d. Notice of lawsuit and request for waiver of service of summons and waiver of summons. 2 FEDFORMS § 3:36.

  e. Complaint. 2 FEDFORMS § 7:14.

  f. Generally. 2B FEDFORMS § 8:10.

  g. Presenting defenses; Official form. 2B FEDFORMS § 8:12.

  h. Denials, admissions and affirmative defenses. 2B FEDFORMS § 8:15.

  i. Denial of particular averment. 2B FEDFORMS § 8:24.

  j. Admission of particular averment. 2B FEDFORMS § 8:25.

  k. Denial of all averments of paragraph. 2B FEDFORMS § 8:26.

  l. Admission of all averments of paragraph. 2B FEDFORMS § 8:27.

    m.   Denial in part and admission in part of paragraph. 2B FEDFORMS § 8:28.

    n.   Notice of amended complaint. 2C FEDFORMS § 14:10.

    o.   Amendment to complaint. 2C FEDFORMS § 14:47.

    p.   Amendment to complaint; Short version. 2C FEDFORMS § 14:48.

    q.   Amendment to complaint; As of course. 2C FEDFORMS § 14:49.

    r.   Complaint; Single count. FEDPROF § 1:68.

    s.   Complaint; Multiple counts; With same jurisdictional basis. FEDPROF § 1:69.

    t.   Amendment of pleading; As matter of course. FEDPROF § 1:220.

    u.   Notice of filing amended pleading; Where amendment is matter of course. FEDPROF § 1:221.

    v.   Amendment of pleading; Particular clauses. FEDPROF § 1:224.

    w.   Amendment of pleading; Clause; Change in title of action. FEDPROF § 1:225.

    x.   Amendment of pleading; Clause; To show amount in controversy. FEDPROF § 1:227.

    y.   Amendment of pleading; Clause; To show diversity of citizenship. FEDPROF § 1:228.

    z.   Amendment of pleading; Clause; Prayer for relief. FEDPROF § 1:229.

## I. Applicable Rules

  1.  *Federal rules*

    a.   Serving and filing pleadings and other papers. FRCP 5.

    b.   Constitutional challenge to a statute; Notice, certification, and intervention. FRCP 5.1.

    c.   Privacy protection for filings made with the court. FRCP 5.2.

    d.   Computing and extending time; Time for motion papers. FRCP 6.

    e.   Pleadings allowed; Form of motions and other papers. FRCP 7.

    f.   General rules of pleading. FRCP 8.

    g.   Pleading special matters. FRCP 9.

    h.   Form of pleadings. FRCP 10.

    i.   Signing pleadings, motions, and other papers; Representations to the court; Sanctions. FRCP 11.

    j.   Defenses and objections; When and how presented; Motion for judgment on the pleadings; Consolidating motions; Waiving defenses; Pretrial hearing. FRCP 12.

    k.   Amended and supplemental pleadings. FRCP 15.

    l.   Right to a jury trial; Demand. FRCP 38.

    m.   Determining foreign law. FRCP 44.1.

  2.  *Local rules*

    a.   Night depository. NY R USDCTS&ED Civ Rule 1.2.

    b.   Duty of attorneys in related cases. NY R USDCTS&ED Civ Rule 1.6.

    c.   Electronic service and filing of documents. NY R USDCTS&ED Civ Rule 5.2.

    d.   Service by overnight delivery. NY R USDCTS&ED Civ Rule 5.3.

    e.   Computation of time. NY R USDCTS&ED Civ Rule 6.4.

    f.   Form of pleadings, motions, and other papers. NY R USDCTS&ED Civ Rule 11.1.

    g.   Submission of orders, judgments and decrees. NY R USDCTS&ED Civ Rule 77.1.

    h.   Alternative dispute resolution (Southern District only). NY R USDCTS&ED Civ Rule 83.9.

    i.   Electronic case filing rules and instructions. NY R USDCTSD CM/ECF, S.D.

    j.   Related cases. NY R USDCTSD Div. Bus., Rule 13.

k. Filing at either courthouse. NY R USDCTSD Div. Bus., Rule 22.

## J. Miscellaneous

**NOTE: Individual judges' rules may apply. For available judge-level information, refer to:**

DISTRICT JUDGE RONNIE ABRAMS: NY R USDCTSD Abrams-Civ Prac; NY R USDCTSD Abrams-Crim Prac; NY R USDCTSD Abrams-Pro Se; NY R USDCTSD Abrams-Case Mgt; NY R USDCTSD Abrams-Jury.

DISTRICT JUDGE DEBORAH A. BATTS: NY R USDCTSD Batts-Practices.

DISTRICT JUDGE RICHARD M. BERMAN: NY R USDCTSD Berman-Practices; NY R USDCTSD Berman-Default; NY R USDCTSD Berman-Sentencing; NY R USDCTSD Berman-Media.

DISTRICT JUDGE VINCENT L. BRICCETTI: NY R USDCTSD Briccetti-Practices; NY R USDCTSD Briccetti-Plan; NY R USDCTSD Briccetti-Notice.

DISTRICT JUDGE VERNON S. BRODERICK: NY R USDCTSD Broderick-Civil; NY R USDCTSD Broderick-Crim; NY R USDCTSD Broderick-Case Mgt; NY R USDCTSD Broderick-Jury.

DISTRICT JUDGE NAOMI REICE BUCHWALD: NY R USDCTSD Buchwald-Practices.

DISTRICT JUDGE VALERIE E. CAPRONI: NY R USDCTSD Caproni-Prac; NY R USDCTSD Caproni--Pro Se; NY R USDCTSD Caproni-Case Mgt; NY R USDCTSD Caproni-Crim Prac.

DISTRICT JUDGE ANDREW L. CARTER JR.: NY R USDCTSD Carter-Practices.

DISTRICT JUDGE KEVIN P. CASTEL: NY R USDCTSD Castel-Practices; NY R USDCTSD Castel-Default; NY R USDCTSD Castel-Scheduling; NY R USDCTSD Castel-Complex; NY R USDCTSD Castel-Trials; NY R USDCTSD Castel-Sentencing.

DISTRICT JUDGE DENISE L. COTE: NY R USDCTSD Cote-Civil Practices; NY R USDCTSD Cote-Pro Se; NY R USDCTSD Cote-Maritime Ord; NY R USDCTSD Cote-Crim Practices; NY R USDCTSD Cote-Crim Trials; NY R USDCTSD Cote-Sentencing.

DISTRICT JUDGE PAUL A. CROTTY: NY R USDCTSD Crotty-Practices; NY R USDCTSD Crotty-Sentencing; NY R USDCTSD Crotty-Calls; NY R USDCTSD Crotty-Scheduling.

DISTRICT JUDGE GEORGE B. DANIELS: NY R USDCTSD Daniels-Practices.

DISTRICT JUDGE KEVIN T. DUFFY: NY R USDCTSD Duffy-Practices.

DISTRICT JUDGE PAUL A. ENGELMAYER: NY R USDCTSD Engelmayer-Practices; NY R USDCTSD Engelmayer-Scheduling; NY R USDCTSD Engelmayer-Sentencing; NY R USDCTSD Engelmayer-Pro Se; NY R USDCTSD Engelmayer-Crim.

DISTRICT JUDGE KATHERINE POLK FAILLA: NY R USDCTSD Failla-Civ Prac; NY R USDCTSD Failla-Crim Prac; NY R USDCTSD Failla-Case Mgt.

DISTRICT JUDGE KATHERINE B. FORREST: NY R USDCTSD Forrest-Civil Prac; NY R USDCTSD Forrest-Crim Prac; NY R USDCTSD Forrest-Crim Pretrial; NY R USDCTSD Forrest-Scheduling; NY R USDCTSD Forrest-Patent Scheduling; NY R USDCTSD Forrest-Sentencing; NY R USDCTSD Forrest-Order 1; NY R USDCTSD Forrest-Order 2.

DISTRICT JUDGE JESSE M. FURMAN: NY R USDCTSD Furman-Civil Prac; NY R USDCTSD Furman-Crim Prac; NY R USDCTSD Furman-Pro Se Prac; NY R USDCTSD Furman-Trials; NY R USDCTSD Furman-Scheduling; NY R USDCTSD Furman-Rights.

DISTRICT JUDGE PAUL G. GARDEPHE: NY R USDCTSD Gardephe-Civ Prac; NY R USDCTSD Gardephe-Pretrial; NY R USDCTSD Gardephe-Prot Ord; NY R USDCTSD Gardephe-Maritime; NY R USDCTSD Gardephe-Crim Prac; NY R USDCTSD Gardephe-Trial.

DISTRICT JUDGE THOMAS P. GRIESA: NY R USDCTSD Griesa-Practices.

DISTRICT JUDGE CHARLES S. HAIGHT: NY R USDCTSD Haight-Practices.

DISTRICT JUDGE ALVIN K. HELLERSTEIN: NY R USDCTSD Hellerstein-Practices; NY R USDCTSD Hellerstein--Sept 11.

DISTRICT JUDGE LEWIS A. KAPLAN: NY R USDCTSD Kaplan-Practices; NY R USDCTSD Kaplan-Sentencing.

DISTRICT JUDGE KENNETH M. KARAS: NY R USDCTSD Karas-Practices; NY R USDCTSD Karas-Case Mgt; NY R USDCTSD Karas-Default; NY R USDCTSD Karas-Sentencing; NY R USDCTSD Karas-Rights.

DISTRICT JUDGE JOHN F. KEENAN: NY R USDCTSD Keenan-Practices.

DISTRICT JUDGE JOHN G. KOELTL: NY R USDCTSD Koeltl-Practices.

DISTRICT JUDGE VICTOR MARRERO: NY R USDCTSD Marrero-Practices; NY R USDCTSD Marrero-Scheduling; NY R USDCTSD Marrero-Default; NY R USDCTSD Marrero-Trial Proc.

DISTRICT JUDGE COLLEEN McMAHON: NY R USDCTSD McMahon-Practices; NY R USDCTSD McMahon-RICO; NY R USDCTSD McMahon-Copies; NY R USDCTSD McMahon-Scheduling; NY R USDCTSD McMahon-Elec Disc; NY R USDCTSD McMahon-Sentencing.

DISTRICT JUDGE ALISON J. NATHAN: NY R USDCTSD Nathan-Civ Prac; NY R USDCTSD Nathan-Crim Prac; NY R USDCTSD Nathan-Pro Se; NY R USDCTSD Nathan-Scheduling.

DISTRICT JUDGE J. PAUL OETKEN: NY R USDCTSD Oetken-Civ Prac; NY R USDCTSD Oetken-Case Mgt; NY R USDCTSD Oetken-Crim Prac; NY R USDCTSD Oetken-Pro Se.

DISTRICT JUDGE WILLIAM H. PAULEY, III: NY R USDCTSD Pauley-Crim Cases; NY R USDCTSD Pauley-Practices.

DISTRICT JUDGE LORETTA A. PRESKA: NY R USDCTSD Preska-Practices.

DISTRICT JUDGE JED S. RAKOFF: NY R USDCTSD Rakoff-Practices; NY R USDCTSD Rakoff-Scheduling; NY R USDCTSD Rakoff-Prot Ord; NY R USDCTSD Rakoff-Maritime Ord.

DISTRICT JUDGE EDGARDO RAMOS: NY R USDCTSD Ramos--Practices; NY R USDCTSD Ramos-Case Mgt.

DISTRICT JUDGE NELSON S. ROMAN: NY R USDCTSD Roman-Civ Prac; NY R USDCTSD Roman-Pro Se; NY R USDCTSD Roman-Crim Prac; NY R USDCTSD Roman-Case Mgt.

DISTRICT JUDGE LEONARD B. SAND: NY R USDCTSD Sand-Practices.

DISTRICT JUDGE LORNA G. SCHOFIELD: NY R USDCTSD Schofield-Civ Prac; NY R USDCTSD Schofield-Crim Prac; NY R USDCTSD Schofield-Sched; NY R USDCTSD Schofield-Pro Se; NY R USDCTSD Schofield-Advice.

DISTRICT JUDGE CATHY SEIBEL: NY R USDCTSD Seibel-Practices.

DISTRICT JUDGE LOUIS L. STANTON: NY R USDCTSD Stanton-Practices; NY R USDCTSD Stanton-Pretrial.

DISTRICT JUDGE SIDNEY H. STEIN: NY R USDCTSD Stein-Practices.

DISTRICT JUDGE RICHARD J. SULLIVAN: NY R USDCTSD Sullivan-Practices; NY R USDCTSD Sullivan-Scheduling; NY R USDCTSD Sullivan-Sentencing; NY R USDCTSD Sullivan-Juries; NY R USDCTSD Sullivan-Trial; NY R USDCTSD Sullivan-Default.

DISTRICT JUDGE LAURA TAYLOR SWAIN: NY R USDCTSD Swain-Practices; NY R USDCTSD Swain-Trial; NY R USDCTSD Swain-Crim Trial; NY R USDCTSD Swain-Juries; NY R USDCTSD Swain-Sentencing; NY R USDCTSD Swain-Rights.

DISTRICT JUDGE ROBERT W. SWEET: NY R USDCTSD Sweet-Practices.

DISTRICT JUDGE ANALISA TORRES: NY R USDCTSD Torres-Civ Prac; NY R USDCTSD Torres-Pro Se; NY R USDCTSD Torres-Scheduling.

DISTRICT JUDGE KIMBA M. WOOD: NY R USDCTSD Wood-Practices; NY R USDCTSD Wood-Scheduling; NY R USDCTSD Wood-Discovery; NY R USDCTSD Wood-RICO; NY R USDCTSD Wood-Juries; NY R USDCTSD Wood-Trial; NY R USDCTSD Wood-Media.

DISTRICT JUDGE GREGORY H. WOODS: NY R USDCTSD Woods-Civ Prac; NY R USDCTSD Woods-Pro Se; NY R USDCTSD Woods-Sched; NY R USDCTSD Woods-Crim Prac; NY R USDCTSD Woods-Protect Order; NY R USDCTSD Woods-Speedy Trial.

MAGISTRATE JUDGE JAMES L. COTT: NY R USDCTSD Cott-Practices; NY R USDCTSD Cott-Settlement.

MAGISTRATE JUDGE PAUL E. DAVISON: NY R USDCTSD Davison-Practices.

MAGISTRATE JUDGE RONALD L. ELLIS: NY R USDCTSD Ellis-Practices.

MAGISTRATE JUDGE KEVIN N. FOX: NY R USDCTSD Fox-Practices; NY R USDCTSD Fox-Settlement.

MAGISTRATE JUDGE JAMES C. FRANCIS: NY R USDCTSD Francis-Practices.

MAGISTRATE JUDGE DEBRA FREEMAN: NY R USDCTSD Freeman-Practices; NY R USDCTSD Freeman-Settlement.

MAGISTRATE JUDGE GABRIEL W. GORENSTEIN: NY R USDCTSD Gorenstein-Practices; NY R US-DCTSD Gorenstein-Ackn.

MAGISTRATE JUDGE FRANK MAAS: NY R USDCTSD Maas-Practices; NY R USDCTSD Maas-Discontinuance; NY R USDCTSD Maas-Conf; NY R USDCTSD Maas-Settlement.

MAGISTRATE JUDGE JUDITH C. McCARTHY: NY R USDCTSD McCarthy-Practices; NY R USDCTSD McCarthy-Conduct.

MAGISTRATE JUDGE BARBARA MOSES: NY R USDCTSD Moses-Practices.

MAGISTRATE JUDGE SARAH NETBURN: NY R USDCTSD Netburn-Civil; NY R USDCTSD Netburn-Settlement; NY R USDCTSD Netburn-Case Mgt; NY R USDCTSD Netburn--Pro Se.

MAGISTRATE JUDGE ANDREW J. PECK: NY R USDCTSD Peck-Practices; NY R USDCTSD Peck-Order; NY R USDCTSD Peck-Rule 502(d).

MAGISTRATE JUDGE HENRY PITMAN: NY R USDCTSD Pitman-Practices.

MAGISTRATE JUDGE LISA MARGARET SMITH: NY R USDCTSD Smith-Practices; NY R USDCTSD Smith-Trials.

## Motions, Oppositions and Replies
## Motion to Strike

### Document Last Updated September 2016

**A. Checklist**

- (I) ☐ Matters to be considered by moving party
  - (a) ☐ Required documents
    - (1) ☐ Notice of motion and motion
    - (2) ☐ Memorandum of law
    - (3) ☐ Certificate of service
  - (b) ☐ Supplemental documents
    - (1) ☐ Deposition
    - (2) ☐ Notice of constitutional question
    - (3) ☐ Nongovernmental corporate disclosure statement
    - (4) ☐ Copies of authorities
    - (5) ☐ Proposed order
    - (6) ☐ Statement explaining untimely electronic filing
    - (7) ☐ Courtesy copies
  - (c) ☐ Timing
    - (1) ☐ The court may act on motion made by a party either before responding to the pleading or, if a response is not allowed, within twenty-one (21) days after being served with the pleading
    - (2) ☐ A written motion and notice of the hearing must be served at least fourteen (14) days before the time specified for the hearing, with the following exceptions: (i) when the motion may be heard ex parte; (ii) when the Federal Rules of Civil Procedure set a different time; or (iii)

when a court order—which a party may, for good cause, apply for ex parte—sets a different time

(3) ❑ Any affidavit supporting a motion must be served with the motion

(II) ❑ Matters to be considered by opposing party

    (a) ❑ Required documents

        (1) ❑ Answering memorandum of law

        (2) ❑ Certificate of service

    (b) ❑ Supplemental documents

        (1) ❑ Deposition

        (2) ❑ Notice of constitutional question

        (3) ❑ Copies of authorities

        (4) ❑ Statement explaining untimely electronic filing

        (5) ❑ Courtesy copies

    (c) ❑ Timing

        (1) ❑ Any opposing affidavits and answering memoranda shall be served within fourteen (14) days after service of the moving papers

        (2) ❑ Except as FRCP 59(c) provides otherwise, any opposing affidavit must be served at least seven (7) days before the hearing, unless the court permits service at another time

## B. Timing

1. *Motion to strike.* The court may act on motion made by a party either before responding to the pleading or, if a response is not allowed, within twenty-one (21) days after being served with the pleading. FRCP 12(f)(2).

2. *Timing of motions, generally*

    a. *Motion and notice of hearing.* Except for letter-motions as permitted by NY R USDCTS&ED Civ Rule 7.1(d), and unless otherwise provided by statute or rule or by the Court in a Judge's Individual Practice or in a direction in a particular case, upon any motion, the notice of motion, supporting affidavits, and memoranda shall be served and filed as follows: on all civil motions, petitions, and applications, other than those described in NY R USDCTS&ED Civ Rule 6.1(a), and other than petitions for writs of habeas corpus, the notice of motion, supporting affidavits, and memoranda of law shall be served by the moving party on all other parties that have appeared in the action. NY R USDCTS&ED Civ Rule 6.1(b)(1). A written motion and notice of the hearing must be served at least fourteen (14) days before the time specified for the hearing, with the following exceptions:

        i. When the motion may be heard ex parte;

        ii. When the Federal Rules of Civil Procedure set a different time; or

        iii. When a court order—which a party may, for good cause, apply for ex parte—sets a different time. FRCP 6(c)(1).

    b. *Supporting affidavit.* Any affidavit supporting a motion must be served with the motion. FRCP 6(c)(2).

3. *Timing of opposing papers.* Except for letter-motions as permitted by NY R USDCTS&ED Civ Rule 7.1(d), and unless otherwise provided by statute or rule or by the Court in a Judge's Individual Practice or in a direction in a particular case, upon any motion, the notice of motion, supporting affidavits, and memoranda shall be served and filed as follows: on all civil motions, petitions, and applications, other than those described in NY R USDCTS&ED Civ Rule 6.1(a), and other than petitions for writs of habeas corpus, any opposing affidavits and answering memoranda shall be served within fourteen (14) days after service of the moving papers. NY R USDCTS&ED Civ Rule 6.1(b)(2).

    a. *Opposing affidavit.* Except as FRCP 59(c) provides otherwise, any opposing affidavit must be served

at least seven (7) days before the hearing, unless the court permits service at another time. FRCP 6(c)(2).

4. *Timing of reply papers.* Where the respondent files an answering affidavit setting up a new matter, the moving party ordinarily is allowed a reasonable time to file a reply affidavit since failure to deny the new matter by affidavit may operate as an admission of its truth. AMJUR MOTIONS § 25.

   a. *Reply affidavits and reply memoranda of law.* Except for letter-motions as permitted by NY R USDCTS&ED Civ Rule 7.1(d), and unless otherwise provided by statute or rule or by the Court in a Judge's Individual Practice or in a direction in a particular case, upon any motion, the notice of motion, supporting affidavits, and memoranda shall be served and filed as follows: on all civil motions, petitions, and applications, other than those described in NY R USDCTS&ED Civ Rule 6.1(a), and other than petitions for writs of habeas corpus, any reply affidavits and memoranda of law shall be served within seven (7) days after service of the answering papers. NY R USDCTS&ED Civ Rule 6.1(b)(3).

5. *Effect of a FRCP 12 motion on the time to serve a responsive pleading.* Unless the court sets a different time, serving a motion under FRCP 12 alters the periods in FRCP 12(a) as follows:

   a. If the court denies the motion or postpones its disposition until trial, the responsive pleading must be served within fourteen (14) days after notice of the court's action; or

   b. If the court grants a motion for a more definite statement, the responsive pleading must be served within fourteen (14) days after the more definite statement is served. FRCP 12(a)(4).

6. *Computation of time*

   a. *Computing time.* FRCP 6 applies in computing any time period specified in the Federal Rules of Civil Procedure, in any local rule or court order, or in any statute that does not specify a method of computing time. FRCP 6(a). In computing any period of time prescribed or allowed by the Local Civil Rules of the United States District Courts for the Southern and Eastern Districts of New York or the Local Admiralty and Maritime Rules, the provisions of FRCP 6 shall apply unless otherwise stated. NY R USDCTS&ED Civ Rule 6.4.

      i. *Period stated in days or a longer unit.* In computing periods of days, refer to FRCP 6 and NY R USDCTS&ED Civ Rule 6.4. NY R USDCTS&ED Civ Rule 6.1(b). When the period is stated in days or a longer unit of time:

         • Exclude the day of the event that triggers the period;

         • Count every day, including intermediate Saturdays, Sundays, and legal holidays; and

         • Include the last day of the period, but if the last day is a Saturday, Sunday, or legal holiday, the period continues to run until the end of the next day that is not a Saturday, Sunday, or legal holiday. FRCP 6(a)(1). In the Local Civil Rules of the United States District Courts for the Southern and Eastern Districts of New York, as in the Federal Rules of Civil Procedure as amended effective December 1, 2009, Saturdays, Sundays, and legal holidays are no longer excluded in computing periods of time. If the last day of the period is a Saturday, Sunday, or legal holiday, the period continues to run until the end of the next day that is not a Saturday, Sunday, or legal holiday. NY R USDCTS&ED Civ Rule 6.4.

      ii. *Period stated in hours.* When the period is stated in hours:

         • Begin counting immediately on the occurrence of the event that triggers the period;

         • Count every hour, including hours during intermediate Saturdays, Sundays, and legal holidays; and

         • If the period would end on a Saturday, Sunday, or legal holiday, the period continues to run until the same time on the next day that is not a Saturday, Sunday, or legal holiday. FRCP 6(a)(2). In the Local Civil Rules of the United States District Courts for the Southern and Eastern Districts of New York, as in the Federal Rules of Civil Procedure as amended effective December 1, 2009, Saturdays, Sundays, and legal holidays are no longer excluded in computing periods of time. If the last day of the period is a Saturday, Sunday, or legal holiday, the period continues to run until the end of the next day that is not a Saturday, Sunday, or legal holiday. NY R USDCTS&ED Civ Rule 6.4.

iii. *Inaccessibility of the clerk's office.* Unless the court orders otherwise, if the clerk's office is inaccessible:

- On the last day for filing under FRCP 6(a)(1), then the time for filing is extended to the first accessible day that is not a Saturday, Sunday, or legal holiday; or

- During the last hour for filing under FRCP 6(a)(2), then the time for filing is extended to the same time on the first accessible day that is not a Saturday, Sunday, or legal holiday. FRCP 6(a)(3).

iv. *"Last day" defined.* Unless a different time is set by a statute, local rule, or court order, the last day ends:

- For electronic filing, at midnight in the court's time zone; and

- For filing by other means, when the clerk's office is scheduled to close. FRCP 6(a)(4).

v. *"Next day" defined.* The "next day" is determined by continuing to count forward when the period is measured after an event and backward when measured before an event. FRCP 6(a)(5).

vi. *"Legal holiday" defined.* "Legal holiday" means:

- The day set aside by statute for observing New Year's Day, Martin Luther King Jr.'s Birthday, Washington's Birthday, Memorial Day, Independence Day, Labor Day, Columbus Day, Veterans' Day, Thanksgiving Day, or Christmas Day;

- Any day declared a holiday by the President or Congress; and

- For periods that are measured after an event, any other day declared a holiday by the state where the district court is located. FRCP 6(a)(6).

b. *Computation of electronic filing deadlines.* You can file electronically twenty-four (24) hours a day, seven (7) days a week, three hundred sixty-five (365) days a year. NY R USDCTSD CM/ECF, S.D.(II)(13)(13.10). Electronic filing must be completed before midnight local time where the Court is located in order to be considered timely filed that day. NY R USDCTSD CM/ECF, S.D.(I)(3)(3.3); NY R USDCTSD CM/ECF, S.D.(II)(13)(13.10); NY R USDCTSD CM/ECF, S.D.(II)(19)(19.4). An electronically filed document is deemed filed on the "filed on" date indicated on the Notice of Electronic Filing (NEF). NY R USDCTSD CM/ECF, S.D.(II)(13)(13.11).

i. *Technical failures.* A Filing User whose filing is made untimely as the result of a technical failure may seek appropriate relief from the Court. NY R USDCTSD CM/ECF, S.D.(I)(11). If you missed a filing deadline when the ECF system was out of order, attach a statement to your filing explaining how the interruption in service prevented you from filing in a timely fashion. NY R USDCTSD CM/ECF, S.D.(II)(23)(23.5).

c. *Extending time*

i. *In general.* When an act may or must be done within a specified time, the court may, for good cause, extend the time:

- With or without motion or notice if the court acts, or if a request is made, before the original time or its extension expires; or

- On motion made after the time has expired if the party failed to act because of excusable neglect. FRCP 6(b)(1).

ii. *Exceptions.* A court must not extend the time to act under FRCP 50(b), FRCP 50(d), FRCP 52(b), FRCP 59(b), FRCP 59(d), FRCP 59(e), and FRCP 60(b). FRCP 6(b)(2).

iii. Refer to the United States District Court for the Southern District of New York KeyRules Motion for Continuance/Extension of Time document for more information on extending time.

d. *Additional time after certain kinds of service.* When a party may or must act within a specified time after service and service is made under FRCP 5(b)(2)(C), FRCP 5(b)(2)(D), FRCP 5(b)(2)(E), or FRCP 5(b)(2)(F), three (3) days are added after the period would otherwise expire under FRCP 6(a). FRCP 6(d). Overnight delivery service shall be deemed service by mail for purposes of FRCP 5 and FRCP 6. NY R USDCTS&ED Civ Rule 5.3.

7. *Individual judge practices.* Refer to the Miscellaneous section of this document for information on individual judge practices on timing of documents.

## C. General Requirements

1. *Motions, generally*

   a. *Requirements.* A request for a court order must be made by motion. The motion must:

      i. Be in writing unless made during a hearing or trial;

      ii. State with particularity the grounds for seeking the order; and

      iii. State the relief sought. FRCP 7(b)(1).

   b. *Notice of motion.* A party interested in resisting the relief sought by a motion has a right to notice thereof, and an opportunity to be heard. AMJUR MOTIONS § 12.

      i. In addition to statutory or court rule provisions requiring notice of a motion—the purpose of such a notice requirement having been said to be to prevent a party from being prejudicially surprised by a motion—principles of natural justice dictate that an adverse party generally must be given notice that a motion will be presented to the court. AMJUR MOTIONS § 12.

      ii. "Notice," in this regard, means reasonable notice, including a meaningful opportunity to prepare and to defend against allegations of a motion. AMJUR MOTIONS § 12.

   c. *Writing requirement.* The writing requirement is intended to insure that the adverse parties are informed and have a record of both the motion's pendency and the grounds on which the movant seeks an order. FPP § 1191; Feldberg v. Quechee Lakes Corp., 463 F.3d 195 (2d Cir. 2006).

      i. It is sufficient "if the motion is stated in a written notice of the hearing of the motion." FPP § 1191.

   d. *Particularity requirement.* The particularity requirement insures that the opposing parties will have notice of their opponent's contentions. FEDPROC § 62:364; Goodman v. 1973 26 Foot Trojan Vessel, Arkansas Registration No. AR1439SN, 859 F.2d 71, 12 Fed.R.Serv.3d 645 (8th Cir. 1988). That requirement ensures that notice of the basis for the motion is provided to the court and to the opposing party so as to avoid prejudice, provide the opponent with a meaningful opportunity to respond, and provide the court with enough information to process the motion correctly. FEDPROC § 62:364; Andreas v. Volkswagen of America, Inc., 336 F.3d 789, 56 Fed.R.Serv.3d 6 (8th Cir. 2003).

      i. Reasonable specification of the grounds for a motion is sufficient. However, where a movant fails to state even one ground for granting the motion in question, the movant has failed to meet the minimal standard of "reasonable specification." FEDPROC § 62:364; Martinez v. Trainor, 556 F.2d 818, 23 Fed.R.Serv.2d 403 (7th Cir. 1977).

      ii. The court may excuse the failure to comply with the particularity requirement if it is inadvertent, and where no prejudice is shown by the opposing party. FEDPROC § 62:364.

   e. *Ex parte orders or orders to show cause to bring on a motion.* No ex parte order, or order to show cause to bring on a motion, will be granted except upon a clear and specific showing by affidavit of good and sufficient reasons why a procedure other than by notice of motion is necessary, and stating whether a previous application for similar relief has been made. NY R USDCTS&ED Civ Rule 6.1(d).

   f. *Letter-motions.* Applications for extensions or adjournments, applications for a pre-motion conference, and similar non-dispositive matters as permitted by the instructions regarding ECF published on the website of each respective Court and any pertinent Individual Judge's Practices, may be brought by letter-motion filed via ECF pursuant to NY R USDCTS&ED Civ Rule 5.2(b). NY R USDCTS&ED Civ Rule 7.1(d).

      i. The following list of motions. . .may be made by LETTER-MOTION: (1) Motion to Adjourn Conference; (2) Motion to Change Attorney Name on Roll; (3) Motion to Compel; (4) Motion for Conference; (5) Motion to Consolidate Cases; (6) Motion to Continue; (7) Motion re: Discovery; (8) Motion to Expedite; (9) Motion for Extension of Time; (10) Motion for Extension of Time to Amend; (11) Motion for Extension of Time to Answer; (12) Motion for

Extension of Time to Complete Discovery; (13) Motion for Extension of Time to File Document; (14) Motion for Extension of Time to File Response/Reply; (15) Motion for Extension of Time re Transcript; (16) Motion to File Amicus Brief; (17) Motion for Leave to File Document; (18) Motion for Leave to File Excess Pages; (19) Motion for Local Rule 37.2 Conference; (20) Motion for Oral Argument; (21) Motion to Reopen; (22) Motion to Reopen Case; (23) Motion to Seal Document; (24) Motion to Stay; (25) Motion to Substitute Attorney. NY R USDCTSD CM/ECF, S.D.(II)(13)(13.1).

    ii.   If the Filing User is making a type of motion that does not appear in this list, the motion may not be made by letter. NY R USDCTSD CM/ECF, S.D.(II)(13)(13.1).

    iii.   For more information on letter motions, refer to NY R USDCTSD CM/ECF, S.D.(II)(13)(13.1).

2.   *Motion to strike.* The court may strike from a pleading an insufficient defense or any redundant, immaterial, impertinent, or scandalous matter. The court may act: (1) on its own; or (2) on motion made by a party either before responding to the pleading or, if a response is not allowed, within twenty-one (21) days after being served with the pleading. FRCP 12(f). FRCP 12(f) also is designed to reinforce the requirement in FRCP 8(e) that pleadings be simple, concise, and direct. However, as the cases make clear, it is neither an authorized nor a proper way to procure the dismissal of all or a part of a complaint, or a counterclaim, or to strike an opponent's affidavits. FPP § 1380.

   a.   *Practice on a motion to strike.* All well-pleaded facts are taken as admitted on a motion to strike but conclusions of law or conclusions drawn from the facts do not have to be treated in that fashion by the district judge. FPP § 1380. Both because striking a portion of a pleading is a drastic remedy and because it often is sought by the movant simply as a dilatory or harassing tactic, numerous judicial decisions make it clear that motions under FRCP 12(f) are viewed with disfavor by the federal courts and are infrequently granted. FPP § 1380.

   b.   *Striking an insufficient defense.* Only if a defense is insufficient as a matter of law will it be stricken. If a defense cannot succeed under any set of circumstances alleged, the defense may be deemed insufficient as a matter of law. In other words, a defense may be stricken if, on the face of the pleadings, it is patently frivolous, or if it is clearly invalid as a matter of law. FEDPROC § 62:412.

    i.   A defense will be stricken if it could not possibly prevent recovery by the plaintiff on its claim. FEDPROC § 62:413. In addition, a defense may be stricken if:

- The defense requires separate statements;
- The defense has been previously advanced and rejected; or
- The defense cannot be waived. FEDPROC § 62:413.

   c.   *Striking immaterial or impertinent matter.* Immaterial or impertinent matter will be stricken from a pleading if it is clear that it can have no possible bearing upon the subject matter of the litigation, and that its inclusion will prejudice the movant. If there is any doubt as to whether under any contingency the matter may raise an issue, the motion should be denied. FEDPROC § 62:415.

    i.   "Immaterial matter," for purposes of FRCP 12(f), is matter which has no essential or important relationship to the claim for relief or the defenses being pleaded. FEDPROC § 62:414. A statement of unnecessary particulars in connection with and descriptive of that which is material may be stricken as immaterial matter. FEDPROC § 62:416.

    ii.   "Impertinent matter," for purposes of FRCP 12(f), consists of statements that do not pertain, and are not necessary, to the issues in question. FEDPROC § 62:414.

   d.   *Striking redundant matter.* "Redundant matter," for purposes of FRCP 12(f), consists of allegations that constitute a needless repetition of other averments or which are wholly foreign to the issue to be decided. However, even if allegations are redundant, they need not be stricken if their presence in the pleading cannot prejudice the moving party. FEDPROC § 62:417.

    i.   Merely duplicative remedies do not necessarily make claims "redundant," within the meaning of FRCP 12(f), if the claims otherwise require proof of different elements, but a claim that merely recasts the same elements under the guise of a different theory may be stricken as redundant. FEDPROC § 62:417.

e. *Striking scandalous matter.* A matter is deemed scandalous, for purposes of FRCP 12(f), when it improperly casts a derogatory light on someone, usually a party to the action. Scandalous matter also consists of any unnecessary allegation which reflects cruelly upon the moral character of an individual, or states anything in repulsive language which detracts from the dignity of the court. To be scandalous, degrading charges must be irrelevant, or, if relevant, must go into in unnecessary detail. FEDPROC § 62:418.

    i. Allegations may be stricken as scandalous if the matter bears no possible relation to the controversy or may cause the objecting party prejudice. FEDPROC § 62:418.

    ii. But there are several limitations on the court's willingness to strike scandalous allegations. For example, it is not enough that the matter offends the sensibilities of the objecting party or the person who is the subject of the statements in the pleading, if the challenged allegations describe acts or events that are relevant to the action. FPP § 1382.

f. *Striking sham or false matter.* FRCP 12(f) does not authorize a motion to strike part or all of a pleading on the ground that it is sham, and the grounds for a motion to strike similarly do not include falsity of the matter alleged. FEDPROC § 62:419; PAE Government Services, Inc. v. MPRI, Inc., 514 F.3d 856 (9th Cir. 2007). However, it has been said that a court will strike a pleading according to FRCP 12(f) when it appears beyond peradventure that it is a sham and false and that its allegations are devoid of factual basis. FEDPROC § 62:419.

g. *Striking conclusions of law.* Unwarranted conclusions of law may be stricken from a pleading pursuant to FRCP 12(f), but ordinarily an allegation is not subject to being stricken merely because it is a conclusion of law. To the contrary, the Federal Rules of Civil Procedure do not condemn conclusions of law, but rather encourage them as at times the clearest and simplest way of stating a claim for relief. Conclusions of law must be unwarranted enough to justify a motion to strike, such as when a plaintiff states causes of action under a federal statute which provides no explicit private right of action. FEDPROC § 62:420.

h. *Striking other particular matter.* Under FRCP 12(f), which permits a court to order stricken from any pleading any redundant, immaterial, impertinent, or scandalous matter, courts have the authority to strike a prayer for relief seeking damages that are not recoverable as a matter of law. A motion to strike may be used to remove an excessive or unauthorized claim for damages. Furthermore, a motion to strike a demand for punitive damages under FRCP 12(f) may be proper if such damages are clearly not collectible, such as in an ordinary breach of contract action. However, there are other ways to raise this issue, and in a particular case, one of these other methods may be more appropriate, such as a motion to dismiss for failure to state a claim pursuant to FRCP 12(b)(6). FEDPROC § 62:421.

i. *Form.* On a motion to strike portions of a pleading, the movant must indicate what paragraphs are being challenged in order to fulfill the particularity requirement; the movant cannot merely state the conclusion that the allegations are too indefinite and insufficient to state a claim or defense. FPP § 1192.

j. *Joining motions*

    i. *Right to join.* A motion under FRCP 12 may be joined with any other motion allowed by FRCP 12. FRCP 12(g)(1).

    ii. *Limitation on further motions.* Except as provided in FRCP 12(h)(2) or FRCP 12(h)(3), a party that makes a motion under FRCP 12 must not make another motion under FRCP 12 raising a defense or objection that was available to the party but omitted from its earlier motion. FRCP 12(g)(2).

3. *Opposing papers.* The Federal Rules of Civil Procedure do not require any formal answer, return, or reply to a motion, except where the Federal Rules of Civil Procedure or local rules may require affidavits, memoranda, or other papers to be filed in opposition to a motion. Such papers are simply to apprise the court of such opposition and the grounds of that opposition. FEDPROC § 62:359. Except for letter-motions as permitted by NY R USDCTS&ED Civ Rule 7.1(d) or as otherwise permitted by the Court, all oppositions and replies with respect to motions shall comply with NY R USDCTS&ED Civ Rule

7.1(a)(2) and NY R USDCTS&ED Civ Rule 7.1(a)(3), and an opposing party who seeks relief that goes beyond the denial of the motion shall comply as well with NY R USDCTS&ED Civ Rule 7.1(a)(1). NY R USDCTS&ED Civ Rule 7.1(b).

a. *Effect of failure to respond to motion.* Although in the absence of statutory provision or court rule, a motion ordinarily does not require a written answer, when a party files a motion and the opposing party fails to respond, the court may construe such failure to respond as nonopposition to the motion or an admission that the motion was meritorious, may take the facts alleged in the motion as true—the rule in some jurisdictions being that the failure to respond to a fact set forth in a motion is deemed an admission—and may grant the motion if the relief requested appears to be justified. AMJUR MOTIONS § 28.

b. *Assent or no opposition not determinative.* However, a motion will not be granted automatically simply because an "assent" or a notation of "no opposition" has been filed; federal judges frequently deny motions that have been assented to when it is thought that justice so dictates. FPP § 1190.

c. *Responsive pleading inappropriate as response to motion.* An attempt to answer or oppose a motion with a responsive pleading usually is not appropriate. FPP § 1190.

4. *Reply papers.* A moving party may be required or permitted to prepare papers in addition to his original motion papers. AMJUR MOTIONS § 25. Papers answering or replying to opposing papers may be appropriate, in the interests of justice, where it appears there is a substantial reason for allowing a reply. Thus, a court may accept reply papers where a party demonstrates that the papers to which it seeks to file a reply raise new issues that are material to the disposition of the question before the court, or where the court determines, sua sponte, that it wishes further briefing of an issue raised in those papers and orders the submission of additional papers. FEDPROC § 62:360. Except for letter-motions as permitted by NY R USDCTS&ED Civ Rule 7.1(d) or as otherwise permitted by the Court, all oppositions and replies with respect to motions shall comply with NY R USDCTS&ED Civ Rule 7.1(a)(2) and NY R USDCTS&ED Civ Rule 7.1(a)(3). NY R USDCTS&ED Civ Rule 7.1(b).

a. *Function of reply papers.* The function of a reply affidavit is to answer the arguments made in opposition to the position taken by the movant and not to permit the movant to introduce new arguments in support of the motion. AMJUR MOTIONS § 25.

b. *Issues raised for the first time in a reply document.* However, the view has been followed in some jurisdictions, that as a matter of judicial economy, where there is no prejudice and where the issues could be raised simply by filing a motion to dismiss, the trial court has discretion to consider arguments raised for the first time in a reply memorandum, and that a trial court may grant a motion to strike issues raised for the first time in a reply memorandum. AMJUR MOTIONS § 26.

5. *Orders on motions.* A memorandum signed by the Court of the decision on a motion that does not finally determine all claims for relief, or an oral decision on such a motion, shall constitute the order unless the memorandum or oral decision directs the submission or settlement of an order in more extended form. The notation in the docket of a memorandum or of an oral decision that does not direct the submission or settlement of an order in more extended form shall constitute the entry of the order. Where an order in more extended form is required to be submitted or settled, the notation in the docket of such order shall constitute the entry of the order. NY R USDCTS&ED Civ Rule 6.2.

6. *Complex civil cases.* For information on procedures for complex civil cases, refer to NY R USDCTSD Order 11 Misc 00388.

7. *Related cases.* It shall be the continuing duty of each attorney appearing in any civil or criminal case to bring promptly to the attention of the Court all facts which said attorney believes are relevant to a determination that said case and one or more pending civil or criminal cases should be heard by the same Judge, in order to avoid unnecessary duplication of judicial effort. As soon as the attorney becomes aware of such relationship, said attorney shall notify the Judges to whom the cases have been assigned. NY R USDCTS&ED Civ Rule 1.6(a). If counsel fails to comply with NY R USDCTS&ED Civ Rule 1.6(a), the Court may assess reasonable costs directly against counsel whose action has obstructed the effective administration of the Court's business. NY R USDCTS&ED Civ Rule 1.6(b).

a. *Determination of relatedness.* Subject to the limitations set forth in NY R USDCTSD Div. Bus., Rule

13(a)(2), a civil case, bankruptcy appeal, or motion to withdraw the bankruptcy reference will be deemed related to one or more civil cases, appeals or motions when the interests of justice and efficiency will be served. In determining relatedness, a judge will consider whether (A) the actions concern the same or substantially similar parties, property, transactions or events; (B) there is substantial factual overlap; (C) the parties could be subjected to conflicting orders; and (D) whether absent a determination of relatedness there would be a substantial duplication of effort and expense, delay, or undue burden on the Court, parties or witnesses. NY R USDCTSD Div. Bus., Rule 13(a)(1). Nothing in this NY R USDCTSD Div. Bus., Rule 13 is intended to preclude parties from moving for consolidated proceedings under FRCP 42. NY R USDCTSD Div. Bus., Rule 13(a)(1). Notwithstanding NY R USDCTSD Div. Bus., Rule 13(a)(1):

    i.   Civil cases shall not be deemed related merely because they involve common legal issues or the same parties. NY R USDCTSD Div. Bus., Rule 13(a)(2)(A).

    ii.   Other than cases subject to NY R USDCTSD Div. Bus., Rule 4(b) and actions seeking the enforcement of a judgment or settlement in or of an earlier case, civil cases presumptively shall not be deemed related unless both cases are pending before the Court (or the earlier case is on appeal). NY R USDCTSD Div. Bus., Rule 13(a)(2)(B).

  b.  *Procedure in regard to cases said to be related*

    i.   *Disclosure of contention of relatedness.* When a civil case is filed or removed or a bankruptcy appeal or motion to withdraw the reference of an adversary proceeding from the bankruptcy court is filed, the person filing or removing shall disclose on form JSC44C any contention of relatedness and shall file a Related Case Statement stating clearly and succinctly the basis for the contention. A copy of the civil cover sheet and Related Case Statement shall be served with the complaint, notice of removal, notice of appeal, or motion. Any party may contest a claim of relatedness by any other in writing addressed to the judge having the case with the lowest docket number of all cases claimed to be related. However, the foregoing shall not delay the assignment process or the operation of NY R USDCTSD Div. Bus., Rule 13. NY R USDCTSD Div. Bus., Rule 13(b)(1). [Editor's note: the reference to form JSC44C is likely meant to be form JS44C-SDNY: Civil Court Cover Sheet].

    ii.   *Claims of relatedness by other parties.* A party other than the one filing a case, bankruptcy appeal or motion to withdraw the reference that contends its case is related to another may so advise in writing the judge assigned in its case and request a transfer of its case to the judge that the party contends has the related case with the lowest docket number. If the assigned judge believes the case is related under NY R USDCTSD Div. Bus., Rule 13(a), he or she shall refer the question to the judge having the case with the lowest docket number. In the event the latter judge agrees, the case shall be transferred to that judge unless the Assignment Committee disagrees. NY R USDCTSD Div. Bus., Rule 13(b)(3).

  c.  For more information on related cases, refer to NY R USDCTSD Div. Bus., Rule 13.

8.  *Alternative dispute resolution (ADR).* The U.S. District Court for the Southern District of New York provides litigants with opportunities to discuss settlement through judicial settlement conferences and mediation. NY R USDCTS&ED Civ Rule 83.9(a).

  a.  *Consideration of alternative dispute resolution.* In all civil cases, including those eligible for mediation pursuant to NY R USDCTS&ED Civ Rule 83.9(e), each party shall consider the use of mediation or a judicial settlement conference and shall report to the assigned Judge at the initial FRCP 16(b) case management conference, or subsequently, whether the party believes mediation or a judicial settlement conference may facilitate the resolution of the lawsuit. Judges are encouraged to note the availability of the mediation program and/or a judicial settlement conference before, at, or after the initial FRCP 16(b) case management conference. NY R USDCTS&ED Civ Rule 83.9(d).

  b.  *Mediation.* In mediation, parties and counsel meet, sometimes collectively and sometimes individually, with a neutral third party (the mediator) who has been trained to facilitate confidential settlement discussions. The parties articulate their respective positions and interests and generate options for a mutually agreeable resolution to the dispute. The mediator assists the parties in reaching their own negotiated settlement by defining the issues, probing and assessing the strengths and weaknesses of each party's legal positions, and identifying areas of agreement and disagreement. The main benefits of mediation are that it can result in an expeditious and less costly resolution of the litigation, and can produce creative solutions to complex disputes often unavailable in traditional litigation. NY R USDCTS&ED Civ Rule 83.9(b).

   i. *Mediation program eligibility.* All civil cases other than Social Security, habeas corpus, and tax cases are eligible for mediation, whether assigned to Manhattan or White Plains. NY R USDCTS&ED Civ Rule 83.9(e)(1).

- The Board of Judges may, by Administrative Order, direct that certain specified categories of cases shall automatically be submitted to the mediation program. The assigned District Judge or Magistrate Judge may issue a written order exempting a particular case with or without the request of the parties. NY R USDCTS&ED Civ Rule 83.9(e)(2).

- For all other cases, the assigned District Judge or Magistrate Judge may determine that a case is appropriate for mediation and may order that case to mediation, with or without the consent of the parties, before, at, or after the initial FRCP 16(b) case management conference. Alternatively, the parties should notify the assigned Judge at any time of their desire to mediate. NY R USDCTS&ED Civ Rule 83.9(e)(3).

  c. *Judicial settlement conferences.* Judicial settlement conferences may be ordered by District Judges or Magistrate Judges with or without the request or consent of the parties. NY R USDCTS&ED Civ Rule 83.9(f).

  d. For more information on alternative dispute resolution (ADR), refer to NY R USDCTS&ED Civ Rule 83.9.

9. *Individual judge practices.* Refer to the Miscellaneous section of this document for information on individual judge practices on general requirements for documents.

## D. Documents

1. *Documents for moving party*

  a. *Required documents*

    i. *Notice of motion and motion.* Except for letter-motions as permitted by NY R USDCTS&ED Civ Rule 7.1(d) or as otherwise permitted by the Court, all motions shall include the following motion papers: a notice of motion, or an order to show cause signed by the Court, which shall specify the applicable rules or statutes pursuant to which the motion is brought, and shall specify the relief sought by the motion. NY R USDCTS&ED Civ Rule 7.1(a)(1). Refer to the General Requirements section of this document for information on the notice of motion and motion.

    ii. *Memorandum of law.* Except for letter-motions as permitted by NY R USDCTS&ED Civ Rule 7.1(d) or as otherwise permitted by the Court, all motions shall include the following motion papers: a memorandum of law, setting forth the cases and other authorities relied upon in support of the motion, and divided, under appropriate headings, into as many parts as there are issues to be determined. NY R USDCTS&ED Civ Rule 7.1(a)(2).

    iii. *Certificate of service.* FRCP 5(d) requires that the person making service under FRCP 5 certify that service has been effected. FRCP 5(Advisory Committee Notes). Having such information on file may be useful for many purposes, including proof of service if an issue arises concerning the effectiveness of the service. FRCP 5(Advisory Committee Notes).

- Such paper service [on attorneys and pro se parties who are not Filing or Receiving Users] must be documented by electronically filing proof of service. NY R USDCTSD CM/ECF, S.D.(I)(9)(9.2); NY R USDCTSD CM/ECF, S.D.(I)(19)(19.3)(b). Pro se parties who are not Filing Users are exempt from that portion of NY R USDCTSD CM/ECF, S.D.(I)(19)(19.3) requiring proof of service to be filed electronically. NY R USDCTSD CM/ECF, S.D.(I)(19)(19.3).

  b. *Supplemental documents.* Matter outside the pleadings normally is not considered on a FRCP 12(f) motion; for example, affidavits in support of or in opposition to the motion typically may not be used. FPP § 1380.

i. *Deposition.* Notwithstanding the general rule that matters outside the pleadings should ordinarily not be considered in passing upon a motion to strike under FRCP 12(f), a court may consider a deposition in deciding a FRCP 12(f) motion if the attorneys for both the plaintiff and the defendant, in their respective briefs, refer to the deposition and to the testimony contained therein. FEDPROC § 62:407.

- *Discovery materials.* A party seeking or opposing relief under FRCP 26 through FRCP 37 inclusive, or making or opposing any other motion or application, shall quote or attach only those portions of the depositions, interrogatories, requests for documents, requests for admissions, or other discovery or disclosure materials, together with the responses and objections thereto, that are the subject of the discovery motion or application, or that are cited in papers submitted in connection with any other motion or application. NY R USDCTS&ED Civ Rule 5.1.

ii. *Notice of constitutional question.* A party that files a pleading, written motion, or other paper drawing into question the constitutionality of a federal or state statute must promptly:

- *File notice.* File a notice of constitutional question stating the question and identifying the paper that raises it, if: (1) a federal statute is questioned and the parties do not include the United States, one of its agencies, or one of its officers or employees in an official capacity; or (2) a state statute is questioned and the parties do not include the state, one of its agencies, or one of its officers or employees in an official capacity; and

- *Serve notice.* Serve the notice and paper on the Attorney General of the United States if a federal statute is questioned—or on the state attorney general if a state statute is questioned—either by certified or registered mail or by sending it to an electronic address designated by the attorney general for this purpose. FRCP 5.1(a).

- *No forfeiture.* A party's failure to file and serve the notice, or the court's failure to certify, does not forfeit a constitutional claim or defense that is otherwise timely asserted. FRCP 5.1(d).

iii. *Nongovernmental corporate disclosure statement*

- *Contents.* A nongovernmental corporate party must file two (2) copies of a disclosure statement that: (1) identifies any parent corporation and any publicly held corporation owning ten percent (10%) or more of its stock; or (2) states that there is no such corporation. FRCP 7.1(a).

- *Time to file; Supplemental filing.* A party must: (1) file the disclosure statement with its first appearance, pleading, petition, motion, response, or other request addressed to the court; and (2) promptly file a supplemental statement if any required information changes. FRCP 7.1(b). For purposes of FRCP 7.1(b)(2), "promptly" shall mean "within fourteen days," that is, parties are required to file a supplemental disclosure statement within fourteen (14) days of the time there is any change in the information required in a disclosure statement filed pursuant to those rules. NY R USDCTS&ED Civ Rule 7.1.1.

iv. *Copies of authorities.* In cases involving a pro se litigant, counsel shall, when serving a memorandum of law (or other submissions to the Court), provide the pro se litigant (but not other counsel or the Court) with copies of cases and other authorities cited therein that are unpublished or reported exclusively on computerized databases. Upon request, counsel shall provide the pro se litigant with copies of such unpublished cases and other authorities as are cited in a decision of the Court and were not previously cited by any party. NY R USDCTS&ED Civ Rule 7.2.

v. *Proposed order.* Refer to the Format section of this document for information on the format of submitting a proposed order to the court.

vi. *Statement explaining untimely electronic filing.* If you missed a filing deadline when the ECF system was out of order, attach a statement to your filing explaining how the interruption in service prevented you from filing in a timely fashion. NY R USDCTSD CM/ECF, S.D.(II)(23)(23.5).

    vii.   *Courtesy copies.* Read the judge's Individual Practices to learn if courtesy copies are required. NY R USDCTSD CM/ECF, S.D.(II)(13)(13.17). Judges' Individual Practices should continue to be followed with respect to delivery of courtesy copies. NY R USDCTSD CM/ECF, S.D.(I)(3)(3.4).

2.  *Documents for opposing party*

  a.  *Required documents*

    i.   *Answering memorandum of law.* Except for letter-motions as permitted by NY R USDCTS&ED Civ Rule 7.1(d) or as otherwise permitted by the Court, all oppositions and replies with respect to motions shall comply with NY R USDCTS&ED Civ Rule 7.1(a)(2). NY R USDCTS&ED Civ Rule 7.1(b). Except for letter-motions as permitted by NY R USDCTS&ED Civ Rule 7.1(d) or as otherwise permitted by the Court, all motions shall include the following motion papers: a memorandum of law, setting forth the cases and other authorities relied upon in support of the motion, and divided, under appropriate headings, into as many parts as there are issues to be determined. NY R USDCTS&ED Civ Rule 7.1(a)(2). Refer to the General Requirements section of this document for information on the opposing papers.

    ii.  *Certificate of service.* FRCP 5(d) requires that the person making service under FRCP 5 certify that service has been effected. FRCP 5(Advisory Committee Notes). Having such information on file may be useful for many purposes, including proof of service if an issue arises concerning the effectiveness of the service. FRCP 5(Advisory Committee Notes).

       • Such paper service [on attorneys and pro se parties who are not Filing or Receiving Users] must be documented by electronically filing proof of service. NY R USDCTSD CM/ECF, S.D.(I)(9)(9.2); NY R USDCTSD CM/ECF, S.D.(I)(19)(19.3)(b). Pro se parties who are not Filing Users are exempt from that portion of NY R USDCTSD CM/ECF, S.D.(I)(19)(19.3) requiring proof of service to be filed electronically. NY R USDCTSD CM/ECF, S.D.(I)(19)(19.3).

  b.  *Supplemental documents.* Matter outside the pleadings normally is not considered on a FRCP 12(f) motion; for example, affidavits in support of or in opposition to the motion typically may not be used. FPP § 1380.

    i.   *Deposition.* Notwithstanding the general rule that matters outside the pleadings should ordinarily not be considered in passing upon a motion to strike under FRCP 12(f), a court may consider a deposition in deciding a FRCP 12(f) motion if the attorneys for both the plaintiff and the defendant, in their respective briefs, refer to the deposition and to the testimony contained therein. FEDPROC § 62:407.

       • *Discovery materials.* A party seeking or opposing relief under FRCP 26 through FRCP 37 inclusive, or making or opposing any other motion or application, shall quote or attach only those portions of the depositions, interrogatories, requests for documents, requests for admissions, or other discovery or disclosure materials, together with the responses and objections thereto, that are the subject of the discovery motion or application, or that are cited in papers submitted in connection with any other motion or application. NY R USDCTS&ED Civ Rule 5.1.

    ii.  *Notice of constitutional question.* A party that files a pleading, written motion, or other paper drawing into question the constitutionality of a federal or state statute must promptly:

       • *File notice.* File a notice of constitutional question stating the question and identifying the paper that raises it, if: (1) a federal statute is questioned and the parties do not include the United States, one of its agencies, or one of its officers or employees in an official capacity; or (2) a state statute is questioned and the parties do not include the state, one of its agencies, or one of its officers or employees in an official capacity; and

       • *Serve notice.* Serve the notice and paper on the Attorney General of the United States if a federal statute is questioned—or on the state attorney general if a state statute is

questioned—either by certified or registered mail or by sending it to an electronic address designated by the attorney general for this purpose. FRCP 5.1(a).

- *No forfeiture.* A party's failure to file and serve the notice, or the court's failure to certify, does not forfeit a constitutional claim or defense that is otherwise timely asserted. FRCP 5.1(d).

iii. *Copies of authorities.* In cases involving a pro se litigant, counsel shall, when serving a memorandum of law (or other submissions to the Court), provide the pro se litigant (but not other counsel or the Court) with copies of cases and other authorities cited therein that are unpublished or reported exclusively on computerized databases. Upon request, counsel shall provide the pro se litigant with copies of such unpublished cases and other authorities as are cited in a decision of the Court and were not previously cited by any party. NY R USDCTS&ED Civ Rule 7.2.

iv. *Statement explaining untimely electronic filing.* If you missed a filing deadline when the ECF system was out of order, attach a statement to your filing explaining how the interruption in service prevented you from filing in a timely fashion. NY R USDCTSD CM/ECF, S.D.(II)(23)(23.5).

v. *Courtesy copies.* Read the judge's Individual Practices to learn if courtesy copies are required. NY R USDCTSD CM/ECF, S.D.(II)(13)(13.17). Judges' Individual Practices should continue to be followed with respect to delivery of courtesy copies. NY R USDCTSD CM/ECF, S.D.(I)(3)(3.4).

3. *Individual judge practices.* Refer to the Miscellaneous section of this document for information on individual judge practices on required documents.

## E. Format

1. *Form of documents.* The rules governing captions and other matters of form in pleadings apply to motions and other papers. FRCP 7(b)(2).

a. *Paper.* Every pleading, written motion, and other paper must: be plainly written, typed, printed, or copied without erasures or interlineations which materially deface it. NY R USDCTS&ED Civ Rule 11.1(a)(1).

b. *Typeface, margin, and spacing.* The typeface, margins, and spacing of all documents presented for filing must meet the following requirements:

i. All text must be twelve (12) point type or larger, except for text in footnotes which may be ten (10) point type;

ii. All documents must have at least one (1) inch margins on all sides;

iii. All text must be double-spaced, except for headings, text in footnotes, or block quotations, which may be single-spaced. NY R USDCTS&ED Civ Rule 11.1(b).

c. *Caption; Names of parties.* Every pleading must have a caption with the court's name, a title, a file number, and a FRCP 7(a) designation. The title of the complaint must name all the parties; the title of other pleadings, after naming the first party on each side, may refer generally to other parties. FRCP 10(a). Every pleading, written motion, and other paper must: bear the docket number and the initials of the District Judge and any Magistrate Judge before whom the action or proceeding is pending, NY R USDCTS&ED Civ Rule 11.1(a)(2).

d. *Paragraphs; Separate statements.* A party must state its claims or defenses in numbered paragraphs, each limited as far as practicable to a single set of circumstances. A later pleading may refer by number to a paragraph in an earlier pleading. If doing so would promote clarity, each claim founded on a separate transaction or occurrence—and each defense other than a denial—must be stated in a separate count or defense. FRCP 10(b).

e. *Adoption by reference; Exhibits.* A statement in a pleading may be adopted by reference elsewhere in the same pleading or in any other pleading or motion. A copy of a written instrument that is an exhibit to a pleading is a part of the pleading for all purposes. FRCP 10(c).

f. *Acceptance by the clerk.* The clerk must not refuse to file a paper solely because it is not in the form prescribed by the Federal Rules of Civil Procedure or by a local rule or practice. FRCP 5(d)(4).

2. *Form of electronic documents*

    a. *PDF-A.* All documents electronically filed on the ECF system must be in PDF-A format (portable document format). A PDF-A file is created using PDF writer software such as Adobe Acrobat (go to the Adobe website for details). PDF-A files cannot be altered, providing security to the filer and the Court. NY R USDCTSD CM/ECF, S.D.(II)(23)(23.2).

    b. *Size limitation.* No single PDF file may be larger than four megabytes (4 MB). If the filing is too large, the ECF system will not allow it to be filed, and you will not see a Notice of Electronic Filing (NEF or filing receipt) screen. To determine the size of an Adobe Acrobat PDF file click on File, Document Properties, Summary. NY R USDCTSD CM/ECF, S.D.(II)(23)(23.3).

        i. Converting documents directly from a word processor to PDF-A format creates the smallest possible file in terms of computer memory. If that is not possible, scan your document at low resolution. Within the Adobe Acrobat program, on the "Scan Manager" screen, adjust the settings for black and white and 200 dpi (dots per inch). This allows more pages to fit into a single PDF-A file. If that does not work, separate an oversized file into 2 or more parts. Simply label each file 1a, 1b, 1c, etc. Only relevant excerpts of exhibits should be electronically filed. NY R USDCTSD CM/ECF, S.D.(II)(23)(23.4).

    c. *Attachments and exhibits.* Filing Users must submit in electronic form all documents referenced as exhibits or attachments, unless the Court permits paper filing. NY R USDCTSD CM/ECF, S.D.(I)(5)(5.1).

        i. A Filing User must submit as exhibits or attachments only those excerpts of the referenced documents that are relevant to the matter under consideration by the Court. Excerpted material must be clearly and prominently identified as such. Filing Users who file excerpts of documents as exhibits or attachments under this procedure do so without prejudice to their right to file timely additional excerpts or the complete document. Responding parties may file timely additional excerpts that they believe are relevant or the complete document. A party may move before the Court for permission to serve and file in hard copy documents that cannot be reasonably scanned. NY R USDCTSD CM/ECF, S.D.(I)(5)(5.2).

        ii. Exhibits must be filed only as attachments to a document, such as a motion or an affidavit. Do not use the ECF Filing Event for "Motion" to file exhibits separately. Exhibits are the only items that should be attached to electronically filed documents. You are limited to electronically filing only relevant excerpts of exhibits. Excerpts must be clearly identified as such. If the exhibit is too large to be scanned and electronically filed you may contact the ECF Help Desk. NY R USDCTSD CM/ECF, S.D.(II)(15)(15.6).

    d. *Letters.* Parties should consult the assigned judge's Individual Practices to determine if the judge accepts letters at all and, if he or she does, whether the judge has any page limitations on letters and/or requires courtesy copies of letters filed on ECF (and, if so, by what means of delivery). All letters addressed to the Court must include a subject line with the case name and docket number (e.g., "Re: Doe v. Smith, 13 Civ. 1234 (ABC)"). NY R USDCTSD CM/ECF, S.D.(II)(13)(13.1).

    e. *Proposed orders, proposed judgments, stipulations and consents.* Any document that requires the signature of a judge should not be electronically filed except as an exhibit to another document. Proposed orders, judgments, stipulations and consents should not be submitted through the ECF system. Instead they should be sent by e-mail to the Clerk. Proposed orders should be submitted in word processing format (WordPerfect or Word) rather than as a PDF document. Stipulations should be submitted in PDF-A format. Stipulations must contain ink signatures not s/. Faxed or emailed signatures are acceptable. Please note that Stipulations of Voluntary Dismissal pursuant to FRCP 41(a)(1)(A)(ii) do not require the signature of a judge and must be electronically filed on the ECF system. Questions may be directed to the Orders and Judgments Clerk at the phone numbers listed in NY R USDCTSD CM/ECF, S.D.(II)(18)(18.3). NY R USDCTSD CM/ECF, S.D.(II)(18)(18.3).

        i. Email the proposed order, judgment or stipulation to the email addresses listed in NY R USDCTSD CM/ECF, S.D.(II)(18)(18.3). NY R USDCTSD CM/ECF, S.D.(II)(18)(18.3).

        ii. Pro se litigants who are not Filing Users are exempt from that portion of NY R USDCTSD

CM/ECF, S.D.(II)(18)(18.3) that requires litigants to email proposed orders, judgments, stipulations and consents, and shall deliver such documents to the Clerk's Office in paper form. NY R USDCTSD CM/ECF, S.D.(II)(18)(18.3).

3. *Signing of pleadings, motions and other papers*

 a. *Signature.* Every pleading, written motion, and other paper must be signed by at least one attorney of record in the attorney's name—or by a party personally if the party is unrepresented. The paper must state the signer's address, e-mail address, and telephone number. FRCP 11(a). Every pleading, written motion, and other paper must: have the name of each person signing it clearly printed or typed directly below the signature. NY R USDCTS&ED Civ Rule 11.1(a)(3).

   i. *Electronic signatures.* The user log-in and password required to submit documents to the ECF system serve as the Filing User's signature on all electronic documents filed with the Court. NY R USDCTSD CM/ECF, S.D.(I)(8)(8.1); NY R USDCTSD CM/ECF, S.D.(II)(13)(13.14). They also serve as a signature for purposes of the Federal Rules of Civil Procedure, including FRCP 11, the Local Civil Rules of the United States District Courts for the Southern and Eastern Districts of New York, and any other purpose for which a signature is required in connection with proceedings before the Court. NY R USDCTSD CM/ECF, S.D.(I)(8)(8.1).

     • *Signature block.* Electronically filed documents must include a signature block and must set forth the name, address, telephone number and e-mail address all in compliance with the Federal Rules of Civil Procedure and NY R USDCTS&ED Civ Rule 11.1. In the absence of a scanned signature image, the name of the Filing User under whose log-in and password the document is submitted must be preceded by an "s/" typed in the space where the signature would otherwise appear. NY R USDCTSD CM/ECF, S.D.(I)(8)(8.2); NY R USDCTSD CM/ECF, S.D.(II)(13)(13.14).

     • *Documents requiring the signature of a party or witness.* A document requiring the signature of a party or witness shall be electronically filed in a scanned format that contains an image of the actual signature. NY R USDCTSD CM/ECF, S.D.(I)(8)(8.4); NY R USDCTSD CM/ECF, S.D.(II)(13)(13.14).

     • *Documents requiring the signature of a judge.* A Filing User submitting a document electronically that requires a judge's signature must promptly deliver the document in such other form, if any, as the Court requires. NY R USDCTSD CM/ECF, S.D.(I)(4)(4.2).

     • *Documents requiring multiple signatures.* Documents requiring signatures of more than one party must be electronically filed either by: (a) submitting a scanned document containing all necessary signatures; (b) representing the consent of the other parties on the document; (c) identifying on the document the parties whose signatures are required and by the submission of a notice of endorsement by the other parties no later than three business days after filing; or (d) in any other manner approved by the Court. NY R USDCTSD CM/ECF, S.D.(I)(8)(8.5).

   ii. *No verification or accompanying affidavit required for pleadings.* Unless a rule or statute specifically states otherwise, a pleading need not be verified or accompanied by an affidavit. FRCP 11(a).

   iii. *Unsigned papers.* The court must strike an unsigned paper unless the omission is promptly corrected after being called to the attorney's or party's attention. FRCP 11(a).

 b. *Representations to the court.* By presenting to the court a pleading, written motion, or other paper—whether by signing, filing, submitting, or later advocating it—an attorney or unrepresented party certifies that to the best of the person's knowledge, information, and belief, formed after an inquiry reasonable under the circumstances:

   i. It is not being presented for any improper purpose, such as to harass, cause unnecessary delay, or needlessly increase the cost of litigation;

   ii. The claims, defenses, and other legal contentions are warranted by existing law or by a nonfrivolous argument for extending, modifying, or reversing existing law or for establishing new law;

iii. The factual contentions have evidentiary support or, if specifically so identified, will likely have evidentiary support after a reasonable opportunity for further investigation or discovery; and

iv. The denials of factual contentions are warranted on the evidence or, if specifically so identified, are reasonably based on belief or a lack of information. FRCP 11(b).

c. *Sanctions.* If, after notice and a reasonable opportunity to respond, the court determines that FRCP 11(b) has been violated, the court may impose an appropriate sanction on any attorney, law firm, or party that violated FRCP 11(b) or is responsible for the violation. FRCP 11(c)(1). Refer to the United States District Court for the Southern District of New York KeyRules Motion for Sanctions document for more information.

4. *Privacy protection for filings made with the court*

a. *Redacted filings.* Unless the court orders otherwise, in an electronic or paper filing with the court that contains an individual's Social Security number, taxpayer-identification number, or birth date, the name of an individual known to be a minor, or a financial-account number, a party or nonparty making the filing may include only:

i. The last four (4) digits of the Social Security number and taxpayer-identification number;

ii. The year of the individual's birth;

iii. The minor's initials; and

iv. The last four (4) digits of the financial-account number. FRCP 5.2(a); NY R USDCTSD CM/ECF, S.D.(II)(21)(21.3).

v. Caution should be exercised when filing documents that contain the following:

- Personal identifying numbers (PIN #'s), such as a driver's license number;
- Medical records, treatment and diagnosis;
- Employment history;
- Individual financial information;
- Proprietary or trade secret information;
- Information regarding an individual's cooperation with the government. NY R US-DCTSD CM/ECF, S.D.(II)(21)(21.4).

b. *Exemptions from the redaction requirement.* The redaction requirement does not apply to the following:

i. A financial-account number that identifies the property allegedly subject to forfeiture in a forfeiture proceeding;

ii. The record of an administrative or agency proceeding;

iii. The official record of a state-court proceeding;

iv. The record of a court or tribunal, if that record was not subject to the redaction requirement when originally filed;

v. A filing covered by FRCP 5.2(c) or FRCP 5.2(d); and

vi. A pro se filing in an action brought under 28 U.S.C.A. § 2241, 28 U.S.C.A. § 2254, or 28 U.S.C.A. § 2255. FRCP 5.2(b).

c. *Limitations on remote access to electronic files; Social Security appeals and immigration cases.* Unless the court orders otherwise, in an action for benefits under the Social Security Act, and in an action or proceeding relating to an order of removal, to relief from removal, or to immigration benefits or detention, access to an electronic file is authorized as follows:

i. The parties and their attorneys may have remote electronic access to any part of the case file, including the administrative record;

ii. Any other person may have electronic access to the full record at the courthouse, but may have remote electronic access only to:

- The docket maintained by the court; and

- An opinion, order, judgment, or other disposition of the court, but not any other part of the case file or the administrative record. FRCP 5.2(c).

d. *Filings made under seal.* The court may order that a filing be made under seal without redaction. The court may later unseal the filing or order the person who made the filing to file a redacted version for the public record. FRCP 5.2(d). For more information on sealing documents, refer to NY R USDCTSD CM/ECF, S.D.(I)(6).

e. *Protective orders.* For good cause, the court may by order in a case:

   i. Require redaction of additional information; or

   ii. Limit or prohibit a nonparty's remote electronic access to a document filed with the court. FRCP 5.2(e).

f. *Option for additional unredacted filing under seal.* A person making a redacted filing may also file an unredacted copy under seal. The court must retain the unredacted copy as part of the record. FRCP 5.2(f); NY R USDCTSD CM/ECF, S.D.(II)(21)(21.5).

g. *Option for filing a reference list.* A filing that contains redacted information may be filed together with a reference list that identifies each item of redacted information and specifies an appropriate identifier that uniquely corresponds to each item listed. The list must be filed under seal and may be amended as of right. Any reference in the case to a listed identifier will be construed to refer to the corresponding item of information. FRCP 5.2(g); NY R USDCTSD CM/ECF, S.D.(II)(21)(21.5).

h. *Responsibility for redaction.* It is the sole responsibility of counsel and the parties to be sure that all documents comply with the rules of this Court requiring redaction of personal identifiers. Neither the judge nor the Clerk of Court will review documents for compliance with these rules. NY R USDCTSD CM/ECF, S.D.(II)(21)(21.2).

i. *Waiver of protection of identifiers.* A person waives the protection of FRCP 5.2(a) as to the person's own information by filing it without redaction and not under seal. FRCP 5.2(h).

j. For more information on privacy and public access to ECF cases, refer to NY R USDCTSD CM/ECF, S.D.(II)(21).

5. *Individual judge practices.* Refer to the Miscellaneous section of this document for information on individual judge practices on formatting documents.

# F. Filing and Service Requirements

1. *Filing requirements.* Any paper after the complaint that is required to be served—together with a certificate of service—must be filed within a reasonable time after service. FRCP 5(d)(1). Complaints and all subsequent papers are accepted at either courthouse, regardless of the place for which the case is designated. NY R USDCTSD Div. Bus., Rule 22. Subject to the instructions regarding ECF published on the website of each respective Court and any pertinent Individual Judge's Practices, letter-motions permitted by NY R USDCTS&ED Civ Rule 7.1(d) and letters addressed to the Court (but not letters between the parties) may be filed via ECF. NY R USDCTS&ED Civ Rule 5.2(b). For information on electronically filing motions, refer to NY R USDCTSD CM/ECF, S.D.(II)(15).

   a. *How filing is made; In general.* A paper is filed by delivering it:

      i. To the clerk; or

      ii. To a judge who agrees to accept it for filing, and who must then note the filing date on the paper and promptly send it to the clerk. FRCP 5(d)(2).

   b. *Night depository.* A night depository with an automatic date stamp shall be maintained by the Clerk of the Southern District in the Pearl Street Courthouse. After regular business hours, papers for the District Court only may be deposited in the night depository. Such papers will be considered as having been filed in the District Court as of the date stamped thereon, which shall be deemed presumptively correct. NY R USDCTS&ED Civ Rule 1.2.

   c. *Electronic filing*

      i. *Authorization of electronic filing program.* A court may, by local rule, allow papers to be filed, signed, or verified by electronic means that are consistent with any technical standards established by the Judicial Conference of the United States. A local rule may require electronic filing only if reasonable exceptions are allowed. A paper filed electronically in compliance with a local rule is a written paper for purposes of the Federal Rules of Civil Procedure. FRCP 5(d)(3).

- The Court will accept for filing documents submitted, signed or verified by electronic means, that comply with the rules in NY R USDCTSD CM/ECF, S.D. NY R USDCTSD CM/ECF, S.D.(I). The information in NY R USDCTSD CM/ECF, S.D. applies only to cases assigned to the ECF system. NY R USDCTSD CM/ECF, S.D.(Introduction).

- Parties serving and filing papers shall follow the instructions regarding Electronic Case Filing (ECF) published on the website of each respective Court. A paper served and filed by electronic means in accordance with such instructions is, for purposes of FRCP 5, served and filed in compliance with the Local Civil Rules of the Southern and Eastern Districts of New York. NY R USDCTS&ED Civ Rule 5.2(a). Parties have an obligation to review the Court's actual order, decree, or judgment (on ECF), which controls, and should not rely on the description on the docket or in the ECF Notice of Electronic Filing (NEF). NY R USDCTS&ED Civ Rule 5.2(c).

- The following should be observed when filing electronically: (1) the Federal Rules of Civil Procedure, (2) the Local Civil Rules of the United States District Courts for the Southern and Eastern Districts of New York, (3) the assigned judge's Individual Practices, and (4) the Court's Electronic Case Filing Rules & Instructions (NY R USDCTSD CM/ECF, S.D.). NY R USDCTSD CM/ECF, S.D.(Introduction).

ii. *Scope of electronic filing.* Except as expressly provided and in exceptional circumstances preventing a party from filing electronically, all documents required to be filed with the Court must be filed electronically. Any party unable to comply with this requirement must seek permission of the Court to file in the traditional manner, on paper. Any such application made after regular business hours may be submitted through the night depository box maintained pursuant to NY R USDCTS&ED Civ Rule 1.2. NY R USDCTSD CM/ECF, S.D.(I)(1)(1.1).

- *Documents filed by pro se litigants.* Unless otherwise ordered by the Court, documents filed by pro se litigants must be filed in the traditional manner, on paper, and will be scanned and docketed by the Clerk's Office into the ECF system. NY R USDCTSD CM/ECF, S.D.(I)(1)(1.1). Pro se litigants must file pleadings and documents in the traditional manner on paper unless the assigned judge has granted permission to electronically file on the ECF system. NY R USDCTSD CM/ECF, S.D.(Introduction).

- *Letters.* Except for letters to be filed under seal, letters addressed to judges who accept letters may be filed electronically. Parties should consult the assigned judge's Individual Practices to determine if the judge accepts letters at all and, if he or she does, whether the judge has any page limitations on letters and/or requires courtesy copies of letters filed on ECF (and, if so, by what means of delivery). NY R USDCTSD CM/ECF, S.D.(II)(13)(13.1). Letters solely between parties or their counsel or otherwise not addressed to the Court may not be filed electronically on ECF (except as exhibits to an otherwise properly filed document). NY R USDCTSD CM/ECF, S.D.(II)(13)(13.1). For more information on filing letters, refer to NY R USDCTSD CM/ECF, S.D.(II)(13)(13.1).

- *Proposed orders, judgments and decrees.* Proposed orders, judgments and decrees shall be presented as directed by the ECF rules published on the website of each respective Court. NY R USDCTS&ED Civ Rule 77.1. For more information, refer to NY R USDCTS&ED Civ Rule 77.1.

iii. *Exceptions to electronic filing.* In an ECF case, the documents that should not be electronically filed include:

- Miscellaneous Case initiating documents, NY R USDCTSD CM/ECF, S.D.(II)(18)(18.2);

- Proposed orders; proposed judgments, stipulations; consents, NY R USDCTSD CM/ECF, S.D.(II)(18)(18.3);

- Orders to show cause / temporary restraining orders, NY R USDCTSD CM/ECF, S.D.(II)(18)(18.4);

- Sealed documents, NY R USDCTSD CM/ECF, S.D.(II)(18)(18.5); and

- Surety bonds, NY R USDCTSD CM/ECF, S.D.(II)(18)(18.6).

- In cases where the record of an administrative or other prior proceeding must be filed with the Court, such record may be served and filed in hard copy without prior motion and order of the Court. NY R USDCTSD CM/ECF, S.D.(I)(5)(5.3).

- For more documents excepted from electronic filing, and for more information on such documents, refer to NY R USDCTSD CM/ECF, S.D.(II)(18).

    iv. *Consequences of electronic filing.* Except as otherwise provided in NY R USDCTSD CM/ECF, S.D.(I)(4), electronic filing of a document in the ECF system consistent with these procedures, together with the transmission of a Notice of Electronic Filing (NEF) from the Court, constitutes filing of the document for all purposes of the Federal Rules of Civil Procedure and the Local Civil Rules of the United States District Courts for the Southern and Eastern Districts of New York and constitutes entry of the document on the docket kept by the Clerk under FRCP 58 and FRCP 79. NY R USDCTSD CM/ECF, S.D.(I)(3)(3.1).

    v. For more information on electronic filing, refer to NY R USDCTSD CM/ECF, S.D.

2. *Service requirements*

  a. *Service; When required*

    i. *In general.* Unless the Federal Rules of Civil Procedure provide otherwise, each of the following papers must be served on every party:

- An order stating that service is required;

- A pleading filed after the original complaint, unless the court orders otherwise under FRCP 5(c) because there are numerous defendants;

- A discovery paper required to be served on a party, unless the court orders otherwise;

- A written motion, except one that may be heard ex parte; and

- A written notice, appearance, demand, or offer of judgment, or any similar paper. FRCP 5(a)(1).

    ii. *If a party fails to appear.* No service is required on a party who is in default for failing to appear. But a pleading that asserts a new claim for relief against such a party must be served on that party under FRCP 4. FRCP 5(a)(2).

    iii. *Seizing property.* If an action is begun by seizing property and no person is or need be named as a defendant, any service required before the filing of an appearance, answer, or claim must be made on the person who had custody or possession of the property when it was seized. FRCP 5(a)(3).

  b. *Service; How made*

    i. *Serving an attorney.* If a party is represented by an attorney, service under FRCP 5 must be made on the attorney unless the court orders service on the party. FRCP 5(b)(1).

    ii. *Service in general.* A paper is served under FRCP 5 by:

- Handing it to the person;

- Leaving it: (1) at the person's office with a clerk or other person in charge or, if no one is in charge, in a conspicuous place in the office; or (2) if the person has no office or the office is closed, at the person's dwelling or usual place of abode with someone of suitable age and discretion who resides there;

- Mailing it to the person's last known address—in which event service is complete upon mailing;

- Leaving it with the court clerk if the person has no known address;

- Sending it by electronic means if the person consented in writing—in which event service is complete upon transmission, but is not effective if the serving party learns that it did not reach the person to be served; or

- Delivering it by any other means that the person consented to in writing—in which event service is complete when the person making service delivers it to the agency designated to make delivery. FRCP 5(b)(2).

iii. *Service by overnight delivery.* Service upon an attorney may be made by overnight delivery service. "Overnight delivery service" means any delivery service which regularly accepts items for overnight delivery. Overnight delivery service shall be deemed service by mail for purposes of FRCP 5 and FRCP 6. NY R USDCTS&ED Civ Rule 5.3.

iv. *Service by electronic means.* Parties serving and filing papers shall follow the instructions regarding Electronic Case Filing (ECF) published on the website of each respective Court. A paper served and filed by electronic means in accordance with such instructions is, for purposes of FRCP 5, served and filed in compliance with the Local Civil Rules of the United States District Courts for the Southern and Eastern Districts of New York. NY R USDCTS&ED Civ Rule 5.2(a). Parties have an obligation to review the Court's actual order, decree, or judgment (on ECF), which controls, and should not rely on the description on the docket or in the ECF Notice of Electronic Filing (NEF). NY R USDCTS&ED Civ Rule 5.2(c).

  - *Notice of electronic filing (NEF).* In cases assigned to the ECF system, service is complete provided all parties receive a Notice of Electronic Filing (NEF), which is sent automatically by email from the Court (see the NEF for a list of who did/did not receive notice electronically). Transmission of the NEF constitutes service upon all Filing and Receiving Users who are listed as recipients of notice by electronic mail. NY R USDCTSD CM/ECF, S.D.(I)(9)(9.1). In cases assigned to the ECF system, if all parties receive a NEF, service is complete upon transmission of the NEF by the Court, and you are not required to serve a paper copy. NY R USDCTSD CM/ECF, S.D.(II)(19)(19.2). It remains the duty of Filing and Receiving Users to maintain current contact information with the court and to regularly review the docket sheet of the case. NY R USDCTSD CM/ECF, S.D.(I)(9)(9.1).

  - *Mailing of court-initiated documents.* The Clerk's Office will no longer mail paper copies of court-initiated documents to Filing and Receiving Users. The Clerk's Office will mail copies of all court-initiated documents to pro se parties who have not registered as Filing or Receiving Users. NY R USDCTSD CM/ECF, S.D.(II)(19)(19.1).

  - *No receipt of a NEF.* If any party does not receive a NEF, you are required to accomplish service on that party in the traditional manner, in paper form. NY R USDCTSD CM/ECF, S.D.(II)(19)(19.2). The NEF receipt will inform you who will receive notice of the filing "electronically" (by e-mail from the Court) and who will receive notice "by other means" (traditional service in paper form). NY R USDCTSD CM/ECF, S.D.(II)(19)(19.2).

  - *Service on non-filing or non-receiving users.* Attorneys and pro se parties who are not Filing or Receiving Users must be served with a paper copy of any electronically filed pleading or other document. Service of such paper copy must be made according to the Federal Rules of Civil Procedure and the Local Civil Rules of the United States District Courts for the Southern and Eastern Districts of New York. NY R USDCTSD CM/ECF, S.D.(I)(9)(9.2). Such paper service must be documented by electronically filing proof of service. NY R USDCTSD CM/ECF, S.D.(I)(9)(9.2); NY R USDCTSD CM/ECF, S.D.(II)(19)(19.2). Where the Clerk scans and electronically files pleadings and documents on behalf of a pro se party, the associated NEF constitutes service. NY R USDCTSD CM/ECF, S.D.(I)(9)(9.2).

  - For more information on service by electronic means, refer to NY R USDCTSD CM/ECF, S.D.(II)(19).

v. *Using court facilities.* If a local rule so authorizes, a party may use the court's transmission facilities to make service under FRCP 5(b)(2)(E). FRCP 5(b)(3).

c. *Serving numerous defendants*

 i. *In general.* If an action involves an unusually large number of defendants, the court may, on motion or on its own, order that:

- Defendants' pleadings and replies to them need not be served on other defendants;

- Any crossclaim, counterclaim, avoidance, or affirmative defense in those pleadings and replies to them will be treated as denied or avoided by all other parties; and

- Filing any such pleading and serving it on the plaintiff constitutes notice of the pleading to all parties. FRCP 5(c)(1).

 ii. *Notifying parties.* A copy of every such order must be served on the parties as the court directs. FRCP 5(c)(2).

3. *Individual judge practices.* Refer to the Miscellaneous section of this document for information on individual judge practices on filing and serving documents.

## G. Hearings

1. *Hearings, generally*

a. *Oral argument.* Due process does not require that oral argument be permitted on a motion and, except as otherwise provided by local rule, the district court has discretion to determine whether it will decide the motion on the papers or hear argument by counsel (and perhaps receive evidence). FPP § 1190; F.D.I.C. v. Deglau, 207 F.3d 153 (3d Cir. 2000). The parties and their attorneys shall only appear to argue the motion if so directed by the Court by order or by a Judge's Individual Practice. NY R USDCTS&ED Civ Rule 6.1(c).

b. *Providing a regular schedule for oral hearings.* A court may establish regular times and places for oral hearings on motions. FRCP 78(a).

c. *Providing for submission on briefs.* By rule or order, the court may provide for submitting and determining motions on briefs, without oral hearings. FRCP 78(b).

2. *Individual judge practices.* Refer to the Miscellaneous section of this document for information on individual judge practices on hearings.

## H. Forms

### 1. Federal Motion to Strike Forms

a. Motion; By plaintiff; To strike insufficient defense from answer. AMJUR PP FEDPRAC § 441.

b. Motion; To strike redundant, immaterial, impertinent, or scandalous matter from pleading. AMJUR PP FEDPRAC § 442.

c. Motion; To strike portions of complaint. AMJUR PP FEDPRAC § 444.

d. Motion to strike insufficient affirmative defenses. 2C FEDFORMS § 11:151.

e. Motion to strike insufficient defense in answer; Stating particular reason. 2C FEDFORMS § 11:153.

f. Notice of motion and motion to strike insufficient affirmative defense. 2C FEDFORMS § 11:155.

g. Motion to strike impertinence and scandal. 2C FEDFORMS § 11:157.

h. Motion to strike impertinence and immateriality. 2C FEDFORMS § 11:158.

i. Motion to strike redundancy and scandal. 2C FEDFORMS § 11:159.

j. Motion to strike immaterial defense. 2C FEDFORMS § 11:160.

k. Motion to strike for immateriality. 2C FEDFORMS § 11:161.

l. Motion to strike counterclaim for lack of evidence. 2C FEDFORMS § 11:162.

m. Opposition; To motion; General form. FEDPROF § 1:750.

n. Affidavit; Supporting or opposing motion. FEDPROF § 1:751.

o. Brief; Supporting or opposing motion. FEDPROF § 1:752.

p. Statement of points and authorities; Opposing motion. FEDPROF § 1:753.

q. Motion; To strike material outside statute of limitations. FEDPROF § 1:773.

r. Opposition to motion; Material not contained in pleading. FEDPROF § 1:774.

s. General form. GOLDLTGFMS § 20:8.

t. General form; Federal form. GOLDLTGFMS § 20:10.

u. Notice and motion to strike immaterial, redundant or scandalous matter. GOLDLTGFMS § 20:13.

v. Motion to strike complaint and dismiss action as to one defendant. GOLDLTGFMS § 20:14.

w. Defendant's motion to strike. GOLDLTGFMS § 20:16.

x. Defendant's motion to strike; Plaintiff's response. GOLDLTGFMS § 20:17.

y. Motion to strike answer. GOLDLTGFMS § 20:19.

z. Objections to motion to strike. GOLDLTGFMS § 20:20.

## I. Applicable Rules

1. *Federal rules*

   a. Serving and filing pleadings and other papers. FRCP 5.

   b. Constitutional challenge to a statute; Notice, certification, and intervention. FRCP 5.1.

   c. Privacy protection for filings made with the court. FRCP 5.2.

   d. Computing and extending time; Time for motion papers. FRCP 6.

   e. Pleadings allowed; Form of motions and other papers. FRCP 7.

   f. Disclosure statement. FRCP 7.1.

   g. Form of pleadings. FRCP 10.

   h. Signing pleadings, motions, and other papers; Representations to the court; Sanctions. FRCP 11.

   i. Defenses and objections; When and how presented; Motion for judgment on the pleadings; Consolidating motions; Waiving defenses; Pretrial hearing. FRCP 12.

   j. Hearing motions; Submission on briefs. FRCP 78.

2. *Local rules*

   a. Night depository. NY R USDCTS&ED Civ Rule 1.2.

   b. Duty of attorneys in related cases. NY R USDCTS&ED Civ Rule 1.6.

   c. Filing of discovery materials. NY R USDCTS&ED Civ Rule 5.1.

   d. Electronic service and filing of documents. NY R USDCTS&ED Civ Rule 5.2.

   e. Service by overnight delivery. NY R USDCTS&ED Civ Rule 5.3.

   f. Service and filing of motion papers. NY R USDCTS&ED Civ Rule 6.1.

   g. Orders on motions. NY R USDCTS&ED Civ Rule 6.2.

   h. Computation of time. NY R USDCTS&ED Civ Rule 6.4.

   i. Motion papers. NY R USDCTS&ED Civ Rule 7.1.

   j. Disclosure statement. NY R USDCTS&ED Civ Rule 7.1.1.

   k. Authorities to be provided to pro se litigants. NY R USDCTS&ED Civ Rule 7.2.

   l. Form of pleadings, motions, and other papers. NY R USDCTS&ED Civ Rule 11.1.

   m. Submission of orders, judgments and decrees. NY R USDCTS&ED Civ Rule 77.1.

   n. Alternative dispute resolution (Southern District only). NY R USDCTS&ED Civ Rule 83.9.

   o. Electronic case filing rules and instructions. NY R USDCTSD CM/ECF, S.D.

   p. Related cases. NY R USDCTSD Div. Bus., Rule 13.

   q. Filing at either courthouse. NY R USDCTSD Div. Bus., Rule 22.

## J.  Miscellaneous

**NOTE: Individual judges' rules may apply. For available judge-level information, refer to:**

DISTRICT JUDGE RONNIE ABRAMS: NY R USDCTSD Abrams-Civ Prac; NY R USDCTSD Abrams-Crim Prac; NY R USDCTSD Abrams-Pro Se; NY R USDCTSD Abrams-Case Mgt; NY R USDCTSD Abrams-Jury.

DISTRICT JUDGE DEBORAH A. BATTS: NY R USDCTSD Batts-Practices.

DISTRICT JUDGE RICHARD M. BERMAN: NY R USDCTSD Berman-Practices; NY R USDCTSD Berman-Default; NY R USDCTSD Berman-Sentencing; NY R USDCTSD Berman-Media.

DISTRICT JUDGE VINCENT L. BRICCETTI: NY R USDCTSD Briccetti-Practices; NY R USDCTSD Briccetti-Plan; NY R USDCTSD Briccetti-Notice.

DISTRICT JUDGE VERNON S. BRODERICK: NY R USDCTSD Broderick-Civil; NY R USDCTSD Broderick-Crim; NY R USDCTSD Broderick-Case Mgt; NY R USDCTSD Broderick-Jury.

DISTRICT JUDGE NAOMI REICE BUCHWALD: NY R USDCTSD Buchwald-Practices.

DISTRICT JUDGE VALERIE E. CAPRONI: NY R USDCTSD Caproni-Prac; NY R USDCTSD Caproni--Pro Se; NY R USDCTSD Caproni-Case Mgt; NY R USDCTSD Caproni-Crim Prac.

DISTRICT JUDGE ANDREW L. CARTER JR.: NY R USDCTSD Carter-Practices.

DISTRICT JUDGE KEVIN P. CASTEL: NY R USDCTSD Castel-Practices; NY R USDCTSD Castel-Default; NY R USDCTSD Castel-Scheduling; NY R USDCTSD Castel-Complex; NY R USDCTSD Castel-Trials; NY R USDCTSD Castel-Sentencing.

DISTRICT JUDGE DENISE L. COTE: NY R USDCTSD Cote-Civil Practices; NY R USDCTSD Cote-Pro Se; NY R USDCTSD Cote-Maritime Ord; NY R USDCTSD Cote-Crim Practices; NY R USDCTSD Cote-Crim Trials; NY R USDCTSD Cote-Sentencing.

DISTRICT JUDGE PAUL A. CROTTY: NY R USDCTSD Crotty-Practices; NY R USDCTSD Crotty-Sentencing; NY R USDCTSD Crotty-Calls; NY R USDCTSD Crotty-Scheduling.

DISTRICT JUDGE GEORGE B. DANIELS: NY R USDCTSD Daniels-Practices.

DISTRICT JUDGE KEVIN T. DUFFY: NY R USDCTSD Duffy-Practices.

DISTRICT JUDGE PAUL A. ENGELMAYER: NY R USDCTSD Engelmayer-Practices; NY R USDCTSD Engelmayer-Scheduling; NY R USDCTSD Engelmayer-Sentencing; NY R USDCTSD Engelmayer-Pro Se; NY R USDCTSD Engelmayer-Crim.

DISTRICT JUDGE KATHERINE POLK FAILLA: NY R USDCTSD Failla-Civ Prac; NY R USDCTSD Failla-Crim Prac; NY R USDCTSD Failla-Case Mgt.

DISTRICT JUDGE KATHERINE B. FORREST: NY R USDCTSD Forrest-Civil Prac; NY R USDCTSD Forrest-Crim Prac; NY R USDCTSD Forrest-Crim Pretrial; NY R USDCTSD Forrest-Scheduling; NY R USDCTSD Forrest-Patent Scheduling; NY R USDCTSD Forrest-Sentencing; NY R USDCTSD Forrest-Order 1; NY R USDCTSD Forrest-Order 2.

DISTRICT JUDGE JESSE M. FURMAN: NY R USDCTSD Furman-Civil Prac; NY R USDCTSD Furman-Crim Prac; NY R USDCTSD Furman-Pro Se Prac; NY R USDCTSD Furman-Trials; NY R USDCTSD Furman-Scheduling; NY R USDCTSD Furman-Rights.

DISTRICT JUDGE PAUL G. GARDEPHE: NY R USDCTSD Gardephe-Civ Prac; NY R USDCTSD Gardephe-Pretrial; NY R USDCTSD Gardephe-Prot Ord; NY R USDCTSD Gardephe-Maritime; NY R USDCTSD Gardephe-Crim Prac; NY R USDCTSD Gardephe-Trial.

DISTRICT JUDGE THOMAS P. GRIESA: NY R USDCTSD Griesa-Practices.

DISTRICT JUDGE CHARLES S. HAIGHT: NY R USDCTSD Haight-Practices.

DISTRICT JUDGE ALVIN K. HELLERSTEIN: NY R USDCTSD Hellerstein-Practices; NY R USDCTSD Hellerstein--Sept 11.

DISTRICT JUDGE LEWIS A. KAPLAN: NY R USDCTSD Kaplan-Practices; NY R USDCTSD Kaplan-Sentencing.

DISTRICT JUDGE KENNETH M. KARAS: NY R USDCTSD Karas-Practices; NY R USDCTSD Karas-Case Mgt; NY R USDCTSD Karas-Default; NY R USDCTSD Karas-Sentencing; NY R USDCTSD Karas-Rights.

DISTRICT JUDGE JOHN F. KEENAN: NY R USDCTSD Keenan-Practices.

DISTRICT JUDGE JOHN G. KOELTL: NY R USDCTSD Koeltl-Practices.

DISTRICT JUDGE VICTOR MARRERO: NY R USDCTSD Marrero-Practices; NY R USDCTSD Marrero-Scheduling; NY R USDCTSD Marrero-Default; NY R USDCTSD Marrero-Trial Proc.

DISTRICT JUDGE COLLEEN McMAHON: NY R USDCTSD McMahon-Practices; NY R USDCTSD McMahon-RICO; NY R USDCTSD McMahon-Copies; NY R USDCTSD McMahon-Scheduling; NY R US-DCTSD McMahon-Elec Disc; NY R USDCTSD McMahon-Sentencing.

DISTRICT JUDGE ALISON J. NATHAN: NY R USDCTSD Nathan-Civ Prac; NY R USDCTSD Nathan-Crim Prac; NY R USDCTSD Nathan-Pro Se; NY R USDCTSD Nathan-Scheduling.

DISTRICT JUDGE J. PAUL OETKEN: NY R USDCTSD Oetken-Civ Prac; NY R USDCTSD Oetken-Case Mgt; NY R USDCTSD Oetken-Crim Prac; NY R USDCTSD Oetken-Pro Se.

DISTRICT JUDGE WILLIAM H. PAULEY, III: NY R USDCTSD Pauley-Crim Cases; NY R USDCTSD Pauley-Practices.

DISTRICT JUDGE LORETTA A. PRESKA: NY R USDCTSD Preska-Practices.

DISTRICT JUDGE JED S. RAKOFF: NY R USDCTSD Rakoff-Practices; NY R USDCTSD Rakoff-Scheduling; NY R USDCTSD Rakoff-Prot Ord; NY R USDCTSD Rakoff-Maritime Ord.

DISTRICT JUDGE EDGARDO RAMOS: NY R USDCTSD Ramos--Practices; NY R USDCTSD Ramos-Case Mgt.

DISTRICT JUDGE NELSON S. ROMAN: NY R USDCTSD Roman-Civ Prac; NY R USDCTSD Roman-Pro Se; NY R USDCTSD Roman-Crim Prac; NY R USDCTSD Roman-Case Mgt.

DISTRICT JUDGE LEONARD B. SAND: NY R USDCTSD Sand-Practices.

DISTRICT JUDGE LORNA G. SCHOFIELD: NY R USDCTSD Schofield-Civ Prac; NY R USDCTSD Schofield-Crim Prac; NY R USDCTSD Schofield-Sched; NY R USDCTSD Schofield-Pro Se; NY R USDCTSD Schofield-Advice.

DISTRICT JUDGE CATHY SEIBEL: NY R USDCTSD Seibel-Practices.

DISTRICT JUDGE LOUIS L. STANTON: NY R USDCTSD Stanton-Practices; NY R USDCTSD Stanton-Pretrial.

DISTRICT JUDGE SIDNEY H. STEIN: NY R USDCTSD Stein-Practices.

DISTRICT JUDGE RICHARD J. SULLIVAN: NY R USDCTSD Sullivan-Practices; NY R USDCTSD Sullivan-Scheduling; NY R USDCTSD Sullivan-Sentencing; NY R USDCTSD Sullivan-Juries; NY R USDCTSD Sullivan-Trial; NY R USDCTSD Sullivan-Default.

DISTRICT JUDGE LAURA TAYLOR SWAIN: NY R USDCTSD Swain-Practices; NY R USDCTSD Swain-Trial; NY R USDCTSD Swain-Crim Trial; NY R USDCTSD Swain-Juries; NY R USDCTSD Swain-Sentencing; NY R USDCTSD Swain-Rights.

DISTRICT JUDGE ROBERT W. SWEET: NY R USDCTSD Sweet-Practices.

DISTRICT JUDGE ANALISA TORRES: NY R USDCTSD Torres-Civ Prac; NY R USDCTSD Torres-Pro Se; NY R USDCTSD Torres-Scheduling.

DISTRICT JUDGE KIMBA M. WOOD: NY R USDCTSD Wood-Practices; NY R USDCTSD Wood-Scheduling; NY R USDCTSD Wood-Discovery; NY R USDCTSD Wood-RICO; NY R USDCTSD Wood-Juries; NY R USDCTSD Wood-Trial; NY R USDCTSD Wood-Media.

DISTRICT JUDGE GREGORY H. WOODS: NY R USDCTSD Woods-Civ Prac; NY R USDCTSD Woods-Pro Se; NY R USDCTSD Woods-Sched; NY R USDCTSD Woods-Crim Prac; NY R USDCTSD Woods-Protect Order; NY R USDCTSD Woods-Speedy Trial.

MAGISTRATE JUDGE JAMES L. COTT: NY R USDCTSD Cott-Practices; NY R USDCTSD Cott-Settlement.

MAGISTRATE JUDGE PAUL E. DAVISON: NY R USDCTSD Davison-Practices.

MAGISTRATE JUDGE RONALD L. ELLIS: NY R USDCTSD Ellis-Practices.

MAGISTRATE JUDGE KEVIN N. FOX: NY R USDCTSD Fox-Practices; NY R USDCTSD Fox-Settlement.

MAGISTRATE JUDGE JAMES C. FRANCIS: NY R USDCTSD Francis-Practices.

MAGISTRATE JUDGE DEBRA FREEMAN: NY R USDCTSD Freeman-Practices; NY R USDCTSD Freeman-Settlement.

MAGISTRATE JUDGE GABRIEL W. GORENSTEIN: NY R USDCTSD Gorenstein-Practices; NY R US-DCTSD Gorenstein-Ackn.

MAGISTRATE JUDGE FRANK MAAS: NY R USDCTSD Maas-Practices; NY R USDCTSD Maas-Discontinuance; NY R USDCTSD Maas-Conf; NY R USDCTSD Maas-Settlement.

MAGISTRATE JUDGE JUDITH C. McCARTHY: NY R USDCTSD McCarthy-Practices; NY R USDCTSD McCarthy-Conduct.

MAGISTRATE JUDGE BARBARA MOSES: NY R USDCTSD Moses-Practices.

MAGISTRATE JUDGE SARAH NETBURN: NY R USDCTSD Netburn-Civil; NY R USDCTSD Netburn-Settlement; NY R USDCTSD Netburn-Case Mgt; NY R USDCTSD Netburn--Pro Se.

MAGISTRATE JUDGE ANDREW J. PECK: NY R USDCTSD Peck-Practices; NY R USDCTSD Peck-Order; NY R USDCTSD Peck-Rule 502(d).

MAGISTRATE JUDGE HENRY PITMAN: NY R USDCTSD Pitman-Practices.

MAGISTRATE JUDGE LISA MARGARET SMITH: NY R USDCTSD Smith-Practices; NY R USDCTSD Smith-Trials.

# Motions, Oppositions and Replies
## Motion for Leave to Amend

**Document Last Updated September 2016**

## A. Checklist

(I) ❑ Matters to be considered by moving party

    (a) ❑ Required documents

        (1) ❑ Notice of motion and motion

        (2) ❑ Memorandum of law

        (3) ❑ Proposed amendment

        (4) ❑ Certificate of service

    (b) ❑ Supplemental documents

        (1) ❑ Supporting evidence

        (2) ❑ Notice of constitutional question

        (3) ❑ Copies of authorities

        (4) ❑ Proposed order

        (5) ❑ Statement explaining untimely electronic filing

        (6) ❑ Courtesy copies

    (c) ❑ Timing

        (1) ❑ Unlike amendments as of course, amendments under FRCP 15(a)(2) may be made at any stage of the litigation

        (2) ❑ A party may move—at any time, even after judgment—to amend the pleadings to conform them to the evidence and to raise an unpleaded issue

        (3) ❑ A written motion and notice of the hearing must be served at least fourteen (14) days before the time specified for the hearing, with the following exceptions: (i) when the motion may be

heard ex parte; (ii) when the Federal Rules of Civil Procedure set a different time; or (iii) when a court order—which a party may, for good cause, apply for ex parte—sets a different time

    (4) ❑ Any affidavit supporting a motion must be served with the motion

(II) ❑ Matters to be considered by opposing party

  (a) ❑ Required documents

    (1) ❑ Answering memorandum of law

    (2) ❑ Certificate of service

  (b) ❑ Supplemental documents

    (1) ❑ Supporting evidence

    (2) ❑ Notice of constitutional question

    (3) ❑ Copies of authorities

    (4) ❑ Statement explaining untimely electronic filing

    (5) ❑ Courtesy copies

  (c) ❑ Timing

    (1) ❑ Any opposing affidavits and answering memoranda shall be served within fourteen (14) days after service of the moving papers

    (2) ❑ Except as FRCP 59(c) provides otherwise, any opposing affidavit must be served at least seven (7) days before the hearing, unless the court permits service at another time

## B. Timing

1. *Motion for leave to amend.* Unlike amendments as of course, amendments under FRCP 15(a)(2) may be made at any stage of the litigation. FPP § 1484.

  a. *Amendments to conform to the evidence.* A party may move—at any time, even after judgment—to amend the pleadings to conform them to the evidence and to raise an unpleaded issue. FRCP 15(b)(2).

  b. *Time to respond to an amended pleading.* Unless the court orders otherwise, any required response to an amended pleading must be made within the time remaining to respond to the original pleading or within fourteen (14) days after service of the amended pleading, whichever is later. FRCP 15(a)(3).

2. *Timing of motions, generally*

  a. *Motion and notice of hearing.* Except for letter-motions as permitted by NY R USDCTS&ED Civ Rule 7.1(d), and unless otherwise provided by statute or rule or by the Court in a Judge's Individual Practice or in a direction in a particular case, upon any motion, the notice of motion, supporting affidavits, and memoranda shall be served and filed as follows: on all civil motions, petitions, and applications, other than those described in NY R USDCTS&ED Civ Rule 6.1(a), and other than petitions for writs of habeas corpus, the notice of motion, supporting affidavits, and memoranda of law shall be served by the moving party on all other parties that have appeared in the action. NY R USDCTS&ED Civ Rule 6.1(b)(1). A written motion and notice of the hearing must be served at least fourteen (14) days before the time specified for the hearing, with the following exceptions:

    i. When the motion may be heard ex parte;

    ii. When the Federal Rules of Civil Procedure set a different time; or

    iii. When a court order—which a party may, for good cause, apply for ex parte—sets a different time. FRCP 6(c)(1).

  b. *Supporting affidavit.* Any affidavit supporting a motion must be served with the motion. FRCP 6(c)(2).

3. *Timing of opposing papers.* Except for letter-motions as permitted by NY R USDCTS&ED Civ Rule

7.1(d), and unless otherwise provided by statute or rule or by the Court in a Judge's Individual Practice or in a direction in a particular case, upon any motion, the notice of motion, supporting affidavits, and memoranda shall be served and filed as follows: on all civil motions, petitions, and applications, other than those described in NY R USDCTS&ED Civ Rule 6.1(a), and other than petitions for writs of habeas corpus, any opposing affidavits and answering memoranda shall be served within fourteen (14) days after service of the moving papers. NY R USDCTS&ED Civ Rule 6.1(b)(2).

a. *Opposing affidavit.* Except as FRCP 59(c) provides otherwise, any opposing affidavit must be served at least seven (7) days before the hearing, unless the court permits service at another time. FRCP 6(c)(2).

4. *Timing of reply papers.* Where the respondent files an answering affidavit setting up a new matter, the moving party ordinarily is allowed a reasonable time to file a reply affidavit since failure to deny the new matter by affidavit may operate as an admission of its truth. AMJUR MOTIONS § 25.

a. *Reply affidavits and reply memoranda of law.* Except for letter-motions as permitted by NY R USDCTS&ED Civ Rule 7.1(d), and unless otherwise provided by statute or rule or by the Court in a Judge's Individual Practice or in a direction in a particular case, upon any motion, the notice of motion, supporting affidavits, and memoranda shall be served and filed as follows: on all civil motions, petitions, and applications, other than those described in NY R USDCTS&ED Civ Rule 6.1(a), and other than petitions for writs of habeas corpus, any reply affidavits and memoranda of law shall be served within seven (7) days after service of the answering papers. NY R USDCTS&ED Civ Rule 6.1(b)(3).

5. *Computation of time*

a. *Computing time.* FRCP 6 applies in computing any time period specified in the Federal Rules of Civil Procedure, in any local rule or court order, or in any statute that does not specify a method of computing time. FRCP 6(a). In computing any period of time prescribed or allowed by the Local Civil Rules of the United States District Courts for the Southern and Eastern Districts of New York or the Local Admiralty and Maritime Rules, the provisions of FRCP 6 shall apply unless otherwise stated. NY R USDCTS&ED Civ Rule 6.4.

i. *Period stated in days or a longer unit.* In computing periods of days, refer to FRCP 6 and NY R USDCTS&ED Civ Rule 6.4. NY R USDCTS&ED Civ Rule 6.1(b). When the period is stated in days or a longer unit of time:

- Exclude the day of the event that triggers the period;
- Count every day, including intermediate Saturdays, Sundays, and legal holidays; and
- Include the last day of the period, but if the last day is a Saturday, Sunday, or legal holiday, the period continues to run until the end of the next day that is not a Saturday, Sunday, or legal holiday. FRCP 6(a)(1). In the Local Civil Rules of the United States District Courts for the Southern and Eastern Districts of New York, as in the Federal Rules of Civil Procedure as amended effective December 1, 2009, Saturdays, Sundays, and legal holidays are no longer excluded in computing periods of time. If the last day of the period is a Saturday, Sunday, or legal holiday, the period continues to run until the end of the next day that is not a Saturday, Sunday, or legal holiday. NY R USDCTS&ED Civ Rule 6.4.

ii. *Period stated in hours.* When the period is stated in hours:

- Begin counting immediately on the occurrence of the event that triggers the period;
- Count every hour, including hours during intermediate Saturdays, Sundays, and legal holidays; and
- If the period would end on a Saturday, Sunday, or legal holiday, the period continues to run until the same time on the next day that is not a Saturday, Sunday, or legal holiday. FRCP 6(a)(2). In the Local Civil Rules of the United States District Courts for the Southern and Eastern Districts of New York, as in the Federal Rules of Civil Procedure as amended effective December 1, 2009, Saturdays, Sundays, and legal holidays are no longer excluded in computing periods of time. If the last day of the period is a Saturday, Sunday,

or legal holiday, the period continues to run until the end of the next day that is not a Saturday, Sunday, or legal holiday. NY R USDCTS&ED Civ Rule 6.4.

iii. *Inaccessibility of the clerk's office.* Unless the court orders otherwise, if the clerk's office is inaccessible:

- On the last day for filing under FRCP 6(a)(1), then the time for filing is extended to the first accessible day that is not a Saturday, Sunday, or legal holiday; or

- During the last hour for filing under FRCP 6(a)(2), then the time for filing is extended to the same time on the first accessible day that is not a Saturday, Sunday, or legal holiday. FRCP 6(a)(3).

iv. *"Last day" defined.* Unless a different time is set by a statute, local rule, or court order, the last day ends:

- For electronic filing, at midnight in the court's time zone; and

- For filing by other means, when the clerk's office is scheduled to close. FRCP 6(a)(4).

v. *"Next day" defined.* The "next day" is determined by continuing to count forward when the period is measured after an event and backward when measured before an event. FRCP 6(a)(5).

vi. *"Legal holiday" defined.* "Legal holiday" means:

- The day set aside by statute for observing New Year's Day, Martin Luther King Jr.'s Birthday, Washington's Birthday, Memorial Day, Independence Day, Labor Day, Columbus Day, Veterans' Day, Thanksgiving Day, or Christmas Day;

- Any day declared a holiday by the President or Congress; and

- For periods that are measured after an event, any other day declared a holiday by the state where the district court is located. FRCP 6(a)(6).

b. *Computation of electronic filing deadlines.* You can file electronically twenty-four (24) hours a day, seven (7) days a week, three hundred sixty-five (365) days a year. NY R USDCTSD CM/ECF, S.D.(II)(13)(13.10). Electronic filing must be completed before midnight local time where the Court is located in order to be considered timely filed that day. NY R USDCTSD CM/ECF, S.D.(I)(3)(3.3); NY R USDCTSD CM/ECF, S.D.(II)(13)(13.10); NY R USDCTSD CM/ECF, S.D.(II)(19)(19.4). An electronically filed document is deemed filed on the "filed on" date indicated on the Notice of Electronic Filing (NEF). NY R USDCTSD CM/ECF, S.D.(II)(13)(13.11).

i. *Technical failures.* A Filing User whose filing is made untimely as the result of a technical failure may seek appropriate relief from the Court. NY R USDCTSD CM/ECF, S.D.(I)(11). If you missed a filing deadline when the ECF system was out of order, attach a statement to your filing explaining how the interruption in service prevented you from filing in a timely fashion. NY R USDCTSD CM/ECF, S.D.(II)(23)(23.5).

c. *Extending time*

i. *In general.* When an act may or must be done within a specified time, the court may, for good cause, extend the time:

- With or without motion or notice if the court acts, or if a request is made, before the original time or its extension expires; or

- On motion made after the time has expired if the party failed to act because of excusable neglect. FRCP 6(b)(1).

ii. *Exceptions.* A court must not extend the time to act under FRCP 50(b), FRCP 50(d), FRCP 52(b), FRCP 59(b), FRCP 59(d), FRCP 59(e), and FRCP 60(b). FRCP 6(b)(2).

iii. Refer to the United States District Court for the Southern District of New York KeyRules Motion for Continuance/Extension of Time document for more information on extending time.

d. *Additional time after certain kinds of service.* When a party may or must act within a specified time after service and service is made under FRCP 5(b)(2)(C), FRCP 5(b)(2)(D), FRCP 5(b)(2)(E), or FRCP 5(b)(2)(F), three (3) days are added after the period would otherwise expire under FRCP 6(a).

FRCP 6(d). Overnight delivery service shall be deemed service by mail for purposes of FRCP 5 and FRCP 6. NY R USDCTS&ED Civ Rule 5.3.

6.  *Individual judge practices.* Refer to the Miscellaneous section of this document for information on individual judge practices on timing of documents.

## C. General Requirements

1.  *Motions, generally*

    a.  *Requirements.* A request for a court order must be made by motion. The motion must:

        i.   Be in writing unless made during a hearing or trial;

        ii.  State with particularity the grounds for seeking the order; and

        iii. State the relief sought. FRCP 7(b)(1).

    b.  *Notice of motion.* A party interested in resisting the relief sought by a motion has a right to notice thereof, and an opportunity to be heard. AMJUR MOTIONS § 12.

        i.   In addition to statutory or court rule provisions requiring notice of a motion—the purpose of such a notice requirement having been said to be to prevent a party from being prejudicially surprised by a motion—principles of natural justice dictate that an adverse party generally must be given notice that a motion will be presented to the court. AMJUR MOTIONS § 12.

        ii.  "Notice," in this regard, means reasonable notice, including a meaningful opportunity to prepare and to defend against allegations of a motion. AMJUR MOTIONS § 12.

    c.  *Writing requirement.* The writing requirement is intended to insure that the adverse parties are informed and have a record of both the motion's pendency and the grounds on which the movant seeks an order. FPP § 1191; Feldberg v. Quechee Lakes Corp., 463 F.3d 195 (2d Cir. 2006).

        i.   It is sufficient "if the motion is stated in a written notice of the hearing of the motion." FPP § 1191.

    d.  *Particularity requirement.* The particularity requirement insures that the opposing parties will have notice of their opponent's contentions. FEDPROC § 62:364; Goodman v. 1973 26 Foot Trojan Vessel, Arkansas Registration No. AR1439SN, 859 F.2d 71, 12 Fed.R.Serv.3d 645 (8th Cir. 1988). That requirement ensures that notice of the basis for the motion is provided to the court and to the opposing party so as to avoid prejudice, provide the opponent with a meaningful opportunity to respond, and provide the court with enough information to process the motion correctly. FEDPROC § 62:364; Andreas v. Volkswagen of America, Inc., 336 F.3d 789, 56 Fed.R.Serv.3d 6 (8th Cir. 2003).

        i.   Reasonable specification of the grounds for a motion is sufficient. However, where a movant fails to state even one ground for granting the motion in question, the movant has failed to meet the minimal standard of "reasonable specification." FEDPROC § 62:364; Martinez v. Trainor, 556 F.2d 818, 23 Fed.R.Serv.2d 403 (7th Cir. 1977).

        ii.  The court may excuse the failure to comply with the particularity requirement if it is inadvertent, and where no prejudice is shown by the opposing party. FEDPROC § 62:364.

    e.  *Ex parte orders or orders to show cause to bring on a motion.* No ex parte order, or order to show cause to bring on a motion, will be granted except upon a clear and specific showing by affidavit of good and sufficient reasons why a procedure other than by notice of motion is necessary, and stating whether a previous application for similar relief has been made. NY R USDCTS&ED Civ Rule 6.1(d).

    f.  *Letter-motions.* Applications for extensions or adjournments, applications for a pre-motion conference, and similar non-dispositive matters as permitted by the instructions regarding ECF published on the website of each respective Court and any pertinent Individual Judge's Practices, may be brought by letter-motion filed via ECF pursuant to NY R USDCTS&ED Civ Rule 5.2(b). NY R USDCTS&ED Civ Rule 7.1(d).

        i.   The following list of motions. . .may be made by LETTER-MOTION: (1) Motion to Adjourn Conference; (2) Motion to Change Attorney Name on Roll; (3) Motion to Compel; (4) Motion for Conference; (5) Motion to Consolidate Cases; (6) Motion to Continue; (7) Motion re:

Discovery; (8) Motion to Expedite; (9) Motion for Extension of Time; (10) Motion for Extension of Time to Amend; (11) Motion for Extension of Time to Answer; (12) Motion for Extension of Time to Complete Discovery; (13) Motion for Extension of Time to File Document; (14) Motion for Extension of Time to File Response/Reply; (15) Motion for Extension of Time re Transcript; (16) Motion to File Amicus Brief; (17) Motion for Leave to File Document; (18) Motion for Leave to File Excess Pages; (19) Motion for Local Rule 37.2 Conference; (20) Motion for Oral Argument; (21) Motion to Reopen; (22) Motion to Reopen Case; (23) Motion to Seal Document; (24) Motion to Stay; (25) Motion to Substitute Attorney. NY R USDCTSD CM/ECF, S.D.(II)(13)(13.1).

  ii.   If the Filing User is making a type of motion that does not appear in this list, the motion may not be made by letter. NY R USDCTSD CM/ECF, S.D.(II)(13)(13.1).

  iii.  For more information on letter motions, refer to NY R USDCTSD CM/ECF, S.D.(II)(13)(13.1).

2. *Motion for leave to amend.* FRCP 15(a)(2) provides that after a party has amended a pleading once as of course or the time for amendments of that type has expired, a party may amend only by obtaining leave of the court or if the adverse party consents to it. FPP § 1484; In re Cessna Distributorship Antitrust Litigation, 532 F.2d 64 (8th Cir. 1976). FRCP 15(a) does not set forth any specific procedure for obtaining leave to amend. Typically, it is sought by a motion addressed to the court's discretion. FPP § 1485.

  a.   *Pleadings to be amended.* As in the case of amendments as of course under FRCP 15(a)(1), any of the pleadings enumerated in FRCP 7(a) may be amended with the court's leave and FRCP 15 does not restrict the purposes for which an amendment may be made or its character. FPP § 1484.

  b.   *Prerequisites for leave to amend.* The only prerequisites are that the district court have jurisdiction over the case and an appeal must not be pending. FPP § 1484. If these two conditions are met, the court will proceed to examine the effect and the timing of the proposed amendments to determine whether they would prejudice the rights of any of the other parties to the suit. FPP § 1484; Nilsen v. City of Moss Point, Miss., 674 F.2d 379, 388 (5th Cir. 1982).

  c.   *When leave or consent is not obtained.* In general, if an amendment that cannot be made as of right is served without obtaining the court's leave or the opposing party's consent, it is without legal effect and any new matter it contains will not be considered unless the amendment is resubmitted for the court's approval. Some courts have held, however, that an untimely amended pleading served without judicial permission may be considered as properly introduced when leave to amend would have been granted had it been sought and when it does not appear that any of the parties will be prejudiced by allowing the change. FPP § 1484.

  d.   *Form.* A motion to amend under FRCP 15(a), as is true of motions generally, is subject to the requirements of FRCP 7(b), and must set forth with particularity the relief or order requested and the grounds supporting the application. In order to satisfy these prerequisites a copy of the amendment should be submitted with the motion so that the court and the adverse party know the precise nature of the pleading changes being proposed. FPP § 1485.

  e.   *Oral motion for leave to amend.* Courts have held that an oral request to amend a pleading that is made before the court in the presence of opposing party's counsel may be sufficient if the adverse party is put on notice of the nature and purpose of the request and is given the same opportunity to present objections to the proposed amendment as would have occurred if a formal motion had been made. FPP § 1485.

  f.   *Conditions imposed on leave to amend.* While FRCP 15(a) does not specifically authorize the district court to impose conditions on its granting of leave to amend, it is well settled that the court may impose such conditions to avoid or minimize any prejudice to the opposing party. FEDPROC § 62:276. Conditions frequently are imposed because the amending party knew of the facts sought to be asserted in the amendment but failed to assert such facts until later, to the prejudice of the opposing party. Conversely, the court may decline to impose conditions where the amendment was asserted with relative promptness. FEDPROC § 62:276.

   i.   The moving party's refusal to comply with the conditions imposed by the court normally will result in a denial of the right to amend. FPP § 1486.

g. *When leave to amend may be granted.* If the underlying facts or circumstances relied upon by a plaintiff may be a proper subject of relief, he ought to be afforded an opportunity to test his claim on the merits. In the absence of any apparent or declared reason—such as undue delay, bad faith or dilatory motive on the part of the movant, repeated failure to cure deficiencies by amendments previously allowed, undue prejudice to the opposing party by virtue of allowance of the amendment, futility of amendment, etc.—the leave sought should, as the rules require, be "freely given." FPP § 1487; Foman v. Davis, 371 U.S. 178, 182, 83 S.Ct. 227, 230, 9 L.Ed.2d 222 (1962).

3. *Amendments, generally*

a. *Amendments before trial.* The function of FRCP 15(a), which provides generally for the amendment of pleadings, is to enable a party to assert matters that were overlooked or were unknown at the time the party interposed the original complaint or answer. FPP § 1473; Smiga v. Dean Witter Reynolds, Inc., 766 F.2d 698, 703 (2d Cir. 1985).

   i. *Matters contained in amended pleading under FRCP 15(a).* Although FRCP 15(a) does not expressly state that an amendment must contain only matters that occurred within a particular time period, FRCP 15(d) provides that any "transaction, occurrence, or event that happened after the date of the pleading" should be set forth in a supplemental pleading. FPP § 1473. Thus, impliedly, an amended pleading, whether prepared with or without leave of court, only should relate to matters that have taken place prior to the date of the earlier pleading. FPP § 1473; Ford Motor Co. v. U.S., 19 C.I.T. 946, 896 F.Supp. 1224, 1230 (1995).

   ii. *Amending as a matter of course.* A party may amend its pleading once as a matter of course within: (1) twenty-one (21) days after serving it, or if the pleading is one to which a responsive pleading is required, twenty-one (21) days after service of a responsive pleading or twenty-one (21) days after service of a motion under FRCP 12(b), FRCP 12(e), or FRCP 12(f), whichever is earlier. FRCP 15(a)(1). Refer to the United States District Court for the Southern District of New York KeyRules Amended Pleading document for more information on amending as a matter of course.

   iii. *Other amendments.* In all other cases, a party may amend its pleading only with the opposing party's written consent or the court's leave. The court should freely give leave when justice so requires. FRCP 15(a)(2).

   iv. *Types of amendments permitted under FRCP 15(a)*

      • *Cure a defective pleading.* Perhaps the most common use of FRCP 15(a) is by a party seeking to amend in order to cure a defective pleading. FPP § 1474.

      • *Correct insufficiently stated claims or defenses.* A more common use of FRCP 15(a) amendments is to correct insufficiently stated claims or defenses. Typically, amendments of this character involve either adding a necessary allegation in order to state a claim for relief or correcting a misnomer of a party to the action. FPP § 1474.

      • *Change nature or theory of claim or capacity of party.* Courts also have allowed a party to amend in order to change the nature or theory of the party's claim or the capacity in which the party is bringing the action. FPP § 1474.

      • *State additional claims or defenses or drop claims or defenses.* Plaintiffs and defendants also have been permitted to amend their pleadings to state additional claims, to assert additional defenses, or to drop claims or defenses. FPP § 1474; Weinberger v. Retail Credit Co., 498 F.2d 552, 554, n.4 (4th Cir. 1974).

      • *Increase amount of damages or elect a different remedy.* A FRCP 15(a) amendment also is appropriate for increasing the amount of damages sought, or for electing a different remedy than the one originally requested. FPP § 1474; McFadden v. Sanchez, 710 F.2d 907 (2d Cir. 1983).

      • *Add, substitute, or drop parties.* Finally, a party may make a FRCP 15(a) amendment to add, substitute, or drop parties to the action. FPP § 1474.

b. *Amendments during and after trial*

   i. *Based on an objection at trial.* If, at trial, a party objects that evidence is not within the issues raised in the pleadings, the court may permit the pleadings to be amended. The court should freely permit an amendment when doing so will aid in presenting the merits and the objecting party fails to satisfy the court that the evidence would prejudice that party's action or defense on the merits. The court may grant a continuance to enable the objecting party to meet the evidence. FRCP 15(b)(1).

ii. *For issues tried by consent.* When an issue not raised by the pleadings is tried by the parties' express or implied consent, it must be treated in all respects as if raised in the pleadings. A party may move—at any time, even after judgment—to amend the pleadings to conform them to the evidence and to raise an unpleaded issue. But failure to amend does not affect the result of the trial of that issue. FRCP 15(b)(2).

c. *Relation back of amendments*

i. *When an amendment relates back.* An amendment to a pleading relates back to the date of the original pleading when:

- The law that provides the applicable statute of limitations allows relation back;

- The amendment asserts a claim or defense that arose out of the conduct, transaction, or occurrence set out—or attempted to be set out—in the original pleading; or

- The amendment changes the party or the naming of the party against whom a claim is asserted, if FRCP 15(c)(1)(B) is satisfied and if, within the period provided by FRCP 4(m) for serving the summons and complaint, the party to be brought in by amendment: (1) received such notice of the action that it will not be prejudiced in defending on the merits; and (2) knew or should have known that the action would have been brought against it, but for a mistake concerning the proper party's identity. FRCP 15(c)(1).

ii. *Notice to the United States.* When the United States or a United States officer or agency is added as a defendant by amendment, the notice requirements of FRCP 15(c)(1)(C)(i) and FRCP 15(c)(1)(C)(ii) are satisfied if, during the stated period, process was delivered or mailed to the United States attorney or the United States attorney's designee, to the Attorney General of the United States, or to the officer or agency. FRCP 15(c)(2).

d. *Effect of an amended pleading.* A pleading that has been amended under FRCP 15(a) supersedes the pleading it modifies and remains in effect throughout the action unless it subsequently is modified. FPP § 1476. Once an amended pleading is interposed, the original pleading no longer performs any function in the case and any subsequent motion made by an opposing party should be directed at the amended pleading. FPP § 1476; Ferdik v. Bonzelet, 963 F.2d 1258, 1262 (9th Cir. 1992); Davis v. TXO Production Corp., 929 F.2d 1515, 1517 (10th Cir. 1991).

4. *Opposing papers.* The Federal Rules of Civil Procedure do not require any formal answer, return, or reply to a motion, except where the Federal Rules of Civil Procedure or local rules may require affidavits, memoranda, or other papers to be filed in opposition to a motion. Such papers are simply to apprise the court of such opposition and the grounds of that opposition. FEDPROC § 62:359. Except for letter-motions as permitted by NY R USDCTS&ED Civ Rule 7.1(d) or as otherwise permitted by the Court, all oppositions and replies with respect to motions shall comply with NY R USDCTS&ED Civ Rule 7.1(a)(2) and NY R USDCTS&ED Civ Rule 7.1(a)(3), and an opposing party who seeks relief that goes beyond the denial of the motion shall comply as well with NY R USDCTS&ED Civ Rule 7.1(a)(1). NY R USDCTS&ED Civ Rule 7.1(b).

a. *Effect of failure to respond to motion.* Although in the absence of statutory provision or court rule, a motion ordinarily does not require a written answer, when a party files a motion and the opposing party fails to respond, the court may construe such failure to respond as nonopposition to the motion or an admission that the motion was meritorious, may take the facts alleged in the motion as true—the rule in some jurisdictions being that the failure to respond to a fact set forth in a motion is deemed an admission—and may grant the motion if the relief requested appears to be justified. AMJUR MOTIONS § 28.

b. *Assent or no opposition not determinative.* However, a motion will not be granted automatically simply because an "assent" or a notation of "no opposition" has been filed; federal judges frequently deny motions that have been assented to when it is thought that justice so dictates. FPP § 1190.

   c. *Responsive pleading inappropriate as response to motion.* An attempt to answer or oppose a motion with a responsive pleading usually is not appropriate. FPP § 1190.

5. *Reply papers.* A moving party may be required or permitted to prepare papers in addition to his original motion papers. AMJUR MOTIONS § 25. Papers answering or replying to opposing papers may be appropriate, in the interests of justice, where it appears there is a substantial reason for allowing a reply. Thus, a court may accept reply papers where a party demonstrates that the papers to which it seeks to file a reply raise new issues that are material to the disposition of the question before the court, or where the court determines, sua sponte, that it wishes further briefing of an issue raised in those papers and orders the submission of additional papers. FEDPROC § 62:360. Except for letter-motions as permitted by NY R USDCTS&ED Civ Rule 7.1(d) or as otherwise permitted by the Court, all oppositions and replies with respect to motions shall comply with NY R USDCTS&ED Civ Rule 7.1(a)(2) and NY R USDCTS&ED Civ Rule 7.1(a)(3). NY R USDCTS&ED Civ Rule 7.1(b).

   a. *Function of reply papers.* The function of a reply affidavit is to answer the arguments made in opposition to the position taken by the movant and not to permit the movant to introduce new arguments in support of the motion. AMJUR MOTIONS § 25.

   b. *Issues raised for the first time in a reply document.* However, the view has been followed in some jurisdictions, that as a matter of judicial economy, where there is no prejudice and where the issues could be raised simply by filing a motion to dismiss, the trial court has discretion to consider arguments raised for the first time in a reply memorandum, and that a trial court may grant a motion to strike issues raised for the first time in a reply memorandum. AMJUR MOTIONS § 26.

6. *Orders on motions.* A memorandum signed by the Court of the decision on a motion that does not finally determine all claims for relief, or an oral decision on such a motion, shall constitute the order unless the memorandum or oral decision directs the submission or settlement of an order in more extended form. The notation in the docket of a memorandum or of an oral decision that does not direct the submission or settlement of an order in more extended form shall constitute the entry of the order. Where an order in more extended form is required to be submitted or settled, the notation in the docket of such order shall constitute the entry of the order. NY R USDCTS&ED Civ Rule 6.2.

7. *Complex civil cases.* For information on procedures for complex civil cases, refer to NY R USDCTSD Order 11 Misc 00388.

8. *Related cases.* It shall be the continuing duty of each attorney appearing in any civil or criminal case to bring promptly to the attention of the Court all facts which said attorney believes are relevant to a determination that said case and one or more pending civil or criminal cases should be heard by the same Judge, in order to avoid unnecessary duplication of judicial effort. As soon as the attorney becomes aware of such relationship, said attorney shall notify the Judges to whom the cases have been assigned. NY R USDCTS&ED Civ Rule 1.6(a). If counsel fails to comply with NY R USDCTS&ED Civ Rule 1.6(a), the Court may assess reasonable costs directly against counsel whose action has obstructed the effective administration of the Court's business. NY R USDCTS&ED Civ Rule 1.6(b).

   a. *Determination of relatedness.* Subject to the limitations set forth in NY R USDCTSD Div. Bus., Rule 13(a)(2), a civil case, bankruptcy appeal, or motion to withdraw the bankruptcy reference will be deemed related to one or more civil cases, appeals or motions when the interests of justice and efficiency will be served. In determining relatedness, a judge will consider whether (A) the actions concern the same or substantially similar parties, property, transactions or events; (B) there is substantial factual overlap; (C) the parties could be subjected to conflicting orders; and (D) whether absent a determination of relatedness there would be a substantial duplication of effort and expense, delay, or undue burden on the Court, parties or witnesses. NY R USDCTSD Div. Bus., Rule 13(a)(1). Nothing in this NY R USDCTSD Div. Bus., Rule 13 is intended to preclude parties from moving for consolidated proceedings under FRCP 42. NY R USDCTSD Div. Bus., Rule 13(a)(1). Notwithstanding NY R USDCTSD Div. Bus., Rule 13(a)(1):

     i. Civil cases shall not be deemed related merely because they involve common legal issues or the same parties. NY R USDCTSD Div. Bus., Rule 13(a)(2)(A).

     ii. Other than cases subject to NY R USDCTSD Div. Bus., Rule 4(b) and actions seeking the enforcement of a judgment or settlement in or of an earlier case, civil cases presumptively shall not be deemed related unless both cases are pending before the Court (or the earlier case is on appeal). NY R USDCTSD Div. Bus., Rule 13(a)(2)(B).

b. *Procedure in regard to cases said to be related*

   i. *Disclosure of contention of relatedness.* When a civil case is filed or removed or a bankruptcy appeal or motion to withdraw the reference of an adversary proceeding from the bankruptcy court is filed, the person filing or removing shall disclose on form JSC44C any contention of relatedness and shall file a Related Case Statement stating clearly and succinctly the basis for the contention. A copy of the civil cover sheet and Related Case Statement shall be served with the complaint, notice of removal, notice of appeal, or motion. Any party may contest a claim of relatedness by any other in writing addressed to the judge having the case with the lowest docket number of all cases claimed to be related. However, the foregoing shall not delay the assignment process or the operation of NY R USDCTSD Div. Bus., Rule 13. NY R USDCTSD Div. Bus., Rule 13(b)(1). [Editor's note: the reference to form JSC44C is likely meant to be form JS44C-SDNY: Civil Court Cover Sheet].

   ii. *Claims of relatedness by other parties.* A party other than the one filing a case, bankruptcy appeal or motion to withdraw the reference that contends its case is related to another may so advise in writing the judge assigned in its case and request a transfer of its case to the judge that the party contends has the related case with the lowest docket number. If the assigned judge believes the case is related under NY R USDCTSD Div. Bus., Rule 13(a), he or she shall refer the question to the judge having the case with the lowest docket number. In the event the latter judge agrees, the case shall be transferred to that judge unless the Assignment Committee disagrees. NY R USDCTSD Div. Bus., Rule 13(b)(3).

c. For more information on related cases, refer to NY R USDCTSD Div. Bus., Rule 13.

9. *Alternative dispute resolution (ADR).* The U.S. District Court for the Southern District of New York provides litigants with opportunities to discuss settlement through judicial settlement conferences and mediation. NY R USDCTS&ED Civ Rule 83.9(a).

   a. *Consideration of alternative dispute resolution.* In all civil cases, including those eligible for mediation pursuant to NY R USDCTS&ED Civ Rule 83.9(e), each party shall consider the use of mediation or a judicial settlement conference and shall report to the assigned Judge at the initial FRCP 16(b) case management conference, or subsequently, whether the party believes mediation or a judicial settlement conference may facilitate the resolution of the lawsuit. Judges are encouraged to note the availability of the mediation program and/or a judicial settlement conference before, at, or after the initial FRCP 16(b) case management conference. NY R USDCTS&ED Civ Rule 83.9(d).

   b. *Mediation.* In mediation, parties and counsel meet, sometimes collectively and sometimes individually, with a neutral third party (the mediator) who has been trained to facilitate confidential settlement discussions. The parties articulate their respective positions and interests and generate options for a mutually agreeable resolution to the dispute. The mediator assists the parties in reaching their own negotiated settlement by defining the issues, probing and assessing the strengths and weaknesses of each party's legal positions, and identifying areas of agreement and disagreement. The main benefits of mediation are that it can result in an expeditious and less costly resolution of the litigation, and can produce creative solutions to complex disputes often unavailable in traditional litigation. NY R USDCTS&ED Civ Rule 83.9(b).

      i. *Mediation program eligibility.* All civil cases other than Social Security, habeas corpus, and tax cases are eligible for mediation, whether assigned to Manhattan or White Plains. NY R USDCTS&ED Civ Rule 83.9(e)(1).

         • The Board of Judges may, by Administrative Order, direct that certain specified categories of cases shall automatically be submitted to the mediation program. The assigned District Judge or Magistrate Judge may issue a written order exempting a particular case with or without the request of the parties. NY R USDCTS&ED Civ Rule 83.9(e)(2).

         • For all other cases, the assigned District Judge or Magistrate Judge may determine that a case is appropriate for mediation and may order that case to mediation, with or without the consent of the parties, before, at, or after the initial FRCP 16(b) case management conference. Alternatively, the parties should notify the assigned Judge at any time of their desire to mediate. NY R USDCTS&ED Civ Rule 83.9(e)(3).

c. *Judicial settlement conferences.* Judicial settlement conferences may be ordered by District Judges or Magistrate Judges with or without the request or consent of the parties. NY R USDCTS&ED Civ Rule 83.9(f).

d. For more information on alternative dispute resolution (ADR), refer to NY R USDCTS&ED Civ Rule 83.9.

10. *Individual judge practices.* Refer to the Miscellaneous section of this document for information on individual judge practices on general requirements for documents.

## D. Documents

1. *Documents for moving party*

   a. *Required documents*

      i. *Notice of motion and motion.* Except for letter-motions as permitted by NY R USDCTS&ED Civ Rule 7.1(d) or as otherwise permitted by the Court, all motions shall include the following motion papers: a notice of motion, or an order to show cause signed by the Court, which shall specify the applicable rules or statutes pursuant to which the motion is brought, and shall specify the relief sought by the motion. NY R USDCTS&ED Civ Rule 7.1(a)(1). Refer to the General Requirements section of this document for information on the notice of motion and motion.

         - *Letter-motion; Alternative procedure.* The following may be made by LETTER-MOTION: Motion for Leave to File Document. NY R USDCTSD CM/ECF, S.D.(II)(13)(13.1).

      ii. *Memorandum of law.* Except for letter-motions as permitted by NY R USDCTS&ED Civ Rule 7.1(d) or as otherwise permitted by the Court, all motions shall include the following motion papers: a memorandum of law, setting forth the cases and other authorities relied upon in support of the motion, and divided, under appropriate headings, into as many parts as there are issues to be determined. NY R USDCTS&ED Civ Rule 7.1(a)(2).

      iii. *Proposed amendment.* In order to satisfy the prerequisites of FRCP 7(b), a copy of the amendment should be submitted with the motion so that the court and the adverse party know the precise nature of the pleading changes being proposed. FPP § 1485. The amending party should submit a copy of the proposed amendment at least by the date of the hearing on the motion for leave to amend. FEDPROC § 62:274; Grombach v. Oerlikon Tool & Arms Corp. of America, 276 F.2d 155 (4th Cir. 1960).

         - The documents accompanying the motion for leave to amend may be an appropriate substitute for a formally proposed amendment, if the documents sufficiently indicate the gist of the amendment. FEDPROC § 62:274.

      iv. *Certificate of service.* FRCP 5(d) requires that the person making service under FRCP 5 certify that service has been effected. FRCP 5(Advisory Committee Notes). Having such information on file may be useful for many purposes, including proof of service if an issue arises concerning the effectiveness of the service. FRCP 5(Advisory Committee Notes).

         - Such paper service [on attorneys and pro se parties who are not Filing or Receiving Users] must be documented by electronically filing proof of service. NY R USDCTSD CM/ECF, S.D.(I)(9)(9.2); NY R USDCTSD CM/ECF, S.D.(I)(19)(19.3)(b). Pro se parties who are not Filing Users are exempt from that portion of NY R USDCTSD CM/ECF, S.D.(I)(19)(19.3) requiring proof of service to be filed electronically. NY R USDCTSD CM/ECF, S.D.(I)(19)(19.3).

   b. *Supplemental documents*

      i. *Supporting evidence.* When a motion relies on facts outside the record, the court may hear the matter on affidavits or may hear it wholly or partly on oral testimony or on depositions. FRCP

43(c). Except for letter-motions as permitted by NY R USDCTS&ED Civ Rule 7.1(d) or as otherwise permitted by the Court, all motions shall include the following motion papers: supporting affidavits and exhibits thereto containing any factual information and portions of the record necessary for the decision of the motion. NY R USDCTS&ED Civ Rule 7.1(a)(3).

- *Discovery materials.* A party seeking or opposing relief under FRCP 26 through FRCP 37 inclusive, or making or opposing any other motion or application, shall quote or attach only those portions of the depositions, interrogatories, requests for documents, requests for admissions, or other discovery or disclosure materials, together with the responses and objections thereto, that are the subject of the discovery motion or application, or that are cited in papers submitted in connection with any other motion or application. NY R USDCTS&ED Civ Rule 5.1.

ii. *Notice of constitutional question.* A party that files a pleading, written motion, or other paper drawing into question the constitutionality of a federal or state statute must promptly:

- *File notice.* File a notice of constitutional question stating the question and identifying the paper that raises it, if: (1) a federal statute is questioned and the parties do not include the United States, one of its agencies, or one of its officers or employees in an official capacity; or (2) a state statute is questioned and the parties do not include the state, one of its agencies, or one of its officers or employees in an official capacity; and

- *Serve notice.* Serve the notice and paper on the Attorney General of the United States if a federal statute is questioned—or on the state attorney general if a state statute is questioned—either by certified or registered mail or by sending it to an electronic address designated by the attorney general for this purpose. FRCP 5.1(a).

- *No forfeiture.* A party's failure to file and serve the notice, or the court's failure to certify, does not forfeit a constitutional claim or defense that is otherwise timely asserted. FRCP 5.1(d).

iii. *Copies of authorities.* In cases involving a pro se litigant, counsel shall, when serving a memorandum of law (or other submissions to the Court), provide the pro se litigant (but not other counsel or the Court) with copies of cases and other authorities cited therein that are unpublished or reported exclusively on computerized databases. Upon request, counsel shall provide the pro se litigant with copies of such unpublished cases and other authorities as are cited in a decision of the Court and were not previously cited by any party. NY R USDCTS&ED Civ Rule 7.2.

iv. *Proposed order.* Refer to the Format section of this document for information on the format of submitting a proposed order to the court.

v. *Statement explaining untimely electronic filing.* If you missed a filing deadline when the ECF system was out of order, attach a statement to your filing explaining how the interruption in service prevented you from filing in a timely fashion. NY R USDCTSD CM/ECF, S.D.(II)(23)(23.5).

vi. *Courtesy copies.* Read the judge's Individual Practices to learn if courtesy copies are required. NY R USDCTSD CM/ECF, S.D.(II)(13)(13.17). Judges' Individual Practices should continue to be followed with respect to delivery of courtesy copies. NY R USDCTSD CM/ECF, S.D.(I)(3)(3.4).

2. *Documents for opposing party*

a. *Required documents*

i. *Answering memorandum of law.* Except for letter-motions as permitted by NY R USDCTS&ED Civ Rule 7.1(d) or as otherwise permitted by the Court, all oppositions and replies with respect to motions shall comply with NY R USDCTS&ED Civ Rule 7.1(a)(2). NY R USDCTS&ED Civ Rule 7.1(b). Except for letter-motions as permitted by NY R USDCTS&ED Civ Rule 7.1(d) or as otherwise permitted by the Court, all motions shall include the following motion papers: a memorandum of law, setting forth the cases and other authorities relied upon in support of the motion, and divided, under appropriate headings, into as many parts as there are issues to be determined. NY R USDCTS&ED Civ Rule 7.1(a)(2). Refer to the General Requirements section of this document for information on the opposing papers.

ii. *Certificate of service.* FRCP 5(d) requires that the person making service under FRCP 5 certify that service has been effected. FRCP 5(Advisory Committee Notes). Having such information on file may be useful for many purposes, including proof of service if an issue arises concerning the effectiveness of the service. FRCP 5(Advisory Committee Notes).

- Such paper service [on attorneys and pro se parties who are not Filing or Receiving Users] must be documented by electronically filing proof of service. NY R USDCTSD CM/ECF, S.D.(I)(9)(9.2); NY R USDCTSD CM/ECF, S.D.(I)(19)(19.3)(b). Pro se parties who are not Filing Users are exempt from that portion of NY R USDCTSD CM/ECF, S.D.(I)(19)(19.3) requiring proof of service to be filed electronically. NY R USDCTSD CM/ECF, S.D.(I)(19)(19.3).

b. *Supplemental documents*

i. *Supporting evidence.* When a motion relies on facts outside the record, the court may hear the matter on affidavits or may hear it wholly or partly on oral testimony or on depositions. FRCP 43(c). Except for letter-motions as permitted by NY R USDCTS&ED Civ Rule 7.1(d) or as otherwise permitted by the Court, all oppositions and replies with respect to motions shall comply with NY R USDCTS&ED Civ Rule 7.1(a)(3). NY R USDCTS&ED Civ Rule 7.1(b). Except for letter-motions as permitted by NY R USDCTS&ED Civ Rule 7.1(d) or as otherwise permitted by the Court, all motions shall include the following motion papers: supporting affidavits and exhibits thereto containing any factual information and portions of the record necessary for the decision of the motion. NY R USDCTS&ED Civ Rule 7.1(a)(3).

- *Discovery materials.* A party seeking or opposing relief under FRCP 26 through FRCP 37 inclusive, or making or opposing any other motion or application, shall quote or attach only those portions of the depositions, interrogatories, requests for documents, requests for admissions, or other discovery or disclosure materials, together with the responses and objections thereto, that are the subject of the discovery motion or application, or that are cited in papers submitted in connection with any other motion or application. NY R USDCTS&ED Civ Rule 5.1.

ii. *Notice of constitutional question.* A party that files a pleading, written motion, or other paper drawing into question the constitutionality of a federal or state statute must promptly:

- *File notice.* File a notice of constitutional question stating the question and identifying the paper that raises it, if: (1) a federal statute is questioned and the parties do not include the United States, one of its agencies, or one of its officers or employees in an official capacity; or (2) a state statute is questioned and the parties do not include the state, one of its agencies, or one of its officers or employees in an official capacity; and

- *Serve notice.* Serve the notice and paper on the Attorney General of the United States if a federal statute is questioned—or on the state attorney general if a state statute is questioned—either by certified or registered mail or by sending it to an electronic address designated by the attorney general for this purpose. FRCP 5.1(a).

- *No forfeiture.* A party's failure to file and serve the notice, or the court's failure to certify, does not forfeit a constitutional claim or defense that is otherwise timely asserted. FRCP 5.1(d).

iii. *Copies of authorities.* In cases involving a pro se litigant, counsel shall, when serving a memorandum of law (or other submissions to the Court), provide the pro se litigant (but not other counsel or the Court) with copies of cases and other authorities cited therein that are unpublished or reported exclusively on computerized databases. Upon request, counsel shall provide the pro se litigant with copies of such unpublished cases and other authorities as are cited in a decision of the Court and were not previously cited by any party. NY R USDCTS&ED Civ Rule 7.2.

iv. *Statement explaining untimely electronic filing.* If you missed a filing deadline when the ECF system was out of order, attach a statement to your filing explaining how the interruption in service prevented you from filing in a timely fashion. NY R USDCTSD CM/ECF, S.D.(II)(23)(23.5).

    v.    *Courtesy copies.* Read the judge's Individual Practices to learn if courtesy copies are required. NY R USDCTSD CM/ECF, S.D.(II)(13)(13.17). Judges' Individual Practices should continue to be followed with respect to delivery of courtesy copies. NY R USDCTSD CM/ECF, S.D.(I)(3)(3.4).

3.    *Individual judge practices.* Refer to the Miscellaneous section of this document for information on individual judge practices on required documents.

## E.  Format

1.    *Form of documents.* The rules governing captions and other matters of form in pleadings apply to motions and other papers. FRCP 7(b)(2).

    a.    *Paper.* Every pleading, written motion, and other paper must: be plainly written, typed, printed, or copied without erasures or interlineations which materially deface it. NY R USDCTS&ED Civ Rule 11.1(a)(1).

    b.    *Typeface, margin, and spacing.* The typeface, margins, and spacing of all documents presented for filing must meet the following requirements:

        i.    All text must be twelve (12) point type or larger, except for text in footnotes which may be ten (10) point type;

        ii.    All documents must have at least one (1) inch margins on all sides;

        iii.    All text must be double-spaced, except for headings, text in footnotes, or block quotations, which may be single-spaced. NY R USDCTS&ED Civ Rule 11.1(b).

    c.    *Caption; Names of parties.* Every pleading must have a caption with the court's name, a title, a file number, and a FRCP 7(a) designation. The title of the complaint must name all the parties; the title of other pleadings, after naming the first party on each side, may refer generally to other parties. FRCP 10(a). Every pleading, written motion, and other paper must: bear the docket number and the initials of the District Judge and any Magistrate Judge before whom the action or proceeding is pending, NY R USDCTS&ED Civ Rule 11.1(a)(2).

    d.    *Paragraphs; Separate statements.* A party must state its claims or defenses in numbered paragraphs, each limited as far as practicable to a single set of circumstances. A later pleading may refer by number to a paragraph in an earlier pleading. If doing so would promote clarity, each claim founded on a separate transaction or occurrence—and each defense other than a denial—must be stated in a separate count or defense. FRCP 10(b).

    e.    *Adoption by reference; Exhibits.* A statement in a pleading may be adopted by reference elsewhere in the same pleading or in any other pleading or motion. A copy of a written instrument that is an exhibit to a pleading is a part of the pleading for all purposes. FRCP 10(c).

    f.    *Acceptance by the clerk.* The clerk must not refuse to file a paper solely because it is not in the form prescribed by the Federal Rules of Civil Procedure or by a local rule or practice. FRCP 5(d)(4).

2.    *Form of electronic documents*

    a.    *PDF-A.* All documents electronically filed on the ECF system must be in PDF-A format (portable document format). A PDF-A file is created using PDF writer software such as Adobe Acrobat (go to the Adobe website for details). PDF-A files cannot be altered, providing security to the filer and the Court. NY R USDCTSD CM/ECF, S.D.(II)(23)(23.2).

    b.    *Size limitation.* No single PDF file may be larger than four megabytes (4 MB). If the filing is too large, the ECF system will not allow it to be filed, and you will not see a Notice of Electronic Filing (NEF or filing receipt) screen. To determine the size of an Adobe Acrobat PDF file click on File, Document Properties, Summary. NY R USDCTSD CM/ECF, S.D.(II)(23)(23.3).

        i.    Converting documents directly from a word processor to PDF-A format creates the smallest possible file in terms of computer memory. If that is not possible, scan your document at low resolution. Within the Adobe Acrobat program, on the "Scan Manager" screen, adjust the settings for black and white and 200 dpi (dots per inch). This allows more pages to fit into a single PDF-A file. If that does not work, separate an oversized file into 2 or more parts. Simply label each file 1a, 1b, 1c, etc. Only relevant excerpts of exhibits should be electronically filed. NY R USDCTSD CM/ECF, S.D.(II)(23)(23.4).

c.   *Attachments and exhibits.* Filing Users must submit in electronic form all documents referenced as exhibits or attachments, unless the Court permits paper filing. NY R USDCTSD CM/ECF, S.D.(I)(5)(5.1).

   i.   A Filing User must submit as exhibits or attachments only those excerpts of the referenced documents that are relevant to the matter under consideration by the Court. Excerpted material must be clearly and prominently identified as such. Filing Users who file excerpts of documents as exhibits or attachments under this procedure do so without prejudice to their right to file timely additional excerpts or the complete document. Responding parties may file timely additional excerpts that they believe are relevant or the complete document. A party may move before the Court for permission to serve and file in hard copy documents that cannot be reasonably scanned. NY R USDCTSD CM/ECF, S.D.(I)(5)(5.2).

   ii.  Exhibits must be filed only as attachments to a document, such as a motion or an affidavit. Do not use the ECF Filing Event for "Motion" to file exhibits separately. Exhibits are the only items that should be attached to electronically filed documents. You are limited to electronically filing only relevant excerpts of exhibits. Excerpts must be clearly identified as such. If the exhibit is too large to be scanned and electronically filed you may contact the ECF Help Desk. NY R USDCTSD CM/ECF, S.D.(II)(15)(15.6).

d.   *Letters.* Parties should consult the assigned judge's Individual Practices to determine if the judge accepts letters at all and, if he or she does, whether the judge has any page limitations on letters and/or requires courtesy copies of letters filed on ECF (and, if so, by what means of delivery). All letters addressed to the Court must include a subject line with the case name and docket number (e.g., "Re: Doe v. Smith, 13 Civ. 1234 (ABC)"). NY R USDCTSD CM/ECF, S.D.(II)(13)(13.1).

e.   *Proposed orders, proposed judgments, stipulations and consents.* Any document that requires the signature of a judge should not be electronically filed except as an exhibit to another document. Proposed orders, judgments, stipulations and consents should not be submitted through the ECF system. Instead they should be sent by e-mail to the Clerk. Proposed orders should be submitted in word processing format (WordPerfect or Word) rather than as a PDF document. Stipulations should be submitted in PDF-A format. Stipulations must contain ink signatures not s/. Faxed or emailed signatures are acceptable. Please note that Stipulations of Voluntary Dismissal pursuant to FRCP 41(a)(1)(A)(ii) do not require the signature of a judge and must be electronically filed on the ECF system. Questions may be directed to the Orders and Judgments Clerk at the phone numbers listed in NY R USDCTSD CM/ECF, S.D.(II)(18)(18.3). NY R USDCTSD CM/ECF, S.D.(II)(18)(18.3).

   i.   Email the proposed order, judgment or stipulation to the email addresses listed in NY R USDCTSD CM/ECF, S.D.(II)(18)(18.3). NY R USDCTSD CM/ECF, S.D.(II)(18)(18.3).

   ii.  Pro se litigants who are not Filing Users are exempt from that portion of NY R USDCTSD CM/ECF, S.D.(II)(18)(18.3) that requires litigants to email proposed orders, judgments, stipulations and consents, and shall deliver such documents to the Clerk's Office in paper form. NY R USDCTSD CM/ECF, S.D.(II)(18)(18.3).

3.   *Signing of pleadings, motions and other papers*

a.   *Signature.* Every pleading, written motion, and other paper must be signed by at least one attorney of record in the attorney's name—or by a party personally if the party is unrepresented. The paper must state the signer's address, e-mail address, and telephone number. FRCP 11(a). Every pleading, written motion, and other paper must: have the name of each person signing it clearly printed or typed directly below the signature. NY R USDCTS&ED Civ Rule 11.1(a)(3).

   i.   *Electronic signatures.* The user log-in and password required to submit documents to the ECF system serve as the Filing User's signature on all electronic documents filed with the Court. NY

R USDCTSD CM/ECF, S.D.(I)(8)(8.1); NY R USDCTSD CM/ECF, S.D.(II)(13)(13.14). They also serve as a signature for purposes of the Federal Rules of Civil Procedure, including FRCP 11, the Local Civil Rules of the United States District Courts for the Southern and Eastern Districts of New York, and any other purpose for which a signature is required in connection with proceedings before the Court. NY R USDCTSD CM/ECF, S.D.(I)(8)(8.1).

- *Signature block.* Electronically filed documents must include a signature block and must set forth the name, address, telephone number and e-mail address all in compliance with the Federal Rules of Civil Procedure and NY R USDCTS&ED Civ Rule 11.1. In the absence of a scanned signature image, the name of the Filing User under whose log-in and password the document is submitted must be preceded by an "s/" typed in the space where the signature would otherwise appear. NY R USDCTSD CM/ECF, S.D.(I)(8)(8.2); NY R USDCTSD CM/ECF, S.D.(II)(13)(13.14).

- *Documents requiring the signature of a party or witness.* A document requiring the signature of a party or witness shall be electronically filed in a scanned format that contains an image of the actual signature. NY R USDCTSD CM/ECF, S.D.(I)(8)(8.4); NY R USDCTSD CM/ECF, S.D.(II)(13)(13.14).

- *Documents requiring the signature of a judge.* A Filing User submitting a document electronically that requires a judge's signature must promptly deliver the document in such other form, if any, as the Court requires. NY R USDCTSD CM/ECF, S.D.(I)(4)(4.2).

- *Documents requiring multiple signatures.* Documents requiring signatures of more than one party must be electronically filed either by: (a) submitting a scanned document containing all necessary signatures; (b) representing the consent of the other parties on the document; (c) identifying on the document the parties whose signatures are required and by the submission of a notice of endorsement by the other parties no later than three business days after filing; or (d) in any other manner approved by the Court. NY R USDCTSD CM/ECF, S.D.(I)(8)(8.5).

 ii. *No verification or accompanying affidavit required for pleadings.* Unless a rule or statute specifically states otherwise, a pleading need not be verified or accompanied by an affidavit. FRCP 11(a).

 iii. *Unsigned papers.* The court must strike an unsigned paper unless the omission is promptly corrected after being called to the attorney's or party's attention. FRCP 11(a).

b. *Representations to the court.* By presenting to the court a pleading, written motion, or other paper—whether by signing, filing, submitting, or later advocating it—an attorney or unrepresented party certifies that to the best of the person's knowledge, information, and belief, formed after an inquiry reasonable under the circumstances:

 i. It is not being presented for any improper purpose, such as to harass, cause unnecessary delay, or needlessly increase the cost of litigation;

 ii. The claims, defenses, and other legal contentions are warranted by existing law or by a nonfrivolous argument for extending, modifying, or reversing existing law or for establishing new law;

 iii. The factual contentions have evidentiary support or, if specifically so identified, will likely have evidentiary support after a reasonable opportunity for further investigation or discovery; and

 iv. The denials of factual contentions are warranted on the evidence or, if specifically so identified, are reasonably based on belief or a lack of information. FRCP 11(b).

c. *Sanctions.* If, after notice and a reasonable opportunity to respond, the court determines that FRCP 11(b) has been violated, the court may impose an appropriate sanction on any attorney, law firm, or party that violated FRCP 11(b) or is responsible for the violation. FRCP 11(c)(1). Refer to the United States District Court for the Southern District of New York KeyRules Motion for Sanctions document for more information.

4. *Privacy protection for filings made with the court*

a. *Redacted filings.* Unless the court orders otherwise, in an electronic or paper filing with the court that

contains an individual's Social Security number, taxpayer-identification number, or birth date, the name of an individual known to be a minor, or a financial-account number, a party or nonparty making the filing may include only:

    i.   The last four (4) digits of the Social Security number and taxpayer-identification number;

    ii.   The year of the individual's birth;

    iii.   The minor's initials; and

    iv.   The last four (4) digits of the financial-account number. FRCP 5.2(a); NY R USDCTSD CM/ECF, S.D.(II)(21)(21.3).

    v.   Caution should be exercised when filing documents that contain the following:

- Personal identifying numbers (PIN #'s), such as a driver's license number;
- Medical records, treatment and diagnosis;
- Employment history;
- Individual financial information;
- Proprietary or trade secret information;
- Information regarding an individual's cooperation with the government. NY R US-DCTSD CM/ECF, S.D.(II)(21)(21.4).

b.   *Exemptions from the redaction requirement.* The redaction requirement does not apply to the following:

    i.   A financial-account number that identifies the property allegedly subject to forfeiture in a forfeiture proceeding;

    ii.   The record of an administrative or agency proceeding;

    iii.   The official record of a state-court proceeding;

    iv.   The record of a court or tribunal, if that record was not subject to the redaction requirement when originally filed;

    v.   A filing covered by FRCP 5.2(c) or FRCP 5.2(d); and

    vi.   A pro se filing in an action brought under 28 U.S.C.A. § 2241, 28 U.S.C.A. § 2254, or 28 U.S.C.A. § 2255. FRCP 5.2(b).

c.   *Limitations on remote access to electronic files; Social Security appeals and immigration cases.* Unless the court orders otherwise, in an action for benefits under the Social Security Act, and in an action or proceeding relating to an order of removal, to relief from removal, or to immigration benefits or detention, access to an electronic file is authorized as follows:

    i.   The parties and their attorneys may have remote electronic access to any part of the case file, including the administrative record;

    ii.   Any other person may have electronic access to the full record at the courthouse, but may have remote electronic access only to:

- The docket maintained by the court; and
- An opinion, order, judgment, or other disposition of the court, but not any other part of the case file or the administrative record. FRCP 5.2(c).

d.   *Filings made under seal.* The court may order that a filing be made under seal without redaction. The court may later unseal the filing or order the person who made the filing to file a redacted version for the public record. FRCP 5.2(d). For more information on sealing documents, refer to NY R USDCTSD CM/ECF, S.D.(I)(6).

e.   *Protective orders.* For good cause, the court may by order in a case:

    i.   Require redaction of additional information; or

    ii.   Limit or prohibit a nonparty's remote electronic access to a document filed with the court. FRCP 5.2(e).

f. *Option for additional unredacted filing under seal.* A person making a redacted filing may also file an unredacted copy under seal. The court must retain the unredacted copy as part of the record. FRCP 5.2(f); NY R USDCTSD CM/ECF, S.D.(II)(21)(21.5).

g. *Option for filing a reference list.* A filing that contains redacted information may be filed together with a reference list that identifies each item of redacted information and specifies an appropriate identifier that uniquely corresponds to each item listed. The list must be filed under seal and may be amended as of right. Any reference in the case to a listed identifier will be construed to refer to the corresponding item of information. FRCP 5.2(g); NY R USDCTSD CM/ECF, S.D.(II)(21)(21.5).

h. *Responsibility for redaction.* It is the sole responsibility of counsel and the parties to be sure that all documents comply with the rules of this Court requiring redaction of personal identifiers. Neither the judge nor the Clerk of Court will review documents for compliance with these rules. NY R USDCTSD CM/ECF, S.D.(II)(21)(21.2).

i. *Waiver of protection of identifiers.* A person waives the protection of FRCP 5.2(a) as to the person's own information by filing it without redaction and not under seal. FRCP 5.2(h).

j. For more information on privacy and public access to ECF cases, refer to NY R USDCTSD CM/ECF, S.D.(II)(21).

5. *Individual judge practices.* Refer to the Miscellaneous section of this document for information on individual judge practices on formatting documents.

## F. Filing and Service Requirements

1. *Filing requirements.* Any paper after the complaint that is required to be served—together with a certificate of service—must be filed within a reasonable time after service. FRCP 5(d)(1). Complaints and all subsequent papers are accepted at either courthouse, regardless of the place for which the case is designated. NY R USDCTSD Div. Bus., Rule 22. Subject to the instructions regarding ECF published on the website of each respective Court and any pertinent Individual Judge's Practices, letter-motions permitted by NY R USDCTS&ED Civ Rule 7.1(d) and letters addressed to the Court (but not letters between the parties) may be filed via ECF. NY R USDCTS&ED Civ Rule 5.2(b). For information on electronically filing motions, refer to NY R USDCTSD CM/ECF, S.D.(II)(15).

a. *How filing is made; In general.* A paper is filed by delivering it:

   i. To the clerk; or

   ii. To a judge who agrees to accept it for filing, and who must then note the filing date on the paper and promptly send it to the clerk. FRCP 5(d)(2).

b. *Night depository.* A night depository with an automatic date stamp shall be maintained by the Clerk of the Southern District in the Pearl Street Courthouse. After regular business hours, papers for the District Court only may be deposited in the night depository. Such papers will be considered as having been filed in the District Court as of the date stamped thereon, which shall be deemed presumptively correct. NY R USDCTS&ED Civ Rule 1.2.

c. *Electronic filing*

   i. *Authorization of electronic filing program.* A court may, by local rule, allow papers to be filed, signed, or verified by electronic means that are consistent with any technical standards established by the Judicial Conference of the United States. A local rule may require electronic filing only if reasonable exceptions are allowed. A paper filed electronically in compliance with a local rule is a written paper for purposes of the Federal Rules of Civil Procedure. FRCP 5(d)(3).

   • The Court will accept for filing documents submitted, signed or verified by electronic means, that comply with the rules in NY R USDCTSD CM/ECF, S.D. NY R USDCTSD CM/ECF, S.D.(I). The information in NY R USDCTSD CM/ECF, S.D. applies only to cases assigned to the ECF system. NY R USDCTSD CM/ECF, S.D.(Introduction).

   • Parties serving and filing papers shall follow the instructions regarding Electronic Case Filing (ECF) published on the website of each respective Court. A paper served and filed by electronic means in accordance with such instructions is, for purposes of FRCP 5, served and filed in compliance with the Local Civil Rules of the Southern and Eastern Districts of New York. NY R USDCTS&ED Civ Rule 5.2(a). Parties have an obligation to review the Court's actual order, decree, or judgment (on ECF), which controls, and should not rely on the description on the docket or in the ECF Notice of Electronic Filing (NEF). NY R USDCTS&ED Civ Rule 5.2(c).

- The following should be observed when filing electronically: (1) the Federal Rules of Civil Procedure, (2) the Local Civil Rules of the United States District Courts for the Southern and Eastern Districts of New York, (3) the assigned judge's Individual Practices, and (4) the Court's Electronic Case Filing Rules & Instructions (NY R USDCTSD CM/ECF, S.D.). NY R USDCTSD CM/ECF, S.D.(Introduction).

ii.  *Scope of electronic filing.* Except as expressly provided and in exceptional circumstances preventing a party from filing electronically, all documents required to be filed with the Court must be filed electronically. Any party unable to comply with this requirement must seek permission of the Court to file in the traditional manner, on paper. Any such application made after regular business hours may be submitted through the night depository box maintained pursuant to NY R USDCTS&ED Civ Rule 1.2. NY R USDCTSD CM/ECF, S.D.(I)(1)(1.1).

- *Documents filed by pro se litigants.* Unless otherwise ordered by the Court, documents filed by pro se litigants must be filed in the traditional manner, on paper, and will be scanned and docketed by the Clerk's Office into the ECF system. NY R USDCTSD CM/ECF, S.D.(I)(1)(1.1). Pro se litigants must file pleadings and documents in the traditional manner on paper unless the assigned judge has granted permission to electronically file on the ECF system. NY R USDCTSD CM/ECF, S.D.(Introduction).

- *Letters.* Except for letters to be filed under seal, letters addressed to judges who accept letters may be filed electronically. Parties should consult the assigned judge's Individual Practices to determine if the judge accepts letters at all and, if he or she does, whether the judge has any page limitations on letters and/or requires courtesy copies of letters filed on ECF (and, if so, by what means of delivery). NY R USDCTSD CM/ECF, S.D.(II)(13)(13.1). Letters solely between parties or their counsel or otherwise not addressed to the Court may not be filed electronically on ECF (except as exhibits to an otherwise properly filed document). NY R USDCTSD CM/ECF, S.D.(II)(13)(13.1). For more information on filing letters, refer to NY R USDCTSD CM/ECF, S.D.(II)(13)(13.1).

- *Proposed orders, judgments and decrees.* Proposed orders, judgments and decrees shall be presented as directed by the ECF rules published on the website of each respective Court. NY R USDCTS&ED Civ Rule 77.1. For more information, refer to NY R USDCTS&ED Civ Rule 77.1.

iii.  *Exceptions to electronic filing.* In an ECF case, the documents that should not be electronically filed include:

- Miscellaneous Case initiating documents, NY R USDCTSD CM/ECF, S.D.(II)(18)(18.2);

- Proposed orders; proposed judgments, stipulations; consents, NY R USDCTSD CM/ECF, S.D.(II)(18)(18.3);

- Orders to show cause / temporary restraining orders, NY R USDCTSD CM/ECF, S.D.(II)(18)(18.4);

- Sealed documents, NY R USDCTSD CM/ECF, S.D.(II)(18)(18.5); and

- Surety bonds, NY R USDCTSD CM/ECF, S.D.(II)(18)(18.6).

- In cases where the record of an administrative or other prior proceeding must be filed with the Court, such record may be served and filed in hard copy without prior motion and order of the Court. NY R USDCTSD CM/ECF, S.D.(I)(5)(5.3).

- For more documents excepted from electronic filing, and for more information on such documents, refer to NY R USDCTSD CM/ECF, S.D.(II)(18).

iv.  *Consequences of electronic filing.* Except as otherwise provided in NY R USDCTSD CM/ECF,

S.D.(I)(4), electronic filing of a document in the ECF system consistent with these procedures, together with the transmission of a Notice of Electronic Filing (NEF) from the Court, constitutes filing of the document for all purposes of the Federal Rules of Civil Procedure and the Local Civil Rules of the United States District Courts for the Southern and Eastern Districts of New York and constitutes entry of the document on the docket kept by the Clerk under FRCP 58 and FRCP 79. NY R USDCTSD CM/ECF, S.D.(I)(3)(3.1).

    v. For more information on electronic filing, refer to NY R USDCTSD CM/ECF, S.D.

2. *Service requirements*

  a. *Service; When required*

    i. *In general.* Unless the Federal Rules of Civil Procedure provide otherwise, each of the following papers must be served on every party:

- An order stating that service is required;
- A pleading filed after the original complaint, unless the court orders otherwise under FRCP 5(c) because there are numerous defendants;
- A discovery paper required to be served on a party, unless the court orders otherwise;
- A written motion, except one that may be heard ex parte; and
- A written notice, appearance, demand, or offer of judgment, or any similar paper. FRCP 5(a)(1).

    ii. *If a party fails to appear.* No service is required on a party who is in default for failing to appear. But a pleading that asserts a new claim for relief against such a party must be served on that party under FRCP 4. FRCP 5(a)(2).

    iii. *Seizing property.* If an action is begun by seizing property and no person is or need be named as a defendant, any service required before the filing of an appearance, answer, or claim must be made on the person who had custody or possession of the property when it was seized. FRCP 5(a)(3).

  b. *Service; How made*

    i. *Serving an attorney.* If a party is represented by an attorney, service under FRCP 5 must be made on the attorney unless the court orders service on the party. FRCP 5(b)(1).

    ii. *Service in general.* A paper is served under FRCP 5 by:

- Handing it to the person;
- Leaving it: (1) at the person's office with a clerk or other person in charge or, if no one is in charge, in a conspicuous place in the office; or (2) if the person has no office or the office is closed, at the person's dwelling or usual place of abode with someone of suitable age and discretion who resides there;
- Mailing it to the person's last known address—in which event service is complete upon mailing;
- Leaving it with the court clerk if the person has no known address;
- Sending it by electronic means if the person consented in writing—in which event service is complete upon transmission, but is not effective if the serving party learns that it did not reach the person to be served; or
- Delivering it by any other means that the person consented to in writing—in which event service is complete when the person making service delivers it to the agency designated to make delivery. FRCP 5(b)(2).

    iii. *Service by overnight delivery.* Service upon an attorney may be made by overnight delivery service. "Overnight delivery service" means any delivery service which regularly accepts items for overnight delivery. Overnight delivery service shall be deemed service by mail for purposes of FRCP 5 and FRCP 6. NY R USDCTS&ED Civ Rule 5.3.

iv. *Service by electronic means.* Parties serving and filing papers shall follow the instructions regarding Electronic Case Filing (ECF) published on the website of each respective Court. A paper served and filed by electronic means in accordance with such instructions is, for purposes of FRCP 5, served and filed in compliance with the Local Civil Rules of the United States District Courts for the Southern and Eastern Districts of New York. NY R USDCTS&ED Civ Rule 5.2(a). Parties have an obligation to review the Court's actual order, decree, or judgment (on ECF), which controls, and should not rely on the description on the docket or in the ECF Notice of Electronic Filing (NEF). NY R USDCTS&ED Civ Rule 5.2(c).

- *Notice of electronic filing (NEF).* In cases assigned to the ECF system, service is complete provided all parties receive a Notice of Electronic Filing (NEF), which is sent automatically by email from the Court (see the NEF for a list of who did/did not receive notice electronically). Transmission of the NEF constitutes service upon all Filing and Receiving Users who are listed as recipients of notice by electronic mail. NY R USDCTSD CM/ECF, S.D.(I)(9)(9.1). In cases assigned to the ECF system, if all parties receive a NEF, service is complete upon transmission of the NEF by the Court, and you are not required to serve a paper copy. NY R USDCTSD CM/ECF, S.D.(II)(19)(19.2). It remains the duty of Filing and Receiving Users to maintain current contact information with the court and to regularly review the docket sheet of the case. NY R USDCTSD CM/ECF, S.D.(I)(9)(9.1).

- *Mailing of court-initiated documents.* The Clerk's Office will no longer mail paper copies of court-initiated documents to Filing and Receiving Users. The Clerk's Office will mail copies of all court-initiated documents to pro se parties who have not registered as Filing or Receiving Users. NY R USDCTSD CM/ECF, S.D.(II)(19)(19.1).

- *No receipt of a NEF.* If any party does not receive a NEF, you are required to accomplish service on that party in the traditional manner, in paper form. NY R USDCTSD CM/ECF, S.D.(II)(19)(19.2). The NEF receipt will inform you who will receive notice of the filing "electronically" (by e-mail from the Court) and who will receive notice "by other means" (traditional service in paper form). NY R USDCTSD CM/ECF, S.D.(II)(19)(19.2).

- *Service on non-filing or non-receiving users.* Attorneys and pro se parties who are not Filing or Receiving Users must be served with a paper copy of any electronically filed pleading or other document. Service of such paper copy must be made according to the Federal Rules of Civil Procedure and the Local Civil Rules of the United States District Courts for the Southern and Eastern Districts of New York. NY R USDCTSD CM/ECF, S.D.(I)(9)(9.2). Such paper service must be documented by electronically filing proof of service. NY R USDCTSD CM/ECF, S.D.(I)(9)(9.2); NY R USDCTSD CM/ECF, S.D.(II)(19)(19.2). Where the Clerk scans and electronically files pleadings and documents on behalf of a pro se party, the associated NEF constitutes service. NY R USDCTSD CM/ECF, S.D.(I)(9)(9.2).

- For more information on service by electronic means, refer to NY R USDCTSD CM/ECF, S.D.(II)(19).

v. *Using court facilities.* If a local rule so authorizes, a party may use the court's transmission facilities to make service under FRCP 5(b)(2)(E). FRCP 5(b)(3).

c. *Serving numerous defendants*

i. *In general.* If an action involves an unusually large number of defendants, the court may, on motion or on its own, order that:

- Defendants' pleadings and replies to them need not be served on other defendants;

- Any crossclaim, counterclaim, avoidance, or affirmative defense in those pleadings and replies to them will be treated as denied or avoided by all other parties; and

- Filing any such pleading and serving it on the plaintiff constitutes notice of the pleading to all parties. FRCP 5(c)(1).

ii. *Notifying parties.* A copy of every such order must be served on the parties as the court directs. FRCP 5(c)(2).

3. *Individual judge practices.* Refer to the Miscellaneous section of this document for information on individual judge practices on filing and serving documents.

## G. Hearings

1. *Hearings, generally*

   a. *Oral argument.* Due process does not require that oral argument be permitted on a motion and, except as otherwise provided by local rule, the district court has discretion to determine whether it will decide the motion on the papers or hear argument by counsel (and perhaps receive evidence). FPP § 1190; F.D.I.C. v. Deglau, 207 F.3d 153 (3d Cir. 2000). The parties and their attorneys shall only appear to argue the motion if so directed by the Court by order or by a Judge's Individual Practice. NY R USDCTS&ED Civ Rule 6.1(c).

   b. *Providing a regular schedule for oral hearings.* A court may establish regular times and places for oral hearings on motions. FRCP 78(a).

   c. *Providing for submission on briefs.* By rule or order, the court may provide for submitting and determining motions on briefs, without oral hearings. FRCP 78(b).

2. *Individual judge practices.* Refer to the Miscellaneous section of this document for information on individual judge practices on hearings.

## H. Forms

### 1. Federal Motion for Leave to Amend Forms

   a. Leave to amend complaint; Attaching copy of amendment. 2C FEDFORMS § 14:18.

   b. Leave to amend complaint; Inserting amendment. 2C FEDFORMS § 14:19.

   c. Leave to amend complaint; Interlineation. 2C FEDFORMS § 14:20.

   d. Leave to amend complaint; Responding to motion to dismiss complaint. 2C FEDFORMS § 14:21.

   e. Leave to amend complaint; Close to trial. 2C FEDFORMS § 14:22.

   f. Leave to amend complaint; Adding new count. 2C FEDFORMS § 14:24.

   g. Leave to amend complaint; Asserting lack of knowledge of facts at time of original complaint. 2C FEDFORMS § 14:25.

   h. Leave to amend complaint; Seeking fourth amendment. 2C FEDFORMS § 14:26.

   i. Leave to amend complaint; Substituting plaintiff and dropping defendant. 2C FEDFORMS § 14:27.

   j. Leave to amend answer. 2C FEDFORMS § 14:30.

   k. Leave to amend answer; With leave endorsed. 2C FEDFORMS § 14:31.

   l. Leave to amend answer; Correcting errors, deleting and interlining. 2C FEDFORMS § 14:32.

   m. Leave to amend answer; Adding paragraph. 2C FEDFORMS § 14:33.

   n. Leave to amend answer; Adding defense. 2C FEDFORMS § 14:34.

   o. Leave to amend answer; During trial. 2C FEDFORMS § 14:35.

   p. Defendant's response to motion for leave to amend complaint a fourth time. 2C FEDFORMS § 14:36.

   q. Motion and notice; For leave to file amended pleading. FEDPROF § 1:222.

   r. Motion; To amend pleading to conform to findings of master. FEDPROF § 1:223.

   s. Affidavit; In support of motion for amendment of pleading. FEDPROF § 1:230.

   t. Opposition; To motion; General form. FEDPROF § 1:750.

   u. Affidavit; Supporting or opposing motion. FEDPROF § 1:751.

   v. Brief; Supporting or opposing motion. FEDPROF § 1:752.

   w. Statement of points and authorities; Opposing motion. FEDPROF § 1:753.

   x. Motion for leave to amend pleading. GOLDLTGFMS § 14:3.

y.  Motion to file second amended complaint on ground of newly discovered evidence. GOLDLTGFMS § 14:20.

z.  Motion for leave to file amended answer. GOLDLTGFMS § 14:22.

## I. Applicable Rules

1. *Federal rules*

   a.  Serving and filing pleadings and other papers. FRCP 5.

   b.  Constitutional challenge to a statute; Notice, certification, and intervention. FRCP 5.1.

   c.  Privacy protection for filings made with the court. FRCP 5.2.

   d.  Computing and extending time; Time for motion papers. FRCP 6.

   e.  Pleadings allowed; Form of motions and other papers. FRCP 7.

   f.  Form of pleadings. FRCP 10.

   g.  Signing pleadings, motions, and other papers; Representations to the court; Sanctions. FRCP 11.

   h.  Amended and supplemental pleadings. FRCP 15.

   i.  Taking testimony. FRCP 43.

   j.  Hearing motions; Submission on briefs. FRCP 78.

2. *Local rules*

   a.  Night depository. NY R USDCTS&ED Civ Rule 1.2.

   b.  Duty of attorneys in related cases. NY R USDCTS&ED Civ Rule 1.6.

   c.  Filing of discovery materials. NY R USDCTS&ED Civ Rule 5.1.

   d.  Electronic service and filing of documents. NY R USDCTS&ED Civ Rule 5.2.

   e.  Service by overnight delivery. NY R USDCTS&ED Civ Rule 5.3.

   f.  Service and filing of motion papers. NY R USDCTS&ED Civ Rule 6.1.

   g.  Orders on motions. NY R USDCTS&ED Civ Rule 6.2.

   h.  Computation of time. NY R USDCTS&ED Civ Rule 6.4.

   i.  Motion papers. NY R USDCTS&ED Civ Rule 7.1.

   j.  Authorities to be provided to pro se litigants. NY R USDCTS&ED Civ Rule 7.2.

   k.  Form of pleadings, motions, and other papers. NY R USDCTS&ED Civ Rule 11.1.

   l.  Submission of orders, judgments and decrees. NY R USDCTS&ED Civ Rule 77.1.

   m.  Alternative dispute resolution (Southern District only). NY R USDCTS&ED Civ Rule 83.9.

   n.  Electronic case filing rules and instructions. NY R USDCTSD CM/ECF, S.D.

   o.  Related cases. NY R USDCTSD Div. Bus., Rule 13.

   p.  Filing at either courthouse. NY R USDCTSD Div. Bus., Rule 22.

## J. Miscellaneous

**NOTE: Individual judges' rules may apply. For available judge-level information, refer to:**

DISTRICT JUDGE RONNIE ABRAMS: NY R USDCTSD Abrams-Civ Prac; NY R USDCTSD Abrams-Crim Prac; NY R USDCTSD Abrams-Pro Se; NY R USDCTSD Abrams-Case Mgt; NY R USDCTSD Abrams-Jury.

DISTRICT JUDGE DEBORAH A. BATTS: NY R USDCTSD Batts-Practices.

DISTRICT JUDGE RICHARD M. BERMAN: NY R USDCTSD Berman-Practices; NY R USDCTSD Berman-Default; NY R USDCTSD Berman-Sentencing; NY R USDCTSD Berman-Media.

DISTRICT JUDGE VINCENT L. BRICCETTI: NY R USDCTSD Briccetti-Practices; NY R USDCTSD Briccetti-Plan; NY R USDCTSD Briccetti-Notice.

DISTRICT JUDGE VERNON S. BRODERICK: NY R USDCTSD Broderick-Civil; NY R USDCTSD Broderick-Crim; NY R USDCTSD Broderick-Case Mgt; NY R USDCTSD Broderick-Jury.

DISTRICT JUDGE NAOMI REICE BUCHWALD: NY R USDCTSD Buchwald-Practices.

DISTRICT JUDGE VALERIE E. CAPRONI: NY R USDCTSD Caproni-Prac; NY R USDCTSD Caproni--Pro Se; NY R USDCTSD Caproni-Case Mgt; NY R USDCTSD Caproni-Crim Prac.

DISTRICT JUDGE ANDREW L. CARTER JR.: NY R USDCTSD Carter-Practices.

DISTRICT JUDGE KEVIN P. CASTEL: NY R USDCTSD Castel-Practices; NY R USDCTSD Castel-Default; NY R USDCTSD Castel-Scheduling; NY R USDCTSD Castel-Complex; NY R USDCTSD Castel-Trials; NY R USDCTSD Castel-Sentencing.

DISTRICT JUDGE DENISE L. COTE: NY R USDCTSD Cote-Civil Practices; NY R USDCTSD Cote-Pro Se; NY R USDCTSD Cote-Maritime Ord; NY R USDCTSD Cote-Crim Practices; NY R USDCTSD Cote-Crim Trials; NY R USDCTSD Cote-Sentencing.

DISTRICT JUDGE PAUL A. CROTTY: NY R USDCTSD Crotty-Practices; NY R USDCTSD Crotty-Sentencing; NY R USDCTSD Crotty-Calls; NY R USDCTSD Crotty-Scheduling.

DISTRICT JUDGE GEORGE B. DANIELS: NY R USDCTSD Daniels-Practices.

DISTRICT JUDGE KEVIN T. DUFFY: NY R USDCTSD Duffy-Practices.

DISTRICT JUDGE PAUL A. ENGELMAYER: NY R USDCTSD Engelmayer-Practices; NY R USDCTSD Engelmayer-Scheduling; NY R USDCTSD Engelmayer-Sentencing; NY R USDCTSD Engelmayer-Pro Se; NY R USDCTSD Engelmayer-Crim.

DISTRICT JUDGE KATHERINE POLK FAILLA: NY R USDCTSD Failla-Civ Prac; NY R USDCTSD Failla-Crim Prac; NY R USDCTSD Failla-Case Mgt.

DISTRICT JUDGE KATHERINE B. FORREST: NY R USDCTSD Forrest-Civil Prac; NY R USDCTSD Forrest-Crim Prac; NY R USDCTSD Forrest-Crim Pretrial; NY R USDCTSD Forrest-Scheduling; NY R US-DCTSD Forrest-Patent Scheduling; NY R USDCTSD Forrest-Sentencing; NY R USDCTSD Forrest-Order 1; NY R USDCTSD Forrest-Order 2.

DISTRICT JUDGE JESSE M. FURMAN: NY R USDCTSD Furman-Civil Prac; NY R USDCTSD Furman-Crim Prac; NY R USDCTSD Furman-Pro Se Prac; NY R USDCTSD Furman-Trials; NY R USDCTSD Furman-Scheduling; NY R USDCTSD Furman-Rights.

DISTRICT JUDGE PAUL G. GARDEPHE: NY R USDCTSD Gardephe-Civ Prac; NY R USDCTSD Gardephe-Pretrial; NY R USDCTSD Gardephe-Prot Ord; NY R USDCTSD Gardephe-Maritime; NY R USDCTSD Gardephe-Crim Prac; NY R USDCTSD Gardephe-Trial.

DISTRICT JUDGE THOMAS P. GRIESA: NY R USDCTSD Griesa-Practices.

DISTRICT JUDGE CHARLES S. HAIGHT: NY R USDCTSD Haight-Practices.

DISTRICT JUDGE ALVIN K. HELLERSTEIN: NY R USDCTSD Hellerstein-Practices; NY R USDCTSD Hellerstein--Sept 11.

DISTRICT JUDGE LEWIS A. KAPLAN: NY R USDCTSD Kaplan-Practices; NY R USDCTSD Kaplan-Sentencing.

DISTRICT JUDGE KENNETH M. KARAS: NY R USDCTSD Karas-Practices; NY R USDCTSD Karas-Case Mgt; NY R USDCTSD Karas-Default; NY R USDCTSD Karas-Sentencing; NY R USDCTSD Karas-Rights.

DISTRICT JUDGE JOHN F. KEENAN: NY R USDCTSD Keenan-Practices.

DISTRICT JUDGE JOHN G. KOELTL: NY R USDCTSD Koeltl-Practices.

DISTRICT JUDGE VICTOR MARRERO: NY R USDCTSD Marrero-Practices; NY R USDCTSD Marrero-Scheduling; NY R USDCTSD Marrero-Default; NY R USDCTSD Marrero-Trial Proc.

DISTRICT JUDGE COLLEEN McMAHON: NY R USDCTSD McMahon-Practices; NY R USDCTSD McMahon-RICO; NY R USDCTSD McMahon-Copies; NY R USDCTSD McMahon-Scheduling; NY R US-DCTSD McMahon-Elec Disc; NY R USDCTSD McMahon-Sentencing.

DISTRICT JUDGE ALISON J. NATHAN: NY R USDCTSD Nathan-Civ Prac; NY R USDCTSD Nathan-Crim Prac; NY R USDCTSD Nathan-Pro Se; NY R USDCTSD Nathan-Scheduling.

DISTRICT JUDGE J. PAUL OETKEN: NY R USDCTSD Oetken-Civ Prac; NY R USDCTSD Oetken-Case Mgt; NY R USDCTSD Oetken-Crim Prac; NY R USDCTSD Oetken-Pro Se.

DISTRICT JUDGE WILLIAM H. PAULEY, III: NY R USDCTSD Pauley-Crim Cases; NY R USDCTSD Pauley-Practices.

DISTRICT JUDGE LORETTA A. PRESKA: NY R USDCTSD Preska-Practices.

DISTRICT JUDGE JED S. RAKOFF: NY R USDCTSD Rakoff-Practices; NY R USDCTSD Rakoff-Scheduling; NY R USDCTSD Rakoff-Prot Ord; NY R USDCTSD Rakoff-Maritime Ord.

DISTRICT JUDGE EDGARDO RAMOS: NY R USDCTSD Ramos--Practices; NY R USDCTSD Ramos-Case Mgt.

DISTRICT JUDGE NELSON S. ROMAN: NY R USDCTSD Roman-Civ Prac; NY R USDCTSD Roman-Pro Se; NY R USDCTSD Roman-Crim Prac; NY R USDCTSD Roman-Case Mgt.

DISTRICT JUDGE LEONARD B. SAND: NY R USDCTSD Sand-Practices.

DISTRICT JUDGE LORNA G. SCHOFIELD: NY R USDCTSD Schofield-Civ Prac; NY R USDCTSD Schofield-Crim Prac; NY R USDCTSD Schofield-Sched; NY R USDCTSD Schofield-Pro Se; NY R USDCTSD Schofield-Advice.

DISTRICT JUDGE CATHY SEIBEL: NY R USDCTSD Seibel-Practices.

DISTRICT JUDGE LOUIS L. STANTON: NY R USDCTSD Stanton-Practices; NY R USDCTSD Stanton-Pretrial.

DISTRICT JUDGE SIDNEY H. STEIN: NY R USDCTSD Stein-Practices.

DISTRICT JUDGE RICHARD J. SULLIVAN: NY R USDCTSD Sullivan-Practices; NY R USDCTSD Sullivan-Scheduling; NY R USDCTSD Sullivan-Sentencing; NY R USDCTSD Sullivan-Juries; NY R USDCTSD Sullivan-Trial; NY R USDCTSD Sullivan-Default.

DISTRICT JUDGE LAURA TAYLOR SWAIN: NY R USDCTSD Swain-Practices; NY R USDCTSD Swain-Trial; NY R USDCTSD Swain-Crim Trial; NY R USDCTSD Swain-Juries; NY R USDCTSD Swain-Sentencing; NY R USDCTSD Swain-Rights.

DISTRICT JUDGE ROBERT W. SWEET: NY R USDCTSD Sweet-Practices.

DISTRICT JUDGE ANALISA TORRES: NY R USDCTSD Torres-Civ Prac; NY R USDCTSD Torres-Pro Se; NY R USDCTSD Torres-Scheduling.

DISTRICT JUDGE KIMBA M. WOOD: NY R USDCTSD Wood-Practices; NY R USDCTSD Wood-Scheduling; NY R USDCTSD Wood-Discovery; NY R USDCTSD Wood-RICO; NY R USDCTSD Wood-Juries; NY R USDCTSD Wood-Trial; NY R USDCTSD Wood-Media.

DISTRICT JUDGE GREGORY H. WOODS: NY R USDCTSD Woods-Civ Prac; NY R USDCTSD Woods-Pro Se; NY R USDCTSD Woods-Sched; NY R USDCTSD Woods-Crim Prac; NY R USDCTSD Woods-Protect Order; NY R USDCTSD Woods-Speedy Trial.

MAGISTRATE JUDGE JAMES L. COTT: NY R USDCTSD Cott-Practices; NY R USDCTSD Cott-Settlement.

MAGISTRATE JUDGE PAUL E. DAVISON: NY R USDCTSD Davison-Practices.

MAGISTRATE JUDGE RONALD L. ELLIS: NY R USDCTSD Ellis-Practices.

MAGISTRATE JUDGE KEVIN N. FOX: NY R USDCTSD Fox-Practices; NY R USDCTSD Fox-Settlement.

MAGISTRATE JUDGE JAMES C. FRANCIS: NY R USDCTSD Francis-Practices.

MAGISTRATE JUDGE DEBRA FREEMAN: NY R USDCTSD Freeman-Practices; NY R USDCTSD Freeman-Settlement.

MAGISTRATE JUDGE GABRIEL W. GORENSTEIN: NY R USDCTSD Gorenstein-Practices; NY R USDCTSD Gorenstein-Ackn.

MAGISTRATE JUDGE FRANK MAAS: NY R USDCTSD Maas-Practices; NY R USDCTSD Maas-Discontinuance; NY R USDCTSD Maas-Conf; NY R USDCTSD Maas-Settlement.

MAGISTRATE JUDGE JUDITH C. McCARTHY: NY R USDCTSD McCarthy-Practices; NY R USDCTSD McCarthy-Conduct.

MAGISTRATE JUDGE BARBARA MOSES: NY R USDCTSD Moses-Practices.

MAGISTRATE JUDGE SARAH NETBURN: NY R USDCTSD Netburn-Civil; NY R USDCTSD Netburn-Settlement; NY R USDCTSD Netburn-Case Mgt; NY R USDCTSD Netburn--Pro Se.

MAGISTRATE JUDGE ANDREW J. PECK: NY R USDCTSD Peck-Practices; NY R USDCTSD Peck-Order; NY R USDCTSD Peck-Rule 502(d).

MAGISTRATE JUDGE HENRY PITMAN: NY R USDCTSD Pitman-Practices.

MAGISTRATE JUDGE LISA MARGARET SMITH: NY R USDCTSD Smith-Practices; NY R USDCTSD Smith-Trials.

# Motions, Oppositions and Replies
# Motion for Continuance/Extension of Time

**Document Last Updated September 2016**

A. **Checklist**

  (I) ❑ Matters to be considered by moving party

    (a) ❑ Required documents

      (1) ❑ Notice of motion and motion

      (2) ❑ Memorandum of law

      (3) ❑ Certificate of service

    (b) ❑ Supplemental documents

      (1) ❑ Supporting evidence

      (2) ❑ Notice of constitutional question

      (3) ❑ Nongovernmental corporate disclosure statement

      (4) ❑ Copies of authorities

      (5) ❑ Proposed order

      (6) ❑ Statement explaining untimely electronic filing

      (7) ❑ Courtesy copies

    (c) ❑ Timing

      (1) ❑ Continuance: there are no specific timing requirements for moving for a continuance

      (2) ❑ Extension of time: when an act may or must be done within a specified time, the court may, for good cause, extend the time:

        (i) ❑ With or without motion or notice if the court acts, or if a request is made, before the original time or its extension expires; or

        (ii) ❑ On motion made after the time has expired if the party failed to act because of excusable neglect

      (3) ❑ A written motion and notice of the hearing must be served at least fourteen (14) days before the time specified for the hearing, with the following exceptions: (i) when the motion may be heard ex parte; (ii) when the Federal Rules of Civil Procedure set a different time; or (iii) when a court order—which a party may, for good cause, apply for ex parte—sets a different time

      (4) ❑ Any affidavit supporting a motion must be served with the motion

  (II) ❑ Matters to be considered by opposing party

    (a) ❑ Required documents

      (1) ❑ Answering memorandum of law

      (2) ❑ Certificate of service

(b) ❑ Supplemental documents

    (1) ❑ Supporting evidence

    (2) ❑ Notice of constitutional question

    (3) ❑ Copies of authorities

    (4) ❑ Statement explaining untimely electronic filing

    (5) ❑ Courtesy copies

(c) ❑ Timing

    (1) ❑ Any opposing affidavits and answering memoranda shall be served within fourteen (14) days after service of the moving papers

    (2) ❑ Except as FRCP 59(c) provides otherwise, any opposing affidavit must be served at least seven (7) days before the hearing, unless the court permits service at another time

## B. Timing

1. *Motion for continuance/extension of time*

    a. *Continuance.* There are no specific timing requirements for moving for a continuance.

    b. *Extension of time.* When an act may or must be done within a specified time, the court may, for good cause, extend the time:

        i. With or without motion or notice if the court acts, or if a request is made, before the original time or its extension expires; or

        ii. On motion made after the time has expired if the party failed to act because of excusable neglect. FRCP 6(b)(1).

2. *Timing of motions, generally*

    a. *Motion and notice of hearing.* Except for letter-motions as permitted by NY R USDCTS&ED Civ Rule 7.1(d), and unless otherwise provided by statute or rule or by the Court in a Judge's Individual Practice or in a direction in a particular case, upon any motion, the notice of motion, supporting affidavits, and memoranda shall be served and filed as follows: on all civil motions, petitions, and applications, other than those described in NY R USDCTS&ED Civ Rule 6.1(a), and other than petitions for writs of habeas corpus, the notice of motion, supporting affidavits, and memoranda of law shall be served by the moving party on all other parties that have appeared in the action. NY R USDCTS&ED Civ Rule 6.1(b)(1). A written motion and notice of the hearing must be served at least fourteen (14) days before the time specified for the hearing, with the following exceptions:

        i. When the motion may be heard ex parte;

        ii. When the Federal Rules of Civil Procedure set a different time; or

        iii. When a court order—which a party may, for good cause, apply for ex parte—sets a different time. FRCP 6(c)(1).

    b. *Supporting affidavit.* Any affidavit supporting a motion must be served with the motion. FRCP 6(c)(2).

3. *Timing of opposing papers.* Except for letter-motions as permitted by NY R USDCTS&ED Civ Rule 7.1(d), and unless otherwise provided by statute or rule or by the Court in a Judge's Individual Practice or in a direction in a particular case, upon any motion, the notice of motion, supporting affidavits, and memoranda shall be served and filed as follows: on all civil motions, petitions, and applications, other than those described in NY R USDCTS&ED Civ Rule 6.1(a), and other than petitions for writs of habeas corpus, any opposing affidavits and answering memoranda shall be served within fourteen (14) days after service of the moving papers. NY R USDCTS&ED Civ Rule 6.1(b)(2).

    a. *Opposing affidavit.* Except as FRCP 59(c) provides otherwise, any opposing affidavit must be served at least seven (7) days before the hearing, unless the court permits service at another time. FRCP 6(c)(2).

4. *Timing of reply papers.* Where the respondent files an answering affidavit setting up a new matter, the

moving party ordinarily is allowed a reasonable time to file a reply affidavit since failure to deny the new matter by affidavit may operate as an admission of its truth. AMJUR MOTIONS § 25.

a. *Reply affidavits and reply memoranda of law.* Except for letter-motions as permitted by NY R USDCTS&ED Civ Rule 7.1(d), and unless otherwise provided by statute or rule or by the Court in a Judge's Individual Practice or in a direction in a particular case, upon any motion, the notice of motion, supporting affidavits, and memoranda shall be served and filed as follows: on all civil motions, petitions, and applications, other than those described in NY R USDCTS&ED Civ Rule 6.1(a), and other than petitions for writs of habeas corpus, any reply affidavits and memoranda of law shall be served within seven (7) days after service of the answering papers. NY R USDCTS&ED Civ Rule 6.1(b)(3).

5. *Computation of time*

   a. *Computing time.* FRCP 6 applies in computing any time period specified in the Federal Rules of Civil Procedure, in any local rule or court order, or in any statute that does not specify a method of computing time. FRCP 6(a). In computing any period of time prescribed or allowed by the Local Civil Rules of the United States District Courts for the Southern and Eastern Districts of New York or the Local Admiralty and Maritime Rules, the provisions of FRCP 6 shall apply unless otherwise stated. NY R USDCTS&ED Civ Rule 6.4.

      i. *Period stated in days or a longer unit.* In computing periods of days, refer to FRCP 6 and NY R USDCTS&ED Civ Rule 6.4. NY R USDCTS&ED Civ Rule 6.1(b). When the period is stated in days or a longer unit of time:

         • Exclude the day of the event that triggers the period;

         • Count every day, including intermediate Saturdays, Sundays, and legal holidays; and

         • Include the last day of the period, but if the last day is a Saturday, Sunday, or legal holiday, the period continues to run until the end of the next day that is not a Saturday, Sunday, or legal holiday. FRCP 6(a)(1). In the Local Civil Rules of the United States District Courts for the Southern and Eastern Districts of New York, as in the Federal Rules of Civil Procedure as amended effective December 1, 2009, Saturdays, Sundays, and legal holidays are no longer excluded in computing periods of time. If the last day of the period is a Saturday, Sunday, or legal holiday, the period continues to run until the end of the next day that is not a Saturday, Sunday, or legal holiday. NY R USDCTS&ED Civ Rule 6.4.

      ii. *Period stated in hours.* When the period is stated in hours:

         • Begin counting immediately on the occurrence of the event that triggers the period;

         • Count every hour, including hours during intermediate Saturdays, Sundays, and legal holidays; and

         • If the period would end on a Saturday, Sunday, or legal holiday, the period continues to run until the same time on the next day that is not a Saturday, Sunday, or legal holiday. FRCP 6(a)(2). In the Local Civil Rules of the United States District Courts for the Southern and Eastern Districts of New York, as in the Federal Rules of Civil Procedure as amended effective December 1, 2009, Saturdays, Sundays, and legal holidays are no longer excluded in computing periods of time. If the last day of the period is a Saturday, Sunday, or legal holiday, the period continues to run until the end of the next day that is not a Saturday, Sunday, or legal holiday. NY R USDCTS&ED Civ Rule 6.4.

      iii. *Inaccessibility of the clerk's office.* Unless the court orders otherwise, if the clerk's office is inaccessible:

         • On the last day for filing under FRCP 6(a)(1), then the time for filing is extended to the first accessible day that is not a Saturday, Sunday, or legal holiday; or

         • During the last hour for filing under FRCP 6(a)(2), then the time for filing is extended to the same time on the first accessible day that is not a Saturday, Sunday, or legal holiday. FRCP 6(a)(3).

    iv.   *"Last day" defined.* Unless a different time is set by a statute, local rule, or court order, the last day ends:

- For electronic filing, at midnight in the court's time zone; and
- For filing by other means, when the clerk's office is scheduled to close. FRCP 6(a)(4).

    v.   *"Next day" defined.* The "next day" is determined by continuing to count forward when the period is measured after an event and backward when measured before an event. FRCP 6(a)(5).

    vi.   *"Legal holiday" defined.* "Legal holiday" means:

- The day set aside by statute for observing New Year's Day, Martin Luther King Jr.'s Birthday, Washington's Birthday, Memorial Day, Independence Day, Labor Day, Columbus Day, Veterans' Day, Thanksgiving Day, or Christmas Day;
- Any day declared a holiday by the President or Congress; and
- For periods that are measured after an event, any other day declared a holiday by the state where the district court is located. FRCP 6(a)(6).

   b.   *Computation of electronic filing deadlines.* You can file electronically twenty-four (24) hours a day, seven (7) days a week, three hundred sixty-five (365) days a year. NY R USDCTSD CM/ECF, S.D.(II)(13)(13.10). Electronic filing must be completed before midnight local time where the Court is located in order to be considered timely filed that day. NY R USDCTSD CM/ECF, S.D.(I)(3)(3.3); NY R USDCTSD CM/ECF, S.D.(II)(13)(13.10); NY R USDCTSD CM/ECF, S.D.(II)(19)(19.4). An electronically filed document is deemed filed on the "filed on" date indicated on the Notice of Electronic Filing (NEF). NY R USDCTSD CM/ECF, S.D.(II)(13)(13.11).

    i.   *Technical failures.* A Filing User whose filing is made untimely as the result of a technical failure may seek appropriate relief from the Court. NY R USDCTSD CM/ECF, S.D.(I)(11). If you missed a filing deadline when the ECF system was out of order, attach a statement to your filing explaining how the interruption in service prevented you from filing in a timely fashion. NY R USDCTSD CM/ECF, S.D.(II)(23)(23.5).

   c.   *Extending time.* Refer to the General Requirements section of this document for information on extending time.

   d.   *Additional time after certain kinds of service.* When a party may or must act within a specified time after service and service is made under FRCP 5(b)(2)(C), FRCP 5(b)(2)(D), FRCP 5(b)(2)(E), or FRCP 5(b)(2)(F), three (3) days are added after the period would otherwise expire under FRCP 6(a). FRCP 6(d). Overnight delivery service shall be deemed service by mail for purposes of FRCP 5 and FRCP 6. NY R USDCTS&ED Civ Rule 5.3.

6.  *Individual judge practices.* Refer to the Miscellaneous section of this document for information on individual judge practices on timing of documents.

## C.  General Requirements

1.  *Motions, generally*

   a.   *Requirements.* A request for a court order must be made by motion. The motion must:

    i.   Be in writing unless made during a hearing or trial;

    ii.   State with particularity the grounds for seeking the order; and

    iii.   State the relief sought. FRCP 7(b)(1).

   b.   *Notice of motion.* A party interested in resisting the relief sought by a motion has a right to notice thereof, and an opportunity to be heard. AMJUR MOTIONS § 12.

    i.   In addition to statutory or court rule provisions requiring notice of a motion—the purpose of such a notice requirement having been said to be to prevent a party from being prejudicially surprised by a motion—principles of natural justice dictate that an adverse party generally must be given notice that a motion will be presented to the court. AMJUR MOTIONS § 12.

    ii.   "Notice," in this regard, means reasonable notice, including a meaningful opportunity to prepare and to defend against allegations of a motion. AMJUR MOTIONS § 12.

c. *Writing requirement.* The writing requirement is intended to insure that the adverse parties are informed and have a record of both the motion's pendency and the grounds on which the movant seeks an order. FPP § 1191; Feldberg v. Quechee Lakes Corp., 463 F.3d 195 (2d Cir. 2006).

    i. It is sufficient "if the motion is stated in a written notice of the hearing of the motion." FPP § 1191.

d. *Particularity requirement.* The particularity requirement insures that the opposing parties will have notice of their opponent's contentions. FEDPROC § 62:364; Goodman v. 1973 26 Foot Trojan Vessel, Arkansas Registration No. AR1439SN, 859 F.2d 71, 12 Fed.R.Serv.3d 645 (8th Cir. 1988). That requirement ensures that notice of the basis for the motion is provided to the court and to the opposing party so as to avoid prejudice, provide the opponent with a meaningful opportunity to respond, and provide the court with enough information to process the motion correctly. FEDPROC § 62:364; Andreas v. Volkswagen of America, Inc., 336 F.3d 789, 56 Fed.R.Serv.3d 6 (8th Cir. 2003).

    i. Reasonable specification of the grounds for a motion is sufficient. However, where a movant fails to state even one ground for granting the motion in question, the movant has failed to meet the minimal standard of "reasonable specification." FEDPROC § 62:364; Martinez v. Trainor, 556 F.2d 818, 23 Fed.R.Serv.2d 403 (7th Cir. 1977).

    ii. The court may excuse the failure to comply with the particularity requirement if it is inadvertent, and where no prejudice is shown by the opposing party. FEDPROC § 62:364.

e. *Ex parte orders or orders to show cause to bring on a motion.* No ex parte order, or order to show cause to bring on a motion, will be granted except upon a clear and specific showing by affidavit of good and sufficient reasons why a procedure other than by notice of motion is necessary, and stating whether a previous application for similar relief has been made. NY R USDCTS&ED Civ Rule 6.1(d).

f. *Letter-motions.* Applications for extensions or adjournments, applications for a pre-motion conference, and similar non-dispositive matters as permitted by the instructions regarding ECF published on the website of each respective Court and any pertinent Individual Judge's Practices, may be brought by letter-motion filed via ECF pursuant to NY R USDCTS&ED Civ Rule 5.2(b). NY R USDCTS&ED Civ Rule 7.1(d).

    i. The following list of motions. . .may be made by LETTER-MOTION: (1) Motion to Adjourn Conference; (2) Motion to Change Attorney Name on Roll; (3) Motion to Compel; (4) Motion for Conference; (5) Motion to Consolidate Cases; (6) Motion to Continue; (7) Motion re: Discovery; (8) Motion to Expedite; (9) Motion for Extension of Time; (10) Motion for Extension of Time to Amend; (11) Motion for Extension of Time to Answer; (12) Motion for Extension of Time to Complete Discovery; (13) Motion for Extension of Time to File Document; (14) Motion for Extension of Time to File Response/Reply; (15) Motion for Extension of Time re Transcript; (16) Motion to File Amicus Brief; (17) Motion for Leave to File Document; (18) Motion for Leave to File Excess Pages; (19) Motion for Local Rule 37.2 Conference; (20) Motion for Oral Argument; (21) Motion to Reopen; (22) Motion to Reopen Case; (23) Motion to Seal Document; (24) Motion to Stay; (25) Motion to Substitute Attorney. NY R USDCTSD CM/ECF, S.D.(II)(13)(13.1).

    ii. If the Filing User is making a type of motion that does not appear in this list, the motion may not be made by letter. NY R USDCTSD CM/ECF, S.D.(II)(13)(13.1).

    iii. For more information on letter motions, refer to NY R USDCTSD CM/ECF, S.D.(II)(13)(13.1).

2. *Motion for continuance/extension of time*

a. *Continuance.* Absent a controlling statute, the grant or denial of a continuance rests in the discretion of the trial judge to whom application is made, taking into consideration not only the facts of the particular case but also all of the demands on counsel's time and the court's. FEDPROC § 77:28; Star Financial Services, Inc. v. AASTAR Mortg. Corp., 89 F.3d 5 (1st Cir. 1996); Streber v. Hunter, 221 F.3d 701, 55 Fed.R.Evid.Serv. 376 (5th Cir. 2000). The grounds upon which a continuance is sought may include the following:

    i. Unpreparedness of a party. FEDPROC § 77:29; U.S. v. 110 Bars of Silver, 3 Crucibles of Silver, 11 Bags of Silver Coins, 508 F.2d 799 (5th Cir. 1975).

ii. Absence of a party. FEDPROC § 77:29. Since it is generally recognized that a party to a civil action ordinarily has a right to attend the trial, an illness severe enough to prevent a party from appearing in court is always a legitimate ground for asking for a continuance. FEDPROC § 77:30; Davis v. Operation Amigo, Inc., 378 F.2d 101 (10th Cir. 1967). However, the failure of the moving party to produce any competent medical evidence of the reasons and necessities for the party's unavailability will result in the denial of the continuance. FEDPROC § 77:30; Weisman v. Alleco, Inc., 925 F.2d 77 (4th Cir. 1991). Some courts, moreover, require a showing that the party has some particular contribution to make to the trial as a material witness or otherwise before granting a continuance due to the party's illness. FEDPROC § 77:30; Johnston v. Harris County Flood Control Dist., 869 F.2d 1565 (5th Cir. 1989).

iii. Absence of counsel. FEDPROC § 77:29. The courts have shown greater leniency when the illness of counsel is the ground for the continuance, especially where the case presents complex issues. FEDPROC § 77:31; Smith-Weik Machinery Corp. v. Murdock Mach. & Engineering Co., 423 F.2d 842 (5th Cir. 1970). However, many courts do not favor the granting of a continuance where counsel is unavailable due to a claimed engagement elsewhere or where it is not clear that counsel's illness was genuine. FEDPROC § 77:31; Community Nat. Life Ins. Co. v. Parker Square Sav. & Loan Ass'n, 406 F.2d 603 (10th Cir. 1969); Williams v. Johanns, 518 F.Supp.2d 205 (D.D.C. 2007).

iv. Absence of a witness or evidence. FEDPROC § 77:29. The moving party must show. . .that the witness's testimony would be competent and material and that there are no other witnesses who can establish the same facts. FEDPROC § 77:32; Krodel v. Houghtaling, 468 F.2d 887 (4th Cir. 1972); Vitarelle v. Long Island R. Co., 415 F.2d 302 (2d Cir. 1969).

v. Surprise and prejudice. FEDPROC § 77:29. The action complained of should not be one which could have been anticipated by due diligence or of which the movant had actual notice. FEDPROC § 77:33; Communications Maintenance, Inc. v. Motorola, Inc., 761 F.2d 1202, 2 Fed.R.Serv.3d 126 (7th Cir. 1985). Surprise and prejudice are often claimed as a result of the court allowing the other party to amend its pleadings under FRCP 15(b). FEDPROC § 77:29.

vi. In determining whether to grant a continuance, the court will consider a variety of factors, including:

- Good faith on the part of the moving party;
- Due diligence of the moving party;
- The likelihood that the need prompting the request for a continuance will be met if the continuance is granted;
- Inconvenience to the court and the nonmoving party, including the witnesses, if the continuance is granted;
- Possible harm to the moving party if the continuance is denied;
- Prior delays in the proceedings;
- The court's prior refusal to grant the opposing party a continuance;
- Judicial economy. FEDPROC § 77:29; Amarin Plastics, Inc. v. Maryland Cup Corp., 946 F.2d 147, 34 Fed.R.Evid.Serv. 528 (1st Cir. 1991); Lewis v. Rawson, 564 F.3d 569 (2d Cir. 2009); U.S. v. 2.61 Acres of Land, More or Less, Situated in Mariposa County, State of Cal., 791 F.2d 666 (9th Cir. 1985); In re Homestore.com, Inc. Securities Litigation, 347 F.Supp.2d 814 (C.D.Cal. 2004).

b. *Extension of time.* When an act may or must be done within a specified time, the court may, for good cause, extend the time:

i. *Before original time or its extension expires.* With or without motion or notice if the court acts, or if a request is made, before the original time or its extension expires. FRCP 6(b)(1)(A).

- An application for the enlargement of time under FRCP 6(b)(1)(A) normally will be granted in the absence of bad faith on the part of the party seeking relief or prejudice to the adverse party. FPP § 1165.

- Neither a formal motion for enlargement nor notice to the adverse party is expressly required by FRCP 6(b). FPP § 1165.

ii. *After the time has expired.* On motion made after the time has expired if the party failed to act because of excusable neglect. FRCP 6(b)(1)(B).

- *Excusable neglect.* Excusable neglect is intended and has proven to be quite elastic in its application. In essence it is an equitable concept that must take account of all relevant circumstances of the party's failure to act within the required time. FPP § 1165.

- *Burden.* The burden is on the movant to establish that the failure to act in a timely manner was the result of excusable neglect. FEDPROC § 77:5. Common sense indicates that among the most important factors are the possibility of prejudice to the other parties, the length of the applicant's delay and its impact on the proceeding, the reason for the delay and whether it was within the control of the movant, and whether the movant has acted in good faith. FPP § 1165; Kettle Range Conservation Group v. U.S. Forest Service, 8 Fed.Appx. 729 (9th Cir. 2001).

- *Motion required.* No relief may be granted under FRCP 6(b)(1)(B) after the expiration of the specified period, even though the failure to act may have been the result of excusable neglect, if no motion is made by the party who failed to act. FEDPROC § 77:3.

iii. *Exceptions.* A court must not extend the time to act under FRCP 50(b), FRCP 50(d), FRCP 52(b), FRCP 59(b), FRCP 59(d), FRCP 59(e), and FRCP 60(b). FRCP 6(b)(2). FRCP 6(b) does not require the district courts to extend a time period where the extension would contravene a local court rule and does not apply to periods of time that are definitely fixed by statute. FEDPROC § 77:4; Truncale v. Universal Pictures Co., 82 F.Supp. 576 (S.D.N.Y. 1949); Lusk v. Lyon Metal Products, 9 F.R.D. 250 (W.D.Mo. 1949).

3. *Opposing papers.* The Federal Rules of Civil Procedure do not require any formal answer, return, or reply to a motion, except where the Federal Rules of Civil Procedure or local rules may require affidavits, memoranda, or other papers to be filed in opposition to a motion. Such papers are simply to apprise the court of such opposition and the grounds of that opposition. FEDPROC § 62:359. Except for letter-motions as permitted by NY R USDCTS&ED Civ Rule 7.1(d) or as otherwise permitted by the Court, all oppositions and replies with respect to motions shall comply with NY R USDCTS&ED Civ Rule 7.1(a)(2) and NY R USDCTS&ED Civ Rule 7.1(a)(3), and an opposing party who seeks relief that goes beyond the denial of the motion shall comply as well with NY R USDCTS&ED Civ Rule 7.1(a)(1). NY R USDCTS&ED Civ Rule 7.1(b).

a. *Effect of failure to respond to motion.* Although in the absence of statutory provision or court rule, a motion ordinarily does not require a written answer, when a party files a motion and the opposing party fails to respond, the court may construe such failure to respond as nonopposition to the motion or an admission that the motion was meritorious, may take the facts alleged in the motion as true—the rule in some jurisdictions being that the failure to respond to a fact set forth in a motion is deemed an admission—and may grant the motion if the relief requested appears to be justified. AMJUR MOTIONS § 28.

b. *Assent or no opposition not determinative.* However, a motion will not be granted automatically simply because an "assent" or a notation of "no opposition" has been filed; federal judges frequently deny motions that have been assented to when it is thought that justice so dictates. FPP § 1190.

c. *Responsive pleading inappropriate as response to motion.* An attempt to answer or oppose a motion with a responsive pleading usually is not appropriate. FPP § 1190.

4. *Reply papers.* A moving party may be required or permitted to prepare papers in addition to his original motion papers. AMJUR MOTIONS § 25. Papers answering or replying to opposing papers may be appropriate, in the interests of justice, where it appears there is a substantial reason for allowing a reply. Thus, a court may accept reply papers where a party demonstrates that the papers to which it seeks to file a reply raise new issues that are material to the disposition of the question before the court, or where the court determines, sua sponte, that it wishes further briefing of an issue raised in those papers and orders the submission of additional papers. FEDPROC § 62:360. Except for letter-motions as permitted by NY

R USDCTS&ED Civ Rule 7.1(d) or as otherwise permitted by the Court, all oppositions and replies with respect to motions shall comply with NY R USDCTS&ED Civ Rule 7.1(a)(2) and NY R USDCTS&ED Civ Rule 7.1(a)(3). NY R USDCTS&ED Civ Rule 7.1(b).

a. *Function of reply papers.* The function of a reply affidavit is to answer the arguments made in opposition to the position taken by the movant and not to permit the movant to introduce new arguments in support of the motion. AMJUR MOTIONS § 25.

b. *Issues raised for the first time in a reply document.* However, the view has been followed in some jurisdictions, that as a matter of judicial economy, where there is no prejudice and where the issues could be raised simply by filing a motion to dismiss, the trial court has discretion to consider arguments raised for the first time in a reply memorandum, and that a trial court may grant a motion to strike issues raised for the first time in a reply memorandum. AMJUR MOTIONS § 26.

5. *Orders on motions.* A memorandum signed by the Court of the decision on a motion that does not finally determine all claims for relief, or an oral decision on such a motion, shall constitute the order unless the memorandum or oral decision directs the submission or settlement of an order in more extended form. The notation in the docket of a memorandum or of an oral decision that does not direct the submission or settlement of an order in more extended form shall constitute the entry of the order. Where an order in more extended form is required to be submitted or settled, the notation in the docket of such order shall constitute the entry of the order. NY R USDCTS&ED Civ Rule 6.2.

6. *Complex civil cases.* For information on procedures for complex civil cases, refer to NY R USDCTSD Order 11 Misc 00388.

7. *Related cases.* It shall be the continuing duty of each attorney appearing in any civil or criminal case to bring promptly to the attention of the Court all facts which said attorney believes are relevant to a determination that said case and one or more pending civil or criminal cases should be heard by the same Judge, in order to avoid unnecessary duplication of judicial effort. As soon as the attorney becomes aware of such relationship, said attorney shall notify the Judges to whom the cases have been assigned. NY R USDCTS&ED Civ Rule 1.6(a). If counsel fails to comply with NY R USDCTS&ED Civ Rule 1.6(a), the Court may assess reasonable costs directly against counsel whose action has obstructed the effective administration of the Court's business. NY R USDCTS&ED Civ Rule 1.6(b).

a. *Determination of relatedness.* Subject to the limitations set forth in NY R USDCTSD Div. Bus., Rule 13(a)(2), a civil case, bankruptcy appeal, or motion to withdraw the bankruptcy reference will be deemed related to one or more civil cases, appeals or motions when the interests of justice and efficiency will be served. In determining relatedness, a judge will consider whether (A) the actions concern the same or substantially similar parties, property, transactions or events; (B) there is substantial factual overlap; (C) the parties could be subjected to conflicting orders; and (D) whether absent a determination of relatedness there would be a substantial duplication of effort and expense, delay, or undue burden on the Court, parties or witnesses. NY R USDCTSD Div. Bus., Rule 13(a)(1). Nothing in this NY R USDCTSD Div. Bus., Rule 13 is intended to preclude parties from moving for consolidated proceedings under FRCP 42. NY R USDCTSD Div. Bus., Rule 13(a)(1). Notwithstanding NY R USDCTSD Div. Bus., Rule 13(a)(1):

    i. Civil cases shall not be deemed related merely because they involve common legal issues or the same parties. NY R USDCTSD Div. Bus., Rule 13(a)(2)(A).

    ii. Other than cases subject to NY R USDCTSD Div. Bus., Rule 4(b) and actions seeking the enforcement of a judgment or settlement in or of an earlier case, civil cases presumptively shall not be deemed related unless both cases are pending before the Court (or the earlier case is on appeal). NY R USDCTSD Div. Bus., Rule 13(a)(2)(B).

b. *Procedure in regard to cases said to be related*

    i. *Disclosure of contention of relatedness.* When a civil case is filed or removed or a bankruptcy appeal or motion to withdraw the reference of an adversary proceeding from the bankruptcy court is filed, the person filing or removing shall disclose on form JSC44C any contention of relatedness and shall file a Related Case Statement stating clearly and succinctly the basis for the contention. A copy of the civil cover sheet and Related Case Statement shall be served with the complaint, notice of removal, notice of appeal, or motion. Any party may contest a claim of relatedness by any other in writing addressed to the judge having the case with the lowest docket number of all cases claimed to be related. However, the foregoing shall not delay the assignment process or the operation of NY R USDCTSD Div. Bus., Rule 13. NY R USDCTSD Div. Bus., Rule 13(b)(1). [Editor's note: the reference to form JSC44C is likely meant to be form JS44C-SDNY: Civil Court Cover Sheet].

ii. *Claims of relatedness by other parties.* A party other than the one filing a case, bankruptcy appeal or motion to withdraw the reference that contends its case is related to another may so advise in writing the judge assigned in its case and request a transfer of its case to the judge that the party contends has the related case with the lowest docket number. If the assigned judge believes the case is related under NY R USDCTSD Div. Bus., Rule 13(a), he or she shall refer the question to the judge having the case with the lowest docket number. In the event the latter judge agrees, the case shall be transferred to that judge unless the Assignment Committee disagrees. NY R USDCTSD Div. Bus., Rule 13(b)(3).

c. For more information on related cases, refer to NY R USDCTSD Div. Bus., Rule 13.

8. *Alternative dispute resolution (ADR).* The U.S. District Court for the Southern District of New York provides litigants with opportunities to discuss settlement through judicial settlement conferences and mediation. NY R USDCTS&ED Civ Rule 83.9(a).

a. *Consideration of alternative dispute resolution.* In all civil cases, including those eligible for mediation pursuant to NY R USDCTS&ED Civ Rule 83.9(e), each party shall consider the use of mediation or a judicial settlement conference and shall report to the assigned Judge at the initial FRCP 16(b) case management conference, or subsequently, whether the party believes mediation or a judicial settlement conference may facilitate the resolution of the lawsuit. Judges are encouraged to note the availability of the mediation program and/or a judicial settlement conference before, at, or after the initial FRCP 16(b) case management conference. NY R USDCTS&ED Civ Rule 83.9(d).

b. *Mediation.* In mediation, parties and counsel meet, sometimes collectively and sometimes individually, with a neutral third party (the mediator) who has been trained to facilitate confidential settlement discussions. The parties articulate their respective positions and interests and generate options for a mutually agreeable resolution to the dispute. The mediator assists the parties in reaching their own negotiated settlement by defining the issues, probing and assessing the strengths and weaknesses of each party's legal positions, and identifying areas of agreement and disagreement. The main benefits of mediation are that it can result in an expeditious and less costly resolution of the litigation, and can produce creative solutions to complex disputes often unavailable in traditional litigation. NY R USDCTS&ED Civ Rule 83.9(b).

i. *Mediation program eligibility.* All civil cases other than Social Security, habeas corpus, and tax cases are eligible for mediation, whether assigned to Manhattan or White Plains. NY R USDCTS&ED Civ Rule 83.9(e)(1).

- The Board of Judges may, by Administrative Order, direct that certain specified categories of cases shall automatically be submitted to the mediation program. The assigned District Judge or Magistrate Judge may issue a written order exempting a particular case with or without the request of the parties. NY R USDCTS&ED Civ Rule 83.9(e)(2).

- For all other cases, the assigned District Judge or Magistrate Judge may determine that a case is appropriate for mediation and may order that case to mediation, with or without the consent of the parties, before, at, or after the initial FRCP 16(b) case management conference. Alternatively, the parties should notify the assigned Judge at any time of their desire to mediate. NY R USDCTS&ED Civ Rule 83.9(e)(3).

c. *Judicial settlement conferences.* Judicial settlement conferences may be ordered by District Judges or Magistrate Judges with or without the request or consent of the parties. NY R USDCTS&ED Civ Rule 83.9(f).

d. For more information on alternative dispute resolution (ADR), refer to NY R USDCTS&ED Civ Rule 83.9.

9. *Individual judge practices.* Refer to the Miscellaneous section of this document for information on individual judge practices on general requirements for documents.

## D. Documents

1. *Documents for moving party*

   a. *Required documents*

      i. *Notice of motion and motion.* Except for letter-motions as permitted by NY R USDCTS&ED Civ Rule 7.1(d) or as otherwise permitted by the Court, all motions shall include the following motion papers: a notice of motion, or an order to show cause signed by the Court, which shall specify the applicable rules or statutes pursuant to which the motion is brought, and shall specify the relief sought by the motion. NY R USDCTS&ED Civ Rule 7.1(a)(1). Refer to the General Requirements section of this document for information on the notice of motion and motion.

         • *Letter-motion; Alternative procedure.* The following may be made by LETTER-MOTION: Motion to Continue, Motion for Extension of Time, Motion for Extension of Time to Amend, Motion for Extension of Time to Answer, Motion for Extension of Time to Complete Discovery, Motion for Extension of Time to File Document, Motion for Extension of Time to File Response/Reply, and Motion for Extension of Time re Transcript. NY R USDCTSD CM/ECF, S.D.(II)(13)(13.1).

      ii. *Memorandum of law.* Except for letter-motions as permitted by NY R USDCTS&ED Civ Rule 7.1(d) or as otherwise permitted by the Court, all motions shall include the following motion papers: a memorandum of law, setting forth the cases and other authorities relied upon in support of the motion, and divided, under appropriate headings, into as many parts as there are issues to be determined. NY R USDCTS&ED Civ Rule 7.1(a)(2).

      iii. *Certificate of service.* FRCP 5(d) requires that the person making service under FRCP 5 certify that service has been effected. FRCP 5(Advisory Committee Notes). Having such information on file may be useful for many purposes, including proof of service if an issue arises concerning the effectiveness of the service. FRCP 5(Advisory Committee Notes).

         • Such paper service [on attorneys and pro se parties who are not Filing or Receiving Users] must be documented by electronically filing proof of service. NY R USDCTSD CM/ECF, S.D.(I)(9)(9.2); NY R USDCTSD CM/ECF, S.D.(I)(19)(19.3)(b). Pro se parties who are not Filing Users are exempt from that portion of NY R USDCTSD CM/ECF, S.D.(I)(19)(19.3) requiring proof of service to be filed electronically. NY R USDCTSD CM/ECF, S.D.(I)(19)(19.3).

   b. *Supplemental documents*

      i. *Supporting evidence.* When a motion relies on facts outside the record, the court may hear the matter on affidavits or may hear it wholly or partly on oral testimony or on depositions. FRCP 43(c). Except for letter-motions as permitted by NY R USDCTS&ED Civ Rule 7.1(d) or as otherwise permitted by the Court, all motions shall include the following motion papers: supporting affidavits and exhibits thereto containing any factual information and portions of the record necessary for the decision of the motion. NY R USDCTS&ED Civ Rule 7.1(a)(3).

         • *Discovery materials.* A party seeking or opposing relief under FRCP 26 through FRCP 37 inclusive, or making or opposing any other motion or application, shall quote or attach only those portions of the depositions, interrogatories, requests for documents, requests for admissions, or other discovery or disclosure materials, together with the responses and objections thereto, that are the subject of the discovery motion or application, or that are cited in papers submitted in connection with any other motion or application. NY R USDCTS&ED Civ Rule 5.1.

      ii. *Notice of constitutional question.* A party that files a pleading, written motion, or other paper drawing into question the constitutionality of a federal or state statute must promptly:

         • *File notice.* File a notice of constitutional question stating the question and identifying the

paper that raises it, if: (1) a federal statute is questioned and the parties do not include the United States, one of its agencies, or one of its officers or employees in an official capacity; or (2) a state statute is questioned and the parties do not include the state, one of its agencies, or one of its officers or employees in an official capacity; and

- *Serve notice.* Serve the notice and paper on the Attorney General of the United States if a federal statute is questioned—or on the state attorney general if a state statute is questioned—either by certified or registered mail or by sending it to an electronic address designated by the attorney general for this purpose. FRCP 5.1(a).

- *No forfeiture.* A party's failure to file and serve the notice, or the court's failure to certify, does not forfeit a constitutional claim or defense that is otherwise timely asserted. FRCP 5.1(d).

iii. *Nongovernmental corporate disclosure statement*

- *Contents.* A nongovernmental corporate party must file two (2) copies of a disclosure statement that: (1) identifies any parent corporation and any publicly held corporation owning ten percent (10%) or more of its stock; or (2) states that there is no such corporation. FRCP 7.1(a).

- *Time to file; Supplemental filing.* A party must: (1) file the disclosure statement with its first appearance, pleading, petition, motion, response, or other request addressed to the court; and (2) promptly file a supplemental statement if any required information changes. FRCP 7.1(b). For purposes of FRCP 7.1(b)(2), "promptly" shall mean "within fourteen days," that is, parties are required to file a supplemental disclosure statement within fourteen (14) days of the time there is any change in the information required in a disclosure statement filed pursuant to those rules. NY R USDCTS&ED Civ Rule 7.1.1.

iv. *Copies of authorities.* In cases involving a pro se litigant, counsel shall, when serving a memorandum of law (or other submissions to the Court), provide the pro se litigant (but not other counsel or the Court) with copies of cases and other authorities cited therein that are unpublished or reported exclusively on computerized databases. Upon request, counsel shall provide the pro se litigant with copies of such unpublished cases and other authorities as are cited in a decision of the Court and were not previously cited by any party. NY R USDCTS&ED Civ Rule 7.2.

v. *Statement explaining untimely electronic filing.* If you missed a filing deadline when the ECF system was out of order, attach a statement to your filing explaining how the interruption in service prevented you from filing in a timely fashion. NY R USDCTSD CM/ECF, S.D.(II)(23)(23.5).

vi. *Courtesy copies.* Read the judge's Individual Practices to learn if courtesy copies are required. NY R USDCTSD CM/ECF, S.D.(II)(13)(13.17). Judges' Individual Practices should continue to be followed with respect to delivery of courtesy copies. NY R USDCTSD CM/ECF, S.D.(I)(3)(3.4).

2. *Documents for opposing party*

a. *Required documents*

i. *Answering memorandum of law.* Except for letter-motions as permitted by NY R USDCTS&ED Civ Rule 7.1(d) or as otherwise permitted by the Court, all oppositions and replies with respect to motions shall comply with NY R USDCTS&ED Civ Rule 7.1(a)(2). NY R USDCTS&ED Civ Rule 7.1(b). Except for letter-motions as permitted by NY R USDCTS&ED Civ Rule 7.1(d) or as otherwise permitted by the Court, all motions shall include the following motion papers: a memorandum of law, setting forth the cases and other authorities relied upon in support of the motion, and divided, under appropriate headings, into as many parts as there are issues to be determined. NY R USDCTS&ED Civ Rule 7.1(a)(2). Refer to the General Requirements section of this document for information on the opposing papers.

ii. *Certificate of service.* FRCP 5(d) requires that the person making service under FRCP 5 certify that service has been effected. FRCP 5(Advisory Committee Notes). Having such information on file may be useful for many purposes, including proof of service if an issue arises concerning the effectiveness of the service. FRCP 5(Advisory Committee Notes).

- Such paper service [on attorneys and pro se parties who are not Filing or Receiving Users] must be documented by electronically filing proof of service. NY R USDCTSD CM/ECF, S.D.(I)(9)(9.2); NY R USDCTSD CM/ECF, S.D.(I)(19)(19.3)(b). Pro se parties who are not Filing Users are exempt from that portion of NY R USDCTSD CM/ECF, S.D.(I)(19)(19.3) requiring proof of service to be filed electronically. NY R USDCTSD CM/ECF, S.D.(I)(19)(19.3).

b. *Supplemental documents*

   i. *Supporting evidence.* When a motion relies on facts outside the record, the court may hear the matter on affidavits or may hear it wholly or partly on oral testimony or on depositions. FRCP 43(c). Except for letter-motions as permitted by NY R USDCTS&ED Civ Rule 7.1(d) or as otherwise permitted by the Court, all oppositions and replies with respect to motions shall comply with NY R USDCTS&ED Civ Rule 7.1(a)(3). NY R USDCTS&ED Civ Rule 7.1(b). Except for letter-motions as permitted by NY R USDCTS&ED Civ Rule 7.1(d) or as otherwise permitted by the Court, all motions shall include the following motion papers: supporting affidavits and exhibits thereto containing any factual information and portions of the record necessary for the decision of the motion. NY R USDCTS&ED Civ Rule 7.1(a)(3).

   - *Discovery materials.* A party seeking or opposing relief under FRCP 26 through FRCP 37 inclusive, or making or opposing any other motion or application, shall quote or attach only those portions of the depositions, interrogatories, requests for documents, requests for admissions, or other discovery or disclosure materials, together with the responses and objections thereto, that are the subject of the discovery motion or application, or that are cited in papers submitted in connection with any other motion or application. NY R USDCTS&ED Civ Rule 5.1.

   ii. *Notice of constitutional question.* A party that files a pleading, written motion, or other paper drawing into question the constitutionality of a federal or state statute must promptly:

   - *File notice.* File a notice of constitutional question stating the question and identifying the paper that raises it, if: (1) a federal statute is questioned and the parties do not include the United States, one of its agencies, or one of its officers or employees in an official capacity; or (2) a state statute is questioned and the parties do not include the state, one of its agencies, or one of its officers or employees in an official capacity; and

   - *Serve notice.* Serve the notice and paper on the Attorney General of the United States if a federal statute is questioned—or on the state attorney general if a state statute is questioned—either by certified or registered mail or by sending it to an electronic address designated by the attorney general for this purpose. FRCP 5.1(a).

   - *No forfeiture.* A party's failure to file and serve the notice, or the court's failure to certify, does not forfeit a constitutional claim or defense that is otherwise timely asserted. FRCP 5.1(d).

   iii. *Copies of authorities.* In cases involving a pro se litigant, counsel shall, when serving a memorandum of law (or other submissions to the Court), provide the pro se litigant (but not other counsel or the Court) with copies of cases and other authorities cited therein that are unpublished or reported exclusively on computerized databases. Upon request, counsel shall provide the pro se litigant with copies of such unpublished cases and other authorities as are cited in a decision of the Court and were not previously cited by any party. NY R USDCTS&ED Civ Rule 7.2.

   iv. *Proposed order.* Refer to the Format section of this document for information on the format of submitting a proposed order to the court.

   v. *Statement explaining untimely electronic filing.* If you missed a filing deadline when the ECF system was out of order, attach a statement to your filing explaining how the interruption in service prevented you from filing in a timely fashion. NY R USDCTSD CM/ECF, S.D.(II)(23)(23.5).

    vi.   *Courtesy copies.* Read the judge's Individual Practices to learn if courtesy copies are required. NY R USDCTSD CM/ECF, S.D.(II)(13)(13.17). Judges' Individual Practices should continue to be followed with respect to delivery of courtesy copies. NY R USDCTSD CM/ECF, S.D.(I)(3)(3.4).

3.   *Individual judge practices.* Refer to the Miscellaneous section of this document for information on individual judge practices on required documents.

## E. Format

1.   *Form of documents.* The rules governing captions and other matters of form in pleadings apply to motions and other papers. FRCP 7(b)(2).

    a.   *Paper.* Every pleading, written motion, and other paper must: be plainly written, typed, printed, or copied without erasures or interlineations which materially deface it. NY R USDCTS&ED Civ Rule 11.1(a)(1).

    b.   *Typeface, margin, and spacing.* The typeface, margins, and spacing of all documents presented for filing must meet the following requirements:

       i.   All text must be twelve (12) point type or larger, except for text in footnotes which may be ten (10) point type;

       ii.   All documents must have at least one (1) inch margins on all sides;

       iii.   All text must be double-spaced, except for headings, text in footnotes, or block quotations, which may be single-spaced. NY R USDCTS&ED Civ Rule 11.1(b).

    c.   *Caption; Names of parties.* Every pleading must have a caption with the court's name, a title, a file number, and a FRCP 7(a) designation. The title of the complaint must name all the parties; the title of other pleadings, after naming the first party on each side, may refer generally to other parties. FRCP 10(a). Every pleading, written motion, and other paper must: bear the docket number and the initials of the District Judge and any Magistrate Judge before whom the action or proceeding is pending, NY R USDCTS&ED Civ Rule 11.1(a)(2).

    d.   *Paragraphs; Separate statements.* A party must state its claims or defenses in numbered paragraphs, each limited as far as practicable to a single set of circumstances. A later pleading may refer by number to a paragraph in an earlier pleading. If doing so would promote clarity, each claim founded on a separate transaction or occurrence—and each defense other than a denial—must be stated in a separate count or defense. FRCP 10(b).

    e.   *Adoption by reference; Exhibits.* A statement in a pleading may be adopted by reference elsewhere in the same pleading or in any other pleading or motion. A copy of a written instrument that is an exhibit to a pleading is a part of the pleading for all purposes. FRCP 10(c).

    f.   *Acceptance by the clerk.* The clerk must not refuse to file a paper solely because it is not in the form prescribed by the Federal Rules of Civil Procedure or by a local rule or practice. FRCP 5(d)(4).

2.   *Form of electronic documents*

    a.   *PDF-A.* All documents electronically filed on the ECF system must be in PDF-A format (portable document format). A PDF-A file is created using PDF writer software such as Adobe Acrobat (go to the Adobe website for details). PDF-A files cannot be altered, providing security to the filer and the Court. NY R USDCTSD CM/ECF, S.D.(II)(23)(23.2).

    b.   *Size limitation.* No single PDF file may be larger than four megabytes (4 MB). If the filing is too large, the ECF system will not allow it to be filed, and you will not see a Notice of Electronic Filing (NEF or filing receipt) screen. To determine the size of an Adobe Acrobat PDF file click on File, Document Properties, Summary. NY R USDCTSD CM/ECF, S.D.(II)(23)(23.3).

       i.   Converting documents directly from a word processor to PDF-A format creates the smallest possible file in terms of computer memory. If that is not possible, scan your document at low resolution. Within the Adobe Acrobat program, on the "Scan Manager" screen, adjust the settings for black and white and 200 dpi (dots per inch). This allows more pages to fit into a single PDF-A file. If that does not work, separate an oversized file into 2 or more parts. Simply label each file 1a, 1b, 1c, etc. Only relevant excerpts of exhibits should be electronically filed. NY R USDCTSD CM/ECF, S.D.(II)(23)(23.4).

c. *Attachments and exhibits.* Filing Users must submit in electronic form all documents referenced as exhibits or attachments, unless the Court permits paper filing. NY R USDCTSD CM/ECF, S.D.(I)(5)(5.1).

    i. A Filing User must submit as exhibits or attachments only those excerpts of the referenced documents that are relevant to the matter under consideration by the Court. Excerpted material must be clearly and prominently identified as such. Filing Users who file excerpts of documents as exhibits or attachments under this procedure do so without prejudice to their right to file timely additional excerpts or the complete document. Responding parties may file timely additional excerpts that they believe are relevant or the complete document. A party may move before the Court for permission to serve and file in hard copy documents that cannot be reasonably scanned. NY R USDCTSD CM/ECF, S.D.(I)(5)(5.2).

    ii. Exhibits must be filed only as attachments to a document, such as a motion or an affidavit. Do not use the ECF Filing Event for "Motion" to file exhibits separately. Exhibits are the only items that should be attached to electronically filed documents. You are limited to electronically filing only relevant excerpts of exhibits. Excerpts must be clearly identified as such. If the exhibit is too large to be scanned and electronically filed you may contact the ECF Help Desk. NY R USDCTSD CM/ECF, S.D.(II)(15)(15.6).

d. *Letters.* Parties should consult the assigned judge's Individual Practices to determine if the judge accepts letters at all and, if he or she does, whether the judge has any page limitations on letters and/or requires courtesy copies of letters filed on ECF (and, if so, by what means of delivery). All letters addressed to the Court must include a subject line with the case name and docket number (e.g., "Re: Doe v. Smith, 13 Civ. 1234 (ABC)"). NY R USDCTSD CM/ECF, S.D.(II)(13)(13.1).

e. *Proposed orders, proposed judgments, stipulations and consents.* Any document that requires the signature of a judge should not be electronically filed except as an exhibit to another document. Proposed orders, judgments, stipulations and consents should not be submitted through the ECF system. Instead they should be sent by e-mail to the Clerk. Proposed orders should be submitted in word processing format (WordPerfect or Word) rather than as a PDF document. Stipulations should be submitted in PDF-A format. Stipulations must contain ink signatures not s/. Faxed or emailed signatures are acceptable. Please note that Stipulations of Voluntary Dismissal pursuant to FRCP 41(a)(1)(A)(ii) do not require the signature of a judge and must be electronically filed on the ECF system. Questions may be directed to the Orders and Judgments Clerk at the phone numbers listed in NY R USDCTSD CM/ECF, S.D.(II)(18)(18.3). NY R USDCTSD CM/ECF, S.D.(II)(18)(18.3).

    i. Email the proposed order, judgment or stipulation to the email addresses listed in NY R USDCTSD CM/ECF, S.D.(II)(18)(18.3). NY R USDCTSD CM/ECF, S.D.(II)(18)(18.3).

    ii. Pro se litigants who are not Filing Users are exempt from that portion of NY R USDCTSD CM/ECF, S.D.(II)(18)(18.3) that requires litigants to email proposed orders, judgments, stipulations and consents, and shall deliver such documents to the Clerk's Office in paper form. NY R USDCTSD CM/ECF, S.D.(II)(18)(18.3).

3. *Signing of pleadings, motions and other papers*

a. *Signature.* Every pleading, written motion, and other paper must be signed by at least one attorney of record in the attorney's name—or by a party personally if the party is unrepresented. The paper must state the signer's address, e-mail address, and telephone number. FRCP 11(a). Every pleading, written motion, and other paper must: have the name of each person signing it clearly printed or typed directly below the signature. NY R USDCTS&ED Civ Rule 11.1(a)(3).

    i. *Electronic signatures.* The user log-in and password required to submit documents to the ECF system serve as the Filing User's signature on all electronic documents filed with the Court. NY R USDCTSD CM/ECF, S.D.(I)(8)(8.1); NY R USDCTSD CM/ECF, S.D.(II)(13)(13.14). They also serve as a signature for purposes of the Federal Rules of Civil Procedure, including FRCP 11, the Local Civil Rules of the United States District Courts for the Southern and Eastern

Districts of New York, and any other purpose for which a signature is required in connection with proceedings before the Court. NY R USDCTSD CM/ECF, S.D.(I)(8)(8.1).

- *Signature block.* Electronically filed documents must include a signature block and must set forth the name, address, telephone number and e-mail address all in compliance with the Federal Rules of Civil Procedure and NY R USDCTS&ED Civ Rule 11.1. In the absence of a scanned signature image, the name of the Filing User under whose log-in and password the document is submitted must be preceded by an "s/" typed in the space where the signature would otherwise appear. NY R USDCTSD CM/ECF, S.D.(I)(8)(8.2); NY R USDCTSD CM/ECF, S.D.(II)(13)(13.14).

- *Documents requiring the signature of a party or witness.* A document requiring the signature of a party or witness shall be electronically filed in a scanned format that contains an image of the actual signature. NY R USDCTSD CM/ECF, S.D.(I)(8)(8.4); NY R USDCTSD CM/ECF, S.D.(II)(13)(13.14).

- *Documents requiring the signature of a judge.* A Filing User submitting a document electronically that requires a judge's signature must promptly deliver the document in such other form, if any, as the Court requires. NY R USDCTSD CM/ECF, S.D.(I)(4)(4.2).

- *Documents requiring multiple signatures.* Documents requiring signatures of more than one party must be electronically filed either by: (a) submitting a scanned document containing all necessary signatures; (b) representing the consent of the other parties on the document; (c) identifying on the document the parties whose signatures are required and by the submission of a notice of endorsement by the other parties no later than three business days after filing; or (d) in any other manner approved by the Court. NY R USDCTSD CM/ECF, S.D.(I)(8)(8.5).

   ii. *No verification or accompanying affidavit required for pleadings.* Unless a rule or statute specifically states otherwise, a pleading need not be verified or accompanied by an affidavit. FRCP 11(a).

   iii. *Unsigned papers.* The court must strike an unsigned paper unless the omission is promptly corrected after being called to the attorney's or party's attention. FRCP 11(a).

b. *Representations to the court.* By presenting to the court a pleading, written motion, or other paper—whether by signing, filing, submitting, or later advocating it—an attorney or unrepresented party certifies that to the best of the person's knowledge, information, and belief, formed after an inquiry reasonable under the circumstances:

   i. It is not being presented for any improper purpose, such as to harass, cause unnecessary delay, or needlessly increase the cost of litigation;

   ii. The claims, defenses, and other legal contentions are warranted by existing law or by a nonfrivolous argument for extending, modifying, or reversing existing law or for establishing new law;

   iii. The factual contentions have evidentiary support or, if specifically so identified, will likely have evidentiary support after a reasonable opportunity for further investigation or discovery; and

   iv. The denials of factual contentions are warranted on the evidence or, if specifically so identified, are reasonably based on belief or a lack of information. FRCP 11(b).

c. *Sanctions.* If, after notice and a reasonable opportunity to respond, the court determines that FRCP 11(b) has been violated, the court may impose an appropriate sanction on any attorney, law firm, or party that violated FRCP 11(b) or is responsible for the violation. FRCP 11(c)(1). Refer to the United States District Court for the Southern District of New York KeyRules Motion for Sanctions document for more information.

4. *Privacy protection for filings made with the court*

a. *Redacted filings.* Unless the court orders otherwise, in an electronic or paper filing with the court that contains an individual's Social Security number, taxpayer-identification number, or birth date, the

name of an individual known to be a minor, or a financial-account number, a party or nonparty making the filing may include only:

i. The last four (4) digits of the Social Security number and taxpayer-identification number;

ii. The year of the individual's birth;

iii. The minor's initials; and

iv. The last four (4) digits of the financial-account number. FRCP 5.2(a); NY R USDCTSD CM/ECF, S.D.(II)(21)(21.3).

v. Caution should be exercised when filing documents that contain the following:

- Personal identifying numbers (PIN #'s), such as a driver's license number;
- Medical records, treatment and diagnosis;
- Employment history;
- Individual financial information;
- Proprietary or trade secret information;
- Information regarding an individual's cooperation with the government. NY R US-DCTSD CM/ECF, S.D.(II)(21)(21.4).

b. *Exemptions from the redaction requirement.* The redaction requirement does not apply to the following:

i. A financial-account number that identifies the property allegedly subject to forfeiture in a forfeiture proceeding;

ii. The record of an administrative or agency proceeding;

iii. The official record of a state-court proceeding;

iv. The record of a court or tribunal, if that record was not subject to the redaction requirement when originally filed;

v. A filing covered by FRCP 5.2(c) or FRCP 5.2(d); and

vi. A pro se filing in an action brought under 28 U.S.C.A. § 2241, 28 U.S.C.A. § 2254, or 28 U.S.C.A. § 2255. FRCP 5.2(b).

c. *Limitations on remote access to electronic files; Social Security appeals and immigration cases.* Unless the court orders otherwise, in an action for benefits under the Social Security Act, and in an action or proceeding relating to an order of removal, to relief from removal, or to immigration benefits or detention, access to an electronic file is authorized as follows:

i. The parties and their attorneys may have remote electronic access to any part of the case file, including the administrative record;

ii. Any other person may have electronic access to the full record at the courthouse, but may have remote electronic access only to:

- The docket maintained by the court; and
- An opinion, order, judgment, or other disposition of the court, but not any other part of the case file or the administrative record. FRCP 5.2(c).

d. *Filings made under seal.* The court may order that a filing be made under seal without redaction. The court may later unseal the filing or order the person who made the filing to file a redacted version for the public record. FRCP 5.2(d). For more information on sealing documents, refer to NY R USDCTSD CM/ECF, S.D.(I)(6).

e. *Protective orders.* For good cause, the court may by order in a case:

i. Require redaction of additional information; or

ii. Limit or prohibit a nonparty's remote electronic access to a document filed with the court. FRCP 5.2(e).

f. *Option for additional unredacted filing under seal.* A person making a redacted filing may also file an unredacted copy under seal. The court must retain the unredacted copy as part of the record. FRCP 5.2(f); NY R USDCTSD CM/ECF, S.D.(II)(21)(21.5).

g. *Option for filing a reference list.* A filing that contains redacted information may be filed together with a reference list that identifies each item of redacted information and specifies an appropriate identifier that uniquely corresponds to each item listed. The list must be filed under seal and may be amended as of right. Any reference in the case to a listed identifier will be construed to refer to the corresponding item of information. FRCP 5.2(g); NY R USDCTSD CM/ECF, S.D.(II)(21)(21.5).

h. *Responsibility for redaction.* It is the sole responsibility of counsel and the parties to be sure that all documents comply with the rules of this Court requiring redaction of personal identifiers. Neither the judge nor the Clerk of Court will review documents for compliance with these rules. NY R USDCTSD CM/ECF, S.D.(II)(21)(21.2).

i. *Waiver of protection of identifiers.* A person waives the protection of FRCP 5.2(a) as to the person's own information by filing it without redaction and not under seal. FRCP 5.2(h).

j. For more information on privacy and public access to ECF cases, refer to NY R USDCTSD CM/ECF, S.D.(II)(21).

5. *Individual judge practices.* Refer to the Miscellaneous section of this document for information on individual judge practices on formatting documents.

## F. Filing and Service Requirements

1. *Filing requirements.* Any paper after the complaint that is required to be served—together with a certificate of service—must be filed within a reasonable time after service. FRCP 5(d)(1). Complaints and all subsequent papers are accepted at either courthouse, regardless of the place for which the case is designated. NY R USDCTSD Div. Bus., Rule 22. Subject to the instructions regarding ECF published on the website of each respective Court and any pertinent Individual Judge's Practices, letter-motions permitted by NY R USDCTS&ED Civ Rule 7.1(d) and letters addressed to the Court (but not letters between the parties) may be filed via ECF. NY R USDCTS&ED Civ Rule 5.2(b). For information on electronically filing motions, refer to NY R USDCTSD CM/ECF, S.D.(II)(15).

a. *How filing is made; In general.* A paper is filed by delivering it:

   i. To the clerk; or

   ii. To a judge who agrees to accept it for filing, and who must then note the filing date on the paper and promptly send it to the clerk. FRCP 5(d)(2).

b. *Night depository.* A night depository with an automatic date stamp shall be maintained by the Clerk of the Southern District in the Pearl Street Courthouse. After regular business hours, papers for the District Court only may be deposited in the night depository. Such papers will be considered as having been filed in the District Court as of the date stamped thereon, which shall be deemed presumptively correct. NY R USDCTS&ED Civ Rule 1.2.

c. *Electronic filing*

   i. *Authorization of electronic filing program.* A court may, by local rule, allow papers to be filed, signed, or verified by electronic means that are consistent with any technical standards established by the Judicial Conference of the United States. A local rule may require electronic filing only if reasonable exceptions are allowed. A paper filed electronically in compliance with a local rule is a written paper for purposes of the Federal Rules of Civil Procedure. FRCP 5(d)(3).

   - The Court will accept for filing documents submitted, signed or verified by electronic means, that comply with the rules in NY R USDCTSD CM/ECF, S.D. NY R USDCTSD CM/ECF, S.D.(I). The information in NY R USDCTSD CM/ECF, S.D. applies only to cases assigned to the ECF system. NY R USDCTSD CM/ECF, S.D.(Introduction).

   - Parties serving and filing papers shall follow the instructions regarding Electronic Case Filing (ECF) published on the website of each respective Court. A paper served and filed by electronic means in accordance with such instructions is, for purposes of FRCP 5, served and filed in compliance with the Local Civil Rules of the Southern and Eastern Districts of New York. NY R USDCTS&ED Civ Rule 5.2(a). Parties have an obligation to review the Court's actual order, decree, or judgment (on ECF), which controls, and should not rely on the description on the docket or in the ECF Notice of Electronic Filing (NEF). NY R USDCTS&ED Civ Rule 5.2(c).

- The following should be observed when filing electronically: (1) the Federal Rules of Civil Procedure, (2) the Local Civil Rules of the United States District Courts for the Southern and Eastern Districts of New York, (3) the assigned judge's Individual Practices, and (4) the Court's Electronic Case Filing Rules & Instructions (NY R USDCTSD CM/ECF, S.D.). NY R USDCTSD CM/ECF, S.D.(Introduction).

ii. *Scope of electronic filing.* Except as expressly provided and in exceptional circumstances preventing a party from filing electronically, all documents required to be filed with the Court must be filed electronically. Any party unable to comply with this requirement must seek permission of the Court to file in the traditional manner, on paper. Any such application made after regular business hours may be submitted through the night depository box maintained pursuant to NY R USDCTS&ED Civ Rule 1.2. NY R USDCTSD CM/ECF, S.D.(I)(1)(1.1).

- *Documents filed by pro se litigants.* Unless otherwise ordered by the Court, documents filed by pro se litigants must be filed in the traditional manner, on paper, and will be scanned and docketed by the Clerk's Office into the ECF system. NY R USDCTSD CM/ECF, S.D.(I)(1)(1.1). Pro se litigants must file pleadings and documents in the traditional manner on paper unless the assigned judge has granted permission to electronically file on the ECF system. NY R USDCTSD CM/ECF, S.D.(Introduction).

- *Letters.* Except for letters to be filed under seal, letters addressed to judges who accept letters may be filed electronically. Parties should consult the assigned judge's Individual Practices to determine if the judge accepts letters at all and, if he or she does, whether the judge has any page limitations on letters and/or requires courtesy copies of letters filed on ECF (and, if so, by what means of delivery). NY R USDCTSD CM/ECF, S.D.(II)(13)(13.1). Letters solely between parties or their counsel or otherwise not addressed to the Court may not be filed electronically on ECF (except as exhibits to an otherwise properly filed document). NY R USDCTSD CM/ECF, S.D.(II)(13)(13.1). For more information on filing letters, refer to NY R USDCTSD CM/ECF, S.D.(II)(13)(13.1).

- *Proposed orders, judgments and decrees.* Proposed orders, judgments and decrees shall be presented as directed by the ECF rules published on the website of each respective Court. NY R USDCTS&ED Civ Rule 77.1. For more information, refer to NY R USDCTS&ED Civ Rule 77.1.

iii. *Exceptions to electronic filing.* In an ECF case, the documents that should not be electronically filed include:

- Miscellaneous Case initiating documents, NY R USDCTSD CM/ECF, S.D.(II)(18)(18.2);

- Proposed orders; proposed judgments, stipulations; consents, NY R USDCTSD CM/ECF, S.D.(II)(18)(18.3);

- Orders to show cause / temporary restraining orders, NY R USDCTSD CM/ECF, S.D.(II)(18)(18.4);

- Sealed documents, NY R USDCTSD CM/ECF, S.D.(II)(18)(18.5); and

- Surety bonds, NY R USDCTSD CM/ECF, S.D.(II)(18)(18.6).

- In cases where the record of an administrative or other prior proceeding must be filed with the Court, such record may be served and filed in hard copy without prior motion and order of the Court. NY R USDCTSD CM/ECF, S.D.(I)(5)(5.3).

- For more documents excepted from electronic filing, and for more information on such documents, refer to NY R USDCTSD CM/ECF, S.D.(II)(18).

iv. *Consequences of electronic filing.* Except as otherwise provided in NY R USDCTSD CM/ECF,

S.D.(I)(4), electronic filing of a document in the ECF system consistent with these procedures, together with the transmission of a Notice of Electronic Filing (NEF) from the Court, constitutes filing of the document for all purposes of the Federal Rules of Civil Procedure and the Local Civil Rules of the United States District Courts for the Southern and Eastern Districts of New York and constitutes entry of the document on the docket kept by the Clerk under FRCP 58 and FRCP 79. NY R USDCTSD CM/ECF, S.D.(I)(3)(3.1).

    v. For more information on electronic filing, refer to NY R USDCTSD CM/ECF, S.D.

2. *Service requirements*

  a. *Service; When required*

    i. *In general.* Unless the Federal Rules of Civil Procedure provide otherwise, each of the following papers must be served on every party:

- An order stating that service is required;

- A pleading filed after the original complaint, unless the court orders otherwise under FRCP 5(c) because there are numerous defendants;

- A discovery paper required to be served on a party, unless the court orders otherwise;

- A written motion, except one that may be heard ex parte; and

- A written notice, appearance, demand, or offer of judgment, or any similar paper. FRCP 5(a)(1).

    ii. *If a party fails to appear.* No service is required on a party who is in default for failing to appear. But a pleading that asserts a new claim for relief against such a party must be served on that party under FRCP 4. FRCP 5(a)(2).

    iii. *Seizing property.* If an action is begun by seizing property and no person is or need be named as a defendant, any service required before the filing of an appearance, answer, or claim must be made on the person who had custody or possession of the property when it was seized. FRCP 5(a)(3).

  b. *Service; How made*

    i. *Serving an attorney.* If a party is represented by an attorney, service under FRCP 5 must be made on the attorney unless the court orders service on the party. FRCP 5(b)(1).

    ii. *Service in general.* A paper is served under FRCP 5 by:

- Handing it to the person;

- Leaving it: (1) at the person's office with a clerk or other person in charge or, if no one is in charge, in a conspicuous place in the office; or (2) if the person has no office or the office is closed, at the person's dwelling or usual place of abode with someone of suitable age and discretion who resides there;

- Mailing it to the person's last known address—in which event service is complete upon mailing;

- Leaving it with the court clerk if the person has no known address;

- Sending it by electronic means if the person consented in writing—in which event service is complete upon transmission, but is not effective if the serving party learns that it did not reach the person to be served; or

- Delivering it by any other means that the person consented to in writing—in which event service is complete when the person making service delivers it to the agency designated to make delivery. FRCP 5(b)(2).

    iii. *Service by overnight delivery.* Service upon an attorney may be made by overnight delivery service. "Overnight delivery service" means any delivery service which regularly accepts items for overnight delivery. Overnight delivery service shall be deemed service by mail for purposes of FRCP 5 and FRCP 6. NY R USDCTS&ED Civ Rule 5.3.

iv. *Service by electronic means.* Parties serving and filing papers shall follow the instructions regarding Electronic Case Filing (ECF) published on the website of each respective Court. A paper served and filed by electronic means in accordance with such instructions is, for purposes of FRCP 5, served and filed in compliance with the Local Civil Rules of the United States District Courts for the Southern and Eastern Districts of New York. NY R USDCTS&ED Civ Rule 5.2(a). Parties have an obligation to review the Court's actual order, decree, or judgment (on ECF), which controls, and should not rely on the description on the docket or in the ECF Notice of Electronic Filing (NEF). NY R USDCTS&ED Civ Rule 5.2(c).

- *Notice of electronic filing (NEF).* In cases assigned to the ECF system, service is complete provided all parties receive a Notice of Electronic Filing (NEF), which is sent automatically by email from the Court (see the NEF for a list of who did/did not receive notice electronically). Transmission of the NEF constitutes service upon all Filing and Receiving Users who are listed as recipients of notice by electronic mail. NY R USDCTSD CM/ECF, S.D.(I)(9)(9.1). In cases assigned to the ECF system, if all parties receive a NEF, service is complete upon transmission of the NEF by the Court, and you are not required to serve a paper copy. NY R USDCTSD CM/ECF, S.D.(II)(19)(19.2). It remains the duty of Filing and Receiving Users to maintain current contact information with the court and to regularly review the docket sheet of the case. NY R USDCTSD CM/ECF, S.D.(I)(9)(9.1).

- *Mailing of court-initiated documents.* The Clerk's Office will no longer mail paper copies of court-initiated documents to Filing and Receiving Users. The Clerk's Office will mail copies of all court-initiated documents to pro se parties who have not registered as Filing or Receiving Users. NY R USDCTSD CM/ECF, S.D.(II)(19)(19.1).

- *No receipt of a NEF.* If any party does not receive a NEF, you are required to accomplish service on that party in the traditional manner, in paper form. NY R USDCTSD CM/ECF, S.D.(II)(19)(19.2). The NEF receipt will inform you who will receive notice of the filing "electronically" (by e-mail from the Court) and who will receive notice "by other means" (traditional service in paper form). NY R USDCTSD CM/ECF, S.D.(II)(19)(19.2).

- *Service on non-filing or non-receiving users.* Attorneys and pro se parties who are not Filing or Receiving Users must be served with a paper copy of any electronically filed pleading or other document. Service of such paper copy must be made according to the Federal Rules of Civil Procedure and the Local Civil Rules of the United States District Courts for the Southern and Eastern Districts of New York. NY R USDCTSD CM/ECF, S.D.(I)(9)(9.2). Such paper service must be documented by electronically filing proof of service. NY R USDCTSD CM/ECF, S.D.(I)(9)(9.2); NY R USDCTSD CM/ECF, S.D.(II)(19)(19.2). Where the Clerk scans and electronically files pleadings and documents on behalf of a pro se party, the associated NEF constitutes service. NY R USDCTSD CM/ECF, S.D.(I)(9)(9.2).

- For more information on service by electronic means, refer to NY R USDCTSD CM/ECF, S.D.(II)(19).

v. *Using court facilities.* If a local rule so authorizes, a party may use the court's transmission facilities to make service under FRCP 5(b)(2)(E). FRCP 5(b)(3).

c. *Serving numerous defendants*

i. *In general.* If an action involves an unusually large number of defendants, the court may, on motion or on its own, order that:

- Defendants' pleadings and replies to them need not be served on other defendants;

- Any crossclaim, counterclaim, avoidance, or affirmative defense in those pleadings and replies to them will be treated as denied or avoided by all other parties; and

- Filing any such pleading and serving it on the plaintiff constitutes notice of the pleading to all parties. FRCP 5(c)(1).

ii. *Notifying parties.* A copy of every such order must be served on the parties as the court directs. FRCP 5(c)(2).

3. *Individual judge practices.* Refer to the Miscellaneous section of this document for information on individual judge practices on filing and serving documents.

## G. Hearings

1. *Hearings, generally*

   a. *Oral argument.* Due process does not require that oral argument be permitted on a motion and, except as otherwise provided by local rule, the district court has discretion to determine whether it will decide the motion on the papers or hear argument by counsel (and perhaps receive evidence). FPP § 1190; F.D.I.C. v. Deglau, 207 F.3d 153 (3d Cir. 2000). The parties and their attorneys shall only appear to argue the motion if so directed by the Court by order or by a Judge's Individual Practice. NY R USDCTS&ED Civ Rule 6.1(c).

   b. *Providing a regular schedule for oral hearings.* A court may establish regular times and places for oral hearings on motions. FRCP 78(a).

   c. *Providing for submission on briefs.* By rule or order, the court may provide for submitting and determining motions on briefs, without oral hearings. FRCP 78(b).

2. *Individual judge practices.* Refer to the Miscellaneous section of this document for information on individual judge practices on hearings.

## H. Forms

### 1. Federal Motion for Continuance/Extension of Time Forms

   a. Opposition in federal district court; To motion for continuance; On ground of additional time required to prepare for trial; No excusable neglect shown. AMJUR PP CONTIN § 79.

   b. Affidavit in opposition to motion for continuance; By plaintiff's attorney; Lack of due diligence in discovery of documents. AMJUR PP CONTIN § 80.

   c. Affidavit in opposition to motion for continuance; By plaintiff's attorney; Defendant's absent witness previously absent; Lack of due diligence in compelling attendance of witness. AMJUR PP CONTIN § 81.

   d. Affidavit in opposition to motion for continuance; By plaintiff; Admission that absent witness of defendant would testify according to affidavit. AMJUR PP CONTIN § 83.

   e. Affidavit in opposition to defendant's motion for continuance; By plaintiff's counsel; Testimony of absent witness merely cumulative. AMJUR PP CONTIN § 85.

   f. Motion for enlargement of time. 2 FEDFORMS § 5:11.

   g. Motion for enlargement of time; By plaintiff. 2 FEDFORMS § 5:12.

   h. Motion for enlargement of time; To answer motion. 2 FEDFORMS § 5:14.

   i. Motion for continuance. 2 FEDFORMS § 5:36.

   j. Motion for continuance; Reciting supporting facts; New allegations in amended answer. 2 FEDFORMS § 5:37.

   k. Motion for continuance; Reciting supporting facts; Absence of witness. 2 FEDFORMS § 5:38.

   l. Motion for continuance; Reciting supporting facts; Absence of witness; Witness outside the country. 2 FEDFORMS § 5:39.

   m. Motion for continuance or in the alternative for change of venue; Hostility against defendant. 2 FEDFORMS § 5:40.

   n. Notice; Of motion; Containing motion. FEDPROF § 1:749.

   o. Brief; Supporting or opposing motion. FEDPROF § 1:752.

   p. Opposition to motion; For continuance; No excusable neglect. FEDPROF § 1:808.

   q. Affidavit; Opposing motion for continuance; Offer to stipulate to testimony of unavailable witness. FEDPROF § 1:813.

   r. Reply to motion for extension of time. GOLDLTGFMS § 10:40.

s. Motions; Extension of time to file jury demand. GOLDLTGFMS § 12:6.

t. Motion for extension of time. GOLDLTGFMS § 25:37.

u. Motion for extension of time to answer. GOLDLTGFMS § 26:13.

v. Motion to extend time for serving answers. GOLDLTGFMS § 26:14.

w. Motion for continuance. GOLDLTGFMS § 43:2.

x. Motion for continuance; Lawyer unavailable. GOLDLTGFMS § 43:3.

y. Motion for continuance; Witness unavailable. GOLDLTGFMS § 43:4.

z. Motion for continuance; Party in military service. GOLDLTGFMS § 43:6.

## I. Applicable Rules

1. *Federal rules*

   a. Serving and filing pleadings and other papers. FRCP 5.

   b. Constitutional challenge to a statute; Notice, certification, and intervention. FRCP 5.1.

   c. Privacy protection for filings made with the court. FRCP 5.2.

   d. Computing and extending time; Time for motion papers. FRCP 6.

   e. Pleadings allowed; Form of motions and other papers. FRCP 7.

   f. Disclosure statement. FRCP 7.1.

   g. Form of pleadings. FRCP 10.

   h. Signing pleadings, motions, and other papers; Representations to the court; Sanctions. FRCP 11.

   i. Taking testimony. FRCP 43.

   j. Hearing motions; Submission on briefs. FRCP 78.

2. *Local rules*

   a. Night depository. NY R USDCTS&ED Civ Rule 1.2.

   b. Duty of attorneys in related cases. NY R USDCTS&ED Civ Rule 1.6.

   c. Filing of discovery materials. NY R USDCTS&ED Civ Rule 5.1.

   d. Electronic service and filing of documents. NY R USDCTS&ED Civ Rule 5.2.

   e. Service by overnight delivery. NY R USDCTS&ED Civ Rule 5.3.

   f. Service and filing of motion papers. NY R USDCTS&ED Civ Rule 6.1.

   g. Orders on motions. NY R USDCTS&ED Civ Rule 6.2.

   h. Computation of time. NY R USDCTS&ED Civ Rule 6.4.

   i. Motion papers. NY R USDCTS&ED Civ Rule 7.1.

   j. Disclosure statement. NY R USDCTS&ED Civ Rule 7.1.1.

   k. Authorities to be provided to pro se litigants. NY R USDCTS&ED Civ Rule 7.2.

   l. Form of pleadings, motions, and other papers. NY R USDCTS&ED Civ Rule 11.1.

   m. Submission of orders, judgments and decrees. NY R USDCTS&ED Civ Rule 77.1.

   n. Alternative dispute resolution (Southern District only). NY R USDCTS&ED Civ Rule 83.9.

   o. Electronic case filing rules and instructions. NY R USDCTSD CM/ECF, S.D.

   p. Related cases. NY R USDCTSD Div. Bus., Rule 13.

   q. Filing at either courthouse. NY R USDCTSD Div. Bus., Rule 22.

## J. Miscellaneous

**NOTE: Individual judges' rules may apply. For available judge-level information, refer to:**

DISTRICT JUDGE RONNIE ABRAMS: NY R USDCTSD Abrams-Civ Prac; NY R USDCTSD Abrams-Crim Prac; NY R USDCTSD Abrams-Pro Se; NY R USDCTSD Abrams-Case Mgt; NY R USDCTSD Abrams-Jury.

DISTRICT JUDGE DEBORAH A. BATTS: NY R USDCTSD Batts-Practices.

DISTRICT JUDGE RICHARD M. BERMAN: NY R USDCTSD Berman-Practices; NY R USDCTSD Berman-Default; NY R USDCTSD Berman-Sentencing; NY R USDCTSD Berman-Media.

DISTRICT JUDGE VINCENT L. BRICCETTI: NY R USDCTSD Briccetti-Practices; NY R USDCTSD Briccetti-Plan; NY R USDCTSD Briccetti-Notice.

DISTRICT JUDGE VERNON S. BRODERICK: NY R USDCTSD Broderick-Civil; NY R USDCTSD Broderick-Crim; NY R USDCTSD Broderick-Case Mgt; NY R USDCTSD Broderick-Jury.

DISTRICT JUDGE NAOMI REICE BUCHWALD: NY R USDCTSD Buchwald-Practices.

DISTRICT JUDGE VALERIE E. CAPRONI: NY R USDCTSD Caproni-Prac; NY R USDCTSD Caproni--Pro Se; NY R USDCTSD Caproni-Case Mgt; NY R USDCTSD Caproni-Crim Prac.

DISTRICT JUDGE ANDREW L. CARTER JR.: NY R USDCTSD Carter-Practices.

DISTRICT JUDGE KEVIN P. CASTEL: NY R USDCTSD Castel-Practices; NY R USDCTSD Castel-Default; NY R USDCTSD Castel-Scheduling; NY R USDCTSD Castel-Complex; NY R USDCTSD Castel-Trials; NY R USDCTSD Castel-Sentencing.

DISTRICT JUDGE DENISE L. COTE: NY R USDCTSD Cote-Civil Practices; NY R USDCTSD Cote-Pro Se; NY R USDCTSD Cote-Maritime Ord; NY R USDCTSD Cote-Crim Practices; NY R USDCTSD Cote-Crim Trials; NY R USDCTSD Cote-Sentencing.

DISTRICT JUDGE PAUL A. CROTTY: NY R USDCTSD Crotty-Practices; NY R USDCTSD Crotty-Sentencing; NY R USDCTSD Crotty-Calls; NY R USDCTSD Crotty-Scheduling.

DISTRICT JUDGE GEORGE B. DANIELS: NY R USDCTSD Daniels-Practices.

DISTRICT JUDGE KEVIN T. DUFFY: NY R USDCTSD Duffy-Practices.

DISTRICT JUDGE PAUL A. ENGELMAYER: NY R USDCTSD Engelmayer-Practices; NY R USDCTSD Engelmayer-Scheduling; NY R USDCTSD Engelmayer-Sentencing; NY R USDCTSD Engelmayer-Pro Se; NY R USDCTSD Engelmayer-Crim.

DISTRICT JUDGE KATHERINE POLK FAILLA: NY R USDCTSD Failla-Civ Prac; NY R USDCTSD Failla-Crim Prac; NY R USDCTSD Failla-Case Mgt.

DISTRICT JUDGE KATHERINE B. FORREST: NY R USDCTSD Forrest-Civil Prac; NY R USDCTSD Forrest-Crim Prac; NY R USDCTSD Forrest-Crim Pretrial; NY R USDCTSD Forrest-Scheduling; NY R US-DCTSD Forrest-Patent Scheduling; NY R USDCTSD Forrest-Sentencing; NY R USDCTSD Forrest-Order 1; NY R USDCTSD Forrest-Order 2.

DISTRICT JUDGE JESSE M. FURMAN: NY R USDCTSD Furman-Civil Prac; NY R USDCTSD Furman-Crim Prac; NY R USDCTSD Furman-Pro Se Prac; NY R USDCTSD Furman-Trials; NY R USDCTSD Furman-Scheduling; NY R USDCTSD Furman-Rights.

DISTRICT JUDGE PAUL G. GARDEPHE: NY R USDCTSD Gardephe-Civ Prac; NY R USDCTSD Gardephe-Pretrial; NY R USDCTSD Gardephe-Prot Ord; NY R USDCTSD Gardephe-Maritime; NY R USDCTSD Gardephe-Crim Prac; NY R USDCTSD Gardephe-Trial.

DISTRICT JUDGE THOMAS P. GRIESA: NY R USDCTSD Griesa-Practices.

DISTRICT JUDGE CHARLES S. HAIGHT: NY R USDCTSD Haight-Practices.

DISTRICT JUDGE ALVIN K. HELLERSTEIN: NY R USDCTSD Hellerstein-Practices; NY R USDCTSD Hellerstein--Sept 11.

DISTRICT JUDGE LEWIS A. KAPLAN: NY R USDCTSD Kaplan-Practices; NY R USDCTSD Kaplan-Sentencing.

DISTRICT JUDGE KENNETH M. KARAS: NY R USDCTSD Karas-Practices; NY R USDCTSD Karas-Case Mgt; NY R USDCTSD Karas-Default; NY R USDCTSD Karas-Sentencing; NY R USDCTSD Karas-Rights.

DISTRICT JUDGE JOHN F. KEENAN: NY R USDCTSD Keenan-Practices.

DISTRICT JUDGE JOHN G. KOELTL: NY R USDCTSD Koeltl-Practices.

DISTRICT JUDGE VICTOR MARRERO: NY R USDCTSD Marrero-Practices; NY R USDCTSD Marrero-Scheduling; NY R USDCTSD Marrero-Default; NY R USDCTSD Marrero-Trial Proc.

DISTRICT JUDGE COLLEEN McMAHON: NY R USDCTSD McMahon-Practices; NY R USDCTSD McMahon-RICO; NY R USDCTSD McMahon-Copies; NY R USDCTSD McMahon-Scheduling; NY R USDCTSD McMahon-Elec Disc; NY R USDCTSD McMahon-Sentencing.

DISTRICT JUDGE ALISON J. NATHAN: NY R USDCTSD Nathan-Civ Prac; NY R USDCTSD Nathan-Crim Prac; NY R USDCTSD Nathan-Pro Se; NY R USDCTSD Nathan-Scheduling.

DISTRICT JUDGE J. PAUL OETKEN: NY R USDCTSD Oetken-Civ Prac; NY R USDCTSD Oetken-Case Mgt; NY R USDCTSD Oetken-Crim Prac; NY R USDCTSD Oetken-Pro Se.

DISTRICT JUDGE WILLIAM H. PAULEY, III: NY R USDCTSD Pauley-Crim Cases; NY R USDCTSD Pauley-Practices.

DISTRICT JUDGE LORETTA A. PRESKA: NY R USDCTSD Preska-Practices.

DISTRICT JUDGE JED S. RAKOFF: NY R USDCTSD Rakoff-Practices; NY R USDCTSD Rakoff-Scheduling; NY R USDCTSD Rakoff-Prot Ord; NY R USDCTSD Rakoff-Maritime Ord.

DISTRICT JUDGE EDGARDO RAMOS: NY R USDCTSD Ramos--Practices; NY R USDCTSD Ramos-Case Mgt.

DISTRICT JUDGE NELSON S. ROMAN: NY R USDCTSD Roman-Civ Prac; NY R USDCTSD Roman-Pro Se; NY R USDCTSD Roman-Crim Prac; NY R USDCTSD Roman-Case Mgt.

DISTRICT JUDGE LEONARD B. SAND: NY R USDCTSD Sand-Practices.

DISTRICT JUDGE LORNA G. SCHOFIELD: NY R USDCTSD Schofield-Civ Prac; NY R USDCTSD Schofield-Crim Prac; NY R USDCTSD Schofield-Sched; NY R USDCTSD Schofield-Pro Se; NY R USDCTSD Schofield-Advice.

DISTRICT JUDGE CATHY SEIBEL: NY R USDCTSD Seibel-Practices.

DISTRICT JUDGE LOUIS L. STANTON: NY R USDCTSD Stanton-Practices; NY R USDCTSD Stanton-Pretrial.

DISTRICT JUDGE SIDNEY H. STEIN: NY R USDCTSD Stein-Practices.

DISTRICT JUDGE RICHARD J. SULLIVAN: NY R USDCTSD Sullivan-Practices; NY R USDCTSD Sullivan-Scheduling; NY R USDCTSD Sullivan-Sentencing; NY R USDCTSD Sullivan-Juries; NY R USDCTSD Sullivan-Trial; NY R USDCTSD Sullivan-Default.

DISTRICT JUDGE LAURA TAYLOR SWAIN: NY R USDCTSD Swain-Practices; NY R USDCTSD Swain-Trial; NY R USDCTSD Swain-Crim Trial; NY R USDCTSD Swain-Juries; NY R USDCTSD Swain-Sentencing; NY R USDCTSD Swain-Rights.

DISTRICT JUDGE ROBERT W. SWEET: NY R USDCTSD Sweet-Practices.

DISTRICT JUDGE ANALISA TORRES: NY R USDCTSD Torres-Civ Prac; NY R USDCTSD Torres-Pro Se; NY R USDCTSD Torres-Scheduling.

DISTRICT JUDGE KIMBA M. WOOD: NY R USDCTSD Wood-Practices; NY R USDCTSD Wood-Scheduling; NY R USDCTSD Wood-Discovery; NY R USDCTSD Wood-RICO; NY R USDCTSD Wood-Juries; NY R USDCTSD Wood-Trial; NY R USDCTSD Wood-Media.

DISTRICT JUDGE GREGORY H. WOODS: NY R USDCTSD Woods-Civ Prac; NY R USDCTSD Woods-Pro Se; NY R USDCTSD Woods-Sched; NY R USDCTSD Woods-Crim Prac; NY R USDCTSD Woods-Protect Order; NY R USDCTSD Woods-Speedy Trial.

MAGISTRATE JUDGE JAMES L. COTT: NY R USDCTSD Cott-Practices; NY R USDCTSD Cott-Settlement.

MAGISTRATE JUDGE PAUL E. DAVISON: NY R USDCTSD Davison-Practices.

MAGISTRATE JUDGE RONALD L. ELLIS: NY R USDCTSD Ellis-Practices.

MAGISTRATE JUDGE KEVIN N. FOX: NY R USDCTSD Fox-Practices; NY R USDCTSD Fox-Settlement.

MAGISTRATE JUDGE JAMES C. FRANCIS: NY R USDCTSD Francis-Practices.

MAGISTRATE JUDGE DEBRA FREEMAN: NY R USDCTSD Freeman-Practices; NY R USDCTSD Freeman-Settlement.

MAGISTRATE JUDGE GABRIEL W. GORENSTEIN: NY R USDCTSD Gorenstein-Practices; NY R US-DCTSD Gorenstein-Ackn.

MAGISTRATE JUDGE FRANK MAAS: NY R USDCTSD Maas-Practices; NY R USDCTSD Maas-Discontinuance; NY R USDCTSD Maas-Conf; NY R USDCTSD Maas-Settlement.

MAGISTRATE JUDGE JUDITH C. McCARTHY: NY R USDCTSD McCarthy-Practices; NY R USDCTSD McCarthy-Conduct.

MAGISTRATE JUDGE BARBARA MOSES: NY R USDCTSD Moses-Practices.

MAGISTRATE JUDGE SARAH NETBURN: NY R USDCTSD Netburn-Civil; NY R USDCTSD Netburn-Settlement; NY R USDCTSD Netburn-Case Mgt; NY R USDCTSD Netburn--Pro Se.

MAGISTRATE JUDGE ANDREW J. PECK: NY R USDCTSD Peck-Practices; NY R USDCTSD Peck-Order; NY R USDCTSD Peck-Rule 502(d).

MAGISTRATE JUDGE HENRY PITMAN: NY R USDCTSD Pitman-Practices.

MAGISTRATE JUDGE LISA MARGARET SMITH: NY R USDCTSD Smith-Practices; NY R USDCTSD Smith-Trials.

## Motions, Oppositions and Replies
## Motion for Summary Judgment

**Document Last Updated September 2016**

### A. Checklist

(I) ❑ Matters to be considered by moving party

    (a) ❑ Required documents

        (1) ❑ Notice of motion and motion

        (2) ❑ Statement of material facts

        (3) ❑ Memorandum of law

        (4) ❑ Certificate of service

    (b) ❑ Supplemental documents

        (1) ❑ Supporting evidence

        (2) ❑ Notice of constitutional question

        (3) ❑ Nongovernmental corporate disclosure statement

        (4) ❑ Notice to pro se litigant who opposes a motion for summary judgment

        (5) ❑ Copies of authorities

        (6) ❑ Proposed order

        (7) ❑ Statement explaining untimely electronic filing

        (8) ❑ Courtesy copies

    (c) ❑ Timing

        (1) ❑ Unless a different time is set by local rule or the court orders otherwise, a party may file a motion for summary judgment at any time until thirty (30) days after the close of all discovery

        (2) ❑ A written motion and notice of the hearing must be served at least fourteen (14) days before the time specified for the hearing, with the following exceptions: (i) when the motion may be heard ex parte; (ii) when the Federal Rules of Civil Procedure set a different time; or (iii) when a court order—which a party may, for good cause, apply for ex parte—sets a different time

        (3) ❑ Any affidavit supporting a motion must be served with the motion

(II) ❏ Matters to be considered by opposing party

    (a) ❏ Required documents

        (1) ❏ Answering memorandum of law

        (2) ❏ Responsive statement of material facts

        (3) ❏ Certificate of service

    (b) ❏ Supplemental documents

        (1) ❏ Supporting evidence

        (2) ❏ Notice of constitutional question

        (3) ❏ Copies of authorities

        (4) ❏ Statement explaining untimely electronic filing

        (5) ❏ Courtesy copies

    (c) ❏ Timing

        (1) ❏ Any opposing affidavits and answering memoranda shall be served within fourteen (14) days after service of the moving papers

        (2) ❏ Except as FRCP 59(c) provides otherwise, any opposing affidavit must be served at least seven (7) days before the hearing, unless the court permits service at another time

## B. Timing

1. *Motion for summary judgment.* Unless a different time is set by local rule or the court orders otherwise, a party may file a motion for summary judgment at any time until thirty (30) days after the close of all discovery. FRCP 56(b).

2. *Timing of motions, generally*

    a. *Motion and notice of hearing.* Except for letter-motions as permitted by NY R USDCTS&ED Civ Rule 7.1(d), and unless otherwise provided by statute or rule or by the Court in a Judge's Individual Practice or in a direction in a particular case, upon any motion, the notice of motion, supporting affidavits, and memoranda shall be served and filed as follows: on all civil motions, petitions, and applications, other than those described in NY R USDCTS&ED Civ Rule 6.1(a), and other than petitions for writs of habeas corpus, the notice of motion, supporting affidavits, and memoranda of law shall be served by the moving party on all other parties that have appeared in the action. NY R USDCTS&ED Civ Rule 6.1(b)(1). A written motion and notice of the hearing must be served at least fourteen (14) days before the time specified for the hearing, with the following exceptions:

        i. When the motion may be heard ex parte;

        ii. When the Federal Rules of Civil Procedure set a different time; or

        iii. When a court order—which a party may, for good cause, apply for ex parte—sets a different time. FRCP 6(c)(1).

    b. *Supporting affidavit.* Any affidavit supporting a motion must be served with the motion. FRCP 6(c)(2).

3. *Timing of opposing papers.* Except for letter-motions as permitted by NY R USDCTS&ED Civ Rule 7.1(d), and unless otherwise provided by statute or rule or by the Court in a Judge's Individual Practice or in a direction in a particular case, upon any motion, the notice of motion, supporting affidavits, and memoranda shall be served and filed as follows: on all civil motions, petitions, and applications, other than those described in NY R USDCTS&ED Civ Rule 6.1(a), and other than petitions for writs of habeas corpus, any opposing affidavits and answering memoranda shall be served within fourteen (14) days after service of the moving papers. NY R USDCTS&ED Civ Rule 6.1(b)(2).

    a. *Opposing affidavit.* Except as FRCP 59(c) provides otherwise, any opposing affidavit must be served at least seven (7) days before the hearing, unless the court permits service at another time. FRCP 6(c)(2).

4. *Timing of reply papers.* Where the respondent files an answering affidavit setting up a new matter, the

moving party ordinarily is allowed a reasonable time to file a reply affidavit since failure to deny the new matter by affidavit may operate as an admission of its truth. AMJUR MOTIONS § 25.

a. *Reply affidavits and reply memoranda of law.* Except for letter-motions as permitted by NY R USDCTS&ED Civ Rule 7.1(d), and unless otherwise provided by statute or rule or by the Court in a Judge's Individual Practice or in a direction in a particular case, upon any motion, the notice of motion, supporting affidavits, and memoranda shall be served and filed as follows: on all civil motions, petitions, and applications, other than those described in NY R USDCTS&ED Civ Rule 6.1(a), and other than petitions for writs of habeas corpus, any reply affidavits and memoranda of law shall be served within seven (7) days after service of the answering papers. NY R USDCTS&ED Civ Rule 6.1(b)(3).

5. *Computation of time*

   a. *Computing time.* FRCP 6 applies in computing any time period specified in the Federal Rules of Civil Procedure, in any local rule or court order, or in any statute that does not specify a method of computing time. FRCP 6(a). In computing any period of time prescribed or allowed by the Local Civil Rules of the United States District Courts for the Southern and Eastern Districts of New York or the Local Admiralty and Maritime Rules, the provisions of FRCP 6 shall apply unless otherwise stated. NY R USDCTS&ED Civ Rule 6.4.

      i. *Period stated in days or a longer unit.* In computing periods of days, refer to FRCP 6 and NY R USDCTS&ED Civ Rule 6.4. NY R USDCTS&ED Civ Rule 6.1(b). When the period is stated in days or a longer unit of time:

         • Exclude the day of the event that triggers the period;

         • Count every day, including intermediate Saturdays, Sundays, and legal holidays; and

         • Include the last day of the period, but if the last day is a Saturday, Sunday, or legal holiday, the period continues to run until the end of the next day that is not a Saturday, Sunday, or legal holiday. FRCP 6(a)(1). In the Local Civil Rules of the United States District Courts for the Southern and Eastern Districts of New York, as in the Federal Rules of Civil Procedure as amended effective December 1, 2009, Saturdays, Sundays, and legal holidays are no longer excluded in computing periods of time. If the last day of the period is a Saturday, Sunday, or legal holiday, the period continues to run until the end of the next day that is not a Saturday, Sunday, or legal holiday. NY R USDCTS&ED Civ Rule 6.4.

      ii. *Period stated in hours.* When the period is stated in hours:

         • Begin counting immediately on the occurrence of the event that triggers the period;

         • Count every hour, including hours during intermediate Saturdays, Sundays, and legal holidays; and

         • If the period would end on a Saturday, Sunday, or legal holiday, the period continues to run until the same time on the next day that is not a Saturday, Sunday, or legal holiday. FRCP 6(a)(2). In the Local Civil Rules of the United States District Courts for the Southern and Eastern Districts of New York, as in the Federal Rules of Civil Procedure as amended effective December 1, 2009, Saturdays, Sundays, and legal holidays are no longer excluded in computing periods of time. If the last day of the period is a Saturday, Sunday, or legal holiday, the period continues to run until the end of the next day that is not a Saturday, Sunday, or legal holiday. NY R USDCTS&ED Civ Rule 6.4.

      iii. *Inaccessibility of the clerk's office.* Unless the court orders otherwise, if the clerk's office is inaccessible:

         • On the last day for filing under FRCP 6(a)(1), then the time for filing is extended to the first accessible day that is not a Saturday, Sunday, or legal holiday; or

         • During the last hour for filing under FRCP 6(a)(2), then the time for filing is extended to the same time on the first accessible day that is not a Saturday, Sunday, or legal holiday. FRCP 6(a)(3).

iv. *"Last day" defined.* Unless a different time is set by a statute, local rule, or court order, the last day ends:

- For electronic filing, at midnight in the court's time zone; and

- For filing by other means, when the clerk's office is scheduled to close. FRCP 6(a)(4).

v. *"Next day" defined.* The "next day" is determined by continuing to count forward when the period is measured after an event and backward when measured before an event. FRCP 6(a)(5).

vi. *"Legal holiday" defined.* "Legal holiday" means:

- The day set aside by statute for observing New Year's Day, Martin Luther King Jr.'s Birthday, Washington's Birthday, Memorial Day, Independence Day, Labor Day, Columbus Day, Veterans' Day, Thanksgiving Day, or Christmas Day;

- Any day declared a holiday by the President or Congress; and

- For periods that are measured after an event, any other day declared a holiday by the state where the district court is located. FRCP 6(a)(6).

b. *Computation of electronic filing deadlines.* You can file electronically twenty-four (24) hours a day, seven (7) days a week, three hundred sixty-five (365) days a year. NY R USDCTSD CM/ECF, S.D.(II)(13)(13.10). Electronic filing must be completed before midnight local time where the Court is located in order to be considered timely filed that day. NY R USDCTSD CM/ECF, S.D.(I)(3)(3.3); NY R USDCTSD CM/ECF, S.D.(II)(13)(13.10); NY R USDCTSD CM/ECF, S.D.(II)(19)(19.4). An electronically filed document is deemed filed on the "filed on" date indicated on the Notice of Electronic Filing (NEF). NY R USDCTSD CM/ECF, S.D.(II)(13)(13.11).

i. *Technical failures.* A Filing User whose filing is made untimely as the result of a technical failure may seek appropriate relief from the Court. NY R USDCTSD CM/ECF, S.D.(I)(11). If you missed a filing deadline when the ECF system was out of order, attach a statement to your filing explaining how the interruption in service prevented you from filing in a timely fashion. NY R USDCTSD CM/ECF, S.D.(II)(23)(23.5).

c. *Extending time*

i. *In general.* When an act may or must be done within a specified time, the court may, for good cause, extend the time:

- With or without motion or notice if the court acts, or if a request is made, before the original time or its extension expires; or

- On motion made after the time has expired if the party failed to act because of excusable neglect. FRCP 6(b)(1).

ii. *Exceptions.* A court must not extend the time to act under FRCP 50(b), FRCP 50(d), FRCP 52(b), FRCP 59(b), FRCP 59(d), FRCP 59(e), and FRCP 60(b). FRCP 6(b)(2).

iii. Refer to the United States District Court for the Southern District of New York KeyRules Motion for Continuance/Extension of Time document for more information on extending time.

d. *Additional time after certain kinds of service.* When a party may or must act within a specified time after service and service is made under FRCP 5(b)(2)(C), FRCP 5(b)(2)(D), FRCP 5(b)(2)(E), or FRCP 5(b)(2)(F), three (3) days are added after the period would otherwise expire under FRCP 6(a). FRCP 6(d). Overnight delivery service shall be deemed service by mail for purposes of FRCP 5 and FRCP 6. NY R USDCTS&ED Civ Rule 5.3.

6. *Individual judge practices.* Refer to the Miscellaneous section of this document for information on individual judge practices on timing of documents.

## C. General Requirements

1. *Motions, generally*

a. *Requirements.* A request for a court order must be made by motion. The motion must:

i. Be in writing unless made during a hearing or trial;

    ii.   State with particularity the grounds for seeking the order; and

    iii.   State the relief sought. FRCP 7(b)(1).

b.  *Notice of motion.* A party interested in resisting the relief sought by a motion has a right to notice thereof, and an opportunity to be heard. AMJUR MOTIONS § 12.

    i.   In addition to statutory or court rule provisions requiring notice of a motion—the purpose of such a notice requirement having been said to be to prevent a party from being prejudicially surprised by a motion—principles of natural justice dictate that an adverse party generally must be given notice that a motion will be presented to the court. AMJUR MOTIONS § 12.

    ii.   "Notice," in this regard, means reasonable notice, including a meaningful opportunity to prepare and to defend against allegations of a motion. AMJUR MOTIONS § 12.

c.  *Writing requirement.* The writing requirement is intended to insure that the adverse parties are informed and have a record of both the motion's pendency and the grounds on which the movant seeks an order. FPP § 1191; Feldberg v. Quechee Lakes Corp., 463 F.3d 195 (2d Cir. 2006).

    i.   It is sufficient "if the motion is stated in a written notice of the hearing of the motion." FPP § 1191.

d.  *Particularity requirement.* The particularity requirement insures that the opposing parties will have notice of their opponent's contentions. FEDPROC § 62:364; Goodman v. 1973 26 Foot Trojan Vessel, Arkansas Registration No. AR1439SN, 859 F.2d 71, 12 Fed.R.Serv.3d 645 (8th Cir. 1988). That requirement ensures that notice of the basis for the motion is provided to the court and to the opposing party so as to avoid prejudice, provide the opponent with a meaningful opportunity to respond, and provide the court with enough information to process the motion correctly. FEDPROC § 62:364; Andreas v. Volkswagen of America, Inc., 336 F.3d 789, 56 Fed.R.Serv.3d 6 (8th Cir. 2003).

    i.   Reasonable specification of the grounds for a motion is sufficient. However, where a movant fails to state even one ground for granting the motion in question, the movant has failed to meet the minimal standard of "reasonable specification." FEDPROC § 62:364; Martinez v. Trainor, 556 F.2d 818, 23 Fed.R.Serv.2d 403 (7th Cir. 1977).

    ii.   The court may excuse the failure to comply with the particularity requirement if it is inadvertent, and where no prejudice is shown by the opposing party. FEDPROC § 62:364.

e.  *Ex parte orders or orders to show cause to bring on a motion.* No ex parte order, or order to show cause to bring on a motion, will be granted except upon a clear and specific showing by affidavit of good and sufficient reasons why a procedure other than by notice of motion is necessary, and stating whether a previous application for similar relief has been made. NY R USDCTS&ED Civ Rule 6.1(d).

f.  *Letter-motions.* Applications for extensions or adjournments, applications for a pre-motion conference, and similar non-dispositive matters as permitted by the instructions regarding ECF published on the website of each respective Court and any pertinent Individual Judge's Practices, may be brought by letter-motion filed via ECF pursuant to NY R USDCTS&ED Civ Rule 5.2(b). NY R USDCTS&ED Civ Rule 7.1(d).

    i.   The following list of motions. . .may be made by LETTER-MOTION: (1) Motion to Adjourn Conference; (2) Motion to Change Attorney Name on Roll; (3) Motion to Compel; (4) Motion for Conference; (5) Motion to Consolidate Cases; (6) Motion to Continue; (7) Motion re: Discovery; (8) Motion to Expedite; (9) Motion for Extension of Time; (10) Motion for Extension of Time to Amend; (11) Motion for Extension of Time to Answer; (12) Motion for Extension of Time to Complete Discovery; (13) Motion for Extension of Time to File Document; (14) Motion for Extension of Time to File Response/Reply; (15) Motion for Extension of Time re Transcript; (16) Motion to File Amicus Brief; (17) Motion for Leave to File Document; (18) Motion for Leave to File Excess Pages; (19) Motion for Local Rule 37.2 Conference; (20) Motion for Oral Argument; (21) Motion to Reopen; (22) Motion to Reopen Case; (23) Motion to Seal Document; (24) Motion to Stay; (25) Motion to Substitute Attorney. NY R USDCTSD CM/ECF, S.D.(II)(13)(13.1).

    ii.   If the Filing User is making a type of motion that does not appear in this list, the motion may not be made by letter. NY R USDCTSD CM/ECF, S.D.(II)(13)(13.1).

      iii.    For more information on letter motions, refer to NY R USDCTSD CM/ECF, S.D.(II)(13)(13.1).

2.   *Motion for summary judgment.* A party may move for summary judgment, identifying each claim or defense—or the part of each claim or defense—on which summary judgment is sought. The court shall grant summary judgment if the movant shows that there is no genuine dispute as to any material fact and the movant is entitled to judgment as a matter of law. The court should state on the record the reasons for granting or denying the motion. FRCP 56(a).

   a.   *Burden of proof and presumptions*

      i.    *Movant's burden.* It is well-settled that the party moving for summary judgment has the burden of demonstrating that the FRCP 56(c) test—"no genuine issue as to any material fact"—is satisfied and that the movant is entitled to judgment as a matter of law. FPP § 2727; Adickes v. S. H. Kress & Co., 398 U.S. 144, 157, 90 S.Ct. 1598, 1608, 26 L.Ed.2d 142 (1970).

- The movant is held to a stringent standard. FPP § 2727. Before summary judgment will be granted it must be clear what the truth is and any doubt as to the existence of a genuine issue of material fact will be resolved against the movant. FPP § 2727; Poller v. Columbia Broadcasting Sys., Inc., 368 U.S. 464, 82 S.Ct. 486, 7 L.Ed.2d 458 (1962); Adickes v. S. H. Kress & Co., 398 U.S. 144, 90 S.Ct. 1598, 26 L.Ed.2d 142 (1970).

- Because the burden is on the movant, the evidence presented to the court always is construed in favor of the party opposing the motion and the opponent is given the benefit of all favorable inferences that can be drawn from it. FPP § 2727; Scott v. Harris, 550 U.S. 372, 127 S.Ct. 1769, 167 L.Ed.2d 686 (2007).

- Finally, facts asserted by the party opposing the motion, if supported by affidavits or other evidentiary material, are regarded as true. FPP § 2727; McLaughlin v. Liu, 849 F.2d 1205, 1208 (9th Cir. 1988).

      ii.   *Opponent's burden.* If the movant makes out a prima facie case that would entitle him to a judgment as a matter of law if uncontroverted at trial, summary judgment will be granted unless the opposing party offers some competent evidence that could be presented at trial showing that there is a genuine issue as to a material fact. FPP § 2727; First Nat. Bank of Arizona v. Cities Serv. Co., 391 U.S. 253, 289, 88 S.Ct. 1575, 1593, 20 L.Ed.2d 569 (1968). In this way the burden of producing evidence is shifted to the party opposing the motion. FPP § 2727; Celotex Corp. v. Catrett, 477 U.S. 317, 331, 106 S.Ct. 2548, 2557, 91 L.Ed.2d 265 (1986).

- The burden on the nonmoving party is not a heavy one; the nonmoving party simply is required to show specific facts, as opposed to general allegations, that present a genuine issue worthy of trial. FPP § 2727; Lujan v. Defenders of Wildlife, 504 U.S. 555, 112 S.Ct. 2130, 119 L.Ed.2d 351 (1992).

- The nonmoving party has two options once the moving party has met its burden of production of evidence demonstrating the absence of a genuine issue of material fact: either come forward with countervailing evidence showing that a genuine issue does exist, or submit an affidavit under FRCP 56(f) demonstrating that more time or further discovery are necessary to enable it to oppose the summary judgment motion. FEDPROC § 62:589.

   b.   *Failing to properly support or address a fact.* If a party fails to properly support an assertion of fact or fails to properly address another party's assertion of fact as required by FRCP 56(c), the court may:

      i.    Give an opportunity to properly support or address the fact;

      ii.   Consider the fact undisputed for purposes of the motion;

     iii.   Grant summary judgment if the motion and supporting materials—including the facts considered undisputed—show that the movant is entitled to it; or

     iv.   Issue any other appropriate order. FRCP 56(e).

   c.   *Judgment independent of the motion.* After giving notice and a reasonable time to respond, the court may:

      i.    Grant summary judgment for a nonmovant;

    ii.   Grant the motion on grounds not raised by a party; or

    iii.   Consider summary judgment on its own after identifying for the parties material facts that may not be genuinely in dispute. FRCP 56(f).

  d.   *Failing to grant all the requested relief.* If the court does not grant all the relief requested by the motion, it may enter an order stating any material fact—including an item of damages or other relief—that is not genuinely in dispute and treating the fact as established in the case. FRCP 56(g).

  e.   *Affidavit or declaration submitted in bad faith.* If satisfied that an affidavit or declaration under FRCP 56 is submitted in bad faith or solely for delay, the court—after notice and a reasonable time to respond—may order the submitting party to pay the other party the reasonable expenses, including attorney's fees, it incurred as a result. An offending party or attorney may also be held in contempt or subjected to other appropriate sanctions. FRCP 56(h).

  f.   *Conversion of motions under FRCP 12(b)(6) and FRCP 12(c).* If, on a motion under FRCP 12(b)(6) or FRCP 12(c), matters outside the pleadings are presented to and not excluded by the court, the motion must be treated as one for summary judgment under FRCP 56. FRCP 12(d).

3.   *Opposing papers*

  a.   *Opposing papers, generally.* The Federal Rules of Civil Procedure do not require any formal answer, return, or reply to a motion, except where the Federal Rules of Civil Procedure or local rules may require affidavits, memoranda, or other papers to be filed in opposition to a motion. Such papers are simply to apprise the court of such opposition and the grounds of that opposition. FEDPROC § 62:359. Except for letter-motions as permitted by NY R USDCTS&ED Civ Rule 7.1(d) or as otherwise permitted by the Court, all oppositions and replies with respect to motions shall comply with NY R USDCTS&ED Civ Rule 7.1(a)(2) and NY R USDCTS&ED Civ Rule 7.1(a)(3), and an opposing party who seeks relief that goes beyond the denial of the motion shall comply as well with NY R USDCTS&ED Civ Rule 7.1(a)(1). NY R USDCTS&ED Civ Rule 7.1(b).

    i.   *Effect of failure to respond to motion.* Although in the absence of statutory provision or court rule, a motion ordinarily does not require a written answer, when a party files a motion and the opposing party fails to respond, the court may construe such failure to respond as nonopposition to the motion or an admission that the motion was meritorious, may take the facts alleged in the motion as true—the rule in some jurisdictions being that the failure to respond to a fact set forth in a motion is deemed an admission—and may grant the motion if the relief requested appears to be justified. AMJUR MOTIONS § 28.

    ii.   *Assent or no opposition not determinative.* However, a motion will not be granted automatically simply because an "assent" or a notation of "no opposition" has been filed; federal judges frequently deny motions that have been assented to when it is thought that justice so dictates. FPP § 1190.

    iii.   *Responsive pleading inappropriate as response to motion.* An attempt to answer or oppose a motion with a responsive pleading usually is not appropriate. FPP § 1190.

  b.   *Opposition to motion for summary judgment.* The party opposing summary judgment does not have a duty to present evidence in opposition to a motion under FRCP 56 in all circumstances. FPP § 2727; Jaroma v. Massey, 873 F.2d 17 (1st Cir. 1989).

    i.   *When facts are unavailable to the nonmovant.* If a nonmovant shows by affidavit or declaration that, for specified reasons, it cannot present facts essential to justify its opposition, the court may:

- Defer considering the motion or deny it;

- Allow time to obtain affidavits or declarations or to take discovery; or

- Issue any other appropriate order. FRCP 56(d).

4.   *Reply papers.* A moving party may be required or permitted to prepare papers in addition to his original motion papers. AMJUR MOTIONS § 25. Papers answering or replying to opposing papers may be appropriate, in the interests of justice, where it appears there is a substantial reason for allowing a reply. Thus, a court may accept reply papers where a party demonstrates that the papers to which it seeks to file

a reply raise new issues that are material to the disposition of the question before the court, or where the court determines, sua sponte, that it wishes further briefing of an issue raised in those papers and orders the submission of additional papers. FEDPROC § 62:360. Except for letter-motions as permitted by NY R USDCTS&ED Civ Rule 7.1(d) or as otherwise permitted by the Court, all oppositions and replies with respect to motions shall comply with NY R USDCTS&ED Civ Rule 7.1(a)(2) and NY R USDCTS&ED Civ Rule 7.1(a)(3). NY R USDCTS&ED Civ Rule 7.1(b).

    a.  *Function of reply papers.* The function of a reply affidavit is to answer the arguments made in opposition to the position taken by the movant and not to permit the movant to introduce new arguments in support of the motion. AMJUR MOTIONS § 25.

    b.  *Issues raised for the first time in a reply document.* However, the view has been followed in some jurisdictions, that as a matter of judicial economy, where there is no prejudice and where the issues could be raised simply by filing a motion to dismiss, the trial court has discretion to consider arguments raised for the first time in a reply memorandum, and that a trial court may grant a motion to strike issues raised for the first time in a reply memorandum. AMJUR MOTIONS § 26.

5.  *Orders on motions.* A memorandum signed by the Court of the decision on a motion that does not finally determine all claims for relief, or an oral decision on such a motion, shall constitute the order unless the memorandum or oral decision directs the submission or settlement of an order in more extended form. The notation in the docket of a memorandum or of an oral decision that does not direct the submission or settlement of an order in more extended form shall constitute the entry of the order. Where an order in more extended form is required to be submitted or settled, the notation in the docket of such order shall constitute the entry of the order. NY R USDCTS&ED Civ Rule 6.2.

6.  *Complex civil cases.* For information on procedures for complex civil cases, refer to NY R USDCTSD Order 11 Misc 00388.

7.  *Related cases.* It shall be the continuing duty of each attorney appearing in any civil or criminal case to bring promptly to the attention of the Court all facts which said attorney believes are relevant to a determination that said case and one or more pending civil or criminal cases should be heard by the same Judge, in order to avoid unnecessary duplication of judicial effort. As soon as the attorney becomes aware of such relationship, said attorney shall notify the Judges to whom the cases have been assigned. NY R USDCTS&ED Civ Rule 1.6(a). If counsel fails to comply with NY R USDCTS&ED Civ Rule 1.6(a), the Court may assess reasonable costs directly against counsel whose action has obstructed the effective administration of the Court's business. NY R USDCTS&ED Civ Rule 1.6(b).

    a.  *Determination of relatedness.* Subject to the limitations set forth in NY R USDCTSD Div. Bus., Rule 13(a)(2), a civil case, bankruptcy appeal, or motion to withdraw the bankruptcy reference will be deemed related to one or more civil cases, appeals or motions when the interests of justice and efficiency will be served. In determining relatedness, a judge will consider whether (A) the actions concern the same or substantially similar parties, property, transactions or events; (B) there is substantial factual overlap; (C) the parties could be subjected to conflicting orders; and (D) whether absent a determination of relatedness there would be a substantial duplication of effort and expense, delay, or undue burden on the Court, parties or witnesses. NY R USDCTSD Div. Bus., Rule 13(a)(1). Nothing in this NY R USDCTSD Div. Bus., Rule 13 is intended to preclude parties from moving for consolidated proceedings under FRCP 42. NY R USDCTSD Div. Bus., Rule 13(a)(1). Notwithstanding NY R USDCTSD Div. Bus., Rule 13(a)(1):

        i.  Civil cases shall not be deemed related merely because they involve common legal issues or the same parties. NY R USDCTSD Div. Bus., Rule 13(a)(2)(A).

        ii.  Other than cases subject to NY R USDCTSD Div. Bus., Rule 4(b) and actions seeking the enforcement of a judgment or settlement in or of an earlier case, civil cases presumptively shall not be deemed related unless both cases are pending before the Court (or the earlier case is on appeal). NY R USDCTSD Div. Bus., Rule 13(a)(2)(B).

    b.  *Procedure in regard to cases said to be related*

        i.  *Disclosure of contention of relatedness.* When a civil case is filed or removed or a bankruptcy appeal or motion to withdraw the reference of an adversary proceeding from the bankruptcy court is filed, the person filing or removing shall disclose on form JSC44C any contention of relatedness and shall file a Related Case Statement stating clearly and succinctly the basis for the contention. A copy of the civil cover sheet and Related Case Statement shall be served with the complaint, notice of removal, notice of appeal, or motion. Any party may contest a claim of relatedness by any other in writing addressed to the judge having the case with the lowest docket number of all cases claimed to be related. However, the foregoing shall not delay the assignment process or the operation of NY R USDCTSD Div. Bus., Rule 13. NY R USDCTSD Div. Bus., Rule 13(b)(1). [Editor's note: the reference to form JSC44C is likely meant to be form JS44C-SDNY: Civil Court Cover Sheet].

    ii.  *Claims of relatedness by other parties.* A party other than the one filing a case, bankruptcy appeal or motion to withdraw the reference that contends its case is related to another may so advise in writing the judge assigned in its case and request a transfer of its case to the judge that the party contends has the related case with the lowest docket number. If the assigned judge believes the case is related under NY R USDCTSD Div. Bus., Rule 13(a), he or she shall refer the question to the judge having the case with the lowest docket number. In the event the latter judge agrees, the case shall be transferred to that judge unless the Assignment Committee disagrees. NY R USDCTSD Div. Bus., Rule 13(b)(3).

  c.  For more information on related cases, refer to NY R USDCTSD Div. Bus., Rule 13.

8.  *Alternative dispute resolution (ADR).* The U.S. District Court for the Southern District of New York provides litigants with opportunities to discuss settlement through judicial settlement conferences and mediation. NY R USDCTS&ED Civ Rule 83.9(a).

  a.  *Consideration of alternative dispute resolution.* In all civil cases, including those eligible for mediation pursuant to NY R USDCTS&ED Civ Rule 83.9(e), each party shall consider the use of mediation or a judicial settlement conference and shall report to the assigned Judge at the initial FRCP 16(b) case management conference, or subsequently, whether the party believes mediation or a judicial settlement conference may facilitate the resolution of the lawsuit. Judges are encouraged to note the availability of the mediation program and/or a judicial settlement conference before, at, or after the initial FRCP 16(b) case management conference. NY R USDCTS&ED Civ Rule 83.9(d).

  b.  *Mediation.* In mediation, parties and counsel meet, sometimes collectively and sometimes individually, with a neutral third party (the mediator) who has been trained to facilitate confidential settlement discussions. The parties articulate their respective positions and interests and generate options for a mutually agreeable resolution to the dispute. The mediator assists the parties in reaching their own negotiated settlement by defining the issues, probing and assessing the strengths and weaknesses of each party's legal positions, and identifying areas of agreement and disagreement. The main benefits of mediation are that it can result in an expeditious and less costly resolution of the litigation, and can produce creative solutions to complex disputes often unavailable in traditional litigation. NY R USDCTS&ED Civ Rule 83.9(b).

    i.  *Mediation program eligibility.* All civil cases other than Social Security, habeas corpus, and tax cases are eligible for mediation, whether assigned to Manhattan or White Plains. NY R USDCTS&ED Civ Rule 83.9(e)(1).

- The Board of Judges may, by Administrative Order, direct that certain specified categories of cases shall automatically be submitted to the mediation program. The assigned District Judge or Magistrate Judge may issue a written order exempting a particular case with or without the request of the parties. NY R USDCTS&ED Civ Rule 83.9(e)(2).

- For all other cases, the assigned District Judge or Magistrate Judge may determine that a case is appropriate for mediation and may order that case to mediation, with or without the consent of the parties, before, at, or after the initial FRCP 16(b) case management conference. Alternatively, the parties should notify the assigned Judge at any time of their desire to mediate. NY R USDCTS&ED Civ Rule 83.9(e)(3).

  c.  *Judicial settlement conferences.* Judicial settlement conferences may be ordered by District Judges or Magistrate Judges with or without the request or consent of the parties. NY R USDCTS&ED Civ Rule 83.9(f).

d. For more information on alternative dispute resolution (ADR), refer to NY R USDCTS&ED Civ Rule 83.9.

9. *Individual judge practices.* Refer to the Miscellaneous section of this document for information on individual judge practices on general requirements for documents.

## D. Documents

1. *Documents for moving party*

   a. *Required documents*

      i. *Notice of motion and motion.* Except for letter-motions as permitted by NY R USDCTS&ED Civ Rule 7.1(d) or as otherwise permitted by the Court, all motions shall include the following motion papers: a notice of motion, or an order to show cause signed by the Court, which shall specify the applicable rules or statutes pursuant to which the motion is brought, and shall specify the relief sought by the motion. NY R USDCTS&ED Civ Rule 7.1(a)(1). Refer to the General Requirements section of this document for information on the notice of motion and motion.

      ii. *Statement of material facts.* Upon any motion for summary judgment pursuant to FRCP 56, there shall be annexed to the notice of motion a separate, short and concise statement, in numbered paragraphs, of the material facts as to which the moving party contends there is no genuine issue to be tried. Failure to submit such a statement may constitute grounds for denial of the motion. NY R USDCTS&ED Civ Rule 56.1(a).

         • Each statement by the movant or opponent pursuant to NY R USDCTS&ED Civ Rule 56.1(a) and NY R USDCTS&ED Civ Rule 56.1(b), including each statement controverting any statement of material fact, must be followed by citation to evidence which would be admissible, set forth as required by FRCP 56(c). NY R USDCTS&ED Civ Rule 56.1(d).

      iii. *Memorandum of law.* Except for letter-motions as permitted by NY R USDCTS&ED Civ Rule 7.1(d) or as otherwise permitted by the Court, all motions shall include the following motion papers: a memorandum of law, setting forth the cases and other authorities relied upon in support of the motion, and divided, under appropriate headings, into as many parts as there are issues to be determined. NY R USDCTS&ED Civ Rule 7.1(a)(2).

      iv. *Certificate of service.* FRCP 5(d) requires that the person making service under FRCP 5 certify that service has been effected. FRCP 5(Advisory Committee Notes). Having such information on file may be useful for many purposes, including proof of service if an issue arises concerning the effectiveness of the service. FRCP 5(Advisory Committee Notes).

         • Such paper service [on attorneys and pro se parties who are not Filing or Receiving Users] must be documented by electronically filing proof of service. NY R USDCTSD CM/ECF, S.D.(I)(9)(9.2); NY R USDCTSD CM/ECF, S.D.(I)(19)(19.3)(b). Pro se parties who are not Filing Users are exempt from that portion of NY R USDCTSD CM/ECF, S.D.(I)(19)(19.3) requiring proof of service to be filed electronically. NY R USDCTSD CM/ECF, S.D.(I)(19)(19.3).

   b. *Supplemental documents*

      i. *Supporting evidence.* When a motion relies on facts outside the record, the court may hear the matter on affidavits or may hear it wholly or partly on oral testimony or on depositions. FRCP 43(c). Except for letter-motions as permitted by NY R USDCTS&ED Civ Rule 7.1(d) or as otherwise permitted by the Court, all motions shall include the following motion papers: supporting affidavits and exhibits thereto containing any factual information and portions of the record necessary for the decision of the motion. NY R USDCTS&ED Civ Rule 7.1(a)(3).

         • *Supporting factual positions.* A party asserting that a fact cannot be or is genuinely disputed must support the assertion by: (1) citing to particular parts of materials in the record, including depositions, documents, electronically stored information, affidavits or declarations, stipulations (including those made for purposes of the motion only), admissions, interrogatory answers, or other materials; or (2) showing that the materials cited do not establish the absence or presence of a genuine dispute, or that an adverse party cannot produce admissible evidence to support the fact. FRCP 56(c)(1).

- *Objection that a fact is not supported by admissible evidence.* A party may object that the material cited to support or dispute a fact cannot be presented in a form that would be admissible in evidence. FRCP 56(c)(2).

- *Materials not cited.* The court need consider only the cited materials, but it may consider other materials in the record. FRCP 56(c)(3).

- *Affidavits or declarations.* An affidavit or declaration used to support or oppose a motion must be made on personal knowledge, set out facts that would be admissible in evidence, and show that the affiant or declarant is competent to testify on the matters stated. FRCP 56(c)(4).

- *Discovery materials.* A party seeking or opposing relief under FRCP 26 through FRCP 37 inclusive, or making or opposing any other motion or application, shall quote or attach only those portions of the depositions, interrogatories, requests for documents, requests for admissions, or other discovery or disclosure materials, together with the responses and objections thereto, that are the subject of the discovery motion or application, or that are cited in papers submitted in connection with any other motion or application. NY R USDCTS&ED Civ Rule 5.1.

ii. *Notice of constitutional question.* A party that files a pleading, written motion, or other paper drawing into question the constitutionality of a federal or state statute must promptly:

- *File notice.* File a notice of constitutional question stating the question and identifying the paper that raises it, if: (1) a federal statute is questioned and the parties do not include the United States, one of its agencies, or one of its officers or employees in an official capacity; or (2) a state statute is questioned and the parties do not include the state, one of its agencies, or one of its officers or employees in an official capacity; and

- *Serve notice.* Serve the notice and paper on the Attorney General of the United States if a federal statute is questioned—or on the state attorney general if a state statute is questioned—either by certified or registered mail or by sending it to an electronic address designated by the attorney general for this purpose. FRCP 5.1(a).

- *No forfeiture.* A party's failure to file and serve the notice, or the court's failure to certify, does not forfeit a constitutional claim or defense that is otherwise timely asserted. FRCP 5.1(d).

iii. *Nongovernmental corporate disclosure statement*

- *Contents.* A nongovernmental corporate party must file two (2) copies of a disclosure statement that: (1) identifies any parent corporation and any publicly held corporation owning ten percent (10%) or more of its stock; or (2) states that there is no such corporation. FRCP 7.1(a).

- *Time to file; Supplemental filing.* A party must: (1) file the disclosure statement with its first appearance, pleading, petition, motion, response, or other request addressed to the court; and (2) promptly file a supplemental statement if any required information changes. FRCP 7.1(b). For purposes of FRCP 7.1(b)(2), "promptly" shall mean "within fourteen days," that is, parties are required to file a supplemental disclosure statement within fourteen (14) days of the time there is any change in the information required in a disclosure statement filed pursuant to those rules. NY R USDCTS&ED Civ Rule 7.1.1.

iv. *Notice to pro se litigant who opposes a motion for summary judgment.* Any represented party moving for summary judgment against a party proceeding pro se shall serve and file as a separate document, together with the papers in support of the motion, the "Notice To Pro Se Litigant Who Opposes a Motion For Summary Judgment" found in NY R USDCTS&ED Civ Rule 56.2 with the full texts of FRCP 56 and NY R USDCTS&ED Civ Rule 56.1 attached. Where the pro se party is not the plaintiff, the movant shall amend the form notice as necessary to reflect that fact. NY R USDCTS&ED Civ Rule 56.2. For the notice, refer to NY R USDCTS&ED Civ Rule 56.2.

v. *Copies of authorities.* In cases involving a pro se litigant, counsel shall, when serving a memorandum of law (or other submissions to the Court), provide the pro se litigant (but not other counsel or the Court) with copies of cases and other authorities cited therein that are unpublished or reported exclusively on computerized databases. Upon request, counsel shall provide the pro se litigant with copies of such unpublished cases and other authorities as are cited in a decision of the Court and were not previously cited by any party. NY R USDCTS&ED Civ Rule 7.2.

vi. *Proposed order.* Refer to the Format section of this document for information on the format of submitting a proposed order to the court.

vii. *Statement explaining untimely electronic filing.* If you missed a filing deadline when the ECF system was out of order, attach a statement to your filing explaining how the interruption in service prevented you from filing in a timely fashion. NY R USDCTSD CM/ECF, S.D.(II)(23)(23.5).

viii. *Courtesy copies.* Read the judge's Individual Practices to learn if courtesy copies are required. NY R USDCTSD CM/ECF, S.D.(II)(13)(13.17). Judges' Individual Practices should continue to be followed with respect to delivery of courtesy copies. NY R USDCTSD CM/ECF, S.D.(I)(3)(3.4).

2. *Documents for opposing party*

a. *Required documents*

i. *Answering memorandum of law.* Except for letter-motions as permitted by NY R USDCTS&ED Civ Rule 7.1(d) or as otherwise permitted by the Court, all oppositions and replies with respect to motions shall comply with NY R USDCTS&ED Civ Rule 7.1(a)(2). NY R USDCTS&ED Civ Rule 7.1(b). Except for letter-motions as permitted by NY R USDCTS&ED Civ Rule 7.1(d) or as otherwise permitted by the Court, all motions shall include the following motion papers: a memorandum of law, setting forth the cases and other authorities relied upon in support of the motion, and divided, under appropriate headings, into as many parts as there are issues to be determined. NY R USDCTS&ED Civ Rule 7.1(a)(2). Refer to the General Requirements section of this document for information on the opposing papers.

ii. *Responsive statement of material facts.* The papers opposing a motion for summary judgment shall include a correspondingly numbered paragraph responding to each numbered paragraph in the statement of the moving party, and if necessary, additional paragraphs containing a separate, short and concise statement of additional material facts as to which it is contended that there exists a genuine issue to be tried. NY R USDCTS&ED Civ Rule 56.1(b).

- Each numbered paragraph in the statement of material facts set forth in the statement required to be served by the moving party will be deemed to be admitted for purposes of the motion unless specifically controverted by a correspondingly numbered paragraph in the statement required to be served by the opposing party. NY R USDCTS&ED Civ Rule 56.1(c).

- Each statement by the movant or opponent pursuant to NY R USDCTS&ED Civ Rule 56.1(a) and NY R USDCTS&ED Civ Rule 56.1(b), including each statement controverting any statement of material fact, must be followed by citation to evidence which would be admissible, set forth as required by FRCP 56(c). NY R USDCTS&ED Civ Rule 56.1(d).

iii. *Certificate of service.* FRCP 5(d) requires that the person making service under FRCP 5 certify that service has been effected. FRCP 5(Advisory Committee Notes). Having such information on file may be useful for many purposes, including proof of service if an issue arises concerning the effectiveness of the service. FRCP 5(Advisory Committee Notes).

- Such paper service [on attorneys and pro se parties who are not Filing or Receiving Users] must be documented by electronically filing proof of service. NY R USDCTSD CM/ECF, S.D.(I)(9)(9.2); NY R USDCTSD CM/ECF, S.D.(I)(19)(19.3)(b). Pro se parties who are not Filing Users are exempt from that portion of NY R USDCTSD CM/ECF, S.D.(I)(19)(19.3) requiring proof of service to be filed electronically. NY R USDCTSD CM/ECF, S.D.(I)(19)(19.3).

b. *Supplemental documents*

    i. *Supporting evidence.* When a motion relies on facts outside the record, the court may hear the matter on affidavits or may hear it wholly or partly on oral testimony or on depositions. FRCP 43(c). Except for letter-motions as permitted by NY R USDCTS&ED Civ Rule 7.1(d) or as otherwise permitted by the Court, all oppositions and replies with respect to motions shall comply with NY R USDCTS&ED Civ Rule 7.1(a)(3). NY R USDCTS&ED Civ Rule 7.1(b). Except for letter-motions as permitted by NY R USDCTS&ED Civ Rule 7.1(d) or as otherwise permitted by the Court, all motions shall include the following motion papers: supporting affidavits and exhibits thereto containing any factual information and portions of the record necessary for the decision of the motion. NY R USDCTS&ED Civ Rule 7.1(a)(3).

- *Supporting factual positions.* A party asserting that a fact cannot be or is genuinely disputed must support the assertion by: (1) citing to particular parts of materials in the record, including depositions, documents, electronically stored information, affidavits or declarations, stipulations (including those made for purposes of the motion only), admissions, interrogatory answers, or other materials; or (2) showing that the materials cited do not establish the absence or presence of a genuine dispute, or that an adverse party cannot produce admissible evidence to support the fact. FRCP 56(c)(1).

- *Objection that a fact is not supported by admissible evidence.* A party may object that the material cited to support or dispute a fact cannot be presented in a form that would be admissible in evidence. FRCP 56(c)(2).

- *Materials not cited.* The court need consider only the cited materials, but it may consider other materials in the record. FRCP 56(c)(3).

- *Affidavits or declarations.* An affidavit or declaration used to support or oppose a motion must be made on personal knowledge, set out facts that would be admissible in evidence, and show that the affiant or declarant is competent to testify on the matters stated. FRCP 56(c)(4).

- *Discovery materials.* A party seeking or opposing relief under FRCP 26 through FRCP 37 inclusive, or making or opposing any other motion or application, shall quote or attach only those portions of the depositions, interrogatories, requests for documents, requests for admissions, or other discovery or disclosure materials, together with the responses and objections thereto, that are the subject of the discovery motion or application, or that are cited in papers submitted in connection with any other motion or application. NY R USDCTS&ED Civ Rule 5.1.

    ii. *Notice of constitutional question.* A party that files a pleading, written motion, or other paper drawing into question the constitutionality of a federal or state statute must promptly:

- *File notice.* File a notice of constitutional question stating the question and identifying the paper that raises it, if: (1) a federal statute is questioned and the parties do not include the United States, one of its agencies, or one of its officers or employees in an official capacity; or (2) a state statute is questioned and the parties do not include the state, one of its agencies, or one of its officers or employees in an official capacity; and

- *Serve notice.* Serve the notice and paper on the Attorney General of the United States if a federal statute is questioned—or on the state attorney general if a state statute is questioned—either by certified or registered mail or by sending it to an electronic address designated by the attorney general for this purpose. FRCP 5.1(a).

- *No forfeiture.* A party's failure to file and serve the notice, or the court's failure to certify, does not forfeit a constitutional claim or defense that is otherwise timely asserted. FRCP 5.1(d).

    iii. *Copies of authorities.* In cases involving a pro se litigant, counsel shall, when serving a memorandum of law (or other submissions to the Court), provide the pro se litigant (but not other counsel or the Court) with copies of cases and other authorities cited therein that are unpublished or reported exclusively on computerized databases. Upon request, counsel shall provide the pro se litigant with copies of such unpublished cases and other authorities as are cited in a decision of the Court and were not previously cited by any party. NY R USDCTS&ED Civ Rule 7.2.

    iv. *Statement explaining untimely electronic filing.* If you missed a filing deadline when the ECF system was out of order, attach a statement to your filing explaining how the interruption in service prevented you from filing in a timely fashion. NY R USDCTSD CM/ECF, S.D.(II)(23)(23.5).

    v. *Courtesy copies.* Read the judge's Individual Practices to learn if courtesy copies are required. NY R USDCTSD CM/ECF, S.D.(II)(13)(13.17). Judges' Individual Practices should continue to be followed with respect to delivery of courtesy copies. NY R USDCTSD CM/ECF, S.D.(I)(3)(3.4).

3. *Individual judge practices.* Refer to the Miscellaneous section of this document for information on individual judge practices on required documents.

## E. Format

1. *Form of documents.* The rules governing captions and other matters of form in pleadings apply to motions and other papers. FRCP 7(b)(2).

    a. *Paper.* Every pleading, written motion, and other paper must: be plainly written, typed, printed, or copied without erasures or interlineations which materially deface it. NY R USDCTS&ED Civ Rule 11.1(a)(1).

    b. *Typeface, margin, and spacing.* The typeface, margins, and spacing of all documents presented for filing must meet the following requirements:

        i. All text must be twelve (12) point type or larger, except for text in footnotes which may be ten (10) point type;

        ii. All documents must have at least one (1) inch margins on all sides;

        iii. All text must be double-spaced, except for headings, text in footnotes, or block quotations, which may be single-spaced. NY R USDCTS&ED Civ Rule 11.1(b).

    c. *Caption; Names of parties.* Every pleading must have a caption with the court's name, a title, a file number, and a FRCP 7(a) designation. The title of the complaint must name all the parties; the title of other pleadings, after naming the first party on each side, may refer generally to other parties. FRCP 10(a). Every pleading, written motion, and other paper must: bear the docket number and the initials of the District Judge and any Magistrate Judge before whom the action or proceeding is pending, NY R USDCTS&ED Civ Rule 11.1(a)(2).

    d. *Paragraphs; Separate statements.* A party must state its claims or defenses in numbered paragraphs, each limited as far as practicable to a single set of circumstances. A later pleading may refer by number to a paragraph in an earlier pleading. If doing so would promote clarity, each claim founded on a separate transaction or occurrence—and each defense other than a denial—must be stated in a separate count or defense. FRCP 10(b).

    e. *Adoption by reference; Exhibits.* A statement in a pleading may be adopted by reference elsewhere in the same pleading or in any other pleading or motion. A copy of a written instrument that is an exhibit to a pleading is a part of the pleading for all purposes. FRCP 10(c).

    f. *Acceptance by the clerk.* The clerk must not refuse to file a paper solely because it is not in the form prescribed by the Federal Rules of Civil Procedure or by a local rule or practice. FRCP 5(d)(4).

2. *Form of electronic documents*

    a. *PDF-A.* All documents electronically filed on the ECF system must be in PDF-A format (portable document format). A PDF-A file is created using PDF writer software such as Adobe Acrobat (go to the Adobe website for details). PDF-A files cannot be altered, providing security to the filer and the Court. NY R USDCTSD CM/ECF, S.D.(II)(23)(23.2).

    b. *Size limitation.* No single PDF file may be larger than four megabytes (4 MB). If the filing is too large, the ECF system will not allow it to be filed, and you will not see a Notice of Electronic Filing

(NEF or filing receipt) screen. To determine the size of an Adobe Acrobat PDF file click on File, Document Properties, Summary. NY R USDCTSD CM/ECF, S.D.(II)(23)(23.3).

    i.   Converting documents directly from a word processor to PDF-A format creates the smallest possible file in terms of computer memory. If that is not possible, scan your document at low resolution. Within the Adobe Acrobat program, on the "Scan Manager" screen, adjust the settings for black and white and 200 dpi (dots per inch). This allows more pages to fit into a single PDF-A file. If that does not work, separate an oversized file into 2 or more parts. Simply label each file 1a, 1b, 1c, etc. Only relevant excerpts of exhibits should be electronically filed. NY R USDCTSD CM/ECF, S.D.(II)(23)(23.4).

  c.  *Attachments and exhibits.* Filing Users must submit in electronic form all documents referenced as exhibits or attachments, unless the Court permits paper filing. NY R USDCTSD CM/ECF, S.D.(I)(5)(5.1).

    i.   A Filing User must submit as exhibits or attachments only those excerpts of the referenced documents that are relevant to the matter under consideration by the Court. Excerpted material must be clearly and prominently identified as such. Filing Users who file excerpts of documents as exhibits or attachments under this procedure do so without prejudice to their right to file timely additional excerpts or the complete document. Responding parties may file timely additional excerpts that they believe are relevant or the complete document. A party may move before the Court for permission to serve and file in hard copy documents that cannot be reasonably scanned. NY R USDCTSD CM/ECF, S.D.(I)(5)(5.2).

    ii.  Exhibits must be filed only as attachments to a document, such as a motion or an affidavit. Do not use the ECF Filing Event for "Motion" to file exhibits separately. Exhibits are the only items that should be attached to electronically filed documents. You are limited to electronically filing only relevant excerpts of exhibits. Excerpts must be clearly identified as such. If the exhibit is too large to be scanned and electronically filed you may contact the ECF Help Desk. NY R USDCTSD CM/ECF, S.D.(II)(15)(15.6).

  d.  *Letters.* Parties should consult the assigned judge's Individual Practices to determine if the judge accepts letters at all and, if he or she does, whether the judge has any page limitations on letters and/or requires courtesy copies of letters filed on ECF (and, if so, by what means of delivery). All letters addressed to the Court must include a subject line with the case name and docket number (e.g., "Re: Doe v. Smith, 13 Civ. 1234 (ABC)"). NY R USDCTSD CM/ECF, S.D.(II)(13)(13.1).

  e.  *Proposed orders, proposed judgments, stipulations and consents.* Any document that requires the signature of a judge should not be electronically filed except as an exhibit to another document. Proposed orders, judgments, stipulations and consents should not be submitted through the ECF system. Instead they should be sent by e-mail to the Clerk. Proposed orders should be submitted in word processing format (WordPerfect or Word) rather than as a PDF document. Stipulations should be submitted in PDF-A format. Stipulations must contain ink signatures not s/. Faxed or emailed signatures are acceptable. Please note that Stipulations of Voluntary Dismissal pursuant to FRCP 41(a)(1)(A)(ii) do not require the signature of a judge and must be electronically filed on the ECF system. Questions may be directed to the Orders and Judgments Clerk at the phone numbers listed in NY R USDCTSD CM/ECF, S.D.(II)(18)(18.3). NY R USDCTSD CM/ECF, S.D.(II)(18)(18.3).

    i.   Email the proposed order, judgment or stipulation to the email addresses listed in NY R USDCTSD CM/ECF, S.D.(II)(18)(18.3). NY R USDCTSD CM/ECF, S.D.(II)(18)(18.3).

    ii.  Pro se litigants who are not Filing Users are exempt from that portion of NY R USDCTSD CM/ECF, S.D.(II)(18)(18.3) that requires litigants to email proposed orders, judgments, stipulations and consents, and shall deliver such documents to the Clerk's Office in paper form. NY R USDCTSD CM/ECF, S.D.(II)(18)(18.3).

3.  *Signing of pleadings, motions and other papers*

  a.  *Signature.* Every pleading, written motion, and other paper must be signed by at least one attorney of record in the attorney's name—or by a party personally if the party is unrepresented. The paper must state the signer's address, e-mail address, and telephone number. FRCP 11(a). Every pleading,

written motion, and other paper must: have the name of each person signing it clearly printed or typed directly below the signature. NY R USDCTS&ED Civ Rule 11.1(a)(3).

i. *Electronic signatures.* The user log-in and password required to submit documents to the ECF system serve as the Filing User's signature on all electronic documents filed with the Court. NY R USDCTSD CM/ECF, S.D.(I)(8)(8.1); NY R USDCTSD CM/ECF, S.D.(II)(13)(13.14). They also serve as a signature for purposes of the Federal Rules of Civil Procedure, including FRCP 11, the Local Civil Rules of the United States District Courts for the Southern and Eastern Districts of New York, and any other purpose for which a signature is required in connection with proceedings before the Court. NY R USDCTSD CM/ECF, S.D.(I)(8)(8.1).

- *Signature block.* Electronically filed documents must include a signature block and must set forth the name, address, telephone number and e-mail address all in compliance with the Federal Rules of Civil Procedure and NY R USDCTS&ED Civ Rule 11.1. In the absence of a scanned signature image, the name of the Filing User under whose log-in and password the document is submitted must be preceded by an "s/" typed in the space where the signature would otherwise appear. NY R USDCTSD CM/ECF, S.D.(I)(8)(8.2); NY R USDCTSD CM/ECF, S.D.(II)(13)(13.14).

- *Documents requiring the signature of a party or witness.* A document requiring the signature of a party or witness shall be electronically filed in a scanned format that contains an image of the actual signature. NY R USDCTSD CM/ECF, S.D.(I)(8)(8.4); NY R USDCTSD CM/ECF, S.D.(II)(13)(13.14).

- *Documents requiring the signature of a judge.* A Filing User submitting a document electronically that requires a judge's signature must promptly deliver the document in such other form, if any, as the Court requires. NY R USDCTSD CM/ECF, S.D.(I)(4)(4.2).

- *Documents requiring multiple signatures.* Documents requiring signatures of more than one party must be electronically filed either by: (a) submitting a scanned document containing all necessary signatures; (b) representing the consent of the other parties on the document; (c) identifying on the document the parties whose signatures are required and by the submission of a notice of endorsement by the other parties no later than three business days after filing; or (d) in any other manner approved by the Court. NY R USDCTSD CM/ECF, S.D.(I)(8)(8.5).

ii. *No verification or accompanying affidavit required for pleadings.* Unless a rule or statute specifically states otherwise, a pleading need not be verified or accompanied by an affidavit. FRCP 11(a).

iii. *Unsigned papers.* The court must strike an unsigned paper unless the omission is promptly corrected after being called to the attorney's or party's attention. FRCP 11(a).

b. *Representations to the court.* By presenting to the court a pleading, written motion, or other paper—whether by signing, filing, submitting, or later advocating it—an attorney or unrepresented party certifies that to the best of the person's knowledge, information, and belief, formed after an inquiry reasonable under the circumstances:

i. It is not being presented for any improper purpose, such as to harass, cause unnecessary delay, or needlessly increase the cost of litigation;

ii. The claims, defenses, and other legal contentions are warranted by existing law or by a nonfrivolous argument for extending, modifying, or reversing existing law or for establishing new law;

iii. The factual contentions have evidentiary support or, if specifically so identified, will likely have evidentiary support after a reasonable opportunity for further investigation or discovery; and

iv. The denials of factual contentions are warranted on the evidence or, if specifically so identified, are reasonably based on belief or a lack of information. FRCP 11(b).

c. *Sanctions.* If, after notice and a reasonable opportunity to respond, the court determines that FRCP 11(b) has been violated, the court may impose an appropriate sanction on any attorney, law firm, or

party that violated FRCP 11(b) or is responsible for the violation. FRCP 11(c)(1). Refer to the United States District Court for the Southern District of New York KeyRules Motion for Sanctions document for more information.

4. *Privacy protection for filings made with the court*

   a. *Redacted filings.* Unless the court orders otherwise, in an electronic or paper filing with the court that contains an individual's Social Security number, taxpayer-identification number, or birth date, the name of an individual known to be a minor, or a financial-account number, a party or nonparty making the filing may include only:

      i. The last four (4) digits of the Social Security number and taxpayer-identification number;

      ii. The year of the individual's birth;

      iii. The minor's initials; and

      iv. The last four (4) digits of the financial-account number. FRCP 5.2(a); NY R USDCTSD CM/ECF, S.D.(II)(21)(21.3).

      v. Caution should be exercised when filing documents that contain the following:

         • Personal identifying numbers (PIN #'s), such as a driver's license number;

         • Medical records, treatment and diagnosis;

         • Employment history;

         • Individual financial information;

         • Proprietary or trade secret information;

         • Information regarding an individual's cooperation with the government. NY R US-DCTSD CM/ECF, S.D.(II)(21)(21.4).

   b. *Exemptions from the redaction requirement.* The redaction requirement does not apply to the following:

      i. A financial-account number that identifies the property allegedly subject to forfeiture in a forfeiture proceeding;

      ii. The record of an administrative or agency proceeding;

      iii. The official record of a state-court proceeding;

      iv. The record of a court or tribunal, if that record was not subject to the redaction requirement when originally filed;

      v. A filing covered by FRCP 5.2(c) or FRCP 5.2(d); and

      vi. A pro se filing in an action brought under 28 U.S.C.A. § 2241, 28 U.S.C.A. § 2254, or 28 U.S.C.A. § 2255. FRCP 5.2(b).

   c. *Limitations on remote access to electronic files; Social Security appeals and immigration cases.* Unless the court orders otherwise, in an action for benefits under the Social Security Act, and in an action or proceeding relating to an order of removal, to relief from removal, or to immigration benefits or detention, access to an electronic file is authorized as follows:

      i. The parties and their attorneys may have remote electronic access to any part of the case file, including the administrative record;

      ii. Any other person may have electronic access to the full record at the courthouse, but may have remote electronic access only to:

         • The docket maintained by the court; and

         • An opinion, order, judgment, or other disposition of the court, but not any other part of the case file or the administrative record. FRCP 5.2(c).

   d. *Filings made under seal.* The court may order that a filing be made under seal without redaction. The court may later unseal the filing or order the person who made the filing to file a redacted version for the public record. FRCP 5.2(d). For more information on sealing documents, refer to NY R USDCTSD CM/ECF, S.D.(I)(6).

e. *Protective orders.* For good cause, the court may by order in a case:

   i.   Require redaction of additional information; or

   ii.  Limit or prohibit a nonparty's remote electronic access to a document filed with the court. FRCP 5.2(e).

f. *Option for additional unredacted filing under seal.* A person making a redacted filing may also file an unredacted copy under seal. The court must retain the unredacted copy as part of the record. FRCP 5.2(f); NY R USDCTSD CM/ECF, S.D.(II)(21)(21.5).

g. *Option for filing a reference list.* A filing that contains redacted information may be filed together with a reference list that identifies each item of redacted information and specifies an appropriate identifier that uniquely corresponds to each item listed. The list must be filed under seal and may be amended as of right. Any reference in the case to a listed identifier will be construed to refer to the corresponding item of information. FRCP 5.2(g); NY R USDCTSD CM/ECF, S.D.(II)(21)(21.5).

h. *Responsibility for redaction.* It is the sole responsibility of counsel and the parties to be sure that all documents comply with the rules of this Court requiring redaction of personal identifiers. Neither the judge nor the Clerk of Court will review documents for compliance with these rules. NY R USDCTSD CM/ECF, S.D.(II)(21)(21.2).

i. *Waiver of protection of identifiers.* A person waives the protection of FRCP 5.2(a) as to the person's own information by filing it without redaction and not under seal. FRCP 5.2(h).

j. For more information on privacy and public access to ECF cases, refer to NY R USDCTSD CM/ECF, S.D.(II)(21).

5. *Individual judge practices.* Refer to the Miscellaneous section of this document for information on individual judge practices on formatting documents.

## F. Filing and Service Requirements

1. *Filing requirements.* Any paper after the complaint that is required to be served—together with a certificate of service—must be filed within a reasonable time after service. FRCP 5(d)(1). Complaints and all subsequent papers are accepted at either courthouse, regardless of the place for which the case is designated. NY R USDCTSD Div. Bus., Rule 22. Subject to the instructions regarding ECF published on the website of each respective Court and any pertinent Individual Judge's Practices, letter-motions permitted by NY R USDCTS&ED Civ Rule 7.1(d) and letters addressed to the Court (but not letters between the parties) may be filed via ECF. NY R USDCTS&ED Civ Rule 5.2(b). For information on electronically filing motions, refer to NY R USDCTSD CM/ECF, S.D.(II)(15).

   a. *How filing is made; In general.* A paper is filed by delivering it:

      i.   To the clerk; or

      ii.  To a judge who agrees to accept it for filing, and who must then note the filing date on the paper and promptly send it to the clerk. FRCP 5(d)(2).

   b. *Night depository.* A night depository with an automatic date stamp shall be maintained by the Clerk of the Southern District in the Pearl Street Courthouse. After regular business hours, papers for the District Court only may be deposited in the night depository. Such papers will be considered as having been filed in the District Court as of the date stamped thereon, which shall be deemed presumptively correct. NY R USDCTS&ED Civ Rule 1.2.

   c. *Electronic filing*

      i.   *Authorization of electronic filing program.* A court may, by local rule, allow papers to be filed, signed, or verified by electronic means that are consistent with any technical standards established by the Judicial Conference of the United States. A local rule may require electronic filing only if reasonable exceptions are allowed. A paper filed electronically in compliance with a local rule is a written paper for purposes of the Federal Rules of Civil Procedure. FRCP 5(d)(3).

           • The Court will accept for filing documents submitted, signed or verified by electronic means, that comply with the rules in NY R USDCTSD CM/ECF, S.D. NY R USDCTSD

CM/ECF, S.D.(I). The information in NY R USDCTSD CM/ECF, S.D. applies only to cases assigned to the ECF system. NY R USDCTSD CM/ECF, S.D.(Introduction).

- Parties serving and filing papers shall follow the instructions regarding Electronic Case Filing (ECF) published on the website of each respective Court. A paper served and filed by electronic means in accordance with such instructions is, for purposes of FRCP 5, served and filed in compliance with the Local Civil Rules of the Southern and Eastern Districts of New York. NY R USDCTS&ED Civ Rule 5.2(a). Parties have an obligation to review the Court's actual order, decree, or judgment (on ECF), which controls, and should not rely on the description on the docket or in the ECF Notice of Electronic Filing (NEF). NY R USDCTS&ED Civ Rule 5.2(c).

- The following should be observed when filing electronically: (1) the Federal Rules of Civil Procedure, (2) the Local Civil Rules of the United States District Courts for the Southern and Eastern Districts of New York, (3) the assigned judge's Individual Practices, and (4) the Court's Electronic Case Filing Rules & Instructions (NY R USDCTSD CM/ECF, S.D.). NY R USDCTSD CM/ECF, S.D.(Introduction).

ii. *Scope of electronic filing.* Except as expressly provided and in exceptional circumstances preventing a party from filing electronically, all documents required to be filed with the Court must be filed electronically. Any party unable to comply with this requirement must seek permission of the Court to file in the traditional manner, on paper. Any such application made after regular business hours may be submitted through the night depository box maintained pursuant to NY R USDCTS&ED Civ Rule 1.2. NY R USDCTSD CM/ECF, S.D.(I)(1)(1.1).

- *Documents filed by pro se litigants.* Unless otherwise ordered by the Court, documents filed by pro se litigants must be filed in the traditional manner, on paper, and will be scanned and docketed by the Clerk's Office into the ECF system. NY R USDCTSD CM/ECF, S.D.(I)(1)(1.1). Pro se litigants must file pleadings and documents in the traditional manner on paper unless the assigned judge has granted permission to electronically file on the ECF system. NY R USDCTSD CM/ECF, S.D.(Introduction).

- *Letters.* Except for letters to be filed under seal, letters addressed to judges who accept letters may be filed electronically. Parties should consult the assigned judge's Individual Practices to determine if the judge accepts letters at all and, if he or she does, whether the judge has any page limitations on letters and/or requires courtesy copies of letters filed on ECF (and, if so, by what means of delivery). NY R USDCTSD CM/ECF, S.D.(II)(13)(13.1). Letters solely between parties or their counsel or otherwise not addressed to the Court may not be filed electronically on ECF (except as exhibits to an otherwise properly filed document). NY R USDCTSD CM/ECF, S.D.(II)(13)(13.1). For more information on filing letters, refer to NY R USDCTSD CM/ECF, S.D.(II)(13)(13.1).

- *Proposed orders, judgments and decrees.* Proposed orders, judgments and decrees shall be presented as directed by the ECF rules published on the website of each respective Court. NY R USDCTS&ED Civ Rule 77.1. For more information, refer to NY R USDCTS&ED Civ Rule 77.1.

iii. *Exceptions to electronic filing.* In an ECF case, the documents that should not be electronically filed include:

- Miscellaneous Case initiating documents, NY R USDCTSD CM/ECF, S.D.(II)(18)(18.2);

- Proposed orders; proposed judgments, stipulations; consents, NY R USDCTSD CM/ECF, S.D.(II)(18)(18.3);

- Orders to show cause / temporary restraining orders, NY R USDCTSD CM/ECF, S.D.(II)(18)(18.4);

- Sealed documents, NY R USDCTSD CM/ECF, S.D.(II)(18)(18.5); and

- Surety bonds, NY R USDCTSD CM/ECF, S.D.(II)(18)(18.6).

- In cases where the record of an administrative or other prior proceeding must be filed with the Court, such record may be served and filed in hard copy without prior motion and order of the Court. NY R USDCTSD CM/ECF, S.D.(I)(5)(5.3).

- For more documents excepted from electronic filing, and for more information on such documents, refer to NY R USDCTSD CM/ECF, S.D.(II)(18).

    iv. *Consequences of electronic filing.* Except as otherwise provided in NY R USDCTSD CM/ECF, S.D.(I)(4), electronic filing of a document in the ECF system consistent with these procedures, together with the transmission of a Notice of Electronic Filing (NEF) from the Court, constitutes filing of the document for all purposes of the Federal Rules of Civil Procedure and the Local Civil Rules of the United States District Courts for the Southern and Eastern Districts of New York and constitutes entry of the document on the docket kept by the Clerk under FRCP 58 and FRCP 79. NY R USDCTSD CM/ECF, S.D.(I)(3)(3.1).

    v. For more information on electronic filing, refer to NY R USDCTSD CM/ECF, S.D.

2. *Service requirements*

  a. *Service; When required*

    i. *In general.* Unless the Federal Rules of Civil Procedure provide otherwise, each of the following papers must be served on every party:

- An order stating that service is required;
- A pleading filed after the original complaint, unless the court orders otherwise under FRCP 5(c) because there are numerous defendants;
- A discovery paper required to be served on a party, unless the court orders otherwise;
- A written motion, except one that may be heard ex parte; and
- A written notice, appearance, demand, or offer of judgment, or any similar paper. FRCP 5(a)(1).

    ii. *If a party fails to appear.* No service is required on a party who is in default for failing to appear. But a pleading that asserts a new claim for relief against such a party must be served on that party under FRCP 4. FRCP 5(a)(2).

    iii. *Seizing property.* If an action is begun by seizing property and no person is or need be named as a defendant, any service required before the filing of an appearance, answer, or claim must be made on the person who had custody or possession of the property when it was seized. FRCP 5(a)(3).

  b. *Service; How made*

    i. *Serving an attorney.* If a party is represented by an attorney, service under FRCP 5 must be made on the attorney unless the court orders service on the party. FRCP 5(b)(1).

    ii. *Service in general.* A paper is served under FRCP 5 by:

- Handing it to the person;
- Leaving it: (1) at the person's office with a clerk or other person in charge or, if no one is in charge, in a conspicuous place in the office; or (2) if the person has no office or the office is closed, at the person's dwelling or usual place of abode with someone of suitable age and discretion who resides there;
- Mailing it to the person's last known address—in which event service is complete upon mailing;
- Leaving it with the court clerk if the person has no known address;
- Sending it by electronic means if the person consented in writing—in which event service is complete upon transmission, but is not effective if the serving party learns that it did not reach the person to be served; or
- Delivering it by any other means that the person consented to in writing—in which event service is complete when the person making service delivers it to the agency designated to make delivery. FRCP 5(b)(2).

iii. *Service by overnight delivery.* Service upon an attorney may be made by overnight delivery service. "Overnight delivery service" means any delivery service which regularly accepts items for overnight delivery. Overnight delivery service shall be deemed service by mail for purposes of FRCP 5 and FRCP 6. NY R USDCTS&ED Civ Rule 5.3.

iv. *Service by electronic means.* Parties serving and filing papers shall follow the instructions regarding Electronic Case Filing (ECF) published on the website of each respective Court. A paper served and filed by electronic means in accordance with such instructions is, for purposes of FRCP 5, served and filed in compliance with the Local Civil Rules of the United States District Courts for the Southern and Eastern Districts of New York. NY R USDCTS&ED Civ Rule 5.2(a). Parties have an obligation to review the Court's actual order, decree, or judgment (on ECF), which controls, and should not rely on the description on the docket or in the ECF Notice of Electronic Filing (NEF). NY R USDCTS&ED Civ Rule 5.2(c).

- *Notice of electronic filing (NEF).* In cases assigned to the ECF system, service is complete provided all parties receive a Notice of Electronic Filing (NEF), which is sent automatically by email from the Court (see the NEF for a list of who did/did not receive notice electronically). Transmission of the NEF constitutes service upon all Filing and Receiving Users who are listed as recipients of notice by electronic mail. NY R USDCTSD CM/ECF, S.D.(I)(9)(9.1). In cases assigned to the ECF system, if all parties receive a NEF, service is complete upon transmission of the NEF by the Court, and you are not required to serve a paper copy. NY R USDCTSD CM/ECF, S.D.(II)(19)(19.2). It remains the duty of Filing and Receiving Users to maintain current contact information with the court and to regularly review the docket sheet of the case. NY R USDCTSD CM/ECF, S.D.(I)(9)(9.1).

- *Mailing of court-initiated documents.* The Clerk's Office will no longer mail paper copies of court-initiated documents to Filing and Receiving Users. The Clerk's Office will mail copies of all court-initiated documents to pro se parties who have not registered as Filing or Receiving Users. NY R USDCTSD CM/ECF, S.D.(II)(19)(19.1).

- *No receipt of a NEF.* If any party does not receive a NEF, you are required to accomplish service on that party in the traditional manner, in paper form. NY R USDCTSD CM/ECF, S.D.(II)(19)(19.2). The NEF receipt will inform you who will receive notice of the filing "electronically" (by e-mail from the Court) and who will receive notice "by other means" (traditional service in paper form). NY R USDCTSD CM/ECF, S.D.(II)(19)(19.2).

- *Service on non-filing or non-receiving users.* Attorneys and pro se parties who are not Filing or Receiving Users must be served with a paper copy of any electronically filed pleading or other document. Service of such paper copy must be made according to the Federal Rules of Civil Procedure and the Local Civil Rules of the United States District Courts for the Southern and Eastern Districts of New York. NY R USDCTSD CM/ECF, S.D.(I)(9)(9.2). Such paper service must be documented by electronically filing proof of service. NY R USDCTSD CM/ECF, S.D.(I)(9)(9.2); NY R USDCTSD CM/ECF, S.D.(II)(19)(19.2). Where the Clerk scans and electronically files pleadings and documents on behalf of a pro se party, the associated NEF constitutes service. NY R USDCTSD CM/ECF, S.D.(I)(9)(9.2).

- For more information on service by electronic means, refer to NY R USDCTSD CM/ECF, S.D.(II)(19).

v. *Using court facilities.* If a local rule so authorizes, a party may use the court's transmission facilities to make service under FRCP 5(b)(2)(E). FRCP 5(b)(3).

c. *Serving numerous defendants*

i. *In general.* If an action involves an unusually large number of defendants, the court may, on motion or on its own, order that:

- Defendants' pleadings and replies to them need not be served on other defendants;

- Any crossclaim, counterclaim, avoidance, or affirmative defense in those pleadings and replies to them will be treated as denied or avoided by all other parties; and

- Filing any such pleading and serving it on the plaintiff constitutes notice of the pleading to all parties. FRCP 5(c)(1).

ii. *Notifying parties.* A copy of every such order must be served on the parties as the court directs. FRCP 5(c)(2).

3. *Individual judge practices.* Refer to the Miscellaneous section of this document for information on individual judge practices on filing and serving documents.

## G. Hearings

1. *Hearings, generally*

   a. *Oral argument.* Due process does not require that oral argument be permitted on a motion and, except as otherwise provided by local rule, the district court has discretion to determine whether it will decide the motion on the papers or hear argument by counsel (and perhaps receive evidence). FPP § 1190; F.D.I.C. v. Deglau, 207 F.3d 153 (3d Cir. 2000). The parties and their attorneys shall only appear to argue the motion if so directed by the Court by order or by a Judge's Individual Practice. NY R USDCTS&ED Civ Rule 6.1(c).

   b. *Providing a regular schedule for oral hearings.* A court may establish regular times and places for oral hearings on motions. FRCP 78(a).

   c. *Providing for submission on briefs.* By rule or order, the court may provide for submitting and determining motions on briefs, without oral hearings. FRCP 78(b).

2. *Hearing on motion for summary judgment.* Even though FRCP 56(c) makes reference to a hearing on the motion for summary judgment, FRCP 56 confers no right to an oral hearing on the summary judgment motion, nor is a hearing required by due process considerations. FEDPROC § 62:673; Forjan v. Leprino Foods, Inc., 209 Fed.Appx. 8, 2006 WL 3623496 (2d Cir. 2006).

   a. *Oral argument.* Oral argument on a motion for summary judgment may be considered ordinarily appropriate, so that as a general rule, a district court should grant a request for oral argument on all but frivolous summary judgment motions, or a nonmovant's request for oral argument must be granted unless summary judgment is also denied, according to some courts. FEDPROC § 62:674; Season-All Industries, Inc. v. Turkiye Sise Ve Cam Fabrikalari, A. S., 425 F.2d 34 (3d Cir. 1970); Houston v. Bryan, 725 F.2d 516 (9th Cir. 1984); Fernhoff v. Tahoe Regional Planning Agency, 803 F.2d 979 (9th Cir. 1986).

      i. Oral argument on a summary judgment motion may be deemed waived where the opposing party does not request it. FEDPROC § 62:674; McCormack v. Citibank, N.A., 100 F.3d 532, 30 UCC Rep.Serv.2d 1175 (8th Cir. 1996).

3. *Individual judge practices.* Refer to the Miscellaneous section of this document for information on individual judge practices on hearings.

## H. Forms

## 1. Federal Motion for Summary Judgment Forms

   a. Answer; To plaintiff's motion for summary judgment. AMJUR PP SUMMARY § 56.

   b. Affidavit opposing defendant's motion for summary judgment; By plaintiff. AMJUR PP SUMMARY § 64.

   c. Affidavit opposing motion for summary judgment; By party; Dispute as to issues of fact. AMJUR PP SUMMARY § 73.

   d. Affidavit opposing motion for summary judgment; By party; Inability to present facts. AMJUR PP SUMMARY § 74.

   e. Affidavit opposing motion for summary judgment; By party; Good defense to part of claim. AMJUR PP SUMMARY § 77.

   f. Statement of disputed and undisputed material facts; In opposition to motion for summary judgment. AMJUR PP SUMMARY § 89.

   g. Motion and notice of motion for summary judgment. 4 FEDFORMS § 4708.

h. Motion for summary judgment by plaintiff. 4 FEDFORMS § 4709.

i. Motion for summary judgment by defendant. 4 FEDFORMS § 4713.

j. Motion for summary judgment by defendant; Claims of plaintiff and counterclaims of defendant. 4 FEDFORMS § 4717.

k. Motion for summary judgment by defendant; Interpleader against another claimant. 4 FEDFORMS § 4718.

l. Motion for summary judgment by defendant; Failure of plaintiff to produce evidence. 4 FED-FORMS § 4719.

m. Motion for summary judgment by defendant; Statute of limitations. 4 FEDFORMS § 4720.

n. Notice of motion for summary judgment. 4 FEDFORMS § 4744.

o. Affidavit in support of motion for summary judgment. 4 FEDFORMS § 4773.

p. Movant's contention there are no genuine issues of material facts. 4 FEDFORMS § 4776.

q. Opposition to statement of uncontested material facts. 4 FEDFORMS § 4777.

r. Response to movant's contention there are no genuine issues with respect to listed material facts. 4 FEDFORMS § 4778.

s. Motion; For summary judgment; By claimant. FEDPROF § 1:1298.

t. Motion; For summary judgment; By defending party. FEDPROF § 1:1302.

u. Motion; By plaintiff; For partial summary judgment. FEDPROF § 1:1305.

v. Notice of cross motion; For summary judgment; By defending party. FEDPROF § 1:1306.

w. Statement of material facts; In support of summary judgment motion. FEDPROF § 1:1311.

x. Statement in support of defendant's summary judgment motion; By codefendant. FEDPROF § 1:1312.

y. Affidavit; Opposing claimant's motion for summary judgment; Witnesses unavailable. FEDPROF § 1:1316.

z. Affidavit; Opposing part of claim. FEDPROF § 1:1317.

**2. Forms for the Southern District of New York**

a. Notice to pro se litigant who opposes a motion for summary judgment. NY R USDCTS&ED Civ Rule 56.2.

## I. Applicable Rules

1. *Federal rules*

a. Serving and filing pleadings and other papers. FRCP 5.

b. Constitutional challenge to a statute; Notice, certification, and intervention. FRCP 5.1.

c. Privacy protection for filings made with the court. FRCP 5.2.

d. Computing and extending time; Time for motion papers. FRCP 6.

e. Pleadings allowed; Form of motions and other papers. FRCP 7.

f. Disclosure statement. FRCP 7.1.

g. Form of pleadings. FRCP 10.

h. Signing pleadings, motions, and other papers; Representations to the court; Sanctions. FRCP 11.

i. Defenses and objections; When and how presented; Motion for judgment on the pleadings; Consolidating motions; Waiving defenses; Pretrial hearing. FRCP 12.

j. Taking testimony. FRCP 43.

k. Summary judgment. FRCP 56.

l. Hearing motions; Submission on briefs. FRCP 78.

2. *Local rules*

    a.   Night depository. NY R USDCTS&ED Civ Rule 1.2.

    b.   Duty of attorneys in related cases. NY R USDCTS&ED Civ Rule 1.6.

    c.   Filing of discovery materials. NY R USDCTS&ED Civ Rule 5.1.

    d.   Electronic service and filing of documents. NY R USDCTS&ED Civ Rule 5.2.

    e.   Service by overnight delivery. NY R USDCTS&ED Civ Rule 5.3.

    f.   Service and filing of motion papers. NY R USDCTS&ED Civ Rule 6.1.

    g.   Orders on motions. NY R USDCTS&ED Civ Rule 6.2.

    h.   Computation of time. NY R USDCTS&ED Civ Rule 6.4.

    i.   Motion papers. NY R USDCTS&ED Civ Rule 7.1.

    j.   Disclosure statement. NY R USDCTS&ED Civ Rule 7.1.1.

    k.   Authorities to be provided to pro se litigants. NY R USDCTS&ED Civ Rule 7.2.

    l.   Form of pleadings, motions, and other papers. NY R USDCTS&ED Civ Rule 11.1.

    m.   Statements of material facts on motion for summary judgment. NY R USDCTS&ED Civ Rule 56.1.

    n.   Notice to pro se litigant who opposes a summary judgment. NY R USDCTS&ED Civ Rule 56.2.

    o.   Submission of orders, judgments and decrees. NY R USDCTS&ED Civ Rule 77.1.

    p.   Alternative dispute resolution (Southern District only). NY R USDCTS&ED Civ Rule 83.9.

    q.   Electronic case filing rules and instructions. NY R USDCTSD CM/ECF, S.D.

    r.   Related cases. NY R USDCTSD Div. Bus., Rule 13.

    s.   Filing at either courthouse. NY R USDCTSD Div. Bus., Rule 22.

## J.  Miscellaneous

**NOTE: Individual judges' rules may apply. For available judge-level information, refer to:**

DISTRICT JUDGE RONNIE ABRAMS: NY R USDCTSD Abrams-Civ Prac; NY R USDCTSD Abrams-Crim Prac; NY R USDCTSD Abrams-Pro Se; NY R USDCTSD Abrams-Case Mgt; NY R USDCTSD Abrams-Jury.

DISTRICT JUDGE DEBORAH A. BATTS: NY R USDCTSD Batts-Practices.

DISTRICT JUDGE RICHARD M. BERMAN: NY R USDCTSD Berman-Practices; NY R USDCTSD Berman-Default; NY R USDCTSD Berman-Sentencing; NY R USDCTSD Berman-Media.

DISTRICT JUDGE VINCENT L. BRICCETTI: NY R USDCTSD Briccetti-Practices; NY R USDCTSD Briccetti-Plan; NY R USDCTSD Briccetti-Notice.

DISTRICT JUDGE VERNON S. BRODERICK: NY R USDCTSD Broderick-Civil; NY R USDCTSD Broderick-Crim; NY R USDCTSD Broderick-Case Mgt; NY R USDCTSD Broderick-Jury.

DISTRICT JUDGE NAOMI REICE BUCHWALD: NY R USDCTSD Buchwald-Practices.

DISTRICT JUDGE VALERIE E. CAPRONI: NY R USDCTSD Caproni-Prac; NY R USDCTSD Caproni--Pro Se; NY R USDCTSD Caproni-Case Mgt; NY R USDCTSD Caproni-Crim Prac.

DISTRICT JUDGE ANDREW L. CARTER JR.: NY R USDCTSD Carter-Practices.

DISTRICT JUDGE KEVIN P. CASTEL: NY R USDCTSD Castel-Practices; NY R USDCTSD Castel-Default; NY R USDCTSD Castel-Scheduling; NY R USDCTSD Castel-Complex; NY R USDCTSD Castel-Trials; NY R USDCTSD Castel-Sentencing.

DISTRICT JUDGE DENISE L. COTE: NY R USDCTSD Cote-Civil Practices; NY R USDCTSD Cote-Pro Se; NY R USDCTSD Cote-Maritime Ord; NY R USDCTSD Cote-Crim Practices; NY R USDCTSD Cote-Crim Trials; NY R USDCTSD Cote-Sentencing.

DISTRICT JUDGE PAUL A. CROTTY: NY R USDCTSD Crotty-Practices; NY R USDCTSD Crotty-Sentencing; NY R USDCTSD Crotty-Calls; NY R USDCTSD Crotty-Scheduling.

DISTRICT JUDGE GEORGE B. DANIELS: NY R USDCTSD Daniels-Practices.

DISTRICT JUDGE KEVIN T. DUFFY: NY R USDCTSD Duffy-Practices.

DISTRICT JUDGE PAUL A. ENGELMAYER: NY R USDCTSD Engelmayer-Practices; NY R USDCTSD Engelmayer-Scheduling; NY R USDCTSD Engelmayer-Sentencing; NY R USDCTSD Engelmayer-Pro Se; NY R USDCTSD Engelmayer-Crim.

DISTRICT JUDGE KATHERINE POLK FAILLA: NY R USDCTSD Failla-Civ Prac; NY R USDCTSD Failla-Crim Prac; NY R USDCTSD Failla-Case Mgt.

DISTRICT JUDGE KATHERINE B. FORREST: NY R USDCTSD Forrest-Civil Prac; NY R USDCTSD Forrest-Crim Prac; NY R USDCTSD Forrest-Crim Pretrial; NY R USDCTSD Forrest-Scheduling; NY R US-DCTSD Forrest-Patent Scheduling; NY R USDCTSD Forrest-Sentencing; NY R USDCTSD Forrest-Order 1; NY R USDCTSD Forrest-Order 2.

DISTRICT JUDGE JESSE M. FURMAN: NY R USDCTSD Furman-Civil Prac; NY R USDCTSD Furman-Crim Prac; NY R USDCTSD Furman-Pro Se Prac; NY R USDCTSD Furman-Trials; NY R USDCTSD Furman-Scheduling; NY R USDCTSD Furman-Rights.

DISTRICT JUDGE PAUL G. GARDEPHE: NY R USDCTSD Gardephe-Civ Prac; NY R USDCTSD Gardephe-Pretrial; NY R USDCTSD Gardephe-Prot Ord; NY R USDCTSD Gardephe-Maritime; NY R USDCTSD Gardephe-Crim Prac; NY R USDCTSD Gardephe-Trial.

DISTRICT JUDGE THOMAS P. GRIESA: NY R USDCTSD Griesa-Practices.

DISTRICT JUDGE CHARLES S. HAIGHT: NY R USDCTSD Haight-Practices.

DISTRICT JUDGE ALVIN K. HELLERSTEIN: NY R USDCTSD Hellerstein-Practices; NY R USDCTSD Hellerstein--Sept 11.

DISTRICT JUDGE LEWIS A. KAPLAN: NY R USDCTSD Kaplan-Practices; NY R USDCTSD Kaplan-Sentencing.

DISTRICT JUDGE KENNETH M. KARAS: NY R USDCTSD Karas-Practices; NY R USDCTSD Karas-Case Mgt; NY R USDCTSD Karas-Default; NY R USDCTSD Karas-Sentencing; NY R USDCTSD Karas-Rights.

DISTRICT JUDGE JOHN F. KEENAN: NY R USDCTSD Keenan-Practices.

DISTRICT JUDGE JOHN G. KOELTL: NY R USDCTSD Koeltl-Practices.

DISTRICT JUDGE VICTOR MARRERO: NY R USDCTSD Marrero-Practices; NY R USDCTSD Marrero-Scheduling; NY R USDCTSD Marrero-Default; NY R USDCTSD Marrero-Trial Proc.

DISTRICT JUDGE COLLEEN McMAHON: NY R USDCTSD McMahon-Practices; NY R USDCTSD McMahon-RICO; NY R USDCTSD McMahon-Copies; NY R USDCTSD McMahon-Scheduling; NY R US-DCTSD McMahon-Elec Disc; NY R USDCTSD McMahon-Sentencing.

DISTRICT JUDGE ALISON J. NATHAN: NY R USDCTSD Nathan-Civ Prac; NY R USDCTSD Nathan-Crim Prac; NY R USDCTSD Nathan-Pro Se; NY R USDCTSD Nathan-Scheduling.

DISTRICT JUDGE J. PAUL OETKEN: NY R USDCTSD Oetken-Civ Prac; NY R USDCTSD Oetken-Case Mgt; NY R USDCTSD Oetken-Crim Prac; NY R USDCTSD Oetken-Pro Se.

DISTRICT JUDGE WILLIAM H. PAULEY, III: NY R USDCTSD Pauley-Crim Cases; NY R USDCTSD Pauley-Practices.

DISTRICT JUDGE LORETTA A. PRESKA: NY R USDCTSD Preska-Practices.

DISTRICT JUDGE JED S. RAKOFF: NY R USDCTSD Rakoff-Practices; NY R USDCTSD Rakoff-Scheduling; NY R USDCTSD Rakoff-Prot Ord; NY R USDCTSD Rakoff-Maritime Ord.

DISTRICT JUDGE EDGARDO RAMOS: NY R USDCTSD Ramos--Practices; NY R USDCTSD Ramos-Case Mgt.

DISTRICT JUDGE NELSON S. ROMAN: NY R USDCTSD Roman-Civ Prac; NY R USDCTSD Roman-Pro Se; NY R USDCTSD Roman-Crim Prac; NY R USDCTSD Roman-Case Mgt.

DISTRICT JUDGE LEONARD B. SAND: NY R USDCTSD Sand-Practices.

DISTRICT JUDGE LORNA G. SCHOFIELD: NY R USDCTSD Schofield-Civ Prac; NY R USDCTSD Schofield-

Crim Prac; NY R USDCTSD Schofield-Sched; NY R USDCTSD Schofield-Pro Se; NY R USDCTSD Schofield-Advice.

DISTRICT JUDGE CATHY SEIBEL: NY R USDCTSD Seibel-Practices.

DISTRICT JUDGE LOUIS L. STANTON: NY R USDCTSD Stanton-Practices; NY R USDCTSD Stanton-Pretrial.

DISTRICT JUDGE SIDNEY H. STEIN: NY R USDCTSD Stein-Practices.

DISTRICT JUDGE RICHARD J. SULLIVAN: NY R USDCTSD Sullivan-Practices; NY R USDCTSD Sullivan-Scheduling; NY R USDCTSD Sullivan-Sentencing; NY R USDCTSD Sullivan-Juries; NY R USDCTSD Sullivan-Trial; NY R USDCTSD Sullivan-Default.

DISTRICT JUDGE LAURA TAYLOR SWAIN: NY R USDCTSD Swain-Practices; NY R USDCTSD Swain-Trial; NY R USDCTSD Swain-Crim Trial; NY R USDCTSD Swain-Juries; NY R USDCTSD Swain-Sentencing; NY R USDCTSD Swain-Rights.

DISTRICT JUDGE ROBERT W. SWEET: NY R USDCTSD Sweet-Practices.

DISTRICT JUDGE ANALISA TORRES: NY R USDCTSD Torres-Civ Prac; NY R USDCTSD Torres-Pro Se; NY R USDCTSD Torres-Scheduling.

DISTRICT JUDGE KIMBA M. WOOD: NY R USDCTSD Wood-Practices; NY R USDCTSD Wood-Scheduling; NY R USDCTSD Wood-Discovery; NY R USDCTSD Wood-RICO; NY R USDCTSD Wood-Juries; NY R USDCTSD Wood-Trial; NY R USDCTSD Wood-Media.

DISTRICT JUDGE GREGORY H. WOODS: NY R USDCTSD Woods-Civ Prac; NY R USDCTSD Woods-Pro Se; NY R USDCTSD Woods-Sched; NY R USDCTSD Woods-Crim Prac; NY R USDCTSD Woods-Protect Order; NY R USDCTSD Woods-Speedy Trial.

MAGISTRATE JUDGE JAMES L. COTT: NY R USDCTSD Cott-Practices; NY R USDCTSD Cott-Settlement.

MAGISTRATE JUDGE PAUL E. DAVISON: NY R USDCTSD Davison-Practices.

MAGISTRATE JUDGE RONALD L. ELLIS: NY R USDCTSD Ellis-Practices.

MAGISTRATE JUDGE KEVIN N. FOX: NY R USDCTSD Fox-Practices; NY R USDCTSD Fox-Settlement.

MAGISTRATE JUDGE JAMES C. FRANCIS: NY R USDCTSD Francis-Practices.

MAGISTRATE JUDGE DEBRA FREEMAN: NY R USDCTSD Freeman-Practices; NY R USDCTSD Freeman-Settlement.

MAGISTRATE JUDGE GABRIEL W. GORENSTEIN: NY R USDCTSD Gorenstein-Practices; NY R USDCTSD Gorenstein-Ackn.

MAGISTRATE JUDGE FRANK MAAS: NY R USDCTSD Maas-Practices; NY R USDCTSD Maas-Discontinuance; NY R USDCTSD Maas-Conf; NY R USDCTSD Maas-Settlement.

MAGISTRATE JUDGE JUDITH C. McCARTHY: NY R USDCTSD McCarthy-Practices; NY R USDCTSD McCarthy-Conduct.

MAGISTRATE JUDGE BARBARA MOSES: NY R USDCTSD Moses-Practices.

MAGISTRATE JUDGE SARAH NETBURN: NY R USDCTSD Netburn-Civil; NY R USDCTSD Netburn-Settlement; NY R USDCTSD Netburn-Case Mgt; NY R USDCTSD Netburn--Pro Se.

MAGISTRATE JUDGE ANDREW J. PECK: NY R USDCTSD Peck-Practices; NY R USDCTSD Peck-Order; NY R USDCTSD Peck-Rule 502(d).

MAGISTRATE JUDGE HENRY PITMAN: NY R USDCTSD Pitman-Practices.

MAGISTRATE JUDGE LISA MARGARET SMITH: NY R USDCTSD Smith-Practices; NY R USDCTSD Smith-Trials.

## Motions, Oppositions and Replies
## Motion to Compel Discovery

### Document Last Updated September 2016

**A. Checklist**

(I) ❏ Matters to be considered by the parties before filing discovery motions

    (a) ❏ Matters to be considered by the moving party

        (1) ❏ Required documents

            (i) ❏ Letter-motion for a pre-motion discovery conference

        (2) ❏ Timing

            (i) ❏ There are no specific timing requirements for submitting a letter-motion for a pre-motion discovery conference to the court

    (b) ❏ Matters to be considered by the opposing party

        (1) ❏ Documents to consider

            (i) ❏ Responsive letter

        (2) ❏ Timing

            (i) ❏ There are no specific timing requirements for submitting a responsive letter to the court

(II) ❏ Matters to be considered by moving party

    (a) ❏ Required documents

        (1) ❏ Notice of motion and motion

        (2) ❏ Certificate of compliance

        (3) ❏ Memorandum of law

        (4) ❏ Certificate of service

    (b) ❏ Supplemental documents

        (1) ❏ Supporting evidence

        (2) ❏ Notice of constitutional question

        (3) ❏ Copies of authorities

        (4) ❏ Proposed order

        (5) ❏ Statement explaining untimely electronic filing

        (6) ❏ Courtesy copies

    (c) ❏ Timing

        (1) ❏ A motion must simply be submitted within a reasonable time; however, a motion to compel discovery filed under FRCP 37(a) is premature if it is filed before any request for discovery is made

        (2) ❏ A written motion and notice of the hearing must be served at least fourteen (14) days before the time specified for the hearing, with the following exceptions: (i) when the motion may be heard ex parte; (ii) when the Federal Rules of Civil Procedure set a different time; or (iii) when a court order—which a party may, for good cause, apply for ex parte—sets a different time

        (3) ❏ Any affidavit supporting a motion must be served with the motion

(III) ❏ Matters to be considered by opposing party

    (a) ❏ Required documents

        (1) ❏ Answering memorandum of law

(2) ❑ Certificate of service

(b) ❑ Supplemental documents

(1) ❑ Supporting evidence

(2) ❑ Notice of constitutional question

(3) ❑ Copies of authorities

(4) ❑ Statement explaining untimely electronic filing

(5) ❑ Courtesy copies

(c) ❑ Timing

(1) ❑ Any opposing affidavits and answering memoranda of law shall be served within seven (7) days after service of the moving papers

(2) ❑ Except as FRCP 59(c) provides otherwise, any opposing affidavit must be served at least seven (7) days before the hearing, unless the court permits service at another time

## B. Timing

1. *Prerequisites to filing a discovery motion*

   a. *Letter-motion for a pre-motion discovery conference.* There are no specific timing requirements for submitting a letter-motion for a pre-motion discovery conference to the court.

   b. *Responsive letter.* There are no specific timing requirements for submitting a responsive letter to the court.

   c. *Reply letter.* There are no specific timing requirements for submitting a reply letter to the court.

2. *Motion to compel discovery.* There is no specific time limit for a motion to compel discovery under FRCP 37(a); rather, a motion must simply be submitted within a reasonable time. FEDPROC § 26:779. However, a motion to compel discovery filed under FRCP 37(a) is premature if it is filed before any request for discovery is made. FEDPROC § 26:779; Bermudez v. Duenas, 936 F.2d 1064, 19 Fed.R.Serv.3d 1443 (9th Cir. 1991).

3. *Timing of motions, generally*

   a. *Motion and notice of hearing.* Except for letter-motions as permitted by NY R USDCTS&ED Civ Rule 7.1(d), and unless otherwise provided by statute or rule or by the Court in a Judge's Individual Practice or in a direction in a particular case, upon any motion, the notice of motion, supporting affidavits, and memoranda shall be served and filed as follows: on all motions and applications under FRCP 26 through FRCP 37 inclusive and FRCP 45(d)(3), the notice of motion, supporting affidavits, and memoranda of law shall be served by the moving party on all other parties that have appeared in the action. NY R USDCTS&ED Civ Rule 6.1(a)(1). A written motion and notice of the hearing must be served at least fourteen (14) days before the time specified for the hearing, with the following exceptions:

      i. When the motion may be heard ex parte;

      ii. When the Federal Rules of Civil Procedure set a different time; or

      iii. When a court order—which a party may, for good cause, apply for ex parte—sets a different time. FRCP 6(c)(1).

   b. *Supporting affidavit.* Any affidavit supporting a motion must be served with the motion. FRCP 6(c)(2).

4. *Timing of opposing papers.* Except for letter-motions as permitted by NY R USDCTS&ED Civ Rule 7.1(d), and unless otherwise provided by statute or rule or by the Court in a Judge's Individual Practice or in a direction in a particular case, upon any motion, the notice of motion, supporting affidavits, and memoranda shall be served and filed as follows: on all motions and applications under FRCP 26 through FRCP 37 inclusive and FRCP 45(d)(3), any opposing affidavits and answering memoranda of law shall be served within seven (7) days after service of the moving papers. NY R USDCTS&ED Civ Rule 6.1(a)(2).

   a. *Opposing affidavit.* Except as FRCP 59(c) provides otherwise, any opposing affidavit must be served

at least seven (7) days before the hearing, unless the court permits service at another time. FRCP 6(c)(2).

5. *Timing of reply papers.* Where the respondent files an answering affidavit setting up a new matter, the moving party ordinarily is allowed a reasonable time to file a reply affidavit since failure to deny the new matter by affidavit may operate as an admission of its truth. AMJUR MOTIONS § 25.

    a. *Reply affidavits and reply memoranda of law.* Except for letter-motions as permitted by NY R USDCTS&ED Civ Rule 7.1(d), and unless otherwise provided by statute or rule or by the Court in a Judge's Individual Practice or in a direction in a particular case, upon any motion, the notice of motion, supporting affidavits, and memoranda shall be served and filed as follows: on all motions and applications under FRCP 26 through FRCP 37 inclusive and FRCP 45(d)(3), any reply affidavits and reply memoranda of law shall be served within two (2) days after service of the answering papers. NY R USDCTS&ED Civ Rule 6.1(a)(3).

6. *Computation of time*

    a. *Computing time.* FRCP 6 applies in computing any time period specified in the Federal Rules of Civil Procedure, in any local rule or court order, or in any statute that does not specify a method of computing time. FRCP 6(a). In computing any period of time prescribed or allowed by the Local Civil Rules of the United States District Courts for the Southern and Eastern Districts of New York or the Local Admiralty and Maritime Rules, the provisions of FRCP 6 shall apply unless otherwise stated. NY R USDCTS&ED Civ Rule 6.4.

        i. *Period stated in days or a longer unit.* In computing periods of days, refer to FRCP 6 and NY R USDCTS&ED Civ Rule 6.4. NY R USDCTS&ED Civ Rule 6.1(a). When the period is stated in days or a longer unit of time:

- Exclude the day of the event that triggers the period;
- Count every day, including intermediate Saturdays, Sundays, and legal holidays; and
- Include the last day of the period, but if the last day is a Saturday, Sunday, or legal holiday, the period continues to run until the end of the next day that is not a Saturday, Sunday, or legal holiday. FRCP 6(a)(1). In the Local Civil Rules of the United States District Courts for the Southern and Eastern Districts of New York, as in the Federal Rules of Civil Procedure as amended effective December 1, 2009, Saturdays, Sundays, and legal holidays are no longer excluded in computing periods of time. If the last day of the period is a Saturday, Sunday, or legal holiday, the period continues to run until the end of the next day that is not a Saturday, Sunday, or legal holiday. NY R USDCTS&ED Civ Rule 6.4.

        ii. *Period stated in hours.* When the period is stated in hours:

- Begin counting immediately on the occurrence of the event that triggers the period;
- Count every hour, including hours during intermediate Saturdays, Sundays, and legal holidays; and
- If the period would end on a Saturday, Sunday, or legal holiday, the period continues to run until the same time on the next day that is not a Saturday, Sunday, or legal holiday. FRCP 6(a)(2). In the Local Civil Rules of the United States District Courts for the Southern and Eastern Districts of New York, as in the Federal Rules of Civil Procedure as amended effective December 1, 2009, Saturdays, Sundays, and legal holidays are no longer excluded in computing periods of time. If the last day of the period is a Saturday, Sunday, or legal holiday, the period continues to run until the end of the next day that is not a Saturday, Sunday, or legal holiday. NY R USDCTS&ED Civ Rule 6.4.

        iii. *Inaccessibility of the clerk's office.* Unless the court orders otherwise, if the clerk's office is inaccessible:

- On the last day for filing under FRCP 6(a)(1), then the time for filing is extended to the first accessible day that is not a Saturday, Sunday, or legal holiday; or
- During the last hour for filing under FRCP 6(a)(2), then the time for filing is extended to the same time on the first accessible day that is not a Saturday, Sunday, or legal holiday. FRCP 6(a)(3).

    iv. *"Last day" defined.* Unless a different time is set by a statute, local rule, or court order, the last day ends:

- For electronic filing, at midnight in the court's time zone; and

- For filing by other means, when the clerk's office is scheduled to close. FRCP 6(a)(4).

    v. *"Next day" defined.* The "next day" is determined by continuing to count forward when the period is measured after an event and backward when measured before an event. FRCP 6(a)(5).

    vi. *"Legal holiday" defined.* "Legal holiday" means:

- The day set aside by statute for observing New Year's Day, Martin Luther King Jr.'s Birthday, Washington's Birthday, Memorial Day, Independence Day, Labor Day, Columbus Day, Veterans' Day, Thanksgiving Day, or Christmas Day;

- Any day declared a holiday by the President or Congress; and

- For periods that are measured after an event, any other day declared a holiday by the state where the district court is located. FRCP 6(a)(6).

  b. *Computation of electronic filing deadlines.* You can file electronically twenty-four (24) hours a day, seven (7) days a week, three hundred sixty-five (365) days a year. NY R USDCTSD CM/ECF, S.D.(II)(13)(13.10). Electronic filing must be completed before midnight local time where the Court is located in order to be considered timely filed that day. NY R USDCTSD CM/ECF, S.D.(I)(3)(3.3); NY R USDCTSD CM/ECF, S.D.(II)(13)(13.10); NY R USDCTSD CM/ECF, S.D.(II)(19)(19.4). An electronically filed document is deemed filed on the "filed on" date indicated on the Notice of Electronic Filing (NEF). NY R USDCTSD CM/ECF, S.D.(II)(13)(13.11).

    i. *Technical failures.* A Filing User whose filing is made untimely as the result of a technical failure may seek appropriate relief from the Court. NY R USDCTSD CM/ECF, S.D.(I)(11). If you missed a filing deadline when the ECF system was out of order, attach a statement to your filing explaining how the interruption in service prevented you from filing in a timely fashion. NY R USDCTSD CM/ECF, S.D.(II)(23)(23.5).

  c. *Extending time*

    i. *In general.* When an act may or must be done within a specified time, the court may, for good cause, extend the time:

- With or without motion or notice if the court acts, or if a request is made, before the original time or its extension expires; or

- On motion made after the time has expired if the party failed to act because of excusable neglect. FRCP 6(b)(1).

    ii. *Exceptions.* A court must not extend the time to act under FRCP 50(b), FRCP 50(d), FRCP 52(b), FRCP 59(b), FRCP 59(d), FRCP 59(e), and FRCP 60(b). FRCP 6(b)(2).

    iii. Refer to the United States District Court for the Southern District of New York KeyRules Motion for Continuance/Extension of Time document for more information on extending time.

  d. *Additional time after certain kinds of service.* When a party may or must act within a specified time after service and service is made under FRCP 5(b)(2)(C), FRCP 5(b)(2)(D), FRCP 5(b)(2)(E), or FRCP 5(b)(2)(F), three (3) days are added after the period would otherwise expire under FRCP 6(a). FRCP 6(d). Overnight delivery service shall be deemed service by mail for purposes of FRCP 5 and FRCP 6. NY R USDCTS&ED Civ Rule 5.3.

7. *Individual judge practices.* Refer to the Miscellaneous section of this document for information on individual judge practices on timing of documents.

## C.  General Requirements

1. *Discovery motion procedure.* No motion under FRCP 26 through FRCP 37 inclusive shall be heard unless counsel for the moving party has first requested an informal conference with the Court by letter-motion for a pre-motion discovery conference (subject to the instructions regarding ECF published on the Court's

website and the Judge's Individual Practices) and such request has either been denied or the discovery dispute has not been resolved as a consequence of such a conference. NY R USDCTS&ED Civ Rule 37.2.

    a.   *Responsive letter.* If a motion is made by letter, the opposing party may file any response in letter form. NY R USDCTSD CM/ECF, S.D.(II)(13)(13.1).

    b.   *Reply letter.* If a motion is made by letter. . .the moving party may file any reply in letter form. NY R USDCTSD CM/ECF, S.D.(II)(13)(13.1).

2.   *Motions, generally*

    a.   *Requirements.* A request for a court order must be made by motion. The motion must:

        i.   Be in writing unless made during a hearing or trial;

        ii.   State with particularity the grounds for seeking the order; and

        iii.   State the relief sought. FRCP 7(b)(1).

    b.   *Notice of motion.* A party interested in resisting the relief sought by a motion has a right to notice thereof, and an opportunity to be heard. AMJUR MOTIONS § 12.

        i.   In addition to statutory or court rule provisions requiring notice of a motion—the purpose of such a notice requirement having been said to be to prevent a party from being prejudicially surprised by a motion—principles of natural justice dictate that an adverse party generally must be given notice that a motion will be presented to the court. AMJUR MOTIONS § 12.

        ii.   "Notice," in this regard, means reasonable notice, including a meaningful opportunity to prepare and to defend against allegations of a motion. AMJUR MOTIONS § 12.

    c.   *Writing requirement.* The writing requirement is intended to insure that the adverse parties are informed and have a record of both the motion's pendency and the grounds on which the movant seeks an order. FPP § 1191; Feldberg v. Quechee Lakes Corp., 463 F.3d 195 (2d Cir. 2006).

        i.   It is sufficient "if the motion is stated in a written notice of the hearing of the motion." FPP § 1191.

    d.   *Particularity requirement.* The particularity requirement insures that the opposing parties will have notice of their opponent's contentions. FEDPROC § 62:364; Goodman v. 1973 26 Foot Trojan Vessel, Arkansas Registration No. AR1439SN, 859 F.2d 71, 12 Fed.R.Serv.3d 645 (8th Cir. 1988). That requirement ensures that notice of the basis for the motion is provided to the court and to the opposing party so as to avoid prejudice, provide the opponent with a meaningful opportunity to respond, and provide the court with enough information to process the motion correctly. FEDPROC § 62:364; Andreas v. Volkswagen of America, Inc., 336 F.3d 789, 56 Fed.R.Serv.3d 6 (8th Cir. 2003).

        i.   Reasonable specification of the grounds for a motion is sufficient. However, where a movant fails to state even one ground for granting the motion in question, the movant has failed to meet the minimal standard of "reasonable specification." FEDPROC § 62:364; Martinez v. Trainor, 556 F.2d 818, 23 Fed.R.Serv.2d 403 (7th Cir. 1977).

        ii.   The court may excuse the failure to comply with the particularity requirement if it is inadvertent, and where no prejudice is shown by the opposing party. FEDPROC § 62:364.

    e.   *Ex parte orders or orders to show cause to bring on a motion.* No ex parte order, or order to show cause to bring on a motion, will be granted except upon a clear and specific showing by affidavit of good and sufficient reasons why a procedure other than by notice of motion is necessary, and stating whether a previous application for similar relief has been made. NY R USDCTS&ED Civ Rule 6.1(d).

    f.   *Letter-motions.* Applications for extensions or adjournments, applications for a pre-motion conference, and similar non-dispositive matters as permitted by the instructions regarding ECF published on the website of each respective Court and any pertinent Individual Judge's Practices, may be brought by letter-motion filed via ECF pursuant to NY R USDCTS&ED Civ Rule 5.2(b). NY R USDCTS&ED Civ Rule 7.1(d).

        i.   The following list of motions. . .may be made by LETTER-MOTION: (1) Motion to Adjourn Conference; (2) Motion to Change Attorney Name on Roll; (3) Motion to Compel; (4) Motion for Conference; (5) Motion to Consolidate Cases; (6) Motion to Continue; (7) Motion re: Discovery; (8) Motion to Expedite; (9) Motion for Extension of Time; (10) Motion for Extension of Time to Amend; (11) Motion for Extension of Time to Answer; (12) Motion for Extension of Time to Complete Discovery; (13) Motion for Extension of Time to File Document; (14) Motion for Extension of Time to File Response/Reply; (15) Motion for Extension of Time re Transcript; (16) Motion to File Amicus Brief; (17) Motion for Leave to File Document; (18) Motion for Leave to File Excess Pages; (19) Motion for Local Rule 37.2 Conference; (20) Motion for Oral Argument; (21) Motion to Reopen; (22) Motion to Reopen Case; (23) Motion to Seal Document; (24) Motion to Stay; (25) Motion to Substitute Attorney. NY R USDCTSD CM/ECF, S.D.(II)(13)(13.1).

ii.  If the Filing User is making a type of motion that does not appear in this list, the motion may not be made by letter. NY R USDCTSD CM/ECF, S.D.(II)(13)(13.1).

iii.  For more information on letter motions, refer to NY R USDCTSD CM/ECF, S.D.(II)(13)(13.1).

3.  *Motion to compel discovery.* On notice to other parties and all affected persons, a party may move for an order compelling disclosure or discovery. FRCP 37(a)(1). A party must request the specific documents in issue from the opposing party before filing a motion to compel the production of documents. FEDPROC § 26:778.

  a.  *Appropriate court.* A motion for an order to a party must be made in the court where the action is pending. A motion for an order to a nonparty must be made in the court where the discovery is or will be taken. FRCP 37(a)(2).

  b.  *Specific motions*

    i.  *To compel disclosure.* If a party fails to make a disclosure required by FRCP 26(a), any other party may move to compel disclosure and for appropriate sanctions. FRCP 37(a)(3)(A). Refer to the United States District Court for the Southern District of New York KeyRules Motion for Discovery Sanctions document for more information on sanctions.

    ii.  *To compel a discovery response.* A party seeking discovery may move for an order compelling an answer, designation, production, or inspection. This motion may be made if:

      • A deponent fails to answer a question asked under FRCP 30 or FRCP 31;

      • A corporation or other entity fails to make a designation under FRCP 30(b)(6) or FRCP 31(a)(4);

      • A party fails to answer an interrogatory submitted under FRCP 33; or

      • A party fails to produce documents or fails to respond that inspection will be permitted—or fails to permit inspection—as requested under FRCP 34. FRCP 37(a)(3)(B).

    iii.  *Related to a deposition.* When taking an oral deposition, the party asking a question may complete or adjourn the examination before moving for an order. FRCP 37(a)(3)(C).

    iv.  *Evasive or incomplete disclosure, answer, or response.* For purposes of FRCP 37(a), an evasive or incomplete disclosure, answer, or response must be treated as a failure to disclose, answer, or respond. FRCP 37(a)(4).

  c.  *Payment of expenses; Protective orders*

    i.  *If the motion is granted (or disclosure or discovery is provided after filing).* If the motion is granted—or if the disclosure or requested discovery is provided after the motion was filed—the court must, after giving an opportunity to be heard, require the party or deponent whose conduct necessitated the motion, the party or attorney advising that conduct, or both to pay the movant's reasonable expenses incurred in making the motion, including attorney's fees. But the court must not order this payment if:

      • The movant filed the motion before attempting in good faith to obtain the disclosure or discovery without court action;

      • The opposing party's nondisclosure, response, or objection was substantially justified; or

- Other circumstances make an award of expenses unjust. FRCP 37(a)(5)(A).

   ii. *If the motion is denied.* If the motion is denied, the court may issue any protective order authorized under FRCP 26(c) and must, after giving an opportunity to be heard, require the movant, the attorney filing the motion, or both to pay the party or deponent who opposed the motion its reasonable expenses incurred in opposing the motion, including attorney's fees. But the court must not order this payment if the motion was substantially justified or other circumstances make an award of expenses unjust. FRCP 37(a)(5)(B).

   iii. *If the motion is granted in part and denied in part.* If the motion is granted in part and denied in part, the court may issue any protective order authorized under FRCP 26(c) and may, after giving an opportunity to be heard, apportion the reasonable expenses for the motion. FRCP 37(a)(5)(C).

4. *Opposing papers.* The Federal Rules of Civil Procedure do not require any formal answer, return, or reply to a motion, except where the Federal Rules of Civil Procedure or local rules may require affidavits, memoranda, or other papers to be filed in opposition to a motion. Such papers are simply to apprise the court of such opposition and the grounds of that opposition. FEDPROC § 62:359. Except for letter-motions as permitted by NY R USDCTS&ED Civ Rule 7.1(d) or as otherwise permitted by the Court, all oppositions and replies with respect to motions shall comply with NY R USDCTS&ED Civ Rule 7.1(a)(2) and NY R USDCTS&ED Civ Rule 7.1(a)(3), and an opposing party who seeks relief that goes beyond the denial of the motion shall comply as well with NY R USDCTS&ED Civ Rule 7.1(a)(1). NY R USDCTS&ED Civ Rule 7.1(b).

   a. *Effect of failure to respond to motion.* Although in the absence of statutory provision or court rule, a motion ordinarily does not require a written answer, when a party files a motion and the opposing party fails to respond, the court may construe such failure to respond as nonopposition to the motion or an admission that the motion was meritorious, may take the facts alleged in the motion as true—the rule in some jurisdictions being that the failure to respond to a fact set forth in a motion is deemed an admission—and may grant the motion if the relief requested appears to be justified. AMJUR MOTIONS § 28.

   b. *Assent or no opposition not determinative.* However, a motion will not be granted automatically simply because an "assent" or a notation of "no opposition" has been filed; federal judges frequently deny motions that have been assented to when it is thought that justice so dictates. FPP § 1190.

   c. *Responsive pleading inappropriate as response to motion.* An attempt to answer or oppose a motion with a responsive pleading usually is not appropriate. FPP § 1190.

5. *Reply papers.* A moving party may be required or permitted to prepare papers in addition to his original motion papers. AMJUR MOTIONS § 25. Papers answering or replying to opposing papers may be appropriate, in the interests of justice, where it appears there is a substantial reason for allowing a reply. Thus, a court may accept reply papers where a party demonstrates that the papers to which it seeks to file a reply raise new issues that are material to the disposition of the question before the court, or where the court determines, sua sponte, that it wishes further briefing of an issue raised in those papers and orders the submission of additional papers. FEDPROC § 62:360. Except for letter-motions as permitted by NY R USDCTS&ED Civ Rule 7.1(d) or as otherwise permitted by the Court, all oppositions and replies with respect to motions shall comply with NY R USDCTS&ED Civ Rule 7.1(a)(2) and NY R USDCTS&ED Civ Rule 7.1(a)(3). NY R USDCTS&ED Civ Rule 7.1(b).

   a. *Function of reply papers.* The function of a reply affidavit is to answer the arguments made in opposition to the position taken by the movant and not to permit the movant to introduce new arguments in support of the motion. AMJUR MOTIONS § 25.

   b. *Issues raised for the first time in a reply document.* However, the view has been followed in some jurisdictions, that as a matter of judicial economy, where there is no prejudice and where the issues could be raised simply by filing a motion to dismiss, the trial court has discretion to consider arguments raised for the first time in a reply memorandum, and that a trial court may grant a motion to strike issues raised for the first time in a reply memorandum. AMJUR MOTIONS § 26.

6. *Orders on motions.* A memorandum signed by the Court of the decision on a motion that does not finally

determine all claims for relief, or an oral decision on such a motion, shall constitute the order unless the memorandum or oral decision directs the submission or settlement of an order in more extended form. The notation in the docket of a memorandum or of an oral decision that does not direct the submission or settlement of an order in more extended form shall constitute the entry of the order. Where an order in more extended form is required to be submitted or settled, the notation in the docket of such order shall constitute the entry of the order. NY R USDCTS&ED Civ Rule 6.2.

7.  *Complex civil cases.* For information on procedures for complex civil cases, refer to NY R USDCTSD Order 11 Misc 00388.

8.  *Related cases.* It shall be the continuing duty of each attorney appearing in any civil or criminal case to bring promptly to the attention of the Court all facts which said attorney believes are relevant to a determination that said case and one or more pending civil or criminal cases should be heard by the same Judge, in order to avoid unnecessary duplication of judicial effort. As soon as the attorney becomes aware of such relationship, said attorney shall notify the Judges to whom the cases have been assigned. NY R USDCTS&ED Civ Rule 1.6(a). If counsel fails to comply with NY R USDCTS&ED Civ Rule 1.6(a), the Court may assess reasonable costs directly against counsel whose action has obstructed the effective administration of the Court's business. NY R USDCTS&ED Civ Rule 1.6(b).

    a.  *Determination of relatedness.* Subject to the limitations set forth in NY R USDCTSD Div. Bus., Rule 13(a)(2), a civil case, bankruptcy appeal, or motion to withdraw the bankruptcy reference will be deemed related to one or more civil cases, appeals or motions when the interests of justice and efficiency will be served. In determining relatedness, a judge will consider whether (A) the actions concern the same or substantially similar parties, property, transactions or events; (B) there is substantial factual overlap; (C) the parties could be subjected to conflicting orders; and (D) whether absent a determination of relatedness there would be a substantial duplication of effort and expense, delay, or undue burden on the Court, parties or witnesses. NY R USDCTSD Div. Bus., Rule 13(a)(1). Nothing in this NY R USDCTSD Div. Bus., Rule 13 is intended to preclude parties from moving for consolidated proceedings under FRCP 42. NY R USDCTSD Div. Bus., Rule 13(a)(1). Notwith-standing NY R USDCTSD Div. Bus., Rule 13(a)(1):

        i.  Civil cases shall not be deemed related merely because they involve common legal issues or the same parties. NY R USDCTSD Div. Bus., Rule 13(a)(2)(A).

        ii. Other than cases subject to NY R USDCTSD Div. Bus., Rule 4(b) and actions seeking the enforcement of a judgment or settlement in or of an earlier case, civil cases presumptively shall not be deemed related unless both cases are pending before the Court (or the earlier case is on appeal). NY R USDCTSD Div. Bus., Rule 13(a)(2)(B).

    b.  *Procedure in regard to cases said to be related*

        i.  *Disclosure of contention of relatedness.* When a civil case is filed or removed or a bankruptcy appeal or motion to withdraw the reference of an adversary proceeding from the bankruptcy court is filed, the person filing or removing shall disclose on form JSC44C any contention of relatedness and shall file a Related Case Statement stating clearly and succinctly the basis for the contention. A copy of the civil cover sheet and Related Case Statement shall be served with the complaint, notice of removal, notice of appeal, or motion. Any party may contest a claim of relatedness by any other in writing addressed to the judge having the case with the lowest docket number of all cases claimed to be related. However, the foregoing shall not delay the assignment process or the operation of NY R USDCTSD Div. Bus., Rule 13. NY R USDCTSD Div. Bus., Rule 13(b)(1). [Editor's note: the reference to form JSC44C is likely meant to be form JS44C-SDNY: Civil Court Cover Sheet].

        ii. *Claims of relatedness by other parties.* A party other than the one filing a case, bankruptcy appeal or motion to withdraw the reference that contends its case is related to another may so advise in writing the judge assigned in its case and request a transfer of its case to the judge that the party contends has the related case with the lowest docket number. If the assigned judge believes the case is related under NY R USDCTSD Div. Bus., Rule 13(a), he or she shall refer the question to the judge having the case with the lowest docket number. In the event the latter judge agrees, the case shall be transferred to that judge unless the Assignment Committee disagrees. NY R USDCTSD Div. Bus., Rule 13(b)(3).

    c.   For more information on related cases, refer to NY R USDCTSD Div. Bus., Rule 13.

9.  *Alternative dispute resolution (ADR).* The U.S. District Court for the Southern District of New York provides litigants with opportunities to discuss settlement through judicial settlement conferences and mediation. NY R USDCTS&ED Civ Rule 83.9(a).

    a.  *Consideration of alternative dispute resolution.* In all civil cases, including those eligible for mediation pursuant to NY R USDCTS&ED Civ Rule 83.9(e), each party shall consider the use of mediation or a judicial settlement conference and shall report to the assigned Judge at the initial FRCP 16(b) case management conference, or subsequently, whether the party believes mediation or a judicial settlement conference may facilitate the resolution of the lawsuit. Judges are encouraged to note the availability of the mediation program and/or a judicial settlement conference before, at, or after the initial FRCP 16(b) case management conference. NY R USDCTS&ED Civ Rule 83.9(d).

    b.  *Mediation.* In mediation, parties and counsel meet, sometimes collectively and sometimes individually, with a neutral third party (the mediator) who has been trained to facilitate confidential settlement discussions. The parties articulate their respective positions and interests and generate options for a mutually agreeable resolution to the dispute. The mediator assists the parties in reaching their own negotiated settlement by defining the issues, probing and assessing the strengths and weaknesses of each party's legal positions, and identifying areas of agreement and disagreement. The main benefits of mediation are that it can result in an expeditious and less costly resolution of the litigation, and can produce creative solutions to complex disputes often unavailable in traditional litigation. NY R USDCTS&ED Civ Rule 83.9(b).

       i.  *Mediation program eligibility.* All civil cases other than Social Security, habeas corpus, and tax cases are eligible for mediation, whether assigned to Manhattan or White Plains. NY R USDCTS&ED Civ Rule 83.9(e)(1).

         &bull;  The Board of Judges may, by Administrative Order, direct that certain specified categories of cases shall automatically be submitted to the mediation program. The assigned District Judge or Magistrate Judge may issue a written order exempting a particular case with or without the request of the parties. NY R USDCTS&ED Civ Rule 83.9(e)(2).

         &bull;  For all other cases, the assigned District Judge or Magistrate Judge may determine that a case is appropriate for mediation and may order that case to mediation, with or without the consent of the parties, before, at, or after the initial FRCP 16(b) case management conference. Alternatively, the parties should notify the assigned Judge at any time of their desire to mediate. NY R USDCTS&ED Civ Rule 83.9(e)(3).

    c.  *Judicial settlement conferences.* Judicial settlement conferences may be ordered by District Judges or Magistrate Judges with or without the request or consent of the parties. NY R USDCTS&ED Civ Rule 83.9(f).

    d.  For more information on alternative dispute resolution (ADR), refer to NY R USDCTS&ED Civ Rule 83.9.

10.  *Individual judge practices.* Refer to the Miscellaneous section of this document for information on individual judge practices on general requirements for documents.

## D.  Documents

    1.  *Documents prior to filing discovery motions*

       a.  *Documents for the moving party*

         i.  *Required documents*

           &bull;  *Letter-motion for a pre-motion discovery conference.* No motion under FRCP 26 through FRCP 37 inclusive shall be heard unless counsel for the moving party has first requested an informal conference with the Court by letter-motion for a pre-motion discovery conference (subject to the instructions regarding ECF published on the Court's website and the Judge's Individual Practices) and such request has either been denied or the discovery dispute has not been resolved as a consequence of such a conference. NY R USDCTS&ED Civ Rule 37.2.

b. *Documents for the opposing party*

    i. *Documents to consider*

- *Responsive letter.* If a motion is made by letter, the opposing party may file any response in letter form. NY R USDCTSD CM/ECF, S.D.(II)(13)(13.1).

2. *Documents for moving party*

a. *Required documents*

    i. *Notice of motion and motion.* Except for letter-motions as permitted by NY R USDCTS&ED Civ Rule 7.1(d) or as otherwise permitted by the Court, all motions shall include the following motion papers: a notice of motion, or an order to show cause signed by the Court, which shall specify the applicable rules or statutes pursuant to which the motion is brought, and shall specify the relief sought by the motion. NY R USDCTS&ED Civ Rule 7.1(a)(1). Refer to the General Requirements section of this document for information on the notice of motion and motion.

- *Quotation or recitation verbatim of discovery materials.* Upon any motion or application involving discovery or disclosure requests or responses under FRCP 37, the moving party shall specify and quote or set forth verbatim in the motion papers each discovery request and response to which the motion or application is addressed. The motion or application shall also set forth the grounds upon which the moving party is entitled to prevail as to each request or response. NY R USDCTS&ED Civ Rule 5.1 also applies to the motion or application. NY R USDCTS&ED Civ Rule 37.1.

    ii. *Certificate of compliance.* The motion must include a certification that the movant has in good faith conferred or attempted to confer with the person or party failing to make disclosure or discovery in an effort to obtain it without court action. FRCP 37(a)(1).

    iii. *Memorandum of law.* Except for letter-motions as permitted by NY R USDCTS&ED Civ Rule 7.1(d) or as otherwise permitted by the Court, all motions shall include the following motion papers: a memorandum of law, setting forth the cases and other authorities relied upon in support of the motion, and divided, under appropriate headings, into as many parts as there are issues to be determined. NY R USDCTS&ED Civ Rule 7.1(a)(2).

    iv. *Certificate of service.* FRCP 5(d) requires that the person making service under FRCP 5 certify that service has been effected. FRCP 5(Advisory Committee Notes). Having such information on file may be useful for many purposes, including proof of service if an issue arises concerning the effectiveness of the service. FRCP 5(Advisory Committee Notes).

- Such paper service [on attorneys and pro se parties who are not Filing or Receiving Users] must be documented by electronically filing proof of service. NY R USDCTSD CM/ECF, S.D.(I)(9)(9.2); NY R USDCTSD CM/ECF, S.D.(I)(19)(19.3)(b). Pro se parties who are not Filing Users are exempt from that portion of NY R USDCTSD CM/ECF, S.D.(I)(19)(19.3) requiring proof of service to be filed electronically. NY R USDCTSD CM/ECF, S.D.(I)(19)(19.3).

b. *Supplemental documents*

    i. *Supporting evidence.* When a motion relies on facts outside the record, the court may hear the matter on affidavits or may hear it wholly or partly on oral testimony or on depositions. FRCP 43(c). Except for letter-motions as permitted by NY R USDCTS&ED Civ Rule 7.1(d) or as otherwise permitted by the Court, all motions shall include the following motion papers: supporting affidavits and exhibits thereto containing any factual information and portions of the record necessary for the decision of the motion. NY R USDCTS&ED Civ Rule 7.1(a)(3).

- *Discovery materials.* A party seeking or opposing relief under FRCP 26 through FRCP 37 inclusive, or making or opposing any other motion or application, shall quote or attach only those portions of the depositions, interrogatories, requests for documents, requests for admissions, or other discovery or disclosure materials, together with the responses and objections thereto, that are the subject of the discovery motion or application, or that are

cited in papers submitted in connection with any other motion or application. NY R USDCTS&ED Civ Rule 5.1.

ii. *Notice of constitutional question.* A party that files a pleading, written motion, or other paper drawing into question the constitutionality of a federal or state statute must promptly:

- *File notice.* File a notice of constitutional question stating the question and identifying the paper that raises it, if: (1) a federal statute is questioned and the parties do not include the United States, one of its agencies, or one of its officers or employees in an official capacity; or (2) a state statute is questioned and the parties do not include the state, one of its agencies, or one of its officers or employees in an official capacity; and

- *Serve notice.* Serve the notice and paper on the Attorney General of the United States if a federal statute is questioned—or on the state attorney general if a state statute is questioned—either by certified or registered mail or by sending it to an electronic address designated by the attorney general for this purpose. FRCP 5.1(a).

- *No forfeiture.* A party's failure to file and serve the notice, or the court's failure to certify, does not forfeit a constitutional claim or defense that is otherwise timely asserted. FRCP 5.1(d).

iii. *Copies of authorities.* In cases involving a pro se litigant, counsel shall, when serving a memorandum of law (or other submissions to the Court), provide the pro se litigant (but not other counsel or the Court) with copies of cases and other authorities cited therein that are unpublished or reported exclusively on computerized databases. Upon request, counsel shall provide the pro se litigant with copies of such unpublished cases and other authorities as are cited in a decision of the Court and were not previously cited by any party. NY R USDCTS&ED Civ Rule 7.2.

iv. *Proposed order.* Refer to the Format section of this document for information on the format of submitting a proposed order to the court.

v. *Statement explaining untimely electronic filing.* If you missed a filing deadline when the ECF system was out of order, attach a statement to your filing explaining how the interruption in service prevented you from filing in a timely fashion. NY R USDCTSD CM/ECF, S.D.(II)(23)(23.5).

vi. *Courtesy copies.* Read the judge's Individual Practices to learn if courtesy copies are required. NY R USDCTSD CM/ECF, S.D.(II)(13)(13.17). Judges' Individual Practices should continue to be followed with respect to delivery of courtesy copies. NY R USDCTSD CM/ECF, S.D.(I)(3)(3.4).

3. *Documents for opposing party*

a. *Required documents*

i. *Answering memorandum of law.* Except for letter-motions as permitted by NY R USDCTS&ED Civ Rule 7.1(d) or as otherwise permitted by the Court, all oppositions and replies with respect to motions shall comply with NY R USDCTS&ED Civ Rule 7.1(a)(2). NY R USDCTS&ED Civ Rule 7.1(b). Except for letter-motions as permitted by NY R USDCTS&ED Civ Rule 7.1(d) or as otherwise permitted by the Court, all motions shall include the following motion papers: a memorandum of law, setting forth the cases and other authorities relied upon in support of the motion, and divided, under appropriate headings, into as many parts as there are issues to be determined. NY R USDCTS&ED Civ Rule 7.1(a)(2). Refer to the General Requirements section of this document for information on the opposing papers.

ii. *Certificate of service.* FRCP 5(d) requires that the person making service under FRCP 5 certify that service has been effected. FRCP 5(Advisory Committee Notes). Having such information on file may be useful for many purposes, including proof of service if an issue arises concerning the effectiveness of the service. FRCP 5(Advisory Committee Notes).

- Such paper service [on attorneys and pro se parties who are not Filing or Receiving Users] must be documented by electronically filing proof of service. NY R USDCTSD CM/ECF,

S.D.(I)(9)(9.2); NY R USDCTSD CM/ECF, S.D.(I)(19)(19.3)(b). Pro se parties who are not Filing Users are exempt from that portion of NY R USDCTSD CM/ECF, S.D.(I)(19)(19.3) requiring proof of service to be filed electronically. NY R USDCTSD CM/ECF, S.D.(I)(19)(19.3).

  b. *Supplemental documents*

    i. *Supporting evidence.* When a motion relies on facts outside the record, the court may hear the matter on affidavits or may hear it wholly or partly on oral testimony or on depositions. FRCP 43(c). Except for letter-motions as permitted by NY R USDCTS&ED Civ Rule 7.1(d) or as otherwise permitted by the Court, all oppositions and replies with respect to motions shall comply with NY R USDCTS&ED Civ Rule 7.1(a)(3). NY R USDCTS&ED Civ Rule 7.1(b). Except for letter-motions as permitted by NY R USDCTS&ED Civ Rule 7.1(d) or as otherwise permitted by the Court, all motions shall include the following motion papers: supporting affidavits and exhibits thereto containing any factual information and portions of the record necessary for the decision of the motion. NY R USDCTS&ED Civ Rule 7.1(a)(3).

- *Discovery materials.* A party seeking or opposing relief under FRCP 26 through FRCP 37 inclusive, or making or opposing any other motion or application, shall quote or attach only those portions of the depositions, interrogatories, requests for documents, requests for admissions, or other discovery or disclosure materials, together with the responses and objections thereto, that are the subject of the discovery motion or application, or that are cited in papers submitted in connection with any other motion or application. NY R USDCTS&ED Civ Rule 5.1.

    ii. *Notice of constitutional question.* A party that files a pleading, written motion, or other paper drawing into question the constitutionality of a federal or state statute must promptly:

- *File notice.* File a notice of constitutional question stating the question and identifying the paper that raises it, if: (1) a federal statute is questioned and the parties do not include the United States, one of its agencies, or one of its officers or employees in an official capacity; or (2) a state statute is questioned and the parties do not include the state, one of its agencies, or one of its officers or employees in an official capacity; and

- *Serve notice.* Serve the notice and paper on the Attorney General of the United States if a federal statute is questioned—or on the state attorney general if a state statute is questioned—either by certified or registered mail or by sending it to an electronic address designated by the attorney general for this purpose. FRCP 5.1(a).

- *No forfeiture.* A party's failure to file and serve the notice, or the court's failure to certify, does not forfeit a constitutional claim or defense that is otherwise timely asserted. FRCP 5.1(d).

    iii. *Copies of authorities.* In cases involving a pro se litigant, counsel shall, when serving a memorandum of law (or other submissions to the Court), provide the pro se litigant (but not other counsel or the Court) with copies of cases and other authorities cited therein that are unpublished or reported exclusively on computerized databases. Upon request, counsel shall provide the pro se litigant with copies of such unpublished cases and other authorities as are cited in a decision of the Court and were not previously cited by any party. NY R USDCTS&ED Civ Rule 7.2.

    iv. *Statement explaining untimely electronic filing.* If you missed a filing deadline when the ECF system was out of order, attach a statement to your filing explaining how the interruption in service prevented you from filing in a timely fashion. NY R USDCTSD CM/ECF, S.D.(II)(23)(23.5).

    v. *Courtesy copies.* Read the judge's Individual Practices to learn if courtesy copies are required. NY R USDCTSD CM/ECF, S.D.(II)(13)(13.17). Judges' Individual Practices should continue to be followed with respect to delivery of courtesy copies. NY R USDCTSD CM/ECF, S.D.(I)(3)(3.4).

4. *Individual judge practices.* Refer to the Miscellaneous section of this document for information on individual judge practices on required documents.

## E. Format

1. *Form of documents.* The rules governing captions and other matters of form in pleadings apply to motions and other papers. FRCP 7(b)(2).

   a. *Paper.* Every pleading, written motion, and other paper must: be plainly written, typed, printed, or copied without erasures or interlineations which materially deface it. NY R USDCTS&ED Civ Rule 11.1(a)(1).

   b. *Typeface, margin, and spacing.* The typeface, margins, and spacing of all documents presented for filing must meet the following requirements:

      i. All text must be twelve (12) point type or larger, except for text in footnotes which may be ten (10) point type;

      ii. All documents must have at least one (1) inch margins on all sides;

      iii. All text must be double-spaced, except for headings, text in footnotes, or block quotations, which may be single-spaced. NY R USDCTS&ED Civ Rule 11.1(b).

   c. *Caption; Names of parties.* Every pleading must have a caption with the court's name, a title, a file number, and a FRCP 7(a) designation. The title of the complaint must name all the parties; the title of other pleadings, after naming the first party on each side, may refer generally to other parties. FRCP 10(a). Every pleading, written motion, and other paper must: bear the docket number and the initials of the District Judge and any Magistrate Judge before whom the action or proceeding is pending, NY R USDCTS&ED Civ Rule 11.1(a)(2).

   d. *Paragraphs; Separate statements.* A party must state its claims or defenses in numbered paragraphs, each limited as far as practicable to a single set of circumstances. A later pleading may refer by number to a paragraph in an earlier pleading. If doing so would promote clarity, each claim founded on a separate transaction or occurrence—and each defense other than a denial—must be stated in a separate count or defense. FRCP 10(b).

   e. *Adoption by reference; Exhibits.* A statement in a pleading may be adopted by reference elsewhere in the same pleading or in any other pleading or motion. A copy of a written instrument that is an exhibit to a pleading is a part of the pleading for all purposes. FRCP 10(c).

   f. *Acceptance by the clerk.* The clerk must not refuse to file a paper solely because it is not in the form prescribed by the Federal Rules of Civil Procedure or by a local rule or practice. FRCP 5(d)(4).

2. *Form of electronic documents*

   a. *PDF-A.* All documents electronically filed on the ECF system must be in PDF-A format (portable document format). A PDF-A file is created using PDF writer software such as Adobe Acrobat (go to the Adobe website for details). PDF-A files cannot be altered, providing security to the filer and the Court. NY R USDCTSD CM/ECF, S.D.(II)(23)(23.2).

   b. *Size limitation.* No single PDF file may be larger than four megabytes (4 MB). If the filing is too large, the ECF system will not allow it to be filed, and you will not see a Notice of Electronic Filing (NEF or filing receipt) screen. To determine the size of an Adobe Acrobat PDF file click on File, Document Properties, Summary. NY R USDCTSD CM/ECF, S.D.(II)(23)(23.3).

      i. Converting documents directly from a word processor to PDF-A format creates the smallest possible file in terms of computer memory. If that is not possible, scan your document at low resolution. Within the Adobe Acrobat program, on the "Scan Manager" screen, adjust the settings for black and white and 200 dpi (dots per inch). This allows more pages to fit into a single PDF-A file. If that does not work, separate an oversized file into 2 or more parts. Simply label each file 1a, 1b, 1c, etc. Only relevant excerpts of exhibits should be electronically filed. NY R USDCTSD CM/ECF, S.D.(II)(23)(23.4).

   c. *Attachments and exhibits.* Filing Users must submit in electronic form all documents referenced as exhibits or attachments, unless the Court permits paper filing. NY R USDCTSD CM/ECF, S.D.(I)(5)(5.1).

      i. A Filing User must submit as exhibits or attachments only those excerpts of the referenced documents that are relevant to the matter under consideration by the Court. Excerpted material must be clearly and prominently identified as such. Filing Users who file excerpts of documents as exhibits or attachments under this procedure do so without prejudice to their right to file timely additional excerpts or the complete document. Responding parties may file timely additional excerpts that they believe are relevant or the complete document. A party may move before the Court for permission to serve and file in hard copy documents that cannot be reasonably scanned. NY R USDCTSD CM/ECF, S.D.(I)(5)(5.2).

ii. Exhibits must be filed only as attachments to a document, such as a motion or an affidavit. Do not use the ECF Filing Event for "Motion" to file exhibits separately. Exhibits are the only items that should be attached to electronically filed documents. You are limited to electronically filing only relevant excerpts of exhibits. Excerpts must be clearly identified as such. If the exhibit is too large to be scanned and electronically filed you may contact the ECF Help Desk. NY R USDCTSD CM/ECF, S.D.(II)(15)(15.6).

d. *Letters.* Parties should consult the assigned judge's Individual Practices to determine if the judge accepts letters at all and, if he or she does, whether the judge has any page limitations on letters and/or requires courtesy copies of letters filed on ECF (and, if so, by what means of delivery). All letters addressed to the Court must include a subject line with the case name and docket number (e.g., "Re: Doe v. Smith, 13 Civ. 1234 (ABC)"). NY R USDCTSD CM/ECF, S.D.(II)(13)(13.1).

e. *Proposed orders, proposed judgments, stipulations and consents.* Any document that requires the signature of a judge should not be electronically filed except as an exhibit to another document. Proposed orders, judgments, stipulations and consents should not be submitted through the ECF system. Instead they should be sent by e-mail to the Clerk. Proposed orders should be submitted in word processing format (WordPerfect or Word) rather than as a PDF document. Stipulations should be submitted in PDF-A format. Stipulations must contain ink signatures not s/. Faxed or emailed signatures are acceptable. Please note that Stipulations of Voluntary Dismissal pursuant to FRCP 41(a)(1)(A)(ii) do not require the signature of a judge and must be electronically filed on the ECF system. Questions may be directed to the Orders and Judgments Clerk at the phone numbers listed in NY R USDCTSD CM/ECF, S.D.(II)(18)(18.3). NY R USDCTSD CM/ECF, S.D.(II)(18)(18.3).

i. Email the proposed order, judgment or stipulation to the email addresses listed in NY R USDCTSD CM/ECF, S.D.(II)(18)(18.3). NY R USDCTSD CM/ECF, S.D.(II)(18)(18.3).

ii. Pro se litigants who are not Filing Users are exempt from that portion of NY R USDCTSD CM/ECF, S.D.(II)(18)(18.3) that requires litigants to email proposed orders, judgments, stipulations and consents, and shall deliver such documents to the Clerk's Office in paper form. NY R USDCTSD CM/ECF, S.D.(II)(18)(18.3).

3. *Signing disclosures and discovery requests, responses, and objections.* FRCP 11 does not apply to disclosures and discovery requests, responses, objections, and motions under FRCP 26 through FRCP 37. FRCP 11(d).

a. *Signature required.* Every disclosure under FRCP 26(a)(1) or FRCP 26(a)(3) and every discovery request, response, or objection must be signed by at least one attorney of record in the attorney's own name—or by the party personally, if unrepresented—and must state the signer's address, e-mail address, and telephone number. FRCP 26(g)(1). Every pleading, written motion, and other paper must: have the name of each person signing it clearly printed or typed directly below the signature. NY R USDCTS&ED Civ Rule 11.1(a)(3).

i. *Electronic signatures.* The user log-in and password required to submit documents to the ECF system serve as the Filing User's signature on all electronic documents filed with the Court. NY R USDCTSD CM/ECF, S.D.(I)(8)(8.1); NY R USDCTSD CM/ECF, S.D.(II)(13)(13.14). They also serve as a signature for purposes of the Federal Rules of Civil Procedure, including FRCP 11, the Local Civil Rules of the United States District Courts for the Southern and Eastern Districts of New York, and any other purpose for which a signature is required in connection with proceedings before the Court. NY R USDCTSD CM/ECF, S.D.(I)(8)(8.1).

- *Signature block.* Electronically filed documents must include a signature block and must set forth the name, address, telephone number and e-mail address all in compliance with the Federal Rules of Civil Procedure and NY R USDCTS&ED Civ Rule 11.1. In the absence of a scanned signature image, the name of the Filing User under whose log-in and password the document is submitted must be preceded by an "s/" typed in the space where the signature would otherwise appear. NY R USDCTSD CM/ECF, S.D.(I)(8)(8.2); NY R USDCTSD CM/ECF, S.D.(II)(13)(13.14).

- *Documents requiring the signature of a party or witness.* A document requiring the signature of a party or witness shall be electronically filed in a scanned format that contains an image of the actual signature. NY R USDCTSD CM/ECF, S.D.(I)(8)(8.4); NY R USDCTSD CM/ECF, S.D.(II)(13)(13.14).

- *Documents requiring the signature of a judge.* A Filing User submitting a document electronically that requires a judge's signature must promptly deliver the document in such other form, if any, as the Court requires. NY R USDCTSD CM/ECF, S.D.(I)(4)(4.2).

- *Documents requiring multiple signatures.* Documents requiring signatures of more than one party must be electronically filed either by: (a) submitting a scanned document containing all necessary signatures; (b) representing the consent of the other parties on the document; (c) identifying on the document the parties whose signatures are required and by the submission of a notice of endorsement by the other parties no later than three business days after filing; or (d) in any other manner approved by the Court. NY R USDCTSD CM/ECF, S.D.(I)(8)(8.5).

b. *Effect of signature.* By signing, an attorney or party certifies that to the best of the person's knowledge, information, and belief formed after a reasonable inquiry:

   i. With respect to a disclosure, it is complete and correct as of the time it is made; and

   ii. With respect to a discovery request, response, or objection, it is:

- Consistent with the Federal Rules of Civil Procedure and warranted by existing law or by a nonfrivolous argument for extending, modifying, or reversing existing law, or for establishing new law;

- Not interposed for any improper purpose, such as to harass, cause unnecessary delay, or needlessly increase the cost of litigation; and

- Neither unreasonable nor unduly burdensome or expensive, considering the needs of the case, prior discovery in the case, the amount in controversy, and the importance of the issues at stake in the action. FRCP 26(g)(1).

c. *Failure to sign.* Other parties have no duty to act on an unsigned disclosure, request, response, or objection until it is signed, and the court must strike it unless a signature is promptly supplied after the omission is called to the attorney's or party's attention. FRCP 26(g)(2).

d. *Sanction for improper certification.* If a certification violates FRCP 26(g) without substantial justification, the court, on motion or on its own, must impose an appropriate sanction on the signer, the party on whose behalf the signer was acting, or both. The sanction may include an order to pay the reasonable expenses, including attorney's fees, caused by the violation. FRCP 26(g)(3). Refer to the United States District Court for the Southern District of New York KeyRules Motion for Discovery Sanctions document for more information.

4. *Privacy protection for filings made with the court*

a. *Redacted filings.* Unless the court orders otherwise, in an electronic or paper filing with the court that contains an individual's Social Security number, taxpayer-identification number, or birth date, the name of an individual known to be a minor, or a financial-account number, a party or nonparty making the filing may include only:

   i. The last four (4) digits of the Social Security number and taxpayer-identification number;

   ii. The year of the individual's birth;

   iii. The minor's initials; and

   iv. The last four (4) digits of the financial-account number. FRCP 5.2(a); NY R USDCTSD CM/ECF, S.D.(II)(21)(21.3).

    v.   Caution should be exercised when filing documents that contain the following:

- Personal identifying numbers (PIN #'s), such as a driver's license number;
- Medical records, treatment and diagnosis;
- Employment history;
- Individual financial information;
- Proprietary or trade secret information;
- Information regarding an individual's cooperation with the government. NY R US-DCTSD CM/ECF, S.D.(II)(21)(21.4).

b.  *Exemptions from the redaction requirement.* The redaction requirement does not apply to the following:

    i.   A financial-account number that identifies the property allegedly subject to forfeiture in a forfeiture proceeding;

    ii.  The record of an administrative or agency proceeding;

    iii.  The official record of a state-court proceeding;

    iv.  The record of a court or tribunal, if that record was not subject to the redaction requirement when originally filed;

    v.   A filing covered by FRCP 5.2(c) or FRCP 5.2(d); and

    vi.  A pro se filing in an action brought under 28 U.S.C.A. § 2241, 28 U.S.C.A. § 2254, or 28 U.S.C.A. § 2255. FRCP 5.2(b).

c.  *Limitations on remote access to electronic files; Social Security appeals and immigration cases.* Unless the court orders otherwise, in an action for benefits under the Social Security Act, and in an action or proceeding relating to an order of removal, to relief from removal, or to immigration benefits or detention, access to an electronic file is authorized as follows:

    i.   The parties and their attorneys may have remote electronic access to any part of the case file, including the administrative record;

    ii.  Any other person may have electronic access to the full record at the courthouse, but may have remote electronic access only to:

- The docket maintained by the court; and
- An opinion, order, judgment, or other disposition of the court, but not any other part of the case file or the administrative record. FRCP 5.2(c).

d.  *Filings made under seal.* The court may order that a filing be made under seal without redaction. The court may later unseal the filing or order the person who made the filing to file a redacted version for the public record. FRCP 5.2(d). For more information on sealing documents, refer to NY R USDCTSD CM/ECF, S.D.(I)(6).

e.  *Protective orders.* For good cause, the court may by order in a case:

    i.   Require redaction of additional information; or

    ii.  Limit or prohibit a nonparty's remote electronic access to a document filed with the court. FRCP 5.2(e).

f.  *Option for additional unredacted filing under seal.* A person making a redacted filing may also file an unredacted copy under seal. The court must retain the unredacted copy as part of the record. FRCP 5.2(f); NY R USDCTSD CM/ECF, S.D.(II)(21)(21.5).

g.  *Option for filing a reference list.* A filing that contains redacted information may be filed together with a reference list that identifies each item of redacted information and specifies an appropriate identifier that uniquely corresponds to each item listed. The list must be filed under seal and may be amended as of right. Any reference in the case to a listed identifier will be construed to refer to the corresponding item of information. FRCP 5.2(g); NY R USDCTSD CM/ECF, S.D.(II)(21)(21.5).

h. *Responsibility for redaction.* It is the sole responsibility of counsel and the parties to be sure that all documents comply with the rules of this Court requiring redaction of personal identifiers. Neither the judge nor the Clerk of Court will review documents for compliance with these rules. NY R USDCTSD CM/ECF, S.D.(II)(21)(21.2).

i. *Waiver of protection of identifiers.* A person waives the protection of FRCP 5.2(a) as to the person's own information by filing it without redaction and not under seal. FRCP 5.2(h).

j. For more information on privacy and public access to ECF cases, refer to NY R USDCTSD CM/ECF, S.D.(II)(21).

5. *Individual judge practices.* Refer to the Miscellaneous section of this document for information on individual judge practices on formatting documents.

## F. Filing and Service Requirements

1. *Filing requirements.* Any paper after the complaint that is required to be served—together with a certificate of service—must be filed within a reasonable time after service. FRCP 5(d)(1). Complaints and all subsequent papers are accepted at either courthouse, regardless of the place for which the case is designated. NY R USDCTSD Div. Bus., Rule 22. Subject to the instructions regarding ECF published on the website of each respective Court and any pertinent Individual Judge's Practices, letter-motions permitted by NY R USDCTS&ED Civ Rule 7.1(d) and letters addressed to the Court (but not letters between the parties) may be filed via ECF. NY R USDCTS&ED Civ Rule 5.2(b). For information on electronically filing motions, refer to NY R USDCTSD CM/ECF, S.D.(II)(15).

a. *How filing is made; In general.* A paper is filed by delivering it:

i. To the clerk; or

ii. To a judge who agrees to accept it for filing, and who must then note the filing date on the paper and promptly send it to the clerk. FRCP 5(d)(2).

b. *Night depository.* A night depository with an automatic date stamp shall be maintained by the Clerk of the Southern District in the Pearl Street Courthouse. After regular business hours, papers for the District Court only may be deposited in the night depository. Such papers will be considered as having been filed in the District Court as of the date stamped thereon, which shall be deemed presumptively correct. NY R USDCTS&ED Civ Rule 1.2.

c. *Electronic filing*

i. *Authorization of electronic filing program.* A court may, by local rule, allow papers to be filed, signed, or verified by electronic means that are consistent with any technical standards established by the Judicial Conference of the United States. A local rule may require electronic filing only if reasonable exceptions are allowed. A paper filed electronically in compliance with a local rule is a written paper for purposes of the Federal Rules of Civil Procedure. FRCP 5(d)(3).

- The Court will accept for filing documents submitted, signed or verified by electronic means, that comply with the rules in NY R USDCTSD CM/ECF, S.D. NY R USDCTSD CM/ECF, S.D.(I). The information in NY R USDCTSD CM/ECF, S.D. applies only to cases assigned to the ECF system. NY R USDCTSD CM/ECF, S.D.(Introduction).

- Parties serving and filing papers shall follow the instructions regarding Electronic Case Filing (ECF) published on the website of each respective Court. A paper served and filed by electronic means in accordance with such instructions is, for purposes of FRCP 5, served and filed in compliance with the Local Civil Rules of the Southern and Eastern Districts of New York. NY R USDCTS&ED Civ Rule 5.2(a). Parties have an obligation to review the Court's actual order, decree, or judgment (on ECF), which controls, and should not rely on the description on the docket or in the ECF Notice of Electronic Filing (NEF). NY R USDCTS&ED Civ Rule 5.2(c).

- The following should be observed when filing electronically: (1) the Federal Rules of Civil Procedure, (2) the Local Civil Rules of the United States District Courts for the Southern and Eastern Districts of New York, (3) the assigned judge's Individual Practices, and (4) the Court's Electronic Case Filing Rules & Instructions (NY R USDCTSD CM/ECF, S.D.). NY R USDCTSD CM/ECF, S.D.(Introduction).

ii. *Scope of electronic filing.* Except as expressly provided and in exceptional circumstances preventing a party from filing electronically, all documents required to be filed with the Court must be filed electronically. Any party unable to comply with this requirement must seek permission of the Court to file in the traditional manner, on paper. Any such application made after regular business hours may be submitted through the night depository box maintained pursuant to NY R USDCTS&ED Civ Rule 1.2. NY R USDCTSD CM/ECF, S.D.(I)(1)(1.1).

- *Documents filed by pro se litigants.* Unless otherwise ordered by the Court, documents filed by pro se litigants must be filed in the traditional manner, on paper, and will be scanned and docketed by the Clerk's Office into the ECF system. NY R USDCTSD CM/ECF, S.D.(I)(1)(1.1). Pro se litigants must file pleadings and documents in the traditional manner on paper unless the assigned judge has granted permission to electronically file on the ECF system. NY R USDCTSD CM/ECF, S.D.(Introduction).

- *Letters.* Except for letters to be filed under seal, letters addressed to judges who accept letters may be filed electronically. Parties should consult the assigned judge's Individual Practices to determine if the judge accepts letters at all and, if he or she does, whether the judge has any page limitations on letters and/or requires courtesy copies of letters filed on ECF (and, if so, by what means of delivery). NY R USDCTSD CM/ECF, S.D.(II)(13)(13.1). Letters solely between parties or their counsel or otherwise not addressed to the Court may not be filed electronically on ECF (except as exhibits to an otherwise properly filed document). NY R USDCTSD CM/ECF, S.D.(II)(13)(13.1). For more information on filing letters, refer to NY R USDCTSD CM/ECF, S.D.(II)(13)(13.1).

- *Proposed orders, judgments and decrees.* Proposed orders, judgments and decrees shall be presented as directed by the ECF rules published on the website of each respective Court. NY R USDCTS&ED Civ Rule 77.1. For more information, refer to NY R USDCTS&ED Civ Rule 77.1.

iii. *Exceptions to electronic filing.* In an ECF case, the documents that should not be electronically filed include:

- Miscellaneous Case initiating documents, NY R USDCTSD CM/ECF, S.D.(II)(18)(18.2);

- Proposed orders; proposed judgments, stipulations; consents, NY R USDCTSD CM/ECF, S.D.(II)(18)(18.3);

- Orders to show cause / temporary restraining orders, NY R USDCTSD CM/ECF, S.D.(II)(18)(18.4);

- Sealed documents, NY R USDCTSD CM/ECF, S.D.(II)(18)(18.5); and

- Surety bonds, NY R USDCTSD CM/ECF, S.D.(II)(18)(18.6).

- In cases where the record of an administrative or other prior proceeding must be filed with the Court, such record may be served and filed in hard copy without prior motion and order of the Court. NY R USDCTSD CM/ECF, S.D.(I)(5)(5.3).

- For more documents excepted from electronic filing, and for more information on such documents, refer to NY R USDCTSD CM/ECF, S.D.(II)(18).

iv. *Consequences of electronic filing.* Except as otherwise provided in NY R USDCTSD CM/ECF, S.D.(I)(4), electronic filing of a document in the ECF system consistent with these procedures, together with the transmission of a Notice of Electronic Filing (NEF) from the Court, constitutes filing of the document for all purposes of the Federal Rules of Civil Procedure and the Local Civil Rules of the United States District Courts for the Southern and Eastern Districts of New York and constitutes entry of the document on the docket kept by the Clerk under FRCP 58 and FRCP 79. NY R USDCTSD CM/ECF, S.D.(I)(3)(3.1).

v. For more information on electronic filing, refer to NY R USDCTSD CM/ECF, S.D.

2. *Service requirements*

   a. *Service; When required*

     i. *In general.* Unless the Federal Rules of Civil Procedure provide otherwise, each of the following papers must be served on every party:

- An order stating that service is required;
- A pleading filed after the original complaint, unless the court orders otherwise under FRCP 5(c) because there are numerous defendants;
- A discovery paper required to be served on a party, unless the court orders otherwise;
- A written motion, except one that may be heard ex parte; and
- A written notice, appearance, demand, or offer of judgment, or any similar paper. FRCP 5(a)(1).

     ii. *If a party fails to appear.* No service is required on a party who is in default for failing to appear. But a pleading that asserts a new claim for relief against such a party must be served on that party under FRCP 4. FRCP 5(a)(2).

     iii. *Seizing property.* If an action is begun by seizing property and no person is or need be named as a defendant, any service required before the filing of an appearance, answer, or claim must be made on the person who had custody or possession of the property when it was seized. FRCP 5(a)(3).

   b. *Service; How made*

     i. *Serving an attorney.* If a party is represented by an attorney, service under FRCP 5 must be made on the attorney unless the court orders service on the party. FRCP 5(b)(1).

     ii. *Service in general.* A paper is served under FRCP 5 by:

- Handing it to the person;
- Leaving it: (1) at the person's office with a clerk or other person in charge or, if no one is in charge, in a conspicuous place in the office; or (2) if the person has no office or the office is closed, at the person's dwelling or usual place of abode with someone of suitable age and discretion who resides there;
- Mailing it to the person's last known address—in which event service is complete upon mailing;
- Leaving it with the court clerk if the person has no known address;
- Sending it by electronic means if the person consented in writing—in which event service is complete upon transmission, but is not effective if the serving party learns that it did not reach the person to be served; or
- Delivering it by any other means that the person consented to in writing—in which event service is complete when the person making service delivers it to the agency designated to make delivery. FRCP 5(b)(2).

     iii. *Service by overnight delivery.* Service upon an attorney may be made by overnight delivery service. "Overnight delivery service" means any delivery service which regularly accepts items for overnight delivery. Overnight delivery service shall be deemed service by mail for purposes of FRCP 5 and FRCP 6. NY R USDCTS&ED Civ Rule 5.3.

     iv. *Service by electronic means.* Parties serving and filing papers shall follow the instructions regarding Electronic Case Filing (ECF) published on the website of each respective Court. A paper served and filed by electronic means in accordance with such instructions is, for purposes of FRCP 5, served and filed in compliance with the Local Civil Rules of the United States District Courts for the Southern and Eastern Districts of New York. NY R USDCTS&ED Civ Rule 5.2(a). Parties have an obligation to review the Court's actual order, decree, or judgment (on ECF), which controls, and should not rely on the description on the docket or in the ECF Notice of Electronic Filing (NEF). NY R USDCTS&ED Civ Rule 5.2(c).

- *Notice of electronic filing (NEF).* In cases assigned to the ECF system, service is complete provided all parties receive a Notice of Electronic Filing (NEF), which is sent automatically by email from the Court (see the NEF for a list of who did/did not receive notice electronically). Transmission of the NEF constitutes service upon all Filing and Receiving Users who are listed as recipients of notice by electronic mail. NY R USDCTSD CM/ECF, S.D.(I)(9)(9.1). In cases assigned to the ECF system, if all parties receive a NEF, service is complete upon transmission of the NEF by the Court, and you are not required to serve a paper copy. NY R USDCTSD CM/ECF, S.D.(II)(19)(19.2). It remains the duty of Filing and Receiving Users to maintain current contact information with the court and to regularly review the docket sheet of the case. NY R USDCTSD CM/ECF, S.D.(I)(9)(9.1).

- *Mailing of court-initiated documents.* The Clerk's Office will no longer mail paper copies of court-initiated documents to Filing and Receiving Users. The Clerk's Office will mail copies of all court-initiated documents to pro se parties who have not registered as Filing or Receiving Users. NY R USDCTSD CM/ECF, S.D.(II)(19)(19.1).

- *No receipt of a NEF.* If any party does not receive a NEF, you are required to accomplish service on that party in the traditional manner, in paper form. NY R USDCTSD CM/ECF, S.D.(II)(19)(19.2). The NEF receipt will inform you who will receive notice of the filing "electronically" (by e-mail from the Court) and who will receive notice "by other means" (traditional service in paper form). NY R USDCTSD CM/ECF, S.D.(II)(19)(19.2).

- *Service on non-filing or non-receiving users.* Attorneys and pro se parties who are not Filing or Receiving Users must be served with a paper copy of any electronically filed pleading or other document. Service of such paper copy must be made according to the Federal Rules of Civil Procedure and the Local Civil Rules of the United States District Courts for the Southern and Eastern Districts of New York. NY R USDCTSD CM/ECF, S.D.(I)(9)(9.2). Such paper service must be documented by electronically filing proof of service. NY R USDCTSD CM/ECF, S.D.(I)(9)(9.2); NY R USDCTSD CM/ECF, S.D.(II)(19)(19.2). Where the Clerk scans and electronically files pleadings and documents on behalf of a pro se party, the associated NEF constitutes service. NY R USDCTSD CM/ECF, S.D.(I)(9)(9.2).

- For more information on service by electronic means, refer to NY R USDCTSD CM/ECF, S.D.(II)(19).

v. *Using court facilities.* If a local rule so authorizes, a party may use the court's transmission facilities to make service under FRCP 5(b)(2)(E). FRCP 5(b)(3).

c. *Serving numerous defendants*

i. *In general.* If an action involves an unusually large number of defendants, the court may, on motion or on its own, order that:

- Defendants' pleadings and replies to them need not be served on other defendants;

- Any crossclaim, counterclaim, avoidance, or affirmative defense in those pleadings and replies to them will be treated as denied or avoided by all other parties; and

- Filing any such pleading and serving it on the plaintiff constitutes notice of the pleading to all parties. FRCP 5(c)(1).

ii. *Notifying parties.* A copy of every such order must be served on the parties as the court directs. FRCP 5(c)(2).

3. *Individual judge practices.* Refer to the Miscellaneous section of this document for information on individual judge practices on filing and serving documents.

## G. Hearings

1. *Hearings, generally*

a. *Oral argument.* Due process does not require that oral argument be permitted on a motion and, except as otherwise provided by local rule, the district court has discretion to determine whether it will decide the motion on the papers or hear argument by counsel (and perhaps receive evidence). FPP § 1190; F.D.I.C. v. Deglau, 207 F.3d 153 (3d Cir. 2000). The parties and their attorneys shall only appear to argue the motion if so directed by the Court by order or by a Judge's Individual Practice. NY R USDCTS&ED Civ Rule 6.1(c).

b. *Providing a regular schedule for oral hearings.* A court may establish regular times and places for oral hearings on motions. FRCP 78(a).

c. *Providing for submission on briefs.* By rule or order, the court may provide for submitting and determining motions on briefs, without oral hearings. FRCP 78(b).

2. *Individual judge practices.* Refer to the Miscellaneous section of this document for information on individual judge practices on hearings.

## H. Forms

### 1. Federal Motion to Compel Discovery Forms

a. Notice of motion; To compel required disclosure of names and addresses of witnesses and persons having knowledge of the claims involved; Civil proceeding. AMJUR PP DEPOSITION § 6.

b. Motion; To compel required disclosure of names and addresses of witnesses and persons having knowledge of the claims involved. AMJUR PP DEPOSITION § 7.

c. Motion; To compel answer to interrogatories; Complete failure to answer. AMJUR PP DEPOSITION § 403.

d. Affidavit; In opposition of motion to compel psychiatric or physical examinations; By attorney. AMJUR PP DEPOSITION § 645.

e. Motion; To compel further responses to interrogatories; Various grounds. AMJUR PP DEPOSITION § 713.

f. Affidavit; In support of motion to compel answers to interrogatories and to impose sanctions. AMJUR PP DEPOSITION § 715.

g. Opposition; To motion to compel electronic discovery; Federal class action. AMJUR PP DEPOSITION § 721.

h. Notice of motion; For order to compel compliance with request to permit entry on real property for inspection. AMJUR PP DEPOSITION § 733.

i. Motion; To compel production of documents; After rejected request; Request for sanctions. AMJUR PP DEPOSITION § 734.

j. Affidavit; In support of motion to compel production of documents; By attorney. AMJUR PP DEPOSITION § 736.

k. Motion; To compel doctor's production of medical records for trial. AMJUR PP DEPOSITION § 744.

l. Notice of motion to compel party to answer deposition questions. 3B FEDFORMS § 3695.

m. Motion to compel deposition, request for sanctions and request for expedited hearing. 3B FEDFORMS § 3698.

n. Motion to compel answer to interrogatories. 3B FEDFORMS § 3699.

o. Affidavit in support of motion. 3B FEDFORMS § 3702.

p. Objection to motion for order requiring witness to answer oral questions on deposition. 3B FEDFORMS § 3705.

q. Motion; To compel answers to outstanding discovery requests. FEDPROF § 23:43.

r. Motion; To compel required disclosure of names and addresses of witnesses and persons having knowledge of the claims involved. FEDPROF § 23:44.

s. Motion; To compel answer to questions asked on oral or written examination. FEDPROF § 23:207.

t. Motion; To compel further answers to questions asked on oral or written examination and to award expenses of motion. FEDPROF § 23:208.

u. Motion; To compel party to produce witness at deposition. FEDPROF § 23:209.

v.   Affidavit; By opposing attorney; In opposition to motion to compel answers asked at deposition; Answers tend to incriminate. FEDPROF § 23:212.

w.   Motion; To compel answer to interrogatories; Complete failure to answer. FEDPROF § 23:375.

x.   Motion; To compel further responses to interrogatories; Various grounds. FEDPROF § 23:376.

y.   Motion to compel discovery. GOLDLTGFMS § 21:2.

## I.  Applicable Rules

1.  *Federal rules*

a.   Serving and filing pleadings and other papers. FRCP 5.

b.   Constitutional challenge to a statute; Notice, certification, and intervention. FRCP 5.1.

c.   Privacy protection for filings made with the court. FRCP 5.2.

d.   Computing and extending time; Time for motion papers. FRCP 6.

e.   Pleadings allowed; Form of motions and other papers. FRCP 7.

f.   Form of pleadings. FRCP 10.

g.   Signing pleadings, motions, and other papers; Representations to the court; Sanctions. FRCP 11.

h.   Duty to disclose; General provisions governing discovery. FRCP 26.

i.   Failure to make disclosures or to cooperate in discovery; Sanctions. FRCP 37.

j.   Taking testimony. FRCP 43.

k.   Hearing motions; Submission on briefs. FRCP 78.

2.  *Local rules*

a.   Night depository. NY R USDCTS&ED Civ Rule 1.2.

b.   Duty of attorneys in related cases. NY R USDCTS&ED Civ Rule 1.6.

c.   Filing of discovery materials. NY R USDCTS&ED Civ Rule 5.1.

d.   Electronic service and filing of documents. NY R USDCTS&ED Civ Rule 5.2.

e.   Service by overnight delivery. NY R USDCTS&ED Civ Rule 5.3.

f.   Service and filing of motion papers. NY R USDCTS&ED Civ Rule 6.1.

g.   Orders on motions. NY R USDCTS&ED Civ Rule 6.2.

h.   Computation of time. NY R USDCTS&ED Civ Rule 6.4.

i.   Motion papers. NY R USDCTS&ED Civ Rule 7.1.

j.   Authorities to be provided to pro se litigants. NY R USDCTS&ED Civ Rule 7.2.

k.   Form of pleadings, motions, and other papers. NY R USDCTS&ED Civ Rule 11.1.

l.   Verbatim quotation of discovery materials. NY R USDCTS&ED Civ Rule 37.1.

m.   Mode of raising discovery disputes with the court (Southern District only). NY R USDCTS&ED Civ Rule 37.2.

n.   Submission of orders, judgments and decrees. NY R USDCTS&ED Civ Rule 77.1.

o.   Alternative dispute resolution (Southern District only). NY R USDCTS&ED Civ Rule 83.9.

p.   Electronic case filing rules and instructions. NY R USDCTSD CM/ECF, S.D.

q.   Related cases. NY R USDCTSD Div. Bus., Rule 13.

r.   Filing at either courthouse. NY R USDCTSD Div. Bus., Rule 22.

## J.  Miscellaneous

**NOTE: Individual judges' rules may apply. For available judge-level information, refer to:**

DISTRICT JUDGE RONNIE ABRAMS: NY R USDCTSD Abrams-Civ Prac; NY R USDCTSD Abrams-Crim Prac; NY R USDCTSD Abrams-Pro Se; NY R USDCTSD Abrams-Case Mgt; NY R USDCTSD Abrams-Jury.

DISTRICT JUDGE DEBORAH A. BATTS: NY R USDCTSD Batts-Practices.

DISTRICT JUDGE RICHARD M. BERMAN: NY R USDCTSD Berman-Practices; NY R USDCTSD Berman-Default; NY R USDCTSD Berman-Sentencing; NY R USDCTSD Berman-Media.

DISTRICT JUDGE VINCENT L. BRICCETTI: NY R USDCTSD Briccetti-Practices; NY R USDCTSD Briccetti-Plan; NY R USDCTSD Briccetti-Notice.

DISTRICT JUDGE VERNON S. BRODERICK: NY R USDCTSD Broderick-Civil; NY R USDCTSD Broderick-Crim; NY R USDCTSD Broderick-Case Mgt; NY R USDCTSD Broderick-Jury.

DISTRICT JUDGE NAOMI REICE BUCHWALD: NY R USDCTSD Buchwald-Practices.

DISTRICT JUDGE VALERIE E. CAPRONI: NY R USDCTSD Caproni-Prac; NY R USDCTSD Caproni--Pro Se; NY R USDCTSD Caproni-Case Mgt; NY R USDCTSD Caproni-Crim Prac.

DISTRICT JUDGE ANDREW L. CARTER JR.: NY R USDCTSD Carter-Practices.

DISTRICT JUDGE KEVIN P. CASTEL: NY R USDCTSD Castel-Practices; NY R USDCTSD Castel-Default; NY R USDCTSD Castel-Scheduling; NY R USDCTSD Castel-Complex; NY R USDCTSD Castel-Trials; NY R USDCTSD Castel-Sentencing.

DISTRICT JUDGE DENISE L. COTE: NY R USDCTSD Cote-Civil Practices; NY R USDCTSD Cote-Pro Se; NY R USDCTSD Cote-Maritime Ord; NY R USDCTSD Cote-Crim Practices; NY R USDCTSD Cote-Crim Trials; NY R USDCTSD Cote-Sentencing.

DISTRICT JUDGE PAUL A. CROTTY: NY R USDCTSD Crotty-Practices; NY R USDCTSD Crotty-Sentencing; NY R USDCTSD Crotty-Calls; NY R USDCTSD Crotty-Scheduling.

DISTRICT JUDGE GEORGE B. DANIELS: NY R USDCTSD Daniels-Practices.

DISTRICT JUDGE KEVIN T. DUFFY: NY R USDCTSD Duffy-Practices.

DISTRICT JUDGE PAUL A. ENGELMAYER: NY R USDCTSD Engelmayer-Practices; NY R USDCTSD Engelmayer-Scheduling; NY R USDCTSD Engelmayer-Sentencing; NY R USDCTSD Engelmayer-Pro Se; NY R USDCTSD Engelmayer-Crim.

DISTRICT JUDGE KATHERINE POLK FAILLA: NY R USDCTSD Failla-Civ Prac; NY R USDCTSD Failla-Crim Prac; NY R USDCTSD Failla-Case Mgt.

DISTRICT JUDGE KATHERINE B. FORREST: NY R USDCTSD Forrest-Civil Prac; NY R USDCTSD Forrest-Crim Prac; NY R USDCTSD Forrest-Crim Pretrial; NY R USDCTSD Forrest-Scheduling; NY R US-DCTSD Forrest-Patent Scheduling; NY R USDCTSD Forrest-Sentencing; NY R USDCTSD Forrest-Order 1; NY R USDCTSD Forrest-Order 2.

DISTRICT JUDGE JESSE M. FURMAN: NY R USDCTSD Furman-Civil Prac; NY R USDCTSD Furman-Crim Prac; NY R USDCTSD Furman-Pro Se Prac; NY R USDCTSD Furman-Trials; NY R USDCTSD Furman-Scheduling; NY R USDCTSD Furman-Rights.

DISTRICT JUDGE PAUL G. GARDEPHE: NY R USDCTSD Gardephe-Civ Prac; NY R USDCTSD Gardephe-Pretrial; NY R USDCTSD Gardephe-Prot Ord; NY R USDCTSD Gardephe-Maritime; NY R USDCTSD Gardephe-Crim Prac; NY R USDCTSD Gardephe-Trial.

DISTRICT JUDGE THOMAS P. GRIESA: NY R USDCTSD Griesa-Practices.

DISTRICT JUDGE CHARLES S. HAIGHT: NY R USDCTSD Haight-Practices.

DISTRICT JUDGE ALVIN K. HELLERSTEIN: NY R USDCTSD Hellerstein-Practices; NY R USDCTSD Hellerstein--Sept 11.

DISTRICT JUDGE LEWIS A. KAPLAN: NY R USDCTSD Kaplan-Practices; NY R USDCTSD Kaplan-Sentencing.

DISTRICT JUDGE KENNETH M. KARAS: NY R USDCTSD Karas-Practices; NY R USDCTSD Karas-Case Mgt; NY R USDCTSD Karas-Default; NY R USDCTSD Karas-Sentencing; NY R USDCTSD Karas-Rights.

DISTRICT JUDGE JOHN F. KEENAN: NY R USDCTSD Keenan-Practices.

DISTRICT JUDGE JOHN G. KOELTL: NY R USDCTSD Koeltl-Practices.

DISTRICT JUDGE VICTOR MARRERO: NY R USDCTSD Marrero-Practices; NY R USDCTSD Marrero-Scheduling; NY R USDCTSD Marrero-Default; NY R USDCTSD Marrero-Trial Proc.

DISTRICT JUDGE COLLEEN McMAHON: NY R USDCTSD McMahon-Practices; NY R USDCTSD McMahon-RICO; NY R USDCTSD McMahon-Copies; NY R USDCTSD McMahon-Scheduling; NY R US-DCTSD McMahon-Elec Disc; NY R USDCTSD McMahon-Sentencing.

DISTRICT JUDGE ALISON J. NATHAN: NY R USDCTSD Nathan-Civ Prac; NY R USDCTSD Nathan-Crim Prac; NY R USDCTSD Nathan-Pro Se; NY R USDCTSD Nathan-Scheduling.

DISTRICT JUDGE J. PAUL OETKEN: NY R USDCTSD Oetken-Civ Prac; NY R USDCTSD Oetken-Case Mgt; NY R USDCTSD Oetken-Crim Prac; NY R USDCTSD Oetken-Pro Se.

DISTRICT JUDGE WILLIAM H. PAULEY, III: NY R USDCTSD Pauley-Crim Cases; NY R USDCTSD Pauley-Practices.

DISTRICT JUDGE LORETTA A. PRESKA: NY R USDCTSD Preska-Practices.

DISTRICT JUDGE JED S. RAKOFF: NY R USDCTSD Rakoff-Practices; NY R USDCTSD Rakoff-Scheduling; NY R USDCTSD Rakoff-Prot Ord; NY R USDCTSD Rakoff-Maritime Ord.

DISTRICT JUDGE EDGARDO RAMOS: NY R USDCTSD Ramos--Practices; NY R USDCTSD Ramos-Case Mgt.

DISTRICT JUDGE NELSON S. ROMAN: NY R USDCTSD Roman-Civ Prac; NY R USDCTSD Roman-Pro Se; NY R USDCTSD Roman-Crim Prac; NY R USDCTSD Roman-Case Mgt.

DISTRICT JUDGE LEONARD B. SAND: NY R USDCTSD Sand-Practices.

DISTRICT JUDGE LORNA G. SCHOFIELD: NY R USDCTSD Schofield-Civ Prac; NY R USDCTSD Schofield-Crim Prac; NY R USDCTSD Schofield-Sched; NY R USDCTSD Schofield-Pro Se; NY R USDCTSD Schofield-Advice.

DISTRICT JUDGE CATHY SEIBEL: NY R USDCTSD Seibel-Practices.

DISTRICT JUDGE LOUIS L. STANTON: NY R USDCTSD Stanton-Practices; NY R USDCTSD Stanton-Pretrial.

DISTRICT JUDGE SIDNEY H. STEIN: NY R USDCTSD Stein-Practices.

DISTRICT JUDGE RICHARD J. SULLIVAN: NY R USDCTSD Sullivan-Practices; NY R USDCTSD Sullivan-Scheduling; NY R USDCTSD Sullivan-Sentencing; NY R USDCTSD Sullivan-Juries; NY R USDCTSD Sullivan-Trial; NY R USDCTSD Sullivan-Default.

DISTRICT JUDGE LAURA TAYLOR SWAIN: NY R USDCTSD Swain-Practices; NY R USDCTSD Swain-Trial; NY R USDCTSD Swain-Crim Trial; NY R USDCTSD Swain-Juries; NY R USDCTSD Swain-Sentencing; NY R USDCTSD Swain-Rights.

DISTRICT JUDGE ROBERT W. SWEET: NY R USDCTSD Sweet-Practices.

DISTRICT JUDGE ANALISA TORRES: NY R USDCTSD Torres-Civ Prac; NY R USDCTSD Torres-Pro Se; NY R USDCTSD Torres-Scheduling.

DISTRICT JUDGE KIMBA M. WOOD: NY R USDCTSD Wood-Practices; NY R USDCTSD Wood-Scheduling; NY R USDCTSD Wood-Discovery; NY R USDCTSD Wood-RICO; NY R USDCTSD Wood-Juries; NY R USDCTSD Wood-Trial; NY R USDCTSD Wood-Media.

DISTRICT JUDGE GREGORY H. WOODS: NY R USDCTSD Woods-Civ Prac; NY R USDCTSD Woods-Pro Se; NY R USDCTSD Woods-Sched; NY R USDCTSD Woods-Crim Prac; NY R USDCTSD Woods-Protect Order; NY R USDCTSD Woods-Speedy Trial.

MAGISTRATE JUDGE JAMES L. COTT: NY R USDCTSD Cott-Practices; NY R USDCTSD Cott-Settlement.

MAGISTRATE JUDGE PAUL E. DAVISON: NY R USDCTSD Davison-Practices.

MAGISTRATE JUDGE RONALD L. ELLIS: NY R USDCTSD Ellis-Practices.

MAGISTRATE JUDGE KEVIN N. FOX: NY R USDCTSD Fox-Practices; NY R USDCTSD Fox-Settlement.

MAGISTRATE JUDGE JAMES C. FRANCIS: NY R USDCTSD Francis-Practices.

MAGISTRATE JUDGE DEBRA FREEMAN: NY R USDCTSD Freeman-Practices; NY R USDCTSD Freeman-Settlement.

MAGISTRATE JUDGE GABRIEL W. GORENSTEIN: NY R USDCTSD Gorenstein-Practices; NY R US-DCTSD Gorenstein-Ackn.

MAGISTRATE JUDGE FRANK MAAS: NY R USDCTSD Maas-Practices; NY R USDCTSD Maas-Discontinuance; NY R USDCTSD Maas-Conf; NY R USDCTSD Maas-Settlement.

MAGISTRATE JUDGE JUDITH C. McCARTHY: NY R USDCTSD McCarthy-Practices; NY R USDCTSD McCarthy-Conduct.

MAGISTRATE JUDGE BARBARA MOSES: NY R USDCTSD Moses-Practices.

MAGISTRATE JUDGE SARAH NETBURN: NY R USDCTSD Netburn-Civil; NY R USDCTSD Netburn-Settlement; NY R USDCTSD Netburn-Case Mgt; NY R USDCTSD Netburn--Pro Se.

MAGISTRATE JUDGE ANDREW J. PECK: NY R USDCTSD Peck-Practices; NY R USDCTSD Peck-Order; NY R USDCTSD Peck-Rule 502(d).

MAGISTRATE JUDGE HENRY PITMAN: NY R USDCTSD Pitman-Practices.

MAGISTRATE JUDGE LISA MARGARET SMITH: NY R USDCTSD Smith-Practices; NY R USDCTSD Smith-Trials.

## Motions, Oppositions and Replies
## Motion for Discovery Sanctions

### Document Last Updated September 2016

A. **Checklist**

(I) ❑ Matters to be considered by the parties before filing discovery motions

  (a) ❑ Matters to be considered by the moving party

    (1) ❑ Required documents

      (i) ❑ Letter-motion for a pre-motion discovery conference

    (2) ❑ Timing

      (i) ❑ There are no specific timing requirements for submitting a letter-motion for a pre-motion discovery conference to the court

  (b) ❑ Matters to be considered by the opposing party

    (1) ❑ Documents to consider

      (i) ❑ Responsive letter

    (2) ❑ Timing

      (i) ❑ There are no specific timing requirements for submitting a responsive letter to the court

(II) ❑ Matters to be considered by moving party

  (a) ❑ Required documents

    (1) ❑ Notice of motion and motion

    (2) ❑ Certificate of compliance

    (3) ❑ Memorandum of law

    (4) ❑ Certificate of service

  (b) ❑ Supplemental documents

    (1) ❑ Supporting evidence

    (2) ❑ Notice of constitutional question

    (3) ❑ Copies of authorities

    (4) ❑ Proposed order

    (5) ❑ Statement explaining untimely electronic filing

    (6) ❑ Courtesy copies

  (c) ❑ Timing

    (1) ❑ A written motion and notice of the hearing must be served at least fourteen (14) days before the time specified for the hearing, with the following exceptions: (i) when the motion may be heard ex parte; (ii) when the Federal Rules of Civil Procedure set a different time; or (iii) when a court order—which a party may, for good cause, apply for ex parte—sets a different time

    (2) ❑ Any affidavit supporting a motion must be served with the motion

(III) ❑ Matters to be considered by opposing party

  (a) ❑ Required documents

    (1) ❑ Answering memorandum of law

    (2) ❑ Certificate of service

  (b) ❑ Supplemental documents

    (1) ❑ Supporting evidence

    (2) ❑ Notice of constitutional question

    (3) ❑ Copies of authorities

    (4) ❑ Statement explaining untimely electronic filing

    (5) ❑ Courtesy copies

  (c) ❑ Timing

    (1) ❑ Any opposing affidavits and answering memoranda of law shall be served within seven (7) days after service of the moving papers

    (2) ❑ Except as FRCP 59(c) provides otherwise, any opposing affidavit must be served at least seven (7) days before the hearing, unless the court permits service at another time

## B. Timing

1. *Prerequisites to filing a discovery motion*

  a. *Letter-motion for a pre-motion discovery conference.* There are no specific timing requirements for submitting a letter-motion for a pre-motion discovery conference to the court.

  b. *Responsive letter.* There are no specific timing requirements for submitting a responsive letter to the court.

  c. *Reply letter.* There are no specific timing requirements for submitting a reply letter to the court.

2. *Motion for discovery sanctions.* There are no specific timing requirements for moving for discovery sanctions.

3. *Timing of motions, generally*

  a. *Motion and notice of hearing.* Except for letter-motions as permitted by NY R USDCTS&ED Civ Rule 7.1(d), and unless otherwise provided by statute or rule or by the Court in a Judge's Individual Practice or in a direction in a particular case, upon any motion, the notice of motion, supporting affidavits, and memoranda shall be served and filed as follows: on all motions and applications under FRCP 26 through FRCP 37 inclusive and FRCP 45(d)(3), the notice of motion, supporting affidavits, and memoranda of law shall be served by the moving party on all other parties that have appeared in the action. NY R USDCTS&ED Civ Rule 6.1(a)(1). A written motion and notice of the hearing must be served at least fourteen (14) days before the time specified for the hearing, with the following exceptions:

    i. When the motion may be heard ex parte;

    ii. When the Federal Rules of Civil Procedure set a different time; or

     iii.   When a court order—which a party may, for good cause, apply for ex parte—sets a different time. FRCP 6(c)(1).

  b.  *Supporting affidavit.* Any affidavit supporting a motion must be served with the motion. FRCP 6(c)(2).

4.  *Timing of opposing papers.* Except for letter-motions as permitted by NY R USDCTS&ED Civ Rule 7.1(d), and unless otherwise provided by statute or rule or by the Court in a Judge's Individual Practice or in a direction in a particular case, upon any motion, the notice of motion, supporting affidavits, and memoranda shall be served and filed as follows: on all motions and applications under FRCP 26 through FRCP 37 inclusive and FRCP 45(d)(3), any opposing affidavits and answering memoranda of law shall be served within seven (7) days after service of the moving papers. NY R USDCTS&ED Civ Rule 6.1(a)(2).

  a.  *Opposing affidavit.* Except as FRCP 59(c) provides otherwise, any opposing affidavit must be served at least seven (7) days before the hearing, unless the court permits service at another time. FRCP 6(c)(2).

5.  *Timing of reply papers.* Where the respondent files an answering affidavit setting up a new matter, the moving party ordinarily is allowed a reasonable time to file a reply affidavit since failure to deny the new matter by affidavit may operate as an admission of its truth. AMJUR MOTIONS § 25.

  a.  *Reply affidavits and reply memoranda of law.* Except for letter-motions as permitted by NY R USDCTS&ED Civ Rule 7.1(d), and unless otherwise provided by statute or rule or by the Court in a Judge's Individual Practice or in a direction in a particular case, upon any motion, the notice of motion, supporting affidavits, and memoranda shall be served and filed as follows: on all motions and applications under FRCP 26 through FRCP 37 inclusive and FRCP 45(d)(3), any reply affidavits and reply memoranda of law shall be served within two (2) days after service of the answering papers. NY R USDCTS&ED Civ Rule 6.1(a)(3).

6.  *Computation of time*

  a.  *Computing time.* FRCP 6 applies in computing any time period specified in the Federal Rules of Civil Procedure, in any local rule or court order, or in any statute that does not specify a method of computing time. FRCP 6(a). In computing any period of time prescribed or allowed by the Local Civil Rules of the United States District Courts for the Southern and Eastern Districts of New York or the Local Admiralty and Maritime Rules, the provisions of FRCP 6 shall apply unless otherwise stated. NY R USDCTS&ED Civ Rule 6.4.

    i.  *Period stated in days or a longer unit.* In computing periods of days, refer to FRCP 6 and NY R USDCTS&ED Civ Rule 6.4. NY R USDCTS&ED Civ Rule 6.1(a). When the period is stated in days or a longer unit of time:

- Exclude the day of the event that triggers the period;
- Count every day, including intermediate Saturdays, Sundays, and legal holidays; and
- Include the last day of the period, but if the last day is a Saturday, Sunday, or legal holiday, the period continues to run until the end of the next day that is not a Saturday, Sunday, or legal holiday. FRCP 6(a)(1). In the Local Civil Rules of the United States District Courts for the Southern and Eastern Districts of New York, as in the Federal Rules of Civil Procedure as amended effective December 1, 2009, Saturdays, Sundays, and legal holidays are no longer excluded in computing periods of time. If the last day of the period is a Saturday, Sunday, or legal holiday, the period continues to run until the end of the next day that is not a Saturday, Sunday, or legal holiday. NY R USDCTS&ED Civ Rule 6.4.

    ii.  *Period stated in hours.* When the period is stated in hours:

- Begin counting immediately on the occurrence of the event that triggers the period;
- Count every hour, including hours during intermediate Saturdays, Sundays, and legal holidays; and
- If the period would end on a Saturday, Sunday, or legal holiday, the period continues to run until the same time on the next day that is not a Saturday, Sunday, or legal holiday. FRCP 6(a)(2). In the Local Civil Rules of the United States District Courts for the Southern and

Eastern Districts of New York, as in the Federal Rules of Civil Procedure as amended effective December 1, 2009, Saturdays, Sundays, and legal holidays are no longer excluded in computing periods of time. If the last day of the period is a Saturday, Sunday, or legal holiday, the period continues to run until the end of the next day that is not a Saturday, Sunday, or legal holiday. NY R USDCTS&ED Civ Rule 6.4.

iii. *Inaccessibility of the clerk's office.* Unless the court orders otherwise, if the clerk's office is inaccessible:

- On the last day for filing under FRCP 6(a)(1), then the time for filing is extended to the first accessible day that is not a Saturday, Sunday, or legal holiday; or

- During the last hour for filing under FRCP 6(a)(2), then the time for filing is extended to the same time on the first accessible day that is not a Saturday, Sunday, or legal holiday. FRCP 6(a)(3).

iv. *"Last day" defined.* Unless a different time is set by a statute, local rule, or court order, the last day ends:

- For electronic filing, at midnight in the court's time zone; and

- For filing by other means, when the clerk's office is scheduled to close. FRCP 6(a)(4).

v. *"Next day" defined.* The "next day" is determined by continuing to count forward when the period is measured after an event and backward when measured before an event. FRCP 6(a)(5).

vi. *"Legal holiday" defined.* "Legal holiday" means:

- The day set aside by statute for observing New Year's Day, Martin Luther King Jr.'s Birthday, Washington's Birthday, Memorial Day, Independence Day, Labor Day, Columbus Day, Veterans' Day, Thanksgiving Day, or Christmas Day;

- Any day declared a holiday by the President or Congress; and

- For periods that are measured after an event, any other day declared a holiday by the state where the district court is located. FRCP 6(a)(6).

b. *Computation of electronic filing deadlines.* You can file electronically twenty-four (24) hours a day, seven (7) days a week, three hundred sixty-five (365) days a year. NY R USDCTSD CM/ECF, S.D.(II)(13)(13.10). Electronic filing must be completed before midnight local time where the Court is located in order to be considered timely filed that day. NY R USDCTSD CM/ECF, S.D.(I)(3)(3.3); NY R USDCTSD CM/ECF, S.D.(II)(13)(13.10); NY R USDCTSD CM/ECF, S.D.(II)(19)(19.4). An electronically filed document is deemed filed on the "filed on" date indicated on the Notice of Electronic Filing (NEF). NY R USDCTSD CM/ECF, S.D.(II)(13)(13.11).

i. *Technical failures.* A Filing User whose filing is made untimely as the result of a technical failure may seek appropriate relief from the Court. NY R USDCTSD CM/ECF, S.D.(I)(11). If you missed a filing deadline when the ECF system was out of order, attach a statement to your filing explaining how the interruption in service prevented you from filing in a timely fashion. NY R USDCTSD CM/ECF, S.D.(II)(23)(23.5).

c. *Extending time*

i. *In general.* When an act may or must be done within a specified time, the court may, for good cause, extend the time:

- With or without motion or notice if the court acts, or if a request is made, before the original time or its extension expires; or

- On motion made after the time has expired if the party failed to act because of excusable neglect. FRCP 6(b)(1).

ii. *Exceptions.* A court must not extend the time to act under FRCP 50(b), FRCP 50(d), FRCP 52(b), FRCP 59(b), FRCP 59(d), FRCP 59(e), and FRCP 60(b). FRCP 6(b)(2).

iii. Refer to the United States District Court for the Southern District of New York KeyRules Motion for Continuance/Extension of Time document for more information on extending time.

d. *Additional time after certain kinds of service.* When a party may or must act within a specified time after service and service is made under FRCP 5(b)(2)(C), FRCP 5(b)(2)(D), FRCP 5(b)(2)(E), or FRCP 5(b)(2)(F), three (3) days are added after the period would otherwise expire under FRCP 6(a). FRCP 6(d). Overnight delivery service shall be deemed service by mail for purposes of FRCP 5 and FRCP 6. NY R USDCTS&ED Civ Rule 5.3.

7. *Individual judge practices.* Refer to the Miscellaneous section of this document for information on individual judge practices on timing of documents.

## C. General Requirements

1. *Discovery motion procedure.* No motion under FRCP 26 through FRCP 37 inclusive shall be heard unless counsel for the moving party has first requested an informal conference with the Court by letter-motion for a pre-motion discovery conference (subject to the instructions regarding ECF published on the Court's website and the Judge's Individual Practices) and such request has either been denied or the discovery dispute has not been resolved as a consequence of such a conference. NY R USDCTS&ED Civ Rule 37.2.

   a. *Responsive letter.* If a motion is made by letter, the opposing party may file any response in letter form. NY R USDCTSD CM/ECF, S.D.(II)(13)(13.1).

   b. *Reply letter.* If a motion is made by letter. . .the moving party may file any reply in letter form. NY R USDCTSD CM/ECF, S.D.(II)(13)(13.1).

2. *Motions, generally*

   a. *Requirements.* A request for a court order must be made by motion. The motion must:

      i. Be in writing unless made during a hearing or trial;

      ii. State with particularity the grounds for seeking the order; and

      iii. State the relief sought. FRCP 7(b)(1).

   b. *Notice of motion.* A party interested in resisting the relief sought by a motion has a right to notice thereof, and an opportunity to be heard. AMJUR MOTIONS § 12.

      i. In addition to statutory or court rule provisions requiring notice of a motion—the purpose of such a notice requirement having been said to be to prevent a party from being prejudicially surprised by a motion—principles of natural justice dictate that an adverse party generally must be given notice that a motion will be presented to the court. AMJUR MOTIONS § 12.

      ii. "Notice," in this regard, means reasonable notice, including a meaningful opportunity to prepare and to defend against allegations of a motion. AMJUR MOTIONS § 12.

   c. *Writing requirement.* The writing requirement is intended to insure that the adverse parties are informed and have a record of both the motion's pendency and the grounds on which the movant seeks an order. FPP § 1191; Feldberg v. Quechee Lakes Corp., 463 F.3d 195 (2d Cir. 2006).

      i. It is sufficient "if the motion is stated in a written notice of the hearing of the motion." FPP § 1191.

   d. *Particularity requirement.* The particularity requirement insures that the opposing parties will have notice of their opponent's contentions. FEDPROC § 62:364; Goodman v. 1973 26 Foot Trojan Vessel, Arkansas Registration No. AR1439SN, 859 F.2d 71, 12 Fed.R.Serv.3d 645 (8th Cir. 1988). That requirement ensures that notice of the basis for the motion is provided to the court and to the opposing party so as to avoid prejudice, provide the opponent with a meaningful opportunity to respond, and provide the court with enough information to process the motion correctly. FEDPROC § 62:364; Andreas v. Volkswagen of America, Inc., 336 F.3d 789, 56 Fed.R.Serv.3d 6 (8th Cir. 2003).

      i. Reasonable specification of the grounds for a motion is sufficient. However, where a movant fails to state even one ground for granting the motion in question, the movant has failed to meet the minimal standard of "reasonable specification." FEDPROC § 62:364; Martinez v. Trainor, 556 F.2d 818, 23 Fed.R.Serv.2d 403 (7th Cir. 1977).

      ii. The court may excuse the failure to comply with the particularity requirement if it is inadvertent, and where no prejudice is shown by the opposing party. FEDPROC § 62:364.

   e. *Ex parte orders or orders to show cause to bring on a motion.* No ex parte order, or order to show cause to bring on a motion, will be granted except upon a clear and specific showing by affidavit of good and sufficient reasons why a procedure other than by notice of motion is necessary, and stating whether a previous application for similar relief has been made. NY R USDCTS&ED Civ Rule 6.1(d).

f. *Letter-motions.* Applications for extensions or adjournments, applications for a pre-motion conference, and similar non-dispositive matters as permitted by the instructions regarding ECF published on the website of each respective Court and any pertinent Individual Judge's Practices, may be brought by letter-motion filed via ECF pursuant to NY R USDCTS&ED Civ Rule 5.2(b). NY R USDCTS&ED Civ Rule 7.1(d).

    i. The following list of motions. . .may be made by LETTER-MOTION: (1) Motion to Adjourn Conference; (2) Motion to Change Attorney Name on Roll; (3) Motion to Compel; (4) Motion for Conference; (5) Motion to Consolidate Cases; (6) Motion to Continue; (7) Motion re: Discovery; (8) Motion to Expedite; (9) Motion for Extension of Time; (10) Motion for Extension of Time to Amend; (11) Motion for Extension of Time to Answer; (12) Motion for Extension of Time to Complete Discovery; (13) Motion for Extension of Time to File Document; (14) Motion for Extension of Time to File Response/Reply; (15) Motion for Extension of Time re Transcript; (16) Motion to File Amicus Brief; (17) Motion for Leave to File Document; (18) Motion for Leave to File Excess Pages; (19) Motion for Local Rule 37.2 Conference; (20) Motion for Oral Argument; (21) Motion to Reopen; (22) Motion to Reopen Case; (23) Motion to Seal Document; (24) Motion to Stay; (25) Motion to Substitute Attorney. NY R USDCTSD CM/ECF, S.D.(II)(13)(13.1).

    ii. If the Filing User is making a type of motion that does not appear in this list, the motion may not be made by letter. NY R USDCTSD CM/ECF, S.D.(II)(13)(13.1).

    iii. For more information on letter motions, refer to NY R USDCTSD CM/ECF, S.D.(II)(13)(13.1).

3. *Motion for discovery sanctions*

a. *Sanctions, generally.* FRCP 37 is flexible. The court is directed to make such orders as are "just" and is not limited in any case of disregard of the discovery rules or court orders under them to a stereotyped response. The sanctions enumerated in FRCP 37 are not exclusive and arbitrary but flexible, selective, and plural. The district court may, within reason, use as many and as varied sanctions as are necessary to hold the scales of justice even. FPP § 2284.

    i. There is one fixed limitation that should be noted. A party may not be imprisoned or otherwise punished for contempt of court for failure to submit to a physical or mental examination, or for failure to produce a person in his or her custody or under his or her control for such an examination. FPP § 2284; Sibbach v. Wilson & Co., 312 U.S. 1, 312 U.S. 655, 61 S.Ct. 422, 85 L.Ed. 479 (1941).

    ii. Although FRCP 37 is very broad, and the courts have considerable discretion in imposing sanctions as authorized by FRCP 37, there are constitutional limits, stemming from the Due Process Clause of U.S.C.A. Const. Amend. V and U.S.C.A. Const. Amend. XIV, on the imposition of sanctions. There are two principal facets of the due process issues:

- First, the court must ask whether there is a sufficient relationship between the discovery and the merits sought to be foreclosed by the sanction to legitimate depriving a party of the opportunity to litigate the merits. FPP § 2283.

- Second, before imposing a serious merits sanction the court should determine whether the party guilty of a failure to provide discovery was unable to comply with the discovery. FPP § 2283.

b. *Sanction for improper certification.* If a certification violates FRCP 26(g) without substantial justification, the court, on motion or on its own, must impose an appropriate sanction on the signer, the party on whose behalf the signer was acting, or both. The sanction may include an order to pay the reasonable expenses, including attorney's fees, caused by the violation. FRCP 26(g)(3).

c. *Motion to compel discovery; Payment of expenses; Protective orders*

    i. *If the motion is granted (or disclosure or discovery is provided after filing).* If the motion is granted—or if the disclosure or requested discovery is provided after the motion was filed—the court must, after giving an opportunity to be heard, require the party or deponent whose conduct necessitated the motion, the party or attorney advising that conduct, or both to pay the movant's reasonable expenses incurred in making the motion, including attorney's fees. But the court must not order this payment if:

- The movant filed the motion before attempting in good faith to obtain the disclosure or discovery without court action;

- The opposing party's nondisclosure, response, or objection was substantially justified; or

- Other circumstances make an award of expenses unjust. FRCP 37(a)(5)(A).

ii. *If the motion is denied.* If the motion is denied, the court may issue any protective order authorized under FRCP 26(c) and must, after giving an opportunity to be heard, require the movant, the attorney filing the motion, or both to pay the party or deponent who opposed the motion its reasonable expenses incurred in opposing the motion, including attorney's fees. But the court must not order this payment if the motion was substantially justified or other circumstances make an award of expenses unjust. FRCP 37(a)(5)(B).

iii. *If the motion is granted in part and denied in part.* If the motion is granted in part and denied in part, the court may issue any protective order authorized under FRCP 26(c) and may, after giving an opportunity to be heard, apportion the reasonable expenses for the motion. FRCP 37(a)(5)(C).

d. *Failure to comply with a court order*

i. *Sanctions in the district where the deposition is taken.* If the court where the discovery is taken orders a deponent to be sworn or to answer a question and the deponent fails to obey, the failure may be treated as contempt of court. If a deposition-related motion is transferred to the court where the action is pending, and that court orders a deponent to be sworn or to answer a question and the deponent fails to obey, the failure may be treated as contempt of either the court where the discovery is taken or the court where the action is pending. FRCP 37(b)(1).

ii. *Sanctions in the district where the action is pending; For not obeying a discovery order.* If a party or a party's officer, director, or managing agent—or a witness designated under FRCP 30(b)(6) or FRCP 31(a)(4)—fails to obey an order to provide or permit discovery, including an order under FRCP 26(f), FRCP 35, or FRCP 37(a), the court where the action is pending may issue further just orders. They may include the following:

- Directing that the matters embraced in the order or other designated facts be taken as established for purposes of the action, as the prevailing party claims;

- Prohibiting the disobedient party from supporting or opposing designated claims or defenses, or from introducing designated matters in evidence;

- Striking pleadings in whole or in part;

- Staying further proceedings until the order is obeyed;

- Dismissing the action or proceeding in whole or in part;

- Rendering a default judgment against the disobedient party; or

- Treating as contempt of court the failure to obey any order except an order to submit to a physical or mental examination. FRCP 37(b)(2)(A).

iii. *Sanctions in the district where the action is pending; For not producing a person for examination.* If a party fails to comply with an order under FRCP 35(a) requiring it to produce another person for examination, the court may issue any of the orders listed in FRCP 37(b)(2)(A)(i) through FRCP 37(b)(2)(A)(vi), unless the disobedient party shows that it cannot produce the other person. FRCP 37(b)(2)(B).

iv. *Sanctions in the district where the action is pending; Payment of expenses.* Instead of or in addition to the orders in FRCP 37(b)(2)(A) and FRCP 37(b)(2)(B), the court must order the disobedient party, the attorney advising that party, or both to pay the reasonable expenses, including attorney's fees, caused by the failure, unless the failure was substantially justified or other circumstances make an award of expenses unjust. FRCP 37(b)(2)(C).

e. *Failure to disclose, to supplement an earlier response, or to admit*

    i. *Failure to disclose or supplement.* If a party fails to provide information or identify a witness as required by FRCP 26(a) or FRCP 26(e), the party is not allowed to use that information or witness to supply evidence on a motion, at a hearing, or at a trial, unless the failure was substantially justified or is harmless. In addition to or instead of this sanction, the court, on motion and after giving an opportunity to be heard:

- May order payment of the reasonable expenses, including attorney's fees, caused by the failure;

- May inform the jury of the party's failure; and

- May impose other appropriate sanctions, including any of the orders listed in FRCP 37(b)(2)(A)(i) through FRCP 37(b)(2)(A)(vi). FRCP 37(c)(1).

    ii. *Failure to admit.* If a party fails to admit what is requested under FRCP 36 and if the requesting party later proves a document to be genuine or the matter true, the requesting party may move that the party who failed to admit pay the reasonable expenses, including attorney's fees, incurred in making that proof. The court must so order unless:

- The request was held objectionable under FRCP 36(a);

- The admission sought was of no substantial importance;

- The party failing to admit had a reasonable ground to believe that it might prevail on the matter; or

- There was other good reason for the failure to admit. FRCP 37(c)(2).

f. *Party's failure to attend its own deposition, serve answers to interrogatories, or respond to a request for inspection*

    i. *Motion; Grounds for sanctions.* The court where the action is pending may, on motion, order sanctions if:

- A party or a party's officer, director, or managing agent—or a person designated under FRCP 30(b)(6) or FRCP 31(a)(4)—fails, after being served with proper notice, to appear for that person's deposition; or

- A party, after being properly served with interrogatories under FRCP 33 or a request for inspection under FRCP 34, fails to serve its answers, objections, or written response. FRCP 37(d)(1)(A).

    ii. *Unacceptable excuse for failing to act.* A failure described in FRCP 37(d)(1)(A) is not excused on the ground that the discovery sought was objectionable, unless the party failing to act has a pending motion for a protective order under FRCP 26(c). FRCP 37(d)(2).

    iii. *Types of sanctions.* Sanctions may include any of the orders listed in FRCP 37(b)(2)(A)(i) through FRCP 37(b)(2)(A)(vi). Instead of or in addition to these sanctions, the court must require the party failing to act, the attorney advising that party, or both to pay the reasonable expenses, including attorney's fees, caused by the failure, unless the failure was substantially justified or other circumstances make an award of expenses unjust. FRCP 37(d)(3).

g. *Failure to provide electronically stored information.* If electronically stored information that should have been preserved in the anticipation or conduct of litigation is lost because a party failed to take reasonable steps to preserve it, and it cannot be restored or replaced through additional discovery, the court:

    i. Upon finding prejudice to another party from loss of the information, may order measures no greater than necessary to cure the prejudice; or

    ii. Only upon finding that the party acted with the intent to deprive another party of the information's use in the litigation may: (1) presume that the lost information was unfavorable to the party; (2) instruct the jury that it may or must presume the information was unfavorable to the party; or (3) dismiss the action or enter a default judgment. FRCP 37(e).

h. *Failure to participate in framing a discovery plan.* If a party or its attorney fails to participate in good faith in developing and submitting a proposed discovery plan as required by FRCP 26(f), the court may, after giving an opportunity to be heard, require that party or attorney to pay to any other party the reasonable expenses, including attorney's fees, caused by the failure. FRCP 37(f).

i. *Counsel's liability for excessive costs.* 28 U.S.C.A. § 1927 is a basis for sanctioning attorney misconduct in discovery proceedings. DISCPROFED § 22:3. Any attorney or other person admitted to conduct cases in any court of the United States or any Territory thereof who so multiplies the proceedings in any case unreasonably and vexatiously may be required by the court to satisfy personally the excess costs, expenses, and attorneys' fees reasonably incurred because of such conduct. 28 U.S.C.A. § 1927.

4. *Opposing papers.* The Federal Rules of Civil Procedure do not require any formal answer, return, or reply to a motion, except where the Federal Rules of Civil Procedure or local rules may require affidavits, memoranda, or other papers to be filed in opposition to a motion. Such papers are simply to apprise the court of such opposition and the grounds of that opposition. FEDPROC § 62:359. Except for letter-motions as permitted by NY R USDCTS&ED Civ Rule 7.1(d) or as otherwise permitted by the Court, all oppositions and replies with respect to motions shall comply with NY R USDCTS&ED Civ Rule 7.1(a)(2) and NY R USDCTS&ED Civ Rule 7.1(a)(3), and an opposing party who seeks relief that goes beyond the denial of the motion shall comply as well with NY R USDCTS&ED Civ Rule 7.1(a)(1). NY R USDCTS&ED Civ Rule 7.1(b).

a. *Effect of failure to respond to motion.* Although in the absence of statutory provision or court rule, a motion ordinarily does not require a written answer, when a party files a motion and the opposing party fails to respond, the court may construe such failure to respond as nonopposition to the motion or an admission that the motion was meritorious, may take the facts alleged in the motion as true—the rule in some jurisdictions being that the failure to respond to a fact set forth in a motion is deemed an admission—and may grant the motion if the relief requested appears to be justified. AMJUR MOTIONS § 28.

b. *Assent or no opposition not determinative.* However, a motion will not be granted automatically simply because an "assent" or a notation of "no opposition" has been filed; federal judges frequently deny motions that have been assented to when it is thought that justice so dictates. FPP § 1190.

c. *Responsive pleading inappropriate as response to motion.* An attempt to answer or oppose a motion with a responsive pleading usually is not appropriate. FPP § 1190.

5. *Reply papers.* A moving party may be required or permitted to prepare papers in addition to his original motion papers. AMJUR MOTIONS § 25. Papers answering or replying to opposing papers may be appropriate, in the interests of justice, where it appears there is a substantial reason for allowing a reply. Thus, a court may accept reply papers where a party demonstrates that the papers to which it seeks to file a reply raise new issues that are material to the disposition of the question before the court, or where the court determines, sua sponte, that it wishes further briefing of an issue raised in those papers and orders the submission of additional papers. FEDPROC § 62:360. Except for letter-motions as permitted by NY R USDCTS&ED Civ Rule 7.1(d) or as otherwise permitted by the Court, all oppositions and replies with respect to motions shall comply with NY R USDCTS&ED Civ Rule 7.1(a)(2) and NY R USDCTS&ED Civ Rule 7.1(a)(3). NY R USDCTS&ED Civ Rule 7.1(b).

a. *Function of reply papers.* The function of a reply affidavit is to answer the arguments made in opposition to the position taken by the movant and not to permit the movant to introduce new arguments in support of the motion. AMJUR MOTIONS § 25.

b. *Issues raised for the first time in a reply document.* However, the view has been followed in some jurisdictions, that as a matter of judicial economy, where there is no prejudice and where the issues could be raised simply by filing a motion to dismiss, the trial court has discretion to consider arguments raised for the first time in a reply memorandum, and that a trial court may grant a motion to strike issues raised for the first time in a reply memorandum. AMJUR MOTIONS § 26.

6. *Orders on motions.* A memorandum signed by the Court of the decision on a motion that does not finally

determine all claims for relief, or an oral decision on such a motion, shall constitute the order unless the memorandum or oral decision directs the submission or settlement of an order in more extended form. The notation in the docket of a memorandum or of an oral decision that does not direct the submission or settlement of an order in more extended form shall constitute the entry of the order. Where an order in more extended form is required to be submitted or settled, the notation in the docket of such order shall constitute the entry of the order. NY R USDCTS&ED Civ Rule 6.2.

7. *Complex civil cases.* For information on procedures for complex civil cases, refer to NY R USDCTSD Order 11 Misc 00388.

8. *Related cases.* It shall be the continuing duty of each attorney appearing in any civil or criminal case to bring promptly to the attention of the Court all facts which said attorney believes are relevant to a determination that said case and one or more pending civil or criminal cases should be heard by the same Judge, in order to avoid unnecessary duplication of judicial effort. As soon as the attorney becomes aware of such relationship, said attorney shall notify the Judges to whom the cases have been assigned. NY R USDCTS&ED Civ Rule 1.6(a). If counsel fails to comply with NY R USDCTS&ED Civ Rule 1.6(a), the Court may assess reasonable costs directly against counsel whose action has obstructed the effective administration of the Court's business. NY R USDCTS&ED Civ Rule 1.6(b).

   a. *Determination of relatedness.* Subject to the limitations set forth in NY R USDCTSD Div. Bus., Rule 13(a)(2), a civil case, bankruptcy appeal, or motion to withdraw the bankruptcy reference will be deemed related to one or more civil cases, appeals or motions when the interests of justice and efficiency will be served. In determining relatedness, a judge will consider whether (A) the actions concern the same or substantially similar parties, property, transactions or events; (B) there is substantial factual overlap; (C) the parties could be subjected to conflicting orders; and (D) whether absent a determination of relatedness there would be a substantial duplication of effort and expense, delay, or undue burden on the Court, parties or witnesses. NY R USDCTSD Div. Bus., Rule 13(a)(1). Nothing in this NY R USDCTSD Div. Bus., Rule 13 is intended to preclude parties from moving for consolidated proceedings under FRCP 42. NY R USDCTSD Div. Bus., Rule 13(a)(1). Notwith-standing NY R USDCTSD Div. Bus., Rule 13(a)(1):

      i. Civil cases shall not be deemed related merely because they involve common legal issues or the same parties. NY R USDCTSD Div. Bus., Rule 13(a)(2)(A).

      ii. Other than cases subject to NY R USDCTSD Div. Bus., Rule 4(b) and actions seeking the enforcement of a judgment or settlement in or of an earlier case, civil cases presumptively shall not be deemed related unless both cases are pending before the Court (or the earlier case is on appeal). NY R USDCTSD Div. Bus., Rule 13(a)(2)(B).

   b. *Procedure in regard to cases said to be related*

      i. *Disclosure of contention of relatedness.* When a civil case is filed or removed or a bankruptcy appeal or motion to withdraw the reference of an adversary proceeding from the bankruptcy court is filed, the person filing or removing shall disclose on form JSC44C any contention of relatedness and shall file a Related Case Statement stating clearly and succinctly the basis for the contention. A copy of the civil cover sheet and Related Case Statement shall be served with the complaint, notice of removal, notice of appeal, or motion. Any party may contest a claim of relatedness by any other in writing addressed to the judge having the case with the lowest docket number of all cases claimed to be related. However, the foregoing shall not delay the assignment process or the operation of NY R USDCTSD Div. Bus., Rule 13. NY R USDCTSD Div. Bus., Rule 13(b)(1). [Editor's note: the reference to form JSC44C is likely meant to be form JS44C-SDNY: Civil Court Cover Sheet].

      ii. *Claims of relatedness by other parties.* A party other than the one filing a case, bankruptcy appeal or motion to withdraw the reference that contends its case is related to another may so advise in writing the judge assigned in its case and request a transfer of its case to the judge that the party contends has the related case with the lowest docket number. If the assigned judge believes the case is related under NY R USDCTSD Div. Bus., Rule 13(a), he or she shall refer the question to the judge having the case with the lowest docket number. In the event the latter judge agrees, the case shall be transferred to that judge unless the Assignment Committee disagrees. NY R USDCTSD Div. Bus., Rule 13(b)(3).

    c.   For more information on related cases, refer to NY R USDCTSD Div. Bus., Rule 13.

9.  *Alternative dispute resolution (ADR).* The U.S. District Court for the Southern District of New York provides litigants with opportunities to discuss settlement through judicial settlement conferences and mediation. NY R USDCTS&ED Civ Rule 83.9(a).

    a.  *Consideration of alternative dispute resolution.* In all civil cases, including those eligible for mediation pursuant to NY R USDCTS&ED Civ Rule 83.9(e), each party shall consider the use of mediation or a judicial settlement conference and shall report to the assigned Judge at the initial FRCP 16(b) case management conference, or subsequently, whether the party believes mediation or a judicial settlement conference may facilitate the resolution of the lawsuit. Judges are encouraged to note the availability of the mediation program and/or a judicial settlement conference before, at, or after the initial FRCP 16(b) case management conference. NY R USDCTS&ED Civ Rule 83.9(d).

    b.  *Mediation.* In mediation, parties and counsel meet, sometimes collectively and sometimes individually, with a neutral third party (the mediator) who has been trained to facilitate confidential settlement discussions. The parties articulate their respective positions and interests and generate options for a mutually agreeable resolution to the dispute. The mediator assists the parties in reaching their own negotiated settlement by defining the issues, probing and assessing the strengths and weaknesses of each party's legal positions, and identifying areas of agreement and disagreement. The main benefits of mediation are that it can result in an expeditious and less costly resolution of the litigation, and can produce creative solutions to complex disputes often unavailable in traditional litigation. NY R USDCTS&ED Civ Rule 83.9(b).

        i.  *Mediation program eligibility.* All civil cases other than Social Security, habeas corpus, and tax cases are eligible for mediation, whether assigned to Manhattan or White Plains. NY R USDCTS&ED Civ Rule 83.9(e)(1).

          &bull;  The Board of Judges may, by Administrative Order, direct that certain specified categories of cases shall automatically be submitted to the mediation program. The assigned District Judge or Magistrate Judge may issue a written order exempting a particular case with or without the request of the parties. NY R USDCTS&ED Civ Rule 83.9(e)(2).

          &bull;  For all other cases, the assigned District Judge or Magistrate Judge may determine that a case is appropriate for mediation and may order that case to mediation, with or without the consent of the parties, before, at, or after the initial FRCP 16(b) case management conference. Alternatively, the parties should notify the assigned Judge at any time of their desire to mediate. NY R USDCTS&ED Civ Rule 83.9(e)(3).

    c.  *Judicial settlement conferences.* Judicial settlement conferences may be ordered by District Judges or Magistrate Judges with or without the request or consent of the parties. NY R USDCTS&ED Civ Rule 83.9(f).

    d.  For more information on alternative dispute resolution (ADR), refer to NY R USDCTS&ED Civ Rule 83.9.

10.  *Individual judge practices.* Refer to the Miscellaneous section of this document for information on individual judge practices on general requirements for documents.

## D. Documents

1.  *Documents prior to filing discovery motions*

    a.  *Documents for the moving party*

        i.  *Required documents*

          &bull;  *Letter-motion for a pre-motion discovery conference.* No motion under FRCP 26 through FRCP 37 inclusive shall be heard unless counsel for the moving party has first requested an informal conference with the Court by letter-motion for a pre-motion discovery conference (subject to the instructions regarding ECF published on the Court's website and the Judge's Individual Practices) and such request has either been denied or the discovery dispute has not been resolved as a consequence of such a conference. NY R USDCTS&ED Civ Rule 37.2.

b. *Documents for the opposing party*

    i. *Documents to consider*

- *Responsive letter.* If a motion is made by letter, the opposing party may file any response in letter form. NY R USDCTSD CM/ECF, S.D.(II)(13)(13.1).

2. *Documents for moving party*

a. *Required documents*

    i. *Notice of motion and motion.* Except for letter-motions as permitted by NY R USDCTS&ED Civ Rule 7.1(d) or as otherwise permitted by the Court, all motions shall include the following motion papers: a notice of motion, or an order to show cause signed by the Court, which shall specify the applicable rules or statutes pursuant to which the motion is brought, and shall specify the relief sought by the motion. NY R USDCTS&ED Civ Rule 7.1(a)(1). Refer to the General Requirements section of this document for information on the notice of motion and motion.

- *Quotation or recitation verbatim of discovery materials.* Upon any motion or application involving discovery or disclosure requests or responses under FRCP 37, the moving party shall specify and quote or set forth verbatim in the motion papers each discovery request and response to which the motion or application is addressed. The motion or application shall also set forth the grounds upon which the moving party is entitled to prevail as to each request or response. NY R USDCTS&ED Civ Rule 5.1 also applies to the motion or application. NY R USDCTS&ED Civ Rule 37.1.

    ii. *Certificate of compliance.* A motion for sanctions for failing to answer or respond must include a certification that the movant has in good faith conferred or attempted to confer with the party failing to act in an effort to obtain the answer or response without court action. FRCP 37(d)(1)(B).

    iii. *Memorandum of law.* Except for letter-motions as permitted by NY R USDCTS&ED Civ Rule 7.1(d) or as otherwise permitted by the Court, all motions shall include the following motion papers: a memorandum of law, setting forth the cases and other authorities relied upon in support of the motion, and divided, under appropriate headings, into as many parts as there are issues to be determined. NY R USDCTS&ED Civ Rule 7.1(a)(2).

    iv. *Certificate of service.* FRCP 5(d) requires that the person making service under FRCP 5 certify that service has been effected. FRCP 5(Advisory Committee Notes). Having such information on file may be useful for many purposes, including proof of service if an issue arises concerning the effectiveness of the service. FRCP 5(Advisory Committee Notes).

- Such paper service [on attorneys and pro se parties who are not Filing or Receiving Users] must be documented by electronically filing proof of service. NY R USDCTSD CM/ECF, S.D.(I)(9)(9.2); NY R USDCTSD CM/ECF, S.D.(I)(19)(19.3)(b). Pro se parties who are not Filing Users are exempt from that portion of NY R USDCTSD CM/ECF, S.D.(I)(19)(19.3) requiring proof of service to be filed electronically. NY R USDCTSD CM/ECF, S.D.(I)(19)(19.3).

b. *Supplemental documents*

    i. *Supporting evidence.* When a motion relies on facts outside the record, the court may hear the matter on affidavits or may hear it wholly or partly on oral testimony or on depositions. FRCP 43(c). Except for letter-motions as permitted by NY R USDCTS&ED Civ Rule 7.1(d) or as otherwise permitted by the Court, all motions shall include the following motion papers: supporting affidavits and exhibits thereto containing any factual information and portions of the record necessary for the decision of the motion. NY R USDCTS&ED Civ Rule 7.1(a)(3).

- *Discovery materials.* A party seeking or opposing relief under FRCP 26 through FRCP 37 inclusive, or making or opposing any other motion or application, shall quote or attach only those portions of the depositions, interrogatories, requests for documents, requests for admissions, or other discovery or disclosure materials, together with the responses and

objections thereto, that are the subject of the discovery motion or application, or that are cited in papers submitted in connection with any other motion or application. NY R USDCTS&ED Civ Rule 5.1.

ii. *Notice of constitutional question.* A party that files a pleading, written motion, or other paper drawing into question the constitutionality of a federal or state statute must promptly:

- *File notice.* File a notice of constitutional question stating the question and identifying the paper that raises it, if: (1) a federal statute is questioned and the parties do not include the United States, one of its agencies, or one of its officers or employees in an official capacity; or (2) a state statute is questioned and the parties do not include the state, one of its agencies, or one of its officers or employees in an official capacity; and

- *Serve notice.* Serve the notice and paper on the Attorney General of the United States if a federal statute is questioned—or on the state attorney general if a state statute is questioned—either by certified or registered mail or by sending it to an electronic address designated by the attorney general for this purpose. FRCP 5.1(a).

- *No forfeiture.* A party's failure to file and serve the notice, or the court's failure to certify, does not forfeit a constitutional claim or defense that is otherwise timely asserted. FRCP 5.1(d).

iii. *Copies of authorities.* In cases involving a pro se litigant, counsel shall, when serving a memorandum of law (or other submissions to the Court), provide the pro se litigant (but not other counsel or the Court) with copies of cases and other authorities cited therein that are unpublished or reported exclusively on computerized databases. Upon request, counsel shall provide the pro se litigant with copies of such unpublished cases and other authorities as are cited in a decision of the Court and were not previously cited by any party. NY R USDCTS&ED Civ Rule 7.2.

iv. *Proposed order.* Refer to the Format section of this document for information on the format of submitting a proposed order to the court.

v. *Statement explaining untimely electronic filing.* If you missed a filing deadline when the ECF system was out of order, attach a statement to your filing explaining how the interruption in service prevented you from filing in a timely fashion. NY R USDCTSD CM/ECF, S.D.(II)(23)(23.5).

vi. *Courtesy copies.* Read the judge's Individual Practices to learn if courtesy copies are required. NY R USDCTSD CM/ECF, S.D.(II)(13)(13.17). Judges' Individual Practices should continue to be followed with respect to delivery of courtesy copies. NY R USDCTSD CM/ECF, S.D.(I)(3)(3.4).

3. *Documents for opposing party*

a. *Required documents*

i. *Answering memorandum of law.* Except for letter-motions as permitted by NY R USDCTS&ED Civ Rule 7.1(d) or as otherwise permitted by the Court, all oppositions and replies with respect to motions shall comply with NY R USDCTS&ED Civ Rule 7.1(a)(2). NY R USDCTS&ED Civ Rule 7.1(b). Except for letter-motions as permitted by NY R USDCTS&ED Civ Rule 7.1(d) or as otherwise permitted by the Court, all motions shall include the following motion papers: a memorandum of law, setting forth the cases and other authorities relied upon in support of the motion, and divided, under appropriate headings, into as many parts as there are issues to be determined. NY R USDCTS&ED Civ Rule 7.1(a)(2). Refer to the General Requirements section of this document for information on the opposing papers.

ii. *Certificate of service.* FRCP 5(d) requires that the person making service under FRCP 5 certify that service has been effected. FRCP 5(Advisory Committee Notes). Having such information on file may be useful for many purposes, including proof of service if an issue arises concerning the effectiveness of the service. FRCP 5(Advisory Committee Notes).

- Such paper service [on attorneys and pro se parties who are not Filing or Receiving Users] must be documented by electronically filing proof of service. NY R USDCTSD CM/ECF, S.D.(I)(9)(9.2); NY R USDCTSD CM/ECF, S.D.(I)(19)(19.3)(b). Pro se parties who are not Filing Users are exempt from that portion of NY R USDCTSD CM/ECF, S.D.(I)(19)(19.3) requiring proof of service to be filed electronically. NY R USDCTSD CM/ECF, S.D.(I)(19)(19.3).

b. *Supplemental documents*

   i. *Supporting evidence.* When a motion relies on facts outside the record, the court may hear the matter on affidavits or may hear it wholly or partly on oral testimony or on depositions. FRCP 43(c). Except for letter-motions as permitted by NY R USDCTS&ED Civ Rule 7.1(d) or as otherwise permitted by the Court, all oppositions and replies with respect to motions shall comply with NY R USDCTS&ED Civ Rule 7.1(a)(3). NY R USDCTS&ED Civ Rule 7.1(b). Except for letter-motions as permitted by NY R USDCTS&ED Civ Rule 7.1(d) or as otherwise permitted by the Court, all motions shall include the following motion papers: supporting affidavits and exhibits thereto containing any factual information and portions of the record necessary for the decision of the motion. NY R USDCTS&ED Civ Rule 7.1(a)(3).

   - *Discovery materials.* A party seeking or opposing relief under FRCP 26 through FRCP 37 inclusive, or making or opposing any other motion or application, shall quote or attach only those portions of the depositions, interrogatories, requests for documents, requests for admissions, or other discovery or disclosure materials, together with the responses and objections thereto, that are the subject of the discovery motion or application, or that are cited in papers submitted in connection with any other motion or application. NY R USDCTS&ED Civ Rule 5.1.

   ii. *Notice of constitutional question.* A party that files a pleading, written motion, or other paper drawing into question the constitutionality of a federal or state statute must promptly:

   - *File notice.* File a notice of constitutional question stating the question and identifying the paper that raises it, if: (1) a federal statute is questioned and the parties do not include the United States, one of its agencies, or one of its officers or employees in an official capacity; or (2) a state statute is questioned and the parties do not include the state, one of its agencies, or one of its officers or employees in an official capacity; and

   - *Serve notice.* Serve the notice and paper on the Attorney General of the United States if a federal statute is questioned—or on the state attorney general if a state statute is questioned—either by certified or registered mail or by sending it to an electronic address designated by the attorney general for this purpose. FRCP 5.1(a).

   - *No forfeiture.* A party's failure to file and serve the notice, or the court's failure to certify, does not forfeit a constitutional claim or defense that is otherwise timely asserted. FRCP 5.1(d).

   iii. *Copies of authorities.* In cases involving a pro se litigant, counsel shall, when serving a memorandum of law (or other submissions to the Court), provide the pro se litigant (but not other counsel or the Court) with copies of cases and other authorities cited therein that are unpublished or reported exclusively on computerized databases. Upon request, counsel shall provide the pro se litigant with copies of such unpublished cases and other authorities as are cited in a decision of the Court and were not previously cited by any party. NY R USDCTS&ED Civ Rule 7.2.

   iv. *Statement explaining untimely electronic filing.* If you missed a filing deadline when the ECF system was out of order, attach a statement to your filing explaining how the interruption in service prevented you from filing in a timely fashion. NY R USDCTSD CM/ECF, S.D.(II)(23)(23.5).

   v. *Courtesy copies.* Read the judge's Individual Practices to learn if courtesy copies are required. NY R USDCTSD CM/ECF, S.D.(II)(13)(13.17). Judges' Individual Practices should continue to be followed with respect to delivery of courtesy copies. NY R USDCTSD CM/ECF, S.D.(I)(3)(3.4).

4. *Individual judge practices.* Refer to the Miscellaneous section of this document for information on individual judge practices on required documents.

# E. Format

1. *Form of documents.* The rules governing captions and other matters of form in pleadings apply to motions and other papers. FRCP 7(b)(2).

   a. *Paper.* Every pleading, written motion, and other paper must: be plainly written, typed, printed, or copied without erasures or interlineations which materially deface it. NY R USDCTS&ED Civ Rule 11.1(a)(1).

   b. *Typeface, margin, and spacing.* The typeface, margins, and spacing of all documents presented for filing must meet the following requirements:

      i. All text must be twelve (12) point type or larger, except for text in footnotes which may be ten (10) point type;

      ii. All documents must have at least one (1) inch margins on all sides;

      iii. All text must be double-spaced, except for headings, text in footnotes, or block quotations, which may be single-spaced. NY R USDCTS&ED Civ Rule 11.1(b).

   c. *Caption; Names of parties.* Every pleading must have a caption with the court's name, a title, a file number, and a FRCP 7(a) designation. The title of the complaint must name all the parties; the title of other pleadings, after naming the first party on each side, may refer generally to other parties. FRCP 10(a). Every pleading, written motion, and other paper must: bear the docket number and the initials of the District Judge and any Magistrate Judge before whom the action or proceeding is pending, NY R USDCTS&ED Civ Rule 11.1(a)(2).

   d. *Paragraphs; Separate statements.* A party must state its claims or defenses in numbered paragraphs, each limited as far as practicable to a single set of circumstances. A later pleading may refer by number to a paragraph in an earlier pleading. If doing so would promote clarity, each claim founded on a separate transaction or occurrence—and each defense other than a denial—must be stated in a separate count or defense. FRCP 10(b).

   e. *Adoption by reference; Exhibits.* A statement in a pleading may be adopted by reference elsewhere in the same pleading or in any other pleading or motion. A copy of a written instrument that is an exhibit to a pleading is a part of the pleading for all purposes. FRCP 10(c).

   f. *Acceptance by the clerk.* The clerk must not refuse to file a paper solely because it is not in the form prescribed by the Federal Rules of Civil Procedure or by a local rule or practice. FRCP 5(d)(4).

2. *Form of electronic documents*

   a. *PDF-A.* All documents electronically filed on the ECF system must be in PDF-A format (portable document format). A PDF-A file is created using PDF writer software such as Adobe Acrobat (go to the Adobe website for details). PDF-A files cannot be altered, providing security to the filer and the Court. NY R USDCTSD CM/ECF, S.D.(II)(23)(23.2).

   b. *Size limitation.* No single PDF file may be larger than four megabytes (4 MB). If the filing is too large, the ECF system will not allow it to be filed, and you will not see a Notice of Electronic Filing (NEF or filing receipt) screen. To determine the size of an Adobe Acrobat PDF file click on File, Document Properties, Summary. NY R USDCTSD CM/ECF, S.D.(II)(23)(23.3).

      i. Converting documents directly from a word processor to PDF-A format creates the smallest possible file in terms of computer memory. If that is not possible, scan your document at low resolution. Within the Adobe Acrobat program, on the "Scan Manager" screen, adjust the settings for black and white and 200 dpi (dots per inch). This allows more pages to fit into a single PDF-A file. If that does not work, separate an oversized file into 2 or more parts. Simply label each file 1a, 1b, 1c, etc. Only relevant excerpts of exhibits should be electronically filed. NY R USDCTSD CM/ECF, S.D.(II)(23)(23.4).

   c. *Attachments and exhibits.* Filing Users must submit in electronic form all documents referenced as exhibits or attachments, unless the Court permits paper filing. NY R USDCTSD CM/ECF, S.D.(I)(5)(5.1).

    i.   A Filing User must submit as exhibits or attachments only those excerpts of the referenced documents that are relevant to the matter under consideration by the Court. Excerpted material must be clearly and prominently identified as such. Filing Users who file excerpts of documents as exhibits or attachments under this procedure do so without prejudice to their right to file timely additional excerpts or the complete document. Responding parties may file timely additional excerpts that they believe are relevant or the complete document. A party may move before the Court for permission to serve and file in hard copy documents that cannot be reasonably scanned. NY R USDCTSD CM/ECF, S.D.(I)(5)(5.2).

    ii.   Exhibits must be filed only as attachments to a document, such as a motion or an affidavit. Do not use the ECF Filing Event for "Motion" to file exhibits separately. Exhibits are the only items that should be attached to electronically filed documents. You are limited to electronically filing only relevant excerpts of exhibits. Excerpts must be clearly identified as such. If the exhibit is too large to be scanned and electronically filed you may contact the ECF Help Desk. NY R USDCTSD CM/ECF, S.D.(II)(15)(15.6).

   d.   *Letters.* Parties should consult the assigned judge's Individual Practices to determine if the judge accepts letters at all and, if he or she does, whether the judge has any page limitations on letters and/or requires courtesy copies of letters filed on ECF (and, if so, by what means of delivery). All letters addressed to the Court must include a subject line with the case name and docket number (e.g., "Re: Doe v. Smith, 13 Civ. 1234 (ABC)"). NY R USDCTSD CM/ECF, S.D.(II)(13)(13.1).

   e.   *Proposed orders, proposed judgments, stipulations and consents.* Any document that requires the signature of a judge should not be electronically filed except as an exhibit to another document. Proposed orders, judgments, stipulations and consents should not be submitted through the ECF system. Instead they should be sent by e-mail to the Clerk. Proposed orders should be submitted in word processing format (WordPerfect or Word) rather than as a PDF document. Stipulations should be submitted in PDF-A format. Stipulations must contain ink signatures not s/. Faxed or emailed signatures are acceptable. Please note that Stipulations of Voluntary Dismissal pursuant to FRCP 41(a)(1)(A)(ii) do not require the signature of a judge and must be electronically filed on the ECF system. Questions may be directed to the Orders and Judgments Clerk at the phone numbers listed in NY R USDCTSD CM/ECF, S.D.(II)(18)(18.3). NY R USDCTSD CM/ECF, S.D.(II)(18)(18.3).

    i.   Email the proposed order, judgment or stipulation to the email addresses listed in NY R USDCTSD CM/ECF, S.D.(II)(18)(18.3). NY R USDCTSD CM/ECF, S.D.(II)(18)(18.3).

    ii.   Pro se litigants who are not Filing Users are exempt from that portion of NY R USDCTSD CM/ECF, S.D.(II)(18)(18.3) that requires litigants to email proposed orders, judgments, stipulations and consents, and shall deliver such documents to the Clerk's Office in paper form. NY R USDCTSD CM/ECF, S.D.(II)(18)(18.3).

3.  *Signing disclosures and discovery requests, responses, and objections.* FRCP 11 does not apply to disclosures and discovery requests, responses, objections, and motions under FRCP 26 through FRCP 37. FRCP 11(d).

   a.   *Signature required.* Every disclosure under FRCP 26(a)(1) or FRCP 26(a)(3) and every discovery request, response, or objection must be signed by at least one attorney of record in the attorney's own name—or by the party personally, if unrepresented—and must state the signer's address, e-mail address, and telephone number. FRCP 26(g)(1). Every pleading, written motion, and other paper must: have the name of each person signing it clearly printed or typed directly below the signature. NY R USDCTS&ED Civ Rule 11.1(a)(3).

    i.   *Electronic signatures.* The user log-in and password required to submit documents to the ECF system serve as the Filing User's signature on all electronic documents filed with the Court. NY R USDCTSD CM/ECF, S.D.(I)(8)(8.1); NY R USDCTSD CM/ECF, S.D.(II)(13)(13.14). They also serve as a signature for purposes of the Federal Rules of Civil Procedure, including FRCP 11, the Local Civil Rules of the United States District Courts for the Southern and Eastern

Districts of New York, and any other purpose for which a signature is required in connection with proceedings before the Court. NY R USDCTSD CM/ECF, S.D.(I)(8)(8.1).

- *Signature block.* Electronically filed documents must include a signature block and must set forth the name, address, telephone number and e-mail address all in compliance with the Federal Rules of Civil Procedure and NY R USDCTS&ED Civ Rule 11.1. In the absence of a scanned signature image, the name of the Filing User under whose log-in and password the document is submitted must be preceded by an "s/" typed in the space where the signature would otherwise appear. NY R USDCTSD CM/ECF, S.D.(I)(8)(8.2); NY R USDCTSD CM/ECF, S.D.(II)(13)(13.14).

- *Documents requiring the signature of a party or witness.* A document requiring the signature of a party or witness shall be electronically filed in a scanned format that contains an image of the actual signature. NY R USDCTSD CM/ECF, S.D.(I)(8)(8.4); NY R USDCTSD CM/ECF, S.D.(II)(13)(13.14).

- *Documents requiring the signature of a judge.* A Filing User submitting a document electronically that requires a judge's signature must promptly deliver the document in such other form, if any, as the Court requires. NY R USDCTSD CM/ECF, S.D.(I)(4)(4.2).

- *Documents requiring multiple signatures.* Documents requiring signatures of more than one party must be electronically filed either by: (a) submitting a scanned document containing all necessary signatures; (b) representing the consent of the other parties on the document; (c) identifying on the document the parties whose signatures are required and by the submission of a notice of endorsement by the other parties no later than three business days after filing; or (d) in any other manner approved by the Court. NY R USDCTSD CM/ECF, S.D.(I)(8)(8.5).

b. *Effect of signature.* By signing, an attorney or party certifies that to the best of the person's knowledge, information, and belief formed after a reasonable inquiry:

   i. With respect to a disclosure, it is complete and correct as of the time it is made; and

   ii. With respect to a discovery request, response, or objection, it is:

- Consistent with the Federal Rules of Civil Procedure and warranted by existing law or by a nonfrivolous argument for extending, modifying, or reversing existing law, or for establishing new law;

- Not interposed for any improper purpose, such as to harass, cause unnecessary delay, or needlessly increase the cost of litigation; and

- Neither unreasonable nor unduly burdensome or expensive, considering the needs of the case, prior discovery in the case, the amount in controversy, and the importance of the issues at stake in the action. FRCP 26(g)(1).

c. *Failure to sign.* Other parties have no duty to act on an unsigned disclosure, request, response, or objection until it is signed, and the court must strike it unless a signature is promptly supplied after the omission is called to the attorney's or party's attention. FRCP 26(g)(2).

d. *Sanction for improper certification.* Refer to the General Requirements section of this document for information on the sanction for improper certification.

4. *Privacy protection for filings made with the court*

a. *Redacted filings.* Unless the court orders otherwise, in an electronic or paper filing with the court that contains an individual's Social Security number, taxpayer-identification number, or birth date, the name of an individual known to be a minor, or a financial-account number, a party or nonparty making the filing may include only:

   i. The last four (4) digits of the Social Security number and taxpayer-identification number;

   ii. The year of the individual's birth;

   iii. The minor's initials; and

   iv. The last four (4) digits of the financial-account number. FRCP 5.2(a); NY R USDCTSD CM/ECF, S.D.(II)(21)(21.3).

   v.   Caution should be exercised when filing documents that contain the following:

   - Personal identifying numbers (PIN #'s), such as a driver's license number;

   - Medical records, treatment and diagnosis;

   - Employment history;

   - Individual financial information;

   - Proprietary or trade secret information;

   - Information regarding an individual's cooperation with the government. NY R US-DCTSD CM/ECF, S.D.(II)(21)(21.4).

b. *Exemptions from the redaction requirement.* The redaction requirement does not apply to the following:

   i.   A financial-account number that identifies the property allegedly subject to forfeiture in a forfeiture proceeding;

   ii.  The record of an administrative or agency proceeding;

   iii. The official record of a state-court proceeding;

   iv.  The record of a court or tribunal, if that record was not subject to the redaction requirement when originally filed;

   v.   A filing covered by FRCP 5.2(c) or FRCP 5.2(d); and

   vi.  A pro se filing in an action brought under 28 U.S.C.A. § 2241, 28 U.S.C.A. § 2254, or 28 U.S.C.A. § 2255. FRCP 5.2(b).

c. *Limitations on remote access to electronic files; Social Security appeals and immigration cases.* Unless the court orders otherwise, in an action for benefits under the Social Security Act, and in an action or proceeding relating to an order of removal, to relief from removal, or to immigration benefits or detention, access to an electronic file is authorized as follows:

   i.   The parties and their attorneys may have remote electronic access to any part of the case file, including the administrative record;

   ii.  Any other person may have electronic access to the full record at the courthouse, but may have remote electronic access only to:

   - The docket maintained by the court; and

   - An opinion, order, judgment, or other disposition of the court, but not any other part of the case file or the administrative record. FRCP 5.2(c).

d. *Filings made under seal.* The court may order that a filing be made under seal without redaction. The court may later unseal the filing or order the person who made the filing to file a redacted version for the public record. FRCP 5.2(d). For more information on sealing documents, refer to NY R USDCTSD CM/ECF, S.D.(I)(6).

e. *Protective orders.* For good cause, the court may by order in a case:

   i.   Require redaction of additional information; or

   ii.  Limit or prohibit a nonparty's remote electronic access to a document filed with the court. FRCP 5.2(e).

f. *Option for additional unredacted filing under seal.* A person making a redacted filing may also file an unredacted copy under seal. The court must retain the unredacted copy as part of the record. FRCP 5.2(f); NY R USDCTSD CM/ECF, S.D.(II)(21)(21.5).

g. *Option for filing a reference list.* A filing that contains redacted information may be filed together with a reference list that identifies each item of redacted information and specifies an appropriate identifier that uniquely corresponds to each item listed. The list must be filed under seal and may be amended as of right. Any reference in the case to a listed identifier will be construed to refer to the corresponding item of information. FRCP 5.2(g); NY R USDCTSD CM/ECF, S.D.(II)(21)(21.5).

h. *Responsibility for redaction.* It is the sole responsibility of counsel and the parties to be sure that all documents comply with the rules of this Court requiring redaction of personal identifiers. Neither the judge nor the Clerk of Court will review documents for compliance with these rules. NY R USDCTSD CM/ECF, S.D.(II)(21)(21.2).

i. *Waiver of protection of identifiers.* A person waives the protection of FRCP 5.2(a) as to the person's own information by filing it without redaction and not under seal. FRCP 5.2(h).

j. For more information on privacy and public access to ECF cases, refer to NY R USDCTSD CM/ECF, S.D.(II)(21).

5. *Individual judge practices.* Refer to the Miscellaneous section of this document for information on individual judge practices on formatting documents.

## F. Filing and Service Requirements

1. *Filing requirements.* Any paper after the complaint that is required to be served—together with a certificate of service—must be filed within a reasonable time after service. FRCP 5(d)(1). Complaints and all subsequent papers are accepted at either courthouse, regardless of the place for which the case is designated. NY R USDCTSD Div. Bus., Rule 22. Subject to the instructions regarding ECF published on the website of each respective Court and any pertinent Individual Judge's Practices, letter-motions permitted by NY R USDCTS&ED Civ Rule 7.1(d) and letters addressed to the Court (but not letters between the parties) may be filed via ECF. NY R USDCTS&ED Civ Rule 5.2(b). For information on electronically filing motions, refer to NY R USDCTSD CM/ECF, S.D.(II)(15).

   a. *How filing is made; In general.* A paper is filed by delivering it:

      i. To the clerk; or

      ii. To a judge who agrees to accept it for filing, and who must then note the filing date on the paper and promptly send it to the clerk. FRCP 5(d)(2).

   b. *Night depository.* A night depository with an automatic date stamp shall be maintained by the Clerk of the Southern District in the Pearl Street Courthouse. After regular business hours, papers for the District Court only may be deposited in the night depository. Such papers will be considered as having been filed in the District Court as of the date stamped thereon, which shall be deemed presumptively correct. NY R USDCTS&ED Civ Rule 1.2.

   c. *Electronic filing*

      i. *Authorization of electronic filing program.* A court may, by local rule, allow papers to be filed, signed, or verified by electronic means that are consistent with any technical standards established by the Judicial Conference of the United States. A local rule may require electronic filing only if reasonable exceptions are allowed. A paper filed electronically in compliance with a local rule is a written paper for purposes of the Federal Rules of Civil Procedure. FRCP 5(d)(3).

         • The Court will accept for filing documents submitted, signed or verified by electronic means, that comply with the rules in NY R USDCTSD CM/ECF, S.D. NY R USDCTSD CM/ECF, S.D.(I). The information in NY R USDCTSD CM/ECF, S.D. applies only to cases assigned to the ECF system. NY R USDCTSD CM/ECF, S.D.(Introduction).

         • Parties serving and filing papers shall follow the instructions regarding Electronic Case Filing (ECF) published on the website of each respective Court. A paper served and filed by electronic means in accordance with such instructions is, for purposes of FRCP 5, served and filed in compliance with the Local Civil Rules of the Southern and Eastern Districts of New York. NY R USDCTS&ED Civ Rule 5.2(a). Parties have an obligation to review the Court's actual order, decree, or judgment (on ECF), which controls, and should not rely on the description on the docket or in the ECF Notice of Electronic Filing (NEF). NY R USDCTS&ED Civ Rule 5.2(c).

         • The following should be observed when filing electronically: (1) the Federal Rules of Civil Procedure, (2) the Local Civil Rules of the United States District Courts for the Southern and Eastern Districts of New York, (3) the assigned judge's Individual Practices, and (4) the Court's Electronic Case Filing Rules & Instructions (NY R USDCTSD CM/ECF, S.D.). NY R USDCTSD CM/ECF, S.D.(Introduction).

ii. *Scope of electronic filing.* Except as expressly provided and in exceptional circumstances preventing a party from filing electronically, all documents required to be filed with the Court must be filed electronically. Any party unable to comply with this requirement must seek permission of the Court to file in the traditional manner, on paper. Any such application made after regular business hours may be submitted through the night depository box maintained pursuant to NY R USDCTS&ED Civ Rule 1.2. NY R USDCTSD CM/ECF, S.D.(I)(1)(1.1).

- *Documents filed by pro se litigants.* Unless otherwise ordered by the Court, documents filed by pro se litigants must be filed in the traditional manner, on paper, and will be scanned and docketed by the Clerk's Office into the ECF system. NY R USDCTSD CM/ECF, S.D.(I)(1)(1.1). Pro se litigants must file pleadings and documents in the traditional manner on paper unless the assigned judge has granted permission to electronically file on the ECF system. NY R USDCTSD CM/ECF, S.D.(Introduction).

- *Letters.* Except for letters to be filed under seal, letters addressed to judges who accept letters may be filed electronically. Parties should consult the assigned judge's Individual Practices to determine if the judge accepts letters at all and, if he or she does, whether the judge has any page limitations on letters and/or requires courtesy copies of letters filed on ECF (and, if so, by what means of delivery). NY R USDCTSD CM/ECF, S.D.(II)(13)(13.1). Letters solely between parties or their counsel or otherwise not addressed to the Court may not be filed electronically on ECF (except as exhibits to an otherwise properly filed document). NY R USDCTSD CM/ECF, S.D.(II)(13)(13.1). For more information on filing letters, refer to NY R USDCTSD CM/ECF, S.D.(II)(13)(13.1).

- *Proposed orders, judgments and decrees.* Proposed orders, judgments and decrees shall be presented as directed by the ECF rules published on the website of each respective Court. NY R USDCTS&ED Civ Rule 77.1. For more information, refer to NY R USDCTS&ED Civ Rule 77.1.

iii. *Exceptions to electronic filing.* In an ECF case, the documents that should not be electronically filed include:

- Miscellaneous Case initiating documents, NY R USDCTSD CM/ECF, S.D.(II)(18)(18.2);

- Proposed orders; proposed judgments, stipulations; consents, NY R USDCTSD CM/ECF, S.D.(II)(18)(18.3);

- Orders to show cause / temporary restraining orders, NY R USDCTSD CM/ECF, S.D.(II)(18)(18.4);

- Sealed documents, NY R USDCTSD CM/ECF, S.D.(II)(18)(18.5); and

- Surety bonds, NY R USDCTSD CM/ECF, S.D.(II)(18)(18.6).

- In cases where the record of an administrative or other prior proceeding must be filed with the Court, such record may be served and filed in hard copy without prior motion and order of the Court. NY R USDCTSD CM/ECF, S.D.(I)(5)(5.3).

- For more documents excepted from electronic filing, and for more information on such documents, refer to NY R USDCTSD CM/ECF, S.D.(II)(18).

iv. *Consequences of electronic filing.* Except as otherwise provided in NY R USDCTSD CM/ECF, S.D.(I)(4), electronic filing of a document in the ECF system consistent with these procedures, together with the transmission of a Notice of Electronic Filing (NEF) from the Court, constitutes filing of the document for all purposes of the Federal Rules of Civil Procedure and the Local Civil Rules of the United States District Courts for the Southern and Eastern Districts of New York and constitutes entry of the document on the docket kept by the Clerk under FRCP 58 and FRCP 79. NY R USDCTSD CM/ECF, S.D.(I)(3)(3.1).

v. For more information on electronic filing, refer to NY R USDCTSD CM/ECF, S.D.

2. *Service requirements*

  a. *Service; When required*

    i. *In general.* Unless the Federal Rules of Civil Procedure provide otherwise, each of the following papers must be served on every party:

- An order stating that service is required;

- A pleading filed after the original complaint, unless the court orders otherwise under FRCP 5(c) because there are numerous defendants;

- A discovery paper required to be served on a party, unless the court orders otherwise;

- A written motion, except one that may be heard ex parte; and

- A written notice, appearance, demand, or offer of judgment, or any similar paper. FRCP 5(a)(1).

    ii. *If a party fails to appear.* No service is required on a party who is in default for failing to appear. But a pleading that asserts a new claim for relief against such a party must be served on that party under FRCP 4. FRCP 5(a)(2).

    iii. *Seizing property.* If an action is begun by seizing property and no person is or need be named as a defendant, any service required before the filing of an appearance, answer, or claim must be made on the person who had custody or possession of the property when it was seized. FRCP 5(a)(3).

  b. *Service; How made*

    i. *Serving an attorney.* If a party is represented by an attorney, service under FRCP 5 must be made on the attorney unless the court orders service on the party. FRCP 5(b)(1).

    ii. *Service in general.* A paper is served under FRCP 5 by:

- Handing it to the person;

- Leaving it: (1) at the person's office with a clerk or other person in charge or, if no one is in charge, in a conspicuous place in the office; or (2) if the person has no office or the office is closed, at the person's dwelling or usual place of abode with someone of suitable age and discretion who resides there;

- Mailing it to the person's last known address—in which event service is complete upon mailing;

- Leaving it with the court clerk if the person has no known address;

- Sending it by electronic means if the person consented in writing—in which event service is complete upon transmission, but is not effective if the serving party learns that it did not reach the person to be served; or

- Delivering it by any other means that the person consented to in writing—in which event service is complete when the person making service delivers it to the agency designated to make delivery. FRCP 5(b)(2).

    iii. *Service by overnight delivery.* Service upon an attorney may be made by overnight delivery service. "Overnight delivery service" means any delivery service which regularly accepts items for overnight delivery. Overnight delivery service shall be deemed service by mail for purposes of FRCP 5 and FRCP 6. NY R USDCTS&ED Civ Rule 5.3.

    iv. *Service by electronic means.* Parties serving and filing papers shall follow the instructions regarding Electronic Case Filing (ECF) published on the website of each respective Court. A paper served and filed by electronic means in accordance with such instructions is, for purposes of FRCP 5, served and filed in compliance with the Local Civil Rules of the United States District Courts for the Southern and Eastern Districts of New York. NY R USDCTS&ED Civ Rule 5.2(a). Parties have an obligation to review the Court's actual order, decree, or judgment (on ECF), which controls, and should not rely on the description on the docket or in the ECF Notice of Electronic Filing (NEF). NY R USDCTS&ED Civ Rule 5.2(c).

- *Notice of electronic filing (NEF).* In cases assigned to the ECF system, service is complete provided all parties receive a Notice of Electronic Filing (NEF), which is sent automatically by email from the Court (see the NEF for a list of who did/did not receive notice electronically). Transmission of the NEF constitutes service upon all Filing and Receiving Users who are listed as recipients of notice by electronic mail. NY R USDCTSD CM/ECF, S.D.(I)(9)(9.1). In cases assigned to the ECF system, if all parties receive a NEF, service is complete upon transmission of the NEF by the Court, and you are not required to serve a paper copy. NY R USDCTSD CM/ECF, S.D.(II)(19)(19.2). It remains the duty of Filing and Receiving Users to maintain current contact information with the court and to regularly review the docket sheet of the case. NY R USDCTSD CM/ECF, S.D.(I)(9)(9.1).

- *Mailing of court-initiated documents.* The Clerk's Office will no longer mail paper copies of court-initiated documents to Filing and Receiving Users. The Clerk's Office will mail copies of all court-initiated documents to pro se parties who have not registered as Filing or Receiving Users. NY R USDCTSD CM/ECF, S.D.(II)(19)(19.1).

- *No receipt of a NEF.* If any party does not receive a NEF, you are required to accomplish service on that party in the traditional manner, in paper form. NY R USDCTSD CM/ECF, S.D.(II)(19)(19.2). The NEF receipt will inform you who will receive notice of the filing "electronically" (by e-mail from the Court) and who will receive notice "by other means" (traditional service in paper form). NY R USDCTSD CM/ECF, S.D.(II)(19)(19.2).

- *Service on non-filing or non-receiving users.* Attorneys and pro se parties who are not Filing or Receiving Users must be served with a paper copy of any electronically filed pleading or other document. Service of such paper copy must be made according to the Federal Rules of Civil Procedure and the Local Civil Rules of the United States District Courts for the Southern and Eastern Districts of New York. NY R USDCTSD CM/ECF, S.D.(I)(9)(9.2). Such paper service must be documented by electronically filing proof of service. NY R USDCTSD CM/ECF, S.D.(I)(9)(9.2); NY R USDCTSD CM/ECF, S.D.(II)(19)(19.2). Where the Clerk scans and electronically files pleadings and documents on behalf of a pro se party, the associated NEF constitutes service. NY R USDCTSD CM/ECF, S.D.(I)(9)(9.2).

- For more information on service by electronic means, refer to NY R USDCTSD CM/ECF, S.D.(II)(19).

v. *Using court facilities.* If a local rule so authorizes, a party may use the court's transmission facilities to make service under FRCP 5(b)(2)(E). FRCP 5(b)(3).

c. *Serving numerous defendants*

i. *In general.* If an action involves an unusually large number of defendants, the court may, on motion or on its own, order that:

- Defendants' pleadings and replies to them need not be served on other defendants;

- Any crossclaim, counterclaim, avoidance, or affirmative defense in those pleadings and replies to them will be treated as denied or avoided by all other parties; and

- Filing any such pleading and serving it on the plaintiff constitutes notice of the pleading to all parties. FRCP 5(c)(1).

ii. *Notifying parties.* A copy of every such order must be served on the parties as the court directs. FRCP 5(c)(2).

3. *Individual judge practices.* Refer to the Miscellaneous section of this document for information on individual judge practices on filing and serving documents.

## G. Hearings

1. *Hearings, generally*

a. *Oral argument.* Due process does not require that oral argument be permitted on a motion and, except as otherwise provided by local rule, the district court has discretion to determine whether it will decide the motion on the papers or hear argument by counsel (and perhaps receive evidence). FPP § 1190; F.D.I.C. v. Deglau, 207 F.3d 153 (3d Cir. 2000). The parties and their attorneys shall only appear to argue the motion if so directed by the Court by order or by a Judge's Individual Practice. NY R USDCTS&ED Civ Rule 6.1(c).

b. *Providing a regular schedule for oral hearings.* A court may establish regular times and places for oral hearings on motions. FRCP 78(a).

c. *Providing for submission on briefs.* By rule or order, the court may provide for submitting and determining motions on briefs, without oral hearings. FRCP 78(b).

2. *Individual judge practices.* Refer to the Miscellaneous section of this document for information on individual judge practices on hearings.

## H. Forms

### 1. Federal Motion for Discovery Sanctions Forms

a. Motion for contempt. 3B FEDFORMS § 3721.

b. Motion for sanctions for failure to appear at deposition. 3B FEDFORMS § 3722.

c. Motion that facts be taken as established for failure to answer questions upon deposition. 3B FEDFORMS § 3723.

d. Motion for order refusing to allow disobedient party to support or oppose designated claims or defenses. 3B FEDFORMS § 3724.

e. Motion for default judgment against defendant for failure to comply with order for production of documents. 3B FEDFORMS § 3725.

f. Motion for award of expenses incurred to prove matter opponent failed to admit under FRCP 36. 3B FEDFORMS § 3726.

g. Motion to strike answer or dismiss action for failure to comply with order requiring answer to interrogatories. 3B FEDFORMS § 3729.

h. Motion to dismiss for failure to comply with previous order requiring answer to interrogatories to party. 3B FEDFORMS § 3732.

i. Motion; For order that facts be taken to be established, and/or prohibiting certain claims, defenses, or evidence in opposition thereto. FEDPROF § 23:595.

j. Affidavit; By attorney; In support of motion for order that facts be taken to be established, etc; Failure to produce documents for inspection. FEDPROF § 23:596.

k. Affidavit; By attorney; In support of motion for order that facts be taken to be established, etc; Failure to obey order to answer questions. FEDPROF § 23:597.

l. Motion; For order striking pleadings, and for default judgment or dismissal of action. FEDPROF § 23:599.

m. Affidavit; By attorney; In support of motion for default judgment for defendant's failure to obey discovery order. FEDPROF § 23:600.

n. Motion; By defendant; For dismissal of action and other sanctions; For failure to comply with orders to complete deposition. FEDPROF § 23:601.

o. Motion; By defendant; For dismissal of action or other sanctions; For failure and refusal to comply with order to produce documents. FEDPROF § 23:602.

p. Motion; By defendant; For dismissal with prejudice; Failure to answer interrogatories as ordered. FEDPROF § 23:603.

q. Motion; For order staying further proceedings until adverse party obeys order compelling discovery. FEDPROF § 23:604.

r. Affidavit; By attorney; Opposing motion for order striking pleading and directing entry of default judgment; Good-faith attempt to obey discovery order; Production of documents illegal under foreign law. FEDPROF § 23:605.

s. Motion; For sanctions for failure to comply with examination order. FEDPROF § 23:610.

    t.    Motion; For order finding person in contempt of court; Refusal, after order, to answer question. FEDPROF § 23:612.

    u.    Affidavit; By attorney; In support of motion for order finding party in contempt. FEDPROF § 23:613.

    v.    Affidavit; By plaintiff; In support of motion for order holding defendant in contempt of court; Defendant disobeyed order for production of documents. FEDPROF § 23:614.

    w.    Motion; For order compelling opposing party to pay expenses incurred in proving facts such party refused to admit. FEDPROF § 23:616.

    x.    Motion; For sanctions; Failure to attend own deposition, serve answers to interrogatories, or respond to request for inspection. FEDPROF § 23:618.

    y.    Motion; For order staying proceedings until required response to discovery request is made. FEDPROF § 23:619.

    z.    Affidavit; By attorney; In support of motion for sanctions; Failure to attend own deposition, serve answers to interrogatories, or respond to request for inspection. FEDPROF § 23:620.

## I. Applicable Rules

  1.  *Federal rules*

    a.    Counsel's liability for excessive costs. 28 U.S.C.A. § 1927.

    b.    Serving and filing pleadings and other papers. FRCP 5.

    c.    Constitutional challenge to a statute; Notice, certification, and intervention. FRCP 5.1.

    d.    Privacy protection for filings made with the court. FRCP 5.2.

    e.    Computing and extending time; Time for motion papers. FRCP 6.

    f.    Pleadings allowed; Form of motions and other papers. FRCP 7.

    g.    Form of pleadings. FRCP 10.

    h.    Signing pleadings, motions, and other papers; Representations to the court; Sanctions. FRCP 11.

    i.    Duty to disclose; General provisions governing discovery. FRCP 26.

    j.    Failure to make disclosures or to cooperate in discovery; Sanctions. FRCP 37.

    k.    Taking testimony. FRCP 43.

    l.    Hearing motions; Submission on briefs. FRCP 78.

  2.  *Local rules*

    a.    Night depository. NY R USDCTS&ED Civ Rule 1.2.

    b.    Duty of attorneys in related cases. NY R USDCTS&ED Civ Rule 1.6.

    c.    Filing of discovery materials. NY R USDCTS&ED Civ Rule 5.1.

    d.    Electronic service and filing of documents. NY R USDCTS&ED Civ Rule 5.2.

    e.    Service by overnight delivery. NY R USDCTS&ED Civ Rule 5.3.

    f.    Service and filing of motion papers. NY R USDCTS&ED Civ Rule 6.1.

    g.    Orders on motions. NY R USDCTS&ED Civ Rule 6.2.

    h.    Computation of time. NY R USDCTS&ED Civ Rule 6.4.

    i.    Motion papers. NY R USDCTS&ED Civ Rule 7.1.

    j.    Authorities to be provided to pro se litigants. NY R USDCTS&ED Civ Rule 7.2.

    k.    Form of pleadings, motions, and other papers. NY R USDCTS&ED Civ Rule 11.1.

    l.    Verbatim quotation of discovery materials. NY R USDCTS&ED Civ Rule 37.1.

    m.    Mode of raising discovery disputes with the court (Southern District only). NY R USDCTS&ED Civ Rule 37.2.

n.  Submission of orders, judgments and decrees. NY R USDCTS&ED Civ Rule 77.1.

o.  Alternative dispute resolution (Southern District only). NY R USDCTS&ED Civ Rule 83.9.

p.  Electronic case filing rules and instructions. NY R USDCTSD CM/ECF, S.D.

q.  Related cases. NY R USDCTSD Div. Bus., Rule 13.

r.  Filing at either courthouse. NY R USDCTSD Div. Bus., Rule 22.

## J.  Miscellaneous

**NOTE: Individual judges' rules may apply. For available judge-level information, refer to:**

DISTRICT JUDGE RONNIE ABRAMS: NY R USDCTSD Abrams-Civ Prac; NY R USDCTSD Abrams-Crim Prac; NY R USDCTSD Abrams-Pro Se; NY R USDCTSD Abrams-Case Mgt; NY R USDCTSD Abrams-Jury.

DISTRICT JUDGE DEBORAH A. BATTS: NY R USDCTSD Batts-Practices.

DISTRICT JUDGE RICHARD M. BERMAN: NY R USDCTSD Berman-Practices; NY R USDCTSD Berman-Default; NY R USDCTSD Berman-Sentencing; NY R USDCTSD Berman-Media.

DISTRICT JUDGE VINCENT L. BRICCETTI: NY R USDCTSD Briccetti-Practices; NY R USDCTSD Briccetti-Plan; NY R USDCTSD Briccetti-Notice.

DISTRICT JUDGE VERNON S. BRODERICK: NY R USDCTSD Broderick-Civil; NY R USDCTSD Broderick-Crim; NY R USDCTSD Broderick-Case Mgt; NY R USDCTSD Broderick-Jury.

DISTRICT JUDGE NAOMI REICE BUCHWALD: NY R USDCTSD Buchwald-Practices.

DISTRICT JUDGE VALERIE E. CAPRONI: NY R USDCTSD Caproni-Prac; NY R USDCTSD Caproni--Pro Se; NY R USDCTSD Caproni-Case Mgt; NY R USDCTSD Caproni-Crim Prac.

DISTRICT JUDGE ANDREW L. CARTER JR.: NY R USDCTSD Carter-Practices.

DISTRICT JUDGE KEVIN P. CASTEL: NY R USDCTSD Castel-Practices; NY R USDCTSD Castel-Default; NY R USDCTSD Castel-Scheduling; NY R USDCTSD Castel-Complex; NY R USDCTSD Castel-Trials; NY R USDCTSD Castel-Sentencing.

DISTRICT JUDGE DENISE L. COTE: NY R USDCTSD Cote-Civil Practices; NY R USDCTSD Cote-Pro Se; NY R USDCTSD Cote-Maritime Ord; NY R USDCTSD Cote-Crim Practices; NY R USDCTSD Cote-Crim Trials; NY R USDCTSD Cote-Sentencing.

DISTRICT JUDGE PAUL A. CROTTY: NY R USDCTSD Crotty-Practices; NY R USDCTSD Crotty-Sentencing; NY R USDCTSD Crotty-Calls; NY R USDCTSD Crotty-Scheduling.

DISTRICT JUDGE GEORGE B. DANIELS: NY R USDCTSD Daniels-Practices.

DISTRICT JUDGE KEVIN T. DUFFY: NY R USDCTSD Duffy-Practices.

DISTRICT JUDGE PAUL A. ENGELMAYER: NY R USDCTSD Engelmayer-Practices; NY R USDCTSD Engelmayer-Scheduling; NY R USDCTSD Engelmayer-Sentencing; NY R USDCTSD Engelmayer-Pro Se; NY R USDCTSD Engelmayer-Crim.

DISTRICT JUDGE KATHERINE POLK FAILLA: NY R USDCTSD Failla-Civ Prac; NY R USDCTSD Failla-Crim Prac; NY R USDCTSD Failla-Case Mgt.

DISTRICT JUDGE KATHERINE B. FORREST: NY R USDCTSD Forrest-Civil Prac; NY R USDCTSD Forrest-Crim Prac; NY R USDCTSD Forrest-Crim Pretrial; NY R USDCTSD Forrest-Scheduling; NY R USDCTSD Forrest-Patent Scheduling; NY R USDCTSD Forrest-Sentencing; NY R USDCTSD Forrest-Order 1; NY R USDCTSD Forrest-Order 2.

DISTRICT JUDGE JESSE M. FURMAN: NY R USDCTSD Furman-Civil Prac; NY R USDCTSD Furman-Crim Prac; NY R USDCTSD Furman-Pro Se Prac; NY R USDCTSD Furman-Trials; NY R USDCTSD Furman-Scheduling; NY R USDCTSD Furman-Rights.

DISTRICT JUDGE PAUL G. GARDEPHE: NY R USDCTSD Gardephe-Civ Prac; NY R USDCTSD Gardephe-Pretrial; NY R USDCTSD Gardephe-Prot Ord; NY R USDCTSD Gardephe-Maritime; NY R USDCTSD Gardephe-Crim Prac; NY R USDCTSD Gardephe-Trial.

DISTRICT JUDGE THOMAS P. GRIESA: NY R USDCTSD Griesa-Practices.

DISTRICT JUDGE CHARLES S. HAIGHT: NY R USDCTSD Haight-Practices.

DISTRICT JUDGE ALVIN K. HELLERSTEIN: NY R USDCTSD Hellerstein-Practices; NY R USDCTSD Hellerstein--Sept 11.

DISTRICT JUDGE LEWIS A. KAPLAN: NY R USDCTSD Kaplan-Practices; NY R USDCTSD Kaplan-Sentencing.

DISTRICT JUDGE KENNETH M. KARAS: NY R USDCTSD Karas-Practices; NY R USDCTSD Karas-Case Mgt; NY R USDCTSD Karas-Default; NY R USDCTSD Karas-Sentencing; NY R USDCTSD Karas-Rights.

DISTRICT JUDGE JOHN F. KEENAN: NY R USDCTSD Keenan-Practices.

DISTRICT JUDGE JOHN G. KOELTL: NY R USDCTSD Koeltl-Practices.

DISTRICT JUDGE VICTOR MARRERO: NY R USDCTSD Marrero-Practices; NY R USDCTSD Marrero-Scheduling; NY R USDCTSD Marrero-Default; NY R USDCTSD Marrero-Trial Proc.

DISTRICT JUDGE COLLEEN McMAHON: NY R USDCTSD McMahon-Practices; NY R USDCTSD McMahon-RICO; NY R USDCTSD McMahon-Copies; NY R USDCTSD McMahon-Scheduling; NY R US-DCTSD McMahon-Elec Disc; NY R USDCTSD McMahon-Sentencing.

DISTRICT JUDGE ALISON J. NATHAN: NY R USDCTSD Nathan-Civ Prac; NY R USDCTSD Nathan-Crim Prac; NY R USDCTSD Nathan-Pro Se; NY R USDCTSD Nathan-Scheduling.

DISTRICT JUDGE J. PAUL OETKEN: NY R USDCTSD Oetken-Civ Prac; NY R USDCTSD Oetken-Case Mgt; NY R USDCTSD Oetken-Crim Prac; NY R USDCTSD Oetken-Pro Se.

DISTRICT JUDGE WILLIAM H. PAULEY, III: NY R USDCTSD Pauley-Crim Cases; NY R USDCTSD Pauley-Practices.

DISTRICT JUDGE LORETTA A. PRESKA: NY R USDCTSD Preska-Practices.

DISTRICT JUDGE JED S. RAKOFF: NY R USDCTSD Rakoff-Practices; NY R USDCTSD Rakoff-Scheduling; NY R USDCTSD Rakoff-Prot Ord; NY R USDCTSD Rakoff-Maritime Ord.

DISTRICT JUDGE EDGARDO RAMOS: NY R USDCTSD Ramos--Practices; NY R USDCTSD Ramos-Case Mgt.

DISTRICT JUDGE NELSON S. ROMAN: NY R USDCTSD Roman-Civ Prac; NY R USDCTSD Roman-Pro Se; NY R USDCTSD Roman-Crim Prac; NY R USDCTSD Roman-Case Mgt.

DISTRICT JUDGE LEONARD B. SAND: NY R USDCTSD Sand-Practices.

DISTRICT JUDGE LORNA G. SCHOFIELD: NY R USDCTSD Schofield-Civ Prac; NY R USDCTSD Schofield-Crim Prac; NY R USDCTSD Schofield-Sched; NY R USDCTSD Schofield-Pro Se; NY R USDCTSD Schofield-Advice.

DISTRICT JUDGE CATHY SEIBEL: NY R USDCTSD Seibel-Practices.

DISTRICT JUDGE LOUIS L. STANTON: NY R USDCTSD Stanton-Practices; NY R USDCTSD Stanton-Pretrial.

DISTRICT JUDGE SIDNEY H. STEIN: NY R USDCTSD Stein-Practices.

DISTRICT JUDGE RICHARD J. SULLIVAN: NY R USDCTSD Sullivan-Practices; NY R USDCTSD Sullivan-Scheduling; NY R USDCTSD Sullivan-Sentencing; NY R USDCTSD Sullivan-Juries; NY R USDCTSD Sullivan-Trial; NY R USDCTSD Sullivan-Default.

DISTRICT JUDGE LAURA TAYLOR SWAIN: NY R USDCTSD Swain-Practices; NY R USDCTSD Swain-Trial; NY R USDCTSD Swain-Crim Trial; NY R USDCTSD Swain-Juries; NY R USDCTSD Swain-Sentencing; NY R USDCTSD Swain-Rights.

DISTRICT JUDGE ROBERT W. SWEET: NY R USDCTSD Sweet-Practices.

DISTRICT JUDGE ANALISA TORRES: NY R USDCTSD Torres-Civ Prac; NY R USDCTSD Torres-Pro Se; NY R USDCTSD Torres-Scheduling.

DISTRICT JUDGE KIMBA M. WOOD: NY R USDCTSD Wood-Practices; NY R USDCTSD Wood-Scheduling; NY R USDCTSD Wood-Discovery; NY R USDCTSD Wood-RICO; NY R USDCTSD Wood-Juries; NY R USDCTSD Wood-Trial; NY R USDCTSD Wood-Media.

DISTRICT JUDGE GREGORY H. WOODS: NY R USDCTSD Woods-Civ Prac; NY R USDCTSD Woods-Pro Se; NY R USDCTSD Woods-Sched; NY R USDCTSD Woods-Crim Prac; NY R USDCTSD Woods-Protect Order; NY R USDCTSD Woods-Speedy Trial.

MAGISTRATE JUDGE JAMES L. COTT: NY R USDCTSD Cott-Practices; NY R USDCTSD Cott-Settlement.

MAGISTRATE JUDGE PAUL E. DAVISON: NY R USDCTSD Davison-Practices.

MAGISTRATE JUDGE RONALD L. ELLIS: NY R USDCTSD Ellis-Practices.

MAGISTRATE JUDGE KEVIN N. FOX: NY R USDCTSD Fox-Practices; NY R USDCTSD Fox-Settlement.

MAGISTRATE JUDGE JAMES C. FRANCIS: NY R USDCTSD Francis-Practices.

MAGISTRATE JUDGE DEBRA FREEMAN: NY R USDCTSD Freeman-Practices; NY R USDCTSD Freeman-Settlement.

MAGISTRATE JUDGE GABRIEL W. GORENSTEIN: NY R USDCTSD Gorenstein-Practices; NY R US-DCTSD Gorenstein-Ackn.

MAGISTRATE JUDGE FRANK MAAS: NY R USDCTSD Maas-Practices; NY R USDCTSD Maas-Discontinuance; NY R USDCTSD Maas-Conf; NY R USDCTSD Maas-Settlement.

MAGISTRATE JUDGE JUDITH C. McCARTHY: NY R USDCTSD McCarthy-Practices; NY R USDCTSD McCarthy-Conduct.

MAGISTRATE JUDGE BARBARA MOSES: NY R USDCTSD Moses-Practices.

MAGISTRATE JUDGE SARAH NETBURN: NY R USDCTSD Netburn-Civil; NY R USDCTSD Netburn-Settlement; NY R USDCTSD Netburn-Case Mgt; NY R USDCTSD Netburn--Pro Se.

MAGISTRATE JUDGE ANDREW J. PECK: NY R USDCTSD Peck-Practices; NY R USDCTSD Peck-Order; NY R USDCTSD Peck-Rule 502(d).

MAGISTRATE JUDGE HENRY PITMAN: NY R USDCTSD Pitman-Practices.

MAGISTRATE JUDGE LISA MARGARET SMITH: NY R USDCTSD Smith-Practices; NY R USDCTSD Smith-Trials.

## Motions, Oppositions and Replies
## Motion for Preliminary Injunction

**Document Last Updated September 2016**

A. **Checklist**

(I) ❑ Matters to be considered by moving party

    (a) ❑ Required documents

        (1) ❑ Notice of motion and motion

        (2) ❑ Memorandum of law

        (3) ❑ Security

        (4) ❑ Certificate of service

    (b) ❑ Supplemental documents

        (1) ❑ Supporting evidence

        (2) ❑ Pleadings

        (3) ❑ Notice of constitutional question

        (4) ❑ Nongovernmental corporate disclosure statement

        (5) ❑ Copies of authorities

        (6) ❑ Proposed order

        (7) ❑ Statement explaining untimely electronic filing

(8) ❑ Courtesy copies

(c) ❑ Timing

    (1) ❑ A written motion and notice of the hearing must be served at least fourteen (14) days before the time specified for the hearing, with the following exceptions: (i) when the motion may be heard ex parte; (ii) when the Federal Rules of Civil Procedure set a different time; or (iii) when a court order—which a party may, for good cause, apply for ex parte—sets a different time

    (2) ❑ Any affidavit supporting a motion must be served with the motion

(II) ❑ Matters to be considered by opposing party

(a) ❑ Required documents

    (1) ❑ Answering memorandum of law

    (2) ❑ Certificate of service

(b) ❑ Supplemental documents

    (1) ❑ Supporting evidence

    (2) ❑ Pleadings

    (3) ❑ Notice of constitutional question

    (4) ❑ Nongovernmental corporate disclosure statement

    (5) ❑ Copies of authorities

    (6) ❑ Statement explaining untimely electronic filing

    (7) ❑ Courtesy copies

(c) ❑ Timing

    (1) ❑ Any opposing affidavits and answering memoranda shall be served within fourteen (14) days after service of the moving papers

    (2) ❑ Except as FRCP 59(c) provides otherwise, any opposing affidavit must be served at least seven (7) days before the hearing, unless the court permits service at another time

## B. Timing

1. *Motion for preliminary injunction.* FRCP 65 is silent about when notice must be given. FPP § 2949.

2. *Timing of motions, generally*

   a. *Motion and notice of hearing.* Except for letter-motions as permitted by NY R USDCTS&ED Civ Rule 7.1(d), and unless otherwise provided by statute or rule or by the Court in a Judge's Individual Practice or in a direction in a particular case, upon any motion, the notice of motion, supporting affidavits, and memoranda shall be served and filed as follows: on all civil motions, petitions, and applications, other than those described in NY R USDCTS&ED Civ Rule 6.1(a), and other than petitions for writs of habeas corpus, the notice of motion, supporting affidavits, and memoranda of law shall be served by the moving party on all other parties that have appeared in the action. NY R USDCTS&ED Civ Rule 6.1(b)(1). A written motion and notice of the hearing must be served at least fourteen (14) days before the time specified for the hearing, with the following exceptions:

     i. When the motion may be heard ex parte;

     ii. When the Federal Rules of Civil Procedure set a different time; or

     iii. When a court order—which a party may, for good cause, apply for ex parte—sets a different time. FRCP 6(c)(1).

   b. *Supporting affidavit.* Any affidavit supporting a motion must be served with the motion. FRCP 6(c)(2).

3. *Timing of opposing papers.* Except for letter-motions as permitted by NY R USDCTS&ED Civ Rule 7.1(d), and unless otherwise provided by statute or rule or by the Court in a Judge's Individual Practice or

in a direction in a particular case, upon any motion, the notice of motion, supporting affidavits, and memoranda shall be served and filed as follows: on all civil motions, petitions, and applications, other than those described in NY R USDCTS&ED Civ Rule 6.1(a), and other than petitions for writs of habeas corpus, any opposing affidavits and answering memoranda shall be served within fourteen (14) days after service of the moving papers. NY R USDCTS&ED Civ Rule 6.1(b)(2).

    a.  *Opposing affidavit.* Except as FRCP 59(c) provides otherwise, any opposing affidavit must be served at least seven (7) days before the hearing, unless the court permits service at another time. FRCP 6(c)(2).

4.  *Timing of reply papers.* Where the respondent files an answering affidavit setting up a new matter, the moving party ordinarily is allowed a reasonable time to file a reply affidavit since failure to deny the new matter by affidavit may operate as an admission of its truth. AMJUR MOTIONS § 25.

    a.  *Reply affidavits and reply memoranda of law.* Except for letter-motions as permitted by NY R USDCTS&ED Civ Rule 7.1(d), and unless otherwise provided by statute or rule or by the Court in a Judge's Individual Practice or in a direction in a particular case, upon any motion, the notice of motion, supporting affidavits, and memoranda shall be served and filed as follows: on all civil motions, petitions, and applications, other than those described in NY R USDCTS&ED Civ Rule 6.1(a), and other than petitions for writs of habeas corpus, any reply affidavits and memoranda of law shall be served within seven (7) days after service of the answering papers. NY R USDCTS&ED Civ Rule 6.1(b)(3).

5.  *Computation of time*

    a.  *Computing time.* FRCP 6 applies in computing any time period specified in the Federal Rules of Civil Procedure, in any local rule or court order, or in any statute that does not specify a method of computing time. FRCP 6(a). In computing any period of time prescribed or allowed by the Local Civil Rules of the United States District Courts for the Southern and Eastern Districts of New York or the Local Admiralty and Maritime Rules, the provisions of FRCP 6 shall apply unless otherwise stated. NY R USDCTS&ED Civ Rule 6.4.

        i.  *Period stated in days or a longer unit.* In computing periods of days, refer to FRCP 6 and NY R USDCTS&ED Civ Rule 6.4. NY R USDCTS&ED Civ Rule 6.1(b). When the period is stated in days or a longer unit of time:

- Exclude the day of the event that triggers the period;

- Count every day, including intermediate Saturdays, Sundays, and legal holidays; and

- Include the last day of the period, but if the last day is a Saturday, Sunday, or legal holiday, the period continues to run until the end of the next day that is not a Saturday, Sunday, or legal holiday. FRCP 6(a)(1). In the Local Civil Rules of the United States District Courts for the Southern and Eastern Districts of New York, as in the Federal Rules of Civil Procedure as amended effective December 1, 2009, Saturdays, Sundays, and legal holidays are no longer excluded in computing periods of time. If the last day of the period is a Saturday, Sunday, or legal holiday, the period continues to run until the end of the next day that is not a Saturday, Sunday, or legal holiday. NY R USDCTS&ED Civ Rule 6.4.

       ii.  *Period stated in hours.* When the period is stated in hours:

- Begin counting immediately on the occurrence of the event that triggers the period;

- Count every hour, including hours during intermediate Saturdays, Sundays, and legal holidays; and

- If the period would end on a Saturday, Sunday, or legal holiday, the period continues to run until the same time on the next day that is not a Saturday, Sunday, or legal holiday. FRCP 6(a)(2). In the Local Civil Rules of the United States District Courts for the Southern and Eastern Districts of New York, as in the Federal Rules of Civil Procedure as amended effective December 1, 2009, Saturdays, Sundays, and legal holidays are no longer excluded in computing periods of time. If the last day of the period is a Saturday, Sunday, or legal holiday, the period continues to run until the end of the next day that is not a Saturday, Sunday, or legal holiday. NY R USDCTS&ED Civ Rule 6.4.

   iii. *Inaccessibility of the clerk's office.* Unless the court orders otherwise, if the clerk's office is inaccessible:

- On the last day for filing under FRCP 6(a)(1), then the time for filing is extended to the first accessible day that is not a Saturday, Sunday, or legal holiday; or

- During the last hour for filing under FRCP 6(a)(2), then the time for filing is extended to the same time on the first accessible day that is not a Saturday, Sunday, or legal holiday. FRCP 6(a)(3).

   iv. *"Last day" defined.* Unless a different time is set by a statute, local rule, or court order, the last day ends:

- For electronic filing, at midnight in the court's time zone; and

- For filing by other means, when the clerk's office is scheduled to close. FRCP 6(a)(4).

   v. *"Next day" defined.* The "next day" is determined by continuing to count forward when the period is measured after an event and backward when measured before an event. FRCP 6(a)(5).

   vi. *"Legal holiday" defined.* "Legal holiday" means:

- The day set aside by statute for observing New Year's Day, Martin Luther King Jr.'s Birthday, Washington's Birthday, Memorial Day, Independence Day, Labor Day, Columbus Day, Veterans' Day, Thanksgiving Day, or Christmas Day;

- Any day declared a holiday by the President or Congress; and

- For periods that are measured after an event, any other day declared a holiday by the state where the district court is located. FRCP 6(a)(6).

  b. *Computation of electronic filing deadlines.* You can file electronically twenty-four (24) hours a day, seven (7) days a week, three hundred sixty-five (365) days a year. NY R USDCTSD CM/ECF, S.D.(II)(13)(13.10). Electronic filing must be completed before midnight local time where the Court is located in order to be considered timely filed that day. NY R USDCTSD CM/ECF, S.D.(I)(3)(3.3); NY R USDCTSD CM/ECF, S.D.(II)(13)(13.10); NY R USDCTSD CM/ECF, S.D.(II)(19)(19.4). An electronically filed document is deemed filed on the "filed on" date indicated on the Notice of Electronic Filing (NEF). NY R USDCTSD CM/ECF, S.D.(II)(13)(13.11).

   i. *Technical failures.* A Filing User whose filing is made untimely as the result of a technical failure may seek appropriate relief from the Court. NY R USDCTSD CM/ECF, S.D.(I)(11). If you missed a filing deadline when the ECF system was out of order, attach a statement to your filing explaining how the interruption in service prevented you from filing in a timely fashion. NY R USDCTSD CM/ECF, S.D.(II)(23)(23.5).

  c. *Extending time*

   i. *In general.* When an act may or must be done within a specified time, the court may, for good cause, extend the time:

- With or without motion or notice if the court acts, or if a request is made, before the original time or its extension expires; or

- On motion made after the time has expired if the party failed to act because of excusable neglect. FRCP 6(b)(1).

   ii. *Exceptions.* A court must not extend the time to act under FRCP 50(b), FRCP 50(d), FRCP 52(b), FRCP 59(b), FRCP 59(d), FRCP 59(e), and FRCP 60(b). FRCP 6(b)(2).

   iii. Refer to the United States District Court for the Southern District of New York KeyRules Motion for Continuance/Extension of Time document for more information on extending time.

  d. *Additional time after certain kinds of service.* When a party may or must act dithin a specified time after service and service is made under FRCP 5(b)(2)(C), FRCP 5(b)(2)(D), FRCP 5(b)(2)(E), or FRCP 5(b)(2)(F), three (3) days are added after the period would otherwise expire under FRCP 6(a). FRCP 6(d). Overnight delivery service shall be deemed service by mail for purposes of FRCP 5 and FRCP 6. NY R USDCTS&ED Civ Rule 5.3.

6. *Individual judge practices.* Refer to the Miscellaneous section of this document for information on individual judge practices on timing of documents.

## C. General Requirements

1. *Motions, generally*

   a. *Requirements.* A request for a court order must be made by motion. The motion must:

      i. Be in writing unless made during a hearing or trial;

      ii. State with particularity the grounds for seeking the order; and

      iii. State the relief sought. FRCP 7(b)(1).

   b. *Notice of motion.* A party interested in resisting the relief sought by a motion has a right to notice thereof, and an opportunity to be heard. AMJUR MOTIONS § 12.

      i. In addition to statutory or court rule provisions requiring notice of a motion—the purpose of such a notice requirement having been said to be to prevent a party from being prejudicially surprised by a motion—principles of natural justice dictate that an adverse party generally must be given notice that a motion will be presented to the court. AMJUR MOTIONS § 12.

      ii. "Notice," in this regard, means reasonable notice, including a meaningful opportunity to prepare and to defend against allegations of a motion. AMJUR MOTIONS § 12.

   c. *Writing requirement.* The writing requirement is intended to insure that the adverse parties are informed and have a record of both the motion's pendency and the grounds on which the movant seeks an order. FPP § 1191; Feldberg v. Quechee Lakes Corp., 463 F.3d 195 (2d Cir. 2006).

      i. It is sufficient "if the motion is stated in a written notice of the hearing of the motion." FPP § 1191.

   d. *Particularity requirement.* The particularity requirement insures that the opposing parties will have notice of their opponent's contentions. FEDPROC § 62:364; Goodman v. 1973 26 Foot Trojan Vessel, Arkansas Registration No. AR1439SN, 859 F.2d 71, 12 Fed.R.Serv.3d 645 (8th Cir. 1988). That requirement ensures that notice of the basis for the motion is provided to the court and to the opposing party so as to avoid prejudice, provide the opponent with a meaningful opportunity to respond, and provide the court with enough information to process the motion correctly. FEDPROC § 62:364; Andreas v. Volkswagen of America, Inc., 336 F.3d 789, 56 Fed.R.Serv.3d 6 (8th Cir. 2003).

      i. Reasonable specification of the grounds for a motion is sufficient. However, where a movant fails to state even one ground for granting the motion in question, the movant has failed to meet the minimal standard of "reasonable specification." FEDPROC § 62:364; Martinez v. Trainor, 556 F.2d 818, 23 Fed.R.Serv.2d 403 (7th Cir. 1977).

      ii. The court may excuse the failure to comply with the particularity requirement if it is inadvertent, and where no prejudice is shown by the opposing party. FEDPROC § 62:364.

   e. *Ex parte orders or orders to show cause to bring on a motion.* No ex parte order, or order to show cause to bring on a motion, will be granted except upon a clear and specific showing by affidavit of good and sufficient reasons why a procedure other than by notice of motion is necessary, and stating whether a previous application for similar relief has been made. NY R USDCTS&ED Civ Rule 6.1(d).

   f. *Letter-motions.* Applications for extensions or adjournments, applications for a pre-motion conference, and similar non-dispositive matters as permitted by the instructions regarding ECF published on the website of each respective Court and any pertinent Individual Judge's Practices, may be brought by letter-motion filed via ECF pursuant to NY R USDCTS&ED Civ Rule 5.2(b). NY R USDCTS&ED Civ Rule 7.1(d).

      i. The following list of motions. . .may be made by LETTER-MOTION: (1) Motion to Adjourn Conference; (2) Motion to Change Attorney Name on Roll; (3) Motion to Compel; (4) Motion for Conference; (5) Motion to Consolidate Cases; (6) Motion to Continue; (7) Motion re: Discovery; (8) Motion to Expedite; (9) Motion for Extension of Time; (10) Motion for Extension of Time to Amend; (11) Motion for Extension of Time to Answer; (12) Motion for

Extension of Time to Complete Discovery; (13) Motion for Extension of Time to File Document; (14) Motion for Extension of Time to File Response/Reply; (15) Motion for Extension of Time re Transcript; (16) Motion to File Amicus Brief; (17) Motion for Leave to File Document; (18) Motion for Leave to File Excess Pages; (19) Motion for Local Rule 37.2 Conference; (20) Motion for Oral Argument; (21) Motion to Reopen; (22) Motion to Reopen Case; (23) Motion to Seal Document; (24) Motion to Stay; (25) Motion to Substitute Attorney. NY R USDCTSD CM/ECF, S.D.(II)(13)(13.1).

    ii.    If the Filing User is making a type of motion that does not appear in this list, the motion may not be made by letter. NY R USDCTSD CM/ECF, S.D.(II)(13)(13.1).

    iii.    For more information on letter motions, refer to NY R USDCTSD CM/ECF, S.D.(II)(13)(13.1).

2.   *Motion for preliminary injunction.* The appropriate procedure for requesting a preliminary injunction is by motion, although it also commonly is requested by an order to show cause. FPP § 2949; James Luterbach Constr. Co. v. Adamkus, 781 F.2d 599, 603 (7th Cir. 1986); Studebaker Corp. v. Gittlin, 360 F.2d 692 (2d. Cir. 1966).

   a.   *Preliminary injunction.* An interim grant of specific relief is a preliminary injunction that may be issued only on notice to the adverse party. FEDPROC § 47:53; Westar Energy, Inc. v. Lake, 552 F.3d 1215 (10th Cir. 2009). Defined broadly, a preliminary injunction is an injunction that is issued to protect plaintiff from irreparable injury and to preserve the court's power to render a meaningful decision after a trial on the merits. FPP § 2947; Evans v. Buchanan, 555 F.2d 373, 387 (3d Cir. 1977).

    i.    *Disfavored injunctions.* There are three types of preliminary injunctions that are disfavored:

- Those that afford the moving party substantially all the relief it might recover after a full trial on the merits;

- Those that disturb the status quo; and

- Those that are mandatory as opposed to prohibitory. FEDPROC § 47:55; Prairie Band of Potawatomi Indians v. Pierce, 253 F.3d 1234, 50 Fed.R.Serv.3d 244 (10th Cir. 2001).

   b.   *Notice.* The court may issue a preliminary injunction only on notice to the adverse party. FRCP 65(a)(1). Although FRCP 65(a)(1) does not define what constitutes proper notice, it has been held that providing a copy of the motion and a specification of the time and place of the hearing are adequate. FPP § 2949.

   c.   *Security.* The court may issue a preliminary injunction or a temporary restraining order only if the movant gives security in an amount that the court considers proper to pay the costs and damages sustained by any party found to have been wrongfully enjoined or restrained. The United States, its officers, and its agencies are not required to give security. FRCP 65(c).

    i.    *Proceedings against a surety.* Whenever the Federal Rules of Civil Procedure (including the Supplemental Rules for Admiralty or Maritime Claims and Asset Forfeiture Actions) require or allow a party to give security, and security is given through a bond or other undertaking with one or more sureties, each surety submits to the court's jurisdiction and irrevocably appoints the court clerk as its agent for receiving service of any papers that affect its liability on the bond or undertaking. The surety's liability may be enforced on motion without an independent action. The motion and any notice that the court orders may be served on the court clerk, who must promptly mail a copy of each to every surety whose address is known. FRCP 65.1.

    ii.    For more information on sureties, refer to NY R USDCTS&ED Civ Rule 65.1.1.

   d.   *Preliminary injunction versus temporary restraining order.* Care should be taken to distinguish preliminary injunctions under FRCP 65(a) from temporary restraining orders under FRCP 65(b). FPP § 2947.

    i.    *Notice and duration.* [Temporary restraining orders] may be issued ex parte without an adversary hearing in order to prevent an immediate, irreparable injury and are of limited duration—they typically remain in effect for a maximum of twenty-eight (28) days. On the other hand, FRCP 65(a)(1) requires that notice be given to the opposing party before a preliminary injunction may be issued. FPP § 2947. Furthermore, a preliminary injunction normally lasts until the completion of the trial on the merits, unless it is dissolved earlier by court order or the consent of the parties. FPP § 2947. Therefore, its duration varies and is controlled by the nature of the situation in which it is utilized. FPP § 2947; Fundicao Tupy S.A. v. U.S., 841 F.2d 1101, 1103 (Fed.Cir. 1988).

ii.   *Hearing.* Some type of a hearing also implicitly is required by FRCP 65(a)(2), which was added in 1966 and provides either for the consolidation of the trial on the merits with the preliminary injunction hearing or the inclusion in the trial record of any evidence received at the FRCP 65(a) hearing. FPP § 2947.

e.   *Grounds for granting or denying a preliminary injunction.* The policies that bear on the propriety of granting a preliminary injunction rarely are discussed directly in the cases. Instead they are taken into account by the court considering a number of factors that have been found useful in deciding whether to grant or deny preliminary injunctions in particular cases. A formulation that has become popular in all kinds of cases, although it originally was devised in connection with stays of administrative orders, is that the four most important factors are: (1) the significance of the threat of irreparable harm to plaintiff if the injunction is not granted; (2) the state of the balance between this harm and the injury that granting the injunction would inflict on defendant; (3) the probability that plaintiff will succeed on the merits; and (4) the public interest. FPP § 2948; Pottgen v. Missouri State High School Activities Ass'n, 40 F.3d 926 (8th Cir. 1994).

i.   *Irreparable harm.* Perhaps the single most important prerequisite for the issuance of a preliminary injunction is a demonstration that if it is not granted the applicant is likely to suffer irreparable harm before a decision on the merits can be rendered. FPP § 2948.1. Only when the threatened harm would impair the court's ability to grant an effective remedy is there really a need for preliminary relief. FPP § 2948.1.

   • There must be a likelihood that irreparable harm will occur. Speculative injury is not sufficient; there must be more than an unfounded fear on the part of the applicant. FPP § 2948.1.

   • Thus, a preliminary injunction will not be issued simply to prevent the possibility of some remote future injury. A presently existing actual threat must be shown. However, the injury need not have been inflicted when application is made or be certain to occur; a strong threat of irreparable injury before trial is an adequate basis. FPP § 2948.1.

ii.   *Balancing hardship to parties.* The second factor bearing on the court's exercise of its discretion as to whether to grant preliminary relief involves an evaluation of the severity of the impact on defendant should the temporary injunction be granted and the hardship that would occur to plaintiff if the injunction should be denied. Two factors that frequently are considered when balancing the hardship on the respective parties of the grant or denial of relief are whether a preliminary injunction would give plaintiff all or most of the relief to which plaintiff would be entitled if successful at trial and whether mandatory relief is being sought. FPP § 2948.2.

iii.   *Likelihood of prevailing on the merits.* The third factor that enters into the preliminary injunction calculus is the likelihood that plaintiff will prevail on the merits. This is relevant because the need for the court to act is, at least in part, a function of the validity of the applicant's claim. The courts use a bewildering variety of formulations of the need for showing some likelihood of success—the most common being that plaintiff must demonstrate a reasonable probability of success. But the verbal differences do not seem to reflect substantive disagreement. All courts agree that plaintiff must present a prima facie case but need not show a certainty of winning. FPP § 2948.3.

iv.   *Public interest.* The final major factor bearing on the court's discretion to issue or deny a preliminary injunction is the public interest. Focusing on this factor is another way of inquiring whether there are policy considerations that bear on whether the order should issue. Thus, when granting preliminary relief, courts frequently emphasize that the public interest will be furthered by the injunction. Conversely, preliminary relief will be denied if the court finds that the public interest would be injured were an injunction to be issued. If the court finds there is no public interest supporting preliminary relief, that conclusion also supports denial of any injunction, even if the public interest would not be harmed by one. FPP § 2948.4. Consequently, an evaluation of the public interest should be given considerable weight in determining whether a motion for a preliminary injunction should be granted. FPP § 2948.4; Yakus v. U.S., 321 U.S. 414, 64 S.Ct. 660, 88 L.Ed. 834 (1944).

  f. *Contents and scope of every injunction and restraining order*

    i. *Contents.* Every order granting an injunction and every restraining order must:

- State the reasons why it issued;
- State its terms specifically; and
- Describe in reasonable detail—and not by referring to the complaint or other document—the act or acts restrained or required. FRCP 65(d)(1).

    ii. *Persons bound.* The order binds only the following who receive actual notice of it by personal service or otherwise:

- The parties;
- The parties' officers, agents, servants, employees, and attorneys; and
- Other persons who are in active concert or participation with anyone described in FRCP 65(d)(2)(A) or FRCP 65(d)(2)(B). FRCP 65(d)(2).

  g. *Other laws not modified.* FRCP 65 does not modify the following:

    i. Any federal statute relating to temporary restraining orders or preliminary injunctions in actions affecting employer and employee;

    ii. 28 U.S.C.A. § 2361, which relates to preliminary injunctions in actions of interpleader or in the nature of interpleader; or

    iii. 28 U.S.C.A. § 2284, which relates to actions that must be heard and decided by a three-judge district court. FRCP 65(e).

  h. *Copyright impoundment.* FRCP 65 applies to copyright-impoundment proceedings. FRCP 65(f).

3. *Opposing papers.* The Federal Rules of Civil Procedure do not require any formal answer, return, or reply to a motion, except where the Federal Rules of Civil Procedure or local rules may require affidavits, memoranda, or other papers to be filed in opposition to a motion. Such papers are simply to apprise the court of such opposition and the grounds of that opposition. FEDPROC § 62:359. Except for letter-motions as permitted by NY R USDCTS&ED Civ Rule 7.1(d) or as otherwise permitted by the Court, all oppositions and replies with respect to motions shall comply with NY R USDCTS&ED Civ Rule 7.1(a)(2) and NY R USDCTS&ED Civ Rule 7.1(a)(3), and an opposing party who seeks relief that goes beyond the denial of the motion shall comply as well with NY R USDCTS&ED Civ Rule 7.1(a)(1). NY R USDCTS&ED Civ Rule 7.1(b).

  a. *Effect of failure to respond to motion.* Although in the absence of statutory provision or court rule, a motion ordinarily does not require a written answer, when a party files a motion and the opposing party fails to respond, the court may construe such failure to respond as nonopposition to the motion or an admission that the motion was meritorious, may take the facts alleged in the motion as true—the rule in some jurisdictions being that the failure to respond to a fact set forth in a motion is deemed an admission—and may grant the motion if the relief requested appears to be justified. AMJUR MOTIONS § 28.

  b. *Assent or no opposition not determinative.* However, a motion will not be granted automatically simply because an "assent" or a notation of "no opposition" has been filed; federal judges frequently deny motions that have been assented to when it is thought that justice so dictates. FPP § 1190.

  c. *Responsive pleading inappropriate as response to motion.* An attempt to answer or oppose a motion with a responsive pleading usually is not appropriate. FPP § 1190.

4. *Reply papers.* A moving party may be required or permitted to prepare papers in addition to his original motion papers. AMJUR MOTIONS § 25. Papers answering or replying to opposing papers may be appropriate, in the interests of justice, where it appears there is a substantial reason for allowing a reply.

Thus, a court may accept reply papers where a party demonstrates that the papers to which it seeks to file a reply raise new issues that are material to the disposition of the question before the court, or where the court determines, sua sponte, that it wishes further briefing of an issue raised in those papers and orders the submission of additional papers. FEDPROC § 62:360. Except for letter-motions as permitted by NY R USDCTS&ED Civ Rule 7.1(d) or as otherwise permitted by the Court, all oppositions and replies with respect to motions shall comply with NY R USDCTS&ED Civ Rule 7.1(a)(2) and NY R USDCTS&ED Civ Rule 7.1(a)(3). NY R USDCTS&ED Civ Rule 7.1(b).

a. *Function of reply papers.* The function of a reply affidavit is to answer the arguments made in opposition to the position taken by the movant and not to permit the movant to introduce new arguments in support of the motion. AMJUR MOTIONS § 25.

b. *Issues raised for the first time in a reply document.* However, the view has been followed in some jurisdictions, that as a matter of judicial economy, where there is no prejudice and where the issues could be raised simply by filing a motion to dismiss, the trial court has discretion to consider arguments raised for the first time in a reply memorandum, and that a trial court may grant a motion to strike issues raised for the first time in a reply memorandum. AMJUR MOTIONS § 26.

5. *Orders on motions.* A memorandum signed by the Court of the decision on a motion that does not finally determine all claims for relief, or an oral decision on such a motion, shall constitute the order unless the memorandum or oral decision directs the submission or settlement of an order in more extended form. The notation in the docket of a memorandum or of an oral decision that does not direct the submission or settlement of an order in more extended form shall constitute the entry of the order. Where an order in more extended form is required to be submitted or settled, the notation in the docket of such order shall constitute the entry of the order. NY R USDCTS&ED Civ Rule 6.2.

6. *Complex civil cases.* For information on procedures for complex civil cases, refer to NY R USDCTSD Order 11 Misc 00388.

7. *Related cases.* It shall be the continuing duty of each attorney appearing in any civil or criminal case to bring promptly to the attention of the Court all facts which said attorney believes are relevant to a determination that said case and one or more pending civil or criminal cases should be heard by the same Judge, in order to avoid unnecessary duplication of judicial effort. As soon as the attorney becomes aware of such relationship, said attorney shall notify the Judges to whom the cases have been assigned. NY R USDCTS&ED Civ Rule 1.6(a). If counsel fails to comply with NY R USDCTS&ED Civ Rule 1.6(a), the Court may assess reasonable costs directly against counsel whose action has obstructed the effective administration of the Court's business. NY R USDCTS&ED Civ Rule 1.6(b).

a. *Determination of relatedness.* Subject to the limitations set forth in NY R USDCTSD Div. Bus., Rule 13(a)(2), a civil case, bankruptcy appeal, or motion to withdraw the bankruptcy reference will be deemed related to one or more civil cases, appeals or motions when the interests of justice and efficiency will be served. In determining relatedness, a judge will consider whether (A) the actions concern the same or substantially similar parties, property, transactions or events; (B) there is substantial factual overlap; (C) the parties could be subjected to conflicting orders; and (D) whether absent a determination of relatedness there would be a substantial duplication of effort and expense, delay, or undue burden on the Court, parties or witnesses. NY R USDCTSD Div. Bus., Rule 13(a)(1). Nothing in this NY R USDCTSD Div. Bus., Rule 13 is intended to preclude parties from moving for consolidated proceedings under FRCP 42. NY R USDCTSD Div. Bus., Rule 13(a)(1). Notwithstanding NY R USDCTSD Div. Bus., Rule 13(a)(1):

i. Civil cases shall not be deemed related merely because they involve common legal issues or the same parties. NY R USDCTSD Div. Bus., Rule 13(a)(2)(A).

ii. Other than cases subject to NY R USDCTSD Div. Bus., Rule 4(b) and actions seeking the enforcement of a judgment or settlement in or of an earlier case, civil cases presumptively shall not be deemed related unless both cases are pending before the Court (or the earlier case is on appeal). NY R USDCTSD Div. Bus., Rule 13(a)(2)(B).

b. *Procedure in regard to cases said to be related*

i. *Disclosure of contention of relatedness.* When a civil case is filed or removed or a bankruptcy appeal or motion to withdraw the reference of an adversary proceeding from the bankruptcy court is filed, the person filing or removing shall disclose on form JSC44C any contention of relatedness and shall file a Related Case Statement stating clearly and succinctly the basis for the contention. A copy of the civil cover sheet and Related Case Statement shall be served with the complaint, notice of removal, notice of appeal, or motion. Any party may contest a claim of relatedness by any other in writing addressed to the judge having the case with the lowest docket number of all cases claimed to be related. However, the foregoing shall not delay the assignment process or the operation of NY R USDCTSD Div. Bus., Rule 13. NY R USDCTSD Div. Bus., Rule 13(b)(1). [Editor's note: the reference to form JSC44C is likely meant to be form JS44C-SDNY: Civil Court Cover Sheet].

ii. *Claims of relatedness by other parties.* A party other than the one filing a case, bankruptcy appeal or motion to withdraw the reference that contends its case is related to another may so advise in writing the judge assigned in its case and request a transfer of its case to the judge that the party contends has the related case with the lowest docket number. If the assigned judge believes the case is related under NY R USDCTSD Div. Bus., Rule 13(a), he or she shall refer the question to the judge having the case with the lowest docket number. In the event the latter judge agrees, the case shall be transferred to that judge unless the Assignment Committee disagrees. NY R USDCTSD Div. Bus., Rule 13(b)(3).

c. For more information on related cases, refer to NY R USDCTSD Div. Bus., Rule 13.

8. *Alternative dispute resolution (ADR).* The U.S. District Court for the Southern District of New York provides litigants with opportunities to discuss settlement through judicial settlement conferences and mediation. NY R USDCTS&ED Civ Rule 83.9(a).

a. *Consideration of alternative dispute resolution.* In all civil cases, including those eligible for mediation pursuant to NY R USDCTS&ED Civ Rule 83.9(e), each party shall consider the use of mediation or a judicial settlement conference and shall report to the assigned Judge at the initial FRCP 16(b) case management conference, or subsequently, whether the party believes mediation or a judicial settlement conference may facilitate the resolution of the lawsuit. Judges are encouraged to note the availability of the mediation program and/or a judicial settlement conference before, at, or after the initial FRCP 16(b) case management conference. NY R USDCTS&ED Civ Rule 83.9(d).

b. *Mediation.* In mediation, parties and counsel meet, sometimes collectively and sometimes individually, with a neutral third party (the mediator) who has been trained to facilitate confidential settlement discussions. The parties articulate their respective positions and interests and generate options for a mutually agreeable resolution to the dispute. The mediator assists the parties in reaching their own negotiated settlement by defining the issues, probing and assessing the strengths and weaknesses of each party's legal positions, and identifying areas of agreement and disagreement. The main benefits of mediation are that it can result in an expeditious and less costly resolution of the litigation, and can produce creative solutions to complex disputes often unavailable in traditional litigation. NY R USDCTS&ED Civ Rule 83.9(b).

i. *Mediation program eligibility.* All civil cases other than Social Security, habeas corpus, and tax cases are eligible for mediation, whether assigned to Manhattan or White Plains. NY R USDCTS&ED Civ Rule 83.9(e)(1).

- The Board of Judges may, by Administrative Order, direct that certain specified categories of cases shall automatically be submitted to the mediation program. The assigned District Judge or Magistrate Judge may issue a written order exempting a particular case with or without the request of the parties. NY R USDCTS&ED Civ Rule 83.9(e)(2).

- For all other cases, the assigned District Judge or Magistrate Judge may determine that a case is appropriate for mediation and may order that case to mediation, with or without the consent of the parties, before, at, or after the initial FRCP 16(b) case management conference. Alternatively, the parties should notify the assigned Judge at any time of their desire to mediate. NY R USDCTS&ED Civ Rule 83.9(e)(3).

c. *Judicial settlement conferences.* Judicial settlement conferences may be ordered by District Judges or Magistrate Judges with or without the request or consent of the parties. NY R USDCTS&ED Civ Rule 83.9(f).

    d.  For more information on alternative dispute resolution (ADR), refer to NY R USDCTS&ED Civ Rule 83.9.

9.  *Individual judge practices.* Refer to the Miscellaneous section of this document for information on individual judge practices on general requirements for documents.

## D. Documents

1.  *Documents for moving party*

    a.  *Required documents*

        i.  *Notice of motion and motion.* Except for letter-motions as permitted by NY R USDCTS&ED Civ Rule 7.1(d) or as otherwise permitted by the Court, all motions shall include the following motion papers: a notice of motion, or an order to show cause signed by the Court, which shall specify the applicable rules or statutes pursuant to which the motion is brought, and shall specify the relief sought by the motion. NY R USDCTS&ED Civ Rule 7.1(a)(1). Refer to the General Requirements section of this document for information on the notice of motion and motion.

        ii.  *Memorandum of law.* Except for letter-motions as permitted by NY R USDCTS&ED Civ Rule 7.1(d) or as otherwise permitted by the Court, all motions shall include the following motion papers: a memorandum of law, setting forth the cases and other authorities relied upon in support of the motion, and divided, under appropriate headings, into as many parts as there are issues to be determined. NY R USDCTS&ED Civ Rule 7.1(a)(2).

        iii.  *Security.* Refer to the General Requirements section of this document for information on the security required.

        iv.  *Certificate of service.* FRCP 5(d) requires that the person making service under FRCP 5 certify that service has been effected. FRCP 5(Advisory Committee Notes). Having such information on file may be useful for many purposes, including proof of service if an issue arises concerning the effectiveness of the service. FRCP 5(Advisory Committee Notes).

            •  Such paper service [on attorneys and pro se parties who are not Filing or Receiving Users] must be documented by electronically filing proof of service. NY R USDCTSD CM/ECF, S.D.(I)(9)(9.2); NY R USDCTSD CM/ECF, S.D.(I)(19)(19.3)(b). Pro se parties who are not Filing Users are exempt from that portion of NY R USDCTSD CM/ECF, S.D.(I)(19)(19.3) requiring proof of service to be filed electronically. NY R USDCTSD CM/ECF, S.D.(I)(19)(19.3).

    b.  *Supplemental documents*

        i.  *Supporting evidence.* When a motion relies on facts outside the record, the court may hear the matter on affidavits or may hear it wholly or partly on oral testimony or on depositions. FRCP 43(c). Evidence that goes beyond the unverified allegations of the pleadings and motion papers must be presented to support or oppose a motion for a preliminary injunction. FPP § 2949. Except for letter-motions as permitted by NY R USDCTS&ED Civ Rule 7.1(d) or as otherwise permitted by the Court, all motions shall include the following motion papers: supporting affidavits and exhibits thereto containing any factual information and portions of the record necessary for the decision of the motion. NY R USDCTS&ED Civ Rule 7.1(a)(3).

            •  *Affidavits.* Affidavits are appropriate on a preliminary injunction motion and typically will be offered by both parties. FPP § 2949. All affidavits should state the facts supporting the litigant's position clearly and specifically. Preliminary injunctions frequently are denied if the affidavits are too vague or conclusory to demonstrate a clear right to relief under FRCP 65. FPP § 2949.

            •  *Discovery materials.* A party seeking or opposing relief under FRCP 26 through FRCP 37 inclusive, or making or opposing any other motion or application, shall quote or attach only those portions of the depositions, interrogatories, requests for documents, requests for admissions, or other discovery or disclosure materials, together with the responses and objections thereto, that are the subject of the discovery motion or application, or that are

cited in papers submitted in connection with any other motion or application. NY R USDCTS&ED Civ Rule 5.1.

ii. *Pleadings.* Pleadings may be considered if they have been verified. FPP § 2949; K-2 Ski Co. v. Head Ski Co., 467 F.2d 1087 (9th Cir. 1972).

iii. *Notice of constitutional question.* A party that files a pleading, written motion, or other paper drawing into question the constitutionality of a federal or state statute must promptly:

- *File notice.* File a notice of constitutional question stating the question and identifying the paper that raises it, if: (1) a federal statute is questioned and the parties do not include the United States, one of its agencies, or one of its officers or employees in an official capacity; or (2) a state statute is questioned and the parties do not include the state, one of its agencies, or one of its officers or employees in an official capacity; and

- *Serve notice.* Serve the notice and paper on the Attorney General of the United States if a federal statute is questioned—or on the state attorney general if a state statute is questioned—either by certified or registered mail or by sending it to an electronic address designated by the attorney general for this purpose. FRCP 5.1(a).

- *No forfeiture.* A party's failure to file and serve the notice, or the court's failure to certify, does not forfeit a constitutional claim or defense that is otherwise timely asserted. FRCP 5.1(d).

iv. *Nongovernmental corporate disclosure statement*

- *Contents.* A nongovernmental corporate party must file two (2) copies of a disclosure statement that: (1) identifies any parent corporation and any publicly held corporation owning ten percent (10%) or more of its stock; or (2) states that there is no such corporation. FRCP 7.1(a).

- *Time to file; Supplemental filing.* A party must: (1) file the disclosure statement with its first appearance, pleading, petition, motion, response, or other request addressed to the court; and (2) promptly file a supplemental statement if any required information changes. FRCP 7.1(b). For purposes of FRCP 7.1(b)(2), "promptly" shall mean "within fourteen days," that is, parties are required to file a supplemental disclosure statement within fourteen (14) days of the time there is any change in the information required in a disclosure statement filed pursuant to those rules. NY R USDCTS&ED Civ Rule 7.1.1.

v. *Copies of authorities.* In cases involving a pro se litigant, counsel shall, when serving a memorandum of law (or other submissions to the Court), provide the pro se litigant (but not other counsel or the Court) with copies of cases and other authorities cited therein that are unpublished or reported exclusively on computerized databases. Upon request, counsel shall provide the pro se litigant with copies of such unpublished cases and other authorities as are cited in a decision of the Court and were not previously cited by any party. NY R USDCTS&ED Civ Rule 7.2.

vi. *Proposed order.* Refer to the Format section of this document for information on the format of submitting a proposed order to the court.

vii. *Statement explaining untimely electronic filing.* If you missed a filing deadline when the ECF system was out of order, attach a statement to your filing explaining how the interruption in service prevented you from filing in a timely fashion. NY R USDCTSD CM/ECF, S.D.(II)(23)(23.5).

viii. *Courtesy copies.* Read the judge's Individual Practices to learn if courtesy copies are required. NY R USDCTSD CM/ECF, S.D.(II)(13)(13.17). Judges' Individual Practices should continue to be followed with respect to delivery of courtesy copies. NY R USDCTSD CM/ECF, S.D.(I)(3)(3.4).

2. *Documents for opposing party*

   a. *Required documents*

      i. *Answering memorandum of law.* Except for letter-motions as permitted by NY R

USDCTS&ED Civ Rule 7.1(d) or as otherwise permitted by the Court, all oppositions and replies with respect to motions shall comply with NY R USDCTS&ED Civ Rule 7.1(a)(2). NY R USDCTS&ED Civ Rule 7.1(b). Except for letter-motions as permitted by NY R USDCTS&ED Civ Rule 7.1(d) or as otherwise permitted by the Court, all motions shall include the following motion papers: a memorandum of law, setting forth the cases and other authorities relied upon in support of the motion, and divided, under appropriate headings, into as many parts as there are issues to be determined. NY R USDCTS&ED Civ Rule 7.1(a)(2). Refer to the General Requirements section of this document for information on the opposing papers.

ii. *Certificate of service.* FRCP 5(d) requires that the person making service under FRCP 5 certify that service has been effected. FRCP 5(Advisory Committee Notes). Having such information on file may be useful for many purposes, including proof of service if an issue arises concerning the effectiveness of the service. FRCP 5(Advisory Committee Notes).

- Such paper service [on attorneys and pro se parties who are not Filing or Receiving Users] must be documented by electronically filing proof of service. NY R USDCTSD CM/ECF, S.D.(I)(9)(9.2); NY R USDCTSD CM/ECF, S.D.(I)(19)(19.3)(b). Pro se parties who are not Filing Users are exempt from that portion of NY R USDCTSD CM/ECF, S.D.(I)(19)(19.3) requiring proof of service to be filed electronically. NY R USDCTSD CM/ECF, S.D.(I)(19)(19.3).

b. *Supplemental documents*

i. *Supporting evidence.* When a motion relies on facts outside the record, the court may hear the matter on affidavits or may hear it wholly or partly on oral testimony or on depositions. FRCP 43(c). Evidence that goes beyond the unverified allegations of the pleadings and motion papers must be presented to support or oppose a motion for a preliminary injunction. FPP § 2949. Except for letter-motions as permitted by NY R USDCTS&ED Civ Rule 7.1(d) or as otherwise permitted by the Court, all oppositions and replies with respect to motions shall comply with NY R USDCTS&ED Civ Rule 7.1(a)(3). NY R USDCTS&ED Civ Rule 7.1(b). Except for letter-motions as permitted by NY R USDCTS&ED Civ Rule 7.1(d) or as otherwise permitted by the Court, all motions shall include the following motion papers: supporting affidavits and exhibits thereto containing any factual information and portions of the record necessary for the decision of the motion. NY R USDCTS&ED Civ Rule 7.1(a)(3).

- *Affidavits.* Affidavits are appropriate on a preliminary injunction motion and typically will be offered by both parties. FPP § 2949. All affidavits should state the facts supporting the litigant's position clearly and specifically. Preliminary injunctions frequently are denied if the affidavits are too vague or conclusory to demonstrate a clear right to relief under FRCP 65. FPP § 2949.

- *Discovery materials.* A party seeking or opposing relief under FRCP 26 through FRCP 37 inclusive, or making or opposing any other motion or application, shall quote or attach only those portions of the depositions, interrogatories, requests for documents, requests for admissions, or other discovery or disclosure materials, together with the responses and objections thereto, that are the subject of the discovery motion or application, or that are cited in papers submitted in connection with any other motion or application. NY R USDCTS&ED Civ Rule 5.1.

ii. *Pleadings.* Pleadings may be considered if they have been verified. FPP § 2949; K-2 Ski Co. v. Head Ski Co., 467 F.2d 1087 (9th Cir. 1972).

iii. *Notice of constitutional question.* A party that files a pleading, written motion, or other paper drawing into question the constitutionality of a federal or state statute must promptly:

- *File notice.* File a notice of constitutional question stating the question and identifying the paper that raises it, if: (1) a federal statute is questioned and the parties do not include the United States, one of its agencies, or one of its officers or employees in an official capacity; or (2) a state statute is questioned and the parties do not include the state, one of its agencies, or one of its officers or employees in an official capacity; and

- *Serve notice.* Serve the notice and paper on the Attorney General of the United States if a federal statute is questioned—or on the state attorney general if a state statute is questioned—either by certified or registered mail or by sending it to an electronic address designated by the attorney general for this purpose. FRCP 5.1(a).

- *No forfeiture.* A party's failure to file and serve the notice, or the court's failure to certify, does not forfeit a constitutional claim or defense that is otherwise timely asserted. FRCP 5.1(d).

    iv. *Nongovernmental corporate disclosure statement*

- *Contents.* A nongovernmental corporate party must file two (2) copies of a disclosure statement that: (1) identifies any parent corporation and any publicly held corporation owning ten percent (10%) or more of its stock; or (2) states that there is no such corporation. FRCP 7.1(a).

- *Time to file; Supplemental filing.* A party must: (1) file the disclosure statement with its first appearance, pleading, petition, motion, response, or other request addressed to the court; and (2) promptly file a supplemental statement if any required information changes. FRCP 7.1(b). For purposes of FRCP 7.1(b)(2), "promptly" shall mean "within fourteen days," that is, parties are required to file a supplemental disclosure statement within fourteen (14) days of the time there is any change in the information required in a disclosure statement filed pursuant to those rules. NY R USDCTS&ED Civ Rule 7.1.1.

    v. *Copies of authorities.* In cases involving a pro se litigant, counsel shall, when serving a memorandum of law (or other submissions to the Court), provide the pro se litigant (but not other counsel or the Court) with copies of cases and other authorities cited therein that are unpublished or reported exclusively on computerized databases. Upon request, counsel shall provide the pro se litigant with copies of such unpublished cases and other authorities as are cited in a decision of the Court and were not previously cited by any party. NY R USDCTS&ED Civ Rule 7.2.

    vi. *Statement explaining untimely electronic filing.* If you missed a filing deadline when the ECF system was out of order, attach a statement to your filing explaining how the interruption in service prevented you from filing in a timely fashion. NY R USDCTSD CM/ECF, S.D.(II)(23)(23.5).

    vii. *Courtesy copies.* Read the judge's Individual Practices to learn if courtesy copies are required. NY R USDCTSD CM/ECF, S.D.(II)(13)(13.17). Judges' Individual Practices should continue to be followed with respect to delivery of courtesy copies. NY R USDCTSD CM/ECF, S.D.(I)(3)(3.4).

3. *Individual judge practices.* Refer to the Miscellaneous section of this document for information on individual judge practices on required documents.

## E. Format

1. *Form of documents.* The rules governing captions and other matters of form in pleadings apply to motions and other papers. FRCP 7(b)(2).

    a. *Paper.* Every pleading, written motion, and other paper must: be plainly written, typed, printed, or copied without erasures or interlineations which materially deface it. NY R USDCTS&ED Civ Rule 11.1(a)(1).

    b. *Typeface, margin, and spacing.* The typeface, margins, and spacing of all documents presented for filing must meet the following requirements:

      i. All text must be twelve (12) point type or larger, except for text in footnotes which may be ten (10) point type;

      ii. All documents must have at least one (1) inch margins on all sides;

      iii. All text must be double-spaced, except for headings, text in footnotes, or block quotations, which may be single-spaced. NY R USDCTS&ED Civ Rule 11.1(b).

    c. *Caption; Names of parties.* Every pleading must have a caption with the court's name, a title, a file

number, and a FRCP 7(a) designation. The title of the complaint must name all the parties; the title of other pleadings, after naming the first party on each side, may refer generally to other parties. FRCP 10(a). Every pleading, written motion, and other paper must: bear the docket number and the initials of the District Judge and any Magistrate Judge before whom the action or proceeding is pending, NY R USDCTS&ED Civ Rule 11.1(a)(2).

d. *Paragraphs; Separate statements.* A party must state its claims or defenses in numbered paragraphs, each limited as far as practicable to a single set of circumstances. A later pleading may refer by number to a paragraph in an earlier pleading. If doing so would promote clarity, each claim founded on a separate transaction or occurrence—and each defense other than a denial—must be stated in a separate count or defense. FRCP 10(b).

e. *Adoption by reference; Exhibits.* A statement in a pleading may be adopted by reference elsewhere in the same pleading or in any other pleading or motion. A copy of a written instrument that is an exhibit to a pleading is a part of the pleading for all purposes. FRCP 10(c).

f. *Acceptance by the clerk.* The clerk must not refuse to file a paper solely because it is not in the form prescribed by the Federal Rules of Civil Procedure or by a local rule or practice. FRCP 5(d)(4).

2. *Form of electronic documents*

a. *PDF-A.* All documents electronically filed on the ECF system must be in PDF-A format (portable document format). A PDF-A file is created using PDF writer software such as Adobe Acrobat (go to the Adobe website for details). PDF-A files cannot be altered, providing security to the filer and the Court. NY R USDCTSD CM/ECF, S.D.(II)(23)(23.2).

b. *Size limitation.* No single PDF file may be larger than four megabytes (4 MB). If the filing is too large, the ECF system will not allow it to be filed, and you will not see a Notice of Electronic Filing (NEF or filing receipt) screen. To determine the size of an Adobe Acrobat PDF file click on File, Document Properties, Summary. NY R USDCTSD CM/ECF, S.D.(II)(23)(23.3).

   i. Converting documents directly from a word processor to PDF-A format creates the smallest possible file in terms of computer memory. If that is not possible, scan your document at low resolution. Within the Adobe Acrobat program, on the "Scan Manager" screen, adjust the settings for black and white and 200 dpi (dots per inch). This allows more pages to fit into a single PDF-A file. If that does not work, separate an oversized file into 2 or more parts. Simply label each file 1a, 1b, 1c, etc. Only relevant excerpts of exhibits should be electronically filed. NY R USDCTSD CM/ECF, S.D.(II)(23)(23.4).

c. *Attachments and exhibits.* Filing Users must submit in electronic form all documents referenced as exhibits or attachments, unless the Court permits paper filing. NY R USDCTSD CM/ECF, S.D.(I)(5)(5.1).

   i. A Filing User must submit as exhibits or attachments only those excerpts of the referenced documents that are relevant to the matter under consideration by the Court. Excerpted material must be clearly and prominently identified as such. Filing Users who file excerpts of documents as exhibits or attachments under this procedure do so without prejudice to their right to file timely additional excerpts or the complete document. Responding parties may file timely additional excerpts that they believe are relevant or the complete document. A party may move before the Court for permission to serve and file in hard copy documents that cannot be reasonably scanned. NY R USDCTSD CM/ECF, S.D.(I)(5)(5.2).

   ii. Exhibits must be filed only as attachments to a document, such as a motion or an affidavit. Do not use the ECF Filing Event for "Motion" to file exhibits separately. Exhibits are the only items that should be attached to electronically filed documents. You are limited to electronically filing only relevant excerpts of exhibits. Excerpts must be clearly identified as such. If the exhibit is too large to be scanned and electronically filed you may contact the ECF Help Desk. NY R USDCTSD CM/ECF, S.D.(II)(15)(15.6).

d. *Letters.* Parties should consult the assigned judge's Individual Practices to determine if the judge accepts letters at all and, if he or she does, whether the judge has any page limitations on letters and/or requires courtesy copies of letters filed on ECF (and, if so, by what means of delivery). All

letters addressed to the Court must include a subject line with the case name and docket number (e.g., "Re: Doe v. Smith, 13 Civ. 1234 (ABC)"). NY R USDCTSD CM/ECF, S.D.(II)(13)(13.1).

e. *Proposed orders, proposed judgments, stipulations and consents.* Any document that requires the signature of a judge should not be electronically filed except as an exhibit to another document. Proposed orders, judgments, stipulations and consents should not be submitted through the ECF system. Instead they should be sent by e-mail to the Clerk. Proposed orders should be submitted in word processing format (WordPerfect or Word) rather than as a PDF document. Stipulations should be submitted in PDF-A format. Stipulations must contain ink signatures not s/. Faxed or emailed signatures are acceptable. Please note that Stipulations of Voluntary Dismissal pursuant to FRCP 41(a)(1)(A)(ii) do not require the signature of a judge and must be electronically filed on the ECF system. Questions may be directed to the Orders and Judgments Clerk at the phone numbers listed in NY R USDCTSD CM/ECF, S.D.(II)(18)(18.3). NY R USDCTSD CM/ECF, S.D.(II)(18)(18.3).

i. Email the proposed order, judgment or stipulation to the email addresses listed in NY R USDCTSD CM/ECF, S.D.(II)(18)(18.3). NY R USDCTSD CM/ECF, S.D.(II)(18)(18.3).

ii. Pro se litigants who are not Filing Users are exempt from that portion of NY R USDCTSD CM/ECF, S.D.(II)(18)(18.3) that requires litigants to email proposed orders, judgments, stipulations and consents, and shall deliver such documents to the Clerk's Office in paper form. NY R USDCTSD CM/ECF, S.D.(II)(18)(18.3).

3. *Signing of pleadings, motions and other papers*

a. *Signature.* Every pleading, written motion, and other paper must be signed by at least one attorney of record in the attorney's name—or by a party personally if the party is unrepresented. The paper must state the signer's address, e-mail address, and telephone number. FRCP 11(a). Every pleading, written motion, and other paper must: have the name of each person signing it clearly printed or typed directly below the signature. NY R USDCTS&ED Civ Rule 11.1(a)(3).

i. *Electronic signatures.* The user log-in and password required to submit documents to the ECF system serve as the Filing User's signature on all electronic documents filed with the Court. NY R USDCTSD CM/ECF, S.D.(I)(8)(8.1); NY R USDCTSD CM/ECF, S.D.(II)(13)(13.14). They also serve as a signature for purposes of the Federal Rules of Civil Procedure, including FRCP 11, the Local Civil Rules of the United States District Courts for the Southern and Eastern Districts of New York, and any other purpose for which a signature is required in connection with proceedings before the Court. NY R USDCTSD CM/ECF, S.D.(I)(8)(8.1).

- *Signature block.* Electronically filed documents must include a signature block and must set forth the name, address, telephone number and e-mail address all in compliance with the Federal Rules of Civil Procedure and NY R USDCTS&ED Civ Rule 11.1. In the absence of a scanned signature image, the name of the Filing User under whose log-in and password the document is submitted must be preceded by an "s/" typed in the space where the signature would otherwise appear. NY R USDCTSD CM/ECF, S.D.(I)(8)(8.2); NY R USDCTSD CM/ECF, S.D.(II)(13)(13.14).

- *Documents requiring the signature of a party or witness.* A document requiring the signature of a party or witness shall be electronically filed in a scanned format that contains an image of the actual signature. NY R USDCTSD CM/ECF, S.D.(I)(8)(8.4); NY R USDCTSD CM/ECF, S.D.(II)(13)(13.14).

- *Documents requiring the signature of a judge.* A Filing User submitting a document electronically that requires a judge's signature must promptly deliver the document in such other form, if any, as the Court requires. NY R USDCTSD CM/ECF, S.D.(I)(4)(4.2).

- *Documents requiring multiple signatures.* Documents requiring signatures of more than one party must be electronically filed either by: (a) submitting a scanned document containing all necessary signatures; (b) representing the consent of the other parties on the document; (c) identifying on the document the parties whose signatures are required and by the submission of a notice of endorsement by the other parties no later than three business days after filing; or (d) in any other manner approved by the Court. NY R USDCTSD CM/ECF, S.D.(I)(8)(8.5).

233

ii.   *No verification or accompanying affidavit required for pleadings.* Unless a rule or statute specifically states otherwise, a pleading need not be verified or accompanied by an affidavit. FRCP 11(a).

iii.  *Unsigned papers.* The court must strike an unsigned paper unless the omission is promptly corrected after being called to the attorney's or party's attention. FRCP 11(a).

b.  *Representations to the court.* By presenting to the court a pleading, written motion, or other paper—whether by signing, filing, submitting, or later advocating it—an attorney or unrepresented party certifies that to the best of the person's knowledge, information, and belief, formed after an inquiry reasonable under the circumstances:

i.   It is not being presented for any improper purpose, such as to harass, cause unnecessary delay, or needlessly increase the cost of litigation;

ii.  The claims, defenses, and other legal contentions are warranted by existing law or by a nonfrivolous argument for extending, modifying, or reversing existing law or for establishing new law;

iii. The factual contentions have evidentiary support or, if specifically so identified, will likely have evidentiary support after a reasonable opportunity for further investigation or discovery; and

iv.  The denials of factual contentions are warranted on the evidence or, if specifically so identified, are reasonably based on belief or a lack of information. FRCP 11(b).

c.  *Sanctions.* If, after notice and a reasonable opportunity to respond, the court determines that FRCP 11(b) has been violated, the court may impose an appropriate sanction on any attorney, law firm, or party that violated FRCP 11(b) or is responsible for the violation. FRCP 11(c)(1). Refer to the United States District Court for the Southern District of New York KeyRules Motion for Sanctions document for more information.

4.  *Privacy protection for filings made with the court*

a.  *Redacted filings.* Unless the court orders otherwise, in an electronic or paper filing with the court that contains an individual's Social Security number, taxpayer-identification number, or birth date, the name of an individual known to be a minor, or a financial-account number, a party or nonparty making the filing may include only:

i.   The last four (4) digits of the Social Security number and taxpayer-identification number;

ii.  The year of the individual's birth;

iii. The minor's initials; and

iv.  The last four (4) digits of the financial-account number. FRCP 5.2(a); NY R USDCTSD CM/ECF, S.D.(II)(21)(21.3).

v.   Caution should be exercised when filing documents that contain the following:

- Personal identifying numbers (PIN #'s), such as a driver's license number;
- Medical records, treatment and diagnosis;
- Employment history;
- Individual financial information;
- Proprietary or trade secret information;
- Information regarding an individual's cooperation with the government. NY R USDCTSD CM/ECF, S.D.(II)(21)(21.4).

b.  *Exemptions from the redaction requirement.* The redaction requirement does not apply to the following:

i.   A financial-account number that identifies the property allegedly subject to forfeiture in a forfeiture proceeding;

ii.  The record of an administrative or agency proceeding;

iii. The official record of a state-court proceeding;

    iv.   The record of a court or tribunal, if that record was not subject to the redaction requirement when originally filed;

    v.   A filing covered by FRCP 5.2(c) or FRCP 5.2(d); and

    vi.   A pro se filing in an action brought under 28 U.S.C.A. § 2241, 28 U.S.C.A. § 2254, or 28 U.S.C.A. § 2255. FRCP 5.2(b).

c.   *Limitations on remote access to electronic files; Social Security appeals and immigration cases.* Unless the court orders otherwise, in an action for benefits under the Social Security Act, and in an action or proceeding relating to an order of removal, to relief from removal, or to immigration benefits or detention, access to an electronic file is authorized as follows:

    i.   The parties and their attorneys may have remote electronic access to any part of the case file, including the administrative record;

    ii.   Any other person may have electronic access to the full record at the courthouse, but may have remote electronic access only to:

- The docket maintained by the court; and

- An opinion, order, judgment, or other disposition of the court, but not any other part of the case file or the administrative record. FRCP 5.2(c).

d.   *Filings made under seal.* The court may order that a filing be made under seal without redaction. The court may later unseal the filing or order the person who made the filing to file a redacted version for the public record. FRCP 5.2(d). For more information on sealing documents, refer to NY R USDCTSD CM/ECF, S.D.(I)(6).

e.   *Protective orders.* For good cause, the court may by order in a case:

    i.   Require redaction of additional information; or

    ii.   Limit or prohibit a nonparty's remote electronic access to a document filed with the court. FRCP 5.2(e).

f.   *Option for additional unredacted filing under seal.* A person making a redacted filing may also file an unredacted copy under seal. The court must retain the unredacted copy as part of the record. FRCP 5.2(f); NY R USDCTSD CM/ECF, S.D.(II)(21)(21.5).

g.   *Option for filing a reference list.* A filing that contains redacted information may be filed together with a reference list that identifies each item of redacted information and specifies an appropriate identifier that uniquely corresponds to each item listed. The list must be filed under seal and may be amended as of right. Any reference in the case to a listed identifier will be construed to refer to the corresponding item of information. FRCP 5.2(g); NY R USDCTSD CM/ECF, S.D.(II)(21)(21.5).

h.   *Responsibility for redaction.* It is the sole responsibility of counsel and the parties to be sure that all documents comply with the rules of this Court requiring redaction of personal identifiers. Neither the judge nor the Clerk of Court will review documents for compliance with these rules. NY R USDCTSD CM/ECF, S.D.(II)(21)(21.2).

i.   *Waiver of protection of identifiers.* A person waives the protection of FRCP 5.2(a) as to the person's own information by filing it without redaction and not under seal. FRCP 5.2(h).

j.   For more information on privacy and public access to ECF cases, refer to NY R USDCTSD CM/ECF, S.D.(II)(21).

5.   *Individual judge practices.* Refer to the Miscellaneous section of this document for information on individual judge practices on formatting documents.

## F.  Filing and Service Requirements

1.   *Filing requirements.* Any paper after the complaint that is required to be served—together with a certificate of service—must be filed within a reasonable time after service. FRCP 5(d)(1). Complaints and all subsequent papers are accepted at either courthouse, regardless of the place for which the case is designated. NY R USDCTSD Div. Bus., Rule 22. Subject to the instructions regarding ECF published on the website of each respective Court and any pertinent Individual Judge's Practices, letter-motions

permitted by NY R USDCTS&ED Civ Rule 7.1(d) and letters addressed to the Court (but not letters between the parties) may be filed via ECF. NY R USDCTS&ED Civ Rule 5.2(b). For information on electronically filing motions, refer to NY R USDCTSD CM/ECF, S.D.(II)(15).

a. *How filing is made; In general.* A paper is filed by delivering it:

    i. To the clerk; or

    ii. To a judge who agrees to accept it for filing, and who must then note the filing date on the paper and promptly send it to the clerk. FRCP 5(d)(2).

b. *Night depository.* A night depository with an automatic date stamp shall be maintained by the Clerk of the Southern District in the Pearl Street Courthouse. After regular business hours, papers for the District Court only may be deposited in the night depository. Such papers will be considered as having been filed in the District Court as of the date stamped thereon, which shall be deemed presumptively correct. NY R USDCTS&ED Civ Rule 1.2.

c. *Electronic filing*

    i. *Authorization of electronic filing program.* A court may, by local rule, allow papers to be filed, signed, or verified by electronic means that are consistent with any technical standards established by the Judicial Conference of the United States. A local rule may require electronic filing only if reasonable exceptions are allowed. A paper filed electronically in compliance with a local rule is a written paper for purposes of the Federal Rules of Civil Procedure. FRCP 5(d)(3).

        • The Court will accept for filing documents submitted, signed or verified by electronic means, that comply with the rules in NY R USDCTSD CM/ECF, S.D. NY R USDCTSD CM/ECF, S.D.(I). The information in NY R USDCTSD CM/ECF, S.D. applies only to cases assigned to the ECF system. NY R USDCTSD CM/ECF, S.D.(Introduction).

        • Parties serving and filing papers shall follow the instructions regarding Electronic Case Filing (ECF) published on the website of each respective Court. A paper served and filed by electronic means in accordance with such instructions is, for purposes of FRCP 5, served and filed in compliance with the Local Civil Rules of the Southern and Eastern Districts of New York. NY R USDCTS&ED Civ Rule 5.2(a). Parties have an obligation to review the Court's actual order, decree, or judgment (on ECF), which controls, and should not rely on the description on the docket or in the ECF Notice of Electronic Filing (NEF). NY R USDCTS&ED Civ Rule 5.2(c).

        • The following should be observed when filing electronically: (1) the Federal Rules of Civil Procedure, (2) the Local Civil Rules of the United States District Courts for the Southern and Eastern Districts of New York, (3) the assigned judge's Individual Practices, and (4) the Court's Electronic Case Filing Rules & Instructions (NY R USDCTSD CM/ECF, S.D.). NY R USDCTSD CM/ECF, S.D.(Introduction).

    ii. *Scope of electronic filing.* Except as expressly provided and in exceptional circumstances preventing a party from filing electronically, all documents required to be filed with the Court must be filed electronically. Any party unable to comply with this requirement must seek permission of the Court to file in the traditional manner, on paper. Any such application made after regular business hours may be submitted through the night depository box maintained pursuant to NY R USDCTS&ED Civ Rule 1.2. NY R USDCTSD CM/ECF, S.D.(I)(1)(1.1).

        • *Documents filed by pro se litigants.* Unless otherwise ordered by the Court, documents filed by pro se litigants must be filed in the traditional manner, on paper, and will be scanned and docketed by the Clerk's Office into the ECF system. NY R USDCTSD CM/ECF, S.D.(I)(1)(1.1). Pro se litigants must file pleadings and documents in the traditional manner on paper unless the assigned judge has granted permission to electronically file on the ECF system. NY R USDCTSD CM/ECF, S.D.(Introduction).

        • *Letters.* Except for letters to be filed under seal, letters addressed to judges who accept letters may be filed electronically. Parties should consult the assigned judge's Individual Practices to determine if the judge accepts letters at all and, if he or she does, whether the

judge has any page limitations on letters and/or requires courtesy copies of letters filed on ECF (and, if so, by what means of delivery). NY R USDCTSD CM/ECF, S.D.(II)(13)(13.1). Letters solely between parties or their counsel or otherwise not addressed to the Court may not be filed electronically on ECF (except as exhibits to an otherwise properly filed document). NY R USDCTSD CM/ECF, S.D.(II)(13)(13.1). For more information on filing letters, refer to NY R USDCTSD CM/ECF, S.D.(II)(13)(13.1).

- *Proposed orders, judgments and decrees.* Proposed orders, judgments and decrees shall be presented as directed by the ECF rules published on the website of each respective Court. NY R USDCTS&ED Civ Rule 77.1. For more information, refer to NY R USDCTS&ED Civ Rule 77.1.

iii. *Exceptions to electronic filing.* In an ECF case, the documents that should not be electronically filed include:

- Miscellaneous Case initiating documents, NY R USDCTSD CM/ECF, S.D.(II)(18)(18.2);

- Proposed orders; proposed judgments, stipulations; consents, NY R USDCTSD CM/ECF, S.D.(II)(18)(18.3);

- Orders to show cause / temporary restraining orders, NY R USDCTSD CM/ECF, S.D.(II)(18)(18.4);

- Sealed documents, NY R USDCTSD CM/ECF, S.D.(II)(18)(18.5); and

- Surety bonds, NY R USDCTSD CM/ECF, S.D.(II)(18)(18.6).

- In cases where the record of an administrative or other prior proceeding must be filed with the Court, such record may be served and filed in hard copy without prior motion and order of the Court. NY R USDCTSD CM/ECF, S.D.(I)(5)(5.3).

- For more documents excepted from electronic filing, and for more information on such documents, refer to NY R USDCTSD CM/ECF, S.D.(II)(18).

iv. *Consequences of electronic filing.* Except as otherwise provided in NY R USDCTSD CM/ECF, S.D.(I)(4), electronic filing of a document in the ECF system consistent with these procedures, together with the transmission of a Notice of Electronic Filing (NEF) from the Court, constitutes filing of the document for all purposes of the Federal Rules of Civil Procedure and the Local Civil Rules of the United States District Courts for the Southern and Eastern Districts of New York and constitutes entry of the document on the docket kept by the Clerk under FRCP 58 and FRCP 79. NY R USDCTSD CM/ECF, S.D.(I)(3)(3.1).

v. For more information on electronic filing, refer to NY R USDCTSD CM/ECF, S.D.

2. *Service requirements*

a. *Service; When required*

i. *In general.* Unless the Federal Rules of Civil Procedure provide otherwise, each of the following papers must be served on every party:

- An order stating that service is required;

- A pleading filed after the original complaint, unless the court orders otherwise under FRCP 5(c) because there are numerous defendants;

- A discovery paper required to be served on a party, unless the court orders otherwise;

- A written motion, except one that may be heard ex parte; and

- A written notice, appearance, demand, or offer of judgment, or any similar paper. FRCP 5(a)(1).

ii. *If a party fails to appear.* No service is required on a party who is in default for failing to appear. But a pleading that asserts a new claim for relief against such a party must be served on that party under FRCP 4. FRCP 5(a)(2).

iii. *Seizing property.* If an action is begun by seizing property and no person is or need be named as

a defendant, any service required before the filing of an appearance, answer, or claim must be made on the person who had custody or possession of the property when it was seized. FRCP 5(a)(3).

b. *Service; How made*

   i. *Serving an attorney.* If a party is represented by an attorney, service under FRCP 5 must be made on the attorney unless the court orders service on the party. FRCP 5(b)(1).

   ii. *Service in general.* A paper is served under FRCP 5 by:

- Handing it to the person;
- Leaving it: (1) at the person's office with a clerk or other person in charge or, if no one is in charge, in a conspicuous place in the office; or (2) if the person has no office or the office is closed, at the person's dwelling or usual place of abode with someone of suitable age and discretion who resides there;
- Mailing it to the person's last known address—in which event service is complete upon mailing;
- Leaving it with the court clerk if the person has no known address;
- Sending it by electronic means if the person consented in writing—in which event service is complete upon transmission, but is not effective if the serving party learns that it did not reach the person to be served; or
- Delivering it by any other means that the person consented to in writing—in which event service is complete when the person making service delivers it to the agency designated to make delivery. FRCP 5(b)(2).

   iii. *Service by overnight delivery.* Service upon an attorney may be made by overnight delivery service. "Overnight delivery service" means any delivery service which regularly accepts items for overnight delivery. Overnight delivery service shall be deemed service by mail for purposes of FRCP 5 and FRCP 6. NY R USDCTS&ED Civ Rule 5.3.

   iv. *Service by electronic means.* Parties serving and filing papers shall follow the instructions regarding Electronic Case Filing (ECF) published on the website of each respective Court. A paper served and filed by electronic means in accordance with such instructions is, for purposes of FRCP 5, served and filed in compliance with the Local Civil Rules of the United States District Courts for the Southern and Eastern Districts of New York. NY R USDCTS&ED Civ Rule 5.2(a). Parties have an obligation to review the Court's actual order, decree, or judgment (on ECF), which controls, and should not rely on the description on the docket or in the ECF Notice of Electronic Filing (NEF). NY R USDCTS&ED Civ Rule 5.2(c).

- *Notice of electronic filing (NEF).* In cases assigned to the ECF system, service is complete provided all parties receive a Notice of Electronic Filing (NEF), which is sent automatically by email from the Court (see the NEF for a list of who did/did not receive notice electronically). Transmission of the NEF constitutes service upon all Filing and Receiving Users who are listed as recipients of notice by electronic mail. NY R USDCTSD CM/ECF, S.D.(I)(9)(9.1). In cases assigned to the ECF system, if all parties receive a NEF, service is complete upon transmission of the NEF by the Court, and you are not required to serve a paper copy. NY R USDCTSD CM/ECF, S.D.(II)(19)(19.2). It remains the duty of Filing and Receiving Users to maintain current contact information with the court and to regularly review the docket sheet of the case. NY R USDCTSD CM/ECF, S.D.(I)(9)(9.1).
- *Mailing of court-initiated documents.* The Clerk's Office will no longer mail paper copies of court-initiated documents to Filing and Receiving Users. The Clerk's Office will mail copies of all court-initiated documents to pro se parties who have not registered as Filing or Receiving Users. NY R USDCTSD CM/ECF, S.D.(II)(19)(19.1).
- *No receipt of a NEF.* If any party does not receive a NEF, you are required to accomplish service on that party in the traditional manner, in paper form. NY R USDCTSD CM/ECF, S.D.(II)(19)(19.2). The NEF receipt will inform you who will receive notice of the filing

"electronically" (by e-mail from the Court) and who will receive notice "by other means" (traditional service in paper form). NY R USDCTSD CM/ECF, S.D.(II)(19)(19.2).

- *Service on non-filing or non-receiving users.* Attorneys and pro se parties who are not Filing or Receiving Users must be served with a paper copy of any electronically filed pleading or other document. Service of such paper copy must be made according to the Federal Rules of Civil Procedure and the Local Civil Rules of the United States District Courts for the Southern and Eastern Districts of New York. NY R USDCTSD CM/ECF, S.D.(I)(9)(9.2). Such paper service must be documented by electronically filing proof of service. NY R USDCTSD CM/ECF, S.D.(I)(9)(9.2); NY R USDCTSD CM/ECF, S.D.(II)(19)(19.2). Where the Clerk scans and electronically files pleadings and documents on behalf of a pro se party, the associated NEF constitutes service. NY R USDCTSD CM/ECF, S.D.(I)(9)(9.2).

- For more information on service by electronic means, refer to NY R USDCTSD CM/ECF, S.D.(II)(19).

   v. *Using court facilities.* If a local rule so authorizes, a party may use the court's transmission facilities to make service under FRCP 5(b)(2)(E). FRCP 5(b)(3).

  c. *Serving numerous defendants*

    i. *In general.* If an action involves an unusually large number of defendants, the court may, on motion or on its own, order that:

- Defendants' pleadings and replies to them need not be served on other defendants;

- Any crossclaim, counterclaim, avoidance, or affirmative defense in those pleadings and replies to them will be treated as denied or avoided by all other parties; and

- Filing any such pleading and serving it on the plaintiff constitutes notice of the pleading to all parties. FRCP 5(c)(1).

    ii. *Notifying parties.* A copy of every such order must be served on the parties as the court directs. FRCP 5(c)(2).

3. *Individual judge practices.* Refer to the Miscellaneous section of this document for information on individual judge practices on filing and serving documents.

## G. Hearings

1. *Hearings, generally*

  a. *Oral argument.* Due process does not require that oral argument be permitted on a motion and, except as otherwise provided by local rule, the district court has discretion to determine whether it will decide the motion on the papers or hear argument by counsel (and perhaps receive evidence). FPP § 1190; F.D.I.C. v. Deglau, 207 F.3d 153 (3d Cir. 2000). The parties and their attorneys shall only appear to argue the motion if so directed by the Court by order or by a Judge's Individual Practice. NY R USDCTS&ED Civ Rule 6.1(c).

  b. *Providing a regular schedule for oral hearings.* A court may establish regular times and places for oral hearings on motions. FRCP 78(a).

  c. *Providing for submission on briefs.* By rule or order, the court may provide for submitting and determining motions on briefs, without oral hearings. FRCP 78(b).

2. *Hearing on motion for preliminary injunction*

  a. *Consolidating the hearing with the trial on the merits.* Before or after beginning the hearing on a motion for a preliminary injunction, the court may advance the trial on the merits and consolidate it with the hearing. Even when consolidation is not ordered, evidence that is received on the motion and that would be admissible at trial becomes part of the trial record and need not be repeated at trial. But the court must preserve any party's right to a jury trial. FRCP 65(a)(2).

  b. *Expediting the hearing after temporary restraining order is issued without notice.* If the order is issued without notice, the motion for a preliminary injunction must be set for hearing at the earliest possible time, taking precedence over all other matters except hearings on older matters of the same character. At the hearing, the party who obtained the order must proceed with the motion; if the party does not, the court must dissolve the order. FRCP 65(b)(3).

3. *Individual judge practices.* Refer to the Miscellaneous section of this document for information on individual judge practices on hearings.

## H. Forms

### 1. Federal Motion for Preliminary Injunction Forms

a. Declaration; In support of motion for preliminary injunction. AMJUR PP INJUNCTION § 38.

b. Memorandum of points and authorities; In support of motion for preliminary injunction. AMJUR PP INJUNCTION § 39.

c. Notice; Motion for preliminary injunction. AMJUR PP INJUNCTION § 40.

d. Motion; For preliminary injunction. AMJUR PP INJUNCTION § 41.

e. Motion; For preliminary injunction; On pleadings and other papers without evidentiary hearing or oral argument. AMJUR PP INJUNCTION § 43.

f. Affidavit; In support of motion for preliminary injunction. AMJUR PP INJUNCTION § 52.

g. Motion for preliminary injunction. 4A FEDFORMS § 5284.

h. Motion enjoining use of information acquired from employment with plaintiff. 4A FEDFORMS § 5287.

i. Motion enjoining interference with public access. 4A FEDFORMS § 5288.

j. Motion enjoining collection of tax assessment. 4A FEDFORMS § 5289.

k. Motion enjoining conducting election or certifying representative. 4A FEDFORMS § 5290.

l. Motion enjoining preventing plaintiff's acting as teacher. 4A FEDFORMS § 5291.

m. Motion enjoining interference with plaintiff's enforcement of judgment in related case. 4A FED-FORMS § 5292.

n. Motion for preliminary injunction in patent infringement action. 4A FEDFORMS § 5293.

o. Motion for preliminary injunction on basis of prayer of complaint and for setting hearing on motion. 4A FEDFORMS § 5294.

p. Notice of motion. 4A FEDFORMS § 5308.

q. Notice of motion and motion. 4A FEDFORMS § 5310.

r. Bond; To obtain preliminary injunction. FEDPROF § 1:701.

s. Opposition; To motion; General form. FEDPROF § 1:750.

t. Brief; Supporting or opposing motion. FEDPROF § 1:752.

u. Motion for temporary restraining order and preliminary injunction. GOLDLTGFMS § 13A:6.

v. Motion for preliminary injunction. GOLDLTGFMS § 13A:18.

w. Motion for preliminary injunction; Based upon pleadings and other papers without evidentiary hearing or oral argument. GOLDLTGFMS § 13A:19.

x. Motion for preliminary injunction; Supporting affidavit. GOLDLTGFMS § 13A:20.

y. Bond. GOLDLTGFMS § 19:2.

z. Bond; In support of injunction. GOLDLTGFMS § 19:3.

## I. Applicable Rules

1. *Federal rules*

a. Serving and filing pleadings and other papers. FRCP 5.

b. Constitutional challenge to a statute; Notice, certification, and intervention. FRCP 5.1.

c. Privacy protection for filings made with the court. FRCP 5.2.

    d.   Computing and extending time; Time for motion papers. FRCP 6.

    e.   Pleadings allowed; Form of motions and other papers. FRCP 7.

    f.   Disclosure statement. FRCP 7.1.

    g.   Form of pleadings. FRCP 10.

    h.   Signing pleadings, motions, and other papers; Representations to the court; Sanctions. FRCP 11.

    i.   Taking testimony. FRCP 43.

    j.   Injunctions and restraining orders. FRCP 65.

    k.   Proceedings against a surety. FRCP 65.1.

    l.   Hearing motions; Submission on briefs. FRCP 78.

2.  *Local rules*

    a.   Night depository. NY R USDCTS&ED Civ Rule 1.2.

    b.   Duty of attorneys in related cases. NY R USDCTS&ED Civ Rule 1.6.

    c.   Filing of discovery materials. NY R USDCTS&ED Civ Rule 5.1.

    d.   Electronic service and filing of documents. NY R USDCTS&ED Civ Rule 5.2.

    e.   Service by overnight delivery. NY R USDCTS&ED Civ Rule 5.3.

    f.   Service and filing of motion papers. NY R USDCTS&ED Civ Rule 6.1.

    g.   Orders on motions. NY R USDCTS&ED Civ Rule 6.2.

    h.   Computation of time. NY R USDCTS&ED Civ Rule 6.4.

    i.   Motion papers. NY R USDCTS&ED Civ Rule 7.1.

    j.   Disclosure statement. NY R USDCTS&ED Civ Rule 7.1.1.

    k.   Authorities to be provided to pro se litigants. NY R USDCTS&ED Civ Rule 7.2.

    l.   Form of pleadings, motions, and other papers. NY R USDCTS&ED Civ Rule 11.1.

    m.   Submission of orders, judgments and decrees. NY R USDCTS&ED Civ Rule 77.1.

    n.   Alternative dispute resolution (Southern District only). NY R USDCTS&ED Civ Rule 83.9.

    o.   Electronic case filing rules and instructions. NY R USDCTSD CM/ECF, S.D.

    p.   Related cases. NY R USDCTSD Div. Bus., Rule 13.

    q.   Filing at either courthouse. NY R USDCTSD Div. Bus., Rule 22.

## J.  Miscellaneous

**NOTE: Individual judges' rules may apply. For available judge-level information, refer to:**

DISTRICT JUDGE RONNIE ABRAMS: NY R USDCTSD Abrams-Civ Prac; NY R USDCTSD Abrams-Crim Prac; NY R USDCTSD Abrams-Pro Se; NY R USDCTSD Abrams-Case Mgt; NY R USDCTSD Abrams-Jury.

DISTRICT JUDGE DEBORAH A. BATTS: NY R USDCTSD Batts-Practices.

DISTRICT JUDGE RICHARD M. BERMAN: NY R USDCTSD Berman-Practices; NY R USDCTSD Berman-Default; NY R USDCTSD Berman-Sentencing; NY R USDCTSD Berman-Media.

DISTRICT JUDGE VINCENT L. BRICCETTI: NY R USDCTSD Briccetti-Practices; NY R USDCTSD Briccetti-Plan; NY R USDCTSD Briccetti-Notice.

DISTRICT JUDGE VERNON S. BRODERICK: NY R USDCTSD Broderick-Civil; NY R USDCTSD Broderick-Crim; NY R USDCTSD Broderick-Case Mgt; NY R USDCTSD Broderick-Jury.

DISTRICT JUDGE NAOMI REICE BUCHWALD: NY R USDCTSD Buchwald-Practices.

DISTRICT JUDGE VALERIE E. CAPRONI: NY R USDCTSD Caproni-Prac; NY R USDCTSD Caproni--Pro Se; NY R USDCTSD Caproni-Case Mgt; NY R USDCTSD Caproni-Crim Prac.

DISTRICT JUDGE ANDREW L. CARTER JR.: NY R USDCTSD Carter-Practices.

DISTRICT JUDGE KEVIN P. CASTEL: NY R USDCTSD Castel-Practices; NY R USDCTSD Castel-Default; NY R USDCTSD Castel-Scheduling; NY R USDCTSD Castel-Complex; NY R USDCTSD Castel-Trials; NY R USDCTSD Castel-Sentencing.

DISTRICT JUDGE DENISE L. COTE: NY R USDCTSD Cote-Civil Practices; NY R USDCTSD Cote-Pro Se; NY R USDCTSD Cote-Maritime Ord; NY R USDCTSD Cote-Crim Practices; NY R USDCTSD Cote-Crim Trials; NY R USDCTSD Cote-Sentencing.

DISTRICT JUDGE PAUL A. CROTTY: NY R USDCTSD Crotty-Practices; NY R USDCTSD Crotty-Sentencing; NY R USDCTSD Crotty-Calls; NY R USDCTSD Crotty-Scheduling.

DISTRICT JUDGE GEORGE B. DANIELS: NY R USDCTSD Daniels-Practices.

DISTRICT JUDGE KEVIN T. DUFFY: NY R USDCTSD Duffy-Practices.

DISTRICT JUDGE PAUL A. ENGELMAYER: NY R USDCTSD Engelmayer-Practices; NY R USDCTSD Engelmayer-Scheduling; NY R USDCTSD Engelmayer-Sentencing; NY R USDCTSD Engelmayer-Pro Se; NY R USDCTSD Engelmayer-Crim.

DISTRICT JUDGE KATHERINE POLK FAILLA: NY R USDCTSD Failla-Civ Prac; NY R USDCTSD Failla-Crim Prac; NY R USDCTSD Failla-Case Mgt.

DISTRICT JUDGE KATHERINE B. FORREST: NY R USDCTSD Forrest-Civil Prac; NY R USDCTSD Forrest-Crim Prac; NY R USDCTSD Forrest-Crim Pretrial; NY R USDCTSD Forrest-Scheduling; NY R USDCTSD Forrest-Patent Scheduling; NY R USDCTSD Forrest-Sentencing; NY R USDCTSD Forrest-Order 1; NY R USDCTSD Forrest-Order 2.

DISTRICT JUDGE JESSE M. FURMAN: NY R USDCTSD Furman-Civil Prac; NY R USDCTSD Furman-Crim Prac; NY R USDCTSD Furman-Pro Se Prac; NY R USDCTSD Furman-Trials; NY R USDCTSD Furman-Scheduling; NY R USDCTSD Furman-Rights.

DISTRICT JUDGE PAUL G. GARDEPHE: NY R USDCTSD Gardephe-Civ Prac; NY R USDCTSD Gardephe-Pretrial; NY R USDCTSD Gardephe-Prot Ord; NY R USDCTSD Gardephe-Maritime; NY R USDCTSD Gardephe-Crim Prac; NY R USDCTSD Gardephe-Trial.

DISTRICT JUDGE THOMAS P. GRIESA: NY R USDCTSD Griesa-Practices.

DISTRICT JUDGE CHARLES S. HAIGHT: NY R USDCTSD Haight-Practices.

DISTRICT JUDGE ALVIN K. HELLERSTEIN: NY R USDCTSD Hellerstein-Practices; NY R USDCTSD Hellerstein--Sept 11.

DISTRICT JUDGE LEWIS A. KAPLAN: NY R USDCTSD Kaplan-Practices; NY R USDCTSD Kaplan-Sentencing.

DISTRICT JUDGE KENNETH M. KARAS: NY R USDCTSD Karas-Practices; NY R USDCTSD Karas-Case Mgt; NY R USDCTSD Karas-Default; NY R USDCTSD Karas-Sentencing; NY R USDCTSD Karas-Rights.

DISTRICT JUDGE JOHN F. KEENAN: NY R USDCTSD Keenan-Practices.

DISTRICT JUDGE JOHN G. KOELTL: NY R USDCTSD Koeltl-Practices.

DISTRICT JUDGE VICTOR MARRERO: NY R USDCTSD Marrero-Practices; NY R USDCTSD Marrero-Scheduling; NY R USDCTSD Marrero-Default; NY R USDCTSD Marrero-Trial Proc.

DISTRICT JUDGE COLLEEN McMAHON: NY R USDCTSD McMahon-Practices; NY R USDCTSD McMahon-RICO; NY R USDCTSD McMahon-Copies; NY R USDCTSD McMahon-Scheduling; NY R USDCTSD McMahon-Elec Disc; NY R USDCTSD McMahon-Sentencing.

DISTRICT JUDGE ALISON J. NATHAN: NY R USDCTSD Nathan-Civ Prac; NY R USDCTSD Nathan-Crim Prac; NY R USDCTSD Nathan-Pro Se; NY R USDCTSD Nathan-Scheduling.

DISTRICT JUDGE J. PAUL OETKEN: NY R USDCTSD Oetken-Civ Prac; NY R USDCTSD Oetken-Case Mgt; NY R USDCTSD Oetken-Crim Prac; NY R USDCTSD Oetken-Pro Se.

DISTRICT JUDGE WILLIAM H. PAULEY, III: NY R USDCTSD Pauley-Crim Cases; NY R USDCTSD Pauley-Practices.

DISTRICT JUDGE LORETTA A. PRESKA: NY R USDCTSD Preska-Practices.

DISTRICT JUDGE JED S. RAKOFF: NY R USDCTSD Rakoff-Practices; NY R USDCTSD Rakoff-Scheduling; NY R USDCTSD Rakoff-Prot Ord; NY R USDCTSD Rakoff-Maritime Ord.

DISTRICT JUDGE EDGARDO RAMOS: NY R USDCTSD Ramos--Practices; NY R USDCTSD Ramos-Case Mgt.

DISTRICT JUDGE NELSON S. ROMAN: NY R USDCTSD Roman-Civ Prac; NY R USDCTSD Roman-Pro Se; NY R USDCTSD Roman-Crim Prac; NY R USDCTSD Roman-Case Mgt.

DISTRICT JUDGE LEONARD B. SAND: NY R USDCTSD Sand-Practices.

DISTRICT JUDGE LORNA G. SCHOFIELD: NY R USDCTSD Schofield-Civ Prac; NY R USDCTSD Schofield-Crim Prac; NY R USDCTSD Schofield-Sched; NY R USDCTSD Schofield-Pro Se; NY R USDCTSD Schofield-Advice.

DISTRICT JUDGE CATHY SEIBEL: NY R USDCTSD Seibel-Practices.

DISTRICT JUDGE LOUIS L. STANTON: NY R USDCTSD Stanton-Practices; NY R USDCTSD Stanton-Pretrial.

DISTRICT JUDGE SIDNEY H. STEIN: NY R USDCTSD Stein-Practices.

DISTRICT JUDGE RICHARD J. SULLIVAN: NY R USDCTSD Sullivan-Practices; NY R USDCTSD Sullivan-Scheduling; NY R USDCTSD Sullivan-Sentencing; NY R USDCTSD Sullivan-Juries; NY R USDCTSD Sullivan-Trial; NY R USDCTSD Sullivan-Default.

DISTRICT JUDGE LAURA TAYLOR SWAIN: NY R USDCTSD Swain-Practices; NY R USDCTSD Swain-Trial; NY R USDCTSD Swain-Crim Trial; NY R USDCTSD Swain-Juries; NY R USDCTSD Swain-Sentencing; NY R USDCTSD Swain-Rights.

DISTRICT JUDGE ROBERT W. SWEET: NY R USDCTSD Sweet-Practices.

DISTRICT JUDGE ANALISA TORRES: NY R USDCTSD Torres-Civ Prac; NY R USDCTSD Torres-Pro Se; NY R USDCTSD Torres-Scheduling.

DISTRICT JUDGE KIMBA M. WOOD: NY R USDCTSD Wood-Practices; NY R USDCTSD Wood-Scheduling; NY R USDCTSD Wood-Discovery; NY R USDCTSD Wood-RICO; NY R USDCTSD Wood-Juries; NY R USDCTSD Wood-Trial; NY R USDCTSD Wood-Media.

DISTRICT JUDGE GREGORY H. WOODS: NY R USDCTSD Woods-Civ Prac; NY R USDCTSD Woods-Pro Se; NY R USDCTSD Woods-Sched; NY R USDCTSD Woods-Crim Prac; NY R USDCTSD Woods-Protect Order; NY R USDCTSD Woods-Speedy Trial.

MAGISTRATE JUDGE JAMES L. COTT: NY R USDCTSD Cott-Practices; NY R USDCTSD Cott-Settlement.

MAGISTRATE JUDGE PAUL E. DAVISON: NY R USDCTSD Davison-Practices.

MAGISTRATE JUDGE RONALD L. ELLIS: NY R USDCTSD Ellis-Practices.

MAGISTRATE JUDGE KEVIN N. FOX: NY R USDCTSD Fox-Practices; NY R USDCTSD Fox-Settlement.

MAGISTRATE JUDGE JAMES C. FRANCIS: NY R USDCTSD Francis-Practices.

MAGISTRATE JUDGE DEBRA FREEMAN: NY R USDCTSD Freeman-Practices; NY R USDCTSD Freeman-Settlement.

MAGISTRATE JUDGE GABRIEL W. GORENSTEIN: NY R USDCTSD Gorenstein-Practices; NY R US-DCTSD Gorenstein-Ackn.

MAGISTRATE JUDGE FRANK MAAS: NY R USDCTSD Maas-Practices; NY R USDCTSD Maas-Discontinuance; NY R USDCTSD Maas-Conf; NY R USDCTSD Maas-Settlement.

MAGISTRATE JUDGE JUDITH C. McCARTHY: NY R USDCTSD McCarthy-Practices; NY R USDCTSD McCarthy-Conduct.

MAGISTRATE JUDGE BARBARA MOSES: NY R USDCTSD Moses-Practices.

MAGISTRATE JUDGE SARAH NETBURN: NY R USDCTSD Netburn-Civil; NY R USDCTSD Netburn-Settlement; NY R USDCTSD Netburn-Case Mgt; NY R USDCTSD Netburn--Pro Se.

MAGISTRATE JUDGE ANDREW J. PECK: NY R USDCTSD Peck-Practices; NY R USDCTSD Peck-Order; NY R USDCTSD Peck-Rule 502(d).

MAGISTRATE JUDGE HENRY PITMAN: NY R USDCTSD Pitman-Practices.

MAGISTRATE JUDGE LISA MARGARET SMITH: NY R USDCTSD Smith-Practices; NY R USDCTSD Smith-Trials.

# Motions, Oppositions and Replies
## Motion to Dismiss for Failure to State a Claim

### Document Last Updated September 2016

## A. Checklist

(I)  ❑  Matters to be considered by moving party

   (a)  ❑  Required documents

      (1)  ❑  Notice of motion and motion

      (2)  ❑  Memorandum of law

      (3)  ❑  Certificate of service

   (b)  ❑  Supplemental documents

      (1)  ❑  Pleading

      (2)  ❑  Notice of constitutional question

      (3)  ❑  Nongovernmental corporate disclosure statement

      (4)  ❑  Notice to pro se litigant who opposes a FRCP 12 motion supported by matters outside the pleadings

      (5)  ❑  Copies of authorities

      (6)  ❑  Proposed order

      (7)  ❑  Statement explaining untimely electronic filing

      (8)  ❑  Courtesy copies

   (c)  ❑  Timing

      (1)  ❑  Failure to state a claim upon which relief can be granted may be raised in any pleading allowed or ordered under FRCP 7(a); every defense to a claim for relief in any pleading must be asserted in the responsive pleading if one is required

      (2)  ❑  A motion asserting any of the defenses in FRCP 12(b) must be made before pleading if a responsive pleading is allowed

      (3)  ❑  Failure to state a claim upon which relief can be granted may be raised by a motion under FRCP 12(c); after the pleadings are closed—but early enough not to delay trial—a party may move for judgment on the pleadings

      (4)  ❑  Failure to state a claim upon which relief can be granted may be raised at trial; if a pleading sets out a claim for relief that does not require a responsive pleading, an opposing party may assert at trial any defense to that claim

      (5)  ❑  A written motion and notice of the hearing must be served at least fourteen (14) days before the time specified for the hearing, with the following exceptions: (i) when the motion may be heard ex parte; (ii) when the Federal Rules of Civil Procedure set a different time; or (iii) when a court order—which a party may, for good cause, apply for ex parte—sets a different time

      (6)  ❑  Any affidavit supporting a motion must be served with the motion

(II)  ❑  Matters to be considered by opposing party

   (a)  ❑  Required documents

      (1)  ❑  Answering memorandum of law

     (2) ❑ Certificate of service

  (b) ❑ Supplemental documents

     (1) ❑ Pleading

     (2) ❑ Notice of constitutional question

     (3) ❑ Copies of authorities

     (4) ❑ Statement explaining untimely electronic filing

     (5) ❑ Courtesy copies

  (c) ❑ Timing

     (1) ❑ Any opposing affidavits and answering memoranda shall be served within fourteen (14) days after service of the moving papers

     (2) ❑ Except as FRCP 59(c) provides otherwise, any opposing affidavit must be served at least seven (7) days before the hearing, unless the court permits service at another time

## B. Timing

1. *Motion to dismiss for failure to state a claim*

    a. *In a pleading under FRCP 7(a).* Failure to state a claim upon which relief can be granted may be raised in any pleading allowed or ordered under FRCP 7(a). FRCP 12(h)(2)(A).

      i. *In a responsive pleading.* Every defense to a claim for relief in any pleading must be asserted in the responsive pleading if one is required. FRCP 12(b).

    b. *By motion.* A motion asserting any of the defenses in FRCP 12(b) must be made before pleading if a responsive pleading is allowed. FRCP 12(b). Although FRCP 12(b) encourages the responsive pleader to file a motion to dismiss before filing the answer, nothing in FRCP 12 prohibits the filing of a motion to dismiss with the answer. An untimely motion to dismiss may be considered if the defense asserted in the motion was previously raised in the responsive pleading. FEDPROC § 62:427.

    c. *By motion under FRCP 12(c).* Failure to state a claim upon which relief can be granted may be raised by a motion under FRCP 12(c). FRCP 12(h)(2)(B). After the pleadings are closed—but early enough not to delay trial—a party may move for judgment on the pleadings. FRCP 12(c).

    d. *At trial.* Failure to state a claim upon which relief can be granted may be raised at trial. FRCP 12(h)(2)(C). If a pleading sets out a claim for relief that does not require a responsive pleading, an opposing party may assert at trial any defense to that claim. FRCP 12(b).

2. *Timing of motions, generally*

    a. *Motion and notice of hearing.* Except for letter-motions as permitted by NY R USDCTS&ED Civ Rule 7.1(d), and unless otherwise provided by statute or rule or by the Court in a Judge's Individual Practice or in a direction in a particular case, upon any motion, the notice of motion, supporting affidavits, and memoranda shall be served and filed as follows: on all civil motions, petitions, and applications, other than those described in NY R USDCTS&ED Civ Rule 6.1(a), and other than petitions for writs of habeas corpus, the notice of motion, supporting affidavits, and memoranda of law shall be served by the moving party on all other parties that have appeared in the action. NY R USDCTS&ED Civ Rule 6.1(b)(1). A written motion and notice of the hearing must be served at least fourteen (14) days before the time specified for the hearing, with the following exceptions:

      i. When the motion may be heard ex parte;

      ii. When the Federal Rules of Civil Procedure set a different time; or

      iii. When a court order—which a party may, for good cause, apply for ex parte—sets a different time. FRCP 6(c)(1).

    b. *Supporting affidavit.* Any affidavit supporting a motion must be served with the motion. FRCP 6(c)(2).

3. *Timing of opposing papers.* Except for letter-motions as permitted by NY R USDCTS&ED Civ Rule

7.1(d), and unless otherwise provided by statute or rule or by the Court in a Judge's Individual Practice or in a direction in a particular case, upon any motion, the notice of motion, supporting affidavits, and memoranda shall be served and filed as follows: on all civil motions, petitions, and applications, other than those described in NY R USDCTS&ED Civ Rule 6.1(a), and other than petitions for writs of habeas corpus, any opposing affidavits and answering memoranda shall be served within fourteen (14) days after service of the moving papers. NY R USDCTS&ED Civ Rule 6.1(b)(2).

a. *Opposing affidavit.* Except as FRCP 59(c) provides otherwise, any opposing affidavit must be served at least seven (7) days before the hearing, unless the court permits service at another time. FRCP 6(c)(2).

4. *Timing of reply papers.* Where the respondent files an answering affidavit setting up a new matter, the moving party ordinarily is allowed a reasonable time to file a reply affidavit since failure to deny the new matter by affidavit may operate as an admission of its truth. AMJUR MOTIONS § 25.

a. *Reply affidavits and reply memoranda of law.* Except for letter-motions as permitted by NY R USDCTS&ED Civ Rule 7.1(d), and unless otherwise provided by statute or rule or by the Court in a Judge's Individual Practice or in a direction in a particular case, upon any motion, the notice of motion, supporting affidavits, and memoranda shall be served and filed as follows: on all civil motions, petitions, and applications, other than those described in NY R USDCTS&ED Civ Rule 6.1(a), and other than petitions for writs of habeas corpus, any reply affidavits and memoranda of law shall be served within seven (7) days after service of the answering papers. NY R USDCTS&ED Civ Rule 6.1(b)(3).

5. *Effect of a FRCP 12 motion on the time to serve a responsive pleading.* Unless the court sets a different time, serving a motion under FRCP 12 alters the periods in FRCP 12(a) as follows:

a. If the court denies the motion or postpones its disposition until trial, the responsive pleading must be served within fourteen (14) days after notice of the court's action; or

b. If the court grants a motion for a more definite statement, the responsive pleading must be served within fourteen (14) days after the more definite statement is served. FRCP 12(a)(4).

6. *Computation of time*

a. *Computing time.* FRCP 6 applies in computing any time period specified in the Federal Rules of Civil Procedure, in any local rule or court order, or in any statute that does not specify a method of computing time. FRCP 6(a). In computing any period of time prescribed or allowed by the Local Civil Rules of the United States District Courts for the Southern and Eastern Districts of New York or the Local Admiralty and Maritime Rules, the provisions of FRCP 6 shall apply unless otherwise stated. NY R USDCTS&ED Civ Rule 6.4.

i. *Period stated in days or a longer unit.* In computing periods of days, refer to FRCP 6 and NY R USDCTS&ED Civ Rule 6.4. NY R USDCTS&ED Civ Rule 6.1(b). When the period is stated in days or a longer unit of time:

- Exclude the day of the event that triggers the period;

- Count every day, including intermediate Saturdays, Sundays, and legal holidays; and

- Include the last day of the period, but if the last day is a Saturday, Sunday, or legal holiday, the period continues to run until the end of the next day that is not a Saturday, Sunday, or legal holiday. FRCP 6(a)(1). In the Local Civil Rules of the United States District Courts for the Southern and Eastern Districts of New York, as in the Federal Rules of Civil Procedure as amended effective December 1, 2009, Saturdays, Sundays, and legal holidays are no longer excluded in computing periods of time. If the last day of the period is a Saturday, Sunday, or legal holiday, the period continues to run until the end of the next day that is not a Saturday, Sunday, or legal holiday. NY R USDCTS&ED Civ Rule 6.4.

ii. *Period stated in hours.* When the period is stated in hours:

- Begin counting immediately on the occurrence of the event that triggers the period;

- Count every hour, including hours during intermediate Saturdays, Sundays, and legal holidays; and

- If the period would end on a Saturday, Sunday, or legal holiday, the period continues to run until the same time on the next day that is not a Saturday, Sunday, or legal holiday. FRCP 6(a)(2). In the Local Civil Rules of the United States District Courts for the Southern and Eastern Districts of New York, as in the Federal Rules of Civil Procedure as amended effective December 1, 2009, Saturdays, Sundays, and legal holidays are no longer excluded in computing periods of time. If the last day of the period is a Saturday, Sunday, or legal holiday, the period continues to run until the end of the next day that is not a Saturday, Sunday, or legal holiday. NY R USDCTS&ED Civ Rule 6.4.

iii. *Inaccessibility of the clerk's office.* Unless the court orders otherwise, if the clerk's office is inaccessible:

- On the last day for filing under FRCP 6(a)(1), then the time for filing is extended to the first accessible day that is not a Saturday, Sunday, or legal holiday; or

- During the last hour for filing under FRCP 6(a)(2), then the time for filing is extended to the same time on the first accessible day that is not a Saturday, Sunday, or legal holiday. FRCP 6(a)(3).

iv. *"Last day" defined.* Unless a different time is set by a statute, local rule, or court order, the last day ends:

- For electronic filing, at midnight in the court's time zone; and

- For filing by other means, when the clerk's office is scheduled to close. FRCP 6(a)(4).

v. *"Next day" defined.* The "next day" is determined by continuing to count forward when the period is measured after an event and backward when measured before an event. FRCP 6(a)(5).

vi. *"Legal holiday" defined.* "Legal holiday" means:

- The day set aside by statute for observing New Year's Day, Martin Luther King Jr.'s Birthday, Washington's Birthday, Memorial Day, Independence Day, Labor Day, Columbus Day, Veterans' Day, Thanksgiving Day, or Christmas Day;

- Any day declared a holiday by the President or Congress; and

- For periods that are measured after an event, any other day declared a holiday by the state where the district court is located. FRCP 6(a)(6).

b. *Computation of electronic filing deadlines.* You can file electronically twenty-four (24) hours a day, seven (7) days a week, three hundred sixty-five (365) days a year. NY R USDCTSD CM/ECF, S.D.(II)(13)(13.10). Electronic filing must be completed before midnight local time where the Court is located in order to be considered timely filed that day. NY R USDCTSD CM/ECF, S.D.(I)(3)(3.3); NY R USDCTSD CM/ECF, S.D.(II)(13)(13.10); NY R USDCTSD CM/ECF, S.D.(II)(19)(19.4). An electronically filed document is deemed filed on the "filed on" date indicated on the Notice of Electronic Filing (NEF). NY R USDCTSD CM/ECF, S.D.(II)(13)(13.11).

i. *Technical failures.* A Filing User whose filing is made untimely as the result of a technical failure may seek appropriate relief from the Court. NY R USDCTSD CM/ECF, S.D.(I)(11). If you missed a filing deadline when the ECF system was out of order, attach a statement to your filing explaining how the interruption in service prevented you from filing in a timely fashion. NY R USDCTSD CM/ECF, S.D.(II)(23)(23.5).

c. *Extending time*

i. *In general.* When an act may or must be done within a specified time, the court may, for good cause, extend the time:

- With or without motion or notice if the court acts, or if a request is made, before the original time or its extension expires; or

- On motion made after the time has expired if the party failed to act because of excusable neglect. FRCP 6(b)(1).

ii. *Exceptions.* A court must not extend the time to act under FRCP 50(b), FRCP 50(d), FRCP 52(b), FRCP 59(b), FRCP 59(d), FRCP 59(e), and FRCP 60(b). FRCP 6(b)(2).

      iii.   Refer to the United States District Court for the Southern District of New York KeyRules Motion for Continuance/Extension of Time document for more information on extending time.

   d.  *Additional time after certain kinds of service.* When a party may or must act within a specified time after service and service is made under FRCP 5(b)(2)(C), FRCP 5(b)(2)(D), FRCP 5(b)(2)(E), or FRCP 5(b)(2)(F), three (3) days are added after the period would otherwise expire under FRCP 6(a). FRCP 6(d). Overnight delivery service shall be deemed service by mail for purposes of FRCP 5 and FRCP 6. NY R USDCTS&ED Civ Rule 5.3.

7.  *Individual judge practices.* Refer to the Miscellaneous section of this document for information on individual judge practices on timing of documents.

## C.  General Requirements

1.  *Motions, generally*

   a.  *Requirements.* A request for a court order must be made by motion. The motion must:

      i.   Be in writing unless made during a hearing or trial;

      ii.   State with particularity the grounds for seeking the order; and

      iii.   State the relief sought. FRCP 7(b)(1).

   b.  *Notice of motion.* A party interested in resisting the relief sought by a motion has a right to notice thereof, and an opportunity to be heard. AMJUR MOTIONS § 12.

      i.   In addition to statutory or court rule provisions requiring notice of a motion—the purpose of such a notice requirement having been said to be to prevent a party from being prejudicially surprised by a motion—principles of natural justice dictate that an adverse party generally must be given notice that a motion will be presented to the court. AMJUR MOTIONS § 12.

      ii.   "Notice," in this regard, means reasonable notice, including a meaningful opportunity to prepare and to defend against allegations of a motion. AMJUR MOTIONS § 12.

   c.  *Writing requirement.* The writing requirement is intended to insure that the adverse parties are informed and have a record of both the motion's pendency and the grounds on which the movant seeks an order. FPP § 1191; Feldberg v. Quechee Lakes Corp., 463 F.3d 195 (2d Cir. 2006).

      i.   It is sufficient "if the motion is stated in a written notice of the hearing of the motion." FPP § 1191.

   d.  *Particularity requirement.* The particularity requirement insures that the opposing parties will have notice of their opponent's contentions. FEDPROC § 62:364; Goodman v. 1973 26 Foot Trojan Vessel, Arkansas Registration No. AR1439SN, 859 F.2d 71, 12 Fed.R.Serv.3d 645 (8th Cir. 1988). That requirement ensures that notice of the basis for the motion is provided to the court and to the opposing party so as to avoid prejudice, provide the opponent with a meaningful opportunity to respond, and provide the court with enough information to process the motion correctly. FEDPROC § 62:364; Andreas v. Volkswagen of America, Inc., 336 F.3d 789, 56 Fed.R.Serv.3d 6 (8th Cir. 2003).

      i.   Reasonable specification of the grounds for a motion is sufficient. However, where a movant fails to state even one ground for granting the motion in question, the movant has failed to meet the minimal standard of "reasonable specification." FEDPROC § 62:364; Martinez v. Trainor, 556 F.2d 818, 23 Fed.R.Serv.2d 403 (7th Cir. 1977).

      ii.   The court may excuse the failure to comply with the particularity requirement if it is inadvertent, and where no prejudice is shown by the opposing party. FEDPROC § 62:364.

   e.  *Ex parte orders or orders to show cause to bring on a motion.* No ex parte order, or order to show cause to bring on a motion, will be granted except upon a clear and specific showing by affidavit of good and sufficient reasons why a procedure other than by notice of motion is necessary, and stating whether a previous application for similar relief has been made. NY R USDCTS&ED Civ Rule 6.1(d).

   f.  *Letter-motions.* Applications for extensions or adjournments, applications for a pre-motion conference, and similar non-dispositive matters as permitted by the instructions regarding ECF published on the website of each respective Court and any pertinent Individual Judge's Practices, may be brought by letter-motion filed via ECF pursuant to NY R USDCTS&ED Civ Rule 5.2(b). NY R USDCTS&ED Civ Rule 7.1(d).

    i.    The following list of motions. . .may be made by LETTER-MOTION: (1) Motion to Adjourn Conference; (2) Motion to Change Attorney Name on Roll; (3) Motion to Compel; (4) Motion for Conference; (5) Motion to Consolidate Cases; (6) Motion to Continue; (7) Motion re: Discovery; (8) Motion to Expedite; (9) Motion for Extension of Time; (10) Motion for Extension of Time to Amend; (11) Motion for Extension of Time to Answer; (12) Motion for Extension of Time to Complete Discovery; (13) Motion for Extension of Time to File Document; (14) Motion for Extension of Time to File Response/Reply; (15) Motion for Extension of Time re Transcript; (16) Motion to File Amicus Brief; (17) Motion for Leave to File Document; (18) Motion for Leave to File Excess Pages; (19) Motion for Local Rule 37.2 Conference; (20) Motion for Oral Argument; (21) Motion to Reopen; (22) Motion to Reopen Case; (23) Motion to Seal Document; (24) Motion to Stay; (25) Motion to Substitute Attorney. NY R USDCTSD CM/ECF, S.D.(II)(13)(13.1).

    ii.    If the Filing User is making a type of motion that does not appear in this list, the motion may not be made by letter. NY R USDCTSD CM/ECF, S.D.(II)(13)(13.1).

    iii.    For more information on letter motions, refer to NY R USDCTSD CM/ECF, S.D.(II)(13)(13.1).

2.    *Motion to dismiss for failure to state a claim.* A party may assert the defense of failure to state a claim upon which relief can be granted by motion. FRCP 12(b)(6). The motion under FRCP 12(b)(6) is available to test a claim for relief in any pleading, whether it be in the plaintiff's original complaint, a defendant's counterclaim, a defendant's cross-claim or counterclaim thereto, or a third-party claim or any other FRCP 14 claim. Most commonly, of course, a FRCP 12(b)(6) motion is directed against the plaintiff's complaint. FPP § 1356.

    a.    *Applicable standard.* The FRCP 12(b)(6) motion is used to test the sufficiency of the complaint. FEDPROC § 62:461; Petruska v. Gannon University, 462 F.3d 294, 212 Ed.Law.Rep. 598 (3d Cir. 2006). In this regard, the applicable standard is stated in FRCP 8(a)(2), which requires that a pleading setting forth a claim for relief contain a short and plain statement of the claim showing that the pleader is entitled to relief. Thus, a complaint must set forth sufficient information to suggest that there is some recognized legal theory upon which relief can be granted. FEDPROC § 62:461. Only when the plaintiff's complaint fails to meet this liberal pleading standard is it subject to dismissal under FRCP 12(b)(6). FPP § 1356.

        i.    In order to withstand a motion to dismiss filed under FRCP 12(b)(6) in response to claims understood to raise a high risk of abusive litigation, addressed by FRCP 9(b), a plaintiff must state factual allegations with greater particularity than that required by FRCP 8. FEDPROC § 62:470; Bell Atlantic Corp. v. Twombly, 550 U.S. 544, 127 S.Ct. 1955, 167 L.Ed.2d 929, 68 Fed.R.Serv.3d 661 (2007).

        ii.    FRCP 12(b)(6) motions are looked on with disfavor by the courts, and are granted sparingly and with care. FEDPROC § 62:464. Even if it is doubtful that the plaintiff would ultimately prevail, if the plaintiff colorably states facts which, if proven, would entitle him or her to relief, a motion to dismiss for failure to state a claim should not be granted. FEDPROC § 62:464.

    b.    *Construction of allegations of complaint (or other pleading).* In considering a FRCP 12(b)(6) motion to dismiss, the complaint is liberally construed and is viewed in the light most favorable to the plaintiff. FEDPROC § 62:467; Bell Atlantic Corp. v. Twombly, 550 U.S. 544, 127 S.Ct. 1955, 167 L.Ed.2d 929, 68 Fed.R.Serv.3d 661 (2007).

        i.    On a motion to dismiss, a federal court presumes that general allegations embrace those specific facts that are necessary to support the claim. FEDPROC § 62:467; Steel Co. v. Citizens for a Better Environment, 523 U.S. 83, 118 S.Ct. 1003, 140 L.Ed.2d 210 (1998).

        ii.    In addition, the well-pleaded allegations of fact contained in the complaint and every inference fairly deducible therefrom are accepted as true for purposes of the motion, including facts alleged on information and belief. FEDPROC § 62:467; Bell Atlantic Corp. v. Twombly, 550 U.S. 544, 127 S.Ct. 1955, 167 L.Ed.2d 929, 68 Fed.R.Serv.3d 661 (2007); Tellabs, Inc. v. Makor Issues & Rights, Ltd., 551 U.S. 308, 127 S.Ct. 2499, 168 L.Ed.2d 179 (2007).

iii. However, the court will not accept as true the plaintiff's bare statements of opinions, conclusory allegations, and unwarranted inferences of fact. FEDPROC § 62:467; Leopoldo Fontanillas, Inc. v. Luis Ayala Colon Sucesores, Inc., 283 F.Supp.2d 579 (D.P.R. 2003); Hopkins v. Women's Div., General Bd. of Global Ministries, 238 F.Supp.2d 174 (D.D.C. 2002). Nor will the court accept as true facts which are legally impossible, facts which the court can take judicial notice of as being other than as alleged by the plaintiff, or facts which by the record or by a document attached to the complaint appear to be unfounded. FEDPROC § 62:467; Cohen v. U.S., 129 F.2d 733 (8th Cir. 1942); Henthorn v. Department of Navy, 29 F.3d 682, 29 Fed.R.Serv.3d 1007 (D.C. Cir. 1994).

c. *Affirmative defenses.* With some exception, it is generally agreed that affirmative defenses can be raised by a FRCP 12(b)(6) motion to dismiss. FEDPROC § 62:471; McCready v. eBay, Inc., 453 F.3d 882 (7th Cir. 2006). However, in order for these defenses to be raised on a FRCP 12(b)(6) motion to dismiss, the complaint must clearly show on its face that the affirmative defense is applicable and bars the action. FEDPROC § 62:471; In re Colonial Mortgage Bankers Corp., 324 F.3d 12 (1st Cir. 2003). Thus, FRCP 12(b)(6) motions may be used to raise the affirmative defenses of: (1) statute of limitations; (2) statute of frauds; (3) res judicata; (4) collateral estoppel; (5) release; (6) waiver; (7) estoppel; (8) sovereign immunity; (9) illegality; and (10) contributory negligence. FEDPROC § 62:471.

d. *Joining motions*

   i. *Right to join.* A motion under FRCP 12 may be joined with any other motion allowed by FRCP 12. FRCP 12(g)(1).

   ii. *Limitation on further motions.* Except as provided in FRCP 12(h)(2) or FRCP 12(h)(3), a party that makes a motion under FRCP 12 must not make another motion under FRCP 12 raising a defense or objection that was available to the party but omitted from its earlier motion. FRCP 12(g)(2).

e. *Waiving and preserving certain defenses.* No defense or objection is waived by joining it with one or more other defenses or objections in a responsive pleading or in a motion. FRCP 12(b).

   i. *When some are waived.* A party waives any defense listed in FRCP 12(b)(2) through FRCP 12(b)(5) by:

- Omitting it from a motion in the circumstances described in FRCP 12(g)(2); or

- Failing to either: (1) make it by motion under FRCP 12; or (2) include it in a responsive pleading or in an amendment allowed by FRCP 15(a)(1) as a matter of course. FRCP 12(h)(1).

   ii. *When to raise others.* Failure to state a claim upon which relief can be granted, to join a person required by FRCP 19(b), or to state a legal defense to a claim may be raised:

- In any pleading allowed or ordered under FRCP 7(a);

- By a motion under FRCP 12(c); or

- At trial. FRCP 12(h)(2).

   iii. *Lack of subject matter jurisdiction.* If the court determines at any time that it lacks subject-matter jurisdiction, the court must dismiss the action. FRCP 12(h)(3).

3. *Opposing papers.* The Federal Rules of Civil Procedure do not require any formal answer, return, or reply to a motion, except where the Federal Rules of Civil Procedure or local rules may require affidavits, memoranda, or other papers to be filed in opposition to a motion. Such papers are simply to apprise the court of such opposition and the grounds of that opposition. FEDPROC § 62:359. Except for letter-motions as permitted by NY R USDCTS&ED Civ Rule 7.1(d) or as otherwise permitted by the Court, all oppositions and replies with respect to motions shall comply with NY R USDCTS&ED Civ Rule 7.1(a)(2) and NY R USDCTS&ED Civ Rule 7.1(a)(3), and an opposing party who seeks relief that goes beyond the denial of the motion shall comply as well with NY R USDCTS&ED Civ Rule 7.1(a)(1). NY R USDCTS&ED Civ Rule 7.1(b).

a. *Effect of failure to respond to motion.* Although in the absence of statutory provision or court rule, a motion ordinarily does not require a written answer, when a party files a motion and the opposing party fails to respond, the court may construe such failure to respond as nonopposition to the motion or an admission that the motion was meritorious, may take the facts alleged in the motion as true—the rule in some jurisdictions being that the failure to respond to a fact set forth in a motion is deemed an admission—and may grant the motion if the relief requested appears to be justified. AMJUR MOTIONS § 28.

b. *Assent or no opposition not determinative.* However, a motion will not be granted automatically simply because an "assent" or a notation of "no opposition" has been filed; federal judges frequently deny motions that have been assented to when it is thought that justice so dictates. FPP § 1190.

c. *Responsive pleading inappropriate as response to motion.* An attempt to answer or oppose a motion with a responsive pleading usually is not appropriate. FPP § 1190.

4. *Reply papers.* A moving party may be required or permitted to prepare papers in addition to his original motion papers. AMJUR MOTIONS § 25. Papers answering or replying to opposing papers may be appropriate, in the interests of justice, where it appears there is a substantial reason for allowing a reply. Thus, a court may accept reply papers where a party demonstrates that the papers to which it seeks to file a reply raise new issues that are material to the disposition of the question before the court, or where the court determines, sua sponte, that it wishes further briefing of an issue raised in those papers and orders the submission of additional papers. FEDPROC § 62:360. Except for letter-motions as permitted by NY R USDCTS&ED Civ Rule 7.1(d) or as otherwise permitted by the Court, all oppositions and replies with respect to motions shall comply with NY R USDCTS&ED Civ Rule 7.1(a)(2) and NY R USDCTS&ED Civ Rule 7.1(a)(3). NY R USDCTS&ED Civ Rule 7.1(b).

a. *Function of reply papers.* The function of a reply affidavit is to answer the arguments made in opposition to the position taken by the movant and not to permit the movant to introduce new arguments in support of the motion. AMJUR MOTIONS § 25.

b. *Issues raised for the first time in a reply document.* However, the view has been followed in some jurisdictions, that as a matter of judicial economy, where there is no prejudice and where the issues could be raised simply by filing a motion to dismiss, the trial court has discretion to consider arguments raised for the first time in a reply memorandum, and that a trial court may grant a motion to strike issues raised for the first time in a reply memorandum. AMJUR MOTIONS § 26.

5. *Orders on motions.* A memorandum signed by the Court of the decision on a motion that does not finally determine all claims for relief, or an oral decision on such a motion, shall constitute the order unless the memorandum or oral decision directs the submission or settlement of an order in more extended form. The notation in the docket of a memorandum or of an oral decision that does not direct the submission or settlement of an order in more extended form shall constitute the entry of the order. Where an order in more extended form is required to be submitted or settled, the notation in the docket of such order shall constitute the entry of the order. NY R USDCTS&ED Civ Rule 6.2.

6. *Complex civil cases.* For information on procedures for complex civil cases, refer to NY R USDCTSD Order 11 Misc 00388.

7. *Related cases.* It shall be the continuing duty of each attorney appearing in any civil or criminal case to bring promptly to the attention of the Court all facts which said attorney believes are relevant to a determination that said case and one or more pending civil or criminal cases should be heard by the same Judge, in order to avoid unnecessary duplication of judicial effort. As soon as the attorney becomes aware of such relationship, said attorney shall notify the Judges to whom the cases have been assigned. NY R USDCTS&ED Civ Rule 1.6(a). If counsel fails to comply with NY R USDCTS&ED Civ Rule 1.6(a), the Court may assess reasonable costs directly against counsel whose action has obstructed the effective administration of the Court's business. NY R USDCTS&ED Civ Rule 1.6(b).

a. *Determination of relatedness.* Subject to the limitations set forth in NY R USDCTSD Div. Bus., Rule 13(a)(2), a civil case, bankruptcy appeal, or motion to withdraw the bankruptcy reference will be deemed related to one or more civil cases, appeals or motions when the interests of justice and efficiency will be served. In determining relatedness, a judge will consider whether (A) the actions concern the same or substantially similar parties, property, transactions or events; (B) there is substantial factual overlap; (C) the parties could be subjected to conflicting orders; and (D) whether absent a determination of relatedness there would be a substantial duplication of effort and expense, delay, or undue burden on the Court, parties or witnesses. NY R USDCTSD Div. Bus., Rule 13(a)(1). Nothing in this NY R USDCTSD Div. Bus., Rule 13 is intended to preclude parties from moving for consolidated proceedings under FRCP 42. NY R USDCTSD Div. Bus., Rule 13(a)(1). Notwithstanding NY R USDCTSD Div. Bus., Rule 13(a)(1):

    i.   Civil cases shall not be deemed related merely because they involve common legal issues or the same parties. NY R USDCTSD Div. Bus., Rule 13(a)(2)(A).

    ii.   Other than cases subject to NY R USDCTSD Div. Bus., Rule 4(b) and actions seeking the enforcement of a judgment or settlement in or of an earlier case, civil cases presumptively shall not be deemed related unless both cases are pending before the Court (or the earlier case is on appeal). NY R USDCTSD Div. Bus., Rule 13(a)(2)(B).

  b.  *Procedure in regard to cases said to be related*

    i.   *Disclosure of contention of relatedness.* When a civil case is filed or removed or a bankruptcy appeal or motion to withdraw the reference of an adversary proceeding from the bankruptcy court is filed, the person filing or removing shall disclose on form JSC44C any contention of relatedness and shall file a Related Case Statement stating clearly and succinctly the basis for the contention. A copy of the civil cover sheet and Related Case Statement shall be served with the complaint, notice of removal, notice of appeal, or motion. Any party may contest a claim of relatedness by any other in writing addressed to the judge having the case with the lowest docket number of all cases claimed to be related. However, the foregoing shall not delay the assignment process or the operation of NY R USDCTSD Div. Bus., Rule 13. NY R USDCTSD Div. Bus., Rule 13(b)(1). [Editor's note: the reference to form JSC44C is likely meant to be form JS44C-SDNY: Civil Court Cover Sheet].

    ii.   *Claims of relatedness by other parties.* A party other than the one filing a case, bankruptcy appeal or motion to withdraw the reference that contends its case is related to another may so advise in writing the judge assigned in its case and request a transfer of its case to the judge that the party contends has the related case with the lowest docket number. If the assigned judge believes the case is related under NY R USDCTSD Div. Bus., Rule 13(a), he or she shall refer the question to the judge having the case with the lowest docket number. In the event the latter judge agrees, the case shall be transferred to that judge unless the Assignment Committee disagrees. NY R USDCTSD Div. Bus., Rule 13(b)(3).

  c.  For more information on related cases, refer to NY R USDCTSD Div. Bus., Rule 13.

8.  *Alternative dispute resolution (ADR).* The U.S. District Court for the Southern District of New York provides litigants with opportunities to discuss settlement through judicial settlement conferences and mediation. NY R USDCTS&ED Civ Rule 83.9(a).

  a.  *Consideration of alternative dispute resolution.* In all civil cases, including those eligible for mediation pursuant to NY R USDCTS&ED Civ Rule 83.9(e), each party shall consider the use of mediation or a judicial settlement conference and shall report to the assigned Judge at the initial FRCP 16(b) case management conference, or subsequently, whether the party believes mediation or a judicial settlement conference may facilitate the resolution of the lawsuit. Judges are encouraged to note the availability of the mediation program and/or a judicial settlement conference before, at, or after the initial FRCP 16(b) case management conference. NY R USDCTS&ED Civ Rule 83.9(d).

  b.  *Mediation.* In mediation, parties and counsel meet, sometimes collectively and sometimes individually, with a neutral third party (the mediator) who has been trained to facilitate confidential settlement discussions. The parties articulate their respective positions and interests and generate options for a mutually agreeable resolution to the dispute. The mediator assists the parties in reaching their own negotiated settlement by defining the issues, probing and assessing the strengths and weaknesses of each party's legal positions, and identifying areas of agreement and disagreement. The main benefits of mediation are that it can result in an expeditious and less costly resolution of the litigation, and can produce creative solutions to complex disputes often unavailable in traditional litigation. NY R USDCTS&ED Civ Rule 83.9(b).

    i.   *Mediation program eligibility.* All civil cases other than Social Security, habeas corpus, and tax cases are eligible for mediation, whether assigned to Manhattan or White Plains. NY R USDCTS&ED Civ Rule 83.9(e)(1).

- The Board of Judges may, by Administrative Order, direct that certain specified categories of cases shall automatically be submitted to the mediation program. The assigned District Judge or Magistrate Judge may issue a written order exempting a particular case with or without the request of the parties. NY R USDCTS&ED Civ Rule 83.9(e)(2).

- For all other cases, the assigned District Judge or Magistrate Judge may determine that a case is appropriate for mediation and may order that case to mediation, with or without the consent of the parties, before, at, or after the initial FRCP 16(b) case management conference. Alternatively, the parties should notify the assigned Judge at any time of their desire to mediate. NY R USDCTS&ED Civ Rule 83.9(e)(3).

c. *Judicial settlement conferences.* Judicial settlement conferences may be ordered by District Judges or Magistrate Judges with or without the request or consent of the parties. NY R USDCTS&ED Civ Rule 83.9(f).

d. For more information on alternative dispute resolution (ADR), refer to NY R USDCTS&ED Civ Rule 83.9.

9. *Individual judge practices.* Refer to the Miscellaneous section of this document for information on individual judge practices on general requirements for documents.

## D. Documents

1. *Documents for moving party*

a. *Required documents*

i. *Notice of motion and motion.* Except for letter-motions as permitted by NY R USDCTS&ED Civ Rule 7.1(d) or as otherwise permitted by the Court, all motions shall include the following motion papers: a notice of motion, or an order to show cause signed by the Court, which shall specify the applicable rules or statutes pursuant to which the motion is brought, and shall specify the relief sought by the motion. NY R USDCTS&ED Civ Rule 7.1(a)(1). Refer to the General Requirements section of this document for information on the notice of motion and motion.

ii. *Memorandum of law.* Except for letter-motions as permitted by NY R USDCTS&ED Civ Rule 7.1(d) or as otherwise permitted by the Court, all motions shall include the following motion papers: a memorandum of law, setting forth the cases and other authorities relied upon in support of the motion, and divided, under appropriate headings, into as many parts as there are issues to be determined. NY R USDCTS&ED Civ Rule 7.1(a)(2).

iii. *Certificate of service.* FRCP 5(d) requires that the person making service under FRCP 5 certify that service has been effected. FRCP 5(Advisory Committee Notes). Having such information on file may be useful for many purposes, including proof of service if an issue arises concerning the effectiveness of the service. FRCP 5(Advisory Committee Notes).

- Such paper service [on attorneys and pro se parties who are not Filing or Receiving Users] must be documented by electronically filing proof of service. NY R USDCTSD CM/ECF, S.D.(I)(9)(9.2); NY R USDCTSD CM/ECF, S.D.(I)(19)(19.3)(b). Pro se parties who are not Filing Users are exempt from that portion of NY R USDCTSD CM/ECF, S.D.(I)(19)(19.3) requiring proof of service to be filed electronically. NY R USDCTSD CM/ECF, S.D.(I)(19)(19.3).

b. *Supplemental documents*

i. *Pleading.* As a general rule, the court may only consider the pleading which is attacked by a FRCP 12(b)(6) motion in determining its sufficiency. FEDPROC § 62:466; Armengau v. Cline, 7 Fed.Appx. 336 (6th Cir. 2001). The plaintiff is not entitled to discovery to obtain information relevant to the motion, and the court is not permitted to look at matters outside the record. FEDPROC § 62:466; Cooperativa de Ahorro y Credito Aguada v. Kidder, Peabody & Co., 993 F.2d 269, 37 Fed.R.Evid.Serv. 904, 25 Fed.R.Serv.3d 982 (1st Cir. 1993).

- *Motion treated as one for summary judgment.* If, on a motion under FRCP 12(b)(6) or

FRCP 12(c), matters outside the pleadings are presented to and not excluded by the court, the motion must be treated as one for summary judgment under FRCP 56. All parties must be given a reasonable opportunity to present all the material that is pertinent to the motion. FRCP 12(d).

- *Documents attached to pleadings.* However, the court may consider documents which are attached to or submitted with the complaint, as well as legal arguments presented in memorandums or briefs and arguments of counsel. FEDPROC § 62:466; Tellabs, Inc. v. Makor Issues & Rights, Ltd., 551 U.S. 308, 127 S.Ct. 2499, 168 L.Ed.2d 179 (2007); E.E.O.C. v. Ohio Edison Co., 7 F.3d 541 (6th Cir. 1993). Documents that the defendant attaches to the motion to dismiss are considered part of the pleadings if they are referred to in the plaintiff's complaint and are central to the claim, and as such may be considered by the court. FEDPROC § 62:466; Hoffman-Pugh v. Ramsey, 312 F.3d 1222 (11th Cir. 2002).

ii. *Notice of constitutional question.* A party that files a pleading, written motion, or other paper drawing into question the constitutionality of a federal or state statute must promptly:

- *File notice.* File a notice of constitutional question stating the question and identifying the paper that raises it, if: (1) a federal statute is questioned and the parties do not include the United States, one of its agencies, or one of its officers or employees in an official capacity; or (2) a state statute is questioned and the parties do not include the state, one of its agencies, or one of its officers or employees in an official capacity; and

- *Serve notice.* Serve the notice and paper on the Attorney General of the United States if a federal statute is questioned—or on the state attorney general if a state statute is questioned—either by certified or registered mail or by sending it to an electronic address designated by the attorney general for this purpose. FRCP 5.1(a).

- *No forfeiture.* A party's failure to file and serve the notice, or the court's failure to certify, does not forfeit a constitutional claim or defense that is otherwise timely asserted. FRCP 5.1(d).

iii. *Nongovernmental corporate disclosure statement*

- *Contents.* A nongovernmental corporate party must file two (2) copies of a disclosure statement that: (1) identifies any parent corporation and any publicly held corporation owning ten percent (10%) or more of its stock; or (2) states that there is no such corporation. FRCP 7.1(a).

- *Time to file; Supplemental filing.* A party must: (1) file the disclosure statement with its first appearance, pleading, petition, motion, response, or other request addressed to the court; and (2) promptly file a supplemental statement if any required information changes. FRCP 7.1(b). For purposes of FRCP 7.1(b)(2), "promptly" shall mean "within fourteen days," that is, parties are required to file a supplemental disclosure statement within fourteen (14) days of the time there is any change in the information required in a disclosure statement filed pursuant to those rules. NY R USDCTS&ED Civ Rule 7.1.1.

iv. *Notice to pro se litigant who opposes a FRCP 12 motion supported by matters outside the pleadings.* A represented party moving to dismiss or for judgment on the pleadings against a party proceeding pro se, who refers in support of the motion to matters outside the pleadings as described in FRCP 12(b) or FRCP 12(c), shall serve and file the notice in NY R USDCTS&ED Civ Rule 12.1 with the full text of FRCP 56 attached at the time the motion is served. If the Court rules that a motion to dismiss or for judgment on the pleadings will be treated as one for summary judgment pursuant to FRCP 56, and the movant has not previously served and filed the notice required by NY R USDCTS&ED Civ Rule 12.1, the movant shall amend the form notice to reflect that fact and shall serve and file the amended notice within fourteen (14) days of the Court's ruling. NY R USDCTS&ED Civ Rule 12.1. For the notice, refer to NY R USDCTS&ED Civ Rule 12.1.

v. *Copies of authorities.* In cases involving a pro se litigant, counsel shall, when serving a memorandum of law (or other submissions to the Court), provide the pro se litigant (but not

other counsel or the Court) with copies of cases and other authorities cited therein that are unpublished or reported exclusively on computerized databases. Upon request, counsel shall provide the pro se litigant with copies of such unpublished cases and other authorities as are cited in a decision of the Court and were not previously cited by any party. NY R USDCTS&ED Civ Rule 7.2.

vi. *Proposed order.* Refer to the Format section of this document for information on the format of submitting a proposed order to the court.

vii. *Statement explaining untimely electronic filing.* If you missed a filing deadline when the ECF system was out of order, attach a statement to your filing explaining how the interruption in service prevented you from filing in a timely fashion. NY R USDCTSD CM/ECF, S.D.(II)(23)(23.5).

viii. *Courtesy copies.* Read the judge's Individual Practices to learn if courtesy copies are required. NY R USDCTSD CM/ECF, S.D.(II)(13)(13.17). Judges' Individual Practices should continue to be followed with respect to delivery of courtesy copies. NY R USDCTSD CM/ECF, S.D.(I)(3)(3.4).

2. *Documents for opposing party*

   a. *Required documents*

      i. *Answering memorandum of law.* Except for letter-motions as permitted by NY R USDCTS&ED Civ Rule 7.1(d) or as otherwise permitted by the Court, all oppositions and replies with respect to motions shall comply with NY R USDCTS&ED Civ Rule 7.1(a)(2). NY R USDCTS&ED Civ Rule 7.1(b). Except for letter-motions as permitted by NY R USDCTS&ED Civ Rule 7.1(d) or as otherwise permitted by the Court, all motions shall include the following motion papers: a memorandum of law, setting forth the cases and other authorities relied upon in support of the motion, and divided, under appropriate headings, into as many parts as there are issues to be determined. NY R USDCTS&ED Civ Rule 7.1(a)(2). Refer to the General Requirements section of this document for information on the opposing papers.

      ii. *Certificate of service.* FRCP 5(d) requires that the person making service under FRCP 5 certify that service has been effected. FRCP 5(Advisory Committee Notes). Having such information on file may be useful for many purposes, including proof of service if an issue arises concerning the effectiveness of the service. FRCP 5(Advisory Committee Notes).

         • Such paper service [on attorneys and pro se parties who are not Filing or Receiving Users] must be documented by electronically filing proof of service. NY R USDCTSD CM/ECF, S.D.(I)(9)(9.2); NY R USDCTSD CM/ECF, S.D.(I)(19)(19.3)(b). Pro se parties who are not Filing Users are exempt from that portion of NY R USDCTSD CM/ECF, S.D.(I)(19)(19.3) requiring proof of service to be filed electronically. NY R USDCTSD CM/ECF, S.D.(I)(19)(19.3).

   b. *Supplemental documents*

      i. *Pleading.* As a general rule, the court may only consider the pleading which is attacked by a FRCP 12(b)(6) motion in determining its sufficiency. FEDPROC § 62:466; Armengau v. Cline, 7 Fed.Appx. 336 (6th Cir. 2001). The plaintiff is not entitled to discovery to obtain information relevant to the motion, and the court is not permitted to look at matters outside the record. FEDPROC § 62:466; Cooperativa de Ahorro y Credito Aguada v. Kidder, Peabody & Co., 993 F.2d 269, 37 Fed.R.Evid.Serv. 904, 25 Fed.R.Serv.3d 982 (1st Cir. 1993).

         • *Motion treated as one for summary judgment.* If, on a motion under FRCP 12(b)(6) or FRCP 12(c), matters outside the pleadings are presented to and not excluded by the court, the motion must be treated as one for summary judgment under FRCP 56. All parties must be given a reasonable opportunity to present all the material that is pertinent to the motion. FRCP 12(d).

         • *Documents attached to pleadings.* However, the court may consider documents which are attached to or submitted with the complaint, as well as legal arguments presented in memorandums or briefs and arguments of counsel. FEDPROC § 62:466; Tellabs, Inc. v.

Makor Issues & Rights, Ltd., 551 U.S. 308, 127 S.Ct. 2499, 168 L.Ed.2d 179 (2007); E.E.O.C. v. Ohio Edison Co., 7 F.3d 541 (6th Cir. 1993). Documents that the defendant attaches to the motion to dismiss are considered part of the pleadings if they are referred to in the plaintiff's complaint and are central to the claim, and as such may be considered by the court. FEDPROC § 62:466; Hoffman-Pugh v. Ramsey, 312 F.3d 1222 (11th Cir. 2002).

ii. *Notice of constitutional question.* A party that files a pleading, written motion, or other paper drawing into question the constitutionality of a federal or state statute must promptly:

- *File notice.* File a notice of constitutional question stating the question and identifying the paper that raises it, if: (1) a federal statute is questioned and the parties do not include the United States, one of its agencies, or one of its officers or employees in an official capacity; or (2) a state statute is questioned and the parties do not include the state, one of its agencies, or one of its officers or employees in an official capacity; and

- *Serve notice.* Serve the notice and paper on the Attorney General of the United States if a federal statute is questioned—or on the state attorney general if a state statute is questioned—either by certified or registered mail or by sending it to an electronic address designated by the attorney general for this purpose. FRCP 5.1(a).

- *No forfeiture.* A party's failure to file and serve the notice, or the court's failure to certify, does not forfeit a constitutional claim or defense that is otherwise timely asserted. FRCP 5.1(d).

iii. *Copies of authorities.* In cases involving a pro se litigant, counsel shall, when serving a memorandum of law (or other submissions to the Court), provide the pro se litigant (but not other counsel or the Court) with copies of cases and other authorities cited therein that are unpublished or reported exclusively on computerized databases. Upon request, counsel shall provide the pro se litigant with copies of such unpublished cases and other authorities as are cited in a decision of the Court and were not previously cited by any party. NY R USDCTS&ED Civ Rule 7.2.

iv. *Statement explaining untimely electronic filing.* If you missed a filing deadline when the ECF system was out of order, attach a statement to your filing explaining how the interruption in service prevented you from filing in a timely fashion. NY R USDCTSD CM/ECF, S.D.(II)(23)(23.5).

v. *Courtesy copies.* Read the judge's Individual Practices to learn if courtesy copies are required. NY R USDCTSD CM/ECF, S.D.(II)(13)(13.17). Judges' Individual Practices should continue to be followed with respect to delivery of courtesy copies. NY R USDCTSD CM/ECF, S.D.(I)(3)(3.4).

3. *Individual judge practices.* Refer to the Miscellaneous section of this document for information on individual judge practices on required documents.

## E. Format

1. *Form of documents.* The rules governing captions and other matters of form in pleadings apply to motions and other papers. FRCP 7(b)(2).

a. *Paper.* Every pleading, written motion, and other paper must: be plainly written, typed, printed, or copied without erasures or interlineations which materially deface it. NY R USDCTS&ED Civ Rule 11.1(a)(1).

b. *Typeface, margin, and spacing.* The typeface, margins, and spacing of all documents presented for filing must meet the following requirements:

i. All text must be twelve (12) point type or larger, except for text in footnotes which may be ten (10) point type;

ii. All documents must have at least one (1) inch margins on all sides;

iii. All text must be double-spaced, except for headings, text in footnotes, or block quotations, which may be single-spaced. NY R USDCTS&ED Civ Rule 11.1(b).

c. *Caption; Names of parties.* Every pleading must have a caption with the court's name, a title, a file

number, and a FRCP 7(a) designation. The title of the complaint must name all the parties; the title of other pleadings, after naming the first party on each side, may refer generally to other parties. FRCP 10(a). Every pleading, written motion, and other paper must: bear the docket number and the initials of the District Judge and any Magistrate Judge before whom the action or proceeding is pending, NY R USDCTS&ED Civ Rule 11.1(a)(2).

d. *Paragraphs; Separate statements.* A party must state its claims or defenses in numbered paragraphs, each limited as far as practicable to a single set of circumstances. A later pleading may refer by number to a paragraph in an earlier pleading. If doing so would promote clarity, each claim founded on a separate transaction or occurrence—and each defense other than a denial—must be stated in a separate count or defense. FRCP 10(b).

e. *Adoption by reference; Exhibits.* A statement in a pleading may be adopted by reference elsewhere in the same pleading or in any other pleading or motion. A copy of a written instrument that is an exhibit to a pleading is a part of the pleading for all purposes. FRCP 10(c).

f. *Acceptance by the clerk.* The clerk must not refuse to file a paper solely because it is not in the form prescribed by the Federal Rules of Civil Procedure or by a local rule or practice. FRCP 5(d)(4).

2. *Form of electronic documents*

a. *PDF-A.* All documents electronically filed on the ECF system must be in PDF-A format (portable document format). A PDF-A file is created using PDF writer software such as Adobe Acrobat (go to the Adobe website for details). PDF-A files cannot be altered, providing security to the filer and the Court. NY R USDCTSD CM/ECF, S.D.(II)(23)(23.2).

b. *Size limitation.* No single PDF file may be larger than four megabytes (4 MB). If the filing is too large, the ECF system will not allow it to be filed, and you will not see a Notice of Electronic Filing (NEF or filing receipt) screen. To determine the size of an Adobe Acrobat PDF file click on File, Document Properties, Summary. NY R USDCTSD CM/ECF, S.D.(II)(23)(23.3).

   i. Converting documents directly from a word processor to PDF-A format creates the smallest possible file in terms of computer memory. If that is not possible, scan your document at low resolution. Within the Adobe Acrobat program, on the "Scan Manager" screen, adjust the settings for black and white and 200 dpi (dots per inch). This allows more pages to fit into a single PDF-A file. If that does not work, separate an oversized file into 2 or more parts. Simply label each file 1a, 1b, 1c, etc. Only relevant excerpts of exhibits should be electronically filed. NY R USDCTSD CM/ECF, S.D.(II)(23)(23.4).

c. *Attachments and exhibits.* Filing Users must submit in electronic form all documents referenced as exhibits or attachments, unless the Court permits paper filing. NY R USDCTSD CM/ECF, S.D.(I)(5)(5.1).

   i. A Filing User must submit as exhibits or attachments only those excerpts of the referenced documents that are relevant to the matter under consideration by the Court. Excerpted material must be clearly and prominently identified as such. Filing Users who file excerpts of documents as exhibits or attachments under this procedure do so without prejudice to their right to file timely additional excerpts or the complete document. Responding parties may file timely additional excerpts that they believe are relevant or the complete document. A party may move before the Court for permission to serve and file in hard copy documents that cannot be reasonably scanned. NY R USDCTSD CM/ECF, S.D.(I)(5)(5.2).

   ii. Exhibits must be filed only as attachments to a document, such as a motion or an affidavit. Do not use the ECF Filing Event for "Motion" to file exhibits separately. Exhibits are the only items that should be attached to electronically filed documents. You are limited to electronically filing only relevant excerpts of exhibits. Excerpts must be clearly identified as such. If the exhibit is too large to be scanned and electronically filed you may contact the ECF Help Desk. NY R USDCTSD CM/ECF, S.D.(II)(15)(15.6).

d. *Letters.* Parties should consult the assigned judge's Individual Practices to determine if the judge accepts letters at all and, if he or she does, whether the judge has any page limitations on letters and/or requires courtesy copies of letters filed on ECF (and, if so, by what means of delivery). All

letters addressed to the Court must include a subject line with the case name and docket number (e.g., "Re: Doe v. Smith, 13 Civ. 1234 (ABC)"). NY R USDCTSD CM/ECF, S.D.(II)(13)(13.1).

e. *Proposed orders, proposed judgments, stipulations and consents.* Any document that requires the signature of a judge should not be electronically filed except as an exhibit to another document. Proposed orders, judgments, stipulations and consents should not be submitted through the ECF system. Instead they should be sent by e-mail to the Clerk. Proposed orders should be submitted in word processing format (WordPerfect or Word) rather than as a PDF document. Stipulations should be submitted in PDF-A format. Stipulations must contain ink signatures not s/. Faxed or emailed signatures are acceptable. Please note that Stipulations of Voluntary Dismissal pursuant to FRCP 41(a)(1)(A)(ii) do not require the signature of a judge and must be electronically filed on the ECF system. Questions may be directed to the Orders and Judgments Clerk at the phone numbers listed in NY R USDCTSD CM/ECF, S.D.(II)(18)(18.3). NY R USDCTSD CM/ECF, S.D.(II)(18)(18.3).

   i. Email the proposed order, judgment or stipulation to the email addresses listed in NY R USDCTSD CM/ECF, S.D.(II)(18)(18.3). NY R USDCTSD CM/ECF, S.D.(II)(18)(18.3).

   ii. Pro se litigants who are not Filing Users are exempt from that portion of NY R USDCTSD CM/ECF, S.D.(II)(18)(18.3) that requires litigants to email proposed orders, judgments, stipulations and consents, and shall deliver such documents to the Clerk's Office in paper form. NY R USDCTSD CM/ECF, S.D.(II)(18)(18.3).

3. *Signing of pleadings, motions and other papers*

  a. *Signature.* Every pleading, written motion, and other paper must be signed by at least one attorney of record in the attorney's name—or by a party personally if the party is unrepresented. The paper must state the signer's address, e-mail address, and telephone number. FRCP 11(a). Every pleading, written motion, and other paper must: have the name of each person signing it clearly printed or typed directly below the signature. NY R USDCTS&ED Civ Rule 11.1(a)(3).

   i. *Electronic signatures.* The user log-in and password required to submit documents to the ECF system serve as the Filing User's signature on all electronic documents filed with the Court. NY R USDCTSD CM/ECF, S.D.(I)(8)(8.1); NY R USDCTSD CM/ECF, S.D.(II)(13)(13.14). They also serve as a signature for purposes of the Federal Rules of Civil Procedure, including FRCP 11, the Local Civil Rules of the United States District Courts for the Southern and Eastern Districts of New York, and any other purpose for which a signature is required in connection with proceedings before the Court. NY R USDCTSD CM/ECF, S.D.(I)(8)(8.1).

     • *Signature block.* Electronically filed documents must include a signature block and must set forth the name, address, telephone number and e-mail address all in compliance with the Federal Rules of Civil Procedure and NY R USDCTS&ED Civ Rule 11.1. In the absence of a scanned signature image, the name of the Filing User under whose log-in and password the document is submitted must be preceded by an "s/" typed in the space where the signature would otherwise appear. NY R USDCTSD CM/ECF, S.D.(I)(8)(8.2); NY R USDCTSD CM/ECF, S.D.(II)(13)(13.14).

     • *Documents requiring the signature of a party or witness.* A document requiring the signature of a party or witness shall be electronically filed in a scanned format that contains an image of the actual signature. NY R USDCTSD CM/ECF, S.D.(I)(8)(8.4); NY R USDCTSD CM/ECF, S.D.(II)(13)(13.14).

     • *Documents requiring the signature of a judge.* A Filing User submitting a document electronically that requires a judge's signature must promptly deliver the document in such other form, if any, as the Court requires. NY R USDCTSD CM/ECF, S.D.(I)(4)(4.2).

     • *Documents requiring multiple signatures.* Documents requiring signatures of more than one party must be electronically filed either by: (a) submitting a scanned document containing all necessary signatures; (b) representing the consent of the other parties on the document; (c) identifying on the document the parties whose signatures are required and by the submission of a notice of endorsement by the other parties no later than three business days after filing; or (d) in any other manner approved by the Court. NY R USDCTSD CM/ECF, S.D.(I)(8)(8.5).

    ii.   *No verification or accompanying affidavit required for pleadings.* Unless a rule or statute specifically states otherwise, a pleading need not be verified or accompanied by an affidavit. FRCP 11(a).

    iii.   *Unsigned papers.* The court must strike an unsigned paper unless the omission is promptly corrected after being called to the attorney's or party's attention. FRCP 11(a).

  b.  *Representations to the court.* By presenting to the court a pleading, written motion, or other paper—whether by signing, filing, submitting, or later advocating it—an attorney or unrepresented party certifies that to the best of the person's knowledge, information, and belief, formed after an inquiry reasonable under the circumstances:

    i.   It is not being presented for any improper purpose, such as to harass, cause unnecessary delay, or needlessly increase the cost of litigation;

    ii.   The claims, defenses, and other legal contentions are warranted by existing law or by a nonfrivolous argument for extending, modifying, or reversing existing law or for establishing new law;

    iii.   The factual contentions have evidentiary support or, if specifically so identified, will likely have evidentiary support after a reasonable opportunity for further investigation or discovery; and

    iv.   The denials of factual contentions are warranted on the evidence or, if specifically so identified, are reasonably based on belief or a lack of information. FRCP 11(b).

  c.  *Sanctions.* If, after notice and a reasonable opportunity to respond, the court determines that FRCP 11(b) has been violated, the court may impose an appropriate sanction on any attorney, law firm, or party that violated FRCP 11(b) or is responsible for the violation. FRCP 11(c)(1). Refer to the United States District Court for the Southern District of New York KeyRules Motion for Sanctions document for more information.

4.  *Privacy protection for filings made with the court*

  a.  *Redacted filings.* Unless the court orders otherwise, in an electronic or paper filing with the court that contains an individual's Social Security number, taxpayer-identification number, or birth date, the name of an individual known to be a minor, or a financial-account number, a party or nonparty making the filing may include only:

    i.   The last four (4) digits of the Social Security number and taxpayer-identification number;

    ii.   The year of the individual's birth;

    iii.   The minor's initials; and

    iv.   The last four (4) digits of the financial-account number. FRCP 5.2(a); NY R USDCTSD CM/ECF, S.D.(II)(21)(21.3).

    v.   Caution should be exercised when filing documents that contain the following:

- Personal identifying numbers (PIN #'s), such as a driver's license number;
- Medical records, treatment and diagnosis;
- Employment history;
- Individual financial information;
- Proprietary or trade secret information;
- Information regarding an individual's cooperation with the government. NY R USDCTSD CM/ECF, S.D.(II)(21)(21.4).

  b.  *Exemptions from the redaction requirement.* The redaction requirement does not apply to the following:

    i.   A financial-account number that identifies the property allegedly subject to forfeiture in a forfeiture proceeding;

    ii.   The record of an administrative or agency proceeding;

    iii.   The official record of a state-court proceeding;

    iv.   The record of a court or tribunal, if that record was not subject to the redaction requirement when originally filed;

    v.   A filing covered by FRCP 5.2(c) or FRCP 5.2(d); and

    vi.   A pro se filing in an action brought under 28 U.S.C.A. § 2241, 28 U.S.C.A. § 2254, or 28 U.S.C.A. § 2255. FRCP 5.2(b).

c.   *Limitations on remote access to electronic files; Social Security appeals and immigration cases.* Unless the court orders otherwise, in an action for benefits under the Social Security Act, and in an action or proceeding relating to an order of removal, to relief from removal, or to immigration benefits or detention, access to an electronic file is authorized as follows:

    i.   The parties and their attorneys may have remote electronic access to any part of the case file, including the administrative record;

    ii.   Any other person may have electronic access to the full record at the courthouse, but may have remote electronic access only to:

       •   The docket maintained by the court; and

       •   An opinion, order, judgment, or other disposition of the court, but not any other part of the case file or the administrative record. FRCP 5.2(c).

d.   *Filings made under seal.* The court may order that a filing be made under seal without redaction. The court may later unseal the filing or order the person who made the filing to file a redacted version for the public record. FRCP 5.2(d). For more information on sealing documents, refer to NY R USDCTSD CM/ECF, S.D.(I)(6).

e.   *Protective orders.* For good cause, the court may by order in a case:

    i.   Require redaction of additional information; or

    ii.   Limit or prohibit a nonparty's remote electronic access to a document filed with the court. FRCP 5.2(e).

f.   *Option for additional unredacted filing under seal.* A person making a redacted filing may also file an unredacted copy under seal. The court must retain the unredacted copy as part of the record. FRCP 5.2(f); NY R USDCTSD CM/ECF, S.D.(II)(21)(21.5).

g.   *Option for filing a reference list.* A filing that contains redacted information may be filed together with a reference list that identifies each item of redacted information and specifies an appropriate identifier that uniquely corresponds to each item listed. The list must be filed under seal and may be amended as of right. Any reference in the case to a listed identifier will be construed to refer to the corresponding item of information. FRCP 5.2(g); NY R USDCTSD CM/ECF, S.D.(II)(21)(21.5).

h.   *Responsibility for redaction.* It is the sole responsibility of counsel and the parties to be sure that all documents comply with the rules of this Court requiring redaction of personal identifiers. Neither the judge nor the Clerk of Court will review documents for compliance with these rules. NY R USDCTSD CM/ECF, S.D.(II)(21)(21.2).

i.   *Waiver of protection of identifiers.* A person waives the protection of FRCP 5.2(a) as to the person's own information by filing it without redaction and not under seal. FRCP 5.2(h).

j.   For more information on privacy and public access to ECF cases, refer to NY R USDCTSD CM/ECF, S.D.(II)(21).

5.   *Individual judge practices.* Refer to the Miscellaneous section of this document for information on individual judge practices on formatting documents.

## F.  Filing and Service Requirements

1.   *Filing requirements.* Any paper after the complaint that is required to be served—together with a certificate of service—must be filed within a reasonable time after service. FRCP 5(d)(1). Complaints and all subsequent papers are accepted at either courthouse, regardless of the place for which the case is designated. NY R USDCTSD Div. Bus., Rule 22. Subject to the instructions regarding ECF published on the website of each respective Court and any pertinent Individual Judge's Practices, letter-motions

permitted by NY R USDCTS&ED Civ Rule 7.1(d) and letters addressed to the Court (but not letters between the parties) may be filed via ECF. NY R USDCTS&ED Civ Rule 5.2(b). For information on electronically filing motions, refer to NY R USDCTSD CM/ECF, S.D.(II)(15).

a. *How filing is made; In general.* A paper is filed by delivering it:

   i. To the clerk; or

   ii. To a judge who agrees to accept it for filing, and who must then note the filing date on the paper and promptly send it to the clerk. FRCP 5(d)(2).

b. *Night depository.* A night depository with an automatic date stamp shall be maintained by the Clerk of the Southern District in the Pearl Street Courthouse. After regular business hours, papers for the District Court only may be deposited in the night depository. Such papers will be considered as having been filed in the District Court as of the date stamped thereon, which shall be deemed presumptively correct. NY R USDCTS&ED Civ Rule 1.2.

c. *Electronic filing*

   i. *Authorization of electronic filing program.* A court may, by local rule, allow papers to be filed, signed, or verified by electronic means that are consistent with any technical standards established by the Judicial Conference of the United States. A local rule may require electronic filing only if reasonable exceptions are allowed. A paper filed electronically in compliance with a local rule is a written paper for purposes of the Federal Rules of Civil Procedure. FRCP 5(d)(3).

- The Court will accept for filing documents submitted, signed or verified by electronic means, that comply with the rules in NY R USDCTSD CM/ECF, S.D. NY R USDCTSD CM/ECF, S.D.(I). The information in NY R USDCTSD CM/ECF, S.D. applies only to cases assigned to the ECF system. NY R USDCTSD CM/ECF, S.D.(Introduction).

- Parties serving and filing papers shall follow the instructions regarding Electronic Case Filing (ECF) published on the website of each respective Court. A paper served and filed by electronic means in accordance with such instructions is, for purposes of FRCP 5, served and filed in compliance with the Local Civil Rules of the Southern and Eastern Districts of New York. NY R USDCTS&ED Civ Rule 5.2(a). Parties have an obligation to review the Court's actual order, decree, or judgment (on ECF), which controls, and should not rely on the description on the docket or in the ECF Notice of Electronic Filing (NEF). NY R USDCTS&ED Civ Rule 5.2(c).

- The following should be observed when filing electronically: (1) the Federal Rules of Civil Procedure, (2) the Local Civil Rules of the United States District Courts for the Southern and Eastern Districts of New York, (3) the assigned judge's Individual Practices, and (4) the Court's Electronic Case Filing Rules & Instructions (NY R USDCTSD CM/ECF, S.D.). NY R USDCTSD CM/ECF, S.D.(Introduction).

   ii. *Scope of electronic filing.* Except as expressly provided and in exceptional circumstances preventing a party from filing electronically, all documents required to be filed with the Court must be filed electronically. Any party unable to comply with this requirement must seek permission of the Court to file in the traditional manner, on paper. Any such application made after regular business hours may be submitted through the night depository box maintained pursuant to NY R USDCTS&ED Civ Rule 1.2. NY R USDCTSD CM/ECF, S.D.(I)(1)(1.1).

- *Documents filed by pro se litigants.* Unless otherwise ordered by the Court, documents filed by pro se litigants must be filed in the traditional manner, on paper, and will be scanned and docketed by the Clerk's Office into the ECF system. NY R USDCTSD CM/ECF, S.D.(I)(1)(1.1). Pro se litigants must file pleadings and documents in the traditional manner on paper unless the assigned judge has granted permission to electronically file on the ECF system. NY R USDCTSD CM/ECF, S.D.(Introduction).

- *Letters.* Except for letters to be filed under seal, letters addressed to judges who accept letters may be filed electronically. Parties should consult the assigned judge's Individual Practices to determine if the judge accepts letters at all and, if he or she does, whether the

judge has any page limitations on letters and/or requires courtesy copies of letters filed on ECF (and, if so, by what means of delivery). NY R USDCTSD CM/ECF, S.D.(II)(13)(13.1). Letters solely between parties or their counsel or otherwise not addressed to the Court may not be filed electronically on ECF (except as exhibits to an otherwise properly filed document). NY R USDCTSD CM/ECF, S.D.(II)(13)(13.1). For more information on filing letters, refer to NY R USDCTSD CM/ECF, S.D.(II)(13)(13.1).

- *Proposed orders, judgments and decrees.* Proposed orders, judgments and decrees shall be presented as directed by the ECF rules published on the website of each respective Court. NY R USDCTS&ED Civ Rule 77.1. For more information, refer to NY R USDCTS&ED Civ Rule 77.1.

iii. *Exceptions to electronic filing.* In an ECF case, the documents that should not be electronically filed include:

- Miscellaneous Case initiating documents, NY R USDCTSD CM/ECF, S.D.(II)(18)(18.2);

- Proposed orders; proposed judgments, stipulations; consents, NY R USDCTSD CM/ECF, S.D.(II)(18)(18.3);

- Orders to show cause / temporary restraining orders, NY R USDCTSD CM/ECF, S.D.(II)(18)(18.4);

- Sealed documents, NY R USDCTSD CM/ECF, S.D.(II)(18)(18.5); and

- Surety bonds, NY R USDCTSD CM/ECF, S.D.(II)(18)(18.6).

- In cases where the record of an administrative or other prior proceeding must be filed with the Court, such record may be served and filed in hard copy without prior motion and order of the Court. NY R USDCTSD CM/ECF, S.D.(I)(5)(5.3).

- For more documents excepted from electronic filing, and for more information on such documents, refer to NY R USDCTSD CM/ECF, S.D.(II)(18).

iv. *Consequences of electronic filing.* Except as otherwise provided in NY R USDCTSD CM/ECF, S.D.(I)(4), electronic filing of a document in the ECF system consistent with these procedures, together with the transmission of a Notice of Electronic Filing (NEF) from the Court, constitutes filing of the document for all purposes of the Federal Rules of Civil Procedure and the Local Civil Rules of the United States District Courts for the Southern and Eastern Districts of New York and constitutes entry of the document on the docket kept by the Clerk under FRCP 58 and FRCP 79. NY R USDCTSD CM/ECF, S.D.(I)(3)(3.1).

v. For more information on electronic filing, refer to NY R USDCTSD CM/ECF, S.D.

2. *Service requirements*

a. *Service; When required*

i. *In general.* Unless the Federal Rules of Civil Procedure provide otherwise, each of the following papers must be served on every party:

- An order stating that service is required;

- A pleading filed after the original complaint, unless the court orders otherwise under FRCP 5(c) because there are numerous defendants;

- A discovery paper required to be served on a party, unless the court orders otherwise;

- A written motion, except one that may be heard ex parte; and

- A written notice, appearance, demand, or offer of judgment, or any similar paper. FRCP 5(a)(1).

ii. *If a party fails to appear.* No service is required on a party who is in default for failing to appear. But a pleading that asserts a new claim for relief against such a party must be served on that party under FRCP 4. FRCP 5(a)(2).

iii. *Seizing property.* If an action is begun by seizing property and no person is or need be named as

a defendant, any service required before the filing of an appearance, answer, or claim must be made on the person who had custody or possession of the property when it was seized. FRCP 5(a)(3).

b. *Service; How made*

   i. *Serving an attorney.* If a party is represented by an attorney, service under FRCP 5 must be made on the attorney unless the court orders service on the party. FRCP 5(b)(1).

   ii. *Service in general.* A paper is served under FRCP 5 by:

- Handing it to the person;

- Leaving it: (1) at the person's office with a clerk or other person in charge or, if no one is in charge, in a conspicuous place in the office; or (2) if the person has no office or the office is closed, at the person's dwelling or usual place of abode with someone of suitable age and discretion who resides there;

- Mailing it to the person's last known address—in which event service is complete upon mailing;

- Leaving it with the court clerk if the person has no known address;

- Sending it by electronic means if the person consented in writing—in which event service is complete upon transmission, but is not effective if the serving party learns that it did not reach the person to be served; or

- Delivering it by any other means that the person consented to in writing—in which event service is complete when the person making service delivers it to the agency designated to make delivery. FRCP 5(b)(2).

   iii. *Service by overnight delivery.* Service upon an attorney may be made by overnight delivery service. "Overnight delivery service" means any delivery service which regularly accepts items for overnight delivery. Overnight delivery service shall be deemed service by mail for purposes of FRCP 5 and FRCP 6. NY R USDCTS&ED Civ Rule 5.3.

   iv. *Service by electronic means.* Parties serving and filing papers shall follow the instructions regarding Electronic Case Filing (ECF) published on the website of each respective Court. A paper served and filed by electronic means in accordance with such instructions is, for purposes of FRCP 5, served and filed in compliance with the Local Civil Rules of the United States District Courts for the Southern and Eastern Districts of New York. NY R USDCTS&ED Civ Rule 5.2(a). Parties have an obligation to review the Court's actual order, decree, or judgment (on ECF), which controls, and should not rely on the description on the docket or in the ECF Notice of Electronic Filing (NEF). NY R USDCTS&ED Civ Rule 5.2(c).

- *Notice of electronic filing (NEF).* In cases assigned to the ECF system, service is complete provided all parties receive a Notice of Electronic Filing (NEF), which is sent automatically by email from the Court (see the NEF for a list of who did/did not receive notice electronically). Transmission of the NEF constitutes service upon all Filing and Receiving Users who are listed as recipients of notice by electronic mail. NY R USDCTSD CM/ECF, S.D.(I)(9)(9.1). In cases assigned to the ECF system, if all parties receive a NEF, service is complete upon transmission of the NEF by the Court, and you are not required to serve a paper copy. NY R USDCTSD CM/ECF, S.D.(II)(19)(19.2). It remains the duty of Filing and Receiving Users to maintain current contact information with the court and to regularly review the docket sheet of the case. NY R USDCTSD CM/ECF, S.D.(I)(9)(9.1).

- *Mailing of court-initiated documents.* The Clerk's Office will no longer mail paper copies of court-initiated documents to Filing and Receiving Users. The Clerk's Office will mail copies of all court-initiated documents to pro se parties who have not registered as Filing or Receiving Users. NY R USDCTSD CM/ECF, S.D.(II)(19)(19.1).

- *No receipt of a NEF.* If any party does not receive a NEF, you are required to accomplish service on that party in the traditional manner, in paper form. NY R USDCTSD CM/ECF, S.D.(II)(19)(19.2). The NEF receipt will inform you who will receive notice of the filing

"electronically" (by e-mail from the Court) and who will receive notice "by other means" (traditional service in paper form). NY R USDCTSD CM/ECF, S.D.(II)(19)(19.2).

- *Service on non-filing or non-receiving users.* Attorneys and pro se parties who are not Filing or Receiving Users must be served with a paper copy of any electronically filed pleading or other document. Service of such paper copy must be made according to the Federal Rules of Civil Procedure and the Local Civil Rules of the United States District Courts for the Southern and Eastern Districts of New York. NY R USDCTSD CM/ECF, S.D.(I)(9)(9.2). Such paper service must be documented by electronically filing proof of service. NY R USDCTSD CM/ECF, S.D.(I)(9)(9.2); NY R USDCTSD CM/ECF, S.D.(II)(19)(19.2). Where the Clerk scans and electronically files pleadings and documents on behalf of a pro se party, the associated NEF constitutes service. NY R USDCTSD CM/ECF, S.D.(I)(9)(9.2).

- For more information on service by electronic means, refer to NY R USDCTSD CM/ECF, S.D.(II)(19).

    v. *Using court facilities.* If a local rule so authorizes, a party may use the court's transmission facilities to make service under FRCP 5(b)(2)(E). FRCP 5(b)(3).

  c. *Serving numerous defendants*

    i. *In general.* If an action involves an unusually large number of defendants, the court may, on motion or on its own, order that:

- Defendants' pleadings and replies to them need not be served on other defendants;

- Any crossclaim, counterclaim, avoidance, or affirmative defense in those pleadings and replies to them will be treated as denied or avoided by all other parties; and

- Filing any such pleading and serving it on the plaintiff constitutes notice of the pleading to all parties. FRCP 5(c)(1).

    ii. *Notifying parties.* A copy of every such order must be served on the parties as the court directs. FRCP 5(c)(2).

3. *Individual judge practices.* Refer to the Miscellaneous section of this document for information on individual judge practices on filing and serving documents.

## G. Hearings

1. *Hearings, generally*

  a. *Oral argument.* Due process does not require that oral argument be permitted on a motion and, except as otherwise provided by local rule, the district court has discretion to determine whether it will decide the motion on the papers or hear argument by counsel (and perhaps receive evidence). FPP § 1190; F.D.I.C. v. Deglau, 207 F.3d 153 (3d Cir. 2000). The parties and their attorneys shall only appear to argue the motion if so directed by the Court by order or by a Judge's Individual Practice. NY R USDCTS&ED Civ Rule 6.1(c).

  b. *Providing a regular schedule for oral hearings.* A court may establish regular times and places for oral hearings on motions. FRCP 78(a).

  c. *Providing for submission on briefs.* By rule or order, the court may provide for submitting and determining motions on briefs, without oral hearings. FRCP 78(b).

2. *Hearing on FRCP 12 defenses before trial.* If a party so moves, any defense listed in FRCP 12(b)(1) through FRCP 12(b)(7)—whether made in a pleading or by motion—and a motion under FRCP 12(c) must be heard and decided before trial unless the court orders a deferral until trial. FRCP 12(i).

3. *Individual judge practices.* Refer to the Miscellaneous section of this document for information on individual judge practices on hearings.

## H. Forms

## 1. Federal Motion to Dismiss for Failure to State a Claim Forms

  a. Notice in federal court; Motion for involuntary dismissal of action without prejudice; Complaint fails to state a claim on which relief can be granted. AMJUR PP DISMISSAL § 109.

b. Motion; To dismiss; Failure to state a claim on which relief can be granted or facts sufficient to constitute cause of action. AMJUR PP LIMITATION § 100.

c. Motion to dismiss; For failure to state a claim, improper service of process, improper venue, and want of jurisdiction. AMJUR PP MOTIONS § 42.

d. Failure to state a claim upon which relief can be granted. 2C FEDFORMS § 11:80.

e. Failure to state a claim upon which relief can be granted; Long version. 2C FEDFORMS § 11:81.

f. Failure to state a claim upon which relief can be granted; Dismissal of certain allegations. 2C FEDFORMS § 11:82.

g. Failure to state a claim upon which relief can be granted; With supporting reasons. 2C FEDFORMS § 11:83.

h. Failure to state a claim upon which relief can be granted; With supporting reasons; Plaintiff not the real party in interest. 2C FEDFORMS § 11:85.

i. Failure to state a claim upon which relief can be granted; With supporting reasons; Failure to show implied contract. 2C FEDFORMS § 11:86.

j. Failure to state a claim upon which relief can be granted; With supporting reasons; Issue not arbitrable. 2C FEDFORMS § 11:87.

k. Failure to state a claim upon which relief can be granted; With supporting affidavits. 2C FED-FORMS § 11:88.

l. Failure to state a claim upon which relief can be granted; In alternative for summary judgment. 2C FEDFORMS § 11:89.

m. Motion; To dismiss; Failure to state sufficient claim; By one of several defendants. FEDPROF § 1:923.

n. Motion to dismiss; Failure to state sufficient claim; By third-party defendant. FEDPROF § 1:924.

o. Motion to dismiss; Failure to state sufficient claim after successive attempts. FEDPROF § 1:925.

p. Motion to dismiss; By individual defendants. FEDPROF § 1:926.

q. Motion to dismiss; By state agency. FEDPROF § 1:927.

r. Motion to dismiss counterclaim. FEDPROF § 1:931.

s. Allegation; In motion to dismiss; Res judicata. FEDPROF § 1:933.

t. Allegation; In motion to dismiss; Statute of limitations. FEDPROF § 1:935.

u. Allegation; In motion to dismiss; Strict liability claim barred by statute. FEDPROF § 1:936.

v. Allegation; In motion to dismiss; By United States; Absence of consent to suit. FEDPROF § 1:938.

w. Reply; To motion to dismiss for failure to state sufficient claim. FEDPROF § 1:939.

x. Motion to dismiss counterclaim. GOLDLTGFMS § 13:10.

y. Motion to dismiss complaint; General form. GOLDLTGFMS § 20:24.

z. Affidavit in support of motion to dismiss complaint. GOLDLTGFMS § 20:32.

## I. Applicable Rules

1. *Federal rules*

    a. Serving and filing pleadings and other papers. FRCP 5.

    b. Constitutional challenge to a statute; Notice, certification, and intervention. FRCP 5.1.

    c. Privacy protection for filings made with the court. FRCP 5.2.

    d. Computing and extending time; Time for motion papers. FRCP 6.

    e. Pleadings allowed; Form of motions and other papers. FRCP 7.

    f. Disclosure statement. FRCP 7.1.

g.  Form of pleadings. FRCP 10.

h.  Signing pleadings, motions, and other papers; Representations to the court; Sanctions. FRCP 11.

i.  Defenses and objections; When and how presented; Motion for judgment on the pleadings; Consolidating motions; Waiving defenses; Pretrial hearing. FRCP 12.

j.  Hearing motions; Submission on briefs. FRCP 78.

2. *Local rules*

a.  Night depository. NY R USDCTS&ED Civ Rule 1.2.

b.  Duty of attorneys in related cases. NY R USDCTS&ED Civ Rule 1.6.

c.  Electronic service and filing of documents. NY R USDCTS&ED Civ Rule 5.2.

d.  Service by overnight delivery. NY R USDCTS&ED Civ Rule 5.3.

e.  Service and filing of motion papers. NY R USDCTS&ED Civ Rule 6.1.

f.  Orders on motions. NY R USDCTS&ED Civ Rule 6.2.

g.  Computation of time. NY R USDCTS&ED Civ Rule 6.4.

h.  Motion papers. NY R USDCTS&ED Civ Rule 7.1.

i.  Disclosure statement. NY R USDCTS&ED Civ Rule 7.1.1.

j.  Authorities to be provided to pro se litigants. NY R USDCTS&ED Civ Rule 7.2.

k.  Form of pleadings, motions, and other papers. NY R USDCTS&ED Civ Rule 11.1.

l.  Notice to pro se litigant who opposes a FRCP 12 motion supported by matters outside the pleadings. NY R USDCTS&ED Civ Rule 12.1.

m.  Submission of orders, judgments and decrees. NY R USDCTS&ED Civ Rule 77.1.

n.  Alternative dispute resolution (Southern District only). NY R USDCTS&ED Civ Rule 83.9.

o.  Electronic case filing rules and instructions. NY R USDCTSD CM/ECF, S.D.

p.  Related cases. NY R USDCTSD Div. Bus., Rule 13.

q.  Filing at either courthouse. NY R USDCTSD Div. Bus., Rule 22.

## J.  Miscellaneous

**NOTE: Individual judges' rules may apply. For available judge-level information, refer to:**

DISTRICT JUDGE RONNIE ABRAMS: NY R USDCTSD Abrams-Civ Prac; NY R USDCTSD Abrams-Crim Prac; NY R USDCTSD Abrams-Pro Se; NY R USDCTSD Abrams-Case Mgt; NY R USDCTSD Abrams-Jury.

DISTRICT JUDGE DEBORAH A. BATTS: NY R USDCTSD Batts-Practices.

DISTRICT JUDGE RICHARD M. BERMAN: NY R USDCTSD Berman-Practices; NY R USDCTSD Berman-Default; NY R USDCTSD Berman-Sentencing; NY R USDCTSD Berman-Media.

DISTRICT JUDGE VINCENT L. BRICCETTI: NY R USDCTSD Briccetti-Practices; NY R USDCTSD Briccetti-Plan; NY R USDCTSD Briccetti-Notice.

DISTRICT JUDGE VERNON S. BRODERICK: NY R USDCTSD Broderick-Civil; NY R USDCTSD Broderick-Crim; NY R USDCTSD Broderick-Case Mgt; NY R USDCTSD Broderick-Jury.

DISTRICT JUDGE NAOMI REICE BUCHWALD: NY R USDCTSD Buchwald-Practices.

DISTRICT JUDGE VALERIE E. CAPRONI: NY R USDCTSD Caproni-Prac; NY R USDCTSD Caproni--Pro Se; NY R USDCTSD Caproni-Case Mgt; NY R USDCTSD Caproni-Crim Prac.

DISTRICT JUDGE ANDREW L. CARTER JR.: NY R USDCTSD Carter-Practices.

DISTRICT JUDGE KEVIN P. CASTEL: NY R USDCTSD Castel-Practices; NY R USDCTSD Castel-Default; NY R USDCTSD Castel-Scheduling; NY R USDCTSD Castel-Complex; NY R USDCTSD Castel-Trials; NY R USDCTSD Castel-Sentencing.

DISTRICT JUDGE DENISE L. COTE: NY R USDCTSD Cote-Civil Practices; NY R USDCTSD Cote-Pro Se;

NY R USDCTSD Cote-Maritime Ord; NY R USDCTSD Cote-Crim Practices; NY R USDCTSD Cote-Crim Trials; NY R USDCTSD Cote-Sentencing.

DISTRICT JUDGE PAUL A. CROTTY: NY R USDCTSD Crotty-Practices; NY R USDCTSD Crotty-Sentencing; NY R USDCTSD Crotty-Calls; NY R USDCTSD Crotty-Scheduling.

DISTRICT JUDGE GEORGE B. DANIELS: NY R USDCTSD Daniels-Practices.

DISTRICT JUDGE KEVIN T. DUFFY: NY R USDCTSD Duffy-Practices.

DISTRICT JUDGE PAUL A. ENGELMAYER: NY R USDCTSD Engelmayer-Practices; NY R USDCTSD Engelmayer-Scheduling; NY R USDCTSD Engelmayer-Sentencing; NY R USDCTSD Engelmayer-Pro Se; NY R USDCTSD Engelmayer-Crim.

DISTRICT JUDGE KATHERINE POLK FAILLA: NY R USDCTSD Failla-Civ Prac; NY R USDCTSD Failla-Crim Prac; NY R USDCTSD Failla-Case Mgt.

DISTRICT JUDGE KATHERINE B. FORREST: NY R USDCTSD Forrest-Civil Prac; NY R USDCTSD Forrest-Crim Prac; NY R USDCTSD Forrest-Crim Pretrial; NY R USDCTSD Forrest-Scheduling; NY R USDCTSD Forrest-Patent Scheduling; NY R USDCTSD Forrest-Sentencing; NY R USDCTSD Forrest-Order 1; NY R USDCTSD Forrest-Order 2.

DISTRICT JUDGE JESSE M. FURMAN: NY R USDCTSD Furman-Civil Prac; NY R USDCTSD Furman-Crim Prac; NY R USDCTSD Furman-Pro Se Prac; NY R USDCTSD Furman-Trials; NY R USDCTSD Furman-Scheduling; NY R USDCTSD Furman-Rights.

DISTRICT JUDGE PAUL G. GARDEPHE: NY R USDCTSD Gardephe-Civ Prac; NY R USDCTSD Gardephe-Pretrial; NY R USDCTSD Gardephe-Prot Ord; NY R USDCTSD Gardephe-Maritime; NY R USDCTSD Gardephe-Crim Prac; NY R USDCTSD Gardephe-Trial.

DISTRICT JUDGE THOMAS P. GRIESA: NY R USDCTSD Griesa-Practices.

DISTRICT JUDGE CHARLES S. HAIGHT: NY R USDCTSD Haight-Practices.

DISTRICT JUDGE ALVIN K. HELLERSTEIN: NY R USDCTSD Hellerstein-Practices; NY R USDCTSD Hellerstein--Sept 11.

DISTRICT JUDGE LEWIS A. KAPLAN: NY R USDCTSD Kaplan-Practices; NY R USDCTSD Kaplan-Sentencing.

DISTRICT JUDGE KENNETH M. KARAS: NY R USDCTSD Karas-Practices; NY R USDCTSD Karas-Case Mgt; NY R USDCTSD Karas-Default; NY R USDCTSD Karas-Sentencing; NY R USDCTSD Karas-Rights.

DISTRICT JUDGE JOHN F. KEENAN: NY R USDCTSD Keenan-Practices.

DISTRICT JUDGE JOHN G. KOELTL: NY R USDCTSD Koeltl-Practices.

DISTRICT JUDGE VICTOR MARRERO: NY R USDCTSD Marrero-Practices; NY R USDCTSD Marrero-Scheduling; NY R USDCTSD Marrero-Default; NY R USDCTSD Marrero-Trial Proc.

DISTRICT JUDGE COLLEEN McMAHON: NY R USDCTSD McMahon-Practices; NY R USDCTSD McMahon-RICO; NY R USDCTSD McMahon-Copies; NY R USDCTSD McMahon-Scheduling; NY R USDCTSD McMahon-Elec Disc; NY R USDCTSD McMahon-Sentencing.

DISTRICT JUDGE ALISON J. NATHAN: NY R USDCTSD Nathan-Civ Prac; NY R USDCTSD Nathan-Crim Prac; NY R USDCTSD Nathan-Pro Se; NY R USDCTSD Nathan-Scheduling.

DISTRICT JUDGE J. PAUL OETKEN: NY R USDCTSD Oetken-Civ Prac; NY R USDCTSD Oetken-Case Mgt; NY R USDCTSD Oetken-Crim Prac; NY R USDCTSD Oetken-Pro Se.

DISTRICT JUDGE WILLIAM H. PAULEY, III: NY R USDCTSD Pauley-Crim Cases; NY R USDCTSD Pauley-Practices.

DISTRICT JUDGE LORETTA A. PRESKA: NY R USDCTSD Preska-Practices.

DISTRICT JUDGE JED S. RAKOFF: NY R USDCTSD Rakoff-Practices; NY R USDCTSD Rakoff-Scheduling; NY R USDCTSD Rakoff-Prot Ord; NY R USDCTSD Rakoff-Maritime Ord.

DISTRICT JUDGE EDGARDO RAMOS: NY R USDCTSD Ramos--Practices; NY R USDCTSD Ramos-Case Mgt.

DISTRICT JUDGE NELSON S. ROMAN: NY R USDCTSD Roman-Civ Prac; NY R USDCTSD Roman-Pro Se; NY R USDCTSD Roman-Crim Prac; NY R USDCTSD Roman-Case Mgt.

DISTRICT JUDGE LEONARD B. SAND: NY R USDCTSD Sand-Practices.

DISTRICT JUDGE LORNA G. SCHOFIELD: NY R USDCTSD Schofield-Civ Prac; NY R USDCTSD Schofield-Crim Prac; NY R USDCTSD Schofield-Sched; NY R USDCTSD Schofield-Pro Se; NY R USDCTSD Schofield-Advice.

DISTRICT JUDGE CATHY SEIBEL: NY R USDCTSD Seibel-Practices.

DISTRICT JUDGE LOUIS L. STANTON: NY R USDCTSD Stanton-Practices; NY R USDCTSD Stanton-Pretrial.

DISTRICT JUDGE SIDNEY H. STEIN: NY R USDCTSD Stein-Practices.

DISTRICT JUDGE RICHARD J. SULLIVAN: NY R USDCTSD Sullivan-Practices; NY R USDCTSD Sullivan-Scheduling; NY R USDCTSD Sullivan-Sentencing; NY R USDCTSD Sullivan-Juries; NY R USDCTSD Sullivan-Trial; NY R USDCTSD Sullivan-Default.

DISTRICT JUDGE LAURA TAYLOR SWAIN: NY R USDCTSD Swain-Practices; NY R USDCTSD Swain-Trial; NY R USDCTSD Swain-Crim Trial; NY R USDCTSD Swain-Juries; NY R USDCTSD Swain-Sentencing; NY R USDCTSD Swain-Rights.

DISTRICT JUDGE ROBERT W. SWEET: NY R USDCTSD Sweet-Practices.

DISTRICT JUDGE ANALISA TORRES: NY R USDCTSD Torres-Civ Prac; NY R USDCTSD Torres-Pro Se; NY R USDCTSD Torres-Scheduling.

DISTRICT JUDGE KIMBA M. WOOD: NY R USDCTSD Wood-Practices; NY R USDCTSD Wood-Scheduling; NY R USDCTSD Wood-Discovery; NY R USDCTSD Wood-RICO; NY R USDCTSD Wood-Juries; NY R USDCTSD Wood-Trial; NY R USDCTSD Wood-Media.

DISTRICT JUDGE GREGORY H. WOODS: NY R USDCTSD Woods-Civ Prac; NY R USDCTSD Woods-Pro Se; NY R USDCTSD Woods-Sched; NY R USDCTSD Woods-Crim Prac; NY R USDCTSD Woods-Protect Order; NY R USDCTSD Woods-Speedy Trial.

MAGISTRATE JUDGE JAMES L. COTT: NY R USDCTSD Cott-Practices; NY R USDCTSD Cott-Settlement.

MAGISTRATE JUDGE PAUL E. DAVISON: NY R USDCTSD Davison-Practices.

MAGISTRATE JUDGE RONALD L. ELLIS: NY R USDCTSD Ellis-Practices.

MAGISTRATE JUDGE KEVIN N. FOX: NY R USDCTSD Fox-Practices; NY R USDCTSD Fox-Settlement.

MAGISTRATE JUDGE JAMES C. FRANCIS: NY R USDCTSD Francis-Practices.

MAGISTRATE JUDGE DEBRA FREEMAN: NY R USDCTSD Freeman-Practices; NY R USDCTSD Freeman-Settlement.

MAGISTRATE JUDGE GABRIEL W. GORENSTEIN: NY R USDCTSD Gorenstein-Practices; NY R USDCTSD Gorenstein-Ackn.

MAGISTRATE JUDGE FRANK MAAS: NY R USDCTSD Maas-Practices; NY R USDCTSD Maas-Discontinuance; NY R USDCTSD Maas-Conf; NY R USDCTSD Maas-Settlement.

MAGISTRATE JUDGE JUDITH C. McCARTHY: NY R USDCTSD McCarthy-Practices; NY R USDCTSD McCarthy-Conduct.

MAGISTRATE JUDGE BARBARA MOSES: NY R USDCTSD Moses-Practices.

MAGISTRATE JUDGE SARAH NETBURN: NY R USDCTSD Netburn-Civil; NY R USDCTSD Netburn-Settlement; NY R USDCTSD Netburn-Case Mgt; NY R USDCTSD Netburn--Pro Se.

MAGISTRATE JUDGE ANDREW J. PECK: NY R USDCTSD Peck-Practices; NY R USDCTSD Peck-Order; NY R USDCTSD Peck-Rule 502(d).

MAGISTRATE JUDGE HENRY PITMAN: NY R USDCTSD Pitman-Practices.

MAGISTRATE JUDGE LISA MARGARET SMITH: NY R USDCTSD Smith-Practices; NY R USDCTSD Smith-Trials.

# Motions, Oppositions and Replies
# Motion to Dismiss for Lack of Subject Matter Jurisdiction

### Document Last Updated September 2016

**A. Checklist**

(I) ❑ Matters to be considered by moving party

    (a) ❑ Required documents

        (1) ❑ Notice of motion and motion

        (2) ❑ Memorandum of law

        (3) ❑ Certificate of service

    (b) ❑ Supplemental documents

        (1) ❑ Supporting evidence

        (2) ❑ Notice of constitutional question

        (3) ❑ Nongovernmental corporate disclosure statement

        (4) ❑ Notice to pro se litigant who opposes a FRCP 12 motion supported by matters outside the pleadings

        (5) ❑ Copies of authorities

        (6) ❑ Proposed order

        (7) ❑ Statement explaining untimely electronic filing

        (8) ❑ Courtesy copies

    (c) ❑ Timing

        (1) ❑ The defense of lack of subject matter jurisdiction can be raised at any time

        (2) ❑ Every defense to a claim for relief in any pleading must be asserted in the responsive pleading if one is required

        (3) ❑ A motion asserting any of the defenses in FRCP 12(b) must be made before pleading if a responsive pleading is allowed

        (4) ❑ If a pleading sets out a claim for relief that does not require a responsive pleading, an opposing party may assert at trial any defense to that claim

        (5) ❑ A written motion and notice of the hearing must be served at least fourteen (14) days before the time specified for the hearing, with the following exceptions: (i) when the motion may be heard ex parte; (ii) when the Federal Rules of Civil Procedure set a different time; or (iii) when a court order—which a party may, for good cause, apply for ex parte—sets a different time

        (6) ❑ Any affidavit supporting a motion must be served with the motion

(II) ❑ Matters to be considered by opposing party

    (a) ❑ Required documents

        (1) ❑ Answering memorandum of law

        (2) ❑ Certificate of service

    (b) ❑ Supplemental documents

        (1) ❑ Supporting evidence

        (2) ❑ Notice of constitutional question

        (3) ❑ Copies of authorities

        (4) ❑ Statement explaining untimely electronic filing

(5) ❑ Courtesy copies

(c) ❑ Timing

(1) ❑ Any opposing affidavits and answering memoranda shall be served within fourteen (14) days after service of the moving papers

(2) ❑ Except as FRCP 59(c) provides otherwise, any opposing affidavit must be served at least seven (7) days before the hearing, unless the court permits service at another time

## B. Timing

1. *Motion to dismiss for lack of subject matter jurisdiction.* [The defense of lack of subject matter jurisdiction] can be raised at any time. FEDPROC § 62:434.

   a. *In a responsive pleading.* Every defense to a claim for relief in any pleading must be asserted in the responsive pleading if one is required. FRCP 12(b).

   b. *By motion.* A motion asserting any of the defenses in FRCP 12(b) must be made before pleading if a responsive pleading is allowed. FRCP 12(b). Although FRCP 12(b) encourages the responsive pleader to file a motion to dismiss before filing the answer, nothing in FRCP 12 prohibits the filing of a motion to dismiss with the answer. An untimely motion to dismiss may be considered if the defense asserted in the motion was previously raised in the responsive pleading. FEDPROC § 62:427.

   c. *At trial.* If a pleading sets out a claim for relief that does not require a responsive pleading, an opposing party may assert at trial any defense to that claim. FRCP 12(b).

2. *Timing of motions, generally*

   a. *Motion and notice of hearing.* Except for letter-motions as permitted by NY R USDCTS&ED Civ Rule 7.1(d), and unless otherwise provided by statute or rule or by the Court in a Judge's Individual Practice or in a direction in a particular case, upon any motion, the notice of motion, supporting affidavits, and memoranda shall be served and filed as follows: on all civil motions, petitions, and applications, other than those described in NY R USDCTS&ED Civ Rule 6.1(a), and other than petitions for writs of habeas corpus, the notice of motion, supporting affidavits, and memoranda of law shall be served by the moving party on all other parties that have appeared in the action. NY R USDCTS&ED Civ Rule 6.1(b)(1). A written motion and notice of the hearing must be served at least fourteen (14) days before the time specified for the hearing, with the following exceptions:

      i. When the motion may be heard ex parte;

      ii. When the Federal Rules of Civil Procedure set a different time; or

      iii. When a court order—which a party may, for good cause, apply for ex parte—sets a different time. FRCP 6(c)(1).

   b. *Supporting affidavit.* Any affidavit supporting a motion must be served with the motion. FRCP 6(c)(2).

3. *Timing of opposing papers.* Except for letter-motions as permitted by NY R USDCTS&ED Civ Rule 7.1(d), and unless otherwise provided by statute or rule or by the Court in a Judge's Individual Practice or in a direction in a particular case, upon any motion, the notice of motion, supporting affidavits, and memoranda shall be served and filed as follows: on all civil motions, petitions, and applications, other than those described in NY R USDCTS&ED Civ Rule 6.1(a), and other than petitions for writs of habeas corpus, any opposing affidavits and answering memoranda shall be served within fourteen (14) days after service of the moving papers. NY R USDCTS&ED Civ Rule 6.1(b)(2).

   a. *Opposing affidavit.* Except as FRCP 59(c) provides otherwise, any opposing affidavit must be served at least seven (7) days before the hearing, unless the court permits service at another time. FRCP 6(c)(2).

4. *Timing of reply papers.* Where the respondent files an answering affidavit setting up a new matter, the moving party ordinarily is allowed a reasonable time to file a reply affidavit since failure to deny the new matter by affidavit may operate as an admission of its truth. AMJUR MOTIONS § 25.

   a. *Reply affidavits and reply memoranda of law.* Except for letter-motions as permitted by NY R

USDCTS&ED Civ Rule 7.1(d), and unless otherwise provided by statute or rule or by the Court in a Judge's Individual Practice or in a direction in a particular case, upon any motion, the notice of motion, supporting affidavits, and memoranda shall be served and filed as follows: on all civil motions, petitions, and applications, other than those described in NY R USDCTS&ED Civ Rule 6.1(a), and other than petitions for writs of habeas corpus, any reply affidavits and memoranda of law shall be served within seven (7) days after service of the answering papers. NY R USDCTS&ED Civ Rule 6.1(b)(3).

5. *Effect of a FRCP 12 motion on the time to serve a responsive pleading.* Unless the court sets a different time, serving a motion under FRCP 12 alters the periods in FRCP 12(a) as follows:

   a. If the court denies the motion or postpones its disposition until trial, the responsive pleading must be served within fourteen (14) days after notice of the court's action; or

   b. If the court grants a motion for a more definite statement, the responsive pleading must be served within fourteen (14) days after the more definite statement is served. FRCP 12(a)(4).

6. *Computation of time*

   a. *Computing time.* FRCP 6 applies in computing any time period specified in the Federal Rules of Civil Procedure, in any local rule or court order, or in any statute that does not specify a method of computing time. FRCP 6(a). In computing any period of time prescribed or allowed by the Local Civil Rules of the United States District Courts for the Southern and Eastern Districts of New York or the Local Admiralty and Maritime Rules, the provisions of FRCP 6 shall apply unless otherwise stated. NY R USDCTS&ED Civ Rule 6.4.

      i. *Period stated in days or a longer unit.* In computing periods of days, refer to FRCP 6 and NY R USDCTS&ED Civ Rule 6.4. NY R USDCTS&ED Civ Rule 6.1(b). When the period is stated in days or a longer unit of time:

         • Exclude the day of the event that triggers the period;

         • Count every day, including intermediate Saturdays, Sundays, and legal holidays; and

         • Include the last day of the period, but if the last day is a Saturday, Sunday, or legal holiday, the period continues to run until the end of the next day that is not a Saturday, Sunday, or legal holiday. FRCP 6(a)(1). In the Local Civil Rules of the United States District Courts for the Southern and Eastern Districts of New York, as in the Federal Rules of Civil Procedure as amended effective December 1, 2009, Saturdays, Sundays, and legal holidays are no longer excluded in computing periods of time. If the last day of the period is a Saturday, Sunday, or legal holiday, the period continues to run until the end of the next day that is not a Saturday, Sunday, or legal holiday. NY R USDCTS&ED Civ Rule 6.4.

      ii. *Period stated in hours.* When the period is stated in hours:

         • Begin counting immediately on the occurrence of the event that triggers the period;

         • Count every hour, including hours during intermediate Saturdays, Sundays, and legal holidays; and

         • If the period would end on a Saturday, Sunday, or legal holiday, the period continues to run until the same time on the next day that is not a Saturday, Sunday, or legal holiday. FRCP 6(a)(2). In the Local Civil Rules of the United States District Courts for the Southern and Eastern Districts of New York, as in the Federal Rules of Civil Procedure as amended effective December 1, 2009, Saturdays, Sundays, and legal holidays are no longer excluded in computing periods of time. If the last day of the period is a Saturday, Sunday, or legal holiday, the period continues to run until the end of the next day that is not a Saturday, Sunday, or legal holiday. NY R USDCTS&ED Civ Rule 6.4.

      iii. *Inaccessibility of the clerk's office.* Unless the court orders otherwise, if the clerk's office is inaccessible:

         • On the last day for filing under FRCP 6(a)(1), then the time for filing is extended to the first accessible day that is not a Saturday, Sunday, or legal holiday; or

         • During the last hour for filing under FRCP 6(a)(2), then the time for filing is extended to

the same time on the first accessible day that is not a Saturday, Sunday, or legal holiday. FRCP 6(a)(3).

    iv. *"Last day" defined.* Unless a different time is set by a statute, local rule, or court order, the last day ends:

- For electronic filing, at midnight in the court's time zone; and

- For filing by other means, when the clerk's office is scheduled to close. FRCP 6(a)(4).

    v. *"Next day" defined.* The "next day" is determined by continuing to count forward when the period is measured after an event and backward when measured before an event. FRCP 6(a)(5).

    vi. *"Legal holiday" defined.* "Legal holiday" means:

- The day set aside by statute for observing New Year's Day, Martin Luther King Jr.'s Birthday, Washington's Birthday, Memorial Day, Independence Day, Labor Day, Columbus Day, Veterans' Day, Thanksgiving Day, or Christmas Day;

- Any day declared a holiday by the President or Congress; and

- For periods that are measured after an event, any other day declared a holiday by the state where the district court is located. FRCP 6(a)(6).

b. *Computation of electronic filing deadlines.* You can file electronically twenty-four (24) hours a day, seven (7) days a week, three hundred sixty-five (365) days a year. NY R USDCTSD CM/ECF, S.D.(II)(13)(13.10). Electronic filing must be completed before midnight local time where the Court is located in order to be considered timely filed that day. NY R USDCTSD CM/ECF, S.D.(I)(3)(3.3); NY R USDCTSD CM/ECF, S.D.(II)(13)(13.10); NY R USDCTSD CM/ECF, S.D.(II)(19)(19.4). An electronically filed document is deemed filed on the "filed on" date indicated on the Notice of Electronic Filing (NEF). NY R USDCTSD CM/ECF, S.D.(II)(13)(13.11).

    i. *Technical failures.* A Filing User whose filing is made untimely as the result of a technical failure may seek appropriate relief from the Court. NY R USDCTSD CM/ECF, S.D.(I)(11). If you missed a filing deadline when the ECF system was out of order, attach a statement to your filing explaining how the interruption in service prevented you from filing in a timely fashion. NY R USDCTSD CM/ECF, S.D.(II)(23)(23.5).

c. *Extending time*

    i. *In general.* When an act may or must be done within a specified time, the court may, for good cause, extend the time:

- With or without motion or notice if the court acts, or if a request is made, before the original time or its extension expires; or

- On motion made after the time has expired if the party failed to act because of excusable neglect. FRCP 6(b)(1).

    ii. *Exceptions.* A court must not extend the time to act under FRCP 50(b), FRCP 50(d), FRCP 52(b), FRCP 59(b), FRCP 59(d), FRCP 59(e), and FRCP 60(b). FRCP 6(b)(2).

    iii. Refer to the United States District Court for the Southern District of New York KeyRules Motion for Continuance/Extension of Time document for more information on extending time.

d. *Additional time after certain kinds of service.* When a party may or must act within a specified time after service and service is made under FRCP 5(b)(2)(C), FRCP 5(b)(2)(D), FRCP 5(b)(2)(E), or FRCP 5(b)(2)(F), three (3) days are added after the period would otherwise expire under FRCP 6(a). FRCP 6(d). Overnight delivery service shall be deemed service by mail for purposes of FRCP 5 and FRCP 6. NY R USDCTS&ED Civ Rule 5.3.

7. *Individual judge practices.* Refer to the Miscellaneous section of this document for information on individual judge practices on timing of documents.

## C. General Requirements

1. *Motions, generally*

    a. *Requirements.* A request for a court order must be made by motion. The motion must:

        i. Be in writing unless made during a hearing or trial;

        ii. State with particularity the grounds for seeking the order; and

        iii. State the relief sought. FRCP 7(b)(1).

    b. *Notice of motion.* A party interested in resisting the relief sought by a motion has a right to notice thereof, and an opportunity to be heard. AMJUR MOTIONS § 12.

        i. In addition to statutory or court rule provisions requiring notice of a motion—the purpose of such a notice requirement having been said to be to prevent a party from being prejudicially surprised by a motion—principles of natural justice dictate that an adverse party generally must be given notice that a motion will be presented to the court. AMJUR MOTIONS § 12.

        ii. "Notice," in this regard, means reasonable notice, including a meaningful opportunity to prepare and to defend against allegations of a motion. AMJUR MOTIONS § 12.

    c. *Writing requirement.* The writing requirement is intended to insure that the adverse parties are informed and have a record of both the motion's pendency and the grounds on which the movant seeks an order. FPP § 1191; Feldberg v. Quechee Lakes Corp., 463 F.3d 195 (2d Cir. 2006).

        i. It is sufficient "if the motion is stated in a written notice of the hearing of the motion." FPP § 1191.

    d. *Particularity requirement.* The particularity requirement insures that the opposing parties will have notice of their opponent's contentions. FEDPROC § 62:364; Goodman v. 1973 26 Foot Trojan Vessel, Arkansas Registration No. AR1439SN, 859 F.2d 71, 12 Fed.R.Serv.3d 645 (8th Cir. 1988). That requirement ensures that notice of the basis for the motion is provided to the court and to the opposing party so as to avoid prejudice, provide the opponent with a meaningful opportunity to respond, and provide the court with enough information to process the motion correctly. FEDPROC § 62:364; Andreas v. Volkswagen of America, Inc., 336 F.3d 789, 56 Fed.R.Serv.3d 6 (8th Cir. 2003).

        i. Reasonable specification of the grounds for a motion is sufficient. However, where a movant fails to state even one ground for granting the motion in question, the movant has failed to meet the minimal standard of "reasonable specification." FEDPROC § 62:364; Martinez v. Trainor, 556 F.2d 818, 23 Fed.R.Serv.2d 403 (7th Cir. 1977).

        ii. The court may excuse the failure to comply with the particularity requirement if it is inadvertent, and where no prejudice is shown by the opposing party. FEDPROC § 62:364.

    e. *Ex parte orders or orders to show cause to bring on a motion.* No ex parte order, or order to show cause to bring on a motion, will be granted except upon a clear and specific showing by affidavit of good and sufficient reasons why a procedure other than by notice of motion is necessary, and stating whether a previous application for similar relief has been made. NY R USDCTS&ED Civ Rule 6.1(d).

    f. *Letter-motions.* Applications for extensions or adjournments, applications for a pre-motion conference, and similar non-dispositive matters as permitted by the instructions regarding ECF published on the website of each respective Court and any pertinent Individual Judge's Practices, may be brought by letter-motion filed via ECF pursuant to NY R USDCTS&ED Civ Rule 5.2(b). NY R USDCTS&ED Civ Rule 7.1(d).

        i. The following list of motions. . .may be made by LETTER-MOTION: (1) Motion to Adjourn Conference; (2) Motion to Change Attorney Name on Roll; (3) Motion to Compel; (4) Motion for Conference; (5) Motion to Consolidate Cases; (6) Motion to Continue; (7) Motion re: Discovery; (8) Motion to Expedite; (9) Motion for Extension of Time; (10) Motion for Extension of Time to Amend; (11) Motion for Extension of Time to Answer; (12) Motion for Extension of Time to Complete Discovery; (13) Motion for Extension of Time to File Document; (14) Motion for Extension of Time to File Response/Reply; (15) Motion for

Extension of Time re Transcript; (16) Motion to File Amicus Brief; (17) Motion for Leave to File Document; (18) Motion for Leave to File Excess Pages; (19) Motion for Local Rule 37.2 Conference; (20) Motion for Oral Argument; (21) Motion to Reopen; (22) Motion to Reopen Case; (23) Motion to Seal Document; (24) Motion to Stay; (25) Motion to Substitute Attorney. NY R USDCTSD CM/ECF, S.D.(II)(13)(13.1).

    ii.    If the Filing User is making a type of motion that does not appear in this list, the motion may not be made by letter. NY R USDCTSD CM/ECF, S.D.(II)(13)(13.1).

    iii.   For more information on letter motions, refer to NY R USDCTSD CM/ECF, S.D.(II)(13)(13.1).

2.   *Motion to dismiss for lack of subject matter jurisdiction.* A party may assert the defense of lack of subject-matter jurisdiction by motion. FRCP 12(b)(1). The objection presented by a motion under FRCP 12(b)(1) challenging the court's subject matter jurisdiction is that the district judge has no authority or competence to hear and decide the case before it. A FRCP 12(b)(1) motion most typically is employed when the movant believes that the claim asserted by the plaintiff does not involve a federal question, and there is no diversity of citizenship between the parties or, in a diversity of citizenship case, the amount in controversy does not exceed the required jurisdictional amount. FPP § 1350.

    a.   *Subject matter jurisdiction.* It always must be remembered that the federal courts are courts of limited jurisdiction and only can adjudicate those cases that fall within Article III of the Constitution (see U.S.C.A. Const. Art. III § 1, et seq.) and a congressional authorization enacted thereunder. FPP § 1350.

       i.   *Federal question.* The district courts shall have original jurisdiction of all civil actions arising under the Constitution, laws, or treaties of the United States. 28 U.S.C.A. § 1331.

       ii.   *Diversity of citizenship; Amount in controversy.* The district courts shall have original jurisdiction of all civil actions where the matter in controversy exceeds the sum or value of seventy-five thousand dollars ($75,000), exclusive of interest and costs, and is between:

- Citizens of different States;

- Citizens of a State and citizens or subjects of a foreign state, except that the district courts shall not have original jurisdiction under 28 U.S.C.A. § 1332 of an action between citizens of a State and citizens or subjects of a foreign state who are lawfully admitted for permanent residence in the United States and are domiciled in the same State;

- Citizens of different States and in which citizens or subjects of a foreign state are additional parties; and

- A foreign state, defined in 28 U.S.C.A. § 1603(a), as plaintiff and citizens of a State or of different States. 28 U.S.C.A. § 1332(a).

    b.   *Types of FRCP 12(b)(1) motions.* There are two separate types of FRCP 12(b)(1) motions to dismiss for lack of subject matter jurisdiction: the "facial attack" and the "factual attack." FEDPROC § 62:440.

       i.   *Facial attack.* The facial attack is addressed to the sufficiency of the allegations of the complaint itself. FEDPROC § 62:440; Stalley ex rel. U.S. v. Orlando Regional Healthcare System, Inc., 524 F.3d 1229 (11th Cir. 2008). On such a motion, the court is merely required to determine whether the plaintiff has sufficiently alleged a basis of subject matter jurisdiction, and the factual allegations of the complaint are taken as true. FEDPROC § 62:440; U.S. ex rel. Atkinson v. PA. Shipbuilding Co., 473 F.3d 506 (3d Cir. 2007).

       ii.   *Factual attack.* The "factual attack," on the other hand, challenges the existence of subject matter jurisdiction in fact, irrespective of the pleadings, and matters outside the pleadings, such as testimony and affidavits, may be considered by the court. FEDPROC § 62:440; Kligman v. I.R.S., 272 Fed.Appx. 166 (3d Cir. 2008); Paper, Allied-Industrial, Chemical and Energy Workers Intern. Union v. Continental Carbon Co., 428 F.3d 1285 (10th Cir. 2005). The trial court in such a situation is free to weigh the evidence and satisfy itself as to the existence of its power to hear the case; therefore, no presumptive truthfulness attaches to the plaintiff's factual allegations. FEDPROC § 62:440; Land v. Dollar, 330 U.S. 731, 67 S.Ct. 1009, 91 L.Ed. 1209 (1947).

c. *Burden.* With the limited exception of the question whether the amount in controversy requirement in diversity of citizenship cases has been satisfied, the extensive case law on the subject makes clear that the burden of proof on a FRCP 12(b)(1) motion is on the party asserting that subject matter jurisdiction exists, which, of course, typically is the plaintiff. FPP § 1350; Thomson v. Gaskill, 315 U.S. 442, 62 S.Ct. 673, 86 L.Ed. 951 (1942). A plaintiff meets the burden of establishing subject matter jurisdiction at the pleading stage by pleading sufficient allegations to show the proper basis for the court to assert subject matter jurisdiction over the action. 2 FEDFORMS § 7:6.

   i. *Federal question.* If subject matter jurisdiction is based on the existence of a federal question, the pleader must show that he or she has alleged a claim for relief arising under federal law and that the claim is not frivolous. FPP § 1350; Baker v. Carr, 369 U.S. 186, 82 S.Ct. 691, 7 L.Ed.2d 663 (1962).

   ii. *Diversity of citizenship.* If jurisdiction is based on diversity of citizenship, on the other hand, the pleader must show that real and complete diversity exists between all of the plaintiffs and all of the defendants, and also that the assertion that the claim exceeds the requisite jurisdictional amount in controversy is made in good faith. FPP § 1350; City of Indianapolis v. Chase Nat. Bank, 314 U.S. 63, 62 S.Ct. 15, 86 L.Ed. 47 (1941). Satisfying this last requirement is a relatively simple task, however, because the claim is deemed to be made in good faith so long as it is not clear to a legal certainty that the claimant could not recover a judgment exceeding the statutorily mandated jurisdictional amount, a matter on which the party challenging the district court's jurisdiction has the burden. FPP § 1350.

d. *Joining motions.* When the motion is based on more than one ground, the cases are legion stating that the district court should consider the FRCP 12(b)(1) challenge first because if it must dismiss the complaint for lack of subject matter jurisdiction, the accompanying defenses and objections become moot and do not need to be determined by the judge. FPP § 1350; Steel Co. v. Citizens for a Better Environment, 523 U.S. 83, 118 S.Ct. 1003, 140 L.Ed.2d 210 (1998). However, there are a number of decisions in which the court has decided one or more defenses in addition to the subject matter jurisdiction question or simply assumed the existence of jurisdiction and gone on to decide another matter. FPP § 1350.

   i. *Right to join.* A motion under FRCP 12 may be joined with any other motion allowed by FRCP 12. FRCP 12(g)(1).

   ii. *Limitation on further motions.* Except as provided in FRCP 12(h)(2) or FRCP 12(h)(3), a party that makes a motion under FRCP 12 must not make another motion under FRCP 12 raising a defense or objection that was available to the party but omitted from its earlier motion. FRCP 12(g)(2).

e. *Waiving and preserving certain defenses.* No defense or objection is waived by joining it with one or more other defenses or objections in a responsive pleading or in a motion. FRCP 12(b).

   i. *Waiver by consent.* The defendant may waive the right to obtain a dismissal prior to trial either by express consent to be sued in a certain district or by some conduct that will be construed as implying consent. FPP § 1352.

   ii. *When some are waived.* A party waives any defense listed in FRCP 12(b)(2) through FRCP 12(b)(5) by:

   - Omitting it from a motion in the circumstances described in FRCP 12(g)(2); or
   - Failing to either: (1) make it by motion under FRCP 12; or (2) include it in a responsive pleading or in an amendment allowed by FRCP 15(a)(1) as a matter of course. FRCP 12(h)(1).

   iii. *When to raise others.* Failure to state a claim upon which relief can be granted, to join a person required by FRCP 19(b), or to state a legal defense to a claim may be raised:

   - In any pleading allowed or ordered under FRCP 7(a);
   - By a motion under FRCP 12(c); or
   - At trial. FRCP 12(h)(2).

    iv. *Lack of subject matter jurisdiction.* If the court determines at any time that it lacks subject-matter jurisdiction, the court must dismiss the action. FRCP 12(h)(3).

3. *Opposing papers.* The Federal Rules of Civil Procedure do not require any formal answer, return, or reply to a motion, except where the Federal Rules of Civil Procedure or local rules may require affidavits, memoranda, or other papers to be filed in opposition to a motion. Such papers are simply to apprise the court of such opposition and the grounds of that opposition. FEDPROC § 62:359. Except for letter-motions as permitted by NY R USDCTS&ED Civ Rule 7.1(d) or as otherwise permitted by the Court, all oppositions and replies with respect to motions shall comply with NY R USDCTS&ED Civ Rule 7.1(a)(2) and NY R USDCTS&ED Civ Rule 7.1(a)(3), and an opposing party who seeks relief that goes beyond the denial of the motion shall comply as well with NY R USDCTS&ED Civ Rule 7.1(a)(1). NY R USDCTS&ED Civ Rule 7.1(b).

    a. *Effect of failure to respond to motion.* Although in the absence of statutory provision or court rule, a motion ordinarily does not require a written answer, when a party files a motion and the opposing party fails to respond, the court may construe such failure to respond as nonopposition to the motion or an admission that the motion was meritorious, may take the facts alleged in the motion as true—the rule in some jurisdictions being that the failure to respond to a fact set forth in a motion is deemed an admission—and may grant the motion if the relief requested appears to be justified. AMJUR MOTIONS § 28.

    b. *Assent or no opposition not determinative.* However, a motion will not be granted automatically simply because an "assent" or a notation of "no opposition" has been filed; federal judges frequently deny motions that have been assented to when it is thought that justice so dictates. FPP § 1190.

    c. *Responsive pleading inappropriate as response to motion.* An attempt to answer or oppose a motion with a responsive pleading usually is not appropriate. FPP § 1190.

4. *Reply papers.* A moving party may be required or permitted to prepare papers in addition to his original motion papers. AMJUR MOTIONS § 25. Papers answering or replying to opposing papers may be appropriate, in the interests of justice, where it appears there is a substantial reason for allowing a reply. Thus, a court may accept reply papers where a party demonstrates that the papers to which it seeks to file a reply raise new issues that are material to the disposition of the question before the court, or where the court determines, sua sponte, that it wishes further briefing of an issue raised in those papers and orders the submission of additional papers. FEDPROC § 62:360. Except for letter-motions as permitted by NY R USDCTS&ED Civ Rule 7.1(d) or as otherwise permitted by the Court, all oppositions and replies with respect to motions shall comply with NY R USDCTS&ED Civ Rule 7.1(a)(2) and NY R USDCTS&ED Civ Rule 7.1(a)(3). NY R USDCTS&ED Civ Rule 7.1(b).

    a. *Function of reply papers.* The function of a reply affidavit is to answer the arguments made in opposition to the position taken by the movant and not to permit the movant to introduce new arguments in support of the motion. AMJUR MOTIONS § 25.

    b. *Issues raised for the first time in a reply document.* However, the view has been followed in some jurisdictions, that as a matter of judicial economy, where there is no prejudice and where the issues could be raised simply by filing a motion to dismiss, the trial court has discretion to consider arguments raised for the first time in a reply memorandum, and that a trial court may grant a motion to strike issues raised for the first time in a reply memorandum. AMJUR MOTIONS § 26.

5. *Orders on motions.* A memorandum signed by the Court of the decision on a motion that does not finally determine all claims for relief, or an oral decision on such a motion, shall constitute the order unless the memorandum or oral decision directs the submission or settlement of an order in more extended form. The notation in the docket of a memorandum or of an oral decision that does not direct the submission or settlement of an order in more extended form shall constitute the entry of the order. Where an order in more extended form is required to be submitted or settled, the notation in the docket of such order shall constitute the entry of the order. NY R USDCTS&ED Civ Rule 6.2.

6. *Complex civil cases.* For information on procedures for complex civil cases, refer to NY R USDCTSD Order 11 Misc 00388.

7. *Related cases.* It shall be the continuing duty of each attorney appearing in any civil or criminal case to

bring promptly to the attention of the Court all facts which said attorney believes are relevant to a determination that said case and one or more pending civil or criminal cases should be heard by the same Judge, in order to avoid unnecessary duplication of judicial effort. As soon as the attorney becomes aware of such relationship, said attorney shall notify the Judges to whom the cases have been assigned. NY R USDCTS&ED Civ Rule 1.6(a). If counsel fails to comply with NY R USDCTS&ED Civ Rule 1.6(a), the Court may assess reasonable costs directly against counsel whose action has obstructed the effective administration of the Court's business. NY R USDCTS&ED Civ Rule 1.6(b).

a. *Determination of relatedness.* Subject to the limitations set forth in NY R USDCTSD Div. Bus., Rule 13(a)(2), a civil case, bankruptcy appeal, or motion to withdraw the bankruptcy reference will be deemed related to one or more civil cases, appeals or motions when the interests of justice and efficiency will be served. In determining relatedness, a judge will consider whether (A) the actions concern the same or substantially similar parties, property, transactions or events; (B) there is substantial factual overlap; (C) the parties could be subjected to conflicting orders; and (D) whether absent a determination of relatedness there would be a substantial duplication of effort and expense, delay, or undue burden on the Court, parties or witnesses. NY R USDCTSD Div. Bus., Rule 13(a)(1). Nothing in this NY R USDCTSD Div. Bus., Rule 13 is intended to preclude parties from moving for consolidated proceedings under FRCP 42. NY R USDCTSD Div. Bus., Rule 13(a)(1). Notwith-standing NY R USDCTSD Div. Bus., Rule 13(a)(1):

   i. Civil cases shall not be deemed related merely because they involve common legal issues or the same parties. NY R USDCTSD Div. Bus., Rule 13(a)(2)(A).

   ii. Other than cases subject to NY R USDCTSD Div. Bus., Rule 4(b) and actions seeking the enforcement of a judgment or settlement in or of an earlier case, civil cases presumptively shall not be deemed related unless both cases are pending before the Court (or the earlier case is on appeal). NY R USDCTSD Div. Bus., Rule 13(a)(2)(B).

b. *Procedure in regard to cases said to be related*

   i. *Disclosure of contention of relatedness.* When a civil case is filed or removed or a bankruptcy appeal or motion to withdraw the reference of an adversary proceeding from the bankruptcy court is filed, the person filing or removing shall disclose on form JSC44C any contention of relatedness and shall file a Related Case Statement stating clearly and succinctly the basis for the contention. A copy of the civil cover sheet and Related Case Statement shall be served with the complaint, notice of removal, notice of appeal, or motion. Any party may contest a claim of relatedness by any other in writing addressed to the judge having the case with the lowest docket number of all cases claimed to be related. However, the foregoing shall not delay the assignment process or the operation of NY R USDCTSD Div. Bus., Rule 13. NY R USDCTSD Div. Bus., Rule 13(b)(1). [Editor's note: the reference to form JSC44C is likely meant to be form JS44C-SDNY: Civil Court Cover Sheet].

   ii. *Claims of relatedness by other parties.* A party other than the one filing a case, bankruptcy appeal or motion to withdraw the reference that contends its case is related to another may so advise in writing the judge assigned in its case and request a transfer of its case to the judge that the party contends has the related case with the lowest docket number. If the assigned judge believes the case is related under NY R USDCTSD Div. Bus., Rule 13(a), he or she shall refer the question to the judge having the case with the lowest docket number. In the event the latter judge agrees, the case shall be transferred to that judge unless the Assignment Committee disagrees. NY R USDCTSD Div. Bus., Rule 13(b)(3).

c. For more information on related cases, refer to NY R USDCTSD Div. Bus., Rule 13.

8. *Alternative dispute resolution (ADR).* The U.S. District Court for the Southern District of New York provides litigants with opportunities to discuss settlement through judicial settlement conferences and mediation. NY R USDCTS&ED Civ Rule 83.9(a).

a. *Consideration of alternative dispute resolution.* In all civil cases, including those eligible for mediation pursuant to NY R USDCTS&ED Civ Rule 83.9(e), each party shall consider the use of mediation or a judicial settlement conference and shall report to the assigned Judge at the initial FRCP 16(b) case management conference, or subsequently, whether the party believes mediation or a judicial settlement conference may facilitate the resolution of the lawsuit. Judges are encouraged to note the availability of the mediation program and/or a judicial settlement conference before, at, or after the initial FRCP 16(b) case management conference. NY R USDCTS&ED Civ Rule 83.9(d).

b. *Mediation.* In mediation, parties and counsel meet, sometimes collectively and sometimes individually, with a neutral third party (the mediator) who has been trained to facilitate confidential settlement discussions. The parties articulate their respective positions and interests and generate options for a mutually agreeable resolution to the dispute. The mediator assists the parties in reaching their own negotiated settlement by defining the issues, probing and assessing the strengths and weaknesses of each party's legal positions, and identifying areas of agreement and disagreement. The main benefits of mediation are that it can result in an expeditious and less costly resolution of the litigation, and can produce creative solutions to complex disputes often unavailable in traditional litigation. NY R USDCTS&ED Civ Rule 83.9(b).

   i. *Mediation program eligibility.* All civil cases other than Social Security, habeas corpus, and tax cases are eligible for mediation, whether assigned to Manhattan or White Plains. NY R USDCTS&ED Civ Rule 83.9(e)(1).

   - The Board of Judges may, by Administrative Order, direct that certain specified categories of cases shall automatically be submitted to the mediation program. The assigned District Judge or Magistrate Judge may issue a written order exempting a particular case with or without the request of the parties. NY R USDCTS&ED Civ Rule 83.9(e)(2).

   - For all other cases, the assigned District Judge or Magistrate Judge may determine that a case is appropriate for mediation and may order that case to mediation, with or without the consent of the parties, before, at, or after the initial FRCP 16(b) case management conference. Alternatively, the parties should notify the assigned Judge at any time of their desire to mediate. NY R USDCTS&ED Civ Rule 83.9(e)(3).

c. *Judicial settlement conferences.* Judicial settlement conferences may be ordered by District Judges or Magistrate Judges with or without the request or consent of the parties. NY R USDCTS&ED Civ Rule 83.9(f).

d. For more information on alternative dispute resolution (ADR), refer to NY R USDCTS&ED Civ Rule 83.9.

9. *Individual judge practices.* Refer to the Miscellaneous section of this document for information on individual judge practices on general requirements for documents.

## D. Documents

1. *Documents for moving party*

   a. *Required documents*

      i. *Notice of motion and motion.* Except for letter-motions as permitted by NY R USDCTS&ED Civ Rule 7.1(d) or as otherwise permitted by the Court, all motions shall include the following motion papers: a notice of motion, or an order to show cause signed by the Court, which shall specify the applicable rules or statutes pursuant to which the motion is brought, and shall specify the relief sought by the motion. NY R USDCTS&ED Civ Rule 7.1(a)(1). Refer to the General Requirements section of this document for information on the notice of motion and motion.

      ii. *Memorandum of law.* Except for letter-motions as permitted by NY R USDCTS&ED Civ Rule 7.1(d) or as otherwise permitted by the Court, all motions shall include the following motion papers: a memorandum of law, setting forth the cases and other authorities relied upon in support of the motion, and divided, under appropriate headings, into as many parts as there are issues to be determined. NY R USDCTS&ED Civ Rule 7.1(a)(2).

      iii. *Certificate of service.* FRCP 5(d) requires that the person making service under FRCP 5 certify that service has been effected. FRCP 5(Advisory Committee Notes). Having such information on file may be useful for many purposes, including proof of service if an issue arises concerning the effectiveness of the service. FRCP 5(Advisory Committee Notes).

      - Such paper service [on attorneys and pro se parties who are not Filing or Receiving Users] must be documented by electronically filing proof of service. NY R USDCTSD CM/ECF, S.D.(I)(9)(9.2); NY R USDCTSD CM/ECF, S.D.(I)(19)(19.3)(b). Pro se parties who are not Filing Users are exempt from that portion of NY R USDCTSD CM/ECF, S.D.(I)(19)(19.3) requiring proof of service to be filed electronically. NY R USDCTSD CM/ECF, S.D.(I)(19)(19.3).

b. *Supplemental documents*

   i. *Supporting evidence.* When a motion relies on facts outside the record, the court may hear the matter on affidavits or may hear it wholly or partly on oral testimony or on depositions. FRCP 43(c). Except for letter-motions as permitted by NY R USDCTS&ED Civ Rule 7.1(d) or as otherwise permitted by the Court, all motions shall include the following motion papers: supporting affidavits and exhibits thereto containing any factual information and portions of the record necessary for the decision of the motion. NY R USDCTS&ED Civ Rule 7.1(a)(3).

   - *Discovery materials.* A party seeking or opposing relief under FRCP 26 through FRCP 37 inclusive, or making or opposing any other motion or application, shall quote or attach only those portions of the depositions, interrogatories, requests for documents, requests for admissions, or other discovery or disclosure materials, together with the responses and objections thereto, that are the subject of the discovery motion or application, or that are cited in papers submitted in connection with any other motion or application. NY R USDCTS&ED Civ Rule 5.1.

   ii. *Notice of constitutional question.* A party that files a pleading, written motion, or other paper drawing into question the constitutionality of a federal or state statute must promptly:

   - *File notice.* File a notice of constitutional question stating the question and identifying the paper that raises it, if: (1) a federal statute is questioned and the parties do not include the United States, one of its agencies, or one of its officers or employees in an official capacity; or (2) a state statute is questioned and the parties do not include the state, one of its agencies, or one of its officers or employees in an official capacity; and

   - *Serve notice.* Serve the notice and paper on the Attorney General of the United States if a federal statute is questioned—or on the state attorney general if a state statute is questioned—either by certified or registered mail or by sending it to an electronic address designated by the attorney general for this purpose. FRCP 5.1(a).

   - *No forfeiture.* A party's failure to file and serve the notice, or the court's failure to certify, does not forfeit a constitutional claim or defense that is otherwise timely asserted. FRCP 5.1(d).

   iii. *Nongovernmental corporate disclosure statement*

   - *Contents.* A nongovernmental corporate party must file two (2) copies of a disclosure statement that: (1) identifies any parent corporation and any publicly held corporation owning ten percent (10%) or more of its stock; or (2) states that there is no such corporation. FRCP 7.1(a).

   - *Time to file; Supplemental filing.* A party must: (1) file the disclosure statement with its first appearance, pleading, petition, motion, response, or other request addressed to the court; and (2) promptly file a supplemental statement if any required information changes. FRCP 7.1(b). For purposes of FRCP 7.1(b)(2), "promptly" shall mean "within fourteen days," that is, parties are required to file a supplemental disclosure statement within fourteen (14) days of the time there is any change in the information required in a disclosure statement filed pursuant to those rules. NY R USDCTS&ED Civ Rule 7.1.1.

   iv. *Notice to pro se litigant who opposes a FRCP 12 motion supported by matters outside the pleadings.* A represented party moving to dismiss or for judgment on the pleadings against a party proceeding pro se, who refers in support of the motion to matters outside the pleadings as described in FRCP 12(b) or FRCP 12(c), shall serve and file the notice in NY R USDCTS&ED Civ Rule 12.1 with the full text of FRCP 56 attached at the time the motion is served. If the Court rules that a motion to dismiss or for judgment on the pleadings will be treated as one for summary judgment pursuant to FRCP 56, and the movant has not previously served and filed the notice required by NY R USDCTS&ED Civ Rule 12.1, the movant shall amend the form notice to reflect that fact and shall serve and file the amended notice within fourteen (14) days of the Court's ruling. NY R USDCTS&ED Civ Rule 12.1. For the notice, refer to NY R USDCTS&ED Civ Rule 12.1.

v.   *Copies of authorities.* In cases involving a pro se litigant, counsel shall, when serving a memorandum of law (or other submissions to the Court), provide the pro se litigant (but not other counsel or the Court) with copies of cases and other authorities cited therein that are unpublished or reported exclusively on computerized databases. Upon request, counsel shall provide the pro se litigant with copies of such unpublished cases and other authorities as are cited in a decision of the Court and were not previously cited by any party. NY R USDCTS&ED Civ Rule 7.2.

vi.  *Proposed order.* Refer to the Format section of this document for information on the format of submitting a proposed order to the court.

vii. *Statement explaining untimely electronic filing.* If you missed a filing deadline when the ECF system was out of order, attach a statement to your filing explaining how the interruption in service prevented you from filing in a timely fashion. NY R USDCTSD CM/ECF, S.D.(II)(23)(23.5).

viii. *Courtesy copies.* Read the judge's Individual Practices to learn if courtesy copies are required. NY R USDCTSD CM/ECF, S.D.(II)(13)(13.17). Judges' Individual Practices should continue to be followed with respect to delivery of courtesy copies. NY R USDCTSD CM/ECF, S.D.(I)(3)(3.4).

2.  *Documents for opposing party*

    a.  *Required documents*

        i.   *Answering memorandum of law.* Except for letter-motions as permitted by NY R USDCTS&ED Civ Rule 7.1(d) or as otherwise permitted by the Court, all oppositions and replies with respect to motions shall comply with NY R USDCTS&ED Civ Rule 7.1(a)(2). NY R USDCTS&ED Civ Rule 7.1(b). Except for letter-motions as permitted by NY R USDCTS&ED Civ Rule 7.1(d) or as otherwise permitted by the Court, all motions shall include the following motion papers: a memorandum of law, setting forth the cases and other authorities relied upon in support of the motion, and divided, under appropriate headings, into as many parts as there are issues to be determined. NY R USDCTS&ED Civ Rule 7.1(a)(2). Refer to the General Requirements section of this document for information on the opposing papers.

        ii.  *Certificate of service.* FRCP 5(d) requires that the person making service under FRCP 5 certify that service has been effected. FRCP 5(Advisory Committee Notes). Having such information on file may be useful for many purposes, including proof of service if an issue arises concerning the effectiveness of the service. FRCP 5(Advisory Committee Notes).

             • Such paper service [on attorneys and pro se parties who are not Filing or Receiving Users] must be documented by electronically filing proof of service. NY R USDCTSD CM/ECF, S.D.(I)(9)(9.2); NY R USDCTSD CM/ECF, S.D.(I)(19)(19.3)(b). Pro se parties who are not Filing Users are exempt from that portion of NY R USDCTSD CM/ECF, S.D.(I)(19)(19.3) requiring proof of service to be filed electronically. NY R USDCTSD CM/ECF, S.D.(I)(19)(19.3).

    b.  *Supplemental documents*

        i.   *Supporting evidence.* When a motion relies on facts outside the record, the court may hear the matter on affidavits or may hear it wholly or partly on oral testimony or on depositions. FRCP 43(c). Except for letter-motions as permitted by NY R USDCTS&ED Civ Rule 7.1(d) or as otherwise permitted by the Court, all oppositions and replies with respect to motions shall comply with NY R USDCTS&ED Civ Rule 7.1(a)(3). NY R USDCTS&ED Civ Rule 7.1(b). Except for letter-motions as permitted by NY R USDCTS&ED Civ Rule 7.1(d) or as otherwise permitted by the Court, all motions shall include the following motion papers: supporting affidavits and exhibits thereto containing any factual information and portions of the record necessary for the decision of the motion. NY R USDCTS&ED Civ Rule 7.1(a)(3).

- *Discovery materials.* A party seeking or opposing relief under FRCP 26 through FRCP 37 inclusive, or making or opposing any other motion or application, shall quote or attach only those portions of the depositions, interrogatories, requests for documents, requests for admissions, or other discovery or disclosure materials, together with the responses and objections thereto, that are the subject of the discovery motion or application, or that are cited in papers submitted in connection with any other motion or application. NY R USDCTS&ED Civ Rule 5.1.

ii. *Notice of constitutional question.* A party that files a pleading, written motion, or other paper drawing into question the constitutionality of a federal or state statute must promptly:

- *File notice.* File a notice of constitutional question stating the question and identifying the paper that raises it, if: (1) a federal statute is questioned and the parties do not include the United States, one of its agencies, or one of its officers or employees in an official capacity; or (2) a state statute is questioned and the parties do not include the state, one of its agencies, or one of its officers or employees in an official capacity; and

- *Serve notice.* Serve the notice and paper on the Attorney General of the United States if a federal statute is questioned—or on the state attorney general if a state statute is questioned—either by certified or registered mail or by sending it to an electronic address designated by the attorney general for this purpose. FRCP 5.1(a).

- *No forfeiture.* A party's failure to file and serve the notice, or the court's failure to certify, does not forfeit a constitutional claim or defense that is otherwise timely asserted. FRCP 5.1(d).

iii. *Copies of authorities.* In cases involving a pro se litigant, counsel shall, when serving a memorandum of law (or other submissions to the Court), provide the pro se litigant (but not other counsel or the Court) with copies of cases and other authorities cited therein that are unpublished or reported exclusively on computerized databases. Upon request, counsel shall provide the pro se litigant with copies of such unpublished cases and other authorities as are cited in a decision of the Court and were not previously cited by any party. NY R USDCTS&ED Civ Rule 7.2.

iv. *Statement explaining untimely electronic filing.* If you missed a filing deadline when the ECF system was out of order, attach a statement to your filing explaining how the interruption in service prevented you from filing in a timely fashion. NY R USDCTSD CM/ECF, S.D.(II)(23)(23.5).

v. *Courtesy copies.* Read the judge's Individual Practices to learn if courtesy copies are required. NY R USDCTSD CM/ECF, S.D.(II)(13)(13.17). Judges' Individual Practices should continue to be followed with respect to delivery of courtesy copies. NY R USDCTSD CM/ECF, S.D.(I)(3)(3.4).

3. *Individual judge practices.* Refer to the Miscellaneous section of this document for information on individual judge practices on required documents.

## E. Format

1. *Form of documents.* The rules governing captions and other matters of form in pleadings apply to motions and other papers. FRCP 7(b)(2).

a. *Paper.* Every pleading, written motion, and other paper must: be plainly written, typed, printed, or copied without erasures or interlineations which materially deface it. NY R USDCTS&ED Civ Rule 11.1(a)(1).

b. *Typeface, margin, and spacing.* The typeface, margins, and spacing of all documents presented for filing must meet the following requirements:

i. All text must be twelve (12) point type or larger, except for text in footnotes which may be ten (10) point type;

    ii.   All documents must have at least one (1) inch margins on all sides;

    iii.   All text must be double-spaced, except for headings, text in footnotes, or block quotations, which may be single-spaced. NY R USDCTS&ED Civ Rule 11.1(b).

c.   *Caption; Names of parties.* Every pleading must have a caption with the court's name, a title, a file number, and a FRCP 7(a) designation. The title of the complaint must name all the parties; the title of other pleadings, after naming the first party on each side, may refer generally to other parties. FRCP 10(a). Every pleading, written motion, and other paper must: bear the docket number and the initials of the District Judge and any Magistrate Judge before whom the action or proceeding is pending, NY R USDCTS&ED Civ Rule 11.1(a)(2).

d.   *Paragraphs; Separate statements.* A party must state its claims or defenses in numbered paragraphs, each limited as far as practicable to a single set of circumstances. A later pleading may refer by number to a paragraph in an earlier pleading. If doing so would promote clarity, each claim founded on a separate transaction or occurrence—and each defense other than a denial—must be stated in a separate count or defense. FRCP 10(b).

e.   *Adoption by reference; Exhibits.* A statement in a pleading may be adopted by reference elsewhere in the same pleading or in any other pleading or motion. A copy of a written instrument that is an exhibit to a pleading is a part of the pleading for all purposes. FRCP 10(c).

f.   *Acceptance by the clerk.* The clerk must not refuse to file a paper solely because it is not in the form prescribed by the Federal Rules of Civil Procedure or by a local rule or practice. FRCP 5(d)(4).

2.   *Form of electronic documents*

a.   *PDF-A.* All documents electronically filed on the ECF system must be in PDF-A format (portable document format). A PDF-A file is created using PDF writer software such as Adobe Acrobat (go to the Adobe website for details). PDF-A files cannot be altered, providing security to the filer and the Court. NY R USDCTSD CM/ECF, S.D.(II)(23)(23.2).

b.   *Size limitation.* No single PDF file may be larger than four megabytes (4 MB). If the filing is too large, the ECF system will not allow it to be filed, and you will not see a Notice of Electronic Filing (NEF or filing receipt) screen. To determine the size of an Adobe Acrobat PDF file click on File, Document Properties, Summary. NY R USDCTSD CM/ECF, S.D.(II)(23)(23.3).

    i.   Converting documents directly from a word processor to PDF-A format creates the smallest possible file in terms of computer memory. If that is not possible, scan your document at low resolution. Within the Adobe Acrobat program, on the "Scan Manager" screen, adjust the settings for black and white and 200 dpi (dots per inch). This allows more pages to fit into a single PDF-A file. If that does not work, separate an oversized file into 2 or more parts. Simply label each file 1a, 1b, 1c, etc. Only relevant excerpts of exhibits should be electronically filed. NY R USDCTSD CM/ECF, S.D.(II)(23)(23.4).

c.   *Attachments and exhibits.* Filing Users must submit in electronic form all documents referenced as exhibits or attachments, unless the Court permits paper filing. NY R USDCTSD CM/ECF, S.D.(I)(5)(5.1).

    i.   A Filing User must submit as exhibits or attachments only those excerpts of the referenced documents that are relevant to the matter under consideration by the Court. Excerpted material must be clearly and prominently identified as such. Filing Users who file excerpts of documents as exhibits or attachments under this procedure do so without prejudice to their right to file timely additional excerpts or the complete document. Responding parties may file timely additional excerpts that they believe are relevant or the complete document. A party may move before the Court for permission to serve and file in hard copy documents that cannot be reasonably scanned. NY R USDCTSD CM/ECF, S.D.(I)(5)(5.2).

    ii.   Exhibits must be filed only as attachments to a document, such as a motion or an affidavit. Do not use the ECF Filing Event for "Motion" to file exhibits separately. Exhibits are the only items that should be attached to electronically filed documents. You are limited to electronically filing only relevant excerpts of exhibits. Excerpts must be clearly identified as such. If the exhibit is too large to be scanned and electronically filed you may contact the ECF Help Desk. NY R USDCTSD CM/ECF, S.D.(II)(15)(15.6).

d. *Letters.* Parties should consult the assigned judge's Individual Practices to determine if the judge accepts letters at all and, if he or she does, whether the judge has any page limitations on letters and/or requires courtesy copies of letters filed on ECF (and, if so, by what means of delivery). All letters addressed to the Court must include a subject line with the case name and docket number (e.g., "Re: Doe v. Smith, 13 Civ. 1234 (ABC)"). NY R USDCTSD CM/ECF, S.D.(II)(13)(13.1).

e. *Proposed orders, proposed judgments, stipulations and consents.* Any document that requires the signature of a judge should not be electronically filed except as an exhibit to another document. Proposed orders, judgments, stipulations and consents should not be submitted through the ECF system. Instead they should be sent by e-mail to the Clerk. Proposed orders should be submitted in word processing format (WordPerfect or Word) rather than as a PDF document. Stipulations should be submitted in PDF-A format. Stipulations must contain ink signatures not s/. Faxed or emailed signatures are acceptable. Please note that Stipulations of Voluntary Dismissal pursuant to FRCP 41(a)(1)(A)(ii) do not require the signature of a judge and must be electronically filed on the ECF system. Questions may be directed to the Orders and Judgments Clerk at the phone numbers listed in NY R USDCTSD CM/ECF, S.D.(II)(18)(18.3). NY R USDCTSD CM/ECF, S.D.(II)(18)(18.3).

   i. Email the proposed order, judgment or stipulation to the email addresses listed in NY R USDCTSD CM/ECF, S.D.(II)(18)(18.3). NY R USDCTSD CM/ECF, S.D.(II)(18)(18.3).

   ii. Pro se litigants who are not Filing Users are exempt from that portion of NY R USDCTSD CM/ECF, S.D.(II)(18)(18.3) that requires litigants to email proposed orders, judgments, stipulations and consents, and shall deliver such documents to the Clerk's Office in paper form. NY R USDCTSD CM/ECF, S.D.(II)(18)(18.3).

3. *Signing of pleadings, motions and other papers*

   a. *Signature.* Every pleading, written motion, and other paper must be signed by at least one attorney of record in the attorney's name—or by a party personally if the party is unrepresented. The paper must state the signer's address, e-mail address, and telephone number. FRCP 11(a). Every pleading, written motion, and other paper must: have the name of each person signing it clearly printed or typed directly below the signature. NY R USDCTS&ED Civ Rule 11.1(a)(3).

      i. *Electronic signatures.* The user log-in and password required to submit documents to the ECF system serve as the Filing User's signature on all electronic documents filed with the Court. NY R USDCTSD CM/ECF, S.D.(I)(8)(8.1); NY R USDCTSD CM/ECF, S.D.(II)(13)(13.14). They also serve as a signature for purposes of the Federal Rules of Civil Procedure, including FRCP 11, the Local Civil Rules of the United States District Courts for the Southern and Eastern Districts of New York, and any other purpose for which a signature is required in connection with proceedings before the Court. NY R USDCTSD CM/ECF, S.D.(I)(8)(8.1).

         • *Signature block.* Electronically filed documents must include a signature block and must set forth the name, address, telephone number and e-mail address all in compliance with the Federal Rules of Civil Procedure and NY R USDCTS&ED Civ Rule 11.1. In the absence of a scanned signature image, the name of the Filing User under whose log-in and password the document is submitted must be preceded by an "s/" typed in the space where the signature would otherwise appear. NY R USDCTSD CM/ECF, S.D.(I)(8)(8.2); NY R USDCTSD CM/ECF, S.D.(II)(13)(13.14).

         • *Documents requiring the signature of a party or witness.* A document requiring the signature of a party or witness shall be electronically filed in a scanned format that contains an image of the actual signature. NY R USDCTSD CM/ECF, S.D.(I)(8)(8.4); NY R USDCTSD CM/ECF, S.D.(II)(13)(13.14).

         • *Documents requiring the signature of a judge.* A Filing User submitting a document electronically that requires a judge's signature must promptly deliver the document in such other form, if any, as the Court requires. NY R USDCTSD CM/ECF, S.D.(I)(4)(4.2).

         • *Documents requiring multiple signatures.* Documents requiring signatures of more than one party must be electronically filed either by: (a) submitting a scanned document containing all necessary signatures; (b) representing the consent of the other parties on the document; (c) identifying on the document the parties whose signatures are required and by the submission of a notice of endorsement by the other parties no later than three business days after filing; or (d) in any other manner approved by the Court. NY R USDCTSD CM/ECF, S.D.(I)(8)(8.5).

    ii. *No verification or accompanying affidavit required for pleadings.* Unless a rule or statute specifically states otherwise, a pleading need not be verified or accompanied by an affidavit. FRCP 11(a).

    iii. *Unsigned papers.* The court must strike an unsigned paper unless the omission is promptly corrected after being called to the attorney's or party's attention. FRCP 11(a).

  b. *Representations to the court.* By presenting to the court a pleading, written motion, or other paper—whether by signing, filing, submitting, or later advocating it—an attorney or unrepresented party certifies that to the best of the person's knowledge, information, and belief, formed after an inquiry reasonable under the circumstances:

    i. It is not being presented for any improper purpose, such as to harass, cause unnecessary delay, or needlessly increase the cost of litigation;

    ii. The claims, defenses, and other legal contentions are warranted by existing law or by a nonfrivolous argument for extending, modifying, or reversing existing law or for establishing new law;

    iii. The factual contentions have evidentiary support or, if specifically so identified, will likely have evidentiary support after a reasonable opportunity for further investigation or discovery; and

    iv. The denials of factual contentions are warranted on the evidence or, if specifically so identified, are reasonably based on belief or a lack of information. FRCP 11(b).

  c. *Sanctions.* If, after notice and a reasonable opportunity to respond, the court determines that FRCP 11(b) has been violated, the court may impose an appropriate sanction on any attorney, law firm, or party that violated FRCP 11(b) or is responsible for the violation. FRCP 11(c)(1). Refer to the United States District Court for the Southern District of New York KeyRules Motion for Sanctions document for more information.

4. *Privacy protection for filings made with the court*

  a. *Redacted filings.* Unless the court orders otherwise, in an electronic or paper filing with the court that contains an individual's Social Security number, taxpayer-identification number, or birth date, the name of an individual known to be a minor, or a financial-account number, a party or nonparty making the filing may include only:

    i. The last four (4) digits of the Social Security number and taxpayer-identification number;

    ii. The year of the individual's birth;

    iii. The minor's initials; and

    iv. The last four (4) digits of the financial-account number. FRCP 5.2(a); NY R USDCTSD CM/ECF, S.D.(II)(21)(21.3).

    v. Caution should be exercised when filing documents that contain the following:

- Personal identifying numbers (PIN #'s), such as a driver's license number;
- Medical records, treatment and diagnosis;
- Employment history;
- Individual financial information;
- Proprietary or trade secret information;
- Information regarding an individual's cooperation with the government. NY R USDCTSD CM/ECF, S.D.(II)(21)(21.4).

b. *Exemptions from the redaction requirement.* The redaction requirement does not apply to the following:

i. A financial-account number that identifies the property allegedly subject to forfeiture in a forfeiture proceeding;

ii. The record of an administrative or agency proceeding;

iii. The official record of a state-court proceeding;

iv. The record of a court or tribunal, if that record was not subject to the redaction requirement when originally filed;

v. A filing covered by FRCP 5.2(c) or FRCP 5.2(d); and

vi. A pro se filing in an action brought under 28 U.S.C.A. § 2241, 28 U.S.C.A. § 2254, or 28 U.S.C.A. § 2255. FRCP 5.2(b).

c. *Limitations on remote access to electronic files; Social Security appeals and immigration cases.* Unless the court orders otherwise, in an action for benefits under the Social Security Act, and in an action or proceeding relating to an order of removal, to relief from removal, or to immigration benefits or detention, access to an electronic file is authorized as follows:

i. The parties and their attorneys may have remote electronic access to any part of the case file, including the administrative record;

ii. Any other person may have electronic access to the full record at the courthouse, but may have remote electronic access only to:

- The docket maintained by the court; and

- An opinion, order, judgment, or other disposition of the court, but not any other part of the case file or the administrative record. FRCP 5.2(c).

d. *Filings made under seal.* The court may order that a filing be made under seal without redaction. The court may later unseal the filing or order the person who made the filing to file a redacted version for the public record. FRCP 5.2(d). For more information on sealing documents, refer to NY R USDCTSD CM/ECF, S.D.(I)(6).

e. *Protective orders.* For good cause, the court may by order in a case:

i. Require redaction of additional information; or

ii. Limit or prohibit a nonparty's remote electronic access to a document filed with the court. FRCP 5.2(e).

f. *Option for additional unredacted filing under seal.* A person making a redacted filing may also file an unredacted copy under seal. The court must retain the unredacted copy as part of the record. FRCP 5.2(f); NY R USDCTSD CM/ECF, S.D.(II)(21)(21.5).

g. *Option for filing a reference list.* A filing that contains redacted information may be filed together with a reference list that identifies each item of redacted information and specifies an appropriate identifier that uniquely corresponds to each item listed. The list must be filed under seal and may be amended as of right. Any reference in the case to a listed identifier will be construed to refer to the corresponding item of information. FRCP 5.2(g); NY R USDCTSD CM/ECF, S.D.(II)(21)(21.5).

h. *Responsibility for redaction.* It is the sole responsibility of counsel and the parties to be sure that all documents comply with the rules of this Court requiring redaction of personal identifiers. Neither the judge nor the Clerk of Court will review documents for compliance with these rules. NY R USDCTSD CM/ECF, S.D.(II)(21)(21.2).

i. *Waiver of protection of identifiers.* A person waives the protection of FRCP 5.2(a) as to the person's own information by filing it without redaction and not under seal. FRCP 5.2(h).

j. For more information on privacy and public access to ECF cases, refer to NY R USDCTSD CM/ECF, S.D.(II)(21).

5. *Individual judge practices.* Refer to the Miscellaneous section of this document for information on individual judge practices on formatting documents.

## F. Filing and Service Requirements

1. *Filing requirements.* Any paper after the complaint that is required to be served—together with a certificate of service—must be filed within a reasonable time after service. FRCP 5(d)(1). Complaints and all subsequent papers are accepted at either courthouse, regardless of the place for which the case is designated. NY R USDCTSD Div. Bus., Rule 22. Subject to the instructions regarding ECF published on the website of each respective Court and any pertinent Individual Judge's Practices, letter-motions permitted by NY R USDCTS&ED Civ Rule 7.1(d) and letters addressed to the Court (but not letters between the parties) may be filed via ECF. NY R USDCTS&ED Civ Rule 5.2(b). For information on electronically filing motions, refer to NY R USDCTSD CM/ECF, S.D.(II)(15).

   a. *How filing is made; In general.* A paper is filed by delivering it:

      i. To the clerk; or

      ii. To a judge who agrees to accept it for filing, and who must then note the filing date on the paper and promptly send it to the clerk. FRCP 5(d)(2).

   b. *Night depository.* A night depository with an automatic date stamp shall be maintained by the Clerk of the Southern District in the Pearl Street Courthouse. After regular business hours, papers for the District Court only may be deposited in the night depository. Such papers will be considered as having been filed in the District Court as of the date stamped thereon, which shall be deemed presumptively correct. NY R USDCTS&ED Civ Rule 1.2.

   c. *Electronic filing*

      i. *Authorization of electronic filing program.* A court may, by local rule, allow papers to be filed, signed, or verified by electronic means that are consistent with any technical standards established by the Judicial Conference of the United States. A local rule may require electronic filing only if reasonable exceptions are allowed. A paper filed electronically in compliance with a local rule is a written paper for purposes of the Federal Rules of Civil Procedure. FRCP 5(d)(3).

         • The Court will accept for filing documents submitted, signed or verified by electronic means, that comply with the rules in NY R USDCTSD CM/ECF, S.D. NY R USDCTSD CM/ECF, S.D.(I). The information in NY R USDCTSD CM/ECF, S.D. applies only to cases assigned to the ECF system. NY R USDCTSD CM/ECF, S.D.(Introduction).

         • Parties serving and filing papers shall follow the instructions regarding Electronic Case Filing (ECF) published on the website of each respective Court. A paper served and filed by electronic means in accordance with such instructions is, for purposes of FRCP 5, served and filed in compliance with the Local Civil Rules of the Southern and Eastern Districts of New York. NY R USDCTS&ED Civ Rule 5.2(a). Parties have an obligation to review the Court's actual order, decree, or judgment (on ECF), which controls, and should not rely on the description on the docket or in the ECF Notice of Electronic Filing (NEF). NY R USDCTS&ED Civ Rule 5.2(c).

         • The following should be observed when filing electronically: (1) the Federal Rules of Civil Procedure, (2) the Local Civil Rules of the United States District Courts for the Southern and Eastern Districts of New York, (3) the assigned judge's Individual Practices, and (4) the Court's Electronic Case Filing Rules & Instructions (NY R USDCTSD CM/ECF, S.D.). NY R USDCTSD CM/ECF, S.D.(Introduction).

      ii. *Scope of electronic filing.* Except as expressly provided and in exceptional circumstances preventing a party from filing electronically, all documents required to be filed with the Court must be filed electronically. Any party unable to comply with this requirement must seek permission of the Court to file in the traditional manner, on paper. Any such application made after regular business hours may be submitted through the night depository box maintained pursuant to NY R USDCTS&ED Civ Rule 1.2. NY R USDCTSD CM/ECF, S.D.(I)(1)(1.1).

         • *Documents filed by pro se litigants.* Unless otherwise ordered by the Court, documents filed by pro se litigants must be filed in the traditional manner, on paper, and will be scanned and docketed by the Clerk's Office into the ECF system. NY R USDCTSD

CM/ECF, S.D.(I)(1)(1.1). Pro se litigants must file pleadings and documents in the traditional manner on paper unless the assigned judge has granted permission to electronically file on the ECF system. NY R USDCTSD CM/ECF, S.D.(Introduction).

- *Letters.* Except for letters to be filed under seal, letters addressed to judges who accept letters may be filed electronically. Parties should consult the assigned judge's Individual Practices to determine if the judge accepts letters at all and, if he or she does, whether the judge has any page limitations on letters and/or requires courtesy copies of letters filed on ECF (and, if so, by what means of delivery). NY R USDCTSD CM/ECF, S.D.(II)(13)(13.1). Letters solely between parties or their counsel or otherwise not addressed to the Court may not be filed electronically on ECF (except as exhibits to an otherwise properly filed document). NY R USDCTSD CM/ECF, S.D.(II)(13)(13.1). For more information on filing letters, refer to NY R USDCTSD CM/ECF, S.D.(II)(13)(13.1).

- *Proposed orders, judgments and decrees.* Proposed orders, judgments and decrees shall be presented as directed by the ECF rules published on the website of each respective Court. NY R USDCTS&ED Civ Rule 77.1. For more information, refer to NY R USDCTS&ED Civ Rule 77.1.

iii. *Exceptions to electronic filing.* In an ECF case, the documents that should not be electronically filed include:

- Miscellaneous Case initiating documents, NY R USDCTSD CM/ECF, S.D.(II)(18)(18.2);

- Proposed orders; proposed judgments, stipulations; consents, NY R USDCTSD CM/ECF, S.D.(II)(18)(18.3);

- Orders to show cause / temporary restraining orders, NY R USDCTSD CM/ECF, S.D.(II)(18)(18.4);

- Sealed documents, NY R USDCTSD CM/ECF, S.D.(II)(18)(18.5); and

- Surety bonds, NY R USDCTSD CM/ECF, S.D.(II)(18)(18.6).

- In cases where the record of an administrative or other prior proceeding must be filed with the Court, such record may be served and filed in hard copy without prior motion and order of the Court. NY R USDCTSD CM/ECF, S.D.(I)(5)(5.3).

- For more documents excepted from electronic filing, and for more information on such documents, refer to NY R USDCTSD CM/ECF, S.D.(II)(18).

iv. *Consequences of electronic filing.* Except as otherwise provided in NY R USDCTSD CM/ECF, S.D.(I)(4), electronic filing of a document in the ECF system consistent with these procedures, together with the transmission of a Notice of Electronic Filing (NEF) from the Court, constitutes filing of the document for all purposes of the Federal Rules of Civil Procedure and the Local Civil Rules of the United States District Courts for the Southern and Eastern Districts of New York and constitutes entry of the document on the docket kept by the Clerk under FRCP 58 and FRCP 79. NY R USDCTSD CM/ECF, S.D.(I)(3)(3.1).

v. For more information on electronic filing, refer to NY R USDCTSD CM/ECF, S.D.

2. *Service requirements*

a. *Service; When required*

i. *In general.* Unless the Federal Rules of Civil Procedure provide otherwise, each of the following papers must be served on every party:

- An order stating that service is required;

- A pleading filed after the original complaint, unless the court orders otherwise under FRCP 5(c) because there are numerous defendants;

- A discovery paper required to be served on a party, unless the court orders otherwise;

- A written motion, except one that may be heard ex parte; and

- A written notice, appearance, demand, or offer of judgment, or any similar paper. FRCP 5(a)(1).

    ii.   *If a party fails to appear.* No service is required on a party who is in default for failing to appear. But a pleading that asserts a new claim for relief against such a party must be served on that party under FRCP 4. FRCP 5(a)(2).

    iii.  *Seizing property.* If an action is begun by seizing property and no person is or need be named as a defendant, any service required before the filing of an appearance, answer, or claim must be made on the person who had custody or possession of the property when it was seized. FRCP 5(a)(3).

b.  *Service; How made*

    i.   *Serving an attorney.* If a party is represented by an attorney, service under FRCP 5 must be made on the attorney unless the court orders service on the party. FRCP 5(b)(1).

    ii.  *Service in general.* A paper is served under FRCP 5 by:

- Handing it to the person;

- Leaving it: (1) at the person's office with a clerk or other person in charge or, if no one is in charge, in a conspicuous place in the office; or (2) if the person has no office or the office is closed, at the person's dwelling or usual place of abode with someone of suitable age and discretion who resides there;

- Mailing it to the person's last known address—in which event service is complete upon mailing;

- Leaving it with the court clerk if the person has no known address;

- Sending it by electronic means if the person consented in writing—in which event service is complete upon transmission, but is not effective if the serving party learns that it did not reach the person to be served; or

- Delivering it by any other means that the person consented to in writing—in which event service is complete when the person making service delivers it to the agency designated to make delivery. FRCP 5(b)(2).

    iii.  *Service by overnight delivery.* Service upon an attorney may be made by overnight delivery service. "Overnight delivery service" means any delivery service which regularly accepts items for overnight delivery. Overnight delivery service shall be deemed service by mail for purposes of FRCP 5 and FRCP 6. NY R USDCTS&ED Civ Rule 5.3.

    iv.  *Service by electronic means.* Parties serving and filing papers shall follow the instructions regarding Electronic Case Filing (ECF) published on the website of each respective Court. A paper served and filed by electronic means in accordance with such instructions is, for purposes of FRCP 5, served and filed in compliance with the Local Civil Rules of the United States District Courts for the Southern and Eastern Districts of New York. NY R USDCTS&ED Civ Rule 5.2(a). Parties have an obligation to review the Court's actual order, decree, or judgment (on ECF), which controls, and should not rely on the description on the docket or in the ECF Notice of Electronic Filing (NEF). NY R USDCTS&ED Civ Rule 5.2(c).

- *Notice of electronic filing (NEF).* In cases assigned to the ECF system, service is complete provided all parties receive a Notice of Electronic Filing (NEF), which is sent automatically by email from the Court (see the NEF for a list of who did/did not receive notice electronically). Transmission of the NEF constitutes service upon all Filing and Receiving Users who are listed as recipients of notice by electronic mail. NY R USDCTSD CM/ECF, S.D.(I)(9)(9.1). In cases assigned to the ECF system, if all parties receive a NEF, service is complete upon transmission of the NEF by the Court, and you are not required to serve a paper copy. NY R USDCTSD CM/ECF, S.D.(II)(19)(19.2). It remains the duty of Filing and Receiving Users to maintain current contact information with the court and to regularly review the docket sheet of the case. NY R USDCTSD CM/ECF, S.D.(I)(9)(9.1).

- *Mailing of court-initiated documents.* The Clerk's Office will no longer mail paper copies of court-initiated documents to Filing and Receiving Users. The Clerk's Office will mail copies of all court-initiated documents to pro se parties who have not registered as Filing or Receiving Users. NY R USDCTSD CM/ECF, S.D.(II)(19)(19.1).

- *No receipt of a NEF.* If any party does not receive a NEF, you are required to accomplish service on that party in the traditional manner, in paper form. NY R USDCTSD CM/ECF, S.D.(II)(19)(19.2). The NEF receipt will inform you who will receive notice of the filing "electronically" (by e-mail from the Court) and who will receive notice "by other means" (traditional service in paper form). NY R USDCTSD CM/ECF, S.D.(II)(19)(19.2).

- *Service on non-filing or non-receiving users.* Attorneys and pro se parties who are not Filing or Receiving Users must be served with a paper copy of any electronically filed pleading or other document. Service of such paper copy must be made according to the Federal Rules of Civil Procedure and the Local Civil Rules of the United States District Courts for the Southern and Eastern Districts of New York. NY R USDCTSD CM/ECF, S.D.(I)(9)(9.2). Such paper service must be documented by electronically filing proof of service. NY R USDCTSD CM/ECF, S.D.(I)(9)(9.2); NY R USDCTSD CM/ECF, S.D.(II)(19)(19.2). Where the Clerk scans and electronically files pleadings and documents on behalf of a pro se party, the associated NEF constitutes service. NY R USDCTSD CM/ECF, S.D.(I)(9)(9.2).

- For more information on service by electronic means, refer to NY R USDCTSD CM/ECF, S.D.(II)(19).

    v. *Using court facilities.* If a local rule so authorizes, a party may use the court's transmission facilities to make service under FRCP 5(b)(2)(E). FRCP 5(b)(3).

  c. *Serving numerous defendants*

    i. *In general.* If an action involves an unusually large number of defendants, the court may, on motion or on its own, order that:

- Defendants' pleadings and replies to them need not be served on other defendants;

- Any crossclaim, counterclaim, avoidance, or affirmative defense in those pleadings and replies to them will be treated as denied or avoided by all other parties; and

- Filing any such pleading and serving it on the plaintiff constitutes notice of the pleading to all parties. FRCP 5(c)(1).

    ii. *Notifying parties.* A copy of every such order must be served on the parties as the court directs. FRCP 5(c)(2).

3. *Individual judge practices.* Refer to the Miscellaneous section of this document for information on individual judge practices on filing and serving documents.

# G. Hearings

1. *Hearings, generally*

  a. *Oral argument.* Due process does not require that oral argument be permitted on a motion and, except as otherwise provided by local rule, the district court has discretion to determine whether it will decide the motion on the papers or hear argument by counsel (and perhaps receive evidence). FPP § 1190; F.D.I.C. v. Deglau, 207 F.3d 153 (3d Cir. 2000). The parties and their attorneys shall only appear to argue the motion if so directed by the Court by order or by a Judge's Individual Practice. NY R USDCTS&ED Civ Rule 6.1(c).

  b. *Providing a regular schedule for oral hearings.* A court may establish regular times and places for oral hearings on motions. FRCP 78(a).

  c. *Providing for submission on briefs.* By rule or order, the court may provide for submitting and determining motions on briefs, without oral hearings. FRCP 78(b).

2. *Hearing on FRCP 12 defenses before trial.* If a party so moves, any defense listed in FRCP 12(b)(1) through FRCP 12(b)(7)—whether made in a pleading or by motion—and a motion under FRCP 12(c) must be heard and decided before trial unless the court orders a deferral until trial. FRCP 12(i).

3. *Hearing on motion to dismiss for lack of subject matter jurisdiction.* It may be error for a court to dismiss a case on the defendant's motion to dismiss for lack of subject matter jurisdiction without first holding a hearing, as FRCP 12(b)(1) requires a preliminary hearing or hearing at trial to determine any disputed facts upon which the motion or opposition to it is predicated. FEDPROC § 62:435.

4. *Individual judge practices.* Refer to the Miscellaneous section of this document for information on individual judge practices on hearings.

## H. Forms

### 1. Federal Motion to Dismiss for Lack of Subject Matter Jurisdiction Forms

a. Motion to dismiss for lack of subject-matter jurisdiction. 2C FEDFORMS § 11:35.

b. Motion to dismiss for lack of subject-matter jurisdiction; Want of diversity of citizenship because requisite diversity not alleged. 2C FEDFORMS § 11:37.

c. Motion to dismiss for lack of subject-matter jurisdiction; Want of diversity on a factual basis and because requisite diversity not alleged. 2C FEDFORMS § 11:38.

d. Motion to dismiss for lack of subject-matter jurisdiction; Want of diversity of citizenship because state of incorporation and principal place of business of defendant not as alleged. 2C FEDFORMS § 11:39.

e. Motion to dismiss for lack of subject-matter jurisdiction; Want of diversity of citizenship because principal place of business of defendant not as alleged. 2C FEDFORMS § 11:40.

f. Motion to dismiss for lack of subject-matter jurisdiction; Failure to comply with procedural requirements. 2C FEDFORMS § 11:41.

g. Motion to dismiss for lack of subject-matter jurisdiction; Want of diversity upon realignment of parties according to interest. 2C FEDFORMS § 11:42.

h. Motion to dismiss for lack of subject-matter jurisdiction; Want of federal question. 2C FEDFORMS § 11:43.

i. Motion to dismiss for lack of subject-matter jurisdiction; Unsubstantial federal question. 2C FEDFORMS § 11:44.

j. Motion to dismiss for lack of subject-matter jurisdiction; Want of amount in controversy. 2C FEDFORMS § 11:45.

k. Motion to dismiss for lack of subject-matter jurisdiction; Want of amount in controversy; Insurance policy limits do not exceed required jurisdictional amount. 2C FEDFORMS § 11:46.

l. Motion to dismiss for lack of subject-matter jurisdiction; Want of amount in controversy; Claim for damages in excess of jurisdictional amount not made in good faith. 2C FEDFORMS § 11:47.

m. Motion to dismiss for lack of subject-matter jurisdiction; Want of amount in controversy; Made after judgment. 2C FEDFORMS § 11:48.

n. Motion to dismiss for lack of subject-matter jurisdiction; Want of consent by the United States to be sued. 2C FEDFORMS § 11:49.

o. Motion to dismiss for lack of subject-matter jurisdiction; Want of consent by United States to be sued; United States indispensable party. 2C FEDFORMS § 11:50.

p. Affidavit; In opposition to motion to dismiss for lack of diversity; Assignment of claim to plaintiff bona fide. FEDPROF § 1:894.

q. Motion; To dismiss; Plaintiff and defendant citizens of same state when action filed. FEDPROF § 1:888.

r. Motion to dismiss; Assignment to nonresident for purpose of invoking federal jurisdiction sham and ineffective to confer jurisdiction. FEDPROF § 1:889.

s. Motion to dismiss; For lack of diversity in third-party complaint. FEDPROF § 1:890.

t. Affidavit; In support of motion to dismiss for want of diversity of citizenship; Plaintiff and defendant citizens of same state on date action filed. FEDPROF § 1:892.

u. Motion; To dismiss; Insufficiency of amount in controversy. FEDPROF § 1:897.

v. Motion to dismiss; Bad faith in claiming jurisdictional amount. FEDPROF § 1:898.

w. Motion; To dismiss; Lack of jurisdiction over subject matter, generally. FEDPROF § 1:903.

x. Motion to dismiss; Absence of federal question. FEDPROF § 1:904.

y. Motion to dismiss; Absence of federal question; Failure to exhaust state remedies. FEDPROF § 1:905.

z. Affidavit; In opposition to motion to dismiss for absence of jurisdiction over subject matter. FEDPROF § 1:906.

## I. Applicable Rules

1. *Federal rules*

   a. Federal question. 28 U.S.C.A. § 1331.

   b. Diversity of citizenship; Amount in controversy; Costs. 28 U.S.C.A. § 1332.

   c. Serving and filing pleadings and other papers. FRCP 5.

   d. Constitutional challenge to a statute; Notice, certification, and intervention. FRCP 5.1.

   e. Privacy protection for filings made with the court. FRCP 5.2.

   f. Computing and extending time; Time for motion papers. FRCP 6.

   g. Pleadings allowed; Form of motions and other papers. FRCP 7.

   h. Disclosure statement. FRCP 7.1.

   i. Form of pleadings. FRCP 10.

   j. Signing pleadings, motions, and other papers; Representations to the court; Sanctions. FRCP 11.

   k. Defenses and objections; When and how presented; Motion for judgment on the pleadings; Consolidating motions; Waiving defenses; Pretrial hearing. FRCP 12.

   l. Taking testimony. FRCP 43.

   m. Hearing motions; Submission on briefs. FRCP 78.

2. *Local rules*

   a. Night depository. NY R USDCTS&ED Civ Rule 1.2.

   b. Duty of attorneys in related cases. NY R USDCTS&ED Civ Rule 1.6.

   c. Filing of discovery materials. NY R USDCTS&ED Civ Rule 5.1.

   d. Electronic service and filing of documents. NY R USDCTS&ED Civ Rule 5.2.

   e. Service by overnight delivery. NY R USDCTS&ED Civ Rule 5.3.

   f. Service and filing of motion papers. NY R USDCTS&ED Civ Rule 6.1.

   g. Orders on motions. NY R USDCTS&ED Civ Rule 6.2.

   h. Computation of time. NY R USDCTS&ED Civ Rule 6.4.

   i. Motion papers. NY R USDCTS&ED Civ Rule 7.1.

   j. Disclosure statement. NY R USDCTS&ED Civ Rule 7.1.1.

   k. Authorities to be provided to pro se litigants. NY R USDCTS&ED Civ Rule 7.2.

   l. Form of pleadings, motions, and other papers. NY R USDCTS&ED Civ Rule 11.1.

   m. Notice to pro se litigant who opposes a FRCP 12 motion supported by matters outside the pleadings. NY R USDCTS&ED Civ Rule 12.1.

   n. Submission of orders, judgments and decrees. NY R USDCTS&ED Civ Rule 77.1.

   o. Alternative dispute resolution (Southern District only). NY R USDCTS&ED Civ Rule 83.9.

   p. Electronic case filing rules and instructions. NY R USDCTSD CM/ECF, S.D.

   q. Related cases. NY R USDCTSD Div. Bus., Rule 13.

   r. Filing at either courthouse. NY R USDCTSD Div. Bus., Rule 22.

## J. Miscellaneous

**NOTE: Individual judges' rules may apply. For available judge-level information, refer to:**

DISTRICT JUDGE RONNIE ABRAMS: NY R USDCTSD Abrams-Civ Prac; NY R USDCTSD Abrams-Crim Prac; NY R USDCTSD Abrams-Pro Se; NY R USDCTSD Abrams-Case Mgt; NY R USDCTSD Abrams-Jury.

DISTRICT JUDGE DEBORAH A. BATTS: NY R USDCTSD Batts-Practices.

DISTRICT JUDGE RICHARD M. BERMAN: NY R USDCTSD Berman-Practices; NY R USDCTSD Berman-Default; NY R USDCTSD Berman-Sentencing; NY R USDCTSD Berman-Media.

DISTRICT JUDGE VINCENT L. BRICCETTI: NY R USDCTSD Briccetti-Practices; NY R USDCTSD Briccetti-Plan; NY R USDCTSD Briccetti-Notice.

DISTRICT JUDGE VERNON S. BRODERICK: NY R USDCTSD Broderick-Civil; NY R USDCTSD Broderick-Crim; NY R USDCTSD Broderick-Case Mgt; NY R USDCTSD Broderick-Jury.

DISTRICT JUDGE NAOMI REICE BUCHWALD: NY R USDCTSD Buchwald-Practices.

DISTRICT JUDGE VALERIE E. CAPRONI: NY R USDCTSD Caproni-Prac; NY R USDCTSD Caproni--Pro Se; NY R USDCTSD Caproni-Case Mgt; NY R USDCTSD Caproni-Crim Prac.

DISTRICT JUDGE ANDREW L. CARTER JR.: NY R USDCTSD Carter-Practices.

DISTRICT JUDGE KEVIN P. CASTEL: NY R USDCTSD Castel-Practices; NY R USDCTSD Castel-Default; NY R USDCTSD Castel-Scheduling; NY R USDCTSD Castel-Complex; NY R USDCTSD Castel-Trials; NY R USDCTSD Castel-Sentencing.

DISTRICT JUDGE DENISE L. COTE: NY R USDCTSD Cote-Civil Practices; NY R USDCTSD Cote-Pro Se; NY R USDCTSD Cote-Maritime Ord; NY R USDCTSD Cote-Crim Practices; NY R USDCTSD Cote-Crim Trials; NY R USDCTSD Cote-Sentencing.

DISTRICT JUDGE PAUL A. CROTTY: NY R USDCTSD Crotty-Practices; NY R USDCTSD Crotty-Sentencing; NY R USDCTSD Crotty-Calls; NY R USDCTSD Crotty-Scheduling.

DISTRICT JUDGE GEORGE B. DANIELS: NY R USDCTSD Daniels-Practices.

DISTRICT JUDGE KEVIN T. DUFFY: NY R USDCTSD Duffy-Practices.

DISTRICT JUDGE PAUL A. ENGELMAYER: NY R USDCTSD Engelmayer-Practices; NY R USDCTSD Engelmayer-Scheduling; NY R USDCTSD Engelmayer-Sentencing; NY R USDCTSD Engelmayer-Pro Se; NY R USDCTSD Engelmayer-Crim.

DISTRICT JUDGE KATHERINE POLK FAILLA: NY R USDCTSD Failla-Civ Prac; NY R USDCTSD Failla-Crim Prac; NY R USDCTSD Failla-Case Mgt.

DISTRICT JUDGE KATHERINE B. FORREST: NY R USDCTSD Forrest-Civil Prac; NY R USDCTSD Forrest-Crim Prac; NY R USDCTSD Forrest-Crim Pretrial; NY R USDCTSD Forrest-Scheduling; NY R USDCTSD Forrest-Patent Scheduling; NY R USDCTSD Forrest-Sentencing; NY R USDCTSD Forrest-Order 1; NY R USDCTSD Forrest-Order 2.

DISTRICT JUDGE JESSE M. FURMAN: NY R USDCTSD Furman-Civil Prac; NY R USDCTSD Furman-Crim Prac; NY R USDCTSD Furman-Pro Se Prac; NY R USDCTSD Furman-Trials; NY R USDCTSD Furman-Scheduling; NY R USDCTSD Furman-Rights.

DISTRICT JUDGE PAUL G. GARDEPHE: NY R USDCTSD Gardephe-Civ Prac; NY R USDCTSD Gardephe-Pretrial; NY R USDCTSD Gardephe-Prot Ord; NY R USDCTSD Gardephe-Maritime; NY R USDCTSD Gardephe-Crim Prac; NY R USDCTSD Gardephe-Trial.

DISTRICT JUDGE THOMAS P. GRIESA: NY R USDCTSD Griesa-Practices.

DISTRICT JUDGE CHARLES S. HAIGHT: NY R USDCTSD Haight-Practices.

DISTRICT JUDGE ALVIN K. HELLERSTEIN: NY R USDCTSD Hellerstein-Practices; NY R USDCTSD Hellerstein--Sept 11.

DISTRICT JUDGE LEWIS A. KAPLAN: NY R USDCTSD Kaplan-Practices; NY R USDCTSD Kaplan-Sentencing.

DISTRICT JUDGE KENNETH M. KARAS: NY R USDCTSD Karas-Practices; NY R USDCTSD Karas-Case Mgt; NY R USDCTSD Karas-Default; NY R USDCTSD Karas-Sentencing; NY R USDCTSD Karas-Rights.

DISTRICT JUDGE JOHN F. KEENAN: NY R USDCTSD Keenan-Practices.

DISTRICT JUDGE JOHN G. KOELTL: NY R USDCTSD Koeltl-Practices.

DISTRICT JUDGE VICTOR MARRERO: NY R USDCTSD Marrero-Practices; NY R USDCTSD Marrero-Scheduling; NY R USDCTSD Marrero-Default; NY R USDCTSD Marrero-Trial Proc.

DISTRICT JUDGE COLLEEN McMAHON: NY R USDCTSD McMahon-Practices; NY R USDCTSD McMahon-RICO; NY R USDCTSD McMahon-Copies; NY R USDCTSD McMahon-Scheduling; NY R US-DCTSD McMahon-Elec Disc; NY R USDCTSD McMahon-Sentencing.

DISTRICT JUDGE ALISON J. NATHAN: NY R USDCTSD Nathan-Civ Prac; NY R USDCTSD Nathan-Crim Prac; NY R USDCTSD Nathan-Pro Se; NY R USDCTSD Nathan-Scheduling.

DISTRICT JUDGE J. PAUL OETKEN: NY R USDCTSD Oetken-Civ Prac; NY R USDCTSD Oetken-Case Mgt; NY R USDCTSD Oetken-Crim Prac; NY R USDCTSD Oetken-Pro Se.

DISTRICT JUDGE WILLIAM H. PAULEY, III: NY R USDCTSD Pauley-Crim Cases; NY R USDCTSD Pauley-Practices.

DISTRICT JUDGE LORETTA A. PRESKA: NY R USDCTSD Preska-Practices.

DISTRICT JUDGE JED S. RAKOFF: NY R USDCTSD Rakoff-Practices; NY R USDCTSD Rakoff-Scheduling; NY R USDCTSD Rakoff-Prot Ord; NY R USDCTSD Rakoff-Maritime Ord.

DISTRICT JUDGE EDGARDO RAMOS: NY R USDCTSD Ramos--Practices; NY R USDCTSD Ramos-Case Mgt.

DISTRICT JUDGE NELSON S. ROMAN: NY R USDCTSD Roman-Civ Prac; NY R USDCTSD Roman-Pro Se; NY R USDCTSD Roman-Crim Prac; NY R USDCTSD Roman-Case Mgt.

DISTRICT JUDGE LEONARD B. SAND: NY R USDCTSD Sand-Practices.

DISTRICT JUDGE LORNA G. SCHOFIELD: NY R USDCTSD Schofield-Civ Prac; NY R USDCTSD Schofield-Crim Prac; NY R USDCTSD Schofield-Sched; NY R USDCTSD Schofield-Pro Se; NY R USDCTSD Schofield-Advice.

DISTRICT JUDGE CATHY SEIBEL: NY R USDCTSD Seibel-Practices.

DISTRICT JUDGE LOUIS L. STANTON: NY R USDCTSD Stanton-Practices; NY R USDCTSD Stanton-Pretrial.

DISTRICT JUDGE SIDNEY H. STEIN: NY R USDCTSD Stein-Practices.

DISTRICT JUDGE RICHARD J. SULLIVAN: NY R USDCTSD Sullivan-Practices; NY R USDCTSD Sullivan-Scheduling; NY R USDCTSD Sullivan-Sentencing; NY R USDCTSD Sullivan-Juries; NY R USDCTSD Sullivan-Trial; NY R USDCTSD Sullivan-Default.

DISTRICT JUDGE LAURA TAYLOR SWAIN: NY R USDCTSD Swain-Practices; NY R USDCTSD Swain-Trial; NY R USDCTSD Swain-Crim Trial; NY R USDCTSD Swain-Juries; NY R USDCTSD Swain-Sentencing; NY R USDCTSD Swain-Rights.

DISTRICT JUDGE ROBERT W. SWEET: NY R USDCTSD Sweet-Practices.

DISTRICT JUDGE ANALISA TORRES: NY R USDCTSD Torres-Civ Prac; NY R USDCTSD Torres-Pro Se; NY R USDCTSD Torres-Scheduling.

DISTRICT JUDGE KIMBA M. WOOD: NY R USDCTSD Wood-Practices; NY R USDCTSD Wood-Scheduling; NY R USDCTSD Wood-Discovery; NY R USDCTSD Wood-RICO; NY R USDCTSD Wood-Juries; NY R USDCTSD Wood-Trial; NY R USDCTSD Wood-Media.

DISTRICT JUDGE GREGORY H. WOODS: NY R USDCTSD Woods-Civ Prac; NY R USDCTSD Woods-Pro Se; NY R USDCTSD Woods-Sched; NY R USDCTSD Woods-Crim Prac; NY R USDCTSD Woods-Protect Order; NY R USDCTSD Woods-Speedy Trial.

MAGISTRATE JUDGE JAMES L. COTT: NY R USDCTSD Cott-Practices; NY R USDCTSD Cott-Settlement.

MAGISTRATE JUDGE PAUL E. DAVISON: NY R USDCTSD Davison-Practices.

MAGISTRATE JUDGE RONALD L. ELLIS: NY R USDCTSD Ellis-Practices.

MAGISTRATE JUDGE KEVIN N. FOX: NY R USDCTSD Fox-Practices; NY R USDCTSD Fox-Settlement.

MAGISTRATE JUDGE JAMES C. FRANCIS: NY R USDCTSD Francis-Practices.

MAGISTRATE JUDGE DEBRA FREEMAN: NY R USDCTSD Freeman-Practices; NY R USDCTSD Freeman-Settlement.

MAGISTRATE JUDGE GABRIEL W. GORENSTEIN: NY R USDCTSD Gorenstein-Practices; NY R USDCTSD Gorenstein-Ackn.

MAGISTRATE JUDGE FRANK MAAS: NY R USDCTSD Maas-Practices; NY R USDCTSD Maas-Discontinuance; NY R USDCTSD Maas-Conf; NY R USDCTSD Maas-Settlement.

MAGISTRATE JUDGE JUDITH C. McCARTHY: NY R USDCTSD McCarthy-Practices; NY R USDCTSD McCarthy-Conduct.

MAGISTRATE JUDGE BARBARA MOSES: NY R USDCTSD Moses-Practices.

MAGISTRATE JUDGE SARAH NETBURN: NY R USDCTSD Netburn-Civil; NY R USDCTSD Netburn-Settlement; NY R USDCTSD Netburn-Case Mgt; NY R USDCTSD Netburn--Pro Se.

MAGISTRATE JUDGE ANDREW J. PECK: NY R USDCTSD Peck-Practices; NY R USDCTSD Peck-Order; NY R USDCTSD Peck-Rule 502(d).

MAGISTRATE JUDGE HENRY PITMAN: NY R USDCTSD Pitman-Practices.

MAGISTRATE JUDGE LISA MARGARET SMITH: NY R USDCTSD Smith-Practices; NY R USDCTSD Smith-Trials.

# Motions, Oppositions and Replies
## Motion to Dismiss for Lack of Personal Jurisdiction

### Document Last Updated September 2016

**A. Checklist**

  (I) ❏ Matters to be considered by moving party

    (a) ❏ Required documents

      (1) ❏ Notice of motion and motion

      (2) ❏ Memorandum of law

      (3) ❏ Certificate of service

    (b) ❏ Supplemental documents

      (1) ❏ Supporting evidence

      (2) ❏ Notice of constitutional question

      (3) ❏ Nongovernmental corporate disclosure statement

      (4) ❏ Notice to pro se litigant who opposes a FRCP 12 motion supported by matters outside the pleadings

      (5) ❏ Copies of authorities

      (6) ❏ Proposed order

      (7) ❏ Statement explaining untimely electronic filing

      (8) ❏ Courtesy copies

    (c) ❏ Timing

      (1) ❏ Every defense to a claim for relief in any pleading must be asserted in the responsive pleading if one is required

      (2) ❏ A motion asserting any of the defenses in FRCP 12(b) must be made before pleading if a responsive pleading is allowed

(3) ❏ If a pleading sets out a claim for relief that does not require a responsive pleading, an opposing party may assert at trial any defense to that claim

(4) ❏ A written motion and notice of the hearing must be served at least fourteen (14) days before the time specified for the hearing, with the following exceptions: (i) when the motion may be heard ex parte; (ii) when the Federal Rules of Civil Procedure set a different time; or (iii) when a court order—which a party may, for good cause, apply for ex parte—sets a different time

(5) ❏ Any affidavit supporting a motion must be served with the motion

(II) ❏ Matters to be considered by opposing party

  (a) ❏ Required documents

    (1) ❏ Answering memorandum of law

    (2) ❏ Certificate of service

  (b) ❏ Supplemental documents

    (1) ❏ Supporting evidence

    (2) ❏ Notice of constitutional question

    (3) ❏ Copies of authorities

    (4) ❏ Statement explaining untimely electronic filing

    (5) ❏ Courtesy copies

  (c) ❏ Timing

    (1) ❏ Any opposing affidavits and answering memoranda shall be served within fourteen (14) days after service of the moving papers

    (2) ❏ Except as FRCP 59(c) provides otherwise, any opposing affidavit must be served at least seven (7) days before the hearing, unless the court permits service at another time

## B. Timing

1. *Motion to dismiss for lack of personal jurisdiction*

  a. *In a responsive pleading.* Every defense to a claim for relief in any pleading must be asserted in the responsive pleading if one is required. FRCP 12(b).

  b. *By motion.* A motion asserting any of the defenses in FRCP 12(b) must be made before pleading if a responsive pleading is allowed. FRCP 12(b). Although FRCP 12(b) encourages the responsive pleader to file a motion to dismiss before filing the answer, nothing in FRCP 12 prohibits the filing of a motion to dismiss with the answer. An untimely motion to dismiss may be considered if the defense asserted in the motion was previously raised in the responsive pleading. FEDPROC § 62:427.

  c. *At trial.* If a pleading sets out a claim for relief that does not require a responsive pleading, an opposing party may assert at trial any defense to that claim. FRCP 12(b).

2. *Timing of motions, generally*

  a. *Motion and notice of hearing.* Except for letter-motions as permitted by NY R USDCTS&ED Civ Rule 7.1(d), and unless otherwise provided by statute or rule or by the Court in a Judge's Individual Practice or in a direction in a particular case, upon any motion, the notice of motion, supporting affidavits, and memoranda shall be served and filed as follows: on all civil motions, petitions, and applications, other than those described in NY R USDCTS&ED Civ Rule 6.1(a), and other than petitions for writs of habeas corpus, the notice of motion, supporting affidavits, and memoranda of law shall be served by the moving party on all other parties that have appeared in the action. NY R USDCTS&ED Civ Rule 6.1(b)(1). A written motion and notice of the hearing must be served at least fourteen (14) days before the time specified for the hearing, with the following exceptions:

    i. When the motion may be heard ex parte;

    ii. When the Federal Rules of Civil Procedure set a different time; or

iii. When a court order—which a party may, for good cause, apply for ex parte—sets a different time. FRCP 6(c)(1).

b. *Supporting affidavit.* Any affidavit supporting a motion must be served with the motion. FRCP 6(c)(2).

3. *Timing of opposing papers.* Except for letter-motions as permitted by NY R USDCTS&ED Civ Rule 7.1(d), and unless otherwise provided by statute or rule or by the Court in a Judge's Individual Practice or in a direction in a particular case, upon any motion, the notice of motion, supporting affidavits, and memoranda shall be served and filed as follows: on all civil motions, petitions, and applications, other than those described in NY R USDCTS&ED Civ Rule 6.1(a), and other than petitions for writs of habeas corpus, any opposing affidavits and answering memoranda shall be served within fourteen (14) days after service of the moving papers. NY R USDCTS&ED Civ Rule 6.1(b)(2).

a. *Opposing affidavit.* Except as FRCP 59(c) provides otherwise, any opposing affidavit must be served at least seven (7) days before the hearing, unless the court permits service at another time. FRCP 6(c)(2).

4. *Timing of reply papers.* Where the respondent files an answering affidavit setting up a new matter, the moving party ordinarily is allowed a reasonable time to file a reply affidavit since failure to deny the new matter by affidavit may operate as an admission of its truth. AMJUR MOTIONS § 25.

a. *Reply affidavits and reply memoranda of law.* Except for letter-motions as permitted by NY R USDCTS&ED Civ Rule 7.1(d), and unless otherwise provided by statute or rule or by the Court in a Judge's Individual Practice or in a direction in a particular case, upon any motion, the notice of motion, supporting affidavits, and memoranda shall be served and filed as follows: on all civil motions, petitions, and applications, other than those described in NY R USDCTS&ED Civ Rule 6.1(a), and other than petitions for writs of habeas corpus, any reply affidavits and memoranda of law shall be served within seven (7) days after service of the answering papers. NY R USDCTS&ED Civ Rule 6.1(b)(3).

5. *Effect of a FRCP 12 motion on the time to serve a responsive pleading.* Unless the court sets a different time, serving a motion under FRCP 12 alters the periods in FRCP 12(a) as follows:

a. If the court denies the motion or postpones its disposition until trial, the responsive pleading must be served within fourteen (14) days after notice of the court's action; or

b. If the court grants a motion for a more definite statement, the responsive pleading must be served within fourteen (14) days after the more definite statement is served. FRCP 12(a)(4).

6. *Computation of time*

a. *Computing time.* FRCP 6 applies in computing any time period specified in the Federal Rules of Civil Procedure, in any local rule or court order, or in any statute that does not specify a method of computing time. FRCP 6(a). In computing any period of time prescribed or allowed by the Local Civil Rules of the United States District Courts for the Southern and Eastern Districts of New York or the Local Admiralty and Maritime Rules, the provisions of FRCP 6 shall apply unless otherwise stated. NY R USDCTS&ED Civ Rule 6.4.

i. *Period stated in days or a longer unit.* In computing periods of days, refer to FRCP 6 and NY R USDCTS&ED Civ Rule 6.4. NY R USDCTS&ED Civ Rule 6.1(b). When the period is stated in days or a longer unit of time:

- Exclude the day of the event that triggers the period;

- Count every day, including intermediate Saturdays, Sundays, and legal holidays; and

- Include the last day of the period, but if the last day is a Saturday, Sunday, or legal holiday, the period continues to run until the end of the next day that is not a Saturday, Sunday, or legal holiday. FRCP 6(a)(1). In the Local Civil Rules of the United States District Courts for the Southern and Eastern Districts of New York, as in the Federal Rules of Civil Procedure as amended effective December 1, 2009, Saturdays, Sundays, and legal holidays are no longer excluded in computing periods of time. If the last day of the period is a Saturday, Sunday, or legal holiday, the period continues to run until the end of the next day that is not a Saturday, Sunday, or legal holiday. NY R USDCTS&ED Civ Rule 6.4.

ii. *Period stated in hours.* When the period is stated in hours:

- Begin counting immediately on the occurrence of the event that triggers the period;

- Count every hour, including hours during intermediate Saturdays, Sundays, and legal holidays; and

- If the period would end on a Saturday, Sunday, or legal holiday, the period continues to run until the same time on the next day that is not a Saturday, Sunday, or legal holiday. FRCP 6(a)(2). In the Local Civil Rules of the United States District Courts for the Southern and Eastern Districts of New York, as in the Federal Rules of Civil Procedure as amended effective December 1, 2009, Saturdays, Sundays, and legal holidays are no longer excluded in computing periods of time. If the last day of the period is a Saturday, Sunday, or legal holiday, the period continues to run until the end of the next day that is not a Saturday, Sunday, or legal holiday. NY R USDCTS&ED Civ Rule 6.4.

iii. *Inaccessibility of the clerk's office.* Unless the court orders otherwise, if the clerk's office is inaccessible:

- On the last day for filing under FRCP 6(a)(1), then the time for filing is extended to the first accessible day that is not a Saturday, Sunday, or legal holiday; or

- During the last hour for filing under FRCP 6(a)(2), then the time for filing is extended to the same time on the first accessible day that is not a Saturday, Sunday, or legal holiday. FRCP 6(a)(3).

iv. *"Last day" defined.* Unless a different time is set by a statute, local rule, or court order, the last day ends:

- For electronic filing, at midnight in the court's time zone; and

- For filing by other means, when the clerk's office is scheduled to close. FRCP 6(a)(4).

v. *"Next day" defined.* The "next day" is determined by continuing to count forward when the period is measured after an event and backward when measured before an event. FRCP 6(a)(5).

vi. *"Legal holiday" defined.* "Legal holiday" means:

- The day set aside by statute for observing New Year's Day, Martin Luther King Jr.'s Birthday, Washington's Birthday, Memorial Day, Independence Day, Labor Day, Columbus Day, Veterans' Day, Thanksgiving Day, or Christmas Day;

- Any day declared a holiday by the President or Congress; and

- For periods that are measured after an event, any other day declared a holiday by the state where the district court is located. FRCP 6(a)(6).

b. *Computation of electronic filing deadlines.* You can file electronically twenty-four (24) hours a day, seven (7) days a week, three hundred sixty-five (365) days a year. NY R USDCTSD CM/ECF, S.D.(II)(13)(13.10). Electronic filing must be completed before midnight local time where the Court is located in order to be considered timely filed that day. NY R USDCTSD CM/ECF, S.D.(I)(3)(3.3); NY R USDCTSD CM/ECF, S.D.(II)(13)(13.10); NY R USDCTSD CM/ECF, S.D.(II)(19)(19.4). An electronically filed document is deemed filed on the "filed on" date indicated on the Notice of Electronic Filing (NEF). NY R USDCTSD CM/ECF, S.D.(II)(13)(13.11).

i. *Technical failures.* A Filing User whose filing is made untimely as the result of a technical failure may seek appropriate relief from the Court. NY R USDCTSD CM/ECF, S.D.(I)(11). If you missed a filing deadline when the ECF system was out of order, attach a statement to your filing explaining how the interruption in service prevented you from filing in a timely fashion. NY R USDCTSD CM/ECF, S.D.(II)(23)(23.5).

c. *Extending time*

i. *In general.* When an act may or must be done within a specified time, the court may, for good cause, extend the time:

- With or without motion or notice if the court acts, or if a request is made, before the original time or its extension expires; or

- On motion made after the time has expired if the party failed to act because of excusable neglect. FRCP 6(b)(1).

    ii. *Exceptions.* A court must not extend the time to act under FRCP 50(b), FRCP 50(d), FRCP 52(b), FRCP 59(b), FRCP 59(d), FRCP 59(e), and FRCP 60(b). FRCP 6(b)(2).

    iii. Refer to the United States District Court for the Southern District of New York KeyRules Motion for Continuance/Extension of Time document for more information on extending time.

  d. *Additional time after certain kinds of service.* When a party may or must act within a specified time after service and service is made under FRCP 5(b)(2)(C), FRCP 5(b)(2)(D), FRCP 5(b)(2)(E), or FRCP 5(b)(2)(F), three (3) days are added after the period would otherwise expire under FRCP 6(a). FRCP 6(d). Overnight delivery service shall be deemed service by mail for purposes of FRCP 5 and FRCP 6. NY R USDCTS&ED Civ Rule 5.3.

7. *Individual judge practices.* Refer to the Miscellaneous section of this document for information on individual judge practices on timing of documents.

## C. General Requirements

1. *Motions, generally*

  a. *Requirements.* A request for a court order must be made by motion. The motion must:

    i. Be in writing unless made during a hearing or trial;

    ii. State with particularity the grounds for seeking the order; and

    iii. State the relief sought. FRCP 7(b)(1).

  b. *Notice of motion.* A party interested in resisting the relief sought by a motion has a right to notice thereof, and an opportunity to be heard. AMJUR MOTIONS § 12.

    i. In addition to statutory or court rule provisions requiring notice of a motion—the purpose of such a notice requirement having been said to be to prevent a party from being prejudicially surprised by a motion—principles of natural justice dictate that an adverse party generally must be given notice that a motion will be presented to the court. AMJUR MOTIONS § 12.

    ii. "Notice," in this regard, means reasonable notice, including a meaningful opportunity to prepare and to defend against allegations of a motion. AMJUR MOTIONS § 12.

  c. *Writing requirement.* The writing requirement is intended to insure that the adverse parties are informed and have a record of both the motion's pendency and the grounds on which the movant seeks an order. FPP § 1191; Feldberg v. Quechee Lakes Corp., 463 F.3d 195 (2d Cir. 2006).

    i. It is sufficient "if the motion is stated in a written notice of the hearing of the motion." FPP § 1191.

  d. *Particularity requirement.* The particularity requirement insures that the opposing parties will have notice of their opponent's contentions. FEDPROC § 62:364; Goodman v. 1973 26 Foot Trojan Vessel, Arkansas Registration No. AR1439SN, 859 F.2d 71, 12 Fed.R.Serv.3d 645 (8th Cir. 1988). That requirement ensures that notice of the basis for the motion is provided to the court and to the opposing party so as to avoid prejudice, provide the opponent with a meaningful opportunity to respond, and provide the court with enough information to process the motion correctly. FEDPROC § 62:364; Andreas v. Volkswagen of America, Inc., 336 F.3d 789, 56 Fed.R.Serv.3d 6 (8th Cir. 2003).

    i. Reasonable specification of the grounds for a motion is sufficient. However, where a movant fails to state even one ground for granting the motion in question, the movant has failed to meet the minimal standard of "reasonable specification." FEDPROC § 62:364; Martinez v. Trainor, 556 F.2d 818, 23 Fed.R.Serv.2d 403 (7th Cir. 1977).

    ii. The court may excuse the failure to comply with the particularity requirement if it is inadvertent, and where no prejudice is shown by the opposing party. FEDPROC § 62:364.

  e. *Ex parte orders or orders to show cause to bring on a motion.* No ex parte order, or order to show cause to bring on a motion, will be granted except upon a clear and specific showing by affidavit of good and sufficient reasons why a procedure other than by notice of motion is necessary, and stating whether a previous application for similar relief has been made. NY R USDCTS&ED Civ Rule 6.1(d).

f. *Letter-motions.* Applications for extensions or adjournments, applications for a pre-motion conference, and similar non-dispositive matters as permitted by the instructions regarding ECF published on the website of each respective Court and any pertinent Individual Judge's Practices, may be brought by letter-motion filed via ECF pursuant to NY R USDCTS&ED Civ Rule 5.2(b). NY R USDCTS&ED Civ Rule 7.1(d).

   i. The following list of motions. . .may be made by LETTER-MOTION: (1) Motion to Adjourn Conference; (2) Motion to Change Attorney Name on Roll; (3) Motion to Compel; (4) Motion for Conference; (5) Motion to Consolidate Cases; (6) Motion to Continue; (7) Motion re: Discovery; (8) Motion to Expedite; (9) Motion for Extension of Time; (10) Motion for Extension of Time to Amend; (11) Motion for Extension of Time to Answer; (12) Motion for Extension of Time to Complete Discovery; (13) Motion for Extension of Time to File Document; (14) Motion for Extension of Time to File Response/Reply; (15) Motion for Extension of Time re Transcript; (16) Motion to File Amicus Brief; (17) Motion for Leave to File Document; (18) Motion for Leave to File Excess Pages; (19) Motion for Local Rule 37.2 Conference; (20) Motion for Oral Argument; (21) Motion to Reopen; (22) Motion to Reopen Case; (23) Motion to Seal Document; (24) Motion to Stay; (25) Motion to Substitute Attorney. NY R USDCTSD CM/ECF, S.D.(II)(13)(13.1).

   ii. If the Filing User is making a type of motion that does not appear in this list, the motion may not be made by letter. NY R USDCTSD CM/ECF, S.D.(II)(13)(13.1).

   iii. For more information on letter motions, refer to NY R USDCTSD CM/ECF, S.D.(II)(13)(13.1).

2. *Motion to dismiss for lack of personal jurisdiction.* A party may assert the defense of lack of subject-matter jurisdiction by motion. FRCP 12(b)(2). The most common use of the FRCP 12(b)(2) motion is to challenge the use of a state long-arm statute in a diversity action. FEDPROC § 62:445; Best Van Lines, Inc. v. Walker, 490 F.3d 239 (2d Cir. 2007). A dismissal pursuant to FRCP 12(b)(2) is proper where it appears that the assertion of jurisdiction over the defendant offends traditional notions of fair play and substantial justice—that is, where neither the defendant nor the controversy has a substantial enough connection with the forum state to make the exercise of jurisdiction reasonable. FEDPROC § 62:445; Neogen Corp. v. Neo Gen Screening, Inc., 282 F.3d 883, 2002 Fed.App. 0080P (6th Cir. 2002).

   a. *Personal jurisdiction, generally*

      i. *Due process limitations.* Due process requires that a court obtain jurisdiction over a defendant before it may adjudicate that defendant's personal rights. FEDPROC § 65:1; Omni Capital Intern., Ltd. v. Rudolf Wolff & Co., Ltd., 484 U.S. 97, 108 S.Ct. 404, 98 L.Ed.2d 415, 9 Fed.R.Serv.3d 691 (1987).

        • Originally it was believed that a judgment in personam could only be entered against a defendant found and served within a state, but the increased flow of commerce between the states and the disuse of the writ of capias ad respondendum, which directed the sheriff to secure the defendant's appearance by taking him into custody, in civil cases led to the liberalization of the concept of personal jurisdiction over nonresidents, and the flexible "minimum contacts" test is now followed. FEDPROC § 65:1.

        • Now the rule is that no binding judgment may be rendered against an individual or corporate defendant unless the defendant has sufficient contacts, ties, or relations with the jurisdiction. FEDPROC § 65:1; Burger King Corp. v. Rudzewicz, 471 U.S. 462, 105 S.Ct. 2174, 85 L.Ed.2d 528 (1985); International Shoe Co. v. State of Wash., Office of Unemployment Compensation and Placement, 326 U.S. 310, 66 S.Ct. 154, 90 L.Ed. 95, 161 A.L.R. 1057 (1945).

        • Moreover, even if the defendant has sufficient contacts with the forum state to satisfy due process, a court nevertheless does not obtain personal jurisdiction over the defendant unless the defendant has notice sufficient to satisfy due process, and, if such notice requires service of a summons, that there is authorization for the type and manner of service used. FEDPROC § 65:1; Omni Capital Intern., Ltd. v. Rudolf Wolff & Co., Ltd., 484 U.S. 97, 108 S.Ct. 404, 98 L.Ed.2d 415, 9 Fed.R.Serv.3d 691 (1987).

- Personal jurisdiction is a prerequisite to the maintenance of an action, and must exist even though subject matter jurisdiction and venue are proper. FEDPROC § 65:1; Bookout v. Beck, 354 F.2d 823 (9th Cir. 1965).

- Personal jurisdiction over a nonresident defendant is appropriate under the due process clause only where the defendant has sufficient minimum contacts with the forum state that are more than random, fortuitous, or attenuated, such that summoning the defendant would not offend traditional notions of fair play and substantial justice. FEDPROC § 65:1; Pecoraro v. Sky Ranch for Boys, Inc., 340 F.3d 558 (8th Cir. 2003).

ii. *Methods of obtaining jurisdiction over an individual.* There are four basic methods of obtaining jurisdiction over an individual:

- Personal service within the jurisdiction. FEDPROC § 65:22.

- Service on a domiciliary of the forum state who is temporarily outside the jurisdiction, on the theory that the authority of a state over one of its citizens is not terminated by the mere fact of his absence. FEDPROC § 65:22; Milliken v. Meyer, 311 U.S. 457, 61 S.Ct. 339, 85 L.Ed. 278, 132 A.L.R. 1357 (1940).

- Service on a nonresident who has sufficient contacts with the forum state, since the test of International Shoe is applicable to individuals. FEDPROC § 65:22; Kulko v. Superior Court of California In and For City and County of San Francisco, 436 U.S. 84, 98 S.Ct. 1690, 56 L.Ed.2d 132 (1978).

- Service on an agent who has been expressly appointed or appointed by operation of law, such as under a nonresident motorist statute. FEDPROC § 65:22; National Equipment Rental, Limited v. Szukhent, 375 U.S. 311, 84 S.Ct. 411, 11 L.Ed.2d 354, 7 Fed.R.Serv.2d 23 (1964).

iii. *Territorial limits of effective service*

- *In general.* Serving a summons or filing a waiver of service establishes personal jurisdiction over a defendant: (1) who is subject to the jurisdiction of a court of general jurisdiction in the state where the district court is located; (2) who is a party joined under FRCP 14 or FRCP 19 and is served within a judicial district of the United States and not more than one hundred (100) miles from where the summons was issued; or (3) when authorized by a federal statute. FRCP 4(k)(1).

- *Federal claim outside state-court jurisdiction.* For a claim that arises under federal law, serving a summons or filing a waiver of service establishes personal jurisdiction over a defendant if: (1) the defendant is not subject to jurisdiction in any state's courts of general jurisdiction; and (2) exercising jurisdiction is consistent with the United States Constitution and laws. FRCP 4(k)(2).

b. *Motion based on lack of in rem or quasi-in-rem jurisdiction.* Although FRCP 12(b)(2) only refers to "jurisdiction over the person," the provision presumably is sufficiently elastic to embrace a defense or objection that the district court lacks in rem or quasi-in-rem jurisdiction, admittedly a subject that rarely arises in contemporary practice. FPP § 1351.

c. *Motion based on insufficient process or insufficient service of process.* FRCP 12(b)(2) motions to dismiss are frequently based on the failure to serve the defendant with process or a defective service of process, on the theory that if the defendant was not properly served with process, the court lacks personal jurisdiction over the defendant. FEDPROC § 62:446; Prokopiou v. Long Island R. Co., 2007 WL 1098696 (S.D.N.Y. 2007).

d. *Independent ground for dismissal.* Lack of overall reasonableness in the assertion of personal jurisdiction constitutes an independent ground for dismissal under FRCP 12(b)(2). FEDPROC § 62:448; Federal Ins. Co. v. Lake Shore Inc., 886 F.2d 654 (4th Cir. 1989).

e. *Burden.* On the motion, the plaintiff bears the burden to establish the court's jurisdiction, which normally is not a heavy one, although the standard of proof may vary depending on the procedure used by the court in making its determination and whether the defendant is successful in rebutting the plaintiff's initial showing. Moreover, the Supreme Court has intimated that in the case of a challenge to the constitutional fairness and reasonableness of the chosen forum, the burden is on the defendant. FPP § 1351; Burger King Corp. v. Rudzewicz, 471 U.S. 462, 105 S.Ct. 2174, 85 L.Ed.2d 528 (1985).

    i.    The most common formulation found in the judicial opinions is that the plaintiff bears the ultimate burden of demonstrating that the court's personal jurisdiction over the defendant exists by a preponderance of the evidence, but needs only make a prima facie showing when the district judge restricts her review of the FRCP 12(b)(2) motion solely to affidavits and other written evidence. FPP § 1351; Mullins v. TestAmerica, Inc., 564 F.3d 386 (5th Cir. 2009).

    ii.    In addition, for purposes of such a review, federal courts will, as they do on other motions under FRCP 12(b), take as true the allegations of the nonmoving party with regard to the jurisdictional issues and resolve all factual disputes in his or her favor. FPP § 1351.

f.    *Motion denied.* A party who has unsuccessfully raised an objection under FRCP 12(b)(2) may proceed to trial on the merits without waiving the ability to renew the objection to the court's jurisdiction. FPP § 1351.

g.    *Joining motions.* As a general rule, when the court is confronted by a motion raising a combination of FRCP 12(b) defenses, it will pass on the jurisdictional issues before considering whether a claim was stated by the complaint. FPP § 1351.

    i.    *Right to join.* A motion under FRCP 12 may be joined with any other motion allowed by FRCP 12. FRCP 12(g)(1).

    ii.    *Limitation on further motions.* Except as provided in FRCP 12(h)(2) or FRCP 12(h)(3), a party that makes a motion under FRCP 12 must not make another motion under FRCP 12 raising a defense or objection that was available to the party but omitted from its earlier motion. FRCP 12(g)(2).

h.    *Waiving and preserving certain defenses.* No defense or objection is waived by joining it with one or more other defenses or objections in a responsive pleading or in a motion. FRCP 12(b).

    i.    *Waiver by consent or stipulation.* A valid consent or a stipulation that the court has jurisdiction prevents the successful assertion of a FRCP 12(b)(2) defense. FPP § 1351.

    ii.    *Waiver by filing permissive counterclaim.* A defendant may be deemed to have waived an objection to personal jurisdiction if he or she files a permissive counterclaim under FRCP 13(b). FPP § 1351.

    iii.    *When some are waived.* A party waives any defense listed in FRCP 12(b)(2) through FRCP 12(b)(5) by:

- Omitting it from a motion in the circumstances described in FRCP 12(g)(2); or
- Failing to either: (1) make it by motion under FRCP 12; or (2) include it in a responsive pleading or in an amendment allowed by FRCP 15(a)(1) as a matter of course. FRCP 12(h)(1).

    iv.    *When to raise others.* Failure to state a claim upon which relief can be granted, to join a person required by FRCP 19(b), or to state a legal defense to a claim may be raised:

- In any pleading allowed or ordered under FRCP 7(a);
- By a motion under FRCP 12(c); or
- At trial. FRCP 12(h)(2).

    v.    *Lack of subject matter jurisdiction.* If the court determines at any time that it lacks subject-matter jurisdiction, the court must dismiss the action. FRCP 12(h)(3).

3.    *Opposing papers.* The Federal Rules of Civil Procedure do not require any formal answer, return, or reply to a motion, except where the Federal Rules of Civil Procedure or local rules may require affidavits, memoranda, or other papers to be filed in opposition to a motion. Such papers are simply to apprise the court of such opposition and the grounds of that opposition. FEDPROC § 62:359. Except for letter-

motions as permitted by NY R USDCTS&ED Civ Rule 7.1(d) or as otherwise permitted by the Court, all oppositions and replies with respect to motions shall comply with NY R USDCTS&ED Civ Rule 7.1(a)(2) and NY R USDCTS&ED Civ Rule 7.1(a)(3), and an opposing party who seeks relief that goes beyond the denial of the motion shall comply as well with NY R USDCTS&ED Civ Rule 7.1(a)(1). NY R USDCTS&ED Civ Rule 7.1(b).

a. *Effect of failure to respond to motion.* Although in the absence of statutory provision or court rule, a motion ordinarily does not require a written answer, when a party files a motion and the opposing party fails to respond, the court may construe such failure to respond as nonopposition to the motion or an admission that the motion was meritorious, may take the facts alleged in the motion as true—the rule in some jurisdictions being that the failure to respond to a fact set forth in a motion is deemed an admission—and may grant the motion if the relief requested appears to be justified. AMJUR MOTIONS § 28.

b. *Assent or no opposition not determinative.* However, a motion will not be granted automatically simply because an "assent" or a notation of "no opposition" has been filed; federal judges frequently deny motions that have been assented to when it is thought that justice so dictates. FPP § 1190.

c. *Responsive pleading inappropriate as response to motion.* An attempt to answer or oppose a motion with a responsive pleading usually is not appropriate. FPP § 1190.

4. *Reply papers.* A moving party may be required or permitted to prepare papers in addition to his original motion papers. AMJUR MOTIONS § 25. Papers answering or replying to opposing papers may be appropriate, in the interests of justice, where it appears there is a substantial reason for allowing a reply. Thus, a court may accept reply papers where a party demonstrates that the papers to which it seeks to file a reply raise new issues that are material to the disposition of the question before the court, or where the court determines, sua sponte, that it wishes further briefing of an issue raised in those papers and orders the submission of additional papers. FEDPROC § 62:360. Except for letter-motions as permitted by NY R USDCTS&ED Civ Rule 7.1(d) or as otherwise permitted by the Court, all oppositions and replies with respect to motions shall comply with NY R USDCTS&ED Civ Rule 7.1(a)(2) and NY R USDCTS&ED Civ Rule 7.1(a)(3). NY R USDCTS&ED Civ Rule 7.1(b).

a. *Function of reply papers.* The function of a reply affidavit is to answer the arguments made in opposition to the position taken by the movant and not to permit the movant to introduce new arguments in support of the motion. AMJUR MOTIONS § 25.

b. *Issues raised for the first time in a reply document.* However, the view has been followed in some jurisdictions, that as a matter of judicial economy, where there is no prejudice and where the issues could be raised simply by filing a motion to dismiss, the trial court has discretion to consider arguments raised for the first time in a reply memorandum, and that a trial court may grant a motion to strike issues raised for the first time in a reply memorandum. AMJUR MOTIONS § 26.

5. *Orders on motions.* A memorandum signed by the Court of the decision on a motion that does not finally determine all claims for relief, or an oral decision on such a motion, shall constitute the order unless the memorandum or oral decision directs the submission or settlement of an order in more extended form. The notation in the docket of a memorandum or of an oral decision that does not direct the submission or settlement of an order in more extended form shall constitute the entry of the order. Where an order in more extended form is required to be submitted or settled, the notation in the docket of such order shall constitute the entry of the order. NY R USDCTS&ED Civ Rule 6.2.

6. *Complex civil cases.* For information on procedures for complex civil cases, refer to NY R USDCTSD Order 11 Misc 00388.

7. *Related cases.* It shall be the continuing duty of each attorney appearing in any civil or criminal case to bring promptly to the attention of the Court all facts which said attorney believes are relevant to a determination that said case and one or more pending civil or criminal cases should be heard by the same Judge, in order to avoid unnecessary duplication of judicial effort. As soon as the attorney becomes aware of such relationship, said attorney shall notify the Judges to whom the cases have been assigned. NY R USDCTS&ED Civ Rule 1.6(a). If counsel fails to comply with NY R USDCTS&ED Civ Rule 1.6(a), the Court may assess reasonable costs directly against counsel whose action has obstructed the effective administration of the Court's business. NY R USDCTS&ED Civ Rule 1.6(b).

a. *Determination of relatedness.* Subject to the limitations set forth in NY R USDCTSD Div. Bus., Rule

13(a)(2), a civil case, bankruptcy appeal, or motion to withdraw the bankruptcy reference will be deemed related to one or more civil cases, appeals or motions when the interests of justice and efficiency will be served. In determining relatedness, a judge will consider whether (A) the actions concern the same or substantially similar parties, property, transactions or events; (B) there is substantial factual overlap; (C) the parties could be subjected to conflicting orders; and (D) whether absent a determination of relatedness there would be a substantial duplication of effort and expense, delay, or undue burden on the Court, parties or witnesses. NY R USDCTSD Div. Bus., Rule 13(a)(1). Nothing in this NY R USDCTSD Div. Bus., Rule 13 is intended to preclude parties from moving for consolidated proceedings under FRCP 42. NY R USDCTSD Div. Bus., Rule 13(a)(1). Notwithstanding NY R USDCTSD Div. Bus., Rule 13(a)(1):

    i.   Civil cases shall not be deemed related merely because they involve common legal issues or the same parties. NY R USDCTSD Div. Bus., Rule 13(a)(2)(A).

    ii.   Other than cases subject to NY R USDCTSD Div. Bus., Rule 4(b) and actions seeking the enforcement of a judgment or settlement in or of an earlier case, civil cases presumptively shall not be deemed related unless both cases are pending before the Court (or the earlier case is on appeal). NY R USDCTSD Div. Bus., Rule 13(a)(2)(B).

  b.  *Procedure in regard to cases said to be related*

    i.   *Disclosure of contention of relatedness.* When a civil case is filed or removed or a bankruptcy appeal or motion to withdraw the reference of an adversary proceeding from the bankruptcy court is filed, the person filing or removing shall disclose on form JSC44C any contention of relatedness and shall file a Related Case Statement stating clearly and succinctly the basis for the contention. A copy of the civil cover sheet and Related Case Statement shall be served with the complaint, notice of removal, notice of appeal, or motion. Any party may contest a claim of relatedness by any other in writing addressed to the judge having the case with the lowest docket number of all cases claimed to be related. However, the foregoing shall not delay the assignment process or the operation of NY R USDCTSD Div. Bus., Rule 13. NY R USDCTSD Div. Bus., Rule 13(b)(1). [Editor's note: the reference to form JSC44C is likely meant to be form JS44C-SDNY: Civil Court Cover Sheet].

    ii.   *Claims of relatedness by other parties.* A party other than the one filing a case, bankruptcy appeal or motion to withdraw the reference that contends its case is related to another may so advise in writing the judge assigned in its case and request a transfer of its case to the judge that the party contends has the related case with the lowest docket number. If the assigned judge believes the case is related under NY R USDCTSD Div. Bus., Rule 13(a), he or she shall refer the question to the judge having the case with the lowest docket number. In the event the latter judge agrees, the case shall be transferred to that judge unless the Assignment Committee disagrees. NY R USDCTSD Div. Bus., Rule 13(b)(3).

  c.  For more information on related cases, refer to NY R USDCTSD Div. Bus., Rule 13.

8.  *Alternative dispute resolution (ADR).* The U.S. District Court for the Southern District of New York provides litigants with opportunities to discuss settlement through judicial settlement conferences and mediation. NY R USDCTS&ED Civ Rule 83.9(a).

  a.  *Consideration of alternative dispute resolution.* In all civil cases, including those eligible for mediation pursuant to NY R USDCTS&ED Civ Rule 83.9(e), each party shall consider the use of mediation or a judicial settlement conference and shall report to the assigned Judge at the initial FRCP 16(b) case management conference, or subsequently, whether the party believes mediation or a judicial settlement conference may facilitate the resolution of the lawsuit. Judges are encouraged to note the availability of the mediation program and/or a judicial settlement conference before, at, or after the initial FRCP 16(b) case management conference. NY R USDCTS&ED Civ Rule 83.9(d).

  b.  *Mediation.* In mediation, parties and counsel meet, sometimes collectively and sometimes individually, with a neutral third party (the mediator) who has been trained to facilitate confidential settlement discussions. The parties articulate their respective positions and interests and generate options for a mutually agreeable resolution to the dispute. The mediator assists the parties in reaching their own negotiated settlement by defining the issues, probing and assessing the strengths and weaknesses of each party's legal positions, and identifying areas of agreement and disagreement. The main benefits of mediation are that it can result in an expeditious and less costly resolution of the litigation, and can produce creative solutions to complex disputes often unavailable in traditional litigation. NY R USDCTS&ED Civ Rule 83.9(b).

    i. *Mediation program eligibility.* All civil cases other than Social Security, habeas corpus, and tax cases are eligible for mediation, whether assigned to Manhattan or White Plains. NY R USDCTS&ED Civ Rule 83.9(e)(1).

- The Board of Judges may, by Administrative Order, direct that certain specified categories of cases shall automatically be submitted to the mediation program. The assigned District Judge or Magistrate Judge may issue a written order exempting a particular case with or without the request of the parties. NY R USDCTS&ED Civ Rule 83.9(e)(2).

- For all other cases, the assigned District Judge or Magistrate Judge may determine that a case is appropriate for mediation and may order that case to mediation, with or without the consent of the parties, before, at, or after the initial FRCP 16(b) case management conference. Alternatively, the parties should notify the assigned Judge at any time of their desire to mediate. NY R USDCTS&ED Civ Rule 83.9(e)(3).

  c. *Judicial settlement conferences.* Judicial settlement conferences may be ordered by District Judges or Magistrate Judges with or without the request or consent of the parties. NY R USDCTS&ED Civ Rule 83.9(f).

  d. For more information on alternative dispute resolution (ADR), refer to NY R USDCTS&ED Civ Rule 83.9.

9. *Individual judge practices.* Refer to the Miscellaneous section of this document for information on individual judge practices on general requirements for documents.

## D. Documents

1. *Documents for moving party*

  a. *Required documents*

    i. *Notice of motion and motion.* Except for letter-motions as permitted by NY R USDCTS&ED Civ Rule 7.1(d) or as otherwise permitted by the Court, all motions shall include the following motion papers: a notice of motion, or an order to show cause signed by the Court, which shall specify the applicable rules or statutes pursuant to which the motion is brought, and shall specify the relief sought by the motion. NY R USDCTS&ED Civ Rule 7.1(a)(1). Refer to the General Requirements section of this document for information on the notice of motion and motion.

    ii. *Memorandum of law.* Except for letter-motions as permitted by NY R USDCTS&ED Civ Rule 7.1(d) or as otherwise permitted by the Court, all motions shall include the following motion papers: a memorandum of law, setting forth the cases and other authorities relied upon in support of the motion, and divided, under appropriate headings, into as many parts as there are issues to be determined. NY R USDCTS&ED Civ Rule 7.1(a)(2).

    iii. *Certificate of service.* FRCP 5(d) requires that the person making service under FRCP 5 certify that service has been effected. FRCP 5(Advisory Committee Notes). Having such information on file may be useful for many purposes, including proof of service if an issue arises concerning the effectiveness of the service. FRCP 5(Advisory Committee Notes).

- Such paper service [on attorneys and pro se parties who are not Filing or Receiving Users] must be documented by electronically filing proof of service. NY R USDCTSD CM/ECF, S.D.(I)(9)(9.2); NY R USDCTSD CM/ECF, S.D.(I)(19)(19.3)(b). Pro se parties who are not Filing Users are exempt from that portion of NY R USDCTSD CM/ECF, S.D.(I)(19)(19.3) requiring proof of service to be filed electronically. NY R USDCTSD CM/ECF, S.D.(I)(19)(19.3).

  b. *Supplemental documents*

    i. *Supporting evidence.* When a motion relies on facts outside the record, the court may hear the

matter on affidavits or may hear it wholly or partly on oral testimony or on depositions. FRCP 43(c). Except for letter-motions as permitted by NY R USDCTS&ED Civ Rule 7.1(d) or as otherwise permitted by the Court, all motions shall include the following motion papers: supporting affidavits and exhibits thereto containing any factual information and portions of the record necessary for the decision of the motion. NY R USDCTS&ED Civ Rule 7.1(a)(3).

- *Discovery materials.* A party seeking or opposing relief under FRCP 26 through FRCP 37 inclusive, or making or opposing any other motion or application, shall quote or attach only those portions of the depositions, interrogatories, requests for documents, requests for admissions, or other discovery or disclosure materials, together with the responses and objections thereto, that are the subject of the discovery motion or application, or that are cited in papers submitted in connection with any other motion or application. NY R USDCTS&ED Civ Rule 5.1.

ii. *Notice of constitutional question.* A party that files a pleading, written motion, or other paper drawing into question the constitutionality of a federal or state statute must promptly:

- *File notice.* File a notice of constitutional question stating the question and identifying the paper that raises it, if: (1) a federal statute is questioned and the parties do not include the United States, one of its agencies, or one of its officers or employees in an official capacity; or (2) a state statute is questioned and the parties do not include the state, one of its agencies, or one of its officers or employees in an official capacity; and

- *Serve notice.* Serve the notice and paper on the Attorney General of the United States if a federal statute is questioned—or on the state attorney general if a state statute is questioned—either by certified or registered mail or by sending it to an electronic address designated by the attorney general for this purpose. FRCP 5.1(a).

- *No forfeiture.* A party's failure to file and serve the notice, or the court's failure to certify, does not forfeit a constitutional claim or defense that is otherwise timely asserted. FRCP 5.1(d).

iii. *Nongovernmental corporate disclosure statement*

- *Contents.* A nongovernmental corporate party must file two (2) copies of a disclosure statement that: (1) identifies any parent corporation and any publicly held corporation owning ten percent (10%) or more of its stock; or (2) states that there is no such corporation. FRCP 7.1(a).

- *Time to file; Supplemental filing.* A party must: (1) file the disclosure statement with its first appearance, pleading, petition, motion, response, or other request addressed to the court; and (2) promptly file a supplemental statement if any required information changes. FRCP 7.1(b). For purposes of FRCP 7.1(b)(2), "promptly" shall mean "within fourteen days," that is, parties are required to file a supplemental disclosure statement within fourteen (14) days of the time there is any change in the information required in a disclosure statement filed pursuant to those rules. NY R USDCTS&ED Civ Rule 7.1.1.

iv. *Notice to pro se litigant who opposes a FRCP 12 motion supported by matters outside the pleadings.* A represented party moving to dismiss or for judgment on the pleadings against a party proceeding pro se, who refers in support of the motion to matters outside the pleadings as described in FRCP 12(b) or FRCP 12(c), shall serve and file the notice in NY R USDCTS&ED Civ Rule 12.1 with the full text of FRCP 56 attached at the time the motion is served. If the Court rules that a motion to dismiss or for judgment on the pleadings will be treated as one for summary judgment pursuant to FRCP 56, and the movant has not previously served and filed the notice required by NY R USDCTS&ED Civ Rule 12.1, the movant shall amend the form notice to reflect that fact and shall serve and file the amended notice within fourteen (14) days of the Court's ruling. NY R USDCTS&ED Civ Rule 12.1. For the notice, refer to NY R USDCTS&ED Civ Rule 12.1.

v. *Copies of authorities.* In cases involving a pro se litigant, counsel shall, when serving a memorandum of law (or other submissions to the Court), provide the pro se litigant (but not

other counsel or the Court) with copies of cases and other authorities cited therein that are unpublished or reported exclusively on computerized databases. Upon request, counsel shall provide the pro se litigant with copies of such unpublished cases and other authorities as are cited in a decision of the Court and were not previously cited by any party. NY R USDCTS&ED Civ Rule 7.2.

vi. *Proposed order.* Refer to the Format section of this document for information on the format of submitting a proposed order to the court.

vii. *Statement explaining untimely electronic filing.* If you missed a filing deadline when the ECF system was out of order, attach a statement to your filing explaining how the interruption in service prevented you from filing in a timely fashion. NY R USDCTSD CM/ECF, S.D.(II)(23)(23.5).

viii. *Courtesy copies.* Read the judge's Individual Practices to learn if courtesy copies are required. NY R USDCTSD CM/ECF, S.D.(II)(13)(13.17). Judges' Individual Practices should continue to be followed with respect to delivery of courtesy copies. NY R USDCTSD CM/ECF, S.D.(I)(3)(3.4).

2. *Documents for opposing party*

  a. *Required documents*

    i. *Answering memorandum of law.* Except for letter-motions as permitted by NY R USDCTS&ED Civ Rule 7.1(d) or as otherwise permitted by the Court, all oppositions and replies with respect to motions shall comply with NY R USDCTS&ED Civ Rule 7.1(a)(2). NY R USDCTS&ED Civ Rule 7.1(b). Except for letter-motions as permitted by NY R USDCTS&ED Civ Rule 7.1(d) or as otherwise permitted by the Court, all motions shall include the following motion papers: a memorandum of law, setting forth the cases and other authorities relied upon in support of the motion, and divided, under appropriate headings, into as many parts as there are issues to be determined. NY R USDCTS&ED Civ Rule 7.1(a)(2). Refer to the General Requirements section of this document for information on the opposing papers.

    ii. *Certificate of service.* FRCP 5(d) requires that the person making service under FRCP 5 certify that service has been effected. FRCP 5(Advisory Committee Notes). Having such information on file may be useful for many purposes, including proof of service if an issue arises concerning the effectiveness of the service. FRCP 5(Advisory Committee Notes).

      • Such paper service [on attorneys and pro se parties who are not Filing or Receiving Users] must be documented by electronically filing proof of service. NY R USDCTSD CM/ECF, S.D.(I)(9)(9.2); NY R USDCTSD CM/ECF, S.D.(I)(19)(19.3)(b). Pro se parties who are not Filing Users are exempt from that portion of NY R USDCTSD CM/ECF, S.D.(I)(19)(19.3) requiring proof of service to be filed electronically. NY R USDCTSD CM/ECF, S.D.(I)(19)(19.3).

  b. *Supplemental documents*

    i. *Supporting evidence.* When a motion relies on facts outside the record, the court may hear the matter on affidavits or may hear it wholly or partly on oral testimony or on depositions. FRCP 43(c). Except for letter-motions as permitted by NY R USDCTS&ED Civ Rule 7.1(d) or as otherwise permitted by the Court, all oppositions and replies with respect to motions shall comply with NY R USDCTS&ED Civ Rule 7.1(a)(3). NY R USDCTS&ED Civ Rule 7.1(b). Except for letter-motions as permitted by NY R USDCTS&ED Civ Rule 7.1(d) or as otherwise permitted by the Court, all motions shall include the following motion papers: supporting affidavits and exhibits thereto containing any factual information and portions of the record necessary for the decision of the motion. NY R USDCTS&ED Civ Rule 7.1(a)(3).

      • *Discovery materials.* A party seeking or opposing relief under FRCP 26 through FRCP 37 inclusive, or making or opposing any other motion or application, shall quote or attach only those portions of the depositions, interrogatories, requests for documents, requests for admissions, or other discovery or disclosure materials, together with the responses and objections thereto, that are the subject of the discovery motion or application, or that are

cited in papers submitted in connection with any other motion or application. NY R USDCTS&ED Civ Rule 5.1.

ii. *Notice of constitutional question.* A party that files a pleading, written motion, or other paper drawing into question the constitutionality of a federal or state statute must promptly:

- *File notice.* File a notice of constitutional question stating the question and identifying the paper that raises it, if: (1) a federal statute is questioned and the parties do not include the United States, one of its agencies, or one of its officers or employees in an official capacity; or (2) a state statute is questioned and the parties do not include the state, one of its agencies, or one of its officers or employees in an official capacity; and

- *Serve notice.* Serve the notice and paper on the Attorney General of the United States if a federal statute is questioned—or on the state attorney general if a state statute is questioned—either by certified or registered mail or by sending it to an electronic address designated by the attorney general for this purpose. FRCP 5.1(a).

- *No forfeiture.* A party's failure to file and serve the notice, or the court's failure to certify, does not forfeit a constitutional claim or defense that is otherwise timely asserted. FRCP 5.1(d).

iii. *Copies of authorities.* In cases involving a pro se litigant, counsel shall, when serving a memorandum of law (or other submissions to the Court), provide the pro se litigant (but not other counsel or the Court) with copies of cases and other authorities cited therein that are unpublished or reported exclusively on computerized databases. Upon request, counsel shall provide the pro se litigant with copies of such unpublished cases and other authorities as are cited in a decision of the Court and were not previously cited by any party. NY R USDCTS&ED Civ Rule 7.2.

iv. *Statement explaining untimely electronic filing.* If you missed a filing deadline when the ECF system was out of order, attach a statement to your filing explaining how the interruption in service prevented you from filing in a timely fashion. NY R USDCTSD CM/ECF, S.D.(II)(23)(23.5).

v. *Courtesy copies.* Read the judge's Individual Practices to learn if courtesy copies are required. NY R USDCTSD CM/ECF, S.D.(II)(13)(13.17). Judges' Individual Practices should continue to be followed with respect to delivery of courtesy copies. NY R USDCTSD CM/ECF, S.D.(I)(3)(3.4).

3. *Individual judge practices.* Refer to the Miscellaneous section of this document for information on individual judge practices on required documents.

# E. Format

1. *Form of documents.* The rules governing captions and other matters of form in pleadings apply to motions and other papers. FRCP 7(b)(2).

   a. *Paper.* Every pleading, written motion, and other paper must: be plainly written, typed, printed, or copied without erasures or interlineations which materially deface it. NY R USDCTS&ED Civ Rule 11.1(a)(1).

   b. *Typeface, margin, and spacing.* The typeface, margins, and spacing of all documents presented for filing must meet the following requirements:

      i. All text must be twelve (12) point type or larger, except for text in footnotes which may be ten (10) point type;

      ii. All documents must have at least one (1) inch margins on all sides;

      iii. All text must be double-spaced, except for headings, text in footnotes, or block quotations, which may be single-spaced. NY R USDCTS&ED Civ Rule 11.1(b).

   c. *Caption; Names of parties.* Every pleading must have a caption with the court's name, a title, a file number, and a FRCP 7(a) designation. The title of the complaint must name all the parties; the title of other pleadings, after naming the first party on each side, may refer generally to other parties.

FRCP 10(a). Every pleading, written motion, and other paper must: bear the docket number and the initials of the District Judge and any Magistrate Judge before whom the action or proceeding is pending, NY R USDCTS&ED Civ Rule 11.1(a)(2).

d. *Paragraphs; Separate statements.* A party must state its claims or defenses in numbered paragraphs, each limited as far as practicable to a single set of circumstances. A later pleading may refer by number to a paragraph in an earlier pleading. If doing so would promote clarity, each claim founded on a separate transaction or occurrence—and each defense other than a denial—must be stated in a separate count or defense. FRCP 10(b).

e. *Adoption by reference; Exhibits.* A statement in a pleading may be adopted by reference elsewhere in the same pleading or in any other pleading or motion. A copy of a written instrument that is an exhibit to a pleading is a part of the pleading for all purposes. FRCP 10(c).

f. *Acceptance by the clerk.* The clerk must not refuse to file a paper solely because it is not in the form prescribed by the Federal Rules of Civil Procedure or by a local rule or practice. FRCP 5(d)(4).

2. *Form of electronic documents*

a. *PDF-A.* All documents electronically filed on the ECF system must be in PDF-A format (portable document format). A PDF-A file is created using PDF writer software such as Adobe Acrobat (go to the Adobe website for details). PDF-A files cannot be altered, providing security to the filer and the Court. NY R USDCTSD CM/ECF, S.D.(II)(23)(23.2).

b. *Size limitation.* No single PDF file may be larger than four megabytes (4 MB). If the filing is too large, the ECF system will not allow it to be filed, and you will not see a Notice of Electronic Filing (NEF or filing receipt) screen. To determine the size of an Adobe Acrobat PDF file click on File, Document Properties, Summary. NY R USDCTSD CM/ECF, S.D.(II)(23)(23.3).

   i. Converting documents directly from a word processor to PDF-A format creates the smallest possible file in terms of computer memory. If that is not possible, scan your document at low resolution. Within the Adobe Acrobat program, on the "Scan Manager" screen, adjust the settings for black and white and 200 dpi (dots per inch). This allows more pages to fit into a single PDF-A file. If that does not work, separate an oversized file into 2 or more parts. Simply label each file 1a, 1b, 1c, etc. Only relevant excerpts of exhibits should be electronically filed. NY R USDCTSD CM/ECF, S.D.(II)(23)(23.4).

c. *Attachments and exhibits.* Filing Users must submit in electronic form all documents referenced as exhibits or attachments, unless the Court permits paper filing. NY R USDCTSD CM/ECF, S.D.(I)(5)(5.1).

   i. A Filing User must submit as exhibits or attachments only those excerpts of the referenced documents that are relevant to the matter under consideration by the Court. Excerpted material must be clearly and prominently identified as such. Filing Users who file excerpts of documents as exhibits or attachments under this procedure do so without prejudice to their right to file timely additional excerpts or the complete document. Responding parties may file timely additional excerpts that they believe are relevant or the complete document. A party may move before the Court for permission to serve and file in hard copy documents that cannot be reasonably scanned. NY R USDCTSD CM/ECF, S.D.(I)(5)(5.2).

   ii. Exhibits must be filed only as attachments to a document, such as a motion or an affidavit. Do not use the ECF Filing Event for "Motion" to file exhibits separately. Exhibits are the only items that should be attached to electronically filed documents. You are limited to electronically filing only relevant excerpts of exhibits. Excerpts must be clearly identified as such. If the exhibit is too large to be scanned and electronically filed you may contact the ECF Help Desk. NY R USDCTSD CM/ECF, S.D.(II)(15)(15.6).

d. *Letters.* Parties should consult the assigned judge's Individual Practices to determine if the judge accepts letters at all and, if he or she does, whether the judge has any page limitations on letters and/or requires courtesy copies of letters filed on ECF (and, if so, by what means of delivery). All letters addressed to the Court must include a subject line with the case name and docket number (e.g., "Re: Doe v. Smith, 13 Civ. 1234 (ABC)"). NY R USDCTSD CM/ECF, S.D.(II)(13)(13.1).

e. *Proposed orders, proposed judgments, stipulations and consents.* Any document that requires the signature of a judge should not be electronically filed except as an exhibit to another document. Proposed orders, judgments, stipulations and consents should not be submitted through the ECF system. Instead they should be sent by e-mail to the Clerk. Proposed orders should be submitted in word processing format (WordPerfect or Word) rather than as a PDF document. Stipulations should be submitted in PDF-A format. Stipulations must contain ink signatures not s/. Faxed or emailed signatures are acceptable. Please note that Stipulations of Voluntary Dismissal pursuant to FRCP 41(a)(1)(A)(ii) do not require the signature of a judge and must be electronically filed on the ECF system. Questions may be directed to the Orders and Judgments Clerk at the phone numbers listed in NY R USDCTSD CM/ECF, S.D.(II)(18)(18.3). NY R USDCTSD CM/ECF, S.D.(II)(18)(18.3).

  i. Email the proposed order, judgment or stipulation to the email addresses listed in NY R USDCTSD CM/ECF, S.D.(II)(18)(18.3). NY R USDCTSD CM/ECF, S.D.(II)(18)(18.3).

  ii. Pro se litigants who are not Filing Users are exempt from that portion of NY R USDCTSD CM/ECF, S.D.(II)(18)(18.3) that requires litigants to email proposed orders, judgments, stipulations and consents, and shall deliver such documents to the Clerk's Office in paper form. NY R USDCTSD CM/ECF, S.D.(II)(18)(18.3).

3. *Signing of pleadings, motions and other papers*

  a. *Signature.* Every pleading, written motion, and other paper must be signed by at least one attorney of record in the attorney's name—or by a party personally if the party is unrepresented. The paper must state the signer's address, e-mail address, and telephone number. FRCP 11(a). Every pleading, written motion, and other paper must: have the name of each person signing it clearly printed or typed directly below the signature. NY R USDCTS&ED Civ Rule 11.1(a)(3).

  i. *Electronic signatures.* The user log-in and password required to submit documents to the ECF system serve as the Filing User's signature on all electronic documents filed with the Court. NY R USDCTSD CM/ECF, S.D.(I)(8)(8.1); NY R USDCTSD CM/ECF, S.D.(II)(13)(13.14). They also serve as a signature for purposes of the Federal Rules of Civil Procedure, including FRCP 11, the Local Civil Rules of the United States District Courts for the Southern and Eastern Districts of New York, and any other purpose for which a signature is required in connection with proceedings before the Court. NY R USDCTSD CM/ECF, S.D.(I)(8)(8.1).

  - *Signature block.* Electronically filed documents must include a signature block and must set forth the name, address, telephone number and e-mail address all in compliance with the Federal Rules of Civil Procedure and NY R USDCTS&ED Civ Rule 11.1. In the absence of a scanned signature image, the name of the Filing User under whose log-in and password the document is submitted must be preceded by an "s/" typed in the space where the signature would otherwise appear. NY R USDCTSD CM/ECF, S.D.(I)(8)(8.2); NY R USDCTSD CM/ECF, S.D.(II)(13)(13.14).

  - *Documents requiring the signature of a party or witness.* A document requiring the signature of a party or witness shall be electronically filed in a scanned format that contains an image of the actual signature. NY R USDCTSD CM/ECF, S.D.(I)(8)(8.4); NY R USDCTSD CM/ECF, S.D.(II)(13)(13.14).

  - *Documents requiring the signature of a judge.* A Filing User submitting a document electronically that requires a judge's signature must promptly deliver the document in such other form, if any, as the Court requires. NY R USDCTSD CM/ECF, S.D.(I)(4)(4.2).

  - *Documents requiring multiple signatures.* Documents requiring signatures of more than one party must be electronically filed either by: (a) submitting a scanned document containing all necessary signatures; (b) representing the consent of the other parties on the document; (c) identifying on the document the parties whose signatures are required and by the submission of a notice of endorsement by the other parties no later than three business days after filing; or (d) in any other manner approved by the Court. NY R USDCTSD CM/ECF, S.D.(I)(8)(8.5).

  ii. *No verification or accompanying affidavit required for pleadings.* Unless a rule or statute specifically states otherwise, a pleading need not be verified or accompanied by an affidavit. FRCP 11(a).

    iii.   *Unsigned papers.* The court must strike an unsigned paper unless the omission is promptly corrected after being called to the attorney's or party's attention. FRCP 11(a).

  b.  *Representations to the court.* By presenting to the court a pleading, written motion, or other paper—whether by signing, filing, submitting, or later advocating it—an attorney or unrepresented party certifies that to the best of the person's knowledge, information, and belief, formed after an inquiry reasonable under the circumstances:

    i.   It is not being presented for any improper purpose, such as to harass, cause unnecessary delay, or needlessly increase the cost of litigation;

    ii.   The claims, defenses, and other legal contentions are warranted by existing law or by a nonfrivolous argument for extending, modifying, or reversing existing law or for establishing new law;

    iii.   The factual contentions have evidentiary support or, if specifically so identified, will likely have evidentiary support after a reasonable opportunity for further investigation or discovery; and

    iv.   The denials of factual contentions are warranted on the evidence or, if specifically so identified, are reasonably based on belief or a lack of information. FRCP 11(b).

  c.  *Sanctions.* If, after notice and a reasonable opportunity to respond, the court determines that FRCP 11(b) has been violated, the court may impose an appropriate sanction on any attorney, law firm, or party that violated FRCP 11(b) or is responsible for the violation. FRCP 11(c)(1). Refer to the United States District Court for the Southern District of New York KeyRules Motion for Sanctions document for more information.

4.  *Privacy protection for filings made with the court*

  a.  *Redacted filings.* Unless the court orders otherwise, in an electronic or paper filing with the court that contains an individual's Social Security number, taxpayer-identification number, or birth date, the name of an individual known to be a minor, or a financial-account number, a party or nonparty making the filing may include only:

    i.   The last four (4) digits of the Social Security number and taxpayer-identification number;

    ii.   The year of the individual's birth;

    iii.   The minor's initials; and

    iv.   The last four (4) digits of the financial-account number. FRCP 5.2(a); NY R USDCTSD CM/ECF, S.D.(II)(21)(21.3).

    v.   Caution should be exercised when filing documents that contain the following:

- Personal identifying numbers (PIN #'s), such as a driver's license number;
- Medical records, treatment and diagnosis;
- Employment history;
- Individual financial information;
- Proprietary or trade secret information;
- Information regarding an individual's cooperation with the government. NY R US-DCTSD CM/ECF, S.D.(II)(21)(21.4).

  b.  *Exemptions from the redaction requirement.* The redaction requirement does not apply to the following:

    i.   A financial-account number that identifies the property allegedly subject to forfeiture in a forfeiture proceeding;

    ii.   The record of an administrative or agency proceeding;

    iii.   The official record of a state-court proceeding;

    iv.  The record of a court or tribunal, if that record was not subject to the redaction requirement when originally filed;

    v.  A filing covered by FRCP 5.2(c) or FRCP 5.2(d); and

    vi.  A pro se filing in an action brought under 28 U.S.C.A. § 2241, 28 U.S.C.A. § 2254, or 28 U.S.C.A. § 2255. FRCP 5.2(b).

c.  *Limitations on remote access to electronic files; Social Security appeals and immigration cases.* Unless the court orders otherwise, in an action for benefits under the Social Security Act, and in an action or proceeding relating to an order of removal, to relief from removal, or to immigration benefits or detention, access to an electronic file is authorized as follows:

    i.  The parties and their attorneys may have remote electronic access to any part of the case file, including the administrative record;

    ii.  Any other person may have electronic access to the full record at the courthouse, but may have remote electronic access only to:

      • The docket maintained by the court; and

      • An opinion, order, judgment, or other disposition of the court, but not any other part of the case file or the administrative record. FRCP 5.2(c).

d.  *Filings made under seal.* The court may order that a filing be made under seal without redaction. The court may later unseal the filing or order the person who made the filing to file a redacted version for the public record. FRCP 5.2(d). For more information on sealing documents, refer to NY R USDCTSD CM/ECF, S.D.(I)(6).

e.  *Protective orders.* For good cause, the court may by order in a case:

    i.  Require redaction of additional information; or

    ii.  Limit or prohibit a nonparty's remote electronic access to a document filed with the court. FRCP 5.2(e).

f.  *Option for additional unredacted filing under seal.* A person making a redacted filing may also file an unredacted copy under seal. The court must retain the unredacted copy as part of the record. FRCP 5.2(f); NY R USDCTSD CM/ECF, S.D.(II)(21)(21.5).

g.  *Option for filing a reference list.* A filing that contains redacted information may be filed together with a reference list that identifies each item of redacted information and specifies an appropriate identifier that uniquely corresponds to each item listed. The list must be filed under seal and may be amended as of right. Any reference in the case to a listed identifier will be construed to refer to the corresponding item of information. FRCP 5.2(g); NY R USDCTSD CM/ECF, S.D.(II)(21)(21.5).

h.  *Responsibility for redaction.* It is the sole responsibility of counsel and the parties to be sure that all documents comply with the rules of this Court requiring redaction of personal identifiers. Neither the judge nor the Clerk of Court will review documents for compliance with these rules. NY R USDCTSD CM/ECF, S.D.(II)(21)(21.2).

i.  *Waiver of protection of identifiers.* A person waives the protection of FRCP 5.2(a) as to the person's own information by filing it without redaction and not under seal. FRCP 5.2(h).

j.  For more information on privacy and public access to ECF cases, refer to NY R USDCTSD CM/ECF, S.D.(II)(21).

5.  *Individual judge practices.* Refer to the Miscellaneous section of this document for information on individual judge practices on formatting documents.

## F. Filing and Service Requirements

1.  *Filing requirements.* Any paper after the complaint that is required to be served—together with a certificate of service—must be filed within a reasonable time after service. FRCP 5(d)(1). Complaints and all subsequent papers are accepted at either courthouse, regardless of the place for which the case is designated. NY R USDCTSD Div. Bus., Rule 22. Subject to the instructions regarding ECF published on the website of each respective Court and any pertinent Individual Judge's Practices, letter-motions

permitted by NY R USDCTS&ED Civ Rule 7.1(d) and letters addressed to the Court (but not letters between the parties) may be filed via ECF. NY R USDCTS&ED Civ Rule 5.2(b). For information on electronically filing motions, refer to NY R USDCTSD CM/ECF, S.D.(II)(15).

a. *How filing is made; In general.* A paper is filed by delivering it:

    i. To the clerk; or

    ii. To a judge who agrees to accept it for filing, and who must then note the filing date on the paper and promptly send it to the clerk. FRCP 5(d)(2).

b. *Night depository.* A night depository with an automatic date stamp shall be maintained by the Clerk of the Southern District in the Pearl Street Courthouse. After regular business hours, papers for the District Court only may be deposited in the night depository. Such papers will be considered as having been filed in the District Court as of the date stamped thereon, which shall be deemed presumptively correct. NY R USDCTS&ED Civ Rule 1.2.

c. *Electronic filing*

    i. *Authorization of electronic filing program.* A court may, by local rule, allow papers to be filed, signed, or verified by electronic means that are consistent with any technical standards established by the Judicial Conference of the United States. A local rule may require electronic filing only if reasonable exceptions are allowed. A paper filed electronically in compliance with a local rule is a written paper for purposes of the Federal Rules of Civil Procedure. FRCP 5(d)(3).

        • The Court will accept for filing documents submitted, signed or verified by electronic means, that comply with the rules in NY R USDCTSD CM/ECF, S.D. NY R USDCTSD CM/ECF, S.D.(I). The information in NY R USDCTSD CM/ECF, S.D. applies only to cases assigned to the ECF system. NY R USDCTSD CM/ECF, S.D.(Introduction).

        • Parties serving and filing papers shall follow the instructions regarding Electronic Case Filing (ECF) published on the website of each respective Court. A paper served and filed by electronic means in accordance with such instructions is, for purposes of FRCP 5, served and filed in compliance with the Local Civil Rules of the Southern and Eastern Districts of New York. NY R USDCTS&ED Civ Rule 5.2(a). Parties have an obligation to review the Court's actual order, decree, or judgment (on ECF), which controls, and should not rely on the description on the docket or in the ECF Notice of Electronic Filing (NEF). NY R USDCTS&ED Civ Rule 5.2(c).

        • The following should be observed when filing electronically: (1) the Federal Rules of Civil Procedure, (2) the Local Civil Rules of the United States District Courts for the Southern and Eastern Districts of New York, (3) the assigned judge's Individual Practices, and (4) the Court's Electronic Case Filing Rules & Instructions (NY R USDCTSD CM/ECF, S.D.). NY R USDCTSD CM/ECF, S.D.(Introduction).

    ii. *Scope of electronic filing.* Except as expressly provided and in exceptional circumstances preventing a party from filing electronically, all documents required to be filed with the Court must be filed electronically. Any party unable to comply with this requirement must seek permission of the Court to file in the traditional manner, on paper. Any such application made after regular business hours may be submitted through the night depository box maintained pursuant to NY R USDCTS&ED Civ Rule 1.2. NY R USDCTSD CM/ECF, S.D.(I)(1)(1.1).

        • *Documents filed by pro se litigants.* Unless otherwise ordered by the Court, documents filed by pro se litigants must be filed in the traditional manner, on paper, and will be scanned and docketed by the Clerk's Office into the ECF system. NY R USDCTSD CM/ECF, S.D.(I)(1)(1.1). Pro se litigants must file pleadings and documents in the traditional manner on paper unless the assigned judge has granted permission to electronically file on the ECF system. NY R USDCTSD CM/ECF, S.D.(Introduction).

        • *Letters.* Except for letters to be filed under seal, letters addressed to judges who accept letters may be filed electronically. Parties should consult the assigned judge's Individual Practices to determine if the judge accepts letters at all and, if he or she does, whether the

judge has any page limitations on letters and/or requires courtesy copies of letters filed on ECF (and, if so, by what means of delivery). NY R USDCTSD CM/ECF, S.D.(II)(13)(13.1). Letters solely between parties or their counsel or otherwise not addressed to the Court may not be filed electronically on ECF (except as exhibits to an otherwise properly filed document). NY R USDCTSD CM/ECF, S.D.(II)(13)(13.1). For more information on filing letters, refer to NY R USDCTSD CM/ECF, S.D.(II)(13)(13.1).

- *Proposed orders, judgments and decrees.* Proposed orders, judgments and decrees shall be presented as directed by the ECF rules published on the website of each respective Court. NY R USDCTS&ED Civ Rule 77.1. For more information, refer to NY R USDCTS&ED Civ Rule 77.1.

iii. *Exceptions to electronic filing.* In an ECF case, the documents that should not be electronically filed include:

- Miscellaneous Case initiating documents, NY R USDCTSD CM/ECF, S.D.(II)(18)(18.2);

- Proposed orders; proposed judgments, stipulations; consents, NY R USDCTSD CM/ECF, S.D.(II)(18)(18.3);

- Orders to show cause / temporary restraining orders, NY R USDCTSD CM/ECF, S.D.(II)(18)(18.4);

- Sealed documents, NY R USDCTSD CM/ECF, S.D.(II)(18)(18.5); and

- Surety bonds, NY R USDCTSD CM/ECF, S.D.(II)(18)(18.6).

- In cases where the record of an administrative or other prior proceeding must be filed with the Court, such record may be served and filed in hard copy without prior motion and order of the Court. NY R USDCTSD CM/ECF, S.D.(I)(5)(5.3).

- For more documents excepted from electronic filing, and for more information on such documents, refer to NY R USDCTSD CM/ECF, S.D.(II)(18).

iv. *Consequences of electronic filing.* Except as otherwise provided in NY R USDCTSD CM/ECF, S.D.(I)(4), electronic filing of a document in the ECF system consistent with these procedures, together with the transmission of a Notice of Electronic Filing (NEF) from the Court, constitutes filing of the document for all purposes of the Federal Rules of Civil Procedure and the Local Civil Rules of the United States District Courts for the Southern and Eastern Districts of New York and constitutes entry of the document on the docket kept by the Clerk under FRCP 58 and FRCP 79. NY R USDCTSD CM/ECF, S.D.(I)(3)(3.1).

v. For more information on electronic filing, refer to NY R USDCTSD CM/ECF, S.D.

2. *Service requirements*

a. *Service; When required*

i. *In general.* Unless the Federal Rules of Civil Procedure provide otherwise, each of the following papers must be served on every party:

- An order stating that service is required;

- A pleading filed after the original complaint, unless the court orders otherwise under FRCP 5(c) because there are numerous defendants;

- A discovery paper required to be served on a party, unless the court orders otherwise;

- A written motion, except one that may be heard ex parte; and

- A written notice, appearance, demand, or offer of judgment, or any similar paper. FRCP 5(a)(1).

ii. *If a party fails to appear.* No service is required on a party who is in default for failing to appear. But a pleading that asserts a new claim for relief against such a party must be served on that party under FRCP 4. FRCP 5(a)(2).

iii. *Seizing property.* If an action is begun by seizing property and no person is or need be named as

a defendant, any service required before the filing of an appearance, answer, or claim must be made on the person who had custody or possession of the property when it was seized. FRCP 5(a)(3).

b. *Service; How made*

   i. *Serving an attorney.* If a party is represented by an attorney, service under FRCP 5 must be made on the attorney unless the court orders service on the party. FRCP 5(b)(1).

   ii. *Service in general.* A paper is served under FRCP 5 by:

   - Handing it to the person;

   - Leaving it: (1) at the person's office with a clerk or other person in charge or, if no one is in charge, in a conspicuous place in the office; or (2) if the person has no office or the office is closed, at the person's dwelling or usual place of abode with someone of suitable age and discretion who resides there;

   - Mailing it to the person's last known address—in which event service is complete upon mailing;

   - Leaving it with the court clerk if the person has no known address;

   - Sending it by electronic means if the person consented in writing—in which event service is complete upon transmission, but is not effective if the serving party learns that it did not reach the person to be served; or

   - Delivering it by any other means that the person consented to in writing—in which event service is complete when the person making service delivers it to the agency designated to make delivery. FRCP 5(b)(2).

   iii. *Service by overnight delivery.* Service upon an attorney may be made by overnight delivery service. "Overnight delivery service" means any delivery service which regularly accepts items for overnight delivery. Overnight delivery service shall be deemed service by mail for purposes of FRCP 5 and FRCP 6. NY R USDCTS&ED Civ Rule 5.3.

   iv. *Service by electronic means.* Parties serving and filing papers shall follow the instructions regarding Electronic Case Filing (ECF) published on the website of each respective Court. A paper served and filed by electronic means in accordance with such instructions is, for purposes of FRCP 5, served and filed in compliance with the Local Civil Rules of the United States District Courts for the Southern and Eastern Districts of New York. NY R USDCTS&ED Civ Rule 5.2(a). Parties have an obligation to review the Court's actual order, decree, or judgment (on ECF), which controls, and should not rely on the description on the docket or in the ECF Notice of Electronic Filing (NEF). NY R USDCTS&ED Civ Rule 5.2(c).

   - *Notice of electronic filing (NEF).* In cases assigned to the ECF system, service is complete provided all parties receive a Notice of Electronic Filing (NEF), which is sent automatically by email from the Court (see the NEF for a list of who did/did not receive notice electronically). Transmission of the NEF constitutes service upon all Filing and Receiving Users who are listed as recipients of notice by electronic mail. NY R USDCTSD CM/ECF, S.D.(I)(9)(9.1). In cases assigned to the ECF system, if all parties receive a NEF, service is complete upon transmission of the NEF by the Court, and you are not required to serve a paper copy. NY R USDCTSD CM/ECF, S.D.(II)(19)(19.2). It remains the duty of Filing and Receiving Users to maintain current contact information with the court and to regularly review the docket sheet of the case. NY R USDCTSD CM/ECF, S.D.(I)(9)(9.1).

   - *Mailing of court-initiated documents.* The Clerk's Office will no longer mail paper copies of court-initiated documents to Filing and Receiving Users. The Clerk's Office will mail copies of all court-initiated documents to pro se parties who have not registered as Filing or Receiving Users. NY R USDCTSD CM/ECF, S.D.(II)(19)(19.1).

   - *No receipt of a NEF.* If any party does not receive a NEF, you are required to accomplish service on that party in the traditional manner, in paper form. NY R USDCTSD CM/ECF, S.D.(II)(19)(19.2). The NEF receipt will inform you who will receive notice of the filing

"electronically" (by e-mail from the Court) and who will receive notice "by other means" (traditional service in paper form). NY R USDCTSD CM/ECF, S.D.(II)(19)(19.2).

- *Service on non-filing or non-receiving users.* Attorneys and pro se parties who are not Filing or Receiving Users must be served with a paper copy of any electronically filed pleading or other document. Service of such paper copy must be made according to the Federal Rules of Civil Procedure and the Local Civil Rules of the United States District Courts for the Southern and Eastern Districts of New York. NY R USDCTSD CM/ECF, S.D.(I)(9)(9.2). Such paper service must be documented by electronically filing proof of service. NY R USDCTSD CM/ECF, S.D.(I)(9)(9.2); NY R USDCTSD CM/ECF, S.D.(II)(19)(19.2). Where the Clerk scans and electronically files pleadings and documents on behalf of a pro se party, the associated NEF constitutes service. NY R USDCTSD CM/ECF, S.D.(I)(9)(9.2).

- For more information on service by electronic means, refer to NY R USDCTSD CM/ECF, S.D.(II)(19).

    v. *Using court facilities.* If a local rule so authorizes, a party may use the court's transmission facilities to make service under FRCP 5(b)(2)(E). FRCP 5(b)(3).

  c. *Serving numerous defendants*

    i. *In general.* If an action involves an unusually large number of defendants, the court may, on motion or on its own, order that:

- Defendants' pleadings and replies to them need not be served on other defendants;

- Any crossclaim, counterclaim, avoidance, or affirmative defense in those pleadings and replies to them will be treated as denied or avoided by all other parties; and

- Filing any such pleading and serving it on the plaintiff constitutes notice of the pleading to all parties. FRCP 5(c)(1).

    ii. *Notifying parties.* A copy of every such order must be served on the parties as the court directs. FRCP 5(c)(2).

3. *Individual judge practices.* Refer to the Miscellaneous section of this document for information on individual judge practices on filing and serving documents.

## G. Hearings

1. *Hearings, generally*

  a. *Oral argument.* Due process does not require that oral argument be permitted on a motion and, except as otherwise provided by local rule, the district court has discretion to determine whether it will decide the motion on the papers or hear argument by counsel (and perhaps receive evidence). FPP § 1190; F.D.I.C. v. Deglau, 207 F.3d 153 (3d Cir. 2000). The parties and their attorneys shall only appear to argue the motion if so directed by the Court by order or by a Judge's Individual Practice. NY R USDCTS&ED Civ Rule 6.1(c).

  b. *Providing a regular schedule for oral hearings.* A court may establish regular times and places for oral hearings on motions. FRCP 78(a).

  c. *Providing for submission on briefs.* By rule or order, the court may provide for submitting and determining motions on briefs, without oral hearings. FRCP 78(b).

2. *Hearing on FRCP 12 defenses before trial.* If a party so moves, any defense listed in FRCP 12(b)(1) through FRCP 12(b)(7)—whether made in a pleading or by motion—and a motion under FRCP 12(c) must be heard and decided before trial unless the court orders a deferral until trial. FRCP 12(i).

3. *Individual judge practices.* Refer to the Miscellaneous section of this document for information on individual judge practices on hearings.

## H. Forms

### 1. Federal Motion to Dismiss for Lack of Personal Jurisdiction Forms

  a. Motion and notice; To dismiss; Defendant not present within state where district court is located. AMJUR PP FEDPRAC § 488.

b.   Motion and notice; To dismiss; Lack of jurisdiction over person. AMJUR PP FEDPRAC § 489.

c.   Motion and notice; To dismiss; Lack of jurisdiction over person; Ineffective service of process on foreign state. AMJUR PP FEDPRAC § 490.

d.   Motion and notice; To dismiss; Lack of jurisdiction over person; Consul not agent of country represented for purpose of receiving service of process. AMJUR PP FEDPRAC § 491.

e.   Motion and notice; To dismiss; Lack of jurisdiction over corporate defendant. AMJUR PP FEDPRAC § 492.

f.   Motion and notice; To dismiss; International organization immune from suit. AMJUR PP FEDPRAC § 493.

g.   Motion and notice; To dismiss; Officer or employee of international organization acting within official capacity; Immune from suit. AMJUR PP FEDPRAC § 494.

h.   Motion and notice; To dismiss; Family member of member of foreign mission immune from suit. AMJUR PP FEDPRAC § 495.

i.   Motion and notice; To dismiss complaint or, in alternative, to quash service of summons; Lack of jurisdiction over corporate defendant. AMJUR PP FEDPRAC § 496.

j.   Motion to dismiss; Lack of personal jurisdiction; No minimum contacts. AMJUR PP FEDPRAC § 497.

k.   Affidavit; Of Consul General; In support of motion to dismiss; Consular immunity and lack of authority to act as agent for service of process. AMJUR PP FEDPRAC § 498.

l.   Motion to dismiss for lack of personal jurisdiction; Corporate defendant. 2C FEDFORMS § 11:52.

m.   Motion to dismiss for lack of personal jurisdiction; By corporate defendant; With citation. 2C FEDFORMS § 11:53.

n.   Motion to dismiss for lack of personal jurisdiction; By a foreign corporation. 2C FEDFORMS § 11:54.

o.   Motion to dismiss for lack of personal jurisdiction; For insufficiency of service. 2C FEDFORMS § 11:55.

p.   Motion to dismiss for lack of personal jurisdiction; Insufficiency of process and insufficiency of service of process. 2C FEDFORMS § 11:56.

q.   Motion; To dismiss; Lack of jurisdiction over person of defendant. FEDPROF § 1:910.

r.   Opposition; To motion; General form. FEDPROF § 1:750.

s.   Affidavit; Supporting or opposing motion. FEDPROF § 1:751.

t.   Brief; Supporting or opposing motion. FEDPROF § 1:752.

u.   Statement of points and authorities; Opposing motion. FEDPROF § 1:753.

v.   Motion to dismiss; Lack of jurisdiction over person of defendant; Short form. FEDPROF § 1:911.

w.   Motion to dismiss; Lack of jurisdiction over person of defendant; Accident in foreign country and defendants have no contacts with forum state. FEDPROF § 1:911.50.

x.   Motion to dismiss; Lack of jurisdiction over corporate defendant. FEDPROF § 1:912.

y.   Motion; To dismiss complaint or, in the alternative, to quash service of summons; Lack of jurisdiction over corporate defendant. FEDPROF § 1:913.

z.   Motion to dismiss complaint; General form. GOLDLTGFMS § 20:24.

## I.  Applicable Rules

1.   *Federal rules*

a.   Summons. FRCP 4.

b.   Serving and filing pleadings and other papers. FRCP 5.

c.   Constitutional challenge to a statute; Notice, certification, and intervention. FRCP 5.1.

    d.   Privacy protection for filings made with the court. FRCP 5.2.

    e.   Computing and extending time; Time for motion papers. FRCP 6.

    f.   Pleadings allowed; Form of motions and other papers. FRCP 7.

    g.   Disclosure statement. FRCP 7.1.

    h.   Form of pleadings. FRCP 10.

    i.   Signing pleadings, motions, and other papers; Representations to the court; Sanctions. FRCP 11.

    j.   Defenses and objections; When and how presented; Motion for judgment on the pleadings; Consolidating motions; Waiving defenses; Pretrial hearing. FRCP 12.

    k.   Taking testimony. FRCP 43.

    l.   Hearing motions; Submission on briefs. FRCP 78.

2.  *Local rules*

    a.   Night depository. NY R USDCTS&ED Civ Rule 1.2.

    b.   Duty of attorneys in related cases. NY R USDCTS&ED Civ Rule 1.6.

    c.   Filing of discovery materials. NY R USDCTS&ED Civ Rule 5.1.

    d.   Electronic service and filing of documents. NY R USDCTS&ED Civ Rule 5.2.

    e.   Service by overnight delivery. NY R USDCTS&ED Civ Rule 5.3.

    f.   Service and filing of motion papers. NY R USDCTS&ED Civ Rule 6.1.

    g.   Orders on motions. NY R USDCTS&ED Civ Rule 6.2.

    h.   Computation of time. NY R USDCTS&ED Civ Rule 6.4.

    i.   Motion papers. NY R USDCTS&ED Civ Rule 7.1.

    j.   Disclosure statement. NY R USDCTS&ED Civ Rule 7.1.1.

    k.   Authorities to be provided to pro se litigants. NY R USDCTS&ED Civ Rule 7.2.

    l.   Form of pleadings, motions, and other papers. NY R USDCTS&ED Civ Rule 11.1.

    m.   Notice to pro se litigant who opposes a FRCP 12 motion supported by matters outside the pleadings. NY R USDCTS&ED Civ Rule 12.1.

    n.   Submission of orders, judgments and decrees. NY R USDCTS&ED Civ Rule 77.1.

    o.   Alternative dispute resolution (Southern District only). NY R USDCTS&ED Civ Rule 83.9.

    p.   Electronic case filing rules and instructions. NY R USDCTSD CM/ECF, S.D.

    q.   Related cases. NY R USDCTSD Div. Bus., Rule 13.

    r.   Filing at either courthouse. NY R USDCTSD Div. Bus., Rule 22.

**J. Miscellaneous**

**NOTE: Individual judges' rules may apply. For available judge-level information, refer to:**

DISTRICT JUDGE RONNIE ABRAMS: NY R USDCTSD Abrams-Civ Prac; NY R USDCTSD Abrams-Crim Prac; NY R USDCTSD Abrams-Pro Se; NY R USDCTSD Abrams-Case Mgt; NY R USDCTSD Abrams-Jury.

DISTRICT JUDGE DEBORAH A. BATTS: NY R USDCTSD Batts-Practices.

DISTRICT JUDGE RICHARD M. BERMAN: NY R USDCTSD Berman-Practices; NY R USDCTSD Berman-Default; NY R USDCTSD Berman-Sentencing; NY R USDCTSD Berman-Media.

DISTRICT JUDGE VINCENT L. BRICCETTI: NY R USDCTSD Briccetti-Practices; NY R USDCTSD Briccetti-Plan; NY R USDCTSD Briccetti-Notice.

DISTRICT JUDGE VERNON S. BRODERICK: NY R USDCTSD Broderick-Civil; NY R USDCTSD Broderick-Crim; NY R USDCTSD Broderick-Case Mgt; NY R USDCTSD Broderick-Jury.

DISTRICT JUDGE NAOMI REICE BUCHWALD: NY R USDCTSD Buchwald-Practices.

DISTRICT JUDGE VALERIE E. CAPRONI: NY R USDCTSD Caproni-Prac; NY R USDCTSD Caproni--Pro Se; NY R USDCTSD Caproni-Case Mgt; NY R USDCTSD Caproni-Crim Prac.

DISTRICT JUDGE ANDREW L. CARTER JR.: NY R USDCTSD Carter-Practices.

DISTRICT JUDGE KEVIN P. CASTEL: NY R USDCTSD Castel-Practices; NY R USDCTSD Castel-Default; NY R USDCTSD Castel-Scheduling; NY R USDCTSD Castel-Complex; NY R USDCTSD Castel-Trials; NY R USDCTSD Castel-Sentencing.

DISTRICT JUDGE DENISE L. COTE: NY R USDCTSD Cote-Civil Practices; NY R USDCTSD Cote-Pro Se; NY R USDCTSD Cote-Maritime Ord; NY R USDCTSD Cote-Crim Practices; NY R USDCTSD Cote-Crim Trials; NY R USDCTSD Cote-Sentencing.

DISTRICT JUDGE PAUL A. CROTTY: NY R USDCTSD Crotty-Practices; NY R USDCTSD Crotty-Sentencing; NY R USDCTSD Crotty-Calls; NY R USDCTSD Crotty-Scheduling.

DISTRICT JUDGE GEORGE B. DANIELS: NY R USDCTSD Daniels-Practices.

DISTRICT JUDGE KEVIN T. DUFFY: NY R USDCTSD Duffy-Practices.

DISTRICT JUDGE PAUL A. ENGELMAYER: NY R USDCTSD Engelmayer-Practices; NY R USDCTSD Engelmayer-Scheduling; NY R USDCTSD Engelmayer-Sentencing; NY R USDCTSD Engelmayer-Pro Se; NY R USDCTSD Engelmayer-Crim.

DISTRICT JUDGE KATHERINE POLK FAILLA: NY R USDCTSD Failla-Civ Prac; NY R USDCTSD Failla-Crim Prac; NY R USDCTSD Failla-Case Mgt.

DISTRICT JUDGE KATHERINE B. FORREST: NY R USDCTSD Forrest-Civil Prac; NY R USDCTSD Forrest-Crim Prac; NY R USDCTSD Forrest-Crim Pretrial; NY R USDCTSD Forrest-Scheduling; NY R USDCTSD Forrest-Patent Scheduling; NY R USDCTSD Forrest-Sentencing; NY R USDCTSD Forrest-Order 1; NY R USDCTSD Forrest-Order 2.

DISTRICT JUDGE JESSE M. FURMAN: NY R USDCTSD Furman-Civil Prac; NY R USDCTSD Furman-Crim Prac; NY R USDCTSD Furman-Pro Se Prac; NY R USDCTSD Furman-Trials; NY R USDCTSD Furman-Scheduling; NY R USDCTSD Furman-Rights.

DISTRICT JUDGE PAUL G. GARDEPHE: NY R USDCTSD Gardephe-Civ Prac; NY R USDCTSD Gardephe-Pretrial; NY R USDCTSD Gardephe-Prot Ord; NY R USDCTSD Gardephe-Maritime; NY R USDCTSD Gardephe-Crim Prac; NY R USDCTSD Gardephe-Trial.

DISTRICT JUDGE THOMAS P. GRIESA: NY R USDCTSD Griesa-Practices.

DISTRICT JUDGE CHARLES S. HAIGHT: NY R USDCTSD Haight-Practices.

DISTRICT JUDGE ALVIN K. HELLERSTEIN: NY R USDCTSD Hellerstein-Practices; NY R USDCTSD Hellerstein--Sept 11.

DISTRICT JUDGE LEWIS A. KAPLAN: NY R USDCTSD Kaplan-Practices; NY R USDCTSD Kaplan-Sentencing.

DISTRICT JUDGE KENNETH M. KARAS: NY R USDCTSD Karas-Practices; NY R USDCTSD Karas-Case Mgt; NY R USDCTSD Karas-Default; NY R USDCTSD Karas-Sentencing; NY R USDCTSD Karas-Rights.

DISTRICT JUDGE JOHN F. KEENAN: NY R USDCTSD Keenan-Practices.

DISTRICT JUDGE JOHN G. KOELTL: NY R USDCTSD Koeltl-Practices.

DISTRICT JUDGE VICTOR MARRERO: NY R USDCTSD Marrero-Practices; NY R USDCTSD Marrero-Scheduling; NY R USDCTSD Marrero-Default; NY R USDCTSD Marrero-Trial Proc.

DISTRICT JUDGE COLLEEN McMAHON: NY R USDCTSD McMahon-Practices; NY R USDCTSD McMahon-RICO; NY R USDCTSD McMahon-Copies; NY R USDCTSD McMahon-Scheduling; NY R USDCTSD McMahon-Elec Disc; NY R USDCTSD McMahon-Sentencing.

DISTRICT JUDGE ALISON J. NATHAN: NY R USDCTSD Nathan-Civ Prac; NY R USDCTSD Nathan-Crim Prac; NY R USDCTSD Nathan-Pro Se; NY R USDCTSD Nathan-Scheduling.

DISTRICT JUDGE J. PAUL OETKEN: NY R USDCTSD Oetken-Civ Prac; NY R USDCTSD Oetken-Case Mgt; NY R USDCTSD Oetken-Crim Prac; NY R USDCTSD Oetken-Pro Se.

DISTRICT JUDGE WILLIAM H. PAULEY, III: NY R USDCTSD Pauley-Crim Cases; NY R USDCTSD Pauley-Practices.

DISTRICT JUDGE LORETTA A. PRESKA: NY R USDCTSD Preska-Practices.

DISTRICT JUDGE JED S. RAKOFF: NY R USDCTSD Rakoff-Practices; NY R USDCTSD Rakoff-Scheduling; NY R USDCTSD Rakoff-Prot Ord; NY R USDCTSD Rakoff-Maritime Ord.

DISTRICT JUDGE EDGARDO RAMOS: NY R USDCTSD Ramos--Practices; NY R USDCTSD Ramos-Case Mgt.

DISTRICT JUDGE NELSON S. ROMAN: NY R USDCTSD Roman-Civ Prac; NY R USDCTSD Roman-Pro Se; NY R USDCTSD Roman-Crim Prac; NY R USDCTSD Roman-Case Mgt.

DISTRICT JUDGE LEONARD B. SAND: NY R USDCTSD Sand-Practices.

DISTRICT JUDGE LORNA G. SCHOFIELD: NY R USDCTSD Schofield-Civ Prac; NY R USDCTSD Schofield-Crim Prac; NY R USDCTSD Schofield-Sched; NY R USDCTSD Schofield-Pro Se; NY R USDCTSD Schofield-Advice.

DISTRICT JUDGE CATHY SEIBEL: NY R USDCTSD Seibel-Practices.

DISTRICT JUDGE LOUIS L. STANTON: NY R USDCTSD Stanton-Practices; NY R USDCTSD Stanton-Pretrial.

DISTRICT JUDGE SIDNEY H. STEIN: NY R USDCTSD Stein-Practices.

DISTRICT JUDGE RICHARD J. SULLIVAN: NY R USDCTSD Sullivan-Practices; NY R USDCTSD Sullivan-Scheduling; NY R USDCTSD Sullivan-Sentencing; NY R USDCTSD Sullivan-Juries; NY R USDCTSD Sullivan-Trial; NY R USDCTSD Sullivan-Default.

DISTRICT JUDGE LAURA TAYLOR SWAIN: NY R USDCTSD Swain-Practices; NY R USDCTSD Swain-Trial; NY R USDCTSD Swain-Crim Trial; NY R USDCTSD Swain-Juries; NY R USDCTSD Swain-Sentencing; NY R USDCTSD Swain-Rights.

DISTRICT JUDGE ROBERT W. SWEET: NY R USDCTSD Sweet-Practices.

DISTRICT JUDGE ANALISA TORRES: NY R USDCTSD Torres-Civ Prac; NY R USDCTSD Torres-Pro Se; NY R USDCTSD Torres-Scheduling.

DISTRICT JUDGE KIMBA M. WOOD: NY R USDCTSD Wood-Practices; NY R USDCTSD Wood-Scheduling; NY R USDCTSD Wood-Discovery; NY R USDCTSD Wood-RICO; NY R USDCTSD Wood-Juries; NY R USDCTSD Wood-Trial; NY R USDCTSD Wood-Media.

DISTRICT JUDGE GREGORY H. WOODS: NY R USDCTSD Woods-Civ Prac; NY R USDCTSD Woods-Pro Se; NY R USDCTSD Woods-Sched; NY R USDCTSD Woods-Crim Prac; NY R USDCTSD Woods-Protect Order; NY R USDCTSD Woods-Speedy Trial.

MAGISTRATE JUDGE JAMES L. COTT: NY R USDCTSD Cott-Practices; NY R USDCTSD Cott-Settlement.

MAGISTRATE JUDGE PAUL E. DAVISON: NY R USDCTSD Davison-Practices.

MAGISTRATE JUDGE RONALD L. ELLIS: NY R USDCTSD Ellis-Practices.

MAGISTRATE JUDGE KEVIN N. FOX: NY R USDCTSD Fox-Practices; NY R USDCTSD Fox-Settlement.

MAGISTRATE JUDGE JAMES C. FRANCIS: NY R USDCTSD Francis-Practices.

MAGISTRATE JUDGE DEBRA FREEMAN: NY R USDCTSD Freeman-Practices; NY R USDCTSD Freeman-Settlement.

MAGISTRATE JUDGE GABRIEL W. GORENSTEIN: NY R USDCTSD Gorenstein-Practices; NY R USDCTSD Gorenstein-Ackn.

MAGISTRATE JUDGE FRANK MAAS: NY R USDCTSD Maas-Practices; NY R USDCTSD Maas-Discontinuance; NY R USDCTSD Maas-Conf; NY R USDCTSD Maas-Settlement.

MAGISTRATE JUDGE JUDITH C. McCARTHY: NY R USDCTSD McCarthy-Practices; NY R USDCTSD McCarthy-Conduct.

MAGISTRATE JUDGE BARBARA MOSES: NY R USDCTSD Moses-Practices.

MAGISTRATE JUDGE SARAH NETBURN: NY R USDCTSD Netburn-Civil; NY R USDCTSD Netburn-Settlement; NY R USDCTSD Netburn-Case Mgt; NY R USDCTSD Netburn--Pro Se.

MAGISTRATE JUDGE ANDREW J. PECK: NY R USDCTSD Peck-Practices; NY R USDCTSD Peck-Order; NY R USDCTSD Peck-Rule 502(d).

MAGISTRATE JUDGE HENRY PITMAN: NY R USDCTSD Pitman-Practices.

MAGISTRATE JUDGE LISA MARGARET SMITH: NY R USDCTSD Smith-Practices; NY R USDCTSD Smith-Trials.

# Motions, Oppositions and Replies
# Motion for Judgment on the Pleadings

### Document Last Updated September 2016

## A. Checklist

(I) ❑ Matters to be considered by moving party

  (a) ❑ Required documents

    (1) ❑ Notice of motion and motion

    (2) ❑ Memorandum of law

    (3) ❑ Certificate of service

  (b) ❑ Supplemental documents

    (1) ❑ Pleadings

    (2) ❑ Notice of constitutional question

    (3) ❑ Nongovernmental corporate disclosure statement

    (4) ❑ Notice to pro se litigant who opposes a FRCP 12 motion supported by matters outside the pleadings

    (5) ❑ Copies of authorities

    (6) ❑ Proposed order

    (7) ❑ Statement explaining untimely electronic filing

    (8) ❑ Courtesy copies

  (c) ❑ Timing

    (1) ❑ After the pleadings are closed—but early enough not to delay trial—a party may move for judgment on the pleadings

    (2) ❑ A written motion and notice of the hearing must be served at least fourteen (14) days before the time specified for the hearing, with the following exceptions: (i) when the motion may be heard ex parte; (ii) when the Federal Rules of Civil Procedure set a different time; or (iii) when a court order—which a party may, for good cause, apply for ex parte—sets a different time

    (3) ❑ Any affidavit supporting a motion must be served with the motion

(II) ❑ Matters to be considered by opposing party

  (a) ❑ Required documents

    (1) ❑ Answering memorandum of law

    (2) ❑ Certificate of service

  (b) ❑ Supplemental documents

    (1) ❑ Pleadings

    (2) ❑ Notice of constitutional question

        (3)  ❏  Copies of authorities

        (4)  ❏  Statement explaining untimely electronic filing

        (5)  ❏  Courtesy copies

   (c)  ❏  Timing

        (1)  ❏  Any opposing affidavits and answering memoranda shall be served within fourteen (14) days after service of the moving papers

        (2)  ❏  Except as FRCP 59(c) provides otherwise, any opposing affidavit must be served at least seven (7) days before the hearing, unless the court permits service at another time

## B. Timing

1. *Motion for judgment on the pleadings.* After the pleadings are closed—but early enough not to delay trial—a party may move for judgment on the pleadings. FRCP 12(c).

   a. *When pleadings are closed.* FRCP 7(a) provides that the pleadings are closed upon the filing of a complaint and an answer (absent a court-ordered reply), unless a counterclaim, cross-claim, or third-party claim is interposed, in which event the filing of a reply to a counterclaim, cross-claim answer, or third-party answer normally will mark the close of the pleadings. FPP § 1367.

   b. *Timeliness and delay.* Ordinarily, a motion for judgment on the pleadings should be made promptly after the close of the pleadings. Generally, however, a FRCP 12(c) motion is considered timely if it is made early enough not to delay trial or cause prejudice to the non-movant. FPP § 1367.

2. *Timing of motions, generally*

   a. *Motion and notice of hearing.* Except for letter-motions as permitted by NY R USDCTS&ED Civ Rule 7.1(d), and unless otherwise provided by statute or rule or by the Court in a Judge's Individual Practice or in a direction in a particular case, upon any motion, the notice of motion, supporting affidavits, and memoranda shall be served and filed as follows: on all civil motions, petitions, and applications, other than those described in NY R USDCTS&ED Civ Rule 6.1(a), and other than petitions for writs of habeas corpus, the notice of motion, supporting affidavits, and memoranda of law shall be served by the moving party on all other parties that have appeared in the action. NY R USDCTS&ED Civ Rule 6.1(b)(1). A written motion and notice of the hearing must be served at least fourteen (14) days before the time specified for the hearing, with the following exceptions:

      i.   When the motion may be heard ex parte;

      ii.  When the Federal Rules of Civil Procedure set a different time; or

      iii. When a court order—which a party may, for good cause, apply for ex parte—sets a different time. FRCP 6(c)(1).

   b. *Supporting affidavit.* Any affidavit supporting a motion must be served with the motion. FRCP 6(c)(2).

3. *Timing of opposing papers.* Except for letter-motions as permitted by NY R USDCTS&ED Civ Rule 7.1(d), and unless otherwise provided by statute or rule or by the Court in a Judge's Individual Practice or in a direction in a particular case, upon any motion, the notice of motion, supporting affidavits, and memoranda shall be served and filed as follows: on all civil motions, petitions, and applications, other than those described in NY R USDCTS&ED Civ Rule 6.1(a), and other than petitions for writs of habeas corpus, any opposing affidavits and answering memoranda shall be served within fourteen (14) days after service of the moving papers. NY R USDCTS&ED Civ Rule 6.1(b)(2).

   a. *Opposing affidavit.* Except as FRCP 59(c) provides otherwise, any opposing affidavit must be served at least seven (7) days before the hearing, unless the court permits service at another time. FRCP 6(c)(2).

4. *Timing of reply papers.* Where the respondent files an answering affidavit setting up a new matter, the moving party ordinarily is allowed a reasonable time to file a reply affidavit since failure to deny the new matter by affidavit may operate as an admission of its truth. AMJUR MOTIONS § 25.

   a. *Reply affidavits and reply memoranda of law.* Except for letter-motions as permitted by NY R

USDCTS&ED Civ Rule 7.1(d), and unless otherwise provided by statute or rule or by the Court in a Judge's Individual Practice or in a direction in a particular case, upon any motion, the notice of motion, supporting affidavits, and memoranda shall be served and filed as follows: on all civil motions, petitions, and applications, other than those described in NY R USDCTS&ED Civ Rule 6.1(a), and other than petitions for writs of habeas corpus, any reply affidavits and memoranda of law shall be served within seven (7) days after service of the answering papers. NY R USDCTS&ED Civ Rule 6.1(b)(3).

5. *Effect of a FRCP 12 motion on the time to serve a responsive pleading.* Unless the court sets a different time, serving a motion under FRCP 12 alters the periods in FRCP 12(a) as follows:

   a. If the court denies the motion or postpones its disposition until trial, the responsive pleading must be served within fourteen (14) days after notice of the court's action; or

   b. If the court grants a motion for a more definite statement, the responsive pleading must be served within fourteen (14) days after the more definite statement is served. FRCP 12(a)(4).

6. *Computation of time*

   a. *Computing time.* FRCP 6 applies in computing any time period specified in the Federal Rules of Civil Procedure, in any local rule or court order, or in any statute that does not specify a method of computing time. FRCP 6(a). In computing any period of time prescribed or allowed by the Local Civil Rules of the United States District Courts for the Southern and Eastern Districts of New York or the Local Admiralty and Maritime Rules, the provisions of FRCP 6 shall apply unless otherwise stated. NY R USDCTS&ED Civ Rule 6.4.

      i. *Period stated in days or a longer unit.* In computing periods of days, refer to FRCP 6 and NY R USDCTS&ED Civ Rule 6.4. NY R USDCTS&ED Civ Rule 6.1(b). When the period is stated in days or a longer unit of time:

         • Exclude the day of the event that triggers the period;

         • Count every day, including intermediate Saturdays, Sundays, and legal holidays; and

         • Include the last day of the period, but if the last day is a Saturday, Sunday, or legal holiday, the period continues to run until the end of the next day that is not a Saturday, Sunday, or legal holiday. FRCP 6(a)(1). In the Local Civil Rules of the United States District Courts for the Southern and Eastern Districts of New York, as in the Federal Rules of Civil Procedure as amended effective December 1, 2009, Saturdays, Sundays, and legal holidays are no longer excluded in computing periods of time. If the last day of the period is a Saturday, Sunday, or legal holiday, the period continues to run until the end of the next day that is not a Saturday, Sunday, or legal holiday. NY R USDCTS&ED Civ Rule 6.4.

      ii. *Period stated in hours.* When the period is stated in hours:

         • Begin counting immediately on the occurrence of the event that triggers the period;

         • Count every hour, including hours during intermediate Saturdays, Sundays, and legal holidays; and

         • If the period would end on a Saturday, Sunday, or legal holiday, the period continues to run until the same time on the next day that is not a Saturday, Sunday, or legal holiday. FRCP 6(a)(2). In the Local Civil Rules of the United States District Courts for the Southern and Eastern Districts of New York, as in the Federal Rules of Civil Procedure as amended effective December 1, 2009, Saturdays, Sundays, and legal holidays are no longer excluded in computing periods of time. If the last day of the period is a Saturday, Sunday, or legal holiday, the period continues to run until the end of the next day that is not a Saturday, Sunday, or legal holiday. NY R USDCTS&ED Civ Rule 6.4.

      iii. *Inaccessibility of the clerk's office.* Unless the court orders otherwise, if the clerk's office is inaccessible:

         • On the last day for filing under FRCP 6(a)(1), then the time for filing is extended to the first accessible day that is not a Saturday, Sunday, or legal holiday; or

         • During the last hour for filing under FRCP 6(a)(2), then the time for filing is extended to

the same time on the first accessible day that is not a Saturday, Sunday, or legal holiday. FRCP 6(a)(3).

iv. *"Last day" defined.* Unless a different time is set by a statute, local rule, or court order, the last day ends:

- For electronic filing, at midnight in the court's time zone; and

- For filing by other means, when the clerk's office is scheduled to close. FRCP 6(a)(4).

v. *"Next day" defined.* The "next day" is determined by continuing to count forward when the period is measured after an event and backward when measured before an event. FRCP 6(a)(5).

vi. *"Legal holiday" defined.* "Legal holiday" means:

- The day set aside by statute for observing New Year's Day, Martin Luther King Jr.'s Birthday, Washington's Birthday, Memorial Day, Independence Day, Labor Day, Columbus Day, Veterans' Day, Thanksgiving Day, or Christmas Day;

- Any day declared a holiday by the President or Congress; and

- For periods that are measured after an event, any other day declared a holiday by the state where the district court is located. FRCP 6(a)(6).

b. *Computation of electronic filing deadlines.* You can file electronically twenty-four (24) hours a day, seven (7) days a week, three hundred sixty-five (365) days a year. NY R USDCTSD CM/ECF, S.D.(II)(13)(13.10). Electronic filing must be completed before midnight local time where the Court is located in order to be considered timely filed that day. NY R USDCTSD CM/ECF, S.D.(I)(3)(3.3); NY R USDCTSD CM/ECF, S.D.(II)(13)(13.10); NY R USDCTSD CM/ECF, S.D.(II)(19)(19.4). An electronically filed document is deemed filed on the "filed on" date indicated on the Notice of Electronic Filing (NEF). NY R USDCTSD CM/ECF, S.D.(II)(13)(13.11).

i. *Technical failures.* A Filing User whose filing is made untimely as the result of a technical failure may seek appropriate relief from the Court. NY R USDCTSD CM/ECF, S.D.(I)(11). If you missed a filing deadline when the ECF system was out of order, attach a statement to your filing explaining how the interruption in service prevented you from filing in a timely fashion. NY R USDCTSD CM/ECF, S.D.(II)(23)(23.5).

c. *Extending time*

i. *In general.* When an act may or must be done within a specified time, the court may, for good cause, extend the time:

- With or without motion or notice if the court acts, or if a request is made, before the original time or its extension expires; or

- On motion made after the time has expired if the party failed to act because of excusable neglect. FRCP 6(b)(1).

ii. *Exceptions.* A court must not extend the time to act under FRCP 50(b), FRCP 50(d), FRCP 52(b), FRCP 59(b), FRCP 59(d), FRCP 59(e), and FRCP 60(b). FRCP 6(b)(2).

iii. Refer to the United States District Court for the Southern District of New York KeyRules Motion for Continuance/Extension of Time document for more information on extending time.

d. *Additional time after certain kinds of service.* When a party may or must act within a specified time after service and service is made under FRCP 5(b)(2)(C), FRCP 5(b)(2)(D), FRCP 5(b)(2)(E), or FRCP 5(b)(2)(F), three (3) days are added after the period would otherwise expire under FRCP 6(a). FRCP 6(d). Overnight delivery service shall be deemed service by mail for purposes of FRCP 5 and FRCP 6. NY R USDCTS&ED Civ Rule 5.3.

7. *Individual judge practices.* Refer to the Miscellaneous section of this document for information on individual judge practices on timing of documents.

## C. General Requirements

1. *Motions, generally*

   a. *Requirements.* A request for a court order must be made by motion. The motion must:

      i. Be in writing unless made during a hearing or trial;

      ii. State with particularity the grounds for seeking the order; and

      iii. State the relief sought. FRCP 7(b)(1).

   b. *Notice of motion.* A party interested in resisting the relief sought by a motion has a right to notice thereof, and an opportunity to be heard. AMJUR MOTIONS § 12.

      i. In addition to statutory or court rule provisions requiring notice of a motion—the purpose of such a notice requirement having been said to be to prevent a party from being prejudicially surprised by a motion—principles of natural justice dictate that an adverse party generally must be given notice that a motion will be presented to the court. AMJUR MOTIONS § 12.

      ii. "Notice," in this regard, means reasonable notice, including a meaningful opportunity to prepare and to defend against allegations of a motion. AMJUR MOTIONS § 12.

   c. *Writing requirement.* The writing requirement is intended to insure that the adverse parties are informed and have a record of both the motion's pendency and the grounds on which the movant seeks an order. FPP § 1191; Feldberg v. Quechee Lakes Corp., 463 F.3d 195 (2d Cir. 2006).

      i. It is sufficient "if the motion is stated in a written notice of the hearing of the motion." FPP § 1191.

   d. *Particularity requirement.* The particularity requirement insures that the opposing parties will have notice of their opponent's contentions. FEDPROC § 62:364; Goodman v. 1973 26 Foot Trojan Vessel, Arkansas Registration No. AR1439SN, 859 F.2d 71, 12 Fed.R.Serv.3d 645 (8th Cir. 1988). That requirement ensures that notice of the basis for the motion is provided to the court and to the opposing party so as to avoid prejudice, provide the opponent with a meaningful opportunity to respond, and provide the court with enough information to process the motion correctly. FEDPROC § 62:364; Andreas v. Volkswagen of America, Inc., 336 F.3d 789, 56 Fed.R.Serv.3d 6 (8th Cir. 2003).

      i. Reasonable specification of the grounds for a motion is sufficient. However, where a movant fails to state even one ground for granting the motion in question, the movant has failed to meet the minimal standard of "reasonable specification." FEDPROC § 62:364; Martinez v. Trainor, 556 F.2d 818, 23 Fed.R.Serv.2d 403 (7th Cir. 1977).

      ii. The court may excuse the failure to comply with the particularity requirement if it is inadvertent, and where no prejudice is shown by the opposing party. FEDPROC § 62:364.

   e. *Ex parte orders or orders to show cause to bring on a motion.* No ex parte order, or order to show cause to bring on a motion, will be granted except upon a clear and specific showing by affidavit of good and sufficient reasons why a procedure other than by notice of motion is necessary, and stating whether a previous application for similar relief has been made. NY R USDCTS&ED Civ Rule 6.1(d).

   f. *Letter-motions.* Applications for extensions or adjournments, applications for a pre-motion conference, and similar non-dispositive matters as permitted by the instructions regarding ECF published on the website of each respective Court and any pertinent Individual Judge's Practices, may be brought by letter-motion filed via ECF pursuant to NY R USDCTS&ED Civ Rule 5.2(b). NY R USDCTS&ED Civ Rule 7.1(d).

      i. The following list of motions. . .may be made by LETTER-MOTION: (1) Motion to Adjourn Conference; (2) Motion to Change Attorney Name on Roll; (3) Motion to Compel; (4) Motion for Conference; (5) Motion to Consolidate Cases; (6) Motion to Continue; (7) Motion re: Discovery; (8) Motion to Expedite; (9) Motion for Extension of Time; (10) Motion for Extension of Time to Amend; (11) Motion for Extension of Time to Answer; (12) Motion for Extension of Time to Complete Discovery; (13) Motion for Extension of Time to File Document; (14) Motion for Extension of Time to File Response/Reply; (15) Motion for

Extension of Time re Transcript; (16) Motion to File Amicus Brief; (17) Motion for Leave to File Document; (18) Motion for Leave to File Excess Pages; (19) Motion for Local Rule 37.2 Conference; (20) Motion for Oral Argument; (21) Motion to Reopen; (22) Motion to Reopen Case; (23) Motion to Seal Document; (24) Motion to Stay; (25) Motion to Substitute Attorney. NY R USDCTSD CM/ECF, S.D.(II)(13)(13.1).

    ii.   If the Filing User is making a type of motion that does not appear in this list, the motion may not be made by letter. NY R USDCTSD CM/ECF, S.D.(II)(13)(13.1).

    iii.   For more information on letter motions, refer to NY R USDCTSD CM/ECF, S.D.(II)(13)(13.1).

2.  *Motion for judgment on the pleadings.* After the pleadings are closed—but early enough not to delay trial—a party may move for judgment on the pleadings. FRCP 12(c).

    a.  *Relationship to other motions*

        i.  *Common law demurrer.* The motion for judgment on the pleadings under FRCP 12(c) has its historical roots in common law practice, which permitted either party, at any point in the proceeding, to demur to his opponent's pleading and secure a dismissal or final judgment on the basis of the pleadings. FPP § 1367.

- The common law demurrer could be used to search the record and raise procedural defects, or it could be employed to resolve the substantive merits of the controversy as disclosed on the face of the pleadings. FPP § 1367.

- In contrast to the common law practice, the FRCP 12(c) judgment on the pleadings procedure primarily is addressed to the latter function of disposing of cases on the basis of the underlying substantive merits of the parties' claims and defenses as they are revealed in the formal pleadings. FPP § 1367. The purpose of FRCP 12(c) is to save time and expense in cases where the ultimate issues of fact are not in dispute, and to prevent the piecemeal process of judicial determination which prevailed under the old common-law practice. FEDPROC § 62:566.

        ii.  *Motions to dismiss.* While FRCP 12(b) motions to dismiss and FRCP 12(c) motions for judgment on the pleadings are to some extent merely interchangeable weapons in a party's arsenal of pretrial challenges, there are differences in the scope and effect of the two motions. A FRCP 12(b) motion to dismiss is directed solely toward the defects of the plaintiff's claim for relief, without concern for the merits of the controversy, while a FRCP 12(c) motion for judgment on the pleadings at least theoretically requires some scrutiny of the merits of the controversy. FEDPROC § 62:568.

        iii.  *Motion to strike.* The FRCP 12(c) motion also should be contrasted with the motion to strike under FRCP 12(f). The latter motion permits either party to strike redundant, immaterial, impertinent, or scandalous matter from an adversary's pleading and may be used to challenge the sufficiency of defenses asserted by that adversary. The motion serves as a pruning device to eliminate objectionable matter from an opponent's pleadings and, unlike the FRCP 12(c) procedure, it is not directed at gaining a final judgment on the merits, although a FRCP 12(f) motion that succeeds in eliminating the defenses to the action may have that purpose and, in some cases, may have that effect. FPP § 1369.

- If a plaintiff seeks to dispute the legal sufficiency of fewer than all of the defenses raised in the defendant's pleading, he should proceed under FRCP 12(f) rather than under FRCP 12(c) because the latter leads to the entry of a judgment. FPP § 1369.

        iv.  *Motion for summary judgment.* In most circumstances a party will find it preferable to proceed under FRCP 56 rather than FRCP 12(c) for a variety of reasons. For example, the summary judgment procedure is available when the defendant fails to file an answer, whereas technically no relief would be available under FRCP 12(c) because the pleadings have not been closed. If a party believes that it will be necessary to introduce evidence outside the formal pleadings in order to demonstrate that no material issue of fact exists and he is clearly entitled to judgment, it is advisable to proceed directly under FRCP 56 rather than taking the circuitous route through FRCP 12(c). Moreover, the FRCP 12(c) path may present certain risks because the court, in its discretion, may refuse to permit the introduction of matters beyond the pleadings and insist on treating the motion as one under FRCP 12(c) or apply the general motion time period set out in FRCP 6(d), rather than the special time provision in FRCP 56. FPP § 1369.

b. *Bringing a FRCP 12(c) motion.* As numerous judicial opinions make clear, a FRCP 12(c) motion is designed to provide a means of disposing of cases when the material facts are not in dispute between the parties and a judgment on the merits can be achieved by focusing on the content of the competing pleadings, exhibits thereto, matters incorporated by reference in the pleadings, whatever is central or integral to the claim for relief or defense, and any facts of which the district court will take judicial notice. FPP § 1367; DiCarlo v. St. Mary Hosp., 530 F.3d 255 (3d Cir. 2008); Buddy Bean Lumber Co. v. Axis Surplus Ins. Co., 715 F.3d 695, 697 (8th Cir. 2013).

   i. The motion for a judgment on the pleadings only has utility when all material allegations of fact are admitted or not controverted in the pleadings and only questions of law remain to be decided by the district court. FPP § 1367; Stafford v. Jewelers Mut. Ins. Co., 554 Fed. Appx. 360, 370 (6th Cir. 2014).

c. *Partial judgment on the pleadings.* Although not provided for by FRCP 12(c), a party may properly move for partial judgment on the pleadings to further the policy goal of efficient resolution of actions when there are no material facts in dispute. This conclusion has been said to be buttressed by FRCP 56(a), which provides that a party may move for summary judgment "on all or part of the claim." FEDPROC § 62:571.

d. *Granting of a motion for judgment on the pleadings.* The federal courts have followed a fairly restrictive standard in ruling on motions for judgment on the pleadings. FPP § 1368. A motion for judgment on the pleadings is a motion for judgment on the merits, and should only be granted if no material issue of fact remains to be resolved and the movant establishes entitlement to judgment as a matter of law. FEDPROC § 62:569; Great Plains Trust Co. v. Morgan Stanley Dean Witter & Co., 313 F.3d 305 (5th Cir. 2002); Sikirica v. Nationwide Ins. Co., 416 F.3d 214 (3d Cir. 2005). A motion for a judgment on the pleadings must be sustained where the undisputed facts appearing in the pleadings, supplemented by any facts of which the court will take judicial notice, show that no relief can be granted. Judgment on the pleadings is not appropriate where the answer raises issues of fact which, if proved, would defeat recovery. FEDPROC § 62:569.

   i. A motion for judgment on the pleadings admits, for purposes of the motion, the truth of all well-pleaded facts in the pleadings of the opposing party, together with all fair inferences to be drawn therefrom, even where the defendant asserts, in the FRCP 12(c) motion, a FRCP 12(b)(6) defense of failure to state a claim upon which relief can be granted. FEDPROC § 62:570; In re World Trade Center Disaster Site Litigation, 521 F.3d 169 (2d Cir. 2008); Massachusetts Nurses Ass'n v. North Adams Regional Hosp., 467 F.3d 27 (1st Cir. 2006). However, all allegations of the moving party which have been denied are taken as false. FEDPROC § 62:570; Volvo Const. Equipment North America, Inc. v. CLM Equipment Company, Inc., 386 F.3d 581 (4th Cir. 2004). In considering a motion for judgment on the pleadings, the trial court is thus required to view the facts presented in the pleadings and inferences to be drawn therefrom in the light most favorable to the nonmoving party. In this fashion the courts hope to insure that the rights of the nonmoving party are decided as fully and fairly on a FRCP 12(c) motion as if there had been a trial. FEDPROC § 62:570.

   ii. On a motion for judgment on the pleadings, the court may consider facts upon the basis of judicial notice. FEDPROC § 62:570; R.G. Financial Corp. v. Vergara-Nunez, 446 F.3d 178 (1st Cir. 2006). However, a motion for judgment on the pleadings does not admit conclusions of law or unwarranted factual inferences. FEDPROC § 62:570; JPMorgan Chase Bank, N.A. v. Winget, 510 F.3d 577 (6th Cir. 2007).

e. *Joining motions*

   i. *Right to join.* A motion under FRCP 12 may be joined with any other motion allowed by FRCP 12. FRCP 12(g)(1).

   ii. *Limitation on further motions.* Except as provided in FRCP 12(h)(2) or FRCP 12(h)(3), a party that makes a motion under FRCP 12 must not make another motion under FRCP 12 raising a defense or objection that was available to the party but omitted from its earlier motion. FRCP 12(g)(2).

    f. *Waiving and preserving certain defenses*

        i. *When some are waived.* A party waives any defense listed in FRCP 12(b)(2) through FRCP 12(b)(5) by:

- Omitting it from a motion in the circumstances described in FRCP 12(g)(2); or

- Failing to either: (1) make it by motion under FRCP 12; or (2) include it in a responsive pleading or in an amendment allowed by FRCP 15(a)(1) as a matter of course. FRCP 12(h)(1).

        ii. *When to raise others.* Failure to state a claim upon which relief can be granted, to join a person required by FRCP 19(b), or to state a legal defense to a claim may be raised:

- In any pleading allowed or ordered under FRCP 7(a);

- By a motion under FRCP 12(c); or

- At trial. FRCP 12(h)(2).

        iii. *Lack of subject matter jurisdiction.* If the court determines at any time that it lacks subject-matter jurisdiction, the court must dismiss the action. FRCP 12(h)(3).

3. *Opposing papers.* The Federal Rules of Civil Procedure do not require any formal answer, return, or reply to a motion, except where the Federal Rules of Civil Procedure or local rules may require affidavits, memoranda, or other papers to be filed in opposition to a motion. Such papers are simply to apprise the court of such opposition and the grounds of that opposition. FEDPROC § 62:359. Except for letter-motions as permitted by NY R USDCTS&ED Civ Rule 7.1(d) or as otherwise permitted by the Court, all oppositions and replies with respect to motions shall comply with NY R USDCTS&ED Civ Rule 7.1(a)(2) and NY R USDCTS&ED Civ Rule 7.1(a)(3), and an opposing party who seeks relief that goes beyond the denial of the motion shall comply as well with NY R USDCTS&ED Civ Rule 7.1(a)(1). NY R USDCTS&ED Civ Rule 7.1(b).

    a. *Effect of failure to respond to motion.* Although in the absence of statutory provision or court rule, a motion ordinarily does not require a written answer, when a party files a motion and the opposing party fails to respond, the court may construe such failure to respond as nonopposition to the motion or an admission that the motion was meritorious, may take the facts alleged in the motion as true—the rule in some jurisdictions being that the failure to respond to a fact set forth in a motion is deemed an admission—and may grant the motion if the relief requested appears to be justified. AMJUR MOTIONS § 28.

    b. *Assent or no opposition not determinative.* However, a motion will not be granted automatically simply because an "assent" or a notation of "no opposition" has been filed; federal judges frequently deny motions that have been assented to when it is thought that justice so dictates. FPP § 1190.

    c. *Responsive pleading inappropriate as response to motion.* An attempt to answer or oppose a motion with a responsive pleading usually is not appropriate. FPP § 1190.

4. *Reply papers.* A moving party may be required or permitted to prepare papers in addition to his original motion papers. AMJUR MOTIONS § 25. Papers answering or replying to opposing papers may be appropriate, in the interests of justice, where it appears there is a substantial reason for allowing a reply. Thus, a court may accept reply papers where a party demonstrates that the papers to which it seeks to file a reply raise new issues that are material to the disposition of the question before the court, or where the court determines, sua sponte, that it wishes further briefing of an issue raised in those papers and orders the submission of additional papers. FEDPROC § 62:360. Except for letter-motions as permitted by NY R USDCTS&ED Civ Rule 7.1(d) or as otherwise permitted by the Court, all oppositions and replies with respect to motions shall comply with NY R USDCTS&ED Civ Rule 7.1(a)(2) and NY R USDCTS&ED Civ Rule 7.1(a)(3). NY R USDCTS&ED Civ Rule 7.1(b).

    a. *Function of reply papers.* The function of a reply affidavit is to answer the arguments made in opposition to the position taken by the movant and not to permit the movant to introduce new arguments in support of the motion. AMJUR MOTIONS § 25.

b. *Issues raised for the first time in a reply document.* However, the view has been followed in some jurisdictions, that as a matter of judicial economy, where there is no prejudice and where the issues could be raised simply by filing a motion to dismiss, the trial court has discretion to consider arguments raised for the first time in a reply memorandum, and that a trial court may grant a motion to strike issues raised for the first time in a reply memorandum. AMJUR MOTIONS § 26.

5. *Orders on motions.* A memorandum signed by the Court of the decision on a motion that does not finally determine all claims for relief, or an oral decision on such a motion, shall constitute the order unless the memorandum or oral decision directs the submission or settlement of an order in more extended form. The notation in the docket of a memorandum or of an oral decision that does not direct the submission or settlement of an order in more extended form shall constitute the entry of the order. Where an order in more extended form is required to be submitted or settled, the notation in the docket of such order shall constitute the entry of the order. NY R USDCTS&ED Civ Rule 6.2.

6. *Complex civil cases.* For information on procedures for complex civil cases, refer to NY R USDCTSD Order 11 Misc 00388.

7. *Related cases.* It shall be the continuing duty of each attorney appearing in any civil or criminal case to bring promptly to the attention of the Court all facts which said attorney believes are relevant to a determination that said case and one or more pending civil or criminal cases should be heard by the same Judge, in order to avoid unnecessary duplication of judicial effort. As soon as the attorney becomes aware of such relationship, said attorney shall notify the Judges to whom the cases have been assigned. NY R USDCTS&ED Civ Rule 1.6(a). If counsel fails to comply with NY R USDCTS&ED Civ Rule 1.6(a), the Court may assess reasonable costs directly against counsel whose action has obstructed the effective administration of the Court's business. NY R USDCTS&ED Civ Rule 1.6(b).

a. *Determination of relatedness.* Subject to the limitations set forth in NY R USDCTSD Div. Bus., Rule 13(a)(2), a civil case, bankruptcy appeal, or motion to withdraw the bankruptcy reference will be deemed related to one or more civil cases, appeals or motions when the interests of justice and efficiency will be served. In determining relatedness, a judge will consider whether (A) the actions concern the same or substantially similar parties, property, transactions or events; (B) there is substantial factual overlap; (C) the parties could be subjected to conflicting orders; and (D) whether absent a determination of relatedness there would be a substantial duplication of effort and expense, delay, or undue burden on the Court, parties or witnesses. NY R USDCTSD Div. Bus., Rule 13(a)(1). Nothing in this NY R USDCTSD Div. Bus., Rule 13 is intended to preclude parties from moving for consolidated proceedings under FRCP 42. NY R USDCTSD Div. Bus., Rule 13(a)(1). Notwithstanding NY R USDCTSD Div. Bus., Rule 13(a)(1):

i. Civil cases shall not be deemed related merely because they involve common legal issues or the same parties. NY R USDCTSD Div. Bus., Rule 13(a)(2)(A).

ii. Other than cases subject to NY R USDCTSD Div. Bus., Rule 4(b) and actions seeking the enforcement of a judgment or settlement in or of an earlier case, civil cases presumptively shall not be deemed related unless both cases are pending before the Court (or the earlier case is on appeal). NY R USDCTSD Div. Bus., Rule 13(a)(2)(B).

b. *Procedure in regard to cases said to be related*

i. *Disclosure of contention of relatedness.* When a civil case is filed or removed or a bankruptcy appeal or motion to withdraw the reference of an adversary proceeding from the bankruptcy court is filed, the person filing or removing shall disclose on form JSC44C any contention of relatedness and shall file a Related Case Statement stating clearly and succinctly the basis for the contention. A copy of the civil cover sheet and Related Case Statement shall be served with the complaint, notice of removal, notice of appeal, or motion. Any party may contest a claim of relatedness by any other in writing addressed to the judge having the case with the lowest docket number of all cases claimed to be related. However, the foregoing shall not delay the assignment process or the operation of NY R USDCTSD Div. Bus., Rule 13. NY R USDCTSD Div. Bus., Rule 13(b)(1). [Editor's note: the reference to form JSC44C is likely meant to be form JS44C-SDNY: Civil Court Cover Sheet].

ii. *Claims of relatedness by other parties.* A party other than the one filing a case, bankruptcy appeal or motion to withdraw the reference that contends its case is related to another may so advise in writing the judge assigned in its case and request a transfer of its case to the judge that the party contends has the related case with the lowest docket number. If the assigned judge believes the case is related under NY R USDCTSD Div. Bus., Rule 13(a), he or she shall refer the question to the judge having the case with the lowest docket number. In the event the latter judge agrees, the case shall be transferred to that judge unless the Assignment Committee disagrees. NY R USDCTSD Div. Bus., Rule 13(b)(3).

   c.  For more information on related cases, refer to NY R USDCTSD Div. Bus., Rule 13.

8.  *Alternative dispute resolution (ADR).* The U.S. District Court for the Southern District of New York provides litigants with opportunities to discuss settlement through judicial settlement conferences and mediation. NY R USDCTS&ED Civ Rule 83.9(a).

   a.  *Consideration of alternative dispute resolution.* In all civil cases, including those eligible for mediation pursuant to NY R USDCTS&ED Civ Rule 83.9(e), each party shall consider the use of mediation or a judicial settlement conference and shall report to the assigned Judge at the initial FRCP 16(b) case management conference, or subsequently, whether the party believes mediation or a judicial settlement conference may facilitate the resolution of the lawsuit. Judges are encouraged to note the availability of the mediation program and/or a judicial settlement conference before, at, or after the initial FRCP 16(b) case management conference. NY R USDCTS&ED Civ Rule 83.9(d).

   b.  *Mediation.* In mediation, parties and counsel meet, sometimes collectively and sometimes individually, with a neutral third party (the mediator) who has been trained to facilitate confidential settlement discussions. The parties articulate their respective positions and interests and generate options for a mutually agreeable resolution to the dispute. The mediator assists the parties in reaching their own negotiated settlement by defining the issues, probing and assessing the strengths and weaknesses of each party's legal positions, and identifying areas of agreement and disagreement. The main benefits of mediation are that it can result in an expeditious and less costly resolution of the litigation, and can produce creative solutions to complex disputes often unavailable in traditional litigation. NY R USDCTS&ED Civ Rule 83.9(b).

      i.  *Mediation program eligibility.* All civil cases other than Social Security, habeas corpus, and tax cases are eligible for mediation, whether assigned to Manhattan or White Plains. NY R USDCTS&ED Civ Rule 83.9(e)(1).

        &bull;  The Board of Judges may, by Administrative Order, direct that certain specified categories of cases shall automatically be submitted to the mediation program. The assigned District Judge or Magistrate Judge may issue a written order exempting a particular case with or without the request of the parties. NY R USDCTS&ED Civ Rule 83.9(e)(2).

        &bull;  For all other cases, the assigned District Judge or Magistrate Judge may determine that a case is appropriate for mediation and may order that case to mediation, with or without the consent of the parties, before, at, or after the initial FRCP 16(b) case management conference. Alternatively, the parties should notify the assigned Judge at any time of their desire to mediate. NY R USDCTS&ED Civ Rule 83.9(e)(3).

   c.  *Judicial settlement conferences.* Judicial settlement conferences may be ordered by District Judges or Magistrate Judges with or without the request or consent of the parties. NY R USDCTS&ED Civ Rule 83.9(f).

   d.  For more information on alternative dispute resolution (ADR), refer to NY R USDCTS&ED Civ Rule 83.9.

9.  *Individual judge practices.* Refer to the Miscellaneous section of this document for information on individual judge practices on general requirements for documents.

# D. Documents

1.  *Documents for moving party*

   a.  *Required documents*

      i.  *Notice of motion and motion.* Except for letter-motions as permitted by NY R USDCTS&ED

Civ Rule 7.1(d) or as otherwise permitted by the Court, all motions shall include the following motion papers: a notice of motion, or an order to show cause signed by the Court, which shall specify the applicable rules or statutes pursuant to which the motion is brought, and shall specify the relief sought by the motion. NY R USDCTS&ED Civ Rule 7.1(a)(1). Refer to the General Requirements section of this document for information on the notice of motion and motion.

ii. *Memorandum of law.* Except for letter-motions as permitted by NY R USDCTS&ED Civ Rule 7.1(d) or as otherwise permitted by the Court, all motions shall include the following motion papers: a memorandum of law, setting forth the cases and other authorities relied upon in support of the motion, and divided, under appropriate headings, into as many parts as there are issues to be determined. NY R USDCTS&ED Civ Rule 7.1(a)(2).

iii. *Certificate of service.* FRCP 5(d) requires that the person making service under FRCP 5 certify that service has been effected. FRCP 5(Advisory Committee Notes). Having such information on file may be useful for many purposes, including proof of service if an issue arises concerning the effectiveness of the service. FRCP 5(Advisory Committee Notes).

- Such paper service [on attorneys and pro se parties who are not Filing or Receiving Users] must be documented by electronically filing proof of service. NY R USDCTSD CM/ECF, S.D.(I)(9)(9.2); NY R USDCTSD CM/ECF, S.D.(I)(19)(19.3)(b). Pro se parties who are not Filing Users are exempt from that portion of NY R USDCTSD CM/ECF, S.D.(I)(19)(19.3) requiring proof of service to be filed electronically. NY R USDCTSD CM/ECF, S.D.(I)(19)(19.3).

b. *Supplemental documents*

i. *Pleadings.* In considering a motion for judgment on the pleadings, the trial court is. . .required to view the facts presented in the pleadings and inferences to be drawn therefrom in the light most favorable to the nonmoving party. FEDPROC § 62:570.

- *Motion treated as one for summary judgment.* If, on a motion under FRCP 12(b)(6) or FRCP 12(c), matters outside the pleadings are presented to and not excluded by the court, the motion must be treated as one for summary judgment under FRCP 56. All parties must be given a reasonable opportunity to present all the material that is pertinent to the motion. FRCP 12(d).

ii. *Notice of constitutional question.* A party that files a pleading, written motion, or other paper drawing into question the constitutionality of a federal or state statute must promptly:

- *File notice.* File a notice of constitutional question stating the question and identifying the paper that raises it, if: (1) a federal statute is questioned and the parties do not include the United States, one of its agencies, or one of its officers or employees in an official capacity; or (2) a state statute is questioned and the parties do not include the state, one of its agencies, or one of its officers or employees in an official capacity; and

- *Serve notice.* Serve the notice and paper on the Attorney General of the United States if a federal statute is questioned—or on the state attorney general if a state statute is questioned—either by certified or registered mail or by sending it to an electronic address designated by the attorney general for this purpose. FRCP 5.1(a).

- *No forfeiture.* A party's failure to file and serve the notice, or the court's failure to certify, does not forfeit a constitutional claim or defense that is otherwise timely asserted. FRCP 5.1(d).

iii. *Nongovernmental corporate disclosure statement*

- *Contents.* A nongovernmental corporate party must file two (2) copies of a disclosure statement that: (1) identifies any parent corporation and any publicly held corporation owning ten percent (10%) or more of its stock; or (2) states that there is no such corporation. FRCP 7.1(a).

- *Time to file; Supplemental filing.* A party must: (1) file the disclosure statement with its first appearance, pleading, petition, motion, response, or other request addressed to the court; and (2) promptly file a supplemental statement if any required information changes. FRCP 7.1(b). For purposes of FRCP 7.1(b)(2), "promptly" shall mean "within fourteen days," that is, parties are required to file a supplemental disclosure statement within fourteen (14) days of the time there is any change in the information required in a disclosure statement filed pursuant to those rules. NY R USDCTS&ED Civ Rule 7.1.1.

iv. *Notice to pro se litigant who opposes a FRCP 12 motion supported by matters outside the pleadings.* A represented party moving to dismiss or for judgment on the pleadings against a party proceeding pro se, who refers in support of the motion to matters outside the pleadings as described in FRCP 12(b) or FRCP 12(c), shall serve and file the notice in NY R USDCTS&ED Civ Rule 12.1 with the full text of FRCP 56 attached at the time the motion is served. If the Court rules that a motion to dismiss or for judgment on the pleadings will be treated as one for summary judgment pursuant to FRCP 56, and the movant has not previously served and filed the notice required by NY R USDCTS&ED Civ Rule 12.1, the movant shall amend the form notice to reflect that fact and shall serve and file the amended notice within fourteen (14) days of the Court's ruling. NY R USDCTS&ED Civ Rule 12.1. For the notice, refer to NY R USDCTS&ED Civ Rule 12.1.

v. *Copies of authorities.* In cases involving a pro se litigant, counsel shall, when serving a memorandum of law (or other submissions to the Court), provide the pro se litigant (but not other counsel or the Court) with copies of cases and other authorities cited therein that are unpublished or reported exclusively on computerized databases. Upon request, counsel shall provide the pro se litigant with copies of such unpublished cases and other authorities as are cited in a decision of the Court and were not previously cited by any party. NY R USDCTS&ED Civ Rule 7.2.

vi. *Proposed order.* Refer to the Format section of this document for information on the format of submitting a proposed order to the court.

vii. *Statement explaining untimely electronic filing.* If you missed a filing deadline when the ECF system was out of order, attach a statement to your filing explaining how the interruption in service prevented you from filing in a timely fashion. NY R USDCTSD CM/ECF, S.D.(II)(23)(23.5).

viii. *Courtesy copies.* Read the judge's Individual Practices to learn if courtesy copies are required. NY R USDCTSD CM/ECF, S.D.(II)(13)(13.17). Judges' Individual Practices should continue to be followed with respect to delivery of courtesy copies. NY R USDCTSD CM/ECF, S.D.(I)(3)(3.4).

2. *Documents for opposing party*

   a. *Required documents*

      i. *Answering memorandum of law.* Except for letter-motions as permitted by NY R USDCTS&ED Civ Rule 7.1(d) or as otherwise permitted by the Court, all oppositions and replies with respect to motions shall comply with NY R USDCTS&ED Civ Rule 7.1(a)(2). NY R USDCTS&ED Civ Rule 7.1(b). Except for letter-motions as permitted by NY R USDCTS&ED Civ Rule 7.1(d) or as otherwise permitted by the Court, all motions shall include the following motion papers: a memorandum of law, setting forth the cases and other authorities relied upon in support of the motion, and divided, under appropriate headings, into as many parts as there are issues to be determined. NY R USDCTS&ED Civ Rule 7.1(a)(2). Refer to the General Requirements section of this document for information on the opposing papers.

      ii. *Certificate of service.* FRCP 5(d) requires that the person making service under FRCP 5 certify that service has been effected. FRCP 5(Advisory Committee Notes). Having such information on file may be useful for many purposes, including proof of service if an issue arises concerning the effectiveness of the service. FRCP 5(Advisory Committee Notes).

         • Such paper service [on attorneys and pro se parties who are not Filing or Receiving Users] must be documented by electronically filing proof of service. NY R USDCTSD CM/ECF,

S.D.(I)(9)(9.2); NY R USDCTSD CM/ECF, S.D.(I)(19)(19.3)(b). Pro se parties who are not Filing Users are exempt from that portion of NY R USDCTSD CM/ECF, S.D.(I)(19)(19.3) requiring proof of service to be filed electronically. NY R USDCTSD CM/ECF, S.D.(I)(19)(19.3).

b. *Supplemental documents*

    i. *Pleadings.* In considering a motion for judgment on the pleadings, the trial court is. . .required to view the facts presented in the pleadings and inferences to be drawn therefrom in the light most favorable to the nonmoving party. FEDPROC § 62:570.

       • *Motion treated as one for summary judgment.* If, on a motion under FRCP 12(b)(6) or FRCP 12(c), matters outside the pleadings are presented to and not excluded by the court, the motion must be treated as one for summary judgment under FRCP 56. All parties must be given a reasonable opportunity to present all the material that is pertinent to the motion. FRCP 12(d).

    ii. *Notice of constitutional question.* A party that files a pleading, written motion, or other paper drawing into question the constitutionality of a federal or state statute must promptly:

       • *File notice.* File a notice of constitutional question stating the question and identifying the paper that raises it, if: (1) a federal statute is questioned and the parties do not include the United States, one of its agencies, or one of its officers or employees in an official capacity; or (2) a state statute is questioned and the parties do not include the state, one of its agencies, or one of its officers or employees in an official capacity; and

       • *Serve notice.* Serve the notice and paper on the Attorney General of the United States if a federal statute is questioned—or on the state attorney general if a state statute is questioned—either by certified or registered mail or by sending it to an electronic address designated by the attorney general for this purpose. FRCP 5.1(a).

       • *No forfeiture.* A party's failure to file and serve the notice, or the court's failure to certify, does not forfeit a constitutional claim or defense that is otherwise timely asserted. FRCP 5.1(d).

    iii. *Copies of authorities.* In cases involving a pro se litigant, counsel shall, when serving a memorandum of law (or other submissions to the Court), provide the pro se litigant (but not other counsel or the Court) with copies of cases and other authorities cited therein that are unpublished or reported exclusively on computerized databases. Upon request, counsel shall provide the pro se litigant with copies of such unpublished cases and other authorities as are cited in a decision of the Court and were not previously cited by any party. NY R USDCTS&ED Civ Rule 7.2.

    iv. *Statement explaining untimely electronic filing.* If you missed a filing deadline when the ECF system was out of order, attach a statement to your filing explaining how the interruption in service prevented you from filing in a timely fashion. NY R USDCTSD CM/ECF, S.D.(II)(23)(23.5).

    v. *Courtesy copies.* Read the judge's Individual Practices to learn if courtesy copies are required. NY R USDCTSD CM/ECF, S.D.(II)(13)(13.17). Judges' Individual Practices should continue to be followed with respect to delivery of courtesy copies. NY R USDCTSD CM/ECF, S.D.(I)(3)(3.4).

3. *Individual judge practices.* Refer to the Miscellaneous section of this document for information on individual judge practices on required documents.

## E. Format

1. *Form of documents.* The rules governing captions and other matters of form in pleadings apply to motions and other papers. FRCP 7(b)(2).

a. *Paper.* Every pleading, written motion, and other paper must: be plainly written, typed, printed, or copied without erasures or interlineations which materially deface it. NY R USDCTS&ED Civ Rule 11.1(a)(1).

b. *Typeface, margin, and spacing.* The typeface, margins, and spacing of all documents presented for filing must meet the following requirements:

    i. All text must be twelve (12) point type or larger, except for text in footnotes which may be ten (10) point type;

    ii. All documents must have at least one (1) inch margins on all sides;

    iii. All text must be double-spaced, except for headings, text in footnotes, or block quotations, which may be single-spaced. NY R USDCTS&ED Civ Rule 11.1(b).

c. *Caption; Names of parties.* Every pleading must have a caption with the court's name, a title, a file number, and a FRCP 7(a) designation. The title of the complaint must name all the parties; the title of other pleadings, after naming the first party on each side, may refer generally to other parties. FRCP 10(a). Every pleading, written motion, and other paper must: bear the docket number and the initials of the District Judge and any Magistrate Judge before whom the action or proceeding is pending, NY R USDCTS&ED Civ Rule 11.1(a)(2).

d. *Paragraphs; Separate statements.* A party must state its claims or defenses in numbered paragraphs, each limited as far as practicable to a single set of circumstances. A later pleading may refer by number to a paragraph in an earlier pleading. If doing so would promote clarity, each claim founded on a separate transaction or occurrence—and each defense other than a denial—must be stated in a separate count or defense. FRCP 10(b).

e. *Adoption by reference; Exhibits.* A statement in a pleading may be adopted by reference elsewhere in the same pleading or in any other pleading or motion. A copy of a written instrument that is an exhibit to a pleading is a part of the pleading for all purposes. FRCP 10(c).

f. *Acceptance by the clerk.* The clerk must not refuse to file a paper solely because it is not in the form prescribed by the Federal Rules of Civil Procedure or by a local rule or practice. FRCP 5(d)(4).

2. *Form of electronic documents*

a. *PDF-A.* All documents electronically filed on the ECF system must be in PDF-A format (portable document format). A PDF-A file is created using PDF writer software such as Adobe Acrobat (go to the Adobe website for details). PDF-A files cannot be altered, providing security to the filer and the Court. NY R USDCTSD CM/ECF, S.D.(II)(23)(23.2).

b. *Size limitation.* No single PDF file may be larger than four megabytes (4 MB). If the filing is too large, the ECF system will not allow it to be filed, and you will not see a Notice of Electronic Filing (NEF or filing receipt) screen. To determine the size of an Adobe Acrobat PDF file click on File, Document Properties, Summary. NY R USDCTSD CM/ECF, S.D.(II)(23)(23.3).

    i. Converting documents directly from a word processor to PDF-A format creates the smallest possible file in terms of computer memory. If that is not possible, scan your document at low resolution. Within the Adobe Acrobat program, on the "Scan Manager" screen, adjust the settings for black and white and 200 dpi (dots per inch). This allows more pages to fit into a single PDF-A file. If that does not work, separate an oversized file into 2 or more parts. Simply label each file 1a, 1b, 1c, etc. Only relevant excerpts of exhibits should be electronically filed. NY R USDCTSD CM/ECF, S.D.(II)(23)(23.4).

c. *Attachments and exhibits.* Filing Users must submit in electronic form all documents referenced as exhibits or attachments, unless the Court permits paper filing. NY R USDCTSD CM/ECF, S.D.(I)(5)(5.1).

    i. A Filing User must submit as exhibits or attachments only those excerpts of the referenced documents that are relevant to the matter under consideration by the Court. Excerpted material must be clearly and prominently identified as such. Filing Users who file excerpts of documents as exhibits or attachments under this procedure do so without prejudice to their right to file timely additional excerpts or the complete document. Responding parties may file timely additional excerpts that they believe are relevant or the complete document. A party may move before the Court for permission to serve and file in hard copy documents that cannot be reasonably scanned. NY R USDCTSD CM/ECF, S.D.(I)(5)(5.2).

    ii.   Exhibits must be filed only as attachments to a document, such as a motion or an affidavit. Do not use the ECF Filing Event for "Motion" to file exhibits separately. Exhibits are the only items that should be attached to electronically filed documents. You are limited to electronically filing only relevant excerpts of exhibits. Excerpts must be clearly identified as such. If the exhibit is too large to be scanned and electronically filed you may contact the ECF Help Desk. NY R USDCTSD CM/ECF, S.D.(II)(15)(15.6).

  d.   *Letters.* Parties should consult the assigned judge's Individual Practices to determine if the judge accepts letters at all and, if he or she does, whether the judge has any page limitations on letters and/or requires courtesy copies of letters filed on ECF (and, if so, by what means of delivery). All letters addressed to the Court must include a subject line with the case name and docket number (e.g., "Re: Doe v. Smith, 13 Civ. 1234 (ABC)"). NY R USDCTSD CM/ECF, S.D.(II)(13)(13.1).

  e.   *Proposed orders, proposed judgments, stipulations and consents.* Any document that requires the signature of a judge should not be electronically filed except as an exhibit to another document. Proposed orders, judgments, stipulations and consents should not be submitted through the ECF system. Instead they should be sent by e-mail to the Clerk. Proposed orders should be submitted in word processing format (WordPerfect or Word) rather than as a PDF document. Stipulations should be submitted in PDF-A format. Stipulations must contain ink signatures not s/. Faxed or emailed signatures are acceptable. Please note that Stipulations of Voluntary Dismissal pursuant to FRCP 41(a)(1)(A)(ii) do not require the signature of a judge and must be electronically filed on the ECF system. Questions may be directed to the Orders and Judgments Clerk at the phone numbers listed in NY R USDCTSD CM/ECF, S.D.(II)(18)(18.3). NY R USDCTSD CM/ECF, S.D.(II)(18)(18.3).

    i.   Email the proposed order, judgment or stipulation to the email addresses listed in NY R USDCTSD CM/ECF, S.D.(II)(18)(18.3). NY R USDCTSD CM/ECF, S.D.(II)(18)(18.3).

    ii.   Pro se litigants who are not Filing Users are exempt from that portion of NY R USDCTSD CM/ECF, S.D.(II)(18)(18.3) that requires litigants to email proposed orders, judgments, stipulations and consents, and shall deliver such documents to the Clerk's Office in paper form. NY R USDCTSD CM/ECF, S.D.(II)(18)(18.3).

3.   *Signing of pleadings, motions and other papers*

  a.   *Signature.* Every pleading, written motion, and other paper must be signed by at least one attorney of record in the attorney's name—or by a party personally if the party is unrepresented. The paper must state the signer's address, e-mail address, and telephone number. FRCP 11(a). Every pleading, written motion, and other paper must: have the name of each person signing it clearly printed or typed directly below the signature. NY R USDCTS&ED Civ Rule 11.1(a)(3).

    i.   *Electronic signatures.* The user log-in and password required to submit documents to the ECF system serve as the Filing User's signature on all electronic documents filed with the Court. NY R USDCTSD CM/ECF, S.D.(I)(8)(8.1); NY R USDCTSD CM/ECF, S.D.(II)(13)(13.14). They also serve as a signature for purposes of the Federal Rules of Civil Procedure, including FRCP 11, the Local Civil Rules of the United States District Courts for the Southern and Eastern Districts of New York, and any other purpose for which a signature is required in connection with proceedings before the Court. NY R USDCTSD CM/ECF, S.D.(I)(8)(8.1).

- *Signature block.* Electronically filed documents must include a signature block and must set forth the name, address, telephone number and e-mail address all in compliance with the Federal Rules of Civil Procedure and NY R USDCTS&ED Civ Rule 11.1. In the absence of a scanned signature image, the name of the Filing User under whose log-in and password the document is submitted must be preceded by an "s/" typed in the space where the signature would otherwise appear. NY R USDCTSD CM/ECF, S.D.(I)(8)(8.2); NY R USDCTSD CM/ECF, S.D.(II)(13)(13.14).

- *Documents requiring the signature of a party or witness.* A document requiring the signature of a party or witness shall be electronically filed in a scanned format that contains an image of the actual signature. NY R USDCTSD CM/ECF, S.D.(I)(8)(8.4); NY R USDCTSD CM/ECF, S.D.(II)(13)(13.14).

- *Documents requiring the signature of a judge.* A Filing User submitting a document electronically that requires a judge's signature must promptly deliver the document in such other form, if any, as the Court requires. NY R USDCTSD CM/ECF, S.D.(I)(4)(4.2).

- *Documents requiring multiple signatures.* Documents requiring signatures of more than one party must be electronically filed either by: (a) submitting a scanned document containing all necessary signatures; (b) representing the consent of the other parties on the document; (c) identifying on the document the parties whose signatures are required and by the submission of a notice of endorsement by the other parties no later than three business days after filing; or (d) in any other manner approved by the Court. NY R USDCTSD CM/ECF, S.D.(I)(8)(8.5).

ii. *No verification or accompanying affidavit required for pleadings.* Unless a rule or statute specifically states otherwise, a pleading need not be verified or accompanied by an affidavit. FRCP 11(a).

iii. *Unsigned papers.* The court must strike an unsigned paper unless the omission is promptly corrected after being called to the attorney's or party's attention. FRCP 11(a).

b. *Representations to the court.* By presenting to the court a pleading, written motion, or other paper—whether by signing, filing, submitting, or later advocating it—an attorney or unrepresented party certifies that to the best of the person's knowledge, information, and belief, formed after an inquiry reasonable under the circumstances:

i. It is not being presented for any improper purpose, such as to harass, cause unnecessary delay, or needlessly increase the cost of litigation;

ii. The claims, defenses, and other legal contentions are warranted by existing law or by a nonfrivolous argument for extending, modifying, or reversing existing law or for establishing new law;

iii. The factual contentions have evidentiary support or, if specifically so identified, will likely have evidentiary support after a reasonable opportunity for further investigation or discovery; and

iv. The denials of factual contentions are warranted on the evidence or, if specifically so identified, are reasonably based on belief or a lack of information. FRCP 11(b).

c. *Sanctions.* If, after notice and a reasonable opportunity to respond, the court determines that FRCP 11(b) has been violated, the court may impose an appropriate sanction on any attorney, law firm, or party that violated FRCP 11(b) or is responsible for the violation. FRCP 11(c)(1). Refer to the United States District Court for the Southern District of New York KeyRules Motion for Sanctions document for more information.

4. *Privacy protection for filings made with the court*

a. *Redacted filings.* Unless the court orders otherwise, in an electronic or paper filing with the court that contains an individual's Social Security number, taxpayer-identification number, or birth date, the name of an individual known to be a minor, or a financial-account number, a party or nonparty making the filing may include only:

i. The last four (4) digits of the Social Security number and taxpayer-identification number;

ii. The year of the individual's birth;

iii. The minor's initials; and

iv. The last four (4) digits of the financial-account number. FRCP 5.2(a); NY R USDCTSD CM/ECF, S.D.(II)(21)(21.3).

v. Caution should be exercised when filing documents that contain the following:

- Personal identifying numbers (PIN #'s), such as a driver's license number;
- Medical records, treatment and diagnosis;
- Employment history;
- Individual financial information;
- Proprietary or trade secret information;

- Information regarding an individual's cooperation with the government. NY R US-DCTSD CM/ECF, S.D.(II)(21)(21.4).

b. *Exemptions from the redaction requirement.* The redaction requirement does not apply to the following:

i. A financial-account number that identifies the property allegedly subject to forfeiture in a forfeiture proceeding;

ii. The record of an administrative or agency proceeding;

iii. The official record of a state-court proceeding;

iv. The record of a court or tribunal, if that record was not subject to the redaction requirement when originally filed;

v. A filing covered by FRCP 5.2(c) or FRCP 5.2(d); and

vi. A pro se filing in an action brought under 28 U.S.C.A. § 2241, 28 U.S.C.A. § 2254, or 28 U.S.C.A. § 2255. FRCP 5.2(b).

c. *Limitations on remote access to electronic files; Social Security appeals and immigration cases.* Unless the court orders otherwise, in an action for benefits under the Social Security Act, and in an action or proceeding relating to an order of removal, to relief from removal, or to immigration benefits or detention, access to an electronic file is authorized as follows:

i. The parties and their attorneys may have remote electronic access to any part of the case file, including the administrative record;

ii. Any other person may have electronic access to the full record at the courthouse, but may have remote electronic access only to:

- The docket maintained by the court; and

- An opinion, order, judgment, or other disposition of the court, but not any other part of the case file or the administrative record. FRCP 5.2(c).

d. *Filings made under seal.* The court may order that a filing be made under seal without redaction. The court may later unseal the filing or order the person who made the filing to file a redacted version for the public record. FRCP 5.2(d). For more information on sealing documents, refer to NY R USDCTSD CM/ECF, S.D.(I)(6).

e. *Protective orders.* For good cause, the court may by order in a case:

i. Require redaction of additional information; or

ii. Limit or prohibit a nonparty's remote electronic access to a document filed with the court. FRCP 5.2(e).

f. *Option for additional unredacted filing under seal.* A person making a redacted filing may also file an unredacted copy under seal. The court must retain the unredacted copy as part of the record. FRCP 5.2(f); NY R USDCTSD CM/ECF, S.D.(II)(21)(21.5).

g. *Option for filing a reference list.* A filing that contains redacted information may be filed together with a reference list that identifies each item of redacted information and specifies an appropriate identifier that uniquely corresponds to each item listed. The list must be filed under seal and may be amended as of right. Any reference in the case to a listed identifier will be construed to refer to the corresponding item of information. FRCP 5.2(g); NY R USDCTSD CM/ECF, S.D.(II)(21)(21.5).

h. *Responsibility for redaction.* It is the sole responsibility of counsel and the parties to be sure that all documents comply with the rules of this Court requiring redaction of personal identifiers. Neither the judge nor the Clerk of Court will review documents for compliance with these rules. NY R USDCTSD CM/ECF, S.D.(II)(21)(21.2).

i. *Waiver of protection of identifiers.* A person waives the protection of FRCP 5.2(a) as to the person's own information by filing it without redaction and not under seal. FRCP 5.2(h).

j. For more information on privacy and public access to ECF cases, refer to NY R USDCTSD CM/ECF, S.D.(II)(21).

5. *Individual judge practices.* Refer to the Miscellaneous section of this document for information on individual judge practices on formatting documents.

## F. Filing and Service Requirements

1. *Filing requirements.* Any paper after the complaint that is required to be served—together with a certificate of service—must be filed within a reasonable time after service. FRCP 5(d)(1). Complaints and all subsequent papers are accepted at either courthouse, regardless of the place for which the case is designated. NY R USDCTSD Div. Bus., Rule 22. Subject to the instructions regarding ECF published on the website of each respective Court and any pertinent Individual Judge's Practices, letter-motions permitted by NY R USDCTS&ED Civ Rule 7.1(d) and letters addressed to the Court (but not letters between the parties) may be filed via ECF. NY R USDCTS&ED Civ Rule 5.2(b). For information on electronically filing motions, refer to NY R USDCTSD CM/ECF, S.D.(II)(15).

   a. *How filing is made; In general.* A paper is filed by delivering it:

      i. To the clerk; or

      ii. To a judge who agrees to accept it for filing, and who must then note the filing date on the paper and promptly send it to the clerk. FRCP 5(d)(2).

   b. *Night depository.* A night depository with an automatic date stamp shall be maintained by the Clerk of the Southern District in the Pearl Street Courthouse. After regular business hours, papers for the District Court only may be deposited in the night depository. Such papers will be considered as having been filed in the District Court as of the date stamped thereon, which shall be deemed presumptively correct. NY R USDCTS&ED Civ Rule 1.2.

   c. *Electronic filing*

      i. *Authorization of electronic filing program.* A court may, by local rule, allow papers to be filed, signed, or verified by electronic means that are consistent with any technical standards established by the Judicial Conference of the United States. A local rule may require electronic filing only if reasonable exceptions are allowed. A paper filed electronically in compliance with a local rule is a written paper for purposes of the Federal Rules of Civil Procedure. FRCP 5(d)(3).

         - The Court will accept for filing documents submitted, signed or verified by electronic means, that comply with the rules in NY R USDCTSD CM/ECF, S.D. NY R USDCTSD CM/ECF, S.D.(I). The information in NY R USDCTSD CM/ECF, S.D. applies only to cases assigned to the ECF system. NY R USDCTSD CM/ECF, S.D.(Introduction).

         - Parties serving and filing papers shall follow the instructions regarding Electronic Case Filing (ECF) published on the website of each respective Court. A paper served and filed by electronic means in accordance with such instructions is, for purposes of FRCP 5, served and filed in compliance with the Local Civil Rules of the Southern and Eastern Districts of New York. NY R USDCTS&ED Civ Rule 5.2(a). Parties have an obligation to review the Court's actual order, decree, or judgment (on ECF), which controls, and should not rely on the description on the docket or in the ECF Notice of Electronic Filing (NEF). NY R USDCTS&ED Civ Rule 5.2(c).

         - The following should be observed when filing electronically: (1) the Federal Rules of Civil Procedure, (2) the Local Civil Rules of the United States District Courts for the Southern and Eastern Districts of New York, (3) the assigned judge's Individual Practices, and (4) the Court's Electronic Case Filing Rules & Instructions (NY R USDCTSD CM/ECF, S.D.). NY R USDCTSD CM/ECF, S.D.(Introduction).

      ii. *Scope of electronic filing.* Except as expressly provided and in exceptional circumstances preventing a party from filing electronically, all documents required to be filed with the Court must be filed electronically. Any party unable to comply with this requirement must seek permission of the Court to file in the traditional manner, on paper. Any such application made after regular business hours may be submitted through the night depository box maintained pursuant to NY R USDCTS&ED Civ Rule 1.2. NY R USDCTSD CM/ECF, S.D.(I)(1)(1.1).

         - *Documents filed by pro se litigants.* Unless otherwise ordered by the Court, documents filed by pro se litigants must be filed in the traditional manner, on paper, and will be scanned and docketed by the Clerk's Office into the ECF system. NY R USDCTSD CM/ECF, S.D.(I)(1)(1.1). Pro se litigants must file pleadings and documents in the traditional manner on paper unless the assigned judge has granted permission to electronically file on the ECF system. NY R USDCTSD CM/ECF, S.D.(Introduction).

- *Letters.* Except for letters to be filed under seal, letters addressed to judges who accept letters may be filed electronically. Parties should consult the assigned judge's Individual Practices to determine if the judge accepts letters at all and, if he or she does, whether the judge has any page limitations on letters and/or requires courtesy copies of letters filed on ECF (and, if so, by what means of delivery). NY R USDCTSD CM/ECF, S.D.(II)(13)(13.1). Letters solely between parties or their counsel or otherwise not addressed to the Court may not be filed electronically on ECF (except as exhibits to an otherwise properly filed document). NY R USDCTSD CM/ECF, S.D.(II)(13)(13.1). For more information on filing letters, refer to NY R USDCTSD CM/ECF, S.D.(II)(13)(13.1).

- *Proposed orders, judgments and decrees.* Proposed orders, judgments and decrees shall be presented as directed by the ECF rules published on the website of each respective Court. NY R USDCTS&ED Civ Rule 77.1. For more information, refer to NY R USDCTS&ED Civ Rule 77.1.

iii. *Exceptions to electronic filing.* In an ECF case, the documents that should not be electronically filed include:

- Miscellaneous Case initiating documents, NY R USDCTSD CM/ECF, S.D.(II)(18)(18.2);

- Proposed orders; proposed judgments, stipulations; consents, NY R USDCTSD CM/ECF, S.D.(II)(18)(18.3);

- Orders to show cause / temporary restraining orders, NY R USDCTSD CM/ECF, S.D.(II)(18)(18.4);

- Sealed documents, NY R USDCTSD CM/ECF, S.D.(II)(18)(18.5); and

- Surety bonds, NY R USDCTSD CM/ECF, S.D.(II)(18)(18.6).

- In cases where the record of an administrative or other prior proceeding must be filed with the Court, such record may be served and filed in hard copy without prior motion and order of the Court. NY R USDCTSD CM/ECF, S.D.(I)(5)(5.3).

- For more documents excepted from electronic filing, and for more information on such documents, refer to NY R USDCTSD CM/ECF, S.D.(II)(18).

iv. *Consequences of electronic filing.* Except as otherwise provided in NY R USDCTSD CM/ECF, S.D.(I)(4), electronic filing of a document in the ECF system consistent with these procedures, together with the transmission of a Notice of Electronic Filing (NEF) from the Court, constitutes filing of the document for all purposes of the Federal Rules of Civil Procedure and the Local Civil Rules of the United States District Courts for the Southern and Eastern Districts of New York and constitutes entry of the document on the docket kept by the Clerk under FRCP 58 and FRCP 79. NY R USDCTSD CM/ECF, S.D.(I)(3)(3.1).

v. For more information on electronic filing, refer to NY R USDCTSD CM/ECF, S.D.

2. *Service requirements*

a. *Service; When required*

i. *In general.* Unless the Federal Rules of Civil Procedure provide otherwise, each of the following papers must be served on every party:

- An order stating that service is required;

- A pleading filed after the original complaint, unless the court orders otherwise under FRCP 5(c) because there are numerous defendants;

- A discovery paper required to be served on a party, unless the court orders otherwise;

- A written motion, except one that may be heard ex parte; and

- A written notice, appearance, demand, or offer of judgment, or any similar paper. FRCP 5(a)(1).

ii. *If a party fails to appear.* No service is required on a party who is in default for failing to appear. But a pleading that asserts a new claim for relief against such a party must be served on that party under FRCP 4. FRCP 5(a)(2).

iii. *Seizing property.* If an action is begun by seizing property and no person is or need be named as a defendant, any service required before the filing of an appearance, answer, or claim must be made on the person who had custody or possession of the property when it was seized. FRCP 5(a)(3).

b. *Service; How made*

i. *Serving an attorney.* If a party is represented by an attorney, service under FRCP 5 must be made on the attorney unless the court orders service on the party. FRCP 5(b)(1).

ii. *Service in general.* A paper is served under FRCP 5 by:

- Handing it to the person;

- Leaving it: (1) at the person's office with a clerk or other person in charge or, if no one is in charge, in a conspicuous place in the office; or (2) if the person has no office or the office is closed, at the person's dwelling or usual place of abode with someone of suitable age and discretion who resides there;

- Mailing it to the person's last known address—in which event service is complete upon mailing;

- Leaving it with the court clerk if the person has no known address;

- Sending it by electronic means if the person consented in writing—in which event service is complete upon transmission, but is not effective if the serving party learns that it did not reach the person to be served; or

- Delivering it by any other means that the person consented to in writing—in which event service is complete when the person making service delivers it to the agency designated to make delivery. FRCP 5(b)(2).

iii. *Service by overnight delivery.* Service upon an attorney may be made by overnight delivery service. "Overnight delivery service" means any delivery service which regularly accepts items for overnight delivery. Overnight delivery service shall be deemed service by mail for purposes of FRCP 5 and FRCP 6. NY R USDCTS&ED Civ Rule 5.3.

iv. *Service by electronic means.* Parties serving and filing papers shall follow the instructions regarding Electronic Case Filing (ECF) published on the website of each respective Court. A paper served and filed by electronic means in accordance with such instructions is, for purposes of FRCP 5, served and filed in compliance with the Local Civil Rules of the United States District Courts for the Southern and Eastern Districts of New York. NY R USDCTS&ED Civ Rule 5.2(a). Parties have an obligation to review the Court's actual order, decree, or judgment (on ECF), which controls, and should not rely on the description on the docket or in the ECF Notice of Electronic Filing (NEF). NY R USDCTS&ED Civ Rule 5.2(c).

- *Notice of electronic filing (NEF).* In cases assigned to the ECF system, service is complete provided all parties receive a Notice of Electronic Filing (NEF), which is sent automatically by email from the Court (see the NEF for a list of who did/did not receive notice electronically). Transmission of the NEF constitutes service upon all Filing and Receiving Users who are listed as recipients of notice by electronic mail. NY R USDCTSD CM/ECF, S.D.(I)(9)(9.1). In cases assigned to the ECF system, if all parties receive a NEF, service is complete upon transmission of the NEF by the Court, and you are not required to serve a paper copy. NY R USDCTSD CM/ECF, S.D.(II)(19)(19.2). It remains the duty of Filing and Receiving Users to maintain current contact information with the court and to regularly review the docket sheet of the case. NY R USDCTSD CM/ECF, S.D.(I)(9)(9.1).

- *Mailing of court-initiated documents.* The Clerk's Office will no longer mail paper copies of court-initiated documents to Filing and Receiving Users. The Clerk's Office will mail copies of all court-initiated documents to pro se parties who have not registered as Filing or Receiving Users. NY R USDCTSD CM/ECF, S.D.(II)(19)(19.1).

- *No receipt of a NEF.* If any party does not receive a NEF, you are required to accomplish service on that party in the traditional manner, in paper form. NY R USDCTSD CM/ECF, S.D.(II)(19)(19.2). The NEF receipt will inform you who will receive notice of the filing "electronically" (by e-mail from the Court) and who will receive notice "by other means" (traditional service in paper form). NY R USDCTSD CM/ECF, S.D.(II)(19)(19.2).

- *Service on non-filing or non-receiving users.* Attorneys and pro se parties who are not Filing or Receiving Users must be served with a paper copy of any electronically filed pleading or other document. Service of such paper copy must be made according to the Federal Rules of Civil Procedure and the Local Civil Rules of the United States District Courts for the Southern and Eastern Districts of New York. NY R USDCTSD CM/ECF, S.D.(I)(9)(9.2). Such paper service must be documented by electronically filing proof of service. NY R USDCTSD CM/ECF, S.D.(I)(9)(9.2); NY R USDCTSD CM/ECF, S.D.(II)(19)(19.2). Where the Clerk scans and electronically files pleadings and documents on behalf of a pro se party, the associated NEF constitutes service. NY R USDCTSD CM/ECF, S.D.(I)(9)(9.2).

- For more information on service by electronic means, refer to NY R USDCTSD CM/ECF, S.D.(II)(19).

    v. *Using court facilities.* If a local rule so authorizes, a party may use the court's transmission facilities to make service under FRCP 5(b)(2)(E). FRCP 5(b)(3).

  c. *Serving numerous defendants*

    i. *In general.* If an action involves an unusually large number of defendants, the court may, on motion or on its own, order that:

- Defendants' pleadings and replies to them need not be served on other defendants;

- Any crossclaim, counterclaim, avoidance, or affirmative defense in those pleadings and replies to them will be treated as denied or avoided by all other parties; and

- Filing any such pleading and serving it on the plaintiff constitutes notice of the pleading to all parties. FRCP 5(c)(1).

    ii. *Notifying parties.* A copy of every such order must be served on the parties as the court directs. FRCP 5(c)(2).

3. *Individual judge practices.* Refer to the Miscellaneous section of this document for information on individual judge practices on filing and serving documents.

## G. Hearings

1. *Hearings, generally*

  a. *Oral argument.* Due process does not require that oral argument be permitted on a motion and, except as otherwise provided by local rule, the district court has discretion to determine whether it will decide the motion on the papers or hear argument by counsel (and perhaps receive evidence). FPP § 1190; F.D.I.C. v. Deglau, 207 F.3d 153 (3d Cir. 2000). The parties and their attorneys shall only appear to argue the motion if so directed by the Court by order or by a Judge's Individual Practice. NY R USDCTS&ED Civ Rule 6.1(c).

  b. *Providing a regular schedule for oral hearings.* A court may establish regular times and places for oral hearings on motions. FRCP 78(a).

  c. *Providing for submission on briefs.* By rule or order, the court may provide for submitting and determining motions on briefs, without oral hearings. FRCP 78(b).

2. *Individual judge practices.* Refer to the Miscellaneous section of this document for information on individual judge practices on hearings.

## H. Forms

### 1. Federal Motion for Judgment on the Pleadings Forms

a. Motion and notice; For judgment on pleadings. AMJUR PP FEDPRAC § 532.

b. Countermotion and notice; For judgment on pleadings; By defendants. AMJUR PP FEDPRAC § 533.

c. Order; For judgment on pleadings; In favor of plaintiff. AMJUR PP FEDPRAC § 534.

d. Order; For judgment on pleadings; In favor of defendant. AMJUR PP FEDPRAC § 535.

e. Motion for judgment on the pleadings. 2C FEDFORMS § 11:131.

f. Motion for judgment on the pleadings; Alternate wording. 2C FEDFORMS § 11:132.

g. Motion for judgment on the pleadings; Long version. 2C FEDFORMS § 11:133.

h. Motion for judgment on the pleadings; Several grounds. 2C FEDFORMS § 11:134.

i. Notice of motion and motion for judgment on the pleadings. 2C FEDFORMS § 11:135.

j. Notice of motion for judgment on the pleadings (partial) or for partial summary judgment. 2C FEDFORMS § 11:136.

k. Order granting judgment on the pleadings. 2C FEDFORMS § 11:137.

l. Order granting judgment on the pleadings; Motion by plaintiff. 2C FEDFORMS § 11:138.

m. Judgment on the pleadings. 2C FEDFORMS § 11:139.

n. Motion; General form. FEDPROF § 1:746.

o. Notice; Of motion; General form. FEDPROF § 1:747.

p. Notice; Of motion; With costs of motion. FEDPROF § 1:748.

q. Notice; Of motion; Containing motion. FEDPROF § 1:749.

r. Opposition; To motion; General form. FEDPROF § 1:750.

s. Affidavit; Supporting or opposing motion. FEDPROF § 1:751.

t. Brief; Supporting or opposing motion. FEDPROF § 1:752.

u. Statement of points and authorities; Opposing motion. FEDPROF § 1:753.

v. Motion; For judgment on the pleadings. FEDPROF § 1:1295.

w. Order; For judgment on the pleadings; In favor of plaintiff. FEDPROF § 1:1296.

x. Order; For judgment on the pleadings; In favor of defendant. FEDPROF § 1:1297.

y. Motion for judgment on pleadings; Plaintiff. GOLDLTGFMS § 20:38.

z. Motion for judgment on pleadings; Defendant. GOLDLTGFMS § 20:39.

## I. Applicable Rules

### 1. *Federal rules*

a. Serving and filing pleadings and other papers. FRCP 5.

b. Constitutional challenge to a statute; Notice, certification, and intervention. FRCP 5.1.

c. Privacy protection for filings made with the court. FRCP 5.2.

d. Computing and extending time; Time for motion papers. FRCP 6.

e. Pleadings allowed; Form of motions and other papers. FRCP 7.

f. Disclosure statement. FRCP 7.1.

g. Form of pleadings. FRCP 10.

h. Signing pleadings, motions, and other papers; Representations to the court; Sanctions. FRCP 11.

i. Defenses and objections; When and how presented; Motion for judgment on the pleadings; Consolidating motions; Waiving defenses; Pretrial hearing. FRCP 12.

    j.  Hearing motions; Submission on briefs. FRCP 78.

2.  *Local rules*

    a.  Night depository. NY R USDCTS&ED Civ Rule 1.2.

    b.  Duty of attorneys in related cases. NY R USDCTS&ED Civ Rule 1.6.

    c.  Electronic service and filing of documents. NY R USDCTS&ED Civ Rule 5.2.

    d.  Service by overnight delivery. NY R USDCTS&ED Civ Rule 5.3.

    e.  Service and filing of motion papers. NY R USDCTS&ED Civ Rule 6.1.

    f.  Orders on motions. NY R USDCTS&ED Civ Rule 6.2.

    g.  Computation of time. NY R USDCTS&ED Civ Rule 6.4.

    h.  Motion papers. NY R USDCTS&ED Civ Rule 7.1.

    i.  Disclosure statement. NY R USDCTS&ED Civ Rule 7.1.1.

    j.  Authorities to be provided to pro se litigants. NY R USDCTS&ED Civ Rule 7.2.

    k.  Form of pleadings, motions, and other papers. NY R USDCTS&ED Civ Rule 11.1.

    l.  Notice to pro se litigant who opposes a FRCP 12 motion supported by matters outside the pleadings. NY R USDCTS&ED Civ Rule 12.1.

    m.  Submission of orders, judgments and decrees. NY R USDCTS&ED Civ Rule 77.1.

    n.  Alternative dispute resolution (Southern District only). NY R USDCTS&ED Civ Rule 83.9.

    o.  Electronic case filing rules and instructions. NY R USDCTSD CM/ECF, S.D.

    p.  Related cases. NY R USDCTSD Div. Bus., Rule 13.

    q.  Filing at either courthouse. NY R USDCTSD Div. Bus., Rule 22.

## J.  Miscellaneous

**NOTE: Individual judges' rules may apply. For available judge-level information, refer to:**

DISTRICT JUDGE RONNIE ABRAMS: NY R USDCTSD Abrams-Civ Prac; NY R USDCTSD Abrams-Crim Prac; NY R USDCTSD Abrams-Pro Se; NY R USDCTSD Abrams-Case Mgt; NY R USDCTSD Abrams-Jury.

DISTRICT JUDGE DEBORAH A. BATTS: NY R USDCTSD Batts-Practices.

DISTRICT JUDGE RICHARD M. BERMAN: NY R USDCTSD Berman-Practices; NY R USDCTSD Berman-Default; NY R USDCTSD Berman-Sentencing; NY R USDCTSD Berman-Media.

DISTRICT JUDGE VINCENT L. BRICCETTI: NY R USDCTSD Briccetti-Practices; NY R USDCTSD Briccetti-Plan; NY R USDCTSD Briccetti-Notice.

DISTRICT JUDGE VERNON S. BRODERICK: NY R USDCTSD Broderick-Civil; NY R USDCTSD Broderick-Crim; NY R USDCTSD Broderick-Case Mgt; NY R USDCTSD Broderick-Jury.

DISTRICT JUDGE NAOMI REICE BUCHWALD: NY R USDCTSD Buchwald-Practices.

DISTRICT JUDGE VALERIE E. CAPRONI: NY R USDCTSD Caproni-Prac; NY R USDCTSD Caproni--Pro Se; NY R USDCTSD Caproni-Case Mgt; NY R USDCTSD Caproni-Crim Prac.

DISTRICT JUDGE ANDREW L. CARTER JR.: NY R USDCTSD Carter-Practices.

DISTRICT JUDGE KEVIN P. CASTEL: NY R USDCTSD Castel-Practices; NY R USDCTSD Castel-Default; NY R USDCTSD Castel-Scheduling; NY R USDCTSD Castel-Complex; NY R USDCTSD Castel-Trials; NY R USDCTSD Castel-Sentencing.

DISTRICT JUDGE DENISE L. COTE: NY R USDCTSD Cote-Civil Practices; NY R USDCTSD Cote-Pro Se; NY R USDCTSD Cote-Maritime Ord; NY R USDCTSD Cote-Crim Practices; NY R USDCTSD Cote-Crim Trials; NY R USDCTSD Cote-Sentencing.

DISTRICT JUDGE PAUL A. CROTTY: NY R USDCTSD Crotty-Practices; NY R USDCTSD Crotty-Sentencing; NY R USDCTSD Crotty-Calls; NY R USDCTSD Crotty-Scheduling.

DISTRICT JUDGE GEORGE B. DANIELS: NY R USDCTSD Daniels-Practices.

DISTRICT JUDGE KEVIN T. DUFFY: NY R USDCTSD Duffy-Practices.

DISTRICT JUDGE PAUL A. ENGELMAYER: NY R USDCTSD Engelmayer-Practices; NY R USDCTSD Engelmayer-Scheduling; NY R USDCTSD Engelmayer-Sentencing; NY R USDCTSD Engelmayer-Pro Se; NY R USDCTSD Engelmayer-Crim.

DISTRICT JUDGE KATHERINE POLK FAILLA: NY R USDCTSD Failla-Civ Prac; NY R USDCTSD Failla-Crim Prac; NY R USDCTSD Failla-Case Mgt.

DISTRICT JUDGE KATHERINE B. FORREST: NY R USDCTSD Forrest-Civil Prac; NY R USDCTSD Forrest-Crim Prac; NY R USDCTSD Forrest-Crim Pretrial; NY R USDCTSD Forrest-Scheduling; NY R USDCTSD Forrest-Patent Scheduling; NY R USDCTSD Forrest-Sentencing; NY R USDCTSD Forrest-Order 1; NY R USDCTSD Forrest-Order 2.

DISTRICT JUDGE JESSE M. FURMAN: NY R USDCTSD Furman-Civil Prac; NY R USDCTSD Furman-Crim Prac; NY R USDCTSD Furman-Pro Se Prac; NY R USDCTSD Furman-Trials; NY R USDCTSD Furman-Scheduling; NY R USDCTSD Furman-Rights.

DISTRICT JUDGE PAUL G. GARDEPHE: NY R USDCTSD Gardephe-Civ Prac; NY R USDCTSD Gardephe-Pretrial; NY R USDCTSD Gardephe-Prot Ord; NY R USDCTSD Gardephe-Maritime; NY R USDCTSD Gardephe-Crim Prac; NY R USDCTSD Gardephe-Trial.

DISTRICT JUDGE THOMAS P. GRIESA: NY R USDCTSD Griesa-Practices.

DISTRICT JUDGE CHARLES S. HAIGHT: NY R USDCTSD Haight-Practices.

DISTRICT JUDGE ALVIN K. HELLERSTEIN: NY R USDCTSD Hellerstein-Practices; NY R USDCTSD Hellerstein--Sept 11.

DISTRICT JUDGE LEWIS A. KAPLAN: NY R USDCTSD Kaplan-Practices; NY R USDCTSD Kaplan-Sentencing.

DISTRICT JUDGE KENNETH M. KARAS: NY R USDCTSD Karas-Practices; NY R USDCTSD Karas-Case Mgt; NY R USDCTSD Karas-Default; NY R USDCTSD Karas-Sentencing; NY R USDCTSD Karas-Rights.

DISTRICT JUDGE JOHN F. KEENAN: NY R USDCTSD Keenan-Practices.

DISTRICT JUDGE JOHN G. KOELTL: NY R USDCTSD Koeltl-Practices.

DISTRICT JUDGE VICTOR MARRERO: NY R USDCTSD Marrero-Practices; NY R USDCTSD Marrero-Scheduling; NY R USDCTSD Marrero-Default; NY R USDCTSD Marrero-Trial Proc.

DISTRICT JUDGE COLLEEN McMAHON: NY R USDCTSD McMahon-Practices; NY R USDCTSD McMahon-RICO; NY R USDCTSD McMahon-Copies; NY R USDCTSD McMahon-Scheduling; NY R USDCTSD McMahon-Elec Disc; NY R USDCTSD McMahon-Sentencing.

DISTRICT JUDGE ALISON J. NATHAN: NY R USDCTSD Nathan-Civ Prac; NY R USDCTSD Nathan-Crim Prac; NY R USDCTSD Nathan-Pro Se; NY R USDCTSD Nathan-Scheduling.

DISTRICT JUDGE J. PAUL OETKEN: NY R USDCTSD Oetken-Civ Prac; NY R USDCTSD Oetken-Case Mgt; NY R USDCTSD Oetken-Crim Prac; NY R USDCTSD Oetken-Pro Se.

DISTRICT JUDGE WILLIAM H. PAULEY, III: NY R USDCTSD Pauley-Crim Cases; NY R USDCTSD Pauley-Practices.

DISTRICT JUDGE LORETTA A. PRESKA: NY R USDCTSD Preska-Practices.

DISTRICT JUDGE JED S. RAKOFF: NY R USDCTSD Rakoff-Practices; NY R USDCTSD Rakoff-Scheduling; NY R USDCTSD Rakoff-Prot Ord; NY R USDCTSD Rakoff-Maritime Ord.

DISTRICT JUDGE EDGARDO RAMOS: NY R USDCTSD Ramos--Practices; NY R USDCTSD Ramos-Case Mgt.

DISTRICT JUDGE NELSON S. ROMAN: NY R USDCTSD Roman-Civ Prac; NY R USDCTSD Roman-Pro Se; NY R USDCTSD Roman-Crim Prac; NY R USDCTSD Roman-Case Mgt.

DISTRICT JUDGE LEONARD B. SAND: NY R USDCTSD Sand-Practices.

DISTRICT JUDGE LORNA G. SCHOFIELD: NY R USDCTSD Schofield-Civ Prac; NY R USDCTSD Schofield-Crim Prac; NY R USDCTSD Schofield-Sched; NY R USDCTSD Schofield-Pro Se; NY R USDCTSD Schofield-Advice.

DISTRICT JUDGE CATHY SEIBEL: NY R USDCTSD Seibel-Practices.

DISTRICT JUDGE LOUIS L. STANTON: NY R USDCTSD Stanton-Practices; NY R USDCTSD Stanton-Pretrial.

DISTRICT JUDGE SIDNEY H. STEIN: NY R USDCTSD Stein-Practices.

DISTRICT JUDGE RICHARD J. SULLIVAN: NY R USDCTSD Sullivan-Practices; NY R USDCTSD Sullivan-Scheduling; NY R USDCTSD Sullivan-Sentencing; NY R USDCTSD Sullivan-Juries; NY R USDCTSD Sullivan-Trial; NY R USDCTSD Sullivan-Default.

DISTRICT JUDGE LAURA TAYLOR SWAIN: NY R USDCTSD Swain-Practices; NY R USDCTSD Swain-Trial; NY R USDCTSD Swain-Crim Trial; NY R USDCTSD Swain-Juries; NY R USDCTSD Swain-Sentencing; NY R USDCTSD Swain-Rights.

DISTRICT JUDGE ROBERT W. SWEET: NY R USDCTSD Sweet-Practices.

DISTRICT JUDGE ANALISA TORRES: NY R USDCTSD Torres-Civ Prac; NY R USDCTSD Torres-Pro Se; NY R USDCTSD Torres-Scheduling.

DISTRICT JUDGE KIMBA M. WOOD: NY R USDCTSD Wood-Practices; NY R USDCTSD Wood-Scheduling; NY R USDCTSD Wood-Discovery; NY R USDCTSD Wood-RICO; NY R USDCTSD Wood-Juries; NY R USDCTSD Wood-Trial; NY R USDCTSD Wood-Media.

DISTRICT JUDGE GREGORY H. WOODS: NY R USDCTSD Woods-Civ Prac; NY R USDCTSD Woods-Pro Se; NY R USDCTSD Woods-Sched; NY R USDCTSD Woods-Crim Prac; NY R USDCTSD Woods-Protect Order; NY R USDCTSD Woods-Speedy Trial.

MAGISTRATE JUDGE JAMES L. COTT: NY R USDCTSD Cott-Practices; NY R USDCTSD Cott-Settlement.

MAGISTRATE JUDGE PAUL E. DAVISON: NY R USDCTSD Davison-Practices.

MAGISTRATE JUDGE RONALD L. ELLIS: NY R USDCTSD Ellis-Practices.

MAGISTRATE JUDGE KEVIN N. FOX: NY R USDCTSD Fox-Practices; NY R USDCTSD Fox-Settlement.

MAGISTRATE JUDGE JAMES C. FRANCIS: NY R USDCTSD Francis-Practices.

MAGISTRATE JUDGE DEBRA FREEMAN: NY R USDCTSD Freeman-Practices; NY R USDCTSD Freeman-Settlement.

MAGISTRATE JUDGE GABRIEL W. GORENSTEIN: NY R USDCTSD Gorenstein-Practices; NY R USDCTSD Gorenstein-Ackn.

MAGISTRATE JUDGE FRANK MAAS: NY R USDCTSD Maas-Practices; NY R USDCTSD Maas-Discontinuance; NY R USDCTSD Maas-Conf; NY R USDCTSD Maas-Settlement.

MAGISTRATE JUDGE JUDITH C. McCARTHY: NY R USDCTSD McCarthy-Practices; NY R USDCTSD McCarthy-Conduct.

MAGISTRATE JUDGE BARBARA MOSES: NY R USDCTSD Moses-Practices.

MAGISTRATE JUDGE SARAH NETBURN: NY R USDCTSD Netburn-Civil; NY R USDCTSD Netburn-Settlement; NY R USDCTSD Netburn-Case Mgt; NY R USDCTSD Netburn--Pro Se.

MAGISTRATE JUDGE ANDREW J. PECK: NY R USDCTSD Peck-Practices; NY R USDCTSD Peck-Order; NY R USDCTSD Peck-Rule 502(d).

MAGISTRATE JUDGE HENRY PITMAN: NY R USDCTSD Pitman-Practices.

MAGISTRATE JUDGE LISA MARGARET SMITH: NY R USDCTSD Smith-Practices; NY R USDCTSD Smith-Trials.

# Requests, Notices and Applications
# Interrogatories

## Document Last Updated September 2016

### A. Checklist

(I) ❑ Matters to be considered by requesting party

    (a) ❑ Required documents

        (1) ❑ Interrogatories

    (b) ❑ Supplemental documents

        (1) ❑ Certificate of service

    (c) ❑ Timing

        (1) ❑ A party may not seek discovery from any source before the parties have conferred as required by FRCP 26(f), except in a proceeding exempted from initial disclosure under FRCP 26(a)(1)(B), or when authorized by the Federal Rules of Civil Procedure, by stipulation, or by court order

        (2) ❑ At the conclusion of other discovery, and at least thirty (30) days prior to the discovery cut-off date, interrogatories seeking the claims and contentions of the opposing party may be served unless the court has ordered otherwise

(II) ❑ Matters to be considered by responding party

    (a) ❑ Required documents

        (1) ❑ Response to interrogatories

    (b) ❑ Supplemental documents

        (1) ❑ Written information regarding assertion of privilege

        (2) ❑ Certificate of service

    (c) ❑ Timing

        (1) ❑ The responding party must serve its answers and any objections within thirty (30) days after being served with the interrogatories

### B. Timing

1. *Interrogatories.* FRCP 33(a) contains no limit on when interrogatories may first be served. FPP § 2170. FRCP 33 is also silent on how late in a case interrogatories may be served. But FRCP 16(b)(3)(A) provides that the scheduling order in the case "must limit the time to . . . complete discovery." Although the scheduling order requirement does not apply to cases exempted by local rule, ordinarily there should be a scheduling order that sets a discovery cutoff. FPP § 2170.

    a. *Interrogatories seeking claims and contentions.* At the conclusion of other discovery, and at least thirty (30) days prior to the discovery cut-off date, interrogatories seeking the claims and contentions of the opposing party may be served unless the Court has ordered otherwise. NY R USDCTS&ED Civ Rule 33.3(c).

2. *Timing of discovery, generally.* A party may not seek discovery from any source before the parties have conferred as required by FRCP 26(f), except in a proceeding exempted from initial disclosure under FRCP 26(a)(1)(B), or when authorized by the Federal Rules of Civil Procedure, by stipulation, or by court order. FRCP 26(d)(1).

3. *Computation of time*

    a. *Computing time.* FRCP 6 applies in computing any time period specified in the Federal Rules of Civil Procedure, in any local rule or court order, or in any statute that does not specify a method of computing time. FRCP 6(a). In computing any period of time prescribed or allowed by the Local Civil Rules of the United States District Courts for the Southern and Eastern Districts of New York or the Local Admiralty and Maritime Rules, the provisions of FRCP 6 shall apply unless otherwise stated. NY R USDCTS&ED Civ Rule 6.4.

i. *Period stated in days or a longer unit.* When the period is stated in days or a longer unit of time:

- Exclude the day of the event that triggers the period;
- Count every day, including intermediate Saturdays, Sundays, and legal holidays; and
- Include the last day of the period, but if the last day is a Saturday, Sunday, or legal holiday, the period continues to run until the end of the next day that is not a Saturday, Sunday, or legal holiday. FRCP 6(a)(1). In the Local Civil Rules of the United States District Courts for the Southern and Eastern Districts of New York, as in the Federal Rules of Civil Procedure as amended effective December 1, 2009, Saturdays, Sundays, and legal holidays are no longer excluded in computing periods of time. If the last day of the period is a Saturday, Sunday, or legal holiday, the period continues to run until the end of the next day that is not a Saturday, Sunday, or legal holiday. NY R USDCTS&ED Civ Rule 6.4.

ii. *Period stated in hours.* When the period is stated in hours:

- Begin counting immediately on the occurrence of the event that triggers the period;
- Count every hour, including hours during intermediate Saturdays, Sundays, and legal holidays; and
- If the period would end on a Saturday, Sunday, or legal holiday, the period continues to run until the same time on the next day that is not a Saturday, Sunday, or legal holiday. FRCP 6(a)(2). In the Local Civil Rules of the United States District Courts for the Southern and Eastern Districts of New York, as in the Federal Rules of Civil Procedure as amended effective December 1, 2009, Saturdays, Sundays, and legal holidays are no longer excluded in computing periods of time. If the last day of the period is a Saturday, Sunday, or legal holiday, the period continues to run until the end of the next day that is not a Saturday, Sunday, or legal holiday. NY R USDCTS&ED Civ Rule 6.4.

iii. *Inaccessibility of the clerk's office.* Unless the court orders otherwise, if the clerk's office is inaccessible:

- On the last day for filing under FRCP 6(a)(1), then the time for filing is extended to the first accessible day that is not a Saturday, Sunday, or legal holiday; or
- During the last hour for filing under FRCP 6(a)(2), then the time for filing is extended to the same time on the first accessible day that is not a Saturday, Sunday, or legal holiday. FRCP 6(a)(3).

iv. *"Last day" defined.* Unless a different time is set by a statute, local rule, or court order, the last day ends:

- For electronic filing, at midnight in the court's time zone; and
- For filing by other means, when the clerk's office is scheduled to close. FRCP 6(a)(4).

v. *"Next day" defined.* The "next day" is determined by continuing to count forward when the period is measured after an event and backward when measured before an event. FRCP 6(a)(5).

vi. *"Legal holiday" defined.* "Legal holiday" means:

- The day set aside by statute for observing New Year's Day, Martin Luther King Jr.'s Birthday, Washington's Birthday, Memorial Day, Independence Day, Labor Day, Columbus Day, Veterans' Day, Thanksgiving Day, or Christmas Day;
- Any day declared a holiday by the President or Congress; and
- For periods that are measured after an event, any other day declared a holiday by the state where the district court is located. FRCP 6(a)(6).

b. *Computation of electronic filing deadlines.* You can file electronically twenty-four (24) hours a day, seven (7) days a week, three hundred sixty-five (365) days a year. NY R USDCTSD CM/ECF, S.D.(II)(13)(13.10). Electronic filing must be completed before midnight local time where the Court is located in order to be considered timely filed that day. NY R USDCTSD CM/ECF, S.D.(I)(3)(3.3); NY R USDCTSD CM/ECF, S.D.(II)(13)(13.10); NY R USDCTSD CM/ECF, S.D.(II)(19)(19.4). An electronically filed document is deemed filed on the "filed on" date indicated on the Notice of Electronic Filing (NEF). NY R USDCTSD CM/ECF, S.D.(II)(13)(13.11).

    i. *Technical failures.* A Filing User whose filing is made untimely as the result of a technical failure may seek appropriate relief from the Court. NY R USDCTSD CM/ECF, S.D.(I)(11). If you missed a filing deadline when the ECF system was out of order, attach a statement to your filing explaining how the interruption in service prevented you from filing in a timely fashion. NY R USDCTSD CM/ECF, S.D.(II)(23)(23.5).

  c. *Extending time*

    i. *In general.* When an act may or must be done within a specified time, the court may, for good cause, extend the time:

- With or without motion or notice if the court acts, or if a request is made, before the original time or its extension expires; or

- On motion made after the time has expired if the party failed to act because of excusable neglect. FRCP 6(b)(1).

    ii. *Exceptions.* A court must not extend the time to act under FRCP 50(b), FRCP 50(d), FRCP 52(b), FRCP 59(b), FRCP 59(d), FRCP 59(e), and FRCP 60(b). FRCP 6(b)(2).

    iii. Refer to the United States District Court for the Southern District of New York KeyRules Motion for Continuance/Extension of Time document for more information on extending time.

  d. *Additional time after certain kinds of service.* When a party may or must act within a specified time after service and service is made under FRCP 5(b)(2)(C), FRCP 5(b)(2)(D), FRCP 5(b)(2)(E), or FRCP 5(b)(2)(F), three (3) days are added after the period would otherwise expire under FRCP 6(a). FRCP 6(d). Overnight delivery service shall be deemed service by mail for purposes of FRCP 5 and FRCP 6. NY R USDCTS&ED Civ Rule 5.3.

4. *Individual judge practices.* Refer to the Miscellaneous section of this document for information on individual judge practices on timing of documents.

## C. General Requirements

1. *General provisions governing discovery*

  a. *Discovery scope and limits*

    i. *Scope in general.* Unless otherwise limited by court order, the scope of discovery is as follows: Parties may obtain discovery regarding any nonprivileged matter that is relevant to any party's claim or defense and proportional to the needs of the case, considering the importance of the issues at stake in the action, the amount in controversy, the parties' relative access to relevant information, the parties' resources, the importance of the discovery in resolving the issues, and whether the burden or expense of the proposed discovery outweighs its likely benefit. Information within this scope of discovery need not be admissible in evidence to be discoverable. FRCP 26(b)(1).

    ii. *Limitations on frequency and extent*

- *When permitted.* By order, the court may alter the limits in the Federal Rules of Civil Procedure on the number of depositions and interrogatories or on the length of depositions under FRCP 30. By order or local rule, the court may also limit the number of requests under FRCP 36. FRCP 26(b)(2)(A).

- *Specific limitations on electronically stored information.* A party need not provide discovery of electronically stored information from sources that the party identifies as not reasonably accessible because of undue burden or cost. On motion to compel discovery or for a protective order, the party from whom discovery is sought must show that the information is not reasonably accessible because of undue burden or cost. If that showing is made, the court may nonetheless order discovery from such sources if the requesting party shows good cause, considering the limitations of FRCP 26(b)(2)(C). The court may specify conditions for the discovery. FRCP 26(b)(2)(B).

- *When required.* On motion or on its own, the court must limit the frequency or extent of discovery otherwise allowed by the Federal Rules of Civil Procedure or by local rule if it determines that: (1) the discovery sought is unreasonably cumulative or duplicative, or can be obtained from some other source that is more convenient, less burdensome, or less expensive; (2) the party seeking discovery has had ample opportunity to obtain the information by discovery in the action; or (3) the proposed discovery is outside the scope permitted by FRCP 26(b)(1). FRCP 26(b)(2)(C).

iii. *Trial preparation; Materials*

- *Documents and tangible things.* Ordinarily, a party may not discover documents and tangible things that are prepared in anticipation of litigation or for trial by or for another party or its representative (including the other party's attorney, consultant, surety, indemnitor, insurer, or agent). But, subject to FRCP 26(b)(4), those materials may be discovered if: (1) they are otherwise discoverable under FRCP 26(b)(1); and (2) the party shows that it has substantial need for the materials to prepare its case and cannot, without undue hardship, obtain their substantial equivalent by other means. FRCP 26(b)(3)(A).

- *Protection against disclosure.* If the court orders discovery of those materials, it must protect against disclosure of the mental impressions, conclusions, opinions, or legal theories of a party's attorney or other representative concerning the litigation. FRCP 26(b)(3)(B).

- *Previous statement.* Any party or other person may, on request and without the required showing, obtain the person's own previous statement about the action or its subject matter. If the request is refused, the person may move for a court order, and FRCP 37(a)(5) applies to the award of expenses. A previous statement is either: (1) a written statement that the person has signed or otherwise adopted or approved; or (2) a contemporaneous stenographic, mechanical, electrical, or other recording—or a transcription of it—that recites substantially verbatim the person's oral statement. FRCP 26(b)(3)(C).

iv. *Trial preparation; Experts*

- *Deposition of an expert who may testify.* A party may depose any person who has been identified as an expert whose opinions may be presented at trial. If FRCP 26(a)(2)(B) requires a report from the expert, the deposition may be conducted only after the report is provided. FRCP 26(b)(4)(A).

- *Trial-preparation protection for draft reports or disclosures.* FRCP 26(b)(3)(A) and FRCP 26(b)(3)(B) protect drafts of any report or disclosure required under FRCP 26(a)(2), regardless of the form in which the draft is recorded. FRCP 26(b)(4)(B).

- *Trial-preparation protection for communications between a party's attorney and expert witnesses.* FRCP 26(b)(3)(A) and FRCP 26(b)(3)(B) protect communications between the party's attorney and any witness required to provide a report under FRCP 26(a)(2)(B), regardless of the form of the communications, except to the extent that the communications: (1) relate to compensation for the expert's study or testimony; (2) identify facts or data that the party's attorney provided and that the expert considered in forming the opinions to be expressed; or (3) identify assumptions that the party's attorney provided and that the expert relied on in forming the opinions to be expressed. FRCP 26(b)(4)(C).

- *Expert employed only for trial preparation.* Ordinarily, a party may not, by interrogatories or deposition, discover facts known or opinions held by an expert who has been retained or specially employed by another party in anticipation of litigation or to prepare for trial and who is not expected to be called as a witness at trial. But a party may do so only: (1) as provided in FRCP 35(b); or (2) on showing exceptional circumstances under which it is impracticable for the party to obtain facts or opinions on the same subject by other means. FRCP 26(b)(4)(D).

- *Payment.* Unless manifest injustice would result, the court must require that the party seeking discovery: (1) pay the expert a reasonable fee for time spent in responding to discovery under FRCP 26(b)(4)(A) or FRCP 26(b)(4)(D); and (2) for discovery FRCP 26(b)(4)(D), also pay the other party a fair portion of the fees and expenses it reasonably incurred in obtaining the expert's facts and opinions. FRCP 26(b)(4)(E).

v. *Claiming privilege or protecting trial-preparation materials*

- *Information withheld.* When a party withholds information otherwise discoverable by claiming that the information is privileged or subject to protection as trial-preparation material, the party must: (1) expressly make the claim; and (2) describe the nature of the documents, communications, or tangible things not produced or disclosed—and do so in a manner that, without revealing information itself privileged or protected, will enable other parties to assess the claim. FRCP 26(b)(5)(A). Unless otherwise agreed by the parties or directed by the Court, where a claim of privilege is asserted in objecting to any means of discovery or disclosure, including but not limited to a deposition, and an answer is not provided on the basis of such assertion, (1) the person asserting the privilege shall identify the nature of the privilege (including work product) which is being claimed and, if the privilege is governed by state law, indicate the state's privilege rule being invoked; and (2) the following information shall be provided in the objection, or (in the case of a deposition) in response to questions by the questioner, unless divulgence of such information would cause disclosure of the allegedly privileged information: (A) for documents: (i) the type of document, e.g., letter or memorandum; (ii) the general subject matter of the document; (iii) the date of the document; and (iv) the author of the document, the addressees of the document, and any other recipients, and, where not apparent, the relationship of the author, addressees, and recipients to each other; (B) for oral communications: (i) the name of the person making the communication and the names of persons present while the communication was made and, where not apparent, the relationship of the persons present to the person making the communication; (ii) the date and place of communication; and (iii) the general subject matter of the communication. NY R USDCTS&ED Civ Rule 26.2(a). Where a claim of privilege is asserted in response to discovery or disclosure other than a deposition, and information is not provided on the basis of such assertion, the information set forth in NY R USDCTS&ED Civ Rule 26.2(a) shall be furnished in writing at the time of the response to such discovery or disclosure, unless otherwise ordered by the Court. NY R USDCTS&ED Civ Rule 26.2(b).

- *Information produced.* If information produced in discovery is subject to a claim of privilege or of protection as trial-preparation material, the party making the claim may notify any party that received the information of the claim and the basis for it. After being notified, a party must promptly return, sequester, or destroy the specified information and any copies it has; must not use or disclose the information until the claim is resolved; must take reasonable steps to retrieve the information if the party disclosed it before being notified; and may promptly present the information to the court under seal for a determination of the claim. The producing party must preserve the information until the claim is resolved. FRCP 26(b)(5)(B).

- *Efficient means of providing information regarding claims of privilege.* Efficient means of providing information regarding claims of privilege are encouraged, and parties are encouraged to agree upon measures that further this end. For example, when asserting privilege on the same basis with respect to multiple documents, it is presumptively proper to provide the information required by NY R USDCTS&ED Civ Rule 26.2 by group or category. A party receiving a privilege log that groups documents or otherwise departs from a document-by-document or communication-by-communication listing may not object solely on that basis, but may object if the substantive information required by NY R USDCTS&ED Civ Rule 26.2 has not been provided in a comprehensible form. NY R USDCTS&ED Civ Rule 26.2(c).

b. *Protective orders.* A party or any person from whom discovery is sought may move for a protective order in the court where the action is pending—or as an alternative on matters relating to a deposition, in the court for the district where the deposition will be taken. FRCP 26(c)(1). Refer to the United States District Court for the Southern District of New York KeyRules Motion for Protective Order document for more information.

c. *Sequence of discovery.* Unless the parties stipulate or the court orders otherwise for the parties' and witnesses' convenience and in the interests of justice: (1) methods of discovery may be used in any sequence; and (2) discovery by one party does not require any other party to delay its discovery. FRCP 26(d)(3).

d. *Uniform definitions in discovery requests.* The full text of the definitions and rules of construction set forth in NY R USDCTS&ED Civ Rule 26.3(c) and NY R USDCTS&ED Civ Rule 26.3(d) is deemed incorporated by reference into all discovery requests. No discovery request shall use broader definitions or rules of construction than those set forth in NY R USDCTS&ED Civ Rule 26.3(c) and NY R USDCTS&ED Civ Rule 26.3(d). NY R USDCTS&ED Civ Rule 26.3 shall not preclude (1) the definition of other terms specific to the particular litigation, (2) the use of abbreviations, or (3) a more narrow definition of a term defined in NY R USDCTS&ED Civ Rule 26.3(c). NY R USDCTS&ED Civ Rule 26.3(a). NY R USDCTS&ED Civ Rule 26.3 is not intended to broaden or narrow the scope of discovery permitted by the Federal Rules of Civil Procedure. NY R USDCTS&ED Civ Rule 26.3(b).

i. *Definitions.* The following definitions apply to all discovery requests:

- *Communication.* The term "communication" means the transmittal of information (in the form of facts, ideas, inquiries or otherwise). NY R USDCTS&ED Civ Rule 26.3(c)(1).

- *Document.* The term "document" is defined to be synonymous in meaning and equal in scope to the usage of the term "documents or electronically stored information" in FRCP 34(a)(1)(A). A draft or non-identical copy is a separate document within the meaning of this term. NY R USDCTS&ED Civ Rule 26.3(c)(2).

- *Identify (with respect to persons).* When referring to a person, "to identify" means to give, to the extent known, the person's full name, present or last known address, and when referring to a natural person, additionally, the present or last known place of employment. Once a person has been identified in accordance with NY R USDCTS&ED Civ Rule 26.3(c)(3), only the name of that person need be listed in response to subsequent discovery requesting the identification of that person. NY R USDCTS&ED Civ Rule 26.3(c)(3).

- *Identify (with respect to documents).* When referring to documents, "to identify" means to give, to the extent known, the (1) type of document; (2) general subject matter; (3) date of the document; and (4) author(s), addressee(s) and recipient(s). In the alternative, the responding party may produce the documents, together with identifying information sufficient to satisfy FRCP 33(d). NY R USDCTS&ED Civ Rule 26.3(c)(4).

- *Parties.* The terms "plaintiff" and "defendant" as well as a party's full or abbreviated name or a pronoun referring to a party mean the party and, where applicable, its officers, directors, employees, partners, corporate parent, subsidiaries or affiliates. This definition is not intended to impose a discovery obligation on any person who is not a party to the litigation. NY R USDCTS&ED Civ Rule 26.3(c)(5).

- *Person.* The term "person" is defined as any natural person or any legal entity, including, without limitation, any business or governmental entity or association. NY R USDCTS&ED Civ Rule 26.3(c)(6).

- *Concerning.* The term "concerning" means relating to, referring to, describing, evidencing or constituting. NY R USDCTS&ED Civ Rule 26.3(c)(7).

ii. *Rules of construction.* The following rules of construction apply to all discovery requests:

- *All/any/each.* The terms "all," "any," and "each" shall each be construed as encompassing any and all. NY R USDCTS&ED Civ Rule 26.3(d)(1).

- *And/or.* The connectives "and" and "or" shall be construed either disjunctively or conjunctively as necessary to bring within the scope of the discovery request all responses that might otherwise be construed to be outside of its scope. NY R USDCTS&ED Civ Rule 26.3(d)(2).

- *Number.* The use of the singular form of any word includes the plural and vice versa. NY R USDCTS&ED Civ Rule 26.3(d)(3).

e. *Cooperation among counsel in discovery.* Counsel are expected to cooperate with each other, consistent with the interests of their clients, in all phases of the discovery process and to be courteous in their dealings with each other, including in matters relating to scheduling and timing of various discovery procedures. NY R USDCTS&ED Civ Rule 26.4(a).

   i. Discovery requests shall be read reasonably in the recognition that the attorney serving them generally does not have the information being sought and the attorney receiving them generally does have such information or can obtain it from the client. NY R USDCTS&ED Civ Rule 26.4(b).

f. *Standard discovery in prisoner pro se actions.* For information on discovery in prisoner pro se actions, refer to NY R USDCTS&ED Civ Rule 33.2.

2. *Interrogatories*

a. *Number.* Unless otherwise stipulated or ordered by the court, a party may serve on any other party no more than twenty-five (25) written interrogatories, including all discrete subparts. Leave to serve additional interrogatories may be granted to the extent consistent with FRCP 26(b)(1) and FRCP 26(b)(2). FRCP 33(a)(1).

b. *Scope.* An interrogatory may relate to any matter that may be inquired into under FRCP 26(b). An interrogatory is not objectionable merely because it asks for an opinion or contention that relates to fact or the application of law to fact, but the court may order that the interrogatory need not be answered until designated discovery is complete, or until a pretrial conference or some other time. FRCP 33(a)(2).

   i. Unless otherwise ordered by the Court, at the commencement of discovery, interrogatories will be restricted to those seeking names of witnesses with knowledge of information relevant to the subject matter of the action, the computation of each category of damage alleged, and the existence, custodian, location and general description of relevant documents, including pertinent insurance agreements, and other physical evidence, or information of a similar nature. NY R USDCTS&ED Civ Rule 33.3(a).

   ii. During discovery, interrogatories other than those seeking information described in NY R USDCTS&ED Civ Rule 33.3(a) may only be served (1) if they are a more practical method of obtaining the information sought than a request for production or a deposition, or (2) if ordered by the Court. NY R USDCTS&ED Civ Rule 33.3(b).

c. *Parties subject to interrogatories.* Depositions may be taken of any person but interrogatories are limited to parties to the litigation. FPP § 2171. Interrogatories may not be directed to the attorney for a party. They must be addressed to the party, who is then required to give all information known to it or its attorney. FPP § 2171; Hickman v. Taylor, 329 U.S. 495, 504, 67 S.Ct. 385, 390, 91 L.Ed. 451 (1947). For more information, refer to FPP § 2171.

d. *Form.* Ideally an interrogatory should be a single direct question phrased in a fashion that will inform the other party what is requested. In fact the courts have given parties considerable latitude in framing interrogatories. Rather general language has been permitted so long as the interrogatory gives the other party a reasonably clear indication of the information to be included in its answer. FPP § 2168.

   i. *Use of definitions.* There is no prohibition against the use of definitions in interrogatories, and definitions may be helpful in clarifying the meaning of obscure terms or avoiding repetitions in a long set of interrogatories. FPP § 2168.

   ii. *Use of standardized form interrogatories.* There have been mixed reactions to the use of standardized form interrogatories. They have been referred to opprobriously as "canned sets of interrogatories of the shotgun variety" and it has been said that their indiscriminate use is an "undesirable practice." FPP § 2168.

e. *Form discovery requests.* Attorneys using form discovery requests shall review them to ascertain that they are consistent with the scope of discovery under FRCP 26(b)(1). Non-compliant requests shall not be used. NY R USDCTS&ED Civ Rule 26.5.

f. *Motion to compel.* The party submitting the interrogatories must attempt to confer with the responding party in an effort to secure the information without court action and, if that fails, move for an order under FRCP 37(a) compelling answers. FPP § 2182. Refer to the United States District Court for the Southern District of New York KeyRules Motion to Compel Discovery document for more information.

3. *Sanctions for failure to cooperate in discovery.* The court where the action is pending may, on motion, order sanctions if a party, after being properly served with interrogatories under FRCP 33 or a request for inspection under FRCP 34, fails to serve its answers, objections, or written response. FRCP 37(d)(1)(A)(ii). If a motion to compel is granted, the court must, after giving an opportunity to be heard, require the party or deponent whose conduct necessitated the motion, the party or attorney advising that conduct, or both to pay the movant's reasonable expenses incurred in making the motion, including attorney's fees. But the court must not order this payment if the opposing party's nondisclosure, response, or objection was substantially justified. FRCP 37(a)(5)(A)(ii). Refer to the United States District Court for the Southern District of New York KeyRules Motion for Discovery Sanctions document for more information.

4. *Stipulations about discovery procedure.* Unless the court orders otherwise, the parties may stipulate that: (1) a deposition may be taken before any person, at any time or place, on any notice, and in the manner specified—in which event it may be used in the same way as any other deposition; and (2) other procedures governing or limiting discovery be modified—but a stipulation extending the time for any form of discovery must have court approval if it would interfere with the time set for completing discovery, for hearing a motion, or for trial. FRCP 29.

5. *Complex civil cases.* For information on procedures for complex civil cases, refer to NY R USDCTSD Order 11 Misc 00388.

6. *Related cases.* It shall be the continuing duty of each attorney appearing in any civil or criminal case to bring promptly to the attention of the Court all facts which said attorney believes are relevant to a determination that said case and one or more pending civil or criminal cases should be heard by the same Judge, in order to avoid unnecessary duplication of judicial effort. As soon as the attorney becomes aware of such relationship, said attorney shall notify the Judges to whom the cases have been assigned. NY R USDCTS&ED Civ Rule 1.6(a). If counsel fails to comply with NY R USDCTS&ED Civ Rule 1.6(a), the Court may assess reasonable costs directly against counsel whose action has obstructed the effective administration of the Court's business. NY R USDCTS&ED Civ Rule 1.6(b).

a. *Determination of relatedness.* Subject to the limitations set forth in NY R USDCTSD Div. Bus., Rule 13(a)(2), a civil case, bankruptcy appeal, or motion to withdraw the bankruptcy reference will be deemed related to one or more civil cases, appeals or motions when the interests of justice and efficiency will be served. In determining relatedness, a judge will consider whether (A) the actions concern the same or substantially similar parties, property, transactions or events; (B) there is substantial factual overlap; (C) the parties could be subjected to conflicting orders; and (D) whether absent a determination of relatedness there would be a substantial duplication of effort and expense, delay, or undue burden on the Court, parties or witnesses. NY R USDCTSD Div. Bus., Rule 13(a)(1). Nothing in this NY R USDCTSD Div. Bus., Rule 13 is intended to preclude parties from moving for consolidated proceedings under FRCP 42. NY R USDCTSD Div. Bus., Rule 13(a)(1). Notwithstanding NY R USDCTSD Div. Bus., Rule 13(a)(1):

   i. Civil cases shall not be deemed related merely because they involve common legal issues or the same parties. NY R USDCTSD Div. Bus., Rule 13(a)(2)(A).

   ii. Other than cases subject to NY R USDCTSD Div. Bus., Rule 4(b) and actions seeking the enforcement of a judgment or settlement in or of an earlier case, civil cases presumptively shall not be deemed related unless both cases are pending before the Court (or the earlier case is on appeal). NY R USDCTSD Div. Bus., Rule 13(a)(2)(B).

b. *Procedure in regard to cases said to be related*

    i. *Disclosure of contention of relatedness.* When a civil case is filed or removed or a bankruptcy appeal or motion to withdraw the reference of an adversary proceeding from the bankruptcy court is filed, the person filing or removing shall disclose on form JSC44C any contention of relatedness and shall file a Related Case Statement stating clearly and succinctly the basis for the contention. A copy of the civil cover sheet and Related Case Statement shall be served with the complaint, notice of removal, notice of appeal, or motion. Any party may contest a claim of relatedness by any other in writing addressed to the judge having the case with the lowest docket number of all cases claimed to be related. However, the foregoing shall not delay the assignment process or the operation of NY R USDCTSD Div. Bus., Rule 13. NY R USDCTSD Div. Bus., Rule 13(b)(1). [Editor's note: the reference to form JSC44C is likely meant to be form JS44C-SDNY: Civil Court Cover Sheet].

    ii. *Claims of relatedness by other parties.* A party other than the one filing a case, bankruptcy appeal or motion to withdraw the reference that contends its case is related to another may so advise in writing the judge assigned in its case and request a transfer of its case to the judge that the party contends has the related case with the lowest docket number. If the assigned judge believes the case is related under NY R USDCTSD Div. Bus., Rule 13(a), he or she shall refer the question to the judge having the case with the lowest docket number. In the event the latter judge agrees, the case shall be transferred to that judge unless the Assignment Committee disagrees. NY R USDCTSD Div. Bus., Rule 13(b)(3).

c. For more information on related cases, refer to NY R USDCTSD Div. Bus., Rule 13.

7. *Alternative dispute resolution (ADR).* The U.S. District Court for the Southern District of New York provides litigants with opportunities to discuss settlement through judicial settlement conferences and mediation. NY R USDCTS&ED Civ Rule 83.9(a).

a. *Consideration of alternative dispute resolution.* In all civil cases, including those eligible for mediation pursuant to NY R USDCTS&ED Civ Rule 83.9(e), each party shall consider the use of mediation or a judicial settlement conference and shall report to the assigned Judge at the initial FRCP 16(b) case management conference, or subsequently, whether the party believes mediation or a judicial settlement conference may facilitate the resolution of the lawsuit. Judges are encouraged to note the availability of the mediation program and/or a judicial settlement conference before, at, or after the initial FRCP 16(b) case management conference. NY R USDCTS&ED Civ Rule 83.9(d).

b. *Mediation.* In mediation, parties and counsel meet, sometimes collectively and sometimes individually, with a neutral third party (the mediator) who has been trained to facilitate confidential settlement discussions. The parties articulate their respective positions and interests and generate options for a mutually agreeable resolution to the dispute. The mediator assists the parties in reaching their own negotiated settlement by defining the issues, probing and assessing the strengths and weaknesses of each party's legal positions, and identifying areas of agreement and disagreement. The main benefits of mediation are that it can result in an expeditious and less costly resolution of the litigation, and can produce creative solutions to complex disputes often unavailable in traditional litigation. NY R USDCTS&ED Civ Rule 83.9(b).

    i. *Mediation program eligibility.* All civil cases other than Social Security, habeas corpus, and tax cases are eligible for mediation, whether assigned to Manhattan or White Plains. NY R USDCTS&ED Civ Rule 83.9(e)(1).

- The Board of Judges may, by Administrative Order, direct that certain specified categories of cases shall automatically be submitted to the mediation program. The assigned District Judge or Magistrate Judge may issue a written order exempting a particular case with or without the request of the parties. NY R USDCTS&ED Civ Rule 83.9(e)(2).

- For all other cases, the assigned District Judge or Magistrate Judge may determine that a case is appropriate for mediation and may order that case to mediation, with or without the consent of the parties, before, at, or after the initial FRCP 16(b) case management conference. Alternatively, the parties should notify the assigned Judge at any time of their desire to mediate. NY R USDCTS&ED Civ Rule 83.9(e)(3).

c. *Judicial settlement conferences.* Judicial settlement conferences may be ordered by District Judges or Magistrate Judges with or without the request or consent of the parties. NY R USDCTS&ED Civ Rule 83.9(f).

d. For more information on alternative dispute resolution (ADR), refer to NY R USDCTS&ED Civ Rule 83.9.

8. *Individual judge practices.* Refer to the Miscellaneous section of this document for information on individual judge practices on general requirements for documents.

## D. Documents

1. *Required documents*

   a. *Interrogatories.* Refer to the General Requirements section of this document for information on interrogatories.

2. *Supplemental documents*

   a. *Certificate of service.* FRCP 5(d) requires that the person making service under FRCP 5 certify that service has been effected. FRCP 5(Advisory Committee Notes). Having such information on file may be useful for many purposes, including proof of service if an issue arises concerning the effectiveness of the service. FRCP 5(Advisory Committee Notes).

3. *Individual judge practices.* Refer to the Miscellaneous section of this document for information on individual judge practices on required documents.

## E. Format

1. *Form of documents.* The rules governing captions and other matters of form in pleadings apply to motions and other papers. FRCP 7(b)(2).

   a. *Paper.* Every pleading, written motion, and other paper must: be plainly written, typed, printed, or copied without erasures or interlineations which materially deface it. NY R USDCTS&ED Civ Rule 11.1(a)(1).

   b. *Typeface, margin, and spacing.* The typeface, margins, and spacing of all documents presented for filing must meet the following requirements:

      i. All text must be twelve (12) point type or larger, except for text in footnotes which may be ten (10) point type;

      ii. All documents must have at least one (1) inch margins on all sides;

      iii. All text must be double-spaced, except for headings, text in footnotes, or block quotations, which may be single-spaced. NY R USDCTS&ED Civ Rule 11.1(b).

   c. *Caption; Names of parties.* Every pleading must have a caption with the court's name, a title, a file number, and a FRCP 7(a) designation. The title of the complaint must name all the parties; the title of other pleadings, after naming the first party on each side, may refer generally to other parties. FRCP 10(a). Every pleading, written motion, and other paper must: bear the docket number and the initials of the District Judge and any Magistrate Judge before whom the action or proceeding is pending, NY R USDCTS&ED Civ Rule 11.1(a)(2).

   d. *Paragraphs; Separate statements.* A party must state its claims or defenses in numbered paragraphs, each limited as far as practicable to a single set of circumstances. A later pleading may refer by number to a paragraph in an earlier pleading. If doing so would promote clarity, each claim founded on a separate transaction or occurrence—and each defense other than a denial—must be stated in a separate count or defense. FRCP 10(b).

   e. *Adoption by reference; Exhibits.* A statement in a pleading may be adopted by reference elsewhere in the same pleading or in any other pleading or motion. A copy of a written instrument that is an exhibit to a pleading is a part of the pleading for all purposes. FRCP 10(c).

   f. *Acceptance by the clerk.* The clerk must not refuse to file a paper solely because it is not in the form prescribed by the Federal Rules of Civil Procedure or by a local rule or practice. FRCP 5(d)(4).

2. *Form of electronic documents*

   a. *PDF-A.* All documents electronically filed on the ECF system must be in PDF-A format (portable document format). A PDF-A file is created using PDF writer software such as Adobe Acrobat (go to the Adobe website for details). PDF-A files cannot be altered, providing security to the filer and the Court. NY R USDCTSD CM/ECF, S.D.(II)(23)(23.2).

b.  *Size limitation.* No single PDF file may be larger than four megabytes (4 MB). If the filing is too large, the ECF system will not allow it to be filed, and you will not see a Notice of Electronic Filing (NEF or filing receipt) screen. To determine the size of an Adobe Acrobat PDF file click on File, Document Properties, Summary. NY R USDCTSD CM/ECF, S.D.(II)(23)(23.3).

   i.  Converting documents directly from a word processor to PDF-A format creates the smallest possible file in terms of computer memory. If that is not possible, scan your document at low resolution. Within the Adobe Acrobat program, on the "Scan Manager" screen, adjust the settings for black and white and 200 dpi (dots per inch). This allows more pages to fit into a single PDF-A file. If that does not work, separate an oversized file into 2 or more parts. Simply label each file 1a, 1b, 1c, etc. Only relevant excerpts of exhibits should be electronically filed. NY R USDCTSD CM/ECF, S.D.(II)(23)(23.4).

c.  *Attachments and exhibits.* Filing Users must submit in electronic form all documents referenced as exhibits or attachments, unless the Court permits paper filing. NY R USDCTSD CM/ECF, S.D.(I)(5)(5.1).

   i.  A Filing User must submit as exhibits or attachments only those excerpts of the referenced documents that are relevant to the matter under consideration by the Court. Excerpted material must be clearly and prominently identified as such. Filing Users who file excerpts of documents as exhibits or attachments under this procedure do so without prejudice to their right to file timely additional excerpts or the complete document. Responding parties may file timely additional excerpts that they believe are relevant or the complete document. A party may move before the Court for permission to serve and file in hard copy documents that cannot be reasonably scanned. NY R USDCTSD CM/ECF, S.D.(I)(5)(5.2).

   ii.  Exhibits must be filed only as attachments to a document, such as a motion or an affidavit. Do not use the ECF Filing Event for "Motion" to file exhibits separately. Exhibits are the only items that should be attached to electronically filed documents. You are limited to electronically filing only relevant excerpts of exhibits. Excerpts must be clearly identified as such. If the exhibit is too large to be scanned and electronically filed you may contact the ECF Help Desk. NY R USDCTSD CM/ECF, S.D.(II)(15)(15.6).

d.  *Letters.* Parties should consult the assigned judge's Individual Practices to determine if the judge accepts letters at all and, if he or she does, whether the judge has any page limitations on letters and/or requires courtesy copies of letters filed on ECF (and, if so, by what means of delivery). All letters addressed to the Court must include a subject line with the case name and docket number (e.g., "Re: Doe v. Smith, 13 Civ. 1234 (ABC)"). NY R USDCTSD CM/ECF, S.D.(II)(13)(13.1).

e.  *Proposed orders, proposed judgments, stipulations and consents.* Any document that requires the signature of a judge should not be electronically filed except as an exhibit to another document. Proposed orders, judgments, stipulations and consents should not be submitted through the ECF system. Instead they should be sent by e-mail to the Clerk. Proposed orders should be submitted in word processing format (WordPerfect or Word) rather than as a PDF document. Stipulations should be submitted in PDF-A format. Stipulations must contain ink signatures not s/. Faxed or emailed signatures are acceptable. Please note that Stipulations of Voluntary Dismissal pursuant to FRCP 41(a)(1)(A)(ii) do not require the signature of a judge and must be electronically filed on the ECF system. Questions may be directed to the Orders and Judgments Clerk at the phone numbers listed in NY R USDCTSD CM/ECF, S.D.(II)(18)(18.3). NY R USDCTSD CM/ECF, S.D.(II)(18)(18.3).

   i.  Email the proposed order, judgment or stipulation to the email addresses listed in NY R USDCTSD CM/ECF, S.D.(II)(18)(18.3). NY R USDCTSD CM/ECF, S.D.(II)(18)(18.3).

   ii.  Pro se litigants who are not Filing Users are exempt from that portion of NY R USDCTSD CM/ECF, S.D.(II)(18)(18.3) that requires litigants to email proposed orders, judgments, stipulations and consents, and shall deliver such documents to the Clerk's Office in paper form. NY R USDCTSD CM/ECF, S.D.(II)(18)(18.3).

3. *Signing disclosures and discovery requests, responses, and objections.* FRCP 11 does not apply to disclosures and discovery requests, responses, objections, and motions under FRCP 26 through FRCP 37. FRCP 11(d).

   a. *Signature required.* Every disclosure under FRCP 26(a)(1) or FRCP 26(a)(3) and every discovery request, response, or objection must be signed by at least one attorney of record in the attorney's own name—or by the party personally, if unrepresented—and must state the signer's address, e-mail address, and telephone number. FRCP 26(g)(1). Every pleading, written motion, and other paper must: have the name of each person signing it clearly printed or typed directly below the signature. NY R USDCTS&ED Civ Rule 11.1(a)(3).

      i. *Electronic signatures.* The user log-in and password required to submit documents to the ECF system serve as the Filing User's signature on all electronic documents filed with the Court. NY R USDCTSD CM/ECF, S.D.(I)(8)(8.1); NY R USDCTSD CM/ECF, S.D.(II)(13)(13.14). They also serve as a signature for purposes of the Federal Rules of Civil Procedure, including FRCP 11, the Local Civil Rules of the United States District Courts for the Southern and Eastern Districts of New York, and any other purpose for which a signature is required in connection with proceedings before the Court. NY R USDCTSD CM/ECF, S.D.(I)(8)(8.1).

         • *Signature block.* Electronically filed documents must include a signature block and must set forth the name, address, telephone number and e-mail address all in compliance with the Federal Rules of Civil Procedure and NY R USDCTS&ED Civ Rule 11.1. In the absence of a scanned signature image, the name of the Filing User under whose log-in and password the document is submitted must be preceded by an "s/" typed in the space where the signature would otherwise appear. NY R USDCTSD CM/ECF, S.D.(I)(8)(8.2); NY R USDCTSD CM/ECF, S.D.(II)(13)(13.14).

         • *Documents requiring the signature of a party or witness.* A document requiring the signature of a party or witness shall be electronically filed in a scanned format that contains an image of the actual signature. NY R USDCTSD CM/ECF, S.D.(I)(8)(8.4); NY R USDCTSD CM/ECF, S.D.(II)(13)(13.14).

         • *Documents requiring the signature of a judge.* A Filing User submitting a document electronically that requires a judge's signature must promptly deliver the document in such other form, if any, as the Court requires. NY R USDCTSD CM/ECF, S.D.(I)(4)(4.2).

         • *Documents requiring multiple signatures.* Documents requiring signatures of more than one party must be electronically filed either by: (a) submitting a scanned document containing all necessary signatures; (b) representing the consent of the other parties on the document; (c) identifying on the document the parties whose signatures are required and by the submission of a notice of endorsement by the other parties no later than three business days after filing; or (d) in any other manner approved by the Court. NY R USDCTSD CM/ECF, S.D.(I)(8)(8.5).

   b. *Effect of signature.* By signing, an attorney or party certifies that to the best of the person's knowledge, information, and belief formed after a reasonable inquiry:

      i. With respect to a disclosure, it is complete and correct as of the time it is made; and

      ii. With respect to a discovery request, response, or objection, it is:

         • Consistent with the Federal Rules of Civil Procedure and warranted by existing law or by a nonfrivolous argument for extending, modifying, or reversing existing law, or for establishing new law;

         • Not interposed for any improper purpose, such as to harass, cause unnecessary delay, or needlessly increase the cost of litigation; and

         • Neither unreasonable nor unduly burdensome or expensive, considering the needs of the case, prior discovery in the case, the amount in controversy, and the importance of the issues at stake in the action. FRCP 26(g)(1).

   c. *Failure to sign.* Other parties have no duty to act on an unsigned disclosure, request, response, or objection until it is signed, and the court must strike it unless a signature is promptly supplied after the omission is called to the attorney's or party's attention. FRCP 26(g)(2).

d. *Sanction for improper certification.* If a certification violates FRCP 26(g) without substantial justification, the court, on motion or on its own, must impose an appropriate sanction on the signer, the party on whose behalf the signer was acting, or both. The sanction may include an order to pay the reasonable expenses, including attorney's fees, caused by the violation. FRCP 26(g)(3). Refer to the United States District Court for the Southern District of New York KeyRules Motion for Discovery Sanctions document for more information.

4. *Privacy protection for filings made with the court*

   a. *Redacted filings.* Unless the court orders otherwise, in an electronic or paper filing with the court that contains an individual's Social Security number, taxpayer-identification number, or birth date, the name of an individual known to be a minor, or a financial-account number, a party or nonparty making the filing may include only:

      i. The last four (4) digits of the Social Security number and taxpayer-identification number;

      ii. The year of the individual's birth;

      iii. The minor's initials; and

      iv. The last four (4) digits of the financial-account number. FRCP 5.2(a); NY R USDCTSD CM/ECF, S.D.(II)(21)(21.3).

      v. Caution should be exercised when filing documents that contain the following:

      - Personal identifying numbers (PIN #'s), such as a driver's license number;
      - Medical records, treatment and diagnosis;
      - Employment history;
      - Individual financial information;
      - Proprietary or trade secret information;
      - Information regarding an individual's cooperation with the government. NY R US-DCTSD CM/ECF, S.D.(II)(21)(21.4).

   b. *Exemptions from the redaction requirement.* The redaction requirement does not apply to the following:

      i. A financial-account number that identifies the property allegedly subject to forfeiture in a forfeiture proceeding;

      ii. The record of an administrative or agency proceeding;

      iii. The official record of a state-court proceeding;

      iv. The record of a court or tribunal, if that record was not subject to the redaction requirement when originally filed;

      v. A filing covered by FRCP 5.2(c) or FRCP 5.2(d); and

      vi. A pro se filing in an action brought under 28 U.S.C.A. § 2241, 28 U.S.C.A. § 2254, or 28 U.S.C.A. § 2255. FRCP 5.2(b).

   c. *Limitations on remote access to electronic files; Social Security appeals and immigration cases.* Unless the court orders otherwise, in an action for benefits under the Social Security Act, and in an action or proceeding relating to an order of removal, to relief from removal, or to immigration benefits or detention, access to an electronic file is authorized as follows:

      i. The parties and their attorneys may have remote electronic access to any part of the case file, including the administrative record;

      ii. Any other person may have electronic access to the full record at the courthouse, but may have remote electronic access only to:

      - The docket maintained by the court; and

- An opinion, order, judgment, or other disposition of the court, but not any other part of the case file or the administrative record. FRCP 5.2(c).

d. *Filings made under seal.* The court may order that a filing be made under seal without redaction. The court may later unseal the filing or order the person who made the filing to file a redacted version for the public record. FRCP 5.2(d). For more information on sealing documents, refer to NY R USDCTSD CM/ECF, S.D.(I)(6).

e. *Protective orders.* For good cause, the court may by order in a case:

    i. Require redaction of additional information; or

    ii. Limit or prohibit a nonparty's remote electronic access to a document filed with the court. FRCP 5.2(e).

f. *Option for additional unredacted filing under seal.* A person making a redacted filing may also file an unredacted copy under seal. The court must retain the unredacted copy as part of the record. FRCP 5.2(f); NY R USDCTSD CM/ECF, S.D.(II)(21)(21.5).

g. *Option for filing a reference list.* A filing that contains redacted information may be filed together with a reference list that identifies each item of redacted information and specifies an appropriate identifier that uniquely corresponds to each item listed. The list must be filed under seal and may be amended as of right. Any reference in the case to a listed identifier will be construed to refer to the corresponding item of information. FRCP 5.2(g); NY R USDCTSD CM/ECF, S.D.(II)(21)(21.5).

h. *Responsibility for redaction.* It is the sole responsibility of counsel and the parties to be sure that all documents comply with the rules of this Court requiring redaction of personal identifiers. Neither the judge nor the Clerk of Court will review documents for compliance with these rules. NY R USDCTSD CM/ECF, S.D.(II)(21)(21.2).

i. *Waiver of protection of identifiers.* A person waives the protection of FRCP 5.2(a) as to the person's own information by filing it without redaction and not under seal. FRCP 5.2(h).

j. For more information on privacy and public access to ECF cases, refer to NY R USDCTSD CM/ECF, S.D.(II)(21).

5. *Individual judge practices.* Refer to the Miscellaneous section of this document for information on individual judge practices on formatting documents.

## F. Filing and Service Requirements

1. *Filing requirements.* Any paper after the complaint that is required to be served—together with a certificate of service—must be filed within a reasonable time after service. But disclosures under FRCP 26(a)(1) or FRCP 26(a)(2) and the following discovery requests and responses must not be filed until they are used in the proceeding or the court orders filing: depositions, interrogatories, requests for documents or tangible things or to permit entry onto land, and requests for admission. FRCP 5(d)(1). Refer to the United States District Court for the Southern District of New York KeyRules pleading and motion documents for information on filing with the court.

2. *Service requirements*

    a. *Service; When required*

        i. *In general.* Unless the Federal Rules of Civil Procedure provide otherwise, each of the following papers must be served on every party:

- An order stating that service is required;
- A pleading filed after the original complaint, unless the court orders otherwise under FRCP 5(c) because there are numerous defendants;
- A discovery paper required to be served on a party, unless the court orders otherwise;
- A written motion, except one that may be heard ex parte; and
- A written notice, appearance, demand, or offer of judgment, or any similar paper. FRCP 5(a)(1).

        ii. *If a party fails to appear.* No service is required on a party who is in default for failing to appear.

But a pleading that asserts a new claim for relief against such a party must be served on that party under FRCP 4. FRCP 5(a)(2).

   iii. *Seizing property.* If an action is begun by seizing property and no person is or need be named as a defendant, any service required before the filing of an appearance, answer, or claim must be made on the person who had custody or possession of the property when it was seized. FRCP 5(a)(3).

b. *Service; How made*

   i. *Serving an attorney.* If a party is represented by an attorney, service under FRCP 5 must be made on the attorney unless the court orders service on the party. FRCP 5(b)(1).

   ii. *Service in general.* A paper is served under FRCP 5 by:

- Handing it to the person;

- Leaving it: (1) at the person's office with a clerk or other person in charge or, if no one is in charge, in a conspicuous place in the office; or (2) if the person has no office or the office is closed, at the person's dwelling or usual place of abode with someone of suitable age and discretion who resides there;

- Mailing it to the person's last known address—in which event service is complete upon mailing;

- Leaving it with the court clerk if the person has no known address;

- Sending it by electronic means if the person consented in writing—in which event service is complete upon transmission, but is not effective if the serving party learns that it did not reach the person to be served; or

- Delivering it by any other means that the person consented to in writing—in which event service is complete when the person making service delivers it to the agency designated to make delivery. FRCP 5(b)(2).

   iii. *Service by overnight delivery.* Service upon an attorney may be made by overnight delivery service. "Overnight delivery service" means any delivery service which regularly accepts items for overnight delivery. Overnight delivery service shall be deemed service by mail for purposes of FRCP 5 and FRCP 6. NY R USDCTS&ED Civ Rule 5.3.

   iv. *Service by electronic means.* Parties serving and filing papers shall follow the instructions regarding Electronic Case Filing (ECF) published on the website of each respective Court. A paper served and filed by electronic means in accordance with such instructions is, for purposes of FRCP 5, served and filed in compliance with the Local Civil Rules of the United States District Courts for the Southern and Eastern Districts of New York. NY R USDCTS&ED Civ Rule 5.2(a). Parties have an obligation to review the Court's actual order, decree, or judgment (on ECF), which controls, and should not rely on the description on the docket or in the ECF Notice of Electronic Filing (NEF). NY R USDCTS&ED Civ Rule 5.2(c).

- *Notice of electronic filing (NEF).* In cases assigned to the ECF system, service is complete provided all parties receive a Notice of Electronic Filing (NEF), which is sent automatically by email from the Court (see the NEF for a list of who did/did not receive notice electronically). Transmission of the NEF constitutes service upon all Filing and Receiving Users who are listed as recipients of notice by electronic mail. NY R USDCTSD CM/ECF, S.D.(I)(9)(9.1). In cases assigned to the ECF system, if all parties receive a NEF, service is complete upon transmission of the NEF by the Court, and you are not required to serve a paper copy. NY R USDCTSD CM/ECF, S.D.(II)(19)(19.2). It remains the duty of Filing and Receiving Users to maintain current contact information with the court and to regularly review the docket sheet of the case. NY R USDCTSD CM/ECF, S.D.(I)(9)(9.1).

- *Mailing of court-initiated documents.* The Clerk's Office will no longer mail paper copies of court-initiated documents to Filing and Receiving Users. The Clerk's Office will mail copies of all court-initiated documents to pro se parties who have not registered as Filing or Receiving Users. NY R USDCTSD CM/ECF, S.D.(II)(19)(19.1).

- *No receipt of a NEF.* If any party does not receive a NEF, you are required to accomplish service on that party in the traditional manner, in paper form. NY R USDCTSD CM/ECF, S.D.(II)(19)(19.2). The NEF receipt will inform you who will receive notice of the filing "electronically" (by e-mail from the Court) and who will receive notice "by other means" (traditional service in paper form). NY R USDCTSD CM/ECF, S.D.(II)(19)(19.2).

- *Service on non-filing or non-receiving users.* Attorneys and pro se parties who are not Filing or Receiving Users must be served with a paper copy of any electronically filed pleading or other document. Service of such paper copy must be made according to the Federal Rules of Civil Procedure and the Local Civil Rules of the United States District Courts for the Southern and Eastern Districts of New York. NY R USDCTSD CM/ECF, S.D.(I)(9)(9.2). Such paper service must be documented by electronically filing proof of service. NY R USDCTSD CM/ECF, S.D.(I)(9)(9.2); NY R USDCTSD CM/ECF, S.D.(II)(19)(19.2). Where the Clerk scans and electronically files pleadings and documents on behalf of a pro se party, the associated NEF constitutes service. NY R USDCTSD CM/ECF, S.D.(I)(9)(9.2).

- For more information on service by electronic means, refer to NY R USDCTSD CM/ECF, S.D.(II)(19).

  v. *Using court facilities.* If a local rule so authorizes, a party may use the court's transmission facilities to make service under FRCP 5(b)(2)(E). FRCP 5(b)(3).

c. *Serving numerous defendants*

  i. *In general.* If an action involves an unusually large number of defendants, the court may, on motion or on its own, order that:

  - Defendants' pleadings and replies to them need not be served on other defendants;

  - Any crossclaim, counterclaim, avoidance, or affirmative defense in those pleadings and replies to them will be treated as denied or avoided by all other parties; and

  - Filing any such pleading and serving it on the plaintiff constitutes notice of the pleading to all parties. FRCP 5(c)(1).

  ii. *Notifying parties.* A copy of every such order must be served on the parties as the court directs. FRCP 5(c)(2).

3. *Individual judge practices.* Refer to the Miscellaneous section of this document for information on individual judge practices on filing and serving documents.

## G. Hearings

1. There is no hearing contemplated in the federal statutes or rules for interrogatories.

## H. Forms

### 1. Federal Interrogatories Forms

a. Introductory statement; Interrogatories to individual. AMJUR PP DEPOSITION § 405.

b. Introductory statement; Interrogatories to corporation. AMJUR PP DEPOSITION § 406.

c. Interrogatories. 3A FEDFORMS § 3488.

d. Interrogatories; Another form. 3A FEDFORMS § 3489.

e. Interrogatories by plaintiff; To corporation. 3A FEDFORMS § 3490.

f. Interrogatories by plaintiff; Complete set. 3A FEDFORMS § 3491.

g. Interrogatories by plaintiff; Requesting identification of documents and production under FRCP 34. 3A FEDFORMS § 3492.

h. Interrogatories by plaintiff; With definition of terms used and instructions for answering. 3A FEDFORMS § 3493.

i. Interrogatories by plaintiff; Employment discrimination case. 3A FEDFORMS § 3494.

j. Interrogatories by defendant. 3A FEDFORMS § 3495.

    k.   Interrogatories by defendant; Complete set. 3A FEDFORMS § 3496.

    l.   Interrogatories by defendant; Complete set; Another form. 3A FEDFORMS § 3497.

    m.  Interrogatories by defendant; Complete set; Another form. 3A FEDFORMS § 3498.

    n.   Interrogatories by defendant; Complete set; Another form. 3A FEDFORMS § 3499.

    o.   Interrogatories by defendant; Follow-up interrogatories to plaintiff after lapse of time since first set of interrogatories or deposition. 3A FEDFORMS § 3500.

    p.   Certificate of service of interrogatories. 3A FEDFORMS § 3501.

    q.   Interrogatories; Outline form. FEDPROF § 23:335.

    r.   Interrogatories; To defendant; Trademark action. FEDPROF § 23:347.

    s.   Interrogatories; With request for documents; To defendant; Collection of royalties. FEDPROF § 23:348.

    t.   Interrogatories; To defendant; Copyright infringement. FEDPROF § 23:350.

    u.   Interrogatories; To plaintiff; Products liability. FEDPROF § 23:352.

    v.   Interrogatories; To plaintiff; Personal injury. FEDPROF § 23:353.

    w.  Interrogatories; To defendant; Premises liability. FEDPROF § 23:356.

    x.   Interrogatories; To defendant; Medical malpractice. FEDPROF § 23:357.

    y.   General forms; Standard interrogatories. GOLDLTGFMS § 26:25.

    z.   General forms; Civil cases. GOLDLTGFMS § 26:26.

## I. Applicable Rules

  1.  *Federal rules*

    a.   Serving and filing pleadings and other papers. FRCP 5.

    b.   Privacy protection for filings made with the court. FRCP 5.2.

    c.   Computing and extending time; Time for motion papers. FRCP 6.

    d.   Pleadings allowed; Form of motions and other papers. FRCP 7.

    e.   Form of pleadings. FRCP 10.

    f.   Signing pleadings, motions, and other papers; Representations to the court; Sanctions. FRCP 11.

    g.   Duty to disclose; General provisions governing discovery. FRCP 26.

    h.   Stipulations about discovery procedure. FRCP 29.

    i.   Interrogatories to parties. FRCP 33.

    j.   Failure to make disclosures or to cooperate in discovery; Sanctions. FRCP 37.

  2.  *Local rules*

    a.   Duty of attorneys in related cases. NY R USDCTS&ED Civ Rule 1.6.

    b.   Electronic service and filing of documents. NY R USDCTS&ED Civ Rule 5.2.

    c.   Service by overnight delivery. NY R USDCTS&ED Civ Rule 5.3.

    d.   Computation of time. NY R USDCTS&ED Civ Rule 6.4.

    e.   Form of pleadings, motions, and other papers. NY R USDCTS&ED Civ Rule 11.1.

    f.   Assertion of claim of privilege. NY R USDCTS&ED Civ Rule 26.2.

    g.   Uniform definitions in discovery requests. NY R USDCTS&ED Civ Rule 26.3.

    h.   Cooperation among counsel in discovery. NY R USDCTS&ED Civ Rule 26.4.

    i.   Form discovery requests. [NY R USDCTS&ED Civ Rule 26.5, as amended by NY ORDER 16-4212, effective September 26, 2016].

    j.   Interrogatories (Southern District only). NY R USDCTS&ED Civ Rule 33.3.

k. Alternative dispute resolution (Southern District only). NY R USDCTS&ED Civ Rule 83.9.

l. Electronic case filing rules and instructions. NY R USDCTSD CM/ECF, S.D.

m. Related cases. NY R USDCTSD Div. Bus., Rule 13.

## J. Miscellaneous

**NOTE: Individual judges' rules may apply. For available judge-level information, refer to:**

DISTRICT JUDGE RONNIE ABRAMS: NY R USDCTSD Abrams-Civ Prac; NY R USDCTSD Abrams-Crim Prac; NY R USDCTSD Abrams-Pro Se; NY R USDCTSD Abrams-Case Mgt; NY R USDCTSD Abrams-Jury.

DISTRICT JUDGE DEBORAH A. BATTS: NY R USDCTSD Batts-Practices.

DISTRICT JUDGE RICHARD M. BERMAN: NY R USDCTSD Berman-Practices; NY R USDCTSD Berman-Default; NY R USDCTSD Berman-Sentencing; NY R USDCTSD Berman-Media.

DISTRICT JUDGE VINCENT L. BRICCETTI: NY R USDCTSD Briccetti-Practices; NY R USDCTSD Briccetti-Plan; NY R USDCTSD Briccetti-Notice.

DISTRICT JUDGE VERNON S. BRODERICK: NY R USDCTSD Broderick-Civil; NY R USDCTSD Broderick-Crim; NY R USDCTSD Broderick-Case Mgt; NY R USDCTSD Broderick-Jury.

DISTRICT JUDGE NAOMI REICE BUCHWALD: NY R USDCTSD Buchwald-Practices.

DISTRICT JUDGE VALERIE E. CAPRONI: NY R USDCTSD Caproni-Prac; NY R USDCTSD Caproni--Pro Se; NY R USDCTSD Caproni-Case Mgt; NY R USDCTSD Caproni-Crim Prac.

DISTRICT JUDGE ANDREW L. CARTER JR.: NY R USDCTSD Carter-Practices.

DISTRICT JUDGE KEVIN P. CASTEL: NY R USDCTSD Castel-Practices; NY R USDCTSD Castel-Default; NY R USDCTSD Castel-Scheduling; NY R USDCTSD Castel-Complex; NY R USDCTSD Castel-Trials; NY R USDCTSD Castel-Sentencing.

DISTRICT JUDGE DENISE L. COTE: NY R USDCTSD Cote-Civil Practices; NY R USDCTSD Cote-Pro Se; NY R USDCTSD Cote-Maritime Ord; NY R USDCTSD Cote-Crim Practices; NY R USDCTSD Cote-Crim Trials; NY R USDCTSD Cote-Sentencing.

DISTRICT JUDGE PAUL A. CROTTY: NY R USDCTSD Crotty-Practices; NY R USDCTSD Crotty-Sentencing; NY R USDCTSD Crotty-Calls; NY R USDCTSD Crotty-Scheduling.

DISTRICT JUDGE GEORGE B. DANIELS: NY R USDCTSD Daniels-Practices.

DISTRICT JUDGE KEVIN T. DUFFY: NY R USDCTSD Duffy-Practices.

DISTRICT JUDGE PAUL A. ENGELMAYER: NY R USDCTSD Engelmayer-Practices; NY R USDCTSD Engelmayer-Scheduling; NY R USDCTSD Engelmayer-Sentencing; NY R USDCTSD Engelmayer-Pro Se; NY R USDCTSD Engelmayer-Crim.

DISTRICT JUDGE KATHERINE POLK FAILLA: NY R USDCTSD Failla-Civ Prac; NY R USDCTSD Failla-Crim Prac; NY R USDCTSD Failla-Case Mgt.

DISTRICT JUDGE KATHERINE B. FORREST: NY R USDCTSD Forrest-Civil Prac; NY R USDCTSD Forrest-Crim Prac; NY R USDCTSD Forrest-Crim Pretrial; NY R USDCTSD Forrest-Scheduling; NY R USDCTSD Forrest-Patent Scheduling; NY R USDCTSD Forrest-Sentencing; NY R USDCTSD Forrest-Order 1; NY R USDCTSD Forrest-Order 2.

DISTRICT JUDGE JESSE M. FURMAN: NY R USDCTSD Furman-Civil Prac; NY R USDCTSD Furman-Crim Prac; NY R USDCTSD Furman-Pro Se Prac; NY R USDCTSD Furman-Trials; NY R USDCTSD Furman-Scheduling; NY R USDCTSD Furman-Rights.

DISTRICT JUDGE PAUL G. GARDEPHE: NY R USDCTSD Gardephe-Civ Prac; NY R USDCTSD Gardephe-Pretrial; NY R USDCTSD Gardephe-Prot Ord; NY R USDCTSD Gardephe-Maritime; NY R USDCTSD Gardephe-Crim Prac; NY R USDCTSD Gardephe-Trial.

DISTRICT JUDGE THOMAS P. GRIESA: NY R USDCTSD Griesa-Practices.

DISTRICT JUDGE CHARLES S. HAIGHT: NY R USDCTSD Haight-Practices.

DISTRICT JUDGE ALVIN K. HELLERSTEIN: NY R USDCTSD Hellerstein-Practices; NY R USDCTSD Hellerstein--Sept 11.

DISTRICT JUDGE LEWIS A. KAPLAN: NY R USDCTSD Kaplan-Practices; NY R USDCTSD Kaplan-Sentencing.

DISTRICT JUDGE KENNETH M. KARAS: NY R USDCTSD Karas-Practices; NY R USDCTSD Karas-Case Mgt; NY R USDCTSD Karas-Default; NY R USDCTSD Karas-Sentencing; NY R USDCTSD Karas-Rights.

DISTRICT JUDGE JOHN F. KEENAN: NY R USDCTSD Keenan-Practices.

DISTRICT JUDGE JOHN G. KOELTL: NY R USDCTSD Koeltl-Practices.

DISTRICT JUDGE VICTOR MARRERO: NY R USDCTSD Marrero-Practices; NY R USDCTSD Marrero-Scheduling; NY R USDCTSD Marrero-Default; NY R USDCTSD Marrero-Trial Proc.

DISTRICT JUDGE COLLEEN McMAHON: NY R USDCTSD McMahon-Practices; NY R USDCTSD McMahon-RICO; NY R USDCTSD McMahon-Copies; NY R USDCTSD McMahon-Scheduling; NY R US-DCTSD McMahon-Elec Disc; NY R USDCTSD McMahon-Sentencing.

DISTRICT JUDGE ALISON J. NATHAN: NY R USDCTSD Nathan-Civ Prac; NY R USDCTSD Nathan-Crim Prac; NY R USDCTSD Nathan-Pro Se; NY R USDCTSD Nathan-Scheduling.

DISTRICT JUDGE J. PAUL OETKEN: NY R USDCTSD Oetken-Civ Prac; NY R USDCTSD Oetken-Case Mgt; NY R USDCTSD Oetken-Crim Prac; NY R USDCTSD Oetken-Pro Se.

DISTRICT JUDGE WILLIAM H. PAULEY, III: NY R USDCTSD Pauley-Crim Cases; NY R USDCTSD Pauley-Practices.

DISTRICT JUDGE LORETTA A. PRESKA: NY R USDCTSD Preska-Practices.

DISTRICT JUDGE JED S. RAKOFF: NY R USDCTSD Rakoff-Practices; NY R USDCTSD Rakoff-Scheduling; NY R USDCTSD Rakoff-Prot Ord; NY R USDCTSD Rakoff-Maritime Ord.

DISTRICT JUDGE EDGARDO RAMOS: NY R USDCTSD Ramos--Practices; NY R USDCTSD Ramos-Case Mgt.

DISTRICT JUDGE NELSON S. ROMAN: NY R USDCTSD Roman-Civ Prac; NY R USDCTSD Roman-Pro Se; NY R USDCTSD Roman-Crim Prac; NY R USDCTSD Roman-Case Mgt.

DISTRICT JUDGE LEONARD B. SAND: NY R USDCTSD Sand-Practices.

DISTRICT JUDGE LORNA G. SCHOFIELD: NY R USDCTSD Schofield-Civ Prac; NY R USDCTSD Schofield-Crim Prac; NY R USDCTSD Schofield-Sched; NY R USDCTSD Schofield-Pro Se; NY R USDCTSD Schofield-Advice.

DISTRICT JUDGE CATHY SEIBEL: NY R USDCTSD Seibel-Practices.

DISTRICT JUDGE LOUIS L. STANTON: NY R USDCTSD Stanton-Practices; NY R USDCTSD Stanton-Pretrial.

DISTRICT JUDGE SIDNEY H. STEIN: NY R USDCTSD Stein-Practices.

DISTRICT JUDGE RICHARD J. SULLIVAN: NY R USDCTSD Sullivan-Practices; NY R USDCTSD Sullivan-Scheduling; NY R USDCTSD Sullivan-Sentencing; NY R USDCTSD Sullivan-Juries; NY R USDCTSD Sullivan-Trial; NY R USDCTSD Sullivan-Default.

DISTRICT JUDGE LAURA TAYLOR SWAIN: NY R USDCTSD Swain-Practices; NY R USDCTSD Swain-Trial; NY R USDCTSD Swain-Crim Trial; NY R USDCTSD Swain-Juries; NY R USDCTSD Swain-Sentencing; NY R USDCTSD Swain-Rights.

DISTRICT JUDGE ROBERT W. SWEET: NY R USDCTSD Sweet-Practices.

DISTRICT JUDGE ANALISA TORRES: NY R USDCTSD Torres-Civ Prac; NY R USDCTSD Torres-Pro Se; NY R USDCTSD Torres-Scheduling.

DISTRICT JUDGE KIMBA M. WOOD: NY R USDCTSD Wood-Practices; NY R USDCTSD Wood-Scheduling; NY R USDCTSD Wood-Discovery; NY R USDCTSD Wood-RICO; NY R USDCTSD Wood-Juries; NY R USDCTSD Wood-Trial; NY R USDCTSD Wood-Media.

DISTRICT JUDGE GREGORY H. WOODS: NY R USDCTSD Woods-Civ Prac; NY R USDCTSD Woods-Pro Se; NY R USDCTSD Woods-Sched; NY R USDCTSD Woods-Crim Prac; NY R USDCTSD Woods-Protect Order; NY R USDCTSD Woods-Speedy Trial.

MAGISTRATE JUDGE JAMES L. COTT: NY R USDCTSD Cott-Practices; NY R USDCTSD Cott-Settlement.

MAGISTRATE JUDGE PAUL E. DAVISON: NY R USDCTSD Davison-Practices.

MAGISTRATE JUDGE RONALD L. ELLIS: NY R USDCTSD Ellis-Practices.

MAGISTRATE JUDGE KEVIN N. FOX: NY R USDCTSD Fox-Practices; NY R USDCTSD Fox-Settlement.

MAGISTRATE JUDGE JAMES C. FRANCIS: NY R USDCTSD Francis-Practices.

MAGISTRATE JUDGE DEBRA FREEMAN: NY R USDCTSD Freeman-Practices; NY R USDCTSD Freeman-Settlement.

MAGISTRATE JUDGE GABRIEL W. GORENSTEIN: NY R USDCTSD Gorenstein-Practices; NY R US-DCTSD Gorenstein-Ackn.

MAGISTRATE JUDGE FRANK MAAS: NY R USDCTSD Maas-Practices; NY R USDCTSD Maas-Discontinuance; NY R USDCTSD Maas-Conf; NY R USDCTSD Maas-Settlement.

MAGISTRATE JUDGE JUDITH C. McCARTHY: NY R USDCTSD McCarthy-Practices; NY R USDCTSD McCarthy-Conduct.

MAGISTRATE JUDGE BARBARA MOSES: NY R USDCTSD Moses-Practices.

MAGISTRATE JUDGE SARAH NETBURN: NY R USDCTSD Netburn-Civil; NY R USDCTSD Netburn-Settlement; NY R USDCTSD Netburn-Case Mgt; NY R USDCTSD Netburn--Pro Se.

MAGISTRATE JUDGE ANDREW J. PECK: NY R USDCTSD Peck-Practices; NY R USDCTSD Peck-Order; NY R USDCTSD Peck-Rule 502(d).

MAGISTRATE JUDGE HENRY PITMAN: NY R USDCTSD Pitman-Practices.

MAGISTRATE JUDGE LISA MARGARET SMITH: NY R USDCTSD Smith-Practices; NY R USDCTSD Smith-Trials.

# Requests, Notices and Applications
## Request for Production of Documents

**Document Last Updated September 2016**

## A. Checklist

(I)  ❏ Matters to be considered by requesting party

   (a)  ❏ Required documents

      (1)  ❏ Request for production of documents

   (b)  ❏ Supplemental documents

      (1)  ❏ Subpoena

      (2)  ❏ Certificate of service

   (c)  ❏ Timing

      (1)  ❏ A party may not seek discovery from any source before the parties have conferred as required by FRCP 26(f), except in a proceeding exempted from initial disclosure under FRCP 26(a)(1)(B), or when authorized by the Federal Rules of Civil Procedure, by stipulation, or by court order

      (2)  ❏ More than twenty-one (21) days after the summons and complaint are served on a party, a request under FRCP 34 may be delivered: (1) to that party by any other party, and (2) by that party to any plaintiff or to any other party that has been served

(II)  ❏ Matters to be considered by responding party

   (a)  ❏ Required documents

      (1)  ❏ Response to request for production of documents

(b) ❑ Supplemental documents

    (1) ❑ Written information regarding assertion of privilege

    (2) ❑ Certificate of service

(c) ❑ Timing

    (1) ❑ The party to whom the request is directed must respond in writing within thirty (30) days after being served or—if the request was delivered under FRCP 26(d)(2)—within thirty (30) days after the parties' first FRCP 26(f) conference

## B. Timing

1. *Request for production of documents.* Without leave of court or written stipulation, a request may not be served before the time specified in FRCP 26(d). FEDPROC § 26:632. Of course, discovery under FRCP 34 should ordinarily precede the trial. FEDPROC § 26:632.

   a. *Early FRCP 34 requests*

     i. *Time to deliver.* More than twenty-one (21) days after the summons and complaint are served on a party, a request under FRCP 34 may be delivered:

- To that party by any other party, and

- By that party to any plaintiff or to any other party that has been served. FRCP 26(d)(2)(A).

     ii. *When considered served.* The request is considered to have been served at the first FRCP 26(f) conference. FRCP 26(d)(2)(B).

2. *Timing of discovery, generally.* A party may not seek discovery from any source before the parties have conferred as required by FRCP 26(f), except in a proceeding exempted from initial disclosure under FRCP 26(a)(1)(B), or when authorized by the Federal Rules of Civil Procedure, by stipulation, or by court order. FRCP 26(d)(1).

3. *Computation of time*

   a. *Computing time.* FRCP 6 applies in computing any time period specified in the Federal Rules of Civil Procedure, in any local rule or court order, or in any statute that does not specify a method of computing time. FRCP 6(a). In computing any period of time prescribed or allowed by the Local Civil Rules of the United States District Courts for the Southern and Eastern Districts of New York or the Local Admiralty and Maritime Rules, the provisions of FRCP 6 shall apply unless otherwise stated. NY R USDCTS&ED Civ Rule 6.4.

     i. *Period stated in days or a longer unit.* When the period is stated in days or a longer unit of time:

- Exclude the day of the event that triggers the period;

- Count every day, including intermediate Saturdays, Sundays, and legal holidays; and

- Include the last day of the period, but if the last day is a Saturday, Sunday, or legal holiday, the period continues to run until the end of the next day that is not a Saturday, Sunday, or legal holiday. FRCP 6(a)(1). In the Local Civil Rules of the United States District Courts for the Southern and Eastern Districts of New York, as in the Federal Rules of Civil Procedure as amended effective December 1, 2009, Saturdays, Sundays, and legal holidays are no longer excluded in computing periods of time. If the last day of the period is a Saturday, Sunday, or legal holiday, the period continues to run until the end of the next day that is not a Saturday, Sunday, or legal holiday. NY R USDCTS&ED Civ Rule 6.4.

     ii. *Period stated in hours.* When the period is stated in hours:

- Begin counting immediately on the occurrence of the event that triggers the period;

- Count every hour, including hours during intermediate Saturdays, Sundays, and legal holidays; and

- If the period would end on a Saturday, Sunday, or legal holiday, the period continues to run until the same time on the next day that is not a Saturday, Sunday, or legal holiday. FRCP 6(a)(2). In the Local Civil Rules of the United States District Courts for the Southern and

Eastern Districts of New York, as in the Federal Rules of Civil Procedure as amended effective December 1, 2009, Saturdays, Sundays, and legal holidays are no longer excluded in computing periods of time. If the last day of the period is a Saturday, Sunday, or legal holiday, the period continues to run until the end of the next day that is not a Saturday, Sunday, or legal holiday. NY R USDCTS&ED Civ Rule 6.4.

iii. *Inaccessibility of the clerk's office.* Unless the court orders otherwise, if the clerk's office is inaccessible:

- On the last day for filing under FRCP 6(a)(1), then the time for filing is extended to the first accessible day that is not a Saturday, Sunday, or legal holiday; or

- During the last hour for filing under FRCP 6(a)(2), then the time for filing is extended to the same time on the first accessible day that is not a Saturday, Sunday, or legal holiday. FRCP 6(a)(3).

iv. *"Last day" defined.* Unless a different time is set by a statute, local rule, or court order, the last day ends:

- For electronic filing, at midnight in the court's time zone; and

- For filing by other means, when the clerk's office is scheduled to close. FRCP 6(a)(4).

v. *"Next day" defined.* The "next day" is determined by continuing to count forward when the period is measured after an event and backward when measured before an event. FRCP 6(a)(5).

vi. *"Legal holiday" defined.* "Legal holiday" means:

- The day set aside by statute for observing New Year's Day, Martin Luther King Jr.'s Birthday, Washington's Birthday, Memorial Day, Independence Day, Labor Day, Columbus Day, Veterans' Day, Thanksgiving Day, or Christmas Day;

- Any day declared a holiday by the President or Congress; and

- For periods that are measured after an event, any other day declared a holiday by the state where the district court is located. FRCP 6(a)(6).

b. *Computation of electronic filing deadlines.* You can file electronically twenty-four (24) hours a day, seven (7) days a week, three hundred sixty-five (365) days a year. NY R USDCTSD CM/ECF, S.D.(II)(13)(13.10). Electronic filing must be completed before midnight local time where the Court is located in order to be considered timely filed that day. NY R USDCTSD CM/ECF, S.D.(I)(3)(3.3); NY R USDCTSD CM/ECF, S.D.(II)(13)(13.10); NY R USDCTSD CM/ECF, S.D.(II)(19)(19.4). An electronically filed document is deemed filed on the "filed on" date indicated on the Notice of Electronic Filing (NEF). NY R USDCTSD CM/ECF, S.D.(II)(13)(13.11).

i. *Technical failures.* A Filing User whose filing is made untimely as the result of a technical failure may seek appropriate relief from the Court. NY R USDCTSD CM/ECF, S.D.(I)(11). If you missed a filing deadline when the ECF system was out of order, attach a statement to your filing explaining how the interruption in service prevented you from filing in a timely fashion. NY R USDCTSD CM/ECF, S.D.(II)(23)(23.5).

c. *Extending time*

i. *In general.* When an act may or must be done within a specified time, the court may, for good cause, extend the time:

- With or without motion or notice if the court acts, or if a request is made, before the original time or its extension expires; or

- On motion made after the time has expired if the party failed to act because of excusable neglect. FRCP 6(b)(1).

ii. *Exceptions.* A court must not extend the time to act under FRCP 50(b), FRCP 50(d), FRCP 52(b), FRCP 59(b), FRCP 59(d), FRCP 59(e), and FRCP 60(b). FRCP 6(b)(2).

iii. Refer to the United States District Court for the Southern District of New York KeyRules Motion for Continuance/Extension of Time document for more information on extending time.

    d. *Additional time after certain kinds of service.* When a party may or must act within a specified time after service and service is made under FRCP 5(b)(2)(C), FRCP 5(b)(2)(D), FRCP 5(b)(2)(E), or FRCP 5(b)(2)(F), three (3) days are added after the period would otherwise expire under FRCP 6(a). FRCP 6(d). Overnight delivery service shall be deemed service by mail for purposes of FRCP 5 and FRCP 6. NY R USDCTS&ED Civ Rule 5.3.

4. *Individual judge practices.* Refer to the Miscellaneous section of this document for information on individual judge practices on timing of documents.

## C. General Requirements

1. *General provisions governing discovery*

    a. *Discovery scope and limits*

        i. *Scope in general.* Unless otherwise limited by court order, the scope of discovery is as follows: Parties may obtain discovery regarding any nonprivileged matter that is relevant to any party's claim or defense and proportional to the needs of the case, considering the importance of the issues at stake in the action, the amount in controversy, the parties' relative access to relevant information, the parties' resources, the importance of the discovery in resolving the issues, and whether the burden or expense of the proposed discovery outweighs its likely benefit. Information within this scope of discovery need not be admissible in evidence to be discoverable. FRCP 26(b)(1).

        ii. *Limitations on frequency and extent*

- *When permitted.* By order, the court may alter the limits in the Federal Rules of Civil Procedure on the number of depositions and interrogatories or on the length of depositions under FRCP 30. By order or local rule, the court may also limit the number of requests under FRCP 36. FRCP 26(b)(2)(A).

- *Specific limitations on electronically stored information.* A party need not provide discovery of electronically stored information from sources that the party identifies as not reasonably accessible because of undue burden or cost. On motion to compel discovery or for a protective order, the party from whom discovery is sought must show that the information is not reasonably accessible because of undue burden or cost. If that showing is made, the court may nonetheless order discovery from such sources if the requesting party shows good cause, considering the limitations of FRCP 26(b)(2)(C). The court may specify conditions for the discovery. FRCP 26(b)(2)(B).

- *When required.* On motion or on its own, the court must limit the frequency or extent of discovery otherwise allowed by the Federal Rules of Civil Procedure or by local rule if it determines that: (1) the discovery sought is unreasonably cumulative or duplicative, or can be obtained from some other source that is more convenient, less burdensome, or less expensive; (2) the party seeking discovery has had ample opportunity to obtain the information by discovery in the action; or (3) the proposed discovery is outside the scope permitted by FRCP 26(b)(1). FRCP 26(b)(2)(C).

        iii. *Trial preparation; Materials*

- *Documents and tangible things.* Ordinarily, a party may not discover documents and tangible things that are prepared in anticipation of litigation or for trial by or for another party or its representative (including the other party's attorney, consultant, surety, indemnitor, insurer, or agent). But, subject to FRCP 26(b)(4), those materials may be discovered if: (1) they are otherwise discoverable under FRCP 26(b)(1); and (2) the party shows that it has substantial need for the materials to prepare its case and cannot, without undue hardship, obtain their substantial equivalent by other means. FRCP 26(b)(3)(A).

- *Protection against disclosure.* If the court orders discovery of those materials, it must protect against disclosure of the mental impressions, conclusions, opinions, or legal theories of a party's attorney or other representative concerning the litigation. FRCP 26(b)(3)(B).

- *Previous statement.* Any party or other person may, on request and without the required showing, obtain the person's own previous statement about the action or its subject matter. If the request is refused, the person may move for a court order, and FRCP 37(a)(5) applies to the award of expenses. A previous statement is either: (1) a written statement that the person has signed or otherwise adopted or approved; or (2) a contemporaneous steno-graphic, mechanical, electrical, or other recording—or a transcription of it—that recites substantially verbatim the person's oral statement. FRCP 26(b)(3)(C).

iv.  *Trial preparation; Experts*

- *Deposition of an expert who may testify.* A party may depose any person who has been identified as an expert whose opinions may be presented at trial. If FRCP 26(a)(2)(B) requires a report from the expert, the deposition may be conducted only after the report is provided. FRCP 26(b)(4)(A).

- *Trial-preparation protection for draft reports or disclosures.* FRCP 26(b)(3)(A) and FRCP 26(b)(3)(B) protect drafts of any report or disclosure required under FRCP 26(a)(2), regardless of the form in which the draft is recorded. FRCP 26(b)(4)(B).

- *Trial-preparation protection for communications between a party's attorney and expert witnesses.* FRCP 26(b)(3)(A) and FRCP 26(b)(3)(B) protect communications between the party's attorney and any witness required to provide a report under FRCP 26(a)(2)(B), regardless of the form of the communications, except to the extent that the communica-tions: (1) relate to compensation for the expert's study or testimony; (2) identify facts or data that the party's attorney provided and that the expert considered in forming the opinions to be expressed; or (3) identify assumptions that the party's attorney provided and that the expert relied on in forming the opinions to be expressed. FRCP 26(b)(4)(C).

- *Expert employed only for trial preparation.* Ordinarily, a party may not, by interrogatories or deposition, discover facts known or opinions held by an expert who has been retained or specially employed by another party in anticipation of litigation or to prepare for trial and who is not expected to be called as a witness at trial. But a party may do so only: (1) as provided in FRCP 35(b); or (2) on showing exceptional circumstances under which it is impracticable for the party to obtain facts or opinions on the same subject by other means. FRCP 26(b)(4)(D).

- *Payment.* Unless manifest injustice would result, the court must require that the party seeking discovery: (1) pay the expert a reasonable fee for time spent in responding to discovery under FRCP 26(b)(4)(A) or FRCP 26(b)(4)(D); and (2) for discovery FRCP 26(b)(4)(D), also pay the other party a fair portion of the fees and expenses it reasonably incurred in obtaining the expert's facts and opinions. FRCP 26(b)(4)(E).

v.  *Claiming privilege or protecting trial-preparation materials*

- *Information withheld.* When a party withholds information otherwise discoverable by claiming that the information is privileged or subject to protection as trial-preparation material, the party must: (1) expressly make the claim; and (2) describe the nature of the documents, communications, or tangible things not produced or disclosed—and do so in a manner that, without revealing information itself privileged or protected, will enable other parties to assess the claim. FRCP 26(b)(5)(A). Unless otherwise agreed by the parties or directed by the Court, where a claim of privilege is asserted in objecting to any means of discovery or disclosure, including but not limited to a deposition, and an answer is not provided on the basis of such assertion, (1) the person asserting the privilege shall identify the nature of the privilege (including work product) which is being claimed and, if the privilege is governed by state law, indicate the state's privilege rule being invoked; and (2) the following information shall be provided in the objection, or (in the case of a deposition) in response to questions by the questioner, unless divulgence of such infor-mation would cause disclosure of the allegedly privileged information: (A) for docu-ments: (i) the type of document, e.g., letter or memorandum; (ii) the general subject matter of the document; (iii) the date of the document; and (iv) the author of the document, the addressees of the document, and any other recipients, and, where not apparent, the relationship of the author, addressees, and recipients to each other; (B) for oral communications: (i) the name of the person making the communication and the names of persons present while the communication was made and, where not apparent, the relationship of the persons present to the person making the communication; (ii) the date and place of communication; and (iii) the general subject matter of the communication. NY R USDCTS&ED Civ Rule 26.2(a). Where a claim of privilege is asserted in response to discovery or disclosure other than a deposition, and information is not provided on the basis of such assertion, the information set forth in NY R USDCTS&ED Civ Rule 26.2(a) shall be furnished in writing at the time of the response to such discovery or disclosure, unless otherwise ordered by the Court. NY R USDCTS&ED Civ Rule 26.2(b).

- *Information produced.* If information produced in discovery is subject to a claim of privilege or of protection as trial-preparation material, the party making the claim may notify any party that received the information of the claim and the basis for it. After being notified, a party must promptly return, sequester, or destroy the specified information and any copies it has; must not use or disclose the information until the claim is resolved; must take reasonable steps to retrieve the information if the party disclosed it before being notified; and may promptly present the information to the court under seal for a determination of the claim. The producing party must preserve the information until the claim is resolved. FRCP 26(b)(5)(B).

- *Efficient means of providing information regarding claims of privilege.* Efficient means of providing information regarding claims of privilege are encouraged, and parties are encouraged to agree upon measures that further this end. For example, when asserting privilege on the same basis with respect to multiple documents, it is presumptively proper to provide the information required by NY R USDCTS&ED Civ Rule 26.2 by group or category. A party receiving a privilege log that groups documents or otherwise departs from a document-by-document or communication-by-communication listing may not object solely on that basis, but may object if the substantive information required by NY R USDCTS&ED Civ Rule 26.2 has not been provided in a comprehensible form. NY R USDCTS&ED Civ Rule 26.2(c).

b.  *Protective orders.* A party or any person from whom discovery is sought may move for a protective order in the court where the action is pending—or as an alternative on matters relating to a deposition, in the court for the district where the deposition will be taken. FRCP 26(c)(1). Refer to the United States District Court for the Southern District of New York KeyRules Motion for Protective Order document for more information.

c.  *Sequence of discovery.* Unless the parties stipulate or the court orders otherwise for the parties' and witnesses' convenience and in the interests of justice: (1) methods of discovery may be used in any sequence; and (2) discovery by one party does not require any other party to delay its discovery. FRCP 26(d)(3).

d.  *Uniform definitions in discovery requests.* The full text of the definitions and rules of construction set forth in NY R USDCTS&ED Civ Rule 26.3(c) and NY R USDCTS&ED Civ Rule 26.3(d) is deemed incorporated by reference into all discovery requests. No discovery request shall use broader definitions or rules of construction than those set forth in NY R USDCTS&ED Civ Rule 26.3(c) and NY R USDCTS&ED Civ Rule 26.3(d). NY R USDCTS&ED Civ Rule 26.3 shall not preclude (1) the definition of other terms specific to the particular litigation, (2) the use of abbreviations, or (3) a more narrow definition of a term defined in NY R USDCTS&ED Civ Rule 26.3(c). NY R USDCTS&ED Civ Rule 26.3(a). NY R USDCTS&ED Civ Rule 26.3 is not intended to broaden or narrow the scope of discovery permitted by the Federal Rules of Civil Procedure. NY R USDCTS&ED Civ Rule 26.3(b).

i.  *Definitions.* The following definitions apply to all discovery requests:

- *Communication.* The term "communication" means the transmittal of information (in the form of facts, ideas, inquiries or otherwise). NY R USDCTS&ED Civ Rule 26.3(c)(1).

- *Document.* The term "document" is defined to be synonymous in meaning and equal in scope to the usage of the term "documents or electronically stored information" in FRCP 34(a)(1)(A). A draft or non-identical copy is a separate document within the meaning of this term. NY R USDCTS&ED Civ Rule 26.3(c)(2).

- *Identify (with respect to persons).* When referring to a person, "to identify" means to give, to the extent known, the person's full name, present or last known address, and when referring to a natural person, additionally, the present or last known place of employment. Once a person has been identified in accordance with NY R USDCTS&ED Civ Rule 26.3(c)(3), only the name of that person need be listed in response to subsequent discovery requesting the identification of that person. NY R USDCTS&ED Civ Rule 26.3(c)(3).

- *Identify (with respect to documents).* When referring to documents, "to identify" means to give, to the extent known, the (1) type of document; (2) general subject matter; (3) date of the document; and (4) author(s), addressee(s) and recipient(s). In the alternative, the responding party may produce the documents, together with identifying information sufficient to satisfy FRCP 33(d). NY R USDCTS&ED Civ Rule 26.3(c)(4).

- *Parties.* The terms "plaintiff" and "defendant" as well as a party's full or abbreviated name or a pronoun referring to a party mean the party and, where applicable, its officers, directors, employees, partners, corporate parent, subsidiaries or affiliates. This definition is not intended to impose a discovery obligation on any person who is not a party to the litigation. NY R USDCTS&ED Civ Rule 26.3(c)(5).

- *Person.* The term "person" is defined as any natural person or any legal entity, including, without limitation, any business or governmental entity or association. NY R USDCTS&ED Civ Rule 26.3(c)(6).

- *Concerning.* The term "concerning" means relating to, referring to, describing, evidencing or constituting. NY R USDCTS&ED Civ Rule 26.3(c)(7).

ii. *Rules of construction.* The following rules of construction apply to all discovery requests:

- *All/any/each.* The terms "all," "any," and "each" shall each be construed as encompassing any and all. NY R USDCTS&ED Civ Rule 26.3(d)(1).

- *And/or.* The connectives "and" and "or" shall be construed either disjunctively or conjunctively as necessary to bring within the scope of the discovery request all responses that might otherwise be construed to be outside of its scope. NY R USDCTS&ED Civ Rule 26.3(d)(2).

- *Number.* The use of the singular form of any word includes the plural and vice versa. NY R USDCTS&ED Civ Rule 26.3(d)(3).

e. *Cooperation among counsel in discovery.* Counsel are expected to cooperate with each other, consistent with the interests of their clients, in all phases of the discovery process and to be courteous in their dealings with each other, including in matters relating to scheduling and timing of various discovery procedures. NY R USDCTS&ED Civ Rule 26.4(a).

i. Discovery requests shall be read reasonably in the recognition that the attorney serving them generally does not have the information being sought and the attorney receiving them generally does have such information or can obtain it from the client. NY R USDCTS&ED Civ Rule 26.4(b).

f. *Standard discovery in prisoner pro se actions.* For information on discovery in prisoner pro se actions, refer to NY R USDCTS&ED Civ Rule 33.2.

2. *Request for production of documents*

a. *In general.* A party may serve on any other party a request within the scope of FRCP 26(b):

i. To produce and permit the requesting party or its representative to inspect, copy, test, or sample the following items in the responding party's possession, custody, or control:

- Any designated documents or electronically stored information—including writings, drawings, graphs, charts, photographs, sound recordings, images, and other data or data compilations—stored in any medium from which information can be obtained either directly or, if necessary, after translation by the responding party into a reasonably usable form; or

- Any designated tangible things; or

ii. To permit entry onto designated land or other property possessed or controlled by the responding party, so that the requesting party may inspect, measure, survey, photograph, test, or sample the property or any designated object or operation on it. FRCP 34(a).

b. *Contents of the request.* The request: (1) must describe with reasonable particularity each item or category of items to be inspected; (2) must specify a reasonable time, place, and manner for the inspection and for performing the related acts; and (3) may specify the form or forms in which electronically stored information is to be produced. FRCP 34(b)(1).

  i. *Description of items.* Although the phrase "reasonable particularity" eludes precise definition and depends on the facts and circumstances in each case, at least two tests have been suggested:

  - The first test is whether the request places a party on "reasonable notice" of what is called for and what is not so that a reasonable person would know what documents or things are called for. FEDPROC § 26:634.

  - The second is whether the request gives a court enough information to enable it to rule intelligently on objections. FEDPROC § 26:634.

c. *Form discovery requests.* Attorneys using form discovery requests shall review them to ascertain that they are consistent with the scope of discovery under FRCP 26(b)(1). Non-compliant requests shall not be used. NY R USDCTS&ED Civ Rule 26.5.

d. *Signature.* Though FRCP 34 does not say so, it is sufficient if the request is signed by the attorney for the party seeking discovery. FPP § 2212. Refer to the Format section of this document for more information on signing of discovery papers.

e. *Other authority on production and inspection*

  i. *Freedom of Information Act.* Although the Freedom of Information Act (FOIA) is fundamentally designed to inform the public about agency action, and not to benefit private litigants, Congress has not acted upon proposals to forbid or limit the use of the FOIA for discovery purposes. FEDPROC § 26:605; National Presto Industries, Inc., 218 Ct.Cl. 696, 1978 WL 8475 (1978). However, a FOIA request may not be used to supplement civil discovery under FRCP 34, as in the case where information is privileged and therefore outside the scope of civil discovery. FEDPROC § 26:605; U.S. v. Weber Aircraft Corp., 465 U.S. 792, 104 S.Ct. 1488, 79 L.Ed.2d 814 (1984).

  ii. *Hague Convention.* Under the Hague Convention, a party seeking evidence abroad must obtain and send a letter of request to the central authority of the country in which the evidence is sought, requesting service of the request on the desired person or entity; if the request complies with the Convention, the central authority will then obtain the desired evidence. FEDPROC § 26:606. [Editor's note: the Hague Convention can be found at T.I.A.S. No. 6638 and is also available in the appendix to FRCP 4].

f. *Motion to compel.* If a party who has been requested to permit discovery under FRCP 34 makes no response to the request, or if its response objects to all or part of the requested discovery, or if it otherwise fails to permit discovery as requested, the party who submitted the request, if it still wishes the discovery that has been refused, may move under FRCP 37(a) for an order compelling inspection in accordance with the request. FPP § 2214. Refer to the United States District Court for the Southern District of New York KeyRules Motion to Compel Discovery document for more information.

3. *Sanctions for failure to cooperate in discovery.* The court where the action is pending may, on motion, order sanctions if a party, after being properly served with interrogatories under FRCP 33 or a request for inspection under FRCP 34, fails to serve its answers, objections, or written response. FRCP 37(d)(1)(A)(ii). If a motion to compel is granted, the court must, after giving an opportunity to be heard, require the party or deponent whose conduct necessitated the motion, the party or attorney advising that

conduct, or both to pay the movant's reasonable expenses incurred in making the motion, including attorney's fees. But the court must not order this payment if the opposing party's nondisclosure, response, or objection was substantially justified. FRCP 37(a)(5)(A)(ii). Refer to the United States District Court for the Southern District of New York KeyRules Motion for Discovery Sanctions document for more information.

4. *Stipulations about discovery procedure.* Unless the court orders otherwise, the parties may stipulate that: (1) a deposition may be taken before any person, at any time or place, on any notice, and in the manner specified—in which event it may be used in the same way as any other deposition; and (2) other procedures governing or limiting discovery be modified—but a stipulation extending the time for any form of discovery must have court approval if it would interfere with the time set for completing discovery, for hearing a motion, or for trial. FRCP 29.

5. *Complex civil cases.* For information on procedures for complex civil cases, refer to NY R USDCTSD Order 11 Misc 00388.

6. *Related cases.* It shall be the continuing duty of each attorney appearing in any civil or criminal case to bring promptly to the attention of the Court all facts which said attorney believes are relevant to a determination that said case and one or more pending civil or criminal cases should be heard by the same Judge, in order to avoid unnecessary duplication of judicial effort. As soon as the attorney becomes aware of such relationship, said attorney shall notify the Judges to whom the cases have been assigned. NY R USDCTS&ED Civ Rule 1.6(a). If counsel fails to comply with NY R USDCTS&ED Civ Rule 1.6(a), the Court may assess reasonable costs directly against counsel whose action has obstructed the effective administration of the Court's business. NY R USDCTS&ED Civ Rule 1.6(b).

   a. *Determination of relatedness.* Subject to the limitations set forth in NY R USDCTSD Div. Bus., Rule 13(a)(2), a civil case, bankruptcy appeal, or motion to withdraw the bankruptcy reference will be deemed related to one or more civil cases, appeals or motions when the interests of justice and efficiency will be served. In determining relatedness, a judge will consider whether (A) the actions concern the same or substantially similar parties, property, transactions or events; (B) there is substantial factual overlap; (C) the parties could be subjected to conflicting orders; and (D) whether absent a determination of relatedness there would be a substantial duplication of effort and expense, delay, or undue burden on the Court, parties or witnesses. NY R USDCTSD Div. Bus., Rule 13(a)(1). Nothing in this NY R USDCTSD Div. Bus., Rule 13 is intended to preclude parties from moving for consolidated proceedings under FRCP 42. NY R USDCTSD Div. Bus., Rule 13(a)(1). Notwithstanding NY R USDCTSD Div. Bus., Rule 13(a)(1):

      i. Civil cases shall not be deemed related merely because they involve common legal issues or the same parties. NY R USDCTSD Div. Bus., Rule 13(a)(2)(A).

      ii. Other than cases subject to NY R USDCTSD Div. Bus., Rule 4(b) and actions seeking the enforcement of a judgment or settlement in or of an earlier case, civil cases presumptively shall not be deemed related unless both cases are pending before the Court (or the earlier case is on appeal). NY R USDCTSD Div. Bus., Rule 13(a)(2)(B).

   b. *Procedure in regard to cases said to be related*

      i. *Disclosure of contention of relatedness.* When a civil case is filed or removed or a bankruptcy appeal or motion to withdraw the reference of an adversary proceeding from the bankruptcy court is filed, the person filing or removing shall disclose on form JSC44C any contention of relatedness and shall file a Related Case Statement stating clearly and succinctly the basis for the contention. A copy of the civil cover sheet and Related Case Statement shall be served with the complaint, notice of removal, notice of appeal, or motion. Any party may contest a claim of relatedness by any other in writing addressed to the judge having the case with the lowest docket number of all cases claimed to be related. However, the foregoing shall not delay the assignment process or the operation of NY R USDCTSD Div. Bus., Rule 13. NY R USDCTSD Div. Bus., Rule 13(b)(1). [Editor's note: the reference to form JSC44C is likely meant to be form JS44C-SDNY: Civil Court Cover Sheet].

      ii. *Claims of relatedness by other parties.* A party other than the one filing a case, bankruptcy appeal or motion to withdraw the reference that contends its case is related to another may so advise in writing the judge assigned in its case and request a transfer of its case to the judge that the party contends has the related case with the lowest docket number. If the assigned judge believes the case is related under NY R USDCTSD Div. Bus., Rule 13(a), he or she shall refer the question to the judge having the case with the lowest docket number. In the event the latter judge agrees, the case shall be transferred to that judge unless the Assignment Committee disagrees. NY R USDCTSD Div. Bus., Rule 13(b)(3).

   c. For more information on related cases, refer to NY R USDCTSD Div. Bus., Rule 13.

7. *Alternative dispute resolution (ADR).* The U.S. District Court for the Southern District of New York provides litigants with opportunities to discuss settlement through judicial settlement conferences and mediation. NY R USDCTS&ED Civ Rule 83.9(a).

   a. *Consideration of alternative dispute resolution.* In all civil cases, including those eligible for mediation pursuant to NY R USDCTS&ED Civ Rule 83.9(e), each party shall consider the use of mediation or a judicial settlement conference and shall report to the assigned Judge at the initial FRCP 16(b) case management conference, or subsequently, whether the party believes mediation or a judicial settlement conference may facilitate the resolution of the lawsuit. Judges are encouraged to note the availability of the mediation program and/or a judicial settlement conference before, at, or after the initial FRCP 16(b) case management conference. NY R USDCTS&ED Civ Rule 83.9(d).

   b. *Mediation.* In mediation, parties and counsel meet, sometimes collectively and sometimes individually, with a neutral third party (the mediator) who has been trained to facilitate confidential settlement discussions. The parties articulate their respective positions and interests and generate options for a mutually agreeable resolution to the dispute. The mediator assists the parties in reaching their own negotiated settlement by defining the issues, probing and assessing the strengths and weaknesses of each party's legal positions, and identifying areas of agreement and disagreement. The main benefits of mediation are that it can result in an expeditious and less costly resolution of the litigation, and can produce creative solutions to complex disputes often unavailable in traditional litigation. NY R USDCTS&ED Civ Rule 83.9(b).

      i. *Mediation program eligibility.* All civil cases other than Social Security, habeas corpus, and tax cases are eligible for mediation, whether assigned to Manhattan or White Plains. NY R USDCTS&ED Civ Rule 83.9(e)(1).

- The Board of Judges may, by Administrative Order, direct that certain specified categories of cases shall automatically be submitted to the mediation program. The assigned District Judge or Magistrate Judge may issue a written order exempting a particular case with or without the request of the parties. NY R USDCTS&ED Civ Rule 83.9(e)(2).

- For all other cases, the assigned District Judge or Magistrate Judge may determine that a case is appropriate for mediation and may order that case to mediation, with or without the consent of the parties, before, at, or after the initial FRCP 16(b) case management conference. Alternatively, the parties should notify the assigned Judge at any time of their desire to mediate. NY R USDCTS&ED Civ Rule 83.9(e)(3).

   c. *Judicial settlement conferences.* Judicial settlement conferences may be ordered by District Judges or Magistrate Judges with or without the request or consent of the parties. NY R USDCTS&ED Civ Rule 83.9(f).

   d. For more information on alternative dispute resolution (ADR), refer to NY R USDCTS&ED Civ Rule 83.9.

8. *Individual judge practices.* Refer to the Miscellaneous section of this document for information on individual judge practices on general requirements for documents.

## D. Documents

1. *Required documents*

   a. *Request for production of documents.* Refer to the General Requirements section of this document for information on the request for production of documents.

2. *Supplemental documents*

   a. *Subpoena.* As provided in FRCP 45, a nonparty may be compelled to produce documents and tangible things or to permit an inspection. FRCP 34(c). For information on the form and contents of the subpoena, refer to FRCP 45.

    b.  *Certificate of service.* FRCP 5(d) requires that the person making service under FRCP 5 certify that service has been effected. FRCP 5(Advisory Committee Notes). Having such information on file may be useful for many purposes, including proof of service if an issue arises concerning the effectiveness of the service. FRCP 5(Advisory Committee Notes).

3.  *Individual judge practices.* Refer to the Miscellaneous section of this document for information on individual judge practices on required documents.

## E. Format

1.  *Form of documents.* The rules governing captions and other matters of form in pleadings apply to motions and other papers. FRCP 7(b)(2).

    a.  *Paper.* Every pleading, written motion, and other paper must: be plainly written, typed, printed, or copied without erasures or interlineations which materially deface it. NY R USDCTS&ED Civ Rule 11.1(a)(1).

    b.  *Typeface, margin, and spacing.* The typeface, margins, and spacing of all documents presented for filing must meet the following requirements:

       i.  All text must be twelve (12) point type or larger, except for text in footnotes which may be ten (10) point type;

      ii.  All documents must have at least one (1) inch margins on all sides;

     iii.  All text must be double-spaced, except for headings, text in footnotes, or block quotations, which may be single-spaced. NY R USDCTS&ED Civ Rule 11.1(b).

    c.  *Caption; Names of parties.* Every pleading must have a caption with the court's name, a title, a file number, and a FRCP 7(a) designation. The title of the complaint must name all the parties; the title of other pleadings, after naming the first party on each side, may refer generally to other parties. FRCP 10(a). Every pleading, written motion, and other paper must: bear the docket number and the initials of the District Judge and any Magistrate Judge before whom the action or proceeding is pending, NY R USDCTS&ED Civ Rule 11.1(a)(2).

    d.  *Paragraphs; Separate statements.* A party must state its claims or defenses in numbered paragraphs, each limited as far as practicable to a single set of circumstances. A later pleading may refer by number to a paragraph in an earlier pleading. If doing so would promote clarity, each claim founded on a separate transaction or occurrence—and each defense other than a denial—must be stated in a separate count or defense. FRCP 10(b).

    e.  *Adoption by reference; Exhibits.* A statement in a pleading may be adopted by reference elsewhere in the same pleading or in any other pleading or motion. A copy of a written instrument that is an exhibit to a pleading is a part of the pleading for all purposes. FRCP 10(c).

    f.  *Acceptance by the clerk.* The clerk must not refuse to file a paper solely because it is not in the form prescribed by the Federal Rules of Civil Procedure or by a local rule or practice. FRCP 5(d)(4).

2.  *Form of electronic documents*

    a.  *PDF-A.* All documents electronically filed on the ECF system must be in PDF-A format (portable document format). A PDF-A file is created using PDF writer software such as Adobe Acrobat (go to the Adobe website for details). PDF-A files cannot be altered, providing security to the filer and the Court. NY R USDCTSD CM/ECF, S.D.(II)(23)(23.2).

    b.  *Size limitation.* No single PDF file may be larger than four megabytes (4 MB). If the filing is too large, the ECF system will not allow it to be filed, and you will not see a Notice of Electronic Filing (NEF or filing receipt) screen. To determine the size of an Adobe Acrobat PDF file click on File, Document Properties, Summary. NY R USDCTSD CM/ECF, S.D.(II)(23)(23.3).

       i.  Converting documents directly from a word processor to PDF-A format creates the smallest possible file in terms of computer memory. If that is not possible, scan your document at low resolution. Within the Adobe Acrobat program, on the "Scan Manager" screen, adjust the settings for black and white and 200 dpi (dots per inch). This allows more pages to fit into a single PDF-A file. If that does not work, separate an oversized file into 2 or more parts. Simply label each file 1a, 1b, 1c, etc. Only relevant excerpts of exhibits should be electronically filed. NY R USDCTSD CM/ECF, S.D.(II)(23)(23.4).

c. *Attachments and exhibits.* Filing Users must submit in electronic form all documents referenced as exhibits or attachments, unless the Court permits paper filing. NY R USDCTSD CM/ECF, S.D.(I)(5)(5.1).

    i. A Filing User must submit as exhibits or attachments only those excerpts of the referenced documents that are relevant to the matter under consideration by the Court. Excerpted material must be clearly and prominently identified as such. Filing Users who file excerpts of documents as exhibits or attachments under this procedure do so without prejudice to their right to file timely additional excerpts or the complete document. Responding parties may file timely additional excerpts that they believe are relevant or the complete document. A party may move before the Court for permission to serve and file in hard copy documents that cannot be reasonably scanned. NY R USDCTSD CM/ECF, S.D.(I)(5)(5.2).

    ii. Exhibits must be filed only as attachments to a document, such as a motion or an affidavit. Do not use the ECF Filing Event for "Motion" to file exhibits separately. Exhibits are the only items that should be attached to electronically filed documents. You are limited to electronically filing only relevant excerpts of exhibits. Excerpts must be clearly identified as such. If the exhibit is too large to be scanned and electronically filed you may contact the ECF Help Desk. NY R USDCTSD CM/ECF, S.D.(II)(15)(15.6).

d. *Letters.* Parties should consult the assigned judge's Individual Practices to determine if the judge accepts letters at all and, if he or she does, whether the judge has any page limitations on letters and/or requires courtesy copies of letters filed on ECF (and, if so, by what means of delivery). All letters addressed to the Court must include a subject line with the case name and docket number (e.g., "Re: Doe v. Smith, 13 Civ. 1234 (ABC)"). NY R USDCTSD CM/ECF, S.D.(II)(13)(13.1).

e. *Proposed orders, proposed judgments, stipulations and consents.* Any document that requires the signature of a judge should not be electronically filed except as an exhibit to another document. Proposed orders, judgments, stipulations and consents should not be submitted through the ECF system. Instead they should be sent by e-mail to the Clerk. Proposed orders should be submitted in word processing format (WordPerfect or Word) rather than as a PDF document. Stipulations should be submitted in PDF-A format. Stipulations must contain ink signatures not s/. Faxed or emailed signatures are acceptable. Please note that Stipulations of Voluntary Dismissal pursuant to FRCP 41(a)(1)(A)(ii) do not require the signature of a judge and must be electronically filed on the ECF system. Questions may be directed to the Orders and Judgments Clerk at the phone numbers listed in NY R USDCTSD CM/ECF, S.D.(II)(18)(18.3). NY R USDCTSD CM/ECF, S.D.(II)(18)(18.3).

    i. Email the proposed order, judgment or stipulation to the email addresses listed in NY R USDCTSD CM/ECF, S.D.(II)(18)(18.3). NY R USDCTSD CM/ECF, S.D.(II)(18)(18.3).

    ii. Pro se litigants who are not Filing Users are exempt from that portion of NY R USDCTSD CM/ECF, S.D.(II)(18)(18.3) that requires litigants to email proposed orders, judgments, stipulations and consents, and shall deliver such documents to the Clerk's Office in paper form. NY R USDCTSD CM/ECF, S.D.(II)(18)(18.3).

3. *Signing disclosures and discovery requests, responses, and objections.* FRCP 11 does not apply to disclosures and discovery requests, responses, objections, and motions under FRCP 26 through FRCP 37. FRCP 11(d).

a. *Signature required.* Every disclosure under FRCP 26(a)(1) or FRCP 26(a)(3) and every discovery request, response, or objection must be signed by at least one attorney of record in the attorney's own name—or by the party personally, if unrepresented—and must state the signer's address, e-mail address, and telephone number. FRCP 26(g)(1). Every pleading, written motion, and other paper must: have the name of each person signing it clearly printed or typed directly below the signature. NY R USDCTS&ED Civ Rule 11.1(a)(3).

    i. *Electronic signatures.* The user log-in and password required to submit documents to the ECF

system serve as the Filing User's signature on all electronic documents filed with the Court. NY R USDCTSD CM/ECF, S.D.(I)(8)(8.1); NY R USDCTSD CM/ECF, S.D.(II)(13)(13.14). They also serve as a signature for purposes of the Federal Rules of Civil Procedure, including FRCP 11, the Local Civil Rules of the United States District Courts for the Southern and Eastern Districts of New York, and any other purpose for which a signature is required in connection with proceedings before the Court. NY R USDCTSD CM/ECF, S.D.(I)(8)(8.1).

- *Signature block.* Electronically filed documents must include a signature block and must set forth the name, address, telephone number and e-mail address all in compliance with the Federal Rules of Civil Procedure and NY R USDCTS&ED Civ Rule 11.1. In the absence of a scanned signature image, the name of the Filing User under whose log-in and password the document is submitted must be preceded by an "s/" typed in the space where the signature would otherwise appear. NY R USDCTSD CM/ECF, S.D.(I)(8)(8.2); NY R USDCTSD CM/ECF, S.D.(II)(13)(13.14).

- *Documents requiring the signature of a party or witness.* A document requiring the signature of a party or witness shall be electronically filed in a scanned format that contains an image of the actual signature. NY R USDCTSD CM/ECF, S.D.(I)(8)(8.4); NY R USDCTSD CM/ECF, S.D.(II)(13)(13.14).

- *Documents requiring the signature of a judge.* A Filing User submitting a document electronically that requires a judge's signature must promptly deliver the document in such other form, if any, as the Court requires. NY R USDCTSD CM/ECF, S.D.(I)(4)(4.2).

- *Documents requiring multiple signatures.* Documents requiring signatures of more than one party must be electronically filed either by: (a) submitting a scanned document containing all necessary signatures; (b) representing the consent of the other parties on the document; (c) identifying on the document the parties whose signatures are required and by the submission of a notice of endorsement by the other parties no later than three business days after filing; or (d) in any other manner approved by the Court. NY R USDCTSD CM/ECF, S.D.(I)(8)(8.5).

b. *Effect of signature.* By signing, an attorney or party certifies that to the best of the person's knowledge, information, and belief formed after a reasonable inquiry:

i. With respect to a disclosure, it is complete and correct as of the time it is made; and

ii. With respect to a discovery request, response, or objection, it is:

- Consistent with the Federal Rules of Civil Procedure and warranted by existing law or by a nonfrivolous argument for extending, modifying, or reversing existing law, or for establishing new law;

- Not interposed for any improper purpose, such as to harass, cause unnecessary delay, or needlessly increase the cost of litigation; and

- Neither unreasonable nor unduly burdensome or expensive, considering the needs of the case, prior discovery in the case, the amount in controversy, and the importance of the issues at stake in the action. FRCP 26(g)(1).

c. *Failure to sign.* Other parties have no duty to act on an unsigned disclosure, request, response, or objection until it is signed, and the court must strike it unless a signature is promptly supplied after the omission is called to the attorney's or party's attention. FRCP 26(g)(2).

d. *Sanction for improper certification.* If a certification violates FRCP 26(g) without substantial justification, the court, on motion or on its own, must impose an appropriate sanction on the signer, the party on whose behalf the signer was acting, or both. The sanction may include an order to pay the reasonable expenses, including attorney's fees, caused by the violation. FRCP 26(g)(3). Refer to the United States District Court for the Southern District of New York KeyRules Motion for Discovery Sanctions document for more information.

4. *Privacy protection for filings made with the court*

a. *Redacted filings.* Unless the court orders otherwise, in an electronic or paper filing with the court that

contains an individual's Social Security number, taxpayer-identification number, or birth date, the name of an individual known to be a minor, or a financial-account number, a party or nonparty making the filing may include only:

i. The last four (4) digits of the Social Security number and taxpayer-identification number;

ii. The year of the individual's birth;

iii. The minor's initials; and

iv. The last four (4) digits of the financial-account number. FRCP 5.2(a); NY R USDCTSD CM/ECF, S.D.(II)(21)(21.3).

v. Caution should be exercised when filing documents that contain the following:

- Personal identifying numbers (PIN #'s), such as a driver's license number;
- Medical records, treatment and diagnosis;
- Employment history;
- Individual financial information;
- Proprietary or trade secret information;
- Information regarding an individual's cooperation with the government. NY R USDCTSD CM/ECF, S.D.(II)(21)(21.4).

b. *Exemptions from the redaction requirement.* The redaction requirement does not apply to the following:

i. A financial-account number that identifies the property allegedly subject to forfeiture in a forfeiture proceeding;

ii. The record of an administrative or agency proceeding;

iii. The official record of a state-court proceeding;

iv. The record of a court or tribunal, if that record was not subject to the redaction requirement when originally filed;

v. A filing covered by FRCP 5.2(c) or FRCP 5.2(d); and

vi. A pro se filing in an action brought under 28 U.S.C.A. § 2241, 28 U.S.C.A. § 2254, or 28 U.S.C.A. § 2255. FRCP 5.2(b).

c. *Limitations on remote access to electronic files; Social Security appeals and immigration cases.* Unless the court orders otherwise, in an action for benefits under the Social Security Act, and in an action or proceeding relating to an order of removal, to relief from removal, or to immigration benefits or detention, access to an electronic file is authorized as follows:

i. The parties and their attorneys may have remote electronic access to any part of the case file, including the administrative record;

ii. Any other person may have electronic access to the full record at the courthouse, but may have remote electronic access only to:

- The docket maintained by the court; and
- An opinion, order, judgment, or other disposition of the court, but not any other part of the case file or the administrative record. FRCP 5.2(c).

d. *Filings made under seal.* The court may order that a filing be made under seal without redaction. The court may later unseal the filing or order the person who made the filing to file a redacted version for the public record. FRCP 5.2(d). For more information on sealing documents, refer to NY R USDCTSD CM/ECF, S.D.(I)(6).

e. *Protective orders.* For good cause, the court may by order in a case:

i. Require redaction of additional information; or

ii. Limit or prohibit a nonparty's remote electronic access to a document filed with the court. FRCP 5.2(e).

f. *Option for additional unredacted filing under seal.* A person making a redacted filing may also file an unredacted copy under seal. The court must retain the unredacted copy as part of the record. FRCP 5.2(f); NY R USDCTSD CM/ECF, S.D.(II)(21)(21.5).

g. *Option for filing a reference list.* A filing that contains redacted information may be filed together with a reference list that identifies each item of redacted information and specifies an appropriate identifier that uniquely corresponds to each item listed. The list must be filed under seal and may be amended as of right. Any reference in the case to a listed identifier will be construed to refer to the corresponding item of information. FRCP 5.2(g); NY R USDCTSD CM/ECF, S.D.(II)(21)(21.5).

h. *Responsibility for redaction.* It is the sole responsibility of counsel and the parties to be sure that all documents comply with the rules of this Court requiring redaction of personal identifiers. Neither the judge nor the Clerk of Court will review documents for compliance with these rules. NY R USDCTSD CM/ECF, S.D.(II)(21)(21.2).

i. *Waiver of protection of identifiers.* A person waives the protection of FRCP 5.2(a) as to the person's own information by filing it without redaction and not under seal. FRCP 5.2(h).

j. For more information on privacy and public access to ECF cases, refer to NY R USDCTSD CM/ECF, S.D.(II)(21).

5. *Individual judge practices.* Refer to the Miscellaneous section of this document for information on individual judge practices on formatting documents.

## F. Filing and Service Requirements

1. *Filing requirements.* Any paper after the complaint that is required to be served—together with a certificate of service—must be filed within a reasonable time after service. But disclosures under FRCP 26(a)(1) or FRCP 26(a)(2) and the following discovery requests and responses must not be filed until they are used in the proceeding or the court orders filing: depositions, interrogatories, requests for documents or tangible things or to permit entry onto land, and requests for admission. FRCP 5(d)(1). Refer to the United States District Court for the Southern District of New York KeyRules pleading and motion documents for information on filing with the court.

2. *Service requirements*

   a. *Service; When required*

      i. *In general.* Unless the Federal Rules of Civil Procedure provide otherwise, each of the following papers must be served on every party:

         • An order stating that service is required;

         • A pleading filed after the original complaint, unless the court orders otherwise under FRCP 5(c) because there are numerous defendants;

         • A discovery paper required to be served on a party, unless the court orders otherwise;

         • A written motion, except one that may be heard ex parte; and

         • A written notice, appearance, demand, or offer of judgment, or any similar paper. FRCP 5(a)(1).

      ii. *If a party fails to appear.* No service is required on a party who is in default for failing to appear. But a pleading that asserts a new claim for relief against such a party must be served on that party under FRCP 4. FRCP 5(a)(2).

      iii. *Seizing property.* If an action is begun by seizing property and no person is or need be named as a defendant, any service required before the filing of an appearance, answer, or claim must be made on the person who had custody or possession of the property when it was seized. FRCP 5(a)(3).

   b. *Service; How made*

      i. *Serving an attorney.* If a party is represented by an attorney, service under FRCP 5 must be made on the attorney unless the court orders service on the party. FRCP 5(b)(1).

      ii. *Service in general.* A paper is served under FRCP 5 by:

         • Handing it to the person;

- Leaving it: (1) at the person's office with a clerk or other person in charge or, if no one is in charge, in a conspicuous place in the office; or (2) if the person has no office or the office is closed, at the person's dwelling or usual place of abode with someone of suitable age and discretion who resides there;

- Mailing it to the person's last known address—in which event service is complete upon mailing;

- Leaving it with the court clerk if the person has no known address;

- Sending it by electronic means if the person consented in writing—in which event service is complete upon transmission, but is not effective if the serving party learns that it did not reach the person to be served; or

- Delivering it by any other means that the person consented to in writing—in which event service is complete when the person making service delivers it to the agency designated to make delivery. FRCP 5(b)(2).

iii. *Service by overnight delivery.* Service upon an attorney may be made by overnight delivery service. "Overnight delivery service" means any delivery service which regularly accepts items for overnight delivery. Overnight delivery service shall be deemed service by mail for purposes of FRCP 5 and FRCP 6. NY R USDCTS&ED Civ Rule 5.3.

iv. *Service by electronic means.* Parties serving and filing papers shall follow the instructions regarding Electronic Case Filing (ECF) published on the website of each respective Court. A paper served and filed by electronic means in accordance with such instructions is, for purposes of FRCP 5, served and filed in compliance with the Local Civil Rules of the United States District Courts for the Southern and Eastern Districts of New York. NY R USDCTS&ED Civ Rule 5.2(a). Parties have an obligation to review the Court's actual order, decree, or judgment (on ECF), which controls, and should not rely on the description on the docket or in the ECF Notice of Electronic Filing (NEF). NY R USDCTS&ED Civ Rule 5.2(c).

- *Notice of electronic filing (NEF).* In cases assigned to the ECF system, service is complete provided all parties receive a Notice of Electronic Filing (NEF), which is sent automatically by email from the Court (see the NEF for a list of who did/did not receive notice electronically). Transmission of the NEF constitutes service upon all Filing and Receiving Users who are listed as recipients of notice by electronic mail. NY R USDCTSD CM/ECF, S.D.(I)(9)(9.1). In cases assigned to the ECF system, if all parties receive a NEF, service is complete upon transmission of the NEF by the Court, and you are not required to serve a paper copy. NY R USDCTSD CM/ECF, S.D.(II)(19)(19.2). It remains the duty of Filing and Receiving Users to maintain current contact information with the court and to regularly review the docket sheet of the case. NY R USDCTSD CM/ECF, S.D.(I)(9)(9.1).

- *Mailing of court-initiated documents.* The Clerk's Office will no longer mail paper copies of court-initiated documents to Filing and Receiving Users. The Clerk's Office will mail copies of all court-initiated documents to pro se parties who have not registered as Filing or Receiving Users. NY R USDCTSD CM/ECF, S.D.(II)(19)(19.1).

- *No receipt of a NEF.* If any party does not receive a NEF, you are required to accomplish service on that party in the traditional manner, in paper form. NY R USDCTSD CM/ECF, S.D.(II)(19)(19.2). The NEF receipt will inform you who will receive notice of the filing "electronically" (by e-mail from the Court) and who will receive notice "by other means" (traditional service in paper form). NY R USDCTSD CM/ECF, S.D.(II)(19)(19.2).

- *Service on non-filing or non-receiving users.* Attorneys and pro se parties who are not Filing or Receiving Users must be served with a paper copy of any electronically filed pleading or other document. Service of such paper copy must be made according to the Federal Rules of Civil Procedure and the Local Civil Rules of the United States District Courts for the Southern and Eastern Districts of New York. NY R USDCTSD CM/ECF, S.D.(I)(9)(9.2). Such paper service must be documented by electronically filing proof of service. NY R USDCTSD CM/ECF, S.D.(I)(9)(9.2); NY R USDCTSD CM/ECF,

S.D.(II)(19)(19.2). Where the Clerk scans and electronically files pleadings and documents on behalf of a pro se party, the associated NEF constitutes service. NY R USDCTSD CM/ECF, S.D.(I)(9)(9.2).

- For more information on service by electronic means, refer to NY R USDCTSD CM/ECF, S.D.(II)(19).

    v. *Using court facilities.* If a local rule so authorizes, a party may use the court's transmission facilities to make service under FRCP 5(b)(2)(E). FRCP 5(b)(3).

  c. *Serving numerous defendants*

    i. *In general.* If an action involves an unusually large number of defendants, the court may, on motion or on its own, order that:

- Defendants' pleadings and replies to them need not be served on other defendants;

- Any crossclaim, counterclaim, avoidance, or affirmative defense in those pleadings and replies to them will be treated as denied or avoided by all other parties; and

- Filing any such pleading and serving it on the plaintiff constitutes notice of the pleading to all parties. FRCP 5(c)(1).

    ii. *Notifying parties.* A copy of every such order must be served on the parties as the court directs. FRCP 5(c)(2).

3. *Individual judge practices.* Refer to the Miscellaneous section of this document for information on individual judge practices on filing and serving documents.

# G. Hearings

1. There is no hearing contemplated in the federal statutes or rules for requests for production of documents.

# H. Forms

## 1. Federal Request for Production of Documents Forms

  a. Request; Production of documents for inspection and copying. AMJUR PP DEPOSITION § 498.

  b. Request for production, inspection and copying of documents, and inspection and photographing of things and real property. 3A FEDFORMS § 3556.

  c. Request for production of documents; Business records. 3A FEDFORMS § 3557.

  d. Request for production of documents; Patent case. 3A FEDFORMS § 3558.

  e. Request for production of documents; Government records and regulations. 3A FEDFORMS § 3559.

  f. Request for production of documents; Government personnel files, memoranda, minutes of meetings, and statistics. 3A FEDFORMS § 3560.

  g. Request for production of documents; Documents to be identified in physically separate but accompanying interrogatories under FRCP 33. 3A FEDFORMS § 3561.

  h. Request for production of documents; Employment discrimination. 3A FEDFORMS § 3562.

  i. Letter requesting production of files. 3A FEDFORMS § 3563.

  j. Request; Production of documents, records, and objects, under FRCP 34. FEDPROF § 23:394.

  k. Request; Production of documents for inspection and copying. FEDPROF § 23:395.

  l. Request; Production of documents for inspection and copying; Business records. FEDPROF § 23:396.

  m. Request; Production of objects for inspection and sampling. FEDPROF § 23:397.

  n. Request; Production of documents for inspection and copying; Government records and files. FEDPROF § 23:398.

  o. Request; Production of documents and things; Patent proceeding. FEDPROF § 23:399.

  p. Request; Production of documents and things; Trademark action. FEDPROF § 23:400.

q. Request; Production of documents; Trademark action; Likelihood of confusion. FEDPROF § 23:401.

r. Request; Production of documents; Automobile negligence. FEDPROF § 23:402.

s. Request; Production of documents; Premises liability. FEDPROF § 23:403.

t. Request; Production of documents for inspection and copying; Wrongful death due to forklift accident. FEDPROF § 23:404.

u. Request; Production of documents; Products liability. FEDPROF § 23:405.

v. Request; Production of documents; Collection of tariff. FEDPROF § 23:406.

w. Request; Production of medical records. FEDPROF § 23:407.

x. Request; Production of employment records. FEDPROF § 23:408.

y. Request; Production of education records. FEDPROF § 23:409.

z. Request; Production of decedent's records. FEDPROF § 23:410.

## I. Applicable Rules

1. *Federal rules*

   a. Serving and filing pleadings and other papers. FRCP 5.

   b. Privacy protection for filings made with the court. FRCP 5.2.

   c. Computing and extending time; Time for motion papers. FRCP 6.

   d. Pleadings allowed; Form of motions and other papers. FRCP 7.

   e. Form of pleadings. FRCP 10.

   f. Signing pleadings, motions, and other papers; Representations to the court; Sanctions. FRCP 11.

   g. Duty to disclose; General provisions governing discovery. FRCP 26.

   h. Stipulations about discovery procedure. FRCP 29.

   i. Producing documents, electronically stored information, and tangible things, or entering onto land, for inspection and other purposes. FRCP 34.

   j. Failure to make disclosures or to cooperate in discovery; Sanctions. FRCP 37.

2. *Local rules*

   a. Duty of attorneys in related cases. NY R USDCTS&ED Civ Rule 1.6.

   b. Electronic service and filing of documents. NY R USDCTS&ED Civ Rule 5.2.

   c. Service by overnight delivery. NY R USDCTS&ED Civ Rule 5.3.

   d. Computation of time. NY R USDCTS&ED Civ Rule 6.4.

   e. Form of pleadings, motions, and other papers. NY R USDCTS&ED Civ Rule 11.1.

   f. Assertion of claim of privilege. NY R USDCTS&ED Civ Rule 26.2.

   g. Uniform definitions in discovery requests. NY R USDCTS&ED Civ Rule 26.3.

   h. Cooperation among counsel in discovery. NY R USDCTS&ED Civ Rule 26.4.

   i. Form discovery requests. [NY R USDCTS&ED Civ Rule 26.5, as amended by NY ORDER 16-4212, effective September 26, 2016].

   j. Alternative dispute resolution (Southern District only). NY R USDCTS&ED Civ Rule 83.9.

   k. Electronic case filing rules and instructions. NY R USDCTSD CM/ECF, S.D.

   l. Related cases. NY R USDCTSD Div. Bus., Rule 13.

## J. Miscellaneous

**NOTE: Individual judges' rules may apply. For available judge-level information, refer to:**

DISTRICT JUDGE RONNIE ABRAMS: NY R USDCTSD Abrams-Civ Prac; NY R USDCTSD Abrams-Crim Prac; NY R USDCTSD Abrams-Pro Se; NY R USDCTSD Abrams-Case Mgt; NY R USDCTSD Abrams-Jury.

DISTRICT JUDGE DEBORAH A. BATTS: NY R USDCTSD Batts-Practices.

DISTRICT JUDGE RICHARD M. BERMAN: NY R USDCTSD Berman-Practices; NY R USDCTSD Berman-Default; NY R USDCTSD Berman-Sentencing; NY R USDCTSD Berman-Media.

DISTRICT JUDGE VINCENT L. BRICCETTI: NY R USDCTSD Briccetti-Practices; NY R USDCTSD Briccetti-Plan; NY R USDCTSD Briccetti-Notice.

DISTRICT JUDGE VERNON S. BRODERICK: NY R USDCTSD Broderick-Civil; NY R USDCTSD Broderick-Crim; NY R USDCTSD Broderick-Case Mgt; NY R USDCTSD Broderick-Jury.

DISTRICT JUDGE NAOMI REICE BUCHWALD: NY R USDCTSD Buchwald-Practices.

DISTRICT JUDGE VALERIE E. CAPRONI: NY R USDCTSD Caproni-Prac; NY R USDCTSD Caproni--Pro Se; NY R USDCTSD Caproni-Case Mgt; NY R USDCTSD Caproni-Crim Prac.

DISTRICT JUDGE ANDREW L. CARTER JR.: NY R USDCTSD Carter-Practices.

DISTRICT JUDGE KEVIN P. CASTEL: NY R USDCTSD Castel-Practices; NY R USDCTSD Castel-Default; NY R USDCTSD Castel-Scheduling; NY R USDCTSD Castel-Complex; NY R USDCTSD Castel-Trials; NY R USDCTSD Castel-Sentencing.

DISTRICT JUDGE DENISE L. COTE: NY R USDCTSD Cote-Civil Practices; NY R USDCTSD Cote-Pro Se; NY R USDCTSD Cote-Maritime Ord; NY R USDCTSD Cote-Crim Practices; NY R USDCTSD Cote-Crim Trials; NY R USDCTSD Cote-Sentencing.

DISTRICT JUDGE PAUL A. CROTTY: NY R USDCTSD Crotty-Practices; NY R USDCTSD Crotty-Sentencing; NY R USDCTSD Crotty-Calls; NY R USDCTSD Crotty-Scheduling.

DISTRICT JUDGE GEORGE B. DANIELS: NY R USDCTSD Daniels-Practices.

DISTRICT JUDGE KEVIN T. DUFFY: NY R USDCTSD Duffy-Practices.

DISTRICT JUDGE PAUL A. ENGELMAYER: NY R USDCTSD Engelmayer-Practices; NY R USDCTSD Engelmayer-Scheduling; NY R USDCTSD Engelmayer-Sentencing; NY R USDCTSD Engelmayer-Pro Se; NY R USDCTSD Engelmayer-Crim.

DISTRICT JUDGE KATHERINE POLK FAILLA: NY R USDCTSD Failla-Civ Prac; NY R USDCTSD Failla-Crim Prac; NY R USDCTSD Failla-Case Mgt.

DISTRICT JUDGE KATHERINE B. FORREST: NY R USDCTSD Forrest-Civil Prac; NY R USDCTSD Forrest-Crim Prac; NY R USDCTSD Forrest-Crim Pretrial; NY R USDCTSD Forrest-Scheduling; NY R US-DCTSD Forrest-Patent Scheduling; NY R USDCTSD Forrest-Sentencing; NY R USDCTSD Forrest-Order 1; NY R USDCTSD Forrest-Order 2.

DISTRICT JUDGE JESSE M. FURMAN: NY R USDCTSD Furman-Civil Prac; NY R USDCTSD Furman-Crim Prac; NY R USDCTSD Furman-Pro Se Prac; NY R USDCTSD Furman-Trials; NY R USDCTSD Furman-Scheduling; NY R USDCTSD Furman-Rights.

DISTRICT JUDGE PAUL G. GARDEPHE: NY R USDCTSD Gardephe-Civ Prac; NY R USDCTSD Gardephe-Pretrial; NY R USDCTSD Gardephe-Prot Ord; NY R USDCTSD Gardephe-Maritime; NY R USDCTSD Gardephe-Crim Prac; NY R USDCTSD Gardephe-Trial.

DISTRICT JUDGE THOMAS P. GRIESA: NY R USDCTSD Griesa-Practices.

DISTRICT JUDGE CHARLES S. HAIGHT: NY R USDCTSD Haight-Practices.

DISTRICT JUDGE ALVIN K. HELLERSTEIN: NY R USDCTSD Hellerstein-Practices; NY R USDCTSD Hellerstein--Sept 11.

DISTRICT JUDGE LEWIS A. KAPLAN: NY R USDCTSD Kaplan-Practices; NY R USDCTSD Kaplan-Sentencing.

DISTRICT JUDGE KENNETH M. KARAS: NY R USDCTSD Karas-Practices; NY R USDCTSD Karas-Case Mgt; NY R USDCTSD Karas-Default; NY R USDCTSD Karas-Sentencing; NY R USDCTSD Karas-Rights.

DISTRICT JUDGE JOHN F. KEENAN: NY R USDCTSD Keenan-Practices.

DISTRICT JUDGE JOHN G. KOELTL: NY R USDCTSD Koeltl-Practices.

DISTRICT JUDGE VICTOR MARRERO: NY R USDCTSD Marrero-Practices; NY R USDCTSD Marrero-Scheduling; NY R USDCTSD Marrero-Default; NY R USDCTSD Marrero-Trial Proc.

DISTRICT JUDGE COLLEEN McMAHON: NY R USDCTSD McMahon-Practices; NY R USDCTSD McMahon-RICO; NY R USDCTSD McMahon-Copies; NY R USDCTSD McMahon-Scheduling; NY R US-DCTSD McMahon-Elec Disc; NY R USDCTSD McMahon-Sentencing.

DISTRICT JUDGE ALISON J. NATHAN: NY R USDCTSD Nathan-Civ Prac; NY R USDCTSD Nathan-Crim Prac; NY R USDCTSD Nathan-Pro Se; NY R USDCTSD Nathan-Scheduling.

DISTRICT JUDGE J. PAUL OETKEN: NY R USDCTSD Oetken-Civ Prac; NY R USDCTSD Oetken-Case Mgt; NY R USDCTSD Oetken-Crim Prac; NY R USDCTSD Oetken-Pro Se.

DISTRICT JUDGE WILLIAM H. PAULEY, III: NY R USDCTSD Pauley-Crim Cases; NY R USDCTSD Pauley-Practices.

DISTRICT JUDGE LORETTA A. PRESKA: NY R USDCTSD Preska-Practices.

DISTRICT JUDGE JED S. RAKOFF: NY R USDCTSD Rakoff-Practices; NY R USDCTSD Rakoff-Scheduling; NY R USDCTSD Rakoff-Prot Ord; NY R USDCTSD Rakoff-Maritime Ord.

DISTRICT JUDGE EDGARDO RAMOS: NY R USDCTSD Ramos--Practices; NY R USDCTSD Ramos-Case Mgt.

DISTRICT JUDGE NELSON S. ROMAN: NY R USDCTSD Roman-Civ Prac; NY R USDCTSD Roman-Pro Se; NY R USDCTSD Roman-Crim Prac; NY R USDCTSD Roman-Case Mgt.

DISTRICT JUDGE LEONARD B. SAND: NY R USDCTSD Sand-Practices.

DISTRICT JUDGE LORNA G. SCHOFIELD: NY R USDCTSD Schofield-Civ Prac; NY R USDCTSD Schofield-Crim Prac; NY R USDCTSD Schofield-Sched; NY R USDCTSD Schofield-Pro Se; NY R USDCTSD Schofield-Advice.

DISTRICT JUDGE CATHY SEIBEL: NY R USDCTSD Seibel-Practices.

DISTRICT JUDGE LOUIS L. STANTON: NY R USDCTSD Stanton-Practices; NY R USDCTSD Stanton-Pretrial.

DISTRICT JUDGE SIDNEY H. STEIN: NY R USDCTSD Stein-Practices.

DISTRICT JUDGE RICHARD J. SULLIVAN: NY R USDCTSD Sullivan-Practices; NY R USDCTSD Sullivan-Scheduling; NY R USDCTSD Sullivan-Sentencing; NY R USDCTSD Sullivan-Juries; NY R USDCTSD Sullivan-Trial; NY R USDCTSD Sullivan-Default.

DISTRICT JUDGE LAURA TAYLOR SWAIN: NY R USDCTSD Swain-Practices; NY R USDCTSD Swain-Trial; NY R USDCTSD Swain-Crim Trial; NY R USDCTSD Swain-Juries; NY R USDCTSD Swain-Sentencing; NY R USDCTSD Swain-Rights.

DISTRICT JUDGE ROBERT W. SWEET: NY R USDCTSD Sweet-Practices.

DISTRICT JUDGE ANALISA TORRES: NY R USDCTSD Torres-Civ Prac; NY R USDCTSD Torres-Pro Se; NY R USDCTSD Torres-Scheduling.

DISTRICT JUDGE KIMBA M. WOOD: NY R USDCTSD Wood-Practices; NY R USDCTSD Wood-Scheduling; NY R USDCTSD Wood-Discovery; NY R USDCTSD Wood-RICO; NY R USDCTSD Wood-Juries; NY R USDCTSD Wood-Trial; NY R USDCTSD Wood-Media.

DISTRICT JUDGE GREGORY H. WOODS: NY R USDCTSD Woods-Civ Prac; NY R USDCTSD Woods-Pro Se; NY R USDCTSD Woods-Sched; NY R USDCTSD Woods-Crim Prac; NY R USDCTSD Woods-Protect Order; NY R USDCTSD Woods-Speedy Trial.

MAGISTRATE JUDGE JAMES L. COTT: NY R USDCTSD Cott-Practices; NY R USDCTSD Cott-Settlement.

MAGISTRATE JUDGE PAUL E. DAVISON: NY R USDCTSD Davison-Practices.

MAGISTRATE JUDGE RONALD L. ELLIS: NY R USDCTSD Ellis-Practices.

MAGISTRATE JUDGE KEVIN N. FOX: NY R USDCTSD Fox-Practices; NY R USDCTSD Fox-Settlement.

MAGISTRATE JUDGE JAMES C. FRANCIS: NY R USDCTSD Francis-Practices.

MAGISTRATE JUDGE DEBRA FREEMAN: NY R USDCTSD Freeman-Practices; NY R USDCTSD Freeman-Settlement.

MAGISTRATE JUDGE GABRIEL W. GORENSTEIN: NY R USDCTSD Gorenstein-Practices; NY R US-DCTSD Gorenstein-Ackn.

MAGISTRATE JUDGE FRANK MAAS: NY R USDCTSD Maas-Practices; NY R USDCTSD Maas-Discontinuance; NY R USDCTSD Maas-Conf; NY R USDCTSD Maas-Settlement.

MAGISTRATE JUDGE JUDITH C. McCARTHY: NY R USDCTSD McCarthy-Practices; NY R USDCTSD McCarthy-Conduct.

MAGISTRATE JUDGE BARBARA MOSES: NY R USDCTSD Moses-Practices.

MAGISTRATE JUDGE SARAH NETBURN: NY R USDCTSD Netburn-Civil; NY R USDCTSD Netburn-Settlement; NY R USDCTSD Netburn-Case Mgt; NY R USDCTSD Netburn--Pro Se.

MAGISTRATE JUDGE ANDREW J. PECK: NY R USDCTSD Peck-Practices; NY R USDCTSD Peck-Order; NY R USDCTSD Peck-Rule 502(d).

MAGISTRATE JUDGE HENRY PITMAN: NY R USDCTSD Pitman-Practices.

MAGISTRATE JUDGE LISA MARGARET SMITH: NY R USDCTSD Smith-Practices; NY R USDCTSD Smith-Trials.

# Requests, Notices and Applications
# Request for Admissions

## Document Last Updated September 2016

### A. Checklist

(I)  ❑ Matters to be considered by requesting party

    (a)  ❑ Required documents

        (1)  ❑ Request for admissions

    (b)  ❑ Supplemental documents

        (1)  ❑ Document(s)

        (2)  ❑ Certificate of service

    (c)  ❑ Timing

        (1)  ❑ A party may not seek discovery from any source before the parties have conferred as required by FRCP 26(f), except in a proceeding exempted from initial disclosure under FRCP 26(a)(1)(B), or when authorized by the Federal Rules of Civil Procedure, by stipulation, or by court order

(II)  ❑ Matters to be considered by responding party

    (a)  ❑ Required documents

        (1)  ❑ Response to request for admissions

    (b)  ❑ Supplemental documents

        (1)  ❑ Written information regarding assertion of privilege

        (2)  ❑ Certificate of service

    (c)  ❑ Timing

        (1)  ❑ A matter is admitted unless, within thirty (30) days after being served, the party to whom the request is directed serves on the requesting party a written answer or objection addressed to the matter and signed by the party or its attorney

### B. Timing

1. *Request for admissions.* Without leave of court or written stipulation, requests for admission may not be served before the time specified in FRCP 26(d). FEDPROC § 26:706.

2. *Timing of discovery, generally.* A party may not seek discovery from any source before the parties have

conferred as required by FRCP 26(f), except in a proceeding exempted from initial disclosure under FRCP 26(a)(1)(B), or when authorized by the Federal Rules of Civil Procedure, by stipulation, or by court order. FRCP 26(d)(1).

3. *Computation of time*

    a. *Computing time.* FRCP 6 applies in computing any time period specified in the Federal Rules of Civil Procedure, in any local rule or court order, or in any statute that does not specify a method of computing time. FRCP 6(a). In computing any period of time prescribed or allowed by the Local Civil Rules of the United States District Courts for the Southern and Eastern Districts of New York or the Local Admiralty and Maritime Rules, the provisions of FRCP 6 shall apply unless otherwise stated. NY R USDCTS&ED Civ Rule 6.4.

        i. *Period stated in days or a longer unit.* When the period is stated in days or a longer unit of time:

- Exclude the day of the event that triggers the period;

- Count every day, including intermediate Saturdays, Sundays, and legal holidays; and

- Include the last day of the period, but if the last day is a Saturday, Sunday, or legal holiday, the period continues to run until the end of the next day that is not a Saturday, Sunday, or legal holiday. FRCP 6(a)(1). In the Local Civil Rules of the United States District Courts for the Southern and Eastern Districts of New York, as in the Federal Rules of Civil Procedure as amended effective December 1, 2009, Saturdays, Sundays, and legal holidays are no longer excluded in computing periods of time. If the last day of the period is a Saturday, Sunday, or legal holiday, the period continues to run until the end of the next day that is not a Saturday, Sunday, or legal holiday. NY R USDCTS&ED Civ Rule 6.4.

        ii. *Period stated in hours.* When the period is stated in hours:

- Begin counting immediately on the occurrence of the event that triggers the period;

- Count every hour, including hours during intermediate Saturdays, Sundays, and legal holidays; and

- If the period would end on a Saturday, Sunday, or legal holiday, the period continues to run until the same time on the next day that is not a Saturday, Sunday, or legal holiday. FRCP 6(a)(2). In the Local Civil Rules of the United States District Courts for the Southern and Eastern Districts of New York, as in the Federal Rules of Civil Procedure as amended effective December 1, 2009, Saturdays, Sundays, and legal holidays are no longer excluded in computing periods of time. If the last day of the period is a Saturday, Sunday, or legal holiday, the period continues to run until the end of the next day that is not a Saturday, Sunday, or legal holiday. NY R USDCTS&ED Civ Rule 6.4.

        iii. *Inaccessibility of the clerk's office.* Unless the court orders otherwise, if the clerk's office is inaccessible:

- On the last day for filing under FRCP 6(a)(1), then the time for filing is extended to the first accessible day that is not a Saturday, Sunday, or legal holiday; or

- During the last hour for filing under FRCP 6(a)(2), then the time for filing is extended to the same time on the first accessible day that is not a Saturday, Sunday, or legal holiday. FRCP 6(a)(3).

        iv. *"Last day" defined.* Unless a different time is set by a statute, local rule, or court order, the last day ends:

- For electronic filing, at midnight in the court's time zone; and

- For filing by other means, when the clerk's office is scheduled to close. FRCP 6(a)(4).

        v. *"Next day" defined.* The "next day" is determined by continuing to count forward when the period is measured after an event and backward when measured before an event. FRCP 6(a)(5).

        vi. *"Legal holiday" defined.* "Legal holiday" means:

- The day set aside by statute for observing New Year's Day, Martin Luther King Jr.'s

Birthday, Washington's Birthday, Memorial Day, Independence Day, Labor Day, Columbus Day, Veterans' Day, Thanksgiving Day, or Christmas Day;

- Any day declared a holiday by the President or Congress; and

- For periods that are measured after an event, any other day declared a holiday by the state where the district court is located. FRCP 6(a)(6).

b. *Computation of electronic filing deadlines.* You can file electronically twenty-four (24) hours a day, seven (7) days a week, three hundred sixty-five (365) days a year. NY R USDCTSD CM/ECF, S.D.(II)(13)(13.10). Electronic filing must be completed before midnight local time where the Court is located in order to be considered timely filed that day. NY R USDCTSD CM/ECF, S.D.(I)(3)(3.3); NY R USDCTSD CM/ECF, S.D.(II)(13)(13.10); NY R USDCTSD CM/ECF, S.D.(II)(19)(19.4). An electronically filed document is deemed filed on the "filed on" date indicated on the Notice of Electronic Filing (NEF). NY R USDCTSD CM/ECF, S.D.(II)(13)(13.11).

   i. *Technical failures.* A Filing User whose filing is made untimely as the result of a technical failure may seek appropriate relief from the Court. NY R USDCTSD CM/ECF, S.D.(I)(11). If you missed a filing deadline when the ECF system was out of order, attach a statement to your filing explaining how the interruption in service prevented you from filing in a timely fashion. NY R USDCTSD CM/ECF, S.D.(II)(23)(23.5).

c. *Extending time*

   i. *In general.* When an act may or must be done within a specified time, the court may, for good cause, extend the time:

- With or without motion or notice if the court acts, or if a request is made, before the original time or its extension expires; or

- On motion made after the time has expired if the party failed to act because of excusable neglect. FRCP 6(b)(1).

   ii. *Exceptions.* A court must not extend the time to act under FRCP 50(b), FRCP 50(d), FRCP 52(b), FRCP 59(b), FRCP 59(d), FRCP 59(e), and FRCP 60(b). FRCP 6(b)(2).

   iii. Refer to the United States District Court for the Southern District of New York KeyRules Motion for Continuance/Extension of Time document for more information on extending time.

d. *Additional time after certain kinds of service.* When a party may or must act within a specified time after service and service is made under FRCP 5(b)(2)(C), FRCP 5(b)(2)(D), FRCP 5(b)(2)(E), or FRCP 5(b)(2)(F), three (3) days are added after the period would otherwise expire under FRCP 6(a). FRCP 6(d). Overnight delivery service shall be deemed service by mail for purposes of FRCP 5 and FRCP 6. NY R USDCTS&ED Civ Rule 5.3.

4. *Individual judge practices.* Refer to the Miscellaneous section of this document for information on individual judge practices on timing of documents.

## C. General Requirements

1. *General provisions governing discovery*

  a. *Discovery scope and limits*

   i. *Scope in general.* Unless otherwise limited by court order, the scope of discovery is as follows: Parties may obtain discovery regarding any nonprivileged matter that is relevant to any party's claim or defense and proportional to the needs of the case, considering the importance of the issues at stake in the action, the amount in controversy, the parties' relative access to relevant information, the parties' resources, the importance of the discovery in resolving the issues, and whether the burden or expense of the proposed discovery outweighs its likely benefit. Information within this scope of discovery need not be admissible in evidence to be discoverable. FRCP 26(b)(1).

   ii. *Limitations on frequency and extent*

- *When permitted.* By order, the court may alter the limits in the Federal Rules of Civil Procedure on the number of depositions and interrogatories or on the length of depositions under FRCP 30. By order or local rule, the court may also limit the number of requests under FRCP 36. FRCP 26(b)(2)(A).

- *Specific limitations on electronically stored information.* A party need not provide discovery of electronically stored information from sources that the party identifies as not reasonably accessible because of undue burden or cost. On motion to compel discovery or for a protective order, the party from whom discovery is sought must show that the information is not reasonably accessible because of undue burden or cost. If that showing is made, the court may nonetheless order discovery from such sources if the requesting party shows good cause, considering the limitations of FRCP 26(b)(2)(C). The court may specify conditions for the discovery. FRCP 26(b)(2)(B).

- *When required.* On motion or on its own, the court must limit the frequency or extent of discovery otherwise allowed by the Federal Rules of Civil Procedure or by local rule if it determines that: (1) the discovery sought is unreasonably cumulative or duplicative, or can be obtained from some other source that is more convenient, less burdensome, or less expensive; (2) the party seeking discovery has had ample opportunity to obtain the information by discovery in the action; or (3) the proposed discovery is outside the scope permitted by FRCP 26(b)(1). FRCP 26(b)(2)(C).

iii.  *Trial preparation; Materials*

- *Documents and tangible things.* Ordinarily, a party may not discover documents and tangible things that are prepared in anticipation of litigation or for trial by or for another party or its representative (including the other party's attorney, consultant, surety, indemnitor, insurer, or agent). But, subject to FRCP 26(b)(4), those materials may be discovered if: (1) they are otherwise discoverable under FRCP 26(b)(1); and (2) the party shows that it has substantial need for the materials to prepare its case and cannot, without undue hardship, obtain their substantial equivalent by other means. FRCP 26(b)(3)(A).

- *Protection against disclosure.* If the court orders discovery of those materials, it must protect against disclosure of the mental impressions, conclusions, opinions, or legal theories of a party's attorney or other representative concerning the litigation. FRCP 26(b)(3)(B).

- *Previous statement.* Any party or other person may, on request and without the required showing, obtain the person's own previous statement about the action or its subject matter. If the request is refused, the person may move for a court order, and FRCP 37(a)(5) applies to the award of expenses. A previous statement is either: (1) a written statement that the person has signed or otherwise adopted or approved; or (2) a contemporaneous stenographic, mechanical, electrical, or other recording—or a transcription of it—that recites substantially verbatim the person's oral statement. FRCP 26(b)(3)(C).

iv.  *Trial preparation; Experts*

- *Deposition of an expert who may testify.* A party may depose any person who has been identified as an expert whose opinions may be presented at trial. If FRCP 26(a)(2)(B) requires a report from the expert, the deposition may be conducted only after the report is provided. FRCP 26(b)(4)(A).

- *Trial-preparation protection for draft reports or disclosures.* FRCP 26(b)(3)(A) and FRCP 26(b)(3)(B) protect drafts of any report or disclosure required under FRCP 26(a)(2), regardless of the form in which the draft is recorded. FRCP 26(b)(4)(B).

- *Trial-preparation protection for communications between a party's attorney and expert witnesses.* FRCP 26(b)(3)(A) and FRCP 26(b)(3)(B) protect communications between the party's attorney and any witness required to provide a report under FRCP 26(a)(2)(B), regardless of the form of the communications, except to the extent that the communications: (1) relate to compensation for the expert's study or testimony; (2) identify facts or data that the party's attorney provided and that the expert considered in forming the opinions to be expressed; or (3) identify assumptions that the party's attorney provided and that the expert relied on in forming the opinions to be expressed. FRCP 26(b)(4)(C).

- *Expert employed only for trial preparation.* Ordinarily, a party may not, by interrogatories or deposition, discover facts known or opinions held by an expert who has been retained or specially employed by another party in anticipation of litigation or to prepare for trial and who is not expected to be called as a witness at trial. But a party may do so only: (1) as provided in FRCP 35(b); or (2) on showing exceptional circumstances under which it is impracticable for the party to obtain facts or opinions on the same subject by other means. FRCP 26(b)(4)(D).

- *Payment.* Unless manifest injustice would result, the court must require that the party seeking discovery: (1) pay the expert a reasonable fee for time spent in responding to discovery under FRCP 26(b)(4)(A) or FRCP 26(b)(4)(D); and (2) for discovery FRCP 26(b)(4)(D), also pay the other party a fair portion of the fees and expenses it reasonably incurred in obtaining the expert's facts and opinions. FRCP 26(b)(4)(E).

v. *Claiming privilege or protecting trial-preparation materials*

- *Information withheld.* When a party withholds information otherwise discoverable by claiming that the information is privileged or subject to protection as trial-preparation material, the party must: (1) expressly make the claim; and (2) describe the nature of the documents, communications, or tangible things not produced or disclosed—and do so in a manner that, without revealing information itself privileged or protected, will enable other parties to assess the claim. FRCP 26(b)(5)(A). Unless otherwise agreed by the parties or directed by the Court, where a claim of privilege is asserted in objecting to any means of discovery or disclosure, including but not limited to a deposition, and an answer is not provided on the basis of such assertion, (1) the person asserting the privilege shall identify the nature of the privilege (including work product) which is being claimed and, if the privilege is governed by state law, indicate the state's privilege rule being invoked; and (2) the following information shall be provided in the objection, or (in the case of a deposition) in response to questions by the questioner, unless divulgence of such information would cause disclosure of the allegedly privileged information: (A) for documents: (i) the type of document, e.g., letter or memorandum; (ii) the general subject matter of the document; (iii) the date of the document; and (iv) the author of the document, the addressees of the document, and any other recipients, and, where not apparent, the relationship of the author, addressees, and recipients to each other; (B) for oral communications: (i) the name of the person making the communication and the names of persons present while the communication was made and, where not apparent, the relationship of the persons present to the person making the communication; (ii) the date and place of communication; and (iii) the general subject matter of the communication. NY R USDCTS&ED Civ Rule 26.2(a). Where a claim of privilege is asserted in response to discovery or disclosure other than a deposition, and information is not provided on the basis of such assertion, the information set forth in NY R USDCTS&ED Civ Rule 26.2(a) shall be furnished in writing at the time of the response to such discovery or disclosure, unless otherwise ordered by the Court. NY R USDCTS&ED Civ Rule 26.2(b).

- *Information produced.* If information produced in discovery is subject to a claim of privilege or of protection as trial-preparation material, the party making the claim may notify any party that received the information of the claim and the basis for it. After being notified, a party must promptly return, sequester, or destroy the specified information and any copies it has; must not use or disclose the information until the claim is resolved; must take reasonable steps to retrieve the information if the party disclosed it before being notified; and may promptly present the information to the court under seal for a determination of the claim. The producing party must preserve the information until the claim is resolved. FRCP 26(b)(5)(B).

- *Efficient means of providing information regarding claims of privilege.* Efficient means of providing information regarding claims of privilege are encouraged, and parties are encouraged to agree upon measures that further this end. For example, when asserting privilege on the same basis with respect to multiple documents, it is presumptively proper to provide the information required by NY R USDCTS&ED Civ Rule 26.2 by group or category. A party receiving a privilege log that groups documents or otherwise departs from a document-by-document or communication-by-communication listing may not object solely on that basis, but may object if the substantive information required by NY R USDCTS&ED Civ Rule 26.2 has not been provided in a comprehensible form. NY R USDCTS&ED Civ Rule 26.2(c).

b. *Protective orders.* A party or any person from whom discovery is sought may move for a protective order in the court where the action is pending—or as an alternative on matters relating to a deposition, in the court for the district where the deposition will be taken. FRCP 26(c)(1). Refer to the United States District Court for the Southern District of New York KeyRules Motion for Protective Order document for more information.

c. *Sequence of discovery.* Unless the parties stipulate or the court orders otherwise for the parties' and witnesses' convenience and in the interests of justice: (1) methods of discovery may be used in any sequence; and (2) discovery by one party does not require any other party to delay its discovery. FRCP 26(d)(3).

d. *Uniform definitions in discovery requests.* The full text of the definitions and rules of construction set forth in NY R USDCTS&ED Civ Rule 26.3(c) and NY R USDCTS&ED Civ Rule 26.3(d) is deemed incorporated by reference into all discovery requests. No discovery request shall use broader definitions or rules of construction than those set forth in NY R USDCTS&ED Civ Rule 26.3(c) and NY R USDCTS&ED Civ Rule 26.3(d). NY R USDCTS&ED Civ Rule 26.3 shall not preclude (1) the definition of other terms specific to the particular litigation, (2) the use of abbreviations, or (3) a more narrow definition of a term defined in NY R USDCTS&ED Civ Rule 26.3(c). NY R USDCTS&ED Civ Rule 26.3(a). NY R USDCTS&ED Civ Rule 26.3 is not intended to broaden or narrow the scope of discovery permitted by the Federal Rules of Civil Procedure. NY R USDCTS&ED Civ Rule 26.3(b).

    i. *Definitions.* The following definitions apply to all discovery requests:

- *Communication.* The term "communication" means the transmittal of information (in the form of facts, ideas, inquiries or otherwise). NY R USDCTS&ED Civ Rule 26.3(c)(1).

- *Document.* The term "document" is defined to be synonymous in meaning and equal in scope to the usage of the term "documents or electronically stored information" in FRCP 34(a)(1)(A). A draft or non-identical copy is a separate document within the meaning of this term. NY R USDCTS&ED Civ Rule 26.3(c)(2).

- *Identify (with respect to persons).* When referring to a person, "to identify" means to give, to the extent known, the person's full name, present or last known address, and when referring to a natural person, additionally, the present or last known place of employment. Once a person has been identified in accordance with NY R USDCTS&ED Civ Rule 26.3(c)(3), only the name of that person need be listed in response to subsequent discovery requesting the identification of that person. NY R USDCTS&ED Civ Rule 26.3(c)(3).

- *Identify (with respect to documents).* When referring to documents, "to identify" means to give, to the extent known, the (1) type of document; (2) general subject matter; (3) date of the document; and (4) author(s), addressee(s) and recipient(s). In the alternative, the responding party may produce the documents, together with identifying information sufficient to satisfy FRCP 33(d). NY R USDCTS&ED Civ Rule 26.3(c)(4).

- *Parties.* The terms "plaintiff" and "defendant" as well as a party's full or abbreviated name or a pronoun referring to a party mean the party and, where applicable, its officers, directors, employees, partners, corporate parent, subsidiaries or affiliates. This definition is not intended to impose a discovery obligation on any person who is not a party to the litigation. NY R USDCTS&ED Civ Rule 26.3(c)(5).

- *Person.* The term "person" is defined as any natural person or any legal entity, including, without limitation, any business or governmental entity or association. NY R USDCTS&ED Civ Rule 26.3(c)(6).

- *Concerning.* The term "concerning" means relating to, referring to, describing, evidencing or constituting. NY R USDCTS&ED Civ Rule 26.3(c)(7).

ii. *Rules of construction.* The following rules of construction apply to all discovery requests:

- *All/any/each.* The terms "all," "any," and "each" shall each be construed as encompassing any and all. NY R USDCTS&ED Civ Rule 26.3(d)(1).

- *And/or.* The connectives "and" and "or" shall be construed either disjunctively or conjunctively as necessary to bring within the scope of the discovery request all responses that might otherwise be construed to be outside of its scope. NY R USDCTS&ED Civ Rule 26.3(d)(2).

- *Number.* The use of the singular form of any word includes the plural and vice versa. NY R USDCTS&ED Civ Rule 26.3(d)(3).

e. *Cooperation among counsel in discovery.* Counsel are expected to cooperate with each other, consistent with the interests of their clients, in all phases of the discovery process and to be courteous in their dealings with each other, including in matters relating to scheduling and timing of various discovery procedures. NY R USDCTS&ED Civ Rule 26.4(a).

  i. Discovery requests shall be read reasonably in the recognition that the attorney serving them generally does not have the information being sought and the attorney receiving them generally does have such information or can obtain it from the client. NY R USDCTS&ED Civ Rule 26.4(b).

f. *Standard discovery in prisoner pro se actions.* For information on discovery in prisoner pro se actions, refer to NY R USDCTS&ED Civ Rule 33.2.

2. *Request for admissions*

a. *Scope.* A party may serve on any other party a written request to admit, for purposes of the pending action only, the truth of any matters within the scope of FRCP 26(b)(1) relating to: (1) facts, the application of law to fact, or opinions about either; and (2) the genuineness of any described documents. FRCP 36(a)(1).

  i. A party may serve a request for admission even though the party has the burden of proving the matters asserted therein because FRCP 36 permits requests for admission to address claims of the party seeking discovery, and generally, the party asserting a claim bears the burden of proof thereon. FEDPROC § 26:715.

b. *Number.* FRCP 36 does not limit a party to a single request, or set of requests, for admissions. But FRCP 26(b)(2)(A) authorizes courts to limit the number of requests by order or local rule. In addition, the court has power to protect a party from harassment by repeated requests for admissions, but will not bar such repeated requests when the circumstances of the case justify them. Even a second request about the same fact or the genuineness of the same document is permissible if circumstances warrant a renewed request. FPP § 2258.

c. *Form.* Each matter must be separately stated. FRCP 36(a)(2). The party called upon to respond should not be required to go through a document and assume the responsibility of determining what facts it is being requested to admit. FPP § 2258. Each request for an admission should be phrased simply and directly so that it can be admitted or denied without explanation. FPP § 2258; United Coal Cos. v. Powell Const. Co., 839 F.2d 958, 968 (3d Cir. 1988).

  i. A request for an admission need not state the source of information about the matter for which the request is made. FPP § 2258.

d. *Form discovery requests.* Attorneys using form discovery requests shall review them to ascertain that they are consistent with the scope of discovery under FRCP 26(b)(1). Non-compliant requests shall not be used. NY R USDCTS&ED Civ Rule 26.5.

e. *Effect of an admission; Withdrawing or amending it.* A matter admitted under FRCP 36 is conclusively established unless the court, on motion, permits the admission to be withdrawn or amended. Subject to FRCP 16(e), the court may permit withdrawal or amendment if it would promote the presentation of the merits of the action and if the court is not persuaded that it would prejudice the requesting party in maintaining or defending the action on the merits. An admission under FRCP 36 is not an admission for any other purpose and cannot be used against the party in any other proceeding. FRCP 36(b).

f. *Motion to compel.* The motion to compel discovery provided by FRCP 37(a) does not apply to a failure to respond to a request for admissions. The automatic admission from a failure to respond is a sufficient remedy for the party who made the request. If, however, a request is objected to, or the requesting party thinks that a response to a request is insufficient, it may move under FRCP 36(a)(6) to determine the sufficiency of the answers or objections. FPP § 2265.

g. *Motion regarding the sufficiency of an answer or objection.* The requesting party may move to determine the sufficiency of an answer or objection. Unless the court finds an objection justified, it must order that an answer be served. On finding that an answer does not comply with FRCP 36, the court may order either that the matter is admitted or that an amended answer be served. The court may defer its final decision until a pretrial conference or a specified time before trial. FRCP 37(a)(5) applies to an award of expenses. FRCP 36(a)(6). Refer to the United States District Court for the Southern District of New York KeyRules Motion for Discovery Sanctions document for more information on sanctions.

3. *Sanctions for failure to cooperate in discovery.* The pattern of sanctions for FRCP 36 is somewhat different from that for the other discovery rules. The most important sanctions are two:

   a. A failure to respond to a request is deemed an admission of the matter to which the request is directed; and

   b. A party who, without good reason, refuses to admit a matter will be required to pay the costs incurred in proving that matter. FPP § 2265. If a party fails to admit what is requested under FRCP 36 and if the requesting party later proves a document to be genuine or the matter true, the requesting party may move that the party who failed to admit pay the reasonable expenses, including attorney's fees, incurred in making that proof. The court must so order unless:

      i. The request was held objectionable under FRCP 36(a);

      ii. The admission sought was of no substantial importance;

      iii. The party failing to admit had a reasonable ground to believe that it might prevail on the matter; or

      iv. There was other good reason for the failure to admit. FRCP 37(c)(2).

   c. Refer to the United States District Court for the Southern District of New York KeyRules Motion for Discovery Sanctions document for more information on sanctions.

4. *Stipulations about discovery procedure.* Unless the court orders otherwise, the parties may stipulate that: (1) a deposition may be taken before any person, at any time or place, on any notice, and in the manner specified—in which event it may be used in the same way as any other deposition; and (2) other procedures governing or limiting discovery be modified—but a stipulation extending the time for any form of discovery must have court approval if it would interfere with the time set for completing discovery, for hearing a motion, or for trial. FRCP 29.

5. *Complex civil cases.* For information on procedures for complex civil cases, refer to NY R USDCTSD Order 11 Misc 00388.

6. *Related cases.* It shall be the continuing duty of each attorney appearing in any civil or criminal case to bring promptly to the attention of the Court all facts which said attorney believes are relevant to a determination that said case and one or more pending civil or criminal cases should be heard by the same Judge, in order to avoid unnecessary duplication of judicial effort. As soon as the attorney becomes aware of such relationship, said attorney shall notify the Judges to whom the cases have been assigned. NY R USDCTS&ED Civ Rule 1.6(a). If counsel fails to comply with NY R USDCTS&ED Civ Rule 1.6(a), the Court may assess reasonable costs directly against counsel whose action has obstructed the effective administration of the Court's business. NY R USDCTS&ED Civ Rule 1.6(b).

   a. *Determination of relatedness.* Subject to the limitations set forth in NY R USDCTSD Div. Bus., Rule 13(a)(2), a civil case, bankruptcy appeal, or motion to withdraw the bankruptcy reference will be deemed related to one or more civil cases, appeals or motions when the interests of justice and efficiency will be served. In determining relatedness, a judge will consider whether (A) the actions concern the same or substantially similar parties, property, transactions or events; (B) there is substantial factual overlap; (C) the parties could be subjected to conflicting orders; and (D) whether absent a determination of relatedness there would be a substantial duplication of effort and expense, delay, or undue burden on the Court, parties or witnesses. NY R USDCTSD Div. Bus., Rule 13(a)(1). Nothing in this NY R USDCTSD Div. Bus., Rule 13 is intended to preclude parties from moving for consolidated proceedings under FRCP 42. NY R USDCTSD Div. Bus., Rule 13(a)(1). Notwithstanding NY R USDCTSD Div. Bus., Rule 13(a)(1):

i. Civil cases shall not be deemed related merely because they involve common legal issues or the same parties. NY R USDCTSD Div. Bus., Rule 13(a)(2)(A).

ii. Other than cases subject to NY R USDCTSD Div. Bus., Rule 4(b) and actions seeking the enforcement of a judgment or settlement in or of an earlier case, civil cases presumptively shall not be deemed related unless both cases are pending before the Court (or the earlier case is on appeal). NY R USDCTSD Div. Bus., Rule 13(a)(2)(B).

b. *Procedure in regard to cases said to be related*

i. *Disclosure of contention of relatedness.* When a civil case is filed or removed or a bankruptcy appeal or motion to withdraw the reference of an adversary proceeding from the bankruptcy court is filed, the person filing or removing shall disclose on form JSC44C any contention of relatedness and shall file a Related Case Statement stating clearly and succinctly the basis for the contention. A copy of the civil cover sheet and Related Case Statement shall be served with the complaint, notice of removal, notice of appeal, or motion. Any party may contest a claim of relatedness by any other in writing addressed to the judge having the case with the lowest docket number of all cases claimed to be related. However, the foregoing shall not delay the assignment process or the operation of NY R USDCTSD Div. Bus., Rule 13. NY R USDCTSD Div. Bus., Rule 13(b)(1). [Editor's note: the reference to form JSC44C is likely meant to be form JS44C-SDNY: Civil Court Cover Sheet].

ii. *Claims of relatedness by other parties.* A party other than the one filing a case, bankruptcy appeal or motion to withdraw the reference that contends its case is related to another may so advise in writing the judge assigned in its case and request a transfer of its case to the judge that the party contends has the related case with the lowest docket number. If the assigned judge believes the case is related under NY R USDCTSD Div. Bus., Rule 13(a), he or she shall refer the question to the judge having the case with the lowest docket number. In the event the latter judge agrees, the case shall be transferred to that judge unless the Assignment Committee disagrees. NY R USDCTSD Div. Bus., Rule 13(b)(3).

c. For more information on related cases, refer to NY R USDCTSD Div. Bus., Rule 13.

7. *Alternative dispute resolution (ADR).* The U.S. District Court for the Southern District of New York provides litigants with opportunities to discuss settlement through judicial settlement conferences and mediation. NY R USDCTS&ED Civ Rule 83.9(a).

a. *Consideration of alternative dispute resolution.* In all civil cases, including those eligible for mediation pursuant to NY R USDCTS&ED Civ Rule 83.9(e), each party shall consider the use of mediation or a judicial settlement conference and shall report to the assigned Judge at the initial FRCP 16(b) case management conference, or subsequently, whether the party believes mediation or a judicial settlement conference may facilitate the resolution of the lawsuit. Judges are encouraged to note the availability of the mediation program and/or a judicial settlement conference before, at, or after the initial FRCP 16(b) case management conference. NY R USDCTS&ED Civ Rule 83.9(d).

b. *Mediation.* In mediation, parties and counsel meet, sometimes collectively and sometimes individually, with a neutral third party (the mediator) who has been trained to facilitate confidential settlement discussions. The parties articulate their respective positions and interests and generate options for a mutually agreeable resolution to the dispute. The mediator assists the parties in reaching their own negotiated settlement by defining the issues, probing and assessing the strengths and weaknesses of each party's legal positions, and identifying areas of agreement and disagreement. The main benefits of mediation are that it can result in an expeditious and less costly resolution of the litigation, and can produce creative solutions to complex disputes often unavailable in traditional litigation. NY R USDCTS&ED Civ Rule 83.9(b).

   i. *Mediation program eligibility.* All civil cases other than Social Security, habeas corpus, and tax cases are eligible for mediation, whether assigned to Manhattan or White Plains. NY R USDCTS&ED Civ Rule 83.9(e)(1).

- The Board of Judges may, by Administrative Order, direct that certain specified categories of cases shall automatically be submitted to the mediation program. The assigned District Judge or Magistrate Judge may issue a written order exempting a particular case with or without the request of the parties. NY R USDCTS&ED Civ Rule 83.9(e)(2).

- For all other cases, the assigned District Judge or Magistrate Judge may determine that a case is appropriate for mediation and may order that case to mediation, with or without the consent of the parties, before, at, or after the initial FRCP 16(b) case management conference. Alternatively, the parties should notify the assigned Judge at any time of their desire to mediate. NY R USDCTS&ED Civ Rule 83.9(e)(3).

  c. *Judicial settlement conferences.* Judicial settlement conferences may be ordered by District Judges or Magistrate Judges with or without the request or consent of the parties. NY R USDCTS&ED Civ Rule 83.9(f).

  d. For more information on alternative dispute resolution (ADR), refer to NY R USDCTS&ED Civ Rule 83.9.

8. *Individual judge practices.* Refer to the Miscellaneous section of this document for information on individual judge practices on general requirements for documents.

## D. Documents

1. *Required documents*

  a. *Request for admissions.* Refer to the General Requirements section of this document for information on the request for admissions.

2. *Supplemental documents*

  a. *Document(s).* A request to admit the genuineness of a document must be accompanied by a copy of the document unless it is, or has been, otherwise furnished or made available for inspection and copying. FRCP 36(a)(2).

  b. *Certificate of service.* FRCP 5(d) requires that the person making service under FRCP 5 certify that service has been effected. FRCP 5(Advisory Committee Notes). Having such information on file may be useful for many purposes, including proof of service if an issue arises concerning the effectiveness of the service. FRCP 5(Advisory Committee Notes).

3. *Individual judge practices.* Refer to the Miscellaneous section of this document for information on individual judge practices on required documents.

## E. Format

1. *Form of documents.* The rules governing captions and other matters of form in pleadings apply to motions and other papers. FRCP 7(b)(2).

  a. *Paper.* Every pleading, written motion, and other paper must: be plainly written, typed, printed, or copied without erasures or interlineations which materially deface it. NY R USDCTS&ED Civ Rule 11.1(a)(1).

  b. *Typeface, margin, and spacing.* The typeface, margins, and spacing of all documents presented for filing must meet the following requirements:

   i. All text must be twelve (12) point type or larger, except for text in footnotes which may be ten (10) point type;

   ii. All documents must have at least one (1) inch margins on all sides;

   iii. All text must be double-spaced, except for headings, text in footnotes, or block quotations, which may be single-spaced. NY R USDCTS&ED Civ Rule 11.1(b).

c. *Caption; Names of parties.* Every pleading must have a caption with the court's name, a title, a file number, and a FRCP 7(a) designation. The title of the complaint must name all the parties; the title of other pleadings, after naming the first party on each side, may refer generally to other parties. FRCP 10(a). Every pleading, written motion, and other paper must: bear the docket number and the initials of the District Judge and any Magistrate Judge before whom the action or proceeding is pending, NY R USDCTS&ED Civ Rule 11.1(a)(2).

d. *Paragraphs; Separate statements.* A party must state its claims or defenses in numbered paragraphs, each limited as far as practicable to a single set of circumstances. A later pleading may refer by number to a paragraph in an earlier pleading. If doing so would promote clarity, each claim founded on a separate transaction or occurrence—and each defense other than a denial—must be stated in a separate count or defense. FRCP 10(b).

e. *Adoption by reference; Exhibits.* A statement in a pleading may be adopted by reference elsewhere in the same pleading or in any other pleading or motion. A copy of a written instrument that is an exhibit to a pleading is a part of the pleading for all purposes. FRCP 10(c).

f. *Acceptance by the clerk.* The clerk must not refuse to file a paper solely because it is not in the form prescribed by the Federal Rules of Civil Procedure or by a local rule or practice. FRCP 5(d)(4).

2. *Form of electronic documents*

a. *PDF-A.* All documents electronically filed on the ECF system must be in PDF-A format (portable document format). A PDF-A file is created using PDF writer software such as Adobe Acrobat (go to the Adobe website for details). PDF-A files cannot be altered, providing security to the filer and the Court. NY R USDCTSD CM/ECF, S.D.(II)(23)(23.2).

b. *Size limitation.* No single PDF file may be larger than four megabytes (4 MB). If the filing is too large, the ECF system will not allow it to be filed, and you will not see a Notice of Electronic Filing (NEF or filing receipt) screen. To determine the size of an Adobe Acrobat PDF file click on File, Document Properties, Summary. NY R USDCTSD CM/ECF, S.D.(II)(23)(23.3).

   i. Converting documents directly from a word processor to PDF-A format creates the smallest possible file in terms of computer memory. If that is not possible, scan your document at low resolution. Within the Adobe Acrobat program, on the "Scan Manager" screen, adjust the settings for black and white and 200 dpi (dots per inch). This allows more pages to fit into a single PDF-A file. If that does not work, separate an oversized file into 2 or more parts. Simply label each file 1a, 1b, 1c, etc. Only relevant excerpts of exhibits should be electronically filed. NY R USDCTSD CM/ECF, S.D.(II)(23)(23.4).

c. *Attachments and exhibits.* Filing Users must submit in electronic form all documents referenced as exhibits or attachments, unless the Court permits paper filing. NY R USDCTSD CM/ECF, S.D.(I)(5)(5.1).

   i. A Filing User must submit as exhibits or attachments only those excerpts of the referenced documents that are relevant to the matter under consideration by the Court. Excerpted material must be clearly and prominently identified as such. Filing Users who file excerpts of documents as exhibits or attachments under this procedure do so without prejudice to their right to file timely additional excerpts or the complete document. Responding parties may file timely additional excerpts that they believe are relevant or the complete document. A party may move before the Court for permission to serve and file in hard copy documents that cannot be reasonably scanned. NY R USDCTSD CM/ECF, S.D.(I)(5)(5.2).

   ii. Exhibits must be filed only as attachments to a document, such as a motion or an affidavit. Do not use the ECF Filing Event for "Motion" to file exhibits separately. Exhibits are the only items that should be attached to electronically filed documents. You are limited to electronically filing only relevant excerpts of exhibits. Excerpts must be clearly identified as such. If the exhibit is too large to be scanned and electronically filed you may contact the ECF Help Desk. NY R USDCTSD CM/ECF, S.D.(II)(15)(15.6).

d. *Letters.* Parties should consult the assigned judge's Individual Practices to determine if the judge accepts letters at all and, if he or she does, whether the judge has any page limitations on letters and/or requires courtesy copies of letters filed on ECF (and, if so, by what means of delivery). All letters addressed to the Court must include a subject line with the case name and docket number (e.g., "Re: Doe v. Smith, 13 Civ. 1234 (ABC)"). NY R USDCTSD CM/ECF, S.D.(II)(13)(13.1).

e. *Proposed orders, proposed judgments, stipulations and consents.* Any document that requires the signature of a judge should not be electronically filed except as an exhibit to another document. Proposed orders, judgments, stipulations and consents should not be submitted through the ECF system. Instead they should be sent by e-mail to the Clerk. Proposed orders should be submitted in word processing format (WordPerfect or Word) rather than as a PDF document. Stipulations should be submitted in PDF-A format. Stipulations must contain ink signatures not s/. Faxed or emailed signatures are acceptable. Please note that Stipulations of Voluntary Dismissal pursuant to FRCP 41(a)(1)(A)(ii) do not require the signature of a judge and must be electronically filed on the ECF system. Questions may be directed to the Orders and Judgments Clerk at the phone numbers listed in NY R USDCTSD CM/ECF, S.D.(II)(18)(18.3). NY R USDCTSD CM/ECF, S.D.(II)(18)(18.3).

    i. Email the proposed order, judgment or stipulation to the email addresses listed in NY R USDCTSD CM/ECF, S.D.(II)(18)(18.3). NY R USDCTSD CM/ECF, S.D.(II)(18)(18.3).

    ii. Pro se litigants who are not Filing Users are exempt from that portion of NY R USDCTSD CM/ECF, S.D.(II)(18)(18.3) that requires litigants to email proposed orders, judgments, stipulations and consents, and shall deliver such documents to the Clerk's Office in paper form. NY R USDCTSD CM/ECF, S.D.(II)(18)(18.3).

3. *Signing disclosures and discovery requests, responses, and objections.* FRCP 11 does not apply to disclosures and discovery requests, responses, objections, and motions under FRCP 26 through FRCP 37. FRCP 11(d).

    a. *Signature required.* Every disclosure under FRCP 26(a)(1) or FRCP 26(a)(3) and every discovery request, response, or objection must be signed by at least one attorney of record in the attorney's own name—or by the party personally, if unrepresented—and must state the signer's address, e-mail address, and telephone number. FRCP 26(g)(1). Every pleading, written motion, and other paper must: have the name of each person signing it clearly printed or typed directly below the signature. NY R USDCTS&ED Civ Rule 11.1(a)(3).

        i. *Electronic signatures.* The user log-in and password required to submit documents to the ECF system serve as the Filing User's signature on all electronic documents filed with the Court. NY R USDCTSD CM/ECF, S.D.(I)(8)(8.1); NY R USDCTSD CM/ECF, S.D.(II)(13)(13.14). They also serve as a signature for purposes of the Federal Rules of Civil Procedure, including FRCP 11, the Local Civil Rules of the United States District Courts for the Southern and Eastern Districts of New York, and any other purpose for which a signature is required in connection with proceedings before the Court. NY R USDCTSD CM/ECF, S.D.(I)(8)(8.1).

- *Signature block.* Electronically filed documents must include a signature block and must set forth the name, address, telephone number and e-mail address all in compliance with the Federal Rules of Civil Procedure and NY R USDCTS&ED Civ Rule 11.1. In the absence of a scanned signature image, the name of the Filing User under whose log-in and password the document is submitted must be preceded by an "s/" typed in the space where the signature would otherwise appear. NY R USDCTSD CM/ECF, S.D.(I)(8)(8.2); NY R USDCTSD CM/ECF, S.D.(II)(13)(13.14).

- *Documents requiring the signature of a party or witness.* A document requiring the signature of a party or witness shall be electronically filed in a scanned format that contains an image of the actual signature. NY R USDCTSD CM/ECF, S.D.(I)(8)(8.4); NY R USDCTSD CM/ECF, S.D.(II)(13)(13.14).

- *Documents requiring the signature of a judge.* A Filing User submitting a document electronically that requires a judge's signature must promptly deliver the document in such other form, if any, as the Court requires. NY R USDCTSD CM/ECF, S.D.(I)(4)(4.2).

- *Documents requiring multiple signatures.* Documents requiring signatures of more than one party must be electronically filed either by: (a) submitting a scanned document containing all necessary signatures; (b) representing the consent of the other parties on the document; (c) identifying on the document the parties whose signatures are required and by the submission of a notice of endorsement by the other parties no later than three business days after filing; or (d) in any other manner approved by the Court. NY R USDCTSD CM/ECF, S.D.(I)(8)(8.5).

b.  *Effect of signature.* By signing, an attorney or party certifies that to the best of the person's knowledge, information, and belief formed after a reasonable inquiry:

 i.   With respect to a disclosure, it is complete and correct as of the time it is made; and

 ii.  With respect to a discovery request, response, or objection, it is:

 - Consistent with the Federal Rules of Civil Procedure and warranted by existing law or by a nonfrivolous argument for extending, modifying, or reversing existing law, or for establishing new law;

 - Not interposed for any improper purpose, such as to harass, cause unnecessary delay, or needlessly increase the cost of litigation; and

 - Neither unreasonable nor unduly burdensome or expensive, considering the needs of the case, prior discovery in the case, the amount in controversy, and the importance of the issues at stake in the action. FRCP 26(g)(1).

c.  *Failure to sign.* Other parties have no duty to act on an unsigned disclosure, request, response, or objection until it is signed, and the court must strike it unless a signature is promptly supplied after the omission is called to the attorney's or party's attention. FRCP 26(g)(2).

d.  *Sanction for improper certification.* If a certification violates FRCP 26(g) without substantial justification, the court, on motion or on its own, must impose an appropriate sanction on the signer, the party on whose behalf the signer was acting, or both. The sanction may include an order to pay the reasonable expenses, including attorney's fees, caused by the violation. FRCP 26(g)(3). Refer to the United States District Court for the Southern District of New York KeyRules Motion for Discovery Sanctions document for more information.

4.  *Privacy protection for filings made with the court*

a.  *Redacted filings.* Unless the court orders otherwise, in an electronic or paper filing with the court that contains an individual's Social Security number, taxpayer-identification number, or birth date, the name of an individual known to be a minor, or a financial-account number, a party or nonparty making the filing may include only:

 i.   The last four (4) digits of the Social Security number and taxpayer-identification number;

 ii.  The year of the individual's birth;

 iii. The minor's initials; and

 iv.  The last four (4) digits of the financial-account number. FRCP 5.2(a); NY R USDCTSD CM/ECF, S.D.(II)(21)(21.3).

 v.   Caution should be exercised when filing documents that contain the following:

 - Personal identifying numbers (PIN #'s), such as a driver's license number;

 - Medical records, treatment and diagnosis;

 - Employment history;

 - Individual financial information;

 - Proprietary or trade secret information;

 - Information regarding an individual's cooperation with the government. NY R USDCTSD CM/ECF, S.D.(II)(21)(21.4).

b.  *Exemptions from the redaction requirement.* The redaction requirement does not apply to the following:

 i.   A financial-account number that identifies the property allegedly subject to forfeiture in a forfeiture proceeding;

    ii.   The record of an administrative or agency proceeding;

    iii.   The official record of a state-court proceeding;

    iv.   The record of a court or tribunal, if that record was not subject to the redaction requirement when originally filed;

    v.   A filing covered by FRCP 5.2(c) or FRCP 5.2(d); and

    vi.   A pro se filing in an action brought under 28 U.S.C.A. § 2241, 28 U.S.C.A. § 2254, or 28 U.S.C.A. § 2255. FRCP 5.2(b).

c.   *Limitations on remote access to electronic files; Social Security appeals and immigration cases.* Unless the court orders otherwise, in an action for benefits under the Social Security Act, and in an action or proceeding relating to an order of removal, to relief from removal, or to immigration benefits or detention, access to an electronic file is authorized as follows:

    i.   The parties and their attorneys may have remote electronic access to any part of the case file, including the administrative record;

    ii.   Any other person may have electronic access to the full record at the courthouse, but may have remote electronic access only to:

      • The docket maintained by the court; and

      • An opinion, order, judgment, or other disposition of the court, but not any other part of the case file or the administrative record. FRCP 5.2(c).

d.   *Filings made under seal.* The court may order that a filing be made under seal without redaction. The court may later unseal the filing or order the person who made the filing to file a redacted version for the public record. FRCP 5.2(d). For more information on sealing documents, refer to NY R USDCTSD CM/ECF, S.D.(I)(6).

e.   *Protective orders.* For good cause, the court may by order in a case:

    i.   Require redaction of additional information; or

    ii.   Limit or prohibit a nonparty's remote electronic access to a document filed with the court. FRCP 5.2(e).

f.   *Option for additional unredacted filing under seal.* A person making a redacted filing may also file an unredacted copy under seal. The court must retain the unredacted copy as part of the record. FRCP 5.2(f); NY R USDCTSD CM/ECF, S.D.(II)(21)(21.5).

g.   *Option for filing a reference list.* A filing that contains redacted information may be filed together with a reference list that identifies each item of redacted information and specifies an appropriate identifier that uniquely corresponds to each item listed. The list must be filed under seal and may be amended as of right. Any reference in the case to a listed identifier will be construed to refer to the corresponding item of information. FRCP 5.2(g); NY R USDCTSD CM/ECF, S.D.(II)(21)(21.5).

h.   *Responsibility for redaction.* It is the sole responsibility of counsel and the parties to be sure that all documents comply with the rules of this Court requiring redaction of personal identifiers. Neither the judge nor the Clerk of Court will review documents for compliance with these rules. NY R USDCTSD CM/ECF, S.D.(II)(21)(21.2).

i.   *Waiver of protection of identifiers.* A person waives the protection of FRCP 5.2(a) as to the person's own information by filing it without redaction and not under seal. FRCP 5.2(h).

j.   For more information on privacy and public access to ECF cases, refer to NY R USDCTSD CM/ECF, S.D.(II)(21).

5.   *Individual judge practices.* Refer to the Miscellaneous section of this document for information on individual judge practices on formatting documents.

## F. Filing and Service Requirements

1.   *Filing requirements.* Any paper after the complaint that is required to be served—together with a certificate of service—must be filed within a reasonable time after service. But disclosures under FRCP

26(a)(1) or FRCP 26(a)(2) and the following discovery requests and responses must not be filed until they are used in the proceeding or the court orders filing: depositions, interrogatories, requests for documents or tangible things or to permit entry onto land, and requests for admission. FRCP 5(d)(1). Refer to the United States District Court for the Southern District of New York KeyRules pleading and motion documents for information on filing with the court.

2. *Service requirements.* [A request for an admission] must be served on the party from whom the admission is requested and, unless the court has otherwise ordered, a copy of the request must be served on every other party. FPP § 2258.

   a. *Service; When required*

      i. *In general.* Unless the Federal Rules of Civil Procedure provide otherwise, each of the following papers must be served on every party:

         - An order stating that service is required;

         - A pleading filed after the original complaint, unless the court orders otherwise under FRCP 5(c) because there are numerous defendants;

         - A discovery paper required to be served on a party, unless the court orders otherwise;

         - A written motion, except one that may be heard ex parte; and

         - A written notice, appearance, demand, or offer of judgment, or any similar paper. FRCP 5(a)(1).

      ii. *If a party fails to appear.* No service is required on a party who is in default for failing to appear. But a pleading that asserts a new claim for relief against such a party must be served on that party under FRCP 4. FRCP 5(a)(2).

      iii. *Seizing property.* If an action is begun by seizing property and no person is or need be named as a defendant, any service required before the filing of an appearance, answer, or claim must be made on the person who had custody or possession of the property when it was seized. FRCP 5(a)(3).

   b. *Service; How made*

      i. *Serving an attorney.* If a party is represented by an attorney, service under FRCP 5 must be made on the attorney unless the court orders service on the party. FRCP 5(b)(1).

      ii. *Service in general.* A paper is served under FRCP 5 by:

         - Handing it to the person;

         - Leaving it: (1) at the person's office with a clerk or other person in charge or, if no one is in charge, in a conspicuous place in the office; or (2) if the person has no office or the office is closed, at the person's dwelling or usual place of abode with someone of suitable age and discretion who resides there;

         - Mailing it to the person's last known address—in which event service is complete upon mailing;

         - Leaving it with the court clerk if the person has no known address;

         - Sending it by electronic means if the person consented in writing—in which event service is complete upon transmission, but is not effective if the serving party learns that it did not reach the person to be served; or

         - Delivering it by any other means that the person consented to in writing—in which event service is complete when the person making service delivers it to the agency designated to make delivery. FRCP 5(b)(2).

      iii. *Service by overnight delivery.* Service upon an attorney may be made by overnight delivery service. "Overnight delivery service" means any delivery service which regularly accepts items for overnight delivery. Overnight delivery service shall be deemed service by mail for purposes of FRCP 5 and FRCP 6. NY R USDCTS&ED Civ Rule 5.3.

      iv. *Service by electronic means.* Parties serving and filing papers shall follow the instructions regarding Electronic Case Filing (ECF) published on the website of each respective Court. A paper served and filed by electronic means in accordance with such instructions is, for purposes of FRCP 5, served and filed in compliance with the Local Civil Rules of the United States District Courts for the Southern and Eastern Districts of New York. NY R USDCTS&ED Civ Rule 5.2(a). Parties have an obligation to review the Court's actual order, decree, or judgment (on ECF), which controls, and should not rely on the description on the docket or in the ECF Notice of Electronic Filing (NEF). NY R USDCTS&ED Civ Rule 5.2(c).

- *Notice of electronic filing (NEF).* In cases assigned to the ECF system, service is complete provided all parties receive a Notice of Electronic Filing (NEF), which is sent automatically by email from the Court (see the NEF for a list of who did/did not receive notice electronically). Transmission of the NEF constitutes service upon all Filing and Receiving Users who are listed as recipients of notice by electronic mail. NY R USDCTSD CM/ECF, S.D.(I)(9)(9.1). In cases assigned to the ECF system, if all parties receive a NEF, service is complete upon transmission of the NEF by the Court, and you are not required to serve a paper copy. NY R USDCTSD CM/ECF, S.D.(II)(19)(19.2). It remains the duty of Filing and Receiving Users to maintain current contact information with the court and to regularly review the docket sheet of the case. NY R USDCTSD CM/ECF, S.D.(I)(9)(9.1).

- *Mailing of court-initiated documents.* The Clerk's Office will no longer mail paper copies of court-initiated documents to Filing and Receiving Users. The Clerk's Office will mail copies of all court-initiated documents to pro se parties who have not registered as Filing or Receiving Users. NY R USDCTSD CM/ECF, S.D.(II)(19)(19.1).

- *No receipt of a NEF.* If any party does not receive a NEF, you are required to accomplish service on that party in the traditional manner, in paper form. NY R USDCTSD CM/ECF, S.D.(II)(19)(19.2). The NEF receipt will inform you who will receive notice of the filing "electronically" (by e-mail from the Court) and who will receive notice "by other means" (traditional service in paper form). NY R USDCTSD CM/ECF, S.D.(II)(19)(19.2).

- *Service on non-filing or non-receiving users.* Attorneys and pro se parties who are not Filing or Receiving Users must be served with a paper copy of any electronically filed pleading or other document. Service of such paper copy must be made according to the Federal Rules of Civil Procedure and the Local Civil Rules of the United States District Courts for the Southern and Eastern Districts of New York. NY R USDCTSD CM/ECF, S.D.(I)(9)(9.2). Such paper service must be documented by electronically filing proof of service. NY R USDCTSD CM/ECF, S.D.(I)(9)(9.2); NY R USDCTSD CM/ECF, S.D.(II)(19)(19.2). Where the Clerk scans and electronically files pleadings and documents on behalf of a pro se party, the associated NEF constitutes service. NY R USDCTSD CM/ECF, S.D.(I)(9)(9.2).

- For more information on service by electronic means, refer to NY R USDCTSD CM/ECF, S.D.(II)(19).

    v. *Using court facilities.* If a local rule so authorizes, a party may use the court's transmission facilities to make service under FRCP 5(b)(2)(E). FRCP 5(b)(3).

  c. *Serving numerous defendants*

    i. *In general.* If an action involves an unusually large number of defendants, the court may, on motion or on its own, order that:

- Defendants' pleadings and replies to them need not be served on other defendants;

- Any crossclaim, counterclaim, avoidance, or affirmative defense in those pleadings and replies to them will be treated as denied or avoided by all other parties; and

- Filing any such pleading and serving it on the plaintiff constitutes notice of the pleading to all parties. FRCP 5(c)(1).

    ii. *Notifying parties.* A copy of every such order must be served on the parties as the court directs. FRCP 5(c)(2).

3. *Individual judge practices.* Refer to the Miscellaneous section of this document for information on individual judge practices on filing and serving documents.

## G. Hearings

1. There is no hearing contemplated in the federal statutes or rules for requests for admissions.

## H. Forms

### 1. Federal Request for Admissions Forms

a. Request; For admission of facts and genuineness of documents. AMJUR PP DEPOSITION § 674.

b. Plaintiff's request for admission. 3B FEDFORMS § 3650.

c. Plaintiff's request for admission; Another form. 3B FEDFORMS § 3651.

d. Plaintiff's request for admission; Statements in documents. 3B FEDFORMS § 3652.

e. Plaintiff's request for admission; Statements in documents; Another form. 3B FEDFORMS § 3653.

f. Plaintiff's request for admission; Specific facts. 3B FEDFORMS § 3654.

g. Plaintiff's request for admission; Specific facts; Another form. 3B FEDFORMS § 3655.

h. Plaintiff's request for admission; Specific documents and facts. 3B FEDFORMS § 3656.

i. Plaintiff's request for admission; Specific documents and facts; Another form. 3B FEDFORMS § 3657.

j. Plaintiff's request for admission; True copies, filing and operational effect of government documents. 3B FEDFORMS § 3658.

k. Plaintiff's request for additional admission. 3B FEDFORMS § 3659.

l. Defendant's request for admission of genuineness; Specific document. 3B FEDFORMS § 3660.

m. Defendant's request for admission of genuineness; Specific document; Another form. 3B FEDFORMS § 3661.

n. Defendant's request for admission of genuineness; Specific document; Another form. 3B FEDFORMS § 3662.

o. Defendant's request for admission; Truth of statement. 3B FEDFORMS § 3663.

p. Request for admissions under FRCP 36. FEDPROF § 23:535.

q. Request for admissions; General form. FEDPROF § 23:536.

r. Request for admissions; Action to collect royalties. FEDPROF § 23:537.

s. Request for admissions; Trademark action. FEDPROF § 23:538.

t. Request for admissions; Automobile negligence action. FEDPROF § 23:539.

u. Request for admissions; Motor vehicle action. FEDPROF § 23:540.

v. Request for admissions; Premises liability action. FEDPROF § 23:541.

w. Request for admissions; Products liability action. FEDPROF § 23:542.

x. Request for admissions; Medical malpractice action. FEDPROF § 23:543.

y. Request for admissions; Genuineness of documents. FEDPROF § 23:544.

z. Request for admissions; Wrongful death due to forklift accident. FEDPROF § 23:545.

## I. Applicable Rules

1. *Federal rules*

a. Serving and filing pleadings and other papers. FRCP 5.

b. Privacy protection for filings made with the court. FRCP 5.2.

c. Computing and extending time; Time for motion papers. FRCP 6.

d. Pleadings allowed; Form of motions and other papers. FRCP 7.

e. Form of pleadings. FRCP 10.

f. Signing pleadings, motions, and other papers; Representations to the court; Sanctions. FRCP 11.

g.   Duty to disclose; General provisions governing discovery. FRCP 26.

h.   Stipulations about discovery procedure. FRCP 29.

i.   Requests for admission. FRCP 36.

j.   Failure to make disclosures or to cooperate in discovery; Sanctions. FRCP 37.

2.   *Local rules*

a.   Duty of attorneys in related cases. NY R USDCTS&ED Civ Rule 1.6.

b.   Electronic service and filing of documents. NY R USDCTS&ED Civ Rule 5.2.

c.   Service by overnight delivery. NY R USDCTS&ED Civ Rule 5.3.

d.   Computation of time. NY R USDCTS&ED Civ Rule 6.4.

e.   Form of pleadings, motions, and other papers. NY R USDCTS&ED Civ Rule 11.1.

f.   Assertion of claim of privilege. NY R USDCTS&ED Civ Rule 26.2.

g.   Uniform definitions in discovery requests. NY R USDCTS&ED Civ Rule 26.3.

h.   Cooperation among counsel in discovery. NY R USDCTS&ED Civ Rule 26.4.

i.   Form discovery requests. [NY R USDCTS&ED Civ Rule 26.5, as amended by NY ORDER 16-4212, effective September 26, 2016].

j.   Alternative dispute resolution (Southern District only). NY R USDCTS&ED Civ Rule 83.9.

k.   Electronic case filing rules and instructions. NY R USDCTSD CM/ECF, S.D.

l.   Related cases. NY R USDCTSD Div. Bus., Rule 13.

## J.  Miscellaneous

**NOTE: Individual judges' rules may apply. For available judge-level information, refer to:**

DISTRICT JUDGE RONNIE ABRAMS: NY R USDCTSD Abrams-Civ Prac; NY R USDCTSD Abrams-Crim Prac; NY R USDCTSD Abrams-Pro Se; NY R USDCTSD Abrams-Case Mgt; NY R USDCTSD Abrams-Jury.

DISTRICT JUDGE DEBORAH A. BATTS: NY R USDCTSD Batts-Practices.

DISTRICT JUDGE RICHARD M. BERMAN: NY R USDCTSD Berman-Practices; NY R USDCTSD Berman-Default; NY R USDCTSD Berman-Sentencing; NY R USDCTSD Berman-Media.

DISTRICT JUDGE VINCENT L. BRICCETTI: NY R USDCTSD Briccetti-Practices; NY R USDCTSD Briccetti-Plan; NY R USDCTSD Briccetti-Notice.

DISTRICT JUDGE VERNON S. BRODERICK: NY R USDCTSD Broderick-Civil; NY R USDCTSD Broderick-Crim; NY R USDCTSD Broderick-Case Mgt; NY R USDCTSD Broderick-Jury.

DISTRICT JUDGE NAOMI REICE BUCHWALD: NY R USDCTSD Buchwald-Practices.

DISTRICT JUDGE VALERIE E. CAPRONI: NY R USDCTSD Caproni-Prac; NY R USDCTSD Caproni--Pro Se; NY R USDCTSD Caproni-Case Mgt; NY R USDCTSD Caproni-Crim Prac.

DISTRICT JUDGE ANDREW L. CARTER JR.: NY R USDCTSD Carter-Practices.

DISTRICT JUDGE KEVIN P. CASTEL: NY R USDCTSD Castel-Practices; NY R USDCTSD Castel-Default; NY R USDCTSD Castel-Scheduling; NY R USDCTSD Castel-Complex; NY R USDCTSD Castel-Trials; NY R USDCTSD Castel-Sentencing.

DISTRICT JUDGE DENISE L. COTE: NY R USDCTSD Cote-Civil Practices; NY R USDCTSD Cote-Pro Se; NY R USDCTSD Cote-Maritime Ord; NY R USDCTSD Cote-Crim Practices; NY R USDCTSD Cote-Crim Trials; NY R USDCTSD Cote-Sentencing.

DISTRICT JUDGE PAUL A. CROTTY: NY R USDCTSD Crotty-Practices; NY R USDCTSD Crotty-Sentencing; NY R USDCTSD Crotty-Calls; NY R USDCTSD Crotty-Scheduling.

DISTRICT JUDGE GEORGE B. DANIELS: NY R USDCTSD Daniels-Practices.

DISTRICT JUDGE KEVIN T. DUFFY: NY R USDCTSD Duffy-Practices.

DISTRICT JUDGE PAUL A. ENGELMAYER: NY R USDCTSD Engelmayer-Practices; NY R USDCTSD

Engelmayer-Scheduling; NY R USDCTSD Engelmayer-Sentencing; NY R USDCTSD Engelmayer-Pro Se; NY R USDCTSD Engelmayer-Crim.

DISTRICT JUDGE KATHERINE POLK FAILLA: NY R USDCTSD Failla-Civ Prac; NY R USDCTSD Failla-Crim Prac; NY R USDCTSD Failla-Case Mgt.

DISTRICT JUDGE KATHERINE B. FORREST: NY R USDCTSD Forrest-Civil Prac; NY R USDCTSD Forrest-Crim Prac; NY R USDCTSD Forrest-Crim Pretrial; NY R USDCTSD Forrest-Scheduling; NY R USDCTSD Forrest-Patent Scheduling; NY R USDCTSD Forrest-Sentencing; NY R USDCTSD Forrest-Order 1; NY R USDCTSD Forrest-Order 2.

DISTRICT JUDGE JESSE M. FURMAN: NY R USDCTSD Furman-Civil Prac; NY R USDCTSD Furman-Crim Prac; NY R USDCTSD Furman-Pro Se Prac; NY R USDCTSD Furman-Trials; NY R USDCTSD Furman-Scheduling; NY R USDCTSD Furman-Rights.

DISTRICT JUDGE PAUL G. GARDEPHE: NY R USDCTSD Gardephe-Civ Prac; NY R USDCTSD Gardephe-Pretrial; NY R USDCTSD Gardephe-Prot Ord; NY R USDCTSD Gardephe-Maritime; NY R USDCTSD Gardephe-Crim Prac; NY R USDCTSD Gardephe-Trial.

DISTRICT JUDGE THOMAS P. GRIESA: NY R USDCTSD Griesa-Practices.

DISTRICT JUDGE CHARLES S. HAIGHT: NY R USDCTSD Haight-Practices.

DISTRICT JUDGE ALVIN K. HELLERSTEIN: NY R USDCTSD Hellerstein-Practices; NY R USDCTSD Hellerstein--Sept 11.

DISTRICT JUDGE LEWIS A. KAPLAN: NY R USDCTSD Kaplan-Practices; NY R USDCTSD Kaplan-Sentencing.

DISTRICT JUDGE KENNETH M. KARAS: NY R USDCTSD Karas-Practices; NY R USDCTSD Karas-Case Mgt; NY R USDCTSD Karas-Default; NY R USDCTSD Karas-Sentencing; NY R USDCTSD Karas-Rights.

DISTRICT JUDGE JOHN F. KEENAN: NY R USDCTSD Keenan-Practices.

DISTRICT JUDGE JOHN G. KOELTL: NY R USDCTSD Koeltl-Practices.

DISTRICT JUDGE VICTOR MARRERO: NY R USDCTSD Marrero-Practices; NY R USDCTSD Marrero-Scheduling; NY R USDCTSD Marrero-Default; NY R USDCTSD Marrero-Trial Proc.

DISTRICT JUDGE COLLEEN McMAHON: NY R USDCTSD McMahon-Practices; NY R USDCTSD McMahon-RICO; NY R USDCTSD McMahon-Copies; NY R USDCTSD McMahon-Scheduling; NY R USDCTSD McMahon-Elec Disc; NY R USDCTSD McMahon-Sentencing.

DISTRICT JUDGE ALISON J. NATHAN: NY R USDCTSD Nathan-Civ Prac; NY R USDCTSD Nathan-Crim Prac; NY R USDCTSD Nathan-Pro Se; NY R USDCTSD Nathan-Scheduling.

DISTRICT JUDGE J. PAUL OETKEN: NY R USDCTSD Oetken-Civ Prac; NY R USDCTSD Oetken-Case Mgt; NY R USDCTSD Oetken-Crim Prac; NY R USDCTSD Oetken-Pro Se.

DISTRICT JUDGE WILLIAM H. PAULEY, III: NY R USDCTSD Pauley-Crim Cases; NY R USDCTSD Pauley-Practices.

DISTRICT JUDGE LORETTA A. PRESKA: NY R USDCTSD Preska-Practices.

DISTRICT JUDGE JED S. RAKOFF: NY R USDCTSD Rakoff-Practices; NY R USDCTSD Rakoff-Scheduling; NY R USDCTSD Rakoff-Prot Ord; NY R USDCTSD Rakoff-Maritime Ord.

DISTRICT JUDGE EDGARDO RAMOS: NY R USDCTSD Ramos--Practices; NY R USDCTSD Ramos-Case Mgt.

DISTRICT JUDGE NELSON S. ROMAN: NY R USDCTSD Roman-Civ Prac; NY R USDCTSD Roman-Pro Se; NY R USDCTSD Roman-Crim Prac; NY R USDCTSD Roman-Case Mgt.

DISTRICT JUDGE LEONARD B. SAND: NY R USDCTSD Sand-Practices.

DISTRICT JUDGE LORNA G. SCHOFIELD: NY R USDCTSD Schofield-Civ Prac; NY R USDCTSD Schofield-Crim Prac; NY R USDCTSD Schofield-Sched; NY R USDCTSD Schofield-Pro Se; NY R USDCTSD Schofield-Advice.

DISTRICT JUDGE CATHY SEIBEL: NY R USDCTSD Seibel-Practices.

DISTRICT JUDGE LOUIS L. STANTON: NY R USDCTSD Stanton-Practices; NY R USDCTSD Stanton-Pretrial.

DISTRICT JUDGE SIDNEY H. STEIN: NY R USDCTSD Stein-Practices.

DISTRICT JUDGE RICHARD J. SULLIVAN: NY R USDCTSD Sullivan-Practices; NY R USDCTSD Sullivan-Scheduling; NY R USDCTSD Sullivan-Sentencing; NY R USDCTSD Sullivan-Juries; NY R USDCTSD Sullivan-Trial; NY R USDCTSD Sullivan-Default.

DISTRICT JUDGE LAURA TAYLOR SWAIN: NY R USDCTSD Swain-Practices; NY R USDCTSD Swain-Trial; NY R USDCTSD Swain-Crim Trial; NY R USDCTSD Swain-Juries; NY R USDCTSD Swain-Sentencing; NY R USDCTSD Swain-Rights.

DISTRICT JUDGE ROBERT W. SWEET: NY R USDCTSD Sweet-Practices.

DISTRICT JUDGE ANALISA TORRES: NY R USDCTSD Torres-Civ Prac; NY R USDCTSD Torres-Pro Se; NY R USDCTSD Torres-Scheduling.

DISTRICT JUDGE KIMBA M. WOOD: NY R USDCTSD Wood-Practices; NY R USDCTSD Wood-Scheduling; NY R USDCTSD Wood-Discovery; NY R USDCTSD Wood-RICO; NY R USDCTSD Wood-Juries; NY R USDCTSD Wood-Trial; NY R USDCTSD Wood-Media.

DISTRICT JUDGE GREGORY H. WOODS: NY R USDCTSD Woods-Civ Prac; NY R USDCTSD Woods-Pro Se; NY R USDCTSD Woods-Sched; NY R USDCTSD Woods-Crim Prac; NY R USDCTSD Woods-Protect Order; NY R USDCTSD Woods-Speedy Trial.

MAGISTRATE JUDGE JAMES L. COTT: NY R USDCTSD Cott-Practices; NY R USDCTSD Cott-Settlement.

MAGISTRATE JUDGE PAUL E. DAVISON: NY R USDCTSD Davison-Practices.

MAGISTRATE JUDGE RONALD L. ELLIS: NY R USDCTSD Ellis-Practices.

MAGISTRATE JUDGE KEVIN N. FOX: NY R USDCTSD Fox-Practices; NY R USDCTSD Fox-Settlement.

MAGISTRATE JUDGE JAMES C. FRANCIS: NY R USDCTSD Francis-Practices.

MAGISTRATE JUDGE DEBRA FREEMAN: NY R USDCTSD Freeman-Practices; NY R USDCTSD Freeman-Settlement.

MAGISTRATE JUDGE GABRIEL W. GORENSTEIN: NY R USDCTSD Gorenstein-Practices; NY R USDCTSD Gorenstein-Ackn.

MAGISTRATE JUDGE FRANK MAAS: NY R USDCTSD Maas-Practices; NY R USDCTSD Maas-Discontinuance; NY R USDCTSD Maas-Conf; NY R USDCTSD Maas-Settlement.

MAGISTRATE JUDGE JUDITH C. McCARTHY: NY R USDCTSD McCarthy-Practices; NY R USDCTSD McCarthy-Conduct.

MAGISTRATE JUDGE BARBARA MOSES: NY R USDCTSD Moses-Practices.

MAGISTRATE JUDGE SARAH NETBURN: NY R USDCTSD Netburn-Civil; NY R USDCTSD Netburn-Settlement; NY R USDCTSD Netburn-Case Mgt; NY R USDCTSD Netburn--Pro Se.

MAGISTRATE JUDGE ANDREW J. PECK: NY R USDCTSD Peck-Practices; NY R USDCTSD Peck-Order; NY R USDCTSD Peck-Rule 502(d).

MAGISTRATE JUDGE HENRY PITMAN: NY R USDCTSD Pitman-Practices.

MAGISTRATE JUDGE LISA MARGARET SMITH: NY R USDCTSD Smith-Practices; NY R USDCTSD Smith-Trials.

## Requests, Notices and Applications
## Notice of Deposition

### Document Last Updated September 2016

**A. Checklist**

(I)  ❑ Matters to be considered by deposing party for depositions by oral examination

    (a)  ❑ Required documents

        (1)  ❑ Notice of deposition

    (b)  ❑ Supplemental documents

        (1)  ❑ Subpoena

        (2)  ❑ Subpoena duces tecum

        (3)  ❑ Request for production of documents

        (4)  ❑ Certificate of service

    (c)  ❑ Timing

        (1)  ❑ A party may, by oral questions, depose any person, including a party, without leave of court except as provided in FRCP 30(a)(2)

        (2)  ❑ A party must obtain leave of court, and the court must grant leave to the extent consistent with FRCP 26(b)(1) and FRCP 26(b)(2):

            (i)  ❑ If the parties have not stipulated to the deposition and: (1) the deposition would result in more than ten (10) depositions being taken under FRCP 30 or FRCP 31 by the plaintiffs, or by the defendants, or by the third-party defendants; (2) the deponent has already been deposed in the case; or (3) the party seeks to take the deposition before the time specified in FRCP 26(d), unless the party certifies in the notice, with supporting facts, that the deponent is expected to leave the United States and be unavailable for examination in this country after that time; or

            (ii)  ❑ If the deponent is confined in prison

        (3)  ❑ A party who wants to depose a person by oral questions must give reasonable written notice to every other party

(II)  ❑ Matters to be considered by deposing party for depositions by written questions

    (a)  ❑ Required documents

        (1)  ❑ Notice of deposition

        (2)  ❑ Written questions

    (b)  ❑ Supplemental documents

        (1)  ❑ Subpoena

        (2)  ❑ Certificate of service

    (c)  ❑ Timing

        (1)  ❑ A party may, by written questions, depose any person, including a party, without leave of court except as provided in FRCP 31(a)(2)

        (2)  ❑ A party must obtain leave of court, and the court must grant leave to the extent consistent with FRCP 26(b)(1) and FRCP 26(b)(2):

            (i)  ❑ If the parties have not stipulated to the deposition and: (1) the deposition would result in more than ten (10) depositions being taken under FRCP 31 or FRCP 30 by the plaintiffs, or by the defendants, or by the third-party defendants; (2) the deponent has already been deposed in the case; or (3) the party seeks to take a deposition before the time specified in FRCP 26(d); or

(ii) ❑ If the deponent is confined in prison

(3) ❑ A party who wants to depose a person by written questions must serve them on every other party, with a notice

## B. Timing

1. *Depositions by oral examination*

   a. *Without leave.* A party may, by oral questions, depose any person, including a party, without leave of court except as provided in FRCP 30(a)(2). FRCP 30(a)(1).

   b. *With leave.* A party must obtain leave of court, and the court must grant leave to the extent consistent with FRCP 26(b)(1) and FRCP 26(b)(2):

      i. If the parties have not stipulated to the deposition and: (1) the deposition would result in more than ten (10) depositions being taken under FRCP 30 or FRCP 31 by the plaintiffs, or by the defendants, or by the third-party defendants; (2) the deponent has already been deposed in the case; or (3) the party seeks to take the deposition before the time specified in FRCP 26(d), unless the party certifies in the notice, with supporting facts, that the deponent is expected to leave the United States and be unavailable for examination in this country after that time; or

      ii. If the deponent is confined in prison. FRCP 30(a)(2).

   c. *Notice of deposition.* A party who wants to depose a person by oral questions must give reasonable written notice to every other party. FRCP 30(b)(1).

2. *Depositions by written questions*

   a. *Without leave.* A party may, by written questions, depose any person, including a party, without leave of court except as provided in FRCP 31(a)(2). FRCP 31(a)(1).

   b. *With leave.* A party must obtain leave of court, and the court must grant leave to the extent consistent with FRCP 26(b)(1) and FRCP 26(b)(2):

      i. If the parties have not stipulated to the deposition and: (1) the deposition would result in more than ten (10) depositions being taken under FRCP 31 or FRCP 30 by the plaintiffs, or by the defendants, or by the third-party defendants; (2) the deponent has already been deposed in the case; or (3) the party seeks to take a deposition before the time specified in FRCP 26(d); or

      ii. If the deponent is confined in prison. FRCP 31(a)(2).

   c. *Notice of deposition with written questions.* A party who wants to depose a person by written questions must serve them on every other party, with a notice. FRCP 31(a)(3). Refer to the General Requirements section of this document for the contents of the notice.

   d. *Questions from other parties.* Any questions to the deponent from other parties must be served on all parties as follows:

      i. *Cross-questions.* Cross-questions, within fourteen (14) days after being served with the notice and direct questions;

      ii. *Redirect questions.* Redirect questions, within seven (7) days after being served with cross-questions; and

      iii. *Recross-questions.* Recross-questions, within seven (7) days after being served with redirect questions. FRCP 31(a)(5).

      iv. *Modification of timing requirements.* The court may, for good cause, extend or shorten these times. FRCP 31(a)(5).

3. *Timing of discovery, generally.* A party may not seek discovery from any source before the parties have conferred as required by FRCP 26(f), except in a proceeding exempted from initial disclosure under FRCP 26(a)(1)(B), or when authorized by the Federal Rules of Civil Procedure, by stipulation, or by court order. FRCP 26(d)(1).

4. *Computation of time*

   a. *Computing time.* FRCP 6 applies in computing any time period specified in the Federal Rules of Civil

Procedure, in any local rule or court order, or in any statute that does not specify a method of computing time. FRCP 6(a). In computing any period of time prescribed or allowed by the Local Civil Rules of the United States District Courts for the Southern and Eastern Districts of New York or the Local Admiralty and Maritime Rules, the provisions of FRCP 6 shall apply unless otherwise stated. NY R USDCTS&ED Civ Rule 6.4.

i.  *Period stated in days or a longer unit.* When the period is stated in days or a longer unit of time:

- Exclude the day of the event that triggers the period;

- Count every day, including intermediate Saturdays, Sundays, and legal holidays; and

- Include the last day of the period, but if the last day is a Saturday, Sunday, or legal holiday, the period continues to run until the end of the next day that is not a Saturday, Sunday, or legal holiday. FRCP 6(a)(1). In the Local Civil Rules of the United States District Courts for the Southern and Eastern Districts of New York, as in the Federal Rules of Civil Procedure as amended effective December 1, 2009, Saturdays, Sundays, and legal holidays are no longer excluded in computing periods of time. If the last day of the period is a Saturday, Sunday, or legal holiday, the period continues to run until the end of the next day that is not a Saturday, Sunday, or legal holiday. NY R USDCTS&ED Civ Rule 6.4.

ii.  *Period stated in hours.* When the period is stated in hours:

- Begin counting immediately on the occurrence of the event that triggers the period;

- Count every hour, including hours during intermediate Saturdays, Sundays, and legal holidays; and

- If the period would end on a Saturday, Sunday, or legal holiday, the period continues to run until the same time on the next day that is not a Saturday, Sunday, or legal holiday. FRCP 6(a)(2). In the Local Civil Rules of the United States District Courts for the Southern and Eastern Districts of New York, as in the Federal Rules of Civil Procedure as amended effective December 1, 2009, Saturdays, Sundays, and legal holidays are no longer excluded in computing periods of time. If the last day of the period is a Saturday, Sunday, or legal holiday, the period continues to run until the end of the next day that is not a Saturday, Sunday, or legal holiday. NY R USDCTS&ED Civ Rule 6.4.

iii.  *Inaccessibility of the clerk's office.* Unless the court orders otherwise, if the clerk's office is inaccessible:

- On the last day for filing under FRCP 6(a)(1), then the time for filing is extended to the first accessible day that is not a Saturday, Sunday, or legal holiday; or

- During the last hour for filing under FRCP 6(a)(2), then the time for filing is extended to the same time on the first accessible day that is not a Saturday, Sunday, or legal holiday. FRCP 6(a)(3).

iv.  *"Last day" defined.* Unless a different time is set by a statute, local rule, or court order, the last day ends:

- For electronic filing, at midnight in the court's time zone; and

- For filing by other means, when the clerk's office is scheduled to close. FRCP 6(a)(4).

v.  *"Next day" defined.* The "next day" is determined by continuing to count forward when the period is measured after an event and backward when measured before an event. FRCP 6(a)(5).

vi.  *"Legal holiday" defined.* "Legal holiday" means:

- The day set aside by statute for observing New Year's Day, Martin Luther King Jr.'s Birthday, Washington's Birthday, Memorial Day, Independence Day, Labor Day, Columbus Day, Veterans' Day, Thanksgiving Day, or Christmas Day;

- Any day declared a holiday by the President or Congress; and

- For periods that are measured after an event, any other day declared a holiday by the state where the district court is located. FRCP 6(a)(6).

    b.  *Computation of electronic filing deadlines.* You can file electronically twenty-four (24) hours a day, seven (7) days a week, three hundred sixty-five (365) days a year. NY R USDCTSD CM/ECF, S.D.(II)(13)(13.10). Electronic filing must be completed before midnight local time where the Court is located in order to be considered timely filed that day. NY R USDCTSD CM/ECF, S.D.(I)(3)(3.3); NY R USDCTSD CM/ECF, S.D.(II)(13)(13.10); NY R USDCTSD CM/ECF, S.D.(II)(19)(19.4). An electronically filed document is deemed filed on the "filed on" date indicated on the Notice of Electronic Filing (NEF). NY R USDCTSD CM/ECF, S.D.(II)(13)(13.11).

        i.  *Technical failures.* A Filing User whose filing is made untimely as the result of a technical failure may seek appropriate relief from the Court. NY R USDCTSD CM/ECF, S.D.(I)(11). If you missed a filing deadline when the ECF system was out of order, attach a statement to your filing explaining how the interruption in service prevented you from filing in a timely fashion. NY R USDCTSD CM/ECF, S.D.(II)(23)(23.5).

    c.  *Extending time*

        i.  *In general.* When an act may or must be done within a specified time, the court may, for good cause, extend the time:

- With or without motion or notice if the court acts, or if a request is made, before the original time or its extension expires; or

- On motion made after the time has expired if the party failed to act because of excusable neglect. FRCP 6(b)(1).

        ii.  *Exceptions.* A court must not extend the time to act under FRCP 50(b), FRCP 50(d), FRCP 52(b), FRCP 59(b), FRCP 59(d), FRCP 59(e), and FRCP 60(b). FRCP 6(b)(2).

        iii.  Refer to the United States District Court for the Southern District of New York KeyRules Motion for Continuance/Extension of Time document for more information on extending time.

    d.  *Additional time after certain kinds of service.* When a party may or must act within a specified time after service and service is made under FRCP 5(b)(2)(C), FRCP 5(b)(2)(D), FRCP 5(b)(2)(E), or FRCP 5(b)(2)(F), three (3) days are added after the period would otherwise expire under FRCP 6(a). FRCP 6(d). Overnight delivery service shall be deemed service by mail for purposes of FRCP 5 and FRCP 6. NY R USDCTS&ED Civ Rule 5.3.

5.  *Individual judge practices.* Refer to the Miscellaneous section of this document for information on individual judge practices on timing of documents.

## C. General Requirements

1.  *General provisions governing discovery*

    a.  *Discovery scope and limits*

        i.  *Scope in general.* Unless otherwise limited by court order, the scope of discovery is as follows: Parties may obtain discovery regarding any nonprivileged matter that is relevant to any party's claim or defense and proportional to the needs of the case, considering the importance of the issues at stake in the action, the amount in controversy, the parties' relative access to relevant information, the parties' resources, the importance of the discovery in resolving the issues, and whether the burden or expense of the proposed discovery outweighs its likely benefit. Information within this scope of discovery need not be admissible in evidence to be discoverable. FRCP 26(b)(1).

        ii.  *Limitations on frequency and extent*

- *When permitted.* By order, the court may alter the limits in the Federal Rules of Civil Procedure on the number of depositions and interrogatories or on the length of depositions under FRCP 30. By order or local rule, the court may also limit the number of requests under FRCP 36. FRCP 26(b)(2)(A).

- *Specific limitations on electronically stored information.* A party need not provide discovery of electronically stored information from sources that the party identifies as not reasonably accessible because of undue burden or cost. On motion to compel discovery or for a protective order, the party from whom discovery is sought must show that the information is not reasonably accessible because of undue burden or cost. If that showing is made, the court may nonetheless order discovery from such sources if the requesting party shows good cause, considering the limitations of FRCP 26(b)(2)(C). The court may specify conditions for the discovery. FRCP 26(b)(2)(B).

- *When required.* On motion or on its own, the court must limit the frequency or extent of discovery otherwise allowed by the Federal Rules of Civil Procedure or by local rule if it determines that: (1) the discovery sought is unreasonably cumulative or duplicative, or can be obtained from some other source that is more convenient, less burdensome, or less expensive; (2) the party seeking discovery has had ample opportunity to obtain the information by discovery in the action; or (3) the proposed discovery is outside the scope permitted by FRCP 26(b)(1). FRCP 26(b)(2)(C).

iii. *Trial preparation; Materials*

- *Documents and tangible things.* Ordinarily, a party may not discover documents and tangible things that are prepared in anticipation of litigation or for trial by or for another party or its representative (including the other party's attorney, consultant, surety, indemnitor, insurer, or agent). But, subject to FRCP 26(b)(4), those materials may be discovered if: (1) they are otherwise discoverable under FRCP 26(b)(1); and (2) the party shows that it has substantial need for the materials to prepare its case and cannot, without undue hardship, obtain their substantial equivalent by other means. FRCP 26(b)(3)(A).

- *Protection against disclosure.* If the court orders discovery of those materials, it must protect against disclosure of the mental impressions, conclusions, opinions, or legal theories of a party's attorney or other representative concerning the litigation. FRCP 26(b)(3)(B).

- *Previous statement.* Any party or other person may, on request and without the required showing, obtain the person's own previous statement about the action or its subject matter. If the request is refused, the person may move for a court order, and FRCP 37(a)(5) applies to the award of expenses. A previous statement is either: (1) a written statement that the person has signed or otherwise adopted or approved; or (2) a contemporaneous stenographic, mechanical, electrical, or other recording—or a transcription of it—that recites substantially verbatim the person's oral statement. FRCP 26(b)(3)(C).

iv. *Trial preparation; Experts*

- *Deposition of an expert who may testify.* A party may depose any person who has been identified as an expert whose opinions may be presented at trial. If FRCP 26(a)(2)(B) requires a report from the expert, the deposition may be conducted only after the report is provided. FRCP 26(b)(4)(A).

- *Trial-preparation protection for draft reports or disclosures.* FRCP 26(b)(3)(A) and FRCP 26(b)(3)(B) protect drafts of any report or disclosure required under FRCP 26(a)(2), regardless of the form in which the draft is recorded. FRCP 26(b)(4)(B).

- *Trial-preparation protection for communications between a party's attorney and expert witnesses.* FRCP 26(b)(3)(A) and FRCP 26(b)(3)(B) protect communications between the party's attorney and any witness required to provide a report under FRCP 26(a)(2)(B), regardless of the form of the communications, except to the extent that the communications: (1) relate to compensation for the expert's study or testimony; (2) identify facts or data that the party's attorney provided and that the expert considered in forming the opinions to be expressed; or (3) identify assumptions that the party's attorney provided and that the expert relied on in forming the opinions to be expressed. FRCP 26(b)(4)(C).

- *Expert employed only for trial preparation.* Ordinarily, a party may not, by interrogatories or deposition, discover facts known or opinions held by an expert who has been retained or specially employed by another party in anticipation of litigation or to prepare for trial and who is not expected to be called as a witness at trial. But a party may do so only: (1)

as provided in FRCP 35(b); or (2) on showing exceptional circumstances under which it is impracticable for the party to obtain facts or opinions on the same subject by other means. FRCP 26(b)(4)(D).

- *Payment.* Unless manifest injustice would result, the court must require that the party seeking discovery: (1) pay the expert a reasonable fee for time spent in responding to discovery under FRCP 26(b)(4)(A) or FRCP 26(b)(4)(D); and (2) for discovery FRCP 26(b)(4)(D), also pay the other party a fair portion of the fees and expenses it reasonably incurred in obtaining the expert's facts and opinions. FRCP 26(b)(4)(E).

v.  *Claiming privilege or protecting trial-preparation materials*

- *Information withheld.* When a party withholds information otherwise discoverable by claiming that the information is privileged or subject to protection as trial-preparation material, the party must: (1) expressly make the claim; and (2) describe the nature of the documents, communications, or tangible things not produced or disclosed—and do so in a manner that, without revealing information itself privileged or protected, will enable other parties to assess the claim. FRCP 26(b)(5)(A). Unless otherwise agreed by the parties or directed by the Court, where a claim of privilege is asserted in objecting to any means of discovery or disclosure, including but not limited to a deposition, and an answer is not provided on the basis of such assertion, (1) the person asserting the privilege shall identify the nature of the privilege (including work product) which is being claimed and, if the privilege is governed by state law, indicate the state's privilege rule being invoked; and (2) the following information shall be provided in the objection, or (in the case of a deposition) in response to questions by the questioner, unless divulgence of such information would cause disclosure of the allegedly privileged information: (A) for documents: (i) the type of document, e.g., letter or memorandum; (ii) the general subject matter of the document; (iii) the date of the document; and (iv) the author of the document, the addressees of the document, and any other recipients, and, where not apparent, the relationship of the author, addressees, and recipients to each other; (B) for oral communications: (i) the name of the person making the communication and the names of persons present while the communication was made and, where not apparent, the relationship of the persons present to the person making the communication; (ii) the date and place of communication; and (iii) the general subject matter of the communication. NY R USDCTS&ED Civ Rule 26.2(a). Where a claim of privilege is asserted in response to discovery or disclosure other than a deposition, and information is not provided on the basis of such assertion, the information set forth in NY R USDCTS&ED Civ Rule 26.2(a) shall be furnished in writing at the time of the response to such discovery or disclosure, unless otherwise ordered by the Court. NY R USDCTS&ED Civ Rule 26.2(b).

- *Information produced.* If information produced in discovery is subject to a claim of privilege or of protection as trial-preparation material, the party making the claim may notify any party that received the information of the claim and the basis for it. After being notified, a party must promptly return, sequester, or destroy the specified information and any copies it has; must not use or disclose the information until the claim is resolved; must take reasonable steps to retrieve the information if the party disclosed it before being notified; and may promptly present the information to the court under seal for a determination of the claim. The producing party must preserve the information until the claim is resolved. FRCP 26(b)(5)(B).

- *Efficient means of providing information regarding claims of privilege.* Efficient means of providing information regarding claims of privilege are encouraged, and parties are encouraged to agree upon measures that further this end. For example, when asserting privilege on the same basis with respect to multiple documents, it is presumptively proper to provide the information required by NY R USDCTS&ED Civ Rule 26.2 by group or category. A party receiving a privilege log that groups documents or otherwise departs from a document-by-document or communication-by-communication listing may not object solely on that basis, but may object if the substantive information required by NY

R USDCTS&ED Civ Rule 26.2 has not been provided in a comprehensible form. NY R USDCTS&ED Civ Rule 26.2(c).

b. *Protective orders.* A party or any person from whom discovery is sought may move for a protective order in the court where the action is pending—or as an alternative on matters relating to a deposition, in the court for the district where the deposition will be taken. FRCP 26(c)(1). Refer to the United States District Court for the Southern District of New York KeyRules Motion for Protective Order document for more information.

c. *Sequence of discovery.* Unless the parties stipulate or the court orders otherwise for the parties' and witnesses' convenience and in the interests of justice: (1) methods of discovery may be used in any sequence; and (2) discovery by one party does not require any other party to delay its discovery. FRCP 26(d)(3).

d. *Uniform definitions in discovery requests.* The full text of the definitions and rules of construction set forth in NY R USDCTS&ED Civ Rule 26.3(c) and NY R USDCTS&ED Civ Rule 26.3(d) is deemed incorporated by reference into all discovery requests. No discovery request shall use broader definitions or rules of construction than those set forth in NY R USDCTS&ED Civ Rule 26.3(c) and NY R USDCTS&ED Civ Rule 26.3(d). NY R USDCTS&ED Civ Rule 26.3 shall not preclude (1) the definition of other terms specific to the particular litigation, (2) the use of abbreviations, or (3) a more narrow definition of a term defined in NY R USDCTS&ED Civ Rule 26.3(c). NY R USDCTS&ED Civ Rule 26.3(a). NY R USDCTS&ED Civ Rule 26.3 is not intended to broaden or narrow the scope of discovery permitted by the Federal Rules of Civil Procedure. NY R USDCTS&ED Civ Rule 26.3(b).

   i. *Definitions.* The following definitions apply to all discovery requests:

- *Communication.* The term "communication" means the transmittal of information (in the form of facts, ideas, inquiries or otherwise). NY R USDCTS&ED Civ Rule 26.3(c)(1).

- *Document.* The term "document" is defined to be synonymous in meaning and equal in scope to the usage of the term "documents or electronically stored information" in FRCP 34(a)(1)(A). A draft or non-identical copy is a separate document within the meaning of this term. NY R USDCTS&ED Civ Rule 26.3(c)(2).

- *Identify (with respect to persons).* When referring to a person, "to identify" means to give, to the extent known, the person's full name, present or last known address, and when referring to a natural person, additionally, the present or last known place of employment. Once a person has been identified in accordance with NY R USDCTS&ED Civ Rule 26.3(c)(3), only the name of that person need be listed in response to subsequent discovery requesting the identification of that person. NY R USDCTS&ED Civ Rule 26.3(c)(3).

- *Identify (with respect to documents).* When referring to documents, "to identify" means to give, to the extent known, the (1) type of document; (2) general subject matter; (3) date of the document; and (4) author(s), addressee(s) and recipient(s). In the alternative, the responding party may produce the documents, together with identifying information sufficient to satisfy FRCP 33(d). NY R USDCTS&ED Civ Rule 26.3(c)(4).

- *Parties.* The terms "plaintiff" and "defendant" as well as a party's full or abbreviated name or a pronoun referring to a party mean the party and, where applicable, its officers, directors, employees, partners, corporate parent, subsidiaries or affiliates. This definition is not intended to impose a discovery obligation on any person who is not a party to the litigation. NY R USDCTS&ED Civ Rule 26.3(c)(5).

- *Person.* The term "person" is defined as any natural person or any legal entity, including, without limitation, any business or governmental entity or association. NY R USDCTS&ED Civ Rule 26.3(c)(6).

- *Concerning.* The term "concerning" means relating to, referring to, describing, evidencing or constituting. NY R USDCTS&ED Civ Rule 26.3(c)(7).

   ii. *Rules of construction.* The following rules of construction apply to all discovery requests:

- *All/any/each.* The terms "all," "any," and "each" shall each be construed as encompassing any and all. NY R USDCTS&ED Civ Rule 26.3(d)(1).

- *And/or.* The connectives "and" and "or" shall be construed either disjunctively or conjunctively as necessary to bring within the scope of the discovery request all responses that might otherwise be construed to be outside of its scope. NY R USDCTS&ED Civ Rule 26.3(d)(2).

- *Number.* The use of the singular form of any word includes the plural and vice versa. NY R USDCTS&ED Civ Rule 26.3(d)(3).

e. *Cooperation among counsel in discovery.* Counsel are expected to cooperate with each other, consistent with the interests of their clients, in all phases of the discovery process and to be courteous in their dealings with each other, including in matters relating to scheduling and timing of various discovery procedures. NY R USDCTS&ED Civ Rule 26.4(a).

　i. Discovery requests shall be read reasonably in the recognition that the attorney serving them generally does not have the information being sought and the attorney receiving them generally does have such information or can obtain it from the client. NY R USDCTS&ED Civ Rule 26.4(b).

f. *Standard discovery in prisoner pro se actions.* For information on discovery in prisoner pro se actions, refer to NY R USDCTS&ED Civ Rule 33.2.

2. *Persons before whom depositions may be taken*

a. *Within the United States.* Within the United States or a territory or insular possession subject to United States jurisdiction, a deposition must be taken before: (1) an officer authorized to administer oaths either by federal law or by the law in the place of examination; or (2) a person appointed by the court where the action is pending to administer oaths and take testimony. FRCP 28(a)(1).

　i. *Definition of "officer".* The term "officer" in FRCP 30, FRCP 31, and FRCP 32 includes a person appointed by the court under FRCP 28 or designated by the parties under FRCP 29(a). FRCP 28(a)(2).

b. *In a foreign country.* A deposition may be taken in a foreign country: (1) under an applicable treaty or convention; (2) under a letter of request, whether or not captioned a "letter rogatory"; (3) on notice, before a person authorized to administer oaths either by federal law or by the law in the place of examination; or (4) before a person commissioned by the court to administer any necessary oath and take testimony. FRCP 28(b)(1).

　i. *Issuing a letter of request or a commission.* A letter of request, a commission, or both may be issued: (1) on appropriate terms after an application and notice of it; and (2) without a showing that taking the deposition in another manner is impracticable or inconvenient. FRCP 28(b)(2).

　ii. *Form of a request, notice, or commission.* When a letter of request or any other device is used according to a treaty or convention, it must be captioned in the form prescribed by that treaty or convention. A letter of request may be addressed "To the Appropriate Authority in [name of country]." A deposition notice or a commission must designate by name or descriptive title the person before whom the deposition is to be taken. FRCP 28(b)(3).

　iii. *Letter of request; Admitting evidence.* Evidence obtained in response to a letter of request need not be excluded merely because it is not a verbatim transcript, because the testimony was not taken under oath, or because of any similar departure from the requirements for depositions taken within the United States. FRCP 28(b)(4).

c. *Disqualification.* A deposition must not be taken before a person who is any party's relative, employee, or attorney; who is related to or employed by any party's attorney; or who is financially interested in the action. FRCP 28(c).

3. *Depositions by oral examination*

a. *Notice of the deposition.* A party who wants to depose a person by oral questions must give reasonable written notice to every other party. The notice must state the time and place of the deposition and, if known, the deponent's name and address. If the name is unknown, the notice must provide a general description sufficient to identify the person or the particular class or group to which the person belongs. FRCP 30(b)(1).

　i. *Notice or subpoena directed to an organization.* In its notice or subpoena, a party may name as

411

the deponent a public or private corporation, a partnership, an association, a governmental agency, or other entity and must describe with reasonable particularity the matters for examination. The named organization must then designate one or more officers, directors, or managing agents, or designate other persons who consent to testify on its behalf; and it may set out the matters on which each person designated will testify. A subpoena must advise a nonparty organization of its duty to make this designation. The persons designated must testify about information known or reasonably available to the organization. FRCP 30(b)(6) does not preclude a deposition by any other procedure allowed by the Federal Rules of Civil Procedure. FRCP 30(b)(6).

b. *Persons attending depositions.* A person who is a party in the action may attend the deposition of a party or witness. A witness or potential witness in the action may attend the deposition of a party or witness unless otherwise ordered by the Court. NY R USDCTS&ED Civ Rule 30.3.

c. *Counsel fees on taking depositions more than 100 miles from courthouse.* When a deposition upon oral examination is to be taken at a place more than one hundred (100) miles from the courthouse, any party may request the Court to issue an order providing that prior to the examination, another party shall pay the expense (including a reasonable counsel fee) of the attendance of one attorney for each other party at the place where the deposition is to be taken. The amounts so paid, unless otherwise directed by the Court, may be taxed as a cost at the conclusion of the action or proceeding. NY R USDCTS&ED Civ Rule 30.1.

d. *Method of recording*

   i. *Method stated in the notice.* The party who notices the deposition must state in the notice the method for recording the testimony. Unless the court orders otherwise, testimony may be recorded by audio, audiovisual, or stenographic means. The noticing party bears the recording costs. Any party may arrange to transcribe a deposition. FRCP 30(b)(3)(A).

   ii. *Additional method.* With prior notice to the deponent and other parties, any party may designate another method for recording the testimony in addition to that specified in the original notice. That party bears the expense of the additional record or transcript unless the court orders otherwise. FRCP 30(b)(3)(B).

e. *By remote means.* The parties may stipulate—or the court may on motion order—that a deposition be taken by telephone or other remote means. For the purpose of FRCP 30 and FRCP 28(a), FRCP 37(a)(2), and FRCP 37(b)(1), the deposition takes place where the deponent answers the questions. FRCP 30(b)(4).

   i. *Telephonic and other remote depositions.* The motion of a party to take the deposition of an adverse party by telephone or other remote means will presumptively be granted. Where the opposing party is a corporation, the term "adverse party" means an officer, director, managing agent or corporate designee pursuant to FRCP 30(b)(6). NY R USDCTS&ED Civ Rule 30.2.

f. *Officer's duties*

   i. *Before the deposition.* Unless the parties stipulate otherwise, a deposition must be conducted before an officer appointed or designated under FRCP 28. The officer must begin the deposition with an on-the-record statement that includes: (1) the officer's name and business address; (2) the date, time, and place of the deposition; (3) the deponent's name; (4) the officer's administration of the oath or affirmation to the deponent; and (5) the identity of all persons present. FRCP 30(b)(5)(A).

   ii. *Conducting the deposition; Avoiding distortion.* If the deposition is recorded non-stenographically, the officer must repeat the items in FRCP 30(b)(5)(A)(i) through FRCP 30(b)(5)(A)(iii) at the beginning of each unit of the recording medium. The deponent's and attorneys' appearance or demeanor must not be distorted through recording techniques. FRCP 30(b)(5)(B).

   iii. *After the deposition.* At the end of a deposition, the officer must state on the record that the deposition is complete and must set out any stipulations made by the attorneys about custody of the transcript or recording and of the exhibits, or about any other pertinent matters. FRCP 30(b)(5)(C).

g. *Examination and cross-examination.* The examination and cross-examination of a deponent proceed as they would at trial under the Federal Rules of Evidence, except FRE 103 and FRE 615. FRCP 30(c)(1).

    i. *Record of the examination.* After putting the deponent under oath or affirmation, the officer must record the testimony by the method designated under FRCP 30(b)(3)(A). The testimony must be recorded by the officer personally or by a person acting in the presence and under the direction of the officer. FRCP 30(c)(1).

    ii. *Objections.* An objection at the time of the examination—whether to evidence, to a party's conduct, to the officer's qualifications, to the manner of taking the deposition, or to any other aspect of the deposition—must be noted on the record, but the examination still proceeds; the testimony is taken subject to any objection. An objection must be stated concisely in a nonargumentative and nonsuggestive manner. A person may instruct a deponent not to answer only when necessary to preserve a privilege, to enforce a limitation ordered by the court, or to present a motion under FRCP 30(d)(3). FRCP 30(c)(2).

    iii. *Participating through written questions.* Instead of participating in the oral examination, a party may serve written questions in a sealed envelope on the party noticing the deposition, who must deliver them to the officer. The officer must ask the deponent those questions and record the answers verbatim. FRCP 30(c)(3).

    iv. *Conferences between deponent and defending attorney.* An attorney for a deponent shall not initiate a private conference with the deponent while a deposition question is pending, except for the purpose of determining whether a privilege should be asserted. NY R USDCTS&ED Civ Rule 30.4.

h. *Duration.* Unless otherwise stipulated or ordered by the court, a deposition is limited to one (1) day of seven (7) hours. The court must allow additional time consistent with FRCP 26(b)(1) and FRCP 26(b)(2) if needed to fairly examine the deponent or if the deponent, another person, or any other circumstance impedes or delays the examination. FRCP 30(d)(1).

i. *Sanction.* The court may impose an appropriate sanction—including the reasonable expenses and attorney's fees incurred by any party—on a person who impedes, delays, or frustrates the fair examination of the deponent. FRCP 30(d)(2). Refer to the United States District Court for the Southern District of New York KeyRules Motion for Discovery Sanctions document for more information on sanctions.

j. *Motion to terminate or limit.* At any time during a deposition, the deponent or a party may move to terminate or limit it on the ground that it is being conducted in bad faith or in a manner that unreasonably annoys, embarrasses, or oppresses the deponent or party. The motion may be filed in the court where the action is pending or the deposition is being taken. If the objecting deponent or party so demands, the deposition must be suspended for the time necessary to obtain an order. FRCP 30(d)(3)(A).

    i. *Order.* The court may order that the deposition be terminated or may limit its scope and manner as provided in FRCP 26(c). If terminated, the deposition may be resumed only by order of the court where the action is pending. FRCP 30(d)(3)(B).

    ii. *Award of expenses.* FRCP 37(a)(5) applies to the award of expenses. FRCP 30(d)(3)(C). Refer to the United States District Court for the Southern District of New York KeyRules Motion for Discovery Sanctions document for more information on sanctions.

k. *Review by the witness; Statement of changes.* On request by the deponent or a party before the deposition is completed, the deponent must be allowed thirty (30) days after being notified by the officer that the transcript or recording is available in which: (1) to review the transcript or recording; and (2) if there are changes in form or substance, to sign a statement listing the changes and the reasons for making them. FRCP 30(e)(1).

    i. *Changes indicated in the officer's certificate.* The officer must note in the certificate prescribed by FRCP 30(f)(1) whether a review was requested and, if so, must attach any changes the deponent makes during the thirty (30) day period. FRCP 30(e)(2).

l.  *Certification and delivery.* The officer must certify in writing that the witness was duly sworn and that the deposition accurately records the witness's testimony. The certificate must accompany the record of the deposition. Unless the court orders otherwise, the officer must seal the deposition in an envelope or package bearing the title of the action and marked "Deposition of [witness's name]" and must promptly send it to the attorney who arranged for the transcript or recording. The attorney must store it under conditions that will protect it against loss, destruction, tampering, or deterioration. FRCP 30(f)(1).

m.  *Documents and tangible things.* Documents and tangible things produced for inspection during a deposition must, on a party's request, be marked for identification and attached to the deposition. Any party may inspect and copy them. But if the person who produced them wants to keep the originals, the person may: (1) offer copies to be marked, attached to the deposition, and then used as originals—after giving all parties a fair opportunity to verify the copies by comparing them with the originals; or (2) give all parties a fair opportunity to inspect and copy the originals after they are marked—in which event the originals may be used as if attached to the deposition. FRCP 30(f)(2)(A).

    i.  *Order regarding the originals.* Any party may move for an order that the originals be attached to the deposition pending final disposition of the case. FRCP 30(f)(2)(B).

n.  *Copies of the transcript or recording.* Unless otherwise stipulated or ordered by the court, the officer must retain the stenographic notes of a deposition taken stenographically or a copy of the recording of a deposition taken by another method. When paid reasonable charges, the officer must furnish a copy of the transcript or recording to any party or the deponent. FRCP 30(f)(3).

o.  *Failure to attend a deposition or serve a subpoena; Expenses.* A party who, expecting a deposition to be taken, attends in person or by an attorney may recover reasonable expenses for attending, including attorney's fees, if the noticing party failed to: (1) attend and proceed with the deposition; or (2) serve a subpoena on a nonparty deponent, who consequently did not attend. FRCP 30(g). Refer to the United States District Court for the Southern District of New York KeyRules Motion for Discovery Sanctions document for more information on sanctions.

4.  *Depositions by written questions*

a.  *Notice of deposition.* A party who wants to depose a person by written questions must serve them on every other party, with a notice stating, if known, the deponent's name and address. If the name is unknown, the notice must provide a general description sufficient to identify the person or the particular class or group to which the person belongs. The notice must also state the name or descriptive title and the address of the officer before whom the deposition will be taken. FRCP 31(a)(3).

b.  *Questions directed to an organization.* A public or private corporation, a partnership, an association, or a governmental agency may be deposed by written questions in accordance with FRCP 30(b)(6). FRCP 31(a)(4).

c.  *Delivery to the officer; Officer's duties.* The party who noticed the deposition must deliver to the officer a copy of all the questions served and of the notice. The officer must promptly proceed in the manner provided in FRCP 30(c), FRCP 30(e), and FRCP 30(f) to:

    i.  Take the deponent's testimony in response to the questions;

    ii.  Prepare and certify the deposition; and

    iii.  Send it to the party, attaching a copy of the questions and of the notice. FRCP 31(b).

d.  *Notice of completion.* The party who noticed the deposition must notify all other parties when it is completed. FRCP 31(c)(1).

5.  *Depositions to perpetuate testimony.* For information on depositions to perpetuate testimony, refer to FRCP 27.

6.  *Stipulations about discovery procedure.* Unless the court orders otherwise, the parties may stipulate that: (1) a deposition may be taken before any person, at any time or place, on any notice, and in the manner specified—in which event it may be used in the same way as any other deposition; and (2) other

procedures governing or limiting discovery be modified—but a stipulation extending the time for any form of discovery must have court approval if it would interfere with the time set for completing discovery, for hearing a motion, or for trial. FRCP 29.

7. *Complex civil cases.* For information on procedures for complex civil cases, refer to NY R USDCTSD Order 11 Misc 00388.

8. *Related cases.* It shall be the continuing duty of each attorney appearing in any civil or criminal case to bring promptly to the attention of the Court all facts which said attorney believes are relevant to a determination that said case and one or more pending civil or criminal cases should be heard by the same Judge, in order to avoid unnecessary duplication of judicial effort. As soon as the attorney becomes aware of such relationship, said attorney shall notify the Judges to whom the cases have been assigned. NY R USDCTS&ED Civ Rule 1.6(a). If counsel fails to comply with NY R USDCTS&ED Civ Rule 1.6(a), the Court may assess reasonable costs directly against counsel whose action has obstructed the effective administration of the Court's business. NY R USDCTS&ED Civ Rule 1.6(b).

a. *Determination of relatedness.* Subject to the limitations set forth in NY R USDCTSD Div. Bus., Rule 13(a)(2), a civil case, bankruptcy appeal, or motion to withdraw the bankruptcy reference will be deemed related to one or more civil cases, appeals or motions when the interests of justice and efficiency will be served. In determining relatedness, a judge will consider whether (A) the actions concern the same or substantially similar parties, property, transactions or events; (B) there is substantial factual overlap; (C) the parties could be subjected to conflicting orders; and (D) whether absent a determination of relatedness there would be a substantial duplication of effort and expense, delay, or undue burden on the Court, parties or witnesses. NY R USDCTSD Div. Bus., Rule 13(a)(1). Nothing in this NY R USDCTSD Div. Bus., Rule 13 is intended to preclude parties from moving for consolidated proceedings under FRCP 42. NY R USDCTSD Div. Bus., Rule 13(a)(1). Notwithstanding NY R USDCTSD Div. Bus., Rule 13(a)(1):

  i. Civil cases shall not be deemed related merely because they involve common legal issues or the same parties. NY R USDCTSD Div. Bus., Rule 13(a)(2)(A).

  ii. Other than cases subject to NY R USDCTSD Div. Bus., Rule 4(b) and actions seeking the enforcement of a judgment or settlement in or of an earlier case, civil cases presumptively shall not be deemed related unless both cases are pending before the Court (or the earlier case is on appeal). NY R USDCTSD Div. Bus., Rule 13(a)(2)(B).

b. *Procedure in regard to cases said to be related*

  i. *Disclosure of contention of relatedness.* When a civil case is filed or removed or a bankruptcy appeal or motion to withdraw the reference of an adversary proceeding from the bankruptcy court is filed, the person filing or removing shall disclose on form JSC44C any contention of relatedness and shall file a Related Case Statement stating clearly and succinctly the basis for the contention. A copy of the civil cover sheet and Related Case Statement shall be served with the complaint, notice of removal, notice of appeal, or motion. Any party may contest a claim of relatedness by any other in writing addressed to the judge having the case with the lowest docket number of all cases claimed to be related. However, the foregoing shall not delay the assignment process or the operation of NY R USDCTSD Div. Bus., Rule 13. NY R USDCTSD Div. Bus., Rule 13(b)(1). [Editor's note: the reference to form JSC44C is likely meant to be form JS44C-SDNY: Civil Court Cover Sheet].

  ii. *Claims of relatedness by other parties.* A party other than the one filing a case, bankruptcy appeal or motion to withdraw the reference that contends its case is related to another may so advise in writing the judge assigned in its case and request a transfer of its case to the judge that the party contends has the related case with the lowest docket number. If the assigned judge believes the case is related under NY R USDCTSD Div. Bus., Rule 13(a), he or she shall refer the question to the judge having the case with the lowest docket number. In the event the latter judge agrees, the case shall be transferred to that judge unless the Assignment Committee disagrees. NY R USDCTSD Div. Bus., Rule 13(b)(3).

c. For more information on related cases, refer to NY R USDCTSD Div. Bus., Rule 13.

9. *Alternative dispute resolution (ADR).* The U.S. District Court for the Southern District of New York

provides litigants with opportunities to discuss settlement through judicial settlement conferences and mediation. NY R USDCTS&ED Civ Rule 83.9(a).

    a. *Consideration of alternative dispute resolution.* In all civil cases, including those eligible for mediation pursuant to NY R USDCTS&ED Civ Rule 83.9(e), each party shall consider the use of mediation or a judicial settlement conference and shall report to the assigned Judge at the initial FRCP 16(b) case management conference, or subsequently, whether the party believes mediation or a judicial settlement conference may facilitate the resolution of the lawsuit. Judges are encouraged to note the availability of the mediation program and/or a judicial settlement conference before, at, or after the initial FRCP 16(b) case management conference. NY R USDCTS&ED Civ Rule 83.9(d).

    b. *Mediation.* In mediation, parties and counsel meet, sometimes collectively and sometimes individually, with a neutral third party (the mediator) who has been trained to facilitate confidential settlement discussions. The parties articulate their respective positions and interests and generate options for a mutually agreeable resolution to the dispute. The mediator assists the parties in reaching their own negotiated settlement by defining the issues, probing and assessing the strengths and weaknesses of each party's legal positions, and identifying areas of agreement and disagreement. The main benefits of mediation are that it can result in an expeditious and less costly resolution of the litigation, and can produce creative solutions to complex disputes often unavailable in traditional litigation. NY R USDCTS&ED Civ Rule 83.9(b).

        i. *Mediation program eligibility.* All civil cases other than Social Security, habeas corpus, and tax cases are eligible for mediation, whether assigned to Manhattan or White Plains. NY R USDCTS&ED Civ Rule 83.9(e)(1).

            • The Board of Judges may, by Administrative Order, direct that certain specified categories of cases shall automatically be submitted to the mediation program. The assigned District Judge or Magistrate Judge may issue a written order exempting a particular case with or without the request of the parties. NY R USDCTS&ED Civ Rule 83.9(e)(2).

            • For all other cases, the assigned District Judge or Magistrate Judge may determine that a case is appropriate for mediation and may order that case to mediation, with or without the consent of the parties, before, at, or after the initial FRCP 16(b) case management conference. Alternatively, the parties should notify the assigned Judge at any time of their desire to mediate. NY R USDCTS&ED Civ Rule 83.9(e)(3).

    c. *Judicial settlement conferences.* Judicial settlement conferences may be ordered by District Judges or Magistrate Judges with or without the request or consent of the parties. NY R USDCTS&ED Civ Rule 83.9(f).

    d. For more information on alternative dispute resolution (ADR), refer to NY R USDCTS&ED Civ Rule 83.9.

  10. *Individual judge practices.* Refer to the Miscellaneous section of this document for information on individual judge practices on general requirements for documents.

## D. Documents

  1. *Depositions by oral examination*

    a. *Required documents*

        i. *Notice of deposition.* Refer to the General Requirements section of this document for the form and contents of the notice of deposition.

    b. *Supplemental documents*

        i. *Subpoena.* The deponent's attendance may be compelled by subpoena under FRCP 45. FRCP 30(a)(1). For more information on subpoenas, refer to FRCP 45.

        ii. *Subpoena duces tecum.* If a subpoena duces tecum is to be served on the deponent, the materials designated for production, as set out in the subpoena, must be listed in the notice or in an attachment. FRCP 30(b)(2). For more information on subpoenas duces tecum, refer to FRCP 45.

        iii. *Request for production of documents.* The notice to a party deponent may be accompanied by a request under FRCP 34 to produce documents and tangible things at the deposition. FRCP 30(b)(2). Refer to the United States District Court for the Southern District of New York KeyRules Request for Production of Documents document for more information.

    iv. *Certificate of service.* FRCP 5(d) requires that the person making service under FRCP 5 certify that service has been effected. FRCP 5(Advisory Committee Notes). Having such information on file may be useful for many purposes, including proof of service if an issue arises concerning the effectiveness of the service. FRCP 5(Advisory Committee Notes).

2. *Depositions by written questions*

  a. *Required documents*

    i. *Notice of deposition.* Refer to the General Requirements section of this document for the form and contents of the notice of deposition.

    ii. *Written questions.* A party who wants to depose a person by written questions must serve them on every other party, with a notice. FRCP 31(a)(3).

  b. *Supplemental documents*

    i. *Subpoena.* The deponent's attendance may be compelled by subpoena under FRCP 45. FRCP 31(a)(1). For more information on subpoenas, refer to FRCP 45.

    ii. *Certificate of service.* FRCP 5(d) requires that the person making service under FRCP 5 certify that service has been effected. FRCP 5(Advisory Committee Notes). Having such information on file may be useful for many purposes, including proof of service if an issue arises concerning the effectiveness of the service. FRCP 5(Advisory Committee Notes).

3. *Individual judge practices.* Refer to the Miscellaneous section of this document for information on individual judge practices on required documents.

## E. Format

1. *Form of documents.* The rules governing captions and other matters of form in pleadings apply to motions and other papers. FRCP 7(b)(2).

  a. *Paper.* Every pleading, written motion, and other paper must: be plainly written, typed, printed, or copied without erasures or interlineations which materially deface it. NY R USDCTS&ED Civ Rule 11.1(a)(1).

  b. *Typeface, margin, and spacing.* The typeface, margins, and spacing of all documents presented for filing must meet the following requirements:

    i. All text must be twelve (12) point type or larger, except for text in footnotes which may be ten (10) point type;

    ii. All documents must have at least one (1) inch margins on all sides;

    iii. All text must be double-spaced, except for headings, text in footnotes, or block quotations, which may be single-spaced. NY R USDCTS&ED Civ Rule 11.1(b).

  c. *Caption; Names of parties.* Every pleading must have a caption with the court's name, a title, a file number, and a FRCP 7(a) designation. The title of the complaint must name all the parties; the title of other pleadings, after naming the first party on each side, may refer generally to other parties. FRCP 10(a). Every pleading, written motion, and other paper must: bear the docket number and the initials of the District Judge and any Magistrate Judge before whom the action or proceeding is pending, NY R USDCTS&ED Civ Rule 11.1(a)(2).

  d. *Paragraphs; Separate statements.* A party must state its claims or defenses in numbered paragraphs, each limited as far as practicable to a single set of circumstances. A later pleading may refer by number to a paragraph in an earlier pleading. If doing so would promote clarity, each claim founded on a separate transaction or occurrence—and each defense other than a denial—must be stated in a separate count or defense. FRCP 10(b).

  e. *Adoption by reference; Exhibits.* A statement in a pleading may be adopted by reference elsewhere in the same pleading or in any other pleading or motion. A copy of a written instrument that is an exhibit to a pleading is a part of the pleading for all purposes. FRCP 10(c).

f. *Acceptance by the clerk.* The clerk must not refuse to file a paper solely because it is not in the form prescribed by the Federal Rules of Civil Procedure or by a local rule or practice. FRCP 5(d)(4).

2. *Form of electronic documents*

a. *PDF-A.* All documents electronically filed on the ECF system must be in PDF-A format (portable document format). A PDF-A file is created using PDF writer software such as Adobe Acrobat (go to the Adobe website for details). PDF-A files cannot be altered, providing security to the filer and the Court. NY R USDCTSD CM/ECF, S.D.(II)(23)(23.2).

b. *Size limitation.* No single PDF file may be larger than four megabytes (4 MB). If the filing is too large, the ECF system will not allow it to be filed, and you will not see a Notice of Electronic Filing (NEF or filing receipt) screen. To determine the size of an Adobe Acrobat PDF file click on File, Document Properties, Summary. NY R USDCTSD CM/ECF, S.D.(II)(23)(23.3).

   i. Converting documents directly from a word processor to PDF-A format creates the smallest possible file in terms of computer memory. If that is not possible, scan your document at low resolution. Within the Adobe Acrobat program, on the "Scan Manager" screen, adjust the settings for black and white and 200 dpi (dots per inch). This allows more pages to fit into a single PDF-A file. If that does not work, separate an oversized file into 2 or more parts. Simply label each file 1a, 1b, 1c, etc. Only relevant excerpts of exhibits should be electronically filed. NY R USDCTSD CM/ECF, S.D.(II)(23)(23.4).

c. *Attachments and exhibits.* Filing Users must submit in electronic form all documents referenced as exhibits or attachments, unless the Court permits paper filing. NY R USDCTSD CM/ECF, S.D.(I)(5)(5.1).

   i. A Filing User must submit as exhibits or attachments only those excerpts of the referenced documents that are relevant to the matter under consideration by the Court. Excerpted material must be clearly and prominently identified as such. Filing Users who file excerpts of documents as exhibits or attachments under this procedure do so without prejudice to their right to file timely additional excerpts or the complete document. Responding parties may file timely additional excerpts that they believe are relevant or the complete document. A party may move before the Court for permission to serve and file in hard copy documents that cannot be reasonably scanned. NY R USDCTSD CM/ECF, S.D.(I)(5)(5.2).

   ii. Exhibits must be filed only as attachments to a document, such as a motion or an affidavit. Do not use the ECF Filing Event for "Motion" to file exhibits separately. Exhibits are the only items that should be attached to electronically filed documents. You are limited to electronically filing only relevant excerpts of exhibits. Excerpts must be clearly identified as such. If the exhibit is too large to be scanned and electronically filed you may contact the ECF Help Desk. NY R USDCTSD CM/ECF, S.D.(II)(15)(15.6).

d. *Letters.* Parties should consult the assigned judge's Individual Practices to determine if the judge accepts letters at all and, if he or she does, whether the judge has any page limitations on letters and/or requires courtesy copies of letters filed on ECF (and, if so, by what means of delivery). All letters addressed to the Court must include a subject line with the case name and docket number (e.g., "Re: Doe v. Smith, 13 Civ. 1234 (ABC)"). NY R USDCTSD CM/ECF, S.D.(II)(13)(13.1).

e. *Proposed orders, proposed judgments, stipulations and consents.* Any document that requires the signature of a judge should not be electronically filed except as an exhibit to another document. Proposed orders, judgments, stipulations and consents should not be submitted through the ECF system. Instead they should be sent by e-mail to the Clerk. Proposed orders should be submitted in word processing format (WordPerfect or Word) rather than as a PDF document. Stipulations should be submitted in PDF-A format. Stipulations must contain ink signatures not s/. Faxed or emailed signatures are acceptable. Please note that Stipulations of Voluntary Dismissal pursuant to FRCP 41(a)(1)(A)(ii) do not require the signature of a judge and must be electronically filed on the ECF system. Questions may be directed to the Orders and Judgments Clerk at the phone numbers listed in NY R USDCTSD CM/ECF, S.D.(II)(18)(18.3). NY R USDCTSD CM/ECF, S.D.(II)(18)(18.3).

   i. Email the proposed order, judgment or stipulation to the email addresses listed in NY R USDCTSD CM/ECF, S.D.(II)(18)(18.3). NY R USDCTSD CM/ECF, S.D.(II)(18)(18.3).

ii. Pro se litigants who are not Filing Users are exempt from that portion of NY R USDCTSD CM/ECF, S.D.(II)(18)(18.3) that requires litigants to email proposed orders, judgments, stipulations and consents, and shall deliver such documents to the Clerk's Office in paper form. NY R USDCTSD CM/ECF, S.D.(II)(18)(18.3).

3. *Signing disclosures and discovery requests, responses, and objections.* FRCP 11 does not apply to disclosures and discovery requests, responses, objections, and motions under FRCP 26 through FRCP 37. FRCP 11(d).

a. *Signature required.* Every disclosure under FRCP 26(a)(1) or FRCP 26(a)(3) and every discovery request, response, or objection must be signed by at least one attorney of record in the attorney's own name—or by the party personally, if unrepresented—and must state the signer's address, e-mail address, and telephone number. FRCP 26(g)(1). Every pleading, written motion, and other paper must: have the name of each person signing it clearly printed or typed directly below the signature. NY R USDCTS&ED Civ Rule 11.1(a)(3).

i. *Electronic signatures.* The user log-in and password required to submit documents to the ECF system serve as the Filing User's signature on all electronic documents filed with the Court. NY R USDCTSD CM/ECF, S.D.(I)(8)(8.1); NY R USDCTSD CM/ECF, S.D.(II)(13)(13.14). They also serve as a signature for purposes of the Federal Rules of Civil Procedure, including FRCP 11, the Local Civil Rules of the United States District Courts for the Southern and Eastern Districts of New York, and any other purpose for which a signature is required in connection with proceedings before the Court. NY R USDCTSD CM/ECF, S.D.(I)(8)(8.1).

- *Signature block.* Electronically filed documents must include a signature block and must set forth the name, address, telephone number and e-mail address all in compliance with the Federal Rules of Civil Procedure and NY R USDCTS&ED Civ Rule 11.1. In the absence of a scanned signature image, the name of the Filing User under whose log-in and password the document is submitted must be preceded by an "s/" typed in the space where the signature would otherwise appear. NY R USDCTSD CM/ECF, S.D.(I)(8)(8.2); NY R USDCTSD CM/ECF, S.D.(II)(13)(13.14).

- *Documents requiring the signature of a party or witness.* A document requiring the signature of a party or witness shall be electronically filed in a scanned format that contains an image of the actual signature. NY R USDCTSD CM/ECF, S.D.(I)(8)(8.4); NY R USDCTSD CM/ECF, S.D.(II)(13)(13.14).

- *Documents requiring the signature of a judge.* A Filing User submitting a document electronically that requires a judge's signature must promptly deliver the document in such other form, if any, as the Court requires. NY R USDCTSD CM/ECF, S.D.(I)(4)(4.2).

- *Documents requiring multiple signatures.* Documents requiring signatures of more than one party must be electronically filed either by: (a) submitting a scanned document containing all necessary signatures; (b) representing the consent of the other parties on the document; (c) identifying on the document the parties whose signatures are required and by the submission of a notice of endorsement by the other parties no later than three business days after filing; or (d) in any other manner approved by the Court. NY R USDCTSD CM/ECF, S.D.(I)(8)(8.5).

b. *Effect of signature.* By signing, an attorney or party certifies that to the best of the person's knowledge, information, and belief formed after a reasonable inquiry:

i. With respect to a disclosure, it is complete and correct as of the time it is made; and

ii. With respect to a discovery request, response, or objection, it is:

- Consistent with the Federal Rules of Civil Procedure and warranted by existing law or by a nonfrivolous argument for extending, modifying, or reversing existing law, or for establishing new law;

- Not interposed for any improper purpose, such as to harass, cause unnecessary delay, or needlessly increase the cost of litigation; and

- Neither unreasonable nor unduly burdensome or expensive, considering the needs of the case, prior discovery in the case, the amount in controversy, and the importance of the issues at stake in the action. FRCP 26(g)(1).

c. *Failure to sign.* Other parties have no duty to act on an unsigned disclosure, request, response, or objection until it is signed, and the court must strike it unless a signature is promptly supplied after the omission is called to the attorney's or party's attention. FRCP 26(g)(2).

d. *Sanction for improper certification.* If a certification violates FRCP 26(g) without substantial justification, the court, on motion or on its own, must impose an appropriate sanction on the signer, the party on whose behalf the signer was acting, or both. The sanction may include an order to pay the reasonable expenses, including attorney's fees, caused by the violation. FRCP 26(g)(3). Refer to the United States District Court for the Southern District of New York KeyRules Motion for Discovery Sanctions document for more information.

4. *Privacy protection for filings made with the court*

a. *Redacted filings.* Unless the court orders otherwise, in an electronic or paper filing with the court that contains an individual's Social Security number, taxpayer-identification number, or birth date, the name of an individual known to be a minor, or a financial-account number, a party or nonparty making the filing may include only:

    i. The last four (4) digits of the Social Security number and taxpayer-identification number;

    ii. The year of the individual's birth;

    iii. The minor's initials; and

    iv. The last four (4) digits of the financial-account number. FRCP 5.2(a); NY R USDCTSD CM/ECF, S.D.(II)(21)(21.3).

    v. Caution should be exercised when filing documents that contain the following:

- Personal identifying numbers (PIN #'s), such as a driver's license number;
- Medical records, treatment and diagnosis;
- Employment history;
- Individual financial information;
- Proprietary or trade secret information;
- Information regarding an individual's cooperation with the government. NY R US-DCTSD CM/ECF, S.D.(II)(21)(21.4).

b. *Exemptions from the redaction requirement.* The redaction requirement does not apply to the following:

    i. A financial-account number that identifies the property allegedly subject to forfeiture in a forfeiture proceeding;

    ii. The record of an administrative or agency proceeding;

    iii. The official record of a state-court proceeding;

    iv. The record of a court or tribunal, if that record was not subject to the redaction requirement when originally filed;

    v. A filing covered by FRCP 5.2(c) or FRCP 5.2(d); and

    vi. A pro se filing in an action brought under 28 U.S.C.A. § 2241, 28 U.S.C.A. § 2254, or 28 U.S.C.A. § 2255. FRCP 5.2(b).

c. *Limitations on remote access to electronic files; Social Security appeals and immigration cases.* Unless the court orders otherwise, in an action for benefits under the Social Security Act, and in an action or proceeding relating to an order of removal, to relief from removal, or to immigration benefits or detention, access to an electronic file is authorized as follows:

    i. The parties and their attorneys may have remote electronic access to any part of the case file, including the administrative record;

     ii.   Any other person may have electronic access to the full record at the courthouse, but may have remote electronic access only to:

        •   The docket maintained by the court; and

        •   An opinion, order, judgment, or other disposition of the court, but not any other part of the case file or the administrative record. FRCP 5.2(c).

   d.   *Filings made under seal.* The court may order that a filing be made under seal without redaction. The court may later unseal the filing or order the person who made the filing to file a redacted version for the public record. FRCP 5.2(d). For more information on sealing documents, refer to NY R USDCTSD CM/ECF, S.D.(I)(6).

   e.   *Protective orders.* For good cause, the court may by order in a case:

     i.   Require redaction of additional information; or

     ii.   Limit or prohibit a nonparty's remote electronic access to a document filed with the court. FRCP 5.2(e).

   f.   *Option for additional unredacted filing under seal.* A person making a redacted filing may also file an unredacted copy under seal. The court must retain the unredacted copy as part of the record. FRCP 5.2(f); NY R USDCTSD CM/ECF, S.D.(II)(21)(21.5).

   g.   *Option for filing a reference list.* A filing that contains redacted information may be filed together with a reference list that identifies each item of redacted information and specifies an appropriate identifier that uniquely corresponds to each item listed. The list must be filed under seal and may be amended as of right. Any reference in the case to a listed identifier will be construed to refer to the corresponding item of information. FRCP 5.2(g); NY R USDCTSD CM/ECF, S.D.(II)(21)(21.5).

   h.   *Responsibility for redaction.* It is the sole responsibility of counsel and the parties to be sure that all documents comply with the rules of this Court requiring redaction of personal identifiers. Neither the judge nor the Clerk of Court will review documents for compliance with these rules. NY R USDCTSD CM/ECF, S.D.(II)(21)(21.2).

   i.   *Waiver of protection of identifiers.* A person waives the protection of FRCP 5.2(a) as to the person's own information by filing it without redaction and not under seal. FRCP 5.2(h).

   j.   For more information on privacy and public access to ECF cases, refer to NY R USDCTSD CM/ECF, S.D.(II)(21).

  5.   *Individual judge practices.* Refer to the Miscellaneous section of this document for information on individual judge practices on formatting documents.

## F.  Filing and Service Requirements

  1.   *Filing requirements.* Any paper after the complaint that is required to be served—together with a certificate of service—must be filed within a reasonable time after service. But disclosures under FRCP 26(a)(1) or FRCP 26(a)(2) and the following discovery requests and responses must not be filed until they are used in the proceeding or the court orders filing: depositions, interrogatories, requests for documents or tangible things or to permit entry onto land, and requests for admission. FRCP 5(d)(1). Refer to the United States District Court for the Southern District of New York KeyRules pleading and motion documents for information on filing with the court.

   a.   *Notice of filing*

     i.   *Depositions by oral examination.* A party who files the deposition must promptly notify all other parties of the filing. FRCP 30(f)(4).

     ii.   *Depositions by written questions.* A party who files the deposition must promptly notify all other parties of the filing. FRCP 31(c)(2).

  2.   *Service requirements*

   a.   *Service; When required*

     i.   *In general.* Unless the Federal Rules of Civil Procedure provide otherwise, each of the following papers must be served on every party:

        •   An order stating that service is required;

- A pleading filed after the original complaint, unless the court orders otherwise under FRCP 5(c) because there are numerous defendants;

- A discovery paper required to be served on a party, unless the court orders otherwise;

- A written motion, except one that may be heard ex parte; and

- A written notice, appearance, demand, or offer of judgment, or any similar paper. FRCP 5(a)(1).

ii. *If a party fails to appear.* No service is required on a party who is in default for failing to appear. But a pleading that asserts a new claim for relief against such a party must be served on that party under FRCP 4. FRCP 5(a)(2).

iii. *Seizing property.* If an action is begun by seizing property and no person is or need be named as a defendant, any service required before the filing of an appearance, answer, or claim must be made on the person who had custody or possession of the property when it was seized. FRCP 5(a)(3).

b. *Service; How made*

i. *Serving an attorney.* If a party is represented by an attorney, service under FRCP 5 must be made on the attorney unless the court orders service on the party. FRCP 5(b)(1).

ii. *Service in general.* A paper is served under FRCP 5 by:

- Handing it to the person;

- Leaving it: (1) at the person's office with a clerk or other person in charge or, if no one is in charge, in a conspicuous place in the office; or (2) if the person has no office or the office is closed, at the person's dwelling or usual place of abode with someone of suitable age and discretion who resides there;

- Mailing it to the person's last known address—in which event service is complete upon mailing;

- Leaving it with the court clerk if the person has no known address;

- Sending it by electronic means if the person consented in writing—in which event service is complete upon transmission, but is not effective if the serving party learns that it did not reach the person to be served; or

- Delivering it by any other means that the person consented to in writing—in which event service is complete when the person making service delivers it to the agency designated to make delivery. FRCP 5(b)(2).

iii. *Service by overnight delivery.* Service upon an attorney may be made by overnight delivery service. "Overnight delivery service" means any delivery service which regularly accepts items for overnight delivery. Overnight delivery service shall be deemed service by mail for purposes of FRCP 5 and FRCP 6. NY R USDCTS&ED Civ Rule 5.3.

iv. *Service by electronic means.* Parties serving and filing papers shall follow the instructions regarding Electronic Case Filing (ECF) published on the website of each respective Court. A paper served and filed by electronic means in accordance with such instructions is, for purposes of FRCP 5, served and filed in compliance with the Local Civil Rules of the United States District Courts for the Southern and Eastern Districts of New York. NY R USDCTS&ED Civ Rule 5.2(a). Parties have an obligation to review the Court's actual order, decree, or judgment (on ECF), which controls, and should not rely on the description on the docket or in the ECF Notice of Electronic Filing (NEF). NY R USDCTS&ED Civ Rule 5.2(c).

- *Notice of electronic filing (NEF).* In cases assigned to the ECF system, service is complete provided all parties receive a Notice of Electronic Filing (NEF), which is sent automatically by email from the Court (see the NEF for a list of who did/did not receive notice electronically). Transmission of the NEF constitutes service upon all Filing and Receiving Users who are listed as recipients of notice by electronic mail. NY R USDCTSD CM/ECF, S.D.(I)(9)(9.1). In cases assigned to the ECF system, if all parties receive a NEF, service is complete upon transmission of the NEF by the Court, and you are not required to serve a paper copy. NY R USDCTSD CM/ECF, S.D.(II)(19)(19.2). It remains the duty of Filing and Receiving Users to maintain current contact information with the court and to regularly review the docket sheet of the case. NY R USDCTSD CM/ECF, S.D.(I)(9)(9.1).

- *Mailing of court-initiated documents.* The Clerk's Office will no longer mail paper copies of court-initiated documents to Filing and Receiving Users. The Clerk's Office will mail copies of all court-initiated documents to pro se parties who have not registered as Filing or Receiving Users. NY R USDCTSD CM/ECF, S.D.(II)(19)(19.1).

- *No receipt of a NEF.* If any party does not receive a NEF, you are required to accomplish service on that party in the traditional manner, in paper form. NY R USDCTSD CM/ECF, S.D.(II)(19)(19.2). The NEF receipt will inform you who will receive notice of the filing "electronically" (by e-mail from the Court) and who will receive notice "by other means" (traditional service in paper form). NY R USDCTSD CM/ECF, S.D.(II)(19)(19.2).

- *Service on non-filing or non-receiving users.* Attorneys and pro se parties who are not Filing or Receiving Users must be served with a paper copy of any electronically filed pleading or other document. Service of such paper copy must be made according to the Federal Rules of Civil Procedure and the Local Civil Rules of the United States District Courts for the Southern and Eastern Districts of New York. NY R USDCTSD CM/ECF, S.D.(I)(9)(9.2). Such paper service must be documented by electronically filing proof of service. NY R USDCTSD CM/ECF, S.D.(I)(9)(9.2); NY R USDCTSD CM/ECF, S.D.(II)(19)(19.2). Where the Clerk scans and electronically files pleadings and documents on behalf of a pro se party, the associated NEF constitutes service. NY R USDCTSD CM/ECF, S.D.(I)(9)(9.2).

- For more information on service by electronic means, refer to NY R USDCTSD CM/ECF, S.D.(II)(19).

  v. *Using court facilities.* If a local rule so authorizes, a party may use the court's transmission facilities to make service under FRCP 5(b)(2)(E). FRCP 5(b)(3).

  c. *Serving numerous defendants*

  i. *In general.* If an action involves an unusually large number of defendants, the court may, on motion or on its own, order that:

- Defendants' pleadings and replies to them need not be served on other defendants;

- Any crossclaim, counterclaim, avoidance, or affirmative defense in those pleadings and replies to them will be treated as denied or avoided by all other parties; and

- Filing any such pleading and serving it on the plaintiff constitutes notice of the pleading to all parties. FRCP 5(c)(1).

  ii. *Notifying parties.* A copy of every such order must be served on the parties as the court directs. FRCP 5(c)(2).

3. *Individual judge practices.* Refer to the Miscellaneous section of this document for information on individual judge practices on filing and serving documents.

## G. Hearings

1. There is no hearing contemplated in the federal statutes or rules for the notice of deposition.

## H. Forms

### 1. Federal Notice of Deposition Forms

a. Notice to take deposition to perpetuate testimony. 3A FEDFORMS § 3339.

b. Notice of taking of deposition to perpetuate testimony pending appeal. 3A FEDFORMS § 3345.

c. Notice of taking deposition upon oral examination. 3A FEDFORMS § 3422.

d. Notice of taking deposition upon oral examination; Party. 3A FEDFORMS § 3423.

e. Notice of taking deposition upon oral examination; Naming and describing person not a party. 3A FEDFORMS § 3424.

f.  Notice of taking deposition upon oral examination; Describing deponents whose names are unknown. 3A FEDFORMS § 3425.

g.  Notice of taking deposition upon oral examination; Pursuant to order granting leave to take deposition. 3A FEDFORMS § 3426.

h.  Notice of taking of deposition of party with notice to produce documents. 3A FEDFORMS § 3427.

i.  Notice of taking of deposition of witness; Including designation of materials in related subpoena duces tecum. 3A FEDFORMS § 3428.

j.  Notice of taking deposition of witness; Including reference to materials designated in attached subpoena. 3A FEDFORMS § 3429.

k.  Notice of taking deposition upon written questions served with notice. 3A FEDFORMS § 3449.

l.  Questions to be attached to notice or served with it. 3A FEDFORMS § 3450.

m.  Notice of return and filing of deposition taken upon written questions. 3A FEDFORMS § 3456.

n.  Notice; Taking of deposition on oral examination. FEDPROF § 23:136.

o.  Notice; Taking of deposition on oral examination; Patent proceedings. FEDPROF § 23:137.

p.  Notice; Taking of deposition on oral examination; Corporate officer. FEDPROF § 23:138.

q.  Notice; Taking of deposition on oral examination; Corporate officers to be designated by corporation. FEDPROF § 23:139.

r.  Notice; Taking of deposition on written questions. FEDPROF § 23:140.

s.  Notice; Taking of deposition on oral examination or on written questions; Pursuant to court order. FEDPROF § 23:141.

t.  Notice; In connection with deposition on written questions; Of cross, redirect, or recross questions. FEDPROF § 23:142.

u.  Attachment to notice; Taking of deposition on written questions; Questions to be propounded. FEDPROF § 23:143.

v.  Attachment to notice; Cross, redirect, or recross questions to be propounded. FEDPROF § 23:144.

w.  Notice; To party taking deposition; Written questions submitted in lieu of participation in oral examination. FEDPROF § 23:145.

x.  Notice of taking deposition; Expert witness; Request for production of supporting documents. FEDPROF § 23:151.

y.  Subpoena; To testify at taking of deposition and to produce documents or things. FEDPROF § 23:152.

z.  Provision in subpoena; Advice to nonparty organization of its duty to designate witness. FEDPROF § 23:155.

## I. Applicable Rules

1. *Federal rules*

   a.  Serving and filing pleadings and other papers. FRCP 5.

   b.  Privacy protection for filings made with the court. FRCP 5.2.

   c.  Computing and extending time; Time for motion papers. FRCP 6.

   d.  Pleadings allowed; Form of motions and other papers. FRCP 7.

   e.  Form of pleadings. FRCP 10.

   f.  Signing pleadings, motions, and other papers; Representations to the court; Sanctions. FRCP 11.

   g.  Duty to disclose; General provisions governing discovery. FRCP 26.

   h.  Persons before whom depositions may be taken. FRCP 28.

   i.  Stipulations about discovery procedure. FRCP 29.

    j.   Depositions by oral examination. FRCP 30.

    k.   Depositions by written questions. FRCP 31.

    l.   Failure to make disclosures or to cooperate in discovery; Sanctions. FRCP 37.

2.  *Local rules*

    a.   Duty of attorneys in related cases. NY R USDCTS&ED Civ Rule 1.6.

    b.   Electronic service and filing of documents. NY R USDCTS&ED Civ Rule 5.2.

    c.   Service by overnight delivery. NY R USDCTS&ED Civ Rule 5.3.

    d.   Computation of time. NY R USDCTS&ED Civ Rule 6.4.

    e.   Form of pleadings, motions, and other papers. NY R USDCTS&ED Civ Rule 11.1.

    f.   Assertion of claim of privilege. NY R USDCTS&ED Civ Rule 26.2.

    g.   Uniform definitions in discovery requests. NY R USDCTS&ED Civ Rule 26.3.

    h.   Cooperation among counsel in discovery. NY R USDCTS&ED Civ Rule 26.4.

    i.   Counsel fees on taking depositions more than 100 miles from courthouse. NY R USDCTS&ED Civ Rule 30.1.

    j.   Telephonic and other remote depositions. NY R USDCTS&ED Civ Rule 30.2.

    k.   Persons attending depositions. NY R USDCTS&ED Civ Rule 30.3.

    l.   Conferences between deponent and defending attorney. NY R USDCTS&ED Civ Rule 30.4.

    m.   Alternative dispute resolution (Southern District only). NY R USDCTS&ED Civ Rule 83.9.

    n.   Electronic case filing rules and instructions. NY R USDCTSD CM/ECF, S.D.

    o.   Related cases. NY R USDCTSD Div. Bus., Rule 13.

## J.  Miscellaneous

**NOTE: Individual judges' rules may apply. For available judge-level information, refer to:**

DISTRICT JUDGE RONNIE ABRAMS: NY R USDCTSD Abrams-Civ Prac; NY R USDCTSD Abrams-Crim Prac; NY R USDCTSD Abrams-Pro Se; NY R USDCTSD Abrams-Case Mgt; NY R USDCTSD Abrams-Jury.

DISTRICT JUDGE DEBORAH A. BATTS: NY R USDCTSD Batts-Practices.

DISTRICT JUDGE RICHARD M. BERMAN: NY R USDCTSD Berman-Practices; NY R USDCTSD Berman-Default; NY R USDCTSD Berman-Sentencing; NY R USDCTSD Berman-Media.

DISTRICT JUDGE VINCENT L. BRICCETTI: NY R USDCTSD Briccetti-Practices; NY R USDCTSD Briccetti-Plan; NY R USDCTSD Briccetti-Notice.

DISTRICT JUDGE VERNON S. BRODERICK: NY R USDCTSD Broderick-Civil; NY R USDCTSD Broderick-Crim; NY R USDCTSD Broderick-Case Mgt; NY R USDCTSD Broderick-Jury.

DISTRICT JUDGE NAOMI REICE BUCHWALD: NY R USDCTSD Buchwald-Practices.

DISTRICT JUDGE VALERIE E. CAPRONI: NY R USDCTSD Caproni-Prac; NY R USDCTSD Caproni--Pro Se; NY R USDCTSD Caproni-Case Mgt; NY R USDCTSD Caproni-Crim Prac.

DISTRICT JUDGE ANDREW L. CARTER JR.: NY R USDCTSD Carter-Practices.

DISTRICT JUDGE KEVIN P. CASTEL: NY R USDCTSD Castel-Practices; NY R USDCTSD Castel-Default; NY R USDCTSD Castel-Scheduling; NY R USDCTSD Castel-Complex; NY R USDCTSD Castel-Trials; NY R USDCTSD Castel-Sentencing.

DISTRICT JUDGE DENISE L. COTE: NY R USDCTSD Cote-Civil Practices; NY R USDCTSD Cote-Pro Se; NY R USDCTSD Cote-Maritime Ord; NY R USDCTSD Cote-Crim Practices; NY R USDCTSD Cote-Crim Trials; NY R USDCTSD Cote-Sentencing.

DISTRICT JUDGE PAUL A. CROTTY: NY R USDCTSD Crotty-Practices; NY R USDCTSD Crotty-Sentencing; NY R USDCTSD Crotty-Calls; NY R USDCTSD Crotty-Scheduling.

DISTRICT JUDGE GEORGE B. DANIELS: NY R USDCTSD Daniels-Practices.

DISTRICT JUDGE KEVIN T. DUFFY: NY R USDCTSD Duffy-Practices.

DISTRICT JUDGE PAUL A. ENGELMAYER: NY R USDCTSD Engelmayer-Practices; NY R USDCTSD Engelmayer-Scheduling; NY R USDCTSD Engelmayer-Sentencing; NY R USDCTSD Engelmayer-Pro Se; NY R USDCTSD Engelmayer-Crim.

DISTRICT JUDGE KATHERINE POLK FAILLA: NY R USDCTSD Failla-Civ Prac; NY R USDCTSD Failla-Crim Prac; NY R USDCTSD Failla-Case Mgt.

DISTRICT JUDGE KATHERINE B. FORREST: NY R USDCTSD Forrest-Civil Prac; NY R USDCTSD Forrest-Crim Prac; NY R USDCTSD Forrest-Crim Pretrial; NY R USDCTSD Forrest-Scheduling; NY R USDCTSD Forrest-Patent Scheduling; NY R USDCTSD Forrest-Sentencing; NY R USDCTSD Forrest-Order 1; NY R USDCTSD Forrest-Order 2.

DISTRICT JUDGE JESSE M. FURMAN: NY R USDCTSD Furman-Civil Prac; NY R USDCTSD Furman-Crim Prac; NY R USDCTSD Furman-Pro Se Prac; NY R USDCTSD Furman-Trials; NY R USDCTSD Furman-Scheduling; NY R USDCTSD Furman-Rights.

DISTRICT JUDGE PAUL G. GARDEPHE: NY R USDCTSD Gardephe-Civ Prac; NY R USDCTSD Gardephe-Pretrial; NY R USDCTSD Gardephe-Prot Ord; NY R USDCTSD Gardephe-Maritime; NY R USDCTSD Gardephe-Crim Prac; NY R USDCTSD Gardephe-Trial.

DISTRICT JUDGE THOMAS P. GRIESA: NY R USDCTSD Griesa-Practices.

DISTRICT JUDGE CHARLES S. HAIGHT: NY R USDCTSD Haight-Practices.

DISTRICT JUDGE ALVIN K. HELLERSTEIN: NY R USDCTSD Hellerstein-Practices; NY R USDCTSD Hellerstein--Sept 11.

DISTRICT JUDGE LEWIS A. KAPLAN: NY R USDCTSD Kaplan-Practices; NY R USDCTSD Kaplan-Sentencing.

DISTRICT JUDGE KENNETH M. KARAS: NY R USDCTSD Karas-Practices; NY R USDCTSD Karas-Case Mgt; NY R USDCTSD Karas-Default; NY R USDCTSD Karas-Sentencing; NY R USDCTSD Karas-Rights.

DISTRICT JUDGE JOHN F. KEENAN: NY R USDCTSD Keenan-Practices.

DISTRICT JUDGE JOHN G. KOELTL: NY R USDCTSD Koeltl-Practices.

DISTRICT JUDGE VICTOR MARRERO: NY R USDCTSD Marrero-Practices; NY R USDCTSD Marrero-Scheduling; NY R USDCTSD Marrero-Default; NY R USDCTSD Marrero-Trial Proc.

DISTRICT JUDGE COLLEEN McMAHON: NY R USDCTSD McMahon-Practices; NY R USDCTSD McMahon-RICO; NY R USDCTSD McMahon-Copies; NY R USDCTSD McMahon-Scheduling; NY R USDCTSD McMahon-Elec Disc; NY R USDCTSD McMahon-Sentencing.

DISTRICT JUDGE ALISON J. NATHAN: NY R USDCTSD Nathan-Civ Prac; NY R USDCTSD Nathan-Crim Prac; NY R USDCTSD Nathan-Pro Se; NY R USDCTSD Nathan-Scheduling.

DISTRICT JUDGE J. PAUL OETKEN: NY R USDCTSD Oetken-Civ Prac; NY R USDCTSD Oetken-Case Mgt; NY R USDCTSD Oetken-Crim Prac; NY R USDCTSD Oetken-Pro Se.

DISTRICT JUDGE WILLIAM H. PAULEY, III: NY R USDCTSD Pauley-Crim Cases; NY R USDCTSD Pauley-Practices.

DISTRICT JUDGE LORETTA A. PRESKA: NY R USDCTSD Preska-Practices.

DISTRICT JUDGE JED S. RAKOFF: NY R USDCTSD Rakoff-Practices; NY R USDCTSD Rakoff-Scheduling; NY R USDCTSD Rakoff-Prot Ord; NY R USDCTSD Rakoff-Maritime Ord.

DISTRICT JUDGE EDGARDO RAMOS: NY R USDCTSD Ramos--Practices; NY R USDCTSD Ramos-Case Mgt.

DISTRICT JUDGE NELSON S. ROMAN: NY R USDCTSD Roman-Civ Prac; NY R USDCTSD Roman-Pro Se; NY R USDCTSD Roman-Crim Prac; NY R USDCTSD Roman-Case Mgt.

DISTRICT JUDGE LEONARD B. SAND: NY R USDCTSD Sand-Practices.

DISTRICT JUDGE LORNA G. SCHOFIELD: NY R USDCTSD Schofield-Civ Prac; NY R USDCTSD Schofield-Crim Prac; NY R USDCTSD Schofield-Sched; NY R USDCTSD Schofield-Pro Se; NY R USDCTSD Schofield-Advice.

NOTICE OF DEPOSITION

DISTRICT JUDGE CATHY SEIBEL: NY R USDCTSD Seibel-Practices.

DISTRICT JUDGE LOUIS L. STANTON: NY R USDCTSD Stanton-Practices; NY R USDCTSD Stanton-Pretrial.

DISTRICT JUDGE SIDNEY H. STEIN: NY R USDCTSD Stein-Practices.

DISTRICT JUDGE RICHARD J. SULLIVAN: NY R USDCTSD Sullivan-Practices; NY R USDCTSD Sullivan-Scheduling; NY R USDCTSD Sullivan-Sentencing; NY R USDCTSD Sullivan-Juries; NY R USDCTSD Sullivan-Trial; NY R USDCTSD Sullivan-Default.

DISTRICT JUDGE LAURA TAYLOR SWAIN: NY R USDCTSD Swain-Practices; NY R USDCTSD Swain-Trial; NY R USDCTSD Swain-Crim Trial; NY R USDCTSD Swain-Juries; NY R USDCTSD Swain-Sentencing; NY R USDCTSD Swain-Rights.

DISTRICT JUDGE ROBERT W. SWEET: NY R USDCTSD Sweet-Practices.

DISTRICT JUDGE ANALISA TORRES: NY R USDCTSD Torres-Civ Prac; NY R USDCTSD Torres-Pro Se; NY R USDCTSD Torres-Scheduling.

DISTRICT JUDGE KIMBA M. WOOD: NY R USDCTSD Wood-Practices; NY R USDCTSD Wood-Scheduling; NY R USDCTSD Wood-Discovery; NY R USDCTSD Wood-RICO; NY R USDCTSD Wood-Juries; NY R USDCTSD Wood-Trial; NY R USDCTSD Wood-Media.

DISTRICT JUDGE GREGORY H. WOODS: NY R USDCTSD Woods-Civ Prac; NY R USDCTSD Woods-Pro Se; NY R USDCTSD Woods-Sched; NY R USDCTSD Woods-Crim Prac; NY R USDCTSD Woods-Protect Order; NY R USDCTSD Woods-Speedy Trial.

MAGISTRATE JUDGE JAMES L. COTT: NY R USDCTSD Cott-Practices; NY R USDCTSD Cott-Settlement.

MAGISTRATE JUDGE PAUL E. DAVISON: NY R USDCTSD Davison-Practices.

MAGISTRATE JUDGE RONALD L. ELLIS: NY R USDCTSD Ellis-Practices.

MAGISTRATE JUDGE KEVIN N. FOX: NY R USDCTSD Fox-Practices; NY R USDCTSD Fox-Settlement.

MAGISTRATE JUDGE JAMES C. FRANCIS: NY R USDCTSD Francis-Practices.

MAGISTRATE JUDGE DEBRA FREEMAN: NY R USDCTSD Freeman-Practices; NY R USDCTSD Freeman-Settlement.

MAGISTRATE JUDGE GABRIEL W. GORENSTEIN: NY R USDCTSD Gorenstein-Practices; NY R USDCTSD Gorenstein-Ackn.

MAGISTRATE JUDGE FRANK MAAS: NY R USDCTSD Maas-Practices; NY R USDCTSD Maas-Discontinuance; NY R USDCTSD Maas-Conf; NY R USDCTSD Maas-Settlement.

MAGISTRATE JUDGE JUDITH C. McCARTHY: NY R USDCTSD McCarthy-Practices; NY R USDCTSD McCarthy-Conduct.

MAGISTRATE JUDGE BARBARA MOSES: NY R USDCTSD Moses-Practices.

MAGISTRATE JUDGE SARAH NETBURN: NY R USDCTSD Netburn-Civil; NY R USDCTSD Netburn-Settlement; NY R USDCTSD Netburn-Case Mgt; NY R USDCTSD Netburn--Pro Se.

MAGISTRATE JUDGE ANDREW J. PECK: NY R USDCTSD Peck-Practices; NY R USDCTSD Peck-Order; NY R USDCTSD Peck-Rule 502(d).

MAGISTRATE JUDGE HENRY PITMAN: NY R USDCTSD Pitman-Practices.

MAGISTRATE JUDGE LISA MARGARET SMITH: NY R USDCTSD Smith-Practices; NY R USDCTSD Smith-Trials.

# Requests, Notices and Applications
# Application for Temporary Restraining Order

## Document Last Updated September 2016

A. **Checklist**

 (I) ❑ Matters to be considered by party applying (with notice)

  (a) ❑ Required documents

   (1) ❑ Notice of motion and motion

   (2) ❑ Memorandum of law

   (3) ❑ Security

   (4) ❑ Certificate of service

  (b) ❑ Supplemental documents

   (1) ❑ Supporting evidence

   (2) ❑ Notice of constitutional question

   (3) ❑ Nongovernmental corporate disclosure statement

   (4) ❑ Copies of authorities

   (5) ❑ Proposed order

   (6) ❑ Statement explaining untimely electronic filing

   (7) ❑ Courtesy copies

  (c) ❑ Timing

   (1) ❑ A written motion and notice of the hearing must be served at least fourteen (14) days before the time specified for the hearing, with the following exceptions: (i) when the motion may be heard ex parte; (ii) when the Federal Rules of Civil Procedure set a different time; or (iii) when a court order—which a party may, for good cause, apply for ex parte—sets a different time

   (2) ❑ Any affidavit supporting a motion must be served with the motion

 (II) ❑ Matters to be considered by party applying (without notice, or "ex parte")

  (a) ❑ Required documents

   (1) ❑ Motion

   (2) ❑ Memorandum of law

   (3) ❑ Affidavit or verified complaint

   (4) ❑ Certificate of attorney

   (5) ❑ Security

  (b) ❑ Supplemental documents

   (1) ❑ Supporting evidence

   (2) ❑ Notice of constitutional question

   (3) ❑ Nongovernmental corporate disclosure statement

   (4) ❑ Copies of authorities

   (5) ❑ Proposed order

   (6) ❑ Statement explaining untimely electronic filing

   (7) ❑ Courtesy copies

(c) ❑ Timing

(1) ❑ There are no specific timing requirements for applying for a temporary restraining order without notice

(2) ❑ Any affidavit supporting a motion must be served with the motion

## B. Timing

1. *Application for temporary restraining order*

   a. *With notice.* There are no specific timing requirements for applying for a temporary restraining order with notice.

   b. *Without notice, or "ex parte."* There are no specific timing requirements for applying for a temporary restraining order without notice, or "ex parte."

2. *Motion to dissolve or modify.* On two (2) days' notice to the party who obtained the order without notice—or on shorter notice set by the court—the adverse party may appear and move to dissolve or modify the order. The court must then hear and decide the motion as promptly as justice requires. FRCP 65(b)(4).

3. *Timing of motions, generally*

   a. *Motion and notice of hearing.* Except for letter-motions as permitted by NY R USDCTS&ED Civ Rule 7.1(d), and unless otherwise provided by statute or rule or by the Court in a Judge's Individual Practice or in a direction in a particular case, upon any motion, the notice of motion, supporting affidavits, and memoranda shall be served and filed as follows: on all civil motions, petitions, and applications, other than those described in NY R USDCTS&ED Civ Rule 6.1(a), and other than petitions for writs of habeas corpus, the notice of motion, supporting affidavits, and memoranda of law shall be served by the moving party on all other parties that have appeared in the action. NY R USDCTS&ED Civ Rule 6.1(b)(1). A written motion and notice of the hearing must be served at least fourteen (14) days before the time specified for the hearing, with the following exceptions:

      i. When the motion may be heard ex parte;

      ii. When the Federal Rules of Civil Procedure set a different time; or

      iii. When a court order—which a party may, for good cause, apply for ex parte—sets a different time. FRCP 6(c)(1).

   b. *Supporting affidavit.* Any affidavit supporting a motion must be served with the motion. FRCP 6(c)(2).

4. *Computation of time*

   a. *Computing time.* FRCP 6 applies in computing any time period specified in the Federal Rules of Civil Procedure, in any local rule or court order, or in any statute that does not specify a method of computing time. FRCP 6(a). In computing any period of time prescribed or allowed by the Local Civil Rules of the United States District Courts for the Southern and Eastern Districts of New York or the Local Admiralty and Maritime Rules, the provisions of FRCP 6 shall apply unless otherwise stated. NY R USDCTS&ED Civ Rule 6.4.

      i. *Period stated in days or a longer unit.* In computing periods of days, refer to FRCP 6 and NY R USDCTS&ED Civ Rule 6.4. NY R USDCTS&ED Civ Rule 6.1(b). When the period is stated in days or a longer unit of time:

         • Exclude the day of the event that triggers the period;

         • Count every day, including intermediate Saturdays, Sundays, and legal holidays; and

         • Include the last day of the period, but if the last day is a Saturday, Sunday, or legal holiday, the period continues to run until the end of the next day that is not a Saturday, Sunday, or legal holiday. FRCP 6(a)(1). In the Local Civil Rules of the United States District Courts for the Southern and Eastern Districts of New York, as in the Federal Rules of Civil Procedure as amended effective December 1, 2009, Saturdays, Sundays, and legal holidays are no longer excluded in computing periods of time. If the last day of the period is a Saturday, Sunday, or legal holiday, the period continues to run until the end of the next day that is not a Saturday, Sunday, or legal holiday. NY R USDCTS&ED Civ Rule 6.4.

ii. *Period stated in hours.* When the period is stated in hours:

- Begin counting immediately on the occurrence of the event that triggers the period;

- Count every hour, including hours during intermediate Saturdays, Sundays, and legal holidays; and

- If the period would end on a Saturday, Sunday, or legal holiday, the period continues to run until the same time on the next day that is not a Saturday, Sunday, or legal holiday. FRCP 6(a)(2). In the Local Civil Rules of the United States District Courts for the Southern and Eastern Districts of New York, as in the Federal Rules of Civil Procedure as amended effective December 1, 2009, Saturdays, Sundays, and legal holidays are no longer excluded in computing periods of time. If the last day of the period is a Saturday, Sunday, or legal holiday, the period continues to run until the end of the next day that is not a Saturday, Sunday, or legal holiday. NY R USDCTS&ED Civ Rule 6.4.

iii. *Inaccessibility of the clerk's office.* Unless the court orders otherwise, if the clerk's office is inaccessible:

- On the last day for filing under FRCP 6(a)(1), then the time for filing is extended to the first accessible day that is not a Saturday, Sunday, or legal holiday; or

- During the last hour for filing under FRCP 6(a)(2), then the time for filing is extended to the same time on the first accessible day that is not a Saturday, Sunday, or legal holiday. FRCP 6(a)(3).

iv. *"Last day" defined.* Unless a different time is set by a statute, local rule, or court order, the last day ends:

- For electronic filing, at midnight in the court's time zone; and

- For filing by other means, when the clerk's office is scheduled to close. FRCP 6(a)(4).

v. *"Next day" defined.* The "next day" is determined by continuing to count forward when the period is measured after an event and backward when measured before an event. FRCP 6(a)(5).

vi. *"Legal holiday" defined.* "Legal holiday" means:

- The day set aside by statute for observing New Year's Day, Martin Luther King Jr.'s Birthday, Washington's Birthday, Memorial Day, Independence Day, Labor Day, Columbus Day, Veterans' Day, Thanksgiving Day, or Christmas Day;

- Any day declared a holiday by the President or Congress; and

- For periods that are measured after an event, any other day declared a holiday by the state where the district court is located. FRCP 6(a)(6).

b. *Computation of electronic filing deadlines.* You can file electronically twenty-four (24) hours a day, seven (7) days a week, three hundred sixty-five (365) days a year. NY R USDCTSD CM/ECF, S.D.(II)(13)(13.10). Electronic filing must be completed before midnight local time where the Court is located in order to be considered timely filed that day. NY R USDCTSD CM/ECF, S.D.(I)(3)(3.3); NY R USDCTSD CM/ECF, S.D.(II)(13)(13.10); NY R USDCTSD CM/ECF, S.D.(II)(19)(19.4). An electronically filed document is deemed filed on the "filed on" date indicated on the Notice of Electronic Filing (NEF). NY R USDCTSD CM/ECF, S.D.(II)(13)(13.11).

i. *Technical failures.* A Filing User whose filing is made untimely as the result of a technical failure may seek appropriate relief from the Court. NY R USDCTSD CM/ECF, S.D.(I)(11). If you missed a filing deadline when the ECF system was out of order, attach a statement to your filing explaining how the interruption in service prevented you from filing in a timely fashion. NY R USDCTSD CM/ECF, S.D.(II)(23)(23.5).

    c.  *Extending time*

        i.  *In general.* When an act may or must be done within a specified time, the court may, for good cause, extend the time:

- With or without motion or notice if the court acts, or if a request is made, before the original time or its extension expires; or

- On motion made after the time has expired if the party failed to act because of excusable neglect. FRCP 6(b)(1).

       ii.  *Exceptions.* A court must not extend the time to act under FRCP 50(b), FRCP 50(d), FRCP 52(b), FRCP 59(b), FRCP 59(d), FRCP 59(e), and FRCP 60(b). FRCP 6(b)(2).

      iii.  Refer to the United States District Court for the Southern District of New York KeyRules Motion for Continuance/Extension of Time document for more information on extending time.

    d.  *Additional time after certain kinds of service.* When a party may or must act within a specified time after service and service is made under FRCP 5(b)(2)(C), FRCP 5(b)(2)(D), FRCP 5(b)(2)(E), or FRCP 5(b)(2)(F), three (3) days are added after the period would otherwise expire under FRCP 6(a). FRCP 6(d). Overnight delivery service shall be deemed service by mail for purposes of FRCP 5 and FRCP 6. NY R USDCTS&ED Civ Rule 5.3.

5.  *Individual judge practices.* Refer to the Miscellaneous section of this document for information on individual judge practices on timing of documents.

## C. General Requirements

1.  *Motions, generally*

    a.  *Requirements.* A request for a court order must be made by motion. The motion must:

        i.  Be in writing unless made during a hearing or trial;

       ii.  State with particularity the grounds for seeking the order; and

      iii.  State the relief sought. FRCP 7(b)(1).

    b.  *Notice of motion.* A party interested in resisting the relief sought by a motion has a right to notice thereof, and an opportunity to be heard. AMJUR MOTIONS § 12.

        i.  In addition to statutory or court rule provisions requiring notice of a motion—the purpose of such a notice requirement having been said to be to prevent a party from being prejudicially surprised by a motion—principles of natural justice dictate that an adverse party generally must be given notice that a motion will be presented to the court. AMJUR MOTIONS § 12.

       ii.  "Notice," in this regard, means reasonable notice, including a meaningful opportunity to prepare and to defend against allegations of a motion. AMJUR MOTIONS § 12.

    c.  *Writing requirement.* The writing requirement is intended to insure that the adverse parties are informed and have a record of both the motion's pendency and the grounds on which the movant seeks an order. FPP § 1191; Feldberg v. Quechee Lakes Corp., 463 F.3d 195 (2d Cir. 2006).

        i.  It is sufficient "if the motion is stated in a written notice of the hearing of the motion." FPP § 1191.

    d.  *Particularity requirement.* The particularity requirement insures that the opposing parties will have notice of their opponent's contentions. FEDPROC § 62:364; Goodman v. 1973 26 Foot Trojan Vessel, Arkansas Registration No. AR1439SN, 859 F.2d 71, 12 Fed.R.Serv.3d 645 (8th Cir. 1988). That requirement ensures that notice of the basis for the motion is provided to the court and to the opposing party so as to avoid prejudice, provide the opponent with a meaningful opportunity to respond, and provide the court with enough information to process the motion correctly. FEDPROC § 62:364; Andreas v. Volkswagen of America, Inc., 336 F.3d 789, 56 Fed.R.Serv.3d 6 (8th Cir. 2003).

        i.  Reasonable specification of the grounds for a motion is sufficient. However, where a movant fails to state even one ground for granting the motion in question, the movant has failed to meet the minimal standard of "reasonable specification." FEDPROC § 62:364; Martinez v. Trainor, 556 F.2d 818, 23 Fed.R.Serv.2d 403 (7th Cir. 1977).

ii. The court may excuse the failure to comply with the particularity requirement if it is inadvertent, and where no prejudice is shown by the opposing party. FEDPROC § 62:364.

e. *Ex parte orders or orders to show cause to bring on a motion.* No ex parte order, or order to show cause to bring on a motion, will be granted except upon a clear and specific showing by affidavit of good and sufficient reasons why a procedure other than by notice of motion is necessary, and stating whether a previous application for similar relief has been made. NY R USDCTS&ED Civ Rule 6.1(d).

f. *Letter-motions.* Applications for extensions or adjournments, applications for a pre-motion conference, and similar non-dispositive matters as permitted by the instructions regarding ECF published on the website of each respective Court and any pertinent Individual Judge's Practices, may be brought by letter-motion filed via ECF pursuant to NY R USDCTS&ED Civ Rule 5.2(b). NY R USDCTS&ED Civ Rule 7.1(d).

   i. The following list of motions. . .may be made by LETTER-MOTION: (1) Motion to Adjourn Conference; (2) Motion to Change Attorney Name on Roll; (3) Motion to Compel; (4) Motion for Conference; (5) Motion to Consolidate Cases; (6) Motion to Continue; (7) Motion re: Discovery; (8) Motion to Expedite; (9) Motion for Extension of Time; (10) Motion for Extension of Time to Amend; (11) Motion for Extension of Time to Answer; (12) Motion for Extension of Time to Complete Discovery; (13) Motion for Extension of Time to File Document; (14) Motion for Extension of Time to File Response/Reply; (15) Motion for Extension of Time re Transcript; (16) Motion to File Amicus Brief; (17) Motion for Leave to File Document; (18) Motion for Leave to File Excess Pages; (19) Motion for Local Rule 37.2 Conference; (20) Motion for Oral Argument; (21) Motion to Reopen; (22) Motion to Reopen Case; (23) Motion to Seal Document; (24) Motion to Stay; (25) Motion to Substitute Attorney. NY R USDCTSD CM/ECF, S.D.(II)(13)(13.1).

   ii. If the Filing User is making a type of motion that does not appear in this list, the motion may not be made by letter. NY R USDCTSD CM/ECF, S.D.(II)(13)(13.1).

   iii. For more information on letter motions, refer to NY R USDCTSD CM/ECF, S.D.(II)(13)(13.1).

2. *Application for temporary restraining order.* Applicants for injunctive relief occasionally are faced with the possibility that irreparable injury will occur before the hearing for a preliminary injunction required by FRCP 65(a) can be held. In that event a temporary restraining order may be available under FRCP 65(b). FPP § 2951. The order is designed to preserve the status quo until there is an opportunity to hold a hearing on the application for a preliminary injunction and may be issued with or without notice to the adverse party. FPP § 2951; Granny Goose Foods, Inc. v. Brotherhood of Teamsters & Auto Truck Drivers Local No. 70 of Alameda County, 415 U.S. 423, 94 S.Ct. 1113, 39 L.Ed.2d 435 (1974).

   a. *Issuing with notice.* When the opposing party actually receives notice of the application for a restraining order, the procedure that is followed does not differ functionally from that on an application for a preliminary injunction and the proceeding is not subject to any special requirements. FPP § 2951; Dilworth v. Riner, 343 F.2d 226 (5th Cir. 1965).

      i. *Duration.* By its terms FRCP 65(b) only governs restraining orders issued without notice or a hearing. But. . .it has been argued that its provisions, at least with regard to the duration of a restraining order, apply even to an order granted when notice has been given to the adverse party but there has been no hearing. FPP § 2951.

   b. *Issuing without notice*

      i. *When available.* The court may issue a temporary restraining order without written or oral notice to the adverse party or its attorney only if:

         • Specific facts in an affidavit or a verified complaint clearly show that immediate and irreparable injury, loss, or damage will result to the movant before the adverse party can be heard in opposition; and

         • The movant's attorney certifies in writing any efforts made to give notice and the reasons why it should not be required. FRCP 65(b)(1).

      ii. *Contents.* Every temporary restraining order issued without notice must state the date and hour it was issued; describe the injury and state why it is irreparable; state why the order was issued without notice; and be promptly filed in the clerk's office and entered in the record. FRCP 65(b)(2).

    iii. *Expiration.* The order expires at the time after entry—not to exceed fourteen (14) days—that the court sets, unless before that time the court, for good cause, extends it for a like period or the adverse party consents to a longer extension. The reasons for an extension must be entered in the record. FRCP 65(b)(2).

c. *Temporary restraining order versus preliminary injunction.* A temporary restraining order differs from a preliminary injunction, the core reasons being that a temporary restraining order is of limited duration and it may issue without notice to the opposing party before the adverse party can be heard in opposition. FEDPROC § 47:80.

d. *Factors considered.* As in the case of an application for a preliminary injunction, four factors must be considered in determining whether a temporary restraining order is to be granted, which are whether the moving party has established: (1) a substantial likelihood of success on the merits; (2) that irreparable injury will be suffered if the relief is not granted; (3) that the threatened injury outweighs the harm the relief would inflict on the nonmoving party; and (4) that entry of the relief would serve the public interest. FEDPROC § 47:84; Schiavo ex rel. Schindler v. Schiavo, 403 F.3d 1223 (11th Cir. 2005).

    i. Plaintiffs are not required to prevail on each of these factors, rather, the factors must be viewed as a continuum, with more of one factor compensating for less of another. In each case, however, all of the factors must be considered to determine whether on balance they weigh toward granting relief. FEDPROC § 47:84.

    ii. In the context of a temporary restraining order, it is particularly important for the moving party to demonstrate a substantial likelihood of success on the merits, because otherwise, there would be no justification for the court's intrusion into the ordinary processes of administration and judicial review. FEDPROC § 47:84.

    iii. Refer to the United States District Court for the Southern District of New York KeyRules Motion for Preliminary Injunction document for more information on the factors considered in moving for a preliminary injunction.

e. *Burden.* As with a preliminary injunction, the burden is on the moving party to establish that relief is appropriate. FEDPROC § 47:84.

f. *Security.* The court may issue a preliminary injunction or a temporary restraining order only if the movant gives security in an amount that the court considers proper to pay the costs and damages sustained by any party found to have been wrongfully enjoined or restrained. The United States, its officers, and its agencies are not required to give security. FRCP 65(c).

    i. *Proceedings against a surety.* Whenever the Federal Rules of Civil Procedure (including the Supplemental Rules for Admiralty or Maritime Claims and Asset Forfeiture Actions) require or allow a party to give security, and security is given through a bond or other undertaking with one or more sureties, each surety submits to the court's jurisdiction and irrevocably appoints the court clerk as its agent for receiving service of any papers that affect its liability on the bond or undertaking. The surety's liability may be enforced on motion without an independent action. The motion and any notice that the court orders may be served on the court clerk, who must promptly mail a copy of each to every surety whose address is known. FRCP 65.1.

    ii. For more information on sureties, refer to NY R USDCTS&ED Civ Rule 65.1.1.

g. *Contents and scope of every injunction and restraining order*

    i. *Contents.* Every order granting an injunction and every restraining order must:

- State the reasons why it issued;

- State its terms specifically; and

- Describe in reasonable detail—and not by referring to the complaint or other document—the act or acts restrained or required. FRCP 65(d)(1).

    ii. *Persons bound.* The order binds only the following who receive actual notice of it by personal service or otherwise:

- The parties;
- The parties' officers, agents, servants, employees, and attorneys; and
- Other persons who are in active concert or participation with anyone described in FRCP 65(d)(2)(A) or FRCP 65(d)(2)(B). FRCP 65(d)(2).

h. *Other laws not modified.* FRCP 65 does not modify the following:

    i. Any federal statute relating to temporary restraining orders or preliminary injunctions in actions affecting employer and employee;

    ii. 28 U.S.C.A. § 2361, which relates to preliminary injunctions in actions of interpleader or in the nature of interpleader; or

    iii. 28 U.S.C.A. § 2284, which relates to actions that must be heard and decided by a three-judge district court. FRCP 65(e).

i. *Copyright impoundment.* FRCP 65 applies to copyright-impoundment proceedings. FRCP 65(f).

3. *Orders on motions.* A memorandum signed by the Court of the decision on a motion that does not finally determine all claims for relief, or an oral decision on such a motion, shall constitute the order unless the memorandum or oral decision directs the submission or settlement of an order in more extended form. The notation in the docket of a memorandum or of an oral decision that does not direct the submission or settlement of an order in more extended form shall constitute the entry of the order. Where an order in more extended form is required to be submitted or settled, the notation in the docket of such order shall constitute the entry of the order. NY R USDCTS&ED Civ Rule 6.2.

4. *Complex civil cases.* For information on procedures for complex civil cases, refer to NY R USDCTSD Order 11 Misc 00388.

5. *Related cases.* It shall be the continuing duty of each attorney appearing in any civil or criminal case to bring promptly to the attention of the Court all facts which said attorney believes are relevant to a determination that said case and one or more pending civil or criminal cases should be heard by the same Judge, in order to avoid unnecessary duplication of judicial effort. As soon as the attorney becomes aware of such relationship, said attorney shall notify the Judges to whom the cases have been assigned. NY R USDCTS&ED Civ Rule 1.6(a). If counsel fails to comply with NY R USDCTS&ED Civ Rule 1.6(a), the Court may assess reasonable costs directly against counsel whose action has obstructed the effective administration of the Court's business. NY R USDCTS&ED Civ Rule 1.6(b).

a. *Determination of relatedness.* Subject to the limitations set forth in NY R USDCTSD Div. Bus., Rule 13(a)(2), a civil case, bankruptcy appeal, or motion to withdraw the bankruptcy reference will be deemed related to one or more civil cases, appeals or motions when the interests of justice and efficiency will be served. In determining relatedness, a judge will consider whether (A) the actions concern the same or substantially similar parties, property, transactions or events; (B) there is substantial factual overlap; (C) the parties could be subjected to conflicting orders; and (D) whether absent a determination of relatedness there would be a substantial duplication of effort and expense, delay, or undue burden on the Court, parties or witnesses. NY R USDCTSD Div. Bus., Rule 13(a)(1). Nothing in this NY R USDCTSD Div. Bus., Rule 13 is intended to preclude parties from moving for consolidated proceedings under FRCP 42. NY R USDCTSD Div. Bus., Rule 13(a)(1). Notwithstanding NY R USDCTSD Div. Bus., Rule 13(a)(1):

    i. Civil cases shall not be deemed related merely because they involve common legal issues or the same parties. NY R USDCTSD Div. Bus., Rule 13(a)(2)(A).

    ii. Other than cases subject to NY R USDCTSD Div. Bus., Rule 4(b) and actions seeking the enforcement of a judgment or settlement in or of an earlier case, civil cases presumptively shall not be deemed related unless both cases are pending before the Court (or the earlier case is on appeal). NY R USDCTSD Div. Bus., Rule 13(a)(2)(B).

b. *Procedure in regard to cases said to be related*

    i. *Disclosure of contention of relatedness.* When a civil case is filed or removed or a bankruptcy appeal or motion to withdraw the reference of an adversary proceeding from the bankruptcy court is filed, the person filing or removing shall disclose on form JSC44C any contention of relatedness and shall file a Related Case Statement stating clearly and succinctly the basis for the contention. A copy of the civil cover sheet and Related Case Statement shall be served with the complaint, notice of removal, notice of appeal, or motion. Any party may contest a claim of relatedness by any other in writing addressed to the judge having the case with the lowest docket number of all cases claimed to be related. However, the foregoing shall not delay the assignment process or the operation of NY R USDCTSD Div. Bus., Rule 13. NY R USDCTSD Div. Bus., Rule 13(b)(1). [Editor's note: the reference to form JSC44C is likely meant to be form JS44C-SDNY: Civil Court Cover Sheet].

ii. *Claims of relatedness by other parties.* A party other than the one filing a case, bankruptcy appeal or motion to withdraw the reference that contends its case is related to another may so advise in writing the judge assigned in its case and request a transfer of its case to the judge that the party contends has the related case with the lowest docket number. If the assigned judge believes the case is related under NY R USDCTSD Div. Bus., Rule 13(a), he or she shall refer the question to the judge having the case with the lowest docket number. In the event the latter judge agrees, the case shall be transferred to that judge unless the Assignment Committee disagrees. NY R USDCTSD Div. Bus., Rule 13(b)(3).

c. For more information on related cases, refer to NY R USDCTSD Div. Bus., Rule 13.

6. *Alternative dispute resolution (ADR).* The U.S. District Court for the Southern District of New York provides litigants with opportunities to discuss settlement through judicial settlement conferences and mediation. NY R USDCTS&ED Civ Rule 83.9(a).

a. *Consideration of alternative dispute resolution.* In all civil cases, including those eligible for mediation pursuant to NY R USDCTS&ED Civ Rule 83.9(e), each party shall consider the use of mediation or a judicial settlement conference and shall report to the assigned Judge at the initial FRCP 16(b) case management conference, or subsequently, whether the party believes mediation or a judicial settlement conference may facilitate the resolution of the lawsuit. Judges are encouraged to note the availability of the mediation program and/or a judicial settlement conference before, at, or after the initial FRCP 16(b) case management conference. NY R USDCTS&ED Civ Rule 83.9(d).

b. *Mediation.* In mediation, parties and counsel meet, sometimes collectively and sometimes individually, with a neutral third party (the mediator) who has been trained to facilitate confidential settlement discussions. The parties articulate their respective positions and interests and generate options for a mutually agreeable resolution to the dispute. The mediator assists the parties in reaching their own negotiated settlement by defining the issues, probing and assessing the strengths and weaknesses of each party's legal positions, and identifying areas of agreement and disagreement. The main benefits of mediation are that it can result in an expeditious and less costly resolution of the litigation, and can produce creative solutions to complex disputes often unavailable in traditional litigation. NY R USDCTS&ED Civ Rule 83.9(b).

i. *Mediation program eligibility.* All civil cases other than Social Security, habeas corpus, and tax cases are eligible for mediation, whether assigned to Manhattan or White Plains. NY R USDCTS&ED Civ Rule 83.9(e)(1).

- The Board of Judges may, by Administrative Order, direct that certain specified categories of cases shall automatically be submitted to the mediation program. The assigned District Judge or Magistrate Judge may issue a written order exempting a particular case with or without the request of the parties. NY R USDCTS&ED Civ Rule 83.9(e)(2).

- For all other cases, the assigned District Judge or Magistrate Judge may determine that a case is appropriate for mediation and may order that case to mediation, with or without the consent of the parties, before, at, or after the initial FRCP 16(b) case management conference. Alternatively, the parties should notify the assigned Judge at any time of their desire to mediate. NY R USDCTS&ED Civ Rule 83.9(e)(3).

c. *Judicial settlement conferences.* Judicial settlement conferences may be ordered by District Judges or Magistrate Judges with or without the request or consent of the parties. NY R USDCTS&ED Civ Rule 83.9(f).

     d.   For more information on alternative dispute resolution (ADR), refer to NY R USDCTS&ED Civ Rule 83.9.

  7.  *Individual judge practices.* Refer to the Miscellaneous section of this document for information on individual judge practices on general requirements for documents.

## D. Documents

  1.  *Application for temporary restraining order (with notice)*

     a.  *Required documents*

        i.  *Notice of motion and motion.* Except for letter-motions as permitted by NY R USDCTS&ED Civ Rule 7.1(d) or as otherwise permitted by the Court, all motions shall include the following motion papers: a notice of motion, or an order to show cause signed by the Court, which shall specify the applicable rules or statutes pursuant to which the motion is brought, and shall specify the relief sought by the motion. NY R USDCTS&ED Civ Rule 7.1(a)(1). Refer to the General Requirements section of this document for information on the notice of motion and motion.

       ii.  *Memorandum of law.* Except for letter-motions as permitted by NY R USDCTS&ED Civ Rule 7.1(d) or as otherwise permitted by the Court, all motions shall include the following motion papers: a memorandum of law, setting forth the cases and other authorities relied upon in support of the motion, and divided, under appropriate headings, into as many parts as there are issues to be determined. NY R USDCTS&ED Civ Rule 7.1(a)(2).

      iii.  *Security.* Refer to the General Requirements section of this document for information on the security required.

      iv.  *Certificate of service.* FRCP 5(d) requires that the person making service under FRCP 5 certify that service has been effected. FRCP 5(Advisory Committee Notes). Having such information on file may be useful for many purposes, including proof of service if an issue arises concerning the effectiveness of the service. FRCP 5(Advisory Committee Notes).

         • Such paper service [on attorneys and pro se parties who are not Filing or Receiving Users] must be documented by electronically filing proof of service. NY R USDCTSD CM/ECF, S.D.(I)(9)(9.2); NY R USDCTSD CM/ECF, S.D.(I)(19)(19.3)(b). Pro se parties who are not Filing Users are exempt from that portion of NY R USDCTSD CM/ECF, S.D.(I)(19)(19.3) requiring proof of service to be filed electronically. NY R USDCTSD CM/ECF, S.D.(I)(19)(19.3).

     b.  *Supplemental documents*

        i.  *Supporting evidence.* When a motion relies on facts outside the record, the court may hear the matter on affidavits or may hear it wholly or partly on oral testimony or on depositions. FRCP 43(c). Except for letter-motions as permitted by NY R USDCTS&ED Civ Rule 7.1(d) or as otherwise permitted by the Court, all motions shall include the following motion papers: supporting affidavits and exhibits thereto containing any factual information and portions of the record necessary for the decision of the motion. NY R USDCTS&ED Civ Rule 7.1(a)(3).

         • *Discovery materials.* A party seeking or opposing relief under FRCP 26 through FRCP 37 inclusive, or making or opposing any other motion or application, shall quote or attach only those portions of the depositions, interrogatories, requests for documents, requests for admissions, or other discovery or disclosure materials, together with the responses and objections thereto, that are the subject of the discovery motion or application, or that are cited in papers submitted in connection with any other motion or application. NY R USDCTS&ED Civ Rule 5.1.

       ii.  *Notice of constitutional question.* A party that files a pleading, written motion, or other paper drawing into question the constitutionality of a federal or state statute must promptly:

         • *File notice.* File a notice of constitutional question stating the question and identifying the paper that raises it, if: (1) a federal statute is questioned and the parties do not include the United States, one of its agencies, or one of its officers or employees in an official capacity;

or (2) a state statute is questioned and the parties do not include the state, one of its agencies, or one of its officers or employees in an official capacity; and

- *Serve notice.* Serve the notice and paper on the Attorney General of the United States if a federal statute is questioned—or on the state attorney general if a state statute is questioned—either by certified or registered mail or by sending it to an electronic address designated by the attorney general for this purpose. FRCP 5.1(a).

- *No forfeiture.* A party's failure to file and serve the notice, or the court's failure to certify, does not forfeit a constitutional claim or defense that is otherwise timely asserted. FRCP 5.1(d).

   iii. *Nongovernmental corporate disclosure statement*

- *Contents.* A nongovernmental corporate party must file two (2) copies of a disclosure statement that: (1) identifies any parent corporation and any publicly held corporation owning ten percent (10%) or more of its stock; or (2) states that there is no such corporation. FRCP 7.1(a).

- *Time to file; Supplemental filing.* A party must: (1) file the disclosure statement with its first appearance, pleading, petition, motion, response, or other request addressed to the court; and (2) promptly file a supplemental statement if any required information changes. FRCP 7.1(b). For purposes of FRCP 7.1(b)(2), "promptly" shall mean "within fourteen days," that is, parties are required to file a supplemental disclosure statement within fourteen (14) days of the time there is any change in the information required in a disclosure statement filed pursuant to those rules. NY R USDCTS&ED Civ Rule 7.1.1.

   iv. *Copies of authorities.* In cases involving a pro se litigant, counsel shall, when serving a memorandum of law (or other submissions to the Court), provide the pro se litigant (but not other counsel or the Court) with copies of cases and other authorities cited therein that are unpublished or reported exclusively on computerized databases. Upon request, counsel shall provide the pro se litigant with copies of such unpublished cases and other authorities as are cited in a decision of the Court and were not previously cited by any party. NY R USDCTS&ED Civ Rule 7.2.

   v. *Proposed order.* Refer to the Format section of this document for information on the format of submitting a proposed order to the court.

   vi. *Statement explaining untimely electronic filing.* If you missed a filing deadline when the ECF system was out of order, attach a statement to your filing explaining how the interruption in service prevented you from filing in a timely fashion. NY R USDCTSD CM/ECF, S.D.(II)(23)(23.5).

   vii. *Courtesy copies.* Read the judge's Individual Practices to learn if courtesy copies are required. NY R USDCTSD CM/ECF, S.D.(II)(13)(13.17). Judges' Individual Practices should continue to be followed with respect to delivery of courtesy copies. NY R USDCTSD CM/ECF, S.D.(I)(3)(3.4).

2. *Application for temporary restraining order (without notice, or "ex parte")*

  a. *Required documents*

   i. *Motion.* Refer to the General Requirements section of this document for information on the motion.

   ii. *Affidavit or verified complaint.* The applicant for an ex parte restraining order must present to the court, in an affidavit or a verified complaint, facts that clearly show irreparable injury. FPP § 2952.

   iii. *Certificate of attorney.* The applicant's attorney must certify in writing any efforts made to give notice and the reasons why it should not be required. FEDPROC § 47:81.

- No ex parte order, or order to show cause to bring on a motion, will be granted except upon a clear and specific showing by affidavit of good and sufficient reasons why a procedure other than by notice of motion is necessary, and stating whether a previous application for similar relief has been made. NY R USDCTS&ED Civ Rule 6.1(d).

iv. *Security.* Refer to the General Requirements section of this document for information on the security required.

b. *Supplemental documents*

    i. *Supporting evidence.* When a motion relies on facts outside the record, the court may hear the matter on affidavits or may hear it wholly or partly on oral testimony or on depositions. FRCP 43(c). Except for letter-motions as permitted by NY R USDCTS&ED Civ Rule 7.1(d) or as otherwise permitted by the Court, all motions shall include the following motion papers: supporting affidavits and exhibits thereto containing any factual information and portions of the record necessary for the decision of the motion. NY R USDCTS&ED Civ Rule 7.1(a)(3).

- *Discovery materials.* A party seeking or opposing relief under FRCP 26 through FRCP 37 inclusive, or making or opposing any other motion or application, shall quote or attach only those portions of the depositions, interrogatories, requests for documents, requests for admissions, or other discovery or disclosure materials, together with the responses and objections thereto, that are the subject of the discovery motion or application, or that are cited in papers submitted in connection with any other motion or application. NY R USDCTS&ED Civ Rule 5.1.

    ii. *Notice of constitutional question.* A party that files a pleading, written motion, or other paper drawing into question the constitutionality of a federal or state statute must promptly:

- *File notice.* File a notice of constitutional question stating the question and identifying the paper that raises it, if: (1) a federal statute is questioned and the parties do not include the United States, one of its agencies, or one of its officers or employees in an official capacity; or (2) a state statute is questioned and the parties do not include the state, one of its agencies, or one of its officers or employees in an official capacity; and

- *Serve notice.* Serve the notice and paper on the Attorney General of the United States if a federal statute is questioned—or on the state attorney general if a state statute is questioned—either by certified or registered mail or by sending it to an electronic address designated by the attorney general for this purpose. FRCP 5.1(a).

- *No forfeiture.* A party's failure to file and serve the notice, or the court's failure to certify, does not forfeit a constitutional claim or defense that is otherwise timely asserted. FRCP 5.1(d).

    iii. *Nongovernmental corporate disclosure statement*

- *Contents.* A nongovernmental corporate party must file two (2) copies of a disclosure statement that: (1) identifies any parent corporation and any publicly held corporation owning ten percent (10%) or more of its stock; or (2) states that there is no such corporation. FRCP 7.1(a).

- *Time to file; Supplemental filing.* A party must: (1) file the disclosure statement with its first appearance, pleading, petition, motion, response, or other request addressed to the court; and (2) promptly file a supplemental statement if any required information changes. FRCP 7.1(b). For purposes of FRCP 7.1(b)(2), "promptly" shall mean "within fourteen days," that is, parties are required to file a supplemental disclosure statement within fourteen (14) days of the time there is any change in the information required in a disclosure statement filed pursuant to those rules. NY R USDCTS&ED Civ Rule 7.1.1.

    iv. *Copies of authorities.* In cases involving a pro se litigant, counsel shall, when serving a memorandum of law (or other submissions to the Court), provide the pro se litigant (but not other counsel or the Court) with copies of cases and other authorities cited therein that are unpublished or reported exclusively on computerized databases. Upon request, counsel shall provide the pro se litigant with copies of such unpublished cases and other authorities as are cited in a decision of the Court and were not previously cited by any party. NY R USDCTS&ED Civ Rule 7.2.

    v. *Proposed order.* Refer to the Format section of this document for information on the format of submitting a proposed order to the court.

    vi.  *Statement explaining untimely electronic filing.* If you missed a filing deadline when the ECF system was out of order, attach a statement to your filing explaining how the interruption in service prevented you from filing in a timely fashion. NY R USDCTSD CM/ECF, S.D.(II)(23)(23.5).

    vii.  *Courtesy copies.* Read the judge's Individual Practices to learn if courtesy copies are required. NY R USDCTSD CM/ECF, S.D.(II)(13)(13.17). Judges' Individual Practices should continue to be followed with respect to delivery of courtesy copies. NY R USDCTSD CM/ECF, S.D.(I)(3)(3.4).

3.  *Individual judge practices.* Refer to the Miscellaneous section of this document for information on individual judge practices on required documents.

## E. Format

1.  *Form of documents.* The rules governing captions and other matters of form in pleadings apply to motions and other papers. FRCP 7(b)(2).

    a.  *Paper.* Every pleading, written motion, and other paper must: be plainly written, typed, printed, or copied without erasures or interlineations which materially deface it. NY R USDCTS&ED Civ Rule 11.1(a)(1).

    b.  *Typeface, margin, and spacing.* The typeface, margins, and spacing of all documents presented for filing must meet the following requirements:

      i.  All text must be twelve (12) point type or larger, except for text in footnotes which may be ten (10) point type;

      ii.  All documents must have at least one (1) inch margins on all sides;

      iii.  All text must be double-spaced, except for headings, text in footnotes, or block quotations, which may be single-spaced. NY R USDCTS&ED Civ Rule 11.1(b).

    c.  *Caption; Names of parties.* Every pleading must have a caption with the court's name, a title, a file number, and a FRCP 7(a) designation. The title of the complaint must name all the parties; the title of other pleadings, after naming the first party on each side, may refer generally to other parties. FRCP 10(a). Every pleading, written motion, and other paper must: bear the docket number and the initials of the District Judge and any Magistrate Judge before whom the action or proceeding is pending, NY R USDCTS&ED Civ Rule 11.1(a)(2).

    d.  *Paragraphs; Separate statements.* A party must state its claims or defenses in numbered paragraphs, each limited as far as practicable to a single set of circumstances. A later pleading may refer by number to a paragraph in an earlier pleading. If doing so would promote clarity, each claim founded on a separate transaction or occurrence—and each defense other than a denial—must be stated in a separate count or defense. FRCP 10(b).

    e.  *Adoption by reference; Exhibits.* A statement in a pleading may be adopted by reference elsewhere in the same pleading or in any other pleading or motion. A copy of a written instrument that is an exhibit to a pleading is a part of the pleading for all purposes. FRCP 10(c).

    f.  *Acceptance by the clerk.* The clerk must not refuse to file a paper solely because it is not in the form prescribed by the Federal Rules of Civil Procedure or by a local rule or practice. FRCP 5(d)(4).

2.  *Form of electronic documents*

    a.  *PDF-A.* All documents electronically filed on the ECF system must be in PDF-A format (portable document format). A PDF-A file is created using PDF writer software such as Adobe Acrobat (go to the Adobe website for details). PDF-A files cannot be altered, providing security to the filer and the Court. NY R USDCTSD CM/ECF, S.D.(II)(23)(23.2).

    b.  *Size limitation.* No single PDF file may be larger than four megabytes (4 MB). If the filing is too large, the ECF system will not allow it to be filed, and you will not see a Notice of Electronic Filing (NEF or filing receipt) screen. To determine the size of an Adobe Acrobat PDF file click on File, Document Properties, Summary. NY R USDCTSD CM/ECF, S.D.(II)(23)(23.3).

      i.  Converting documents directly from a word processor to PDF-A format creates the smallest possible file in terms of computer memory. If that is not possible, scan your document at low resolution. Within the Adobe Acrobat program, on the "Scan Manager" screen, adjust the settings for black and white and 200 dpi (dots per inch). This allows more pages to fit into a single PDF-A file. If that does not work, separate an oversized file into 2 or more parts. Simply label each file 1a, 1b, 1c, etc. Only relevant excerpts of exhibits should be electronically filed. NY R USDCTSD CM/ECF, S.D.(II)(23)(23.4).

c. *Attachments and exhibits.* Filing Users must submit in electronic form all documents referenced as exhibits or attachments, unless the Court permits paper filing. NY R USDCTSD CM/ECF, S.D.(I)(5)(5.1).

   i. A Filing User must submit as exhibits or attachments only those excerpts of the referenced documents that are relevant to the matter under consideration by the Court. Excerpted material must be clearly and prominently identified as such. Filing Users who file excerpts of documents as exhibits or attachments under this procedure do so without prejudice to their right to file timely additional excerpts or the complete document. Responding parties may file timely additional excerpts that they believe are relevant or the complete document. A party may move before the Court for permission to serve and file in hard copy documents that cannot be reasonably scanned. NY R USDCTSD CM/ECF, S.D.(I)(5)(5.2).

   ii. Exhibits must be filed only as attachments to a document, such as a motion or an affidavit. Do not use the ECF Filing Event for "Motion" to file exhibits separately. Exhibits are the only items that should be attached to electronically filed documents. You are limited to electronically filing only relevant excerpts of exhibits. Excerpts must be clearly identified as such. If the exhibit is too large to be scanned and electronically filed you may contact the ECF Help Desk. NY R USDCTSD CM/ECF, S.D.(II)(15)(15.6).

d. *Letters.* Parties should consult the assigned judge's Individual Practices to determine if the judge accepts letters at all and, if he or she does, whether the judge has any page limitations on letters and/or requires courtesy copies of letters filed on ECF (and, if so, by what means of delivery). All letters addressed to the Court must include a subject line with the case name and docket number (e.g., "Re: Doe v. Smith, 13 Civ. 1234 (ABC)"). NY R USDCTSD CM/ECF, S.D.(II)(13)(13.1).

e. *Proposed orders, proposed judgments, stipulations and consents.* Any document that requires the signature of a judge should not be electronically filed except as an exhibit to another document. Proposed orders, judgments, stipulations and consents should not be submitted through the ECF system. Instead they should be sent by e-mail to the Clerk. Proposed orders should be submitted in word processing format (WordPerfect or Word) rather than as a PDF document. Stipulations should be submitted in PDF-A format. Stipulations must contain ink signatures not s/. Faxed or emailed signatures are acceptable. Please note that Stipulations of Voluntary Dismissal pursuant to FRCP 41(a)(1)(A)(ii) do not require the signature of a judge and must be electronically filed on the ECF system. Questions may be directed to the Orders and Judgments Clerk at the phone numbers listed in NY R USDCTSD CM/ECF, S.D.(II)(18)(18.3). NY R USDCTSD CM/ECF, S.D.(II)(18)(18.3).

   i. Email the proposed order, judgment or stipulation to the email addresses listed in NY R USDCTSD CM/ECF, S.D.(II)(18)(18.3). NY R USDCTSD CM/ECF, S.D.(II)(18)(18.3).

   ii. Pro se litigants who are not Filing Users are exempt from that portion of NY R USDCTSD CM/ECF, S.D.(II)(18)(18.3) that requires litigants to email proposed orders, judgments, stipulations and consents, and shall deliver such documents to the Clerk's Office in paper form. NY R USDCTSD CM/ECF, S.D.(II)(18)(18.3).

3. *Signing of pleadings, motions and other papers*

   a. *Signature.* Every pleading, written motion, and other paper must be signed by at least one attorney of record in the attorney's name—or by a party personally if the party is unrepresented. The paper must state the signer's address, e-mail address, and telephone number. FRCP 11(a). Every pleading, written motion, and other paper must: have the name of each person signing it clearly printed or typed directly below the signature. NY R USDCTS&ED Civ Rule 11.1(a)(3).

      i. *Electronic signatures.* The user log-in and password required to submit documents to the ECF

system serve as the Filing User's signature on all electronic documents filed with the Court. NY R USDCTSD CM/ECF, S.D.(I)(8)(8.1); NY R USDCTSD CM/ECF, S.D.(II)(13)(13.14). They also serve as a signature for purposes of the Federal Rules of Civil Procedure, including FRCP 11, the Local Civil Rules of the United States District Courts for the Southern and Eastern Districts of New York, and any other purpose for which a signature is required in connection with proceedings before the Court. NY R USDCTSD CM/ECF, S.D.(I)(8)(8.1).

- *Signature block.* Electronically filed documents must include a signature block and must set forth the name, address, telephone number and e-mail address all in compliance with the Federal Rules of Civil Procedure and NY R USDCTS&ED Civ Rule 11.1. In the absence of a scanned signature image, the name of the Filing User under whose log-in and password the document is submitted must be preceded by an "s/" typed in the space where the signature would otherwise appear. NY R USDCTSD CM/ECF, S.D.(I)(8)(8.2); NY R USDCTSD CM/ECF, S.D.(II)(13)(13.14).

- *Documents requiring the signature of a party or witness.* A document requiring the signature of a party or witness shall be electronically filed in a scanned format that contains an image of the actual signature. NY R USDCTSD CM/ECF, S.D.(I)(8)(8.4); NY R USDCTSD CM/ECF, S.D.(II)(13)(13.14).

- *Documents requiring the signature of a judge.* A Filing User submitting a document electronically that requires a judge's signature must promptly deliver the document in such other form, if any, as the Court requires. NY R USDCTSD CM/ECF, S.D.(I)(4)(4.2).

- *Documents requiring multiple signatures.* Documents requiring signatures of more than one party must be electronically filed either by: (a) submitting a scanned document containing all necessary signatures; (b) representing the consent of the other parties on the document; (c) identifying on the document the parties whose signatures are required and by the submission of a notice of endorsement by the other parties no later than three business days after filing; or (d) in any other manner approved by the Court. NY R USDCTSD CM/ECF, S.D.(I)(8)(8.5).

ii. *No verification or accompanying affidavit required for pleadings.* Unless a rule or statute specifically states otherwise, a pleading need not be verified or accompanied by an affidavit. FRCP 11(a).

iii. *Unsigned papers.* The court must strike an unsigned paper unless the omission is promptly corrected after being called to the attorney's or party's attention. FRCP 11(a).

b. *Representations to the court.* By presenting to the court a pleading, written motion, or other paper—whether by signing, filing, submitting, or later advocating it—an attorney or unrepresented party certifies that to the best of the person's knowledge, information, and belief, formed after an inquiry reasonable under the circumstances:

i. It is not being presented for any improper purpose, such as to harass, cause unnecessary delay, or needlessly increase the cost of litigation;

ii. The claims, defenses, and other legal contentions are warranted by existing law or by a nonfrivolous argument for extending, modifying, or reversing existing law or for establishing new law;

iii. The factual contentions have evidentiary support or, if specifically so identified, will likely have evidentiary support after a reasonable opportunity for further investigation or discovery; and

iv. The denials of factual contentions are warranted on the evidence or, if specifically so identified, are reasonably based on belief or a lack of information. FRCP 11(b).

c. *Sanctions.* If, after notice and a reasonable opportunity to respond, the court determines that FRCP 11(b) has been violated, the court may impose an appropriate sanction on any attorney, law firm, or party that violated FRCP 11(b) or is responsible for the violation. FRCP 11(c)(1). Refer to the United States District Court for the Southern District of New York KeyRules Motion for Sanctions document for more information.

4. *Privacy protection for filings made with the court*

   a. *Redacted filings.* Unless the court orders otherwise, in an electronic or paper filing with the court that contains an individual's Social Security number, taxpayer-identification number, or birth date, the name of an individual known to be a minor, or a financial-account number, a party or nonparty making the filing may include only:

      i. The last four (4) digits of the Social Security number and taxpayer-identification number;

      ii. The year of the individual's birth;

      iii. The minor's initials; and

      iv. The last four (4) digits of the financial-account number. FRCP 5.2(a); NY R USDCTSD CM/ECF, S.D.(II)(21)(21.3).

      v. Caution should be exercised when filing documents that contain the following:

         • Personal identifying numbers (PIN #'s), such as a driver's license number;

         • Medical records, treatment and diagnosis;

         • Employment history;

         • Individual financial information;

         • Proprietary or trade secret information;

         • Information regarding an individual's cooperation with the government. NY R US-DCTSD CM/ECF, S.D.(II)(21)(21.4).

   b. *Exemptions from the redaction requirement.* The redaction requirement does not apply to the following:

      i. A financial-account number that identifies the property allegedly subject to forfeiture in a forfeiture proceeding;

      ii. The record of an administrative or agency proceeding;

      iii. The official record of a state-court proceeding;

      iv. The record of a court or tribunal, if that record was not subject to the redaction requirement when originally filed;

      v. A filing covered by FRCP 5.2(c) or FRCP 5.2(d); and

      vi. A pro se filing in an action brought under 28 U.S.C.A. § 2241, 28 U.S.C.A. § 2254, or 28 U.S.C.A. § 2255. FRCP 5.2(b).

   c. *Limitations on remote access to electronic files; Social Security appeals and immigration cases.* Unless the court orders otherwise, in an action for benefits under the Social Security Act, and in an action or proceeding relating to an order of removal, to relief from removal, or to immigration benefits or detention, access to an electronic file is authorized as follows:

      i. The parties and their attorneys may have remote electronic access to any part of the case file, including the administrative record;

      ii. Any other person may have electronic access to the full record at the courthouse, but may have remote electronic access only to:

         • The docket maintained by the court; and

         • An opinion, order, judgment, or other disposition of the court, but not any other part of the case file or the administrative record. FRCP 5.2(c).

   d. *Filings made under seal.* The court may order that a filing be made under seal without redaction. The court may later unseal the filing or order the person who made the filing to file a redacted version for the public record. FRCP 5.2(d). For more information on sealing documents, refer to NY R USDCTSD CM/ECF, S.D.(I)(6).

   e. *Protective orders.* For good cause, the court may by order in a case:

      i. Require redaction of additional information; or

    ii. Limit or prohibit a nonparty's remote electronic access to a document filed with the court. FRCP 5.2(e).

  f. *Option for additional unredacted filing under seal.* A person making a redacted filing may also file an unredacted copy under seal. The court must retain the unredacted copy as part of the record. FRCP 5.2(f); NY R USDCTSD CM/ECF, S.D.(II)(21)(21.5).

  g. *Option for filing a reference list.* A filing that contains redacted information may be filed together with a reference list that identifies each item of redacted information and specifies an appropriate identifier that uniquely corresponds to each item listed. The list must be filed under seal and may be amended as of right. Any reference in the case to a listed identifier will be construed to refer to the corresponding item of information. FRCP 5.2(g); NY R USDCTSD CM/ECF, S.D.(II)(21)(21.5).

  h. *Responsibility for redaction.* It is the sole responsibility of counsel and the parties to be sure that all documents comply with the rules of this Court requiring redaction of personal identifiers. Neither the judge nor the Clerk of Court will review documents for compliance with these rules. NY R USDCTSD CM/ECF, S.D.(II)(21)(21.2).

  i. *Waiver of protection of identifiers.* A person waives the protection of FRCP 5.2(a) as to the person's own information by filing it without redaction and not under seal. FRCP 5.2(h).

  j. For more information on privacy and public access to ECF cases, refer to NY R USDCTSD CM/ECF, S.D.(II)(21).

5. *Individual judge practices.* Refer to the Miscellaneous section of this document for information on individual judge practices on formatting documents.

## F. Filing and Service Requirements

1. *Filing requirements.* Any paper after the complaint that is required to be served—together with a certificate of service—must be filed within a reasonable time after service. FRCP 5(d)(1). Complaints and all subsequent papers are accepted at either courthouse, regardless of the place for which the case is designated. NY R USDCTSD Div. Bus., Rule 22. Subject to the instructions regarding ECF published on the website of each respective Court and any pertinent Individual Judge's Practices, letter-motions permitted by NY R USDCTS&ED Civ Rule 7.1(d) and letters addressed to the Court (but not letters between the parties) may be filed via ECF. NY R USDCTS&ED Civ Rule 5.2(b). For information on electronically filing motions, refer to NY R USDCTSD CM/ECF, S.D.(II)(15).

  a. *How filing is made; In general.* A paper is filed by delivering it:

    i. To the clerk; or

    ii. To a judge who agrees to accept it for filing, and who must then note the filing date on the paper and promptly send it to the clerk. FRCP 5(d)(2).

  b. *Night depository.* A night depository with an automatic date stamp shall be maintained by the Clerk of the Southern District in the Pearl Street Courthouse. After regular business hours, papers for the District Court only may be deposited in the night depository. Such papers will be considered as having been filed in the District Court as of the date stamped thereon, which shall be deemed presumptively correct. NY R USDCTS&ED Civ Rule 1.2.

  c. *Electronic filing*

    i. *Authorization of electronic filing program.* A court may, by local rule, allow papers to be filed, signed, or verified by electronic means that are consistent with any technical standards established by the Judicial Conference of the United States. A local rule may require electronic filing only if reasonable exceptions are allowed. A paper filed electronically in compliance with a local rule is a written paper for purposes of the Federal Rules of Civil Procedure. FRCP 5(d)(3).

      • The Court will accept for filing documents submitted, signed or verified by electronic means, that comply with the rules in NY R USDCTSD CM/ECF, S.D. NY R USDCTSD CM/ECF, S.D.(I). The information in NY R USDCTSD CM/ECF, S.D. applies only to cases assigned to the ECF system. NY R USDCTSD CM/ECF, S.D.(Introduction).

      • Parties serving and filing papers shall follow the instructions regarding Electronic Case

443

Filing (ECF) published on the website of each respective Court. A paper served and filed by electronic means in accordance with such instructions is, for purposes of FRCP 5, served and filed in compliance with the Local Civil Rules of the Southern and Eastern Districts of New York. NY R USDCTS&ED Civ Rule 5.2(a). Parties have an obligation to review the Court's actual order, decree, or judgment (on ECF), which controls, and should not rely on the description on the docket or in the ECF Notice of Electronic Filing (NEF). NY R USDCTS&ED Civ Rule 5.2(c).

- The following should be observed when filing electronically: (1) the Federal Rules of Civil Procedure, (2) the Local Civil Rules of the United States District Courts for the Southern and Eastern Districts of New York, (3) the assigned judge's Individual Practices, and (4) the Court's Electronic Case Filing Rules & Instructions (NY R USDCTSD CM/ECF, S.D.). NY R USDCTSD CM/ECF, S.D.(Introduction).

ii. *Scope of electronic filing.* Except as expressly provided and in exceptional circumstances preventing a party from filing electronically, all documents required to be filed with the Court must be filed electronically. Any party unable to comply with this requirement must seek permission of the Court to file in the traditional manner, on paper. Any such application made after regular business hours may be submitted through the night depository box maintained pursuant to NY R USDCTS&ED Civ Rule 1.2. NY R USDCTSD CM/ECF, S.D.(I)(1)(1.1).

- *Documents filed by pro se litigants.* Unless otherwise ordered by the Court, documents filed by pro se litigants must be filed in the traditional manner, on paper, and will be scanned and docketed by the Clerk's Office into the ECF system. NY R USDCTSD CM/ECF, S.D.(I)(1)(1.1). Pro se litigants must file pleadings and documents in the traditional manner on paper unless the assigned judge has granted permission to electronically file on the ECF system. NY R USDCTSD CM/ECF, S.D.(Introduction).

- *Letters.* Except for letters to be filed under seal, letters addressed to judges who accept letters may be filed electronically. Parties should consult the assigned judge's Individual Practices to determine if the judge accepts letters at all and, if he or she does, whether the judge has any page limitations on letters and/or requires courtesy copies of letters filed on ECF (and, if so, by what means of delivery). NY R USDCTSD CM/ECF, S.D.(II)(13)(13.1). Letters solely between parties or their counsel or otherwise not addressed to the Court may not be filed electronically on ECF (except as exhibits to an otherwise properly filed document). NY R USDCTSD CM/ECF, S.D.(II)(13)(13.1). For more information on filing letters, refer to NY R USDCTSD CM/ECF, S.D.(II)(13)(13.1).

- *Proposed orders, judgments and decrees.* Proposed orders, judgments and decrees shall be presented as directed by the ECF rules published on the website of each respective Court. NY R USDCTS&ED Civ Rule 77.1. For more information, refer to NY R USDCTS&ED Civ Rule 77.1.

iii. *Exceptions to electronic filing.* In an ECF case, the documents that should not be electronically filed include:

- Miscellaneous Case initiating documents, NY R USDCTSD CM/ECF, S.D.(II)(18)(18.2);

- Proposed orders; proposed judgments, stipulations; consents, NY R USDCTSD CM/ECF, S.D.(II)(18)(18.3);

- Orders to show cause / temporary restraining orders, NY R USDCTSD CM/ECF, S.D.(II)(18)(18.4);

- Sealed documents, NY R USDCTSD CM/ECF, S.D.(II)(18)(18.5); and

- Surety bonds, NY R USDCTSD CM/ECF, S.D.(II)(18)(18.6).

- In cases where the record of an administrative or other prior proceeding must be filed with the Court, such record may be served and filed in hard copy without prior motion and order of the Court. NY R USDCTSD CM/ECF, S.D.(I)(5)(5.3).

- For more documents excepted from electronic filing, and for more information on such documents, refer to NY R USDCTSD CM/ECF, S.D.(II)(18).

iv. *Consequences of electronic filing.* Except as otherwise provided in NY R USDCTSD CM/ECF, S.D.(I)(4), electronic filing of a document in the ECF system consistent with these procedures, together with the transmission of a Notice of Electronic Filing (NEF) from the Court, constitutes filing of the document for all purposes of the Federal Rules of Civil Procedure and the Local Civil Rules of the United States District Courts for the Southern and Eastern Districts of New York and constitutes entry of the document on the docket kept by the Clerk under FRCP 58 and FRCP 79. NY R USDCTSD CM/ECF, S.D.(I)(3)(3.1).

v. For more information on electronic filing, refer to NY R USDCTSD CM/ECF, S.D.

2. *Service requirements*

   a. *Service; When required*

      i. *In general.* Unless the Federal Rules of Civil Procedure provide otherwise, each of the following papers must be served on every party:

         - An order stating that service is required;
         - A pleading filed after the original complaint, unless the court orders otherwise under FRCP 5(c) because there are numerous defendants;
         - A discovery paper required to be served on a party, unless the court orders otherwise;
         - A written motion, except one that may be heard ex parte; and
         - A written notice, appearance, demand, or offer of judgment, or any similar paper. FRCP 5(a)(1).

      ii. *If a party fails to appear.* No service is required on a party who is in default for failing to appear. But a pleading that asserts a new claim for relief against such a party must be served on that party under FRCP 4. FRCP 5(a)(2).

      iii. *Seizing property.* If an action is begun by seizing property and no person is or need be named as a defendant, any service required before the filing of an appearance, answer, or claim must be made on the person who had custody or possession of the property when it was seized. FRCP 5(a)(3).

   b. *Service; How made*

      i. *Serving an attorney.* If a party is represented by an attorney, service under FRCP 5 must be made on the attorney unless the court orders service on the party. FRCP 5(b)(1).

      ii. *Service in general.* A paper is served under FRCP 5 by:

         - Handing it to the person;
         - Leaving it: (1) at the person's office with a clerk or other person in charge or, if no one is in charge, in a conspicuous place in the office; or (2) if the person has no office or the office is closed, at the person's dwelling or usual place of abode with someone of suitable age and discretion who resides there;
         - Mailing it to the person's last known address—in which event service is complete upon mailing;
         - Leaving it with the court clerk if the person has no known address;
         - Sending it by electronic means if the person consented in writing—in which event service is complete upon transmission, but is not effective if the serving party learns that it did not reach the person to be served; or
         - Delivering it by any other means that the person consented to in writing—in which event service is complete when the person making service delivers it to the agency designated to make delivery. FRCP 5(b)(2).

      iii. *Service by overnight delivery.* Service upon an attorney may be made by overnight delivery service. "Overnight delivery service" means any delivery service which regularly accepts items for overnight delivery. Overnight delivery service shall be deemed service by mail for purposes of FRCP 5 and FRCP 6. NY R USDCTS&ED Civ Rule 5.3.

iv. *Service by electronic means.* Parties serving and filing papers shall follow the instructions regarding Electronic Case Filing (ECF) published on the website of each respective Court. A paper served and filed by electronic means in accordance with such instructions is, for purposes of FRCP 5, served and filed in compliance with the Local Civil Rules of the United States District Courts for the Southern and Eastern Districts of New York. NY R USDCTS&ED Civ Rule 5.2(a). Parties have an obligation to review the Court's actual order, decree, or judgment (on ECF), which controls, and should not rely on the description on the docket or in the ECF Notice of Electronic Filing (NEF). NY R USDCTS&ED Civ Rule 5.2(c).

- *Notice of electronic filing (NEF).* In cases assigned to the ECF system, service is complete provided all parties receive a Notice of Electronic Filing (NEF), which is sent automatically by email from the Court (see the NEF for a list of who did/did not receive notice electronically). Transmission of the NEF constitutes service upon all Filing and Receiving Users who are listed as recipients of notice by electronic mail. NY R USDCTSD CM/ECF, S.D.(I)(9)(9.1). In cases assigned to the ECF system, if all parties receive a NEF, service is complete upon transmission of the NEF by the Court, and you are not required to serve a paper copy. NY R USDCTSD CM/ECF, S.D.(II)(19)(19.2). It remains the duty of Filing and Receiving Users to maintain current contact information with the court and to regularly review the docket sheet of the case. NY R USDCTSD CM/ECF, S.D.(I)(9)(9.1).

- *Mailing of court-initiated documents.* The Clerk's Office will no longer mail paper copies of court-initiated documents to Filing and Receiving Users. The Clerk's Office will mail copies of all court-initiated documents to pro se parties who have not registered as Filing or Receiving Users. NY R USDCTSD CM/ECF, S.D.(II)(19)(19.1).

- *No receipt of a NEF.* If any party does not receive a NEF, you are required to accomplish service on that party in the traditional manner, in paper form. NY R USDCTSD CM/ECF, S.D.(II)(19)(19.2). The NEF receipt will inform you who will receive notice of the filing "electronically" (by e-mail from the Court) and who will receive notice "by other means" (traditional service in paper form). NY R USDCTSD CM/ECF, S.D.(II)(19)(19.2).

- *Service on non-filing or non-receiving users.* Attorneys and pro se parties who are not Filing or Receiving Users must be served with a paper copy of any electronically filed pleading or other document. Service of such paper copy must be made according to the Federal Rules of Civil Procedure and the Local Civil Rules of the United States District Courts for the Southern and Eastern Districts of New York. NY R USDCTSD CM/ECF, S.D.(I)(9)(9.2). Such paper service must be documented by electronically filing proof of service. NY R USDCTSD CM/ECF, S.D.(I)(9)(9.2); NY R USDCTSD CM/ECF, S.D.(II)(19)(19.2). Where the Clerk scans and electronically files pleadings and documents on behalf of a pro se party, the associated NEF constitutes service. NY R USDCTSD CM/ECF, S.D.(I)(9)(9.2).

- For more information on service by electronic means, refer to NY R USDCTSD CM/ECF, S.D.(II)(19).

v. *Using court facilities.* If a local rule so authorizes, a party may use the court's transmission facilities to make service under FRCP 5(b)(2)(E). FRCP 5(b)(3).

c. *Serving numerous defendants*

i. *In general.* If an action involves an unusually large number of defendants, the court may, on motion or on its own, order that:

- Defendants' pleadings and replies to them need not be served on other defendants;

- Any crossclaim, counterclaim, avoidance, or affirmative defense in those pleadings and replies to them will be treated as denied or avoided by all other parties; and

- Filing any such pleading and serving it on the plaintiff constitutes notice of the pleading to all parties. FRCP 5(c)(1).

ii. *Notifying parties.* A copy of every such order must be served on the parties as the court directs. FRCP 5(c)(2).

3. *Individual judge practices.* Refer to the Miscellaneous section of this document for information on individual judge practices on filing and serving documents.

## G. Hearings

1. *Hearings, generally*

   a. *Oral argument.* Due process does not require that oral argument be permitted on a motion and, except as otherwise provided by local rule, the district court has discretion to determine whether it will decide the motion on the papers or hear argument by counsel (and perhaps receive evidence). FPP § 1190; F.D.I.C. v. Deglau, 207 F.3d 153 (3d Cir. 2000). The parties and their attorneys shall only appear to argue the motion if so directed by the Court by order or by a Judge's Individual Practice. NY R USDCTS&ED Civ Rule 6.1(c).

   b. *Providing a regular schedule for oral hearings.* A court may establish regular times and places for oral hearings on motions. FRCP 78(a).

   c. *Providing for submission on briefs.* By rule or order, the court may provide for submitting and determining motions on briefs, without oral hearings. FRCP 78(b).

2. *Hearing on motion for preliminary injunction after temporary restraining order is issued without notice*

   a. *Expediting the preliminary injunction hearing.* If the order is issued without notice, the motion for a preliminary injunction must be set for hearing at the earliest possible time, taking precedence over all other matters except hearings on older matters of the same character. At the hearing, the party who obtained the order must proceed with the motion; if the party does not, the court must dissolve the order. FRCP 65(b)(3). Refer to the United States District Court for the Southern District of New York KeyRules Motion for Preliminary Injunction document for more information on the hearing on the motion for preliminary injunction.

3. *Individual judge practices.* Refer to the Miscellaneous section of this document for information on individual judge practices on hearings.

## H. Forms

### 1. Federal Application for Temporary Restraining Order Forms

   a. Ex parte motion; For temporary restraining order and order to show cause; Interference with property rights. AMJUR PP INJUNCTION § 42.

   b. Affidavit; In support of ex parte motion for temporary restraining order. AMJUR PP INJUNCTION § 48.

   c. Certificate of attorney; In support of ex parte motion for temporary restraining order. AMJUR PP INJUNCTION § 50.

   d. Affidavit; In support of ex parte motion for temporary restraining order; Interference with property rights. AMJUR PP INJUNCTION § 51.

   e. Motion. 4A FEDFORMS § 5344.

   f. Motion; Another form. 4A FEDFORMS § 5345.

   g. Motion; Another form. 4A FEDFORMS § 5346.

   h. Motion without notice. 4A FEDFORMS § 5347.

   i. Motion without notice; Another form. 4A FEDFORMS § 5348.

   j. Motion without notice; Another form. 4A FEDFORMS § 5349.

   k. Motion without notice; Another form. 4A FEDFORMS § 5350.

   l. Motion without notice; Another form. 4A FEDFORMS § 5351.

   m. Motion without notice; Another form. 4A FEDFORMS § 5352.

   n. Certificate of attorney's efforts to give notice. 4A FEDFORMS § 5353.

   o. Certificate of attorney's efforts to give notice; Another form. 4A FEDFORMS § 5354.

   p. Certificate of attorney's efforts to give notice; Another form. 4A FEDFORMS § 5355.

q. Certificate of attorney's efforts to give notice; Another form. 4A FEDFORMS § 5356.

r. Motion requesting expedited hearing. 4A FEDFORMS § 5357.

s. Motion seeking temporary restraining order. 4A FEDFORMS § 5359.

t. Motion to dissolve or modify temporary restraining order. 4A FEDFORMS § 5361.

u.\ Motion for temporary restraining order and preliminary injunction. GOLDLTGFMS § 13A:6.

v. Motion for temporary restraining order; General form. GOLDLTGFMS § 13A:11.

w. Motion for temporary restraining order; Ex parte application. GOLDLTGFMS § 13A:12.

x. Motion for temporary restraining order; Ex parte application; Supporting affidavit by party. GOLDLTGFMS § 13A:13.

y. Motion for temporary restraining order; Ex parte application; Supporting affidavit by party; Copyright infringement. GOLDLTGFMS § 13A:14.

z. Motion for temporary restraining order; Ex parte application; Certificate by counsel. GOLDLTGFMS § 13A:15.

## I. Applicable Rules

1. *Federal rules*

   a. Serving and filing pleadings and other papers. FRCP 5.

   b. Constitutional challenge to a statute; Notice, certification, and intervention. FRCP 5.1.

   c. Privacy protection for filings made with the court. FRCP 5.2.

   d. Computing and extending time; Time for motion papers. FRCP 6.

   e. Pleadings allowed; Form of motions and other papers. FRCP 7.

   f. Disclosure statement. FRCP 7.1.

   g. Form of pleadings. FRCP 10.

   h. Signing pleadings, motions, and other papers; Representations to the court; Sanctions. FRCP 11.

   i. Taking testimony. FRCP 43.

   j. Injunctions and restraining orders. FRCP 65.

   k. Proceedings against a surety. FRCP 65.1.

   l. Hearing motions; Submission on briefs. FRCP 78.

2. *Local rules*

   a. Night depository. NY R USDCTS&ED Civ Rule 1.2.

   b. Duty of attorneys in related cases. NY R USDCTS&ED Civ Rule 1.6.

   c. Filing of discovery materials. NY R USDCTS&ED Civ Rule 5.1.

   d. Electronic service and filing of documents. NY R USDCTS&ED Civ Rule 5.2.

   e. Service by overnight delivery. NY R USDCTS&ED Civ Rule 5.3.

   f. Service and filing of motion papers. NY R USDCTS&ED Civ Rule 6.1.

   g. Orders on motions. NY R USDCTS&ED Civ Rule 6.2.

   h. Computation of time. NY R USDCTS&ED Civ Rule 6.4.

   i. Motion papers. NY R USDCTS&ED Civ Rule 7.1.

   j. Disclosure statement. NY R USDCTS&ED Civ Rule 7.1.1.

   k. Authorities to be provided to pro se litigants. NY R USDCTS&ED Civ Rule 7.2.

   l. Form of pleadings, motions, and other papers. NY R USDCTS&ED Civ Rule 11.1.

   m. Submission of orders, judgments and decrees. NY R USDCTS&ED Civ Rule 77.1.

   n. Alternative dispute resolution (Southern District only). NY R USDCTS&ED Civ Rule 83.9.

o. Electronic case filing rules and instructions. NY R USDCTSD CM/ECF, S.D.

p. Related cases. NY R USDCTSD Div. Bus., Rule 13.

q. Filing at either courthouse. NY R USDCTSD Div. Bus., Rule 22.

## J. Miscellaneous

**NOTE: Individual judges' rules may apply. For available judge-level information, refer to:**

DISTRICT JUDGE RONNIE ABRAMS: NY R USDCTSD Abrams-Civ Prac; NY R USDCTSD Abrams-Crim Prac; NY R USDCTSD Abrams-Pro Se; NY R USDCTSD Abrams-Case Mgt; NY R USDCTSD Abrams-Jury.

DISTRICT JUDGE DEBORAH A. BATTS: NY R USDCTSD Batts-Practices.

DISTRICT JUDGE RICHARD M. BERMAN: NY R USDCTSD Berman-Practices; NY R USDCTSD Berman-Default; NY R USDCTSD Berman-Sentencing; NY R USDCTSD Berman-Media.

DISTRICT JUDGE VINCENT L. BRICCETTI: NY R USDCTSD Briccetti-Practices; NY R USDCTSD Briccetti-Plan; NY R USDCTSD Briccetti-Notice.

DISTRICT JUDGE VERNON S. BRODERICK: NY R USDCTSD Broderick-Civil; NY R USDCTSD Broderick-Crim; NY R USDCTSD Broderick-Case Mgt; NY R USDCTSD Broderick-Jury.

DISTRICT JUDGE NAOMI REICE BUCHWALD: NY R USDCTSD Buchwald-Practices.

DISTRICT JUDGE VALERIE E. CAPRONI: NY R USDCTSD Caproni-Prac; NY R USDCTSD Caproni--Pro Se; NY R USDCTSD Caproni-Case Mgt; NY R USDCTSD Caproni-Crim Prac.

DISTRICT JUDGE ANDREW L. CARTER JR.: NY R USDCTSD Carter-Practices.

DISTRICT JUDGE KEVIN P. CASTEL: NY R USDCTSD Castel-Practices; NY R USDCTSD Castel-Default; NY R USDCTSD Castel-Scheduling; NY R USDCTSD Castel-Complex; NY R USDCTSD Castel-Trials; NY R USDCTSD Castel-Sentencing.

DISTRICT JUDGE DENISE L. COTE: NY R USDCTSD Cote-Civil Practices; NY R USDCTSD Cote-Pro Se; NY R USDCTSD Cote-Maritime Ord; NY R USDCTSD Cote-Crim Practices; NY R USDCTSD Cote-Crim Trials; NY R USDCTSD Cote-Sentencing.

DISTRICT JUDGE PAUL A. CROTTY: NY R USDCTSD Crotty-Practices; NY R USDCTSD Crotty-Sentencing; NY R USDCTSD Crotty-Calls; NY R USDCTSD Crotty-Scheduling.

DISTRICT JUDGE GEORGE B. DANIELS: NY R USDCTSD Daniels-Practices.

DISTRICT JUDGE KEVIN T. DUFFY: NY R USDCTSD Duffy-Practices.

DISTRICT JUDGE PAUL A. ENGELMAYER: NY R USDCTSD Engelmayer-Practices; NY R USDCTSD Engelmayer-Scheduling; NY R USDCTSD Engelmayer-Sentencing; NY R USDCTSD Engelmayer-Pro Se; NY R USDCTSD Engelmayer-Crim.

DISTRICT JUDGE KATHERINE POLK FAILLA: NY R USDCTSD Failla-Civ Prac; NY R USDCTSD Failla-Crim Prac; NY R USDCTSD Failla-Case Mgt.

DISTRICT JUDGE KATHERINE B. FORREST: NY R USDCTSD Forrest-Civil Prac; NY R USDCTSD Forrest-Crim Prac; NY R USDCTSD Forrest-Crim Pretrial; NY R USDCTSD Forrest-Scheduling; NY R USDCTSD Forrest-Patent Scheduling; NY R USDCTSD Forrest-Sentencing; NY R USDCTSD Forrest-Order 1; NY R USDCTSD Forrest-Order 2.

DISTRICT JUDGE JESSE M. FURMAN: NY R USDCTSD Furman-Civil Prac; NY R USDCTSD Furman-Crim Prac; NY R USDCTSD Furman-Pro Se Prac; NY R USDCTSD Furman-Trials; NY R USDCTSD Furman-Scheduling; NY R USDCTSD Furman-Rights.

DISTRICT JUDGE PAUL G. GARDEPHE: NY R USDCTSD Gardephe-Civ Prac; NY R USDCTSD Gardephe-Pretrial; NY R USDCTSD Gardephe-Prot Ord; NY R USDCTSD Gardephe-Maritime; NY R USDCTSD Gardephe-Crim Prac; NY R USDCTSD Gardephe-Trial.

DISTRICT JUDGE THOMAS P. GRIESA: NY R USDCTSD Griesa-Practices.

DISTRICT JUDGE CHARLES S. HAIGHT: NY R USDCTSD Haight-Practices.

DISTRICT JUDGE ALVIN K. HELLERSTEIN: NY R USDCTSD Hellerstein-Practices; NY R USDCTSD Hellerstein--Sept 11.

DISTRICT JUDGE LEWIS A. KAPLAN: NY R USDCTSD Kaplan-Practices; NY R USDCTSD Kaplan-Sentencing.

DISTRICT JUDGE KENNETH M. KARAS: NY R USDCTSD Karas-Practices; NY R USDCTSD Karas-Case Mgt; NY R USDCTSD Karas-Default; NY R USDCTSD Karas-Sentencing; NY R USDCTSD Karas-Rights.

DISTRICT JUDGE JOHN F. KEENAN: NY R USDCTSD Keenan-Practices.

DISTRICT JUDGE JOHN G. KOELTL: NY R USDCTSD Koeltl-Practices.

DISTRICT JUDGE VICTOR MARRERO: NY R USDCTSD Marrero-Practices; NY R USDCTSD Marrero-Scheduling; NY R USDCTSD Marrero-Default; NY R USDCTSD Marrero-Trial Proc.

DISTRICT JUDGE COLLEEN McMAHON: NY R USDCTSD McMahon-Practices; NY R USDCTSD McMahon-RICO; NY R USDCTSD McMahon-Copies; NY R USDCTSD McMahon-Scheduling; NY R US-DCTSD McMahon-Elec Disc; NY R USDCTSD McMahon-Sentencing.

DISTRICT JUDGE ALISON J. NATHAN: NY R USDCTSD Nathan-Civ Prac; NY R USDCTSD Nathan-Crim Prac; NY R USDCTSD Nathan-Pro Se; NY R USDCTSD Nathan-Scheduling.

DISTRICT JUDGE J. PAUL OETKEN: NY R USDCTSD Oetken-Civ Prac; NY R USDCTSD Oetken-Case Mgt; NY R USDCTSD Oetken-Crim Prac; NY R USDCTSD Oetken-Pro Se.

DISTRICT JUDGE WILLIAM H. PAULEY, III: NY R USDCTSD Pauley-Crim Cases; NY R USDCTSD Pauley-Practices.

DISTRICT JUDGE LORETTA A. PRESKA: NY R USDCTSD Preska-Practices.

DISTRICT JUDGE JED S. RAKOFF: NY R USDCTSD Rakoff-Practices; NY R USDCTSD Rakoff-Scheduling; NY R USDCTSD Rakoff-Prot Ord; NY R USDCTSD Rakoff-Maritime Ord.

DISTRICT JUDGE EDGARDO RAMOS: NY R USDCTSD Ramos--Practices; NY R USDCTSD Ramos-Case Mgt.

DISTRICT JUDGE NELSON S. ROMAN: NY R USDCTSD Roman-Civ Prac; NY R USDCTSD Roman-Pro Se; NY R USDCTSD Roman-Crim Prac; NY R USDCTSD Roman-Case Mgt.

DISTRICT JUDGE LEONARD B. SAND: NY R USDCTSD Sand-Practices.

DISTRICT JUDGE LORNA G. SCHOFIELD: NY R USDCTSD Schofield-Civ Prac; NY R USDCTSD Schofield-Crim Prac; NY R USDCTSD Schofield-Sched; NY R USDCTSD Schofield-Pro Se; NY R USDCTSD Schofield-Advice.

DISTRICT JUDGE CATHY SEIBEL: NY R USDCTSD Seibel-Practices.

DISTRICT JUDGE LOUIS L. STANTON: NY R USDCTSD Stanton-Practices; NY R USDCTSD Stanton-Pretrial.

DISTRICT JUDGE SIDNEY H. STEIN: NY R USDCTSD Stein-Practices.

DISTRICT JUDGE RICHARD J. SULLIVAN: NY R USDCTSD Sullivan-Practices; NY R USDCTSD Sullivan-Scheduling; NY R USDCTSD Sullivan-Sentencing; NY R USDCTSD Sullivan-Juries; NY R USDCTSD Sullivan-Trial; NY R USDCTSD Sullivan-Default.

DISTRICT JUDGE LAURA TAYLOR SWAIN: NY R USDCTSD Swain-Practices; NY R USDCTSD Swain-Trial; NY R USDCTSD Swain-Crim Trial; NY R USDCTSD Swain-Juries; NY R USDCTSD Swain-Sentencing; NY R USDCTSD Swain-Rights.

DISTRICT JUDGE ROBERT W. SWEET: NY R USDCTSD Sweet-Practices.

DISTRICT JUDGE ANALISA TORRES: NY R USDCTSD Torres-Civ Prac; NY R USDCTSD Torres-Pro Se; NY R USDCTSD Torres-Scheduling.

DISTRICT JUDGE KIMBA M. WOOD: NY R USDCTSD Wood-Practices; NY R USDCTSD Wood-Scheduling; NY R USDCTSD Wood-Discovery; NY R USDCTSD Wood-RICO; NY R USDCTSD Wood-Juries; NY R USDCTSD Wood-Trial; NY R USDCTSD Wood-Media.

DISTRICT JUDGE GREGORY H. WOODS: NY R USDCTSD Woods-Civ Prac; NY R USDCTSD Woods-Pro Se; NY R USDCTSD Woods-Sched; NY R USDCTSD Woods-Crim Prac; NY R USDCTSD Woods-Protect Order; NY R USDCTSD Woods-Speedy Trial.

MAGISTRATE JUDGE JAMES L. COTT: NY R USDCTSD Cott-Practices; NY R USDCTSD Cott-Settlement.

MAGISTRATE JUDGE PAUL E. DAVISON: NY R USDCTSD Davison-Practices.

MAGISTRATE JUDGE RONALD L. ELLIS: NY R USDCTSD Ellis-Practices.

MAGISTRATE JUDGE KEVIN N. FOX: NY R USDCTSD Fox-Practices; NY R USDCTSD Fox-Settlement.

MAGISTRATE JUDGE JAMES C. FRANCIS: NY R USDCTSD Francis-Practices.

MAGISTRATE JUDGE DEBRA FREEMAN: NY R USDCTSD Freeman-Practices; NY R USDCTSD Freeman-Settlement.

MAGISTRATE JUDGE GABRIEL W. GORENSTEIN: NY R USDCTSD Gorenstein-Practices; NY R USDCTSD Gorenstein-Ackn.

MAGISTRATE JUDGE FRANK MAAS: NY R USDCTSD Maas-Practices; NY R USDCTSD Maas-Discontinuance; NY R USDCTSD Maas-Conf; NY R USDCTSD Maas-Settlement.

MAGISTRATE JUDGE JUDITH C. McCARTHY: NY R USDCTSD McCarthy-Practices; NY R USDCTSD McCarthy-Conduct.

MAGISTRATE JUDGE BARBARA MOSES: NY R USDCTSD Moses-Practices.

MAGISTRATE JUDGE SARAH NETBURN: NY R USDCTSD Netburn-Civil; NY R USDCTSD Netburn-Settlement; NY R USDCTSD Netburn-Case Mgt; NY R USDCTSD Netburn--Pro Se.

MAGISTRATE JUDGE ANDREW J. PECK: NY R USDCTSD Peck-Practices; NY R USDCTSD Peck-Order; NY R USDCTSD Peck-Rule 502(d).

MAGISTRATE JUDGE HENRY PITMAN: NY R USDCTSD Pitman-Practices.

MAGISTRATE JUDGE LISA MARGARET SMITH: NY R USDCTSD Smith-Practices; NY R USDCTSD Smith-Trials.

# Requests, Notices and Applications
# Pretrial Conferences, Scheduling, Management

### Document Last Updated September 2016

## A. Checklist

(I) ❑ Matters to be considered by parties for the pretrial conference

    (a) ❑ Documents to consider

        (1) ❑ Pretrial memorandum or statement

        (2) ❑ Statement explaining untimely electronic filing

        (3) ❑ Courtesy copies

    (b) ❑ Timing

        (1) ❑ The court determines at what stage in the action to hold a pretrial conference

(II) ❑ Matters to be considered by parties for the scheduling conference

    (a) ❑ Documents to consider

        (1) ❑ Request for scheduling conference

        (2) ❑ Statement explaining untimely electronic filing

        (3) ❑ Courtesy copies

    (b) ❑ Timing

        (1) ❑ If a scheduling conference is called, it is important to recognize that, unlike the ordinary pretrial conference, the scheduling conference occurs before the substantive issues have been defined and is directed toward organizing the processing of the action by setting deadlines for the completion of the various pretrial phases

(III)  ❑ Matters to be considered by parties for the discovery planning conference

    (a)  ❑ Required documents

        (1)  ❑ Written report outlining proposed discovery plan

    (b)  ❑ Supplemental documents

        (1)  ❑ Statement explaining untimely electronic filing

        (2)  ❑ Courtesy copies

    (c)  ❑ Timing

        (1)  ❑ Except in a proceeding exempted from initial disclosure under FRCP 26(a)(1)(B) or when the court orders otherwise, the parties must confer as soon as practicable—and in any event at least twenty-one (21) days before a scheduling conference is to be held or a scheduling order is due under FRCP 16(b)

        (2)  ❑ Within fourteen (14) days after the conference, the attorneys of record are responsible for submitting a written report outlining the plan

## B. Timing

1.  *Pretrial conferences, generally.* The court determines at what stage in the action to hold a pretrial conference. When only one conference is involved, the most favored practice seems to be to wait until after the case has been prepared for trial. FPP § 1524. Although there rarely will be any need to hold a conference in a relatively simple case until after the preliminary motions have been disposed of, the only inherently logical limitation on the court's discretion as to when to hold a conference is that it should not be held before all the necessary and indispensable parties are served. FPP § 1524.

2.  *Scheduling conference.* If a scheduling conference is called, it is important to recognize that, unlike the ordinary pretrial conference, the scheduling conference occurs before the substantive issues have been defined and is directed toward organizing the processing of the action by setting deadlines for the completion of the various pretrial phases. FPP § 1522.1.

3.  *Discovery planning conference.* Except in a proceeding exempted from initial disclosure under FRCP 26(a)(1)(B) or when the court orders otherwise, the parties must confer as soon as practicable—and in any event at least twenty-one (21) days before a scheduling conference is to be held or a scheduling order is due under FRCP 16(b). FRCP 26(f)(1).

    a.  *Submission of written report outlining proposed discovery plan.* The attorneys of record and all unrepresented parties that have appeared in the case are jointly responsible for arranging the conference, for attempting in good faith to agree on the proposed discovery plan, and for submitting to the court within fourteen (14) days after the conference a written report outlining the plan. FRCP 26(f)(2).

    b.  *Expedited schedule.* If necessary to comply with its expedited schedule for FRCP 16(b) conferences, a court may by local rule: (1) require the parties' conference to occur less than twenty-one (21) days before the scheduling conference is held or a scheduling order is due under FRCP 16(b); and (2) require the written report outlining the discovery plan to be filed less than fourteen (14) days after the parties' conference, or excuse the parties from submitting a written report and permit them to report orally on their discovery plan at the FRCP 16(b) conference. FRCP 26(f)(4).

4.  *Computation of time*

    a.  *Computing time.* FRCP 6 applies in computing any time period specified in the Federal Rules of Civil Procedure, in any local rule or court order, or in any statute that does not specify a method of computing time. FRCP 6(a). In computing any period of time prescribed or allowed by the Local Civil Rules of the United States District Courts for the Southern and Eastern Districts of New York or the Local Admiralty and Maritime Rules, the provisions of FRCP 6 shall apply unless otherwise stated. NY R USDCTS&ED Civ Rule 6.4.

        i.  *Period stated in days or a longer unit.* When the period is stated in days or a longer unit of time:

            • Exclude the day of the event that triggers the period;

            • Count every day, including intermediate Saturdays, Sundays, and legal holidays; and

- Include the last day of the period, but if the last day is a Saturday, Sunday, or legal holiday, the period continues to run until the end of the next day that is not a Saturday, Sunday, or legal holiday. FRCP 6(a)(1). In the Local Civil Rules of the United States District Courts for the Southern and Eastern Districts of New York, as in the Federal Rules of Civil Procedure as amended effective December 1, 2009, Saturdays, Sundays, and legal holidays are no longer excluded in computing periods of time. If the last day of the period is a Saturday, Sunday, or legal holiday, the period continues to run until the end of the next day that is not a Saturday, Sunday, or legal holiday. NY R USDCTS&ED Civ Rule 6.4.

ii. *Period stated in hours.* When the period is stated in hours:

- Begin counting immediately on the occurrence of the event that triggers the period;

- Count every hour, including hours during intermediate Saturdays, Sundays, and legal holidays; and

- If the period would end on a Saturday, Sunday, or legal holiday, the period continues to run until the same time on the next day that is not a Saturday, Sunday, or legal holiday. FRCP 6(a)(2). In the Local Civil Rules of the United States District Courts for the Southern and Eastern Districts of New York, as in the Federal Rules of Civil Procedure as amended effective December 1, 2009, Saturdays, Sundays, and legal holidays are no longer excluded in computing periods of time. If the last day of the period is a Saturday, Sunday, or legal holiday, the period continues to run until the end of the next day that is not a Saturday, Sunday, or legal holiday. NY R USDCTS&ED Civ Rule 6.4.

iii. *Inaccessibility of the clerk's office.* Unless the court orders otherwise, if the clerk's office is inaccessible:

- On the last day for filing under FRCP 6(a)(1), then the time for filing is extended to the first accessible day that is not a Saturday, Sunday, or legal holiday; or

- During the last hour for filing under FRCP 6(a)(2), then the time for filing is extended to the same time on the first accessible day that is not a Saturday, Sunday, or legal holiday. FRCP 6(a)(3).

iv. *"Last day" defined.* Unless a different time is set by a statute, local rule, or court order, the last day ends:

- For electronic filing, at midnight in the court's time zone; and

- For filing by other means, when the clerk's office is scheduled to close. FRCP 6(a)(4).

v. *"Next day" defined.* The "next day" is determined by continuing to count forward when the period is measured after an event and backward when measured before an event. FRCP 6(a)(5).

vi. *"Legal holiday" defined.* "Legal holiday" means:

- The day set aside by statute for observing New Year's Day, Martin Luther King Jr.'s Birthday, Washington's Birthday, Memorial Day, Independence Day, Labor Day, Columbus Day, Veterans' Day, Thanksgiving Day, or Christmas Day;

- Any day declared a holiday by the President or Congress; and

- For periods that are measured after an event, any other day declared a holiday by the state where the district court is located. FRCP 6(a)(6).

b. *Computation of electronic filing deadlines.* You can file electronically twenty-four (24) hours a day, seven (7) days a week, three hundred sixty-five (365) days a year. NY R USDCTSD CM/ECF, S.D.(II)(13)(13.10). Electronic filing must be completed before midnight local time where the Court is located in order to be considered timely filed that day. NY R USDCTSD CM/ECF, S.D.(I)(3)(3.3); NY R USDCTSD CM/ECF, S.D.(II)(13)(13.10); NY R USDCTSD CM/ECF, S.D.(II)(19)(19.4). An electronically filed document is deemed filed on the "filed on" date indicated on the Notice of Electronic Filing (NEF). NY R USDCTSD CM/ECF, S.D.(II)(13)(13.11).

i. *Technical failures.* A Filing User whose filing is made untimely as the result of a technical failure may seek appropriate relief from the Court. NY R USDCTSD CM/ECF, S.D.(I)(11). If you missed a filing deadline when the ECF system was out of order, attach a statement to your filing explaining how the interruption in service prevented you from filing in a timely fashion. NY R USDCTSD CM/ECF, S.D.(II)(23)(23.5).

c. *Extending time*

    i. *In general.* When an act may or must be done within a specified time, the court may, for good cause, extend the time:

- With or without motion or notice if the court acts, or if a request is made, before the original time or its extension expires; or

- On motion made after the time has expired if the party failed to act because of excusable neglect. FRCP 6(b)(1).

    ii. *Exceptions.* A court must not extend the time to act under FRCP 50(b), FRCP 50(d), FRCP 52(b), FRCP 59(b), FRCP 59(d), FRCP 59(e), and FRCP 60(b). FRCP 6(b)(2).

    iii. Refer to the United States District Court for the Southern District of New York KeyRules Motion for Continuance/Extension of Time document for more information on extending time.

d. *Additional time after certain kinds of service.* When a party may or must act within a specified time after service and service is made under FRCP 5(b)(2)(C), FRCP 5(b)(2)(D), FRCP 5(b)(2)(E), or FRCP 5(b)(2)(F), three (3) days are added after the period would otherwise expire under FRCP 6(a). FRCP 6(d). Overnight delivery service shall be deemed service by mail for purposes of FRCP 5 and FRCP 6. NY R USDCTS&ED Civ Rule 5.3.

5. *Individual judge practices.* Refer to the Miscellaneous section of this document for information on individual judge practices on timing of documents.

## C. General Requirements

1. *Pretrial conferences, generally*

a. *Purposes of a pretrial conference.* FRCP 16 provides an important mechanism for carrying out one of the basic policies of the Federal Rules of Civil Procedure—the determination of disputes on their merits rather than on the basis of procedural niceties or tactical advantage. FPP § 1522. In any action, the court may order the attorneys and any unrepresented parties to appear for one or more pretrial conferences for such purposes as:

    i. Expediting disposition of the action;

    ii. Establishing early and continuing control so that the case will not be protracted because of lack of management;

    iii. Discouraging wasteful pretrial activities;

    iv. Improving the quality of the trial through more thorough preparation; and

    v. Facilitating settlement. FRCP 16(a).

b. *When appropriate.* FRCP 16 specifically provides that the court "may order the attorneys and any unrepresented parties to appear for one or more pretrial conferences." This language makes it clear that the utilization of the pretrial conference procedure lies within the discretion of the district court both as a matter of general policy and in terms of whether and when the rule should be invoked in a particular case. FPP § 1523; Mizwicki v. Helwig, 196 F.3d 828 (7th Cir. 1999). There is no requirement that any pretrial conferences be held or not held in certain types of actions. FPP § 1523.

c. *Attendance at a pretrial conference.* A represented party must authorize at least one of its attorneys to make stipulations and admissions about all matters that can reasonably be anticipated for discussion at a pretrial conference. If appropriate, the court may require that a party or its representative be present or reasonably available by other means to consider possible settlement. FRCP 16(c)(1).

d. *Matters for consideration at a pretrial conference.* At any pretrial conference, the court may consider and take appropriate action on the following matters:

    i. Formulating and simplifying the issues, and eliminating frivolous claims or defenses;

    ii.   Amending the pleadings if necessary or desirable;

    iii.   Obtaining admissions and stipulations about facts and documents to avoid unnecessary proof, and ruling in advance on the admissibility of evidence;

    iv.   Avoiding unnecessary proof and cumulative evidence, and limiting the use of testimony under FRE 702;

    v.   Determining the appropriateness and timing of summary adjudication under FRCP 56;

    vi.   Controlling and scheduling discovery, including orders affecting disclosures and discovery under FRCP 26 and FRCP 29 through FRCP 37;

    vii.   Identifying witnesses and documents, scheduling the filing and exchange of any pretrial briefs, and setting dates for further conferences and for trial;

    viii.   Referring matters to a magistrate judge or a master;

    ix.   Settling the case and using special procedures to assist in resolving the dispute when authorized by statute or local rule;

    x.   Determining the form and content of the pretrial order;

    xi.   Disposing of pending motions;

    xii.   Adopting special procedures for managing potentially difficult or protracted actions that may involve complex issues, multiple parties, difficult legal questions, or unusual proof problems;

    xiii.   Ordering a separate trial under FRCP 42(b) of a claim, counterclaim, crossclaim, third-party claim, or particular issue;

    xiv.   Ordering the presentation of evidence early in the trial on a manageable issue that might, on the evidence, be the basis for a judgment as a matter of law under FRCP 50(a) or a judgment on partial findings under FRCP 52(c);

    xv.   Establishing a reasonable limit on the time allowed to present evidence; and

    xvi.   Facilitating in other ways the just, speedy, and inexpensive disposition of the action. FRCP 16(c)(2).

  e.  *Pretrial orders.* After any conference under FRCP 16, the court should issue an order reciting the action taken. This order controls the course of the action unless the court modifies it. FRCP 16(d).

  f.  *Sanctions.* On motion or on its own, the court may issue any just orders, including those authorized by FRCP 37(b)(2)(A)(ii) through FRCP 37(b)(2)(A)(vii), if a party or its attorney: (1) fails to appear at a scheduling or other pretrial conference; (2) is substantially unprepared to participate—or does not participate in good faith—in the conference; or (3) fails to obey a scheduling or other pretrial order. FRCP 16(f)(1).

    i.  *Imposing fees and costs.* Instead of or in addition to any other sanction, the court must order the party, its attorney, or both to pay the reasonable expenses—including attorney's fees—incurred because of any noncompliance with FRCP 16, unless the noncompliance was substantially justified or other circumstances make an award of expenses unjust. FRCP 16(f)(2).

2.  *Scheduling conference.* A scheduling conference may be requested by the judge or by the parties, but it is not mandatory. FPP § 1522.1.

  a.  *Scheduling order.* Except in categories of actions exempted by local rule, the district judge—or a magistrate judge when authorized by local rule—must issue a scheduling order: (1) after receiving the parties' report under FRCP 26(f); or (2) after consulting with the parties' attorneys and any unrepresented parties at a scheduling conference. FRCP 16(b)(1). In any case referred to a Magistrate Judge, the Magistrate Judge may issue or modify scheduling orders pursuant to FRCP 16(b). NY R USDCTS&ED Civ Rule 16.2.

    i.  *Exemptions.* Matters involving habeas corpus petitions, Social Security disability cases, motions to vacate sentences, forfeitures, and reviews from administrative agencies are exempted from the mandatory scheduling order required by FRCP 16(b). NY R USDCTS&ED Civ Rule 16.1.

    ii.  *Required contents of the order.* The scheduling order must limit the time to join other parties, amend the pleadings, complete discovery, and file motions. FRCP 16(b)(3)(A).

    iii.  *Permitted contents of the order.* The scheduling order may:

- Modify the timing of disclosures under FRCP 26(a) and FRCP 26(e)(1);

- Modify the extent of discovery;

- Provide for disclosure, discovery, or preservation of electronically stored information;

- Include any agreements the parties reach for asserting claims of privilege or of protection as trial-preparation material after information is produced, including agreements reached under FRE 502;

- Direct that before moving for an order relating to discovery, the movant must request a conference with the court;

- Set dates for pretrial conferences and for trial; and

- Include other appropriate matters. FRCP 16(b)(3)(B).

  b.  *Time to issue.* The judge must issue the scheduling order as soon as practicable, but unless the judge finds good cause for delay, the judge must issue it within the earlier of ninety (90) days after any defendant has been served with the complaint or sixty (60) days after any defendant has appeared. FRCP 16(b)(2).

  c.  *Modifying a schedule.* A schedule may be modified only for good cause and with the judge's consent. FRCP 16(b)(4).

3.  *Final pretrial conference.* The court may hold a final pretrial conference to formulate a trial plan, including a plan to facilitate the admission of evidence. FRCP 16(e).

  a.  *Timing and attendance.* The conference must be held as close to the start of trial as is reasonable, and must be attended by at least one attorney who will conduct the trial for each party and by any unrepresented party. FRCP 16(e).

  b.  *Modification of final pretrial order.* The court may modify the order issued after a final pretrial conference only to prevent manifest injustice. FRCP 16(e).

4.  *Discovery planning conference*

  a.  *Conference content.* In conferring, the parties must consider the nature and basis of their claims and defenses and the possibilities for promptly settling or resolving the case; make or arrange for the disclosures required by FRCP 26(a)(1); discuss any issues about preserving discoverable information; and develop a proposed discovery plan. FRCP 26(f)(2).

  b.  *Parties' responsibilities.* The attorneys of record and all unrepresented parties that have appeared in the case are jointly responsible for arranging the conference, for attempting in good faith to agree on the proposed discovery plan, and for submitting to the court within fourteen (14) days after the conference a written report outlining the plan. The court may order the parties or attorneys to attend the conference in person. FRCP 26(f)(2).

  c.  *Discovery plan.* A discovery plan must state the parties' views and proposals on:

    i.  What changes should be made in the timing, form, or requirement for disclosures under FRCP 26(a), including a statement of when initial disclosures were made or will be made;

    ii.  The subjects on which discovery may be needed, when discovery should be completed, and whether discovery should be conducted in phases or be limited to or focused on particular issues;

    iii.  Any issues about disclosure, discovery, or preservation of electronically stored information, including the form or forms in which it should be produced;

    iv.  Any issues about claims of privilege or of protection as trial-preparation materials, including—if the parties agree on a procedure to assert these claims after production—whether to ask the court to include their agreement in an order under FRE 502;

     v.    What changes should be made in the limitations on discovery imposed under the Federal Rules of Civil Procedure or by local rule, and what other limitations should be imposed; and

     vi.   Any other orders that the court should issue under FRCP 26(c) or under FRCP 16(b) and FRCP 26(c). FRCP 26(f)(3).

5.  *Complex civil cases.* For information on procedures for complex civil cases, refer to NY R USDCTSD Order 11 Misc 00388.

6.  *Related cases.* It shall be the continuing duty of each attorney appearing in any civil or criminal case to bring promptly to the attention of the Court all facts which said attorney believes are relevant to a determination that said case and one or more pending civil or criminal cases should be heard by the same Judge, in order to avoid unnecessary duplication of judicial effort. As soon as the attorney becomes aware of such relationship, said attorney shall notify the Judges to whom the cases have been assigned. NY R USDCTS&ED Civ Rule 1.6(a). If counsel fails to comply with NY R USDCTS&ED Civ Rule 1.6(a), the Court may assess reasonable costs directly against counsel whose action has obstructed the effective administration of the Court's business. NY R USDCTS&ED Civ Rule 1.6(b).

    a.  *Determination of relatedness.* Subject to the limitations set forth in NY R USDCTSD Div. Bus., Rule 13(a)(2), a civil case, bankruptcy appeal, or motion to withdraw the bankruptcy reference will be deemed related to one or more civil cases, appeals or motions when the interests of justice and efficiency will be served. In determining relatedness, a judge will consider whether (A) the actions concern the same or substantially similar parties, property, transactions or events; (B) there is substantial factual overlap; (C) the parties could be subjected to conflicting orders; and (D) whether absent a determination of relatedness there would be a substantial duplication of effort and expense, delay, or undue burden on the Court, parties or witnesses. NY R USDCTSD Div. Bus., Rule 13(a)(1). Nothing in this NY R USDCTSD Div. Bus., Rule 13 is intended to preclude parties from moving for consolidated proceedings under FRCP 42. NY R USDCTSD Div. Bus., Rule 13(a)(1). Notwithstanding NY R USDCTSD Div. Bus., Rule 13(a)(1):

       i.   Civil cases shall not be deemed related merely because they involve common legal issues or the same parties. NY R USDCTSD Div. Bus., Rule 13(a)(2)(A).

       ii.  Other than cases subject to NY R USDCTSD Div. Bus., Rule 4(b) and actions seeking the enforcement of a judgment or settlement in or of an earlier case, civil cases presumptively shall not be deemed related unless both cases are pending before the Court (or the earlier case is on appeal). NY R USDCTSD Div. Bus., Rule 13(a)(2)(B).

    b.  *Procedure in regard to cases said to be related*

       i.   *Disclosure of contention of relatedness.* When a civil case is filed or removed or a bankruptcy appeal or motion to withdraw the reference of an adversary proceeding from the bankruptcy court is filed, the person filing or removing shall disclose on form JSC44C any contention of relatedness and shall file a Related Case Statement stating clearly and succinctly the basis for the contention. A copy of the civil cover sheet and Related Case Statement shall be served with the complaint, notice of removal, notice of appeal, or motion. Any party may contest a claim of relatedness by any other in writing addressed to the judge having the case with the lowest docket number of all cases claimed to be related. However, the foregoing shall not delay the assignment process or the operation of NY R USDCTSD Div. Bus., Rule 13. NY R USDCTSD Div. Bus., Rule 13(b)(1). [Editor's note: the reference to form JSC44C is likely meant to be form JS44C-SDNY: Civil Court Cover Sheet].

       ii.  *Claims of relatedness by other parties.* A party other than the one filing a case, bankruptcy appeal or motion to withdraw the reference that contends its case is related to another may so advise in writing the judge assigned in its case and request a transfer of its case to the judge that the party contends has the related case with the lowest docket number. If the assigned judge believes the case is related under NY R USDCTSD Div. Bus., Rule 13(a), he or she shall refer the question to the judge having the case with the lowest docket number. In the event the latter judge agrees, the case shall be transferred to that judge unless the Assignment Committee disagrees. NY R USDCTSD Div. Bus., Rule 13(b)(3).

    c.  For more information on related cases, refer to NY R USDCTSD Div. Bus., Rule 13.

7. *Alternative dispute resolution (ADR).* The U.S. District Court for the Southern District of New York provides litigants with opportunities to discuss settlement through judicial settlement conferences and mediation. NY R USDCTS&ED Civ Rule 83.9(a).

   a. *Consideration of alternative dispute resolution.* In all civil cases, including those eligible for mediation pursuant to NY R USDCTS&ED Civ Rule 83.9(e), each party shall consider the use of mediation or a judicial settlement conference and shall report to the assigned Judge at the initial FRCP 16(b) case management conference, or subsequently, whether the party believes mediation or a judicial settlement conference may facilitate the resolution of the lawsuit. Judges are encouraged to note the availability of the mediation program and/or a judicial settlement conference before, at, or after the initial FRCP 16(b) case management conference. NY R USDCTS&ED Civ Rule 83.9(d).

   b. *Mediation.* In mediation, parties and counsel meet, sometimes collectively and sometimes individually, with a neutral third party (the mediator) who has been trained to facilitate confidential settlement discussions. The parties articulate their respective positions and interests and generate options for a mutually agreeable resolution to the dispute. The mediator assists the parties in reaching their own negotiated settlement by defining the issues, probing and assessing the strengths and weaknesses of each party's legal positions, and identifying areas of agreement and disagreement. The main benefits of mediation are that it can result in an expeditious and less costly resolution of the litigation, and can produce creative solutions to complex disputes often unavailable in traditional litigation. NY R USDCTS&ED Civ Rule 83.9(b).

      i. *Mediation program eligibility.* All civil cases other than Social Security, habeas corpus, and tax cases are eligible for mediation, whether assigned to Manhattan or White Plains. NY R USDCTS&ED Civ Rule 83.9(e)(1).

         - The Board of Judges may, by Administrative Order, direct that certain specified categories of cases shall automatically be submitted to the mediation program. The assigned District Judge or Magistrate Judge may issue a written order exempting a particular case with or without the request of the parties. NY R USDCTS&ED Civ Rule 83.9(e)(2).

         - For all other cases, the assigned District Judge or Magistrate Judge may determine that a case is appropriate for mediation and may order that case to mediation, with or without the consent of the parties, before, at, or after the initial FRCP 16(b) case management conference. Alternatively, the parties should notify the assigned Judge at any time of their desire to mediate. NY R USDCTS&ED Civ Rule 83.9(e)(3).

   c. *Judicial settlement conferences.* Judicial settlement conferences may be ordered by District Judges or Magistrate Judges with or without the request or consent of the parties. NY R USDCTS&ED Civ Rule 83.9(f).

   d. For more information on alternative dispute resolution (ADR), refer to NY R USDCTS&ED Civ Rule 83.9.

8. *Individual judge practices.* Refer to the Miscellaneous section of this document for information on individual judge practices on general requirements for documents.

# D. Documents

1. *Pretrial conference*

   a. *Documents to consider*

      i. *Pretrial memorandum or statement.* Even though it is not specifically mentioned in FRCP 16, most courts require the attorney for each side to file a pretrial memorandum or statement prior to the conference, which, if adopted by the court, may be binding at trial. FPP § 1524. The purpose of the memorandum is to reveal the lawyer's theory of the case and the issues counsel believes are in contention in order to aid the court in determining what matters should be considered at the conference itself. FPP § 1524; Manbeck v. Ostrowski, 384 F.2d 970 (D.C. Cir. 1967).

      ii. *Statement explaining untimely electronic filing.* If you missed a filing deadline when the ECF system was out of order, attach a statement to your filing explaining how the interruption in service prevented you from filing in a timely fashion. NY R USDCTSD CM/ECF, S.D.(II)(23)(23.5).

   iii. *Courtesy copies.* Read the judge's Individual Practices to learn if courtesy copies are required. NY R USDCTSD CM/ECF, S.D.(II)(13)(13.17). Judges' Individual Practices should continue to be followed with respect to delivery of courtesy copies. NY R USDCTSD CM/ECF, S.D.(I)(3)(3.4).

2. *Scheduling conference*

  a. *Documents to consider*

    i. *Request for scheduling conference.* A scheduling conference may be requested by the judge or by the parties, but it is not mandatory. FPP § 1522.1.

    ii. *Statement explaining untimely electronic filing.* If you missed a filing deadline when the ECF system was out of order, attach a statement to your filing explaining how the interruption in service prevented you from filing in a timely fashion. NY R USDCTSD CM/ECF, S.D.(II)(23)(23.5).

    iii. *Courtesy copies.* Read the judge's Individual Practices to learn if courtesy copies are required. NY R USDCTSD CM/ECF, S.D.(II)(13)(13.17). Judges' Individual Practices should continue to be followed with respect to delivery of courtesy copies. NY R USDCTSD CM/ECF, S.D.(I)(3)(3.4).

3. *Discovery planning conference*

  a. *Required documents*

    i. *Written report outlining proposed discovery plan.* Refer to the General Requirements section of this document for information on the parties' responsibilities for submitting a written report outlining the proposed discovery plan.

  b. *Supplemental documents*

    i. *Statement explaining untimely electronic filing.* If you missed a filing deadline when the ECF system was out of order, attach a statement to your filing explaining how the interruption in service prevented you from filing in a timely fashion. NY R USDCTSD CM/ECF, S.D.(II)(23)(23.5).

    ii. *Courtesy copies.* Read the judge's Individual Practices to learn if courtesy copies are required. NY R USDCTSD CM/ECF, S.D.(II)(13)(13.17). Judges' Individual Practices should continue to be followed with respect to delivery of courtesy copies. NY R USDCTSD CM/ECF, S.D.(I)(3)(3.4).

4. *Individual judge practices.* Refer to the Miscellaneous section of this document for information on individual judge practices on required documents.

## E. Format

1. *Form of documents.* The rules governing captions and other matters of form in pleadings apply to motions and other papers. FRCP 7(b)(2).

  a. *Paper.* Every pleading, written motion, and other paper must: be plainly written, typed, printed, or copied without erasures or interlineations which materially deface it. NY R USDCTS&ED Civ Rule 11.1(a)(1).

  b. *Typeface, margin, and spacing.* The typeface, margins, and spacing of all documents presented for filing must meet the following requirements:

    i. All text must be twelve (12) point type or larger, except for text in footnotes which may be ten (10) point type;

    ii. All documents must have at least one (1) inch margins on all sides;

    iii. All text must be double-spaced, except for headings, text in footnotes, or block quotations, which may be single-spaced. NY R USDCTS&ED Civ Rule 11.1(b).

  c. *Caption; Names of parties.* Every pleading must have a caption with the court's name, a title, a file

number, and a FRCP 7(a) designation. The title of the complaint must name all the parties; the title of other pleadings, after naming the first party on each side, may refer generally to other parties. FRCP 10(a). Every pleading, written motion, and other paper must: bear the docket number and the initials of the District Judge and any Magistrate Judge before whom the action or proceeding is pending, NY R USDCTS&ED Civ Rule 11.1(a)(2).

d. *Paragraphs; Separate statements.* A party must state its claims or defenses in numbered paragraphs, each limited as far as practicable to a single set of circumstances. A later pleading may refer by number to a paragraph in an earlier pleading. If doing so would promote clarity, each claim founded on a separate transaction or occurrence—and each defense other than a denial—must be stated in a separate count or defense. FRCP 10(b).

e. *Adoption by reference; Exhibits.* A statement in a pleading may be adopted by reference elsewhere in the same pleading or in any other pleading or motion. A copy of a written instrument that is an exhibit to a pleading is a part of the pleading for all purposes. FRCP 10(c).

f. *Acceptance by the clerk.* The clerk must not refuse to file a paper solely because it is not in the form prescribed by the Federal Rules of Civil Procedure or by a local rule or practice. FRCP 5(d)(4).

2. *Form of electronic documents*

a. *PDF-A.* All documents electronically filed on the ECF system must be in PDF-A format (portable document format). A PDF-A file is created using PDF writer software such as Adobe Acrobat (go to the Adobe website for details). PDF-A files cannot be altered, providing security to the filer and the Court. NY R USDCTSD CM/ECF, S.D.(II)(23)(23.2).

b. *Size limitation.* No single PDF file may be larger than four megabytes (4 MB). If the filing is too large, the ECF system will not allow it to be filed, and you will not see a Notice of Electronic Filing (NEF or filing receipt) screen. To determine the size of an Adobe Acrobat PDF file click on File, Document Properties, Summary. NY R USDCTSD CM/ECF, S.D.(II)(23)(23.3).

  i. Converting documents directly from a word processor to PDF-A format creates the smallest possible file in terms of computer memory. If that is not possible, scan your document at low resolution. Within the Adobe Acrobat program, on the "Scan Manager" screen, adjust the settings for black and white and 200 dpi (dots per inch). This allows more pages to fit into a single PDF-A file. If that does not work, separate an oversized file into 2 or more parts. Simply label each file 1a, 1b, 1c, etc. Only relevant excerpts of exhibits should be electronically filed. NY R USDCTSD CM/ECF, S.D.(II)(23)(23.4).

c. *Attachments and exhibits.* Filing Users must submit in electronic form all documents referenced as exhibits or attachments, unless the Court permits paper filing. NY R USDCTSD CM/ECF, S.D.(I)(5)(5.1).

  i. A Filing User must submit as exhibits or attachments only those excerpts of the referenced documents that are relevant to the matter under consideration by the Court. Excerpted material must be clearly and prominently identified as such. Filing Users who file excerpts of documents as exhibits or attachments under this procedure do so without prejudice to their right to file timely additional excerpts or the complete document. Responding parties may file timely additional excerpts that they believe are relevant or the complete document. A party may move before the Court for permission to serve and file in hard copy documents that cannot be reasonably scanned. NY R USDCTSD CM/ECF, S.D.(I)(5)(5.2).

  ii. Exhibits must be filed only as attachments to a document, such as a motion or an affidavit. Do not use the ECF Filing Event for "Motion" to file exhibits separately. Exhibits are the only items that should be attached to electronically filed documents. You are limited to electronically filing only relevant excerpts of exhibits. Excerpts must be clearly identified as such. If the exhibit is too large to be scanned and electronically filed you may contact the ECF Help Desk. NY R USDCTSD CM/ECF, S.D.(II)(15)(15.6).

d. *Letters.* Parties should consult the assigned judge's Individual Practices to determine if the judge accepts letters at all and, if he or she does, whether the judge has any page limitations on letters and/or requires courtesy copies of letters filed on ECF (and, if so, by what means of delivery). All

letters addressed to the Court must include a subject line with the case name and docket number (e.g., "Re: Doe v. Smith, 13 Civ. 1234 (ABC)"). NY R USDCTSD CM/ECF, S.D.(II)(13)(13.1).

e. *Proposed orders, proposed judgments, stipulations and consents.* Any document that requires the signature of a judge should not be electronically filed except as an exhibit to another document. Proposed orders, judgments, stipulations and consents should not be submitted through the ECF system. Instead they should be sent by e-mail to the Clerk. Proposed orders should be submitted in word processing format (WordPerfect or Word) rather than as a PDF document. Stipulations should be submitted in PDF-A format. Stipulations must contain ink signatures not s/. Faxed or emailed signatures are acceptable. Please note that Stipulations of Voluntary Dismissal pursuant to FRCP 41(a)(1)(A)(ii) do not require the signature of a judge and must be electronically filed on the ECF system. Questions may be directed to the Orders and Judgments Clerk at the phone numbers listed in NY R USDCTSD CM/ECF, S.D.(II)(18)(18.3). NY R USDCTSD CM/ECF, S.D.(II)(18)(18.3).

  i. Email the proposed order, judgment or stipulation to the email addresses listed in NY R USDCTSD CM/ECF, S.D.(II)(18)(18.3). NY R USDCTSD CM/ECF, S.D.(II)(18)(18.3).

  ii. Pro se litigants who are not Filing Users are exempt from that portion of NY R USDCTSD CM/ECF, S.D.(II)(18)(18.3) that requires litigants to email proposed orders, judgments, stipulations and consents, and shall deliver such documents to the Clerk's Office in paper form. NY R USDCTSD CM/ECF, S.D.(II)(18)(18.3).

3. *Signing of pleadings, motions and other papers*

  a. *Signature.* Every pleading, written motion, and other paper must be signed by at least one attorney of record in the attorney's name—or by a party personally if the party is unrepresented. The paper must state the signer's address, e-mail address, and telephone number. FRCP 11(a). Every pleading, written motion, and other paper must: have the name of each person signing it clearly printed or typed directly below the signature. NY R USDCTS&ED Civ Rule 11.1(a)(3).

    i. *Electronic signatures.* The user log-in and password required to submit documents to the ECF system serve as the Filing User's signature on all electronic documents filed with the Court. NY R USDCTSD CM/ECF, S.D.(I)(8)(8.1); NY R USDCTSD CM/ECF, S.D.(II)(13)(13.14). They also serve as a signature for purposes of the Federal Rules of Civil Procedure, including FRCP 11, the Local Civil Rules of the United States District Courts for the Southern and Eastern Districts of New York, and any other purpose for which a signature is required in connection with proceedings before the Court. NY R USDCTSD CM/ECF, S.D.(I)(8)(8.1).

      - *Signature block.* Electronically filed documents must include a signature block and must set forth the name, address, telephone number and e-mail address all in compliance with the Federal Rules of Civil Procedure and NY R USDCTS&ED Civ Rule 11.1. In the absence of a scanned signature image, the name of the Filing User under whose log-in and password the document is submitted must be preceded by an "s/" typed in the space where the signature would otherwise appear. NY R USDCTSD CM/ECF, S.D.(I)(8)(8.2); NY R USDCTSD CM/ECF, S.D.(II)(13)(13.14).

      - *Documents requiring the signature of a party or witness.* A document requiring the signature of a party or witness shall be electronically filed in a scanned format that contains an image of the actual signature. NY R USDCTSD CM/ECF, S.D.(I)(8)(8.4); NY R USDCTSD CM/ECF, S.D.(II)(13)(13.14).

      - *Documents requiring the signature of a judge.* A Filing User submitting a document electronically that requires a judge's signature must promptly deliver the document in such other form, if any, as the Court requires. NY R USDCTSD CM/ECF, S.D.(I)(4)(4.2).

      - *Documents requiring multiple signatures.* Documents requiring signatures of more than one party must be electronically filed either by: (a) submitting a scanned document containing all necessary signatures; (b) representing the consent of the other parties on the document; (c) identifying on the document the parties whose signatures are required and by the submission of a notice of endorsement by the other parties no later than three business days after filing; or (d) in any other manner approved by the Court. NY R USDCTSD CM/ECF, S.D.(I)(8)(8.5).

    ii.   *No verification or accompanying affidavit required for pleadings.* Unless a rule or statute specifically states otherwise, a pleading need not be verified or accompanied by an affidavit. FRCP 11(a).

    iii.   *Unsigned papers.* The court must strike an unsigned paper unless the omission is promptly corrected after being called to the attorney's or party's attention. FRCP 11(a).

  b.  *Representations to the court.* By presenting to the court a pleading, written motion, or other paper—whether by signing, filing, submitting, or later advocating it—an attorney or unrepresented party certifies that to the best of the person's knowledge, information, and belief, formed after an inquiry reasonable under the circumstances:

    i.   It is not being presented for any improper purpose, such as to harass, cause unnecessary delay, or needlessly increase the cost of litigation;

    ii.   The claims, defenses, and other legal contentions are warranted by existing law or by a nonfrivolous argument for extending, modifying, or reversing existing law or for establishing new law;

    iii.   The factual contentions have evidentiary support or, if specifically so identified, will likely have evidentiary support after a reasonable opportunity for further investigation or discovery; and

    iv.   The denials of factual contentions are warranted on the evidence or, if specifically so identified, are reasonably based on belief or a lack of information. FRCP 11(b).

  c.  *Sanctions.* If, after notice and a reasonable opportunity to respond, the court determines that FRCP 11(b) has been violated, the court may impose an appropriate sanction on any attorney, law firm, or party that violated FRCP 11(b) or is responsible for the violation. FRCP 11(c)(1). Refer to the United States District Court for the Southern District of New York KeyRules Motion for Sanctions document for more information.

4.  *Privacy protection for filings made with the court*

  a.  *Redacted filings.* Unless the court orders otherwise, in an electronic or paper filing with the court that contains an individual's Social Security number, taxpayer-identification number, or birth date, the name of an individual known to be a minor, or a financial-account number, a party or nonparty making the filing may include only:

    i.   The last four (4) digits of the Social Security number and taxpayer-identification number;

    ii.   The year of the individual's birth;

    iii.   The minor's initials; and

    iv.   The last four (4) digits of the financial-account number. FRCP 5.2(a); NY R USDCTSD CM/ECF, S.D.(II)(21)(21.3).

    v.   Caution should be exercised when filing documents that contain the following:

- Personal identifying numbers (PIN #'s), such as a driver's license number;
- Medical records, treatment and diagnosis;
- Employment history;
- Individual financial information;
- Proprietary or trade secret information;
- Information regarding an individual's cooperation with the government. NY R US-DCTSD CM/ECF, S.D.(II)(21)(21.4).

  b.  *Exemptions from the redaction requirement.* The redaction requirement does not apply to the following:

    i.   A financial-account number that identifies the property allegedly subject to forfeiture in a forfeiture proceeding;

    ii.   The record of an administrative or agency proceeding;

    iii.   The official record of a state-court proceeding;

    iv.  The record of a court or tribunal, if that record was not subject to the redaction requirement when originally filed;

    v.  A filing covered by FRCP 5.2(c) or FRCP 5.2(d); and

    vi.  A pro se filing in an action brought under 28 U.S.C.A. § 2241, 28 U.S.C.A. § 2254, or 28 U.S.C.A. § 2255. FRCP 5.2(b).

  c.  *Limitations on remote access to electronic files; Social Security appeals and immigration cases.* Unless the court orders otherwise, in an action for benefits under the Social Security Act, and in an action or proceeding relating to an order of removal, to relief from removal, or to immigration benefits or detention, access to an electronic file is authorized as follows:

    i.  The parties and their attorneys may have remote electronic access to any part of the case file, including the administrative record;

    ii.  Any other person may have electronic access to the full record at the courthouse, but may have remote electronic access only to:

- The docket maintained by the court; and

- An opinion, order, judgment, or other disposition of the court, but not any other part of the case file or the administrative record. FRCP 5.2(c).

  d.  *Filings made under seal.* The court may order that a filing be made under seal without redaction. The court may later unseal the filing or order the person who made the filing to file a redacted version for the public record. FRCP 5.2(d). For more information on sealing documents, refer to NY R USDCTSD CM/ECF, S.D.(I)(6).

  e.  *Protective orders.* For good cause, the court may by order in a case:

    i.  Require redaction of additional information; or

    ii.  Limit or prohibit a nonparty's remote electronic access to a document filed with the court. FRCP 5.2(e).

  f.  *Option for additional unredacted filing under seal.* A person making a redacted filing may also file an unredacted copy under seal. The court must retain the unredacted copy as part of the record. FRCP 5.2(f); NY R USDCTSD CM/ECF, S.D.(II)(21)(21.5).

  g.  *Option for filing a reference list.* A filing that contains redacted information may be filed together with a reference list that identifies each item of redacted information and specifies an appropriate identifier that uniquely corresponds to each item listed. The list must be filed under seal and may be amended as of right. Any reference in the case to a listed identifier will be construed to refer to the corresponding item of information. FRCP 5.2(g); NY R USDCTSD CM/ECF, S.D.(II)(21)(21.5).

  h.  *Responsibility for redaction.* It is the sole responsibility of counsel and the parties to be sure that all documents comply with the rules of this Court requiring redaction of personal identifiers. Neither the judge nor the Clerk of Court will review documents for compliance with these rules. NY R USDCTSD CM/ECF, S.D.(II)(21)(21.2).

  i.  *Waiver of protection of identifiers.* A person waives the protection of FRCP 5.2(a) as to the person's own information by filing it without redaction and not under seal. FRCP 5.2(h).

  j.  For more information on privacy and public access to ECF cases, refer to NY R USDCTSD CM/ECF, S.D.(II)(21).

5.  *Individual judge practices.* Refer to the Miscellaneous section of this document for information on individual judge practices on formatting documents.

## F. Filing and Service Requirements

1.  *Filing requirements.* Any paper after the complaint that is required to be served—together with a certificate of service—must be filed within a reasonable time after service. FRCP 5(d)(1). Complaints and all subsequent papers are accepted at either courthouse, regardless of the place for which the case is designated. NY R USDCTSD Div. Bus., Rule 22.

  a.  *How filing is made; In general.* A paper is filed by delivering it:

    i.  To the clerk; or

ii.   To a judge who agrees to accept it for filing, and who must then note the filing date on the paper and promptly send it to the clerk. FRCP 5(d)(2).

b.   *Night depository.* A night depository with an automatic date stamp shall be maintained by the Clerk of the Southern District in the Pearl Street Courthouse. After regular business hours, papers for the District Court only may be deposited in the night depository. Such papers will be considered as having been filed in the District Court as of the date stamped thereon, which shall be deemed presumptively correct. NY R USDCTS&ED Civ Rule 1.2.

c.   *Electronic filing*

   i.   *Authorization of electronic filing program.* A court may, by local rule, allow papers to be filed, signed, or verified by electronic means that are consistent with any technical standards established by the Judicial Conference of the United States. A local rule may require electronic filing only if reasonable exceptions are allowed. A paper filed electronically in compliance with a local rule is a written paper for purposes of the Federal Rules of Civil Procedure. FRCP 5(d)(3).

   - The Court will accept for filing documents submitted, signed or verified by electronic means, that comply with the rules in NY R USDCTSD CM/ECF, S.D. NY R USDCTSD CM/ECF, S.D.(I). The information in NY R USDCTSD CM/ECF, S.D. applies only to cases assigned to the ECF system. NY R USDCTSD CM/ECF, S.D.(Introduction).

   - Parties serving and filing papers shall follow the instructions regarding Electronic Case Filing (ECF) published on the website of each respective Court. A paper served and filed by electronic means in accordance with such instructions is, for purposes of FRCP 5, served and filed in compliance with the Local Civil Rules of the Southern and Eastern Districts of New York. NY R USDCTS&ED Civ Rule 5.2(a). Parties have an obligation to review the Court's actual order, decree, or judgment (on ECF), which controls, and should not rely on the description on the docket or in the ECF Notice of Electronic Filing (NEF). NY R USDCTS&ED Civ Rule 5.2(c).

   - The following should be observed when filing electronically: (1) the Federal Rules of Civil Procedure, (2) the Local Civil Rules of the United States District Courts for the Southern and Eastern Districts of New York, (3) the assigned judge's Individual Practices, and (4) the Court's Electronic Case Filing Rules & Instructions (NY R USDCTSD CM/ECF, S.D.). NY R USDCTSD CM/ECF, S.D.(Introduction).

   ii.   *Scope of electronic filing.* Except as expressly provided and in exceptional circumstances preventing a party from filing electronically, all documents required to be filed with the Court must be filed electronically. Any party unable to comply with this requirement must seek permission of the Court to file in the traditional manner, on paper. Any such application made after regular business hours may be submitted through the night depository box maintained pursuant to NY R USDCTS&ED Civ Rule 1.2. NY R USDCTSD CM/ECF, S.D.(I)(1)(1.1).

   - *Documents filed by pro se litigants.* Unless otherwise ordered by the Court, documents filed by pro se litigants must be filed in the traditional manner, on paper, and will be scanned and docketed by the Clerk's Office into the ECF system. NY R USDCTSD CM/ECF, S.D.(I)(1)(1.1). Pro se litigants must file pleadings and documents in the traditional manner on paper unless the assigned judge has granted permission to electronically file on the ECF system. NY R USDCTSD CM/ECF, S.D.(Introduction).

   - *Letters.* Except for letters to be filed under seal, letters addressed to judges who accept letters may be filed electronically. Parties should consult the assigned judge's Individual Practices to determine if the judge accepts letters at all and, if he or she does, whether the judge has any page limitations on letters and/or requires courtesy copies of letters filed on ECF (and, if so, by what means of delivery). NY R USDCTSD CM/ECF, S.D.(II)(13)(13.1). Letters solely between parties or their counsel or otherwise not addressed to the Court may not be filed electronically on ECF (except as exhibits to an otherwise properly filed document). NY R USDCTSD CM/ECF, S.D.(II)(13)(13.1). For more information on filing letters, refer to NY R USDCTSD CM/ECF, S.D.(II)(13)(13.1).

- *Proposed orders, judgments and decrees.* Proposed orders, judgments and decrees shall be presented as directed by the ECF rules published on the website of each respective Court. NY R USDCTS&ED Civ Rule 77.1. For more information, refer to NY R USDCTS&ED Civ Rule 77.1.

iii. *Exceptions to electronic filing.* In an ECF case, the documents that should not be electronically filed include:

- Miscellaneous Case initiating documents, NY R USDCTSD CM/ECF, S.D.(II)(18)(18.2);

- Proposed orders; proposed judgments, stipulations; consents, NY R USDCTSD CM/ECF, S.D.(II)(18)(18.3);

- Orders to show cause / temporary restraining orders, NY R USDCTSD CM/ECF, S.D.(II)(18)(18.4);

- Sealed documents, NY R USDCTSD CM/ECF, S.D.(II)(18)(18.5); and

- Surety bonds, NY R USDCTSD CM/ECF, S.D.(II)(18)(18.6).

- In cases where the record of an administrative or other prior proceeding must be filed with the Court, such record may be served and filed in hard copy without prior motion and order of the Court. NY R USDCTSD CM/ECF, S.D.(I)(5)(5.3).

- For more documents excepted from electronic filing, and for more information on such documents, refer to NY R USDCTSD CM/ECF, S.D.(II)(18).

iv. *Consequences of electronic filing.* Except as otherwise provided in NY R USDCTSD CM/ECF, S.D.(I)(4), electronic filing of a document in the ECF system consistent with these procedures, together with the transmission of a Notice of Electronic Filing (NEF) from the Court, constitutes filing of the document for all purposes of the Federal Rules of Civil Procedure and the Local Civil Rules of the United States District Courts for the Southern and Eastern Districts of New York and constitutes entry of the document on the docket kept by the Clerk under FRCP 58 and FRCP 79. NY R USDCTSD CM/ECF, S.D.(I)(3)(3.1).

v. For more information on electronic filing, refer to NY R USDCTSD CM/ECF, S.D.

2. *Service requirements*

a. *Service; When required*

i. *In general.* Unless the Federal Rules of Civil Procedure provide otherwise, each of the following papers must be served on every party:

- An order stating that service is required;

- A pleading filed after the original complaint, unless the court orders otherwise under FRCP 5(c) because there are numerous defendants;

- A discovery paper required to be served on a party, unless the court orders otherwise;

- A written motion, except one that may be heard ex parte; and

- A written notice, appearance, demand, or offer of judgment, or any similar paper. FRCP 5(a)(1).

ii. *If a party fails to appear.* No service is required on a party who is in default for failing to appear. But a pleading that asserts a new claim for relief against such a party must be served on that party under FRCP 4. FRCP 5(a)(2).

iii. *Seizing property.* If an action is begun by seizing property and no person is or need be named as a defendant, any service required before the filing of an appearance, answer, or claim must be made on the person who had custody or possession of the property when it was seized. FRCP 5(a)(3).

b. *Service; How made*

i. *Serving an attorney.* If a party is represented by an attorney, service under FRCP 5 must be made on the attorney unless the court orders service on the party. FRCP 5(b)(1).

ii. *Service in general.* A paper is served under FRCP 5 by:

- Handing it to the person;

- Leaving it: (1) at the person's office with a clerk or other person in charge or, if no one is in charge, in a conspicuous place in the office; or (2) if the person has no office or the office is closed, at the person's dwelling or usual place of abode with someone of suitable age and discretion who resides there;

- Mailing it to the person's last known address—in which event service is complete upon mailing;

- Leaving it with the court clerk if the person has no known address;

- Sending it by electronic means if the person consented in writing—in which event service is complete upon transmission, but is not effective if the serving party learns that it did not reach the person to be served; or

- Delivering it by any other means that the person consented to in writing—in which event service is complete when the person making service delivers it to the agency designated to make delivery. FRCP 5(b)(2).

iii. *Service by overnight delivery.* Service upon an attorney may be made by overnight delivery service. "Overnight delivery service" means any delivery service which regularly accepts items for overnight delivery. Overnight delivery service shall be deemed service by mail for purposes of FRCP 5 and FRCP 6. NY R USDCTS&ED Civ Rule 5.3.

iv. *Service by electronic means.* Parties serving and filing papers shall follow the instructions regarding Electronic Case Filing (ECF) published on the website of each respective Court. A paper served and filed by electronic means in accordance with such instructions is, for purposes of FRCP 5, served and filed in compliance with the Local Civil Rules of the United States District Courts for the Southern and Eastern Districts of New York. NY R USDCTS&ED Civ Rule 5.2(a). Parties have an obligation to review the Court's actual order, decree, or judgment (on ECF), which controls, and should not rely on the description on the docket or in the ECF Notice of Electronic Filing (NEF). NY R USDCTS&ED Civ Rule 5.2(c).

- *Notice of electronic filing (NEF).* In cases assigned to the ECF system, service is complete provided all parties receive a Notice of Electronic Filing (NEF), which is sent automatically by email from the Court (see the NEF for a list of who did/did not receive notice electronically). Transmission of the NEF constitutes service upon all Filing and Receiving Users who are listed as recipients of notice by electronic mail. NY R USDCTSD CM/ECF, S.D.(I)(9)(9.1). In cases assigned to the ECF system, if all parties receive a NEF, service is complete upon transmission of the NEF by the Court, and you are not required to serve a paper copy. NY R USDCTSD CM/ECF, S.D.(II)(19)(19.2). It remains the duty of Filing and Receiving Users to maintain current contact information with the court and to regularly review the docket sheet of the case. NY R USDCTSD CM/ECF, S.D.(I)(9)(9.1).

- *Mailing of court-initiated documents.* The Clerk's Office will no longer mail paper copies of court-initiated documents to Filing and Receiving Users. The Clerk's Office will mail copies of all court-initiated documents to pro se parties who have not registered as Filing or Receiving Users. NY R USDCTSD CM/ECF, S.D.(II)(19)(19.1).

- *No receipt of a NEF.* If any party does not receive a NEF, you are required to accomplish service on that party in the traditional manner, in paper form. NY R USDCTSD CM/ECF, S.D.(II)(19)(19.2). The NEF receipt will inform you who will receive notice of the filing "electronically" (by e-mail from the Court) and who will receive notice "by other means" (traditional service in paper form). NY R USDCTSD CM/ECF, S.D.(II)(19)(19.2).

- *Service on non-filing or non-receiving users.* Attorneys and pro se parties who are not Filing or Receiving Users must be served with a paper copy of any electronically filed pleading or other document. Service of such paper copy must be made according to the Federal Rules of Civil Procedure and the Local Civil Rules of the United States District Courts for the Southern and Eastern Districts of New York. NY R USDCTSD CM/ECF,

S.D.(I)(9)(9.2). Such paper service must be documented by electronically filing proof of service. NY R USDCTSD CM/ECF, S.D.(I)(9)(9.2); NY R USDCTSD CM/ECF, S.D.(II)(19)(19.2). Where the Clerk scans and electronically files pleadings and documents on behalf of a pro se party, the associated NEF constitutes service. NY R USDCTSD CM/ECF, S.D.(I)(9)(9.2).

- For more information on service by electronic means, refer to NY R USDCTSD CM/ECF, S.D.(II)(19).

  v. *Using court facilities.* If a local rule so authorizes, a party may use the court's transmission facilities to make service under FRCP 5(b)(2)(E). FRCP 5(b)(3).

c. *Serving numerous defendants*

  i. *In general.* If an action involves an unusually large number of defendants, the court may, on motion or on its own, order that:

  - Defendants' pleadings and replies to them need not be served on other defendants;

  - Any crossclaim, counterclaim, avoidance, or affirmative defense in those pleadings and replies to them will be treated as denied or avoided by all other parties; and

  - Filing any such pleading and serving it on the plaintiff constitutes notice of the pleading to all parties. FRCP 5(c)(1).

  ii. *Notifying parties.* A copy of every such order must be served on the parties as the court directs. FRCP 5(c)(2).

3. *Individual judge practices.* Refer to the Miscellaneous section of this document for information on individual judge practices on filing and serving documents.

## G. Hearings

1. Refer to the General Requirements section of this document for information on pretrial conferences, scheduling conferences, and discovery planning conferences.

## H. Forms

### 1. Federal Pretrial Conferences, Scheduling, Management Forms

a. Plaintiff's informal summary of status of case to judge prior to pretrial conference in complex case. 2C FEDFORMS § 2807.

b. Joint pretrial report. 2C FEDFORMS § 2807.10.

c. Joint statement of undisputed facts. 2C FEDFORMS § 2807.20.

d. Joint statement of disputed facts. 2C FEDFORMS § 2807.30.

e. Joint report of counsel prior to pretrial conference. 2C FEDFORMS § 2807.40.

f. Plaintiff's pretrial conference statement; Insurance case. 2C FEDFORMS § 2807.50.

g. Defendant's pretrial conference statement; Insurance case. 2C FEDFORMS § 2807.60.

h. Plaintiff's list of exhibits to be offered at trial. 2C FEDFORMS § 2811.

i. Defendant's list of prospective witnesses. 2C FEDFORMS § 2811.10.

j. Designation of witnesses whom plaintiff intends to call at trial pursuant to pretrial conference oral stipulation. 2C FEDFORMS § 2811.20.

k. Defendant's list of prospective exhibits. 2C FEDFORMS § 2811.40.

l. Report of parties' planning meeting. 3A FEDFORMS § 3314.

m. Report of parties' discovery conference; Another form. 3A FEDFORMS § 3315.

n. Report of parties' discovery conference; Another form. 3A FEDFORMS § 3316.

o. Joint scheduling report. 3A FEDFORMS § 3316.5.

p. Stipulation and order regarding discovery conference discussions. 3A FEDFORMS § 3316.6.

q. Pretrial statement; By plaintiff; Automobile collision involving corporate defendant. FEDPROF § 1:658.

r. Pretrial statement; By defendant; Automobile collision. FEDPROF § 1:659.

s. Pretrial statement; By parties jointly; Automobile collision. FEDPROF § 1:660.

t. Pretrial statement; Provision; Waiver of abandoned claims or defenses. FEDPROF § 1:661.

u. Status report. GOLDLTGFMS § 34:2.

v. Preliminary pretrial checklist. GOLDLTGFMS § 34:3.

w. Pretrial memorandum. GOLDLTGFMS § 34:4.

x. Pretrial memorandum; Short form. GOLDLTGFMS § 34:5.

y. Pretrial memorandum; Civil action. GOLDLTGFMS § 34:6.

z. Pretrial memorandum; Worker's compensation case. GOLDLTGFMS § 34:7.

## I. Applicable Rules

1. *Federal rules*

   a. Serving and filing pleadings and other papers. FRCP 5.

   b. Privacy protection for filings made with the court. FRCP 5.2.

   c. Computing and extending time; Time for motion papers. FRCP 6.

   d. Pleadings allowed; Form of motions and other papers. FRCP 7.

   e. Form of pleadings. FRCP 10.

   f. Signing pleadings, motions, and other papers; Representations to the court; Sanctions. FRCP 11.

   g. Pretrial conferences; Scheduling; Management. FRCP 16.

   h. Duty to disclose; General provisions governing discovery. FRCP 26.

2. *Local rules*

   a. Night depository. NY R USDCTS&ED Civ Rule 1.2.

   b. Duty of attorneys in related cases. NY R USDCTS&ED Civ Rule 1.6.

   c. Electronic service and filing of documents. NY R USDCTS&ED Civ Rule 5.2.

   d. Service by overnight delivery. NY R USDCTS&ED Civ Rule 5.3.

   e. Computation of time. NY R USDCTS&ED Civ Rule 6.4.

   f. Form of pleadings, motions, and other papers. NY R USDCTS&ED Civ Rule 11.1.

   g. Exemptions from mandatory scheduling order. NY R USDCTS&ED Civ Rule 16.1.

   h. Entry and modification of mandatory scheduling orders by magistrate judges. NY R USDCTS&ED Civ Rule 16.2.

   i. Submission of orders, judgments and decrees. NY R USDCTS&ED Civ Rule 77.1.

   j. Alternative dispute resolution (Southern District only). NY R USDCTS&ED Civ Rule 83.9.

   k. Electronic case filing rules and instructions. NY R USDCTSD CM/ECF, S.D.

   l. Related cases. NY R USDCTSD Div. Bus., Rule 13.

   m. Filing at either courthouse. NY R USDCTSD Div. Bus., Rule 22.

## J. Miscellaneous

**NOTE: Individual judges' rules may apply. For available judge-level information, refer to:**

DISTRICT JUDGE RONNIE ABRAMS: NY R USDCTSD Abrams-Civ Prac; NY R USDCTSD Abrams-Crim Prac; NY R USDCTSD Abrams-Pro Se; NY R USDCTSD Abrams-Case Mgt; NY R USDCTSD Abrams-Jury.

DISTRICT JUDGE DEBORAH A. BATTS: NY R USDCTSD Batts-Practices.

DISTRICT JUDGE RICHARD M. BERMAN: NY R USDCTSD Berman-Practices; NY R USDCTSD Berman-Default; NY R USDCTSD Berman-Sentencing; NY R USDCTSD Berman-Media.

DISTRICT JUDGE VINCENT L. BRICCETTI: NY R USDCTSD Briccetti-Practices; NY R USDCTSD Briccetti-Plan; NY R USDCTSD Briccetti-Notice.

DISTRICT JUDGE VERNON S. BRODERICK: NY R USDCTSD Broderick-Civil; NY R USDCTSD Broderick-Crim; NY R USDCTSD Broderick-Case Mgt; NY R USDCTSD Broderick-Jury.

DISTRICT JUDGE NAOMI REICE BUCHWALD: NY R USDCTSD Buchwald-Practices.

DISTRICT JUDGE VALERIE E. CAPRONI: NY R USDCTSD Caproni-Prac; NY R USDCTSD Caproni--Pro Se; NY R USDCTSD Caproni-Case Mgt; NY R USDCTSD Caproni-Crim Prac.

DISTRICT JUDGE ANDREW L. CARTER JR.: NY R USDCTSD Carter-Practices.

DISTRICT JUDGE KEVIN P. CASTEL: NY R USDCTSD Castel-Practices; NY R USDCTSD Castel-Default; NY R USDCTSD Castel-Scheduling; NY R USDCTSD Castel-Complex; NY R USDCTSD Castel-Trials; NY R USDCTSD Castel-Sentencing.

DISTRICT JUDGE DENISE L. COTE: NY R USDCTSD Cote-Civil Practices; NY R USDCTSD Cote-Pro Se; NY R USDCTSD Cote-Maritime Ord; NY R USDCTSD Cote-Crim Practices; NY R USDCTSD Cote-Crim Trials; NY R USDCTSD Cote-Sentencing.

DISTRICT JUDGE PAUL A. CROTTY: NY R USDCTSD Crotty-Practices; NY R USDCTSD Crotty-Sentencing; NY R USDCTSD Crotty-Calls; NY R USDCTSD Crotty-Scheduling.

DISTRICT JUDGE GEORGE B. DANIELS: NY R USDCTSD Daniels-Practices.

DISTRICT JUDGE KEVIN T. DUFFY: NY R USDCTSD Duffy-Practices.

DISTRICT JUDGE PAUL A. ENGELMAYER: NY R USDCTSD Engelmayer-Practices; NY R USDCTSD Engelmayer-Scheduling; NY R USDCTSD Engelmayer-Sentencing; NY R USDCTSD Engelmayer-Pro Se; NY R USDCTSD Engelmayer-Crim.

DISTRICT JUDGE KATHERINE POLK FAILLA: NY R USDCTSD Failla-Civ Prac; NY R USDCTSD Failla-Crim Prac; NY R USDCTSD Failla-Case Mgt.

DISTRICT JUDGE KATHERINE B. FORREST: NY R USDCTSD Forrest-Civil Prac; NY R USDCTSD Forrest-Crim Prac; NY R USDCTSD Forrest-Crim Pretrial; NY R USDCTSD Forrest-Scheduling; NY R USDCTSD Forrest-Patent Scheduling; NY R USDCTSD Forrest-Sentencing; NY R USDCTSD Forrest-Order 1; NY R USDCTSD Forrest-Order 2.

DISTRICT JUDGE JESSE M. FURMAN: NY R USDCTSD Furman-Civil Prac; NY R USDCTSD Furman-Crim Prac; NY R USDCTSD Furman-Pro Se Prac; NY R USDCTSD Furman-Trials; NY R USDCTSD Furman-Scheduling; NY R USDCTSD Furman-Rights.

DISTRICT JUDGE PAUL G. GARDEPHE: NY R USDCTSD Gardephe-Civ Prac; NY R USDCTSD Gardephe-Pretrial; NY R USDCTSD Gardephe-Prot Ord; NY R USDCTSD Gardephe-Maritime; NY R USDCTSD Gardephe-Crim Prac; NY R USDCTSD Gardephe-Trial.

DISTRICT JUDGE THOMAS P. GRIESA: NY R USDCTSD Griesa-Practices.

DISTRICT JUDGE CHARLES S. HAIGHT: NY R USDCTSD Haight-Practices.

DISTRICT JUDGE ALVIN K. HELLERSTEIN: NY R USDCTSD Hellerstein-Practices; NY R USDCTSD Hellerstein--Sept 11.

DISTRICT JUDGE LEWIS A. KAPLAN: NY R USDCTSD Kaplan-Practices; NY R USDCTSD Kaplan-Sentencing.

DISTRICT JUDGE KENNETH M. KARAS: NY R USDCTSD Karas-Practices; NY R USDCTSD Karas-Case Mgt; NY R USDCTSD Karas-Default; NY R USDCTSD Karas-Sentencing; NY R USDCTSD Karas-Rights.

DISTRICT JUDGE JOHN F. KEENAN: NY R USDCTSD Keenan-Practices.

DISTRICT JUDGE JOHN G. KOELTL: NY R USDCTSD Koeltl-Practices.

DISTRICT JUDGE VICTOR MARRERO: NY R USDCTSD Marrero-Practices; NY R USDCTSD Marrero-Scheduling; NY R USDCTSD Marrero-Default; NY R USDCTSD Marrero-Trial Proc.

DISTRICT JUDGE COLLEEN McMAHON: NY R USDCTSD McMahon-Practices; NY R USDCTSD McMahon-RICO; NY R USDCTSD McMahon-Copies; NY R USDCTSD McMahon-Scheduling; NY R US-DCTSD McMahon-Elec Disc; NY R USDCTSD McMahon-Sentencing.

DISTRICT JUDGE ALISON J. NATHAN: NY R USDCTSD Nathan-Civ Prac; NY R USDCTSD Nathan-Crim Prac; NY R USDCTSD Nathan-Pro Se; NY R USDCTSD Nathan-Scheduling.

DISTRICT JUDGE J. PAUL OETKEN: NY R USDCTSD Oetken-Civ Prac; NY R USDCTSD Oetken-Case Mgt; NY R USDCTSD Oetken-Crim Prac; NY R USDCTSD Oetken-Pro Se.

DISTRICT JUDGE WILLIAM H. PAULEY, III: NY R USDCTSD Pauley-Crim Cases; NY R USDCTSD Pauley-Practices.

DISTRICT JUDGE LORETTA A. PRESKA: NY R USDCTSD Preska-Practices.

DISTRICT JUDGE JED S. RAKOFF: NY R USDCTSD Rakoff-Practices; NY R USDCTSD Rakoff-Scheduling; NY R USDCTSD Rakoff-Prot Ord; NY R USDCTSD Rakoff-Maritime Ord.

DISTRICT JUDGE EDGARDO RAMOS: NY R USDCTSD Ramos--Practices; NY R USDCTSD Ramos-Case Mgt.

DISTRICT JUDGE NELSON S. ROMAN: NY R USDCTSD Roman-Civ Prac; NY R USDCTSD Roman-Pro Se; NY R USDCTSD Roman-Crim Prac; NY R USDCTSD Roman-Case Mgt.

DISTRICT JUDGE LEONARD B. SAND: NY R USDCTSD Sand-Practices.

DISTRICT JUDGE LORNA G. SCHOFIELD: NY R USDCTSD Schofield-Civ Prac; NY R USDCTSD Schofield-Crim Prac; NY R USDCTSD Schofield-Sched; NY R USDCTSD Schofield-Pro Se; NY R USDCTSD Schofield-Advice.

DISTRICT JUDGE CATHY SEIBEL: NY R USDCTSD Seibel-Practices.

DISTRICT JUDGE LOUIS L. STANTON: NY R USDCTSD Stanton-Practices; NY R USDCTSD Stanton-Pretrial.

DISTRICT JUDGE SIDNEY H. STEIN: NY R USDCTSD Stein-Practices.

DISTRICT JUDGE RICHARD J. SULLIVAN: NY R USDCTSD Sullivan-Practices; NY R USDCTSD Sullivan-Scheduling; NY R USDCTSD Sullivan-Sentencing; NY R USDCTSD Sullivan-Juries; NY R USDCTSD Sullivan-Trial; NY R USDCTSD Sullivan-Default.

DISTRICT JUDGE LAURA TAYLOR SWAIN: NY R USDCTSD Swain-Practices; NY R USDCTSD Swain-Trial; NY R USDCTSD Swain-Crim Trial; NY R USDCTSD Swain-Juries; NY R USDCTSD Swain-Sentencing; NY R USDCTSD Swain-Rights.

DISTRICT JUDGE ROBERT W. SWEET: NY R USDCTSD Sweet-Practices.

DISTRICT JUDGE ANALISA TORRES: NY R USDCTSD Torres-Civ Prac; NY R USDCTSD Torres-Pro Se; NY R USDCTSD Torres-Scheduling.

DISTRICT JUDGE KIMBA M. WOOD: NY R USDCTSD Wood-Practices; NY R USDCTSD Wood-Scheduling; NY R USDCTSD Wood-Discovery; NY R USDCTSD Wood-RICO; NY R USDCTSD Wood-Juries; NY R USDCTSD Wood-Trial; NY R USDCTSD Wood-Media.

DISTRICT JUDGE GREGORY H. WOODS: NY R USDCTSD Woods-Civ Prac; NY R USDCTSD Woods-Pro Se; NY R USDCTSD Woods-Sched; NY R USDCTSD Woods-Crim Prac; NY R USDCTSD Woods-Protect Order; NY R USDCTSD Woods-Speedy Trial.

MAGISTRATE JUDGE JAMES L. COTT: NY R USDCTSD Cott-Practices; NY R USDCTSD Cott-Settlement.

MAGISTRATE JUDGE PAUL E. DAVISON: NY R USDCTSD Davison-Practices.

MAGISTRATE JUDGE RONALD L. ELLIS: NY R USDCTSD Ellis-Practices.

MAGISTRATE JUDGE KEVIN N. FOX: NY R USDCTSD Fox-Practices; NY R USDCTSD Fox-Settlement.

MAGISTRATE JUDGE JAMES C. FRANCIS: NY R USDCTSD Francis-Practices.

MAGISTRATE JUDGE DEBRA FREEMAN: NY R USDCTSD Freeman-Practices; NY R USDCTSD Freeman-Settlement.

MAGISTRATE JUDGE GABRIEL W. GORENSTEIN: NY R USDCTSD Gorenstein-Practices; NY R US-DCTSD Gorenstein-Ackn.

MAGISTRATE JUDGE FRANK MAAS: NY R USDCTSD Maas-Practices; NY R USDCTSD Maas-Discontinuance; NY R USDCTSD Maas-Conf; NY R USDCTSD Maas-Settlement.

MAGISTRATE JUDGE JUDITH C. McCARTHY: NY R USDCTSD McCarthy-Practices; NY R USDCTSD McCarthy-Conduct.

MAGISTRATE JUDGE BARBARA MOSES: NY R USDCTSD Moses-Practices.

MAGISTRATE JUDGE SARAH NETBURN: NY R USDCTSD Netburn-Civil; NY R USDCTSD Netburn-Settlement; NY R USDCTSD Netburn-Case Mgt; NY R USDCTSD Netburn--Pro Se.

MAGISTRATE JUDGE ANDREW J. PECK: NY R USDCTSD Peck-Practices; NY R USDCTSD Peck-Order; NY R USDCTSD Peck-Rule 502(d).

MAGISTRATE JUDGE HENRY PITMAN: NY R USDCTSD Pitman-Practices.

MAGISTRATE JUDGE LISA MARGARET SMITH: NY R USDCTSD Smith-Practices; NY R USDCTSD Smith-Trials.

# EASTERN DISTRICT OF NEW YORK

## Pleadings
## Complaint

**Document Last Updated September 2016**

**A. Checklist**

- (I) ❑ Matters to be considered by plaintiff
  - (a) ❑ Required documents
    - (1) ❑ Civil cover sheet
    - (2) ❑ Complaint
    - (3) ❑ Summons
    - (4) ❑ Information sheet
    - (5) ❑ Notice, consent, and reference of a civil action to a magistrate judge
    - (6) ❑ Filing fee
    - (7) ❑ Affidavit proving service
  - (b) ❑ Supplemental documents
    - (1) ❑ Notice and request for waiver of service
    - (2) ❑ Notice of constitutional question
    - (3) ❑ Notice of issue concerning foreign law
    - (4) ❑ Nongovernmental corporate disclosure statement
    - (5) ❑ Notice regarding availability of electronic filing
    - (6) ❑ Certification of amount of damages
  - (c) ❑ Timing
    - (1) ❑ A civil action is commenced by filing a complaint with the court
    - (2) ❑ If a defendant is not served within ninety (90) days after the complaint is filed, the court—on motion or on its own after notice to the plaintiff—must dismiss the action without prejudice against that defendant or order that service be made within a specified time
- (II) ❑ Matters to be considered by defendant
  - (a) ❑ Required documents
    - (1) ❑ Answer
    - (2) ❑ Certificate of service
  - (b) ❑ Supplemental documents
    - (1) ❑ Waiver of the service of summons
    - (2) ❑ Notice of constitutional question
    - (3) ❑ Notice of issue concerning foreign law
    - (4) ❑ Nongovernmental corporate disclosure statement
    - (5) ❑ Certification of amount of damages
  - (c) ❑ Timing
    - (1) ❑ A defendant must serve an answer:
      - (i) ❑ Within twenty-one (21) days after being served with the summons and complaint; or

        (ii)    ❑  If it has timely waived service under FRCP 4(d), within sixty (60) days after the request for a waiver was sent, or within ninety (90) days after it was sent to the defendant outside any judicial district of the United States

    (2)   ❑  The United States, a United States agency, or a United States officer or employee sued only in an official capacity must serve an answer to a complaint, counterclaim, or crossclaim within sixty (60) days after service on the United States attorney

    (3)   ❑  A United States officer or employee sued in an individual capacity for an act or omission occurring in connection with duties performed on the United States' behalf must serve an answer to a complaint, counterclaim, or crossclaim within sixty (60) days after service on the officer or employee or service on the United States attorney, whichever is later

    (4)   ❑  Unless the court sets a different time, serving a motion under FRCP 12 alters these periods as follows:

        (i)    ❑  If the court denies the motion or postpones its disposition until trial, the responsive pleading must be served within fourteen (14) days after notice of the court's action; or

        (ii)    ❑  If the court grants a motion for a more definite statement, the responsive pleading must be served within fourteen (14) days after the more definite statement is served

    (5)   ❑  Defendant is given a reasonable time of at least thirty (30) days after a waiver of service request is sent—or at least sixty (60) days if sent to defendant outside any judicial district of the United States—to return the waiver

## B.  Timing

1.  *Commencing an action.* A civil action is commenced by filing a complaint with the court. FRCP 3.

    a.  *Statute of limitations.* An action will be barred if it is not commenced within the period set forth in the applicable statute of limitations. Under the Federal Rules of Civil Procedure (FRCP), an action is commenced by filing a complaint with the court. Thus, in a suit on a right created by federal law, filing a complaint suffices to satisfy the statute of limitations. FEDPROF § 61:2.

        i.  *Federal question cases.* Absent a specific statutory provision for tolling the statute of limitations, in federal question cases, the filing of the complaint will toll the statute, even if not all filing fees have been paid, although some courts have added the requirement of reasonable diligence in effecting service. FEDPROF § 61:2.

        ii.  *Diversity cases.* In diversity actions the matter is less clear. In the landmark Ragan case, the Supreme Court held in construing FRCP 3 that if, under local law, an action is not commenced until the defendant has been served, the statute is not tolled until service has been accomplished. FEDPROF § 61:2; Ragan v. Merchants Transfer & Warehouse Co., 337 U.S. 530, 69 S.Ct. 1233, 93 L.Ed. 1520 (1949). However, in a subsequent case, the Supreme Court distinguished Ragan in holding that the provision of FRCP 4 governing methods of service prevails over a conflicting state rule requiring personal service. FEDPROF § 61:2; Hanna v. Plumer, 380 U.S. 460, 85 S.Ct. 1136, 14 L.Ed.2d 8 (1965). The court reaffirmed Ragan and held that (1) a state law mandating actual service of a summons to toll the statute of limitations must be followed in a diversity case, and (2) FRCP 3 only governs other timing requirements in the federal rules. FEDPROF § 61:2; Walker v. Armco Steel Corp., 446 U.S. 740, 100 S.Ct. 1978, 64 L.Ed.2d 659 (1980).

2.  *Service of summons and complaint.* If a defendant is not served within ninety (90) days after the complaint is filed, the court—on motion or on its own after notice to the plaintiff—must dismiss the action without prejudice against that defendant or order that service be made within a specified time. But if the plaintiff shows good cause for the failure, the court must extend the time for service for an appropriate period. FRCP 4(m) does not apply to service in a foreign country under FRCP 4(f) or FRCP 4(j)(1) or to service of a notice under FRCP 71.1(d)(3)(A). FRCP 4(m).

3.  *Computation of time*

    a.  *Computing time.* FRCP 6 applies in computing any time period specified in the Federal Rules of Civil Procedure, in any local rule or court order, or in any statute that does not specify a method of computing time. FRCP 6(a). In computing any period of time prescribed or allowed by the Local Civil Rules of the United States District Courts for the Southern and Eastern Districts of New York or the Local Admiralty and Maritime Rules, the provisions of FRCP 6 shall apply unless otherwise stated. NY R USDCTS&ED Civ Rule 6.4.

i.   *Period stated in days or a longer unit.* When the period is stated in days or a longer unit of time:

- Exclude the day of the event that triggers the period;

- Count every day, including intermediate Saturdays, Sundays, and legal holidays; and

- Include the last day of the period, but if the last day is a Saturday, Sunday, or legal holiday, the period continues to run until the end of the next day that is not a Saturday, Sunday, or legal holiday. FRCP 6(a)(1). In the Local Civil Rules of the United States District Courts for the Southern and Eastern Districts of New York, as in the Federal Rules of Civil Procedure as amended effective December 1, 2009, Saturdays, Sundays, and legal holidays are no longer excluded in computing periods of time. If the last day of the period is a Saturday, Sunday, or legal holiday, the period continues to run until the end of the next day that is not a Saturday, Sunday, or legal holiday. NY R USDCTS&ED Civ Rule 6.4.

ii.  *Period stated in hours.* When the period is stated in hours:

- Begin counting immediately on the occurrence of the event that triggers the period;

- Count every hour, including hours during intermediate Saturdays, Sundays, and legal holidays; and

- If the period would end on a Saturday, Sunday, or legal holiday, the period continues to run until the same time on the next day that is not a Saturday, Sunday, or legal holiday. FRCP 6(a)(2). In the Local Civil Rules of the United States District Courts for the Southern and Eastern Districts of New York, as in the Federal Rules of Civil Procedure as amended effective December 1, 2009, Saturdays, Sundays, and legal holidays are no longer excluded in computing periods of time. If the last day of the period is a Saturday, Sunday, or legal holiday, the period continues to run until the end of the next day that is not a Saturday, Sunday, or legal holiday. NY R USDCTS&ED Civ Rule 6.4.

iii. *Inaccessibility of the clerk's office.* Unless the court orders otherwise, if the clerk's office is inaccessible:

- On the last day for filing under FRCP 6(a)(1), then the time for filing is extended to the first accessible day that is not a Saturday, Sunday, or legal holiday; or

- During the last hour for filing under FRCP 6(a)(2), then the time for filing is extended to the same time on the first accessible day that is not a Saturday, Sunday, or legal holiday. FRCP 6(a)(3).

iv.  *"Last day" defined.* Unless a different time is set by a statute, local rule, or court order, the last day ends:

- For electronic filing, at midnight in the court's time zone; and

- For filing by other means, when the clerk's office is scheduled to close. FRCP 6(a)(4).

v.   *"Next day" defined.* The "next day" is determined by continuing to count forward when the period is measured after an event and backward when measured before an event. FRCP 6(a)(5).

vi.  *"Legal holiday" defined.* "Legal holiday" means:

- The day set aside by statute for observing New Year's Day, Martin Luther King Jr.'s Birthday, Washington's Birthday, Memorial Day, Independence Day, Labor Day, Columbus Day, Veterans' Day, Thanksgiving Day, or Christmas Day;

- Any day declared a holiday by the President or Congress; and

- For periods that are measured after an event, any other day declared a holiday by the state where the district court is located. FRCP 6(a)(6).

b. *Extending time*

　　i. *In general.* When an act may or must be done within a specified time, the court may, for good cause, extend the time:

- With or without motion or notice if the court acts, or if a request is made, before the original time or its extension expires; or

- On motion made after the time has expired if the party failed to act because of excusable neglect. FRCP 6(b)(1).

　　ii. *Exceptions.* A court must not extend the time to act under FRCP 50(b), FRCP 50(d), FRCP 52(b), FRCP 59(b), FRCP 59(d), FRCP 59(e), and FRCP 60(b). FRCP 6(b)(2).

　　iii. Refer to the United States District Court for the Eastern District of New York KeyRules Motion for Continuance/Extension of Time document for more information on extending time.

4. *Individual judge practices.* Refer to the Miscellaneous section of this document for information on individual judge practices on timing of documents.

## C. General Requirements

1. *Pleading, generally*

a. *Pleadings allowed.* Only these pleadings are allowed: (1) a complaint; (2) an answer to a complaint; (3) an answer to a counterclaim designated as a counterclaim; (4) an answer to a crossclaim; (5) a third-party complaint; (6) an answer to a third-party complaint; and (7) if the court orders one, a reply to an answer. FRCP 7(a).

b. *Pleading to be concise and direct.* Each allegation must be simple, concise, and direct. No technical form is required. FRCP 8(d)(1).

c. *Alternative statements of a claim or defense.* A party may set out two or more statements of a claim or defense alternatively or hypothetically, either in a single count or defense or in separate ones. If a party makes alternative statements, the pleading is sufficient if any one of them is sufficient. FRCP 8(d)(2).

d. *Inconsistent claims or defenses.* A party may state as many separate claims or defenses as it has, regardless of consistency. FRCP 8(d)(3).

e. *Construing pleadings.* Pleadings must be construed so as to do justice. FRCP 8(e).

2. *Pleading special matters*

a. *Capacity or authority to sue; Legal existence*

　　i. *In general.* Except when required to show that the court has jurisdiction, a pleading need not allege:

- A party's capacity to sue or be sued;

- A party's authority to sue or be sued in a representative capacity; or

- The legal existence of an organized association of persons that is made a party. FRCP 9(a)(1).

　　ii. *Raising those issues.* To raise any of those issues, a party must do so by a specific denial, which must state any supporting facts that are peculiarly within the party's knowledge. FRCP 9(a)(2).

b. *Fraud or mistake; Conditions of mind.* In alleging fraud or mistake, a party must state with particularity the circumstances constituting fraud or mistake. Malice, intent, knowledge, and other conditions of a person's mind may be alleged generally. FRCP 9(b).

c. *Conditions precedent.* In pleading conditions precedent, it suffices to allege generally that all conditions precedent have occurred or been performed. But when denying that a condition precedent has occurred or been performed, a party must do so with particularity. FRCP 9(c).

d. *Official document or act.* In pleading an official document or official act, it suffices to allege that the document was legally issued or the act legally done. FRCP 9(d).

e. *Judgment.* In pleading a judgment or decision of a domestic or foreign court, a judicial or quasi-judicial tribunal, or a board or officer, it suffices to plead the judgment or decision without showing jurisdiction to render it. FRCP 9(e).

f. *Time and place.* An allegation of time or place is material when testing the sufficiency of a pleading. FRCP 9(f).

g. *Special damages.* If an item of special damage is claimed, it must be specifically stated. FRCP 9(g).

h. *Admiralty or maritime claim*

    i. *How designated.* If a claim for relief is within the admiralty or maritime jurisdiction and also within the court's subject-matter jurisdiction on some other ground, the pleading may designate the claim as an admiralty or maritime claim for purposes of FRCP 14(c), FRCP 38(e), and FRCP 82 and the Supplemental Rules for Admiralty or Maritime Claims and Asset Forfeiture Actions. A claim cognizable only in the admiralty or maritime jurisdiction is an admiralty or maritime claim for those purposes, whether or not so designated. FRCP 9(h)(1).

    ii. *Designation for appeal.* A case that includes an admiralty or maritime claim within FRCP 9(h) is an admiralty case within 28 U.S.C.A. § 1292(a)(3). FRCP 9(h)(2).

3. *Complaint.* A pleading that states a claim for relief must contain: (1) a short and plain statement of the grounds for the court's jurisdiction, unless the court already has jurisdiction and the claim needs no new jurisdictional support; (2) a short and plain statement of the claim showing that the pleader is entitled to relief; and (3) a demand for the relief sought, which may include relief in the alternative or different types of relief. FRCP 8(a).

    a. *Statement of jurisdiction.* Federal courts are courts of limited jurisdiction, and it is presumed that they are without jurisdiction unless the contrary affirmatively appears. FEDPROC § 62:38; Kirkland Masonry, Inc. v. C.I.R., 614 F.2d 532 (5th Cir. 1980). Therefore, in order for a complaint to comply with the requirement that it contain a short and plain statement of the grounds upon which the court's jurisdiction depends, the jurisdictional basis must be alleged affirmatively and distinctly on the face of the complaint. FEDPROC § 62:38; Spain v. U.S. Through Atomic Nuclear Regulatory Commission Through U.S. Atomic Safety and Licensing Bd., 397 F.Supp. 15 (M.D.La. 1975).

    i. Although it has been said that the jurisdictional statement requirement contemplates reference to a federal statute, a sufficient jurisdictional statement is not made by simply citing a federal statute without alleging facts which bring the plaintiff within the purview of the statute. FEDPROC § 62:38; Atkins v. School Bd. of Halifax County, 379 F.Supp. 1060 (W.D.Va. 1974); Sims v. Mercy Hospital of Monroe, 451 F.2d 171 (6th Cir. 1971).

    ii. Improper venue is an affirmative defense, and a complaint need not include allegations showing venue to be proper. FEDPROC § 62:38; Ripperger v. A.C. Allyn & Co., 113 F.2d 332 (2d Cir. 1940).

    b. *Statement of claim*

    i. *Notice pleading.* Because the only function left exclusively to the pleadings by the Federal Rules of Civil Procedure is that of giving notice, federal courts frequently have said that the Federal Rules of Civil Procedure have adopted a system of "notice pleading." FPP § 1202; Swierkiewicz v. Sorema N.A., 534 U.S. 506, 122 S.Ct. 992, 152 L.Ed.2d 1 (2002). To comply with the requirement that a complaint contain a short and plain statement of the claim, a pleading must give the opposing party fair notice of the nature of a claim and of the basis or grounds for it, so that the defendant will at least be notified as to which of its actions gave rise to the claim upon which the complaint is based. FEDPROC § 62:45.

       • *Plausibility standard.* Bell Atlantic Corporation v. Twombly and Ashcroft v. Iqbal have paved the way for a heightened "plausibility" pleading standard that requires plaintiffs to provide greater factual development in their complaints in order to survive a FRCP 12(b)(6) motion to dismiss. FPP § 1202; Bell Atlantic Corp. v. Twombly, 550 U.S. 544, 127 S.Ct. 1955, 167 L.Ed.2d 929, 68 Fed.R.Serv.3d 661 (2007); Ashcroft v. Iqbal, 556 U.S. 662, 129 S.Ct. 1937, 173 L.Ed.2d 868 (2009). In discussing what appears to be the new plausibility standard, the Court [in Bell Atlantic Corp. v. Twombly] stated: "While a complaint attacked by a FRCP 12(b)(6) motion to dismiss does not need detailed factual allegations. . . .a plaintiff's obligation to provide the 'grounds' of his 'entitle[ment] to relief' requires more than labels and conclusions, and a formulaic recitation of the elements of a cause of action will not do. . . .Factual allegations must be enough to raise a right to relief above the speculative level." FPP § 1216; Bell Atlantic Corp. v. Twombly, 550 U.S. 544, 127 S.Ct. 1955, 167 L.Ed.2d 929, 68 Fed.R.Serv.3d 661 (2007).

ii. *Facts and evidence.* The complaint need only state enough facts to raise a reasonable expectation that discovery will reveal evidence of the necessary elements. FEDPROC § 62:52; Phillips v. County of Allegheny, 515 F.3d 224 (3d Cir. 2008). A complaint is not intended to formulate issues or fully summarize the facts involved. FEDPROC § 62:52; Hill v. MCI WorldCom Communications, Inc., 141 F.Supp.2d 1205 (S.D.Iowa 2001). Under notice pleading, the full development of the facts and the narrowing of contested issues are accomplished through discovery and other pretrial procedures. FEDPROC § 62:52.

iii. *Particularity.* The claim should be particularized sufficiently for the defendant to prepare an adequate defense, file a responsive pleading, determine whether the defense of res judicata is appropriate, and commence discovery, and should insure that the court is sufficiently informed to determine the issue presented and to decide whether the complaint states a claim upon which relief can be had. FEDPROC § 62:45; Kelly v. Schmidberger, 806 F.2d 44, 6 Fed.R.Serv.3d 798 (2d Cir. 1986); Frank v. Mracek, 58 F.R.D. 365 (M.D.Ala. 1973); Barlow v. Pep Boys, Inc., 625 F.Supp. 130 (E.D.Pa. 1985); Philadelphia Dressed Beef Co. v. Wilson & Co., 19 F.R.D. 198 (E.D.Pa. 1956); Luckett v. Cohen, 145 F.Supp. 155 (S.D.N.Y. 1956).

c. *Demand for relief sought.* FRCP 8(a)(3) does not require a party to frame the demand for judgment according to a prescribed form or set of particular words; any concise statement identifying the remedies and the parties against whom relief is sought will be sufficient. FPP § 1255; Chandler v. McKee Foods Corp., 2009 WL 210858 (W.D.Va. 2009). Moreover, the pleader need only make one demand for relief regardless of the number of claims that are asserted. FPP § 1255; Liberty Mut. Ins. Co. v. Wetzel, 424 U.S. 737, 96 S.Ct. 1202, 47 L.Ed.2d 435 (1976).

i. Relief must be requested as to each defendant. FEDPROC § 62:58; RKO-Stanley Warner Theatres, Inc. v. Mellon Nat. Bank & Trust Co., 436 F.2d 1297 (3d Cir. 1970).

4. *Joinder*

a. *Joinder of claims.* A party asserting a claim, counterclaim, crossclaim, or third-party claim may join, as independent or alternative claims, as many claims as it has against an opposing party. FRCP 18(a).

i. *Joinder of contingent claims.* A party may join two claims even though one of them is contingent on the disposition of the other; but the court may grant relief only in accordance with the parties' relative substantive rights. In particular, a plaintiff may state a claim for money and a claim to set aside a conveyance that is fraudulent as to that plaintiff, without first obtaining a judgment for the money. FRCP 18(b).

b. *Joinder of parties; Required*

i. *Persons required to be joined if feasible; Required party.* A person who is subject to service of process and whose joinder will not deprive the court of subject-matter jurisdiction must be joined as a party if:

- In that person's absence, the court cannot accord complete relief among existing parties; or

- That person claims an interest relating to the subject of the action and is so situated that disposing of the action in the person's absence may: (1) as a practical matter impair or impede the person's ability to protect the interest; or (2) leave an existing party subject to a substantial risk of incurring double, multiple, or otherwise inconsistent obligations because of the interest. FRCP 19(a)(1).

ii. *Joinder of parties by court order.* If a person has not been joined as required, the court must order that the person be made a party. A person who refuses to join as a plaintiff may be made either a defendant or, in a proper case, an involuntary plaintiff. FRCP 19(a)(2).

iii. *Venue.* If a joined party objects to venue and the joinder would make venue improper, the court must dismiss that party. FRCP 19(a)(3).

    iv.  *When joinder of parties is not feasible.* If a person who is required to be joined if feasible cannot be joined, the court must determine whether, in equity and good conscience, the action should proceed among the existing parties or should be dismissed. FRCP 19(b). For a list of the factors for the court to consider in determining whether joinder of parties is feasible, refer to FRCP 19(b)(1) through FRCP 19(b)(4).

    v.  *Pleading the reasons for nonjoinder.* When asserting a claim for relief, a party must state:

- The name, if known, of any person who is required to be joined if feasible but is not joined; and

- The reasons for not joining that person. FRCP 19(c).

    vi.  *Exception for class actions.* FRCP 19 is subject to FRCP 23. FRCP 19(d). For information on class actions, refer to FRCP 23.

  c.  *Joinder of parties; Permissible*

    i.  *Persons who may join or be joined*

- *Plaintiffs.* Persons may join in one action as plaintiffs if: (1) they assert any right to relief jointly, severally, or in the alternative with respect to or arising out of the same transaction, occurrence, or series of transactions or occurrences; and (2) any question of law or fact common to all plaintiffs will arise in the action. FRCP 20(a)(1).

- *Defendants.* Persons—as well as a vessel, cargo, or other property subject to admiralty process in rem—may be joined in one action as defendants if: (1) any right to relief is asserted against them jointly, severally, or in the alternative with respect to or arising out of the same transaction, occurrence, or series of transactions or occurrences; and (2) any question of law or fact common to all defendants will arise in the action. FRCP 20(a)(2).

- *Extent of relief.* Neither a plaintiff nor a defendant need be interested in obtaining or defending against all the relief demanded. The court may grant judgment to one or more plaintiffs according to their rights, and against one or more defendants according to their liabilities. FRCP 20(a)(3).

    ii.  *Protective measures.* The court may issue orders—including an order for separate trials—to protect a party against embarrassment, delay, expense, or other prejudice that arises from including a person against whom the party asserts no claim and who asserts no claim against the party. FRCP 20(b).

  d.  *Misjoinder and nonjoinder of parties.* Misjoinder of parties is not a ground for dismissing an action. On motion or on its own, the court may at any time, on just terms, add or drop a party. The court may also sever any claim against a party. FRCP 21.

5.  *Right to a jury trial; Demand*

  a.  *Right preserved.* The right of trial by jury as declared by U.S.C.A. Const. Amend. VII, or as provided by a federal statute, is preserved to the parties inviolate. FRCP 38(a).

  b.  *Demand.* On any issue triable of right by a jury, a party may demand a jury trial by:

    i.  Serving the other parties with a written demand—which may be included in a pleading—no later than fourteen (14) days after the last pleading directed to the issue is served; and

    ii.  Filing the demand in accordance with FRCP 5(d). FRCP 38(b).

  c.  *Specifying issues.* In its demand, a party may specify the issues that it wishes to have tried by a jury; otherwise, it is considered to have demanded a jury trial on all the issues so triable. If the party has demanded a jury trial on only some issues, any other party may—within fourteen (14) days after being served with the demand or within a shorter time ordered by the court—serve a demand for a jury trial on any other or all factual issues triable by jury, FRCP 38(c).

  d.  *Waiver; Withdrawal.* A party waives a jury trial unless its demand is properly served and filed. A proper demand may be withdrawn only if the parties consent. FRCP 38(d).

  e.  *Admiralty and maritime claims.* The rules in FRCP 38 do not create a right to a jury trial on issues in a claim that is an admiralty or maritime claim under FRCP 9(h). FRCP 38(e).

6. *Related cases.* It shall be the continuing duty of each attorney appearing in any civil or criminal case to bring promptly to the attention of the Court all facts which said attorney believes are relevant to a determination that said case and one or more pending civil or criminal cases should be heard by the same Judge, in order to avoid unnecessary duplication of judicial effort. As soon as the attorney becomes aware of such relationship, said attorney shall notify the Judges to whom the cases have been assigned. NY R USDCTS&ED Civ Rule 1.6(a). If counsel fails to comply with NY R USDCTS&ED Civ Rule 1.6(a), the Court may assess reasonable costs directly against counsel whose action has obstructed the effective administration of the Court's business. NY R USDCTS&ED Civ Rule 1.6(b).

7. *Alternative dispute resolution (ADR)*

  a. *Court-annexed arbitration*

    i. *Civil cases eligible for compulsory arbitration.* The Clerk of Court shall, as to all cases filed after January 1, 1986, designate and process for compulsory arbitration all civil cases (excluding Social Security cases, tax matters, prisoners' civil rights cases and any action based on an alleged violation of a right secured by the Constitution of the United States or if jurisdiction is based in whole or in part on 28 U.S.C.A. § 1343) wherein money damages only are being sought in an amount not in excess of one hundred fifty thousand dollars ($150,000) exclusive of interest and costs. NY R USDCTS&ED Civ Rule 83.7(d)(1).

      • The parties may by written stipulation agree that the Clerk of Court shall designate and process for court-annexed arbitration any civil case that is not subject to compulsory arbitration in NY R USDCTS&ED Civ Rule 83.7. NY R USDCTS&ED Civ Rule 83.7(d)(2).

      • For purposes of NY R USDCTS&ED Civ Rule 83.7 only, in all civil cases damages shall be presumed to be not in excess of one hundred fifty thousand dollars ($150,000) exclusive of interest and costs, unless: (1) counsel for plaintiff, at the time of filing the complaint, or in the event of the removal of a case from state court or transfer of a case from another district to this Court, within thirty (30) days of the docketing of the case in this district, files a certification with the Court that the damages sought exceed one hundred fifty thousand dollars ($150,000), exclusive of interest and costs; or (2) counsel for a defendant, at the time of filing a counterclaim or cross-claim files a certification with the court that the damages sought by the counter-claim or cross-claim exceed one hundred fifty thousand dollars ($150,000) exclusive of interest and costs. NY R USDCTS&ED Civ Rule 83.7(d)(3).

    ii. *Exemption from arbitration.* The Court shall, sua sponte, or on motion of a party, exempt any case from arbitration in which the objectives of arbitration would not be realized (1) because the case involves complex or novel issues, (2) because legal issues predominate over factual issues, or (3) for other good cause. NY R USDCTS&ED Civ Rule 83.7(e)(2). For information on applying for an exemption, refer to NY R USDCTS&ED Civ Rule 83.7

    iii. *Referral to arbitration.* Cases not originally designated as eligible for compulsory arbitration, but which in the discretion of the assigned Judge, are later found to qualify, may be referred to arbitration. A U.S. District Judge or a U.S. Magistrate Judge, in cases that exceed the arbitration ceiling of one hundred fifty thousand dollars ($150,000) exclusive of interest and costs, in their discretion, may suggest that the parties should consider arbitration. If the parties are agreeable, an appropriate consent form signed by all parties or their representatives may be entered and filed in the case prior to scheduling an arbitration hearing. NY R USDCTS&ED Civ Rule 83.7(e)(3).

    iv. For more information on arbitration, refer to NY R USDCTS&ED Civ Rule 83.7.

  b. *Court-annexed mediation.* Mediation is a process in which parties and counsel agree to meet with a neutral mediator trained to assist them in settling disputes. The mediator improves communication across party lines, helps parties articulate their interests and understand those of the other party, probes the strengths and weaknesses of each party's legal positions, and identifies areas of agreement and helps generate options for a mutually agreeable resolution to the dispute. In all cases, mediation provides an opportunity to explore a wide range of potential solutions and to address interests that may be outside the scope of the stated controversy or which could not be addressed by judicial action. A hallmark of mediation is its capacity to expand traditional settlement discussions and broaden resolution options, often by exploring litigant needs and interests that may be formally independent of the legal issues in controversy. NY R USDCTS&ED Civ Rule 83.8(a).

   i. *Eligible cases.* Judges and Magistrate Judges may designate civil cases for inclusion in the mediation program, and when doing so shall prepare an order to that effect. Alternatively, and subject to the availability of qualified mediators, the parties may consent to participation in the mediation program by preparing and executing a stipulation signed by all parties to the action and so-ordered by the Court. NY R USDCTS&ED Civ Rule 83.8(b)(1).

   ii. For more information on mediation, refer to NY R USDCTS&ED Civ Rule 83.8.

8. *Individual judge practices.* Refer to the Miscellaneous section of this document for information on individual judge practices on general requirements for documents.

## D. Documents

1. *Required documents*

   a. *Civil cover sheet.* A civil cover sheet is submitted with each civil complaint filed in the district court. Copies of the cover sheet may be obtained from the Clerk of Court. 2 FEDFORMS § 3:29(Comment).

   b. *Complaint.* Refer to the General Requirements section of this document for the form and contents of the complaint.

   c. *Summons.* A summons must be served with a copy of the complaint. FRCP 4(c)(1). A summons must:

     i. Name the court and the parties;

     ii. Be directed to the defendant;

     iii. State the name and address of the plaintiff's attorney or—if unrepresented—of the plaintiff;

     iv. State the time within which the defendant must appear and defend;

     v. Notify the defendant that a failure to appear and defend will result in a default judgment against the defendant for the relief demanded in the complaint;

     vi. Be signed by the clerk; and

     vii. Bear the court's seal. FRCP 4(a)(1).

   d. *Information sheet.* The party filing the initial paper in a civil or criminal case shall complete and attach an information sheet. The information sheet shall be placed in the case file. NY R USDCTED Div. Bus., Rule 50.1(b).

   e. *Notice, consent, and reference of a civil action to a magistrate judge.* When a civil action is filed with the Clerk, the Clerk shall give the filing party notice of the Magistrate Judge's consent jurisdiction in a form approved by the Court, with sufficient copies to be served with the complaint on adversary parties. A copy of such notice shall be attached to any third-party complaint served by a defendant. NY R USDCTS&ED Civ Rule 73.1(a). For more information on consent jurisdiction procedure, refer to NY R USDCTS&ED Civ Rule 73.1.

   f. *Filing fee.* The clerk of each district court shall require the parties instituting any civil action, suit or proceeding in such court, whether by original process, removal or otherwise, to pay a filing fee. 28 U.S.C.A. § 1914(a). Each district court by rule or standing order may require advance payment of fees. 28 U.S.C.A. § 1914(c). The Clerk shall not be required to render any service for which a fee is prescribed by statute or by the Judicial Conference of the United States unless the fee for the particular service is paid to the Clerk in advance or the Court orders otherwise. NY R USDCTS&ED Civ Rule 1.7(a). For information on filing fees and the District Court Miscellaneous Fee Schedule, refer to 28 U.S.C.A. § 1914.

   g. *Affidavit proving service.* Unless service is waived, proof of service must be made to the court. Except for service by a United States marshal or deputy marshal, proof must be by the server's affidavit. FRCP 4(l)(1). Refer to the Filing and Service Requirements section of this document for more information.

2. *Supplemental documents*

    a. *Notice and request for waiver of service.* An individual, corporation, or association that is subject to service under FRCP 4(e), FRCP 4(f), or FRCP 4(h) has a duty to avoid unnecessary expenses of serving the summons. The plaintiff may notify such a defendant that an action has been commenced and request that the defendant waive service of a summons. The notice and request must:

        i. Be in writing and be addressed:

- To the individual defendant; or

- For a defendant subject to service under FRCP 4(h), to an officer, a managing or general agent, or any other agent authorized by appointment or by law to receive service of process;

        ii. Name the court where the complaint was filed;

       iii. Be accompanied by a copy of the complaint, two (2) copies of a waiver form appended to FRCP 4, and a prepaid means for returning the form;

       iv. Inform the defendant, using the form appended to FRCP 4, of the consequences of waiving and not waiving service;

       v. State the date when the request is sent;

       vi. Give the defendant a reasonable time of at least thirty (30) days after the request was sent—or at least sixty (60) days if sent to the defendant outside any judicial district of the United States—to return the waiver; and

       vii. Be sent by first-class mail or other reliable means. FRCP 4(d)(1).

    b. *Notice of constitutional question.* A party that files a pleading, written motion, or other paper drawing into question the constitutionality of a federal or state statute must promptly:

        i. *File notice.* File a notice of constitutional question stating the question and identifying the paper that raises it, if:

- A federal statute is questioned and the parties do not include the United States, one of its agencies, or one of its officers or employees in an official capacity; or

- A state statute is questioned and the parties do not include the state, one of its agencies, or one of its officers or employees in an official capacity; and

        ii. *Serve notice.* Serve the notice and paper on the Attorney General of the United States if a federal statute is questioned—or on the state attorney general if a state statute is questioned—either by certified or registered mail or by sending it to an electronic address designated by the attorney general for this purpose. FRCP 5.1(a).

       iii. *No forfeiture.* A party's failure to file and serve the notice, or the court's failure to certify, does not forfeit a constitutional claim or defense that is otherwise timely asserted. FRCP 5.1(d).

    c. *Notice of issue concerning foreign law.* A party who intends to raise an issue about a foreign country's law must give notice by a pleading or other writing. In determining foreign law, the court may consider any relevant material or source, including testimony, whether or not submitted by a party or admissible under the Federal Rules of Evidence. The court's determination must be treated as a ruling on a question of law. FRCP 44.1.

    d. *Nongovernmental corporate disclosure statement.* To enable judges and magistrates to evaluate possible disqualification or recusal, counsel for a private (nongovernmental) party shall submit at the time of initial pleading a certificate identifying any corporate parent, subsidiaries, or affiliates of that party. NY R USDCTED Div. Bus., Rule 50.1(c).

        i. *Contents.* A nongovernmental corporate party must file two (2) copies of a disclosure statement that:

- Identifies any parent corporation and any publicly held corporation owning ten percent (10%) or more of its stock; or

- States that there is no such corporation. FRCP 7.1(a).

      ii.   *Time to file; Supplemental filing.* A party must:

- File the disclosure statement with its first appearance, pleading, petition, motion, response, or other request addressed to the court; and

- Promptly file a supplemental statement if any required information changes. FRCP 7.1(b). For purposes of FRCP 7.1(b)(2), "promptly" shall mean "within fourteen days," that is, parties are required to file a supplemental disclosure statement within fourteen (14) days of the time there is any change in the information required in a disclosure statement filed pursuant to those rules. NY R USDCTS&ED Civ Rule 7.1.1.

     e.   *Certification of amount of damages.* For purposes of NY R USDCTS&ED Civ Rule 83.7 only, in all civil cases damages shall be presumed to be not in excess of one hundred fifty thousand dollars ($150,000) exclusive of interest and costs, unless counsel for plaintiff, at the time of filing the complaint, or in the event of the removal of a case from state court or transfer of a case from another district to this Court, within thirty (30) days of the docketing of the case in this district, files a certification with the Court that the damages sought exceed one hundred fifty thousand dollars ($150,000), exclusive of interest and costs. NY R USDCTS&ED Civ Rule 83.7(d)(3)(A).

3.   *Individual judge practices.* Refer to the Miscellaneous section of this document for information on individual judge practices on required documents.

## E.  Format

1.   *Form of documents*

     a.   *Paper.* Every pleading, written motion, and other paper must: be plainly written, typed, printed, or copied without erasures or interlineations which materially deface it. NY R USDCTS&ED Civ Rule 11.1(a)(1).

     b.   *Typeface, margin, and spacing.* The typeface, margins, and spacing of all documents presented for filing must meet the following requirements:

        i.   All text must be twelve (12) point type or larger, except for text in footnotes which may be ten (10) point type;

       ii.   All documents must have at least one (1) inch margins on all sides;

      iii.   All text must be double-spaced, except for headings, text in footnotes, or block quotations, which may be single-spaced. NY R USDCTS&ED Civ Rule 11.1(b).

     c.   *Caption; Names of parties.* Every pleading must have a caption with the court's name, a title, a file number, and a FRCP 7(a) designation. The title of the complaint must name all the parties; the title of other pleadings, after naming the first party on each side, may refer generally to other parties. FRCP 10(a). Every pleading, written motion, and other paper must: bear the docket number and the initials of the District Judge and any Magistrate Judge before whom the action or proceeding is pending, NY R USDCTS&ED Civ Rule 11.1(a)(2).

     d.   *Paragraphs; Separate statements.* A party must state its claims or defenses in numbered paragraphs, each limited as far as practicable to a single set of circumstances. A later pleading may refer by number to a paragraph in an earlier pleading. If doing so would promote clarity, each claim founded on a separate transaction or occurrence—and each defense other than a denial—must be stated in a separate count or defense. FRCP 10(b).

     e.   *Adoption by reference; Exhibits.* A statement in a pleading may be adopted by reference elsewhere in the same pleading or in any other pleading or motion. A copy of a written instrument that is an exhibit to a pleading is a part of the pleading for all purposes. FRCP 10(c).

     f.   *Acceptance by the clerk.* The clerk must not refuse to file a paper solely because it is not in the form prescribed by the Federal Rules of Civil Procedure or by a local rule or practice. FRCP 5(d)(4).

2.   *Signing of pleadings, motions and other papers*

     a.   *Signature.* Every pleading, written motion, and other paper must be signed by at least one attorney of record in the attorney's name—or by a party personally if the party is unrepresented. The paper must state the signer's address, e-mail address, and telephone number. FRCP 11(a). Every pleading,

written motion, and other paper must: have the name of each person signing it clearly printed or typed directly below the signature. NY R USDCTS&ED Civ Rule 11.1(a)(3).

   i. *No verification or accompanying affidavit required for pleadings.* Unless a rule or statute specifically states otherwise, a pleading need not be verified or accompanied by an affidavit. FRCP 11(a).

   ii. *Unsigned papers.* The court must strike an unsigned paper unless the omission is promptly corrected after being called to the attorney's or party's attention. FRCP 11(a).

b. *Representations to the court.* By presenting to the court a pleading, written motion, or other paper—whether by signing, filing, submitting, or later advocating it—an attorney or unrepresented party certifies that to the best of the person's knowledge, information, and belief, formed after an inquiry reasonable under the circumstances:

   i. It is not being presented for any improper purpose, such as to harass, cause unnecessary delay, or needlessly increase the cost of litigation;

   ii. The claims, defenses, and other legal contentions are warranted by existing law or by a nonfrivolous argument for extending, modifying, or reversing existing law or for establishing new law;

   iii. The factual contentions have evidentiary support or, if specifically so identified, will likely have evidentiary support after a reasonable opportunity for further investigation or discovery; and

   iv. The denials of factual contentions are warranted on the evidence or, if specifically so identified, are reasonably based on belief or a lack of information. FRCP 11(b).

c. *Sanctions.* If, after notice and a reasonable opportunity to respond, the court determines that FRCP 11(b) has been violated, the court may impose an appropriate sanction on any attorney, law firm, or party that violated FRCP 11(b) or is responsible for the violation. FRCP 11(c)(1). Refer to the United States District Court for the Eastern District of New York KeyRules Motion for Sanctions document for more information.

3. *Privacy protection for filings made with the court*

a. *Redacted filings.* Unless the court orders otherwise, in an electronic or paper filing with the court that contains an individual's Social Security number, taxpayer-identification number, or birth date, the name of an individual known to be a minor, or a financial-account number, a party or nonparty making the filing may include only:

   i. The last four (4) digits of the Social Security number and taxpayer-identification number;

   ii. The year of the individual's birth;

   iii. The minor's initials; and

   iv. The last four (4) digits of the financial-account number. FRCP 5.2(a); NY R USDCTED Order 2004-09.

   v. In addition, exercise caution when filing documents that contain the following:

- Personal identifying number, such as driver's license number;
- Medical records, treatment and diagnosis;
- Employment history;
- Individual financial information; and
- Proprietary or trade secret information. NY R USDCTED Order 2004-09.

b. *Exemptions from the redaction requirement.* The redaction requirement does not apply to the following:

   i. A financial-account number that identifies the property allegedly subject to forfeiture in a forfeiture proceeding;

   ii. The record of an administrative or agency proceeding;

   iii. The official record of a state-court proceeding;

    iv.   The record of a court or tribunal, if that record was not subject to the redaction requirement when originally filed;

    v.   A filing covered by FRCP 5.2(c) or FRCP 5.2(d); and

    vi.   A pro se filing in an action brought under 28 U.S.C.A. § 2241, 28 U.S.C.A. § 2254, or 28 U.S.C.A. § 2255. FRCP 5.2(b).

c.   *Limitations on remote access to electronic files; Social Security appeals and immigration cases.* Unless the court orders otherwise, in an action for benefits under the Social Security Act, and in an action or proceeding relating to an order of removal, to relief from removal, or to immigration benefits or detention, access to an electronic file is authorized as follows:

    i.   The parties and their attorneys may have remote electronic access to any part of the case file, including the administrative record;

    ii.   Any other person may have electronic access to the full record at the courthouse, but may have remote electronic access only to:

- The docket maintained by the court; and

- An opinion, order, judgment, or other disposition of the court, but not any other part of the case file or the administrative record. FRCP 5.2(c).

d.   *Filings made under seal.* The court may order that a filing be made under seal without redaction. The court may later unseal the filing or order the person who made the filing to file a redacted version for the public record. FRCP 5.2(d).

e.   *Protective orders.* For good cause, the court may by order in a case:

    i.   Require redaction of additional information; or

    ii.   Limit or prohibit a nonparty's remote electronic access to a document filed with the court. FRCP 5.2(e).

f.   *Option for additional unredacted filing under seal.* A person making a redacted filing may also file an unredacted copy under seal. The court must retain the unredacted copy as part of the record. FRCP 5.2(f); NY R USDCTED Order 2004-09. The unredacted version of the document or the reference list shall be retained by the court as part of the record. The court may, however, still require the party to file a redacted copy for the public file. NY R USDCTED Order 2004-09.

g.   *Option for filing a reference list.* A filing that contains redacted information may be filed together with a reference list that identifies each item of redacted information and specifies an appropriate identifier that uniquely corresponds to each item listed. The list must be filed under seal and may be amended as of right. Any reference in the case to a listed identifier will be construed to refer to the corresponding item of information. FRCP 5.2(g); NY R USDCTED Order 2004-09. The unredacted version of the document or the reference list shall be retained by the court as part of the record. The court may, however, still require the party to file a redacted copy for the public file. NY R USDCTED Order 2004-09.

h.   *Responsibility for redaction.* The responsibility for redacting these personal identifiers rests solely with counsel and the parties. The Clerk will not review each pleading for compliance with NY R USDCTED Order 2004-09. NY R USDCTED Order 2004-09.

    i.   Counsel is strongly urged to share this notice with all clients so that an informed decision about the inclusion of certain materials may be made. If a redacted document is filed, it is the sole responsibility of counsel and the parties to be sure that all pleadings comply with the rules of this court requiring redaction of personal data identifiers. The clerk will not review each pleading for redaction. NY R USDCTED Order 2004-09.

i.   *Waiver of protection of identifiers.* A person waives the protection of FRCP 5.2(a) as to the person's own information by filing it without redaction and not under seal. FRCP 5.2(h).

4.   *Individual judge practices.* Refer to the Miscellaneous section of this document for information on individual judge practices on formatting documents.

## F.  Filing and Service Requirements

1.   *Filing requirements.* A civil action is commenced by filing a complaint with the court. FRCP 3. The first

step in a civil action in a United States district court is the filing of the complaint with the clerk or the judge. FPP § 1052. Filing a complaint requires nothing more than delivery of the document to a court officer authorized to receive it. FPP § 1052; *Central States, Southeast & Southwest Areas Pension Fund v. Paramount Liquor Co.*, 34 F.Supp.2d 1092 (N.D.Ill. 1999).

a. *Pro se incarcerated litigants.* Individuals who are incarcerated and are filing their legal documents pro se may benefit from a special "mailbox rule," which fixes the time of commencement of an action at the point when the complaint enters the prison mail system, rather than when it reaches the court clerk. FPP § 1052; *Houston v. Lack*, 487 U.S. 266, 276, 108 S.Ct. 2379, 2385, 101 L.Ed.2d 245 (1988).

b. *Night depository.* A night depository with an automatic date stamp shall be maintained. . .by the Clerk of the Eastern District in the Brooklyn Courthouse. After regular business hours, papers for the District Court only may be deposited in the night depository. Such papers will be considered as having been filed in the District Court as of the date stamped thereon, which shall be deemed presumptively correct. NY R USDCTS&ED Civ Rule 1.2.

c. *Electronic filing*

    i. *Authorization of electronic filing program.* A court may, by local rule, allow papers to be filed, signed, or verified by electronic means that are consistent with any technical standards established by the Judicial Conference of the United States. A local rule may require electronic filing only if reasonable exceptions are allowed. A paper filed electronically in compliance with a local rule is a written paper for purposes of the Federal Rules of Civil Procedure. FRCP 5(d)(3).

- Parties serving and filing papers shall follow the instructions regarding Electronic Case Filing (ECF) published on the website of each respective Court. A paper served and filed by electronic means in accordance with such instructions is, for purposes of FRCP 5, served and filed in compliance with the Local Civil Rules of the Southern and Eastern Districts of New York. NY R USDCTS&ED Civ Rule 5.2(a). Parties have an obligation to review the Court's actual order, decree, or judgment (on ECF), which controls, and should not rely on the description on the docket or in the ECF Notice of Electronic Filing (NEF). NY R USDCTS&ED Civ Rule 5.2(c).

    ii. *Mandatory electronic filing.* Beginning on August 2, 2004, electronic case filing will be mandatory for all civil cases other than pro se cases. NY R USDCTED Order 2004-08.

- *Letter-motions and letters addressed to the court.* Subject to the instructions regarding ECF published on the website of each respective Court and any pertinent Individual Judge's Practices, letter-motions permitted by NY R USDCTS&ED Civ Rule 7.1(d) and letters addressed to the Court (but not letters between the parties) may be filed via ECF. NY R USDCTS&ED Civ Rule 5.2(b).

- *Proposed orders, judgments and decrees.* Proposed orders, judgments and decrees shall be presented as directed by the ECF rules published on the website of each respective Court. NY R USDCTS&ED Civ Rule 77.1. For more information, refer to NY R USDCTS&ED Civ Rule 77.1.

- *Request for exemption.* Requests by attorneys for an exemption to the mandatory policy will be considered for good cause hardship reasons only, and will be reviewed on an individual basis by the assigned United States Magistrate Judge. The Clerk's Office provides an electronic filing training program to assist attorneys filing electronically. Before seeking a hardship exemption, attorneys are advised to participate in the training program or otherwise seek the assistance of the Clerk's Office. NY R USDCTED Order 2004-08.

    iii. For more information on electronic filing, refer to the court's website.

2. *Issuance of summons.* On or after filing the complaint, the plaintiff may present a summons to the clerk for signature and seal. If the summons is properly completed, the clerk must sign, seal, and issue it to the

plaintiff for service on the defendant. A summons—or a copy of a summons that is addressed to multiple defendants—must be issued for each defendant to be served. FRCP 4(b).

   a.  *Amendments.* The court may permit a summons to be amended. FRCP 4(a)(2).

3.  *Service requirements.* A summons must be served with a copy of the complaint. The plaintiff is responsible for having the summons and complaint served within the time allowed by FRCP 4(m) and must furnish the necessary copies to the person who makes service. FRCP 4(c)(1).

   a.  *By whom served.* Any person who is at least 18 years old and not a party may serve a summons and complaint. FRCP 4(c)(2).

      i.  *By a marshal or someone specially appointed.* At the plaintiff's request, the court may order that service be made by a United States marshal or deputy marshal or by a person specially appointed by the court. The court must so order if the plaintiff is authorized to proceed in forma pauperis under 28 U.S.C.A. § 1915 or as a seaman under 28 U.S.C.A. § 1916. FRCP 4(c)(3).

   b.  *Serving an individual within a judicial district of the United States.* Unless federal law provides otherwise, an individual—other than a minor, an incompetent person, or a person whose waiver has been filed—may be served in a judicial district of the United States by:

      i.  Following state law for serving a summons in an action brought in courts of general jurisdiction in the state where the district court is located or where service is made; or

      ii.  Doing any of the following:

- Delivering a copy of the summons and of the complaint to the individual personally;

- Leaving a copy of each at the individual's dwelling or usual place of abode with someone of suitable age and discretion who resides there; or

- Delivering a copy of each to an agent authorized by appointment or by law to receive service of process. FRCP 4(e).

   c.  *Serving an individual in a foreign country.* Unless federal law provides otherwise, an individual—other than a minor, an incompetent person, or a person whose waiver has been filed—may be served at a place not within any judicial district of the United States:

      i.  By any internationally agreed means of service that is reasonably calculated to give notice, such as those authorized by the Hague Convention on the Service Abroad of Judicial and Extrajudicial Documents;

      ii.  If there is no internationally agreed means, or if an international agreement allows but does not specify other means, by a method that is reasonably calculated to give notice:

- As prescribed by the foreign country's law for service in that country in an action in its courts of general jurisdiction;

- As the foreign authority directs in response to a letter rogatory or letter of request; or

- Unless prohibited by the foreign country's law, by: (1) delivering a copy of the summons and of the complaint to the individual personally; or (2) using any form of mail that the clerk addresses and sends to the individual and that requires a signed receipt; or

- By other means not prohibited by international agreement, as the court orders. FRCP 4(f).

   d.  *Serving a minor or an incompetent person.* A minor or an incompetent person in a judicial district of the United States must be served by following state law for serving a summons or like process on such a defendant in an action brought in the courts of general jurisdiction of the state where service is made. A minor or an incompetent person who is not within any judicial district of the United States must be served in the manner prescribed by FRCP 4(f)(2)(A), FRCP 4(f)(2)(B), or FRCP 4(f)(3). FRCP 4(g).

   e.  *Serving a corporation, partnership, or association.* Unless federal law provides otherwise or the defendant's waiver has been filed, a domestic or foreign corporation, or a partnership or other unincorporated association that is subject to suit under a common name, must be served:

      i.  In a judicial district of the United States:

- In the manner prescribed by FRCP 4(e)(1) for serving an individual; or

- By delivering a copy of the summons and of the complaint to an officer, a managing or general agent, or any other agent authorized by appointment or by law to receive service of process and—if the agent is one authorized by statute and the statute so requires—by also mailing a copy of each to the defendant; or

ii. At a place not within any judicial district of the United States, in any manner prescribed by FRCP 4(f) for serving an individual, except personal delivery under FRCP 4(f)(2)(C)(i). FRCP 4(h).

f. *Serving the United States and its agencies, corporations, officers, or employees*

   i. *United States.* To serve the United States, a party must:

- Deliver a copy of the summons and of the complaint to the United States attorney for the district where the action is brought—or to an assistant United States attorney or clerical employee whom the United States attorney designates in a writing filed with the court clerk—or send a copy of each by registered or certified mail to the civil-process clerk at the United States attorney's office;

- Send a copy of each by registered or certified mail to the Attorney General of the United States at Washington, D.C.; and

- If the action challenges an order of a nonparty agency or officer of the United States, send a copy of each by registered or certified mail to the agency or officer. FRCP 4(i)(1).

   ii. *Agency; Corporation; Officer or employee sued in an official capacity.* To serve a United States agency or corporation, or a United States officer or employee sued only in an official capacity, a party must serve the United States and also send a copy of the summons and of the complaint by registered or certified mail to the agency, corporation, officer, or employee. FRCP 4(i)(2).

   iii. *Officer or employee sued individually.* To serve a United States officer or employee sued in an individual capacity for an act or omission occurring in connection with duties performed on the United States' behalf (whether or not the officer or employee is also sued in an official capacity), a party must serve the United States and also serve the officer or employee under FRCP 4(e), FRCP 4(f), or FRCP 4(g). FRCP 4(i)(3).

   iv. *Extending time.* The court must allow a party a reasonable time to cure its failure to:

- Serve a person required to be served under FRCP 4(i)(2), if the party has served either the United States attorney or the Attorney General of the United States; or

- Serve the United States under FRCP 4(i)(3), if the party has served the United States officer or employee. FRCP 4(i)(4).

g. *Serving a foreign, state, or local government*

   i. *Foreign state.* A foreign state or its political subdivision, agency, or instrumentality must be served in accordance with 28 U.S.C.A. § 1608. FRCP 4(j)(1).

   ii. *State or local government.* A state, a municipal corporation, or any other state-created governmental organization that is subject to suit must be served by:

- Delivering a copy of the summons and of the complaint to its chief executive officer; or

- Serving a copy of each in the manner prescribed by that state's law for serving a summons or like process on such a defendant. FRCP 4(j)(2).

h. *Territorial limits of effective service*

   i. *In general.* Serving a summons or filing a waiver of service establishes personal jurisdiction over a defendant:

- Who is subject to the jurisdiction of a court of general jurisdiction in the state where the district court is located;

- Who is a party joined under FRCP 14 or FRCP 19 and is served within a judicial district of the United States and not more than one hundred (100) miles from where the summons was issued; or

- When authorized by a federal statute. FRCP 4(k)(1).

    ii. *Federal claim outside state-court jurisdiction.* For a claim that arises under federal law, serving a summons or filing a waiver of service establishes personal jurisdiction over a defendant if:

- The defendant is not subject to jurisdiction in any state's courts of general jurisdiction; and
- Exercising jurisdiction is consistent with the United States Constitution and laws. FRCP 4(k)(2).

  i. *Asserting jurisdiction over property or assets*

    i. *Federal law.* The court may assert jurisdiction over property if authorized by a federal statute. Notice to claimants of the property must be given as provided in the statute or by serving a summons under FRCP 4. FRCP 4(n)(1).

    ii. *State law.* On a showing that personal jurisdiction over a defendant cannot be obtained in the district where the action is brought by reasonable efforts to serve a summons under FRCP 4, the court may assert jurisdiction over the defendant's assets found in the district. Jurisdiction is acquired by seizing the assets under the circumstances and in the manner provided by state law in that district. FRCP 4(n)(2).

  j. *Proving service*

    i. *Affidavit required.* Unless service is waived, proof of service must be made to the court. Except for service by a United States marshal or deputy marshal, proof must be by the server's affidavit. FRCP 4(l)(1).

    ii. *Service outside the United States.* Service not within any judicial district of the United States must be proved as follows:

- If made under FRCP 4(f)(1), as provided in the applicable treaty or convention; or
- If made under FRCP 4(f)(2) or FRCP 4(f)(3), by a receipt signed by the addressee, or by other evidence satisfying the court that the summons and complaint were delivered to the addressee. FRCP 4(l)(2).

    iii. *Validity of service; Amending proof.* Failure to prove service does not affect the validity of service. The court may permit proof of service to be amended. FRCP 4(l)(3).

    iv. *Results of filing a waiver of service.* When the plaintiff files a waiver, proof of service is not required and FRCP 4 applies as if a summons and complaint had been served at the time of filing the waiver. FRCP 4(d)(4).

  k. *Service of other process.* For information on service of other process, refer to FRCP 4.1.

4. *Individual judge practices.* Refer to the Miscellaneous section of this document for information on individual judge practices on filing and serving documents.

## G. Hearings

1. There is no hearing contemplated in the federal statutes or rules for the complaint and summons.

## H. Forms

### 1. Official Federal Complaint and Summons Forms

  a. Rule 4 notice of a lawsuit and request to waive service of summons. FRCP 4.

### 2. Federal Complaint and Summons Forms

  a. Summons. 2 FEDFORMS § 3:23.

  b. Summons; With proof of service. 2 FEDFORMS § 3:24.

  c. Summons; Suit against officers of the United States. 2 FEDFORMS § 3:26.

  d. Request for summons. 2 FEDFORMS § 3:27.

  e. Civil cover sheet. 2 FEDFORMS § 3:29.

  f. Motion for appointment of person to serve process. 2 FEDFORMS § 3:30.

g.  Motion for appointment of United States marshal to serve process. 2 FEDFORMS § 3:34.

h.  Notice of lawsuit and request for waiver of service of summons and waiver of summons. 2 FEDFORMS § 3:36.

i.  Motion for payment of costs of personal service. 2 FEDFORMS § 3:37.

j.  Affidavit of personal service; Delivery to individual. 2 FEDFORMS § 3:54.

k.  Declaration of service; Delivery to individual. 2 FEDFORMS § 3:55.

l.  Declaration of service; Delivery at usual place of abode or residence. 2 FEDFORMS § 3:56.

m.  Declaration of service; Service on corporation; Delivery to officer. 2 FEDFORMS § 3:57.

n.  Declaration of service; Service on United States. 2 FEDFORMS § 3:69.

o.  Declaration of service; Service on officer of United States. 2 FEDFORMS § 3:71.

p.  Complaint. 2 FEDFORMS § 7:14.

q.  Introductory clause; Single claim stated. 2 FEDFORMS § 7:16.

r.  Introductory clause; Several claims stated in separate counts. 2 FEDFORMS § 7:18.

s.  Allegations on information and belief. 2 FEDFORMS § 7:19.

t.  General prayer for relief. 2 FEDFORMS § 7:21.

u.  Disparate treatment; Sex discrimination; Sexual harassment and constructive discharge. 2A FEDFORMS § 7:143.

v.  Against manufacturer for negligent design and manufacture. 2B FEDFORMS § 7:426.

w.  Complaint; Single count. FEDPROF § 1:68.

x.  Complaint; Multiple counts; With same jurisdictional basis. FEDPROF § 1:69.

y.  Complaint; Multiple counts; With different jurisdictional basis for each. FEDPROF § 1:70.

z.  Civil cover sheet; General form. FEDPROF § 1:144.

# I. Applicable Rules

1.  *Federal rules*

    a.  District court; Filing and miscellaneous fees; Rules of court. 28 U.S.C.A. § 1914.

    b.  Commencing an action. FRCP 3.

    c.  Summons. FRCP 4.

    d.  Serving and filing pleadings and other papers. FRCP 5.

    e.  Constitutional challenge to a statute; Notice, certification, and intervention. FRCP 5.1.

    f.  Privacy protection for filings made with the court. FRCP 5.2.

    g.  Computing and extending time; Time for motion papers. FRCP 6.

    h.  Pleadings allowed; Form of motions and other papers. FRCP 7.

    i.  Disclosure statement. FRCP 7.1.

    j.  General rules of pleading. FRCP 8.

    k.  Pleading special matters. FRCP 9.

    l.  Form of pleadings. FRCP 10.

    m.  Signing pleadings, motions, and other papers; Representations to the court; Sanctions. FRCP 11.

    n.  Joinder of claims. FRCP 18.

    o.  Required joinder of parties. FRCP 19.

    p.  Permissive joinder of parties. FRCP 20.

    q.  Misjoinder and nonjoinder of parties. FRCP 21.

    r.   Right to a jury trial; Demand. FRCP 38.

    s.   Determining foreign law. FRCP 44.1.

2.  *Local rules*

    a.   Night depository. NY R USDCTS&ED Civ Rule 1.2.

    b.   Duty of attorneys in related cases. NY R USDCTS&ED Civ Rule 1.6.

    c.   Fees of court clerks and reporters. NY R USDCTS&ED Civ Rule 1.7.

    d.   Electronic service and filing of documents. NY R USDCTS&ED Civ Rule 5.2.

    e.   Computation of time. NY R USDCTS&ED Civ Rule 6.4.

    f.   Disclosure statement. NY R USDCTS&ED Civ Rule 7.1.1.

    g.   Form of pleadings, motions, and other papers. NY R USDCTS&ED Civ Rule 11.1.

    h.   Submission of orders, judgments and decrees. NY R USDCTS&ED Civ Rule 77.1.

    i.   Court-annexed arbitration (Eastern District only). NY R USDCTS&ED Civ Rule 83.7.

    j.   Court-annexed mediation (Eastern District only). NY R USDCTS&ED Civ Rule 83.8.

    k.   Electronic case filing. NY R USDCTED Order 2004-08.

    l.   The August 2, 2004 amendment to the E-Government Act of 2002. NY R USDCTED Order 2004-09.

    m.   Categories and classification of cases; Information on cases and parties. NY R USDCTED Div. Bus., Rule 50.1.

## J.  Miscellaneous

**NOTE: Individual judges' rules may apply. For available judge-level information, refer to:**

DISTRICT JUDGE CAROL BAGLEY AMON: NY R USDCTED Amon-Practices.

DISTRICT JUDGE JOAN M. AZRACK: NY R USDCTED Azrack-Practices.

DISTRICT JUDGE JOSEPH F. BIANCO: NY R USDCTED Bianco-Practices.

DISTRICT JUDGE FREDERIC BLOCK: NY R USDCTED Block-Practices.

DISTRICT JUDGE MARGO K. BRODIE: NY R USDCTED Brodie-Practices.

DISTRICT JUDGE PAMELA K. CHEN: NY R USDCTED Chen-Practices.

DISTRICT JUDGE BRIAN M. COGAN: NY R USDCTED Cogan-Practices; NY R USDCTED Cogan-Pretrial.

DISTRICT JUDGE LaSHANN DeARCY HALL: NY R USDCTED DeArcy Hall-Practices.

DISTRICT JUDGE RAYMOND J. DEARIE: NY R USDCTED Dearie-Practices.

DISTRICT JUDGE ANN M. DONNELLY: NY R USDCTED Donnelly-Practices.

DISTRICT JUDGE SANDRA J. FEUERSTEIN: NY R USDCTED Feuerstein-Practices; NY R USDCTED Feuerstein-Pretrial.

DISTRICT JUDGE NICHOLAS G. GARAUIFIS: NY R USDCTED Garaufis-Practices; NY R USDCTED Garaufis-Pretrial.

DISTRICT JUDGE NINA GERSHON: NY R USDCTED Gershon-Practices.

DISTRICT JUDGE I. LEO GLASSER: NY R USDCTED Glasser-Practices; NY R USDCTED Glasser-Crim.

DISTRICT JUDGE DENIS R. HURLEY: NY R USDCTED Hurley-Practices; [NY R USDCTED Hurley-Pro Cooperation Info, as added by NY ORDER 16-4188, effective July 22, 2016]; [NY R USDCTED Hurley-Pro Cooperation Info Stay, as added by NY ORDER 16-4188, effective July 22, 2016].

DISTRICT JUDGE DORA L. IRIZARRY: NY R USDCTED Irizarry-Practices; NY R USDCTED Irizarry-Pretrial; NY R USDCTED Irizarry-Crim.

DISTRICT JUDGE STERLING JOHNSON, JR.: NY R USDCTED Johnson-Practices.

DISTRICT JUDGE EDWARD R. KORMAN: NY R USDCTED Korman-Practices; NY R USDCTED Korman-Pretrial.

DISTRICT JUDGE WILLIAM F. KUNTZ: NY R USDCTED Kuntz-Practices.

DISTRICT JUDGE KIYO A. MATSUMOTO: NY R USDCTED Matsumoto-Practices.

DISTRICT JUDGE ROSLYNN R. MAUSKOPF: NY R USDCTED Mauskopf-Practices; NY R USDCTED Mauskopf-Recusal.

DISTRICT JUDGE THOMAS C. PLATT: NY R USDCTED Platt-Practices.

DISTRICT JUDGE ALLYNE R. ROSS: NY R USDCTED Ross-Practices.

DISTRICT JUDGE JOANNA SEYBERT: NY R USDCTED Seybert-Practices.

DISTRICT JUDGE ARTHUR D. SPATT: NY R USDCTED Spatt-Practices.

DISTRICT JUDGE SANDRA L. TOWNES: NY R USDCTED Townes-Practices.

DISTRICT JUDGE ERIC N. VITALIANO: NY R USDCTED Vitaliano-Practices.

DISTRICT JUDGE JACK B. WEINSTEIN: NY R USDCTED Weinstein-Practices.

DISTRICT JUDGE LEONARD D. WEXLER: NY R USDCTED Wexler-Practices; NY R USDCTED Wexler-Rules.

MAGISTRATE JUDGE LOIS BLOOM: NY R USDCTED Bloom-Practices.

MAGISTRATE JUDGE GARY R. BROWN: NY R USDCTED Brown-Practices.

MAGISTRATE JUDGE MARILYN D. GO: NY R USDCTED Go-Practices.

MAGISTRATE JUDGE STEVEN M. GOLD: NY R USDCTED Gold-Practices.

MAGISTRATE JUDGE PEGGY KUO: NY R USDCTED Kuo-Practices; NY R USDCTED Kuo-Scheduling Order.

MAGISTRATE JUDGE ROBERT M. LEVY: NY R USDCTED Levy-Practices.

MAGISTRATE JUDGE ARLENE R. LINDSAY: NY R USDCTED Lindsay-Practices.

MAGISTRATE JUDGE STEVEN I. LOCKE: NY R USDCTED Locke-Practices.

MAGISTRATE JUDGE ROANNE L. MANN: NY R USDCTED Mann-Practices.

MAGISTRATE JUDGE JAMES ORENSTEIN: NY R USDCTED Jorenstein--Practices.

MAGISTRATE JUDGE VIKTOR V. POHORELSKY: NY R USDCTED Pohorelsky-Practices.

MAGISTRATE JUDGE CHERYL L. POLLAK: NY R USDCTED Pollak-Practices; NY R USDCTED Pollak-Pretrial.

MAGISTRATE JUDGE RAMON E. REYES, JR.: NY R USDCTED Reyes-Practices.

MAGISTRATE JUDGE VERA M. SCANLON: NY R USDCTED Scanlon-Practices.

MAGISTRATE JUDGE ANNE Y. SHIELDS: NY R USDCTED Shields-Practices.

MAGISTRATE JUDGE STEVEN L. TISCIONE: NY R USDCTED Tiscione-Practices.

MAGISTRATE JUDGE A. KATHLEEN TOMILINSON: NY R USDCTED Tomlinson-Practices.

# Pleadings
## Answer

**Document Last Updated September 2016**

A. **Checklist**

    (I) ❑ Matters to be considered by plaintiff

        (a) ❑ Required documents

            (1) ❑ Civil cover sheet

            (2) ❑ Complaint

      (3)  ❑  Summons

      (4)  ❑  Information sheet

      (5)  ❑  Notice, consent, and reference of a civil action to a magistrate judge

      (6)  ❑  Filing fee

      (7)  ❑  Affidavit proving service

  (b)  ❑  Supplemental documents

      (1)  ❑  Notice and request for waiver of service

      (2)  ❑  Notice of constitutional question

      (3)  ❑  Notice of issue concerning foreign law

      (4)  ❑  Nongovernmental corporate disclosure statement

      (5)  ❑  Notice regarding availability of electronic filing

      (6)  ❑  Certification of amount of damages

  (c)  ❑  Timing

      (1)  ❑  A civil action is commenced by filing a complaint with the court

      (2)  ❑  If a defendant is not served within ninety (90) days after the complaint is filed, the court—on motion or on its own after notice to the plaintiff—must dismiss the action without prejudice against that defendant or order that service be made within a specified time

(II)  ❑  Matters to be considered by defendant

  (a)  ❑  Required documents

      (1)  ❑  Answer

      (2)  ❑  Certificate of service

  (b)  ❑  Supplemental documents

      (1)  ❑  Waiver of the service of summons

      (2)  ❑  Notice of constitutional question

      (3)  ❑  Notice of issue concerning foreign law

      (4)  ❑  Nongovernmental corporate disclosure statement

      (5)  ❑  Certification of amount of damages

  (c)  ❑  Timing

      (1)  ❑  A defendant must serve an answer:

         (i)  ❑  Within twenty-one (21) days after being served with the summons and complaint; or

        (ii)  ❑  If it has timely waived service under FRCP 4(d), within sixty (60) days after the request for a waiver was sent, or within ninety (90) days after it was sent to the defendant outside any judicial district of the United States

      (2)  ❑  The United States, a United States agency, or a United States officer or employee sued only in an official capacity must serve an answer to a complaint, counterclaim, or crossclaim within sixty (60) days after service on the United States attorney

      (3)  ❑  A United States officer or employee sued in an individual capacity for an act or omission occurring in connection with duties performed on the United States' behalf must serve an answer to a complaint, counterclaim, or crossclaim within sixty (60) days after service on the officer or employee or service on the United States attorney, whichever is later

      (4)  ❑  Unless the court sets a different time, serving a motion under FRCP 12 alters these periods as follows:

         (i)  ❑  If the court denies the motion or postpones its disposition until trial, the responsive pleading must be served within fourteen (14) days after notice of the court's action; or

      (ii)  ❑  If the court grants a motion for a more definite statement, the responsive pleading must be served within fourteen (14) days after the more definite statement is served

  (5)  ❑  Defendant is given a reasonable time of at least thirty (30) days after a waiver of service request is sent—or at least sixty (60) days if sent to defendant outside any judicial district of the United States—to return the waiver

## B. Timing

1. *Answer.* Unless another time is specified by FRCP 12 or a federal statute. . .a defendant must serve an answer: (1) within twenty-one (21) days after being served with the summons and complaint; or (2) if it has timely waived service under FRCP 4(d), within sixty (60) days after the request for a waiver was sent, or within ninety (90) days after it was sent to the defendant outside any judicial district of the United States. FRCP 12(a)(1)(A).

   a. *Time to serve other responsive pleadings.* Unless another time is specified by FRCP 12 or a federal statute, the time for serving a responsive pleading is as follows:

      i. *Answer to counterclaim or crossclaim.* A party must serve an answer to a counterclaim or crossclaim within twenty-one (21) days after being served with the pleading that states the counterclaim or crossclaim. FRCP 12(a)(1)(B).

      ii. *Reply to an answer.* A party must serve a reply to an answer within twenty-one (21) days after being served with an order to reply, unless the order specifies a different time. FRCP 12(a)(1)(C).

   b. *United States and its agencies, officers, or employees sued in an official capacity.* The United States, a United States agency, or a United States officer or employee sued only in an official capacity must serve an answer to a complaint, counterclaim, or crossclaim within sixty (60) days after service on the United States attorney. FRCP 12(a)(2).

   c. *United States officers or employees sued in an individual capacity.* A United States officer or employee sued in an individual capacity for an act or omission occurring in connection with duties performed on the United States' behalf must serve an answer to a complaint, counterclaim, or crossclaim within sixty (60) days after service on the officer or employee or service on the United States attorney, whichever is later. FRCP 12(a)(3).

   d. *Effect of a FRCP 12 motion on the time to serve a responsive pleading.* Unless the court sets a different time, serving a motion under FRCP 12 alters the periods in FRCP 12(a) as follows:

      i. If the court denies the motion or postpones its disposition until trial, the responsive pleading must be served within fourteen (14) days after notice of the court's action; or

      ii. If the court grants a motion for a more definite statement, the responsive pleading must be served within fourteen (14) days after the more definite statement is served. FRCP 12(a)(4).

2. *Waiver of service.* The notice and request for waiver must give the defendant a reasonable time of at least thirty (30) days after the request was sent—or at least sixty (60) days if sent to defendant outside any judicial district of the United States—to return the waiver. FRCP 4(d)(1)(F).

   a. *Time to answer after a waiver.* A defendant who, before being served with process, timely returns a waiver need not serve an answer to the complaint until sixty (60) days after the request was sent—or until ninety (90) days after it was sent to the defendant outside any judicial district of the United States. FRCP 4(d)(3).

3. *Computation of time*

   a. *Computing time.* FRCP 6 applies in computing any time period specified in the Federal Rules of Civil Procedure, in any local rule or court order, or in any statute that does not specify a method of computing time. FRCP 6(a). In computing any period of time prescribed or allowed by the Local Civil Rules of the United States District Courts for the Southern and Eastern Districts of New York or the Local Admiralty and Maritime Rules, the provisions of FRCP 6 shall apply unless otherwise stated. NY R USDCTS&ED Civ Rule 6.4.

      i. *Period stated in days or a longer unit.* When the period is stated in days or a longer unit of time:

         • Exclude the day of the event that triggers the period;

- Count every day, including intermediate Saturdays, Sundays, and legal holidays; and

- Include the last day of the period, but if the last day is a Saturday, Sunday, or legal holiday, the period continues to run until the end of the next day that is not a Saturday, Sunday, or legal holiday. FRCP 6(a)(1). In the Local Civil Rules of the United States District Courts for the Southern and Eastern Districts of New York, as in the Federal Rules of Civil Procedure as amended effective December 1, 2009, Saturdays, Sundays, and legal holidays are no longer excluded in computing periods of time. If the last day of the period is a Saturday, Sunday, or legal holiday, the period continues to run until the end of the next day that is not a Saturday, Sunday, or legal holiday. NY R USDCTS&ED Civ Rule 6.4.

ii. *Period stated in hours.* When the period is stated in hours:

- Begin counting immediately on the occurrence of the event that triggers the period;

- Count every hour, including hours during intermediate Saturdays, Sundays, and legal holidays; and

- If the period would end on a Saturday, Sunday, or legal holiday, the period continues to run until the same time on the next day that is not a Saturday, Sunday, or legal holiday. FRCP 6(a)(2). In the Local Civil Rules of the United States District Courts for the Southern and Eastern Districts of New York, as in the Federal Rules of Civil Procedure as amended effective December 1, 2009, Saturdays, Sundays, and legal holidays are no longer excluded in computing periods of time. If the last day of the period is a Saturday, Sunday, or legal holiday, the period continues to run until the end of the next day that is not a Saturday, Sunday, or legal holiday. NY R USDCTS&ED Civ Rule 6.4.

iii. *Inaccessibility of the clerk's office.* Unless the court orders otherwise, if the clerk's office is inaccessible:

- On the last day for filing under FRCP 6(a)(1), then the time for filing is extended to the first accessible day that is not a Saturday, Sunday, or legal holiday; or

- During the last hour for filing under FRCP 6(a)(2), then the time for filing is extended to the same time on the first accessible day that is not a Saturday, Sunday, or legal holiday. FRCP 6(a)(3).

iv. *"Last day" defined.* Unless a different time is set by a statute, local rule, or court order, the last day ends:

- For electronic filing, at midnight in the court's time zone; and

- For filing by other means, when the clerk's office is scheduled to close. FRCP 6(a)(4).

v. *"Next day" defined.* The "next day" is determined by continuing to count forward when the period is measured after an event and backward when measured before an event. FRCP 6(a)(5).

vi. *"Legal holiday" defined.* "Legal holiday" means:

- The day set aside by statute for observing New Year's Day, Martin Luther King Jr.'s Birthday, Washington's Birthday, Memorial Day, Independence Day, Labor Day, Columbus Day, Veterans' Day, Thanksgiving Day, or Christmas Day;

- Any day declared a holiday by the President or Congress; and

- For periods that are measured after an event, any other day declared a holiday by the state where the district court is located. FRCP 6(a)(6).

b. *Extending time*

i. *In general.* When an act may or must be done within a specified time, the court may, for good cause, extend the time:

- With or without motion or notice if the court acts, or if a request is made, before the original time or its extension expires; or

- On motion made after the time has expired if the party failed to act because of excusable neglect. FRCP 6(b)(1).

    ii.   *Exceptions.* A court must not extend the time to act under FRCP 50(b), FRCP 50(d), FRCP 52(b), FRCP 59(b), FRCP 59(d), FRCP 59(e), and FRCP 60(b). FRCP 6(b)(2).

    iii.  Refer to the United States District Court for the Eastern District of New York KeyRules Motion for Continuance/Extension of Time document for more information on extending time.

  c.  *Additional time after certain kinds of service.* When a party may or must act within a specified time after service and service is made under FRCP 5(b)(2)(C), FRCP 5(b)(2)(D), FRCP 5(b)(2)(E), or FRCP 5(b)(2)(F), three (3) days are added after the period would otherwise expire under FRCP 6(a). FRCP 6(d). Overnight delivery service shall be deemed service by mail for purposes of FRCP 5 and FRCP 6. NY R USDCTS&ED Civ Rule 5.3.

4.  *Individual judge practices.* Refer to the Miscellaneous section of this document for information on individual judge practices on timing of documents.

## C. General Requirements

1.  *Pleading, generally*

  a.  *Pleadings allowed.* Only these pleadings are allowed: (1) a complaint; (2) an answer to a complaint; (3) an answer to a counterclaim designated as a counterclaim; (4) an answer to a crossclaim; (5) a third-party complaint; (6) an answer to a third-party complaint; and (7) if the court orders one, a reply to an answer. FRCP 7(a).

  b.  *Pleading to be concise and direct.* Each allegation must be simple, concise, and direct. No technical form is required. FRCP 8(d)(1).

  c.  *Alternative statements of a claim or defense.* A party may set out two or more statements of a claim or defense alternatively or hypothetically, either in a single count or defense or in separate ones. If a party makes alternative statements, the pleading is sufficient if any one of them is sufficient. FRCP 8(d)(2).

  d.  *Inconsistent claims or defenses.* A party may state as many separate claims or defenses as it has, regardless of consistency. FRCP 8(d)(3).

  e.  *Construing pleadings.* Pleadings must be construed so as to do justice. FRCP 8(e).

2.  *Pleading special matters*

  a.  *Capacity or authority to sue; Legal existence*

    i.   *In general.* Except when required to show that the court has jurisdiction, a pleading need not allege:

- A party's capacity to sue or be sued;
- A party's authority to sue or be sued in a representative capacity; or
- The legal existence of an organized association of persons that is made a party. FRCP 9(a)(1).

    ii.  *Raising those issues.* To raise any of those issues, a party must do so by a specific denial, which must state any supporting facts that are peculiarly within the party's knowledge. FRCP 9(a)(2).

  b.  *Fraud or mistake; Conditions of mind.* In alleging fraud or mistake, a party must state with particularity the circumstances constituting fraud or mistake. Malice, intent, knowledge, and other conditions of a person's mind may be alleged generally. FRCP 9(b).

  c.  *Conditions precedent.* In pleading conditions precedent, it suffices to allege generally that all conditions precedent have occurred or been performed. But when denying that a condition precedent has occurred or been performed, a party must do so with particularity. FRCP 9(c).

  d.  *Official document or act.* In pleading an official document or official act, it suffices to allege that the document was legally issued or the act legally done. FRCP 9(d).

  e.  *Judgment.* In pleading a judgment or decision of a domestic or foreign court, a judicial or quasi-judicial tribunal, or a board or officer, it suffices to plead the judgment or decision without showing jurisdiction to render it. FRCP 9(e).

f. *Time and place.* An allegation of time or place is material when testing the sufficiency of a pleading. FRCP 9(f).

g. *Special damages.* If an item of special damage is claimed, it must be specifically stated. FRCP 9(g).

h. *Admiralty or maritime claim*

    i. *How designated.* If a claim for relief is within the admiralty or maritime jurisdiction and also within the court's subject-matter jurisdiction on some other ground, the pleading may designate the claim as an admiralty or maritime claim for purposes of FRCP 14(c), FRCP 38(e), and FRCP 82 and the Supplemental Rules for Admiralty or Maritime Claims and Asset Forfeiture Actions. A claim cognizable only in the admiralty or maritime jurisdiction is an admiralty or maritime claim for those purposes, whether or not so designated. FRCP 9(h)(1).

    ii. *Designation for appeal.* A case that includes an admiralty or maritime claim within FRCP 9(h) is an admiralty case within 28 U.S.C.A. § 1292(a)(3). FRCP 9(h)(2).

3. *Answer*

a. *Defenses; Admissions and denials*

    i. *In general.* In responding to a pleading, a party must: (1) state in short and plain terms its defenses to each claim asserted against it; and (2) admit or deny the allegations asserted against it by an opposing party. FRCP 8(b)(1).

       • The purpose of an answer is to formulate issues by means of defenses addressed to the allegations of the complaint, and to give the plaintiff notice of the defenses he or she will be called upon to meet. FEDPROC § 62:70; Lopez v. U.S. Fidelity & Guaranty Co., 15 Alaska 633, 18 F.R.D. 59 (1955); Moriarty v. Curran, 18 F.R.D. 461 (S.D.N.Y. 1956).

       • An answer is adequate where it accomplishes these purposes, even if it contains general and specific denials and at the same time asserts additional facts by way of justification or explanation, and even if it sets forth conclusions of law. FEDPROC § 62:70; Johnston v. Jones, 178 F.2d 481 (3d Cir. 1949); Burke v. Mesta Mach. Co., 5 F.R.D. 134 (W.D.Pa. 1946).

    ii. *Denials; Responding to the substance.* A denial must fairly respond to the substance of the allegation. FRCP 8(b)(2).

    iii. *General and specific denials.* A party that intends in good faith to deny all the allegations of a pleading—including the jurisdictional grounds—may do so by a general denial. A party that does not intend to deny all the allegations must either specifically deny designated allegations or generally deny all except those specifically admitted. FRCP 8(b)(3).

    iv. *Denying part of an allegation.* A party that intends in good faith to deny only part of an allegation must admit the part that is true and deny the rest. FRCP 8(b)(4).

    v. *Lacking knowledge or information.* A party that lacks knowledge or information sufficient to form a belief about the truth of an allegation must so state, and the statement has the effect of a denial. FRCP 8(b)(5).

       • An answer merely stating that the defendant lacks knowledge to form a belief as to the plaintiff's allegations, and making no statement as to his or her lack of information, has been held to be insufficient, the court suggesting that the phrase might be used in an attempt to mask the defendant's inability to make a good-faith denial of the allegations. FEDPROC § 62:73; Gilbert v. Johnston, 127 F.R.D. 145 (N.D.Ill. 1989).

    vi. *Effect of failing to deny.* An allegation—other than one relating to the amount of damages—is admitted if a responsive pleading is required and the allegation is not denied. If a responsive pleading is not required, an allegation is considered denied or avoided. FRCP 8(b)(6).

b. *Affirmative defenses.* In responding to a pleading, a party must affirmatively state any avoidance or affirmative defense, including: (1) accord and satisfaction; (2) arbitration and award; (3) assumption of risk; (4) contributory negligence; (5) duress; (6) estoppel; (7) failure of consideration; (8) fraud;

(9) illegality; (10) injury by fellow servant; (11) laches; (12) license; (13) payment; (14) release; (15) res judicata; (16) statute of frauds; (17) statute of limitations; and (18) waiver. FRCP 8(c)(1).

    i. *Mistaken designation.* If a party mistakenly designates a defense as a counterclaim, or a counterclaim as a defense, the court must, if justice requires, treat the pleading as though it were correctly designated, and may impose terms for doing so. FRCP 8(c)(2).

  c. *How to present defenses.* Every defense to a claim for relief in any pleading must be asserted in the responsive pleading if one is required. But a party may assert the following defenses by motion: (1) lack of subject-matter jurisdiction; (2) lack of personal jurisdiction; (3) improper venue; (4) insufficient process; (5) insufficient service of process; (6) failure to state a claim upon which relief can be granted; and (7) failure to join a party under FRCP 19. FRCP 12(b).

    i. A motion asserting any of these defenses must be made before pleading if a responsive pleading is allowed. If a pleading sets out a claim for relief that does not require a responsive pleading, an opposing party may assert at trial any defense to that claim. FRCP 12(b).

    ii. Refer to the United States District Court for the Eastern District of New York KeyRules Motion to Dismiss for Lack of Subject Matter Jurisdiction, Motion to Dismiss for Lack of Personal Jurisdiction, Motion to Dismiss for Improper Venue, and Motion to Dismiss for Failure to State a Claim documents for more information on motions under FRCP 12(b)(1), FRCP 12(b)(2), FRCP 12(b)(3), and FRCP 12(b)(6).

  d. *Waiving and preserving certain defenses.* No defense or objection is waived by joining it with one or more other defenses or objections in a responsive pleading or in a motion. FRCP 12(b).

    i. *When some are waived.* A party waives any defense listed in FRCP 12(b)(2) through FRCP 12(b)(5) by:

- Omitting it from a motion in the circumstances described in FRCP 12(g)(2); or
- Failing to either: (1) make it by motion under FRCP 12; or (2) include it in a responsive pleading or in an amendment allowed by FRCP 15(a)(1) as a matter of course. FRCP 12(h)(1).

    ii. *When to raise others.* Failure to state a claim upon which relief can be granted, to join a person required by FRCP 19(b), or to state a legal defense to a claim may be raised:

- In any pleading allowed or ordered under FRCP 7(a);
- By a motion under FRCP 12(c); or
- At trial. FRCP 12(h)(2).

    iii. *Lack of subject matter jurisdiction.* If the court determines at any time that it lacks subject-matter jurisdiction, the court must dismiss the action. FRCP 12(h)(3).

4. *Counterclaim and crossclaim*

  a. *Compulsory counterclaim*

    i. *In general.* A pleading must state as a counterclaim any claim that—at the time of its service—the pleader has against an opposing party if the claim:

- Arises out of the transaction or occurrence that is the subject matter of the opposing party's claim; and
- Does not require adding another party over whom the court cannot acquire jurisdiction. FRCP 13(a)(1).

    ii. *Exceptions.* The pleader need not state the claim if:

- When the action was commenced, the claim was the subject of another pending action; or
- The opposing party sued on its claim by attachment or other process that did not establish personal jurisdiction over the pleader on that claim, and the pleader does not assert any counterclaim under FRCP 13. FRCP 13(a)(2).

  b. *Permissive counterclaim.* A pleading may state as a counterclaim against an opposing party any claim that is not compulsory. FRCP 13(b).

   c.  *Relief sought in a counterclaim.* A counterclaim need not diminish or defeat the recovery sought by the opposing party. It may request relief that exceeds in amount or differs in kind from the relief sought by the opposing party. FRCP 13(c).

   d.  *Counterclaim against the United States.* The Federal Rules of Civil Procedure do not expand the right to assert a counterclaim—or to claim a credit—against the United States or a United States officer or agency. FRCP 13(d).

   e.  *Counterclaim maturing or acquired after pleading.* The court may permit a party to file a supplemental pleading asserting a counterclaim that matured or was acquired by the party after serving an earlier pleading. FRCP 13(e).

   f.  *Crossclaim against a coparty.* A pleading may state as a crossclaim any claim by one party against a coparty if the claim arises out of the transaction or occurrence that is the subject matter of the original action or of a counterclaim, or if the claim relates to any property that is the subject matter of the original action. The crossclaim may include a claim that the coparty is or may be liable to the cross-claimant for all or part of a claim asserted in the action against the cross-claimant. FRCP 13(g).

   g.  *Joining additional parties.* FRCP 19 and FRCP 20 govern the addition of a person as a party to a counterclaim or crossclaim. FRCP 13(h).

   h.  *Separate trials; Separate judgments.* If the court orders separate trials under FRCP 42(b), it may enter judgment on a counterclaim or crossclaim under FRCP 54(b) when it has jurisdiction to do so, even if the opposing party's claims have been dismissed or otherwise resolved. FRCP 13(i).

5.  *Third-party practice*

   a.  *Timing of the summons and complaint.* A defending party may, as third-party plaintiff, serve a summons and complaint on a nonparty who is or may be liable to it for all or part of the claim against it. But the third-party plaintiff must, by motion, obtain the court's leave if it files the third-party complaint more than fourteen (14) days after serving its original answer. FRCP 14(a)(1).

   b.  *Third-party defendant's claims and defenses.* The person served with the summons and third-party complaint—the "third-party defendant":

      i.  Must assert any defense against the third-party plaintiff's claim under FRCP 12;

      ii.  Must assert any counterclaim against the third-party plaintiff under FRCP 13(a), and may assert any counterclaim against the third-party plaintiff under FRCP 13(b) or any crossclaim against another third-party defendant under FRCP 13(g);

      iii.  May assert against the plaintiff any defense that the third-party plaintiff has to the plaintiff's claim; and

      iv.  May also assert against the plaintiff any claim arising out of the transaction or occurrence that is the subject matter of the plaintiff's claim against the third-party plaintiff. FRCP 14(a)(2).

   c.  For more information on third-party practice, refer to FRCP 14.

6.  *Right to a jury trial; Demand*

   a.  *Right preserved.* The right of trial by jury as declared by U.S.C.A. Const. Amend. VII, or as provided by a federal statute, is preserved to the parties inviolate. FRCP 38(a).

   b.  *Demand.* On any issue triable of right by a jury, a party may demand a jury trial by:

      i.  Serving the other parties with a written demand—which may be included in a pleading—no later than fourteen (14) days after the last pleading directed to the issue is served; and

      ii.  Filing the demand in accordance with FRCP 5(d). FRCP 38(b).

   c.  *Specifying issues.* In its demand, a party may specify the issues that it wishes to have tried by a jury; otherwise, it is considered to have demanded a jury trial on all the issues so triable. If the party has demanded a jury trial on only some issues, any other party may—within fourteen (14) days after being served with the demand or within a shorter time ordered by the court—serve a demand for a jury trial on any other or all factual issues triable by jury. FRCP 38(c).

   d.  *Waiver; Withdrawal.* A party waives a jury trial unless its demand is properly served and filed. A proper demand may be withdrawn only if the parties consent. FRCP 38(d).

e. *Admiralty and maritime claims.* The rules in FRCP 38 do not create a right to a jury trial on issues in a claim that is an admiralty or maritime claim under FRCP 9(h). FRCP 38(e).

7. *Related cases.* It shall be the continuing duty of each attorney appearing in any civil or criminal case to bring promptly to the attention of the Court all facts which said attorney believes are relevant to a determination that said case and one or more pending civil or criminal cases should be heard by the same Judge, in order to avoid unnecessary duplication of judicial effort. As soon as the attorney becomes aware of such relationship, said attorney shall notify the Judges to whom the cases have been assigned. NY R USDCTS&ED Civ Rule 1.6(a). If counsel fails to comply with NY R USDCTS&ED Civ Rule 1.6(a), the Court may assess reasonable costs directly against counsel whose action has obstructed the effective administration of the Court's business. NY R USDCTS&ED Civ Rule 1.6(b).

8. *Alternative dispute resolution (ADR)*

   a. *Court-annexed arbitration*

      i. *Civil cases eligible for compulsory arbitration.* The Clerk of Court shall, as to all cases filed after January 1, 1986, designate and process for compulsory arbitration all civil cases (excluding Social Security cases, tax matters, prisoners' civil rights cases and any action based on an alleged violation of a right secured by the Constitution of the United States or if jurisdiction is based in whole or in part on 28 U.S.C.A. § 1343) wherein money damages only are being sought in an amount not in excess of one hundred fifty thousand dollars ($150,000) exclusive of interest and costs. NY R USDCTS&ED Civ Rule 83.7(d)(1).

         • The parties may by written stipulation agree that the Clerk of Court shall designate and process for court-annexed arbitration any civil case that is not subject to compulsory arbitration in NY R USDCTS&ED Civ Rule 83.7. NY R USDCTS&ED Civ Rule 83.7(d)(2).

         • For purposes of NY R USDCTS&ED Civ Rule 83.7 only, in all civil cases damages shall be presumed to be not in excess of one hundred fifty thousand dollars ($150,000) exclusive of interest and costs, unless: (1) counsel for plaintiff, at the time of filing the complaint, or in the event of the removal of a case from state court or transfer of a case from another district to this Court, within thirty (30) days of the docketing of the case in this district, files a certification with the Court that the damages sought exceed one hundred fifty thousand dollars ($150,000), exclusive of interest and costs; or (2) counsel for a defendant, at the time of filing a counterclaim or cross-claim files a certification with the court that the damages sought by the counter-claim or cross-claim exceed one hundred fifty thousand dollars ($150,000) exclusive of interest and costs. NY R USDCTS&ED Civ Rule 83.7(d)(3).

      ii. *Exemption from arbitration.* The Court shall, sua sponte, or on motion of a party, exempt any case from arbitration in which the objectives of arbitration would not be realized (1) because the case involves complex or novel issues, (2) because legal issues predominate over factual issues, or (3) for other good cause. NY R USDCTS&ED Civ Rule 83.7(e)(2). For information on applying for an exemption, refer to NY R USDCTS&ED Civ Rule 83.7

      iii. *Referral to arbitration.* Cases not originally designated as eligible for compulsory arbitration, but which in the discretion of the assigned Judge, are later found to qualify, may be referred to arbitration. A U.S. District Judge or a U.S. Magistrate Judge, in cases that exceed the arbitration ceiling of one hundred fifty thousand dollars ($150,000) exclusive of interest and costs, in their discretion, may suggest that the parties should consider arbitration. If the parties are agreeable, an appropriate consent form signed by all parties or their representatives may be entered and filed in the case prior to scheduling an arbitration hearing. NY R USDCTS&ED Civ Rule 83.7(e)(3).

      iv. For more information on arbitration, refer to NY R USDCTS&ED Civ Rule 83.7.

   b. *Court-annexed mediation.* Mediation is a process in which parties and counsel agree to meet with a neutral mediator trained to assist them in settling disputes. The mediator improves communication across party lines, helps parties articulate their interests and understand those of the other party, probes the strengths and weaknesses of each party's legal positions, and identifies areas of agreement and helps generate options for a mutually agreeable resolution to the dispute. In all cases, mediation provides an opportunity to explore a wide range of potential solutions and to address interests that may be outside the scope of the stated controversy or which could not be addressed by judicial action. A hallmark of mediation is its capacity to expand traditional settlement discussions and broaden resolution options, often by exploring litigant needs and interests that may be formally independent of the legal issues in controversy. NY R USDCTS&ED Civ Rule 83.8(a).

    i. *Eligible cases.* Judges and Magistrate Judges may designate civil cases for inclusion in the mediation program, and when doing so shall prepare an order to that effect. Alternatively, and subject to the availability of qualified mediators, the parties may consent to participation in the mediation program by preparing and executing a stipulation signed by all parties to the action and so-ordered by the Court. NY R USDCTS&ED Civ Rule 83.8(b)(1).

    ii. For more information on mediation, refer to NY R USDCTS&ED Civ Rule 83.8.

9. *Individual judge practices.* Refer to the Miscellaneous section of this document for information on individual judge practices on general requirements for documents.

## D. Documents

1. *Required documents*

   a. *Answer.* Refer to the General Requirements section of this document for information on the form and contents of the answer.

   b. *Certificate of service.* FRCP 5(d) requires that the person making service under FRCP 5 certify that service has been effected. FRCP 5(Advisory Committee Notes). Having such information on file may be useful for many purposes, including proof of service if an issue arises concerning the effectiveness of the service. FRCP 5(Advisory Committee Notes).

2. *Supplemental documents*

   a. *Waiver of the service of summons.* An individual, corporation, or association that is subject to service under FRCP 4(e), FRCP 4(f), or FRCP 4(h) has a duty to avoid unnecessary expenses of serving the summons. FRCP 4(d)(1). Waiving service of a summons does not waive any objection to personal jurisdiction or to venue. FRCP 4(d)(5). If a defendant located within the United States fails, without good cause, to sign and return a waiver requested by a plaintiff located within the United States, the court must impose on the defendant:

      i. The expenses later incurred in making service; and

      ii. The reasonable expenses, including attorney's fees, of any motion required to collect those service expenses. FRCP 4(d)(2).

   b. *Notice of constitutional question.* A party that files a pleading, written motion, or other paper drawing into question the constitutionality of a federal or state statute must promptly:

      i. *File notice.* File a notice of constitutional question stating the question and identifying the paper that raises it, if:

         • A federal statute is questioned and the parties do not include the United States, one of its agencies, or one of its officers or employees in an official capacity; or

         • A state statute is questioned and the parties do not include the state, one of its agencies, or one of its officers or employees in an official capacity; and

      ii. *Serve notice.* Serve the notice and paper on the Attorney General of the United States if a federal statute is questioned—or on the state attorney general if a state statute is questioned—either by certified or registered mail or by sending it to an electronic address designated by the attorney general for this purpose. FRCP 5.1(a).

      iii. *No forfeiture.* A party's failure to file and serve the notice, or the court's failure to certify, does not forfeit a constitutional claim or defense that is otherwise timely asserted. FRCP 5.1(d).

   c. *Notice of issue concerning foreign law.* A party who intends to raise an issue about a foreign country's law must give notice by a pleading or other writing. In determining foreign law, the court may consider any relevant material or source, including testimony, whether or not submitted by a party or admissible under the Federal Rules of Evidence. The court's determination must be treated as a ruling on a question of law. FRCP 44.1.

d. *Nongovernmental corporate disclosure statement.* To enable judges and magistrates to evaluate possible disqualification or recusal, counsel for a private (nongovernmental) party shall submit at the time of initial pleading a certificate identifying any corporate parent, subsidiaries, or affiliates of that party. NY R USDCTED Div. Bus., Rule 50.1(c).

   i. *Contents.* A nongovernmental corporate party must file two (2) copies of a disclosure statement that:

   - Identifies any parent corporation and any publicly held corporation owning ten percent (10%) or more of its stock; or

   - States that there is no such corporation. FRCP 7.1(a).

   ii. *Time to file; Supplemental filing.* A party must:

   - File the disclosure statement with its first appearance, pleading, petition, motion, response, or other request addressed to the court; and

   - Promptly file a supplemental statement if any required information changes. FRCP 7.1(b). For purposes of FRCP 7.1(b)(2), "promptly" shall mean "within fourteen days," that is, parties are required to file a supplemental disclosure statement within fourteen (14) days of the time there is any change in the information required in a disclosure statement filed pursuant to those rules. NY R USDCTS&ED Civ Rule 7.1.1.

e. *Certification of amount of damages.* For purposes of NY R USDCTS&ED Civ Rule 83.7 only, in all civil cases damages shall be presumed to be not in excess of one hundred fifty thousand dollars ($150,000) exclusive of interest and costs, unless counsel for a defendant, at the time of filing a counterclaim or cross-claim files a certification with the court that the damages sought by the counter-claim or cross-claim exceed one hundred fifty thousand dollars ($150,000) exclusive of interest and costs. NY R USDCTS&ED Civ Rule 83.7(d)(3)(B).

3. *Individual judge practices.* Refer to the Miscellaneous section of this document for information on individual judge practices on required documents.

## E. Format

1. *Form of documents*

   a. *Paper.* Every pleading, written motion, and other paper must: be plainly written, typed, printed, or copied without erasures or interlineations which materially deface it. NY R USDCTS&ED Civ Rule 11.1(a)(1).

   b. *Typeface, margin, and spacing.* The typeface, margins, and spacing of all documents presented for filing must meet the following requirements:

   i. All text must be twelve (12) point type or larger, except for text in footnotes which may be ten (10) point type;

   ii. All documents must have at least one (1) inch margins on all sides;

   iii. All text must be double-spaced, except for headings, text in footnotes, or block quotations, which may be single-spaced. NY R USDCTS&ED Civ Rule 11.1(b).

   c. *Caption; Names of parties.* Every pleading must have a caption with the court's name, a title, a file number, and a FRCP 7(a) designation. The title of the complaint must name all the parties; the title of other pleadings, after naming the first party on each side, may refer generally to other parties. FRCP 10(a). Every pleading, written motion, and other paper must: bear the docket number and the initials of the District Judge and any Magistrate Judge before whom the action or proceeding is pending, NY R USDCTS&ED Civ Rule 11.1(a)(2).

   d. *Paragraphs; Separate statements.* A party must state its claims or defenses in numbered paragraphs, each limited as far as practicable to a single set of circumstances. A later pleading may refer by number to a paragraph in an earlier pleading. If doing so would promote clarity, each claim founded on a separate transaction or occurrence—and each defense other than a denial—must be stated in a separate count or defense. FRCP 10(b).

e. *Adoption by reference; Exhibits.* A statement in a pleading may be adopted by reference elsewhere in the same pleading or in any other pleading or motion. A copy of a written instrument that is an exhibit to a pleading is a part of the pleading for all purposes. FRCP 10(c).

f. *Acceptance by the clerk.* The clerk must not refuse to file a paper solely because it is not in the form prescribed by the Federal Rules of Civil Procedure or by a local rule or practice. FRCP 5(d)(4).

2. *Signing of pleadings, motions and other papers*

   a. *Signature.* Every pleading, written motion, and other paper must be signed by at least one attorney of record in the attorney's name—or by a party personally if the party is unrepresented. The paper must state the signer's address, e-mail address, and telephone number. FRCP 11(a). Every pleading, written motion, and other paper must: have the name of each person signing it clearly printed or typed directly below the signature. NY R USDCTS&ED Civ Rule 11.1(a)(3).

      i. *No verification or accompanying affidavit required for pleadings.* Unless a rule or statute specifically states otherwise, a pleading need not be verified or accompanied by an affidavit. FRCP 11(a).

      ii. *Unsigned papers.* The court must strike an unsigned paper unless the omission is promptly corrected after being called to the attorney's or party's attention. FRCP 11(a).

   b. *Representations to the court.* By presenting to the court a pleading, written motion, or other paper—whether by signing, filing, submitting, or later advocating it—an attorney or unrepresented party certifies that to the best of the person's knowledge, information, and belief, formed after an inquiry reasonable under the circumstances:

      i. It is not being presented for any improper purpose, such as to harass, cause unnecessary delay, or needlessly increase the cost of litigation;

      ii. The claims, defenses, and other legal contentions are warranted by existing law or by a nonfrivolous argument for extending, modifying, or reversing existing law or for establishing new law;

      iii. The factual contentions have evidentiary support or, if specifically so identified, will likely have evidentiary support after a reasonable opportunity for further investigation or discovery; and

      iv. The denials of factual contentions are warranted on the evidence or, if specifically so identified, are reasonably based on belief or a lack of information. FRCP 11(b).

   c. *Sanctions.* If, after notice and a reasonable opportunity to respond, the court determines that FRCP 11(b) has been violated, the court may impose an appropriate sanction on any attorney, law firm, or party that violated FRCP 11(b) or is responsible for the violation. FRCP 11(c)(1). Refer to the United States District Court for the Eastern District of New York KeyRules Motion for Sanctions document for more information.

3. *Privacy protection for filings made with the court*

   a. *Redacted filings.* Unless the court orders otherwise, in an electronic or paper filing with the court that contains an individual's Social Security number, taxpayer-identification number, or birth date, the name of an individual known to be a minor, or a financial-account number, a party or nonparty making the filing may include only:

      i. The last four (4) digits of the Social Security number and taxpayer-identification number;

      ii. The year of the individual's birth;

      iii. The minor's initials; and

      iv. The last four (4) digits of the financial-account number. FRCP 5.2(a); NY R USDCTED Order 2004-09.

      v. In addition, exercise caution when filing documents that contain the following:

         • Personal identifying number, such as driver's license number;

- Medical records, treatment and diagnosis;
- Employment history;
- Individual financial information; and
- Proprietary or trade secret information. NY R USDCTED Order 2004-09.

b. *Exemptions from the redaction requirement.* The redaction requirement does not apply to the following:

    i. A financial-account number that identifies the property allegedly subject to forfeiture in a forfeiture proceeding;

    ii. The record of an administrative or agency proceeding;

    iii. The official record of a state-court proceeding;

    iv. The record of a court or tribunal, if that record was not subject to the redaction requirement when originally filed;

    v. A filing covered by FRCP 5.2(c) or FRCP 5.2(d); and

    vi. A pro se filing in an action brought under 28 U.S.C.A. § 2241, 28 U.S.C.A. § 2254, or 28 U.S.C.A. § 2255. FRCP 5.2(b).

c. *Limitations on remote access to electronic files; Social Security appeals and immigration cases.* Unless the court orders otherwise, in an action for benefits under the Social Security Act, and in an action or proceeding relating to an order of removal, to relief from removal, or to immigration benefits or detention, access to an electronic file is authorized as follows:

    i. The parties and their attorneys may have remote electronic access to any part of the case file, including the administrative record;

    ii. Any other person may have electronic access to the full record at the courthouse, but may have remote electronic access only to:

- The docket maintained by the court; and
- An opinion, order, judgment, or other disposition of the court, but not any other part of the case file or the administrative record. FRCP 5.2(c).

d. *Filings made under seal.* The court may order that a filing be made under seal without redaction. The court may later unseal the filing or order the person who made the filing to file a redacted version for the public record. FRCP 5.2(d).

e. *Protective orders.* For good cause, the court may by order in a case:

    i. Require redaction of additional information; or

    ii. Limit or prohibit a nonparty's remote electronic access to a document filed with the court. FRCP 5.2(e).

f. *Option for additional unredacted filing under seal.* A person making a redacted filing may also file an unredacted copy under seal. The court must retain the unredacted copy as part of the record. FRCP 5.2(f); NY R USDCTED Order 2004-09. The unredacted version of the document or the reference list shall be retained by the court as part of the record. The court may, however, still require the party to file a redacted copy for the public file. NY R USDCTED Order 2004-09.

g. *Option for filing a reference list.* A filing that contains redacted information may be filed together with a reference list that identifies each item of redacted information and specifies an appropriate identifier that uniquely corresponds to each item listed. The list must be filed under seal and may be amended as of right. Any reference in the case to a listed identifier will be construed to refer to the corresponding item of information. FRCP 5.2(g); NY R USDCTED Order 2004-09. The unredacted version of the document or the reference list shall be retained by the court as part of the record. The court may, however, still require the party to file a redacted copy for the public file. NY R USDCTED Order 2004-09.

h. *Responsibility for redaction.* The responsibility for redacting these personal identifiers rests solely with counsel and the parties. The Clerk will not review each pleading for compliance with NY R USDCTED Order 2004-09. NY R USDCTED Order 2004-09.

    i.   Counsel is strongly urged to share this notice with all clients so that an informed decision about the inclusion of certain materials may be made. If a redacted document is filed, it is the sole responsibility of counsel and the parties to be sure that all pleadings comply with the rules of this court requiring redaction of personal data identifiers. The clerk will not review each pleading for redaction. NY R USDCTED Order 2004-09.

  i.   *Waiver of protection of identifiers.* A person waives the protection of FRCP 5.2(a) as to the person's own information by filing it without redaction and not under seal. FRCP 5.2(h).

4.  *Individual judge practices.* Refer to the Miscellaneous section of this document for information on individual judge practices on formatting documents.

## F.  Filing and Service Requirements

1.  *Filing requirements.* Any paper after the complaint that is required to be served—together with a certificate of service—must be filed within a reasonable time after service. FRCP 5(d)(1).

  a.  *How filing is made; In general.* A paper is filed by delivering it:

    i.   To the clerk; or

    ii.  To a judge who agrees to accept it for filing, and who must then note the filing date on the paper and promptly send it to the clerk. FRCP 5(d)(2).

  b.  *Night depository.* A night depository with an automatic date stamp shall be maintained. . .by the Clerk of the Eastern District in the Brooklyn Courthouse. After regular business hours, papers for the District Court only may be deposited in the night depository. Such papers will be considered as having been filed in the District Court as of the date stamped thereon, which shall be deemed presumptively correct. NY R USDCTS&ED Civ Rule 1.2.

  c.  *Electronic filing*

    i.   *Authorization of electronic filing program.* A court may, by local rule, allow papers to be filed, signed, or verified by electronic means that are consistent with any technical standards established by the Judicial Conference of the United States. A local rule may require electronic filing only if reasonable exceptions are allowed. A paper filed electronically in compliance with a local rule is a written paper for purposes of the Federal Rules of Civil Procedure. FRCP 5(d)(3).

       •  Parties serving and filing papers shall follow the instructions regarding Electronic Case Filing (ECF) published on the website of each respective Court. A paper served and filed by electronic means in accordance with such instructions is, for purposes of FRCP 5, served and filed in compliance with the Local Civil Rules of the Southern and Eastern Districts of New York. NY R USDCTS&ED Civ Rule 5.2(a). Parties have an obligation to review the Court's actual order, decree, or judgment (on ECF), which controls, and should not rely on the description on the docket or in the ECF Notice of Electronic Filing (NEF). NY R USDCTS&ED Civ Rule 5.2(c).

    ii.  *Mandatory electronic filing.* Beginning on August 2, 2004, electronic case filing will be mandatory for all civil cases other than pro se cases. NY R USDCTED Order 2004-08.

       •  *Letter-motions and letters addressed to the court.* Subject to the instructions regarding ECF published on the website of each respective Court and any pertinent Individual Judge's Practices, letter-motions permitted by NY R USDCTS&ED Civ Rule 7.1(d) and letters addressed to the Court (but not letters between the parties) may be filed via ECF. NY R USDCTS&ED Civ Rule 5.2(b).

       •  *Proposed orders, judgments and decrees.* Proposed orders, judgments and decrees shall be presented as directed by the ECF rules published on the website of each respective Court. NY R USDCTS&ED Civ Rule 77.1. For more information, refer to NY R USDCTS&ED Civ Rule 77.1.

       •  *Request for exemption.* Requests by attorneys for an exemption to the mandatory policy will be considered for good cause hardship reasons only, and will be reviewed on an individual basis by the assigned United States Magistrate Judge. The Clerk's Office provides an electronic filing training program to assist attorneys filing electronically. Before seeking a hardship exemption, attorneys are advised to participate in the training program or otherwise seek the assistance of the Clerk's Office. NY R USDCTED Order 2004-08.

iii.  For more information on electronic filing, refer to the court's website.

2. *Service requirements*

  a. *Service; When required*

  i.  *In general.* Unless the Federal Rules of Civil Procedure provide otherwise, each of the following papers must be served on every party:

  - An order stating that service is required;

  - A pleading filed after the original complaint, unless the court orders otherwise under FRCP 5(c) because there are numerous defendants;

  - A discovery paper required to be served on a party, unless the court orders otherwise;

  - A written motion, except one that may be heard ex parte; and

  - A written notice, appearance, demand, or offer of judgment, or any similar paper. FRCP 5(a)(1).

  ii.  *If a party fails to appear.* No service is required on a party who is in default for failing to appear. But a pleading that asserts a new claim for relief against such a party must be served on that party under FRCP 4. FRCP 5(a)(2).

  iii.  *Seizing property.* If an action is begun by seizing property and no person is or need be named as a defendant, any service required before the filing of an appearance, answer, or claim must be made on the person who had custody or possession of the property when it was seized. FRCP 5(a)(3).

  b. *Service; How made*

  i.  *Serving an attorney.* If a party is represented by an attorney, service under FRCP 5 must be made on the attorney unless the court orders service on the party. FRCP 5(b)(1).

  ii.  *Service in general.* A paper is served under FRCP 5 by:

  - Handing it to the person;

  - Leaving it: (1) at the person's office with a clerk or other person in charge or, if no one is in charge, in a conspicuous place in the office; or (2) if the person has no office or the office is closed, at the person's dwelling or usual place of abode with someone of suitable age and discretion who resides there;

  - Mailing it to the person's last known address—in which event service is complete upon mailing;

  - Leaving it with the court clerk if the person has no known address;

  - Sending it by electronic means if the person consented in writing—in which event service is complete upon transmission, but is not effective if the serving party learns that it did not reach the person to be served; or

  - Delivering it by any other means that the person consented to in writing—in which event service is complete when the person making service delivers it to the agency designated to make delivery. FRCP 5(b)(2).

  iii.  *Service by overnight delivery.* Service upon an attorney may be made by overnight delivery service. "Overnight delivery service" means any delivery service which regularly accepts items for overnight delivery. Overnight delivery service shall be deemed service by mail for purposes of FRCP 5 and FRCP 6. NY R USDCTS&ED Civ Rule 5.3.

    iv.  *Service by electronic means.* Parties serving and filing papers shall follow the instructions regarding Electronic Case Filing (ECF) published on the website of each respective Court. A paper served and filed by electronic means in accordance with such instructions is, for purposes of FRCP 5, served and filed in compliance with the Local Civil Rules of the United States District Courts for the Southern and Eastern Districts of New York. NY R USDCTS&ED Civ Rule 5.2(a). Parties have an obligation to review the Court's actual order, decree, or judgment (on ECF), which controls, and should not rely on the description on the docket or in the ECF Notice of Electronic Filing (NEF). NY R USDCTS&ED Civ Rule 5.2(c).

    v.  *Using court facilities.* If a local rule so authorizes, a party may use the court's transmission facilities to make service under FRCP 5(b)(2)(E). FRCP 5(b)(3).

  c.  *Serving numerous defendants*

    i.  *In general.* If an action involves an unusually large number of defendants, the court may, on motion or on its own, order that:

- Defendants' pleadings and replies to them need not be served on other defendants;
- Any crossclaim, counterclaim, avoidance, or affirmative defense in those pleadings and replies to them will be treated as denied or avoided by all other parties; and
- Filing any such pleading and serving it on the plaintiff constitutes notice of the pleading to all parties. FRCP 5(c)(1).

    ii.  *Notifying parties.* A copy of every such order must be served on the parties as the court directs. FRCP 5(c)(2).

3.  *Individual judge practices.* Refer to the Miscellaneous section of this document for information on individual judge practices on filing and serving documents.

## G. Hearings

1.  *Hearing on FRCP 12 defenses before trial.* If a party so moves, any defense listed in FRCP 12(b)(1) through FRCP 12(b)(7)—whether made in a pleading or by motion—and a motion under FRCP 12(c) must be heard and decided before trial unless the court orders a deferral until trial. FRCP 12(i).

2.  *Individual judge practices.* Refer to the Miscellaneous section of this document for information on individual judge practices on hearings.

## H. Forms

### 1. Official Federal Answer Forms

  a.  Rule 4 waiver of the service of summons. FRCP 4.

### 2. Federal Answer Forms

  a.  Generally. 2B FEDFORMS § 8:10.

  b.  Introduction to separate defenses. 2B FEDFORMS § 8:11.

  c.  Presenting defenses. 2B FEDFORMS § 8:12.

  d.  With counterclaim for interpleader. 2B FEDFORMS § 8:13.

  e.  Denials and admissions. 2B FEDFORMS § 8:14.

  f.  Denials, admissions and affirmative defenses. 2B FEDFORMS § 8:15.

  g.  Separate answer of two defendants; Duty of fair representation. 2B FEDFORMS § 8:16.

  h.  Separate answer of third defendant. 2B FEDFORMS § 8:17.

  i.  Reciting paragraphs and subparagraphs of complaint; Account malpractice. 2B FEDFORMS § 8:18.

  j.  One of multiple defendants. 2B FEDFORMS § 8:21.

  k.  Answer to complaint for employment discrimination. 2B FEDFORMS § 8:22.

  l.  Denial of particular averment. 2B FEDFORMS § 8:24.

  m.  Admission of particular averment. 2B FEDFORMS § 8:25.

n.  Denial of all averments of paragraph. 2B FEDFORMS § 8:26.

o.  Admission of all averments of paragraph. 2B FEDFORMS § 8:27.

p.  Denial in part and admission in part of paragraph. 2B FEDFORMS § 8:28.

q.  General denial. 2B FEDFORMS § 8:29.

r.  Qualified general denial. 2B FEDFORMS § 8:30.

s.  Denial of knowledge or information sufficient to form a belief. 2B FEDFORMS § 8:31.

t.  Denial of jurisdictional allegations; Jurisdictional amount. 2B FEDFORMS § 8:32.

u.  Denial of jurisdictional allegations; Federal question. 2B FEDFORMS § 8:34.

v.  Denial of jurisdictional allegations; Diversity of citizenship. 2B FEDFORMS § 8:37.

w.  Contributory negligence. 2B FEDFORMS § 8:58.

x.  Fraud. 2B FEDFORMS § 8:74.

y.  Mistake. 2B FEDFORMS § 8:85.

z.  Statute of limitations. 2B FEDFORMS § 8:103.

## I. Applicable Rules

1.  *Federal rules*

    a.  Summons. FRCP 4.

    b.  Serving and filing pleadings and other papers. FRCP 5.

    c.  Constitutional challenge to a statute; Notice, certification, and intervention. FRCP 5.1.

    d.  Privacy protection for filings made with the court. FRCP 5.2.

    e.  Computing and extending time; Time for motion papers. FRCP 6.

    f.  Pleadings allowed; Form of motions and other papers. FRCP 7.

    g.  Disclosure statement. FRCP 7.1.

    h.  General rules of pleading. FRCP 8.

    i.  Pleading special matters. FRCP 9.

    j.  Form of pleadings. FRCP 10.

    k.  Signing pleadings, motions, and other papers; Representations to the court; Sanctions. FRCP 11.

    l.  Defenses and objections; When and how presented; Motion for judgment on the pleadings; Consolidating motions; Waiving defenses; Pretrial hearing. FRCP 12.

    m.  Counterclaim and crossclaim. FRCP 13.

    n.  Third-party practice. FRCP 14.

    o.  Right to a jury trial; Demand. FRCP 38.

    p.  Determining foreign law. FRCP 44.1.

2.  *Local rules*

    a.  Night depository. NY R USDCTS&ED Civ Rule 1.2.

    b.  Duty of attorneys in related cases. NY R USDCTS&ED Civ Rule 1.6.

    c.  Electronic service and filing of documents. NY R USDCTS&ED Civ Rule 5.2.

    d.  Service by overnight delivery. NY R USDCTS&ED Civ Rule 5.3.

    e.  Computation of time. NY R USDCTS&ED Civ Rule 6.4.

    f.  Disclosure statement. NY R USDCTS&ED Civ Rule 7.1.1.

    g.  Form of pleadings, motions, and other papers. NY R USDCTS&ED Civ Rule 11.1.

    h.  Submission of orders, judgments and decrees. NY R USDCTS&ED Civ Rule 77.1.

    i.    Court-annexed arbitration (Eastern District only). NY R USDCTS&ED Civ Rule 83.7.

    j.    Court-annexed mediation (Eastern District only). NY R USDCTS&ED Civ Rule 83.8.

    k.    Electronic case filing. NY R USDCTED Order 2004-08.

    l.    The August 2, 2004 amendment to the E-Government Act of 2002. NY R USDCTED Order 2004-09.

    m.    Categories and classification of cases; Information on cases and parties. NY R USDCTED Div. Bus., Rule 50.1.

## J. Miscellaneous

**NOTE: Individual judges' rules may apply. For available judge-level information, refer to:**

DISTRICT JUDGE CAROL BAGLEY AMON: NY R USDCTED Amon-Practices.

DISTRICT JUDGE JOAN M. AZRACK: NY R USDCTED Azrack-Practices.

DISTRICT JUDGE JOSEPH F. BIANCO: NY R USDCTED Bianco-Practices.

DISTRICT JUDGE FREDERIC BLOCK: NY R USDCTED Block-Practices.

DISTRICT JUDGE MARGO K. BRODIE: NY R USDCTED Brodie-Practices.

DISTRICT JUDGE PAMELA K. CHEN: NY R USDCTED Chen-Practices.

DISTRICT JUDGE BRIAN M. COGAN: NY R USDCTED Cogan-Practices; NY R USDCTED Cogan-Pretrial.

DISTRICT JUDGE LaSHANN DeARCY HALL: NY R USDCTED DeArcy Hall-Practices.

DISTRICT JUDGE RAYMOND J. DEARIE: NY R USDCTED Dearie-Practices.

DISTRICT JUDGE ANN M. DONNELLY: NY R USDCTED Donnelly-Practices.

DISTRICT JUDGE SANDRA J. FEUERSTEIN: NY R USDCTED Feuerstein-Practices; NY R USDCTED Feuerstein-Pretrial.

DISTRICT JUDGE NICHOLAS G. GARAUIFIS: NY R USDCTED Garaufis-Practices; NY R USDCTED Garaufis-Pretrial.

DISTRICT JUDGE NINA GERSHON: NY R USDCTED Gershon-Practices.

DISTRICT JUDGE I. LEO GLASSER: NY R USDCTED Glasser-Practices; NY R USDCTED Glasser-Crim.

DISTRICT JUDGE DENIS R. HURLEY: NY R USDCTED Hurley-Practices; [NY R USDCTED Hurley-Pro Cooperation Info, as added by NY ORDER 16-4188, effective July 22, 2016]; [NY R USDCTED Hurley-Pro Cooperation Info Stay, as added by NY ORDER 16-4188, effective July 22, 2016].

DISTRICT JUDGE DORA L. IRIZARRY: NY R USDCTED Irizarry-Practices; NY R USDCTED Irizarry-Pretrial; NY R USDCTED Irizarry-Crim.

DISTRICT JUDGE STERLING JOHNSON, JR.: NY R USDCTED Johnson-Practices.

DISTRICT JUDGE EDWARD R. KORMAN: NY R USDCTED Korman-Practices; NY R USDCTED Korman-Pretrial.

DISTRICT JUDGE WILLIAM F. KUNTZ: NY R USDCTED Kuntz-Practices.

DISTRICT JUDGE KIYO A. MATSUMOTO: NY R USDCTED Matsumoto-Practices.

DISTRICT JUDGE ROSLYNN R. MAUSKOPF: NY R USDCTED Mauskopf-Practices; NY R USDCTED Mauskopf-Recusal.

DISTRICT JUDGE THOMAS C. PLATT: NY R USDCTED Platt-Practices.

DISTRICT JUDGE ALLYNE R. ROSS: NY R USDCTED Ross-Practices.

DISTRICT JUDGE JOANNA SEYBERT: NY R USDCTED Seybert-Practices.

DISTRICT JUDGE ARTHUR D. SPATT: NY R USDCTED Spatt-Practices.

DISTRICT JUDGE SANDRA L. TOWNES: NY R USDCTED Townes-Practices.

DISTRICT JUDGE ERIC N. VITALIANO: NY R USDCTED Vitaliano-Practices.

DISTRICT JUDGE JACK B. WEINSTEIN: NY R USDCTED Weinstein-Practices.

DISTRICT JUDGE LEONARD D. WEXLER: NY R USDCTED Wexler-Practices; NY R USDCTED Wexler-Rules.

MAGISTRATE JUDGE LOIS BLOOM: NY R USDCTED Bloom-Practices.

MAGISTRATE JUDGE GARY R. BROWN: NY R USDCTED Brown-Practices.

MAGISTRATE JUDGE MARILYN D. GO: NY R USDCTED Go-Practices.

MAGISTRATE JUDGE STEVEN M. GOLD: NY R USDCTED Gold-Practices.

MAGISTRATE JUDGE PEGGY KUO: NY R USDCTED Kuo-Practices; NY R USDCTED Kuo-Scheduling Order.

MAGISTRATE JUDGE ROBERT M. LEVY: NY R USDCTED Levy-Practices.

MAGISTRATE JUDGE ARLENE R. LINDSAY: NY R USDCTED Lindsay-Practices.

MAGISTRATE JUDGE STEVEN I. LOCKE: NY R USDCTED Locke-Practices.

MAGISTRATE JUDGE ROANNE L. MANN: NY R USDCTED Mann-Practices.

MAGISTRATE JUDGE JAMES ORENSTEIN: NY R USDCTED Jorenstein--Practices.

MAGISTRATE JUDGE VIKTOR V. POHORELSKY: NY R USDCTED Pohorelsky-Practices.

MAGISTRATE JUDGE CHERYL L. POLLAK: NY R USDCTED Pollak-Practices; NY R USDCTED Pollak-Pretrial.

MAGISTRATE JUDGE RAMON E. REYES, JR.: NY R USDCTED Reyes-Practices.

MAGISTRATE JUDGE VERA M. SCANLON: NY R USDCTED Scanlon-Practices.

MAGISTRATE JUDGE ANNE Y. SHIELDS: NY R USDCTED Shields-Practices.

MAGISTRATE JUDGE STEVEN L. TISCIONE: NY R USDCTED Tiscione-Practices.

MAGISTRATE JUDGE A. KATHLEEN TOMILINSON: NY R USDCTED Tomlinson-Practices.

# Pleadings
# Amended Pleading

## Document Last Updated September 2016

**A. Checklist**

(I)  ❑ Matters to be considered by plaintiff or defendant

    (a)  ❑ Required documents

        (1)  ❑ Amended pleading

        (2)  ❑ Certificate of service

    (b)  ❑ Supplemental documents

        (1)  ❑ Notice of constitutional question

        (2)  ❑ Notice of issue concerning foreign law

    (c)  ❑ Timing

        (1)  ❑ A party may amend its pleading once as a matter of course within:

            (i)  ❑ Twenty-one (21) days after serving it, or

            (ii)  ❑ If the pleading is one to which a responsive pleading is required, twenty-one (21) days after service of a responsive pleading or twenty-one (21) days after service of a motion under FRCP 12(b), FRCP 12(e), or FRCP 12(f), whichever is earlier

**B. Timing**

1. *Amended pleading*

   a. *Amending as a matter of course.* A party may amend its pleading once as a matter of course within:

      i. Twenty-one (21) days after serving it, or

      ii. If the pleading is one to which a responsive pleading is required, twenty-one (21) days after service of a responsive pleading or twenty-one (21) days after service of a motion under FRCP 12(b), FRCP 12(e), or FRCP 12(f), whichever is earlier. FRCP 15(a)(1).

   b. *Extension of time.* If the time for serving the responsive pleading is extended by a motion for enlargement of time under FRCP 6(b), or by a stipulation, the period for amending as of right also may be enlarged. FPP § 1480.

   c. *Other amendments.* In all other cases, a party may amend its pleading only with the opposing party's written consent or the court's leave. The court should freely give leave when justice so requires. FRCP 15(a)(2). Refer to the United States District Court for the Eastern District of New York KeyRules Motion for Leave to Amend document for more information.

2. *Time to respond to an amended pleading.* Unless the court orders otherwise, any required response to an amended pleading must be made within the time remaining to respond to the original pleading or within fourteen (14) days after service of the amended pleading, whichever is later. FRCP 15(a)(3).

3. *Computation of time*

   a. *Computing time.* FRCP 6 applies in computing any time period specified in the Federal Rules of Civil Procedure, in any local rule or court order, or in any statute that does not specify a method of computing time. FRCP 6(a). In computing any period of time prescribed or allowed by the Local Civil Rules of the United States District Courts for the Southern and Eastern Districts of New York or the Local Admiralty and Maritime Rules, the provisions of FRCP 6 shall apply unless otherwise stated. NY R USDCTS&ED Civ Rule 6.4.

      i. *Period stated in days or a longer unit.* When the period is stated in days or a longer unit of time:

         • Exclude the day of the event that triggers the period;

         • Count every day, including intermediate Saturdays, Sundays, and legal holidays; and

         • Include the last day of the period, but if the last day is a Saturday, Sunday, or legal holiday, the period continues to run until the end of the next day that is not a Saturday, Sunday, or legal holiday. FRCP 6(a)(1). In the Local Civil Rules of the United States District Courts for the Southern and Eastern Districts of New York, as in the Federal Rules of Civil Procedure as amended effective December 1, 2009, Saturdays, Sundays, and legal holidays are no longer excluded in computing periods of time. If the last day of the period is a Saturday, Sunday, or legal holiday, the period continues to run until the end of the next day that is not a Saturday, Sunday, or legal holiday. NY R USDCTS&ED Civ Rule 6.4.

      ii. *Period stated in hours.* When the period is stated in hours:

         • Begin counting immediately on the occurrence of the event that triggers the period;

         • Count every hour, including hours during intermediate Saturdays, Sundays, and legal holidays; and

         • If the period would end on a Saturday, Sunday, or legal holiday, the period continues to run until the same time on the next day that is not a Saturday, Sunday, or legal holiday. FRCP 6(a)(2). In the Local Civil Rules of the United States District Courts for the Southern and Eastern Districts of New York, as in the Federal Rules of Civil Procedure as amended effective December 1, 2009, Saturdays, Sundays, and legal holidays are no longer excluded in computing periods of time. If the last day of the period is a Saturday, Sunday, or legal holiday, the period continues to run until the end of the next day that is not a Saturday, Sunday, or legal holiday. NY R USDCTS&ED Civ Rule 6.4.

     iii.  *Inaccessibility of the clerk's office.* Unless the court orders otherwise, if the clerk's office is inaccessible:

- On the last day for filing under FRCP 6(a)(1), then the time for filing is extended to the first accessible day that is not a Saturday, Sunday, or legal holiday; or

- During the last hour for filing under FRCP 6(a)(2), then the time for filing is extended to the same time on the first accessible day that is not a Saturday, Sunday, or legal holiday. FRCP 6(a)(3).

     iv.  *"Last day" defined.* Unless a different time is set by a statute, local rule, or court order, the last day ends:

- For electronic filing, at midnight in the court's time zone; and

- For filing by other means, when the clerk's office is scheduled to close. FRCP 6(a)(4).

     v.  *"Next day" defined.* The "next day" is determined by continuing to count forward when the period is measured after an event and backward when measured before an event. FRCP 6(a)(5).

     vi.  *"Legal holiday" defined.* "Legal holiday" means:

- The day set aside by statute for observing New Year's Day, Martin Luther King Jr.'s Birthday, Washington's Birthday, Memorial Day, Independence Day, Labor Day, Columbus Day, Veterans' Day, Thanksgiving Day, or Christmas Day;

- Any day declared a holiday by the President or Congress; and

- For periods that are measured after an event, any other day declared a holiday by the state where the district court is located. FRCP 6(a)(6).

  b.  *Extending time*

     i.  *In general.* When an act may or must be done within a specified time, the court may, for good cause, extend the time:

- With or without motion or notice if the court acts, or if a request is made, before the original time or its extension expires; or

- On motion made after the time has expired if the party failed to act because of excusable neglect. FRCP 6(b)(1).

     ii.  *Exceptions.* A court must not extend the time to act under FRCP 50(b), FRCP 50(d), FRCP 52(b), FRCP 59(b), FRCP 59(d), FRCP 59(e), and FRCP 60(b). FRCP 6(b)(2).

     iii.  Refer to the United States District Court for the Eastern District of New York KeyRules Motion for Continuance/Extension of Time document for more information on extending time.

  c.  *Additional time after certain kinds of service.* When a party may or must act within a specified time after service and service is made under FRCP 5(b)(2)(C), FRCP 5(b)(2)(D), FRCP 5(b)(2)(E), or FRCP 5(b)(2)(F), three (3) days are added after the period would otherwise expire under FRCP 6(a). FRCP 6(d). Overnight delivery service shall be deemed service by mail for purposes of FRCP 5 and FRCP 6. NY R USDCTS&ED Civ Rule 5.3.

4.  *Individual judge practices.* Refer to the Miscellaneous section of this document for information on individual judge practices on timing of documents.

## C. General Requirements

1.  *Pleading, generally*

  a.  *Pleadings allowed.* Only these pleadings are allowed: (1) a complaint; (2) an answer to a complaint; (3) an answer to a counterclaim designated as a counterclaim; (4) an answer to a crossclaim; (5) a third-party complaint; (6) an answer to a third-party complaint; and (7) if the court orders one, a reply to an answer. FRCP 7(a).

  b.  *Pleading to be concise and direct.* Each allegation must be simple, concise, and direct. No technical form is required. FRCP 8(d)(1).

  c.  *Alternative statements of a claim or defense.* A party may set out two or more statements of a claim or defense alternatively or hypothetically, either in a single count or defense or in separate ones. If a party makes alternative statements, the pleading is sufficient if any one of them is sufficient. FRCP 8(d)(2).

d. *Inconsistent claims or defenses.* A party may state as many separate claims or defenses as it has, regardless of consistency. FRCP 8(d)(3).

e. *Construing pleadings.* Pleadings must be construed so as to do justice. FRCP 8(e).

2. *Pleading special matters*

a. *Capacity or authority to sue; Legal existence*

   i. *In general.* Except when required to show that the court has jurisdiction, a pleading need not allege:

   - A party's capacity to sue or be sued;

   - A party's authority to sue or be sued in a representative capacity; or

   - The legal existence of an organized association of persons that is made a party. FRCP 9(a)(1).

   ii. *Raising those issues.* To raise any of those issues, a party must do so by a specific denial, which must state any supporting facts that are peculiarly within the party's knowledge. FRCP 9(a)(2).

b. *Fraud or mistake; Conditions of mind.* In alleging fraud or mistake, a party must state with particularity the circumstances constituting fraud or mistake. Malice, intent, knowledge, and other conditions of a person's mind may be alleged generally. FRCP 9(b).

c. *Conditions precedent.* In pleading conditions precedent, it suffices to allege generally that all conditions precedent have occurred or been performed. But when denying that a condition precedent has occurred or been performed, a party must do so with particularity. FRCP 9(c).

d. *Official document or act.* In pleading an official document or official act, it suffices to allege that the document was legally issued or the act legally done. FRCP 9(d).

e. *Judgment.* In pleading a judgment or decision of a domestic or foreign court, a judicial or quasi-judicial tribunal, or a board or officer, it suffices to plead the judgment or decision without showing jurisdiction to render it. FRCP 9(e).

f. *Time and place.* An allegation of time or place is material when testing the sufficiency of a pleading. FRCP 9(f).

g. *Special damages.* If an item of special damage is claimed, it must be specifically stated. FRCP 9(g).

h. *Admiralty or maritime claim*

   i. *How designated.* If a claim for relief is within the admiralty or maritime jurisdiction and also within the court's subject-matter jurisdiction on some other ground, the pleading may designate the claim as an admiralty or maritime claim for purposes of FRCP 14(c), FRCP 38(e), and FRCP 82 and the Supplemental Rules for Admiralty or Maritime Claims and Asset Forfeiture Actions. A claim cognizable only in the admiralty or maritime jurisdiction is an admiralty or maritime claim for those purposes, whether or not so designated. FRCP 9(h)(1).

   ii. *Designation for appeal.* A case that includes an admiralty or maritime claim within FRCP 9(h) is an admiralty case within 28 U.S.C.A. § 1292(a)(3). FRCP 9(h)(2).

3. *Amended pleading*

a. *Amendments before trial.* The function of FRCP 15(a), which provides generally for the amendment of pleadings, is to enable a party to assert matters that were overlooked or were unknown at the time the party interposed the original complaint or answer. FPP § 1473; Smiga v. Dean Witter Reynolds, Inc., 766 F.2d 698, 703 (2d Cir. 1985).

   i. *Matters contained in amended pleading under FRCP 15(a).* Although FRCP 15(a) does not expressly state that an amendment must contain only matters that occurred within a particular time period, FRCP 15(d) provides that any "transaction, occurrence, or event that happened after the date of the pleading" should be set forth in a supplemental pleading. FPP § 1473. Thus, impliedly, an amended pleading, whether prepared with or without leave of court, only should relate to matters that have taken place prior to the date of the earlier pleading. FPP § 1473; Ford Motor Co. v. U.S., 19 C.I.T. 946, 896 F.Supp. 1224, 1230 (1995).

ii. *Amending as a matter of course.* The right to amend as of course is not restricted to any particular litigant or pleading. FPP § 1480. It is a right conferred on all of the parties to an action and thus extends to persons who were not original parties to the litigation, but are brought into the action by way of counterclaim, crossclaim, third-party claim, or defensive interpleader. FPP § 1480; Johnson v. Walsh, 65 F.Supp. 157 (W.D.Mo. 1946).

- *Amending a complaint with multiple defendants.* When a number of defendants are involved in an action, some of whom have answered and some of whom have filed no responsive pleading, the plaintiff can amend as a matter of course as to those defendants who have not answered. FEDPROC § 62:267; Pallant v. Sinatra, 7 F.R.D. 293 (S.D.N.Y. 1945). A plaintiff may not file an amended complaint as of right against those defendants who have not yet answered, if he or she has amended the complaint once already as a matter of course. FEDPROC § 62:267; Glaros v. Perse, 628 F.2d 679 (1st Cir. 1980).

iii. *Amending with leave of court.* Refer to the United States District Court for the Eastern District of New York KeyRules Motion for Leave to Amend document for information on amending the pleadings with leave of court.

iv. *Types of amendments permitted under FRCP 15(a)*

- *Cure a defective pleading.* Perhaps the most common use of FRCP 15(a) is by a party seeking to amend in order to cure a defective pleading. FPP § 1474.

- *Correct insufficiently stated claims or defenses.* A more common use of FRCP 15(a) amendments is to correct insufficiently stated claims or defenses. Typically, amendments of this character involve either adding a necessary allegation in order to state a claim for relief or correcting a misnomer of a party to the action. FPP § 1474.

- *Change nature or theory of claim or capacity of party.* Courts also have allowed a party to amend in order to change the nature or theory of the party's claim or the capacity in which the party is bringing the action. FPP § 1474.

- *State additional claims or defenses or drop claims or defenses.* Plaintiffs and defendants also have been permitted to amend their pleadings to state additional claims, to assert additional defenses, or to drop claims or defenses. FPP § 1474; Weinberger v. Retail Credit Co., 498 F.2d 552, 554, n.4 (4th Cir. 1974).

- *Increase amount of damages or elect a different remedy.* A FRCP 15(a) amendment also is appropriate for increasing the amount of damages sought, or for electing a different remedy than the one originally requested. FPP § 1474; McFadden v. Sanchez, 710 F.2d 907 (2d Cir. 1983).

- *Add, substitute, or drop parties.* Finally, a party may make a FRCP 15(a) amendment to add, substitute, or drop parties to the action. FPP § 1474.

b. *Amendments during and after trial*

i. *Based on an objection at trial.* If, at trial, a party objects that evidence is not within the issues raised in the pleadings, the court may permit the pleadings to be amended. The court should freely permit an amendment when doing so will aid in presenting the merits and the objecting party fails to satisfy the court that the evidence would prejudice that party's action or defense on the merits. The court may grant a continuance to enable the objecting party to meet the evidence. FRCP 15(b)(1).

ii. *For issues tried by consent.* When an issue not raised by the pleadings is tried by the parties' express or implied consent, it must be treated in all respects as if raised in the pleadings. A party may move—at any time, even after judgment—to amend the pleadings to conform them to the evidence and to raise an unpleaded issue. But failure to amend does not affect the result of the trial of that issue. FRCP 15(b)(2).

      iii.  Refer to the United States District Court for the Eastern District of New York KeyRules Motion for Leave to Amend document for more information on moving to amend the pleadings.

   c.  *Relation back of amendments*

      i.  *When an amendment relates back.* An amendment to a pleading relates back to the date of the original pleading when:

- The law that provides the applicable statute of limitations allows relation back;

- The amendment asserts a claim or defense that arose out of the conduct, transaction, or occurrence set out—or attempted to be set out—in the original pleading; or

- The amendment changes the party or the naming of the party against whom a claim is asserted, if FRCP 15(c)(1)(B) is satisfied and if, within the period provided by FRCP 4(m) for serving the summons and complaint, the party to be brought in by amendment: (1) received such notice of the action that it will not be prejudiced in defending on the merits; and (2) knew or should have known that the action would have been brought against it, but for a mistake concerning the proper party's identity. FRCP 15(c)(1).

      ii.  *Notice to the United States.* When the United States or a United States officer or agency is added as a defendant by amendment, the notice requirements of FRCP 15(c)(1)(C)(i) and FRCP 15(c)(1)(C)(ii) are satisfied if, during the stated period, process was delivered or mailed to the United States attorney or the United States attorney's designee, to the Attorney General of the United States, or to the officer or agency. FRCP 15(c)(2).

   d.  *Effect of an amended pleading.* A pleading that has been amended under FRCP 15(a) supersedes the pleading it modifies and remains in effect throughout the action unless it subsequently is modified. FPP § 1476. Once an amended pleading is interposed, the original pleading no longer performs any function in the case and any subsequent motion made by an opposing party should be directed at the amended pleading. FPP § 1476; Ferdik v. Bonzelet, 963 F.2d 1258, 1262 (9th Cir. 1992); Davis v. TXO Production Corp., 929 F.2d 1515, 1517 (10th Cir. 1991).

4.  *Amended complaint.* Refer to the United States District Court for the Eastern District of New York KeyRules Complaint document for the requirements specific to the amended complaint.

5.  *Amended answer.* Refer to the United States District Court for the Eastern District of New York KeyRules Answer document for the requirements specific to the amended answer.

6.  *Right to a jury trial; Demand*

   a.  *Right preserved.* The right of trial by jury as declared by U.S.C.A. Const. Amend. VII, or as provided by a federal statute, is preserved to the parties inviolate. FRCP 38(a).

   b.  *Demand.* On any issue triable of right by a jury, a party may demand a jury trial by:

      i.  Serving the other parties with a written demand—which may be included in a pleading—no later than fourteen (14) days after the last pleading directed to the issue is served; and

      ii.  Filing the demand in accordance with FRCP 5(d). FRCP 38(b).

   c.  *Specifying issues.* In its demand, a party may specify the issues that it wishes to have tried by a jury; otherwise, it is considered to have demanded a jury trial on all the issues so triable. If the party has demanded a jury trial on only some issues, any other party may—within fourteen (14) days after being served with the demand or within a shorter time ordered by the court—serve a demand for a jury trial on any other or all factual issues triable by jury. FRCP 38(c).

   d.  *Waiver; Withdrawal.* A party waives a jury trial unless its demand is properly served and filed. A proper demand may be withdrawn only if the parties consent. FRCP 38(d).

   e.  *Admiralty and maritime claims.* The rules in FRCP 38 do not create a right to a jury trial on issues in a claim that is an admiralty or maritime claim under FRCP 9(h). FRCP 38(e).

7.  *Related cases.* It shall be the continuing duty of each attorney appearing in any civil or criminal case to bring promptly to the attention of the Court all facts which said attorney believes are relevant to a determination that said case and one or more pending civil or criminal cases should be heard by the same Judge, in order to avoid unnecessary duplication of judicial effort. As soon as the attorney becomes aware

of such relationship, said attorney shall notify the Judges to whom the cases have been assigned. NY R USDCTS&ED Civ Rule 1.6(a). If counsel fails to comply with NY R USDCTS&ED Civ Rule 1.6(a), the Court may assess reasonable costs directly against counsel whose action has obstructed the effective administration of the Court's business. NY R USDCTS&ED Civ Rule 1.6(b).

8. *Alternative dispute resolution (ADR)*

   a. *Court-annexed arbitration*

      i. *Civil cases eligible for compulsory arbitration.* The Clerk of Court shall, as to all cases filed after January 1, 1986, designate and process for compulsory arbitration all civil cases (excluding Social Security cases, tax matters, prisoners' civil rights cases and any action based on an alleged violation of a right secured by the Constitution of the United States or if jurisdiction is based in whole or in part on 28 U.S.C.A. § 1343) wherein money damages only are being sought in an amount not in excess of one hundred fifty thousand dollars ($150,000) exclusive of interest and costs. NY R USDCTS&ED Civ Rule 83.7(d)(1).

         - The parties may by written stipulation agree that the Clerk of Court shall designate and process for court-annexed arbitration any civil case that is not subject to compulsory arbitration in NY R USDCTS&ED Civ Rule 83.7. NY R USDCTS&ED Civ Rule 83.7(d)(2).

         - For purposes of NY R USDCTS&ED Civ Rule 83.7 only, in all civil cases damages shall be presumed to be not in excess of one hundred fifty thousand dollars ($150,000) exclusive of interest and costs, unless: (1) counsel for plaintiff, at the time of filing the complaint, or in the event of the removal of a case from state court or transfer of a case from another district to this Court, within thirty (30) days of the docketing of the case in this district, files a certification with the Court that the damages sought exceed one hundred fifty thousand dollars ($150,000), exclusive of interest and costs; or (2) counsel for a defendant, at the time of filing a counterclaim or cross-claim files a certification with the court that the damages sought by the counter-claim or cross-claim exceed one hundred fifty thousand dollars ($150,000) exclusive of interest and costs. NY R USDCTS&ED Civ Rule 83.7(d)(3).

      ii. *Exemption from arbitration.* The Court shall, sua sponte, or on motion of a party, exempt any case from arbitration in which the objectives of arbitration would not be realized (1) because the case involves complex or novel issues, (2) because legal issues predominate over factual issues, or (3) for other good cause. NY R USDCTS&ED Civ Rule 83.7(e)(2). For information on applying for an exemption, refer to NY R USDCTS&ED Civ Rule 83.7

      iii. *Referral to arbitration.* Cases not originally designated as eligible for compulsory arbitration, but which in the discretion of the assigned Judge, are later found to qualify, may be referred to arbitration. A U.S. District Judge or a U.S. Magistrate Judge, in cases that exceed the arbitration ceiling of one hundred fifty thousand dollars ($150,000) exclusive of interest and costs, in their discretion, may suggest that the parties should consider arbitration. If the parties are agreeable, an appropriate consent form signed by all parties or their representatives may be entered and filed in the case prior to scheduling an arbitration hearing. NY R USDCTS&ED Civ Rule 83.7(e)(3).

      iv. For more information on arbitration, refer to NY R USDCTS&ED Civ Rule 83.7.

   b. *Court-annexed mediation.* Mediation is a process in which parties and counsel agree to meet with a neutral mediator trained to assist them in settling disputes. The mediator improves communication across party lines, helps parties articulate their interests and understand those of the other party, probes the strengths and weaknesses of each party's legal positions, and identifies areas of agreement and helps generate options for a mutually agreeable resolution to the dispute. In all cases, mediation provides an opportunity to explore a wide range of potential solutions and to address interests that may be outside the scope of the stated controversy or which could not be addressed by judicial action. A hallmark of mediation is its capacity to expand traditional settlement discussions and broaden resolution options, often by exploring litigant needs and interests that may be formally independent of the legal issues in controversy. NY R USDCTS&ED Civ Rule 83.8(a).

      i. *Eligible cases.* Judges and Magistrate Judges may designate civil cases for inclusion in the mediation program, and when doing so shall prepare an order to that effect. Alternatively, and subject to the availability of qualified mediators, the parties may consent to participation in the mediation program by preparing and executing a stipulation signed by all parties to the action and so-ordered by the Court. NY R USDCTS&ED Civ Rule 83.8(b)(1).

    ii.   For more information on mediation, refer to NY R USDCTS&ED Civ Rule 83.8.

9.  *Individual judge practices.* Refer to the Miscellaneous section of this document for information on individual judge practices on general requirements for documents.

## D. Documents

1.  *Required documents*

    a.  *Amended pleading.* Refer to the General Requirements section of this document for the form and contents of the amended pleading.

    b.  *Certificate of service.* FRCP 5(d) requires that the person making service under FRCP 5 certify that service has been effected. FRCP 5(Advisory Committee Notes). Having such information on file may be useful for many purposes, including proof of service if an issue arises concerning the effectiveness of the service. FRCP 5(Advisory Committee Notes).

2.  *Supplemental documents*

    a.  *Notice of constitutional question.* A party that files a pleading, written motion, or other paper drawing into question the constitutionality of a federal or state statute must promptly:

        i.   *File notice.* File a notice of constitutional question stating the question and identifying the paper that raises it, if:

- A federal statute is questioned and the parties do not include the United States, one of its agencies, or one of its officers or employees in an official capacity; or

- A state statute is questioned and the parties do not include the state, one of its agencies, or one of its officers or employees in an official capacity; and

        ii.  *Serve notice.* Serve the notice and paper on the Attorney General of the United States if a federal statute is questioned—or on the state attorney general if a state statute is questioned—either by certified or registered mail or by sending it to an electronic address designated by the attorney general for this purpose. FRCP 5.1(a).

      iii.  *No forfeiture.* A party's failure to file and serve the notice, or the court's failure to certify, does not forfeit a constitutional claim or defense that is otherwise timely asserted. FRCP 5.1(d).

    b.  *Notice of issue concerning foreign law.* A party who intends to raise an issue about a foreign country's law must give notice by a pleading or other writing. In determining foreign law, the court may consider any relevant material or source, including testimony, whether or not submitted by a party or admissible under the Federal Rules of Evidence. The court's determination must be treated as a ruling on a question of law. FRCP 44.1.

3.  *Documents required for an amended complaint adding a new claim for relief or new party.* Refer to the United States District Court for the Eastern District of New York KeyRules Complaint document for the documents for an amended complaint adding a new claim for relief or being filed and served against a new party.

4.  *Individual judge practices.* Refer to the Miscellaneous section of this document for information on individual judge practices on required documents.

## E. Format

1.  *Form of documents*

    a.  *Paper.* Every pleading, written motion, and other paper must: be plainly written, typed, printed, or copied without erasures or interlineations which materially deface it. NY R USDCTS&ED Civ Rule 11.1(a)(1).

b. *Typeface, margin, and spacing.* The typeface, margins, and spacing of all documents presented for filing must meet the following requirements:

    i. All text must be twelve (12) point type or larger, except for text in footnotes which may be ten (10) point type;

    ii. All documents must have at least one (1) inch margins on all sides;

    iii. All text must be double-spaced, except for headings, text in footnotes, or block quotations, which may be single-spaced. NY R USDCTS&ED Civ Rule 11.1(b).

c. *Caption; Names of parties.* Every pleading must have a caption with the court's name, a title, a file number, and a FRCP 7(a) designation. The title of the complaint must name all the parties; the title of other pleadings, after naming the first party on each side, may refer generally to other parties. FRCP 10(a). Every pleading, written motion, and other paper must: bear the docket number and the initials of the District Judge and any Magistrate Judge before whom the action or proceeding is pending, NY R USDCTS&ED Civ Rule 11.1(a)(2).

d. *Paragraphs; Separate statements.* A party must state its claims or defenses in numbered paragraphs, each limited as far as practicable to a single set of circumstances. A later pleading may refer by number to a paragraph in an earlier pleading. If doing so would promote clarity, each claim founded on a separate transaction or occurrence—and each defense other than a denial—must be stated in a separate count or defense. FRCP 10(b).

e. *Adoption by reference; Exhibits.* A statement in a pleading may be adopted by reference elsewhere in the same pleading or in any other pleading or motion. A copy of a written instrument that is an exhibit to a pleading is a part of the pleading for all purposes. FRCP 10(c).

f. *Acceptance by the clerk.* The clerk must not refuse to file a paper solely because it is not in the form prescribed by the Federal Rules of Civil Procedure or by a local rule or practice. FRCP 5(d)(4).

2. *Signing of pleadings, motions and other papers*

a. *Signature.* Every pleading, written motion, and other paper must be signed by at least one attorney of record in the attorney's name—or by a party personally if the party is unrepresented. The paper must state the signer's address, e-mail address, and telephone number. FRCP 11(a). Every pleading, written motion, and other paper must: have the name of each person signing it clearly printed or typed directly below the signature. NY R USDCTS&ED Civ Rule 11.1(a)(3).

    i. *No verification or accompanying affidavit required for pleadings.* Unless a rule or statute specifically states otherwise, a pleading need not be verified or accompanied by an affidavit. FRCP 11(a).

    ii. *Unsigned papers.* The court must strike an unsigned paper unless the omission is promptly corrected after being called to the attorney's or party's attention. FRCP 11(a).

b. *Representations to the court.* By presenting to the court a pleading, written motion, or other paper—whether by signing, filing, submitting, or later advocating it—an attorney or unrepresented party certifies that to the best of the person's knowledge, information, and belief, formed after an inquiry reasonable under the circumstances:

    i. It is not being presented for any improper purpose, such as to harass, cause unnecessary delay, or needlessly increase the cost of litigation;

    ii. The claims, defenses, and other legal contentions are warranted by existing law or by a nonfrivolous argument for extending, modifying, or reversing existing law or for establishing new law;

    iii. The factual contentions have evidentiary support or, if specifically so identified, will likely have evidentiary support after a reasonable opportunity for further investigation or discovery; and

    iv. The denials of factual contentions are warranted on the evidence or, if specifically so identified, are reasonably based on belief or a lack of information. FRCP 11(b).

c. *Sanctions.* If, after notice and a reasonable opportunity to respond, the court determines that FRCP 11(b) has been violated, the court may impose an appropriate sanction on any attorney, law firm, or

party that violated FRCP 11(b) or is responsible for the violation. FRCP 11(c)(1). Refer to the United States District Court for the Eastern District of New York KeyRules Motion for Sanctions document for more information.

3. *Privacy protection for filings made with the court*

a. *Redacted filings.* Unless the court orders otherwise, in an electronic or paper filing with the court that contains an individual's Social Security number, taxpayer-identification number, or birth date, the name of an individual known to be a minor, or a financial-account number, a party or nonparty making the filing may include only:

   i. The last four (4) digits of the Social Security number and taxpayer-identification number;

   ii. The year of the individual's birth;

   iii. The minor's initials; and

   iv. The last four (4) digits of the financial-account number. FRCP 5.2(a); NY R USDCTED Order 2004-09.

   v. In addition, exercise caution when filing documents that contain the following:

   - Personal identifying number, such as driver's license number;
   - Medical records, treatment and diagnosis;
   - Employment history;
   - Individual financial information; and
   - Proprietary or trade secret information. NY R USDCTED Order 2004-09.

b. *Exemptions from the redaction requirement.* The redaction requirement does not apply to the following:

   i. A financial-account number that identifies the property allegedly subject to forfeiture in a forfeiture proceeding;

   ii. The record of an administrative or agency proceeding;

   iii. The official record of a state-court proceeding;

   iv. The record of a court or tribunal, if that record was not subject to the redaction requirement when originally filed;

   v. A filing covered by FRCP 5.2(c) or FRCP 5.2(d); and

   vi. A pro se filing in an action brought under 28 U.S.C.A. § 2241, 28 U.S.C.A. § 2254, or 28 U.S.C.A. § 2255. FRCP 5.2(b).

c. *Limitations on remote access to electronic files; Social Security appeals and immigration cases.* Unless the court orders otherwise, in an action for benefits under the Social Security Act, and in an action or proceeding relating to an order of removal, to relief from removal, or to immigration benefits or detention, access to an electronic file is authorized as follows:

   i. The parties and their attorneys may have remote electronic access to any part of the case file, including the administrative record;

   ii. Any other person may have electronic access to the full record at the courthouse, but may have remote electronic access only to:

   - The docket maintained by the court; and
   - An opinion, order, judgment, or other disposition of the court, but not any other part of the case file or the administrative record. FRCP 5.2(c).

d. *Filings made under seal.* The court may order that a filing be made under seal without redaction. The court may later unseal the filing or order the person who made the filing to file a redacted version for the public record. FRCP 5.2(d).

e. *Protective orders.* For good cause, the court may by order in a case:

   i. Require redaction of additional information; or

518

      ii.   Limit or prohibit a nonparty's remote electronic access to a document filed with the court. FRCP 5.2(e).

   f.   *Option for additional unredacted filing under seal.* A person making a redacted filing may also file an unredacted copy under seal. The court must retain the unredacted copy as part of the record. FRCP 5.2(f); NY R USDCTED Order 2004-09. The unredacted version of the document or the reference list shall be retained by the court as part of the record. The court may, however, still require the party to file a redacted copy for the public file. NY R USDCTED Order 2004-09.

   g.   *Option for filing a reference list.* A filing that contains redacted information may be filed together with a reference list that identifies each item of redacted information and specifies an appropriate identifier that uniquely corresponds to each item listed. The list must be filed under seal and may be amended as of right. Any reference in the case to a listed identifier will be construed to refer to the corresponding item of information. FRCP 5.2(g); NY R USDCTED Order 2004-09. The unredacted version of the document or the reference list shall be retained by the court as part of the record. The court may, however, still require the party to file a redacted copy for the public file. NY R USDCTED Order 2004-09.

   h.   *Responsibility for redaction.* The responsibility for redacting these personal identifiers rests solely with counsel and the parties. The Clerk will not review each pleading for compliance with NY R USDCTED Order 2004-09. NY R USDCTED Order 2004-09.

      i.   Counsel is strongly urged to share this notice with all clients so that an informed decision about the inclusion of certain materials may be made. If a redacted document is filed, it is the sole responsibility of counsel and the parties to be sure that all pleadings comply with the rules of this court requiring redaction of personal data identifiers. The clerk will not review each pleading for redaction. NY R USDCTED Order 2004-09.

   i.   *Waiver of protection of identifiers.* A person waives the protection of FRCP 5.2(a) as to the person's own information by filing it without redaction and not under seal. FRCP 5.2(h).

4.   *Individual judge practices.* Refer to the Miscellaneous section of this document for information on individual judge practices on formatting documents.

## F. Filing and Service Requirements

1.   *Filing requirements.* Any paper after the complaint that is required to be served—together with a certificate of service—must be filed within a reasonable time after service. FRCP 5(d)(1).

   a.   *How filing is made; In general.* A paper is filed by delivering it:

      i.   To the clerk; or

      ii.   To a judge who agrees to accept it for filing, and who must then note the filing date on the paper and promptly send it to the clerk. FRCP 5(d)(2).

   b.   *Night depository.* A night depository with an automatic date stamp shall be maintained. . .by the Clerk of the Eastern District in the Brooklyn Courthouse. After regular business hours, papers for the District Court only may be deposited in the night depository. Such papers will be considered as having been filed in the District Court as of the date stamped thereon, which shall be deemed presumptively correct. NY R USDCTS&ED Civ Rule 1.2.

   c.   *Electronic filing*

      i.   *Authorization of electronic filing program.* A court may, by local rule, allow papers to be filed, signed, or verified by electronic means that are consistent with any technical standards established by the Judicial Conference of the United States. A local rule may require electronic filing only if reasonable exceptions are allowed. A paper filed electronically in compliance with a local rule is a written paper for purposes of the Federal Rules of Civil Procedure. FRCP 5(d)(3).

         •   Parties serving and filing papers shall follow the instructions regarding Electronic Case Filing (ECF) published on the website of each respective Court. A paper served and filed by electronic means in accordance with such instructions is, for purposes of FRCP 5, served and filed in compliance with the Local Civil Rules of the Southern and Eastern

Districts of New York. NY R USDCTS&ED Civ Rule 5.2(a). Parties have an obligation to review the Court's actual order, decree, or judgment (on ECF), which controls, and should not rely on the description on the docket or in the ECF Notice of Electronic Filing (NEF). NY R USDCTS&ED Civ Rule 5.2(c).

ii. *Mandatory electronic filing.* Beginning on August 2, 2004, electronic case filing will be mandatory for all civil cases other than pro se cases. NY R USDCTED Order 2004-08.

- *Letter-motions and letters addressed to the court.* Subject to the instructions regarding ECF published on the website of each respective Court and any pertinent Individual Judge's Practices, letter-motions permitted by NY R USDCTS&ED Civ Rule 7.1(d) and letters addressed to the Court (but not letters between the parties) may be filed via ECF. NY R USDCTS&ED Civ Rule 5.2(b).

- *Proposed orders, judgments and decrees.* Proposed orders, judgments and decrees shall be presented as directed by the ECF rules published on the website of each respective Court. NY R USDCTS&ED Civ Rule 77.1. For more information, refer to NY R USDCTS&ED Civ Rule 77.1.

- *Request for exemption.* Requests by attorneys for an exemption to the mandatory policy will be considered for good cause hardship reasons only, and will be reviewed on an individual basis by the assigned United States Magistrate Judge. The Clerk's Office provides an electronic filing training program to assist attorneys filing electronically. Before seeking a hardship exemption, attorneys are advised to participate in the training program or otherwise seek the assistance of the Clerk's Office. NY R USDCTED Order 2004-08.

iii. For more information on electronic filing, refer to the court's website.

2. *Service requirements*

a. *Service; When required*

i. *In general.* Unless the Federal Rules of Civil Procedure provide otherwise, each of the following papers must be served on every party:

- An order stating that service is required;

- A pleading filed after the original complaint, unless the court orders otherwise under FRCP 5(c) because there are numerous defendants;

- A discovery paper required to be served on a party, unless the court orders otherwise;

- A written motion, except one that may be heard ex parte; and

- A written notice, appearance, demand, or offer of judgment, or any similar paper. FRCP 5(a)(1).

ii. *If a party fails to appear.* No service is required on a party who is in default for failing to appear. But a pleading that asserts a new claim for relief against such a party must be served on that party under FRCP 4. FRCP 5(a)(2).

iii. *Seizing property.* If an action is begun by seizing property and no person is or need be named as a defendant, any service required before the filing of an appearance, answer, or claim must be made on the person who had custody or possession of the property when it was seized. FRCP 5(a)(3).

b. *Service; How made*

i. *Serving an attorney.* If a party is represented by an attorney, service under FRCP 5 must be made on the attorney unless the court orders service on the party. FRCP 5(b)(1).

ii. *Service in general.* A paper is served under FRCP 5 by:

- Handing it to the person;

- Leaving it: (1) at the person's office with a clerk or other person in charge or, if no one is in charge, in a conspicuous place in the office; or (2) if the person has no office or the office is closed, at the person's dwelling or usual place of abode with someone of suitable age and discretion who resides there;

- Mailing it to the person's last known address—in which event service is complete upon mailing;

- Leaving it with the court clerk if the person has no known address;

- Sending it by electronic means if the person consented in writing—in which event service is complete upon transmission, but is not effective if the serving party learns that it did not reach the person to be served; or

- Delivering it by any other means that the person consented to in writing—in which event service is complete when the person making service delivers it to the agency designated to make delivery. FRCP 5(b)(2).

   iii. *Service by overnight delivery.* Service upon an attorney may be made by overnight delivery service. "Overnight delivery service" means any delivery service which regularly accepts items for overnight delivery. Overnight delivery service shall be deemed service by mail for purposes of FRCP 5 and FRCP 6. NY R USDCTS&ED Civ Rule 5.3.

   iv. *Service by electronic means.* Parties serving and filing papers shall follow the instructions regarding Electronic Case Filing (ECF) published on the website of each respective Court. A paper served and filed by electronic means in accordance with such instructions is, for purposes of FRCP 5, served and filed in compliance with the Local Civil Rules of the United States District Courts for the Southern and Eastern Districts of New York. NY R USDCTS&ED Civ Rule 5.2(a). Parties have an obligation to review the Court's actual order, decree, or judgment (on ECF), which controls, and should not rely on the description on the docket or in the ECF Notice of Electronic Filing (NEF). NY R USDCTS&ED Civ Rule 5.2(c).

   v. *Using court facilities.* If a local rule so authorizes, a party may use the court's transmission facilities to make service under FRCP 5(b)(2)(E). FRCP 5(b)(3).

  c. *Serving numerous defendants*

   i. *In general.* If an action involves an unusually large number of defendants, the court may, on motion or on its own, order that:

- Defendants' pleadings and replies to them need not be served on other defendants;

- Any crossclaim, counterclaim, avoidance, or affirmative defense in those pleadings and replies to them will be treated as denied or avoided by all other parties; and

- Filing any such pleading and serving it on the plaintiff constitutes notice of the pleading to all parties. FRCP 5(c)(1).

   ii. *Notifying parties.* A copy of every such order must be served on the parties as the court directs. FRCP 5(c)(2).

3. *Service requirements of an amended complaint asserting new or additional claims for relief.* The service of amended pleadings is generally governed by FRCP 5. Thus, except for an amended pleading against a defaulting party that does not assert new or additional claims for relief, an amended pleading must be served in accordance with FRCP 5. FEDPROC § 62:263; International Controls Corp. v. Vesco, 556 F.2d 665, 23 Fed.R.Serv.2d 923 (2d Cir. 1977). However, while FRCP 5 permits service of an amended complaint on counsel, where the amended complaint contains an entirely different cause of action that could not have been properly served originally by the method used in serving the original complaint, the amended complaint must be served in accordance with the terms of FRCP 4. FEDPROC § 62:263; Lasch v. Antkies, 161 F.Supp. 851 (E.D.Pa. 1958). Refer to the United States District Court for the Eastern District of New York KeyRules Complaint document for more information on serving the amended complaint in accordance with FRCP 4.

4. *Individual judge practices.* Refer to the Miscellaneous section of this document for information on individual judge practices on filing and serving documents.

## G. Hearings

1. *Hearings, generally.* Generally, there is no hearing contemplated in the federal statutes or rules for the amended pleading.

    a. *Amended answer; Hearing on FRCP 12 defenses before trial.* If a party so moves, any defense listed in FRCP 12(b)(1) through FRCP 12(b)(7)—whether made in a pleading or by motion—and a motion under FRCP 12(c) must be heard and decided before trial unless the court orders a deferral until trial. FRCP 12(i).

2. *Individual judge practices.* Refer to the Miscellaneous section of this document for information on individual judge practices on hearings.

## H. Forms

### 1. Federal Amended Pleading Forms

   a. Notice; Of filing amended pleading as of course. AMJUR PP FEDPRAC § 153.

   b. Amendment; Of pleading as of course. AMJUR PP FEDPRAC § 154.

   c. Civil cover sheet. 2 FEDFORMS § 3:29.

   d. Notice of lawsuit and request for waiver of service of summons and waiver of summons. 2 FEDFORMS § 3:36.

   e. Complaint. 2 FEDFORMS § 7:14.

   f. Generally. 2B FEDFORMS § 8:10.

   g. Presenting defenses; Official form. 2B FEDFORMS § 8:12.

   h. Denials, admissions and affirmative defenses. 2B FEDFORMS § 8:15.

   i. Denial of particular averment. 2B FEDFORMS § 8:24.

   j. Admission of particular averment. 2B FEDFORMS § 8:25.

   k. Denial of all averments of paragraph. 2B FEDFORMS § 8:26.

   l. Admission of all averments of paragraph. 2B FEDFORMS § 8:27.

   m. Denial in part and admission in part of paragraph. 2B FEDFORMS § 8:28.

   n. Notice of amended complaint. 2C FEDFORMS § 14:10.

   o. Amendment to complaint. 2C FEDFORMS § 14:47.

   p. Amendment to complaint; Short version. 2C FEDFORMS § 14:48.

   q. Amendment to complaint; As of course. 2C FEDFORMS § 14:49.

   r. Complaint; Single count. FEDPROF § 1:68.

   s. Complaint; Multiple counts; With same jurisdictional basis. FEDPROF § 1:69.

   t. Amendment of pleading; As matter of course. FEDPROF § 1:220.

   u. Notice of filing amended pleading; Where amendment is matter of course. FEDPROF § 1:221.

   v. Amendment of pleading; Particular clauses. FEDPROF § 1:224.

   w. Amendment of pleading; Clause; Change in title of action. FEDPROF § 1:225.

   x. Amendment of pleading; Clause; To show amount in controversy. FEDPROF § 1:227.

   y. Amendment of pleading; Clause; To show diversity of citizenship. FEDPROF § 1:228.

   z. Amendment of pleading; Clause; Prayer for relief. FEDPROF § 1:229.

## I. Applicable Rules

1. *Federal rules*

   a. Serving and filing pleadings and other papers. FRCP 5.

   b. Constitutional challenge to a statute; Notice, certification, and intervention. FRCP 5.1.

   c.   Privacy protection for filings made with the court. FRCP 5.2.

   d.   Computing and extending time; Time for motion papers. FRCP 6.

   e.   Pleadings allowed; Form of motions and other papers. FRCP 7.

   f.   General rules of pleading. FRCP 8.

   g.   Pleading special matters. FRCP 9.

   h.   Form of pleadings. FRCP 10.

   i.   Signing pleadings, motions, and other papers; Representations to the court; Sanctions. FRCP 11.

   j.   Defenses and objections; When and how presented; Motion for judgment on the pleadings; Consolidating motions; Waiving defenses; Pretrial hearing. FRCP 12.

   k.   Amended and supplemental pleadings. FRCP 15.

   l.   Right to a jury trial; Demand. FRCP 38.

   m.   Determining foreign law. FRCP 44.1.

2.  *Local rules*

   a.   Night depository. NY R USDCTS&ED Civ Rule 1.2.

   b.   Duty of attorneys in related cases. NY R USDCTS&ED Civ Rule 1.6.

   c.   Electronic service and filing of documents. NY R USDCTS&ED Civ Rule 5.2.

   d.   Service by overnight delivery. NY R USDCTS&ED Civ Rule 5.3.

   e.   Computation of time. NY R USDCTS&ED Civ Rule 6.4.

   f.   Form of pleadings, motions, and other papers. NY R USDCTS&ED Civ Rule 11.1.

   g.   Submission of orders, judgments and decrees. NY R USDCTS&ED Civ Rule 77.1.

   h.   Court-annexed arbitration (Eastern District only). NY R USDCTS&ED Civ Rule 83.7.

   i.   Court-annexed mediation (Eastern District only). NY R USDCTS&ED Civ Rule 83.8.

   j.   Electronic case filing. NY R USDCTED Order 2004-08.

   k.   The August 2, 2004 amendment to the E-Government Act of 2002. NY R USDCTED Order 2004-09.

## J. Miscellaneous

**NOTE: Individual judges' rules may apply. For available judge-level information, refer to:**

DISTRICT JUDGE CAROL BAGLEY AMON: NY R USDCTED Amon-Practices.

DISTRICT JUDGE JOAN M. AZRACK: NY R USDCTED Azrack-Practices.

DISTRICT JUDGE JOSEPH F. BIANCO: NY R USDCTED Bianco-Practices.

DISTRICT JUDGE FREDERIC BLOCK: NY R USDCTED Block-Practices.

DISTRICT JUDGE MARGO K. BRODIE: NY R USDCTED Brodie-Practices.

DISTRICT JUDGE PAMELA K. CHEN: NY R USDCTED Chen-Practices.

DISTRICT JUDGE BRIAN M. COGAN: NY R USDCTED Cogan-Practices; NY R USDCTED Cogan-Pretrial.

DISTRICT JUDGE LaSHANN DeARCY HALL: NY R USDCTED DeArcy Hall-Practices.

DISTRICT JUDGE RAYMOND J. DEARIE: NY R USDCTED Dearie-Practices.

DISTRICT JUDGE ANN M. DONNELLY: NY R USDCTED Donnelly-Practices.

DISTRICT JUDGE SANDRA J. FEUERSTEIN: NY R USDCTED Feuerstein-Practices; NY R USDCTED Feuerstein-Pretrial.

DISTRICT JUDGE NICHOLAS G. GARAUIFIS: NY R USDCTED Garaufis-Practices; NY R USDCTED Garaufis-Pretrial.

DISTRICT JUDGE NINA GERSHON: NY R USDCTED Gershon-Practices.

DISTRICT JUDGE I. LEO GLASSER: NY R USDCTED Glasser-Practices; NY R USDCTED Glasser-Crim.

DISTRICT JUDGE DENIS R. HURLEY: NY R USDCTED Hurley-Practices; [NY R USDCTED Hurley-Pro Cooperation Info, as added by NY ORDER 16-4188, effective July 22, 2016]; [NY R USDCTED Hurley-Pro Cooperation Info Stay, as added by NY ORDER 16-4188, effective July 22, 2016].

DISTRICT JUDGE DORA L. IRIZARRY: NY R USDCTED Irizarry-Practices; NY R USDCTED Irizarry-Pretrial; NY R USDCTED Irizarry-Crim.

DISTRICT JUDGE STERLING JOHNSON, JR.: NY R USDCTED Johnson-Practices.

DISTRICT JUDGE EDWARD R. KORMAN: NY R USDCTED Korman-Practices; NY R USDCTED Korman-Pretrial.

DISTRICT JUDGE WILLIAM F. KUNTZ: NY R USDCTED Kuntz-Practices.

DISTRICT JUDGE KIYO A. MATSUMOTO: NY R USDCTED Matsumoto-Practices.

DISTRICT JUDGE ROSLYNN R. MAUSKOPF: NY R USDCTED Mauskopf-Practices; NY R USDCTED Mauskopf-Recusal.

DISTRICT JUDGE THOMAS C. PLATT: NY R USDCTED Platt-Practices.

DISTRICT JUDGE ALLYNE R. ROSS: NY R USDCTED Ross-Practices.

DISTRICT JUDGE JOANNA SEYBERT: NY R USDCTED Seybert-Practices.

DISTRICT JUDGE ARTHUR D. SPATT: NY R USDCTED Spatt-Practices.

DISTRICT JUDGE SANDRA L. TOWNES: NY R USDCTED Townes-Practices.

DISTRICT JUDGE ERIC N. VITALIANO: NY R USDCTED Vitaliano-Practices.

DISTRICT JUDGE JACK B. WEINSTEIN: NY R USDCTED Weinstein-Practices.

DISTRICT JUDGE LEONARD D. WEXLER: NY R USDCTED Wexler-Practices; NY R USDCTED Wexler-Rules.

MAGISTRATE JUDGE LOIS BLOOM: NY R USDCTED Bloom-Practices.

MAGISTRATE JUDGE GARY R. BROWN: NY R USDCTED Brown-Practices.

MAGISTRATE JUDGE MARILYN D. GO: NY R USDCTED Go-Practices.

MAGISTRATE JUDGE STEVEN M. GOLD: NY R USDCTED Gold-Practices.

MAGISTRATE JUDGE PEGGY KUO: NY R USDCTED Kuo-Practices; NY R USDCTED Kuo-Scheduling Order.

MAGISTRATE JUDGE ROBERT M. LEVY: NY R USDCTED Levy-Practices.

MAGISTRATE JUDGE ARLENE R. LINDSAY: NY R USDCTED Lindsay-Practices.

MAGISTRATE JUDGE STEVEN I. LOCKE: NY R USDCTED Locke-Practices.

MAGISTRATE JUDGE ROANNE L. MANN: NY R USDCTED Mann-Practices.

MAGISTRATE JUDGE JAMES ORENSTEIN: NY R USDCTED Jorenstein--Practices.

MAGISTRATE JUDGE VIKTOR V. POHORELSKY: NY R USDCTED Pohorelsky-Practices.

MAGISTRATE JUDGE CHERYL L. POLLAK: NY R USDCTED Pollak-Practices; NY R USDCTED Pollak-Pretrial.

MAGISTRATE JUDGE RAMON E. REYES, JR.: NY R USDCTED Reyes-Practices.

MAGISTRATE JUDGE VERA M. SCANLON: NY R USDCTED Scanlon-Practices.

MAGISTRATE JUDGE ANNE Y. SHIELDS: NY R USDCTED Shields-Practices.

MAGISTRATE JUDGE STEVEN L. TISCIONE: NY R USDCTED Tiscione-Practices.

MAGISTRATE JUDGE A. KATHLEEN TOMILINSON: NY R USDCTED Tomlinson-Practices.

# Motions, Oppositions and Replies
## Motion to Strike

### Document Last Updated September 2016

**A. Checklist**

(I) ❑ Matters to be considered by moving party

    (a) ❑ Required documents

        (1) ❑ Letter-motion

    (b) ❑ Supplemental documents

        (1) ❑ Deposition

        (2) ❑ Notice of constitutional question

        (3) ❑ Nongovernmental corporate disclosure statement

        (4) ❑ Copies of authorities

        (5) ❑ Notice of motion and motion

        (6) ❑ Memorandum of law

        (7) ❑ Certificate of service

    (c) ❑ Timing

        (1) ❑ There are no specific timing requirements for submitting a letter-motion to the court

        (2) ❑ The court may act on motion made by a party either before responding to the pleading or, if a response is not allowed, within twenty-one (21) days after being served with the pleading

        (3) ❑ A written motion and notice of the hearing must be served at least fourteen (14) days before the time specified for the hearing, with the following exceptions: (i) when the motion may be heard ex parte; (ii) when the Federal Rules of Civil Procedure set a different time; or (iii) when a court order—which a party may, for good cause, apply for ex parte—sets a different time

        (4) ❑ Any affidavit supporting a motion must be served with the motion

(II) ❑ Matters to be considered by opposing party

    (a) ❑ Required documents

        (1) ❑ Responsive letter

    (b) ❑ Supplemental documents

        (1) ❑ Deposition

        (2) ❑ Notice of constitutional question

        (3) ❑ Copies of authorities

        (4) ❑ Answering memorandum of law

        (5) ❑ Certificate of service

    (c) ❑ Timing

        (1) ❑ Within four (4) days of receiving such a letter, any opposing affected party or non-party witness may submit a responsive letter not exceeding three (3) pages attaching relevant materials

        (2) ❑ Any opposing affidavits and answering memoranda shall be served within fourteen (14) days after service of the moving papers

        (3) ❑ Except as FRCP 59(c) provides otherwise, any opposing affidavit must be served at least seven (7) days before the hearing, unless the court permits service at another time

## B. Timing

1. *Mode of raising discovery and other non-dispositive pretrial disputes with the court*

   a. *Letter-motion.* There are no specific timing requirements for submitting a letter-motion to the court.

   b. *Responsive letter.* Within four (4) days of receiving such a letter, any opposing affected party or non-party witness may submit a responsive letter not exceeding three (3) pages attaching relevant materials. NY R USDCTS&ED Civ Rule 37.3(c).

2. *Motion to strike.* The court may act on motion made by a party either before responding to the pleading or, if a response is not allowed, within twenty-one (21) days after being served with the pleading. FRCP 12(f)(2).

3. *Timing of motions, generally*

   a. *Motion and notice of hearing.* Except for letter-motions as permitted by NY R USDCTS&ED Civ Rule 7.1(d), and unless otherwise provided by statute or rule or by the Court in a Judge's Individual Practice or in a direction in a particular case, upon any motion, the notice of motion, supporting affidavits, and memoranda shall be served and filed as follows: on all civil motions, petitions, and applications, other than those described in NY R USDCTS&ED Civ Rule 6.1(a), and other than petitions for writs of habeas corpus, the notice of motion, supporting affidavits, and memoranda of law shall be served by the moving party on all other parties that have appeared in the action. NY R USDCTS&ED Civ Rule 6.1(b)(1). A written motion and notice of the hearing must be served at least fourteen (14) days before the time specified for the hearing, with the following exceptions:

      i. When the motion may be heard ex parte;

      ii. When the Federal Rules of Civil Procedure set a different time; or

      iii. When a court order—which a party may, for good cause, apply for ex parte—sets a different time. FRCP 6(c)(1).

   b. *Supporting affidavit.* Any affidavit supporting a motion must be served with the motion. FRCP 6(c)(2).

4. *Timing of opposing papers.* Except for letter-motions as permitted by NY R USDCTS&ED Civ Rule 7.1(d), and unless otherwise provided by statute or rule or by the Court in a Judge's Individual Practice or in a direction in a particular case, upon any motion, the notice of motion, supporting affidavits, and memoranda shall be served and filed as follows: on all civil motions, petitions, and applications, other than those described in NY R USDCTS&ED Civ Rule 6.1(a), and other than petitions for writs of habeas corpus, any opposing affidavits and answering memoranda shall be served within fourteen (14) days after service of the moving papers. NY R USDCTS&ED Civ Rule 6.1(b)(2).

   a. *Opposing affidavit.* Except as FRCP 59(c) provides otherwise, any opposing affidavit must be served at least seven (7) days before the hearing, unless the court permits service at another time. FRCP 6(c)(2).

5. *Timing of reply papers.* Where the respondent files an answering affidavit setting up a new matter, the moving party ordinarily is allowed a reasonable time to file a reply affidavit since failure to deny the new matter by affidavit may operate as an admission of its truth. AMJUR MOTIONS § 25.

   a. *Reply affidavits and reply memoranda of law.* Except for letter-motions as permitted by NY R USDCTS&ED Civ Rule 7.1(d), and unless otherwise provided by statute or rule or by the Court in a Judge's Individual Practice or in a direction in a particular case, upon any motion, the notice of motion, supporting affidavits, and memoranda shall be served and filed as follows: on all civil motions, petitions, and applications, other than those described in NY R USDCTS&ED Civ Rule 6.1(a), and other than petitions for writs of habeas corpus, any reply affidavits and memoranda of law shall be served within seven (7) days after service of the answering papers. NY R USDCTS&ED Civ Rule 6.1(b)(3).

6. *Effect of a FRCP 12 motion on the time to serve a responsive pleading.* Unless the court sets a different time, serving a motion under FRCP 12 alters the periods in FRCP 12(a) as follows:

   a. If the court denies the motion or postpones its disposition until trial, the responsive pleading must be served within fourteen (14) days after notice of the court's action; or

b. If the court grants a motion for a more definite statement, the responsive pleading must be served within fourteen (14) days after the more definite statement is served. FRCP 12(a)(4).

7. *Computation of time*

a. *Computing time.* FRCP 6 applies in computing any time period specified in the Federal Rules of Civil Procedure, in any local rule or court order, or in any statute that does not specify a method of computing time. FRCP 6(a). In computing any period of time prescribed or allowed by the Local Civil Rules of the United States District Courts for the Southern and Eastern Districts of New York or the Local Admiralty and Maritime Rules, the provisions of FRCP 6 shall apply unless otherwise stated. NY R USDCTS&ED Civ Rule 6.4.

i. *Period stated in days or a longer unit.* In computing periods of days, refer to FRCP 6 and NY R USDCTS&ED Civ Rule 6.4. NY R USDCTS&ED Civ Rule 6.1(b). When the period is stated in days or a longer unit of time:

- Exclude the day of the event that triggers the period;

- Count every day, including intermediate Saturdays, Sundays, and legal holidays; and

- Include the last day of the period, but if the last day is a Saturday, Sunday, or legal holiday, the period continues to run until the end of the next day that is not a Saturday, Sunday, or legal holiday. FRCP 6(a)(1). In the Local Civil Rules of the United States District Courts for the Southern and Eastern Districts of New York, as in the Federal Rules of Civil Procedure as amended effective December 1, 2009, Saturdays, Sundays, and legal holidays are no longer excluded in computing periods of time. If the last day of the period is a Saturday, Sunday, or legal holiday, the period continues to run until the end of the next day that is not a Saturday, Sunday, or legal holiday. NY R USDCTS&ED Civ Rule 6.4.

ii. *Period stated in hours.* When the period is stated in hours:

- Begin counting immediately on the occurrence of the event that triggers the period;

- Count every hour, including hours during intermediate Saturdays, Sundays, and legal holidays; and

- If the period would end on a Saturday, Sunday, or legal holiday, the period continues to run until the same time on the next day that is not a Saturday, Sunday, or legal holiday. FRCP 6(a)(2). In the Local Civil Rules of the United States District Courts for the Southern and Eastern Districts of New York, as in the Federal Rules of Civil Procedure as amended effective December 1, 2009, Saturdays, Sundays, and legal holidays are no longer excluded in computing periods of time. If the last day of the period is a Saturday, Sunday, or legal holiday, the period continues to run until the end of the next day that is not a Saturday, Sunday, or legal holiday. NY R USDCTS&ED Civ Rule 6.4.

iii. *Inaccessibility of the clerk's office.* Unless the court orders otherwise, if the clerk's office is inaccessible:

- On the last day for filing under FRCP 6(a)(1), then the time for filing is extended to the first accessible day that is not a Saturday, Sunday, or legal holiday; or

- During the last hour for filing under FRCP 6(a)(2), then the time for filing is extended to the same time on the first accessible day that is not a Saturday, Sunday, or legal holiday. FRCP 6(a)(3).

iv. *"Last day" defined.* Unless a different time is set by a statute, local rule, or court order, the last day ends:

- For electronic filing, at midnight in the court's time zone; and

- For filing by other means, when the clerk's office is scheduled to close. FRCP 6(a)(4).

v. *"Next day" defined.* The "next day" is determined by continuing to count forward when the period is measured after an event and backward when measured before an event. FRCP 6(a)(5).

vi. *"Legal holiday" defined.* "Legal holiday" means:

- The day set aside by statute for observing New Year's Day, Martin Luther King Jr.'s

Birthday, Washington's Birthday, Memorial Day, Independence Day, Labor Day, Columbus Day, Veterans' Day, Thanksgiving Day, or Christmas Day;

- Any day declared a holiday by the President or Congress; and

- For periods that are measured after an event, any other day declared a holiday by the state where the district court is located. FRCP 6(a)(6).

b. *Extending time*

    i. *In general.* When an act may or must be done within a specified time, the court may, for good cause, extend the time:

- With or without motion or notice if the court acts, or if a request is made, before the original time or its extension expires; or

- On motion made after the time has expired if the party failed to act because of excusable neglect. FRCP 6(b)(1).

    ii. *Exceptions.* A court must not extend the time to act under FRCP 50(b), FRCP 50(d), FRCP 52(b), FRCP 59(b), FRCP 59(d), FRCP 59(e), and FRCP 60(b). FRCP 6(b)(2).

    iii. Refer to the United States District Court for the Eastern District of New York KeyRules Motion for Continuance/Extension of Time document for more information on extending time.

c. *Additional time after certain kinds of service.* When a party may or must act within a specified time after service and service is made under FRCP 5(b)(2)(C), FRCP 5(b)(2)(D), FRCP 5(b)(2)(E), or FRCP 5(b)(2)(F), three (3) days are added after the period would otherwise expire under FRCP 6(a). FRCP 6(d). Overnight delivery service shall be deemed service by mail for purposes of FRCP 5 and FRCP 6. NY R USDCTS&ED Civ Rule 5.3.

8. *Individual judge practices.* Refer to the Miscellaneous section of this document for information on individual judge practices on timing of documents.

## C. General Requirements

1. *Mode of raising discovery and other non-dispositive pretrial disputes with the court.* Prior to seeking judicial resolution of a discovery or non-dispositive pretrial dispute, the attorneys for the affected parties or non-party witness shall attempt to confer in good faith in person or by telephone in an effort to resolve the dispute, in conformity with FRCP 37(a)(1). NY R USDCTS&ED Civ Rule 37.3(a). Refer to the Documents section of this document for the procedure to follow when the attorneys for the affected parties or non-party witness cannot agree on a resolution of the discovery or other non-dispositive pretrial dispute.

a. *Motion for reconsideration.* A ruling made exclusively as a result of a telephone conference may be the subject of de novo reconsideration by a letter not exceeding five (5) pages in length attaching relevant materials submitted by any affected party or non-party witness. Within four (4) days of receiving such a letter, any other affected party or non-party witness may submit a responsive letter not exceeding five (5) pages in length attaching relevant materials. NY R USDCTS&ED Civ Rule 37.3(d).

b. *Decision of the court.* The Court shall record or arrange for the recording of the Court's decision in writing. Such written order may take the form of an oral order read into the record of a deposition or other proceeding, a handwritten memorandum, a handwritten marginal notation on a letter or other document, or any other form the Court deems appropriate. NY R USDCTS&ED Civ Rule 37.3(e).

2. *Motions, generally*

a. *Requirements.* A request for a court order must be made by motion. The motion must:

    i. Be in writing unless made during a hearing or trial;

    ii. State with particularity the grounds for seeking the order; and

    iii. State the relief sought. FRCP 7(b)(1).

b. *Notice of motion.* A party interested in resisting the relief sought by a motion has a right to notice thereof, and an opportunity to be heard. AMJUR MOTIONS § 12.

    i. In addition to statutory or court rule provisions requiring notice of a motion—the purpose of

such a notice requirement having been said to be to prevent a party from being prejudicially surprised by a motion—principles of natural justice dictate that an adverse party generally must be given notice that a motion will be presented to the court. AMJUR MOTIONS § 12.

    ii.   "Notice," in this regard, means reasonable notice, including a meaningful opportunity to prepare and to defend against allegations of a motion. AMJUR MOTIONS § 12.

c.  *Writing requirement.* The writing requirement is intended to insure that the adverse parties are informed and have a record of both the motion's pendency and the grounds on which the movant seeks an order. FPP § 1191; Feldberg v. Quechee Lakes Corp., 463 F.3d 195 (2d Cir. 2006).

    i.   It is sufficient "if the motion is stated in a written notice of the hearing of the motion." FPP § 1191.

d.  *Particularity requirement.* The particularity requirement insures that the opposing parties will have notice of their opponent's contentions. FEDPROC § 62:364; Goodman v. 1973 26 Foot Trojan Vessel, Arkansas Registration No. AR1439SN, 859 F.2d 71, 12 Fed.R.Serv.3d 645 (8th Cir. 1988). That requirement ensures that notice of the basis for the motion is provided to the court and to the opposing party so as to avoid prejudice, provide the opponent with a meaningful opportunity to respond, and provide the court with enough information to process the motion correctly. FEDPROC § 62:364; Andreas v. Volkswagen of America, Inc., 336 F.3d 789, 56 Fed.R.Serv.3d 6 (8th Cir. 2003).

    i.   Reasonable specification of the grounds for a motion is sufficient. However, where a movant fails to state even one ground for granting the motion in question, the movant has failed to meet the minimal standard of "reasonable specification." FEDPROC § 62:364; Martinez v. Trainor, 556 F.2d 818, 23 Fed.R.Serv.2d 403 (7th Cir. 1977).

    ii.   The court may excuse the failure to comply with the particularity requirement if it is inadvertent, and where no prejudice is shown by the opposing party. FEDPROC § 62:364.

e.  *Ex parte orders or orders to show cause to bring on a motion.* No ex parte order, or order to show cause to bring on a motion, will be granted except upon a clear and specific showing by affidavit of good and sufficient reasons why a procedure other than by notice of motion is necessary, and stating whether a previous application for similar relief has been made. NY R USDCTS&ED Civ Rule 6.1(d).

f.  *Letter-motions.* Applications for extensions or adjournments, applications for a pre-motion conference, and similar non-dispositive matters as permitted by the instructions regarding ECF published on the website of each respective Court and any pertinent Individual Judge's Practices, may be brought by letter-motion filed via ECF pursuant to NY R USDCTS&ED Civ Rule 5.2(b). NY R USDCTS&ED Civ Rule 7.1(d).

3.  *Motion to strike.* The court may strike from a pleading an insufficient defense or any redundant, immaterial, impertinent, or scandalous matter. The court may act: (1) on its own; or (2) on motion made by a party either before responding to the pleading or, if a response is not allowed, within twenty-one (21) days after being served with the pleading. FRCP 12(f). FRCP 12(f) also is designed to reinforce the requirement in FRCP 8(e) that pleadings be simple, concise, and direct. However, as the cases make clear, it is neither an authorized nor a proper way to procure the dismissal of all or a part of a complaint, or a counterclaim, or to strike an opponent's affidavits. FPP § 1380.

a.  *Practice on a motion to strike.* All well-pleaded facts are taken as admitted on a motion to strike but conclusions of law or conclusions drawn from the facts do not have to be treated in that fashion by the district judge. FPP § 1380. Both because striking a portion of a pleading is a drastic remedy and because it often is sought by the movant simply as a dilatory or harassing tactic, numerous judicial decisions make it clear that motions under FRCP 12(f) are viewed with disfavor by the federal courts and are infrequently granted. FPP § 1380.

b.  *Striking an insufficient defense.* Only if a defense is insufficient as a matter of law will it be stricken. If a defense cannot succeed under any set of circumstances alleged, the defense may be deemed insufficient as a matter of law. In other words, a defense may be stricken if, on the face of the pleadings, it is patently frivolous, or if it is clearly invalid as a matter of law. FEDPROC § 62:412.

    i.   A defense will be stricken if it could not possibly prevent recovery by the plaintiff on its claim. FEDPROC § 62:413. In addition, a defense may be stricken if:

- The defense requires separate statements;
- The defense has been previously advanced and rejected; or
- The defense cannot be waived. FEDPROC § 62:413.

c.  *Striking immaterial or impertinent matter.* Immaterial or impertinent matter will be stricken from a pleading if it is clear that it can have no possible bearing upon the subject matter of the litigation, and that its inclusion will prejudice the movant. If there is any doubt as to whether under any contingency the matter may raise an issue, the motion should be denied. FEDPROC § 62:415.

    i.   "Immaterial matter," for purposes of FRCP 12(f), is matter which has no essential or important relationship to the claim for relief or the defenses being pleaded. FEDPROC § 62:414. A statement of unnecessary particulars in connection with and descriptive of that which is material may be stricken as immaterial matter. FEDPROC § 62:416.

    ii.  "Impertinent matter," for purposes of FRCP 12(f), consists of statements that do not pertain, and are not necessary, to the issues in question. FEDPROC § 62:414.

d.  *Striking redundant matter.* "Redundant matter," for purposes of FRCP 12(f), consists of allegations that constitute a needless repetition of other averments or which are wholly foreign to the issue to be decided. However, even if allegations are redundant, they need not be stricken if their presence in the pleading cannot prejudice the moving party. FEDPROC § 62:417.

    i.   Merely duplicative remedies do not necessarily make claims "redundant," within the meaning of FRCP 12(f), if the claims otherwise require proof of different elements, but a claim that merely recasts the same elements under the guise of a different theory may be stricken as redundant. FEDPROC § 62:417.

e.  *Striking scandalous matter.* A matter is deemed scandalous, for purposes of FRCP 12(f), when it improperly casts a derogatory light on someone, usually a party to the action. Scandalous matter also consists of any unnecessary allegation which reflects cruelly upon the moral character of an individual, or states anything in repulsive language which detracts from the dignity of the court. To be scandalous, degrading charges must be irrelevant, or, if relevant, must go into in unnecessary detail. FEDPROC § 62:418.

    i.   Allegations may be stricken as scandalous if the matter bears no possible relation to the controversy or may cause the objecting party prejudice. FEDPROC § 62:418.

    ii.  But there are several limitations on the court's willingness to strike scandalous allegations. For example, it is not enough that the matter offends the sensibilities of the objecting party or the person who is the subject of the statements in the pleading, if the challenged allegations describe acts or events that are relevant to the action. FPP § 1382.

f.  *Striking sham or false matter.* FRCP 12(f) does not authorize a motion to strike part or all of a pleading on the ground that it is sham, and the grounds for a motion to strike similarly do not include falsity of the matter alleged. FEDPROC § 62:419; PAE Government Services, Inc. v. MPRI, Inc., 514 F.3d 856 (9th Cir. 2007). However, it has been said that a court will strike a pleading according to FRCP 12(f) when it appears beyond peradventure that it is a sham and false and that its allegations are devoid of factual basis. FEDPROC § 62:419.

g.  *Striking conclusions of law.* Unwarranted conclusions of law may be stricken from a pleading pursuant to FRCP 12(f), but ordinarily an allegation is not subject to being stricken merely because it is a conclusion of law. To the contrary, the Federal Rules of Civil Procedure do not condemn conclusions of law, but rather encourage them as at times the clearest and simplest way of stating a claim for relief. Conclusions of law must be unwarranted enough to justify a motion to strike, such as when a plaintiff states causes of action under a federal statute which provides no explicit private right of action. FEDPROC § 62:420.

h. *Striking other particular matter.* Under FRCP 12(f), which permits a court to order stricken from any pleading any redundant, immaterial, impertinent, or scandalous matter, courts have the authority to strike a prayer for relief seeking damages that are not recoverable as a matter of law. A motion to strike may be used to remove an excessive or unauthorized claim for damages. Furthermore, a motion to strike a demand for punitive damages under FRCP 12(f) may be proper if such damages are clearly not collectible, such as in an ordinary breach of contract action. However, there are other ways to raise this issue, and in a particular case, one of these other methods may be more appropriate, such as a motion to dismiss for failure to state a claim pursuant to FRCP 12(b)(6). FEDPROC § 62:421.

i. *Form.* On a motion to strike portions of a pleading, the movant must indicate what paragraphs are being challenged in order to fulfill the particularity requirement; the movant cannot merely state the conclusion that the allegations are too indefinite and insufficient to state a claim or defense. FPP § 1192.

j. *Joining motions*

   i. *Right to join.* A motion under FRCP 12 may be joined with any other motion allowed by FRCP 12. FRCP 12(g)(1).

   ii. *Limitation on further motions.* Except as provided in FRCP 12(h)(2) or FRCP 12(h)(3), a party that makes a motion under FRCP 12 must not make another motion under FRCP 12 raising a defense or objection that was available to the party but omitted from its earlier motion. FRCP 12(g)(2).

4. *Opposing papers.* The Federal Rules of Civil Procedure do not require any formal answer, return, or reply to a motion, except where the Federal Rules of Civil Procedure or local rules may require affidavits, memoranda, or other papers to be filed in opposition to a motion. Such papers are simply to apprise the court of such opposition and the grounds of that opposition. FEDPROC § 62:359. Except for letter-motions as permitted by NY R USDCTS&ED Civ Rule 7.1(d) or as otherwise permitted by the Court, all oppositions and replies with respect to motions shall comply with NY R USDCTS&ED Civ Rule 7.1(a)(2) and NY R USDCTS&ED Civ Rule 7.1(a)(3), and an opposing party who seeks relief that goes beyond the denial of the motion shall comply as well with NY R USDCTS&ED Civ Rule 7.1(a)(1). NY R USDCTS&ED Civ Rule 7.1(b).

a. *Effect of failure to respond to motion.* Although in the absence of statutory provision or court rule, a motion ordinarily does not require a written answer, when a party files a motion and the opposing party fails to respond, the court may construe such failure to respond as nonopposition to the motion or an admission that the motion was meritorious, may take the facts alleged in the motion as true—the rule in some jurisdictions being that the failure to respond to a fact set forth in a motion is deemed an admission—and may grant the motion if the relief requested appears to be justified. AMJUR MOTIONS § 28.

b. *Assent or no opposition not determinative.* However, a motion will not be granted automatically simply because an "assent" or a notation of "no opposition" has been filed; federal judges frequently deny motions that have been assented to when it is thought that justice so dictates. FPP § 1190.

c. *Responsive pleading inappropriate as response to motion.* An attempt to answer or oppose a motion with a responsive pleading usually is not appropriate. FPP § 1190.

5. *Reply papers.* A moving party may be required or permitted to prepare papers in addition to his original motion papers. AMJUR MOTIONS § 25. Papers answering or replying to opposing papers may be appropriate, in the interests of justice, where it appears there is a substantial reason for allowing a reply. Thus, a court may accept reply papers where a party demonstrates that the papers to which it seeks to file a reply raise new issues that are material to the disposition of the question before the court, or where the court determines, sua sponte, that it wishes further briefing of an issue raised in those papers and orders the submission of additional papers. FEDPROC § 62:360. Except for letter-motions as permitted by NY R USDCTS&ED Civ Rule 7.1(d) or as otherwise permitted by the Court, all oppositions and replies with respect to motions shall comply with NY R USDCTS&ED Civ Rule 7.1(a)(2) and NY R USDCTS&ED Civ Rule 7.1(a)(3). NY R USDCTS&ED Civ Rule 7.1(b).

a. *Function of reply papers.* The function of a reply affidavit is to answer the arguments made in opposition to the position taken by the movant and not to permit the movant to introduce new arguments in support of the motion. AMJUR MOTIONS § 25.

b. *Issues raised for the first time in a reply document.* However, the view has been followed in some jurisdictions, that as a matter of judicial economy, where there is no prejudice and where the issues could be raised simply by filing a motion to dismiss, the trial court has discretion to consider arguments raised for the first time in a reply memorandum, and that a trial court may grant a motion to strike issues raised for the first time in a reply memorandum. AMJUR MOTIONS § 26.

6. *Orders on motions.* A memorandum signed by the Court of the decision on a motion that does not finally determine all claims for relief, or an oral decision on such a motion, shall constitute the order unless the memorandum or oral decision directs the submission or settlement of an order in more extended form. The notation in the docket of a memorandum or of an oral decision that does not direct the submission or settlement of an order in more extended form shall constitute the entry of the order. Where an order in more extended form is required to be submitted or settled, the notation in the docket of such order shall constitute the entry of the order. NY R USDCTS&ED Civ Rule 6.2.

7. *Related cases.* It shall be the continuing duty of each attorney appearing in any civil or criminal case to bring promptly to the attention of the Court all facts which said attorney believes are relevant to a determination that said case and one or more pending civil or criminal cases should be heard by the same Judge, in order to avoid unnecessary duplication of judicial effort. As soon as the attorney becomes aware of such relationship, said attorney shall notify the Judges to whom the cases have been assigned. NY R USDCTS&ED Civ Rule 1.6(a). If counsel fails to comply with NY R USDCTS&ED Civ Rule 1.6(a), the Court may assess reasonable costs directly against counsel whose action has obstructed the effective administration of the Court's business. NY R USDCTS&ED Civ Rule 1.6(b).

8. *Alternative dispute resolution (ADR)*

   a. *Court-annexed arbitration*

      i. *Civil cases eligible for compulsory arbitration.* The Clerk of Court shall, as to all cases filed after January 1, 1986, designate and process for compulsory arbitration all civil cases (excluding Social Security cases, tax matters, prisoners' civil rights cases and any action based on an alleged violation of a right secured by the Constitution of the United States or if jurisdiction is based in whole or in part on 28 U.S.C.A. § 1343) wherein money damages only are being sought in an amount not in excess of one hundred fifty thousand dollars ($150,000) exclusive of interest and costs. NY R USDCTS&ED Civ Rule 83.7(d)(1).

         • The parties may by written stipulation agree that the Clerk of Court shall designate and process for court-annexed arbitration any civil case that is not subject to compulsory arbitration in NY R USDCTS&ED Civ Rule 83.7. NY R USDCTS&ED Civ Rule 83.7(d)(2).

         • For purposes of NY R USDCTS&ED Civ Rule 83.7 only, in all civil cases damages shall be presumed to be not in excess of one hundred fifty thousand dollars ($150,000) exclusive of interest and costs, unless: (1) counsel for plaintiff, at the time of filing the complaint, or in the event of the removal of a case from state court or transfer of a case from another district to this Court, within thirty (30) days of the docketing of the case in this district, files a certification with the Court that the damages sought exceed one hundred fifty thousand dollars ($150,000), exclusive of interest and costs; or (2) counsel for a defendant, at the time of filing a counterclaim or cross-claim files a certification with the court that the damages sought by the counter-claim or cross-claim exceed one hundred fifty thousand dollars ($150,000) exclusive of interest and costs. NY R USDCTS&ED Civ Rule 83.7(d)(3).

      ii. *Exemption from arbitration.* The Court shall, sua sponte, or on motion of a party, exempt any case from arbitration in which the objectives of arbitration would not be realized (1) because the case involves complex or novel issues, (2) because legal issues predominate over factual issues, or (3) for other good cause. NY R USDCTS&ED Civ Rule 83.7(e)(2). For information on applying for an exemption, refer to NY R USDCTS&ED Civ Rule 83.7

      iii. *Referral to arbitration.* Cases not originally designated as eligible for compulsory arbitration, but which in the discretion of the assigned Judge, are later found to qualify, may be referred to arbitration. A U.S. District Judge or a U.S. Magistrate Judge, in cases that exceed the arbitration ceiling of one hundred fifty thousand dollars ($150,000) exclusive of interest and costs, in their discretion, may suggest that the parties should consider arbitration. If the parties are agreeable, an appropriate consent form signed by all parties or their representatives may be entered and filed in the case prior to scheduling an arbitration hearing. NY R USDCTS&ED Civ Rule 83.7(e)(3).

    iv.   For more information on arbitration, refer to NY R USDCTS&ED Civ Rule 83.7.

  b.  *Court-annexed mediation.* Mediation is a process in which parties and counsel agree to meet with a neutral mediator trained to assist them in settling disputes. The mediator improves communication across party lines, helps parties articulate their interests and understand those of the other party, probes the strengths and weaknesses of each party's legal positions, and identifies areas of agreement and helps generate options for a mutually agreeable resolution to the dispute. In all cases, mediation provides an opportunity to explore a wide range of potential solutions and to address interests that may be outside the scope of the stated controversy or which could not be addressed by judicial action. A hallmark of mediation is its capacity to expand traditional settlement discussions and broaden resolution options, often by exploring litigant needs and interests that may be formally independent of the legal issues in controversy. NY R USDCTS&ED Civ Rule 83.8(a).

    i.   *Eligible cases.* Judges and Magistrate Judges may designate civil cases for inclusion in the mediation program, and when doing so shall prepare an order to that effect. Alternatively, and subject to the availability of qualified mediators, the parties may consent to participation in the mediation program by preparing and executing a stipulation signed by all parties to the action and so-ordered by the Court. NY R USDCTS&ED Civ Rule 83.8(b)(1).

    ii.   For more information on mediation, refer to NY R USDCTS&ED Civ Rule 83.8.

9.  *Individual judge practices.* Refer to the Miscellaneous section of this document for information on individual judge practices on general requirements for documents.

## D. Documents

1.  *Documents for moving party*

  a.  *Required documents*

    i.   *Letter-motion.* Where the attorneys for the affected parties or non-party witness cannot agree on a resolution of any other discovery dispute or non-dispositive pretrial dispute, or if they are unable to obtain a telephonic ruling on a discovery dispute that arises during a deposition as provided in NY R USDCTS&ED Civ Rule 37.3(b), they shall notify the Court by letter not exceeding three (3) pages in length outlining the nature of the dispute and attaching relevant materials. NY R USDCTS&ED Civ Rule 37.3(c).

  b.  *Supplemental documents.* Except for the letters and attachments authorized herein, or where a ruling which was made exclusively as a result of a telephone conference is the subject of de novo review pursuant to NY R USDCTS&ED Civ Rule 37.3(d), papers shall not be submitted with respect to a dispute governed by NY R USDCTS&ED Civ Rule 37.3 unless the Court has so directed. NY R USDCTS&ED Civ Rule 37.3(c). Matter outside the pleadings normally is not considered on a FRCP 12(f) motion; for example, affidavits in support of or in opposition to the motion typically may not be used. FPP § 1380.

    i.   *Deposition.* Notwithstanding the general rule that matters outside the pleadings should ordinarily not be considered in passing upon a motion to strike under FRCP 12(f), a court may consider a deposition in deciding a FRCP 12(f) motion if the attorneys for both the plaintiff and the defendant, in their respective briefs, refer to the deposition and to the testimony contained therein. FEDPROC § 62:407.

      •  *Discovery materials.* A party seeking or opposing relief under FRCP 26 through FRCP 37 inclusive, or making or opposing any other motion or application, shall quote or attach only those portions of the depositions, interrogatories, requests for documents, requests for admissions, or other discovery or disclosure materials, together with the responses and

objections thereto, that are the subject of the discovery motion or application, or that are cited in papers submitted in connection with any other motion or application. NY R USDCTS&ED Civ Rule 5.1.

ii. *Notice of constitutional question.* A party that files a pleading, written motion, or other paper drawing into question the constitutionality of a federal or state statute must promptly:

- *File notice.* File a notice of constitutional question stating the question and identifying the paper that raises it, if: (1) a federal statute is questioned and the parties do not include the United States, one of its agencies, or one of its officers or employees in an official capacity; or (2) a state statute is questioned and the parties do not include the state, one of its agencies, or one of its officers or employees in an official capacity; and

- *Serve notice.* Serve the notice and paper on the Attorney General of the United States if a federal statute is questioned—or on the state attorney general if a state statute is questioned—either by certified or registered mail or by sending it to an electronic address designated by the attorney general for this purpose. FRCP 5.1(a).

- *No forfeiture.* A party's failure to file and serve the notice, or the court's failure to certify, does not forfeit a constitutional claim or defense that is otherwise timely asserted. FRCP 5.1(d).

iii. *Nongovernmental corporate disclosure statement.* To enable judges and magistrates to evaluate possible disqualification or recusal, counsel for a private (nongovernmental) party shall submit at the time of initial pleading a certificate identifying any corporate parent, subsidiaries, or affiliates of that party. NY R USDCTED Div. Bus., Rule 50.1(c).

- *Contents.* A nongovernmental corporate party must file two (2) copies of a disclosure statement that: (1) identifies any parent corporation and any publicly held corporation owning ten percent (10%) or more of its stock; or (2) states that there is no such corporation. FRCP 7.1(a).

- *Time to file; Supplemental filing.* A party must: (1) file the disclosure statement with its first appearance, pleading, petition, motion, response, or other request addressed to the court; and (2) promptly file a supplemental statement if any required information changes. FRCP 7.1(b). For purposes of FRCP 7.1(b)(2), "promptly" shall mean "within fourteen days," that is, parties are required to file a supplemental disclosure statement within fourteen (14) days of the time there is any change in the information required in a disclosure statement filed pursuant to those rules. NY R USDCTS&ED Civ Rule 7.1.1.

iv. *Copies of authorities.* In cases involving a pro se litigant, counsel shall, when serving a memorandum of law (or other submissions to the Court), provide the pro se litigant (but not other counsel or the Court) with copies of cases and other authorities cited therein that are unpublished or reported exclusively on computerized databases. Upon request, counsel shall provide the pro se litigant with copies of such unpublished cases and other authorities as are cited in a decision of the Court and were not previously cited by any party. NY R USDCTS&ED Civ Rule 7.2.

v. *Notice of motion and motion.* Except for letter-motions as permitted by NY R USDCTS&ED Civ Rule 7.1(d) or as otherwise permitted by the Court, all motions shall include the following motion papers: a notice of motion, or an order to show cause signed by the Court, which shall specify the applicable rules or statutes pursuant to which the motion is brought, and shall specify the relief sought by the motion. NY R USDCTS&ED Civ Rule 7.1(a)(1). Refer to the General Requirements section of this document for information on the notice of motion and motion.

vi. *Memorandum of law.* Except for letter-motions as permitted by NY R USDCTS&ED Civ Rule 7.1(d) or as otherwise permitted by the Court, all motions shall include the following motion papers: a memorandum of law, setting forth the cases and other authorities relied upon in support of the motion, and divided, under appropriate headings, into as many parts as there are issues to be determined. NY R USDCTS&ED Civ Rule 7.1(a)(2).

vii. *Certificate of service.* FRCP 5(d) requires that the person making service under FRCP 5 certify that service has been effected. FRCP 5(Advisory Committee Notes). Having such information on file may be useful for many purposes, including proof of service if an issue arises concerning the effectiveness of the service. FRCP 5(Advisory Committee Notes).

2. *Documents for opposing party*

   a. *Required documents*

      i. *Responsive letter.* Within four (4) days of receiving such a letter, any opposing affected party or non-party witness may submit a responsive letter not exceeding three (3) pages attaching relevant materials. NY R USDCTS&ED Civ Rule 37.3(c).

   b. *Supplemental documents.* Except for the letters and attachments authorized herein, or where a ruling which was made exclusively as a result of a telephone conference is the subject of de novo review pursuant to NY R USDCTS&ED Civ Rule 37.3(d), papers shall not be submitted with respect to a dispute governed by NY R USDCTS&ED Civ Rule 37.3 unless the Court has so directed. NY R USDCTS&ED Civ Rule 37.3(c). Matter outside the pleadings normally is not considered on a FRCP 12(f) motion; for example, affidavits in support of or in opposition to the motion typically may not be used. FPP § 1380.

      i. *Deposition.* Notwithstanding the general rule that matters outside the pleadings should ordinarily not be considered in passing upon a motion to strike under FRCP 12(f), a court may consider a deposition in deciding a FRCP 12(f) motion if the attorneys for both the plaintiff and the defendant, in their respective briefs, refer to the deposition and to the testimony contained therein. FEDPROC § 62:407.

- *Discovery materials.* A party seeking or opposing relief under FRCP 26 through FRCP 37 inclusive, or making or opposing any other motion or application, shall quote or attach only those portions of the depositions, interrogatories, requests for documents, requests for admissions, or other discovery or disclosure materials, together with the responses and objections thereto, that are the subject of the discovery motion or application, or that are cited in papers submitted in connection with any other motion or application. NY R USDCTS&ED Civ Rule 5.1.

      ii. *Notice of constitutional question.* A party that files a pleading, written motion, or other paper drawing into question the constitutionality of a federal or state statute must promptly:

- *File notice.* File a notice of constitutional question stating the question and identifying the paper that raises it, if: (1) a federal statute is questioned and the parties do not include the United States, one of its agencies, or one of its officers or employees in an official capacity; or (2) a state statute is questioned and the parties do not include the state, one of its agencies, or one of its officers or employees in an official capacity; and

- *Serve notice.* Serve the notice and paper on the Attorney General of the United States if a federal statute is questioned—or on the state attorney general if a state statute is questioned—either by certified or registered mail or by sending it to an electronic address designated by the attorney general for this purpose. FRCP 5.1(a).

- *No forfeiture.* A party's failure to file and serve the notice, or the court's failure to certify, does not forfeit a constitutional claim or defense that is otherwise timely asserted. FRCP 5.1(d).

      iii. *Copies of authorities.* In cases involving a pro se litigant, counsel shall, when serving a memorandum of law (or other submissions to the Court), provide the pro se litigant (but not other counsel or the Court) with copies of cases and other authorities cited therein that are unpublished or reported exclusively on computerized databases. Upon request, counsel shall provide the pro se litigant with copies of such unpublished cases and other authorities as are cited in a decision of the Court and were not previously cited by any party. NY R USDCTS&ED Civ Rule 7.2.

      iv. *Answering memorandum of law.* Except for letter-motions as permitted by NY R USDCTS&ED Civ Rule 7.1(d) or as otherwise permitted by the Court, all oppositions and replies with respect to motions shall comply with NY R USDCTS&ED Civ Rule 7.1(a)(2). NY R USDCTS&ED Civ Rule 7.1(b). Except for letter-motions as permitted by NY R USDCTS&ED Civ Rule 7.1(d) or as otherwise permitted by the Court, all motions shall include the following motion papers: a memorandum of law, setting forth the cases and other authorities relied upon in support of the motion, and divided, under appropriate headings, into as many parts as there are issues to be determined. NY R USDCTS&ED Civ Rule 7.1(a)(2). Refer to the General Requirements section of this document for information on the opposing papers.

    v. *Certificate of service.* FRCP 5(d) requires that the person making service under FRCP 5 certify that service has been effected. FRCP 5(Advisory Committee Notes). Having such information on file may be useful for many purposes, including proof of service if an issue arises concerning the effectiveness of the service. FRCP 5(Advisory Committee Notes).

3. *Individual judge practices.* Refer to the Miscellaneous section of this document for information on individual judge practices on required documents.

## E. Format

1. *Form of documents.* The rules governing captions and other matters of form in pleadings apply to motions and other papers. FRCP 7(b)(2).

    a. *Paper.* Every pleading, written motion, and other paper must: be plainly written, typed, printed, or copied without erasures or interlineations which materially deface it. NY R USDCTS&ED Civ Rule 11.1(a)(1).

    b. *Typeface, margin, and spacing.* The typeface, margins, and spacing of all documents presented for filing must meet the following requirements:

        i. All text must be twelve (12) point type or larger, except for text in footnotes which may be ten (10) point type;

        ii. All documents must have at least one (1) inch margins on all sides;

        iii. All text must be double-spaced, except for headings, text in footnotes, or block quotations, which may be single-spaced. NY R USDCTS&ED Civ Rule 11.1(b).

    c. *Caption; Names of parties.* Every pleading must have a caption with the court's name, a title, a file number, and a FRCP 7(a) designation. The title of the complaint must name all the parties; the title of other pleadings, after naming the first party on each side, may refer generally to other parties. FRCP 10(a). Every pleading, written motion, and other paper must: bear the docket number and the initials of the District Judge and any Magistrate Judge before whom the action or proceeding is pending, NY R USDCTS&ED Civ Rule 11.1(a)(2).

    d. *Paragraphs; Separate statements.* A party must state its claims or defenses in numbered paragraphs, each limited as far as practicable to a single set of circumstances. A later pleading may refer by number to a paragraph in an earlier pleading. If doing so would promote clarity, each claim founded on a separate transaction or occurrence—and each defense other than a denial—must be stated in a separate count or defense. FRCP 10(b).

    e. *Adoption by reference; Exhibits.* A statement in a pleading may be adopted by reference elsewhere in the same pleading or in any other pleading or motion. A copy of a written instrument that is an exhibit to a pleading is a part of the pleading for all purposes. FRCP 10(c).

    f. *Acceptance by the clerk.* The clerk must not refuse to file a paper solely because it is not in the form prescribed by the Federal Rules of Civil Procedure or by a local rule or practice. FRCP 5(d)(4).

2. *Signing of pleadings, motions and other papers*

    a. *Signature.* Every pleading, written motion, and other paper must be signed by at least one attorney of record in the attorney's name—or by a party personally if the party is unrepresented. The paper must state the signer's address, e-mail address, and telephone number. FRCP 11(a). Every pleading, written motion, and other paper must: have the name of each person signing it clearly printed or typed directly below the signature. NY R USDCTS&ED Civ Rule 11.1(a)(3).

        i. *No verification or accompanying affidavit required for pleadings.* Unless a rule or statute specifically states otherwise, a pleading need not be verified or accompanied by an affidavit. FRCP 11(a).

    ii.   *Unsigned papers.* The court must strike an unsigned paper unless the omission is promptly corrected after being called to the attorney's or party's attention. FRCP 11(a).

  b.  *Representations to the court.* By presenting to the court a pleading, written motion, or other paper—whether by signing, filing, submitting, or later advocating it—an attorney or unrepresented party certifies that to the best of the person's knowledge, information, and belief, formed after an inquiry reasonable under the circumstances:

    i.   It is not being presented for any improper purpose, such as to harass, cause unnecessary delay, or needlessly increase the cost of litigation;

    ii.   The claims, defenses, and other legal contentions are warranted by existing law or by a nonfrivolous argument for extending, modifying, or reversing existing law or for establishing new law;

    iii.   The factual contentions have evidentiary support or, if specifically so identified, will likely have evidentiary support after a reasonable opportunity for further investigation or discovery; and

    iv.   The denials of factual contentions are warranted on the evidence or, if specifically so identified, are reasonably based on belief or a lack of information. FRCP 11(b).

  c.  *Sanctions.* If, after notice and a reasonable opportunity to respond, the court determines that FRCP 11(b) has been violated, the court may impose an appropriate sanction on any attorney, law firm, or party that violated FRCP 11(b) or is responsible for the violation. FRCP 11(c)(1). Refer to the United States District Court for the Eastern District of New York KeyRules Motion for Sanctions document for more information.

3.  *Privacy protection for filings made with the court*

  a.  *Redacted filings.* Unless the court orders otherwise, in an electronic or paper filing with the court that contains an individual's Social Security number, taxpayer-identification number, or birth date, the name of an individual known to be a minor, or a financial-account number, a party or nonparty making the filing may include only:

    i.   The last four (4) digits of the Social Security number and taxpayer-identification number;

    ii.   The year of the individual's birth;

    iii.   The minor's initials; and

    iv.   The last four (4) digits of the financial-account number. FRCP 5.2(a); NY R USDCTED Order 2004-09.

    v.   In addition, exercise caution when filing documents that contain the following:

- Personal identifying number, such as driver's license number;

- Medical records, treatment and diagnosis;

- Employment history;

- Individual financial information; and

- Proprietary or trade secret information. NY R USDCTED Order 2004-09.

  b.  *Exemptions from the redaction requirement.* The redaction requirement does not apply to the following:

    i.   A financial-account number that identifies the property allegedly subject to forfeiture in a forfeiture proceeding;

    ii.   The record of an administrative or agency proceeding;

    iii.   The official record of a state-court proceeding;

    iv.   The record of a court or tribunal, if that record was not subject to the redaction requirement when originally filed;

    v.   A filing covered by FRCP 5.2(c) or FRCP 5.2(d); and

    vi.  A pro se filing in an action brought under 28 U.S.C.A. § 2241, 28 U.S.C.A. § 2254, or 28 U.S.C.A. § 2255. FRCP 5.2(b).

c.   *Limitations on remote access to electronic files; Social Security appeals and immigration cases.* Unless the court orders otherwise, in an action for benefits under the Social Security Act, and in an action or proceeding relating to an order of removal, to relief from removal, or to immigration benefits or detention, access to an electronic file is authorized as follows:

    i.   The parties and their attorneys may have remote electronic access to any part of the case file, including the administrative record;

    ii.  Any other person may have electronic access to the full record at the courthouse, but may have remote electronic access only to:

- The docket maintained by the court; and

- An opinion, order, judgment, or other disposition of the court, but not any other part of the case file or the administrative record. FRCP 5.2(c).

d.   *Filings made under seal.* The court may order that a filing be made under seal without redaction. The court may later unseal the filing or order the person who made the filing to file a redacted version for the public record. FRCP 5.2(d).

e.   *Protective orders.* For good cause, the court may by order in a case:

    i.   Require redaction of additional information; or

    ii.  Limit or prohibit a nonparty's remote electronic access to a document filed with the court. FRCP 5.2(e).

f.   *Option for additional unredacted filing under seal.* A person making a redacted filing may also file an unredacted copy under seal. The court must retain the unredacted copy as part of the record. FRCP 5.2(f); NY R USDCTED Order 2004-09. The unredacted version of the document or the reference list shall be retained by the court as part of the record. The court may, however, still require the party to file a redacted copy for the public file. NY R USDCTED Order 2004-09.

g.   *Option for filing a reference list.* A filing that contains redacted information may be filed together with a reference list that identifies each item of redacted information and specifies an appropriate identifier that uniquely corresponds to each item listed. The list must be filed under seal and may be amended as of right. Any reference in the case to a listed identifier will be construed to refer to the corresponding item of information. FRCP 5.2(g); NY R USDCTED Order 2004-09. The unredacted version of the document or the reference list shall be retained by the court as part of the record. The court may, however, still require the party to file a redacted copy for the public file. NY R USDCTED Order 2004-09.

h.   *Responsibility for redaction.* The responsibility for redacting these personal identifiers rests solely with counsel and the parties. The Clerk will not review each pleading for compliance with NY R USDCTED Order 2004-09. NY R USDCTED Order 2004-09.

    i.   Counsel is strongly urged to share this notice with all clients so that an informed decision about the inclusion of certain materials may be made. If a redacted document is filed, it is the sole responsibility of counsel and the parties to be sure that all pleadings comply with the rules of this court requiring redaction of personal data identifiers. The clerk will not review each pleading for redaction. NY R USDCTED Order 2004-09.

i.   *Waiver of protection of identifiers.* A person waives the protection of FRCP 5.2(a) as to the person's own information by filing it without redaction and not under seal. FRCP 5.2(h).

4.  *Individual judge practices.* Refer to the Miscellaneous section of this document for information on individual judge practices on formatting documents.

## F. Filing and Service Requirements

1. *Filing requirements.* Any paper after the complaint that is required to be served—together with a certificate of service—must be filed within a reasonable time after service. FRCP 5(d)(1).

   a. *How filing is made; In general.* A paper is filed by delivering it:

      i. To the clerk; or

      ii. To a judge who agrees to accept it for filing, and who must then note the filing date on the paper and promptly send it to the clerk. FRCP 5(d)(2).

   b. *Night depository.* A night depository with an automatic date stamp shall be maintained. . .by the Clerk of the Eastern District in the Brooklyn Courthouse. After regular business hours, papers for the District Court only may be deposited in the night depository. Such papers will be considered as having been filed in the District Court as of the date stamped thereon, which shall be deemed presumptively correct. NY R USDCTS&ED Civ Rule 1.2.

   c. *Electronic filing*

      i. *Authorization of electronic filing program.* A court may, by local rule, allow papers to be filed, signed, or verified by electronic means that are consistent with any technical standards established by the Judicial Conference of the United States. A local rule may require electronic filing only if reasonable exceptions are allowed. A paper filed electronically in compliance with a local rule is a written paper for purposes of the Federal Rules of Civil Procedure. FRCP 5(d)(3).

         • Parties serving and filing papers shall follow the instructions regarding Electronic Case Filing (ECF) published on the website of each respective Court. A paper served and filed by electronic means in accordance with such instructions is, for purposes of FRCP 5, served and filed in compliance with the Local Civil Rules of the Southern and Eastern Districts of New York. NY R USDCTS&ED Civ Rule 5.2(a). Parties have an obligation to review the Court's actual order, decree, or judgment (on ECF), which controls, and should not rely on the description on the docket or in the ECF Notice of Electronic Filing (NEF). NY R USDCTS&ED Civ Rule 5.2(c).

      ii. *Mandatory electronic filing.* Beginning on August 2, 2004, electronic case filing will be mandatory for all civil cases other than pro se cases. NY R USDCTED Order 2004-08.

         • *Letter-motions and letters addressed to the court.* Subject to the instructions regarding ECF published on the website of each respective Court and any pertinent Individual Judge's Practices, letter-motions permitted by NY R USDCTS&ED Civ Rule 7.1(d) and letters addressed to the Court (but not letters between the parties) may be filed via ECF. NY R USDCTS&ED Civ Rule 5.2(b).

         • *Proposed orders, judgments and decrees.* Proposed orders, judgments and decrees shall be presented as directed by the ECF rules published on the website of each respective Court. NY R USDCTS&ED Civ Rule 77.1. For more information, refer to NY R USDCTS&ED Civ Rule 77.1.

         • *Request for exemption.* Requests by attorneys for an exemption to the mandatory policy will be considered for good cause hardship reasons only, and will be reviewed on an individual basis by the assigned United States Magistrate Judge. The Clerk's Office provides an electronic filing training program to assist attorneys filing electronically. Before seeking a hardship exemption, attorneys are advised to participate in the training program or otherwise seek the assistance of the Clerk's Office. NY R USDCTED Order 2004-08.

      iii. For more information on electronic filing, refer to the court's website.

2.   *Service requirements*

   a.   *Service; When required*

   i.   *In general.* Unless the Federal Rules of Civil Procedure provide otherwise, each of the following papers must be served on every party:

   • An order stating that service is required;

   • A pleading filed after the original complaint, unless the court orders otherwise under FRCP 5(c) because there are numerous defendants;

   • A discovery paper required to be served on a party, unless the court orders otherwise;

   • A written motion, except one that may be heard ex parte; and

   • A written notice, appearance, demand, or offer of judgment, or any similar paper. FRCP 5(a)(1).

   ii.  *If a party fails to appear.* No service is required on a party who is in default for failing to appear. But a pleading that asserts a new claim for relief against such a party must be served on that party under FRCP 4. FRCP 5(a)(2).

   iii. *Seizing property.* If an action is begun by seizing property and no person is or need be named as a defendant, any service required before the filing of an appearance, answer, or claim must be made on the person who had custody or possession of the property when it was seized. FRCP 5(a)(3).

   b.   *Service; How made*

   i.   *Serving an attorney.* If a party is represented by an attorney, service under FRCP 5 must be made on the attorney unless the court orders service on the party. FRCP 5(b)(1).

   ii.  *Service in general.* A paper is served under FRCP 5 by:

   • Handing it to the person;

   • Leaving it: (1) at the person's office with a clerk or other person in charge or, if no one is in charge, in a conspicuous place in the office; or (2) if the person has no office or the office is closed, at the person's dwelling or usual place of abode with someone of suitable age and discretion who resides there;

   • Mailing it to the person's last known address—in which event service is complete upon mailing;

   • Leaving it with the court clerk if the person has no known address;

   • Sending it by electronic means if the person consented in writing—in which event service is complete upon transmission, but is not effective if the serving party learns that it did not reach the person to be served; or

   • Delivering it by any other means that the person consented to in writing—in which event service is complete when the person making service delivers it to the agency designated to make delivery. FRCP 5(b)(2).

   iii. *Service by overnight delivery.* Service upon an attorney may be made by overnight delivery service. "Overnight delivery service" means any delivery service which regularly accepts items for overnight delivery. Overnight delivery service shall be deemed service by mail for purposes of FRCP 5 and FRCP 6. NY R USDCTS&ED Civ Rule 5.3.

   iv.  *Service by electronic means.* Parties serving and filing papers shall follow the instructions regarding Electronic Case Filing (ECF) published on the website of each respective Court. A paper served and filed by electronic means in accordance with such instructions is, for purposes of FRCP 5, served and filed in compliance with the Local Civil Rules of the United States District Courts for the Southern and Eastern Districts of New York. NY R USDCTS&ED Civ Rule 5.2(a). Parties have an obligation to review the Court's actual order, decree, or judgment (on ECF), which controls, and should not rely on the description on the docket or in the ECF Notice of Electronic Filing (NEF). NY R USDCTS&ED Civ Rule 5.2(c).

v. *Using court facilities.* If a local rule so authorizes, a party may use the court's transmission facilities to make service under FRCP 5(b)(2)(E). FRCP 5(b)(3).

c. *Serving numerous defendants*

  i. *In general.* If an action involves an unusually large number of defendants, the court may, on motion or on its own, order that:

- Defendants' pleadings and replies to them need not be served on other defendants;
- Any crossclaim, counterclaim, avoidance, or affirmative defense in those pleadings and replies to them will be treated as denied or avoided by all other parties; and
- Filing any such pleading and serving it on the plaintiff constitutes notice of the pleading to all parties. FRCP 5(c)(1).

  ii. *Notifying parties.* A copy of every such order must be served on the parties as the court directs. FRCP 5(c)(2).

3. *Individual judge practices.* Refer to the Miscellaneous section of this document for information on individual judge practices on filing and serving documents.

## G. Hearings

1. *Hearings, generally*

a. *Oral argument.* Due process does not require that oral argument be permitted on a motion and, except as otherwise provided by local rule, the district court has discretion to determine whether it will decide the motion on the papers or hear argument by counsel (and perhaps receive evidence). FPP § 1190; F.D.I.C. v. Deglau, 207 F.3d 153 (3d Cir. 2000). The parties and their attorneys shall only appear to argue the motion if so directed by the Court by order or by a Judge's Individual Practice. NY R USDCTS&ED Civ Rule 6.1(c).

b. *Providing a regular schedule for oral hearings.* A court may establish regular times and places for oral hearings on motions. FRCP 78(a).

c. *Providing for submission on briefs.* By rule or order, the court may provide for submitting and determining motions on briefs, without oral hearings. FRCP 78(b).

2. *Individual judge practices.* Refer to the Miscellaneous section of this document for information on individual judge practices on hearings.

## H. Forms

### 1. Federal Motion to Strike Forms

a. Motion; By plaintiff; To strike insufficient defense from answer. AMJUR PP FEDPRAC § 441.

b. Motion; To strike redundant, immaterial, impertinent, or scandalous matter from pleading. AMJUR PP FEDPRAC § 442.

c. Motion; To strike portions of complaint. AMJUR PP FEDPRAC § 444.

d. Motion to strike insufficient affirmative defenses. 2C FEDFORMS § 11:151.

e. Motion to strike insufficient defense in answer; Stating particular reason. 2C FEDFORMS § 11:153.

f. Notice of motion and motion to strike insufficient affirmative defense. 2C FEDFORMS § 11:155.

g. Motion to strike impertinence and scandal. 2C FEDFORMS § 11:157.

h. Motion to strike impertinence and immateriality. 2C FEDFORMS § 11:158.

i. Motion to strike redundancy and scandal. 2C FEDFORMS § 11:159.

j. Motion to strike immaterial defense. 2C FEDFORMS § 11:160.

k. Motion to strike for immateriality. 2C FEDFORMS § 11:161.

l. Motion to strike counterclaim for lack of evidence. 2C FEDFORMS § 11:162.

m. Opposition; To motion; General form. FEDPROF § 1:750.

n. Affidavit; Supporting or opposing motion. FEDPROF § 1:751.

o.   Brief; Supporting or opposing motion. FEDPROF § 1:752.

p.   Statement of points and authorities; Opposing motion. FEDPROF § 1:753.

q.   Motion; To strike material outside statute of limitations. FEDPROF § 1:773.

r.   Opposition to motion; Material not contained in pleading. FEDPROF § 1:774.

s.   General form. GOLDLTGFMS § 20:8.

t.   General form; Federal form. GOLDLTGFMS § 20:10.

u.   Notice and motion to strike immaterial, redundant or scandalous matter. GOLDLTGFMS § 20:13.

v.   Motion to strike complaint and dismiss action as to one defendant. GOLDLTGFMS § 20:14.

w.   Defendant's motion to strike. GOLDLTGFMS § 20:16.

x.   Defendant's motion to strike; Plaintiff's response. GOLDLTGFMS § 20:17.

y.   Motion to strike answer. GOLDLTGFMS § 20:19.

z.   Objections to motion to strike. GOLDLTGFMS § 20:20.

## I.  Applicable Rules

1.  *Federal rules*

a.   Serving and filing pleadings and other papers. FRCP 5.

b.   Constitutional challenge to a statute; Notice, certification, and intervention. FRCP 5.1.

c.   Privacy protection for filings made with the court. FRCP 5.2.

d.   Computing and extending time; Time for motion papers. FRCP 6.

e.   Pleadings allowed; Form of motions and other papers. FRCP 7.

f.   Disclosure statement. FRCP 7.1.

g.   Form of pleadings. FRCP 10.

h.   Signing pleadings, motions, and other papers; Representations to the court; Sanctions. FRCP 11.

i.   Defenses and objections; When and how presented; Motion for judgment on the pleadings; Consolidating motions; Waiving defenses; Pretrial hearing. FRCP 12.

j.   Hearing motions; Submission on briefs. FRCP 78.

2.  *Local rules*

a.   Night depository. NY R USDCTS&ED Civ Rule 1.2.

b.   Duty of attorneys in related cases. NY R USDCTS&ED Civ Rule 1.6.

c.   Filing of discovery materials. NY R USDCTS&ED Civ Rule 5.1.

d.   Electronic service and filing of documents. NY R USDCTS&ED Civ Rule 5.2.

e.   Service by overnight delivery. NY R USDCTS&ED Civ Rule 5.3.

f.   Service and filing of motion papers. NY R USDCTS&ED Civ Rule 6.1.

g.   Orders on motions. NY R USDCTS&ED Civ Rule 6.2.

h.   Computation of time. NY R USDCTS&ED Civ Rule 6.4.

i.   Motion papers. NY R USDCTS&ED Civ Rule 7.1.

j.   Disclosure statement. NY R USDCTS&ED Civ Rule 7.1.1.

k.   Authorities to be provided to pro se litigants. NY R USDCTS&ED Civ Rule 7.2.

l.   Form of pleadings, motions, and other papers. NY R USDCTS&ED Civ Rule 11.1.

m.   Mode of raising discovery and other non-dispositive pretrial disputes with the court (Eastern District only). NY R USDCTS&ED Civ Rule 37.3.

n.   Submission of orders, judgments and decrees. NY R USDCTS&ED Civ Rule 77.1.

o.   Court-annexed arbitration (Eastern District only). NY R USDCTS&ED Civ Rule 83.7.

p.   Court-annexed mediation (Eastern District only). NY R USDCTS&ED Civ Rule 83.8.

q.   Electronic case filing. NY R USDCTED Order 2004-08.

r.   The August 2, 2004 amendment to the E-Government Act of 2002. NY R USDCTED Order 2004-09.

s.   Categories and classification of cases; Information on cases and parties. NY R USDCTED Div. Bus., Rule 50.1.

## J.  Miscellaneous

**NOTE: Individual judges' rules may apply. For available judge-level information, refer to:**

DISTRICT JUDGE CAROL BAGLEY AMON: NY R USDCTED Amon-Practices.

DISTRICT JUDGE JOAN M. AZRACK: NY R USDCTED Azrack-Practices.

DISTRICT JUDGE JOSEPH F. BIANCO: NY R USDCTED Bianco-Practices.

DISTRICT JUDGE FREDERIC BLOCK: NY R USDCTED Block-Practices.

DISTRICT JUDGE MARGO K. BRODIE: NY R USDCTED Brodie-Practices.

DISTRICT JUDGE PAMELA K. CHEN: NY R USDCTED Chen-Practices.

DISTRICT JUDGE BRIAN M. COGAN: NY R USDCTED Cogan-Practices; NY R USDCTED Cogan-Pretrial.

DISTRICT JUDGE LaSHANN DeARCY HALL: NY R USDCTED DeArcy Hall-Practices.

DISTRICT JUDGE RAYMOND J. DEARIE: NY R USDCTED Dearie-Practices.

DISTRICT JUDGE ANN M. DONNELLY: NY R USDCTED Donnelly-Practices.

DISTRICT JUDGE SANDRA J. FEUERSTEIN: NY R USDCTED Feuerstein-Practices; NY R USDCTED Feuerstein-Pretrial.

DISTRICT JUDGE NICHOLAS G. GARAUIFIS: NY R USDCTED Garaufis-Practices; NY R USDCTED Garaufis-Pretrial.

DISTRICT JUDGE NINA GERSHON: NY R USDCTED Gershon-Practices.

DISTRICT JUDGE I. LEO GLASSER: NY R USDCTED Glasser-Practices; NY R USDCTED Glasser-Crim.

DISTRICT JUDGE DENIS R. HURLEY: NY R USDCTED Hurley-Practices; [NY R USDCTED Hurley-Pro Cooperation Info, as added by NY ORDER 16-4188, effective July 22, 2016]; [NY R USDCTED Hurley-Pro Cooperation Info Stay, as added by NY ORDER 16-4188, effective July 22, 2016].

DISTRICT JUDGE DORA L. IRIZARRY: NY R USDCTED Irizarry-Practices; NY R USDCTED Irizarry-Pretrial; NY R USDCTED Irizarry-Crim.

DISTRICT JUDGE STERLING JOHNSON, JR.: NY R USDCTED Johnson-Practices.

DISTRICT JUDGE EDWARD R. KORMAN: NY R USDCTED Korman-Practices; NY R USDCTED Korman-Pretrial.

DISTRICT JUDGE WILLIAM F. KUNTZ: NY R USDCTED Kuntz-Practices.

DISTRICT JUDGE KIYO A. MATSUMOTO: NY R USDCTED Matsumoto-Practices.

DISTRICT JUDGE ROSLYNN R. MAUSKOPF: NY R USDCTED Mauskopf-Practices; NY R USDCTED Mauskopf-Recusal.

DISTRICT JUDGE THOMAS C. PLATT: NY R USDCTED Platt-Practices.

DISTRICT JUDGE ALLYNE R. ROSS: NY R USDCTED Ross-Practices.

DISTRICT JUDGE JOANNA SEYBERT: NY R USDCTED Seybert-Practices.

DISTRICT JUDGE ARTHUR D. SPATT: NY R USDCTED Spatt-Practices.

DISTRICT JUDGE SANDRA L. TOWNES: NY R USDCTED Townes-Practices.

DISTRICT JUDGE ERIC N. VITALIANO: NY R USDCTED Vitaliano-Practices.

DISTRICT JUDGE JACK B. WEINSTEIN: NY R USDCTED Weinstein-Practices.

DISTRICT JUDGE LEONARD D. WEXLER: NY R USDCTED Wexler-Practices; NY R USDCTED Wexler-Rules.

MAGISTRATE JUDGE LOIS BLOOM: NY R USDCTED Bloom-Practices.

MAGISTRATE JUDGE GARY R. BROWN: NY R USDCTED Brown-Practices.

MAGISTRATE JUDGE MARILYN D. GO: NY R USDCTED Go-Practices.

MAGISTRATE JUDGE STEVEN M. GOLD: NY R USDCTED Gold-Practices.

MAGISTRATE JUDGE PEGGY KUO: NY R USDCTED Kuo-Practices; NY R USDCTED Kuo-Scheduling Order.

MAGISTRATE JUDGE ROBERT M. LEVY: NY R USDCTED Levy-Practices.

MAGISTRATE JUDGE ARLENE R. LINDSAY: NY R USDCTED Lindsay-Practices.

MAGISTRATE JUDGE STEVEN I. LOCKE: NY R USDCTED Locke-Practices.

MAGISTRATE JUDGE ROANNE L. MANN: NY R USDCTED Mann-Practices.

MAGISTRATE JUDGE JAMES ORENSTEIN: NY R USDCTED Jorenstein--Practices.

MAGISTRATE JUDGE VIKTOR V. POHORELSKY: NY R USDCTED Pohorelsky-Practices.

MAGISTRATE JUDGE CHERYL L. POLLAK: NY R USDCTED Pollak-Practices; NY R USDCTED Pollak-Pretrial.

MAGISTRATE JUDGE RAMON E. REYES, JR.: NY R USDCTED Reyes-Practices.

MAGISTRATE JUDGE VERA M. SCANLON: NY R USDCTED Scanlon-Practices.

MAGISTRATE JUDGE ANNE Y. SHIELDS: NY R USDCTED Shields-Practices.

MAGISTRATE JUDGE STEVEN L. TISCIONE: NY R USDCTED Tiscione-Practices.

MAGISTRATE JUDGE A. KATHLEEN TOMILINSON: NY R USDCTED Tomlinson-Practices.

## Motions, Oppositions and Replies
## Motion for Leave to Amend

### Document Last Updated September 2016

**A. Checklist**

(I) ❑ Matters to be considered by moving party

    (a) ❑ Required documents

        (1) ❑ Letter-motion

        (2) ❑ Proposed amendment

    (b) ❑ Supplemental documents

        (1) ❑ Supporting evidence

        (2) ❑ Notice of constitutional question

        (3) ❑ Copies of authorities

        (4) ❑ Notice of motion and motion

        (5) ❑ Memorandum of law

        (6) ❑ Certificate of service

    (c) ❑ Timing

        (1) ❑ There are no specific timing requirements for submitting a letter-motion to the court

        (2) ❑ Unlike amendments as of course, amendments under FRCP 15(a)(2) may be made at any stage of the litigation

(3) ❑ A party may move—at any time, even after judgment—to amend the pleadings to conform them to the evidence and to raise an unpleaded issue

(4) ❑ A written motion and notice of the hearing must be served at least fourteen (14) days before the time specified for the hearing, with the following exceptions: (i) when the motion may be heard ex parte; (ii) when the Federal Rules of Civil Procedure set a different time; or (iii) when a court order—which a party may, for good cause, apply for ex parte—sets a different time

(5) ❑ Any affidavit supporting a motion must be served with the motion

(II) ❑ Matters to be considered by opposing party

   (a) ❑ Required documents

     (1) ❑ Responsive letter

   (b) ❑ Supplemental documents

     (1) ❑ Supporting evidence

     (2) ❑ Notice of constitutional question

     (3) ❑ Copies of authorities

     (4) ❑ Answering memorandum of law

     (5) ❑ Certificate of service

   (c) ❑ Timing

     (1) ❑ Within four (4) days of receiving such a letter, any opposing affected party or non-party witness may submit a responsive letter not exceeding three (3) pages attaching relevant materials

     (2) ❑ Any opposing affidavits and answering memoranda shall be served within fourteen (14) days after service of the moving papers

     (3) ❑ Except as FRCP 59(c) provides otherwise, any opposing affidavit must be served at least seven (7) days before the hearing, unless the court permits service at another time

## B. Timing

1. *Mode of raising discovery and other non-dispositive pretrial disputes with the court*

   a. *Letter-motion.* There are no specific timing requirements for submitting a letter-motion to the court.

   b. *Responsive letter.* Within four (4) days of receiving such a letter, any opposing affected party or non-party witness may submit a responsive letter not exceeding three (3) pages attaching relevant materials. NY R USDCTS&ED Civ Rule 37.3(c).

2. *Motion for leave to amend.* Unlike amendments as of course, amendments under FRCP 15(a)(2) may be made at any stage of the litigation. FPP § 1484.

   a. *Amendments to conform to the evidence.* A party may move—at any time, even after judgment—to amend the pleadings to conform them to the evidence and to raise an unpleaded issue. FRCP 15(b)(2).

   b. *Time to respond to an amended pleading.* Unless the court orders otherwise, any required response to an amended pleading must be made within the time remaining to respond to the original pleading or within fourteen (14) days after service of the amended pleading, whichever is later. FRCP 15(a)(3).

3. *Timing of motions, generally*

   a. *Motion and notice of hearing.* Except for letter-motions as permitted by NY R USDCTS&ED Civ Rule 7.1(d), and unless otherwise provided by statute or rule or by the Court in a Judge's Individual Practice or in a direction in a particular case, upon any motion, the notice of motion, supporting affidavits, and memoranda shall be served and filed as follows: on all civil motions, petitions, and applications, other than those described in NY R USDCTS&ED Civ Rule 6.1(a), and other than petitions for writs of habeas corpus, the notice of motion, supporting affidavits, and memoranda of law shall be served by the moving party on all other parties that have appeared in the action. NY R USDCTS&ED Civ Rule 6.1(b)(1). A written motion and notice of the hearing must be served at least fourteen (14) days before the time specified for the hearing, with the following exceptions:

    i.   When the motion may be heard ex parte;

    ii.  When the Federal Rules of Civil Procedure set a different time; or

    iii. When a court order—which a party may, for good cause, apply for ex parte—sets a different time. FRCP 6(c)(1).

  b.  *Supporting affidavit.* Any affidavit supporting a motion must be served with the motion. FRCP 6(c)(2).

4.  *Timing of opposing papers.* Except for letter-motions as permitted by NY R USDCTS&ED Civ Rule 7.1(d), and unless otherwise provided by statute or rule or by the Court in a Judge's Individual Practice or in a direction in a particular case, upon any motion, the notice of motion, supporting affidavits, and memoranda shall be served and filed as follows: on all civil motions, petitions, and applications, other than those described in NY R USDCTS&ED Civ Rule 6.1(a), and other than petitions for writs of habeas corpus, any opposing affidavits and answering memoranda shall be served within fourteen (14) days after service of the moving papers. NY R USDCTS&ED Civ Rule 6.1(b)(2).

  a.  *Opposing affidavit.* Except as FRCP 59(c) provides otherwise, any opposing affidavit must be served at least seven (7) days before the hearing, unless the court permits service at another time. FRCP 6(c)(2).

5.  *Timing of reply papers.* Where the respondent files an answering affidavit setting up a new matter, the moving party ordinarily is allowed a reasonable time to file a reply affidavit since failure to deny the new matter by affidavit may operate as an admission of its truth. AMJUR MOTIONS § 25.

  a.  *Reply affidavits and reply memoranda of law.* Except for letter-motions as permitted by NY R USDCTS&ED Civ Rule 7.1(d), and unless otherwise provided by statute or rule or by the Court in a Judge's Individual Practice or in a direction in a particular case, upon any motion, the notice of motion, supporting affidavits, and memoranda shall be served and filed as follows: on all civil motions, petitions, and applications, other than those described in NY R USDCTS&ED Civ Rule 6.1(a), and other than petitions for writs of habeas corpus, any reply affidavits and memoranda of law shall be served within seven (7) days after service of the answering papers. NY R USDCTS&ED Civ Rule 6.1(b)(3).

6.  *Computation of time*

  a.  *Computing time.* FRCP 6 applies in computing any time period specified in the Federal Rules of Civil Procedure, in any local rule or court order, or in any statute that does not specify a method of computing time. FRCP 6(a). In computing any period of time prescribed or allowed by the Local Civil Rules of the United States District Courts for the Southern and Eastern Districts of New York or the Local Admiralty and Maritime Rules, the provisions of FRCP 6 shall apply unless otherwise stated. NY R USDCTS&ED Civ Rule 6.4.

    i.   *Period stated in days or a longer unit.* In computing periods of days, refer to FRCP 6 and NY R USDCTS&ED Civ Rule 6.4. NY R USDCTS&ED Civ Rule 6.1(b). When the period is stated in days or a longer unit of time:

- Exclude the day of the event that triggers the period;
- Count every day, including intermediate Saturdays, Sundays, and legal holidays; and
- Include the last day of the period, but if the last day is a Saturday, Sunday, or legal holiday, the period continues to run until the end of the next day that is not a Saturday, Sunday, or legal holiday. FRCP 6(a)(1). In the Local Civil Rules of the United States District Courts for the Southern and Eastern Districts of New York, as in the Federal Rules of Civil Procedure as amended effective December 1, 2009, Saturdays, Sundays, and legal holidays are no longer excluded in computing periods of time. If the last day of the period is a Saturday, Sunday, or legal holiday, the period continues to run until the end of the next day that is not a Saturday, Sunday, or legal holiday. NY R USDCTS&ED Civ Rule 6.4.

ii. *Period stated in hours.* When the period is stated in hours:

- Begin counting immediately on the occurrence of the event that triggers the period;

- Count every hour, including hours during intermediate Saturdays, Sundays, and legal holidays; and

- If the period would end on a Saturday, Sunday, or legal holiday, the period continues to run until the same time on the next day that is not a Saturday, Sunday, or legal holiday. FRCP 6(a)(2). In the Local Civil Rules of the United States District Courts for the Southern and Eastern Districts of New York, as in the Federal Rules of Civil Procedure as amended effective December 1, 2009, Saturdays, Sundays, and legal holidays are no longer excluded in computing periods of time. If the last day of the period is a Saturday, Sunday, or legal holiday, the period continues to run until the end of the next day that is not a Saturday, Sunday, or legal holiday. NY R USDCTS&ED Civ Rule 6.4.

iii. *Inaccessibility of the clerk's office.* Unless the court orders otherwise, if the clerk's office is inaccessible:

- On the last day for filing under FRCP 6(a)(1), then the time for filing is extended to the first accessible day that is not a Saturday, Sunday, or legal holiday; or

- During the last hour for filing under FRCP 6(a)(2), then the time for filing is extended to the same time on the first accessible day that is not a Saturday, Sunday, or legal holiday. FRCP 6(a)(3).

iv. *"Last day" defined.* Unless a different time is set by a statute, local rule, or court order, the last day ends:

- For electronic filing, at midnight in the court's time zone; and

- For filing by other means, when the clerk's office is scheduled to close. FRCP 6(a)(4).

v. *"Next day" defined.* The "next day" is determined by continuing to count forward when the period is measured after an event and backward when measured before an event. FRCP 6(a)(5).

vi. *"Legal holiday" defined.* "Legal holiday" means:

- The day set aside by statute for observing New Year's Day, Martin Luther King Jr.'s Birthday, Washington's Birthday, Memorial Day, Independence Day, Labor Day, Columbus Day, Veterans' Day, Thanksgiving Day, or Christmas Day;

- Any day declared a holiday by the President or Congress; and

- For periods that are measured after an event, any other day declared a holiday by the state where the district court is located. FRCP 6(a)(6).

b. *Extending time*

i. *In general.* When an act may or must be done within a specified time, the court may, for good cause, extend the time:

- With or without motion or notice if the court acts, or if a request is made, before the original time or its extension expires; or

- On motion made after the time has expired if the party failed to act because of excusable neglect. FRCP 6(b)(1).

ii. *Exceptions.* A court must not extend the time to act under FRCP 50(b), FRCP 50(d), FRCP 52(b), FRCP 59(b), FRCP 59(d), FRCP 59(e), and FRCP 60(b). FRCP 6(b)(2).

iii. Refer to the United States District Court for the Eastern District of New York KeyRules Motion for Continuance/Extension of Time document for more information on extending time.

c. *Additional time after certain kinds of service.* When a party may or must act within a specified time after service and service is made under FRCP 5(b)(2)(C), FRCP 5(b)(2)(D), FRCP 5(b)(2)(E), or FRCP 5(b)(2)(F), three (3) days are added after the period would otherwise expire under FRCP 6(a). FRCP 6(d). Overnight delivery service shall be deemed service by mail for purposes of FRCP 5 and FRCP 6. NY R USDCTS&ED Civ Rule 5.3.

7. *Individual judge practices.* Refer to the Miscellaneous section of this document for information on individual judge practices on timing of documents.

## C. General Requirements

1. *Mode of raising discovery and other non-dispositive pretrial disputes with the court.* Prior to seeking judicial resolution of a discovery or non-dispositive pretrial dispute, the attorneys for the affected parties or non-party witness shall attempt to confer in good faith in person or by telephone in an effort to resolve the dispute, in conformity with FRCP 37(a)(1). NY R USDCTS&ED Civ Rule 37.3(a). Refer to the Documents section of this document for the procedure to follow when the attorneys for the affected parties or non-party witness cannot agree on a resolution of the discovery or other non-dispositive pretrial dispute.

   a. *Motion for reconsideration.* A ruling made exclusively as a result of a telephone conference may be the subject of de novo reconsideration by a letter not exceeding five (5) pages in length attaching relevant materials submitted by any affected party or non-party witness. Within four (4) days of receiving such a letter, any other affected party or non-party witness may submit a responsive letter not exceeding five (5) pages in length attaching relevant materials. NY R USDCTS&ED Civ Rule 37.3(d).

   b. *Decision of the court.* The Court shall record or arrange for the recording of the Court's decision in writing. Such written order may take the form of an oral order read into the record of a deposition or other proceeding, a handwritten memorandum, a handwritten marginal notation on a letter or other document, or any other form the Court deems appropriate. NY R USDCTS&ED Civ Rule 37.3(e).

2. *Motions, generally*

   a. *Requirements.* A request for a court order must be made by motion. The motion must:

      i. Be in writing unless made during a hearing or trial;

      ii. State with particularity the grounds for seeking the order; and

      iii. State the relief sought. FRCP 7(b)(1).

   b. *Notice of motion.* A party interested in resisting the relief sought by a motion has a right to notice thereof, and an opportunity to be heard. AMJUR MOTIONS § 12.

      i. In addition to statutory or court rule provisions requiring notice of a motion—the purpose of such a notice requirement having been said to be to prevent a party from being prejudicially surprised by a motion—principles of natural justice dictate that an adverse party generally must be given notice that a motion will be presented to the court. AMJUR MOTIONS § 12.

      ii. "Notice," in this regard, means reasonable notice, including a meaningful opportunity to prepare and to defend against allegations of a motion. AMJUR MOTIONS § 12.

   c. *Writing requirement.* The writing requirement is intended to insure that the adverse parties are informed and have a record of both the motion's pendency and the grounds on which the movant seeks an order. FPP § 1191; Feldberg v. Quechee Lakes Corp., 463 F.3d 195 (2d Cir. 2006).

      i. It is sufficient "if the motion is stated in a written notice of the hearing of the motion." FPP § 1191.

   d. *Particularity requirement.* The particularity requirement insures that the opposing parties will have notice of their opponent's contentions. FEDPROC § 62:364; Goodman v. 1973 26 Foot Trojan Vessel, Arkansas Registration No. AR1439SN, 859 F.2d 71, 12 Fed.R.Serv.3d 645 (8th Cir. 1988). That requirement ensures that notice of the basis for the motion is provided to the court and to the opposing party so as to avoid prejudice, provide the opponent with a meaningful opportunity to respond, and provide the court with enough information to process the motion correctly. FEDPROC § 62:364; Andreas v. Volkswagen of America, Inc., 336 F.3d 789, 56 Fed.R.Serv.3d 6 (8th Cir. 2003).

      i. Reasonable specification of the grounds for a motion is sufficient. However, where a movant fails to state even one ground for granting the motion in question, the movant has failed to meet the minimal standard of "reasonable specification." FEDPROC § 62:364; Martinez v. Trainor, 556 F.2d 818, 23 Fed.R.Serv.2d 403 (7th Cir. 1977).

    ii.   The court may excuse the failure to comply with the particularity requirement if it is inadvertent, and where no prejudice is shown by the opposing party. FEDPROC § 62:364.

  e.  *Ex parte orders or orders to show cause to bring on a motion.* No ex parte order, or order to show cause to bring on a motion, will be granted except upon a clear and specific showing by affidavit of good and sufficient reasons why a procedure other than by notice of motion is necessary, and stating whether a previous application for similar relief has been made. NY R USDCTS&ED Civ Rule 6.1(d).

  f.  *Letter-motions.* Applications for extensions or adjournments, applications for a pre-motion conference, and similar non-dispositive matters as permitted by the instructions regarding ECF published on the website of each respective Court and any pertinent Individual Judge's Practices, may be brought by letter-motion filed via ECF pursuant to NY R USDCTS&ED Civ Rule 5.2(b). NY R USDCTS&ED Civ Rule 7.1(d).

3.  *Motion for leave to amend.* FRCP 15(a)(2) provides that after a party has amended a pleading once as of course or the time for amendments of that type has expired, a party may amend only by obtaining leave of the court or if the adverse party consents to it. FPP § 1484; In re Cessna Distributorship Antitrust Litigation, 532 F.2d 64 (8th Cir. 1976). FRCP 15(a) does not set forth any specific procedure for obtaining leave to amend. Typically, it is sought by a motion addressed to the court's discretion. FPP § 1485.

  a.  *Pleadings to be amended.* As in the case of amendments as of course under FRCP 15(a)(1), any of the pleadings enumerated in FRCP 7(a) may be amended with the court's leave and FRCP 15 does not restrict the purposes for which an amendment may be made or its character. FPP § 1484.

  b.  *Prerequisites for leave to amend.* The only prerequisites are that the district court have jurisdiction over the case and an appeal must not be pending. FPP § 1484. If these two conditions are met, the court will proceed to examine the effect and the timing of the proposed amendments to determine whether they would prejudice the rights of any of the other parties to the suit. FPP § 1484; Nilsen v. City of Moss Point, Miss., 674 F.2d 379, 388 (5th Cir. 1982).

  c.  *When leave or consent is not obtained.* In general, if an amendment that cannot be made as of right is served without obtaining the court's leave or the opposing party's consent, it is without legal effect and any new matter it contains will not be considered unless the amendment is resubmitted for the court's approval. Some courts have held, however, that an untimely amended pleading served without judicial permission may be considered as properly introduced when leave to amend would have been granted had it been sought and when it does not appear that any of the parties will be prejudiced by allowing the change. FPP § 1484.

  d.  *Form.* A motion to amend under FRCP 15(a), as is true of motions generally, is subject to the requirements of FRCP 7(b), and must set forth with particularity the relief or order requested and the grounds supporting the application. In order to satisfy these prerequisites a copy of the amendment should be submitted with the motion so that the court and the adverse party know the precise nature of the pleading changes being proposed. FPP § 1485.

  e.  *Oral motion for leave to amend.* Courts have held that an oral request to amend a pleading that is made before the court in the presence of opposing party's counsel may be sufficient if the adverse party is put on notice of the nature and purpose of the request and is given the same opportunity to present objections to the proposed amendment as would have occurred if a formal motion had been made. FPP § 1485.

  f.  *Conditions imposed on leave to amend.* While FRCP 15(a) does not specifically authorize the district court to impose conditions on its granting of leave to amend, it is well settled that the court may impose such conditions to avoid or minimize any prejudice to the opposing party. FEDPROC § 62:276. Conditions frequently are imposed because the amending party knew of the facts sought to be asserted in the amendment but failed to assert such facts until later, to the prejudice of the opposing party. Conversely, the court may decline to impose conditions where the amendment was asserted with relative promptness. FEDPROC § 62:276.

    i.   The moving party's refusal to comply with the conditions imposed by the court normally will result in a denial of the right to amend. FPP § 1486.

g. *When leave to amend may be granted.* If the underlying facts or circumstances relied upon by a plaintiff may be a proper subject of relief, he ought to be afforded an opportunity to test his claim on the merits. In the absence of any apparent or declared reason—such as undue delay, bad faith or dilatory motive on the part of the movant, repeated failure to cure deficiencies by amendments previously allowed, undue prejudice to the opposing party by virtue of allowance of the amendment, futility of amendment, etc.—the leave sought should, as the rules require, be "freely given." FPP § 1487; Foman v. Davis, 371 U.S. 178, 182, 83 S.Ct. 227, 230, 9 L.Ed.2d 222 (1962).

4. *Amendments, generally*

   a. *Amendments before trial.* The function of FRCP 15(a), which provides generally for the amendment of pleadings, is to enable a party to assert matters that were overlooked or were unknown at the time the party interposed the original complaint or answer. FPP § 1473; Smiga v. Dean Witter Reynolds, Inc., 766 F.2d 698, 703 (2d Cir. 1985).

      i. *Matters contained in amended pleading under FRCP 15(a).* Although FRCP 15(a) does not expressly state that an amendment must contain only matters that occurred within a particular time period, FRCP 15(d) provides that any "transaction, occurrence, or event that happened after the date of the pleading" should be set forth in a supplemental pleading. FPP § 1473. Thus, impliedly, an amended pleading, whether prepared with or without leave of court, only should relate to matters that have taken place prior to the date of the earlier pleading. FPP § 1473; Ford Motor Co. v. U.S., 19 C.I.T. 946, 896 F.Supp. 1224, 1230 (1995).

      ii. *Amending as a matter of course.* A party may amend its pleading once as a matter of course within: (1) twenty-one (21) days after serving it, or if the pleading is one to which a responsive pleading is required, twenty-one (21) days after service of a responsive pleading or twenty-one (21) days after service of a motion under FRCP 12(b), FRCP 12(e), or FRCP 12(f), whichever is earlier. FRCP 15(a)(1). Refer to the United States District Court for the Eastern District of New York KeyRules Amended Pleading document for more information on amending as a matter of course.

      iii. *Other amendments.* In all other cases, a party may amend its pleading only with the opposing party's written consent or the court's leave. The court should freely give leave when justice so requires. FRCP 15(a)(2).

      iv. *Types of amendments permitted under FRCP 15(a)*

          • *Cure a defective pleading.* Perhaps the most common use of FRCP 15(a) is by a party seeking to amend in order to cure a defective pleading. FPP § 1474.

          • *Correct insufficiently stated claims or defenses.* A more common use of FRCP 15(a) amendments is to correct insufficiently stated claims or defenses. Typically, amendments of this character involve either adding a necessary allegation in order to state a claim for relief or correcting a misnomer of a party to the action. FPP § 1474.

          • *Change nature or theory of claim or capacity of party.* Courts also have allowed a party to amend in order to change the nature or theory of the party's claim or the capacity in which the party is bringing the action. FPP § 1474.

          • *State additional claims or defenses or drop claims or defenses.* Plaintiffs and defendants also have been permitted to amend their pleadings to state additional claims, to assert additional defenses, or to drop claims or defenses. FPP § 1474; Weinberger v. Retail Credit Co., 498 F.2d 552, 554, n.4 (4th Cir. 1974).

          • *Increase amount of damages or elect a different remedy.* A FRCP 15(a) amendment also is appropriate for increasing the amount of damages sought, or for electing a different remedy than the one originally requested. FPP § 1474; McFadden v. Sanchez, 710 F.2d 907 (2d Cir. 1983).

          • *Add, substitute, or drop parties.* Finally, a party may make a FRCP 15(a) amendment to add, substitute, or drop parties to the action. FPP § 1474.

   b. *Amendments during and after trial*

      i. *Based on an objection at trial.* If, at trial, a party objects that evidence is not within the issues raised in the pleadings, the court may permit the pleadings to be amended. The court should freely permit an amendment when doing so will aid in presenting the merits and the objecting party fails to satisfy the court that the evidence would prejudice that party's action or defense on the merits. The court may grant a continuance to enable the objecting party to meet the evidence. FRCP 15(b)(1).

ii. *For issues tried by consent.* When an issue not raised by the pleadings is tried by the parties' express or implied consent, it must be treated in all respects as if raised in the pleadings. A party may move—at any time, even after judgment—to amend the pleadings to conform them to the evidence and to raise an unpleaded issue. But failure to amend does not affect the result of the trial of that issue. FRCP 15(b)(2).

c. *Relation back of amendments*

i. *When an amendment relates back.* An amendment to a pleading relates back to the date of the original pleading when:

- The law that provides the applicable statute of limitations allows relation back;

- The amendment asserts a claim or defense that arose out of the conduct, transaction, or occurrence set out—or attempted to be set out—in the original pleading; or

- The amendment changes the party or the naming of the party against whom a claim is asserted, if FRCP 15(c)(1)(B) is satisfied and if, within the period provided by FRCP 4(m) for serving the summons and complaint, the party to be brought in by amendment: (1) received such notice of the action that it will not be prejudiced in defending on the merits; and (2) knew or should have known that the action would have been brought against it, but for a mistake concerning the proper party's identity. FRCP 15(c)(1).

ii. *Notice to the United States.* When the United States or a United States officer or agency is added as a defendant by amendment, the notice requirements of FRCP 15(c)(1)(C)(i) and FRCP 15(c)(1)(C)(ii) are satisfied if, during the stated period, process was delivered or mailed to the United States attorney or the United States attorney's designee, to the Attorney General of the United States, or to the officer or agency. FRCP 15(c)(2).

d. *Effect of an amended pleading.* A pleading that has been amended under FRCP 15(a) supersedes the pleading it modifies and remains in effect throughout the action unless it subsequently is modified. FPP § 1476. Once an amended pleading is interposed, the original pleading no longer performs any function in the case and any subsequent motion made by an opposing party should be directed at the amended pleading. FPP § 1476; Ferdik v. Bonzelet, 963 F.2d 1258, 1262 (9th Cir. 1992); Davis v. TXO Production Corp., 929 F.2d 1515, 1517 (10th Cir. 1991).

5. *Opposing papers.* The Federal Rules of Civil Procedure do not require any formal answer, return, or reply to a motion, except where the Federal Rules of Civil Procedure or local rules may require affidavits, memoranda, or other papers to be filed in opposition to a motion. Such papers are simply to apprise the court of such opposition and the grounds of that opposition. FEDPROC § 62:359. Except for letter-motions as permitted by NY R USDCTS&ED Civ Rule 7.1(d) or as otherwise permitted by the Court, all oppositions and replies with respect to motions shall comply with NY R USDCTS&ED Civ Rule 7.1(a)(2) and NY R USDCTS&ED Civ Rule 7.1(a)(3), and an opposing party who seeks relief that goes beyond the denial of the motion shall comply as well with NY R USDCTS&ED Civ Rule 7.1(a)(1). NY R USDCTS&ED Civ Rule 7.1(b).

a. *Effect of failure to respond to motion.* Although in the absence of statutory provision or court rule, a motion ordinarily does not require a written answer, when a party files a motion and the opposing party fails to respond, the court may construe such failure to respond as nonopposition to the motion or an admission that the motion was meritorious, may take the facts alleged in the motion as true—the rule in some jurisdictions being that the failure to respond to a fact set forth in a motion is deemed an admission—and may grant the motion if the relief requested appears to be justified. AMJUR MOTIONS § 28.

b. *Assent or no opposition not determinative.* However, a motion will not be granted automatically simply because an "assent" or a notation of "no opposition" has been filed; federal judges frequently deny motions that have been assented to when it is thought that justice so dictates. FPP § 1190.

c. *Responsive pleading inappropriate as response to motion.* An attempt to answer or oppose a motion with a responsive pleading usually is not appropriate. FPP § 1190.

6. *Reply papers.* A moving party may be required or permitted to prepare papers in addition to his original motion papers. AMJUR MOTIONS § 25. Papers answering or replying to opposing papers may be appropriate, in the interests of justice, where it appears there is a substantial reason for allowing a reply. Thus, a court may accept reply papers where a party demonstrates that the papers to which it seeks to file a reply raise new issues that are material to the disposition of the question before the court, or where the court determines, sua sponte, that it wishes further briefing of an issue raised in those papers and orders the submission of additional papers. FEDPROC § 62:360. Except for letter-motions as permitted by NY R USDCTS&ED Civ Rule 7.1(d) or as otherwise permitted by the Court, all oppositions and replies with respect to motions shall comply with NY R USDCTS&ED Civ Rule 7.1(a)(2) and NY R USDCTS&ED Civ Rule 7.1(a)(3). NY R USDCTS&ED Civ Rule 7.1(b).

a. *Function of reply papers.* The function of a reply affidavit is to answer the arguments made in opposition to the position taken by the movant and not to permit the movant to introduce new arguments in support of the motion. AMJUR MOTIONS § 25.

b. *Issues raised for the first time in a reply document.* However, the view has been followed in some jurisdictions, that as a matter of judicial economy, where there is no prejudice and where the issues could be raised simply by filing a motion to dismiss, the trial court has discretion to consider arguments raised for the first time in a reply memorandum, and that a trial court may grant a motion to strike issues raised for the first time in a reply memorandum. AMJUR MOTIONS § 26.

7. *Orders on motions.* A memorandum signed by the Court of the decision on a motion that does not finally determine all claims for relief, or an oral decision on such a motion, shall constitute the order unless the memorandum or oral decision directs the submission or settlement of an order in more extended form. The notation in the docket of a memorandum or of an oral decision that does not direct the submission or settlement of an order in more extended form shall constitute the entry of the order. Where an order in more extended form is required to be submitted or settled, the notation in the docket of such order shall constitute the entry of the order. NY R USDCTS&ED Civ Rule 6.2.

8. *Related cases.* It shall be the continuing duty of each attorney appearing in any civil or criminal case to bring promptly to the attention of the Court all facts which said attorney believes are relevant to a determination that said case and one or more pending civil or criminal cases should be heard by the same Judge, in order to avoid unnecessary duplication of judicial effort. As soon as the attorney becomes aware of such relationship, said attorney shall notify the Judges to whom the cases have been assigned. NY R USDCTS&ED Civ Rule 1.6(a). If counsel fails to comply with NY R USDCTS&ED Civ Rule 1.6(a), the Court may assess reasonable costs directly against counsel whose action has obstructed the effective administration of the Court's business. NY R USDCTS&ED Civ Rule 1.6(b).

9. *Alternative dispute resolution (ADR)*

a. *Court-annexed arbitration*

i. *Civil cases eligible for compulsory arbitration.* The Clerk of Court shall, as to all cases filed after January 1, 1986, designate and process for compulsory arbitration all civil cases (excluding Social Security cases, tax matters, prisoners' civil rights cases and any action based on an alleged violation of a right secured by the Constitution of the United States or if jurisdiction is based in whole or in part on 28 U.S.C.A. § 1343) wherein money damages only are being sought in an amount not in excess of one hundred fifty thousand dollars ($150,000) exclusive of interest and costs. NY R USDCTS&ED Civ Rule 83.7(d)(1).

- The parties may by written stipulation agree that the Clerk of Court shall designate and process for court-annexed arbitration any civil case that is not subject to compulsory arbitration in NY R USDCTS&ED Civ Rule 83.7. NY R USDCTS&ED Civ Rule 83.7(d)(2).

- For purposes of NY R USDCTS&ED Civ Rule 83.7 only, in all civil cases damages shall be presumed to be not in excess of one hundred fifty thousand dollars ($150,000) exclusive of interest and costs, unless: (1) counsel for plaintiff, at the time of filing the complaint, or in the event of the removal of a case from state court or transfer of a case from another district to this Court, within thirty (30) days of the docketing of the case in this district, files a certification with the Court that the damages sought exceed one hundred fifty thousand dollars ($150,000), exclusive of interest and costs; or (2) counsel for a defendant, at the time of filing a counterclaim or cross-claim files a certification with the court that the damages sought by the counter-claim or cross-claim exceed one hundred fifty thousand dollars ($150,000) exclusive of interest and costs. NY R USDCTS&ED Civ Rule 83.7(d)(3).

    ii.   *Exemption from arbitration.* The Court shall, sua sponte, or on motion of a party, exempt any case from arbitration in which the objectives of arbitration would not be realized (1) because the case involves complex or novel issues, (2) because legal issues predominate over factual issues, or (3) for other good cause. NY R USDCTS&ED Civ Rule 83.7(e)(2). For information on applying for an exemption, refer to NY R USDCTS&ED Civ Rule 83.7

    iii.   *Referral to arbitration.* Cases not originally designated as eligible for compulsory arbitration, but which in the discretion of the assigned Judge, are later found to qualify, may be referred to arbitration. A U.S. District Judge or a U.S. Magistrate Judge, in cases that exceed the arbitration ceiling of one hundred fifty thousand dollars ($150,000) exclusive of interest and costs, in their discretion, may suggest that the parties should consider arbitration. If the parties are agreeable, an appropriate consent form signed by all parties or their representatives may be entered and filed in the case prior to scheduling an arbitration hearing. NY R USDCTS&ED Civ Rule 83.7(e)(3).

    iv.   For more information on arbitration, refer to NY R USDCTS&ED Civ Rule 83.7.

  b.  *Court-annexed mediation.* Mediation is a process in which parties and counsel agree to meet with a neutral mediator trained to assist them in settling disputes. The mediator improves communication across party lines, helps parties articulate their interests and understand those of the other party, probes the strengths and weaknesses of each party's legal positions, and identifies areas of agreement and helps generate options for a mutually agreeable resolution to the dispute. In all cases, mediation provides an opportunity to explore a wide range of potential solutions and to address interests that may be outside the scope of the stated controversy or which could not be addressed by judicial action. A hallmark of mediation is its capacity to expand traditional settlement discussions and broaden resolution options, often by exploring litigant needs and interests that may be formally independent of the legal issues in controversy. NY R USDCTS&ED Civ Rule 83.8(a).

    i.   *Eligible cases.* Judges and Magistrate Judges may designate civil cases for inclusion in the mediation program, and when doing so shall prepare an order to that effect. Alternatively, and subject to the availability of qualified mediators, the parties may consent to participation in the mediation program by preparing and executing a stipulation signed by all parties to the action and so-ordered by the Court. NY R USDCTS&ED Civ Rule 83.8(b)(1).

    ii.   For more information on mediation, refer to NY R USDCTS&ED Civ Rule 83.8.

10.  *Individual judge practices.* Refer to the Miscellaneous section of this document for information on individual judge practices on general requirements for documents.

## D. Documents

1.  *Documents for moving party*

  a.  *Required documents*

    i.   *Letter-motion.* Where the attorneys for the affected parties or non-party witness cannot agree on a resolution of any other discovery dispute or non-dispositive pretrial dispute, or if they are unable to obtain a telephonic ruling on a discovery dispute that arises during a deposition as provided in NY R USDCTS&ED Civ Rule 37.3(b), they shall notify the Court by letter not exceeding three (3) pages in length outlining the nature of the dispute and attaching relevant materials. NY R USDCTS&ED Civ Rule 37.3(c).

    ii.   *Proposed amendment.* In order to satisfy the prerequisites of FRCP 7(b), a copy of the amendment should be submitted with the motion so that the court and the adverse party know the precise nature of the pleading changes being proposed. FPP § 1485. The amending party should submit a copy of the proposed amendment at least by the date of the hearing on the motion for leave to amend. FEDPROC § 62:274; Grombach v. Oerlikon Tool & Arms Corp. of America, 276 F.2d 155 (4th Cir. 1960).

- The documents accompanying the motion for leave to amend may be an appropriate substitute for a formally proposed amendment, if the documents sufficiently indicate the gist of the amendment. FEDPROC § 62:274.

b. *Supplemental documents.* Except for the letters and attachments authorized herein, or where a ruling which was made exclusively as a result of a telephone conference is the subject of de novo review pursuant to NY R USDCTS&ED Civ Rule 37.3(d), papers shall not be submitted with respect to a dispute governed by NY R USDCTS&ED Civ Rule 37.3 unless the Court has so directed. NY R USDCTS&ED Civ Rule 37.3(c).

i. *Supporting evidence.* When a motion relies on facts outside the record, the court may hear the matter on affidavits or may hear it wholly or partly on oral testimony or on depositions. FRCP 43(c). Except for letter-motions as permitted by NY R USDCTS&ED Civ Rule 7.1(d) or as otherwise permitted by the Court, all motions shall include the following motion papers: supporting affidavits and exhibits thereto containing any factual information and portions of the record necessary for the decision of the motion. NY R USDCTS&ED Civ Rule 7.1(a)(3).

- *Discovery materials.* A party seeking or opposing relief under FRCP 26 through FRCP 37 inclusive, or making or opposing any other motion or application, shall quote or attach only those portions of the depositions, interrogatories, requests for documents, requests for admissions, or other discovery or disclosure materials, together with the responses and objections thereto, that are the subject of the discovery motion or application, or that are cited in papers submitted in connection with any other motion or application. NY R USDCTS&ED Civ Rule 5.1.

ii. *Notice of constitutional question.* A party that files a pleading, written motion, or other paper drawing into question the constitutionality of a federal or state statute must promptly:

- *File notice.* File a notice of constitutional question stating the question and identifying the paper that raises it, if: (1) a federal statute is questioned and the parties do not include the United States, one of its agencies, or one of its officers or employees in an official capacity; or (2) a state statute is questioned and the parties do not include the state, one of its agencies, or one of its officers or employees in an official capacity; and

- *Serve notice.* Serve the notice and paper on the Attorney General of the United States if a federal statute is questioned—or on the state attorney general if a state statute is questioned—either by certified or registered mail or by sending it to an electronic address designated by the attorney general for this purpose. FRCP 5.1(a).

- *No forfeiture.* A party's failure to file and serve the notice, or the court's failure to certify, does not forfeit a constitutional claim or defense that is otherwise timely asserted. FRCP 5.1(d).

iii. *Copies of authorities.* In cases involving a pro se litigant, counsel shall, when serving a memorandum of law (or other submissions to the Court), provide the pro se litigant (but not other counsel or the Court) with copies of cases and other authorities cited therein that are unpublished or reported exclusively on computerized databases. Upon request, counsel shall provide the pro se litigant with copies of such unpublished cases and other authorities as are cited in a decision of the Court and were not previously cited by any party. NY R USDCTS&ED Civ Rule 7.2.

iv. *Notice of motion and motion.* Except for letter-motions as permitted by NY R USDCTS&ED Civ Rule 7.1(d) or as otherwise permitted by the Court, all motions shall include the following motion papers: a notice of motion, or an order to show cause signed by the Court, which shall specify the applicable rules or statutes pursuant to which the motion is brought, and shall specify the relief sought by the motion. NY R USDCTS&ED Civ Rule 7.1(a)(1). Refer to the

General Requirements section of this document for information on the notice of motion and motion.

v. *Memorandum of law.* Except for letter-motions as permitted by NY R USDCTS&ED Civ Rule 7.1(d) or as otherwise permitted by the Court, all motions shall include the following motion papers: a memorandum of law, setting forth the cases and other authorities relied upon in support of the motion, and divided, under appropriate headings, into as many parts as there are issues to be determined. NY R USDCTS&ED Civ Rule 7.1(a)(2).

vi. *Certificate of service.* FRCP 5(d) requires that the person making service under FRCP 5 certify that service has been effected. FRCP 5(Advisory Committee Notes). Having such information on file may be useful for many purposes, including proof of service if an issue arises concerning the effectiveness of the service. FRCP 5(Advisory Committee Notes).

2. *Documents for opposing party*

a. *Required documents*

i. *Responsive letter.* Within four (4) days of receiving such a letter, any opposing affected party or non-party witness may submit a responsive letter not exceeding three (3) pages attaching relevant materials. NY R USDCTS&ED Civ Rule 37.3(c).

b. *Supplemental documents.* Except for the letters and attachments authorized herein, or where a ruling which was made exclusively as a result of a telephone conference is the subject of de novo review pursuant to NY R USDCTS&ED Civ Rule 37.3(d), papers shall not be submitted with respect to a dispute governed by NY R USDCTS&ED Civ Rule 37.3 unless the Court has so directed. NY R USDCTS&ED Civ Rule 37.3(c).

i. *Supporting evidence.* When a motion relies on facts outside the record, the court may hear the matter on affidavits or may hear it wholly or partly on oral testimony or on depositions. FRCP 43(c). Except for letter-motions as permitted by NY R USDCTS&ED Civ Rule 7.1(d) or as otherwise permitted by the Court, all oppositions and replies with respect to motions shall comply with NY R USDCTS&ED Civ Rule 7.1(a)(3). NY R USDCTS&ED Civ Rule 7.1(b). Except for letter-motions as permitted by NY R USDCTS&ED Civ Rule 7.1(d) or as otherwise permitted by the Court, all motions shall include the following motion papers: supporting affidavits and exhibits thereto containing any factual information and portions of the record necessary for the decision of the motion. NY R USDCTS&ED Civ Rule 7.1(a)(3).

- *Discovery materials.* A party seeking or opposing relief under FRCP 26 through FRCP 37 inclusive, or making or opposing any other motion or application, shall quote or attach only those portions of the depositions, interrogatories, requests for documents, requests for admissions, or other discovery or disclosure materials, together with the responses and objections thereto, that are the subject of the discovery motion or application, or that are cited in papers submitted in connection with any other motion or application. NY R USDCTS&ED Civ Rule 5.1.

ii. *Notice of constitutional question.* A party that files a pleading, written motion, or other paper drawing into question the constitutionality of a federal or state statute must promptly:

- *File notice.* File a notice of constitutional question stating the question and identifying the paper that raises it, if: (1) a federal statute is questioned and the parties do not include the United States, one of its agencies, or one of its officers or employees in an official capacity; or (2) a state statute is questioned and the parties do not include the state, one of its agencies, or one of its officers or employees in an official capacity; and

- *Serve notice.* Serve the notice and paper on the Attorney General of the United States if a federal statute is questioned—or on the state attorney general if a state statute is questioned—either by certified or registered mail or by sending it to an electronic address designated by the attorney general for this purpose. FRCP 5.1(a).

- *No forfeiture.* A party's failure to file and serve the notice, or the court's failure to certify, does not forfeit a constitutional claim or defense that is otherwise timely asserted. FRCP 5.1(d).

iii. *Copies of authorities.* In cases involving a pro se litigant, counsel shall, when serving a memorandum of law (or other submissions to the Court), provide the pro se litigant (but not other counsel or the Court) with copies of cases and other authorities cited therein that are unpublished or reported exclusively on computerized databases. Upon request, counsel shall provide the pro se litigant with copies of such unpublished cases and other authorities as are cited in a decision of the Court and were not previously cited by any party. NY R USDCTS&ED Civ Rule 7.2.

iv. *Answering memorandum of law.* Except for letter-motions as permitted by NY R USDCTS&ED Civ Rule 7.1(d) or as otherwise permitted by the Court, all oppositions and replies with respect to motions shall comply with NY R USDCTS&ED Civ Rule 7.1(a)(2). NY R USDCTS&ED Civ Rule 7.1(b). Except for letter-motions as permitted by NY R USDCTS&ED Civ Rule 7.1(d) or as otherwise permitted by the Court, all motions shall include the following motion papers: a memorandum of law, setting forth the cases and other authorities relied upon in support of the motion, and divided, under appropriate headings, into as many parts as there are issues to be determined. NY R USDCTS&ED Civ Rule 7.1(a)(2). Refer to the General Requirements section of this document for information on the opposing papers.

v. *Certificate of service.* FRCP 5(d) requires that the person making service under FRCP 5 certify that service has been effected. FRCP 5(Advisory Committee Notes). Having such information on file may be useful for many purposes, including proof of service if an issue arises concerning the effectiveness of the service. FRCP 5(Advisory Committee Notes).

3. *Individual judge practices.* Refer to the Miscellaneous section of this document for information on individual judge practices on required documents.

## E. Format

1. *Form of documents.* The rules governing captions and other matters of form in pleadings apply to motions and other papers. FRCP 7(b)(2).

   a. *Paper.* Every pleading, written motion, and other paper must: be plainly written, typed, printed, or copied without erasures or interlineations which materially deface it. NY R USDCTS&ED Civ Rule 11.1(a)(1).

   b. *Typeface, margin, and spacing.* The typeface, margins, and spacing of all documents presented for filing must meet the following requirements:

      i. All text must be twelve (12) point type or larger, except for text in footnotes which may be ten (10) point type;

      ii. All documents must have at least one (1) inch margins on all sides;

      iii. All text must be double-spaced, except for headings, text in footnotes, or block quotations, which may be single-spaced. NY R USDCTS&ED Civ Rule 11.1(b).

   c. *Caption; Names of parties.* Every pleading must have a caption with the court's name, a title, a file number, and a FRCP 7(a) designation. The title of the complaint must name all the parties; the title of other pleadings, after naming the first party on each side, may refer generally to other parties. FRCP 10(a). Every pleading, written motion, and other paper must: bear the docket number and the initials of the District Judge and any Magistrate Judge before whom the action or proceeding is pending, NY R USDCTS&ED Civ Rule 11.1(a)(2).

   d. *Paragraphs; Separate statements.* A party must state its claims or defenses in numbered paragraphs, each limited as far as practicable to a single set of circumstances. A later pleading may refer by number to a paragraph in an earlier pleading. If doing so would promote clarity, each claim founded on a separate transaction or occurrence—and each defense other than a denial—must be stated in a separate count or defense. FRCP 10(b).

   e. *Adoption by reference; Exhibits.* A statement in a pleading may be adopted by reference elsewhere in the same pleading or in any other pleading or motion. A copy of a written instrument that is an exhibit to a pleading is a part of the pleading for all purposes. FRCP 10(c).

   f. *Acceptance by the clerk.* The clerk must not refuse to file a paper solely because it is not in the form prescribed by the Federal Rules of Civil Procedure or by a local rule or practice. FRCP 5(d)(4).

2. *Signing of pleadings, motions and other papers*

    a. *Signature.* Every pleading, written motion, and other paper must be signed by at least one attorney of record in the attorney's name—or by a party personally if the party is unrepresented. The paper must state the signer's address, e-mail address, and telephone number. FRCP 11(a). Every pleading, written motion, and other paper must: have the name of each person signing it clearly printed or typed directly below the signature. NY R USDCTS&ED Civ Rule 11.1(a)(3).

        i. *No verification or accompanying affidavit required for pleadings.* Unless a rule or statute specifically states otherwise, a pleading need not be verified or accompanied by an affidavit. FRCP 11(a).

        ii. *Unsigned papers.* The court must strike an unsigned paper unless the omission is promptly corrected after being called to the attorney's or party's attention. FRCP 11(a).

    b. *Representations to the court.* By presenting to the court a pleading, written motion, or other paper—whether by signing, filing, submitting, or later advocating it—an attorney or unrepresented party certifies that to the best of the person's knowledge, information, and belief, formed after an inquiry reasonable under the circumstances:

        i. It is not being presented for any improper purpose, such as to harass, cause unnecessary delay, or needlessly increase the cost of litigation;

        ii. The claims, defenses, and other legal contentions are warranted by existing law or by a nonfrivolous argument for extending, modifying, or reversing existing law or for establishing new law;

        iii. The factual contentions have evidentiary support or, if specifically so identified, will likely have evidentiary support after a reasonable opportunity for further investigation or discovery; and

        iv. The denials of factual contentions are warranted on the evidence or, if specifically so identified, are reasonably based on belief or a lack of information. FRCP 11(b).

    c. *Sanctions.* If, after notice and a reasonable opportunity to respond, the court determines that FRCP 11(b) has been violated, the court may impose an appropriate sanction on any attorney, law firm, or party that violated FRCP 11(b) or is responsible for the violation. FRCP 11(c)(1). Refer to the United States District Court for the Eastern District of New York KeyRules Motion for Sanctions document for more information.

3. *Privacy protection for filings made with the court*

    a. *Redacted filings.* Unless the court orders otherwise, in an electronic or paper filing with the court that contains an individual's Social Security number, taxpayer-identification number, or birth date, the name of an individual known to be a minor, or a financial-account number, a party or nonparty making the filing may include only:

        i. The last four (4) digits of the Social Security number and taxpayer-identification number;

        ii. The year of the individual's birth;

        iii. The minor's initials; and

        iv. The last four (4) digits of the financial-account number. FRCP 5.2(a); NY R USDCTED Order 2004-09.

        v. In addition, exercise caution when filing documents that contain the following:

          • Personal identifying number, such as driver's license number;

          • Medical records, treatment and diagnosis;

          • Employment history;

          • Individual financial information; and

          • Proprietary or trade secret information. NY R USDCTED Order 2004-09.

b. *Exemptions from the redaction requirement.* The redaction requirement does not apply to the following:

    i. A financial-account number that identifies the property allegedly subject to forfeiture in a forfeiture proceeding;

    ii. The record of an administrative or agency proceeding;

    iii. The official record of a state-court proceeding;

    iv. The record of a court or tribunal, if that record was not subject to the redaction requirement when originally filed;

    v. A filing covered by FRCP 5.2(c) or FRCP 5.2(d); and

    vi. A pro se filing in an action brought under 28 U.S.C.A. § 2241, 28 U.S.C.A. § 2254, or 28 U.S.C.A. § 2255. FRCP 5.2(b).

c. *Limitations on remote access to electronic files; Social Security appeals and immigration cases.* Unless the court orders otherwise, in an action for benefits under the Social Security Act, and in an action or proceeding relating to an order of removal, to relief from removal, or to immigration benefits or detention, access to an electronic file is authorized as follows:

    i. The parties and their attorneys may have remote electronic access to any part of the case file, including the administrative record;

    ii. Any other person may have electronic access to the full record at the courthouse, but may have remote electronic access only to:

- The docket maintained by the court; and

- An opinion, order, judgment, or other disposition of the court, but not any other part of the case file or the administrative record. FRCP 5.2(c).

d. *Filings made under seal.* The court may order that a filing be made under seal without redaction. The court may later unseal the filing or order the person who made the filing to file a redacted version for the public record. FRCP 5.2(d).

e. *Protective orders.* For good cause, the court may by order in a case:

    i. Require redaction of additional information; or

    ii. Limit or prohibit a nonparty's remote electronic access to a document filed with the court. FRCP 5.2(e).

f. *Option for additional unredacted filing under seal.* A person making a redacted filing may also file an unredacted copy under seal. The court must retain the unredacted copy as part of the record. FRCP 5.2(f); NY R USDCTED Order 2004-09. The unredacted version of the document or the reference list shall be retained by the court as part of the record. The court may, however, still require the party to file a redacted copy for the public file. NY R USDCTED Order 2004-09.

g. *Option for filing a reference list.* A filing that contains redacted information may be filed together with a reference list that identifies each item of redacted information and specifies an appropriate identifier that uniquely corresponds to each item listed. The list must be filed under seal and may be amended as of right. Any reference in the case to a listed identifier will be construed to refer to the corresponding item of information. FRCP 5.2(g); NY R USDCTED Order 2004-09. The unredacted version of the document or the reference list shall be retained by the court as part of the record. The court may, however, still require the party to file a redacted copy for the public file. NY R USDCTED Order 2004-09.

h. *Responsibility for redaction.* The responsibility for redacting these personal identifiers rests solely with counsel and the parties. The Clerk will not review each pleading for compliance with NY R USDCTED Order 2004-09. NY R USDCTED Order 2004-09.

    i. Counsel is strongly urged to share this notice with all clients so that an informed decision about the inclusion of certain materials may be made. If a redacted document is filed, it is the sole responsibility of counsel and the parties to be sure that all pleadings comply with the rules of

this court requiring redaction of personal data identifiers. The clerk will not review each pleading for redaction. NY R USDCTED Order 2004-09.

   i. *Waiver of protection of identifiers.* A person waives the protection of FRCP 5.2(a) as to the person's own information by filing it without redaction and not under seal. FRCP 5.2(h).

4. *Individual judge practices.* Refer to the Miscellaneous section of this document for information on individual judge practices on formatting documents.

## F. Filing and Service Requirements

1. *Filing requirements.* Any paper after the complaint that is required to be served—together with a certificate of service—must be filed within a reasonable time after service. FRCP 5(d)(1).

   a. *How filing is made; In general.* A paper is filed by delivering it:

      i. To the clerk; or

      ii. To a judge who agrees to accept it for filing, and who must then note the filing date on the paper and promptly send it to the clerk. FRCP 5(d)(2).

   b. *Night depository.* A night depository with an automatic date stamp shall be maintained. . .by the Clerk of the Eastern District in the Brooklyn Courthouse. After regular business hours, papers for the District Court only may be deposited in the night depository. Such papers will be considered as having been filed in the District Court as of the date stamped thereon, which shall be deemed presumptively correct. NY R USDCTS&ED Civ Rule 1.2.

   c. *Electronic filing*

      i. *Authorization of electronic filing program.* A court may, by local rule, allow papers to be filed, signed, or verified by electronic means that are consistent with any technical standards established by the Judicial Conference of the United States. A local rule may require electronic filing only if reasonable exceptions are allowed. A paper filed electronically in compliance with a local rule is a written paper for purposes of the Federal Rules of Civil Procedure. FRCP 5(d)(3).

        • Parties serving and filing papers shall follow the instructions regarding Electronic Case Filing (ECF) published on the website of each respective Court. A paper served and filed by electronic means in accordance with such instructions is, for purposes of FRCP 5, served and filed in compliance with the Local Civil Rules of the Southern and Eastern Districts of New York. NY R USDCTS&ED Civ Rule 5.2(a). Parties have an obligation to review the Court's actual order, decree, or judgment (on ECF), which controls, and should not rely on the description on the docket or in the ECF Notice of Electronic Filing (NEF). NY R USDCTS&ED Civ Rule 5.2(c).

      ii. *Mandatory electronic filing.* Beginning on August 2, 2004, electronic case filing will be mandatory for all civil cases other than pro se cases. NY R USDCTED Order 2004-08.

        • *Letter-motions and letters addressed to the court.* Subject to the instructions regarding ECF published on the website of each respective Court and any pertinent Individual Judge's Practices, letter-motions permitted by NY R USDCTS&ED Civ Rule 7.1(d) and letters addressed to the Court (but not letters between the parties) may be filed via ECF. NY R USDCTS&ED Civ Rule 5.2(b).

        • *Proposed orders, judgments and decrees.* Proposed orders, judgments and decrees shall be presented as directed by the ECF rules published on the website of each respective Court. NY R USDCTS&ED Civ Rule 77.1. For more information, refer to NY R USDCTS&ED Civ Rule 77.1.

        • *Request for exemption.* Requests by attorneys for an exemption to the mandatory policy will be considered for good cause hardship reasons only, and will be reviewed on an individual basis by the assigned United States Magistrate Judge. The Clerk's Office provides an electronic filing training program to assist attorneys filing electronically. Before seeking a hardship exemption, attorneys are advised to participate in the training program or otherwise seek the assistance of the Clerk's Office. NY R USDCTED Order 2004-08.

iii. For more information on electronic filing, refer to the court's website.

2. *Service requirements*

  a. *Service; When required*

    i. *In general.* Unless the Federal Rules of Civil Procedure provide otherwise, each of the following papers must be served on every party:

- An order stating that service is required;
- A pleading filed after the original complaint, unless the court orders otherwise under FRCP 5(c) because there are numerous defendants;
- A discovery paper required to be served on a party, unless the court orders otherwise;
- A written motion, except one that may be heard ex parte; and
- A written notice, appearance, demand, or offer of judgment, or any similar paper. FRCP 5(a)(1).

    ii. *If a party fails to appear.* No service is required on a party who is in default for failing to appear. But a pleading that asserts a new claim for relief against such a party must be served on that party under FRCP 4. FRCP 5(a)(2).

    iii. *Seizing property.* If an action is begun by seizing property and no person is or need be named as a defendant, any service required before the filing of an appearance, answer, or claim must be made on the person who had custody or possession of the property when it was seized. FRCP 5(a)(3).

  b. *Service; How made*

    i. *Serving an attorney.* If a party is represented by an attorney, service under FRCP 5 must be made on the attorney unless the court orders service on the party. FRCP 5(b)(1).

    ii. *Service in general.* A paper is served under FRCP 5 by:

- Handing it to the person;
- Leaving it: (1) at the person's office with a clerk or other person in charge or, if no one is in charge, in a conspicuous place in the office; or (2) if the person has no office or the office is closed, at the person's dwelling or usual place of abode with someone of suitable age and discretion who resides there;
- Mailing it to the person's last known address—in which event service is complete upon mailing;
- Leaving it with the court clerk if the person has no known address;
- Sending it by electronic means if the person consented in writing—in which event service is complete upon transmission, but is not effective if the serving party learns that it did not reach the person to be served; or
- Delivering it by any other means that the person consented to in writing—in which event service is complete when the person making service delivers it to the agency designated to make delivery. FRCP 5(b)(2).

    iii. *Service by overnight delivery.* Service upon an attorney may be made by overnight delivery service. "Overnight delivery service" means any delivery service which regularly accepts items for overnight delivery. Overnight delivery service shall be deemed service by mail for purposes of FRCP 5 and FRCP 6. NY R USDCTS&ED Civ Rule 5.3.

    iv. *Service by electronic means.* Parties serving and filing papers shall follow the instructions regarding Electronic Case Filing (ECF) published on the website of each respective Court. A paper served and filed by electronic means in accordance with such instructions is, for purposes of FRCP 5, served and filed in compliance with the Local Civil Rules of the United States District Courts for the Southern and Eastern Districts of New York. NY R USDCTS&ED Civ Rule 5.2(a). Parties have an obligation to review the Court's actual order, decree, or judgment

(on ECF), which controls, and should not rely on the description on the docket or in the ECF Notice of Electronic Filing (NEF). NY R USDCTS&ED Civ Rule 5.2(c).

    v. *Using court facilities.* If a local rule so authorizes, a party may use the court's transmission facilities to make service under FRCP 5(b)(2)(E). FRCP 5(b)(3).

  c. *Serving numerous defendants*

    i. *In general.* If an action involves an unusually large number of defendants, the court may, on motion or on its own, order that:

- Defendants' pleadings and replies to them need not be served on other defendants;

- Any crossclaim, counterclaim, avoidance, or affirmative defense in those pleadings and replies to them will be treated as denied or avoided by all other parties; and

- Filing any such pleading and serving it on the plaintiff constitutes notice of the pleading to all parties. FRCP 5(c)(1).

    ii. *Notifying parties.* A copy of every such order must be served on the parties as the court directs. FRCP 5(c)(2).

3. *Individual judge practices.* Refer to the Miscellaneous section of this document for information on individual judge practices on filing and serving documents.

## G. Hearings

1. *Hearings, generally*

  a. *Oral argument.* Due process does not require that oral argument be permitted on a motion and, except as otherwise provided by local rule, the district court has discretion to determine whether it will decide the motion on the papers or hear argument by counsel (and perhaps receive evidence). FPP § 1190; F.D.I.C. v. Deglau, 207 F.3d 153 (3d Cir. 2000). The parties and their attorneys shall only appear to argue the motion if so directed by the Court by order or by a Judge's Individual Practice. NY R USDCTS&ED Civ Rule 6.1(c).

  b. *Providing a regular schedule for oral hearings.* A court may establish regular times and places for oral hearings on motions. FRCP 78(a).

  c. *Providing for submission on briefs.* By rule or order, the court may provide for submitting and determining motions on briefs, without oral hearings. FRCP 78(b).

2. *Individual judge practices.* Refer to the Miscellaneous section of this document for information on individual judge practices on hearings.

## H. Forms

### 1. Federal Motion for Leave to Amend Forms

  a. Leave to amend complaint; Attaching copy of amendment. 2C FEDFORMS § 14:18.

  b. Leave to amend complaint; Inserting amendment. 2C FEDFORMS § 14:19.

  c. Leave to amend complaint; Interlineation. 2C FEDFORMS § 14:20.

  d. Leave to amend complaint; Responding to motion to dismiss complaint. 2C FEDFORMS § 14:21.

  e. Leave to amend complaint; Close to trial. 2C FEDFORMS § 14:22.

  f. Leave to amend complaint; Adding new count. 2C FEDFORMS § 14:24.

  g. Leave to amend complaint; Asserting lack of knowledge of facts at time of original complaint. 2C FEDFORMS § 14:25.

  h. Leave to amend complaint; Seeking fourth amendment. 2C FEDFORMS § 14:26.

  i. Leave to amend complaint; Substituting plaintiff and dropping defendant. 2C FEDFORMS § 14:27.

  j. Leave to amend answer. 2C FEDFORMS § 14:30.

  k. Leave to amend answer; With leave endorsed. 2C FEDFORMS § 14:31.

  l. Leave to amend answer; Correcting errors, deleting and interlining. 2C FEDFORMS § 14:32.

m. Leave to amend answer; Adding paragraph. 2C FEDFORMS § 14:33.

n. Leave to amend answer; Adding defense. 2C FEDFORMS § 14:34.

o. Leave to amend answer; During trial. 2C FEDFORMS § 14:35.

p. Defendant's response to motion for leave to amend complaint a fourth time. 2C FEDFORMS § 14:36.

q. Motion and notice; For leave to file amended pleading. FEDPROF § 1:222.

r. Motion; To amend pleading to conform to findings of master. FEDPROF § 1:223.

s. Affidavit; In support of motion for amendment of pleading. FEDPROF § 1:230.

t. Opposition; To motion; General form. FEDPROF § 1:750.

u. Affidavit; Supporting or opposing motion. FEDPROF § 1:751.

v. Brief; Supporting or opposing motion. FEDPROF § 1:752.

w. Statement of points and authorities; Opposing motion. FEDPROF § 1:753.

x. Motion for leave to amend pleading. GOLDLTGFMS § 14:3.

y. Motion to file second amended complaint on ground of newly discovered evidence. GOLDLTGFMS § 14:20.

z. Motion for leave to file amended answer. GOLDLTGFMS § 14:22.

## I. Applicable Rules

1. *Federal rules*

   a. Serving and filing pleadings and other papers. FRCP 5.

   b. Constitutional challenge to a statute; Notice, certification, and intervention. FRCP 5.1.

   c. Privacy protection for filings made with the court. FRCP 5.2.

   d. Computing and extending time; Time for motion papers. FRCP 6.

   e. Pleadings allowed; Form of motions and other papers. FRCP 7.

   f. Form of pleadings. FRCP 10.

   g. Signing pleadings, motions, and other papers; Representations to the court; Sanctions. FRCP 11.

   h. Amended and supplemental pleadings. FRCP 15.

   i. Taking testimony. FRCP 43.

   j. Hearing motions; Submission on briefs. FRCP 78.

2. *Local rules*

   a. Night depository. NY R USDCTS&ED Civ Rule 1.2.

   b. Duty of attorneys in related cases. NY R USDCTS&ED Civ Rule 1.6.

   c. Filing of discovery materials. NY R USDCTS&ED Civ Rule 5.1.

   d. Electronic service and filing of documents. NY R USDCTS&ED Civ Rule 5.2.

   e. Service by overnight delivery. NY R USDCTS&ED Civ Rule 5.3.

   f. Service and filing of motion papers. NY R USDCTS&ED Civ Rule 6.1.

   g. Orders on motions. NY R USDCTS&ED Civ Rule 6.2.

   h. Computation of time. NY R USDCTS&ED Civ Rule 6.4.

   i. Motion papers. NY R USDCTS&ED Civ Rule 7.1.

   j. Authorities to be provided to pro se litigants. NY R USDCTS&ED Civ Rule 7.2.

   k. Form of pleadings, motions, and other papers. NY R USDCTS&ED Civ Rule 11.1.

   l. Mode of raising discovery and other non-dispositive pretrial disputes with the court (Eastern District only). NY R USDCTS&ED Civ Rule 37.3.

m.   Submission of orders, judgments and decrees. NY R USDCTS&ED Civ Rule 77.1.

n.   Court-annexed arbitration (Eastern District only). NY R USDCTS&ED Civ Rule 83.7.

o.   Court-annexed mediation (Eastern District only). NY R USDCTS&ED Civ Rule 83.8.

p.   Electronic case filing. NY R USDCTED Order 2004-08.

q.   The August 2, 2004 amendment to the E-Government Act of 2002. NY R USDCTED Order 2004-09.

## J.  Miscellaneous

**NOTE: Individual judges' rules may apply. For available judge-level information, refer to:**

DISTRICT JUDGE CAROL BAGLEY AMON: NY R USDCTED Amon-Practices.

DISTRICT JUDGE JOAN M. AZRACK: NY R USDCTED Azrack-Practices.

DISTRICT JUDGE JOSEPH F. BIANCO: NY R USDCTED Bianco-Practices.

DISTRICT JUDGE FREDERIC BLOCK: NY R USDCTED Block-Practices.

DISTRICT JUDGE MARGO K. BRODIE: NY R USDCTED Brodie-Practices.

DISTRICT JUDGE PAMELA K. CHEN: NY R USDCTED Chen-Practices.

DISTRICT JUDGE BRIAN M. COGAN: NY R USDCTED Cogan-Practices; NY R USDCTED Cogan-Pretrial.

DISTRICT JUDGE LaSHANN DeARCY HALL: NY R USDCTED DeArcy Hall-Practices.

DISTRICT JUDGE RAYMOND J. DEARIE: NY R USDCTED Dearie-Practices.

DISTRICT JUDGE ANN M. DONNELLY: NY R USDCTED Donnelly-Practices.

DISTRICT JUDGE SANDRA J. FEUERSTEIN: NY R USDCTED Feuerstein-Practices; NY R USDCTED Feuerstein-Pretrial.

DISTRICT JUDGE NICHOLAS G. GARAUIFIS: NY R USDCTED Garaufis-Practices; NY R USDCTED Garaufis-Pretrial.

DISTRICT JUDGE NINA GERSHON: NY R USDCTED Gershon-Practices.

DISTRICT JUDGE I. LEO GLASSER: NY R USDCTED Glasser-Practices; NY R USDCTED Glasser-Crim.

DISTRICT JUDGE DENIS R. HURLEY: NY R USDCTED Hurley-Practices; [NY R USDCTED Hurley-Pro Cooperation Info, as added by NY ORDER 16-4188, effective July 22, 2016]; [NY R USDCTED Hurley-Pro Cooperation Info Stay, as added by NY ORDER 16-4188, effective July 22, 2016].

DISTRICT JUDGE DORA L. IRIZARRY: NY R USDCTED Irizarry-Practices; NY R USDCTED Irizarry-Pretrial; NY R USDCTED Irizarry-Crim.

DISTRICT JUDGE STERLING JOHNSON, JR.: NY R USDCTED Johnson-Practices.

DISTRICT JUDGE EDWARD R. KORMAN: NY R USDCTED Korman-Practices; NY R USDCTED Korman-Pretrial.

DISTRICT JUDGE WILLIAM F. KUNTZ: NY R USDCTED Kuntz-Practices.

DISTRICT JUDGE KIYO A. MATSUMOTO: NY R USDCTED Matsumoto-Practices.

DISTRICT JUDGE ROSLYNN R. MAUSKOPF: NY R USDCTED Mauskopf-Practices; NY R USDCTED Mauskopf-Recusal.

DISTRICT JUDGE THOMAS C. PLATT: NY R USDCTED Platt-Practices.

DISTRICT JUDGE ALLYNE R. ROSS: NY R USDCTED Ross-Practices.

DISTRICT JUDGE JOANNA SEYBERT: NY R USDCTED Seybert-Practices.

DISTRICT JUDGE ARTHUR D. SPATT: NY R USDCTED Spatt-Practices.

DISTRICT JUDGE SANDRA L. TOWNES: NY R USDCTED Townes-Practices.

DISTRICT JUDGE ERIC N. VITALIANO: NY R USDCTED Vitaliano-Practices.

DISTRICT JUDGE JACK B. WEINSTEIN: NY R USDCTED Weinstein-Practices.

DISTRICT JUDGE LEONARD D. WEXLER: NY R USDCTED Wexler-Practices; NY R USDCTED Wexler-Rules.

MAGISTRATE JUDGE LOIS BLOOM: NY R USDCTED Bloom-Practices.

MAGISTRATE JUDGE GARY R. BROWN: NY R USDCTED Brown-Practices.

MAGISTRATE JUDGE MARILYN D. GO: NY R USDCTED Go-Practices.

MAGISTRATE JUDGE STEVEN M. GOLD: NY R USDCTED Gold-Practices.

MAGISTRATE JUDGE PEGGY KUO: NY R USDCTED Kuo-Practices; NY R USDCTED Kuo-Scheduling Order.

MAGISTRATE JUDGE ROBERT M. LEVY: NY R USDCTED Levy-Practices.

MAGISTRATE JUDGE ARLENE R. LINDSAY: NY R USDCTED Lindsay-Practices.

MAGISTRATE JUDGE STEVEN I. LOCKE: NY R USDCTED Locke-Practices.

MAGISTRATE JUDGE ROANNE L. MANN: NY R USDCTED Mann-Practices.

MAGISTRATE JUDGE JAMES ORENSTEIN: NY R USDCTED Jorenstein--Practices.

MAGISTRATE JUDGE VIKTOR V. POHORELSKY: NY R USDCTED Pohorelsky-Practices.

MAGISTRATE JUDGE CHERYL L. POLLAK: NY R USDCTED Pollak-Practices; NY R USDCTED Pollak-Pretrial.

MAGISTRATE JUDGE RAMON E. REYES, JR.: NY R USDCTED Reyes-Practices.

MAGISTRATE JUDGE VERA M. SCANLON: NY R USDCTED Scanlon-Practices.

MAGISTRATE JUDGE ANNE Y. SHIELDS: NY R USDCTED Shields-Practices.

MAGISTRATE JUDGE STEVEN L. TISCIONE: NY R USDCTED Tiscione-Practices.

MAGISTRATE JUDGE A. KATHLEEN TOMILINSON: NY R USDCTED Tomlinson-Practices.

# Motions, Oppositions and Replies
# Motion for Continuance/Extension of Time

### Document Last Updated September 2016

**A. Checklist**

(I)  ❑ Matters to be considered by moving party

   (a)  ❑ Required documents

      (1)  ❑ Letter-motion

   (b)  ❑ Supplemental documents

      (1)  ❑ Supporting evidence

      (2)  ❑ Notice of constitutional question

      (3)  ❑ Nongovernmental corporate disclosure statement

      (4)  ❑ Copies of authorities

      (5)  ❑ Notice of motion and motion

      (6)  ❑ Memorandum of law

      (7)  ❑ Certificate of service

   (c)  ❑ Timing

      (1)  ❑ There are no specific timing requirements for submitting a letter-motion to the court

      (2)  ❑ Continuance: there are no specific timing requirements for moving for a continuance

(3) ❏ Extension of time: when an act may or must be done within a specified time, the court may, for good cause, extend the time:

    (i) ❏ With or without motion or notice if the court acts, or if a request is made, before the original time or its extension expires; or

    (ii) ❏ On motion made after the time has expired if the party failed to act because of excusable neglect

(4) ❏ A written motion and notice of the hearing must be served at least fourteen (14) days before the time specified for the hearing, with the following exceptions: (i) when the motion may be heard ex parte; (ii) when the Federal Rules of Civil Procedure set a different time; or (iii) when a court order—which a party may, for good cause, apply for ex parte—sets a different time

(5) ❏ Any affidavit supporting a motion must be served with the motion

(II) ❏ Matters to be considered by opposing party

  (a) ❏ Required documents

    (1) ❏ Responsive letter

  (b) ❏ Supplemental documents

    (1) ❏ Supporting evidence

    (2) ❏ Notice of constitutional question

    (3) ❏ Copies of authorities

    (4) ❏ Answering memorandum of law

    (5) ❏ Certificate of service

  (c) ❏ Timing

    (1) ❏ Within four (4) days of receiving such a letter, any opposing affected party or non-party witness may submit a responsive letter not exceeding three (3) pages attaching relevant materials

    (2) ❏ Any opposing affidavits and answering memoranda shall be served within fourteen (14) days after service of the moving papers

    (3) ❏ Except as FRCP 59(c) provides otherwise, any opposing affidavit must be served at least seven (7) days before the hearing, unless the court permits service at another time

## B. Timing

1. *Mode of raising discovery and other non-dispositive pretrial disputes with the court*

  a. *Letter-motion.* There are no specific timing requirements for submitting a letter-motion to the court.

  b. *Responsive letter.* Within four (4) days of receiving such a letter, any opposing affected party or non-party witness may submit a responsive letter not exceeding three (3) pages attaching relevant materials. NY R USDCTS&ED Civ Rule 37.3(c).

2. *Motion for continuance/extension of time*

  a. *Continuance.* There are no specific timing requirements for moving for a continuance.

  b. *Extension of time.* When an act may or must be done within a specified time, the court may, for good cause, extend the time:

    i. With or without motion or notice if the court acts, or if a request is made, before the original time or its extension expires; or

    ii. On motion made after the time has expired if the party failed to act because of excusable neglect. FRCP 6(b)(1).

3. *Timing of motions, generally*

  a. *Motion and notice of hearing.* Except for letter-motions as permitted by NY R USDCTS&ED Civ

Rule 7.1(d), and unless otherwise provided by statute or rule or by the Court in a Judge's Individual Practice or in a direction in a particular case, upon any motion, the notice of motion, supporting affidavits, and memoranda shall be served and filed as follows: on all civil motions, petitions, and applications, other than those described in NY R USDCTS&ED Civ Rule 6.1(a), and other than petitions for writs of habeas corpus, the notice of motion, supporting affidavits, and memoranda of law shall be served by the moving party on all other parties that have appeared in the action. NY R USDCTS&ED Civ Rule 6.1(b)(1). A written motion and notice of the hearing must be served at least fourteen (14) days before the time specified for the hearing, with the following exceptions:

    i. When the motion may be heard ex parte;

    ii. When the Federal Rules of Civil Procedure set a different time; or

    iii. When a court order—which a party may, for good cause, apply for ex parte—sets a different time. FRCP 6(c)(1).

  b. *Supporting affidavit.* Any affidavit supporting a motion must be served with the motion. FRCP 6(c)(2).

4. *Timing of opposing papers.* Except for letter-motions as permitted by NY R USDCTS&ED Civ Rule 7.1(d), and unless otherwise provided by statute or rule or by the Court in a Judge's Individual Practice or in a direction in a particular case, upon any motion, the notice of motion, supporting affidavits, and memoranda shall be served and filed as follows: on all civil motions, petitions, and applications, other than those described in NY R USDCTS&ED Civ Rule 6.1(a), and other than petitions for writs of habeas corpus, any opposing affidavits and answering memoranda shall be served within fourteen (14) days after service of the moving papers. NY R USDCTS&ED Civ Rule 6.1(b)(2).

  a. *Opposing affidavit.* Except as FRCP 59(c) provides otherwise, any opposing affidavit must be served at least seven (7) days before the hearing, unless the court permits service at another time. FRCP 6(c)(2).

5. *Timing of reply papers.* Where the respondent files an answering affidavit setting up a new matter, the moving party ordinarily is allowed a reasonable time to file a reply affidavit since failure to deny the new matter by affidavit may operate as an admission of its truth. AMJUR MOTIONS § 25.

  a. *Reply affidavits and reply memoranda of law.* Except for letter-motions as permitted by NY R USDCTS&ED Civ Rule 7.1(d), and unless otherwise provided by statute or rule or by the Court in a Judge's Individual Practice or in a direction in a particular case, upon any motion, the notice of motion, supporting affidavits, and memoranda shall be served and filed as follows: on all civil motions, petitions, and applications, other than those described in NY R USDCTS&ED Civ Rule 6.1(a), and other than petitions for writs of habeas corpus, any reply affidavits and memoranda of law shall be served within seven (7) days after service of the answering papers. NY R USDCTS&ED Civ Rule 6.1(b)(3).

6. *Computation of time*

  a. *Computing time.* FRCP 6 applies in computing any time period specified in the Federal Rules of Civil Procedure, in any local rule or court order, or in any statute that does not specify a method of computing time. FRCP 6(a). In computing any period of time prescribed or allowed by the Local Civil Rules of the United States District Courts for the Southern and Eastern Districts of New York or the Local Admiralty and Maritime Rules, the provisions of FRCP 6 shall apply unless otherwise stated. NY R USDCTS&ED Civ Rule 6.4.

    i. *Period stated in days or a longer unit.* In computing periods of days, refer to FRCP 6 and NY R USDCTS&ED Civ Rule 6.4. NY R USDCTS&ED Civ Rule 6.1(b). When the period is stated in days or a longer unit of time:

      • Exclude the day of the event that triggers the period;

      • Count every day, including intermediate Saturdays, Sundays, and legal holidays; and

      • Include the last day of the period, but if the last day is a Saturday, Sunday, or legal holiday, the period continues to run until the end of the next day that is not a Saturday, Sunday, or legal holiday. FRCP 6(a)(1). In the Local Civil Rules of the United States District Courts for the Southern and Eastern Districts of New York, as in the Federal Rules of Civil Procedure as amended effective December 1, 2009, Saturdays, Sundays, and legal holidays are no longer excluded in computing periods of time. If the last day of the period is a Saturday, Sunday, or legal holiday, the period continues to run until the end of the next day that is not a Saturday, Sunday, or legal holiday. NY R USDCTS&ED Civ Rule 6.4.

ii.  *Period stated in hours.* When the period is stated in hours:

- Begin counting immediately on the occurrence of the event that triggers the period;
- Count every hour, including hours during intermediate Saturdays, Sundays, and legal holidays; and
- If the period would end on a Saturday, Sunday, or legal holiday, the period continues to run until the same time on the next day that is not a Saturday, Sunday, or legal holiday. FRCP 6(a)(2). In the Local Civil Rules of the United States District Courts for the Southern and Eastern Districts of New York, as in the Federal Rules of Civil Procedure as amended effective December 1, 2009, Saturdays, Sundays, and legal holidays are no longer excluded in computing periods of time. If the last day of the period is a Saturday, Sunday, or legal holiday, the period continues to run until the end of the next day that is not a Saturday, Sunday, or legal holiday. NY R USDCTS&ED Civ Rule 6.4.

iii.  *Inaccessibility of the clerk's office.* Unless the court orders otherwise, if the clerk's office is inaccessible:

- On the last day for filing under FRCP 6(a)(1), then the time for filing is extended to the first accessible day that is not a Saturday, Sunday, or legal holiday; or
- During the last hour for filing under FRCP 6(a)(2), then the time for filing is extended to the same time on the first accessible day that is not a Saturday, Sunday, or legal holiday. FRCP 6(a)(3).

iv.  *"Last day" defined.* Unless a different time is set by a statute, local rule, or court order, the last day ends:

- For electronic filing, at midnight in the court's time zone; and
- For filing by other means, when the clerk's office is scheduled to close. FRCP 6(a)(4).

v.  *"Next day" defined.* The "next day" is determined by continuing to count forward when the period is measured after an event and backward when measured before an event. FRCP 6(a)(5).

vi.  *"Legal holiday" defined.* "Legal holiday" means:

- The day set aside by statute for observing New Year's Day, Martin Luther King Jr.'s Birthday, Washington's Birthday, Memorial Day, Independence Day, Labor Day, Columbus Day, Veterans' Day, Thanksgiving Day, or Christmas Day;
- Any day declared a holiday by the President or Congress; and
- For periods that are measured after an event, any other day declared a holiday by the state where the district court is located. FRCP 6(a)(6).

b.  *Extending time.* Refer to the General Requirements section of this document for information on extending time.

c.  *Additional time after certain kinds of service.* When a party may or must act within a specified time after service and service is made under FRCP 5(b)(2)(C), FRCP 5(b)(2)(D), FRCP 5(b)(2)(E), or FRCP 5(b)(2)(F), three (3) days are added after the period would otherwise expire under FRCP 6(a). FRCP 6(d). Overnight delivery service shall be deemed service by mail for purposes of FRCP 5 and FRCP 6. NY R USDCTS&ED Civ Rule 5.3.

7.  *Individual judge practices.* Refer to the Miscellaneous section of this document for information on individual judge practices on timing of documents.

## C.  General Requirements

1.  *Mode of raising discovery and other non-dispositive pretrial disputes with the court.* Prior to seeking

judicial resolution of a discovery or non-dispositive pretrial dispute, the attorneys for the affected parties or non-party witness shall attempt to confer in good faith in person or by telephone in an effort to resolve the dispute, in conformity with FRCP 37(a)(1). NY R USDCTS&ED Civ Rule 37.3(a). Refer to the Documents section of this document for the procedure to follow when the attorneys for the affected parties or non-party witness cannot agree on a resolution of the discovery or other non-dispositive pretrial dispute.

a. *Motion for reconsideration.* A ruling made exclusively as a result of a telephone conference may be the subject of de novo reconsideration by a letter not exceeding five (5) pages in length attaching relevant materials submitted by any affected party or non-party witness. Within four (4) days of receiving such a letter, any other affected party or non-party witness may submit a responsive letter not exceeding five (5) pages in length attaching relevant materials. NY R USDCTS&ED Civ Rule 37.3(d).

b. *Decision of the court.* The Court shall record or arrange for the recording of the Court's decision in writing. Such written order may take the form of an oral order read into the record of a deposition or other proceeding, a handwritten memorandum, a handwritten marginal notation on a letter or other document, or any other form the Court deems appropriate. NY R USDCTS&ED Civ Rule 37.3(e).

2. *Motions, generally*

a. *Requirements.* A request for a court order must be made by motion. The motion must:

   i. Be in writing unless made during a hearing or trial;

   ii. State with particularity the grounds for seeking the order; and

   iii. State the relief sought. FRCP 7(b)(1).

b. *Notice of motion.* A party interested in resisting the relief sought by a motion has a right to notice thereof, and an opportunity to be heard. AMJUR MOTIONS § 12.

   i. In addition to statutory or court rule provisions requiring notice of a motion—the purpose of such a notice requirement having been said to be to prevent a party from being prejudicially surprised by a motion—principles of natural justice dictate that an adverse party generally must be given notice that a motion will be presented to the court. AMJUR MOTIONS § 12.

   ii. "Notice," in this regard, means reasonable notice, including a meaningful opportunity to prepare and to defend against allegations of a motion. AMJUR MOTIONS § 12.

c. *Writing requirement.* The writing requirement is intended to insure that the adverse parties are informed and have a record of both the motion's pendency and the grounds on which the movant seeks an order. FPP § 1191; Feldberg v. Quechee Lakes Corp., 463 F.3d 195 (2d Cir. 2006).

   i. It is sufficient "if the motion is stated in a written notice of the hearing of the motion." FPP § 1191.

d. *Particularity requirement.* The particularity requirement insures that the opposing parties will have notice of their opponent's contentions. FEDPROC § 62:364; Goodman v. 1973 26 Foot Trojan Vessel, Arkansas Registration No. AR1439SN, 859 F.2d 71, 12 Fed.R.Serv.3d 645 (8th Cir. 1988). That requirement ensures that notice of the basis for the motion is provided to the court and to the opposing party so as to avoid prejudice, provide the opponent with a meaningful opportunity to respond, and provide the court with enough information to process the motion correctly. FEDPROC § 62:364; Andreas v. Volkswagen of America, Inc., 336 F.3d 789, 56 Fed.R.Serv.3d 6 (8th Cir. 2003).

   i. Reasonable specification of the grounds for a motion is sufficient. However, where a movant fails to state even one ground for granting the motion in question, the movant has failed to meet the minimal standard of "reasonable specification." FEDPROC § 62:364; Martinez v. Trainor, 556 F.2d 818, 23 Fed.R.Serv.2d 403 (7th Cir. 1977).

   ii. The court may excuse the failure to comply with the particularity requirement if it is inadvertent, and where no prejudice is shown by the opposing party. FEDPROC § 62:364.

e. *Ex parte orders or orders to show cause to bring on a motion.* No ex parte order, or order to show cause to bring on a motion, will be granted except upon a clear and specific showing by affidavit of good and sufficient reasons why a procedure other than by notice of motion is necessary, and stating whether a previous application for similar relief has been made. NY R USDCTS&ED Civ Rule 6.1(d).

f. *Letter-motions.* Applications for extensions or adjournments, applications for a pre-motion conference, and similar non-dispositive matters as permitted by the instructions regarding ECF published on the website of each respective Court and any pertinent Individual Judge's Practices, may be brought by letter-motion filed via ECF pursuant to NY R USDCTS&ED Civ Rule 5.2(b). NY R USDCTS&ED Civ Rule 7.1(d).

3. *Motion for continuance/extension of time*

a. *Continuance.* Absent a controlling statute, the grant or denial of a continuance rests in the discretion of the trial judge to whom application is made, taking into consideration not only the facts of the particular case but also all of the demands on counsel's time and the court's. FEDPROC § 77:28; Star Financial Services, Inc. v. AASTAR Mortg. Corp., 89 F.3d 5 (1st Cir. 1996); Streber v. Hunter, 221 F.3d 701, 55 Fed.R.Evid.Serv. 376 (5th Cir. 2000). The grounds upon which a continuance is sought may include the following:

i. Unpreparedness of a party. FEDPROC § 77:29; U.S. v. 110 Bars of Silver, 3 Crucibles of Silver, 11 Bags of Silver Coins, 508 F.2d 799 (5th Cir. 1975).

ii. Absence of a party. FEDPROC § 77:29. Since it is generally recognized that a party to a civil action ordinarily has a right to attend the trial, an illness severe enough to prevent a party from appearing in court is always a legitimate ground for asking for a continuance. FEDPROC § 77:30; Davis v. Operation Amigo, Inc., 378 F.2d 101 (10th Cir. 1967). However, the failure of the moving party to produce any competent medical evidence of the reasons and necessities for the party's unavailability will result in the denial of the continuance. FEDPROC § 77:30; Weisman v. Alleco, Inc., 925 F.2d 77 (4th Cir. 1991). Some courts, moreover, require a showing that the party has some particular contribution to make to the trial as a material witness or otherwise before granting a continuance due to the party's illness. FEDPROC § 77:30; Johnston v. Harris County Flood Control Dist., 869 F.2d 1565 (5th Cir. 1989).

iii. Absence of counsel. FEDPROC § 77:29. The courts have shown greater leniency when the illness of counsel is the ground for the continuance, especially where the case presents complex issues. FEDPROC § 77:31; Smith-Weik Machinery Corp. v. Murdock Mach. & Engineering Co., 423 F.2d 842 (5th Cir. 1970). However, many courts do not favor the granting of a continuance where counsel is unavailable due to a claimed engagement elsewhere or where it is not clear that counsel's illness was genuine. FEDPROC § 77:31; Community Nat. Life Ins. Co. v. Parker Square Sav. & Loan Ass'n, 406 F.2d 603 (10th Cir. 1969); Williams v. Johanns, 518 F.Supp.2d 205 (D.D.C. 2007).

iv. Absence of a witness or evidence. FEDPROC § 77:29. The moving party must show. . .that the witness's testimony would be competent and material and that there are no other witnesses who can establish the same facts. FEDPROC § 77:32; Krodel v. Houghtaling, 468 F.2d 887 (4th Cir. 1972); Vitarelle v. Long Island R. Co., 415 F.2d 302 (2d Cir. 1969).

v. Surprise and prejudice. FEDPROC § 77:29. The action complained of should not be one which could have been anticipated by due diligence or of which the movant had actual notice. FEDPROC § 77:33; Communications Maintenance, Inc. v. Motorola, Inc., 761 F.2d 1202, 2 Fed.R.Serv.3d 126 (7th Cir. 1985). Surprise and prejudice are often claimed as a result of the court allowing the other party to amend its pleadings under FRCP 15(b). FEDPROC § 77:29.

vi. In determining whether to grant a continuance, the court will consider a variety of factors, including:

- Good faith on the part of the moving party;
- Due diligence of the moving party;
- The likelihood that the need prompting the request for a continuance will be met if the continuance is granted;
- Inconvenience to the court and the nonmoving party, including the witnesses, if the continuance is granted;

- Possible harm to the moving party if the continuance is denied;

- Prior delays in the proceedings;

- The court's prior refusal to grant the opposing party a continuance;

- Judicial economy. FEDPROC § 77:29; Amarin Plastics, Inc. v. Maryland Cup Corp., 946 F.2d 147, 34 Fed.R.Evid.Serv. 528 (1st Cir. 1991); Lewis v. Rawson, 564 F.3d 569 (2d Cir. 2009); U.S. v. 2.61 Acres of Land, More or Less, Situated in Mariposa County, State of Cal., 791 F.2d 666 (9th Cir. 1985); In re Homestore.com, Inc. Securities Litigation, 347 F.Supp.2d 814 (C.D.Cal. 2004).

b. *Extension of time.* When an act may or must be done within a specified time, the court may, for good cause, extend the time:

   i. *Before original time or its extension expires.* With or without motion or notice if the court acts, or if a request is made, before the original time or its extension expires. FRCP 6(b)(1)(A).

   - An application for the enlargement of time under FRCP 6(b)(1)(A) normally will be granted in the absence of bad faith on the part of the party seeking relief or prejudice to the adverse party. FPP § 1165.

   - Neither a formal motion for enlargement nor notice to the adverse party is expressly required by FRCP 6(b). FPP § 1165.

   ii. *After the time has expired.* On motion made after the time has expired if the party failed to act because of excusable neglect. FRCP 6(b)(1)(B).

   - *Excusable neglect.* Excusable neglect is intended and has proven to be quite elastic in its application. In essence it is an equitable concept that must take account of all relevant circumstances of the party's failure to act within the required time. FPP § 1165.

   - *Burden.* The burden is on the movant to establish that the failure to act in a timely manner was the result of excusable neglect. FEDPROC § 77:5. Common sense indicates that among the most important factors are the possibility of prejudice to the other parties, the length of the applicant's delay and its impact on the proceeding, the reason for the delay and whether it was within the control of the movant, and whether the movant has acted in good faith. FPP § 1165; Kettle Range Conservation Group v. U.S. Forest Service, 8 Fed.Appx. 729 (9th Cir. 2001).

   - *Motion required.* No relief may be granted under FRCP 6(b)(1)(B) after the expiration of the specified period, even though the failure to act may have been the result of excusable neglect, if no motion is made by the party who failed to act. FEDPROC § 77:3.

   iii. *Exceptions.* A court must not extend the time to act under FRCP 50(b), FRCP 50(d), FRCP 52(b), FRCP 59(b), FRCP 59(d), FRCP 59(e), and FRCP 60(b). FRCP 6(b)(2). FRCP 6(b) does not require the district courts to extend a time period where the extension would contravene a local court rule and does not apply to periods of time that are definitely fixed by statute. FEDPROC § 77:4; Truncale v. Universal Pictures Co., 82 F.Supp. 576 (S.D.N.Y. 1949); Lusk v. Lyon Metal Products, 9 F.R.D. 250 (W.D.Mo. 1949).

4. *Opposing papers.* The Federal Rules of Civil Procedure do not require any formal answer, return, or reply to a motion, except where the Federal Rules of Civil Procedure or local rules may require affidavits, memoranda, or other papers to be filed in opposition to a motion. Such papers are simply to apprise the court of such opposition and the grounds of that opposition. FEDPROC § 62:359. Except for letter-motions as permitted by NY R USDCTS&ED Civ Rule 7.1(d) or as otherwise permitted by the Court, all oppositions and replies with respect to motions shall comply with NY R USDCTS&ED Civ Rule 7.1(a)(2) and NY R USDCTS&ED Civ Rule 7.1(a)(3), and an opposing party who seeks relief that goes beyond the denial of the motion shall comply as well with NY R USDCTS&ED Civ Rule 7.1(a)(1). NY R USDCTS&ED Civ Rule 7.1(b).

a. *Effect of failure to respond to motion.* Although in the absence of statutory provision or court rule, a motion ordinarily does not require a written answer, when a party files a motion and the opposing party fails to respond, the court may construe such failure to respond as nonopposition to the motion or an admission that the motion was meritorious, may take the facts alleged in the motion as true—the rule in some jurisdictions being that the failure to respond to a fact set forth in a motion is deemed an admission—and may grant the motion if the relief requested appears to be justified. AMJUR MOTIONS § 28.

    b.    *Assent or no opposition not determinative.* However, a motion will not be granted automatically simply because an "assent" or a notation of "no opposition" has been filed; federal judges frequently deny motions that have been assented to when it is thought that justice so dictates. FPP § 1190.

    c.    *Responsive pleading inappropriate as response to motion.* An attempt to answer or oppose a motion with a responsive pleading usually is not appropriate. FPP § 1190.

5.    *Reply papers.* A moving party may be required or permitted to prepare papers in addition to his original motion papers. AMJUR MOTIONS § 25. Papers answering or replying to opposing papers may be appropriate, in the interests of justice, where it appears there is a substantial reason for allowing a reply. Thus, a court may accept reply papers where a party demonstrates that the papers to which it seeks to file a reply raise new issues that are material to the disposition of the question before the court, or where the court determines, sua sponte, that it wishes further briefing of an issue raised in those papers and orders the submission of additional papers. FEDPROC § 62:360. Except for letter-motions as permitted by NY R USDCTS&ED Civ Rule 7.1(d) or as otherwise permitted by the Court, all oppositions and replies with respect to motions shall comply with NY R USDCTS&ED Civ Rule 7.1(a)(2) and NY R USDCTS&ED Civ Rule 7.1(a)(3). NY R USDCTS&ED Civ Rule 7.1(b).

    a.    *Function of reply papers.* The function of a reply affidavit is to answer the arguments made in opposition to the position taken by the movant and not to permit the movant to introduce new arguments in support of the motion. AMJUR MOTIONS § 25.

    b.    *Issues raised for the first time in a reply document.* However, the view has been followed in some jurisdictions, that as a matter of judicial economy, where there is no prejudice and where the issues could be raised simply by filing a motion to dismiss, the trial court has discretion to consider arguments raised for the first time in a reply memorandum, and that a trial court may grant a motion to strike issues raised for the first time in a reply memorandum. AMJUR MOTIONS § 26.

6.    *Orders on motions.* A memorandum signed by the Court of the decision on a motion that does not finally determine all claims for relief, or an oral decision on such a motion, shall constitute the order unless the memorandum or oral decision directs the submission or settlement of an order in more extended form. The notation in the docket of a memorandum or of an oral decision that does not direct the submission or settlement of an order in more extended form shall constitute the entry of the order. Where an order in more extended form is required to be submitted or settled, the notation in the docket of such order shall constitute the entry of the order. NY R USDCTS&ED Civ Rule 6.2.

7.    *Related cases.* It shall be the continuing duty of each attorney appearing in any civil or criminal case to bring promptly to the attention of the Court all facts which said attorney believes are relevant to a determination that said case and one or more pending civil or criminal cases should be heard by the same Judge, in order to avoid unnecessary duplication of judicial effort. As soon as the attorney becomes aware of such relationship, said attorney shall notify the Judges to whom the cases have been assigned. NY R USDCTS&ED Civ Rule 1.6(a). If counsel fails to comply with NY R USDCTS&ED Civ Rule 1.6(a), the Court may assess reasonable costs directly against counsel whose action has obstructed the effective administration of the Court's business. NY R USDCTS&ED Civ Rule 1.6(b).

8.    *Alternative dispute resolution (ADR)*

    a.    *Court-annexed arbitration*

        i.    *Civil cases eligible for compulsory arbitration.* The Clerk of Court shall, as to all cases filed after January 1, 1986, designate and process for compulsory arbitration all civil cases (excluding Social Security cases, tax matters, prisoners' civil rights cases and any action based on an alleged violation of a right secured by the Constitution of the United States or if jurisdiction is based in whole or in part on 28 U.S.C.A. § 1343) wherein money damages only are being sought in an amount not in excess of one hundred fifty thousand dollars ($150,000) exclusive of interest and costs. NY R USDCTS&ED Civ Rule 83.7(d)(1).

           •    The parties may by written stipulation agree that the Clerk of Court shall designate and process for court-annexed arbitration any civil case that is not subject to compulsory arbitration in NY R USDCTS&ED Civ Rule 83.7. NY R USDCTS&ED Civ Rule 83.7(d)(2).

- For purposes of NY R USDCTS&ED Civ Rule 83.7 only, in all civil cases damages shall be presumed to be not in excess of one hundred fifty thousand dollars ($150,000) exclusive of interest and costs, unless: (1) counsel for plaintiff, at the time of filing the complaint, or in the event of the removal of a case from state court or transfer of a case from another district to this Court, within thirty (30) days of the docketing of the case in this district, files a certification with the Court that the damages sought exceed one hundred fifty thousand dollars ($150,000), exclusive of interest and costs; or (2) counsel for a defendant, at the time of filing a counterclaim or cross-claim files a certification with the court that the damages sought by the counter-claim or cross-claim exceed one hundred fifty thousand dollars ($150,000) exclusive of interest and costs. NY R USDCTS&ED Civ Rule 83.7(d)(3).

ii. *Exemption from arbitration.* The Court shall, sua sponte, or on motion of a party, exempt any case from arbitration in which the objectives of arbitration would not be realized (1) because the case involves complex or novel issues, (2) because legal issues predominate over factual issues, or (3) for other good cause. NY R USDCTS&ED Civ Rule 83.7(e)(2). For information on applying for an exemption, refer to NY R USDCTS&ED Civ Rule 83.7

iii. *Referral to arbitration.* Cases not originally designated as eligible for compulsory arbitration, but which in the discretion of the assigned Judge, are later found to qualify, may be referred to arbitration. A U.S. District Judge or a U.S. Magistrate Judge, in cases that exceed the arbitration ceiling of one hundred fifty thousand dollars ($150,000) exclusive of interest and costs, in their discretion, may suggest that the parties should consider arbitration. If the parties are agreeable, an appropriate consent form signed by all parties or their representatives may be entered and filed in the case prior to scheduling an arbitration hearing. NY R USDCTS&ED Civ Rule 83.7(e)(3).

iv. For more information on arbitration, refer to NY R USDCTS&ED Civ Rule 83.7.

b. *Court-annexed mediation.* Mediation is a process in which parties and counsel agree to meet with a neutral mediator trained to assist them in settling disputes. The mediator improves communication across party lines, helps parties articulate their interests and understand those of the other party, probes the strengths and weaknesses of each party's legal positions, and identifies areas of agreement and helps generate options for a mutually agreeable resolution to the dispute. In all cases, mediation provides an opportunity to explore a wide range of potential solutions and to address interests that may be outside the scope of the stated controversy or which could not be addressed by judicial action. A hallmark of mediation is its capacity to expand traditional settlement discussions and broaden resolution options, often by exploring litigant needs and interests that may be formally independent of the legal issues in controversy. NY R USDCTS&ED Civ Rule 83.8(a).

i. *Eligible cases.* Judges and Magistrate Judges may designate civil cases for inclusion in the mediation program, and when doing so shall prepare an order to that effect. Alternatively, and subject to the availability of qualified mediators, the parties may consent to participation in the mediation program by preparing and executing a stipulation signed by all parties to the action and so-ordered by the Court. NY R USDCTS&ED Civ Rule 83.8(b)(1).

ii. For more information on mediation, refer to NY R USDCTS&ED Civ Rule 83.8.

9. *Individual judge practices.* Refer to the Miscellaneous section of this document for information on individual judge practices on general requirements for documents.

## D. Documents

1. *Documents for moving party*

   a. *Required documents*

      i. *Letter-motion.* Where the attorneys for the affected parties or non-party witness cannot agree on a resolution of any other discovery dispute or non-dispositive pretrial dispute, or if they are unable to obtain a telephonic ruling on a discovery dispute that arises during a deposition as provided in NY R USDCTS&ED Civ Rule 37.3(b), they shall notify the Court by letter not exceeding three (3) pages in length outlining the nature of the dispute and attaching relevant materials. NY R USDCTS&ED Civ Rule 37.3(c).

b.  *Supplemental documents.* Except for the letters and attachments authorized herein, or where a ruling which was made exclusively as a result of a telephone conference is the subject of de novo review pursuant to NY R USDCTS&ED Civ Rule 37.3(d), papers shall not be submitted with respect to a dispute governed by NY R USDCTS&ED Civ Rule 37.3 unless the Court has so directed. NY R USDCTS&ED Civ Rule 37.3(c).

    i.  *Supporting evidence.* When a motion relies on facts outside the record, the court may hear the matter on affidavits or may hear it wholly or partly on oral testimony or on depositions. FRCP 43(c). Except for letter-motions as permitted by NY R USDCTS&ED Civ Rule 7.1(d) or as otherwise permitted by the Court, all motions shall include the following motion papers: supporting affidavits and exhibits thereto containing any factual information and portions of the record necessary for the decision of the motion. NY R USDCTS&ED Civ Rule 7.1(a)(3).

        • *Discovery materials.* A party seeking or opposing relief under FRCP 26 through FRCP 37 inclusive, or making or opposing any other motion or application, shall quote or attach only those portions of the depositions, interrogatories, requests for documents, requests for admissions, or other discovery or disclosure materials, together with the responses and objections thereto, that are the subject of the discovery motion or application, or that are cited in papers submitted in connection with any other motion or application. NY R USDCTS&ED Civ Rule 5.1.

    ii.  *Notice of constitutional question.* A party that files a pleading, written motion, or other paper drawing into question the constitutionality of a federal or state statute must promptly:

        • *File notice.* File a notice of constitutional question stating the question and identifying the paper that raises it, if: (1) a federal statute is questioned and the parties do not include the United States, one of its agencies, or one of its officers or employees in an official capacity; or (2) a state statute is questioned and the parties do not include the state, one of its agencies, or one of its officers or employees in an official capacity; and

        • *Serve notice.* Serve the notice and paper on the Attorney General of the United States if a federal statute is questioned—or on the state attorney general if a state statute is questioned—either by certified or registered mail or by sending it to an electronic address designated by the attorney general for this purpose. FRCP 5.1(a).

        • *No forfeiture.* A party's failure to file and serve the notice, or the court's failure to certify, does not forfeit a constitutional claim or defense that is otherwise timely asserted. FRCP 5.1(d).

    iii.  *Nongovernmental corporate disclosure statement.* To enable judges and magistrates to evaluate possible disqualification or recusal, counsel for a private (nongovernmental) party shall submit at the time of initial pleading a certificate identifying any corporate parent, subsidiaries, or affiliates of that party. NY R USDCTED Div. Bus., Rule 50.1(c).

        • *Contents.* A nongovernmental corporate party must file two (2) copies of a disclosure statement that: (1) identifies any parent corporation and any publicly held corporation owning ten percent (10%) or more of its stock; or (2) states that there is no such corporation. FRCP 7.1(a).

        • *Time to file; Supplemental filing.* A party must: (1) file the disclosure statement with its first appearance, pleading, petition, motion, response, or other request addressed to the court; and (2) promptly file a supplemental statement if any required information changes. FRCP 7.1(b). For purposes of FRCP 7.1(b)(2), "promptly" shall mean "within fourteen days," that is, parties are required to file a supplemental disclosure statement within fourteen (14) days of the time there is any change in the information required in a disclosure statement filed pursuant to those rules. NY R USDCTS&ED Civ Rule 7.1.1.

iv. *Copies of authorities.* In cases involving a pro se litigant, counsel shall, when serving a memorandum of law (or other submissions to the Court), provide the pro se litigant (but not other counsel or the Court) with copies of cases and other authorities cited therein that are unpublished or reported exclusively on computerized databases. Upon request, counsel shall provide the pro se litigant with copies of such unpublished cases and other authorities as are cited in a decision of the Court and were not previously cited by any party. NY R USDCTS&ED Civ Rule 7.2.

v. *Notice of motion and motion.* Except for letter-motions as permitted by NY R USDCTS&ED Civ Rule 7.1(d) or as otherwise permitted by the Court, all motions shall include the following motion papers: a notice of motion, or an order to show cause signed by the Court, which shall specify the applicable rules or statutes pursuant to which the motion is brought, and shall specify the relief sought by the motion. NY R USDCTS&ED Civ Rule 7.1(a)(1). Refer to the General Requirements section of this document for information on the notice of motion and motion.

vi. *Memorandum of law.* Except for letter-motions as permitted by NY R USDCTS&ED Civ Rule 7.1(d) or as otherwise permitted by the Court, all motions shall include the following motion papers: a memorandum of law, setting forth the cases and other authorities relied upon in support of the motion, and divided, under appropriate headings, into as many parts as there are issues to be determined. NY R USDCTS&ED Civ Rule 7.1(a)(2).

vii. *Certificate of service.* FRCP 5(d) requires that the person making service under FRCP 5 certify that service has been effected. FRCP 5(Advisory Committee Notes). Having such information on file may be useful for many purposes, including proof of service if an issue arises concerning the effectiveness of the service. FRCP 5(Advisory Committee Notes).

2. *Documents for opposing party*

   a. *Required documents*

      i. *Responsive letter.* Within four (4) days of receiving such a letter, any opposing affected party or non-party witness may submit a responsive letter not exceeding three (3) pages attaching relevant materials. NY R USDCTS&ED Civ Rule 37.3(c).

   b. *Supplemental documents.* Except for the letters and attachments authorized herein, or where a ruling which was made exclusively as a result of a telephone conference is the subject of de novo review pursuant to NY R USDCTS&ED Civ Rule 37.3(d), papers shall not be submitted with respect to a dispute governed by NY R USDCTS&ED Civ Rule 37.3 unless the Court has so directed. NY R USDCTS&ED Civ Rule 37.3(c).

      i. *Supporting evidence.* When a motion relies on facts outside the record, the court may hear the matter on affidavits or may hear it wholly or partly on oral testimony or on depositions. FRCP 43(c). Except for letter-motions as permitted by NY R USDCTS&ED Civ Rule 7.1(d) or as otherwise permitted by the Court, all oppositions and replies with respect to motions shall comply with NY R USDCTS&ED Civ Rule 7.1(a)(3). NY R USDCTS&ED Civ Rule 7.1(b). Except for letter-motions as permitted by NY R USDCTS&ED Civ Rule 7.1(d) or as otherwise permitted by the Court, all motions shall include the following motion papers: supporting affidavits and exhibits thereto containing any factual information and portions of the record necessary for the decision of the motion. NY R USDCTS&ED Civ Rule 7.1(a)(3).

         • *Discovery materials.* A party seeking or opposing relief under FRCP 26 through FRCP 37 inclusive, or making or opposing any other motion or application, shall quote or attach only those portions of the depositions, interrogatories, requests for documents, requests for admissions, or other discovery or disclosure materials, together with the responses and objections thereto, that are the subject of the discovery motion or application, or that are cited in papers submitted in connection with any other motion or application. NY R USDCTS&ED Civ Rule 5.1.

      ii. *Notice of constitutional question.* A party that files a pleading, written motion, or other paper drawing into question the constitutionality of a federal or state statute must promptly:

         • *File notice.* File a notice of constitutional question stating the question and identifying the

paper that raises it, if: (1) a federal statute is questioned and the parties do not include the United States, one of its agencies, or one of its officers or employees in an official capacity; or (2) a state statute is questioned and the parties do not include the state, one of its agencies, or one of its officers or employees in an official capacity; and

- *Serve notice.* Serve the notice and paper on the Attorney General of the United States if a federal statute is questioned—or on the state attorney general if a state statute is questioned—either by certified or registered mail or by sending it to an electronic address designated by the attorney general for this purpose. FRCP 5.1(a).

- *No forfeiture.* A party's failure to file and serve the notice, or the court's failure to certify, does not forfeit a constitutional claim or defense that is otherwise timely asserted. FRCP 5.1(d).

iii.   *Copies of authorities.* In cases involving a pro se litigant, counsel shall, when serving a memorandum of law (or other submissions to the Court), provide the pro se litigant (but not other counsel or the Court) with copies of cases and other authorities cited therein that are unpublished or reported exclusively on computerized databases. Upon request, counsel shall provide the pro se litigant with copies of such unpublished cases and other authorities as are cited in a decision of the Court and were not previously cited by any party. NY R USDCTS&ED Civ Rule 7.2.

iv.   *Answering memorandum of law.* Except for letter-motions as permitted by NY R USDCTS&ED Civ Rule 7.1(d) or as otherwise permitted by the Court, all oppositions and replies with respect to motions shall comply with NY R USDCTS&ED Civ Rule 7.1(a)(2). NY R USDCTS&ED Civ Rule 7.1(b). Except for letter-motions as permitted by NY R USDCTS&ED Civ Rule 7.1(d) or as otherwise permitted by the Court, all motions shall include the following motion papers: a memorandum of law, setting forth the cases and other authorities relied upon in support of the motion, and divided, under appropriate headings, into as many parts as there are issues to be determined. NY R USDCTS&ED Civ Rule 7.1(a)(2). Refer to the General Requirements section of this document for information on the opposing papers.

v.   *Certificate of service.* FRCP 5(d) requires that the person making service under FRCP 5 certify that service has been effected. FRCP 5(Advisory Committee Notes). Having such information on file may be useful for many purposes, including proof of service if an issue arises concerning the effectiveness of the service. FRCP 5(Advisory Committee Notes).

3.   *Individual judge practices.* Refer to the Miscellaneous section of this document for information on individual judge practices on required documents.

## E.  Format

1.   *Form of documents.* The rules governing captions and other matters of form in pleadings apply to motions and other papers. FRCP 7(b)(2).

a.   *Paper.* Every pleading, written motion, and other paper must: be plainly written, typed, printed, or copied without erasures or interlineations which materially deface it. NY R USDCTS&ED Civ Rule 11.1(a)(1).

b.   *Typeface, margin, and spacing.* The typeface, margins, and spacing of all documents presented for filing must meet the following requirements:

i.   All text must be twelve (12) point type or larger, except for text in footnotes which may be ten (10) point type;

ii.   All documents must have at least one (1) inch margins on all sides;

iii.   All text must be double-spaced, except for headings, text in footnotes, or block quotations, which may be single-spaced. NY R USDCTS&ED Civ Rule 11.1(b).

c.   *Caption; Names of parties.* Every pleading must have a caption with the court's name, a title, a file number, and a FRCP 7(a) designation. The title of the complaint must name all the parties; the title of other pleadings, after naming the first party on each side, may refer generally to other parties. FRCP 10(a). Every pleading, written motion, and other paper must: bear the docket number and the initials of the District Judge and any Magistrate Judge before whom the action or proceeding is pending, NY R USDCTS&ED Civ Rule 11.1(a)(2).

d. *Paragraphs; Separate statements.* A party must state its claims or defenses in numbered paragraphs, each limited as far as practicable to a single set of circumstances. A later pleading may refer by number to a paragraph in an earlier pleading. If doing so would promote clarity, each claim founded on a separate transaction or occurrence—and each defense other than a denial—must be stated in a separate count or defense. FRCP 10(b).

e. *Adoption by reference; Exhibits.* A statement in a pleading may be adopted by reference elsewhere in the same pleading or in any other pleading or motion. A copy of a written instrument that is an exhibit to a pleading is a part of the pleading for all purposes. FRCP 10(c).

f. *Acceptance by the clerk.* The clerk must not refuse to file a paper solely because it is not in the form prescribed by the Federal Rules of Civil Procedure or by a local rule or practice. FRCP 5(d)(4).

2. *Signing of pleadings, motions and other papers*

a. *Signature.* Every pleading, written motion, and other paper must be signed by at least one attorney of record in the attorney's name—or by a party personally if the party is unrepresented. The paper must state the signer's address, e-mail address, and telephone number. FRCP 11(a). Every pleading, written motion, and other paper must: have the name of each person signing it clearly printed or typed directly below the signature. NY R USDCTS&ED Civ Rule 11.1(a)(3).

i. *No verification or accompanying affidavit required for pleadings.* Unless a rule or statute specifically states otherwise, a pleading need not be verified or accompanied by an affidavit. FRCP 11(a).

ii. *Unsigned papers.* The court must strike an unsigned paper unless the omission is promptly corrected after being called to the attorney's or party's attention. FRCP 11(a).

b. *Representations to the court.* By presenting to the court a pleading, written motion, or other paper—whether by signing, filing, submitting, or later advocating it—an attorney or unrepresented party certifies that to the best of the person's knowledge, information, and belief, formed after an inquiry reasonable under the circumstances:

i. It is not being presented for any improper purpose, such as to harass, cause unnecessary delay, or needlessly increase the cost of litigation;

ii. The claims, defenses, and other legal contentions are warranted by existing law or by a nonfrivolous argument for extending, modifying, or reversing existing law or for establishing new law;

iii. The factual contentions have evidentiary support or, if specifically so identified, will likely have evidentiary support after a reasonable opportunity for further investigation or discovery; and

iv. The denials of factual contentions are warranted on the evidence or, if specifically so identified, are reasonably based on belief or a lack of information. FRCP 11(b).

c. *Sanctions.* If, after notice and a reasonable opportunity to respond, the court determines that FRCP 11(b) has been violated, the court may impose an appropriate sanction on any attorney, law firm, or party that violated FRCP 11(b) or is responsible for the violation. FRCP 11(c)(1). Refer to the United States District Court for the Eastern District of New York KeyRules Motion for Sanctions document for more information.

3. *Privacy protection for filings made with the court*

a. *Redacted filings.* Unless the court orders otherwise, in an electronic or paper filing with the court that contains an individual's Social Security number, taxpayer-identification number, or birth date, the name of an individual known to be a minor, or a financial-account number, a party or nonparty making the filing may include only:

i. The last four (4) digits of the Social Security number and taxpayer-identification number;

ii. The year of the individual's birth;

iii. The minor's initials; and

iv. The last four (4) digits of the financial-account number. FRCP 5.2(a); NY R USDCTED Order 2004-09.

v. In addition, exercise caution when filing documents that contain the following:

- Personal identifying number, such as driver's license number;

- Medical records, treatment and diagnosis;

- Employment history;

- Individual financial information; and

- Proprietary or trade secret information. NY R USDCTED Order 2004-09.

b. *Exemptions from the redaction requirement.* The redaction requirement does not apply to the following:

i. A financial-account number that identifies the property allegedly subject to forfeiture in a forfeiture proceeding;

ii. The record of an administrative or agency proceeding;

iii. The official record of a state-court proceeding;

iv. The record of a court or tribunal, if that record was not subject to the redaction requirement when originally filed;

v. A filing covered by FRCP 5.2(c) or FRCP 5.2(d); and

vi. A pro se filing in an action brought under 28 U.S.C.A. § 2241, 28 U.S.C.A. § 2254, or 28 U.S.C.A. § 2255. FRCP 5.2(b).

c. *Limitations on remote access to electronic files; Social Security appeals and immigration cases.* Unless the court orders otherwise, in an action for benefits under the Social Security Act, and in an action or proceeding relating to an order of removal, to relief from removal, or to immigration benefits or detention, access to an electronic file is authorized as follows:

i. The parties and their attorneys may have remote electronic access to any part of the case file, including the administrative record;

ii. Any other person may have electronic access to the full record at the courthouse, but may have remote electronic access only to:

- The docket maintained by the court; and

- An opinion, order, judgment, or other disposition of the court, but not any other part of the case file or the administrative record. FRCP 5.2(c).

d. *Filings made under seal.* The court may order that a filing be made under seal without redaction. The court may later unseal the filing or order the person who made the filing to file a redacted version for the public record. FRCP 5.2(d).

e. *Protective orders.* For good cause, the court may by order in a case:

i. Require redaction of additional information; or

ii. Limit or prohibit a nonparty's remote electronic access to a document filed with the court. FRCP 5.2(e).

f. *Option for additional unredacted filing under seal.* A person making a redacted filing may also file an unredacted copy under seal. The court must retain the unredacted copy as part of the record. FRCP 5.2(f); NY R USDCTED Order 2004-09. The unredacted version of the document or the reference list shall be retained by the court as part of the record. The court may, however, still require the party to file a redacted copy for the public file. NY R USDCTED Order 2004-09.

g. *Option for filing a reference list.* A filing that contains redacted information may be filed together with a reference list that identifies each item of redacted information and specifies an appropriate identifier that uniquely corresponds to each item listed. The list must be filed under seal and may be amended as of right. Any reference in the case to a listed identifier will be construed to refer to the corresponding item of information. FRCP 5.2(g); NY R USDCTED Order 2004-09. The unredacted version of the document or the reference list shall be retained by the court as part of the record. The court may, however, still require the party to file a redacted copy for the public file. NY R USDCTED Order 2004-09.

    h.   *Responsibility for redaction.* The responsibility for redacting these personal identifiers rests solely with counsel and the parties. The Clerk will not review each pleading for compliance with NY R USDCTED Order 2004-09. NY R USDCTED Order 2004-09.

        i.   Counsel is strongly urged to share this notice with all clients so that an informed decision about the inclusion of certain materials may be made. If a redacted document is filed, it is the sole responsibility of counsel and the parties to be sure that all pleadings comply with the rules of this court requiring redaction of personal data identifiers. The clerk will not review each pleading for redaction. NY R USDCTED Order 2004-09.

    i.   *Waiver of protection of identifiers.* A person waives the protection of FRCP 5.2(a) as to the person's own information by filing it without redaction and not under seal. FRCP 5.2(h).

4.   *Individual judge practices.* Refer to the Miscellaneous section of this document for information on individual judge practices on formatting documents.

# F.  Filing and Service Requirements

1.   *Filing requirements.* Any paper after the complaint that is required to be served—together with a certificate of service—must be filed within a reasonable time after service. FRCP 5(d)(1).

    a.   *How filing is made; In general.* A paper is filed by delivering it:

        i.   To the clerk; or

       ii.   To a judge who agrees to accept it for filing, and who must then note the filing date on the paper and promptly send it to the clerk. FRCP 5(d)(2).

    b.   *Night depository.* A night depository with an automatic date stamp shall be maintained. . .by the Clerk of the Eastern District in the Brooklyn Courthouse. After regular business hours, papers for the District Court only may be deposited in the night depository. Such papers will be considered as having been filed in the District Court as of the date stamped thereon, which shall be deemed presumptively correct. NY R USDCTS&ED Civ Rule 1.2.

    c.   *Electronic filing*

        i.   *Authorization of electronic filing program.* A court may, by local rule, allow papers to be filed, signed, or verified by electronic means that are consistent with any technical standards established by the Judicial Conference of the United States. A local rule may require electronic filing only if reasonable exceptions are allowed. A paper filed electronically in compliance with a local rule is a written paper for purposes of the Federal Rules of Civil Procedure. FRCP 5(d)(3).

           ●   Parties serving and filing papers shall follow the instructions regarding Electronic Case Filing (ECF) published on the website of each respective Court. A paper served and filed by electronic means in accordance with such instructions is, for purposes of FRCP 5, served and filed in compliance with the Local Civil Rules of the Southern and Eastern Districts of New York. NY R USDCTS&ED Civ Rule 5.2(a). Parties have an obligation to review the Court's actual order, decree, or judgment (on ECF), which controls, and should not rely on the description on the docket or in the ECF Notice of Electronic Filing (NEF). NY R USDCTS&ED Civ Rule 5.2(c).

        ii.   *Mandatory electronic filing.* Beginning on August 2, 2004, electronic case filing will be mandatory for all civil cases other than pro se cases. NY R USDCTED Order 2004-08.

           ●   *Letter-motions and letters addressed to the court.* Subject to the instructions regarding ECF published on the website of each respective Court and any pertinent Individual Judge's Practices, letter-motions permitted by NY R USDCTS&ED Civ Rule 7.1(d) and letters addressed to the Court (but not letters between the parties) may be filed via ECF. NY R USDCTS&ED Civ Rule 5.2(b).

- *Proposed orders, judgments and decrees.* Proposed orders, judgments and decrees shall be presented as directed by the ECF rules published on the website of each respective Court. NY R USDCTS&ED Civ Rule 77.1. For more information, refer to NY R USDCTS&ED Civ Rule 77.1.

- *Request for exemption.* Requests by attorneys for an exemption to the mandatory policy will be considered for good cause hardship reasons only, and will be reviewed on an individual basis by the assigned United States Magistrate Judge. The Clerk's Office provides an electronic filing training program to assist attorneys filing electronically. Before seeking a hardship exemption, attorneys are advised to participate in the training program or otherwise seek the assistance of the Clerk's Office. NY R USDCTED Order 2004-08.

  iii. For more information on electronic filing, refer to the court's website.

2. *Service requirements*

 a. *Service; When required*

  i. *In general.* Unless the Federal Rules of Civil Procedure provide otherwise, each of the following papers must be served on every party:

- An order stating that service is required;

- A pleading filed after the original complaint, unless the court orders otherwise under FRCP 5(c) because there are numerous defendants;

- A discovery paper required to be served on a party, unless the court orders otherwise;

- A written motion, except one that may be heard ex parte; and

- A written notice, appearance, demand, or offer of judgment, or any similar paper. FRCP 5(a)(1).

  ii. *If a party fails to appear.* No service is required on a party who is in default for failing to appear. But a pleading that asserts a new claim for relief against such a party must be served on that party under FRCP 4. FRCP 5(a)(2).

  iii. *Seizing property.* If an action is begun by seizing property and no person is or need be named as a defendant, any service required before the filing of an appearance, answer, or claim must be made on the person who had custody or possession of the property when it was seized. FRCP 5(a)(3).

 b. *Service; How made*

  i. *Serving an attorney.* If a party is represented by an attorney, service under FRCP 5 must be made on the attorney unless the court orders service on the party. FRCP 5(b)(1).

  ii. *Service in general.* A paper is served under FRCP 5 by:

- Handing it to the person;

- Leaving it: (1) at the person's office with a clerk or other person in charge or, if no one is in charge, in a conspicuous place in the office; or (2) if the person has no office or the office is closed, at the person's dwelling or usual place of abode with someone of suitable age and discretion who resides there;

- Mailing it to the person's last known address—in which event service is complete upon mailing;

- Leaving it with the court clerk if the person has no known address;

- Sending it by electronic means if the person consented in writing—in which event service is complete upon transmission, but is not effective if the serving party learns that it did not reach the person to be served; or

- Delivering it by any other means that the person consented to in writing—in which event service is complete when the person making service delivers it to the agency designated to make delivery. FRCP 5(b)(2).

    iii. *Service by overnight delivery.* Service upon an attorney may be made by overnight delivery service. "Overnight delivery service" means any delivery service which regularly accepts items for overnight delivery. Overnight delivery service shall be deemed service by mail for purposes of FRCP 5 and FRCP 6. NY R USDCTS&ED Civ Rule 5.3.

    iv. *Service by electronic means.* Parties serving and filing papers shall follow the instructions regarding Electronic Case Filing (ECF) published on the website of each respective Court. A paper served and filed by electronic means in accordance with such instructions is, for purposes of FRCP 5, served and filed in compliance with the Local Civil Rules of the United States District Courts for the Southern and Eastern Districts of New York. NY R USDCTS&ED Civ Rule 5.2(a). Parties have an obligation to review the Court's actual order, decree, or judgment (on ECF), which controls, and should not rely on the description on the docket or in the ECF Notice of Electronic Filing (NEF). NY R USDCTS&ED Civ Rule 5.2(c).

    v. *Using court facilities.* If a local rule so authorizes, a party may use the court's transmission facilities to make service under FRCP 5(b)(2)(E). FRCP 5(b)(3).

  c. *Serving numerous defendants*

    i. *In general.* If an action involves an unusually large number of defendants, the court may, on motion or on its own, order that:

- Defendants' pleadings and replies to them need not be served on other defendants;
- Any crossclaim, counterclaim, avoidance, or affirmative defense in those pleadings and replies to them will be treated as denied or avoided by all other parties; and
- Filing any such pleading and serving it on the plaintiff constitutes notice of the pleading to all parties. FRCP 5(c)(1).

    ii. *Notifying parties.* A copy of every such order must be served on the parties as the court directs. FRCP 5(c)(2).

3. *Individual judge practices.* Refer to the Miscellaneous section of this document for information on individual judge practices on filing and serving documents.

## G. Hearings

1. *Hearings, generally*

  a. *Oral argument.* Due process does not require that oral argument be permitted on a motion and, except as otherwise provided by local rule, the district court has discretion to determine whether it will decide the motion on the papers or hear argument by counsel (and perhaps receive evidence). FPP § 1190; F.D.I.C. v. Deglau, 207 F.3d 153 (3d Cir. 2000). The parties and their attorneys shall only appear to argue the motion if so directed by the Court by order or by a Judge's Individual Practice. NY R USDCTS&ED Civ Rule 6.1(c).

  b. *Providing a regular schedule for oral hearings.* A court may establish regular times and places for oral hearings on motions. FRCP 78(a).

  c. *Providing for submission on briefs.* By rule or order, the court may provide for submitting and determining motions on briefs, without oral hearings. FRCP 78(b).

2. *Individual judge practices.* Refer to the Miscellaneous section of this document for information on individual judge practices on hearings.

## H. Forms

### 1. Federal Motion for Continuance/Extension of Time Forms

  a. Opposition in federal district court; To motion for continuance; On ground of additional time required to prepare for trial; No excusable neglect shown. AMJUR PP CONTIN § 79.

  b. Affidavit in opposition to motion for continuance; By plaintiff's attorney; Lack of due diligence in discovery of documents. AMJUR PP CONTIN § 80.

  c. Affidavit in opposition to motion for continuance; By plaintiff's attorney; Defendant's absent witness previously absent; Lack of due diligence in compelling attendance of witness. AMJUR PP CONTIN § 81.

    d.   Affidavit in opposition to motion for continuance; By plaintiff; Admission that absent witness of defendant would testify according to affidavit. AMJUR PP CONTIN § 83.

    e.   Affidavit in opposition to defendant's motion for continuance; By plaintiff's counsel; Testimony of absent witness merely cumulative. AMJUR PP CONTIN § 85.

    f.   Motion for enlargement of time. 2 FEDFORMS § 5:11.

    g.   Motion for enlargement of time; By plaintiff. 2 FEDFORMS § 5:12.

    h.   Motion for enlargement of time; To answer motion. 2 FEDFORMS § 5:14.

    i.   Motion for continuance. 2 FEDFORMS § 5:36.

    j.   Motion for continuance; Reciting supporting facts; New allegations in amended answer. 2 FEDFORMS § 5:37.

    k.   Motion for continuance; Reciting supporting facts; Absence of witness. 2 FEDFORMS § 5:38.

    l.   Motion for continuance; Reciting supporting facts; Absence of witness; Witness outside the country. 2 FEDFORMS § 5:39.

    m.   Motion for continuance or in the alternative for change of venue; Hostility against defendant. 2 FEDFORMS § 5:40.

    n.   Notice; Of motion; Containing motion. FEDPROF § 1:749.

    o.   Brief; Supporting or opposing motion. FEDPROF § 1:752.

    p.   Opposition to motion; For continuance; No excusable neglect. FEDPROF § 1:808.

    q.   Affidavit; Opposing motion for continuance; Offer to stipulate to testimony of unavailable witness. FEDPROF § 1:813.

    r.   Reply to motion for extension of time. GOLDLTGFMS § 10:40.

    s.   Motions; Extension of time to file jury demand. GOLDLTGFMS § 12:6.

    t.   Motion for extension of time. GOLDLTGFMS § 25:37.

    u.   Motion for extension of time to answer. GOLDLTGFMS § 26:13.

    v.   Motion to extend time for serving answers. GOLDLTGFMS § 26:14.

    w.   Motion for continuance. GOLDLTGFMS § 43:2.

    x.   Motion for continuance; Lawyer unavailable. GOLDLTGFMS § 43:3.

    y.   Motion for continuance; Witness unavailable. GOLDLTGFMS § 43:4.

    z.   Motion for continuance; Party in military service. GOLDLTGFMS § 43:6.

## I.  Applicable Rules

  1.  *Federal rules*

    a.   Serving and filing pleadings and other papers. FRCP 5.

    b.   Constitutional challenge to a statute; Notice, certification, and intervention. FRCP 5.1.

    c.   Privacy protection for filings made with the court. FRCP 5.2.

    d.   Computing and extending time; Time for motion papers. FRCP 6.

    e.   Pleadings allowed; Form of motions and other papers. FRCP 7.

    f.   Disclosure statement. FRCP 7.1.

    g.   Form of pleadings. FRCP 10.

    h.   Signing pleadings, motions, and other papers; Representations to the court; Sanctions. FRCP 11.

    i.   Taking testimony. FRCP 43.

    j.   Hearing motions; Submission on briefs. FRCP 78.

  2.  *Local rules*

    a.   Night depository. NY R USDCTS&ED Civ Rule 1.2.

b.  Duty of attorneys in related cases. NY R USDCTS&ED Civ Rule 1.6.

c.  Filing of discovery materials. NY R USDCTS&ED Civ Rule 5.1.

d.  Electronic service and filing of documents. NY R USDCTS&ED Civ Rule 5.2.

e.  Service by overnight delivery. NY R USDCTS&ED Civ Rule 5.3.

f.  Service and filing of motion papers. NY R USDCTS&ED Civ Rule 6.1.

g.  Orders on motions. NY R USDCTS&ED Civ Rule 6.2.

h.  Computation of time. NY R USDCTS&ED Civ Rule 6.4.

i.  Motion papers. NY R USDCTS&ED Civ Rule 7.1.

j.  Disclosure statement. NY R USDCTS&ED Civ Rule 7.1.1.

k.  Authorities to be provided to pro se litigants. NY R USDCTS&ED Civ Rule 7.2.

l.  Form of pleadings, motions, and other papers. NY R USDCTS&ED Civ Rule 11.1.

m.  Mode of raising discovery and other non-dispositive pretrial disputes with the court (Eastern District only). NY R USDCTS&ED Civ Rule 37.3.

n.  Submission of orders, judgments and decrees. NY R USDCTS&ED Civ Rule 77.1.

o.  Court-annexed arbitration (Eastern District only). NY R USDCTS&ED Civ Rule 83.7.

p.  Court-annexed mediation (Eastern District only). NY R USDCTS&ED Civ Rule 83.8.

q.  Electronic case filing. NY R USDCTED Order 2004-08.

r.  The August 2, 2004 amendment to the E-Government Act of 2002. NY R USDCTED Order 2004-09.

s.  Categories and classification of cases; Information on cases and parties. NY R USDCTED Div. Bus., Rule 50.1.

## J.  Miscellaneous

**NOTE: Individual judges' rules may apply. For available judge-level information, refer to:**

DISTRICT JUDGE CAROL BAGLEY AMON: NY R USDCTED Amon-Practices.

DISTRICT JUDGE JOAN M. AZRACK: NY R USDCTED Azrack-Practices.

DISTRICT JUDGE JOSEPH F. BIANCO: NY R USDCTED Bianco-Practices.

DISTRICT JUDGE FREDERIC BLOCK: NY R USDCTED Block-Practices.

DISTRICT JUDGE MARGO K. BRODIE: NY R USDCTED Brodie-Practices.

DISTRICT JUDGE PAMELA K. CHEN: NY R USDCTED Chen-Practices.

DISTRICT JUDGE BRIAN M. COGAN: NY R USDCTED Cogan-Practices; NY R USDCTED Cogan-Pretrial.

DISTRICT JUDGE LaSHANN DeARCY HALL: NY R USDCTED DeArcy Hall-Practices.

DISTRICT JUDGE RAYMOND J. DEARIE: NY R USDCTED Dearie-Practices.

DISTRICT JUDGE ANN M. DONNELLY: NY R USDCTED Donnelly-Practices.

DISTRICT JUDGE SANDRA J. FEUERSTEIN: NY R USDCTED Feuerstein-Practices; NY R USDCTED Feuerstein-Pretrial.

DISTRICT JUDGE NICHOLAS G. GARAUIFIS: NY R USDCTED Garaufis-Practices; NY R USDCTED Garaufis-Pretrial.

DISTRICT JUDGE NINA GERSHON: NY R USDCTED Gershon-Practices.

DISTRICT JUDGE I. LEO GLASSER: NY R USDCTED Glasser-Practices; NY R USDCTED Glasser-Crim.

DISTRICT JUDGE DENIS R. HURLEY: NY R USDCTED Hurley-Practices; [NY R USDCTED Hurley-Pro Cooperation Info, as added by NY ORDER 16-4188, effective July 22, 2016]; [NY R USDCTED Hurley-Pro Cooperation Info Stay, as added by NY ORDER 16-4188, effective July 22, 2016].

DISTRICT JUDGE DORA L. IRIZARRY: NY R USDCTED Irizarry-Practices; NY R USDCTED Irizarry-Pretrial; NY R USDCTED Irizarry-Crim.

DISTRICT JUDGE STERLING JOHNSON, JR.: NY R USDCTED Johnson-Practices.

DISTRICT JUDGE EDWARD R. KORMAN: NY R USDCTED Korman-Practices; NY R USDCTED Korman-Pretrial.

DISTRICT JUDGE WILLIAM F. KUNTZ: NY R USDCTED Kuntz-Practices.

DISTRICT JUDGE KIYO A. MATSUMOTO: NY R USDCTED Matsumoto-Practices.

DISTRICT JUDGE ROSLYNN R. MAUSKOPF: NY R USDCTED Mauskopf-Practices; NY R USDCTED Mauskopf-Recusal.

DISTRICT JUDGE THOMAS C. PLATT: NY R USDCTED Platt-Practices.

DISTRICT JUDGE ALLYNE R. ROSS: NY R USDCTED Ross-Practices.

DISTRICT JUDGE JOANNA SEYBERT: NY R USDCTED Seybert-Practices.

DISTRICT JUDGE ARTHUR D. SPATT: NY R USDCTED Spatt-Practices.

DISTRICT JUDGE SANDRA L. TOWNES: NY R USDCTED Townes-Practices.

DISTRICT JUDGE ERIC N. VITALIANO: NY R USDCTED Vitaliano-Practices.

DISTRICT JUDGE JACK B. WEINSTEIN: NY R USDCTED Weinstein-Practices.

DISTRICT JUDGE LEONARD D. WEXLER: NY R USDCTED Wexler-Practices; NY R USDCTED Wexler-Rules.

MAGISTRATE JUDGE LOIS BLOOM: NY R USDCTED Bloom-Practices.

MAGISTRATE JUDGE GARY R. BROWN: NY R USDCTED Brown-Practices.

MAGISTRATE JUDGE MARILYN D. GO: NY R USDCTED Go-Practices.

MAGISTRATE JUDGE STEVEN M. GOLD: NY R USDCTED Gold-Practices.

MAGISTRATE JUDGE PEGGY KUO: NY R USDCTED Kuo-Practices; NY R USDCTED Kuo-Scheduling Order.

MAGISTRATE JUDGE ROBERT M. LEVY: NY R USDCTED Levy-Practices.

MAGISTRATE JUDGE ARLENE R. LINDSAY: NY R USDCTED Lindsay-Practices.

MAGISTRATE JUDGE STEVEN I. LOCKE: NY R USDCTED Locke-Practices.

MAGISTRATE JUDGE ROANNE L. MANN: NY R USDCTED Mann-Practices.

MAGISTRATE JUDGE JAMES ORENSTEIN: NY R USDCTED Jorenstein--Practices.

MAGISTRATE JUDGE VIKTOR V. POHORELSKY: NY R USDCTED Pohorelsky-Practices.

MAGISTRATE JUDGE CHERYL L. POLLAK: NY R USDCTED Pollak-Practices; NY R USDCTED Pollak-Pretrial.

MAGISTRATE JUDGE RAMON E. REYES, JR.: NY R USDCTED Reyes-Practices.

MAGISTRATE JUDGE VERA M. SCANLON: NY R USDCTED Scanlon-Practices.

MAGISTRATE JUDGE ANNE Y. SHIELDS: NY R USDCTED Shields-Practices.

MAGISTRATE JUDGE STEVEN L. TISCIONE: NY R USDCTED Tiscione-Practices.

MAGISTRATE JUDGE A. KATHLEEN TOMILINSON: NY R USDCTED Tomlinson-Practices.

## Motions, Oppositions and Replies
## Motion for Summary Judgment

### Document Last Updated September 2016

**A. Checklist**

(I) ❏ Matters to be considered by moving party

    (a) ❏ Required documents

        (1) ❏ Notice of motion and motion

        (2) ❏ Statement of material facts

        (3) ❏ Memorandum of law

        (4) ❏ Certificate of service

    (b) ❏ Supplemental documents

        (1) ❏ Supporting evidence

        (2) ❏ Notice of constitutional question

        (3) ❏ Nongovernmental corporate disclosure statement

        (4) ❏ Notice to pro se litigant who opposes a motion for summary judgment

        (5) ❏ Copies of authorities

    (c) ❏ Timing

        (1) ❏ Unless a different time is set by local rule or the court orders otherwise, a party may file a motion for summary judgment at any time until thirty (30) days after the close of all discovery

        (2) ❏ A written motion and notice of the hearing must be served at least fourteen (14) days before the time specified for the hearing, with the following exceptions: (i) when the motion may be heard ex parte; (ii) when the Federal Rules of Civil Procedure set a different time; or (iii) when a court order—which a party may, for good cause, apply for ex parte—sets a different time

        (3) ❏ Any affidavit supporting a motion must be served with the motion

(II) ❏ Matters to be considered by opposing party

    (a) ❏ Required documents

        (1) ❏ Answering memorandum of law

        (2) ❏ Responsive statement of material facts

        (3) ❏ Certificate of service

    (b) ❏ Supplemental documents

        (1) ❏ Supporting evidence

        (2) ❏ Notice of constitutional question

        (3) ❏ Copies of authorities

    (c) ❏ Timing

        (1) ❏ Any opposing affidavits and answering memoranda shall be served within fourteen (14) days after service of the moving papers

        (2) ❏ Except as FRCP 59(c) provides otherwise, any opposing affidavit must be served at least seven (7) days before the hearing, unless the court permits service at another time

**B. Timing**

1. *Motion for summary judgment.* Unless a different time is set by local rule or the court orders otherwise,

a party may file a motion for summary judgment at any time until thirty (30) days after the close of all discovery. FRCP 56(b).

2. *Timing of motions, generally*

   a. *Motion and notice of hearing.* Except for letter-motions as permitted by NY R USDCTS&ED Civ Rule 7.1(d), and unless otherwise provided by statute or rule or by the Court in a Judge's Individual Practice or in a direction in a particular case, upon any motion, the notice of motion, supporting affidavits, and memoranda shall be served and filed as follows: on all civil motions, petitions, and applications, other than those described in NY R USDCTS&ED Civ Rule 6.1(a), and other than petitions for writs of habeas corpus, the notice of motion, supporting affidavits, and memoranda of law shall be served by the moving party on all other parties that have appeared in the action. NY R USDCTS&ED Civ Rule 6.1(b)(1). A written motion and notice of the hearing must be served at least fourteen (14) days before the time specified for the hearing, with the following exceptions:

      i. When the motion may be heard ex parte;

      ii. When the Federal Rules of Civil Procedure set a different time; or

      iii. When a court order—which a party may, for good cause, apply for ex parte—sets a different time. FRCP 6(c)(1).

   b. *Supporting affidavit.* Any affidavit supporting a motion must be served with the motion. FRCP 6(c)(2).

3. *Timing of opposing papers.* Except for letter-motions as permitted by NY R USDCTS&ED Civ Rule 7.1(d), and unless otherwise provided by statute or rule or by the Court in a Judge's Individual Practice or in a direction in a particular case, upon any motion, the notice of motion, supporting affidavits, and memoranda shall be served and filed as follows: on all civil motions, petitions, and applications, other than those described in NY R USDCTS&ED Civ Rule 6.1(a), and other than petitions for writs of habeas corpus, any opposing affidavits and answering memoranda shall be served within fourteen (14) days after service of the moving papers. NY R USDCTS&ED Civ Rule 6.1(b)(2).

   a. *Opposing affidavit.* Except as FRCP 59(c) provides otherwise, any opposing affidavit must be served at least seven (7) days before the hearing, unless the court permits service at another time. FRCP 6(c)(2).

4. *Timing of reply papers.* Where the respondent files an answering affidavit setting up a new matter, the moving party ordinarily is allowed a reasonable time to file a reply affidavit since failure to deny the new matter by affidavit may operate as an admission of its truth. AMJUR MOTIONS § 25.

   a. *Reply affidavits and reply memoranda of law.* Except for letter-motions as permitted by NY R USDCTS&ED Civ Rule 7.1(d), and unless otherwise provided by statute or rule or by the Court in a Judge's Individual Practice or in a direction in a particular case, upon any motion, the notice of motion, supporting affidavits, and memoranda shall be served and filed as follows: on all civil motions, petitions, and applications, other than those described in NY R USDCTS&ED Civ Rule 6.1(a), and other than petitions for writs of habeas corpus, any reply affidavits and memoranda of law shall be served within seven (7) days after service of the answering papers. NY R USDCTS&ED Civ Rule 6.1(b)(3).

5. *Computation of time*

   a. *Computing time.* FRCP 6 applies in computing any time period specified in the Federal Rules of Civil Procedure, in any local rule or court order, or in any statute that does not specify a method of computing time. FRCP 6(a). In computing any period of time prescribed or allowed by the Local Civil Rules of the United States District Courts for the Southern and Eastern Districts of New York or the Local Admiralty and Maritime Rules, the provisions of FRCP 6 shall apply unless otherwise stated. NY R USDCTS&ED Civ Rule 6.4.

      i. *Period stated in days or a longer unit.* In computing periods of days, refer to FRCP 6 and NY R USDCTS&ED Civ Rule 6.4. NY R USDCTS&ED Civ Rule 6.1(b). When the period is stated in days or a longer unit of time:

         • Exclude the day of the event that triggers the period;

- Count every day, including intermediate Saturdays, Sundays, and legal holidays; and

- Include the last day of the period, but if the last day is a Saturday, Sunday, or legal holiday, the period continues to run until the end of the next day that is not a Saturday, Sunday, or legal holiday. FRCP 6(a)(1). In the Local Civil Rules of the United States District Courts for the Southern and Eastern Districts of New York, as in the Federal Rules of Civil Procedure as amended effective December 1, 2009, Saturdays, Sundays, and legal holidays are no longer excluded in computing periods of time. If the last day of the period is a Saturday, Sunday, or legal holiday, the period continues to run until the end of the next day that is not a Saturday, Sunday, or legal holiday. NY R USDCTS&ED Civ Rule 6.4.

ii. *Period stated in hours.* When the period is stated in hours:

- Begin counting immediately on the occurrence of the event that triggers the period;

- Count every hour, including hours during intermediate Saturdays, Sundays, and legal holidays; and

- If the period would end on a Saturday, Sunday, or legal holiday, the period continues to run until the same time on the next day that is not a Saturday, Sunday, or legal holiday. FRCP 6(a)(2). In the Local Civil Rules of the United States District Courts for the Southern and Eastern Districts of New York, as in the Federal Rules of Civil Procedure as amended effective December 1, 2009, Saturdays, Sundays, and legal holidays are no longer excluded in computing periods of time. If the last day of the period is a Saturday, Sunday, or legal holiday, the period continues to run until the end of the next day that is not a Saturday, Sunday, or legal holiday. NY R USDCTS&ED Civ Rule 6.4.

iii. *Inaccessibility of the clerk's office.* Unless the court orders otherwise, if the clerk's office is inaccessible:

- On the last day for filing under FRCP 6(a)(1), then the time for filing is extended to the first accessible day that is not a Saturday, Sunday, or legal holiday; or

- During the last hour for filing under FRCP 6(a)(2), then the time for filing is extended to the same time on the first accessible day that is not a Saturday, Sunday, or legal holiday. FRCP 6(a)(3).

iv. *"Last day" defined.* Unless a different time is set by a statute, local rule, or court order, the last day ends:

- For electronic filing, at midnight in the court's time zone; and

- For filing by other means, when the clerk's office is scheduled to close. FRCP 6(a)(4).

v. *"Next day" defined.* The "next day" is determined by continuing to count forward when the period is measured after an event and backward when measured before an event. FRCP 6(a)(5).

vi. *"Legal holiday" defined.* "Legal holiday" means:

- The day set aside by statute for observing New Year's Day, Martin Luther King Jr.'s Birthday, Washington's Birthday, Memorial Day, Independence Day, Labor Day, Columbus Day, Veterans' Day, Thanksgiving Day, or Christmas Day;

- Any day declared a holiday by the President or Congress; and

- For periods that are measured after an event, any other day declared a holiday by the state where the district court is located. FRCP 6(a)(6).

b. *Extending time*

i. *In general.* When an act may or must be done within a specified time, the court may, for good cause, extend the time:

- With or without motion or notice if the court acts, or if a request is made, before the original time or its extension expires; or

- On motion made after the time has expired if the party failed to act because of excusable neglect. FRCP 6(b)(1).

ii. *Exceptions.* A court must not extend the time to act under FRCP 50(b), FRCP 50(d), FRCP 52(b), FRCP 59(b), FRCP 59(d), FRCP 59(e), and FRCP 60(b). FRCP 6(b)(2).

iii. Refer to the United States District Court for the Eastern District of New York KeyRules Motion for Continuance/Extension of Time document for more information on extending time.

c. *Additional time after certain kinds of service.* When a party may or must act within a specified time after service and service is made under FRCP 5(b)(2)(C), FRCP 5(b)(2)(D), FRCP 5(b)(2)(E), or FRCP 5(b)(2)(F), three (3) days are added after the period would otherwise expire under FRCP 6(a). FRCP 6(d). Overnight delivery service shall be deemed service by mail for purposes of FRCP 5 and FRCP 6. NY R USDCTS&ED Civ Rule 5.3.

6. *Individual judge practices.* Refer to the Miscellaneous section of this document for information on individual judge practices on timing of documents.

## C. General Requirements

1. *Motions, generally*

a. *Requirements.* A request for a court order must be made by motion. The motion must:

i. Be in writing unless made during a hearing or trial;

ii. State with particularity the grounds for seeking the order; and

iii. State the relief sought. FRCP 7(b)(1).

b. *Notice of motion.* A party interested in resisting the relief sought by a motion has a right to notice thereof, and an opportunity to be heard. AMJUR MOTIONS § 12.

i. In addition to statutory or court rule provisions requiring notice of a motion—the purpose of such a notice requirement having been said to be to prevent a party from being prejudicially surprised by a motion—principles of natural justice dictate that an adverse party generally must be given notice that a motion will be presented to the court. AMJUR MOTIONS § 12.

ii. "Notice," in this regard, means reasonable notice, including a meaningful opportunity to prepare and to defend against allegations of a motion. AMJUR MOTIONS § 12.

c. *Writing requirement.* The writing requirement is intended to insure that the adverse parties are informed and have a record of both the motion's pendency and the grounds on which the movant seeks an order. FPP § 1191; Feldberg v. Quechee Lakes Corp., 463 F.3d 195 (2d Cir. 2006).

i. It is sufficient "if the motion is stated in a written notice of the hearing of the motion." FPP § 1191.

d. *Particularity requirement.* The particularity requirement insures that the opposing parties will have notice of their opponent's contentions. FEDPROC § 62:364; Goodman v. 1973 26 Foot Trojan Vessel, Arkansas Registration No. AR1439SN, 859 F.2d 71, 12 Fed.R.Serv.3d 645 (8th Cir. 1988). That requirement ensures that notice of the basis for the motion is provided to the court and to the opposing party so as to avoid prejudice, provide the opponent with a meaningful opportunity to respond, and provide the court with enough information to process the motion correctly. FEDPROC § 62:364; Andreas v. Volkswagen of America, Inc., 336 F.3d 789, 56 Fed.R.Serv.3d 6 (8th Cir. 2003).

i. Reasonable specification of the grounds for a motion is sufficient. However, where a movant fails to state even one ground for granting the motion in question, the movant has failed to meet the minimal standard of "reasonable specification." FEDPROC § 62:364; Martinez v. Trainor, 556 F.2d 818, 23 Fed.R.Serv.2d 403 (7th Cir. 1977).

ii. The court may excuse the failure to comply with the particularity requirement if it is inadvertent, and where no prejudice is shown by the opposing party. FEDPROC § 62:364.

e. *Ex parte orders or orders to show cause to bring on a motion.* No ex parte order, or order to show cause to bring on a motion, will be granted except upon a clear and specific showing by affidavit of good and sufficient reasons why a procedure other than by notice of motion is necessary, and stating whether a previous application for similar relief has been made. NY R USDCTS&ED Civ Rule 6.1(d).

f. *Letter-motions.* Applications for extensions or adjournments, applications for a pre-motion conference, and similar non-dispositive matters as permitted by the instructions regarding ECF published on the website of each respective Court and any pertinent Individual Judge's Practices, may be brought by letter-motion filed via ECF pursuant to NY R USDCTS&ED Civ Rule 5.2(b). NY R USDCTS&ED Civ Rule 7.1(d).

2.  *Motion for summary judgment.* A party may move for summary judgment, identifying each claim or defense—or the part of each claim or defense—on which summary judgment is sought. The court shall grant summary judgment if the movant shows that there is no genuine dispute as to any material fact and the movant is entitled to judgment as a matter of law. The court should state on the record the reasons for granting or denying the motion. FRCP 56(a).

    a.  *Burden of proof and presumptions*

        i.  *Movant's burden.* It is well-settled that the party moving for summary judgment has the burden of demonstrating that the FRCP 56(c) test—"no genuine issue as to any material fact"—is satisfied and that the movant is entitled to judgment as a matter of law. FPP § 2727; Adickes v. S. H. Kress & Co., 398 U.S. 144, 157, 90 S.Ct. 1598, 1608, 26 L.Ed.2d 142 (1970).

            •  The movant is held to a stringent standard. FPP § 2727. Before summary judgment will be granted it must be clear what the truth is and any doubt as to the existence of a genuine issue of material fact will be resolved against the movant. FPP § 2727; Poller v. Columbia Broadcasting Sys., Inc., 368 U.S. 464, 82 S.Ct. 486, 7 L.Ed.2d 458 (1962); Adickes v. S. H. Kress & Co., 398 U.S. 144, 90 S.Ct. 1598, 26 L.Ed.2d 142 (1970).

            •  Because the burden is on the movant, the evidence presented to the court always is construed in favor of the party opposing the motion and the opponent is given the benefit of all favorable inferences that can be drawn from it. FPP § 2727; Scott v. Harris, 550 U.S. 372, 127 S.Ct. 1769, 167 L.Ed.2d 686 (2007).

            •  Finally, facts asserted by the party opposing the motion, if supported by affidavits or other evidentiary material, are regarded as true. FPP § 2727; McLaughlin v. Liu, 849 F.2d 1205, 1208 (9th Cir. 1988).

        ii.  *Opponent's burden.* If the movant makes out a prima facie case that would entitle him to a judgment as a matter of law if uncontroverted at trial, summary judgment will be granted unless the opposing party offers some competent evidence that could be presented at trial showing that there is a genuine issue as to a material fact. FPP § 2727; First Nat. Bank of Arizona v. Cities Serv. Co., 391 U.S. 253, 289, 88 S.Ct. 1575, 1593, 20 L.Ed.2d 569 (1968). In this way the burden of producing evidence is shifted to the party opposing the motion. FPP § 2727; Celotex Corp. v. Catrett, 477 U.S. 317, 331, 106 S.Ct. 2548, 2557, 91 L.Ed.2d 265 (1986).

            •  The burden on the nonmoving party is not a heavy one; the nonmoving party simply is required to show specific facts, as opposed to general allegations, that present a genuine issue worthy of trial. FPP § 2727; Lujan v. Defenders of Wildlife, 504 U.S. 555, 112 S.Ct. 2130, 119 L.Ed.2d 351 (1992).

            •  The nonmoving party has two options once the moving party has met its burden of production of evidence demonstrating the absence of a genuine issue of material fact: either come forward with countervailing evidence showing that a genuine issue does exist, or submit an affidavit under FRCP 56(f) demonstrating that more time or further discovery are necessary to enable it to oppose the summary judgment motion. FEDPROC § 62:589.

    b.  *Failing to properly support or address a fact.* If a party fails to properly support an assertion of fact or fails to properly address another party's assertion of fact as required by FRCP 56(c), the court may:

        i.  Give an opportunity to properly support or address the fact;

        ii.  Consider the fact undisputed for purposes of the motion;

        iii.  Grant summary judgment if the motion and supporting materials—including the facts considered undisputed—show that the movant is entitled to it; or

        iv.  Issue any other appropriate order. FRCP 56(e).

    c. *Judgment independent of the motion.* After giving notice and a reasonable time to respond, the court may:

        i. Grant summary judgment for a nonmovant;

        ii. Grant the motion on grounds not raised by a party; or

        iii. Consider summary judgment on its own after identifying for the parties material facts that may not be genuinely in dispute. FRCP 56(f).

    d. *Failing to grant all the requested relief.* If the court does not grant all the relief requested by the motion, it may enter an order stating any material fact—including an item of damages or other relief—that is not genuinely in dispute and treating the fact as established in the case. FRCP 56(g).

    e. *Affidavit or declaration submitted in bad faith.* If satisfied that an affidavit or declaration under FRCP 56 is submitted in bad faith or solely for delay, the court—after notice and a reasonable time to respond—may order the submitting party to pay the other party the reasonable expenses, including attorney's fees, it incurred as a result. An offending party or attorney may also be held in contempt or subjected to other appropriate sanctions. FRCP 56(h).

    f. *Conversion of motions under FRCP 12(b)(6) and FRCP 12(c).* If, on a motion under FRCP 12(b)(6) or FRCP 12(c), matters outside the pleadings are presented to and not excluded by the court, the motion must be treated as one for summary judgment under FRCP 56. FRCP 12(d).

3. *Opposing papers*

    a. *Opposing papers, generally.* The Federal Rules of Civil Procedure do not require any formal answer, return, or reply to a motion, except where the Federal Rules of Civil Procedure or local rules may require affidavits, memoranda, or other papers to be filed in opposition to a motion. Such papers are simply to apprise the court of such opposition and the grounds of that opposition. FEDPROC § 62:359. Except for letter-motions as permitted by NY R USDCTS&ED Civ Rule 7.1(d) or as otherwise permitted by the Court, all oppositions and replies with respect to motions shall comply with NY R USDCTS&ED Civ Rule 7.1(a)(2) and NY R USDCTS&ED Civ Rule 7.1(a)(3), and an opposing party who seeks relief that goes beyond the denial of the motion shall comply as well with NY R USDCTS&ED Civ Rule 7.1(a)(1). NY R USDCTS&ED Civ Rule 7.1(b).

        i. *Effect of failure to respond to motion.* Although in the absence of statutory provision or court rule, a motion ordinarily does not require a written answer, when a party files a motion and the opposing party fails to respond, the court may construe such failure to respond as nonopposition to the motion or an admission that the motion was meritorious, may take the facts alleged in the motion as true—the rule in some jurisdictions being that the failure to respond to a fact set forth in a motion is deemed an admission—and may grant the motion if the relief requested appears to be justified. AMJUR MOTIONS § 28.

        ii. *Assent or no opposition not determinative.* However, a motion will not be granted automatically simply because an "assent" or a notation of "no opposition" has been filed; federal judges frequently deny motions that have been assented to when it is thought that justice so dictates. FPP § 1190.

        iii. *Responsive pleading inappropriate as response to motion.* An attempt to answer or oppose a motion with a responsive pleading usually is not appropriate. FPP § 1190.

    b. *Opposition to motion for summary judgment.* The party opposing summary judgment does not have a duty to present evidence in opposition to a motion under FRCP 56 in all circumstances. FPP § 2727; Jaroma v. Massey, 873 F.2d 17 (1st Cir. 1989).

        i. *When facts are unavailable to the nonmovant.* If a nonmovant shows by affidavit or declaration that, for specified reasons, it cannot present facts essential to justify its opposition, the court may:

            • Defer considering the motion or deny it;

            • Allow time to obtain affidavits or declarations or to take discovery; or

            • Issue any other appropriate order. FRCP 56(d).

4.  *Reply papers.* A moving party may be required or permitted to prepare papers in addition to his original motion papers. AMJUR MOTIONS § 25. Papers answering or replying to opposing papers may be appropriate, in the interests of justice, where it appears there is a substantial reason for allowing a reply. Thus, a court may accept reply papers where a party demonstrates that the papers to which it seeks to file a reply raise new issues that are material to the disposition of the question before the court, or where the court determines, sua sponte, that it wishes further briefing of an issue raised in those papers and orders the submission of additional papers. FEDPROC § 62:360. Except for letter-motions as permitted by NY R USDCTS&ED Civ Rule 7.1(d) or as otherwise permitted by the Court, all oppositions and replies with respect to motions shall comply with NY R USDCTS&ED Civ Rule 7.1(a)(2) and NY R USDCTS&ED Civ Rule 7.1(a)(3). NY R USDCTS&ED Civ Rule 7.1(b).

    a.  *Function of reply papers.* The function of a reply affidavit is to answer the arguments made in opposition to the position taken by the movant and not to permit the movant to introduce new arguments in support of the motion. AMJUR MOTIONS § 25.

    b.  *Issues raised for the first time in a reply document.* However, the view has been followed in some jurisdictions, that as a matter of judicial economy, where there is no prejudice and where the issues could be raised simply by filing a motion to dismiss, the trial court has discretion to consider arguments raised for the first time in a reply memorandum, and that a trial court may grant a motion to strike issues raised for the first time in a reply memorandum. AMJUR MOTIONS § 26.

5.  *Orders on motions.* A memorandum signed by the Court of the decision on a motion that does not finally determine all claims for relief, or an oral decision on such a motion, shall constitute the order unless the memorandum or oral decision directs the submission or settlement of an order in more extended form. The notation in the docket of a memorandum or of an oral decision that does not direct the submission or settlement of an order in more extended form shall constitute the entry of the order. Where an order in more extended form is required to be submitted or settled, the notation in the docket of such order shall constitute the entry of the order. NY R USDCTS&ED Civ Rule 6.2.

6.  *Related cases.* It shall be the continuing duty of each attorney appearing in any civil or criminal case to bring promptly to the attention of the Court all facts which said attorney believes are relevant to a determination that said case and one or more pending civil or criminal cases should be heard by the same Judge, in order to avoid unnecessary duplication of judicial effort. As soon as the attorney becomes aware of such relationship, said attorney shall notify the Judges to whom the cases have been assigned. NY R USDCTS&ED Civ Rule 1.6(a). If counsel fails to comply with NY R USDCTS&ED Civ Rule 1.6(a), the Court may assess reasonable costs directly against counsel whose action has obstructed the effective administration of the Court's business. NY R USDCTS&ED Civ Rule 1.6(b).

7.  *Alternative dispute resolution (ADR)*

    a.  *Court-annexed arbitration*

        i.  *Civil cases eligible for compulsory arbitration.* The Clerk of Court shall, as to all cases filed after January 1, 1986, designate and process for compulsory arbitration all civil cases (excluding Social Security cases, tax matters, prisoners' civil rights cases and any action based on an alleged violation of a right secured by the Constitution of the United States or if jurisdiction is based in whole or in part on 28 U.S.C.A. § 1343) wherein money damages only are being sought in an amount not in excess of one hundred fifty thousand dollars ($150,000) exclusive of interest and costs. NY R USDCTS&ED Civ Rule 83.7(d)(1).

            • The parties may by written stipulation agree that the Clerk of Court shall designate and process for court-annexed arbitration any civil case that is not subject to compulsory arbitration in NY R USDCTS&ED Civ Rule 83.7. NY R USDCTS&ED Civ Rule 83.7(d)(2).

            • For purposes of NY R USDCTS&ED Civ Rule 83.7 only, in all civil cases damages shall be presumed to be not in excess of one hundred fifty thousand dollars ($150,000) exclusive of interest and costs, unless: (1) counsel for plaintiff, at the time of filing the complaint, or in the event of the removal of a case from state court or transfer of a case from another district to this Court, within thirty (30) days of the docketing of the case in this district, files a certification with the Court that the damages sought exceed one hundred fifty thousand dollars ($150,000), exclusive of interest and costs; or (2) counsel for a defendant, at the time of filing a counterclaim or cross-claim files a certification with the court that the damages sought by the counter-claim or cross-claim exceed one hundred fifty thousand dollars ($150,000) exclusive of interest and costs. NY R USDCTS&ED Civ Rule 83.7(d)(3).

ii. *Exemption from arbitration.* The Court shall, sua sponte, or on motion of a party, exempt any case from arbitration in which the objectives of arbitration would not be realized (1) because the case involves complex or novel issues, (2) because legal issues predominate over factual issues, or (3) for other good cause. NY R USDCTS&ED Civ Rule 83.7(e)(2). For information on applying for an exemption, refer to NY R USDCTS&ED Civ Rule 83.7

iii. *Referral to arbitration.* Cases not originally designated as eligible for compulsory arbitration, but which in the discretion of the assigned Judge, are later found to qualify, may be referred to arbitration. A U.S. District Judge or a U.S. Magistrate Judge, in cases that exceed the arbitration ceiling of one hundred fifty thousand dollars ($150,000) exclusive of interest and costs, in their discretion, may suggest that the parties should consider arbitration. If the parties are agreeable, an appropriate consent form signed by all parties or their representatives may be entered and filed in the case prior to scheduling an arbitration hearing. NY R USDCTS&ED Civ Rule 83.7(e)(3).

iv. For more information on arbitration, refer to NY R USDCTS&ED Civ Rule 83.7.

b. *Court-annexed mediation.* Mediation is a process in which parties and counsel agree to meet with a neutral mediator trained to assist them in settling disputes. The mediator improves communication across party lines, helps parties articulate their interests and understand those of the other party, probes the strengths and weaknesses of each party's legal positions, and identifies areas of agreement and helps generate options for a mutually agreeable resolution to the dispute. In all cases, mediation provides an opportunity to explore a wide range of potential solutions and to address interests that may be outside the scope of the stated controversy or which could not be addressed by judicial action. A hallmark of mediation is its capacity to expand traditional settlement discussions and broaden resolution options, often by exploring litigant needs and interests that may be formally independent of the legal issues in controversy. NY R USDCTS&ED Civ Rule 83.8(a).

i. *Eligible cases.* Judges and Magistrate Judges may designate civil cases for inclusion in the mediation program, and when doing so shall prepare an order to that effect. Alternatively, and subject to the availability of qualified mediators, the parties may consent to participation in the mediation program by preparing and executing a stipulation signed by all parties to the action and so-ordered by the Court. NY R USDCTS&ED Civ Rule 83.8(b)(1).

ii. For more information on mediation, refer to NY R USDCTS&ED Civ Rule 83.8.

8. *Individual judge practices.* Refer to the Miscellaneous section of this document for information on individual judge practices on general requirements for documents.

## D. Documents

1. *Documents for moving party*

   a. *Required documents*

   i. *Notice of motion and motion.* Except for letter-motions as permitted by NY R USDCTS&ED Civ Rule 7.1(d) or as otherwise permitted by the Court, all motions shall include the following motion papers: a notice of motion, or an order to show cause signed by the Court, which shall specify the applicable rules or statutes pursuant to which the motion is brought, and shall specify the relief sought by the motion. NY R USDCTS&ED Civ Rule 7.1(a)(1). Refer to the General Requirements section of this document for information on the notice of motion and motion.

   ii. *Statement of material facts.* Upon any motion for summary judgment pursuant to FRCP 56, there shall be annexed to the notice of motion a separate, short and concise statement, in numbered paragraphs, of the material facts as to which the moving party contends there is no genuine issue to be tried. Failure to submit such a statement may constitute grounds for denial of the motion. NY R USDCTS&ED Civ Rule 56.1(a).

- Each statement by the movant or opponent pursuant to NY R USDCTS&ED Civ Rule 56.1(a) and NY R USDCTS&ED Civ Rule 56.1(b), including each statement controverting any statement of material fact, must be followed by citation to evidence which would be admissible, set forth as required by FRCP 56(c). NY R USDCTS&ED Civ Rule 56.1(d).

iii. *Memorandum of law.* Except for letter-motions as permitted by NY R USDCTS&ED Civ Rule 7.1(d) or as otherwise permitted by the Court, all motions shall include the following motion papers: a memorandum of law, setting forth the cases and other authorities relied upon in support of the motion, and divided, under appropriate headings, into as many parts as there are issues to be determined. NY R USDCTS&ED Civ Rule 7.1(a)(2).

iv. *Certificate of service.* FRCP 5(d) requires that the person making service under FRCP 5 certify that service has been effected. FRCP 5(Advisory Committee Notes). Having such information on file may be useful for many purposes, including proof of service if an issue arises concerning the effectiveness of the service. FRCP 5(Advisory Committee Notes).

b. *Supplemental documents*

i. *Supporting evidence.* When a motion relies on facts outside the record, the court may hear the matter on affidavits or may hear it wholly or partly on oral testimony or on depositions. FRCP 43(c). Except for letter-motions as permitted by NY R USDCTS&ED Civ Rule 7.1(d) or as otherwise permitted by the Court, all motions shall include the following motion papers: supporting affidavits and exhibits thereto containing any factual information and portions of the record necessary for the decision of the motion. NY R USDCTS&ED Civ Rule 7.1(a)(3).

- *Supporting factual positions.* A party asserting that a fact cannot be or is genuinely disputed must support the assertion by: (1) citing to particular parts of materials in the record, including depositions, documents, electronically stored information, affidavits or declarations, stipulations (including those made for purposes of the motion only), admissions, interrogatory answers, or other materials; or (2) showing that the materials cited do not establish the absence or presence of a genuine dispute, or that an adverse party cannot produce admissible evidence to support the fact. FRCP 56(c)(1).

- *Objection that a fact is not supported by admissible evidence.* A party may object that the material cited to support or dispute a fact cannot be presented in a form that would be admissible in evidence. FRCP 56(c)(2).

- *Materials not cited.* The court need consider only the cited materials, but it may consider other materials in the record. FRCP 56(c)(3).

- *Affidavits or declarations.* An affidavit or declaration used to support or oppose a motion must be made on personal knowledge, set out facts that would be admissible in evidence, and show that the affiant or declarant is competent to testify on the matters stated. FRCP 56(c)(4).

- *Discovery materials.* A party seeking or opposing relief under FRCP 26 through FRCP 37 inclusive, or making or opposing any other motion or application, shall quote or attach only those portions of the depositions, interrogatories, requests for documents, requests for admissions, or other discovery or disclosure materials, together with the responses and objections thereto, that are the subject of the discovery motion or application, or that are cited in papers submitted in connection with any other motion or application. NY R USDCTS&ED Civ Rule 5.1.

ii. *Notice of constitutional question.* A party that files a pleading, written motion, or other paper drawing into question the constitutionality of a federal or state statute must promptly:

- *File notice.* File a notice of constitutional question stating the question and identifying the paper that raises it, if: (1) a federal statute is questioned and the parties do not include the United States, one of its agencies, or one of its officers or employees in an official capacity; or (2) a state statute is questioned and the parties do not include the state, one of its agencies, or one of its officers or employees in an official capacity; and

- *Serve notice.* Serve the notice and paper on the Attorney General of the United States if a federal statute is questioned—or on the state attorney general if a state statute is questioned—either by certified or registered mail or by sending it to an electronic address designated by the attorney general for this purpose. FRCP 5.1(a).

- *No forfeiture.* A party's failure to file and serve the notice, or the court's failure to certify, does not forfeit a constitutional claim or defense that is otherwise timely asserted. FRCP 5.1(d).

iii. *Nongovernmental corporate disclosure statement.* To enable judges and magistrates to evaluate possible disqualification or recusal, counsel for a private (nongovernmental) party shall submit at the time of initial pleading a certificate identifying any corporate parent, subsidiaries, or affiliates of that party. NY R USDCTED Div. Bus., Rule 50.1(c).

- *Contents.* A nongovernmental corporate party must file two (2) copies of a disclosure statement that: (1) identifies any parent corporation and any publicly held corporation owning ten percent (10%) or more of its stock; or (2) states that there is no such corporation. FRCP 7.1(a).

- *Time to file; Supplemental filing.* A party must: (1) file the disclosure statement with its first appearance, pleading, petition, motion, response, or other request addressed to the court; and (2) promptly file a supplemental statement if any required information changes. FRCP 7.1(b). For purposes of FRCP 7.1(b)(2), "promptly" shall mean "within fourteen days," that is, parties are required to file a supplemental disclosure statement within fourteen (14) days of the time there is any change in the information required in a disclosure statement filed pursuant to those rules. NY R USDCTS&ED Civ Rule 7.1.1.

iv. *Notice to pro se litigant who opposes a motion for summary judgment.* Any represented party moving for summary judgment against a party proceeding pro se shall serve and file as a separate document, together with the papers in support of the motion, the "Notice To Pro Se Litigant Who Opposes a Motion For Summary Judgment" found in NY R USDCTS&ED Civ Rule 56.2 with the full texts of FRCP 56 and NY R USDCTS&ED Civ Rule 56.1 attached. Where the pro se party is not the plaintiff, the movant shall amend the form notice as necessary to reflect that fact. NY R USDCTS&ED Civ Rule 56.2. For the notice, refer to NY R USDCTS&ED Civ Rule 56.2.

v. *Copies of authorities.* In cases involving a pro se litigant, counsel shall, when serving a memorandum of law (or other submissions to the Court), provide the pro se litigant (but not other counsel or the Court) with copies of cases and other authorities cited therein that are unpublished or reported exclusively on computerized databases. Upon request, counsel shall provide the pro se litigant with copies of such unpublished cases and other authorities as are cited in a decision of the Court and were not previously cited by any party. NY R USDCTS&ED Civ Rule 7.2.

2. *Documents for opposing party*

a. *Required documents*

i. *Answering memorandum of law.* Except for letter-motions as permitted by NY R USDCTS&ED Civ Rule 7.1(d) or as otherwise permitted by the Court, all oppositions and replies with respect to motions shall comply with NY R USDCTS&ED Civ Rule 7.1(a)(2). NY R USDCTS&ED Civ Rule 7.1(b). Except for letter-motions as permitted by NY R USDCTS&ED Civ Rule 7.1(d) or as otherwise permitted by the Court, all motions shall include the following motion papers: a memorandum of law, setting forth the cases and other authorities relied upon in support of the motion, and divided, under appropriate headings, into as many parts as there are issues to be determined. NY R USDCTS&ED Civ Rule 7.1(a)(2). Refer to the General Requirements section of this document for information on the opposing papers.

ii. *Responsive statement of material facts.* The papers opposing a motion for summary judgment shall include a correspondingly numbered paragraph responding to each numbered paragraph in the statement of the moving party, and if necessary, additional paragraphs containing a separate, short and concise statement of additional material facts as to which it is contended that there exists a genuine issue to be tried. NY R USDCTS&ED Civ Rule 56.1(b).

- Each numbered paragraph in the statement of material facts set forth in the statement required to be served by the moving party will be deemed to be admitted for purposes of the motion unless specifically controverted by a correspondingly numbered paragraph in the statement required to be served by the opposing party. NY R USDCTS&ED Civ Rule 56.1(c).

- Each statement by the movant or opponent pursuant to NY R USDCTS&ED Civ Rule 56.1(a) and NY R USDCTS&ED Civ Rule 56.1(b), including each statement controverting any statement of material fact, must be followed by citation to evidence which would be admissible, set forth as required by FRCP 56(c). NY R USDCTS&ED Civ Rule 56.1(d).

iii. *Certificate of service.* FRCP 5(d) requires that the person making service under FRCP 5 certify that service has been effected. FRCP 5(Advisory Committee Notes). Having such information on file may be useful for many purposes, including proof of service if an issue arises concerning the effectiveness of the service. FRCP 5(Advisory Committee Notes).

b. *Supplemental documents*

i. *Supporting evidence.* When a motion relies on facts outside the record, the court may hear the matter on affidavits or may hear it wholly or partly on oral testimony or on depositions. FRCP 43(c). Except for letter-motions as permitted by NY R USDCTS&ED Civ Rule 7.1(d) or as otherwise permitted by the Court, all oppositions and replies with respect to motions shall comply with NY R USDCTS&ED Civ Rule 7.1(a)(3). NY R USDCTS&ED Civ Rule 7.1(b). Except for letter-motions as permitted by NY R USDCTS&ED Civ Rule 7.1(d) or as otherwise permitted by the Court, all motions shall include the following motion papers: supporting affidavits and exhibits thereto containing any factual information and portions of the record necessary for the decision of the motion. NY R USDCTS&ED Civ Rule 7.1(a)(3).

- *Supporting factual positions.* A party asserting that a fact cannot be or is genuinely disputed must support the assertion by: (1) citing to particular parts of materials in the record, including depositions, documents, electronically stored information, affidavits or declarations, stipulations (including those made for purposes of the motion only), admissions, interrogatory answers, or other materials; or (2) showing that the materials cited do not establish the absence or presence of a genuine dispute, or that an adverse party cannot produce admissible evidence to support the fact. FRCP 56(c)(1).

- *Objection that a fact is not supported by admissible evidence.* A party may object that the material cited to support or dispute a fact cannot be presented in a form that would be admissible in evidence. FRCP 56(c)(2).

- *Materials not cited.* The court need consider only the cited materials, but it may consider other materials in the record. FRCP 56(c)(3).

- *Affidavits or declarations.* An affidavit or declaration used to support or oppose a motion must be made on personal knowledge, set out facts that would be admissible in evidence, and show that the affiant or declarant is competent to testify on the matters stated. FRCP 56(c)(4).

- *Discovery materials.* A party seeking or opposing relief under FRCP 26 through FRCP 37 inclusive, or making or opposing any other motion or application, shall quote or attach only those portions of the depositions, interrogatories, requests for documents, requests for admissions, or other discovery or disclosure materials, together with the responses and objections thereto, that are the subject of the discovery motion or application, or that are cited in papers submitted in connection with any other motion or application. NY R USDCTS&ED Civ Rule 5.1.

ii. *Notice of constitutional question.* A party that files a pleading, written motion, or other paper drawing into question the constitutionality of a federal or state statute must promptly:

- *File notice.* File a notice of constitutional question stating the question and identifying the

paper that raises it, if: (1) a federal statute is questioned and the parties do not include the United States, one of its agencies, or one of its officers or employees in an official capacity; or (2) a state statute is questioned and the parties do not include the state, one of its agencies, or one of its officers or employees in an official capacity; and

- *Serve notice.* Serve the notice and paper on the Attorney General of the United States if a federal statute is questioned—or on the state attorney general if a state statute is questioned—either by certified or registered mail or by sending it to an electronic address designated by the attorney general for this purpose. FRCP 5.1(a).

- *No forfeiture.* A party's failure to file and serve the notice, or the court's failure to certify, does not forfeit a constitutional claim or defense that is otherwise timely asserted. FRCP 5.1(d).

iii. *Copies of authorities.* In cases involving a pro se litigant, counsel shall, when serving a memorandum of law (or other submissions to the Court), provide the pro se litigant (but not other counsel or the Court) with copies of cases and other authorities cited therein that are unpublished or reported exclusively on computerized databases. Upon request, counsel shall provide the pro se litigant with copies of such unpublished cases and other authorities as are cited in a decision of the Court and were not previously cited by any party. NY R USDCTS&ED Civ Rule 7.2.

3. *Individual judge practices.* Refer to the Miscellaneous section of this document for information on individual judge practices on required documents.

## E. Format

1. *Form of documents.* The rules governing captions and other matters of form in pleadings apply to motions and other papers. FRCP 7(b)(2).

   a. *Paper.* Every pleading, written motion, and other paper must: be plainly written, typed, printed, or copied without erasures or interlineations which materially deface it. NY R USDCTS&ED Civ Rule 11.1(a)(1).

   b. *Typeface, margin, and spacing.* The typeface, margins, and spacing of all documents presented for filing must meet the following requirements:

      i. All text must be twelve (12) point type or larger, except for text in footnotes which may be ten (10) point type;

      ii. All documents must have at least one (1) inch margins on all sides;

      iii. All text must be double-spaced, except for headings, text in footnotes, or block quotations, which may be single-spaced. NY R USDCTS&ED Civ Rule 11.1(b).

   c. *Caption; Names of parties.* Every pleading must have a caption with the court's name, a title, a file number, and a FRCP 7(a) designation. The title of the complaint must name all the parties; the title of other pleadings, after naming the first party on each side, may refer generally to other parties. FRCP 10(a). Every pleading, written motion, and other paper must: bear the docket number and the initials of the District Judge and any Magistrate Judge before whom the action or proceeding is pending, NY R USDCTS&ED Civ Rule 11.1(a)(2).

   d. *Paragraphs; Separate statements.* A party must state its claims or defenses in numbered paragraphs, each limited as far as practicable to a single set of circumstances. A later pleading may refer by number to a paragraph in an earlier pleading. If doing so would promote clarity, each claim founded on a separate transaction or occurrence—and each defense other than a denial—must be stated in a separate count or defense. FRCP 10(b).

   e. *Adoption by reference; Exhibits.* A statement in a pleading may be adopted by reference elsewhere in the same pleading or in any other pleading or motion. A copy of a written instrument that is an exhibit to a pleading is a part of the pleading for all purposes. FRCP 10(c).

   f. *Acceptance by the clerk.* The clerk must not refuse to file a paper solely because it is not in the form prescribed by the Federal Rules of Civil Procedure or by a local rule or practice. FRCP 5(d)(4).

2. *Signing of pleadings, motions and other papers*

    a. *Signature.* Every pleading, written motion, and other paper must be signed by at least one attorney of record in the attorney's name—or by a party personally if the party is unrepresented. The paper must state the signer's address, e-mail address, and telephone number. FRCP 11(a). Every pleading, written motion, and other paper must: have the name of each person signing it clearly printed or typed directly below the signature. NY R USDCTS&ED Civ Rule 11.1(a)(3).

        i. *No verification or accompanying affidavit required for pleadings.* Unless a rule or statute specifically states otherwise, a pleading need not be verified or accompanied by an affidavit. FRCP 11(a).

        ii. *Unsigned papers.* The court must strike an unsigned paper unless the omission is promptly corrected after being called to the attorney's or party's attention. FRCP 11(a).

    b. *Representations to the court.* By presenting to the court a pleading, written motion, or other paper—whether by signing, filing, submitting, or later advocating it—an attorney or unrepresented party certifies that to the best of the person's knowledge, information, and belief, formed after an inquiry reasonable under the circumstances:

        i. It is not being presented for any improper purpose, such as to harass, cause unnecessary delay, or needlessly increase the cost of litigation;

        ii. The claims, defenses, and other legal contentions are warranted by existing law or by a nonfrivolous argument for extending, modifying, or reversing existing law or for establishing new law;

        iii. The factual contentions have evidentiary support or, if specifically so identified, will likely have evidentiary support after a reasonable opportunity for further investigation or discovery; and

        iv. The denials of factual contentions are warranted on the evidence or, if specifically so identified, are reasonably based on belief or a lack of information. FRCP 11(b).

    c. *Sanctions.* If, after notice and a reasonable opportunity to respond, the court determines that FRCP 11(b) has been violated, the court may impose an appropriate sanction on any attorney, law firm, or party that violated FRCP 11(b) or is responsible for the violation. FRCP 11(c)(1). Refer to the United States District Court for the Eastern District of New York KeyRules Motion for Sanctions document for more information.

3. *Privacy protection for filings made with the court*

    a. *Redacted filings.* Unless the court orders otherwise, in an electronic or paper filing with the court that contains an individual's Social Security number, taxpayer-identification number, or birth date, the name of an individual known to be a minor, or a financial-account number, a party or nonparty making the filing may include only:

        i. The last four (4) digits of the Social Security number and taxpayer-identification number;

        ii. The year of the individual's birth;

        iii. The minor's initials; and

        iv. The last four (4) digits of the financial-account number. FRCP 5.2(a); NY R USDCTED Order 2004-09.

        v. In addition, exercise caution when filing documents that contain the following:

           • Personal identifying number, such as driver's license number;

           • Medical records, treatment and diagnosis;

           • Employment history;

           • Individual financial information; and

           • Proprietary or trade secret information. NY R USDCTED Order 2004-09.

b. *Exemptions from the redaction requirement.* The redaction requirement does not apply to the following:

    i. A financial-account number that identifies the property allegedly subject to forfeiture in a forfeiture proceeding;

    ii. The record of an administrative or agency proceeding;

    iii. The official record of a state-court proceeding;

    iv. The record of a court or tribunal, if that record was not subject to the redaction requirement when originally filed;

    v. A filing covered by FRCP 5.2(c) or FRCP 5.2(d); and

    vi. A pro se filing in an action brought under 28 U.S.C.A. § 2241, 28 U.S.C.A. § 2254, or 28 U.S.C.A. § 2255. FRCP 5.2(b).

c. *Limitations on remote access to electronic files; Social Security appeals and immigration cases.* Unless the court orders otherwise, in an action for benefits under the Social Security Act, and in an action or proceeding relating to an order of removal, to relief from removal, or to immigration benefits or detention, access to an electronic file is authorized as follows:

    i. The parties and their attorneys may have remote electronic access to any part of the case file, including the administrative record;

    ii. Any other person may have electronic access to the full record at the courthouse, but may have remote electronic access only to:

        • The docket maintained by the court; and

        • An opinion, order, judgment, or other disposition of the court, but not any other part of the case file or the administrative record. FRCP 5.2(c).

d. *Filings made under seal.* The court may order that a filing be made under seal without redaction. The court may later unseal the filing or order the person who made the filing to file a redacted version for the public record. FRCP 5.2(d).

e. *Protective orders.* For good cause, the court may by order in a case:

    i. Require redaction of additional information; or

    ii. Limit or prohibit a nonparty's remote electronic access to a document filed with the court. FRCP 5.2(e).

f. *Option for additional unredacted filing under seal.* A person making a redacted filing may also file an unredacted copy under seal. The court must retain the unredacted copy as part of the record. FRCP 5.2(f); NY R USDCTED Order 2004-09. The unredacted version of the document or the reference list shall be retained by the court as part of the record. The court may, however, still require the party to file a redacted copy for the public file. NY R USDCTED Order 2004-09.

g. *Option for filing a reference list.* A filing that contains redacted information may be filed together with a reference list that identifies each item of redacted information and specifies an appropriate identifier that uniquely corresponds to each item listed. The list must be filed under seal and may be amended as of right. Any reference in the case to a listed identifier will be construed to refer to the corresponding item of information. FRCP 5.2(g); NY R USDCTED Order 2004-09. The unredacted version of the document or the reference list shall be retained by the court as part of the record. The court may, however, still require the party to file a redacted copy for the public file. NY R USDCTED Order 2004-09.

h. *Responsibility for redaction.* The responsibility for redacting these personal identifiers rests solely with counsel and the parties. The Clerk will not review each pleading for compliance with NY R USDCTED Order 2004-09. NY R USDCTED Order 2004-09.

    i. Counsel is strongly urged to share this notice with all clients so that an informed decision about the inclusion of certain materials may be made. If a redacted document is filed, it is the sole responsibility of counsel and the parties to be sure that all pleadings comply with the rules of

this court requiring redaction of personal data identifiers. The clerk will not review each pleading for redaction. NY R USDCTED Order 2004-09.

    i. *Waiver of protection of identifiers.* A person waives the protection of FRCP 5.2(a) as to the person's own information by filing it without redaction and not under seal. FRCP 5.2(h).

4. *Individual judge practices.* Refer to the Miscellaneous section of this document for information on individual judge practices on formatting documents.

## F. Filing and Service Requirements

1. *Filing requirements.* Any paper after the complaint that is required to be served—together with a certificate of service—must be filed within a reasonable time after service. FRCP 5(d)(1).

    a. *How filing is made; In general.* A paper is filed by delivering it:

        i. To the clerk; or

        ii. To a judge who agrees to accept it for filing, and who must then note the filing date on the paper and promptly send it to the clerk. FRCP 5(d)(2).

    b. *Night depository.* A night depository with an automatic date stamp shall be maintained. . .by the Clerk of the Eastern District in the Brooklyn Courthouse. After regular business hours, papers for the District Court only may be deposited in the night depository. Such papers will be considered as having been filed in the District Court as of the date stamped thereon, which shall be deemed presumptively correct. NY R USDCTS&ED Civ Rule 1.2.

    c. *Electronic filing*

        i. *Authorization of electronic filing program.* A court may, by local rule, allow papers to be filed, signed, or verified by electronic means that are consistent with any technical standards established by the Judicial Conference of the United States. A local rule may require electronic filing only if reasonable exceptions are allowed. A paper filed electronically in compliance with a local rule is a written paper for purposes of the Federal Rules of Civil Procedure. FRCP 5(d)(3).

          • Parties serving and filing papers shall follow the instructions regarding Electronic Case Filing (ECF) published on the website of each respective Court. A paper served and filed by electronic means in accordance with such instructions is, for purposes of FRCP 5, served and filed in compliance with the Local Civil Rules of the Southern and Eastern Districts of New York. NY R USDCTS&ED Civ Rule 5.2(a). Parties have an obligation to review the Court's actual order, decree, or judgment (on ECF), which controls, and should not rely on the description on the docket or in the ECF Notice of Electronic Filing (NEF). NY R USDCTS&ED Civ Rule 5.2(c).

        ii. *Mandatory electronic filing.* Beginning on August 2, 2004, electronic case filing will be mandatory for all civil cases other than pro se cases. NY R USDCTED Order 2004-08.

          • *Letter-motions and letters addressed to the court.* Subject to the instructions regarding ECF published on the website of each respective Court and any pertinent Individual Judge's Practices, letter-motions permitted by NY R USDCTS&ED Civ Rule 7.1(d) and letters addressed to the Court (but not letters between the parties) may be filed via ECF. NY R USDCTS&ED Civ Rule 5.2(b).

          • *Proposed orders, judgments and decrees.* Proposed orders, judgments and decrees shall be presented as directed by the ECF rules published on the website of each respective Court. NY R USDCTS&ED Civ Rule 77.1. For more information, refer to NY R USDCTS&ED Civ Rule 77.1.

          • *Request for exemption.* Requests by attorneys for an exemption to the mandatory policy will be considered for good cause hardship reasons only, and will be reviewed on an individual basis by the assigned United States Magistrate Judge. The Clerk's Office provides an electronic filing training program to assist attorneys filing electronically. Before seeking a hardship exemption, attorneys are advised to participate in the training program or otherwise seek the assistance of the Clerk's Office. NY R USDCTED Order 2004-08.

      iii.   For more information on electronic filing, refer to the court's website.

2.  *Service requirements*

   a.  *Service; When required*

      i.   *In general.* Unless the Federal Rules of Civil Procedure provide otherwise, each of the following papers must be served on every party:

- An order stating that service is required;

- A pleading filed after the original complaint, unless the court orders otherwise under FRCP 5(c) because there are numerous defendants;

- A discovery paper required to be served on a party, unless the court orders otherwise;

- A written motion, except one that may be heard ex parte; and

- A written notice, appearance, demand, or offer of judgment, or any similar paper. FRCP 5(a)(1).

      ii.  *If a party fails to appear.* No service is required on a party who is in default for failing to appear. But a pleading that asserts a new claim for relief against such a party must be served on that party under FRCP 4. FRCP 5(a)(2).

     iii.  *Seizing property.* If an action is begun by seizing property and no person is or need be named as a defendant, any service required before the filing of an appearance, answer, or claim must be made on the person who had custody or possession of the property when it was seized. FRCP 5(a)(3).

   b.  *Service; How made*

      i.   *Serving an attorney.* If a party is represented by an attorney, service under FRCP 5 must be made on the attorney unless the court orders service on the party. FRCP 5(b)(1).

      ii.  *Service in general.* A paper is served under FRCP 5 by:

- Handing it to the person;

- Leaving it: (1) at the person's office with a clerk or other person in charge or, if no one is in charge, in a conspicuous place in the office; or (2) if the person has no office or the office is closed, at the person's dwelling or usual place of abode with someone of suitable age and discretion who resides there;

- Mailing it to the person's last known address—in which event service is complete upon mailing;

- Leaving it with the court clerk if the person has no known address;

- Sending it by electronic means if the person consented in writing—in which event service is complete upon transmission, but is not effective if the serving party learns that it did not reach the person to be served; or

- Delivering it by any other means that the person consented to in writing—in which event service is complete when the person making service delivers it to the agency designated to make delivery. FRCP 5(b)(2).

     iii.  *Service by overnight delivery.* Service upon an attorney may be made by overnight delivery service. "Overnight delivery service" means any delivery service which regularly accepts items for overnight delivery. Overnight delivery service shall be deemed service by mail for purposes of FRCP 5 and FRCP 6. NY R USDCTS&ED Civ Rule 5.3.

     iv.  *Service by electronic means.* Parties serving and filing papers shall follow the instructions regarding Electronic Case Filing (ECF) published on the website of each respective Court. A paper served and filed by electronic means in accordance with such instructions is, for purposes of FRCP 5, served and filed in compliance with the Local Civil Rules of the United States District Courts for the Southern and Eastern Districts of New York. NY R USDCTS&ED Civ Rule 5.2(a). Parties have an obligation to review the Court's actual order, decree, or judgment

(on ECF), which controls, and should not rely on the description on the docket or in the ECF Notice of Electronic Filing (NEF). NY R USDCTS&ED Civ Rule 5.2(c).

    v. *Using court facilities.* If a local rule so authorizes, a party may use the court's transmission facilities to make service under FRCP 5(b)(2)(E). FRCP 5(b)(3).

  c. *Serving numerous defendants*

    i. *In general.* If an action involves an unusually large number of defendants, the court may, on motion or on its own, order that:

- Defendants' pleadings and replies to them need not be served on other defendants;

- Any crossclaim, counterclaim, avoidance, or affirmative defense in those pleadings and replies to them will be treated as denied or avoided by all other parties; and

- Filing any such pleading and serving it on the plaintiff constitutes notice of the pleading to all parties. FRCP 5(c)(1).

    ii. *Notifying parties.* A copy of every such order must be served on the parties as the court directs. FRCP 5(c)(2).

3. *Individual judge practices.* Refer to the Miscellaneous section of this document for information on individual judge practices on filing and serving documents.

## G. Hearings

1. *Hearings, generally*

  a. *Oral argument.* Due process does not require that oral argument be permitted on a motion and, except as otherwise provided by local rule, the district court has discretion to determine whether it will decide the motion on the papers or hear argument by counsel (and perhaps receive evidence). FPP § 1190; F.D.I.C. v. Deglau, 207 F.3d 153 (3d Cir. 2000). The parties and their attorneys shall only appear to argue the motion if so directed by the Court by order or by a Judge's Individual Practice. NY R USDCTS&ED Civ Rule 6.1(c).

  b. *Providing a regular schedule for oral hearings.* A court may establish regular times and places for oral hearings on motions. FRCP 78(a).

  c. *Providing for submission on briefs.* By rule or order, the court may provide for submitting and determining motions on briefs, without oral hearings. FRCP 78(b).

2. *Hearing on motion for summary judgment.* Even though FRCP 56(c) makes reference to a hearing on the motion for summary judgment, FRCP 56 confers no right to an oral hearing on the summary judgment motion, nor is a hearing required by due process considerations. FEDPROC § 62:673; Forjan v. Leprino Foods, Inc., 209 Fed.Appx. 8, 2006 WL 3623496 (2d Cir. 2006).

  a. *Oral argument.* Oral argument on a motion for summary judgment may be considered ordinarily appropriate, so that as a general rule, a district court should grant a request for oral argument on all but frivolous summary judgment motions, or a nonmovant's request for oral argument must be granted unless summary judgment is also denied, according to some courts. FEDPROC § 62:674; Season-All Industries, Inc. v. Turkiye Sise Ve Cam Fabrikalari, A. S., 425 F.2d 34 (3d Cir. 1970); Houston v. Bryan, 725 F.2d 516 (9th Cir. 1984); Fernhoff v. Tahoe Regional Planning Agency, 803 F.2d 979 (9th Cir. 1986).

    i. Oral argument on a summary judgment motion may be deemed waived where the opposing party does not request it. FEDPROC § 62:674; McCormack v. Citibank, N.A., 100 F.3d 532, 30 UCC Rep.Serv.2d 1175 (8th Cir. 1996).

3. *Individual judge practices.* Refer to the Miscellaneous section of this document for information on individual judge practices on hearings.

## H. Forms

### 1. Federal Motion for Summary Judgment Forms

  a. Answer; To plaintiff's motion for summary judgment. AMJUR PP SUMMARY § 56.

  b. Affidavit opposing defendant's motion for summary judgment; By plaintiff. AMJUR PP SUMMARY § 64.

c.  Affidavit opposing motion for summary judgment; By party; Dispute as to issues of fact. AMJUR PP SUMMARY § 73.

d.  Affidavit opposing motion for summary judgment; By party; Inability to present facts. AMJUR PP SUMMARY § 74.

e.  Affidavit opposing motion for summary judgment; By party; Good defense to part of claim. AMJUR PP SUMMARY § 77.

f.  Statement of disputed and undisputed material facts; In opposition to motion for summary judgment. AMJUR PP SUMMARY § 89.

g.  Motion and notice of motion for summary judgment. 4 FEDFORMS § 4708.

h.  Motion for summary judgment by plaintiff. 4 FEDFORMS § 4709.

i.  Motion for summary judgment by defendant. 4 FEDFORMS § 4713.

j.  Motion for summary judgment by defendant; Claims of plaintiff and counterclaims of defendant. 4 FEDFORMS § 4717.

k.  Motion for summary judgment by defendant; Interpleader against another claimant. 4 FEDFORMS § 4718.

l.  Motion for summary judgment by defendant; Failure of plaintiff to produce evidence. 4 FED-FORMS § 4719.

m.  Motion for summary judgment by defendant; Statute of limitations. 4 FEDFORMS § 4720.

n.  Notice of motion for summary judgment. 4 FEDFORMS § 4744.

o.  Affidavit in support of motion for summary judgment. 4 FEDFORMS § 4773.

p.  Movant's contention there are no genuine issues of material facts. 4 FEDFORMS § 4776.

q.  Opposition to statement of uncontested material facts. 4 FEDFORMS § 4777.

r.  Response to movant's contention there are no genuine issues with respect to listed material facts. 4 FEDFORMS § 4778.

s.  Motion; For summary judgment; By claimant. FEDPROF § 1:1298.

t.  Motion; For summary judgment; By defending party. FEDPROF § 1:1302.

u.  Motion; By plaintiff; For partial summary judgment. FEDPROF § 1:1305.

v.  Notice of cross motion; For summary judgment; By defending party. FEDPROF § 1:1306.

w.  Statement of material facts; In support of summary judgment motion. FEDPROF § 1:1311.

x.  Statement in support of defendant's summary judgment motion; By codefendant. FEDPROF § 1:1312.

y.  Affidavit; Opposing claimant's motion for summary judgment; Witnesses unavailable. FEDPROF § 1:1316.

z.  Affidavit; Opposing part of claim. FEDPROF § 1:1317.

**2.  Forms for the Eastern District of New York**

a.  Notice to pro se litigant who opposes a summary judgment. NY R USDCTS&ED Civ Rule 56.2.

# I.  Applicable Rules

1.  *Federal rules*

a.  Serving and filing pleadings and other papers. FRCP 5.

b.  Constitutional challenge to a statute; Notice, certification, and intervention. FRCP 5.1.

c.  Privacy protection for filings made with the court. FRCP 5.2.

d.  Computing and extending time; Time for motion papers. FRCP 6.

e.  Pleadings allowed; Form of motions and other papers. FRCP 7.

    f.    Disclosure statement. FRCP 7.1.

    g.    Form of pleadings. FRCP 10.

    h.    Signing pleadings, motions, and other papers; Representations to the court; Sanctions. FRCP 11.

    i.    Defenses and objections; When and how presented; Motion for judgment on the pleadings; Consolidating motions; Waiving defenses; Pretrial hearing. FRCP 12.

    j.    Taking testimony. FRCP 43.

    k.    Summary judgment. FRCP 56.

    l.    Hearing motions; Submission on briefs. FRCP 78.

2.  *Local rules*

    a.    Night depository. NY R USDCTS&ED Civ Rule 1.2.

    b.    Duty of attorneys in related cases. NY R USDCTS&ED Civ Rule 1.6.

    c.    Filing of discovery materials. NY R USDCTS&ED Civ Rule 5.1.

    d.    Electronic service and filing of documents. NY R USDCTS&ED Civ Rule 5.2.

    e.    Service by overnight delivery. NY R USDCTS&ED Civ Rule 5.3.

    f.    Service and filing of motion papers. NY R USDCTS&ED Civ Rule 6.1.

    g.    Orders on motions. NY R USDCTS&ED Civ Rule 6.2.

    h.    Computation of time. NY R USDCTS&ED Civ Rule 6.4.

    i.    Motion papers. NY R USDCTS&ED Civ Rule 7.1.

    j.    Disclosure statement. NY R USDCTS&ED Civ Rule 7.1.1.

    k.    Authorities to be provided to pro se litigants. NY R USDCTS&ED Civ Rule 7.2.

    l.    Form of pleadings, motions, and other papers. NY R USDCTS&ED Civ Rule 11.1.

    m.    Statements of material facts on motion for summary judgment. NY R USDCTS&ED Civ Rule 56.1.

    n.    Notice to pro se litigant who opposes a summary judgment. NY R USDCTS&ED Civ Rule 56.2.

    o.    Submission of orders, judgments and decrees. NY R USDCTS&ED Civ Rule 77.1.

    p.    Court-annexed arbitration (Eastern District only). NY R USDCTS&ED Civ Rule 83.7.

    q.    Court-annexed mediation (Eastern District only). NY R USDCTS&ED Civ Rule 83.8.

    r.    Electronic case filing. NY R USDCTED Order 2004-08.

    s.    The August 2, 2004 amendment to the E-Government Act of 2002. NY R USDCTED Order 2004-09.

    t.    Categories and classification of cases; Information on cases and parties. NY R USDCTED Div. Bus., Rule 50.1.

## J.  Miscellaneous

**NOTE: Individual judges' rules may apply. For available judge-level information, refer to:**

DISTRICT JUDGE CAROL BAGLEY AMON: NY R USDCTED Amon-Practices.

DISTRICT JUDGE JOAN M. AZRACK: NY R USDCTED Azrack-Practices.

DISTRICT JUDGE JOSEPH F. BIANCO: NY R USDCTED Bianco-Practices.

DISTRICT JUDGE FREDERIC BLOCK: NY R USDCTED Block-Practices.

DISTRICT JUDGE MARGO K. BRODIE: NY R USDCTED Brodie-Practices.

DISTRICT JUDGE PAMELA K. CHEN: NY R USDCTED Chen-Practices.

DISTRICT JUDGE BRIAN M. COGAN: NY R USDCTED Cogan-Practices; NY R USDCTED Cogan-Pretrial.

DISTRICT JUDGE LaSHANN DeARCY HALL: NY R USDCTED DeArcy Hall-Practices.

DISTRICT JUDGE RAYMOND J. DEARIE: NY R USDCTED Dearie-Practices.

DISTRICT JUDGE ANN M. DONNELLY: NY R USDCTED Donnelly-Practices.

DISTRICT JUDGE SANDRA J. FEUERSTEIN: NY R USDCTED Feuerstein-Practices; NY R USDCTED Feuerstein-Pretrial.

DISTRICT JUDGE NICHOLAS G. GARAUIFIS: NY R USDCTED Garaufis-Practices; NY R USDCTED Garaufis-Pretrial.

DISTRICT JUDGE NINA GERSHON: NY R USDCTED Gershon-Practices.

DISTRICT JUDGE I. LEO GLASSER: NY R USDCTED Glasser-Practices; NY R USDCTED Glasser-Crim.

DISTRICT JUDGE DENIS R. HURLEY: NY R USDCTED Hurley-Practices; [NY R USDCTED Hurley-Pro Cooperation Info, as added by NY ORDER 16-4188, effective July 22, 2016]; [NY R USDCTED Hurley-Pro Cooperation Info Stay, as added by NY ORDER 16-4188, effective July 22, 2016].

DISTRICT JUDGE DORA L. IRIZARRY: NY R USDCTED Irizarry-Practices; NY R USDCTED Irizarry-Pretrial; NY R USDCTED Irizarry-Crim.

DISTRICT JUDGE STERLING JOHNSON, JR.: NY R USDCTED Johnson-Practices.

DISTRICT JUDGE EDWARD R. KORMAN: NY R USDCTED Korman-Practices; NY R USDCTED Korman-Pretrial.

DISTRICT JUDGE WILLIAM F. KUNTZ: NY R USDCTED Kuntz-Practices.

DISTRICT JUDGE KIYO A. MATSUMOTO: NY R USDCTED Matsumoto-Practices.

DISTRICT JUDGE ROSLYNN R. MAUSKOPF: NY R USDCTED Mauskopf-Practices; NY R USDCTED Mauskopf-Recusal.

DISTRICT JUDGE THOMAS C. PLATT: NY R USDCTED Platt-Practices.

DISTRICT JUDGE ALLYNE R. ROSS: NY R USDCTED Ross-Practices.

DISTRICT JUDGE JOANNA SEYBERT: NY R USDCTED Seybert-Practices.

DISTRICT JUDGE ARTHUR D. SPATT: NY R USDCTED Spatt-Practices.

DISTRICT JUDGE SANDRA L. TOWNES: NY R USDCTED Townes-Practices.

DISTRICT JUDGE ERIC N. VITALIANO: NY R USDCTED Vitaliano-Practices.

DISTRICT JUDGE JACK B. WEINSTEIN: NY R USDCTED Weinstein-Practices.

DISTRICT JUDGE LEONARD D. WEXLER: NY R USDCTED Wexler-Practices; NY R USDCTED Wexler-Rules.

MAGISTRATE JUDGE LOIS BLOOM: NY R USDCTED Bloom-Practices.

MAGISTRATE JUDGE GARY R. BROWN: NY R USDCTED Brown-Practices.

MAGISTRATE JUDGE MARILYN D. GO: NY R USDCTED Go-Practices.

MAGISTRATE JUDGE STEVEN M. GOLD: NY R USDCTED Gold-Practices.

MAGISTRATE JUDGE PEGGY KUO: NY R USDCTED Kuo-Practices; NY R USDCTED Kuo-Scheduling Order.

MAGISTRATE JUDGE ROBERT M. LEVY: NY R USDCTED Levy-Practices.

MAGISTRATE JUDGE ARLENE R. LINDSAY: NY R USDCTED Lindsay-Practices.

MAGISTRATE JUDGE STEVEN I. LOCKE: NY R USDCTED Locke-Practices.

MAGISTRATE JUDGE ROANNE L. MANN: NY R USDCTED Mann-Practices.

MAGISTRATE JUDGE JAMES ORENSTEIN: NY R USDCTED Jorenstein--Practices.

MAGISTRATE JUDGE VIKTOR V. POHORELSKY: NY R USDCTED Pohorelsky-Practices.

MAGISTRATE JUDGE CHERYL L. POLLAK: NY R USDCTED Pollak-Practices; NY R USDCTED Pollak-Pretrial.

MAGISTRATE JUDGE RAMON E. REYES, JR.: NY R USDCTED Reyes-Practices.

MAGISTRATE JUDGE VERA M. SCANLON: NY R USDCTED Scanlon-Practices.

MAGISTRATE JUDGE ANNE Y. SHIELDS: NY R USDCTED Shields-Practices.

MAGISTRATE JUDGE STEVEN L. TISCIONE: NY R USDCTED Tiscione-Practices.

MAGISTRATE JUDGE A. KATHLEEN TOMILINSON: NY R USDCTED Tomlinson-Practices.

## Motions, Oppositions and Replies
## Motion to Compel Discovery

### Document Last Updated September 2016

**A. Checklist**

(I) ❏ Matters to be considered by moving party

    (a) ❏ Required documents

        (1) ❏ Letter-motion

        (2) ❏ Certificate of compliance

    (b) ❏ Supplemental documents

        (1) ❏ Supporting evidence

        (2) ❏ Notice of constitutional question

        (3) ❏ Copies of authorities

        (4) ❏ Notice of motion and motion

        (5) ❏ Memorandum of law

        (6) ❏ Certificate of service

    (c) ❏ Timing

        (1) ❏ There are no specific timing requirements for submitting a letter-motion to the court

        (2) ❏ A motion must simply be submitted within a reasonable time; however, a motion to compel discovery filed under FRCP 37(a) is premature if it is filed before any request for discovery is made

        (3) ❏ A written motion and notice of the hearing must be served at least fourteen (14) days before the time specified for the hearing, with the following exceptions: (i) when the motion may be heard ex parte; (ii) when the Federal Rules of Civil Procedure set a different time; or (iii) when a court order—which a party may, for good cause, apply for ex parte—sets a different time

        (4) ❏ Any affidavit supporting a motion must be served with the motion

(II) ❏ Matters to be considered by opposing party

    (a) ❏ Required documents

        (1) ❏ Responsive letter

    (b) ❏ Supplemental documents

        (1) ❏ Supporting evidence

        (2) ❏ Notice of constitutional question

        (3) ❏ Copies of authorities

        (4) ❏ Answering memorandum of law

        (5) ❏ Certificate of service

    (c) ❏ Timing

        (1) ❏ Within four (4) days of receiving such a letter, any opposing affected party or non-party

witness may submit a responsive letter not exceeding three (3) pages attaching relevant materials

(2) ❑ Any opposing affidavits and answering memoranda of law shall be served within seven (7) days after service of the moving papers

(3) ❑ Except as FRCP 59(c) provides otherwise, any opposing affidavit must be served at least seven (7) days before the hearing, unless the court permits service at another time

## B. Timing

1. *Mode of raising discovery and other non-dispositive pretrial disputes with the court*

   a. *Letter-motion.* There are no specific timing requirements for submitting a letter-motion to the court.

   b. *Responsive letter.* Within four (4) days of receiving such a letter, any opposing affected party or non-party witness may submit a responsive letter not exceeding three (3) pages attaching relevant materials. NY R USDCTS&ED Civ Rule 37.3(c).

2. *Motion to compel discovery.* There is no specific time limit for a motion to compel discovery under FRCP 37(a); rather, a motion must simply be submitted within a reasonable time. FEDPROC § 26:779. However, a motion to compel discovery filed under FRCP 37(a) is premature if it is filed before any request for discovery is made. FEDPROC § 26:779; Bermudez v. Duenas, 936 F.2d 1064, 19 Fed.R.Serv.3d 1443 (9th Cir. 1991).

3. *Timing of motions, generally*

   a. *Motion and notice of hearing.* Except for letter-motions as permitted by NY R USDCTS&ED Civ Rule 7.1(d), and unless otherwise provided by statute or rule or by the Court in a Judge's Individual Practice or in a direction in a particular case, upon any motion, the notice of motion, supporting affidavits, and memoranda shall be served and filed as follows: on all motions and applications under FRCP 26 through FRCP 37 inclusive and FRCP 45(d)(3), the notice of motion, supporting affidavits, and memoranda of law shall be served by the moving party on all other parties that have appeared in the action. NY R USDCTS&ED Civ Rule 6.1(a)(1). A written motion and notice of the hearing must be served at least fourteen (14) days before the time specified for the hearing, with the following exceptions:

      i. When the motion may be heard ex parte;

      ii. When the Federal Rules of Civil Procedure set a different time; or

      iii. When a court order—which a party may, for good cause, apply for ex parte—sets a different time. FRCP 6(c)(1).

   b. *Supporting affidavit.* Any affidavit supporting a motion must be served with the motion. FRCP 6(c)(2).

4. *Timing of opposing papers.* Except for letter-motions as permitted by NY R USDCTS&ED Civ Rule 7.1(d), and unless otherwise provided by statute or rule or by the Court in a Judge's Individual Practice or in a direction in a particular case, upon any motion, the notice of motion, supporting affidavits, and memoranda shall be served and filed as follows: on all motions and applications under FRCP 26 through FRCP 37 inclusive and FRCP 45(d)(3), any opposing affidavits and answering memoranda of law shall be served within seven (7) days after service of the moving papers. NY R USDCTS&ED Civ Rule 6.1(a)(2).

   a. *Opposing affidavit.* Except as FRCP 59(c) provides otherwise, any opposing affidavit must be served at least seven (7) days before the hearing, unless the court permits service at another time. FRCP 6(c)(2).

5. *Timing of reply papers.* Where the respondent files an answering affidavit setting up a new matter, the moving party ordinarily is allowed a reasonable time to file a reply affidavit since failure to deny the new matter by affidavit may operate as an admission of its truth. AMJUR MOTIONS § 25.

   a. *Reply affidavits and reply memoranda of law.* Except for letter-motions as permitted by NY R USDCTS&ED Civ Rule 7.1(d), and unless otherwise provided by statute or rule or by the Court in a Judge's Individual Practice or in a direction in a particular case, upon any motion, the notice of motion, supporting affidavits, and memoranda shall be served and filed as follows: on all motions and applications under FRCP 26 through FRCP 37 inclusive and FRCP 45(d)(3), any reply affidavits and reply memoranda of law shall be served within two (2) days after service of the answering papers. NY R USDCTS&ED Civ Rule 6.1(a)(3).

6. *Computation of time*

   a. *Computing time.* FRCP 6 applies in computing any time period specified in the Federal Rules of Civil Procedure, in any local rule or court order, or in any statute that does not specify a method of computing time. FRCP 6(a). In computing any period of time prescribed or allowed by the Local Civil Rules of the United States District Courts for the Southern and Eastern Districts of New York or the Local Admiralty and Maritime Rules, the provisions of FRCP 6 shall apply unless otherwise stated. NY R USDCTS&ED Civ Rule 6.4.

      i. *Period stated in days or a longer unit.* In computing periods of days, refer to FRCP 6 and NY R USDCTS&ED Civ Rule 6.4. NY R USDCTS&ED Civ Rule 6.1(a). When the period is stated in days or a longer unit of time:

         • Exclude the day of the event that triggers the period;

         • Count every day, including intermediate Saturdays, Sundays, and legal holidays; and

         • Include the last day of the period, but if the last day is a Saturday, Sunday, or legal holiday, the period continues to run until the end of the next day that is not a Saturday, Sunday, or legal holiday. FRCP 6(a)(1). In the Local Civil Rules of the United States District Courts for the Southern and Eastern Districts of New York, as in the Federal Rules of Civil Procedure as amended effective December 1, 2009, Saturdays, Sundays, and legal holidays are no longer excluded in computing periods of time. If the last day of the period is a Saturday, Sunday, or legal holiday, the period continues to run until the end of the next day that is not a Saturday, Sunday, or legal holiday. NY R USDCTS&ED Civ Rule 6.4.

      ii. *Period stated in hours.* When the period is stated in hours:

         • Begin counting immediately on the occurrence of the event that triggers the period;

         • Count every hour, including hours during intermediate Saturdays, Sundays, and legal holidays; and

         • If the period would end on a Saturday, Sunday, or legal holiday, the period continues to run until the same time on the next day that is not a Saturday, Sunday, or legal holiday. FRCP 6(a)(2). In the Local Civil Rules of the United States District Courts for the Southern and Eastern Districts of New York, as in the Federal Rules of Civil Procedure as amended effective December 1, 2009, Saturdays, Sundays, and legal holidays are no longer excluded in computing periods of time. If the last day of the period is a Saturday, Sunday, or legal holiday, the period continues to run until the end of the next day that is not a Saturday, Sunday, or legal holiday. NY R USDCTS&ED Civ Rule 6.4.

      iii. *Inaccessibility of the clerk's office.* Unless the court orders otherwise, if the clerk's office is inaccessible:

         • On the last day for filing under FRCP 6(a)(1), then the time for filing is extended to the first accessible day that is not a Saturday, Sunday, or legal holiday; or

         • During the last hour for filing under FRCP 6(a)(2), then the time for filing is extended to the same time on the first accessible day that is not a Saturday, Sunday, or legal holiday. FRCP 6(a)(3).

      iv. *"Last day" defined.* Unless a different time is set by a statute, local rule, or court order, the last day ends:

         • For electronic filing, at midnight in the court's time zone; and

         • For filing by other means, when the clerk's office is scheduled to close. FRCP 6(a)(4).

      v. *"Next day" defined.* The "next day" is determined by continuing to count forward when the period is measured after an event and backward when measured before an event. FRCP 6(a)(5).

      vi. *"Legal holiday" defined.* "Legal holiday" means:

         • The day set aside by statute for observing New Year's Day, Martin Luther King Jr.'s

Birthday, Washington's Birthday, Memorial Day, Independence Day, Labor Day, Columbus Day, Veterans' Day, Thanksgiving Day, or Christmas Day;

- Any day declared a holiday by the President or Congress; and

- For periods that are measured after an event, any other day declared a holiday by the state
where the district court is located. FRCP 6(a)(6).

b. *Extending time*

  i. *In general.* When an act may or must be done within a specified time, the court may, for good
  cause, extend the time:

  - With or without motion or notice if the court acts, or if a request is made, before the
  original time or its extension expires; or

  - On motion made after the time has expired if the party failed to act because of excusable
  neglect. FRCP 6(b)(1).

  ii. *Exceptions.* A court must not extend the time to act under FRCP 50(b), FRCP 50(d), FRCP
  52(b), FRCP 59(b), FRCP 59(d), FRCP 59(e), and FRCP 60(b). FRCP 6(b)(2).

  iii. Refer to the United States District Court for the Eastern District of New York KeyRules Motion
  for Continuance/Extension of Time document for more information on extending time.

c. *Additional time after certain kinds of service.* When a party may or must act within a specified time
after service and service is made under FRCP 5(b)(2)(C), FRCP 5(b)(2)(D), FRCP 5(b)(2)(E), or
FRCP 5(b)(2)(F), three (3) days are added after the period would otherwise expire under FRCP 6(a).
FRCP 6(d). Overnight delivery service shall be deemed service by mail for purposes of FRCP 5 and
FRCP 6. NY R USDCTS&ED Civ Rule 5.3.

7. *Individual judge practices.* Refer to the Miscellaneous section of this document for information on
individual judge practices on timing of documents.

## C. General Requirements

1. *Mode of raising discovery and other non-dispositive pretrial disputes with the court.* Prior to seeking
judicial resolution of a discovery or non-dispositive pretrial dispute, the attorneys for the affected parties
or non-party witness shall attempt to confer in good faith in person or by telephone in an effort to resolve
the dispute, in conformity with FRCP 37(a)(1). NY R USDCTS&ED Civ Rule 37.3(a). Refer to the
Documents section of this document for the procedure to follow when the attorneys for the affected
parties or non-party witness cannot agree on a resolution of the discovery or other non-dispositive pretrial
dispute.

  a. *Motion for reconsideration.* A ruling made exclusively as a result of a telephone conference may be
  the subject of de novo reconsideration by a letter not exceeding five (5) pages in length attaching
  relevant materials submitted by any affected party or non-party witness. Within four (4) days of
  receiving such a letter, any other affected party or non-party witness may submit a responsive letter
  not exceeding five (5) pages in length attaching relevant materials. NY R USDCTS&ED Civ Rule
  37.3(d).

  b. *Decision of the court.* The Court shall record or arrange for the recording of the Court's decision in
  writing. Such written order may take the form of an oral order read into the record of a deposition or
  other proceeding, a handwritten memorandum, a handwritten marginal notation on a letter or other
  document, or any other form the Court deems appropriate. NY R USDCTS&ED Civ Rule 37.3(e).

2. *Motions, generally*

  a. *Requirements.* A request for a court order must be made by motion. The motion must:

  i. Be in writing unless made during a hearing or trial;

  ii. State with particularity the grounds for seeking the order; and

  iii. State the relief sought. FRCP 7(b)(1).

  b. *Notice of motion.* A party interested in resisting the relief sought by a motion has a right to notice
  thereof, and an opportunity to be heard. AMJUR MOTIONS § 12.

  i. In addition to statutory or court rule provisions requiring notice of a motion—the purpose of

such a notice requirement having been said to be to prevent a party from being prejudicially surprised by a motion—principles of natural justice dictate that an adverse party generally must be given notice that a motion will be presented to the court. AMJUR MOTIONS § 12.

ii.   "Notice," in this regard, means reasonable notice, including a meaningful opportunity to prepare and to defend against allegations of a motion. AMJUR MOTIONS § 12.

c.   *Writing requirement.* The writing requirement is intended to insure that the adverse parties are informed and have a record of both the motion's pendency and the grounds on which the movant seeks an order. FPP § 1191; Feldberg v. Quechee Lakes Corp., 463 F.3d 195 (2d Cir. 2006).

i.   It is sufficient "if the motion is stated in a written notice of the hearing of the motion." FPP § 1191.

d.   *Particularity requirement.* The particularity requirement insures that the opposing parties will have notice of their opponent's contentions. FEDPROC § 62:364; Goodman v. 1973 26 Foot Trojan Vessel, Arkansas Registration No. AR1439SN, 859 F.2d 71, 12 Fed.R.Serv.3d 645 (8th Cir. 1988). That requirement ensures that notice of the basis for the motion is provided to the court and to the opposing party so as to avoid prejudice, provide the opponent with a meaningful opportunity to respond, and provide the court with enough information to process the motion correctly. FEDPROC § 62:364; Andreas v. Volkswagen of America, Inc., 336 F.3d 789, 56 Fed.R.Serv.3d 6 (8th Cir. 2003).

i.   Reasonable specification of the grounds for a motion is sufficient. However, where a movant fails to state even one ground for granting the motion in question, the movant has failed to meet the minimal standard of "reasonable specification." FEDPROC § 62:364; Martinez v. Trainor, 556 F.2d 818, 23 Fed.R.Serv.2d 403 (7th Cir. 1977).

ii.   The court may excuse the failure to comply with the particularity requirement if it is inadvertent, and where no prejudice is shown by the opposing party. FEDPROC § 62:364.

e.   *Ex parte orders or orders to show cause to bring on a motion.* No ex parte order, or order to show cause to bring on a motion, will be granted except upon a clear and specific showing by affidavit of good and sufficient reasons why a procedure other than by notice of motion is necessary, and stating whether a previous application for similar relief has been made. NY R USDCTS&ED Civ Rule 6.1(d).

f.   *Letter-motions.* Applications for extensions or adjournments, applications for a pre-motion conference, and similar non-dispositive matters as permitted by the instructions regarding ECF published on the website of each respective Court and any pertinent Individual Judge's Practices, may be brought by letter-motion filed via ECF pursuant to NY R USDCTS&ED Civ Rule 5.2(b). NY R USDCTS&ED Civ Rule 7.1(d).

3.   *Motion to compel discovery.* On notice to other parties and all affected persons, a party may move for an order compelling disclosure or discovery. FRCP 37(a)(1). A party must request the specific documents in issue from the opposing party before filing a motion to compel the production of documents. FEDPROC § 26:778.

a.   *Appropriate court.* A motion for an order to a party must be made in the court where the action is pending. A motion for an order to a nonparty must be made in the court where the discovery is or will be taken. FRCP 37(a)(2).

b.   *Specific motions*

i.   *To compel disclosure.* If a party fails to make a disclosure required by FRCP 26(a), any other party may move to compel disclosure and for appropriate sanctions. FRCP 37(a)(3)(A). Refer to the United States District Court for the Eastern District of New York KeyRules Motion for Discovery Sanctions document for more information on sanctions.

ii.   *To compel a discovery response.* A party seeking discovery may move for an order compelling an answer, designation, production, or inspection. This motion may be made if:

●   A deponent fails to answer a question asked under FRCP 30 or FRCP 31;

●   A corporation or other entity fails to make a designation under FRCP 30(b)(6) or FRCP 31(a)(4);

- A party fails to answer an interrogatory submitted under FRCP 33; or
- A party fails to produce documents or fails to respond that inspection will be permitted—or fails to permit inspection—as requested under FRCP 34. FRCP 37(a)(3)(B).

  iii. *Related to a deposition.* When taking an oral deposition, the party asking a question may complete or adjourn the examination before moving for an order. FRCP 37(a)(3)(C).

  iv. *Evasive or incomplete disclosure, answer, or response.* For purposes of FRCP 37(a), an evasive or incomplete disclosure, answer, or response must be treated as a failure to disclose, answer, or respond. FRCP 37(a)(4).

 c. *Payment of expenses; Protective orders*

  i. *If the motion is granted (or disclosure or discovery is provided after filing).* If the motion is granted—or if the disclosure or requested discovery is provided after the motion was filed—the court must, after giving an opportunity to be heard, require the party or deponent whose conduct necessitated the motion, the party or attorney advising that conduct, or both to pay the movant's reasonable expenses incurred in making the motion, including attorney's fees. But the court must not order this payment if:

- The movant filed the motion before attempting in good faith to obtain the disclosure or discovery without court action;
- The opposing party's nondisclosure, response, or objection was substantially justified; or
- Other circumstances make an award of expenses unjust. FRCP 37(a)(5)(A).

  ii. *If the motion is denied.* If the motion is denied, the court may issue any protective order authorized under FRCP 26(c) and must, after giving an opportunity to be heard, require the movant, the attorney filing the motion, or both to pay the party or deponent who opposed the motion its reasonable expenses incurred in opposing the motion, including attorney's fees. But the court must not order this payment if the motion was substantially justified or other circumstances make an award of expenses unjust. FRCP 37(a)(5)(B).

  iii. *If the motion is granted in part and denied in part.* If the motion is granted in part and denied in part, the court may issue any protective order authorized under FRCP 26(c) and may, after giving an opportunity to be heard, apportion the reasonable expenses for the motion. FRCP 37(a)(5)(C).

4. *Opposing papers.* The Federal Rules of Civil Procedure do not require any formal answer, return, or reply to a motion, except where the Federal Rules of Civil Procedure or local rules may require affidavits, memoranda, or other papers to be filed in opposition to a motion. Such papers are simply to apprise the court of such opposition and the grounds of that opposition. FEDPROC § 62:359. Except for letter-motions as permitted by NY R USDCTS&ED Civ Rule 7.1(d) or as otherwise permitted by the Court, all oppositions and replies with respect to motions shall comply with NY R USDCTS&ED Civ Rule 7.1(a)(2) and NY R USDCTS&ED Civ Rule 7.1(a)(3), and an opposing party who seeks relief that goes beyond the denial of the motion shall comply as well with NY R USDCTS&ED Civ Rule 7.1(a)(1). NY R USDCTS&ED Civ Rule 7.1(b).

 a. *Effect of failure to respond to motion.* Although in the absence of statutory provision or court rule, a motion ordinarily does not require a written answer, when a party files a motion and the opposing party fails to respond, the court may construe such failure to respond as nonopposition to the motion or an admission that the motion was meritorious, may take the facts alleged in the motion as true—the rule in some jurisdictions being that the failure to respond to a fact set forth in a motion is deemed an admission—and may grant the motion if the relief requested appears to be justified. AMJUR MOTIONS § 28.

 b. *Assent or no opposition not determinative.* However, a motion will not be granted automatically simply because an "assent" or a notation of "no opposition" has been filed; federal judges frequently deny motions that have been assented to when it is thought that justice so dictates. FPP § 1190.

 c. *Responsive pleading inappropriate as response to motion.* An attempt to answer or oppose a motion with a responsive pleading usually is not appropriate. FPP § 1190.

5. *Reply papers.* A moving party may be required or permitted to prepare papers in addition to his original motion papers. AMJUR MOTIONS § 25. Papers answering or replying to opposing papers may be appropriate, in the interests of justice, where it appears there is a substantial reason for allowing a reply. Thus, a court may accept reply papers where a party demonstrates that the papers to which it seeks to file a reply raise new issues that are material to the disposition of the question before the court, or where the court determines, sua sponte, that it wishes further briefing of an issue raised in those papers and orders the submission of additional papers. FEDPROC § 62:360. Except for letter-motions as permitted by NY R USDCTS&ED Civ Rule 7.1(d) or as otherwise permitted by the Court, all oppositions and replies with respect to motions shall comply with NY R USDCTS&ED Civ Rule 7.1(a)(2) and NY R USDCTS&ED Civ Rule 7.1(a)(3). NY R USDCTS&ED Civ Rule 7.1(b).

    a. *Function of reply papers.* The function of a reply affidavit is to answer the arguments made in opposition to the position taken by the movant and not to permit the movant to introduce new arguments in support of the motion. AMJUR MOTIONS § 25.

    b. *Issues raised for the first time in a reply document.* However, the view has been followed in some jurisdictions, that as a matter of judicial economy, where there is no prejudice and where the issues could be raised simply by filing a motion to dismiss, the trial court has discretion to consider arguments raised for the first time in a reply memorandum, and that a trial court may grant a motion to strike issues raised for the first time in a reply memorandum. AMJUR MOTIONS § 26.

6. *Orders on motions.* A memorandum signed by the Court of the decision on a motion that does not finally determine all claims for relief, or an oral decision on such a motion, shall constitute the order unless the memorandum or oral decision directs the submission or settlement of an order in more extended form. The notation in the docket of a memorandum or of an oral decision that does not direct the submission or settlement of an order in more extended form shall constitute the entry of the order. Where an order in more extended form is required to be submitted or settled, the notation in the docket of such order shall constitute the entry of the order. NY R USDCTS&ED Civ Rule 6.2.

7. *Related cases.* It shall be the continuing duty of each attorney appearing in any civil or criminal case to bring promptly to the attention of the Court all facts which said attorney believes are relevant to a determination that said case and one or more pending civil or criminal cases should be heard by the same Judge, in order to avoid unnecessary duplication of judicial effort. As soon as the attorney becomes aware of such relationship, said attorney shall notify the Judges to whom the cases have been assigned. NY R USDCTS&ED Civ Rule 1.6(a). If counsel fails to comply with NY R USDCTS&ED Civ Rule 1.6(a), the Court may assess reasonable costs directly against counsel whose action has obstructed the effective administration of the Court's business. NY R USDCTS&ED Civ Rule 1.6(b).

8. *Alternative dispute resolution (ADR)*

    a. *Court-annexed arbitration*

        i. *Civil cases eligible for compulsory arbitration.* The Clerk of Court shall, as to all cases filed after January 1, 1986, designate and process for compulsory arbitration all civil cases (excluding Social Security cases, tax matters, prisoners' civil rights cases and any action based on an alleged violation of a right secured by the Constitution of the United States or if jurisdiction is based in whole or in part on 28 U.S.C.A. § 1343) wherein money damages only are being sought in an amount not in excess of one hundred fifty thousand dollars ($150,000) exclusive of interest and costs. NY R USDCTS&ED Civ Rule 83.7(d)(1).

           • The parties may by written stipulation agree that the Clerk of Court shall designate and process for court-annexed arbitration any civil case that is not subject to compulsory arbitration in NY R USDCTS&ED Civ Rule 83.7. NY R USDCTS&ED Civ Rule 83.7(d)(2).

           • For purposes of NY R USDCTS&ED Civ Rule 83.7 only, in all civil cases damages shall be presumed to be not in excess of one hundred fifty thousand dollars ($150,000) exclusive of interest and costs, unless: (1) counsel for plaintiff, at the time of filing the complaint, or in the event of the removal of a case from state court or transfer of a case from another district to this Court, within thirty (30) days of the docketing of the case in this district, files a certification with the Court that the damages sought exceed one hundred fifty thousand dollars ($150,000), exclusive of interest and costs; or (2) counsel for a defendant, at the time of filing a counterclaim or cross-claim files a certification with the court that the damages sought by the counter-claim or cross-claim exceed one hundred fifty thousand dollars ($150,000) exclusive of interest and costs. NY R USDCTS&ED Civ Rule 83.7(d)(3).

ii. *Exemption from arbitration.* The Court shall, sua sponte, or on motion of a party, exempt any case from arbitration in which the objectives of arbitration would not be realized (1) because the case involves complex or novel issues, (2) because legal issues predominate over factual issues, or (3) for other good cause. NY R USDCTS&ED Civ Rule 83.7(e)(2). For information on applying for an exemption, refer to NY R USDCTS&ED Civ Rule 83.7

iii. *Referral to arbitration.* Cases not originally designated as eligible for compulsory arbitration, but which in the discretion of the assigned Judge, are later found to qualify, may be referred to arbitration. A U.S. District Judge or a U.S. Magistrate Judge, in cases that exceed the arbitration ceiling of one hundred fifty thousand dollars ($150,000) exclusive of interest and costs, in their discretion, may suggest that the parties should consider arbitration. If the parties are agreeable, an appropriate consent form signed by all parties or their representatives may be entered and filed in the case prior to scheduling an arbitration hearing. NY R USDCTS&ED Civ Rule 83.7(e)(3).

iv. For more information on arbitration, refer to NY R USDCTS&ED Civ Rule 83.7.

b. *Court-annexed mediation.* Mediation is a process in which parties and counsel agree to meet with a neutral mediator trained to assist them in settling disputes. The mediator improves communication across party lines, helps parties articulate their interests and understand those of the other party, probes the strengths and weaknesses of each party's legal positions, and identifies areas of agreement and helps generate options for a mutually agreeable resolution to the dispute. In all cases, mediation provides an opportunity to explore a wide range of potential solutions and to address interests that may be outside the scope of the stated controversy or which could not be addressed by judicial action. A hallmark of mediation is its capacity to expand traditional settlement discussions and broaden resolution options, often by exploring litigant needs and interests that may be formally independent of the legal issues in controversy. NY R USDCTS&ED Civ Rule 83.8(a).

i. *Eligible cases.* Judges and Magistrate Judges may designate civil cases for inclusion in the mediation program, and when doing so shall prepare an order to that effect. Alternatively, and subject to the availability of qualified mediators, the parties may consent to participation in the mediation program by preparing and executing a stipulation signed by all parties to the action and so-ordered by the Court. NY R USDCTS&ED Civ Rule 83.8(b)(1).

ii. For more information on mediation, refer to NY R USDCTS&ED Civ Rule 83.8.

9. *Individual judge practices.* Refer to the Miscellaneous section of this document for information on individual judge practices on general requirements for documents.

## D. Documents

1. *Documents for moving party*

   a. *Required documents*

      i. *Letter-motion.* Where the attorneys for the affected parties or non-party witness cannot agree on a resolution of any other discovery dispute or non-dispositive pretrial dispute, or if they are unable to obtain a telephonic ruling on a discovery dispute that arises during a deposition as provided in NY R USDCTS&ED Civ Rule 37.3(b), they shall notify the Court by letter not exceeding three (3) pages in length outlining the nature of the dispute and attaching relevant materials. NY R USDCTS&ED Civ Rule 37.3(c).

      - *Quotation or recitation verbatim of discovery materials.* Upon any motion or application involving discovery or disclosure requests or responses under FRCP 37, the moving party shall specify and quote or set forth verbatim in the motion papers each discovery request and response to which the motion or application is addressed. The motion or application shall also set forth the grounds upon which the moving party is entitled to prevail as to each request or response. NY R USDCTS&ED Civ Rule 5.1 also applies to the motion or application. NY R USDCTS&ED Civ Rule 37.1.

ii. *Certificate of compliance.* The motion must include a certification that the movant has in good faith conferred or attempted to confer with the person or party failing to make disclosure or discovery in an effort to obtain it without court action. FRCP 37(a)(1).

b. *Supplemental documents.* Except for the letters and attachments authorized herein, or where a ruling which was made exclusively as a result of a telephone conference is the subject of de novo review pursuant to NY R USDCTS&ED Civ Rule 37.3(d), papers shall not be submitted with respect to a dispute governed by NY R USDCTS&ED Civ Rule 37.3 unless the Court has so directed. NY R USDCTS&ED Civ Rule 37.3(c).

   i. *Supporting evidence.* When a motion relies on facts outside the record, the court may hear the matter on affidavits or may hear it wholly or partly on oral testimony or on depositions. FRCP 43(c). Except for letter-motions as permitted by NY R USDCTS&ED Civ Rule 7.1(d) or as otherwise permitted by the Court, all motions shall include the following motion papers: supporting affidavits and exhibits thereto containing any factual information and portions of the record necessary for the decision of the motion. NY R USDCTS&ED Civ Rule 7.1(a)(3).

   - *Discovery materials.* A party seeking or opposing relief under FRCP 26 through FRCP 37 inclusive, or making or opposing any other motion or application, shall quote or attach only those portions of the depositions, interrogatories, requests for documents, requests for admissions, or other discovery or disclosure materials, together with the responses and objections thereto, that are the subject of the discovery motion or application, or that are cited in papers submitted in connection with any other motion or application. NY R USDCTS&ED Civ Rule 5.1.

   ii. *Notice of constitutional question.* A party that files a pleading, written motion, or other paper drawing into question the constitutionality of a federal or state statute must promptly:

   - *File notice.* File a notice of constitutional question stating the question and identifying the paper that raises it, if: (1) a federal statute is questioned and the parties do not include the United States, one of its agencies, or one of its officers or employees in an official capacity; or (2) a state statute is questioned and the parties do not include the state, one of its agencies, or one of its officers or employees in an official capacity; and

   - *Serve notice.* Serve the notice and paper on the Attorney General of the United States if a federal statute is questioned—or on the state attorney general if a state statute is questioned—either by certified or registered mail or by sending it to an electronic address designated by the attorney general for this purpose. FRCP 5.1(a).

   - *No forfeiture.* A party's failure to file and serve the notice, or the court's failure to certify, does not forfeit a constitutional claim or defense that is otherwise timely asserted. FRCP 5.1(d).

   iii. *Copies of authorities.* In cases involving a pro se litigant, counsel shall, when serving a memorandum of law (or other submissions to the Court), provide the pro se litigant (but not other counsel or the Court) with copies of cases and other authorities cited therein that are unpublished or reported exclusively on computerized databases. Upon request, counsel shall provide the pro se litigant with copies of such unpublished cases and other authorities as are cited in a decision of the Court and were not previously cited by any party. NY R USDCTS&ED Civ Rule 7.2.

   iv. *Notice of motion and motion.* Except for letter-motions as permitted by NY R USDCTS&ED Civ Rule 7.1(d) or as otherwise permitted by the Court, all motions shall include the following motion papers: a notice of motion, or an order to show cause signed by the Court, which shall specify the applicable rules or statutes pursuant to which the motion is brought, and shall specify the relief sought by the motion. NY R USDCTS&ED Civ Rule 7.1(a)(1). Refer to the General Requirements section of this document for information on the notice of motion and motion.

    v.   *Memorandum of law.* Except for letter-motions as permitted by NY R USDCTS&ED Civ Rule 7.1(d) or as otherwise permitted by the Court, all motions shall include the following motion papers: a memorandum of law, setting forth the cases and other authorities relied upon in support of the motion, and divided, under appropriate headings, into as many parts as there are issues to be determined. NY R USDCTS&ED Civ Rule 7.1(a)(2).

    vi.   *Certificate of service.* FRCP 5(d) requires that the person making service under FRCP 5 certify that service has been effected. FRCP 5(Advisory Committee Notes). Having such information on file may be useful for many purposes, including proof of service if an issue arises concerning the effectiveness of the service. FRCP 5(Advisory Committee Notes).

2.   *Documents for opposing party*

  a.  *Required documents*

    i.   *Responsive letter.* Within four (4) days of receiving such a letter, any opposing affected party or non-party witness may submit a responsive letter not exceeding three (3) pages attaching relevant materials. NY R USDCTS&ED Civ Rule 37.3(c).

  b.  *Supplemental documents.* Except for the letters and attachments authorized herein, or where a ruling which was made exclusively as a result of a telephone conference is the subject of de novo review pursuant to NY R USDCTS&ED Civ Rule 37.3(d), papers shall not be submitted with respect to a dispute governed by NY R USDCTS&ED Civ Rule 37.3 unless the Court has so directed. NY R USDCTS&ED Civ Rule 37.3(c).

    i.   *Supporting evidence.* When a motion relies on facts outside the record, the court may hear the matter on affidavits or may hear it wholly or partly on oral testimony or on depositions. FRCP 43(c). Except for letter-motions as permitted by NY R USDCTS&ED Civ Rule 7.1(d) or as otherwise permitted by the Court, all oppositions and replies with respect to motions shall comply with NY R USDCTS&ED Civ Rule 7.1(a)(3). NY R USDCTS&ED Civ Rule 7.1(b). Except for letter-motions as permitted by NY R USDCTS&ED Civ Rule 7.1(d) or as otherwise permitted by the Court, all motions shall include the following motion papers: supporting affidavits and exhibits thereto containing any factual information and portions of the record necessary for the decision of the motion. NY R USDCTS&ED Civ Rule 7.1(a)(3).

      •  *Discovery materials.* A party seeking or opposing relief under FRCP 26 through FRCP 37 inclusive, or making or opposing any other motion or application, shall quote or attach only those portions of the depositions, interrogatories, requests for documents, requests for admissions, or other discovery or disclosure materials, together with the responses and objections thereto, that are the subject of the discovery motion or application, or that are cited in papers submitted in connection with any other motion or application. NY R USDCTS&ED Civ Rule 5.1.

    ii.  *Notice of constitutional question.* A party that files a pleading, written motion, or other paper drawing into question the constitutionality of a federal or state statute must promptly:

      •  *File notice.* File a notice of constitutional question stating the question and identifying the paper that raises it, if: (1) a federal statute is questioned and the parties do not include the United States, one of its agencies, or one of its officers or employees in an official capacity; or (2) a state statute is questioned and the parties do not include the state, one of its agencies, or one of its officers or employees in an official capacity; and

      •  *Serve notice.* Serve the notice and paper on the Attorney General of the United States if a federal statute is questioned—or on the state attorney general if a state statute is questioned—either by certified or registered mail or by sending it to an electronic address designated by the attorney general for this purpose. FRCP 5.1(a).

      •  *No forfeiture.* A party's failure to file and serve the notice, or the court's failure to certify, does not forfeit a constitutional claim or defense that is otherwise timely asserted. FRCP 5.1(d).

    iii.  *Copies of authorities.* In cases involving a pro se litigant, counsel shall, when serving a memorandum of law (or other submissions to the Court), provide the pro se litigant (but not

other counsel or the Court) with copies of cases and other authorities cited therein that are unpublished or reported exclusively on computerized databases. Upon request, counsel shall provide the pro se litigant with copies of such unpublished cases and other authorities as are cited in a decision of the Court and were not previously cited by any party. NY R USDCTS&ED Civ Rule 7.2.

    iv.   *Answering memorandum of law.* Except for letter-motions as permitted by NY R USDCTS&ED Civ Rule 7.1(d) or as otherwise permitted by the Court, all oppositions and replies with respect to motions shall comply with NY R USDCTS&ED Civ Rule 7.1(a)(2). NY R USDCTS&ED Civ Rule 7.1(b). Except for letter-motions as permitted by NY R USDCTS&ED Civ Rule 7.1(d) or as otherwise permitted by the Court, all motions shall include the following motion papers: a memorandum of law, setting forth the cases and other authorities relied upon in support of the motion, and divided, under appropriate headings, into as many parts as there are issues to be determined. NY R USDCTS&ED Civ Rule 7.1(a)(2). Refer to the General Requirements section of this document for information on the opposing papers.

    v.   *Certificate of service.* FRCP 5(d) requires that the person making service under FRCP 5 certify that service has been effected. FRCP 5(Advisory Committee Notes). Having such information on file may be useful for many purposes, including proof of service if an issue arises concerning the effectiveness of the service. FRCP 5(Advisory Committee Notes).

3.  *Individual judge practices.* Refer to the Miscellaneous section of this document for information on individual judge practices on required documents.

## E. Format

1.  *Form of documents.* The rules governing captions and other matters of form in pleadings apply to motions and other papers. FRCP 7(b)(2).

    a.  *Paper.* Every pleading, written motion, and other paper must: be plainly written, typed, printed, or copied without erasures or interlineations which materially deface it. NY R USDCTS&ED Civ Rule 11.1(a)(1).

    b.  *Typeface, margin, and spacing.* The typeface, margins, and spacing of all documents presented for filing must meet the following requirements:

        i.   All text must be twelve (12) point type or larger, except for text in footnotes which may be ten (10) point type;

        ii.   All documents must have at least one (1) inch margins on all sides;

        iii.   All text must be double-spaced, except for headings, text in footnotes, or block quotations, which may be single-spaced. NY R USDCTS&ED Civ Rule 11.1(b).

    c.  *Caption; Names of parties.* Every pleading must have a caption with the court's name, a title, a file number, and a FRCP 7(a) designation. The title of the complaint must name all the parties; the title of other pleadings, after naming the first party on each side, may refer generally to other parties. FRCP 10(a). Every pleading, written motion, and other paper must: bear the docket number and the initials of the District Judge and any Magistrate Judge before whom the action or proceeding is pending, NY R USDCTS&ED Civ Rule 11.1(a)(2).

    d.  *Paragraphs; Separate statements.* A party must state its claims or defenses in numbered paragraphs, each limited as far as practicable to a single set of circumstances. A later pleading may refer by number to a paragraph in an earlier pleading. If doing so would promote clarity, each claim founded on a separate transaction or occurrence—and each defense other than a denial—must be stated in a separate count or defense. FRCP 10(b).

    e.  *Adoption by reference; Exhibits.* A statement in a pleading may be adopted by reference elsewhere in the same pleading or in any other pleading or motion. A copy of a written instrument that is an exhibit to a pleading is a part of the pleading for all purposes. FRCP 10(c).

    f.  *Acceptance by the clerk.* The clerk must not refuse to file a paper solely because it is not in the form prescribed by the Federal Rules of Civil Procedure or by a local rule or practice. FRCP 5(d)(4).

2.  *Signing disclosures and discovery requests, responses, and objections.* FRCP 11 does not apply to

disclosures and discovery requests, responses, objections, and motions under FRCP 26 through FRCP 37. FRCP 11(d).

a. *Signature required.* Every disclosure under FRCP 26(a)(1) or FRCP 26(a)(3) and every discovery request, response, or objection must be signed by at least one attorney of record in the attorney's own name—or by the party personally, if unrepresented—and must state the signer's address, e-mail address, and telephone number. FRCP 26(g)(1). Every pleading, written motion, and other paper must: have the name of each person signing it clearly printed or typed directly below the signature. NY R USDCTS&ED Civ Rule 11.1(a)(3).

b. *Effect of signature.* By signing, an attorney or party certifies that to the best of the person's knowledge, information, and belief formed after a reasonable inquiry:

   i. With respect to a disclosure, it is complete and correct as of the time it is made; and

   ii. With respect to a discovery request, response, or objection, it is:

- Consistent with the Federal Rules of Civil Procedure and warranted by existing law or by a nonfrivolous argument for extending, modifying, or reversing existing law, or for establishing new law;

- Not interposed for any improper purpose, such as to harass, cause unnecessary delay, or needlessly increase the cost of litigation; and

- Neither unreasonable nor unduly burdensome or expensive, considering the needs of the case, prior discovery in the case, the amount in controversy, and the importance of the issues at stake in the action. FRCP 26(g)(1).

c. *Failure to sign.* Other parties have no duty to act on an unsigned disclosure, request, response, or objection until it is signed, and the court must strike it unless a signature is promptly supplied after the omission is called to the attorney's or party's attention. FRCP 26(g)(2).

d. *Sanction for improper certification.* If a certification violates FRCP 26(g) without substantial justification, the court, on motion or on its own, must impose an appropriate sanction on the signer, the party on whose behalf the signer was acting, or both. The sanction may include an order to pay the reasonable expenses, including attorney's fees, caused by the violation. FRCP 26(g)(3). Refer to the United States District Court for the Eastern District of New York KeyRules Motion for Discovery Sanctions document for more information.

3. *Privacy protection for filings made with the court*

a. *Redacted filings.* Unless the court orders otherwise, in an electronic or paper filing with the court that contains an individual's Social Security number, taxpayer-identification number, or birth date, the name of an individual known to be a minor, or a financial-account number, a party or nonparty making the filing may include only:

   i. The last four (4) digits of the Social Security number and taxpayer-identification number;

   ii. The year of the individual's birth;

   iii. The minor's initials; and

   iv. The last four (4) digits of the financial-account number. FRCP 5.2(a); NY R USDCTED Order 2004-09.

   v. In addition, exercise caution when filing documents that contain the following:

- Personal identifying number, such as driver's license number;

- Medical records, treatment and diagnosis;

- Employment history;

- Individual financial information; and

- Proprietary or trade secret information. NY R USDCTED Order 2004-09.

b. *Exemptions from the redaction requirement.* The redaction requirement does not apply to the following:

    i. A financial-account number that identifies the property allegedly subject to forfeiture in a forfeiture proceeding;

    ii. The record of an administrative or agency proceeding;

    iii. The official record of a state-court proceeding;

    iv. The record of a court or tribunal, if that record was not subject to the redaction requirement when originally filed;

    v. A filing covered by FRCP 5.2(c) or FRCP 5.2(d); and

    vi. A pro se filing in an action brought under 28 U.S.C.A. § 2241, 28 U.S.C.A. § 2254, or 28 U.S.C.A. § 2255. FRCP 5.2(b).

c. *Limitations on remote access to electronic files; Social Security appeals and immigration cases.* Unless the court orders otherwise, in an action for benefits under the Social Security Act, and in an action or proceeding relating to an order of removal, to relief from removal, or to immigration benefits or detention, access to an electronic file is authorized as follows:

    i. The parties and their attorneys may have remote electronic access to any part of the case file, including the administrative record;

    ii. Any other person may have electronic access to the full record at the courthouse, but may have remote electronic access only to:

        • The docket maintained by the court; and

        • An opinion, order, judgment, or other disposition of the court, but not any other part of the case file or the administrative record. FRCP 5.2(c).

d. *Filings made under seal.* The court may order that a filing be made under seal without redaction. The court may later unseal the filing or order the person who made the filing to file a redacted version for the public record. FRCP 5.2(d).

e. *Protective orders.* For good cause, the court may by order in a case:

    i. Require redaction of additional information; or

    ii. Limit or prohibit a nonparty's remote electronic access to a document filed with the court. FRCP 5.2(e).

f. *Option for additional unredacted filing under seal.* A person making a redacted filing may also file an unredacted copy under seal. The court must retain the unredacted copy as part of the record. FRCP 5.2(f); NY R USDCTED Order 2004-09. The unredacted version of the document or the reference list shall be retained by the court as part of the record. The court may, however, still require the party to file a redacted copy for the public file. NY R USDCTED Order 2004-09.

g. *Option for filing a reference list.* A filing that contains redacted information may be filed together with a reference list that identifies each item of redacted information and specifies an appropriate identifier that uniquely corresponds to each item listed. The list must be filed under seal and may be amended as of right. Any reference in the case to a listed identifier will be construed to refer to the corresponding item of information. FRCP 5.2(g); NY R USDCTED Order 2004-09. The unredacted version of the document or the reference list shall be retained by the court as part of the record. The court may, however, still require the party to file a redacted copy for the public file. NY R USDCTED Order 2004-09.

h. *Responsibility for redaction.* The responsibility for redacting these personal identifiers rests solely with counsel and the parties. The Clerk will not review each pleading for compliance with NY R USDCTED Order 2004-09. NY R USDCTED Order 2004-09.

    i. Counsel is strongly urged to share this notice with all clients so that an informed decision about the inclusion of certain materials may be made. If a redacted document is filed, it is the sole responsibility of counsel and the parties to be sure that all pleadings comply with the rules of

this court requiring redaction of personal data identifiers. The clerk will not review each pleading for redaction. NY R USDCTED Order 2004-09.

    i. *Waiver of protection of identifiers.* A person waives the protection of FRCP 5.2(a) as to the person's own information by filing it without redaction and not under seal. FRCP 5.2(h).

4. *Individual judge practices.* Refer to the Miscellaneous section of this document for information on individual judge practices on formatting documents.

## F. Filing and Service Requirements

1. *Filing requirements.* Any paper after the complaint that is required to be served—together with a certificate of service—must be filed within a reasonable time after service. FRCP 5(d)(1).

    a. *How filing is made; In general.* A paper is filed by delivering it:

        i. To the clerk; or

        ii. To a judge who agrees to accept it for filing, and who must then note the filing date on the paper and promptly send it to the clerk. FRCP 5(d)(2).

    b. *Night depository.* A night depository with an automatic date stamp shall be maintained. . .by the Clerk of the Eastern District in the Brooklyn Courthouse. After regular business hours, papers for the District Court only may be deposited in the night depository. Such papers will be considered as having been filed in the District Court as of the date stamped thereon, which shall be deemed presumptively correct. NY R USDCTS&ED Civ Rule 1.2.

    c. *Electronic filing*

        i. *Authorization of electronic filing program.* A court may, by local rule, allow papers to be filed, signed, or verified by electronic means that are consistent with any technical standards established by the Judicial Conference of the United States. A local rule may require electronic filing only if reasonable exceptions are allowed. A paper filed electronically in compliance with a local rule is a written paper for purposes of the Federal Rules of Civil Procedure. FRCP 5(d)(3).

- Parties serving and filing papers shall follow the instructions regarding Electronic Case Filing (ECF) published on the website of each respective Court. A paper served and filed by electronic means in accordance with such instructions is, for purposes of FRCP 5, served and filed in compliance with the Local Civil Rules of the Southern and Eastern Districts of New York. NY R USDCTS&ED Civ Rule 5.2(a). Parties have an obligation to review the Court's actual order, decree, or judgment (on ECF), which controls, and should not rely on the description on the docket or in the ECF Notice of Electronic Filing (NEF). NY R USDCTS&ED Civ Rule 5.2(c).

        ii. *Mandatory electronic filing.* Beginning on August 2, 2004, electronic case filing will be mandatory for all civil cases other than pro se cases. NY R USDCTED Order 2004-08.

- *Letter-motions and letters addressed to the court.* Subject to the instructions regarding ECF published on the website of each respective Court and any pertinent Individual Judge's Practices, letter-motions permitted by NY R USDCTS&ED Civ Rule 7.1(d) and letters addressed to the Court (but not letters between the parties) may be filed via ECF. NY R USDCTS&ED Civ Rule 5.2(b).

- *Proposed orders, judgments and decrees.* Proposed orders, judgments and decrees shall be presented as directed by the ECF rules published on the website of each respective Court. NY R USDCTS&ED Civ Rule 77.1. For more information, refer to NY R USDCTS&ED Civ Rule 77.1.

- *Request for exemption.* Requests by attorneys for an exemption to the mandatory policy will be considered for good cause hardship reasons only, and will be reviewed on an individual basis by the assigned United States Magistrate Judge. The Clerk's Office provides an electronic filing training program to assist attorneys filing electronically. Before seeking a hardship exemption, attorneys are advised to participate in the training program or otherwise seek the assistance of the Clerk's Office. NY R USDCTED Order 2004-08.

iii. For more information on electronic filing, refer to the court's website.

2. *Service requirements*

  a. *Service; When required*

    i. *In general.* Unless the Federal Rules of Civil Procedure provide otherwise, each of the following papers must be served on every party:

- An order stating that service is required;

- A pleading filed after the original complaint, unless the court orders otherwise under FRCP 5(c) because there are numerous defendants;

- A discovery paper required to be served on a party, unless the court orders otherwise;

- A written motion, except one that may be heard ex parte; and

- A written notice, appearance, demand, or offer of judgment, or any similar paper. FRCP 5(a)(1).

    ii. *If a party fails to appear.* No service is required on a party who is in default for failing to appear. But a pleading that asserts a new claim for relief against such a party must be served on that party under FRCP 4. FRCP 5(a)(2).

    iii. *Seizing property.* If an action is begun by seizing property and no person is or need be named as a defendant, any service required before the filing of an appearance, answer, or claim must be made on the person who had custody or possession of the property when it was seized. FRCP 5(a)(3).

  b. *Service; How made*

    i. *Serving an attorney.* If a party is represented by an attorney, service under FRCP 5 must be made on the attorney unless the court orders service on the party. FRCP 5(b)(1).

    ii. *Service in general.* A paper is served under FRCP 5 by:

- Handing it to the person;

- Leaving it: (1) at the person's office with a clerk or other person in charge or, if no one is in charge, in a conspicuous place in the office; or (2) if the person has no office or the office is closed, at the person's dwelling or usual place of abode with someone of suitable age and discretion who resides there;

- Mailing it to the person's last known address—in which event service is complete upon mailing;

- Leaving it with the court clerk if the person has no known address;

- Sending it by electronic means if the person consented in writing—in which event service is complete upon transmission, but is not effective if the serving party learns that it did not reach the person to be served; or

- Delivering it by any other means that the person consented to in writing—in which event service is complete when the person making service delivers it to the agency designated to make delivery. FRCP 5(b)(2).

    iii. *Service by overnight delivery.* Service upon an attorney may be made by overnight delivery service. "Overnight delivery service" means any delivery service which regularly accepts items for overnight delivery. Overnight delivery service shall be deemed service by mail for purposes of FRCP 5 and FRCP 6. NY R USDCTS&ED Civ Rule 5.3.

    iv. *Service by electronic means.* Parties serving and filing papers shall follow the instructions regarding Electronic Case Filing (ECF) published on the website of each respective Court. A paper served and filed by electronic means in accordance with such instructions is, for purposes of FRCP 5, served and filed in compliance with the Local Civil Rules of the United States District Courts for the Southern and Eastern Districts of New York. NY R USDCTS&ED Civ Rule 5.2(a). Parties have an obligation to review the Court's actual order, decree, or judgment

(on ECF), which controls, and should not rely on the description on the docket or in the ECF Notice of Electronic Filing (NEF). NY R USDCTS&ED Civ Rule 5.2(c).

    v. *Using court facilities.* If a local rule so authorizes, a party may use the court's transmission facilities to make service under FRCP 5(b)(2)(E). FRCP 5(b)(3).

  c. *Serving numerous defendants*

    i. *In general.* If an action involves an unusually large number of defendants, the court may, on motion or on its own, order that:

- Defendants' pleadings and replies to them need not be served on other defendants;

- Any crossclaim, counterclaim, avoidance, or affirmative defense in those pleadings and replies to them will be treated as denied or avoided by all other parties; and

- Filing any such pleading and serving it on the plaintiff constitutes notice of the pleading to all parties. FRCP 5(c)(1).

    ii. *Notifying parties.* A copy of every such order must be served on the parties as the court directs. FRCP 5(c)(2).

3. *Individual judge practices.* Refer to the Miscellaneous section of this document for information on individual judge practices on filing and serving documents.

## G. Hearings

1. *Hearings, generally*

  a. *Oral argument.* Due process does not require that oral argument be permitted on a motion and, except as otherwise provided by local rule, the district court has discretion to determine whether it will decide the motion on the papers or hear argument by counsel (and perhaps receive evidence). FPP § 1190; F.D.I.C. v. Deglau, 207 F.3d 153 (3d Cir. 2000). The parties and their attorneys shall only appear to argue the motion if so directed by the Court by order or by a Judge's Individual Practice. NY R USDCTS&ED Civ Rule 6.1(c).

  b. *Providing a regular schedule for oral hearings.* A court may establish regular times and places for oral hearings on motions. FRCP 78(a).

  c. *Providing for submission on briefs.* By rule or order, the court may provide for submitting and determining motions on briefs, without oral hearings. FRCP 78(b).

2. *Individual judge practices.* Refer to the Miscellaneous section of this document for information on individual judge practices on hearings.

## H. Forms

### 1. Federal Motion to Compel Discovery Forms

  a. Notice of motion; To compel required disclosure of names and addresses of witnesses and persons having knowledge of the claims involved; Civil proceeding. AMJUR PP DEPOSITION § 6.

  b. Motion; To compel required disclosure of names and addresses of witnesses and persons having knowledge of the claims involved. AMJUR PP DEPOSITION § 7.

  c. Motion; To compel answer to interrogatories; Complete failure to answer. AMJUR PP DEPOSITION § 403.

  d. Affidavit; In opposition of motion to compel psychiatric or physical examinations; By attorney. AMJUR PP DEPOSITION § 645.

  e. Motion; To compel further responses to interrogatories; Various grounds. AMJUR PP DEPOSITION § 713.

  f. Affidavit; In support of motion to compel answers to interrogatories and to impose sanctions. AMJUR PP DEPOSITION § 715.

  g. Opposition; To motion to compel electronic discovery; Federal class action. AMJUR PP DEPOSITION § 721.

  h. Notice of motion; For order to compel compliance with request to permit entry on real property for inspection. AMJUR PP DEPOSITION § 733.

    i.    Motion; To compel production of documents; After rejected request; Request for sanctions. AMJUR PP DEPOSITION § 734.

    j.    Affidavit; In support of motion to compel production of documents; By attorney. AMJUR PP DEPOSITION § 736.

    k.    Motion; To compel doctor's production of medical records for trial. AMJUR PP DEPOSITION § 744.

    l.    Notice of motion to compel party to answer deposition questions. 3B FEDFORMS § 3695.

    m.    Motion to compel deposition, request for sanctions and request for expedited hearing. 3B FEDFORMS § 3698.

    n.    Motion to compel answer to interrogatories. 3B FEDFORMS § 3699.

    o.    Affidavit in support of motion. 3B FEDFORMS § 3702.

    p.    Objection to motion for order requiring witness to answer oral questions on deposition. 3B FEDFORMS § 3705.

    q.    Motion; To compel answers to outstanding discovery requests. FEDPROF § 23:43.

    r.    Motion; To compel required disclosure of names and addresses of witnesses and persons having knowledge of the claims involved. FEDPROF § 23:44.

    s.    Motion; To compel answer to questions asked on oral or written examination. FEDPROF § 23:207.

    t.    Motion; To compel further answers to questions asked on oral or written examination and to award expenses of motion. FEDPROF § 23:208.

    u.    Motion; To compel party to produce witness at deposition. FEDPROF § 23:209.

    v.    Affidavit; By opposing attorney; In opposition to motion to compel answers asked at deposition; Answers tend to incriminate. FEDPROF § 23:212.

    w.    Motion; To compel answer to interrogatories; Complete failure to answer. FEDPROF § 23:375.

    x.    Motion; To compel further responses to interrogatories; Various grounds. FEDPROF § 23:376.

    y.    Motion to compel discovery. GOLDLTGFMS § 21:2.

## I.  Applicable Rules

1. *Federal rules*

    a.    Serving and filing pleadings and other papers. FRCP 5.

    b.    Constitutional challenge to a statute; Notice, certification, and intervention. FRCP 5.1.

    c.    Privacy protection for filings made with the court. FRCP 5.2.

    d.    Computing and extending time; Time for motion papers. FRCP 6.

    e.    Pleadings allowed; Form of motions and other papers. FRCP 7.

    f.    Form of pleadings. FRCP 10.

    g.    Signing pleadings, motions, and other papers; Representations to the court; Sanctions. FRCP 11.

    h.    Duty to disclose; General provisions governing discovery. FRCP 26.

    i.    Failure to make disclosures or to cooperate in discovery; Sanctions. FRCP 37.

    j.    Taking testimony. FRCP 43.

    k.    Hearing motions; Submission on briefs. FRCP 78.

2. *Local rules*

    a.    Night depository. NY R USDCTS&ED Civ Rule 1.2.

    b.    Duty of attorneys in related cases. NY R USDCTS&ED Civ Rule 1.6.

    c.    Filing of discovery materials. NY R USDCTS&ED Civ Rule 5.1.

    d.    Electronic service and filing of documents. NY R USDCTS&ED Civ Rule 5.2.

e.  Service by overnight delivery. NY R USDCTS&ED Civ Rule 5.3.

f.  Service and filing of motion papers. NY R USDCTS&ED Civ Rule 6.1.

g.  Orders on motions. NY R USDCTS&ED Civ Rule 6.2.

h.  Computation of time. NY R USDCTS&ED Civ Rule 6.4.

i.  Motion papers. NY R USDCTS&ED Civ Rule 7.1.

j.  Authorities to be provided to pro se litigants. NY R USDCTS&ED Civ Rule 7.2.

k.  Form of pleadings, motions, and other papers. NY R USDCTS&ED Civ Rule 11.1.

l.  Mode of raising discovery and other non-dispositive pretrial disputes with the court (Eastern District only). NY R USDCTS&ED Civ Rule 37.3.

m.  Verbatim quotation of discovery materials. NY R USDCTS&ED Civ Rule 37.1.

n.  Submission of orders, judgments and decrees. NY R USDCTS&ED Civ Rule 77.1.

o.  Court-annexed arbitration (Eastern District only). NY R USDCTS&ED Civ Rule 83.7.

p.  Court-annexed mediation (Eastern District only). NY R USDCTS&ED Civ Rule 83.8.

q.  Electronic case filing. NY R USDCTED Order 2004-08.

r.  The August 2, 2004 amendment to the E-Government Act of 2002. NY R USDCTED Order 2004-09.

## J.  Miscellaneous

**NOTE: Individual judges' rules may apply. For available judge-level information, refer to:**

DISTRICT JUDGE CAROL BAGLEY AMON: NY R USDCTED Amon-Practices.

DISTRICT JUDGE JOAN M. AZRACK: NY R USDCTED Azrack-Practices.

DISTRICT JUDGE JOSEPH F. BIANCO: NY R USDCTED Bianco-Practices.

DISTRICT JUDGE FREDERIC BLOCK: NY R USDCTED Block-Practices.

DISTRICT JUDGE MARGO K. BRODIE: NY R USDCTED Brodie-Practices.

DISTRICT JUDGE PAMELA K. CHEN: NY R USDCTED Chen-Practices.

DISTRICT JUDGE BRIAN M. COGAN: NY R USDCTED Cogan-Practices; NY R USDCTED Cogan-Pretrial.

DISTRICT JUDGE LaSHANN DeARCY HALL: NY R USDCTED DeArcy Hall-Practices.

DISTRICT JUDGE RAYMOND J. DEARIE: NY R USDCTED Dearie-Practices.

DISTRICT JUDGE ANN M. DONNELLY: NY R USDCTED Donnelly-Practices.

DISTRICT JUDGE SANDRA J. FEUERSTEIN: NY R USDCTED Feuerstein-Practices; NY R USDCTED Feuerstein-Pretrial.

DISTRICT JUDGE NICHOLAS G. GARAUIFIS: NY R USDCTED Garaufis-Practices; NY R USDCTED Garaufis-Pretrial.

DISTRICT JUDGE NINA GERSHON: NY R USDCTED Gershon-Practices.

DISTRICT JUDGE I. LEO GLASSER: NY R USDCTED Glasser-Practices; NY R USDCTED Glasser-Crim.

DISTRICT JUDGE DENIS R. HURLEY: NY R USDCTED Hurley-Practices; [NY R USDCTED Hurley-Pro Cooperation Info, as added by NY ORDER 16-4188, effective July 22, 2016]; [NY R USDCTED Hurley-Pro Cooperation Info Stay, as added by NY ORDER 16-4188, effective July 22, 2016].

DISTRICT JUDGE DORA L. IRIZARRY: NY R USDCTED Irizarry-Practices; NY R USDCTED Irizarry-Pretrial; NY R USDCTED Irizarry-Crim.

DISTRICT JUDGE STERLING JOHNSON, JR.: NY R USDCTED Johnson-Practices.

DISTRICT JUDGE EDWARD R. KORMAN: NY R USDCTED Korman-Practices; NY R USDCTED Korman-Pretrial.

DISTRICT JUDGE WILLIAM F. KUNTZ: NY R USDCTED Kuntz-Practices.

DISTRICT JUDGE KIYO A. MATSUMOTO: NY R USDCTED Matsumoto-Practices.

DISTRICT JUDGE ROSLYNN R. MAUSKOPF: NY R USDCTED Mauskopf-Practices; NY R USDCTED Mauskopf-Recusal.

DISTRICT JUDGE THOMAS C. PLATT: NY R USDCTED Platt-Practices.

DISTRICT JUDGE ALLYNE R. ROSS: NY R USDCTED Ross-Practices.

DISTRICT JUDGE JOANNA SEYBERT: NY R USDCTED Seybert-Practices.

DISTRICT JUDGE ARTHUR D. SPATT: NY R USDCTED Spatt-Practices.

DISTRICT JUDGE SANDRA L. TOWNES: NY R USDCTED Townes-Practices.

DISTRICT JUDGE ERIC N. VITALIANO: NY R USDCTED Vitaliano-Practices.

DISTRICT JUDGE JACK B. WEINSTEIN: NY R USDCTED Weinstein-Practices.

DISTRICT JUDGE LEONARD D. WEXLER: NY R USDCTED Wexler-Practices; NY R USDCTED Wexler-Rules.

MAGISTRATE JUDGE LOIS BLOOM: NY R USDCTED Bloom-Practices.

MAGISTRATE JUDGE GARY R. BROWN: NY R USDCTED Brown-Practices.

MAGISTRATE JUDGE MARILYN D. GO: NY R USDCTED Go-Practices.

MAGISTRATE JUDGE STEVEN M. GOLD: NY R USDCTED Gold-Practices.

MAGISTRATE JUDGE PEGGY KUO: NY R USDCTED Kuo-Practices; NY R USDCTED Kuo-Scheduling Order.

MAGISTRATE JUDGE ROBERT M. LEVY: NY R USDCTED Levy-Practices.

MAGISTRATE JUDGE ARLENE R. LINDSAY: NY R USDCTED Lindsay-Practices.

MAGISTRATE JUDGE STEVEN I. LOCKE: NY R USDCTED Locke-Practices.

MAGISTRATE JUDGE ROANNE L. MANN: NY R USDCTED Mann-Practices.

MAGISTRATE JUDGE JAMES ORENSTEIN: NY R USDCTED Jorenstein--Practices.

MAGISTRATE JUDGE VIKTOR V. POHORELSKY: NY R USDCTED Pohorelsky-Practices.

MAGISTRATE JUDGE CHERYL L. POLLAK: NY R USDCTED Pollak-Practices; NY R USDCTED Pollak-Pretrial.

MAGISTRATE JUDGE RAMON E. REYES, JR.: NY R USDCTED Reyes-Practices.

MAGISTRATE JUDGE VERA M. SCANLON: NY R USDCTED Scanlon-Practices.

MAGISTRATE JUDGE ANNE Y. SHIELDS: NY R USDCTED Shields-Practices.

MAGISTRATE JUDGE STEVEN L. TISCIONE: NY R USDCTED Tiscione-Practices.

MAGISTRATE JUDGE A. KATHLEEN TOMILINSON: NY R USDCTED Tomlinson-Practices.

## Motions, Oppositions and Replies
## Motion for Discovery Sanctions

**Document Last Updated September 2016**

A. **Checklist**

    (I)   ❏ Matters to be considered by moving party

        (a)  ❏ Required documents

            (1)  ❏ Letter-motion

            (2)  ❏ Certificate of compliance

        (b)  ❏ Supplemental documents

            (1)  ❏ Supporting evidence

    (2)  ❑ Notice of constitutional question

    (3)  ❑ Copies of authorities

    (4)  ❑ Notice of motion and motion

    (5)  ❑ Memorandum of law

    (6)  ❑ Certificate of service

  (c)  ❑ Timing

    (1)  ❑ There are no specific timing requirements for submitting a letter-motion to the court

    (2)  ❑ A written motion and notice of the hearing must be served at least fourteen (14) days before the time specified for the hearing, with the following exceptions: (i) when the motion may be heard ex parte; (ii) when the Federal Rules of Civil Procedure set a different time; or (iii) when a court order—which a party may, for good cause, apply for ex parte—sets a different time

    (3)  ❑ Any affidavit supporting a motion must be served with the motion

(II)  ❑ Matters to be considered by opposing party

  (a)  ❑ Required documents

    (1)  ❑ Responsive letter

  (b)  ❑ Supplemental documents

    (1)  ❑ Supporting evidence

    (2)  ❑ Notice of constitutional question

    (3)  ❑ Copies of authorities

    (4)  ❑ Answering memorandum of law

    (5)  ❑ Certificate of service

  (c)  ❑ Timing

    (1)  ❑ Within four (4) days of receiving such a letter, any opposing affected party or non-party witness may submit a responsive letter not exceeding three (3) pages attaching relevant materials

    (2)  ❑ Any opposing affidavits and answering memoranda of law shall be served within seven (7) days after service of the moving papers

    (3)  ❑ Except as FRCP 59(c) provides otherwise, any opposing affidavit must be served at least seven (7) days before the hearing, unless the court permits service at another time

## B. Timing

1. *Mode of raising discovery and other non-dispositive pretrial disputes with the court*

  a.  *Letter-motion.* There are no specific timing requirements for submitting a letter-motion to the court.

  b.  *Responsive letter.* Within four (4) days of receiving such a letter, any opposing affected party or non-party witness may submit a responsive letter not exceeding three (3) pages attaching relevant materials. NY R USDCTS&ED Civ Rule 37.3(c).

2. *Motion for discovery sanctions.* There are no specific timing requirements for moving for discovery sanctions.

3. *Timing of motions, generally*

  a.  *Motion and notice of hearing.* Except for letter-motions as permitted by NY R USDCTS&ED Civ Rule 7.1(d), and unless otherwise provided by statute or rule or by the Court in a Judge's Individual Practice or in a direction in a particular case, upon any motion, the notice of motion, supporting affidavits, and memoranda shall be served and filed as follows: on all motions and applications under FRCP 26 through FRCP 37 inclusive and FRCP 45(d)(3), the notice of motion, supporting affidavits, and memoranda of law shall be served by the moving party on all other parties that have appeared in the action. NY R USDCTS&ED Civ Rule 6.1(a)(1). A written motion and notice of the hearing must be served at least fourteen (14) days before the time specified for the hearing, with the following exceptions:

   i.   When the motion may be heard ex parte;

   ii.  When the Federal Rules of Civil Procedure set a different time; or

   iii. When a court order—which a party may, for good cause, apply for ex parte—sets a different time. FRCP 6(c)(1).

   b.   *Supporting affidavit.* Any affidavit supporting a motion must be served with the motion. FRCP 6(c)(2).

4. *Timing of opposing papers.* Except for letter-motions as permitted by NY R USDCTS&ED Civ Rule 7.1(d), and unless otherwise provided by statute or rule or by the Court in a Judge's Individual Practice or in a direction in a particular case, upon any motion, the notice of motion, supporting affidavits, and memoranda shall be served and filed as follows: on all motions and applications under FRCP 26 through FRCP 37 inclusive and FRCP 45(d)(3), any opposing affidavits and answering memoranda of law shall be served within seven (7) days after service of the moving papers. NY R USDCTS&ED Civ Rule 6.1(a)(2).

   a.   *Opposing affidavit.* Except as FRCP 59(c) provides otherwise, any opposing affidavit must be served at least seven (7) days before the hearing, unless the court permits service at another time. FRCP 6(c)(2).

5. *Timing of reply papers.* Where the respondent files an answering affidavit setting up a new matter, the moving party ordinarily is allowed a reasonable time to file a reply affidavit since failure to deny the new matter by affidavit may operate as an admission of its truth. AMJUR MOTIONS § 25.

   a.   *Reply affidavits and reply memoranda of law.* Except for letter-motions as permitted by NY R USDCTS&ED Civ Rule 7.1(d), and unless otherwise provided by statute or rule or by the Court in a Judge's Individual Practice or in a direction in a particular case, upon any motion, the notice of motion, supporting affidavits, and memoranda shall be served and filed as follows: on all motions and applications under FRCP 26 through FRCP 37 inclusive and FRCP 45(d)(3), any reply affidavits and reply memoranda of law shall be served within two (2) days after service of the answering papers. NY R USDCTS&ED Civ Rule 6.1(a)(3).

6. *Computation of time*

   a.   *Computing time.* FRCP 6 applies in computing any time period specified in the Federal Rules of Civil Procedure, in any local rule or court order, or in any statute that does not specify a method of computing time. FRCP 6(a). In computing any period of time prescribed or allowed by the Local Civil Rules of the United States District Courts for the Southern and Eastern Districts of New York or the Local Admiralty and Maritime Rules, the provisions of FRCP 6 shall apply unless otherwise stated. NY R USDCTS&ED Civ Rule 6.4.

      i.   *Period stated in days or a longer unit.* In computing periods of days, refer to FRCP 6 and NY R USDCTS&ED Civ Rule 6.4. NY R USDCTS&ED Civ Rule 6.1(a). When the period is stated in days or a longer unit of time:

         • Exclude the day of the event that triggers the period;

         • Count every day, including intermediate Saturdays, Sundays, and legal holidays; and

         • Include the last day of the period, but if the last day is a Saturday, Sunday, or legal holiday, the period continues to run until the end of the next day that is not a Saturday, Sunday, or legal holiday. FRCP 6(a)(1). In the Local Civil Rules of the United States District Courts for the Southern and Eastern Districts of New York, as in the Federal Rules of Civil Procedure as amended effective December 1, 2009, Saturdays, Sundays, and legal holidays are no longer excluded in computing periods of time. If the last day of the period is a Saturday, Sunday, or legal holiday, the period continues to run until the end of the next day that is not a Saturday, Sunday, or legal holiday. NY R USDCTS&ED Civ Rule 6.4.

      ii.  *Period stated in hours.* When the period is stated in hours:

         • Begin counting immediately on the occurrence of the event that triggers the period;

- Count every hour, including hours during intermediate Saturdays, Sundays, and legal holidays; and
- If the period would end on a Saturday, Sunday, or legal holiday, the period continues to run until the same time on the next day that is not a Saturday, Sunday, or legal holiday. FRCP 6(a)(2). In the Local Civil Rules of the United States District Courts for the Southern and Eastern Districts of New York, as in the Federal Rules of Civil Procedure as amended effective December 1, 2009, Saturdays, Sundays, and legal holidays are no longer excluded in computing periods of time. If the last day of the period is a Saturday, Sunday, or legal holiday, the period continues to run until the end of the next day that is not a Saturday, Sunday, or legal holiday. NY R USDCTS&ED Civ Rule 6.4.

iii. *Inaccessibility of the clerk's office.* Unless the court orders otherwise, if the clerk's office is inaccessible:

- On the last day for filing under FRCP 6(a)(1), then the time for filing is extended to the first accessible day that is not a Saturday, Sunday, or legal holiday; or
- During the last hour for filing under FRCP 6(a)(2), then the time for filing is extended to the same time on the first accessible day that is not a Saturday, Sunday, or legal holiday. FRCP 6(a)(3).

iv. *"Last day" defined.* Unless a different time is set by a statute, local rule, or court order, the last day ends:

- For electronic filing, at midnight in the court's time zone; and
- For filing by other means, when the clerk's office is scheduled to close. FRCP 6(a)(4).

v. *"Next day" defined.* The "next day" is determined by continuing to count forward when the period is measured after an event and backward when measured before an event. FRCP 6(a)(5).

vi. *"Legal holiday" defined.* "Legal holiday" means:

- The day set aside by statute for observing New Year's Day, Martin Luther King Jr.'s Birthday, Washington's Birthday, Memorial Day, Independence Day, Labor Day, Columbus Day, Veterans' Day, Thanksgiving Day, or Christmas Day;
- Any day declared a holiday by the President or Congress; and
- For periods that are measured after an event, any other day declared a holiday by the state where the district court is located. FRCP 6(a)(6).

b. *Extending time*

i. *In general.* When an act may or must be done within a specified time, the court may, for good cause, extend the time:

- With or without motion or notice if the court acts, or if a request is made, before the original time or its extension expires; or
- On motion made after the time has expired if the party failed to act because of excusable neglect. FRCP 6(b)(1).

ii. *Exceptions.* A court must not extend the time to act under FRCP 50(b), FRCP 50(d), FRCP 52(b), FRCP 59(b), FRCP 59(d), FRCP 59(e), and FRCP 60(b). FRCP 6(b)(2).

iii. Refer to the United States District Court for the Eastern District of New York KeyRules Motion for Continuance/Extension of Time document for more information on extending time.

c. *Additional time after certain kinds of service.* When a party may or must act within a specified time after service and service is made under FRCP 5(b)(2)(C), FRCP 5(b)(2)(D), FRCP 5(b)(2)(E), or FRCP 5(b)(2)(F), three (3) days are added after the period would otherwise expire under FRCP 6(a). FRCP 6(d). Overnight delivery service shall be deemed service by mail for purposes of FRCP 5 and FRCP 6. NY R USDCTS&ED Civ Rule 5.3.

7. *Individual judge practices.* Refer to the Miscellaneous section of this document for information on individual judge practices on timing of documents.

## C. General Requirements

1. *Mode of raising discovery and other non-dispositive pretrial disputes with the court.* Prior to seeking judicial resolution of a discovery or non-dispositive pretrial dispute, the attorneys for the affected parties or non-party witness shall attempt to confer in good faith in person or by telephone in an effort to resolve the dispute, in conformity with FRCP 37(a)(1). NY R USDCTS&ED Civ Rule 37.3(a). Refer to the Documents section of this document for the procedure to follow when the attorneys for the affected parties or non-party witness cannot agree on a resolution of the discovery or other non-dispositive pretrial dispute.

   a. *Motion for reconsideration.* A ruling made exclusively as a result of a telephone conference may be the subject of de novo reconsideration by a letter not exceeding five (5) pages in length attaching relevant materials submitted by any affected party or non-party witness. Within four (4) days of receiving such a letter, any other affected party or non-party witness may submit a responsive letter not exceeding five (5) pages in length attaching relevant materials. NY R USDCTS&ED Civ Rule 37.3(d).

   b. *Decision of the court.* The Court shall record or arrange for the recording of the Court's decision in writing. Such written order may take the form of an oral order read into the record of a deposition or other proceeding, a handwritten memorandum, a handwritten marginal notation on a letter or other document, or any other form the Court deems appropriate. NY R USDCTS&ED Civ Rule 37.3(e).

2. *Motions, generally*

   a. *Requirements.* A request for a court order must be made by motion. The motion must:

      i. Be in writing unless made during a hearing or trial;

      ii. State with particularity the grounds for seeking the order; and

      iii. State the relief sought. FRCP 7(b)(1).

   b. *Notice of motion.* A party interested in resisting the relief sought by a motion has a right to notice thereof, and an opportunity to be heard. AMJUR MOTIONS § 12.

      i. In addition to statutory or court rule provisions requiring notice of a motion—the purpose of such a notice requirement having been said to be to prevent a party from being prejudicially surprised by a motion—principles of natural justice dictate that an adverse party generally must be given notice that a motion will be presented to the court. AMJUR MOTIONS § 12.

      ii. "Notice," in this regard, means reasonable notice, including a meaningful opportunity to prepare and to defend against allegations of a motion. AMJUR MOTIONS § 12.

   c. *Writing requirement.* The writing requirement is intended to insure that the adverse parties are informed and have a record of both the motion's pendency and the grounds on which the movant seeks an order. FPP § 1191; Feldberg v. Quechee Lakes Corp., 463 F.3d 195 (2d Cir. 2006).

      i. It is sufficient "if the motion is stated in a written notice of the hearing of the motion." FPP § 1191.

   d. *Particularity requirement.* The particularity requirement insures that the opposing parties will have notice of their opponent's contentions. FEDPROC § 62:364; Goodman v. 1973 26 Foot Trojan Vessel, Arkansas Registration No. AR1439SN, 859 F.2d 71, 12 Fed.R.Serv.3d 645 (8th Cir. 1988). That requirement ensures that notice of the basis for the motion is provided to the court and to the opposing party so as to avoid prejudice, provide the opponent with a meaningful opportunity to respond, and provide the court with enough information to process the motion correctly. FEDPROC § 62:364; Andreas v. Volkswagen of America, Inc., 336 F.3d 789, 56 Fed.R.Serv.3d 6 (8th Cir. 2003).

      i. Reasonable specification of the grounds for a motion is sufficient. However, where a movant fails to state even one ground for granting the motion in question, the movant has failed to meet the minimal standard of "reasonable specification." FEDPROC § 62:364; Martinez v. Trainor, 556 F.2d 818, 23 Fed.R.Serv.2d 403 (7th Cir. 1977).

      ii. The court may excuse the failure to comply with the particularity requirement if it is inadvertent, and where no prejudice is shown by the opposing party. FEDPROC § 62:364.

e. *Ex parte orders or orders to show cause to bring on a motion.* No ex parte order, or order to show cause to bring on a motion, will be granted except upon a clear and specific showing by affidavit of good and sufficient reasons why a procedure other than by notice of motion is necessary, and stating whether a previous application for similar relief has been made. NY R USDCTS&ED Civ Rule 6.1(d).

f. *Letter-motions.* Applications for extensions or adjournments, applications for a pre-motion conference, and similar non-dispositive matters as permitted by the instructions regarding ECF published on the website of each respective Court and any pertinent Individual Judge's Practices, may be brought by letter-motion filed via ECF pursuant to NY R USDCTS&ED Civ Rule 5.2(b). NY R USDCTS&ED Civ Rule 7.1(d).

3. *Motion for discovery sanctions*

   a. *Sanctions, generally.* FRCP 37 is flexible. The court is directed to make such orders as are "just" and is not limited in any case of disregard of the discovery rules or court orders under them to a stereotyped response. The sanctions enumerated in FRCP 37 are not exclusive and arbitrary but flexible, selective, and plural. The district court may, within reason, use as many and as varied sanctions as are necessary to hold the scales of justice even. FPP § 2284.

      i. There is one fixed limitation that should be noted. A party may not be imprisoned or otherwise punished for contempt of court for failure to submit to a physical or mental examination, or for failure to produce a person in his or her custody or under his or her control for such an examination. FPP § 2284; Sibbach v. Wilson & Co., 312 U.S. 1, 312 U.S. 655, 61 S.Ct. 422, 85 L.Ed. 479 (1941).

      ii. Although FRCP 37 is very broad, and the courts have considerable discretion in imposing sanctions as authorized by FRCP 37, there are constitutional limits, stemming from the Due Process Clause of U.S.C.A. Const. Amend. V and U.S.C.A. Const. Amend. XIV, on the imposition of sanctions. There are two principal facets of the due process issues:

         • First, the court must ask whether there is a sufficient relationship between the discovery and the merits sought to be foreclosed by the sanction to legitimate depriving a party of the opportunity to litigate the merits. FPP § 2283.

         • Second, before imposing a serious merits sanction the court should determine whether the party guilty of a failure to provide discovery was unable to comply with the discovery. FPP § 2283.

   b. *Sanction for improper certification.* If a certification violates FRCP 26(g) without substantial justification, the court, on motion or on its own, must impose an appropriate sanction on the signer, the party on whose behalf the signer was acting, or both. The sanction may include an order to pay the reasonable expenses, including attorney's fees, caused by the violation. FRCP 26(g)(3).

   c. *Motion to compel discovery; Payment of expenses; Protective orders*

      i. *If the motion is granted (or disclosure or discovery is provided after filing).* If the motion is granted—or if the disclosure or requested discovery is provided after the motion was filed—the court must, after giving an opportunity to be heard, require the party or deponent whose conduct necessitated the motion, the party or attorney advising that conduct, or both to pay the movant's reasonable expenses incurred in making the motion, including attorney's fees. But the court must not order this payment if:

         • The movant filed the motion before attempting in good faith to obtain the disclosure or discovery without court action;

         • The opposing party's nondisclosure, response, or objection was substantially justified; or

         • Other circumstances make an award of expenses unjust. FRCP 37(a)(5)(A).

      ii. *If the motion is denied.* If the motion is denied, the court may issue any protective order authorized under FRCP 26(c) and must, after giving an opportunity to be heard, require the movant, the attorney filing the motion, or both to pay the party or deponent who opposed the motion its reasonable expenses incurred in opposing the motion, including attorney's fees. But the court must not order this payment if the motion was substantially justified or other circumstances make an award of expenses unjust. FRCP 37(a)(5)(B).

iii. *If the motion is granted in part and denied in part.* If the motion is granted in part and denied in part, the court may issue any protective order authorized under FRCP 26(c) and may, after giving an opportunity to be heard, apportion the reasonable expenses for the motion. FRCP 37(a)(5)(C).

d. *Failure to comply with a court order*

i. *Sanctions in the district where the deposition is taken.* If the court where the discovery is taken orders a deponent to be sworn or to answer a question and the deponent fails to obey, the failure may be treated as contempt of court. If a deposition-related motion is transferred to the court where the action is pending, and that court orders a deponent to be sworn or to answer a question and the deponent fails to obey, the failure may be treated as contempt of either the court where the discovery is taken or the court where the action is pending. FRCP 37(b)(1).

ii. *Sanctions in the district where the action is pending; For not obeying a discovery order.* If a party or a party's officer, director, or managing agent—or a witness designated under FRCP 30(b)(6) or FRCP 31(a)(4)—fails to obey an order to provide or permit discovery, including an order under FRCP 26(f), FRCP 35, or FRCP 37(a), the court where the action is pending may issue further just orders. They may include the following:

- Directing that the matters embraced in the order or other designated facts be taken as established for purposes of the action, as the prevailing party claims;

- Prohibiting the disobedient party from supporting or opposing designated claims or defenses, or from introducing designated matters in evidence;

- Striking pleadings in whole or in part;

- Staying further proceedings until the order is obeyed;

- Dismissing the action or proceeding in whole or in part;

- Rendering a default judgment against the disobedient party; or

- Treating as contempt of court the failure to obey any order except an order to submit to a physical or mental examination. FRCP 37(b)(2)(A).

iii. *Sanctions in the district where the action is pending; For not producing a person for examination.* If a party fails to comply with an order under FRCP 35(a) requiring it to produce another person for examination, the court may issue any of the orders listed in FRCP 37(b)(2)(A)(i) through FRCP 37(b)(2)(A)(vi), unless the disobedient party shows that it cannot produce the other person. FRCP 37(b)(2)(B).

iv. *Sanctions in the district where the action is pending; Payment of expenses.* Instead of or in addition to the orders in FRCP 37(b)(2)(A) and FRCP 37(b)(2)(B), the court must order the disobedient party, the attorney advising that party, or both to pay the reasonable expenses, including attorney's fees, caused by the failure, unless the failure was substantially justified or other circumstances make an award of expenses unjust. FRCP 37(b)(2)(C).

e. *Failure to disclose, to supplement an earlier response, or to admit*

i. *Failure to disclose or supplement.* If a party fails to provide information or identify a witness as required by FRCP 26(a) or FRCP 26(e), the party is not allowed to use that information or witness to supply evidence on a motion, at a hearing, or at a trial, unless the failure was substantially justified or is harmless. In addition to or instead of this sanction, the court, on motion and after giving an opportunity to be heard:

- May order payment of the reasonable expenses, including attorney's fees, caused by the failure;

- May inform the jury of the party's failure; and

- May impose other appropriate sanctions, including any of the orders listed in FRCP 37(b)(2)(A)(i) through FRCP 37(b)(2)(A)(vi). FRCP 37(c)(1).

    ii.   *Failure to admit.* If a party fails to admit what is requested under FRCP 36 and if the requesting party later proves a document to be genuine or the matter true, the requesting party may move that the party who failed to admit pay the reasonable expenses, including attorney's fees, incurred in making that proof. The court must so order unless:

- The request was held objectionable under FRCP 36(a);
- The admission sought was of no substantial importance;
- The party failing to admit had a reasonable ground to believe that it might prevail on the matter; or
- There was other good reason for the failure to admit. FRCP 37(c)(2).

f.   *Party's failure to attend its own deposition, serve answers to interrogatories, or respond to a request for inspection*

    i.   *Motion; Grounds for sanctions.* The court where the action is pending may, on motion, order sanctions if:

- A party or a party's officer, director, or managing agent—or a person designated under FRCP 30(b)(6) or FRCP 31(a)(4)—fails, after being served with proper notice, to appear for that person's deposition; or
- A party, after being properly served with interrogatories under FRCP 33 or a request for inspection under FRCP 34, fails to serve its answers, objections, or written response. FRCP 37(d)(1)(A).

    ii.   *Unacceptable excuse for failing to act.* A failure described in FRCP 37(d)(1)(A) is not excused on the ground that the discovery sought was objectionable, unless the party failing to act has a pending motion for a protective order under FRCP 26(c). FRCP 37(d)(2).

    iii.   *Types of sanctions.* Sanctions may include any of the orders listed in FRCP 37(b)(2)(A)(i) through FRCP 37(b)(2)(A)(vi). Instead of or in addition to these sanctions, the court must require the party failing to act, the attorney advising that party, or both to pay the reasonable expenses, including attorney's fees, caused by the failure, unless the failure was substantially justified or other circumstances make an award of expenses unjust. FRCP 37(d)(3).

g.   *Failure to provide electronically stored information.* If electronically stored information that should have been preserved in the anticipation or conduct of litigation is lost because a party failed to take reasonable steps to preserve it, and it cannot be restored or replaced through additional discovery, the court:

    i.   Upon finding prejudice to another party from loss of the information, may order measures no greater than necessary to cure the prejudice; or

    ii.   Only upon finding that the party acted with the intent to deprive another party of the information's use in the litigation may: (1) presume that the lost information was unfavorable to the party; (2) instruct the jury that it may or must presume the information was unfavorable to the party; or (3) dismiss the action or enter a default judgment. FRCP 37(e).

h.   *Failure to participate in framing a discovery plan.* If a party or its attorney fails to participate in good faith in developing and submitting a proposed discovery plan as required by FRCP 26(f), the court may, after giving an opportunity to be heard, require that party or attorney to pay to any other party the reasonable expenses, including attorney's fees, caused by the failure. FRCP 37(f).

i.   *Counsel's liability for excessive costs.* 28 U.S.C.A. § 1927 is a basis for sanctioning attorney misconduct in discovery proceedings. DISCPROFED § 22:3. Any attorney or other person admitted to conduct cases in any court of the United States or any Territory thereof who so multiplies the proceedings in any case unreasonably and vexatiously may be required by the court to satisfy personally the excess costs, expenses, and attorneys' fees reasonably incurred because of such conduct. 28 U.S.C.A. § 1927.

4.   *Opposing papers.* The Federal Rules of Civil Procedure do not require any formal answer, return, or reply to a motion, except where the Federal Rules of Civil Procedure or local rules may require affidavits,

memoranda, or other papers to be filed in opposition to a motion. Such papers are simply to apprise the court of such opposition and the grounds of that opposition. FEDPROC § 62:359. Except for letter-motions as permitted by NY R USDCTS&ED Civ Rule 7.1(d) or as otherwise permitted by the Court, all oppositions and replies with respect to motions shall comply with NY R USDCTS&ED Civ Rule 7.1(a)(2) and NY R USDCTS&ED Civ Rule 7.1(a)(3), and an opposing party who seeks relief that goes beyond the denial of the motion shall comply as well with NY R USDCTS&ED Civ Rule 7.1(a)(1). NY R USDCTS&ED Civ Rule 7.1(b).

   a. *Effect of failure to respond to motion.* Although in the absence of statutory provision or court rule, a motion ordinarily does not require a written answer, when a party files a motion and the opposing party fails to respond, the court may construe such failure to respond as nonopposition to the motion or an admission that the motion was meritorious, may take the facts alleged in the motion as true—the rule in some jurisdictions being that the failure to respond to a fact set forth in a motion is deemed an admission—and may grant the motion if the relief requested appears to be justified. AMJUR MOTIONS § 28.

   b. *Assent or no opposition not determinative.* However, a motion will not be granted automatically simply because an "assent" or a notation of "no opposition" has been filed; federal judges frequently deny motions that have been assented to when it is thought that justice so dictates. FPP § 1190.

   c. *Responsive pleading inappropriate as response to motion.* An attempt to answer or oppose a motion with a responsive pleading usually is not appropriate. FPP § 1190.

5. *Reply papers.* A moving party may be required or permitted to prepare papers in addition to his original motion papers. AMJUR MOTIONS § 25. Papers answering or replying to opposing papers may be appropriate, in the interests of justice, where it appears there is a substantial reason for allowing a reply. Thus, a court may accept reply papers where a party demonstrates that the papers to which it seeks to file a reply raise new issues that are material to the disposition of the question before the court, or where the court determines, sua sponte, that it wishes further briefing of an issue raised in those papers and orders the submission of additional papers. FEDPROC § 62:360. Except for letter-motions as permitted by NY R USDCTS&ED Civ Rule 7.1(d) or as otherwise permitted by the Court, all oppositions and replies with respect to motions shall comply with NY R USDCTS&ED Civ Rule 7.1(a)(2) and NY R USDCTS&ED Civ Rule 7.1(a)(3). NY R USDCTS&ED Civ Rule 7.1(b).

   a. *Function of reply papers.* The function of a reply affidavit is to answer the arguments made in opposition to the position taken by the movant and not to permit the movant to introduce new arguments in support of the motion. AMJUR MOTIONS § 25.

   b. *Issues raised for the first time in a reply document.* However, the view has been followed in some jurisdictions, that as a matter of judicial economy, where there is no prejudice and where the issues could be raised simply by filing a motion to dismiss, the trial court has discretion to consider arguments raised for the first time in a reply memorandum, and that a trial court may grant a motion to strike issues raised for the first time in a reply memorandum. AMJUR MOTIONS § 26.

6. *Orders on motions.* A memorandum signed by the Court of the decision on a motion that does not finally determine all claims for relief, or an oral decision on such a motion, shall constitute the order unless the memorandum or oral decision directs the submission or settlement of an order in more extended form. The notation in the docket of a memorandum or of an oral decision that does not direct the submission or settlement of an order in more extended form shall constitute the entry of the order. Where an order in more extended form is required to be submitted or settled, the notation in the docket of such order shall constitute the entry of the order. NY R USDCTS&ED Civ Rule 6.2.

7. *Related cases.* It shall be the continuing duty of each attorney appearing in any civil or criminal case to bring promptly to the attention of the Court all facts which said attorney believes are relevant to a determination that said case and one or more pending civil or criminal cases should be heard by the same Judge, in order to avoid unnecessary duplication of judicial effort. As soon as the attorney becomes aware of such relationship, said attorney shall notify the Judges to whom the cases have been assigned. NY R USDCTS&ED Civ Rule 1.6(a). If counsel fails to comply with NY R USDCTS&ED Civ Rule 1.6(a), the Court may assess reasonable costs directly against counsel whose action has obstructed the effective administration of the Court's business. NY R USDCTS&ED Civ Rule 1.6(b).

8. *Alternative dispute resolution (ADR)*

   a. *Court-annexed arbitration*

      i. *Civil cases eligible for compulsory arbitration.* The Clerk of Court shall, as to all cases filed after January 1, 1986, designate and process for compulsory arbitration all civil cases (excluding Social Security cases, tax matters, prisoners' civil rights cases and any action based on an alleged violation of a right secured by the Constitution of the United States or if jurisdiction is based in whole or in part on 28 U.S.C.A. § 1343) wherein money damages only are being sought in an amount not in excess of one hundred fifty thousand dollars ($150,000) exclusive of interest and costs. NY R USDCTS&ED Civ Rule 83.7(d)(1).

         • The parties may by written stipulation agree that the Clerk of Court shall designate and process for court-annexed arbitration any civil case that is not subject to compulsory arbitration in NY R USDCTS&ED Civ Rule 83.7. NY R USDCTS&ED Civ Rule 83.7(d)(2).

         • For purposes of NY R USDCTS&ED Civ Rule 83.7 only, in all civil cases damages shall be presumed to be not in excess of one hundred fifty thousand dollars ($150,000) exclusive of interest and costs, unless: (1) counsel for plaintiff, at the time of filing the complaint, or in the event of the removal of a case from state court or transfer of a case from another district to this Court, within thirty (30) days of the docketing of the case in this district, files a certification with the Court that the damages sought exceed one hundred fifty thousand dollars ($150,000), exclusive of interest and costs; or (2) counsel for a defendant, at the time of filing a counterclaim or cross-claim files a certification with the court that the damages sought by the counter-claim or cross-claim exceed one hundred fifty thousand dollars ($150,000) exclusive of interest and costs. NY R USDCTS&ED Civ Rule 83.7(d)(3).

      ii. *Exemption from arbitration.* The Court shall, sua sponte, or on motion of a party, exempt any case from arbitration in which the objectives of arbitration would not be realized (1) because the case involves complex or novel issues, (2) because legal issues predominate over factual issues, or (3) for other good cause. NY R USDCTS&ED Civ Rule 83.7(e)(2). For information on applying for an exemption, refer to NY R USDCTS&ED Civ Rule 83.7

      iii. *Referral to arbitration.* Cases not originally designated as eligible for compulsory arbitration, but which in the discretion of the assigned Judge, are later found to qualify, may be referred to arbitration. A U.S. District Judge or a U.S. Magistrate Judge, in cases that exceed the arbitration ceiling of one hundred fifty thousand dollars ($150,000) exclusive of interest and costs, in their discretion, may suggest that the parties should consider arbitration. If the parties are agreeable, an appropriate consent form signed by all parties or their representatives may be entered and filed in the case prior to scheduling an arbitration hearing. NY R USDCTS&ED Civ Rule 83.7(e)(3).

      iv. For more information on arbitration, refer to NY R USDCTS&ED Civ Rule 83.7.

   b. *Court-annexed mediation.* Mediation is a process in which parties and counsel agree to meet with a neutral mediator trained to assist them in settling disputes. The mediator improves communication across party lines, helps parties articulate their interests and understand those of the other party, probes the strengths and weaknesses of each party's legal positions, and identifies areas of agreement and helps generate options for a mutually agreeable resolution to the dispute. In all cases, mediation provides an opportunity to explore a wide range of potential solutions and to address interests that may be outside the scope of the stated controversy or which could not be addressed by judicial action. A hallmark of mediation is its capacity to expand traditional settlement discussions and broaden resolution options, often by exploring litigant needs and interests that may be formally independent of the legal issues in controversy. NY R USDCTS&ED Civ Rule 83.8(a).

      i. *Eligible cases.* Judges and Magistrate Judges may designate civil cases for inclusion in the mediation program, and when doing so shall prepare an order to that effect. Alternatively, and subject to the availability of qualified mediators, the parties may consent to participation in the mediation program by preparing and executing a stipulation signed by all parties to the action and so-ordered by the Court. NY R USDCTS&ED Civ Rule 83.8(b)(1).

ii.   For more information on mediation, refer to NY R USDCTS&ED Civ Rule 83.8.

9.   *Individual judge practices.* Refer to the Miscellaneous section of this document for information on individual judge practices on general requirements for documents.

## D.   Documents

1.   *Documents for moving party*

   a.   *Required documents*

   i.   *Letter-motion.* Where the attorneys for the affected parties or non-party witness cannot agree on a resolution of any other discovery dispute or non-dispositive pretrial dispute, or if they are unable to obtain a telephonic ruling on a discovery dispute that arises during a deposition as provided in NY R USDCTS&ED Civ Rule 37.3(b), they shall notify the Court by letter not exceeding three (3) pages in length outlining the nature of the dispute and attaching relevant materials. NY R USDCTS&ED Civ Rule 37.3(c).

   - *Quotation or recitation verbatim of discovery materials.* Upon any motion or application involving discovery or disclosure requests or responses under FRCP 37, the moving party shall specify and quote or set forth verbatim in the motion papers each discovery request and response to which the motion or application is addressed. The motion or application shall also set forth the grounds upon which the moving party is entitled to prevail as to each request or response. NY R USDCTS&ED Civ Rule 5.1 also applies to the motion or application. NY R USDCTS&ED Civ Rule 37.1.

   ii.   *Certificate of compliance.* A motion for sanctions for failing to answer or respond must include a certification that the movant has in good faith conferred or attempted to confer with the party failing to act in an effort to obtain the answer or response without court action. FRCP 37(d)(1)(B).

   b.   *Supplemental documents.* Except for the letters and attachments authorized herein, or where a ruling which was made exclusively as a result of a telephone conference is the subject of de novo review pursuant to NY R USDCTS&ED Civ Rule 37.3(d), papers shall not be submitted with respect to a dispute governed by NY R USDCTS&ED Civ Rule 37.3 unless the Court has so directed. NY R USDCTS&ED Civ Rule 37.3(c).

   i.   *Supporting evidence.* When a motion relies on facts outside the record, the court may hear the matter on affidavits or may hear it wholly or partly on oral testimony or on depositions. FRCP 43(c). Except for letter-motions as permitted by NY R USDCTS&ED Civ Rule 7.1(d) or as otherwise permitted by the Court, all motions shall include the following motion papers: supporting affidavits and exhibits thereto containing any factual information and portions of the record necessary for the decision of the motion. NY R USDCTS&ED Civ Rule 7.1(a)(3).

   - *Discovery materials.* A party seeking or opposing relief under FRCP 26 through FRCP 37 inclusive, or making or opposing any other motion or application, shall quote or attach only those portions of the depositions, interrogatories, requests for documents, requests for admissions, or other discovery or disclosure materials, together with the responses and objections thereto, that are the subject of the discovery motion or application, or that are cited in papers submitted in connection with any other motion or application. NY R USDCTS&ED Civ Rule 5.1.

   ii.   *Notice of constitutional question.* A party that files a pleading, written motion, or other paper drawing into question the constitutionality of a federal or state statute must promptly:

   - *File notice.* File a notice of constitutional question stating the question and identifying the paper that raises it, if: (1) a federal statute is questioned and the parties do not include the United States, one of its agencies, or one of its officers or employees in an official capacity; or (2) a state statute is questioned and the parties do not include the state, one of its agencies, or one of its officers or employees in an official capacity; and

   - *Serve notice.* Serve the notice and paper on the Attorney General of the United States if a federal statute is questioned—or on the state attorney general if a state statute is

questioned—either by certified or registered mail or by sending it to an electronic address designated by the attorney general for this purpose. FRCP 5.1(a).

- *No forfeiture.* A party's failure to file and serve the notice, or the court's failure to certify, does not forfeit a constitutional claim or defense that is otherwise timely asserted. FRCP 5.1(d).

iii. *Copies of authorities.* In cases involving a pro se litigant, counsel shall, when serving a memorandum of law (or other submissions to the Court), provide the pro se litigant (but not other counsel or the Court) with copies of cases and other authorities cited therein that are unpublished or reported exclusively on computerized databases. Upon request, counsel shall provide the pro se litigant with copies of such unpublished cases and other authorities as are cited in a decision of the Court and were not previously cited by any party. NY R USDCTS&ED Civ Rule 7.2.

iv. *Notice of motion and motion.* Except for letter-motions as permitted by NY R USDCTS&ED Civ Rule 7.1(d) or as otherwise permitted by the Court, all motions shall include the following motion papers: a notice of motion, or an order to show cause signed by the Court, which shall specify the applicable rules or statutes pursuant to which the motion is brought, and shall specify the relief sought by the motion. NY R USDCTS&ED Civ Rule 7.1(a)(1). Refer to the General Requirements section of this document for information on the notice of motion and motion.

v. *Memorandum of law.* Except for letter-motions as permitted by NY R USDCTS&ED Civ Rule 7.1(d) or as otherwise permitted by the Court, all motions shall include the following motion papers: a memorandum of law, setting forth the cases and other authorities relied upon in support of the motion, and divided, under appropriate headings, into as many parts as there are issues to be determined. NY R USDCTS&ED Civ Rule 7.1(a)(2).

vi. *Certificate of service.* FRCP 5(d) requires that the person making service under FRCP 5 certify that service has been effected. FRCP 5(Advisory Committee Notes). Having such information on file may be useful for many purposes, including proof of service if an issue arises concerning the effectiveness of the service. FRCP 5(Advisory Committee Notes).

2. *Documents for opposing party*

a. *Required documents*

i. *Responsive letter.* Within four (4) days of receiving such a letter, any opposing affected party or non-party witness may submit a responsive letter not exceeding three (3) pages attaching relevant materials. NY R USDCTS&ED Civ Rule 37.3(c).

b. *Supplemental documents.* Except for the letters and attachments authorized herein, or where a ruling which was made exclusively as a result of a telephone conference is the subject of de novo review pursuant to NY R USDCTS&ED Civ Rule 37.3(d), papers shall not be submitted with respect to a dispute governed by NY R USDCTS&ED Civ Rule 37.3 unless the Court has so directed. NY R USDCTS&ED Civ Rule 37.3(c).

i. *Supporting evidence.* When a motion relies on facts outside the record, the court may hear the matter on affidavits or may hear it wholly or partly on oral testimony or on depositions. FRCP 43(c). Except for letter-motions as permitted by NY R USDCTS&ED Civ Rule 7.1(d) or as otherwise permitted by the Court, all oppositions and replies with respect to motions shall comply with NY R USDCTS&ED Civ Rule 7.1(a)(3). NY R USDCTS&ED Civ Rule 7.1(b). Except for letter-motions as permitted by NY R USDCTS&ED Civ Rule 7.1(d) or as otherwise permitted by the Court, all motions shall include the following motion papers: supporting affidavits and exhibits thereto containing any factual information and portions of the record necessary for the decision of the motion. NY R USDCTS&ED Civ Rule 7.1(a)(3).

- *Discovery materials.* A party seeking or opposing relief under FRCP 26 through FRCP 37 inclusive, or making or opposing any other motion or application, shall quote or attach only those portions of the depositions, interrogatories, requests for documents, requests for admissions, or other discovery or disclosure materials, together with the responses and

objections thereto, that are the subject of the discovery motion or application, or that are cited in papers submitted in connection with any other motion or application. NY R USDCTS&ED Civ Rule 5.1.

ii. *Notice of constitutional question.* A party that files a pleading, written motion, or other paper drawing into question the constitutionality of a federal or state statute must promptly:

- *File notice.* File a notice of constitutional question stating the question and identifying the paper that raises it, if: (1) a federal statute is questioned and the parties do not include the United States, one of its agencies, or one of its officers or employees in an official capacity; or (2) a state statute is questioned and the parties do not include the state, one of its agencies, or one of its officers or employees in an official capacity; and

- *Serve notice.* Serve the notice and paper on the Attorney General of the United States if a federal statute is questioned—or on the state attorney general if a state statute is questioned—either by certified or registered mail or by sending it to an electronic address designated by the attorney general for this purpose. FRCP 5.1(a).

- *No forfeiture.* A party's failure to file and serve the notice, or the court's failure to certify, does not forfeit a constitutional claim or defense that is otherwise timely asserted. FRCP 5.1(d).

iii. *Copies of authorities.* In cases involving a pro se litigant, counsel shall, when serving a memorandum of law (or other submissions to the Court), provide the pro se litigant (but not other counsel or the Court) with copies of cases and other authorities cited therein that are unpublished or reported exclusively on computerized databases. Upon request, counsel shall provide the pro se litigant with copies of such unpublished cases and other authorities as are cited in a decision of the Court and were not previously cited by any party. NY R USDCTS&ED Civ Rule 7.2.

iv. *Answering memorandum of law.* Except for letter-motions as permitted by NY R USDCTS&ED Civ Rule 7.1(d) or as otherwise permitted by the Court, all oppositions and replies with respect to motions shall comply with NY R USDCTS&ED Civ Rule 7.1(a)(2). NY R USDCTS&ED Civ Rule 7.1(b). Except for letter-motions as permitted by NY R USDCTS&ED Civ Rule 7.1(d) or as otherwise permitted by the Court, all motions shall include the following motion papers: a memorandum of law, setting forth the cases and other authorities relied upon in support of the motion, and divided, under appropriate headings, into as many parts as there are issues to be determined. NY R USDCTS&ED Civ Rule 7.1(a)(2). Refer to the General Requirements section of this document for information on the opposing papers.

v. *Certificate of service.* FRCP 5(d) requires that the person making service under FRCP 5 certify that service has been effected. FRCP 5(Advisory Committee Notes). Having such information on file may be useful for many purposes, including proof of service if an issue arises concerning the effectiveness of the service. FRCP 5(Advisory Committee Notes).

3. *Individual judge practices.* Refer to the Miscellaneous section of this document for information on individual judge practices on required documents.

## E. Format

1. *Form of documents.* The rules governing captions and other matters of form in pleadings apply to motions and other papers. FRCP 7(b)(2).

   a. *Paper.* Every pleading, written motion, and other paper must: be plainly written, typed, printed, or copied without erasures or interlineations which materially deface it. NY R USDCTS&ED Civ Rule 11.1(a)(1).

   b. *Typeface, margin, and spacing.* The typeface, margins, and spacing of all documents presented for filing must meet the following requirements:

      i. All text must be twelve (12) point type or larger, except for text in footnotes which may be ten (10) point type;

      ii. All documents must have at least one (1) inch margins on all sides;

      iii.  All text must be double-spaced, except for headings, text in footnotes, or block quotations, which may be single-spaced. NY R USDCTS&ED Civ Rule 11.1(b).

  c.  *Caption; Names of parties.* Every pleading must have a caption with the court's name, a title, a file number, and a FRCP 7(a) designation. The title of the complaint must name all the parties; the title of other pleadings, after naming the first party on each side, may refer generally to other parties. FRCP 10(a). Every pleading, written motion, and other paper must: bear the docket number and the initials of the District Judge and any Magistrate Judge before whom the action or proceeding is pending, NY R USDCTS&ED Civ Rule 11.1(a)(2).

  d.  *Paragraphs; Separate statements.* A party must state its claims or defenses in numbered paragraphs, each limited as far as practicable to a single set of circumstances. A later pleading may refer by number to a paragraph in an earlier pleading. If doing so would promote clarity, each claim founded on a separate transaction or occurrence—and each defense other than a denial—must be stated in a separate count or defense. FRCP 10(b).

  e.  *Adoption by reference; Exhibits.* A statement in a pleading may be adopted by reference elsewhere in the same pleading or in any other pleading or motion. A copy of a written instrument that is an exhibit to a pleading is a part of the pleading for all purposes. FRCP 10(c).

  f.  *Acceptance by the clerk.* The clerk must not refuse to file a paper solely because it is not in the form prescribed by the Federal Rules of Civil Procedure or by a local rule or practice. FRCP 5(d)(4).

2.  *Signing disclosures and discovery requests, responses, and objections.* FRCP 11 does not apply to disclosures and discovery requests, responses, objections, and motions under FRCP 26 through FRCP 37. FRCP 11(d).

  a.  *Signature required.* Every disclosure under FRCP 26(a)(1) or FRCP 26(a)(3) and every discovery request, response, or objection must be signed by at least one attorney of record in the attorney's own name—or by the party personally, if unrepresented—and must state the signer's address, e-mail address, and telephone number. FRCP 26(g)(1). Every pleading, written motion, and other paper must: have the name of each person signing it clearly printed or typed directly below the signature. NY R USDCTS&ED Civ Rule 11.1(a)(3).

  b.  *Effect of signature.* By signing, an attorney or party certifies that to the best of the person's knowledge, information, and belief formed after a reasonable inquiry:

      i.  With respect to a disclosure, it is complete and correct as of the time it is made; and

      ii.  With respect to a discovery request, response, or objection, it is:

- Consistent with the Federal Rules of Civil Procedure and warranted by existing law or by a nonfrivolous argument for extending, modifying, or reversing existing law, or for establishing new law;

- Not interposed for any improper purpose, such as to harass, cause unnecessary delay, or needlessly increase the cost of litigation; and

- Neither unreasonable nor unduly burdensome or expensive, considering the needs of the case, prior discovery in the case, the amount in controversy, and the importance of the issues at stake in the action. FRCP 26(g)(1).

  c.  *Failure to sign.* Other parties have no duty to act on an unsigned disclosure, request, response, or objection until it is signed, and the court must strike it unless a signature is promptly supplied after the omission is called to the attorney's or party's attention. FRCP 26(g)(2).

  d.  *Sanction for improper certification.* Refer to the General Requirements section of this document for information on the sanction for improper certification.

3.  *Privacy protection for filings made with the court*

  a.  *Redacted filings.* Unless the court orders otherwise, in an electronic or paper filing with the court that contains an individual's Social Security number, taxpayer-identification number, or birth date, the name of an individual known to be a minor, or a financial-account number, a party or nonparty making the filing may include only:

      i.  The last four (4) digits of the Social Security number and taxpayer-identification number;

    ii.    The year of the individual's birth;

    iii.   The minor's initials; and

    iv.   The last four (4) digits of the financial-account number. FRCP 5.2(a); NY R USDCTED Order 2004-09.

    v.    In addition, exercise caution when filing documents that contain the following:

- Personal identifying number, such as driver's license number;
- Medical records, treatment and diagnosis;
- Employment history;
- Individual financial information; and
- Proprietary or trade secret information. NY R USDCTED Order 2004-09.

b.   *Exemptions from the redaction requirement.* The redaction requirement does not apply to the following:

    i.    A financial-account number that identifies the property allegedly subject to forfeiture in a forfeiture proceeding;

    ii.   The record of an administrative or agency proceeding;

    iii.   The official record of a state-court proceeding;

    iv.   The record of a court or tribunal, if that record was not subject to the redaction requirement when originally filed;

    v.    A filing covered by FRCP 5.2(c) or FRCP 5.2(d); and

    vi.   A pro se filing in an action brought under 28 U.S.C.A. § 2241, 28 U.S.C.A. § 2254, or 28 U.S.C.A. § 2255. FRCP 5.2(b).

c.   *Limitations on remote access to electronic files; Social Security appeals and immigration cases.* Unless the court orders otherwise, in an action for benefits under the Social Security Act, and in an action or proceeding relating to an order of removal, to relief from removal, or to immigration benefits or detention, access to an electronic file is authorized as follows:

    i.    The parties and their attorneys may have remote electronic access to any part of the case file, including the administrative record;

    ii.   Any other person may have electronic access to the full record at the courthouse, but may have remote electronic access only to:

- The docket maintained by the court; and
- An opinion, order, judgment, or other disposition of the court, but not any other part of the case file or the administrative record. FRCP 5.2(c).

d.   *Filings made under seal.* The court may order that a filing be made under seal without redaction. The court may later unseal the filing or order the person who made the filing to file a redacted version for the public record. FRCP 5.2(d).

e.   *Protective orders.* For good cause, the court may by order in a case:

    i.    Require redaction of additional information; or

    ii.   Limit or prohibit a nonparty's remote electronic access to a document filed with the court. FRCP 5.2(e).

f.   *Option for additional unredacted filing under seal.* A person making a redacted filing may also file an unredacted copy under seal. The court must retain the unredacted copy as part of the record. FRCP 5.2(f); NY R USDCTED Order 2004-09. The unredacted version of the document or the reference list shall be retained by the court as part of the record. The court may, however, still require the party to file a redacted copy for the public file. NY R USDCTED Order 2004-09.

g.   *Option for filing a reference list.* A filing that contains redacted information may be filed together with a reference list that identifies each item of redacted information and specifies an appropriate

identifier that uniquely corresponds to each item listed. The list must be filed under seal and may be amended as of right. Any reference in the case to a listed identifier will be construed to refer to the corresponding item of information. FRCP 5.2(g); NY R USDCTED Order 2004-09. The unredacted version of the document or the reference list shall be retained by the court as part of the record. The court may, however, still require the party to file a redacted copy for the public file. NY R USDCTED Order 2004-09.

   h. *Responsibility for redaction.* The responsibility for redacting these personal identifiers rests solely with counsel and the parties. The Clerk will not review each pleading for compliance with NY R USDCTED Order 2004-09. NY R USDCTED Order 2004-09.

      i. Counsel is strongly urged to share this notice with all clients so that an informed decision about the inclusion of certain materials may be made. If a redacted document is filed, it is the sole responsibility of counsel and the parties to be sure that all pleadings comply with the rules of this court requiring redaction of personal data identifiers. The clerk will not review each pleading for redaction. NY R USDCTED Order 2004-09.

   i. *Waiver of protection of identifiers.* A person waives the protection of FRCP 5.2(a) as to the person's own information by filing it without redaction and not under seal. FRCP 5.2(h).

4. *Individual judge practices.* Refer to the Miscellaneous section of this document for information on individual judge practices on formatting documents.

## F. Filing and Service Requirements

1. *Filing requirements.* Any paper after the complaint that is required to be served—together with a certificate of service—must be filed within a reasonable time after service. FRCP 5(d)(1).

   a. *How filing is made; In general.* A paper is filed by delivering it:

      i. To the clerk; or

      ii. To a judge who agrees to accept it for filing, and who must then note the filing date on the paper and promptly send it to the clerk. FRCP 5(d)(2).

   b. *Night depository.* A night depository with an automatic date stamp shall be maintained. . .by the Clerk of the Eastern District in the Brooklyn Courthouse. After regular business hours, papers for the District Court only may be deposited in the night depository. Such papers will be considered as having been filed in the District Court as of the date stamped thereon, which shall be deemed presumptively correct. NY R USDCTS&ED Civ Rule 1.2.

   c. *Electronic filing*

      i. *Authorization of electronic filing program.* A court may, by local rule, allow papers to be filed, signed, or verified by electronic means that are consistent with any technical standards established by the Judicial Conference of the United States. A local rule may require electronic filing only if reasonable exceptions are allowed. A paper filed electronically in compliance with a local rule is a written paper for purposes of the Federal Rules of Civil Procedure. FRCP 5(d)(3).

        • Parties serving and filing papers shall follow the instructions regarding Electronic Case Filing (ECF) published on the website of each respective Court. A paper served and filed by electronic means in accordance with such instructions is, for purposes of FRCP 5, served and filed in compliance with the Local Civil Rules of the Southern and Eastern Districts of New York. NY R USDCTS&ED Civ Rule 5.2(a). Parties have an obligation to review the Court's actual order, decree, or judgment (on ECF), which controls, and should not rely on the description on the docket or in the ECF Notice of Electronic Filing (NEF). NY R USDCTS&ED Civ Rule 5.2(c).

      ii. *Mandatory electronic filing.* Beginning on August 2, 2004, electronic case filing will be mandatory for all civil cases other than pro se cases. NY R USDCTED Order 2004-08.

        • *Letter-motions and letters addressed to the court.* Subject to the instructions regarding ECF published on the website of each respective Court and any pertinent Individual Judge's Practices, letter-motions permitted by NY R USDCTS&ED Civ Rule 7.1(d) and letters addressed to the Court (but not letters between the parties) may be filed via ECF. NY R USDCTS&ED Civ Rule 5.2(b).

- *Proposed orders, judgments and decrees.* Proposed orders, judgments and decrees shall be presented as directed by the ECF rules published on the website of each respective Court. NY R USDCTS&ED Civ Rule 77.1. For more information, refer to NY R USDCTS&ED Civ Rule 77.1.

- *Request for exemption.* Requests by attorneys for an exemption to the mandatory policy will be considered for good cause hardship reasons only, and will be reviewed on an individual basis by the assigned United States Magistrate Judge. The Clerk's Office provides an electronic filing training program to assist attorneys filing electronically. Before seeking a hardship exemption, attorneys are advised to participate in the training program or otherwise seek the assistance of the Clerk's Office. NY R USDCTED Order 2004-08.

    iii. For more information on electronic filing, refer to the court's website.

2. *Service requirements*

  a. *Service; When required*

    i. *In general.* Unless the Federal Rules of Civil Procedure provide otherwise, each of the following papers must be served on every party:

- An order stating that service is required;

- A pleading filed after the original complaint, unless the court orders otherwise under FRCP 5(c) because there are numerous defendants;

- A discovery paper required to be served on a party, unless the court orders otherwise;

- A written motion, except one that may be heard ex parte; and

- A written notice, appearance, demand, or offer of judgment, or any similar paper. FRCP 5(a)(1).

    ii. *If a party fails to appear.* No service is required on a party who is in default for failing to appear. But a pleading that asserts a new claim for relief against such a party must be served on that party under FRCP 4. FRCP 5(a)(2).

    iii. *Seizing property.* If an action is begun by seizing property and no person is or need be named as a defendant, any service required before the filing of an appearance, answer, or claim must be made on the person who had custody or possession of the property when it was seized. FRCP 5(a)(3).

  b. *Service; How made*

    i. *Serving an attorney.* If a party is represented by an attorney, service under FRCP 5 must be made on the attorney unless the court orders service on the party. FRCP 5(b)(1).

    ii. *Service in general.* A paper is served under FRCP 5 by:

- Handing it to the person;

- Leaving it: (1) at the person's office with a clerk or other person in charge or, if no one is in charge, in a conspicuous place in the office; or (2) if the person has no office or the office is closed, at the person's dwelling or usual place of abode with someone of suitable age and discretion who resides there;

- Mailing it to the person's last known address—in which event service is complete upon mailing;

- Leaving it with the court clerk if the person has no known address;

- Sending it by electronic means if the person consented in writing—in which event service is complete upon transmission, but is not effective if the serving party learns that it did not reach the person to be served; or

- Delivering it by any other means that the person consented to in writing—in which event service is complete when the person making service delivers it to the agency designated to make delivery. FRCP 5(b)(2).

iii. *Service by overnight delivery.* Service upon an attorney may be made by overnight delivery service. "Overnight delivery service" means any delivery service which regularly accepts items for overnight delivery. Overnight delivery service shall be deemed service by mail for purposes of FRCP 5 and FRCP 6. NY R USDCTS&ED Civ Rule 5.3.

iv. *Service by electronic means.* Parties serving and filing papers shall follow the instructions regarding Electronic Case Filing (ECF) published on the website of each respective Court. A paper served and filed by electronic means in accordance with such instructions is, for purposes of FRCP 5, served and filed in compliance with the Local Civil Rules of the United States District Courts for the Southern and Eastern Districts of New York. NY R USDCTS&ED Civ Rule 5.2(a). Parties have an obligation to review the Court's actual order, decree, or judgment (on ECF), which controls, and should not rely on the description on the docket or in the ECF Notice of Electronic Filing (NEF). NY R USDCTS&ED Civ Rule 5.2(c).

v. *Using court facilities.* If a local rule so authorizes, a party may use the court's transmission facilities to make service under FRCP 5(b)(2)(E). FRCP 5(b)(3).

c. *Serving numerous defendants*

i. *In general.* If an action involves an unusually large number of defendants, the court may, on motion or on its own, order that:

- Defendants' pleadings and replies to them need not be served on other defendants;

- Any crossclaim, counterclaim, avoidance, or affirmative defense in those pleadings and replies to them will be treated as denied or avoided by all other parties; and

- Filing any such pleading and serving it on the plaintiff constitutes notice of the pleading to all parties. FRCP 5(c)(1).

ii. *Notifying parties.* A copy of every such order must be served on the parties as the court directs. FRCP 5(c)(2).

3. *Individual judge practices.* Refer to the Miscellaneous section of this document for information on individual judge practices on filing and serving documents.

## G. Hearings

1. *Hearings, generally*

a. *Oral argument.* Due process does not require that oral argument be permitted on a motion and, except as otherwise provided by local rule, the district court has discretion to determine whether it will decide the motion on the papers or hear argument by counsel (and perhaps receive evidence). FPP § 1190; F.D.I.C. v. Deglau, 207 F.3d 153 (3d Cir. 2000). The parties and their attorneys shall only appear to argue the motion if so directed by the Court by order or by a Judge's Individual Practice. NY R USDCTS&ED Civ Rule 6.1(c).

b. *Providing a regular schedule for oral hearings.* A court may establish regular times and places for oral hearings on motions. FRCP 78(a).

c. *Providing for submission on briefs.* By rule or order, the court may provide for submitting and determining motions on briefs, without oral hearings. FRCP 78(b).

2. *Individual judge practices.* Refer to the Miscellaneous section of this document for information on individual judge practices on hearings.

## H. Forms

### 1. Federal Motion for Discovery Sanctions Forms

a. Motion for contempt. 3B FEDFORMS § 3721.

b. Motion for sanctions for failure to appear at deposition. 3B FEDFORMS § 3722.

c. Motion that facts be taken as established for failure to answer questions upon deposition. 3B FEDFORMS § 3723.

d.  Motion for order refusing to allow disobedient party to support or oppose designated claims or defenses. 3B FEDFORMS § 3724.

e.  Motion for default judgment against defendant for failure to comply with order for production of documents. 3B FEDFORMS § 3725.

f.  Motion for award of expenses incurred to prove matter opponent failed to admit under FRCP 36. 3B FEDFORMS § 3726.

g.  Motion to strike answer or dismiss action for failure to comply with order requiring answer to interrogatories. 3B FEDFORMS § 3729.

h.  Motion to dismiss for failure to comply with previous order requiring answer to interrogatories to party. 3B FEDFORMS § 3732.

i.  Motion; For order that facts be taken to be established, and/or prohibiting certain claims, defenses, or evidence in opposition thereto. FEDPROF § 23:595.

j.  Affidavit; By attorney; In support of motion for order that facts be taken to be established, etc; Failure to produce documents for inspection. FEDPROF § 23:596.

k.  Affidavit; By attorney; In support of motion for order that facts be taken to be established, etc; Failure to obey order to answer questions. FEDPROF § 23:597.

l.  Motion; For order striking pleadings, and for default judgment or dismissal of action. FEDPROF § 23:599.

m.  Affidavit; By attorney; In support of motion for default judgment for defendant's failure to obey discovery order. FEDPROF § 23:600.

n.  Motion; By defendant; For dismissal of action and other sanctions; For failure to comply with orders to complete deposition. FEDPROF § 23:601.

o.  Motion; By defendant; For dismissal of action or other sanctions; For failure and refusal to comply with order to produce documents. FEDPROF § 23:602.

p.  Motion; By defendant; For dismissal with prejudice; Failure to answer interrogatories as ordered. FEDPROF § 23:603.

q.  Motion; For order staying further proceedings until adverse party obeys order compelling discovery. FEDPROF § 23:604.

r.  Affidavit; By attorney; Opposing motion for order striking pleading and directing entry of default judgment; Good-faith attempt to obey discovery order; Production of documents illegal under foreign law. FEDPROF § 23:605.

s.  Motion; For sanctions for failure to comply with examination order. FEDPROF § 23:610.

t.  Motion; For order finding person in contempt of court; Refusal, after order, to answer question. FEDPROF § 23:612.

u.  Affidavit; By attorney; In support of motion for order finding party in contempt. FEDPROF § 23:613.

v.  Affidavit; By plaintiff; In support of motion for order holding defendant in contempt of court; Defendant disobeyed order for production of documents. FEDPROF § 23:614.

w.  Motion; For order compelling opposing party to pay expenses incurred in proving facts such party refused to admit. FEDPROF § 23:616.

x.  Motion; For sanctions; Failure to attend own deposition, serve answers to interrogatories, or respond to request for inspection. FEDPROF § 23:618.

y.  Motion; For order staying proceedings until required response to discovery request is made. FEDPROF § 23:619.

z.  Affidavit; By attorney; In support of motion for sanctions; Failure to attend own deposition, serve answers to interrogatories, or respond to request for inspection. FEDPROF § 23:620.

## I. Applicable Rules

1. *Federal rules*

   a. Counsel's liability for excessive costs. 28 U.S.C.A. § 1927.

   b. Serving and filing pleadings and other papers. FRCP 5.

   c. Constitutional challenge to a statute; Notice, certification, and intervention. FRCP 5.1.

   d. Privacy protection for filings made with the court. FRCP 5.2.

   e. Computing and extending time; Time for motion papers. FRCP 6.

   f. Pleadings allowed; Form of motions and other papers. FRCP 7.

   g. Form of pleadings. FRCP 10.

   h. Signing pleadings, motions, and other papers; Representations to the court; Sanctions. FRCP 11.

   i. Duty to disclose; General provisions governing discovery. FRCP 26.

   j. Failure to make disclosures or to cooperate in discovery; Sanctions. FRCP 37.

   k. Taking testimony. FRCP 43.

   l. Hearing motions; Submission on briefs. FRCP 78.

2. *Local rules*

   a. Night depository. NY R USDCTS&ED Civ Rule 1.2.

   b. Duty of attorneys in related cases. NY R USDCTS&ED Civ Rule 1.6.

   c. Filing of discovery materials. NY R USDCTS&ED Civ Rule 5.1.

   d. Electronic service and filing of documents. NY R USDCTS&ED Civ Rule 5.2.

   e. Service by overnight delivery. NY R USDCTS&ED Civ Rule 5.3.

   f. Service and filing of motion papers. NY R USDCTS&ED Civ Rule 6.1.

   g. Orders on motions. NY R USDCTS&ED Civ Rule 6.2.

   h. Computation of time. NY R USDCTS&ED Civ Rule 6.4.

   i. Motion papers. NY R USDCTS&ED Civ Rule 7.1.

   j. Authorities to be provided to pro se litigants. NY R USDCTS&ED Civ Rule 7.2.

   k. Form of pleadings, motions, and other papers. NY R USDCTS&ED Civ Rule 11.1.

   l. Mode of raising discovery and other non-dispositive pretrial disputes with the court (Eastern District only). NY R USDCTS&ED Civ Rule 37.3.

   m. Verbatim quotation of discovery materials. NY R USDCTS&ED Civ Rule 37.1.

   n. Submission of orders, judgments and decrees. NY R USDCTS&ED Civ Rule 77.1.

   o. Court-annexed arbitration (Eastern District only). NY R USDCTS&ED Civ Rule 83.7.

   p. Court-annexed mediation (Eastern District only). NY R USDCTS&ED Civ Rule 83.8.

   q. Electronic case filing. NY R USDCTED Order 2004-08.

   r. The August 2, 2004 amendment to the E-Government Act of 2002. NY R USDCTED Order 2004-09.

## J. Miscellaneous

**NOTE: Individual judges' rules may apply. For available judge-level information, refer to:**

DISTRICT JUDGE CAROL BAGLEY AMON: NY R USDCTED Amon-Practices.

DISTRICT JUDGE JOAN M. AZRACK: NY R USDCTED Azrack-Practices.

DISTRICT JUDGE JOSEPH F. BIANCO: NY R USDCTED Bianco-Practices.

DISTRICT JUDGE FREDERIC BLOCK: NY R USDCTED Block-Practices.

DISTRICT JUDGE MARGO K. BRODIE: NY R USDCTED Brodie-Practices.

DISTRICT JUDGE PAMELA K. CHEN: NY R USDCTED Chen-Practices.

DISTRICT JUDGE BRIAN M. COGAN: NY R USDCTED Cogan-Practices; NY R USDCTED Cogan-Pretrial.

DISTRICT JUDGE LaSHANN DeARCY HALL: NY R USDCTED DeArcy Hall-Practices.

DISTRICT JUDGE RAYMOND J. DEARIE: NY R USDCTED Dearie-Practices.

DISTRICT JUDGE ANN M. DONNELLY: NY R USDCTED Donnelly-Practices.

DISTRICT JUDGE SANDRA J. FEUERSTEIN: NY R USDCTED Feuerstein-Practices; NY R USDCTED Feuerstein-Pretrial.

DISTRICT JUDGE NICHOLAS G. GARAUIFIS: NY R USDCTED Garaufis-Practices; NY R USDCTED Garaufis-Pretrial.

DISTRICT JUDGE NINA GERSHON: NY R USDCTED Gershon-Practices.

DISTRICT JUDGE I. LEO GLASSER: NY R USDCTED Glasser-Practices; NY R USDCTED Glasser-Crim.

DISTRICT JUDGE DENIS R. HURLEY: NY R USDCTED Hurley-Practices; [NY R USDCTED Hurley-Pro Cooperation Info, as added by NY ORDER 16-4188, effective July 22, 2016]; [NY R USDCTED Hurley-Pro Cooperation Info Stay, as added by NY ORDER 16-4188, effective July 22, 2016].

DISTRICT JUDGE DORA L. IRIZARRY: NY R USDCTED Irizarry-Practices; NY R USDCTED Irizarry-Pretrial; NY R USDCTED Irizarry-Crim.

DISTRICT JUDGE STERLING JOHNSON, JR.: NY R USDCTED Johnson-Practices.

DISTRICT JUDGE EDWARD R. KORMAN: NY R USDCTED Korman-Practices; NY R USDCTED Korman-Pretrial.

DISTRICT JUDGE WILLIAM F. KUNTZ: NY R USDCTED Kuntz-Practices.

DISTRICT JUDGE KIYO A. MATSUMOTO: NY R USDCTED Matsumoto-Practices.

DISTRICT JUDGE ROSLYNN R. MAUSKOPF: NY R USDCTED Mauskopf-Practices; NY R USDCTED Mauskopf-Recusal.

DISTRICT JUDGE THOMAS C. PLATT: NY R USDCTED Platt-Practices.

DISTRICT JUDGE ALLYNE R. ROSS: NY R USDCTED Ross-Practices.

DISTRICT JUDGE JOANNA SEYBERT: NY R USDCTED Seybert-Practices.

DISTRICT JUDGE ARTHUR D. SPATT: NY R USDCTED Spatt-Practices.

DISTRICT JUDGE SANDRA L. TOWNES: NY R USDCTED Townes-Practices.

DISTRICT JUDGE ERIC N. VITALIANO: NY R USDCTED Vitaliano-Practices.

DISTRICT JUDGE JACK B. WEINSTEIN: NY R USDCTED Weinstein-Practices.

DISTRICT JUDGE LEONARD D. WEXLER: NY R USDCTED Wexler-Practices; NY R USDCTED Wexler-Rules.

MAGISTRATE JUDGE LOIS BLOOM: NY R USDCTED Bloom-Practices.

MAGISTRATE JUDGE GARY R. BROWN: NY R USDCTED Brown-Practices.

MAGISTRATE JUDGE MARILYN D. GO: NY R USDCTED Go-Practices.

MAGISTRATE JUDGE STEVEN M. GOLD: NY R USDCTED Gold-Practices.

MAGISTRATE JUDGE PEGGY KUO: NY R USDCTED Kuo-Practices; NY R USDCTED Kuo-Scheduling Order.

MAGISTRATE JUDGE ROBERT M. LEVY: NY R USDCTED Levy-Practices.

MAGISTRATE JUDGE ARLENE R. LINDSAY: NY R USDCTED Lindsay-Practices.

MAGISTRATE JUDGE STEVEN I. LOCKE: NY R USDCTED Locke-Practices.

MAGISTRATE JUDGE ROANNE L. MANN: NY R USDCTED Mann-Practices.

MAGISTRATE JUDGE JAMES ORENSTEIN: NY R USDCTED Jorenstein--Practices.

MAGISTRATE JUDGE VIKTOR V. POHORELSKY: NY R USDCTED Pohorelsky-Practices.

MAGISTRATE JUDGE CHERYL L. POLLAK: NY R USDCTED Pollak-Practices; NY R USDCTED Pollak-Pretrial.

MAGISTRATE JUDGE RAMON E. REYES, JR.: NY R USDCTED Reyes-Practices.

MAGISTRATE JUDGE VERA M. SCANLON: NY R USDCTED Scanlon-Practices.

MAGISTRATE JUDGE ANNE Y. SHIELDS: NY R USDCTED Shields-Practices.

MAGISTRATE JUDGE STEVEN L. TISCIONE: NY R USDCTED Tiscione-Practices.

MAGISTRATE JUDGE A. KATHLEEN TOMILINSON: NY R USDCTED Tomlinson-Practices.

# Motions, Oppositions and Replies
# Motion for Preliminary Injunction

## Document Last Updated September 2016

## A. Checklist

(I) ❏ Matters to be considered by moving party

    (a) ❏ Required documents

        (1) ❏ Letter-motion

        (2) ❏ Security

    (b) ❏ Supplemental documents

        (1) ❏ Supporting evidence

        (2) ❏ Pleadings

        (3) ❏ Notice of constitutional question

        (4) ❏ Nongovernmental corporate disclosure statement

        (5) ❏ Copies of authorities

        (6) ❏ Notice of motion and motion

        (7) ❏ Memorandum of law

        (8) ❏ Certificate of service

    (c) ❏ Timing

        (1) ❏ There are no specific timing requirements for submitting a letter-motion to the court

        (2) ❏ A written motion and notice of the hearing must be served at least fourteen (14) days before the time specified for the hearing, with the following exceptions: (i) when the motion may be heard ex parte; (ii) when the Federal Rules of Civil Procedure set a different time; or (iii) when a court order—which a party may, for good cause, apply for ex parte—sets a different time

        (3) ❏ Any affidavit supporting a motion must be served with the motion

(II) ❏ Matters to be considered by opposing party

    (a) ❏ Required documents

        (1) ❏ Responsive letter

    (b) ❏ Supplemental documents

        (1) ❏ Supporting evidence

        (2) ❏ Pleadings

        (3) ❏ Notice of constitutional question

        (4) ❏ Nongovernmental corporate disclosure statement

      (5)  ❑  Copies of authorities

      (6)  ❑  Answering memorandum of law

      (7)  ❑  Certificate of service

  (c)  ❑  Timing

      (1)  ❑  Within four (4) days of receiving such a letter, any opposing affected party or non-party witness may submit a responsive letter not exceeding three (3) pages attaching relevant materials

      (2)  ❑  Any opposing affidavits and answering memoranda shall be served within fourteen (14) days after service of the moving papers

      (3)  ❑  Except as FRCP 59(c) provides otherwise, any opposing affidavit must be served at least seven (7) days before the hearing, unless the court permits service at another time

## B.  Timing

1. *Mode of raising discovery and other non-dispositive pretrial disputes with the court*

   a. *Letter-motion.* There are no specific timing requirements for submitting a letter-motion to the court.

   b. *Responsive letter.* Within four (4) days of receiving such a letter, any opposing affected party or non-party witness may submit a responsive letter not exceeding three (3) pages attaching relevant materials. NY R USDCTS&ED Civ Rule 37.3(c).

2. *Motion for preliminary injunction.* FRCP 65 is silent about when notice must be given. FPP § 2949.

3. *Timing of motions, generally*

   a. *Motion and notice of hearing.* Except for letter-motions as permitted by NY R USDCTS&ED Civ Rule 7.1(d), and unless otherwise provided by statute or rule or by the Court in a Judge's Individual Practice or in a direction in a particular case, upon any motion, the notice of motion, supporting affidavits, and memoranda shall be served and filed as follows: on all civil motions, petitions, and applications, other than those described in NY R USDCTS&ED Civ Rule 6.1(a), and other than petitions for writs of habeas corpus, the notice of motion, supporting affidavits, and memoranda of law shall be served by the moving party on all other parties that have appeared in the action. NY R USDCTS&ED Civ Rule 6.1(b)(1). A written motion and notice of the hearing must be served at least fourteen (14) days before the time specified for the hearing, with the following exceptions:

     i.  When the motion may be heard ex parte;

     ii.  When the Federal Rules of Civil Procedure set a different time; or

     iii.  When a court order—which a party may, for good cause, apply for ex parte—sets a different time. FRCP 6(c)(1).

   b. *Supporting affidavit.* Any affidavit supporting a motion must be served with the motion. FRCP 6(c)(2).

4. *Timing of opposing papers.* Except for letter-motions as permitted by NY R USDCTS&ED Civ Rule 7.1(d), and unless otherwise provided by statute or rule or by the Court in a Judge's Individual Practice or in a direction in a particular case, upon any motion, the notice of motion, supporting affidavits, and memoranda shall be served and filed as follows: on all civil motions, petitions, and applications, other than those described in NY R USDCTS&ED Civ Rule 6.1(a), and other than petitions for writs of habeas corpus, any opposing affidavits and answering memoranda shall be served within fourteen (14) days after service of the moving papers. NY R USDCTS&ED Civ Rule 6.1(b)(2).

   a. *Opposing affidavit.* Except as FRCP 59(c) provides otherwise, any opposing affidavit must be served at least seven (7) days before the hearing, unless the court permits service at another time. FRCP 6(c)(2).

5. *Timing of reply papers.* Where the respondent files an answering affidavit setting up a new matter, the moving party ordinarily is allowed a reasonable time to file a reply affidavit since failure to deny the new matter by affidavit may operate as an admission of its truth. AMJUR MOTIONS § 25.

   a. *Reply affidavits and reply memoranda of law.* Except for letter-motions as permitted by NY R

USDCTS&ED Civ Rule 7.1(d), and unless otherwise provided by statute or rule or by the Court in a Judge's Individual Practice or in a direction in a particular case, upon any motion, the notice of motion, supporting affidavits, and memoranda shall be served and filed as follows: on all civil motions, petitions, and applications, other than those described in NY R USDCTS&ED Civ Rule 6.1(a), and other than petitions for writs of habeas corpus, any reply affidavits and memoranda of law shall be served within seven (7) days after service of the answering papers. NY R USDCTS&ED Civ Rule 6.1(b)(3).

6. *Computation of time*

   a. *Computing time.* FRCP 6 applies in computing any time period specified in the Federal Rules of Civil Procedure, in any local rule or court order, or in any statute that does not specify a method of computing time. FRCP 6(a). In computing any period of time prescribed or allowed by the Local Civil Rules of the United States District Courts for the Southern and Eastern Districts of New York or the Local Admiralty and Maritime Rules, the provisions of FRCP 6 shall apply unless otherwise stated. NY R USDCTS&ED Civ Rule 6.4.

      i. *Period stated in days or a longer unit.* In computing periods of days, refer to FRCP 6 and NY R USDCTS&ED Civ Rule 6.4. NY R USDCTS&ED Civ Rule 6.1(b). When the period is stated in days or a longer unit of time:

         • Exclude the day of the event that triggers the period;

         • Count every day, including intermediate Saturdays, Sundays, and legal holidays; and

         • Include the last day of the period, but if the last day is a Saturday, Sunday, or legal holiday, the period continues to run until the end of the next day that is not a Saturday, Sunday, or legal holiday. FRCP 6(a)(1). In the Local Civil Rules of the United States District Courts for the Southern and Eastern Districts of New York, as in the Federal Rules of Civil Procedure as amended effective December 1, 2009, Saturdays, Sundays, and legal holidays are no longer excluded in computing periods of time. If the last day of the period is a Saturday, Sunday, or legal holiday, the period continues to run until the end of the next day that is not a Saturday, Sunday, or legal holiday. NY R USDCTS&ED Civ Rule 6.4.

      ii. *Period stated in hours.* When the period is stated in hours:

         • Begin counting immediately on the occurrence of the event that triggers the period;

         • Count every hour, including hours during intermediate Saturdays, Sundays, and legal holidays; and

         • If the period would end on a Saturday, Sunday, or legal holiday, the period continues to run until the same time on the next day that is not a Saturday, Sunday, or legal holiday. FRCP 6(a)(2). In the Local Civil Rules of the United States District Courts for the Southern and Eastern Districts of New York, as in the Federal Rules of Civil Procedure as amended effective December 1, 2009, Saturdays, Sundays, and legal holidays are no longer excluded in computing periods of time. If the last day of the period is a Saturday, Sunday, or legal holiday, the period continues to run until the end of the next day that is not a Saturday, Sunday, or legal holiday. NY R USDCTS&ED Civ Rule 6.4.

      iii. *Inaccessibility of the clerk's office.* Unless the court orders otherwise, if the clerk's office is inaccessible:

         • On the last day for filing under FRCP 6(a)(1), then the time for filing is extended to the first accessible day that is not a Saturday, Sunday, or legal holiday; or

         • During the last hour for filing under FRCP 6(a)(2), then the time for filing is extended to the same time on the first accessible day that is not a Saturday, Sunday, or legal holiday. FRCP 6(a)(3).

      iv. *"Last day" defined.* Unless a different time is set by a statute, local rule, or court order, the last day ends:

         • For electronic filing, at midnight in the court's time zone; and

         • For filing by other means, when the clerk's office is scheduled to close. FRCP 6(a)(4).

    v.   *"Next day" defined.* The "next day" is determined by continuing to count forward when the period is measured after an event and backward when measured before an event. FRCP 6(a)(5).

    vi.  *"Legal holiday" defined.* "Legal holiday" means:

- The day set aside by statute for observing New Year's Day, Martin Luther King Jr.'s Birthday, Washington's Birthday, Memorial Day, Independence Day, Labor Day, Columbus Day, Veterans' Day, Thanksgiving Day, or Christmas Day;

- Any day declared a holiday by the President or Congress; and

- For periods that are measured after an event, any other day declared a holiday by the state where the district court is located. FRCP 6(a)(6).

  b.  *Extending time*

    i.  *In general.* When an act may or must be done within a specified time, the court may, for good cause, extend the time:

- With or without motion or notice if the court acts, or if a request is made, before the original time or its extension expires; or

- On motion made after the time has expired if the party failed to act because of excusable neglect. FRCP 6(b)(1).

    ii.  *Exceptions.* A court must not extend the time to act under FRCP 50(b), FRCP 50(d), FRCP 52(b), FRCP 59(b), FRCP 59(d), FRCP 59(e), and FRCP 60(b). FRCP 6(b)(2).

    iii.  Refer to the United States District Court for the Eastern District of New York KeyRules Motion for Continuance/Extension of Time document for more information on extending time.

  c.  *Additional time after certain kinds of service.* When a party may or must act within a specified time after service and service is made under FRCP 5(b)(2)(C), FRCP 5(b)(2)(D), FRCP 5(b)(2)(E), or FRCP 5(b)(2)(F), three (3) days are added after the period would otherwise expire under FRCP 6(a). FRCP 6(d). Overnight delivery service shall be deemed service by mail for purposes of FRCP 5 and FRCP 6. NY R USDCTS&ED Civ Rule 5.3.

7.  *Individual judge practices.* Refer to the Miscellaneous section of this document for information on individual judge practices on timing of documents.

## C.  General Requirements

1.  *Mode of raising discovery and other non-dispositive pretrial disputes with the court.* Prior to seeking judicial resolution of a discovery or non-dispositive pretrial dispute, the attorneys for the affected parties or non-party witness shall attempt to confer in good faith in person or by telephone in an effort to resolve the dispute, in conformity with FRCP 37(a)(1). NY R USDCTS&ED Civ Rule 37.3(a). Refer to the Documents section of this document for the procedure to follow when the attorneys for the affected parties or non-party witness cannot agree on a resolution of the discovery or other non-dispositive pretrial dispute.

  a.  *Motion for reconsideration.* A ruling made exclusively as a result of a telephone conference may be the subject of de novo reconsideration by a letter not exceeding five (5) pages in length attaching relevant materials submitted by any affected party or non-party witness. Within four (4) days of receiving such a letter, any other affected party or non-party witness may submit a responsive letter not exceeding five (5) pages in length attaching relevant materials. NY R USDCTS&ED Civ Rule 37.3(d).

  b.  *Decision of the court.* The Court shall record or arrange for the recording of the Court's decision in writing. Such written order may take the form of an oral order read into the record of a deposition or other proceeding, a handwritten memorandum, a handwritten marginal notation on a letter or other document, or any other form the Court deems appropriate. NY R USDCTS&ED Civ Rule 37.3(e).

2.  *Motions, generally*

  a.  *Requirements.* A request for a court order must be made by motion. The motion must:

    i.  Be in writing unless made during a hearing or trial;

   ii. State with particularity the grounds for seeking the order; and

   iii. State the relief sought. FRCP 7(b)(1).

 b. *Notice of motion.* A party interested in resisting the relief sought by a motion has a right to notice thereof, and an opportunity to be heard. AMJUR MOTIONS § 12.

   i. In addition to statutory or court rule provisions requiring notice of a motion—the purpose of such a notice requirement having been said to be to prevent a party from being prejudicially surprised by a motion—principles of natural justice dictate that an adverse party generally must be given notice that a motion will be presented to the court. AMJUR MOTIONS § 12.

   ii. "Notice," in this regard, means reasonable notice, including a meaningful opportunity to prepare and to defend against allegations of a motion. AMJUR MOTIONS § 12.

 c. *Writing requirement.* The writing requirement is intended to insure that the adverse parties are informed and have a record of both the motion's pendency and the grounds on which the movant seeks an order. FPP § 1191; Feldberg v. Quechee Lakes Corp., 463 F.3d 195 (2d Cir. 2006).

   i. It is sufficient "if the motion is stated in a written notice of the hearing of the motion." FPP § 1191.

 d. *Particularity requirement.* The particularity requirement insures that the opposing parties will have notice of their opponent's contentions. FEDPROC § 62:364; Goodman v. 1973 26 Foot Trojan Vessel, Arkansas Registration No. AR1439SN, 859 F.2d 71, 12 Fed.R.Serv.3d 645 (8th Cir. 1988). That requirement ensures that notice of the basis for the motion is provided to the court and to the opposing party so as to avoid prejudice, provide the opponent with a meaningful opportunity to respond, and provide the court with enough information to process the motion correctly. FEDPROC § 62:364; Andreas v. Volkswagen of America, Inc., 336 F.3d 789, 56 Fed.R.Serv.3d 6 (8th Cir. 2003).

   i. Reasonable specification of the grounds for a motion is sufficient. However, where a movant fails to state even one ground for granting the motion in question, the movant has failed to meet the minimal standard of "reasonable specification." FEDPROC § 62:364; Martinez v. Trainor, 556 F.2d 818, 23 Fed.R.Serv.2d 403 (7th Cir. 1977).

   ii. The court may excuse the failure to comply with the particularity requirement if it is inadvertent, and where no prejudice is shown by the opposing party. FEDPROC § 62:364.

 e. *Ex parte orders or orders to show cause to bring on a motion.* No ex parte order, or order to show cause to bring on a motion, will be granted except upon a clear and specific showing by affidavit of good and sufficient reasons why a procedure other than by notice of motion is necessary, and stating whether a previous application for similar relief has been made. NY R USDCTS&ED Civ Rule 6.1(d).

 f. *Letter-motions.* Applications for extensions or adjournments, applications for a pre-motion conference, and similar non-dispositive matters as permitted by the instructions regarding ECF published on the website of each respective Court and any pertinent Individual Judge's Practices, may be brought by letter-motion filed via ECF pursuant to NY R USDCTS&ED Civ Rule 5.2(b). NY R USDCTS&ED Civ Rule 7.1(d).

3. *Motion for preliminary injunction.* The appropriate procedure for requesting a preliminary injunction is by motion, although it also commonly is requested by an order to show cause. FPP § 2949; James Luterbach Constr. Co. v. Adamkus, 781 F.2d 599, 603 (7th Cir. 1986); Studebaker Corp. v. Gittlin, 360 F.2d 692 (2d. Cir. 1966).

 a. *Preliminary injunction.* An interim grant of specific relief is a preliminary injunction that may be issued only on notice to the adverse party. FEDPROC § 47:53; Westar Energy, Inc. v. Lake, 552 F.3d 1215 (10th Cir. 2009). Defined broadly, a preliminary injunction is an injunction that is issued to protect plaintiff from irreparable injury and to preserve the court's power to render a meaningful decision after a trial on the merits. FPP § 2947; Evans v. Buchanan, 555 F.2d 373, 387 (3d Cir. 1977).

   i. *Disfavored injunctions.* There are three types of preliminary injunctions that are disfavored:

    • Those that afford the moving party substantially all the relief it might recover after a full trial on the merits;

- Those that disturb the status quo; and

- Those that are mandatory as opposed to prohibitory. FEDPROC § 47:55; Prairie Band of Potawatomi Indians v. Pierce, 253 F.3d 1234, 50 Fed.R.Serv.3d 244 (10th Cir. 2001).

b. *Notice.* The court may issue a preliminary injunction only on notice to the adverse party. FRCP 65(a)(1). Although FRCP 65(a)(1) does not define what constitutes proper notice, it has been held that providing a copy of the motion and a specification of the time and place of the hearing are adequate. FPP § 2949.

c. *Security.* The court may issue a preliminary injunction or a temporary restraining order only if the movant gives security in an amount that the court considers proper to pay the costs and damages sustained by any party found to have been wrongfully enjoined or restrained. The United States, its officers, and its agencies are not required to give security. FRCP 65(c).

  i. *Proceedings against a surety.* Whenever the Federal Rules of Civil Procedure (including the Supplemental Rules for Admiralty or Maritime Claims and Asset Forfeiture Actions) require or allow a party to give security, and security is given through a bond or other undertaking with one or more sureties, each surety submits to the court's jurisdiction and irrevocably appoints the court clerk as its agent for receiving service of any papers that affect its liability on the bond or undertaking. The surety's liability may be enforced on motion without an independent action. The motion and any notice that the court orders may be served on the court clerk, who must promptly mail a copy of each to every surety whose address is known. FRCP 65.1.

  ii. For more information on sureties, refer to NY R USDCTS&ED Civ Rule 65.1.1.

d. *Preliminary injunction versus temporary restraining order.* Care should be taken to distinguish preliminary injunctions under FRCP 65(a) from temporary restraining orders under FRCP 65(b). FPP § 2947.

  i. *Notice and duration.* [Temporary restraining orders] may be issued ex parte without an adversary hearing in order to prevent an immediate, irreparable injury and are of limited duration—they typically remain in effect for a maximum of twenty-eight (28) days. On the other hand, FRCP 65(a)(1) requires that notice be given to the opposing party before a preliminary injunction may be issued. FPP § 2947. Furthermore, a preliminary injunction normally lasts until the completion of the trial on the merits, unless it is dissolved earlier by court order or the consent of the parties. FPP § 2947. Therefore, its duration varies and is controlled by the nature of the situation in which it is utilized. FPP § 2947; Fundicao Tupy S.A. v. U.S., 841 F.2d 1101, 1103 (Fed.Cir. 1988).

  ii. *Hearing.* Some type of a hearing also implicitly is required by FRCP 65(a)(2), which was added in 1966 and provides either for the consolidation of the trial on the merits with the preliminary injunction hearing or the inclusion in the trial record of any evidence received at the FRCP 65(a) hearing. FPP § 2947.

e. *Grounds for granting or denying a preliminary injunction.* The policies that bear on the propriety of granting a preliminary injunction rarely are discussed directly in the cases. Instead they are taken into account by the court considering a number of factors that have been found useful in deciding whether to grant or deny preliminary injunctions in particular cases. A formulation that has become popular in all kinds of cases, although it originally was devised in connection with stays of administrative orders, is that the four most important factors are: (1) the significance of the threat of irreparable harm to plaintiff if the injunction is not granted; (2) the state of the balance between this harm and the injury that granting the injunction would inflict on defendant; (3) the probability that plaintiff will succeed on the merits; and (4) the public interest. FPP § 2948; Pottgen v. Missouri State High School Activities Ass'n, 40 F.3d 926 (8th Cir. 1994).

  i. *Irreparable harm.* Perhaps the single most important prerequisite for the issuance of a preliminary injunction is a demonstration that if it is not granted the applicant is likely to suffer irreparable harm before a decision on the merits can be rendered. FPP § 2948.1. Only when the threatened harm would impair the court's ability to grant an effective remedy is there really a need for preliminary relief. FPP § 2948.1.

    - There must be a likelihood that irreparable harm will occur. Speculative injury is not sufficient; there must be more than an unfounded fear on the part of the applicant. FPP § 2948.1.

- Thus, a preliminary injunction will not be issued simply to prevent the possibility of some remote future injury. A presently existing actual threat must be shown. However, the injury need not have been inflicted when application is made or be certain to occur; a strong threat of irreparable injury before trial is an adequate basis. FPP § 2948.1.

ii. *Balancing hardship to parties.* The second factor bearing on the court's exercise of its discretion as to whether to grant preliminary relief involves an evaluation of the severity of the impact on defendant should the temporary injunction be granted and the hardship that would occur to plaintiff if the injunction should be denied. Two factors that frequently are considered when balancing the hardship on the respective parties of the grant or denial of relief are whether a preliminary injunction would give plaintiff all or most of the relief to which plaintiff would be entitled if successful at trial and whether mandatory relief is being sought. FPP § 2948.2.

iii. *Likelihood of prevailing on the merits.* The third factor that enters into the preliminary injunction calculus is the likelihood that plaintiff will prevail on the merits. This is relevant because the need for the court to act is, at least in part, a function of the validity of the applicant's claim. The courts use a bewildering variety of formulations of the need for showing some likelihood of success—the most common being that plaintiff must demonstrate a reasonable probability of success. But the verbal differences do not seem to reflect substantive disagreement. All courts agree that plaintiff must present a prima facie case but need not show a certainty of winning. FPP § 2948.3.

iv. *Public interest.* The final major factor bearing on the court's discretion to issue or deny a preliminary injunction is the public interest. Focusing on this factor is another way of inquiring whether there are policy considerations that bear on whether the order should issue. Thus, when granting preliminary relief, courts frequently emphasize that the public interest will be furthered by the injunction. Conversely, preliminary relief will be denied if the court finds that the public interest would be injured were an injunction to be issued. If the court finds there is no public interest supporting preliminary relief, that conclusion also supports denial of any injunction, even if the public interest would not be harmed by one. FPP § 2948.4. Consequently, an evaluation of the public interest should be given considerable weight in determining whether a motion for a preliminary injunction should be granted. FPP § 2948.4; Yakus v. U.S., 321 U.S. 414, 64 S.Ct. 660, 88 L.Ed. 834 (1944).

f. *Contents and scope of every injunction and restraining order*

i. *Contents.* Every order granting an injunction and every restraining order must:

- State the reasons why it issued;

- State its terms specifically; and

- Describe in reasonable detail—and not by referring to the complaint or other document—the act or acts restrained or required. FRCP 65(d)(1).

ii. *Persons bound.* The order binds only the following who receive actual notice of it by personal service or otherwise:

- The parties;

- The parties' officers, agents, servants, employees, and attorneys; and

- Other persons who are in active concert or participation with anyone described in FRCP 65(d)(2)(A) or FRCP 65(d)(2)(B). FRCP 65(d)(2).

g. *Other laws not modified.* FRCP 65 does not modify the following:

i. Any federal statute relating to temporary restraining orders or preliminary injunctions in actions affecting employer and employee;

ii. 28 U.S.C.A. § 2361, which relates to preliminary injunctions in actions of interpleader or in the nature of interpleader; or

    iii.  28 U.S.C.A. § 2284, which relates to actions that must be heard and decided by a three-judge district court. FRCP 65(e).

  h.  *Copyright impoundment.* FRCP 65 applies to copyright-impoundment proceedings. FRCP 65(f).

4.  *Opposing papers.* The Federal Rules of Civil Procedure do not require any formal answer, return, or reply to a motion, except where the Federal Rules of Civil Procedure or local rules may require affidavits, memoranda, or other papers to be filed in opposition to a motion. Such papers are simply to apprise the court of such opposition and the grounds of that opposition. FEDPROC § 62:359. Except for letter-motions as permitted by NY R USDCTS&ED Civ Rule 7.1(d) or as otherwise permitted by the Court, all oppositions and replies with respect to motions shall comply with NY R USDCTS&ED Civ Rule 7.1(a)(2) and NY R USDCTS&ED Civ Rule 7.1(a)(3), and an opposing party who seeks relief that goes beyond the denial of the motion shall comply as well with NY R USDCTS&ED Civ Rule 7.1(a)(1). NY R USDCTS&ED Civ Rule 7.1(b).

  a.  *Effect of failure to respond to motion.* Although in the absence of statutory provision or court rule, a motion ordinarily does not require a written answer, when a party files a motion and the opposing party fails to respond, the court may construe such failure to respond as nonopposition to the motion or an admission that the motion was meritorious, may take the facts alleged in the motion as true—the rule in some jurisdictions being that the failure to respond to a fact set forth in a motion is deemed an admission—and may grant the motion if the relief requested appears to be justified. AMJUR MOTIONS § 28.

  b.  *Assent or no opposition not determinative.* However, a motion will not be granted automatically simply because an "assent" or a notation of "no opposition" has been filed; federal judges frequently deny motions that have been assented to when it is thought that justice so dictates. FPP § 1190.

  c.  *Responsive pleading inappropriate as response to motion.* An attempt to answer or oppose a motion with a responsive pleading usually is not appropriate. FPP § 1190.

5.  *Reply papers.* A moving party may be required or permitted to prepare papers in addition to his original motion papers. AMJUR MOTIONS § 25. Papers answering or replying to opposing papers may be appropriate, in the interests of justice, where it appears there is a substantial reason for allowing a reply. Thus, a court may accept reply papers where a party demonstrates that the papers to which it seeks to file a reply raise new issues that are material to the disposition of the question before the court, or where the court determines, sua sponte, that it wishes further briefing of an issue raised in those papers and orders the submission of additional papers. FEDPROC § 62:360. Except for letter-motions as permitted by NY R USDCTS&ED Civ Rule 7.1(d) or as otherwise permitted by the Court, all oppositions and replies with respect to motions shall comply with NY R USDCTS&ED Civ Rule 7.1(a)(2) and NY R USDCTS&ED Civ Rule 7.1(a)(3). NY R USDCTS&ED Civ Rule 7.1(b).

  a.  *Function of reply papers.* The function of a reply affidavit is to answer the arguments made in opposition to the position taken by the movant and not to permit the movant to introduce new arguments in support of the motion. AMJUR MOTIONS § 25.

  b.  *Issues raised for the first time in a reply document.* However, the view has been followed in some jurisdictions, that as a matter of judicial economy, where there is no prejudice and where the issues could be raised simply by filing a motion to dismiss, the trial court has discretion to consider arguments raised for the first time in a reply memorandum, and that a trial court may grant a motion to strike issues raised for the first time in a reply memorandum. AMJUR MOTIONS § 26.

6.  *Orders on motions.* A memorandum signed by the Court of the decision on a motion that does not finally determine all claims for relief, or an oral decision on such a motion, shall constitute the order unless the memorandum or oral decision directs the submission or settlement of an order in more extended form. The notation in the docket of a memorandum or of an oral decision that does not direct the submission or settlement of an order in more extended form shall constitute the entry of the order. Where an order in more extended form is required to be submitted or settled, the notation in the docket of such order shall constitute the entry of the order. NY R USDCTS&ED Civ Rule 6.2.

7.  *Related cases.* It shall be the continuing duty of each attorney appearing in any civil or criminal case to bring promptly to the attention of the Court all facts which said attorney believes are relevant to a

determination that said case and one or more pending civil or criminal cases should be heard by the same Judge, in order to avoid unnecessary duplication of judicial effort. As soon as the attorney becomes aware of such relationship, said attorney shall notify the Judges to whom the cases have been assigned. NY R USDCTS&ED Civ Rule 1.6(a). If counsel fails to comply with NY R USDCTS&ED Civ Rule 1.6(a), the Court may assess reasonable costs directly against counsel whose action has obstructed the effective administration of the Court's business. NY R USDCTS&ED Civ Rule 1.6(b).

8. *Alternative dispute resolution (ADR)*

   a. *Court-annexed arbitration*

      i. *Civil cases eligible for compulsory arbitration.* The Clerk of Court shall, as to all cases filed after January 1, 1986, designate and process for compulsory arbitration all civil cases (excluding Social Security cases, tax matters, prisoners' civil rights cases and any action based on an alleged violation of a right secured by the Constitution of the United States or if jurisdiction is based in whole or in part on 28 U.S.C.A. § 1343) wherein money damages only are being sought in an amount not in excess of one hundred fifty thousand dollars ($150,000) exclusive of interest and costs. NY R USDCTS&ED Civ Rule 83.7(d)(1).

         • The parties may by written stipulation agree that the Clerk of Court shall designate and process for court-annexed arbitration any civil case that is not subject to compulsory arbitration in NY R USDCTS&ED Civ Rule 83.7. NY R USDCTS&ED Civ Rule 83.7(d)(2).

         • For purposes of NY R USDCTS&ED Civ Rule 83.7 only, in all civil cases damages shall be presumed to be not in excess of one hundred fifty thousand dollars ($150,000) exclusive of interest and costs, unless: (1) counsel for plaintiff, at the time of filing the complaint, or in the event of the removal of a case from state court or transfer of a case from another district to this Court, within thirty (30) days of the docketing of the case in this district, files a certification with the Court that the damages sought exceed one hundred fifty thousand dollars ($150,000), exclusive of interest and costs; or (2) counsel for a defendant, at the time of filing a counterclaim or cross-claim files a certification with the court that the damages sought by the counter-claim or cross-claim exceed one hundred fifty thousand dollars ($150,000) exclusive of interest and costs. NY R USDCTS&ED Civ Rule 83.7(d)(3).

      ii. *Exemption from arbitration.* The Court shall, sua sponte, or on motion of a party, exempt any case from arbitration in which the objectives of arbitration would not be realized (1) because the case involves complex or novel issues, (2) because legal issues predominate over factual issues, or (3) for other good cause. NY R USDCTS&ED Civ Rule 83.7(e)(2). For information on applying for an exemption, refer to NY R USDCTS&ED Civ Rule 83.7

      iii. *Referral to arbitration.* Cases not originally designated as eligible for compulsory arbitration, but which in the discretion of the assigned Judge, are later found to qualify, may be referred to arbitration. A U.S. District Judge or a U.S. Magistrate Judge, in cases that exceed the arbitration ceiling of one hundred fifty thousand dollars ($150,000) exclusive of interest and costs, in their discretion, may suggest that the parties should consider arbitration. If the parties are agreeable, an appropriate consent form signed by all parties or their representatives may be entered and filed in the case prior to scheduling an arbitration hearing. NY R USDCTS&ED Civ Rule 83.7(e)(3).

      iv. For more information on arbitration, refer to NY R USDCTS&ED Civ Rule 83.7.

   b. *Court-annexed mediation.* Mediation is a process in which parties and counsel agree to meet with a neutral mediator trained to assist them in settling disputes. The mediator improves communication across party lines, helps parties articulate their interests and understand those of the other party, probes the strengths and weaknesses of each party's legal positions, and identifies areas of agreement and helps generate options for a mutually agreeable resolution to the dispute. In all cases, mediation provides an opportunity to explore a wide range of potential solutions and to address interests that may be outside the scope of the stated controversy or which could not be addressed by judicial action. A hallmark of mediation is its capacity to expand traditional settlement discussions

651

and broaden resolution options, often by exploring litigant needs and interests that may be formally independent of the legal issues in controversy. NY R USDCTS&ED Civ Rule 83.8(a).

    i. *Eligible cases.* Judges and Magistrate Judges may designate civil cases for inclusion in the mediation program, and when doing so shall prepare an order to that effect. Alternatively, and subject to the availability of qualified mediators, the parties may consent to participation in the mediation program by preparing and executing a stipulation signed by all parties to the action and so-ordered by the Court. NY R USDCTS&ED Civ Rule 83.8(b)(1).

    ii. For more information on mediation, refer to NY R USDCTS&ED Civ Rule 83.8.

9. *Individual judge practices.* Refer to the Miscellaneous section of this document for information on individual judge practices on general requirements for documents.

## D. Documents

1. *Documents for moving party*

  a. *Required documents*

    i. *Letter-motion.* Where the attorneys for the affected parties or non-party witness cannot agree on a resolution of any other discovery dispute or non-dispositive pretrial dispute, or if they are unable to obtain a telephonic ruling on a discovery dispute that arises during a deposition as provided in NY R USDCTS&ED Civ Rule 37.3(b), they shall notify the Court by letter not exceeding three (3) pages in length outlining the nature of the dispute and attaching relevant materials. NY R USDCTS&ED Civ Rule 37.3(c).

    ii. *Security.* Refer to the General Requirements section of this document for information on the security required.

  b. *Supplemental documents.* Except for the letters and attachments authorized herein, or where a ruling which was made exclusively as a result of a telephone conference is the subject of de novo review pursuant to NY R USDCTS&ED Civ Rule 37.3(d), papers shall not be submitted with respect to a dispute governed by NY R USDCTS&ED Civ Rule 37.3 unless the Court has so directed. NY R USDCTS&ED Civ Rule 37.3(c).

    i. *Supporting evidence.* When a motion relies on facts outside the record, the court may hear the matter on affidavits or may hear it wholly or partly on oral testimony or on depositions. FRCP 43(c). Evidence that goes beyond the unverified allegations of the pleadings and motion papers must be presented to support or oppose a motion for a preliminary injunction. FPP § 2949. Except for letter-motions as permitted by NY R USDCTS&ED Civ Rule 7.1(d) or as otherwise permitted by the Court, all motions shall include the following motion papers: supporting affidavits and exhibits thereto containing any factual information and portions of the record necessary for the decision of the motion. NY R USDCTS&ED Civ Rule 7.1(a)(3).

      • *Affidavits.* Affidavits are appropriate on a preliminary injunction motion and typically will be offered by both parties. FPP § 2949. All affidavits should state the facts supporting the litigant's position clearly and specifically. Preliminary injunctions frequently are denied if the affidavits are too vague or conclusory to demonstrate a clear right to relief under FRCP 65. FPP § 2949.

      • *Discovery materials.* A party seeking or opposing relief under FRCP 26 through FRCP 37 inclusive, or making or opposing any other motion or application, shall quote or attach only those portions of the depositions, interrogatories, requests for documents, requests for admissions, or other discovery or disclosure materials, together with the responses and objections thereto, that are the subject of the discovery motion or application, or that are cited in papers submitted in connection with any other motion or application. NY R USDCTS&ED Civ Rule 5.1.

    ii. *Pleadings.* Pleadings may be considered if they have been verified. FPP § 2949; K-2 Ski Co. v. Head Ski Co., 467 F.2d 1087 (9th Cir. 1972).

    iii. *Notice of constitutional question.* A party that files a pleading, written motion, or other paper drawing into question the constitutionality of a federal or state statute must promptly:

      • *File notice.* File a notice of constitutional question stating the question and identifying the

paper that raises it, if: (1) a federal statute is questioned and the parties do not include the United States, one of its agencies, or one of its officers or employees in an official capacity; or (2) a state statute is questioned and the parties do not include the state, one of its agencies, or one of its officers or employees in an official capacity; and

- *Serve notice.* Serve the notice and paper on the Attorney General of the United States if a federal statute is questioned—or on the state attorney general if a state statute is questioned—either by certified or registered mail or by sending it to an electronic address designated by the attorney general for this purpose. FRCP 5.1(a).

- *No forfeiture.* A party's failure to file and serve the notice, or the court's failure to certify, does not forfeit a constitutional claim or defense that is otherwise timely asserted. FRCP 5.1(d).

iv. *Nongovernmental corporate disclosure statement.* To enable judges and magistrates to evaluate possible disqualification or recusal, counsel for a private (nongovernmental) party shall submit at the time of initial pleading a certificate identifying any corporate parent, subsidiaries, or affiliates of that party. NY R USDCTED Div. Bus., Rule 50.1(c).

- *Contents.* A nongovernmental corporate party must file two (2) copies of a disclosure statement that: (1) identifies any parent corporation and any publicly held corporation owning ten percent (10%) or more of its stock; or (2) states that there is no such corporation. FRCP 7.1(a).

- *Time to file; Supplemental filing.* A party must: (1) file the disclosure statement with its first appearance, pleading, petition, motion, response, or other request addressed to the court; and (2) promptly file a supplemental statement if any required information changes. FRCP 7.1(b). For purposes of FRCP 7.1(b)(2), "promptly" shall mean "within fourteen days," that is, parties are required to file a supplemental disclosure statement within fourteen (14) days of the time there is any change in the information required in a disclosure statement filed pursuant to those rules. NY R USDCTS&ED Civ Rule 7.1.1.

v. *Copies of authorities.* In cases involving a pro se litigant, counsel shall, when serving a memorandum of law (or other submissions to the Court), provide the pro se litigant (but not other counsel or the Court) with copies of cases and other authorities cited therein that are unpublished or reported exclusively on computerized databases. Upon request, counsel shall provide the pro se litigant with copies of such unpublished cases and other authorities as are cited in a decision of the Court and were not previously cited by any party. NY R USDCTS&ED Civ Rule 7.2.

vi. *Notice of motion and motion.* Except for letter-motions as permitted by NY R USDCTS&ED Civ Rule 7.1(d) or as otherwise permitted by the Court, all motions shall include the following motion papers: a notice of motion, or an order to show cause signed by the Court, which shall specify the applicable rules or statutes pursuant to which the motion is brought, and shall specify the relief sought by the motion. NY R USDCTS&ED Civ Rule 7.1(a)(1). Refer to the General Requirements section of this document for information on the notice of motion and motion.

vii. *Memorandum of law.* Except for letter-motions as permitted by NY R USDCTS&ED Civ Rule 7.1(d) or as otherwise permitted by the Court, all motions shall include the following motion papers: a memorandum of law, setting forth the cases and other authorities relied upon in support of the motion, and divided, under appropriate headings, into as many parts as there are issues to be determined. NY R USDCTS&ED Civ Rule 7.1(a)(2).

viii. *Certificate of service.* FRCP 5(d) requires that the person making service under FRCP 5 certify that service has been effected. FRCP 5(Advisory Committee Notes). Having such information on file may be useful for many purposes, including proof of service if an issue arises concerning the effectiveness of the service. FRCP 5(Advisory Committee Notes).

2. *Documents for opposing party*

   a. *Required documents*

      i. *Responsive letter.* Within four (4) days of receiving such a letter, any opposing affected party or non-party witness may submit a responsive letter not exceeding three (3) pages attaching relevant materials. NY R USDCTS&ED Civ Rule 37.3(c).

b. *Supplemental documents.* Except for the letters and attachments authorized herein, or where a ruling which was made exclusively as a result of a telephone conference is the subject of de novo review pursuant to NY R USDCTS&ED Civ Rule 37.3(d), papers shall not be submitted with respect to a dispute governed by NY R USDCTS&ED Civ Rule 37.3 unless the Court has so directed. NY R USDCTS&ED Civ Rule 37.3(c).

    i. *Supporting evidence.* When a motion relies on facts outside the record, the court may hear the matter on affidavits or may hear it wholly or partly on oral testimony or on depositions. FRCP 43(c). Evidence that goes beyond the unverified allegations of the pleadings and motion papers must be presented to support or oppose a motion for a preliminary injunction. FPP § 2949. Except for letter-motions as permitted by NY R USDCTS&ED Civ Rule 7.1(d) or as otherwise permitted by the Court, all oppositions and replies with respect to motions shall comply with NY R USDCTS&ED Civ Rule 7.1(a)(3). NY R USDCTS&ED Civ Rule 7.1(b). Except for letter-motions as permitted by NY R USDCTS&ED Civ Rule 7.1(d) or as otherwise permitted by the Court, all motions shall include the following motion papers: supporting affidavits and exhibits thereto containing any factual information and portions of the record necessary for the decision of the motion. NY R USDCTS&ED Civ Rule 7.1(a)(3).

- *Affidavits.* Affidavits are appropriate on a preliminary injunction motion and typically will be offered by both parties. FPP § 2949. All affidavits should state the facts supporting the litigant's position clearly and specifically. Preliminary injunctions frequently are denied if the affidavits are too vague or conclusory to demonstrate a clear right to relief under FRCP 65. FPP § 2949.

- *Discovery materials.* A party seeking or opposing relief under FRCP 26 through FRCP 37 inclusive, or making or opposing any other motion or application, shall quote or attach only those portions of the depositions, interrogatories, requests for documents, requests for admissions, or other discovery or disclosure materials, together with the responses and objections thereto, that are the subject of the discovery motion or application, or that are cited in papers submitted in connection with any other motion or application. NY R USDCTS&ED Civ Rule 5.1.

    ii. *Pleadings.* Pleadings may be considered if they have been verified. FPP § 2949; K-2 Ski Co. v. Head Ski Co., 467 F.2d 1087 (9th Cir. 1972).

    iii. *Notice of constitutional question.* A party that files a pleading, written motion, or other paper drawing into question the constitutionality of a federal or state statute must promptly:

- *File notice.* File a notice of constitutional question stating the question and identifying the paper that raises it, if: (1) a federal statute is questioned and the parties do not include the United States, one of its agencies, or one of its officers or employees in an official capacity; or (2) a state statute is questioned and the parties do not include the state, one of its agencies, or one of its officers or employees in an official capacity; and

- *Serve notice.* Serve the notice and paper on the Attorney General of the United States if a federal statute is questioned—or on the state attorney general if a state statute is questioned—either by certified or registered mail or by sending it to an electronic address designated by the attorney general for this purpose. FRCP 5.1(a).

- *No forfeiture.* A party's failure to file and serve the notice, or the court's failure to certify, does not forfeit a constitutional claim or defense that is otherwise timely asserted. FRCP 5.1(d).

    iv. *Nongovernmental corporate disclosure statement.* To enable judges and magistrates to evaluate possible disqualification or recusal, counsel for a private (nongovernmental) party shall submit at the time of initial pleading a certificate identifying any corporate parent, subsidiaries, or affiliates of that party. NY R USDCTED Div. Bus., Rule 50.1(c).

- *Contents.* A nongovernmental corporate party must file two (2) copies of a disclosure statement that: (1) identifies any parent corporation and any publicly held corporation owning ten percent (10%) or more of its stock; or (2) states that there is no such corporation. FRCP 7.1(a).

- *Time to file; Supplemental filing.* A party must: (1) file the disclosure statement with its first appearance, pleading, petition, motion, response, or other request addressed to the court; and (2) promptly file a supplemental statement if any required information changes. FRCP 7.1(b). For purposes of FRCP 7.1(b)(2), "promptly" shall mean "within fourteen days," that is, parties are required to file a supplemental disclosure statement within fourteen (14) days of the time there is any change in the information required in a disclosure statement filed pursuant to those rules. NY R USDCTS&ED Civ Rule 7.1.1.

v. *Copies of authorities.* In cases involving a pro se litigant, counsel shall, when serving a memorandum of law (or other submissions to the Court), provide the pro se litigant (but not other counsel or the Court) with copies of cases and other authorities cited therein that are unpublished or reported exclusively on computerized databases. Upon request, counsel shall provide the pro se litigant with copies of such unpublished cases and other authorities as are cited in a decision of the Court and were not previously cited by any party. NY R USDCTS&ED Civ Rule 7.2.

vi. *Answering memorandum of law.* Except for letter-motions as permitted by NY R USDCTS&ED Civ Rule 7.1(d) or as otherwise permitted by the Court, all oppositions and replies with respect to motions shall comply with NY R USDCTS&ED Civ Rule 7.1(a)(2). NY R USDCTS&ED Civ Rule 7.1(b). Except for letter-motions as permitted by NY R USDCTS&ED Civ Rule 7.1(d) or as otherwise permitted by the Court, all motions shall include the following motion papers: a memorandum of law, setting forth the cases and other authorities relied upon in support of the motion, and divided, under appropriate headings, into as many parts as there are issues to be determined. NY R USDCTS&ED Civ Rule 7.1(a)(2). Refer to the General Requirements section of this document for information on the opposing papers.

vii. *Certificate of service.* FRCP 5(d) requires that the person making service under FRCP 5 certify that service has been effected. FRCP 5(Advisory Committee Notes). Having such information on file may be useful for many purposes, including proof of service if an issue arises concerning the effectiveness of the service. FRCP 5(Advisory Committee Notes).

3. *Individual judge practices.* Refer to the Miscellaneous section of this document for information on individual judge practices on required documents.

## E. Format

1. *Form of documents.* The rules governing captions and other matters of form in pleadings apply to motions and other papers. FRCP 7(b)(2).

   a. *Paper.* Every pleading, written motion, and other paper must: be plainly written, typed, printed, or copied without erasures or interlineations which materially deface it. NY R USDCTS&ED Civ Rule 11.1(a)(1).

   b. *Typeface, margin, and spacing.* The typeface, margins, and spacing of all documents presented for filing must meet the following requirements:

      i. All text must be twelve (12) point type or larger, except for text in footnotes which may be ten (10) point type;

      ii. All documents must have at least one (1) inch margins on all sides;

      iii. All text must be double-spaced, except for headings, text in footnotes, or block quotations, which may be single-spaced. NY R USDCTS&ED Civ Rule 11.1(b).

   c. *Caption; Names of parties.* Every pleading must have a caption with the court's name, a title, a file number, and a FRCP 7(a) designation. The title of the complaint must name all the parties; the title of other pleadings, after naming the first party on each side, may refer generally to other parties. FRCP 10(a). Every pleading, written motion, and other paper must: bear the docket number and the initials of the District Judge and any Magistrate Judge before whom the action or proceeding is pending, NY R USDCTS&ED Civ Rule 11.1(a)(2).

d. *Paragraphs; Separate statements.* A party must state its claims or defenses in numbered paragraphs, each limited as far as practicable to a single set of circumstances. A later pleading may refer by number to a paragraph in an earlier pleading. If doing so would promote clarity, each claim founded on a separate transaction or occurrence—and each defense other than a denial—must be stated in a separate count or defense. FRCP 10(b).

e. *Adoption by reference; Exhibits.* A statement in a pleading may be adopted by reference elsewhere in the same pleading or in any other pleading or motion. A copy of a written instrument that is an exhibit to a pleading is a part of the pleading for all purposes. FRCP 10(c).

f. *Acceptance by the clerk.* The clerk must not refuse to file a paper solely because it is not in the form prescribed by the Federal Rules of Civil Procedure or by a local rule or practice. FRCP 5(d)(4).

2. *Signing of pleadings, motions and other papers*

a. *Signature.* Every pleading, written motion, and other paper must be signed by at least one attorney of record in the attorney's name—or by a party personally if the party is unrepresented. The paper must state the signer's address, e-mail address, and telephone number. FRCP 11(a). Every pleading, written motion, and other paper must: have the name of each person signing it clearly printed or typed directly below the signature. NY R USDCTS&ED Civ Rule 11.1(a)(3).

   i. *No verification or accompanying affidavit required for pleadings.* Unless a rule or statute specifically states otherwise, a pleading need not be verified or accompanied by an affidavit. FRCP 11(a).

   ii. *Unsigned papers.* The court must strike an unsigned paper unless the omission is promptly corrected after being called to the attorney's or party's attention. FRCP 11(a).

b. *Representations to the court.* By presenting to the court a pleading, written motion, or other paper—whether by signing, filing, submitting, or later advocating it—an attorney or unrepresented party certifies that to the best of the person's knowledge, information, and belief, formed after an inquiry reasonable under the circumstances:

   i. It is not being presented for any improper purpose, such as to harass, cause unnecessary delay, or needlessly increase the cost of litigation;

   ii. The claims, defenses, and other legal contentions are warranted by existing law or by a nonfrivolous argument for extending, modifying, or reversing existing law or for establishing new law;

   iii. The factual contentions have evidentiary support or, if specifically so identified, will likely have evidentiary support after a reasonable opportunity for further investigation or discovery; and

   iv. The denials of factual contentions are warranted on the evidence or, if specifically so identified, are reasonably based on belief or a lack of information. FRCP 11(b).

c. *Sanctions.* If, after notice and a reasonable opportunity to respond, the court determines that FRCP 11(b) has been violated, the court may impose an appropriate sanction on any attorney, law firm, or party that violated FRCP 11(b) or is responsible for the violation. FRCP 11(c)(1). Refer to the United States District Court for the Eastern District of New York KeyRules Motion for Sanctions document for more information.

3. *Privacy protection for filings made with the court*

a. *Redacted filings.* Unless the court orders otherwise, in an electronic or paper filing with the court that contains an individual's Social Security number, taxpayer-identification number, or birth date, the name of an individual known to be a minor, or a financial-account number, a party or nonparty making the filing may include only:

   i. The last four (4) digits of the Social Security number and taxpayer-identification number;

   ii. The year of the individual's birth;

   iii. The minor's initials; and

   iv. The last four (4) digits of the financial-account number. FRCP 5.2(a); NY R USDCTED Order 2004-09.

    v.   In addition, exercise caution when filing documents that contain the following:

- Personal identifying number, such as driver's license number;
- Medical records, treatment and diagnosis;
- Employment history;
- Individual financial information; and
- Proprietary or trade secret information. NY R USDCTED Order 2004-09.

b.  *Exemptions from the redaction requirement.* The redaction requirement does not apply to the following:

    i.   A financial-account number that identifies the property allegedly subject to forfeiture in a forfeiture proceeding;

    ii.   The record of an administrative or agency proceeding;

    iii.   The official record of a state-court proceeding;

    iv.   The record of a court or tribunal, if that record was not subject to the redaction requirement when originally filed;

    v.   A filing covered by FRCP 5.2(c) or FRCP 5.2(d); and

    vi.   A pro se filing in an action brought under 28 U.S.C.A. § 2241, 28 U.S.C.A. § 2254, or 28 U.S.C.A. § 2255. FRCP 5.2(b).

c.  *Limitations on remote access to electronic files; Social Security appeals and immigration cases.* Unless the court orders otherwise, in an action for benefits under the Social Security Act, and in an action or proceeding relating to an order of removal, to relief from removal, or to immigration benefits or detention, access to an electronic file is authorized as follows:

    i.   The parties and their attorneys may have remote electronic access to any part of the case file, including the administrative record;

    ii.   Any other person may have electronic access to the full record at the courthouse, but may have remote electronic access only to:

- The docket maintained by the court; and
- An opinion, order, judgment, or other disposition of the court, but not any other part of the case file or the administrative record. FRCP 5.2(c).

d.  *Filings made under seal.* The court may order that a filing be made under seal without redaction. The court may later unseal the filing or order the person who made the filing to file a redacted version for the public record. FRCP 5.2(d).

e.  *Protective orders.* For good cause, the court may by order in a case:

    i.   Require redaction of additional information; or

    ii.   Limit or prohibit a nonparty's remote electronic access to a document filed with the court. FRCP 5.2(e).

f.  *Option for additional unredacted filing under seal.* A person making a redacted filing may also file an unredacted copy under seal. The court must retain the unredacted copy as part of the record. FRCP 5.2(f); NY R USDCTED Order 2004-09. The unredacted version of the document or the reference list shall be retained by the court as part of the record. The court may, however, still require the party to file a redacted copy for the public file. NY R USDCTED Order 2004-09.

g.  *Option for filing a reference list.* A filing that contains redacted information may be filed together with a reference list that identifies each item of redacted information and specifies an appropriate identifier that uniquely corresponds to each item listed. The list must be filed under seal and may be amended as of right. Any reference in the case to a listed identifier will be construed to refer to the corresponding item of information. FRCP 5.2(g); NY R USDCTED Order 2004-09. The unredacted version of the document or the reference list shall be retained by the court as part of the record. The court may, however, still require the party to file a redacted copy for the public file. NY R USDCTED Order 2004-09.

h. *Responsibility for redaction.* The responsibility for redacting these personal identifiers rests solely with counsel and the parties. The Clerk will not review each pleading for compliance with NY R USDCTED Order 2004-09. NY R USDCTED Order 2004-09.

  i. Counsel is strongly urged to share this notice with all clients so that an informed decision about the inclusion of certain materials may be made. If a redacted document is filed, it is the sole responsibility of counsel and the parties to be sure that all pleadings comply with the rules of this court requiring redaction of personal data identifiers. The clerk will not review each pleading for redaction. NY R USDCTED Order 2004-09.

i. *Waiver of protection of identifiers.* A person waives the protection of FRCP 5.2(a) as to the person's own information by filing it without redaction and not under seal. FRCP 5.2(h).

4. *Individual judge practices.* Refer to the Miscellaneous section of this document for information on individual judge practices on formatting documents.

## F. Filing and Service Requirements

1. *Filing requirements.* Any paper after the complaint that is required to be served—together with a certificate of service—must be filed within a reasonable time after service. FRCP 5(d)(1).

a. *How filing is made; In general.* A paper is filed by delivering it:

  i. To the clerk; or

  ii. To a judge who agrees to accept it for filing, and who must then note the filing date on the paper and promptly send it to the clerk. FRCP 5(d)(2).

b. *Night depository.* A night depository with an automatic date stamp shall be maintained. . .by the Clerk of the Eastern District in the Brooklyn Courthouse. After regular business hours, papers for the District Court only may be deposited in the night depository. Such papers will be considered as having been filed in the District Court as of the date stamped thereon, which shall be deemed presumptively correct. NY R USDCTS&ED Civ Rule 1.2.

c. *Electronic filing*

  i. *Authorization of electronic filing program.* A court may, by local rule, allow papers to be filed, signed, or verified by electronic means that are consistent with any technical standards established by the Judicial Conference of the United States. A local rule may require electronic filing only if reasonable exceptions are allowed. A paper filed electronically in compliance with a local rule is a written paper for purposes of the Federal Rules of Civil Procedure. FRCP 5(d)(3).

  • Parties serving and filing papers shall follow the instructions regarding Electronic Case Filing (ECF) published on the website of each respective Court. A paper served and filed by electronic means in accordance with such instructions is, for purposes of FRCP 5, served and filed in compliance with the Local Civil Rules of the Southern and Eastern Districts of New York. NY R USDCTS&ED Civ Rule 5.2(a). Parties have an obligation to review the Court's actual order, decree, or judgment (on ECF), which controls, and should not rely on the description on the docket or in the ECF Notice of Electronic Filing (NEF). NY R USDCTS&ED Civ Rule 5.2(c).

  ii. *Mandatory electronic filing.* Beginning on August 2, 2004, electronic case filing will be mandatory for all civil cases other than pro se cases. NY R USDCTED Order 2004-08.

  • *Letter-motions and letters addressed to the court.* Subject to the instructions regarding ECF published on the website of each respective Court and any pertinent Individual Judge's Practices, letter-motions permitted by NY R USDCTS&ED Civ Rule 7.1(d) and letters addressed to the Court (but not letters between the parties) may be filed via ECF. NY R USDCTS&ED Civ Rule 5.2(b).

  • *Proposed orders, judgments and decrees.* Proposed orders, judgments and decrees shall be presented as directed by the ECF rules published on the website of each respective Court. NY R USDCTS&ED Civ Rule 77.1. For more information, refer to NY R USDCTS&ED Civ Rule 77.1.

- *Request for exemption.* Requests by attorneys for an exemption to the mandatory policy will be considered for good cause hardship reasons only, and will be reviewed on an individual basis by the assigned United States Magistrate Judge. The Clerk's Office provides an electronic filing training program to assist attorneys filing electronically. Before seeking a hardship exemption, attorneys are advised to participate in the training program or otherwise seek the assistance of the Clerk's Office. NY R USDCTED Order 2004-08.

   iii.   For more information on electronic filing, refer to the court's website.

2. *Service requirements*

   a.   *Service; When required*

      i.   *In general.* Unless the Federal Rules of Civil Procedure provide otherwise, each of the following papers must be served on every party:

- An order stating that service is required;
- A pleading filed after the original complaint, unless the court orders otherwise under FRCP 5(c) because there are numerous defendants;
- A discovery paper required to be served on a party, unless the court orders otherwise;
- A written motion, except one that may be heard ex parte; and
- A written notice, appearance, demand, or offer of judgment, or any similar paper. FRCP 5(a)(1).

      ii.   *If a party fails to appear.* No service is required on a party who is in default for failing to appear. But a pleading that asserts a new claim for relief against such a party must be served on that party under FRCP 4. FRCP 5(a)(2).

      iii.   *Seizing property.* If an action is begun by seizing property and no person is or need be named as a defendant, any service required before the filing of an appearance, answer, or claim must be made on the person who had custody or possession of the property when it was seized. FRCP 5(a)(3).

   b.   *Service; How made*

      i.   *Serving an attorney.* If a party is represented by an attorney, service under FRCP 5 must be made on the attorney unless the court orders service on the party. FRCP 5(b)(1).

      ii.   *Service in general.* A paper is served under FRCP 5 by:

- Handing it to the person;
- Leaving it: (1) at the person's office with a clerk or other person in charge or, if no one is in charge, in a conspicuous place in the office; or (2) if the person has no office or the office is closed, at the person's dwelling or usual place of abode with someone of suitable age and discretion who resides there;
- Mailing it to the person's last known address—in which event service is complete upon mailing;
- Leaving it with the court clerk if the person has no known address;
- Sending it by electronic means if the person consented in writing—in which event service is complete upon transmission, but is not effective if the serving party learns that it did not reach the person to be served; or
- Delivering it by any other means that the person consented to in writing—in which event service is complete when the person making service delivers it to the agency designated to make delivery. FRCP 5(b)(2).

      iii.   *Service by overnight delivery.* Service upon an attorney may be made by overnight delivery service. "Overnight delivery service" means any delivery service which regularly accepts items for overnight delivery. Overnight delivery service shall be deemed service by mail for purposes of FRCP 5 and FRCP 6. NY R USDCTS&ED Civ Rule 5.3.

iv. *Service by electronic means.* Parties serving and filing papers shall follow the instructions regarding Electronic Case Filing (ECF) published on the website of each respective Court. A paper served and filed by electronic means in accordance with such instructions is, for purposes of FRCP 5, served and filed in compliance with the Local Civil Rules of the United States District Courts for the Southern and Eastern Districts of New York. NY R USDCTS&ED Civ Rule 5.2(a). Parties have an obligation to review the Court's actual order, decree, or judgment (on ECF), which controls, and should not rely on the description on the docket or in the ECF Notice of Electronic Filing (NEF). NY R USDCTS&ED Civ Rule 5.2(c).

v. *Using court facilities.* If a local rule so authorizes, a party may use the court's transmission facilities to make service under FRCP 5(b)(2)(E). FRCP 5(b)(3).

c. *Serving numerous defendants*

i. *In general.* If an action involves an unusually large number of defendants, the court may, on motion or on its own, order that:

- Defendants' pleadings and replies to them need not be served on other defendants;

- Any crossclaim, counterclaim, avoidance, or affirmative defense in those pleadings and replies to them will be treated as denied or avoided by all other parties; and

- Filing any such pleading and serving it on the plaintiff constitutes notice of the pleading to all parties. FRCP 5(c)(1).

ii. *Notifying parties.* A copy of every such order must be served on the parties as the court directs. FRCP 5(c)(2).

3. *Individual judge practices.* Refer to the Miscellaneous section of this document for information on individual judge practices on filing and serving documents.

## G. Hearings

1. *Hearings, generally*

a. *Oral argument.* Due process does not require that oral argument be permitted on a motion and, except as otherwise provided by local rule, the district court has discretion to determine whether it will decide the motion on the papers or hear argument by counsel (and perhaps receive evidence). FPP § 1190; F.D.I.C. v. Deglau, 207 F.3d 153 (3d Cir. 2000). The parties and their attorneys shall only appear to argue the motion if so directed by the Court by order or by a Judge's Individual Practice. NY R USDCTS&ED Civ Rule 6.1(c).

b. *Providing a regular schedule for oral hearings.* A court may establish regular times and places for oral hearings on motions. FRCP 78(a).

c. *Providing for submission on briefs.* By rule or order, the court may provide for submitting and determining motions on briefs, without oral hearings. FRCP 78(b).

2. *Hearing on motion for preliminary injunction*

a. *Consolidating the hearing with the trial on the merits.* Before or after beginning the hearing on a motion for a preliminary injunction, the court may advance the trial on the merits and consolidate it with the hearing. Even when consolidation is not ordered, evidence that is received on the motion and that would be admissible at trial becomes part of the trial record and need not be repeated at trial. But the court must preserve any party's right to a jury trial. FRCP 65(a)(2).

b. *Expediting the hearing after temporary restraining order is issued without notice.* If the order is issued without notice, the motion for a preliminary injunction must be set for hearing at the earliest possible time, taking precedence over all other matters except hearings on older matters of the same character. At the hearing, the party who obtained the order must proceed with the motion; if the party does not, the court must dissolve the order. FRCP 65(b)(3).

3. *Individual judge practices.* Refer to the Miscellaneous section of this document for information on individual judge practices on hearings.

## H. Forms

### 1. Federal Motion for Preliminary Injunction Forms

a. Declaration; In support of motion for preliminary injunction. AMJUR PP INJUNCTION § 38.

b. Memorandum of points and authorities; In support of motion for preliminary injunction. AMJUR PP INJUNCTION § 39.

c. Notice; Motion for preliminary injunction. AMJUR PP INJUNCTION § 40.

d. Motion; For preliminary injunction. AMJUR PP INJUNCTION § 41.

e. Motion; For preliminary injunction; On pleadings and other papers without evidentiary hearing or oral argument. AMJUR PP INJUNCTION § 43.

f. Affidavit; In support of motion for preliminary injunction. AMJUR PP INJUNCTION § 52.

g. Motion for preliminary injunction. 4A FEDFORMS § 5284.

h. Motion enjoining use of information acquired from employment with plaintiff. 4A FEDFORMS § 5287.

i. Motion enjoining interference with public access. 4A FEDFORMS § 5288.

j. Motion enjoining collection of tax assessment. 4A FEDFORMS § 5289.

k. Motion enjoining conducting election or certifying representative. 4A FEDFORMS § 5290.

l. Motion enjoining preventing plaintiff's acting as teacher. 4A FEDFORMS § 5291.

m. Motion enjoining interference with plaintiff's enforcement of judgment in related case. 4A FED-FORMS § 5292.

n. Motion for preliminary injunction in patent infringement action. 4A FEDFORMS § 5293.

o. Motion for preliminary injunction on basis of prayer of complaint and for setting hearing on motion. 4A FEDFORMS § 5294.

p. Notice of motion. 4A FEDFORMS § 5308.

q. Notice of motion and motion. 4A FEDFORMS § 5310.

r. Bond; To obtain preliminary injunction. FEDPROF § 1:701.

s. Opposition; To motion; General form. FEDPROF § 1:750.

t. Brief; Supporting or opposing motion. FEDPROF § 1:752.

u. Motion for temporary restraining order and preliminary injunction. GOLDLTGFMS § 13A:6.

v. Motion for preliminary injunction. GOLDLTGFMS § 13A:18.

w. Motion for preliminary injunction; Based upon pleadings and other papers without evidentiary hearing or oral argument. GOLDLTGFMS § 13A:19.

x. Motion for preliminary injunction; Supporting affidavit. GOLDLTGFMS § 13A:20.

y. Bond. GOLDLTGFMS § 19:2.

z. Bond; In support of injunction. GOLDLTGFMS § 19:3.

## I. Applicable Rules

### 1. *Federal rules*

a. Serving and filing pleadings and other papers. FRCP 5.

b. Constitutional challenge to a statute; Notice, certification, and intervention. FRCP 5.1.

c. Privacy protection for filings made with the court. FRCP 5.2.

d. Computing and extending time; Time for motion papers. FRCP 6.

e. Pleadings allowed; Form of motions and other papers. FRCP 7.

f. Disclosure statement. FRCP 7.1.

g.  Form of pleadings. FRCP 10.

h.  Signing pleadings, motions, and other papers; Representations to the court; Sanctions. FRCP 11.

i.  Taking testimony. FRCP 43.

j.  Injunctions and restraining orders. FRCP 65.

k.  Proceedings against a surety. FRCP 65.1.

l.  Hearing motions; Submission on briefs. FRCP 78.

2.  *Local rules*

a.  Night depository. NY R USDCTS&ED Civ Rule 1.2.

b.  Duty of attorneys in related cases. NY R USDCTS&ED Civ Rule 1.6.

c.  Filing of discovery materials. NY R USDCTS&ED Civ Rule 5.1.

d.  Electronic service and filing of documents. NY R USDCTS&ED Civ Rule 5.2.

e.  Service by overnight delivery. NY R USDCTS&ED Civ Rule 5.3.

f.  Service and filing of motion papers. NY R USDCTS&ED Civ Rule 6.1.

g.  Orders on motions. NY R USDCTS&ED Civ Rule 6.2.

h.  Computation of time. NY R USDCTS&ED Civ Rule 6.4.

i.  Motion papers. NY R USDCTS&ED Civ Rule 7.1.

j.  Disclosure statement. NY R USDCTS&ED Civ Rule 7.1.1.

k.  Authorities to be provided to pro se litigants. NY R USDCTS&ED Civ Rule 7.2.

l.  Form of pleadings, motions, and other papers. NY R USDCTS&ED Civ Rule 11.1.

m.  Mode of raising discovery and other non-dispositive pretrial disputes with the court (Eastern District only). NY R USDCTS&ED Civ Rule 37.3.

n.  Submission of orders, judgments and decrees. NY R USDCTS&ED Civ Rule 77.1.

o.  Court-annexed arbitration (Eastern District only). NY R USDCTS&ED Civ Rule 83.7.

p.  Court-annexed mediation (Eastern District only). NY R USDCTS&ED Civ Rule 83.8.

q.  Electronic case filing. NY R USDCTED Order 2004-08.

r.  The August 2, 2004 amendment to the E-Government Act of 2002. NY R USDCTED Order 2004-09.

s.  Categories and classification of cases; Information on cases and parties. NY R USDCTED Div. Bus., Rule 50.1.

## J.  Miscellaneous

**NOTE: Individual judges' rules may apply. For available judge-level information, refer to:**

DISTRICT JUDGE CAROL BAGLEY AMON: NY R USDCTED Amon-Practices.

DISTRICT JUDGE JOAN M. AZRACK: NY R USDCTED Azrack-Practices.

DISTRICT JUDGE JOSEPH F. BIANCO: NY R USDCTED Bianco-Practices.

DISTRICT JUDGE FREDERIC BLOCK: NY R USDCTED Block-Practices.

DISTRICT JUDGE MARGO K. BRODIE: NY R USDCTED Brodie-Practices.

DISTRICT JUDGE PAMELA K. CHEN: NY R USDCTED Chen-Practices.

DISTRICT JUDGE BRIAN M. COGAN: NY R USDCTED Cogan-Practices; NY R USDCTED Cogan-Pretrial.

DISTRICT JUDGE LaSHANN DeARCY HALL: NY R USDCTED DeArcy Hall-Practices.

DISTRICT JUDGE RAYMOND J. DEARIE: NY R USDCTED Dearie-Practices.

DISTRICT JUDGE ANN M. DONNELLY: NY R USDCTED Donnelly-Practices.

DISTRICT JUDGE SANDRA J. FEUERSTEIN: NY R USDCTED Feuerstein-Practices; NY R USDCTED Feuerstein-Pretrial.

DISTRICT JUDGE NICHOLAS G. GARAUIFIS: NY R USDCTED Garaufis-Practices; NY R USDCTED Garaufis-Pretrial.

DISTRICT JUDGE NINA GERSHON: NY R USDCTED Gershon-Practices.

DISTRICT JUDGE I. LEO GLASSER: NY R USDCTED Glasser-Practices; NY R USDCTED Glasser-Crim.

DISTRICT JUDGE DENIS R. HURLEY: NY R USDCTED Hurley-Practices; [NY R USDCTED Hurley-Pro Cooperation Info, as added by NY ORDER 16-4188, effective July 22, 2016]; [NY R USDCTED Hurley-Pro Cooperation Info Stay, as added by NY ORDER 16-4188, effective July 22, 2016].

DISTRICT JUDGE DORA L. IRIZARRY: NY R USDCTED Irizarry-Practices; NY R USDCTED Irizarry-Pretrial; NY R USDCTED Irizarry-Crim.

DISTRICT JUDGE STERLING JOHNSON, JR.: NY R USDCTED Johnson-Practices.

DISTRICT JUDGE EDWARD R. KORMAN: NY R USDCTED Korman-Practices; NY R USDCTED Korman-Pretrial.

DISTRICT JUDGE WILLIAM F. KUNTZ: NY R USDCTED Kuntz-Practices.

DISTRICT JUDGE KIYO A. MATSUMOTO: NY R USDCTED Matsumoto-Practices.

DISTRICT JUDGE ROSLYNN R. MAUSKOPF: NY R USDCTED Mauskopf-Practices; NY R USDCTED Mauskopf-Recusal.

DISTRICT JUDGE THOMAS C. PLATT: NY R USDCTED Platt-Practices.

DISTRICT JUDGE ALLYNE R. ROSS: NY R USDCTED Ross-Practices.

DISTRICT JUDGE JOANNA SEYBERT: NY R USDCTED Seybert-Practices.

DISTRICT JUDGE ARTHUR D. SPATT: NY R USDCTED Spatt-Practices.

DISTRICT JUDGE SANDRA L. TOWNES: NY R USDCTED Townes-Practices.

DISTRICT JUDGE ERIC N. VITALIANO: NY R USDCTED Vitaliano-Practices.

DISTRICT JUDGE JACK B. WEINSTEIN: NY R USDCTED Weinstein-Practices.

DISTRICT JUDGE LEONARD D. WEXLER: NY R USDCTED Wexler-Practices; NY R USDCTED Wexler-Rules.

MAGISTRATE JUDGE LOIS BLOOM: NY R USDCTED Bloom-Practices.

MAGISTRATE JUDGE GARY R. BROWN: NY R USDCTED Brown-Practices.

MAGISTRATE JUDGE MARILYN D. GO: NY R USDCTED Go-Practices.

MAGISTRATE JUDGE STEVEN M. GOLD: NY R USDCTED Gold-Practices.

MAGISTRATE JUDGE PEGGY KUO: NY R USDCTED Kuo-Practices; NY R USDCTED Kuo-Scheduling Order.

MAGISTRATE JUDGE ROBERT M. LEVY: NY R USDCTED Levy-Practices.

MAGISTRATE JUDGE ARLENE R. LINDSAY: NY R USDCTED Lindsay-Practices.

MAGISTRATE JUDGE STEVEN I. LOCKE: NY R USDCTED Locke-Practices.

MAGISTRATE JUDGE ROANNE L. MANN: NY R USDCTED Mann-Practices.

MAGISTRATE JUDGE JAMES ORENSTEIN: NY R USDCTED Jorenstein--Practices.

MAGISTRATE JUDGE VIKTOR V. POHORELSKY: NY R USDCTED Pohorelsky-Practices.

MAGISTRATE JUDGE CHERYL L. POLLAK: NY R USDCTED Pollak-Practices; NY R USDCTED Pollak-Pretrial.

MAGISTRATE JUDGE RAMON E. REYES, JR.: NY R USDCTED Reyes-Practices.

MAGISTRATE JUDGE VERA M. SCANLON: NY R USDCTED Scanlon-Practices.

MAGISTRATE JUDGE ANNE Y. SHIELDS: NY R USDCTED Shields-Practices.

MAGISTRATE JUDGE STEVEN L. TISCIONE: NY R USDCTED Tiscione-Practices.

MAGISTRATE JUDGE A. KATHLEEN TOMILINSON: NY R USDCTED Tomlinson-Practices.

## Motions, Oppositions and Replies
## Motion to Dismiss for Failure to State a Claim

### Document Last Updated September 2016

**A. Checklist**

(I) ❑ Matters to be considered by moving party

    (a) ❑ Required documents

        (1) ❑ Notice of motion and motion

        (2) ❑ Memorandum of law

        (3) ❑ Certificate of service

    (b) ❑ Supplemental documents

        (1) ❑ Pleading

        (2) ❑ Notice of constitutional question

        (3) ❑ Nongovernmental corporate disclosure statement

        (4) ❑ Notice to pro se litigant who opposes a FRCP 12 motion supported by matters outside the pleadings

        (5) ❑ Copies of authorities

    (c) ❑ Timing

        (1) ❑ Failure to state a claim upon which relief can be granted may be raised in any pleading allowed or ordered under FRCP 7(a); every defense to a claim for relief in any pleading must be asserted in the responsive pleading if one is required

        (2) ❑ A motion asserting any of the defenses in FRCP 12(b) must be made before pleading if a responsive pleading is allowed

        (3) ❑ Failure to state a claim upon which relief can be granted may be raised by a motion under FRCP 12(c); after the pleadings are closed—but early enough not to delay trial—a party may move for judgment on the pleadings

        (4) ❑ Failure to state a claim upon which relief can be granted may be raised at trial; if a pleading sets out a claim for relief that does not require a responsive pleading, an opposing party may assert at trial any defense to that claim

        (5) ❑ A written motion and notice of the hearing must be served at least fourteen (14) days before the time specified for the hearing, with the following exceptions: (i) when the motion may be heard ex parte; (ii) when the Federal Rules of Civil Procedure set a different time; or (iii) when a court order—which a party may, for good cause, apply for ex parte—sets a different time

        (6) ❑ Any affidavit supporting a motion must be served with the motion

(II) ❑ Matters to be considered by opposing party

    (a) ❑ Required documents

        (1) ❑ Answering memorandum of law

        (2) ❑ Certificate of service

    (b) ❑ Supplemental documents

        (1) ❑ Pleading

        (2) ❑ Notice of constitutional question

        (3) ❑ Copies of authorities

(c) ❑ Timing

    (1) ❑ Any opposing affidavits and answering memoranda shall be served within fourteen (14) days after service of the moving papers

    (2) ❑ Except as FRCP 59(c) provides otherwise, any opposing affidavit must be served at least seven (7) days before the hearing, unless the court permits service at another time

## B. Timing

1. *Motion to dismiss for failure to state a claim*

    a. *In a pleading under FRCP 7(a).* Failure to state a claim upon which relief can be granted may be raised in any pleading allowed or ordered under FRCP 7(a). FRCP 12(h)(2)(A).

        i. *In a responsive pleading.* Every defense to a claim for relief in any pleading must be asserted in the responsive pleading if one is required. FRCP 12(b).

    b. *By motion.* A motion asserting any of the defenses in FRCP 12(b) must be made before pleading if a responsive pleading is allowed. FRCP 12(b). Although FRCP 12(b) encourages the responsive pleader to file a motion to dismiss before filing the answer, nothing in FRCP 12 prohibits the filing of a motion to dismiss with the answer. An untimely motion to dismiss may be considered if the defense asserted in the motion was previously raised in the responsive pleading. FEDPROC § 62:427.

    c. *By motion under FRCP 12(c).* Failure to state a claim upon which relief can be granted may be raised by a motion under FRCP 12(c). FRCP 12(h)(2)(B). After the pleadings are closed—but early enough not to delay trial—a party may move for judgment on the pleadings. FRCP 12(c).

    d. *At trial.* Failure to state a claim upon which relief can be granted may be raised at trial. FRCP 12(h)(2)(C). If a pleading sets out a claim for relief that does not require a responsive pleading, an opposing party may assert at trial any defense to that claim. FRCP 12(b).

2. *Timing of motions, generally*

    a. *Motion and notice of hearing.* Except for letter-motions as permitted by NY R USDCTS&ED Civ Rule 7.1(d), and unless otherwise provided by statute or rule or by the Court in a Judge's Individual Practice or in a direction in a particular case, upon any motion, the notice of motion, supporting affidavits, and memoranda shall be served and filed as follows: on all civil motions, petitions, and applications, other than those described in NY R USDCTS&ED Civ Rule 6.1(a), and other than petitions for writs of habeas corpus, the notice of motion, supporting affidavits, and memoranda of law shall be served by the moving party on all other parties that have appeared in the action. NY R USDCTS&ED Civ Rule 6.1(b)(1). A written motion and notice of the hearing must be served at least fourteen (14) days before the time specified for the hearing, with the following exceptions:

        i. When the motion may be heard ex parte;

        ii. When the Federal Rules of Civil Procedure set a different time; or

        iii. When a court order—which a party may, for good cause, apply for ex parte—sets a different time. FRCP 6(c)(1).

    b. *Supporting affidavit.* Any affidavit supporting a motion must be served with the motion. FRCP 6(c)(2).

3. *Timing of opposing papers.* Except for letter-motions as permitted by NY R USDCTS&ED Civ Rule 7.1(d), and unless otherwise provided by statute or rule or by the Court in a Judge's Individual Practice or in a direction in a particular case, upon any motion, the notice of motion, supporting affidavits, and memoranda shall be served and filed as follows: on all civil motions, petitions, and applications, other than those described in NY R USDCTS&ED Civ Rule 6.1(a), and other than petitions for writs of habeas corpus, any opposing affidavits and answering memoranda shall be served within fourteen (14) days after service of the moving papers. NY R USDCTS&ED Civ Rule 6.1(b)(2).

    a. *Opposing affidavit.* Except as FRCP 59(c) provides otherwise, any opposing affidavit must be served at least seven (7) days before the hearing, unless the court permits service at another time. FRCP 6(c)(2).

4. *Timing of reply papers.* Where the respondent files an answering affidavit setting up a new matter, the moving party ordinarily is allowed a reasonable time to file a reply affidavit since failure to deny the new matter by affidavit may operate as an admission of its truth. AMJUR MOTIONS § 25.

   a. *Reply affidavits and reply memoranda of law.* Except for letter-motions as permitted by NY R USDCTS&ED Civ Rule 7.1(d), and unless otherwise provided by statute or rule or by the Court in a Judge's Individual Practice or in a direction in a particular case, upon any motion, the notice of motion, supporting affidavits, and memoranda shall be served and filed as follows: on all civil motions, petitions, and applications, other than those described in NY R USDCTS&ED Civ Rule 6.1(a), and other than petitions for writs of habeas corpus, any reply affidavits and memoranda of law shall be served within seven (7) days after service of the answering papers. NY R USDCTS&ED Civ Rule 6.1(b)(3).

5. *Effect of a FRCP 12 motion on the time to serve a responsive pleading.* Unless the court sets a different time, serving a motion under FRCP 12 alters the periods in FRCP 12(a) as follows:

   a. If the court denies the motion or postpones its disposition until trial, the responsive pleading must be served within fourteen (14) days after notice of the court's action; or

   b. If the court grants a motion for a more definite statement, the responsive pleading must be served within fourteen (14) days after the more definite statement is served. FRCP 12(a)(4).

6. *Computation of time*

   a. *Computing time.* FRCP 6 applies in computing any time period specified in the Federal Rules of Civil Procedure, in any local rule or court order, or in any statute that does not specify a method of computing time. FRCP 6(a). In computing any period of time prescribed or allowed by the Local Civil Rules of the United States District Courts for the Southern and Eastern Districts of New York or the Local Admiralty and Maritime Rules, the provisions of FRCP 6 shall apply unless otherwise stated. NY R USDCTS&ED Civ Rule 6.4.

      i. *Period stated in days or a longer unit.* In computing periods of days, refer to FRCP 6 and NY R USDCTS&ED Civ Rule 6.4. NY R USDCTS&ED Civ Rule 6.1(b). When the period is stated in days or a longer unit of time:

         • Exclude the day of the event that triggers the period;

         • Count every day, including intermediate Saturdays, Sundays, and legal holidays; and

         • Include the last day of the period, but if the last day is a Saturday, Sunday, or legal holiday, the period continues to run until the end of the next day that is not a Saturday, Sunday, or legal holiday. FRCP 6(a)(1). In the Local Civil Rules of the United States District Courts for the Southern and Eastern Districts of New York, as in the Federal Rules of Civil Procedure as amended effective December 1, 2009, Saturdays, Sundays, and legal holidays are no longer excluded in computing periods of time. If the last day of the period is a Saturday, Sunday, or legal holiday, the period continues to run until the end of the next day that is not a Saturday, Sunday, or legal holiday. NY R USDCTS&ED Civ Rule 6.4.

      ii. *Period stated in hours.* When the period is stated in hours:

         • Begin counting immediately on the occurrence of the event that triggers the period;

         • Count every hour, including hours during intermediate Saturdays, Sundays, and legal holidays; and

         • If the period would end on a Saturday, Sunday, or legal holiday, the period continues to run until the same time on the next day that is not a Saturday, Sunday, or legal holiday. FRCP 6(a)(2). In the Local Civil Rules of the United States District Courts for the Southern and Eastern Districts of New York, as in the Federal Rules of Civil Procedure as amended effective December 1, 2009, Saturdays, Sundays, and legal holidays are no longer excluded in computing periods of time. If the last day of the period is a Saturday, Sunday, or legal holiday, the period continues to run until the end of the next day that is not a Saturday, Sunday, or legal holiday. NY R USDCTS&ED Civ Rule 6.4.

    iii.  *Inaccessibility of the clerk's office.* Unless the court orders otherwise, if the clerk's office is inaccessible:

- On the last day for filing under FRCP 6(a)(1), then the time for filing is extended to the first accessible day that is not a Saturday, Sunday, or legal holiday; or

- During the last hour for filing under FRCP 6(a)(2), then the time for filing is extended to the same time on the first accessible day that is not a Saturday, Sunday, or legal holiday. FRCP 6(a)(3).

    iv.  *"Last day" defined.* Unless a different time is set by a statute, local rule, or court order, the last day ends:

- For electronic filing, at midnight in the court's time zone; and

- For filing by other means, when the clerk's office is scheduled to close. FRCP 6(a)(4).

    v.  *"Next day" defined.* The "next day" is determined by continuing to count forward when the period is measured after an event and backward when measured before an event. FRCP 6(a)(5).

    vi.  *"Legal holiday" defined.* "Legal holiday" means:

- The day set aside by statute for observing New Year's Day, Martin Luther King Jr.'s Birthday, Washington's Birthday, Memorial Day, Independence Day, Labor Day, Columbus Day, Veterans' Day, Thanksgiving Day, or Christmas Day;

- Any day declared a holiday by the President or Congress; and

- For periods that are measured after an event, any other day declared a holiday by the state where the district court is located. FRCP 6(a)(6).

  b.  *Extending time*

    i.  *In general.* When an act may or must be done within a specified time, the court may, for good cause, extend the time:

- With or without motion or notice if the court acts, or if a request is made, before the original time or its extension expires; or

- On motion made after the time has expired if the party failed to act because of excusable neglect. FRCP 6(b)(1).

    ii.  *Exceptions.* A court must not extend the time to act under FRCP 50(b), FRCP 50(d), FRCP 52(b), FRCP 59(b), FRCP 59(d), FRCP 59(e), and FRCP 60(b). FRCP 6(b)(2).

    iii.  Refer to the United States District Court for the Eastern District of New York KeyRules Motion for Continuance/Extension of Time document for more information on extending time.

  c.  *Additional time after certain kinds of service.* When a party may or must act within a specified time after service and service is made under FRCP 5(b)(2)(C), FRCP 5(b)(2)(D), FRCP 5(b)(2)(E), or FRCP 5(b)(2)(F), three (3) days are added after the period would otherwise expire under FRCP 6(a). FRCP 6(d). Overnight delivery service shall be deemed service by mail for purposes of FRCP 5 and FRCP 6. NY R USDCTS&ED Civ Rule 5.3.

7.  *Individual judge practices.* Refer to the Miscellaneous section of this document for information on individual judge practices on timing of documents.

## C. General Requirements

1.  *Motions, generally*

  a.  *Requirements.* A request for a court order must be made by motion. The motion must:

    i.  Be in writing unless made during a hearing or trial;

    ii.  State with particularity the grounds for seeking the order; and

    iii.  State the relief sought. FRCP 7(b)(1).

  b.  *Notice of motion.* A party interested in resisting the relief sought by a motion has a right to notice thereof, and an opportunity to be heard. AMJUR MOTIONS § 12.

    i.  In addition to statutory or court rule provisions requiring notice of a motion—the purpose of

such a notice requirement having been said to be to prevent a party from being prejudicially surprised by a motion—principles of natural justice dictate that an adverse party generally must be given notice that a motion will be presented to the court. AMJUR MOTIONS § 12.

ii. "Notice," in this regard, means reasonable notice, including a meaningful opportunity to prepare and to defend against allegations of a motion. AMJUR MOTIONS § 12.

c. *Writing requirement.* The writing requirement is intended to insure that the adverse parties are informed and have a record of both the motion's pendency and the grounds on which the movant seeks an order. FPP § 1191; Feldberg v. Quechee Lakes Corp., 463 F.3d 195 (2d Cir. 2006).

i. It is sufficient "if the motion is stated in a written notice of the hearing of the motion." FPP § 1191.

d. *Particularity requirement.* The particularity requirement insures that the opposing parties will have notice of their opponent's contentions. FEDPROC § 62:364; Goodman v. 1973 26 Foot Trojan Vessel, Arkansas Registration No. AR1439SN, 859 F.2d 71, 12 Fed.R.Serv.3d 645 (8th Cir. 1988). That requirement ensures that notice of the basis for the motion is provided to the court and to the opposing party so as to avoid prejudice, provide the opponent with a meaningful opportunity to respond, and provide the court with enough information to process the motion correctly. FEDPROC § 62:364; Andreas v. Volkswagen of America, Inc., 336 F.3d 789, 56 Fed.R.Serv.3d 6 (8th Cir. 2003).

i. Reasonable specification of the grounds for a motion is sufficient. However, where a movant fails to state even one ground for granting the motion in question, the movant has failed to meet the minimal standard of "reasonable specification." FEDPROC § 62:364; Martinez v. Trainor, 556 F.2d 818, 23 Fed.R.Serv.2d 403 (7th Cir. 1977).

ii. The court may excuse the failure to comply with the particularity requirement if it is inadvertent, and where no prejudice is shown by the opposing party. FEDPROC § 62:364.

e. *Ex parte orders or orders to show cause to bring on a motion.* No ex parte order, or order to show cause to bring on a motion, will be granted except upon a clear and specific showing by affidavit of good and sufficient reasons why a procedure other than by notice of motion is necessary, and stating whether a previous application for similar relief has been made. NY R USDCTS&ED Civ Rule 6.1(d).

f. *Letter-motions.* Applications for extensions or adjournments, applications for a pre-motion conference, and similar non-dispositive matters as permitted by the instructions regarding ECF published on the website of each respective Court and any pertinent Individual Judge's Practices, may be brought by letter-motion filed via ECF pursuant to NY R USDCTS&ED Civ Rule 5.2(b). NY R USDCTS&ED Civ Rule 7.1(d).

2. *Motion to dismiss for failure to state a claim.* A party may assert the defense of failure to state a claim upon which relief can be granted by motion. FRCP 12(b)(6). The motion under FRCP 12(b)(6) is available to test a claim for relief in any pleading, whether it be in the plaintiff's original complaint, a defendant's counterclaim, a defendant's cross-claim or counterclaim thereto, or a third-party claim or any other FRCP 14 claim. Most commonly, of course, a FRCP 12(b)(6) motion is directed against the plaintiff's complaint. FPP § 1356.

a. *Applicable standard.* The FRCP 12(b)(6) motion is used to test the sufficiency of the complaint. FEDPROC § 62:461; Petruska v. Gannon University, 462 F.3d 294, 212 Ed.Law.Rep. 598 (3d Cir. 2006). In this regard, the applicable standard is stated in FRCP 8(a)(2), which requires that a pleading setting forth a claim for relief contain a short and plain statement of the claim showing that the pleader is entitled to relief. Thus, a complaint must set forth sufficient information to suggest that there is some recognized legal theory upon which relief can be granted. FEDPROC § 62:461. Only when the plaintiff's complaint fails to meet this liberal pleading standard is it subject to dismissal under FRCP 12(b)(6). FPP § 1356.

i. In order to withstand a motion to dismiss filed under FRCP 12(b)(6) in response to claims understood to raise a high risk of abusive litigation, addressed by FRCP 9(b), a plaintiff must state factual allegations with greater particularity than that required by FRCP 8. FEDPROC § 62:470; Bell Atlantic Corp. v. Twombly, 550 U.S. 544, 127 S.Ct. 1955, 167 L.Ed.2d 929, 68 Fed.R.Serv.3d 661 (2007).

    ii.    FRCP 12(b)(6) motions are looked on with disfavor by the courts, and are granted sparingly and with care. FEDPROC § 62:464. Even if it is doubtful that the plaintiff would ultimately prevail, if the plaintiff colorably states facts which, if proven, would entitle him or her to relief, a motion to dismiss for failure to state a claim should not be granted. FEDPROC § 62:464.

b.    *Construction of allegations of complaint (or other pleading).* In considering a FRCP 12(b)(6) motion to dismiss, the complaint is liberally construed and is viewed in the light most favorable to the plaintiff. FEDPROC § 62:467; Bell Atlantic Corp. v. Twombly, 550 U.S. 544, 127 S.Ct. 1955, 167 L.Ed.2d 929, 68 Fed.R.Serv.3d 661 (2007).

    i.    On a motion to dismiss, a federal court presumes that general allegations embrace those specific facts that are necessary to support the claim. FEDPROC § 62:467; Steel Co. v. Citizens for a Better Environment, 523 U.S. 83, 118 S.Ct. 1003, 140 L.Ed.2d 210 (1998).

    ii.    In addition, the well-pleaded allegations of fact contained in the complaint and every inference fairly deducible therefrom are accepted as true for purposes of the motion, including facts alleged on information and belief. FEDPROC § 62:467; Bell Atlantic Corp. v. Twombly, 550 U.S. 544, 127 S.Ct. 1955, 167 L.Ed.2d 929, 68 Fed.R.Serv.3d 661 (2007); Tellabs, Inc. v. Makor Issues & Rights, Ltd., 551 U.S. 308, 127 S.Ct. 2499, 168 L.Ed.2d 179 (2007).

    iii.    However, the court will not accept as true the plaintiff's bare statements of opinions, conclusory allegations, and unwarranted inferences of fact. FEDPROC § 62:467; Leopoldo Fontanillas, Inc. v. Luis Ayala Colon Sucesores, Inc., 283 F.Supp.2d 579 (D.P.R. 2003); Hopkins v. Women's Div., General Bd. of Global Ministries, 238 F.Supp.2d 174 (D.D.C. 2002). Nor will the court accept as true facts which are legally impossible, facts which the court can take judicial notice of as being other than as alleged by the plaintiff, or facts which by the record or by a document attached to the complaint appear to be unfounded. FEDPROC § 62:467; Cohen v. U.S., 129 F.2d 733 (8th Cir. 1942); Henthorn v. Department of Navy, 29 F.3d 682, 29 Fed.R.Serv.3d 1007 (D.C. Cir. 1994).

c.    *Affirmative defenses.* With some exception, it is generally agreed that affirmative defenses can be raised by a FRCP 12(b)(6) motion to dismiss. FEDPROC § 62:471; McCready v. eBay, Inc., 453 F.3d 882 (7th Cir. 2006). However, in order for these defenses to be raised on a FRCP 12(b)(6) motion to dismiss, the complaint must clearly show on its face that the affirmative defense is applicable and bars the action. FEDPROC § 62:471; In re Colonial Mortgage Bankers Corp., 324 F.3d 12 (1st Cir. 2003). Thus, FRCP 12(b)(6) motions may be used to raise the affirmative defenses of: (1) statute of limitations; (2) statute of frauds; (3) res judicata; (4) collateral estoppel; (5) release; (6) waiver; (7) estoppel; (8) sovereign immunity; (9) illegality; and (10) contributory negligence. FEDPROC § 62:471.

d.    *Joining motions*

    i.    *Right to join.* A motion under FRCP 12 may be joined with any other motion allowed by FRCP 12. FRCP 12(g)(1).

    ii.    *Limitation on further motions.* Except as provided in FRCP 12(h)(2) or FRCP 12(h)(3), a party that makes a motion under FRCP 12 must not make another motion under FRCP 12 raising a defense or objection that was available to the party but omitted from its earlier motion. FRCP 12(g)(2).

e.    *Waiving and preserving certain defenses.* No defense or objection is waived by joining it with one or more other defenses or objections in a responsive pleading or in a motion. FRCP 12(b).

    i.    *When some are waived.* A party waives any defense listed in FRCP 12(b)(2) through FRCP 12(b)(5) by:

        •    Omitting it from a motion in the circumstances described in FRCP 12(g)(2); or

        •    Failing to either: (1) make it by motion under FRCP 12; or (2) include it in a responsive pleading or in an amendment allowed by FRCP 15(a)(1) as a matter of course. FRCP 12(h)(1).

    ii.   *When to raise others.* Failure to state a claim upon which relief can be granted, to join a person required by FRCP 19(b), or to state a legal defense to a claim may be raised:

- In any pleading allowed or ordered under FRCP 7(a);
- By a motion under FRCP 12(c); or
- At trial. FRCP 12(h)(2).

    iii.  *Lack of subject matter jurisdiction.* If the court determines at any time that it lacks subject-matter jurisdiction, the court must dismiss the action. FRCP 12(h)(3).

3. *Opposing papers.* The Federal Rules of Civil Procedure do not require any formal answer, return, or reply to a motion, except where the Federal Rules of Civil Procedure or local rules may require affidavits, memoranda, or other papers to be filed in opposition to a motion. Such papers are simply to apprise the court of such opposition and the grounds of that opposition. FEDPROC § 62:359. Except for letter-motions as permitted by NY R USDCTS&ED Civ Rule 7.1(d) or as otherwise permitted by the Court, all oppositions and replies with respect to motions shall comply with NY R USDCTS&ED Civ Rule 7.1(a)(2) and NY R USDCTS&ED Civ Rule 7.1(a)(3), and an opposing party who seeks relief that goes beyond the denial of the motion shall comply as well with NY R USDCTS&ED Civ Rule 7.1(a)(1). NY R USDCTS&ED Civ Rule 7.1(b).

    a.   *Effect of failure to respond to motion.* Although in the absence of statutory provision or court rule, a motion ordinarily does not require a written answer, when a party files a motion and the opposing party fails to respond, the court may construe such failure to respond as nonopposition to the motion or an admission that the motion was meritorious, may take the facts alleged in the motion as true—the rule in some jurisdictions being that the failure to respond to a fact set forth in a motion is deemed an admission—and may grant the motion if the relief requested appears to be justified. AMJUR MOTIONS § 28.

    b.   *Assent or no opposition not determinative.* However, a motion will not be granted automatically simply because an "assent" or a notation of "no opposition" has been filed; federal judges frequently deny motions that have been assented to when it is thought that justice so dictates. FPP § 1190.

    c.   *Responsive pleading inappropriate as response to motion.* An attempt to answer or oppose a motion with a responsive pleading usually is not appropriate. FPP § 1190.

4. *Reply papers.* A moving party may be required or permitted to prepare papers in addition to his original motion papers. AMJUR MOTIONS § 25. Papers answering or replying to opposing papers may be appropriate, in the interests of justice, where it appears there is a substantial reason for allowing a reply. Thus, a court may accept reply papers where a party demonstrates that the papers to which it seeks to file a reply raise new issues that are material to the disposition of the question before the court, or where the court determines, sua sponte, that it wishes further briefing of an issue raised in those papers and orders the submission of additional papers. FEDPROC § 62:360. Except for letter-motions as permitted by NY R USDCTS&ED Civ Rule 7.1(d) or as otherwise permitted by the Court, all oppositions and replies with respect to motions shall comply with NY R USDCTS&ED Civ Rule 7.1(a)(2) and NY R USDCTS&ED Civ Rule 7.1(a)(3). NY R USDCTS&ED Civ Rule 7.1(b).

    a.   *Function of reply papers.* The function of a reply affidavit is to answer the arguments made in opposition to the position taken by the movant and not to permit the movant to introduce new arguments in support of the motion. AMJUR MOTIONS § 25.

    b.   *Issues raised for the first time in a reply document.* However, the view has been followed in some jurisdictions, that as a matter of judicial economy, where there is no prejudice and where the issues could be raised simply by filing a motion to dismiss, the trial court has discretion to consider arguments raised for the first time in a reply memorandum, and that a trial court may grant a motion to strike issues raised for the first time in a reply memorandum. AMJUR MOTIONS § 26.

5. *Orders on motions.* A memorandum signed by the Court of the decision on a motion that does not finally determine all claims for relief, or an oral decision on such a motion, shall constitute the order unless the memorandum or oral decision directs the submission or settlement of an order in more extended form. The notation in the docket of a memorandum or of an oral decision that does not direct the submission or settlement of an order in more extended form shall constitute the entry of the order. Where an order in

more extended form is required to be submitted or settled, the notation in the docket of such order shall constitute the entry of the order. NY R USDCTS&ED Civ Rule 6.2.

6. *Related cases.* It shall be the continuing duty of each attorney appearing in any civil or criminal case to bring promptly to the attention of the Court all facts which said attorney believes are relevant to a determination that said case and one or more pending civil or criminal cases should be heard by the same Judge, in order to avoid unnecessary duplication of judicial effort. As soon as the attorney becomes aware of such relationship, said attorney shall notify the Judges to whom the cases have been assigned. NY R USDCTS&ED Civ Rule 1.6(a). If counsel fails to comply with NY R USDCTS&ED Civ Rule 1.6(a), the Court may assess reasonable costs directly against counsel whose action has obstructed the effective administration of the Court's business. NY R USDCTS&ED Civ Rule 1.6(b).

7. *Alternative dispute resolution (ADR)*

   a. *Court-annexed arbitration*

      i. *Civil cases eligible for compulsory arbitration.* The Clerk of Court shall, as to all cases filed after January 1, 1986, designate and process for compulsory arbitration all civil cases (excluding Social Security cases, tax matters, prisoners' civil rights cases and any action based on an alleged violation of a right secured by the Constitution of the United States or if jurisdiction is based in whole or in part on 28 U.S.C.A. § 1343) wherein money damages only are being sought in an amount not in excess of one hundred fifty thousand dollars ($150,000) exclusive of interest and costs. NY R USDCTS&ED Civ Rule 83.7(d)(1).

         • The parties may by written stipulation agree that the Clerk of Court shall designate and process for court-annexed arbitration any civil case that is not subject to compulsory arbitration in NY R USDCTS&ED Civ Rule 83.7. NY R USDCTS&ED Civ Rule 83.7(d)(2).

         • For purposes of NY R USDCTS&ED Civ Rule 83.7 only, in all civil cases damages shall be presumed to be not in excess of one hundred fifty thousand dollars ($150,000) exclusive of interest and costs, unless: (1) counsel for plaintiff, at the time of filing the complaint, or in the event of the removal of a case from state court or transfer of a case from another district to this Court, within thirty (30) days of the docketing of the case in this district, files a certification with the Court that the damages sought exceed one hundred fifty thousand dollars ($150,000), exclusive of interest and costs; or (2) counsel for a defendant, at the time of filing a counterclaim or cross-claim files a certification with the court that the damages sought by the counter-claim or cross-claim exceed one hundred fifty thousand dollars ($150,000) exclusive of interest and costs. NY R USDCTS&ED Civ Rule 83.7(d)(3).

      ii. *Exemption from arbitration.* The Court shall, sua sponte, or on motion of a party, exempt any case from arbitration in which the objectives of arbitration would not be realized (1) because the case involves complex or novel issues, (2) because legal issues predominate over factual issues, or (3) for other good cause. NY R USDCTS&ED Civ Rule 83.7(e)(2). For information on applying for an exemption, refer to NY R USDCTS&ED Civ Rule 83.7

      iii. *Referral to arbitration.* Cases not originally designated as eligible for compulsory arbitration, but which in the discretion of the assigned Judge, are later found to qualify, may be referred to arbitration. A U.S. District Judge or a U.S. Magistrate Judge, in cases that exceed the arbitration ceiling of one hundred fifty thousand dollars ($150,000) exclusive of interest and costs, in their discretion, may suggest that the parties should consider arbitration. If the parties are agreeable, an appropriate consent form signed by all parties or their representatives may be entered and filed in the case prior to scheduling an arbitration hearing. NY R USDCTS&ED Civ Rule 83.7(e)(3).

      iv. For more information on arbitration, refer to NY R USDCTS&ED Civ Rule 83.7.

   b. *Court-annexed mediation.* Mediation is a process in which parties and counsel agree to meet with a neutral mediator trained to assist them in settling disputes. The mediator improves communication across party lines, helps parties articulate their interests and understand those of the other party, probes the strengths and weaknesses of each party's legal positions, and identifies areas of agreement and helps generate options for a mutually agreeable resolution to the dispute. In all cases, mediation provides an opportunity to explore a wide range of potential solutions and to address interests that may be outside the scope of the stated controversy or which could not be addressed by judicial action. A hallmark of mediation is its capacity to expand traditional settlement discussions and broaden resolution options, often by exploring litigant needs and interests that may be formally independent of the legal issues in controversy. NY R USDCTS&ED Civ Rule 83.8(a).

    i. *Eligible cases.* Judges and Magistrate Judges may designate civil cases for inclusion in the mediation program, and when doing so shall prepare an order to that effect. Alternatively, and subject to the availability of qualified mediators, the parties may consent to participation in the mediation program by preparing and executing a stipulation signed by all parties to the action and so-ordered by the Court. NY R USDCTS&ED Civ Rule 83.8(b)(1).

    ii. For more information on mediation, refer to NY R USDCTS&ED Civ Rule 83.8.

8. *Individual judge practices.* Refer to the Miscellaneous section of this document for information on individual judge practices on general requirements for documents.

## D. Documents

1. *Documents for moving party*

  a. *Required documents*

    i. *Notice of motion and motion.* Except for letter-motions as permitted by NY R USDCTS&ED Civ Rule 7.1(d) or as otherwise permitted by the Court, all motions shall include the following motion papers: a notice of motion, or an order to show cause signed by the Court, which shall specify the applicable rules or statutes pursuant to which the motion is brought, and shall specify the relief sought by the motion. NY R USDCTS&ED Civ Rule 7.1(a)(1). Refer to the General Requirements section of this document for information on the notice of motion and motion.

    ii. *Memorandum of law.* Except for letter-motions as permitted by NY R USDCTS&ED Civ Rule 7.1(d) or as otherwise permitted by the Court, all motions shall include the following motion papers: a memorandum of law, setting forth the cases and other authorities relied upon in support of the motion, and divided, under appropriate headings, into as many parts as there are issues to be determined. NY R USDCTS&ED Civ Rule 7.1(a)(2).

    iii. *Certificate of service.* FRCP 5(d) requires that the person making service under FRCP 5 certify that service has been effected. FRCP 5(Advisory Committee Notes). Having such information on file may be useful for many purposes, including proof of service if an issue arises concerning the effectiveness of the service. FRCP 5(Advisory Committee Notes).

  b. *Supplemental documents*

    i. *Pleading.* As a general rule, the court may only consider the pleading which is attacked by a FRCP 12(b)(6) motion in determining its sufficiency. FEDPROC § 62:466; Armengau v. Cline, 7 Fed.Appx. 336 (6th Cir. 2001). The plaintiff is not entitled to discovery to obtain information relevant to the motion, and the court is not permitted to look at matters outside the record. FEDPROC § 62:466; Cooperativa de Ahorro y Credito Aguada v. Kidder, Peabody & Co., 993 F.2d 269, 37 Fed.R.Evid.Serv. 904, 25 Fed.R.Serv.3d 982 (1st Cir. 1993).

      • *Motion treated as one for summary judgment.* If, on a motion under FRCP 12(b)(6) or FRCP 12(c), matters outside the pleadings are presented to and not excluded by the court, the motion must be treated as one for summary judgment under FRCP 56. All parties must be given a reasonable opportunity to present all the material that is pertinent to the motion. FRCP 12(d).

      • *Documents attached to pleadings.* However, the court may consider documents which are attached to or submitted with the complaint, as well as legal arguments presented in memorandums or briefs and arguments of counsel. FEDPROC § 62:466; Tellabs, Inc. v. Makor Issues & Rights, Ltd., 551 U.S. 308, 127 S.Ct. 2499, 168 L.Ed.2d 179 (2007);

E.E.O.C. v. Ohio Edison Co., 7 F.3d 541 (6th Cir. 1993). Documents that the defendant attaches to the motion to dismiss are considered part of the pleadings if they are referred to in the plaintiff's complaint and are central to the claim, and as such may be considered by the court. FEDPROC § 62:466; Hoffman-Pugh v. Ramsey, 312 F.3d 1222 (11th Cir. 2002).

ii. *Notice of constitutional question.* A party that files a pleading, written motion, or other paper drawing into question the constitutionality of a federal or state statute must promptly:

- *File notice.* File a notice of constitutional question stating the question and identifying the paper that raises it, if: (1) a federal statute is questioned and the parties do not include the United States, one of its agencies, or one of its officers or employees in an official capacity; or (2) a state statute is questioned and the parties do not include the state, one of its agencies, or one of its officers or employees in an official capacity; and

- *Serve notice.* Serve the notice and paper on the Attorney General of the United States if a federal statute is questioned—or on the state attorney general if a state statute is questioned—either by certified or registered mail or by sending it to an electronic address designated by the attorney general for this purpose. FRCP 5.1(a).

- *No forfeiture.* A party's failure to file and serve the notice, or the court's failure to certify, does not forfeit a constitutional claim or defense that is otherwise timely asserted. FRCP 5.1(d).

iii. *Nongovernmental corporate disclosure statement.* To enable judges and magistrates to evaluate possible disqualification or recusal, counsel for a private (nongovernmental) party shall submit at the time of initial pleading a certificate identifying any corporate parent, subsidiaries, or affiliates of that party. NY R USDCTED Div. Bus., Rule 50.1(c).

- *Contents.* A nongovernmental corporate party must file two (2) copies of a disclosure statement that: (1) identifies any parent corporation and any publicly held corporation owning ten percent (10%) or more of its stock; or (2) states that there is no such corporation. FRCP 7.1(a).

- *Time to file; Supplemental filing.* A party must: (1) file the disclosure statement with its first appearance, pleading, petition, motion, response, or other request addressed to the court; and (2) promptly file a supplemental statement if any required information changes. FRCP 7.1(b). For purposes of FRCP 7.1(b)(2), "promptly" shall mean "within fourteen days," that is, parties are required to file a supplemental disclosure statement within fourteen (14) days of the time there is any change in the information required in a disclosure statement filed pursuant to those rules. NY R USDCTS&ED Civ Rule 7.1.1.

iv. *Notice to pro se litigant who opposes a FRCP 12 motion supported by matters outside the pleadings.* A represented party moving to dismiss or for judgment on the pleadings against a party proceeding pro se, who refers in support of the motion to matters outside the pleadings as described in FRCP 12(b) or FRCP 12(c), shall serve and file the notice in NY R USDCTS&ED Civ Rule 12.1 with the full text of FRCP 56 attached at the time the motion is served. If the Court rules that a motion to dismiss or for judgment on the pleadings will be treated as one for summary judgment pursuant to FRCP 56, and the movant has not previously served and filed the notice required by NY R USDCTS&ED Civ Rule 12.1, the movant shall amend the form notice to reflect that fact and shall serve and file the amended notice within fourteen (14) days of the Court's ruling. NY R USDCTS&ED Civ Rule 12.1. For the notice, refer to NY R USDCTS&ED Civ Rule 12.1.

v. *Copies of authorities.* In cases involving a pro se litigant, counsel shall, when serving a memorandum of law (or other submissions to the Court), provide the pro se litigant (but not other counsel or the Court) with copies of cases and other authorities cited therein that are unpublished or reported exclusively on computerized databases. Upon request, counsel shall provide the pro se litigant with copies of such unpublished cases and other authorities as are cited in a decision of the Court and were not previously cited by any party. NY R USDCTS&ED Civ Rule 7.2.

2. *Documents for opposing party*

    a. *Required documents*

        i. *Answering memorandum of law.* Except for letter-motions as permitted by NY R USDCTS&ED Civ Rule 7.1(d) or as otherwise permitted by the Court, all oppositions and replies with respect to motions shall comply with NY R USDCTS&ED Civ Rule 7.1(a)(2). NY R USDCTS&ED Civ Rule 7.1(b). Except for letter-motions as permitted by NY R USDCTS&ED Civ Rule 7.1(d) or as otherwise permitted by the Court, all motions shall include the following motion papers: a memorandum of law, setting forth the cases and other authorities relied upon in support of the motion, and divided, under appropriate headings, into as many parts as there are issues to be determined. NY R USDCTS&ED Civ Rule 7.1(a)(2). Refer to the General Requirements section of this document for information on the opposing papers.

        ii. *Certificate of service.* FRCP 5(d) requires that the person making service under FRCP 5 certify that service has been effected. FRCP 5(Advisory Committee Notes). Having such information on file may be useful for many purposes, including proof of service if an issue arises concerning the effectiveness of the service. FRCP 5(Advisory Committee Notes).

    b. *Supplemental documents*

        i. *Pleading.* As a general rule, the court may only consider the pleading which is attacked by a FRCP 12(b)(6) motion in determining its sufficiency. FEDPROC § 62:466; Armengau v. Cline, 7 Fed.Appx. 336 (6th Cir. 2001). The plaintiff is not entitled to discovery to obtain information relevant to the motion, and the court is not permitted to look at matters outside the record. FEDPROC § 62:466; Cooperativa de Ahorro y Credito Aguada v. Kidder, Peabody & Co., 993 F.2d 269, 37 Fed.R.Evid.Serv. 904, 25 Fed.R.Serv.3d 982 (1st Cir. 1993).

            • *Motion treated as one for summary judgment.* If, on a motion under FRCP 12(b)(6) or FRCP 12(c), matters outside the pleadings are presented to and not excluded by the court, the motion must be treated as one for summary judgment under FRCP 56. All parties must be given a reasonable opportunity to present all the material that is pertinent to the motion. FRCP 12(d).

            • *Documents attached to pleadings.* However, the court may consider documents which are attached to or submitted with the complaint, as well as legal arguments presented in memorandums or briefs and arguments of counsel. FEDPROC § 62:466; Tellabs, Inc. v. Makor Issues & Rights, Ltd., 551 U.S. 308, 127 S.Ct. 2499, 168 L.Ed.2d 179 (2007); E.E.O.C. v. Ohio Edison Co., 7 F.3d 541 (6th Cir. 1993). Documents that the defendant attaches to the motion to dismiss are considered part of the pleadings if they are referred to in the plaintiff's complaint and are central to the claim, and as such may be considered by the court. FEDPROC § 62:466; Hoffman-Pugh v. Ramsey, 312 F.3d 1222 (11th Cir. 2002).

        ii. *Notice of constitutional question.* A party that files a pleading, written motion, or other paper drawing into question the constitutionality of a federal or state statute must promptly:

            • *File notice.* File a notice of constitutional question stating the question and identifying the paper that raises it, if: (1) a federal statute is questioned and the parties do not include the United States, one of its agencies, or one of its officers or employees in an official capacity; or (2) a state statute is questioned and the parties do not include the state, one of its agencies, or one of its officers or employees in an official capacity; and

            • *Serve notice.* Serve the notice and paper on the Attorney General of the United States if a federal statute is questioned—or on the state attorney general if a state statute is questioned—either by certified or registered mail or by sending it to an electronic address designated by the attorney general for this purpose. FRCP 5.1(a).

            • *No forfeiture.* A party's failure to file and serve the notice, or the court's failure to certify, does not forfeit a constitutional claim or defense that is otherwise timely asserted. FRCP 5.1(d).

        iii. *Copies of authorities.* In cases involving a pro se litigant, counsel shall, when serving a memorandum of law (or other submissions to the Court), provide the pro se litigant (but not

other counsel or the Court) with copies of cases and other authorities cited therein that are unpublished or reported exclusively on computerized databases. Upon request, counsel shall provide the pro se litigant with copies of such unpublished cases and other authorities as are cited in a decision of the Court and were not previously cited by any party. NY R USDCTS&ED Civ Rule 7.2.

3. *Individual judge practices.* Refer to the Miscellaneous section of this document for information on individual judge practices on required documents.

## E. Format

1. *Form of documents.* The rules governing captions and other matters of form in pleadings apply to motions and other papers. FRCP 7(b)(2).

   a. *Paper.* Every pleading, written motion, and other paper must: be plainly written, typed, printed, or copied without erasures or interlineations which materially deface it. NY R USDCTS&ED Civ Rule 11.1(a)(1).

   b. *Typeface, margin, and spacing.* The typeface, margins, and spacing of all documents presented for filing must meet the following requirements:

      i. All text must be twelve (12) point type or larger, except for text in footnotes which may be ten (10) point type;

      ii. All documents must have at least one (1) inch margins on all sides;

      iii. All text must be double-spaced, except for headings, text in footnotes, or block quotations, which may be single-spaced. NY R USDCTS&ED Civ Rule 11.1(b).

   c. *Caption; Names of parties.* Every pleading must have a caption with the court's name, a title, a file number, and a FRCP 7(a) designation. The title of the complaint must name all the parties; the title of other pleadings, after naming the first party on each side, may refer generally to other parties. FRCP 10(a). Every pleading, written motion, and other paper must: bear the docket number and the initials of the District Judge and any Magistrate Judge before whom the action or proceeding is pending, NY R USDCTS&ED Civ Rule 11.1(a)(2).

   d. *Paragraphs; Separate statements.* A party must state its claims or defenses in numbered paragraphs, each limited as far as practicable to a single set of circumstances. A later pleading may refer by number to a paragraph in an earlier pleading. If doing so would promote clarity, each claim founded on a separate transaction or occurrence—and each defense other than a denial—must be stated in a separate count or defense. FRCP 10(b).

   e. *Adoption by reference; Exhibits.* A statement in a pleading may be adopted by reference elsewhere in the same pleading or in any other pleading or motion. A copy of a written instrument that is an exhibit to a pleading is a part of the pleading for all purposes. FRCP 10(c).

   f. *Acceptance by the clerk.* The clerk must not refuse to file a paper solely because it is not in the form prescribed by the Federal Rules of Civil Procedure or by a local rule or practice. FRCP 5(d)(4).

2. *Signing of pleadings, motions and other papers*

   a. *Signature.* Every pleading, written motion, and other paper must be signed by at least one attorney of record in the attorney's name—or by a party personally if the party is unrepresented. The paper must state the signer's address, e-mail address, and telephone number. FRCP 11(a). Every pleading, written motion, and other paper must: have the name of each person signing it clearly printed or typed directly below the signature. NY R USDCTS&ED Civ Rule 11.1(a)(3).

      i. *No verification or accompanying affidavit required for pleadings.* Unless a rule or statute specifically states otherwise, a pleading need not be verified or accompanied by an affidavit. FRCP 11(a).

      ii. *Unsigned papers.* The court must strike an unsigned paper unless the omission is promptly corrected after being called to the attorney's or party's attention. FRCP 11(a).

   b. *Representations to the court.* By presenting to the court a pleading, written motion, or other paper—whether by signing, filing, submitting, or later advocating it—an attorney or unrepresented party certifies that to the best of the person's knowledge, information, and belief, formed after an inquiry reasonable under the circumstances:

    i.   It is not being presented for any improper purpose, such as to harass, cause unnecessary delay, or needlessly increase the cost of litigation;

    ii.   The claims, defenses, and other legal contentions are warranted by existing law or by a nonfrivolous argument for extending, modifying, or reversing existing law or for establishing new law;

    iii.   The factual contentions have evidentiary support or, if specifically so identified, will likely have evidentiary support after a reasonable opportunity for further investigation or discovery; and

    iv.   The denials of factual contentions are warranted on the evidence or, if specifically so identified, are reasonably based on belief or a lack of information. FRCP 11(b).

  c.  *Sanctions.* If, after notice and a reasonable opportunity to respond, the court determines that FRCP 11(b) has been violated, the court may impose an appropriate sanction on any attorney, law firm, or party that violated FRCP 11(b) or is responsible for the violation. FRCP 11(c)(1). Refer to the United States District Court for the Eastern District of New York KeyRules Motion for Sanctions document for more information.

3.  *Privacy protection for filings made with the court*

  a.  *Redacted filings.* Unless the court orders otherwise, in an electronic or paper filing with the court that contains an individual's Social Security number, taxpayer-identification number, or birth date, the name of an individual known to be a minor, or a financial-account number, a party or nonparty making the filing may include only:

    i.   The last four (4) digits of the Social Security number and taxpayer-identification number;

    ii.   The year of the individual's birth;

    iii.   The minor's initials; and

    iv.   The last four (4) digits of the financial-account number. FRCP 5.2(a); NY R USDCTED Order 2004-09.

    v.   In addition, exercise caution when filing documents that contain the following:

- Personal identifying number, such as driver's license number;
- Medical records, treatment and diagnosis;
- Employment history;
- Individual financial information; and
- Proprietary or trade secret information. NY R USDCTED Order 2004-09.

  b.  *Exemptions from the redaction requirement.* The redaction requirement does not apply to the following:

    i.   A financial-account number that identifies the property allegedly subject to forfeiture in a forfeiture proceeding;

    ii.   The record of an administrative or agency proceeding;

    iii.   The official record of a state-court proceeding;

    iv.   The record of a court or tribunal, if that record was not subject to the redaction requirement when originally filed;

    v.   A filing covered by FRCP 5.2(c) or FRCP 5.2(d); and

    vi.   A pro se filing in an action brought under 28 U.S.C.A. § 2241, 28 U.S.C.A. § 2254, or 28 U.S.C.A. § 2255. FRCP 5.2(b).

  c.  *Limitations on remote access to electronic files; Social Security appeals and immigration cases.* Unless the court orders otherwise, in an action for benefits under the Social Security Act, and in an action or proceeding relating to an order of removal, to relief from removal, or to immigration benefits or detention, access to an electronic file is authorized as follows:

    i.   The parties and their attorneys may have remote electronic access to any part of the case file, including the administrative record;

    ii.   Any other person may have electronic access to the full record at the courthouse, but may have remote electronic access only to:

- The docket maintained by the court; and

- An opinion, order, judgment, or other disposition of the court, but not any other part of the case file or the administrative record. FRCP 5.2(c).

d.  *Filings made under seal.* The court may order that a filing be made under seal without redaction. The court may later unseal the filing or order the person who made the filing to file a redacted version for the public record. FRCP 5.2(d).

e.  *Protective orders.* For good cause, the court may by order in a case:

    i.   Require redaction of additional information; or

    ii.   Limit or prohibit a nonparty's remote electronic access to a document filed with the court. FRCP 5.2(e).

f.  *Option for additional unredacted filing under seal.* A person making a redacted filing may also file an unredacted copy under seal. The court must retain the unredacted copy as part of the record. FRCP 5.2(f); NY R USDCTED Order 2004-09. The unredacted version of the document or the reference list shall be retained by the court as part of the record. The court may, however, still require the party to file a redacted copy for the public file. NY R USDCTED Order 2004-09.

g.  *Option for filing a reference list.* A filing that contains redacted information may be filed together with a reference list that identifies each item of redacted information and specifies an appropriate identifier that uniquely corresponds to each item listed. The list must be filed under seal and may be amended as of right. Any reference in the case to a listed identifier will be construed to refer to the corresponding item of information. FRCP 5.2(g); NY R USDCTED Order 2004-09. The unredacted version of the document or the reference list shall be retained by the court as part of the record. The court may, however, still require the party to file a redacted copy for the public file. NY R USDCTED Order 2004-09.

h.  *Responsibility for redaction.* The responsibility for redacting these personal identifiers rests solely with counsel and the parties. The Clerk will not review each pleading for compliance with NY R USDCTED Order 2004-09. NY R USDCTED Order 2004-09.

    i.   Counsel is strongly urged to share this notice with all clients so that an informed decision about the inclusion of certain materials may be made. If a redacted document is filed, it is the sole responsibility of counsel and the parties to be sure that all pleadings comply with the rules of this court requiring redaction of personal data identifiers. The clerk will not review each pleading for redaction. NY R USDCTED Order 2004-09.

i.  *Waiver of protection of identifiers.* A person waives the protection of FRCP 5.2(a) as to the person's own information by filing it without redaction and not under seal. FRCP 5.2(h).

4.  *Individual judge practices.* Refer to the Miscellaneous section of this document for information on individual judge practices on formatting documents.

## F. Filing and Service Requirements

1.  *Filing requirements.* Any paper after the complaint that is required to be served—together with a certificate of service—must be filed within a reasonable time after service. FRCP 5(d)(1).

a.  *How filing is made; In general.* A paper is filed by delivering it:

    i.   To the clerk; or

    ii.   To a judge who agrees to accept it for filing, and who must then note the filing date on the paper and promptly send it to the clerk. FRCP 5(d)(2).

b. *Night depository.* A night depository with an automatic date stamp shall be maintained. . .by the Clerk of the Eastern District in the Brooklyn Courthouse. After regular business hours, papers for the District Court only may be deposited in the night depository. Such papers will be considered as having been filed in the District Court as of the date stamped thereon, which shall be deemed presumptively correct. NY R USDCTS&ED Civ Rule 1.2.

c. *Electronic filing*

 i. *Authorization of electronic filing program.* A court may, by local rule, allow papers to be filed, signed, or verified by electronic means that are consistent with any technical standards established by the Judicial Conference of the United States. A local rule may require electronic filing only if reasonable exceptions are allowed. A paper filed electronically in compliance with a local rule is a written paper for purposes of the Federal Rules of Civil Procedure. FRCP 5(d)(3).

- Parties serving and filing papers shall follow the instructions regarding Electronic Case Filing (ECF) published on the website of each respective Court. A paper served and filed by electronic means in accordance with such instructions is, for purposes of FRCP 5, served and filed in compliance with the Local Civil Rules of the Southern and Eastern Districts of New York. NY R USDCTS&ED Civ Rule 5.2(a). Parties have an obligation to review the Court's actual order, decree, or judgment (on ECF), which controls, and should not rely on the description on the docket or in the ECF Notice of Electronic Filing (NEF). NY R USDCTS&ED Civ Rule 5.2(c).

 ii. *Mandatory electronic filing.* Beginning on August 2, 2004, electronic case filing will be mandatory for all civil cases other than pro se cases. NY R USDCTED Order 2004-08.

- *Letter-motions and letters addressed to the court.* Subject to the instructions regarding ECF published on the website of each respective Court and any pertinent Individual Judge's Practices, letter-motions permitted by NY R USDCTS&ED Civ Rule 7.1(d) and letters addressed to the Court (but not letters between the parties) may be filed via ECF. NY R USDCTS&ED Civ Rule 5.2(b).

- *Proposed orders, judgments and decrees.* Proposed orders, judgments and decrees shall be presented as directed by the ECF rules published on the website of each respective Court. NY R USDCTS&ED Civ Rule 77.1. For more information, refer to NY R USDCTS&ED Civ Rule 77.1.

- *Request for exemption.* Requests by attorneys for an exemption to the mandatory policy will be considered for good cause hardship reasons only, and will be reviewed on an individual basis by the assigned United States Magistrate Judge. The Clerk's Office provides an electronic filing training program to assist attorneys filing electronically. Before seeking a hardship exemption, attorneys are advised to participate in the training program or otherwise seek the assistance of the Clerk's Office. NY R USDCTED Order 2004-08.

 iii. For more information on electronic filing, refer to the court's website.

2. *Service requirements*

a. *Service; When required*

 i. *In general.* Unless the Federal Rules of Civil Procedure provide otherwise, each of the following papers must be served on every party:

- An order stating that service is required;

- A pleading filed after the original complaint, unless the court orders otherwise under FRCP 5(c) because there are numerous defendants;

- A discovery paper required to be served on a party, unless the court orders otherwise;

- A written motion, except one that may be heard ex parte; and

- A written notice, appearance, demand, or offer of judgment, or any similar paper. FRCP 5(a)(1).

    ii.   *If a party fails to appear.* No service is required on a party who is in default for failing to appear. But a pleading that asserts a new claim for relief against such a party must be served on that party under FRCP 4. FRCP 5(a)(2).

    iii.  *Seizing property.* If an action is begun by seizing property and no person is or need be named as a defendant, any service required before the filing of an appearance, answer, or claim must be made on the person who had custody or possession of the property when it was seized. FRCP 5(a)(3).

b.  *Service; How made*

    i.   *Serving an attorney.* If a party is represented by an attorney, service under FRCP 5 must be made on the attorney unless the court orders service on the party. FRCP 5(b)(1).

    ii.  *Service in general.* A paper is served under FRCP 5 by:

- Handing it to the person;

- Leaving it: (1) at the person's office with a clerk or other person in charge or, if no one is in charge, in a conspicuous place in the office; or (2) if the person has no office or the office is closed, at the person's dwelling or usual place of abode with someone of suitable age and discretion who resides there;

- Mailing it to the person's last known address—in which event service is complete upon mailing;

- Leaving it with the court clerk if the person has no known address;

- Sending it by electronic means if the person consented in writing—in which event service is complete upon transmission, but is not effective if the serving party learns that it did not reach the person to be served; or

- Delivering it by any other means that the person consented to in writing—in which event service is complete when the person making service delivers it to the agency designated to make delivery. FRCP 5(b)(2).

    iii.  *Service by overnight delivery.* Service upon an attorney may be made by overnight delivery service. "Overnight delivery service" means any delivery service which regularly accepts items for overnight delivery. Overnight delivery service shall be deemed service by mail for purposes of FRCP 5 and FRCP 6. NY R USDCTS&ED Civ Rule 5.3.

    iv.  *Service by electronic means.* Parties serving and filing papers shall follow the instructions regarding Electronic Case Filing (ECF) published on the website of each respective Court. A paper served and filed by electronic means in accordance with such instructions is, for purposes of FRCP 5, served and filed in compliance with the Local Civil Rules of the United States District Courts for the Southern and Eastern Districts of New York. NY R USDCTS&ED Civ Rule 5.2(a). Parties have an obligation to review the Court's actual order, decree, or judgment (on ECF), which controls, and should not rely on the description on the docket or in the ECF Notice of Electronic Filing (NEF). NY R USDCTS&ED Civ Rule 5.2(c).

    v.   *Using court facilities.* If a local rule so authorizes, a party may use the court's transmission facilities to make service under FRCP 5(b)(2)(E). FRCP 5(b)(3).

c.  *Serving numerous defendants*

    i.   *In general.* If an action involves an unusually large number of defendants, the court may, on motion or on its own, order that:

- Defendants' pleadings and replies to them need not be served on other defendants;

- Any crossclaim, counterclaim, avoidance, or affirmative defense in those pleadings and replies to them will be treated as denied or avoided by all other parties; and

- Filing any such pleading and serving it on the plaintiff constitutes notice of the pleading to all parties. FRCP 5(c)(1).

    ii.  *Notifying parties.* A copy of every such order must be served on the parties as the court directs. FRCP 5(c)(2).

3. *Individual judge practices.* Refer to the Miscellaneous section of this document for information on individual judge practices on filing and serving documents.

## G. Hearings

1. *Hearings, generally*

   a. *Oral argument.* Due process does not require that oral argument be permitted on a motion and, except as otherwise provided by local rule, the district court has discretion to determine whether it will decide the motion on the papers or hear argument by counsel (and perhaps receive evidence). FPP § 1190; F.D.I.C. v. Deglau, 207 F.3d 153 (3d Cir. 2000). The parties and their attorneys shall only appear to argue the motion if so directed by the Court by order or by a Judge's Individual Practice. NY R USDCTS&ED Civ Rule 6.1(c).

   b. *Providing a regular schedule for oral hearings.* A court may establish regular times and places for oral hearings on motions. FRCP 78(a).

   c. *Providing for submission on briefs.* By rule or order, the court may provide for submitting and determining motions on briefs, without oral hearings. FRCP 78(b).

2. *Hearing on FRCP 12 defenses before trial.* If a party so moves, any defense listed in FRCP 12(b)(1) through FRCP 12(b)(7)—whether made in a pleading or by motion—and a motion under FRCP 12(c) must be heard and decided before trial unless the court orders a deferral until trial. FRCP 12(i).

3. *Individual judge practices.* Refer to the Miscellaneous section of this document for information on individual judge practices on hearings.

## H. Forms

### 1. Federal Motion to Dismiss for Failure to State a Claim Forms

   a. Notice in federal court; Motion for involuntary dismissal of action without prejudice; Complaint fails to state a claim on which relief can be granted. AMJUR PP DISMISSAL § 109.

   b. Motion; To dismiss; Failure to state a claim on which relief can be granted or facts sufficient to constitute cause of action. AMJUR PP LIMITATION § 100.

   c. Motion to dismiss; For failure to state a claim, improper service of process, improper venue, and want of jurisdiction. AMJUR PP MOTIONS § 42.

   d. Failure to state a claim upon which relief can be granted. 2C FEDFORMS § 11:80.

   e. Failure to state a claim upon which relief can be granted; Long version. 2C FEDFORMS § 11:81.

   f. Failure to state a claim upon which relief can be granted; Dismissal of certain allegations. 2C FEDFORMS § 11:82.

   g. Failure to state a claim upon which relief can be granted; With supporting reasons. 2C FEDFORMS § 11:83.

   h. Failure to state a claim upon which relief can be granted; With supporting reasons; Plaintiff not the real party in interest. 2C FEDFORMS § 11:85.

   i. Failure to state a claim upon which relief can be granted; With supporting reasons; Failure to show implied contract. 2C FEDFORMS § 11:86.

   j. Failure to state a claim upon which relief can be granted; With supporting reasons; Issue not arbitrable. 2C FEDFORMS § 11:87.

   k. Failure to state a claim upon which relief can be granted; With supporting affidavits. 2C FED-FORMS § 11:88.

   l. Failure to state a claim upon which relief can be granted; In alternative for summary judgment. 2C FEDFORMS § 11:89.

   m. Motion; To dismiss; Failure to state sufficient claim; By one of several defendants. FEDPROF § 1:923.

   n. Motion to dismiss; Failure to state sufficient claim; By third-party defendant. FEDPROF § 1:924.

   o. Motion to dismiss; Failure to state sufficient claim after successive attempts. FEDPROF § 1:925.

p.   Motion to dismiss; By individual defendants. FEDPROF § 1:926.

q.   Motion to dismiss; By state agency. FEDPROF § 1:927.

r.   Motion to dismiss counterclaim. FEDPROF § 1:931.

s.   Allegation; In motion to dismiss; Res judicata. FEDPROF § 1:933.

t.   Allegation; In motion to dismiss; Statute of limitations. FEDPROF § 1:935.

u.   Allegation; In motion to dismiss; Strict liability claim barred by statute. FEDPROF § 1:936.

v.   Allegation; In motion to dismiss; By United States; Absence of consent to suit. FEDPROF § 1:938.

w.   Reply; To motion to dismiss for failure to state sufficient claim. FEDPROF § 1:939.

x.   Motion to dismiss counterclaim. GOLDLTGFMS § 13:10.

y.   Motion to dismiss complaint; General form. GOLDLTGFMS § 20:24.

z.   Affidavit in support of motion to dismiss complaint. GOLDLTGFMS § 20:32.

# I.  Applicable Rules

1.  *Federal rules*

a.   Serving and filing pleadings and other papers. FRCP 5.

b.   Constitutional challenge to a statute; Notice, certification, and intervention. FRCP 5.1.

c.   Privacy protection for filings made with the court. FRCP 5.2.

d.   Computing and extending time; Time for motion papers. FRCP 6.

e.   Pleadings allowed; Form of motions and other papers. FRCP 7.

f.   Disclosure statement. FRCP 7.1.

g.   Form of pleadings. FRCP 10.

h.   Signing pleadings, motions, and other papers; Representations to the court; Sanctions. FRCP 11.

i.   Defenses and objections; When and how presented; Motion for judgment on the pleadings; Consolidating motions; Waiving defenses; Pretrial hearing. FRCP 12.

j.   Hearing motions; Submission on briefs. FRCP 78.

2.  *Local rules*

a.   Night depository. NY R USDCTS&ED Civ Rule 1.2.

b.   Duty of attorneys in related cases. NY R USDCTS&ED Civ Rule 1.6.

c.   Electronic service and filing of documents. NY R USDCTS&ED Civ Rule 5.2.

d.   Service by overnight delivery. NY R USDCTS&ED Civ Rule 5.3.

e.   Service and filing of motion papers. NY R USDCTS&ED Civ Rule 6.1.

f.   Orders on motions. NY R USDCTS&ED Civ Rule 6.2.

g.   Computation of time. NY R USDCTS&ED Civ Rule 6.4.

h.   Motion papers. NY R USDCTS&ED Civ Rule 7.1.

i.   Disclosure statement. NY R USDCTS&ED Civ Rule 7.1.1.

j.   Authorities to be provided to pro se litigants. NY R USDCTS&ED Civ Rule 7.2.

k.   Form of pleadings, motions, and other papers. NY R USDCTS&ED Civ Rule 11.1.

l.   Notice to pro se litigant who opposes a FRCP 12 motion supported by matters outside the pleadings. NY R USDCTS&ED Civ Rule 12.1.

m.   Submission of orders, judgments and decrees. NY R USDCTS&ED Civ Rule 77.1.

n.   Court-annexed arbitration (Eastern District only). NY R USDCTS&ED Civ Rule 83.7.

o.   Court-annexed mediation (Eastern District only). NY R USDCTS&ED Civ Rule 83.8.

    p.    Electronic case filing. NY R USDCTED Order 2004-08.

    q.    The August 2, 2004 amendment to the E-Government Act of 2002. NY R USDCTED Order 2004-09.

    r.    Categories and classification of cases; Information on cases and parties. NY R USDCTED Div. Bus., Rule 50.1.

## J.  Miscellaneous

**NOTE: Individual judges' rules may apply. For available judge-level information, refer to:**

DISTRICT JUDGE CAROL BAGLEY AMON: NY R USDCTED Amon-Practices.

DISTRICT JUDGE JOAN M. AZRACK: NY R USDCTED Azrack-Practices.

DISTRICT JUDGE JOSEPH F. BIANCO: NY R USDCTED Bianco-Practices.

DISTRICT JUDGE FREDERIC BLOCK: NY R USDCTED Block-Practices.

DISTRICT JUDGE MARGO K. BRODIE: NY R USDCTED Brodie-Practices.

DISTRICT JUDGE PAMELA K. CHEN: NY R USDCTED Chen-Practices.

DISTRICT JUDGE BRIAN M. COGAN: NY R USDCTED Cogan-Practices; NY R USDCTED Cogan-Pretrial.

DISTRICT JUDGE LaSHANN DeARCY HALL: NY R USDCTED DeArcy Hall-Practices.

DISTRICT JUDGE RAYMOND J. DEARIE: NY R USDCTED Dearie-Practices.

DISTRICT JUDGE ANN M. DONNELLY: NY R USDCTED Donnelly-Practices.

DISTRICT JUDGE SANDRA J. FEUERSTEIN: NY R USDCTED Feuerstein-Practices; NY R USDCTED Feuerstein-Pretrial.

DISTRICT JUDGE NICHOLAS G. GARAUIFIS: NY R USDCTED Garaufis-Practices; NY R USDCTED Garaufis-Pretrial.

DISTRICT JUDGE NINA GERSHON: NY R USDCTED Gershon-Practices.

DISTRICT JUDGE I. LEO GLASSER: NY R USDCTED Glasser-Practices; NY R USDCTED Glasser-Crim.

DISTRICT JUDGE DENIS R. HURLEY: NY R USDCTED Hurley-Practices; [NY R USDCTED Hurley-Pro Cooperation Info, as added by NY ORDER 16-4188, effective July 22, 2016]; [NY R USDCTED Hurley-Pro Cooperation Info Stay, as added by NY ORDER 16-4188, effective July 22, 2016].

DISTRICT JUDGE DORA L. IRIZARRY: NY R USDCTED Irizarry-Practices; NY R USDCTED Irizarry-Pretrial; NY R USDCTED Irizarry-Crim.

DISTRICT JUDGE STERLING JOHNSON, JR.: NY R USDCTED Johnson-Practices.

DISTRICT JUDGE EDWARD R. KORMAN: NY R USDCTED Korman-Practices; NY R USDCTED Korman-Pretrial.

DISTRICT JUDGE WILLIAM F. KUNTZ: NY R USDCTED Kuntz-Practices.

DISTRICT JUDGE KIYO A. MATSUMOTO: NY R USDCTED Matsumoto-Practices.

DISTRICT JUDGE ROSLYNN R. MAUSKOPF: NY R USDCTED Mauskopf-Practices; NY R USDCTED Mauskopf-Recusal.

DISTRICT JUDGE THOMAS C. PLATT: NY R USDCTED Platt-Practices.

DISTRICT JUDGE ALLYNE R. ROSS: NY R USDCTED Ross-Practices.

DISTRICT JUDGE JOANNA SEYBERT: NY R USDCTED Seybert-Practices.

DISTRICT JUDGE ARTHUR D. SPATT: NY R USDCTED Spatt-Practices.

DISTRICT JUDGE SANDRA L. TOWNES: NY R USDCTED Townes-Practices.

DISTRICT JUDGE ERIC N. VITALIANO: NY R USDCTED Vitaliano-Practices.

DISTRICT JUDGE JACK B. WEINSTEIN: NY R USDCTED Weinstein-Practices.

DISTRICT JUDGE LEONARD D. WEXLER: NY R USDCTED Wexler-Practices; NY R USDCTED Wexler-Rules.

MAGISTRATE JUDGE LOIS BLOOM: NY R USDCTED Bloom-Practices.

MAGISTRATE JUDGE GARY R. BROWN: NY R USDCTED Brown-Practices.

MAGISTRATE JUDGE MARILYN D. GO: NY R USDCTED Go-Practices.

MAGISTRATE JUDGE STEVEN M. GOLD: NY R USDCTED Gold-Practices.

MAGISTRATE JUDGE PEGGY KUO: NY R USDCTED Kuo-Practices; NY R USDCTED Kuo-Scheduling Order.

MAGISTRATE JUDGE ROBERT M. LEVY: NY R USDCTED Levy-Practices.

MAGISTRATE JUDGE ARLENE R. LINDSAY: NY R USDCTED Lindsay-Practices.

MAGISTRATE JUDGE STEVEN I. LOCKE: NY R USDCTED Locke-Practices.

MAGISTRATE JUDGE ROANNE L. MANN: NY R USDCTED Mann-Practices.

MAGISTRATE JUDGE JAMES ORENSTEIN: NY R USDCTED Jorenstein--Practices.

MAGISTRATE JUDGE VIKTOR V. POHORELSKY: NY R USDCTP Pohorelsky-Practices.

MAGISTRATE JUDGE CHERYL L. POLLAK: NY R USDCTED Pollak-Practices; NY R USDCTED Pollak-Pretrial.

MAGISTRATE JUDGE RAMON E. REYES, JR.: NY R USDCTED Reyes-Practices.

MAGISTRATE JUDGE VERA M. SCANLON: NY R USDCTED Scanlon-Practices.

MAGISTRATE JUDGE ANNE Y. SHIELDS: NY R USDCTED Shields-Practices.

MAGISTRATE JUDGE STEVEN L. TISCIONE: NY R USDCTED Tiscione-Practices.

MAGISTRATE JUDGE A. KATHLEEN TOMILINSON: NY R USDCTED Tomlinson-Practices.

# Motions, Oppositions and Replies
# Motion to Dismiss for Lack of Subject Matter Jurisdiction

### Document Last Updated September 2016

A. **Checklist**

(I) ❑ Matters to be considered by moving party

    (a) ❑ Required documents

        (1) ❑ Notice of motion and motion

        (2) ❑ Memorandum of law

        (3) ❑ Certificate of service

    (b) ❑ Supplemental documents

        (1) ❑ Supporting evidence

        (2) ❑ Notice of constitutional question

        (3) ❑ Nongovernmental corporate disclosure statement

        (4) ❑ Notice to pro se litigant who opposes a FRCP 12 motion supported by matters outside the pleadings

        (5) ❑ Copies of authorities

    (c) ❑ Timing

        (1) ❑ The defense of lack of subject matter jurisdiction can be raised at any time

        (2) ❑ Every defense to a claim for relief in any pleading must be asserted in the responsive pleading if one is required

        (3) ❑ A motion asserting any of the defenses in FRCP 12(b) must be made before pleading if a responsive pleading is allowed

(4) ❏ If a pleading sets out a claim for relief that does not require a responsive pleading, an opposing party may assert at trial any defense to that claim

(5) ❏ A written motion and notice of the hearing must be served at least fourteen (14) days before the time specified for the hearing, with the following exceptions: (i) when the motion may be heard ex parte; (ii) when the Federal Rules of Civil Procedure set a different time; or (iii) when a court order—which a party may, for good cause, apply for ex parte—sets a different time

(6) ❏ Any affidavit supporting a motion must be served with the motion

(II) ❏ Matters to be considered by opposing party

  (a) ❏ Required documents

    (1) ❏ Answering memorandum of law

    (2) ❏ Certificate of service

  (b) ❏ Supplemental documents

    (1) ❏ Supporting evidence

    (2) ❏ Notice of constitutional question

    (3) ❏ Copies of authorities

  (c) ❏ Timing

    (1) ❏ Any opposing affidavits and answering memoranda shall be served within fourteen (14) days after service of the moving papers

    (2) ❏ Except as FRCP 59(c) provides otherwise, any opposing affidavit must be served at least seven (7) days before the hearing, unless the court permits service at another time

## B. Timing

1. *Motion to dismiss for lack of subject matter jurisdiction.* [The defense of lack of subject matter jurisdiction] can be raised at any time. FEDPROC § 62:434.

  a. *In a responsive pleading.* Every defense to a claim for relief in any pleading must be asserted in the responsive pleading if one is required. FRCP 12(b).

  b. *By motion.* A motion asserting any of the defenses in FRCP 12(b) must be made before pleading if a responsive pleading is allowed. FRCP 12(b). Although FRCP 12(b) encourages the responsive pleader to file a motion to dismiss before filing the answer, nothing in FRCP 12 prohibits the filing of a motion to dismiss with the answer. An untimely motion to dismiss may be considered if the defense asserted in the motion was previously raised in the responsive pleading. FEDPROC § 62:427.

  c. *At trial.* If a pleading sets out a claim for relief that does not require a responsive pleading, an opposing party may assert at trial any defense to that claim. FRCP 12(b).

2. *Timing of motions, generally*

  a. *Motion and notice of hearing.* Except for letter-motions as permitted by NY R USDCTS&ED Civ Rule 7.1(d), and unless otherwise provided by statute or rule or by the Court in a Judge's Individual Practice or in a direction in a particular case, upon any motion, the notice of motion, supporting affidavits, and memoranda shall be served and filed as follows: on all civil motions, petitions, and applications, other than those described in NY R USDCTS&ED Civ Rule 6.1(a), and other than petitions for writs of habeas corpus, the notice of motion, supporting affidavits, and memoranda of law shall be served by the moving party on all other parties that have appeared in the action. NY R USDCTS&ED Civ Rule 6.1(b)(1). A written motion and notice of the hearing must be served at least fourteen (14) days before the time specified for the hearing, with the following exceptions:

    i. When the motion may be heard ex parte;

    ii. When the Federal Rules of Civil Procedure set a different time; or

    iii. When a court order—which a party may, for good cause, apply for ex parte—sets a different time. FRCP 6(c)(1).

    b.   *Supporting affidavit.* Any affidavit supporting a motion must be served with the motion. FRCP 6(c)(2).

3.   *Timing of opposing papers.* Except for letter-motions as permitted by NY R USDCTS&ED Civ Rule 7.1(d), and unless otherwise provided by statute or rule or by the Court in a Judge's Individual Practice or in a direction in a particular case, upon any motion, the notice of motion, supporting affidavits, and memoranda shall be served and filed as follows: on all civil motions, petitions, and applications, other than those described in NY R USDCTS&ED Civ Rule 6.1(a), and other than petitions for writs of habeas corpus, any opposing affidavits and answering memoranda shall be served within fourteen (14) days after service of the moving papers. NY R USDCTS&ED Civ Rule 6.1(b)(2).

    a.   *Opposing affidavit.* Except as FRCP 59(c) provides otherwise, any opposing affidavit must be served at least seven (7) days before the hearing, unless the court permits service at another time. FRCP 6(c)(2).

4.   *Timing of reply papers.* Where the respondent files an answering affidavit setting up a new matter, the moving party ordinarily is allowed a reasonable time to file a reply affidavit since failure to deny the new matter by affidavit may operate as an admission of its truth. AMJUR MOTIONS § 25.

    a.   *Reply affidavits and reply memoranda of law.* Except for letter-motions as permitted by NY R USDCTS&ED Civ Rule 7.1(d), and unless otherwise provided by statute or rule or by the Court in a Judge's Individual Practice or in a direction in a particular case, upon any motion, the notice of motion, supporting affidavits, and memoranda shall be served and filed as follows: on all civil motions, petitions, and applications, other than those described in NY R USDCTS&ED Civ Rule 6.1(a), and other than petitions for writs of habeas corpus, any reply affidavits and memoranda of law shall be served within seven (7) days after service of the answering papers. NY R USDCTS&ED Civ Rule 6.1(b)(3).

5.   *Effect of a FRCP 12 motion on the time to serve a responsive pleading.* Unless the court sets a different time, serving a motion under FRCP 12 alters the periods in FRCP 12(a) as follows:

    a.   If the court denies the motion or postpones its disposition until trial, the responsive pleading must be served within fourteen (14) days after notice of the court's action; or

    b.   If the court grants a motion for a more definite statement, the responsive pleading must be served within fourteen (14) days after the more definite statement is served. FRCP 12(a)(4).

6.   *Computation of time*

    a.   *Computing time.* FRCP 6 applies in computing any time period specified in the Federal Rules of Civil Procedure, in any local rule or court order, or in any statute that does not specify a method of computing time. FRCP 6(a). In computing any period of time prescribed or allowed by the Local Civil Rules of the United States District Courts for the Southern and Eastern Districts of New York or the Local Admiralty and Maritime Rules, the provisions of FRCP 6 shall apply unless otherwise stated. NY R USDCTS&ED Civ Rule 6.4.

       i.   *Period stated in days or a longer unit.* In computing periods of days, refer to FRCP 6 and NY R USDCTS&ED Civ Rule 6.4. NY R USDCTS&ED Civ Rule 6.1(b). When the period is stated in days or a longer unit of time:

          • Exclude the day of the event that triggers the period;

          • Count every day, including intermediate Saturdays, Sundays, and legal holidays; and

          • Include the last day of the period, but if the last day is a Saturday, Sunday, or legal holiday, the period continues to run until the end of the next day that is not a Saturday, Sunday, or legal holiday. FRCP 6(a)(1). In the Local Civil Rules of the United States District Courts for the Southern and Eastern Districts of New York, as in the Federal Rules of Civil Procedure as amended effective December 1, 2009, Saturdays, Sundays, and legal holidays are no longer excluded in computing periods of time. If the last day of the period is a Saturday, Sunday, or legal holiday, the period continues to run until the end of the next day that is not a Saturday, Sunday, or legal holiday. NY R USDCTS&ED Civ Rule 6.4.

       ii.   *Period stated in hours.* When the period is stated in hours:

          • Begin counting immediately on the occurrence of the event that triggers the period;

- Count every hour, including hours during intermediate Saturdays, Sundays, and legal holidays; and

- If the period would end on a Saturday, Sunday, or legal holiday, the period continues to run until the same time on the next day that is not a Saturday, Sunday, or legal holiday. FRCP 6(a)(2). In the Local Civil Rules of the United States District Courts for the Southern and Eastern Districts of New York, as in the Federal Rules of Civil Procedure as amended effective December 1, 2009, Saturdays, Sundays, and legal holidays are no longer excluded in computing periods of time. If the last day of the period is a Saturday, Sunday, or legal holiday, the period continues to run until the end of the next day that is not a Saturday, Sunday, or legal holiday. NY R USDCTS&ED Civ Rule 6.4.

iii. *Inaccessibility of the clerk's office.* Unless the court orders otherwise, if the clerk's office is inaccessible:

- On the last day for filing under FRCP 6(a)(1), then the time for filing is extended to the first accessible day that is not a Saturday, Sunday, or legal holiday; or

- During the last hour for filing under FRCP 6(a)(2), then the time for filing is extended to the same time on the first accessible day that is not a Saturday, Sunday, or legal holiday. FRCP 6(a)(3).

iv. *"Last day" defined.* Unless a different time is set by a statute, local rule, or court order, the last day ends:

- For electronic filing, at midnight in the court's time zone; and

- For filing by other means, when the clerk's office is scheduled to close. FRCP 6(a)(4).

v. *"Next day" defined.* The "next day" is determined by continuing to count forward when the period is measured after an event and backward when measured before an event. FRCP 6(a)(5).

vi. *"Legal holiday" defined.* "Legal holiday" means:

- The day set aside by statute for observing New Year's Day, Martin Luther King Jr.'s Birthday, Washington's Birthday, Memorial Day, Independence Day, Labor Day, Columbus Day, Veterans' Day, Thanksgiving Day, or Christmas Day;

- Any day declared a holiday by the President or Congress; and

- For periods that are measured after an event, any other day declared a holiday by the state where the district court is located. FRCP 6(a)(6).

b. *Extending time*

i. *In general.* When an act may or must be done within a specified time, the court may, for good cause, extend the time:

- With or without motion or notice if the court acts, or if a request is made, before the original time or its extension expires; or

- On motion made after the time has expired if the party failed to act because of excusable neglect. FRCP 6(b)(1).

ii. *Exceptions.* A court must not extend the time to act under FRCP 50(b), FRCP 50(d), FRCP 52(b), FRCP 59(b), FRCP 59(d), FRCP 59(e), and FRCP 60(b). FRCP 6(b)(2).

iii. Refer to the United States District Court for the Eastern District of New York KeyRules Motion for Continuance/Extension of Time document for more information on extending time.

c. *Additional time after certain kinds of service.* When a party may or must act within a specified time after service and service is made under FRCP 5(b)(2)(C), FRCP 5(b)(2)(D), FRCP 5(b)(2)(E), or FRCP 5(b)(2)(F), three (3) days are added after the period would otherwise expire under FRCP 6(a). FRCP 6(d). Overnight delivery service shall be deemed service by mail for purposes of FRCP 5 and FRCP 6. NY R USDCTS&ED Civ Rule 5.3.

7. *Individual judge practices.* Refer to the Miscellaneous section of this document for information on individual judge practices on timing of documents.

## C. General Requirements

1. *Motions, generally*

   a. *Requirements.* A request for a court order must be made by motion. The motion must:

      i. Be in writing unless made during a hearing or trial;

      ii. State with particularity the grounds for seeking the order; and

      iii. State the relief sought. FRCP 7(b)(1).

   b. *Notice of motion.* A party interested in resisting the relief sought by a motion has a right to notice thereof, and an opportunity to be heard. AMJUR MOTIONS § 12.

      i. In addition to statutory or court rule provisions requiring notice of a motion—the purpose of such a notice requirement having been said to be to prevent a party from being prejudicially surprised by a motion—principles of natural justice dictate that an adverse party generally must be given notice that a motion will be presented to the court. AMJUR MOTIONS § 12.

      ii. "Notice," in this regard, means reasonable notice, including a meaningful opportunity to prepare and to defend against allegations of a motion. AMJUR MOTIONS § 12.

   c. *Writing requirement.* The writing requirement is intended to insure that the adverse parties are informed and have a record of both the motion's pendency and the grounds on which the movant seeks an order. FPP § 1191; Feldberg v. Quechee Lakes Corp., 463 F.3d 195 (2d Cir. 2006).

      i. It is sufficient "if the motion is stated in a written notice of the hearing of the motion." FPP § 1191.

   d. *Particularity requirement.* The particularity requirement insures that the opposing parties will have notice of their opponent's contentions. FEDPROC § 62:364; Goodman v. 1973 26 Foot Trojan Vessel, Arkansas Registration No. AR1439SN, 859 F.2d 71, 12 Fed.R.Serv.3d 645 (8th Cir. 1988). That requirement ensures that notice of the basis for the motion is provided to the court and to the opposing party so as to avoid prejudice, provide the opponent with a meaningful opportunity to respond, and provide the court with enough information to process the motion correctly. FEDPROC § 62:364; Andreas v. Volkswagen of America, Inc., 336 F.3d 789, 56 Fed.R.Serv.3d 6 (8th Cir. 2003).

      i. Reasonable specification of the grounds for a motion is sufficient. However, where a movant fails to state even one ground for granting the motion in question, the movant has failed to meet the minimal standard of "reasonable specification." FEDPROC § 62:364; Martinez v. Trainor, 556 F.2d 818, 23 Fed.R.Serv.2d 403 (7th Cir. 1977).

      ii. The court may excuse the failure to comply with the particularity requirement if it is inadvertent, and where no prejudice is shown by the opposing party. FEDPROC § 62:364.

   e. *Ex parte orders or orders to show cause to bring on a motion.* No ex parte order, or order to show cause to bring on a motion, will be granted except upon a clear and specific showing by affidavit of good and sufficient reasons why a procedure other than by notice of motion is necessary, and stating whether a previous application for similar relief has been made. NY R USDCTS&ED Civ Rule 6.1(d).

   f. *Letter-motions.* Applications for extensions or adjournments, applications for a pre-motion conference, and similar non-dispositive matters as permitted by the instructions regarding ECF published on the website of each respective Court and any pertinent Individual Judge's Practices, may be brought by letter-motion filed via ECF pursuant to NY R USDCTS&ED Civ Rule 5.2(b). NY R USDCTS&ED Civ Rule 7.1(d).

2. *Motion to dismiss for lack of subject matter jurisdiction.* A party may assert the defense of lack of subject-matter jurisdiction by motion. FRCP 12(b)(1). The objection presented by a motion under FRCP 12(b)(1) challenging the court's subject matter jurisdiction is that the district judge has no authority or competence to hear and decide the case before it. A FRCP 12(b)(1) motion most typically is employed when the movant believes that the claim asserted by the plaintiff does not involve a federal question, and there is no diversity of citizenship between the parties or, in a diversity of citizenship case, the amount in controversy does not exceed the required jurisdictional amount. FPP § 1350.

   a. *Subject matter jurisdiction.* It always must be remembered that the federal courts are courts of limited jurisdiction and only can adjudicate those cases that fall within Article III of the Constitution (see U.S.C.A. Const. Art. III § 1, et seq.) and a congressional authorization enacted thereunder. FPP § 1350.

    i.  *Federal question.* The district courts shall have original jurisdiction of all civil actions arising under the Constitution, laws, or treaties of the United States. 28 U.S.C.A. § 1331.

    ii.  *Diversity of citizenship; Amount in controversy.* The district courts shall have original jurisdiction of all civil actions where the matter in controversy exceeds the sum or value of seventy-five thousand dollars ($75,000), exclusive of interest and costs, and is between:

- Citizens of different States;

- Citizens of a State and citizens or subjects of a foreign state, except that the district courts shall not have original jurisdiction under 28 U.S.C.A. § 1332 of an action between citizens of a State and citizens or subjects of a foreign state who are lawfully admitted for permanent residence in the United States and are domiciled in the same State;

- Citizens of different States and in which citizens or subjects of a foreign state are additional parties; and

- A foreign state, defined in 28 U.S.C.A. § 1603(a), as plaintiff and citizens of a State or of different States. 28 U.S.C.A. § 1332(a).

b.  *Types of FRCP 12(b)(1) motions.* There are two separate types of FRCP 12(b)(1) motions to dismiss for lack of subject matter jurisdiction: the "facial attack" and the "factual attack." FEDPROC § 62:440.

    i.  *Facial attack.* The facial attack is addressed to the sufficiency of the allegations of the complaint itself. FEDPROC § 62:440; Stalley ex rel. U.S. v. Orlando Regional Healthcare System, Inc., 524 F.3d 1229 (11th Cir. 2008). On such a motion, the court is merely required to determine whether the plaintiff has sufficiently alleged a basis of subject matter jurisdiction, and the factual allegations of the complaint are taken as true. FEDPROC § 62:440; U.S. ex rel. Atkinson v. PA. Shipbuilding Co., 473 F.3d 506 (3d Cir. 2007).

    ii.  *Factual attack.* The "factual attack," on the other hand, challenges the existence of subject matter jurisdiction in fact, irrespective of the pleadings, and matters outside the pleadings, such as testimony and affidavits, may be considered by the court. FEDPROC § 62:440; Kligman v. I.R.S., 272 Fed.Appx. 166 (3d Cir. 2008); Paper, Allied-Industrial, Chemical and Energy Workers Intern. Union v. Continental Carbon Co., 428 F.3d 1285 (10th Cir. 2005). The trial court in such a situation is free to weigh the evidence and satisfy itself as to the existence of its power to hear the case; therefore, no presumptive truthfulness attaches to the plaintiff's factual allegations. FEDPROC § 62:440; Land v. Dollar, 330 U.S. 731, 67 S.Ct. 1009, 91 L.Ed. 1209 (1947).

c.  *Burden.* With the limited exception of the question whether the amount in controversy requirement in diversity of citizenship cases has been satisfied, the extensive case law on the subject makes clear that the burden of proof on a FRCP 12(b)(1) motion is on the party asserting that subject matter jurisdiction exists, which, of course, typically is the plaintiff. FPP § 1350; Thomson v. Gaskill, 315 U.S. 442, 62 S.Ct. 673, 86 L.Ed. 951 (1942). A plaintiff meets the burden of establishing subject matter jurisdiction at the pleading stage by pleading sufficient allegations to show the proper basis for the court to assert subject matter jurisdiction over the action. 2 FEDFORMS § 7:6.

    i.  *Federal question.* If subject matter jurisdiction is based on the existence of a federal question, the pleader must show that he or she has alleged a claim for relief arising under federal law and that the claim is not frivolous. FPP § 1350; Baker v. Carr, 369 U.S. 186, 82 S.Ct. 691, 7 L.Ed.2d 663 (1962).

    ii.  *Diversity of citizenship.* If jurisdiction is based on diversity of citizenship, on the other hand, the pleader must show that real and complete diversity exists between all of the plaintiffs and all of the defendants, and also that the assertion that the claim exceeds the requisite jurisdictional amount in controversy is made in good faith. FPP § 1350; City of Indianapolis v. Chase Nat. Bank, 314 U.S. 63, 62 S.Ct. 15, 86 L.Ed. 47 (1941). Satisfying this last requirement is a relatively simple task, however, because the claim is deemed to be made in good faith so long as it is not clear to a legal certainty that the claimant could not recover a judgment exceeding the statutorily mandated jurisdictional amount, a matter on which the party challenging the district court's jurisdiction has the burden. FPP § 1350.

d. *Joining motions.* When the motion is based on more than one ground, the cases are legion stating that the district court should consider the FRCP 12(b)(1) challenge first because if it must dismiss the complaint for lack of subject matter jurisdiction, the accompanying defenses and objections become moot and do not need to be determined by the judge. FPP § 1350; Steel Co. v. Citizens for a Better Environment, 523 U.S. 83, 118 S.Ct. 1003, 140 L.Ed.2d 210 (1998). However, there are a number of decisions in which the court has decided one or more defenses in addition to the subject matter jurisdiction question or simply assumed the existence of jurisdiction and gone on to decide another matter. FPP § 1350.

    i. *Right to join.* A motion under FRCP 12 may be joined with any other motion allowed by FRCP 12. FRCP 12(g)(1).

    ii. *Limitation on further motions.* Except as provided in FRCP 12(h)(2) or FRCP 12(h)(3), a party that makes a motion under FRCP 12 must not make another motion under FRCP 12 raising a defense or objection that was available to the party but omitted from its earlier motion. FRCP 12(g)(2).

e. *Waiving and preserving certain defenses.* No defense or objection is waived by joining it with one or more other defenses or objections in a responsive pleading or in a motion. FRCP 12(b).

    i. *Waiver by consent.* The defendant may waive the right to obtain a dismissal prior to trial either by express consent to be sued in a certain district or by some conduct that will be construed as implying consent. FPP § 1352.

    ii. *When some are waived.* A party waives any defense listed in FRCP 12(b)(2) through FRCP 12(b)(5) by:

- Omitting it from a motion in the circumstances described in FRCP 12(g)(2); or

- Failing to either: (1) make it by motion under FRCP 12; or (2) include it in a responsive pleading or in an amendment allowed by FRCP 15(a)(1) as a matter of course. FRCP 12(h)(1).

    iii. *When to raise others.* Failure to state a claim upon which relief can be granted, to join a person required by FRCP 19(b), or to state a legal defense to a claim may be raised:

- In any pleading allowed or ordered under FRCP 7(a);

- By a motion under FRCP 12(c); or

- At trial. FRCP 12(h)(2).

    iv. *Lack of subject matter jurisdiction.* If the court determines at any time that it lacks subject-matter jurisdiction, the court must dismiss the action. FRCP 12(h)(3).

3. *Opposing papers.* The Federal Rules of Civil Procedure do not require any formal answer, return, or reply to a motion, except where the Federal Rules of Civil Procedure or local rules may require affidavits, memoranda, or other papers to be filed in opposition to a motion. Such papers are simply to apprise the court of such opposition and the grounds of that opposition. FEDPROC § 62:359. Except for letter-motions as permitted by NY R USDCTS&ED Civ Rule 7.1(d) or as otherwise permitted by the Court, all oppositions and replies with respect to motions shall comply with NY R USDCTS&ED Civ Rule 7.1(a)(2) and NY R USDCTS&ED Civ Rule 7.1(a)(3), and an opposing party who seeks relief that goes beyond the denial of the motion shall comply as well with NY R USDCTS&ED Civ Rule 7.1(a)(1). NY R USDCTS&ED Civ Rule 7.1(b).

a. *Effect of failure to respond to motion.* Although in the absence of statutory provision or court rule, a motion ordinarily does not require a written answer, when a party files a motion and the opposing party fails to respond, the court may construe such failure to respond as nonopposition to the motion or an admission that the motion was meritorious, may take the facts alleged in the motion as true—the rule in some jurisdictions being that the failure to respond to a fact set forth in a motion is deemed an admission—and may grant the motion if the relief requested appears to be justified. AMJUR MOTIONS § 28.

b.  *Assent or no opposition not determinative.* However, a motion will not be granted automatically simply because an "assent" or a notation of "no opposition" has been filed; federal judges frequently deny motions that have been assented to when it is thought that justice so dictates. FPP § 1190.

c.  *Responsive pleading inappropriate as response to motion.* An attempt to answer or oppose a motion with a responsive pleading usually is not appropriate. FPP § 1190.

4.  *Reply papers.* A moving party may be required or permitted to prepare papers in addition to his original motion papers. AMJUR MOTIONS § 25. Papers answering or replying to opposing papers may be appropriate, in the interests of justice, where it appears there is a substantial reason for allowing a reply. Thus, a court may accept reply papers where a party demonstrates that the papers to which it seeks to file a reply raise new issues that are material to the disposition of the question before the court, or where the court determines, sua sponte, that it wishes further briefing of an issue raised in those papers and orders the submission of additional papers. FEDPROC § 62:360. Except for letter-motions as permitted by NY R USDCTS&ED Civ Rule 7.1(d) or as otherwise permitted by the Court, all oppositions and replies with respect to motions shall comply with NY R USDCTS&ED Civ Rule 7.1(a)(2) and NY R USDCTS&ED Civ Rule 7.1(a)(3). NY R USDCTS&ED Civ Rule 7.1(b).

a.  *Function of reply papers.* The function of a reply affidavit is to answer the arguments made in opposition to the position taken by the movant and not to permit the movant to introduce new arguments in support of the motion. AMJUR MOTIONS § 25.

b.  *Issues raised for the first time in a reply document.* However, the view has been followed in some jurisdictions, that as a matter of judicial economy, where there is no prejudice and where the issues could be raised simply by filing a motion to dismiss, the trial court has discretion to consider arguments raised for the first time in a reply memorandum, and that a trial court may grant a motion to strike issues raised for the first time in a reply memorandum. AMJUR MOTIONS § 26.

5.  *Orders on motions.* A memorandum signed by the Court of the decision on a motion that does not finally determine all claims for relief, or an oral decision on such a motion, shall constitute the order unless the memorandum or oral decision directs the submission or settlement of an order in more extended form. The notation in the docket of a memorandum or of an oral decision that does not direct the submission or settlement of an order in more extended form shall constitute the entry of the order. Where an order in more extended form is required to be submitted or settled, the notation in the docket of such order shall constitute the entry of the order. NY R USDCTS&ED Civ Rule 6.2.

6.  *Related cases.* It shall be the continuing duty of each attorney appearing in any civil or criminal case to bring promptly to the attention of the Court all facts which said attorney believes are relevant to a determination that said case and one or more pending civil or criminal cases should be heard by the same Judge, in order to avoid unnecessary duplication of judicial effort. As soon as the attorney becomes aware of such relationship, said attorney shall notify the Judges to whom the cases have been assigned. NY R USDCTS&ED Civ Rule 1.6(a). If counsel fails to comply with NY R USDCTS&ED Civ Rule 1.6(a), the Court may assess reasonable costs directly against counsel whose action has obstructed the effective administration of the Court's business. NY R USDCTS&ED Civ Rule 1.6(b).

7.  *Alternative dispute resolution (ADR)*

a.  *Court-annexed arbitration*

i.  *Civil cases eligible for compulsory arbitration.* The Clerk of Court shall, as to all cases filed after January 1, 1986, designate and process for compulsory arbitration all civil cases (excluding Social Security cases, tax matters, prisoners' civil rights cases and any action based on an alleged violation of a right secured by the Constitution of the United States or if jurisdiction is based in whole or in part on 28 U.S.C.A. § 1343) wherein money damages only are being sought in an amount not in excess of one hundred fifty thousand dollars ($150,000) exclusive of interest and costs. NY R USDCTS&ED Civ Rule 83.7(d)(1).

• The parties may by written stipulation agree that the Clerk of Court shall designate and process for court-annexed arbitration any civil case that is not subject to compulsory arbitration in NY R USDCTS&ED Civ Rule 83.7. NY R USDCTS&ED Civ Rule 83.7(d)(2).

- For purposes of NY R USDCTS&ED Civ Rule 83.7 only, in all civil cases damages shall be presumed to be not in excess of one hundred fifty thousand dollars ($150,000) exclusive of interest and costs, unless: (1) counsel for plaintiff, at the time of filing the complaint, or in the event of the removal of a case from state court or transfer of a case from another district to this Court, within thirty (30) days of the docketing of the case in this district, files a certification with the Court that the damages sought exceed one hundred fifty thousand dollars ($150,000), exclusive of interest and costs; or (2) counsel for a defendant, at the time of filing a counterclaim or cross-claim files a certification with the court that the damages sought by the counter-claim or cross-claim exceed one hundred fifty thousand dollars ($150,000) exclusive of interest and costs. NY R USDCTS&ED Civ Rule 83.7(d)(3).

    ii. *Exemption from arbitration.* The Court shall, sua sponte, or on motion of a party, exempt any case from arbitration in which the objectives of arbitration would not be realized (1) because the case involves complex or novel issues, (2) because legal issues predominate over factual issues, or (3) for other good cause. NY R USDCTS&ED Civ Rule 83.7(e)(2). For information on applying for an exemption, refer to NY R USDCTS&ED Civ Rule 83.7

    iii. *Referral to arbitration.* Cases not originally designated as eligible for compulsory arbitration, but which in the discretion of the assigned Judge, are later found to qualify, may be referred to arbitration. A U.S. District Judge or a U.S. Magistrate Judge, in cases that exceed the arbitration ceiling of one hundred fifty thousand dollars ($150,000) exclusive of interest and costs, in their discretion, may suggest that the parties should consider arbitration. If the parties are agreeable, an appropriate consent form signed by all parties or their representatives may be entered and filed in the case prior to scheduling an arbitration hearing. NY R USDCTS&ED Civ Rule 83.7(e)(3).

    iv. For more information on arbitration, refer to NY R USDCTS&ED Civ Rule 83.7.

  b. *Court-annexed mediation.* Mediation is a process in which parties and counsel agree to meet with a neutral mediator trained to assist them in settling disputes. The mediator improves communication across party lines, helps parties articulate their interests and understand those of the other party, probes the strengths and weaknesses of each party's legal positions, and identifies areas of agreement and helps generate options for a mutually agreeable resolution to the dispute. In all cases, mediation provides an opportunity to explore a wide range of potential solutions and to address interests that may be outside the scope of the stated controversy or which could not be addressed by judicial action. A hallmark of mediation is its capacity to expand traditional settlement discussions and broaden resolution options, often by exploring litigant needs and interests that may be formally independent of the legal issues in controversy. NY R USDCTS&ED Civ Rule 83.8(a).

    i. *Eligible cases.* Judges and Magistrate Judges may designate civil cases for inclusion in the mediation program, and when doing so shall prepare an order to that effect. Alternatively, and subject to the availability of qualified mediators, the parties may consent to participation in the mediation program by preparing and executing a stipulation signed by all parties to the action and so-ordered by the Court. NY R USDCTS&ED Civ Rule 83.8(b)(1).

    ii. For more information on mediation, refer to NY R USDCTS&ED Civ Rule 83.8.

8. *Individual judge practices.* Refer to the Miscellaneous section of this document for information on individual judge practices on general requirements for documents.

## D. Documents

1. *Documents for moving party*

  a. *Required documents*

    i. *Notice of motion and motion.* Except for letter-motions as permitted by NY R USDCTS&ED Civ Rule 7.1(d) or as otherwise permitted by the Court, all motions shall include the following motion papers: a notice of motion, or an order to show cause signed by the Court, which shall specify the applicable rules or statutes pursuant to which the motion is brought, and shall specify the relief sought by the motion. NY R USDCTS&ED Civ Rule 7.1(a)(1). Refer to the General Requirements section of this document for information on the notice of motion and motion.

ii. *Memorandum of law.* Except for letter-motions as permitted by NY R USDCTS&ED Civ Rule 7.1(d) or as otherwise permitted by the Court, all motions shall include the following motion papers: a memorandum of law, setting forth the cases and other authorities relied upon in support of the motion, and divided, under appropriate headings, into as many parts as there are issues to be determined. NY R USDCTS&ED Civ Rule 7.1(a)(2).

iii. *Certificate of service.* FRCP 5(d) requires that the person making service under FRCP 5 certify that service has been effected. FRCP 5(Advisory Committee Notes). Having such information on file may be useful for many purposes, including proof of service if an issue arises concerning the effectiveness of the service. FRCP 5(Advisory Committee Notes).

b. *Supplemental documents*

i. *Supporting evidence.* When a motion relies on facts outside the record, the court may hear the matter on affidavits or may hear it wholly or partly on oral testimony or on depositions. FRCP 43(c). Except for letter-motions as permitted by NY R USDCTS&ED Civ Rule 7.1(d) or as otherwise permitted by the Court, all motions shall include the following motion papers: supporting affidavits and exhibits thereto containing any factual information and portions of the record necessary for the decision of the motion. NY R USDCTS&ED Civ Rule 7.1(a)(3).

- *Discovery materials.* A party seeking or opposing relief under FRCP 26 through FRCP 37 inclusive, or making or opposing any other motion or application, shall quote or attach only those portions of the depositions, interrogatories, requests for documents, requests for admissions, or other discovery or disclosure materials, together with the responses and objections thereto, that are the subject of the discovery motion or application, or that are cited in papers submitted in connection with any other motion or application. NY R USDCTS&ED Civ Rule 5.1.

ii. *Notice of constitutional question.* A party that files a pleading, written motion, or other paper drawing into question the constitutionality of a federal or state statute must promptly:

- *File notice.* File a notice of constitutional question stating the question and identifying the paper that raises it, if: (1) a federal statute is questioned and the parties do not include the United States, one of its agencies, or one of its officers or employees in an official capacity; or (2) a state statute is questioned and the parties do not include the state, one of its agencies, or one of its officers or employees in an official capacity; and

- *Serve notice.* Serve the notice and paper on the Attorney General of the United States if a federal statute is questioned—or on the state attorney general if a state statute is questioned—either by certified or registered mail or by sending it to an electronic address designated by the attorney general for this purpose. FRCP 5.1(a).

- *No forfeiture.* A party's failure to file and serve the notice, or the court's failure to certify, does not forfeit a constitutional claim or defense that is otherwise timely asserted. FRCP 5.1(d).

iii. *Nongovernmental corporate disclosure statement.* To enable judges and magistrates to evaluate possible disqualification or recusal, counsel for a private (nongovernmental) party shall submit at the time of initial pleading a certificate identifying any corporate parent, subsidiaries, or affiliates of that party. NY R USDCTED Div. Bus., Rule 50.1(c).

- *Contents.* A nongovernmental corporate party must file two (2) copies of a disclosure statement that: (1) identifies any parent corporation and any publicly held corporation owning ten percent (10%) or more of its stock; or (2) states that there is no such corporation. FRCP 7.1(a).

- *Time to file; Supplemental filing.* A party must: (1) file the disclosure statement with its first appearance, pleading, petition, motion, response, or other request addressed to the court;

and (2) promptly file a supplemental statement if any required information changes. FRCP 7.1(b). For purposes of FRCP 7.1(b)(2), "promptly" shall mean "within fourteen days," that is, parties are required to file a supplemental disclosure statement within fourteen (14) days of the time there is any change in the information required in a disclosure statement filed pursuant to those rules. NY R USDCTS&ED Civ Rule 7.1.1.

iv. *Notice to pro se litigant who opposes a FRCP 12 motion supported by matters outside the pleadings.* A represented party moving to dismiss or for judgment on the pleadings against a party proceeding pro se, who refers in support of the motion to matters outside the pleadings as described in FRCP 12(b) or FRCP 12(c), shall serve and file the notice in NY R USDCTS&ED Civ Rule 12.1 with the full text of FRCP 56 attached at the time the motion is served. If the Court rules that a motion to dismiss or for judgment on the pleadings will be treated as one for summary judgment pursuant to FRCP 56, and the movant has not previously served and filed the notice required by NY R USDCTS&ED Civ Rule 12.1, the movant shall amend the form notice to reflect that fact and shall serve and file the amended notice within fourteen (14) days of the Court's ruling. NY R USDCTS&ED Civ Rule 12.1. For the notice, refer to NY R USDCTS&ED Civ Rule 12.1.

v. *Copies of authorities.* In cases involving a pro se litigant, counsel shall, when serving a memorandum of law (or other submissions to the Court), provide the pro se litigant (but not other counsel or the Court) with copies of cases and other authorities cited therein that are unpublished or reported exclusively on computerized databases. Upon request, counsel shall provide the pro se litigant with copies of such unpublished cases and other authorities as are cited in a decision of the Court and were not previously cited by any party. NY R USDCTS&ED Civ Rule 7.2.

2. *Documents for opposing party*

   a. *Required documents*

      i. *Answering memorandum of law.* Except for letter-motions as permitted by NY R USDCTS&ED Civ Rule 7.1(d) or as otherwise permitted by the Court, all oppositions and replies with respect to motions shall comply with NY R USDCTS&ED Civ Rule 7.1(a)(2). NY R USDCTS&ED Civ Rule 7.1(b). Except for letter-motions as permitted by NY R USDCTS&ED Civ Rule 7.1(d) or as otherwise permitted by the Court, all motions shall include the following motion papers: a memorandum of law, setting forth the cases and other authorities relied upon in support of the motion, and divided, under appropriate headings, into as many parts as there are issues to be determined. NY R USDCTS&ED Civ Rule 7.1(a)(2). Refer to the General Requirements section of this document for information on the opposing papers.

      ii. *Certificate of service.* FRCP 5(d) requires that the person making service under FRCP 5 certify that service has been effected. FRCP 5(Advisory Committee Notes). Having such information on file may be useful for many purposes, including proof of service if an issue arises concerning the effectiveness of the service. FRCP 5(Advisory Committee Notes).

   b. *Supplemental documents*

      i. *Supporting evidence.* When a motion relies on facts outside the record, the court may hear the matter on affidavits or may hear it wholly or partly on oral testimony or on depositions. FRCP 43(c). Except for letter-motions as permitted by NY R USDCTS&ED Civ Rule 7.1(d) or as otherwise permitted by the Court, all oppositions and replies with respect to motions shall comply with NY R USDCTS&ED Civ Rule 7.1(a)(3). NY R USDCTS&ED Civ Rule 7.1(b). Except for letter-motions as permitted by NY R USDCTS&ED Civ Rule 7.1(d) or as otherwise permitted by the Court, all motions shall include the following motion papers: supporting affidavits and exhibits thereto containing any factual information and portions of the record necessary for the decision of the motion. NY R USDCTS&ED Civ Rule 7.1(a)(3).

         • *Discovery materials.* A party seeking or opposing relief under FRCP 26 through FRCP 37 inclusive, or making or opposing any other motion or application, shall quote or attach only those portions of the depositions, interrogatories, requests for documents, requests for admissions, or other discovery or disclosure materials, together with the responses and

objections thereto, that are the subject of the discovery motion or application, or that are cited in papers submitted in connection with any other motion or application. NY R USDCTS&ED Civ Rule 5.1.

ii. *Notice of constitutional question.* A party that files a pleading, written motion, or other paper drawing into question the constitutionality of a federal or state statute must promptly:

- *File notice.* File a notice of constitutional question stating the question and identifying the paper that raises it, if: (1) a federal statute is questioned and the parties do not include the United States, one of its agencies, or one of its officers or employees in an official capacity; or (2) a state statute is questioned and the parties do not include the state, one of its agencies, or one of its officers or employees in an official capacity; and

- *Serve notice.* Serve the notice and paper on the Attorney General of the United States if a federal statute is questioned—or on the state attorney general if a state statute is questioned—either by certified or registered mail or by sending it to an electronic address designated by the attorney general for this purpose. FRCP 5.1(a).

- *No forfeiture.* A party's failure to file and serve the notice, or the court's failure to certify, does not forfeit a constitutional claim or defense that is otherwise timely asserted. FRCP 5.1(d).

iii. *Copies of authorities.* In cases involving a pro se litigant, counsel shall, when serving a memorandum of law (or other submissions to the Court), provide the pro se litigant (but not other counsel or the Court) with copies of cases and other authorities cited therein that are unpublished or reported exclusively on computerized databases. Upon request, counsel shall provide the pro se litigant with copies of such unpublished cases and other authorities as are cited in a decision of the Court and were not previously cited by any party. NY R USDCTS&ED Civ Rule 7.2.

3. *Individual judge practices.* Refer to the Miscellaneous section of this document for information on individual judge practices on required documents.

## E. Format

1. *Form of documents.* The rules governing captions and other matters of form in pleadings apply to motions and other papers. FRCP 7(b)(2).

   a. *Paper.* Every pleading, written motion, and other paper must: be plainly written, typed, printed, or copied without erasures or interlineations which materially deface it. NY R USDCTS&ED Civ Rule 11.1(a)(1).

   b. *Typeface, margin, and spacing.* The typeface, margins, and spacing of all documents presented for filing must meet the following requirements:

      i. All text must be twelve (12) point type or larger, except for text in footnotes which may be ten (10) point type;

      ii. All documents must have at least one (1) inch margins on all sides;

      iii. All text must be double-spaced, except for headings, text in footnotes, or block quotations, which may be single-spaced. NY R USDCTS&ED Civ Rule 11.1(b).

   c. *Caption; Names of parties.* Every pleading must have a caption with the court's name, a title, a file number, and a FRCP 7(a) designation. The title of the complaint must name all the parties; the title of other pleadings, after naming the first party on each side, may refer generally to other parties. FRCP 10(a). Every pleading, written motion, and other paper must: bear the docket number and the initials of the District Judge and any Magistrate Judge before whom the action or proceeding is pending, NY R USDCTS&ED Civ Rule 11.1(a)(2).

   d. *Paragraphs; Separate statements.* A party must state its claims or defenses in numbered paragraphs, each limited as far as practicable to a single set of circumstances. A later pleading may refer by number to a paragraph in an earlier pleading. If doing so would promote clarity, each claim founded on a separate transaction or occurrence—and each defense other than a denial—must be stated in a separate count or defense. FRCP 10(b).

e. *Adoption by reference; Exhibits.* A statement in a pleading may be adopted by reference elsewhere in the same pleading or in any other pleading or motion. A copy of a written instrument that is an exhibit to a pleading is a part of the pleading for all purposes. FRCP 10(c).

f. *Acceptance by the clerk.* The clerk must not refuse to file a paper solely because it is not in the form prescribed by the Federal Rules of Civil Procedure or by a local rule or practice. FRCP 5(d)(4).

2. *Signing of pleadings, motions and other papers*

a. *Signature.* Every pleading, written motion, and other paper must be signed by at least one attorney of record in the attorney's name—or by a party personally if the party is unrepresented. The paper must state the signer's address, e-mail address, and telephone number. FRCP 11(a). Every pleading, written motion, and other paper must: have the name of each person signing it clearly printed or typed directly below the signature. NY R USDCTS&ED Civ Rule 11.1(a)(3).

    i. *No verification or accompanying affidavit required for pleadings.* Unless a rule or statute specifically states otherwise, a pleading need not be verified or accompanied by an affidavit. FRCP 11(a).

    ii. *Unsigned papers.* The court must strike an unsigned paper unless the omission is promptly corrected after being called to the attorney's or party's attention. FRCP 11(a).

b. *Representations to the court.* By presenting to the court a pleading, written motion, or other paper—whether by signing, filing, submitting, or later advocating it—an attorney or unrepresented party certifies that to the best of the person's knowledge, information, and belief, formed after an inquiry reasonable under the circumstances:

    i. It is not being presented for any improper purpose, such as to harass, cause unnecessary delay, or needlessly increase the cost of litigation;

    ii. The claims, defenses, and other legal contentions are warranted by existing law or by a nonfrivolous argument for extending, modifying, or reversing existing law or for establishing new law;

    iii. The factual contentions have evidentiary support or, if specifically so identified, will likely have evidentiary support after a reasonable opportunity for further investigation or discovery; and

    iv. The denials of factual contentions are warranted on the evidence or, if specifically so identified, are reasonably based on belief or a lack of information. FRCP 11(b).

c. *Sanctions.* If, after notice and a reasonable opportunity to respond, the court determines that FRCP 11(b) has been violated, the court may impose an appropriate sanction on any attorney, law firm, or party that violated FRCP 11(b) or is responsible for the violation. FRCP 11(c)(1). Refer to the United States District Court for the Eastern District of New York KeyRules Motion for Sanctions document for more information.

3. *Privacy protection for filings made with the court*

a. *Redacted filings.* Unless the court orders otherwise, in an electronic or paper filing with the court that contains an individual's Social Security number, taxpayer-identification number, or birth date, the name of an individual known to be a minor, or a financial-account number, a party or nonparty making the filing may include only:

    i. The last four (4) digits of the Social Security number and taxpayer-identification number;

    ii. The year of the individual's birth;

    iii. The minor's initials; and

    iv. The last four (4) digits of the financial-account number. FRCP 5.2(a); NY R USDCTED Order 2004-09.

    v. In addition, exercise caution when filing documents that contain the following:

    - Personal identifying number, such as driver's license number;

    - Medical records, treatment and diagnosis;

    - Employment history;

- Individual financial information; and
- Proprietary or trade secret information. NY R USDCTED Order 2004-09.

b. *Exemptions from the redaction requirement.* The redaction requirement does not apply to the following:

    i. A financial-account number that identifies the property allegedly subject to forfeiture in a forfeiture proceeding;

    ii. The record of an administrative or agency proceeding;

    iii. The official record of a state-court proceeding;

    iv. The record of a court or tribunal, if that record was not subject to the redaction requirement when originally filed;

    v. A filing covered by FRCP 5.2(c) or FRCP 5.2(d); and

    vi. A pro se filing in an action brought under 28 U.S.C.A. § 2241, 28 U.S.C.A. § 2254, or 28 U.S.C.A. § 2255. FRCP 5.2(b).

c. *Limitations on remote access to electronic files; Social Security appeals and immigration cases.* Unless the court orders otherwise, in an action for benefits under the Social Security Act, and in an action or proceeding relating to an order of removal, to relief from removal, or to immigration benefits or detention, access to an electronic file is authorized as follows:

    i. The parties and their attorneys may have remote electronic access to any part of the case file, including the administrative record;

    ii. Any other person may have electronic access to the full record at the courthouse, but may have remote electronic access only to:

        - The docket maintained by the court; and

        - An opinion, order, judgment, or other disposition of the court, but not any other part of the case file or the administrative record. FRCP 5.2(c).

d. *Filings made under seal.* The court may order that a filing be made under seal without redaction. The court may later unseal the filing or order the person who made the filing to file a redacted version for the public record. FRCP 5.2(d).

e. *Protective orders.* For good cause, the court may by order in a case:

    i. Require redaction of additional information; or

    ii. Limit or prohibit a nonparty's remote electronic access to a document filed with the court. FRCP 5.2(e).

f. *Option for additional unredacted filing under seal.* A person making a redacted filing may also file an unredacted copy under seal. The court must retain the unredacted copy as part of the record. FRCP 5.2(f); NY R USDCTED Order 2004-09. The unredacted version of the document or the reference list shall be retained by the court as part of the record. The court may, however, still require the party to file a redacted copy for the public file. NY R USDCTED Order 2004-09.

g. *Option for filing a reference list.* A filing that contains redacted information may be filed together with a reference list that identifies each item of redacted information and specifies an appropriate identifier that uniquely corresponds to each item listed. The list must be filed under seal and may be amended as of right. Any reference in the case to a listed identifier will be construed to refer to the corresponding item of information. FRCP 5.2(g); NY R USDCTED Order 2004-09. The unredacted version of the document or the reference list shall be retained by the court as part of the record. The court may, however, still require the party to file a redacted copy for the public file. NY R USDCTED Order 2004-09.

h. *Responsibility for redaction.* The responsibility for redacting these personal identifiers rests solely with counsel and the parties. The Clerk will not review each pleading for compliance with NY R USDCTED Order 2004-09. NY R USDCTED Order 2004-09.

    i. Counsel is strongly urged to share this notice with all clients so that an informed decision about the inclusion of certain materials may be made. If a redacted document is filed, it is the sole responsibility of counsel and the parties to be sure that all pleadings comply with the rules of this court requiring redaction of personal data identifiers. The clerk will not review each pleading for redaction. NY R USDCTED Order 2004-09.

    i.  *Waiver of protection of identifiers.* A person waives the protection of FRCP 5.2(a) as to the person's own information by filing it without redaction and not under seal. FRCP 5.2(h).

4.  *Individual judge practices.* Refer to the Miscellaneous section of this document for information on individual judge practices on formatting documents.

## F.  Filing and Service Requirements

1.  *Filing requirements.* Any paper after the complaint that is required to be served—together with a certificate of service—must be filed within a reasonable time after service. FRCP 5(d)(1).

    a.  *How filing is made; In general.* A paper is filed by delivering it:

        i.  To the clerk; or

        ii.  To a judge who agrees to accept it for filing, and who must then note the filing date on the paper and promptly send it to the clerk. FRCP 5(d)(2).

    b.  *Night depository.* A night depository with an automatic date stamp shall be maintained. . .by the Clerk of the Eastern District in the Brooklyn Courthouse. After regular business hours, papers for the District Court only may be deposited in the night depository. Such papers will be considered as having been filed in the District Court as of the date stamped thereon, which shall be deemed presumptively correct. NY R USDCTS&ED Civ Rule 1.2.

    c.  *Electronic filing*

        i.  *Authorization of electronic filing program.* A court may, by local rule, allow papers to be filed, signed, or verified by electronic means that are consistent with any technical standards established by the Judicial Conference of the United States. A local rule may require electronic filing only if reasonable exceptions are allowed. A paper filed electronically in compliance with a local rule is a written paper for purposes of the Federal Rules of Civil Procedure. FRCP 5(d)(3).

          • Parties serving and filing papers shall follow the instructions regarding Electronic Case Filing (ECF) published on the website of each respective Court. A paper served and filed by electronic means in accordance with such instructions is, for purposes of FRCP 5, served and filed in compliance with the Local Civil Rules of the Southern and Eastern Districts of New York. NY R USDCTS&ED Civ Rule 5.2(a). Parties have an obligation to review the Court's actual order, decree, or judgment (on ECF), which controls, and should not rely on the description on the docket or in the ECF Notice of Electronic Filing (NEF). NY R USDCTS&ED Civ Rule 5.2(c).

        ii.  *Mandatory electronic filing.* Beginning on August 2, 2004, electronic case filing will be mandatory for all civil cases other than pro se cases. NY R USDCTED Order 2004-08.

          • *Letter-motions and letters addressed to the court.* Subject to the instructions regarding ECF published on the website of each respective Court and any pertinent Individual Judge's Practices, letter-motions permitted by NY R USDCTS&ED Civ Rule 7.1(d) and letters addressed to the Court (but not letters between the parties) may be filed via ECF. NY R USDCTS&ED Civ Rule 5.2(b).

          • *Proposed orders, judgments and decrees.* Proposed orders, judgments and decrees shall be presented as directed by the ECF rules published on the website of each respective Court. NY R USDCTS&ED Civ Rule 77.1. For more information, refer to NY R USDCTS&ED Civ Rule 77.1.

          • *Request for exemption.* Requests by attorneys for an exemption to the mandatory policy will be considered for good cause hardship reasons only, and will be reviewed on an individual basis by the assigned United States Magistrate Judge. The Clerk's Office provides an electronic filing training program to assist attorneys filing electronically.

> Before seeking a hardship exemption, attorneys are advised to participate in the training program or otherwise seek the assistance of the Clerk's Office. NY R USDCTED Order 2004-08.

   iii.  For more information on electronic filing, refer to the court's website.

2. *Service requirements*

  a.  *Service; When required*

    i.  *In general.* Unless the Federal Rules of Civil Procedure provide otherwise, each of the following papers must be served on every party:

- An order stating that service is required;
- A pleading filed after the original complaint, unless the court orders otherwise under FRCP 5(c) because there are numerous defendants;
- A discovery paper required to be served on a party, unless the court orders otherwise;
- A written motion, except one that may be heard ex parte; and
- A written notice, appearance, demand, or offer of judgment, or any similar paper. FRCP 5(a)(1).

    ii.  *If a party fails to appear.* No service is required on a party who is in default for failing to appear. But a pleading that asserts a new claim for relief against such a party must be served on that party under FRCP 4. FRCP 5(a)(2).

   iii.  *Seizing property.* If an action is begun by seizing property and no person is or need be named as a defendant, any service required before the filing of an appearance, answer, or claim must be made on the person who had custody or possession of the property when it was seized. FRCP 5(a)(3).

  b.  *Service; How made*

    i.  *Serving an attorney.* If a party is represented by an attorney, service under FRCP 5 must be made on the attorney unless the court orders service on the party. FRCP 5(b)(1).

    ii.  *Service in general.* A paper is served under FRCP 5 by:

- Handing it to the person;
- Leaving it: (1) at the person's office with a clerk or other person in charge or, if no one is in charge, in a conspicuous place in the office; or (2) if the person has no office or the office is closed, at the person's dwelling or usual place of abode with someone of suitable age and discretion who resides there;
- Mailing it to the person's last known address—in which event service is complete upon mailing;
- Leaving it with the court clerk if the person has no known address;
- Sending it by electronic means if the person consented in writing—in which event service is complete upon transmission, but is not effective if the serving party learns that it did not reach the person to be served; or
- Delivering it by any other means that the person consented to in writing—in which event service is complete when the person making service delivers it to the agency designated to make delivery. FRCP 5(b)(2).

   iii.  *Service by overnight delivery.* Service upon an attorney may be made by overnight delivery service. "Overnight delivery service" means any delivery service which regularly accepts items for overnight delivery. Overnight delivery service shall be deemed service by mail for purposes of FRCP 5 and FRCP 6. NY R USDCTS&ED Civ Rule 5.3.

   iv.  *Service by electronic means.* Parties serving and filing papers shall follow the instructions regarding Electronic Case Filing (ECF) published on the website of each respective Court. A paper served and filed by electronic means in accordance with such instructions is, for purposes of FRCP 5, served and filed in compliance with the Local Civil Rules of the United States District Courts for the Southern and Eastern Districts of New York. NY R USDCTS&ED Civ Rule 5.2(a). Parties have an obligation to review the Court's actual order, decree, or judgment (on ECF), which controls, and should not rely on the description on the docket or in the ECF Notice of Electronic Filing (NEF). NY R USDCTS&ED Civ Rule 5.2(c).

     v.  *Using court facilities.* If a local rule so authorizes, a party may use the court's transmission facilities to make service under FRCP 5(b)(2)(E). FRCP 5(b)(3).

  c.  *Serving numerous defendants*

     i.  *In general.* If an action involves an unusually large number of defendants, the court may, on motion or on its own, order that:

- Defendants' pleadings and replies to them need not be served on other defendants;

- Any crossclaim, counterclaim, avoidance, or affirmative defense in those pleadings and replies to them will be treated as denied or avoided by all other parties; and

- Filing any such pleading and serving it on the plaintiff constitutes notice of the pleading to all parties. FRCP 5(c)(1).

     ii.  *Notifying parties.* A copy of every such order must be served on the parties as the court directs. FRCP 5(c)(2).

3.  *Individual judge practices.* Refer to the Miscellaneous section of this document for information on individual judge practices on filing and serving documents.

## G. Hearings

1.  *Hearings, generally*

  a.  *Oral argument.* Due process does not require that oral argument be permitted on a motion and, except as otherwise provided by local rule, the district court has discretion to determine whether it will decide the motion on the papers or hear argument by counsel (and perhaps receive evidence). FPP § 1190; F.D.I.C. v. Deglau, 207 F.3d 153 (3d Cir. 2000). The parties and their attorneys shall only appear to argue the motion if so directed by the Court by order or by a Judge's Individual Practice. NY R USDCTS&ED Civ Rule 6.1(c).

  b.  *Providing a regular schedule for oral hearings.* A court may establish regular times and places for oral hearings on motions. FRCP 78(a).

  c.  *Providing for submission on briefs.* By rule or order, the court may provide for submitting and determining motions on briefs, without oral hearings. FRCP 78(b).

2.  *Hearing on FRCP 12 defenses before trial.* If a party so moves, any defense listed in FRCP 12(b)(1) through FRCP 12(b)(7)—whether made in a pleading or by motion—and a motion under FRCP 12(c) must be heard and decided before trial unless the court orders a deferral until trial. FRCP 12(i).

3.  *Hearing on motion to dismiss for lack of subject matter jurisdiction.* It may be error for a court to dismiss a case on the defendant's motion to dismiss for lack of subject matter jurisdiction without first holding a hearing, as FRCP 12(b)(1) requires a preliminary hearing or hearing at trial to determine any disputed facts upon which the motion or opposition to it is predicated. FEDPROC § 62:435.

4.  *Individual judge practices.* Refer to the Miscellaneous section of this document for information on individual judge practices on hearings.

## H. Forms

**1. Federal Motion to Dismiss for Lack of Subject Matter Jurisdiction Forms**

  a.  Motion to dismiss for lack of subject-matter jurisdiction. 2C FEDFORMS § 11:35.

  b.  Motion to dismiss for lack of subject-matter jurisdiction; Want of diversity of citizenship because requisite diversity not alleged. 2C FEDFORMS § 11:37.

  c.  Motion to dismiss for lack of subject-matter jurisdiction; Want of diversity on a factual basis and because requisite diversity not alleged. 2C FEDFORMS § 11:38.

d. Motion to dismiss for lack of subject-matter jurisdiction; Want of diversity of citizenship because state of incorporation and principal place of business of defendant not as alleged. 2C FEDFORMS § 11:39.

e. Motion to dismiss for lack of subject-matter jurisdiction; Want of diversity of citizenship because principal place of business of defendant not as alleged. 2C FEDFORMS § 11:40.

f. Motion to dismiss for lack of subject-matter jurisdiction; Failure to comply with procedural requirements. 2C FEDFORMS § 11:41.

g. Motion to dismiss for lack of subject-matter jurisdiction; Want of diversity upon realignment of parties according to interest. 2C FEDFORMS § 11:42.

h. Motion to dismiss for lack of subject-matter jurisdiction; Want of federal question. 2C FEDFORMS § 11:43.

i. Motion to dismiss for lack of subject-matter jurisdiction; Unsubstantial federal question. 2C FEDFORMS § 11:44.

j. Motion to dismiss for lack of subject-matter jurisdiction; Want of amount in controversy. 2C FEDFORMS § 11:45.

k. Motion to dismiss for lack of subject-matter jurisdiction; Want of amount in controversy; Insurance policy limits do not exceed required jurisdictional amount. 2C FEDFORMS § 11:46.

l. Motion to dismiss for lack of subject-matter jurisdiction; Want of amount in controversy; Claim for damages in excess of jurisdictional amount not made in good faith. 2C FEDFORMS § 11:47.

m. Motion to dismiss for lack of subject-matter jurisdiction; Want of amount in controversy; Made after judgment. 2C FEDFORMS § 11:48.

n. Motion to dismiss for lack of subject-matter jurisdiction; Want of consent by the United States to be sued. 2C FEDFORMS § 11:49.

o. Motion to dismiss for lack of subject-matter jurisdiction; Want of consent by United States to be sued; United States indispensable party. 2C FEDFORMS § 11:50.

p. Affidavit; In opposition to motion to dismiss for lack of diversity; Assignment of claim to plaintiff bona fide. FEDPROF § 1:894.

q. Motion; To dismiss; Plaintiff and defendant citizens of same state when action filed. FEDPROF § 1:888.

r. Motion to dismiss; Assignment to nonresident for purpose of invoking federal jurisdiction sham and ineffective to confer jurisdiction. FEDPROF § 1:889.

s. Motion to dismiss; For lack of diversity in third-party complaint. FEDPROF § 1:890.

t. Affidavit; In support of motion to dismiss for want of diversity of citizenship; Plaintiff and defendant citizens of same state on date action filed. FEDPROF § 1:892.

u. Motion; To dismiss; Insufficiency of amount in controversy. FEDPROF § 1:897.

v. Motion to dismiss; Bad faith in claiming jurisdictional amount. FEDPROF § 1:898.

w. Motion; To dismiss; Lack of jurisdiction over subject matter, generally. FEDPROF § 1:903.

x. Motion to dismiss; Absence of federal question. FEDPROF § 1:904.

y. Motion to dismiss; Absence of federal question; Failure to exhaust state remedies. FEDPROF § 1:905.

z. Affidavit; In opposition to motion to dismiss for absence of jurisdiction over subject matter. FEDPROF § 1:906.

## I. Applicable Rules

1. *Federal rules*

   a. Federal question. 28 U.S.C.A. § 1331.

   b. Diversity of citizenship; Amount in controversy; Costs. 28 U.S.C.A. § 1332.

    c. Serving and filing pleadings and other papers. FRCP 5.

    d. Constitutional challenge to a statute; Notice, certification, and intervention. FRCP 5.1.

    e. Privacy protection for filings made with the court. FRCP 5.2.

    f. Computing and extending time; Time for motion papers. FRCP 6.

    g. Pleadings allowed; Form of motions and other papers. FRCP 7.

    h. Disclosure statement. FRCP 7.1.

    i. Form of pleadings. FRCP 10.

    j. Signing pleadings, motions, and other papers; Representations to the court; Sanctions. FRCP 11.

    k. Defenses and objections; When and how presented; Motion for judgment on the pleadings; Consolidating motions; Waiving defenses; Pretrial hearing. FRCP 12.

    l. Taking testimony. FRCP 43.

    m. Hearing motions; Submission on briefs. FRCP 78.

2. *Local rules*

    a. Night depository. NY R USDCTS&ED Civ Rule 1.2.

    b. Duty of attorneys in related cases. NY R USDCTS&ED Civ Rule 1.6.

    c. Filing of discovery materials. NY R USDCTS&ED Civ Rule 5.1.

    d. Electronic service and filing of documents. NY R USDCTS&ED Civ Rule 5.2.

    e. Service by overnight delivery. NY R USDCTS&ED Civ Rule 5.3.

    f. Service and filing of motion papers. NY R USDCTS&ED Civ Rule 6.1.

    g. Orders on motions. NY R USDCTS&ED Civ Rule 6.2.

    h. Computation of time. NY R USDCTS&ED Civ Rule 6.4.

    i. Motion papers. NY R USDCTS&ED Civ Rule 7.1.

    j. Disclosure statement. NY R USDCTS&ED Civ Rule 7.1.1.

    k. Authorities to be provided to pro se litigants. NY R USDCTS&ED Civ Rule 7.2.

    l. Form of pleadings, motions, and other papers. NY R USDCTS&ED Civ Rule 11.1.

    m. Notice to pro se litigant who opposes a FRCP 12 motion supported by matters outside the pleadings. NY R USDCTS&ED Civ Rule 12.1.

    n. Submission of orders, judgments and decrees. NY R USDCTS&ED Civ Rule 77.1.

    o. Court-annexed arbitration (Eastern District only). NY R USDCTS&ED Civ Rule 83.7.

    p. Court-annexed mediation (Eastern District only). NY R USDCTS&ED Civ Rule 83.8.

    q. Electronic case filing. NY R USDCTED Order 2004-08.

    r. The August 2, 2004 amendment to the E-Government Act of 2002. NY R USDCTED Order 2004-09.

    s. Categories and classification of cases; Information on cases and parties. NY R USDCTED Div. Bus., Rule 50.1.

## J. Miscellaneous

**NOTE: Individual judges' rules may apply. For available judge-level information, refer to:**

DISTRICT JUDGE CAROL BAGLEY AMON: NY R USDCTED Amon-Practices.

DISTRICT JUDGE JOAN M. AZRACK: NY R USDCTED Azrack-Practices.

DISTRICT JUDGE JOSEPH F. BIANCO: NY R USDCTED Bianco-Practices.

DISTRICT JUDGE FREDERIC BLOCK: NY R USDCTED Block-Practices.

DISTRICT JUDGE MARGO K. BRODIE: NY R USDCTED Brodie-Practices.

DISTRICT JUDGE PAMELA K. CHEN: NY R USDCTED Chen-Practices.

DISTRICT JUDGE BRIAN M. COGAN: NY R USDCTED Cogan-Practices; NY R USDCTED Cogan-Pretrial.

DISTRICT JUDGE LaSHANN DeARCY HALL: NY R USDCTED DeArcy Hall-Practices.

DISTRICT JUDGE RAYMOND J. DEARIE: NY R USDCTED Dearie-Practices.

DISTRICT JUDGE ANN M. DONNELLY: NY R USDCTED Donnelly-Practices.

DISTRICT JUDGE SANDRA J. FEUERSTEIN: NY R USDCTED Feuerstein-Practices; NY R USDCTED Feuerstein-Pretrial.

DISTRICT JUDGE NICHOLAS G. GARAUIFIS: NY R USDCTED Garaufis-Practices; NY R USDCTED Garaufis-Pretrial.

DISTRICT JUDGE NINA GERSHON: NY R USDCTED Gershon-Practices.

DISTRICT JUDGE I. LEO GLASSER: NY R USDCTED Glasser-Practices; NY R USDCTED Glasser-Crim.

DISTRICT JUDGE DENIS R. HURLEY: NY R USDCTED Hurley-Practices; [NY R USDCTED Hurley-Pro Cooperation Info, as added by NY ORDER 16-4188, effective July 22, 2016]; [NY R USDCTED Hurley-Pro Cooperation Info Stay, as added by NY ORDER 16-4188, effective July 22, 2016].

DISTRICT JUDGE DORA L. IRIZARRY: NY R USDCTED Irizarry-Practices; NY R USDCTED Irizarry-Pretrial; NY R USDCTED Irizarry-Crim.

DISTRICT JUDGE STERLING JOHNSON, JR.: NY R USDCTED Johnson-Practices.

DISTRICT JUDGE EDWARD R. KORMAN: NY R USDCTED Korman-Practices; NY R USDCTED Korman-Pretrial.

DISTRICT JUDGE WILLIAM F. KUNTZ: NY R USDCTED Kuntz-Practices.

DISTRICT JUDGE KIYO A. MATSUMOTO: NY R USDCTED Matsumoto-Practices.

DISTRICT JUDGE ROSLYNN R. MAUSKOPF: NY R USDCTED Mauskopf-Practices; NY R USDCTED Mauskopf-Recusal.

DISTRICT JUDGE THOMAS C. PLATT: NY R USDCTED Platt-Practices.

DISTRICT JUDGE ALLYNE R. ROSS: NY R USDCTED Ross-Practices.

DISTRICT JUDGE JOANNA SEYBERT: NY R USDCTED Seybert-Practices.

DISTRICT JUDGE ARTHUR D. SPATT: NY R USDCTED Spatt-Practices.

DISTRICT JUDGE SANDRA L. TOWNES: NY R USDCTED Townes-Practices.

DISTRICT JUDGE ERIC N. VITALIANO: NY R USDCTED Vitaliano-Practices.

DISTRICT JUDGE JACK B. WEINSTEIN: NY R USDCTED Weinstein-Practices.

DISTRICT JUDGE LEONARD D. WEXLER: NY R USDCTED Wexler-Practices; NY R USDCTED Wexler-Rules.

MAGISTRATE JUDGE LOIS BLOOM: NY R USDCTED Bloom-Practices.

MAGISTRATE JUDGE GARY R. BROWN: NY R USDCTED Brown-Practices.

MAGISTRATE JUDGE MARILYN D. GO: NY R USDCTED Go-Practices.

MAGISTRATE JUDGE STEVEN M. GOLD: NY R USDCTED Gold-Practices.

MAGISTRATE JUDGE PEGGY KUO: NY R USDCTED Kuo-Practices; NY R USDCTED Kuo-Scheduling Order.

MAGISTRATE JUDGE ROBERT M. LEVY: NY R USDCTED Levy-Practices.

MAGISTRATE JUDGE ARLENE R. LINDSAY: NY R USDCTED Lindsay-Practices.

MAGISTRATE JUDGE STEVEN I. LOCKE: NY R USDCTED Locke-Practices.

MAGISTRATE JUDGE ROANNE L. MANN: NY R USDCTED Mann-Practices.

MAGISTRATE JUDGE JAMES ORENSTEIN: NY R USDCTED Jorenstein--Practices.

MAGISTRATE JUDGE VIKTOR V. POHORELSKY: NY R USDCTED Pohorelsky-Practices.

MAGISTRATE JUDGE CHERYL L. POLLAK: NY R USDCTED Pollak-Practices; NY R USDCTED Pollak-Pretrial.

MAGISTRATE JUDGE RAMON E. REYES, JR.: NY R USDCTED Reyes-Practices.

MAGISTRATE JUDGE VERA M. SCANLON: NY R USDCTED Scanlon-Practices.

MAGISTRATE JUDGE ANNE Y. SHIELDS: NY R USDCTED Shields-Practices.

MAGISTRATE JUDGE STEVEN L. TISCIONE: NY R USDCTED Tiscione-Practices.

MAGISTRATE JUDGE A. KATHLEEN TOMILINSON: NY R USDCTED Tomlinson-Practices.

# Motions, Oppositions and Replies
## Motion to Dismiss for Lack of Personal Jurisdiction

### Document Last Updated September 2016

A.  **Checklist**

  (I)  ❑ Matters to be considered by moving party

  (a)  ❑ Required documents

  (1)  ❑ Notice of motion and motion

  (2)  ❑ Memorandum of law

  (3)  ❑ Certificate of service

  (b)  ❑ Supplemental documents

  (1)  ❑ Supporting evidence

  (2)  ❑ Notice of constitutional question

  (3)  ❑ Nongovernmental corporate disclosure statement

  (4)  ❑ Notice to pro se litigant who opposes a FRCP 12 motion supported by matters outside the pleadings

  (5)  ❑ Copies of authorities

  (c)  ❑ Timing

  (1)  ❑ Every defense to a claim for relief in any pleading must be asserted in the responsive pleading if one is required

  (2)  ❑ A motion asserting any of the defenses in FRCP 12(b) must be made before pleading if a responsive pleading is allowed

  (3)  ❑ If a pleading sets out a claim for relief that does not require a responsive pleading, an opposing party may assert at trial any defense to that claim

  (4)  ❑ A written motion and notice of the hearing must be served at least fourteen (14) days before the time specified for the hearing, with the following exceptions: (i) when the motion may be heard ex parte; (ii) when the Federal Rules of Civil Procedure set a different time; or (iii) when a court order—which a party may, for good cause, apply for ex parte—sets a different time

  (5)  ❑ Any affidavit supporting a motion must be served with the motion

  (II)  ❑ Matters to be considered by opposing party

  (a)  ❑ Required documents

  (1)  ❑ Answering memorandum of law

  (2)  ❑ Certificate of service

  (b)  ❑ Supplemental documents

  (1)  ❑ Supporting evidence

    (2) ❏ Notice of constitutional question

    (3) ❏ Copies of authorities

  (c) ❏ Timing

    (1) ❏ Any opposing affidavits and answering memoranda shall be served within fourteen (14) days after service of the moving papers

    (2) ❏ Except as FRCP 59(c) provides otherwise, any opposing affidavit must be served at least seven (7) days before the hearing, unless the court permits service at another time

## B. Timing

1. *Motion to dismiss for lack of personal jurisdiction*

  a. *In a responsive pleading.* Every defense to a claim for relief in any pleading must be asserted in the responsive pleading if one is required. FRCP 12(b).

  b. *By motion.* A motion asserting any of the defenses in FRCP 12(b) must be made before pleading if a responsive pleading is allowed. FRCP 12(b). Although FRCP 12(b) encourages the responsive pleader to file a motion to dismiss before filing the answer, nothing in FRCP 12 prohibits the filing of a motion to dismiss with the answer. An untimely motion to dismiss may be considered if the defense asserted in the motion was previously raised in the responsive pleading. FEDPROC § 62:427.

  c. *At trial.* If a pleading sets out a claim for relief that does not require a responsive pleading, an opposing party may assert at trial any defense to that claim. FRCP 12(b).

2. *Timing of motions, generally*

  a. *Motion and notice of hearing.* Except for letter-motions as permitted by NY R USDCTS&ED Civ Rule 7.1(d), and unless otherwise provided by statute or rule or by the Court in a Judge's Individual Practice or in a direction in a particular case, upon any motion, the notice of motion, supporting affidavits, and memoranda shall be served and filed as follows: on all civil motions, petitions, and applications, other than those described in NY R USDCTS&ED Civ Rule 6.1(a), and other than petitions for writs of habeas corpus, the notice of motion, supporting affidavits, and memoranda of law shall be served by the moving party on all other parties that have appeared in the action. NY R USDCTS&ED Civ Rule 6.1(b)(1). A written motion and notice of the hearing must be served at least fourteen (14) days before the time specified for the hearing, with the following exceptions:

    i. When the motion may be heard ex parte;

    ii. When the Federal Rules of Civil Procedure set a different time; or

    iii. When a court order—which a party may, for good cause, apply for ex parte—sets a different time. FRCP 6(c)(1).

  b. *Supporting affidavit.* Any affidavit supporting a motion must be served with the motion. FRCP 6(c)(2).

3. *Timing of opposing papers.* Except for letter-motions as permitted by NY R USDCTS&ED Civ Rule 7.1(d), and unless otherwise provided by statute or rule or by the Court in a Judge's Individual Practice or in a direction in a particular case, upon any motion, the notice of motion, supporting affidavits, and memoranda shall be served and filed as follows: on all civil motions, petitions, and applications, other than those described in NY R USDCTS&ED Civ Rule 6.1(a), and other than petitions for writs of habeas corpus, any opposing affidavits and answering memoranda shall be served within fourteen (14) days after service of the moving papers. NY R USDCTS&ED Civ Rule 6.1(b)(2).

  a. *Opposing affidavit.* Except as FRCP 59(c) provides otherwise, any opposing affidavit must be served at least seven (7) days before the hearing, unless the court permits service at another time. FRCP 6(c)(2).

4. *Timing of reply papers.* Where the respondent files an answering affidavit setting up a new matter, the moving party ordinarily is allowed a reasonable time to file a reply affidavit since failure to deny the new matter by affidavit may operate as an admission of its truth. AMJUR MOTIONS § 25.

  a. *Reply affidavits and reply memoranda of law.* Except for letter-motions as permitted by NY R

USDCTS&ED Civ Rule 7.1(d), and unless otherwise provided by statute or rule or by the Court in a Judge's Individual Practice or in a direction in a particular case, upon any motion, the notice of motion, supporting affidavits, and memoranda shall be served and filed as follows: on all civil motions, petitions, and applications, other than those described in NY R USDCTS&ED Civ Rule 6.1(a), and other than petitions for writs of habeas corpus, any reply affidavits and memoranda of law shall be served within seven (7) days after service of the answering papers. NY R USDCTS&ED Civ Rule 6.1(b)(3).

5. *Effect of a FRCP 12 motion on the time to serve a responsive pleading.* Unless the court sets a different time, serving a motion under FRCP 12 alters the periods in FRCP 12(a) as follows:

   a. If the court denies the motion or postpones its disposition until trial, the responsive pleading must be served within fourteen (14) days after notice of the court's action; or

   b. If the court grants a motion for a more definite statement, the responsive pleading must be served within fourteen (14) days after the more definite statement is served. FRCP 12(a)(4).

6. *Computation of time*

   a. *Computing time.* FRCP 6 applies in computing any time period specified in the Federal Rules of Civil Procedure, in any local rule or court order, or in any statute that does not specify a method of computing time. FRCP 6(a). In computing any period of time prescribed or allowed by the Local Civil Rules of the United States District Courts for the Southern and Eastern Districts of New York or the Local Admiralty and Maritime Rules, the provisions of FRCP 6 shall apply unless otherwise stated. NY R USDCTS&ED Civ Rule 6.4.

      i. *Period stated in days or a longer unit.* In computing periods of days, refer to FRCP 6 and NY R USDCTS&ED Civ Rule 6.4. NY R USDCTS&ED Civ Rule 6.1(b). When the period is stated in days or a longer unit of time:

         • Exclude the day of the event that triggers the period;

         • Count every day, including intermediate Saturdays, Sundays, and legal holidays; and

         • Include the last day of the period, but if the last day is a Saturday, Sunday, or legal holiday, the period continues to run until the end of the next day that is not a Saturday, Sunday, or legal holiday. FRCP 6(a)(1). In the Local Civil Rules of the United States District Courts for the Southern and Eastern Districts of New York, as in the Federal Rules of Civil Procedure as amended effective December 1, 2009, Saturdays, Sundays, and legal holidays are no longer excluded in computing periods of time. If the last day of the period is a Saturday, Sunday, or legal holiday, the period continues to run until the end of the next day that is not a Saturday, Sunday, or legal holiday. NY R USDCTS&ED Civ Rule 6.4.

      ii. *Period stated in hours.* When the period is stated in hours:

         • Begin counting immediately on the occurrence of the event that triggers the period;

         • Count every hour, including hours during intermediate Saturdays, Sundays, and legal holidays; and

         • If the period would end on a Saturday, Sunday, or legal holiday, the period continues to run until the same time on the next day that is not a Saturday, Sunday, or legal holiday. FRCP 6(a)(2). In the Local Civil Rules of the United States District Courts for the Southern and Eastern Districts of New York, as in the Federal Rules of Civil Procedure as amended effective December 1, 2009, Saturdays, Sundays, and legal holidays are no longer excluded in computing periods of time. If the last day of the period is a Saturday, Sunday, or legal holiday, the period continues to run until the end of the next day that is not a Saturday, Sunday, or legal holiday. NY R USDCTS&ED Civ Rule 6.4.

      iii. *Inaccessibility of the clerk's office.* Unless the court orders otherwise, if the clerk's office is inaccessible:

         • On the last day for filing under FRCP 6(a)(1), then the time for filing is extended to the first accessible day that is not a Saturday, Sunday, or legal holiday; or

         • During the last hour for filing under FRCP 6(a)(2), then the time for filing is extended to

the same time on the first accessible day that is not a Saturday, Sunday, or legal holiday. FRCP 6(a)(3).

    iv. *"Last day" defined.* Unless a different time is set by a statute, local rule, or court order, the last day ends:

- For electronic filing, at midnight in the court's time zone; and

- For filing by other means, when the clerk's office is scheduled to close. FRCP 6(a)(4).

    v. *"Next day" defined.* The "next day" is determined by continuing to count forward when the period is measured after an event and backward when measured before an event. FRCP 6(a)(5).

    vi. *"Legal holiday" defined.* "Legal holiday" means:

- The day set aside by statute for observing New Year's Day, Martin Luther King Jr.'s Birthday, Washington's Birthday, Memorial Day, Independence Day, Labor Day, Columbus Day, Veterans' Day, Thanksgiving Day, or Christmas Day;

- Any day declared a holiday by the President or Congress; and

- For periods that are measured after an event, any other day declared a holiday by the state where the district court is located. FRCP 6(a)(6).

  b. *Extending time*

    i. *In general.* When an act may or must be done within a specified time, the court may, for good cause, extend the time:

- With or without motion or notice if the court acts, or if a request is made, before the original time or its extension expires; or

- On motion made after the time has expired if the party failed to act because of excusable neglect. FRCP 6(b)(1).

    ii. *Exceptions.* A court must not extend the time to act under FRCP 50(b), FRCP 50(d), FRCP 52(b), FRCP 59(b), FRCP 59(d), FRCP 59(e), and FRCP 60(b). FRCP 6(b)(2).

    iii. Refer to the United States District Court for the Eastern District of New York KeyRules Motion for Continuance/Extension of Time document for more information on extending time.

  c. *Additional time after certain kinds of service.* When a party may or must act within a specified time after service and service is made under FRCP 5(b)(2)(C), FRCP 5(b)(2)(D), FRCP 5(b)(2)(E), or FRCP 5(b)(2)(F), three (3) days are added after the period would otherwise expire under FRCP 6(a). FRCP 6(d). Overnight delivery service shall be deemed service by mail for purposes of FRCP 5 and FRCP 6. NY R USDCTS&ED Civ Rule 5.3.

7. *Individual judge practices.* Refer to the Miscellaneous section of this document for information on individual judge practices on timing of documents.

## C. General Requirements

1. *Motions, generally*

  a. *Requirements.* A request for a court order must be made by motion. The motion must:

    i. Be in writing unless made during a hearing or trial;

    ii. State with particularity the grounds for seeking the order; and

    iii. State the relief sought. FRCP 7(b)(1).

  b. *Notice of motion.* A party interested in resisting the relief sought by a motion has a right to notice thereof, and an opportunity to be heard. AMJUR MOTIONS § 12.

    i. In addition to statutory or court rule provisions requiring notice of a motion—the purpose of such a notice requirement having been said to be to prevent a party from being prejudicially surprised by a motion—principles of natural justice dictate that an adverse party generally must be given notice that a motion will be presented to the court. AMJUR MOTIONS § 12.

    ii. "Notice," in this regard, means reasonable notice, including a meaningful opportunity to prepare and to defend against allegations of a motion. AMJUR MOTIONS § 12.

c. *Writing requirement.* The writing requirement is intended to insure that the adverse parties are informed and have a record of both the motion's pendency and the grounds on which the movant seeks an order. FPP § 1191; Feldberg v. Quechee Lakes Corp., 463 F.3d 195 (2d Cir. 2006).

   i. It is sufficient "if the motion is stated in a written notice of the hearing of the motion." FPP § 1191.

d. *Particularity requirement.* The particularity requirement insures that the opposing parties will have notice of their opponent's contentions. FEDPROC § 62:364; Goodman v. 1973 26 Foot Trojan Vessel, Arkansas Registration No. AR1439SN, 859 F.2d 71, 12 Fed.R.Serv.3d 645 (8th Cir. 1988). That requirement ensures that notice of the basis for the motion is provided to the court and to the opposing party so as to avoid prejudice, provide the opponent with a meaningful opportunity to respond, and provide the court with enough information to process the motion correctly. FEDPROC § 62:364; Andreas v. Volkswagen of America, Inc., 336 F.3d 789, 56 Fed.R.Serv.3d 6 (8th Cir. 2003).

   i. Reasonable specification of the grounds for a motion is sufficient. However, where a movant fails to state even one ground for granting the motion in question, the movant has failed to meet the minimal standard of "reasonable specification." FEDPROC § 62:364; Martinez v. Trainor, 556 F.2d 818, 23 Fed.R.Serv.2d 403 (7th Cir. 1977).

   ii. The court may excuse the failure to comply with the particularity requirement if it is inadvertent, and where no prejudice is shown by the opposing party. FEDPROC § 62:364.

e. *Ex parte orders or orders to show cause to bring on a motion.* No ex parte order, or order to show cause to bring on a motion, will be granted except upon a clear and specific showing by affidavit of good and sufficient reasons why a procedure other than by notice of motion is necessary, and stating whether a previous application for similar relief has been made. NY R USDCTS&ED Civ Rule 6.1(d).

f. *Letter-motions.* Applications for extensions or adjournments, applications for a pre-motion conference, and similar non-dispositive matters as permitted by the instructions regarding ECF published on the website of each respective Court and any pertinent Individual Judge's Practices, may be brought by letter-motion filed via ECF pursuant to NY R USDCTS&ED Civ Rule 5.2(b). NY R USDCTS&ED Civ Rule 7.1(d).

2. *Motion to dismiss for lack of personal jurisdiction.* A party may assert the defense of lack of subject-matter jurisdiction by motion. FRCP 12(b)(2). The most common use of the FRCP 12(b)(2) motion is to challenge the use of a state long-arm statute in a diversity action. FEDPROC § 62:445; Best Van Lines, Inc. v. Walker, 490 F.3d 239 (2d Cir. 2007). A dismissal pursuant to FRCP 12(b)(2) is proper where it appears that the assertion of jurisdiction over the defendant offends traditional notions of fair play and substantial justice—that is, where neither the defendant nor the controversy has a substantial enough connection with the forum state to make the exercise of jurisdiction reasonable. FEDPROC § 62:445; Neogen Corp. v. Neo Gen Screening, Inc., 282 F.3d 883, 2002 Fed.App. 0080P (6th Cir. 2002).

a. *Personal jurisdiction, generally*

   i. *Due process limitations.* Due process requires that a court obtain jurisdiction over a defendant before it may adjudicate that defendant's personal rights. FEDPROC § 65:1; Omni Capital Intern., Ltd. v. Rudolf Wolff & Co., Ltd., 484 U.S. 97, 108 S.Ct. 404, 98 L.Ed.2d 415, 9 Fed.R.Serv.3d 691 (1987).

   • Originally it was believed that a judgment in personam could only be entered against a defendant found and served within a state, but the increased flow of commerce between the states and the disuse of the writ of capias ad respondendum, which directed the sheriff to secure the defendant's appearance by taking him into custody, in civil cases led to the liberalization of the concept of personal jurisdiction over nonresidents, and the flexible "minimum contacts" test is now followed. FEDPROC § 65:1.

   • Now the rule is that no binding judgment may be rendered against an individual or corporate defendant unless the defendant has sufficient contacts, ties, or relations with the jurisdiction. FEDPROC § 65:1; Burger King Corp. v. Rudzewicz, 471 U.S. 462, 105 S.Ct. 2174, 85 L.Ed.2d 528 (1985); International Shoe Co. v. State of Wash., Office of

Unemployment Compensation and Placement, 326 U.S. 310, 66 S.Ct. 154, 90 L.Ed. 95, 161 A.L.R. 1057 (1945).

- Moreover, even if the defendant has sufficient contacts with the forum state to satisfy due process, a court nevertheless does not obtain personal jurisdiction over the defendant unless the defendant has notice sufficient to satisfy due process, and, if such notice requires service of a summons, that there is authorization for the type and manner of service used. FEDPROC § 65:1; Omni Capital Intern., Ltd. v. Rudolf Wolff & Co., Ltd., 484 U.S. 97, 108 S.Ct. 404, 98 L.Ed.2d 415, 9 Fed.R.Serv.3d 691 (1987).

- Personal jurisdiction is a prerequisite to the maintenance of an action, and must exist even though subject matter jurisdiction and venue are proper. FEDPROC § 65:1; Bookout v. Beck, 354 F.2d 823 (9th Cir. 1965).

- Personal jurisdiction over a nonresident defendant is appropriate under the due process clause only where the defendant has sufficient minimum contacts with the forum state that are more than random, fortuitous, or attenuated, such that summoning the defendant would not offend traditional notions of fair play and substantial justice. FEDPROC § 65:1; Pecoraro v. Sky Ranch for Boys, Inc., 340 F.3d 558 (8th Cir. 2003).

ii. *Methods of obtaining jurisdiction over an individual.* There are four basic methods of obtaining jurisdiction over an individual:

- Personal service within the jurisdiction. FEDPROC § 65:22.

- Service on a domiciliary of the forum state who is temporarily outside the jurisdiction, on the theory that the authority of a state over one of its citizens is not terminated by the mere fact of his absence. FEDPROC § 65:22; Milliken v. Meyer, 311 U.S. 457, 61 S.Ct. 339, 85 L.Ed. 278, 132 A.L.R. 1357 (1940).

- Service on a nonresident who has sufficient contacts with the forum state, since the test of International Shoe is applicable to individuals. FEDPROC § 65:22; Kulko v. Superior Court of California In and For City and County of San Francisco, 436 U.S. 84, 98 S.Ct. 1690, 56 L.Ed.2d 132 (1978).

- Service on an agent who has been expressly appointed or appointed by operation of law, such as under a nonresident motorist statute. FEDPROC § 65:22; National Equipment Rental, Limited v. Szukhent, 375 U.S. 311, 84 S.Ct. 411, 11 L.Ed.2d 354, 7 Fed.R.Serv.2d 23 (1964).

iii. *Territorial limits of effective service*

- *In general.* Serving a summons or filing a waiver of service establishes personal jurisdiction over a defendant: (1) who is subject to the jurisdiction of a court of general jurisdiction in the state where the district court is located; (2) who is a party joined under FRCP 14 or FRCP 19 and is served within a judicial district of the United States and not more than one hundred (100) miles from where the summons was issued; or (3) when authorized by a federal statute. FRCP 4(k)(1).

- *Federal claim outside state-court jurisdiction.* For a claim that arises under federal law, serving a summons or filing a waiver of service establishes personal jurisdiction over a defendant if: (1) the defendant is not subject to jurisdiction in any state's courts of general jurisdiction; and (2) exercising jurisdiction is consistent with the United States Constitution and laws. FRCP 4(k)(2).

b. *Motion based on lack of in rem or quasi-in-rem jurisdiction.* Although FRCP 12(b)(2) only refers to "jurisdiction over the person," the provision presumably is sufficiently elastic to embrace a defense or objection that the district court lacks in rem or quasi-in-rem jurisdiction, admittedly a subject that rarely arises in contemporary practice. FPP § 1351.

c. *Motion based on insufficient process or insufficient service of process.* FRCP 12(b)(2) motions to dismiss are frequently based on the failure to serve the defendant with process or a defective service of process, on the theory that if the defendant was not properly served with process, the court lacks personal jurisdiction over the defendant. FEDPROC § 62:446; Prokopiou v. Long Island R. Co., 2007 WL 1098696 (S.D.N.Y. 2007).

d. *Independent ground for dismissal.* Lack of overall reasonableness in the assertion of personal jurisdiction constitutes an independent ground for dismissal under FRCP 12(b)(2). FEDPROC § 62:448; Federal Ins. Co. v. Lake Shore Inc., 886 F.2d 654 (4th Cir. 1989).

e. *Burden.* On the motion, the plaintiff bears the burden to establish the court's jurisdiction, which normally is not a heavy one, although the standard of proof may vary depending on the procedure used by the court in making its determination and whether the defendant is successful in rebutting the plaintiff's initial showing. Moreover, the Supreme Court has intimated that in the case of a challenge to the constitutional fairness and reasonableness of the chosen forum, the burden is on the defendant. FPP § 1351; Burger King Corp. v. Rudzewicz, 471 U.S. 462, 105 S.Ct. 2174, 85 L.Ed.2d 528 (1985).

   i. The most common formulation found in the judicial opinions is that the plaintiff bears the ultimate burden of demonstrating that the court's personal jurisdiction over the defendant exists by a preponderance of the evidence, but needs only make a prima facie showing when the district judge restricts her review of the FRCP 12(b)(2) motion solely to affidavits and other written evidence. FPP § 1351; Mullins v. TestAmerica, Inc., 564 F.3d 386 (5th Cir. 2009).

   ii. In addition, for purposes of such a review, federal courts will, as they do on other motions under FRCP 12(b), take as true the allegations of the nonmoving party with regard to the jurisdictional issues and resolve all factual disputes in his or her favor. FPP § 1351.

f. *Motion denied.* A party who has unsuccessfully raised an objection under FRCP 12(b)(2) may proceed to trial on the merits without waiving the ability to renew the objection to the court's jurisdiction. FPP § 1351.

g. *Joining motions.* As a general rule, when the court is confronted by a motion raising a combination of FRCP 12(b) defenses, it will pass on the jurisdictional issues before considering whether a claim was stated by the complaint. FPP § 1351.

   i. *Right to join.* A motion under FRCP 12 may be joined with any other motion allowed by FRCP 12. FRCP 12(g)(1).

   ii. *Limitation on further motions.* Except as provided in FRCP 12(h)(2) or FRCP 12(h)(3), a party that makes a motion under FRCP 12 must not make another motion under FRCP 12 raising a defense or objection that was available to the party but omitted from its earlier motion. FRCP 12(g)(2).

h. *Waiving and preserving certain defenses.* No defense or objection is waived by joining it with one or more other defenses or objections in a responsive pleading or in a motion. FRCP 12(b).

   i. *Waiver by consent or stipulation.* A valid consent or a stipulation that the court has jurisdiction prevents the successful assertion of a FRCP 12(b)(2) defense. FPP § 1351.

   ii. *Waiver by filing permissive counterclaim.* A defendant may be deemed to have waived an objection to personal jurisdiction if he or she files a permissive counterclaim under FRCP 13(b). FPP § 1351.

   iii. *When some are waived.* A party waives any defense listed in FRCP 12(b)(2) through FRCP 12(b)(5) by:

   - Omitting it from a motion in the circumstances described in FRCP 12(g)(2); or

   - Failing to either: (1) make it by motion under FRCP 12; or (2) include it in a responsive pleading or in an amendment allowed by FRCP 15(a)(1) as a matter of course. FRCP 12(h)(1).

   iv. *When to raise others.* Failure to state a claim upon which relief can be granted, to join a person required by FRCP 19(b), or to state a legal defense to a claim may be raised:

   - In any pleading allowed or ordered under FRCP 7(a);

   - By a motion under FRCP 12(c); or

   - At trial. FRCP 12(h)(2).

    v.   *Lack of subject matter jurisdiction.* If the court determines at any time that it lacks subject-matter jurisdiction, the court must dismiss the action. FRCP 12(h)(3).

3.  *Opposing papers.* The Federal Rules of Civil Procedure do not require any formal answer, return, or reply to a motion, except where the Federal Rules of Civil Procedure or local rules may require affidavits, memoranda, or other papers to be filed in opposition to a motion. Such papers are simply to apprise the court of such opposition and the grounds of that opposition. FEDPROC § 62:359. Except for letter-motions as permitted by NY R USDCTS&ED Civ Rule 7.1(d) or as otherwise permitted by the Court, all oppositions and replies with respect to motions shall comply with NY R USDCTS&ED Civ Rule 7.1(a)(2) and NY R USDCTS&ED Civ Rule 7.1(a)(3), and an opposing party who seeks relief that goes beyond the denial of the motion shall comply as well with NY R USDCTS&ED Civ Rule 7.1(a)(1). NY R USDCTS&ED Civ Rule 7.1(b).

    a.  *Effect of failure to respond to motion.* Although in the absence of statutory provision or court rule, a motion ordinarily does not require a written answer, when a party files a motion and the opposing party fails to respond, the court may construe such failure to respond as nonopposition to the motion or an admission that the motion was meritorious, may take the facts alleged in the motion as true—the rule in some jurisdictions being that the failure to respond to a fact set forth in a motion is deemed an admission—and may grant the motion if the relief requested appears to be justified. AMJUR MOTIONS § 28.

    b.  *Assent or no opposition not determinative.* However, a motion will not be granted automatically simply because an "assent" or a notation of "no opposition" has been filed; federal judges frequently deny motions that have been assented to when it is thought that justice so dictates. FPP § 1190.

    c.  *Responsive pleading inappropriate as response to motion.* An attempt to answer or oppose a motion with a responsive pleading usually is not appropriate. FPP § 1190.

4.  *Reply papers.* A moving party may be required or permitted to prepare papers in addition to his original motion papers. AMJUR MOTIONS § 25. Papers answering or replying to opposing papers may be appropriate, in the interests of justice, where it appears there is a substantial reason for allowing a reply. Thus, a court may accept reply papers where a party demonstrates that the papers to which it seeks to file a reply raise new issues that are material to the disposition of the question before the court, or where the court determines, sua sponte, that it wishes further briefing of an issue raised in those papers and orders the submission of additional papers. FEDPROC § 62:360. Except for letter-motions as permitted by NY R USDCTS&ED Civ Rule 7.1(d) or as otherwise permitted by the Court, all oppositions and replies with respect to motions shall comply with NY R USDCTS&ED Civ Rule 7.1(a)(2) and NY R USDCTS&ED Civ Rule 7.1(a)(3). NY R USDCTS&ED Civ Rule 7.1(b).

    a.  *Function of reply papers.* The function of a reply affidavit is to answer the arguments made in opposition to the position taken by the movant and not to permit the movant to introduce new arguments in support of the motion. AMJUR MOTIONS § 25.

    b.  *Issues raised for the first time in a reply document.* However, the view has been followed in some jurisdictions, that as a matter of judicial economy, where there is no prejudice and where the issues could be raised simply by filing a motion to dismiss, the trial court has discretion to consider arguments raised for the first time in a reply memorandum, and that a trial court may grant a motion to strike issues raised for the first time in a reply memorandum. AMJUR MOTIONS § 26.

5.  *Orders on motions.* A memorandum signed by the Court of the decision on a motion that does not finally determine all claims for relief, or an oral decision on such a motion, shall constitute the order unless the memorandum or oral decision directs the submission or settlement of an order in more extended form. The notation in the docket of a memorandum or of an oral decision that does not direct the submission or settlement of an order in more extended form shall constitute the entry of the order. Where an order in more extended form is required to be submitted or settled, the notation in the docket of such order shall constitute the entry of the order. NY R USDCTS&ED Civ Rule 6.2.

6.  *Related cases.* It shall be the continuing duty of each attorney appearing in any civil or criminal case to bring promptly to the attention of the Court all facts which said attorney believes are relevant to a determination that said case and one or more pending civil or criminal cases should be heard by the same Judge, in order to avoid unnecessary duplication of judicial effort. As soon as the attorney becomes aware

of such relationship, said attorney shall notify the Judges to whom the cases have been assigned. NY R USDCTS&ED Civ Rule 1.6(a). If counsel fails to comply with NY R USDCTS&ED Civ Rule 1.6(a), the Court may assess reasonable costs directly against counsel whose action has obstructed the effective administration of the Court's business. NY R USDCTS&ED Civ Rule 1.6(b).

7. *Alternative dispute resolution (ADR)*

   a. *Court-annexed arbitration*

      i. *Civil cases eligible for compulsory arbitration.* The Clerk of Court shall, as to all cases filed after January 1, 1986, designate and process for compulsory arbitration all civil cases (excluding Social Security cases, tax matters, prisoners' civil rights cases and any action based on an alleged violation of a right secured by the Constitution of the United States or if jurisdiction is based in whole or in part on 28 U.S.C.A. § 1343) wherein money damages only are being sought in an amount not in excess of one hundred fifty thousand dollars ($150,000) exclusive of interest and costs. NY R USDCTS&ED Civ Rule 83.7(d)(1).

         • The parties may by written stipulation agree that the Clerk of Court shall designate and process for court-annexed arbitration any civil case that is not subject to compulsory arbitration in NY R USDCTS&ED Civ Rule 83.7. NY R USDCTS&ED Civ Rule 83.7(d)(2).

         • For purposes of NY R USDCTS&ED Civ Rule 83.7 only, in all civil cases damages shall be presumed to be not in excess of one hundred fifty thousand dollars ($150,000) exclusive of interest and costs, unless: (1) counsel for plaintiff, at the time of filing the complaint, or in the event of the removal of a case from state court or transfer of a case from another district to this Court, within thirty (30) days of the docketing of the case in this district, files a certification with the Court that the damages sought exceed one hundred fifty thousand dollars ($150,000), exclusive of interest and costs; or (2) counsel for a defendant, at the time of filing a counterclaim or cross-claim files a certification with the court that the damages sought by the counter-claim or cross-claim exceed one hundred fifty thousand dollars ($150,000) exclusive of interest and costs. NY R USDCTS&ED Civ Rule 83.7(d)(3).

      ii. *Exemption from arbitration.* The Court shall, sua sponte, or on motion of a party, exempt any case from arbitration in which the objectives of arbitration would not be realized (1) because the case involves complex or novel issues, (2) because legal issues predominate over factual issues, or (3) for other good cause. NY R USDCTS&ED Civ Rule 83.7(e)(2). For information on applying for an exemption, refer to NY R USDCTS&ED Civ Rule 83.7

      iii. *Referral to arbitration.* Cases not originally designated as eligible for compulsory arbitration, but which in the discretion of the assigned Judge, are later found to qualify, may be referred to arbitration. A U.S. District Judge or a U.S. Magistrate Judge, in cases that exceed the arbitration ceiling of one hundred fifty thousand dollars ($150,000) exclusive of interest and costs, in their discretion, may suggest that the parties should consider arbitration. If the parties are agreeable, an appropriate consent form signed by all parties or their representatives may be entered and filed in the case prior to scheduling an arbitration hearing. NY R USDCTS&ED Civ Rule 83.7(e)(3).

      iv. For more information on arbitration, refer to NY R USDCTS&ED Civ Rule 83.7.

   b. *Court-annexed mediation.* Mediation is a process in which parties and counsel agree to meet with a neutral mediator trained to assist them in settling disputes. The mediator improves communication across party lines, helps parties articulate their interests and understand those of the other party, probes the strengths and weaknesses of each party's legal positions, and identifies areas of agreement and helps generate options for a mutually agreeable resolution to the dispute. In all cases, mediation provides an opportunity to explore a wide range of potential solutions and to address interests that may be outside the scope of the stated controversy or which could not be addressed by judicial action. A hallmark of mediation is its capacity to expand traditional settlement discussions and broaden resolution options, often by exploring litigant needs and interests that may be formally independent of the legal issues in controversy. NY R USDCTS&ED Civ Rule 83.8(a).

      i. *Eligible cases.* Judges and Magistrate Judges may designate civil cases for inclusion in the mediation program, and when doing so shall prepare an order to that effect. Alternatively, and subject to the availability of qualified mediators, the parties may consent to participation in the mediation program by preparing and executing a stipulation signed by all parties to the action and so-ordered by the Court. NY R USDCTS&ED Civ Rule 83.8(b)(1).

    ii.  For more information on mediation, refer to NY R USDCTS&ED Civ Rule 83.8.

8. *Individual judge practices.* Refer to the Miscellaneous section of this document for information on individual judge practices on general requirements for documents.

## D. Documents

1. *Documents for moving party*

    a.  *Required documents*

        i.  *Notice of motion and motion.* Except for letter-motions as permitted by NY R USDCTS&ED Civ Rule 7.1(d) or as otherwise permitted by the Court, all motions shall include the following motion papers: a notice of motion, or an order to show cause signed by the Court, which shall specify the applicable rules or statutes pursuant to which the motion is brought, and shall specify the relief sought by the motion. NY R USDCTS&ED Civ Rule 7.1(a)(1). Refer to the General Requirements section of this document for information on the notice of motion and motion.

        ii.  *Memorandum of law.* Except for letter-motions as permitted by NY R USDCTS&ED Civ Rule 7.1(d) or as otherwise permitted by the Court, all motions shall include the following motion papers: a memorandum of law, setting forth the cases and other authorities relied upon in support of the motion, and divided, under appropriate headings, into as many parts as there are issues to be determined. NY R USDCTS&ED Civ Rule 7.1(a)(2).

        iii.  *Certificate of service.* FRCP 5(d) requires that the person making service under FRCP 5 certify that service has been effected. FRCP 5(Advisory Committee Notes). Having such information on file may be useful for many purposes, including proof of service if an issue arises concerning the effectiveness of the service. FRCP 5(Advisory Committee Notes).

    b.  *Supplemental documents*

        i.  *Supporting evidence.* When a motion relies on facts outside the record, the court may hear the matter on affidavits or may hear it wholly or partly on oral testimony or on depositions. FRCP 43(c). Except for letter-motions as permitted by NY R USDCTS&ED Civ Rule 7.1(d) or as otherwise permitted by the Court, all motions shall include the following motion papers: supporting affidavits and exhibits thereto containing any factual information and portions of the record necessary for the decision of the motion. NY R USDCTS&ED Civ Rule 7.1(a)(3).

- *Discovery materials.* A party seeking or opposing relief under FRCP 26 through FRCP 37 inclusive, or making or opposing any other motion or application, shall quote or attach only those portions of the depositions, interrogatories, requests for documents, requests for admissions, or other discovery or disclosure materials, together with the responses and objections thereto, that are the subject of the discovery motion or application, or that are cited in papers submitted in connection with any other motion or application. NY R USDCTS&ED Civ Rule 5.1.

        ii.  *Notice of constitutional question.* A party that files a pleading, written motion, or other paper drawing into question the constitutionality of a federal or state statute must promptly:

- *File notice.* File a notice of constitutional question stating the question and identifying the paper that raises it, if: (1) a federal statute is questioned and the parties do not include the United States, one of its agencies, or one of its officers or employees in an official capacity; or (2) a state statute is questioned and the parties do not include the state, one of its agencies, or one of its officers or employees in an official capacity; and

- *Serve notice.* Serve the notice and paper on the Attorney General of the United States if a federal statute is questioned—or on the state attorney general if a state statute is questioned—either by certified or registered mail or by sending it to an electronic address designated by the attorney general for this purpose. FRCP 5.1(a).

- *No forfeiture.* A party's failure to file and serve the notice, or the court's failure to certify, does not forfeit a constitutional claim or defense that is otherwise timely asserted. FRCP 5.1(d).

iii. *Nongovernmental corporate disclosure statement.* To enable judges and magistrates to evaluate possible disqualification or recusal, counsel for a private (nongovernmental) party shall submit at the time of initial pleading a certificate identifying any corporate parent, subsidiaries, or affiliates of that party. NY R USDCTED Div. Bus., Rule 50.1(c).

- *Contents.* A nongovernmental corporate party must file two (2) copies of a disclosure statement that: (1) identifies any parent corporation and any publicly held corporation owning ten percent (10%) or more of its stock; or (2) states that there is no such corporation. FRCP 7.1(a).

- *Time to file; Supplemental filing.* A party must: (1) file the disclosure statement with its first appearance, pleading, petition, motion, response, or other request addressed to the court; and (2) promptly file a supplemental statement if any required information changes. FRCP 7.1(b). For purposes of FRCP 7.1(b)(2), "promptly" shall mean "within fourteen days," that is, parties are required to file a supplemental disclosure statement within fourteen (14) days of the time there is any change in the information required in a disclosure statement filed pursuant to those rules. NY R USDCTS&ED Civ Rule 7.1.1.

iv. *Notice to pro se litigant who opposes a FRCP 12 motion supported by matters outside the pleadings.* A represented party moving to dismiss or for judgment on the pleadings against a party proceeding pro se, who refers in support of the motion to matters outside the pleadings as described in FRCP 12(b) or FRCP 12(c), shall serve and file the notice in NY R USDCTS&ED Civ Rule 12.1 with the full text of FRCP 56 attached at the time the motion is served. If the Court rules that a motion to dismiss or for judgment on the pleadings will be treated as one for summary judgment pursuant to FRCP 56, and the movant has not previously served and filed the notice required by NY R USDCTS&ED Civ Rule 12.1, the movant shall amend the form notice to reflect that fact and shall serve and file the amended notice within fourteen (14) days of the Court's ruling. NY R USDCTS&ED Civ Rule 12.1. For the notice, refer to NY R USDCTS&ED Civ Rule 12.1.

v. *Copies of authorities.* In cases involving a pro se litigant, counsel shall, when serving a memorandum of law (or other submissions to the Court), provide the pro se litigant (but not other counsel or the Court) with copies of cases and other authorities cited therein that are unpublished or reported exclusively on computerized databases. Upon request, counsel shall provide the pro se litigant with copies of such unpublished cases and other authorities as are cited in a decision of the Court and were not previously cited by any party. NY R USDCTS&ED Civ Rule 7.2.

2. *Documents for opposing party*

   a. *Required documents*

      i. *Answering memorandum of law.* Except for letter-motions as permitted by NY R USDCTS&ED Civ Rule 7.1(d) or as otherwise permitted by the Court, all oppositions and replies with respect to motions shall comply with NY R USDCTS&ED Civ Rule 7.1(a)(2). NY R USDCTS&ED Civ Rule 7.1(b). Except for letter-motions as permitted by NY R USDCTS&ED Civ Rule 7.1(d) or as otherwise permitted by the Court, all motions shall include the following motion papers: a memorandum of law, setting forth the cases and other authorities relied upon in support of the motion, and divided, under appropriate headings, into as many parts as there are issues to be determined. NY R USDCTS&ED Civ Rule 7.1(a)(2). Refer to the General Requirements section of this document for information on the opposing papers.

      ii. *Certificate of service.* FRCP 5(d) requires that the person making service under FRCP 5 certify that service has been effected. FRCP 5(Advisory Committee Notes). Having such information on file may be useful for many purposes, including proof of service if an issue arises concerning the effectiveness of the service. FRCP 5(Advisory Committee Notes).

   b. *Supplemental documents*

      i. *Supporting evidence.* When a motion relies on facts outside the record, the court may hear the

matter on affidavits or may hear it wholly or partly on oral testimony or on depositions. FRCP 43(c). Except for letter-motions as permitted by NY R USDCTS&ED Civ Rule 7.1(d) or as otherwise permitted by the Court, all oppositions and replies with respect to motions shall comply with NY R USDCTS&ED Civ Rule 7.1(a)(3). NY R USDCTS&ED Civ Rule 7.1(b). Except for letter-motions as permitted by NY R USDCTS&ED Civ Rule 7.1(d) or as otherwise permitted by the Court, all motions shall include the following motion papers: supporting affidavits and exhibits thereto containing any factual information and portions of the record necessary for the decision of the motion. NY R USDCTS&ED Civ Rule 7.1(a)(3).

- *Discovery materials.* A party seeking or opposing relief under FRCP 26 through FRCP 37 inclusive, or making or opposing any other motion or application, shall quote or attach only those portions of the depositions, interrogatories, requests for documents, requests for admissions, or other discovery or disclosure materials, together with the responses and objections thereto, that are the subject of the discovery motion or application, or that are cited in papers submitted in connection with any other motion or application. NY R USDCTS&ED Civ Rule 5.1.

ii. *Notice of constitutional question.* A party that files a pleading, written motion, or other paper drawing into question the constitutionality of a federal or state statute must promptly:

- *File notice.* File a notice of constitutional question stating the question and identifying the paper that raises it, if: (1) a federal statute is questioned and the parties do not include the United States, one of its agencies, or one of its officers or employees in an official capacity; or (2) a state statute is questioned and the parties do not include the state, one of its agencies, or one of its officers or employees in an official capacity; and

- *Serve notice.* Serve the notice and paper on the Attorney General of the United States if a federal statute is questioned—or on the state attorney general if a state statute is questioned—either by certified or registered mail or by sending it to an electronic address designated by the attorney general for this purpose. FRCP 5.1(a).

- *No forfeiture.* A party's failure to file and serve the notice, or the court's failure to certify, does not forfeit a constitutional claim or defense that is otherwise timely asserted. FRCP 5.1(d).

iii. *Copies of authorities.* In cases involving a pro se litigant, counsel shall, when serving a memorandum of law (or other submissions to the Court), provide the pro se litigant (but not other counsel or the Court) with copies of cases and other authorities cited therein that are unpublished or reported exclusively on computerized databases. Upon request, counsel shall provide the pro se litigant with copies of such unpublished cases and other authorities as are cited in a decision of the Court and were not previously cited by any party. NY R USDCTS&ED Civ Rule 7.2.

3. *Individual judge practices.* Refer to the Miscellaneous section of this document for information on individual judge practices on required documents.

## E. Format

1. *Form of documents.* The rules governing captions and other matters of form in pleadings apply to motions and other papers. FRCP 7(b)(2).

a. *Paper.* Every pleading, written motion, and other paper must: be plainly written, typed, printed, or copied without erasures or interlineations which materially deface it. NY R USDCTS&ED Civ Rule 11.1(a)(1).

b. *Typeface, margin, and spacing.* The typeface, margins, and spacing of all documents presented for filing must meet the following requirements:

i. All text must be twelve (12) point type or larger, except for text in footnotes which may be ten (10) point type;

ii. All documents must have at least one (1) inch margins on all sides;

iii. All text must be double-spaced, except for headings, text in footnotes, or block quotations, which may be single-spaced. NY R USDCTS&ED Civ Rule 11.1(b).

c. *Caption; Names of parties.* Every pleading must have a caption with the court's name, a title, a file number, and a FRCP 7(a) designation. The title of the complaint must name all the parties; the title of other pleadings, after naming the first party on each side, may refer generally to other parties. FRCP 10(a). Every pleading, written motion, and other paper must: bear the docket number and the initials of the District Judge and any Magistrate Judge before whom the action or proceeding is pending, NY R USDCTS&ED Civ Rule 11.1(a)(2).

d. *Paragraphs; Separate statements.* A party must state its claims or defenses in numbered paragraphs, each limited as far as practicable to a single set of circumstances. A later pleading may refer by number to a paragraph in an earlier pleading. If doing so would promote clarity, each claim founded on a separate transaction or occurrence—and each defense other than a denial—must be stated in a separate count or defense. FRCP 10(b).

e. *Adoption by reference; Exhibits.* A statement in a pleading may be adopted by reference elsewhere in the same pleading or in any other pleading or motion. A copy of a written instrument that is an exhibit to a pleading is a part of the pleading for all purposes. FRCP 10(c).

f. *Acceptance by the clerk.* The clerk must not refuse to file a paper solely because it is not in the form prescribed by the Federal Rules of Civil Procedure or by a local rule or practice. FRCP 5(d)(4).

2. *Signing of pleadings, motions and other papers*

a. *Signature.* Every pleading, written motion, and other paper must be signed by at least one attorney of record in the attorney's name—or by a party personally if the party is unrepresented. The paper must state the signer's address, e-mail address, and telephone number. FRCP 11(a). Every pleading, written motion, and other paper must: have the name of each person signing it clearly printed or typed directly below the signature. NY R USDCTS&ED Civ Rule 11.1(a)(3).

   i. *No verification or accompanying affidavit required for pleadings.* Unless a rule or statute specifically states otherwise, a pleading need not be verified or accompanied by an affidavit. FRCP 11(a).

   ii. *Unsigned papers.* The court must strike an unsigned paper unless the omission is promptly corrected after being called to the attorney's or party's attention. FRCP 11(a).

b. *Representations to the court.* By presenting to the court a pleading, written motion, or other paper—whether by signing, filing, submitting, or later advocating it—an attorney or unrepresented party certifies that to the best of the person's knowledge, information, and belief, formed after an inquiry reasonable under the circumstances:

   i. It is not being presented for any improper purpose, such as to harass, cause unnecessary delay, or needlessly increase the cost of litigation;

   ii. The claims, defenses, and other legal contentions are warranted by existing law or by a nonfrivolous argument for extending, modifying, or reversing existing law or for establishing new law;

   iii. The factual contentions have evidentiary support or, if specifically so identified, will likely have evidentiary support after a reasonable opportunity for further investigation or discovery; and

   iv. The denials of factual contentions are warranted on the evidence or, if specifically so identified, are reasonably based on belief or a lack of information. FRCP 11(b).

c. *Sanctions.* If, after notice and a reasonable opportunity to respond, the court determines that FRCP 11(b) has been violated, the court may impose an appropriate sanction on any attorney, law firm, or party that violated FRCP 11(b) or is responsible for the violation. FRCP 11(c)(1). Refer to the United States District Court for the Eastern District of New York KeyRules Motion for Sanctions document for more information.

3. *Privacy protection for filings made with the court*

a. *Redacted filings.* Unless the court orders otherwise, in an electronic or paper filing with the court that contains an individual's Social Security number, taxpayer-identification number, or birth date, the name of an individual known to be a minor, or a financial-account number, a party or nonparty making the filing may include only:

   i. The last four (4) digits of the Social Security number and taxpayer-identification number;

    ii.   The year of the individual's birth;

    iii.  The minor's initials; and

    iv.  The last four (4) digits of the financial-account number. FRCP 5.2(a); NY R USDCTED Order 2004-09.

    v.   In addition, exercise caution when filing documents that contain the following:

- Personal identifying number, such as driver's license number;

- Medical records, treatment and diagnosis;

- Employment history;

- Individual financial information; and

- Proprietary or trade secret information. NY R USDCTED Order 2004-09.

b.  *Exemptions from the redaction requirement.* The redaction requirement does not apply to the following:

    i.   A financial-account number that identifies the property allegedly subject to forfeiture in a forfeiture proceeding;

    ii.  The record of an administrative or agency proceeding;

    iii.  The official record of a state-court proceeding;

    iv.  The record of a court or tribunal, if that record was not subject to the redaction requirement when originally filed;

    v.   A filing covered by FRCP 5.2(c) or FRCP 5.2(d); and

    vi.  A pro se filing in an action brought under 28 U.S.C.A. § 2241, 28 U.S.C.A. § 2254, or 28 U.S.C.A. § 2255. FRCP 5.2(b).

c.  *Limitations on remote access to electronic files; Social Security appeals and immigration cases.* Unless the court orders otherwise, in an action for benefits under the Social Security Act, and in an action or proceeding relating to an order of removal, to relief from removal, or to immigration benefits or detention, access to an electronic file is authorized as follows:

    i.   The parties and their attorneys may have remote electronic access to any part of the case file, including the administrative record;

    ii.  Any other person may have electronic access to the full record at the courthouse, but may have remote electronic access only to:

- The docket maintained by the court; and

- An opinion, order, judgment, or other disposition of the court, but not any other part of the case file or the administrative record. FRCP 5.2(c).

d.  *Filings made under seal.* The court may order that a filing be made under seal without redaction. The court may later unseal the filing or order the person who made the filing to file a redacted version for the public record. FRCP 5.2(d).

e.  *Protective orders.* For good cause, the court may by order in a case:

    i.   Require redaction of additional information; or

    ii.  Limit or prohibit a nonparty's remote electronic access to a document filed with the court. FRCP 5.2(e).

f.  *Option for additional unredacted filing under seal.* A person making a redacted filing may also file an unredacted copy under seal. The court must retain the unredacted copy as part of the record. FRCP 5.2(f); NY R USDCTED Order 2004-09. The unredacted version of the document or the reference list shall be retained by the court as part of the record. The court may, however, still require the party to file a redacted copy for the public file. NY R USDCTED Order 2004-09.

g.  *Option for filing a reference list.* A filing that contains redacted information may be filed together with a reference list that identifies each item of redacted information and specifies an appropriate

identifier that uniquely corresponds to each item listed. The list must be filed under seal and may be amended as of right. Any reference in the case to a listed identifier will be construed to refer to the corresponding item of information. FRCP 5.2(g); NY R USDCTED Order 2004-09. The unredacted version of the document or the reference list shall be retained by the court as part of the record. The court may, however, still require the party to file a redacted copy for the public file. NY R USDCTED Order 2004-09.

h. *Responsibility for redaction.* The responsibility for redacting these personal identifiers rests solely with counsel and the parties. The Clerk will not review each pleading for compliance with NY R USDCTED Order 2004-09. NY R USDCTED Order 2004-09.

   i. Counsel is strongly urged to share this notice with all clients so that an informed decision about the inclusion of certain materials may be made. If a redacted document is filed, it is the sole responsibility of counsel and the parties to be sure that all pleadings comply with the rules of this court requiring redaction of personal data identifiers. The clerk will not review each pleading for redaction. NY R USDCTED Order 2004-09.

i. *Waiver of protection of identifiers.* A person waives the protection of FRCP 5.2(a) as to the person's own information by filing it without redaction and not under seal. FRCP 5.2(h).

4. *Individual judge practices.* Refer to the Miscellaneous section of this document for information on individual judge practices on formatting documents.

## F. Filing and Service Requirements

1. *Filing requirements.* Any paper after the complaint that is required to be served—together with a certificate of service—must be filed within a reasonable time after service. FRCP 5(d)(1).

   a. *How filing is made; In general.* A paper is filed by delivering it:

      i. To the clerk; or

      ii. To a judge who agrees to accept it for filing, and who must then note the filing date on the paper and promptly send it to the clerk. FRCP 5(d)(2).

   b. *Night depository.* A night depository with an automatic date stamp shall be maintained. . .by the Clerk of the Eastern District in the Brooklyn Courthouse. After regular business hours, papers for the District Court only may be deposited in the night depository. Such papers will be considered as having been filed in the District Court as of the date stamped thereon, which shall be deemed presumptively correct. NY R USDCTS&ED Civ Rule 1.2.

   c. *Electronic filing*

      i. *Authorization of electronic filing program.* A court may, by local rule, allow papers to be filed, signed, or verified by electronic means that are consistent with any technical standards established by the Judicial Conference of the United States. A local rule may require electronic filing only if reasonable exceptions are allowed. A paper filed electronically in compliance with a local rule is a written paper for purposes of the Federal Rules of Civil Procedure. FRCP 5(d)(3).

         • Parties serving and filing papers shall follow the instructions regarding Electronic Case Filing (ECF) published on the website of each respective Court. A paper served and filed by electronic means in accordance with such instructions is, for purposes of FRCP 5, served and filed in compliance with the Local Civil Rules of the Southern and Eastern Districts of New York. NY R USDCTS&ED Civ Rule 5.2(a). Parties have an obligation to review the Court's actual order, decree, or judgment (on ECF), which controls, and should not rely on the description on the docket or in the ECF Notice of Electronic Filing (NEF). NY R USDCTS&ED Civ Rule 5.2(c).

      ii. *Mandatory electronic filing.* Beginning on August 2, 2004, electronic case filing will be mandatory for all civil cases other than pro se cases. NY R USDCTED Order 2004-08.

         • *Letter-motions and letters addressed to the court.* Subject to the instructions regarding ECF published on the website of each respective Court and any pertinent Individual Judge's Practices, letter-motions permitted by NY R USDCTS&ED Civ Rule 7.1(d) and letters addressed to the Court (but not letters between the parties) may be filed via ECF. NY R USDCTS&ED Civ Rule 5.2(b).

- *Proposed orders, judgments and decrees.* Proposed orders, judgments and decrees shall be presented as directed by the ECF rules published on the website of each respective Court. NY R USDCTS&ED Civ Rule 77.1. For more information, refer to NY R USDCTS&ED Civ Rule 77.1.

- *Request for exemption.* Requests by attorneys for an exemption to the mandatory policy will be considered for good cause hardship reasons only, and will be reviewed on an individual basis by the assigned United States Magistrate Judge. The Clerk's Office provides an electronic filing training program to assist attorneys filing electronically. Before seeking a hardship exemption, attorneys are advised to participate in the training program or otherwise seek the assistance of the Clerk's Office. NY R USDCTED Order 2004-08.

    iii.  For more information on electronic filing, refer to the court's website.

2. *Service requirements*

  a.  *Service; When required*

    i.  *In general.* Unless the Federal Rules of Civil Procedure provide otherwise, each of the following papers must be served on every party:

- An order stating that service is required;

- A pleading filed after the original complaint, unless the court orders otherwise under FRCP 5(c) because there are numerous defendants;

- A discovery paper required to be served on a party, unless the court orders otherwise;

- A written motion, except one that may be heard ex parte; and

- A written notice, appearance, demand, or offer of judgment, or any similar paper. FRCP 5(a)(1).

    ii.  *If a party fails to appear.* No service is required on a party who is in default for failing to appear. But a pleading that asserts a new claim for relief against such a party must be served on that party under FRCP 4. FRCP 5(a)(2).

    iii.  *Seizing property.* If an action is begun by seizing property and no person is or need be named as a defendant, any service required before the filing of an appearance, answer, or claim must be made on the person who had custody or possession of the property when it was seized. FRCP 5(a)(3).

  b.  *Service; How made*

    i.  *Serving an attorney.* If a party is represented by an attorney, service under FRCP 5 must be made on the attorney unless the court orders service on the party. FRCP 5(b)(1).

    ii.  *Service in general.* A paper is served under FRCP 5 by:

- Handing it to the person;

- Leaving it: (1) at the person's office with a clerk or other person in charge or, if no one is in charge, in a conspicuous place in the office; or (2) if the person has no office or the office is closed, at the person's dwelling or usual place of abode with someone of suitable age and discretion who resides there;

- Mailing it to the person's last known address—in which event service is complete upon mailing;

- Leaving it with the court clerk if the person has no known address;

- Sending it by electronic means if the person consented in writing—in which event service is complete upon transmission, but is not effective if the serving party learns that it did not reach the person to be served; or

- Delivering it by any other means that the person consented to in writing—in which event service is complete when the person making service delivers it to the agency designated to make delivery. FRCP 5(b)(2).

   iii. *Service by overnight delivery.* Service upon an attorney may be made by overnight delivery service. "Overnight delivery service" means any delivery service which regularly accepts items for overnight delivery. Overnight delivery service shall be deemed service by mail for purposes of FRCP 5 and FRCP 6. NY R USDCTS&ED Civ Rule 5.3.

   iv. *Service by electronic means.* Parties serving and filing papers shall follow the instructions regarding Electronic Case Filing (ECF) published on the website of each respective Court. A paper served and filed by electronic means in accordance with such instructions is, for purposes of FRCP 5, served and filed in compliance with the Local Civil Rules of the United States District Courts for the Southern and Eastern Districts of New York. NY R USDCTS&ED Civ Rule 5.2(a). Parties have an obligation to review the Court's actual order, decree, or judgment (on ECF), which controls, and should not rely on the description on the docket or in the ECF Notice of Electronic Filing (NEF). NY R USDCTS&ED Civ Rule 5.2(c).

   v. *Using court facilities.* If a local rule so authorizes, a party may use the court's transmission facilities to make service under FRCP 5(b)(2)(E). FRCP 5(b)(3).

 c. *Serving numerous defendants*

   i. *In general.* If an action involves an unusually large number of defendants, the court may, on motion or on its own, order that:

   - Defendants' pleadings and replies to them need not be served on other defendants;
   - Any crossclaim, counterclaim, avoidance, or affirmative defense in those pleadings and replies to them will be treated as denied or avoided by all other parties; and
   - Filing any such pleading and serving it on the plaintiff constitutes notice of the pleading to all parties. FRCP 5(c)(1).

   ii. *Notifying parties.* A copy of every such order must be served on the parties as the court directs. FRCP 5(c)(2).

3. *Individual judge practices.* Refer to the Miscellaneous section of this document for information on individual judge practices on filing and serving documents.

# G. Hearings

1. *Hearings, generally*

 a. *Oral argument.* Due process does not require that oral argument be permitted on a motion and, except as otherwise provided by local rule, the district court has discretion to determine whether it will decide the motion on the papers or hear argument by counsel (and perhaps receive evidence). FPP § 1190; F.D.I.C. v. Deglau, 207 F.3d 153 (3d Cir. 2000). The parties and their attorneys shall only appear to argue the motion if so directed by the Court by order or by a Judge's Individual Practice. NY R USDCTS&ED Civ Rule 6.1(c).

 b. *Providing a regular schedule for oral hearings.* A court may establish regular times and places for oral hearings on motions. FRCP 78(a).

 c. *Providing for submission on briefs.* By rule or order, the court may provide for submitting and determining motions on briefs, without oral hearings. FRCP 78(b).

2. *Hearing on FRCP 12 defenses before trial.* If a party so moves, any defense listed in FRCP 12(b)(1) through FRCP 12(b)(7)—whether made in a pleading or by motion—and a motion under FRCP 12(c) must be heard and decided before trial unless the court orders a deferral until trial. FRCP 12(i).

3. *Individual judge practices.* Refer to the Miscellaneous section of this document for information on individual judge practices on hearings.

## H. Forms

### 1. Federal Motion to Dismiss for Lack of Personal Jurisdiction Forms

a. Motion and notice; To dismiss; Defendant not present within state where district court is located. AMJUR PP FEDPRAC § 488.

b. Motion and notice; To dismiss; Lack of jurisdiction over person. AMJUR PP FEDPRAC § 489.

c. Motion and notice; To dismiss; Lack of jurisdiction over person; Ineffective service of process on foreign state. AMJUR PP FEDPRAC § 490.

d. Motion and notice; To dismiss; Lack of jurisdiction over person; Consul not agent of country represented for purpose of receiving service of process. AMJUR PP FEDPRAC § 491.

e. Motion and notice; To dismiss; Lack of jurisdiction over corporate defendant. AMJUR PP FEDPRAC § 492.

f. Motion and notice; To dismiss; International organization immune from suit. AMJUR PP FEDPRAC § 493.

g. Motion and notice; To dismiss; Officer or employee of international organization acting within official capacity; Immune from suit. AMJUR PP FEDPRAC § 494.

h. Motion and notice; To dismiss; Family member of member of foreign mission immune from suit. AMJUR PP FEDPRAC § 495.

i. Motion and notice; To dismiss complaint or, in alternative, to quash service of summons; Lack of jurisdiction over corporate defendant. AMJUR PP FEDPRAC § 496.

j. Motion to dismiss; Lack of personal jurisdiction; No minimum contacts. AMJUR PP FEDPRAC § 497.

k. Affidavit; Of Consul General; In support of motion to dismiss; Consular immunity and lack of authority to act as agent for service of process. AMJUR PP FEDPRAC § 498.

l. Motion to dismiss for lack of personal jurisdiction; Corporate defendant. 2C FEDFORMS § 11:52.

m. Motion to dismiss for lack of personal jurisdiction; By corporate defendant; With citation. 2C FEDFORMS § 11:53.

n. Motion to dismiss for lack of personal jurisdiction; By a foreign corporation. 2C FEDFORMS § 11:54.

o. Motion to dismiss for lack of personal jurisdiction; For insufficiency of service. 2C FEDFORMS § 11:55.

p. Motion to dismiss for lack of personal jurisdiction; Insufficiency of process and insufficiency of service of process. 2C FEDFORMS § 11:56.

q. Motion; To dismiss; Lack of jurisdiction over person of defendant. FEDPROF § 1:910.

r. Opposition; To motion; General form. FEDPROF § 1:750.

s. Affidavit; Supporting or opposing motion. FEDPROF § 1:751.

t. Brief; Supporting or opposing motion. FEDPROF § 1:752.

u. Statement of points and authorities; Opposing motion. FEDPROF § 1:753.

v. Motion to dismiss; Lack of jurisdiction over person of defendant; Short form. FEDPROF § 1:911.

w. Motion to dismiss; Lack of jurisdiction over person of defendant; Accident in foreign country and defendants have no contacts with forum state. FEDPROF § 1:911.50.

x. Motion to dismiss; Lack of jurisdiction over corporate defendant. FEDPROF § 1:912.

y. Motion; To dismiss complaint or, in the alternative, to quash service of summons; Lack of jurisdiction over corporate defendant. FEDPROF § 1:913.

z. Motion to dismiss complaint; General form. GOLDLTGFMS § 20:24.

MOTION TO DISMISS FOR LACK OF PERSONAL JURISDICTION

## I. Applicable Rules

1. *Federal rules*

   a. Summons. FRCP 4.

   b. Serving and filing pleadings and other papers. FRCP 5.

   c. Constitutional challenge to a statute; Notice, certification, and intervention. FRCP 5.1.

   d. Privacy protection for filings made with the court. FRCP 5.2.

   e. Computing and extending time; Time for motion papers. FRCP 6.

   f. Pleadings allowed; Form of motions and other papers. FRCP 7.

   g. Disclosure statement. FRCP 7.1.

   h. Form of pleadings. FRCP 10.

   i. Signing pleadings, motions, and other papers; Representations to the court; Sanctions. FRCP 11.

   j. Defenses and objections; When and how presented; Motion for judgment on the pleadings; Consolidating motions; Waiving defenses; Pretrial hearing. FRCP 12.

   k. Taking testimony. FRCP 43.

   l. Hearing motions; Submission on briefs. FRCP 78.

2. *Local rules*

   a. Night depository. NY R USDCTS&ED Civ Rule 1.2.

   b. Duty of attorneys in related cases. NY R USDCTS&ED Civ Rule 1.6.

   c. Filing of discovery materials. NY R USDCTS&ED Civ Rule 5.1.

   d. Electronic service and filing of documents. NY R USDCTS&ED Civ Rule 5.2.

   e. Service by overnight delivery. NY R USDCTS&ED Civ Rule 5.3.

   f. Service and filing of motion papers. NY R USDCTS&ED Civ Rule 6.1.

   g. Orders on motions. NY R USDCTS&ED Civ Rule 6.2.

   h. Computation of time. NY R USDCTS&ED Civ Rule 6.4.

   i. Motion papers. NY R USDCTS&ED Civ Rule 7.1.

   j. Disclosure statement. NY R USDCTS&ED Civ Rule 7.1.1.

   k. Authorities to be provided to pro se litigants. NY R USDCTS&ED Civ Rule 7.2.

   l. Form of pleadings, motions, and other papers. NY R USDCTS&ED Civ Rule 11.1.

   m. Notice to pro se litigant who opposes a FRCP 12 motion supported by matters outside the pleadings. NY R USDCTS&ED Civ Rule 12.1.

   n. Submission of orders, judgments and decrees. NY R USDCTS&ED Civ Rule 77.1.

   o. Court-annexed arbitration (Eastern District only). NY R USDCTS&ED Civ Rule 83.7.

   p. Court-annexed mediation (Eastern District only). NY R USDCTS&ED Civ Rule 83.8.

   q. Electronic case filing. NY R USDCTED Order 2004-08.

   r. The August 2, 2004 amendment to the E-Government Act of 2002. NY R USDCTED Order 2004-09.

   s. Categories and classification of cases; Information on cases and parties. NY R USDCTED Div. Bus., Rule 50.1.

## J. Miscellaneous

**NOTE: Individual judges' rules may apply. For available judge-level information, refer to:**

DISTRICT JUDGE CAROL BAGLEY AMON: NY R USDCTED Amon-Practices.

DISTRICT JUDGE JOAN M. AZRACK: NY R USDCTED Azrack-Practices.

DISTRICT JUDGE JOSEPH F. BIANCO: NY R USDCTED Bianco-Practices.

DISTRICT JUDGE FREDERIC BLOCK: NY R USDCTED Block-Practices.

DISTRICT JUDGE MARGO K. BRODIE: NY R USDCTED Brodie-Practices.

DISTRICT JUDGE PAMELA K. CHEN: NY R USDCTED Chen-Practices.

DISTRICT JUDGE BRIAN M. COGAN: NY R USDCTED Cogan-Practices; NY R USDCTED Cogan-Pretrial.

DISTRICT JUDGE LaSHANN DeARCY HALL: NY R USDCTED DeArcy Hall-Practices.

DISTRICT JUDGE RAYMOND J. DEARIE: NY R USDCTED Dearie-Practices.

DISTRICT JUDGE ANN M. DONNELLY: NY R USDCTED Donnelly-Practices.

DISTRICT JUDGE SANDRA J. FEUERSTEIN: NY R USDCTED Feuerstein-Practices; NY R USDCTED Feuerstein-Pretrial.

DISTRICT JUDGE NICHOLAS G. GARAUIFIS: NY R USDCTED Garaufis-Practices; NY R USDCTED Garaufis-Pretrial.

DISTRICT JUDGE NINA GERSHON: NY R USDCTED Gershon-Practices.

DISTRICT JUDGE I. LEO GLASSER: NY R USDCTED Glasser-Practices; NY R USDCTED Glasser-Crim.

DISTRICT JUDGE DENIS R. HURLEY: NY R USDCTED Hurley-Practices; [NY R USDCTED Hurley-Pro Cooperation Info, as added by NY ORDER 16-4188, effective July 22, 2016]; [NY R USDCTED Hurley-Pro Cooperation Info Stay, as added by NY ORDER 16-4188, effective July 22, 2016].

DISTRICT JUDGE DORA L. IRIZARRY: NY R USDCTED Irizarry-Practices; NY R USDCTED Irizarry-Pretrial; NY R USDCTED Irizarry-Crim.

DISTRICT JUDGE STERLING JOHNSON, JR.: NY R USDCTED Johnson-Practices.

DISTRICT JUDGE EDWARD R. KORMAN: NY R USDCTED Korman-Practices; NY R USDCTED Korman-Pretrial.

DISTRICT JUDGE WILLIAM F. KUNTZ: NY R USDCTED Kuntz-Practices.

DISTRICT JUDGE KIYO A. MATSUMOTO: NY R USDCTED Matsumoto-Practices.

DISTRICT JUDGE ROSLYNN R. MAUSKOPF: NY R USDCTED Mauskopf-Practices; NY R USDCTED Mauskopf-Recusal.

DISTRICT JUDGE THOMAS C. PLATT: NY R USDCTED Platt-Practices.

DISTRICT JUDGE ALLYNE R. ROSS: NY R USDCTED Ross-Practices.

DISTRICT JUDGE JOANNA SEYBERT: NY R USDCTED Seybert-Practices.

DISTRICT JUDGE ARTHUR D. SPATT: NY R USDCTED Spatt-Practices.

DISTRICT JUDGE SANDRA L. TOWNES: NY R USDCTED Townes-Practices.

DISTRICT JUDGE ERIC N. VITALIANO: NY R USDCTED Vitaliano-Practices.

DISTRICT JUDGE JACK B. WEINSTEIN: NY R USDCTED Weinstein-Practices.

DISTRICT JUDGE LEONARD D. WEXLER: NY R USDCTED Wexler-Practices; NY R USDCTED Wexler-Rules.

MAGISTRATE JUDGE LOIS BLOOM: NY R USDCTED Bloom-Practices.

MAGISTRATE JUDGE GARY R. BROWN: NY R USDCTED Brown-Practices.

MAGISTRATE JUDGE MARILYN D. GO: NY R USDCTED Go-Practices.

MAGISTRATE JUDGE STEVEN M. GOLD: NY R USDCTED Gold-Practices.

MAGISTRATE JUDGE PEGGY KUO: NY R USDCTED Kuo-Practices; NY R USDCTED Kuo-Scheduling Order.

MAGISTRATE JUDGE ROBERT M. LEVY: NY R USDCTED Levy-Practices.

MAGISTRATE JUDGE ARLENE R. LINDSAY: NY R USDCTED Lindsay-Practices.

MAGISTRATE JUDGE STEVEN I. LOCKE: NY R USDCTED Locke-Practices.

MAGISTRATE JUDGE ROANNE L. MANN: NY R USDCTED Mann-Practices.

MAGISTRATE JUDGE JAMES ORENSTEIN: NY R USDCTED Jorenstein--Practices.

MAGISTRATE JUDGE VIKTOR V. POHORELSKY: NY R USDCTED Pohorelsky-Practices.

MAGISTRATE JUDGE CHERYL L. POLLAK: NY R USDCTED Pollak-Practices; NY R USDCTED Pollak-Pretrial.

MAGISTRATE JUDGE RAMON E. REYES, JR.: NY R USDCTED Reyes-Practices.

MAGISTRATE JUDGE VERA M. SCANLON: NY R USDCTED Scanlon-Practices.

MAGISTRATE JUDGE ANNE Y. SHIELDS: NY R USDCTED Shields-Practices.

MAGISTRATE JUDGE STEVEN L. TISCIONE: NY R USDCTED Tiscione-Practices.

MAGISTRATE JUDGE A. KATHLEEN TOMILINSON: NY R USDCTED Tomlinson-Practices.

# Motions, Oppositions and Replies
# Motion for Judgment on the Pleadings

### Document Last Updated September 2016

## A.  Checklist

(I)  ❑ Matters to be considered by moving party

   (a)  ❑ Required documents

      (1)  ❑ Notice of motion and motion

      (2)  ❑ Memorandum of law

      (3)  ❑ Certificate of service

   (b)  ❑ Supplemental documents

      (1)  ❑ Pleadings

      (2)  ❑ Notice of constitutional question

      (3)  ❑ Nongovernmental corporate disclosure statement

      (4)  ❑ Notice to pro se litigant who opposes a FRCP 12 motion supported by matters outside the pleadings

      (5)  ❑ Copies of authorities

   (c)  ❑ Timing

      (1)  ❑ After the pleadings are closed—but early enough not to delay trial—a party may move for judgment on the pleadings

      (2)  ❑ A written motion and notice of the hearing must be served at least fourteen (14) days before the time specified for the hearing, with the following exceptions: (i) when the motion may be heard ex parte; (ii) when the Federal Rules of Civil Procedure set a different time; or (iii) when a court order—which a party may, for good cause, apply for ex parte—sets a different time

      (3)  ❑ Any affidavit supporting a motion must be served with the motion

(II)  ❑ Matters to be considered by opposing party

   (a)  ❑ Required documents

      (1)  ❑ Answering memorandum of law

      (2)  ❑ Certificate of service

   (b)  ❑ Supplemental documents

      (1)  ❑ Pleadings

(2) ❑ Notice of constitutional question

(3) ❑ Copies of authorities

(c) ❑ Timing

(1) ❑ Any opposing affidavits and answering memoranda shall be served within fourteen (14) days after service of the moving papers

(2) ❑ Except as FRCP 59(c) provides otherwise, any opposing affidavit must be served at least seven (7) days before the hearing, unless the court permits service at another time

## B. Timing

1. *Motion for judgment on the pleadings.* After the pleadings are closed—but early enough not to delay trial—a party may move for judgment on the pleadings. FRCP 12(c).

   a. *When pleadings are closed.* FRCP 7(a) provides that the pleadings are closed upon the filing of a complaint and an answer (absent a court-ordered reply), unless a counterclaim, cross-claim, or third-party claim is interposed, in which event the filing of a reply to a counterclaim, cross-claim answer, or third-party answer normally will mark the close of the pleadings. FPP § 1367.

   b. *Timeliness and delay.* Ordinarily, a motion for judgment on the pleadings should be made promptly after the close of the pleadings. Generally, however, a FRCP 12(c) motion is considered timely if it is made early enough not to delay trial or cause prejudice to the non-movant. FPP § 1367.

2. *Timing of motions, generally*

   a. *Motion and notice of hearing.* Except for letter-motions as permitted by NY R USDCTS&ED Civ Rule 7.1(d), and unless otherwise provided by statute or rule or by the Court in a Judge's Individual Practice or in a direction in a particular case, upon any motion, the notice of motion, supporting affidavits, and memoranda shall be served and filed as follows: on all civil motions, petitions, and applications, other than those described in NY R USDCTS&ED Civ Rule 6.1(a), and other than petitions for writs of habeas corpus, the notice of motion, supporting affidavits, and memoranda of law shall be served by the moving party on all other parties that have appeared in the action. NY R USDCTS&ED Civ Rule 6.1(b)(1). A written motion and notice of the hearing must be served at least fourteen (14) days before the time specified for the hearing, with the following exceptions:

      i. When the motion may be heard ex parte;

      ii. When the Federal Rules of Civil Procedure set a different time; or

      iii. When a court order—which a party may, for good cause, apply for ex parte—sets a different time. FRCP 6(c)(1).

   b. *Supporting affidavit.* Any affidavit supporting a motion must be served with the motion. FRCP 6(c)(2).

3. *Timing of opposing papers.* Except for letter-motions as permitted by NY R USDCTS&ED Civ Rule 7.1(d), and unless otherwise provided by statute or rule or by the Court in a Judge's Individual Practice or in a direction in a particular case, upon any motion, the notice of motion, supporting affidavits, and memoranda shall be served and filed as follows: on all civil motions, petitions, and applications, other than those described in NY R USDCTS&ED Civ Rule 6.1(a), and other than petitions for writs of habeas corpus, any opposing affidavits and answering memoranda shall be served within fourteen (14) days after service of the moving papers. NY R USDCTS&ED Civ Rule 6.1(b)(2).

   a. *Opposing affidavit.* Except as FRCP 59(c) provides otherwise, any opposing affidavit must be served at least seven (7) days before the hearing, unless the court permits service at another time. FRCP 6(c)(2).

4. *Timing of reply papers.* Where the respondent files an answering affidavit setting up a new matter, the moving party ordinarily is allowed a reasonable time to file a reply affidavit since failure to deny the new matter by affidavit may operate as an admission of its truth. AMJUR MOTIONS § 25.

   a. *Reply affidavits and reply memoranda of law.* Except for letter-motions as permitted by NY R USDCTS&ED Civ Rule 7.1(d), and unless otherwise provided by statute or rule or by the Court in a Judge's Individual Practice or in a direction in a particular case, upon any motion, the notice of motion, supporting affidavits, and memoranda shall be served and filed as follows: on all civil motions, petitions, and applications, other than those described in NY R USDCTS&ED Civ Rule 6.1(a), and other than petitions for writs of habeas corpus, any reply affidavits and memoranda of law shall be served within seven (7) days after service of the answering papers. NY R USDCTS&ED Civ Rule 6.1(b)(3).

5. *Effect of a FRCP 12 motion on the time to serve a responsive pleading.* Unless the court sets a different time, serving a motion under FRCP 12 alters the periods in FRCP 12(a) as follows:

   a. If the court denies the motion or postpones its disposition until trial, the responsive pleading must be served within fourteen (14) days after notice of the court's action; or

   b. If the court grants a motion for a more definite statement, the responsive pleading must be served within fourteen (14) days after the more definite statement is served. FRCP 12(a)(4).

6. *Computation of time*

   a. *Computing time.* FRCP 6 applies in computing any time period specified in the Federal Rules of Civil Procedure, in any local rule or court order, or in any statute that does not specify a method of computing time. FRCP 6(a). In computing any period of time prescribed or allowed by the Local Civil Rules of the United States District Courts for the Southern and Eastern Districts of New York or the Local Admiralty and Maritime Rules, the provisions of FRCP 6 shall apply unless otherwise stated. NY R USDCTS&ED Civ Rule 6.4.

      i. *Period stated in days or a longer unit.* In computing periods of days, refer to FRCP 6 and NY R USDCTS&ED Civ Rule 6.4. NY R USDCTS&ED Civ Rule 6.1(b). When the period is stated in days or a longer unit of time:

         • Exclude the day of the event that triggers the period;

         • Count every day, including intermediate Saturdays, Sundays, and legal holidays; and

         • Include the last day of the period, but if the last day is a Saturday, Sunday, or legal holiday, the period continues to run until the end of the next day that is not a Saturday, Sunday, or legal holiday. FRCP 6(a)(1). In the Local Civil Rules of the United States District Courts for the Southern and Eastern Districts of New York, as in the Federal Rules of Civil Procedure as amended effective December 1, 2009, Saturdays, Sundays, and legal holidays are no longer excluded in computing periods of time. If the last day of the period is a Saturday, Sunday, or legal holiday, the period continues to run until the end of the next day that is not a Saturday, Sunday, or legal holiday. NY R USDCTS&ED Civ Rule 6.4.

      ii. *Period stated in hours.* When the period is stated in hours:

         • Begin counting immediately on the occurrence of the event that triggers the period;

         • Count every hour, including hours during intermediate Saturdays, Sundays, and legal holidays; and

         • If the period would end on a Saturday, Sunday, or legal holiday, the period continues to run until the same time on the next day that is not a Saturday, Sunday, or legal holiday. FRCP 6(a)(2). In the Local Civil Rules of the United States District Courts for the Southern and Eastern Districts of New York, as in the Federal Rules of Civil Procedure as amended effective December 1, 2009, Saturdays, Sundays, and legal holidays are no longer excluded in computing periods of time. If the last day of the period is a Saturday, Sunday, or legal holiday, the period continues to run until the end of the next day that is not a Saturday, Sunday, or legal holiday. NY R USDCTS&ED Civ Rule 6.4.

      iii. *Inaccessibility of the clerk's office.* Unless the court orders otherwise, if the clerk's office is inaccessible:

         • On the last day for filing under FRCP 6(a)(1), then the time for filing is extended to the first accessible day that is not a Saturday, Sunday, or legal holiday; or

         • During the last hour for filing under FRCP 6(a)(2), then the time for filing is extended to the same time on the first accessible day that is not a Saturday, Sunday, or legal holiday. FRCP 6(a)(3).

iv. *"Last day" defined.* Unless a different time is set by a statute, local rule, or court order, the last day ends:

- For electronic filing, at midnight in the court's time zone; and
- For filing by other means, when the clerk's office is scheduled to close. FRCP 6(a)(4).

v. *"Next day" defined.* The "next day" is determined by continuing to count forward when the period is measured after an event and backward when measured before an event. FRCP 6(a)(5).

vi. *"Legal holiday" defined.* "Legal holiday" means:

- The day set aside by statute for observing New Year's Day, Martin Luther King Jr.'s Birthday, Washington's Birthday, Memorial Day, Independence Day, Labor Day, Columbus Day, Veterans' Day, Thanksgiving Day, or Christmas Day;
- Any day declared a holiday by the President or Congress; and
- For periods that are measured after an event, any other day declared a holiday by the state where the district court is located. FRCP 6(a)(6).

b. *Extending time*

i. *In general.* When an act may or must be done within a specified time, the court may, for good cause, extend the time:

- With or without motion or notice if the court acts, or if a request is made, before the original time or its extension expires; or
- On motion made after the time has expired if the party failed to act because of excusable neglect. FRCP 6(b)(1).

ii. *Exceptions.* A court must not extend the time to act under FRCP 50(b), FRCP 50(d), FRCP 52(b), FRCP 59(b), FRCP 59(d), FRCP 59(e), and FRCP 60(b). FRCP 6(b)(2).

iii. Refer to the United States District Court for the Eastern District of New York KeyRules Motion for Continuance/Extension of Time document for more information on extending time.

c. *Additional time after certain kinds of service.* When a party may or must act within a specified time after service and service is made under FRCP 5(b)(2)(C), FRCP 5(b)(2)(D), FRCP 5(b)(2)(E), or FRCP 5(b)(2)(F), three (3) days are added after the period would otherwise expire under FRCP 6(a). FRCP 6(d). Overnight delivery service shall be deemed service by mail for purposes of FRCP 5 and FRCP 6. NY R USDCTS&ED Civ Rule 5.3.

7. *Individual judge practices.* Refer to the Miscellaneous section of this document for information on individual judge practices on timing of documents.

## C. General Requirements

1. *Motions, generally*

a. *Requirements.* A request for a court order must be made by motion. The motion must:

i. Be in writing unless made during a hearing or trial;

ii. State with particularity the grounds for seeking the order; and

iii. State the relief sought. FRCP 7(b)(1).

b. *Notice of motion.* A party interested in resisting the relief sought by a motion has a right to notice thereof, and an opportunity to be heard. AMJUR MOTIONS § 12.

i. In addition to statutory or court rule provisions requiring notice of a motion—the purpose of such a notice requirement having been said to be to prevent a party from being prejudicially surprised by a motion—principles of natural justice dictate that an adverse party generally must be given notice that a motion will be presented to the court. AMJUR MOTIONS § 12.

ii. "Notice," in this regard, means reasonable notice, including a meaningful opportunity to prepare and to defend against allegations of a motion. AMJUR MOTIONS § 12.

c. *Writing requirement.* The writing requirement is intended to insure that the adverse parties are

informed and have a record of both the motion's pendency and the grounds on which the movant seeks an order. FPP § 1191; Feldberg v. Quechee Lakes Corp., 463 F.3d 195 (2d Cir. 2006).

    i.   It is sufficient "if the motion is stated in a written notice of the hearing of the motion." FPP § 1191.

  d.  *Particularity requirement.* The particularity requirement insures that the opposing parties will have notice of their opponent's contentions. FEDPROC § 62:364; Goodman v. 1973 26 Foot Trojan Vessel, Arkansas Registration No. AR1439SN, 859 F.2d 71, 12 Fed.R.Serv.3d 645 (8th Cir. 1988). That requirement ensures that notice of the basis for the motion is provided to the court and to the opposing party so as to avoid prejudice, provide the opponent with a meaningful opportunity to respond, and provide the court with enough information to process the motion correctly. FEDPROC § 62:364; Andreas v. Volkswagen of America, Inc., 336 F.3d 789, 56 Fed.R.Serv.3d 6 (8th Cir. 2003).

    i.   Reasonable specification of the grounds for a motion is sufficient. However, where a movant fails to state even one ground for granting the motion in question, the movant has failed to meet the minimal standard of "reasonable specification." FEDPROC § 62:364; Martinez v. Trainor, 556 F.2d 818, 23 Fed.R.Serv.2d 403 (7th Cir. 1977).

    ii.   The court may excuse the failure to comply with the particularity requirement if it is inadvertent, and where no prejudice is shown by the opposing party. FEDPROC § 62:364.

  e.  *Ex parte orders or orders to show cause to bring on a motion.* No ex parte order, or order to show cause to bring on a motion, will be granted except upon a clear and specific showing by affidavit of good and sufficient reasons why a procedure other than by notice of motion is necessary, and stating whether a previous application for similar relief has been made. NY R USDCTS&ED Civ Rule 6.1(d).

  f.  *Letter-motions.* Applications for extensions or adjournments, applications for a pre-motion conference, and similar non-dispositive matters as permitted by the instructions regarding ECF published on the website of each respective Court and any pertinent Individual Judge's Practices, may be brought by letter-motion filed via ECF pursuant to NY R USDCTS&ED Civ Rule 5.2(b). NY R USDCTS&ED Civ Rule 7.1(d).

2.  *Motion for judgment on the pleadings.* After the pleadings are closed—but early enough not to delay trial—a party may move for judgment on the pleadings. FRCP 12(c).

  a.  *Relationship to other motions*

    i.   *Common law demurrer.* The motion for judgment on the pleadings under FRCP 12(c) has its historical roots in common law practice, which permitted either party, at any point in the proceeding, to demur to his opponent's pleading and secure a dismissal or final judgment on the basis of the pleadings. FPP § 1367.

       •  The common law demurrer could be used to search the record and raise procedural defects, or it could be employed to resolve the substantive merits of the controversy as disclosed on the face of the pleadings. FPP § 1367.

       •  In contrast to the common law practice, the FRCP 12(c) judgment on the pleadings procedure primarily is addressed to the latter function of disposing of cases on the basis of the underlying substantive merits of the parties' claims and defenses as they are revealed in the formal pleadings. FPP § 1367. The purpose of FRCP 12(c) is to save time and expense in cases where the ultimate issues of fact are not in dispute, and to prevent the piecemeal process of judicial determination which prevailed under the old common-law practice. FEDPROC § 62:566.

    ii.   *Motions to dismiss.* While FRCP 12(b) motions to dismiss and FRCP 12(c) motions for judgment on the pleadings are to some extent merely interchangeable weapons in a party's arsenal of pretrial challenges, there are differences in the scope and effect of the two motions. A FRCP 12(b) motion to dismiss is directed solely toward the defects of the plaintiff's claim for relief, without concern for the merits of the controversy, while a FRCP 12(c) motion for judgment on the pleadings at least theoretically requires some scrutiny of the merits of the controversy. FEDPROC § 62:568.

iii.   *Motion to strike.* The FRCP 12(c) motion also should be contrasted with the motion to strike under FRCP 12(f). The latter motion permits either party to strike redundant, immaterial, impertinent, or scandalous matter from an adversary's pleading and may be used to challenge the sufficiency of defenses asserted by that adversary. The motion serves as a pruning device to eliminate objectionable matter from an opponent's pleadings and, unlike the FRCP 12(c) procedure, it is not directed at gaining a final judgment on the merits, although a FRCP 12(f) motion that succeeds in eliminating the defenses to the action may have that purpose and, in some cases, may have that effect. FPP § 1369.

- If a plaintiff seeks to dispute the legal sufficiency of fewer than all of the defenses raised in the defendant's pleading, he should proceed under FRCP 12(f) rather than under FRCP 12(c) because the latter leads to the entry of a judgment. FPP § 1369.

iv.   *Motion for summary judgment.* In most circumstances a party will find it preferable to proceed under FRCP 56 rather than FRCP 12(c) for a variety of reasons. For example, the summary judgment procedure is available when the defendant fails to file an answer, whereas technically no relief would be available under FRCP 12(c) because the pleadings have not been closed. If a party believes that it will be necessary to introduce evidence outside the formal pleadings in order to demonstrate that no material issue of fact exists and he is clearly entitled to judgment, it is advisable to proceed directly under FRCP 56 rather than taking the circuitous route through FRCP 12(c). Moreover, the FRCP 12(c) path may present certain risks because the court, in its discretion, may refuse to permit the introduction of matters beyond the pleadings and insist on treating the motion as one under FRCP 12(c) or apply the general motion time period set out in FRCP 6(d), rather than the special time provision in FRCP 56. FPP § 1369.

b.   *Bringing a FRCP 12(c) motion.* As numerous judicial opinions make clear, a FRCP 12(c) motion is designed to provide a means of disposing of cases when the material facts are not in dispute between the parties and a judgment on the merits can be achieved by focusing on the content of the competing pleadings, exhibits thereto, matters incorporated by reference in the pleadings, whatever is central or integral to the claim for relief or defense, and any facts of which the district court will take judicial notice. FPP § 1367; DiCarlo v. St. Mary Hosp., 530 F.3d 255 (3d Cir. 2008); Buddy Bean Lumber Co. v. Axis Surplus Ins. Co., 715 F.3d 695, 697 (8th Cir. 2013).

i.   The motion for a judgment on the pleadings only has utility when all material allegations of fact are admitted or not controverted in the pleadings and only questions of law remain to be decided by the district court. FPP § 1367; Stafford v. Jewelers Mut. Ins. Co., 554 Fed. Appx. 360, 370 (6th Cir. 2014).

c.   *Partial judgment on the pleadings.* Although not provided for by FRCP 12(c), a party may properly move for partial judgment on the pleadings to further the policy goal of efficient resolution of actions when there are no material facts in dispute. This conclusion has been said to be buttressed by FRCP 56(a), which provides that a party may move for summary judgment "on all or part of the claim." FEDPROC § 62:571.

d.   *Granting of a motion for judgment on the pleadings.* The federal courts have followed a fairly restrictive standard in ruling on motions for judgment on the pleadings. FPP § 1368. A motion for judgment on the pleadings is a motion for judgment on the merits, and should only be granted if no material issue of fact remains to be resolved and the movant establishes entitlement to judgment as a matter of law. FEDPROC § 62:569; Great Plains Trust Co. v. Morgan Stanley Dean Witter & Co., 313 F.3d 305 (5th Cir. 2002); Sikirica v. Nationwide Ins. Co., 416 F.3d 214 (3d Cir. 2005). A motion for a judgment on the pleadings must be sustained where the undisputed facts appearing in the pleadings, supplemented by any facts of which the court will take judicial notice, show that no relief can be granted. Judgment on the pleadings is not appropriate where the answer raises issues of fact which, if proved, would defeat recovery. FEDPROC § 62:569.

i.   A motion for judgment on the pleadings admits, for purposes of the motion, the truth of all well-pleaded facts in the pleadings of the opposing party, together with all fair inferences to be drawn therefrom, even where the defendant asserts, in the FRCP 12(c) motion, a FRCP 12(b)(6) defense of failure to state a claim upon which relief can be granted. FEDPROC § 62:570; In re World Trade Center Disaster Site Litigation, 521 F.3d 169 (2d Cir. 2008); Massachusetts Nurses

Ass'n v. North Adams Regional Hosp., 467 F.3d 27 (1st Cir. 2006). However, all allegations of the moving party which have been denied are taken as false. FEDPROC § 62:570; Volvo Const. Equipment North America, Inc. v. CLM Equipment Company, Inc., 386 F.3d 581 (4th Cir. 2004). In considering a motion for judgment on the pleadings, the trial court is thus required to view the facts presented in the pleadings and inferences to be drawn therefrom in the light most favorable to the nonmoving party. In this fashion the courts hope to insure that the rights of the nonmoving party are decided as fully and fairly on a FRCP 12(c) motion as if there had been a trial. FEDPROC § 62:570.

    ii.  On a motion for judgment on the pleadings, the court may consider facts upon the basis of judicial notice. FEDPROC § 62:570; R.G. Financial Corp. v. Vergara-Nunez, 446 F.3d 178 (1st Cir. 2006). However, a motion for judgment on the pleadings does not admit conclusions of law or unwarranted factual inferences. FEDPROC § 62:570; JPMorgan Chase Bank, N.A. v. Winget, 510 F.3d 577 (6th Cir. 2007).

e.  *Joining motions*

    i.  *Right to join.* A motion under FRCP 12 may be joined with any other motion allowed by FRCP 12. FRCP 12(g)(1).

    ii.  *Limitation on further motions.* Except as provided in FRCP 12(h)(2) or FRCP 12(h)(3), a party that makes a motion under FRCP 12 must not make another motion under FRCP 12 raising a defense or objection that was available to the party but omitted from its earlier motion. FRCP 12(g)(2).

f.  *Waiving and preserving certain defenses*

    i.  *When some are waived.* A party waives any defense listed in FRCP 12(b)(2) through FRCP 12(b)(5) by:

- Omitting it from a motion in the circumstances described in FRCP 12(g)(2); or

- Failing to either: (1) make it by motion under FRCP 12; or (2) include it in a responsive pleading or in an amendment allowed by FRCP 15(a)(1) as a matter of course. FRCP 12(h)(1).

    ii.  *When to raise others.* Failure to state a claim upon which relief can be granted, to join a person required by FRCP 19(b), or to state a legal defense to a claim may be raised:

- In any pleading allowed or ordered under FRCP 7(a);

- By a motion under FRCP 12(c); or

- At trial. FRCP 12(h)(2).

    iii.  *Lack of subject matter jurisdiction.* If the court determines at any time that it lacks subject-matter jurisdiction, the court must dismiss the action. FRCP 12(h)(3).

3.  *Opposing papers.* The Federal Rules of Civil Procedure do not require any formal answer, return, or reply to a motion, except where the Federal Rules of Civil Procedure or local rules may require affidavits, memoranda, or other papers to be filed in opposition to a motion. Such papers are simply to apprise the court of such opposition and the grounds of that opposition. FEDPROC § 62:359. Except for letter-motions as permitted by NY R USDCTS&ED Civ Rule 7.1(d) or as otherwise permitted by the Court, all oppositions and replies with respect to motions shall comply with NY R USDCTS&ED Civ Rule 7.1(a)(2) and NY R USDCTS&ED Civ Rule 7.1(a)(3), and an opposing party who seeks relief that goes beyond the denial of the motion shall comply as well with NY R USDCTS&ED Civ Rule 7.1(a)(1). NY R USDCTS&ED Civ Rule 7.1(b).

a.  *Effect of failure to respond to motion.* Although in the absence of statutory provision or court rule, a motion ordinarily does not require a written answer, when a party files a motion and the opposing party fails to respond, the court may construe such failure to respond as nonopposition to the motion or an admission that the motion was meritorious, may take the facts alleged in the motion as true—the rule in some jurisdictions being that the failure to respond to a fact set forth in a motion is deemed an admission—and may grant the motion if the relief requested appears to be justified. AMJUR MOTIONS § 28.

b. *Assent or no opposition not determinative.* However, a motion will not be granted automatically simply because an "assent" or a notation of "no opposition" has been filed; federal judges frequently deny motions that have been assented to when it is thought that justice so dictates. FPP § 1190.

c. *Responsive pleading inappropriate as response to motion.* An attempt to answer or oppose a motion with a responsive pleading usually is not appropriate. FPP § 1190.

4. *Reply papers.* A moving party may be required or permitted to prepare papers in addition to his original motion papers. AMJUR MOTIONS § 25. Papers answering or replying to opposing papers may be appropriate, in the interests of justice, where it appears there is a substantial reason for allowing a reply. Thus, a court may accept reply papers where a party demonstrates that the papers to which it seeks to file a reply raise new issues that are material to the disposition of the question before the court, or where the court determines, sua sponte, that it wishes further briefing of an issue raised in those papers and orders the submission of additional papers. FEDPROC § 62:360. Except for letter-motions as permitted by NY R USDCTS&ED Civ Rule 7.1(d) or as otherwise permitted by the Court, all oppositions and replies with respect to motions shall comply with NY R USDCTS&ED Civ Rule 7.1(a)(2) and NY R USDCTS&ED Civ Rule 7.1(a)(3). NY R USDCTS&ED Civ Rule 7.1(b).

   a. *Function of reply papers.* The function of a reply affidavit is to answer the arguments made in opposition to the position taken by the movant and not to permit the movant to introduce new arguments in support of the motion. AMJUR MOTIONS § 25.

   b. *Issues raised for the first time in a reply document.* However, the view has been followed in some jurisdictions, that as a matter of judicial economy, where there is no prejudice and where the issues could be raised simply by filing a motion to dismiss, the trial court has discretion to consider arguments raised for the first time in a reply memorandum, and that a trial court may grant a motion to strike issues raised for the first time in a reply memorandum. AMJUR MOTIONS § 26.

5. *Orders on motions.* A memorandum signed by the Court of the decision on a motion that does not finally determine all claims for relief, or an oral decision on such a motion, shall constitute the order unless the memorandum or oral decision directs the submission or settlement of an order in more extended form. The notation in the docket of a memorandum or of an oral decision that does not direct the submission or settlement of an order in more extended form shall constitute the entry of the order. Where an order in more extended form is required to be submitted or settled, the notation in the docket of such order shall constitute the entry of the order. NY R USDCTS&ED Civ Rule 6.2.

6. *Related cases.* It shall be the continuing duty of each attorney appearing in any civil or criminal case to bring promptly to the attention of the Court all facts which said attorney believes are relevant to a determination that said case and one or more pending civil or criminal cases should be heard by the same Judge, in order to avoid unnecessary duplication of judicial effort. As soon as the attorney becomes aware of such relationship, said attorney shall notify the Judges to whom the cases have been assigned. NY R USDCTS&ED Civ Rule 1.6(a). If counsel fails to comply with NY R USDCTS&ED Civ Rule 1.6(a), the Court may assess reasonable costs directly against counsel whose action has obstructed the effective administration of the Court's business. NY R USDCTS&ED Civ Rule 1.6(b).

7. *Alternative dispute resolution (ADR)*

   a. *Court-annexed arbitration*

      i. *Civil cases eligible for compulsory arbitration.* The Clerk of Court shall, as to all cases filed after January 1, 1986, designate and process for compulsory arbitration all civil cases (excluding Social Security cases, tax matters, prisoners' civil rights cases and any action based on an alleged violation of a right secured by the Constitution of the United States or if jurisdiction is based in whole or in part on 28 U.S.C.A. § 1343) wherein money damages only are being sought in an amount not in excess of one hundred fifty thousand dollars ($150,000) exclusive of interest and costs. NY R USDCTS&ED Civ Rule 83.7(d)(1).

         • The parties may by written stipulation agree that the Clerk of Court shall designate and process for court-annexed arbitration any civil case that is not subject to compulsory arbitration in NY R USDCTS&ED Civ Rule 83.7. NY R USDCTS&ED Civ Rule 83.7(d)(2).

- For purposes of NY R USDCTS&ED Civ Rule 83.7 only, in all civil cases damages shall be presumed to be not in excess of one hundred fifty thousand dollars ($150,000) exclusive of interest and costs, unless: (1) counsel for plaintiff, at the time of filing the complaint, or in the event of the removal of a case from state court or transfer of a case from another district to this Court, within thirty (30) days of the docketing of the case in this district, files a certification with the Court that the damages sought exceed one hundred fifty thousand dollars ($150,000), exclusive of interest and costs; or (2) counsel for a defendant, at the time of filing a counterclaim or cross-claim files a certification with the court that the damages sought by the counter-claim or cross-claim exceed one hundred fifty thousand dollars ($150,000) exclusive of interest and costs. NY R USDCTS&ED Civ Rule 83.7(d)(3).

ii. *Exemption from arbitration.* The Court shall, sua sponte, or on motion of a party, exempt any case from arbitration in which the objectives of arbitration would not be realized (1) because the case involves complex or novel issues, (2) because legal issues predominate over factual issues, or (3) for other good cause. NY R USDCTS&ED Civ Rule 83.7(e)(2). For information on applying for an exemption, refer to NY R USDCTS&ED Civ Rule 83.7

iii. *Referral to arbitration.* Cases not originally designated as eligible for compulsory arbitration, but which in the discretion of the assigned Judge, are later found to qualify, may be referred to arbitration. A U.S. District Judge or a U.S. Magistrate Judge, in cases that exceed the arbitration ceiling of one hundred fifty thousand dollars ($150,000) exclusive of interest and costs, in their discretion, may suggest that the parties should consider arbitration. If the parties are agreeable, an appropriate consent form signed by all parties or their representatives may be entered and filed in the case prior to scheduling an arbitration hearing. NY R USDCTS&ED Civ Rule 83.7(e)(3).

iv. For more information on arbitration, refer to NY R USDCTS&ED Civ Rule 83.7.

b. *Court-annexed mediation.* Mediation is a process in which parties and counsel agree to meet with a neutral mediator trained to assist them in settling disputes. The mediator improves communication across party lines, helps parties articulate their interests and understand those of the other party, probes the strengths and weaknesses of each party's legal positions, and identifies areas of agreement and helps generate options for a mutually agreeable resolution to the dispute. In all cases, mediation provides an opportunity to explore a wide range of potential solutions and to address interests that may be outside the scope of the stated controversy or which could not be addressed by judicial action. A hallmark of mediation is its capacity to expand traditional settlement discussions and broaden resolution options, often by exploring litigant needs and interests that may be formally independent of the legal issues in controversy. NY R USDCTS&ED Civ Rule 83.8(a).

i. *Eligible cases.* Judges and Magistrate Judges may designate civil cases for inclusion in the mediation program, and when doing so shall prepare an order to that effect. Alternatively, and subject to the availability of qualified mediators, the parties may consent to participation in the mediation program by preparing and executing a stipulation signed by all parties to the action and so-ordered by the Court. NY R USDCTS&ED Civ Rule 83.8(b)(1).

ii. For more information on mediation, refer to NY R USDCTS&ED Civ Rule 83.8.

8. *Individual judge practices.* Refer to the Miscellaneous section of this document for information on individual judge practices on general requirements for documents.

## D. Documents

1. *Documents for moving party*

a. *Required documents*

i. *Notice of motion and motion.* Except for letter-motions as permitted by NY R USDCTS&ED Civ Rule 7.1(d) or as otherwise permitted by the Court, all motions shall include the following motion papers: a notice of motion, or an order to show cause signed by the Court, which shall specify the applicable rules or statutes pursuant to which the motion is brought, and shall specify the relief sought by the motion. NY R USDCTS&ED Civ Rule 7.1(a)(1). Refer to the

General Requirements section of this document for information on the notice of motion and motion.

ii.   *Memorandum of law.* Except for letter-motions as permitted by NY R USDCTS&ED Civ Rule 7.1(d) or as otherwise permitted by the Court, all motions shall include the following motion papers: a memorandum of law, setting forth the cases and other authorities relied upon in support of the motion, and divided, under appropriate headings, into as many parts as there are issues to be determined. NY R USDCTS&ED Civ Rule 7.1(a)(2).

iii.   *Certificate of service.* FRCP 5(d) requires that the person making service under FRCP 5 certify that service has been effected. FRCP 5(Advisory Committee Notes). Having such information on file may be useful for many purposes, including proof of service if an issue arises concerning the effectiveness of the service. FRCP 5(Advisory Committee Notes).

b.   *Supplemental documents*

i.   *Pleadings.* In considering a motion for judgment on the pleadings, the trial court is. . .required to view the facts presented in the pleadings and inferences to be drawn therefrom in the light most favorable to the nonmoving party. FEDPROC § 62:570.

- *Motion treated as one for summary judgment.* If, on a motion under FRCP 12(b)(6) or FRCP 12(c), matters outside the pleadings are presented to and not excluded by the court, the motion must be treated as one for summary judgment under FRCP 56. All parties must be given a reasonable opportunity to present all the material that is pertinent to the motion. FRCP 12(d).

ii.   *Notice of constitutional question.* A party that files a pleading, written motion, or other paper drawing into question the constitutionality of a federal or state statute must promptly:

- *File notice.* File a notice of constitutional question stating the question and identifying the paper that raises it, if: (1) a federal statute is questioned and the parties do not include the United States, one of its agencies, or one of its officers or employees in an official capacity; or (2) a state statute is questioned and the parties do not include the state, one of its agencies, or one of its officers or employees in an official capacity; and

- *Serve notice.* Serve the notice and paper on the Attorney General of the United States if a federal statute is questioned—or on the state attorney general if a state statute is questioned—either by certified or registered mail or by sending it to an electronic address designated by the attorney general for this purpose. FRCP 5.1(a).

- *No forfeiture.* A party's failure to file and serve the notice, or the court's failure to certify, does not forfeit a constitutional claim or defense that is otherwise timely asserted. FRCP 5.1(d).

iii.   *Nongovernmental corporate disclosure statement.* To enable judges and magistrates to evaluate possible disqualification or recusal, counsel for a private (nongovernmental) party shall submit at the time of initial pleading a certificate identifying any corporate parent, subsidiaries, or affiliates of that party. NY R USDCTED Div. Bus., Rule 50.1(c).

- *Contents.* A nongovernmental corporate party must file two (2) copies of a disclosure statement that: (1) identifies any parent corporation and any publicly held corporation owning ten percent (10%) or more of its stock; or (2) states that there is no such corporation. FRCP 7.1(a).

- *Time to file; Supplemental filing.* A party must: (1) file the disclosure statement with its first appearance, pleading, petition, motion, response, or other request addressed to the court; and (2) promptly file a supplemental statement if any required information changes. FRCP 7.1(b). For purposes of FRCP 7.1(b)(2), "promptly" shall mean "within fourteen days," that is, parties are required to file a supplemental disclosure statement within fourteen (14) days of the time there is any change in the information required in a disclosure statement filed pursuant to those rules. NY R USDCTS&ED Civ Rule 7.1.1.

iv.   *Notice to pro se litigant who opposes a FRCP 12 motion supported by matters outside the*

732

*pleadings.* A represented party moving to dismiss or for judgment on the pleadings against a party proceeding pro se, who refers in support of the motion to matters outside the pleadings as described in FRCP 12(b) or FRCP 12(c), shall serve and file the notice in NY R USDCTS&ED Civ Rule 12.1 with the full text of FRCP 56 attached at the time the motion is served. If the Court rules that a motion to dismiss or for judgment on the pleadings will be treated as one for summary judgment pursuant to FRCP 56, and the movant has not previously served and filed the notice required by NY R USDCTS&ED Civ Rule 12.1, the movant shall amend the form notice to reflect that fact and shall serve and file the amended notice within fourteen (14) days of the Court's ruling. NY R USDCTS&ED Civ Rule 12.1. For the notice, refer to NY R USDCTS&ED Civ Rule 12.1.

v. *Copies of authorities.* In cases involving a pro se litigant, counsel shall, when serving a memorandum of law (or other submissions to the Court), provide the pro se litigant (but not other counsel or the Court) with copies of cases and other authorities cited therein that are unpublished or reported exclusively on computerized databases. Upon request, counsel shall provide the pro se litigant with copies of such unpublished cases and other authorities as are cited in a decision of the Court and were not previously cited by any party. NY R USDCTS&ED Civ Rule 7.2.

2. *Documents for opposing party*

   a. *Required documents*

      i. *Answering memorandum of law.* Except for letter-motions as permitted by NY R USDCTS&ED Civ Rule 7.1(d) or as otherwise permitted by the Court, all oppositions and replies with respect to motions shall comply with NY R USDCTS&ED Civ Rule 7.1(a)(2). NY R USDCTS&ED Civ Rule 7.1(b). Except for letter-motions as permitted by NY R USDCTS&ED Civ Rule 7.1(d) or as otherwise permitted by the Court, all motions shall include the following motion papers: a memorandum of law, setting forth the cases and other authorities relied upon in support of the motion, and divided, under appropriate headings, into as many parts as there are issues to be determined. NY R USDCTS&ED Civ Rule 7.1(a)(2). Refer to the General Requirements section of this document for information on the opposing papers.

      ii. *Certificate of service.* FRCP 5(d) requires that the person making service under FRCP 5 certify that service has been effected. FRCP 5(Advisory Committee Notes). Having such information on file may be useful for many purposes, including proof of service if an issue arises concerning the effectiveness of the service. FRCP 5(Advisory Committee Notes).

   b. *Supplemental documents*

      i. *Pleadings.* In considering a motion for judgment on the pleadings, the trial court is. . .required to view the facts presented in the pleadings and inferences to be drawn therefrom in the light most favorable to the nonmoving party. FEDPROC § 62:570.

         • *Motion treated as one for summary judgment.* If, on a motion under FRCP 12(b)(6) or FRCP 12(c), matters outside the pleadings are presented to and not excluded by the court, the motion must be treated as one for summary judgment under FRCP 56. All parties must be given a reasonable opportunity to present all the material that is pertinent to the motion. FRCP 12(d).

      ii. *Notice of constitutional question.* A party that files a pleading, written motion, or other paper drawing into question the constitutionality of a federal or state statute must promptly:

         • *File notice.* File a notice of constitutional question stating the question and identifying the paper that raises it, if: (1) a federal statute is questioned and the parties do not include the United States, one of its agencies, or one of its officers or employees in an official capacity; or (2) a state statute is questioned and the parties do not include the state, one of its agencies, or one of its officers or employees in an official capacity; and

         • *Serve notice.* Serve the notice and paper on the Attorney General of the United States if a federal statute is questioned—or on the state attorney general if a state statute is questioned—either by certified or registered mail or by sending it to an electronic address designated by the attorney general for this purpose. FRCP 5.1(a).

- *No forfeiture.* A party's failure to file and serve the notice, or the court's failure to certify, does not forfeit a constitutional claim or defense that is otherwise timely asserted. FRCP 5.1(d).

   iii.   *Copies of authorities.* In cases involving a pro se litigant, counsel shall, when serving a memorandum of law (or other submissions to the Court), provide the pro se litigant (but not other counsel or the Court) with copies of cases and other authorities cited therein that are unpublished or reported exclusively on computerized databases. Upon request, counsel shall provide the pro se litigant with copies of such unpublished cases and other authorities as are cited in a decision of the Court and were not previously cited by any party. NY R USDCTS&ED Civ Rule 7.2.

3.   *Individual judge practices.* Refer to the Miscellaneous section of this document for information on individual judge practices on required documents.

## E. Format

1.   *Form of documents.* The rules governing captions and other matters of form in pleadings apply to motions and other papers. FRCP 7(b)(2).

   a.   *Paper.* Every pleading, written motion, and other paper must: be plainly written, typed, printed, or copied without erasures or interlineations which materially deface it. NY R USDCTS&ED Civ Rule 11.1(a)(1).

   b.   *Typeface, margin, and spacing.* The typeface, margins, and spacing of all documents presented for filing must meet the following requirements:

      i.   All text must be twelve (12) point type or larger, except for text in footnotes which may be ten (10) point type;

      ii.   All documents must have at least one (1) inch margins on all sides;

      iii.   All text must be double-spaced, except for headings, text in footnotes, or block quotations, which may be single-spaced. NY R USDCTS&ED Civ Rule 11.1(b).

   c.   *Caption; Names of parties.* Every pleading must have a caption with the court's name, a title, a file number, and a FRCP 7(a) designation. The title of the complaint must name all the parties; the title of other pleadings, after naming the first party on each side, may refer generally to other parties. FRCP 10(a). Every pleading, written motion, and other paper must: bear the docket number and the initials of the District Judge and any Magistrate Judge before whom the action or proceeding is pending, NY R USDCTS&ED Civ Rule 11.1(a)(2).

   d.   *Paragraphs; Separate statements.* A party must state its claims or defenses in numbered paragraphs, each limited as far as practicable to a single set of circumstances. A later pleading may refer by number to a paragraph in an earlier pleading. If doing so would promote clarity, each claim founded on a separate transaction or occurrence—and each defense other than a denial—must be stated in a separate count or defense. FRCP 10(b).

   e.   *Adoption by reference; Exhibits.* A statement in a pleading may be adopted by reference elsewhere in the same pleading or in any other pleading or motion. A copy of a written instrument that is an exhibit to a pleading is a part of the pleading for all purposes. FRCP 10(c).

   f.   *Acceptance by the clerk.* The clerk must not refuse to file a paper solely because it is not in the form prescribed by the Federal Rules of Civil Procedure or by a local rule or practice. FRCP 5(d)(4).

2.   *Signing of pleadings, motions and other papers*

   a.   *Signature.* Every pleading, written motion, and other paper must be signed by at least one attorney of record in the attorney's name—or by a party personally if the party is unrepresented. The paper must state the signer's address, e-mail address, and telephone number. FRCP 11(a). Every pleading, written motion, and other paper must: have the name of each person signing it clearly printed or typed directly below the signature. NY R USDCTS&ED Civ Rule 11.1(a)(3).

      i.   *No verification or accompanying affidavit required for pleadings.* Unless a rule or statute specifically states otherwise, a pleading need not be verified or accompanied by an affidavit. FRCP 11(a).

      ii.  *Unsigned papers.* The court must strike an unsigned paper unless the omission is promptly corrected after being called to the attorney's or party's attention. FRCP 11(a).

  b.  *Representations to the court.* By presenting to the court a pleading, written motion, or other paper—whether by signing, filing, submitting, or later advocating it—an attorney or unrepresented party certifies that to the best of the person's knowledge, information, and belief, formed after an inquiry reasonable under the circumstances:

      i.  It is not being presented for any improper purpose, such as to harass, cause unnecessary delay, or needlessly increase the cost of litigation;

      ii.  The claims, defenses, and other legal contentions are warranted by existing law or by a nonfrivolous argument for extending, modifying, or reversing existing law or for establishing new law;

      iii.  The factual contentions have evidentiary support or, if specifically so identified, will likely have evidentiary support after a reasonable opportunity for further investigation or discovery; and

      iv.  The denials of factual contentions are warranted on the evidence or, if specifically so identified, are reasonably based on belief or a lack of information. FRCP 11(b).

  c.  *Sanctions.* If, after notice and a reasonable opportunity to respond, the court determines that FRCP 11(b) has been violated, the court may impose an appropriate sanction on any attorney, law firm, or party that violated FRCP 11(b) or is responsible for the violation. FRCP 11(c)(1). Refer to the United States District Court for the Eastern District of New York KeyRules Motion for Sanctions document for more information.

3.  *Privacy protection for filings made with the court*

  a.  *Redacted filings.* Unless the court orders otherwise, in an electronic or paper filing with the court that contains an individual's Social Security number, taxpayer-identification number, or birth date, the name of an individual known to be a minor, or a financial-account number, a party or nonparty making the filing may include only:

      i.  The last four (4) digits of the Social Security number and taxpayer-identification number;

      ii.  The year of the individual's birth;

      iii.  The minor's initials; and

      iv.  The last four (4) digits of the financial-account number. FRCP 5.2(a); NY R USDCTED Order 2004-09.

      v.  In addition, exercise caution when filing documents that contain the following:

- Personal identifying number, such as driver's license number;

- Medical records, treatment and diagnosis;

- Employment history;

- Individual financial information; and

- Proprietary or trade secret information. NY R USDCTED Order 2004-09.

  b.  *Exemptions from the redaction requirement.* The redaction requirement does not apply to the following:

      i.  A financial-account number that identifies the property allegedly subject to forfeiture in a forfeiture proceeding;

      ii.  The record of an administrative or agency proceeding;

      iii.  The official record of a state-court proceeding;

      iv.  The record of a court or tribunal, if that record was not subject to the redaction requirement when originally filed;

      v.  A filing covered by FRCP 5.2(c) or FRCP 5.2(d); and

      vi.  A pro se filing in an action brought under 28 U.S.C.A. § 2241, 28 U.S.C.A. § 2254, or 28 U.S.C.A. § 2255. FRCP 5.2(b).

c. *Limitations on remote access to electronic files; Social Security appeals and immigration cases.* Unless the court orders otherwise, in an action for benefits under the Social Security Act, and in an action or proceeding relating to an order of removal, to relief from removal, or to immigration benefits or detention, access to an electronic file is authorized as follows:

    i. The parties and their attorneys may have remote electronic access to any part of the case file, including the administrative record;

    ii. Any other person may have electronic access to the full record at the courthouse, but may have remote electronic access only to:

       • The docket maintained by the court; and

       • An opinion, order, judgment, or other disposition of the court, but not any other part of the case file or the administrative record. FRCP 5.2(c).

d. *Filings made under seal.* The court may order that a filing be made under seal without redaction. The court may later unseal the filing or order the person who made the filing to file a redacted version for the public record. FRCP 5.2(d).

e. *Protective orders.* For good cause, the court may by order in a case:

    i. Require redaction of additional information; or

    ii. Limit or prohibit a nonparty's remote electronic access to a document filed with the court. FRCP 5.2(e).

f. *Option for additional unredacted filing under seal.* A person making a redacted filing may also file an unredacted copy under seal. The court must retain the unredacted copy as part of the record. FRCP 5.2(f); NY R USDCTED Order 2004-09. The unredacted version of the document or the reference list shall be retained by the court as part of the record. The court may, however, still require the party to file a redacted copy for the public file. NY R USDCTED Order 2004-09.

g. *Option for filing a reference list.* A filing that contains redacted information may be filed together with a reference list that identifies each item of redacted information and specifies an appropriate identifier that uniquely corresponds to each item listed. The list must be filed under seal and may be amended as of right. Any reference in the case to a listed identifier will be construed to refer to the corresponding item of information. FRCP 5.2(g); NY R USDCTED Order 2004-09. The unredacted version of the document or the reference list shall be retained by the court as part of the record. The court may, however, still require the party to file a redacted copy for the public file. NY R USDCTED Order 2004-09.

h. *Responsibility for redaction.* The responsibility for redacting these personal identifiers rests solely with counsel and the parties. The Clerk will not review each pleading for compliance with NY R USDCTED Order 2004-09. NY R USDCTED Order 2004-09.

    i. Counsel is strongly urged to share this notice with all clients so that an informed decision about the inclusion of certain materials may be made. If a redacted document is filed, it is the sole responsibility of counsel and the parties to be sure that all pleadings comply with the rules of this court requiring redaction of personal data identifiers. The clerk will not review each pleading for redaction. NY R USDCTED Order 2004-09.

i. *Waiver of protection of identifiers.* A person waives the protection of FRCP 5.2(a) as to the person's own information by filing it without redaction and not under seal. FRCP 5.2(h).

4. *Individual judge practices.* Refer to the Miscellaneous section of this document for information on individual judge practices on formatting documents.

## F. Filing and Service Requirements

1. *Filing requirements.* Any paper after the complaint that is required to be served—together with a certificate of service—must be filed within a reasonable time after service. FRCP 5(d)(1).

    a. *How filing is made; In general.* A paper is filed by delivering it:

      i. To the clerk; or

      ii. To a judge who agrees to accept it for filing, and who must then note the filing date on the paper and promptly send it to the clerk. FRCP 5(d)(2).

b. *Night depository.* A night depository with an automatic date stamp shall be maintained. . .by the Clerk of the Eastern District in the Brooklyn Courthouse. After regular business hours, papers for the District Court only may be deposited in the night depository. Such papers will be considered as having been filed in the District Court as of the date stamped thereon, which shall be deemed presumptively correct. NY R USDCTS&ED Civ Rule 1.2.

c. *Electronic filing*

   i. *Authorization of electronic filing program.* A court may, by local rule, allow papers to be filed, signed, or verified by electronic means that are consistent with any technical standards established by the Judicial Conference of the United States. A local rule may require electronic filing only if reasonable exceptions are allowed. A paper filed electronically in compliance with a local rule is a written paper for purposes of the Federal Rules of Civil Procedure. FRCP 5(d)(3).

   - Parties serving and filing papers shall follow the instructions regarding Electronic Case Filing (ECF) published on the website of each respective Court. A paper served and filed by electronic means in accordance with such instructions is, for purposes of FRCP 5, served and filed in compliance with the Local Civil Rules of the Southern and Eastern Districts of New York. NY R USDCTS&ED Civ Rule 5.2(a). Parties have an obligation to review the Court's actual order, decree, or judgment (on ECF), which controls, and should not rely on the description on the docket or in the ECF Notice of Electronic Filing (NEF). NY R USDCTS&ED Civ Rule 5.2(c).

   ii. *Mandatory electronic filing.* Beginning on August 2, 2004, electronic case filing will be mandatory for all civil cases other than pro se cases. NY R USDCTED Order 2004-08.

   - *Letter-motions and letters addressed to the court.* Subject to the instructions regarding ECF published on the website of each respective Court and any pertinent Individual Judge's Practices, letter-motions permitted by NY R USDCTS&ED Civ Rule 7.1(d) and letters addressed to the Court (but not letters between the parties) may be filed via ECF. NY R USDCTS&ED Civ Rule 5.2(b).

   - *Proposed orders, judgments and decrees.* Proposed orders, judgments and decrees shall be presented as directed by the ECF rules published on the website of each respective Court. NY R USDCTS&ED Civ Rule 77.1. For more information, refer to NY R USDCTS&ED Civ Rule 77.1.

   - *Request for exemption.* Requests by attorneys for an exemption to the mandatory policy will be considered for good cause hardship reasons only, and will be reviewed on an individual basis by the assigned United States Magistrate Judge. The Clerk's Office provides an electronic filing training program to assist attorneys filing electronically. Before seeking a hardship exemption, attorneys are advised to participate in the training program or otherwise seek the assistance of the Clerk's Office. NY R USDCTED Order 2004-08.

   iii. For more information on electronic filing, refer to the court's website.

2. *Service requirements*

   a. *Service; When required*

      i. *In general.* Unless the Federal Rules of Civil Procedure provide otherwise, each of the following papers must be served on every party:

      - An order stating that service is required;
      - A pleading filed after the original complaint, unless the court orders otherwise under FRCP 5(c) because there are numerous defendants;
      - A discovery paper required to be served on a party, unless the court orders otherwise;
      - A written motion, except one that may be heard ex parte; and
      - A written notice, appearance, demand, or offer of judgment, or any similar paper. FRCP 5(a)(1).

    ii.  *If a party fails to appear.* No service is required on a party who is in default for failing to appear. But a pleading that asserts a new claim for relief against such a party must be served on that party under FRCP 4. FRCP 5(a)(2).

    iii.  *Seizing property.* If an action is begun by seizing property and no person is or need be named as a defendant, any service required before the filing of an appearance, answer, or claim must be made on the person who had custody or possession of the property when it was seized. FRCP 5(a)(3).

b.  *Service; How made*

    i.  *Serving an attorney.* If a party is represented by an attorney, service under FRCP 5 must be made on the attorney unless the court orders service on the party. FRCP 5(b)(1).

    ii.  *Service in general.* A paper is served under FRCP 5 by:

- Handing it to the person;
- Leaving it: (1) at the person's office with a clerk or other person in charge or, if no one is in charge, in a conspicuous place in the office; or (2) if the person has no office or the office is closed, at the person's dwelling or usual place of abode with someone of suitable age and discretion who resides there;
- Mailing it to the person's last known address—in which event service is complete upon mailing;
- Leaving it with the court clerk if the person has no known address;
- Sending it by electronic means if the person consented in writing—in which event service is complete upon transmission, but is not effective if the serving party learns that it did not reach the person to be served; or
- Delivering it by any other means that the person consented to in writing—in which event service is complete when the person making service delivers it to the agency designated to make delivery. FRCP 5(b)(2).

    iii.  *Service by overnight delivery.* Service upon an attorney may be made by overnight delivery service. "Overnight delivery service" means any delivery service which regularly accepts items for overnight delivery. Overnight delivery service shall be deemed service by mail for purposes of FRCP 5 and FRCP 6. NY R USDCTS&ED Civ Rule 5.3.

    iv.  *Service by electronic means.* Parties serving and filing papers shall follow the instructions regarding Electronic Case Filing (ECF) published on the website of each respective Court. A paper served and filed by electronic means in accordance with such instructions is, for purposes of FRCP 5, served and filed in compliance with the Local Civil Rules of the United States District Courts for the Southern and Eastern Districts of New York. NY R USDCTS&ED Civ Rule 5.2(a). Parties have an obligation to review the Court's actual order, decree, or judgment (on ECF), which controls, and should not rely on the description on the docket or in the ECF Notice of Electronic Filing (NEF). NY R USDCTS&ED Civ Rule 5.2(c).

    v.  *Using court facilities.* If a local rule so authorizes, a party may use the court's transmission facilities to make service under FRCP 5(b)(2)(E). FRCP 5(b)(3).

c.  *Serving numerous defendants*

    i.  *In general.* If an action involves an unusually large number of defendants, the court may, on motion or on its own, order that:

- Defendants' pleadings and replies to them need not be served on other defendants;
- Any crossclaim, counterclaim, avoidance, or affirmative defense in those pleadings and replies to them will be treated as denied or avoided by all other parties; and
- Filing any such pleading and serving it on the plaintiff constitutes notice of the pleading to all parties. FRCP 5(c)(1).

    ii.  *Notifying parties.* A copy of every such order must be served on the parties as the court directs. FRCP 5(c)(2).

3. *Individual judge practices.* Refer to the Miscellaneous section of this document for information on individual judge practices on filing and serving documents.

## G. Hearings

1. *Hearings, generally*

   a. *Oral argument.* Due process does not require that oral argument be permitted on a motion and, except as otherwise provided by local rule, the district court has discretion to determine whether it will decide the motion on the papers or hear argument by counsel (and perhaps receive evidence). FPP § 1190; F.D.I.C. v. Deglau, 207 F.3d 153 (3d Cir. 2000). The parties and their attorneys shall only appear to argue the motion if so directed by the Court by order or by a Judge's Individual Practice. NY R USDCTS&ED Civ Rule 6.1(c).

   b. *Providing a regular schedule for oral hearings.* A court may establish regular times and places for oral hearings on motions. FRCP 78(a).

   c. *Providing for submission on briefs.* By rule or order, the court may provide for submitting and determining motions on briefs, without oral hearings. FRCP 78(b).

2. *Individual judge practices.* Refer to the Miscellaneous section of this document for information on individual judge practices on hearings.

## H. Forms

### 1. Federal Motion for Judgment on the Pleadings Forms

   a. Motion and notice; For judgment on pleadings. AMJUR PP FEDPRAC § 532.

   b. Countermotion and notice; For judgment on pleadings; By defendants. AMJUR PP FEDPRAC § 533.

   c. Order; For judgment on pleadings; In favor of plaintiff. AMJUR PP FEDPRAC § 534.

   d. Order; For judgment on pleadings; In favor of defendant. AMJUR PP FEDPRAC § 535.

   e. Motion for judgment on the pleadings. 2C FEDFORMS § 11:131.

   f. Motion for judgment on the pleadings; Alternate wording. 2C FEDFORMS § 11:132.

   g. Motion for judgment on the pleadings; Long version. 2C FEDFORMS § 11:133.

   h. Motion for judgment on the pleadings; Several grounds. 2C FEDFORMS § 11:134.

   i. Notice of motion and motion for judgment on the pleadings. 2C FEDFORMS § 11:135.

   j. Notice of motion for judgment on the pleadings (partial) or for partial summary judgment. 2C FEDFORMS § 11:136.

   k. Order granting judgment on the pleadings. 2C FEDFORMS § 11:137.

   l. Order granting judgment on the pleadings; Motion by plaintiff. 2C FEDFORMS § 11:138.

   m. Judgment on the pleadings. 2C FEDFORMS § 11:139.

   n. Motion; General form. FEDPROF § 1:746.

   o. Notice; Of motion; General form. FEDPROF § 1:747.

   p. Notice; Of motion; With costs of motion. FEDPROF § 1:748.

   q. Notice; Of motion; Containing motion. FEDPROF § 1:749.

   r. Opposition; To motion; General form. FEDPROF § 1:750.

   s. Affidavit; Supporting or opposing motion. FEDPROF § 1:751.

   t. Brief; Supporting or opposing motion. FEDPROF § 1:752.

   u. Statement of points and authorities; Opposing motion. FEDPROF § 1:753.

   v. Motion; For judgment on the pleadings. FEDPROF § 1:1295.

   w. Order; For judgment on the pleadings; In favor of plaintiff. FEDPROF § 1:1296.

   x. Order; For judgment on the pleadings; In favor of defendant. FEDPROF § 1:1297.

y. Motion for judgment on pleadings; Plaintiff. GOLDLTGFMS § 20:38.

z. Motion for judgment on pleadings; Defendant. GOLDLTGFMS § 20:39.

## I. Applicable Rules

1. *Federal rules*

   a. Serving and filing pleadings and other papers. FRCP 5.

   b. Constitutional challenge to a statute; Notice, certification, and intervention. FRCP 5.1.

   c. Privacy protection for filings made with the court. FRCP 5.2.

   d. Computing and extending time; Time for motion papers. FRCP 6.

   e. Pleadings allowed; Form of motions and other papers. FRCP 7.

   f. Disclosure statement. FRCP 7.1.

   g. Form of pleadings. FRCP 10.

   h. Signing pleadings, motions, and other papers; Representations to the court; Sanctions. FRCP 11.

   i. Defenses and objections; When and how presented; Motion for judgment on the pleadings; Consolidating motions; Waiving defenses; Pretrial hearing. FRCP 12.

   j. Hearing motions; Submission on briefs. FRCP 78.

2. *Local rules*

   a. Night depository. NY R USDCTS&ED Civ Rule 1.2.

   b. Duty of attorneys in related cases. NY R USDCTS&ED Civ Rule 1.6.

   c. Electronic service and filing of documents. NY R USDCTS&ED Civ Rule 5.2.

   d. Service by overnight delivery. NY R USDCTS&ED Civ Rule 5.3.

   e. Service and filing of motion papers. NY R USDCTS&ED Civ Rule 6.1.

   f. Orders on motions. NY R USDCTS&ED Civ Rule 6.2.

   g. Computation of time. NY R USDCTS&ED Civ Rule 6.4.

   h. Motion papers. NY R USDCTS&ED Civ Rule 7.1.

   i. Disclosure statement. NY R USDCTS&ED Civ Rule 7.1.1.

   j. Authorities to be provided to pro se litigants. NY R USDCTS&ED Civ Rule 7.2.

   k. Form of pleadings, motions, and other papers. NY R USDCTS&ED Civ Rule 11.1.

   l. Notice to pro se litigant who opposes a FRCP 12 motion supported by matters outside the pleadings. NY R USDCTS&ED Civ Rule 12.1.

   m. Submission of orders, judgments and decrees. NY R USDCTS&ED Civ Rule 77.1.

   n. Court-annexed arbitration (Eastern District only). NY R USDCTS&ED Civ Rule 83.7.

   o. Court-annexed mediation (Eastern District only). NY R USDCTS&ED Civ Rule 83.8.

   p. Electronic case filing. NY R USDCTED Order 2004-08.

   q. The August 2, 2004 amendment to the E-Government Act of 2002. NY R USDCTED Order 2004-09.

   r. Categories and classification of cases; Information on cases and parties. NY R USDCTED Div. Bus., Rule 50.1.

## J. Miscellaneous

**NOTE: Individual judges' rules may apply. For available judge-level information, refer to:**

DISTRICT JUDGE CAROL BAGLEY AMON: NY R USDCTED Amon-Practices.

DISTRICT JUDGE JOAN M. AZRACK: NY R USDCTED Azrack-Practices.

DISTRICT JUDGE JOSEPH F. BIANCO: NY R USDCTED Bianco-Practices.

DISTRICT JUDGE FREDERIC BLOCK: NY R USDCTED Block-Practices.

DISTRICT JUDGE MARGO K. BRODIE: NY R USDCTED Brodie-Practices.

DISTRICT JUDGE PAMELA K. CHEN: NY R USDCTED Chen-Practices.

DISTRICT JUDGE BRIAN M. COGAN: NY R USDCTED Cogan-Practices; NY R USDCTED Cogan-Pretrial.

DISTRICT JUDGE LaSHANN DeARCY HALL: NY R USDCTED DeArcy Hall-Practices.

DISTRICT JUDGE RAYMOND J. DEARIE: NY R USDCTED Dearie-Practices.

DISTRICT JUDGE ANN M. DONNELLY: NY R USDCTED Donnelly-Practices.

DISTRICT JUDGE SANDRA J. FEUERSTEIN: NY R USDCTED Feuerstein-Practices; NY R USDCTED Feuerstein-Pretrial.

DISTRICT JUDGE NICHOLAS G. GARAUIFIS: NY R USDCTED Garaufis-Practices; NY R USDCTED Garaufis-Pretrial.

DISTRICT JUDGE NINA GERSHON: NY R USDCTED Gershon-Practices.

DISTRICT JUDGE I. LEO GLASSER: NY R USDCTED Glasser-Practices; NY R USDCTED Glasser-Crim.

DISTRICT JUDGE DENIS R. HURLEY: NY R USDCTED Hurley-Practices; [NY R USDCTED Hurley-Pro Cooperation Info, as added by NY ORDER 16-4188, effective July 22, 2016]; [NY R USDCTED Hurley-Pro Cooperation Info Stay, as added by NY ORDER 16-4188, effective July 22, 2016].

DISTRICT JUDGE DORA L. IRIZARRY: NY R USDCTED Irizarry-Practices; NY R USDCTED Irizarry-Pretrial; NY R USDCTED Irizarry-Crim.

DISTRICT JUDGE STERLING JOHNSON, JR.: NY R USDCTED Johnson-Practices.

DISTRICT JUDGE EDWARD R. KORMAN: NY R USDCTED Korman-Practices; NY R USDCTED Korman-Pretrial.

DISTRICT JUDGE WILLIAM F. KUNTZ: NY R USDCTED Kuntz-Practices.

DISTRICT JUDGE KIYO A. MATSUMOTO: NY R USDCTED Matsumoto-Practices.

DISTRICT JUDGE ROSLYNN R. MAUSKOPF: NY R USDCTED Mauskopf-Practices; NY R USDCTED Mauskopf-Recusal.

DISTRICT JUDGE THOMAS C. PLATT: NY R USDCTED Platt-Practices.

DISTRICT JUDGE ALLYNE R. ROSS: NY R USDCTED Ross-Practices.

DISTRICT JUDGE JOANNA SEYBERT: NY R USDCTED Seybert-Practices.

DISTRICT JUDGE ARTHUR D. SPATT: NY R USDCTED Spatt-Practices.

DISTRICT JUDGE SANDRA L. TOWNES: NY R USDCTED Townes-Practices.

DISTRICT JUDGE ERIC N. VITALIANO: NY R USDCTED Vitaliano-Practices.

DISTRICT JUDGE JACK B. WEINSTEIN: NY R USDCTED Weinstein-Practices.

DISTRICT JUDGE LEONARD D. WEXLER: NY R USDCTED Wexler-Practices; NY R USDCTED Wexler-Rules.

MAGISTRATE JUDGE LOIS BLOOM: NY R USDCTED Bloom-Practices.

MAGISTRATE JUDGE GARY R. BROWN: NY R USDCTED Brown-Practices.

MAGISTRATE JUDGE MARILYN D. GO: NY R USDCTED Go-Practices.

MAGISTRATE JUDGE STEVEN M. GOLD: NY R USDCTED Gold-Practices.

MAGISTRATE JUDGE PEGGY KUO: NY R USDCTED Kuo-Practices; NY R USDCTED Kuo-Scheduling Order.

MAGISTRATE JUDGE ROBERT M. LEVY: NY R USDCTED Levy-Practices.

MAGISTRATE JUDGE ARLENE R. LINDSAY: NY R USDCTED Lindsay-Practices.

MAGISTRATE JUDGE STEVEN I. LOCKE: NY R USDCTED Locke-Practices.

MAGISTRATE JUDGE ROANNE L. MANN: NY R USDCTED Mann-Practices.

EASTERN DISTRICT OF NEW YORK

MAGISTRATE JUDGE JAMES ORENSTEIN: NY R USDCTED Jorenstein--Practices.

MAGISTRATE JUDGE VIKTOR V. POHORELSKY: NY R USDCTED Pohorelsky-Practices.

MAGISTRATE JUDGE CHERYL L. POLLAK: NY R USDCTED Pollak-Practices; NY R USDCTED Pollak-Pretrial.

MAGISTRATE JUDGE RAMON E. REYES, JR.: NY R USDCTED Reyes-Practices.

MAGISTRATE JUDGE VERA M. SCANLON: NY R USDCTED Scanlon-Practices.

MAGISTRATE JUDGE ANNE Y. SHIELDS: NY R USDCTED Shields-Practices.

MAGISTRATE JUDGE STEVEN L. TISCIONE: NY R USDCTED Tiscione-Practices.

MAGISTRATE JUDGE A. KATHLEEN TOMILINSON: NY R USDCTED Tomlinson-Practices.

## Requests, Notices and Applications
## Interrogatories

### Document Last Updated September 2016

**A. Checklist**

  (I)  ❑ Matters to be considered by requesting party

    (a)  ❑ Required documents

      (1)  ❑ Interrogatories

    (b)  ❑ Supplemental documents

      (1)  ❑ Certificate of service

    (c)  ❑ Timing

      (1)  ❑ A party may not seek discovery from any source before the parties have conferred as required by FRCP 26(f), except in a proceeding exempted from initial disclosure under FRCP 26(a)(1)(B), or when authorized by the Federal Rules of Civil Procedure, by stipulation, or by court order

  (II)  ❑ Matters to be considered by responding party

    (a)  ❑ Required documents

      (1)  ❑ Response to interrogatories

    (b)  ❑ Supplemental documents

      (1)  ❑ Written information regarding assertion of privilege

      (2)  ❑ Certificate of service

    (c)  ❑ Timing

      (1)  ❑ The responding party must serve its answers and any objections within thirty (30) days after being served with the interrogatories

**B. Timing**

1. *Interrogatories.* FRCP 33(a) contains no limit on when interrogatories may first be served. FPP § 2170. FRCP 33 is also silent on how late in a case interrogatories may be served. But FRCP 16(b)(3)(A) provides that the scheduling order in the case "must limit the time to . . . complete discovery." Although the scheduling order requirement does not apply to cases exempted by local rule, ordinarily there should be a scheduling order that sets a discovery cutoff. FPP § 2170.

2. *Timing of discovery, generally.* A party may not seek discovery from any source before the parties have conferred as required by FRCP 26(f), except in a proceeding exempted from initial disclosure under FRCP 26(a)(1)(B), or when authorized by the Federal Rules of Civil Procedure, by stipulation, or by court order. FRCP 26(d)(1).

742

3. *Computation of time*

    a. *Computing time.* FRCP 6 applies in computing any time period specified in the Federal Rules of Civil Procedure, in any local rule or court order, or in any statute that does not specify a method of computing time. FRCP 6(a). In computing any period of time prescribed or allowed by the Local Civil Rules of the United States District Courts for the Southern and Eastern Districts of New York or the Local Admiralty and Maritime Rules, the provisions of FRCP 6 shall apply unless otherwise stated. NY R USDCTS&ED Civ Rule 6.4.

        i. *Period stated in days or a longer unit.* When the period is stated in days or a longer unit of time:

- Exclude the day of the event that triggers the period;

- Count every day, including intermediate Saturdays, Sundays, and legal holidays; and

- Include the last day of the period, but if the last day is a Saturday, Sunday, or legal holiday, the period continues to run until the end of the next day that is not a Saturday, Sunday, or legal holiday. FRCP 6(a)(1). In the Local Civil Rules of the United States District Courts for the Southern and Eastern Districts of New York, as in the Federal Rules of Civil Procedure as amended effective December 1, 2009, Saturdays, Sundays, and legal holidays are no longer excluded in computing periods of time. If the last day of the period is a Saturday, Sunday, or legal holiday, the period continues to run until the end of the next day that is not a Saturday, Sunday, or legal holiday. NY R USDCTS&ED Civ Rule 6.4.

        ii. *Period stated in hours.* When the period is stated in hours:

- Begin counting immediately on the occurrence of the event that triggers the period;

- Count every hour, including hours during intermediate Saturdays, Sundays, and legal holidays; and

- If the period would end on a Saturday, Sunday, or legal holiday, the period continues to run until the same time on the next day that is not a Saturday, Sunday, or legal holiday. FRCP 6(a)(2). In the Local Civil Rules of the United States District Courts for the Southern and Eastern Districts of New York, as in the Federal Rules of Civil Procedure as amended effective December 1, 2009, Saturdays, Sundays, and legal holidays are no longer excluded in computing periods of time. If the last day of the period is a Saturday, Sunday, or legal holiday, the period continues to run until the end of the next day that is not a Saturday, Sunday, or legal holiday. NY R USDCTS&ED Civ Rule 6.4.

        iii. *Inaccessibility of the clerk's office.* Unless the court orders otherwise, if the clerk's office is inaccessible:

- On the last day for filing under FRCP 6(a)(1), then the time for filing is extended to the first accessible day that is not a Saturday, Sunday, or legal holiday; or

- During the last hour for filing under FRCP 6(a)(2), then the time for filing is extended to the same time on the first accessible day that is not a Saturday, Sunday, or legal holiday. FRCP 6(a)(3).

        iv. *"Last day" defined.* Unless a different time is set by a statute, local rule, or court order, the last day ends:

- For electronic filing, at midnight in the court's time zone; and

- For filing by other means, when the clerk's office is scheduled to close. FRCP 6(a)(4).

        v. *"Next day" defined.* The "next day" is determined by continuing to count forward when the period is measured after an event and backward when measured before an event. FRCP 6(a)(5).

        vi. *"Legal holiday" defined.* "Legal holiday" means:

- The day set aside by statute for observing New Year's Day, Martin Luther King Jr.'s Birthday, Washington's Birthday, Memorial Day, Independence Day, Labor Day, Columbus Day, Veterans' Day, Thanksgiving Day, or Christmas Day;

- Any day declared a holiday by the President or Congress; and

- For periods that are measured after an event, any other day declared a holiday by the state where the district court is located. FRCP 6(a)(6).

b. *Extending time*

    i. *In general.* When an act may or must be done within a specified time, the court may, for good cause, extend the time:

- With or without motion or notice if the court acts, or if a request is made, before the original time or its extension expires; or

- On motion made after the time has expired if the party failed to act because of excusable neglect. FRCP 6(b)(1).

    ii. *Exceptions.* A court must not extend the time to act under FRCP 50(b), FRCP 50(d), FRCP 52(b), FRCP 59(b), FRCP 59(d), FRCP 59(e), and FRCP 60(b). FRCP 6(b)(2).

    iii. Refer to the United States District Court for the Eastern District of New York KeyRules Motion for Continuance/Extension of Time document for more information on extending time.

c. *Additional time after certain kinds of service.* When a party may or must act within a specified time after service and service is made under FRCP 5(b)(2)(C), FRCP 5(b)(2)(D), FRCP 5(b)(2)(E), or FRCP 5(b)(2)(F), three (3) days are added after the period would otherwise expire under FRCP 6(a). FRCP 6(d). Overnight delivery service shall be deemed service by mail for purposes of FRCP 5 and FRCP 6. NY R USDCTS&ED Civ Rule 5.3.

4. *Individual judge practices.* Refer to the Miscellaneous section of this document for information on individual judge practices on timing of documents.

## C. General Requirements

1. *General provisions governing discovery*

a. *Discovery scope and limits*

    i. *Scope in general.* Unless otherwise limited by court order, the scope of discovery is as follows: Parties may obtain discovery regarding any nonprivileged matter that is relevant to any party's claim or defense and proportional to the needs of the case, considering the importance of the issues at stake in the action, the amount in controversy, the parties' relative access to relevant information, the parties' resources, the importance of the discovery in resolving the issues, and whether the burden or expense of the proposed discovery outweighs its likely benefit. Information within this scope of discovery need not be admissible in evidence to be discoverable. FRCP 26(b)(1).

    ii. *Limitations on frequency and extent*

- *When permitted.* By order, the court may alter the limits in the Federal Rules of Civil Procedure on the number of depositions and interrogatories or on the length of depositions under FRCP 30. By order or local rule, the court may also limit the number of requests under FRCP 36. FRCP 26(b)(2)(A).

- *Specific limitations on electronically stored information.* A party need not provide discovery of electronically stored information from sources that the party identifies as not reasonably accessible because of undue burden or cost. On motion to compel discovery or for a protective order, the party from whom discovery is sought must show that the information is not reasonably accessible because of undue burden or cost. If that showing is made, the court may nonetheless order discovery from such sources if the requesting party shows good cause, considering the limitations of FRCP 26(b)(2)(C). The court may specify conditions for the discovery. FRCP 26(b)(2)(B).

- *When required.* On motion or on its own, the court must limit the frequency or extent of discovery otherwise allowed by the Federal Rules of Civil Procedure or by local rule if it determines that: (1) the discovery sought is unreasonably cumulative or duplicative, or can be obtained from some other source that is more convenient, less burdensome, or less expensive; (2) the party seeking discovery has had ample opportunity to obtain the information by discovery in the action; or (3) the proposed discovery is outside the scope permitted by FRCP 26(b)(1). FRCP 26(b)(2)(C).

iii. *Trial preparation; Materials*

- *Documents and tangible things.* Ordinarily, a party may not discover documents and tangible things that are prepared in anticipation of litigation or for trial by or for another party or its representative (including the other party's attorney, consultant, surety, indemnitor, insurer, or agent). But, subject to FRCP 26(b)(4), those materials may be discovered if: (1) they are otherwise discoverable under FRCP 26(b)(1); and (2) the party shows that it has substantial need for the materials to prepare its case and cannot, without undue hardship, obtain their substantial equivalent by other means. FRCP 26(b)(3)(A).

- *Protection against disclosure.* If the court orders discovery of those materials, it must protect against disclosure of the mental impressions, conclusions, opinions, or legal theories of a party's attorney or other representative concerning the litigation. FRCP 26(b)(3)(B).

- *Previous statement.* Any party or other person may, on request and without the required showing, obtain the person's own previous statement about the action or its subject matter. If the request is refused, the person may move for a court order, and FRCP 37(a)(5) applies to the award of expenses. A previous statement is either: (1) a written statement that the person has signed or otherwise adopted or approved; or (2) a contemporaneous stenographic, mechanical, electrical, or other recording—or a transcription of it—that recites substantially verbatim the person's oral statement. FRCP 26(b)(3)(C).

iv. *Trial preparation; Experts*

- *Deposition of an expert who may testify.* A party may depose any person who has been identified as an expert whose opinions may be presented at trial. If FRCP 26(a)(2)(B) requires a report from the expert, the deposition may be conducted only after the report is provided. FRCP 26(b)(4)(A).

- *Trial-preparation protection for draft reports or disclosures.* FRCP 26(b)(3)(A) and FRCP 26(b)(3)(B) protect drafts of any report or disclosure required under FRCP 26(a)(2), regardless of the form in which the draft is recorded. FRCP 26(b)(4)(B).

- *Trial-preparation protection for communications between a party's attorney and expert witnesses.* FRCP 26(b)(3)(A) and FRCP 26(b)(3)(B) protect communications between the party's attorney and any witness required to provide a report under FRCP 26(a)(2)(B), regardless of the form of the communications, except to the extent that the communications: (1) relate to compensation for the expert's study or testimony; (2) identify facts or data that the party's attorney provided and that the expert considered in forming the opinions to be expressed; or (3) identify assumptions that the party's attorney provided and that the expert relied on in forming the opinions to be expressed. FRCP 26(b)(4)(C).

- *Expert employed only for trial preparation.* Ordinarily, a party may not, by interrogatories or deposition, discover facts known or opinions held by an expert who has been retained or specially employed by another party in anticipation of litigation or to prepare for trial and who is not expected to be called as a witness at trial. But a party may do so only: (1) as provided in FRCP 35(b); or (2) on showing exceptional circumstances under which it is impracticable for the party to obtain facts or opinions on the same subject by other means. FRCP 26(b)(4)(D).

- *Payment.* Unless manifest injustice would result, the court must require that the party seeking discovery: (1) pay the expert a reasonable fee for time spent in responding to discovery under FRCP 26(b)(4)(A) or FRCP 26(b)(4)(D); and (2) for discovery FRCP 26(b)(4)(D), also pay the other party a fair portion of the fees and expenses it reasonably incurred in obtaining the expert's facts and opinions. FRCP 26(b)(4)(E).

v. *Claiming privilege or protecting trial-preparation materials*

- *Information withheld.* When a party withholds information otherwise discoverable by claiming that the information is privileged or subject to protection as trial-preparation material, the party must: (1) expressly make the claim; and (2) describe the nature of the documents, communications, or tangible things not produced or disclosed—and do so in a manner that, without revealing information itself privileged or protected, will enable other parties to assess the claim. FRCP 26(b)(5)(A). Unless otherwise agreed by the parties or directed by the Court, where a claim of privilege is asserted in objecting to any means of discovery or disclosure, including but not limited to a deposition, and an answer is not provided on the basis of such assertion, (1) the person asserting the privilege shall identify the nature of the privilege (including work product) which is being claimed and, if the privilege is governed by state law, indicate the state's privilege rule being invoked; and (2) the following information shall be provided in the objection, or (in the case of a deposition) in response to questions by the questioner, unless divulgence of such information would cause disclosure of the allegedly privileged information: (A) for documents: (i) the type of document, e.g., letter or memorandum; (ii) the general subject matter of the document; (iii) the date of the document; and (iv) the author of the document, the addressees of the document, and any other recipients, and, where not apparent, the relationship of the author, addressees, and recipients to each other; (B) for oral communications: (i) the name of the person making the communication and the names of persons present while the communication was made and, where not apparent, the relationship of the persons present to the person making the communication; (ii) the date and place of communication; and (iii) the general subject matter of the communication. NY R USDCTS&ED Civ Rule 26.2(a). Where a claim of privilege is asserted in response to discovery or disclosure other than a deposition, and information is not provided on the basis of such assertion, the information set forth in NY R USDCTS&ED Civ Rule 26.2(a) shall be furnished in writing at the time of the response to such discovery or disclosure, unless otherwise ordered by the Court. NY R USDCTS&ED Civ Rule 26.2(b).

- *Information produced.* If information produced in discovery is subject to a claim of privilege or of protection as trial-preparation material, the party making the claim may notify any party that received the information of the claim and the basis for it. After being notified, a party must promptly return, sequester, or destroy the specified information and any copies it has; must not use or disclose the information until the claim is resolved; must take reasonable steps to retrieve the information if the party disclosed it before being notified; and may promptly present the information to the court under seal for a determination of the claim. The producing party must preserve the information until the claim is resolved. FRCP 26(b)(5)(B).

- *Efficient means of providing information regarding claims of privilege.* Efficient means of providing information regarding claims of privilege are encouraged, and parties are encouraged to agree upon measures that further this end. For example, when asserting privilege on the same basis with respect to multiple documents, it is presumptively proper to provide the information required by NY R USDCTS&ED Civ Rule 26.2 by group or category. A party receiving a privilege log that groups documents or otherwise departs from a document-by-document or communication-by-communication listing may not object solely on that basis, but may object if the substantive information required by NY R USDCTS&ED Civ Rule 26.2 has not been provided in a comprehensible form. NY R USDCTS&ED Civ Rule 26.2(c).

b. *Protective orders.* A party or any person from whom discovery is sought may move for a protective order in the court where the action is pending—or as an alternative on matters relating to a deposition, in the court for the district where the deposition will be taken. FRCP 26(c)(1). Refer to the United States District Court for the Eastern District of New York KeyRules Motion for Protective Order document for more information.

c. *Sequence of discovery.* Unless the parties stipulate or the court orders otherwise for the parties' and witnesses' convenience and in the interests of justice: (1) methods of discovery may be used in any sequence; and (2) discovery by one party does not require any other party to delay its discovery. FRCP 26(d)(3).

d. *Uniform definitions in discovery requests.* The full text of the definitions and rules of construction set forth in NY R USDCTS&ED Civ Rule 26.3(c) and NY R USDCTS&ED Civ Rule 26.3(d) is deemed incorporated by reference into all discovery requests. No discovery request shall use broader definitions or rules of construction than those set forth in NY R USDCTS&ED Civ Rule 26.3(c) and NY R USDCTS&ED Civ Rule 26.3(d). NY R USDCTS&ED Civ Rule 26.3 shall not preclude (1) the definition of other terms specific to the particular litigation, (2) the use of abbreviations, or (3) a more narrow definition of a term defined in NY R USDCTS&ED Civ Rule 26.3(c). NY R USDCTS&ED Civ Rule 26.3(a). NY R USDCTS&ED Civ Rule 26.3 is not intended to broaden or narrow the scope of discovery permitted by the Federal Rules of Civil Procedure. NY R USDCTS&ED Civ Rule 26.3(b).

    i. *Definitions.* The following definitions apply to all discovery requests:

- *Communication.* The term "communication" means the transmittal of information (in the form of facts, ideas, inquiries or otherwise). NY R USDCTS&ED Civ Rule 26.3(c)(1).

- *Document.* The term "document" is defined to be synonymous in meaning and equal in scope to the usage of the term "documents or electronically stored information" in FRCP 34(a)(1)(A). A draft or non-identical copy is a separate document within the meaning of this term. NY R USDCTS&ED Civ Rule 26.3(c)(2).

- *Identify (with respect to persons).* When referring to a person, "to identify" means to give, to the extent known, the person's full name, present or last known address, and when referring to a natural person, additionally, the present or last known place of employment. Once a person has been identified in accordance with NY R USDCTS&ED Civ Rule 26.3(c)(3), only the name of that person need be listed in response to subsequent discovery requesting the identification of that person. NY R USDCTS&ED Civ Rule 26.3(c)(3).

- *Identify (with respect to documents).* When referring to documents, "to identify" means to give, to the extent known, the (1) type of document; (2) general subject matter; (3) date of the document; and (4) author(s), addressee(s) and recipient(s). In the alternative, the responding party may produce the documents, together with identifying information sufficient to satisfy FRCP 33(d). NY R USDCTS&ED Civ Rule 26.3(c)(4).

- *Parties.* The terms "plaintiff" and "defendant" as well as a party's full or abbreviated name or a pronoun referring to a party mean the party and, where applicable, its officers, directors, employees, partners, corporate parent, subsidiaries or affiliates. This definition is not intended to impose a discovery obligation on any person who is not a party to the litigation. NY R USDCTS&ED Civ Rule 26.3(c)(5).

- *Person.* The term "person" is defined as any natural person or any legal entity, including, without limitation, any business or governmental entity or association. NY R USDCTS&ED Civ Rule 26.3(c)(6).

- *Concerning.* The term "concerning" means relating to, referring to, describing, evidencing or constituting. NY R USDCTS&ED Civ Rule 26.3(c)(7).

    ii. *Rules of construction.* The following rules of construction apply to all discovery requests:

- *All/any/each.* The terms "all," "any," and "each" shall each be construed as encompassing any and all. NY R USDCTS&ED Civ Rule 26.3(d)(1).

- *And/or.* The connectives "and" and "or" shall be construed either disjunctively or conjunctively as necessary to bring within the scope of the discovery request all responses that might otherwise be construed to be outside of its scope. NY R USDCTS&ED Civ Rule 26.3(d)(2).

- *Number.* The use of the singular form of any word includes the plural and vice versa. NY R USDCTS&ED Civ Rule 26.3(d)(3).

e. *Cooperation among counsel in discovery.* Counsel are expected to cooperate with each other, consistent with the interests of their clients, in all phases of the discovery process and to be courteous in their dealings with each other, including in matters relating to scheduling and timing of various discovery procedures. NY R USDCTS&ED Civ Rule 26.4(a).

    i.  Discovery requests shall be read reasonably in the recognition that the attorney serving them generally does not have the information being sought and the attorney receiving them generally does have such information or can obtain it from the client. NY R USDCTS&ED Civ Rule 26.4(b).

f.  *Standard discovery in prisoner pro se actions.* For information on discovery in prisoner pro se actions, refer to NY R USDCTS&ED Civ Rule 33.2.

2.  *Interrogatories*

    a.  *Number.* Unless otherwise stipulated or ordered by the court, a party may serve on any other party no more than twenty-five (25) written interrogatories, including all discrete subparts. Leave to serve additional interrogatories may be granted to the extent consistent with FRCP 26(b)(1) and FRCP 26(b)(2). FRCP 33(a)(1).

    b.  *Scope.* An interrogatory may relate to any matter that may be inquired into under FRCP 26(b). An interrogatory is not objectionable merely because it asks for an opinion or contention that relates to fact or the application of law to fact, but the court may order that the interrogatory need not be answered until designated discovery is complete, or until a pretrial conference or some other time. FRCP 33(a)(2).

    c.  *Parties subject to interrogatories.* Depositions may be taken of any person but interrogatories are limited to parties to the litigation. FPP § 2171. Interrogatories may not be directed to the attorney for a party. They must be addressed to the party, who is then required to give all information known to it or its attorney. FPP § 2171; Hickman v. Taylor, 329 U.S. 495, 504, 67 S.Ct. 385, 390, 91 L.Ed. 451 (1947). For more information, refer to FPP § 2171.

    d.  *Form.* Ideally an interrogatory should be a single direct question phrased in a fashion that will inform the other party what is requested. In fact the courts have given parties considerable latitude in framing interrogatories. Rather general language has been permitted so long as the interrogatory gives the other party a reasonably clear indication of the information to be included in its answer. FPP § 2168.

        i.  *Use of definitions.* There is no prohibition against the use of definitions in interrogatories, and definitions may be helpful in clarifying the meaning of obscure terms or avoiding repetitions in a long set of interrogatories. FPP § 2168.

        ii.  *Use of standardized form interrogatories.* There have been mixed reactions to the use of standardized form interrogatories. They have been referred to opprobriously as "canned sets of interrogatories of the shotgun variety" and it has been said that their indiscriminate use is an "undesirable practice." FPP § 2168.

    e.  *Form discovery requests.* Attorneys using form discovery requests shall review them to ascertain that they are consistent with the scope of discovery under FRCP 26(b)(1). Non-compliant requests shall not be used. NY R USDCTS&ED Civ Rule 26.5.

    f.  *Motion to compel.* The party submitting the interrogatories must attempt to confer with the responding party in an effort to secure the information without court action and, if that fails, move for an order under FRCP 37(a) compelling answers. FPP § 2182. Refer to the United States District Court for the Eastern District of New York KeyRules Motion to Compel Discovery document for more information.

3.  *Sanctions for failure to cooperate in discovery.* The court where the action is pending may, on motion, order sanctions if a party, after being properly served with interrogatories under FRCP 33 or a request for inspection under FRCP 34, fails to serve its answers, objections, or written response. FRCP 37(d)(1)(A)(ii). If a motion to compel is granted, the court must, after giving an opportunity to be heard, require the party or deponent whose conduct necessitated the motion, the party or attorney advising that conduct, or both to pay the movant's reasonable expenses incurred in making the motion, including attorney's fees. But the court must not order this payment if the opposing party's nondisclosure, response, or objection was substantially justified. FRCP 37(a)(5)(A)(ii). Refer to the United States District Court for

the Eastern District of New York KeyRules Motion for Discovery Sanctions document for more information.

4. *Stipulations about discovery procedure.* Unless the court orders otherwise, the parties may stipulate that: (1) a deposition may be taken before any person, at any time or place, on any notice, and in the manner specified—in which event it may be used in the same way as any other deposition; and (2) other procedures governing or limiting discovery be modified—but a stipulation extending the time for any form of discovery must have court approval if it would interfere with the time set for completing discovery, for hearing a motion, or for trial. FRCP 29.

5. *Related cases.* It shall be the continuing duty of each attorney appearing in any civil or criminal case to bring promptly to the attention of the Court all facts which said attorney believes are relevant to a determination that said case and one or more pending civil or criminal cases should be heard by the same Judge, in order to avoid unnecessary duplication of judicial effort. As soon as the attorney becomes aware of such relationship, said attorney shall notify the Judges to whom the cases have been assigned. NY R USDCTS&ED Civ Rule 1.6(a). If counsel fails to comply with NY R USDCTS&ED Civ Rule 1.6(a), the Court may assess reasonable costs directly against counsel whose action has obstructed the effective administration of the Court's business. NY R USDCTS&ED Civ Rule 1.6(b).

6. *Alternative dispute resolution (ADR)*

   a. *Court-annexed arbitration*

      i. *Civil cases eligible for compulsory arbitration.* The Clerk of Court shall, as to all cases filed after January 1, 1986, designate and process for compulsory arbitration all civil cases (excluding Social Security cases, tax matters, prisoners' civil rights cases and any action based on an alleged violation of a right secured by the Constitution of the United States or if jurisdiction is based in whole or in part on 28 U.S.C.A. § 1343) wherein money damages only are being sought in an amount not in excess of one hundred fifty thousand dollars ($150,000) exclusive of interest and costs. NY R USDCTS&ED Civ Rule 83.7(d)(1).

         • The parties may by written stipulation agree that the Clerk of Court shall designate and process for court-annexed arbitration any civil case that is not subject to compulsory arbitration in NY R USDCTS&ED Civ Rule 83.7. NY R USDCTS&ED Civ Rule 83.7(d)(2).

         • For purposes of NY R USDCTS&ED Civ Rule 83.7 only, in all civil cases damages shall be presumed to be not in excess of one hundred fifty thousand dollars ($150,000) exclusive of interest and costs, unless: (1) counsel for plaintiff, at the time of filing the complaint, or in the event of the removal of a case from state court or transfer of a case from another district to this Court, within thirty (30) days of the docketing of the case in this district, files a certification with the Court that the damages sought exceed one hundred fifty thousand dollars ($150,000), exclusive of interest and costs; or (2) counsel for a defendant, at the time of filing a counterclaim or cross-claim files a certification with the court that the damages sought by the counter-claim or cross-claim exceed one hundred fifty thousand dollars ($150,000) exclusive of interest and costs. NY R USDCTS&ED Civ Rule 83.7(d)(3).

      ii. *Exemption from arbitration.* The Court shall, sua sponte, or on motion of a party, exempt any case from arbitration in which the objectives of arbitration would not be realized (1) because the case involves complex or novel issues, (2) because legal issues predominate over factual issues, or (3) for other good cause. NY R USDCTS&ED Civ Rule 83.7(e)(2). For information on applying for an exemption, refer to NY R USDCTS&ED Civ Rule 83.7

      iii. *Referral to arbitration.* Cases not originally designated as eligible for compulsory arbitration, but which in the discretion of the assigned Judge, are later found to qualify, may be referred to arbitration. A U.S. District Judge or a U.S. Magistrate Judge, in cases that exceed the arbitration ceiling of one hundred fifty thousand dollars ($150,000) exclusive of interest and costs, in their discretion, may suggest that the parties should consider arbitration. If the parties are agreeable, an appropriate consent form signed by all parties or their representatives may be entered and filed in the case prior to scheduling an arbitration hearing. NY R USDCTS&ED Civ Rule 83.7(e)(3).

    iv.   For more information on arbitration, refer to NY R USDCTS&ED Civ Rule 83.7.

  b.  *Court-annexed mediation.* Mediation is a process in which parties and counsel agree to meet with a neutral mediator trained to assist them in settling disputes. The mediator improves communication across party lines, helps parties articulate their interests and understand those of the other party, probes the strengths and weaknesses of each party's legal positions, and identifies areas of agreement and helps generate options for a mutually agreeable resolution to the dispute. In all cases, mediation provides an opportunity to explore a wide range of potential solutions and to address interests that may be outside the scope of the stated controversy or which could not be addressed by judicial action. A hallmark of mediation is its capacity to expand traditional settlement discussions and broaden resolution options, often by exploring litigant needs and interests that may be formally independent of the legal issues in controversy. NY R USDCTS&ED Civ Rule 83.8(a).

    i.   *Eligible cases.* Judges and Magistrate Judges may designate civil cases for inclusion in the mediation program, and when doing so shall prepare an order to that effect. Alternatively, and subject to the availability of qualified mediators, the parties may consent to participation in the mediation program by preparing and executing a stipulation signed by all parties to the action and so-ordered by the Court. NY R USDCTS&ED Civ Rule 83.8(b)(1).

    ii.  For more information on mediation, refer to NY R USDCTS&ED Civ Rule 83.8.

7.  *Individual judge practices.* Refer to the Miscellaneous section of this document for information on individual judge practices on general requirements for documents.

## D.  Documents

1.  *Required documents*

  a.  *Interrogatories.* Refer to the General Requirements section of this document for information on interrogatories.

2.  *Supplemental documents*

  a.  *Certificate of service.* FRCP 5(d) requires that the person making service under FRCP 5 certify that service has been effected. FRCP 5(Advisory Committee Notes). Having such information on file may be useful for many purposes, including proof of service if an issue arises concerning the effectiveness of the service. FRCP 5(Advisory Committee Notes).

3.  *Individual judge practices.* Refer to the Miscellaneous section of this document for information on individual judge practices on required documents.

## E.  Format

1.  *Form of documents.* The rules governing captions and other matters of form in pleadings apply to motions and other papers. FRCP 7(b)(2).

  a.  *Paper.* Every pleading, written motion, and other paper must: be plainly written, typed, printed, or copied without erasures or interlineations which materially deface it. NY R USDCTS&ED Civ Rule 11.1(a)(1).

  b.  *Typeface, margin, and spacing.* The typeface, margins, and spacing of all documents presented for filing must meet the following requirements:

    i.   All text must be twelve (12) point type or larger, except for text in footnotes which may be ten (10) point type;

    ii.  All documents must have at least one (1) inch margins on all sides;

    iii. All text must be double-spaced, except for headings, text in footnotes, or block quotations, which may be single-spaced. NY R USDCTS&ED Civ Rule 11.1(b).

  c.  *Caption; Names of parties.* Every pleading must have a caption with the court's name, a title, a file number, and a FRCP 7(a) designation. The title of the complaint must name all the parties; the title of other pleadings, after naming the first party on each side, may refer generally to other parties. FRCP 10(a). Every pleading, written motion, and other paper must: bear the docket number and the initials of the District Judge and any Magistrate Judge before whom the action or proceeding is pending, NY R USDCTS&ED Civ Rule 11.1(a)(2).

d. *Paragraphs; Separate statements.* A party must state its claims or defenses in numbered paragraphs, each limited as far as practicable to a single set of circumstances. A later pleading may refer by number to a paragraph in an earlier pleading. If doing so would promote clarity, each claim founded on a separate transaction or occurrence—and each defense other than a denial—must be stated in a separate count or defense. FRCP 10(b).

e. *Adoption by reference; Exhibits.* A statement in a pleading may be adopted by reference elsewhere in the same pleading or in any other pleading or motion. A copy of a written instrument that is an exhibit to a pleading is a part of the pleading for all purposes. FRCP 10(c).

f. *Acceptance by the clerk.* The clerk must not refuse to file a paper solely because it is not in the form prescribed by the Federal Rules of Civil Procedure or by a local rule or practice. FRCP 5(d)(4).

2. *Signing disclosures and discovery requests, responses, and objections.* FRCP 11 does not apply to disclosures and discovery requests, responses, objections, and motions under FRCP 26 through FRCP 37. FRCP 11(d).

a. *Signature required.* Every disclosure under FRCP 26(a)(1) or FRCP 26(a)(3) and every discovery request, response, or objection must be signed by at least one attorney of record in the attorney's own name—or by the party personally, if unrepresented—and must state the signer's address, e-mail address, and telephone number. FRCP 26(g)(1). Every pleading, written motion, and other paper must: have the name of each person signing it clearly printed or typed directly below the signature. NY R USDCTS&ED Civ Rule 11.1(a)(3).

b. *Effect of signature.* By signing, an attorney or party certifies that to the best of the person's knowledge, information, and belief formed after a reasonable inquiry:

   i. With respect to a disclosure, it is complete and correct as of the time it is made; and

   ii. With respect to a discovery request, response, or objection, it is:

   - Consistent with the Federal Rules of Civil Procedure and warranted by existing law or by a nonfrivolous argument for extending, modifying, or reversing existing law, or for establishing new law;

   - Not interposed for any improper purpose, such as to harass, cause unnecessary delay, or needlessly increase the cost of litigation; and

   - Neither unreasonable nor unduly burdensome or expensive, considering the needs of the case, prior discovery in the case, the amount in controversy, and the importance of the issues at stake in the action. FRCP 26(g)(1).

c. *Failure to sign.* Other parties have no duty to act on an unsigned disclosure, request, response, or objection until it is signed, and the court must strike it unless a signature is promptly supplied after the omission is called to the attorney's or party's attention. FRCP 26(g)(2).

d. *Sanction for improper certification.* If a certification violates FRCP 26(g) without substantial justification, the court, on motion or on its own, must impose an appropriate sanction on the signer, the party on whose behalf the signer was acting, or both. The sanction may include an order to pay the reasonable expenses, including attorney's fees, caused by the violation. FRCP 26(g)(3). Refer to the United States District Court for the Eastern District of New York KeyRules Motion for Discovery Sanctions document for more information.

3. *Privacy protection for filings made with the court*

a. *Redacted filings.* Unless the court orders otherwise, in an electronic or paper filing with the court that contains an individual's Social Security number, taxpayer-identification number, or birth date, the name of an individual known to be a minor, or a financial-account number, a party or nonparty making the filing may include only:

   i. The last four (4) digits of the Social Security number and taxpayer-identification number;

   ii. The year of the individual's birth;

   iii. The minor's initials; and

   iv. The last four (4) digits of the financial-account number. FRCP 5.2(a); NY R USDCTED Order 2004-09.

    v.   In addition, exercise caution when filing documents that contain the following:

- Personal identifying number, such as driver's license number;
- Medical records, treatment and diagnosis;
- Employment history;
- Individual financial information; and
- Proprietary or trade secret information. NY R USDCTED Order 2004-09.

b.  *Exemptions from the redaction requirement.* The redaction requirement does not apply to the following:

    i.   A financial-account number that identifies the property allegedly subject to forfeiture in a forfeiture proceeding;

    ii.  The record of an administrative or agency proceeding;

    iii.  The official record of a state-court proceeding;

    iv.  The record of a court or tribunal, if that record was not subject to the redaction requirement when originally filed;

    v.   A filing covered by FRCP 5.2(c) or FRCP 5.2(d); and

    vi.  A pro se filing in an action brought under 28 U.S.C.A. § 2241, 28 U.S.C.A. § 2254, or 28 U.S.C.A. § 2255. FRCP 5.2(b).

c.  *Limitations on remote access to electronic files; Social Security appeals and immigration cases.* Unless the court orders otherwise, in an action for benefits under the Social Security Act, and in an action or proceeding relating to an order of removal, to relief from removal, or to immigration benefits or detention, access to an electronic file is authorized as follows:

    i.   The parties and their attorneys may have remote electronic access to any part of the case file, including the administrative record;

    ii.  Any other person may have electronic access to the full record at the courthouse, but may have remote electronic access only to:

- The docket maintained by the court; and
- An opinion, order, judgment, or other disposition of the court, but not any other part of the case file or the administrative record. FRCP 5.2(c).

d.  *Filings made under seal.* The court may order that a filing be made under seal without redaction. The court may later unseal the filing or order the person who made the filing to file a redacted version for the public record. FRCP 5.2(d).

e.  *Protective orders.* For good cause, the court may by order in a case:

    i.   Require redaction of additional information; or

    ii.  Limit or prohibit a nonparty's remote electronic access to a document filed with the court. FRCP 5.2(e).

f.  *Option for additional unredacted filing under seal.* A person making a redacted filing may also file an unredacted copy under seal. The court must retain the unredacted copy as part of the record. FRCP 5.2(f); NY R USDCTED Order 2004-09. The unredacted version of the document or the reference list shall be retained by the court as part of the record. The court may, however, still require the party to file a redacted copy for the public file. NY R USDCTED Order 2004-09.

g.  *Option for filing a reference list.* A filing that contains redacted information may be filed together with a reference list that identifies each item of redacted information and specifies an appropriate identifier that uniquely corresponds to each item listed. The list must be filed under seal and may be amended as of right. Any reference in the case to a listed identifier will be construed to refer to the corresponding item of information. FRCP 5.2(g); NY R USDCTED Order 2004-09. The unredacted version of the document or the reference list shall be retained by the court as part of the record. The court may, however, still require the party to file a redacted copy for the public file. NY R USDCTED Order 2004-09.

h. *Responsibility for redaction.* The responsibility for redacting these personal identifiers rests solely with counsel and the parties. The Clerk will not review each pleading for compliance with NY R USDCTED Order 2004-09. NY R USDCTED Order 2004-09.

    i. Counsel is strongly urged to share this notice with all clients so that an informed decision about the inclusion of certain materials may be made. If a redacted document is filed, it is the sole responsibility of counsel and the parties to be sure that all pleadings comply with the rules of this court requiring redaction of personal data identifiers. The clerk will not review each pleading for redaction. NY R USDCTED Order 2004-09.

i. *Waiver of protection of identifiers.* A person waives the protection of FRCP 5.2(a) as to the person's own information by filing it without redaction and not under seal. FRCP 5.2(h).

4. *Individual judge practices.* Refer to the Miscellaneous section of this document for information on individual judge practices on formatting documents.

## F. Filing and Service Requirements

1. *Filing requirements.* Any paper after the complaint that is required to be served—together with a certificate of service—must be filed within a reasonable time after service. But disclosures under FRCP 26(a)(1) or FRCP 26(a)(2) and the following discovery requests and responses must not be filed until they are used in the proceeding or the court orders filing: depositions, interrogatories, requests for documents or tangible things or to permit entry onto land, and requests for admission. FRCP 5(d)(1). Refer to the United States District Court for the Eastern District of New York KeyRules pleading and motion documents for information on filing with the court.

2. *Service requirements*

  a. *Service; When required*

    i. *In general.* Unless the Federal Rules of Civil Procedure provide otherwise, each of the following papers must be served on every party:

- An order stating that service is required;
- A pleading filed after the original complaint, unless the court orders otherwise under FRCP 5(c) because there are numerous defendants;
- A discovery paper required to be served on a party, unless the court orders otherwise;
- A written motion, except one that may be heard ex parte; and
- A written notice, appearance, demand, or offer of judgment, or any similar paper. FRCP 5(a)(1).

    ii. *If a party fails to appear.* No service is required on a party who is in default for failing to appear. But a pleading that asserts a new claim for relief against such a party must be served on that party under FRCP 4. FRCP 5(a)(2).

    iii. *Seizing property.* If an action is begun by seizing property and no person is or need be named as a defendant, any service required before the filing of an appearance, answer, or claim must be made on the person who had custody or possession of the property when it was seized. FRCP 5(a)(3).

  b. *Service; How made*

    i. *Serving an attorney.* If a party is represented by an attorney, service under FRCP 5 must be made on the attorney unless the court orders service on the party. FRCP 5(b)(1).

    ii. *Service in general.* A paper is served under FRCP 5 by:

- Handing it to the person;
- Leaving it: (1) at the person's office with a clerk or other person in charge or, if no one is in charge, in a conspicuous place in the office; or (2) if the person has no office or the office is closed, at the person's dwelling or usual place of abode with someone of suitable age and discretion who resides there;
- Mailing it to the person's last known address—in which event service is complete upon mailing;

- Leaving it with the court clerk if the person has no known address;

- Sending it by electronic means if the person consented in writing—in which event service is complete upon transmission, but is not effective if the serving party learns that it did not reach the person to be served; or

- Delivering it by any other means that the person consented to in writing—in which event service is complete when the person making service delivers it to the agency designated to make delivery. FRCP 5(b)(2).

   iii. *Service by overnight delivery.* Service upon an attorney may be made by overnight delivery service. "Overnight delivery service" means any delivery service which regularly accepts items for overnight delivery. Overnight delivery service shall be deemed service by mail for purposes of FRCP 5 and FRCP 6. NY R USDCTS&ED Civ Rule 5.3.

   iv. *Service by electronic means.* Parties serving and filing papers shall follow the instructions regarding Electronic Case Filing (ECF) published on the website of each respective Court. A paper served and filed by electronic means in accordance with such instructions is, for purposes of FRCP 5, served and filed in compliance with the Local Civil Rules of the United States District Courts for the Southern and Eastern Districts of New York. NY R USDCTS&ED Civ Rule 5.2(a). Parties have an obligation to review the Court's actual order, decree, or judgment (on ECF), which controls, and should not rely on the description on the docket or in the ECF Notice of Electronic Filing (NEF). NY R USDCTS&ED Civ Rule 5.2(c).

   v. *Using court facilities.* If a local rule so authorizes, a party may use the court's transmission facilities to make service under FRCP 5(b)(2)(E). FRCP 5(b)(3).

  c. *Serving numerous defendants*

   i. *In general.* If an action involves an unusually large number of defendants, the court may, on motion or on its own, order that:

- Defendants' pleadings and replies to them need not be served on other defendants;

- Any crossclaim, counterclaim, avoidance, or affirmative defense in those pleadings and replies to them will be treated as denied or avoided by all other parties; and

- Filing any such pleading and serving it on the plaintiff constitutes notice of the pleading to all parties. FRCP 5(c)(1).

   ii. *Notifying parties.* A copy of every such order must be served on the parties as the court directs. FRCP 5(c)(2).

3. *Individual judge practices.* Refer to the Miscellaneous section of this document for information on individual judge practices on filing and serving documents.

## G. Hearings

1. There is no hearing contemplated in the federal statutes or rules for interrogatories.

## H. Forms

### 1. Federal Interrogatories Forms

  a. Introductory statement; Interrogatories to individual. AMJUR PP DEPOSITION § 405.

  b. Introductory statement; Interrogatories to corporation. AMJUR PP DEPOSITION § 406.

  c. Interrogatories. 3A FEDFORMS § 3488.

  d. Interrogatories; Another form. 3A FEDFORMS § 3489.

  e. Interrogatories by plaintiff; To corporation. 3A FEDFORMS § 3490.

  f. Interrogatories by plaintiff; Complete set. 3A FEDFORMS § 3491.

  g. Interrogatories by plaintiff; Requesting identification of documents and production under FRCP 34. 3A FEDFORMS § 3492.

  h. Interrogatories by plaintiff; With definition of terms used and instructions for answering. 3A FEDFORMS § 3493.

i.  Interrogatories by plaintiff; Employment discrimination case. 3A FEDFORMS § 3494.

j.  Interrogatories by defendant. 3A FEDFORMS § 3495.

k.  Interrogatories by defendant; Complete set. 3A FEDFORMS § 3496.

l.  Interrogatories by defendant; Complete set; Another form. 3A FEDFORMS § 3497.

m.  Interrogatories by defendant; Complete set; Another form. 3A FEDFORMS § 3498.

n.  Interrogatories by defendant; Complete set; Another form. 3A FEDFORMS § 3499.

o.  Interrogatories by defendant; Follow-up interrogatories to plaintiff after lapse of time since first set of interrogatories or deposition. 3A FEDFORMS § 3500.

p.  Certificate of service of interrogatories. 3A FEDFORMS § 3501.

q.  Interrogatories; Outline form. FEDPROF § 23:335.

r.  Interrogatories; To defendant; Trademark action. FEDPROF § 23:347.

s.  Interrogatories; With request for documents; To defendant; Collection of royalties. FEDPROF § 23:348.

t.  Interrogatories; To defendant; Copyright infringement. FEDPROF § 23:350.

u.  Interrogatories; To plaintiff; Products liability. FEDPROF § 23:352.

v.  Interrogatories; To plaintiff; Personal injury. FEDPROF § 23:353.

w.  Interrogatories; To defendant; Premises liability. FEDPROF § 23:356.

x.  Interrogatories; To defendant; Medical malpractice. FEDPROF § 23:357.

y.  General forms; Standard interrogatories. GOLDLTGFMS § 26:25.

z.  General forms; Civil cases. GOLDLTGFMS § 26:26.

## I. Applicable Rules

1. *Federal rules*

   a.  Serving and filing pleadings and other papers. FRCP 5.

   b.  Privacy protection for filings made with the court. FRCP 5.2.

   c.  Computing and extending time; Time for motion papers. FRCP 6.

   d.  Pleadings allowed; Form of motions and other papers. FRCP 7.

   e.  Form of pleadings. FRCP 10.

   f.  Signing pleadings, motions, and other papers; Representations to the court; Sanctions. FRCP 11.

   g.  Duty to disclose; General provisions governing discovery. FRCP 26.

   h.  Stipulations about discovery procedure. FRCP 29.

   i.  Interrogatories to parties. FRCP 33.

   j.  Failure to make disclosures or to cooperate in discovery; Sanctions. FRCP 37.

2. *Local rules*

   a.  Duty of attorneys in related cases. NY R USDCTS&ED Civ Rule 1.6.

   b.  Electronic service and filing of documents. NY R USDCTS&ED Civ Rule 5.2.

   c.  Service by overnight delivery. NY R USDCTS&ED Civ Rule 5.3.

   d.  Computation of time. NY R USDCTS&ED Civ Rule 6.4.

   e.  Form of pleadings, motions, and other papers. NY R USDCTS&ED Civ Rule 11.1.

   f.  Assertion of claim of privilege. NY R USDCTS&ED Civ Rule 26.2.

   g.  Uniform definitions in discovery requests. NY R USDCTS&ED Civ Rule 26.3.

   h.  Cooperation among counsel in discovery. NY R USDCTS&ED Civ Rule 26.4.

    i.    Form discovery requests. [NY R USDCTS&ED Civ Rule 26.5, as amended by NY ORDER 16-4212, effective September 26, 2016].

    j.    Court-annexed arbitration (Eastern District only). NY R USDCTS&ED Civ Rule 83.7.

    k.    Court-annexed mediation (Eastern District only). NY R USDCTS&ED Civ Rule 83.8.

    l.    The August 2, 2004 amendment to the E-Government Act of 2002. NY R USDCTED Order 2004-09.

## J.  Miscellaneous

**NOTE: Individual judges' rules may apply. For available judge-level information, refer to:**

DISTRICT JUDGE CAROL BAGLEY AMON: NY R USDCTED Amon-Practices.

DISTRICT JUDGE JOAN M. AZRACK: NY R USDCTED Azrack-Practices.

DISTRICT JUDGE JOSEPH F. BIANCO: NY R USDCTED Bianco-Practices.

DISTRICT JUDGE FREDERIC BLOCK: NY R USDCTED Block-Practices.

DISTRICT JUDGE MARGO K. BRODIE: NY R USDCTED Brodie-Practices.

DISTRICT JUDGE PAMELA K. CHEN: NY R USDCTED Chen-Practices.

DISTRICT JUDGE BRIAN M. COGAN: NY R USDCTED Cogan-Practices; NY R USDCTED Cogan-Pretrial.

DISTRICT JUDGE LaSHANN DeARCY HALL: NY R USDCTED DeArcy Hall-Practices.

DISTRICT JUDGE RAYMOND J. DEARIE: NY R USDCTED Dearie-Practices.

DISTRICT JUDGE ANN M. DONNELLY: NY R USDCTED Donnelly-Practices.

DISTRICT JUDGE SANDRA J. FEUERSTEIN: NY R USDCTED Feuerstein-Practices; NY R USDCTED Feuerstein-Pretrial.

DISTRICT JUDGE NICHOLAS G. GARAUIFIS: NY R USDCTED Garaufis-Practices; NY R USDCTED Garaufis-Pretrial.

DISTRICT JUDGE NINA GERSHON: NY R USDCTED Gershon-Practices.

DISTRICT JUDGE I. LEO GLASSER: NY R USDCTED Glasser-Practices; NY R USDCTED Glasser-Crim.

DISTRICT JUDGE DENIS R. HURLEY: NY R USDCTED Hurley-Practices; [NY R USDCTED Hurley-Pro Cooperation Info, as added by NY ORDER 16-4188, effective July 22, 2016]; [NY R USDCTED Hurley-Pro Cooperation Info Stay, as added by NY ORDER 16-4188, effective July 22, 2016].

DISTRICT JUDGE DORA L. IRIZARRY: NY R USDCTED Irizarry-Practices; NY R USDCTED Irizarry-Pretrial; NY R USDCTED Irizarry-Crim.

DISTRICT JUDGE STERLING JOHNSON, JR.: NY R USDCTED Johnson-Practices.

DISTRICT JUDGE EDWARD R. KORMAN: NY R USDCTED Korman-Practices; NY R USDCTED Korman-Pretrial.

DISTRICT JUDGE WILLIAM F. KUNTZ: NY R USDCTED Kuntz-Practices.

DISTRICT JUDGE KIYO A. MATSUMOTO: NY R USDCTED Matsumoto-Practices.

DISTRICT JUDGE ROSLYNN R. MAUSKOPF: NY R USDCTED Mauskopf-Practices; NY R USDCTED Mauskopf-Recusal.

DISTRICT JUDGE THOMAS C. PLATT: NY R USDCTED Platt-Practices.

DISTRICT JUDGE ALLYNE R. ROSS: NY R USDCTED Ross-Practices.

DISTRICT JUDGE JOANNA SEYBERT: NY R USDCTED Seybert-Practices.

DISTRICT JUDGE ARTHUR D. SPATT: NY R USDCTED Spatt-Practices.

DISTRICT JUDGE SANDRA L. TOWNES: NY R USDCTED Townes-Practices.

DISTRICT JUDGE ERIC N. VITALIANO: NY R USDCTED Vitaliano-Practices.

DISTRICT JUDGE JACK B. WEINSTEIN: NY R USDCTED Weinstein-Practices.

DISTRICT JUDGE LEONARD D. WEXLER: NY R USDCTED Wexler-Practices; NY R USDCTED Wexler-Rules.

MAGISTRATE JUDGE LOIS BLOOM: NY R USDCTED Bloom-Practices.

MAGISTRATE JUDGE GARY R. BROWN: NY R USDCTED Brown-Practices.

MAGISTRATE JUDGE MARILYN D. GO: NY R USDCTED Go-Practices.

MAGISTRATE JUDGE STEVEN M. GOLD: NY R USDCTED Gold-Practices.

MAGISTRATE JUDGE PEGGY KUO: NY R USDCTED Kuo-Practices; NY R USDCTED Kuo-Scheduling Order.

MAGISTRATE JUDGE ROBERT M. LEVY: NY R USDCTED Levy-Practices.

MAGISTRATE JUDGE ARLENE R. LINDSAY: NY R USDCTED Lindsay-Practices.

MAGISTRATE JUDGE STEVEN I. LOCKE: NY R USDCTED Locke-Practices.

MAGISTRATE JUDGE ROANNE L. MANN: NY R USDCTED Mann-Practices.

MAGISTRATE JUDGE JAMES ORENSTEIN: NY R USDCTED Jorenstein--Practices.

MAGISTRATE JUDGE VIKTOR V. POHORELSKY: NY R USDCTED Pohorelsky-Practices.

MAGISTRATE JUDGE CHERYL L. POLLAK: NY R USDCTED Pollak-Practices; NY R USDCTED Pollak-Pretrial.

MAGISTRATE JUDGE RAMON E. REYES, JR.: NY R USDCTED Reyes-Practices.

MAGISTRATE JUDGE VERA M. SCANLON: NY R USDCTED Scanlon-Practices.

MAGISTRATE JUDGE ANNE Y. SHIELDS: NY R USDCTED Shields-Practices.

MAGISTRATE JUDGE STEVEN L. TISCIONE: NY R USDCTED Tiscione-Practices.

MAGISTRATE JUDGE A. KATHLEEN TOMILINSON: NY R USDCTED Tomlinson-Practices.

# Requests, Notices and Applications
## Request for Production of Documents

### Document Last Updated September 2016

A. **Checklist**

  (I)  ❑ Matters to be considered by requesting party

      (a)  ❑ Required documents

          (1)  ❑ Request for production of documents

      (b)  ❑ Supplemental documents

          (1)  ❑ Subpoena

          (2)  ❑ Certificate of service

      (c)  ❑ Timing

          (1)  ❑ A party may not seek discovery from any source before the parties have conferred as required by FRCP 26(f), except in a proceeding exempted from initial disclosure under FRCP 26(a)(1)(B), or when authorized by the Federal Rules of Civil Procedure, by stipulation, or by court order

          (2)  ❑ More than twenty-one (21) days after the summons and complaint are served on a party, a request under FRCP 34 may be delivered: (1) to that party by any other party, and (2) by that party to any plaintiff or to any other party that has been served

  (II)  ❑ Matters to be considered by responding party

      (a)  ❑ Required documents

          (1)  ❑ Response to request for production of documents

      (b)  ❑ Supplemental documents

          (1)  ❑ Written information regarding assertion of privilege

      (2)  ❑  Certificate of service

  (c)  ❑  Timing

      (1)  ❑  The party to whom the request is directed must respond in writing within thirty (30) days after being served or—if the request was delivered under FRCP 26(d)(2)—within thirty (30) days after the parties' first FRCP 26(f) conference

## B. Timing

1. *Request for production of documents.* Without leave of court or written stipulation, a request may not be served before the time specified in FRCP 26(d). FEDPROC § 26:632. Of course, discovery under FRCP 34 should ordinarily precede the trial. FEDPROC § 26:632.

    a.  *Early FRCP 34 requests*

      i.  *Time to deliver.* More than twenty-one (21) days after the summons and complaint are served on a party, a request under FRCP 34 may be delivered:

- To that party by any other party, and

- By that party to any plaintiff or to any other party that has been served. FRCP 26(d)(2)(A).

      ii.  *When considered served.* The request is considered to have been served at the first FRCP 26(f) conference. FRCP 26(d)(2)(B).

2. *Timing of discovery, generally.* A party may not seek discovery from any source before the parties have conferred as required by FRCP 26(f), except in a proceeding exempted from initial disclosure under FRCP 26(a)(1)(B), or when authorized by the Federal Rules of Civil Procedure, by stipulation, or by court order. FRCP 26(d)(1).

3. *Computation of time*

    a.  *Computing time.* FRCP 6 applies in computing any time period specified in the Federal Rules of Civil Procedure, in any local rule or court order, or in any statute that does not specify a method of computing time. FRCP 6(a). In computing any period of time prescribed or allowed by the Local Civil Rules of the United States District Courts for the Southern and Eastern Districts of New York or the Local Admiralty and Maritime Rules, the provisions of FRCP 6 shall apply unless otherwise stated. NY R USDCTS&ED Civ Rule 6.4.

      i.  *Period stated in days or a longer unit.* When the period is stated in days or a longer unit of time:

- Exclude the day of the event that triggers the period;

- Count every day, including intermediate Saturdays, Sundays, and legal holidays; and

- Include the last day of the period, but if the last day is a Saturday, Sunday, or legal holiday, the period continues to run until the end of the next day that is not a Saturday, Sunday, or legal holiday. FRCP 6(a)(1). In the Local Civil Rules of the United States District Courts for the Southern and Eastern Districts of New York, as in the Federal Rules of Civil Procedure as amended effective December 1, 2009, Saturdays, Sundays, and legal holidays are no longer excluded in computing periods of time. If the last day of the period is a Saturday, Sunday, or legal holiday, the period continues to run until the end of the next day that is not a Saturday, Sunday, or legal holiday. NY R USDCTS&ED Civ Rule 6.4.

      ii.  *Period stated in hours.* When the period is stated in hours:

- Begin counting immediately on the occurrence of the event that triggers the period;

- Count every hour, including hours during intermediate Saturdays, Sundays, and legal holidays; and

- If the period would end on a Saturday, Sunday, or legal holiday, the period continues to run until the same time on the next day that is not a Saturday, Sunday, or legal holiday. FRCP 6(a)(2). In the Local Civil Rules of the United States District Courts for the Southern and Eastern Districts of New York, as in the Federal Rules of Civil Procedure as amended effective December 1, 2009, Saturdays, Sundays, and legal holidays are no longer excluded in computing periods of time. If the last day of the period is a Saturday, Sunday, or legal holiday, the period continues to run until the end of the next day that is not a Saturday, Sunday, or legal holiday. NY R USDCTS&ED Civ Rule 6.4.

    iii. *Inaccessibility of the clerk's office.* Unless the court orders otherwise, if the clerk's office is inaccessible:

- On the last day for filing under FRCP 6(a)(1), then the time for filing is extended to the first accessible day that is not a Saturday, Sunday, or legal holiday; or

- During the last hour for filing under FRCP 6(a)(2), then the time for filing is extended to the same time on the first accessible day that is not a Saturday, Sunday, or legal holiday. FRCP 6(a)(3).

    iv. *"Last day" defined.* Unless a different time is set by a statute, local rule, or court order, the last day ends:

- For electronic filing, at midnight in the court's time zone; and

- For filing by other means, when the clerk's office is scheduled to close. FRCP 6(a)(4).

    v. *"Next day" defined.* The "next day" is determined by continuing to count forward when the period is measured after an event and backward when measured before an event. FRCP 6(a)(5).

    vi. *"Legal holiday" defined.* "Legal holiday" means:

- The day set aside by statute for observing New Year's Day, Martin Luther King Jr.'s Birthday, Washington's Birthday, Memorial Day, Independence Day, Labor Day, Columbus Day, Veterans' Day, Thanksgiving Day, or Christmas Day;

- Any day declared a holiday by the President or Congress; and

- For periods that are measured after an event, any other day declared a holiday by the state where the district court is located. FRCP 6(a)(6).

  b. *Extending time*

    i. *In general.* When an act may or must be done within a specified time, the court may, for good cause, extend the time:

- With or without motion or notice if the court acts, or if a request is made, before the original time or its extension expires; or

- On motion made after the time has expired if the party failed to act because of excusable neglect. FRCP 6(b)(1).

    ii. *Exceptions.* A court must not extend the time to act under FRCP 50(b), FRCP 50(d), FRCP 52(b), FRCP 59(b), FRCP 59(d), FRCP 59(e), and FRCP 60(b). FRCP 6(b)(2).

    iii. Refer to the United States District Court for the Eastern District of New York KeyRules Motion for Continuance/Extension of Time document for more information on extending time.

  c. *Additional time after certain kinds of service.* When a party may or must act within a specified time after service and service is made under FRCP 5(b)(2)(C), FRCP 5(b)(2)(D), FRCP 5(b)(2)(E), or FRCP 5(b)(2)(F), three (3) days are added after the period would otherwise expire under FRCP 6(a). FRCP 6(d). Overnight delivery service shall be deemed service by mail for purposes of FRCP 5 and FRCP 6. NY R USDCTS&ED Civ Rule 5.3.

4. *Individual judge practices.* Refer to the Miscellaneous section of this document for information on individual judge practices on timing of documents.

## C. General Requirements

1. *General provisions governing discovery*

  a. *Discovery scope and limits*

    i. *Scope in general.* Unless otherwise limited by court order, the scope of discovery is as follows: Parties may obtain discovery regarding any nonprivileged matter that is relevant to any party's claim or defense and proportional to the needs of the case, considering the importance of the issues at stake in the action, the amount in controversy, the parties' relative access to relevant information, the parties' resources, the importance of the discovery in resolving the issues, and whether the burden or expense of the proposed discovery outweighs its likely benefit. Information within this scope of discovery need not be admissible in evidence to be discoverable. FRCP 26(b)(1).

ii. *Limitations on frequency and extent*

- *When permitted.* By order, the court may alter the limits in the Federal Rules of Civil Procedure on the number of depositions and interrogatories or on the length of depositions under FRCP 30. By order or local rule, the court may also limit the number of requests under FRCP 36. FRCP 26(b)(2)(A).

- *Specific limitations on electronically stored information.* A party need not provide discovery of electronically stored information from sources that the party identifies as not reasonably accessible because of undue burden or cost. On motion to compel discovery or for a protective order, the party from whom discovery is sought must show that the information is not reasonably accessible because of undue burden or cost. If that showing is made, the court may nonetheless order discovery from such sources if the requesting party shows good cause, considering the limitations of FRCP 26(b)(2)(C). The court may specify conditions for the discovery. FRCP 26(b)(2)(B).

- *When required.* On motion or on its own, the court must limit the frequency or extent of discovery otherwise allowed by the Federal Rules of Civil Procedure or by local rule if it determines that: (1) the discovery sought is unreasonably cumulative or duplicative, or can be obtained from some other source that is more convenient, less burdensome, or less expensive; (2) the party seeking discovery has had ample opportunity to obtain the information by discovery in the action; or (3) the proposed discovery is outside the scope permitted by FRCP 26(b)(1). FRCP 26(b)(2)(C).

iii. *Trial preparation; Materials*

- *Documents and tangible things.* Ordinarily, a party may not discover documents and tangible things that are prepared in anticipation of litigation or for trial by or for another party or its representative (including the other party's attorney, consultant, surety, indemnitor, insurer, or agent). But, subject to FRCP 26(b)(4), those materials may be discovered if: (1) they are otherwise discoverable under FRCP 26(b)(1); and (2) the party shows that it has substantial need for the materials to prepare its case and cannot, without undue hardship, obtain their substantial equivalent by other means. FRCP 26(b)(3)(A).

- *Protection against disclosure.* If the court orders discovery of those materials, it must protect against disclosure of the mental impressions, conclusions, opinions, or legal theories of a party's attorney or other representative concerning the litigation. FRCP 26(b)(3)(B).

- *Previous statement.* Any party or other person may, on request and without the required showing, obtain the person's own previous statement about the action or its subject matter. If the request is refused, the person may move for a court order, and FRCP 37(a)(5) applies to the award of expenses. A previous statement is either: (1) a written statement that the person has signed or otherwise adopted or approved; or (2) a contemporaneous stenographic, mechanical, electrical, or other recording—or a transcription of it—that recites substantially verbatim the person's oral statement. FRCP 26(b)(3)(C).

iv. *Trial preparation; Experts*

- *Deposition of an expert who may testify.* A party may depose any person who has been identified as an expert whose opinions may be presented at trial. If FRCP 26(a)(2)(B) requires a report from the expert, the deposition may be conducted only after the report is provided. FRCP 26(b)(4)(A).

- *Trial-preparation protection for draft reports or disclosures.* FRCP 26(b)(3)(A) and FRCP 26(b)(3)(B) protect drafts of any report or disclosure required under FRCP 26(a)(2), regardless of the form in which the draft is recorded. FRCP 26(b)(4)(B).

- *Trial-preparation protection for communications between a party's attorney and expert witnesses.* FRCP 26(b)(3)(A) and FRCP 26(b)(3)(B) protect communications between the party's attorney and any witness required to provide a report under FRCP 26(a)(2)(B), regardless of the form of the communications, except to the extent that the communications: (1) relate to compensation for the expert's study or testimony; (2) identify facts or data that the party's attorney provided and that the expert considered in forming the opinions to be expressed; or (3) identify assumptions that the party's attorney provided and that the expert relied on in forming the opinions to be expressed. FRCP 26(b)(4)(C).

- *Expert employed only for trial preparation.* Ordinarily, a party may not, by interrogatories or deposition, discover facts known or opinions held by an expert who has been retained or specially employed by another party in anticipation of litigation or to prepare for trial and who is not expected to be called as a witness at trial. But a party may do so only: (1) as provided in FRCP 35(b); or (2) on showing exceptional circumstances under which it is impracticable for the party to obtain facts or opinions on the same subject by other means. FRCP 26(b)(4)(D).

- *Payment.* Unless manifest injustice would result, the court must require that the party seeking discovery: (1) pay the expert a reasonable fee for time spent in responding to discovery under FRCP 26(b)(4)(A) or FRCP 26(b)(4)(D); and (2) for discovery FRCP 26(b)(4)(D), also pay the other party a fair portion of the fees and expenses it reasonably incurred in obtaining the expert's facts and opinions. FRCP 26(b)(4)(E).

v. *Claiming privilege or protecting trial-preparation materials*

- *Information withheld.* When a party withholds information otherwise discoverable by claiming that the information is privileged or subject to protection as trial-preparation material, the party must: (1) expressly make the claim; and (2) describe the nature of the documents, communications, or tangible things not produced or disclosed—and do so in a manner that, without revealing information itself privileged or protected, will enable other parties to assess the claim. FRCP 26(b)(5)(A). Unless otherwise agreed by the parties or directed by the Court, where a claim of privilege is asserted in objecting to any means of discovery or disclosure, including but not limited to a deposition, and an answer is not provided on the basis of such assertion, (1) the person asserting the privilege shall identify the nature of the privilege (including work product) which is being claimed and, if the privilege is governed by state law, indicate the state's privilege rule being invoked; and (2) the following information shall be provided in the objection, or (in the case of a deposition) in response to questions by the questioner, unless divulgence of such information would cause disclosure of the allegedly privileged information: (A) for documents: (i) the type of document, e.g., letter or memorandum; (ii) the general subject matter of the document; (iii) the date of the document; and (iv) the author of the document, the addressees of the document, and any other recipients, and, where not apparent, the relationship of the author, addressees, and recipients to each other; (B) for oral communications: (i) the name of the person making the communication and the names of persons present while the communication was made and, where not apparent, the relationship of the persons present to the person making the communication; (ii) the date and place of communication; and (iii) the general subject matter of the communication. NY R USDCTS&ED Civ Rule 26.2(a). Where a claim of privilege is asserted in response to discovery or disclosure other than a deposition, and information is not provided on the basis of such assertion, the information set forth in NY R USDCTS&ED Civ Rule 26.2(a) shall be furnished in writing at the time of the response to such discovery or disclosure, unless otherwise ordered by the Court. NY R USDCTS&ED Civ Rule 26.2(b).

- *Information produced.* If information produced in discovery is subject to a claim of privilege or of protection as trial-preparation material, the party making the claim may notify any party that received the information of the claim and the basis for it. After being notified, a party must promptly return, sequester, or destroy the specified information and any copies it has; must not use or disclose the information until the claim is resolved; must take reasonable steps to retrieve the information if the party disclosed it before being notified; and may promptly present the information to the court under seal for a determination of the claim. The producing party must preserve the information until the claim is resolved. FRCP 26(b)(5)(B).

- *Efficient means of providing information regarding claims of privilege.* Efficient means of providing information regarding claims of privilege are encouraged, and parties are encouraged to agree upon measures that further this end. For example, when asserting privilege on the same basis with respect to multiple documents, it is presumptively proper to provide the information required by NY R USDCTS&ED Civ Rule 26.2 by group or category. A party receiving a privilege log that groups documents or otherwise departs from a document-by-document or communication-by-communication listing may not object solely on that basis, but may object if the substantive information required by NY R USDCTS&ED Civ Rule 26.2 has not been provided in a comprehensible form. NY R USDCTS&ED Civ Rule 26.2(c).

b. *Protective orders.* A party or any person from whom discovery is sought may move for a protective order in the court where the action is pending—or as an alternative on matters relating to a deposition, in the court for the district where the deposition will be taken. FRCP 26(c)(1). Refer to the United States District Court for the Eastern District of New York KeyRules Motion for Protective Order document for more information.

c. *Sequence of discovery.* Unless the parties stipulate or the court orders otherwise for the parties' and witnesses' convenience and in the interests of justice: (1) methods of discovery may be used in any sequence; and (2) discovery by one party does not require any other party to delay its discovery. FRCP 26(d)(3).

d. *Uniform definitions in discovery requests.* The full text of the definitions and rules of construction set forth in NY R USDCTS&ED Civ Rule 26.3(c) and NY R USDCTS&ED Civ Rule 26.3(d) is deemed incorporated by reference into all discovery requests. No discovery request shall use broader definitions or rules of construction than those set forth in NY R USDCTS&ED Civ Rule 26.3(c) and NY R USDCTS&ED Civ Rule 26.3(d). NY R USDCTS&ED Civ Rule 26.3 shall not preclude (1) the definition of other terms specific to the particular litigation, (2) the use of abbreviations, or (3) a more narrow definition of a term defined in NY R USDCTS&ED Civ Rule 26.3(c). NY R USDCTS&ED Civ Rule 26.3(a). NY R USDCTS&ED Civ Rule 26.3 is not intended to broaden or narrow the scope of discovery permitted by the Federal Rules of Civil Procedure. NY R USDCTS&ED Civ Rule 26.3(b).

   i. *Definitions.* The following definitions apply to all discovery requests:

      - *Communication.* The term "communication" means the transmittal of information (in the form of facts, ideas, inquiries or otherwise). NY R USDCTS&ED Civ Rule 26.3(c)(1).

      - *Document.* The term "document" is defined to be synonymous in meaning and equal in scope to the usage of the term "documents or electronically stored information" in FRCP 34(a)(1)(A). A draft or non-identical copy is a separate document within the meaning of this term. NY R USDCTS&ED Civ Rule 26.3(c)(2).

      - *Identify (with respect to persons).* When referring to a person, "to identify" means to give, to the extent known, the person's full name, present or last known address, and when referring to a natural person, additionally, the present or last known place of employment. Once a person has been identified in accordance with NY R USDCTS&ED Civ Rule 26.3(c)(3), only the name of that person need be listed in response to subsequent discovery requesting the identification of that person. NY R USDCTS&ED Civ Rule 26.3(c)(3).

      - *Identify (with respect to documents).* When referring to documents, "to identify" means to give, to the extent known, the (1) type of document; (2) general subject matter; (3) date of the document; and (4) author(s), addressee(s) and recipient(s). In the alternative, the responding party may produce the documents, together with identifying information sufficient to satisfy FRCP 33(d). NY R USDCTS&ED Civ Rule 26.3(c)(4).

      - *Parties.* The terms "plaintiff" and "defendant" as well as a party's full or abbreviated name or a pronoun referring to a party mean the party and, where applicable, its officers, directors, employees, partners, corporate parent, subsidiaries or affiliates. This definition is not intended to impose a discovery obligation on any person who is not a party to the litigation. NY R USDCTS&ED Civ Rule 26.3(c)(5).

- *Person.* The term "person" is defined as any natural person or any legal entity, including, without limitation, any business or governmental entity or association. NY R USDCTS&ED Civ Rule 26.3(c)(6).

- *Concerning.* The term "concerning" means relating to, referring to, describing, evidencing or constituting. NY R USDCTS&ED Civ Rule 26.3(c)(7).

   ii. *Rules of construction.* The following rules of construction apply to all discovery requests:

- *All/any/each.* The terms "all," "any," and "each" shall each be construed as encompassing any and all. NY R USDCTS&ED Civ Rule 26.3(d)(1).

- *And/or.* The connectives "and" and "or" shall be construed either disjunctively or conjunctively as necessary to bring within the scope of the discovery request all responses that might otherwise be construed to be outside of its scope. NY R USDCTS&ED Civ Rule 26.3(d)(2).

- *Number.* The use of the singular form of any word includes the plural and vice versa. NY R USDCTS&ED Civ Rule 26.3(d)(3).

e. *Cooperation among counsel in discovery.* Counsel are expected to cooperate with each other, consistent with the interests of their clients, in all phases of the discovery process and to be courteous in their dealings with each other, including in matters relating to scheduling and timing of various discovery procedures. NY R USDCTS&ED Civ Rule 26.4(a).

   i. Discovery requests shall be read reasonably in the recognition that the attorney serving them generally does not have the information being sought and the attorney receiving them generally does have such information or can obtain it from the client. NY R USDCTS&ED Civ Rule 26.4(b).

f. *Standard discovery in prisoner pro se actions.* For information on discovery in prisoner pro se actions, refer to NY R USDCTS&ED Civ Rule 33.2.

2. *Request for production of documents*

a. *In general.* A party may serve on any other party a request within the scope of FRCP 26(b):

   i. To produce and permit the requesting party or its representative to inspect, copy, test, or sample the following items in the responding party's possession, custody, or control:

- Any designated documents or electronically stored information—including writings, drawings, graphs, charts, photographs, sound recordings, images, and other data or data compilations—stored in any medium from which information can be obtained either directly or, if necessary, after translation by the responding party into a reasonably usable form; or

- Any designated tangible things; or

   ii. To permit entry onto designated land or other property possessed or controlled by the responding party, so that the requesting party may inspect, measure, survey, photograph, test, or sample the property or any designated object or operation on it. FRCP 34(a).

b. *Contents of the request.* The request: (1) must describe with reasonable particularity each item or category of items to be inspected; (2) must specify a reasonable time, place, and manner for the inspection and for performing the related acts; and (3) may specify the form or forms in which electronically stored information is to be produced. FRCP 34(b)(1).

   i. *Description of items.* Although the phrase "reasonable particularity" eludes precise definition and depends on the facts and circumstances in each case, at least two tests have been suggested:

- The first test is whether the request places a party on "reasonable notice" of what is called for and what is not so that a reasonable person would know what documents or things are called for. FEDPROC § 26:634.

- The second is whether the request gives a court enough information to enable it to rule intelligently on objections. FEDPROC § 26:634.

c. *Form discovery requests.* Attorneys using form discovery requests shall review them to ascertain that they are consistent with the scope of discovery under FRCP 26(b)(1). Non-compliant requests shall not be used. NY R USDCTS&ED Civ Rule 26.5.

d. *Signature.* Though FRCP 34 does not say so, it is sufficient if the request is signed by the attorney for the party seeking discovery. FPP § 2212. Refer to the Format section of this document for more information on signing of discovery papers.

e. *Other authority on production and inspection*

   i. *Freedom of Information Act.* Although the Freedom of Information Act (FOIA) is fundamentally designed to inform the public about agency action, and not to benefit private litigants, Congress has not acted upon proposals to forbid or limit the use of the FOIA for discovery purposes. FEDPROC § 26:605; National Presto Industries, Inc., 218 Ct.Cl. 696, 1978 WL 8475 (1978). However, a FOIA request may not be used to supplement civil discovery under FRCP 34, as in the case where information is privileged and therefore outside the scope of civil discovery. FEDPROC § 26:605; U.S. v. Weber Aircraft Corp., 465 U.S. 792, 104 S.Ct. 1488, 79 L.Ed.2d 814 (1984).

   ii. *Hague Convention.* Under the Hague Convention, a party seeking evidence abroad must obtain and send a letter of request to the central authority of the country in which the evidence is sought, requesting service of the request on the desired person or entity; if the request complies with the Convention, the central authority will then obtain the desired evidence. FEDPROC § 26:606. [Editor's note: the Hague Convention can be found at T.I.A.S. No. 6638 and is also available in the appendix to FRCP 4].

f. *Motion to compel.* If a party who has been requested to permit discovery under FRCP 34 makes no response to the request, or if its response objects to all or part of the requested discovery, or if it otherwise fails to permit discovery as requested, the party who submitted the request, if it still wishes the discovery that has been refused, may move under FRCP 37(a) for an order compelling inspection in accordance with the request. FPP § 2214. Refer to the United States District Court for the Eastern District of New York KeyRules Motion to Compel Discovery document for more information.

3. *Sanctions for failure to cooperate in discovery.* The court where the action is pending may, on motion, order sanctions if a party, after being properly served with interrogatories under FRCP 33 or a request for inspection under FRCP 34, fails to serve its answers, objections, or written response. FRCP 37(d)(1)(A)(ii). If a motion to compel is granted, the court must, after giving an opportunity to be heard, require the party or deponent whose conduct necessitated the motion, the party or attorney advising that conduct, or both to pay the movant's reasonable expenses incurred in making the motion, including attorney's fees. But the court must not order this payment if the opposing party's nondisclosure, response, or objection was substantially justified. FRCP 37(a)(5)(A)(ii). Refer to the United States District Court for the Eastern District of New York KeyRules Motion for Discovery Sanctions document for more information.

4. *Stipulations about discovery procedure.* Unless the court orders otherwise, the parties may stipulate that: (1) a deposition may be taken before any person, at any time or place, on any notice, and in the manner specified—in which event it may be used in the same way as any other deposition; and (2) other procedures governing or limiting discovery be modified—but a stipulation extending the time for any form of discovery must have court approval if it would interfere with the time set for completing discovery, for hearing a motion, or for trial. FRCP 29.

5. *Related cases.* It shall be the continuing duty of each attorney appearing in any civil or criminal case to bring promptly to the attention of the Court all facts which said attorney believes are relevant to a determination that said case and one or more pending civil or criminal cases should be heard by the same Judge, in order to avoid unnecessary duplication of judicial effort. As soon as the attorney becomes aware of such relationship, said attorney shall notify the Judges to whom the cases have been assigned. NY R USDCTS&ED Civ Rule 1.6(a). If counsel fails to comply with NY R USDCTS&ED Civ Rule 1.6(a), the Court may assess reasonable costs directly against counsel whose action has obstructed the effective administration of the Court's business. NY R USDCTS&ED Civ Rule 1.6(b).

6. *Alternative dispute resolution (ADR)*

   a. *Court-annexed arbitration*

      i. *Civil cases eligible for compulsory arbitration.* The Clerk of Court shall, as to all cases filed after January 1, 1986, designate and process for compulsory arbitration all civil cases (excluding Social Security cases, tax matters, prisoners' civil rights cases and any action based on an alleged violation of a right secured by the Constitution of the United States or if jurisdiction is based in whole or in part on 28 U.S.C.A. § 1343) wherein money damages only are being sought in an amount not in excess of one hundred fifty thousand dollars ($150,000) exclusive of interest and costs. NY R USDCTS&ED Civ Rule 83.7(d)(1).

         • The parties may by written stipulation agree that the Clerk of Court shall designate and process for court-annexed arbitration any civil case that is not subject to compulsory arbitration in NY R USDCTS&ED Civ Rule 83.7. NY R USDCTS&ED Civ Rule 83.7(d)(2).

         • For purposes of NY R USDCTS&ED Civ Rule 83.7 only, in all civil cases damages shall be presumed to be not in excess of one hundred fifty thousand dollars ($150,000) exclusive of interest and costs, unless: (1) counsel for plaintiff, at the time of filing the complaint, or in the event of the removal of a case from state court or transfer of a case from another district to this Court, within thirty (30) days of the docketing of the case in this district, files a certification with the Court that the damages sought exceed one hundred fifty thousand dollars ($150,000), exclusive of interest and costs; or (2) counsel for a defendant, at the time of filing a counterclaim or cross-claim files a certification with the court that the damages sought by the counter-claim or cross-claim exceed one hundred fifty thousand dollars ($150,000) exclusive of interest and costs. NY R USDCTS&ED Civ Rule 83.7(d)(3).

      ii. *Exemption from arbitration.* The Court shall, sua sponte, or on motion of a party, exempt any case from arbitration in which the objectives of arbitration would not be realized (1) because the case involves complex or novel issues, (2) because legal issues predominate over factual issues, or (3) for other good cause. NY R USDCTS&ED Civ Rule 83.7(e)(2). For information on applying for an exemption, refer to NY R USDCTS&ED Civ Rule 83.7

      iii. *Referral to arbitration.* Cases not originally designated as eligible for compulsory arbitration, but which in the discretion of the assigned Judge, are later found to qualify, may be referred to arbitration. A U.S. District Judge or a U.S. Magistrate Judge, in cases that exceed the arbitration ceiling of one hundred fifty thousand dollars ($150,000) exclusive of interest and costs, in their discretion, may suggest that the parties should consider arbitration. If the parties are agreeable, an appropriate consent form signed by all parties or their representatives may be entered and filed in the case prior to scheduling an arbitration hearing. NY R USDCTS&ED Civ Rule 83.7(e)(3).

      iv. For more information on arbitration, refer to NY R USDCTS&ED Civ Rule 83.7.

   b. *Court-annexed mediation.* Mediation is a process in which parties and counsel agree to meet with a neutral mediator trained to assist them in settling disputes. The mediator improves communication across party lines, helps parties articulate their interests and understand those of the other party, probes the strengths and weaknesses of each party's legal positions, and identifies areas of agreement and helps generate options for a mutually agreeable resolution to the dispute. In all cases, mediation provides an opportunity to explore a wide range of potential solutions and to address interests that may be outside the scope of the stated controversy or which could not be addressed by judicial action. A hallmark of mediation is its capacity to expand traditional settlement discussions and broaden resolution options, often by exploring litigant needs and interests that may be formally independent of the legal issues in controversy. NY R USDCTS&ED Civ Rule 83.8(a).

      i. *Eligible cases.* Judges and Magistrate Judges may designate civil cases for inclusion in the mediation program, and when doing so shall prepare an order to that effect. Alternatively, and subject to the availability of qualified mediators, the parties may consent to participation in the mediation program by preparing and executing a stipulation signed by all parties to the action and so-ordered by the Court. NY R USDCTS&ED Civ Rule 83.8(b)(1).

    ii.   For more information on mediation, refer to NY R USDCTS&ED Civ Rule 83.8.

7.  *Individual judge practices.* Refer to the Miscellaneous section of this document for information on individual judge practices on general requirements for documents.

## D. Documents

1.  *Required documents*

    a.  *Request for production of documents.* Refer to the General Requirements section of this document for information on the request for production of documents.

2.  *Supplemental documents*

    a.  *Subpoena.* As provided in FRCP 45, a nonparty may be compelled to produce documents and tangible things or to permit an inspection. FRCP 34(c). For information on the form and contents of the subpoena, refer to FRCP 45.

    b.  *Certificate of service.* FRCP 5(d) requires that the person making service under FRCP 5 certify that service has been effected. FRCP 5(Advisory Committee Notes). Having such information on file may be useful for many purposes, including proof of service if an issue arises concerning the effectiveness of the service. FRCP 5(Advisory Committee Notes).

3.  *Individual judge practices.* Refer to the Miscellaneous section of this document for information on individual judge practices on required documents.

## E. Format

1.  *Form of documents.* The rules governing captions and other matters of form in pleadings apply to motions and other papers. FRCP 7(b)(2).

    a.  *Paper.* Every pleading, written motion, and other paper must: be plainly written, typed, printed, or copied without erasures or interlineations which materially deface it. NY R USDCTS&ED Civ Rule 11.1(a)(1).

    b.  *Typeface, margin, and spacing.* The typeface, margins, and spacing of all documents presented for filing must meet the following requirements:

        i.   All text must be twelve (12) point type or larger, except for text in footnotes which may be ten (10) point type;

        ii.   All documents must have at least one (1) inch margins on all sides;

        iii.   All text must be double-spaced, except for headings, text in footnotes, or block quotations, which may be single-spaced. NY R USDCTS&ED Civ Rule 11.1(b).

    c.  *Caption; Names of parties.* Every pleading must have a caption with the court's name, a title, a file number, and a FRCP 7(a) designation. The title of the complaint must name all the parties; the title of other pleadings, after naming the first party on each side, may refer generally to other parties. FRCP 10(a). Every pleading, written motion, and other paper must: bear the docket number and the initials of the District Judge and any Magistrate Judge before whom the action or proceeding is pending, NY R USDCTS&ED Civ Rule 11.1(a)(2).

    d.  *Paragraphs; Separate statements.* A party must state its claims or defenses in numbered paragraphs, each limited as far as practicable to a single set of circumstances. A later pleading may refer by number to a paragraph in an earlier pleading. If doing so would promote clarity, each claim founded on a separate transaction or occurrence—and each defense other than a denial—must be stated in a separate count or defense. FRCP 10(b).

    e.  *Adoption by reference; Exhibits.* A statement in a pleading may be adopted by reference elsewhere in the same pleading or in any other pleading or motion. A copy of a written instrument that is an exhibit to a pleading is a part of the pleading for all purposes. FRCP 10(c).

    f.  *Acceptance by the clerk.* The clerk must not refuse to file a paper solely because it is not in the form prescribed by the Federal Rules of Civil Procedure or by a local rule or practice. FRCP 5(d)(4).

2.  *Signing disclosures and discovery requests, responses, and objections.* FRCP 11 does not apply to

disclosures and discovery requests, responses, objections, and motions under FRCP 26 through FRCP 37. FRCP 11(d).

    a.  *Signature required.* Every disclosure under FRCP 26(a)(1) or FRCP 26(a)(3) and every discovery request, response, or objection must be signed by at least one attorney of record in the attorney's own name—or by the party personally, if unrepresented—and must state the signer's address, e-mail address, and telephone number. FRCP 26(g)(1). Every pleading, written motion, and other paper must: have the name of each person signing it clearly printed or typed directly below the signature. NY R USDCTS&ED Civ Rule 11.1(a)(3).

    b.  *Effect of signature.* By signing, an attorney or party certifies that to the best of the person's knowledge, information, and belief formed after a reasonable inquiry:

       i.  With respect to a disclosure, it is complete and correct as of the time it is made; and

      ii.  With respect to a discovery request, response, or objection, it is:

- Consistent with the Federal Rules of Civil Procedure and warranted by existing law or by a nonfrivolous argument for extending, modifying, or reversing existing law, or for establishing new law;

- Not interposed for any improper purpose, such as to harass, cause unnecessary delay, or needlessly increase the cost of litigation; and

- Neither unreasonable nor unduly burdensome or expensive, considering the needs of the case, prior discovery in the case, the amount in controversy, and the importance of the issues at stake in the action. FRCP 26(g)(1).

    c.  *Failure to sign.* Other parties have no duty to act on an unsigned disclosure, request, response, or objection until it is signed, and the court must strike it unless a signature is promptly supplied after the omission is called to the attorney's or party's attention. FRCP 26(g)(2).

    d.  *Sanction for improper certification.* If a certification violates FRCP 26(g) without substantial justification, the court, on motion or on its own, must impose an appropriate sanction on the signer, the party on whose behalf the signer was acting, or both. The sanction may include an order to pay the reasonable expenses, including attorney's fees, caused by the violation. FRCP 26(g)(3). Refer to the United States District Court for the Eastern District of New York KeyRules Motion for Discovery Sanctions document for more information.

3.  *Privacy protection for filings made with the court*

    a.  *Redacted filings.* Unless the court orders otherwise, in an electronic or paper filing with the court that contains an individual's Social Security number, taxpayer-identification number, or birth date, the name of an individual known to be a minor, or a financial-account number, a party or nonparty making the filing may include only:

       i.  The last four (4) digits of the Social Security number and taxpayer-identification number;

      ii.  The year of the individual's birth;

     iii.  The minor's initials; and

     iv.  The last four (4) digits of the financial-account number. FRCP 5.2(a); NY R USDCTED Order 2004-09.

      v.  In addition, exercise caution when filing documents that contain the following:

- Personal identifying number, such as driver's license number;

- Medical records, treatment and diagnosis;

- Employment history;

- Individual financial information; and

- Proprietary or trade secret information. NY R USDCTED Order 2004-09.

b. *Exemptions from the redaction requirement.* The redaction requirement does not apply to the following:

    i. A financial-account number that identifies the property allegedly subject to forfeiture in a forfeiture proceeding;

    ii. The record of an administrative or agency proceeding;

    iii. The official record of a state-court proceeding;

    iv. The record of a court or tribunal, if that record was not subject to the redaction requirement when originally filed;

    v. A filing covered by FRCP 5.2(c) or FRCP 5.2(d); and

    vi. A pro se filing in an action brought under 28 U.S.C.A. § 2241, 28 U.S.C.A. § 2254, or 28 U.S.C.A. § 2255. FRCP 5.2(b).

c. *Limitations on remote access to electronic files; Social Security appeals and immigration cases.* Unless the court orders otherwise, in an action for benefits under the Social Security Act, and in an action or proceeding relating to an order of removal, to relief from removal, or to immigration benefits or detention, access to an electronic file is authorized as follows:

    i. The parties and their attorneys may have remote electronic access to any part of the case file, including the administrative record;

    ii. Any other person may have electronic access to the full record at the courthouse, but may have remote electronic access only to:

        • The docket maintained by the court; and

        • An opinion, order, judgment, or other disposition of the court, but not any other part of the case file or the administrative record. FRCP 5.2(c).

d. *Filings made under seal.* The court may order that a filing be made under seal without redaction. The court may later unseal the filing or order the person who made the filing to file a redacted version for the public record. FRCP 5.2(d).

e. *Protective orders.* For good cause, the court may by order in a case:

    i. Require redaction of additional information; or

    ii. Limit or prohibit a nonparty's remote electronic access to a document filed with the court. FRCP 5.2(e).

f. *Option for additional unredacted filing under seal.* A person making a redacted filing may also file an unredacted copy under seal. The court must retain the unredacted copy as part of the record. FRCP 5.2(f); NY R USDCTED Order 2004-09. The unredacted version of the document or the reference list shall be retained by the court as part of the record. The court may, however, still require the party to file a redacted copy for the public file. NY R USDCTED Order 2004-09.

g. *Option for filing a reference list.* A filing that contains redacted information may be filed together with a reference list that identifies each item of redacted information and specifies an appropriate identifier that uniquely corresponds to each item listed. The list must be filed under seal and may be amended as of right. Any reference in the case to a listed identifier will be construed to refer to the corresponding item of information. FRCP 5.2(g); NY R USDCTED Order 2004-09. The unredacted version of the document or the reference list shall be retained by the court as part of the record. The court may, however, still require the party to file a redacted copy for the public file. NY R USDCTED Order 2004-09.

h. *Responsibility for redaction.* The responsibility for redacting these personal identifiers rests solely with counsel and the parties. The Clerk will not review each pleading for compliance with NY R USDCTED Order 2004-09. NY R USDCTED Order 2004-09.

    i. Counsel is strongly urged to share this notice with all clients so that an informed decision about the inclusion of certain materials may be made. If a redacted document is filed, it is the sole responsibility of counsel and the parties to be sure that all pleadings comply with the rules of

this court requiring redaction of personal data identifiers. The clerk will not review each pleading for redaction. NY R USDCTED Order 2004-09.

    i.  *Waiver of protection of identifiers.* A person waives the protection of FRCP 5.2(a) as to the person's own information by filing it without redaction and not under seal. FRCP 5.2(h).

4.  *Individual judge practices.* Refer to the Miscellaneous section of this document for information on individual judge practices on formatting documents.

## F. Filing and Service Requirements

1.  *Filing requirements.* Any paper after the complaint that is required to be served—together with a certificate of service—must be filed within a reasonable time after service. But disclosures under FRCP 26(a)(1) or FRCP 26(a)(2) and the following discovery requests and responses must not be filed until they are used in the proceeding or the court orders filing: depositions, interrogatories, requests for documents or tangible things or to permit entry onto land, and requests for admission. FRCP 5(d)(1). Refer to the United States District Court for the Eastern District of New York KeyRules pleading and motion documents for information on filing with the court.

2.  *Service requirements*

  a.  *Service; When required*

    i.  *In general.* Unless the Federal Rules of Civil Procedure provide otherwise, each of the following papers must be served on every party:

- An order stating that service is required;
- A pleading filed after the original complaint, unless the court orders otherwise under FRCP 5(c) because there are numerous defendants;
- A discovery paper required to be served on a party, unless the court orders otherwise;
- A written motion, except one that may be heard ex parte; and
- A written notice, appearance, demand, or offer of judgment, or any similar paper. FRCP 5(a)(1).

    ii.  *If a party fails to appear.* No service is required on a party who is in default for failing to appear. But a pleading that asserts a new claim for relief against such a party must be served on that party under FRCP 4. FRCP 5(a)(2).

    iii.  *Seizing property.* If an action is begun by seizing property and no person is or need be named as a defendant, any service required before the filing of an appearance, answer, or claim must be made on the person who had custody or possession of the property when it was seized. FRCP 5(a)(3).

  b.  *Service; How made*

    i.  *Serving an attorney.* If a party is represented by an attorney, service under FRCP 5 must be made on the attorney unless the court orders service on the party. FRCP 5(b)(1).

    ii.  *Service in general.* A paper is served under FRCP 5 by:

- Handing it to the person;
- Leaving it: (1) at the person's office with a clerk or other person in charge or, if no one is in charge, in a conspicuous place in the office; or (2) if the person has no office or the office is closed, at the person's dwelling or usual place of abode with someone of suitable age and discretion who resides there;
- Mailing it to the person's last known address—in which event service is complete upon mailing;
- Leaving it with the court clerk if the person has no known address;
- Sending it by electronic means if the person consented in writing—in which event service is complete upon transmission, but is not effective if the serving party learns that it did not reach the person to be served; or

- Delivering it by any other means that the person consented to in writing—in which event service is complete when the person making service delivers it to the agency designated to make delivery. FRCP 5(b)(2).

    iii. *Service by overnight delivery.* Service upon an attorney may be made by overnight delivery service. "Overnight delivery service" means any delivery service which regularly accepts items for overnight delivery. Overnight delivery service shall be deemed service by mail for purposes of FRCP 5 and FRCP 6. NY R USDCTS&ED Civ Rule 5.3.

    iv. *Service by electronic means.* Parties serving and filing papers shall follow the instructions regarding Electronic Case Filing (ECF) published on the website of each respective Court. A paper served and filed by electronic means in accordance with such instructions is, for purposes of FRCP 5, served and filed in compliance with the Local Civil Rules of the United States District Courts for the Southern and Eastern Districts of New York. NY R USDCTS&ED Civ Rule 5.2(a). Parties have an obligation to review the Court's actual order, decree, or judgment (on ECF), which controls, and should not rely on the description on the docket or in the ECF Notice of Electronic Filing (NEF). NY R USDCTS&ED Civ Rule 5.2(c).

    v. *Using court facilities.* If a local rule so authorizes, a party may use the court's transmission facilities to make service under FRCP 5(b)(2)(E). FRCP 5(b)(3).

  c. *Serving numerous defendants*

    i. *In general.* If an action involves an unusually large number of defendants, the court may, on motion or on its own, order that:

      - Defendants' pleadings and replies to them need not be served on other defendants;

      - Any crossclaim, counterclaim, avoidance, or affirmative defense in those pleadings and replies to them will be treated as denied or avoided by all other parties; and

      - Filing any such pleading and serving it on the plaintiff constitutes notice of the pleading to all parties. FRCP 5(c)(1).

    ii. *Notifying parties.* A copy of every such order must be served on the parties as the court directs. FRCP 5(c)(2).

3. *Individual judge practices.* Refer to the Miscellaneous section of this document for information on individual judge practices on filing and serving documents.

## G. Hearings

1. There is no hearing contemplated in the federal statutes or rules for requests for production of documents.

## H. Forms

### 1. Federal Request for Production of Documents Forms

  a. Request; Production of documents for inspection and copying. AMJUR PP DEPOSITION § 498.

  b. Request for production, inspection and copying of documents, and inspection and photographing of things and real property. 3A FEDFORMS § 3556.

  c. Request for production of documents; Business records. 3A FEDFORMS § 3557.

  d. Request for production of documents; Patent case. 3A FEDFORMS § 3558.

  e. Request for production of documents; Government records and regulations. 3A FEDFORMS § 3559.

  f. Request for production of documents; Government personnel files, memoranda, minutes of meetings, and statistics. 3A FEDFORMS § 3560.

  g. Request for production of documents; Documents to be identified in physically separate but accompanying interrogatories under FRCP 33. 3A FEDFORMS § 3561.

  h. Request for production of documents; Employment discrimination. 3A FEDFORMS § 3562.

  i. Letter requesting production of files. 3A FEDFORMS § 3563.

  j. Request; Production of documents, records, and objects, under FRCP 34. FEDPROF § 23:394.

k. Request; Production of documents for inspection and copying. FEDPROF § 23:395.

l. Request; Production of documents for inspection and copying; Business records. FEDPROF § 23:396.

m. Request; Production of objects for inspection and sampling. FEDPROF § 23:397.

n. Request; Production of documents for inspection and copying; Government records and files. FEDPROF § 23:398.

o. Request; Production of documents and things; Patent proceeding. FEDPROF § 23:399.

p. Request; Production of documents and things; Trademark action. FEDPROF § 23:400.

q. Request; Production of documents; Trademark action; Likelihood of confusion. FEDPROF § 23:401.

r. Request; Production of documents; Automobile negligence. FEDPROF § 23:402.

s. Request; Production of documents; Premises liability. FEDPROF § 23:403.

t. Request; Production of documents for inspection and copying; Wrongful death due to forklift accident. FEDPROF § 23:404.

u. Request; Production of documents; Products liability. FEDPROF § 23:405.

v. Request; Production of documents; Collection of tariff. FEDPROF § 23:406.

w. Request; Production of medical records. FEDPROF § 23:407.

x. Request; Production of employment records. FEDPROF § 23:408.

y. Request; Production of education records. FEDPROF § 23:409.

z. Request; Production of decedent's records. FEDPROF § 23:410.

## I. Applicable Rules

1. *Federal rules*

   a. Serving and filing pleadings and other papers. FRCP 5.

   b. Privacy protection for filings made with the court. FRCP 5.2.

   c. Computing and extending time; Time for motion papers. FRCP 6.

   d. Pleadings allowed; Form of motions and other papers. FRCP 7.

   e. Form of pleadings. FRCP 10.

   f. Signing pleadings, motions, and other papers; Representations to the court; Sanctions. FRCP 11.

   g. Duty to disclose; General provisions governing discovery. FRCP 26.

   h. Stipulations about discovery procedure. FRCP 29.

   i. Producing documents, electronically stored information, and tangible things, or entering onto land, for inspection and other purposes. FRCP 34.

   j. Failure to make disclosures or to cooperate in discovery; Sanctions. FRCP 37.

2. *Local rules*

   a. Duty of attorneys in related cases. NY R USDCTS&ED Civ Rule 1.6.

   b. Electronic service and filing of documents. NY R USDCTS&ED Civ Rule 5.2.

   c. Service by overnight delivery. NY R USDCTS&ED Civ Rule 5.3.

   d. Computation of time. NY R USDCTS&ED Civ Rule 6.4.

   e. Form of pleadings, motions, and other papers. NY R USDCTS&ED Civ Rule 11.1.

   f. Assertion of claim of privilege. NY R USDCTS&ED Civ Rule 26.2.

   g. Uniform definitions in discovery requests. NY R USDCTS&ED Civ Rule 26.3.

   h. Cooperation among counsel in discovery. NY R USDCTS&ED Civ Rule 26.4.

    i.   Form discovery requests. [NY R USDCTS&ED Civ Rule 26.5, as amended by NY ORDER 16-4212, effective September 26, 2016].

    j.   Court-annexed arbitration (Eastern District only). NY R USDCTS&ED Civ Rule 83.7.

    k.   Court-annexed mediation (Eastern District only). NY R USDCTS&ED Civ Rule 83.8.

    l.   The August 2, 2004 amendment to the E-Government Act of 2002. NY R USDCTED Order 2004-09.

## J.  Miscellaneous

**NOTE: Individual judges' rules may apply. For available judge-level information, refer to:**

DISTRICT JUDGE CAROL BAGLEY AMON: NY R USDCTED Amon-Practices.

DISTRICT JUDGE JOAN M. AZRACK: NY R USDCTED Azrack-Practices.

DISTRICT JUDGE JOSEPH F. BIANCO: NY R USDCTED Bianco-Practices.

DISTRICT JUDGE FREDERIC BLOCK: NY R USDCTED Block-Practices.

DISTRICT JUDGE MARGO K. BRODIE: NY R USDCTED Brodie-Practices.

DISTRICT JUDGE PAMELA K. CHEN: NY R USDCTED Chen-Practices.

DISTRICT JUDGE BRIAN M. COGAN: NY R USDCTED Cogan-Practices; NY R USDCTED Cogan-Pretrial.

DISTRICT JUDGE LaSHANN DeARCY HALL: NY R USDCTED DeArcy Hall-Practices.

DISTRICT JUDGE RAYMOND J. DEARIE: NY R USDCTED Dearie-Practices.

DISTRICT JUDGE ANN M. DONNELLY: NY R USDCTED Donnelly-Practices.

DISTRICT JUDGE SANDRA J. FEUERSTEIN: NY R USDCTED Feuerstein-Practices; NY R USDCTED Feuerstein-Pretrial.

DISTRICT JUDGE NICHOLAS G. GARAUIFIS: NY R USDCTED Garaufis-Practices; NY R USDCTED Garaufis-Pretrial.

DISTRICT JUDGE NINA GERSHON: NY R USDCTED Gershon-Practices.

DISTRICT JUDGE I. LEO GLASSER: NY R USDCTED Glasser-Practices; NY R USDCTED Glasser-Crim.

DISTRICT JUDGE DENIS R. HURLEY: NY R USDCTED Hurley-Practices; [NY R USDCTED Hurley-Pro Cooperation Info, as added by NY ORDER 16-4188, effective July 22, 2016]; [NY R USDCTED Hurley-Pro Cooperation Info Stay, as added by NY ORDER 16-4188, effective July 22, 2016].

DISTRICT JUDGE DORA L. IRIZARRY: NY R USDCTED Irizarry-Practices; NY R USDCTED Irizarry-Pretrial; NY R USDCTED Irizarry-Crim.

DISTRICT JUDGE STERLING JOHNSON, JR.: NY R USDCTED Johnson-Practices.

DISTRICT JUDGE EDWARD R. KORMAN: NY R USDCTED Korman-Practices; NY R USDCTED Korman-Pretrial.

DISTRICT JUDGE WILLIAM F. KUNTZ: NY R USDCTED Kuntz-Practices.

DISTRICT JUDGE KIYO A. MATSUMOTO: NY R USDCTED Matsumoto-Practices.

DISTRICT JUDGE ROSLYNN R. MAUSKOPF: NY R USDCTED Mauskopf-Practices; NY R USDCTED Mauskopf-Recusal.

DISTRICT JUDGE THOMAS C. PLATT: NY R USDCTED Platt-Practices.

DISTRICT JUDGE ALLYNE R. ROSS: NY R USDCTED Ross-Practices.

DISTRICT JUDGE JOANNA SEYBERT: NY R USDCTED Seybert-Practices.

DISTRICT JUDGE ARTHUR D. SPATT: NY R USDCTED Spatt-Practices.

DISTRICT JUDGE SANDRA L. TOWNES: NY R USDCTED Townes-Practices.

DISTRICT JUDGE ERIC N. VITALIANO: NY R USDCTED Vitaliano-Practices.

DISTRICT JUDGE JACK B. WEINSTEIN: NY R USDCTED Weinstein-Practices.

DISTRICT JUDGE LEONARD D. WEXLER: NY R USDCTED Wexler-Practices; NY R USDCTED Wexler-Rules.

MAGISTRATE JUDGE LOIS BLOOM: NY R USDCTED Bloom-Practices.

MAGISTRATE JUDGE GARY R. BROWN: NY R USDCTED Brown-Practices.

MAGISTRATE JUDGE MARILYN D. GO: NY R USDCTED Go-Practices.

MAGISTRATE JUDGE STEVEN M. GOLD: NY R USDCTED Gold-Practices.

MAGISTRATE JUDGE PEGGY KUO: NY R USDCTED Kuo-Practices; NY R USDCTED Kuo-Scheduling Order.

MAGISTRATE JUDGE ROBERT M. LEVY: NY R USDCTED Levy-Practices.

MAGISTRATE JUDGE ARLENE R. LINDSAY: NY R USDCTED Lindsay-Practices.

MAGISTRATE JUDGE STEVEN I. LOCKE: NY R USDCTED Locke-Practices.

MAGISTRATE JUDGE ROANNE L. MANN: NY R USDCTED Mann-Practices.

MAGISTRATE JUDGE JAMES ORENSTEIN: NY R USDCTED Jorenstein--Practices.

MAGISTRATE JUDGE VIKTOR V. POHORELSKY: NY R USDCTED Pohorelsky-Practices.

MAGISTRATE JUDGE CHERYL L. POLLAK: NY R USDCTED Pollak-Practices; NY R USDCTED Pollak-Pretrial.

MAGISTRATE JUDGE RAMON E. REYES, JR.: NY R USDCTED Reyes-Practices.

MAGISTRATE JUDGE VERA M. SCANLON: NY R USDCTED Scanlon-Practices.

MAGISTRATE JUDGE ANNE Y. SHIELDS: NY R USDCTED Shields-Practices.

MAGISTRATE JUDGE STEVEN L. TISCIONE: NY R USDCTED Tiscione-Practices.

MAGISTRATE JUDGE A. KATHLEEN TOMILINSON: NY R USDCTED Tomlinson-Practices.

# Requests, Notices and Applications
# Request for Admissions

### Document Last Updated September 2016

**A. Checklist**

   (I) ❏ Matters to be considered by requesting party

      (a) ❏ Required documents

         (1) ❏ Request for admissions

      (b) ❏ Supplemental documents

         (1) ❏ Document(s)

         (2) ❏ Certificate of service

      (c) ❏ Timing

         (1) ❏ A party may not seek discovery from any source before the parties have conferred as required by FRCP 26(f), except in a proceeding exempted from initial disclosure under FRCP 26(a)(1)(B), or when authorized by the Federal Rules of Civil Procedure, by stipulation, or by court order

   (II) ❏ Matters to be considered by responding party

      (a) ❏ Required documents

         (1) ❏ Response to request for admissions

      (b) ❏ Supplemental documents

         (1) ❏ Written information regarding assertion of privilege

         (2) ❏ Certificate of service

(c) ❏ Timing

    (1)   ❏ A matter is admitted unless, within thirty (30) days after being served, the party to whom the request is directed serves on the requesting party a written answer or objection addressed to the matter and signed by the party or its attorney

## B. Timing

1. *Request for admissions.* Without leave of court or written stipulation, requests for admission may not be served before the time specified in FRCP 26(d). FEDPROC § 26:706.

2. *Timing of discovery, generally.* A party may not seek discovery from any source before the parties have conferred as required by FRCP 26(f), except in a proceeding exempted from initial disclosure under FRCP 26(a)(1)(B), or when authorized by the Federal Rules of Civil Procedure, by stipulation, or by court order. FRCP 26(d)(1).

3. *Computation of time*

    a.  *Computing time.* FRCP 6 applies in computing any time period specified in the Federal Rules of Civil Procedure, in any local rule or court order, or in any statute that does not specify a method of computing time. FRCP 6(a). In computing any period of time prescribed or allowed by the Local Civil Rules of the United States District Courts for the Southern and Eastern Districts of New York or the Local Admiralty and Maritime Rules, the provisions of FRCP 6 shall apply unless otherwise stated. NY R USDCTS&ED Civ Rule 6.4.

        i.  *Period stated in days or a longer unit.* When the period is stated in days or a longer unit of time:

- Exclude the day of the event that triggers the period;

- Count every day, including intermediate Saturdays, Sundays, and legal holidays; and

- Include the last day of the period, but if the last day is a Saturday, Sunday, or legal holiday, the period continues to run until the end of the next day that is not a Saturday, Sunday, or legal holiday. FRCP 6(a)(1). In the Local Civil Rules of the United States District Courts for the Southern and Eastern Districts of New York, as in the Federal Rules of Civil Procedure as amended effective December 1, 2009, Saturdays, Sundays, and legal holidays are no longer excluded in computing periods of time. If the last day of the period is a Saturday, Sunday, or legal holiday, the period continues to run until the end of the next day that is not a Saturday, Sunday, or legal holiday. NY R USDCTS&ED Civ Rule 6.4.

        ii.  *Period stated in hours.* When the period is stated in hours:

- Begin counting immediately on the occurrence of the event that triggers the period;

- Count every hour, including hours during intermediate Saturdays, Sundays, and legal holidays; and

- If the period would end on a Saturday, Sunday, or legal holiday, the period continues to run until the same time on the next day that is not a Saturday, Sunday, or legal holiday. FRCP 6(a)(2). In the Local Civil Rules of the United States District Courts for the Southern and Eastern Districts of New York, as in the Federal Rules of Civil Procedure as amended effective December 1, 2009, Saturdays, Sundays, and legal holidays are no longer excluded in computing periods of time. If the last day of the period is a Saturday, Sunday, or legal holiday, the period continues to run until the end of the next day that is not a Saturday, Sunday, or legal holiday. NY R USDCTS&ED Civ Rule 6.4.

        iii.  *Inaccessibility of the clerk's office.* Unless the court orders otherwise, if the clerk's office is inaccessible:

- On the last day for filing under FRCP 6(a)(1), then the time for filing is extended to the first accessible day that is not a Saturday, Sunday, or legal holiday; or

- During the last hour for filing under FRCP 6(a)(2), then the time for filing is extended to the same time on the first accessible day that is not a Saturday, Sunday, or legal holiday. FRCP 6(a)(3).

iv. *"Last day" defined.* Unless a different time is set by a statute, local rule, or court order, the last day ends:

- For electronic filing, at midnight in the court's time zone; and

- For filing by other means, when the clerk's office is scheduled to close. FRCP 6(a)(4).

v. *"Next day" defined.* The "next day" is determined by continuing to count forward when the period is measured after an event and backward when measured before an event. FRCP 6(a)(5).

vi. *"Legal holiday" defined.* "Legal holiday" means:

- The day set aside by statute for observing New Year's Day, Martin Luther King Jr.'s Birthday, Washington's Birthday, Memorial Day, Independence Day, Labor Day, Columbus Day, Veterans' Day, Thanksgiving Day, or Christmas Day;

- Any day declared a holiday by the President or Congress; and

- For periods that are measured after an event, any other day declared a holiday by the state where the district court is located. FRCP 6(a)(6).

b. *Extending time*

i. *In general.* When an act may or must be done within a specified time, the court may, for good cause, extend the time:

- With or without motion or notice if the court acts, or if a request is made, before the original time or its extension expires; or

- On motion made after the time has expired if the party failed to act because of excusable neglect. FRCP 6(b)(1).

ii. *Exceptions.* A court must not extend the time to act under FRCP 50(b), FRCP 50(d), FRCP 52(b), FRCP 59(b), FRCP 59(d), FRCP 59(e), and FRCP 60(b). FRCP 6(b)(2).

iii. Refer to the United States District Court for the Eastern District of New York KeyRules Motion for Continuance/Extension of Time document for more information on extending time.

c. *Additional time after certain kinds of service.* When a party may or must act within a specified time after service and service is made under FRCP 5(b)(2)(C), FRCP 5(b)(2)(D), FRCP 5(b)(2)(E), or FRCP 5(b)(2)(F), three (3) days are added after the period would otherwise expire under FRCP 6(a). FRCP 6(d). Overnight delivery service shall be deemed service by mail for purposes of FRCP 5 and FRCP 6. NY R USDCTS&ED Civ Rule 5.3.

4. *Individual judge practices.* Refer to the Miscellaneous section of this document for information on individual judge practices on timing of documents.

## C. General Requirements

1. *General provisions governing discovery*

a. *Discovery scope and limits*

i. *Scope in general.* Unless otherwise limited by court order, the scope of discovery is as follows: Parties may obtain discovery regarding any nonprivileged matter that is relevant to any party's claim or defense and proportional to the needs of the case, considering the importance of the issues at stake in the action, the amount in controversy, the parties' relative access to relevant information, the parties' resources, the importance of the discovery in resolving the issues, and whether the burden or expense of the proposed discovery outweighs its likely benefit. Information within this scope of discovery need not be admissible in evidence to be discoverable. FRCP 26(b)(1).

ii. *Limitations on frequency and extent*

- *When permitted.* By order, the court may alter the limits in the Federal Rules of Civil Procedure on the number of depositions and interrogatories or on the length of depositions under FRCP 30. By order or local rule, the court may also limit the number of requests under FRCP 36. FRCP 26(b)(2)(A).

- *Specific limitations on electronically stored information.* A party need not provide discovery of electronically stored information from sources that the party identifies as not reasonably accessible because of undue burden or cost. On motion to compel discovery or for a protective order, the party from whom discovery is sought must show that the information is not reasonably accessible because of undue burden or cost. If that showing is made, the court may nonetheless order discovery from such sources if the requesting party shows good cause, considering the limitations of FRCP 26(b)(2)(C). The court may specify conditions for the discovery. FRCP 26(b)(2)(B).

- *When required.* On motion or on its own, the court must limit the frequency or extent of discovery otherwise allowed by the Federal Rules of Civil Procedure or by local rule if it determines that: (1) the discovery sought is unreasonably cumulative or duplicative, or can be obtained from some other source tha° is more convenient, less burdensome, or less expensive; (2) the party seeking discovery has had ample opportunity to obtain the information by discovery in the action; or (3) the proposed discovery is outside the scope permitted by FRCP 26(b)(1). FRCP 26(b)(2)(C).

iii. *Trial preparation; Materials*

- *Documents and tangible things.* Ordinarily, a party may not discover documents and tangible things that are prepared in anticipation of litigation or for trial by or for another party or its representative (including the other party's attorney, consultant, surety, indemnitor, insurer, or agent). But, subject to FRCP 26(b)(4), those materials may be discovered if: (1) they are otherwise discoverable under FRCP 26(b)(1); and (2) the party shows that it has substantial need for the materials to prepare its case and cannot, without undue hardship, obtain their substantial equivalent by other means. FRCP 26(b)(3)(A).

- *Protection against disclosure.* If the court orders discovery of those materials, it must protect against disclosure of the mental impressions, conclusions, opinions, or legal theories of a party's attorney or other representative concerning the litigation. FRCP 26(b)(3)(B).

- *Previous statement.* Any party or other person may, on request and without the required showing, obtain the person's own previous statement about the action or its subject matter. If the request is refused, the person may move for a court order, and FRCP 37(a)(5) applies to the award of expenses. A previous statement is either: (1) a written statement that the person has signed or otherwise adopted or approved; or (2) a contemporaneous stenographic, mechanical, electrical, or other recording—or a transcription of it—that recites substantially verbatim the person's oral statement. FRCP 26(b)(3)(C).

iv. *Trial preparation; Experts*

- *Deposition of an expert who may testify.* A party may depose any person who has been identified as an expert whose opinions may be presented at trial. If FRCP 26(a)(2)(B) requires a report from the expert, the deposition may be conducted only after the report is provided. FRCP 26(b)(4)(A).

- *Trial-preparation protection for draft reports or disclosures.* FRCP 26(b)(3)(A) and FRCP 26(b)(3)(B) protect drafts of any report or disclosure required under FRCP 26(a)(2), regardless of the form in which the draft is recorded. FRCP 26(b)(4)(B).

- *Trial-preparation protection for communications between a party's attorney and expert witnesses.* FRCP 26(b)(3)(A) and FRCP 26(b)(3)(B) protect communications between the party's attorney and any witness required to provide a report under FRCP 26(a)(2)(B), regardless of the form of the communications, except to the extent that the communications: (1) relate to compensation for the expert's study or testimony; (2) identify facts or data that the party's attorney provided and that the expert considered in forming the opinions to be expressed; or (3) identify assumptions that the party's attorney provided and that the expert relied on in forming the opinions to be expressed. FRCP 26(b)(4)(C).

- *Expert employed only for trial preparation.* Ordinarily, a party may not, by interrogatories or deposition, discover facts known or opinions held by an expert who has been retained or specially employed by another party in anticipation of litigation or to prepare for trial and who is not expected to be called as a witness at trial. But a party may do so only: (1) as provided in FRCP 35(b); or (2) on showing exceptional circumstances under which it is impracticable for the party to obtain facts or opinions on the same subject by other means. FRCP 26(b)(4)(D).

- *Payment.* Unless manifest injustice would result, the court must require that the party seeking discovery: (1) pay the expert a reasonable fee for time spent in responding to discovery under FRCP 26(b)(4)(A) or FRCP 26(b)(4)(D); and (2) for discovery FRCP 26(b)(4)(D), also pay the other party a fair portion of the fees and expenses it reasonably incurred in obtaining the expert's facts and opinions. FRCP 26(b)(4)(E).

v. *Claiming privilege or protecting trial-preparation materials*

- *Information withheld.* When a party withholds information otherwise discoverable by claiming that the information is privileged or subject to protection as trial-preparation material, the party must: (1) expressly make the claim; and (2) describe the nature of the documents, communications, or tangible things not produced or disclosed—and do so in a manner that, without revealing information itself privileged or protected, will enable other parties to assess the claim. FRCP 26(b)(5)(A). Unless otherwise agreed by the parties or directed by the Court, where a claim of privilege is asserted in objecting to any means of discovery or disclosure, including but not limited to a deposition, and an answer is not provided on the basis of such assertion, (1) the person asserting the privilege shall identify the nature of the privilege (including work product) which is being claimed and, if the privilege is governed by state law, indicate the state's privilege rule being invoked; and (2) the following information shall be provided in the objection, or (in the case of a deposition) in response to questions by the questioner, unless divulgence of such information would cause disclosure of the allegedly privileged information: (A) for documents: (i) the type of document, e.g., letter or memorandum; (ii) the general subject matter of the document; (iii) the date of the document; and (iv) the author of the document, the addressees of the document, and any other recipients, and, where not apparent, the relationship of the author, addressees, and recipients to each other; (B) for oral communications: (i) the name of the person making the communication and the names of persons present while the communication was made and, where not apparent, the relationship of the persons present to the person making the communication; (ii) the date and place of communication; and (iii) the general subject matter of the communication. NY R USDCTS&ED Civ Rule 26.2(a). Where a claim of privilege is asserted in response to discovery or disclosure other than a deposition, and information is not provided on the basis of such assertion, the information set forth in NY R USDCTS&ED Civ Rule 26.2(a) shall be furnished in writing at the time of the response to such discovery or disclosure, unless otherwise ordered by the Court. NY R USDCTS&ED Civ Rule 26.2(b).

- *Information produced.* If information produced in discovery is subject to a claim of privilege or of protection as trial-preparation material, the party making the claim may notify any party that received the information of the claim and the basis for it. After being notified, a party must promptly return, sequester, or destroy the specified information and any copies it has; must not use or disclose the information until the claim is resolved; must take reasonable steps to retrieve the information if the party disclosed it before being notified; and may promptly present the information to the court under seal for a determination of the claim. The producing party must preserve the information until the claim is resolved. FRCP 26(b)(5)(B).

- *Efficient means of providing information regarding claims of privilege.* Efficient means of providing information regarding claims of privilege are encouraged, and parties are encouraged to agree upon measures that further this end. For example, when asserting privilege on the same basis with respect to multiple documents, it is presumptively proper to provide the information required by NY R USDCTS&ED Civ Rule 26.2 by group or category. A party receiving a privilege log that groups documents or otherwise departs from a document-by-document or communication-by-communication listing may not object solely on that basis, but may object if the substantive information required by NY R USDCTS&ED Civ Rule 26.2 has not been provided in a comprehensible form. NY R USDCTS&ED Civ Rule 26.2(c).

b. *Protective orders.* A party or any person from whom discovery is sought may move for a protective order in the court where the action is pending—or as an alternative on matters relating to a deposition, in the court for the district where the deposition will be taken. FRCP 26(c)(1). Refer to the United States District Court for the Eastern District of New York KeyRules Motion for Protective Order document for more information.

c. *Sequence of discovery.* Unless the parties stipulate or the court orders otherwise for the parties' and witnesses' convenience and in the interests of justice: (1) methods of discovery may be used in any sequence; and (2) discovery by one party does not require any other party to delay its discovery. FRCP 26(d)(3).

d. *Uniform definitions in discovery requests.* The full text of the definitions and rules of construction set forth in NY R USDCTS&ED Civ Rule 26.3(c) and NY R USDCTS&ED Civ Rule 26.3(d) is deemed incorporated by reference into all discovery requests. No discovery request shall use broader definitions or rules of construction than those set forth in NY R USDCTS&ED Civ Rule 26.3(c) and NY R USDCTS&ED Civ Rule 26.3(d). NY R USDCTS&ED Civ Rule 26.3 shall not preclude (1) the definition of other terms specific to the particular litigation, (2) the use of abbreviations, or (3) a more narrow definition of a term defined in NY R USDCTS&ED Civ Rule 26.3(c). NY R USDCTS&ED Civ Rule 26.3(a). NY R USDCTS&ED Civ Rule 26.3 is not intended to broaden or narrow the scope of discovery permitted by the Federal Rules of Civil Procedure. NY R USDCTS&ED Civ Rule 26.3(b).

i. *Definitions.* The following definitions apply to all discovery requests:

- *Communication.* The term "communication" means the transmittal of information (in the form of facts, ideas, inquiries or otherwise). NY R USDCTS&ED Civ Rule 26.3(c)(1).

- *Document.* The term "document" is defined to be synonymous in meaning and equal in scope to the usage of the term "documents or electronically stored information" in FRCP 34(a)(1)(A). A draft or non-identical copy is a separate document within the meaning of this term. NY R USDCTS&ED Civ Rule 26.3(c)(2).

- *Identify (with respect to persons).* When referring to a person, "to identify" means to give, to the extent known, the person's full name, present or last known address, and when referring to a natural person, additionally, the present or last known place of employment. Once a person has been identified in accordance with NY R USDCTS&ED Civ Rule 26.3(c)(3), only the name of that person need be listed in response to subsequent discovery requesting the identification of that person. NY R USDCTS&ED Civ Rule 26.3(c)(3).

- *Identify (with respect to documents).* When referring to documents, "to identify" means to give, to the extent known, the (1) type of document; (2) general subject matter; (3) date of the document; and (4) author(s), addressee(s) and recipient(s). In the alternative, the responding party may produce the documents, together with identifying information sufficient to satisfy FRCP 33(d). NY R USDCTS&ED Civ Rule 26.3(c)(4).

- *Parties.* The terms "plaintiff" and "defendant" as well as a party's full or abbreviated name or a pronoun referring to a party mean the party and, where applicable, its officers, directors, employees, partners, corporate parent, subsidiaries or affiliates. This definition is not intended to impose a discovery obligation on any person who is not a party to the litigation. NY R USDCTS&ED Civ Rule 26.3(c)(5).

- *Person.* The term "person" is defined as any natural person or any legal entity, including, without limitation, any business or governmental entity or association. NY R USDCTS&ED Civ Rule 26.3(c)(6).

- *Concerning.* The term "concerning" means relating to, referring to, describing, evidencing or constituting. NY R USDCTS&ED Civ Rule 26.3(c)(7).

      ii.  *Rules of construction.* The following rules of construction apply to all discovery requests:

- *All/any/each.* The terms "all," "any," and "each" shall each be construed as encompassing any and all. NY R USDCTS&ED Civ Rule 26.3(d)(1).

- *And/or.* The connectives "and" and "or" shall be construed either disjunctively or conjunctively as necessary to bring within the scope of the discovery request all responses that might otherwise be construed to be outside of its scope. NY R USDCTS&ED Civ Rule 26.3(d)(2).

- *Number.* The use of the singular form of any word includes the plural and vice versa. NY R USDCTS&ED Civ Rule 26.3(d)(3).

e.  *Cooperation among counsel in discovery.* Counsel are expected to cooperate with each other, consistent with the interests of their clients, in all phases of the discovery process and to be courteous in their dealings with each other, including in matters relating to scheduling and timing of various discovery procedures. NY R USDCTS&ED Civ Rule 26.4(a).

      i.  Discovery requests shall be read reasonably in the recognition that the attorney serving them generally does not have the information being sought and the attorney receiving them generally does have such information or can obtain it from the client. NY R USDCTS&ED Civ Rule 26.4(b).

f.  *Standard discovery in prisoner pro se actions.* For information on discovery in prisoner pro se actions, refer to NY R USDCTS&ED Civ Rule 33.2.

2.  *Request for admissions*

a.  *Scope.* A party may serve on any other party a written request to admit, for purposes of the pending action only, the truth of any matters within the scope of FRCP 26(b)(1) relating to: (1) facts, the application of law to fact, or opinions about either; and (2) the genuineness of any described documents. FRCP 36(a)(1).

      i.  A party may serve a request for admission even though the party has the burden of proving the matters asserted therein because FRCP 36 permits requests for admission to address claims of the party seeking discovery, and generally, the party asserting a claim bears the burden of proof thereon. FEDPROC § 26:715.

b.  *Number.* FRCP 36 does not limit a party to a single request, or set of requests, for admissions. But FRCP 26(b)(2)(A) authorizes courts to limit the number of requests by order or local rule. In addition, the court has power to protect a party from harassment by repeated requests for admissions, but will not bar such repeated requests when the circumstances of the case justify them. Even a second request about the same fact or the genuineness of the same document is permissible if circumstances warrant a renewed request. FPP § 2258.

c.  *Form.* Each matter must be separately stated. FRCP 36(a)(2). The party called upon to respond should not be required to go through a document and assume the responsibility of determining what facts it is being requested to admit. FPP § 2258. Each request for an admission should be phrased simply and directly so that it can be admitted or denied without explanation. FPP § 2258; United Coal Cos. v. Powell Const. Co., 839 F.2d 958, 968 (3d Cir. 1988).

      i.  A request for an admission need not state the source of information about the matter for which the request is made. FPP § 2258.

d.  *Form discovery requests.* Attorneys using form discovery requests shall review them to ascertain that they are consistent with the scope of discovery under FRCP 26(b)(1). Non-compliant requests shall not be used. NY R USDCTS&ED Civ Rule 26.5.

e.  *Effect of an admission; Withdrawing or amending it.* A matter admitted under FRCP 36 is conclusively established unless the court, on motion, permits the admission to be withdrawn or amended. Subject to FRCP 16(e), the court may permit withdrawal or amendment if it would promote the presentation of the merits of the action and if the court is not persuaded that it would prejudice the requesting party in maintaining or defending the action on the merits. An admission under FRCP 36 is not an admission for any other purpose and cannot be used against the party in any other proceeding. FRCP 36(b).

f. *Motion to compel.* The motion to compel discovery provided by FRCP 37(a) does not apply to a failure to respond to a request for admissions. The automatic admission from a failure to respond is a sufficient remedy for the party who made the request. If, however, a request is objected to, or the requesting party thinks that a response to a request is insufficient, it may move under FRCP 36(a)(6) to determine the sufficiency of the answers or objections. FPP § 2265.

g. *Motion regarding the sufficiency of an answer or objection.* The requesting party may move to determine the sufficiency of an answer or objection. Unless the court finds an objection justified, it must order that an answer be served. On finding that an answer does not comply with FRCP 36, the court may order either that the matter is admitted or that an amended answer be served. The court may defer its final decision until a pretrial conference or a specified time before trial. FRCP 37(a)(5) applies to an award of expenses. FRCP 36(a)(6). Refer to the United States District Court for the Eastern District of New York KeyRules Motion for Discovery Sanctions document for more information on sanctions.

3. *Sanctions for failure to cooperate in discovery.* The pattern of sanctions for FRCP 36 is somewhat different from that for the other discovery rules. The most important sanctions are two:

   a. A failure to respond to a request is deemed an admission of the matter to which the request is directed; and

   b. A party who, without good reason, refuses to admit a matter will be required to pay the costs incurred in proving that matter. FPP § 2265. If a party fails to admit what is requested under FRCP 36 and if the requesting party later proves a document to be genuine or the matter true, the requesting party may move that the party who failed to admit pay the reasonable expenses, including attorney's fees, incurred in making that proof. The court must so order unless:

      i. The request was held objectionable under FRCP 36(a);

      ii. The admission sought was of no substantial importance;

      iii. The party failing to admit had a reasonable ground to believe that it might prevail on the matter; or

      iv. There was other good reason for the failure to admit. FRCP 37(c)(2).

   c. Refer to the United States District Court for the Eastern District of New York KeyRules Motion for Discovery Sanctions document for more information on sanctions.

4. *Stipulations about discovery procedure.* Unless the court orders otherwise, the parties may stipulate that: (1) a deposition may be taken before any person, at any time or place, on any notice, and in the manner specified—in which event it may be used in the same way as any other deposition; and (2) other procedures governing or limiting discovery be modified—but a stipulation extending the time for any form of discovery must have court approval if it would interfere with the time set for completing discovery, for hearing a motion, or for trial. FRCP 29.

5. *Related cases.* It shall be the continuing duty of each attorney appearing in any civil or criminal case to bring promptly to the attention of the Court all facts which said attorney believes are relevant to a determination that said case and one or more pending civil or criminal cases should be heard by the same Judge, in order to avoid unnecessary duplication of judicial effort. As soon as the attorney becomes aware of such relationship, said attorney shall notify the Judges to whom the cases have been assigned. NY R USDCTS&ED Civ Rule 1.6(a). If counsel fails to comply with NY R USDCTS&ED Civ Rule 1.6(a), the Court may assess reasonable costs directly against counsel whose action has obstructed the effective administration of the Court's business. NY R USDCTS&ED Civ Rule 1.6(b).

6. *Alternative dispute resolution (ADR)*

   a. *Court-annexed arbitration*

      i. *Civil cases eligible for compulsory arbitration.* The Clerk of Court shall, as to all cases filed after January 1, 1986, designate and process for compulsory arbitration all civil cases (excluding Social Security cases, tax matters, prisoners' civil rights cases and any action based on an alleged violation of a right secured by the Constitution of the United States or if jurisdiction is based in whole or in part on 28 U.S.C.A. § 1343) wherein money damages only are being sought in an amount not in excess of one hundred fifty thousand dollars ($150,000) exclusive of interest and costs. NY R USDCTS&ED Civ Rule 83.7(d)(1).

- The parties may by written stipulation agree that the Clerk of Court shall designate and process for court-annexed arbitration any civil case that is not subject to compulsory arbitration in NY R USDCTS&ED Civ Rule 83.7. NY R USDCTS&ED Civ Rule 83.7(d)(2).

- For purposes of NY R USDCTS&ED Civ Rule 83.7 only, in all civil cases damages shall be presumed to be not in excess of one hundred fifty thousand dollars ($150,000) exclusive of interest and costs, unless: (1) counsel for plaintiff, at the time of filing the complaint, or in the event of the removal of a case from state court or transfer of a case from another district to this Court, within thirty (30) days of the docketing of the case in this district, files a certification with the Court that the damages sought exceed one hundred fifty thousand dollars ($150,000), exclusive of interest and costs; or (2) counsel for a defendant, at the time of filing a counterclaim or cross-claim files a certification with the court that the damages sought by the counter-claim or cross-claim exceed one hundred fifty thousand dollars ($150,000) exclusive of interest and costs. NY R USDCTS&ED Civ Rule 83.7(d)(3).

ii. *Exemption from arbitration.* The Court shall, sua sponte, or on motion of a party, exempt any case from arbitration in which the objectives of arbitration would not be realized (1) because the case involves complex or novel issues, (2) because legal issues predominate over factual issues, or (3) for other good cause. NY R USDCTS&ED Civ Rule 83.7(e)(2). For information on applying for an exemption, refer to NY R USDCTS&ED Civ Rule 83.7

iii. *Referral to arbitration.* Cases not originally designated as eligible for compulsory arbitration, but which in the discretion of the assigned Judge, are later found to qualify, may be referred to arbitration. A U.S. District Judge or a U.S. Magistrate Judge, in cases that exceed the arbitration ceiling of one hundred fifty thousand dollars ($150,000) exclusive of interest and costs, in their discretion, may suggest that the parties should consider arbitration. If the parties are agreeable, an appropriate consent form signed by all parties or their representatives may be entered and filed in the case prior to scheduling an arbitration hearing. NY R USDCTS&ED Civ Rule 83.7(e)(3).

iv. For more information on arbitration, refer to NY R USDCTS&ED Civ Rule 83.7.

b. *Court-annexed mediation.* Mediation is a process in which parties and counsel agree to meet with a neutral mediator trained to assist them in settling disputes. The mediator improves communication across party lines, helps parties articulate their interests and understand those of the other party, probes the strengths and weaknesses of each party's legal positions, and identifies areas of agreement and helps generate options for a mutually agreeable resolution to the dispute. In all cases, mediation provides an opportunity to explore a wide range of potential solutions and to address interests that may be outside the scope of the stated controversy or which could not be addressed by judicial action. A hallmark of mediation is its capacity to expand traditional settlement discussions and broaden resolution options, often by exploring litigant needs and interests that may be formally independent of the legal issues in controversy. NY R USDCTS&ED Civ Rule 83.8(a).

i. *Eligible cases.* Judges and Magistrate Judges may designate civil cases for inclusion in the mediation program, and when doing so shall prepare an order to that effect. Alternatively, and subject to the availability of qualified mediators, the parties may consent to participation in the mediation program by preparing and executing a stipulation signed by all parties to the action and so-ordered by the Court. NY R USDCTS&ED Civ Rule 83.8(b)(1).

ii. For more information on mediation, refer to NY R USDCTS&ED Civ Rule 83.8.

7. *Individual judge practices.* Refer to the Miscellaneous section of this document for information on individual judge practices on general requirements for documents.

## D. Documents

1. *Required documents*

   a. *Request for admissions.* Refer to the General Requirements section of this document for information on the request for admissions.

2. *Supplemental documents*

   a. *Document(s).* A request to admit the genuineness of a document must be accompanied by a copy of the document unless it is, or has been, otherwise furnished or made available for inspection and copying. FRCP 36(a)(2).

   b. *Certificate of service.* FRCP 5(d) requires that the person making service under FRCP 5 certify that service has been effected. FRCP 5(Advisory Committee Notes). Having such information on file may be useful for many purposes, including proof of service if an issue arises concerning the effectiveness of the service. FRCP 5(Advisory Committee Notes).

3. *Individual judge practices.* Refer to the Miscellaneous section of this document for information on individual judge practices on required documents.

## E. Format

1. *Form of documents.* The rules governing captions and other matters of form in pleadings apply to motions and other papers. FRCP 7(b)(2).

   a. *Paper.* Every pleading, written motion, and other paper must: be plainly written, typed, printed, or copied without erasures or interlineations which materially deface it. NY R USDCTS&ED Civ Rule 11.1(a)(1).

   b. *Typeface, margin, and spacing.* The typeface, margins, and spacing of all documents presented for filing must meet the following requirements:

      i. All text must be twelve (12) point type or larger, except for text in footnotes which may be ten (10) point type;

      ii. All documents must have at least one (1) inch margins on all sides;

      iii. All text must be double-spaced, except for headings, text in footnotes, or block quotations, which may be single-spaced. NY R USDCTS&ED Civ Rule 11.1(b).

   c. *Caption; Names of parties.* Every pleading must have a caption with the court's name, a title, a file number, and a FRCP 7(a) designation. The title of the complaint must name all the parties; the title of other pleadings, after naming the first party on each side, may refer generally to other parties. FRCP 10(a). Every pleading, written motion, and other paper must: bear the docket number and the initials of the District Judge and any Magistrate Judge before whom the action or proceeding is pending, NY R USDCTS&ED Civ Rule 11.1(a)(2).

   d. *Paragraphs; Separate statements.* A party must state its claims or defenses in numbered paragraphs, each limited as far as practicable to a single set of circumstances. A later pleading may refer by number to a paragraph in an earlier pleading. If doing so would promote clarity, each claim founded on a separate transaction or occurrence—and each defense other than a denial—must be stated in a separate count or defense. FRCP 10(b).

   e. *Adoption by reference; Exhibits.* A statement in a pleading may be adopted by reference elsewhere in the same pleading or in any other pleading or motion. A copy of a written instrument that is an exhibit to a pleading is a part of the pleading for all purposes. FRCP 10(c).

   f. *Acceptance by the clerk.* The clerk must not refuse to file a paper solely because it is not in the form prescribed by the Federal Rules of Civil Procedure or by a local rule or practice. FRCP 5(d)(4).

2. *Signing disclosures and discovery requests, responses, and objections.* FRCP 11 does not apply to disclosures and discovery requests, responses, objections, and motions under FRCP 26 through FRCP 37. FRCP 11(d).

   a. *Signature required.* Every disclosure under FRCP 26(a)(1) or FRCP 26(a)(3) and every discovery request, response, or objection must be signed by at least one attorney of record in the attorney's own name—or by the party personally, if unrepresented—and must state the signer's address, e-mail address, and telephone number. FRCP 26(g)(1). Every pleading, written motion, and other paper must: have the name of each person signing it clearly printed or typed directly below the signature. NY R USDCTS&ED Civ Rule 11.1(a)(3).

b. *Effect of signature.* By signing, an attorney or party certifies that to the best of the person's knowledge, information, and belief formed after a reasonable inquiry:

   i. With respect to a disclosure, it is complete and correct as of the time it is made; and

   ii. With respect to a discovery request, response, or objection, it is:

   • Consistent with the Federal Rules of Civil Procedure and warranted by existing law or by a nonfrivolous argument for extending, modifying, or reversing existing law, or for establishing new law;

   • Not interposed for any improper purpose, such as to harass, cause unnecessary delay, or needlessly increase the cost of litigation; and

   • Neither unreasonable nor unduly burdensome or expensive, considering the needs of the case, prior discovery in the case, the amount in controversy, and the importance of the issues at stake in the action. FRCP 26(g)(1).

c. *Failure to sign.* Other parties have no duty to act on an unsigned disclosure, request, response, or objection until it is signed, and the court must strike it unless a signature is promptly supplied after the omission is called to the attorney's or party's attention. FRCP 26(g)(2).

d. *Sanction for improper certification.* If a certification violates FRCP 26(g) without substantial justification, the court, on motion or on its own, must impose an appropriate sanction on the signer, the party on whose behalf the signer was acting, or both. The sanction may include an order to pay the reasonable expenses, including attorney's fees, caused by the violation. FRCP 26(g)(3). Refer to the United States District Court for the Eastern District of New York KeyRules Motion for Discovery Sanctions document for more information.

3. *Privacy protection for filings made with the court*

   a. *Redacted filings.* Unless the court orders otherwise, in an electronic or paper filing with the court that contains an individual's Social Security number, taxpayer-identification number, or birth date, the name of an individual known to be a minor, or a financial-account number, a party or nonparty making the filing may include only:

      i. The last four (4) digits of the Social Security number and taxpayer-identification number;

      ii. The year of the individual's birth;

      iii. The minor's initials; and

      iv. The last four (4) digits of the financial-account number. FRCP 5.2(a); NY R USDCTED Order 2004-09.

      v. In addition, exercise caution when filing documents that contain the following:

      • Personal identifying number, such as driver's license number;

      • Medical records, treatment and diagnosis;

      • Employment history;

      • Individual financial information; and

      • Proprietary or trade secret information. NY R USDCTED Order 2004-09.

   b. *Exemptions from the redaction requirement.* The redaction requirement does not apply to the following:

      i. A financial-account number that identifies the property allegedly subject to forfeiture in a forfeiture proceeding;

      ii. The record of an administrative or agency proceeding;

      iii. The official record of a state-court proceeding;

    iv.   The record of a court or tribunal, if that record was not subject to the redaction requirement when originally filed;

    v.   A filing covered by FRCP 5.2(c) or FRCP 5.2(d); and

    vi.   A pro se filing in an action brought under 28 U.S.C.A. § 2241, 28 U.S.C.A. § 2254, or 28 U.S.C.A. § 2255. FRCP 5.2(b).

c.   *Limitations on remote access to electronic files; Social Security appeals and immigration cases.* Unless the court orders otherwise, in an action for benefits under the Social Security Act, and in an action or proceeding relating to an order of removal, to relief from removal, or to immigration benefits or detention, access to an electronic file is authorized as follows:

    i.   The parties and their attorneys may have remote electronic access to any part of the case file, including the administrative record;

    ii.   Any other person may have electronic access to the full record at the courthouse, but may have remote electronic access only to:

- The docket maintained by the court; and
- An opinion, order, judgment, or other disposition of the court, but not any other part of the case file or the administrative record. FRCP 5.2(c).

d.   *Filings made under seal.* The court may order that a filing be made under seal without redaction. The court may later unseal the filing or order the person who made the filing to file a redacted version for the public record. FRCP 5.2(d).

e.   *Protective orders.* For good cause, the court may by order in a case:

    i.   Require redaction of additional information; or

    ii.   Limit or prohibit a nonparty's remote electronic access to a document filed with the court. FRCP 5.2(e).

f.   *Option for additional unredacted filing under seal.* A person making a redacted filing may also file an unredacted copy under seal. The court must retain the unredacted copy as part of the record. FRCP 5.2(f); NY R USDCTED Order 2004-09. The unredacted version of the document or the reference list shall be retained by the court as part of the record. The court may, however, still require the party to file a redacted copy for the public file. NY R USDCTED Order 2004-09.

g.   *Option for filing a reference list.* A filing that contains redacted information may be filed together with a reference list that identifies each item of redacted information and specifies an appropriate identifier that uniquely corresponds to each item listed. The list must be filed under seal and may be amended as of right. Any reference in the case to a listed identifier will be construed to refer to the corresponding item of information. FRCP 5.2(g); NY R USDCTED Order 2004-09. The unredacted version of the document or the reference list shall be retained by the court as part of the record. The court may, however, still require the party to file a redacted copy for the public file. NY R USDCTED Order 2004-09.

h.   *Responsibility for redaction.* The responsibility for redacting these personal identifiers rests solely with counsel and the parties. The Clerk will not review each pleading for compliance with NY R USDCTED Order 2004-09. NY R USDCTED Order 2004-09.

    i.   Counsel is strongly urged to share this notice with all clients so that an informed decision about the inclusion of certain materials may be made. If a redacted document is filed, it is the sole responsibility of counsel and the parties to be sure that all pleadings comply with the rules of this court requiring redaction of personal data identifiers. The clerk will not review each pleading for redaction. NY R USDCTED Order 2004-09.

i.   *Waiver of protection of identifiers.* A person waives the protection of FRCP 5.2(a) as to the person's own information by filing it without redaction and not under seal. FRCP 5.2(h).

4.   *Individual judge practices.* Refer to the Miscellaneous section of this document for information on individual judge practices on formatting documents.

# F.  Filing and Service Requirements

1.   *Filing requirements.* Any paper after the complaint that is required to be served—together with a

certificate of service—must be filed within a reasonable time after service. But disclosures under FRCP 26(a)(1) or FRCP 26(a)(2) and the following discovery requests and responses must not be filed until they are used in the proceeding or the court orders filing: depositions, interrogatories, requests for documents or tangible things or to permit entry onto land, and requests for admission. FRCP 5(d)(1). Refer to the United States District Court for the Eastern District of New York KeyRules pleading and motion documents for information on filing with the court.

2. *Service requirements.* [A request for an admission] must be served on the party from whom the admission is requested and, unless the court has otherwise ordered, a copy of the request must be served on every other party. FPP § 2258.

  a. *Service; When required*

    i. *In general.* Unless the Federal Rules of Civil Procedure provide otherwise, each of the following papers must be served on every party:

- An order stating that service is required;

- A pleading filed after the original complaint, unless the court orders otherwise under FRCP 5(c) because there are numerous defendants;

- A discovery paper required to be served on a party, unless the court orders otherwise;

- A written motion, except one that may be heard ex parte; and

- A written notice, appearance, demand, or offer of judgment, or any similar paper. FRCP 5(a)(1).

    ii. *If a party fails to appear.* No service is required on a party who is in default for failing to appear. But a pleading that asserts a new claim for relief against such a party must be served on that party under FRCP 4. FRCP 5(a)(2).

    iii. *Seizing property.* If an action is begun by seizing property and no person is or need be named as a defendant, any service required before the filing of an appearance, answer, or claim must be made on the person who had custody or possession of the property when it was seized. FRCP 5(a)(3).

  b. *Service; How made*

    i. *Serving an attorney.* If a party is represented by an attorney, service under FRCP 5 must be made on the attorney unless the court orders service on the party. FRCP 5(b)(1).

    ii. *Service in general.* A paper is served under FRCP 5 by:

- Handing it to the person;

- Leaving it: (1) at the person's office with a clerk or other person in charge or, if no one is in charge, in a conspicuous place in the office; or (2) if the person has no office or the office is closed, at the person's dwelling or usual place of abode with someone of suitable age and discretion who resides there;

- Mailing it to the person's last known address—in which event service is complete upon mailing;

- Leaving it with the court clerk if the person has no known address;

- Sending it by electronic means if the person consented in writing—in which event service is complete upon transmission, but is not effective if the serving party learns that it did not reach the person to be served; or

- Delivering it by any other means that the person consented to in writing—in which event service is complete when the person making service delivers it to the agency designated to make delivery. FRCP 5(b)(2).

    iii. *Service by overnight delivery.* Service upon an attorney may be made by overnight delivery service. "Overnight delivery service" means any delivery service which regularly accepts items for overnight delivery. Overnight delivery service shall be deemed service by mail for purposes of FRCP 5 and FRCP 6. NY R USDCTS&ED Civ Rule 5.3.

iv. *Service by electronic means.* Parties serving and filing papers shall follow the instructions regarding Electronic Case Filing (ECF) published on the website of each respective Court. A paper served and filed by electronic means in accordance with such instructions is, for purposes of FRCP 5, served and filed in compliance with the Local Civil Rules of the United States District Courts for the Southern and Eastern Districts of New York. NY R USDCTS&ED Civ Rule 5.2(a). Parties have an obligation to review the Court's actual order, decree, or judgment (on ECF), which controls, and should not rely on the description on the docket or in the ECF Notice of Electronic Filing (NEF). NY R USDCTS&ED Civ Rule 5.2(c).

v. *Using court facilities.* If a local rule so authorizes, a party may use the court's transmission facilities to make service under FRCP 5(b)(2)(E). FRCP 5(b)(3).

c. *Serving numerous defendants*

i. *In general.* If an action involves an unusually large number of defendants, the court may, on motion or on its own, order that:

- Defendants' pleadings and replies to them need not be served on other defendants;

- Any crossclaim, counterclaim, avoidance, or affirmative defense in those pleadings and replies to them will be treated as denied or avoided by all other parties; and

- Filing any such pleading and serving it on the plaintiff constitutes notice of the pleading to all parties. FRCP 5(c)(1).

ii. *Notifying parties.* A copy of every such order must be served on the parties as the court directs. FRCP 5(c)(2).

3. *Individual judge practices.* Refer to the Miscellaneous section of this document for information on individual judge practices on filing and serving documents.

## G. Hearings

1. There is no hearing contemplated in the federal statutes or rules for requests for admissions.

## H. Forms

### 1. Federal Request for Admissions Forms

a. Request; For admission of facts and genuineness of documents. AMJUR PP DEPOSITION § 674.

b. Plaintiff's request for admission. 3B FEDFORMS § 3650.

c. Plaintiff's request for admission; Another form. 3B FEDFORMS § 3651.

d. Plaintiff's request for admission; Statements in documents. 3B FEDFORMS § 3652.

e. Plaintiff's request for admission; Statements in documents; Another form. 3B FEDFORMS § 3653.

f. Plaintiff's request for admission; Specific facts. 3B FEDFORMS § 3654.

g. Plaintiff's request for admission; Specific facts; Another form. 3B FEDFORMS § 3655.

h. Plaintiff's request for admission; Specific documents and facts. 3B FEDFORMS § 3656.

i. Plaintiff's request for admission; Specific documents and facts; Another form. 3B FEDFORMS § 3657.

j. Plaintiff's request for admission; True copies, filing and operational effect of government documents. 3B FEDFORMS § 3658.

k. Plaintiff's request for additional admission. 3B FEDFORMS § 3659.

l. Defendant's request for admission of genuineness; Specific document. 3B FEDFORMS § 3660.

m. Defendant's request for admission of genuineness; Specific document; Another form. 3B FED-FORMS § 3661.

n. Defendant's request for admission of genuineness; Specific document; Another form. 3B FED-FORMS § 3662.

o. Defendant's request for admission; Truth of statement. 3B FEDFORMS § 3663.

p. Request for admissions under FRCP 36. FEDPROF § 23:535.

q. Request for admissions; General form. FEDPROF § 23:536.

r. Request for admissions; Action to collect royalties. FEDPROF § 23:537.

s. Request for admissions; Trademark action. FEDPROF § 23:538.

t. Request for admissions; Automobile negligence action. FEDPROF § 23:539.

u. Request for admissions; Motor vehicle action. FEDPROF § 23:540.

v. Request for admissions; Premises liability action. FEDPROF § 23:541.

w. Request for admissions; Products liability action. FEDPROF § 23:542.

x. Request for admissions; Medical malpractice action. FEDPROF § 23:543.

y. Request for admissions; Genuineness of documents. FEDPROF § 23:544.

z. Request for admissions; Wrongful death due to forklift accident. FEDPROF § 23:545.

## I. Applicable Rules

1. *Federal rules*

   a. Serving and filing pleadings and other papers. FRCP 5.

   b. Privacy protection for filings made with the court. FRCP 5.2.

   c. Computing and extending time; Time for motion papers. FRCP 6.

   d. Pleadings allowed; Form of motions and other papers. FRCP 7.

   e. Form of pleadings. FRCP 10.

   f. Signing pleadings, motions, and other papers; Representations to the court; Sanctions. FRCP 11.

   g. Duty to disclose; General provisions governing discovery. FRCP 26.

   h. Stipulations about discovery procedure. FRCP 29.

   i. Requests for admission. FRCP 36.

   j. Failure to make disclosures or to cooperate in discovery; Sanctions. FRCP 37.

2. *Local rules*

   a. Duty of attorneys in related cases. NY R USDCTS&ED Civ Rule 1.6.

   b. Electronic service and filing of documents. NY R USDCTS&ED Civ Rule 5.2.

   c. Service by overnight delivery. NY R USDCTS&ED Civ Rule 5.3.

   d. Computation of time. NY R USDCTS&ED Civ Rule 6.4.

   e. Form of pleadings, motions, and other papers. NY R USDCTS&ED Civ Rule 11.1.

   f. Assertion of claim of privilege. NY R USDCTS&ED Civ Rule 26.2.

   g. Uniform definitions in discovery requests. NY R USDCTS&ED Civ Rule 26.3.

   h. Cooperation among counsel in discovery. NY R USDCTS&ED Civ Rule 26.4.

   i. Form discovery requests. [NY R USDCTS&ED Civ Rule 26.5, as amended by NY ORDER 16-4212, effective September 26, 2016].

   j. Court-annexed arbitration (Eastern District only). NY R USDCTS&ED Civ Rule 83.7.

   k. Court-annexed mediation (Eastern District only). NY R USDCTS&ED Civ Rule 83.8.

   l. The August 2, 2004 amendment to the E-Government Act of 2002. NY R USDCTED Order 2004-09.

## J. Miscellaneous

**NOTE: Individual judges' rules may apply. For available judge-level information, refer to:**

DISTRICT JUDGE CAROL BAGLEY AMON: NY R USDCTED Amon-Practices.

DISTRICT JUDGE JOAN M. AZRACK: NY R USDCTED Azrack-Practices.

DISTRICT JUDGE JOSEPH F. BIANCO: NY R USDCTED Bianco-Practices.

DISTRICT JUDGE FREDERIC BLOCK: NY R USDCTED Block-Practices.

DISTRICT JUDGE MARGO K. BRODIE: NY R USDCTED Brodie-Practices.

DISTRICT JUDGE PAMELA K. CHEN: NY R USDCTED Chen-Practices.

DISTRICT JUDGE BRIAN M. COGAN: NY R USDCTED Cogan-Practices; NY R USDCTED Cogan-Pretrial.

DISTRICT JUDGE LaSHANN DeARCY HALL: NY R USDCTED DeArcy Hall-Practices.

DISTRICT JUDGE RAYMOND J. DEARIE: NY R USDCTED Dearie-Practices.

DISTRICT JUDGE ANN M. DONNELLY: NY R USDCTED Donnelly-Practices.

DISTRICT JUDGE SANDRA J. FEUERSTEIN: NY R USDCTED Feuerstein-Practices; NY R USDCTED Feuerstein-Pretrial.

DISTRICT JUDGE NICHOLAS G. GARAUIFIS: NY R USDCTED Garaufis-Practices; NY R USDCTED Garaufis-Pretrial.

DISTRICT JUDGE NINA GERSHON: NY R USDCTED Gershon-Practices.

DISTRICT JUDGE I. LEO GLASSER: NY R USDCTED Glasser-Practices; NY R USDCTED Glasser-Crim.

DISTRICT JUDGE DENIS R. HURLEY: NY R USDCTED Hurley-Practices; [NY R USDCTED Hurley-Pro Cooperation Info, as added by NY ORDER 16-4188, effective July 22, 2016]; [NY R USDCTED Hurley-Pro Cooperation Info Stay, as added by NY ORDER 16-4188, effective July 22, 2016].

DISTRICT JUDGE DORA L. IRIZARRY: NY R USDCTED Irizarry-Practices; NY R USDCTED Irizarry-Pretrial; NY R USDCTED Irizarry-Crim.

DISTRICT JUDGE STERLING JOHNSON, JR.: NY R USDCTED Johnson-Practices.

DISTRICT JUDGE EDWARD R. KORMAN: NY R USDCTED Korman-Practices; NY R USDCTED Korman-Pretrial.

DISTRICT JUDGE WILLIAM F. KUNTZ: NY R USDCTED Kuntz-Practices.

DISTRICT JUDGE KIYO A. MATSUMOTO: NY R USDCTED Matsumoto-Practices.

DISTRICT JUDGE ROSLYNN R. MAUSKOPF: NY R USDCTED Mauskopf-Practices; NY R USDCTED Mauskopf-Recusal.

DISTRICT JUDGE THOMAS C. PLATT: NY R USDCTED Platt-Practices.

DISTRICT JUDGE ALLYNE R. ROSS: NY R USDCTED Ross-Practices.

DISTRICT JUDGE JOANNA SEYBERT: NY R USDCTED Seybert-Practices.

DISTRICT JUDGE ARTHUR D. SPATT: NY R USDCTED Spatt-Practices.

DISTRICT JUDGE SANDRA L. TOWNES: NY R USDCTED Townes-Practices.

DISTRICT JUDGE ERIC N. VITALIANO: NY R USDCTED Vitaliano-Practices.

DISTRICT JUDGE JACK B. WEINSTEIN: NY R USDCTED Weinstein-Practices.

DISTRICT JUDGE LEONARD D. WEXLER: NY R USDCTED Wexler-Practices; NY R USDCTED Wexler-Rules.

MAGISTRATE JUDGE LOIS BLOOM: NY R USDCTED Bloom-Practices.

MAGISTRATE JUDGE GARY R. BROWN: NY R USDCTED Brown-Practices.

MAGISTRATE JUDGE MARILYN D. GO: NY R USDCTED Go-Practices.

MAGISTRATE JUDGE STEVEN M. GOLD: NY R USDCTED Gold-Practices.

MAGISTRATE JUDGE PEGGY KUO: NY R USDCTED Kuo-Practices; NY R USDCTED Kuo-Scheduling Order.

MAGISTRATE JUDGE ROBERT M. LEVY: NY R USDCTED Levy-Practices.

MAGISTRATE JUDGE ARLENE R. LINDSAY: NY R USDCTED Lindsay-Practices.

MAGISTRATE JUDGE STEVEN I. LOCKE: NY R USDCTED Locke-Practices.

MAGISTRATE JUDGE ROANNE L. MANN: NY R USDCTED Mann-Practices.

MAGISTRATE JUDGE JAMES ORENSTEIN: NY R USDCTED Jorenstein--Practices.

MAGISTRATE JUDGE VIKTOR V. POHORELSKY: NY R USDCTED Pohorelsky-Practices.

MAGISTRATE JUDGE CHERYL L. POLLAK: NY R USDCTED Pollak-Practices; NY R USDCTED Pollak-Pretrial.

MAGISTRATE JUDGE RAMON E. REYES, JR.: NY R USDCTED Reyes-Practices.

MAGISTRATE JUDGE VERA M. SCANLON: NY R USDCTED Scanlon-Practices.

MAGISTRATE JUDGE ANNE Y. SHIELDS: NY R USDCTED Shields-Practices.

MAGISTRATE JUDGE STEVEN L. TISCIONE: NY R USDCTED Tiscione-Practices.

MAGISTRATE JUDGE A. KATHLEEN TOMILINSON: NY R USDCTED Tomlinson-Practices.

# Requests, Notices and Applications
# Notice of Deposition

## Document Last Updated September 2016

**A. Checklist**

(I) ❑ Matters to be considered by deposing party for depositions by oral examination

   (a) ❑ Required documents

      (1) ❑ Notice of deposition

   (b) ❑ Supplemental documents

      (1) ❑ Subpoena

      (2) ❑ Subpoena duces tecum

      (3) ❑ Request for production of documents

      (4) ❑ Certificate of service

   (c) ❑ Timing

      (1) ❑ A party may, by oral questions, depose any person, including a party, without leave of court except as provided in FRCP 30(a)(2)

      (2) ❑ A party must obtain leave of court, and the court must grant leave to the extent consistent with FRCP 26(b)(1) and FRCP 26(b)(2):

         (i) ❑ If the parties have not stipulated to the deposition and: (1) the deposition would result in more than ten (10) depositions being taken under FRCP 30 or FRCP 31 by the plaintiffs, or by the defendants, or by the third-party defendants; (2) the deponent has already been deposed in the case; or (3) the party seeks to take the deposition before the time specified in FRCP 26(d), unless the party certifies in the notice, with supporting facts, that the deponent is expected to leave the United States and be unavailable for examination in this country after that time; or

         (ii) ❑ If the deponent is confined in prison

      (3) ❑ A party who wants to depose a person by oral questions must give reasonable written notice to every other party

(II) ❑ Matters to be considered by deposing party for depositions by written questions

   (a) ❑ Required documents

      (1) ❑ Notice of deposition

      (2) ❑ Written questions

(b) ❑ Supplemental documents

    (1) ❑ Subpoena

    (2) ❑ Certificate of service

(c) ❑ Timing

    (1) ❑ A party may, by written questions, depose any person, including a party, without leave of court except as provided in FRCP 31(a)(2)

    (2) ❑ A party must obtain leave of court, and the court must grant leave to the extent consistent with FRCP 26(b)(1) and FRCP 26(b)(2):

        (i) ❑ If the parties have not stipulated to the deposition and: (1) the deposition would result in more than ten (10) depositions being taken under FRCP 31 or FRCP 30 by the plaintiffs, or by the defendants, or by the third-party defendants; (2) the deponent has already been deposed in the case; or (3) the party seeks to take a deposition before the time specified in FRCP 26(d); or

        (ii) ❑ If the deponent is confined in prison

    (3) ❑ A party who wants to depose a person by written questions must serve them on every other party, with a notice

## B. Timing

1. *Depositions by oral examination*

    a. *Without leave.* A party may, by oral questions, depose any person, including a party, without leave of court except as provided in FRCP 30(a)(2). FRCP 30(a)(1).

    b. *With leave.* A party must obtain leave of court, and the court must grant leave to the extent consistent with FRCP 26(b)(1) and FRCP 26(b)(2):

        i. If the parties have not stipulated to the deposition and: (1) the deposition would result in more than ten (10) depositions being taken under FRCP 30 or FRCP 31 by the plaintiffs, or by the defendants, or by the third-party defendants; (2) the deponent has already been deposed in the case; or (3) the party seeks to take the deposition before the time specified in FRCP 26(d), unless the party certifies in the notice, with supporting facts, that the deponent is expected to leave the United States and be unavailable for examination in this country after that time; or

        ii. If the deponent is confined in prison. FRCP 30(a)(2).

    c. *Notice of deposition.* A party who wants to depose a person by oral questions must give reasonable written notice to every other party. FRCP 30(b)(1).

2. *Depositions by written questions*

    a. *Without leave.* A party may, by written questions, depose any person, including a party, without leave of court except as provided in FRCP 31(a)(2). FRCP 31(a)(1).

    b. *With leave.* A party must obtain leave of court, and the court must grant leave to the extent consistent with FRCP 26(b)(1) and FRCP 26(b)(2):

        i. If the parties have not stipulated to the deposition and: (1) the deposition would result in more than ten (10) depositions being taken under FRCP 31 or FRCP 30 by the plaintiffs, or by the defendants, or by the third-party defendants; (2) the deponent has already been deposed in the case; or (3) the party seeks to take a deposition before the time specified in FRCP 26(d); or

        ii. If the deponent is confined in prison. FRCP 31(a)(2).

    c. *Notice of deposition with written questions.* A party who wants to depose a person by written questions must serve them on every other party, with a notice. FRCP 31(a)(3). Refer to the General Requirements section of this document for the contents of the notice.

    d. *Questions from other parties.* Any questions to the deponent from other parties must be served on all parties as follows:

        i. *Cross-questions.* Cross-questions, within fourteen (14) days after being served with the notice and direct questions;

ii. *Redirect questions.* Redirect questions, within seven (7) days after being served with cross-questions; and

iii. *Recross-questions.* Recross-questions, within seven (7) days after being served with redirect questions. FRCP 31(a)(5).

iv. *Modification of timing requirements.* The court may, for good cause, extend or shorten these times. FRCP 31(a)(5).

3. *Timing of discovery, generally.* A party may not seek discovery from any source before the parties have conferred as required by FRCP 26(f), except in a proceeding exempted from initial disclosure under FRCP 26(a)(1)(B), or when authorized by the Federal Rules of Civil Procedure, by stipulation, or by court order. FRCP 26(d)(1).

4. *Computation of time*

a. *Computing time.* FRCP 6 applies in computing any time period specified in the Federal Rules of Civil Procedure, in any local rule or court order, or in any statute that does not specify a method of computing time. FRCP 6(a). In computing any period of time prescribed or allowed by the Local Civil Rules of the United States District Courts for the Southern and Eastern Districts of New York or the Local Admiralty and Maritime Rules, the provisions of FRCP 6 shall apply unless otherwise stated. NY R USDCTS&ED Civ Rule 6.4.

   i. *Period stated in days or a longer unit.* When the period is stated in days or a longer unit of time:

   • Exclude the day of the event that triggers the period;

   • Count every day, including intermediate Saturdays, Sundays, and legal holidays; and

   • Include the last day of the period, but if the last day is a Saturday, Sunday, or legal holiday, the period continues to run until the end of the next day that is not a Saturday, Sunday, or legal holiday. FRCP 6(a)(1). In the Local Civil Rules of the United States District Courts for the Southern and Eastern Districts of New York, as in the Federal Rules of Civil Procedure as amended effective December 1, 2009, Saturdays, Sundays, and legal holidays are no longer excluded in computing periods of time. If the last day of the period is a Saturday, Sunday, or legal holiday, the period continues to run until the end of the next day that is not a Saturday, Sunday, or legal holiday. NY R USDCTS&ED Civ Rule 6.4.

   ii. *Period stated in hours.* When the period is stated in hours:

   • Begin counting immediately on the occurrence of the event that triggers the period;

   • Count every hour, including hours during intermediate Saturdays, Sundays, and legal holidays; and

   • If the period would end on a Saturday, Sunday, or legal holiday, the period continues to run until the same time on the next day that is not a Saturday, Sunday, or legal holiday. FRCP 6(a)(2). In the Local Civil Rules of the United States District Courts for the Southern and Eastern Districts of New York, as in the Federal Rules of Civil Procedure as amended effective December 1, 2009, Saturdays, Sundays, and legal holidays are no longer excluded in computing periods of time. If the last day of the period is a Saturday, Sunday, or legal holiday, the period continues to run until the end of the next day that is not a Saturday, Sunday, or legal holiday. NY R USDCTS&ED Civ Rule 6.4.

   iii. *Inaccessibility of the clerk's office.* Unless the court orders otherwise, if the clerk's office is inaccessible:

   • On the last day for filing under FRCP 6(a)(1), then the time for filing is extended to the first accessible day that is not a Saturday, Sunday, or legal holiday; or

   • During the last hour for filing under FRCP 6(a)(2), then the time for filing is extended to the same time on the first accessible day that is not a Saturday, Sunday, or legal holiday. FRCP 6(a)(3).

   iv. *"Last day" defined.* Unless a different time is set by a statute, local rule, or court order, the last day ends:

   • For electronic filing, at midnight in the court's time zone; and

- For filing by other means, when the clerk's office is scheduled to close. FRCP 6(a)(4).

v. *"Next day" defined.* The "next day" is determined by continuing to count forward when the period is measured after an event and backward when measured before an event. FRCP 6(a)(5).

vi. *"Legal holiday" defined.* "Legal holiday" means:

- The day set aside by statute for observing New Year's Day, Martin Luther King Jr.'s Birthday, Washington's Birthday, Memorial Day, Independence Day, Labor Day, Columbus Day, Veterans' Day, Thanksgiving Day, or Christmas Day;

- Any day declared a holiday by the President or Congress; and

- For periods that are measured after an event, any other day declared a holiday by the state where the district court is located. FRCP 6(a)(6).

b. *Extending time*

i. *In general.* When an act may or must be done within a specified time, the court may, for good cause, extend the time:

- With or without motion or notice if the court acts, or if a request is made, before the original time or its extension expires; or

- On motion made after the time has expired if the party failed to act because of excusable neglect. FRCP 6(b)(1).

ii. *Exceptions.* A court must not extend the time to act under FRCP 50(b), FRCP 50(d), FRCP 52(b), FRCP 59(b), FRCP 59(d), FRCP 59(e), and FRCP 60(b). FRCP 6(b)(2).

iii. Refer to the United States District Court for the Eastern District of New York KeyRules Motion for Continuance/Extension of Time document for more information on extending time.

c. *Additional time after certain kinds of service.* When a party may or must act within a specified time after service and service is made under FRCP 5(b)(2)(C), FRCP 5(b)(2)(D), FRCP 5(b)(2)(E), or FRCP 5(b)(2)(F), three (3) days are added after the period would otherwise expire under FRCP 6(a). FRCP 6(d). Overnight delivery service shall be deemed service by mail for purposes of FRCP 5 and FRCP 6. NY R USDCTS&ED Civ Rule 5.3.

5. *Individual judge practices.* Refer to the Miscellaneous section of this document for information on individual judge practices on timing of documents.

## C. General Requirements

1. *General provisions governing discovery*

a. *Discovery scope and limits*

i. *Scope in general.* Unless otherwise limited by court order, the scope of discovery is as follows: Parties may obtain discovery regarding any nonprivileged matter that is relevant to any party's claim or defense and proportional to the needs of the case, considering the importance of the issues at stake in the action, the amount in controversy, the parties' relative access to relevant information, the parties' resources, the importance of the discovery in resolving the issues, and whether the burden or expense of the proposed discovery outweighs its likely benefit. Information within this scope of discovery need not be admissible in evidence to be discoverable. FRCP 26(b)(1).

ii. *Limitations on frequency and extent*

- *When permitted.* By order, the court may alter the limits in the Federal Rules of Civil Procedure on the number of depositions and interrogatories or on the length of depositions under FRCP 30. By order or local rule, the court may also limit the number of requests under FRCP 36. FRCP 26(b)(2)(A).

- *Specific limitations on electronically stored information.* A party need not provide discovery of electronically stored information from sources that the party identifies as not reasonably accessible because of undue burden or cost. On motion to compel discovery or for a protective order, the party from whom discovery is sought must show that the information is not reasonably accessible because of undue burden or cost. If that showing is made, the court may nonetheless order discovery from such sources if the requesting party shows good cause, considering the limitations of FRCP 26(b)(2)(C). The court may specify conditions for the discovery. FRCP 26(b)(2)(B).

- *When required.* On motion or on its own, the court must limit the frequency or extent of discovery otherwise allowed by the Federal Rules of Civil Procedure or by local rule if it determines that: (1) the discovery sought is unreasonably cumulative or duplicative, or can be obtained from some other source that is more convenient, less burdensome, or less expensive; (2) the party seeking discovery has had ample opportunity to obtain the information by discovery in the action; or (3) the proposed discovery is outside the scope permitted by FRCP 26(b)(1). FRCP 26(b)(2)(C).

iii. *Trial preparation; Materials*

- *Documents and tangible things.* Ordinarily, a party may not discover documents and tangible things that are prepared in anticipation of litigation or for trial by or for another party or its representative (including the other party's attorney, consultant, surety, indemnitor, insurer, or agent). But, subject to FRCP 26(b)(4), those materials may be discovered if: (1) they are otherwise discoverable under FRCP 26(b)(1); and (2) the party shows that it has substantial need for the materials to prepare its case and cannot, without undue hardship, obtain their substantial equivalent by other means. FRCP 26(b)(3)(A).

- *Protection against disclosure.* If the court orders discovery of those materials, it must protect against disclosure of the mental impressions, conclusions, opinions, or legal theories of a party's attorney or other representative concerning the litigation. FRCP 26(b)(3)(B).

- *Previous statement.* Any party or other person may, on request and without the required showing, obtain the person's own previous statement about the action or its subject matter. If the request is refused, the person may move for a court order, and FRCP 37(a)(5) applies to the award of expenses. A previous statement is either: (1) a written statement that the person has signed or otherwise adopted or approved; or (2) a contemporaneous stenographic, mechanical, electrical, or other recording—or a transcription of it—that recites substantially verbatim the person's oral statement. FRCP 26(b)(3)(C).

iv. *Trial preparation; Experts*

- *Deposition of an expert who may testify.* A party may depose any person who has been identified as an expert whose opinions may be presented at trial. If FRCP 26(a)(2)(B) requires a report from the expert, the deposition may be conducted only after the report is provided. FRCP 26(b)(4)(A).

- *Trial-preparation protection for draft reports or disclosures.* FRCP 26(b)(3)(A) and FRCP 26(b)(3)(B) protect drafts of any report or disclosure required under FRCP 26(a)(2), regardless of the form in which the draft is recorded. FRCP 26(b)(4)(B).

- *Trial-preparation protection for communications between a party's attorney and expert witnesses.* FRCP 26(b)(3)(A) and FRCP 26(b)(3)(B) protect communications between the party's attorney and any witness required to provide a report under FRCP 26(a)(2)(B), regardless of the form of the communications, except to the extent that the communications: (1) relate to compensation for the expert's study or testimony; (2) identify facts or data that the party's attorney provided and that the expert considered in forming the opinions to be expressed; or (3) identify assumptions that the party's attorney provided and that the expert relied on in forming the opinions to be expressed. FRCP 26(b)(4)(C).

- *Expert employed only for trial preparation.* Ordinarily, a party may not, by interrogatories or deposition, discover facts known or opinions held by an expert who has been retained or specially employed by another party in anticipation of litigation or to prepare for trial and who is not expected to be called as a witness at trial. But a party may do so only: (1) as provided in FRCP 35(b); or (2) on showing exceptional circumstances under which it is impracticable for the party to obtain facts or opinions on the same subject by other means. FRCP 26(b)(4)(D).

- *Payment.* Unless manifest injustice would result, the court must require that the party seeking discovery: (1) pay the expert a reasonable fee for time spent in responding to discovery under FRCP 26(b)(4)(A) or FRCP 26(b)(4)(D); and (2) for discovery FRCP 26(b)(4)(D), also pay the other party a fair portion of the fees and expenses it reasonably incurred in obtaining the expert's facts and opinions. FRCP 26(b)(4)(E).

v. *Claiming privilege or protecting trial-preparation materials*

- *Information withheld.* When a party withholds information otherwise discoverable by claiming that the information is privileged or subject to protection as trial-preparation material, the party must: (1) expressly make the claim; and (2) describe the nature of the documents, communications, or tangible things not produced or disclosed—and do so in a manner that, without revealing information itself privileged or protected, will enable other parties to assess the claim. FRCP 26(b)(5)(A). Unless otherwise agreed by the parties or directed by the Court, where a claim of privilege is asserted in objecting to any means of discovery or disclosure, including but not limited to a deposition, and an answer is not provided on the basis of such assertion, (1) the person asserting the privilege shall identify the nature of the privilege (including work product) which is being claimed and, if the privilege is governed by state law, indicate the state's privilege rule being invoked; and (2) the following information shall be provided in the objection, or (in the case of a deposition) in response to questions by the questioner, unless divulgence of such information would cause disclosure of the allegedly privileged information: (A) for documents: (i) the type of document, e.g., letter or memorandum; (ii) the general subject matter of the document; (iii) the date of the document; and (iv) the author of the document, the addressees of the document, and any other recipients, and, where not apparent, the relationship of the author, addressees, and recipients to each other; (B) for oral communications: (i) the name of the person making the communication and the names of persons present while the communication was made and, where not apparent, the relationship of the persons present to the person making the communication; (ii) the date and place of communication; and (iii) the general subject matter of the communication. NY R USDCTS&ED Civ Rule 26.2(a). Where a claim of privilege is asserted in response to discovery or disclosure other than a deposition, and information is not provided on the basis of such assertion, the information set forth in NY R USDCTS&ED Civ Rule 26.2(a) shall be furnished in writing at the time of the response to such discovery or disclosure, unless otherwise ordered by the Court. NY R USDCTS&ED Civ Rule 26.2(b).

- *Information produced.* If information produced in discovery is subject to a claim of privilege or of protection as trial-preparation material, the party making the claim may notify any party that received the information of the claim and the basis for it. After being notified, a party must promptly return, sequester, or destroy the specified information and any copies it has; must not use or disclose the information until the claim is resolved; must take reasonable steps to retrieve the information if the party disclosed it before being notified; and may promptly present the information to the court under seal for a determination of the claim. The producing party must preserve the information until the claim is resolved. FRCP 26(b)(5)(B).

- *Efficient means of providing information regarding claims of privilege.* Efficient means of providing information regarding claims of privilege are encouraged, and parties are encouraged to agree upon measures that further this end. For example, when asserting privilege on the same basis with respect to multiple documents, it is presumptively proper to provide the information required by NY R USDCTS&ED Civ Rule 26.2 by group or category. A party receiving a privilege log that groups documents or otherwise departs from a document-by-document or communication-by-communication listing may not object solely on that basis, but may object if the substantive information required by NY R USDCTS&ED Civ Rule 26.2 has not been provided in a comprehensible form. NY R USDCTS&ED Civ Rule 26.2(c).

b. *Protective orders.* A party or any person from whom discovery is sought may move for a protective order in the court where the action is pending—or as an alternative on matters relating to a deposition, in the court for the district where the deposition will be taken. FRCP 26(c)(1). Refer to the United States District Court for the Eastern District of New York KeyRules Motion for Protective Order document for more information.

c. *Sequence of discovery.* Unless the parties stipulate or the court orders otherwise for the parties' and witnesses' convenience and in the interests of justice: (1) methods of discovery may be used in any sequence; and (2) discovery by one party does not require any other party to delay its discovery. FRCP 26(d)(3).

d. *Uniform definitions in discovery requests.* The full text of the definitions and rules of construction set forth in NY R USDCTS&ED Civ Rule 26.3(c) and NY R USDCTS&ED Civ Rule 26.3(d) is deemed incorporated by reference into all discovery requests. No discovery request shall use broader definitions or rules of construction than those set forth in NY R USDCTS&ED Civ Rule 26.3(c) and NY R USDCTS&ED Civ Rule 26.3(d). NY R USDCTS&ED Civ Rule 26.3 shall not preclude (1) the definition of other terms specific to the particular litigation, (2) the use of abbreviations, or (3) a more narrow definition of a term defined in NY R USDCTS&ED Civ Rule 26.3(c). NY R USDCTS&ED Civ Rule 26.3(a). NY R USDCTS&ED Civ Rule 26.3 is not intended to broaden or narrow the scope of discovery permitted by the Federal Rules of Civil Procedure. NY R USDCTS&ED Civ Rule 26.3(b).

    i. *Definitions.* The following definitions apply to all discovery requests:

- *Communication.* The term "communication" means the transmittal of information (in the form of facts, ideas, inquiries or otherwise). NY R USDCTS&ED Civ Rule 26.3(c)(1).

- *Document.* The term "document" is defined to be synonymous in meaning and equal in scope to the usage of the term "documents or electronically stored information" in FRCP 34(a)(1)(A). A draft or non-identical copy is a separate document within the meaning of this term. NY R USDCTS&ED Civ Rule 26.3(c)(2).

- *Identify (with respect to persons).* When referring to a person, "to identify" means to give, to the extent known, the person's full name, present or last known address, and when referring to a natural person, additionally, the present or last known place of employment. Once a person has been identified in accordance with NY R USDCTS&ED Civ Rule 26.3(c)(3), only the name of that person need be listed in response to subsequent discovery requesting the identification of that person. NY R USDCTS&ED Civ Rule 26.3(c)(3).

- *Identify (with respect to documents).* When referring to documents, "to identify" means to give, to the extent known, the (1) type of document; (2) general subject matter; (3) date of the document; and (4) author(s), addressee(s) and recipient(s). In the alternative, the responding party may produce the documents, together with identifying information sufficient to satisfy FRCP 33(d). NY R USDCTS&ED Civ Rule 26.3(c)(4).

- *Parties.* The terms "plaintiff" and "defendant" as well as a party's full or abbreviated name or a pronoun referring to a party mean the party and, where applicable, its officers, directors, employees, partners, corporate parent, subsidiaries or affiliates. This definition is not intended to impose a discovery obligation on any person who is not a party to the litigation. NY R USDCTS&ED Civ Rule 26.3(c)(5).

- *Person.* The term "person" is defined as any natural person or any legal entity, including, without limitation, any business or governmental entity or association. NY R USDCTS&ED Civ Rule 26.3(c)(6).

- *Concerning.* The term "concerning" means relating to, referring to, describing, evidencing or constituting. NY R USDCTS&ED Civ Rule 26.3(c)(7).

    ii. *Rules of construction.* The following rules of construction apply to all discovery requests:

- *All/any/each.* The terms "all," "any," and "each" shall each be construed as encompassing any and all. NY R USDCTS&ED Civ Rule 26.3(d)(1).

- *And/or.* The connectives "and" and "or" shall be construed either disjunctively or conjunctively as necessary to bring within the scope of the discovery request all responses that might otherwise be construed to be outside of its scope. NY R USDCTS&ED Civ Rule 26.3(d)(2).

- *Number.* The use of the singular form of any word includes the plural and vice versa. NY R USDCTS&ED Civ Rule 26.3(d)(3).

e. *Cooperation among counsel in discovery.* Counsel are expected to cooperate with each other, consistent with the interests of their clients, in all phases of the discovery process and to be courteous in their dealings with each other, including in matters relating to scheduling and timing of various discovery procedures. NY R USDCTS&ED Civ Rule 26.4(a).

  i. Discovery requests shall be read reasonably in the recognition that the attorney serving them generally does not have the information being sought and the attorney receiving them generally does have such information or can obtain it from the client. NY R USDCTS&ED Civ Rule 26.4(b).

f. *Standard discovery in prisoner pro se actions.* For information on discovery in prisoner pro se actions, refer to NY R USDCTS&ED Civ Rule 33.2.

2. *Persons before whom depositions may be taken*

a. *Within the United States.* Within the United States or a territory or insular possession subject to United States jurisdiction, a deposition must be taken before: (1) an officer authorized to administer oaths either by federal law or by the law in the place of examination; or (2) a person appointed by the court where the action is pending to administer oaths and take testimony. FRCP 28(a)(1).

  i. *Definition of "officer".* The term "officer" in FRCP 30, FRCP 31, and FRCP 32 includes a person appointed by the court under FRCP 28 or designated by the parties under FRCP 29(a). FRCP 28(a)(2).

b. *In a foreign country.* A deposition may be taken in a foreign country: (1) under an applicable treaty or convention; (2) under a letter of request, whether or not captioned a "letter rogatory"; (3) on notice, before a person authorized to administer oaths either by federal law or by the law in the place of examination; or (4) before a person commissioned by the court to administer any necessary oath and take testimony. FRCP 28(b)(1).

  i. *Issuing a letter of request or a commission.* A letter of request, a commission, or both may be issued: (1) on appropriate terms after an application and notice of it; and (2) without a showing that taking the deposition in another manner is impracticable or inconvenient. FRCP 28(b)(2).

  ii. *Form of a request, notice, or commission.* When a letter of request or any other device is used according to a treaty or convention, it must be captioned in the form prescribed by that treaty or convention. A letter of request may be addressed "To the Appropriate Authority in [name of country]." A deposition notice or a commission must designate by name or descriptive title the person before whom the deposition is to be taken. FRCP 28(b)(3).

  iii. *Letter of request; Admitting evidence.* Evidence obtained in response to a letter of request need not be excluded merely because it is not a verbatim transcript, because the testimony was not taken under oath, or because of any similar departure from the requirements for depositions taken within the United States. FRCP 28(b)(4).

c. *Disqualification.* A deposition must not be taken before a person who is any party's relative, employee, or attorney; who is related to or employed by any party's attorney; or who is financially interested in the action. FRCP 28(c).

3. *Depositions by oral examination*

a. *Notice of the deposition.* A party who wants to depose a person by oral questions must give reasonable written notice to every other party. The notice must state the time and place of the deposition and, if known, the deponent's name and address. If the name is unknown, the notice must provide a general description sufficient to identify the person or the particular class or group to which the person belongs. FRCP 30(b)(1).

  i. *Notice or subpoena directed to an organization.* In its notice or subpoena, a party may name as the deponent a public or private corporation, a partnership, an association, a governmental agency, or other entity and must describe with reasonable particularity the matters for examination. The named organization must then designate one or more officers, directors, or managing agents, or designate other persons who consent to testify on its behalf; and it may set out the matters on which each person designated will testify. A subpoena must advise a nonparty organization of its duty to make this designation. The persons designated must testify about information known or reasonably available to the organization. FRCP 30(b)(6) does not preclude a deposition by any other procedure allowed by the Federal Rules of Civil Procedure. FRCP 30(b)(6).

b. *Persons attending depositions.* A person who is a party in the action may attend the deposition of a party or witness. A witness or potential witness in the action may attend the deposition of a party or witness unless otherwise ordered by the Court. NY R USDCTS&ED Civ Rule 30.3.

c. *Counsel fees on taking depositions more than 100 miles from courthouse.* When a deposition upon oral examination is to be taken at a place more than one hundred (100) miles from the courthouse, any party may request the Court to issue an order providing that prior to the examination, another party shall pay the expense (including a reasonable counsel fee) of the attendance of one attorney for each other party at the place where the deposition is to be taken. The amounts so paid, unless otherwise directed by the Court, may be taxed as a cost at the conclusion of the action or proceeding. NY R USDCTS&ED Civ Rule 30.1.

d. *Method of recording*

    i. *Method stated in the notice.* The party who notices the deposition must state in the notice the method for recording the testimony. Unless the court orders otherwise, testimony may be recorded by audio, audiovisual, or stenographic means. The noticing party bears the recording costs. Any party may arrange to transcribe a deposition. FRCP 30(b)(3)(A).

    ii. *Additional method.* With prior notice to the deponent and other parties, any party may designate another method for recording the testimony in addition to that specified in the original notice. That party bears the expense of the additional record or transcript unless the court orders otherwise. FRCP 30(b)(3)(B).

e. *By remote means.* The parties may stipulate—or the court may on motion order—that a deposition be taken by telephone or other remote means. For the purpose of FRCP 30 and FRCP 28(a), FRCP 37(a)(2), and FRCP 37(b)(1), the deposition takes place where the deponent answers the questions. FRCP 30(b)(4).

    i. *Telephonic and other remote depositions.* The motion of a party to take the deposition of an adverse party by telephone or other remote means will presumptively be granted. Where the opposing party is a corporation, the term "adverse party" means an officer, director, managing agent or corporate designee pursuant to FRCP 30(b)(6). NY R USDCTS&ED Civ Rule 30.2.

f. *Officer's duties*

    i. *Before the deposition.* Unless the parties stipulate otherwise, a deposition must be conducted before an officer appointed or designated under FRCP 28. The officer must begin the deposition with an on-the-record statement that includes: (1) the officer's name and business address; (2) the date, time, and place of the deposition; (3) the deponent's name; (4) the officer's administration of the oath or affirmation to the deponent; and (5) the identity of all persons present. FRCP 30(b)(5)(A).

    ii. *Conducting the deposition; Avoiding distortion.* If the deposition is recorded non-stenographically, the officer must repeat the items in FRCP 30(b)(5)(A)(i) through FRCP 30(b)(5)(A)(iii) at the beginning of each unit of the recording medium. The deponent's and attorneys' appearance or demeanor must not be distorted through recording techniques. FRCP 30(b)(5)(B).

    iii. *After the deposition.* At the end of a deposition, the officer must state on the record that the deposition is complete and must set out any stipulations made by the attorneys about custody of the transcript or recording and of the exhibits, or about any other pertinent matters. FRCP 30(b)(5)(C).

g. *Examination and cross-examination.* The examination and cross-examination of a deponent proceed as they would at trial under the Federal Rules of Evidence, except FRE 103 and FRE 615. FRCP 30(c)(1).

    i. *Record of the examination.* After putting the deponent under oath or affirmation, the officer must record the testimony by the method designated under FRCP 30(b)(3)(A). The testimony must be recorded by the officer personally or by a person acting in the presence and under the direction of the officer. FRCP 30(c)(1).

    ii. *Objections.* An objection at the time of the examination—whether to evidence, to a party's conduct, to the officer's qualifications, to the manner of taking the deposition, or to any other aspect of the deposition—must be noted on the record, but the examination still proceeds; the testimony is taken subject to any objection. An objection must be stated concisely in a nonargumentative and nonsuggestive manner. A person may instruct a deponent not to answer only when necessary to preserve a privilege, to enforce a limitation ordered by the court, or to present a motion under FRCP 30(d)(3). FRCP 30(c)(2).

    iii. *Disputes arising during depositions.* Where the attorneys for the affected parties or a non-party witness cannot agree on a resolution of a discovery dispute that arises during a deposition, they shall, to the extent practicable, notify the Court by telephone and seek a ruling while the deposition is in progress. If a prompt ruling cannot be obtained, and the dispute involves an instruction to the witness not to answer a question, the instruction not to answer may stand and the deposition shall continue until a ruling is obtained pursuant to the procedure set forth in NY R USDCTS&ED Civ Rule 37.3(c). NY R USDCTS&ED Civ Rule 37.3(b). For more information, refer to NY R USDCTS&ED Civ Rule 37.3.

    iv. *Participating through written questions.* Instead of participating in the oral examination, a party may serve written questions in a sealed envelope on the party noticing the deposition, who must deliver them to the officer. The officer must ask the deponent those questions and record the answers verbatim. FRCP 30(c)(3).

    v. *Conferences between deponent and defending attorney.* An attorney for a deponent shall not initiate a private conference with the deponent while a deposition question is pending, except for the purpose of determining whether a privilege should be asserted. NY R USDCTS&ED Civ Rule 30.4.

h. *Duration.* Unless otherwise stipulated or ordered by the court, a deposition is limited to one (1) day of seven (7) hours. The court must allow additional time consistent with FRCP 26(b)(1) and FRCP 26(b)(2) if needed to fairly examine the deponent or if the deponent, another person, or any other circumstance impedes or delays the examination. FRCP 30(d)(1).

i. *Sanction.* The court may impose an appropriate sanction—including the reasonable expenses and attorney's fees incurred by any party—on a person who impedes, delays, or frustrates the fair examination of the deponent. FRCP 30(d)(2). Refer to the United States District Court for the Eastern District of New York KeyRules Motion for Discovery Sanctions document for more information on sanctions.

j. *Motion to terminate or limit.* At any time during a deposition, the deponent or a party may move to terminate or limit it on the ground that it is being conducted in bad faith or in a manner that unreasonably annoys, embarrasses, or oppresses the deponent or party. The motion may be filed in the court where the action is pending or the deposition is being taken. If the objecting deponent or party so demands, the deposition must be suspended for the time necessary to obtain an order. FRCP 30(d)(3)(A).

    i. *Order.* The court may order that the deposition be terminated or may limit its scope and manner as provided in FRCP 26(c). If terminated, the deposition may be resumed only by order of the court where the action is pending. FRCP 30(d)(3)(B).

    ii. *Award of expenses.* FRCP 37(a)(5) applies to the award of expenses. FRCP 30(d)(3)(C). Refer to the United States District Court for the Eastern District of New York KeyRules Motion for Discovery Sanctions document for more information on sanctions.

k. *Review by the witness; Statement of changes.* On request by the deponent or a party before the deposition is completed, the deponent must be allowed thirty (30) days after being notified by the officer that the transcript or recording is available in which: (1) to review the transcript or recording; and (2) if there are changes in form or substance, to sign a statement listing the changes and the reasons for making them. FRCP 30(e)(1).

   i. *Changes indicated in the officer's certificate.* The officer must note in the certificate prescribed by FRCP 30(f)(1) whether a review was requested and, if so, must attach any changes the deponent makes during the thirty (30) day period. FRCP 30(e)(2).

l. *Certification and delivery.* The officer must certify in writing that the witness was duly sworn and that the deposition accurately records the witness's testimony. The certificate must accompany the record of the deposition. Unless the court orders otherwise, the officer must seal the deposition in an envelope or package bearing the title of the action and marked "Deposition of [witness's name]" and must promptly send it to the attorney who arranged for the transcript or recording. The attorney must store it under conditions that will protect it against loss, destruction, tampering, or deterioration. FRCP 30(f)(1).

m. *Documents and tangible things.* Documents and tangible things produced for inspection during a deposition must, on a party's request, be marked for identification and attached to the deposition. Any party may inspect and copy them. But if the person who produced them wants to keep the originals, the person may: (1) offer copies to be marked, attached to the deposition, and then used as originals—after giving all parties a fair opportunity to verify the copies by comparing them with the originals; or (2) give all parties a fair opportunity to inspect and copy the originals after they are marked—in which event the originals may be used as if attached to the deposition. FRCP 30(f)(2)(A).

   i. *Order regarding the originals.* Any party may move for an order that the originals be attached to the deposition pending final disposition of the case. FRCP 30(f)(2)(B).

n. *Copies of the transcript or recording.* Unless otherwise stipulated or ordered by the court, the officer must retain the stenographic notes of a deposition taken stenographically or a copy of the recording of a deposition taken by another method. When paid reasonable charges, the officer must furnish a copy of the transcript or recording to any party or the deponent. FRCP 30(f)(3).

o. *Failure to attend a deposition or serve a subpoena; Expenses.* A party who, expecting a deposition to be taken, attends in person or by an attorney may recover reasonable expenses for attending, including attorney's fees, if the noticing party failed to: (1) attend and proceed with the deposition; or (2) serve a subpoena on a nonparty deponent, who consequently did not attend. FRCP 30(g). Refer to the United States District Court for the Eastern District of New York KeyRules Motion for Discovery Sanctions document for more information on sanctions.

4. *Depositions by written questions*

   a. *Notice of deposition.* A party who wants to depose a person by written questions must serve them on every other party, with a notice stating, if known, the deponent's name and address. If the name is unknown, the notice must provide a general description sufficient to identify the person or the particular class or group to which the person belongs. The notice must also state the name or descriptive title and the address of the officer before whom the deposition will be taken. FRCP 31(a)(3).

   b. *Questions directed to an organization.* A public or private corporation, a partnership, an association, or a governmental agency may be deposed by written questions in accordance with FRCP 30(b)(6). FRCP 31(a)(4).

   c. *Delivery to the officer; Officer's duties.* The party who noticed the deposition must deliver to the officer a copy of all the questions served and of the notice. The officer must promptly proceed in the manner provided in FRCP 30(c), FRCP 30(e), and FRCP 30(f) to:

      i. Take the deponent's testimony in response to the questions;

      ii. Prepare and certify the deposition; and

      iii. Send it to the party, attaching a copy of the questions and of the notice. FRCP 31(b).

d.  *Notice of completion.* The party who noticed the deposition must notify all other parties when it is completed. FRCP 31(c)(1).

5.  *Depositions to perpetuate testimony.* For information on depositions to perpetuate testimony, refer to FRCP 27.

6.  *Stipulations about discovery procedure.* Unless the court orders otherwise, the parties may stipulate that: (1) a deposition may be taken before any person, at any time or place, on any notice, and in the manner specified—in which event it may be used in the same way as any other deposition; and (2) other procedures governing or limiting discovery be modified—but a stipulation extending the time for any form of discovery must have court approval if it would interfere with the time set for completing discovery, for hearing a motion, or for trial. FRCP 29.

7.  *Related cases.* It shall be the continuing duty of each attorney appearing in any civil or criminal case to bring promptly to the attention of the Court all facts which said attorney believes are relevant to a determination that said case and one or more pending civil or criminal cases should be heard by the same Judge, in order to avoid unnecessary duplication of judicial effort. As soon as the attorney becomes aware of such relationship, said attorney shall notify the Judges to whom the cases have been assigned. NY R USDCTS&ED Civ Rule 1.6(a). If counsel fails to comply with NY R USDCTS&ED Civ Rule 1.6(a), the Court may assess reasonable costs directly against counsel whose action has obstructed the effective administration of the Court's business. NY R USDCTS&ED Civ Rule 1.6(b).

8.  *Alternative dispute resolution (ADR)*

    a.  *Court-annexed arbitration*

        i.   *Civil cases eligible for compulsory arbitration.* The Clerk of Court shall, as to all cases filed after January 1, 1986, designate and process for compulsory arbitration all civil cases (excluding Social Security cases, tax matters, prisoners' civil rights cases and any action based on an alleged violation of a right secured by the Constitution of the United States or if jurisdiction is based in whole or in part on 28 U.S.C.A. § 1343) wherein money damages only are being sought in an amount not in excess of one hundred fifty thousand dollars ($150,000) exclusive of interest and costs. NY R USDCTS&ED Civ Rule 83.7(d)(1).

            • The parties may by written stipulation agree that the Clerk of Court shall designate and process for court-annexed arbitration any civil case that is not subject to compulsory arbitration in NY R USDCTS&ED Civ Rule 83.7. NY R USDCTS&ED Civ Rule 83.7(d)(2).

            • For purposes of NY R USDCTS&ED Civ Rule 83.7 only, in all civil cases damages shall be presumed to be not in excess of one hundred fifty thousand dollars ($150,000) exclusive of interest and costs, unless: (1) counsel for plaintiff, at the time of filing the complaint, or in the event of the removal of a case from state court or transfer of a case from another district to this Court, within thirty (30) days of the docketing of the case in this district, files a certification with the Court that the damages sought exceed one hundred fifty thousand dollars ($150,000), exclusive of interest and costs; or (2) counsel for a defendant, at the time of filing a counterclaim or cross-claim files a certification with the court that the damages sought by the counter-claim or cross-claim exceed one hundred fifty thousand dollars ($150,000) exclusive of interest and costs. NY R USDCTS&ED Civ Rule 83.7(d)(3).

        ii.  *Exemption from arbitration.* The Court shall, sua sponte, or on motion of a party, exempt any case from arbitration in which the objectives of arbitration would not be realized (1) because the case involves complex or novel issues, (2) because legal issues predominate over factual issues, or (3) for other good cause. NY R USDCTS&ED Civ Rule 83.7(e)(2). For information on applying for an exemption, refer to NY R USDCTS&ED Civ Rule 83.7

        iii. *Referral to arbitration.* Cases not originally designated as eligible for compulsory arbitration, but which in the discretion of the assigned Judge, are later found to qualify, may be referred to arbitration. A U.S. District Judge or a U.S. Magistrate Judge, in cases that exceed the arbitration ceiling of one hundred fifty thousand dollars ($150,000) exclusive of interest and costs, in their discretion, may suggest that the parties should consider arbitration. If the parties are agreeable, an appropriate consent form signed by all parties or their representatives may be entered and filed in the case prior to scheduling an arbitration hearing. NY R USDCTS&ED Civ Rule 83.7(e)(3).

    iv. For more information on arbitration, refer to NY R USDCTS&ED Civ Rule 83.7.

  b. *Court-annexed mediation.* Mediation is a process in which parties and counsel agree to meet with a neutral mediator trained to assist them in settling disputes. The mediator improves communication across party lines, helps parties articulate their interests and understand those of the other party, probes the strengths and weaknesses of each party's legal positions, and identifies areas of agreement and helps generate options for a mutually agreeable resolution to the dispute. In all cases, mediation provides an opportunity to explore a wide range of potential solutions and to address interests that may be outside the scope of the stated controversy or which could not be addressed by judicial action. A hallmark of mediation is its capacity to expand traditional settlement discussions and broaden resolution options, often by exploring litigant needs and interests that may be formally independent of the legal issues in controversy. NY R USDCTS&ED Civ Rule 83.8(a).

    i. *Eligible cases.* Judges and Magistrate Judges may designate civil cases for inclusion in the mediation program, and when doing so shall prepare an order to that effect. Alternatively, and subject to the availability of qualified mediators, the parties may consent to participation in the mediation program by preparing and executing a stipulation signed by all parties to the action and so-ordered by the Court. NY R USDCTS&ED Civ Rule 83.8(b)(1).

    ii. For more information on mediation, refer to NY R USDCTS&ED Civ Rule 83.8.

9. *Individual judge practices.* Refer to the Miscellaneous section of this document for information on individual judge practices on general requirements for documents.

## D. Documents

1. *Depositions by oral examination*

  a. *Required documents*

    i. *Notice of deposition.* Refer to the General Requirements section of this document for the form and contents of the notice of deposition.

  b. *Supplemental documents*

    i. *Subpoena.* The deponent's attendance may be compelled by subpoena under FRCP 45. FRCP 30(a)(1). For more information on subpoenas, refer to FRCP 45.

    ii. *Subpoena duces tecum.* If a subpoena duces tecum is to be served on the deponent, the materials designated for production, as set out in the subpoena, must be listed in the notice or in an attachment. FRCP 30(b)(2). For more information on subpoenas duces tecum, refer to FRCP 45.

    iii. *Request for production of documents.* The notice to a party deponent may be accompanied by a request under FRCP 34 to produce documents and tangible things at the deposition. FRCP 30(b)(2). Refer to the United States District Court for the Eastern District of New York KeyRules Request for Production of Documents document for more information.

    iv. *Certificate of service.* FRCP 5(d) requires that the person making service under FRCP 5 certify that service has been effected. FRCP 5(Advisory Committee Notes). Having such information on file may be useful for many purposes, including proof of service if an issue arises concerning the effectiveness of the service. FRCP 5(Advisory Committee Notes).

2. *Depositions by written questions*

  a. *Required documents*

    i. *Notice of deposition.* Refer to the General Requirements section of this document for the form and contents of the notice of deposition.

    ii. *Written questions.* A party who wants to depose a person by written questions must serve them on every other party, with a notice. FRCP 31(a)(3).

    b.   *Supplemental documents*

        i.   *Subpoena.* The deponent's attendance may be compelled by subpoena under FRCP 45. FRCP 31(a)(1). For more information on subpoenas, refer to FRCP 45.

        ii.   *Certificate of service.* FRCP 5(d) requires that the person making service under FRCP 5 certify that service has been effected. FRCP 5(Advisory Committee Notes). Having such information on file may be useful for many purposes, including proof of service if an issue arises concerning the effectiveness of the service. FRCP 5(Advisory Committee Notes).

  3.  *Individual judge practices.* Refer to the Miscellaneous section of this document for information on individual judge practices on required documents.

## E.  Format

  1.  *Form of documents.* The rules governing captions and other matters of form in pleadings apply to motions and other papers. FRCP 7(b)(2).

    a.   *Paper.* Every pleading, written motion, and other paper must: be plainly written, typed, printed, or copied without erasures or interlineations which materially deface it. NY R USDCTS&ED Civ Rule 11.1(a)(1).

    b.   *Typeface, margin, and spacing.* The typeface, margins, and spacing of all documents presented for filing must meet the following requirements:

        i.   All text must be twelve (12) point type or larger, except for text in footnotes which may be ten (10) point type;

        ii.   All documents must have at least one (1) inch margins on all sides;

        iii.   All text must be double-spaced, except for headings, text in footnotes, or block quotations, which may be single-spaced. NY R USDCTS&ED Civ Rule 11.1(b).

    c.   *Caption; Names of parties.* Every pleading must have a caption with the court's name, a title, a file number, and a FRCP 7(a) designation. The title of the complaint must name all the parties; the title of other pleadings, after naming the first party on each side, may refer generally to other parties. FRCP 10(a). Every pleading, written motion, and other paper must: bear the docket number and the initials of the District Judge and any Magistrate Judge before whom the action or proceeding is pending, NY R USDCTS&ED Civ Rule 11.1(a)(2).

    d.   *Paragraphs; Separate statements.* A party must state its claims or defenses in numbered paragraphs, each limited as far as practicable to a single set of circumstances. A later pleading may refer by number to a paragraph in an earlier pleading. If doing so would promote clarity, each claim founded on a separate transaction or occurrence—and each defense other than a denial—must be stated in a separate count or defense. FRCP 10(b).

    e.   *Adoption by reference; Exhibits.* A statement in a pleading may be adopted by reference elsewhere in the same pleading or in any other pleading or motion. A copy of a written instrument that is an exhibit to a pleading is a part of the pleading for all purposes. FRCP 10(c).

    f.   *Acceptance by the clerk.* The clerk must not refuse to file a paper solely because it is not in the form prescribed by the Federal Rules of Civil Procedure or by a local rule or practice. FRCP 5(d)(4).

  2.  *Signing disclosures and discovery requests, responses, and objections.* FRCP 11 does not apply to disclosures and discovery requests, responses, objections, and motions under FRCP 26 through FRCP 37. FRCP 11(d).

    a.   *Signature required.* Every disclosure under FRCP 26(a)(1) or FRCP 26(a)(3) and every discovery request, response, or objection must be signed by at least one attorney of record in the attorney's own name—or by the party personally, if unrepresented—and must state the signer's address, e-mail address, and telephone number. FRCP 26(g)(1). Every pleading, written motion, and other paper must: have the name of each person signing it clearly printed or typed directly below the signature. NY R USDCTS&ED Civ Rule 11.1(a)(3).

    b.   *Effect of signature.* By signing, an attorney or party certifies that to the best of the person's knowledge, information, and belief formed after a reasonable inquiry:

        i.   With respect to a disclosure, it is complete and correct as of the time it is made; and

    ii.    With respect to a discovery request, response, or objection, it is:

- Consistent with the Federal Rules of Civil Procedure and warranted by existing law or by a nonfrivolous argument for extending, modifying, or reversing existing law, or for establishing new law;

- Not interposed for any improper purpose, such as to harass, cause unnecessary delay, or needlessly increase the cost of litigation; and

- Neither unreasonable nor unduly burdensome or expensive, considering the needs of the case, prior discovery in the case, the amount in controversy, and the importance of the issues at stake in the action. FRCP 26(g)(1).

    c.    *Failure to sign.* Other parties have no duty to act on an unsigned disclosure, request, response, or objection until it is signed, and the court must strike it unless a signature is promptly supplied after the omission is called to the attorney's or party's attention. FRCP 26(g)(2).

    d.    *Sanction for improper certification.* If a certification violates FRCP 26(g) without substantial justification, the court, on motion or on its own, must impose an appropriate sanction on the signer, the party on whose behalf the signer was acting, or both. The sanction may include an order to pay the reasonable expenses, including attorney's fees, caused by the violation. FRCP 26(g)(3). Refer to the United States District Court for the Eastern District of New York KeyRules Motion for Discovery Sanctions document for more information.

3.   *Privacy protection for filings made with the court*

    a.    *Redacted filings.* Unless the court orders otherwise, in an electronic or paper filing with the court that contains an individual's Social Security number, taxpayer-identification number, or birth date, the name of an individual known to be a minor, or a financial-account number, a party or nonparty making the filing may include only:

    i.    The last four (4) digits of the Social Security number and taxpayer-identification number;

    ii.    The year of the individual's birth;

    iii.    The minor's initials; and

    iv.    The last four (4) digits of the financial-account number. FRCP 5.2(a); NY R USDCTED Order 2004-09.

    v.    In addition, exercise caution when filing documents that contain the following:

- Personal identifying number, such as driver's license number;

- Medical records, treatment and diagnosis;

- Employment history;

- Individual financial information; and

- Proprietary or trade secret information. NY R USDCTED Order 2004-09.

    b.    *Exemptions from the redaction requirement.* The redaction requirement does not apply to the following:

    i.    A financial-account number that identifies the property allegedly subject to forfeiture in a forfeiture proceeding;

    ii.    The record of an administrative or agency proceeding;

    iii.    The official record of a state-court proceeding;

    iv.    The record of a court or tribunal, if that record was not subject to the redaction requirement when originally filed;

    v.    A filing covered by FRCP 5.2(c) or FRCP 5.2(d); and

    vi.    A pro se filing in an action brought under 28 U.S.C.A. § 2241, 28 U.S.C.A. § 2254, or 28 U.S.C.A. § 2255. FRCP 5.2(b).

    c.    *Limitations on remote access to electronic files; Social Security appeals and immigration cases.*

Unless the court orders otherwise, in an action for benefits under the Social Security Act, and in an action or proceeding relating to an order of removal, to relief from removal, or to immigration benefits or detention, access to an electronic file is authorized as follows:

i.   The parties and their attorneys may have remote electronic access to any part of the case file, including the administrative record;

ii.  Any other person may have electronic access to the full record at the courthouse, but may have remote electronic access only to:

- The docket maintained by the court; and

- An opinion, order, judgment, or other disposition of the court, but not any other part of the case file or the administrative record. FRCP 5.2(c).

d.   *Filings made under seal.* The court may order that a filing be made under seal without redaction. The court may later unseal the filing or order the person who made the filing to file a redacted version for the public record. FRCP 5.2(d).

e.   *Protective orders.* For good cause, the court may by order in a case:

i.   Require redaction of additional information; or

ii.  Limit or prohibit a nonparty's remote electronic access to a document filed with the court. FRCP 5.2(e).

f.   *Option for additional unredacted filing under seal.* A person making a redacted filing may also file an unredacted copy under seal. The court must retain the unredacted copy as part of the record. FRCP 5.2(f); NY R USDCTED Order 2004-09. The unredacted version of the document or the reference list shall be retained by the court as part of the record. The court may, however, still require the party to file a redacted copy for the public file. NY R USDCTED Order 2004-09.

g.   *Option for filing a reference list.* A filing that contains redacted information may be filed together with a reference list that identifies each item of redacted information and specifies an appropriate identifier that uniquely corresponds to each item listed. The list must be filed under seal and may be amended as of right. Any reference in the case to a listed identifier will be construed to refer to the corresponding item of information. FRCP 5.2(g); NY R USDCTED Order 2004-09. The unredacted version of the document or the reference list shall be retained by the court as part of the record. The court may, however, still require the party to file a redacted copy for the public file. NY R USDCTED Order 2004-09.

h.   *Responsibility for redaction.* The responsibility for redacting these personal identifiers rests solely with counsel and the parties. The Clerk will not review each pleading for compliance with NY R USDCTED Order 2004-09. NY R USDCTED Order 2004-09.

i.   Counsel is strongly urged to share this notice with all clients so that an informed decision about the inclusion of certain materials may be made. If a redacted document is filed, it is the sole responsibility of counsel and the parties to be sure that all pleadings comply with the rules of this court requiring redaction of personal data identifiers. The clerk will not review each pleading for redaction. NY R USDCTED Order 2004-09.

i.   *Waiver of protection of identifiers.* A person waives the protection of FRCP 5.2(a) as to the person's own information by filing it without redaction and not under seal. FRCP 5.2(h).

4.   *Individual judge practices.* Refer to the Miscellaneous section of this document for information on individual judge practices on formatting documents.

## F.   Filing and Service Requirements

1.   *Filing requirements.* Any paper after the complaint that is required to be served—together with a certificate of service—must be filed within a reasonable time after service. But disclosures under FRCP 26(a)(1) or FRCP 26(a)(2) and the following discovery requests and responses must not be filed until they are used in the proceeding or the court orders filing: depositions, interrogatories, requests for documents or tangible things or to permit entry onto land, and requests for admission. FRCP 5(d)(1). Refer to the

United States District Court for the Eastern District of New York KeyRules pleading and motion documents for information on filing with the court.

a. *Notice of filing*

    i. *Depositions by oral examination.* A party who files the deposition must promptly notify all other parties of the filing. FRCP 30(f)(4).

    ii. *Depositions by written questions.* A party who files the deposition must promptly notify all other parties of the filing. FRCP 31(c)(2).

2. *Service requirements*

a. *Service; When required*

    i. *In general.* Unless the Federal Rules of Civil Procedure provide otherwise, each of the following papers must be served on every party:

- An order stating that service is required;
- A pleading filed after the original complaint, unless the court orders otherwise under FRCP 5(c) because there are numerous defendants;
- A discovery paper required to be served on a party, unless the court orders otherwise;
- A written motion, except one that may be heard ex parte; and
- A written notice, appearance, demand, or offer of judgment, or any similar paper. FRCP 5(a)(1).

    ii. *If a party fails to appear.* No service is required on a party who is in default for failing to appear. But a pleading that asserts a new claim for relief against such a party must be served on that party under FRCP 4. FRCP 5(a)(2).

    iii. *Seizing property.* If an action is begun by seizing property and no person is or need be named as a defendant, any service required before the filing of an appearance, answer, or claim must be made on the person who had custody or possession of the property when it was seized. FRCP 5(a)(3).

b. *Service; How made*

    i. *Serving an attorney.* If a party is represented by an attorney, service under FRCP 5 must be made on the attorney unless the court orders service on the party. FRCP 5(b)(1).

    ii. *Service in general.* A paper is served under FRCP 5 by:

- Handing it to the person;
- Leaving it: (1) at the person's office with a clerk or other person in charge or, if no one is in charge, in a conspicuous place in the office; or (2) if the person has no office or the office is closed, at the person's dwelling or usual place of abode with someone of suitable age and discretion who resides there;
- Mailing it to the person's last known address—in which event service is complete upon mailing;
- Leaving it with the court clerk if the person has no known address;
- Sending it by electronic means if the person consented in writing—in which event service is complete upon transmission, but is not effective if the serving party learns that it did not reach the person to be served; or
- Delivering it by any other means that the person consented to in writing—in which event service is complete when the person making service delivers it to the agency designated to make delivery. FRCP 5(b)(2).

    iii. *Service by overnight delivery.* Service upon an attorney may be made by overnight delivery service. "Overnight delivery service" means any delivery service which regularly accepts items for overnight delivery. Overnight delivery service shall be deemed service by mail for purposes of FRCP 5 and FRCP 6. NY R USDCTS&ED Civ Rule 5.3.

iv. *Service by electronic means.* Parties serving and filing papers shall follow the instructions regarding Electronic Case Filing (ECF) published on the website of each respective Court. A paper served and filed by electronic means in accordance with such instructions is, for purposes of FRCP 5, served and filed in compliance with the Local Civil Rules of the United States District Courts for the Southern and Eastern Districts of New York. NY R USDCTS&ED Civ Rule 5.2(a). Parties have an obligation to review the Court's actual order, decree, or judgment (on ECF), which controls, and should not rely on the description on the docket or in the ECF Notice of Electronic Filing (NEF). NY R USDCTS&ED Civ Rule 5.2(c).

v. *Using court facilities.* If a local rule so authorizes, a party may use the court's transmission facilities to make service under FRCP 5(b)(2)(E). FRCP 5(b)(3).

c. *Serving numerous defendants*

i. *In general.* If an action involves an unusually large number of defendants, the court may, on motion or on its own, order that:

- Defendants' pleadings and replies to them need not be served on other defendants;

- Any crossclaim, counterclaim, avoidance, or affirmative defense in those pleadings and replies to them will be treated as denied or avoided by all other parties; and

- Filing any such pleading and serving it on the plaintiff constitutes notice of the pleading to all parties. FRCP 5(c)(1).

ii. *Notifying parties.* A copy of every such order must be served on the parties as the court directs. FRCP 5(c)(2).

3. *Individual judge practices.* Refer to the Miscellaneous section of this document for information on individual judge practices on filing and serving documents.

## G. Hearings

1. There is no hearing contemplated in the federal statutes or rules for the notice of deposition.

## H. Forms

### 1. Federal Notice of Deposition Forms

a. Notice to take deposition to perpetuate testimony. 3A FEDFORMS § 3339.

b. Notice of taking of deposition to perpetuate testimony pending appeal. 3A FEDFORMS § 3345.

c. Notice of taking deposition upon oral examination. 3A FEDFORMS § 3422.

d. Notice of taking deposition upon oral examination; Party. 3A FEDFORMS § 3423.

e. Notice of taking deposition upon oral examination; Naming and describing person not a party. 3A FEDFORMS § 3424.

f. Notice of taking deposition upon oral examination; Describing deponents whose names are unknown. 3A FEDFORMS § 3425.

g. Notice of taking deposition upon oral examination; Pursuant to order granting leave to take deposition. 3A FEDFORMS § 3426.

h. Notice of taking of deposition of party with notice to produce documents. 3A FEDFORMS § 3427.

i. Notice of taking of deposition of witness; Including designation of materials in related subpoena duces tecum. 3A FEDFORMS § 3428.

j. Notice of taking of deposition of witness; Including reference to materials designated in attached subpoena. 3A FEDFORMS § 3429.

k. Notice of taking deposition upon written questions served with notice. 3A FEDFORMS § 3449.

l. Questions to be attached to notice or served with it. 3A FEDFORMS § 3450.

m. Notice of return and filing of deposition taken upon written questions. 3A FEDFORMS § 3456.

n. Notice; Taking of deposition on oral examination. FEDPROF § 23:136.

o. Notice; Taking of deposition on oral examination; Patent proceedings. FEDPROF § 23:137.

p.   Notice; Taking of deposition on oral examination; Corporate officer. FEDPROF § 23:138.

q.   Notice; Taking of deposition on oral examination; Corporate officers to be designated by corporation. FEDPROF § 23:139.

r.   Notice; Taking of deposition on written questions. FEDPROF § 23:140.

s.   Notice; Taking of deposition on oral examination or on written questions; Pursuant to court order. FEDPROF § 23:141.

t.   Notice; In connection with deposition on written questions; Of cross, redirect, or recross questions. FEDPROF § 23:142.

u.   Attachment to notice; Taking of deposition on written questions; Questions to be propounded. FEDPROF § 23:143.

v.   Attachment to notice; Cross, redirect, or recross questions to be propounded. FEDPROF § 23:144.

w.   Notice; To party taking deposition; Written questions submitted in lieu of participation in oral examination. FEDPROF § 23:145.

x.   Notice of taking deposition; Expert witness; Request for production of supporting documents. FEDPROF § 23:151.

y.   Subpoena; To testify at taking of deposition and to produce documents or things. FEDPROF § 23:152.

z.   Provision in subpoena; Advice to nonparty organization of its duty to designate witness. FEDPROF § 23:155.

## I.  Applicable Rules

1.  *Federal rules*

   a.   Serving and filing pleadings and other papers. FRCP 5.

   b.   Privacy protection for filings made with the court. FRCP 5.2.

   c.   Computing and extending time; Time for motion papers. FRCP 6.

   d.   Pleadings allowed; Form of motions and other papers. FRCP 7.

   e.   Form of pleadings. FRCP 10.

   f.   Signing pleadings, motions, and other papers; Representations to the court; Sanctions. FRCP 11.

   g.   Duty to disclose; General provisions governing discovery. FRCP 26.

   h.   Persons before whom depositions may be taken. FRCP 28.

   i.   Stipulations about discovery procedure. FRCP 29.

   j.   Depositions by oral examination. FRCP 30.

   k.   Depositions by written questions. FRCP 31.

   l.   Failure to make disclosures or to cooperate in discovery; Sanctions. FRCP 37.

2.  *Local rules*

   a.   Duty of attorneys in related cases. NY R USDCTS&ED Civ Rule 1.6.

   b.   Electronic service and filing of documents. NY R USDCTS&ED Civ Rule 5.2.

   c.   Service by overnight delivery. NY R USDCTS&ED Civ Rule 5.3.

   d.   Computation of time. NY R USDCTS&ED Civ Rule 6.4.

   e.   Form of pleadings, motions, and other papers. NY R USDCTS&ED Civ Rule 11.1.

   f.   Assertion of claim of privilege. NY R USDCTS&ED Civ Rule 26.2.

   g.   Uniform definitions in discovery requests. NY R USDCTS&ED Civ Rule 26.3.

   h.   Cooperation among counsel in discovery. NY R USDCTS&ED Civ Rule 26.4.

   i.   Counsel fees on taking depositions more than 100 miles from courthouse. NY R USDCTS&ED Civ Rule 30.1.

j. Telephonic and other remote depositions. NY R USDCTS&ED Civ Rule 30.2.

k. Persons attending depositions. NY R USDCTS&ED Civ Rule 30.3.

l. Conferences between deponent and defending attorney. NY R USDCTS&ED Civ Rule 30.4.

m. Mode of raising discovery and other non-dispositive pretrial disputes with the court (Eastern District only). NY R USDCTS&ED Civ Rule 37.3.

n. Court-annexed arbitration (Eastern District only). NY R USDCTS&ED Civ Rule 83.7.

o. Court-annexed mediation (Eastern District only). NY R USDCTS&ED Civ Rule 83.8.

p. The August 2, 2004 amendment to the E-Government Act of 2002. NY R USDCTED Order 2004-09.

## J. Miscellaneous

**NOTE: Individual judges' rules may apply. For available judge-level information, refer to:**

DISTRICT JUDGE CAROL BAGLEY AMON: NY R USDCTED Amon-Practices.

DISTRICT JUDGE JOAN M. AZRACK: NY R USDCTED Azrack-Practices.

DISTRICT JUDGE JOSEPH F. BIANCO: NY R USDCTED Bianco-Practices.

DISTRICT JUDGE FREDERIC BLOCK: NY R USDCTED Block-Practices.

DISTRICT JUDGE MARGO K. BRODIE: NY R USDCTED Brodie-Practices.

DISTRICT JUDGE PAMELA K. CHEN: NY R USDCTED Chen-Practices.

DISTRICT JUDGE BRIAN M. COGAN: NY R USDCTED Cogan-Practices; NY R USDCTED Cogan-Pretrial.

DISTRICT JUDGE LaSHANN DeARCY HALL: NY R USDCTED DeArcy Hall-Practices.

DISTRICT JUDGE RAYMOND J. DEARIE: NY R USDCTED Dearie-Practices.

DISTRICT JUDGE ANN M. DONNELLY: NY R USDCTED Donnelly-Practices.

DISTRICT JUDGE SANDRA J. FEUERSTEIN: NY R USDCTED Feuerstein-Practices; NY R USDCTED Feuerstein-Pretrial.

DISTRICT JUDGE NICHOLAS G. GARAUIFIS: NY R USDCTED Garaufis-Practices; NY R USDCTED Garaufis-Pretrial.

DISTRICT JUDGE NINA GERSHON: NY R USDCTED Gershon-Practices.

DISTRICT JUDGE I. LEO GLASSER: NY R USDCTED Glasser-Practices; NY R USDCTED Glasser-Crim.

DISTRICT JUDGE DENIS R. HURLEY: NY R USDCTED Hurley-Practices; [NY R USDCTED Hurley-Pro Cooperation Info, as added by NY ORDER 16-4188, effective July 22, 2016]; [NY R USDCTED Hurley-Pro Cooperation Info Stay, as added by NY ORDER 16-4188, effective July 22, 2016].

DISTRICT JUDGE DORA L. IRIZARRY: NY R USDCTED Irizarry-Practices; NY R USDCTED Irizarry-Pretrial; NY R USDCTED Irizarry-Crim.

DISTRICT JUDGE STERLING JOHNSON, JR.: NY R USDCTED Johnson-Practices.

DISTRICT JUDGE EDWARD R. KORMAN: NY R USDCTED Korman-Practices; NY R USDCTED Korman-Pretrial.

DISTRICT JUDGE WILLIAM F. KUNTZ: NY R USDCTED Kuntz-Practices.

DISTRICT JUDGE KIYO A. MATSUMOTO: NY R USDCTED Matsumoto-Practices.

DISTRICT JUDGE ROSLYNN R. MAUSKOPF: NY R USDCTED Mauskopf-Practices; NY R USDCTED Mauskopf-Recusal.

DISTRICT JUDGE THOMAS C. PLATT: NY R USDCTED Platt-Practices.

DISTRICT JUDGE ALLYNE R. ROSS: NY R USDCTED Ross-Practices.

DISTRICT JUDGE JOANNA SEYBERT: NY R USDCTED Seybert-Practices.

DISTRICT JUDGE ARTHUR D. SPATT: NY R USDCTED Spatt-Practices.

DISTRICT JUDGE SANDRA L. TOWNES: NY R USDCTED Townes-Practices.

DISTRICT JUDGE ERIC N. VITALIANO: NY R USDCTED Vitaliano-Practices.

DISTRICT JUDGE JACK B. WEINSTEIN: NY R USDCTED Weinstein-Practices.

DISTRICT JUDGE LEONARD D. WEXLER: NY R USDCTED Wexler-Practices; NY R USDCTED Wexler-Rules.

MAGISTRATE JUDGE LOIS BLOOM: NY R USDCTED Bloom-Practices.

MAGISTRATE JUDGE GARY R. BROWN: NY R USDCTED Brown-Practices.

MAGISTRATE JUDGE MARILYN D. GO: NY R USDCTED Go-Practices.

MAGISTRATE JUDGE STEVEN M. GOLD: NY R USDCTED Gold-Practices.

MAGISTRATE JUDGE PEGGY KUO: NY R USDCTED Kuo-Practices; NY R USDCTED Kuo-Scheduling Order.

MAGISTRATE JUDGE ROBERT M. LEVY: NY R USDCTED Levy-Practices.

MAGISTRATE JUDGE ARLENE R. LINDSAY: NY R USDCTED Lindsay-Practices.

MAGISTRATE JUDGE STEVEN I. LOCKE: NY R USDCTED Locke-Practices.

MAGISTRATE JUDGE ROANNE L. MANN: NY R USDCTED Mann-Practices.

MAGISTRATE JUDGE JAMES ORENSTEIN: NY R USDCTED Jorenstein--Practices.

MAGISTRATE JUDGE VIKTOR V. POHORELSKY: NY R USDCTED Pohorelsky-Practices.

MAGISTRATE JUDGE CHERYL L. POLLAK: NY R USDCTED Pollak-Practices; NY R USDCTED Pollak-Pretrial.

MAGISTRATE JUDGE RAMON E. REYES, JR.: NY R USDCTED Reyes-Practices.

MAGISTRATE JUDGE VERA M. SCANLON: NY R USDCTED Scanlon-Practices.

MAGISTRATE JUDGE ANNE Y. SHIELDS: NY R USDCTED Shields-Practices.

MAGISTRATE JUDGE STEVEN L. TISCIONE: NY R USDCTED Tiscione-Practices.

MAGISTRATE JUDGE A. KATHLEEN TOMILINSON: NY R USDCTED Tomlinson-Practices.

# Requests, Notices and Applications
## Application for Temporary Restraining Order

### Document Last Updated September 2016

**A. Checklist**

    (I)  ❑ Matters to be considered by party applying (with notice)

        (a)  ❑ Required documents

            (1)  ❑ Letter-motion

            (2)  ❑ Security

        (b)  ❑ Supplemental documents

            (1)  ❑ Supporting evidence

            (2)  ❑ Notice of constitutional question

            (3)  ❑ Nongovernmental corporate disclosure statement

            (4)  ❑ Copies of authorities

            (5)  ❑ Notice of motion and motion

            (6)  ❑ Memorandum of law

            (7)  ❑ Certificate of service

        (c)  ❑ Timing

            (1)  ❑ There are no specific timing requirements for submitting a letter-motion to the court

(2) ☐ A written motion and notice of the hearing must be served at least fourteen (14) days before the time specified for the hearing, with the following exceptions: (i) when the motion may be heard ex parte; (ii) when the Federal Rules of Civil Procedure set a different time; or (iii) when a court order—which a party may, for good cause, apply for ex parte—sets a different time

(3) ☐ Any affidavit supporting a motion must be served with the motion

(II) ☐ Matters to be considered by party applying (without notice, or "ex parte")

  (a) ☐ Required documents

    (1) ☐ Letter-motion

    (2) ☐ Affidavit or verified complaint

    (3) ☐ Certificate of attorney

    (4) ☐ Security

  (b) ☐ Supplemental documents

    (1) ☐ Supporting evidence

    (2) ☐ Notice of constitutional question

    (3) ☐ Nongovernmental corporate disclosure statement

    (4) ☐ Copies of authorities

    (5) ☐ Motion

    (6) ☐ Memorandum of law

  (c) ☐ Timing

    (1) ☐ There are no specific timing requirements for submitting a letter-motion to the court

    (2) ☐ There are no specific timing requirements for applying for a temporary restraining order without notice

    (3) ☐ Any affidavit supporting a motion must be served with the motion

## B. Timing

1. *Mode of raising discovery and other non-dispositive pretrial disputes with the court*

   a. *Letter-motion.* There are no specific timing requirements for submitting a letter-motion to the court.

   b. *Responsive letter.* Within four (4) days of receiving such a letter, any opposing affected party or non-party witness may submit a responsive letter not exceeding three (3) pages attaching relevant materials. NY R USDCTS&ED Civ Rule 37.3(c).

2. *Application for temporary restraining order*

   a. *With notice.* There are no specific timing requirements for applying for a temporary restraining order with notice.

   b. *Without notice, or "ex parte."* There are no specific timing requirements for applying for a temporary restraining order without notice, or "ex parte."

3. *Motion to dissolve or modify.* On two (2) days' notice to the party who obtained the order without notice—or on shorter notice set by the court—the adverse party may appear and move to dissolve or modify the order. The court must then hear and decide the motion as promptly as justice requires. FRCP 65(b)(4).

4. *Timing of motions, generally*

   a. *Motion and notice of hearing.* Except for letter-motions as permitted by NY R USDCTS&ED Civ Rule 7.1(d), and unless otherwise provided by statute or rule or by the Court in a Judge's Individual Practice or in a direction in a particular case, upon any motion, the notice of motion, supporting affidavits, and memoranda shall be served and filed as follows: on all civil motions, petitions, and applications, other than those described in NY R USDCTS&ED Civ Rule 6.1(a), and other than petitions for writs of habeas corpus, the notice of motion, supporting affidavits, and memoranda of law shall be served by the moving party on all other parties that have appeared in the action. NY R USDCTS&ED Civ Rule 6.1(b)(1). A written motion and notice of the hearing must be served at least fourteen (14) days before the time specified for the hearing, with the following exceptions:

    i.   When the motion may be heard ex parte;

    ii.   When the Federal Rules of Civil Procedure set a different time; or

    iii.   When a court order—which a party may, for good cause, apply for ex parte—sets a different time. FRCP 6(c)(1).

b.  *Supporting affidavit.* Any affidavit supporting a motion must be served with the motion. FRCP 6(c)(2).

5.  *Computation of time*

    a.  *Computing time.* FRCP 6 applies in computing any time period specified in the Federal Rules of Civil Procedure, in any local rule or court order, or in any statute that does not specify a method of computing time. FRCP 6(a). In computing any period of time prescribed or allowed by the Local Civil Rules of the United States District Courts for the Southern and Eastern Districts of New York or the Local Admiralty and Maritime Rules, the provisions of FRCP 6 shall apply unless otherwise stated. NY R USDCTS&ED Civ Rule 6.4.

        i.  *Period stated in days or a longer unit.* In computing periods of days, refer to FRCP 6 and NY R USDCTS&ED Civ Rule 6.4. NY R USDCTS&ED Civ Rule 6.1(b). When the period is stated in days or a longer unit of time:

- Exclude the day of the event that triggers the period;

- Count every day, including intermediate Saturdays, Sundays, and legal holidays; and

- Include the last day of the period, but if the last day is a Saturday, Sunday, or legal holiday, the period continues to run until the end of the next day that is not a Saturday, Sunday, or legal holiday. FRCP 6(a)(1). In the Local Civil Rules of the United States District Courts for the Southern and Eastern Districts of New York, as in the Federal Rules of Civil Procedure as amended effective December 1, 2009, Saturdays, Sundays, and legal holidays are no longer excluded in computing periods of time. If the last day of the period is a Saturday, Sunday, or legal holiday, the period continues to run until the end of the next day that is not a Saturday, Sunday, or legal holiday. NY R USDCTS&ED Civ Rule 6.4.

        ii.  *Period stated in hours.* When the period is stated in hours:

- Begin counting immediately on the occurrence of the event that triggers the period;

- Count every hour, including hours during intermediate Saturdays, Sundays, and legal holidays; and

- If the period would end on a Saturday, Sunday, or legal holiday, the period continues to run until the same time on the next day that is not a Saturday, Sunday, or legal holiday. FRCP 6(a)(2). In the Local Civil Rules of the United States District Courts for the Southern and Eastern Districts of New York, as in the Federal Rules of Civil Procedure as amended effective December 1, 2009, Saturdays, Sundays, and legal holidays are no longer excluded in computing periods of time. If the last day of the period is a Saturday, Sunday, or legal holiday, the period continues to run until the end of the next day that is not a Saturday, Sunday, or legal holiday. NY R USDCTS&ED Civ Rule 6.4.

        iii.  *Inaccessibility of the clerk's office.* Unless the court orders otherwise, if the clerk's office is inaccessible:

- On the last day for filing under FRCP 6(a)(1), then the time for filing is extended to the first accessible day that is not a Saturday, Sunday, or legal holiday; or

- During the last hour for filing under FRCP 6(a)(2), then the time for filing is extended to the same time on the first accessible day that is not a Saturday, Sunday, or legal holiday. FRCP 6(a)(3).

    iv. *"Last day" defined.* Unless a different time is set by a statute, local rule, or court order, the last day ends:

- For electronic filing, at midnight in the court's time zone; and

- For filing by other means, when the clerk's office is scheduled to close. FRCP 6(a)(4).

    v. *"Next day" defined.* The "next day" is determined by continuing to count forward when the period is measured after an event and backward when measured before an event. FRCP 6(a)(5).

    vi. *"Legal holiday" defined.* "Legal holiday" means:

- The day set aside by statute for observing New Year's Day, Martin Luther King Jr.'s Birthday, Washington's Birthday, Memorial Day, Independence Day, Labor Day, Columbus Day, Veterans' Day, Thanksgiving Day, or Christmas Day;

- Any day declared a holiday by the President or Congress; and

- For periods that are measured after an event, any other day declared a holiday by the state where the district court is located. FRCP 6(a)(6).

  b. *Extending time*

    i. *In general.* When an act may or must be done within a specified time, the court may, for good cause, extend the time:

- With or without motion or notice if the court acts, or if a request is made, before the original time or its extension expires; or

- On motion made after the time has expired if the party failed to act because of excusable neglect. FRCP 6(b)(1).

    ii. *Exceptions.* A court must not extend the time to act under FRCP 50(b), FRCP 50(d), FRCP 52(b), FRCP 59(b), FRCP 59(d), FRCP 59(e), and FRCP 60(b). FRCP 6(b)(2).

    iii. Refer to the United States District Court for the Eastern District of New York KeyRules Motion for Continuance/Extension of Time document for more information on extending time.

  c. *Additional time after certain kinds of service.* When a party may or must act within a specified time after service and service is made under FRCP 5(b)(2)(C), FRCP 5(b)(2)(D), FRCP 5(b)(2)(E), or FRCP 5(b)(2)(F), three (3) days are added after the period would otherwise expire under FRCP 6(a). FRCP 6(d). Overnight delivery service shall be deemed service by mail for purposes of FRCP 5 and FRCP 6. NY R USDCTS&ED Civ Rule 5.3.

6. *Individual judge practices.* Refer to the Miscellaneous section of this document for information on individual judge practices on timing of documents.

## C. General Requirements

1. *Mode of raising discovery and other non-dispositive pretrial disputes with the court.* Prior to seeking judicial resolution of a discovery or non-dispositive pretrial dispute, the attorneys for the affected parties or non-party witness shall attempt to confer in good faith in person or by telephone in an effort to resolve the dispute, in conformity with FRCP 37(a)(1). NY R USDCTS&ED Civ Rule 37.3(a). Refer to the Documents section of this document for the procedure to follow when the attorneys for the affected parties or non-party witness cannot agree on a resolution of the discovery or other non-dispositive pretrial dispute.

  a. *Motion for reconsideration.* A ruling made exclusively as a result of a telephone conference may be the subject of de novo reconsideration by a letter not exceeding five (5) pages in length attaching relevant materials submitted by any affected party or non-party witness. Within four (4) days of receiving such a letter, any other affected party or non-party witness may submit a responsive letter not exceeding five (5) pages in length attaching relevant materials. NY R USDCTS&ED Civ Rule 37.3(d).

  b. *Decision of the court.* The Court shall record or arrange for the recording of the Court's decision in writing. Such written order may take the form of an oral order read into the record of a deposition or other proceeding, a handwritten memorandum, a handwritten marginal notation on a letter or other document, or any other form the Court deems appropriate. NY R USDCTS&ED Civ Rule 37.3(e).

2. *Motions, generally*

    a. *Requirements.* A request for a court order must be made by motion. The motion must:

        i. Be in writing unless made during a hearing or trial;

        ii. State with particularity the grounds for seeking the order; and

        iii. State the relief sought. FRCP 7(b)(1).

    b. *Notice of motion.* A party interested in resisting the relief sought by a motion has a right to notice thereof, and an opportunity to be heard. AMJUR MOTIONS § 12.

        i. In addition to statutory or court rule provisions requiring notice of a motion—the purpose of such a notice requirement having been said to be to prevent a party from being prejudicially surprised by a motion—principles of natural justice dictate that an adverse party generally must be given notice that a motion will be presented to the court. AMJUR MOTIONS § 12.

        ii. "Notice," in this regard, means reasonable notice, including a meaningful opportunity to prepare and to defend against allegations of a motion. AMJUR MOTIONS § 12.

    c. *Writing requirement.* The writing requirement is intended to insure that the adverse parties are informed and have a record of both the motion's pendency and the grounds on which the movant seeks an order. FPP § 1191; Feldberg v. Quechee Lakes Corp., 463 F.3d 195 (2d Cir. 2006).

        i. It is sufficient "if the motion is stated in a written notice of the hearing of the motion." FPP § 1191.

    d. *Particularity requirement.* The particularity requirement insures that the opposing parties will have notice of their opponent's contentions. FEDPROC § 62:364; Goodman v. 1973 26 Foot Trojan Vessel, Arkansas Registration No. AR1439SN, 859 F.2d 71, 12 Fed.R.Serv.3d 645 (8th Cir. 1988). That requirement ensures that notice of the basis for the motion is provided to the court and to the opposing party so as to avoid prejudice, provide the opponent with a meaningful opportunity to respond, and provide the court with enough information to process the motion correctly. FEDPROC § 62:364; Andreas v. Volkswagen of America, Inc., 336 F.3d 789, 56 Fed.R.Serv.3d 6 (8th Cir. 2003).

        i. Reasonable specification of the grounds for a motion is sufficient. However, where a movant fails to state even one ground for granting the motion in question, the movant has failed to meet the minimal standard of "reasonable specification." FEDPROC § 62:364; Martinez v. Trainor, 556 F.2d 818, 23 Fed.R.Serv.2d 403 (7th Cir. 1977).

        ii. The court may excuse the failure to comply with the particularity requirement if it is inadvertent, and where no prejudice is shown by the opposing party. FEDPROC § 62:364.

    e. *Ex parte orders or orders to show cause to bring on a motion.* No ex parte order, or order to show cause to bring on a motion, will be granted except upon a clear and specific showing by affidavit of good and sufficient reasons why a procedure other than by notice of motion is necessary, and stating whether a previous application for similar relief has been made. NY R USDCTS&ED Civ Rule 6.1(d).

    f. *Letter-motions.* Applications for extensions or adjournments, applications for a pre-motion conference, and similar non-dispositive matters as permitted by the instructions regarding ECF published on the website of each respective Court and any pertinent Individual Judge's Practices, may be brought by letter-motion filed via ECF pursuant to NY R USDCTS&ED Civ Rule 5.2(b). NY R USDCTS&ED Civ Rule 7.1(d).

3. *Application for temporary restraining order.* Applicants for injunctive relief occasionally are faced with the possibility that irreparable injury will occur before the hearing for a preliminary injunction required by FRCP 65(a) can be held. In that event a temporary restraining order may be available under FRCP 65(b). FPP § 2951. The order is designed to preserve the status quo until there is an opportunity to hold a hearing on the application for a preliminary injunction and may be issued with or without notice to the adverse party. FPP § 2951; Granny Goose Foods, Inc. v. Brotherhood of Teamsters & Auto Truck Drivers Local No. 70 of Alameda County, 415 U.S. 423, 94 S.Ct. 1113, 39 L.Ed.2d 435 (1974).

    a. *Issuing with notice.* When the opposing party actually receives notice of the application for a restraining order, the procedure that is followed does not differ functionally from that on an application for a preliminary injunction and the proceeding is not subject to any special requirements. FPP § 2951; Dilworth v. Riner, 343 F.2d 226 (5th Cir. 1965).

    i.   *Duration.* By its terms FRCP 65(b) only governs restraining orders issued without notice or a hearing. But. . .it has been argued that its provisions, at least with regard to the duration of a restraining order, apply even to an order granted when notice has been given to the adverse party but there has been no hearing. FPP § 2951.

b.  *Issuing without notice*

    i.   *When available.* The court may issue a temporary restraining order without written or oral notice to the adverse party or its attorney only if:

- Specific facts in an affidavit or a verified complaint clearly show that immediate and irreparable injury, loss, or damage will result to the movant before the adverse party can be heard in opposition; and

- The movant's attorney certifies in writing any efforts made to give notice and the reasons why it should not be required. FRCP 65(b)(1).

    ii.  *Contents.* Every temporary restraining order issued without notice must state the date and hour it was issued; describe the injury and state why it is irreparable; state why the order was issued without notice; and be promptly filed in the clerk's office and entered in the record. FRCP 65(b)(2).

    iii.  *Expiration.* The order expires at the time after entry—not to exceed fourteen (14) days—that the court sets, unless before that time the court, for good cause, extends it for a like period or the adverse party consents to a longer extension. The reasons for an extension must be entered in the record. FRCP 65(b)(2).

c.  *Temporary restraining order versus preliminary injunction.* A temporary restraining order differs from a preliminary injunction, the core reasons being that a temporary restraining order is of limited duration and it may issue without notice to the opposing party before the adverse party can be heard in opposition. FEDPROC § 47:80.

d.  *Factors considered.* As in the case of an application for a preliminary injunction, four factors must be considered in determining whether a temporary restraining order is to be granted, which are whether the moving party has established: (1) a substantial likelihood of success on the merits; (2) that irreparable injury will be suffered if the relief is not granted; (3) that the threatened injury outweighs the harm the relief would inflict on the nonmoving party; and (4) that entry of the relief would serve the public interest. FEDPROC § 47:84; Schiavo ex rel. Schindler v. Schiavo, 403 F.3d 1223 (11th Cir. 2005).

    i.   Plaintiffs are not required to prevail on each of these factors, rather, the factors must be viewed as a continuum, with more of one factor compensating for less of another. In each case, however, all of the factors must be considered to determine whether on balance they weigh toward granting relief. FEDPROC § 47:84.

    ii.  In the context of a temporary restraining order, it is particularly important for the moving party to demonstrate a substantial likelihood of success on the merits, because otherwise, there would be no justification for the court's intrusion into the ordinary processes of administration and judicial review. FEDPROC § 47:84.

    iii.  Refer to the United States District Court for the Eastern District of New York KeyRules Motion for Preliminary Injunction document for more information on the factors considered in moving for a preliminary injunction.

e.  *Burden.* As with a preliminary injunction, the burden is on the moving party to establish that relief is appropriate. FEDPROC § 47:84.

f.  *Security.* The court may issue a preliminary injunction or a temporary restraining order only if the movant gives security in an amount that the court considers proper to pay the costs and damages sustained by any party found to have been wrongfully enjoined or restrained. The United States, its officers, and its agencies are not required to give security. FRCP 65(c).

    i.   *Proceedings against a surety.* Whenever the Federal Rules of Civil Procedure (including the Supplemental Rules for Admiralty or Maritime Claims and Asset Forfeiture Actions) require or allow a party to give security, and security is given through a bond or other undertaking with one or more sureties, each surety submits to the court's jurisdiction and irrevocably appoints the court clerk as its agent for receiving service of any papers that affect its liability on the bond or undertaking. The surety's liability may be enforced on motion without an independent action. The motion and any notice that the court orders may be served on the court clerk, who must promptly mail a copy of each to every surety whose address is known. FRCP 65.1.

    ii.   For more information on sureties, refer to NY R USDCTS&ED Civ Rule 65.1.1.

  g.   *Contents and scope of every injunction and restraining order*

    i.   *Contents.* Every order granting an injunction and every restraining order must:

- State the reasons why it issued;
- State its terms specifically; and
- Describe in reasonable detail—and not by referring to the complaint or other document—the act or acts restrained or required. FRCP 65(d)(1).

    ii.   *Persons bound.* The order binds only the following who receive actual notice of it by personal service or otherwise:

- The parties;
- The parties' officers, agents, servants, employees, and attorneys; and
- Other persons who are in active concert or participation with anyone described in FRCP 65(d)(2)(A) or FRCP 65(d)(2)(B). FRCP 65(d)(2).

  h.   *Other laws not modified.* FRCP 65 does not modify the following:

    i.   Any federal statute relating to temporary restraining orders or preliminary injunctions in actions affecting employer and employee;

    ii.   28 U.S.C.A. § 2361, which relates to preliminary injunctions in actions of interpleader or in the nature of interpleader; or

    iii.   28 U.S.C.A. § 2284, which relates to actions that must be heard and decided by a three-judge district court. FRCP 65(e).

  i.   *Copyright impoundment.* FRCP 65 applies to copyright-impoundment proceedings. FRCP 65(f).

4.  *Orders on motions.* A memorandum signed by the Court of the decision on a motion that does not finally determine all claims for relief, or an oral decision on such a motion, shall constitute the order unless the memorandum or oral decision directs the submission or settlement of an order in more extended form. The notation in the docket of a memorandum or of an oral decision that does not direct the submission or settlement of an order in more extended form shall constitute the entry of the order. Where an order in more extended form is required to be submitted or settled, the notation in the docket of such order shall constitute the entry of the order. NY R USDCTS&ED Civ Rule 6.2.

5.  *Related cases.* It shall be the continuing duty of each attorney appearing in any civil or criminal case to bring promptly to the attention of the Court all facts which said attorney believes are relevant to a determination that said case and one or more pending civil or criminal cases should be heard by the same Judge, in order to avoid unnecessary duplication of judicial effort. As soon as the attorney becomes aware of such relationship, said attorney shall notify the Judges to whom the cases have been assigned. NY R USDCTS&ED Civ Rule 1.6(a). If counsel fails to comply with NY R USDCTS&ED Civ Rule 1.6(a), the Court may assess reasonable costs directly against counsel whose action has obstructed the effective administration of the Court's business. NY R USDCTS&ED Civ Rule 1.6(b).

6.  *Alternative dispute resolution (ADR)*

  a.   *Court-annexed arbitration*

    i.   *Civil cases eligible for compulsory arbitration.* The Clerk of Court shall, as to all cases filed after January 1, 1986, designate and process for compulsory arbitration all civil cases (excluding Social Security cases, tax matters, prisoners' civil rights cases and any action based on an alleged violation of a right secured by the Constitution of the United States or if jurisdiction is based in whole or in part on 28 U.S.C.A. § 1343) wherein money damages only are being sought in an amount not in excess of one hundred fifty thousand dollars ($150,000) exclusive of interest and costs. NY R USDCTS&ED Civ Rule 83.7(d)(1).

- The parties may by written stipulation agree that the Clerk of Court shall designate and process for court-annexed arbitration any civil case that is not subject to compulsory arbitration in NY R USDCTS&ED Civ Rule 83.7. NY R USDCTS&ED Civ Rule 83.7(d)(2).

- For purposes of NY R USDCTS&ED Civ Rule 83.7 only, in all civil cases damages shall be presumed to be not in excess of one hundred fifty thousand dollars ($150,000) exclusive of interest and costs, unless: (1) counsel for plaintiff, at the time of filing the complaint, or in the event of the removal of a case from state court or transfer of a case from another district to this Court, within thirty (30) days of the docketing of the case in this district, files a certification with the Court that the damages sought exceed one hundred fifty thousand dollars ($150,000), exclusive of interest and costs; or (2) counsel for a defendant, at the time of filing a counterclaim or cross-claim files a certification with the court that the damages sought by the counter-claim or cross-claim exceed one hundred fifty thousand dollars ($150,000) exclusive of interest and costs. NY R USDCTS&ED Civ Rule 83.7(d)(3).

ii. *Exemption from arbitration.* The Court shall, sua sponte, or on motion of a party, exempt any case from arbitration in which the objectives of arbitration would not be realized (1) because the case involves complex or novel issues, (2) because legal issues predominate over factual issues, or (3) for other good cause. NY R USDCTS&ED Civ Rule 83.7(e)(2). For information on applying for an exemption, refer to NY R USDCTS&ED Civ Rule 83.7

iii. *Referral to arbitration.* Cases not originally designated as eligible for compulsory arbitration, but which in the discretion of the assigned Judge, are later found to qualify, may be referred to arbitration. A U.S. District Judge or a U.S. Magistrate Judge, in cases that exceed the arbitration ceiling of one hundred fifty thousand dollars ($150,000) exclusive of interest and costs, in their discretion, may suggest that the parties should consider arbitration. If the parties are agreeable, an appropriate consent form signed by all parties or their representatives may be entered and filed in the case prior to scheduling an arbitration hearing. NY R USDCTS&ED Civ Rule 83.7(e)(3).

iv. For more information on arbitration, refer to NY R USDCTS&ED Civ Rule 83.7.

b. *Court-annexed mediation.* Mediation is a process in which parties and counsel agree to meet with a neutral mediator trained to assist them in settling disputes. The mediator improves communication across party lines, helps parties articulate their interests and understand those of the other party, probes the strengths and weaknesses of each party's legal positions, and identifies areas of agreement and helps generate options for a mutually agreeable resolution to the dispute. In all cases, mediation provides an opportunity to explore a wide range of potential solutions and to address interests that may be outside the scope of the stated controversy or which could not be addressed by judicial action. A hallmark of mediation is its capacity to expand traditional settlement discussions and broaden resolution options, often by exploring litigant needs and interests that may be formally independent of the legal issues in controversy. NY R USDCTS&ED Civ Rule 83.8(a).

i. *Eligible cases.* Judges and Magistrate Judges may designate civil cases for inclusion in the mediation program, and when doing so shall prepare an order to that effect. Alternatively, and subject to the availability of qualified mediators, the parties may consent to participation in the mediation program by preparing and executing a stipulation signed by all parties to the action and so-ordered by the Court. NY R USDCTS&ED Civ Rule 83.8(b)(1).

ii. For more information on mediation, refer to NY R USDCTS&ED Civ Rule 83.8.

7. *Individual judge practices.* Refer to the Miscellaneous section of this document for information on individual judge practices on general requirements for documents.

## D. Documents

1. *Application for temporary restraining order (with notice)*

   a. *Required documents*

      i. *Letter-motion.* Where the attorneys for the affected parties or non-party witness cannot agree on a resolution of any other discovery dispute or non-dispositive pretrial dispute, or if they are unable to obtain a telephonic ruling on a discovery dispute that arises during a deposition as provided in NY R USDCTS&ED Civ Rule 37.3(b), they shall notify the Court by letter not exceeding three (3) pages in length outlining the nature of the dispute and attaching relevant materials. NY R USDCTS&ED Civ Rule 37.3(c).

      ii. *Security.* Refer to the General Requirements section of this document for information on the security required.

   b. *Supplemental documents.* Except for the letters and attachments authorized NY R USDCTS&ED Civ Rule 37.3, or where a ruling which was made exclusively as a result of a telephone conference is the subject of de novo review pursuant to NY R USDCTS&ED Civ Rule 37.3(d), papers shall not be submitted with respect to a dispute governed by NY R USDCTS&ED Civ Rule 37.3 unless the Court has so directed. NY R USDCTS&ED Civ Rule 37.3(c).

      i. *Supporting evidence.* When a motion relies on facts outside the record, the court may hear the matter on affidavits or may hear it wholly or partly on oral testimony or on depositions. FRCP 43(c). Except for letter-motions as permitted by NY R USDCTS&ED Civ Rule 7.1(d) or as otherwise permitted by the Court, all motions shall include the following motion papers: supporting affidavits and exhibits thereto containing any factual information and portions of the record necessary for the decision of the motion. NY R USDCTS&ED Civ Rule 7.1(a)(3).

         • *Discovery materials.* A party seeking or opposing relief under FRCP 26 through FRCP 37 inclusive, or making or opposing any other motion or application, shall quote or attach only those portions of the depositions, interrogatories, requests for documents, requests for admissions, or other discovery or disclosure materials, together with the responses and objections thereto, that are the subject of the discovery motion or application, or that are cited in papers submitted in connection with any other motion or application. NY R USDCTS&ED Civ Rule 5.1.

      ii. *Notice of constitutional question.* A party that files a pleading, written motion, or other paper drawing into question the constitutionality of a federal or state statute must promptly:

         • *File notice.* File a notice of constitutional question stating the question and identifying the paper that raises it, if: (1) a federal statute is questioned and the parties do not include the United States, one of its agencies, or one of its officers or employees in an official capacity; or (2) a state statute is questioned and the parties do not include the state, one of its agencies, or one of its officers or employees in an official capacity; and

         • *Serve notice.* Serve the notice and paper on the Attorney General of the United States if a federal statute is questioned—or on the state attorney general if a state statute is questioned—either by certified or registered mail or by sending it to an electronic address designated by the attorney general for this purpose. FRCP 5.1(a).

         • *No forfeiture.* A party's failure to file and serve the notice, or the court's failure to certify, does not forfeit a constitutional claim or defense that is otherwise timely asserted. FRCP 5.1(d).

      iii. *Nongovernmental corporate disclosure statement.* To enable judges and magistrates to evaluate possible disqualification or recusal, counsel for a private (nongovernmental) party shall submit at the time of initial pleading a certificate identifying any corporate parent, subsidiaries, or affiliates of that party. NY R USDCTED Div. Bus., Rule 50.1(c).

         • *Contents.* A nongovernmental corporate party must file two (2) copies of a disclosure statement that: (1) identifies any parent corporation and any publicly held corporation owning ten percent (10%) or more of its stock; or (2) states that there is no such corporation. FRCP 7.1(a).

- *Time to file; Supplemental filing.* A party must: (1) file the disclosure statement with its first appearance, pleading, petition, motion, response, or other request addressed to the court; and (2) promptly file a supplemental statement if any required information changes. FRCP 7.1(b). For purposes of FRCP 7.1(b)(2), "promptly" shall mean "within fourteen days," that is, parties are required to file a supplemental disclosure statement within fourteen (14) days of the time there is any change in the information required in a disclosure statement filed pursuant to those rules. NY R USDCTS&ED Civ Rule 7.1.1.

iv. *Copies of authorities.* In cases involving a pro se litigant, counsel shall, when serving a memorandum of law (or other submissions to the Court), provide the pro se litigant (but not other counsel or the Court) with copies of cases and other authorities cited therein that are unpublished or reported exclusively on computerized databases. Upon request, counsel shall provide the pro se litigant with copies of such unpublished cases and other authorities as are cited in a decision of the Court and were not previously cited by any party. NY R USDCTS&ED Civ Rule 7.2.

v. *Notice of motion and motion.* Except for letter-motions as permitted by NY R USDCTS&ED Civ Rule 7.1(d) or as otherwise permitted by the Court, all motions shall include the following motion papers: a notice of motion, or an order to show cause signed by the Court, which shall specify the applicable rules or statutes pursuant to which the motion is brought, and shall specify the relief sought by the motion. NY R USDCTS&ED Civ Rule 7.1(a)(1). Refer to the General Requirements section of this document for information on the notice of motion and motion.

vi. *Memorandum of law.* Except for letter-motions as permitted by NY R USDCTS&ED Civ Rule 7.1(d) or as otherwise permitted by the Court, all motions shall include the following motion papers: a memorandum of law, setting forth the cases and other authorities relied upon in support of the motion, and divided, under appropriate headings, into as many parts as there are issues to be determined. NY R USDCTS&ED Civ Rule 7.1(a)(2).

vii. *Certificate of service.* FRCP 5(d) requires that the person making service under FRCP 5 certify that service has been effected. FRCP 5(Advisory Committee Notes). Having such information on file may be useful for many purposes, including proof of service if an issue arises concerning the effectiveness of the service. FRCP 5(Advisory Committee Notes).

2. *Application for temporary restraining order (without notice, or "ex parte")*

   a. *Required documents*

   i. *Letter-motion.* Where the attorneys for the affected parties or non-party witness cannot agree on a resolution of any other discovery dispute or non-dispositive pretrial dispute, or if they are unable to obtain a telephonic ruling on a discovery dispute that arises during a deposition as provided in NY R USDCTS&ED Civ Rule 37.3(b), they shall notify the Court by letter not exceeding three (3) pages in length outlining the nature of the dispute and attaching relevant materials. NY R USDCTS&ED Civ Rule 37.3(c).

   ii. *Affidavit or verified complaint.* The applicant for an ex parte restraining order must present to the court, in an affidavit or a verified complaint, facts that clearly show irreparable injury. FPP § 2952.

   iii. *Certificate of attorney.* The applicant's attorney must certify in writing any efforts made to give notice and the reasons why it should not be required. FEDPROC § 47:81.

   - No ex parte order, or order to show cause to bring on a motion, will be granted except upon a clear and specific showing by affidavit of good and sufficient reasons why a procedure other than by notice of motion is necessary, and stating whether a previous application for similar relief has been made. NY R USDCTS&ED Civ Rule 6.1(d).

   iv. *Security.* Refer to the General Requirements section of this document for information on the security required.

   b. *Supplemental documents.* Except for the letters and attachments authorized NY R USDCTS&ED Civ Rule 37.3, or where a ruling which was made exclusively as a result of a telephone conference is the subject of de novo review pursuant to NY R USDCTS&ED Civ Rule 37.3(d), papers shall not be submitted with respect to a dispute governed by NY R USDCTS&ED Civ Rule 37.3 unless the Court has so directed. NY R USDCTS&ED Civ Rule 37.3(c).

i.   *Supporting evidence.* When a motion relies on facts outside the record, the court may hear the matter on affidavits or may hear it wholly or partly on oral testimony or on depositions. FRCP 43(c). Except for letter-motions as permitted by NY R USDCTS&ED Civ Rule 7.1(d) or as otherwise permitted by the Court, all motions shall include the following motion papers: supporting affidavits and exhibits thereto containing any factual information and portions of the record necessary for the decision of the motion. NY R USDCTS&ED Civ Rule 7.1(a)(3).

   - *Discovery materials.* A party seeking or opposing relief under FRCP 26 through FRCP 37 inclusive, or making or opposing any other motion or application, shall quote or attach only those portions of the depositions, interrogatories, requests for documents, requests for admissions, or other discovery or disclosure materials, together with the responses and objections thereto, that are the subject of the discovery motion or application, or that are cited in papers submitted in connection with any other motion or application. NY R USDCTS&ED Civ Rule 5.1.

ii.  *Notice of constitutional question.* A party that files a pleading, written motion, or other paper drawing into question the constitutionality of a federal or state statute must promptly:

   - *File notice.* File a notice of constitutional question stating the question and identifying the paper that raises it, if: (1) a federal statute is questioned and the parties do not include the United States, one of its agencies, or one of its officers or employees in an official capacity; or (2) a state statute is questioned and the parties do not include the state, one of its agencies, or one of its officers or employees in an official capacity; and

   - *Serve notice.* Serve the notice and paper on the Attorney General of the United States if a federal statute is questioned—or on the state attorney general if a state statute is questioned—either by certified or registered mail or by sending it to an electronic address designated by the attorney general for this purpose. FRCP 5.1(a).

   - *No forfeiture.* A party's failure to file and serve the notice, or the court's failure to certify, does not forfeit a constitutional claim or defense that is otherwise timely asserted. FRCP 5.1(d).

iii. *Nongovernmental corporate disclosure statement.* To enable judges and magistrates to evaluate possible disqualification or recusal, counsel for a private (nongovernmental) party shall submit at the time of initial pleading a certificate identifying any corporate parent, subsidiaries, or affiliates of that party. NY R USDCTED Div. Bus., Rule 50.1(c).

   - *Contents.* A nongovernmental corporate party must file two (2) copies of a disclosure statement that: (1) identifies any parent corporation and any publicly held corporation owning ten percent (10%) or more of its stock; or (2) states that there is no such corporation. FRCP 7.1(a).

   - *Time to file; Supplemental filing.* A party must: (1) file the disclosure statement with its first appearance, pleading, petition, motion, response, or other request addressed to the court; and (2) promptly file a supplemental statement if any required information changes. FRCP 7.1(b). For purposes of FRCP 7.1(b)(2), "promptly" shall mean "within fourteen days," that is, parties are required to file a supplemental disclosure statement within fourteen (14) days of the time there is any change in the information required in a disclosure statement filed pursuant to those rules. NY R USDCTS&ED Civ Rule 7.1.1.

iv.  *Copies of authorities.* In cases involving a pro se litigant, counsel shall, when serving a memorandum of law (or other submissions to the Court), provide the pro se litigant (but not other counsel or the Court) with copies of cases and other authorities cited therein that are unpublished or reported exclusively on computerized databases. Upon request, counsel shall provide the pro se litigant with copies of such unpublished cases and other authorities as are cited in a decision of the Court and were not previously cited by any party. NY R USDCTS&ED Civ Rule 7.2.

    v.   *Motion.* Refer to the General Requirements section of this document for information on the motion.

    vi.   *Memorandum of law.* Except for letter-motions as permitted by NY R USDCTS&ED Civ Rule 7.1(d) or as otherwise permitted by the Court, all motions shall include the following motion papers: a memorandum of law, setting forth the cases and other authorities relied upon in support of the motion, and divided, under appropriate headings, into as many parts as there are issues to be determined. NY R USDCTS&ED Civ Rule 7.1(a)(2).

3.   *Individual judge practices.* Refer to the Miscellaneous section of this document for information on individual judge practices on required documents.

## E. Format

1.   *Form of documents.* The rules governing captions and other matters of form in pleadings apply to motions and other papers. FRCP 7(b)(2).

    a.   *Paper.* Every pleading, written motion, and other paper must: be plainly written, typed, printed, or copied without erasures or interlineations which materially deface it. NY R USDCTS&ED Civ Rule 11.1(a)(1).

    b.   *Typeface, margin, and spacing.* The typeface, margins, and spacing of all documents presented for filing must meet the following requirements:

        i.   All text must be twelve (12) point type or larger, except for text in footnotes which may be ten (10) point type;

        ii.   All documents must have at least one (1) inch margins on all sides;

        iii.   All text must be double-spaced, except for headings, text in footnotes, or block quotations, which may be single-spaced. NY R USDCTS&ED Civ Rule 11.1(b).

    c.   *Caption; Names of parties.* Every pleading must have a caption with the court's name, a title, a file number, and a FRCP 7(a) designation. The title of the complaint must name all the parties; the title of other pleadings, after naming the first party on each side, may refer generally to other parties. FRCP 10(a). Every pleading, written motion, and other paper must: bear the docket number and the initials of the District Judge and any Magistrate Judge before whom the action or proceeding is pending, NY R USDCTS&ED Civ Rule 11.1(a)(2).

    d.   *Paragraphs; Separate statements.* A party must state its claims or defenses in numbered paragraphs, each limited as far as practicable to a single set of circumstances. A later pleading may refer by number to a paragraph in an earlier pleading. If doing so would promote clarity, each claim founded on a separate transaction or occurrence—and each defense other than a denial—must be stated in a separate count or defense. FRCP 10(b).

    e.   *Adoption by reference; Exhibits.* A statement in a pleading may be adopted by reference elsewhere in the same pleading or in any other pleading or motion. A copy of a written instrument that is an exhibit to a pleading is a part of the pleading for all purposes. FRCP 10(c).

    f.   *Acceptance by the clerk.* The clerk must not refuse to file a paper solely because it is not in the form prescribed by the Federal Rules of Civil Procedure or by a local rule or practice. FRCP 5(d)(4).

2.   *Signing of pleadings, motions and other papers*

    a.   *Signature.* Every pleading, written motion, and other paper must be signed by at least one attorney of record in the attorney's name—or by a party personally if the party is unrepresented. The paper must state the signer's address, e-mail address, and telephone number. FRCP 11(a). Every pleading, written motion, and other paper must: have the name of each person signing it clearly printed or typed directly below the signature. NY R USDCTS&ED Civ Rule 11.1(a)(3).

        i.   *No verification or accompanying affidavit required for pleadings.* Unless a rule or statute specifically states otherwise, a pleading need not be verified or accompanied by an affidavit. FRCP 11(a).

        ii.   *Unsigned papers.* The court must strike an unsigned paper unless the omission is promptly corrected after being called to the attorney's or party's attention. FRCP 11(a).

b. *Representations to the court.* By presenting to the court a pleading, written motion, or other paper—whether by signing, filing, submitting, or later advocating it—an attorney or unrepresented party certifies that to the best of the person's knowledge, information, and belief, formed after an inquiry reasonable under the circumstances:

    i. It is not being presented for any improper purpose, such as to harass, cause unnecessary delay, or needlessly increase the cost of litigation;

    ii. The claims, defenses, and other legal contentions are warranted by existing law or by a nonfrivolous argument for extending, modifying, or reversing existing law or for establishing new law;

    iii. The factual contentions have evidentiary support or, if specifically so identified, will likely have evidentiary support after a reasonable opportunity for further investigation or discovery; and

    iv. The denials of factual contentions are warranted on the evidence or, if specifically so identified, are reasonably based on belief or a lack of information. FRCP 11(b).

c. *Sanctions.* If, after notice and a reasonable opportunity to respond, the court determines that FRCP 11(b) has been violated, the court may impose an appropriate sanction on any attorney, law firm, or party that violated FRCP 11(b) or is responsible for the violation. FRCP 11(c)(1). Refer to the United States District Court for the Eastern District of New York KeyRules Motion for Sanctions document for more information.

3. *Privacy protection for filings made with the court*

a. *Redacted filings.* Unless the court orders otherwise, in an electronic or paper filing with the court that contains an individual's Social Security number, taxpayer-identification number, or birth date, the name of an individual known to be a minor, or a financial-account number, a party or nonparty making the filing may include only:

    i. The last four (4) digits of the Social Security number and taxpayer-identification number;

    ii. The year of the individual's birth;

    iii. The minor's initials; and

    iv. The last four (4) digits of the financial-account number. FRCP 5.2(a); NY R USDCTED Order 2004-09.

    v. In addition, exercise caution when filing documents that contain the following:

- Personal identifying number, such as driver's license number;

- Medical records, treatment and diagnosis;

- Employment history;

- Individual financial information; and

- Proprietary or trade secret information. NY R USDCTED Order 2004-09.

b. *Exemptions from the redaction requirement.* The redaction requirement does not apply to the following:

    i. A financial-account number that identifies the property allegedly subject to forfeiture in a forfeiture proceeding;

    ii. The record of an administrative or agency proceeding;

    iii. The official record of a state-court proceeding;

    iv. The record of a court or tribunal, if that record was not subject to the redaction requirement when originally filed;

    v. A filing covered by FRCP 5.2(c) or FRCP 5.2(d); and

    vi. A pro se filing in an action brought under 28 U.S.C.A. § 2241, 28 U.S.C.A. § 2254, or 28 U.S.C.A. § 2255. FRCP 5.2(b).

c. *Limitations on remote access to electronic files; Social Security appeals and immigration cases.*

821

Unless the court orders otherwise, in an action for benefits under the Social Security Act, and in an action or proceeding relating to an order of removal, to relief from removal, or to immigration benefits or detention, access to an electronic file is authorized as follows:

    i.    The parties and their attorneys may have remote electronic access to any part of the case file, including the administrative record;

    ii.    Any other person may have electronic access to the full record at the courthouse, but may have remote electronic access only to:

        • The docket maintained by the court; and

        • An opinion, order, judgment, or other disposition of the court, but not any other part of the case file or the administrative record. FRCP 5.2(c).

  d.    *Filings made under seal.* The court may order that a filing be made under seal without redaction. The court may later unseal the filing or order the person who made the filing to file a redacted version for the public record. FRCP 5.2(d).

  e.    *Protective orders.* For good cause, the court may by order in a case:

    i.    Require redaction of additional information; or

    ii.    Limit or prohibit a nonparty's remote electronic access to a document filed with the court. FRCP 5.2(e).

  f.    *Option for additional unredacted filing under seal.* A person making a redacted filing may also file an unredacted copy under seal. The court must retain the unredacted copy as part of the record. FRCP 5.2(f); NY R USDCTED Order 2004-09. The unredacted version of the document or the reference list shall be retained by the court as part of the record. The court may, however, still require the party to file a redacted copy for the public file. NY R USDCTED Order 2004-09.

  g.    *Option for filing a reference list.* A filing that contains redacted information may be filed together with a reference list that identifies each item of redacted information and specifies an appropriate identifier that uniquely corresponds to each item listed. The list must be filed under seal and may be amended as of right. Any reference in the case to a listed identifier will be construed to refer to the corresponding item of information. FRCP 5.2(g); NY R USDCTED Order 2004-09. The unredacted version of the document or the reference list shall be retained by the court as part of the record. The court may, however, still require the party to file a redacted copy for the public file. NY R USDCTED Order 2004-09.

  h.    *Responsibility for redaction.* The responsibility for redacting these personal identifiers rests solely with counsel and the parties. The Clerk will not review each pleading for compliance with NY R USDCTED Order 2004-09. NY R USDCTED Order 2004-09.

    i.    Counsel is strongly urged to share this notice with all clients so that an informed decision about the inclusion of certain materials may be made. If a redacted document is filed, it is the sole responsibility of counsel and the parties to be sure that all pleadings comply with the rules of this court requiring redaction of personal data identifiers. The clerk will not review each pleading for redaction. NY R USDCTED Order 2004-09.

  i.    *Waiver of protection of identifiers.* A person waives the protection of FRCP 5.2(a) as to the person's own information by filing it without redaction and not under seal. FRCP 5.2(h).

4.    *Individual judge practices.* Refer to the Miscellaneous section of this document for information on individual judge practices on formatting documents.

## F.  Filing and Service Requirements

1.    *Filing requirements.* Any paper after the complaint that is required to be served—together with a certificate of service—must be filed within a reasonable time after service. FRCP 5(d)(1).

  a.    *How filing is made; In general.* A paper is filed by delivering it:

    i.    To the clerk; or

    ii.    To a judge who agrees to accept it for filing, and who must then note the filing date on the paper and promptly send it to the clerk. FRCP 5(d)(2).

b. *Night depository.* A night depository with an automatic date stamp shall be maintained. . .by the Clerk of the Eastern District in the Brooklyn Courthouse. After regular business hours, papers for the District Court only may be deposited in the night depository. Such papers will be considered as having been filed in the District Court as of the date stamped thereon, which shall be deemed presumptively correct. NY R USDCTS&ED Civ Rule 1.2.

c. *Electronic filing*

   i. *Authorization of electronic filing program.* A court may, by local rule, allow papers to be filed, signed, or verified by electronic means that are consistent with any technical standards established by the Judicial Conference of the United States. A local rule may require electronic filing only if reasonable exceptions are allowed. A paper filed electronically in compliance with a local rule is a written paper for purposes of the Federal Rules of Civil Procedure. FRCP 5(d)(3).

- Parties serving and filing papers shall follow the instructions regarding Electronic Case Filing (ECF) published on the website of each respective Court. A paper served and filed by electronic means in accordance with such instructions is, for purposes of FRCP 5, served and filed in compliance with the Local Civil Rules of the Southern and Eastern Districts of New York. NY R USDCTS&ED Civ Rule 5.2(a). Parties have an obligation to review the Court's actual order, decree, or judgment (on ECF), which controls, and should not rely on the description on the docket or in the ECF Notice of Electronic Filing (NEF). NY R USDCTS&ED Civ Rule 5.2(c).

   ii. *Mandatory electronic filing.* Beginning on August 2, 2004, electronic case filing will be mandatory for all civil cases other than pro se cases. NY R USDCTED Order 2004-08.

- *Letter-motions and letters addressed to the court.* Subject to the instructions regarding ECF published on the website of each respective Court and any pertinent Individual Judge's Practices, letter-motions permitted by NY R USDCTS&ED Civ Rule 7.1(d) and letters addressed to the Court (but not letters between the parties) may be filed via ECF. NY R USDCTS&ED Civ Rule 5.2(b).

- *Proposed orders, judgments and decrees.* Proposed orders, judgments and decrees shall be presented as directed by the ECF rules published on the website of each respective Court. NY R USDCTS&ED Civ Rule 77.1. For more information, refer to NY R USDCTS&ED Civ Rule 77.1.

- *Request for exemption.* Requests by attorneys for an exemption to the mandatory policy will be considered for good cause hardship reasons only, and will be reviewed on an individual basis by the assigned United States Magistrate Judge. The Clerk's Office provides an electronic filing training program to assist attorneys filing electronically. Before seeking a hardship exemption, attorneys are advised to participate in the training program or otherwise seek the assistance of the Clerk's Office. NY R USDCTED Order 2004-08.

   iii. For more information on electronic filing, refer to the court's website.

2. *Service requirements*

a. *Service; When required*

   i. *In general.* Unless the Federal Rules of Civil Procedure provide otherwise, each of the following papers must be served on every party:

- An order stating that service is required;

- A pleading filed after the original complaint, unless the court orders otherwise under FRCP 5(c) because there are numerous defendants;

- A discovery paper required to be served on a party, unless the court orders otherwise;

- A written motion, except one that may be heard ex parte; and

- A written notice, appearance, demand, or offer of judgment, or any similar paper. FRCP 5(a)(1).

    ii.   *If a party fails to appear.* No service is required on a party who is in default for failing to appear. But a pleading that asserts a new claim for relief against such a party must be served on that party under FRCP 4. FRCP 5(a)(2).

    iii.   *Seizing property.* If an action is begun by seizing property and no person is or need be named as a defendant, any service required before the filing of an appearance, answer, or claim must be made on the person who had custody or possession of the property when it was seized. FRCP 5(a)(3).

  b.  *Service; How made*

    i.   *Serving an attorney.* If a party is represented by an attorney, service under FRCP 5 must be made on the attorney unless the court orders service on the party. FRCP 5(b)(1).

    ii.   *Service in general.* A paper is served under FRCP 5 by:

- Handing it to the person;
- Leaving it: (1) at the person's office with a clerk or other person in charge or, if no one is in charge, in a conspicuous place in the office; or (2) if the person has no office or the office is closed, at the person's dwelling or usual place of abode with someone of suitable age and discretion who resides there;
- Mailing it to the person's last known address—in which event service is complete upon mailing;
- Leaving it with the court clerk if the person has no known address;
- Sending it by electronic means if the person consented in writing—in which event service is complete upon transmission, but is not effective if the serving party learns that it did not reach the person to be served; or
- Delivering it by any other means that the person consented to in writing—in which event service is complete when the person making service delivers it to the agency designated to make delivery. FRCP 5(b)(2).

    iii.   *Service by overnight delivery.* Service upon an attorney may be made by overnight delivery service. "Overnight delivery service" means any delivery service which regularly accepts items for overnight delivery. Overnight delivery service shall be deemed service by mail for purposes of FRCP 5 and FRCP 6. NY R USDCTS&ED Civ Rule 5.3.

    iv.   *Service by electronic means.* Parties serving and filing papers shall follow the instructions regarding Electronic Case Filing (ECF) published on the website of each respective Court. A paper served and filed by electronic means in accordance with such instructions is, for purposes of FRCP 5, served and filed in compliance with the Local Civil Rules of the United States District Courts for the Southern and Eastern Districts of New York. NY R USDCTS&ED Civ Rule 5.2(a). Parties have an obligation to review the Court's actual order, decree, or judgment (on ECF), which controls, and should not rely on the description on the docket or in the ECF Notice of Electronic Filing (NEF). NY R USDCTS&ED Civ Rule 5.2(c).

    v.   *Using court facilities.* If a local rule so authorizes, a party may use the court's transmission facilities to make service under FRCP 5(b)(2)(E). FRCP 5(b)(3).

  c.  *Serving numerous defendants*

    i.   *In general.* If an action involves an unusually large number of defendants, the court may, on motion or on its own, order that:

- Defendants' pleadings and replies to them need not be served on other defendants;
- Any crossclaim, counterclaim, avoidance, or affirmative defense in those pleadings and replies to them will be treated as denied or avoided by all other parties; and
- Filing any such pleading and serving it on the plaintiff constitutes notice of the pleading to all parties. FRCP 5(c)(1).

    ii.   *Notifying parties.* A copy of every such order must be served on the parties as the court directs. FRCP 5(c)(2).

3. *Individual judge practices.* Refer to the Miscellaneous section of this document for information on individual judge practices on filing and serving documents.

## G. Hearings

1. *Hearings, generally*

   a. *Oral argument.* Due process does not require that oral argument be permitted on a motion and, except as otherwise provided by local rule, the district court has discretion to determine whether it will decide the motion on the papers or hear argument by counsel (and perhaps receive evidence). FPP § 1190; F.D.I.C. v. Deglau, 207 F.3d 153 (3d Cir. 2000). The parties and their attorneys shall only appear to argue the motion if so directed by the Court by order or by a Judge's Individual Practice. NY R USDCTS&ED Civ Rule 6.1(c).

   b. *Providing a regular schedule for oral hearings.* A court may establish regular times and places for oral hearings on motions. FRCP 78(a).

   c. *Providing for submission on briefs.* By rule or order, the court may provide for submitting and determining motions on briefs, without oral hearings. FRCP 78(b).

2. *Hearing on motion for preliminary injunction after temporary restraining order is issued without notice*

   a. *Expediting the preliminary injunction hearing.* If the order is issued without notice, the motion for a preliminary injunction must be set for hearing at the earliest possible time, taking precedence over all other matters except hearings on older matters of the same character. At the hearing, the party who obtained the order must proceed with the motion; if the party does not, the court must dissolve the order. FRCP 65(b)(3). Refer to the United States District Court for the Eastern District of New York KeyRules Motion for Preliminary Injunction document for more information on the hearing on the motion for preliminary injunction.

3. *Individual judge practices.* Refer to the Miscellaneous section of this document for information on individual judge practices on hearings.

## H. Forms

1. **Federal Application for Temporary Restraining Order Forms**

   a. Ex parte motion; For temporary restraining order and order to show cause; Interference with property rights. AMJUR PP INJUNCTION § 42.

   b. Affidavit; In support of ex parte motion for temporary restraining order. AMJUR PP INJUNCTION § 48.

   c. Certificate of attorney; In support of ex parte motion for temporary restraining order. AMJUR PP INJUNCTION § 50.

   d. Affidavit; In support of ex parte motion for temporary restraining order; Interference with property rights. AMJUR PP INJUNCTION § 51.

   e. Motion. 4A FEDFORMS § 5344.

   f. Motion; Another form. 4A FEDFORMS § 5345.

   g. Motion; Another form. 4A FEDFORMS § 5346.

   h. Motion without notice. 4A FEDFORMS § 5347.

   i. Motion without notice; Another form. 4A FEDFORMS § 5348.

   j. Motion without notice; Another form. 4A FEDFORMS § 5349.

   k. Motion without notice; Another form. 4A FEDFORMS § 5350.

   l. Motion without notice; Another form. 4A FEDFORMS § 5351.

   m. Motion without notice; Another form. 4A FEDFORMS § 5352.

   n. Certificate of attorney's efforts to give notice. 4A FEDFORMS § 5353.

   o. Certificate of attorney's efforts to give notice; Another form. 4A FEDFORMS § 5354.

   p. Certificate of attorney's efforts to give notice; Another form. 4A FEDFORMS § 5355.

q.  Certificate of attorney's efforts to give notice; Another form. 4A FEDFORMS § 5356.

r.  Motion requesting expedited hearing. 4A FEDFORMS § 5357.

s.  Motion seeking temporary restraining order. 4A FEDFORMS § 5359.

t.  Motion to dissolve or modify temporary restraining order. 4A FEDFORMS § 5361.

u.  Motion for temporary restraining order and preliminary injunction. GOLDLTGFMS § 13A:6.

v.  Motion for temporary restraining order; General form. GOLDLTGFMS § 13A:11.

w.  Motion for temporary restraining order; Ex parte application. GOLDLTGFMS § 13A:12.

x.  Motion for temporary restraining order; Ex parte application; Supporting affidavit by party. GOLDLTGFMS § 13A:13.

y.  Motion for temporary restraining order; Ex parte application; Supporting affidavit by party; Copyright infringement. GOLDLTGFMS § 13A:14.

z.  Motion for temporary restraining order; Ex parte application; Certificate by counsel. GOLDLTGFMS § 13A:15.

## I.  Applicable Rules

1.  *Federal rules*

    a.  Serving and filing pleadings and other papers. FRCP 5.

    b.  Constitutional challenge to a statute; Notice, certification, and intervention. FRCP 5.1.

    c.  Privacy protection for filings made with the court. FRCP 5.2.

    d.  Computing and extending time; Time for motion papers. FRCP 6.

    e.  Pleadings allowed; Form of motions and other papers. FRCP 7.

    f.  Disclosure statement. FRCP 7.1.

    g.  Form of pleadings. FRCP 10.

    h.  Signing pleadings, motions, and other papers; Representations to the court; Sanctions. FRCP 11.

    i.  Taking testimony. FRCP 43.

    j.  Injunctions and restraining orders. FRCP 65.

    k.  Proceedings against a surety. FRCP 65.1.

    l.  Hearing motions; Submission on briefs. FRCP 78.

2.  *Local rules*

    a.  Night depository. NY R USDCTS&ED Civ Rule 1.2.

    b.  Duty of attorneys in related cases. NY R USDCTS&ED Civ Rule 1.6.

    c.  Filing of discovery materials. NY R USDCTS&ED Civ Rule 5.1.

    d.  Electronic service and filing of documents. NY R USDCTS&ED Civ Rule 5.2.

    e.  Service by overnight delivery. NY R USDCTS&ED Civ Rule 5.3.

    f.  Service and filing of motion papers. NY R USDCTS&ED Civ Rule 6.1.

    g.  Orders on motions. NY R USDCTS&ED Civ Rule 6.2.

    h.  Computation of time. NY R USDCTS&ED Civ Rule 6.4.

    i.  Motion papers. NY R USDCTS&ED Civ Rule 7.1.

    j.  Disclosure statement. NY R USDCTS&ED Civ Rule 7.1.1.

    k.  Authorities to be provided to pro se litigants. NY R USDCTS&ED Civ Rule 7.2.

    l.  Form of pleadings, motions, and other papers. NY R USDCTS&ED Civ Rule 11.1.

    m.  Mode of raising discovery and other non-dispositive pretrial disputes with the court (Eastern District only). NY R USDCTS&ED Civ Rule 37.3.

n.  Submission of orders, judgments and decrees. NY R USDCTS&ED Civ Rule 77.1.

o.  Court-annexed arbitration (Eastern District only). NY R USDCTS&ED Civ Rule 83.7.

p.  Court-annexed mediation (Eastern District only). NY R USDCTS&ED Civ Rule 83.8.

q.  Electronic case filing. NY R USDCTED Order 2004-08.

r.  The August 2, 2004 amendment to the E-Government Act of 2002. NY R USDCTED Order 2004-09.

s.  Categories and classification of cases; Information on cases and parties. NY R USDCTED Div. Bus., Rule 50.1.

## J.  Miscellaneous

**NOTE: Individual judges' rules may apply. For available judge-level information, refer to:**

DISTRICT JUDGE CAROL BAGLEY AMON: NY R USDCTED Amon-Practices.

DISTRICT JUDGE JOAN M. AZRACK: NY R USDCTED Azrack-Practices.

DISTRICT JUDGE JOSEPH F. BIANCO: NY R USDCTED Bianco-Practices.

DISTRICT JUDGE FREDERIC BLOCK: NY R USDCTED Block-Practices.

DISTRICT JUDGE MARGO K. BRODIE: NY R USDCTED Brodie-Practices.

DISTRICT JUDGE PAMELA K. CHEN: NY R USDCTED Chen-Practices.

DISTRICT JUDGE BRIAN M. COGAN: NY R USDCTED Cogan-Practices; NY R USDCTED Cogan-Pretrial.

DISTRICT JUDGE LaSHANN DeARCY HALL: NY R USDCTED DeArcy Hall-Practices.

DISTRICT JUDGE RAYMOND J. DEARIE: NY R USDCTED Dearie-Practices.

DISTRICT JUDGE ANN M. DONNELLY: NY R USDCTED Donnelly-Practices.

DISTRICT JUDGE SANDRA J. FEUERSTEIN: NY R USDCTED Feuerstein-Practices; NY R USDCTED Feuerstein-Pretrial.

DISTRICT JUDGE NICHOLAS G. GARAUIFIS: NY R USDCTED Garaufis-Practices; NY R USDCTED Garaufis-Pretrial.

DISTRICT JUDGE NINA GERSHON: NY R USDCTED Gershon-Practices.

DISTRICT JUDGE I. LEO GLASSER: NY R USDCTED Glasser-Practices; NY R USDCTED Glasser-Crim.

DISTRICT JUDGE DENIS R. HURLEY: NY R USDCTED Hurley-Practices; [NY R USDCTED Hurley-Pro Cooperation Info, as added by NY ORDER 16-4188, effective July 22, 2016]; [NY R USDCTED Hurley-Pro Cooperation Info Stay, as added by NY ORDER 16-4188, effective July 22, 2016].

DISTRICT JUDGE DORA L. IRIZARRY: NY R USDCTED Irizarry-Practices; NY R USDCTED Irizarry-Pretrial; NY R USDCTED Irizarry-Crim.

DISTRICT JUDGE STERLING JOHNSON, JR.: NY R USDCTED Johnson-Practices.

DISTRICT JUDGE EDWARD R. KORMAN: NY R USDCTED Korman-Practices; NY R USDCTED Korman-Pretrial.

DISTRICT JUDGE WILLIAM F. KUNTZ: NY R USDCTED Kuntz-Practices.

DISTRICT JUDGE KIYO A. MATSUMOTO: NY R USDCTED Matsumoto-Practices.

DISTRICT JUDGE ROSLYNN R. MAUSKOPF: NY R USDCTED Mauskopf-Practices; NY R USDCTED Mauskopf-Recusal.

DISTRICT JUDGE THOMAS C. PLATT: NY R USDCTED Platt-Practices.

DISTRICT JUDGE ALLYNE R. ROSS: NY R USDCTED Ross-Practices.

DISTRICT JUDGE JOANNA SEYBERT: NY R USDCTED Seybert-Practices.

DISTRICT JUDGE ARTHUR D. SPATT: NY R USDCTED Spatt-Practices.

DISTRICT JUDGE SANDRA L. TOWNES: NY R USDCTED Townes-Practices.

DISTRICT JUDGE ERIC N. VITALIANO: NY R USDCTED Vitaliano-Practices.

DISTRICT JUDGE JACK B. WEINSTEIN: NY R USDCTED Weinstein-Practices.

DISTRICT JUDGE LEONARD D. WEXLER: NY R USDCTED Wexler-Practices; NY R USDCTED Wexler-Rules.

MAGISTRATE JUDGE LOIS BLOOM: NY R USDCTED Bloom-Practices.

MAGISTRATE JUDGE GARY R. BROWN: NY R USDCTED Brown-Practices.

MAGISTRATE JUDGE MARILYN D. GO: NY R USDCTED Go-Practices.

MAGISTRATE JUDGE STEVEN M. GOLD: NY R USDCTED Gold-Practices.

MAGISTRATE JUDGE PEGGY KUO: NY R USDCTED Kuo-Practices; NY R USDCTED Kuo-Scheduling Order.

MAGISTRATE JUDGE ROBERT M. LEVY: NY R USDCTED Levy-Practices.

MAGISTRATE JUDGE ARLENE R. LINDSAY: NY R USDCTED Lindsay-Practices.

MAGISTRATE JUDGE STEVEN I. LOCKE: NY R USDCTED Locke-Practices.

MAGISTRATE JUDGE ROANNE L. MANN: NY R USDCTED Mann-Practices.

MAGISTRATE JUDGE JAMES ORENSTEIN: NY R USDCTED Jorenstein--Practices.

MAGISTRATE JUDGE VIKTOR V. POHORELSKY: NY R USDCTED Pohorelsky-Practices.

MAGISTRATE JUDGE CHERYL L. POLLAK: NY R USDCTED Pollak-Practices; NY R USDCTED Pollak-Pretrial.

MAGISTRATE JUDGE RAMON E. REYES, JR.: NY R USDCTED Reyes-Practices.

MAGISTRATE JUDGE VERA M. SCANLON: NY R USDCTED Scanlon-Practices.

MAGISTRATE JUDGE ANNE Y. SHIELDS: NY R USDCTED Shields-Practices.

MAGISTRATE JUDGE STEVEN L. TISCIONE: NY R USDCTED Tiscione-Practices.

MAGISTRATE JUDGE A. KATHLEEN TOMILINSON: NY R USDCTED Tomlinson-Practices.

# Requests, Notices and Applications
# Pretrial Conferences, Scheduling, Management

## Document Last Updated September 2016

**A. Checklist**

(I) ❑ Matters to be considered by parties for the pretrial conference

    (a) ❑ Documents to consider

        (1) ❑ Pretrial memorandum or statement

    (b) ❑ Timing

        (1) ❑ The court determines at what stage in the action to hold a pretrial conference

(II) ❑ Matters to be considered by parties for the scheduling conference

    (a) ❑ Documents to consider

        (1) ❑ Request for scheduling conference

    (b) ❑ Timing

        (1) ❑ If a scheduling conference is called, it is important to recognize that, unlike the ordinary pretrial conference, the scheduling conference occurs before the substantive issues have been defined and is directed toward organizing the processing of the action by setting deadlines for the completion of the various pretrial phases

(III) ❏ Matters to be considered by parties for the discovery planning conference

    (a) ❏ Required documents

        (1) ❏ Written report outlining proposed discovery plan

    (b) ❏ Timing

        (1) ❏ Except in a proceeding exempted from initial disclosure under FRCP 26(a)(1)(B) or when the court orders otherwise, the parties must confer as soon as practicable—and in any event at least twenty-one (21) days before a scheduling conference is to be held or a scheduling order is due under FRCP 16(b)

        (2) ❏ Within fourteen (14) days after the conference, the attorneys of record are responsible for submitting a written report outlining the plan

## B. Timing

1. *Pretrial conferences, generally.* The court determines at what stage in the action to hold a pretrial conference. When only one conference is involved, the most favored practice seems to be to wait until after the case has been prepared for trial. FPP § 1524. Although there rarely will be any need to hold a conference in a relatively simple case until after the preliminary motions have been disposed of, the only inherently logical limitation on the court's discretion as to when to hold a conference is that it should not be held before all the necessary and indispensable parties are served. FPP § 1524.

2. *Scheduling conference.* If a scheduling conference is called, it is important to recognize that, unlike the ordinary pretrial conference, the scheduling conference occurs before the substantive issues have been defined and is directed toward organizing the processing of the action by setting deadlines for the completion of the various pretrial phases. FPP § 1522.1.

3. *Discovery planning conference.* Except in a proceeding exempted from initial disclosure under FRCP 26(a)(1)(B) or when the court orders otherwise, the parties must confer as soon as practicable—and in any event at least twenty-one (21) days before a scheduling conference is to be held or a scheduling order is due under FRCP 16(b). FRCP 26(f)(1).

    a. *Submission of written report outlining proposed discovery plan.* The attorneys of record and all unrepresented parties that have appeared in the case are jointly responsible for arranging the conference, for attempting in good faith to agree on the proposed discovery plan, and for submitting to the court within fourteen (14) days after the conference a written report outlining the plan. FRCP 26(f)(2).

    b. *Expedited schedule.* If necessary to comply with its expedited schedule for FRCP 16(b) conferences, a court may by local rule: (1) require the parties' conference to occur less than twenty-one (21) days before the scheduling conference is held or a scheduling order is due under FRCP 16(b); and (2) require the written report outlining the discovery plan to be filed less than fourteen (14) days after the parties' conference, or excuse the parties from submitting a written report and permit them to report orally on their discovery plan at the FRCP 16(b) conference. FRCP 26(f)(4).

4. *Computation of time*

    a. *Computing time.* FRCP 6 applies in computing any time period specified in the Federal Rules of Civil Procedure, in any local rule or court order, or in any statute that does not specify a method of computing time. FRCP 6(a). In computing any period of time prescribed or allowed by the Local Civil Rules of the United States District Courts for the Southern and Eastern Districts of New York or the Local Admiralty and Maritime Rules, the provisions of FRCP 6 shall apply unless otherwise stated. NY R USDCTS&ED Civ Rule 6.4.

        i. *Period stated in days or a longer unit.* When the period is stated in days or a longer unit of time:

            • Exclude the day of the event that triggers the period;

            • Count every day, including intermediate Saturdays, Sundays, and legal holidays; and

            • Include the last day of the period, but if the last day is a Saturday, Sunday, or legal holiday, the period continues to run until the end of the next day that is not a Saturday, Sunday, or legal holiday. FRCP 6(a)(1). In the Local Civil Rules of the United States District Courts for the Southern and Eastern Districts of New York, as in the Federal Rules of Civil Procedure as amended effective December 1, 2009, Saturdays, Sundays, and legal holidays are no longer excluded in computing periods of time. If the last day of the period is a Saturday, Sunday, or legal holiday, the period continues to run until the end of the next day that is not a Saturday, Sunday, or legal holiday. NY R USDCTS&ED Civ Rule 6.4.

ii. *Period stated in hours.* When the period is stated in hours:

- Begin counting immediately on the occurrence of the event that triggers the period;

- Count every hour, including hours during intermediate Saturdays, Sundays, and legal holidays; and

- If the period would end on a Saturday, Sunday, or legal holiday, the period continues to run until the same time on the next day that is not a Saturday, Sunday, or legal holiday. FRCP 6(a)(2). In the Local Civil Rules of the United States District Courts for the Southern and Eastern Districts of New York, as in the Federal Rules of Civil Procedure as amended effective December 1, 2009, Saturdays, Sundays, and legal holidays are no longer excluded in computing periods of time. If the last day of the period is a Saturday, Sunday, or legal holiday, the period continues to run until the end of the next day that is not a Saturday, Sunday, or legal holiday. NY R USDCTS&ED Civ Rule 6.4.

iii. *Inaccessibility of the clerk's office.* Unless the court orders otherwise, if the clerk's office is inaccessible:

- On the last day for filing under FRCP 6(a)(1), then the time for filing is extended to the first accessible day that is not a Saturday, Sunday, or legal holiday; or

- During the last hour for filing under FRCP 6(a)(2), then the time for filing is extended to the same time on the first accessible day that is not a Saturday, Sunday, or legal holiday. FRCP 6(a)(3).

iv. *"Last day" defined.* Unless a different time is set by a statute, local rule, or court order, the last day ends:

- For electronic filing, at midnight in the court's time zone; and

- For filing by other means, when the clerk's office is scheduled to close. FRCP 6(a)(4).

v. *"Next day" defined.* The "next day" is determined by continuing to count forward when the period is measured after an event and backward when measured before an event. FRCP 6(a)(5).

vi. *"Legal holiday" defined.* "Legal holiday" means:

- The day set aside by statute for observing New Year's Day, Martin Luther King Jr.'s Birthday, Washington's Birthday, Memorial Day, Independence Day, Labor Day, Columbus Day, Veterans' Day, Thanksgiving Day, or Christmas Day;

- Any day declared a holiday by the President or Congress; and

- For periods that are measured after an event, any other day declared a holiday by the state where the district court is located. FRCP 6(a)(6).

b. *Extending time*

i. *In general.* When an act may or must be done within a specified time, the court may, for good cause, extend the time:

- With or without motion or notice if the court acts, or if a request is made, before the original time or its extension expires; or

- On motion made after the time has expired if the party failed to act because of excusable neglect. FRCP 6(b)(1).

ii. *Exceptions.* A court must not extend the time to act under FRCP 50(b), FRCP 50(d), FRCP 52(b), FRCP 59(b), FRCP 59(d), FRCP 59(e), and FRCP 60(b). FRCP 6(b)(2).

iii. Refer to the United States District Court for the Eastern District of New York KeyRules Motion for Continuance/Extension of Time document for more information on extending time.

    c. *Additional time after certain kinds of service.* When a party may or must act within a specified time after service and service is made under FRCP 5(b)(2)(C), FRCP 5(b)(2)(D), FRCP 5(b)(2)(E), or FRCP 5(b)(2)(F), three (3) days are added after the period would otherwise expire under FRCP 6(a). FRCP 6(d). Overnight delivery service shall be deemed service by mail for purposes of FRCP 5 and FRCP 6. NY R USDCTS&ED Civ Rule 5.3.

5. *Individual judge practices.* Refer to the Miscellaneous section of this document for information on individual judge practices on timing of documents.

## C. General Requirements

1. *Pretrial conferences, generally*

    a. *Purposes of a pretrial conference.* FRCP 16 provides an important mechanism for carrying out one of the basic policies of the Federal Rules of Civil Procedure—the determination of disputes on their merits rather than on the basis of procedural niceties or tactical advantage. FPP § 1522. In any action, the court may order the attorneys and any unrepresented parties to appear for one or more pretrial conferences for such purposes as:

        i. Expediting disposition of the action;

        ii. Establishing early and continuing control so that the case will not be protracted because of lack of management;

        iii. Discouraging wasteful pretrial activities;

        iv. Improving the quality of the trial through more thorough preparation; and

        v. Facilitating settlement. FRCP 16(a).

    b. *When appropriate.* FRCP 16 specifically provides that the court "may order the attorneys and any unrepresented parties to appear for one or more pretrial conferences." This language makes it clear that the utilization of the pretrial conference procedure lies within the discretion of the district court both as a matter of general policy and in terms of whether and when the rule should be invoked in a particular case. FPP § 1523; Mizwicki v. Helwig, 196 F.3d 828 (7th Cir. 1999). There is no requirement that any pretrial conferences be held or not held in certain types of actions. FPP § 1523.

    c. *Attendance at a pretrial conference.* A represented party must authorize at least one of its attorneys to make stipulations and admissions about all matters that can reasonably be anticipated for discussion at a pretrial conference. If appropriate, the court may require that a party or its representative be present or reasonably available by other means to consider possible settlement. FRCP 16(c)(1).

    d. *Matters for consideration at a pretrial conference.* At any pretrial conference, the court may consider and take appropriate action on the following matters:

        i. Formulating and simplifying the issues, and eliminating frivolous claims or defenses;

        ii. Amending the pleadings if necessary or desirable;

        iii. Obtaining admissions and stipulations about facts and documents to avoid unnecessary proof, and ruling in advance on the admissibility of evidence;

        iv. Avoiding unnecessary proof and cumulative evidence, and limiting the use of testimony under FRE 702;

        v. Determining the appropriateness and timing of summary adjudication under FRCP 56;

        vi. Controlling and scheduling discovery, including orders affecting disclosures and discovery under FRCP 26 and FRCP 29 through FRCP 37;

        vii. Identifying witnesses and documents, scheduling the filing and exchange of any pretrial briefs, and setting dates for further conferences and for trial;

        viii. Referring matters to a magistrate judge or a master;

        ix. Settling the case and using special procedures to assist in resolving the dispute when authorized by statute or local rule;

x. Determining the form and content of the pretrial order;

xi. Disposing of pending motions;

xii. Adopting special procedures for managing potentially difficult or protracted actions that may involve complex issues, multiple parties, difficult legal questions, or unusual proof problems;

xiii. Ordering a separate trial under FRCP 42(b) of a claim, counterclaim, crossclaim, third-party claim, or particular issue;

xiv. Ordering the presentation of evidence early in the trial on a manageable issue that might, on the evidence, be the basis for a judgment as a matter of law under FRCP 50(a) or a judgment on partial findings under FRCP 52(c);

xv. Establishing a reasonable limit on the time allowed to present evidence; and

xvi. Facilitating in other ways the just, speedy, and inexpensive disposition of the action. FRCP 16(c)(2).

e. *Pretrial orders.* After any conference under FRCP 16, the court should issue an order reciting the action taken. This order controls the course of the action unless the court modifies it. FRCP 16(d).

f. *Sanctions.* On motion or on its own, the court may issue any just orders, including those authorized by FRCP 37(b)(2)(A)(ii) through FRCP 37(b)(2)(A)(vii), if a party or its attorney: (1) fails to appear at a scheduling or other pretrial conference; (2) is substantially unprepared to participate—or does not participate in good faith—in the conference; or (3) fails to obey a scheduling or other pretrial order. FRCP 16(f)(1).

i. *Imposing fees and costs.* Instead of or in addition to any other sanction, the court must order the party, its attorney, or both to pay the reasonable expenses—including attorney's fees—incurred because of any noncompliance with FRCP 16, unless the noncompliance was substantially justified or other circumstances make an award of expenses unjust. FRCP 16(f)(2).

2. *Scheduling conference.* A scheduling conference may be requested by the judge or by the parties, but it is not mandatory. FPP § 1522.1.

a. *Scheduling order.* Except in categories of actions exempted by local rule, the district judge—or a magistrate judge when authorized by local rule—must issue a scheduling order: (1) after receiving the parties' report under FRCP 26(f); or (2) after consulting with the parties' attorneys and any unrepresented parties at a scheduling conference. FRCP 16(b)(1). In any case referred to a Magistrate Judge, the Magistrate Judge may issue or modify scheduling orders pursuant to FRCP 16(b). NY R USDCTS&ED Civ Rule 16.2.

i. *Exemptions.* Matters involving habeas corpus petitions, Social Security disability cases, motions to vacate sentences, forfeitures, and reviews from administrative agencies are exempted from the mandatory scheduling order required by FRCP 16(b). NY R USDCTS&ED Civ Rule 16.1.

ii. *Required contents of the order.* The scheduling order must limit the time to join other parties, amend the pleadings, complete discovery, and file motions. FRCP 16(b)(3)(A).

iii. *Permitted contents of the order.* The scheduling order may:

- Modify the timing of disclosures under FRCP 26(a) and FRCP 26(e)(1);

- Modify the extent of discovery;

- Provide for disclosure, discovery, or preservation of electronically stored information;

- Include any agreements the parties reach for asserting claims of privilege or of protection as trial-preparation material after information is produced, including agreements reached under FRE 502;

- Direct that before moving for an order relating to discovery, the movant must request a conference with the court;

- Set dates for pretrial conferences and for trial; and

- Include other appropriate matters. FRCP 16(b)(3)(B).

b. *Time to issue.* The judge must issue the scheduling order as soon as practicable, but unless the judge finds good cause for delay, the judge must issue it within the earlier of ninety (90) days after any defendant has been served with the complaint or sixty (60) days after any defendant has appeared. FRCP 16(b)(2).

c. *Modifying a schedule.* A schedule may be modified only for good cause and with the judge's consent. FRCP 16(b)(4).

3. *Final pretrial conference.* The court may hold a final pretrial conference to formulate a trial plan, including a plan to facilitate the admission of evidence. FRCP 16(e).

a. *Timing and attendance.* The conference must be held as close to the start of trial as is reasonable, and must be attended by at least one attorney who will conduct the trial for each party and by any unrepresented party. FRCP 16(e).

b. *Modification of final pretrial order.* The court may modify the order issued after a final pretrial conference only to prevent manifest injustice. FRCP 16(e).

4. *Discovery planning conference*

a. *Conference content.* In conferring, the parties must consider the nature and basis of their claims and defenses and the possibilities for promptly settling or resolving the case; make or arrange for the disclosures required by FRCP 26(a)(1); discuss any issues about preserving discoverable information; and develop a proposed discovery plan. FRCP 26(f)(2).

b. *Parties' responsibilities.* The attorneys of record and all unrepresented parties that have appeared in the case are jointly responsible for arranging the conference, for attempting in good faith to agree on the proposed discovery plan, and for submitting to the court within fourteen (14) days after the conference a written report outlining the plan. The court may order the parties or attorneys to attend the conference in person. FRCP 26(f)(2).

c. *Discovery plan.* A discovery plan must state the parties' views and proposals on:

   i. What changes should be made in the timing, form, or requirement for disclosures under FRCP 26(a), including a statement of when initial disclosures were made or will be made;

   ii. The subjects on which discovery may be needed, when discovery should be completed, and whether discovery should be conducted in phases or be limited to or focused on particular issues;

   iii. Any issues about disclosure, discovery, or preservation of electronically stored information, including the form or forms in which it should be produced;

   iv. Any issues about claims of privilege or of protection as trial-preparation materials, including—if the parties agree on a procedure to assert these claims after production—whether to ask the court to include their agreement in an order under FRE 502;

   v. What changes should be made in the limitations on discovery imposed under the Federal Rules of Civil Procedure or by local rule, and what other limitations should be imposed; and

   vi. Any other orders that the court should issue under FRCP 26(c) or under FRCP 16(b) and FRCP 26(c). FRCP 26(f)(3).

5. *Related cases.* It shall be the continuing duty of each attorney appearing in any civil or criminal case to bring promptly to the attention of the Court all facts which said attorney believes are relevant to a determination that said case and one or more pending civil or criminal cases should be heard by the same Judge, in order to avoid unnecessary duplication of judicial effort. As soon as the attorney becomes aware of such relationship, said attorney shall notify the Judges to whom the cases have been assigned. NY R USDCTS&ED Civ Rule 1.6(a). If counsel fails to comply with NY R USDCTS&ED Civ Rule 1.6(a), the Court may assess reasonable costs directly against counsel whose action has obstructed the effective administration of the Court's business. NY R USDCTS&ED Civ Rule 1.6(b).

6. *Alternative dispute resolution (ADR)*

a. *Court-annexed arbitration*

   i. *Civil cases eligible for compulsory arbitration.* The Clerk of Court shall, as to all cases filed after January 1, 1986, designate and process for compulsory arbitration all civil cases (excluding Social Security cases, tax matters, prisoners' civil rights cases and any action based on an alleged violation of a right secured by the Constitution of the United States or if jurisdiction is based in whole or in part on 28 U.S.C.A. § 1343) wherein money damages only are being sought in an amount not in excess of one hundred fifty thousand dollars ($150,000) exclusive of interest and costs. NY R USDCTS&ED Civ Rule 83.7(d)(1).

- The parties may by written stipulation agree that the Clerk of Court shall designate and process for court-annexed arbitration any civil case that is not subject to compulsory arbitration in NY R USDCTS&ED Civ Rule 83.7. NY R USDCTS&ED Civ Rule 83.7(d)(2).

- For purposes of NY R USDCTS&ED Civ Rule 83.7 only, in all civil cases damages shall be presumed to be not in excess of one hundred fifty thousand dollars ($150,000) exclusive of interest and costs, unless: (1) counsel for plaintiff, at the time of filing the complaint, or in the event of the removal of a case from state court or transfer of a case from another district to this Court, within thirty (30) days of the docketing of the case in this district, files a certification with the Court that the damages sought exceed one hundred fifty thousand dollars ($150,000), exclusive of interest and costs; or (2) counsel for a defendant, at the time of filing a counterclaim or cross-claim files a certification with the court that the damages sought by the counter-claim or cross-claim exceed one hundred fifty thousand dollars ($150,000) exclusive of interest and costs. NY R USDCTS&ED Civ Rule 83.7(d)(3).

ii. *Exemption from arbitration.* The Court shall, sua sponte, or on motion of a party, exempt any case from arbitration in which the objectives of arbitration would not be realized (1) because the case involves complex or novel issues, (2) because legal issues predominate over factual issues, or (3) for other good cause. NY R USDCTS&ED Civ Rule 83.7(e)(2). For information on applying for an exemption, refer to NY R USDCTS&ED Civ Rule 83.7

iii. *Referral to arbitration.* Cases not originally designated as eligible for compulsory arbitration, but which in the discretion of the assigned Judge, are later found to qualify, may be referred to arbitration. A U.S. District Judge or a U.S. Magistrate Judge, in cases that exceed the arbitration ceiling of one hundred fifty thousand dollars ($150,000) exclusive of interest and costs, in their discretion, may suggest that the parties should consider arbitration. If the parties are agreeable, an appropriate consent form signed by all parties or their representatives may be entered and filed in the case prior to scheduling an arbitration hearing. NY R USDCTS&ED Civ Rule 83.7(e)(3).

iv. For more information on arbitration, refer to NY R USDCTS&ED Civ Rule 83.7.

b. *Court-annexed mediation.* Mediation is a process in which parties and counsel agree to meet with a neutral mediator trained to assist them in settling disputes. The mediator improves communication across party lines, helps parties articulate their interests and understand those of the other party, probes the strengths and weaknesses of each party's legal positions, and identifies areas of agreement and helps generate options for a mutually agreeable resolution to the dispute. In all cases, mediation provides an opportunity to explore a wide range of potential solutions and to address interests that may be outside the scope of the stated controversy or which could not be addressed by judicial action. A hallmark of mediation is its capacity to expand traditional settlement discussions and broaden resolution options, often by exploring litigant needs and interests that may be formally independent of the legal issues in controversy. NY R USDCTS&ED Civ Rule 83.8(a).

i. *Eligible cases.* Judges and Magistrate Judges may designate civil cases for inclusion in the mediation program, and when doing so shall prepare an order to that effect. Alternatively, and subject to the availability of qualified mediators, the parties may consent to participation in the mediation program by preparing and executing a stipulation signed by all parties to the action and so-ordered by the Court. NY R USDCTS&ED Civ Rule 83.8(b)(1).

ii. For more information on mediation, refer to NY R USDCTS&ED Civ Rule 83.8.

7. *Individual judge practices.* Refer to the Miscellaneous section of this document for information on individual judge practices on general requirements for documents.

## D. Documents

1. *Pretrial conference*

   a. *Documents to consider*

      i. *Pretrial memorandum or statement.* Even though it is not specifically mentioned in FRCP 16, most courts require the attorney for each side to file a pretrial memorandum or statement prior to the conference, which, if adopted by the court, may be binding at trial. FPP § 1524. The purpose of the memorandum is to reveal the lawyer's theory of the case and the issues counsel believes are in contention in order to aid the court in determining what matters should be considered at the conference itself. FPP § 1524; Manbeck v. Ostrowski, 384 F.2d 970 (D.C. Cir. 1967).

2. *Scheduling conference*

   a. *Documents to consider*

      i. *Request for scheduling conference.* A scheduling conference may be requested by the judge or by the parties, but it is not mandatory. FPP § 1522.1.

3. *Discovery planning conference*

   a. *Required documents*

      i. *Written report outlining proposed discovery plan.* Refer to the General Requirements section of this document for information on the parties' responsibilities for submitting a written report outlining the proposed discovery plan.

4. *Individual judge practices.* Refer to the Miscellaneous section of this document for information on individual judge practices on required documents.

## E. Format

1. *Form of documents.* The rules governing captions and other matters of form in pleadings apply to motions and other papers. FRCP 7(b)(2).

   a. *Paper.* Every pleading, written motion, and other paper must: be plainly written, typed, printed, or copied without erasures or interlineations which materially deface it. NY R USDCTS&ED Civ Rule 11.1(a)(1).

   b. *Typeface, margin, and spacing.* The typeface, margins, and spacing of all documents presented for filing must meet the following requirements:

      i. All text must be twelve (12) point type or larger, except for text in footnotes which may be ten (10) point type;

      ii. All documents must have at least one (1) inch margins on all sides;

      iii. All text must be double-spaced, except for headings, text in footnotes, or block quotations, which may be single-spaced. NY R USDCTS&ED Civ Rule 11.1(b).

   c. *Caption; Names of parties.* Every pleading must have a caption with the court's name, a title, a file number, and a FRCP 7(a) designation. The title of the complaint must name all the parties; the title of other pleadings, after naming the first party on each side, may refer generally to other parties. FRCP 10(a). Every pleading, written motion, and other paper must: bear the docket number and the initials of the District Judge and any Magistrate Judge before whom the action or proceeding is pending, NY R USDCTS&ED Civ Rule 11.1(a)(2).

   d. *Paragraphs; Separate statements.* A party must state its claims or defenses in numbered paragraphs, each limited as far as practicable to a single set of circumstances. A later pleading may refer by number to a paragraph in an earlier pleading. If doing so would promote clarity, each claim founded on a separate transaction or occurrence—and each defense other than a denial—must be stated in a separate count or defense. FRCP 10(b).

   e. *Adoption by reference; Exhibits.* A statement in a pleading may be adopted by reference elsewhere in the same pleading or in any other pleading or motion. A copy of a written instrument that is an exhibit to a pleading is a part of the pleading for all purposes. FRCP 10(c).

f. *Acceptance by the clerk.* The clerk must not refuse to file a paper solely because it is not in the form prescribed by the Federal Rules of Civil Procedure or by a local rule or practice. FRCP 5(d)(4).

2. *Signing of pleadings, motions and other papers*

   a. *Signature.* Every pleading, written motion, and other paper must be signed by at least one attorney of record in the attorney's name—or by a party personally if the party is unrepresented. The paper must state the signer's address, e-mail address, and telephone number. FRCP 11(a). Every pleading, written motion, and other paper must: have the name of each person signing it clearly printed or typed directly below the signature. NY R USDCTS&ED Civ Rule 11.1(a)(3).

      i. *No verification or accompanying affidavit required for pleadings.* Unless a rule or statute specifically states otherwise, a pleading need not be verified or accompanied by an affidavit. FRCP 11(a).

      ii. *Unsigned papers.* The court must strike an unsigned paper unless the omission is promptly corrected after being called to the attorney's or party's attention. FRCP 11(a).

   b. *Representations to the court.* By presenting to the court a pleading, written motion, or other paper—whether by signing, filing, submitting, or later advocating it—an attorney or unrepresented party certifies that to the best of the person's knowledge, information, and belief, formed after an inquiry reasonable under the circumstances:

      i. It is not being presented for any improper purpose, such as to harass, cause unnecessary delay, or needlessly increase the cost of litigation;

      ii. The claims, defenses, and other legal contentions are warranted by existing law or by a nonfrivolous argument for extending, modifying, or reversing existing law or for establishing new law;

      iii. The factual contentions have evidentiary support or, if specifically so identified, will likely have evidentiary support after a reasonable opportunity for further investigation or discovery; and

      iv. The denials of factual contentions are warranted on the evidence or, if specifically so identified, are reasonably based on belief or a lack of information. FRCP 11(b).

   c. *Sanctions.* If, after notice and a reasonable opportunity to respond, the court determines that FRCP 11(b) has been violated, the court may impose an appropriate sanction on any attorney, law firm, or party that violated FRCP 11(b) or is responsible for the violation. FRCP 11(c)(1). Refer to the United States District Court for the Eastern District of New York KeyRules Motion for Sanctions document for more information.

3. *Privacy protection for filings made with the court*

   a. *Redacted filings.* Unless the court orders otherwise, in an electronic or paper filing with the court that contains an individual's Social Security number, taxpayer-identification number, or birth date, the name of an individual known to be a minor, or a financial-account number, a party or nonparty making the filing may include only:

      i. The last four (4) digits of the Social Security number and taxpayer-identification number;

      ii. The year of the individual's birth;

      iii. The minor's initials; and

      iv. The last four (4) digits of the financial-account number. FRCP 5.2(a); NY R USDCTED Order 2004-09.

      v. In addition, exercise caution when filing documents that contain the following:

        • Personal identifying number, such as driver's license number;

        • Medical records, treatment and diagnosis;

        • Employment history;

        • Individual financial information; and

        • Proprietary or trade secret information. NY R USDCTED Order 2004-09.

b. *Exemptions from the redaction requirement.* The redaction requirement does not apply to the following:

    i. A financial-account number that identifies the property allegedly subject to forfeiture in a forfeiture proceeding;

    ii. The record of an administrative or agency proceeding;

    iii. The official record of a state-court proceeding;

    iv. The record of a court or tribunal, if that record was not subject to the redaction requirement when originally filed;

    v. A filing covered by FRCP 5.2(c) or FRCP 5.2(d); and

    vi. A pro se filing in an action brought under 28 U.S.C.A. § 2241, 28 U.S.C.A. § 2254, or 28 U.S.C.A. § 2255. FRCP 5.2(b).

c. *Limitations on remote access to electronic files; Social Security appeals and immigration cases.* Unless the court orders otherwise, in an action for benefits under the Social Security Act, and in an action or proceeding relating to an order of removal, to relief from removal, or to immigration benefits or detention, access to an electronic file is authorized as follows:

    i. The parties and their attorneys may have remote electronic access to any part of the case file, including the administrative record;

    ii. Any other person may have electronic access to the full record at the courthouse, but may have remote electronic access only to:

        • The docket maintained by the court; and

        • An opinion, order, judgment, or other disposition of the court, but not any other part of the case file or the administrative record. FRCP 5.2(c).

d. *Filings made under seal.* The court may order that a filing be made under seal without redaction. The court may later unseal the filing or order the person who made the filing to file a redacted version for the public record. FRCP 5.2(d).

e. *Protective orders.* For good cause, the court may by order in a case:

    i. Require redaction of additional information; or

    ii. Limit or prohibit a nonparty's remote electronic access to a document filed with the court. FRCP 5.2(e).

f. *Option for additional unredacted filing under seal.* A person making a redacted filing may also file an unredacted copy under seal. The court must retain the unredacted copy as part of the record. FRCP 5.2(f); NY R USDCTED Order 2004-09. The unredacted version of the document or the reference list shall be retained by the court as part of the record. The court may, however, still require the party to file a redacted copy for the public file. NY R USDCTED Order 2004-09.

g. *Option for filing a reference list.* A filing that contains redacted information may be filed together with a reference list that identifies each item of redacted information and specifies an appropriate identifier that uniquely corresponds to each item listed. The list must be filed under seal and may be amended as of right. Any reference in the case to a listed identifier will be construed to refer to the corresponding item of information. FRCP 5.2(g); NY R USDCTED Order 2004-09. The unredacted version of the document or the reference list shall be retained by the court as part of the record. The court may, however, still require the party to file a redacted copy for the public file. NY R USDCTED Order 2004-09.

h. *Responsibility for redaction.* The responsibility for redacting these personal identifiers rests solely with counsel and the parties. The Clerk will not review each pleading for compliance with NY R USDCTED Order 2004-09. NY R USDCTED Order 2004-09.

    i. Counsel is strongly urged to share this notice with all clients so that an informed decision about the inclusion of certain materials may be made. If a redacted document is filed, it is the sole responsibility of counsel and the parties to be sure that all pleadings comply with the rules of

this court requiring redaction of personal data identifiers. The clerk will not review each pleading for redaction. NY R USDCTED Order 2004-09.

    i. *Waiver of protection of identifiers.* A person waives the protection of FRCP 5.2(a) as to the person's own information by filing it without redaction and not under seal. FRCP 5.2(h).

4. *Individual judge practices.* Refer to the Miscellaneous section of this document for information on individual judge practices on formatting documents.

## F. Filing and Service Requirements

1. *Filing requirements.* Any paper after the complaint that is required to be served—together with a certificate of service—must be filed within a reasonable time after service. FRCP 5(d)(1).

    a. *How filing is made; In general.* A paper is filed by delivering it:

        i. To the clerk; or

        ii. To a judge who agrees to accept it for filing, and who must then note the filing date on the paper and promptly send it to the clerk. FRCP 5(d)(2).

    b. *Night depository.* A night depository with an automatic date stamp shall be maintained. . .by the Clerk of the Eastern District in the Brooklyn Courthouse. After regular business hours, papers for the District Court only may be deposited in the night depository. Such papers will be considered as having been filed in the District Court as of the date stamped thereon, which shall be deemed presumptively correct. NY R USDCTS&ED Civ Rule 1.2.

    c. *Electronic filing*

        i. *Authorization of electronic filing program.* A court may, by local rule, allow papers to be filed, signed, or verified by electronic means that are consistent with any technical standards established by the Judicial Conference of the United States. A local rule may require electronic filing only if reasonable exceptions are allowed. A paper filed electronically in compliance with a local rule is a written paper for purposes of the Federal Rules of Civil Procedure. FRCP 5(d)(3).

- Parties serving and filing papers shall follow the instructions regarding Electronic Case Filing (ECF) published on the website of each respective Court. A paper served and filed by electronic means in accordance with such instructions is, for purposes of FRCP 5, served and filed in compliance with the Local Civil Rules of the Southern and Eastern Districts of New York. NY R USDCTS&ED Civ Rule 5.2(a). Parties have an obligation to review the Court's actual order, decree, or judgment (on ECF), which controls, and should not rely on the description on the docket or in the ECF Notice of Electronic Filing (NEF). NY R USDCTS&ED Civ Rule 5.2(c).

        ii. *Mandatory electronic filing.* Beginning on August 2, 2004, electronic case filing will be mandatory for all civil cases other than pro se cases. NY R USDCTED Order 2004-08.

- *Letter-motions and letters addressed to the court.* Subject to the instructions regarding ECF published on the website of each respective Court and any pertinent Individual Judge's Practices, letter-motions permitted by NY R USDCTS&ED Civ Rule 7.1(d) and letters addressed to the Court (but not letters between the parties) may be filed via ECF. NY R USDCTS&ED Civ Rule 5.2(b).

- *Proposed orders, judgments and decrees.* Proposed orders, judgments and decrees shall be presented as directed by the ECF rules published on the website of each respective Court. NY R USDCTS&ED Civ Rule 77.1. For more information, refer to NY R USDCTS&ED Civ Rule 77.1.

- *Request for exemption.* Requests by attorneys for an exemption to the mandatory policy will be considered for good cause hardship reasons only, and will be reviewed on an individual basis by the assigned United States Magistrate Judge. The Clerk's Office provides an electronic filing training program to assist attorneys filing electronically. Before seeking a hardship exemption, attorneys are advised to participate in the training program or otherwise seek the assistance of the Clerk's Office. NY R USDCTED Order 2004-08.

iii. For more information on electronic filing, refer to the court's website.

2. *Service requirements*

  a. *Service; When required*

    i. *In general.* Unless the Federal Rules of Civil Procedure provide otherwise, each of the following papers must be served on every party:

    - An order stating that service is required;

    - A pleading filed after the original complaint, unless the court orders otherwise under FRCP 5(c) because there are numerous defendants;

    - A discovery paper required to be served on a party, unless the court orders otherwise;

    - A written motion, except one that may be heard ex parte; and

    - A written notice, appearance, demand, or offer of judgment, or any similar paper. FRCP 5(a)(1).

    ii. *If a party fails to appear.* No service is required on a party who is in default for failing to appear. But a pleading that asserts a new claim for relief against such a party must be served on that party under FRCP 4. FRCP 5(a)(2).

    iii. *Seizing property.* If an action is begun by seizing property and no person is or need be named as a defendant, any service required before the filing of an appearance, answer, or claim must be made on the person who had custody or possession of the property when it was seized. FRCP 5(a)(3).

  b. *Service; How made*

    i. *Serving an attorney.* If a party is represented by an attorney, service under FRCP 5 must be made on the attorney unless the court orders service on the party. FRCP 5(b)(1).

    ii. *Service in general.* A paper is served under FRCP 5 by:

    - Handing it to the person;

    - Leaving it: (1) at the person's office with a clerk or other person in charge or, if no one is in charge, in a conspicuous place in the office; or (2) if the person has no office or the office is closed, at the person's dwelling or usual place of abode with someone of suitable age and discretion who resides there;

    - Mailing it to the person's last known address—in which event service is complete upon mailing;

    - Leaving it with the court clerk if the person has no known address;

    - Sending it by electronic means if the person consented in writing—in which event service is complete upon transmission, but is not effective if the serving party learns that it did not reach the person to be served; or

    - Delivering it by any other means that the person consented to in writing—in which event service is complete when the person making service delivers it to the agency designated to make delivery. FRCP 5(b)(2).

    iii. *Service by overnight delivery.* Service upon an attorney may be made by overnight delivery service. "Overnight delivery service" means any delivery service which regularly accepts items for overnight delivery. Overnight delivery service shall be deemed service by mail for purposes of FRCP 5 and FRCP 6. NY R USDCTS&ED Civ Rule 5.3.

    iv. *Service by electronic means.* Parties serving and filing papers shall follow the instructions regarding Electronic Case Filing (ECF) published on the website of each respective Court. A paper served and filed by electronic means in accordance with such instructions is, for purposes of FRCP 5, served and filed in compliance with the Local Civil Rules of the United States District Courts for the Southern and Eastern Districts of New York. NY R USDCTS&ED Civ Rule 5.2(a). Parties have an obligation to review the Court's actual order, decree, or judgment

(on ECF), which controls, and should not rely on the description on the docket or in the ECF Notice of Electronic Filing (NEF). NY R USDCTS&ED Civ Rule 5.2(c).

    v. *Using court facilities.* If a local rule so authorizes, a party may use the court's transmission facilities to make service under FRCP 5(b)(2)(E). FRCP 5(b)(3).

  c. *Serving numerous defendants*

    i. *In general.* If an action involves an unusually large number of defendants, the court may, on motion or on its own, order that:

- Defendants' pleadings and replies to them need not be served on other defendants;

- Any crossclaim, counterclaim, avoidance, or affirmative defense in those pleadings and replies to them will be treated as denied or avoided by all other parties; and

- Filing any such pleading and serving it on the plaintiff constitutes notice of the pleading to all parties. FRCP 5(c)(1).

    ii. *Notifying parties.* A copy of every such order must be served on the parties as the court directs. FRCP 5(c)(2).

3. *Individual judge practices.* Refer to the Miscellaneous section of this document for information on individual judge practices on filing and serving documents.

## G. Hearings

1. Refer to the General Requirements section of this document for information on pretrial conferences, scheduling conferences, and discovery planning conferences.

## H. Forms

### 1. Federal Pretrial Conferences, Scheduling, Management Forms

  a. Plaintiff's informal summary of status of case to judge prior to pretrial conference in complex case. 2C FEDFORMS § 2807.

  b. Joint pretrial report. 2C FEDFORMS § 2807.10.

  c. Joint statement of undisputed facts. 2C FEDFORMS § 2807.20.

  d. Joint statement of disputed facts. 2C FEDFORMS § 2807.30.

  e. Joint report of counsel prior to pretrial conference. 2C FEDFORMS § 2807.40.

  f. Plaintiff's pretrial conference statement; Insurance case. 2C FEDFORMS § 2807.50.

  g. Defendant's pretrial conference statement; Insurance case. 2C FEDFORMS § 2807.60.

  h. Plaintiff's list of exhibits to be offered at trial. 2C FEDFORMS § 2811.

  i. Defendant's list of prospective witnesses. 2C FEDFORMS § 2811.10.

  j. Designation of witnesses whom plaintiff intends to call at trial pursuant to pretrial conference oral stipulation. 2C FEDFORMS § 2811.20.

  k. Defendant's list of prospective exhibits. 2C FEDFORMS § 2811.40.

  l. Report of parties' planning meeting. 3A FEDFORMS § 3314.

  m. Report of parties' discovery conference; Another form. 3A FEDFORMS § 3315.

  n. Report of parties' discovery conference; Another form. 3A FEDFORMS § 3316.

  o. Joint scheduling report. 3A FEDFORMS § 3316.5.

  p. Stipulation and order regarding discovery conference discussions. 3A FEDFORMS § 3316.6.

  q. Pretrial statement; By plaintiff; Automobile collision involving corporate defendant. FEDPROF § 1:658.

  r. Pretrial statement; By defendant; Automobile collision. FEDPROF § 1:659.

  s. Pretrial statement; By parties jointly; Automobile collision. FEDPROF § 1:660.

  t. Pretrial statement; Provision; Waiver of abandoned claims or defenses. FEDPROF § 1:661.

u.  Status report. GOLDLTGFMS § 34:2.

v.  Preliminary pretrial checklist. GOLDLTGFMS § 34:3.

w.  Pretrial memorandum. GOLDLTGFMS § 34:4.

x.  Pretrial memorandum; Short form. GOLDLTGFMS § 34:5.

y.  Pretrial memorandum; Civil action. GOLDLTGFMS § 34:6.

z.  Pretrial memorandum; Worker's compensation case. GOLDLTGFMS § 34:7.

## I.  Applicable Rules

1.  *Federal rules*

a.  Serving and filing pleadings and other papers. FRCP 5.

b.  Privacy protection for filings made with the court. FRCP 5.2.

c.  Computing and extending time; Time for motion papers. FRCP 6.

d.  Pleadings allowed; Form of motions and other papers. FRCP 7.

e.  Form of pleadings. FRCP 10.

f.  Signing pleadings, motions, and other papers; Representations to the court; Sanctions. FRCP 11.

g.  Pretrial conferences; Scheduling; Management. FRCP 16.

h.  Duty to disclose; General provisions governing discovery. FRCP 26.

2.  *Local rules*

a.  Night depository. NY R USDCTS&ED Civ Rule 1.2.

b.  Duty of attorneys in related cases. NY R USDCTS&ED Civ Rule 1.6.

c.  Electronic service and filing of documents. NY R USDCTS&ED Civ Rule 5.2.

d.  Service by overnight delivery. NY R USDCTS&ED Civ Rule 5.3.

e.  Computation of time. NY R USDCTS&ED Civ Rule 6.4.

f.  Form of pleadings, motions, and other papers. NY R USDCTS&ED Civ Rule 11.1.

g.  Exemptions from mandatory scheduling order. NY R USDCTS&ED Civ Rule 16.1.

h.  Entry and modification of mandatory scheduling orders by magistrate judges. NY R USDCTS&ED Civ Rule 16.2.

i.  Submission of orders, judgments and decrees. NY R USDCTS&ED Civ Rule 77.1.

j.  Court-annexed arbitration (Eastern District only). NY R USDCTS&ED Civ Rule 83.7.

k.  Court-annexed mediation (Eastern District only). NY R USDCTS&ED Civ Rule 83.8.

l.  Electronic case filing. NY R USDCTED Order 2004-08.

m.  The August 2, 2004 amendment to the E-Government Act of 2002. NY R USDCTED Order 2004-09.

## J.  Miscellaneous

**NOTE: Individual judges' rules may apply. For available judge-level information, refer to:**

DISTRICT JUDGE CAROL BAGLEY AMON: NY R USDCTED Amon-Practices.

DISTRICT JUDGE JOAN M. AZRACK: NY R USDCTED Azrack-Practices.

DISTRICT JUDGE JOSEPH F. BIANCO: NY R USDCTED Bianco-Practices.

DISTRICT JUDGE FREDERIC BLOCK: NY R USDCTED Block-Practices.

DISTRICT JUDGE MARGO K. BRODIE: NY R USDCTED Brodie-Practices.

DISTRICT JUDGE PAMELA K, CHEN: NY R USDCTED Chen-Practices.

DISTRICT JUDGE BRIAN M. COGAN: NY R USDCTED Cogan-Practices; NY R USDCTED Cogan-Pretrial.

DISTRICT JUDGE LaSHANN DeARCY HALL: NY R USDCTED DeArcy Hall-Practices.

DISTRICT JUDGE RAYMOND J. DEARIE: NY R USDCTED Dearie-Practices.

DISTRICT JUDGE ANN M. DONNELLY: NY R USDCTED Donnelly-Practices.

DISTRICT JUDGE SANDRA J. FEUERSTEIN: NY R USDCTED Feuerstein-Practices; NY R USDCTED Feuerstein-Pretrial.

DISTRICT JUDGE NICHOLAS G. GARAUIFIS: NY R USDCTED Garaufis-Practices; NY R USDCTED Garaufis-Pretrial.

DISTRICT JUDGE NINA GERSHON: NY R USDCTED Gershon-Practices.

DISTRICT JUDGE I. LEO GLASSER: NY R USDCTED Glasser-Practices; NY R USDCTED Glasser-Crim.

DISTRICT JUDGE DENIS R. HURLEY: NY R USDCTED Hurley-Practices; [NY R USDCTED Hurley-Pro Cooperation Info, as added by NY ORDER 16-4188, effective July 22, 2016]; [NY R USDCTED Hurley-Pro Cooperation Info Stay, as added by NY ORDER 16-4188, effective July 22, 2016].

DISTRICT JUDGE DORA L. IRIZARRY: NY R USDCTED Irizarry-Practices; NY R USDCTED Irizarry-Pretrial; NY R USDCTED Irizarry-Crim.

DISTRICT JUDGE STERLING JOHNSON, JR.: NY R USDCTED Johnson-Practices.

DISTRICT JUDGE EDWARD R. KORMAN: NY R USDCTED Korman-Practices; NY R USDCTED Korman-Pretrial.

DISTRICT JUDGE WILLIAM F. KUNTZ: NY R USDCTED Kuntz-Practices.

DISTRICT JUDGE KIYO A. MATSUMOTO: NY R USDCTED Matsumoto-Practices.

DISTRICT JUDGE ROSLYNN R. MAUSKOPF: NY R USDCTED Mauskopf-Practices; NY R USDCTED Mauskopf-Recusal.

DISTRICT JUDGE THOMAS C. PLATT: NY R USDCTED Platt-Practices.

DISTRICT JUDGE ALLYNE R. ROSS: NY R USDCTED Ross-Practices.

DISTRICT JUDGE JOANNA SEYBERT: NY R USDCTED Seybert-Practices.

DISTRICT JUDGE ARTHUR D. SPATT: NY R USDCTED Spatt-Practices.

DISTRICT JUDGE SANDRA L. TOWNES: NY R USDCTED Townes-Practices.

DISTRICT JUDGE ERIC N. VITALIANO: NY R USDCTED Vitaliano-Practices.

DISTRICT JUDGE JACK B. WEINSTEIN: NY R USDCTED Weinstein-Practices.

DISTRICT JUDGE LEONARD D. WEXLER: NY R USDCTED Wexler-Practices; NY R USDCTED Wexler-Rules.

MAGISTRATE JUDGE LOIS BLOOM: NY R USDCTED Bloom-Practices.

MAGISTRATE JUDGE GARY R. BROWN: NY R USDCTED Brown-Practices.

MAGISTRATE JUDGE MARILYN D. GO: NY R USDCTED Go-Practices.

MAGISTRATE JUDGE STEVEN M. GOLD: NY R USDCTED Gold-Practices.

MAGISTRATE JUDGE PEGGY KUO: NY R USDCTED Kuo-Practices; NY R USDCTED Kuo-Scheduling Order.

MAGISTRATE JUDGE ROBERT M. LEVY: NY R USDCTED Levy-Practices.

MAGISTRATE JUDGE ARLENE R. LINDSAY: NY R USDCTED Lindsay-Practices.

MAGISTRATE JUDGE STEVEN I. LOCKE: NY R USDCTED Locke-Practices.

MAGISTRATE JUDGE ROANNE L. MANN: NY R USDCTED Mann-Practices.

MAGISTRATE JUDGE JAMES ORENSTEIN: NY R USDCTED Jorenstein--Practices.

MAGISTRATE JUDGE VIKTOR V. POHORELSKY: NY R USDCTED Pohorelsky-Practices.

MAGISTRATE JUDGE CHERYL L. POLLAK: NY R USDCTED Pollak-Practices; NY R USDCTED Pollak-Pretrial.

MAGISTRATE JUDGE RAMON E. REYES, JR.: NY R USDCTED Reyes-Practices.

MAGISTRATE JUDGE VERA M. SCANLON: NY R USDCTED Scanlon-Practices.

MAGISTRATE JUDGE ANNE Y. SHIELDS: NY R USDCTED Shields-Practices.

MAGISTRATE JUDGE STEVEN L. TISCIONE: NY R USDCTED Tiscione-Practices.

MAGISTRATE JUDGE A. KATHLEEN TOMILINSON: NY R USDCTED Tomlinson-Practices.

# NORTHERN DISTRICT OF NEW YORK

## Pleadings
## Complaint

**Document Last Updated September 2016**

A. **Checklist**

(I) ❑ Matters to be considered by plaintiff

    (a) ❑ Required documents

        (1) ❑ Civil cover sheet

        (2) ❑ Complaint

        (3) ❑ Summons

        (4) ❑ Judicial case assignment form

        (5) ❑ Judicial civil case management plan containing notice of initial pretrial conference

        (6) ❑ Notice and consent form to proceed before a United States magistrate judge

        (7) ❑ Notice and consent form for the court sponsored alternative dispute resolution procedures

        (8) ❑ General Order 25 (NY R USDCTND Order 25)

        (9) ❑ Filing fee

       (10) ❑ Affidavit proving service

    (b) ❑ Supplemental documents

        (1) ❑ Notice and request for waiver of service

        (2) ❑ Service by mail forms

        (3) ❑ Notice of constitutional question

        (4) ❑ Notice of issue concerning foreign law

        (5) ❑ Nongovernmental corporate disclosure statement

        (6) ❑ Application to convene a three-judge court

        (7) ❑ Application to proceed in forma pauperis

        (8) ❑ Motion for TRO and supporting documents

        (9) ❑ Cover letter authorizing e-mail or facsimile filing

       (10) ❑ Affidavit attesting to failed attempts to file electronically

       (11) ❑ Notice of conventional filing

       (12) ❑ CD/ROM with PDF of document(s)

       (13) ❑ English translation

       (14) ❑ Courtesy copies

       (15) ❑ Copies for three-judge court

    (c) ❑ Timing

        (1) ❑ A civil action is commenced by filing a complaint with the court

        (2) ❑ If a defendant is not served within ninety (90) days after the complaint is filed, the court—on motion or on its own after notice to the plaintiff—must dismiss the action without prejudice against that defendant or order that service be made within a specified time

          (i) ❑ Local variation: upon the filing of a complaint, the clerk shall issue to the plaintiff NY

R USDCTND Order 25, which requires, among other things, service of process upon all defendants within sixty (60) days of the filing of the complaint

(3) ❑ Proof(s) of service of process are to be filed with the clerk's office no later than five (5) days after service of the complaint or notice of removal with a copy of NY R USDCTND Order 25

(II) ❑ Matters to be considered by defendant

  (a) ❑ Required documents

    (1) ❑ Answer

    (2) ❑ Certificate of service

  (b) ❑ Supplemental documents

    (1) ❑ Waiver of the service of summons

    (2) ❑ Notice of constitutional question

    (3) ❑ Notice of issue concerning foreign law

    (4) ❑ Nongovernmental corporate disclosure statement

    (5) ❑ Cover letter authorizing e-mail or facsimile filing

    (6) ❑ Affidavit attesting to failed attempts to file electronically

    (7) ❑ Notice of conventional filing

    (8) ❑ CD/ROM with PDF of document(s)

    (9) ❑ English translation

   (10) ❑ Courtesy copies

   (11) ❑ Copies for three-judge court

  (c) ❑ Timing

    (1) ❑ A defendant must serve an answer:

      (i) ❑ Within twenty-one (21) days after being served with the summons and complaint; or

     (ii) ❑ If it has timely waived service under FRCP 4(d), within sixty (60) days after the request for a waiver was sent, or within ninety (90) days after it was sent to the defendant outside any judicial district of the United States

    (2) ❑ The United States, a United States agency, or a United States officer or employee sued only in an official capacity must serve an answer to a complaint, counterclaim, or crossclaim within sixty (60) days after service on the United States attorney

    (3) ❑ A United States officer or employee sued in an individual capacity for an act or omission occurring in connection with duties performed on the United States' behalf must serve an answer to a complaint, counterclaim, or crossclaim within sixty (60) days after service on the officer or employee or service on the United States attorney, whichever is later

    (4) ❑ Unless the court sets a different time, serving a motion under FRCP 12 alters these periods as follows:

      (i) ❑ If the court denies the motion or postpones its disposition until trial, the responsive pleading must be served within fourteen (14) days after notice of the court's action; or

     (ii) ❑ If the court grants a motion for a more definite statement, the responsive pleading must be served within fourteen (14) days after the more definite statement is served

    (5) ❑ Defendant is given a reasonable time of at least thirty (30) days after a waiver of service request is sent—or at least sixty (60) days if sent to defendant outside any judicial district of the United States—to return the waiver

## B. Timing

1. *Commencing an action.* A civil action is commenced by filing a complaint with the court. FRCP 3.

    a. *Statute of limitations.* An action will be barred if it is not commenced within the period set forth in the applicable statute of limitations. Under the Federal Rules of Civil Procedure (FRCP), an action is commenced by filing a complaint with the court. Thus, in a suit on a right created by federal law, filing a complaint suffices to satisfy the statute of limitations. FEDPROF § 61:2.

        i. *Federal question cases.* Absent a specific statutory provision for tolling the statute of limitations, in federal question cases, the filing of the complaint will toll the statute, even if not all filing fees have been paid, although some courts have added the requirement of reasonable diligence in effecting service. FEDPROF § 61:2.

        ii. *Diversity cases.* In diversity actions the matter is less clear. In the landmark Ragan case, the Supreme Court held in construing FRCP 3 that if, under local law, an action is not commenced until the defendant has been served, the statute is not tolled until service has been accomplished. FEDPROF § 61:2; Ragan v. Merchants Transfer & Warehouse Co., 337 U.S. 530, 69 S.Ct. 1233, 93 L.Ed. 1520 (1949). However, in a subsequent case, the Supreme Court distinguished Ragan in holding that the provision of FRCP 4 governing methods of service prevails over a conflicting state rule requiring personal service. FEDPROF § 61:2; Hanna v. Plumer, 380 U.S. 460, 85 S.Ct. 1136, 14 L.Ed.2d 8 (1965). The court reaffirmed Ragan and held that (1) a state law mandating actual service of a summons to toll the statute of limitations must be followed in a diversity case, and (2) FRCP 3 only governs other timing requirements in the federal rules. FEDPROF § 61:2; Walker v. Armco Steel Corp., 446 U.S. 740, 100 S.Ct. 1978, 64 L.Ed.2d 659 (1980).

2. *Service of summons and complaint.* If a defendant is not served within ninety (90) days after the complaint is filed, the court—on motion or on its own after notice to the plaintiff—must dismiss the action without prejudice against that defendant or order that service be made within a specified time. But if the plaintiff shows good cause for the failure, the court must extend the time for service for an appropriate period. FRCP 4(m) does not apply to service in a foreign country under FRCP 4(f) or FRCP 4(j)(1) or to service of a notice under FRCP 71.1(d)(3)(A). FRCP 4(m).

    a. *Local variation.* Upon the filing of a complaint, the Clerk shall issue to the plaintiff NY R USDCTND Order 25, which requires, among other things, service of process upon all defendants within sixty (60) days of the filing of the complaint. This expedited service requirement is necessary to ensure adequate time for pretrial discovery and motion practice. NY R USDCTND L.R. 16.1(a); NY R USDCTND Order 25(III)(A). However, in no event shall service of process be completed after the time specified in FRCP 4, or any other Rule or Statute which may govern service of process in a given action. NY R USDCTND Order 25(III)(A).

        i. *Non compliance with sixty (60) day service requirement.* In the event that the filing party cannot comply with the Sixty (60) day service requirement, that party shall immediately notify the assigned Magistrate Judge and request an adjournment of the initial FRCP 16 case management conference date contained in the attached Civil Case Management Plan. NY R USDCTND Order 25(III)(C). If an adjournment of the conference date is granted, it shall be the responsibility of the filing party to notify all parties to the action of the new date, time and location for the case management conference. Proof of service of such notice shall then be immediately filed with the clerk's office. NY R USDCTND Order 25(III)(C).

    b. *Proof of service of process.* Proof(s) of service of process are to be filed with the clerk's office no later than five (5) days after service of the complaint or notice of removal with a copy of NY R USDCTND Order 25. NY R USDCTND Order 25(III)(B).

3. *Computation of time*

    a. *Computing time.* FRCP 6 applies in computing any time period specified in the Federal Rules of Civil Procedure, in any local rule or court order, or in any statute that does not specify a method of computing time. FRCP 6(a).

        i. *Period stated in days or a longer unit.* When the period is stated in days or a longer unit of time:
            - Exclude the day of the event that triggers the period;

- Count every day, including intermediate Saturdays, Sundays, and legal holidays; and

- Include the last day of the period, but if the last day is a Saturday, Sunday, or legal holiday, the period continues to run until the end of the next day that is not a Saturday, Sunday, or legal holiday. FRCP 6(a)(1).

    ii. *Period stated in hours.* When the period is stated in hours:

- Begin counting immediately on the occurrence of the event that triggers the period;

- Count every hour, including hours during intermediate Saturdays, Sundays, and legal holidays; and

- If the period would end on a Saturday, Sunday, or legal holiday, the period continues to run until the same time on the next day that is not a Saturday, Sunday, or legal holiday. FRCP 6(a)(2).

    iii. *Inaccessibility of the clerk's office.* Unless the court orders otherwise, if the clerk's office is inaccessible:

- On the last day for filing under FRCP 6(a)(1), then the time for filing is extended to the first accessible day that is not a Saturday, Sunday, or legal holiday; or

- During the last hour for filing under FRCP 6(a)(2), then the time for filing is extended to the same time on the first accessible day that is not a Saturday, Sunday, or legal holiday. FRCP 6(a)(3).

    iv. *"Last day" defined.* Unless a different time is set by a statute, local rule, or court order, the last day ends:

- For electronic filing, at midnight in the court's time zone; and

- For filing by other means, when the clerk's office is scheduled to close. FRCP 6(a)(4).

    v. *"Next day" defined.* The "next day" is determined by continuing to count forward when the period is measured after an event and backward when measured before an event. FRCP 6(a)(5).

    vi. *"Legal holiday" defined.* "Legal holiday" means:

- The day set aside by statute for observing New Year's Day, Martin Luther King Jr.'s Birthday, Washington's Birthday, Memorial Day, Independence Day, Labor Day, Columbus Day, Veterans' Day, Thanksgiving Day, or Christmas Day;

- Any day declared a holiday by the President or Congress; and

- For periods that are measured after an event, any other day declared a holiday by the state where the district court is located. FRCP 6(a)(6).

  b. *Computation of electronic filing deadlines.* A document will be deemed timely filed if electronically filed prior to midnight Eastern Time. However, if the time of day is of the essence, the assigned judge may order that the document be filed by a time certain. NY R USDCTND CM/ECF(4)(4.3).

    i. *Technical failures.* A Filing User, whose filing is untimely as the result of a technical failure of the Court's CM/ECF site, may seek appropriate relief from the Court. However, Filing Users are cautioned that, in some circumstances, the Court lacks the authority to grant an extension of time to file (e.g., FRCP 6(b) of the Federal Rules of Civil Procedure). NY R USDCTND CM/ECF(10)(10.1).

- *Technical failure of the filing user's system.* Problems with the Filing User's system, such as phone line problems, problems with the Filing User's Internet Service Provider ("ISP"), or hardware or software problems, will not constitute a technical failure under these Administrative Procedures nor excuse an untimely filing. A Filing User who cannot file documents electronically because of a problem on the Filing User's system must file the documents' conventionally along with an affidavit explaining the reason for not filing the documents electronically. NY R USDCTND CM/ECF(10)(10.2).

    c. *Extending time*

        i. *In general.* When an act may or must be done within a specified time, the court may, for good cause, extend the time:

- With or without motion or notice if the court acts, or if a request is made, before the original time or its extension expires; or

- On motion made after the time has expired if the party failed to act because of excusable neglect. FRCP 6(b)(1).

        ii. *Exceptions.* A court must not extend the time to act under FRCP 50(b), FRCP 50(d), FRCP 52(b), FRCP 59(b), FRCP 59(d), FRCP 59(e), and FRCP 60(b). FRCP 6(b)(2).

        iii. Refer to the United States District Court for the Northern District of New York KeyRules Motion for Continuance/Extension of Time document for more information on extending time.

4. *Individual judge practices.* Refer to the Miscellaneous section of this document for information on individual judge practices on timing of documents.

## C. General Requirements

1. *Pleading, generally*

    a. *Pleadings allowed.* Only these pleadings are allowed: (1) a complaint; (2) an answer to a complaint; (3) an answer to a counterclaim designated as a counterclaim; (4) an answer to a crossclaim; (5) a third-party complaint; (6) an answer to a third-party complaint; and (7) if the court orders one, a reply to an answer. FRCP 7(a).

    b. *Pleading to be concise and direct.* Each allegation must be simple, concise, and direct. No technical form is required. FRCP 8(d)(1).

    c. *Alternative statements of a claim or defense.* A party may set out two or more statements of a claim or defense alternatively or hypothetically, either in a single count or defense or in separate ones. If a party makes alternative statements, the pleading is sufficient if any one of them is sufficient. FRCP 8(d)(2).

    d. *Inconsistent claims or defenses.* A party may state as many separate claims or defenses as it has, regardless of consistency. FRCP 8(d)(3).

    e. *Construing pleadings.* Pleadings must be construed so as to do justice. FRCP 8(e).

2. *Pleading special matters*

    a. *Capacity or authority to sue; Legal existence*

        i. *In general.* Except when required to show that the court has jurisdiction, a pleading need not allege:

- A party's capacity to sue or be sued;

- A party's authority to sue or be sued in a representative capacity; or

- The legal existence of an organized association of persons that is made a party. FRCP 9(a)(1).

        ii. *Raising those issues.* To raise any of those issues, a party must do so by a specific denial, which must state any supporting facts that are peculiarly within the party's knowledge. FRCP 9(a)(2).

    b. *Fraud or mistake; Conditions of mind.* In alleging fraud or mistake, a party must state with particularity the circumstances constituting fraud or mistake. Malice, intent, knowledge, and other conditions of a person's mind may be alleged generally. FRCP 9(b).

    c. *Conditions precedent.* In pleading conditions precedent, it suffices to allege generally that all conditions precedent have occurred or been performed. But when denying that a condition precedent has occurred or been performed, a party must do so with particularity. FRCP 9(c).

    d. *Official document or act.* In pleading an official document or official act, it suffices to allege that the document was legally issued or the act legally done. FRCP 9(d).

    e. *Judgment.* In pleading a judgment or decision of a domestic or foreign court, a judicial or quasi-judicial tribunal, or a board or officer, it suffices to plead the judgment or decision without showing jurisdiction to render it. FRCP 9(e).

f. *Time and place.* An allegation of time or place is material when testing the sufficiency of a pleading. FRCP 9(f).

g. *Special damages.* If an item of special damage is claimed, it must be specifically stated. FRCP 9(g).

h. *Admiralty or maritime claim*

   i. *How designated.* If a claim for relief is within the admiralty or maritime jurisdiction and also within the court's subject-matter jurisdiction on some other ground, the pleading may designate the claim as an admiralty or maritime claim for purposes of FRCP 14(c), FRCP 38(e), and FRCP 82 and the Supplemental Rules for Admiralty or Maritime Claims and Asset Forfeiture Actions. A claim cognizable only in the admiralty or maritime jurisdiction is an admiralty or maritime claim for those purposes, whether or not so designated. FRCP 9(h)(1).

   ii. *Designation for appeal.* A case that includes an admiralty or maritime claim within FRCP 9(h) is an admiralty case within 28 U.S.C.A. § 1292(a)(3). FRCP 9(h)(2).

3. *Complaint.* A pleading that states a claim for relief must contain: (1) a short and plain statement of the grounds for the court's jurisdiction, unless the court already has jurisdiction and the claim needs no new jurisdictional support; (2) a short and plain statement of the claim showing that the pleader is entitled to relief; and (3) a demand for the relief sought, which may include relief in the alternative or different types of relief. FRCP 8(a).

   a. *Statement of jurisdiction.* Federal courts are courts of limited jurisdiction, and it is presumed that they are without jurisdiction unless the contrary affirmatively appears. FEDPROC § 62:38; Kirkland Masonry, Inc. v. C.I.R., 614 F.2d 532 (5th Cir. 1980). Therefore, in order for a complaint to comply with the requirement that it contain a short and plain statement of the grounds upon which the court's jurisdiction depends, the jurisdictional basis must be alleged affirmatively and distinctly on the face of the complaint. FEDPROC § 62:38; Spain v. U.S. Through Atomic Nuclear Regulatory Commission Through U.S. Atomic Safety and Licensing Bd., 397 F.Supp. 15 (M.D.La. 1975).

      i. Although it has been said that the jurisdictional statement requirement contemplates reference to a federal statute, a sufficient jurisdictional statement is not made by simply citing a federal statute without alleging facts which bring the plaintiff within the purview of the statute. FEDPROC § 62:38; Atkins v. School Bd. of Halifax County, 379 F.Supp. 1060 (W.D.Va. 1974); Sims v. Mercy Hospital of Monroe, 451 F.2d 171 (6th Cir. 1971).

      ii. Improper venue is an affirmative defense, and a complaint need not include allegations showing venue to be proper. FEDPROC § 62:38; Ripperger v. A.C. Allyn & Co., 113 F.2d 332 (2d Cir. 1940).

   b. *Statement of claim*

      i. *Notice pleading.* Because the only function left exclusively to the pleadings by the Federal Rules of Civil Procedure is that of giving notice, federal courts frequently have said that the Federal Rules of Civil Procedure have adopted a system of "notice pleading." FPP § 1202; Swierkiewicz v. Sorema N.A., 534 U.S. 506, 122 S.Ct. 992, 152 L.Ed.2d 1 (2002). To comply with the requirement that a complaint contain a short and plain statement of the claim, a pleading must give the opposing party fair notice of the nature of a claim and of the basis or grounds for it, so that the defendant will at least be notified as to which of its actions gave rise to the claim upon which the complaint is based. FEDPROC § 62:45.

         • *Plausibility standard.* Bell Atlantic Corporation v. Twombly and Ashcroft v. Iqbal have paved the way for a heightened "plausibility" pleading standard that requires plaintiffs to provide greater factual development in their complaints in order to survive a FRCP 12(b)(6) motion to dismiss. FPP § 1202; Bell Atlantic Corp. v. Twombly, 550 U.S. 544, 127 S.Ct. 1955, 167 L.Ed.2d 929, 68 Fed.R.Serv.3d 661 (2007); Ashcroft v. Iqbal, 556 U.S. 662, 129 S.Ct. 1937, 173 L.Ed.2d 868 (2009). In discussing what appears to be the new plausibility standard, the Court [in Bell Atlantic Corp. v. Twombly] stated: "While a complaint attacked by a FRCP 12(b)(6) motion to dismiss does not need detailed factual allegations. . .a plaintiff's obligation to provide the 'grounds' of his 'entitle[ment] to relief' requires more than labels and conclusions, and a formulaic recitation of the elements of a cause of action will not do. . .Factual allegations must be enough to raise a right to relief above the speculative level." FPP § 1216; Bell Atlantic Corp. v. Twombly, 550 U.S. 544, 127 S.Ct. 1955, 167 L.Ed.2d 929, 68 Fed.R.Serv.3d 661 (2007).

ii.   *Facts and evidence.* The complaint need only state enough facts to raise a reasonable expectation that discovery will reveal evidence of the necessary elements. FEDPROC § 62:52; Phillips v. County of Allegheny, 515 F.3d 224 (3d Cir. 2008). A complaint is not intended to formulate issues or fully summarize the facts involved. FEDPROC § 62:52; Hill v. MCI WorldCom Communications, Inc., 141 F.Supp.2d 1205 (S.D.Iowa 2001). Under notice pleading, the full development of the facts and the narrowing of contested issues are accomplished through discovery and other pretrial procedures. FEDPROC § 62:52.

iii.  *Particularity.* The claim should be particularized sufficiently for the defendant to prepare an adequate defense, file a responsive pleading, determine whether the defense of res judicata is appropriate, and commence discovery, and should insure that the court is sufficiently informed to determine the issue presented and to decide whether the complaint states a claim upon which relief can be had. FEDPROC § 62:45; Kelly v. Schmidberger, 806 F.2d 44, 6 Fed.R.Serv.3d 798 (2d Cir. 1986); Frank v. Mracek, 58 F.R.D. 365 (M.D.Ala. 1973); Barlow v. Pep Boys, Inc., 625 F.Supp. 130 (E.D.Pa. 1985); Philadelphia Dressed Beef Co. v. Wilson & Co., 19 F.R.D. 198 (E.D.Pa. 1956); Luckett v. Cohen, 145 F.Supp. 155 (S.D.N.Y. 1956).

iv.   *Requirement to file a civil RICO statement.* In any action in which a party asserts a claim under the Racketeer Influenced and Corrupt Organizations Act ("RICO"), 18 U.S.C.A. § 1961 et seq., the party asserting such a claim shall file a RICO statement within thirty (30) days of the filing of the pleading containing such claim. This statement shall conform to the format that the Court has adopted and shall be entitled "RICO Statement." Parties may obtain copies of NY R USDCTND Order 14--CIVIL RICO STATEMENT FILING REQUIREMENTS from the Clerk's office or at the Court's webpage. This statement shall state in detail and with specificity the information requested in the RICO Statement. The Court shall construe the RICO Statement as an amendment to the pleadings. NY R USDCTND L.R. 9.2.

c.  *Demand for relief sought.* FRCP 8(a)(3) does not require a party to frame the demand for judgment according to a prescribed form or set of particular words; any concise statement identifying the remedies and the parties against whom relief is sought will be sufficient. FPP § 1255; Chandler v. McKee Foods Corp., 2009 WL 210858 (W.D.Va. 2009). Moreover, the pleader need only make one demand for relief regardless of the number of claims that are asserted. FPP § 1255; Liberty Mut. Ins. Co. v. Wetzel, 424 U.S. 737, 96 S.Ct. 1202, 47 L.Ed.2d 435 (1976).

i.   Relief must be requested as to each defendant. FEDPROC § 62:58; RKO-Stanley Warner Theatres, Inc. v. Mellon Nat. Bank & Trust Co., 436 F.2d 1297 (3d Cir. 1970).

4.  *Joinder*

a.  *Joinder of claims.* A party asserting a claim, counterclaim, crossclaim, or third-party claim may join, as independent or alternative claims, as many claims as it has against an opposing party. FRCP 18(a).

i.   *Joinder of contingent claims.* A party may join two claims even though one of them is contingent on the disposition of the other; but the court may grant relief only in accordance with the parties' relative substantive rights. In particular, a plaintiff may state a claim for money and a claim to set aside a conveyance that is fraudulent as to that plaintiff, without first obtaining a judgment for the money. FRCP 18(b).

b.  *Joinder of parties; Required*

i.   *Persons required to be joined if feasible; Required party.* A person who is subject to service of process and whose joinder will not deprive the court of subject-matter jurisdiction must be joined as a party if:

- In that person's absence, the court cannot accord complete relief among existing parties; or

850

- That person claims an interest relating to the subject of the action and is so situated that disposing of the action in the person's absence may: (1) as a practical matter impair or impede the person's ability to protect the interest; or (2) leave an existing party subject to a substantial risk of incurring double, multiple, or otherwise inconsistent obligations because of the interest. FRCP 19(a)(1).

ii. *Joinder of parties by court order.* If a person has not been joined as required, the court must order that the person be made a party. A person who refuses to join as a plaintiff may be made either a defendant or, in a proper case, an involuntary plaintiff. FRCP 19(a)(2).

iii. *Venue.* If a joined party objects to venue and the joinder would make venue improper, the court must dismiss that party. FRCP 19(a)(3).

iv. *When joinder of parties is not feasible.* If a person who is required to be joined if feasible cannot be joined, the court must determine whether, in equity and good conscience, the action should proceed among the existing parties or should be dismissed. FRCP 19(b). For a list of the factors for the court to consider in determining whether joinder of parties is feasible, refer to FRCP 19(b)(1) through FRCP 19(b)(4).

v. *Pleading the reasons for nonjoinder.* When asserting a claim for relief, a party must state:

- The name, if known, of any person who is required to be joined if feasible but is not joined; and

- The reasons for not joining that person. FRCP 19(c).

vi. *Exception for class actions.* FRCP 19 is subject to FRCP 23. FRCP 19(d). For information on class actions, refer to FRCP 23.

c. *Joinder of parties; Permissible*

i. *Persons who may join or be joined*

- *Plaintiffs.* Persons may join in one action as plaintiffs if: (1) they assert any right to relief jointly, severally, or in the alternative with respect to or arising out of the same transaction, occurrence, or series of transactions or occurrences; and (2) any question of law or fact common to all plaintiffs will arise in the action. FRCP 20(a)(1).

- *Defendants.* Persons—as well as a vessel, cargo, or other property subject to admiralty process in rem—may be joined in one action as defendants if: (1) any right to relief is asserted against them jointly, severally, or in the alternative with respect to or arising out of the same transaction, occurrence, or series of transactions or occurrences; and (2) any question of law or fact common to all defendants will arise in the action. FRCP 20(a)(2).

- *Extent of relief.* Neither a plaintiff nor a defendant need be interested in obtaining or defending against all the relief demanded. The court may grant judgment to one or more plaintiffs according to their rights, and against one or more defendants according to their liabilities. FRCP 20(a)(3).

ii. *Protective measures.* The court may issue orders—including an order for separate trials—to protect a party against embarrassment, delay, expense, or other prejudice that arises from including a person against whom the party asserts no claim and who asserts no claim against the party. FRCP 20(b).

d. *Misjoinder and nonjoinder of parties.* Misjoinder of parties is not a ground for dismissing an action. On motion or on its own, the court may at any time, on just terms, add or drop a party. The court may also sever any claim against a party. FRCP 21.

5. *Right to a jury trial; Demand*

a. *Right preserved.* The right of trial by jury as declared by U.S.C.A. Const. Amend. VII, or as provided by a federal statute, is preserved to the parties inviolate. FRCP 38(a).

b. *Demand.* On any issue triable of right by a jury, a party may demand a jury trial by:

i. Serving the other parties with a written demand—which may be included in a pleading—no later than fourteen (14) days after the last pleading directed to the issue is served; and

    ii.   Filing the demand in accordance with FRCP 5(d). FRCP 38(b).

    iii.  In cases removed from state court, a party may file a "Demand for Jury Trial" that is separate from the initial pleading. See FRCP 81(c); NY R USDCTND L.R. 81.3. NY R USDCTND L.R. 38.1(b).

  c.  *Specifying issues.* In its demand, a party may specify the issues that it wishes to have tried by a jury; otherwise, it is considered to have demanded a jury trial on all the issues so triable. If the party has demanded a jury trial on only some issues, any other party may—within fourteen (14) days after being served with the demand or within a shorter time ordered by the court—serve a demand for a jury trial on any other or all factual issues triable by jury. FRCP 38(c).

  d.  *Waiver; Withdrawal.* A party waives a jury trial unless its demand is properly served and filed. A proper demand may be withdrawn only if the parties consent. FRCP 38(d).

  e.  *Admiralty and maritime claims.* The rules in FRCP 38 do not create a right to a jury trial on issues in a claim that is an admiralty or maritime claim under FRCP 9(h). FRCP 38(e).

6.  *Complex and multi-district litigation.* If the assigned judge determines, in his or her discretion, that the case is of such a complex nature that it cannot reasonably be trial ready within eighteen (18) months from the date the complaint is filed, the assigned judge may design and issue a particularized case management order that will move the case to trial as quickly as the complexity of the case allows. NY R USDCTND L.R. 3.3(a). The parties shall promptly notify the Court in writing if any action commenced is appropriate for multi-district litigation. NY R USDCTND L.R. 3.3(b).

7.  *Appearances.* An attorney appearing for a party in a civil case shall promptly file with the Clerk a written notice of appearance; however, an attorney does not need to file a notice of appearance if the attorney who would be filing the notice of appearance is the same individual who has signed the complaint, notice of removal, pre-answer motion, or answer. NY R USDCTND L.R. 83.2(a). For more information, refer to NY R USDCTND L.R. 83.2.

8.  *Related cases.* A civil case is "related" to another civil case for purposes of this guideline when, because of the similarity of facts and legal issues or because the cases arise from the same transactions or events, a substantial saving of judicial resources is likely to result from assigning the cases to the same Judge and Magistrate Judge. NY R USDCTND Order 12(G)(2). A civil case shall not be deemed related to another civil case merely because the civil case: (1) involves similar legal issues, or (2) involves the same parties. NY R USDCTND Order 12(G)(3). Presumptively, and subject to the power of a Judge to determine otherwise pursuant to NY R USDCTND Order 12(G)(5), civil cases shall not be deemed to be "related" unless both cases are still pending before the Court. NY R USDCTND Order 12(G)(4).

  a.  *New filings.* If an attorney or filing party indicates on the Civil Cover Sheet that a case is related to an earlier filed case, the Clerk shall instruct the filing party to file a notice of related cases. The allegedly related cases will be submitted by the Clerk to the Judge to whom the earliest filed case is assigned, who shall advise the Clerk whether such cases are related. NY R USDCTND Order 12(G)(1).

  b.  *Judicial determination that civil cases are "related."* Except for the cases described in the final sentence of NY R USDCTND Order 12(G)(6), all civil cases shall be randomly assigned when they are filed. Other than the cases described in the final sentence of NY R USDCTND Order 12(G)(6), civil cases shall not be deemed to be "related" for purposes of this guideline at the instance of any litigant or attorney unless and until there has been a determination by a Judge of this Court that the standard of NY R USDCTND Order 12(G)(2) is met. NY R USDCTND Order 12(G)(5).

    i.   *Notice of related filing.* Any party may apply for such a determination by filing with the Clerk a notice of related filing, which should include an explanation as to why the standard of NY R USDCTND Order 12(G)(2) is met. A form for this purpose is available on the Court's website. A copy of the notice shall be served on all other parties who have appeared. Such an application must be made after the date when at least a majority of the defendants have been served with the complaint. Before making such an application, the applicant must confer in good faith with all other parties in an effort to reach an agreement on whether or not the case is "related". After such an application is made, any other party may serve and file within seven (7) calendar days a letter of no more than two (2) pages supporting or opposing the application. The application to have the case assigned to another Judge shall be presented to the Judge with the earliest filed case for decision on whether the action(s) should be reassigned as related cases. The Judge with the earliest filed case may then enter an order in the case at bar, either deeming the case to be related and directing the Clerk to reassign the action, or denying the application for reassignment. Any disputes concerning the assignment of related cases will be referred to the Chief Judge for resolution. NY R USDCTND Order 12(G)(5).

   c.   For more information on related cases, refer to NY R USDCTND Order 12(G).

9.   *Alternative dispute resolution (ADR).* It is the mission of this court to do everything it can to help parties resolve their disputes as fairly, quickly, and efficiently as possible. NY R USDCTND Order 25(VIII).

   a.   *Arbitration.* NY R USDCTND L.R. 83.7 governs the consensual arbitration program for referral of civil actions to court-annexed arbitration. It may remain in effect until further order of the Court. Its purpose is to establish a less formal procedure for the just, efficient and economical resolution of disputes, while preserving the right to a full trial on demand. NY R USDCTND L.R. 83.7-1.

      i.   *Actions subject to arbitration.* The Clerk shall notify the parties in all civil cases, except as the Local Rules of Practice for the United States District Court for the Northern District of New York otherwise direct, that they may consent to non-binding arbitration under NY R US-DCTND L.R. 83.7. The notice shall be furnished to the parties at pretrial/scheduling conferences or shall be included with pretrial conference notices and instructions. Consent to arbitration under NY R USDCTND L.R. 83.7 shall be discussed at the pretrial/scheduling conference. No party or attorney shall be prejudiced for refusing to participate in arbitration. The Court shall allow the referral of any civil action pending before it to the arbitration process if the parties consent. The plaintiff shall be responsible for securing the execution of a consent form by the parties and for filing the form with the Clerk within fourteen (14) days after the parties receive the form. The parties shall freely and knowingly enter into the consent. NY R USDCTND L.R. 83.7-2.

      ii.   *Referral to arbitration.* The Clerk shall refer every action subject to NY R USDCTND L.R. 83.7 to arbitration in accordance with the procedures under NY R USDCTND L.R. 83.7 twenty-one (21) days after the filing of the last responsive pleading or within twenty-one (21) days of the filing of a stipulated consent order referring the action to arbitration, whichever event occurs last, except as otherwise provided. If any party notices a motion to dismiss under the provisions of FRCP 12(a) and/or FRCP 12(b), or a motion to join necessary parties pursuant to the Federal Rules of Civil Procedure prior to the expiration of the twenty-one (21) day period, the assigned judge shall hear the motion and further proceedings under NY R USDCTND L.R. 83.7 shall be deferred pending decision on the motion. If the Court does not dismiss the action on the motion, the Court shall refer the action to arbitration twenty-one (21) days after the filing of the decision. NY R USDCTND L.R. 83.7-3(a). Motions for summary judgment pursuant to FRCP 56 shall be filed and served within twenty-one (21) days following the close of discovery. The filing of a FRCP 56 motion shall defer further proceedings under NY R USDCTND L.R. 83.7 pending decision on the motion. NY R USDCTND L.R. 83.7-3(a).

         &bull;   *Relief from referral.* Any party shall request relief from the operation of NY R USDCTND L.R. 83.7 by filing with the Court a motion for the relief within twenty-one (21) days after entry of the initial stipulated consent order which refers the case for arbitration. The assigned judge shall, sua sponte, exempt an action from the application of NY R USDCTND L.R. 83.7 where the objectives of arbitration would not be realized because (1) the case involves complex or novel legal issues, (2) legal issues predominate over factual issues, or (3) for other good cause. NY R USDCTND L.R. 83.7-3(c).

      iii.   For more information on arbitration, refer to NY R USDCTND L.R. 83.7.

   b.   *Mediation.* The purpose of NY R USDCTND L.R. 83.11 is to provide a supplementary procedure to the Court's existing alternative dispute resolution procedures. NY R USDCTND L.R. 83.11 provides for an earlier resolution of civil disputes resulting in savings of time and cost to litigants and the Court without sacrificing the quality of justice rendered or the right of litigants to a full trial on all issues not resolved through mediation. NY R USDCTND L.R. 83.11-1(a). Mediation is a process by which an impartial person, the mediator, facilitates communication between disputing parties to promote understanding, reconciliation and settlement. The mediator is an advocate for settlement and uses the mediation process to help the parties fully explore any potential area of agreement. The mediator does not serve as a judge or arbitrator and has no authority to render any decision on any disputed issue or to force a settlement. The parties themselves are responsible for negotiating any resolution(s) to their dispute. NY R USDCTND L.R. 83.11-1(b).

i.   *Actions subject to mediation.* The Court may refer any civil action (or any portion thereof) to mediation under NY R USDCTND L.R. 83.11: (1) by order of referral; or (2) on the motion of any party; or (3) by consent of the parties. NY R USDCTND L.R. 83.11-3(a).

  - *Withdrawal from mediation.* The parties may withdraw from mediation any civil action or claim that the Court refers to mediation pursuant to NY R USDCTND L.R. 83.11-3 by application to the assigned judge at least ten (10) days prior to the scheduled mediation session. NY R USDCTND L.R. 83.11-3(b).

ii.   *Mandatory mediation program.* The United States District Court for the Northern District of New York has adopted this Mandatory Mediation Plan. The paid Mediation Program is designed to provide quicker, less expensive and potentially more satisfying alternatives to continuing litigation, without impairing the quality of justice or the right to trial. NY R USDCTND Order 47(1)(1.2)(A). This Mandatory Mediation Plan applies to civil actions pending as well as newly filed actions, except as otherwise indicated in NY R USDCTND Order 47. The Local Rules for voluntary mediation will apply only to Pro Se Cases that proceed through the Assisted Mediation Program. NY R USDCTND Order 47(1)(1.2)(B).

  - *Referral into the pilot mandatory mediation program for new cases.* All civil cases shall be referred automatically into the Mandatory Mediation Program. Notice of the Mandatory Mediation requirements will be provided to all parties immediately upon the filing of a complaint and answer or a notice of removal. ADR intervention will be scheduled at the conference held pursuant to NY R USDCTND L.R. 16.1. NY R USDCTND Order 47(2)(2.1)(A). For a list of categories of actions exempted from automatic referral, refer to NY R USDCTND Order 47(2)(2.1)(A).

  - *Referral into the pilot mandatory mediation program for pending cases.* The assigned Judge or Magistrate Judge on any pending civil case may, sua sponte or with status conference, issue an order referring the case into the Mandatory Mediation Program. The order shall specify a date on which the ADR intervention is to be completed. NY R USDCTND Order 47(2)(2.1)(B).

  - *Referral into the pilot mandatory mediation program by stipulation.* A case may be referred into the Mandatory Mediation Program by stipulation of all parties. Stipulations shall be filed and shall designate the time frame within which the ADR process will be completed. Stipulations are presumed acceptable unless the assigned Judge or Magistrate Judge determines that the interests of justice are not served. NY R USDCTND Order 47(2)(2.1)(C).

  - *Relief from referral.* Motions to opt out of the program will be addressed by the assigned Magistrate Judge at the FRCP 16 conference. NY R USDCTND Order 47(2)(2.2)(A). Opting Out Motions shall be granted only for "good cause" shown. Inconvenience, travel costs, attorney fees or other costs shall not constitute "good cause." A party seeking relief from the Mandatory Mediation Program must set forth the reasons why Mandatory Mediation has no reasonable chance of being productive. NY R USDCTND Order 47(2)(2.2)(B). The assigned Magistrate Judge may, sua sponte, exempt any case from the Court's Mandatory Mediation Program. NY R USDCTND Order 47(2)(2.2)(C).

iii.   *Assisted mediation program.* The Court may assign specially trained pro bono Special Media-tion Counsel to assist pro se civilian litigants with preparing for and participating in mediation. The Assisted Mediation Program is open to civilian pro se parties to actions in the Northern District of New York. The assigned judge or magistrate judge determines if the case would benefit from mediation and would also benefit from the assignment of Special Mediation Counsel to assist the pro se party with the mediation process. NY R USDCTND L.R. 83.8(a). Appointment of Special Mediation Counsel is in no way guaranteed, even if the action is referred to the court-annexed mediation program. Appointment is at the sole discretion of the presiding judge. NY R USDCTND L.R. 83.8(a).

- *Referral to assisted mediation program.* If the court determines that referral to the Assisted Mediation Program is appropriate, the Court shall enter an order of reference to the Assisted Mediation Program. NY R USDCTND L.R. 83.8(b).

iv.  For more information on mediation, refer to NY R USDCTND L.R. 83.11 and NY R USDCTND Order 47.

c.  *Early neutral evaluation (ENE).* Early neutral evaluation (ENE) is a process in which parties obtain from an experienced neutral (an "evaluator") a nonbinding, reasoned, oral evaluation of the merits of the case. The first step in the ENE process involves the Court appointing an evaluator who has expertise in the area of law in the case. After the parties exchange essential information and position statements early in the pretrial period (usually within one hundred fifty (150) to two hundred (200) days after a complaint has been filed), the evaluator convenes an ENE session that typically lasts about two hours. At the ENE meeting, each side briefly presents the factual and legal basis of its position. The evaluator may ask questions of the parties and help them identify the main issues in dispute and the areas of agreement. The evaluator may also help the parties explore options for settlement. If settlement does not occur, the evaluator then offers an opinion as to the settlement value of the case, including the likelihood of liability and the likely range of damages. With the benefit of this assessment, the parties are again encouraged to discuss settlement, with or without the evaluator's assistance. The parties may also explore ways to narrow the issues in dispute, exchange information about the case or otherwise prepare efficiently for trial. NY R USDCTND L.R. 83.12-1.

i.  *Actions subject to early neutral evaluation.* The Court may refer any civil action (or any portion thereof) to ENE under NY R USDCTND L.R. 83.12: (1) by order of referral; (2) on the motion of any party; or (3) by consent of the parties. NY R USDCTND L.R. 83.12-3(a).

- *Withdrawal from the ENE process.* The parties may withdraw any civil action or claim that the Court has referred to the ENE Process pursuant to NY R USDCTND L.R. 83.12-3 by application to the assigned judge at least ten (10) days before the scheduled evaluation session. NY R USDCTND L.R. 83.12-3(b).

ii.  For more information on early neutral evaluation (ENE), refer to NY R USDCTND L.R. 83.12.

10.  *Settlement procedures.* On notice to the Court or the Clerk that the parties have settled an action, and upon confirmation of the settlement by all parties, the Court may issue a judgment dismissing the action by reason of settlement. The Court shall issue the order without prejudice to the parties' right to secure reinstatement of the case within thirty (30) days after the date of judgment by making a showing that the settlement was not, in fact, consummated. NY R USDCTND L.R. 68.2(a). If the Court decides not to follow the procedures set forth in NY R USDCTND L.R. 68.2(a), the parties shall file within thirty (30) days of the notification to the Court, unless otherwise directed by written order, such notices, stipulations and/or motions as are necessary to terminate the action. If the required documents are not filed within the thirty (30) day period, the Clerk shall place the action on the dismissal calendar. NY R USDCTND L.R. 68.2(b).

11.  *Sanctions and penalties for noncompliance.* Failure of an attorney or of a party to comply with any provision of the Local Rules of Practice for the United States District Court for the Northern District of New York, General Orders of this District, Orders of the Court, or the Federal Rules of Civil Procedure shall be a ground for imposition of sanctions. NY R USDCTND L.R. 1.1(d).

12.  *Individual judge practices.* Refer to the Miscellaneous section of this document for information on individual judge practices on general requirements for documents.

## D.  Documents

1.  *Required documents*

a.  *Civil cover sheet.* A completed civil cover sheet on a form available from the Clerk shall be submitted with every complaint, notice of removal, or other document initiating a civil action. This requirement is solely for administrative purposes, and matters appearing on the civil cover sheet have no legal effect in the action. NY R USDCTND L.R. 3.1. A civil cover sheet is submitted with each civil complaint filed in the district court. Copies of the cover sheet may be obtained from the Clerk of Court. 2 FEDFORMS § 3:29(Comment).

    i. *Class action.* The plaintiff also [in addition to including the words "Class Action" next to the caption] shall check the appropriate box on the Civil Cover Sheet at the time of filing the action. NY R USDCTND L.R. 23.1(b). For more information on class actions, refer to NY R USDCTND L.R. 23.2.

b. *Complaint.* All civil complaints submitted to the Clerk for filing shall be accompanied by a summons or, if electing to serve by mail, the approved service by mail forms, together with sufficient copies of the complaint for service on each of the named defendants. NY R USDCTND L.R. 5.1(f). Refer to the General Requirements section of this document for the form and contents of the complaint.

c. *Summons.* All civil complaints submitted to the Clerk for filing shall be accompanied by a summons. NY R USDCTND L.R. 5.1(f). A summons must be served with a copy of the complaint. FRCP 4(c)(1). A summons must:

    i. Name the court and the parties;

    ii. Be directed to the defendant;

    iii. State the name and address of the plaintiff's attorney or—if unrepresented—of the plaintiff;

    iv. State the time within which the defendant must appear and defend;

    v. Notify the defendant that a failure to appear and defend will result in a default judgment against the defendant for the relief demanded in the complaint;

    vi. Be signed by the clerk; and

    vii. Bear the court's seal. FRCP 4(a)(1).

d. *Judicial case assignment form.* At the time the complaint or notice of removal is served, the party seeking to invoke the jurisdiction of this Court shall also serve on all parties the following: Judicial Case Assignment Form. NY R USDCTND L.R. 4.1(c)(1).

e. *Judicial civil case management plan containing notice of initial pretrial conference.* At the time the complaint or notice of removal is served, the party seeking to invoke the jurisdiction of this Court shall also serve on all parties the following: Joint Civil Case Management Plan Containing Notice of Initial Pretrial Conference. NY R USDCTND L.R. 4.1(c)(2).

f. *Notice and consent form to proceed before a United States magistrate judge.* At the time the complaint or notice of removal is served, the party seeking to invoke the jurisdiction of this Court shall also serve on all parties the following: Notice and Consent Form to Proceed Before a United States Magistrate Judge. NY R USDCTND L.R. 4.1(c)(3).

g. *Notice and consent form for the court sponsored alternative dispute resolution procedures.* At the time the complaint or notice of removal is served, the party seeking to invoke the jurisdiction of this Court shall also serve on all parties the following: Notice and Consent Form for the Court Sponsored Alternative Dispute Resolution Procedures. NY R USDCTND L.R. 4.1(c)(4).

h. *General Order 25 (NY R USDCTND Order 25).* Proof(s) of service of process are to be filed with the clerk's office no later than five (5) days after service of the complaint or notice of removal with a copy of NY R USDCTND Order 25. NY R USDCTND Order 25(III)(B).

i. *Filing fee.* The clerk of each district court shall require the parties instituting any civil action, suit or proceeding in such court, whether by original process, removal or otherwise, to pay a filing fee. 28 U.S.C.A. § 1914(a). Each district court by rule or standing order may require advance payment of fees. 28 U.S.C.A. § 1914(c). A party commencing an action or removing an action from a state court must pay to the Clerk the statutory filing fee before the case will be docketed and process issued. Title 28 U.S.C.A. § 1915 and NY R USDCTND L.R. 5.4 govern in forma pauperis proceedings. NY R USDCTND L.R. 5.2(a). The Clerk is not required to render any service for which a fee is prescribed by statute or by the Judicial Conference of the United States unless the fee for the service is paid in advance. NY R USDCTND L.R. 5.2(b). The payment of the filing fee will be made through a secure United States Treasury Internet Credit Card site. NY R USDCTND CM/ECF(4)(4.2). Fee schedules are available at the Clerk's office or at the Court's webpage. NY R USDCTND L.R. 5.3. For information on filing fees and the District Court Miscellaneous Fee Schedule, refer to 28 U.S.C.A. § 1914.

j. *Affidavit proving service.* Unless service is waived, proof of service must be made to the court. Except for service by a United States marshal or deputy marshal, proof must be by the server's affidavit. FRCP 4(l)(1). Refer to the Filing and Service Requirements section of this document for more information.

2. *Supplemental documents*

a. *Notice and request for waiver of service.* An individual, corporation, or association that is subject to service under FRCP 4(e), FRCP 4(f), or FRCP 4(h) has a duty to avoid unnecessary expenses of serving the summons. The plaintiff may notify such a defendant that an action has been commenced and request that the defendant waive service of a summons. The notice and request must:

   i. Be in writing and be addressed:
      - To the individual defendant; or
      - For a defendant subject to service under FRCP 4(h), to an officer, a managing or general agent, or any other agent authorized by appointment or by law to receive service of process;

   ii. Name the court where the complaint was filed;

   iii. Be accompanied by a copy of the complaint, two (2) copies of a waiver form appended to FRCP 4, and a prepaid means for returning the form;

   iv. Inform the defendant, using the form appended to FRCP 4, of the consequences of waiving and not waiving service;

   v. State the date when the request is sent;

   vi. Give the defendant a reasonable time of at least thirty (30) days after the request was sent—or at least sixty (60) days if sent to the defendant outside any judicial district of the United States—to return the waiver; and

   vii. Be sent by first-class mail or other reliable means. FRCP 4(d)(1).

b. *Service by mail forms.* All civil complaints submitted to the Clerk for filing shall be accompanied by a summons or, if electing to serve by mail, the approved service by mail forms. NY R USDCTND L.R. 5.1(f).

c. *Notice of constitutional question.* A party that files a pleading, written motion, or other paper drawing into question the constitutionality of a federal or state statute must promptly:

   i. *File notice.* File a notice of constitutional question stating the question and identifying the paper that raises it, if:
      - A federal statute is questioned and the parties do not include the United States, one of its agencies, or one of its officers or employees in an official capacity; or
      - A state statute is questioned and the parties do not include the state, one of its agencies, or one of its officers or employees in an official capacity; and

   ii. *Serve notice.* Serve the notice and paper on the Attorney General of the United States if a federal statute is questioned—or on the state attorney general if a state statute is questioned—either by certified or registered mail or by sending it to an electronic address designated by the attorney general for this purpose. FRCP 5.1(a).

   iii. *No forfeiture.* A party's failure to file and serve the notice, or the court's failure to certify, does not forfeit a constitutional claim or defense that is otherwise timely asserted. FRCP 5.1(d).

d. *Notice of issue concerning foreign law.* A party who intends to raise an issue about a foreign country's law must give notice by a pleading or other writing. In determining foreign law, the court may consider any relevant material or source, including testimony, whether or not submitted by a party or admissible under the Federal Rules of Evidence. The court's determination must be treated as a ruling on a question of law. FRCP 44.1.

e. *Nongovernmental corporate disclosure statement*

    i. *Contents.* A nongovernmental corporate party must file two (2) copies of a disclosure statement that:

- Identifies any parent corporation and any publicly held corporation owning ten percent (10%) or more of its stock; or

- States that there is no such corporation. FRCP 7.1(a).

    ii. *Time to file; Supplemental filing.* A party must:

- File the disclosure statement with its first appearance, pleading, petition, motion, response, or other request addressed to the court; and

- Promptly file a supplemental statement if any required information changes. FRCP 7.1(b).

f. *Application to convene a three-judge court.* Whenever a party believes that only a three-judge court is required, the party shall submit a separate application to convene a three-judge court along with the first pleading in which the party asserts the cause of action requiring a three-judge court. On the convening of a three-judge court, the parties shall make three copies of all non-electronically filed pleadings, motion papers, and memoranda of law available to the Clerk for distribution. NY R USDCTND L.R. 9.1.

g. *Application to proceed in forma pauperis.* If the filing attorney is seeking to have the filing fee waived, an In Forma Pauperis application should be filed as an attachment to the electronically filed civil complaint and the filing attorney would answer "yes" at the IFP screen. NY R USDCTND CM/ECF(4)(4.2).

h. *Motion for TRO and supporting documents.* If the initial complaint includes a motion for a TRO, please file the complaint with summons and civil cover sheet, motion for TRO and supporting documents as attachments, and call the Clerk's Office to notify of the filing. NY R USDCTND CM/ECF(4)(4.2). Refer to the United States District Court for the Northern District of New York Application for Temporary Restraining Order document for more information on applying for a temporary restraining order.

i. *Cover letter authorizing e-mail or facsimile filing.* Neither the Court nor the Clerk's Office will accept for filing any facsimile or e-mail transmission without prior authorization from the Court. The party using facsimile or e-mail transmissions to file its papers must accompany any such documents with a cover letter stating that the Court authorized such transmissions and the date on which the Court provided that authorization. Violations of NY R USDCTND L.R. 5.5 subject the offending party to the Court's full disciplinary powers. NY R USDCTND L.R. 5.5.

j. *Affidavit attesting to failed attempts to file electronically.* If the Court's CM/ECF site experiences a technical failure, a Filing User may submit documents to the Court that day in an alternate manner provided that the documents are accompanied by the Filing User's affidavit stating that the Filing User attempted to file electronically at least two times in one (1) hour increments after 10:00 a.m. that day. The following methods are acceptable alternate means for filing documents in case of a technical failure: (1) via electronic mail in a PDF attachment sent to the e-mail address for technical failures; or (2) in person, by bringing the document to the Clerk's Office on paper accompanied by a CD/ROM that contains the document in .pdf format. NY R USDCTND CM/ECF(10)(10.1).

    i. A Filing User who cannot file documents electronically because of a problem on the Filing User's system must file the documents' conventionally along with an affidavit explaining the reason for not filing the documents electronically. NY R USDCTND CM/ECF(10)(10.2).

k. *Notice of conventional filing.* If the Clerk's Office grants permission to conventionally file the document, the Filing User shall electronically file a notice of conventional filing for the documents. More information regarding this process can be obtained from the Court's web page. NY R USDCTND CM/ECF(4)(4.5).

l. *CD/ROM with PDF of document(s).* If the Court grants permission to file a document traditionally, the attorney must submit the documents for filing to the Clerk's Office on CD/ROM in .pdf or pdf.A format. NY R USDCTND CM/ECF(2).

m. *English translation.* The Court conducts its reviews and deliberations in English. Unless otherwise directed by the Court, any document that a party transmits to the Court (including one in the record on appeal) that is in a language other than English must be accompanied by an English translation that the translator has certified as true and accurate, pursuant to 28 U.S.C.A. § 1746. NY R USDCTND L.R. 10.1(e). For more information, refer to NY R USDCTND L.R. 10.1(e).

n. *Courtesy copies.* The Court may require that courtesy copies of electronically filed documents be submitted for its review and may amend these Administrative Procedures (NY R USDCTND CM/ECF) at any time without prior notice. NY R USDCTND CM/ECF(2).

o. *Copies for three-judge court.* On the convening of a three-judge court, the parties shall make three (3) copies of all non-electronically filed pleadings, motion papers, and memoranda of law available to the Clerk for distribution. NY R USDCTND L.R. 9.1.

3. *Individual judge practices.* Refer to the Miscellaneous section of this document for information on individual judge practices on required documents.

## E. Format

1. *Form of documents.* All pleadings and other papers shall be served and filed in accordance with the Federal Rules of Civil Procedure and shall be in the form prescribed by NY R USDCTND L.R. 10.1. NY R USDCTND L.R. 5.1(a).

   a. *Form, generally.* All pleadings, motions, and other documents that a party presents for filing, whether in paper form or in electronic form, shall meet the following requirements:

      i. *Font size.* All text, whether in the body of the document or in footnotes, must be a minimum of twelve (12) point type. NY R USDCTND L.R. 10.1(a)(1).

      ii. *Margins.* All documents must have one (1) inch margins on all four sides of the page. NY R USDCTND L.R. 10.1(a)(2).

      iii. *Spacing.* All text in the body of the document must be double-spaced. NY R USDCTND L.R. 10.1(a)(3).

         • The text in block quotations and footnotes may be single-spaced. NY R USDCTND L.R. 10.1(a)(4).

      iv. *Page numbering.* Pages must be consecutively numbered. NY R USDCTND L.R. 10.1(a)(7).

      v. *Circumventing formatting limitations*

         • Extensive footnotes must not be used to circumvent page limitations. NY R USDCTND L.R. 10.1(a)(5).

         • Compacted or other compressed printing features must not be used. NY R USDCTND L.R. 10.1(a)(6).

   b. *Additional requirements for paper filing.* Additional requirements for all pleadings, motions, and other documents that a party presents for filing in paper form:

      i. *Paper size.* All documents must be on eight and one-half by eleven (8-1/2 x 11) inch white paper of good quality. NY R USDCTND L.R. 10.1(b)(1).

      ii. *Text.* All text must be plainly and legibly written, typewritten, printed or reproduced without erasures or interlineations materially defacing them. NY R USDCTND L.R. 10.1(b)(2).

      iii. *Ink.* All documents must be in black or blue ink. NY R USDCTND L.R. 10.1(b)(3).

      iv. *Binding.* Pages of all documents must be stapled (or in some other way fastened) together. NY R USDCTND L.R. 10.1(b)(4).

      v. *Single-sided paper.* All documents must be single-sided. NY R USDCTND L.R. 10.1(b)(5).

      vi. *Electronic submission.* The Court, at its discretion, may require the electronic submission of any document in a WordPerfect-compatible format. NY R USDCTND L.R. 10.1(b)(6).

vii. *Rejection of document.* The Court may reject documents that do not comply with the above-listed requirements. NY R USDCTND L.R. 10.1(b).

c. *Caption; Names of parties.* Every pleading must have a caption with the court's name, a title, a file number, and a FRCP 7(a) designation. The title of the complaint must name all the parties; the title of other pleadings, after naming the first party on each side, may refer generally to other parties. FRCP 10(a). Each document must contain a caption for the specific case to which it pertains. The caption must include the title of the Court, the title of the action, the civil action number of the case, the initials of the assigned judge(s), and the name or nature of the paper in sufficient detail for identification. If a litigant has more than one action pending in this Court, any and all papers filed in a case must contain and pertain to one civil action number, unless the civil actions have been consolidated by the Court. Any motion or other papers purporting to relate to more than one action will not be accepted for filing and may be stricken by the Court. NY R USDCTND L.R. 10.1(c)(1) shall not apply, as noted in NY R USDCTND L.R. 10.1(c), to notices of change of address filed by attorneys of record and pro se litigants. The parties must separately caption affidavits and declarations and must not physically attach them to the Notice of Motion or Memorandum of Law. NY R USDCTND L.R. 10.1(c)(1).

   i. *Demand for jury trial.* If a party demands a jury trial as FRCP 38(b) permits, the party shall place a notation on the front page of the initial pleading which that party signed, stating "Demand for Jury Trial" or an equivalent statement. This notation shall serve as a sufficient demand under FRCP 38(b). NY R USDCTND L.R. 38.1(a).

   ii. *Class action.* If a party seeks to maintain a case as a class action pursuant to FRCP 23, the party shall include the words "Class Action" in the complaint or other pleading asserting a class action next to its caption. NY R USDCTND L.R. 23.1(a).

d. *Paragraphs; Separate statements.* A party must state its claims or defenses in numbered paragraphs, each limited as far as practicable to a single set of circumstances. A later pleading may refer by number to a paragraph in an earlier pleading. If doing so would promote clarity, each claim founded on a separate transaction or occurrence—and each defense other than a denial—must be stated in a separate count or defense. FRCP 10(b).

e. *Adoption by reference; Exhibits.* A statement in a pleading may be adopted by reference elsewhere in the same pleading or in any other pleading or motion. A copy of a written instrument that is an exhibit to a pleading is a part of the pleading for all purposes. FRCP 10(c).

f. *Citation of local rules.* These are the Local Rules of Practice for the United States District Court for the Northern District of New York. They shall be cited as "L.R. ___." NY R USDCTND L.R. 1.1(a).

g. *Acceptance by the clerk.* The clerk must not refuse to file a paper solely because it is not in the form prescribed by the Federal Rules of Civil Procedure or by a local rule or practice. FRCP 5(d)(4).

2. *Form of electronic documents.* All pleadings, motions, and other documents that a party presents for filing, whether in paper form or in electronic form, shall meet the requirements in NY R USDCTND L.R. 10.1(a). NY R USDCTND L.R. 10.1(a). Refer above for more information.

a. *Attachments and exhibits.* A Filing User must submit in electronic form all documents referenced as exhibits or attachments in accordance with the Court's CM/ECF Users Manual unless the Court otherwise orders. A Filing User shall submit as exhibits or attachments only those excerpts of the referenced documents that are directly germane to the matter under the Court's consideration. Excerpted material must be clearly and prominently identified as such. Filing Users who file excerpts of documents as exhibits or attachments under these Administrative Procedures (NY R USDCTND CM/ECF) do so without prejudice to their right to timely file additional excerpts or the complete document. Responding parties may also timely file the complete document or additional excerpts that they believe are directly germane to the matter under the Court's consideration. NY R USDCTND CM/ECF(4)(4.4).

   i. All attachments must be described in sufficient detail so the Court and opposing counsel can easily identify and distinguish the filed attachments. Vague or general descriptions are insufficient (i.e., "Exhibit 1"). Rather, each attachment shall have a descriptive title identifying, with specificity, the document that is being filed (i.e., "Exhibit 12 Mulligan County Fire Investigation Report.") Failure to adequately describe attachments may result in the document being rejected by the Court. NY R USDCTND CM/ECF(4)(4.4).

b. *Large documents.* For information on the electronic filing of large documents, please consult the Court's CM/ECF Users Manual, which is available on the Court's web page. NY R USDCTND CM/ECF(4)(4.5).

    i. A party who believes a document is too lengthy to electronically image, i.e., "scan," may contact the Clerk's Office for permission to file that document conventionally. If the Clerk's Office grants permission to conventionally file the document, the Filing User shall electronically file a notice of conventional filing for the documents. More information regarding this process can be obtained from the Court's web page. Exhibits submitted conventionally shall be served on other parties as if they were not subject to these Administrative Procedures (NY R USDCTND CM/ECF). For a list of hints and tips for scanning large documents, please consult the Court's web page. NY R USDCTND CM/ECF(4)(4.5).

c. *Legibility.* It shall be the Filing User's responsibility to verify the legibility of scanned documents before filing them electronically with the Court. NY R USDCTND CM/ECF(4)(4.6).

d. *Color documents.* Since documents scanned in color or containing a graphic take much longer to upload, Filing Users are encouraged to configure their scanners to scan documents at 300 dpi and preferably in black and white rather than in color. NY R USDCTND CM/ECF(4)(4.7).

e. *Items not in .PDF format.* Parties wishing to file items not amenable to .pdf format (i.e. CD's, DVD's), shall file such items conventionally with the Clerk's Office. The Filing User shall electronically file a notice of conventional filing indicating that these items have been submitted to the clerk and shall serve copies of these items on other parties as if they were not subject to these Administrative Procedures (NY R USDCTND CM/ECF). These item(s) will be maintained by the Clerk's Office until the case is disposed, at which time they will be returned to the filing party for retention consistent with NY R USDCTND CM/ECF(4)(4.9). NY R USDCTND CM/ECF(4)(4.8).

3. *Signing of pleadings, motions and other papers*

a. *Signature.* Every pleading, written motion, and other paper must be signed by at least one attorney of record in the attorney's name—or by a party personally if the party is unrepresented. The paper must state the signer's address, e-mail address, and telephone number. FRCP 11(a). Each document must identify the person filing the document. This identification must include an original signature of the attorney or pro se litigant; the typewritten name of that person; the address of a pro se litigant; and the bar roll number, office address, telephone number, e-mail address and fax number of the attorney. Telephone numbers of non-prisoner pro se parties may be provided voluntarily or upon request of the Court. See General Order #22 (NY R USDCTND CM/ECF) for signature requirements. NY R USDCTND L.R. 10.1(c)(2).

    i. *Electronic signatures.* Documents filed under an attorney's login and password shall constitute that attorney's signature for purposes of the Local Rules of Practice for the United States District Court for the Northern District of New York and Federal Rules of Civil Procedure, including but not limited to FRCP 11. A pleading or other document requiring an attorney's signature shall be signed in the following manner, whether filed electronically or submitted on disk or CD/ROM to the Clerk's Office: "s/ (attorney name)." The correct format for an attorney signature is found in NY R USDCTND CM/ECF(6)(6.1). NY R USDCTND CM/ECF(6)(6.1).

- *Non-attorney signature.* If an original document requires the signature of a non-attorney, the Filing User may scan the original document containing the original signature(s), then electronically file it on the System. Alternatively, the Filing User may convert the document into .pdf text format and submit the document using "s/" for the signature of the non-attorney. NY R USDCTND CM/ECF(6)(6.2).

- *Multiple signatures.* A document requiring signatures of more than one party must be filed electronically either by (1) submitting a scanned document containing all necessary signatures; (2) representing the consent of the other parties on the document; or (3) in any other manner that the Court approves. NY R USDCTND CM/ECF(6)(6.3).

    ii. *No verification or accompanying affidavit required for pleadings.* Unless a rule or statute specifically states otherwise, a pleading need not be verified or accompanied by an affidavit. FRCP 11(a).

    iii. *Unsigned papers.* The court must strike an unsigned paper unless the omission is promptly corrected after being called to the attorney's or party's attention. FRCP 11(a).

b. *Representations to the court.* By presenting to the court a pleading, written motion, or other paper—whether by signing, filing, submitting, or later advocating it—an attorney or unrepresented party certifies that to the best of the person's knowledge, information, and belief, formed after an inquiry reasonable under the circumstances:

    i. It is not being presented for any improper purpose, such as to harass, cause unnecessary delay, or needlessly increase the cost of litigation;

    ii. The claims, defenses, and other legal contentions are warranted by existing law or by a nonfrivolous argument for extending, modifying, or reversing existing law or for establishing new law;

    iii. The factual contentions have evidentiary support or, if specifically so identified, will likely have evidentiary support after a reasonable opportunity for further investigation or discovery; and

    iv. The denials of factual contentions are warranted on the evidence or, if specifically so identified, are reasonably based on belief or a lack of information. FRCP 11(b).

c. *Sanctions.* If, after notice and a reasonable opportunity to respond, the court determines that FRCP 11(b) has been violated, the court may impose an appropriate sanction on any attorney, law firm, or party that violated FRCP 11(b) or is responsible for the violation. FRCP 11(c)(1). Refer to the United States District Court for the Northern District of New York KeyRules Motion for Sanctions document for more information.

4. *Privacy protection for filings made with the court*

a. *Redacted filings.* Unless the court orders otherwise, in an electronic or paper filing with the court that contains an individual's Social Security number, taxpayer-identification number, or birth date, the name of an individual known to be a minor, or a financial-account number, a party or nonparty making the filing may include only:

    i. The last four (4) digits of the Social Security number and taxpayer-identification number;

    ii. The year of the individual's birth;

    iii. The minor's initials; and

    iv. The last four (4) digits of the financial-account number. FRCP 5.2(a); NY R USDCTND L.R. 8.1; NY R USDCTND CM/ECF(11)(11.2).

    v. If a home address must be used, use only the City and State. NY R USDCTND L.R. 8.1; NY R USDCTND CM/ECF(11)(11.2).

    vi. If the victim of a sexual assault must be referenced, redact the name to 'Victim.' NY R USDCTND CM/ECF(11)(11.2); NY R USDCTND L.R. 8.1.

    vii. In addition, caution shall be exercised when filing documents that contain the following:

- Personal identifying number, such as a driver's license number;
- Medical records, treatment and diagnosis;
- Employment history;
- Individual financial information; and
- Proprietary or trade secret information. NY R USDCTND L.R. 8.1; NY R USDCTND CM/ECF(11)(11.2).

b. *Exemptions from the redaction requirement.* The redaction requirement does not apply to the following:

    i. A financial-account number that identifies the property allegedly subject to forfeiture in a forfeiture proceeding;

ii. The record of an administrative or agency proceeding;

iii. The official record of a state-court proceeding;

iv. The record of a court or tribunal, if that record was not subject to the redaction requirement when originally filed;

v. A filing covered by FRCP 5.2(c) or FRCP 5.2(d); and

vi. A pro se filing in an action brought under 28 U.S.C.A. § 2241, 28 U.S.C.A. § 2254, or 28 U.S.C.A. § 2255. FRCP 5.2(b).

vii. Transcripts of the administrative record in social security proceedings are exempt from this requirement. State court records and other documents filed in habeas corpus proceedings are exempt from this requirement except for proceedings that involve victims of sex crimes. In habeas corpus cases involving sex crimes, the parties must redact the record and supporting papers, or may move to seal, if appropriate. NY R USDCTND L.R. 8.1.

c. *Limitations on remote access to electronic files; Social Security appeals and immigration cases.* Unless the court orders otherwise, in an action for benefits under the Social Security Act, and in an action or proceeding relating to an order of removal, to relief from removal, or to immigration benefits or detention, access to an electronic file is authorized as follows:

i. The parties and their attorneys may have remote electronic access to any part of the case file, including the administrative record;

ii. Any other person may have electronic access to the full record at the courthouse, but may have remote electronic access only to:

- The docket maintained by the court; and
- An opinion, order, judgment, or other disposition of the court, but not any other part of the case file or the administrative record. FRCP 5.2(c).

d. *Filings made under seal.* The court may order that a filing be made under seal without redaction. The court may later unseal the filing or order the person who made the filing to file a redacted version for the public record. FRCP 5.2(d); NY R USDCTND L.R. 8.1. For information on sealed matters, refer to NY R USDCTND L.R. 83.13 and NY R USDCTND CM/ECF(12).

e. *Protective orders.* For good cause, the court may by order in a case:

i. Require redaction of additional information; or

ii. Limit or prohibit a nonparty's remote electronic access to a document filed with the court. FRCP 5.2(e).

f. *Option for additional unredacted filing under seal.* A person making a redacted filing may also file an unredacted copy under seal. The court must retain the unredacted copy as part of the record. FRCP 5.2(f); NY R USDCTND L.R. 8.1; NY R USDCTND CM/ECF(11)(11.3).

g. *Option for filing a reference list.* A filing that contains redacted information may be filed together with a reference list that identifies each item of redacted information and specifies an appropriate identifier that uniquely corresponds to each item listed. The list must be filed under seal and may be amended as of right. Any reference in the case to a listed identifier will be construed to refer to the corresponding item of information. FRCP 5.2(g); NY R USDCTND L.R. 8.1; NY R USDCTND CM/ECF(11)(11.3).

h. *Responsibility for redaction.* Counsel is strongly urged to discuss this issue with all their clients so that they can make an informed decision about the inclusion of certain information. The responsibility for redacting these personal identifiers rests solely with counsel and the parties. The Clerk will not review each filing for compliance with NY R USDCTND L.R. 8.1. Counsel and the parties are cautioned that failure to redact these personal identifiers may subject them to the Court's full disciplinary power. NY R USDCTND L.R. 8.1; NY R USDCTND CM/ECF(11)(11.3).

i. *Waiver of protection of identifiers.* A person waives the protection of FRCP 5.2(a) as to the person's own information by filing it without redaction and not under seal. FRCP 5.2(h).

5. *Individual judge practices.* Refer to the Miscellaneous section of this document for information on individual judge practices on formatting documents.

## F. Filing and Service Requirements

1.  *Filing requirements.* A civil action is commenced by filing a complaint with the court. FRCP 3. The first step in a civil action in a United States district court is the filing of the complaint with the clerk or the judge. FPP § 1052. Filing a complaint requires nothing more than delivery of the document to a court officer authorized to receive it. FPP § 1052; Central States, Southeast & Southwest Areas Pension Fund v. Paramount Liquor Co., 34 F.Supp.2d 1092 (N.D.Ill. 1999).

    a.  *Opening a civil case.* All civil actions commenced by members of the Bar must be filed electronically in CM/ECF. The payment of the filing fee will be made through a secure United States Treasury Internet Credit Card site. The attorney will log into CM/ECF and submit all initiating documents in .pdf format to a universal shell case "5:00-at-99999." The Clerk will transfer the case from the shell file, and assign a case number, district court judge and magistrate judge. Once the new case is opened by the Clerk the filing attorney will receive a Notice of Electronic Filing (NEF). Please note--the action will be filed as of the date that the filing fee was paid and the complaint was uploaded into the shell case. NY R USDCTND CM/ECF(4)(4.2). New cases are deemed filed the day the Clerk's Office receives the complaint and required filing fee. NY R USDCTND CM/ECF(4)(4.3).

    b.  *Venue.* The Court's Civil Case Assignment Plan as set forth in NY R USDCTND Order 12 shall control venue for civil cases filed in the Northern District of New York. When filing a related action, parties must comply with NY R USDCTND Order 12(G). NY R USDCTND L.R. 3.2.

    c.  *Pro se incarcerated litigants.* Individuals who are incarcerated and are filing their legal documents pro se may benefit from a special "mailbox rule," which fixes the time of commencement of an action at the point when the complaint enters the prison mail system, rather than when it reaches the court clerk. FPP § 1052; Houston v. Lack, 487 U.S. 266, 276, 108 S.Ct. 2379, 2385, 101 L.Ed.2d 245 (1988).

    d.  *Electronic filing*

        i.  *Authorization of electronic filing program.* A court may, by local rule, allow papers to be filed, signed, or verified by electronic means that are consistent with any technical standards established by the Judicial Conference of the United States. A local rule may require electronic filing only if reasonable exceptions are allowed. A paper filed electronically in compliance with a local rule is a written paper for purposes of the Federal Rules of Civil Procedure. FRCP 5(d)(3).

            *   All cases filed in this Court may be assigned to the Electronic Case Files System ("ECF") in accordance with the Procedural Order on Electronic Case Filing (General Order #22 (NY R USDCTND CM/ECF)), the provisions of which are incorporated herein by reference, and which the Court may amend from time to time. Copies of General Order #22 (NY R USDCTND CM/ECF) are available at the Clerk's office or at the Court's webpage. NY R USDCTND L.R. 5.1.1; NY R USDCTND Order 25(XII).

            *   The Court may deviate from these Administrative Procedures (NY R USDCTND CM/ECF) in specific cases, without prior notice, if deemed appropriate in the exercise of discretion, considering the need for the just, speedy, and inexpensive determination of matters pending before the Court. NY R USDCTND CM/ECF(2).

        ii. *Scope of electronic filing.* After January 1, 2004, all documents that attorneys admitted to practice in the Northern District of New York submit for filing shall be filed electronically using the System or shall be scanned and uploaded to the System, no matter when a case was originally filed, unless these Administrative Procedures (NY R USDCTND CM/ECF) otherwise permit or unless the assigned judge otherwise authorizes. An attorney who is not a Filing User by January 1, 2004, must show good cause to the assigned judge to file and serve pleadings and other papers in the traditional manner. NY R USDCTND CM/ECF(2).

        iii. *Exceptions and/or waivers from mandatory electronic filing.* The following types of cases and/or documents are not required to be filed electronically:

            *   If you are seeking to have your complaint filed under seal, please file your complaint and proposed sealing order traditionally at the Clerk's Office. NY R USDCTND CM/ECF(2)(2.1)(1).

- Any document that a party proceeding pro se files. (See NY R USDCTND CM/ECF(12)(12.1) for procedural details). NY R USDCTND CM/ECF(2)(2.1)(2). A non-prisoner who is a party to a civil action and who is not represented by an attorney may file a motion to obtain an Electronic Case Filing (ECF) login and password on a form prescribed by the Clerk's Office. The Pro Se CM/ECF Registration Form shall be submitted with the motion. If during the course of the action an attorney appears on behalf of the pro se party, the Clerk's Office shall terminate the pro se party's registration based upon the attorney's appearance. NY R USDCTND CM/ECF(12)(12.1). Absent permission to file electronically, pro se filers shall file paper originals of all complaints, pleadings, motions, affidavits, briefs, and other documents which must be signed or which require either verification or an unsworn declaration under any rule or statute. The Clerk's Office will scan these original documents into an electronic file in the System but will also maintain a paper file. NY R USDCTND CM/ECF(12)(12.1). A pro se party may also seek permission to receive immediate notice of all public documents filed in their cases. Notices of Electronic Filing (NEF) and attached documents would be transmitted to a non-prisoner pro se party who selects this option. Note: The pro se party would continue to file their documents with the Clerk's Office in paper form. NY R USDCTND CM/ECF(12)(12.1).

- Sealed documents, sealed cases, documents for in camera review, documents lodged with the Court, ex parte documents, confidential agreements, Qui Tam actions and Grand Jury material and warrants must be filed traditionally. (See NY R USDCTND CM/ECF(12)(12.2) for further information the filing of the above-referenced documents). NY R USDCTND CM/ECF(2)(2.1)(3).

- Discovery: In accordance with NY R USDCTND L.R. 26.2, parties shall not file discovery, provided, however, that discovery material to be used at trial or in support of any motion, including a motion to compel or for summary judgment, shall be filed electronically with the Court prior to the trial or with the motion. Any motion pursuant to FRCP 37 shall be accompanied by the electronically filed discovery materials to which the motion relates if those materials have not previously been filed with the Court. NY R USDCTND CM/ECF(2)(2.1)(4).

- Transport Orders: All orders requesting that an incarcerated individual be transported that a judicial officer of the Northern District of New York signs shall be filed traditionally. These Orders will not be filed with the case or uploaded to the docket but rather will be processed in accordance with the procedures that the Clerk of Court promulgates. NY R USDCTND CM/ECF(2)(2.1)(5).

iv. *Filing defined.* Electronic transmission of a document to the System in accordance with these Administrative Procedures, together with the transmission of a Notice of Electronic Filing from the Court, constitutes filing of the document for all purposes of the Federal Rules of Civil Procedure and the Local Rules of Practice for the United States District Court for the Northern District of New York and constitutes entry of the document on the docket that the Clerk's Office keeps under FRCP 58 and FRCP 79. E-mailing a document to the Clerk's Office or to the assigned judge shall not constitute "filing" of the document. NY R USDCTND CM/ECF(4)(4.1).

v. *Filing fees.* Any fee required for filing a pleading or paper in this Court is payable to the Clerk of the Court. The Court will not maintain electronic billing or debit accounts for attorneys or law firms. Effective January 1, 2007, payment for filing fees will be mandatory through CM/ECF's Internet Credit Card Payment site--a secure Treasury Site. The Filing User will be prompted to enter either Bank Account Debit (ACH) or credit card information while filing the initial pleading. Any document that requires a filing fee (e.g., Notice of Appeal, Motion for Pro Hac Vice Admission) may also be paid through the federal electronic payment website. NY R USDCTND CM/ECF(7).

vi. For more information on electronic filing, refer to NY R USDCTND CM/ECF.

e. *E-mail or facsimile filing.* Neither the Court nor the Clerk's Office will accept for filing any facsimile or e-mail transmission without prior authorization from the Court. The party using facsimile or e-mail transmissions to file its papers must accompany any such documents with a cover letter stating that the Court authorized such transmissions and the date on which the Court provided that authorization. Violations of NY R USDCTND L.R. 5.5 subject the offending party to the Court's full disciplinary powers. NY R USDCTND L.R. 5.5.

2. *Issuance of summons.* On or after filing the complaint, the plaintiff may present a summons to the clerk for signature and seal. If the summons is properly completed, the clerk must sign, seal, and issue it to the plaintiff for service on the defendant. A summons—or a copy of a summons that is addressed to multiple defendants—must be issued for each defendant to be served. FRCP 4(b).

   a. *Amendments.* The court may permit a summons to be amended. FRCP 4(a)(2).

3. *Issuance of other documents.* Upon the filing of a complaint, the Clerk shall issue to the plaintiff NY R USDCTND Order 25 which requires, among other things, service of process upon all defendants within sixty (60) days of the filing of the complaint. This expedited service requirement is necessary to ensure adequate time for pretrial discovery and motion practice. In no event shall service of process be completed after the time specified in FRCP 4. NY R USDCTND L.R. 4.1(b). The Clerk shall furnish the materials in NY R USDCTND L.R. 4.1(c) to the party seeking to invoke the jurisdiction of the Court at the time the complaint or notice of removal is filed. NY R USDCTND L.R. 4.1(c).

4. *Service requirements.* A summons must be served with a copy of the complaint. The plaintiff is responsible for having the summons and complaint served within the time allowed by FRCP 4(m) and must furnish the necessary copies to the person who makes service. FRCP 4(c)(1). FRCP 5(b) does not permit electronic service of process for purposes of obtaining personal jurisdiction, i.e., FRCP 4 Service. Therefore, service of process must be effected in the traditional manner. NY R USDCTND CM/ECF(5)(5.1). Service shall be made in the manner specified in the Federal Rules of Civil Procedure or as required or permitted by statute. The party seeking service of papers shall be responsible for arranging the service. The Clerk is authorized to sign orders appointing persons to serve process. NY R USDCTND L.R. 4.1(a).

   a. *By whom served.* Any person who is at least 18 years old and not a party may serve a summons and complaint. FRCP 4(c)(2).

      i. *By a private process server.* A private process server shall serve every summons, except as otherwise required by statute or rule or as the Court directs for good cause shown. A private process server is any person authorized to serve process in an action brought in the New York State Supreme Court or in the court of general jurisdiction of the State in which service is made. NY R USDCTND L.R. 5.1(g).

      ii. *By a marshal or someone specially appointed.* At the plaintiff's request, the court may order that service be made by a United States marshal or deputy marshal or by a person specially appointed by the court. The court must so order if the plaintiff is authorized to proceed in forma pauperis under 28 U.S.C.A. § 1915 or as a seaman under 28 U.S.C.A. § 1916. FRCP 4(c)(3).

   b. *Serving an individual within a judicial district of the United States.* Unless federal law provides otherwise, an individual—other than a minor, an incompetent person, or a person whose waiver has been filed—may be served in a judicial district of the United States by:

      i. Following state law for serving a summons in an action brought in courts of general jurisdiction in the state where the district court is located or where service is made; or

      ii. Doing any of the following:

         • Delivering a copy of the summons and of the complaint to the individual personally;

         • Leaving a copy of each at the individual's dwelling or usual place of abode with someone of suitable age and discretion who resides there; or

         • Delivering a copy of each to an agent authorized by appointment or by law to receive service of process. FRCP 4(e).

   c. *Serving an individual in a foreign country.* Unless federal law provides otherwise, an individual—

other than a minor, an incompetent person, or a person whose waiver has been filed—may be served at a place not within any judicial district of the United States:

i. By any internationally agreed means of service that is reasonably calculated to give notice, such as those authorized by the Hague Convention on the Service Abroad of Judicial and Extrajudicial Documents;

ii. If there is no internationally agreed means, or if an international agreement allows but does not specify other means, by a method that is reasonably calculated to give notice:

- As prescribed by the foreign country's law for service in that country in an action in its courts of general jurisdiction;

- As the foreign authority directs in response to a letter rogatory or letter of request; or

- Unless prohibited by the foreign country's law, by: (1) delivering a copy of the summons and of the complaint to the individual personally; or (2) using any form of mail that the clerk addresses and sends to the individual and that requires a signed receipt; or

- By other means not prohibited by international agreement, as the court orders. FRCP 4(f).

d. *Serving a minor or an incompetent person.* A minor or an incompetent person in a judicial district of the United States must be served by following state law for serving a summons or like process on such a defendant in an action brought in the courts of general jurisdiction of the state where service is made. A minor or an incompetent person who is not within any judicial district of the United States must be served in the manner prescribed by FRCP 4(f)(2)(A), FRCP 4(f)(2)(B), or FRCP 4(f)(3). FRCP 4(g).

e. *Serving a corporation, partnership, or association.* Unless federal law provides otherwise or the defendant's waiver has been filed, a domestic or foreign corporation, or a partnership or other unincorporated association that is subject to suit under a common name, must be served:

i. In a judicial district of the United States:

- In the manner prescribed by FRCP 4(e)(1) for serving an individual; or

- By delivering a copy of the summons and of the complaint to an officer, a managing or general agent, or any other agent authorized by appointment or by law to receive service of process and—if the agent is one authorized by statute and the statute so requires—by also mailing a copy of each to the defendant; or

ii. At a place not within any judicial district of the United States, in any manner prescribed by FRCP 4(f) for serving an individual, except personal delivery under FRCP 4(f)(2)(C)(i). FRCP 4(h).

f. *Serving the United States and its agencies, corporations, officers, or employees*

i. *United States.* To serve the United States, a party must:

- Deliver a copy of the summons and of the complaint to the United States attorney for the district where the action is brought—or to an assistant United States attorney or clerical employee whom the United States attorney designates in a writing filed with the court clerk—or send a copy of each by registered or certified mail to the civil-process clerk at the United States attorney's office;

- Send a copy of each by registered or certified mail to the Attorney General of the United States at Washington, D.C.; and

- If the action challenges an order of a nonparty agency or officer of the United States, send a copy of each by registered or certified mail to the agency or officer. FRCP 4(i)(1).

ii. *Agency; Corporation; Officer or employee sued in an official capacity.* To serve a United States agency or corporation, or a United States officer or employee sued only in an official capacity, a party must serve the United States and also send a copy of the summons and of the complaint by registered or certified mail to the agency, corporation, officer, or employee. FRCP 4(i)(2).

iii. *Officer or employee sued individually.* To serve a United States officer or employee sued in an individual capacity for an act or omission occurring in connection with duties performed on the United States' behalf (whether or not the officer or employee is also sued in an official capacity), a party must serve the United States and also serve the officer or employee under FRCP 4(e), FRCP 4(f), or FRCP 4(g). FRCP 4(i)(3).

  iv.  *Extending time.* The court must allow a party a reasonable time to cure its failure to:

  - Serve a person required to be served under FRCP 4(i)(2), if the party has served either the United States attorney or the Attorney General of the United States; or

  - Serve the United States under FRCP 4(i)(3), if the party has served the United States officer or employee. FRCP 4(i)(4).

g.  *Serving a foreign, state, or local government*

  i.  *Foreign state.* A foreign state or its political subdivision, agency, or instrumentality must be served in accordance with 28 U.S.C.A. § 1608. FRCP 4(j)(1).

  ii.  *State or local government.* A state, a municipal corporation, or any other state-created governmental organization that is subject to suit must be served by:

  - Delivering a copy of the summons and of the complaint to its chief executive officer; or

  - Serving a copy of each in the manner prescribed by that state's law for serving a summons or like process on such a defendant. FRCP 4(j)(2).

h.  *Territorial limits of effective service*

  i.  *In general.* Serving a summons or filing a waiver of service establishes personal jurisdiction over a defendant:

  - Who is subject to the jurisdiction of a court of general jurisdiction in the state where the district court is located;

  - Who is a party joined under FRCP 14 or FRCP 19 and is served within a judicial district of the United States and not more than one hundred (100) miles from where the summons was issued; or

  - When authorized by a federal statute. FRCP 4(k)(1).

  ii.  *Federal claim outside state-court jurisdiction.* For a claim that arises under federal law, serving a summons or filing a waiver of service establishes personal jurisdiction over a defendant if:

  - The defendant is not subject to jurisdiction in any state's courts of general jurisdiction; and

  - Exercising jurisdiction is consistent with the United States Constitution and laws. FRCP 4(k)(2).

i.  *Asserting jurisdiction over property or assets*

  i.  *Federal law.* The court may assert jurisdiction over property if authorized by a federal statute. Notice to claimants of the property must be given as provided in the statute or by serving a summons under FRCP 4. FRCP 4(n)(1).

  ii.  *State law.* On a showing that personal jurisdiction over a defendant cannot be obtained in the district where the action is brought by reasonable efforts to serve a summons under FRCP 4, the court may assert jurisdiction over the defendant's assets found in the district. Jurisdiction is acquired by seizing the assets under the circumstances and in the manner provided by state law in that district. FRCP 4(n)(2).

j.  *Proving service*

  i.  *Affidavit required.* Unless service is waived, proof of service must be made to the court. Except for service by a United States marshal or deputy marshal, proof must be by the server's affidavit. FRCP 4(l)(1).

  ii.  *Service outside the United States.* Service not within any judicial district of the United States must be proved as follows:

  - If made under FRCP 4(f)(1), as provided in the applicable treaty or convention; or

- If made under FRCP 4(f)(2) or FRCP 4(f)(3), by a receipt signed by the addressee, or by other evidence satisfying the court that the summons and complaint were delivered to the addressee. FRCP 4(l)(2).

    iii. *Validity of service; Amending proof.* Failure to prove service does not affect the validity of service. The court may permit proof of service to be amended. FRCP 4(l)(3).

    iv. *Results of filing a waiver of service.* When the plaintiff files a waiver, proof of service is not required and FRCP 4 applies as if a summons and complaint had been served at the time of filing the waiver. FRCP 4(d)(4).

  k. *Service of other process.* For information on service of other process, refer to FRCP 4.1.

5. *Individual judge practices.* Refer to the Miscellaneous section of this document for information on individual judge practices on filing and serving documents.

## G. Hearings

1. There is no hearing contemplated in the federal statutes or rules for the complaint and summons.

## H. Forms

### 1. Official Federal Complaint and Summons Forms

  a. Rule 4 notice of a lawsuit and request to waive service of summons. FRCP 4.

### 2. Federal Complaint and Summons Forms

  a. Summons. 2 FEDFORMS § 3:23.

  b. Summons; With proof of service. 2 FEDFORMS § 3:24.

  c. Summons; Suit against officers of the United States. 2 FEDFORMS § 3:26.

  d. Request for summons. 2 FEDFORMS § 3:27.

  e. Civil cover sheet. 2 FEDFORMS § 3:29.

  f. Motion for appointment of person to serve process. 2 FEDFORMS § 3:30.

  g. Motion for appointment of United States marshal to serve process. 2 FEDFORMS § 3:34.

  h. Notice of lawsuit and request for waiver of service of summons and waiver of summons. 2 FEDFORMS § 3:36.

  i. Motion for payment of costs of personal service. 2 FEDFORMS § 3:37.

  j. Affidavit of personal service; Delivery to individual. 2 FEDFORMS § 3:54.

  k. Declaration of service; Delivery to individual. 2 FEDFORMS § 3:55.

  l. Declaration of service; Delivery at usual place of abode or residence. 2 FEDFORMS § 3:56.

  m. Declaration of service; Service on corporation; Delivery to officer. 2 FEDFORMS § 3:57.

  n. Declaration of service; Service on United States. 2 FEDFORMS § 3:69.

  o. Declaration of service; Service on officer of United States. 2 FEDFORMS § 3:71.

  p. Complaint. 2 FEDFORMS § 7:14.

  q. Introductory clause; Single claim stated. 2 FEDFORMS § 7:16.

  r. Introductory clause; Several claims stated in separate counts. 2 FEDFORMS § 7:18.

  s. Allegations on information and belief. 2 FEDFORMS § 7:19.

  t. General prayer for relief. 2 FEDFORMS § 7:21.

  u. Disparate treatment; Sex discrimination; Sexual harassment and constructive discharge. 2A FEDFORMS § 7:143.

  v. Against manufacturer for negligent design and manufacture. 2B FEDFORMS § 7:426.

  w. Complaint; Single count. FEDPROF § 1:68.

  x. Complaint; Multiple counts; With same jurisdictional basis. FEDPROF § 1:69.

y. Complaint; Multiple counts; With different jurisdictional basis for each. FEDPROF § 1:70.

z. Civil cover sheet; General form. FEDPROF § 1:144.

## I. Applicable Rules

1. *Federal rules*

   a. District court; Filing and miscellaneous fees; Rules of court. 28 U.S.C.A. § 1914.

   b. Commencing an action. FRCP 3.

   c. Summons. FRCP 4.

   d. Serving and filing pleadings and other papers. FRCP 5.

   e. Constitutional challenge to a statute; Notice, certification, and intervention. FRCP 5.1.

   f. Privacy protection for filings made with the court. FRCP 5.2.

   g. Computing and extending time; Time for motion papers. FRCP 6.

   h. Pleadings allowed; Form of motions and other papers. FRCP 7.

   i. Disclosure statement. FRCP 7.1.

   j. General rules of pleading. FRCP 8.

   k. Pleading special matters. FRCP 9.

   l. Form of pleadings. FRCP 10.

   m. Signing pleadings, motions, and other papers; Representations to the court; Sanctions. FRCP 11.

   n. Joinder of claims. FRCP 18.

   o. Required joinder of parties. FRCP 19.

   p. Permissive joinder of parties. FRCP 20.

   q. Misjoinder and nonjoinder of parties. FRCP 21.

   r. Right to a jury trial; Demand. FRCP 38.

   s. Determining foreign law. FRCP 44.1.

2. *Local rules*

   a. Scope of the rules. NY R USDCTND L.R. 1.1.

   b. Civil cover sheet. NY R USDCTND L.R. 3.1.

   c. Venue. NY R USDCTND L.R. 3.2.

   d. Complex and multi-district litigation. NY R USDCTND L.R. 3.3.

   e. Service of process. NY R USDCTND L.R. 4.1.

   f. Service and filing of papers. NY R USDCTND L.R. 5.1.

   g. Prepayment of fees. NY R USDCTND L.R. 5.2.

   h. Schedule of fees. NY R USDCTND L.R. 5.3.

   i. Filing by facsimile or e-mail. NY R USDCTND L.R. 5.5.

   j. Personal privacy protection. NY R USDCTND L.R. 8.1.

   k. Request for three-judge court. NY R USDCTND L.R. 9.1.

   l. Requirement to file a civil RICO statement. NY R USDCTND L.R. 9.2.

   m. Form of papers. NY R USDCTND L.R. 10.1.

   n. Civil case management. NY R USDCTND L.R. 16.1.

   o. Designation of "class action" in the caption. NY R USDCTND L.R. 23.1.

   p. Notation of "jury demand" in the pleading. NY R USDCTND L.R. 38.1.

   q. Settlement procedures. NY R USDCTND L.R. 68.2.

r.   Appearance and withdrawal of attorney. NY R USDCTND L.R. 83.2.

s.   Arbitration. NY R USDCTND L.R. 83.7-1; NY R USDCTND L.R. 83.7-2; NY R USDCTND L.R. 83.7-3.

t.   Assisted mediation program. NY R USDCTND L.R. 83.8.

u.   Mediation. NY R USDCTND L.R. 83.11-1; NY R USDCTND L.R. 83.11-3.

v.   Early neutral evaluation. NY R USDCTND L.R. 83.12-1; NY R USDCTND L.R. 83.12-3.

w.   Administrative procedures for electronic case filing. NY R USDCTND CM/ECF.

x.   Case assignment plan for the Northern District of New York. [NY R USDCTND Order 12, as amended by NY ORDER 16-4201, effective March 24, 2015].

y.   Directing the expedited service of the summons and complaint and further directing the completion of FRCP 16 stipulation for the timely progression of civil actions. [NY R USDCTND Order 25, as amended by NY ORDER 16-4187, effective June 23, 2016].

z.   Mandatory mediation program. NY R USDCTND Order 47.

## J.  Miscellaneous

**NOTE: Individual judges' rules may apply. For available judge-level information, refer to:**

DISTRICT JUDGE MAE A. D'AGOSTINO: [NY R USDCTND D'Agostino-Rules and Practices, as added by NY ORDER 16-4200, effective April 4, 2016].

DISTRICT JUDGE THOMAS J. McAVOY: NY R USDCTND McAvoy-Order.

# Pleadings
# Answer

### Document Last Updated September 2016

## A.  Checklist

(I)   ❑  Matters to be considered by plaintiff

(a)   ❑  Required documents

(1)   ❑  Civil cover sheet

(2)   ❑  Complaint

(3)   ❑  Summons

(4)   ❑  Judicial case assignment form

(5)   ❑  Judicial civil case management plan containing notice of initial pretrial conference

(6)   ❑  Notice and consent form to proceed before a United States magistrate judge

(7)   ❑  Notice and consent form for the court sponsored alternative dispute resolution procedures

(8)   ❑  General Order 25 (NY R USDCTND Order 25)

(9)   ❑  Filing fee

(10)  ❑  Affidavit proving service

(b)   ❑  Supplemental documents

(1)   ❑  Notice and request for waiver of service

(2)   ❑  Service by mail forms

(3)   ❑  Notice of constitutional question

(4)   ❑  Notice of issue concerning foreign law

(5)   ❑  Nongovernmental corporate disclosure statement

(6)   ❑  Application to convene a three-judge court

      (7)  ❏  Application to proceed in forma pauperis

      (8)  ❏  Motion for TRO and supporting documents

      (9)  ❏  Cover letter authorizing e-mail or facsimile filing

    (10)  ❏  Affidavit attesting to failed attempts to file electronically

    (11)  ❏  Notice of conventional filing

    (12)  ❏  CD/ROM with PDF of document(s)

    (13)  ❏  English translation

    (14)  ❏  Courtesy copies

    (15)  ❏  Copies for three-judge court

(c)  ❏  Timing

      (1)  ❏  A civil action is commenced by filing a complaint with the court

      (2)  ❏  If a defendant is not served within ninety (90) days after the complaint is filed, the court—on motion or on its own after notice to the plaintiff—must dismiss the action without prejudice against that defendant or order that service be made within a specified time

          (i)  ❏  Local variation: upon the filing of a complaint, the clerk shall issue to the plaintiff NY R USDCTND Order 25, which requires, among other things, service of process upon all defendants within sixty (60) days of the filing of the complaint

      (3)  ❏  Proof(s) of service of process are to be filed with the clerk's office no later than five (5) days after service of the complaint or notice of removal with a copy of NY R USDCTND Order 25

(II)  ❏  Matters to be considered by defendant

  (a)  ❏  Required documents

      (1)  ❏  Answer

      (2)  ❏  Certificate of service

  (b)  ❏  Supplemental documents

      (1)  ❏  Waiver of the service of summons

      (2)  ❏  Notice of constitutional question

      (3)  ❏  Notice of issue concerning foreign law

      (4)  ❏  Nongovernmental corporate disclosure statement

      (5)  ❏  Cover letter authorizing e-mail or facsimile filing

      (6)  ❏  Affidavit attesting to failed attempts to file electronically

      (7)  ❏  Notice of conventional filing

      (8)  ❏  CD/ROM with PDF of document(s)

      (9)  ❏  English translation

    (10)  ❏  Courtesy copies

    (11)  ❏  Copies for three-judge court

  (c)  ❏  Timing

      (1)  ❏  A defendant must serve an answer:

          (i)  ❏  Within twenty-one (21) days after being served with the summons and complaint; or

         (ii)  ❏  If it has timely waived service under FRCP 4(d), within sixty (60) days after the request for a waiver was sent, or within ninety (90) days after it was sent to the defendant outside any judicial district of the United States

      (2)  ❏  The United States, a United States agency, or a United States officer or employee sued only

in an official capacity must serve an answer to a complaint, counterclaim, or crossclaim within sixty (60) days after service on the United States attorney

(3)  ❑ A United States officer or employee sued in an individual capacity for an act or omission occurring in connection with duties performed on the United States' behalf must serve an answer to a complaint, counterclaim, or crossclaim within sixty (60) days after service on the officer or employee or service on the United States attorney, whichever is later

(4)  ❑ Unless the court sets a different time, serving a motion under FRCP 12 alters these periods as follows:

    (i)  ❑ If the court denies the motion or postpones its disposition until trial, the responsive pleading must be served within fourteen (14) days after notice of the court's action; or

    (ii)  ❑ If the court grants a motion for a more definite statement, the responsive pleading must be served within fourteen (14) days after the more definite statement is served

(5)  ❑ Defendant is given a reasonable time of at least thirty (30) days after a waiver of service request is sent—or at least sixty (60) days if sent to defendant outside any judicial district of the United States—to return the waiver

## B. Timing

1. *Answer.* Unless another time is specified by FRCP 12 or a federal statute. . .a defendant must serve an answer: (1) within twenty-one (21) days after being served with the summons and complaint; or (2) if it has timely waived service under FRCP 4(d), within sixty (60) days after the request for a waiver was sent, or within ninety (90) days after it was sent to the defendant outside any judicial district of the United States. FRCP 12(a)(1)(A).

    a. *Time to serve other responsive pleadings.* Unless another time is specified by FRCP 12 or a federal statute, the time for serving a responsive pleading is as follows:

        i. *Answer to counterclaim or crossclaim.* A party must serve an answer to a counterclaim or crossclaim within twenty-one (21) days after being served with the pleading that states the counterclaim or crossclaim. FRCP 12(a)(1)(B).

        ii. *Reply to an answer.* A party must serve a reply to an answer within twenty-one (21) days after being served with an order to reply, unless the order specifies a different time. FRCP 12(a)(1)(C).

    b. *United States and its agencies, officers, or employees sued in an official capacity.* The United States, a United States agency, or a United States officer or employee sued only in an official capacity must serve an answer to a complaint, counterclaim, or crossclaim within sixty (60) days after service on the United States attorney. FRCP 12(a)(2).

    c. *United States officers or employees sued in an individual capacity.* A United States officer or employee sued in an individual capacity for an act or omission occurring in connection with duties performed on the United States' behalf must serve an answer to a complaint, counterclaim, or crossclaim within sixty (60) days after service on the officer or employee or service on the United States attorney, whichever is later. FRCP 12(a)(3).

    d. *Effect of a FRCP 12 motion on the time to serve a responsive pleading.* Unless the court sets a different time, serving a motion under FRCP 12 alters the periods in FRCP 12(a) as follows:

        i. If the court denies the motion or postpones its disposition until trial, the responsive pleading must be served within fourteen (14) days after notice of the court's action; or

        ii. If the court grants a motion for a more definite statement, the responsive pleading must be served within fourteen (14) days after the more definite statement is served. FRCP 12(a)(4).

2. *Waiver of service.* The notice and request for waiver must give the defendant a reasonable time of at least thirty (30) days after the request was sent—or at least sixty (60) days if sent to defendant outside any judicial district of the United States—to return the waiver. FRCP 4(d)(1)(F).

    a. *Time to answer after a waiver.* A defendant who, before being served with process, timely returns a waiver need not serve an answer to the complaint until sixty (60) days after the request was sent—or until ninety (90) days after it was sent to the defendant outside any judicial district of the United States. FRCP 4(d)(3).

3. *Computation of time*

a. *Computing time.* FRCP 6 applies in computing any time period specified in the Federal Rules of Civil Procedure, in any local rule or court order, or in any statute that does not specify a method of computing time. FRCP 6(a).

   i. *Period stated in days or a longer unit.* When the period is stated in days or a longer unit of time:

   - Exclude the day of the event that triggers the period;

   - Count every day, including intermediate Saturdays, Sundays, and legal holidays; and

   - Include the last day of the period, but if the last day is a Saturday, Sunday, or legal holiday, the period continues to run until the end of the next day that is not a Saturday, Sunday, or legal holiday. FRCP 6(a)(1).

   ii. *Period stated in hours.* When the period is stated in hours:

   - Begin counting immediately on the occurrence of the event that triggers the period;

   - Count every hour, including hours during intermediate Saturdays, Sundays, and legal holidays; and

   - If the period would end on a Saturday, Sunday, or legal holiday, the period continues to run until the same time on the next day that is not a Saturday, Sunday, or legal holiday. FRCP 6(a)(2).

   iii. *Inaccessibility of the clerk's office.* Unless the court orders otherwise, if the clerk's office is inaccessible:

   - On the last day for filing under FRCP 6(a)(1), then the time for filing is extended to the first accessible day that is not a Saturday, Sunday, or legal holiday; or

   - During the last hour for filing under FRCP 6(a)(2), then the time for filing is extended to the same time on the first accessible day that is not a Saturday, Sunday, or legal holiday. FRCP 6(a)(3).

   iv. *"Last day" defined.* Unless a different time is set by a statute, local rule, or court order, the last day ends:

   - For electronic filing, at midnight in the court's time zone; and

   - For filing by other means, when the clerk's office is scheduled to close. FRCP 6(a)(4).

   v. *"Next day" defined.* The "next day" is determined by continuing to count forward when the period is measured after an event and backward when measured before an event. FRCP 6(a)(5).

   vi. *"Legal holiday" defined.* "Legal holiday" means:

   - The day set aside by statute for observing New Year's Day, Martin Luther King Jr.'s Birthday, Washington's Birthday, Memorial Day, Independence Day, Labor Day, Columbus Day, Veterans' Day, Thanksgiving Day, or Christmas Day;

   - Any day declared a holiday by the President or Congress; and

   - For periods that are measured after an event, any other day declared a holiday by the state where the district court is located. FRCP 6(a)(6).

b. *Computation of electronic filing deadlines.* A document will be deemed timely filed if electronically filed prior to midnight Eastern Time. However, if the time of day is of the essence, the assigned judge may order that the document be filed by a time certain. NY R USDCTND CM/ECF(4)(4.3).

   i. *Technical failures.* A Filing User, whose filing is untimely as the result of a technical failure of the Court's CM/ECF site, may seek appropriate relief from the Court. However, Filing Users are cautioned that, in some circumstances, the Court lacks the authority to grant an extension of time to file (e.g., FRCP 6(b) of the Federal Rules of Civil Procedure). NY R USDCTND CM/ECF(10)(10.1).

   - *Technical failure of the filing user's system.* Problems with the Filing User's system, such as phone line problems, problems with the Filing User's Internet Service Provider ("ISP"), or hardware or software problems, will not constitute a technical failure under these Administrative Procedures nor excuse an untimely filing. A Filing User who cannot file documents electronically because of a problem on the Filing User's system must file the documents' conventionally along with an affidavit explaining the reason for not filing the documents electronically. NY R USDCTND CM/ECF(10)(10.2).

   c. *Extending time*

      i. *In general.* When an act may or must be done within a specified time, the court may, for good cause, extend the time:

- With or without motion or notice if the court acts, or if a request is made, before the original time or its extension expires; or

- On motion made after the time has expired if the party failed to act because of excusable neglect. FRCP 6(b)(1).

      ii. *Exceptions.* A court must not extend the time to act under FRCP 50(b), FRCP 50(d), FRCP 52(b), FRCP 59(b), FRCP 59(d), FRCP 59(e), and FRCP 60(b). FRCP 6(b)(2).

      iii. Refer to the United States District Court for the Northern District of New York KeyRules Motion for Continuance/Extension of Time document for more information on extending time.

   d. *Additional time after certain kinds of service.* When a party may or must act within a specified time after service and service is made under FRCP 5(b)(2)(C), FRCP 5(b)(2)(D), FRCP 5(b)(2)(E), or FRCP 5(b)(2)(F), three (3) days are added after the period would otherwise expire under FRCP 6(a). FRCP 6(d).

      i. In accordance with FRCP 6(e), service by electronic means is treated the same as service by mail for purposes of adding three (3) days to the prescribed period to respond. NY R USDCTND CM/ECF(5)(5.4). [Editor's note: the reference to FRCP 6(e) is likely meant to be a reference to FRCP 6(d)].

4. *Individual judge practices.* Refer to the Miscellaneous section of this document for information on individual judge practices on timing of documents.

## C. General Requirements

1. *Pleading, generally*

   a. *Pleadings allowed.* Only these pleadings are allowed: (1) a complaint; (2) an answer to a complaint; (3) an answer to a counterclaim designated as a counterclaim; (4) an answer to a crossclaim; (5) a third-party complaint; (6) an answer to a third-party complaint; and (7) if the court orders one, a reply to an answer. FRCP 7(a).

   b. *Pleading to be concise and direct.* Each allegation must be simple, concise, and direct. No technical form is required. FRCP 8(d)(1).

   c. *Alternative statements of a claim or defense.* A party may set out two or more statements of a claim or defense alternatively or hypothetically, either in a single count or defense or in separate ones. If a party makes alternative statements, the pleading is sufficient if any one of them is sufficient. FRCP 8(d)(2).

   d. *Inconsistent claims or defenses.* A party may state as many separate claims or defenses as it has, regardless of consistency. FRCP 8(d)(3).

   e. *Construing pleadings.* Pleadings must be construed so as to do justice. FRCP 8(e).

2. *Pleading special matters*

   a. *Capacity or authority to sue; Legal existence*

      i. *In general.* Except when required to show that the court has jurisdiction, a pleading need not allege:

- A party's capacity to sue or be sued;

- A party's authority to sue or be sued in a representative capacity; or

- The legal existence of an organized association of persons that is made a party. FRCP 9(a)(1).

ii. *Raising those issues.* To raise any of those issues, a party must do so by a specific denial, which must state any supporting facts that are peculiarly within the party's knowledge. FRCP 9(a)(2).

b. *Fraud or mistake; Conditions of mind.* In alleging fraud or mistake, a party must state with particularity the circumstances constituting fraud or mistake. Malice, intent, knowledge, and other conditions of a person's mind may be alleged generally. FRCP 9(b).

c. *Conditions precedent.* In pleading conditions precedent, it suffices to allege generally that all conditions precedent have occurred or been performed. But when denying that a condition precedent has occurred or been performed, a party must do so with particularity. FRCP 9(c).

d. *Official document or act.* In pleading an official document or official act, it suffices to allege that the document was legally issued or the act legally done. FRCP 9(d).

e. *Judgment.* In pleading a judgment or decision of a domestic or foreign court, a judicial or quasi-judicial tribunal, or a board or officer, it suffices to plead the judgment or decision without showing jurisdiction to render it. FRCP 9(e).

f. *Time and place.* An allegation of time or place is material when testing the sufficiency of a pleading. FRCP 9(f).

g. *Special damages.* If an item of special damage is claimed, it must be specifically stated. FRCP 9(g).

h. *Admiralty or maritime claim*

   i. *How designated.* If a claim for relief is within the admiralty or maritime jurisdiction and also within the court's subject-matter jurisdiction on some other ground, the pleading may designate the claim as an admiralty or maritime claim for purposes of FRCP 14(c), FRCP 38(e), and FRCP 82 and the Supplemental Rules for Admiralty or Maritime Claims and Asset Forfeiture Actions. A claim cognizable only in the admiralty or maritime jurisdiction is an admiralty or maritime claim for those purposes, whether or not so designated. FRCP 9(h)(1).

   ii. *Designation for appeal.* A case that includes an admiralty or maritime claim within FRCP 9(h) is an admiralty case within 28 U.S.C.A. § 1292(a)(3). FRCP 9(h)(2).

3. *Answer*

   a. *Defenses; Admissions and denials*

      i. *In general.* In responding to a pleading, a party must: (1) state in short and plain terms its defenses to each claim asserted against it; and (2) admit or deny the allegations asserted against it by an opposing party. FRCP 8(b)(1).

         - The purpose of an answer is to formulate issues by means of defenses addressed to the allegations of the complaint, and to give the plaintiff notice of the defenses he or she will be called upon to meet. FEDPROC § 62:70; Lopez v. U.S. Fidelity & Guaranty Co., 15 Alaska 633, 18 F.R.D. 59 (1955); Moriarty v. Curran, 18 F.R.D. 461 (S.D.N.Y. 1956).

         - An answer is adequate where it accomplishes these purposes, even if it contains general and specific denials and at the same time asserts additional facts by way of justification or explanation, and even if it sets forth conclusions of law. FEDPROC § 62:70; Johnston v. Jones, 178 F.2d 481 (3d Cir. 1949); Burke v. Mesta Mach. Co., 5 F.R.D. 134 (W.D.Pa. 1946).

      ii. *Denials; Responding to the substance.* A denial must fairly respond to the substance of the allegation. FRCP 8(b)(2).

      iii. *General and specific denials.* A party that intends in good faith to deny all the allegations of a pleading—including the jurisdictional grounds—may do so by a general denial. A party that does not intend to deny all the allegations must either specifically deny designated allegations or generally deny all except those specifically admitted. FRCP 8(b)(3).

      iv. *Denying part of an allegation.* A party that intends in good faith to deny only part of an allegation must admit the part that is true and deny the rest. FRCP 8(b)(4).

v. *Lacking knowledge or information.* A party that lacks knowledge or information sufficient to form a belief about the truth of an allegation must so state, and the statement has the effect of a denial. FRCP 8(b)(5).

- An answer merely stating that the defendant lacks knowledge to form a belief as to the plaintiff's allegations, and making no statement as to his or her lack of information, has been held to be insufficient, the court suggesting that the phrase might be used in an attempt to mask the defendant's inability to make a good-faith denial of the allegations. FEDPROC § 62:73; Gilbert v. Johnston, 127 F.R.D. 145 (N.D.Ill. 1989).

vi. *Effect of failing to deny.* An allegation—other than one relating to the amount of damages—is admitted if a responsive pleading is required and the allegation is not denied. If a responsive pleading is not required, an allegation is considered denied or avoided. FRCP 8(b)(6).

b. *Affirmative defenses.* In responding to a pleading, a party must affirmatively state any avoidance or affirmative defense, including: (1) accord and satisfaction; (2) arbitration and award; (3) assumption of risk; (4) contributory negligence; (5) duress; (6) estoppel; (7) failure of consideration; (8) fraud; (9) illegality; (10) injury by fellow servant; (11) laches; (12) license; (13) payment; (14) release; (15) res judicata; (16) statute of frauds; (17) statute of limitations; and (18) waiver. FRCP 8(c)(1).

i. *Mistaken designation.* If a party mistakenly designates a defense as a counterclaim, or a counterclaim as a defense, the court must, if justice requires, treat the pleading as though it were correctly designated, and may impose terms for doing so. FRCP 8(c)(2).

c. *How to present defenses.* Every defense to a claim for relief in any pleading must be asserted in the responsive pleading if one is required. But a party may assert the following defenses by motion: (1) lack of subject-matter jurisdiction; (2) lack of personal jurisdiction; (3) improper venue; (4) insufficient process; (5) insufficient service of process; (6) failure to state a claim upon which relief can be granted; and (7) failure to join a party under FRCP 19. FRCP 12(b).

i. A motion asserting any of these defenses must be made before pleading if a responsive pleading is allowed. If a pleading sets out a claim for relief that does not require a responsive pleading, an opposing party may assert at trial any defense to that claim. FRCP 12(b).

ii. Refer to the United States District Court for the Northern District of New York KeyRules Motion to Dismiss for Lack of Subject Matter Jurisdiction, Motion to Dismiss for Lack of Personal Jurisdiction, Motion to Dismiss for Improper Venue, and Motion to Dismiss for Failure to State a Claim documents for more information on motions under FRCP 12(b)(1), FRCP 12(b)(2), FRCP 12(b)(3), and FRCP 12(b)(6).

d. *Waiving and preserving certain defenses.* No defense or objection is waived by joining it with one or more other defenses or objections in a responsive pleading or in a motion. FRCP 12(b).

i. *When some are waived.* A party waives any defense listed in FRCP 12(b)(2) through FRCP 12(b)(5) by:

- Omitting it from a motion in the circumstances described in FRCP 12(g)(2); or
- Failing to either: (1) make it by motion under FRCP 12; or (2) include it in a responsive pleading or in an amendment allowed by FRCP 15(a)(1) as a matter of course. FRCP 12(h)(1).

ii. *When to raise others.* Failure to state a claim upon which relief can be granted, to join a person required by FRCP 19(b), or to state a legal defense to a claim may be raised:

- In any pleading allowed or ordered under FRCP 7(a);
- By a motion under FRCP 12(c); or
- At trial. FRCP 12(h)(2).

iii. *Lack of subject matter jurisdiction.* If the court determines at any time that it lacks subject-matter jurisdiction, the court must dismiss the action. FRCP 12(h)(3).

4. *Counterclaim and crossclaim*

   a. *Compulsory counterclaim*

      i. *In general.* A pleading must state as a counterclaim any claim that—at the time of its service—the pleader has against an opposing party if the claim:

         • Arises out of the transaction or occurrence that is the subject matter of the opposing party's claim; and

         • Does not require adding another party over whom the court cannot acquire jurisdiction. FRCP 13(a)(1).

      ii. *Exceptions.* The pleader need not state the claim if:

         • When the action was commenced, the claim was the subject of another pending action; or

         • The opposing party sued on its claim by attachment or other process that did not establish personal jurisdiction over the pleader on that claim, and the pleader does not assert any counterclaim under FRCP 13. FRCP 13(a)(2).

   b. *Permissive counterclaim.* A pleading may state as a counterclaim against an opposing party any claim that is not compulsory. FRCP 13(b).

   c. *Relief sought in a counterclaim.* A counterclaim need not diminish or defeat the recovery sought by the opposing party. It may request relief that exceeds in amount or differs in kind from the relief sought by the opposing party. FRCP 13(c).

   d. *Counterclaim against the United States.* The Federal Rules of Civil Procedure do not expand the right to assert a counterclaim—or to claim a credit—against the United States or a United States officer or agency. FRCP 13(d).

   e. *Counterclaim maturing or acquired after pleading.* The court may permit a party to file a supplemental pleading asserting a counterclaim that matured or was acquired by the party after serving an earlier pleading. FRCP 13(e).

   f. *Crossclaim against a coparty.* A pleading may state as a crossclaim any claim by one party against a coparty if the claim arises out of the transaction or occurrence that is the subject matter of the original action or of a counterclaim, or if the claim relates to any property that is the subject matter of the original action. The crossclaim may include a claim that the coparty is or may be liable to the cross-claimant for all or part of a claim asserted in the action against the cross-claimant. FRCP 13(g).

   g. *Joining additional parties.* FRCP 19 and FRCP 20 govern the addition of a person as a party to a counterclaim or crossclaim. FRCP 13(h).

   h. *Separate trials; Separate judgments.* If the court orders separate trials under FRCP 42(b), it may enter judgment on a counterclaim or crossclaim under FRCP 54(b) when it has jurisdiction to do so, even if the opposing party's claims have been dismissed or otherwise resolved. FRCP 13(i).

5. *Third-party practice*

   a. *Timing of the summons and complaint.* A defending party may, as third-party plaintiff, serve a summons and complaint on a nonparty who is or may be liable to it for all or part of the claim against it. But the third-party plaintiff must, by motion, obtain the court's leave if it files the third-party complaint more than fourteen (14) days after serving its original answer. FRCP 14(a)(1).

   b. *Third-party defendant's claims and defenses.* The person served with the summons and third-party complaint—the "third-party defendant":

      i. Must assert any defense against the third-party plaintiff's claim under FRCP 12;

      ii. Must assert any counterclaim against the third-party plaintiff under FRCP 13(a), and may assert any counterclaim against the third-party plaintiff under FRCP 13(b) or any crossclaim against another third-party defendant under FRCP 13(g);

      iii. May assert against the plaintiff any defense that the third-party plaintiff has to the plaintiff's claim; and

      iv. May also assert against the plaintiff any claim arising out of the transaction or occurrence that is the subject matter of the plaintiff's claim against the third-party plaintiff. FRCP 14(a)(2).

c.  For more information on third-party practice, refer to FRCP 14.

6.  *Right to a jury trial; Demand*

    a.  *Right preserved.* The right of trial by jury as declared by U.S.C.A. Const. Amend. VII, or as provided by a federal statute, is preserved to the parties inviolate. FRCP 38(a).

    b.  *Demand.* On any issue triable of right by a jury, a party may demand a jury trial by:

        i.  Serving the other parties with a written demand—which may be included in a pleading—no later than fourteen (14) days after the last pleading directed to the issue is served; and

        ii.  Filing the demand in accordance with FRCP 5(d). FRCP 38(b).

        iii.  In cases removed from state court, a party may file a "Demand for Jury Trial" that is separate from the initial pleading. See FRCP 81(c); NY R USDCTND L.R. 81.3. NY R USDCTND L.R. 38.1(b).

    c.  *Specifying issues.* In its demand, a party may specify the issues that it wishes to have tried by a jury; otherwise, it is considered to have demanded a jury trial on all the issues so triable. If the party has demanded a jury trial on only some issues, any other party may—within fourteen (14) days after being served with the demand or within a shorter time ordered by the court—serve a demand for a jury trial on any other or all factual issues triable by jury. FRCP 38(c).

    d.  *Waiver; Withdrawal.* A party waives a jury trial unless its demand is properly served and filed. A proper demand may be withdrawn only if the parties consent. FRCP 38(d).

    e.  *Admiralty and maritime claims.* The rules in FRCP 38 do not create a right to a jury trial on issues in a claim that is an admiralty or maritime claim under FRCP 9(h). FRCP 38(e).

7.  *Complex and multi-district litigation.* If the assigned judge determines, in his or her discretion, that the case is of such a complex nature that it cannot reasonably be trial ready within eighteen (18) months from the date the complaint is filed, the assigned judge may design and issue a particularized case management order that will move the case to trial as quickly as the complexity of the case allows. NY R USDCTND L.R. 3.3(a). The parties shall promptly notify the Court in writing if any action commenced is appropriate for multi-district litigation. NY R USDCTND L.R. 3.3(b).

8.  *Appearances.* An attorney appearing for a party in a civil case shall promptly file with the Clerk a written notice of appearance; however, an attorney does not need to file a notice of appearance if the attorney who would be filing the notice of appearance is the same individual who has signed the complaint, notice of removal, pre-answer motion, or answer. NY R USDCTND L.R. 83.2(a). For more information, refer to NY R USDCTND L.R. 83.2.

9.  *Related cases.* A civil case is "related" to another civil case for purposes of this guideline when, because of the similarity of facts and legal issues or because the cases arise from the same transactions or events, a substantial saving of judicial resources is likely to result from assigning the cases to the same Judge and Magistrate Judge. NY R USDCTND Order 12(G)(2). A civil case shall not be deemed related to another civil case merely because the civil case: (1) involves similar legal issues, or (2) involves the same parties. NY R USDCTND Order 12(G)(3). Presumptively, and subject to the power of a Judge to determine otherwise pursuant to NY R USDCTND Order 12(G)(5), civil cases shall not be deemed to be "related" unless both cases are still pending before the Court. NY R USDCTND Order 12(G)(4).

    a.  *New filings.* If an attorney or filing party indicates on the Civil Cover Sheet that a case is related to an earlier filed case, the Clerk shall instruct the filing party to file a notice of related cases. The allegedly related cases will be submitted by the Clerk to the Judge to whom the earliest filed case is assigned, who shall advise the Clerk whether such cases are related. NY R USDCTND Order 12(G)(1).

    b.  *Judicial determination that civil cases are "related."* Except for the cases described in the final sentence of NY R USDCTND Order 12(G)(6), all civil cases shall be randomly assigned when they are filed. Other than the cases described in the final sentence of NY R USDCTND Order 12(G)(6), civil cases shall not be deemed to be "related" for purposes of this guideline at the instance of any litigant or attorney unless and until there has been a determination by a Judge of this Court that the standard of NY R USDCTND Order 12(G)(2) is met. NY R USDCTND Order 12(G)(5).

        i.  *Notice of related filing.* Any party may apply for such a determination by filing with the Clerk a notice of related filing, which should include an explanation as to why the standard of NY R USDCTND Order 12(G)(2) is met. A form for this purpose is available on the Court's website. A copy of the notice shall be served on all other parties who have appeared. Such an application must be made after the date when at least a majority of the defendants have been served with the complaint. Before making such an application, the applicant must confer in good faith with all other parties in an effort to reach an agreement on whether or not the case is "related". After such an application is made, any other party may serve and file within seven (7) calendar days a letter of no more than two (2) pages supporting or opposing the application. The application to have the case assigned to another Judge shall be presented to the Judge with the earliest filed case for decision on whether the action(s) should be reassigned as related cases. The Judge with the earliest filed case may then enter an order in the case at bar, either deeming the case to be related and directing the Clerk to reassign the action, or denying the application for reassignment. Any disputes concerning the assignment of related cases will be referred to the Chief Judge for resolution. NY R USDCTND Order 12(G)(5).

   c.   For more information on related cases, refer to NY R USDCTND Order 12(G).

10.  *Alternative dispute resolution (ADR).* It is the mission of this court to do everything it can to help parties resolve their disputes as fairly, quickly, and efficiently as possible. NY R USDCTND Order 25(VIII).

   a.  *Arbitration.* NY R USDCTND L.R. 83.7 governs the consensual arbitration program for referral of civil actions to court-annexed arbitration. It may remain in effect until further order of the Court. Its purpose is to establish a less formal procedure for the just, efficient and economical resolution of disputes, while preserving the right to a full trial on demand. NY R USDCTND L.R. 83.7-1.

      i.  *Actions subject to arbitration.* The Clerk shall notify the parties in all civil cases, except as the Local Rules of Practice for the United States District Court for the Northern District of New York otherwise direct, that they may consent to non-binding arbitration under NY R US-DCTND L.R. 83.7. The notice shall be furnished to the parties at pretrial/scheduling conferences or shall be included with pretrial conference notices and instructions. Consent to arbitration under NY R USDCTND L.R. 83.7 shall be discussed at the pretrial/scheduling conference. No party or attorney shall be prejudiced for refusing to participate in arbitration. The Court shall allow the referral of any civil action pending before it to the arbitration process if the parties consent. The plaintiff shall be responsible for securing the execution of a consent form by the parties and for filing the form with the Clerk within fourteen (14) days after the parties receive the form. The parties shall freely and knowingly enter into the consent. NY R USDCTND L.R. 83.7-2.

     ii.  *Referral to arbitration.* The Clerk shall refer every action subject to NY R USDCTND L.R. 83.7 to arbitration in accordance with the procedures under NY R USDCTND L.R. 83.7 twenty-one (21) days after the filing of the last responsive pleading or within twenty-one (21) days of the filing of a stipulated consent order referring the action to arbitration, whichever event occurs last, except as otherwise provided. If any party notices a motion to dismiss under the provisions of FRCP 12(a) and/or FRCP 12(b), or a motion to join necessary parties pursuant to the Federal Rules of Civil Procedure prior to the expiration of the twenty-one (21) day period, the assigned judge shall hear the motion and further proceedings under NY R USDCTND L.R. 83.7 shall be deferred pending decision on the motion. If the Court does not dismiss the action on the motion, the Court shall refer the action to arbitration twenty-one (21) days after the filing of the decision. NY R USDCTND L.R. 83.7-3(a). Motions for summary judgment pursuant to FRCP 56 shall be filed and served within twenty-one (21) days following the close of discovery. The filing of a FRCP 56 motion shall defer further proceedings under NY R USDCTND L.R. 83.7 pending decision on the motion. NY R USDCTND L.R. 83.7-3(a).

       •  *Relief from referral.* Any party shall request relief from the operation of NY R USDCTND L.R. 83.7 by filing with the Court a motion for the relief within twenty-one (21) days after entry of the initial stipulated consent order which refers the case for arbitration. The assigned judge shall, sua sponte, exempt an action from the application of NY R USDCTND L.R. 83.7 where the objectives of arbitration would not be realized because (1) the case involves complex or novel legal issues, (2) legal issues predominate over factual issues, or (3) for other good cause. NY R USDCTND L.R. 83.7-3(c).

iii. For more information on arbitration, refer to NY R USDCTND L.R. 83.7.

b. *Mediation.* The purpose of NY R USDCTND L.R. 83.11 is to provide a supplementary procedure to the Court's existing alternative dispute resolution procedures. NY R USDCTND L.R. 83.11 provides for an earlier resolution of civil disputes resulting in savings of time and cost to litigants and the Court without sacrificing the quality of justice rendered or the right of litigants to a full trial on all issues not resolved through mediation. NY R USDCTND L.R. 83.11-1(a). Mediation is a process by which an impartial person, the mediator, facilitates communication between disputing parties to promote understanding, reconciliation and settlement. The mediator is an advocate for settlement and uses the mediation process to help the parties fully explore any potential area of agreement. The mediator does not serve as a judge or arbitrator and has no authority to render any decision on any disputed issue or to force a settlement. The parties themselves are responsible for negotiating any resolution(s) to their dispute. NY R USDCTND L.R. 83.11-1(b).

i. *Actions subject to mediation.* The Court may refer any civil action (or any portion thereof) to mediation under NY R USDCTND L.R. 83.11: (1) by order of referral; or (2) on the motion of any party; or (3) by consent of the parties. NY R USDCTND L.R. 83.11-3(a).

- *Withdrawal from mediation.* The parties may withdraw from mediation any civil action or claim that the Court refers to mediation pursuant to NY R USDCTND L.R. 83.11-3 by application to the assigned judge at least ten (10) days prior to the scheduled mediation session. NY R USDCTND L.R. 83.11-3(b).

ii. *Mandatory mediation program.* The United States District Court for the Northern District of New York has adopted this Mandatory Mediation Plan. The paid Mediation Program is designed to provide quicker, less expensive and potentially more satisfying alternatives to continuing litigation, without impairing the quality of justice or the right to trial. NY R USDCTND Order 47(1)(1.2)(A). This Mandatory Mediation Plan applies to civil actions pending as well as newly filed actions, except as otherwise indicated in NY R USDCTND Order 47. The Local Rules for voluntary mediation will apply only to Pro Se Cases that proceed through the Assisted Mediation Program. NY R USDCTND Order 47(1)(1.2)(B).

- *Referral into the pilot mandatory mediation program for new cases.* All civil cases shall be referred automatically into the Mandatory Mediation Program. Notice of the Mandatory Mediation requirements will be provided to all parties immediately upon the filing of a complaint and answer or a notice of removal. ADR intervention will be scheduled at the conference held pursuant to NY R USDCTND L.R. 16.1. NY R USDCTND Order 47(2)(2.1)(A). For a list of categories of actions exempted from automatic referral, refer to NY R USDCTND Order 47(2)(2.1)(A).

- *Referral into the pilot mandatory mediation program for pending cases.* The assigned Judge or Magistrate Judge on any pending civil case may, sua sponte or with status conference, issue an order referring the case into the Mandatory Mediation Program. The order shall specify a date on which the ADR intervention is to be completed. NY R USDCTND Order 47(2)(2.1)(B).

- *Referral into the pilot mandatory mediation program by stipulation.* A case may be referred into the Mandatory Mediation Program by stipulation of all parties. Stipulations shall be filed and shall designate the time frame within which the ADR process will be completed. Stipulations are presumed acceptable unless the assigned Judge or Magistrate Judge determines that the interests of justice are not served. NY R USDCTND Order 47(2)(2.1)(C).

- *Relief from referral.* Motions to opt out of the program will be addressed by the assigned Magistrate Judge at the FRCP 16 conference. NY R USDCTND Order 47(2)(2.2)(A). Opting Out Motions shall be granted only for "good cause" shown. Inconvenience, travel costs, attorney fees or other costs shall not constitute "good cause." A party seeking relief from the Mandatory Mediation Program must set forth the reasons why Mandatory Mediation has no reasonable chance of being productive. NY R USDCTND Order 47(2)(2.2)(B). The assigned Magistrate Judge may, sua sponte, exempt any case from the Court's Mandatory Mediation Program. NY R USDCTND Order 47(2)(2.2)(C).

iii. *Assisted mediation program.* The Court may assign specially trained pro bono Special Media-
tion Counsel to assist pro se civilian litigants with preparing for and participating in mediation.
The Assisted Mediation Program is open to civilian pro se parties to actions in the Northern
District of New York. The assigned judge or magistrate judge determines if the case would
benefit from mediation and would also benefit from the assignment of Special Mediation
Counsel to assist the pro se party with the mediation process. NY R USDCTND L.R. 83.8(a).
Appointment of Special Mediation Counsel is in no way guaranteed, even if the action is
referred to the court-annexed mediation program. Appointment is at the sole discretion of the
presiding judge. NY R USDCTND L.R. 83.8(a).

- *Referral to assisted mediation program.* If the court determines that referral to the Assisted
Mediation Program is appropriate, the Court shall enter an order of reference to the
Assisted Mediation Program. NY R USDCTND L.R. 83.8(b).

iv. For more information on mediation, refer to NY R USDCTND L.R. 83.11 and NY R
USDCTND Order 47.

c. *Early neutral evaluation (ENE).* Early neutral evaluation (ENE) is a process in which parties obtain
from an experienced neutral (an "evaluator") a nonbinding, reasoned, oral evaluation of the merits of
the case. The first step in the ENE process involves the Court appointing an evaluator who has
expertise in the area of law in the case. After the parties exchange essential information and position
statements early in the pretrial period (usually within one hundred fifty (150) to two hundred (200)
days after a complaint has been filed), the evaluator convenes an ENE session that typically lasts
about two hours. At the ENE meeting, each side briefly presents the factual and legal basis of its
position. The evaluator may ask questions of the parties and help them identify the main issues in
dispute and the areas of agreement. The evaluator may also help the parties explore options for
settlement. If settlement does not occur, the evaluator then offers an opinion as to the settlement
value of the case, including the likelihood of liability and the likely range of damages. With the
benefit of this assessment, the parties are again encouraged to discuss settlement, with or without the
evaluator's assistance. The parties may also explore ways to narrow the issues in dispute, exchange
information about the case or otherwise prepare efficiently for trial. NY R USDCTND L.R. 83.12-1.

i. *Actions subject to early neutral evaluation.* The Court may refer any civil action (or any portion
thereof) to ENE under NY R USDCTND L.R. 83.12: (1) by order of referral; (2) on the motion
of any party; or (3) by consent of the parties. NY R USDCTND L.R. 83.12-3(a).

- *Withdrawal from the ENE process.* The parties may withdraw any civil action or claim that
the Court has referred to the ENE Process pursuant to NY R USDCTND L.R. 83.12-3 by
application to the assigned judge at least ten (10) days before the scheduled evaluation
session. NY R USDCTND L.R. 83.12-3(b).

ii. For more information on early neutral evaluation (ENE), refer to NY R USDCTND L.R. 83.12.

11. *Settlement procedures.* On notice to the Court or the Clerk that the parties have settled an action, and upon
confirmation of the settlement by all parties, the Court may issue a judgment dismissing the action by
reason of settlement. The Court shall issue the order without prejudice to the parties' right to secure
reinstatement of the case within thirty (30) days after the date of judgment by making a showing that the
settlement was not, in fact, consummated. NY R USDCTND L.R. 68.2(a). If the Court decides not to
follow the procedures set forth in NY R USDCTND L.R. 68.2(a), the parties shall file within thirty (30)
days of the notification to the Court, unless otherwise directed by written order, such notices, stipulations
and/or motions as are necessary to terminate the action. If the required documents are not filed within the
thirty (30) day period, the Clerk shall place the action on the dismissal calendar. NY R USDCTND L.R.
68.2(b).

12. *Sanctions and penalties for noncompliance.* Failure of an attorney or of a party to comply with any
provision of the Local Rules of Practice for the United States District Court for the Northern District of
New York, General Orders of this District, Orders of the Court, or the Federal Rules of Civil Procedure
shall be a ground for imposition of sanctions. NY R USDCTND L.R. 1.1(d).

13. *Individual judge practices.* Refer to the Miscellaneous section of this document for information on
individual judge practices on general requirements for documents.

## D. Documents

1. *Required documents*

   a. *Answer.* Refer to the General Requirements section of this document for information on the form and contents of the answer.

   b. *Certificate of service.* FRCP 5(d) requires that the person making service under FRCP 5 certify that service has been effected. FRCP 5(Advisory Committee Notes). Having such information on file may be useful for many purposes, including proof of service if an issue arises concerning the effectiveness of the service. FRCP 5(Advisory Committee Notes). The party or its designee shall declare, by affidavit or certification, that it has provided all other parties in the action with all documents it has filed with the Court. NY R USDCTND L.R. 5.1(a).

      i. Attorneys and pro se parties who are not Filing or Receiving Users must be served with a paper copy of any electronically filed pleading or other document. NY R USDCTND CM/ECF(5)(5.2). Such paper service must be documented by electronically filing a certificate of service. NY R USDCTND CM/ECF(5)(5.2).

2. *Supplemental documents*

   a. *Waiver of the service of summons.* An individual, corporation, or association that is subject to service under FRCP 4(e), FRCP 4(f), or FRCP 4(h) has a duty to avoid unnecessary expenses of serving the summons. FRCP 4(d)(1). Waiving service of a summons does not waive any objection to personal jurisdiction or to venue. FRCP 4(d)(5). If a defendant located within the United States fails, without good cause, to sign and return a waiver requested by a plaintiff located within the United States, the court must impose on the defendant:

      i. The expenses later incurred in making service; and

      ii. The reasonable expenses, including attorney's fees, of any motion required to collect those service expenses. FRCP 4(d)(2).

   b. *Notice of constitutional question.* A party that files a pleading, written motion, or other paper drawing into question the constitutionality of a federal or state statute must promptly:

      i. *File notice.* File a notice of constitutional question stating the question and identifying the paper that raises it, if:

         • A federal statute is questioned and the parties do not include the United States, one of its agencies, or one of its officers or employees in an official capacity; or

         • A state statute is questioned and the parties do not include the state, one of its agencies, or one of its officers or employees in an official capacity; and

      ii. *Serve notice.* Serve the notice and paper on the Attorney General of the United States if a federal statute is questioned—or on the state attorney general if a state statute is questioned—either by certified or registered mail or by sending it to an electronic address designated by the attorney general for this purpose. FRCP 5.1(a).

      iii. *No forfeiture.* A party's failure to file and serve the notice, or the court's failure to certify, does not forfeit a constitutional claim or defense that is otherwise timely asserted. FRCP 5.1(d).

   c. *Notice of issue concerning foreign law.* A party who intends to raise an issue about a foreign country's law must give notice by a pleading or other writing. In determining foreign law, the court may consider any relevant material or source, including testimony, whether or not submitted by a party or admissible under the Federal Rules of Evidence. The court's determination must be treated as a ruling on a question of law. FRCP 44.1.

   d. *Nongovernmental corporate disclosure statement*

      i. *Contents.* A nongovernmental corporate party must file two (2) copies of a disclosure statement that:

         • Identifies any parent corporation and any publicly held corporation owning ten percent (10%) or more of its stock; or

         • States that there is no such corporation. FRCP 7.1(a).

    ii.  *Time to file; Supplemental filing.* A party must:

- File the disclosure statement with its first appearance, pleading, petition, motion, response, or other request addressed to the court; and

- Promptly file a supplemental statement if any required information changes. FRCP 7.1(b).

e.  *Cover letter authorizing e-mail or facsimile filing.* Neither the Court nor the Clerk's Office will accept for filing any facsimile or e-mail transmission without prior authorization from the Court. The party using facsimile or e-mail transmissions to file its papers must accompany any such documents with a cover letter stating that the Court authorized such transmissions and the date on which the Court provided that authorization. Violations of NY R USDCTND L.R. 5.5 subject the offending party to the Court's full disciplinary powers. NY R USDCTND L.R. 5.5.

f.  *Affidavit attesting to failed attempts to file electronically.* If the Court's CM/ECF site experiences a technical failure, a Filing User may submit documents to the Court that day in an alternate manner provided that the documents are accompanied by the Filing User's affidavit stating that the Filing User attempted to file electronically at least two times in one (1) hour increments after 10:00 a.m. that day. The following methods are acceptable alternate means for filing documents in case of a technical failure: (1) via electronic mail in a PDF attachment sent to the e-mail address for technical failures; or (2) in person, by bringing the document to the Clerk's Office on paper accompanied by a CD/ROM that contains the document in .pdf format. NY R USDCTND CM/ECF(10)(10.1).

    i.  A Filing User who cannot file documents electronically because of a problem on the Filing User's system must file the documents' conventionally along with an affidavit explaining the reason for not filing the documents electronically. NY R USDCTND CM/ECF(10)(10.2).

g.  *Notice of conventional filing.* If the Clerk's Office grants permission to conventionally file the document, the Filing User shall electronically file a notice of conventional filing for the documents. More information regarding this process can be obtained from the Court's web page. NY R USDCTND CM/ECF(4)(4.5).

h.  *CD/ROM with PDF of document(s).* If the Court grants permission to file a document traditionally, the attorney must submit the documents for filing to the Clerk's Office on CD/ROM in .pdf or pdf.A format. NY R USDCTND CM/ECF(2).

i.  *English translation.* The Court conducts its reviews and deliberations in English. Unless otherwise directed by the Court, any document that a party transmits to the Court (including one in the record on appeal) that is in a language other than English must be accompanied by an English translation that the translator has certified as true and accurate, pursuant to 28 U.S.C.A. § 1746. NY R USDCTND L.R. 10.1(e). For more information, refer to NY R USDCTND L.R. 10.1(e).

j.  *Courtesy copies.* The Court may require that courtesy copies of electronically filed documents be submitted for its review and may amend these Administrative Procedures (NY R USDCTND CM/ECF) at any time without prior notice. NY R USDCTND CM/ECF(2).

k.  *Copies for three-judge court.* On the convening of a three-judge court, the parties shall make three (3) copies of all non-electronically filed pleadings, motion papers, and memoranda of law available to the Clerk for distribution. NY R USDCTND L.R. 9.1.

3.  *Individual judge practices.* Refer to the Miscellaneous section of this document for information on individual judge practices on required documents.

## E.  Format

1.  *Form of documents.* All pleadings and other papers shall be served and filed in accordance with the Federal Rules of Civil Procedure and shall be in the form prescribed by NY R USDCTND L.R. 10.1. NY R USDCTND L.R. 5.1(a).

a.  *Form, generally.* All pleadings, motions, and other documents that a party presents for filing, whether in paper form or in electronic form, shall meet the following requirements:

    i.  *Font size.* All text, whether in the body of the document or in footnotes, must be a minimum of twelve (12) point type. NY R USDCTND L.R. 10.1(a)(1).

    ii.  *Margins.* All documents must have one (1) inch margins on all four sides of the page. NY R USDCTND L.R. 10.1(a)(2).

    iii.  *Spacing.* All text in the body of the document must be double-spaced. NY R USDCTND L.R. 10.1(a)(3).

        • The text in block quotations and footnotes may be single-spaced. NY R USDCTND L.R. 10.1(a)(4).

    iv.  *Page numbering.* Pages must be consecutively numbered. NY R USDCTND L.R. 10.1(a)(7).

    v.  *Circumventing formatting limitations*

        • Extensive footnotes must not be used to circumvent page limitations. NY R USDCTND L.R. 10.1(a)(5).

        • Compacted or other compressed printing features must not be used. NY R USDCTND L.R. 10.1(a)(6).

b.  *Additional requirements for paper filing.* Additional requirements for all pleadings, motions, and other documents that a party presents for filing in paper form:

    i.  *Paper size.* All documents must be on eight and one-half by eleven (8-1/2 x 11) inch white paper of good quality. NY R USDCTND L.R. 10.1(b)(1).

    ii.  *Text.* All text must be plainly and legibly written, typewritten, printed or reproduced without erasures or interlineations materially defacing them. NY R USDCTND L.R. 10.1(b)(2).

    iii.  *Ink.* All documents must be in black or blue ink. NY R USDCTND L.R. 10.1(b)(3).

    iv.  *Binding.* Pages of all documents must be stapled (or in some other way fastened) together. NY R USDCTND L.R. 10.1(b)(4).

    v.  *Single-sided paper.* All documents must be single-sided. NY R USDCTND L.R. 10.1(b)(5).

    vi.  *Electronic submission.* The Court, at its discretion, may require the electronic submission of any document in a WordPerfect-compatible format. NY R USDCTND L.R. 10.1(b)(6).

    vii.  *Rejection of document.* The Court may reject documents that do not comply with the above-listed requirements. NY R USDCTND L.R. 10.1(b).

c.  *Caption; Names of parties.* Every pleading must have a caption with the court's name, a title, a file number, and a FRCP 7(a) designation. The title of the complaint must name all the parties; the title of other pleadings, after naming the first party on each side, may refer generally to other parties. FRCP 10(a). Each document must contain a caption for the specific case to which it pertains. The caption must include the title of the Court, the title of the action, the civil action number of the case, the initials of the assigned judge(s), and the name or nature of the paper in sufficient detail for identification. If a litigant has more than one action pending in this Court, any and all papers filed in a case must contain and pertain to one civil action number, unless the civil actions have been consolidated by the Court. Any motion or other papers purporting to relate to more than one action will not be accepted for filing and may be stricken by the Court. NY R USDCTND L.R. 10.1(c)(1) shall not apply, as noted in NY R USDCTND L.R. 10.1(c), to notices of change of address filed by attorneys of record and pro se litigants. The parties must separately caption affidavits and declarations and must not physically attach them to the Notice of Motion or Memorandum of Law. NY R USDCTND L.R. 10.1(c)(1).

    i.  *Demand for jury trial.* If a party demands a jury trial as FRCP 38(b) permits, the party shall place a notation on the front page of the initial pleading which that party signed, stating "Demand for Jury Trial" or an equivalent statement. This notation shall serve as a sufficient demand under FRCP 38(b). NY R USDCTND L.R. 38.1(a).

    ii.  *Class action.* If a party seeks to maintain a case as a class action pursuant to FRCP 23, the party shall include the words "Class Action" in the complaint or other pleading asserting a class action next to its caption. NY R USDCTND L.R. 23.1(a).

d.  *Paragraphs; Separate statements.* A party must state its claims or defenses in numbered paragraphs, each limited as far as practicable to a single set of circumstances. A later pleading may refer by number to a paragraph in an earlier pleading. If doing so would promote clarity, each claim founded on a separate transaction or occurrence—and each defense other than a denial—must be stated in a separate count or defense. FRCP 10(b).

e.  *Adoption by reference; Exhibits.* A statement in a pleading may be adopted by reference elsewhere in the same pleading or in any other pleading or motion. A copy of a written instrument that is an exhibit to a pleading is a part of the pleading for all purposes. FRCP 10(c).

f.  *Citation of local rules.* These are the Local Rules of Practice for the United States District Court for the Northern District of New York. They shall be cited as "L.R. ___." NY R USDCTND L.R. 1.1(a).

g.  *Acceptance by the clerk.* The clerk must not refuse to file a paper solely because it is not in the form prescribed by the Federal Rules of Civil Procedure or by a local rule or practice. FRCP 5(d)(4).

2.  *Form of electronic documents.* All pleadings, motions, and other documents that a party presents for filing, whether in paper form or in electronic form, shall meet the requirements in NY R USDCTND L.R. 10.1(a). NY R USDCTND L.R. 10.1(a). Refer above for more information.

   a.  *Attachments and exhibits.* A Filing User must submit in electronic form all documents referenced as exhibits or attachments in accordance with the Court's CM/ECF Users Manual unless the Court otherwise orders. A Filing User shall submit as exhibits or attachments only those excerpts of the referenced documents that are directly germane to the matter under the Court's consideration. Excerpted material must be clearly and prominently identified as such. Filing Users who file excerpts of documents as exhibits or attachments under these Administrative Procedures (NY R USDCTND CM/ECF) do so without prejudice to their right to timely file additional excerpts or the complete document. Responding parties may also timely file the complete document or additional excerpts that they believe are directly germane to the matter under the Court's consideration. NY R USDCTND CM/ECF(4)(4.4).

      i.  All attachments must be described in sufficient detail so the Court and opposing counsel can easily identify and distinguish the filed attachments. Vague or general descriptions are insufficient (i.e., "Exhibit 1"). Rather, each attachment shall have a descriptive title identifying, with specificity, the document that is being filed (i.e., "Exhibit 12 Mulligan County Fire Investigation Report.") Failure to adequately describe attachments may result in the document being rejected by the Court. NY R USDCTND CM/ECF(4)(4.4).

   b.  *Large documents.* For information on the electronic filing of large documents, please consult the Court's CM/ECF Users Manual, which is available on the Court's web page. NY R USDCTND CM/ECF(4)(4.5).

      i.  A party who believes a document is too lengthy to electronically image, i.e., "scan," may contact the Clerk's Office for permission to file that document conventionally. If the Clerk's Office grants permission to conventionally file the document, the Filing User shall electronically file a notice of conventional filing for the documents. More information regarding this process can be obtained from the Court's web page. Exhibits submitted conventionally shall be served on other parties as if they were not subject to these Administrative Procedures (NY R USDCTND CM/ECF). For a list of hints and tips for scanning large documents, please consult the Court's web page. NY R USDCTND CM/ECF(4)(4.5).

   c.  *Legibility.* It shall be the Filing User's responsibility to verify the legibility of scanned documents before filing them electronically with the Court. NY R USDCTND CM/ECF(4)(4.6).

   d.  *Color documents.* Since documents scanned in color or containing a graphic take much longer to upload, Filing Users are encouraged to configure their scanners to scan documents at 300 dpi and preferably in black and white rather than in color. NY R USDCTND CM/ECF(4)(4.7).

   e.  *Items not in .PDF format.* Parties wishing to file items not amenable to .pdf format (i.e. CD's, DVD's), shall file such items conventionally with the Clerk's Office. The Filing User shall electronically file a notice of conventional filing indicating that these items have been submitted to the clerk and shall serve copies of these items on other parties as if they were not subject to these Administrative Procedures (NY R USDCTND CM/ECF). These item(s) will be maintained by the Clerk's Office until the case is disposed, at which time they will be returned to the filing party for retention consistent with NY R USDCTND CM/ECF(4)(4.9). NY R USDCTND CM/ECF(4)(4.8).

3.  *Signing of pleadings, motions and other papers*

   a.  *Signature.* Every pleading, written motion, and other paper must be signed by at least one attorney of record in the attorney's name—or by a party personally if the party is unrepresented. The paper must state the signer's address, e-mail address, and telephone number. FRCP 11(a). Each document must identify the person filing the document. This identification must include an original signature of the attorney or pro se litigant; the typewritten name of that person; the address of a pro se litigant; and the bar roll number, office address, telephone number, e-mail address and fax number of the attorney. Telephone numbers of non-prisoner pro se parties may be provided voluntarily or upon request of the Court. See General Order #22 (NY R USDCTND CM/ECF) for signature requirements. NY R USDCTND L.R. 10.1(c)(2).

    i.  *Electronic signatures.* Documents filed under an attorney's login and password shall constitute that attorney's signature for purposes of the Local Rules of Practice for the United States District Court for the Northern District of New York and Federal Rules of Civil Procedure, including but not limited to FRCP 11. A pleading or other document requiring an attorney's signature shall be signed in the following manner, whether filed electronically or submitted on disk or CD/ROM to the Clerk's Office: "s/ (attorney name)." The correct format for an attorney signature is found in NY R USDCTND CM/ECF(6)(6.1). NY R USDCTND CM/ECF(6)(6.1).

        • *Non-attorney signature.* If an original document requires the signature of a non-attorney, the Filing User may scan the original document containing the original signature(s), then electronically file it on the System. Alternatively, the Filing User may convert the document into .pdf text format and submit the document using "s/" for the signature of the non-attorney. NY R USDCTND CM/ECF(6)(6.2).

        • *Multiple signatures.* A document requiring signatures of more than one party must be filed electronically either by (1) submitting a scanned document containing all necessary signatures; (2) representing the consent of the other parties on the document; or (3) in any other manner that the Court approves. NY R USDCTND CM/ECF(6)(6.3).

    ii.  *No verification or accompanying affidavit required for pleadings.* Unless a rule or statute specifically states otherwise, a pleading need not be verified or accompanied by an affidavit. FRCP 11(a).

    iii.  *Unsigned papers.* The court must strike an unsigned paper unless the omission is promptly corrected after being called to the attorney's or party's attention. FRCP 11(a).

b.  *Representations to the court.* By presenting to the court a pleading, written motion, or other paper—whether by signing, filing, submitting, or later advocating it—an attorney or unrepresented party certifies that to the best of the person's knowledge, information, and belief, formed after an inquiry reasonable under the circumstances:

    i.  It is not being presented for any improper purpose, such as to harass, cause unnecessary delay, or needlessly increase the cost of litigation;

    ii.  The claims, defenses, and other legal contentions are warranted by existing law or by a nonfrivolous argument for extending, modifying, or reversing existing law or for establishing new law;

    iii.  The factual contentions have evidentiary support or, if specifically so identified, will likely have evidentiary support after a reasonable opportunity for further investigation or discovery; and

    iv.  The denials of factual contentions are warranted on the evidence or, if specifically so identified, are reasonably based on belief or a lack of information. FRCP 11(b).

c.  *Sanctions.* If, after notice and a reasonable opportunity to respond, the court determines that FRCP 11(b) has been violated, the court may impose an appropriate sanction on any attorney, law firm, or party that violated FRCP 11(b) or is responsible for the violation. FRCP 11(c)(1). Refer to the United States District Court for the Northern District of New York KeyRules Motion for Sanctions document for more information.

4.  *Privacy protection for filings made with the court*

    a.  *Redacted filings.* Unless the court orders otherwise, in an electronic or paper filing with the court that contains an individual's Social Security number, taxpayer-identification number, or birth date, the

name of an individual known to be a minor, or a financial-account number, a party or nonparty making the filing may include only:

i. The last four (4) digits of the Social Security number and taxpayer-identification number;

ii. The year of the individual's birth;

iii. The minor's initials; and

iv. The last four (4) digits of the financial-account number. FRCP 5.2(a); NY R USDCTND L.R. 8.1; NY R USDCTND CM/ECF(11)(11.2).

v. If a home address must be used, use only the City and State. NY R USDCTND L.R. 8.1; NY R USDCTND CM/ECF(11)(11.2).

vi. If the victim of a sexual assault must be referenced, redact the name to 'Victim.' NY R USDCTND CM/ECF(11)(11.2); NY R USDCTND L.R. 8.1.

vii. In addition, caution shall be exercised when filing documents that contain the following:

- Personal identifying number, such as a driver's license number;
- Medical records, treatment and diagnosis;
- Employment history;
- Individual financial information; and
- Proprietary or trade secret information. NY R USDCTND L.R. 8.1; NY R USDCTND CM/ECF(11)(11.2).

b. *Exemptions from the redaction requirement.* The redaction requirement does not apply to the following:

i. A financial-account number that identifies the property allegedly subject to forfeiture in a forfeiture proceeding;

ii. The record of an administrative or agency proceeding;

iii. The official record of a state-court proceeding;

iv. The record of a court or tribunal, if that record was not subject to the redaction requirement when originally filed;

v. A filing covered by FRCP 5.2(c) or FRCP 5.2(d); and

vi. A pro se filing in an action brought under 28 U.S.C.A. § 2241, 28 U.S.C.A. § 2254, or 28 U.S.C.A. § 2255. FRCP 5.2(b).

vii. Transcripts of the administrative record in social security proceedings are exempt from this requirement. State court records and other documents filed in habeas corpus proceedings are exempt from this requirement except for proceedings that involve victims of sex crimes. In habeas corpus cases involving sex crimes, the parties must redact the record and supporting papers, or may move to seal, if appropriate. NY R USDCTND L.R. 8.1.

c. *Limitations on remote access to electronic files; Social Security appeals and immigration cases.* Unless the court orders otherwise, in an action for benefits under the Social Security Act, and in an action or proceeding relating to an order of removal, to relief from removal, or to immigration benefits or detention, access to an electronic file is authorized as follows:

i. The parties and their attorneys may have remote electronic access to any part of the case file, including the administrative record;

ii. Any other person may have electronic access to the full record at the courthouse, but may have remote electronic access only to:

- The docket maintained by the court; and
- An opinion, order, judgment, or other disposition of the court, but not any other part of the case file or the administrative record. FRCP 5.2(c).

d. *Filings made under seal.* The court may order that a filing be made under seal without redaction. The court may later unseal the filing or order the person who made the filing to file a redacted version for the public record. FRCP 5.2(d); NY R USDCTND L.R. 8.1. For information on sealed matters, refer to NY R USDCTND L.R. 83.13 and NY R USDCTND CM/ECF(12).

e. *Protective orders.* For good cause, the court may by order in a case:

    i.   Require redaction of additional information; or

    ii.  Limit or prohibit a nonparty's remote electronic access to a document filed with the court. FRCP 5.2(e).

f. *Option for additional unredacted filing under seal.* A person making a redacted filing may also file an unredacted copy under seal. The court must retain the unredacted copy as part of the record. FRCP 5.2(f); NY R USDCTND L.R. 8.1; NY R USDCTND CM/ECF(11)(11.3).

g. *Option for filing a reference list.* A filing that contains redacted information may be filed together with a reference list that identifies each item of redacted information and specifies an appropriate identifier that uniquely corresponds to each item listed. The list must be filed under seal and may be amended as of right. Any reference in the case to a listed identifier will be construed to refer to the corresponding item of information. FRCP 5.2(g); NY R USDCTND L.R. 8.1; NY R USDCTND CM/ECF(11)(11.3).

h. *Responsibility for redaction.* Counsel is strongly urged to discuss this issue with all their clients so that they can make an informed decision about the inclusion of certain information. The responsibility for redacting these personal identifiers rests solely with counsel and the parties. The Clerk will not review each filing for compliance with NY R USDCTND L.R. 8.1. Counsel and the parties are cautioned that failure to redact these personal identifiers may subject them to the Court's full disciplinary power. NY R USDCTND L.R. 8.1; NY R USDCTND CM/ECF(11)(11.3).

i. *Waiver of protection of identifiers.* A person waives the protection of FRCP 5.2(a) as to the person's own information by filing it without redaction and not under seal. FRCP 5.2(h).

5. *Individual judge practices.* Refer to the Miscellaneous section of this document for information on individual judge practices on formatting documents.

## F. Filing and Service Requirements

1. *Filing requirements.* Any paper after the complaint that is required to be served—together with a certificate of service—must be filed within a reasonable time after service. FRCP 5(d)(1).

    a. *How filing is made; In general.* A paper is filed by delivering it:

        i.   To the clerk; or

        ii.  To a judge who agrees to accept it for filing, and who must then note the filing date on the paper and promptly send it to the clerk. FRCP 5(d)(2).

    b. *Electronic filing*

        i. *Authorization of electronic filing program.* A court may, by local rule, allow papers to be filed, signed, or verified by electronic means that are consistent with any technical standards established by the Judicial Conference of the United States. A local rule may require electronic filing only if reasonable exceptions are allowed. A paper filed electronically in compliance with a local rule is a written paper for purposes of the Federal Rules of Civil Procedure. FRCP 5(d)(3).

            • All cases filed in this Court may be assigned to the Electronic Case Files System ("ECF") in accordance with the Procedural Order on Electronic Case Filing (General Order #22 (NY R USDCTND CM/ECF)), the provisions of which are incorporated herein by reference, and which the Court may amend from time to time. Copies of General Order #22 (NY R USDCTND CM/ECF) are available at the Clerk's office or at the Court's webpage. NY R USDCTND L.R. 5.1.1; NY R USDCTND Order 25(XII).

            • The Court may deviate from these Administrative Procedures (NY R USDCTND CM/ECF) in specific cases, without prior notice, if deemed appropriate in the exercise of discretion, considering the need for the just, speedy, and inexpensive determination of matters pending before the Court. NY R USDCTND CM/ECF(2).

ii. *Scope of electronic filing.* After January 1, 2004, all documents that attorneys admitted to practice in the Northern District of New York submit for filing shall be filed electronically using the System or shall be scanned and uploaded to the System, no matter when a case was originally filed, unless these Administrative Procedures (NY R USDCTND CM/ECF) otherwise permit or unless the assigned judge otherwise authorizes. An attorney who is not a Filing User by January 1, 2004, must show good cause to the assigned judge to file and serve pleadings and other papers in the traditional manner. NY R USDCTND CM/ECF(2).

iii. *Exceptions and/or waivers from mandatory electronic filing.* The following types of cases and/or documents are not required to be filed electronically:

- If you are seeking to have your complaint filed under seal, please file your complaint and proposed sealing order traditionally at the Clerk's Office. NY R USDCTND CM/ECF(2)(2.1)(1).

- Any document that a party proceeding pro se files. (See NY R USDCTND CM/ECF(12)(12.1) for procedural details). NY R USDCTND CM/ECF(2)(2.1)(2). A non-prisoner who is a party to a civil action and who is not represented by an attorney may file a motion to obtain an Electronic Case Filing (ECF) login and password on a form prescribed by the Clerk's Office. The Pro Se CM/ECF Registration Form shall be submitted with the motion. If during the course of the action an attorney appears on behalf of the pro se party, the Clerk's Office shall terminate the pro se party's registration based upon the attorney's appearance. NY R USDCTND CM/ECF(12)(12.1). Absent permission to file electronically, pro se filers shall file paper originals of all complaints, pleadings, motions, affidavits, briefs, and other documents which must be signed or which require either verification or an unsworn declaration under any rule or statute. The Clerk's Office will scan these original documents into an electronic file in the System but will also maintain a paper file. NY R USDCTND CM/ECF(12)(12.1). A pro se party may also seek permission to receive immediate notice of all public documents filed in their cases. Notices of Electronic Filing (NEF) and attached documents would be transmitted to a non-prisoner pro se party who selects this option. Note: The pro se party would continue to file their documents with the Clerk's Office in paper form. NY R USDCTND CM/ECF(12)(12.1).

- Sealed documents, sealed cases, documents for in camera review, documents lodged with the Court, ex parte documents, confidential agreements, Qui Tam actions and Grand Jury material and warrants must be filed traditionally. (See NY R USDCTND CM/ECF(12)(12.2) for further information the filing of the above-referenced documents). NY R USDCTND CM/ECF(2)(2.1)(3).

- Discovery: In accordance with NY R USDCTND L.R. 26.2, parties shall not file discovery, provided, however, that discovery material to be used at trial or in support of any motion, including a motion to compel or for summary judgment, shall be filed electronically with the Court prior to the trial or with the motion. Any motion pursuant to FRCP 37 shall be accompanied by the electronically filed discovery materials to which the motion relates if those materials have not previously been filed with the Court. NY R USDCTND CM/ECF(2)(2.1)(4).

- Transport Orders: All orders requesting that an incarcerated individual be transported that a judicial officer of the Northern District of New York signs shall be filed traditionally. These Orders will not be filed with the case or uploaded to the docket but rather will be processed in accordance with the procedures that the Clerk of Court promulgates. NY R USDCTND CM/ECF(2)(2.1)(5).

iv. *Filing defined.* Electronic transmission of a document to the System in accordance with these Administrative Procedures, together with the transmission of a Notice of Electronic Filing from the Court, constitutes filing of the document for all purposes of the Federal Rules of Civil Procedure and the Local Rules of Practice for the United States District Court for the Northern District of New York and constitutes entry of the document on the docket that the Clerk's Office keeps under FRCP 58 and FRCP 79. E-mailing a document to the Clerk's Office or to the assigned judge shall not constitute "filing" of the document. NY R USDCTND CM/ECF(4)(4.1).

v. *Filing fees.* Any fee required for filing a pleading or paper in this Court is payable to the Clerk of the Court. The Court will not maintain electronic billing or debit accounts for attorneys or law firms. Effective January 1, 2007, payment for filing fees will be mandatory through CM/ECF's Internet Credit Card Payment site--a secure Treasury Site. The Filing User will be prompted to enter either Bank Account Debit (ACH) or credit card information while filing the initial pleading. Any document that requires a filing fee (e.g., Notice of Appeal, Motion for Pro Hac Vice Admission) may also be paid through the federal electronic payment website. NY R USDCTND CM/ECF(7).

vi. For more information on electronic filing, refer to NY R USDCTND CM/ECF.

c. *E-mail or facsimile filing.* Neither the Court nor the Clerk's Office will accept for filing any facsimile or e-mail transmission without prior authorization from the Court. The party using facsimile or e-mail transmissions to file its papers must accompany any such documents with a cover letter stating that the Court authorized such transmissions and the date on which the Court provided that authorization. Violations of NY R USDCTND L.R. 5.5 subject the offending party to the Court's full disciplinary powers. NY R USDCTND L.R. 5.5.

2. *Service requirements*

a. *Service; When required*

i. *In general.* Unless the Federal Rules of Civil Procedure provide otherwise, each of the following papers must be served on every party:

- An order stating that service is required;
- A pleading filed after the original complaint, unless the court orders otherwise under FRCP 5(c) because there are numerous defendants;
- A discovery paper required to be served on a party, unless the court orders otherwise;
- A written motion, except one that may be heard ex parte; and
- A written notice, appearance, demand, or offer of judgment, or any similar paper. FRCP 5(a)(1).

ii. *If a party fails to appear.* No service is required on a party who is in default for failing to appear. But a pleading that asserts a new claim for relief against such a party must be served on that party under FRCP 4. FRCP 5(a)(2).

iii. *Seizing property.* If an action is begun by seizing property and no person is or need be named as a defendant, any service required before the filing of an appearance, answer, or claim must be made on the person who had custody or possession of the property when it was seized. FRCP 5(a)(3).

b. *Service; How made*

i. *Serving an attorney.* If a party is represented by an attorney, service under FRCP 5 must be made on the attorney unless the court orders service on the party. FRCP 5(b)(1).

ii. *Service in general.* A paper is served under FRCP 5 by:

- Handing it to the person;
- Leaving it: (1) at the person's office with a clerk or other person in charge or, if no one is in charge, in a conspicuous place in the office; or (2) if the person has no office or the office is closed, at the person's dwelling or usual place of abode with someone of suitable age and discretion who resides there;
- Mailing it to the person's last known address—in which event service is complete upon mailing;
- Leaving it with the court clerk if the person has no known address;
- Sending it by electronic means if the person consented in writing—in which event service

is complete upon transmission, but is not effective if the serving party learns that it did not reach the person to be served; or

- Delivering it by any other means that the person consented to in writing—in which event service is complete when the person making service delivers it to the agency designated to make delivery. FRCP 5(b)(2).

    iii. *Service of electronically-filed documents.* Service is complete provided all parties receive a Notice of Electronic Filing (NEF), which is sent automatically by email from the Court (see the NEF for a list of who did/did not receive notice electronically). Transmission of the NEF constitutes service upon all Filing and Receiving Users who are listed as recipients of notice by electronic mail. It remains the responsibility of Filing and Receiving Users to maintain current contact information with the court and to regularly review the docket sheet of the case. NY R USDCTND CM/ECF(5)(5.2).

- *Non-filing or receiving users.* Attorneys and pro se parties who are not Filing or Receiving Users must be served with a paper copy of any electronically filed pleading or other document. Service of such paper copy must be made according to the Federal Rules of Civil Procedure and the Local Rules of Practice for the United States District Court for the Northern District of New York. Such paper service must be documented by electronically filing a certificate of service. NY R USDCTND CM/ECF(5)(5.2). A party who is not a Filing User of the System is entitled to a paper copy of any electronically-filed pleading, document, or order. The Filing User must therefore provide the non-Filing User with the pleading or document according to the Federal Rules of Civil Procedure. NY R US-DCTND CM/ECF(5)(5.3).

    iv. *Using court facilities.* If a local rule so authorizes, a party may use the court's transmission facilities to make service under FRCP 5(b)(2)(E). FRCP 5(b)(3).

  c. *Serving numerous defendants*

    i. *In general.* If an action involves an unusually large number of defendants, the court may, on motion or on its own, order that:

- Defendants' pleadings and replies to them need not be served on other defendants;

- Any crossclaim, counterclaim, avoidance, or affirmative defense in those pleadings and replies to them will be treated as denied or avoided by all other parties; and

- Filing any such pleading and serving it on the plaintiff constitutes notice of the pleading to all parties. FRCP 5(c)(1).

    ii. *Notifying parties.* A copy of every such order must be served on the parties as the court directs. FRCP 5(c)(2).

3. *Individual judge practices.* Refer to the Miscellaneous section of this document for information on individual judge practices on filing and serving documents.

## G. Hearings

1. *Hearing on FRCP 12 defenses before trial.* If a party so moves, any defense listed in FRCP 12(b)(1) through FRCP 12(b)(7)—whether made in a pleading or by motion—and a motion under FRCP 12(c) must be heard and decided before trial unless the court orders a deferral until trial. FRCP 12(i).

2. *Individual judge practices.* Refer to the Miscellaneous section of this document for information on individual judge practices on hearings.

## H. Forms

### 1. Official Federal Answer Forms

  a. Rule 4 waiver of the service of summons. FRCP 4.

### 2. Federal Answer Forms

  a. Generally. 2B FEDFORMS § 8:10.

  b. Introduction to separate defenses. 2B FEDFORMS § 8:11.

    c.   Presenting defenses. 2B FEDFORMS § 8:12.

    d.   With counterclaim for interpleader. 2B FEDFORMS § 8:13.

    e.   Denials and admissions. 2B FEDFORMS § 8:14.

    f.   Denials, admissions and affirmative defenses. 2B FEDFORMS § 8:15.

    g.   Separate answer of two defendants; Duty of fair representation. 2B FEDFORMS § 8:16.

    h.   Separate answer of third defendant. 2B FEDFORMS § 8:17.

    i.   Reciting paragraphs and subparagraphs of complaint; Account malpractice. 2B FEDFORMS § 8:18.

    j.   One of multiple defendants. 2B FEDFORMS § 8:21.

    k.   Answer to complaint for employment discrimination. 2B FEDFORMS § 8:22.

    l.   Denial of particular averment. 2B FEDFORMS § 8:24.

    m.   Admission of particular averment. 2B FEDFORMS § 8:25.

    n.   Denial of all averments of paragraph. 2B FEDFORMS § 8:26.

    o.   Admission of all averments of paragraph. 2B FEDFORMS § 8:27.

    p.   Denial in part and admission in part of paragraph. 2B FEDFORMS § 8:28.

    q.   General denial. 2B FEDFORMS § 8:29.

    r.   Qualified general denial. 2B FEDFORMS § 8:30.

    s.   Denial of knowledge or information sufficient to form a belief. 2B FEDFORMS § 8:31.

    t.   Denial of jurisdictional allegations; Jurisdictional amount. 2B FEDFORMS § 8:32.

    u.   Denial of jurisdictional allegations; Federal question. 2B FEDFORMS § 8:34.

    v.   Denial of jurisdictional allegations; Diversity of citizenship. 2B FEDFORMS § 8:37.

    w.   Contributory negligence. 2B FEDFORMS § 8:58.

    x.   Fraud. 2B FEDFORMS § 8:74.

    y.   Mistake. 2B FEDFORMS § 8:85.

    z.   Statute of limitations. 2B FEDFORMS § 8:103.

## I. Applicable Rules

  1.  *Federal rules*

    a.   Summons. FRCP 4.

    b.   Serving and filing pleadings and other papers. FRCP 5.

    c.   Constitutional challenge to a statute; Notice, certification, and intervention. FRCP 5.1.

    d.   Privacy protection for filings made with the court. FRCP 5.2.

    e.   Computing and extending time; Time for motion papers. FRCP 6.

    f.   Pleadings allowed; Form of motions and other papers. FRCP 7.

    g.   Disclosure statement. FRCP 7.1.

    h.   General rules of pleading. FRCP 8.

    i.   Pleading special matters. FRCP 9.

    j.   Form of pleadings. FRCP 10.

    k.   Signing pleadings, motions, and other papers; Representations to the court; Sanctions. FRCP 11.

    l.   Defenses and objections; When and how presented; Motion for judgment on the pleadings; Consolidating motions; Waiving defenses; Pretrial hearing. FRCP 12.

    m.   Counterclaim and crossclaim. FRCP 13.

    n.   Third-party practice. FRCP 14.

o. Right to a jury trial; Demand. FRCP 38.

p. Determining foreign law. FRCP 44.1.

2. *Local rules*

a. Scope of the rules. NY R USDCTND L.R. 1.1.

b. Complex and multi-district litigation. NY R USDCTND L.R. 3.3.

c. Service and filing of papers. NY R USDCTND L.R. 5.1.

d. Filing by facsimile or e-mail. NY R USDCTND L.R. 5.5.

e. Personal privacy protection. NY R USDCTND L.R. 8.1.

f. Request for three-judge court. NY R USDCTND L.R. 9.1.

g. Form of papers. NY R USDCTND L.R. 10.1.

h. Designation of "class action" in the caption. NY R USDCTND L.R. 23.1.

i. Notation of "jury demand" in the pleading. NY R USDCTND L.R. 38.1.

j. Settlement procedures. NY R USDCTND L.R. 68.2.

k. Appearance and withdrawal of attorney. NY R USDCTND L.R. 83.2.

l. Arbitration. NY R USDCTND L.R. 83.7-1; NY R USDCTND L.R. 83.7-2; NY R USDCTND L.R. 83.7-3.

m. Assisted mediation program. NY R USDCTND L.R. 83.8.

n. Mediation. NY R USDCTND L.R. 83.11-1; NY R USDCTND L.R. 83.11-3.

o. Early neutral evaluation. NY R USDCTND L.R. 83.12-1; NY R USDCTND L.R. 83.12-3.

p. Administrative procedures for electronic case filing. NY R USDCTND CM/ECF.

q. Case assignment plan for the Northern District of New York. [NY R USDCTND Order 12, as amended by NY ORDER 16-4201, effective March 24, 2015].

r. Directing the expedited service of the summons and complaint and further directing the completion of FRCP 16 stipulation for the timely progression of civil actions. [NY R USDCTND Order 25, as amended by NY ORDER 16-4187, effective June 23, 2016].

s. Mandatory mediation program. NY R USDCTND Order 47.

**J. Miscellaneous**

**NOTE: Individual judges' rules may apply. For available judge-level information, refer to:**

DISTRICT JUDGE MAE A. D'AGOSTINO: [NY R USDCTND D'Agostino-Rules and Practices, as added by NY ORDER 16-4200, effective April 4, 2016].

DISTRICT JUDGE THOMAS J. McAVOY: NY R USDCTND McAvoy-Order.

# Pleadings
## Amended Pleading

### Document Last Updated September 2016

**A. Checklist**

(I) ❑ Matters to be considered by plaintiff or defendant

    (a) ❑ Required documents

        (1) ❑ Amended pleading

        (2) ❑ Certificate of service

    (b) ❑ Supplemental documents

        (1) ❑ Notice of constitutional question

    (2) ❑ Notice of issue concerning foreign law

    (3) ❑ Cover letter authorizing e-mail or facsimile filing

    (4) ❑ Affidavit attesting to failed attempts to file electronically

    (5) ❑ Notice of conventional filing

    (6) ❑ CD/ROM with PDF of document(s)

    (7) ❑ English translation

    (8) ❑ Courtesy copies

    (9) ❑ Copies for three-judge court

(c) ❑ Timing

    (1) ❑ A party may amend its pleading once as a matter of course within:

        (i) ❑ Twenty-one (21) days after serving it, or

        (ii) ❑ If the pleading is one to which a responsive pleading is required, twenty-one (21) days after service of a responsive pleading or twenty-one (21) days after service of a motion under FRCP 12(b), FRCP 12(e), or FRCP 12(f), whichever is earlier

## B. Timing

1. *Amended pleading*

   a. *Amending as a matter of course.* A party may amend its pleading once as a matter of course within:

      i. Twenty-one (21) days after serving it, or

      ii. If the pleading is one to which a responsive pleading is required, twenty-one (21) days after service of a responsive pleading or twenty-one (21) days after service of a motion under FRCP 12(b), FRCP 12(e), or FRCP 12(f), whichever is earlier. FRCP 15(a)(1).

   b. *Extension of time.* If the time for serving the responsive pleading is extended by a motion for enlargement of time under FRCP 6(b), or by a stipulation, the period for amending as of right also may be enlarged. FPP § 1480.

   c. *Other amendments.* In all other cases, a party may amend its pleading only with the opposing party's written consent or the court's leave. The court should freely give leave when justice so requires. FRCP 15(a)(2). Refer to the United States District Court for the Northern District of New York KeyRules Motion for Leave to Amend document for more information.

2. *Time to respond to an amended pleading.* Unless the court orders otherwise, any required response to an amended pleading must be made within the time remaining to respond to the original pleading or within fourteen (14) days after service of the amended pleading, whichever is later. FRCP 15(a)(3).

3. *Computation of time*

   a. *Computing time.* FRCP 6 applies in computing any time period specified in the Federal Rules of Civil Procedure, in any local rule or court order, or in any statute that does not specify a method of computing time. FRCP 6(a).

      i. *Period stated in days or a longer unit.* When the period is stated in days or a longer unit of time:

- Exclude the day of the event that triggers the period;

- Count every day, including intermediate Saturdays, Sundays, and legal holidays; and

- Include the last day of the period, but if the last day is a Saturday, Sunday, or legal holiday, the period continues to run until the end of the next day that is not a Saturday, Sunday, or legal holiday. FRCP 6(a)(1).

      ii. *Period stated in hours.* When the period is stated in hours:

- Begin counting immediately on the occurrence of the event that triggers the period;

- Count every hour, including hours during intermediate Saturdays, Sundays, and legal holidays; and

- If the period would end on a Saturday, Sunday, or legal holiday, the period continues to run until the same time on the next day that is not a Saturday, Sunday, or legal holiday. FRCP 6(a)(2).

iii. *Inaccessibility of the clerk's office.* Unless the court orders otherwise, if the clerk's office is inaccessible:

- On the last day for filing under FRCP 6(a)(1), then the time for filing is extended to the first accessible day that is not a Saturday, Sunday, or legal holiday; or

- During the last hour for filing under FRCP 6(a)(2), then the time for filing is extended to the same time on the first accessible day that is not a Saturday, Sunday, or legal holiday. FRCP 6(a)(3).

iv. *"Last day" defined.* Unless a different time is set by a statute, local rule, or court order, the last day ends:

- For electronic filing, at midnight in the court's time zone; and

- For filing by other means, when the clerk's office is scheduled to close. FRCP 6(a)(4).

v. *"Next day" defined.* The "next day" is determined by continuing to count forward when the period is measured after an event and backward when measured before an event. FRCP 6(a)(5).

vi. *"Legal holiday" defined.* "Legal holiday" means:

- The day set aside by statute for observing New Year's Day, Martin Luther King Jr.'s Birthday, Washington's Birthday, Memorial Day, Independence Day, Labor Day, Columbus Day, Veterans' Day, Thanksgiving Day, or Christmas Day;

- Any day declared a holiday by the President or Congress; and

- For periods that are measured after an event, any other day declared a holiday by the state where the district court is located. FRCP 6(a)(6).

b. *Computation of electronic filing deadlines.* A document will be deemed timely filed if electronically filed prior to midnight Eastern Time. However, if the time of day is of the essence, the assigned judge may order that the document be filed by a time certain. NY R USDCTND CM/ECF(4)(4.3).

   i. *Technical failures.* A Filing User, whose filing is untimely as the result of a technical failure of the Court's CM/ECF site, may seek appropriate relief from the Court. However, Filing Users are cautioned that, in some circumstances, the Court lacks the authority to grant an extension of time to file (e.g., FRCP 6(b) of the Federal Rules of Civil Procedure). NY R USDCTND CM/ECF(10)(10.1).

   - *Technical failure of the filing user's system.* Problems with the Filing User's system, such as phone line problems, problems with the Filing User's Internet Service Provider ("ISP"), or hardware or software problems, will not constitute a technical failure under these Administrative Procedures nor excuse an untimely filing. A Filing User who cannot file documents electronically because of a problem on the Filing User's system must file the documents' conventionally along with an affidavit explaining the reason for not filing the documents electronically. NY R USDCTND CM/ECF(10)(10.2).

c. *Extending time*

   i. *In general.* When an act may or must be done within a specified time, the court may, for good cause, extend the time:

   - With or without motion or notice if the court acts, or if a request is made, before the original time or its extension expires; or

   - On motion made after the time has expired if the party failed to act because of excusable neglect. FRCP 6(b)(1).

   ii. *Exceptions.* A court must not extend the time to act under FRCP 50(b), FRCP 50(d), FRCP 52(b), FRCP 59(b), FRCP 59(d), FRCP 59(e), and FRCP 60(b). FRCP 6(b)(2).

   iii. Refer to the United States District Court for the Northern District of New York KeyRules Motion for Continuance/Extension of Time document for more information on extending time.

    d.  *Additional time after certain kinds of service.* When a party may or must act within a specified time after service and service is made under FRCP 5(b)(2)(C), FRCP 5(b)(2)(D), FRCP 5(b)(2)(E), or FRCP 5(b)(2)(F), three (3) days are added after the period would otherwise expire under FRCP 6(a). FRCP 6(d).

        i.  In accordance with FRCP 6(e), service by electronic means is treated the same as service by mail for purposes of adding three (3) days to the prescribed period to respond. NY R USDCTND CM/ECF(5)(5.4). [Editor's note: the reference to FRCP 6(e) is likely meant to be a reference to FRCP 6(d)].

  4.  *Individual judge practices.* Refer to the Miscellaneous section of this document for information on individual judge practices on timing of documents.

## C.  General Requirements

  1.  *Pleading, generally*

    a.  *Pleadings allowed.* Only these pleadings are allowed: (1) a complaint; (2) an answer to a complaint; (3) an answer to a counterclaim designated as a counterclaim; (4) an answer to a crossclaim; (5) a third-party complaint; (6) an answer to a third-party complaint; and (7) if the court orders one, a reply to an answer. FRCP 7(a).

    b.  *Pleading to be concise and direct.* Each allegation must be simple, concise, and direct. No technical form is required. FRCP 8(d)(1).

    c.  *Alternative statements of a claim or defense.* A party may set out two or more statements of a claim or defense alternatively or hypothetically, either in a single count or defense or in separate ones. If a party makes alternative statements, the pleading is sufficient if any one of them is sufficient. FRCP 8(d)(2).

    d.  *Inconsistent claims or defenses.* A party may state as many separate claims or defenses as it has, regardless of consistency. FRCP 8(d)(3).

    e.  *Construing pleadings.* Pleadings must be construed so as to do justice. FRCP 8(e).

  2.  *Pleading special matters*

    a.  *Capacity or authority to sue; Legal existence*

        i.  *In general.* Except when required to show that the court has jurisdiction, a pleading need not allege:

- A party's capacity to sue or be sued;

- A party's authority to sue or be sued in a representative capacity; or

- The legal existence of an organized association of persons that is made a party. FRCP 9(a)(1).

       ii.  *Raising those issues.* To raise any of those issues, a party must do so by a specific denial, which must state any supporting facts that are peculiarly within the party's knowledge. FRCP 9(a)(2).

    b.  *Fraud or mistake; Conditions of mind.* In alleging fraud or mistake, a party must state with particularity the circumstances constituting fraud or mistake. Malice, intent, knowledge, and other conditions of a person's mind may be alleged generally. FRCP 9(b).

    c.  *Conditions precedent.* In pleading conditions precedent, it suffices to allege generally that all conditions precedent have occurred or been performed. But when denying that a condition precedent has occurred or been performed, a party must do so with particularity. FRCP 9(c).

    d.  *Official document or act.* In pleading an official document or official act, it suffices to allege that the document was legally issued or the act legally done. FRCP 9(d).

    e.  *Judgment.* In pleading a judgment or decision of a domestic or foreign court, a judicial or quasi-judicial tribunal, or a board or officer, it suffices to plead the judgment or decision without showing jurisdiction to render it. FRCP 9(e).

    f.  *Time and place.* An allegation of time or place is material when testing the sufficiency of a pleading. FRCP 9(f).

g. *Special damages.* If an item of special damage is claimed, it must be specifically stated. FRCP 9(g).

h. *Admiralty or maritime claim*

    i. *How designated.* If a claim for relief is within the admiralty or maritime jurisdiction and also within the court's subject-matter jurisdiction on some other ground, the pleading may designate the claim as an admiralty or maritime claim for purposes of FRCP 14(c), FRCP 38(e), and FRCP 82 and the Supplemental Rules for Admiralty or Maritime Claims and Asset Forfeiture Actions. A claim cognizable only in the admiralty or maritime jurisdiction is an admiralty or maritime claim for those purposes, whether or not so designated. FRCP 9(h)(1).

    ii. *Designation for appeal.* A case that includes an admiralty or maritime claim within FRCP 9(h) is an admiralty case within 28 U.S.C.A. § 1292(a)(3). FRCP 9(h)(2).

3. *Amended pleading*

a. *Amendments before trial.* The function of FRCP 15(a), which provides generally for the amendment of pleadings, is to enable a party to assert matters that were overlooked or were unknown at the time the party interposed the original complaint or answer. FPP § 1473; Smiga v. Dean Witter Reynolds, Inc., 766 F.2d 698, 703 (2d Cir. 1985).

    i. *Matters contained in amended pleading under FRCP 15(a).* Although FRCP 15(a) does not expressly state that an amendment must contain only matters that occurred within a particular time period, FRCP 15(d) provides that any "transaction, occurrence, or event that happened after the date of the pleading" should be set forth in a supplemental pleading. FPP § 1473. Thus, impliedly, an amended pleading, whether prepared with or without leave of court, only should relate to matters that have taken place prior to the date of the earlier pleading. FPP § 1473; Ford Motor Co. v. U.S., 19 C.I.T. 946, 896 F.Supp. 1224, 1230 (1995).

    ii. *Amending as a matter of course.* The right to amend as of course is not restricted to any particular litigant or pleading. FPP § 1480. It is a right conferred on all of the parties to an action and thus extends to persons who were not original parties to the litigation, but are brought into the action by way of counterclaim, crossclaim, third-party claim, or defensive interpleader. FPP § 1480; Johnson v. Walsh, 65 F.Supp. 157 (W.D.Mo. 1946).

- *Amending a complaint with multiple defendants.* When a number of defendants are involved in an action, some of whom have answered and some of whom have filed no responsive pleading, the plaintiff can amend as a matter of course as to those defendants who have not answered. FEDPROC § 62:267; Pallant v. Sinatra, 7 F.R.D. 293 (S.D.N.Y. 1945). A plaintiff may not file an amended complaint as of right against those defendants who have not yet answered, if he or she has amended the complaint once already as a matter of course. FEDPROC § 62:267; Glaros v. Perse, 628 F.2d 679 (1st Cir. 1980).

    iii. *Amending with leave of court.* Refer to the United States District Court for the Northern District of New York KeyRules Motion for Leave to Amend document for information on amending the pleadings with leave of court.

    iv. *Types of amendments permitted under FRCP 15(a)*

- *Cure a defective pleading.* Perhaps the most common use of FRCP 15(a) is by a party seeking to amend in order to cure a defective pleading. FPP § 1474.

- *Correct insufficiently stated claims or defenses.* A more common use of FRCP 15(a) amendments is to correct insufficiently stated claims or defenses. Typically, amendments of this character involve either adding a necessary allegation in order to state a claim for relief or correcting a misnomer of a party to the action. FPP § 1474.

- *Change nature or theory of claim or capacity of party.* Courts also have allowed a party to amend in order to change the nature or theory of the party's claim or the capacity in which the party is bringing the action. FPP § 1474.

- *State additional claims or defenses or drop claims or defenses.* Plaintiffs and defendants also have been permitted to amend their pleadings to state additional claims, to assert additional defenses, or to drop claims or defenses. FPP § 1474; Weinberger v. Retail Credit Co., 498 F.2d 552, 554, n.4 (4th Cir. 1974).

- *Increase amount of damages or elect a different remedy.* A FRCP 15(a) amendment also is appropriate for increasing the amount of damages sought, or for electing a different remedy than the one originally requested. FPP § 1474; McFadden v. Sanchez, 710 F.2d 907 (2d Cir. 1983).

- *Add, substitute, or drop parties.* Finally, a party may make a FRCP 15(a) amendment to add, substitute, or drop parties to the action. FPP § 1474.

   b.  *Amendments during and after trial*

      i.  *Based on an objection at trial.* If, at trial, a party objects that evidence is not within the issues raised in the pleadings, the court may permit the pleadings to be amended. The court should freely permit an amendment when doing so will aid in presenting the merits and the objecting party fails to satisfy the court that the evidence would prejudice that party's action or defense on the merits. The court may grant a continuance to enable the objecting party to meet the evidence. FRCP 15(b)(1).

      ii.  *For issues tried by consent.* When an issue not raised by the pleadings is tried by the parties' express or implied consent, it must be treated in all respects as if raised in the pleadings. A party may move—at any time, even after judgment—to amend the pleadings to conform them to the evidence and to raise an unpleaded issue. But failure to amend does not affect the result of the trial of that issue. FRCP 15(b)(2).

      iii.  Refer to the United States District Court for the Northern District of New York KeyRules Motion for Leave to Amend document for more information on moving to amend the pleadings.

   c.  *Relation back of amendments*

      i.  *When an amendment relates back.* An amendment to a pleading relates back to the date of the original pleading when:

- The law that provides the applicable statute of limitations allows relation back;

- The amendment asserts a claim or defense that arose out of the conduct, transaction, or occurrence set out—or attempted to be set out—in the original pleading; or

- The amendment changes the party or the naming of the party against whom a claim is asserted, if FRCP 15(c)(1)(B) is satisfied and if, within the period provided by FRCP 4(m) for serving the summons and complaint, the party to be brought in by amendment: (1) received such notice of the action that it will not be prejudiced in defending on the merits; and (2) knew or should have known that the action would have been brought against it, but for a mistake concerning the proper party's identity. FRCP 15(c)(1).

      ii.  *Notice to the United States.* When the United States or a United States officer or agency is added as a defendant by amendment, the notice requirements of FRCP 15(c)(1)(C)(i) and FRCP 15(c)(1)(C)(ii) are satisfied if, during the stated period, process was delivered or mailed to the United States attorney or the United States attorney's designee, to the Attorney General of the United States, or to the officer or agency. FRCP 15(c)(2).

   d.  *Effect of an amended pleading.* A pleading that has been amended under FRCP 15(a) supersedes the pleading it modifies and remains in effect throughout the action unless it subsequently is modified. FPP § 1476. Once an amended pleading is interposed, the original pleading no longer performs any function in the case and any subsequent motion made by an opposing party should be directed at the amended pleading. FPP § 1476; Ferdik v. Bonzelet, 963 F.2d 1258, 1262 (9th Cir. 1992); Davis v. TXO Production Corp., 929 F.2d 1515, 1517 (10th Cir. 1991).

4.  *Amended complaint.* Refer to the United States District Court for the Northern District of New York KeyRules Complaint document for the requirements specific to the amended complaint.

5.  *Amended answer.* Refer to the United States District Court for the Northern District of New York KeyRules Answer document for the requirements specific to the amended answer.

6.  *Right to a jury trial; Demand*

   a.  *Right preserved.* The right of trial by jury as declared by U.S.C.A. Const. Amend. VII, or as provided by a federal statute, is preserved to the parties inviolate. FRCP 38(a).

b. *Demand.* On any issue triable of right by a jury, a party may demand a jury trial by:

    i. Serving the other parties with a written demand—which may be included in a pleading—no later than fourteen (14) days after the last pleading directed to the issue is served; and

    ii. Filing the demand in accordance with FRCP 5(d). FRCP 38(b).

    iii. In cases removed from state court, a party may file a "Demand for Jury Trial" that is separate from the initial pleading. See FRCP 81(c); NY R USDCTND L.R. 81.3. NY R USDCTND L.R. 38.1(b).

c. *Specifying issues.* In its demand, a party may specify the issues that it wishes to have tried by a jury; otherwise, it is considered to have demanded a jury trial on all the issues so triable. If the party has demanded a jury trial on only some issues, any other party may—within fourteen (14) days after being served with the demand or within a shorter time ordered by the court—serve a demand for a jury trial on any other or all factual issues triable by jury. FRCP 38(c).

d. *Waiver; Withdrawal.* A party waives a jury trial unless its demand is properly served and filed. A proper demand may be withdrawn only if the parties consent. FRCP 38(d).

e. *Admiralty and maritime claims.* The rules in FRCP 38 do not create a right to a jury trial on issues in a claim that is an admiralty or maritime claim under FRCP 9(h). FRCP 38(e).

7. *Complex and multi-district litigation.* If the assigned judge determines, in his or her discretion, that the case is of such a complex nature that it cannot reasonably be trial ready within eighteen (18) months from the date the complaint is filed, the assigned judge may design and issue a particularized case management order that will move the case to trial as quickly as the complexity of the case allows. NY R USDCTND L.R. 3.3(a). The parties shall promptly notify the Court in writing if any action commenced is appropriate for multi-district litigation. NY R USDCTND L.R. 3.3(b).

8. *Appearances.* An attorney appearing for a party in a civil case shall promptly file with the Clerk a written notice of appearance; however, an attorney does not need to file a notice of appearance if the attorney who would be filing the notice of appearance is the same individual who has signed the complaint, notice of removal, pre-answer motion, or answer. NY R USDCTND L.R. 83.2(a). For more information, refer to NY R USDCTND L.R. 83.2.

9. *Related cases.* A civil case is "related" to another civil case for purposes of this guideline when, because of the similarity of facts and legal issues or because the cases arise from the same transactions or events, a substantial saving of judicial resources is likely to result from assigning the cases to the same Judge and Magistrate Judge. NY R USDCTND Order 12(G)(2). A civil case shall not be deemed related to another civil case merely because the civil case: (1) involves similar legal issues, or (2) involves the same parties. NY R USDCTND Order 12(G)(3). Presumptively, and subject to the power of a Judge to determine otherwise pursuant to NY R USDCTND Order 12(G)(5), civil cases shall not be deemed to be "related" unless both cases are still pending before the Court. NY R USDCTND Order 12(G)(4).

a. *New filings.* If an attorney or filing party indicates on the Civil Cover Sheet that a case is related to an earlier filed case, the Clerk shall instruct the filing party to file a notice of related cases. The allegedly related cases will be submitted by the Clerk to the Judge to whom the earliest filed case is assigned, who shall advise the Clerk whether such cases are related. NY R USDCTND Order 12(G)(1).

b. *Judicial determination that civil cases are "related."* Except for the cases described in the final sentence of NY R USDCTND Order 12(G)(6), all civil cases shall be randomly assigned when they are filed. Other than the cases described in the final sentence of NY R USDCTND Order 12(G)(6), civil cases shall not be deemed to be "related" for purposes of this guideline at the instance of any litigant or attorney unless and until there has been a determination by a Judge of this Court that the standard of NY R USDCTND Order 12(G)(2) is met. NY R USDCTND Order 12(G)(5).

    i. *Notice of related filing.* Any party may apply for such a determination by filing with the Clerk a notice of related filing, which should include an explanation as to why the standard of NY R USDCTND Order 12(G)(2) is met. A form for this purpose is available on the Court's website. A copy of the notice shall be served on all other parties who have appeared. Such an application must be made after the date when at least a majority of the defendants have been served with the complaint. Before making such an application, the applicant must confer in good faith with all other parties in an effort to reach an agreement on whether or not the case is "related". After such an application is made, any other party may serve and file within seven (7) calendar days a letter of no more than two (2) pages supporting or opposing the application. The application to have the case assigned to another Judge shall be presented to the Judge with the earliest filed case for decision on whether the action(s) should be reassigned as related cases. The Judge with the earliest filed case may then enter an order in the case at bar, either deeming the case to be related and directing the Clerk to reassign the action, or denying the application for reassignment. Any disputes concerning the assignment of related cases will be referred to the Chief Judge for resolution. NY R USDCTND Order 12(G)(5).

    c.    For more information on related cases, refer to NY R USDCTND Order 12(G).

10.    *Alternative dispute resolution (ADR).* It is the mission of this court to do everything it can to help parties resolve their disputes as fairly, quickly, and efficiently as possible. NY R USDCTND Order 25(VIII).

    a.    *Arbitration.* NY R USDCTND L.R. 83.7 governs the consensual arbitration program for referral of civil actions to court-annexed arbitration. It may remain in effect until further order of the Court. Its purpose is to establish a less formal procedure for the just, efficient and economical resolution of disputes, while preserving the right to a full trial on demand. NY R USDCTND L.R. 83.7-1.

        i.    *Actions subject to arbitration.* The Clerk shall notify the parties in all civil cases, except as the Local Rules of Practice for the United States District Court for the Northern District of New York otherwise direct, that they may consent to non-binding arbitration under NY R US-DCTND L.R. 83.7. The notice shall be furnished to the parties at pretrial/scheduling conferences or shall be included with pretrial conference notices and instructions. Consent to arbitration under NY R USDCTND L.R. 83.7 shall be discussed at the pretrial/scheduling conference. No party or attorney shall be prejudiced for refusing to participate in arbitration. The Court shall allow the referral of any civil action pending before it to the arbitration process if the parties consent. The plaintiff shall be responsible for securing the execution of a consent form by the parties and for filing the form with the Clerk within fourteen (14) days after the parties receive the form. The parties shall freely and knowingly enter into the consent. NY R USDCTND L.R. 83.7-2.

        ii.    *Referral to arbitration.* The Clerk shall refer every action subject to NY R USDCTND L.R. 83.7 to arbitration in accordance with the procedures under NY R USDCTND L.R. 83.7 twenty-one (21) days after the filing of the last responsive pleading or within twenty-one (21) days of the filing of a stipulated consent order referring the action to arbitration, whichever event occurs last, except as otherwise provided. If any party notices a motion to dismiss under the provisions of FRCP 12(a) and/or FRCP 12(b), or a motion to join necessary parties pursuant to the Federal Rules of Civil Procedure prior to the expiration of the twenty-one (21) day period, the assigned judge shall hear the motion and further proceedings under NY R USDCTND L.R. 83.7 shall be deferred pending decision on the motion. If the Court does not dismiss the action on the motion, the Court shall refer the action to arbitration twenty-one (21) days after the filing of the decision. NY R USDCTND L.R. 83.7-3(a). Motions for summary judgment pursuant to FRCP 56 shall be filed and served within twenty-one (21) days following the close of discovery. The filing of a FRCP 56 motion shall defer further proceedings under NY R USDCTND L.R. 83.7 pending decision on the motion. NY R USDCTND L.R. 83.7-3(a).

            ●    *Relief from referral.* Any party shall request relief from the operation of NY R USDCTND L.R. 83.7 by filing with the Court a motion for the relief within twenty-one (21) days after entry of the initial stipulated consent order which refers the case for arbitration. The assigned judge shall, sua sponte, exempt an action from the application of NY R USDCTND L.R. 83.7 where the objectives of arbitration would not be realized because (1) the case involves complex or novel legal issues, (2) legal issues predominate over factual issues, or (3) for other good cause. NY R USDCTND L.R. 83.7-3(c).

        iii.    For more information on arbitration, refer to NY R USDCTND L.R. 83.7.

    b.    *Mediation.* The purpose of NY R USDCTND L.R. 83.11 is to provide a supplementary procedure to the Court's existing alternative dispute resolution procedures. NY R USDCTND L.R. 83.11 provides for an earlier resolution of civil disputes resulting in savings of time and cost to litigants and the Court without sacrificing the quality of justice rendered or the right of litigants to a full trial on all issues not resolved through mediation. NY R USDCTND L.R. 83.11-1(a). Mediation is a process by which an impartial person, the mediator, facilitates communication between disputing parties to promote understanding, reconciliation and settlement. The mediator is an advocate for settlement and uses the mediation process to help the parties fully explore any potential area of agreement. The mediator does not serve as a judge or arbitrator and has no authority to render any decision on any disputed issue or to force a settlement. The parties themselves are responsible for negotiating any resolution(s) to their dispute. NY R USDCTND L.R. 83.11-1(b).

i.   *Actions subject to mediation.* The Court may refer any civil action (or any portion thereof) to mediation under NY R USDCTND L.R. 83.11: (1) by order of referral; or (2) on the motion of any party; or (3) by consent of the parties. NY R USDCTND L.R. 83.11-3(a).

- *Withdrawal from mediation.* The parties may withdraw from mediation any civil action or claim that the Court refers to mediation pursuant to NY R USDCTND L.R. 83.11-3 by application to the assigned judge at least ten (10) days prior to the scheduled mediation session. NY R USDCTND L.R. 83.11-3(b).

ii.  *Mandatory mediation program.* The United States District Court for the Northern District of New York has adopted this Mandatory Mediation Plan. The paid Mediation Program is designed to provide quicker, less expensive and potentially more satisfying alternatives to continuing litigation, without impairing the quality of justice or the right to trial. NY R USDCTND Order 47(1)(1.2)(A). This Mandatory Mediation Plan applies to civil actions pending as well as newly filed actions, except as otherwise indicated in NY R USDCTND Order 47. The Local Rules for voluntary mediation will apply only to Pro Se Cases that proceed through the Assisted Mediation Program. NY R USDCTND Order 47(1)(1.2)(B).

- *Referral into the pilot mandatory mediation program for new cases.* All civil cases shall be referred automatically into the Mandatory Mediation Program. Notice of the Mandatory Mediation requirements will be provided to all parties immediately upon the filing of a complaint and answer or a notice of removal. ADR intervention will be scheduled at the conference held pursuant to NY R USDCTND L.R. 16.1. NY R USDCTND Order 47(2)(2.1)(A). For a list of categories of actions exempted from automatic referral, refer to NY R USDCTND Order 47(2)(2.1)(A).

- *Referral into the pilot mandatory mediation program for pending cases.* The assigned Judge or Magistrate Judge on any pending civil case may, sua sponte or with status conference, issue an order referring the case into the Mandatory Mediation Program. The order shall specify a date on which the ADR intervention is to be completed. NY R USDCTND Order 47(2)(2.1)(B).

- *Referral into the pilot mandatory mediation program by stipulation.* A case may be referred into the Mandatory Mediation Program by stipulation of all parties. Stipulations shall be filed and shall designate the time frame within which the ADR process will be completed. Stipulations are presumed acceptable unless the assigned Judge or Magistrate Judge determines that the interests of justice are not served. NY R USDCTND Order 47(2)(2.1)(C).

- *Relief from referral.* Motions to opt out of the program will be addressed by the assigned Magistrate Judge at the FRCP 16 conference. NY R USDCTND Order 47(2)(2.2)(A). Opting Out Motions shall be granted only for "good cause" shown. Inconvenience, travel costs, attorney fees or other costs shall not constitute "good cause." A party seeking relief from the Mandatory Mediation Program must set forth the reasons why Mandatory Mediation has no reasonable chance of being productive. NY R USDCTND Order 47(2)(2.2)(B). The assigned Magistrate Judge may, sua sponte, exempt any case from the Court's Mandatory Mediation Program. NY R USDCTND Order 47(2)(2.2)(C).

iii. *Assisted mediation program.* The Court may assign specially trained pro bono Special Media-

tion Counsel to assist pro se civilian litigants with preparing for and participating in mediation. The Assisted Mediation Program is open to civilian pro se parties to actions in the Northern District of New York. The assigned judge or magistrate judge determines if the case would benefit from mediation and would also benefit from the assignment of Special Mediation Counsel to assist the pro se party with the mediation process. NY R USDCTND L.R. 83.8(a). Appointment of Special Mediation Counsel is in no way guaranteed, even if the action is referred to the court-annexed mediation program. Appointment is at the sole discretion of the presiding judge. NY R USDCTND L.R. 83.8(a).

- *Referral to assisted mediation program.* If the court determines that referral to the Assisted Mediation Program is appropriate, the Court shall enter an order of reference to the Assisted Mediation Program. NY R USDCTND L.R. 83.8(b).

iv. For more information on mediation, refer to NY R USDCTND L.R. 83.11 and NY R USDCTND Order 47.

c. *Early neutral evaluation (ENE).* Early neutral evaluation (ENE) is a process in which parties obtain from an experienced neutral (an "evaluator") a nonbinding, reasoned, oral evaluation of the merits of the case. The first step in the ENE process involves the Court appointing an evaluator who has expertise in the area of law in the case. After the parties exchange essential information and position statements early in the pretrial period (usually within one hundred fifty (150) to two hundred (200) days after a complaint has been filed), the evaluator convenes an ENE session that typically lasts about two hours. At the ENE meeting, each side briefly presents the factual and legal basis of its position. The evaluator may ask questions of the parties and help them identify the main issues in dispute and the areas of agreement. The evaluator may also help the parties explore options for settlement. If settlement does not occur, the evaluator then offers an opinion as to the settlement value of the case, including the likelihood of liability and the likely range of damages. With the benefit of this assessment, the parties are again encouraged to discuss settlement, with or without the evaluator's assistance. The parties may also explore ways to narrow the issues in dispute, exchange information about the case or otherwise prepare efficiently for trial. NY R USDCTND L.R. 83.12-1.

i. *Actions subject to early neutral evaluation.* The Court may refer any civil action (or any portion thereof) to ENE under NY R USDCTND L.R. 83.12: (1) by order of referral; (2) on the motion of any party; or (3) by consent of the parties. NY R USDCTND L.R. 83.12-3(a).

- *Withdrawal from the ENE process.* The parties may withdraw any civil action or claim that the Court has referred to the ENE Process pursuant to NY R USDCTND L.R. 83.12-3 by application to the assigned judge at least ten (10) days before the scheduled evaluation session. NY R USDCTND L.R. 83.12-3(b).

ii. For more information on early neutral evaluation (ENE), refer to NY R USDCTND L.R. 83.12.

11. *Settlement procedures.* On notice to the Court or the Clerk that the parties have settled an action, and upon confirmation of the settlement by all parties, the Court may issue a judgment dismissing the action by reason of settlement. The Court shall issue the order without prejudice to the parties' right to secure reinstatement of the case within thirty (30) days after the date of judgment by making a showing that the settlement was not, in fact, consummated. NY R USDCTND L.R. 68.2(a). If the Court decides not to follow the procedures set forth in NY R USDCTND L.R. 68.2(a), the parties shall file within thirty (30) days of the notification to the Court, unless otherwise directed by written order, such notices, stipulations and/or motions as are necessary to terminate the action. If the required documents are not filed within the thirty (30) day period, the Clerk shall place the action on the dismissal calendar. NY R USDCTND L.R. 68.2(b).

12. *Sanctions and penalties for noncompliance.* Failure of an attorney or of a party to comply with any provision of the Local Rules of Practice for the United States District Court for the Northern District of New York, General Orders of this District, Orders of the Court, or the Federal Rules of Civil Procedure shall be a ground for imposition of sanctions. NY R USDCTND L.R. 1.1(d).

13. *Individual judge practices.* Refer to the Miscellaneous section of this document for information on individual judge practices on general requirements for documents.

## D. Documents

1. *Required documents*

    a. *Amended pleading.* Refer to the General Requirements section of this document for the form and contents of the amended pleading.

    b. *Certificate of service.* FRCP 5(d) requires that the person making service under FRCP 5 certify that service has been effected. FRCP 5(Advisory Committee Notes). Having such information on file may be useful for many purposes, including proof of service if an issue arises concerning the effectiveness of the service. FRCP 5(Advisory Committee Notes). The party or its designee shall declare, by affidavit or certification, that it has provided all other parties in the action with all documents it has filed with the Court. NY R USDCTND L.R. 5.1(a).

        i. Attorneys and pro se parties who are not Filing or Receiving Users must be served with a paper copy of any electronically filed pleading or other document. NY R USDCTND CM/ECF(5)(5.2). Such paper service must be documented by electronically filing a certificate of service. NY R USDCTND CM/ECF(5)(5.2).

2. *Supplemental documents*

    a. *Notice of constitutional question.* A party that files a pleading, written motion, or other paper drawing into question the constitutionality of a federal or state statute must promptly:

        i. *File notice.* File a notice of constitutional question stating the question and identifying the paper that raises it, if:

            • A federal statute is questioned and the parties do not include the United States, one of its agencies, or one of its officers or employees in an official capacity; or

            • A state statute is questioned and the parties do not include the state, one of its agencies, or one of its officers or employees in an official capacity; and

        ii. *Serve notice.* Serve the notice and paper on the Attorney General of the United States if a federal statute is questioned—or on the state attorney general if a state statute is questioned—either by certified or registered mail or by sending it to an electronic address designated by the attorney general for this purpose. FRCP 5.1(a).

        iii. *No forfeiture.* A party's failure to file and serve the notice, or the court's failure to certify, does not forfeit a constitutional claim or defense that is otherwise timely asserted. FRCP 5.1(d).

    b. *Notice of issue concerning foreign law.* A party who intends to raise an issue about a foreign country's law must give notice by a pleading or other writing. In determining foreign law, the court may consider any relevant material or source, including testimony, whether or not submitted by a party or admissible under the Federal Rules of Evidence. The court's determination must be treated as a ruling on a question of law. FRCP 44.1.

    c. *Cover letter authorizing e-mail or facsimile filing.* Neither the Court nor the Clerk's Office will accept for filing any facsimile or e-mail transmission without prior authorization from the Court. The party using facsimile or e-mail transmissions to file its papers must accompany any such documents with a cover letter stating that the Court authorized such transmissions and the date on which the Court provided that authorization. Violations of NY R USDCTND L.R. 5.5 subject the offending party to the Court's full disciplinary powers. NY R USDCTND L.R. 5.5.

    d. *Affidavit attesting to failed attempts to file electronically.* If the Court's CM/ECF site experiences a technical failure, a Filing User may submit documents to the Court that day in an alternate manner provided that the documents are accompanied by the Filing User's affidavit stating that the Filing User attempted to file electronically at least two times in one (1) hour increments after 10:00 a.m. that day. The following methods are acceptable alternate means for filing documents in case of a technical failure: (1) via electronic mail in a PDF attachment sent to the e-mail address for technical failures; or (2) in person, by bringing the document to the Clerk's Office on paper accompanied by a CD/ROM that contains the document in .pdf format. NY R USDCTND CM/ECF(10)(10.1).

        i. A Filing User who cannot file documents electronically because of a problem on the Filing User's system must file the documents' conventionally along with an affidavit explaining the reason for not filing the documents electronically. NY R USDCTND CM/ECF(10)(10.2).

e. *Notice of conventional filing.* If the Clerk's Office grants permission to conventionally file the document, the Filing User shall electronically file a notice of conventional filing for the documents. More information regarding this process can be obtained from the Court's web page. NY R USDCTND CM/ECF(4)(4.5).

f. *CD/ROM with PDF of document(s).* If the Court grants permission to file a document traditionally, the attorney must submit the documents for filing to the Clerk's Office on CD/ROM in .pdf or pdf.A format. NY R USDCTND CM/ECF(2).

g. *English translation.* The Court conducts its reviews and deliberations in English. Unless otherwise directed by the Court, any document that a party transmits to the Court (including one in the record on appeal) that is in a language other than English must be accompanied by an English translation that the translator has certified as true and accurate, pursuant to 28 U.S.C.A. § 1746. NY R USDCTND L.R. 10.1(e). For more information, refer to NY R USDCTND L.R. 10.1(e).

h. *Courtesy copies.* The Court may require that courtesy copies of electronically filed documents be submitted for its review and may amend these Administrative Procedures (NY R USDCTND CM/ECF) at any time without prior notice. NY R USDCTND CM/ECF(2).

i. *Copies for three-judge court.* On the convening of a three-judge court, the parties shall make three (3) copies of all non-electronically filed pleadings, motion papers, and memoranda of law available to the Clerk for distribution. NY R USDCTND L.R. 9.1.

3. *Documents required for an amended complaint adding a new claim for relief or new party.* Refer to the United States District Court for the Northern District of New York KeyRules Complaint document for the documents for an amended complaint adding a new claim for relief or being filed and served against a new party.

4. *Individual judge practices.* Refer to the Miscellaneous section of this document for information on individual judge practices on required documents.

## E. Format

1. *Form of documents.* All pleadings and other papers shall be served and filed in accordance with the Federal Rules of Civil Procedure and shall be in the form prescribed by NY R USDCTND L.R. 10.1. NY R USDCTND L.R. 5.1(a).

   a. *Form, generally.* All pleadings, motions, and other documents that a party presents for filing, whether in paper form or in electronic form, shall meet the following requirements:

      i. *Font size.* All text, whether in the body of the document or in footnotes, must be a minimum of twelve (12) point type. NY R USDCTND L.R. 10.1(a)(1).

      ii. *Margins.* All documents must have one (1) inch margins on all four sides of the page. NY R USDCTND L.R. 10.1(a)(2).

      iii. *Spacing.* All text in the body of the document must be double-spaced. NY R USDCTND L.R. 10.1(a)(3).

      - The text in block quotations and footnotes may be single-spaced. NY R USDCTND L.R. 10.1(a)(4).

      iv. *Page numbering.* Pages must be consecutively numbered. NY R USDCTND L.R. 10.1(a)(7).

      v. *Circumventing formatting limitations*

      - Extensive footnotes must not be used to circumvent page limitations. NY R USDCTND L.R. 10.1(a)(5).

      - Compacted or other compressed printing features must not be used. NY R USDCTND L.R. 10.1(a)(6).

   b. *Additional requirements for paper filing.* Additional requirements for all pleadings, motions, and other documents that a party presents for filing in paper form:

      i. *Paper size.* All documents must be on eight and one-half by eleven (8-1/2 x 11) inch white paper of good quality. NY R USDCTND L.R. 10.1(b)(1).

ii. *Text.* All text must be plainly and legibly written, typewritten, printed or reproduced without erasures or interlineations materially defacing them. NY R USDCTND L.R. 10.1(b)(2).

iii. *Ink.* All documents must be in black or blue ink. NY R USDCTND L.R. 10.1(b)(3).

iv. *Binding.* Pages of all documents must be stapled (or in some other way fastened) together. NY R USDCTND L.R. 10.1(b)(4).

v. *Single-sided paper.* All documents must be single-sided. NY R USDCTND L.R. 10.1(b)(5).

vi. *Electronic submission.* The Court, at its discretion, may require the electronic submission of any document in a WordPerfect-compatible format. NY R USDCTND L.R. 10.1(b)(6).

vii. *Rejection of document.* The Court may reject documents that do not comply with the above-listed requirements. NY R USDCTND L.R. 10.1(b).

c. *Caption; Names of parties.* Every pleading must have a caption with the court's name, a title, a file number, and a FRCP 7(a) designation. The title of the complaint must name all the parties; the title of other pleadings, after naming the first party on each side, may refer generally to other parties. FRCP 10(a). Each document must contain a caption for the specific case to which it pertains. The caption must include the title of the Court, the title of the action, the civil action number of the case, the initials of the assigned judge(s), and the name or nature of the paper in sufficient detail for identification. If a litigant has more than one action pending in this Court, any and all papers filed in a case must contain and pertain to one civil action number, unless the civil actions have been consolidated by the Court. Any motion or other papers purporting to relate to more than one action will not be accepted for filing and may be stricken by the Court. NY R USDCTND L.R. 10.1(c)(1) shall not apply, as noted in NY R USDCTND L.R. 10.1(c), to notices of change of address filed by attorneys of record and pro se litigants. The parties must separately caption affidavits and declarations and must not physically attach them to the Notice of Motion or Memorandum of Law. NY R USDCTND L.R. 10.1(c)(1).

i. *Demand for jury trial.* If a party demands a jury trial as FRCP 38(b) permits, the party shall place a notation on the front page of the initial pleading which that party signed, stating "Demand for Jury Trial" or an equivalent statement. This notation shall serve as a sufficient demand under FRCP 38(b). NY R USDCTND L.R. 38.1(a).

ii. *Class action.* If a party seeks to maintain a case as a class action pursuant to FRCP 23, the party shall include the words "Class Action" in the complaint or other pleading asserting a class action next to its caption. NY R USDCTND L.R. 23.1(a).

d. *Paragraphs; Separate statements.* A party must state its claims or defenses in numbered paragraphs, each limited as far as practicable to a single set of circumstances. A later pleading may refer by number to a paragraph in an earlier pleading. If doing so would promote clarity, each claim founded on a separate transaction or occurrence—and each defense other than a denial—must be stated in a separate count or defense. FRCP 10(b).

e. *Adoption by reference; Exhibits.* A statement in a pleading may be adopted by reference elsewhere in the same pleading or in any other pleading or motion. A copy of a written instrument that is an exhibit to a pleading is a part of the pleading for all purposes. FRCP 10(c).

f. *Citation of local rules.* These are the Local Rules of Practice for the United States District Court for the Northern District of New York. They shall be cited as "L.R. ___." NY R USDCTND L.R. 1.1(a).

g. *Acceptance by the clerk.* The clerk must not refuse to file a paper solely because it is not in the form prescribed by the Federal Rules of Civil Procedure or by a local rule or practice. FRCP 5(d)(4).

2. *Form of electronic documents.* All pleadings, motions, and other documents that a party presents for filing, whether in paper form or in electronic form, shall meet the requirements in NY R USDCTND L.R. 10.1(a). NY R USDCTND L.R. 10.1(a). Refer above for more information.

a. *Attachments and exhibits.* A Filing User must submit in electronic form all documents referenced as exhibits or attachments in accordance with the Court's CM/ECF Users Manual unless the Court otherwise orders. A Filing User shall submit as exhibits or attachments only those excerpts of the referenced documents that are directly germane to the matter under the Court's consideration.

Excerpted material must be clearly and prominently identified as such. Filing Users who file excerpts of documents as exhibits or attachments under these Administrative Procedures (NY R USDCTND CM/ECF) do so without prejudice to their right to timely file additional excerpts or the complete document. Responding parties may also timely file the complete document or additional excerpts that they believe are directly germane to the matter under the Court's consideration. NY R USDCTND CM/ECF(4)(4.4).

   i.   All attachments must be described in sufficient detail so the Court and opposing counsel can easily identify and distinguish the filed attachments. Vague or general descriptions are insufficient (i.e., "Exhibit 1"). Rather, each attachment shall have a descriptive title identifying, with specificity, the document that is being filed (i.e., "Exhibit 12 Mulligan County Fire Investigation Report.") Failure to adequately describe attachments may result in the document being rejected by the Court. NY R USDCTND CM/ECF(4)(4.4).

b.   *Large documents.* For information on the electronic filing of large documents, please consult the Court's CM/ECF Users Manual, which is available on the Court's web page. NY R USDCTND CM/ECF(4)(4.5).

   i.   A party who believes a document is too lengthy to electronically image, i.e., "scan," may contact the Clerk's Office for permission to file that document conventionally. If the Clerk's Office grants permission to conventionally file the document, the Filing User shall electronically file a notice of conventional filing for the documents. More information regarding this process can be obtained from the Court's web page. Exhibits submitted conventionally shall be served on other parties as if they were not subject to these Administrative Procedures (NY R USDCTND CM/ECF). For a list of hints and tips for scanning large documents, please consult the Court's web page. NY R USDCTND CM/ECF(4)(4.5).

c.   *Legibility.* It shall be the Filing User's responsibility to verify the legibility of scanned documents before filing them electronically with the Court. NY R USDCTND CM/ECF(4)(4.6).

d.   *Color documents.* Since documents scanned in color or containing a graphic take much longer to upload, Filing Users are encouraged to configure their scanners to scan documents at 300 dpi and preferably in black and white rather than in color. NY R USDCTND CM/ECF(4)(4.7).

e.   *Items not in .PDF format.* Parties wishing to file items not amenable to .pdf format (i.e. CD's, DVD's), shall file such items conventionally with the Clerk's Office. The Filing User shall electronically file a notice of conventional filing indicating that these items have been submitted to the clerk and shall serve copies of these items on other parties as if they were not subject to these Administrative Procedures (NY R USDCTND CM/ECF). These item(s) will be maintained by the Clerk's Office until the case is disposed, at which time they will be returned to the filing party for retention consistent with NY R USDCTND CM/ECF(4)(4.9). NY R USDCTND CM/ECF(4)(4.8).

3.   *Signing of pleadings, motions and other papers*

a.   *Signature.* Every pleading, written motion, and other paper must be signed by at least one attorney of record in the attorney's name—or by a party personally if the party is unrepresented. The paper must state the signer's address, e-mail address, and telephone number. FRCP 11(a). Each document must identify the person filing the document. This identification must include an original signature of the attorney or pro se litigant; the typewritten name of that person; the address of a pro se litigant; and the bar roll number, office address, telephone number, e-mail address and fax number of the attorney. Telephone numbers of non-prisoner pro se parties may be provided voluntarily or upon request of the Court. See General Order #22 (NY R USDCTND CM/ECF) for signature requirements. NY R USDCTND L.R. 10.1(c)(2).

   i.   *Electronic signatures.* Documents filed under an attorney's login and password shall constitute that attorney's signature for purposes of the Local Rules of Practice for the United States District Court for the Northern District of New York and Federal Rules of Civil Procedure, including but not limited to FRCP 11. A pleading or other document requiring an attorney's signature shall be signed in the following manner, whether filed electronically or submitted on disk or CD/ROM to the Clerk's Office: "s/ (attorney name)." The correct format for an attorney signature is found in NY R USDCTND CM/ECF(6)(6.1). NY R USDCTND CM/ECF(6)(6.1).

     •   *Non-attorney signature.* If an original document requires the signature of a non-attorney, the Filing User may scan the original document containing the original signature(s), then electronically file it on the System. Alternatively, the Filing User may convert the document into .pdf text format and submit the document using "s/" for the signature of the non-attorney. NY R USDCTND CM/ECF(6)(6.2).

- *Multiple signatures.* A document requiring signatures of more than one party must be filed electronically either by (1) submitting a scanned document containing all necessary signatures; (2) representing the consent of the other parties on the document; or (3) in any other manner that the Court approves. NY R USDCTND CM/ECF(6)(6.3).

ii. *No verification or accompanying affidavit required for pleadings.* Unless a rule or statute specifically states otherwise, a pleading need not be verified or accompanied by an affidavit. FRCP 11(a).

iii. *Unsigned papers.* The court must strike an unsigned paper unless the omission is promptly corrected after being called to the attorney's or party's attention. FRCP 11(a).

b. *Representations to the court.* By presenting to the court a pleading, written motion, or other paper—whether by signing, filing, submitting, or later advocating it—an attorney or unrepresented party certifies that to the best of the person's knowledge, information, and belief, formed after an inquiry reasonable under the circumstances:

i. It is not being presented for any improper purpose, such as to harass, cause unnecessary delay, or needlessly increase the cost of litigation;

ii. The claims, defenses, and other legal contentions are warranted by existing law or by a nonfrivolous argument for extending, modifying, or reversing existing law or for establishing new law;

iii. The factual contentions have evidentiary support or, if specifically so identified, will likely have evidentiary support after a reasonable opportunity for further investigation or discovery; and

iv. The denials of factual contentions are warranted on the evidence or, if specifically so identified, are reasonably based on belief or a lack of information. FRCP 11(b).

c. *Sanctions.* If, after notice and a reasonable opportunity to respond, the court determines that FRCP 11(b) has been violated, the court may impose an appropriate sanction on any attorney, law firm, or party that violated FRCP 11(b) or is responsible for the violation. FRCP 11(c)(1). Refer to the United States District Court for the Northern District of New York KeyRules Motion for Sanctions document for more information.

4. *Privacy protection for filings made with the court*

a. *Redacted filings.* Unless the court orders otherwise, in an electronic or paper filing with the court that contains an individual's Social Security number, taxpayer-identification number, or birth date, the name of an individual known to be a minor, or a financial-account number, a party or nonparty making the filing may include only:

i. The last four (4) digits of the Social Security number and taxpayer-identification number;

ii. The year of the individual's birth;

iii. The minor's initials; and

iv. The last four (4) digits of the financial-account number. FRCP 5.2(a); NY R USDCTND L.R. 8.1; NY R USDCTND CM/ECF(11)(11.2).

v. If a home address must be used, use only the City and State. NY R USDCTND L.R. 8.1; NY R USDCTND CM/ECF(11)(11.2).

vi. If the victim of a sexual assault must be referenced, redact the name to 'Victim.' NY R USDCTND CM/ECF(11)(11.2); NY R USDCTND L.R. 8.1.

vii. In addition, caution shall be exercised when filing documents that contain the following:

- Personal identifying number, such as a driver's license number;
- Medical records, treatment and diagnosis;

- Employment history;

- Individual financial information; and

- Proprietary or trade secret information. NY R USDCTND L.R. 8.1; NY R USDCTND CM/ECF(11)(11.2).

b. *Exemptions from the redaction requirement.* The redaction requirement does not apply to the following:

  i. A financial-account number that identifies the property allegedly subject to forfeiture in a forfeiture proceeding;

  ii. The record of an administrative or agency proceeding;

  iii. The official record of a state-court proceeding;

  iv. The record of a court or tribunal, if that record was not subject to the redaction requirement when originally filed;

  v. A filing covered by FRCP 5.2(c) or FRCP 5.2(d); and

  vi. A pro se filing in an action brought under 28 U.S.C.A. § 2241, 28 U.S.C.A. § 2254, or 28 U.S.C.A. § 2255. FRCP 5.2(b).

  vii. Transcripts of the administrative record in social security proceedings are exempt from this requirement. State court records and other documents filed in habeas corpus proceedings are exempt from this requirement except for proceedings that involve victims of sex crimes. In habeas corpus cases involving sex crimes, the parties must redact the record and supporting papers, or may move to seal, if appropriate. NY R USDCTND L.R. 8.1.

c. *Limitations on remote access to electronic files; Social Security appeals and immigration cases.* Unless the court orders otherwise, in an action for benefits under the Social Security Act, and in an action or proceeding relating to an order of removal, to relief from removal, or to immigration benefits or detention, access to an electronic file is authorized as follows:

  i. The parties and their attorneys may have remote electronic access to any part of the case file, including the administrative record;

  ii. Any other person may have electronic access to the full record at the courthouse, but may have remote electronic access only to:

    - The docket maintained by the court; and

    - An opinion, order, judgment, or other disposition of the court, but not any other part of the case file or the administrative record. FRCP 5.2(c).

d. *Filings made under seal.* The court may order that a filing be made under seal without redaction. The court may later unseal the filing or order the person who made the filing to file a redacted version for the public record. FRCP 5.2(d); NY R USDCTND L.R. 8.1. For information on sealed matters, refer to NY R USDCTND L.R. 83.13 and NY R USDCTND CM/ECF(12).

e. *Protective orders.* For good cause, the court may by order in a case:

  i. Require redaction of additional information; or

  ii. Limit or prohibit a nonparty's remote electronic access to a document filed with the court. FRCP 5.2(e).

f. *Option for additional unredacted filing under seal.* A person making a redacted filing may also file an unredacted copy under seal. The court must retain the unredacted copy as part of the record. FRCP 5.2(f); NY R USDCTND L.R. 8.1; NY R USDCTND CM/ECF(11)(11.3).

g. *Option for filing a reference list.* A filing that contains redacted information may be filed together with a reference list that identifies each item of redacted information and specifies an appropriate identifier that uniquely corresponds to each item listed. The list must be filed under seal and may be amended as of right. Any reference in the case to a listed identifier will be construed to refer to the corresponding item of information. FRCP 5.2(g); NY R USDCTND L.R. 8.1; NY R USDCTND CM/ECF(11)(11.3).

h. *Responsibility for redaction.* Counsel is strongly urged to discuss this issue with all their clients so that they can make an informed decision about the inclusion of certain information. The responsibility for redacting these personal identifiers rests solely with counsel and the parties. The Clerk will not review each filing for compliance with NY R USDCTND L.R. 8.1. Counsel and the parties are cautioned that failure to redact these personal identifiers may subject them to the Court's full disciplinary power. NY R USDCTND L.R. 8.1; NY R USDCTND CM/ECF(11)(11.3).

i. *Waiver of protection of identifiers.* A person waives the protection of FRCP 5.2(a) as to the person's own information by filing it without redaction and not under seal. FRCP 5.2(h).

5. *Individual judge practices.* Refer to the Miscellaneous section of this document for information on individual judge practices on formatting documents.

## F. Filing and Service Requirements

1. *Filing requirements.* Any paper after the complaint that is required to be served—together with a certificate of service—must be filed within a reasonable time after service. FRCP 5(d)(1).

   a. *How filing is made; In general.* A paper is filed by delivering it:

      i. To the clerk; or

      ii. To a judge who agrees to accept it for filing, and who must then note the filing date on the paper and promptly send it to the clerk. FRCP 5(d)(2).

   b. *Electronic filing*

      i. *Authorization of electronic filing program.* A court may, by local rule, allow papers to be filed, signed, or verified by electronic means that are consistent with any technical standards established by the Judicial Conference of the United States. A local rule may require electronic filing only if reasonable exceptions are allowed. A paper filed electronically in compliance with a local rule is a written paper for purposes of the Federal Rules of Civil Procedure. FRCP 5(d)(3).

         • All cases filed in this Court may be assigned to the Electronic Case Files System ("ECF") in accordance with the Procedural Order on Electronic Case Filing (General Order #22 (NY R USDCTND CM/ECF)), the provisions of which are incorporated herein by reference, and which the Court may amend from time to time. Copies of General Order #22 (NY R USDCTND CM/ECF) are available at the Clerk's office or at the Court's webpage. NY R USDCTND L.R. 5.1.1; NY R USDCTND Order 25(XII).

         • The Court may deviate from these Administrative Procedures (NY R USDCTND CM/ECF) in specific cases, without prior notice, if deemed appropriate in the exercise of discretion, considering the need for the just, speedy, and inexpensive determination of matters pending before the Court. NY R USDCTND CM/ECF(2).

      ii. *Scope of electronic filing.* After January 1, 2004, all documents that attorneys admitted to practice in the Northern District of New York submit for filing shall be filed electronically using the System or shall be scanned and uploaded to the System, no matter when a case was originally filed, unless these Administrative Procedures (NY R USDCTND CM/ECF) otherwise permit or unless the assigned judge otherwise authorizes. An attorney who is not a Filing User by January 1, 2004, must show good cause to the assigned judge to file and serve pleadings and other papers in the traditional manner. NY R USDCTND CM/ECF(2).

      iii. *Exceptions and/or waivers from mandatory electronic filing.* The following types of cases and/or documents are not required to be filed electronically:

         • If you are seeking to have your complaint filed under seal, please file your complaint and proposed sealing order traditionally at the Clerk's Office. NY R USDCTND CM/ECF(2)(2.1)(1).

         • Any document that a party proceeding pro se files. (See NY R USDCTND CM/ECF(12)(12.1) for procedural details). NY R USDCTND CM/ECF(2)(2.1)(2). A non-prisoner who is a party to a civil action and who is not represented by an attorney may file a motion to obtain an Electronic Case Filing (ECF) login and password on a form prescribed by the Clerk's Office. The Pro Se CM/ECF Registration Form shall be submitted with the motion. If during the course of the action an attorney appears on behalf of the pro se party, the Clerk's Office shall terminate the pro se party's registration based upon the attorney's appearance. NY R USDCTND CM/ECF(12)(12.1). Absent permission to file electronically, pro se filers shall file paper originals of all complaints, pleadings, motions, affidavits, briefs, and other documents which must be signed or which require either verification or an unsworn declaration under any rule or statute. The Clerk's Office will scan these original documents into an electronic file in the System but will also maintain a paper file. NY R USDCTND CM/ECF(12)(12.1). A pro se party may also seek permission to receive immediate notice of all public documents filed in their cases. Notices of Electronic Filing (NEF) and attached documents would be transmitted to a non-prisoner pro se party who selects this option. Note: The pro se party would continue to file their documents with the Clerk's Office in paper form. NY R USDCTND CM/ECF(12)(12.1).

- Sealed documents, sealed cases, documents for in camera review, documents lodged with the Court, ex parte documents, confidential agreements, Qui Tam actions and Grand Jury material and warrants must be filed traditionally. (See NY R USDCTND CM/ECF(12)(12.2) for further information the filing of the above-referenced documents). NY R USDCTND CM/ECF(2)(2.1)(3).

- Discovery: In accordance with NY R USDCTND L.R. 26.2, parties shall not file discovery, provided, however, that discovery material to be used at trial or in support of any motion, including a motion to compel or for summary judgment, shall be filed electronically with the Court prior to the trial or with the motion. Any motion pursuant to FRCP 37 shall be accompanied by the electronically filed discovery materials to which the motion relates if those materials have not previously been filed with the Court. NY R USDCTND CM/ECF(2)(2.1)(4).

- Transport Orders: All orders requesting that an incarcerated individual be transported that a judicial officer of the Northern District of New York signs shall be filed traditionally. These Orders will not be filed with the case or uploaded to the docket but rather will be processed in accordance with the procedures that the Clerk of Court promulgates. NY R USDCTND CM/ECF(2)(2.1)(5).

iv. *Filing defined.* Electronic transmission of a document to the System in accordance with these Administrative Procedures, together with the transmission of a Notice of Electronic Filing from the Court, constitutes filing of the document for all purposes of the Federal Rules of Civil Procedure and the Local Rules of Practice for the United States District Court for the Northern District of New York and constitutes entry of the document on the docket that the Clerk's Office keeps under FRCP 58 and FRCP 79. E-mailing a document to the Clerk's Office or to the assigned judge shall not constitute "filing" of the document. NY R USDCTND CM/ECF(4)(4.1).

v. *Filing fees.* Any fee required for filing a pleading or paper in this Court is payable to the Clerk of the Court. The Court will not maintain electronic billing or debit accounts for attorneys or law firms. Effective January 1, 2007, payment for filing fees will be mandatory through CM/ECF's Internet Credit Card Payment site--a secure Treasury Site. The Filing User will be prompted to enter either Bank Account Debit (ACH) or credit card information while filing the initial pleading. Any document that requires a filing fee (e.g., Notice of Appeal, Motion for Pro Hac Vice Admission) may also be paid through the federal electronic payment website. NY R USDCTND CM/ECF(7).

vi. For more information on electronic filing, refer to NY R USDCTND CM/ECF.

c. *E-mail or facsimile filing.* Neither the Court nor the Clerk's Office will accept for filing any facsimile or e-mail transmission without prior authorization from the Court. The party using facsimile or e-mail transmissions to file its papers must accompany any such documents with a cover letter stating that the Court authorized such transmissions and the date on which the Court provided that authorization. Violations of NY R USDCTND L.R. 5.5 subject the offending party to the Court's full disciplinary powers. NY R USDCTND L.R. 5.5.

2. *Service requirements*

   a. *Service; When required*

      i. *In general.* Unless the Federal Rules of Civil Procedure provide otherwise, each of the following papers must be served on every party:

- An order stating that service is required;

- A pleading filed after the original complaint, unless the court orders otherwise under FRCP 5(c) because there are numerous defendants;

- A discovery paper required to be served on a party, unless the court orders otherwise;

- A written motion, except one that may be heard ex parte; and

- A written notice, appearance, demand, or offer of judgment, or any similar paper. FRCP 5(a)(1).

      ii. *If a party fails to appear.* No service is required on a party who is in default for failing to appear. But a pleading that asserts a new claim for relief against such a party must be served on that party under FRCP 4. FRCP 5(a)(2).

      iii. *Seizing property.* If an action is begun by seizing property and no person is or need be named as a defendant, any service required before the filing of an appearance, answer, or claim must be made on the person who had custody or possession of the property when it was seized. FRCP 5(a)(3).

   b. *Service; How made*

      i. *Serving an attorney.* If a party is represented by an attorney, service under FRCP 5 must be made on the attorney unless the court orders service on the party. FRCP 5(b)(1).

      ii. *Service in general.* A paper is served under FRCP 5 by:

- Handing it to the person;

- Leaving it: (1) at the person's office with a clerk or other person in charge or, if no one is in charge, in a conspicuous place in the office; or (2) if the person has no office or the office is closed, at the person's dwelling or usual place of abode with someone of suitable age and discretion who resides there;

- Mailing it to the person's last known address—in which event service is complete upon mailing;

- Leaving it with the court clerk if the person has no known address;

- Sending it by electronic means if the person consented in writing—in which event service is complete upon transmission, but is not effective if the serving party learns that it did not reach the person to be served; or

- Delivering it by any other means that the person consented to in writing—in which event service is complete when the person making service delivers it to the agency designated to make delivery. FRCP 5(b)(2).

      iii. *Service of electronically-filed documents.* Service is complete provided all parties receive a Notice of Electronic Filing (NEF), which is sent automatically by email from the Court (see the NEF for a list of who did/did not receive notice electronically). Transmission of the NEF constitutes service upon all Filing and Receiving Users who are listed as recipients of notice by electronic mail. It remains the responsibility of Filing and Receiving Users to maintain current contact information with the court and to regularly review the docket sheet of the case. NY R USDCTND CM/ECF(5)(5.2).

- *Non-filing or receiving users.* Attorneys and pro se parties who are not Filing or Receiving Users must be served with a paper copy of any electronically filed pleading or other document. Service of such paper copy must be made according to the Federal Rules of Civil Procedure and the Local Rules of Practice for the United States District Court for the Northern District of New York. Such paper service must be documented by electronically filing a certificate of service. NY R USDCTND CM/ECF(5)(5.2). A party who is not a Filing User of the System is entitled to a paper copy of any electronically-filed pleading, document, or order. The Filing User must therefore provide the non-Filing User with the pleading or document according to the Federal Rules of Civil Procedure. NY R US-DCTND CM/ECF(5)(5.3).

 iv. *Using court facilities.* If a local rule so authorizes, a party may use the court's transmission facilities to make service under FRCP 5(b)(2)(E). FRCP 5(b)(3).

 c. *Serving numerous defendants*

  i. *In general.* If an action involves an unusually large number of defendants, the court may, on motion or on its own, order that:

- Defendants' pleadings and replies to them need not be served on other defendants;

- Any crossclaim, counterclaim, avoidance, or affirmative defense in those pleadings and replies to them will be treated as denied or avoided by all other parties; and

- Filing any such pleading and serving it on the plaintiff constitutes notice of the pleading to all parties. FRCP 5(c)(1).

  ii. *Notifying parties.* A copy of every such order must be served on the parties as the court directs. FRCP 5(c)(2).

3. *Service requirements of an amended complaint asserting new or additional claims for relief.* The service of amended pleadings is generally governed by FRCP 5. Thus, except for an amended pleading against a defaulting party that does not assert new or additional claims for relief, an amended pleading must be served in accordance with FRCP 5. FEDPROC § 62:263; International Controls Corp. v. Vesco, 556 F.2d 665, 23 Fed.R.Serv.2d 923 (2d Cir. 1977). However, while FRCP 5 permits service of an amended complaint on counsel, where the amended complaint contains an entirely different cause of action that could not have been properly served originally by the method used in serving the original complaint, the amended complaint must be served in accordance with the terms of FRCP 4. FEDPROC § 62:263; Lasch v. Antkies, 161 F.Supp. 851 (E.D.Pa. 1958). Refer to the United States District Court for the Northern District of New York KeyRules Complaint document for more information on serving the amended complaint in accordance with FRCP 4.

4. *Individual judge practices.* Refer to the Miscellaneous section of this document for information on individual judge practices on filing and serving documents.

## G. Hearings

1. *Hearings, generally.* Generally, there is no hearing contemplated in the federal statutes or rules for the amended pleading.

 a. *Amended answer; Hearing on FRCP 12 defenses before trial.* If a party so moves, any defense listed in FRCP 12(b)(1) through FRCP 12(b)(7)—whether made in a pleading or by motion—and a motion under FRCP 12(c) must be heard and decided before trial unless the court orders a deferral until trial. FRCP 12(i).

2. *Individual judge practices.* Refer to the Miscellaneous section of this document for information on individual judge practices on hearings.

## H. Forms

### 1. Federal Amended Pleading Forms

 a. Notice; Of filing amended pleading as of course. AMJUR PP FEDPRAC § 153.

 b. Amendment; Of pleading as of course. AMJUR PP FEDPRAC § 154.

 c. Civil cover sheet. 2 FEDFORMS § 3:29.

 d. Notice of lawsuit and request for waiver of service of summons and waiver of summons. 2 FEDFORMS § 3:36.

 e. Complaint. 2 FEDFORMS § 7:14.

 f. Generally. 2B FEDFORMS § 8:10.

g.   Presenting defenses; Official form. 2B FEDFORMS § 8:12.

h.   Denials, admissions and affirmative defenses. 2B FEDFORMS § 8:15.

i.   Denial of particular averment. 2B FEDFORMS § 8:24.

j.   Admission of particular averment. 2B FEDFORMS § 8:25.

k.   Denial of all averments of paragraph. 2B FEDFORMS § 8:26.

l.   Admission of all averments of paragraph. 2B FEDFORMS § 8:27.

m.   Denial in part and admission in part of paragraph. 2B FEDFORMS § 8:28.

n.   Notice of amended complaint. 2C FEDFORMS § 14:10.

o.   Amendment to complaint. 2C FEDFORMS § 14:47.

p.   Amendment to complaint; Short version. 2C FEDFORMS § 14:48.

q.   Amendment to complaint; As of course. 2C FEDFORMS § 14:49.

r.   Complaint; Single count. FEDPROF § 1:68.

s.   Complaint; Multiple counts; With same jurisdictional basis. FEDPROF § 1:69.

t.   Amendment of pleading; As matter of course. FEDPROF § 1:220.

u.   Notice of filing amended pleading; Where amendment is matter of course. FEDPROF § 1:221.

v.   Amendment of pleading; Particular clauses. FEDPROF § 1:224.

w.   Amendment of pleading; Clause; Change in title of action. FEDPROF § 1:225.

x.   Amendment of pleading; Clause; To show amount in controversy. FEDPROF § 1:227.

y.   Amendment of pleading; Clause; To show diversity of citizenship. FEDPROF § 1:228.

z.   Amendment of pleading; Clause; Prayer for relief. FEDPROF § 1:229.

## I.  Applicable Rules

1.  *Federal rules*

a.   Serving and filing pleadings and other papers. FRCP 5.

b.   Constitutional challenge to a statute; Notice, certification, and intervention. FRCP 5.1.

c.   Privacy protection for filings made with the court. FRCP 5.2.

d.   Computing and extending time; Time for motion papers. FRCP 6.

e.   Pleadings allowed; Form of motions and other papers. FRCP 7.

f.   General rules of pleading. FRCP 8.

g.   Pleading special matters. FRCP 9.

h.   Form of pleadings. FRCP 10.

i.   Signing pleadings, motions, and other papers; Representations to the court; Sanctions. FRCP 11.

j.   Defenses and objections; When and how presented; Motion for judgment on the pleadings; Consolidating motions; Waiving defenses; Pretrial hearing. FRCP 12.

k.   Amended and supplemental pleadings. FRCP 15.

l.   Right to a jury trial; Demand. FRCP 38.

m.   Determining foreign law. FRCP 44.1.

2.  *Local rules*

a.   Scope of the rules. NY R USDCTND L.R. 1.1.

b.   Complex and multi-district litigation. NY R USDCTND L.R. 3.3.

c.   Service and filing of papers. NY R USDCTND L.R. 5.1.

d.   Filing by facsimile or e-mail. NY R USDCTND L.R. 5.5.

MOTION TO STRIKE

e.  Personal privacy protection. NY R USDCTND L.R. 8.1.

f.  Request for three-judge court. NY R USDCTND L.R. 9.1.

g.  Form of papers. NY R USDCTND L.R. 10.1.

h.  Designation of "class action" in the caption. NY R USDCTND L.R. 23.1.

i.  Notation of "jury demand" in the pleading. NY R USDCTND L.R. 38.1.

j.  Settlement procedures. NY R USDCTND L.R. 68.2.

k.  Appearance and withdrawal of attorney. NY R USDCTND L.R. 83.2.

l.  Arbitration. NY R USDCTND L.R. 83.7-1; NY R USDCTND L.R. 83.7-2; NY R USDCTND L.R. 83.7-3.

m.  Assisted mediation program. NY R USDCTND L.R. 83.8.

n.  Mediation. NY R USDCTND L.R. 83.11-1; NY R USDCTND L.R. 83.11-3.

o.  Early neutral evaluation. NY R USDCTND L.R. 83.12-1; NY R USDCTND L.R. 83.12-3.

p.  Administrative procedures for electronic case filing. NY R USDCTND CM/ECF.

q.  Case assignment plan for the Northern District of New York. [NY R USDCTND Order 12, as amended by NY ORDER 16-4201, effective March 24, 2015].

r.  Directing the expedited service of the summons and complaint and further directing the completion of FRCP 16 stipulation for the timely progression of civil actions. [NY R USDCTND Order 25, as amended by NY ORDER 16-4187, effective June 23, 2016].

s.  Mandatory mediation program. NY R USDCTND Order 47.

**J. Miscellaneous**

**NOTE: Individual judges' rules may apply. For available judge-level information, refer to:**

DISTRICT JUDGE MAE A. D'AGOSTINO: [NY R USDCTND D'Agostino-Rules and Practices, as added by NY ORDER 16-4200, effective April 4, 2016].

DISTRICT JUDGE THOMAS J. McAVOY: NY R USDCTND McAvoy-Order.

# Motions, Oppositions and Replies
# Motion to Strike

**Document Last Updated September 2016**

**A. Checklist**

(I)  ❑ Matters to be considered by moving party

  (a)  ❑ Required documents

    (1)  ❑ Notice of motion and motion

    (2)  ❑ Memorandum of law

    (3)  ❑ Certificate of service

  (b)  ❑ Supplemental documents

    (1)  ❑ Deposition

    (2)  ❑ Notice of constitutional question

    (3)  ❑ Nongovernmental corporate disclosure statement

    (4)  ❑ Copies of authorities

    (5)  ❑ Proposed order

    (6)  ❑ Cover letter authorizing e-mail or facsimile filing

    (7)  ❑ Affidavit attesting to failed attempts to file electronically

915

      (8)  ❑  Notice of conventional filing

      (9)  ❑  CD/ROM with PDF of document(s)

     (10)  ❑  English translation

     (11)  ❑  Courtesy copies

     (12)  ❑  Copies for three-judge court

   (c)  ❑  Timing

      (1)  ❑  The court may act on motion made by a party either before responding to the pleading or, if a response is not allowed, within twenty-one (21) days after being served with the pleading

      (2)  ❑  Unless the court orders otherwise, the moving party must file all motion papers with the court and serve them upon the other parties not less than thirty-one (31) days prior to the return date of the motion

      (3)  ❑  A written motion and notice of the hearing must be served at least fourteen (14) days before the time specified for the hearing, with the following exceptions: (i) when the motion may be heard ex parte; (ii) when the Federal Rules of Civil Procedure set a different time; or (iii) when a court order—which a party may, for good cause, apply for ex parte—sets a different time

      (4)  ❑  Any affidavit supporting a motion must be served with the motion

  (II)  ❑  Matters to be considered by opposing party

   (a)  ❑  Required documents

      (1)  ❑  Opposition

      (2)  ❑  Memorandum of law

      (3)  ❑  Certificate of service

   (b)  ❑  Supplemental documents

      (1)  ❑  Deposition

      (2)  ❑  Notice of constitutional question

      (3)  ❑  Cross-motion

      (4)  ❑  Copies of authorities

      (5)  ❑  Cover letter authorizing e-mail or facsimile filing

      (6)  ❑  Affidavit attesting to failed attempts to file electronically

      (7)  ❑  Notice of conventional filing

      (8)  ❑  CD/ROM with PDF of document(s)

      (9)  ❑  English translation

     (10)  ❑  Courtesy copies

     (11)  ❑  Copies for three-judge court

   (c)  ❑  Timing

      (1)  ❑  The party opposing the motion must file its opposition papers with the court and serve them upon the other parties not less than seventeen (17) days prior to the return date of the motion

      (2)  ❑  Except as FRCP 59(c) provides otherwise, any opposing affidavit must be served at least seven (7) days before the hearing, unless the court permits service at another time

      (3)  ❑  A party may file and serve a cross-motion (meaning a competing request for relief or order similar to that requested by another party against the cross-moving party) at the time it files and serves its opposition papers to the original motion, i.e., not less than seventeen (17) days prior to the return date of the motion

## B.  Timing

  1.  *Motion to strike.* The court may act on motion made by a party either before responding to the pleading

or, if a response is not allowed, within twenty-one (21) days after being served with the pleading. FRCP 12(f)(2).

2. *Timing of motions, generally.* Unless the Court orders otherwise, the moving party must file all motion papers with the Court and serve them upon the other parties not less than THIRTY-ONE (31) DAYS prior to the return date of the motion. NY R USDCTND L.R. 7.1(b)(2).

   a. *Motion and notice of hearing.* A written motion and notice of the hearing must be served at least fourteen (14) days before the time specified for the hearing, with the following exceptions:

      i. When the motion may be heard ex parte;

      ii. When the Federal Rules of Civil Procedure set a different time; or

      iii. When a court order—which a party may, for good cause, apply for ex parte—sets a different time. FRCP 6(c)(1).

   b. *Supporting affidavit.* Any affidavit supporting a motion must be served with the motion. FRCP 6(c)(2).

3. *Timing of opposing papers.* The party opposing the motion must file its Opposition papers with the Court and serve them upon the other parties not less than SEVENTEEN (17) DAYS prior to the return date of the motion. NY R USDCTND L.R. 7.1(b)(2).

   a. *Opposing affidavit.* Except as FRCP 59(c) provides otherwise, any opposing affidavit must be served at least seven (7) days before the hearing, unless the court permits service at another time. FRCP 6(c)(2).

   b. *Cross-motion.* A party may file and serve a cross-motion (meaning a competing request for relief or order similar to that requested by another party against the cross-moving party) at the time it files and serves its opposition papers to the original motion, i.e., not less than SEVENTEEN (17) DAYS prior to the return date of the motion. NY R USDCTND L.R. 7.1(c).

4. *Timing of reply papers.* Where the respondent files an answering affidavit setting up a new matter, the moving party ordinarily is allowed a reasonable time to file a reply affidavit since failure to deny the new matter by affidavit may operate as an admission of its truth. AMJUR MOTIONS § 25.

   a. *Reply papers.* Reply papers and adjournments are not permitted without the Court's prior permission. Permission to file a reply does not exist simply because CM/ECF generates a deadline for a reply on a nondispositive motion. NY R USDCTND L.R. 7.1(b)(2).

   b. *Opposition to cross-motion.* The original moving party must file its reply/opposition papers with the Court and serve them on the other parties not less than ELEVEN (11) DAYS prior to the return date of the original motion. NY R USDCTND L.R. 7.1(c).

5. *Effect of a FRCP 12 motion on the time to serve a responsive pleading.* Unless the court sets a different time, serving a motion under FRCP 12 alters the periods in FRCP 12(a) as follows:

   a. If the court denies the motion or postpones its disposition until trial, the responsive pleading must be served within fourteen (14) days after notice of the court's action; or

   b. If the court grants a motion for a more definite statement, the responsive pleading must be served within fourteen (14) days after the more definite statement is served. FRCP 12(a)(4).

6. *Computation of time*

   a. *Computing time.* FRCP 6 applies in computing any time period specified in the Federal Rules of Civil Procedure, in any local rule or court order, or in any statute that does not specify a method of computing time. FRCP 6(a).

      i. *Period stated in days or a longer unit.* When the period is stated in days or a longer unit of time:

        • Exclude the day of the event that triggers the period;

        • Count every day, including intermediate Saturdays, Sundays, and legal holidays; and

        • Include the last day of the period, but if the last day is a Saturday, Sunday, or legal holiday, the period continues to run until the end of the next day that is not a Saturday, Sunday, or legal holiday. FRCP 6(a)(1).

ii. *Period stated in hours.* When the period is stated in hours:

- Begin counting immediately on the occurrence of the event that triggers the period;
- Count every hour, including hours during intermediate Saturdays, Sundays, and legal holidays; and
- If the period would end on a Saturday, Sunday, or legal holiday, the period continues to run until the same time on the next day that is not a Saturday, Sunday, or legal holiday. FRCP 6(a)(2).

iii. *Inaccessibility of the clerk's office.* Unless the court orders otherwise, if the clerk's office is inaccessible:

- On the last day for filing under FRCP 6(a)(1), then the time for filing is extended to the first accessible day that is not a Saturday, Sunday, or legal holiday; or
- During the last hour for filing under FRCP 6(a)(2), then the time for filing is extended to the same time on the first accessible day that is not a Saturday, Sunday, or legal holiday. FRCP 6(a)(3).

iv. *"Last day" defined.* Unless a different time is set by a statute, local rule, or court order, the last day ends:

- For electronic filing, at midnight in the court's time zone; and
- For filing by other means, when the clerk's office is scheduled to close. FRCP 6(a)(4).

v. *"Next day" defined.* The "next day" is determined by continuing to count forward when the period is measured after an event and backward when measured before an event. FRCP 6(a)(5).

vi. *"Legal holiday" defined.* "Legal holiday" means:

- The day set aside by statute for observing New Year's Day, Martin Luther King Jr.'s Birthday, Washington's Birthday, Memorial Day, Independence Day, Labor Day, Columbus Day, Veterans' Day, Thanksgiving Day, or Christmas Day;
- Any day declared a holiday by the President or Congress; and
- For periods that are measured after an event, any other day declared a holiday by the state where the district court is located. FRCP 6(a)(6).

b. *Computation of electronic filing deadlines.* A document will be deemed timely filed if electronically filed prior to midnight Eastern Time. However, if the time of day is of the essence, the assigned judge may order that the document be filed by a time certain. NY R USDCTND CM/ECF(4)(4.3).

i. *Technical failures.* A Filing User, whose filing is untimely as the result of a technical failure of the Court's CM/ECF site, may seek appropriate relief from the Court. However, Filing Users are cautioned that, in some circumstances, the Court lacks the authority to grant an extension of time to file (e.g., FRCP 6(b) of the Federal Rules of Civil Procedure). NY R USDCTND CM/ECF(10)(10.1).

- *Technical failure of the filing user's system.* Problems with the Filing User's system, such as phone line problems, problems with the Filing User's Internet Service Provider ("ISP"), or hardware or software problems, will not constitute a technical failure under these Administrative Procedures nor excuse an untimely filing. A Filing User who cannot file documents electronically because of a problem on the Filing User's system must file the documents' conventionally along with an affidavit explaining the reason for not filing the documents electronically. NY R USDCTND CM/ECF(10)(10.2).

c. *Extending time*

i. *In general.* When an act may or must be done within a specified time, the court may, for good cause, extend the time:

- With or without motion or notice if the court acts, or if a request is made, before the original time or its extension expires; or
- On motion made after the time has expired if the party failed to act because of excusable neglect. FRCP 6(b)(1).

    ii.    *Exceptions.* A court must not extend the time to act under FRCP 50(b), FRCP 50(d), FRCP 52(b), FRCP 59(b), FRCP 59(d), FRCP 59(e), and FRCP 60(b). FRCP 6(b)(2).

    iii.    Refer to the United States District Court for the Northern District of New York KeyRules Motion for Continuance/Extension of Time document for more information on extending time.

  d.  *Additional time after certain kinds of service.* When a party may or must act within a specified time after service and service is made under FRCP 5(b)(2)(C), FRCP 5(b)(2)(D), FRCP 5(b)(2)(E), or FRCP 5(b)(2)(F), three (3) days are added after the period would otherwise expire under FRCP 6(a). FRCP 6(d).

    i.    In accordance with FRCP 6(e), service by electronic means is treated the same as service by mail for purposes of adding three (3) days to the prescribed period to respond. NY R USDCTND CM/ECF(5)(5.4). [Editor's note: the reference to FRCP 6(e) is likely meant to be a reference to FRCP 6(d)].

7.  *Individual judge practices.* Refer to the Miscellaneous section of this document for information on individual judge practices on timing of documents.

## C. General Requirements

1.  *Court conference for non-dispositive motions.* Prior to making any non-dispositive motion before the assigned Magistrate Judge, the parties must make good faith efforts among themselves to resolve or reduce all differences relating to the non-dispositive issue. If, after conferring, the parties are unable to arrive at a mutually satisfactory resolution, the party seeking relief must then request a court conference with the assigned Magistrate Judge. NY R USDCTND L.R. 7.1(b)(2). A court conference is a prerequisite to filing a non-dispositive motion before the assigned Magistrate Judge. NY R USDCTND L.R. 7.1(b)(2). In addition, no non-dispositive or discovery motions should be presented to the Court unless authorized by the Magistrate Judge after communication with the Magistrate Judge's chambers. NY R USDCTND Order 25(IX)(A). Actions which involve an incarcerated, pro se party are not subject to the requirement that a court conference be held prior to filing a non-dispositive motion. NY R USDCTND L.R. 7.1(b)(2).

2.  *Motions, generally*

  a.  *Requirements.* A request for a court order must be made by motion. The motion must:

    i.    Be in writing unless made during a hearing or trial;

    ii.    State with particularity the grounds for seeking the order; and

    iii.    State the relief sought. FRCP 7(b)(1).

    iv.    When a moving party makes a motion based upon a rule or statute, the moving party must specify in its moving papers the rule or statute upon which it bases its motion. NY R USDCTND L.R. 7.1(a)(1).

  b.  *Notice of motion.* A party interested in resisting the relief sought by a motion has a right to notice thereof, and an opportunity to be heard. AMJUR MOTIONS § 12.

    i.    In addition to statutory or court rule provisions requiring notice of a motion—the purpose of such a notice requirement having been said to be to prevent a party from being prejudicially surprised by a motion—principles of natural justice dictate that an adverse party generally must be given notice that a motion will be presented to the court. AMJUR MOTIONS § 12.

    ii.    "Notice," in this regard, means reasonable notice, including a meaningful opportunity to prepare and to defend against allegations of a motion. AMJUR MOTIONS § 12.

  c.  *Writing requirement.* The writing requirement is intended to insure that the adverse parties are informed and have a record of both the motion's pendency and the grounds on which the movant seeks an order. FPP § 1191; Feldberg v. Quechee Lakes Corp., 463 F.3d 195 (2d Cir. 2006).

    i.    It is sufficient "if the motion is stated in a written notice of the hearing of the motion." FPP § 1191.

  d.  *Particularity requirement.* The particularity requirement insures that the opposing parties will have notice of their opponent's contentions. FEDPROC § 62:364; Goodman v. 1973 26 Foot Trojan Vessel, Arkansas Registration No. AR1439SN, 859 F.2d 71, 12 Fed.R.Serv.3d 645 (8th Cir. 1988).

That requirement ensures that notice of the basis for the motion is provided to the court and to the opposing party so as to avoid prejudice, provide the opponent with a meaningful opportunity to respond, and provide the court with enough information to process the motion correctly. FEDPROC § 62:364; Andreas v. Volkswagen of America, Inc., 336 F.3d 789, 56 Fed.R.Serv.3d 6 (8th Cir. 2003).

    i.   Reasonable specification of the grounds for a motion is sufficient. However, where a movant fails to state even one ground for granting the motion in question, the movant has failed to meet the minimal standard of "reasonable specification." FEDPROC § 62:364; Martinez v. Trainor, 556 F.2d 818, 23 Fed.R.Serv.2d 403 (7th Cir. 1977).

    ii.   The court may excuse the failure to comply with the particularity requirement if it is inadvertent, and where no prejudice is shown by the opposing party. FEDPROC § 62:364.

e.   *Order to show cause.* All motions that a party brings by Order to Show Cause shall conform to the requirements set forth in NY R USDCTND L.R. 7.1(a)(1) and NY R USDCTND L.R. 7.1(a)(2). Immediately after filing an Order to Show Cause, the moving party must telephone the Chambers of the presiding judicial officer and inform Chambers staff that it has filed an Order to Show Cause. Parties may obtain the telephone numbers for all Chambers from the Clerk's office or at the Court's webpage. The Court shall determine the briefing schedule and return date applicable to motions brought by Order to Show Cause. NY R USDCTND L.R. 7.1(e).

    i.   In addition to the requirements set forth in NY R USDCTND L.R. 7.1(a)(1) and NY R USDCTND L.R. 7.1(a)(2), a motion brought by Order to Show Cause must include an affidavit clearly and specifically showing good and sufficient cause why the standard Notice of Motion procedure cannot be used. The moving party must give reasonable advance notice of the application for an Order to Show Cause to the other parties, except in those circumstances where the movant can demonstrate, in a detailed and specific affidavit, good cause and substantial prejudice that would result from the requirement of reasonable notice. NY R USDCTND L.R. 7.1(e).

    ii.   An Order to Show Cause must contain a space for the assigned judge to set forth:

- The deadline for filing and serving supporting papers,
- The deadline for filing and serving opposing papers, and
- The date and time for the hearing. NY R USDCTND L.R. 7.1(e).

3.   *Motion to strike.* The court may strike from a pleading an insufficient defense or any redundant, immaterial, impertinent, or scandalous matter. The court may act: (1) on its own; or (2) on motion made by a party either before responding to the pleading or, if a response is not allowed, within twenty-one (21) days after being served with the pleading. FRCP 12(f). FRCP 12(f) also is designed to reinforce the requirement in FRCP 8(e) that pleadings be simple, concise, and direct. However, as the cases make clear, it is neither an authorized nor a proper way to procure the dismissal of all or a part of a complaint, or a counterclaim, or to strike an opponent's affidavits. FPP § 1380.

a.   *Practice on a motion to strike.* All well-pleaded facts are taken as admitted on a motion to strike but conclusions of law or conclusions drawn from the facts do not have to be treated in that fashion by the district judge. FPP § 1380. Both because striking a portion of a pleading is a drastic remedy and because it often is sought by the movant simply as a dilatory or harassing tactic, numerous judicial decisions make it clear that motions under FRCP 12(f) are viewed with disfavor by the federal courts and are infrequently granted. FPP § 1380.

b.   *Striking an insufficient defense.* Only if a defense is insufficient as a matter of law will it be stricken. If a defense cannot succeed under any set of circumstances alleged, the defense may be deemed insufficient as a matter of law. In other words, a defense may be stricken if, on the face of the pleadings, it is patently frivolous, or if it is clearly invalid as a matter of law. FEDPROC § 62:412.

    i.   A defense will be stricken if it could not possibly prevent recovery by the plaintiff on its claim. FEDPROC § 62:413. In addition, a defense may be stricken if:

- The defense requires separate statements;
- The defense has been previously advanced and rejected; or

- The defense cannot be waived. FEDPROC § 62:413.

c. *Striking immaterial or impertinent matter.* Immaterial or impertinent matter will be stricken from a pleading if it is clear that it can have no possible bearing upon the subject matter of the litigation, and that its inclusion will prejudice the movant. If there is any doubt as to whether under any contingency the matter may raise an issue, the motion should be denied. FEDPROC § 62:415.

   i. "Immaterial matter," for purposes of FRCP 12(f), is matter which has no essential or important relationship to the claim for relief or the defenses being pleaded. FEDPROC § 62:414. A statement of unnecessary particulars in connection with and descriptive of that which is material may be stricken as immaterial matter. FEDPROC § 62:416.

   ii. "Impertinent matter," for purposes of FRCP 12(f), consists of statements that do not pertain, and are not necessary, to the issues in question. FEDPROC § 62:414.

d. *Striking redundant matter.* "Redundant matter," for purposes of FRCP 12(f), consists of allegations that constitute a needless repetition of other averments or which are wholly foreign to the issue to be decided. However, even if allegations are redundant, they need not be stricken if their presence in the pleading cannot prejudice the moving party. FEDPROC § 62:417.

   i. Merely duplicative remedies do not necessarily make claims "redundant," within the meaning of FRCP 12(f), if the claims otherwise require proof of different elements, but a claim that merely recasts the same elements under the guise of a different theory may be stricken as redundant. FEDPROC § 62:417.

e. *Striking scandalous matter.* A matter is deemed scandalous, for purposes of FRCP 12(f), when it improperly casts a derogatory light on someone, usually a party to the action. Scandalous matter also consists of any unnecessary allegation which reflects cruelly upon the moral character of an individual, or states anything in repulsive language which detracts from the dignity of the court. To be scandalous, degrading charges must be irrelevant, or, if relevant, must go into in unnecessary detail. FEDPROC § 62:418.

   i. Allegations may be stricken as scandalous if the matter bears no possible relation to the controversy or may cause the objecting party prejudice. FEDPROC § 62:418.

   ii. But there are several limitations on the court's willingness to strike scandalous allegations. For example, it is not enough that the matter offends the sensibilities of the objecting party or the person who is the subject of the statements in the pleading, if the challenged allegations describe acts or events that are relevant to the action. FPP § 1382.

f. *Striking sham or false matter.* FRCP 12(f) does not authorize a motion to strike part or all of a pleading on the ground that it is sham, and the grounds for a motion to strike similarly do not include falsity of the matter alleged. FEDPROC § 62:419; PAE Government Services, Inc. v. MPRI, Inc., 514 F.3d 856 (9th Cir. 2007). However, it has been said that a court will strike a pleading according to FRCP 12(f) when it appears beyond peradventure that it is a sham and false and that its allegations are devoid of factual basis. FEDPROC § 62:419.

g. *Striking conclusions of law.* Unwarranted conclusions of law may be stricken from a pleading pursuant to FRCP 12(f), but ordinarily an allegation is not subject to being stricken merely because it is a conclusion of law. To the contrary, the Federal Rules of Civil Procedure do not condemn conclusions of law, but rather encourage them as at times the clearest and simplest way of stating a claim for relief. Conclusions of law must be unwarranted enough to justify a motion to strike, such as when a plaintiff states causes of action under a federal statute which provides no explicit private right of action. FEDPROC § 62:420.

h. *Striking other particular matter.* Under FRCP 12(f), which permits a court to order stricken from any pleading any redundant, immaterial, impertinent, or scandalous matter, courts have the authority to strike a prayer for relief seeking damages that are not recoverable as a matter of law. A motion to strike may be used to remove an excessive or unauthorized claim for damages. Furthermore, a motion to strike a demand for punitive damages under FRCP 12(f) may be proper if such damages are clearly not collectible, such as in an ordinary breach of contract action. However, there are other ways to raise this issue, and in a particular case, one of these other methods may be more appropriate, such as a motion to dismiss for failure to state a claim pursuant to FRCP 12(b)(6). FEDPROC § 62:421.

   i. *Form.* On a motion to strike portions of a pleading, the movant must indicate what paragraphs are being challenged in order to fulfill the particularity requirement; the movant cannot merely state the conclusion that the allegations are too indefinite and insufficient to state a claim or defense. FPP § 1192.

   j. *Joining motions*

     i. *Right to join.* A motion under FRCP 12 may be joined with any other motion allowed by FRCP 12. FRCP 12(g)(1).

     ii. *Limitation on further motions.* Except as provided in FRCP 12(h)(2) or FRCP 12(h)(3), a party that makes a motion under FRCP 12 must not make another motion under FRCP 12 raising a defense or objection that was available to the party but omitted from its earlier motion. FRCP 12(g)(2).

4. *Opposing papers.* The Federal Rules of Civil Procedure do not require any formal answer, return, or reply to a motion, except where the Federal Rules of Civil Procedure or local rules may require affidavits, memoranda, or other papers to be filed in opposition to a motion. Such papers are simply to apprise the court of such opposition and the grounds of that opposition. FEDPROC § 62:359.

   a. *Effect of failure to respond to motion.* Although in the absence of statutory provision or court rule, a motion ordinarily does not require a written answer, when a party files a motion and the opposing party fails to respond, the court may construe such failure to respond as nonopposition to the motion or an admission that the motion was meritorious, may take the facts alleged in the motion as true—the rule in some jurisdictions being that the failure to respond to a fact set forth in a motion is deemed an admission—and may grant the motion if the relief requested appears to be justified. AMJUR MOTIONS § 28.

   b. *Assent or no opposition not determinative.* However, a motion will not be granted automatically simply because an "assent" or a notation of "no opposition" has been filed; federal judges frequently deny motions that have been assented to when it is thought that justice so dictates. FPP § 1190.

   c. *Responsive pleading inappropriate as response to motion.* An attempt to answer or oppose a motion with a responsive pleading usually is not appropriate. FPP § 1190.

5. *Reply papers.* Reply papers and adjournments are not permitted without the Court's prior permission. Permission to file a reply does not exist simply because CM/ECF generates a deadline for a reply on a nondispositive motion. NY R USDCTND L.R. 7.1(b)(2). A moving party may be required or permitted to prepare papers in addition to his original motion papers. AMJUR MOTIONS § 25. Papers answering or replying to opposing papers may be appropriate, in the interests of justice, where it appears there is a substantial reason for allowing a reply. Thus, a court may accept reply papers where a party demonstrates that the papers to which it seeks to file a reply raise new issues that are material to the disposition of the question before the court, or where the court determines, sua sponte, that it wishes further briefing of an issue raised in those papers and orders the submission of additional papers. FEDPROC § 62:360.

   a. *Function of reply papers.* The function of a reply affidavit is to answer the arguments made in opposition to the position taken by the movant and not to permit the movant to introduce new arguments in support of the motion. AMJUR MOTIONS § 25.

   b. *Issues raised for the first time in a reply document.* However, the view has been followed in some jurisdictions, that as a matter of judicial economy, where there is no prejudice and where the issues could be raised simply by filing a motion to dismiss, the trial court has discretion to consider arguments raised for the first time in a reply memorandum, and that a trial court may grant a motion to strike issues raised for the first time in a reply memorandum. AMJUR MOTIONS § 26.

   c. *Opposition to cross-motion.* The original moving party may reply in further support of the original motion and in opposition to the cross-motion with a reply/opposition brief that does not exceed twenty-five (25) pages in length, exclusive of exhibits. NY R USDCTND L.R. 7.1(c).

6. *Surreply in support of cross-motion.* The cross-moving party may not reply in further support of its cross-motion without the Court's prior permission. NY R USDCTND L.R. 7.1(c).

7. *Submission of proposed order by prevailing party.* If the assigned judge instructs the prevailing party to do so, the prevailing party shall submit a proposed order which the opposing party has approved and which contains the endorsement of the opposing party: "Approved as to form." NY R USDCTND L.R. 77.2(b). In civil actions where the Court has directed a party to submit an order or judgment, that party shall file all such orders or judgments in duplicate, and the Clerk's entry of such duplicate in the proper record book shall be deemed in compliance with FRCP 79(b). Such party shall also furnish the Clerk with a sufficient number of additional copies for each party to the action, which the Clerk shall mail with notice of entry in accordance with FRCP 77(d). NY R USDCTND L.R. 5.1(b).

    a. *Disagreement as to form of proposed order.* When the parties are unable to agree as to the form of the proposed order, the prevailing party shall, on seven (7) days notice to all other parties, submit a proposed order and a written explanation for the form of that order. The Court may award costs and attorney's fees against a party whose unreasonable conduct the Court deemed to have required the bringing of the motion. The provisions of NY R USDCTND L.R. 7.1 shall not apply to such motion, and the Court shall not hear oral argument. NY R USDCTND L.R. 77.2(b).

    b. For more information on orders, refer to NY R USDCTND L.R. 77.2.

8. *Sanctions for vexatious or frivolous motions or failure to comply with* NY R USDCTND L.R. 7.1. A party who presents vexatious or frivolous motion papers or fails to comply with NY R USDCTND L.R. 7.1 is subject to discipline as the Court deems appropriate, including sanctions and the imposition of costs and attorney's fees to the opposing party. NY R USDCTND L.R. 7.1(i).

9. *Complex and multi-district litigation.* If the assigned judge determines, in his or her discretion, that the case is of such a complex nature that it cannot reasonably be trial ready within eighteen (18) months from the date the complaint is filed, the assigned judge may design and issue a particularized case management order that will move the case to trial as quickly as the complexity of the case allows. NY R USDCTND L.R. 3.3(a). The parties shall promptly notify the Court in writing if any action commenced is appropriate for multi-district litigation. NY R USDCTND L.R. 3.3(b).

10. *Appearances.* An attorney appearing for a party in a civil case shall promptly file with the Clerk a written notice of appearance; however, an attorney does not need to file a notice of appearance if the attorney who would be filing the notice of appearance is the same individual who has signed the complaint, notice of removal, pre-answer motion, or answer. NY R USDCTND L.R. 83.2(a). For more information, refer to NY R USDCTND L.R. 83.2.

11. *Related cases.* A civil case is "related" to another civil case for purposes of this guideline when, because of the similarity of facts and legal issues or because the cases arise from the same transactions or events, a substantial saving of judicial resources is likely to result from assigning the cases to the same Judge and Magistrate Judge. NY R USDCTND Order 12(G)(2). A civil case shall not be deemed related to another civil case merely because the civil case: (1) involves similar legal issues, or (2) involves the same parties. NY R USDCTND Order 12(G)(3). Presumptively, and subject to the power of a Judge to determine otherwise pursuant to NY R USDCTND Order 12(G)(5), civil cases shall not be deemed to be "related" unless both cases are still pending before the Court. NY R USDCTND Order 12(G)(4).

    a. *New filings.* If an attorney or filing party indicates on the Civil Cover Sheet that a case is related to an earlier filed case, the Clerk shall instruct the filing party to file a notice of related cases. The allegedly related cases will be submitted by the Clerk to the Judge to whom the earliest filed case is assigned, who shall advise the Clerk whether such cases are related. NY R USDCTND Order 12(G)(1).

    b. *Judicial determination that civil cases are "related."* Except for the cases described in the final sentence of NY R USDCTND Order 12(G)(6), all civil cases shall be randomly assigned when they are filed. Other than the cases described in the final sentence of NY R USDCTND Order 12(G)(6), civil cases shall not be deemed to be "related" for purposes of this guideline at the instance of any litigant or attorney unless and until there has been a determination by a Judge of this Court that the standard of NY R USDCTND Order 12(G)(2) is met. NY R USDCTND Order 12(G)(5).

        i. *Notice of related filing.* Any party may apply for such a determination by filing with the Clerk a notice of related filing, which should include an explanation as to why the standard of NY R USDCTND Order 12(G)(2) is met. A form for this purpose is available on the Court's website.

A copy of the notice shall be served on all other parties who have appeared. Such an application must be made after the date when at least a majority of the defendants have been served with the complaint. Before making such an application, the applicant must confer in good faith with all other parties in an effort to reach an agreement on whether or not the case is "related". After such an application is made, any other party may serve and file within seven (7) calendar days a letter of no more than two (2) pages supporting or opposing the application. The application to have the case assigned to another Judge shall be presented to the Judge with the earliest filed case for decision on whether the action(s) should be reassigned as related cases. The Judge with the earliest filed case may then enter an order in the case at bar, either deeming the case to be related and directing the Clerk to reassign the action, or denying the application for reassignment. Any disputes concerning the assignment of related cases will be referred to the Chief Judge for resolution. NY R USDCTND Order 12(G)(5).

   c.   For more information on related cases, refer to NY R USDCTND Order 12(G).

12.   *Alternative dispute resolution (ADR).* It is the mission of this court to do everything it can to help parties resolve their disputes as fairly, quickly, and efficiently as possible. NY R USDCTND Order 25(VIII).

   a.   *Arbitration.* NY R USDCTND L.R. 83.7 governs the consensual arbitration program for referral of civil actions to court-annexed arbitration. It may remain in effect until further order of the Court. Its purpose is to establish a less formal procedure for the just, efficient and economical resolution of disputes, while preserving the right to a full trial on demand. NY R USDCTND L.R. 83.7-1.

      i.   *Actions subject to arbitration.* The Clerk shall notify the parties in all civil cases, except as the Local Rules of Practice for the United States District Court for the Northern District of New York otherwise direct, that they may consent to non-binding arbitration under NY R US-DCTND L.R. 83.7. The notice shall be furnished to the parties at pretrial/scheduling conferences or shall be included with pretrial conference notices and instructions. Consent to arbitration under NY R USDCTND L.R. 83.7 shall be discussed at the pretrial/scheduling conference. No party or attorney shall be prejudiced for refusing to participate in arbitration. The Court shall allow the referral of any civil action pending before it to the arbitration process if the parties consent. The plaintiff shall be responsible for securing the execution of a consent form by the parties and for filing the form with the Clerk within fourteen (14) days after the parties receive the form. The parties shall freely and knowingly enter into the consent. NY R USDCTND L.R. 83.7-2.

      ii.   *Referral to arbitration.* The Clerk shall refer every action subject to NY R USDCTND L.R. 83.7 to arbitration in accordance with the procedures under NY R USDCTND L.R. 83.7 twenty-one (21) days after the filing of the last responsive pleading or within twenty-one (21) days of the filing of a stipulated consent order referring the action to arbitration, whichever event occurs last, except as otherwise provided. If any party notices a motion to dismiss under the provisions of FRCP 12(a) and/or FRCP 12(b), or a motion to join necessary parties pursuant to the Federal Rules of Civil Procedure prior to the expiration of the twenty-one (21) day period, the assigned judge shall hear the motion and further proceedings under NY R USDCTND L.R. 83.7 shall be deferred pending decision on the motion. If the Court does not dismiss the action on the motion, the Court shall refer the action to arbitration twenty-one (21) days after the filing of the decision. NY R USDCTND L.R. 83.7-3(a). Motions for summary judgment pursuant to FRCP 56 shall be filed and served within twenty-one (21) days following the close of discovery. The filing of a FRCP 56 motion shall defer further proceedings under NY R USDCTND L.R. 83.7 pending decision on the motion. NY R USDCTND L.R. 83.7-3(a).

         •   *Relief from referral.* Any party shall request relief from the operation of NY R USDCTND L.R. 83.7 by filing with the Court a motion for the relief within twenty-one (21) days after entry of the initial stipulated consent order which refers the case for arbitration. The assigned judge shall, sua sponte, exempt an action from the application of NY R USDCTND L.R. 83.7 where the objectives of arbitration would not be realized because (1) the case involves complex or novel legal issues, (2) legal issues predominate over factual issues, or (3) for other good cause. NY R USDCTND L.R. 83.7-3(c).

      iii.   For more information on arbitration, refer to NY R USDCTND L.R. 83.7.

b.  *Mediation.* The purpose of NY R USDCTND L.R. 83.11 is to provide a supplementary procedure to the Court's existing alternative dispute resolution procedures. NY R USDCTND L.R. 83.11 provides for an earlier resolution of civil disputes resulting in savings of time and cost to litigants and the Court without sacrificing the quality of justice rendered or the right of litigants to a full trial on all issues not resolved through mediation. NY R USDCTND L.R. 83.11-1(a). Mediation is a process by which an impartial person, the mediator, facilitates communication between disputing parties to promote understanding, reconciliation and settlement. The mediator is an advocate for settlement and uses the mediation process to help the parties fully explore any potential area of agreement. The mediator does not serve as a judge or arbitrator and has no authority to render any decision on any disputed issue or to force a settlement. The parties themselves are responsible for negotiating any resolution(s) to their dispute. NY R USDCTND L.R. 83.11-1(b).

   i.  *Actions subject to mediation.* The Court may refer any civil action (or any portion thereof) to mediation under NY R USDCTND L.R. 83.11: (1) by order of referral; or (2) on the motion of any party; or (3) by consent of the parties. NY R USDCTND L.R. 83.11-3(a).

   - *Withdrawal from mediation.* The parties may withdraw from mediation any civil action or claim that the Court refers to mediation pursuant to NY R USDCTND L.R. 83.11-3 by application to the assigned judge at least ten (10) days prior to the scheduled mediation session. NY R USDCTND L.R. 83.11-3(b).

   ii.  *Mandatory mediation program.* The United States District Court for the Northern District of New York has adopted this Mandatory Mediation Plan. The paid Mediation Program is designed to provide quicker, less expensive and potentially more satisfying alternatives to continuing litigation, without impairing the quality of justice or the right to trial. NY R USDCTND Order 47(1)(1.2)(A). This Mandatory Mediation Plan applies to civil actions pending as well as newly filed actions, except as otherwise indicated in NY R USDCTND Order 47. The Local Rules for voluntary mediation will apply only to Pro Se Cases that proceed through the Assisted Mediation Program. NY R USDCTND Order 47(1)(1.2)(B).

   - *Referral into the pilot mandatory mediation program for new cases.* All civil cases shall be referred automatically into the Mandatory Mediation Program. Notice of the Mandatory Mediation requirements will be provided to all parties immediately upon the filing of a complaint and answer or a notice of removal. ADR intervention will be scheduled at the conference held pursuant to NY R USDCTND L.R. 16.1. NY R USDCTND Order 47(2)(2.1)(A). For a list of categories of actions exempted from automatic referral, refer to NY R USDCTND Order 47(2)(2.1)(A).

   - *Referral into the pilot mandatory mediation program for pending cases.* The assigned Judge or Magistrate Judge on any pending civil case may, sua sponte or with status conference, issue an order referring the case into the Mandatory Mediation Program. The order shall specify a date on which the ADR intervention is to be completed. NY R USDCTND Order 47(2)(2.1)(B).

   - *Referral into the pilot mandatory mediation program by stipulation.* A case may be referred into the Mandatory Mediation Program by stipulation of all parties. Stipulations shall be filed and shall designate the time frame within which the ADR process will be completed. Stipulations are presumed acceptable unless the assigned Judge or Magistrate Judge determines that the interests of justice are not served. NY R USDCTND Order 47(2)(2.1)(C).

   - *Relief from referral.* Motions to opt out of the program will be addressed by the assigned Magistrate Judge at the FRCP 16 conference. NY R USDCTND Order 47(2)(2.2)(A). Opting Out Motions shall be granted only for "good cause" shown. Inconvenience, travel costs, attorney fees or other costs shall not constitute "good cause." A party seeking relief from the Mandatory Mediation Program must set forth the reasons why Mandatory Mediation has no reasonable chance of being productive. NY R USDCTND Order 47(2)(2.2)(B). The assigned Magistrate Judge may, sua sponte, exempt any case from the Court's Mandatory Mediation Program. NY R USDCTND Order 47(2)(2.2)(C).

   iii.  *Assisted mediation program.* The Court may assign specially trained pro bono Special Media-

tion Counsel to assist pro se civilian litigants with preparing for and participating in mediation. The Assisted Mediation Program is open to civilian pro se parties to actions in the Northern District of New York. The assigned judge or magistrate judge determines if the case would benefit from mediation and would also benefit from the assignment of Special Mediation Counsel to assist the pro se party with the mediation process. NY R USDCTND L.R. 83.8(a). Appointment of Special Mediation Counsel is in no way guaranteed, even if the action is referred to the court-annexed mediation program. Appointment is at the sole discretion of the presiding judge. NY R USDCTND L.R. 83.8(a).

- *Referral to assisted mediation program.* If the court determines that referral to the Assisted Mediation Program is appropriate, the Court shall enter an order of reference to the Assisted Mediation Program. NY R USDCTND L.R. 83.8(b).

iv. For more information on mediation, refer to NY R USDCTND L.R. 83.11 and NY R USDCTND Order 47.

c. *Early neutral evaluation (ENE).* Early neutral evaluation (ENE) is a process in which parties obtain from an experienced neutral (an "evaluator") a nonbinding, reasoned, oral evaluation of the merits of the case. The first step in the ENE process involves the Court appointing an evaluator who has expertise in the area of law in the case. After the parties exchange essential information and position statements early in the pretrial period (usually within one hundred fifty (150) to two hundred (200) days after a complaint has been filed), the evaluator convenes an ENE session that typically lasts about two hours. At the ENE meeting, each side briefly presents the factual and legal basis of its position. The evaluator may ask questions of the parties and help them identify the main issues in dispute and the areas of agreement. The evaluator may also help the parties explore options for settlement. If settlement does not occur, the evaluator then offers an opinion as to the settlement value of the case, including the likelihood of liability and the likely range of damages. With the benefit of this assessment, the parties are again encouraged to discuss settlement, with or without the evaluator's assistance. The parties may also explore ways to narrow the issues in dispute, exchange information about the case or otherwise prepare efficiently for trial. NY R USDCTND L.R. 83.12-1.

i. *Actions subject to early neutral evaluation.* The Court may refer any civil action (or any portion thereof) to ENE under NY R USDCTND L.R. 83.12: (1) by order of referral; (2) on the motion of any party; or (3) by consent of the parties. NY R USDCTND L.R. 83.12-3(a).

- *Withdrawal from the ENE process.* The parties may withdraw any civil action or claim that the Court has referred to the ENE Process pursuant to NY R USDCTND L.R. 83.12-3 by application to the assigned judge at least ten (10) days before the scheduled evaluation session. NY R USDCTND L.R. 83.12-3(b).

ii. For more information on early neutral evaluation (ENE), refer to NY R USDCTND L.R. 83.12.

13. *Settlement procedures.* On notice to the Court or the Clerk that the parties have settled an action, and upon confirmation of the settlement by all parties, the Court may issue a judgment dismissing the action by reason of settlement. The Court shall issue the order without prejudice to the parties' right to secure reinstatement of the case within thirty (30) days after the date of judgment by making a showing that the settlement was not, in fact, consummated. NY R USDCTND L.R. 68.2(a). If the Court decides not to follow the procedures set forth in NY R USDCTND L.R. 68.2(a), the parties shall file within thirty (30) days of the notification to the Court, unless otherwise directed by written order, such notices, stipulations and/or motions as are necessary to terminate the action. If the required documents are not filed within the thirty (30) day period, the Clerk shall place the action on the dismissal calendar. NY R USDCTND L.R. 68.2(b).

14. *Sanctions and penalties for noncompliance.* Failure of an attorney or of a party to comply with any provision of the Local Rules of Practice for the United States District Court for the Northern District of New York, General Orders of this District, Orders of the Court, or the Federal Rules of Civil Procedure shall be a ground for imposition of sanctions. NY R USDCTND L.R. 1.1(d).

15. *Individual judge practices.* Refer to the Miscellaneous section of this document for information on individual judge practices on general requirements for documents.

## D. Documents

1. *Documents for moving party*

   a. *Required documents*

      i. *Notice of motion and motion.* In the Notice of Motion, the moving party is required to set forth the date that the court conference with the Magistrate Judge was held regarding the issues being presented in the motion. Failure to include this information in the Notice of Motion may result in the Court rejecting the motion papers. NY R USDCTND L.R. 7.1(b)(2). Refer to the General Requirements section of this document for information on the notice of motion and motion.

         - *Order to show cause.* Refer to the General Requirements section of this document for information on bringing a motion by order to show cause.

      ii. *Memorandum of law.* Except as otherwise provided in NY R USDCTND L.R. 7.1(a), all motions. . .require a memorandum of law. NY R USDCTND L.R. 7.1(a). Refer to the Format section of this document for the formatting requirements for memoranda of law.

      iii. *Certificate of service.* Except as otherwise provided in NY R USDCTND L.R. 7.1(a), all motions. . .require. . .proof of service on all the parties. See NY R USDCTND L.R. 5.1(a). NY R USDCTND L.R. 7.1(a). FRCP 5(d) requires that the person making service under FRCP 5 certify that service has been effected. FRCP 5(Advisory Committee Notes). Having such information on file may be useful for many purposes, including proof of service if an issue arises concerning the effectiveness of the service. FRCP 5(Advisory Committee Notes). The party or its designee shall declare, by affidavit or certification, that it has provided all other parties in the action with all documents it has filed with the Court. NY R USDCTND L.R. 5.1(a).

         - Attorneys and pro se parties who are not Filing or Receiving Users must be served with a paper copy of any electronically filed pleading or other document. NY R USDCTND CM/ECF(5)(5.2). Such paper service must be documented by electronically filing a certificate of service. NY R USDCTND CM/ECF(5)(5.2).

   b. *Supplemental documents.* Matter outside the pleadings normally is not considered on a FRCP 12(f) motion; for example, affidavits in support of or in opposition to the motion typically may not be used. FPP § 1380.

      i. *Deposition.* Notwithstanding the general rule that matters outside the pleadings should ordinarily not be considered in passing upon a motion to strike under FRCP 12(f), a court may consider a deposition in deciding a FRCP 12(f) motion if the attorneys for both the plaintiff and the defendant, in their respective briefs, refer to the deposition and to the testimony contained therein. FEDPROC § 62:407.

      ii. *Notice of constitutional question.* A party that files a pleading, written motion, or other paper drawing into question the constitutionality of a federal or state statute must promptly:

         - *File notice.* File a notice of constitutional question stating the question and identifying the paper that raises it, if: (1) a federal statute is questioned and the parties do not include the United States, one of its agencies, or one of its officers or employees in an official capacity; or (2) a state statute is questioned and the parties do not include the state, one of its agencies, or one of its officers or employees in an official capacity; and

         - *Serve notice.* Serve the notice and paper on the Attorney General of the United States if a federal statute is questioned—or on the state attorney general if a state statute is questioned—either by certified or registered mail or by sending it to an electronic address designated by the attorney general for this purpose. FRCP 5.1(a).

         - *No forfeiture.* A party's failure to file and serve the notice, or the court's failure to certify, does not forfeit a constitutional claim or defense that is otherwise timely asserted. FRCP 5.1(d).

      iii. *Nongovernmental corporate disclosure statement*

         - *Contents.* A nongovernmental corporate party must file two (2) copies of a disclosure statement that: (1) identifies any parent corporation and any publicly held corporation owning ten percent (10%) or more of its stock; or (2) states that there is no such corporation. FRCP 7.1(a).

- *Time to file; Supplemental filing.* A party must: (1) file the disclosure statement with its first appearance, pleading, petition, motion, response, or other request addressed to the court; and (2) promptly file a supplemental statement if any required information changes. FRCP 7.1(b).

iv. *Copies of authorities.* When serving a pro se litigant with a memorandum of law or any other paper which contains citations to authorities that are unpublished or published exclusively on electronic databases, counsel shall include a hard copy of those authorities. Although copies of authorities published only on electronic databases are not required to be filed, copies shall be provided upon request to opposing counsel who lack access to electronic databases. NY R USDCTND L.R. 7.1(a)(1).

v. *Proposed order.* A document that is submitted in .pdf format cannot be modified; therefore, a proposed order or stipulation must be in a word processing format. The chambers of the assigned judge may request that a proposed order and/or a stipulation be e-mailed to the courtroom deputy for the presiding judge in either WordPerfect or Microsoft Word format. Please attach your proposed order and/or stipulation to an Internet e-mail sent to the appropriate e-mail address listed in NY R USDCTND CM/ECF(8)(8.2). NY R USDCTND CM/ECF(8)(8.2).

vi. *Cover letter authorizing e-mail or facsimile filing.* Neither the Court nor the Clerk's Office will accept for filing any facsimile or e-mail transmission without prior authorization from the Court. The party using facsimile or e-mail transmissions to file its papers must accompany any such documents with a cover letter stating that the Court authorized such transmissions and the date on which the Court provided that authorization. Violations of NY R USDCTND L.R. 5.5 subject the offending party to the Court's full disciplinary powers. NY R USDCTND L.R. 5.5.

vii. *Affidavit attesting to failed attempts to file electronically.* If the Court's CM/ECF site experiences a technical failure, a Filing User may submit documents to the Court that day in an alternate manner provided that the documents are accompanied by the Filing User's affidavit stating that the Filing User attempted to file electronically at least two times in one (1) hour increments after 10:00 a.m. that day. The following methods are acceptable alternate means for filing documents in case of a technical failure: (1) via electronic mail in a PDF attachment sent to the e-mail address for technical failures; or (2) in person, by bringing the document to the Clerk's Office on paper accompanied by a CD/ROM that contains the document in .pdf format. NY R USDCTND CM/ECF(10)(10.1).

- A Filing User who cannot file documents electronically because of a problem on the Filing User's system must file the documents' conventionally along with an affidavit explaining the reason for not filing the documents electronically. NY R USDCTND CM/ECF(10)(10.2).

viii. *Notice of conventional filing.* If the Clerk's Office grants permission to conventionally file the document, the Filing User shall electronically file a notice of conventional filing for the documents. More information regarding this process can be obtained from the Court's web page. NY R USDCTND CM/ECF(4)(4.5).

ix. *CD/ROM with PDF of document(s).* If the Court grants permission to file a document traditionally, the attorney must submit the documents for filing to the Clerk's Office on CD/ROM in .pdf or pdf.A format. NY R USDCTND CM/ECF(2).

x. *English translation.* The Court conducts its reviews and deliberations in English. Unless otherwise directed by the Court, any document that a party transmits to the Court (including one in the record on appeal) that is in a language other than English must be accompanied by an English translation that the translator has certified as true and accurate, pursuant to 28 U.S.C.A. § 1746. NY R USDCTND L.R. 10.1(e). For more information, refer to NY R USDCTND L.R. 10.1(e).

    xi.  *Courtesy copies.* The Court may require that courtesy copies of electronically filed documents be submitted for its review and may amend these Administrative Procedures (NY R USDCTND CM/ECF) at any time without prior notice. NY R USDCTND CM/ECF(2).

    xii.  *Copies for three-judge court.* On the convening of a three-judge court, the parties shall make three (3) copies of all non-electronically filed pleadings, motion papers, and memoranda of law available to the Clerk for distribution. NY R USDCTND L.R. 9.1.

2.  *Documents for opposing party*

  a.  *Required documents*

    i.  *Opposition.* Refer to the General Requirements section of this document for information on the opposing papers.

    ii.  *Memorandum of law.* Except as otherwise provided in NY R USDCTND L.R. 7.1(a), all. . .opposition to motions require a memorandum of law. NY R USDCTND L.R. 7.1(a).

- *Cross-motion brief.* If a party makes a cross-motion, it must join its cross motion brief with its opposition brief, and this combined brief may not exceed twenty-five (25) pages in length, exclusive of exhibits. A separate brief in opposition to the original motion is not permissible. NY R USDCTND L.R. 7.1(c).

- Refer to the Format section of this document for the formatting requirements for memoranda of law.

    iii.  *Certificate of service.* Except as otherwise provided in NY R USDCTND L.R. 7.1(a), all. . .opposition to motions require. . .proof of service on all the parties. See NY R USDCTND L.R. 5.1(a). NY R USDCTND L.R. 7.1(a). FRCP 5(d) requires that the person making service under FRCP 5 certify that service has been effected. FRCP 5(Advisory Committee Notes). Having such information on file may be useful for many purposes, including proof of service if an issue arises concerning the effectiveness of the service. FRCP 5(Advisory Committee Notes). The party or its designee shall declare, by affidavit or certification, that it has provided all other parties in the action with all documents it has filed with the Court. NY R USDCTND L.R. 5.1(a).

- Attorneys and pro se parties who are not Filing or Receiving Users must be served with a paper copy of any electronically filed pleading or other document. NY R USDCTND CM/ECF(5)(5.2). Such paper service must be documented by electronically filing a certificate of service. NY R USDCTND CM/ECF(5)(5.2).

  b.  *Supplemental documents.* Matter outside the pleadings normally is not considered on a FRCP 12(f) motion; for example, affidavits in support of or in opposition to the motion typically may not be used. FPP § 1380.

    i.  *Deposition.* Notwithstanding the general rule that matters outside the pleadings should ordinarily not be considered in passing upon a motion to strike under FRCP 12(f), a court may consider a deposition in deciding a FRCP 12(f) motion if the attorneys for both the plaintiff and the defendant, in their respective briefs, refer to the deposition and to the testimony contained therein. FEDPROC § 62:407.

    ii.  *Notice of constitutional question.* A party that files a pleading, written motion, or other paper drawing into question the constitutionality of a federal or state statute must promptly:

- *File notice.* File a notice of constitutional question stating the question and identifying the paper that raises it, if: (1) a federal statute is questioned and the parties do not include the United States, one of its agencies, or one of its officers or employees in an official capacity; or (2) a state statute is questioned and the parties do not include the state, one of its agencies, or one of its officers or employees in an official capacity; and

- *Serve notice.* Serve the notice and paper on the Attorney General of the United States if a federal statute is questioned—or on the state attorney general if a state statute is questioned—either by certified or registered mail or by sending it to an electronic address designated by the attorney general for this purpose. FRCP 5.1(a).

- *No forfeiture.* A party's failure to file and serve the notice, or the court's failure to certify, does not forfeit a constitutional claim or defense that is otherwise timely asserted. FRCP 5.1(d).

iii. *Cross-motion.* A party may file and serve a cross-motion (meaning a competing request for relief or order similar to that requested by another party against the cross-moving party) at the time it files and serves its opposition papers to the original motion, i.e., not less than SEVENTEEN (17) DAYS prior to the return date of the motion. NY R USDCTND L.R. 7.1(c).

iv. *Copies of authorities.* When serving a pro se litigant with a memorandum of law or any other paper which contains citations to authorities that are unpublished or published exclusively on electronic databases, counsel shall include a hard copy of those authorities. Although copies of authorities published only on electronic databases are not required to be filed, copies shall be provided upon request to opposing counsel who lack access to electronic databases. NY R USDCTND L.R. 7.1(a)(1).

v. *Cover letter authorizing e-mail or facsimile filing.* Neither the Court nor the Clerk's Office will accept for filing any facsimile or e-mail transmission without prior authorization from the Court. The party using facsimile or e-mail transmissions to file its papers must accompany any such documents with a cover letter stating that the Court authorized such transmissions and the date on which the Court provided that authorization. Violations of NY R USDCTND L.R. 5.5 subject the offending party to the Court's full disciplinary powers. NY R USDCTND L.R. 5.5.

vi. *Affidavit attesting to failed attempts to file electronically.* If the Court's CM/ECF site experiences a technical failure, a Filing User may submit documents to the Court that day in an alternate manner provided that the documents are accompanied by the Filing User's affidavit stating that the Filing User attempted to file electronically at least two times in one (1) hour increments after 10:00 a.m. that day. The following methods are acceptable alternate means for filing documents in case of a technical failure: (1) via electronic mail in a PDF attachment sent to the e-mail address for technical failures; or (2) in person, by bringing the document to the Clerk's Office on paper accompanied by a CD/ROM that contains the document in .pdf format. NY R USDCTND CM/ECF(10)(10.1).

  - A Filing User who cannot file documents electronically because of a problem on the Filing User's system must file the documents' conventionally along with an affidavit explaining the reason for not filing the documents electronically. NY R USDCTND CM/ECF(10)(10.2).

vii. *Notice of conventional filing.* If the Clerk's Office grants permission to conventionally file the document, the Filing User shall electronically file a notice of conventional filing for the documents. More information regarding this process can be obtained from the Court's web page. NY R USDCTND CM/ECF(4)(4.5).

viii. *CD/ROM with PDF of document(s).* If the Court grants permission to file a document traditionally, the attorney must submit the documents for filing to the Clerk's Office on CD/ROM in .pdf or pdf.A format. NY R USDCTND CM/ECF(2).

ix. *English translation.* The Court conducts its reviews and deliberations in English. Unless otherwise directed by the Court, any document that a party transmits to the Court (including one in the record on appeal) that is in a language other than English must be accompanied by an English translation that the translator has certified as true and accurate, pursuant to 28 U.S.C.A. § 1746. NY R USDCTND L.R. 10.1(e). For more information, refer to NY R USDCTND L.R. 10.1(e).

x. *Courtesy copies.* The Court may require that courtesy copies of electronically filed documents be submitted for its review and may amend these Administrative Procedures (NY R USDCTND CM/ECF) at any time without prior notice. NY R USDCTND CM/ECF(2).

xi. *Copies for three-judge court.* On the convening of a three-judge court, the parties shall make three (3) copies of all non-electronically filed pleadings, motion papers, and memoranda of law available to the Clerk for distribution. NY R USDCTND L.R. 9.1.

3. *Individual judge practices.* Refer to the Miscellaneous section of this document for information on individual judge practices on required documents.

## E. Format

1. *Form of documents.* The rules governing captions and other matters of form in pleadings apply to motions and other papers. FRCP 7(b)(2). All pleadings and other papers shall be served and filed in accordance with the Federal Rules of Civil Procedure and shall be in the form prescribed by NY R USDCTND L.R. 10.1. NY R USDCTND L.R. 5.1(a).

   a. *Form, generally.* All pleadings, motions, and other documents that a party presents for filing, whether in paper form or in electronic form, shall meet the following requirements:

      i. *Font size.* All text, whether in the body of the document or in footnotes, must be a minimum of twelve (12) point type. NY R USDCTND L.R. 10.1(a)(1).

      ii. *Margins.* All documents must have one (1) inch margins on all four sides of the page. NY R USDCTND L.R. 10.1(a)(2).

      iii. *Spacing.* All text in the body of the document must be double-spaced. NY R USDCTND L.R. 10.1(a)(3).

         • The text in block quotations and footnotes may be single-spaced. NY R USDCTND L.R. 10.1(a)(4).

      iv. *Page numbering.* Pages must be consecutively numbered. NY R USDCTND L.R. 10.1(a)(7).

      v. *Circumventing formatting limitations*

         • Extensive footnotes must not be used to circumvent page limitations. NY R USDCTND L.R. 10.1(a)(5).

         • Compacted or other compressed printing features must not be used. NY R USDCTND L.R. 10.1(a)(6).

   b. *Additional requirements for paper filing.* Additional requirements for all pleadings, motions, and other documents that a party presents for filing in paper form:

      i. *Paper size.* All documents must be on eight and one-half by eleven (8-1/2 x 11) inch white paper of good quality. NY R USDCTND L.R. 10.1(b)(1).

      ii. *Text.* All text must be plainly and legibly written, typewritten, printed or reproduced without erasures or interlineations materially defacing them. NY R USDCTND L.R. 10.1(b)(2).

      iii. *Ink.* All documents must be in black or blue ink. NY R USDCTND L.R. 10.1(b)(3).

      iv. *Binding.* Pages of all documents must be stapled (or in some other way fastened) together. NY R USDCTND L.R. 10.1(b)(4).

      v. *Single-sided paper.* All documents must be single-sided. NY R USDCTND L.R. 10.1(b)(5).

      vi. *Electronic submission.* The Court, at its discretion, may require the electronic submission of any document in a WordPerfect-compatible format. NY R USDCTND L.R. 10.1(b)(6).

      vii. *Rejection of document.* The Court may reject documents that do not comply with the above-listed requirements. NY R USDCTND L.R. 10.1(b).

   c. *Caption; Names of parties.* Every pleading must have a caption with the court's name, a title, a file number, and a FRCP 7(a) designation. The title of the complaint must name all the parties; the title of other pleadings, after naming the first party on each side, may refer generally to other parties. FRCP 10(a). Each document must contain a caption for the specific case to which it pertains. The caption must include the title of the Court, the title of the action, the civil action number of the case, the initials of the assigned judge(s), and the name or nature of the paper in sufficient detail for identification. If a litigant has more than one action pending in this Court, any and all papers filed in a case must contain and pertain to one civil action number, unless the civil actions have been consolidated by the Court. Any motion or other papers purporting to relate to more than one action will not be accepted for filing and may be stricken by the Court. NY R USDCTND L.R. 10.1(c)(1) shall not apply, as noted in NY R USDCTND L.R. 10.1(c), to notices of change of address filed by attorneys of record and pro se litigants. The parties must separately caption affidavits and declarations and must not physically attach them to the Notice of Motion or Memorandum of Law. NY R USDCTND L.R. 10.1(c)(1).

d. *Paragraphs; Separate statements.* A party must state its claims or defenses in numbered paragraphs, each limited as far as practicable to a single set of circumstances. A later pleading may refer by number to a paragraph in an earlier pleading. If doing so would promote clarity, each claim founded on a separate transaction or occurrence—and each defense other than a denial—must be stated in a separate count or defense. FRCP 10(b).

e. *Adoption by reference; Exhibits.* A statement in a pleading may be adopted by reference elsewhere in the same pleading or in any other pleading or motion. A copy of a written instrument that is an exhibit to a pleading is a part of the pleading for all purposes. FRCP 10(c).

f. *Citation of local rules.* These are the Local Rules of Practice for the United States District Court for the Northern District of New York. They shall be cited as "L.R. ___." NY R USDCTND L.R. 1.1(a).

g. *Acceptance by the clerk.* The clerk must not refuse to file a paper solely because it is not in the form prescribed by the Federal Rules of Civil Procedure or by a local rule or practice. FRCP 5(d)(4).

2. *Form of electronic documents.* All pleadings, motions, and other documents that a party presents for filing, whether in paper form or in electronic form, shall meet the requirements in NY R USDCTND L.R. 10.1(a). NY R USDCTND L.R. 10.1(a). Refer above for more information.

a. *Attachments and exhibits.* A Filing User must submit in electronic form all documents referenced as exhibits or attachments in accordance with the Court's CM/ECF Users Manual unless the Court otherwise orders. A Filing User shall submit as exhibits or attachments only those excerpts of the referenced documents that are directly germane to the matter under the Court's consideration. Excerpted material must be clearly and prominently identified as such. Filing Users who file excerpts of documents as exhibits or attachments under these Administrative Procedures (NY R USDCTND CM/ECF) do so without prejudice to their right to timely file additional excerpts or the complete document. Responding parties may also timely file the complete document or additional excerpts that they believe are directly germane to the matter under the Court's consideration. NY R USDCTND CM/ECF(4)(4.4).

   i. All attachments must be described in sufficient detail so the Court and opposing counsel can easily identify and distinguish the filed attachments. Vague or general descriptions are insufficient (i.e., "Exhibit 1"). Rather, each attachment shall have a descriptive title identifying, with specificity, the document that is being filed (i.e., "Exhibit 12 Mulligan County Fire Investigation Report.") Failure to adequately describe attachments may result in the document being rejected by the Court. NY R USDCTND CM/ECF(4)(4.4).

b. *Large documents.* For information on the electronic filing of large documents, please consult the Court's CM/ECF Users Manual, which is available on the Court's web page. NY R USDCTND CM/ECF(4)(4.5).

   i. A party who believes a document is too lengthy to electronically image, i.e., "scan," may contact the Clerk's Office for permission to file that document conventionally. If the Clerk's Office grants permission to conventionally file the document, the Filing User shall electronically file a notice of conventional filing for the documents. More information regarding this process can be obtained from the Court's web page. Exhibits submitted conventionally shall be served on other parties as if they were not subject to these Administrative Procedures (NY R USDCTND CM/ECF). For a list of hints and tips for scanning large documents, please consult the Court's web page. NY R USDCTND CM/ECF(4)(4.5).

c. *Legibility.* It shall be the Filing User's responsibility to verify the legibility of scanned documents before filing them electronically with the Court. NY R USDCTND CM/ECF(4)(4.6).

d. *Color documents.* Since documents scanned in color or containing a graphic take much longer to upload, Filing Users are encouraged to configure their scanners to scan documents at 300 dpi and preferably in black and white rather than in color. NY R USDCTND CM/ECF(4)(4.7).

e. *Items not in .PDF format.* Parties wishing to file items not amenable to .pdf format (i.e. CD's,

DVD's), shall file such items conventionally with the Clerk's Office. The Filing User shall electronically file a notice of conventional filing indicating that these items have been submitted to the clerk and shall serve copies of these items on other parties as if they were not subject to these Administrative Procedures (NY R USDCTND CM/ECF). These item(s) will be maintained by the Clerk's Office until the case is disposed, at which time they will be returned to the filing party for retention consistent with NY R USDCTND CM/ECF(4)(4.9). NY R USDCTND CM/ECF(4)(4.8).

3. *Form of memoranda of law*

   a. *Length limitation.* No party shall file or serve a memorandum of law that exceeds twenty-five (25) pages in length, unless that party obtains leave of the judge hearing the motion prior to filing. NY R USDCTND L.R. 7.1(a)(1).

   b. *Table of contents.* All memoranda of law shall contain a table of contents. NY R USDCTND L.R. 7.1(a)(1).

4. *Signing of pleadings, motions and other papers*

   a. *Signature.* Every pleading, written motion, and other paper must be signed by at least one attorney of record in the attorney's name—or by a party personally if the party is unrepresented. The paper must state the signer's address, e-mail address, and telephone number. FRCP 11(a). Each document must identify the person filing the document. This identification must include an original signature of the attorney or pro se litigant; the typewritten name of that person; the address of a pro se litigant; and the bar roll number, office address, telephone number, e-mail address and fax number of the attorney. Telephone numbers of non-prisoner pro se parties may be provided voluntarily or upon request of the Court. See General Order #22 (NY R USDCTND CM/ECF) for signature requirements. NY R USDCTND L.R. 10.1(c)(2).

      i. *Electronic signatures.* Documents filed under an attorney's login and password shall constitute that attorney's signature for purposes of the Local Rules of Practice for the United States District Court for the Northern District of New York and Federal Rules of Civil Procedure, including but not limited to FRCP 11. A pleading or other document requiring an attorney's signature shall be signed in the following manner, whether filed electronically or submitted on disk or CD/ROM to the Clerk's Office: "s/ (attorney name)." The correct format for an attorney signature is found in NY R USDCTND CM/ECF(6)(6.1). NY R USDCTND CM/ECF(6)(6.1).

         • *Non-attorney signature.* If an original document requires the signature of a non-attorney, the Filing User may scan the original document containing the original signature(s), then electronically file it on the System. Alternatively, the Filing User may convert the document into .pdf text format and submit the document using "s/" for the signature of the non-attorney. NY R USDCTND CM/ECF(6)(6.2).

         • *Multiple signatures.* A document requiring signatures of more than one party must be filed electronically either by (1) submitting a scanned document containing all necessary signatures; (2) representing the consent of the other parties on the document; or (3) in any other manner that the Court approves. NY R USDCTND CM/ECF(6)(6.3).

      ii. *No verification or accompanying affidavit required for pleadings.* Unless a rule or statute specifically states otherwise, a pleading need not be verified or accompanied by an affidavit. FRCP 11(a).

      iii. *Unsigned papers.* The court must strike an unsigned paper unless the omission is promptly corrected after being called to the attorney's or party's attention. FRCP 11(a).

   b. *Representations to the court.* By presenting to the court a pleading, written motion, or other paper—whether by signing, filing, submitting, or later advocating it—an attorney or unrepresented party certifies that to the best of the person's knowledge, information, and belief, formed after an inquiry reasonable under the circumstances:

      i. It is not being presented for any improper purpose, such as to harass, cause unnecessary delay, or needlessly increase the cost of litigation;

      ii. The claims, defenses, and other legal contentions are warranted by existing law or by a nonfrivolous argument for extending, modifying, or reversing existing law or for establishing new law;

    iii.   The factual contentions have evidentiary support or, if specifically so identified, will likely have evidentiary support after a reasonable opportunity for further investigation or discovery; and

    iv.   The denials of factual contentions are warranted on the evidence or, if specifically so identified, are reasonably based on belief or a lack of information. FRCP 11(b).

  c.   *Sanctions.* If, after notice and a reasonable opportunity to respond, the court determines that FRCP 11(b) has been violated, the court may impose an appropriate sanction on any attorney, law firm, or party that violated FRCP 11(b) or is responsible for the violation. FRCP 11(c)(1). Refer to the United States District Court for the Northern District of New York KeyRules Motion for Sanctions document for more information.

5.  *Privacy protection for filings made with the court*

  a.   *Redacted filings.* Unless the court orders otherwise, in an electronic or paper filing with the court that contains an individual's Social Security number, taxpayer-identification number, or birth date, the name of an individual known to be a minor, or a financial-account number, a party or nonparty making the filing may include only:

    i.   The last four (4) digits of the Social Security number and taxpayer-identification number;

    ii.   The year of the individual's birth;

    iii.   The minor's initials; and

    iv.   The last four (4) digits of the financial-account number. FRCP 5.2(a); NY R USDCTND L.R. 8.1; NY R USDCTND CM/ECF(11)(11.2).

    v.   If a home address must be used, use only the City and State. NY R USDCTND L.R. 8.1; NY R USDCTND CM/ECF(11)(11.2).

    vi.   If the victim of a sexual assault must be referenced, redact the name to 'Victim.' NY R USDCTND CM/ECF(11)(11.2); NY R USDCTND L.R. 8.1.

    vii.   In addition, caution shall be exercised when filing documents that contain the following:

- Personal identifying number, such as a driver's license number;

- Medical records, treatment and diagnosis;

- Employment history;

- Individual financial information; and

- Proprietary or trade secret information. NY R USDCTND L.R. 8.1; NY R USDCTND CM/ECF(11)(11.2).

  b.   *Exemptions from the redaction requirement.* The redaction requirement does not apply to the following:

    i.   A financial-account number that identifies the property allegedly subject to forfeiture in a forfeiture proceeding;

    ii.   The record of an administrative or agency proceeding;

    iii.   The official record of a state-court proceeding;

    iv.   The record of a court or tribunal, if that record was not subject to the redaction requirement when originally filed;

    v.   A filing covered by FRCP 5.2(c) or FRCP 5.2(d); and

    vi.   A pro se filing in an action brought under 28 U.S.C.A. § 2241, 28 U.S.C.A. § 2254, or 28 U.S.C.A. § 2255. FRCP 5.2(b).

    vii.   Transcripts of the administrative record in social security proceedings are exempt from this requirement. State court records and other documents filed in habeas corpus proceedings are exempt from this requirement except for proceedings that involve victims of sex crimes. In habeas corpus cases involving sex crimes, the parties must redact the record and supporting papers, or may move to seal, if appropriate. NY R USDCTND L.R. 8.1.

c. *Limitations on remote access to electronic files; Social Security appeals and immigration cases.* Unless the court orders otherwise, in an action for benefits under the Social Security Act, and in an action or proceeding relating to an order of removal, to relief from removal, or to immigration benefits or detention, access to an electronic file is authorized as follows:

   i. The parties and their attorneys may have remote electronic access to any part of the case file, including the administrative record;

   ii. Any other person may have electronic access to the full record at the courthouse, but may have remote electronic access only to:

      • The docket maintained by the court; and

      • An opinion, order, judgment, or other disposition of the court, but not any other part of the case file or the administrative record. FRCP 5.2(c).

d. *Filings made under seal.* The court may order that a filing be made under seal without redaction. The court may later unseal the filing or order the person who made the filing to file a redacted version for the public record. FRCP 5.2(d); NY R USDCTND L.R. 8.1. For information on sealed matters, refer to NY R USDCTND L.R. 83.13 and NY R USDCTND CM/ECF(12).

e. *Protective orders.* For good cause, the court may by order in a case:

   i. Require redaction of additional information; or

   ii. Limit or prohibit a nonparty's remote electronic access to a document filed with the court. FRCP 5.2(e).

f. *Option for additional unredacted filing under seal.* A person making a redacted filing may also file an unredacted copy under seal. The court must retain the unredacted copy as part of the record. FRCP 5.2(f); NY R USDCTND L.R. 8.1; NY R USDCTND CM/ECF(11)(11.3).

g. *Option for filing a reference list.* A filing that contains redacted information may be filed together with a reference list that identifies each item of redacted information and specifies an appropriate identifier that uniquely corresponds to each item listed. The list must be filed under seal and may be amended as of right. Any reference in the case to a listed identifier will be construed to refer to the corresponding item of information. FRCP 5.2(g); NY R USDCTND L.R. 8.1; NY R USDCTND CM/ECF(11)(11.3).

h. *Responsibility for redaction.* Counsel is strongly urged to discuss this issue with all their clients so that they can make an informed decision about the inclusion of certain information. The responsibility for redacting these personal identifiers rests solely with counsel and the parties. The Clerk will not review each filing for compliance with NY R USDCTND L.R. 8.1. Counsel and the parties are cautioned that failure to redact these personal identifiers may subject them to the Court's full disciplinary power. NY R USDCTND L.R. 8.1; NY R USDCTND CM/ECF(11)(11.3).

i. *Waiver of protection of identifiers.* A person waives the protection of FRCP 5.2(a) as to the person's own information by filing it without redaction and not under seal. FRCP 5.2(h).

6. *Individual judge practices.* Refer to the Miscellaneous section of this document for information on individual judge practices on formatting documents.

## F. Filing and Service Requirements

1. *Filing requirements.* Any paper after the complaint that is required to be served—together with a certificate of service—must be filed within a reasonable time after service. FRCP 5(d)(1).

a. *How filing is made; In general.* A paper is filed by delivering it:

   i. To the clerk; or

   ii. To a judge who agrees to accept it for filing, and who must then note the filing date on the paper and promptly send it to the clerk. FRCP 5(d)(2).

b. *Electronic filing*

   i. *Authorization of electronic filing program.* A court may, by local rule, allow papers to be filed, signed, or verified by electronic means that are consistent with any technical standards established by the Judicial Conference of the United States. A local rule may require electronic filing only if reasonable exceptions are allowed. A paper filed electronically in compliance with a local rule is a written paper for purposes of the Federal Rules of Civil Procedure. FRCP 5(d)(3).

- All cases filed in this Court may be assigned to the Electronic Case Files System ("ECF") in accordance with the Procedural Order on Electronic Case Filing (General Order #22 (NY R USDCTND CM/ECF)), the provisions of which are incorporated herein by reference, and which the Court may amend from time to time. Copies of General Order #22 (NY R USDCTND CM/ECF) are available at the Clerk's office or at the Court's webpage. NY R USDCTND L.R. 5.1.1; NY R USDCTND Order 25(XII).

- The Court may deviate from these Administrative Procedures (NY R USDCTND CM/ECF) in specific cases, without prior notice, if deemed appropriate in the exercise of discretion, considering the need for the just, speedy, and inexpensive determination of matters pending before the Court. NY R USDCTND CM/ECF(2).

ii. *Scope of electronic filing.* After January 1, 2004, all documents that attorneys admitted to practice in the Northern District of New York submit for filing shall be filed electronically using the System or shall be scanned and uploaded to the System, no matter when a case was originally filed, unless these Administrative Procedures (NY R USDCTND CM/ECF) otherwise permit or unless the assigned judge otherwise authorizes. An attorney who is not a Filing User by January 1, 2004, must show good cause to the assigned judge to file and serve pleadings and other papers in the traditional manner. NY R USDCTND CM/ECF(2).

iii. *Exceptions and/or waivers from mandatory electronic filing.* The following types of cases and/or documents are not required to be filed electronically:

- If you are seeking to have your complaint filed under seal, please file your complaint and proposed sealing order traditionally at the Clerk's Office. NY R USDCTND CM/ECF(2)(2.1)(1).

- Any document that a party proceeding pro se files. (See NY R USDCTND CM/ECF(12)(12.1) for procedural details). NY R USDCTND CM/ECF(2)(2.1)(2). A non-prisoner who is a party to a civil action and who is not represented by an attorney may file a motion to obtain an Electronic Case Filing (ECF) login and password on a form prescribed by the Clerk's Office. The Pro Se CM/ECF Registration Form shall be submitted with the motion. If during the course of the action an attorney appears on behalf of the pro se party, the Clerk's Office shall terminate the pro se party's registration based upon the attorney's appearance. NY R USDCTND CM/ECF(12)(12.1). Absent permission to file electronically, pro se filers shall file paper originals of all complaints, pleadings, motions, affidavits, briefs, and other documents which must be signed or which require either verification or an unsworn declaration under any rule or statute. The Clerk's Office will scan these original documents into an electronic file in the System but will also maintain a paper file. NY R USDCTND CM/ECF(12)(12.1). A pro se party may also seek permission to receive immediate notice of all public documents filed in their cases. Notices of Electronic Filing (NEF) and attached documents would be transmitted to a non-prisoner pro se party who selects this option. Note: The pro se party would continue to file their documents with the Clerk's Office in paper form. NY R USDCTND CM/ECF(12)(12.1).

- Sealed documents, sealed cases, documents for in camera review, documents lodged with the Court, ex parte documents, confidential agreements, Qui Tam actions and Grand Jury material and warrants must be filed traditionally. (See NY R USDCTND CM/ECF(12)(12.2) for further information the filing of the above-referenced documents). NY R USDCTND CM/ECF(2)(2.1)(3).

- Discovery: In accordance with NY R USDCTND L.R. 26.2, parties shall not file discovery, provided, however, that discovery material to be used at trial or in support of any motion, including a motion to compel or for summary judgment, shall be filed electronically with the Court prior to the trial or with the motion. Any motion pursuant to FRCP 37 shall be accompanied by the electronically filed discovery materials to which the motion relates if those materials have not previously been filed with the Court. NY R USDCTND CM/ECF(2)(2.1)(4).

- Transport Orders: All orders requesting that an incarcerated individual be transported that a judicial officer of the Northern District of New York signs shall be filed traditionally. These Orders will not be filed with the case or uploaded to the docket but rather will be processed in accordance with the procedures that the Clerk of Court promulgates. NY R USDCTND CM/ECF(2)(2.1)(5).

iv. *Filing defined.* Electronic transmission of a document to the System in accordance with these Administrative Procedures, together with the transmission of a Notice of Electronic Filing from the Court, constitutes filing of the document for all purposes of the Federal Rules of Civil Procedure and the Local Rules of Practice for the United States District Court for the Northern District of New York and constitutes entry of the document on the docket that the Clerk's Office keeps under FRCP 58 and FRCP 79. E-mailing a document to the Clerk's Office or to the assigned judge shall not constitute "filing" of the document. NY R USDCTND CM/ECF(4)(4.1).

v. *Filing fees.* Any fee required for filing a pleading or paper in this Court is payable to the Clerk of the Court. The Court will not maintain electronic billing or debit accounts for attorneys or law firms. Effective January 1, 2007, payment for filing fees will be mandatory through CM/ECF's Internet Credit Card Payment site--a secure Treasury Site. The Filing User will be prompted to enter either Bank Account Debit (ACH) or credit card information while filing the initial pleading. Any document that requires a filing fee (e.g., Notice of Appeal, Motion for Pro Hac Vice Admission) may also be paid through the federal electronic payment website. NY R USDCTND CM/ECF(7).

vi. For more information on electronic filing, refer to NY R USDCTND CM/ECF.

c. *E-mail or facsimile filing.* Neither the Court nor the Clerk's Office will accept for filing any facsimile or e-mail transmission without prior authorization from the Court. The party using facsimile or e-mail transmissions to file its papers must accompany any such documents with a cover letter stating that the Court authorized such transmissions and the date on which the Court provided that authorization. Violations of NY R USDCTND L.R. 5.5 subject the offending party to the Court's full disciplinary powers. NY R USDCTND L.R. 5.5.

2. *Service requirements*

a. *Service; When required*

i. *In general.* Unless the Federal Rules of Civil Procedure provide otherwise, each of the following papers must be served on every party:

- An order stating that service is required;
- A pleading filed after the original complaint, unless the court orders otherwise under FRCP 5(c) because there are numerous defendants;
- A discovery paper required to be served on a party, unless the court orders otherwise;
- A written motion, except one that may be heard ex parte; and
- A written notice, appearance, demand, or offer of judgment, or any similar paper. FRCP 5(a)(1).

ii. *If a party fails to appear.* No service is required on a party who is in default for failing to appear. But a pleading that asserts a new claim for relief against such a party must be served on that party under FRCP 4. FRCP 5(a)(2).

iii. *Seizing property.* If an action is begun by seizing property and no person is or need be named as a defendant, any service required before the filing of an appearance, answer, or claim must be made on the person who had custody or possession of the property when it was seized. FRCP 5(a)(3).

b. *Service; How made*

    i. *Serving an attorney.* If a party is represented by an attorney, service under FRCP 5 must be made on the attorney unless the court orders service on the party. FRCP 5(b)(1).

    ii. *Service in general.* A paper is served under FRCP 5 by:

- Handing it to the person;

- Leaving it: (1) at the person's office with a clerk or other person in charge or, if no one is in charge, in a conspicuous place in the office; or (2) if the person has no office or the office is closed, at the person's dwelling or usual place of abode with someone of suitable age and discretion who resides there;

- Mailing it to the person's last known address—in which event service is complete upon mailing;

- Leaving it with the court clerk if the person has no known address;

- Sending it by electronic means if the person consented in writing—in which event service is complete upon transmission, but is not effective if the serving party learns that it did not reach the person to be served; or

- Delivering it by any other means that the person consented to in writing—in which event service is complete when the person making service delivers it to the agency designated to make delivery. FRCP 5(b)(2).

    iii. *Service of electronically-filed documents.* Service is complete provided all parties receive a Notice of Electronic Filing (NEF), which is sent automatically by email from the Court (see the NEF for a list of who did/did not receive notice electronically). Transmission of the NEF constitutes service upon all Filing and Receiving Users who are listed as recipients of notice by electronic mail. It remains the responsibility of Filing and Receiving Users to maintain current contact information with the court and to regularly review the docket sheet of the case. NY R USDCTND CM/ECF(5)(5.2).

- *Non-filing or receiving users.* Attorneys and pro se parties who are not Filing or Receiving Users must be served with a paper copy of any electronically filed pleading or other document. Service of such paper copy must be made according to the Federal Rules of Civil Procedure and the Local Rules of Practice for the United States District Court for the Northern District of New York. Such paper service must be documented by electronically filing a certificate of service. NY R USDCTND CM/ECF(5)(5.2). A party who is not a Filing User of the System is entitled to a paper copy of any electronically-filed pleading, document, or order. The Filing User must therefore provide the non-Filing User with the pleading or document according to the Federal Rules of Civil Procedure. NY R US-DCTND CM/ECF(5)(5.3).

    iv. *Using court facilities.* If a local rule so authorizes, a party may use the court's transmission facilities to make service under FRCP 5(b)(2)(E). FRCP 5(b)(3).

c. *Serving numerous defendants*

    i. *In general.* If an action involves an unusually large number of defendants, the court may, on motion or on its own, order that:

- Defendants' pleadings and replies to them need not be served on other defendants;

- Any crossclaim, counterclaim, avoidance, or affirmative defense in those pleadings and replies to them will be treated as denied or avoided by all other parties; and

- Filing any such pleading and serving it on the plaintiff constitutes notice of the pleading to all parties. FRCP 5(c)(1).

    ii. *Notifying parties.* A copy of every such order must be served on the parties as the court directs. FRCP 5(c)(2).

3. *Individual judge practices.* Refer to the Miscellaneous section of this document for information on individual judge practices on filing and serving documents.

## G. Hearings

1. *Hearings, generally*

   a. *Oral argument.* Due process does not require that oral argument be permitted on a motion a. Motion days. Listings of the regularly scheduled motion days for all judges shall be available at each Clerk's office and are available on the Court's webpage. The Clerk shall provide notice of the regular motion days for all judges to the parties at the time an action is commenced. NY R USDCTND L.R. 78.1.

   b. *Return date.* Unless the Court directs otherwise, the moving party shall make its motion returnable at the next regularly scheduled motion date at least thirty-one (31) days from the date the moving party files and serves its motion. The moving party shall select a return date in accordance with the procedures set forth in NY R USDCTND L.R. 7.1(b). If the return date the moving party selects is not the next regularly scheduled motion date, or if the moving party selects no return date, the Clerk will set the proper return date and notify the parties. NY R USDCTND L.R. 7.1.

      i. Information regarding motion dates and times is specified on the case assignment form that the Court provides to the parties at the commencement of the litigation or the parties may obtain this form from the Clerk's office or at the Court's webpage. NY R USDCTND L.R. 7.1.

      ii. The Court hereby directs the Clerk to set a proper return date in motions that pro se litigants submit for filing that do not specify a return date or fail to allow for sufficient time pursuant to NY R USDCTND L.R. 7.1. Generally, the return date that the Clerk selects should not exceed thirty (30) days from the date of filing. Furthermore, the Clerk shall forward a copy of the revised or corrected notice of motion to the parties. NY R USDCTND L.R. 7.1.

   c. *Oral argument.* Due process does not require that oral argument be permitted on a motion and, except as otherwise provided by local rule, the district court has discretion to determine whether it will decide the motion on the papers or hear argument by counsel (and perhaps receive evidence). FPP § 1190; F.D.I.C. v. Deglau, 207 F.3d 153 (3d Cir. 2000).

      i. The parties shall appear for oral argument on all motions that they make returnable before a district court judge, except motions for reconsideration, on the scheduled return date of the motion. A motion may be disposed of without oral argument as described in NY R USDCTND Order 25, on consideration of a request of any party, or otherwise at the discretion of the presiding judge. Thus, the parties should be prepared to have their motion papers serve as the sole method of argument on the motion. NY R USDCTND L.R. 7.1(h).

      ii. The parties shall not appear for oral argument on motions that they make returnable before a Magistrate Judge on the scheduled return date of the motion unless the Magistrate Judge sua sponte directs or grants the request of any party for oral argument. NY R USDCTND L.R. 7.1(h).

   d. *Providing a regular schedule for oral hearings.* A court may establish regular times and places for oral hearings on motions. FRCP 78(a).

   e. *Providing for submission on briefs.* By rule or order, the court may provide for submitting and determining motions on briefs, without oral hearings. FRCP 78(b).

2. *Individual judge practices.* Refer to the Miscellaneous section of this document for information on individual judge practices on hearings.

## H. Forms

1. **Federal Motion to Strike Forms**

   a. Motion; By plaintiff; To strike insufficient defense from answer. AMJUR PP FEDPRAC § 441.

   b. Motion; To strike redundant, immaterial, impertinent, or scandalous matter from pleading. AMJUR PP FEDPRAC § 442.

   c. Motion; To strike portions of complaint. AMJUR PP FEDPRAC § 444.

   d. Motion to strike insufficient affirmative defenses. 2C FEDFORMS § 11:151.

   e. Motion to strike insufficient defense in answer; Stating particular reason. 2C FEDFORMS § 11:153.

   f. Notice of motion and motion to strike insufficient affirmative defense. 2C FEDFORMS § 11:155.

g. Motion to strike impertinence and scandal. 2C FEDFORMS § 11:157.

h. Motion to strike impertinence and immateriality. 2C FEDFORMS § 11:158.

i. Motion to strike redundancy and scandal. 2C FEDFORMS § 11:159.

j. Motion to strike immaterial defense. 2C FEDFORMS § 11:160.

k. Motion to strike for immateriality. 2C FEDFORMS § 11:161.

l. Motion to strike counterclaim for lack of evidence. 2C FEDFORMS § 11:162.

m. Opposition; To motion; General form. FEDPROF § 1:750.

n. Affidavit; Supporting or opposing motion. FEDPROF § 1:751.

o. Brief; Supporting or opposing motion. FEDPROF § 1:752.

p. Statement of points and authorities; Opposing motion. FEDPROF § 1:753.

q. Motion; To strike material outside statute of limitations. FEDPROF § 1:773.

r. Opposition to motion; Material not contained in pleading. FEDPROF § 1:774.

s. General form. GOLDLTGFMS § 20:8.

t. General form; Federal form. GOLDLTGFMS § 20:10.

u. Notice and motion to strike immaterial, redundant or scandalous matter. GOLDLTGFMS § 20:13.

v. Motion to strike complaint and dismiss action as to one defendant. GOLDLTGFMS § 20:14.

w. Defendant's motion to strike. GOLDLTGFMS § 20:16.

x. Defendant's motion to strike; Plaintiff's response. GOLDLTGFMS § 20:17.

y. Motion to strike answer. GOLDLTGFMS § 20:19.

z. Objections to motion to strike. GOLDLTGFMS § 20:20.

## I. Applicable Rules

1. *Federal rules*

   a. Serving and filing pleadings and other papers. FRCP 5.

   b. Constitutional challenge to a statute; Notice, certification, and intervention. FRCP 5.1.

   c. Privacy protection for filings made with the court. FRCP 5.2.

   d. Computing and extending time; Time for motion papers. FRCP 6.

   e. Pleadings allowed; Form of motions and other papers. FRCP 7.

   f. Disclosure statement. FRCP 7.1.

   g. Form of pleadings. FRCP 10.

   h. Signing pleadings, motions, and other papers; Representations to the court; Sanctions. FRCP 11.

   i. Defenses and objections; When and how presented; Motion for judgment on the pleadings; Consolidating motions; Waiving defenses; Pretrial hearing. FRCP 12.

   j. Hearing motions; Submission on briefs. FRCP 78.

2. *Local rules*

   a. Scope of the rules. NY R USDCTND L.R. 1.1.

   b. Complex and multi-district litigation. NY R USDCTND L.R. 3.3.

   c. Service and filing of papers. NY R USDCTND L.R. 5.1.

   d. Filing by facsimile or e-mail. NY R USDCTND L.R. 5.5.

   e. Motion practice. NY R USDCTND L.R. 7.1.

   f. Personal privacy protection. NY R USDCTND L.R. 8.1.

   g. Request for three-judge court. NY R USDCTND L.R. 9.1.

h.    Form of papers. NY R USDCTND L.R. 10.1.

i.    Settlement procedures. NY R USDCTND L.R. 68.2.

j.    Orders. NY R USDCTND L.R. 77.2.

k.    Motion days. NY R USDCTND L.R. 78.1.

l.    Appearance and withdrawal of attorney. NY R USDCTND L.R. 83.2.

m.    Arbitration. NY R USDCTND L.R. 83.7-1; NY R USDCTND L.R. 83.7-2; NY R USDCTND L.R. 83.7-3.

n.    Assisted mediation program. NY R USDCTND L.R. 83.8.

o.    Mediation. NY R USDCTND L.R. 83.11-1; NY R USDCTND L.R. 83.11-3.

p.    Early neutral evaluation. NY R USDCTND L.R. 83.12-1; NY R USDCTND L.R. 83.12-3.

q.    Administrative procedures for electronic case filing. NY R USDCTND CM/ECF.

r.    Case assignment plan for the Northern District of New York. [NY R USDCTND Order 12, as amended by NY ORDER 16-4201, effective March 24, 2015].

s.    Directing the expedited service of the summons and complaint and further directing the completion of FRCP 16 stipulation for the timely progression of civil actions. [NY R USDCTND Order 25, as amended by NY ORDER 16-4187, effective June 23, 2016].

t.    Mandatory mediation program. NY R USDCTND Order 47.

**J.  Miscellaneous**

**NOTE: Individual judges' rules may apply. For available judge-level information, refer to:**

DISTRICT JUDGE MAE A. D'AGOSTINO: [NY R USDCTND D'Agostino-Rules and Practices, as added by NY ORDER 16-4200, effective April 4, 2016].

DISTRICT JUDGE THOMAS J. McAVOY: NY R USDCTND McAvoy-Order.

## Motions, Oppositions and Replies
## Motion for Leave to Amend

### Document Last Updated September 2016

**A.  Checklist**

(I)    ❑  Matters to be considered by moving party

(a)    ❑  Required documents

(1)    ❑  Notice of motion and motion

(2)    ❑  Memorandum of law

(3)    ❑  Supporting affidavit

(4)    ❑  Redline/strikeout version of the amended pleading

(5)    ❑  Proposed amended pleading

(6)    ❑  Certificate of service

(b)    ❑  Supplemental documents

(1)    ❑  Supporting evidence

(2)    ❑  Notice of constitutional question

(3)    ❑  Copies of authorities

(4)    ❑  Proposed order

(5)    ❑  Cover letter authorizing e-mail or facsimile filing

(6)    ❑  Affidavit attesting to failed attempts to file electronically

(7) ❑ Notice of conventional filing

(8) ❑ CD/ROM with PDF of document(s)

(9) ❑ English translation

(10) ❑ Courtesy copies

(11) ❑ Copies for three-judge court

(c) ❑ Timing

    (1) ❑ Unlike amendments as of course, amendments under FRCP 15(a)(2) may be made at any stage of the litigation

    (2) ❑ A party may move—at any time, even after judgment—to amend the pleadings to conform them to the evidence and to raise an unpleaded issue

    (3) ❑ Unless the court orders otherwise, the moving party must file all motion papers with the court and serve them upon the other parties not less than thirty-one (31) days prior to the return date of the motion

    (4) ❑ A written motion and notice of the hearing must be served at least fourteen (14) days before the time specified for the hearing, with the following exceptions: (i) when the motion may be heard ex parte; (ii) when the Federal Rules of Civil Procedure set a different time; or (iii) when a court order—which a party may, for good cause, apply for ex parte—sets a different time

    (5) ❑ Any affidavit supporting a motion must be served with the motion

(II) ❑ Matters to be considered by opposing party

(a) ❑ Required documents

    (1) ❑ Opposition

    (2) ❑ Memorandum of law

    (3) ❑ Supporting affidavit

    (4) ❑ Certificate of service

(b) ❑ Supplemental documents

    (1) ❑ Supporting evidence

    (2) ❑ Notice of constitutional question

    (3) ❑ Cross-motion

    (4) ❑ Copies of authorities

    (5) ❑ Cover letter authorizing e-mail or facsimile filing

    (6) ❑ Affidavit attesting to failed attempts to file electronically

    (7) ❑ Notice of conventional filing

    (8) ❑ CD/ROM with PDF of document(s)

    (9) ❑ English translation

    (10) ❑ Courtesy copies

    (11) ❑ Copies for three-judge court

(c) ❑ Timing

    (1) ❑ The party opposing the motion must file its opposition papers with the court and serve them upon the other parties not less than seventeen (17) days prior to the return date of the motion

    (2) ❑ Except as FRCP 59(c) provides otherwise, any opposing affidavit must be served at least seven (7) days before the hearing, unless the court permits service at another time

    (3) ❑ A party may file and serve a cross-motion (meaning a competing request for relief or order

similar to that requested by another party against the cross-moving party) at the time it files and serves its opposition papers to the original motion, i.e., not less than seventeen (17) days prior to the return date of the motion

## B. Timing

1.  *Motion for leave to amend.* Unlike amendments as of course, amendments under FRCP 15(a)(2) may be made at any stage of the litigation. FPP § 1484.

    a.  *Amendments to conform to the evidence.* A party may move—at any time, even after judgment—to amend the pleadings to conform them to the evidence and to raise an unpleaded issue. FRCP 15(b)(2).

    b.  *Time to respond to an amended pleading.* Unless the court orders otherwise, any required response to an amended pleading must be made within the time remaining to respond to the original pleading or within fourteen (14) days after service of the amended pleading, whichever is later. FRCP 15(a)(3).

2.  *Timing of motions, generally.* Unless the Court orders otherwise, the moving party must file all motion papers with the Court and serve them upon the other parties not less than THIRTY-ONE (31) DAYS prior to the return date of the motion. NY R USDCTND L.R. 7.1(b)(2).

    a.  *Motion and notice of hearing.* A written motion and notice of the hearing must be served at least fourteen (14) days before the time specified for the hearing, with the following exceptions:

        i.  When the motion may be heard ex parte;

        ii. When the Federal Rules of Civil Procedure set a different time; or

        iii. When a court order—which a party may, for good cause, apply for ex parte—sets a different time. FRCP 6(c)(1).

    b.  *Supporting affidavit.* Any affidavit supporting a motion must be served with the motion. FRCP 6(c)(2).

3.  *Timing of opposing papers.* The party opposing the motion must file its Opposition papers with the Court and serve them upon the other parties not less than SEVENTEEN (17) DAYS prior to the return date of the motion. NY R USDCTND L.R. 7.1(b)(2).

    a.  *Opposing affidavit.* Except as FRCP 59(c) provides otherwise, any opposing affidavit must be served at least seven (7) days before the hearing, unless the court permits service at another time. FRCP 6(c)(2).

    b.  *Cross-motion.* A party may file and serve a cross-motion (meaning a competing request for relief or order similar to that requested by another party against the cross-moving party) at the time it files and serves its opposition papers to the original motion, i.e., not less than SEVENTEEN (17) DAYS prior to the return date of the motion. NY R USDCTND L.R. 7.1(c).

4.  *Timing of reply papers.* Where the respondent files an answering affidavit setting up a new matter, the moving party ordinarily is allowed a reasonable time to file a reply affidavit since failure to deny the new matter by affidavit may operate as an admission of its truth. AMJUR MOTIONS § 25.

    a.  *Reply papers.* Reply papers and adjournments are not permitted without the Court's prior permission. Permission to file a reply does not exist simply because CM/ECF generates a deadline for a reply on a nondispositive motion. NY R USDCTND L.R. 7.1(b)(2).

    b.  *Opposition to cross-motion.* The original moving party must file its reply/opposition papers with the Court and serve them on the other parties not less than ELEVEN (11) DAYS prior to the return date of the original motion. NY R USDCTND L.R. 7.1(c).

5.  *Computation of time*

    a.  *Computing time.* FRCP 6 applies in computing any time period specified in the Federal Rules of Civil Procedure, in any local rule or court order, or in any statute that does not specify a method of computing time. FRCP 6(a).

        i.  *Period stated in days or a longer unit.* When the period is stated in days or a longer unit of time:

            • Exclude the day of the event that triggers the period;

- Count every day, including intermediate Saturdays, Sundays, and legal holidays; and

- Include the last day of the period, but if the last day is a Saturday, Sunday, or legal holiday, the period continues to run until the end of the next day that is not a Saturday, Sunday, or legal holiday. FRCP 6(a)(1).

ii. *Period stated in hours.* When the period is stated in hours:

- Begin counting immediately on the occurrence of the event that triggers the period;

- Count every hour, including hours during intermediate Saturdays, Sundays, and legal holidays; and

- If the period would end on a Saturday, Sunday, or legal holiday, the period continues to run until the same time on the next day that is not a Saturday, Sunday, or legal holiday. FRCP 6(a)(2).

iii. *Inaccessibility of the clerk's office.* Unless the court orders otherwise, if the clerk's office is inaccessible:

- On the last day for filing under FRCP 6(a)(1), then the time for filing is extended to the first accessible day that is not a Saturday, Sunday, or legal holiday; or

- During the last hour for filing under FRCP 6(a)(2), then the time for filing is extended to the same time on the first accessible day that is not a Saturday, Sunday, or legal holiday. FRCP 6(a)(3).

iv. *"Last day" defined.* Unless a different time is set by a statute, local rule, or court order, the last day ends:

- For electronic filing, at midnight in the court's time zone; and

- For filing by other means, when the clerk's office is scheduled to close. FRCP 6(a)(4).

v. *"Next day" defined.* The "next day" is determined by continuing to count forward when the period is measured after an event and backward when measured before an event. FRCP 6(a)(5).

vi. *"Legal holiday" defined.* "Legal holiday" means:

- The day set aside by statute for observing New Year's Day, Martin Luther King Jr.'s Birthday, Washington's Birthday, Memorial Day, Independence Day, Labor Day, Columbus Day, Veterans' Day, Thanksgiving Day, or Christmas Day;

- Any day declared a holiday by the President or Congress; and

- For periods that are measured after an event, any other day declared a holiday by the state where the district court is located. FRCP 6(a)(6).

b. *Computation of electronic filing deadlines.* A document will be deemed timely filed if electronically filed prior to midnight Eastern Time. However, if the time of day is of the essence, the assigned judge may order that the document be filed by a time certain. NY R USDCTND CM/ECF(4)(4.3).

i. *Technical failures.* A Filing User, whose filing is untimely as the result of a technical failure of the Court's CM/ECF site, may seek appropriate relief from the Court. However, Filing Users are cautioned that, in some circumstances, the Court lacks the authority to grant an extension of time to file (e.g., FRCP 6(b) of the Federal Rules of Civil Procedure). NY R USDCTND CM/ECF(10)(10.1).

- *Technical failure of the filing user's system.* Problems with the Filing User's system, such as phone line problems, problems with the Filing User's Internet Service Provider ("ISP"), or hardware or software problems, will not constitute a technical failure under these Administrative Procedures nor excuse an untimely filing. A Filing User who cannot file documents electronically because of a problem on the Filing User's system must file the documents' conventionally along with an affidavit explaining the reason for not filing the documents electronically. NY R USDCTND CM/ECF(10)(10.2).

944

c. *Extending time*

    i. *In general.* When an act may or must be done within a specified time, the court may, for good cause, extend the time:

- With or without motion or notice if the court acts, or if a request is made, before the original time or its extension expires; or

- On motion made after the time has expired if the party failed to act because of excusable neglect. FRCP 6(b)(1).

    ii. *Exceptions.* A court must not extend the time to act under FRCP 50(b), FRCP 50(d), FRCP 52(b), FRCP 59(b), FRCP 59(d), FRCP 59(e), and FRCP 60(b). FRCP 6(b)(2).

    iii. Refer to the United States District Court for the Northern District of New York KeyRules Motion for Continuance/Extension of Time document for more information on extending time.

d. *Additional time after certain kinds of service.* When a party may or must act within a specified time after service and service is made under FRCP 5(b)(2)(C), FRCP 5(b)(2)(D), FRCP 5(b)(2)(E), or FRCP 5(b)(2)(F), three (3) days are added after the period would otherwise expire under FRCP 6(a). FRCP 6(d).

    i. In accordance with FRCP 6(e), service by electronic means is treated the same as service by mail for purposes of adding three (3) days to the prescribed period to respond. NY R USDCTND CM/ECF(5)(5.4). [Editor's note: the reference to FRCP 6(e) is likely meant to be a reference to FRCP 6(d)].

6. *Individual judge practices.* Refer to the Miscellaneous section of this document for information on individual judge practices on timing of documents.

## C. General Requirements

1. *Court conference for non-dispositive motions.* Prior to making any non-dispositive motion before the assigned Magistrate Judge, the parties must make good faith efforts among themselves to resolve or reduce all differences relating to the non-dispositive issue. If, after conferring, the parties are unable to arrive at a mutually satisfactory resolution, the party seeking relief must then request a court conference with the assigned Magistrate Judge. NY R USDCTND L.R. 7.1(b)(2). A court conference is a prerequisite to filing a non-dispositive motion before the assigned Magistrate Judge. NY R USDCTND L.R. 7.1(b)(2). In addition, no non-dispositive or discovery motions should be presented to the Court unless authorized by the Magistrate Judge after communication with the Magistrate Judge's chambers. NY R USDCTND Order 25(IX)(A). Actions which involve an incarcerated, pro se party are not subject to the requirement that a court conference be held prior to filing a non-dispositive motion. NY R USDCTND L.R. 7.1(b)(2).

2. *Motions, generally*

a. *Requirements.* A request for a court order must be made by motion. The motion must:

    i. Be in writing unless made during a hearing or trial;

    ii. State with particularity the grounds for seeking the order; and

    iii. State the relief sought. FRCP 7(b)(1).

    iv. When a moving party makes a motion based upon a rule or statute, the moving party must specify in its moving papers the rule or statute upon which it bases its motion. NY R USDCTND L.R. 7.1(a)(1).

b. *Notice of motion.* A party interested in resisting the relief sought by a motion has a right to notice thereof, and an opportunity to be heard. AMJUR MOTIONS § 12.

    i. In addition to statutory or court rule provisions requiring notice of a motion—the purpose of such a notice requirement having been said to be to prevent a party from being prejudicially surprised by a motion—principles of natural justice dictate that an adverse party generally must be given notice that a motion will be presented to the court. AMJUR MOTIONS § 12.

    ii. "Notice," in this regard, means reasonable notice, including a meaningful opportunity to prepare and to defend against allegations of a motion. AMJUR MOTIONS § 12.

c. *Writing requirement.* The writing requirement is intended to insure that the adverse parties are informed and have a record of both the motion's pendency and the grounds on which the movant seeks an order. FPP § 1191; Feldberg v. Quechee Lakes Corp., 463 F.3d 195 (2d Cir. 2006).

   i. It is sufficient "if the motion is stated in a written notice of the hearing of the motion." FPP § 1191.

d. *Particularity requirement.* The particularity requirement insures that the opposing parties will have notice of their opponent's contentions. FEDPROC § 62:364; Goodman v. 1973 26 Foot Trojan Vessel, Arkansas Registration No. AR1439SN, 859 F.2d 71, 12 Fed.R.Serv.3d 645 (8th Cir. 1988). That requirement ensures that notice of the basis for the motion is provided to the court and to the opposing party so as to avoid prejudice, provide the opponent with a meaningful opportunity to respond, and provide the court with enough information to process the motion correctly. FEDPROC § 62:364; Andreas v. Volkswagen of America, Inc., 336 F.3d 789, 56 Fed.R.Serv.3d 6 (8th Cir. 2003).

   i. Reasonable specification of the grounds for a motion is sufficient. However, where a movant fails to state even one ground for granting the motion in question, the movant has failed to meet the minimal standard of "reasonable specification." FEDPROC § 62:364; Martinez v. Trainor, 556 F.2d 818, 23 Fed.R.Serv.2d 403 (7th Cir. 1977).

   ii. The court may excuse the failure to comply with the particularity requirement if it is inadvertent, and where no prejudice is shown by the opposing party. FEDPROC § 62:364.

e. *Order to show cause.* All motions that a party brings by Order to Show Cause shall conform to the requirements set forth in NY R USDCTND L.R. 7.1(a)(1) and NY R USDCTND L.R. 7.1(a)(2). Immediately after filing an Order to Show Cause, the moving party must telephone the Chambers of the presiding judicial officer and inform Chambers staff that it has filed an Order to Show Cause. Parties may obtain the telephone numbers for all Chambers from the Clerk's office or at the Court's webpage. The Court shall determine the briefing schedule and return date applicable to motions brought by Order to Show Cause. NY R USDCTND L.R. 7.1(e).

   i. In addition to the requirements set forth in NY R USDCTND L.R. 7.1(a)(1) and NY R USDCTND L.R. 7.1(a)(2), a motion brought by Order to Show Cause must include an affidavit clearly and specifically showing good and sufficient cause why the standard Notice of Motion procedure cannot be used. The moving party must give reasonable advance notice of the application for an Order to Show Cause to the other parties, except in those circumstances where the movant can demonstrate, in a detailed and specific affidavit, good cause and substantial prejudice that would result from the requirement of reasonable notice. NY R USDCTND L.R. 7.1(e).

   ii. An Order to Show Cause must contain a space for the assigned judge to set forth:

   - The deadline for filing and serving supporting papers,
   - The deadline for filing and serving opposing papers, and
   - The date and time for the hearing. NY R USDCTND L.R. 7.1(e).

3. *Motion for leave to amend.* FRCP 15(a)(2) provides that after a party has amended a pleading once as of course or the time for amendments of that type has expired, a party may amend only by obtaining leave of the court or if the adverse party consents to it. FPP § 1484; In re Cessna Distributorship Antitrust Litigation, 532 F.2d 64 (8th Cir. 1976). FRCP 15(a) does not set forth any specific procedure for obtaining leave to amend. Typically, it is sought by a motion addressed to the court's discretion. FPP § 1485.

   a. *Pleadings to be amended.* As in the case of amendments as of course under FRCP 15(a)(1), any of the pleadings enumerated in FRCP 7(a) may be amended with the court's leave and FRCP 15 does not restrict the purposes for which an amendment may be made or its character. FPP § 1484.

   b. *Prerequisites for leave to amend.* The only prerequisites are that the district court have jurisdiction over the case and an appeal must not be pending. FPP § 1484. If these two conditions are met, the court will proceed to examine the effect and the timing of the proposed amendments to determine whether they would prejudice the rights of any of the other parties to the suit. FPP § 1484; Nilsen v. City of Moss Point, Miss., 674 F.2d 379, 388 (5th Cir. 1982).

c. *When leave or consent is not obtained.* In general, if an amendment that cannot be made as of right is served without obtaining the court's leave or the opposing party's consent, it is without legal effect and any new matter it contains will not be considered unless the amendment is resubmitted for the court's approval. Some courts have held, however, that an untimely amended pleading served without judicial permission may be considered as properly introduced when leave to amend would have been granted had it been sought and when it does not appear that any of the parties will be prejudiced by allowing the change. FPP § 1484.

d. *Form.* A motion to amend under FRCP 15(a), as is true of motions generally, is subject to the requirements of FRCP 7(b), and must set forth with particularity the relief or order requested and the grounds supporting the application. In order to satisfy these prerequisites a copy of the amendment should be submitted with the motion so that the court and the adverse party know the precise nature of the pleading changes being proposed. FPP § 1485.

e. *Oral motion for leave to amend.* Courts have held that an oral request to amend a pleading that is made before the court in the presence of opposing party's counsel may be sufficient if the adverse party is put on notice of the nature and purpose of the request and is given the same opportunity to present objections to the proposed amendment as would have occurred if a formal motion had been made. FPP § 1485.

f. *Conditions imposed on leave to amend.* While FRCP 15(a) does not specifically authorize the district court to impose conditions on its granting of leave to amend, it is well settled that the court may impose such conditions to avoid or minimize any prejudice to the opposing party. FEDPROC § 62:276. Conditions frequently are imposed because the amending party knew of the facts sought to be asserted in the amendment but failed to assert such facts until later, to the prejudice of the opposing party. Conversely, the court may decline to impose conditions where the amendment was asserted with relative promptness. FEDPROC § 62:276.

    i. The moving party's refusal to comply with the conditions imposed by the court normally will result in a denial of the right to amend. FPP § 1486.

g. *When leave to amend may be granted.* If the underlying facts or circumstances relied upon by a plaintiff may be a proper subject of relief, he ought to be afforded an opportunity to test his claim on the merits. In the absence of any apparent or declared reason—such as undue delay, bad faith or dilatory motive on the part of the movant, repeated failure to cure deficiencies by amendments previously allowed, undue prejudice to the opposing party by virtue of allowance of the amendment, futility of amendment, etc.—the leave sought should, as the rules require, be "freely given." FPP § 1487; Foman v. Davis, 371 U.S. 178, 182, 83 S.Ct. 227, 230, 9 L.Ed.2d 222 (1962).

4. *Amendments, generally*

a. *Amendments before trial.* The function of FRCP 15(a), which provides generally for the amendment of pleadings, is to enable a party to assert matters that were overlooked or were unknown at the time the party interposed the original complaint or answer. FPP § 1473; Smiga v. Dean Witter Reynolds, Inc., 766 F.2d 698, 703 (2d Cir. 1985).

    i. *Matters contained in amended pleading under FRCP 15(a).* Although FRCP 15(a) does not expressly state that an amendment must contain only matters that occurred within a particular time period, FRCP 15(d) provides that any "transaction, occurrence, or event that happened after the date of the pleading" should be set forth in a supplemental pleading. FPP § 1473. Thus, impliedly, an amended pleading, whether prepared with or without leave of court, only should relate to matters that have taken place prior to the date of the earlier pleading. FPP § 1473; Ford Motor Co. v. U.S., 19 C.I.T. 946, 896 F.Supp. 1224, 1230 (1995).

    ii. *Amending as a matter of course.* A party may amend its pleading once as a matter of course within: (1) twenty-one (21) days after serving it, or if the pleading is one to which a responsive pleading is required, twenty-one (21) days after service of a responsive pleading or twenty-one (21) days after service of a motion under FRCP 12(b), FRCP 12(e), or FRCP 12(f), whichever is earlier. FRCP 15(a)(1). Refer to the United States District Court for the Northern District of New York KeyRules Amended Pleading document for more information on amending as a matter of course.

iii.  *Other amendments.* In all other cases, a party may amend its pleading only with the opposing party's written consent or the court's leave. The court should freely give leave when justice so requires. FRCP 15(a)(2).

iv.  *Types of amendments permitted under FRCP 15(a)*

- *Cure a defective pleading.* Perhaps the most common use of FRCP 15(a) is by a party seeking to amend in order to cure a defective pleading. FPP § 1474.

- *Correct insufficiently stated claims or defenses.* A more common use of FRCP 15(a) amendments is to correct insufficiently stated claims or defenses. Typically, amendments of this character involve either adding a necessary allegation in order to state a claim for relief or correcting a misnomer of a party to the action. FPP § 1474.

- *Change nature or theory of claim or capacity of party.* Courts also have allowed a party to amend in order to change the nature or theory of the party's claim or the capacity in which the party is bringing the action. FPP § 1474.

- *State additional claims or defenses or drop claims or defenses.* Plaintiffs and defendants also have been permitted to amend their pleadings to state additional claims, to assert additional defenses, or to drop claims or defenses. FPP § 1474; Weinberger v. Retail Credit Co., 498 F.2d 552, 554, n.4 (4th Cir. 1974).

- *Increase amount of damages or elect a different remedy.* A FRCP 15(a) amendment also is appropriate for increasing the amount of damages sought, or for electing a different remedy than the one originally requested. FPP § 1474; McFadden v. Sanchez, 710 F.2d 907 (2d Cir. 1983).

- *Add, substitute, or drop parties.* Finally, a party may make a FRCP 15(a) amendment to add, substitute, or drop parties to the action. FPP § 1474.

b.  *Amendments during and after trial*

i.  *Based on an objection at trial.* If, at trial, a party objects that evidence is not within the issues raised in the pleadings, the court may permit the pleadings to be amended. The court should freely permit an amendment when doing so will aid in presenting the merits and the objecting party fails to satisfy the court that the evidence would prejudice that party's action or defense on the merits. The court may grant a continuance to enable the objecting party to meet the evidence. FRCP 15(b)(1).

ii.  *For issues tried by consent.* When an issue not raised by the pleadings is tried by the parties' express or implied consent, it must be treated in all respects as if raised in the pleadings. A party may move—at any time, even after judgment—to amend the pleadings to conform them to the evidence and to raise an unpleaded issue. But failure to amend does not affect the result of the trial of that issue. FRCP 15(b)(2).

c.  *Relation back of amendments*

i.  *When an amendment relates back.* An amendment to a pleading relates back to the date of the original pleading when:

- The law that provides the applicable statute of limitations allows relation back;

- The amendment asserts a claim or defense that arose out of the conduct, transaction, or occurrence set out—or attempted to be set out—in the original pleading; or

- The amendment changes the party or the naming of the party against whom a claim is asserted, if FRCP 15(c)(1)(B) is satisfied and if, within the period provided by FRCP 4(m) for serving the summons and complaint, the party to be brought in by amendment: (1) received such notice of the action that it will not be prejudiced in defending on the merits; and (2) knew or should have known that the action would have been brought against it, but for a mistake concerning the proper party's identity. FRCP 15(c)(1).

ii.  *Notice to the United States.* When the United States or a United States officer or agency is added as a defendant by amendment, the notice requirements of FRCP 15(c)(1)(C)(i) and FRCP

15(c)(1)(C)(ii) are satisfied if, during the stated period, process was delivered or mailed to the United States attorney or the United States attorney's designee, to the Attorney General of the United States, or to the officer or agency. FRCP 15(c)(2).

d. *Effect of an amended pleading.* A pleading that has been amended under FRCP 15(a) supersedes the pleading it modifies and remains in effect throughout the action unless it subsequently is modified. FPP § 1476. Once an amended pleading is interposed, the original pleading no longer performs any function in the case and any subsequent motion made by an opposing party should be directed at the amended pleading. FPP § 1476; Ferdik v. Bonzelet, 963 F.2d 1258, 1262 (9th Cir. 1992); Davis v. TXO Production Corp., 929 F.2d 1515, 1517 (10th Cir. 1991).

5. *Opposing papers.* The Federal Rules of Civil Procedure do not require any formal answer, return, or reply to a motion, except where the Federal Rules of Civil Procedure or local rules may require affidavits, memoranda, or other papers to be filed in opposition to a motion. Such papers are simply to apprise the court of such opposition and the grounds of that opposition. FEDPROC § 62:359.

a. *Effect of failure to respond to motion.* Although in the absence of statutory provision or court rule, a motion ordinarily does not require a written answer, when a party files a motion and the opposing party fails to respond, the court may construe such failure to respond as nonopposition to the motion or an admission that the motion was meritorious, may take the facts alleged in the motion as true—the rule in some jurisdictions being that the failure to respond to a fact set forth in a motion is deemed an admission—and may grant the motion if the relief requested appears to be justified. AMJUR MOTIONS § 28.

b. *Assent or no opposition not determinative.* However, a motion will not be granted automatically simply because an "assent" or a notation of "no opposition" has been filed; federal judges frequently deny motions that have been assented to when it is thought that justice so dictates. FPP § 1190.

c. *Responsive pleading inappropriate as response to motion.* An attempt to answer or oppose a motion with a responsive pleading usually is not appropriate. FPP § 1190.

6. *Reply papers.* Reply papers and adjournments are not permitted without the Court's prior permission. Permission to file a reply does not exist simply because CM/ECF generates a deadline for a reply on a nondispositive motion. NY R USDCTND L.R. 7.1(b)(2). A moving party may be required or permitted to prepare papers in addition to his original motion papers. AMJUR MOTIONS § 25. Papers answering or replying to opposing papers may be appropriate, in the interests of justice, where it appears there is a substantial reason for allowing a reply. Thus, a court may accept reply papers where a party demonstrates that the papers to which it seeks to file a reply raise new issues that are material to the disposition of the question before the court, or where the court determines, sua sponte, that it wishes further briefing of an issue raised in those papers and orders the submission of additional papers. FEDPROC § 62:360.

a. *Function of reply papers.* The function of a reply affidavit is to answer the arguments made in opposition to the position taken by the movant and not to permit the movant to introduce new arguments in support of the motion. AMJUR MOTIONS § 25.

b. *Issues raised for the first time in a reply document.* However, the view has been followed in some jurisdictions, that as a matter of judicial economy, where there is no prejudice and where the issues could be raised simply by filing a motion to dismiss, the trial court has discretion to consider arguments raised for the first time in a reply memorandum, and that a trial court may grant a motion to strike issues raised for the first time in a reply memorandum. AMJUR MOTIONS § 26.

c. *Opposition to cross-motion.* The original moving party may reply in further support of the original motion and in opposition to the cross-motion with a reply/opposition brief that does not exceed twenty-five (25) pages in length, exclusive of exhibits. NY R USDCTND L.R. 7.1(c).

7. *Surreply in support of cross-motion.* The cross-moving party may not reply in further support of its cross-motion without the Court's prior permission. NY R USDCTND L.R. 7.1(c).

8. *Submission of proposed order by prevailing party.* If the assigned judge instructs the prevailing party to do so, the prevailing party shall submit a proposed order which the opposing party has approved and which contains the endorsement of the opposing party: "Approved as to form." NY R USDCTND L.R. 77.2(b). In civil actions where the Court has directed a party to submit an order or judgment, that party

shall file all such orders or judgments in duplicate, and the Clerk's entry of such duplicate in the proper record book shall be deemed in compliance with FRCP 79(b). Such party shall also furnish the Clerk with a sufficient number of additional copies for each party to the action, which the Clerk shall mail with notice of entry in accordance with FRCP 77(d). NY R USDCTND L.R. 5.1(b).

a. *Disagreement as to form of proposed order.* When the parties are unable to agree as to the form of the proposed order, the prevailing party shall, on seven (7) days notice to all other parties, submit a proposed order and a written explanation for the form of that order. The Court may award costs and attorney's fees against a party whose unreasonable conduct the Court deemed to have required the bringing of the motion. The provisions of NY R USDCTND L.R. 7.1 shall not apply to such motion, and the Court shall not hear oral argument. NY R USDCTND L.R. 77.2(b).

b. For more information on orders, refer to NY R USDCTND L.R. 77.2.

9. *Sanctions for vexatious or frivolous motions or failure to comply with* NY R USDCTND L.R. 7.1. A party who presents vexatious or frivolous motion papers or fails to comply with NY R USDCTND L.R. 7.1 is subject to discipline as the Court deems appropriate, including sanctions and the imposition of costs and attorney's fees to the opposing party. NY R USDCTND L.R. 7.1(i).

10. *Complex and multi-district litigation.* If the assigned judge determines, in his or her discretion, that the case is of such a complex nature that it cannot reasonably be trial ready within eighteen (18) months from the date the complaint is filed, the assigned judge may design and issue a particularized case management order that will move the case to trial as quickly as the complexity of the case allows. NY R USDCTND L.R. 3.3(a). The parties shall promptly notify the Court in writing if any action commenced is appropriate for multi-district litigation. NY R USDCTND L.R. 3.3(b).

11. *Appearances.* An attorney appearing for a party in a civil case shall promptly file with the Clerk a written notice of appearance; however, an attorney does not need to file a notice of appearance if the attorney who would be filing the notice of appearance is the same individual who has signed the complaint, notice of removal, pre-answer motion, or answer. NY R USDCTND L.R. 83.2(a). For more information, refer to NY R USDCTND L.R. 83.2.

12. *Related cases.* A civil case is "related" to another civil case for purposes of this guideline when, because of the similarity of facts and legal issues or because the cases arise from the same transactions or events, a substantial saving of judicial resources is likely to result from assigning the cases to the same Judge and Magistrate Judge. NY R USDCTND Order 12(G)(2). A civil case shall not be deemed related to another civil case merely because the civil case: (1) involves similar legal issues, or (2) involves the same parties. NY R USDCTND Order 12(G)(3). Presumptively, and subject to the power of a Judge to determine otherwise pursuant to NY R USDCTND Order 12(G)(5), civil cases shall not be deemed to be "related" unless both cases are still pending before the Court. NY R USDCTND Order 12(G)(4).

a. *New filings.* If an attorney or filing party indicates on the Civil Cover Sheet that a case is related to an earlier filed case, the Clerk shall instruct the filing party to file a notice of related cases. The allegedly related cases will be submitted by the Clerk to the Judge to whom the earliest filed case is assigned, who shall advise the Clerk whether such cases are related. NY R USDCTND Order 12(G)(1).

b. *Judicial determination that civil cases are "related."* Except for the cases described in the final sentence of NY R USDCTND Order 12(G)(6), all civil cases shall be randomly assigned when they are filed. Other than the cases described in the final sentence of NY R USDCTND Order 12(G)(6), civil cases shall not be deemed to be "related" for purposes of this guideline at the instance of any litigant or attorney unless and until there has been a determination by a Judge of this Court that the standard of NY R USDCTND Order 12(G)(2) is met. NY R USDCTND Order 12(G)(5).

i. *Notice of related filing.* Any party may apply for such a determination by filing with the Clerk a notice of related filing, which should include an explanation as to why the standard of NY R USDCTND Order 12(G)(2) is met. A form for this purpose is available on the Court's website. A copy of the notice shall be served on all other parties who have appeared. Such an application must be made after the date when at least a majority of the defendants have been served with the complaint. Before making such an application, the applicant must confer in good faith with all other parties in an effort to reach an agreement on whether or not the case is "related". After such an application is made, any other party may serve and file within seven (7) calendar days a letter of no more than two (2) pages supporting or opposing the application. The application to have the case assigned to another Judge shall be presented to the Judge with the earliest filed case for decision on whether the action(s) should be reassigned as related cases. The Judge with the earliest filed case may then enter an order in the case at bar, either deeming the case to be related and directing the Clerk to reassign the action, or denying the application for reassignment. Any disputes concerning the assignment of related cases will be referred to the Chief Judge for resolution. NY R USDCTND Order 12(G)(5).

   c.    For more information on related cases, refer to NY R USDCTND Order 12(G).

13.    *Alternative dispute resolution (ADR).* It is the mission of this court to do everything it can to help parties resolve their disputes as fairly, quickly, and efficiently as possible. NY R USDCTND Order 25(VIII).

   a.    *Arbitration.* NY R USDCTND L.R. 83.7 governs the consensual arbitration program for referral of civil actions to court-annexed arbitration. It may remain in effect until further order of the Court. Its purpose is to establish a less formal procedure for the just, efficient and economical resolution of disputes, while preserving the right to a full trial on demand. NY R USDCTND L.R. 83.7-1.

     i.    *Actions subject to arbitration.* The Clerk shall notify the parties in all civil cases, except as the Local Rules of Practice for the United States District Court for the Northern District of New York otherwise direct, that they may consent to non-binding arbitration under NY R US-DCTND L.R. 83.7. The notice shall be furnished to the parties at pretrial/scheduling conferences or shall be included with pretrial conference notices and instructions. Consent to arbitration under NY R USDCTND L.R. 83.7 shall be discussed at the pretrial/scheduling conference. No party or attorney shall be prejudiced for refusing to participate in arbitration. The Court shall allow the referral of any civil action pending before it to the arbitration process if the parties consent. The plaintiff shall be responsible for securing the execution of a consent form by the parties and for filing the form with the Clerk within fourteen (14) days after the parties receive the form. The parties shall freely and knowingly enter into the consent. NY R USDCTND L.R. 83.7-2.

     ii.    *Referral to arbitration.* The Clerk shall refer every action subject to NY R USDCTND L.R. 83.7 to arbitration in accordance with the procedures under NY R USDCTND L.R. 83.7 twenty-one (21) days after the filing of the last responsive pleading or within twenty-one (21) days of the filing of a stipulated consent order referring the action to arbitration, whichever event occurs last, except as otherwise provided. If any party notices a motion to dismiss under the provisions of FRCP 12(a) and/or FRCP 12(b), or a motion to join necessary parties pursuant to the Federal Rules of Civil Procedure prior to the expiration of the twenty-one (21) day period, the assigned judge shall hear the motion and further proceedings under NY R USDCTND L.R. 83.7 shall be deferred pending decision on the motion. If the Court does not dismiss the action on the motion, the Court shall refer the action to arbitration twenty-one (21) days after the filing of the decision. NY R USDCTND L.R. 83.7-3(a). Motions for summary judgment pursuant to FRCP 56 shall be filed and served within twenty-one (21) days following the close of discovery. The filing of a FRCP 56 motion shall defer further proceedings under NY R USDCTND L.R. 83.7 pending decision on the motion. NY R USDCTND L.R. 83.7-3(a).

       &bull;    *Relief from referral.* Any party shall request relief from the operation of NY R USDCTND L.R. 83.7 by filing with the Court a motion for the relief within twenty-one (21) days after entry of the initial stipulated consent order which refers the case for arbitration. The assigned judge shall, sua sponte, exempt an action from the application of NY R USDCTND L.R. 83.7 where the objectives of arbitration would not be realized because (1) the case involves complex or novel legal issues, (2) legal issues predominate over factual issues, or (3) for other good cause. NY R USDCTND L.R. 83.7-3(c).

     iii.    For more information on arbitration, refer to NY R USDCTND L.R. 83.7.

   b.    *Mediation.* The purpose of NY R USDCTND L.R. 83.11 is to provide a supplementary procedure to the Court's existing alternative dispute resolution procedures. NY R USDCTND L.R. 83.11 provides for an earlier resolution of civil disputes resulting in savings of time and cost to litigants and the Court without sacrificing the quality of justice rendered or the right of litigants to a full trial on all issues not resolved through mediation. NY R USDCTND L.R. 83.11-1(a). Mediation is a process by which an impartial person, the mediator, facilitates communication between disputing parties to promote understanding, reconciliation and settlement. The mediator is an advocate for settlement and uses the mediation process to help the parties fully explore any potential area of agreement. The mediator does not serve as a judge or arbitrator and has no authority to render any decision on any disputed issue or to force a settlement. The parties themselves are responsible for negotiating any resolution(s) to their dispute. NY R USDCTND L.R. 83.11-1(b).

i.   *Actions subject to mediation.* The Court may refer any civil action (or any portion thereof) to mediation under NY R USDCTND L.R. 83.11: (1) by order of referral; or (2) on the motion of any party; or (3) by consent of the parties. NY R USDCTND L.R. 83.11-3(a).

- *Withdrawal from mediation.* The parties may withdraw from mediation any civil action or claim that the Court refers to mediation pursuant to NY R USDCTND L.R. 83.11-3 by application to the assigned judge at least ten (10) days prior to the scheduled mediation session. NY R USDCTND L.R. 83.11-3(b).

ii.  *Mandatory mediation program.* The United States District Court for the Northern District of New York has adopted this Mandatory Mediation Plan. The paid Mediation Program is designed to provide quicker, less expensive and potentially more satisfying alternatives to continuing litigation, without impairing the quality of justice or the right to trial. NY R USDCTND Order 47(1)(1.2)(A). This Mandatory Mediation Plan applies to civil actions pending as well as newly filed actions, except as otherwise indicated in NY R USDCTND Order 47. The Local Rules for voluntary mediation will apply only to Pro Se Cases that proceed through the Assisted Mediation Program. NY R USDCTND Order 47(1)(1.2)(B).

- *Referral into the pilot mandatory mediation program for new cases.* All civil cases shall be referred automatically into the Mandatory Mediation Program. Notice of the Mandatory Mediation requirements will be provided to all parties immediately upon the filing of a complaint and answer or a notice of removal. ADR intervention will be scheduled at the conference held pursuant to NY R USDCTND L.R. 16.1. NY R USDCTND Order 47(2)(2.1)(A). For a list of categories of actions exempted from automatic referral, refer to NY R USDCTND Order 47(2)(2.1)(A).

- *Referral into the pilot mandatory mediation program for pending cases.* The assigned Judge or Magistrate Judge on any pending civil case may, sua sponte or with status conference, issue an order referring the case into the Mandatory Mediation Program. The order shall specify a date on which the ADR intervention is to be completed. NY R USDCTND Order 47(2)(2.1)(B).

- *Referral into the pilot mandatory mediation program by stipulation.* A case may be referred into the Mandatory Mediation Program by stipulation of all parties. Stipulations shall be filed and shall designate the time frame within which the ADR process will be completed. Stipulations are presumed acceptable unless the assigned Judge or Magistrate Judge determines that the interests of justice are not served. NY R USDCTND Order 47(2)(2.1)(C).

- *Relief from referral.* Motions to opt out of the program will be addressed by the assigned Magistrate Judge at the FRCP 16 conference. NY R USDCTND Order 47(2)(2.2)(A). Opting Out Motions shall be granted only for "good cause" shown. Inconvenience, travel costs, attorney fees or other costs shall not constitute "good cause." A party seeking relief from the Mandatory Mediation Program must set forth the reasons why Mandatory Mediation has no reasonable chance of being productive. NY R USDCTND Order 47(2)(2.2)(B). The assigned Magistrate Judge may, sua sponte, exempt any case from the Court's Mandatory Mediation Program. NY R USDCTND Order 47(2)(2.2)(C).

iii. *Assisted mediation program.* The Court may assign specially trained pro bono Special Mediation Counsel to assist pro se civilian litigants with preparing for and participating in mediation. The Assisted Mediation Program is open to civilian pro se parties to actions in the Northern

District of New York. The assigned judge or magistrate judge determines if the case would benefit from mediation and would also benefit from the assignment of Special Mediation Counsel to assist the pro se party with the mediation process. NY R USDCTND L.R. 83.8(a). Appointment of Special Mediation Counsel is in no way guaranteed, even if the action is referred to the court-annexed mediation program. Appointment is at the sole discretion of the presiding judge. NY R USDCTND L.R. 83.8(a).

- *Referral to assisted mediation program.* If the court determines that referral to the Assisted Mediation Program is appropriate, the Court shall enter an order of reference to the Assisted Mediation Program. NY R USDCTND L.R. 83.8(b).

    iv.  For more information on mediation, refer to NY R USDCTND L.R. 83.11 and NY R USDCTND Order 47.

  c.  *Early neutral evaluation (ENE).* Early neutral evaluation (ENE) is a process in which parties obtain from an experienced neutral (an "evaluator") a nonbinding, reasoned, oral evaluation of the merits of the case. The first step in the ENE process involves the Court appointing an evaluator who has expertise in the area of law in the case. After the parties exchange essential information and position statements early in the pretrial period (usually within one hundred fifty (150) to two hundred (200) days after a complaint has been filed), the evaluator convenes an ENE session that typically lasts about two hours. At the ENE meeting, each side briefly presents the factual and legal basis of its position. The evaluator may ask questions of the parties and help them identify the main issues in dispute and the areas of agreement. The evaluator may also help the parties explore options for settlement. If settlement does not occur, the evaluator then offers an opinion as to the settlement value of the case, including the likelihood of liability and the likely range of damages. With the benefit of this assessment, the parties are again encouraged to discuss settlement, with or without the evaluator's assistance. The parties may also explore ways to narrow the issues in dispute, exchange information about the case or otherwise prepare efficiently for trial. NY R USDCTND L.R. 83.12-1.

    i.  *Actions subject to early neutral evaluation.* The Court may refer any civil action (or any portion thereof) to ENE under NY R USDCTND L.R. 83.12: (1) by order of referral; (2) on the motion of any party; or (3) by consent of the parties. NY R USDCTND L.R. 83.12-3(a).

- *Withdrawal from the ENE process.* The parties may withdraw any civil action or claim that the Court has referred to the ENE Process pursuant to NY R USDCTND L.R. 83.12-3 by application to the assigned judge at least ten (10) days before the scheduled evaluation session. NY R USDCTND L.R. 83.12-3(b).

    ii.  For more information on early neutral evaluation (ENE), refer to NY R USDCTND L.R. 83.12.

14.  *Settlement procedures.* On notice to the Court or the Clerk that the parties have settled an action, and upon confirmation of the settlement by all parties, the Court may issue a judgment dismissing the action by reason of settlement. The Court shall issue the order without prejudice to the parties' right to secure reinstatement of the case within thirty (30) days after the date of judgment by making a showing that the settlement was not, in fact, consummated. NY R USDCTND L.R. 68.2(a). If the Court decides not to follow the procedures set forth in NY R USDCTND L.R. 68.2(a), the parties shall file within thirty (30) days of the notification to the Court, unless otherwise directed by written order, such notices, stipulations and/or motions as are necessary to terminate the action. If the required documents are not filed within the thirty (30) day period, the Clerk shall place the action on the dismissal calendar. NY R USDCTND L.R. 68.2(b).

15.  *Sanctions and penalties for noncompliance.* Failure of an attorney or of a party to comply with any provision of the Local Rules of Practice for the United States District Court for the Northern District of New York, General Orders of this District, Orders of the Court, or the Federal Rules of Civil Procedure shall be a ground for imposition of sanctions. NY R USDCTND L.R. 1.1(d).

16.  *Individual judge practices.* Refer to the Miscellaneous section of this document for information on individual judge practices on general requirements for documents.

**D. Documents**

1. *Documents for moving party*

    a. *Required documents*

        i. *Notice of motion and motion.* In the Notice of Motion, the moving party is required to set forth the date that the court conference with the Magistrate Judge was held regarding the issues being presented in the motion. Failure to include this information in the Notice of Motion may result in the Court rejecting the motion papers. NY R USDCTND L.R. 7.1(b)(2). Refer to the General Requirements section of this document for information on the notice of motion and motion.

            • *Order to show cause.* Refer to the General Requirements section of this document for information on bringing a motion by order to show cause.

        ii. *Memorandum of law.* Except as otherwise provided in NY R USDCTND L.R. 7.1(a), all motions. . .require a memorandum of law. NY R USDCTND L.R. 7.1(a). Refer to the Format section of this document for the formatting requirements for memoranda of law.

        iii. *Supporting affidavit.* Except as otherwise provided in NY R USDCTND L.R. 7.1(a), all motions. . .require a. . .supporting affidavit. NY R USDCTND L.R. 7.1(a). An affidavit must not contain legal arguments but must contain factual and procedural background that is relevant to the motion the affidavit supports. NY R USDCTND L.R. 7.1(a)(2).

        iv. *Redline/strikeout version of the amended pleading.* The motion must set forth specifically the proposed insertions and deletions of language and identify the amendments in the proposed pleading, either through the submission of a redline/strikeout version of the pleading sought to be amended or through other equivalent means. NY R USDCTND L.R. 7.1(a)(4).

        v. *Proposed amended pleading.* A party moving to amend a pleading pursuant to FRCP 14, FRCP 15, FRCP 19 through FRCP 22 must attach an unsigned copy of the proposed amended pleading to its motion papers. Except if the Court otherwise orders, the proposed amended pleading must be a complete pleading, which will supersede the pleading sought to be amended in all respects. A party shall not incorporate any portion of its prior pleading into the proposed amended pleading by reference. NY R USDCTND L.R. 7.1(a)(4). In order to satisfy the prerequisites of FRCP 7(b), a copy of the amendment should be submitted with the motion so that the court and the adverse party know the precise nature of the pleading changes being proposed. FPP § 1485. The amending party should submit a copy of the proposed amendment at least by the date of the hearing on the motion for leave to amend. FEDPROC § 62:274; Grombach v. Oerlikon Tool & Arms Corp. of America, 276 F.2d 155 (4th Cir. 1960).

            • The documents accompanying the motion for leave to amend may be an appropriate substitute for a formally proposed amendment, if the documents sufficiently indicate the gist of the amendment. FEDPROC § 62:274.

            • The granting of the motion does not constitute the filing of the amended pleading. After the Court grants leave, unless the Court otherwise orders, the moving party must file and serve the original signed amended pleading within fourteen (14) days of the Order granting the motion. NY R USDCTND L.R. 7.1(a)(4).

        vi. *Certificate of service.* Except as otherwise provided in NY R USDCTND L.R. 7.1(a), all motions. . .require. . .proof of service on all the parties. See NY R USDCTND L.R. 5.1(a). NY R USDCTND L.R. 7.1(a). FRCP 5(d) requires that the person making service under FRCP 5 certify that service has been effected. FRCP 5(Advisory Committee Notes). Having such information on file may be useful for many purposes, including proof of service if an issue arises concerning the effectiveness of the service. FRCP 5(Advisory Committee Notes). The party or its designee shall declare, by affidavit or certification, that it has provided all other parties in the action with all documents it has filed with the Court. NY R USDCTND L.R. 5.1(a).

            • Attorneys and pro se parties who are not Filing or Receiving Users must be served with a paper copy of any electronically filed pleading or other document. NY R USDCTND CM/ECF(5)(5.2). Such paper service must be documented by electronically filing a certificate of service. NY R USDCTND CM/ECF(5)(5.2).

b. *Supplemental documents*

    i.   *Supporting evidence.* When a motion relies on facts outside the record, the court may hear the matter on affidavits or may hear it wholly or partly on oral testimony or on depositions. FRCP 43(c).

    ii.   *Notice of constitutional question.* A party that files a pleading, written motion, or other paper drawing into question the constitutionality of a federal or state statute must promptly:

- *File notice.* File a notice of constitutional question stating the question and identifying the paper that raises it, if: (1) a federal statute is questioned and the parties do not include the United States, one of its agencies, or one of its officers or employees in an official capacity; or (2) a state statute is questioned and the parties do not include the state, one of its agencies, or one of its officers or employees in an official capacity; and

- *Serve notice.* Serve the notice and paper on the Attorney General of the United States if a federal statute is questioned—or on the state attorney general if a state statute is questioned—either by certified or registered mail or by sending it to an electronic address designated by the attorney general for this purpose. FRCP 5.1(a).

- *No forfeiture.* A party's failure to file and serve the notice, or the court's failure to certify, does not forfeit a constitutional claim or defense that is otherwise timely asserted. FRCP 5.1(d).

    iii.   *Copies of authorities.* When serving a pro se litigant with a memorandum of law or any other paper which contains citations to authorities that are unpublished or published exclusively on electronic databases, counsel shall include a hard copy of those authorities. Although copies of authorities published only on electronic databases are not required to be filed, copies shall be provided upon request to opposing counsel who lack access to electronic databases. NY R USDCTND L.R. 7.1(a)(1).

    iv.   *Proposed order.* A document that is submitted in .pdf format cannot be modified; therefore, a proposed order or stipulation must be in a word processing format. The chambers of the assigned judge may request that a proposed order and/or a stipulation be e-mailed to the courtroom deputy for the presiding judge in either WordPerfect or Microsoft Word format. Please attach your proposed order and/or stipulation to an Internet e-mail sent to the appropriate e-mail address listed in NY R USDCTND CM/ECF(8)(8.2). NY R USDCTND CM/ECF(8)(8.2).

    v.   *Cover letter authorizing e-mail or facsimile filing.* Neither the Court nor the Clerk's Office will accept for filing any facsimile or e-mail transmission without prior authorization from the Court. The party using facsimile or e-mail transmissions to file its papers must accompany any such documents with a cover letter stating that the Court authorized such transmissions and the date on which the Court provided that authorization. Violations of NY R USDCTND L.R. 5.5 subject the offending party to the Court's full disciplinary powers. NY R USDCTND L.R. 5.5.

    vi.   *Affidavit attesting to failed attempts to file electronically.* If the Court's CM/ECF site experiences a technical failure, a Filing User may submit documents to the Court that day in an alternate manner provided that the documents are accompanied by the Filing User's affidavit stating that the Filing User attempted to file electronically at least two times in one (1) hour increments after 10:00 a.m. that day. The following methods are acceptable alternate means for filing documents in case of a technical failure: (1) via electronic mail in a PDF attachment sent to the e-mail address for technical failures; or (2) in person, by bringing the document to the Clerk's Office on paper accompanied by a CD/ROM that contains the document in .pdf format. NY R USDCTND CM/ECF(10)(10.1).

- A Filing User who cannot file documents electronically because of a problem on the Filing User's system must file the documents' conventionally along with an affidavit explaining the reason for not filing the documents electronically. NY R USDCTND CM/ECF(10)(10.2).

    vii.   *Notice of conventional filing.* If the Clerk's Office grants permission to conventionally file the

document, the Filing User shall electronically file a notice of conventional filing for the documents. More information regarding this process can be obtained from the Court's web page. NY R USDCTND CM/ECF(4)(4.5).

viii. *CD/ROM with PDF of document(s).* If the Court grants permission to file a document traditionally, the attorney must submit the documents for filing to the Clerk's Office on CD/ROM in .pdf or pdf.A format. NY R USDCTND CM/ECF(2).

ix. *English translation.* The Court conducts its reviews and deliberations in English. Unless otherwise directed by the Court, any document that a party transmits to the Court (including one in the record on appeal) that is in a language other than English must be accompanied by an English translation that the translator has certified as true and accurate, pursuant to 28 U.S.C.A. § 1746. NY R USDCTND L.R. 10.1(e). For more information, refer to NY R USDCTND L.R. 10.1(e).

x. *Courtesy copies.* The Court may require that courtesy copies of electronically filed documents be submitted for its review and may amend these Administrative Procedures (NY R USDCTND CM/ECF) at any time without prior notice. NY R USDCTND CM/ECF(2).

xi. *Copies for three-judge court.* On the convening of a three-judge court, the parties shall make three (3) copies of all non-electronically filed pleadings, motion papers, and memoranda of law available to the Clerk for distribution. NY R USDCTND L.R. 9.1.

2. *Documents for opposing party*

  a. *Required documents*

    i. *Opposition.* Refer to the General Requirements section of this document for information on the opposing papers.

    ii. *Memorandum of law.* Except as otherwise provided in NY R USDCTND L.R. 7.1(a), all. . .opposition to motions require a memorandum of law. NY R USDCTND L.R. 7.1(a).

      - *Cross-motion brief.* If a party makes a cross-motion, it must join its cross motion brief with its opposition brief, and this combined brief may not exceed twenty-five (25) pages in length, exclusive of exhibits. A separate brief in opposition to the original motion is not permissible. NY R USDCTND L.R. 7.1(c).

      - Refer to the Format section of this document for the formatting requirements for memoranda of law.

    iii. *Supporting affidavit.* Except as otherwise provided in NY R USDCTND L.R. 7.1(a), all. . .opposition to motions require a. . .supporting affidavit. NY R USDCTND L.R. 7.1(a). An affidavit must not contain legal arguments but must contain factual and procedural background that is relevant to the motion the affidavit supports. NY R USDCTND L.R. 7.1(a)(2).

    iv. *Certificate of service.* Except as otherwise provided in NY R USDCTND L.R. 7.1(a), all. . .opposition to motions require. . .proof of service on all the parties. See NY R USDCTND L.R. 5.1(a). NY R USDCTND L.R. 7.1(a). FRCP 5(d) requires that the person making service under FRCP 5 certify that service has been effected. FRCP 5(Advisory Committee Notes). Having such information on file may be useful for many purposes, including proof of service if an issue arises concerning the effectiveness of the service. FRCP 5(Advisory Committee Notes). The party or its designee shall declare, by affidavit or certification, that it has provided all other parties in the action with all documents it has filed with the Court. NY R USDCTND L.R. 5.1(a).

      - Attorneys and pro se parties who are not Filing or Receiving Users must be served with a paper copy of any electronically filed pleading or other document. NY R USDCTND CM/ECF(5)(5.2). Such paper service must be documented by electronically filing a certificate of service. NY R USDCTND CM/ECF(5)(5.2).

  b. *Supplemental documents*

    i. *Supporting evidence.* When a motion relies on facts outside the record, the court may hear the

matter on affidavits or may hear it wholly or partly on oral testimony or on depositions. FRCP 43(c).

ii.  *Notice of constitutional question.* A party that files a pleading, written motion, or other paper drawing into question the constitutionality of a federal or state statute must promptly:

   - *File notice.* File a notice of constitutional question stating the question and identifying the paper that raises it, if: (1) a federal statute is questioned and the parties do not include the United States, one of its agencies, or one of its officers or employees in an official capacity; or (2) a state statute is questioned and the parties do not include the state, one of its agencies, or one of its officers or employees in an official capacity; and

   - *Serve notice.* Serve the notice and paper on the Attorney General of the United States if a federal statute is questioned—or on the state attorney general if a state statute is questioned—either by certified or registered mail or by sending it to an electronic address designated by the attorney general for this purpose. FRCP 5.1(a).

   - *No forfeiture.* A party's failure to file and serve the notice, or the court's failure to certify, does not forfeit a constitutional claim or defense that is otherwise timely asserted. FRCP 5.1(d).

iii.  *Cross-motion.* A party may file and serve a cross-motion (meaning a competing request for relief or order similar to that requested by another party against the cross-moving party) at the time it files and serves its opposition papers to the original motion, i.e., not less than SEVENTEEN (17) DAYS prior to the return date of the motion. NY R USDCTND L.R. 7.1(c).

iv.  *Copies of authorities.* When serving a pro se litigant with a memorandum of law or any other paper which contains citations to authorities that are unpublished or published exclusively on electronic databases, counsel shall include a hard copy of those authorities. Although copies of authorities published only on electronic databases are not required to be filed, copies shall be provided upon request to opposing counsel who lack access to electronic databases. NY R USDCTND L.R. 7.1(a)(1).

v.  *Cover letter authorizing e-mail or facsimile filing.* Neither the Court nor the Clerk's Office will accept for filing any facsimile or e-mail transmission without prior authorization from the Court. The party using facsimile or e-mail transmissions to file its papers must accompany any such documents with a cover letter stating that the Court authorized such transmissions and the date on which the Court provided that authorization. Violations of NY R USDCTND L.R. 5.5 subject the offending party to the Court's full disciplinary powers. NY R USDCTND L.R. 5.5.

vi.  *Affidavit attesting to failed attempts to file electronically.* If the Court's CM/ECF site experiences a technical failure, a Filing User may submit documents to the Court that day in an alternate manner provided that the documents are accompanied by the Filing User's affidavit stating that the Filing User attempted to file electronically at least two times in one (1) hour increments after 10:00 a.m. that day. The following methods are acceptable alternate means for filing documents in case of a technical failure: (1) via electronic mail in a PDF attachment sent to the e-mail address for technical failures; or (2) in person, by bringing the document to the Clerk's Office on paper accompanied by a CD/ROM that contains the document in .pdf format. NY R USDCTND CM/ECF(10)(10.1).

   - A Filing User who cannot file documents electronically because of a problem on the Filing User's system must file the documents' conventionally along with an affidavit explaining the reason for not filing the documents electronically. NY R USDCTND CM/ECF(10)(10.2).

vii.  *Notice of conventional filing.* If the Clerk's Office grants permission to conventionally file the document, the Filing User shall electronically file a notice of conventional filing for the documents. More information regarding this process can be obtained from the Court's web page. NY R USDCTND CM/ECF(4)(4.5).

viii.  *CD/ROM with PDF of document(s).* If the Court grants permission to file a document traditionally, the attorney must submit the documents for filing to the Clerk's Office on CD/ROM in .pdf or pdf.A format. NY R USDCTND CM/ECF(2).

ix. *English translation.* The Court conducts its reviews and deliberations in English. Unless otherwise directed by the Court, any document that a party transmits to the Court (including one in the record on appeal) that is in a language other than English must be accompanied by an English translation that the translator has certified as true and accurate, pursuant to 28 U.S.C.A. § 1746. NY R USDCTND L.R. 10.1(e). For more information, refer to NY R USDCTND L.R. 10.1(e).

x. *Courtesy copies.* The Court may require that courtesy copies of electronically filed documents be submitted for its review and may amend these Administrative Procedures (NY R USDCTND CM/ECF) at any time without prior notice. NY R USDCTND CM/ECF(2).

xi. *Copies for three-judge court.* On the convening of a three-judge court, the parties shall make three (3) copies of all non-electronically filed pleadings, motion papers, and memoranda of law available to the Clerk for distribution. NY R USDCTND L.R. 9.1.

3. *Individual judge practices.* Refer to the Miscellaneous section of this document for information on individual judge practices on required documents.

## E. Format

1. *Form of documents.* The rules governing captions and other matters of form in pleadings apply to motions and other papers. FRCP 7(b)(2). All pleadings and other papers shall be served and filed in accordance with the Federal Rules of Civil Procedure and shall be in the form prescribed by NY R USDCTND L.R. 10.1. NY R USDCTND L.R. 5.1(a).

a. *Form, generally.* All pleadings, motions, and other documents that a party presents for filing, whether in paper form or in electronic form, shall meet the following requirements:

i. *Font size.* All text, whether in the body of the document or in footnotes, must be a minimum of twelve (12) point type. NY R USDCTND L.R. 10.1(a)(1).

ii. *Margins.* All documents must have one (1) inch margins on all four sides of the page. NY R USDCTND L.R. 10.1(a)(2).

iii. *Spacing.* All text in the body of the document must be double-spaced. NY R USDCTND L.R. 10.1(a)(3).

- The text in block quotations and footnotes may be single-spaced. NY R USDCTND L.R. 10.1(a)(4).

iv. *Page numbering.* Pages must be consecutively numbered. NY R USDCTND L.R. 10.1(a)(7).

v. *Circumventing formatting limitations*

- Extensive footnotes must not be used to circumvent page limitations. NY R USDCTND L.R. 10.1(a)(5).
- Compacted or other compressed printing features must not be used. NY R USDCTND L.R. 10.1(a)(6).

b. *Additional requirements for paper filing.* Additional requirements for all pleadings, motions, and other documents that a party presents for filing in paper form:

i. *Paper size.* All documents must be on eight and one-half by eleven (8-1/2 x 11) inch white paper of good quality. NY R USDCTND L.R. 10.1(b)(1).

ii. *Text.* All text must be plainly and legibly written, typewritten, printed or reproduced without erasures or interlineations materially defacing them. NY R USDCTND L.R. 10.1(b)(2).

iii. *Ink.* All documents must be in black or blue ink. NY R USDCTND L.R. 10.1(b)(3).

iv. *Binding.* Pages of all documents must be stapled (or in some other way fastened) together. NY R USDCTND L.R. 10.1(b)(4).

v. *Single-sided paper.* All documents must be single-sided. NY R USDCTND L.R. 10.1(b)(5).

vi. *Electronic submission.* The Court, at its discretion, may require the electronic submission of any document in a WordPerfect-compatible format. NY R USDCTND L.R. 10.1(b)(6).

vii. *Rejection of document.* The Court may reject documents that do not comply with the above-listed requirements. NY R USDCTND L.R. 10.1(b).

c. *Caption; Names of parties.* Every pleading must have a caption with the court's name, a title, a file number, and a FRCP 7(a) designation. The title of the complaint must name all the parties; the title of other pleadings, after naming the first party on each side, may refer generally to other parties. FRCP 10(a). Each document must contain a caption for the specific case to which it pertains. The caption must include the title of the Court, the title of the action, the civil action number of the case, the initials of the assigned judge(s), and the name or nature of the paper in sufficient detail for identification. If a litigant has more than one action pending in this Court, any and all papers filed in a case must contain and pertain to one civil action number, unless the civil actions have been consolidated by the Court. Any motion or other papers purporting to relate to more than one action will not be accepted for filing and may be stricken by the Court. NY R USDCTND L.R. 10.1(c)(1) shall not apply, as noted in NY R USDCTND L.R. 10.1(c), to notices of change of address filed by attorneys of record and pro se litigants. The parties must separately caption affidavits and declarations and must not physically attach them to the Notice of Motion or Memorandum of Law. NY R USDCTND L.R. 10.1(c)(1).

d. *Paragraphs; Separate statements.* A party must state its claims or defenses in numbered paragraphs, each limited as far as practicable to a single set of circumstances. A later pleading may refer by number to a paragraph in an earlier pleading. If doing so would promote clarity, each claim founded on a separate transaction or occurrence—and each defense other than a denial—must be stated in a separate count or defense. FRCP 10(b).

e. *Adoption by reference; Exhibits.* A statement in a pleading may be adopted by reference elsewhere in the same pleading or in any other pleading or motion. A copy of a written instrument that is an exhibit to a pleading is a part of the pleading for all purposes. FRCP 10(c).

f. *Citation of local rules.* These are the Local Rules of Practice for the United States District Court for the Northern District of New York. They shall be cited as "L.R. ___." NY R USDCTND L.R. 1.1(a).

g. *Acceptance by the clerk.* The clerk must not refuse to file a paper solely because it is not in the form prescribed by the Federal Rules of Civil Procedure or by a local rule or practice. FRCP 5(d)(4).

2. *Form of electronic documents.* All pleadings, motions, and other documents that a party presents for filing, whether in paper form or in electronic form, shall meet the requirements in NY R USDCTND L.R. 10.1(a). NY R USDCTND L.R. 10.1(a). Refer above for more information.

a. *Attachments and exhibits.* A Filing User must submit in electronic form all documents referenced as exhibits or attachments in accordance with the Court's CM/ECF Users Manual unless the Court otherwise orders. A Filing User shall submit as exhibits or attachments only those excerpts of the referenced documents that are directly germane to the matter under the Court's consideration. Excerpted material must be clearly and prominently identified as such. Filing Users who file excerpts of documents as exhibits or attachments under these Administrative Procedures (NY R USDCTND CM/ECF) do so without prejudice to their right to timely file additional excerpts or the complete document. Responding parties may also timely file the complete document or additional excerpts that they believe are directly germane to the matter under the Court's consideration. NY R USDCTND CM/ECF(4)(4.4).

i. All attachments must be described in sufficient detail so the Court and opposing counsel can easily identify and distinguish the filed attachments. Vague or general descriptions are insufficient (i.e., "Exhibit 1"). Rather, each attachment shall have a descriptive title identifying, with specificity, the document that is being filed (i.e., "Exhibit 12 Mulligan County Fire Investigation Report.") Failure to adequately describe attachments may result in the document being rejected by the Court. NY R USDCTND CM/ECF(4)(4.4).

b. *Large documents.* For information on the electronic filing of large documents, please consult the Court's CM/ECF Users Manual, which is available on the Court's web page. NY R USDCTND CM/ECF(4)(4.5).

i. A party who believes a document is too lengthy to electronically image, i.e., "scan," may contact the Clerk's Office for permission to file that document conventionally. If the Clerk's Office grants permission to conventionally file the document, the Filing User shall electronically file a notice of conventional filing for the documents. More information regarding this process can be obtained from the Court's web page. Exhibits submitted conventionally shall be served on other parties as if they were not subject to these Administrative Procedures (NY R USDCTND CM/ECF). For a list of hints and tips for scanning large documents, please consult the Court's web page. NY R USDCTND CM/ECF(4)(4.5).

c. *Legibility.* It shall be the Filing User's responsibility to verify the legibility of scanned documents before filing them electronically with the Court. NY R USDCTND CM/ECF(4)(4.6).

d. *Color documents.* Since documents scanned in color or containing a graphic take much longer to upload, Filing Users are encouraged to configure their scanners to scan documents at 300 dpi and preferably in black and white rather than in color. NY R USDCTND CM/ECF(4)(4.7).

e. *Items not in .PDF format.* Parties wishing to file items not amenable to .pdf format (i.e. CD's, DVD's), shall file such items conventionally with the Clerk's Office. The Filing User shall electronically file a notice of conventional filing indicating that these items have been submitted to the clerk and shall serve copies of these items on other parties as if they were not subject to these Administrative Procedures (NY R USDCTND CM/ECF). These item(s) will be maintained by the Clerk's Office until the case is disposed, at which time they will be returned to the filing party for retention consistent with NY R USDCTND CM/ECF(4)(4.9). NY R USDCTND CM/ECF(4)(4.8).

3. *Form of memoranda of law*

   a. *Length limitation.* No party shall file or serve a memorandum of law that exceeds twenty-five (25) pages in length, unless that party obtains leave of the judge hearing the motion prior to filing. NY R USDCTND L.R. 7.1(a)(1).

   b. *Table of contents.* All memoranda of law shall contain a table of contents. NY R USDCTND L.R. 7.1(a)(1).

4. *Signing of pleadings, motions and other papers*

   a. *Signature.* Every pleading, written motion, and other paper must be signed by at least one attorney of record in the attorney's name—or by a party personally if the party is unrepresented. The paper must state the signer's address, e-mail address, and telephone number. FRCP 11(a). Each document must identify the person filing the document. This identification must include an original signature of the attorney or pro se litigant; the typewritten name of that person; the address of a pro se litigant; and the bar roll number, office address, telephone number, e-mail address and fax number of the attorney. Telephone numbers of non-prisoner pro se parties may be provided voluntarily or upon request of the Court. See General Order #22 (NY R USDCTND CM/ECF) for signature requirements. NY R USDCTND L.R. 10.1(c)(2).

      i. *Electronic signatures.* Documents filed under an attorney's login and password shall constitute that attorney's signature for purposes of the Local Rules of Practice for the United States District Court for the Northern District of New York and Federal Rules of Civil Procedure, including but not limited to FRCP 11. A pleading or other document requiring an attorney's signature shall be signed in the following manner, whether filed electronically or submitted on disk or CD/ROM to the Clerk's Office: "s/ (attorney name)." The correct format for an attorney signature is found in NY R USDCTND CM/ECF(6)(6.1). NY R USDCTND CM/ECF(6)(6.1).

         • *Non-attorney signature.* If an original document requires the signature of a non-attorney, the Filing User may scan the original document containing the original signature(s), then electronically file it on the System. Alternatively, the Filing User may convert the document into .pdf text format and submit the document using "s/" for the signature of the non-attorney. NY R USDCTND CM/ECF(6)(6.2).

         • *Multiple signatures.* A document requiring signatures of more than one party must be filed electronically either by (1) submitting a scanned document containing all necessary signatures; (2) representing the consent of the other parties on the document; or (3) in any other manner that the Court approves. NY R USDCTND CM/ECF(6)(6.3).

ii. *No verification or accompanying affidavit required for pleadings.* Unless a rule or statute specifically states otherwise, a pleading need not be verified or accompanied by an affidavit. FRCP 11(a).

iii. *Unsigned papers.* The court must strike an unsigned paper unless the omission is promptly corrected after being called to the attorney's or party's attention. FRCP 11(a).

b. *Representations to the court.* By presenting to the court a pleading, written motion, or other paper—whether by signing, filing, submitting, or later advocating it—an attorney or unrepresented party certifies that to the best of the person's knowledge, information, and belief, formed after an inquiry reasonable under the circumstances:

i. It is not being presented for any improper purpose, such as to harass, cause unnecessary delay, or needlessly increase the cost of litigation;

ii. The claims, defenses, and other legal contentions are warranted by existing law or by a nonfrivolous argument for extending, modifying, or reversing existing law or for establishing new law;

iii. The factual contentions have evidentiary support or, if specifically so identified, will likely have evidentiary support after a reasonable opportunity for further investigation or discovery; and

iv. The denials of factual contentions are warranted on the evidence or, if specifically so identified, are reasonably based on belief or a lack of information. FRCP 11(b).

c. *Sanctions.* If, after notice and a reasonable opportunity to respond, the court determines that FRCP 11(b) has been violated, the court may impose an appropriate sanction on any attorney, law firm, or party that violated FRCP 11(b) or is responsible for the violation. FRCP 11(c)(1). Refer to the United States District Court for the Northern District of New York KeyRules Motion for Sanctions document for more information.

5. *Privacy protection for filings made with the court*

a. *Redacted filings.* Unless the court orders otherwise, in an electronic or paper filing with the court that contains an individual's Social Security number, taxpayer-identification number, or birth date, the name of an individual known to be a minor, or a financial-account number, a party or nonparty making the filing may include only:

i. The last four (4) digits of the Social Security number and taxpayer-identification number;

ii. The year of the individual's birth;

iii. The minor's initials; and

iv. The last four (4) digits of the financial-account number. FRCP 5.2(a); NY R USDCTND L.R. 8.1; NY R USDCTND CM/ECF(11)(11.2).

v. If a home address must be used, use only the City and State. NY R USDCTND L.R. 8.1; NY R USDCTND CM/ECF(11)(11.2).

vi. If the victim of a sexual assault must be referenced, redact the name to 'Victim.' NY R USDCTND CM/ECF(11)(11.2); NY R USDCTND L.R. 8.1.

vii. In addition, caution shall be exercised when filing documents that contain the following:

- Personal identifying number, such as a driver's license number;

- Medical records, treatment and diagnosis;

- Employment history;

- Individual financial information; and

- Proprietary or trade secret information. NY R USDCTND L.R. 8.1; NY R USDCTND CM/ECF(11)(11.2).

b. *Exemptions from the redaction requirement.* The redaction requirement does not apply to the following:

i. A financial-account number that identifies the property allegedly subject to forfeiture in a forfeiture proceeding;

  ii. The record of an administrative or agency proceeding;

  iii. The official record of a state-court proceeding;

  iv. The record of a court or tribunal, if that record was not subject to the redaction requirement when originally filed;

  v. A filing covered by FRCP 5.2(c) or FRCP 5.2(d); and

  vi. A pro se filing in an action brought under 28 U.S.C.A. § 2241, 28 U.S.C.A. § 2254, or 28 U.S.C.A. § 2255. FRCP 5.2(b).

  vii. Transcripts of the administrative record in social security proceedings are exempt from this requirement. State court records and other documents filed in habeas corpus proceedings are exempt from this requirement except for proceedings that involve victims of sex crimes. In habeas corpus cases involving sex crimes, the parties must redact the record and supporting papers, or may move to seal, if appropriate. NY R USDCTND L.R. 8.1.

 c. *Limitations on remote access to electronic files; Social Security appeals and immigration cases.* Unless the court orders otherwise, in an action for benefits under the Social Security Act, and in an action or proceeding relating to an order of removal, to relief from removal, or to immigration benefits or detention, access to an electronic file is authorized as follows:

  i. The parties and their attorneys may have remote electronic access to any part of the case file, including the administrative record;

  ii. Any other person may have electronic access to the full record at the courthouse, but may have remote electronic access only to:

   • The docket maintained by the court; and

   • An opinion, order, judgment, or other disposition of the court, but not any other part of the case file or the administrative record. FRCP 5.2(c).

 d. *Filings made under seal.* The court may order that a filing be made under seal without redaction. The court may later unseal the filing or order the person who made the filing to file a redacted version for the public record. FRCP 5.2(d); NY R USDCTND L.R. 8.1. For information on sealed matters, refer to NY R USDCTND L.R. 83.13 and NY R USDCTND CM/ECF(12).

 e. *Protective orders.* For good cause, the court may by order in a case:

  i. Require redaction of additional information; or

  ii. Limit or prohibit a nonparty's remote electronic access to a document filed with the court. FRCP 5.2(e).

 f. *Option for additional unredacted filing under seal.* A person making a redacted filing may also file an unredacted copy under seal. The court must retain the unredacted copy as part of the record. FRCP 5.2(f); NY R USDCTND L.R. 8.1; NY R USDCTND CM/ECF(11)(11.3).

 g. *Option for filing a reference list.* A filing that contains redacted information may be filed together with a reference list that identifies each item of redacted information and specifies an appropriate identifier that uniquely corresponds to each item listed. The list must be filed under seal and may be amended as of right. Any reference in the case to a listed identifier will be construed to refer to the corresponding item of information. FRCP 5.2(g); NY R USDCTND L.R. 8.1; NY R USDCTND CM/ECF(11)(11.3).

 h. *Responsibility for redaction.* Counsel is strongly urged to discuss this issue with all their clients so that they can make an informed decision about the inclusion of certain information. The responsibility for redacting these personal identifiers rests solely with counsel and the parties. The Clerk will not review each filing for compliance with NY R USDCTND L.R. 8.1. Counsel and the parties are cautioned that failure to redact these personal identifiers may subject them to the Court's full disciplinary power. NY R USDCTND L.R. 8.1; NY R USDCTND CM/ECF(11)(11.3).

 i. *Waiver of protection of identifiers.* A person waives the protection of FRCP 5.2(a) as to the person's own information by filing it without redaction and not under seal. FRCP 5.2(h).

6. *Individual judge practices.* Refer to the Miscellaneous section of this document for information on individual judge practices on formatting documents.

## F. Filing and Service Requirements

1. *Filing requirements.* Any paper after the complaint that is required to be served—together with a certificate of service—must be filed within a reasonable time after service. FRCP 5(d)(1).

    a. *How filing is made; In general.* A paper is filed by delivering it:

        i. To the clerk; or

        ii. To a judge who agrees to accept it for filing, and who must then note the filing date on the paper and promptly send it to the clerk. FRCP 5(d)(2).

    b. *Electronic filing*

        i. *Authorization of electronic filing program.* A court may, by local rule, allow papers to be filed, signed, or verified by electronic means that are consistent with any technical standards established by the Judicial Conference of the United States. A local rule may require electronic filing only if reasonable exceptions are allowed. A paper filed electronically in compliance with a local rule is a written paper for purposes of the Federal Rules of Civil Procedure. FRCP 5(d)(3).

            • All cases filed in this Court may be assigned to the Electronic Case Files System ("ECF") in accordance with the Procedural Order on Electronic Case Filing (General Order #22 (NY R USDCTND CM/ECF)), the provisions of which are incorporated herein by reference, and which the Court may amend from time to time. Copies of General Order #22 (NY R USDCTND CM/ECF) are available at the Clerk's office or at the Court's webpage. NY R USDCTND L.R. 5.1.1; NY R USDCTND Order 25(XII).

            • The Court may deviate from these Administrative Procedures (NY R USDCTND CM/ECF) in specific cases, without prior notice, if deemed appropriate in the exercise of discretion, considering the need for the just, speedy, and inexpensive determination of matters pending before the Court. NY R USDCTND CM/ECF(2).

        ii. *Scope of electronic filing.* After January 1, 2004, all documents that attorneys admitted to practice in the Northern District of New York submit for filing shall be filed electronically using the System or shall be scanned and uploaded to the System, no matter when a case was originally filed, unless these Administrative Procedures (NY R USDCTND CM/ECF) other-wise permit or unless the assigned judge otherwise authorizes. An attorney who is not a Filing User by January 1, 2004, must show good cause to the assigned judge to file and serve pleadings and other papers in the traditional manner. NY R USDCTND CM/ECF(2).

        iii. *Exceptions and/or waivers from mandatory electronic filing.* The following types of cases and/or documents are not required to be filed electronically:

            • If you are seeking to have your complaint filed under seal, please file your complaint and proposed sealing order traditionally at the Clerk's Office. NY R USDCTND CM/ECF(2)(2.1)(1).

            • Any document that a party proceeding pro se files. (See NY R USDCTND CM/ECF(12)(12.1) for procedural details). NY R USDCTND CM/ECF(2)(2.1)(2). A non-prisoner who is a party to a civil action and who is not represented by an attorney may file a motion to obtain an Electronic Case Filing (ECF) login and password on a form prescribed by the Clerk's Office. The Pro Se CM/ECF Registration Form shall be submitted with the motion. If during the course of the action an attorney appears on behalf of the pro se party, the Clerk's Office shall terminate the pro se party's registration based upon the attorney's appearance. NY R USDCTND CM/ECF(12)(12.1). Absent permis-sion to file electronically, pro se filers shall file paper originals of all complaints, pleadings, motions, affidavits, briefs, and other documents which must be signed or which require either verification or an unsworn declaration under any rule or statute. The Clerk's Office will scan these original documents into an electronic file in the System but will also maintain a paper file. NY R USDCTND CM/ECF(12)(12.1). A pro se party may also seek permission to receive immediate notice of all public documents filed in their cases. Notices of Electronic Filing (NEF) and attached documents would be transmitted to a non-prisoner pro se party who selects this option. Note: The pro se party would continue to file their documents with the Clerk's Office in paper form. NY R USDCTND CM/ECF(12)(12.1).

- Sealed documents, sealed cases, documents for in camera review, documents lodged with the Court, ex parte documents, confidential agreements, Qui Tam actions and Grand Jury material and warrants must be filed traditionally. (See NY R USDCTND CM/ECF(12)(12.2) for further information the filing of the above-referenced documents). NY R USDCTND CM/ECF(2)(2.1)(3).

- Discovery: In accordance with NY R USDCTND L.R. 26.2, parties shall not file discovery, provided, however, that discovery material to be used at trial or in support of any motion, including a motion to compel or for summary judgment, shall be filed electronically with the Court prior to the trial or with the motion. Any motion pursuant to FRCP 37 shall be accompanied by the electronically filed discovery materials to which the motion relates if those materials have not previously been filed with the Court. NY R USDCTND CM/ECF(2)(2.1)(4).

- Transport Orders: All orders requesting that an incarcerated individual be transported that a judicial officer of the Northern District of New York signs shall be filed traditionally. These Orders will not be filed with the case or uploaded to the docket but rather will be processed in accordance with the procedures that the Clerk of Court promulgates. NY R USDCTND CM/ECF(2)(2.1)(5).

iv. *Filing defined.* Electronic transmission of a document to the System in accordance with these Administrative Procedures, together with the transmission of a Notice of Electronic Filing from the Court, constitutes filing of the document for all purposes of the Federal Rules of Civil Procedure and the Local Rules of Practice for the United States District Court for the Northern District of New York and constitutes entry of the document on the docket that the Clerk's Office keeps under FRCP 58 and FRCP 79. E-mailing a document to the Clerk's Office or to the assigned judge shall not constitute "filing" of the document. NY R USDCTND CM/ECF(4)(4.1).

v. *Filing fees.* Any fee required for filing a pleading or paper in this Court is payable to the Clerk of the Court. The Court will not maintain electronic billing or debit accounts for attorneys or law firms. Effective January 1, 2007, payment for filing fees will be mandatory through CM/ECF's Internet Credit Card Payment site--a secure Treasury Site. The Filing User will be prompted to enter either Bank Account Debit (ACH) or credit card information while filing the initial pleading. Any document that requires a filing fee (e.g., Notice of Appeal, Motion for Pro Hac Vice Admission) may also be paid through the federal electronic payment website. NY R USDCTND CM/ECF(7).

vi. For more information on electronic filing, refer to NY R USDCTND CM/ECF.

c. *E-mail or facsimile filing.* Neither the Court nor the Clerk's Office will accept for filing any facsimile or e-mail transmission without prior authorization from the Court. The party using facsimile or e-mail transmissions to file its papers must accompany any such documents with a cover letter stating that the Court authorized such transmissions and the date on which the Court provided that authorization. Violations of NY R USDCTND L.R. 5.5 subject the offending party to the Court's full disciplinary powers. NY R USDCTND L.R. 5.5.

2. *Service requirements*

a. *Service; When required*

i. *In general.* Unless the Federal Rules of Civil Procedure provide otherwise, each of the following papers must be served on every party:

- An order stating that service is required;

- A pleading filed after the original complaint, unless the court orders otherwise under FRCP 5(c) because there are numerous defendants;

- A discovery paper required to be served on a party, unless the court orders otherwise;

- A written motion, except one that may be heard ex parte; and

- A written notice, appearance, demand, or offer of judgment, or any similar paper. FRCP 5(a)(1).

ii. *If a party fails to appear.* No service is required on a party who is in default for failing to appear. But a pleading that asserts a new claim for relief against such a party must be served on that party under FRCP 4. FRCP 5(a)(2).

iii. *Seizing property.* If an action is begun by seizing property and no person is or need be named as a defendant, any service required before the filing of an appearance, answer, or claim must be made on the person who had custody or possession of the property when it was seized. FRCP 5(a)(3).

b. *Service; How made*

i. *Serving an attorney.* If a party is represented by an attorney, service under FRCP 5 must be made on the attorney unless the court orders service on the party. FRCP 5(b)(1).

ii. *Service in general.* A paper is served under FRCP 5 by:

- Handing it to the person;

- Leaving it: (1) at the person's office with a clerk or other person in charge or, if no one is in charge, in a conspicuous place in the office; or (2) if the person has no office or the office is closed, at the person's dwelling or usual place of abode with someone of suitable age and discretion who resides there;

- Mailing it to the person's last known address—in which event service is complete upon mailing;

- Leaving it with the court clerk if the person has no known address;

- Sending it by electronic means if the person consented in writing—in which event service is complete upon transmission, but is not effective if the serving party learns that it did not reach the person to be served; or

- Delivering it by any other means that the person consented to in writing—in which event service is complete when the person making service delivers it to the agency designated to make delivery. FRCP 5(b)(2).

iii. *Service of electronically-filed documents.* Service is complete provided all parties receive a Notice of Electronic Filing (NEF), which is sent automatically by email from the Court (see the NEF for a list of who did/did not receive notice electronically). Transmission of the NEF constitutes service upon all Filing and Receiving Users who are listed as recipients of notice by electronic mail. It remains the responsibility of Filing and Receiving Users to maintain current contact information with the court and to regularly review the docket sheet of the case. NY R USDCTND CM/ECF(5)(5.2).

- *Non-filing or receiving users.* Attorneys and pro se parties who are not Filing or Receiving Users must be served with a paper copy of any electronically filed pleading or other document. Service of such paper copy must be made according to the Federal Rules of Civil Procedure and the Local Rules of Practice for the United States District Court for the Northern District of New York. Such paper service must be documented by electronically filing a certificate of service. NY R USDCTND CM/ECF(5)(5.2). A party who is not a Filing User of the System is entitled to a paper copy of any electronically-filed pleading, document, or order. The Filing User must therefore provide the non-Filing User with the pleading or document according to the Federal Rules of Civil Procedure. NY R US-DCTND CM/ECF(5)(5.3).

iv. *Using court facilities.* If a local rule so authorizes, a party may use the court's transmission facilities to make service under FRCP 5(b)(2)(E). FRCP 5(b)(3).

c. *Serving numerous defendants*

    i. *In general.* If an action involves an unusually large number of defendants, the court may, on motion or on its own, order that:

- Defendants' pleadings and replies to them need not be served on other defendants;

- Any crossclaim, counterclaim, avoidance, or affirmative defense in those pleadings and replies to them will be treated as denied or avoided by all other parties; and

- Filing any such pleading and serving it on the plaintiff constitutes notice of the pleading to all parties. FRCP 5(c)(1).

    ii. *Notifying parties.* A copy of every such order must be served on the parties as the court directs. FRCP 5(c)(2).

3. *Individual judge practices.* Refer to the Miscellaneous section of this document for information on individual judge practices on filing and serving documents.

## G. Hearings

1. *Hearings, generally*

    a. *Motion days.* Listings of the regularly scheduled motion days for all judges shall be available at each Clerk's office and are available on the Court's webpage. The Clerk shall provide notice of the regular motion days for all judges to the parties at the time an action is commenced. NY R USDCTND L.R. 78.1.

    b. *Return date.* Unless the Court directs otherwise, the moving party shall make its motion returnable at the next regularly scheduled motion date at least thirty-one (31) days from the date the moving party files and serves its motion. The moving party shall select a return date in accordance with the procedures set forth in NY R USDCTND L.R. 7.1(b). If the return date the moving party selects is not the next regularly scheduled motion date, or if the moving party selects no return date, the Clerk will set the proper return date and notify the parties. NY R USDCTND L.R. 7.1.

    i. Information regarding motion dates and times is specified on the case assignment form that the Court provides to the parties at the commencement of the litigation or the parties may obtain this form from the Clerk's office or at the Court's webpage. NY R USDCTND L.R. 7.1.

    ii. The Court hereby directs the Clerk to set a proper return date in motions that pro se litigants submit for filing that do not specify a return date or fail to allow for sufficient time pursuant to NY R USDCTND L.R. 7.1. Generally, the return date that the Clerk selects should not exceed thirty (30) days from the date of filing. Furthermore, the Clerk shall forward a copy of the revised or corrected notice of motion to the parties. NY R USDCTND L.R. 7.1.

    c. *Oral argument.* Due process does not require that oral argument be permitted on a motion and, except as otherwise provided by local rule, the district court has discretion to determine whether it will decide the motion on the papers or hear argument by counsel (and perhaps receive evidence). FPP § 1190; F.D.I.C. v. Deglau, 207 F.3d 153 (3d Cir. 2000).

    i. The parties shall appear for oral argument on all motions that they make returnable before a district court judge, except motions for reconsideration, on the scheduled return date of the motion. A motion may be disposed of without oral argument as described in NY R USDCTND Order 25, on consideration of a request of any party, or otherwise at the discretion of the presiding judge. Thus, the parties should be prepared to have their motion papers serve as the sole method of argument on the motion. NY R USDCTND L.R. 7.1(h).

    ii. The parties shall not appear for oral argument on motions that they make returnable before a Magistrate Judge on the scheduled return date of the motion unless the Magistrate Judge sua sponte directs or grants the request of any party for oral argument. NY R USDCTND L.R. 7.1(h).

    d. *Providing a regular schedule for oral hearings.* A court may establish regular times and places for oral hearings on motions. FRCP 78(a).

    e. *Providing for submission on briefs.* By rule or order, the court may provide for submitting and determining motions on briefs, without oral hearings. FRCP 78(b).

2. *Individual judge practices.* Refer to the Miscellaneous section of this document for information on individual judge practices on hearings.

## H. Forms

### 1. Federal Motion for Leave to Amend Forms

a. Leave to amend complaint; Attaching copy of amendment. 2C FEDFORMS § 14:18.

b. Leave to amend complaint; Inserting amendment. 2C FEDFORMS § 14:19.

c. Leave to amend complaint; Interlineation. 2C FEDFORMS § 14:20.

d. Leave to amend complaint; Responding to motion to dismiss complaint. 2C FEDFORMS § 14:21.

e. Leave to amend complaint; Close to trial. 2C FEDFORMS § 14:22.

f. Leave to amend complaint; Adding new count. 2C FEDFORMS § 14:24.

g. Leave to amend complaint; Asserting lack of knowledge of facts at time of original complaint. 2C FEDFORMS § 14:25.

h. Leave to amend complaint; Seeking fourth amendment. 2C FEDFORMS § 14:26.

i. Leave to amend complaint; Substituting plaintiff and dropping defendant. 2C FEDFORMS § 14:27.

j. Leave to amend answer. 2C FEDFORMS § 14:30.

k. Leave to amend answer; With leave endorsed. 2C FEDFORMS § 14:31.

l. Leave to amend answer; Correcting errors, deleting and interlining. 2C FEDFORMS § 14:32.

m. Leave to amend answer; Adding paragraph. 2C FEDFORMS § 14:33.

n. Leave to amend answer; Adding defense. 2C FEDFORMS § 14:34.

o. Leave to amend answer; During trial. 2C FEDFORMS § 14:35.

p. Defendant's response to motion for leave to amend complaint a fourth time. 2C FEDFORMS § 14:36.

q. Motion and notice; For leave to file amended pleading. FEDPROF § 1:222.

r. Motion; To amend pleading to conform to findings of master. FEDPROF § 1:223.

s. Affidavit; In support of motion for amendment of pleading. FEDPROF § 1:230.

t. Opposition; To motion; General form. FEDPROF § 1:750.

u. Affidavit; Supporting or opposing motion. FEDPROF § 1:751.

v. Brief; Supporting or opposing motion. FEDPROF § 1:752.

w. Statement of points and authorities; Opposing motion. FEDPROF § 1:753.

x. Motion for leave to amend pleading. GOLDLTGFMS § 14:3.

y. Motion to file second amended complaint on ground of newly discovered evidence. GOLDLTGFMS § 14:20.

z. Motion for leave to file amended answer. GOLDLTGFMS § 14:22.

## I. Applicable Rules

1. *Federal rules*

a. Serving and filing pleadings and other papers. FRCP 5.

b. Constitutional challenge to a statute; Notice, certification, and intervention. FRCP 5.1.

c. Privacy protection for filings made with the court. FRCP 5.2.

d. Computing and extending time; Time for motion papers. FRCP 6.

e. Pleadings allowed; Form of motions and other papers. FRCP 7.

f. Form of pleadings. FRCP 10.

g. Signing pleadings, motions, and other papers; Representations to the court; Sanctions. FRCP 11.

    h.   Amended and supplemental pleadings. FRCP 15.

    i.   Taking testimony. FRCP 43.

    j.   Hearing motions; Submission on briefs. FRCP 78.

2.  *Local rules*

    a.   Scope of the rules. NY R USDCTND L.R. 1.1.

    b.   Complex and multi-district litigation. NY R USDCTND L.R. 3.3.

    c.   Service and filing of papers. NY R USDCTND L.R. 5.1.

    d.   Filing by facsimile or e-mail. NY R USDCTND L.R. 5.5.

    e.   Motion practice. NY R USDCTND L.R. 7.1.

    f.   Personal privacy protection. NY R USDCTND L.R. 8.1.

    g.   Request for three-judge court. NY R USDCTND L.R. 9.1.

    h.   Form of papers. NY R USDCTND L.R. 10.1.

    i.   Settlement procedures. NY R USDCTND L.R. 68.2.

    j.   Orders. NY R USDCTND L.R. 77.2.

    k.   Motion days. NY R USDCTND L.R. 78.1.

    l.   Appearance and withdrawal of attorney. NY R USDCTND L.R. 83.2.

    m.   Arbitration. NY R USDCTND L.R. 83.7-1; NY R USDCTND L.R. 83.7-2; NY R USDCTND L.R. 83.7-3.

    n.   Assisted mediation program. NY R USDCTND L.R. 83.8.

    o.   Mediation. NY R USDCTND L.R. 83.11-1; NY R USDCTND L.R. 83.11-3.

    p.   Early neutral evaluation. NY R USDCTND L.R. 83.12-1; NY R USDCTND L.R. 83.12-3.

    q.   Administrative procedures for electronic case filing. NY R USDCTND CM/ECF.

    r.   Case assignment plan for the Northern District of New York. [NY R USDCTND Order 12, as amended by NY ORDER 16-4201, effective March 24, 2015].

    s.   Directing the expedited service of the summons and complaint and further directing the completion of FRCP 16 stipulation for the timely progression of civil actions. [NY R USDCTND Order 25, as amended by NY ORDER 16-4187, effective June 23, 2016].

    t.   Mandatory mediation program. NY R USDCTND Order 47.

**J.  Miscellaneous**

**NOTE: Individual judges' rules may apply. For available judge-level information, refer to:**

DISTRICT JUDGE MAE A. D'AGOSTINO: [NY R USDCTND D'Agostino-Rules and Practices, as added by NY ORDER 16-4200, effective April 4, 2016].

DISTRICT JUDGE THOMAS J. McAVOY: NY R USDCTND McAvoy-Order.

# Motions, Oppositions and Replies
# Motion for Continuance/Extension of Time

**Document Last Updated September 2016**

**A.  Checklist**

  (I)  ❏  Matters to be considered by moving party

      (a)  ❏  Required documents

          (1)  ❏  Notice of motion and motion

          (2)  ❏  Memorandum of law

      (3)  ❑  Supporting affidavit

      (4)  ❑  Certificate of service

  (b)  ❑  Supplemental documents

      (1)  ❑  Supporting evidence

      (2)  ❑  Notice of constitutional question

      (3)  ❑  Nongovernmental corporate disclosure statement

      (4)  ❑  Copies of authorities

      (5)  ❑  Proposed order

      (6)  ❑  Cover letter authorizing e-mail or facsimile filing

      (7)  ❑  Affidavit attesting to failed attempts to file electronically

      (8)  ❑  Notice of conventional filing

      (9)  ❑  CD/ROM with PDF of document(s)

     (10)  ❑  English translation

     (11)  ❑  Courtesy copies

     (12)  ❑  Copies for three-judge court

  (c)  ❑  Timing

      (1)  ❑  Continuance: there are no specific timing requirements for moving for a continuance

      (2)  ❑  Extension of time: when an act may or must be done within a specified time, the court may, for good cause, extend the time:

         (i)  ❑  With or without motion or notice if the court acts, or if a request is made, before the original time or its extension expires; or

        (ii)  ❑  On motion made after the time has expired if the party failed to act because of excusable neglect

      (3)  ❑  Unless the court orders otherwise, the moving party must file all motion papers with the court and serve them upon the other parties not less than thirty-one (31) days prior to the return date of the motion

      (4)  ❑  A written motion and notice of the hearing must be served at least fourteen (14) days before the time specified for the hearing, with the following exceptions: (i) when the motion may be heard ex parte; (ii) when the Federal Rules of Civil Procedure set a different time; or (iii) when a court order—which a party may, for good cause, apply for ex parte—sets a different time

      (5)  ❑  Any affidavit supporting a motion must be served with the motion

(II)  ❑  Matters to be considered by opposing party

  (a)  ❑  Required documents

      (1)  ❑  Opposition

      (2)  ❑  Memorandum of law

      (3)  ❑  Supporting affidavit

      (4)  ❑  Certificate of service

  (b)  ❑  Supplemental documents

      (1)  ❑  Supporting evidence

      (2)  ❑  Notice of constitutional question

      (3)  ❑  Cross-motion

      (4)  ❑  Copies of authorities

(5) ❏ Cover letter authorizing e-mail or facsimile filing

(6) ❏ Affidavit attesting to failed attempts to file electronically

(7) ❏ Notice of conventional filing

(8) ❏ CD/ROM with PDF of document(s)

(9) ❏ English translation

(10) ❏ Courtesy copies

(11) ❏ Copies for three-judge court

(c) ❏ Timing

(1) ❏ The party opposing the motion must file its opposition papers with the court and serve them upon the other parties not less than seventeen (17) days prior to the return date of the motion

(2) ❏ Except as FRCP 59(c) provides otherwise, any opposing affidavit must be served at least seven (7) days before the hearing, unless the court permits service at another time

(3) ❏ A party may file and serve a cross-motion (meaning a competing request for relief or order similar to that requested by another party against the cross-moving party) at the time it files and serves its opposition papers to the original motion, i.e., not less than seventeen (17) days prior to the return date of the motion

## B. Timing

1. *Motion for continuance/extension of time*

   a. *Continuance.* There are no specific timing requirements for moving for a continuance.

   b. *Extension of time.* When an act may or must be done within a specified time, the court may, for good cause, extend the time:

      i. With or without motion or notice if the court acts, or if a request is made, before the original time or its extension expires; or

      ii. On motion made after the time has expired if the party failed to act because of excusable neglect. FRCP 6(b)(1).

2. *Timing of motions, generally.* Unless the Court orders otherwise, the moving party must file all motion papers with the Court and serve them upon the other parties not less than THIRTY-ONE (31) DAYS prior to the return date of the motion. NY R USDCTND L.R. 7.1(b)(2).

   a. *Motion and notice of hearing.* A written motion and notice of the hearing must be served at least fourteen (14) days before the time specified for the hearing, with the following exceptions:

      i. When the motion may be heard ex parte;

      ii. When the Federal Rules of Civil Procedure set a different time; or

      iii. When a court order—which a party may, for good cause, apply for ex parte—sets a different time. FRCP 6(c)(1).

   b. *Supporting affidavit.* Any affidavit supporting a motion must be served with the motion. FRCP 6(c)(2).

3. *Timing of opposing papers.* The party opposing the motion must file its Opposition papers with the Court and serve them upon the other parties not less than SEVENTEEN (17) DAYS prior to the return date of the motion. NY R USDCTND L.R. 7.1(b)(2).

   a. *Opposing affidavit.* Except as FRCP 59(c) provides otherwise, any opposing affidavit must be served at least seven (7) days before the hearing, unless the court permits service at another time. FRCP 6(c)(2).

   b. *Cross-motion.* A party may file and serve a cross-motion (meaning a competing request for relief or order similar to that requested by another party against the cross-moving party) at the time it files and serves its opposition papers to the original motion, i.e., not less than SEVENTEEN (17) DAYS prior to the return date of the motion. NY R USDCTND L.R. 7.1(c).

4. *Timing of reply papers.* Where the respondent files an answering affidavit setting up a new matter, the moving party ordinarily is allowed a reasonable time to file a reply affidavit since failure to deny the new matter by affidavit may operate as an admission of its truth. AMJUR MOTIONS § 25.

   a. *Reply papers.* Reply papers and adjournments are not permitted without the Court's prior permission. Permission to file a reply does not exist simply because CM/ECF generates a deadline for a reply on a nondispositive motion. NY R USDCTND L.R. 7.1(b)(2).

   b. *Opposition to cross-motion.* The original moving party must file its reply/opposition papers with the Court and serve them on the other parties not less than ELEVEN (11) DAYS prior to the return date of the original motion. NY R USDCTND L.R. 7.1(c).

5. *Computation of time*

   a. *Computing time.* FRCP 6 applies in computing any time period specified in the Federal Rules of Civil Procedure, in any local rule or court order, or in any statute that does not specify a method of computing time. FRCP 6(a).

      i. *Period stated in days or a longer unit.* When the period is stated in days or a longer unit of time:

         • Exclude the day of the event that triggers the period;

         • Count every day, including intermediate Saturdays, Sundays, and legal holidays; and

         • Include the last day of the period, but if the last day is a Saturday, Sunday, or legal holiday, the period continues to run until the end of the next day that is not a Saturday, Sunday, or legal holiday. FRCP 6(a)(1).

      ii. *Period stated in hours.* When the period is stated in hours:

         • Begin counting immediately on the occurrence of the event that triggers the period;

         • Count every hour, including hours during intermediate Saturdays, Sundays, and legal holidays; and

         • If the period would end on a Saturday, Sunday, or legal holiday, the period continues to run until the same time on the next day that is not a Saturday, Sunday, or legal holiday. FRCP 6(a)(2).

      iii. *Inaccessibility of the clerk's office.* Unless the court orders otherwise, if the clerk's office is inaccessible:

         • On the last day for filing under FRCP 6(a)(1), then the time for filing is extended to the first accessible day that is not a Saturday, Sunday, or legal holiday; or

         • During the last hour for filing under FRCP 6(a)(2), then the time for filing is extended to the same time on the first accessible day that is not a Saturday, Sunday, or legal holiday. FRCP 6(a)(3).

      iv. *"Last day" defined.* Unless a different time is set by a statute, local rule, or court order, the last day ends:

         • For electronic filing, at midnight in the court's time zone; and

         • For filing by other means, when the clerk's office is scheduled to close. FRCP 6(a)(4).

      v. *"Next day" defined.* The "next day" is determined by continuing to count forward when the period is measured after an event and backward when measured before an event. FRCP 6(a)(5).

      vi. *"Legal holiday" defined.* "Legal holiday" means:

         • The day set aside by statute for observing New Year's Day, Martin Luther King Jr.'s Birthday, Washington's Birthday, Memorial Day, Independence Day, Labor Day, Columbus Day, Veterans' Day, Thanksgiving Day, or Christmas Day;

         • Any day declared a holiday by the President or Congress; and

         • For periods that are measured after an event, any other day declared a holiday by the state where the district court is located. FRCP 6(a)(6).

   b. *Computation of electronic filing deadlines.* A document will be deemed timely filed if electronically filed prior to midnight Eastern Time. However, if the time of day is of the essence, the assigned judge may order that the document be filed by a time certain. NY R USDCTND CM/ECF(4)(4.3).

    i.   *Technical failures.* A Filing User, whose filing is untimely as the result of a technical failure of the Court's CM/ECF site, may seek appropriate relief from the Court. However, Filing Users are cautioned that, in some circumstances, the Court lacks the authority to grant an extension of time to file (e.g., FRCP 6(b) of the Federal Rules of Civil Procedure). NY R USDCTND CM/ECF(10)(10.1).

        •   *Technical failure of the filing user's system.* Problems with the Filing User's system, such as phone line problems, problems with the Filing User's Internet Service Provider ("ISP"), or hardware or software problems, will not constitute a technical failure under these Administrative Procedures nor excuse an untimely filing. A Filing User who cannot file documents electronically because of a problem on the Filing User's system must file the documents' conventionally along with an affidavit explaining the reason for not filing the documents electronically. NY R USDCTND CM/ECF(10)(10.2).

    c.   *Extending time.* Refer to the General Requirements section of this document for information on extending time.

    d.   *Additional time after certain kinds of service.* When a party may or must act within a specified time after service and service is made under FRCP 5(b)(2)(C), FRCP 5(b)(2)(D), FRCP 5(b)(2)(E), or FRCP 5(b)(2)(F), three (3) days are added after the period would otherwise expire under FRCP 6(a). FRCP 6(d).

        i.   In accordance with FRCP 6(e), service by electronic means is treated the same as service by mail for purposes of adding three (3) days to the prescribed period to respond. NY R USDCTND CM/ECF(5)(5.4). [Editor's note: the reference to FRCP 6(e) is likely meant to be a reference to FRCP 6(d)].

6.   *Individual judge practices.* Refer to the Miscellaneous section of this document for information on individual judge practices on timing of documents.

## C.  General Requirements

1.   *Court conference for non-dispositive motions.* Prior to making any non-dispositive motion before the assigned Magistrate Judge, the parties must make good faith efforts among themselves to resolve or reduce all differences relating to the non-dispositive issue. If, after conferring, the parties are unable to arrive at a mutually satisfactory resolution, the party seeking relief must then request a court conference with the assigned Magistrate Judge. NY R USDCTND L.R. 7.1(b)(2). A court conference is a prerequisite to filing a non-dispositive motion before the assigned Magistrate Judge. NY R USDCTND L.R. 7.1(b)(2). In addition, no non-dispositive or discovery motions should be presented to the Court unless authorized by the Magistrate Judge after communication with the Magistrate Judge's chambers. NY R USDCTND Order 25(IX)(A). Actions which involve an incarcerated, pro se party are not subject to the requirement that a court conference be held prior to filing a non-dispositive motion. NY R USDCTND L.R. 7.1(b)(2).

2.   *Motions, generally*

    a.   *Requirements.* A request for a court order must be made by motion. The motion must:

        i.   Be in writing unless made during a hearing or trial;

        ii.   State with particularity the grounds for seeking the order; and

        iii.   State the relief sought. FRCP 7(b)(1).

        iv.   When a moving party makes a motion based upon a rule or statute, the moving party must specify in its moving papers the rule or statute upon which it bases its motion. NY R USDCTND L.R. 7.1(a)(1).

    b.   *Notice of motion.* A party interested in resisting the relief sought by a motion has a right to notice thereof, and an opportunity to be heard. AMJUR MOTIONS § 12.

        i.   In addition to statutory or court rule provisions requiring notice of a motion—the purpose of such a notice requirement having been said to be to prevent a party from being prejudicially surprised by a motion—principles of natural justice dictate that an adverse party generally must be given notice that a motion will be presented to the court. AMJUR MOTIONS § 12.

    ii.  "Notice," in this regard, means reasonable notice, including a meaningful opportunity to prepare and to defend against allegations of a motion. AMJUR MOTIONS § 12.

c.  *Writing requirement.* The writing requirement is intended to insure that the adverse parties are informed and have a record of both the motion's pendency and the grounds on which the movant seeks an order. FPP § 1191; Feldberg v. Quechee Lakes Corp., 463 F.3d 195 (2d Cir. 2006).

    i.  It is sufficient "if the motion is stated in a written notice of the hearing of the motion." FPP § 1191.

d.  *Particularity requirement.* The particularity requirement insures that the opposing parties will have notice of their opponent's contentions. FEDPROC § 62:364; Goodman v. 1973 26 Foot Trojan Vessel, Arkansas Registration No. AR1439SN, 859 F.2d 71, 12 Fed.R.Serv.3d 645 (8th Cir. 1988). That requirement ensures that notice of the basis for the motion is provided to the court and to the opposing party so as to avoid prejudice, provide the opponent with a meaningful opportunity to respond, and provide the court with enough information to process the motion correctly. FEDPROC § 62:364; Andreas v. Volkswagen of America, Inc., 336 F.3d 789, 56 Fed.R.Serv.3d 6 (8th Cir. 2003).

    i.  Reasonable specification of the grounds for a motion is sufficient. However, where a movant fails to state even one ground for granting the motion in question, the movant has failed to meet the minimal standard of "reasonable specification." FEDPROC § 62:364; Martinez v. Trainor, 556 F.2d 818, 23 Fed.R.Serv.2d 403 (7th Cir. 1977).

    ii.  The court may excuse the failure to comply with the particularity requirement if it is inadvertent, and where no prejudice is shown by the opposing party. FEDPROC § 62:364.

e.  *Order to show cause.* All motions that a party brings by Order to Show Cause shall conform to the requirements set forth in NY R USDCTND L.R. 7.1(a)(1) and NY R USDCTND L.R. 7.1(a)(2). Immediately after filing an Order to Show Cause, the moving party must telephone the Chambers of the presiding judicial officer and inform Chambers staff that it has filed an Order to Show Cause. Parties may obtain the telephone numbers for all Chambers from the Clerk's office or at the Court's webpage. The Court shall determine the briefing schedule and return date applicable to motions brought by Order to Show Cause. NY R USDCTND L.R. 7.1(e).

    i.  In addition to the requirements set forth in NY R USDCTND L.R. 7.1(a)(1) and NY R USDCTND L.R. 7.1(a)(2), a motion brought by Order to Show Cause must include an affidavit clearly and specifically showing good and sufficient cause why the standard Notice of Motion procedure cannot be used. The moving party must give reasonable advance notice of the application for an Order to Show Cause to the other parties, except in those circumstances where the movant can demonstrate, in a detailed and specific affidavit, good cause and substantial prejudice that would result from the requirement of reasonable notice. NY R USDCTND L.R. 7.1(e).

    ii.  An Order to Show Cause must contain a space for the assigned judge to set forth:

- The deadline for filing and serving supporting papers,
- The deadline for filing and serving opposing papers, and
- The date and time for the hearing. NY R USDCTND L.R. 7.1(e).

3.  *Motion for continuance/extension of time*

a.  *Continuance.* Absent a controlling statute, the grant or denial of a continuance rests in the discretion of the trial judge to whom application is made, taking into consideration not only the facts of the particular case but also all of the demands on counsel's time and the court's. FEDPROC § 77:28; Star Financial Services, Inc. v. AASTAR Mortg. Corp., 89 F.3d 5 (1st Cir. 1996); Streber v. Hunter, 221 F.3d 701, 55 Fed.R.Evid.Serv. 376 (5th Cir. 2000). The grounds upon which a continuance is sought may include the following:

    i.  Unpreparedness of a party. FEDPROC § 77:29; U.S. v. 110 Bars of Silver, 3 Crucibles of Silver, 11 Bags of Silver Coins, 508 F.2d 799 (5th Cir. 1975).

ii.  Absence of a party. FEDPROC § 77:29. Since it is generally recognized that a party to a civil action ordinarily has a right to attend the trial, an illness severe enough to prevent a party from appearing in court is always a legitimate ground for asking for a continuance. FEDPROC § 77:30; Davis v. Operation Amigo, Inc., 378 F.2d 101 (10th Cir. 1967). However, the failure of the moving party to produce any competent medical evidence of the reasons and necessities for the party's unavailability will result in the denial of the continuance. FEDPROC § 77:30; Weisman v. Alleco, Inc., 925 F.2d 77 (4th Cir. 1991). Some courts, moreover, require a showing that the party has some particular contribution to make to the trial as a material witness or otherwise before granting a continuance due to the party's illness. FEDPROC § 77:30; Johnston v. Harris County Flood Control Dist., 869 F.2d 1565 (5th Cir. 1989).

iii. Absence of counsel. FEDPROC § 77:29. The courts have shown greater leniency when the illness of counsel is the ground for the continuance, especially where the case presents complex issues. FEDPROC § 77:31; Smith-Weik Machinery Corp. v. Murdock Mach. & Engineering Co., 423 F.2d 842 (5th Cir. 1970). However, many courts do not favor the granting of a continuance where counsel is unavailable due to a claimed engagement elsewhere or where it is not clear that counsel's illness was genuine. FEDPROC § 77:31; Community Nat. Life Ins. Co. v. Parker Square Sav. & Loan Ass'n, 406 F.2d 603 (10th Cir. 1969); Williams v. Johanns, 518 F.Supp.2d 205 (D.D.C. 2007).

iv.  Absence of a witness or evidence. FEDPROC § 77:29. The moving party must show. . .that the witness's testimony would be competent and material and that there are no other witnesses who can establish the same facts. FEDPROC § 77:32; Krodel v. Houghtaling, 468 F.2d 887 (4th Cir. 1972); Vitarelle v. Long Island R. Co., 415 F.2d 302 (2d Cir. 1969).

v.   Surprise and prejudice. FEDPROC § 77:29. The action complained of should not be one which could have been anticipated by due diligence or of which the movant had actual notice. FEDPROC § 77:33; Communications Maintenance, Inc. v. Motorola, Inc., 761 F.2d 1202, 2 Fed.R.Serv.3d 126 (7th Cir. 1985). Surprise and prejudice are often claimed as a result of the court allowing the other party to amend its pleadings under FRCP 15(b). FEDPROC § 77:29.

vi.  In determining whether to grant a continuance, the court will consider a variety of factors, including:

- Good faith on the part of the moving party;
- Due diligence of the moving party;
- The likelihood that the need prompting the request for a continuance will be met if the continuance is granted;
- Inconvenience to the court and the nonmoving party, including the witnesses, if the continuance is granted;
- Possible harm to the moving party if the continuance is denied;
- Prior delays in the proceedings;
- The court's prior refusal to grant the opposing party a continuance;
- Judicial economy. FEDPROC § 77:29; Amarin Plastics, Inc. v. Maryland Cup Corp., 946 F.2d 147, 34 Fed.R.Evid.Serv. 528 (1st Cir. 1991); Lewis v. Rawson, 564 F.3d 569 (2d Cir. 2009); U.S. v. 2.61 Acres of Land, More or Less, Situated in Mariposa County, State of Cal., 791 F.2d 666 (9th Cir. 1985); In re Homestore.com, Inc. Securities Litigation, 347 F.Supp.2d 814 (C.D.Cal. 2004).

b.  *Extension of time.* When an act may or must be done within a specified time, the court may, for good cause, extend the time:

i.  *Before original time or its extension expires.* With or without motion or notice if the court acts, or if a request is made, before the original time or its extension expires. FRCP 6(b)(1)(A).

- An application for the enlargement of time under FRCP 6(b)(1)(A) normally will be granted in the absence of bad faith on the part of the party seeking relief or prejudice to the adverse party. FPP § 1165.

- Neither a formal motion for enlargement nor notice to the adverse party is expressly required by FRCP 6(b). FPP § 1165.

ii. *After the time has expired.* On motion made after the time has expired if the party failed to act because of excusable neglect. FRCP 6(b)(1)(B).

- *Excusable neglect.* Excusable neglect is intended and has proven to be quite elastic in its application. In essence it is an equitable concept that must take account of all relevant circumstances of the party's failure to act within the required time. FPP § 1165.

- *Burden.* The burden is on the movant to establish that the failure to act in a timely manner was the result of excusable neglect. FEDPROC § 77:5. Common sense indicates that among the most important factors are the possibility of prejudice to the other parties, the length of the applicant's delay and its impact on the proceeding, the reason for the delay and whether it was within the control of the movant, and whether the movant has acted in good faith. FPP § 1165; Kettle Range Conservation Group v. U.S. Forest Service, 8 Fed.Appx. 729 (9th Cir. 2001).

- *Motion required.* No relief may be granted under FRCP 6(b)(1)(B) after the expiration of the specified period, even though the failure to act may have been the result of excusable neglect, if no motion is made by the party who failed to act. FEDPROC § 77:3.

iii. *Exceptions.* A court must not extend the time to act under FRCP 50(b), FRCP 50(d), FRCP 52(b), FRCP 59(b), FRCP 59(d), FRCP 59(e), and FRCP 60(b). FRCP 6(b)(2). FRCP 6(b) does not require the district courts to extend a time period where the extension would contravene a local court rule and does not apply to periods of time that are definitely fixed by statute. FEDPROC § 77:4; Truncale v. Universal Pictures Co., 82 F.Supp. 576 (S.D.N.Y. 1949); Lusk v. Lyon Metal Products, 9 F.R.D. 250 (W.D.Mo. 1949).

4. *Opposing papers.* The Federal Rules of Civil Procedure do not require any formal answer, return, or reply to a motion, except where the Federal Rules of Civil Procedure or local rules may require affidavits, memoranda, or other papers to be filed in opposition to a motion. Such papers are simply to apprise the court of such opposition and the grounds of that opposition. FEDPROC § 62:359.

a. *Effect of failure to respond to motion.* Although in the absence of statutory provision or court rule, a motion ordinarily does not require a written answer, when a party files a motion and the opposing party fails to respond, the court may construe such failure to respond as nonopposition to the motion or an admission that the motion was meritorious, may take the facts alleged in the motion as true—the rule in some jurisdictions being that the failure to respond to a fact set forth in a motion is deemed an admission—and may grant the motion if the relief requested appears to be justified. AMJUR MOTIONS § 28.

b. *Assent or no opposition not determinative.* However, a motion will not be granted automatically simply because an "assent" or a notation of "no opposition" has been filed; federal judges frequently deny motions that have been assented to when it is thought that justice so dictates. FPP § 1190.

c. *Responsive pleading inappropriate as response to motion.* An attempt to answer or oppose a motion with a responsive pleading usually is not appropriate. FPP § 1190.

5. *Reply papers.* Reply papers and adjournments are not permitted without the Court's prior permission. Permission to file a reply does not exist simply because CM/ECF generates a deadline for a reply on a nondispositive motion. NY R USDCTND L.R. 7.1(b)(2). A moving party may be required or permitted to prepare papers in addition to his original motion papers. AMJUR MOTIONS § 25. Papers answering or replying to opposing papers may be appropriate, in the interests of justice, where it appears there is a substantial reason for allowing a reply. Thus, a court may accept reply papers where a party demonstrates that the papers to which it seeks to file a reply raise new issues that are material to the disposition of the question before the court, or where the court determines, sua sponte, that it wishes further briefing of an issue raised in those papers and orders the submission of additional papers. FEDPROC § 62:360.

a. *Function of reply papers.* The function of a reply affidavit is to answer the arguments made in opposition to the position taken by the movant and not to permit the movant to introduce new arguments in support of the motion. AMJUR MOTIONS § 25.

b. *Issues raised for the first time in a reply document.* However, the view has been followed in some jurisdictions, that as a matter of judicial economy, where there is no prejudice and where the issues could be raised simply by filing a motion to dismiss, the trial court has discretion to consider arguments raised for the first time in a reply memorandum, and that a trial court may grant a motion to strike issues raised for the first time in a reply memorandum. AMJUR MOTIONS § 26.

c. *Opposition to cross-motion.* The original moving party may reply in further support of the original motion and in opposition to the cross-motion with a reply/opposition brief that does not exceed twenty-five (25) pages in length, exclusive of exhibits. NY R USDCTND L.R. 7.1(c).

6. *Surreply in support of cross-motion.* The cross-moving party may not reply in further support of its cross-motion without the Court's prior permission. NY R USDCTND L.R. 7.1(c).

7. *Submission of proposed order by prevailing party.* If the assigned judge instructs the prevailing party to do so, the prevailing party shall submit a proposed order which the opposing party has approved and which contains the endorsement of the opposing party: "Approved as to form." NY R USDCTND L.R. 77.2(b). In civil actions where the Court has directed a party to submit an order or judgment, that party shall file all such orders or judgments in duplicate, and the Clerk's entry of such duplicate in the proper record book shall be deemed in compliance with FRCP 79(b). Such party shall also furnish the Clerk with a sufficient number of additional copies for each party to the action, which the Clerk shall mail with notice of entry in accordance with FRCP 77(d). NY R USDCTND L.R. 5.1(b).

a. *Disagreement as to form of proposed order.* When the parties are unable to agree as to the form of the proposed order, the prevailing party shall, on seven (7) days notice to all other parties, submit a proposed order and a written explanation for the form of that order. The Court may award costs and attorney's fees against a party whose unreasonable conduct the Court deemed to have required the bringing of the motion. The provisions of NY R USDCTND L.R. 7.1 shall not apply to such motion, and the Court shall not hear oral argument. NY R USDCTND L.R. 77.2(b).

b. For more information on orders, refer to NY R USDCTND L.R. 77.2.

8. *Sanctions for vexatious or frivolous motions or failure to comply with* NY R USDCTND L.R. 7.1. A party who presents vexatious or frivolous motion papers or fails to comply with NY R USDCTND L.R. 7.1 is subject to discipline as the Court deems appropriate, including sanctions and the imposition of costs and attorney's fees to the opposing party. NY R USDCTND L.R. 7.1(i).

9. *Complex and multi-district litigation.* If the assigned judge determines, in his or her discretion, that the case is of such a complex nature that it cannot reasonably be trial ready within eighteen (18) months from the date the complaint is filed, the assigned judge may design and issue a particularized case management order that will move the case to trial as quickly as the complexity of the case allows. NY R USDCTND L.R. 3.3(a). The parties shall promptly notify the Court in writing if any action commenced is appropriate for multi-district litigation. NY R USDCTND L.R. 3.3(b).

10. *Appearances.* An attorney appearing for a party in a civil case shall promptly file with the Clerk a written notice of appearance; however, an attorney does not need to file a notice of appearance if the attorney who would be filing the notice of appearance is the same individual who has signed the complaint, notice of removal, pre-answer motion, or answer. NY R USDCTND L.R. 83.2(a). For more information, refer to NY R USDCTND L.R. 83.2.

11. *Related cases.* A civil case is "related" to another civil case for purposes of this guideline when, because of the similarity of facts and legal issues or because the cases arise from the same transactions or events, a substantial saving of judicial resources is likely to result from assigning the cases to the same Judge and Magistrate Judge. NY R USDCTND Order 12(G)(2). A civil case shall not be deemed related to another civil case merely because the civil case: (1) involves similar legal issues, or (2) involves the same parties. NY R USDCTND Order 12(G)(3). Presumptively, and subject to the power of a Judge to determine otherwise pursuant to NY R USDCTND Order 12(G)(5), civil cases shall not be deemed to be "related" unless both cases are still pending before the Court. NY R USDCTND Order 12(G)(4).

a. *New filings.* If an attorney or filing party indicates on the Civil Cover Sheet that a case is related to an earlier filed case, the Clerk shall instruct the filing party to file a notice of related cases. The allegedly related cases will be submitted by the Clerk to the Judge to whom the earliest filed case is assigned, who shall advise the Clerk whether such cases are related. NY R USDCTND Order 12(G)(1).

b. *Judicial determination that civil cases are "related."* Except for the cases described in the final sentence of NY R USDCTND Order 12(G)(6), all civil cases shall be randomly assigned when they are filed. Other than the cases described in the final sentence of NY R USDCTND Order 12(G)(6), civil cases shall not be deemed to be "related" for purposes of this guideline at the instance of any litigant or attorney unless and until there has been a determination by a Judge of this Court that the standard of NY R USDCTND Order 12(G)(2) is met. NY R USDCTND Order 12(G)(5).

 i. *Notice of related filing.* Any party may apply for such a determination by filing with the Clerk a notice of related filing, which should include an explanation as to why the standard of NY R USDCTND Order 12(G)(2) is met. A form for this purpose is available on the Court's website. A copy of the notice shall be served on all other parties who have appeared. Such an application must be made after the date when at least a majority of the defendants have been served with the complaint. Before making such an application, the applicant must confer in good faith with all other parties in an effort to reach an agreement on whether or not the case is "related". After such an application is made, any other party may serve and file within seven (7) calendar days a letter of no more than two (2) pages supporting or opposing the application. The application to have the case assigned to another Judge shall be presented to the Judge with the earliest filed case for decision on whether the action(s) should be reassigned as related cases. The Judge with the earliest filed case may then enter an order in the case at bar, either deeming the case to be related and directing the Clerk to reassign the action, or denying the application for reassignment. Any disputes concerning the assignment of related cases will be referred to the Chief Judge for resolution. NY R USDCTND Order 12(G)(5).

c. For more information on related cases, refer to NY R USDCTND Order 12(G).

12. *Alternative dispute resolution (ADR).* It is the mission of this court to do everything it can to help parties resolve their disputes as fairly, quickly, and efficiently as possible. NY R USDCTND Order 25(VIII).

a. *Arbitration.* NY R USDCTND L.R. 83.7 governs the consensual arbitration program for referral of civil actions to court-annexed arbitration. It may remain in effect until further order of the Court. Its purpose is to establish a less formal procedure for the just, efficient and economical resolution of disputes, while preserving the right to a full trial on demand. NY R USDCTND L.R. 83.7-1.

 i. *Actions subject to arbitration.* The Clerk shall notify the parties in all civil cases, except as the Local Rules of Practice for the United States District Court for the Northern District of New York otherwise direct, that they may consent to non-binding arbitration under NY R US-DCTND L.R. 83.7. The notice shall be furnished to the parties at pretrial/scheduling conferences or shall be included with pretrial conference notices and instructions. Consent to arbitration under NY R USDCTND L.R. 83.7 shall be discussed at the pretrial/scheduling conference. No party or attorney shall be prejudiced for refusing to participate in arbitration. The Court shall allow the referral of any civil action pending before it to the arbitration process if the parties consent. The plaintiff shall be responsible for securing the execution of a consent form by the parties and for filing the form with the Clerk within fourteen (14) days after the parties receive the form. The parties shall freely and knowingly enter into the consent. NY R USDCTND L.R. 83.7-2.

 ii. *Referral to arbitration.* The Clerk shall refer every action subject to NY R USDCTND L.R. 83.7 to arbitration in accordance with the procedures under NY R USDCTND L.R. 83.7 twenty-one (21) days after the filing of the last responsive pleading or within twenty-one (21) days of the filing of a stipulated consent order referring the action to arbitration, whichever event occurs last, except as otherwise provided. If any party notices a motion to dismiss under the provisions of FRCP 12(a) and/or FRCP 12(b), or a motion to join necessary parties pursuant to the Federal Rules of Civil Procedure prior to the expiration of the twenty-one (21) day period, the assigned judge shall hear the motion and further proceedings under NY R USDCTND L.R. 83.7 shall be deferred pending decision on the motion. If the Court does not dismiss the action on the motion, the Court shall refer the action to arbitration twenty-one (21) days after the filing of the decision. NY R USDCTND L.R. 83.7-3(a). Motions for summary judgment pursuant to

FRCP 56 shall be filed and served within twenty-one (21) days following the close of discovery. The filing of a FRCP 56 motion shall defer further proceedings under NY R USDCTND L.R. 83.7 pending decision on the motion. NY R USDCTND L.R. 83.7-3(a).

- *Relief from referral.* Any party shall request relief from the operation of NY R USDCTND L.R. 83.7 by filing with the Court a motion for the relief within twenty-one (21) days after entry of the initial stipulated consent order which refers the case for arbitration. The assigned judge shall, sua sponte, exempt an action from the application of NY R USDCTND L.R. 83.7 where the objectives of arbitration would not be realized because (1) the case involves complex or novel legal issues, (2) legal issues predominate over factual issues, or (3) for other good cause. NY R USDCTND L.R. 83.7-3(c).

iii. For more information on arbitration, refer to NY R USDCTND L.R. 83.7.

b. *Mediation.* The purpose of NY R USDCTND L.R. 83.11 is to provide a supplementary procedure to the Court's existing alternative dispute resolution procedures. NY R USDCTND L.R. 83.11 provides for an earlier resolution of civil disputes resulting in savings of time and cost to litigants and the Court without sacrificing the quality of justice rendered or the right of litigants to a full trial on all issues not resolved through mediation. NY R USDCTND L.R. 83.11-1(a). Mediation is a process by which an impartial person, the mediator, facilitates communication between disputing parties to promote understanding, reconciliation and settlement. The mediator is an advocate for settlement and uses the mediation process to help the parties fully explore any potential area of agreement. The mediator does not serve as a judge or arbitrator and has no authority to render any decision on any disputed issue or to force a settlement. The parties themselves are responsible for negotiating any resolution(s) to their dispute. NY R USDCTND L.R. 83.11-1(b).

i. *Actions subject to mediation.* The Court may refer any civil action (or any portion thereof) to mediation under NY R USDCTND L.R. 83.11: (1) by order of referral; or (2) on the motion of any party; or (3) by consent of the parties. NY R USDCTND L.R. 83.11-3(a).

- *Withdrawal from mediation.* The parties may withdraw from mediation any civil action or claim that the Court refers to mediation pursuant to NY R USDCTND L.R. 83.11-3 by application to the assigned judge at least ten (10) days prior to the scheduled mediation session. NY R USDCTND L.R. 83.11-3(b).

ii. *Mandatory mediation program.* The United States District Court for the Northern District of New York has adopted this Mandatory Mediation Plan. The paid Mediation Program is designed to provide quicker, less expensive and potentially more satisfying alternatives to continuing litigation, without impairing the quality of justice or the right to trial. NY R USDCTND Order 47(1)(1.2)(A). This Mandatory Mediation Plan applies to civil actions pending as well as newly filed actions, except as otherwise indicated in NY R USDCTND Order 47. The Local Rules for voluntary mediation will apply only to Pro Se Cases that proceed through the Assisted Mediation Program. NY R USDCTND Order 47(1)(1.2)(B).

- *Referral into the pilot mandatory mediation program for new cases.* All civil cases shall be referred automatically into the Mandatory Mediation Program. Notice of the Mandatory Mediation requirements will be provided to all parties immediately upon the filing of a complaint and answer or a notice of removal. ADR intervention will be scheduled at the conference held pursuant to NY R USDCTND L.R. 16.1. NY R USDCTND Order 47(2)(2.1)(A). For a list of categories of actions exempted from automatic referral, refer to NY R USDCTND Order 47(2)(2.1)(A).

- *Referral into the pilot mandatory mediation program for pending cases.* The assigned Judge or Magistrate Judge on any pending civil case may, sua sponte or with status conference, issue an order referring the case into the Mandatory Mediation Program. The order shall specify a date on which the ADR intervention is to be completed. NY R USDCTND Order 47(2)(2.1)(B).

- *Referral into the pilot mandatory mediation program by stipulation.* A case may be referred into the Mandatory Mediation Program by stipulation of all parties. Stipulations shall be filed and shall designate the time frame within which the ADR process will be completed. Stipulations are presumed acceptable unless the assigned Judge or Magistrate Judge determines that the interests of justice are not served. NY R USDCTND Order 47(2)(2.1)(C).

- *Relief from referral.* Motions to opt out of the program will be addressed by the assigned Magistrate Judge at the FRCP 16 conference. NY R USDCTND Order 47(2)(2.2)(A). Opting Out Motions shall be granted only for "good cause" shown. Inconvenience, travel costs, attorney fees or other costs shall not constitute "good cause." A party seeking relief from the Mandatory Mediation Program must set forth the reasons why Mandatory Mediation has no reasonable chance of being productive. NY R USDCTND Order 47(2)(2.2)(B). The assigned Magistrate Judge may, sua sponte, exempt any case from the Court's Mandatory Mediation Program. NY R USDCTND Order 47(2)(2.2)(C).

iii. *Assisted mediation program.* The Court may assign specially trained pro bono Special Mediation Counsel to assist pro se civilian litigants with preparing for and participating in mediation. The Assisted Mediation Program is open to civilian pro se parties to actions in the Northern District of New York. The assigned judge or magistrate judge determines if the case would benefit from mediation and would also benefit from the assignment of Special Mediation Counsel to assist the pro se party with the mediation process. NY R USDCTND L.R. 83.8(a). Appointment of Special Mediation Counsel is in no way guaranteed, even if the action is referred to the court-annexed mediation program. Appointment is at the sole discretion of the presiding judge. NY R USDCTND L.R. 83.8(a).

- *Referral to assisted mediation program.* If the court determines that referral to the Assisted Mediation Program is appropriate, the Court shall enter an order of reference to the Assisted Mediation Program. NY R USDCTND L.R. 83.8(b).

iv. For more information on mediation, refer to NY R USDCTND L.R. 83.11 and NY R USDCTND Order 47.

c. *Early neutral evaluation (ENE).* Early neutral evaluation (ENE) is a process in which parties obtain from an experienced neutral (an "evaluator") a nonbinding, reasoned, oral evaluation of the merits of the case. The first step in the ENE process involves the Court appointing an evaluator who has expertise in the area of law in the case. After the parties exchange essential information and position statements early in the pretrial period (usually within one hundred fifty (150) to two hundred (200) days after a complaint has been filed), the evaluator convenes an ENE session that typically lasts about two hours. At the ENE meeting, each side briefly presents the factual and legal basis of its position. The evaluator may ask questions of the parties and help them identify the main issues in dispute and the areas of agreement. The evaluator may also help the parties explore options for settlement. If settlement does not occur, the evaluator then offers an opinion as to the settlement value of the case, including the likelihood of liability and the likely range of damages. With the benefit of this assessment, the parties are again encouraged to discuss settlement, with or without the evaluator's assistance. The parties may also explore ways to narrow the issues in dispute, exchange information about the case or otherwise prepare efficiently for trial. NY R USDCTND L.R. 83.12-1.

i. *Actions subject to early neutral evaluation.* The Court may refer any civil action (or any portion thereof) to ENE under NY R USDCTND L.R. 83.12: (1) by order of referral; (2) on the motion of any party; or (3) by consent of the parties. NY R USDCTND L.R. 83.12-3(a).

- *Withdrawal from the ENE process.* The parties may withdraw any civil action or claim that the Court has referred to the ENE Process pursuant to NY R USDCTND L.R. 83.12-3 by application to the assigned judge at least ten (10) days before the scheduled evaluation session. NY R USDCTND L.R. 83.12-3(b).

ii. For more information on early neutral evaluation (ENE), refer to NY R USDCTND L.R. 83.12.

13. *Settlement procedures.* On notice to the Court or the Clerk that the parties have settled an action, and upon confirmation of the settlement by all parties, the Court may issue a judgment dismissing the action by reason of settlement. The Court shall issue the order without prejudice to the parties' right to secure reinstatement of the case within thirty (30) days after the date of judgment by making a showing that the settlement was not, in fact, consummated. NY R USDCTND L.R. 68.2(a). If the Court decides not to

follow the procedures set forth in NY R USDCTND L.R. 68.2(a), the parties shall file within thirty (30) days of the notification to the Court, unless otherwise directed by written order, such notices, stipulations and/or motions as are necessary to terminate the action. If the required documents are not filed within the thirty (30) day period, the Clerk shall place the action on the dismissal calendar. NY R USDCTND L.R. 68.2(b).

14. *Sanctions and penalties for noncompliance.* Failure of an attorney or of a party to comply with any provision of the Local Rules of Practice for the United States District Court for the Northern District of New York, General Orders of this District, Orders of the Court, or the Federal Rules of Civil Procedure shall be a ground for imposition of sanctions. NY R USDCTND L.R. 1.1(d).

15. *Individual judge practices.* Refer to the Miscellaneous section of this document for information on individual judge practices on general requirements for documents.

## D. Documents

1. *Documents for moving party*

   a. *Required documents*

      i. *Notice of motion and motion.* In the Notice of Motion, the moving party is required to set forth the date that the court conference with the Magistrate Judge was held regarding the issues being presented in the motion. Failure to include this information in the Notice of Motion may result in the Court rejecting the motion papers. NY R USDCTND L.R. 7.1(b)(2). Refer to the General Requirements section of this document for information on the notice of motion and motion.

         • *Order to show cause.* Refer to the General Requirements section of this document for information on bringing a motion by order to show cause.

      ii. *Memorandum of law.* Except as otherwise provided in NY R USDCTND L.R. 7.1(a), all motions. . .require a memorandum of law. NY R USDCTND L.R. 7.1(a). Refer to the Format section of this document for the formatting requirements for memoranda of law.

      iii. *Supporting affidavit.* Except as otherwise provided in NY R USDCTND L.R. 7.1(a), all motions. . .require a. . .supporting affidavit. NY R USDCTND L.R. 7.1(a). An affidavit must not contain legal arguments but must contain factual and procedural background that is relevant to the motion the affidavit supports. NY R USDCTND L.R. 7.1(a)(2).

      iv. *Certificate of service.* Except as otherwise provided in NY R USDCTND L.R. 7.1(a), all motions. . .require. . .proof of service on all the parties. See NY R USDCTND L.R. 5.1(a). NY R USDCTND L.R. 7.1(a). FRCP 5(d) requires that the person making service under FRCP 5 certify that service has been effected. FRCP 5(Advisory Committee Notes). Having such information on file may be useful for many purposes, including proof of service if an issue arises concerning the effectiveness of the service. FRCP 5(Advisory Committee Notes). The party or its designee shall declare, by affidavit or certification, that it has provided all other parties in the action with all documents it has filed with the Court. NY R USDCTND L.R. 5.1(a).

         • Attorneys and pro se parties who are not Filing or Receiving Users must be served with a paper copy of any electronically filed pleading or other document. NY R USDCTND CM/ECF(5)(5.2). Such paper service must be documented by electronically filing a certificate of service. NY R USDCTND CM/ECF(5)(5.2).

   b. *Supplemental documents*

      i. *Supporting evidence.* When a motion relies on facts outside the record, the court may hear the matter on affidavits or may hear it wholly or partly on oral testimony or on depositions. FRCP 43(c).

      ii. *Notice of constitutional question.* A party that files a pleading, written motion, or other paper drawing into question the constitutionality of a federal or state statute must promptly:

         • *File notice.* File a notice of constitutional question stating the question and identifying the paper that raises it, if: (1) a federal statute is questioned and the parties do not include the United States, one of its agencies, or one of its officers or employees in an official capacity;

or (2) a state statute is questioned and the parties do not include the state, one of its agencies, or one of its officers or employees in an official capacity; and

- *Serve notice.* Serve the notice and paper on the Attorney General of the United States if a federal statute is questioned—or on the state attorney general if a state statute is questioned—either by certified or registered mail or by sending it to an electronic address designated by the attorney general for this purpose. FRCP 5.1(a).

- *No forfeiture.* A party's failure to file and serve the notice, or the court's failure to certify, does not forfeit a constitutional claim or defense that is otherwise timely asserted. FRCP 5.1(d).

iii. *Nongovernmental corporate disclosure statement*

- *Contents.* A nongovernmental corporate party must file two (2) copies of a disclosure statement that: (1) identifies any parent corporation and any publicly held corporation owning ten percent (10%) or more of its stock; or (2) states that there is no such corporation. FRCP 7.1(a).

- *Time to file; Supplemental filing.* A party must: (1) file the disclosure statement with its first appearance, pleading, petition, motion, response, or other request addressed to the court; and (2) promptly file a supplemental statement if any required information changes. FRCP 7.1(b).

iv. *Copies of authorities.* When serving a pro se litigant with a memorandum of law or any other paper which contains citations to authorities that are unpublished or published exclusively on electronic databases, counsel shall include a hard copy of those authorities. Although copies of authorities published only on electronic databases are not required to be filed, copies shall be provided upon request to opposing counsel who lack access to electronic databases. NY R USDCTND L.R. 7.1(a)(1).

v. *Proposed order.* A document that is submitted in .pdf format cannot be modified; therefore, a proposed order or stipulation must be in a word processing format. The chambers of the assigned judge may request that a proposed order and/or a stipulation be e-mailed to the courtroom deputy for the presiding judge in either WordPerfect or Microsoft Word format. Please attach your proposed order and/or stipulation to an Internet e-mail sent to the appropriate e-mail address listed in NY R USDCTND CM/ECF(8)(8.2). NY R USDCTND CM/ECF(8)(8.2).

vi. *Cover letter authorizing e-mail or facsimile filing.* Neither the Court nor the Clerk's Office will accept for filing any facsimile or e-mail transmission without prior authorization from the Court. The party using facsimile or e-mail transmissions to file its papers must accompany any such documents with a cover letter stating that the Court authorized such transmissions and the date on which the Court provided that authorization. Violations of NY R USDCTND L.R. 5.5 subject the offending party to the Court's full disciplinary powers. NY R USDCTND L.R. 5.5.

vii. *Affidavit attesting to failed attempts to file electronically.* If the Court's CM/ECF site experiences a technical failure, a Filing User may submit documents to the Court that day in an alternate manner provided that the documents are accompanied by the Filing User's affidavit stating that the Filing User attempted to file electronically at least two times in one (1) hour increments after 10:00 a.m. that day. The following methods are acceptable alternate means for filing documents in case of a technical failure: (1) via electronic mail in a PDF attachment sent to the e-mail address for technical failures; or (2) in person, by bringing the document to the Clerk's Office on paper accompanied by a CD/ROM that contains the document in .pdf format. NY R USDCTND CM/ECF(10)(10.1).

- A Filing User who cannot file documents electronically because of a problem on the Filing User's system must file the documents' conventionally along with an affidavit explaining the reason for not filing the documents electronically. NY R USDCTND CM/ECF(10)(10.2).

viii. *Notice of conventional filing.* If the Clerk's Office grants permission to conventionally file the

document, the Filing User shall electronically file a notice of conventional filing for the documents. More information regarding this process can be obtained from the Court's web page. NY R USDCTND CM/ECF(4)(4.5).

ix. *CD/ROM with PDF of document(s).* If the Court grants permission to file a document traditionally, the attorney must submit the documents for filing to the Clerk's Office on CD/ROM in .pdf or pdf.A format. NY R USDCTND CM/ECF(2).

x. *English translation.* The Court conducts its reviews and deliberations in English. Unless otherwise directed by the Court, any document that a party transmits to the Court (including one in the record on appeal) that is in a language other than English must be accompanied by an English translation that the translator has certified as true and accurate, pursuant to 28 U.S.C.A. § 1746. NY R USDCTND L.R. 10.1(e). For more information, refer to NY R USDCTND L.R. 10.1(e).

xi. *Courtesy copies.* The Court may require that courtesy copies of electronically filed documents be submitted for its review and may amend these Administrative Procedures (NY R USDCTND CM/ECF) at any time without prior notice. NY R USDCTND CM/ECF(2).

xii. *Copies for three-judge court.* On the convening of a three-judge court, the parties shall make three (3) copies of all non-electronically filed pleadings, motion papers, and memoranda of law available to the Clerk for distribution. NY R USDCTND L.R. 9.1.

2. *Documents for opposing party*

   a. *Required documents*

      i. *Opposition.* Refer to the General Requirements section of this document for information on the opposing papers.

      ii. *Memorandum of law.* Except as otherwise provided in NY R USDCTND L.R. 7.1(a), all. . .opposition to motions require a memorandum of law. NY R USDCTND L.R. 7.1(a).

         • *Cross-motion brief.* If a party makes a cross-motion, it must join its cross motion brief with its opposition brief, and this combined brief may not exceed twenty-five (25) pages in length, exclusive of exhibits. A separate brief in opposition to the original motion is not permissible. NY R USDCTND L.R. 7.1(c).

         • Refer to the Format section of this document for the formatting requirements for memoranda of law.

      iii. *Supporting affidavit.* Except as otherwise provided in NY R USDCTND L.R. 7.1(a), all. . .opposition to motions require a. . .supporting affidavit. NY R USDCTND L.R. 7.1(a). An affidavit must not contain legal arguments but must contain factual and procedural background that is relevant to the motion the affidavit supports. NY R USDCTND L.R. 7.1(a)(2).

      iv. *Certificate of service.* Except as otherwise provided in NY R USDCTND L.R. 7.1(a), all. . .opposition to motions require. . .proof of service on all the parties. See NY R US-DCTND L.R. 5.1(a). NY R USDCTND L.R. 7.1(a). FRCP 5(d) requires that the person making service under FRCP 5 certify that service has been effected. FRCP 5(Advisory Committee Notes). Having such information on file may be useful for many purposes, including proof of service if an issue arises concerning the effectiveness of the service. FRCP 5(Advisory Committee Notes). The party or its designee shall declare, by affidavit or certification, that it has provided all other parties in the action with all documents it has filed with the Court. NY R USDCTND L.R. 5.1(a).

         • Attorneys and pro se parties who are not Filing or Receiving Users must be served with a paper copy of any electronically filed pleading or other document. NY R USDCTND CM/ECF(5)(5.2). Such paper service must be documented by electronically filing a certificate of service. NY R USDCTND CM/ECF(5)(5.2).

   b. *Supplemental documents*

      i. *Supporting evidence.* When a motion relies on facts outside the record, the court may hear the

matter on affidavits or may hear it wholly or partly on oral testimony or on depositions. FRCP 43(c).

ii.   *Notice of constitutional question.* A party that files a pleading, written motion, or other paper drawing into question the constitutionality of a federal or state statute must promptly:

- *File notice.* File a notice of constitutional question stating the question and identifying the paper that raises it, if: (1) a federal statute is questioned and the parties do not include the United States, one of its agencies, or one of its officers or employees in an official capacity; or (2) a state statute is questioned and the parties do not include the state, one of its agencies, or one of its officers or employees in an official capacity; and

- *Serve notice.* Serve the notice and paper on the Attorney General of the United States if a federal statute is questioned—or on the state attorney general if a state statute is questioned—either by certified or registered mail or by sending it to an electronic address designated by the attorney general for this purpose. FRCP 5.1(a).

- *No forfeiture.* A party's failure to file and serve the notice, or the court's failure to certify, does not forfeit a constitutional claim or defense that is otherwise timely asserted. FRCP 5.1(d).

iii.  *Cross-motion.* A party may file and serve a cross-motion (meaning a competing request for relief or order similar to that requested by another party against the cross-moving party) at the time it files and serves its opposition papers to the original motion, i.e., not less than SEVENTEEN (17) DAYS prior to the return date of the motion. NY R USDCTND L.R. 7.1(c).

iv.   *Copies of authorities.* When serving a pro se litigant with a memorandum of law or any other paper which contains citations to authorities that are unpublished or published exclusively on electronic databases, counsel shall include a hard copy of those authorities. Although copies of authorities published only on electronic databases are not required to be filed, copies shall be provided upon request to opposing counsel who lack access to electronic databases. NY R USDCTND L.R. 7.1(a)(1).

v.    *Cover letter authorizing e-mail or facsimile filing.* Neither the Court nor the Clerk's Office will accept for filing any facsimile or e-mail transmission without prior authorization from the Court. The party using facsimile or e-mail transmissions to file its papers must accompany any such documents with a cover letter stating that the Court authorized such transmissions and the date on which the Court provided that authorization. Violations of NY R USDCTND L.R. 5.5 subject the offending party to the Court's full disciplinary powers. NY R USDCTND L.R. 5.5.

vi.   *Affidavit attesting to failed attempts to file electronically.* If the Court's CM/ECF site experiences a technical failure, a Filing User may submit documents to the Court that day in an alternate manner provided that the documents are accompanied by the Filing User's affidavit stating that the Filing User attempted to file electronically at least two times in one (1) hour increments after 10:00 a.m. that day. The following methods are acceptable alternate means for filing documents in case of a technical failure: (1) via electronic mail in a PDF attachment sent to the e-mail address for technical failures; or (2) in person, by bringing the document to the Clerk's Office on paper accompanied by a CD/ROM that contains the document in .pdf format. NY R USDCTND CM/ECF(10)(10.1).

- A Filing User who cannot file documents electronically because of a problem on the Filing User's system must file the documents' conventionally along with an affidavit explaining the reason for not filing the documents electronically. NY R USDCTND CM/ECF(10)(10.2).

vii.  *Notice of conventional filing.* If the Clerk's Office grants permission to conventionally file the document, the Filing User shall electronically file a notice of conventional filing for the documents. More information regarding this process can be obtained from the Court's web page. NY R USDCTND CM/ECF(4)(4.5).

viii. *CD/ROM with PDF of document(s).* If the Court grants permission to file a document traditionally, the attorney must submit the documents for filing to the Clerk's Office on CD/ROM in .pdf or pdf.A format. NY R USDCTND CM/ECF(2).

ix. *English translation.* The Court conducts its reviews and deliberations in English. Unless otherwise directed by the Court, any document that a party transmits to the Court (including one in the record on appeal) that is in a language other than English must be accompanied by an English translation that the translator has certified as true and accurate, pursuant to 28 U.S.C.A. § 1746. NY R USDCTND L.R. 10.1(e). For more information, refer to NY R USDCTND L.R. 10.1(e).

x. *Courtesy copies.* The Court may require that courtesy copies of electronically filed documents be submitted for its review and may amend these Administrative Procedures (NY R USDCTND CM/ECF) at any time without prior notice. NY R USDCTND CM/ECF(2).

xi. *Copies for three-judge court.* On the convening of a three-judge court, the parties shall make three (3) copies of all non-electronically filed pleadings, motion papers, and memoranda of law available to the Clerk for distribution. NY R USDCTND L.R. 9.1.

3. *Individual judge practices.* Refer to the Miscellaneous section of this document for information on individual judge practices on required documents.

## E. Format

1. *Form of documents.* The rules governing captions and other matters of form in pleadings apply to motions and other papers. FRCP 7(b)(2). All pleadings and other papers shall be served and filed in accordance with the Federal Rules of Civil Procedure and shall be in the form prescribed by NY R USDCTND L.R. 10.1. NY R USDCTND L.R. 5.1(a).

   a. *Form, generally.* All pleadings, motions, and other documents that a party presents for filing, whether in paper form or in electronic form, shall meet the following requirements:

      i. *Font size.* All text, whether in the body of the document or in footnotes, must be a minimum of twelve (12) point type. NY R USDCTND L.R. 10.1(a)(1).

      ii. *Margins.* All documents must have one (1) inch margins on all four sides of the page. NY R USDCTND L.R. 10.1(a)(2).

      iii. *Spacing.* All text in the body of the document must be double-spaced. NY R USDCTND L.R. 10.1(a)(3).

         • The text in block quotations and footnotes may be single-spaced. NY R USDCTND L.R. 10.1(a)(4).

      iv. *Page numbering.* Pages must be consecutively numbered. NY R USDCTND L.R. 10.1(a)(7).

      v. *Circumventing formatting limitations*

         • Extensive footnotes must not be used to circumvent page limitations. NY R USDCTND L.R. 10.1(a)(5).

         • Compacted or other compressed printing features must not be used. NY R USDCTND L.R. 10.1(a)(6).

   b. *Additional requirements for paper filing.* Additional requirements for all pleadings, motions, and other documents that a party presents for filing in paper form:

      i. *Paper size.* All documents must be on eight and one-half by eleven (8-1/2 x 11) inch white paper of good quality. NY R USDCTND L.R. 10.1(b)(1).

      ii. *Text.* All text must be plainly and legibly written, typewritten, printed or reproduced without erasures or interlineations materially defacing them. NY R USDCTND L.R. 10.1(b)(2).

      iii. *Ink.* All documents must be in black or blue ink. NY R USDCTND L.R. 10.1(b)(3).

      iv. *Binding.* Pages of all documents must be stapled (or in some other way fastened) together. NY R USDCTND L.R. 10.1(b)(4).

      v. *Single-sided paper.* All documents must be single-sided. NY R USDCTND L.R. 10.1(b)(5).

      vi. *Electronic submission.* The Court, at its discretion, may require the electronic submission of any document in a WordPerfect-compatible format. NY R USDCTND L.R. 10.1(b)(6).

vii. *Rejection of document.* The Court may reject documents that do not comply with the above-listed requirements. NY R USDCTND L.R. 10.1(b).

c. *Caption; Names of parties.* Every pleading must have a caption with the court's name, a title, a file number, and a FRCP 7(a) designation. The title of the complaint must name all the parties; the title of other pleadings, after naming the first party on each side, may refer generally to other parties. FRCP 10(a). Each document must contain a caption for the specific case to which it pertains. The caption must include the title of the Court, the title of the action, the civil action number of the case, the initials of the assigned judge(s), and the name or nature of the paper in sufficient detail for identification. If a litigant has more than one action pending in this Court, any and all papers filed in a case must contain and pertain to one civil action number, unless the civil actions have been consolidated by the Court. Any motion or other papers purporting to relate to more than one action will not be accepted for filing and may be stricken by the Court. NY R USDCTND L.R. 10.1(c)(1) shall not apply, as noted in NY R USDCTND L.R. 10.1(c), to notices of change of address filed by attorneys of record and pro se litigants. The parties must separately caption affidavits and declarations and must not physically attach them to the Notice of Motion or Memorandum of Law. NY R USDCTND L.R. 10.1(c)(1).

d. *Paragraphs; Separate statements.* A party must state its claims or defenses in numbered paragraphs, each limited as far as practicable to a single set of circumstances. A later pleading may refer by number to a paragraph in an earlier pleading. If doing so would promote clarity, each claim founded on a separate transaction or occurrence—and each defense other than a denial—must be stated in a separate count or defense. FRCP 10(b).

e. *Adoption by reference; Exhibits.* A statement in a pleading may be adopted by reference elsewhere in the same pleading or in any other pleading or motion. A copy of a written instrument that is an exhibit to a pleading is a part of the pleading for all purposes. FRCP 10(c).

f. *Citation of local rules.* These are the Local Rules of Practice for the United States District Court for the Northern District of New York. They shall be cited as "L.R. ___." NY R USDCTND L.R. 1.1(a).

g. *Acceptance by the clerk.* The clerk must not refuse to file a paper solely because it is not in the form prescribed by the Federal Rules of Civil Procedure or by a local rule or practice. FRCP 5(d)(4).

2. *Form of electronic documents.* All pleadings, motions, and other documents that a party presents for filing, whether in paper form or in electronic form, shall meet the requirements in NY R USDCTND L.R. 10.1(a). NY R USDCTND L.R. 10.1(a). Refer above for more information.

a. *Attachments and exhibits.* A Filing User must submit in electronic form all documents referenced as exhibits or attachments in accordance with the Court's CM/ECF Users Manual unless the Court otherwise orders. A Filing User shall submit as exhibits or attachments only those excerpts of the referenced documents that are directly germane to the matter under the Court's consideration. Excerpted material must be clearly and prominently identified as such. Filing Users who file excerpts of documents as exhibits or attachments under these Administrative Procedures (NY R USDCTND CM/ECF) do so without prejudice to their right to timely file additional excerpts or the complete document. Responding parties may also timely file the complete document or additional excerpts that they believe are directly germane to the matter under the Court's consideration. NY R USDCTND CM/ECF(4)(4.4).

i. All attachments must be described in sufficient detail so the Court and opposing counsel can easily identify and distinguish the filed attachments. Vague or general descriptions are insufficient (i.e., "Exhibit 1"). Rather, each attachment shall have a descriptive title identifying, with specificity, the document that is being filed (i.e., "Exhibit 12 Mulligan County Fire Investigation Report.") Failure to adequately describe attachments may result in the document being rejected by the Court. NY R USDCTND CM/ECF(4)(4.4).

b. *Large documents.* For information on the electronic filing of large documents, please consult the Court's CM/ECF Users Manual, which is available on the Court's web page. NY R USDCTND CM/ECF(4)(4.5).

i. A party who believes a document is too lengthy to electronically image, i.e., "scan," may contact the Clerk's Office for permission to file that document conventionally. If the Clerk's Office grants permission to conventionally file the document, the Filing User shall electronically file a notice of conventional filing for the documents. More information regarding this process can be obtained from the Court's web page. Exhibits submitted conventionally shall be served on other parties as if they were not subject to these Administrative Procedures (NY R USDCTND CM/ECF). For a list of hints and tips for scanning large documents, please consult the Court's web page. NY R USDCTND CM/ECF(4)(4.5).

c.  *Legibility.* It shall be the Filing User's responsibility to verify the legibility of scanned documents before filing them electronically with the Court. NY R USDCTND CM/ECF(4)(4.6).

d.  *Color documents.* Since documents scanned in color or containing a graphic take much longer to upload, Filing Users are encouraged to configure their scanners to scan documents at 300 dpi and preferably in black and white rather than in color. NY R USDCTND CM/ECF(4)(4.7).

e.  *Items not in .PDF format.* Parties wishing to file items not amenable to .pdf format (i.e. CD's, DVD's), shall file such items conventionally with the Clerk's Office. The Filing User shall electronically file a notice of conventional filing indicating that these items have been submitted to the clerk and shall serve copies of these items on other parties as if they were not subject to these Administrative Procedures (NY R USDCTND CM/ECF). These item(s) will be maintained by the Clerk's Office until the case is disposed, at which time they will be returned to the filing party for retention consistent with NY R USDCTND CM/ECF(4)(4.9). NY R USDCTND CM/ECF(4)(4.8).

3.  *Form of memoranda of law*

a.  *Length limitation.* No party shall file or serve a memorandum of law that exceeds twenty-five (25) pages in length, unless that party obtains leave of the judge hearing the motion prior to filing. NY R USDCTND L.R. 7.1(a)(1).

b.  *Table of contents.* All memoranda of law shall contain a table of contents. NY R USDCTND L.R. 7.1(a)(1).

4.  *Signing of pleadings, motions and other papers*

a.  *Signature.* Every pleading, written motion, and other paper must be signed by at least one attorney of record in the attorney's name—or by a party personally if the party is unrepresented. The paper must state the signer's address, e-mail address, and telephone number. FRCP 11(a). Each document must identify the person filing the document. This identification must include an original signature of the attorney or pro se litigant; the typewritten name of that person; the address of a pro se litigant; and the bar roll number, office address, telephone number, e-mail address and fax number of the attorney. Telephone numbers of non-prisoner pro se parties may be provided voluntarily or upon request of the Court. See General Order #22 (NY R USDCTND CM/ECF) for signature requirements. NY R USDCTND L.R. 10.1(c)(2).

  i.  *Electronic signatures.* Documents filed under an attorney's login and password shall constitute that attorney's signature for purposes of the Local Rules of Practice for the United States District Court for the Northern District of New York and Federal Rules of Civil Procedure, including but not limited to FRCP 11. A pleading or other document requiring an attorney's signature shall be signed in the following manner, whether filed electronically or submitted on disk or CD/ROM to the Clerk's Office: "s/ (attorney name)." The correct format for an attorney signature is found in NY R USDCTND CM/ECF(6)(6.1). NY R USDCTND CM/ECF(6)(6.1).

   - *Non-attorney signature.* If an original document requires the signature of a non-attorney, the Filing User may scan the original document containing the original signature(s), then electronically file it on the System. Alternatively, the Filing User may convert the document into .pdf text format and submit the document using "s/" for the signature of the non-attorney. NY R USDCTND CM/ECF(6)(6.2).

   - *Multiple signatures.* A document requiring signatures of more than one party must be filed electronically either by (1) submitting a scanned document containing all necessary signatures; (2) representing the consent of the other parties on the document; or (3) in any other manner that the Court approves. NY R USDCTND CM/ECF(6)(6.3).

    ii.   *No verification or accompanying affidavit required for pleadings.* Unless a rule or statute specifically states otherwise, a pleading need not be verified or accompanied by an affidavit. FRCP 11(a).

    iii.   *Unsigned papers.* The court must strike an unsigned paper unless the omission is promptly corrected after being called to the attorney's or party's attention. FRCP 11(a).

  b.  *Representations to the court.* By presenting to the court a pleading, written motion, or other paper—whether by signing, filing, submitting, or later advocating it—an attorney or unrepresented party certifies that to the best of the person's knowledge, information, and belief, formed after an inquiry reasonable under the circumstances:

    i.   It is not being presented for any improper purpose, such as to harass, cause unnecessary delay, or needlessly increase the cost of litigation;

    ii.   The claims, defenses, and other legal contentions are warranted by existing law or by a nonfrivolous argument for extending, modifying, or reversing existing law or for establishing new law;

    iii.   The factual contentions have evidentiary support or, if specifically so identified, will likely have evidentiary support after a reasonable opportunity for further investigation or discovery; and

    iv.   The denials of factual contentions are warranted on the evidence or, if specifically so identified, are reasonably based on belief or a lack of information. FRCP 11(b).

  c.  *Sanctions.* If, after notice and a reasonable opportunity to respond, the court determines that FRCP 11(b) has been violated, the court may impose an appropriate sanction on any attorney, law firm, or party that violated FRCP 11(b) or is responsible for the violation. FRCP 11(c)(1). Refer to the United States District Court for the Northern District of New York KeyRules Motion for Sanctions document for more information.

5.  *Privacy protection for filings made with the court*

  a.  *Redacted filings.* Unless the court orders otherwise, in an electronic or paper filing with the court that contains an individual's Social Security number, taxpayer-identification number, or birth date, the name of an individual known to be a minor, or a financial-account number, a party or nonparty making the filing may include only:

    i.   The last four (4) digits of the Social Security number and taxpayer-identification number;

    ii.   The year of the individual's birth;

    iii.   The minor's initials; and

    iv.   The last four (4) digits of the financial-account number. FRCP 5.2(a); NY R USDCTND L.R. 8.1; NY R USDCTND CM/ECF(11)(11.2).

    v.   If a home address must be used, use only the City and State. NY R USDCTND L.R. 8.1; NY R USDCTND CM/ECF(11)(11.2).

    vi.   If the victim of a sexual assault must be referenced, redact the name to 'Victim.' NY R USDCTND CM/ECF(11)(11.2); NY R USDCTND L.R. 8.1.

    vii.   In addition, caution shall be exercised when filing documents that contain the following:

      • Personal identifying number, such as a driver's license number;

      • Medical records, treatment and diagnosis;

      • Employment history;

      • Individual financial information; and

      • Proprietary or trade secret information. NY R USDCTND L.R. 8.1; NY R USDCTND CM/ECF(11)(11.2).

  b.  *Exemptions from the redaction requirement.* The redaction requirement does not apply to the following:

    i.   A financial-account number that identifies the property allegedly subject to forfeiture in a forfeiture proceeding;

    ii.   The record of an administrative or agency proceeding;

    iii.   The official record of a state-court proceeding;

    iv.   The record of a court or tribunal, if that record was not subject to the redaction requirement when originally filed;

    v.   A filing covered by FRCP 5.2(c) or FRCP 5.2(d); and

    vi.   A pro se filing in an action brought under 28 U.S.C.A. § 2241, 28 U.S.C.A. § 2254, or 28 U.S.C.A. § 2255. FRCP 5.2(b).

    vii.   Transcripts of the administrative record in social security proceedings are exempt from this requirement. State court records and other documents filed in habeas corpus proceedings are exempt from this requirement except for proceedings that involve victims of sex crimes. In habeas corpus cases involving sex crimes, the parties must redact the record and supporting papers, or may move to seal, if appropriate. NY R USDCTND L.R. 8.1.

c.   *Limitations on remote access to electronic files; Social Security appeals and immigration cases.* Unless the court orders otherwise, in an action for benefits under the Social Security Act, and in an action or proceeding relating to an order of removal, to relief from removal, or to immigration benefits or detention, access to an electronic file is authorized as follows:

    i.   The parties and their attorneys may have remote electronic access to any part of the case file, including the administrative record;

    ii.   Any other person may have electronic access to the full record at the courthouse, but may have remote electronic access only to:

       •   The docket maintained by the court; and

       •   An opinion, order, judgment, or other disposition of the court, but not any other part of the case file or the administrative record. FRCP 5.2(c).

d.   *Filings made under seal.* The court may order that a filing be made under seal without redaction. The court may later unseal the filing or order the person who made the filing to file a redacted version for the public record. FRCP 5.2(d); NY R USDCTND L.R. 8.1. For information on sealed matters, refer to NY R USDCTND L.R. 83.13 and NY R USDCTND CM/ECF(12).

e.   *Protective orders.* For good cause, the court may by order in a case:

    i.   Require redaction of additional information; or

    ii.   Limit or prohibit a nonparty's remote electronic access to a document filed with the court. FRCP 5.2(e).

f.   *Option for additional unredacted filing under seal.* A person making a redacted filing may also file an unredacted copy under seal. The court must retain the unredacted copy as part of the record. FRCP 5.2(f); NY R USDCTND L.R. 8.1; NY R USDCTND CM/ECF(11)(11.3).

g.   *Option for filing a reference list.* A filing that contains redacted information may be filed together with a reference list that identifies each item of redacted information and specifies an appropriate identifier that uniquely corresponds to each item listed. The list must be filed under seal and may be amended as of right. Any reference in the case to a listed identifier will be construed to refer to the corresponding item of information. FRCP 5.2(g); NY R USDCTND L.R. 8.1; NY R USDCTND CM/ECF(11)(11.3).

h.   *Responsibility for redaction.* Counsel is strongly urged to discuss this issue with all their clients so that they can make an informed decision about the inclusion of certain information. The responsibility for redacting these personal identifiers rests solely with counsel and the parties. The Clerk will not review each filing for compliance with NY R USDCTND L.R. 8.1. Counsel and the parties are cautioned that failure to redact these personal identifiers may subject them to the Court's full disciplinary power. NY R USDCTND L.R. 8.1; NY R USDCTND CM/ECF(11)(11.3).

i.   *Waiver of protection of identifiers.* A person waives the protection of FRCP 5.2(a) as to the person's own information by filing it without redaction and not under seal. FRCP 5.2(h).

6.   *Individual judge practices.* Refer to the Miscellaneous section of this document for information on individual judge practices on formatting documents.

## F. Filing and Service Requirements

1. *Filing requirements.* Any paper after the complaint that is required to be served—together with a certificate of service—must be filed within a reasonable time after service. FRCP 5(d)(1).

    a. *How filing is made; In general.* A paper is filed by delivering it:

      i. To the clerk; or

      ii. To a judge who agrees to accept it for filing, and who must then note the filing date on the paper and promptly send it to the clerk. FRCP 5(d)(2).

    b. *Electronic filing*

      i. *Authorization of electronic filing program.* A court may, by local rule, allow papers to be filed, signed, or verified by electronic means that are consistent with any technical standards established by the Judicial Conference of the United States. A local rule may require electronic filing only if reasonable exceptions are allowed. A paper filed electronically in compliance with a local rule is a written paper for purposes of the Federal Rules of Civil Procedure. FRCP 5(d)(3).

        • All cases filed in this Court may be assigned to the Electronic Case Files System ("ECF") in accordance with the Procedural Order on Electronic Case Filing (General Order #22 (NY R USDCTND CM/ECF)), the provisions of which are incorporated herein by reference, and which the Court may amend from time to time. Copies of General Order #22 (NY R USDCTND CM/ECF) are available at the Clerk's office or at the Court's webpage. NY R USDCTND L.R. 5.1.1; NY R USDCTND Order 25(XII).

        • The Court may deviate from these Administrative Procedures (NY R USDCTND CM/ECF) in specific cases, without prior notice, if deemed appropriate in the exercise of discretion, considering the need for the just, speedy, and inexpensive determination of matters pending before the Court. NY R USDCTND CM/ECF(2).

      ii. *Scope of electronic filing.* After January 1, 2004, all documents that attorneys admitted to practice in the Northern District of New York submit for filing shall be filed electronically using the System or shall be scanned and uploaded to the System, no matter when a case was originally filed, unless these Administrative Procedures (NY R USDCTND CM/ECF) otherwise permit or unless the assigned judge otherwise authorizes. An attorney who is not a Filing User by January 1, 2004, must show good cause to the assigned judge to file and serve pleadings and other papers in the traditional manner. NY R USDCTND CM/ECF(2).

      iii. *Exceptions and/or waivers from mandatory electronic filing.* The following types of cases and/or documents are not required to be filed electronically:

        • If you are seeking to have your complaint filed under seal, please file your complaint and proposed sealing order traditionally at the Clerk's Office. NY R USDCTND CM/ECF(2)(2.1)(1).

        • Any document that a party proceeding pro se files. (See NY R USDCTND CM/ECF(12)(12.1) for procedural details). NY R USDCTND CM/ECF(2)(2.1)(2). A non-prisoner who is a party to a civil action and who is not represented by an attorney may file a motion to obtain an Electronic Case Filing (ECF) login and password on a form prescribed by the Clerk's Office. The Pro Se CM/ECF Registration Form shall be submitted with the motion. If during the course of the action an attorney appears on behalf of the pro se party, the Clerk's Office shall terminate the pro se party's registration based upon the attorney's appearance. NY R USDCTND CM/ECF(12)(12.1). Absent permission to file electronically, pro se filers shall file paper originals of all complaints, pleadings, motions, affidavits, briefs, and other documents which must be signed or which require either verification or an unsworn declaration under any rule or statute. The Clerk's Office will scan these original documents into an electronic file in the System but will also maintain a paper file. NY R USDCTND CM/ECF(12)(12.1). A pro se party may also seek permission to receive immediate notice of all public documents filed in their cases. Notices of Electronic Filing (NEF) and attached documents would be transmitted to a non-prisoner pro se party who selects this option. Note: The pro se party would continue to file their documents with the Clerk's Office in paper form. NY R USDCTND CM/ECF(12)(12.1).

- Sealed documents, sealed cases, documents for in camera review, documents lodged with the Court, ex parte documents, confidential agreements, Qui Tam actions and Grand Jury material and warrants must be filed traditionally. (See NY R USDCTND CM/ECF(12)(12.2) for further information the filing of the above-referenced documents). NY R USDCTND CM/ECF(2)(2.1)(3).

- Discovery: In accordance with NY R USDCTND L.R. 26.2, parties shall not file discovery, provided, however, that discovery material to be used at trial or in support of any motion, including a motion to compel or for summary judgment, shall be filed electronically with the Court prior to the trial or with the motion. Any motion pursuant to FRCP 37 shall be accompanied by the electronically filed discovery materials to which the motion relates if those materials have not previously been filed with the Court. NY R USDCTND CM/ECF(2)(2.1)(4).

- Transport Orders: All orders requesting that an incarcerated individual be transported that a judicial officer of the Northern District of New York signs shall be filed traditionally. These Orders will not be filed with the case or uploaded to the docket but rather will be processed in accordance with the procedures that the Clerk of Court promulgates. NY R USDCTND CM/ECF(2)(2.1)(5).

iv. *Filing defined.* Electronic transmission of a document to the System in accordance with these Administrative Procedures, together with the transmission of a Notice of Electronic Filing from the Court, constitutes filing of the document for all purposes of the Federal Rules of Civil Procedure and the Local Rules of Practice for the United States District Court for the Northern District of New York and constitutes entry of the document on the docket that the Clerk's Office keeps under FRCP 58 and FRCP 79. E-mailing a document to the Clerk's Office or to the assigned judge shall not constitute "filing" of the document. NY R USDCTND CM/ECF(4)(4.1).

v. *Filing fees.* Any fee required for filing a pleading or paper in this Court is payable to the Clerk of the Court. The Court will not maintain electronic billing or debit accounts for attorneys or law firms. Effective January 1, 2007, payment for filing fees will be mandatory through CM/ECF's Internet Credit Card Payment site--a secure Treasury Site. The Filing User will be prompted to enter either Bank Account Debit (ACH) or credit card information while filing the initial pleading. Any document that requires a filing fee (e.g., Notice of Appeal, Motion for Pro Hac Vice Admission) may also be paid through the federal electronic payment website. NY R USDCTND CM/ECF(7).

vi. For more information on electronic filing, refer to NY R USDCTND CM/ECF.

c. *E-mail or facsimile filing.* Neither the Court nor the Clerk's Office will accept for filing any facsimile or e-mail transmission without prior authorization from the Court. The party using facsimile or e-mail transmissions to file its papers must accompany any such documents with a cover letter stating that the Court authorized such transmissions and the date on which the Court provided that authorization. Violations of NY R USDCTND L.R. 5.5 subject the offending party to the Court's full disciplinary powers. NY R USDCTND L.R. 5.5.

2. *Service requirements*

a. *Service; When required*

i. *In general.* Unless the Federal Rules of Civil Procedure provide otherwise, each of the following papers must be served on every party:

- An order stating that service is required;

- A pleading filed after the original complaint, unless the court orders otherwise under FRCP 5(c) because there are numerous defendants;

- A discovery paper required to be served on a party, unless the court orders otherwise;

- A written motion, except one that may be heard ex parte; and

- A written notice, appearance, demand, or offer of judgment, or any similar paper. FRCP 5(a)(1).

ii. *If a party fails to appear.* No service is required on a party who is in default for failing to appear. But a pleading that asserts a new claim for relief against such a party must be served on that party under FRCP 4. FRCP 5(a)(2).

iii. *Seizing property.* If an action is begun by seizing property and no person is or need be named as a defendant, any service required before the filing of an appearance, answer, or claim must be made on the person who had custody or possession of the property when it was seized. FRCP 5(a)(3).

b. *Service; How made*

i. *Serving an attorney.* If a party is represented by an attorney, service under FRCP 5 must be made on the attorney unless the court orders service on the party. FRCP 5(b)(1).

ii. *Service in general.* A paper is served under FRCP 5 by:

- Handing it to the person;

- Leaving it: (1) at the person's office with a clerk or other person in charge or, if no one is in charge, in a conspicuous place in the office; or (2) if the person has no office or the office is closed, at the person's dwelling or usual place of abode with someone of suitable age and discretion who resides there;

- Mailing it to the person's last known address—in which event service is complete upon mailing;

- Leaving it with the court clerk if the person has no known address;

- Sending it by electronic means if the person consented in writing—in which event service is complete upon transmission, but is not effective if the serving party learns that it did not reach the person to be served; or

- Delivering it by any other means that the person consented to in writing—in which event service is complete when the person making service delivers it to the agency designated to make delivery. FRCP 5(b)(2).

iii. *Service of electronically-filed documents.* Service is complete provided all parties receive a Notice of Electronic Filing (NEF), which is sent automatically by email from the Court (see the NEF for a list of who did/did not receive notice electronically). Transmission of the NEF constitutes service upon all Filing and Receiving Users who are listed as recipients of notice by electronic mail. It remains the responsibility of Filing and Receiving Users to maintain current contact information with the court and to regularly review the docket sheet of the case. NY R USDCTND CM/ECF(5)(5.2).

- *Non-filing or receiving users.* Attorneys and pro se parties who are not Filing or Receiving Users must be served with a paper copy of any electronically filed pleading or other document. Service of such paper copy must be made according to the Federal Rules of Civil Procedure and the Local Rules of Practice for the United States District Court for the Northern District of New York. Such paper service must be documented by electronically filing a certificate of service. NY R USDCTND CM/ECF(5)(5.2). A party who is not a Filing User of the System is entitled to a paper copy of any electronically-filed pleading, document, or order. The Filing User must therefore provide the non-Filing User with the pleading or document according to the Federal Rules of Civil Procedure. NY R US-DCTND CM/ECF(5)(5.3).

iv. *Using court facilities.* If a local rule so authorizes, a party may use the court's transmission facilities to make service under FRCP 5(b)(2)(E). FRCP 5(b)(3).

c. *Serving numerous defendants*

    i. *In general.* If an action involves an unusually large number of defendants, the court may, on motion or on its own, order that:

- Defendants' pleadings and replies to them need not be served on other defendants;

- Any crossclaim, counterclaim, avoidance, or affirmative defense in those pleadings and replies to them will be treated as denied or avoided by all other parties; and

- Filing any such pleading and serving it on the plaintiff constitutes notice of the pleading to all parties. FRCP 5(c)(1).

    ii. *Notifying parties.* A copy of every such order must be served on the parties as the court directs. FRCP 5(c)(2).

3. *Individual judge practices.* Refer to the Miscellaneous section of this document for information on individual judge practices on filing and serving documents.

## G. Hearings

1. *Hearings, generally*

a. *Motion days.* Listings of the regularly scheduled motion days for all judges shall be available at each Clerk's office and are available on the Court's webpage. The Clerk shall provide notice of the regular motion days for all judges to the parties at the time an action is commenced. NY R USDCTND L.R. 78.1.

b. *Return date.* Unless the Court directs otherwise, the moving party shall make its motion returnable at the next regularly scheduled motion date at least thirty-one (31) days from the date the moving party files and serves its motion. The moving party shall select a return date in accordance with the procedures set forth in NY R USDCTND L.R. 7.1(b). If the return date the moving party selects is not the next regularly scheduled motion date, or if the moving party selects no return date, the Clerk will set the proper return date and notify the parties. NY R USDCTND L.R. 7.1.

    i. Information regarding motion dates and times is specified on the case assignment form that the Court provides to the parties at the commencement of the litigation or the parties may obtain this form from the Clerk's office or at the Court's webpage. NY R USDCTND L.R. 7.1.

    ii. The Court hereby directs the Clerk to set a proper return date in motions that pro se litigants submit for filing that do not specify a return date or fail to allow for sufficient time pursuant to NY R USDCTND L.R. 7.1. Generally, the return date that the Clerk selects should not exceed thirty (30) days from the date of filing. Furthermore, the Clerk shall forward a copy of the revised or corrected notice of motion to the parties. NY R USDCTND L.R. 7.1.

c. *Oral argument.* Due process does not require that oral argument be permitted on a motion and, except as otherwise provided by local rule, the district court has discretion to determine whether it will decide the motion on the papers or hear argument by counsel (and perhaps receive evidence). FPP § 1190; F.D.I.C. v. Deglau, 207 F.3d 153 (3d Cir. 2000).

    i. The parties shall appear for oral argument on all motions that they make returnable before a district court judge, except motions for reconsideration, on the scheduled return date of the motion. A motion may be disposed of without oral argument as described in NY R USDCTND Order 25, on consideration of a request of any party, or otherwise at the discretion of the presiding judge. Thus, the parties should be prepared to have their motion papers serve as the sole method of argument on the motion. NY R USDCTND L.R. 7.1(h).

    ii. The parties shall not appear for oral argument on motions that they make returnable before a Magistrate Judge on the scheduled return date of the motion unless the Magistrate Judge sua sponte directs or grants the request of any party for oral argument. NY R USDCTND L.R. 7.1(h).

d. *Providing a regular schedule for oral hearings.* A court may establish regular times and places for oral hearings on motions. FRCP 78(a).

e. *Providing for submission on briefs.* By rule or order, the court may provide for submitting and determining motions on briefs, without oral hearings. FRCP 78(b).

2. *Individual judge practices.* Refer to the Miscellaneous section of this document for information on individual judge practices on hearings.

## H. Forms

### 1. Federal Motion for Continuance/Extension of Time Forms

a.  Opposition in federal district court; To motion for continuance; On ground of additional time required to prepare for trial; No excusable neglect shown. AMJUR PP CONTIN § 79.

b.  Affidavit in opposition to motion for continuance; By plaintiff's attorney; Lack of due diligence in discovery of documents. AMJUR PP CONTIN § 80.

c.  Affidavit in opposition to motion for continuance; By plaintiff's attorney; Defendant's absent witness previously absent; Lack of due diligence in compelling attendance of witness. AMJUR PP CONTIN § 81.

d.  Affidavit in opposition to motion for continuance; By plaintiff; Admission that absent witness of defendant would testify according to affidavit. AMJUR PP CONTIN § 83.

e.  Affidavit in opposition to defendant's motion for continuance; By plaintiff's counsel; Testimony of absent witness merely cumulative. AMJUR PP CONTIN § 85.

f.  Motion for enlargement of time. 2 FEDFORMS § 5:11.

g.  Motion for enlargement of time; By plaintiff. 2 FEDFORMS § 5:12.

h.  Motion for enlargement of time; To answer motion. 2 FEDFORMS § 5:14.

i.  Motion for continuance. 2 FEDFORMS § 5:36.

j.  Motion for continuance; Reciting supporting facts; New allegations in amended answer. 2 FEDFORMS § 5:37.

k.  Motion for continuance; Reciting supporting facts; Absence of witness. 2 FEDFORMS § 5:38.

l.  Motion for continuance; Reciting supporting facts; Absence of witness; Witness outside the country. 2 FEDFORMS § 5:39.

m.  Motion for continuance or in the alternative for change of venue; Hostility against defendant. 2 FEDFORMS § 5:40.

n.  Notice; Of motion; Containing motion. FEDPROF § 1:749.

o.  Brief; Supporting or opposing motion. FEDPROF § 1:752.

p.  Opposition to motion; For continuance; No excusable neglect. FEDPROF § 1:808.

q.  Affidavit; Opposing motion for continuance; Offer to stipulate to testimony of unavailable witness. FEDPROF § 1:813.

r.  Reply to motion for extension of time. GOLDLTGFMS § 10:40.

s.  Motions; Extension of time to file jury demand. GOLDLTGFMS § 12:6.

t.  Motion for extension of time. GOLDLTGFMS § 25:37.

u.  Motion for extension of time to answer. GOLDLTGFMS § 26:13.

v.  Motion to extend time for serving answers. GOLDLTGFMS § 26:14.

w.  Motion for continuance. GOLDLTGFMS § 43:2.

x.  Motion for continuance; Lawyer unavailable. GOLDLTGFMS § 43:3.

y.  Motion for continuance; Witness unavailable. GOLDLTGFMS § 43:4.

z.  Motion for continuance; Party in military service. GOLDLTGFMS § 43:6.

## I. Applicable Rules

1. *Federal rules*

a.  Serving and filing pleadings and other papers. FRCP 5.

b.  Constitutional challenge to a statute; Notice, certification, and intervention. FRCP 5.1.

    c.  Privacy protection for filings made with the court. FRCP 5.2.

    d.  Computing and extending time; Time for motion papers. FRCP 6.

    e.  Pleadings allowed; Form of motions and other papers. FRCP 7.

    f.  Disclosure statement. FRCP 7.1.

    g.  Form of pleadings. FRCP 10.

    h.  Signing pleadings, motions, and other papers; Representations to the court; Sanctions. FRCP 11.

    i.  Taking testimony. FRCP 43.

    j.  Hearing motions; Submission on briefs. FRCP 78.

2.  *Local rules*

    a.  Scope of the rules. NY R USDCTND L.R. 1.1.

    b.  Complex and multi-district litigation. NY R USDCTND L.R. 3.3.

    c.  Service and filing of papers. NY R USDCTND L.R. 5.1.

    d.  Filing by facsimile or e-mail. NY R USDCTND L.R. 5.5.

    e.  Motion practice. NY R USDCTND L.R. 7.1.

    f.  Personal privacy protection. NY R USDCTND L.R. 8.1.

    g.  Request for three-judge court. NY R USDCTND L.R. 9.1.

    h.  Form of papers. NY R USDCTND L.R. 10.1.

    i.  Settlement procedures. NY R USDCTND L.R. 68.2.

    j.  Orders. NY R USDCTND L.R. 77.2.

    k.  Motion days. NY R USDCTND L.R. 78.1.

    l.  Appearance and withdrawal of attorney. NY R USDCTND L.R. 83.2.

    m.  Arbitration. NY R USDCTND L.R. 83.7-1; NY R USDCTND L.R. 83.7-2; NY R USDCTND L.R. 83.7-3.

    n.  Assisted mediation program. NY R USDCTND L.R. 83.8.

    o.  Mediation. NY R USDCTND L.R. 83.11-1; NY R USDCTND L.R. 83.11-3.

    p.  Early neutral evaluation. NY R USDCTND L.R. 83.12-1; NY R USDCTND L.R. 83.12-3.

    q.  Administrative procedures for electronic case filing. NY R USDCTND CM/ECF.

    r.  Case assignment plan for the Northern District of New York. [NY R USDCTND Order 12, as amended by NY ORDER 16-4201, effective March 24, 2015].

    s.  Directing the expedited service of the summons and complaint and further directing the completion of FRCP 16 stipulation for the timely progression of civil actions. [NY R USDCTND Order 25, as amended by NY ORDER 16-4187, effective June 23, 2016].

    t.  Mandatory mediation program. NY R USDCTND Order 47.

## J.  Miscellaneous

**NOTE: Individual judges' rules may apply. For available judge-level information, refer to:**

DISTRICT JUDGE MAE A. D'AGOSTINO: [NY R USDCTND D'Agostino-Rules and Practices, as added by NY ORDER 16-4200, effective April 4, 2016].

DISTRICT JUDGE THOMAS J. McAVOY: NY R USDCTND McAvoy-Order.

# Motions, Oppositions and Replies
# Motion for Summary Judgment

### Document Last Updated September 2016

**A. Checklist**

(I) ❑ Matters to be considered by moving party

    (a) ❑ Required documents

        (1) ❑ Notice of motion and motion

        (2) ❑ Statement of material facts

        (3) ❑ Memorandum of law

        (4) ❑ Supporting affidavit

        (5) ❑ Certificate of service

    (b) ❑ Supplemental documents

        (1) ❑ Supporting evidence

        (2) ❑ Notice of constitutional question

        (3) ❑ Nongovernmental corporate disclosure statement

        (4) ❑ Notice to pro se litigants of the consequences of failing to respond to a summary judgment motion

        (5) ❑ Copies of authorities

        (6) ❑ Proposed order

        (7) ❑ Cover letter authorizing e-mail or facsimile filing

        (8) ❑ Affidavit attesting to failed attempts to file electronically

        (9) ❑ Notice of conventional filing

        (10) ❑ CD/ROM with PDF of document(s)

        (11) ❑ English translation

        (12) ❑ Courtesy copies

        (13) ❑ Copies for three-judge court

    (c) ❑ Timing

        (1) ❑ Unless a different time is set by local rule or the court orders otherwise, a party may file a motion for summary judgment at any time until thirty (30) days after the close of all discovery

            (i) ❑ Local variation: motions for summary judgment pursuant to FRCP 56 shall be filed and served within twenty-one (21) days following the close of discovery

        (2) ❑ The moving party must file all motion papers with the court and serve them upon the other parties not less than thirty-one (31) days prior to the return date of the motion

        (3) ❑ A written motion and notice of the hearing must be served at least fourteen (14) days before the time specified for the hearing, with the following exceptions: (i) when the motion may be heard ex parte; (ii) when the Federal Rules of Civil Procedure set a different time; or (iii) when a court order—which a party may, for good cause, apply for ex parte—sets a different time

        (4) ❑ Any affidavit supporting a motion must be served with the motion

(II) ❑ Matters to be considered by opposing party

    (a) ❑ Required documents

        (1) ❑ Opposition

    (2)  ❑  Response to the statement of material facts

    (3)  ❑  Memorandum of law

    (4)  ❑  Supporting affidavit

    (5)  ❑  Certificate of service

  (b)  ❑  Supplemental documents

    (1)  ❑  Supporting evidence

    (2)  ❑  Notice of constitutional question

    (3)  ❑  Cross-motion

    (4)  ❑  Copies of authorities

    (5)  ❑  Cover letter authorizing e-mail or facsimile filing

    (6)  ❑  Affidavit attesting to failed attempts to file electronically

    (7)  ❑  Notice of conventional filing

    (8)  ❑  CD/ROM with PDF of document(s)

    (9)  ❑  English translation

   (10)  ❑  Courtesy copies

   (11)  ❑  Copies for three-judge court

  (c)  ❑  Timing

    (1)  ❑  The party opposing the motion must file its opposition papers with the court and serve them upon the other parties not less than seventeen (17) days prior to the return date of the motion

    (2)  ❑  Except as FRCP 59(c) provides otherwise, any opposing affidavit must be served at least seven (7) days before the hearing, unless the court permits service at another time

    (3)  ❑  A party may file and serve a cross-motion (meaning a competing request for relief or order similar to that requested by another party against the cross-moving party) at the time it files and serves its opposition papers to the original motion, i.e., not less than seventeen (17) days prior to the return date of the motion

## B. Timing

1. *Motion for summary judgment.* Unless a different time is set by local rule or the court orders otherwise, a party may file a motion for summary judgment at any time until thirty (30) days after the close of all discovery. FRCP 56(b).

  a.  *Local variation.* Motions for summary judgment pursuant to FRCP 56 shall be filed and served within twenty-one (21) days following the close of discovery. NY R USDCTND L.R. 83.7-3(a).

2. *Timing of motions, generally.* The moving party must file all motion papers with the Court and serve them upon the other parties not less than THIRTY-ONE (31) DAYS prior to the return date of the motion. NY R USDCTND L.R. 7.1(b)(1).

  a.  *Motion and notice of hearing.* A written motion and notice of the hearing must be served at least fourteen (14) days before the time specified for the hearing, with the following exceptions:

    i.  When the motion may be heard ex parte;

    ii.  When the Federal Rules of Civil Procedure set a different time; or

    iii.  When a court order—which a party may, for good cause, apply for ex parte—sets a different time. FRCP 6(c)(1).

  b.  *Supporting affidavit.* Any affidavit supporting a motion must be served with the motion. FRCP 6(c)(2).

3. *Timing of opposing papers.* The party opposing the motion must file its opposition papers with the Court

and serve them upon the other parties not less than SEVENTEEN (17) DAYS prior to the return date of the motion. NY R USDCTND L.R. 7.1(b)(1).

a. *Opposing affidavit.* Except as FRCP 59(c) provides otherwise, any opposing affidavit must be served at least seven (7) days before the hearing, unless the court permits service at another time. FRCP 6(c)(2).

b. *Cross-motion.* A party may file and serve a cross-motion (meaning a competing request for relief or order similar to that requested by another party against the cross-moving party) at the time it files and serves its opposition papers to the original motion, i.e., not less than SEVENTEEN (17) DAYS prior to the return date of the motion. NY R USDCTND L.R. 7.1(c).

4. *Timing of reply papers.* Where the respondent files an answering affidavit setting up a new matter, the moving party ordinarily is allowed a reasonable time to file a reply affidavit since failure to deny the new matter by affidavit may operate as an admission of its truth. AMJUR MOTIONS § 25.

a. *Reply papers.* The moving party must file its reply papers, which may not exceed (10) pages with the Court and serve them upon the other parties not less than ELEVEN (11) DAYS prior to the return date of the motion. NY R USDCTND L.R. 7.1(b)(1).

b. *Opposition to cross-motion.* The original moving party must file its reply/opposition papers with the Court and serve them on the other parties not less than ELEVEN (11) DAYS prior to the return date of the original motion. NY R USDCTND L.R. 7.1(c).

5. *Computation of time*

a. *Computing time.* FRCP 6 applies in computing any time period specified in the Federal Rules of Civil Procedure, in any local rule or court order, or in any statute that does not specify a method of computing time. FRCP 6(a).

  i. *Period stated in days or a longer unit.* When the period is stated in days or a longer unit of time:
  - Exclude the day of the event that triggers the period;
  - Count every day, including intermediate Saturdays, Sundays, and legal holidays; and
  - Include the last day of the period, but if the last day is a Saturday, Sunday, or legal holiday, the period continues to run until the end of the next day that is not a Saturday, Sunday, or legal holiday. FRCP 6(a)(1).

  ii. *Period stated in hours.* When the period is stated in hours:
  - Begin counting immediately on the occurrence of the event that triggers the period;
  - Count every hour, including hours during intermediate Saturdays, Sundays, and legal holidays; and
  - If the period would end on a Saturday, Sunday, or legal holiday, the period continues to run until the same time on the next day that is not a Saturday, Sunday, or legal holiday. FRCP 6(a)(2).

  iii. *Inaccessibility of the clerk's office.* Unless the court orders otherwise, if the clerk's office is inaccessible:
  - On the last day for filing under FRCP 6(a)(1), then the time for filing is extended to the first accessible day that is not a Saturday, Sunday, or legal holiday; or
  - During the last hour for filing under FRCP 6(a)(2), then the time for filing is extended to the same time on the first accessible day that is not a Saturday, Sunday, or legal holiday. FRCP 6(a)(3).

  iv. *"Last day" defined.* Unless a different time is set by a statute, local rule, or court order, the last day ends:
  - For electronic filing, at midnight in the court's time zone; and
  - For filing by other means, when the clerk's office is scheduled to close. FRCP 6(a)(4).

  v. *"Next day" defined.* The "next day" is determined by continuing to count forward when the period is measured after an event and backward when measured before an event. FRCP 6(a)(5).

vi. *"Legal holiday" defined.* "Legal holiday" means:

- The day set aside by statute for observing New Year's Day, Martin Luther King Jr.'s Birthday, Washington's Birthday, Memorial Day, Independence Day, Labor Day, Columbus Day, Veterans' Day, Thanksgiving Day, or Christmas Day;

- Any day declared a holiday by the President or Congress; and

- For periods that are measured after an event, any other day declared a holiday by the state where the district court is located. FRCP 6(a)(6).

b. *Computation of electronic filing deadlines.* A document will be deemed timely filed if electronically filed prior to midnight Eastern Time. However, if the time of day is of the essence, the assigned judge may order that the document be filed by a time certain. NY R USDCTND CM/ECF(4)(4.3).

i. *Technical failures.* A Filing User, whose filing is untimely as the result of a technical failure of the Court's CM/ECF site, may seek appropriate relief from the Court. However, Filing Users are cautioned that, in some circumstances, the Court lacks the authority to grant an extension of time to file (e.g., FRCP 6(b) of the Federal Rules of Civil Procedure). NY R USDCTND CM/ECF(10)(10.1).

- *Technical failure of the filing user's system.* Problems with the Filing User's system, such as phone line problems, problems with the Filing User's Internet Service Provider ("ISP"), or hardware or software problems, will not constitute a technical failure under these Administrative Procedures nor excuse an untimely filing. A Filing User who cannot file documents electronically because of a problem on the Filing User's system must file the documents' conventionally along with an affidavit explaining the reason for not filing the documents electronically. NY R USDCTND CM/ECF(10)(10.2).

c. *Extending time*

i. *In general.* When an act may or must be done within a specified time, the court may, for good cause, extend the time:

- With or without motion or notice if the court acts, or if a request is made, before the original time or its extension expires; or

- On motion made after the time has expired if the party failed to act because of excusable neglect. FRCP 6(b)(1).

ii. *Exceptions.* A court must not extend the time to act under FRCP 50(b), FRCP 50(d), FRCP 52(b), FRCP 59(b), FRCP 59(d), FRCP 59(e), and FRCP 60(b). FRCP 6(b)(2).

iii. Refer to the United States District Court for the Northern District of New York KeyRules Motion for Continuance/Extension of Time document for more information on extending time.

d. *Additional time after certain kinds of service.* When a party may or must act within a specified time after service and service is made under FRCP 5(b)(2)(C), FRCP 5(b)(2)(D), FRCP 5(b)(2)(E), or FRCP 5(b)(2)(F), three (3) days are added after the period would otherwise expire under FRCP 6(a). FRCP 6(d).

i. In accordance with FRCP 6(e), service by electronic means is treated the same as service by mail for purposes of adding three (3) days to the prescribed period to respond. NY R USDCTND CM/ECF(5)(5.4). [Editor's note: the reference to FRCP 6(e) is likely meant to be a reference to FRCP 6(d)].

6. *Individual judge practices.* Refer to the Miscellaneous section of this document for information on individual judge practices on timing of documents.

## C. General Requirements

1. *Motions, generally*

a. *Requirements.* A request for a court order must be made by motion. The motion must:

i. Be in writing unless made during a hearing or trial;

ii. State with particularity the grounds for seeking the order; and

    iii.   State the relief sought. FRCP 7(b)(1).

    iv.   When a moving party makes a motion based upon a rule or statute, the moving party must specify in its moving papers the rule or statute upon which it bases its motion. NY R USDCTND L.R. 7.1(a)(1).

  b.  *Notice of motion.* A party interested in resisting the relief sought by a motion has a right to notice thereof, and an opportunity to be heard. AMJUR MOTIONS § 12.

    i.   In addition to statutory or court rule provisions requiring notice of a motion—the purpose of such a notice requirement having been said to be to prevent a party from being prejudicially surprised by a motion—principles of natural justice dictate that an adverse party generally must be given notice that a motion will be presented to the court. AMJUR MOTIONS § 12.

    ii.   "Notice," in this regard, means reasonable notice, including a meaningful opportunity to prepare and to defend against allegations of a motion. AMJUR MOTIONS § 12.

  c.  *Writing requirement.* The writing requirement is intended to insure that the adverse parties are informed and have a record of both the motion's pendency and the grounds on which the movant seeks an order. FPP § 1191; Feldberg v. Quechee Lakes Corp., 463 F.3d 195 (2d Cir. 2006).

    i.   It is sufficient "if the motion is stated in a written notice of the hearing of the motion." FPP § 1191.

  d.  *Particularity requirement.* The particularity requirement insures that the opposing parties will have notice of their opponent's contentions. FEDPROC § 62:364; Goodman v. 1973 26 Foot Trojan Vessel, Arkansas Registration No. AR1439SN, 859 F.2d 71, 12 Fed.R.Serv.3d 645 (8th Cir. 1988). That requirement ensures that notice of the basis for the motion is provided to the court and to the opposing party so as to avoid prejudice, provide the opponent with a meaningful opportunity to respond, and provide the court with enough information to process the motion correctly. FEDPROC § 62:364; Andreas v. Volkswagen of America, Inc., 336 F.3d 789, 56 Fed.R.Serv.3d 6 (8th Cir. 2003).

    i.   Reasonable specification of the grounds for a motion is sufficient. However, where a movant fails to state even one ground for granting the motion in question, the movant has failed to meet the minimal standard of "reasonable specification." FEDPROC § 62:364; Martinez v. Trainor, 556 F.2d 818, 23 Fed.R.Serv.2d 403 (7th Cir. 1977).

    ii.   The court may excuse the failure to comply with the particularity requirement if it is inadvertent, and where no prejudice is shown by the opposing party. FEDPROC § 62:364.

  e.  *Order to show cause.* All motions that a party brings by Order to Show Cause shall conform to the requirements set forth in NY R USDCTND L.R. 7.1(a)(1) and NY R USDCTND L.R. 7.1(a)(2). Immediately after filing an Order to Show Cause, the moving party must telephone the Chambers of the presiding judicial officer and inform Chambers staff that it has filed an Order to Show Cause. Parties may obtain the telephone numbers for all Chambers from the Clerk's office or at the Court's webpage. The Court shall determine the briefing schedule and return date applicable to motions brought by Order to Show Cause. NY R USDCTND L.R. 7.1(e).

    i.   In addition to the requirements set forth in NY R USDCTND L.R. 7.1(a)(1) and NY R USDCTND L.R. 7.1(a)(2), a motion brought by Order to Show Cause must include an affidavit clearly and specifically showing good and sufficient cause why the standard Notice of Motion procedure cannot be used. The moving party must give reasonable advance notice of the application for an Order to Show Cause to the other parties, except in those circumstances where the movant can demonstrate, in a detailed and specific affidavit, good cause and substantial prejudice that would result from the requirement of reasonable notice. NY R USDCTND L.R. 7.1(e).

    ii.   An Order to Show Cause must contain a space for the assigned judge to set forth:

- The deadline for filing and serving supporting papers,
- The deadline for filing and serving opposing papers, and
- The date and time for the hearing. NY R USDCTND L.R. 7.1(e).

2.  *Motion for summary judgment.* A party may move for summary judgment, identifying each claim or

defense—or the part of each claim or defense—on which summary judgment is sought. The court shall grant summary judgment if the movant shows that there is no genuine dispute as to any material fact and the movant is entitled to judgment as a matter of law. The court should state on the record the reasons for granting or denying the motion. FRCP 56(a).

a. *Burden of proof and presumptions*

    i. *Movant's burden.* It is well-settled that the party moving for summary judgment has the burden of demonstrating that the FRCP 56(c) test—"no genuine issue as to any material fact"—is satisfied and that the movant is entitled to judgment as a matter of law. FPP § 2727; Adickes v. S. H. Kress & Co., 398 U.S. 144, 157, 90 S.Ct. 1598, 1608, 26 L.Ed.2d 142 (1970).

- The movant is held to a stringent standard. FPP § 2727. Before summary judgment will be granted it must be clear what the truth is and any doubt as to the existence of a genuine issue of material fact will be resolved against the movant. FPP § 2727; Poller v. Columbia Broadcasting Sys., Inc., 368 U.S. 464, 82 S.Ct. 486, 7 L.Ed.2d 458 (1962); Adickes v. S. H. Kress & Co., 398 U.S. 144, 90 S.Ct. 1598, 26 L.Ed.2d 142 (1970).

- Because the burden is on the movant, the evidence presented to the court always is construed in favor of the party opposing the motion and the opponent is given the benefit of all favorable inferences that can be drawn from it. FPP § 2727; Scott v. Harris, 550 U.S. 372, 127 S.Ct. 1769, 167 L.Ed.2d 686 (2007).

- Finally, facts asserted by the party opposing the motion, if supported by affidavits or other evidentiary material, are regarded as true. FPP § 2727; McLaughlin v. Liu, 849 F.2d 1205, 1208 (9th Cir. 1988).

    ii. *Opponent's burden.* If the movant makes out a prima facie case that would entitle him to a judgment as a matter of law if uncontroverted at trial, summary judgment will be granted unless the opposing party offers some competent evidence that could be presented at trial showing that there is a genuine issue as to a material fact. FPP § 2727; First Nat. Bank of Arizona v. Cities Serv. Co., 391 U.S. 253, 289, 88 S.Ct. 1575, 1593, 20 L.Ed.2d 569 (1968). In this way the burden of producing evidence is shifted to the party opposing the motion. FPP § 2727; Celotex Corp. v. Catrett, 477 U.S. 317, 331, 106 S.Ct. 2548, 2557, 91 L.Ed.2d 265 (1986).

- The burden on the nonmoving party is not a heavy one; the nonmoving party simply is required to show specific facts, as opposed to general allegations, that present a genuine issue worthy of trial. FPP § 2727; Lujan v. Defenders of Wildlife, 504 U.S. 555, 112 S.Ct. 2130, 119 L.Ed.2d 351 (1992).

- The nonmoving party has two options once the moving party has met its burden of production of evidence demonstrating the absence of a genuine issue of material fact: either come forward with countervailing evidence showing that a genuine issue does exist, or submit an affidavit under FRCP 56(f) demonstrating that more time or further discovery are necessary to enable it to oppose the summary judgment motion. FEDPROC § 62:589.

b. *Failing to properly support or address a fact.* If a party fails to properly support an assertion of fact or fails to properly address another party's assertion of fact as required by FRCP 56(c), the court may:

    i. Give an opportunity to properly support or address the fact;

    ii. Consider the fact undisputed for purposes of the motion;

    iii. Grant summary judgment if the motion and supporting materials—including the facts considered undisputed—show that the movant is entitled to it; or

    iv. Issue any other appropriate order. FRCP 56(e).

c. *Judgment independent of the motion.* After giving notice and a reasonable time to respond, the court may:

    i. Grant summary judgment for a nonmovant;

    ii. Grant the motion on grounds not raised by a party; or

iii. Consider summary judgment on its own after identifying for the parties material facts that may not be genuinely in dispute. FRCP 56(f).

d. *Failing to grant all the requested relief.* If the court does not grant all the relief requested by the motion, it may enter an order stating any material fact—including an item of damages or other relief—that is not genuinely in dispute and treating the fact as established in the case. FRCP 56(g).

e. *Affidavit or declaration submitted in bad faith.* If satisfied that an affidavit or declaration under FRCP 56 is submitted in bad faith or solely for delay, the court—after notice and a reasonable time to respond—may order the submitting party to pay the other party the reasonable expenses, including attorney's fees, it incurred as a result. An offending party or attorney may also be held in contempt or subjected to other appropriate sanctions. FRCP 56(h).

f. *Conversion of motions under FRCP 12(b)(6) and FRCP 12(c).* If, on a motion under FRCP 12(b)(6) or FRCP 12(c), matters outside the pleadings are presented to and not excluded by the court, the motion must be treated as one for summary judgment under FRCP 56. FRCP 12(d).

3. *Opposing papers*

a. *Opposing papers, generally.* The Federal Rules of Civil Procedure do not require any formal answer, return, or reply to a motion, except where the Federal Rules of Civil Procedure or local rules may require affidavits, memoranda, or other papers to be filed in opposition to a motion. Such papers are simply to apprise the court of such opposition and the grounds of that opposition. FEDPROC § 62:359.

i. *Effect of failure to respond to motion.* Although in the absence of statutory provision or court rule, a motion ordinarily does not require a written answer, when a party files a motion and the opposing party fails to respond, the court may construe such failure to respond as nonopposition to the motion or an admission that the motion was meritorious, may take the facts alleged in the motion as true—the rule in some jurisdictions being that the failure to respond to a fact set forth in a motion is deemed an admission—and may grant the motion if the relief requested appears to be justified. AMJUR MOTIONS § 28.

ii. *Assent or no opposition not determinative.* However, a motion will not be granted automatically simply because an "assent" or a notation of "no opposition" has been filed; federal judges frequently deny motions that have been assented to when it is thought that justice so dictates. FPP § 1190.

iii. *Responsive pleading inappropriate as response to motion.* An attempt to answer or oppose a motion with a responsive pleading usually is not appropriate. FPP § 1190.

b. *Opposition to motion for summary judgment.* The party opposing summary judgment does not have a duty to present evidence in opposition to a motion under FRCP 56 in all circumstances. FPP § 2727; Jaroma v. Massey, 873 F.2d 17 (1st Cir. 1989).

i. *When facts are unavailable to the nonmovant.* If a nonmovant shows by affidavit or declaration that, for specified reasons, it cannot present facts essential to justify its opposition, the court may:

- Defer considering the motion or deny it;

- Allow time to obtain affidavits or declarations or to take discovery; or

- Issue any other appropriate order. FRCP 56(d).

4. *Reply papers.* A moving party may be required or permitted to prepare papers in addition to his original motion papers. AMJUR MOTIONS § 25. Papers answering or replying to opposing papers may be appropriate, in the interests of justice, where it appears there is a substantial reason for allowing a reply. Thus, a court may accept reply papers where a party demonstrates that the papers to which it seeks to file a reply raise new issues that are material to the disposition of the question before the court, or where the court determines, sua sponte, that it wishes further briefing of an issue raised in those papers and orders the submission of additional papers. FEDPROC § 62:360.

a. *Function of reply papers.* The function of a reply affidavit is to answer the arguments made in opposition to the position taken by the movant and not to permit the movant to introduce new arguments in support of the motion. AMJUR MOTIONS § 25.

b. *Issues raised for the first time in a reply document.* However, the view has been followed in some jurisdictions, that as a matter of judicial economy, where there is no prejudice and where the issues could be raised simply by filing a motion to dismiss, the trial court has discretion to consider arguments raised for the first time in a reply memorandum, and that a trial court may grant a motion to strike issues raised for the first time in a reply memorandum. AMJUR MOTIONS § 26.

c. *Opposition to cross-motion.* The original moving party may reply in further support of the original motion and in opposition to the cross-motion with a reply/opposition brief that does not exceed twenty-five (25) pages in length, exclusive of exhibits. NY R USDCTND L.R. 7.1(c).

5. *Surreply.* A surreply is not permitted. NY R USDCTND L.R. 7.1(b)(1).

a. *Surreply in support of cross-motion.* The cross-moving party may not reply in further support of its cross-motion without the Court's prior permission. NY R USDCTND L.R. 7.1(c).

6. *Submission of proposed order by prevailing party.* If the assigned judge instructs the prevailing party to do so, the prevailing party shall submit a proposed order which the opposing party has approved and which contains the endorsement of the opposing party: "Approved as to form." NY R USDCTND L.R. 77.2(b). In civil actions where the Court has directed a party to submit an order or judgment, that party shall file all such orders or judgments in duplicate, and the Clerk's entry of such duplicate in the proper record book shall be deemed in compliance with FRCP 79(b). Such party shall also furnish the Clerk with a sufficient number of additional copies for each party to the action, which the Clerk shall mail with notice of entry in accordance with FRCP 77(d). NY R USDCTND L.R. 5.1(b).

a. *Disagreement as to form of proposed order.* When the parties are unable to agree as to the form of the proposed order, the prevailing party shall, on seven (7) days notice to all other parties, submit a proposed order and a written explanation for the form of that order. The Court may award costs and attorney's fees against a party whose unreasonable conduct the Court deemed to have required the bringing of the motion. The provisions of NY R USDCTND L.R. 7.1 shall not apply to such motion, and the Court shall not hear oral argument. NY R USDCTND L.R. 77.2(b).

b. For more information on orders, refer to NY R USDCTND L.R. 77.2.

7. *Sanctions for vexatious or frivolous motions or failure to comply with* NY R USDCTND L.R. 7.1. A party who presents vexatious or frivolous motion papers or fails to comply with NY R USDCTND L.R. 7.1 is subject to discipline as the Court deems appropriate, including sanctions and the imposition of costs and attorney's fees to the opposing party. NY R USDCTND L.R. 7.1(i).

8. *Complex and multi-district litigation.* If the assigned judge determines, in his or her discretion, that the case is of such a complex nature that it cannot reasonably be trial ready within eighteen (18) months from the date the complaint is filed, the assigned judge may design and issue a particularized case management order that will move the case to trial as quickly as the complexity of the case allows. NY R USDCTND L.R. 3.3(a). The parties shall promptly notify the Court in writing if any action commenced is appropriate for multi-district litigation. NY R USDCTND L.R. 3.3(b).

9. *Appearances.* An attorney appearing for a party in a civil case shall promptly file with the Clerk a written notice of appearance; however, an attorney does not need to file a notice of appearance if the attorney who would be filing the notice of appearance is the same individual who has signed the complaint, notice of removal, pre-answer motion, or answer. NY R USDCTND L.R. 83.2(a). For more information, refer to NY R USDCTND L.R. 83.2.

10. *Related cases.* A civil case is "related" to another civil case for purposes of this guideline when, because of the similarity of facts and legal issues or because the cases arise from the same transactions or events, a substantial saving of judicial resources is likely to result from assigning the cases to the same Judge and Magistrate Judge. NY R USDCTND Order 12(G)(2). A civil case shall not be deemed related to another civil case merely because the civil case: (1) involves similar legal issues, or (2) involves the same parties. NY R USDCTND Order 12(G)(3). Presumptively, and subject to the power of a Judge to determine otherwise pursuant to NY R USDCTND Order 12(G)(5), civil cases shall not be deemed to be "related" unless both cases are still pending before the Court. NY R USDCTND Order 12(G)(4).

a. *New filings.* If an attorney or filing party indicates on the Civil Cover Sheet that a case is related to an earlier filed case, the Clerk shall instruct the filing party to file a notice of related cases. The allegedly related cases will be submitted by the Clerk to the Judge to whom the earliest filed case is assigned, who shall advise the Clerk whether such cases are related. NY R USDCTND Order 12(G)(1).

b. *Judicial determination that civil cases are "related."* Except for the cases described in the final sentence of NY R USDCTND Order 12(G)(6), all civil cases shall be randomly assigned when they are filed. Other than the cases described in the final sentence of NY R USDCTND Order 12(G)(6), civil cases shall not be deemed to be "related" for purposes of this guideline at the instance of any litigant or attorney unless and until there has been a determination by a Judge of this Court that the standard of NY R USDCTND Order 12(G)(2) is met. NY R USDCTND Order 12(G)(5).

   i. *Notice of related filing.* Any party may apply for such a determination by filing with the Clerk a notice of related filing, which should include an explanation as to why the standard of NY R USDCTND Order 12(G)(2) is met. A form for this purpose is available on the Court's website. A copy of the notice shall be served on all other parties who have appeared. Such an application must be made after the date when at least a majority of the defendants have been served with the complaint. Before making such an application, the applicant must confer in good faith with all other parties in an effort to reach an agreement on whether or not the case is "related". After such an application is made, any other party may serve and file within seven (7) calendar days a letter of no more than two (2) pages supporting or opposing the application. The application to have the case assigned to another Judge shall be presented to the Judge with the earliest filed case for decision on whether the action(s) should be reassigned as related cases. The Judge with the earliest filed case may then enter an order in the case at bar, either deeming the case to be related and directing the Clerk to reassign the action, or denying the application for reassignment. Any disputes concerning the assignment of related cases will be referred to the Chief Judge for resolution. NY R USDCTND Order 12(G)(5).

c. For more information on related cases, refer to NY R USDCTND Order 12(G).

11. *Alternative dispute resolution (ADR).* It is the mission of this court to do everything it can to help parties resolve their disputes as fairly, quickly, and efficiently as possible. NY R USDCTND Order 25(VIII).

a. *Arbitration.* NY R USDCTND L.R. 83.7 governs the consensual arbitration program for referral of civil actions to court-annexed arbitration. It may remain in effect until further order of the Court. Its purpose is to establish a less formal procedure for the just, efficient and economical resolution of disputes, while preserving the right to a full trial on demand. NY R USDCTND L.R. 83.7-1.

   i. *Actions subject to arbitration.* The Clerk shall notify the parties in all civil cases, except as the Local Rules of Practice for the United States District Court for the Northern District of New York otherwise direct, that they may consent to non-binding arbitration under NY R US-DCTND L.R. 83.7. The notice shall be furnished to the parties at pretrial/scheduling conferences or shall be included with pretrial conference notices and instructions. Consent to arbitration under NY R USDCTND L.R. 83.7 shall be discussed at the pretrial/scheduling conference. No party or attorney shall be prejudiced for refusing to participate in arbitration. The Court shall allow the referral of any civil action pending before it to the arbitration process if the parties consent. The plaintiff shall be responsible for securing the execution of a consent form by the parties and for filing the form with the Clerk within fourteen (14) days after the parties receive the form. The parties shall freely and knowingly enter into the consent. NY R USDCTND L.R. 83.7-2.

   ii. *Referral to arbitration.* The Clerk shall refer every action subject to NY R USDCTND L.R. 83.7 to arbitration in accordance with the procedures under NY R USDCTND L.R. 83.7 twenty-one (21) days after the filing of the last responsive pleading or within twenty-one (21) days of the filing of a stipulated consent order referring the action to arbitration, whichever event occurs last, except as otherwise provided. If any party notices a motion to dismiss under the provisions of FRCP 12(a) and/or FRCP 12(b), or a motion to join necessary parties pursuant to the Federal Rules of Civil Procedure prior to the expiration of the twenty-one (21) day period, the assigned judge shall hear the motion and further proceedings under NY R USDCTND L.R. 83.7 shall be deferred pending decision on the motion. If the Court does not dismiss the action on the motion, the Court shall refer the action to arbitration twenty-one (21) days after the filing of the decision. NY R USDCTND L.R. 83.7-3(a). Motions for summary judgment pursuant to FRCP 56 shall be filed and served within twenty-one (21) days following the close of discovery. The filing of a FRCP 56 motion shall defer further proceedings under NY R USDCTND L.R. 83.7 pending decision on the motion. NY R USDCTND L.R. 83.7-3(a).

- *Relief from referral.* Any party shall request relief from the operation of NY R USDCTND L.R. 83.7 by filing with the Court a motion for the relief within twenty-one (21) days after entry of the initial stipulated consent order which refers the case for arbitration. The assigned judge shall, sua sponte, exempt an action from the application of NY R USDCTND L.R. 83.7 where the objectives of arbitration would not be realized because (1) the case involves complex or novel legal issues, (2) legal issues predominate over factual issues, or (3) for other good cause. NY R USDCTND L.R. 83.7-3(c).

iii. For more information on arbitration, refer to NY R USDCTND L.R. 83.7.

b. *Mediation.* The purpose of NY R USDCTND L.R. 83.11 is to provide a supplementary procedure to the Court's existing alternative dispute resolution procedures. NY R USDCTND L.R. 83.11 provides for an earlier resolution of civil disputes resulting in savings of time and cost to litigants and the Court without sacrificing the quality of justice rendered or the right of litigants to a full trial on all issues not resolved through mediation. NY R USDCTND L.R. 83.11-1(a). Mediation is a process by which an impartial person, the mediator, facilitates communication between disputing parties to promote understanding, reconciliation and settlement. The mediator is an advocate for settlement and uses the mediation process to help the parties fully explore any potential area of agreement. The mediator does not serve as a judge or arbitrator and has no authority to render any decision on any disputed issue or to force a settlement. The parties themselves are responsible for negotiating any resolution(s) to their dispute. NY R USDCTND L.R. 83.11-1(b).

i. *Actions subject to mediation.* The Court may refer any civil action (or any portion thereof) to mediation under NY R USDCTND L.R. 83.11: (1) by order of referral; or (2) on the motion of any party; or (3) by consent of the parties. NY R USDCTND L.R. 83.11-3(a).

- *Withdrawal from mediation.* The parties may withdraw from mediation any civil action or claim that the Court refers to mediation pursuant to NY R USDCTND L.R. 83.11-3 by application to the assigned judge at least ten (10) days prior to the scheduled mediation session. NY R USDCTND L.R. 83.11-3(b).

ii. *Mandatory mediation program.* The United States District Court for the Northern District of New York has adopted this Mandatory Mediation Plan. The paid Mediation Program is designed to provide quicker, less expensive and potentially more satisfying alternatives to continuing litigation, without impairing the quality of justice or the right to trial. NY R USDCTND Order 47(1)(1.2)(A). This Mandatory Mediation Plan applies to civil actions pending as well as newly filed actions, except as otherwise indicated in NY R USDCTND Order 47. The Local Rules for voluntary mediation will apply only to Pro Se Cases that proceed through the Assisted Mediation Program. NY R USDCTND Order 47(1)(1.2)(B).

- *Referral into the pilot mandatory mediation program for new cases.* All civil cases shall be referred automatically into the Mandatory Mediation Program. Notice of the Mandatory Mediation requirements will be provided to all parties immediately upon the filing of a complaint and answer or a notice of removal. ADR intervention will be scheduled at the conference held pursuant to NY R USDCTND L.R. 16.1. NY R USDCTND Order 47(2)(2.1)(A). For a list of categories of actions exempted from automatic referral, refer to NY R USDCTND Order 47(2)(2.1)(A).

- *Referral into the pilot mandatory mediation program for pending cases.* The assigned Judge or Magistrate Judge on any pending civil case may, sua sponte or with status conference, issue an order referring the case into the Mandatory Mediation Program. The order shall specify a date on which the ADR intervention is to be completed. NY R USDCTND Order 47(2)(2.1)(B).

- *Referral into the pilot mandatory mediation program by stipulation.* A case may be referred into the Mandatory Mediation Program by stipulation of all parties. Stipulations shall be filed and shall designate the time frame within which the ADR process will be completed. Stipulations are presumed acceptable unless the assigned Judge or Magistrate Judge determines that the interests of justice are not served. NY R USDCTND Order 47(2)(2.1)(C).

- *Relief from referral.* Motions to opt out of the program will be addressed by the assigned Magistrate Judge at the FRCP 16 conference. NY R USDCTND Order 47(2)(2.2)(A). Opting Out Motions shall be granted only for "good cause" shown. Inconvenience, travel costs, attorney fees or other costs shall not constitute "good cause." A party seeking relief from the Mandatory Mediation Program must set forth the reasons why Mandatory Mediation has no reasonable chance of being productive. NY R USDCTND Order 47(2)(2.2)(B). The assigned Magistrate Judge may, sua sponte, exempt any case from the Court's Mandatory Mediation Program. NY R USDCTND Order 47(2)(2.2)(C).

iii. *Assisted mediation program.* The Court may assign specially trained pro bono Special Mediation Counsel to assist pro se civilian litigants with preparing for and participating in mediation. The Assisted Mediation Program is open to civilian pro se parties to actions in the Northern District of New York. The assigned judge or magistrate judge determines if the case would benefit from mediation and would also benefit from the assignment of Special Mediation Counsel to assist the pro se party with the mediation process. NY R USDCTND L.R. 83.8(a). Appointment of Special Mediation Counsel is in no way guaranteed, even if the action is referred to the court-annexed mediation program. Appointment is at the sole discretion of the presiding judge. NY R USDCTND L.R. 83.8(a).

- *Referral to assisted mediation program.* If the court determines that referral to the Assisted Mediation Program is appropriate, the Court shall enter an order of reference to the Assisted Mediation Program. NY R USDCTND L.R. 83.8(b).

iv. For more information on mediation, refer to NY R USDCTND L.R. 83.11 and NY R USDCTND Order 47.

c. *Early neutral evaluation (ENE).* Early neutral evaluation (ENE) is a process in which parties obtain from an experienced neutral (an "evaluator") a nonbinding, reasoned, oral evaluation of the merits of the case. The first step in the ENE process involves the Court appointing an evaluator who has expertise in the area of law in the case. After the parties exchange essential information and position statements early in the pretrial period (usually within one hundred fifty (150) to two hundred (200) days after a complaint has been filed), the evaluator convenes an ENE session that typically lasts about two hours. At the ENE meeting, each side briefly presents the factual and legal basis of its position. The evaluator may ask questions of the parties and help them identify the main issues in dispute and the areas of agreement. The evaluator may also help the parties explore options for settlement. If settlement does not occur, the evaluator then offers an opinion as to the settlement value of the case, including the likelihood of liability and the likely range of damages. With the benefit of this assessment, the parties are again encouraged to discuss settlement, with or without the evaluator's assistance. The parties may also explore ways to narrow the issues in dispute, exchange information about the case or otherwise prepare efficiently for trial. NY R USDCTND L.R. 83.12-1.

i. *Actions subject to early neutral evaluation.* The Court may refer any civil action (or any portion thereof) to ENE under NY R USDCTND L.R. 83.12: (1) by order of referral; (2) on the motion of any party; or (3) by consent of the parties. NY R USDCTND L.R. 83.12-3(a).

- *Withdrawal from the ENE process.* The parties may withdraw any civil action or claim that the Court has referred to the ENE Process pursuant to NY R USDCTND L.R. 83.12-3 by application to the assigned judge at least ten (10) days before the scheduled evaluation session. NY R USDCTND L.R. 83.12-3(b).

ii. For more information on early neutral evaluation (ENE), refer to NY R USDCTND L.R. 83.12.

12. *Settlement procedures.* On notice to the Court or the Clerk that the parties have settled an action, and upon confirmation of the settlement by all parties, the Court may issue a judgment dismissing the action by reason of settlement. The Court shall issue the order without prejudice to the parties' right to secure reinstatement of the case within thirty (30) days after the date of judgment by making a showing that the

settlement was not, in fact, consummated. NY R USDCTND L.R. 68.2(a). If the Court decides not to follow the procedures set forth in NY R USDCTND L.R. 68.2(a), the parties shall file within thirty (30) days of the notification to the Court, unless otherwise directed by written order, such notices, stipulations and/or motions as are necessary to terminate the action. If the required documents are not filed within the thirty (30) day period, the Clerk shall place the action on the dismissal calendar. NY R USDCTND L.R. 68.2(b).

13. *Sanctions and penalties for noncompliance.* Failure of an attorney or of a party to comply with any provision of the Local Rules of Practice for the United States District Court for the Northern District of New York, General Orders of this District, Orders of the Court, or the Federal Rules of Civil Procedure shall be a ground for imposition of sanctions. NY R USDCTND L.R. 1.1(d).

14. *Individual judge practices.* Refer to the Miscellaneous section of this document for information on individual judge practices on general requirements for documents.

## D. Documents

1. *Documents for moving party*

   a. *Required documents*

      i. *Notice of motion and motion.* The Notice of Motion must state the return date that the moving party has selected. NY R USDCTND L.R. 7.1(b)(1). Refer to the General Requirements section of this document for information on the notice of motion and motion.

         • *Order to show cause.* Refer to the General Requirements section of this document for information on bringing a motion by order to show cause.

      ii. *Statement of material facts.* Any motion for summary judgment shall contain a Statement of Material Facts. The Statement of Material Facts shall set forth, in numbered paragraphs, each material fact about which the moving party contends there exists no genuine issue. Each fact listed shall set forth a specific citation to the record where the fact is established. The record for purposes of the Statement of Material Facts includes the pleadings, depositions, answers to interrogatories, admissions and affidavits. It does not, however, include attorney's affidavits. Failure of the moving party to submit an accurate and complete Statement of Material Facts shall result in a denial of the motion. NY R USDCTND L.R. 7.1(a)(3).

      iii. *Memorandum of law.* Except as otherwise provided in NY R USDCTND L.R. 7.1(a), all motions. . .require a memorandum of law. NY R USDCTND L.R. 7.1(a). Refer to the Format section of this document for the formatting requirements for memoranda of law.

      iv. *Supporting affidavit.* Except as otherwise provided in NY R USDCTND L.R. 7.1(a), all motions. . .require a. . .supporting affidavit. NY R USDCTND L.R. 7.1(a). An affidavit must not contain legal arguments but must contain factual and procedural background that is relevant to the motion the affidavit supports. NY R USDCTND L.R. 7.1(a)(2).

      v. *Certificate of service.* Except as otherwise provided in NY R USDCTND L.R. 7.1(a), all motions. . .require. . .proof of service on all the parties. See NY R USDCTND L.R. 5.1(a). NY R USDCTND L.R. 7.1(a). FRCP 5(d) requires that the person making service under FRCP 5 certify that service has been effected. FRCP 5(Advisory Committee Notes). Having such information on file may be useful for many purposes, including proof of service if an issue arises concerning the effectiveness of the service. FRCP 5(Advisory Committee Notes). The party or its designee shall declare, by affidavit or certification, that it has provided all other parties in the action with all documents it has filed with the Court. NY R USDCTND L.R. 5.1(a).

         • Attorneys and pro se parties who are not Filing or Receiving Users must be served with a paper copy of any electronically filed pleading or other document. NY R USDCTND CM/ECF(5)(5.2). Such paper service must be documented by electronically filing a certificate of service. NY R USDCTND CM/ECF(5)(5.2).

   b. *Supplemental documents*

      i. *Supporting evidence.* When a motion relies on facts outside the record, the court may hear the

matter on affidavits or may hear it wholly or partly on oral testimony or on depositions. FRCP 43(c).

- *Supporting factual positions.* A party asserting that a fact cannot be or is genuinely disputed must support the assertion by: (1) citing to particular parts of materials in the record, including depositions, documents, electronically stored information, affidavits or declarations, stipulations (including those made for purposes of the motion only), admissions, interrogatory answers, or other materials; or (2) showing that the materials cited do not establish the absence or presence of a genuine dispute, or that an adverse party cannot produce admissible evidence to support the fact. FRCP 56(c)(1).

- *Objection that a fact is not supported by admissible evidence.* A party may object that the material cited to support or dispute a fact cannot be presented in a form that would be admissible in evidence. FRCP 56(c)(2).

- *Materials not cited.* The court need consider only the cited materials, but it may consider other materials in the record. FRCP 56(c)(3).

- *Affidavits or declarations.* An affidavit or declaration used to support or oppose a motion must be made on personal knowledge, set out facts that would be admissible in evidence, and show that the affiant or declarant is competent to testify on the matters stated. FRCP 56(c)(4).

ii. *Notice of constitutional question.* A party that files a pleading, written motion, or other paper drawing into question the constitutionality of a federal or state statute must promptly:

- *File notice.* File a notice of constitutional question stating the question and identifying the paper that raises it, if: (1) a federal statute is questioned and the parties do not include the United States, one of its agencies, or one of its officers or employees in an official capacity; or (2) a state statute is questioned and the parties do not include the state, one of its agencies, or one of its officers or employees in an official capacity; and

- *Serve notice.* Serve the notice and paper on the Attorney General of the United States if a federal statute is questioned—or on the state attorney general if a state statute is questioned—either by certified or registered mail or by sending it to an electronic address designated by the attorney general for this purpose. FRCP 5.1(a).

- *No forfeiture.* A party's failure to file and serve the notice, or the court's failure to certify, does not forfeit a constitutional claim or defense that is otherwise timely asserted. FRCP 5.1(d).

iii. *Nongovernmental corporate disclosure statement*

- *Contents.* A nongovernmental corporate party must file two (2) copies of a disclosure statement that: (1) identifies any parent corporation and any publicly held corporation owning ten percent (10%) or more of its stock; or (2) states that there is no such corporation. FRCP 7.1(a).

- *Time to file; Supplemental filing.* A party must: (1) file the disclosure statement with its first appearance, pleading, petition, motion, response, or other request addressed to the court; and (2) promptly file a supplemental statement if any required information changes. FRCP 7.1(b).

iv. *Notice to pro se litigants of the consequences of failing to respond to a summary judgment motion.* The moving party shall also advise pro se litigants about the consequences of their failure to respond to a motion for summary judgment. See also NY R USDCTND L.R. 56.2. NY R USDCTND L.R. 7.1(a)(3). When moving for summary judgment against a pro se litigant, the moving party shall inform the pro se litigant of the consequences of failing to respond to the summary judgment motion. Counsel for the moving party shall send a notice to the pro se litigant that a motion for summary judgment seeks dismissal of some or all of the claims or defenses asserted in their complaint or answer and that the pro se litigant's failure to respond to the motion may result in the Court entering a judgment against the pro se litigant. Parties can obtain a sample notice from the Court's webpage. NY R USDCTND L.R. 56.2.

v. *Copies of authorities.* When serving a pro se litigant with a memorandum of law or any other paper which contains citations to authorities that are unpublished or published exclusively on electronic databases, counsel shall include a hard copy of those authorities. Although copies of authorities published only on electronic databases are not required to be filed, copies shall be provided upon request to opposing counsel who lack access to electronic databases. NY R USDCTND L.R. 7.1(a)(1).

vi. *Proposed order.* A document that is submitted in .pdf format cannot be modified; therefore, a proposed order or stipulation must be in a word processing format. The chambers of the assigned judge may request that a proposed order and/or a stipulation be e-mailed to the courtroom deputy for the presiding judge in either WordPerfect or Microsoft Word format. Please attach your proposed order and/or stipulation to an Internet e-mail sent to the appropriate e-mail address listed in NY R USDCTND CM/ECF(8)(8.2). NY R USDCTND CM/ECF(8)(8.2).

vii. *Cover letter authorizing e-mail or facsimile filing.* Neither the Court nor the Clerk's Office will accept for filing any facsimile or e-mail transmission without prior authorization from the Court. The party using facsimile or e-mail transmissions to file its papers must accompany any such documents with a cover letter stating that the Court authorized such transmissions and the date on which the Court provided that authorization. Violations of NY R USDCTND L.R. 5.5 subject the offending party to the Court's full disciplinary powers. NY R USDCTND L.R. 5.5.

viii. *Affidavit attesting to failed attempts to file electronically.* If the Court's CM/ECF site experiences a technical failure, a Filing User may submit documents to the Court that day in an alternate manner provided that the documents are accompanied by the Filing User's affidavit stating that the Filing User attempted to file electronically at least two times in one (1) hour increments after 10:00 a.m. that day. The following methods are acceptable alternate means for filing documents in case of a technical failure: (1) via electronic mail in a PDF attachment sent to the e-mail address for technical failures; or (2) in person, by bringing the document to the Clerk's Office on paper accompanied by a CD/ROM that contains the document in .pdf format. NY R USDCTND CM/ECF(10)(10.1).

- A Filing User who cannot file documents electronically because of a problem on the Filing User's system must file the documents' conventionally along with an affidavit explaining the reason for not filing the documents electronically. NY R USDCTND CM/ECF(10)(10.2).

ix. *Notice of conventional filing.* If the Clerk's Office grants permission to conventionally file the document, the Filing User shall electronically file a notice of conventional filing for the documents. More information regarding this process can be obtained from the Court's web page. NY R USDCTND CM/ECF(4)(4.5).

x. *CD/ROM with PDF of document(s).* If the Court grants permission to file a document traditionally, the attorney must submit the documents for filing to the Clerk's Office on CD/ROM in .pdf or pdf.A format. NY R USDCTND CM/ECF(2).

xi. *English translation.* The Court conducts its reviews and deliberations in English. Unless otherwise directed by the Court, any document that a party transmits to the Court (including one in the record on appeal) that is in a language other than English must be accompanied by an English translation that the translator has certified as true and accurate, pursuant to 28 U.S.C.A. § 1746. NY R USDCTND L.R. 10.1(e). For more information, refer to NY R USDCTND L.R. 10.1(e).

xii. *Courtesy copies.* The Court may require that courtesy copies of electronically filed documents be submitted for its review and may amend these Administrative Procedures (NY R USDCTND CM/ECF) at any time without prior notice. NY R USDCTND CM/ECF(2).

- The parties need not provide a courtesy copy of their motion papers to the assigned judge unless the assigned judge requests a copy. NY R USDCTND L.R. 7.1(b)(1).

xiii. *Copies for three-judge court.* On the convening of a three-judge court, the parties shall make three (3) copies of all non-electronically filed pleadings, motion papers, and memoranda of law available to the Clerk for distribution. NY R USDCTND L.R. 9.1.

2. *Documents for opposing party*

   a. *Required documents*

      i. *Opposition.* Refer to the General Requirements section of this document for information on the opposing papers.

      ii. *Response to the statement of material facts.* The opposing party shall file a response to the Statement of Material Facts. The non-movant's response shall mirror the movant's Statement of Material Facts by admitting and/or denying each of the movant's assertions in matching numbered paragraphs. Each denial shall set forth a specific citation to the record where the factual issue arises. The Court shall deem admitted any properly supported facts set forth in the Statement of Material Facts that the opposing party does not specifically controvert. The non-movant's response may also set forth any additional material facts that the non-movant contends are in dispute in separately numbered paragraphs, followed by a specific citation to the record where the fact is established. NY R USDCTND L.R. 7.1(a)(3).

      iii. *Memorandum of law.* Except as otherwise provided in NY R USDCTND L.R. 7.1(a), all. . .opposition to motions require a memorandum of law. NY R USDCTND L.R. 7.1(a).

         • *Cross-motion brief.* If a party makes a cross-motion, it must join its cross motion brief with its opposition brief, and this combined brief may not exceed twenty-five (25) pages in length, exclusive of exhibits. A separate brief in opposition to the original motion is not permissible. NY R USDCTND L.R. 7.1(c).

         • Refer to the Format section of this document for the formatting requirements for memoranda of law.

      iv. *Supporting affidavit.* Except as otherwise provided in NY R USDCTND L.R. 7.1(a), all. . .opposition to motions require a. . .supporting affidavit. NY R USDCTND L.R. 7.1(a). An affidavit must not contain legal arguments but must contain factual and procedural background that is relevant to the motion the affidavit supports. NY R USDCTND L.R. 7.1(a)(2).

      v. *Certificate of service.* Except as otherwise provided in NY R USDCTND L.R. 7.1(a), all. . .opposition to motions require. . .proof of service on all the parties. See NY R USDCTND L.R. 5.1(a). NY R USDCTND L.R. 7.1(a). FRCP 5(d) requires that the person making service under FRCP 5 certify that service has been effected. FRCP 5(Advisory Committee Notes). Having such information on file may be useful for many purposes, including proof of service if an issue arises concerning the effectiveness of the service. FRCP 5(Advisory Committee Notes). The party or its designee shall declare, by affidavit or certification, that it has provided all other parties in the action with all documents it has filed with the Court. NY R USDCTND L.R. 5.1(a).

         • Attorneys and pro se parties who are not Filing or Receiving Users must be served with a paper copy of any electronically filed pleading or other document. NY R USDCTND CM/ECF(5)(5.2). Such paper service must be documented by electronically filing a certificate of service. NY R USDCTND CM/ECF(5)(5.2).

   b. *Supplemental documents*

      i. *Supporting evidence.* When a motion relies on facts outside the record, the court may hear the matter on affidavits or may hear it wholly or partly on oral testimony or on depositions. FRCP 43(c).

         • *Supporting factual positions.* A party asserting that a fact cannot be or is genuinely disputed must support the assertion by: (1) citing to particular parts of materials in the record, including depositions, documents, electronically stored information, affidavits or declarations, stipulations (including those made for purposes of the motion only), admissions, interrogatory answers, or other materials; or (2) showing that the materials cited do not establish the absence or presence of a genuine dispute, or that an adverse party cannot produce admissible evidence to support the fact. FRCP 56(c)(1).

- *Objection that a fact is not supported by admissible evidence.* A party may object that the material cited to support or dispute a fact cannot be presented in a form that would be admissible in evidence. FRCP 56(c)(2).

- *Materials not cited.* The court need consider only the cited materials, but it may consider other materials in the record. FRCP 56(c)(3).

- *Affidavits or declarations.* An affidavit or declaration used to support or oppose a motion must be made on personal knowledge, set out facts that would be admissible in evidence, and show that the affiant or declarant is competent to testify on the matters stated. FRCP 56(c)(4).

ii. *Notice of constitutional question.* A party that files a pleading, written motion, or other paper drawing into question the constitutionality of a federal or state statute must promptly:

- *File notice.* File a notice of constitutional question stating the question and identifying the paper that raises it, if: (1) a federal statute is questioned and the parties do not include the United States, one of its agencies, or one of its officers or employees in an official capacity; or (2) a state statute is questioned and the parties do not include the state, one of its agencies, or one of its officers or employees in an official capacity; and

- *Serve notice.* Serve the notice and paper on the Attorney General of the United States if a federal statute is questioned—or on the state attorney general if a state statute is questioned—either by certified or registered mail or by sending it to an electronic address designated by the attorney general for this purpose. FRCP 5.1(a).

- *No forfeiture.* A party's failure to file and serve the notice, or the court's failure to certify, does not forfeit a constitutional claim or defense that is otherwise timely asserted. FRCP 5.1(d).

iii. *Cross-motion.* A party may file and serve a cross-motion (meaning a competing request for relief or order similar to that requested by another party against the cross-moving party) at the time it files and serves its opposition papers to the original motion, i.e., not less than SEVENTEEN (17) DAYS prior to the return date of the motion. NY R USDCTND L.R. 7.1(c).

iv. *Copies of authorities.* When serving a pro se litigant with a memorandum of law or any other paper which contains citations to authorities that are unpublished or published exclusively on electronic databases, counsel shall include a hard copy of those authorities. Although copies of authorities published only on electronic databases are not required to be filed, copies shall be provided upon request to opposing counsel who lack access to electronic databases. NY R USDCTND L.R. 7.1(a)(1).

v. *Cover letter authorizing e-mail or facsimile filing.* Neither the Court nor the Clerk's Office will accept for filing any facsimile or e-mail transmission without prior authorization from the Court. The party using facsimile or e-mail transmissions to file its papers must accompany any such documents with a cover letter stating that the Court authorized such transmissions and the date on which the Court provided that authorization. Violations of NY R USDCTND L.R. 5.5 subject the offending party to the Court's full disciplinary powers. NY R USDCTND L.R. 5.5.

vi. *Affidavit attesting to failed attempts to file electronically.* If the Court's CM/ECF site experiences a technical failure, a Filing User may submit documents to the Court that day in an alternate manner provided that the documents are accompanied by the Filing User's affidavit stating that the Filing User attempted to file electronically at least two times in one (1) hour increments after 10:00 a.m. that day. The following methods are acceptable alternate means for filing documents in case of a technical failure: (1) via electronic mail in a PDF attachment sent to the e-mail address for technical failures; or (2) in person, by bringing the document to the Clerk's Office on paper accompanied by a CD/ROM that contains the document in .pdf format. NY R USDCTND CM/ECF(10)(10.1).

- A Filing User who cannot file documents electronically because of a problem on the Filing

User's system must file the documents' conventionally along with an affidavit explaining the reason for not filing the documents electronically. NY R USDCTND CM/ECF(10)(10.2).

vii. *Notice of conventional filing.* If the Clerk's Office grants permission to conventionally file the document, the Filing User shall electronically file a notice of conventional filing for the documents. More information regarding this process can be obtained from the Court's web page. NY R USDCTND CM/ECF(4)(4.5).

viii. *CD/ROM with PDF of document(s).* If the Court grants permission to file a document traditionally, the attorney must submit the documents for filing to the Clerk's Office on CD/ROM in .pdf or pdf.A format. NY R USDCTND CM/ECF(2).

ix. *English translation.* The Court conducts its reviews and deliberations in English. Unless otherwise directed by the Court, any document that a party transmits to the Court (including one in the record on appeal) that is in a language other than English must be accompanied by an English translation that the translator has certified as true and accurate, pursuant to 28 U.S.C.A. § 1746. NY R USDCTND L.R. 10.1(e). For more information, refer to NY R USDCTND L.R. 10.1(e).

x. *Courtesy copies.* The Court may require that courtesy copies of electronically filed documents be submitted for its review and may amend these Administrative Procedures (NY R USDCTND CM/ECF) at any time without prior notice. NY R USDCTND CM/ECF(2).

- The parties need not provide a courtesy copy of their motion papers to the assigned judge unless the assigned judge requests a copy. NY R USDCTND L.R. 7.1(b)(1).

xi. *Copies for three-judge court.* On the convening of a three-judge court, the parties shall make three (3) copies of all non-electronically filed pleadings, motion papers, and memoranda of law available to the Clerk for distribution. NY R USDCTND L.R. 9.1.

3. *Individual judge practices.* Refer to the Miscellaneous section of this document for information on individual judge practices on required documents.

## E. Format

1. *Form of documents.* The rules governing captions and other matters of form in pleadings apply to motions and other papers. FRCP 7(b)(2). All pleadings and other papers shall be served and filed in accordance with the Federal Rules of Civil Procedure and shall be in the form prescribed by NY R USDCTND L.R. 10.1. NY R USDCTND L.R. 5.1(a).

a. *Form, generally.* All pleadings, motions, and other documents that a party presents for filing, whether in paper form or in electronic form, shall meet the following requirements:

i. *Font size.* All text, whether in the body of the document or in footnotes, must be a minimum of twelve (12) point type. NY R USDCTND L.R. 10.1(a)(1).

ii. *Margins.* All documents must have one (1) inch margins on all four sides of the page. NY R USDCTND L.R. 10.1(a)(2).

iii. *Spacing.* All text in the body of the document must be double-spaced. NY R USDCTND L.R. 10.1(a)(3).

- The text in block quotations and footnotes may be single-spaced. NY R USDCTND L.R. 10.1(a)(4).

iv. *Page numbering.* Pages must be consecutively numbered. NY R USDCTND L.R. 10.1(a)(7).

v. *Circumventing formatting limitations*

- Extensive footnotes must not be used to circumvent page limitations. NY R USDCTND L.R. 10.1(a)(5).

- Compacted or other compressed printing features must not be used. NY R USDCTND L.R. 10.1(a)(6).

b. *Additional requirements for paper filing.* Additional requirements for all pleadings, motions, and other documents that a party presents for filing in paper form:

   i. *Paper size.* All documents must be on eight and one-half by eleven (8-1/2 x 11) inch white paper of good quality. NY R USDCTND L.R. 10.1(b)(1).

   ii. *Text.* All text must be plainly and legibly written, typewritten, printed or reproduced without erasures or interlineations materially defacing them. NY R USDCTND L.R. 10.1(b)(2).

   iii. *Ink.* All documents must be in black or blue ink. NY R USDCTND L.R. 10.1(b)(3).

   iv. *Binding.* Pages of all documents must be stapled (or in some other way fastened) together. NY R USDCTND L.R. 10.1(b)(4).

   v. *Single-sided paper.* All documents must be single-sided. NY R USDCTND L.R. 10.1(b)(5).

   vi. *Electronic submission.* The Court, at its discretion, may require the electronic submission of any document in a WordPerfect-compatible format. NY R USDCTND L.R. 10.1(b)(6).

   vii. *Rejection of document.* The Court may reject documents that do not comply with the above-listed requirements. NY R USDCTND L.R. 10.1(b).

c. *Caption; Names of parties.* Every pleading must have a caption with the court's name, a title, a file number, and a FRCP 7(a) designation. The title of the complaint must name all the parties; the title of other pleadings, after naming the first party on each side, may refer generally to other parties. FRCP 10(a). Each document must contain a caption for the specific case to which it pertains. The caption must include the title of the Court, the title of the action, the civil action number of the case, the initials of the assigned judge(s), and the name or nature of the paper in sufficient detail for identification. If a litigant has more than one action pending in this Court, any and all papers filed in a case must contain and pertain to one civil action number, unless the civil actions have been consolidated by the Court. Any motion or other papers purporting to relate to more than one action will not be accepted for filing and may be stricken by the Court. NY R USDCTND L.R. 10.1(c)(1) shall not apply, as noted in NY R USDCTND L.R. 10.1(c), to notices of change of address filed by attorneys of record and pro se litigants. The parties must separately caption affidavits and declarations and must not physically attach them to the Notice of Motion or Memorandum of Law. NY R USDCTND L.R. 10.1(c)(1).

d. *Paragraphs; Separate statements.* A party must state its claims or defenses in numbered paragraphs, each limited as far as practicable to a single set of circumstances. A later pleading may refer by number to a paragraph in an earlier pleading. If doing so would promote clarity, each claim founded on a separate transaction or occurrence—and each defense other than a denial—must be stated in a separate count or defense. FRCP 10(b).

e. *Adoption by reference; Exhibits.* A statement in a pleading may be adopted by reference elsewhere in the same pleading or in any other pleading or motion. A copy of a written instrument that is an exhibit to a pleading is a part of the pleading for all purposes. FRCP 10(c).

f. *Citation of local rules.* These are the Local Rules of Practice for the United States District Court for the Northern District of New York. They shall be cited as "L.R. ___." NY R USDCTND L.R. 1.1(a).

g. *Acceptance by the clerk.* The clerk must not refuse to file a paper solely because it is not in the form prescribed by the Federal Rules of Civil Procedure or by a local rule or practice. FRCP 5(d)(4).

2. *Form of electronic documents.* All pleadings, motions, and other documents that a party presents for filing, whether in paper form or in electronic form, shall meet the requirements in NY R USDCTND L.R. 10.1(a). NY R USDCTND L.R. 10.1(a). Refer above for more information.

a. *Attachments and exhibits.* A Filing User must submit in electronic form all documents referenced as exhibits or attachments in accordance with the Court's CM/ECF Users Manual unless the Court otherwise orders. A Filing User shall submit as exhibits or attachments only those excerpts of the referenced documents that are directly germane to the matter under the Court's consideration. Excerpted material must be clearly and prominently identified as such. Filing Users who file excerpts of documents as exhibits or attachments under these Administrative Procedures (NY R USDCTND CM/ECF) do so without prejudice to their right to timely file additional excerpts or the complete document. Responding parties may also timely file the complete document or additional excerpts that they believe are directly germane to the matter under the Court's consideration. NY R USDCTND CM/ECF(4)(4.4).

    i.   All attachments must be described in sufficient detail so the Court and opposing counsel can easily identify and distinguish the filed attachments. Vague or general descriptions are insufficient (i.e., "Exhibit 1"). Rather, each attachment shall have a descriptive title identifying, with specificity, the document that is being filed (i.e., "Exhibit 12 Mulligan County Fire Investigation Report.") Failure to adequately describe attachments may result in the document being rejected by the Court. NY R USDCTND CM/ECF(4)(4.4).

  b.  *Large documents.* For information on the electronic filing of large documents, please consult the Court's CM/ECF Users Manual, which is available on the Court's web page. NY R USDCTND CM/ECF(4)(4.5).

    i.   A party who believes a document is too lengthy to electronically image, i.e., "scan," may contact the Clerk's Office for permission to file that document conventionally. If the Clerk's Office grants permission to conventionally file the document, the Filing User shall electronically file a notice of conventional filing for the documents. More information regarding this process can be obtained from the Court's web page. Exhibits submitted conventionally shall be served on other parties as if they were not subject to these Administrative Procedures (NY R USDCTND CM/ECF). For a list of hints and tips for scanning large documents, please consult the Court's web page. NY R USDCTND CM/ECF(4)(4.5).

  c.  *Legibility.* It shall be the Filing User's responsibility to verify the legibility of scanned documents before filing them electronically with the Court. NY R USDCTND CM/ECF(4)(4.6).

  d.  *Color documents.* Since documents scanned in color or containing a graphic take much longer to upload, Filing Users are encouraged to configure their scanners to scan documents at 300 dpi and preferably in black and white rather than in color. NY R USDCTND CM/ECF(4)(4.7).

  e.  *Items not in .PDF format.* Parties wishing to file items not amenable to .pdf format (i.e. CD's, DVD's), shall file such items conventionally with the Clerk's Office. The Filing User shall electronically file a notice of conventional filing indicating that these items have been submitted to the clerk and shall serve copies of these items on other parties as if they were not subject to these Administrative Procedures (NY R USDCTND CM/ECF). These item(s) will be maintained by the Clerk's Office until the case is disposed, at which time they will be returned to the filing party for retention consistent with NY R USDCTND CM/ECF(4)(4.9). NY R USDCTND CM/ECF(4)(4.8).

3.  *Form of memoranda of law*

  a.  *Length limitation.* No party shall file or serve a memorandum of law that exceeds twenty-five (25) pages in length, unless that party obtains leave of the judge hearing the motion prior to filing. NY R USDCTND L.R. 7.1(a)(1).

  b.  *Table of contents.* All memoranda of law shall contain a table of contents. NY R USDCTND L.R. 7.1(a)(1).

4.  *Signing of pleadings, motions and other papers*

  a.  *Signature.* Every pleading, written motion, and other paper must be signed by at least one attorney of record in the attorney's name—or by a party personally if the party is unrepresented. The paper must state the signer's address, e-mail address, and telephone number. FRCP 11(a). Each document must identify the person filing the document. This identification must include an original signature of the attorney or pro se litigant; the typewritten name of that person; the address of a pro se litigant; and the bar roll number, office address, telephone number, e-mail address and fax number of the attorney. Telephone numbers of non-prisoner pro se parties may be provided voluntarily or upon request of the Court. See General Order #22 (NY R USDCTND CM/ECF) for signature requirements. NY R USDCTND L.R. 10.1(c)(2).

    i.   *Electronic signatures.* Documents filed under an attorney's login and password shall constitute that attorney's signature for purposes of the Local Rules of Practice for the United States District Court for the Northern District of New York and Federal Rules of Civil Procedure, including but not limited to FRCP 11. A pleading or other document requiring an attorney's signature shall be signed in the following manner, whether filed electronically or submitted on disk or CD/ROM to the Clerk's Office: "s/ (attorney name)." The correct format for an attorney signature is found in NY R USDCTND CM/ECF(6)(6.1). NY R USDCTND CM/ECF(6)(6.1).

- *Non-attorney signature.* If an original document requires the signature of a non-attorney, the Filing User may scan the original document containing the original signature(s), then electronically file it on the System. Alternatively, the Filing User may convert the document into .pdf text format and submit the document using "s/" for the signature of the non-attorney. NY R USDCTND CM/ECF(6)(6.2).

- *Multiple signatures.* A document requiring signatures of more than one party must be filed electronically either by (1) submitting a scanned document containing all necessary signatures; (2) representing the consent of the other parties on the document; or (3) in any other manner that the Court approves. NY R USDCTND CM/ECF(6)(6.3).

  ii.  *No verification or accompanying affidavit required for pleadings.* Unless a rule or statute specifically states otherwise, a pleading need not be verified or accompanied by an affidavit. FRCP 11(a).

  iii.  *Unsigned papers.* The court must strike an unsigned paper unless the omission is promptly corrected after being called to the attorney's or party's attention. FRCP 11(a).

b.  *Representations to the court.* By presenting to the court a pleading, written motion, or other paper—whether by signing, filing, submitting, or later advocating it—an attorney or unrepresented party certifies that to the best of the person's knowledge, information, and belief, formed after an inquiry reasonable under the circumstances:

  i.  It is not being presented for any improper purpose, such as to harass, cause unnecessary delay, or needlessly increase the cost of litigation;

  ii.  The claims, defenses, and other legal contentions are warranted by existing law or by a nonfrivolous argument for extending, modifying, or reversing existing law or for establishing new law;

  iii.  The factual contentions have evidentiary support or, if specifically so identified, will likely have evidentiary support after a reasonable opportunity for further investigation or discovery; and

  iv.  The denials of factual contentions are warranted on the evidence or, if specifically so identified, are reasonably based on belief or a lack of information. FRCP 11(b).

c.  *Sanctions.* If, after notice and a reasonable opportunity to respond, the court determines that FRCP 11(b) has been violated, the court may impose an appropriate sanction on any attorney, law firm, or party that violated FRCP 11(b) or is responsible for the violation. FRCP 11(c)(1). Refer to the United States District Court for the Northern District of New York KeyRules Motion for Sanctions document for more information.

5.  *Privacy protection for filings made with the court*

a.  *Redacted filings.* Unless the court orders otherwise, in an electronic or paper filing with the court that contains an individual's Social Security number, taxpayer-identification number, or birth date, the name of an individual known to be a minor, or a financial-account number, a party or nonparty making the filing may include only:

  i.  The last four (4) digits of the Social Security number and taxpayer-identification number;

  ii.  The year of the individual's birth;

  iii.  The minor's initials; and

  iv.  The last four (4) digits of the financial-account number. FRCP 5.2(a); NY R USDCTND L.R. 8.1; NY R USDCTND CM/ECF(11)(11.2).

  v.  If a home address must be used, use only the City and State. NY R USDCTND L.R. 8.1; NY R USDCTND CM/ECF(11)(11.2).

  vi.  If the victim of a sexual assault must be referenced, redact the name to 'Victim.' NY R USDCTND CM/ECF(11)(11.2); NY R USDCTND L.R. 8.1.

vii.    In addition, caution shall be exercised when filing documents that contain the following:

- Personal identifying number, such as a driver's license number;

- Medical records, treatment and diagnosis;

- Employment history;

- Individual financial information; and

- Proprietary or trade secret information. NY R USDCTND L.R. 8.1; NY R USDCTND CM/ECF(11)(11.2).

b.  *Exemptions from the redaction requirement.* The redaction requirement does not apply to the following:

i.    A financial-account number that identifies the property allegedly subject to forfeiture in a forfeiture proceeding;

ii.   The record of an administrative or agency proceeding;

iii.  The official record of a state-court proceeding;

iv.   The record of a court or tribunal, if that record was not subject to the redaction requirement when originally filed;

v.    A filing covered by FRCP 5.2(c) or FRCP 5.2(d); and

vi.   A pro se filing in an action brought under 28 U.S.C.A. § 2241, 28 U.S.C.A. § 2254, or 28 U.S.C.A. § 2255. FRCP 5.2(b).

vii.  Transcripts of the administrative record in social security proceedings are exempt from this requirement. State court records and other documents filed in habeas corpus proceedings are exempt from this requirement except for proceedings that involve victims of sex crimes. In habeas corpus cases involving sex crimes, the parties must redact the record and supporting papers, or may move to seal, if appropriate. NY R USDCTND L.R. 8.1.

c.  *Limitations on remote access to electronic files; Social Security appeals and immigration cases.* Unless the court orders otherwise, in an action for benefits under the Social Security Act, and in an action or proceeding relating to an order of removal, to relief from removal, or to immigration benefits or detention, access to an electronic file is authorized as follows:

i.    The parties and their attorneys may have remote electronic access to any part of the case file, including the administrative record;

ii.   Any other person may have electronic access to the full record at the courthouse, but may have remote electronic access only to:

- The docket maintained by the court; and

- An opinion, order, judgment, or other disposition of the court, but not any other part of the case file or the administrative record. FRCP 5.2(c).

d.  *Filings made under seal.* The court may order that a filing be made under seal without redaction. The court may later unseal the filing or order the person who made the filing to file a redacted version for the public record. FRCP 5.2(d); NY R USDCTND L.R. 8.1. For information on sealed matters, refer to NY R USDCTND L.R. 83.13 and NY R USDCTND CM/ECF(12).

e.  *Protective orders.* For good cause, the court may by order in a case:

i.    Require redaction of additional information; or

ii.   Limit or prohibit a nonparty's remote electronic access to a document filed with the court. FRCP 5.2(e).

f.  *Option for additional unredacted filing under seal.* A person making a redacted filing may also file an unredacted copy under seal. The court must retain the unredacted copy as part of the record. FRCP 5.2(f); NY R USDCTND L.R. 8.1; NY R USDCTND CM/ECF(11)(11.3).

g.  *Option for filing a reference list.* A filing that contains redacted information may be filed together

with a reference list that identifies each item of redacted information and specifies an appropriate identifier that uniquely corresponds to each item listed. The list must be filed under seal and may be amended as of right. Any reference in the case to a listed identifier will be construed to refer to the corresponding item of information. FRCP 5.2(g); NY R USDCTND L.R. 8.1; NY R USDCTND CM/ECF(11)(11.3).

h. *Responsibility for redaction.* Counsel is strongly urged to discuss this issue with all their clients so that they can make an informed decision about the inclusion of certain information. The responsibility for redacting these personal identifiers rests solely with counsel and the parties. The Clerk will not review each filing for compliance with NY R USDCTND L.R. 8.1. Counsel and the parties are cautioned that failure to redact these personal identifiers may subject them to the Court's full disciplinary power. NY R USDCTND L.R. 8.1; NY R USDCTND CM/ECF(11)(11.3).

i. *Waiver of protection of identifiers.* A person waives the protection of FRCP 5.2(a) as to the person's own information by filing it without redaction and not under seal. FRCP 5.2(h).

6. *Individual judge practices.* Refer to the Miscellaneous section of this document for information on individual judge practices on formatting documents.

## F. Filing and Service Requirements

1. *Filing requirements.* Any paper after the complaint that is required to be served—together with a certificate of service—must be filed within a reasonable time after service. FRCP 5(d)(1). Parties shall file all original motion papers, including memoranda of law and supporting affidavits, if any, in accordance with the Administrative Procedures for Electronic Case Filing (General Order #22 (NY R USDCTND CM/ECF)) and/or the case assignment form provided to the parties at the commencement of the litigation. NY R USDCTND L.R. 7.1(b)(1).

   a. *How filing is made; In general.* A paper is filed by delivering it:

      i. To the clerk; or

      ii. To a judge who agrees to accept it for filing, and who must then note the filing date on the paper and promptly send it to the clerk. FRCP 5(d)(2).

   b. *Electronic filing*

      i. *Authorization of electronic filing program.* A court may, by local rule, allow papers to be filed, signed, or verified by electronic means that are consistent with any technical standards established by the Judicial Conference of the United States. A local rule may require electronic filing only if reasonable exceptions are allowed. A paper filed electronically in compliance with a local rule is a written paper for purposes of the Federal Rules of Civil Procedure. FRCP 5(d)(3).

         • All cases filed in this Court may be assigned to the Electronic Case Files System ("ECF") in accordance with the Procedural Order on Electronic Case Filing (General Order #22 (NY R USDCTND CM/ECF)), the provisions of which are incorporated herein by reference, and which the Court may amend from time to time. Copies of General Order #22 (NY R USDCTND CM/ECF) are available at the Clerk's office or at the Court's webpage. NY R USDCTND L.R. 5.1.1; NY R USDCTND Order 25(XII).

         • The Court may deviate from these Administrative Procedures (NY R USDCTND CM/ECF) in specific cases, without prior notice, if deemed appropriate in the exercise of discretion, considering the need for the just, speedy, and inexpensive determination of matters pending before the Court. NY R USDCTND CM/ECF(2).

      ii. *Scope of electronic filing.* After January 1, 2004, all documents that attorneys admitted to practice in the Northern District of New York submit for filing shall be filed electronically using the System or shall be scanned and uploaded to the System, no matter when a case was originally filed, unless these Administrative Procedures (NY R USDCTND CM/ECF) otherwise permit or unless the assigned judge otherwise authorizes. An attorney who is not a Filing User by January 1, 2004, must show good cause to the assigned judge to file and serve pleadings and other papers in the traditional manner. NY R USDCTND CM/ECF(2).

iii. *Exceptions and/or waivers from mandatory electronic filing.* The following types of cases and/or documents are not required to be filed electronically:

- If you are seeking to have your complaint filed under seal, please file your complaint and proposed sealing order traditionally at the Clerk's Office. NY R USDCTND CM/ECF(2)(2.1)(1).

- Any document that a party proceeding pro se files. (See NY R USDCTND CM/ECF(12)(12.1) for procedural details). NY R USDCTND CM/ECF(2)(2.1)(2). A non-prisoner who is a party to a civil action and who is not represented by an attorney may file a motion to obtain an Electronic Case Filing (ECF) login and password on a form prescribed by the Clerk's Office. The Pro Se CM/ECF Registration Form shall be submitted with the motion. If during the course of the action an attorney appears on behalf of the pro se party, the Clerk's Office shall terminate the pro se party's registration based upon the attorney's appearance. NY R USDCTND CM/ECF(12)(12.1). Absent permission to file electronically, pro se filers shall file paper originals of all complaints, pleadings, motions, affidavits, briefs, and other documents which must be signed or which require either verification or an unsworn declaration under any rule or statute. The Clerk's Office will scan these original documents into an electronic file in the System but will also maintain a paper file. NY R USDCTND CM/ECF(12)(12.1). A pro se party may also seek permission to receive immediate notice of all public documents filed in their cases. Notices of Electronic Filing (NEF) and attached documents would be transmitted to a non-prisoner pro se party who selects this option. Note: The pro se party would continue to file their documents with the Clerk's Office in paper form. NY R USDCTND CM/ECF(12)(12.1).

- Sealed documents, sealed cases, documents for in camera review, documents lodged with the Court, ex parte documents, confidential agreements, Qui Tam actions and Grand Jury material and warrants must be filed traditionally. (See NY R USDCTND CM/ECF(12)(12.2) for further information the filing of the above-referenced documents). NY R USDCTND CM/ECF(2)(2.1)(3).

- Discovery: In accordance with NY R USDCTND L.R. 26.2, parties shall not file discovery, provided, however, that discovery material to be used at trial or in support of any motion, including a motion to compel or for summary judgment, shall be filed electronically with the Court prior to the trial or with the motion. Any motion pursuant to FRCP 37 shall be accompanied by the electronically filed discovery materials to which the motion relates if those materials have not previously been filed with the Court. NY R USDCTND CM/ECF(2)(2.1)(4).

- Transport Orders: All orders requesting that an incarcerated individual be transported that a judicial officer of the Northern District of New York signs shall be filed traditionally. These Orders will not be filed with the case or uploaded to the docket but rather will be processed in accordance with the procedures that the Clerk of Court promulgates. NY R USDCTND CM/ECF(2)(2.1)(5).

iv. *Filing defined.* Electronic transmission of a document to the System in accordance with these Administrative Procedures, together with the transmission of a Notice of Electronic Filing from the Court, constitutes filing of the document for all purposes of the Federal Rules of Civil Procedure and the Local Rules of Practice for the United States District Court for the Northern District of New York and constitutes entry of the document on the docket that the Clerk's Office keeps under FRCP 58 and FRCP 79. E-mailing a document to the Clerk's Office or to the assigned judge shall not constitute "filing" of the document. NY R USDCTND CM/ECF(4)(4.1).

v. *Filing fees.* Any fee required for filing a pleading or paper in this Court is payable to the Clerk of the Court. The Court will not maintain electronic billing or debit accounts for attorneys or law firms. Effective January 1, 2007, payment for filing fees will be mandatory through CM/ECF's Internet Credit Card Payment site--a secure Treasury Site. The Filing User will be prompted to enter either Bank Account Debit (ACH) or credit card information while filing the initial pleading. Any document that requires a filing fee (e.g., Notice of Appeal, Motion for Pro Hac Vice Admission) may also be paid through the federal electronic payment website. NY R USDCTND CM/ECF(7).

vi. For more information on electronic filing, refer to NY R USDCTND CM/ECF.

c. *E-mail or facsimile filing.* Neither the Court nor the Clerk's Office will accept for filing any facsimile or e-mail transmission without prior authorization from the Court. The party using facsimile or e-mail transmissions to file its papers must accompany any such documents with a cover letter stating that the Court authorized such transmissions and the date on which the Court provided that authorization. Violations of NY R USDCTND L.R. 5.5 subject the offending party to the Court's full disciplinary powers. NY R USDCTND L.R. 5.5.

2. *Service requirements*

a. *Service; When required*

i. *In general.* Unless the Federal Rules of Civil Procedure provide otherwise, each of the following papers must be served on every party:

- An order stating that service is required;
- A pleading filed after the original complaint, unless the court orders otherwise under FRCP 5(c) because there are numerous defendants;
- A discovery paper required to be served on a party, unless the court orders otherwise;
- A written motion, except one that may be heard ex parte; and
- A written notice, appearance, demand, or offer of judgment, or any similar paper. FRCP 5(a)(1).

ii. *If a party fails to appear.* No service is required on a party who is in default for failing to appear. But a pleading that asserts a new claim for relief against such a party must be served on that party under FRCP 4. FRCP 5(a)(2).

iii. *Seizing property.* If an action is begun by seizing property and no person is or need be named as a defendant, any service required before the filing of an appearance, answer, or claim must be made on the person who had custody or possession of the property when it was seized. FRCP 5(a)(3).

b. *Service; How made*

i. *Serving an attorney.* If a party is represented by an attorney, service under FRCP 5 must be made on the attorney unless the court orders service on the party. FRCP 5(b)(1).

ii. *Service in general.* A paper is served under FRCP 5 by:

- Handing it to the person;
- Leaving it: (1) at the person's office with a clerk or other person in charge or, if no one is in charge, in a conspicuous place in the office; or (2) if the person has no office or the office is closed, at the person's dwelling or usual place of abode with someone of suitable age and discretion who resides there;
- Mailing it to the person's last known address—in which event service is complete upon mailing;
- Leaving it with the court clerk if the person has no known address;
- Sending it by electronic means if the person consented in writing—in which event service is complete upon transmission, but is not effective if the serving party learns that it did not reach the person to be served; or
- Delivering it by any other means that the person consented to in writing—in which event service is complete when the person making service delivers it to the agency designated to make delivery. FRCP 5(b)(2).

iii. *Service of electronically-filed documents.* Service is complete provided all parties receive a

Notice of Electronic Filing (NEF), which is sent automatically by email from the Court (see the NEF for a list of who did/did not receive notice electronically). Transmission of the NEF constitutes service upon all Filing and Receiving Users who are listed as recipients of notice by electronic mail. It remains the responsibility of Filing and Receiving Users to maintain current contact information with the court and to regularly review the docket sheet of the case. NY R USDCTND CM/ECF(5)(5.2).

- *Non-filing or receiving users.* Attorneys and pro se parties who are not Filing or Receiving Users must be served with a paper copy of any electronically filed pleading or other document. Service of such paper copy must be made according to the Federal Rules of Civil Procedure and the Local Rules of Practice for the United States District Court for the Northern District of New York. Such paper service must be documented by electronically filing a certificate of service. NY R USDCTND CM/ECF(5)(5.2). A party who is not a Filing User of the System is entitled to a paper copy of any electronically-filed pleading, document, or order. The Filing User must therefore provide the non-Filing User with the pleading or document according to the Federal Rules of Civil Procedure. NY R US-DCTND CM/ECF(5)(5.3).

 iv. *Using court facilities.* If a local rule so authorizes, a party may use the court's transmission facilities to make service under FRCP 5(b)(2)(E). FRCP 5(b)(3).

 c. *Serving numerous defendants*

  i. *In general.* If an action involves an unusually large number of defendants, the court may, on motion or on its own, order that:

- Defendants' pleadings and replies to them need not be served on other defendants;

- Any crossclaim, counterclaim, avoidance, or affirmative defense in those pleadings and replies to them will be treated as denied or avoided by all other parties; and

- Filing any such pleading and serving it on the plaintiff constitutes notice of the pleading to all parties. FRCP 5(c)(1).

  ii. *Notifying parties.* A copy of every such order must be served on the parties as the court directs. FRCP 5(c)(2).

3. *Individual judge practices.* Refer to the Miscellaneous section of this document for information on individual judge practices on filing and serving documents.

## G. Hearings

1. *Hearings, generally*

 a. *Motion days.* Listings of the regularly scheduled motion days for all judges shall be available at each Clerk's office and are available on the Court's webpage. The Clerk shall provide notice of the regular motion days for all judges to the parties at the time an action is commenced. NY R USDCTND L.R. 78.1.

 b. *Return date.* Unless the Court directs otherwise, the moving party shall make its motion returnable at the next regularly scheduled motion date at least thirty-one (31) days from the date the moving party files and serves its motion. The moving party shall select a return date in accordance with the procedures set forth in NY R USDCTND L.R. 7.1(b). If the return date the moving party selects is not the next regularly scheduled motion date, or if the moving party selects no return date, the Clerk will set the proper return date and notify the parties. NY R USDCTND L.R. 7.1.

  i. Information regarding motion dates and times is specified on the case assignment form that the Court provides to the parties at the commencement of the litigation or the parties may obtain this form from the Clerk's office or at the Court's webpage. NY R USDCTND L.R. 7.1.

  ii. The Court hereby directs the Clerk to set a proper return date in motions that pro se litigants submit for filing that do not specify a return date or fail to allow for sufficient time pursuant to NY R USDCTND L.R. 7.1. Generally, the return date that the Clerk selects should not exceed thirty (30) days from the date of filing. Furthermore, the Clerk shall forward a copy of the revised or corrected notice of motion to the parties. NY R USDCTND L.R. 7.1.

   c.   *Oral argument.* Due process does not require that oral argument be permitted on a motion and, except as otherwise provided by local rule, the district court has discretion to determine whether it will decide the motion on the papers or hear argument by counsel (and perhaps receive evidence). FPP § 1190; F.D.I.C. v. Deglau, 207 F.3d 153 (3d Cir. 2000).

      i.   The parties shall appear for oral argument on all motions that they make returnable before a district court judge, except motions for reconsideration, on the scheduled return date of the motion. A motion may be disposed of without oral argument as described in NY R USDCTND Order 25, on consideration of a request of any party, or otherwise at the discretion of the presiding judge. Thus, the parties should be prepared to have their motion papers serve as the sole method of argument on the motion. NY R USDCTND L.R. 7.1(h).

      ii.   The parties shall not appear for oral argument on motions that they make returnable before a Magistrate Judge on the scheduled return date of the motion unless the Magistrate Judge sua sponte directs or grants the request of any party for oral argument. NY R USDCTND L.R. 7.1(h).

   d.   *Providing a regular schedule for oral hearings.* A court may establish regular times and places for oral hearings on motions. FRCP 78(a).

   e.   *Providing for submission on briefs.* By rule or order, the court may provide for submitting and determining motions on briefs, without oral hearings. FRCP 78(b).

2.   *Adjournments of dispositive motions.* After the moving party files and serves its motion papers requesting dispositive relief, but before the time that the opposing party must file and serve its opposing papers, the parties may agree to an adjournment of the return date for the motion. However, any such adjournment may not be for more than THIRTY-ONE (31) DAYS from the return date that the moving party selected. In addition, the parties may agree to new dates for the filing and service of opposition and reply papers. However, the parties must file all papers with the Court and serve them upon the other parties not less than ELEVEN (11) DAYS prior to the newly selected return date of the motion. If the parties agree to such an adjournment, they must file a letter with the Court stating the following: (1) that they have agreed to an adjournment of the return date for the motion, (2) the new return date, (3) the date on which the opposing party must file and serve its opposition papers, and (4) the date on which the moving party must file and serve its reply papers. The parties may not agree to any further adjournment. NY R USDCTND L.R. 7.1(j).

   a.   *Procedure when only one party seeks an adjournment.* If one of the parties seeks an adjournment of not more than THIRTY-ONE (31) DAYS from the return date that the moving party selected, but the other parties will not agree to such an adjournment, the party seeking the adjournment must file a letter request with the Court and serve the same upon the other parties, stating the following: (1) that the parties cannot agree to an adjournment, (2) the reason that the party is seeking the adjournment, and (3) the suggested return date for the motion. Within three days of receiving this letter request, the parties who have not agreed to an adjournment may file a letter with the Court and serve the same upon the other parties, setting forth the reasons that they do not agree to the requested adjournment. The Court will then take the request under advisement and, as soon as practicable, will enter an order granting or denying the request and, if granting the request, will set forth new dates for the filing and serving of opposition and reply papers. NY R USDCTND L.R. 7.1(j).

   b.   *Procedure when adjournment is more than thirty-one (31) days from the return date.* If any party seeks an adjournment of the return date that is more than THIRTY-ONE DAYS from the return date that the moving party selected, that party must file a letter request with the Court stating the following: (1) why the party needs a longer adjournment and (2) a suggested return date for the motion. The Court will grant such an adjournment only upon a showing of exceptional circumstances. In the alternative or if the Court denies the request for an adjournment, the moving party may withdraw its motion without prejudice to refile at a later date. The moving party must refile its motion within the time frame set in the Uniform Pretrial Scheduling Order unless either the assigned District Judge or the assigned Magistrate Judge has granted an extension of the motion-filing deadline. NY R USDCTND L.R. 7.1(j).

3.   *Hearing on motion for summary judgment.* Even though FRCP 56(c) makes reference to a hearing on the

motion for summary judgment, FRCP 56 confers no right to an oral hearing on the summary judgment motion, nor is a hearing required by due process considerations. FEDPROC § 62:673; Forjan v. Leprino Foods, Inc., 209 Fed.Appx. 8, 2006 WL 3623496 (2d Cir. 2006).

    a.   *Oral argument.* Oral argument on a motion for summary judgment may be considered ordinarily appropriate, so that as a general rule, a district court should grant a request for oral argument on all but frivolous summary judgment motions, or a nonmovant's request for oral argument must be granted unless summary judgment is also denied, according to some courts. FEDPROC § 62:674; Season-All Industries, Inc. v. Turkiye Sise Ve Cam Fabrikalari, A. S., 425 F.2d 34 (3d Cir. 1970); Houston v. Bryan, 725 F.2d 516 (9th Cir. 1984); Fernhoff v. Tahoe Regional Planning Agency, 803 F.2d 979 (9th Cir. 1986).

        i.   Oral argument on a summary judgment motion may be deemed waived where the opposing party does not request it. FEDPROC § 62:674; McCormack v. Citibank, N.A., 100 F.3d 532, 30 UCC Rep.Serv.2d 1175 (8th Cir. 1996).

4.   *Individual judge practices.* Refer to the Miscellaneous section of this document for information on individual judge practices on hearings.

## H.  Forms

### 1.  Federal Motion for Summary Judgment Forms

    a.   Answer; To plaintiff's motion for summary judgment. AMJUR PP SUMMARY § 56.

    b.   Affidavit opposing defendant's motion for summary judgment; By plaintiff. AMJUR PP SUMMARY § 64.

    c.   Affidavit opposing motion for summary judgment; By party; Dispute as to issues of fact. AMJUR PP SUMMARY § 73.

    d.   Affidavit opposing motion for summary judgment; By party; Inability to present facts. AMJUR PP SUMMARY § 74.

    e.   Affidavit opposing motion for summary judgment; By party; Good defense to part of claim. AMJUR PP SUMMARY § 77.

    f.   Statement of disputed and undisputed material facts; In opposition to motion for summary judgment. AMJUR PP SUMMARY § 89.

    g.   Motion and notice of motion for summary judgment. 4 FEDFORMS § 4708.

    h.   Motion for summary judgment by plaintiff. 4 FEDFORMS § 4709.

    i.   Motion for summary judgment by defendant. 4 FEDFORMS § 4713.

    j.   Motion for summary judgment by defendant; Claims of plaintiff and counterclaims of defendant. 4 FEDFORMS § 4717.

    k.   Motion for summary judgment by defendant; Interpleader against another claimant. 4 FEDFORMS § 4718.

    l.   Motion for summary judgment by defendant; Failure of plaintiff to produce evidence. 4 FEDFORMS § 4719.

    m.   Motion for summary judgment by defendant; Statute of limitations. 4 FEDFORMS § 4720.

    n.   Notice of motion for summary judgment. 4 FEDFORMS § 4744.

    o.   Affidavit in support of motion for summary judgment. 4 FEDFORMS § 4773.

    p.   Movant's contention there are no genuine issues of material facts. 4 FEDFORMS § 4776.

    q.   Opposition to statement of uncontested material facts. 4 FEDFORMS § 4777.

    r.   Response to movant's contention there are no genuine issues with respect to listed material facts. 4 FEDFORMS § 4778.

    s.   Motion; For summary judgment; By claimant. FEDPROF § 1:1298.

    t.   Motion; For summary judgment; By defending party. FEDPROF § 1:1302.

u.  Motion; By plaintiff; For partial summary judgment. FEDPROF § 1:1305.

v.  Notice of cross motion; For summary judgment; By defending party. FEDPROF § 1:1306.

w.  Statement of material facts; In support of summary judgment motion. FEDPROF § 1:1311.

x.  Statement in support of defendant's summary judgment motion; By codefendant. FEDPROF § 1:1312.

y.  Affidavit; Opposing claimant's motion for summary judgment; Witnesses unavailable. FEDPROF § 1:1316.

z.  Affidavit; Opposing part of claim. FEDPROF § 1:1317.

## I.  Applicable Rules

1.  *Federal rules*

    a.  Serving and filing pleadings and other papers. FRCP 5.

    b.  Constitutional challenge to a statute; Notice, certification, and intervention. FRCP 5.1.

    c.  Privacy protection for filings made with the court. FRCP 5.2.

    d.  Computing and extending time; Time for motion papers. FRCP 6.

    e.  Pleadings allowed; Form of motions and other papers. FRCP 7.

    f.  Disclosure statement. FRCP 7.1.

    g.  Form of pleadings. FRCP 10.

    h.  Signing pleadings, motions, and other papers; Representations to the court; Sanctions. FRCP 11.

    i.  Defenses and objections; When and how presented; Motion for judgment on the pleadings; Consolidating motions; Waiving defenses; Pretrial hearing. FRCP 12.

    j.  Taking testimony. FRCP 43.

    k.  Summary judgment. FRCP 56.

    l.  Hearing motions; Submission on briefs. FRCP 78.

2.  *Local rules*

    a.  Scope of the rules. NY R USDCTND L.R. 1.1.

    b.  Complex and multi-district litigation. NY R USDCTND L.R. 3.3.

    c.  Service and filing of papers. NY R USDCTND L.R. 5.1.

    d.  Filing by facsimile or e-mail. NY R USDCTND L.R. 5.5.

    e.  Motion practice. NY R USDCTND L.R. 7.1.

    f.  Personal privacy protection. NY R USDCTND L.R. 8.1.

    g.  Request for three-judge court. NY R USDCTND L.R. 9.1.

    h.  Form of papers. NY R USDCTND L.R. 10.1.

    i.  Notice to pro se litigants of the consequences of failing to respond to a summary judgment motion. NY R USDCTND L.R. 56.2.

    j.  Settlement procedures. NY R USDCTND L.R. 68.2.

    k.  Orders. NY R USDCTND L.R. 77.2.

    l.  Motion days. NY R USDCTND L.R. 78.1.

    m.  Appearance and withdrawal of attorney. NY R USDCTND L.R. 83.2.

    n.  Arbitration. NY R USDCTND L.R. 83.7-1; NY R USDCTND L.R. 83.7-2; NY R USDCTND L.R. 83.7-3.

    o.  Assisted mediation program. NY R USDCTND L.R. 83.8.

    p.  Mediation. NY R USDCTND L.R. 83.11-1; NY R USDCTND L.R. 83.11-3.

q.   Early neutral evaluation. NY R USDCTND L.R. 83.12-1; NY R USDCTND L.R. 83.12-3.

r.   Administrative procedures for electronic case filing. NY R USDCTND CM/ECF.

s.   Case assignment plan for the Northern District of New York. [NY R USDCTND Order 12, as amended by NY ORDER 16-4201, effective March 24, 2015].

t.   Directing the expedited service of the summons and complaint and further directing the completion of FRCP 16 stipulation for the timely progression of civil actions. [NY R USDCTND Order 25, as amended by NY ORDER 16-4187, effective June 23, 2016].

u.   Mandatory mediation program. NY R USDCTND Order 47.

**J.  Miscellaneous**

**NOTE: Individual judges' rules may apply. For available judge-level information, refer to:**

DISTRICT JUDGE MAE A. D'AGOSTINO: [NY R USDCTND D'Agostino-Rules and Practices, as added by NY ORDER 16-4200, effective April 4, 2016].

DISTRICT JUDGE THOMAS J. McAVOY: NY R USDCTND McAvoy-Order.

## Motions, Oppositions and Replies
## Motion to Compel Discovery

### Document Last Updated September 2016

**A.  Checklist**

(I)   ❏  Matters to be considered by moving party

   (a)   ❏  Required documents

      (1)   ❏  Notice of motion and motion

      (2)   ❏  Certificate of compliance

      (3)   ❏  Supporting affidavit

      (4)   ❏  Certificate of service

   (b)   ❏  Supplemental documents

      (1)   ❏  Memorandum of law

      (2)   ❏  Supporting evidence

      (3)   ❏  Notice of constitutional question

      (4)   ❏  Copies of authorities

      (5)   ❏  Proposed order

      (6)   ❏  Cover letter authorizing e-mail or facsimile filing

      (7)   ❏  Affidavit attesting to failed attempts to file electronically

      (8)   ❏  Notice of conventional filing

      (9)   ❏  CD/ROM with PDF of document(s)

      (10)  ❏  English translation

      (11)  ❏  Courtesy copies

      (12)  ❏  Copies for three-judge court

   (c)   ❏  Timing

      (1)   ❏  A motion must simply be submitted within a reasonable time; however, a motion to compel discovery filed under FRCP 37(a) is premature if it is filed before any request for discovery is made

      (2)   ❏  The parties shall file any motion to compel discovery that the Local Rules of Practice for the

United States District Court for the Northern District of New York authorize no later than fourteen (14) days after the discovery cut-off date

(3) ❑ Unless the court orders otherwise, the moving party must file all motion papers with the court and serve them upon the other parties not less than thirty-one (31) days prior to the return date of the motion

(4) ❑ A written motion and notice of the hearing must be served at least fourteen (14) days before the time specified for the hearing, with the following exceptions: (i) when the motion may be heard ex parte; (ii) when the Federal Rules of Civil Procedure set a different time; or (iii) when a court order—which a party may, for good cause, apply for ex parte—sets a different time

(5) ❑ Any affidavit supporting a motion must be served with the motion

(II) ❑ Matters to be considered by opposing party

  (a) ❑ Required documents

    (1) ❑ Opposition

    (2) ❑ Supporting affidavit

    (3) ❑ Certificate of service

  (b) ❑ Supplemental documents

    (1) ❑ Memorandum of law

    (2) ❑ Supporting evidence

    (3) ❑ Notice of constitutional question

    (4) ❑ Cross-motion

    (5) ❑ Copies of authorities

    (6) ❑ Cover letter authorizing e-mail or facsimile filing

    (7) ❑ Affidavit attesting to failed attempts to file electronically

    (8) ❑ Notice of conventional filing

    (9) ❑ CD/ROM with PDF of document(s)

    (10) ❑ English translation

    (11) ❑ Courtesy copies

    (12) ❑ Copies for three-judge court

  (c) ❑ Timing

    (1) ❑ The party opposing the motion must file its opposition papers with the court and serve them upon the other parties not less than seventeen (17) days prior to the return date of the motion

    (2) ❑ Except as FRCP 59(c) provides otherwise, any opposing affidavit must be served at least seven (7) days before the hearing, unless the court permits service at another time

    (3) ❑ A party may file and serve a cross-motion (meaning a competing request for relief or order similar to that requested by another party against the cross-moving party) at the time it files and serves its opposition papers to the original motion, i.e., not less than seventeen (17) days prior to the return date of the motion

## B. Timing

1. *Motion to compel discovery.* There is no specific time limit for a motion to compel discovery under FRCP 37(a); rather, a motion must simply be submitted within a reasonable time. FEDPROC § 26:779. However, a motion to compel discovery filed under FRCP 37(a) is premature if it is filed before any request for discovery is made. FEDPROC § 26:779; Bermudez v. Duenas, 936 F.2d 1064, 19 Fed.R.Serv.3d 1443 (9th Cir. 1991). The parties shall file any motion to compel discovery that the Local Rules of Practice for the United States District Court for the Northern District of New York authorize no

later than FOURTEEN (14) DAYS after the discovery cut-off date. See NY R USDCTND L.R. 16.2. NY R USDCTND L.R. 7.1(d)(8).

2. *Timing of motions, generally.* Unless the Court orders otherwise, the moving party must file all motion papers with the Court and serve them upon the other parties not less than THIRTY-ONE (31) DAYS prior to the return date of the motion. NY R USDCTND L.R. 7.1(b)(2).

   a. *Motion and notice of hearing.* A written motion and notice of the hearing must be served at least fourteen (14) days before the time specified for the hearing, with the following exceptions:

      i.   When the motion may be heard ex parte;

      ii.  When the Federal Rules of Civil Procedure set a different time; or

      iii. When a court order—which a party may, for good cause, apply for ex parte—sets a different time. FRCP 6(c)(1).

   b. *Supporting affidavit.* Any affidavit supporting a motion must be served with the motion. FRCP 6(c)(2).

3. *Timing of opposing papers.* The party opposing the motion must file its Opposition papers with the Court and serve them upon the other parties not less than SEVENTEEN (17) DAYS prior to the return date of the motion. NY R USDCTND L.R. 7.1(b)(2).

   a. *Opposing affidavit.* Except as FRCP 59(c) provides otherwise, any opposing affidavit must be served at least seven (7) days before the hearing, unless the court permits service at another time. FRCP 6(c)(2).

   b. *Cross-motion.* A party may file and serve a cross-motion (meaning a competing request for relief or order similar to that requested by another party against the cross-moving party) at the time it files and serves its opposition papers to the original motion, i.e., not less than SEVENTEEN (17) DAYS prior to the return date of the motion. NY R USDCTND L.R. 7.1(c).

4. *Timing of reply papers.* Where the respondent files an answering affidavit setting up a new matter, the moving party ordinarily is allowed a reasonable time to file a reply affidavit since failure to deny the new matter by affidavit may operate as an admission of its truth. AMJUR MOTIONS § 25.

   a. *Reply papers.* Reply papers and adjournments are not permitted without the Court's prior permission. Permission to file a reply does not exist simply because CM/ECF generates a deadline for a reply on a nondispositive motion. NY R USDCTND L.R. 7.1(b)(2).

   b. *Opposition to cross-motion.* The original moving party must file its reply/opposition papers with the Court and serve them on the other parties not less than ELEVEN (11) DAYS prior to the return date of the original motion. NY R USDCTND L.R. 7.1(c).

5. *Computation of time*

   a. *Computing time.* FRCP 6 applies in computing any time period specified in the Federal Rules of Civil Procedure, in any local rule or court order, or in any statute that does not specify a method of computing time. FRCP 6(a).

      i. *Period stated in days or a longer unit.* When the period is stated in days or a longer unit of time:

         • Exclude the day of the event that triggers the period;

         • Count every day, including intermediate Saturdays, Sundays, and legal holidays; and

         • Include the last day of the period, but if the last day is a Saturday, Sunday, or legal holiday, the period continues to run until the end of the next day that is not a Saturday, Sunday, or legal holiday. FRCP 6(a)(1).

      ii. *Period stated in hours.* When the period is stated in hours:

         • Begin counting immediately on the occurrence of the event that triggers the period;

         • Count every hour, including hours during intermediate Saturdays, Sundays, and legal holidays; and

         • If the period would end on a Saturday, Sunday, or legal holiday, the period continues to run until the same time on the next day that is not a Saturday, Sunday, or legal holiday. FRCP 6(a)(2).

iii. *Inaccessibility of the clerk's office.* Unless the court orders otherwise, if the clerk's office is inaccessible:

- On the last day for filing under FRCP 6(a)(1), then the time for filing is extended to the first accessible day that is not a Saturday, Sunday, or legal holiday; or

- During the last hour for filing under FRCP 6(a)(2), then the time for filing is extended to the same time on the first accessible day that is not a Saturday, Sunday, or legal holiday. FRCP 6(a)(3).

iv. *"Last day" defined.* Unless a different time is set by a statute, local rule, or court order, the last day ends:

- For electronic filing, at midnight in the court's time zone; and

- For filing by other means, when the clerk's office is scheduled to close. FRCP 6(a)(4).

v. *"Next day" defined.* The "next day" is determined by continuing to count forward when the period is measured after an event and backward when measured before an event. FRCP 6(a)(5).

vi. *"Legal holiday" defined.* "Legal holiday" means:

- The day set aside by statute for observing New Year's Day, Martin Luther King Jr.'s Birthday, Washington's Birthday, Memorial Day, Independence Day, Labor Day, Columbus Day, Veterans' Day, Thanksgiving Day, or Christmas Day;

- Any day declared a holiday by the President or Congress; and

- For periods that are measured after an event, any other day declared a holiday by the state where the district court is located. FRCP 6(a)(6).

b. *Computation of electronic filing deadlines.* A document will be deemed timely filed if electronically filed prior to midnight Eastern Time. However, if the time of day is of the essence, the assigned judge may order that the document be filed by a time certain. NY R USDCTND CM/ECF(4)(4.3).

i. *Technical failures.* A Filing User, whose filing is untimely as the result of a technical failure of the Court's CM/ECF site, may seek appropriate relief from the Court. However, Filing Users are cautioned that, in some circumstances, the Court lacks the authority to grant an extension of time to file (e.g., FRCP 6(b) of the Federal Rules of Civil Procedure). NY R USDCTND CM/ECF(10)(10.1).

- *Technical failure of the filing user's system.* Problems with the Filing User's system, such as phone line problems, problems with the Filing User's Internet Service Provider ("ISP"), or hardware or software problems, will not constitute a technical failure under these Administrative Procedures nor excuse an untimely filing. A Filing User who cannot file documents electronically because of a problem on the Filing User's system must file the documents' conventionally along with an affidavit explaining the reason for not filing the documents electronically. NY R USDCTND CM/ECF(10)(10.2).

c. *Extending time*

i. *In general.* When an act may or must be done within a specified time, the court may, for good cause, extend the time:

- With or without motion or notice if the court acts, or if a request is made, before the original time or its extension expires; or

- On motion made after the time has expired if the party failed to act because of excusable neglect. FRCP 6(b)(1).

ii. *Exceptions.* A court must not extend the time to act under FRCP 50(b), FRCP 50(d), FRCP 52(b), FRCP 59(b), FRCP 59(d), FRCP 59(e), and FRCP 60(b). FRCP 6(b)(2).

iii. Refer to the United States District Court for the Northern District of New York KeyRules Motion for Continuance/Extension of Time document for more information on extending time.

    d.   *Additional time after certain kinds of service.* When a party may or must act within a specified time after service and service is made under FRCP 5(b)(2)(C), FRCP 5(b)(2)(D), FRCP 5(b)(2)(E), or FRCP 5(b)(2)(F), three (3) days are added after the period would otherwise expire under FRCP 6(a). FRCP 6(d).

       i.   In accordance with FRCP 6(e), service by electronic means is treated the same as service by mail for purposes of adding three (3) days to the prescribed period to respond. NY R USDCTND CM/ECF(5)(5.4). [Editor's note: the reference to FRCP 6(e) is likely meant to be a reference to FRCP 6(d)].

6.   *Individual judge practices.* Refer to the Miscellaneous section of this document for information on individual judge practices on timing of documents.

## C.  General Requirements

1.   *Prerequisites to making a discovery motion.* The following steps are required prior to making any discovery motion pursuant to FRCP 26 through FRCP 37. NY R USDCTND L.R. 7.1(d).

    a.   *Efforts to resolve or reduce differences.* Parties must make good faith efforts among themselves to resolve or reduce all differences relating to discovery prior to seeking court intervention. NY R USDCTND L.R. 7.1(d)(1). Prior to bringing a discovery dispute to a Magistrate Judge, the parties must confer in good faith in accordance with the provisions of NY R USDCTND L.R. 7.1(d). NY R USDCTND Order 25(IX)(A).

    b.   *Conference of the parties.* The moving party must confer in detail with the opposing party concerning the discovery issues between them in a good faith effort to eliminate or reduce the area of controversy and to arrive at a mutually satisfactory resolution. Failure to do so may result in denial of a motion to compel discovery and/or imposition of sanctions. NY R USDCTND L.R. 7.1(d)(2).

    c.   *Conference with the court.* If the parties' conference does not fully resolve the discovery issues, the party seeking relief must then request a court conference with the assigned Magistrate Judge. Incarcerated, pro se parties are not subject to the court conference requirement prior to filing a motion to compel discovery. The assigned Magistrate Judge may direct the party making the request for a court conference to file an affidavit setting forth the date(s) and mode(s) of the consultation(s) with the opposing party and a letter that concisely sets forth the nature of the dispute and a specific listing of each of the items of discovery sought or opposed. Immediately following each disputed item, the party must set forth the reason why the Court should allow or disallow that item. NY R USDCTND L.R. 7.1(d)(3).

       i.   Following a request for a discovery conference, the Court may schedule a conference and advise all parties of a date and time. The assigned Magistrate Judge may, in his or her discretion, conduct the discovery conference by telephone conference call, initiated by the party making the request for the conference, by video conference, or by personal appearance. NY R USDCTND L.R. 7.1(d)(4).

    d.   *Proposed order.* Following a discovery conference, the Court may direct the prevailing party to submit a proposed order on notice to the other parties. NY R USDCTND L.R. 7.1(d)(5).

    e.   *Sanctions.* If a party fails or refuses to confer in good faith with the requesting party, thus requiring the request for a discovery conference, the Court, at its discretion, may subject the resisting party to the sanction of the imposition of costs, including the attorney's fees of opposing party in accordance with FRCP 37. NY R USDCTND L.R. 7.1(d)(6).

    f.   *Claim of privilege.* A party claiming privilege with respect to a communication or other item must specifically identify the privilege and the grounds for the claimed privilege. The parties may not make any generalized claims of privilege. NY R USDCTND L.R. 7.1(d)(7).

2.   *Court conference for non-dispositive motions.* Prior to making any non-dispositive motion before the assigned Magistrate Judge, the parties must make good faith efforts among themselves to resolve or reduce all differences relating to the non-dispositive issue. If, after conferring, the parties are unable to arrive at a mutually satisfactory resolution, the party seeking relief must then request a court conference with the assigned Magistrate Judge. NY R USDCTND L.R. 7.1(b)(2). A court conference is a prerequisite to filing a non-dispositive motion before the assigned Magistrate Judge. NY R USDCTND L.R. 7.1(b)(2).

In addition, no non-dispositive or discovery motions should be presented to the Court unless authorized by the Magistrate Judge after communication with the Magistrate Judge's chambers. NY R USDCTND Order 25(IX)(A). Actions which involve an incarcerated, pro se party are not subject to the requirement that a court conference be held prior to filing a non-dispositive motion. NY R USDCTND L.R. 7.1(b)(2).

3. *Motions, generally*

    a. *Requirements.* A request for a court order must be made by motion. The motion must:

        i. Be in writing unless made during a hearing or trial;

        ii. State with particularity the grounds for seeking the order; and

        iii. State the relief sought. FRCP 7(b)(1).

        iv. When a moving party makes a motion based upon a rule or statute, the moving party must specify in its moving papers the rule or statute upon which it bases its motion. NY R USDCTND L.R. 7.1(a)(1).

    b. *Notice of motion.* A party interested in resisting the relief sought by a motion has a right to notice thereof, and an opportunity to be heard. AMJUR MOTIONS § 12.

        i. In addition to statutory or court rule provisions requiring notice of a motion—the purpose of such a notice requirement having been said to be to prevent a party from being prejudicially surprised by a motion—principles of natural justice dictate that an adverse party generally must be given notice that a motion will be presented to the court. AMJUR MOTIONS § 12.

        ii. "Notice," in this regard, means reasonable notice, including a meaningful opportunity to prepare and to defend against allegations of a motion. AMJUR MOTIONS § 12.

    c. *Writing requirement.* The writing requirement is intended to insure that the adverse parties are informed and have a record of both the motion's pendency and the grounds on which the movant seeks an order. FPP § 1191; Feldberg v. Quechee Lakes Corp., 463 F.3d 195 (2d Cir. 2006).

        i. It is sufficient "if the motion is stated in a written notice of the hearing of the motion." FPP § 1191.

    d. *Particularity requirement.* The particularity requirement insures that the opposing parties will have notice of their opponent's contentions. FEDPROC § 62:364; Goodman v. 1973 26 Foot Trojan Vessel, Arkansas Registration No. AR1439SN, 859 F.2d 71, 12 Fed.R.Serv.3d 645 (8th Cir. 1988). That requirement ensures that notice of the basis for the motion is provided to the court and to the opposing party so as to avoid prejudice, provide the opponent with a meaningful opportunity to respond, and provide the court with enough information to process the motion correctly. FEDPROC § 62:364; Andreas v. Volkswagen of America, Inc., 336 F.3d 789, 56 Fed.R.Serv.3d 6 (8th Cir. 2003).

        i. Reasonable specification of the grounds for a motion is sufficient. However, where a movant fails to state even one ground for granting the motion in question, the movant has failed to meet the minimal standard of "reasonable specification." FEDPROC § 62:364; Martinez v. Trainor, 556 F.2d 818, 23 Fed.R.Serv.2d 403 (7th Cir. 1977).

        ii. The court may excuse the failure to comply with the particularity requirement if it is inadvertent, and where no prejudice is shown by the opposing party. FEDPROC § 62:364.

    e. *Order to show cause.* All motions that a party brings by Order to Show Cause shall conform to the requirements set forth in NY R USDCTND L.R. 7.1(a)(1) and NY R USDCTND L.R. 7.1(a)(2). Immediately after filing an Order to Show Cause, the moving party must telephone the Chambers of the presiding judicial officer and inform Chambers staff that it has filed an Order to Show Cause. Parties may obtain the telephone numbers for all Chambers from the Clerk's office or at the Court's webpage. The Court shall determine the briefing schedule and return date applicable to motions brought by Order to Show Cause. NY R USDCTND L.R. 7.1(e).

        i. In addition to the requirements set forth in NY R USDCTND L.R. 7.1(a)(1) and NY R USDCTND L.R. 7.1(a)(2), a motion brought by Order to Show Cause must include an affidavit clearly and specifically showing good and sufficient cause why the standard Notice of Motion procedure cannot be used. The moving party must give reasonable advance notice of the application for an Order to Show Cause to the other parties, except in those circumstances where the movant can demonstrate, in a detailed and specific affidavit, good cause and substantial prejudice that would result from the requirement of reasonable notice. NY R USDCTND L.R. 7.1(e).

    ii.  An Order to Show Cause must contain a space for the assigned judge to set forth:

- The deadline for filing and serving supporting papers,
- The deadline for filing and serving opposing papers, and
- The date and time for the hearing. NY R USDCTND L.R. 7.1(e).

4.  *Motion to compel discovery.* On notice to other parties and all affected persons, a party may move for an order compelling disclosure or discovery. FRCP 37(a)(1). A party must request the specific documents in issue from the opposing party before filing a motion to compel the production of documents. FEDPROC § 26:778.

  a.  *Appropriate court.* A motion for an order to a party must be made in the court where the action is pending. A motion for an order to a nonparty must be made in the court where the discovery is or will be taken. FRCP 37(a)(2).

  b.  *Specific motions*

    i.  *To compel disclosure.* If a party fails to make a disclosure required by FRCP 26(a), any other party may move to compel disclosure and for appropriate sanctions. FRCP 37(a)(3)(A). Refer to the United States District Court for the Northern District of New York KeyRules Motion for Discovery Sanctions document for more information on sanctions.

    ii.  *To compel a discovery response.* A party seeking discovery may move for an order compelling an answer, designation, production, or inspection. This motion may be made if:

- A deponent fails to answer a question asked under FRCP 30 or FRCP 31;
- A corporation or other entity fails to make a designation under FRCP 30(b)(6) or FRCP 31(a)(4);
- A party fails to answer an interrogatory submitted under FRCP 33; or
- A party fails to produce documents or fails to respond that inspection will be permitted—or fails to permit inspection—as requested under FRCP 34. FRCP 37(a)(3)(B).

    iii.  *Related to a deposition.* When taking an oral deposition, the party asking a question may complete or adjourn the examination before moving for an order. FRCP 37(a)(3)(C).

    iv.  *Evasive or incomplete disclosure, answer, or response.* For purposes of FRCP 37(a), an evasive or incomplete disclosure, answer, or response must be treated as a failure to disclose, answer, or respond. FRCP 37(a)(4).

  c.  *Payment of expenses; Protective orders*

    i.  *If the motion is granted (or disclosure or discovery is provided after filing).* If the motion is granted—or if the disclosure or requested discovery is provided after the motion was filed—the court must, after giving an opportunity to be heard, require the party or deponent whose conduct necessitated the motion, the party or attorney advising that conduct, or both to pay the movant's reasonable expenses incurred in making the motion, including attorney's fees. But the court must not order this payment if:

- The movant filed the motion before attempting in good faith to obtain the disclosure or discovery without court action;
- The opposing party's nondisclosure, response, or objection was substantially justified; or
- Other circumstances make an award of expenses unjust. FRCP 37(a)(5)(A).

    ii.  *If the motion is denied.* If the motion is denied, the court may issue any protective order authorized under FRCP 26(c) and must, after giving an opportunity to be heard, require the movant, the attorney filing the motion, or both to pay the party or deponent who opposed the motion its reasonable expenses incurred in opposing the motion, including attorney's fees. But the court must not order this payment if the motion was substantially justified or other circumstances make an award of expenses unjust. FRCP 37(a)(5)(B).

 iii. *If the motion is granted in part and denied in part.* If the motion is granted in part and denied in part, the court may issue any protective order authorized under FRCP 26(c) and may, after giving an opportunity to be heard, apportion the reasonable expenses for the motion. FRCP 37(a)(5)(C).

5. *Opposing papers.* The Federal Rules of Civil Procedure do not require any formal answer, return, or reply to a motion, except where the Federal Rules of Civil Procedure or local rules may require affidavits, memoranda, or other papers to be filed in opposition to a motion. Such papers are simply to apprise the court of such opposition and the grounds of that opposition. FEDPROC § 62:359.

 a. *Effect of failure to respond to motion.* Although in the absence of statutory provision or court rule, a motion ordinarily does not require a written answer, when a party files a motion and the opposing party fails to respond, the court may construe such failure to respond as nonopposition to the motion or an admission that the motion was meritorious, may take the facts alleged in the motion as true—the rule in some jurisdictions being that the failure to respond to a fact set forth in a motion is deemed an admission—and may grant the motion if the relief requested appears to be justified. AMJUR MOTIONS § 28.

 b. *Assent or no opposition not determinative.* However, a motion will not be granted automatically simply because an "assent" or a notation of "no opposition" has been filed; federal judges frequently deny motions that have been assented to when it is thought that justice so dictates. FPP § 1190.

 c. *Responsive pleading inappropriate as response to motion.* An attempt to answer or oppose a motion with a responsive pleading usually is not appropriate. FPP § 1190.

6. *Reply papers.* Reply papers and adjournments are not permitted without the Court's prior permission. Permission to file a reply does not exist simply because CM/ECF generates a deadline for a reply on a nondispositive motion. NY R USDCTND L.R. 7.1(b)(2). A moving party may be required or permitted to prepare papers in addition to his original motion papers. AMJUR MOTIONS § 25. Papers answering or replying to opposing papers may be appropriate, in the interests of justice, where it appears there is a substantial reason for allowing a reply. Thus, a court may accept reply papers where a party demonstrates that the papers to which it seeks to file a reply raise new issues that are material to the disposition of the question before the court, or where the court determines, sua sponte, that it wishes further briefing of an issue raised in those papers and orders the submission of additional papers. FEDPROC § 62:360.

 a. *Function of reply papers.* The function of a reply affidavit is to answer the arguments made in opposition to the position taken by the movant and not to permit the movant to introduce new arguments in support of the motion. AMJUR MOTIONS § 25.

 b. *Issues raised for the first time in a reply document.* However, the view has been followed in some jurisdictions, that as a matter of judicial economy, where there is no prejudice and where the issues could be raised simply by filing a motion to dismiss, the trial court has discretion to consider arguments raised for the first time in a reply memorandum, and that a trial court may grant a motion to strike issues raised for the first time in a reply memorandum. AMJUR MOTIONS § 26.

 c. *Opposition to cross-motion.* The original moving party may reply in further support of the original motion and in opposition to the cross-motion with a reply/opposition brief that does not exceed twenty-five (25) pages in length, exclusive of exhibits. NY R USDCTND L.R. 7.1(c).

7. *Surreply in support of cross-motion.* The cross-moving party may not reply in further support of its cross-motion without the Court's prior permission. NY R USDCTND L.R. 7.1(c).

8. *Submission of proposed order by prevailing party.* If the assigned judge instructs the prevailing party to do so, the prevailing party shall submit a proposed order which the opposing party has approved and which contains the endorsement of the opposing party: "Approved as to form." NY R USDCTND L.R. 77.2(b). In civil actions where the Court has directed a party to submit an order or judgment, that party shall file all such orders or judgments in duplicate, and the Clerk's entry of such duplicate in the proper

record book shall be deemed in compliance with FRCP 79(b). Such party shall also furnish the Clerk with a sufficient number of additional copies for each party to the action, which the Clerk shall mail with notice of entry in accordance with FRCP 77(d). NY R USDCTND L.R. 5.1(b).

a. *Disagreement as to form of proposed order.* When the parties are unable to agree as to the form of the proposed order, the prevailing party shall, on seven (7) days notice to all other parties, submit a proposed order and a written explanation for the form of that order. The Court may award costs and attorney's fees against a party whose unreasonable conduct the Court deemed to have required the bringing of the motion. The provisions of NY R USDCTND L.R. 7.1 shall not apply to such motion, and the Court shall not hear oral argument. NY R USDCTND L.R. 77.2(b).

b. For more information on orders, refer to NY R USDCTND L.R. 77.2.

9. *Sanctions for vexatious or frivolous motions or failure to comply with* NY R USDCTND L.R. 7.1. A party who presents vexatious or frivolous motion papers or fails to comply with NY R USDCTND L.R. 7.1 is subject to discipline as the Court deems appropriate, including sanctions and the imposition of costs and attorney's fees to the opposing party. NY R USDCTND L.R. 7.1(i).

10. *Complex and multi-district litigation.* If the assigned judge determines, in his or her discretion, that the case is of such a complex nature that it cannot reasonably be trial ready within eighteen (18) months from the date the complaint is filed, the assigned judge may design and issue a particularized case management order that will move the case to trial as quickly as the complexity of the case allows. NY R USDCTND L.R. 3.3(a). The parties shall promptly notify the Court in writing if any action commenced is appropriate for multi-district litigation. NY R USDCTND L.R. 3.3(b).

11. *Appearances.* An attorney appearing for a party in a civil case shall promptly file with the Clerk a written notice of appearance; however, an attorney does not need to file a notice of appearance if the attorney who would be filing the notice of appearance is the same individual who has signed the complaint, notice of removal, pre-answer motion, or answer. NY R USDCTND L.R. 83.2(a). For more information, refer to NY R USDCTND L.R. 83.2.

12. *Related cases.* A civil case is "related" to another civil case for purposes of this guideline when, because of the similarity of facts and legal issues or because the cases arise from the same transactions or events, a substantial saving of judicial resources is likely to result from assigning the cases to the same Judge and Magistrate Judge. NY R USDCTND Order 12(G)(2). A civil case shall not be deemed related to another civil case merely because the civil case: (1) involves similar legal issues, or (2) involves the same parties. NY R USDCTND Order 12(G)(3). Presumptively, and subject to the power of a Judge to determine otherwise pursuant to NY R USDCTND Order 12(G)(5), civil cases shall not be deemed to be "related" unless both cases are still pending before the Court. NY R USDCTND Order 12(G)(4).

a. *New filings.* If an attorney or filing party indicates on the Civil Cover Sheet that a case is related to an earlier filed case, the Clerk shall instruct the filing party to file a notice of related cases. The allegedly related cases will be submitted by the Clerk to the Judge to whom the earliest filed case is assigned, who shall advise the Clerk whether such cases are related. NY R USDCTND Order 12(G)(1).

b. *Judicial determination that civil cases are "related."* Except for the cases described in the final sentence of NY R USDCTND Order 12(G)(6), all civil cases shall be randomly assigned when they are filed. Other than the cases described in the final sentence of NY R USDCTND Order 12(G)(6), civil cases shall not be deemed to be "related" for purposes of this guideline at the instance of any litigant or attorney unless and until there has been a determination by a Judge of this Court that the standard of NY R USDCTND Order 12(G)(2) is met. NY R USDCTND Order 12(G)(5).

i. *Notice of related filing.* Any party may apply for such a determination by filing with the Clerk a notice of related filing, which should include an explanation as to why the standard of NY R USDCTND Order 12(G)(2) is met. A form for this purpose is available on the Court's website. A copy of the notice shall be served on all other parties who have appeared. Such an application must be made after the date when at least a majority of the defendants have been served with the complaint. Before making such an application, the applicant must confer in good faith with all other parties in an effort to reach an agreement on whether or not the case is "related". After such an application is made, any other party may serve and file within seven (7) calendar days a letter of no more than two (2) pages supporting or opposing the application. The application to have the case assigned to another Judge shall be presented to the Judge with the earliest filed case for decision on whether the action(s) should be reassigned as related cases. The Judge with the earliest filed case may then enter an order in the case at bar, either deeming the case to be related and directing the Clerk to reassign the action, or denying the application for reassignment. Any disputes concerning the assignment of related cases will be referred to the Chief Judge for resolution. NY R USDCTND Order 12(G)(5).

c. For more information on related cases, refer to NY R USDCTND Order 12(G).

13. *Alternative dispute resolution (ADR).* It is the mission of this court to do everything it can to help parties resolve their disputes as fairly, quickly, and efficiently as possible. NY R USDCTND Order 25(VIII).

a. *Arbitration.* NY R USDCTND L.R. 83.7 governs the consensual arbitration program for referral of civil actions to court-annexed arbitration. It may remain in effect until further order of the Court. Its purpose is to establish a less formal procedure for the just, efficient and economical resolution of disputes, while preserving the right to a full trial on demand. NY R USDCTND L.R. 83.7-1.

   i. *Actions subject to arbitration.* The Clerk shall notify the parties in all civil cases, except as the Local Rules of Practice for the United States District Court for the Northern District of New York otherwise direct, that they may consent to non-binding arbitration under NY R US-DCTND L.R. 83.7. The notice shall be furnished to the parties at pretrial/scheduling conferences or shall be included with pretrial conference notices and instructions. Consent to arbitration under NY R USDCTND L.R. 83.7 shall be discussed at the pretrial/scheduling conference. No party or attorney shall be prejudiced for refusing to participate in arbitration. The Court shall allow the referral of any civil action pending before it to the arbitration process if the parties consent. The plaintiff shall be responsible for securing the execution of a consent form by the parties and for filing the form with the Clerk within fourteen (14) days after the parties receive the form. The parties shall freely and knowingly enter into the consent. NY R USDCTND L.R. 83.7-2.

   ii. *Referral to arbitration.* The Clerk shall refer every action subject to NY R USDCTND L.R. 83.7 to arbitration in accordance with the procedures under NY R USDCTND L.R. 83.7 twenty-one (21) days after the filing of the last responsive pleading or within twenty-one (21) days of the filing of a stipulated consent order referring the action to arbitration, whichever event occurs last, except as otherwise provided. If any party notices a motion to dismiss under the provisions of FRCP 12(a) and/or FRCP 12(b), or a motion to join necessary parties pursuant to the Federal Rules of Civil Procedure prior to the expiration of the twenty-one (21) day period, the assigned judge shall hear the motion and further proceedings under NY R USDCTND L.R. 83.7 shall be deferred pending decision on the motion. If the Court does not dismiss the action on the motion, the Court shall refer the action to arbitration twenty-one (21) days after the filing of the decision. NY R USDCTND L.R. 83.7-3(a). Motions for summary judgment pursuant to FRCP 56 shall be filed and served within twenty-one (21) days following the close of discovery. The filing of a FRCP 56 motion shall defer further proceedings under NY R USDCTND L.R. 83.7 pending decision on the motion. NY R USDCTND L.R. 83.7-3(a).

   - *Relief from referral.* Any party shall request relief from the operation of NY R USDCTND L.R. 83.7 by filing with the Court a motion for the relief within twenty-one (21) days after entry of the initial stipulated consent order which refers the case for arbitration. The assigned judge shall, sua sponte, exempt an action from the application of NY R USDCTND L.R. 83.7 where the objectives of arbitration would not be realized because (1) the case involves complex or novel legal issues, (2) legal issues predominate over factual issues, or (3) for other good cause. NY R USDCTND L.R. 83.7-3(c).

   iii. For more information on arbitration, refer to NY R USDCTND L.R. 83.7.

b. *Mediation.* The purpose of NY R USDCTND L.R. 83.11 is to provide a supplementary procedure to the Court's existing alternative dispute resolution procedures. NY R USDCTND L.R. 83.11 provides for an earlier resolution of civil disputes resulting in savings of time and cost to litigants and the Court without sacrificing the quality of justice rendered or the right of litigants to a full trial on all issues not resolved through mediation. NY R USDCTND L.R. 83.11-1(a). Mediation is a process by which an impartial person, the mediator, facilitates communication between disputing parties to promote understanding, reconciliation and settlement. The mediator is an advocate for settlement and uses the mediation process to help the parties fully explore any potential area of agreement. The mediator does not serve as a judge or arbitrator and has no authority to render any decision on any disputed issue or to force a settlement. The parties themselves are responsible for negotiating any resolution(s) to their dispute. NY R USDCTND L.R. 83.11-1(b).

i.   *Actions subject to mediation.* The Court may refer any civil action (or any portion thereof) to mediation under NY R USDCTND L.R. 83.11: (1) by order of referral; or (2) on the motion of any party; or (3) by consent of the parties. NY R USDCTND L.R. 83.11-3(a).

   - *Withdrawal from mediation.* The parties may withdraw from mediation any civil action or claim that the Court refers to mediation pursuant to NY R USDCTND L.R. 83.11-3 by application to the assigned judge at least ten (10) days prior to the scheduled mediation session. NY R USDCTND L.R. 83.11-3(b).

ii.  *Mandatory mediation program.* The United States District Court for the Northern District of New York has adopted this Mandatory Mediation Plan. The paid Mediation Program is designed to provide quicker, less expensive and potentially more satisfying alternatives to continuing litigation, without impairing the quality of justice or the right to trial. NY R USDCTND Order 47(1)(1.2)(A). This Mandatory Mediation Plan applies to civil actions pending as well as newly filed actions, except as otherwise indicated in NY R USDCTND Order 47. The Local Rules for voluntary mediation will apply only to Pro Se Cases that proceed through the Assisted Mediation Program. NY R USDCTND Order 47(1)(1.2)(B).

   - *Referral into the pilot mandatory mediation program for new cases.* All civil cases shall be referred automatically into the Mandatory Mediation Program. Notice of the Mandatory Mediation requirements will be provided to all parties immediately upon the filing of a complaint and answer or a notice of removal. ADR intervention will be scheduled at the conference held pursuant to NY R USDCTND L.R. 16.1. NY R USDCTND Order 47(2)(2.1)(A). For a list of categories of actions exempted from automatic referral, refer to NY R USDCTND Order 47(2)(2.1)(A).

   - *Referral into the pilot mandatory mediation program for pending cases.* The assigned Judge or Magistrate Judge on any pending civil case may, sua sponte or with status conference, issue an order referring the case into the Mandatory Mediation Program. The order shall specify a date on which the ADR intervention is to be completed. NY R USDCTND Order 47(2)(2.1)(B).

   - *Referral into the pilot mandatory mediation program by stipulation.* A case may be referred into the Mandatory Mediation Program by stipulation of all parties. Stipulations shall be filed and shall designate the time frame within which the ADR process will be completed. Stipulations are presumed acceptable unless the assigned Judge or Magistrate Judge determines that the interests of justice are not served. NY R USDCTND Order 47(2)(2.1)(C).

   - *Relief from referral.* Motions to opt out of the program will be addressed by the assigned Magistrate Judge at the FRCP 16 conference. NY R USDCTND Order 47(2)(2.2)(A). Opting Out Motions shall be granted only for "good cause" shown. Inconvenience, travel costs, attorney fees or other costs shall not constitute "good cause." A party seeking relief from the Mandatory Mediation Program must set forth the reasons why Mandatory Mediation has no reasonable chance of being productive. NY R USDCTND Order 47(2)(2.2)(B). The assigned Magistrate Judge may, sua sponte, exempt any case from the Court's Mandatory Mediation Program. NY R USDCTND Order 47(2)(2.2)(C).

iii. *Assisted mediation program.* The Court may assign specially trained pro bono Special Mediation Counsel to assist pro se civilian litigants with preparing for and participating in mediation. The Assisted Mediation Program is open to civilian pro se parties to actions in the Northern District of New York. The assigned judge or magistrate judge determines if the case would benefit from mediation and would also benefit from the assignment of Special Mediation Counsel to assist the pro se party with the mediation process. NY R USDCTND L.R. 83.8(a). Appointment of Special Mediation Counsel is in no way guaranteed, even if the action is referred to the court-annexed mediation program. Appointment is at the sole discretion of the presiding judge. NY R USDCTND L.R. 83.8(a).

- *Referral to assisted mediation program.* If the court determines that referral to the Assisted Mediation Program is appropriate, the Court shall enter an order of reference to the Assisted Mediation Program. NY R USDCTND L.R. 83.8(b).

    iv. For more information on mediation, refer to NY R USDCTND L.R. 83.11 and NY R USDCTND Order 47.

  c. *Early neutral evaluation (ENE).* Early neutral evaluation (ENE) is a process in which parties obtain from an experienced neutral (an "evaluator") a nonbinding, reasoned, oral evaluation of the merits of the case. The first step in the ENE process involves the Court appointing an evaluator who has expertise in the area of law in the case. After the parties exchange essential information and position statements early in the pretrial period (usually within one hundred fifty (150) to two hundred (200) days after a complaint has been filed), the evaluator convenes an ENE session that typically lasts about two hours. At the ENE meeting, each side briefly presents the factual and legal basis of its position. The evaluator may ask questions of the parties and help them identify the main issues in dispute and the areas of agreement. The evaluator may also help the parties explore options for settlement. If settlement does not occur, the evaluator then offers an opinion as to the settlement value of the case, including the likelihood of liability and the likely range of damages. With the benefit of this assessment, the parties are again encouraged to discuss settlement, with or without the evaluator's assistance. The parties may also explore ways to narrow the issues in dispute, exchange information about the case or otherwise prepare efficiently for trial. NY R USDCTND L.R. 83.12-1.

    i. *Actions subject to early neutral evaluation.* The Court may refer any civil action (or any portion thereof) to ENE under NY R USDCTND L.R. 83.12: (1) by order of referral; (2) on the motion of any party; or (3) by consent of the parties. NY R USDCTND L.R. 83.12-3(a).

- *Withdrawal from the ENE process.* The parties may withdraw any civil action or claim that the Court has referred to the ENE Process pursuant to NY R USDCTND L.R. 83.12-3 by application to the assigned judge at least ten (10) days before the scheduled evaluation session. NY R USDCTND L.R. 83.12-3(b).

    ii. For more information on early neutral evaluation (ENE), refer to NY R USDCTND L.R. 83.12.

14. *Settlement procedures.* On notice to the Court or the Clerk that the parties have settled an action, and upon confirmation of the settlement by all parties, the Court may issue a judgment dismissing the action by reason of settlement. The Court shall issue the order without prejudice to the parties' right to secure reinstatement of the case within thirty (30) days after the date of judgment by making a showing that the settlement was not, in fact, consummated. NY R USDCTND L.R. 68.2(a). If the Court decides not to follow the procedures set forth in NY R USDCTND L.R. 68.2(a), the parties shall file within thirty (30) days of the notification to the Court, unless otherwise directed by written order, such notices, stipulations and/or motions as are necessary to terminate the action. If the required documents are not filed within the thirty (30) day period, the Clerk shall place the action on the dismissal calendar. NY R USDCTND L.R. 68.2(b).

15. *Sanctions and penalties for noncompliance.* Failure of an attorney or of a party to comply with any provision of the Local Rules of Practice for the United States District Court for the Northern District of New York, General Orders of this District, Orders of the Court, or the Federal Rules of Civil Procedure shall be a ground for imposition of sanctions. NY R USDCTND L.R. 1.1(d).

16. *Individual judge practices.* Refer to the Miscellaneous section of this document for information on individual judge practices on general requirements for documents.

## D. Documents

1. *Documents for moving party*

  a. *Required documents*

    i. *Notice of motion and motion.* In the Notice of Motion, the moving party is required to set forth the date that the court conference with the Magistrate Judge was held regarding the issues being presented in the motion. Failure to include this information in the Notice of Motion may result in the Court rejecting the motion papers. NY R USDCTND L.R. 7.1(b)(2). Refer to the General Requirements section of this document for information on the notice of motion and motion.

- *Order to show cause.* Refer to the General Requirements section of this document for information on bringing a motion by order to show cause.

    ii. *Certificate of compliance.* The motion must include a certification that the movant has in good faith conferred or attempted to confer with the person or party failing to make disclosure or discovery in an effort to obtain it without court action. FRCP 37(a)(1).

    iii. *Supporting affidavit.* Except as otherwise provided in NY R USDCTND L.R. 7.1(a), all motions. . .require a. . .supporting affidavit. NY R USDCTND L.R. 7.1(a). An affidavit must not contain legal arguments but must contain factual and procedural background that is relevant to the motion the affidavit supports. NY R USDCTND L.R. 7.1(a)(2).

    iv. *Certificate of service.* Except as otherwise provided in NY R USDCTND L.R. 7.1(a), all motions. . .require. . .proof of service on all the parties. See NY R USDCTND L.R. 5.1(a). NY R USDCTND L.R. 7.1(a). FRCP 5(d) requires that the person making service under FRCP 5 certify that service has been effected. FRCP 5(Advisory Committee Notes). Having such information on file may be useful for many purposes, including proof of service if an issue arises concerning the effectiveness of the service. FRCP 5(Advisory Committee Notes). The party or its designee shall declare, by affidavit or certification, that it has provided all other parties in the action with all documents it has filed with the Court. NY R USDCTND L.R. 5.1(a).

- Attorneys and pro se parties who are not Filing or Receiving Users must be served with a paper copy of any electronically filed pleading or other document. NY R USDCTND CM/ECF(5)(5.2). Such paper service must be documented by electronically filing a certificate of service. NY R USDCTND CM/ECF(5)(5.2).

 b. *Supplemental documents*

    i. *Memorandum of law.* A memorandum of law is required for all motions except: a motion pursuant to FRCP 37 to compel discovery. NY R USDCTND L.R. 7.1(a)(1)(D). Refer to the Format section of this document for the formatting requirements for memoranda of law.

    ii. *Supporting evidence.* When a motion relies on facts outside the record, the court may hear the matter on affidavits or may hear it wholly or partly on oral testimony or on depositions. FRCP 43(c).

- *Discovery materials.* A party shall accompany any motion that it files pursuant to FRCP 37 with the discovery materials to which the motion relates if the parties have not previously filed those materials with the Court. NY R USDCTND L.R. 7.1(d)(8); NY R USDCTND L.R. 26.2; NY R USDCTND CM/ECF(2)(2.1)(4).

    iii. *Notice of constitutional question.* A party that files a pleading, written motion, or other paper drawing into question the constitutionality of a federal or state statute must promptly:

- *File notice.* File a notice of constitutional question stating the question and identifying the paper that raises it, if: (1) a federal statute is questioned and the parties do not include the United States, one of its agencies, or one of its officers or employees in an official capacity; or (2) a state statute is questioned and the parties do not include the state, one of its agencies, or one of its officers or employees in an official capacity; and

- *Serve notice.* Serve the notice and paper on the Attorney General of the United States if a federal statute is questioned—or on the state attorney general if a state statute is questioned—either by certified or registered mail or by sending it to an electronic address designated by the attorney general for this purpose. FRCP 5.1(a).

- *No forfeiture.* A party's failure to file and serve the notice, or the court's failure to certify, does not forfeit a constitutional claim or defense that is otherwise timely asserted. FRCP 5.1(d).

iv. *Copies of authorities.* When serving a pro se litigant with a memorandum of law or any other paper which contains citations to authorities that are unpublished or published exclusively on electronic databases, counsel shall include a hard copy of those authorities. Although copies of authorities published only on electronic databases are not required to be filed, copies shall be provided upon request to opposing counsel who lack access to electronic databases. NY R USDCTND L.R. 7.1(a)(1).

v. *Proposed order.* A document that is submitted in .pdf format cannot be modified; therefore, a proposed order or stipulation must be in a word processing format. The chambers of the assigned judge may request that a proposed order and/or a stipulation be e-mailed to the courtroom deputy for the presiding judge in either WordPerfect or Microsoft Word format. Please attach your proposed order and/or stipulation to an Internet e-mail sent to the appropriate e-mail address listed in NY R USDCTND CM/ECF(8)(8.2). NY R USDCTND CM/ECF(8)(8.2).

vi. *Cover letter authorizing e-mail or facsimile filing.* Neither the Court nor the Clerk's Office will accept for filing any facsimile or e-mail transmission without prior authorization from the Court. The party using facsimile or e-mail transmissions to file its papers must accompany any such documents with a cover letter stating that the Court authorized such transmissions and the date on which the Court provided that authorization. Violations of NY R USDCTND L.R. 5.5 subject the offending party to the Court's full disciplinary powers. NY R USDCTND L.R. 5.5.

vii. *Affidavit attesting to failed attempts to file electronically.* If the Court's CM/ECF site experiences a technical failure, a Filing User may submit documents to the Court that day in an alternate manner provided that the documents are accompanied by the Filing User's affidavit stating that the Filing User attempted to file electronically at least two times in one (1) hour increments after 10:00 a.m. that day. The following methods are acceptable alternate means for filing documents in case of a technical failure: (1) via electronic mail in a PDF attachment sent to the e-mail address for technical failures; or (2) in person, by bringing the document to the Clerk's Office on paper accompanied by a CD/ROM that contains the document in .pdf format. NY R USDCTND CM/ECF(10)(10.1).

- A Filing User who cannot file documents electronically because of a problem on the Filing User's system must file the documents' conventionally along with an affidavit explaining the reason for not filing the documents electronically. NY R USDCTND CM/ECF(10)(10.2).

viii. *Notice of conventional filing.* If the Clerk's Office grants permission to conventionally file the document, the Filing User shall electronically file a notice of conventional filing for the documents. More information regarding this process can be obtained from the Court's web page. NY R USDCTND CM/ECF(4)(4.5).

ix. *CD/ROM with PDF of document(s).* If the Court grants permission to file a document traditionally, the attorney must submit the documents for filing to the Clerk's Office on CD/ROM in .pdf or pdf.A format. NY R USDCTND CM/ECF(2).

x. *English translation.* The Court conducts its reviews and deliberations in English. Unless otherwise directed by the Court, any document that a party transmits to the Court (including one in the record on appeal) that is in a language other than English must be accompanied by an English translation that the translator has certified as true and accurate, pursuant to 28 U.S.C.A. § 1746. NY R USDCTND L.R. 10.1(e). For more information, refer to NY R USDCTND L.R. 10.1(e).

xi. *Courtesy copies.* The Court may require that courtesy copies of electronically filed documents be submitted for its review and may amend these Administrative Procedures (NY R USDCTND CM/ECF) at any time without prior notice. NY R USDCTND CM/ECF(2).

xii. *Copies for three-judge court.* On the convening of a three-judge court, the parties shall make three (3) copies of all non-electronically filed pleadings, motion papers, and memoranda of law available to the Clerk for distribution. NY R USDCTND L.R. 9.1.

2. *Documents for opposing party*

  a. *Required documents*

    i. *Opposition.* Refer to the General Requirements section of this document for information on the opposing papers.

    ii. *Supporting affidavit.* Except as otherwise provided in NY R USDCTND L.R. 7.1(a), all. . .opposition to motions require a. . .supporting affidavit. NY R USDCTND L.R. 7.1(a). An affidavit must not contain legal arguments but must contain factual and procedural background that is relevant to the motion the affidavit supports. NY R USDCTND L.R. 7.1(a)(2).

    iii. *Certificate of service.* Except as otherwise provided in NY R USDCTND L.R. 7.1(a), all. . .opposition to motions require. . .proof of service on all the parties. See NY R USDCTND L.R. 5.1(a). NY R USDCTND L.R. 7.1(a). FRCP 5(d) requires that the person making service under FRCP 5 certify that service has been effected. FRCP 5(Advisory Committee Notes). Having such information on file may be useful for many purposes, including proof of service if an issue arises concerning the effectiveness of the service. FRCP 5(Advisory Committee Notes). The party or its designee shall declare, by affidavit or certification, that it has provided all other parties in the action with all documents it has filed with the Court. NY R USDCTND L.R. 5.1(a).

      ● Attorneys and pro se parties who are not Filing or Receiving Users must be served with a paper copy of any electronically filed pleading or other document. NY R USDCTND CM/ECF(5)(5.2). Such paper service must be documented by electronically filing a certificate of service. NY R USDCTND CM/ECF(5)(5.2).

  b. *Supplemental documents*

    i. *Memorandum of law.* A memorandum of law is required for all motions except: a motion pursuant to FRCP 37 to compel discovery. NY R USDCTND L.R. 7.1(a)(1)(D).

      ● *Cross-motion brief.* If a party makes a cross-motion, it must join its cross motion brief with its opposition brief, and this combined brief may not exceed twenty-five (25) pages in length, exclusive of exhibits. A separate brief in opposition to the original motion is not permissible. NY R USDCTND L.R. 7.1(c).

      ● Refer to the Format section of this document for the formatting requirements for memoranda of law.

    ii. *Supporting evidence.* When a motion relies on facts outside the record, the court may hear the matter on affidavits or may hear it wholly or partly on oral testimony or on depositions. FRCP 43(c).

    iii. *Notice of constitutional question.* A party that files a pleading, written motion, or other paper drawing into question the constitutionality of a federal or state statute must promptly:

      ● *File notice.* File a notice of constitutional question stating the question and identifying the paper that raises it, if: (1) a federal statute is questioned and the parties do not include the United States, one of its agencies, or one of its officers or employees in an official capacity; or (2) a state statute is questioned and the parties do not include the state, one of its agencies, or one of its officers or employees in an official capacity; and

      ● *Serve notice.* Serve the notice and paper on the Attorney General of the United States if a federal statute is questioned—or on the state attorney general if a state statute is questioned—either by certified or registered mail or by sending it to an electronic address designated by the attorney general for this purpose. FRCP 5.1(a).

      ● *No forfeiture.* A party's failure to file and serve the notice, or the court's failure to certify, does not forfeit a constitutional claim or defense that is otherwise timely asserted. FRCP 5.1(d).

    iv. *Cross-motion.* A party may file and serve a cross-motion (meaning a competing request for relief or order similar to that requested by another party against the cross-moving party) at the time it files and serves its opposition papers to the original motion, i.e., not less than SEVENTEEN (17) DAYS prior to the return date of the motion. NY R USDCTND L.R. 7.1(c).

v. *Copies of authorities.* When serving a pro se litigant with a memorandum of law or any other paper which contains citations to authorities that are unpublished or published exclusively on electronic databases, counsel shall include a hard copy of those authorities. Although copies of authorities published only on electronic databases are not required to be filed, copies shall be provided upon request to opposing counsel who lack access to electronic databases. NY R USDCTND L.R. 7.1(a)(1).

vi. *Cover letter authorizing e-mail or facsimile filing.* Neither the Court nor the Clerk's Office will accept for filing any facsimile or e-mail transmission without prior authorization from the Court. The party using facsimile or e-mail transmissions to file its papers must accompany any such documents with a cover letter stating that the Court authorized such transmissions and the date on which the Court provided that authorization. Violations of NY R USDCTND L.R. 5.5 subject the offending party to the Court's full disciplinary powers. NY R USDCTND L.R. 5.5.

vii. *Affidavit attesting to failed attempts to file electronically.* If the Court's CM/ECF site experiences a technical failure, a Filing User may submit documents to the Court that day in an alternate manner provided that the documents are accompanied by the Filing User's affidavit stating that the Filing User attempted to file electronically at least two times in one (1) hour increments after 10:00 a.m. that day. The following methods are acceptable alternate means for filing documents in case of a technical failure: (1) via electronic mail in a PDF attachment sent to the e-mail address for technical failures; or (2) in person, by bringing the document to the Clerk's Office on paper accompanied by a CD/ROM that contains the document in .pdf format. NY R USDCTND CM/ECF(10)(10.1).

- A Filing User who cannot file documents electronically because of a problem on the Filing User's system must file the documents' conventionally along with an affidavit explaining the reason for not filing the documents electronically. NY R USDCTND CM/ECF(10)(10.2).

viii. *Notice of conventional filing.* If the Clerk's Office grants permission to conventionally file the document, the Filing User shall electronically file a notice of conventional filing for the documents. More information regarding this process can be obtained from the Court's web page. NY R USDCTND CM/ECF(4)(4.5).

ix. *CD/ROM with PDF of document(s).* If the Court grants permission to file a document traditionally, the attorney must submit the documents for filing to the Clerk's Office on CD/ROM in .pdf or pdf.A format. NY R USDCTND CM/ECF(2).

x. *English translation.* The Court conducts its reviews and deliberations in English. Unless otherwise directed by the Court, any document that a party transmits to the Court (including one in the record on appeal) that is in a language other than English must be accompanied by an English translation that the translator has certified as true and accurate, pursuant to 28 U.S.C.A. § 1746. NY R USDCTND L.R. 10.1(e). For more information, refer to NY R USDCTND L.R. 10.1(e).

xi. *Courtesy copies.* The Court may require that courtesy copies of electronically filed documents be submitted for its review and may amend these Administrative Procedures (NY R USDCTND CM/ECF) at any time without prior notice. NY R USDCTND CM/ECF(2).

xii. *Copies for three-judge court.* On the convening of a three-judge court, the parties shall make three (3) copies of all non-electronically filed pleadings, motion papers, and memoranda of law available to the Clerk for distribution. NY R USDCTND L.R. 9.1.

3. *Individual judge practices.* Refer to the Miscellaneous section of this document for information on individual judge practices on required documents.

# E. Format

1. *Form of documents.* The rules governing captions and other matters of form in pleadings apply to motions and other papers. FRCP 7(b)(2). All pleadings and other papers shall be served and filed in accordance

with the Federal Rules of Civil Procedure and shall be in the form prescribed by NY R USDCTND L.R. 10.1. NY R USDCTND L.R. 5.1(a).

a. *Form, generally.* All pleadings, motions, and other documents that a party presents for filing, whether in paper form or in electronic form, shall meet the following requirements:

    i. *Font size.* All text, whether in the body of the document or in footnotes, must be a minimum of twelve (12) point type. NY R USDCTND L.R. 10.1(a)(1).

    ii. *Margins.* All documents must have one (1) inch margins on all four sides of the page. NY R USDCTND L.R. 10.1(a)(2).

    iii. *Spacing.* All text in the body of the document must be double-spaced. NY R USDCTND L.R. 10.1(a)(3).

        • The text in block quotations and footnotes may be single-spaced. NY R USDCTND L.R. 10.1(a)(4).

    iv. *Page numbering.* Pages must be consecutively numbered. NY R USDCTND L.R. 10.1(a)(7).

    v. *Circumventing formatting limitations*

        • Extensive footnotes must not be used to circumvent page limitations. NY R USDCTND L.R. 10.1(a)(5).

        • Compacted or other compressed printing features must not be used. NY R USDCTND L.R. 10.1(a)(6).

b. *Additional requirements for paper filing.* Additional requirements for all pleadings, motions, and other documents that a party presents for filing in paper form:

    i. *Paper size.* All documents must be on eight and one-half by eleven (8-1/2 x 11) inch white paper of good quality. NY R USDCTND L.R. 10.1(b)(1).

    ii. *Text.* All text must be plainly and legibly written, typewritten, printed or reproduced without erasures or interlineations materially defacing them. NY R USDCTND L.R. 10.1(b)(2).

    iii. *Ink.* All documents must be in black or blue ink. NY R USDCTND L.R. 10.1(b)(3).

    iv. *Binding.* Pages of all documents must be stapled (or in some other way fastened) together. NY R USDCTND L.R. 10.1(b)(4).

    v. *Single-sided paper.* All documents must be single-sided. NY R USDCTND L.R. 10.1(b)(5).

    vi. *Electronic submission.* The Court, at its discretion, may require the electronic submission of any document in a WordPerfect-compatible format. NY R USDCTND L.R. 10.1(b)(6).

    vii. *Rejection of document.* The Court may reject documents that do not comply with the above-listed requirements. NY R USDCTND L.R. 10.1(b).

c. *Caption; Names of parties.* Every pleading must have a caption with the court's name, a title, a file number, and a FRCP 7(a) designation. The title of the complaint must name all the parties; the title of other pleadings, after naming the first party on each side, may refer generally to other parties. FRCP 10(a). Each document must contain a caption for the specific case to which it pertains. The caption must include the title of the Court, the title of the action, the civil action number of the case, the initials of the assigned judge(s), and the name or nature of the paper in sufficient detail for identification. If a litigant has more than one action pending in this Court, any and all papers filed in a case must contain and pertain to one civil action number, unless the civil actions have been consolidated by the Court. Any motion or other papers purporting to relate to more than one action will not be accepted for filing and may be stricken by the Court. NY R USDCTND L.R. 10.1(c)(1) shall not apply, as noted in NY R USDCTND L.R. 10.1(c), to notices of change of address filed by attorneys of record and pro se litigants. The parties must separately caption affidavits and declarations and must not physically attach them to the Notice of Motion or Memorandum of Law. NY R USDCTND L.R. 10.1(c)(1).

d. *Paragraphs; Separate statements.* A party must state its claims or defenses in numbered paragraphs, each limited as far as practicable to a single set of circumstances. A later pleading may refer by

number to a paragraph in an earlier pleading. If doing so would promote clarity, each claim founded on a separate transaction or occurrence—and each defense other than a denial—must be stated in a separate count or defense. FRCP 10(b).

e. *Adoption by reference; Exhibits.* A statement in a pleading may be adopted by reference elsewhere in the same pleading or in any other pleading or motion. A copy of a written instrument that is an exhibit to a pleading is a part of the pleading for all purposes. FRCP 10(c).

f. *Citation of local rules.* These are the Local Rules of Practice for the United States District Court for the Northern District of New York. They shall be cited as "L.R. ___." NY R USDCTND L.R. 1.1(a).

g. *Acceptance by the clerk.* The clerk must not refuse to file a paper solely because it is not in the form prescribed by the Federal Rules of Civil Procedure or by a local rule or practice. FRCP 5(d)(4).

2. *Form of electronic documents.* All pleadings, motions, and other documents that a party presents for filing, whether in paper form or in electronic form, shall meet the requirements in NY R USDCTND L.R. 10.1(a). NY R USDCTND L.R. 10.1(a). Refer above for more information.

a. *Attachments and exhibits.* A Filing User must submit in electronic form all documents referenced as exhibits or attachments in accordance with the Court's CM/ECF Users Manual unless the Court otherwise orders. A Filing User shall submit as exhibits or attachments only those excerpts of the referenced documents that are directly germane to the matter under the Court's consideration. Excerpted material must be clearly and prominently identified as such. Filing Users who file excerpts of documents as exhibits or attachments under these Administrative Procedures (NY R USDCTND CM/ECF) do so without prejudice to their right to timely file additional excerpts or the complete document. Responding parties may also timely file the complete document or additional excerpts that they believe are directly germane to the matter under the Court's consideration. NY R USDCTND CM/ECF(4)(4.4).

i. All attachments must be described in sufficient detail so the Court and opposing counsel can easily identify and distinguish the filed attachments. Vague or general descriptions are insufficient (i.e., "Exhibit 1"). Rather, each attachment shall have a descriptive title identifying, with specificity, the document that is being filed (i.e., "Exhibit 12 Mulligan County Fire Investigation Report.") Failure to adequately describe attachments may result in the document being rejected by the Court. NY R USDCTND CM/ECF(4)(4.4).

b. *Large documents.* For information on the electronic filing of large documents, please consult the Court's CM/ECF Users Manual, which is available on the Court's web page. NY R USDCTND CM/ECF(4)(4.5).

i. A party who believes a document is too lengthy to electronically image, i.e., "scan," may contact the Clerk's Office for permission to file that document conventionally. If the Clerk's Office grants permission to conventionally file the document, the Filing User shall electronically file a notice of conventional filing for the documents. More information regarding this process can be obtained from the Court's web page. Exhibits submitted conventionally shall be served on other parties as if they were not subject to these Administrative Procedures (NY R USDCTND CM/ECF). For a list of hints and tips for scanning large documents, please consult the Court's web page. NY R USDCTND CM/ECF(4)(4.5).

c. *Legibility.* It shall be the Filing User's responsibility to verify the legibility of scanned documents before filing them electronically with the Court. NY R USDCTND CM/ECF(4)(4.6).

d. *Color documents.* Since documents scanned in color or containing a graphic take much longer to upload, Filing Users are encouraged to configure their scanners to scan documents at 300 dpi and preferably in black and white rather than in color. NY R USDCTND CM/ECF(4)(4.7).

e. *Items not in .PDF format.* Parties wishing to file items not amenable to .pdf format (i.e. CD's, DVD's), shall file such items conventionally with the Clerk's Office. The Filing User shall electronically file a notice of conventional filing indicating that these items have been submitted to the clerk and shall serve copies of these items on other parties as if they were not subject to these Administrative Procedures (NY R USDCTND CM/ECF). These item(s) will be maintained by the Clerk's Office until the case is disposed, at which time they will be returned to the filing party for retention consistent with NY R USDCTND CM/ECF(4)(4.9). NY R USDCTND CM/ECF(4)(4.8).

3. *Form of memoranda of law*

    a. *Length limitation.* No party shall file or serve a memorandum of law that exceeds twenty-five (25) pages in length, unless that party obtains leave of the judge hearing the motion prior to filing. NY R USDCTND L.R. 7.1(a)(1).

    b. *Table of contents.* All memoranda of law shall contain a table of contents. NY R USDCTND L.R. 7.1(a)(1).

4. *Signing disclosures and discovery requests, responses, and objections.* FRCP 11 does not apply to disclosures and discovery requests, responses, objections, and motions under FRCP 26 through FRCP 37. FRCP 11(d).

    a. *Signature required.* Every disclosure under FRCP 26(a)(1) or FRCP 26(a)(3) and every discovery request, response, or objection must be signed by at least one attorney of record in the attorney's own name—or by the party personally, if unrepresented—and must state the signer's address, e-mail address, and telephone number. FRCP 26(g)(1). Each document must identify the person filing the document. This identification must include an original signature of the attorney or pro se litigant; the typewritten name of that person; the address of a pro se litigant; and the bar roll number, office address, telephone number, e-mail address and fax number of the attorney. Telephone numbers of non-prisoner pro se parties may be provided voluntarily or upon request of the Court. See General Order #22 (NY R USDCTND CM/ECF) for signature requirements. NY R USDCTND L.R. 10.1(c)(2).

        i. *Electronic signatures.* Documents filed under an attorney's login and password shall constitute that attorney's signature for purposes of the Local Rules of Practice for the United States District Court for the Northern District of New York and Federal Rules of Civil Procedure, including but not limited to FRCP 11. A pleading or other document requiring an attorney's signature shall be signed in the following manner, whether filed electronically or submitted on disk or CD/ROM to the Clerk's Office: "s/ (attorney name)." The correct format for an attorney signature is found in NY R USDCTND CM/ECF(6)(6.1). NY R USDCTND CM/ECF(6)(6.1).

            • *Non-attorney signature.* If an original document requires the signature of a non-attorney, the Filing User may scan the original document containing the original signature(s), then electronically file it on the System. Alternatively, the Filing User may convert the document into .pdf text format and submit the document using "s/" for the signature of the non-attorney. NY R USDCTND CM/ECF(6)(6.2).

            • *Multiple signatures.* A document requiring signatures of more than one party must be filed electronically either by (1) submitting a scanned document containing all necessary signatures; (2) representing the consent of the other parties on the document; or (3) in any other manner that the Court approves. NY R USDCTND CM/ECF(6)(6.3).

    b. *Effect of signature.* By signing, an attorney or party certifies that to the best of the person's knowledge, information, and belief formed after a reasonable inquiry:

        i. With respect to a disclosure, it is complete and correct as of the time it is made; and

        ii. With respect to a discovery request, response, or objection, it is:

            • Consistent with the Federal Rules of Civil Procedure and warranted by existing law or by a nonfrivolous argument for extending, modifying, or reversing existing law, or for establishing new law;

            • Not interposed for any improper purpose, such as to harass, cause unnecessary delay, or needlessly increase the cost of litigation; and

            • Neither unreasonable nor unduly burdensome or expensive, considering the needs of the case, prior discovery in the case, the amount in controversy, and the importance of the issues at stake in the action. FRCP 26(g)(1).

    c. *Failure to sign.* Other parties have no duty to act on an unsigned disclosure, request, response, or objection until it is signed, and the court must strike it unless a signature is promptly supplied after the omission is called to the attorney's or party's attention. FRCP 26(g)(2).

d. *Sanction for improper certification.* If a certification violates FRCP 26(g) without substantial justification, the court, on motion or on its own, must impose an appropriate sanction on the signer, the party on whose behalf the signer was acting, or both. The sanction may include an order to pay the reasonable expenses, including attorney's fees, caused by the violation. FRCP 26(g)(3). Refer to the United States District Court for the Northern District of New York KeyRules Motion for Discovery Sanctions document for more information.

5. *Privacy protection for filings made with the court*

   a. *Redacted filings.* Unless the court orders otherwise, in an electronic or paper filing with the court that contains an individual's Social Security number, taxpayer-identification number, or birth date, the name of an individual known to be a minor, or a financial-account number, a party or nonparty making the filing may include only:

      i. The last four (4) digits of the Social Security number and taxpayer-identification number;

      ii. The year of the individual's birth;

      iii. The minor's initials; and

      iv. The last four (4) digits of the financial-account number. FRCP 5.2(a); NY R USDCTND L.R. 8.1; NY R USDCTND CM/ECF(11)(11.2).

      v. If a home address must be used, use only the City and State. NY R USDCTND L.R. 8.1; NY R USDCTND CM/ECF(11)(11.2).

      vi. If the victim of a sexual assault must be referenced, redact the name to 'Victim.' NY R USDCTND CM/ECF(11)(11.2); NY R USDCTND L.R. 8.1.

      vii. In addition, caution shall be exercised when filing documents that contain the following:

      - Personal identifying number, such as a driver's license number;
      - Medical records, treatment and diagnosis;
      - Employment history;
      - Individual financial information; and
      - Proprietary or trade secret information. NY R USDCTND L.R. 8.1; NY R USDCTND CM/ECF(11)(11.2).

   b. *Exemptions from the redaction requirement.* The redaction requirement does not apply to the following:

      i. A financial-account number that identifies the property allegedly subject to forfeiture in a forfeiture proceeding;

      ii. The record of an administrative or agency proceeding;

      iii. The official record of a state-court proceeding;

      iv. The record of a court or tribunal, if that record was not subject to the redaction requirement when originally filed;

      v. A filing covered by FRCP 5.2(c) or FRCP 5.2(d); and

      vi. A pro se filing in an action brought under 28 U.S.C.A. § 2241, 28 U.S.C.A. § 2254, or 28 U.S.C.A. § 2255. FRCP 5.2(b).

      vii. Transcripts of the administrative record in social security proceedings are exempt from this requirement. State court records and other documents filed in habeas corpus proceedings are exempt from this requirement except for proceedings that involve victims of sex crimes. In habeas corpus cases involving sex crimes, the parties must redact the record and supporting papers, or may move to seal, if appropriate. NY R USDCTND L.R. 8.1.

   c. *Limitations on remote access to electronic files; Social Security appeals and immigration cases.* Unless the court orders otherwise, in an action for benefits under the Social Security Act, and in an action or proceeding relating to an order of removal, to relief from removal, or to immigration benefits or detention, access to an electronic file is authorized as follows:

   i. The parties and their attorneys may have remote electronic access to any part of the case file, including the administrative record;

   ii. Any other person may have electronic access to the full record at the courthouse, but may have remote electronic access only to:

- The docket maintained by the court; and

- An opinion, order, judgment, or other disposition of the court, but not any other part of the case file or the administrative record. FRCP 5.2(c).

  d. *Filings made under seal.* The court may order that a filing be made under seal without redaction. The court may later unseal the filing or order the person who made the filing to file a redacted version for the public record. FRCP 5.2(d); NY R USDCTND L.R. 8.1. For information on sealed matters, refer to NY R USDCTND L.R. 83.13 and NY R USDCTND CM/ECF(12).

  e. *Protective orders.* For good cause, the court may by order in a case:

   i. Require redaction of additional information; or

   ii. Limit or prohibit a nonparty's remote electronic access to a document filed with the court. FRCP 5.2(e).

  f. *Option for additional unredacted filing under seal.* A person making a redacted filing may also file an unredacted copy under seal. The court must retain the unredacted copy as part of the record. FRCP 5.2(f); NY R USDCTND L.R. 8.1; NY R USDCTND CM/ECF(11)(11.3).

  g. *Option for filing a reference list.* A filing that contains redacted information may be filed together with a reference list that identifies each item of redacted information and specifies an appropriate identifier that uniquely corresponds to each item listed. The list must be filed under seal and may be amended as of right. Any reference in the case to a listed identifier will be construed to refer to the corresponding item of information. FRCP 5.2(g); NY R USDCTND L.R. 8.1; NY R USDCTND CM/ECF(11)(11.3).

  h. *Responsibility for redaction.* Counsel is strongly urged to discuss this issue with all their clients so that they can make an informed decision about the inclusion of certain information. The responsibility for redacting these personal identifiers rests solely with counsel and the parties. The Clerk will not review each filing for compliance with NY R USDCTND L.R. 8.1. Counsel and the parties are cautioned that failure to redact these personal identifiers may subject them to the Court's full disciplinary power. NY R USDCTND L.R. 8.1; NY R USDCTND CM/ECF(11)(11.3).

  i. *Waiver of protection of identifiers.* A person waives the protection of FRCP 5.2(a) as to the person's own information by filing it without redaction and not under seal. FRCP 5.2(h).

6. *Individual judge practices.* Refer to the Miscellaneous section of this document for information on individual judge practices on formatting documents.

## F. Filing and Service Requirements

1. *Filing requirements.* Any paper after the complaint that is required to be served—together with a certificate of service—must be filed within a reasonable time after service. FRCP 5(d)(1).

  a. *How filing is made; In general.* A paper is filed by delivering it:

   i. To the clerk; or

   ii. To a judge who agrees to accept it for filing, and who must then note the filing date on the paper and promptly send it to the clerk. FRCP 5(d)(2).

  b. *Electronic filing*

   i. *Authorization of electronic filing program.* A court may, by local rule, allow papers to be filed, signed, or verified by electronic means that are consistent with any technical standards established by the Judicial Conference of the United States. A local rule may require electronic filing only if reasonable exceptions are allowed. A paper filed electronically in compliance with a local rule is a written paper for purposes of the Federal Rules of Civil Procedure. FRCP 5(d)(3).

- All cases filed in this Court may be assigned to the Electronic Case Files System ("ECF") in accordance with the Procedural Order on Electronic Case Filing (General Order #22 (NY R USDCTND CM/ECF)), the provisions of which are incorporated herein by reference, and which the Court may amend from time to time. Copies of General Order #22 (NY R USDCTND CM/ECF) are available at the Clerk's office or at the Court's webpage. NY R USDCTND L.R. 5.1.1; NY R USDCTND Order 25(XII).

- The Court may deviate from these Administrative Procedures (NY R USDCTND CM/ECF) in specific cases, without prior notice, if deemed appropriate in the exercise of discretion, considering the need for the just, speedy, and inexpensive determination of matters pending before the Court. NY R USDCTND CM/ECF(2).

ii. *Scope of electronic filing.* After January 1, 2004, all documents that attorneys admitted to practice in the Northern District of New York submit for filing shall be filed electronically using the System or shall be scanned and uploaded to the System, no matter when a case was originally filed, unless these Administrative Procedures (NY R USDCTND CM/ECF) otherwise permit or unless the assigned judge otherwise authorizes. An attorney who is not a Filing User by January 1, 2004, must show good cause to the assigned judge to file and serve pleadings and other papers in the traditional manner. NY R USDCTND CM/ECF(2).

iii. *Exceptions and/or waivers from mandatory electronic filing.* The following types of cases and/or documents are not required to be filed electronically:

- If you are seeking to have your complaint filed under seal, please file your complaint and proposed sealing order traditionally at the Clerk's Office. NY R USDCTND CM/ECF(2)(2.1)(1).

- Any document that a party proceeding pro se files. (See NY R USDCTND CM/ECF(12)(12.1) for procedural details). NY R USDCTND CM/ECF(2)(2.1)(2). A non-prisoner who is a party to a civil action and who is not represented by an attorney may file a motion to obtain an Electronic Case Filing (ECF) login and password on a form prescribed by the Clerk's Office. The Pro Se CM/ECF Registration Form shall be submitted with the motion. If during the course of the action an attorney appears on behalf of the pro se party, the Clerk's Office shall terminate the pro se party's registration based upon the attorney's appearance. NY R USDCTND CM/ECF(12)(12.1). Absent permission to file electronically, pro se filers shall file paper originals of all complaints, pleadings, motions, affidavits, briefs, and other documents which must be signed or which require either verification or an unsworn declaration under any rule or statute. The Clerk's Office will scan these original documents into an electronic file in the System but will also maintain a paper file. NY R USDCTND CM/ECF(12)(12.1). A pro se party may also seek permission to receive immediate notice of all public documents filed in their cases. Notices of Electronic Filing (NEF) and attached documents would be transmitted to a non-prisoner pro se party who selects this option. Note: The pro se party would continue to file their documents with the Clerk's Office in paper form. NY R USDCTND CM/ECF(12)(12.1).

- Sealed documents, sealed cases, documents for in camera review, documents lodged with the Court, ex parte documents, confidential agreements, Qui Tam actions and Grand Jury material and warrants must be filed traditionally. (See NY R USDCTND CM/ECF(12)(12.2) for further information the filing of the above-referenced documents). NY R USDCTND CM/ECF(2)(2.1)(3).

- Discovery: In accordance with NY R USDCTND L.R. 26.2, parties shall not file discovery, provided, however, that discovery material to be used at trial or in support of any motion, including a motion to compel or for summary judgment, shall be filed electronically with the Court prior to the trial or with the motion. Any motion pursuant to FRCP 37 shall be accompanied by the electronically filed discovery materials to which the motion relates if those materials have not previously been filed with the Court. NY R USDCTND CM/ECF(2)(2.1)(4).

- Transport Orders: All orders requesting that an incarcerated individual be transported that a judicial officer of the Northern District of New York signs shall be filed traditionally. These Orders will not be filed with the case or uploaded to the docket but rather will be processed in accordance with the procedures that the Clerk of Court promulgates. NY R USDCTND CM/ECF(2)(2.1)(5).

iv. *Filing defined.* Electronic transmission of a document to the System in accordance with these Administrative Procedures, together with the transmission of a Notice of Electronic Filing from the Court, constitutes filing of the document for all purposes of the Federal Rules of Civil Procedure and the Local Rules of Practice for the United States District Court for the Northern District of New York and constitutes entry of the document on the docket that the Clerk's Office keeps under FRCP 58 and FRCP 79. E-mailing a document to the Clerk's Office or to the assigned judge shall not constitute "filing" of the document. NY R USDCTND CM/ECF(4)(4.1).

v. *Filing fees.* Any fee required for filing a pleading or paper in this Court is payable to the Clerk of the Court. The Court will not maintain electronic billing or debit accounts for attorneys or law firms. Effective January 1, 2007, payment for filing fees will be mandatory through CM/ECF's Internet Credit Card Payment site--a secure Treasury Site. The Filing User will be prompted to enter either Bank Account Debit (ACH) or credit card information while filing the initial pleading. Any document that requires a filing fee (e.g., Notice of Appeal, Motion for Pro Hac Vice Admission) may also be paid through the federal electronic payment website. NY R USDCTND CM/ECF(7).

vi. For more information on electronic filing, refer to NY R USDCTND CM/ECF.

c. *E-mail or facsimile filing.* Neither the Court nor the Clerk's Office will accept for filing any facsimile or e-mail transmission without prior authorization from the Court. The party using facsimile or e-mail transmissions to file its papers must accompany any such documents with a cover letter stating that the Court authorized such transmissions and the date on which the Court provided that authorization. Violations of NY R USDCTND L.R. 5.5 subject the offending party to the Court's full disciplinary powers. NY R USDCTND L.R. 5.5.

2. *Service requirements*

a. *Service; When required*

i. *In general.* Unless the Federal Rules of Civil Procedure provide otherwise, each of the following papers must be served on every party:

- An order stating that service is required;
- A pleading filed after the original complaint, unless the court orders otherwise under FRCP 5(c) because there are numerous defendants;
- A discovery paper required to be served on a party, unless the court orders otherwise;
- A written motion, except one that may be heard ex parte; and
- A written notice, appearance, demand, or offer of judgment, or any similar paper. FRCP 5(a)(1).

ii. *If a party fails to appear.* No service is required on a party who is in default for failing to appear. But a pleading that asserts a new claim for relief against such a party must be served on that party under FRCP 4. FRCP 5(a)(2).

iii. *Seizing property.* If an action is begun by seizing property and no person is or need be named as a defendant, any service required before the filing of an appearance, answer, or claim must be made on the person who had custody or possession of the property when it was seized. FRCP 5(a)(3).

b. *Service; How made*

   i. *Serving an attorney.* If a party is represented by an attorney, service under FRCP 5 must be made on the attorney unless the court orders service on the party. FRCP 5(b)(1).

   ii. *Service in general.* A paper is served under FRCP 5 by:

- Handing it to the person;

- Leaving it: (1) at the person's office with a clerk or other person in charge or, if no one is in charge, in a conspicuous place in the office; or (2) if the person has no office or the office is closed, at the person's dwelling or usual place of abode with someone of suitable age and discretion who resides there;

- Mailing it to the person's last known address—in which event service is complete upon mailing;

- Leaving it with the court clerk if the person has no known address;

- Sending it by electronic means if the person consented in writing—in which event service is complete upon transmission, but is not effective if the serving party learns that it did not reach the person to be served; or

- Delivering it by any other means that the person consented to in writing—in which event service is complete when the person making service delivers it to the agency designated to make delivery. FRCP 5(b)(2).

   iii. *Service of electronically-filed documents.* Service is complete provided all parties receive a Notice of Electronic Filing (NEF), which is sent automatically by email from the Court (see the NEF for a list of who did/did not receive notice electronically). Transmission of the NEF constitutes service upon all Filing and Receiving Users who are listed as recipients of notice by electronic mail. It remains the responsibility of Filing and Receiving Users to maintain current contact information with the court and to regularly review the docket sheet of the case. NY R USDCTND CM/ECF(5)(5.2).

- *Non-filing or receiving users.* Attorneys and pro se parties who are not Filing or Receiving Users must be served with a paper copy of any electronically filed pleading or other document. Service of such paper copy must be made according to the Federal Rules of Civil Procedure and the Local Rules of Practice for the United States District Court for the Northern District of New York. Such paper service must be documented by electronically filing a certificate of service. NY R USDCTND CM/ECF(5)(5.2). A party who is not a Filing User of the System is entitled to a paper copy of any electronically-filed pleading, document, or order. The Filing User must therefore provide the non-Filing User with the pleading or document according to the Federal Rules of Civil Procedure. NY R US-DCTND CM/ECF(5)(5.3).

   iv. *Using court facilities.* If a local rule so authorizes, a party may use the court's transmission facilities to make service under FRCP 5(b)(2)(E). FRCP 5(b)(3).

c. *Serving numerous defendants*

   i. *In general.* If an action involves an unusually large number of defendants, the court may, on motion or on its own, order that:

- Defendants' pleadings and replies to them need not be served on other defendants;

- Any crossclaim, counterclaim, avoidance, or affirmative defense in those pleadings and replies to them will be treated as denied or avoided by all other parties; and

- Filing any such pleading and serving it on the plaintiff constitutes notice of the pleading to all parties. FRCP 5(c)(1).

   ii. *Notifying parties.* A copy of every such order must be served on the parties as the court directs. FRCP 5(c)(2).

3. *Individual judge practices.* Refer to the Miscellaneous section of this document for information on individual judge practices on filing and serving documents.

## G. Hearings

1. *Hearings, generally*

   a. *Motion days.* Listings of the regularly scheduled motion days for all judges shall be available at each Clerk's office and are available on the Court's webpage. The Clerk shall provide notice of the regular motion days for all judges to the parties at the time an action is commenced. NY R USDCTND L.R. 78.1.

   b. *Return date.* Unless the Court directs otherwise, the moving party shall make its motion returnable at the next regularly scheduled motion date at least thirty-one (31) days from the date the moving party files and serves its motion. The moving party shall select a return date in accordance with the procedures set forth in NY R USDCTND L.R. 7.1(b). If the return date the moving party selects is not the next regularly scheduled motion date, or if the moving party selects no return date, the Clerk will set the proper return date and notify the parties. NY R USDCTND L.R. 7.1.

      i. Information regarding motion dates and times is specified on the case assignment form that the Court provides to the parties at the commencement of the litigation or the parties may obtain this form from the Clerk's office or at the Court's webpage. NY R USDCTND L.R. 7.1.

      ii. The Court hereby directs the Clerk to set a proper return date in motions that pro se litigants submit for filing that do not specify a return date or fail to allow for sufficient time pursuant to NY R USDCTND L.R. 7.1. Generally, the return date that the Clerk selects should not exceed thirty (30) days from the date of filing. Furthermore, the Clerk shall forward a copy of the revised or corrected notice of motion to the parties. NY R USDCTND L.R. 7.1.

   c. *Oral argument.* Due process does not require that oral argument be permitted on a motion and, except as otherwise provided by local rule, the district court has discretion to determine whether it will decide the motion on the papers or hear argument by counsel (and perhaps receive evidence). FPP § 1190; F.D.I.C. v. Deglau, 207 F.3d 153 (3d Cir. 2000).

      i. The parties shall appear for oral argument on all motions that they make returnable before a district court judge, except motions for reconsideration, on the scheduled return date of the motion. A motion may be disposed of without oral argument as described in NY R USDCTND Order 25, on consideration of a request of any party, or otherwise at the discretion of the presiding judge. Thus, the parties should be prepared to have their motion papers serve as the sole method of argument on the motion. NY R USDCTND L.R. 7.1(h).

      ii. The parties shall not appear for oral argument on motions that they make returnable before a Magistrate Judge on the scheduled return date of the motion unless the Magistrate Judge sua sponte directs or grants the request of any party for oral argument. NY R USDCTND L.R. 7.1(h).

   d. *Providing a regular schedule for oral hearings.* A court may establish regular times and places for oral hearings on motions. FRCP 78(a).

   e. *Providing for submission on briefs.* By rule or order, the court may provide for submitting and determining motions on briefs, without oral hearings. FRCP 78(b).

2. *Individual judge practices.* Refer to the Miscellaneous section of this document for information on individual judge practices on hearings.

## H. Forms

### 1. Federal Motion to Compel Discovery Forms

   a. Notice of motion; To compel required disclosure of names and addresses of witnesses and persons having knowledge of the claims involved; Civil proceeding. AMJUR PP DEPOSITION § 6.

   b. Motion; To compel required disclosure of names and addresses of witnesses and persons having knowledge of the claims involved. AMJUR PP DEPOSITION § 7.

   c. Motion; To compel answer to interrogatories; Complete failure to answer. AMJUR PP DEPOSITION § 403.

   d. Affidavit; In opposition of motion to compel psychiatric or physical examinations; By attorney. AMJUR PP DEPOSITION § 645.

e.  Motion; To compel further responses to interrogatories; Various grounds. AMJUR PP DEPOSITION § 713.

f.  Affidavit; In support of motion to compel answers to interrogatories and to impose sanctions. AMJUR PP DEPOSITION § 715.

g.  Opposition; To motion to compel electronic discovery; Federal class action. AMJUR PP DEPOSITION § 721.

h.  Notice of motion; For order to compel compliance with request to permit entry on real property for inspection. AMJUR PP DEPOSITION § 733.

i.  Motion; To compel production of documents; After rejected request; Request for sanctions. AMJUR PP DEPOSITION § 734.

j.  Affidavit; In support of motion to compel production of documents; By attorney. AMJUR PP DEPOSITION § 736.

k.  Motion; To compel doctor's production of medical records for trial. AMJUR PP DEPOSITION § 744.

l.  Notice of motion to compel party to answer deposition questions. 3B FEDFORMS § 3695.

m.  Motion to compel deposition, request for sanctions and request for expedited hearing. 3B FEDFORMS § 3698.

n.  Motion to compel answer to interrogatories. 3B FEDFORMS § 3699.

o.  Affidavit in support of motion. 3B FEDFORMS § 3702.

p.  Objection to motion for order requiring witness to answer oral questions on deposition. 3B FEDFORMS § 3705.

q.  Motion; To compel answers to outstanding discovery requests. FEDPROF § 23:43.

r.  Motion; To compel required disclosure of names and addresses of witnesses and persons having knowledge of the claims involved. FEDPROF § 23:44.

s.  Motion; To compel answer to questions asked on oral or written examination. FEDPROF § 23:207.

t.  Motion; To compel further answers to questions asked on oral or written examination and to award expenses of motion. FEDPROF § 23:208.

u.  Motion; To compel party to produce witness at deposition. FEDPROF § 23:209.

v.  Affidavit; By opposing attorney; In opposition to motion to compel answers asked at deposition; Answers tend to incriminate. FEDPROF § 23:212.

w.  Motion; To compel answer to interrogatories; Complete failure to answer. FEDPROF § 23:375.

x.  Motion; To compel further responses to interrogatories; Various grounds. FEDPROF § 23:376.

y.  Motion to compel discovery. GOLDLTGFMS § 21:2.

# I.  Applicable Rules

1.  *Federal rules*

    a.  Serving and filing pleadings and other papers. FRCP 5.

    b.  Constitutional challenge to a statute; Notice, certification, and intervention. FRCP 5.1.

    c.  Privacy protection for filings made with the court. FRCP 5.2.

    d.  Computing and extending time; Time for motion papers. FRCP 6.

    e.  Pleadings allowed; Form of motions and other papers. FRCP 7.

    f.  Form of pleadings. FRCP 10.

    g.  Signing pleadings, motions, and other papers; Representations to the court; Sanctions. FRCP 11.

    h.  Duty to disclose; General provisions governing discovery. FRCP 26.

    i.  Failure to make disclosures or to cooperate in discovery; Sanctions. FRCP 37.

    j.   Taking testimony. FRCP 43.

    k.   Hearing motions; Submission on briefs. FRCP 78.

2.  *Local rules*

    a.   Scope of the rules. NY R USDCTND L.R. 1.1.

    b.   Complex and multi-district litigation. NY R USDCTND L.R. 3.3.

    c.   Service and filing of papers. NY R USDCTND L.R. 5.1.

    d.   Filing by facsimile or e-mail. NY R USDCTND L.R. 5.5.

    e.   Motion practice. NY R USDCTND L.R. 7.1.

    f.   Personal privacy protection. NY R USDCTND L.R. 8.1.

    g.   Request for three-judge court. NY R USDCTND L.R. 9.1.

    h.   Form of papers. NY R USDCTND L.R. 10.1.

    i.   Filing discovery. NY R USDCTND L.R. 26.2.

    j.   Settlement procedures. NY R USDCTND L.R. 68.2.

    k.   Orders. NY R USDCTND L.R. 77.2.

    l.   Motion days. NY R USDCTND L.R. 78.1.

    m.   Appearance and withdrawal of attorney. NY R USDCTND L.R. 83.2.

    n.   Arbitration. NY R USDCTND L.R. 83.7-1; NY R USDCTND L.R. 83.7-2; NY R USDCTND L.R. 83.7-3.

    o.   Assisted mediation program. NY R USDCTND L.R. 83.8.

    p.   Mediation. NY R USDCTND L.R. 83.11-1; NY R USDCTND L.R. 83.11-3.

    q.   Early neutral evaluation. NY R USDCTND L.R. 83.12-1; NY R USDCTND L.R. 83.12-3.

    r.   Administrative procedures for electronic case filing. NY R USDCTND CM/ECF.

    s.   Case assignment plan for the Northern District of New York. [NY R USDCTND Order 12, as amended by NY ORDER 16-4201, effective March 24, 2015].

    t.   Directing the expedited service of the summons and complaint and further directing the completion of FRCP 16 stipulation for the timely progression of civil actions. [NY R USDCTND Order 25, as amended by NY ORDER 16-4187, effective June 23, 2016].

    u.   Mandatory mediation program. NY R USDCTND Order 47.

**J.  Miscellaneous**

**NOTE: Individual judges' rules may apply. For available judge-level information, refer to:**

DISTRICT JUDGE MAE A. D'AGOSTINO: [NY R USDCTND D'Agostino-Rules and Practices, as added by NY ORDER 16-4200, effective April 4, 2016].

DISTRICT JUDGE THOMAS J. McAVOY: NY R USDCTND McAvoy-Order.

# Motions, Oppositions and Replies
# Motion for Discovery Sanctions

**Document Last Updated September 2016**

**A.  Checklist**

  (I)  ❑  Matters to be considered by moving party

    (a)  ❑  Required documents

      (1)  ❑  Notice of motion and motion

      (2)  ❑  Certificate of compliance

  (3) ❑ Memorandum of law

  (4) ❑ Supporting affidavit

  (5) ❑ Certificate of service

 (b) ❑ Supplemental documents

  (1) ❑ Supporting evidence

  (2) ❑ Notice of constitutional question

  (3) ❑ Copies of authorities

  (4) ❑ Proposed order

  (5) ❑ Cover letter authorizing e-mail or facsimile filing

  (6) ❑ Affidavit attesting to failed attempts to file electronically

  (7) ❑ Notice of conventional filing

  (8) ❑ CD/ROM with PDF of document(s)

  (9) ❑ English translation

  (10) ❑ Courtesy copies

  (11) ❑ Copies for three-judge court

 (c) ❑ Timing

  (1) ❑ Unless the court orders otherwise, the moving party must file all motion papers with the court and serve them upon the other parties not less than thirty-one (31) days prior to the return date of the motion

  (2) ❑ A written motion and notice of the hearing must be served at least fourteen (14) days before the time specified for the hearing, with the following exceptions: (i) when the motion may be heard ex parte; (ii) when the Federal Rules of Civil Procedure set a different time; or (iii) when a court order—which a party may, for good cause, apply for ex parte—sets a different time

  (3) ❑ Any affidavit supporting a motion must be served with the motion

(II) ❑ Matters to be considered by opposing party

 (a) ❑ Required documents

  (1) ❑ Opposition

  (2) ❑ Memorandum of law

  (3) ❑ Supporting affidavit

  (4) ❑ Certificate of service

 (b) ❑ Supplemental documents

  (1) ❑ Supporting evidence

  (2) ❑ Notice of constitutional question

  (3) ❑ Cross-motion

  (4) ❑ Demand for jury trial

  (5) ❑ Copies of authorities

  (6) ❑ Cover letter authorizing e-mail or facsimile filing

  (7) ❑ Affidavit attesting to failed attempts to file electronically

  (8) ❑ Notice of conventional filing

  (9) ❑ CD/ROM with PDF of document(s)

  (10) ❑ English translation

(11) ❑ Courtesy copies

(12) ❑ Copies for three-judge court

(c) ❑ Timing

    (1) ❑ The party opposing the motion must file its opposition papers with the court and serve them upon the other parties not less than seventeen (17) days prior to the return date of the motion

    (2) ❑ Except as FRCP 59(c) provides otherwise, any opposing affidavit must be served at least seven (7) days before the hearing, unless the court permits service at another time

    (3) ❑ A party may file and serve a cross-motion (meaning a competing request for relief or order similar to that requested by another party against the cross-moving party) at the time it files and serves its opposition papers to the original motion, i.e., not less than seventeen (17) days prior to the return date of the motion

## B. Timing

1. *Motion for discovery sanctions.* There are no specific timing requirements for moving for discovery sanctions.

2. *Timing of motions, generally.* Unless the Court orders otherwise, the moving party must file all motion papers with the Court and serve them upon the other parties not less than THIRTY-ONE (31) DAYS prior to the return date of the motion. NY R USDCTND L.R. 7.1(b)(2).

    a. *Motion and notice of hearing.* A written motion and notice of the hearing must be served at least fourteen (14) days before the time specified for the hearing, with the following exceptions:

        i. When the motion may be heard ex parte;

        ii. When the Federal Rules of Civil Procedure set a different time; or

        iii. When a court order—which a party may, for good cause, apply for ex parte—sets a different time. FRCP 6(c)(1).

    b. *Supporting affidavit.* Any affidavit supporting a motion must be served with the motion. FRCP 6(c)(2).

3. *Timing of opposing papers.* The party opposing the motion must file its Opposition papers with the Court and serve them upon the other parties not less than SEVENTEEN (17) DAYS prior to the return date of the motion. NY R USDCTND L.R. 7.1(b)(2).

    a. *Opposing affidavit.* Except as FRCP 59(c) provides otherwise, any opposing affidavit must be served at least seven (7) days before the hearing, unless the court permits service at another time. FRCP 6(c)(2).

    b. *Cross-motion.* A party may file and serve a cross-motion (meaning a competing request for relief or order similar to that requested by another party against the cross-moving party) at the time it files and serves its opposition papers to the original motion, i.e., not less than SEVENTEEN (17) DAYS prior to the return date of the motion. NY R USDCTND L.R. 7.1(c).

4. *Timing of reply papers.* Where the respondent files an answering affidavit setting up a new matter, the moving party ordinarily is allowed a reasonable time to file a reply affidavit since failure to deny the new matter by affidavit may operate as an admission of its truth. AMJUR MOTIONS § 25.

    a. *Reply papers.* Reply papers and adjournments are not permitted without the Court's prior permission. Permission to file a reply does not exist simply because CM/ECF generates a deadline for a reply on a nondispositive motion. NY R USDCTND L.R. 7.1(b)(2).

    b. *Opposition to cross-motion.* The original moving party must file its reply/opposition papers with the Court and serve them on the other parties not less than ELEVEN (11) DAYS prior to the return date of the original motion. NY R USDCTND L.R. 7.1(c).

5. *Computation of time*

    a. *Computing time.* FRCP 6 applies in computing any time period specified in the Federal Rules of Civil

Procedure, in any local rule or court order, or in any statute that does not specify a method of computing time. FRCP 6(a).

i. *Period stated in days or a longer unit.* When the period is stated in days or a longer unit of time:

- Exclude the day of the event that triggers the period;
- Count every day, including intermediate Saturdays, Sundays, and legal holidays; and
- Include the last day of the period, but if the last day is a Saturday, Sunday, or legal holiday, the period continues to run until the end of the next day that is not a Saturday, Sunday, or legal holiday. FRCP 6(a)(1).

ii. *Period stated in hours.* When the period is stated in hours:

- Begin counting immediately on the occurrence of the event that triggers the period;
- Count every hour, including hours during intermediate Saturdays, Sundays, and legal holidays; and
- If the period would end on a Saturday, Sunday, or legal holiday, the period continues to run until the same time on the next day that is not a Saturday, Sunday, or legal holiday. FRCP 6(a)(2).

iii. *Inaccessibility of the clerk's office.* Unless the court orders otherwise, if the clerk's office is inaccessible:

- On the last day for filing under FRCP 6(a)(1), then the time for filing is extended to the first accessible day that is not a Saturday, Sunday, or legal holiday; or
- During the last hour for filing under FRCP 6(a)(2), then the time for filing is extended to the same time on the first accessible day that is not a Saturday, Sunday, or legal holiday. FRCP 6(a)(3).

iv. *"Last day" defined.* Unless a different time is set by a statute, local rule, or court order, the last day ends:

- For electronic filing, at midnight in the court's time zone; and
- For filing by other means, when the clerk's office is scheduled to close. FRCP 6(a)(4).

v. *"Next day" defined.* The "next day" is determined by continuing to count forward when the period is measured after an event and backward when measured before an event. FRCP 6(a)(5).

vi. *"Legal holiday" defined.* "Legal holiday" means:

- The day set aside by statute for observing New Year's Day, Martin Luther King Jr.'s Birthday, Washington's Birthday, Memorial Day, Independence Day, Labor Day, Columbus Day, Veterans' Day, Thanksgiving Day, or Christmas Day;
- Any day declared a holiday by the President or Congress; and
- For periods that are measured after an event, any other day declared a holiday by the state where the district court is located. FRCP 6(a)(6).

b. *Computation of electronic filing deadlines.* A document will be deemed timely filed if electronically filed prior to midnight Eastern Time. However, if the time of day is of the essence, the assigned judge may order that the document be filed by a time certain. NY R USDCTND CM/ECF(4)(4.3).

i. *Technical failures.* A Filing User, whose filing is untimely as the result of a technical failure of the Court's CM/ECF site, may seek appropriate relief from the Court. However, Filing Users are cautioned that, in some circumstances, the Court lacks the authority to grant an extension of time to file (e.g., FRCP 6(b) of the Federal Rules of Civil Procedure). NY R USDCTND CM/ECF(10)(10.1).

- *Technical failure of the filing user's system.* Problems with the Filing User's system, such as phone line problems, problems with the Filing User's Internet Service Provider ("ISP"), or hardware or software problems, will not constitute a technical failure under these Administrative Procedures nor excuse an untimely filing. A Filing User who cannot file

documents electronically because of a problem on the Filing User's system must file the documents' conventionally along with an affidavit explaining the reason for not filing the documents electronically. NY R USDCTND CM/ECF(10)(10.2).

   c. *Extending time*

      i. *In general.* When an act may or must be done within a specified time, the court may, for good cause, extend the time:

- With or without motion or notice if the court acts, or if a request is made, before the original time or its extension expires; or

- On motion made after the time has expired if the party failed to act because of excusable neglect. FRCP 6(b)(1).

      ii. *Exceptions.* A court must not extend the time to act under FRCP 50(b), FRCP 50(d), FRCP 52(b), FRCP 59(b), FRCP 59(d), FRCP 59(e), and FRCP 60(b). FRCP 6(b)(2).

      iii. Refer to the United States District Court for the Northern District of New York KeyRules Motion for Continuance/Extension of Time document for more information on extending time.

   d. *Additional time after certain kinds of service.* When a party may or must act within a specified time after service and service is made under FRCP 5(b)(2)(C), FRCP 5(b)(2)(D), FRCP 5(b)(2)(E), or FRCP 5(b)(2)(F), three (3) days are added after the period would otherwise expire under FRCP 6(a). FRCP 6(d).

      i. In accordance with FRCP 6(e), service by electronic means is treated the same as service by mail for purposes of adding three (3) days to the prescribed period to respond. NY R USDCTND CM/ECF(5)(5.4). [Editor's note: the reference to FRCP 6(e) is likely meant to be a reference to FRCP 6(d)].

6. *Individual judge practices.* Refer to the Miscellaneous section of this document for information on individual judge practices on timing of documents.

## C. General Requirements

1. *Prerequisites to making a discovery motion.* The following steps are required prior to making any discovery motion pursuant to FRCP 26 through FRCP 37. NY R USDCTND L.R. 7.1(d).

   a. *Efforts to resolve or reduce differences.* Parties must make good faith efforts among themselves to resolve or reduce all differences relating to discovery prior to seeking court intervention. NY R USDCTND L.R. 7.1(d)(1). Prior to bringing a discovery dispute to a Magistrate Judge, the parties must confer in good faith in accordance with the provisions of NY R USDCTND L.R. 7.1(d). NY R USDCTND Order 25(IX)(A).

   b. *Conference of the parties.* The moving party must confer in detail with the opposing party concerning the discovery issues between them in a good faith effort to eliminate or reduce the area of controversy and to arrive at a mutually satisfactory resolution. Failure to do so may result in denial of a motion to compel discovery and/or imposition of sanctions. NY R USDCTND L.R. 7.1(d)(2).

   c. *Conference with the court.* If the parties' conference does not fully resolve the discovery issues, the party seeking relief must then request a court conference with the assigned Magistrate Judge. Incarcerated, pro se parties are not subject to the court conference requirement prior to filing a motion to compel discovery. The assigned Magistrate Judge may direct the party making the request for a court conference to file an affidavit setting forth the date(s) and mode(s) of the consultation(s) with the opposing party and a letter that concisely sets forth the nature of the dispute and a specific listing of each of the items of discovery sought or opposed. Immediately following each disputed item, the party must set forth the reason why the Court should allow or disallow that item. NY R USDCTND L.R. 7.1(d)(3).

      i. Following a request for a discovery conference, the Court may schedule a conference and advise all parties of a date and time. The assigned Magistrate Judge may, in his or her discretion, conduct the discovery conference by telephone conference call, initiated by the party making the request for the conference, by video conference, or by personal appearance. NY R USDCTND L.R. 7.1(d)(4).

d. *Proposed order.* Following a discovery conference, the Court may direct the prevailing party to submit a proposed order on notice to the other parties. NY R USDCTND L.R. 7.1(d)(5).

e. *Sanctions.* If a party fails or refuses to confer in good faith with the requesting party, thus requiring the request for a discovery conference, the Court, at its discretion, may subject the resisting party to the sanction of the imposition of costs, including the attorney's fees of opposing party in accordance with FRCP 37. NY R USDCTND L.R. 7.1(d)(6).

f. *Claim of privilege.* A party claiming privilege with respect to a communication or other item must specifically identify the privilege and the grounds for the claimed privilege. The parties may not make any generalized claims of privilege. NY R USDCTND L.R. 7.1(d)(7).

2. *Court conference for non-dispositive motions.* Prior to making any non-dispositive motion before the assigned Magistrate Judge, the parties must make good faith efforts among themselves to resolve or reduce all differences relating to the non-dispositive issue. If, after conferring, the parties are unable to arrive at a mutually satisfactory resolution, the party seeking relief must then request a court conference with the assigned Magistrate Judge. NY R USDCTND L.R. 7.1(b)(2). A court conference is a prerequisite to filing a non-dispositive motion before the assigned Magistrate Judge. NY R USDCTND L.R. 7.1(b)(2). In addition, no non-dispositive or discovery motions should be presented to the Court unless authorized by the Magistrate Judge after communication with the Magistrate Judge's chambers. NY R USDCTND Order 25(IX)(A). Actions which involve an incarcerated, pro se party are not subject to the requirement that a court conference be held prior to filing a non-dispositive motion. NY R USDCTND L.R. 7.1(b)(2).

3. *Motions, generally*

    a. *Requirements.* A request for a court order must be made by motion. The motion must:

        i. Be in writing unless made during a hearing or trial;

        ii. State with particularity the grounds for seeking the order; and

        iii. State the relief sought. FRCP 7(b)(1).

        iv. When a moving party makes a motion based upon a rule or statute, the moving party must specify in its moving papers the rule or statute upon which it bases its motion. NY R USDCTND L.R. 7.1(a)(1).

    b. *Notice of motion.* A party interested in resisting the relief sought by a motion has a right to notice thereof, and an opportunity to be heard. AMJUR MOTIONS § 12.

        i. In addition to statutory or court rule provisions requiring notice of a motion—the purpose of such a notice requirement having been said to be to prevent a party from being prejudicially surprised by a motion—principles of natural justice dictate that an adverse party generally must be given notice that a motion will be presented to the court. AMJUR MOTIONS § 12.

        ii. "Notice," in this regard, means reasonable notice, including a meaningful opportunity to prepare and to defend against allegations of a motion. AMJUR MOTIONS § 12.

    c. *Writing requirement.* The writing requirement is intended to insure that the adverse parties are informed and have a record of both the motion's pendency and the grounds on which the movant seeks an order. FPP § 1191; Feldberg v. Quechee Lakes Corp., 463 F.3d 195 (2d Cir. 2006).

        i. It is sufficient "if the motion is stated in a written notice of the hearing of the motion." FPP § 1191.

    d. *Particularity requirement.* The particularity requirement insures that the opposing parties will have notice of their opponent's contentions. FEDPROC § 62:364; Goodman v. 1973 26 Foot Trojan Vessel, Arkansas Registration No. AR1439SN, 859 F.2d 71, 12 Fed.R.Serv.3d 645 (8th Cir. 1988). That requirement ensures that notice of the basis for the motion is provided to the court and to the opposing party so as to avoid prejudice, provide the opponent with a meaningful opportunity to respond, and provide the court with enough information to process the motion correctly. FEDPROC § 62:364; Andreas v. Volkswagen of America, Inc., 336 F.3d 789, 56 Fed.R.Serv.3d 6 (8th Cir. 2003).

        i. Reasonable specification of the grounds for a motion is sufficient. However, where a movant fails to state even one ground for granting the motion in question, the movant has failed to meet the minimal standard of "reasonable specification." FEDPROC § 62:364; Martinez v. Trainor, 556 F.2d 818, 23 Fed.R.Serv.2d 403 (7th Cir. 1977).

    ii.    The court may excuse the failure to comply with the particularity requirement if it is inadvertent, and where no prejudice is shown by the opposing party. FEDPROC § 62:364.

  e.  *Order to show cause.* All motions that a party brings by Order to Show Cause shall conform to the requirements set forth in NY R USDCTND L.R. 7.1(a)(1) and NY R USDCTND L.R. 7.1(a)(2). Immediately after filing an Order to Show Cause, the moving party must telephone the Chambers of the presiding judicial officer and inform Chambers staff that it has filed an Order to Show Cause. Parties may obtain the telephone numbers for all Chambers from the Clerk's office or at the Court's webpage. The Court shall determine the briefing schedule and return date applicable to motions brought by Order to Show Cause. NY R USDCTND L.R. 7.1(e).

    i.    In addition to the requirements set forth in NY R USDCTND L.R. 7.1(a)(1) and NY R USDCTND L.R. 7.1(a)(2), a motion brought by Order to Show Cause must include an affidavit clearly and specifically showing good and sufficient cause why the standard Notice of Motion procedure cannot be used. The moving party must give reasonable advance notice of the application for an Order to Show Cause to the other parties, except in those circumstances where the movant can demonstrate, in a detailed and specific affidavit, good cause and substantial prejudice that would result from the requirement of reasonable notice. NY R USDCTND L.R. 7.1(e).

    ii.    An Order to Show Cause must contain a space for the assigned judge to set forth:

- The deadline for filing and serving supporting papers,
- The deadline for filing and serving opposing papers, and
- The date and time for the hearing. NY R USDCTND L.R. 7.1(e).

4.  *Motion for discovery sanctions*

  a.  *Sanctions, generally.* FRCP 37 is flexible. The court is directed to make such orders as are "just" and is not limited in any case of disregard of the discovery rules or court orders under them to a stereotyped response. The sanctions enumerated in FRCP 37 are not exclusive and arbitrary but flexible, selective, and plural. The district court may, within reason, use as many and as varied sanctions as are necessary to hold the scales of justice even. FPP § 2284.

    i.    There is one fixed limitation that should be noted. A party may not be imprisoned or otherwise punished for contempt of court for failure to submit to a physical or mental examination, or for failure to produce a person in his or her custody or under his or her control for such an examination. FPP § 2284; Sibbach v. Wilson & Co., 312 U.S. 1, 312 U.S. 655, 61 S.Ct. 422, 85 L.Ed. 479 (1941).

    ii.    Although FRCP 37 is very broad, and the courts have considerable discretion in imposing sanctions as authorized by FRCP 37, there are constitutional limits, stemming from the Due Process Clause of U.S.C.A. Const. Amend. V and U.S.C.A. Const. Amend. XIV, on the imposition of sanctions. There are two principal facets of the due process issues:

- First, the court must ask whether there is a sufficient relationship between the discovery and the merits sought to be foreclosed by the sanction to legitimate depriving a party of the opportunity to litigate the merits. FPP § 2283.
- Second, before imposing a serious merits sanction the court should determine whether the party guilty of a failure to provide discovery was unable to comply with the discovery. FPP § 2283.

  b.  *Sanction for improper certification.* If a certification violates FRCP 26(g) without substantial justification, the court, on motion or on its own, must impose an appropriate sanction on the signer, the party on whose behalf the signer was acting, or both. The sanction may include an order to pay the reasonable expenses, including attorney's fees, caused by the violation. FRCP 26(g)(3).

  c.  *Sanctions for failure to produce expert witness information.* There shall be binding disclosure of the identity of expert witnesses. The parties shall make such disclosure, including a curriculum vitae and, unless waived by the other parties, service of the expert's written report pursuant to FRCP 26(a)(2)(B), before the completion of discovery in accordance with the deadlines contained in the Uniform Pretrial Scheduling Order or any other Court order. Failure to comply with these deadlines may result in the imposition of sanctions, including the preclusion of testimony, pursuant to FRCP 16(f). NY R USDCTND L.R. 26.3.

d. *Motion to compel discovery; Payment of expenses; Protective orders*

  i. *If the motion is granted (or disclosure or discovery is provided after filing).* If the motion is granted—or if the disclosure or requested discovery is provided after the motion was filed—the court must, after giving an opportunity to be heard, require the party or deponent whose conduct necessitated the motion, the party or attorney advising that conduct, or both to pay the movant's reasonable expenses incurred in making the motion, including attorney's fees. But the court must not order this payment if:

   • The movant filed the motion before attempting in good faith to obtain the disclosure or discovery without court action;

   • The opposing party's nondisclosure, response, or objection was substantially justified; or

   • Other circumstances make an award of expenses unjust. FRCP 37(a)(5)(A).

  ii. *If the motion is denied.* If the motion is denied, the court may issue any protective order authorized under FRCP 26(c) and must, after giving an opportunity to be heard, require the movant, the attorney filing the motion, or both to pay the party or deponent who opposed the motion its reasonable expenses incurred in opposing the motion, including attorney's fees. But the court must not order this payment if the motion was substantially justified or other circumstances make an award of expenses unjust. FRCP 37(a)(5)(B).

  iii. *If the motion is granted in part and denied in part.* If the motion is granted in part and denied in part, the court may issue any protective order authorized under FRCP 26(c) and may, after giving an opportunity to be heard, apportion the reasonable expenses for the motion. FRCP 37(a)(5)(C).

e. *Failure to comply with a court order*

  i. *Sanctions in the district where the deposition is taken.* If the court where the discovery is taken orders a deponent to be sworn or to answer a question and the deponent fails to obey, the failure may be treated as contempt of court. If a deposition-related motion is transferred to the court where the action is pending, and that court orders a deponent to be sworn or to answer a question and the deponent fails to obey, the failure may be treated as contempt of either the court where the discovery is taken or the court where the action is pending. FRCP 37(b)(1).

  ii. *Sanctions in the district where the action is pending; For not obeying a discovery order.* If a party or a party's officer, director, or managing agent—or a witness designated under FRCP 30(b)(6) or FRCP 31(a)(4)—fails to obey an order to provide or permit discovery, including an order under FRCP 26(f), FRCP 35, or FRCP 37(a), the court where the action is pending may issue further just orders. They may include the following:

   • Directing that the matters embraced in the order or other designated facts be taken as established for purposes of the action, as the prevailing party claims;

   • Prohibiting the disobedient party from supporting or opposing designated claims or defenses, or from introducing designated matters in evidence;

   • Striking pleadings in whole or in part;

   • Staying further proceedings until the order is obeyed;

   • Dismissing the action or proceeding in whole or in part;

   • Rendering a default judgment against the disobedient party; or

   • Treating as contempt of court the failure to obey any order except an order to submit to a physical or mental examination. FRCP 37(b)(2)(A).

  iii. *Sanctions in the district where the action is pending; For not producing a person for examination.* If a party fails to comply with an order under FRCP 35(a) requiring it to produce another person for examination, the court may issue any of the orders listed in FRCP 37(b)(2)(A)(i) through FRCP 37(b)(2)(A)(vi), unless the disobedient party shows that it cannot produce the other person. FRCP 37(b)(2)(B).

iv. *Sanctions in the district where the action is pending; Payment of expenses.* Instead of or in addition to the orders in FRCP 37(b)(2)(A) and FRCP 37(b)(2)(B), the court must order the disobedient party, the attorney advising that party, or both to pay the reasonable expenses, including attorney's fees, caused by the failure, unless the failure was substantially justified or other circumstances make an award of expenses unjust. FRCP 37(b)(2)(C).

v. *Contempt.* A proceeding to adjudicate a person in civil contempt of court, including a case provided for in FRCP 37(b), shall be commenced by the service of a notice of motion or order to show cause. NY R USDCTND L.R. 83.5(a).

- *Alleged contemnor found guilty.* If the Court finds that the alleged contemnor is in contempt of the Court, the Court shall issue and enter an order: (1) reciting or referring to the verdict or findings of fact on which the adjudication is based; (2) setting forth the amount of the damages to which the complainant is entitled; (3) fixing the fine, if any, imposed by the Court, which fine shall include the damages found and naming the person to whom the fine shall be payable; (4) stating any other conditions, the performance of which shall operate to purge the contempt; (5) directing, in the Court's discretion, the Marshal to arrest and confine the contemnor until the performance of the condition fixed in the order and payment of the fine or until the contemnor is otherwise discharged pursuant to law. The order shall specify the place of confinement. No party shall be required to pay or to advance to the Marshal any expenses for the upkeep of the prisoner. On an order of contempt, no person shall be detained in prison by reason of the non-payment of the fine for a period exceeding six (6) months. A certified copy of the order committing the contemnor shall be sufficient warrant to the Marshal for the arrest and confinement. The aggrieved party shall also have the same remedies against the property of the contemnor as if the order awarding the fine were a final judgment. NY R USDCTND L.R. 83.5(c).

- *Alleged contemnor found not guilty.* If the alleged contemnor is found not guilty of the charges, the contemnor shall be discharged from the proceeding and, in the discretion of the Court, shall have judgment against the complainant for costs, disbursements and a reasonable attorney's fee. NY R USDCTND L.R. 83.5(d).

f. *Failure to disclose, to supplement an earlier response, or to admit*

i. *Failure to disclose or supplement.* If a party fails to provide information or identify a witness as required by FRCP 26(a) or FRCP 26(e), the party is not allowed to use that information or witness to supply evidence on a motion, at a hearing, or at a trial, unless the failure was substantially justified or is harmless. In addition to or instead of this sanction, the court, on motion and after giving an opportunity to be heard:

- May order payment of the reasonable expenses, including attorney's fees, caused by the failure;

- May inform the jury of the party's failure; and

- May impose other appropriate sanctions, including any of the orders listed in FRCP 37(b)(2)(A)(i) through FRCP 37(b)(2)(A)(vi). FRCP 37(c)(1).

ii. *Failure to admit.* If a party fails to admit what is requested under FRCP 36 and if the requesting party later proves a document to be genuine or the matter true, the requesting party may move that the party who failed to admit pay the reasonable expenses, including attorney's fees, incurred in making that proof. The court must so order unless:

- The request was held objectionable under FRCP 36(a);

- The admission sought was of no substantial importance;

- The party failing to admit had a reasonable ground to believe that it might prevail on the matter; or

- There was other good reason for the failure to admit. FRCP 37(c)(2).

g. *Party's failure to attend its own deposition, serve answers to interrogatories, or respond to a request for inspection*

    i. *Motion; Grounds for sanctions.* The court where the action is pending may, on motion, order sanctions if:

- A party or a party's officer, director, or managing agent—or a person designated under FRCP 30(b)(6) or FRCP 31(a)(4)—fails, after being served with proper notice, to appear for that person's deposition; or

- A party, after being properly served with interrogatories under FRCP 33 or a request for inspection under FRCP 34, fails to serve its answers, objections, or written response. FRCP 37(d)(1)(A).

    ii. *Unacceptable excuse for failing to act.* A failure described in FRCP 37(d)(1)(A) is not excused on the ground that the discovery sought was objectionable, unless the party failing to act has a pending motion for a protective order under FRCP 26(c). FRCP 37(d)(2).

    iii. *Types of sanctions.* Sanctions may include any of the orders listed in FRCP 37(b)(2)(A)(i) through FRCP 37(b)(2)(A)(vi). Instead of or in addition to these sanctions, the court must require the party failing to act, the attorney advising that party, or both to pay the reasonable expenses, including attorney's fees, caused by the failure, unless the failure was substantially justified or other circumstances make an award of expenses unjust. FRCP 37(d)(3).

h. *Failure to provide electronically stored information.* If electronically stored information that should have been preserved in the anticipation or conduct of litigation is lost because a party failed to take reasonable steps to preserve it, and it cannot be restored or replaced through additional discovery, the court:

    i. Upon finding prejudice to another party from loss of the information, may order measures no greater than necessary to cure the prejudice; or

    ii. Only upon finding that the party acted with the intent to deprive another party of the information's use in the litigation may: (1) presume that the lost information was unfavorable to the party; (2) instruct the jury that it may or must presume the information was unfavorable to the party; or (3) dismiss the action or enter a default judgment. FRCP 37(e).

i. *Failure to participate in framing a discovery plan.* If a party or its attorney fails to participate in good faith in developing and submitting a proposed discovery plan as required by FRCP 26(f), the court may, after giving an opportunity to be heard, require that party or attorney to pay to any other party the reasonable expenses, including attorney's fees, caused by the failure. FRCP 37(f).

j. *Counsel's liability for excessive costs.* 28 U.S.C.A. § 1927 is a basis for sanctioning attorney misconduct in discovery proceedings. DISCPROFED § 22:3. Any attorney or other person admitted to conduct cases in any court of the United States or any Territory thereof who so multiplies the proceedings in any case unreasonably and vexatiously may be required by the court to satisfy personally the excess costs, expenses, and attorneys' fees reasonably incurred because of such conduct. 28 U.S.C.A. § 1927.

5. *Opposing papers.* The Federal Rules of Civil Procedure do not require any formal answer, return, or reply to a motion, except where the Federal Rules of Civil Procedure or local rules may require affidavits, memoranda, or other papers to be filed in opposition to a motion. Such papers are simply to apprise the court of such opposition and the grounds of that opposition. FEDPROC § 62:359.

a. *Effect of failure to respond to motion.* Although in the absence of statutory provision or court rule, a motion ordinarily does not require a written answer, when a party files a motion and the opposing party fails to respond, the court may construe such failure to respond as nonopposition to the motion or an admission that the motion was meritorious, may take the facts alleged in the motion as true—the rule in some jurisdictions being that the failure to respond to a fact set forth in a motion is deemed an admission—and may grant the motion if the relief requested appears to be justified. AMJUR MOTIONS § 28.

b. *Assent or no opposition not determinative.* However, a motion will not be granted automatically simply because an "assent" or a notation of "no opposition" has been filed; federal judges frequently deny motions that have been assented to when it is thought that justice so dictates. FPP § 1190.

c. *Responsive pleading inappropriate as response to motion.* An attempt to answer or oppose a motion with a responsive pleading usually is not appropriate. FPP § 1190.

6. *Reply papers.* Reply papers and adjournments are not permitted without the Court's prior permission. Permission to file a reply does not exist simply because CM/ECF generates a deadline for a reply on a nondispositive motion. NY R USDCTND L.R. 7.1(b)(2). A moving party may be required or permitted to prepare papers in addition to his original motion papers. AMJUR MOTIONS § 25. Papers answering or replying to opposing papers may be appropriate, in the interests of justice, where it appears there is a substantial reason for allowing a reply. Thus, a court may accept reply papers where a party demonstrates that the papers to which it seeks to file a reply raise new issues that are material to the disposition of the question before the court, or where the court determines, sua sponte, that it wishes further briefing of an issue raised in those papers and orders the submission of additional papers. FEDPROC § 62:360.

a. *Function of reply papers.* The function of a reply affidavit is to answer the arguments made in opposition to the position taken by the movant and not to permit the movant to introduce new arguments in support of the motion. AMJUR MOTIONS § 25.

b. *Issues raised for the first time in a reply document.* However, the view has been followed in some jurisdictions, that as a matter of judicial economy, where there is no prejudice and where the issues could be raised simply by filing a motion to dismiss, the trial court has discretion to consider arguments raised for the first time in a reply memorandum, and that a trial court may grant a motion to strike issues raised for the first time in a reply memorandum. AMJUR MOTIONS § 26.

c. *Opposition to cross-motion.* The original moving party may reply in further support of the original motion and in opposition to the cross-motion with a reply/opposition brief that does not exceed twenty-five (25) pages in length, exclusive of exhibits. NY R USDCTND L.R. 7.1(c).

7. *Surreply in support of cross-motion.* The cross-moving party may not reply in further support of its cross-motion without the Court's prior permission. NY R USDCTND L.R. 7.1(c).

8. *Submission of proposed order by prevailing party.* If the assigned judge instructs the prevailing party to do so, the prevailing party shall submit a proposed order which the opposing party has approved and which contains the endorsement of the opposing party: "Approved as to form." NY R USDCTND L.R. 77.2(b). In civil actions where the Court has directed a party to submit an order or judgment, that party shall file all such orders or judgments in duplicate, and the Clerk's entry of such duplicate in the proper record book shall be deemed in compliance with FRCP 79(b). Such party shall also furnish the Clerk with a sufficient number of additional copies for each party to the action, which the Clerk shall mail with notice of entry in accordance with FRCP 77(d). NY R USDCTND L.R. 5.1(b).

a. *Disagreement as to form of proposed order.* When the parties are unable to agree as to the form of the proposed order, the prevailing party shall, on seven (7) days notice to all other parties, submit a proposed order and a written explanation for the form of that order. The Court may award costs and attorney's fees against a party whose unreasonable conduct the Court deemed to have required the bringing of the motion. The provisions of NY R USDCTND L.R. 7.1 shall not apply to such motion, and the Court shall not hear oral argument. NY R USDCTND L.R. 77.2(b).

b. For more information on orders, refer to NY R USDCTND L.R. 77.2.

9. *Sanctions for vexatious or frivolous motions or failure to comply with* NY R USDCTND L.R. 7.1. A party who presents vexatious or frivolous motion papers or fails to comply with NY R USDCTND L.R. 7.1 is subject to discipline as the Court deems appropriate, including sanctions and the imposition of costs and attorney's fees to the opposing party. NY R USDCTND L.R. 7.1(i).

10. *Complex and multi-district litigation.* If the assigned judge determines, in his or her discretion, that the case is of such a complex nature that it cannot reasonably be trial ready within eighteen (18) months from the date the complaint is filed, the assigned judge may design and issue a particularized case management order that will move the case to trial as quickly as the complexity of the case allows. NY R USDCTND L.R. 3.3(a). The parties shall promptly notify the Court in writing if any action commenced is appropriate for multi-district litigation. NY R USDCTND L.R. 3.3(b).

11.  *Appearances.* An attorney appearing for a party in a civil case shall promptly file with the Clerk a written notice of appearance; however, an attorney does not need to file a notice of appearance if the attorney who would be filing the notice of appearance is the same individual who has signed the complaint, notice of removal, pre-answer motion, or answer. NY R USDCTND L.R. 83.2(a). For more information, refer to NY R USDCTND L.R. 83.2.

12.  *Related cases.* A civil case is "related" to another civil case for purposes of this guideline when, because of the similarity of facts and legal issues or because the cases arise from the same transactions or events, a substantial saving of judicial resources is likely to result from assigning the cases to the same Judge and Magistrate Judge. NY R USDCTND Order 12(G)(2). A civil case shall not be deemed related to another civil case merely because the civil case: (1) involves similar legal issues, or (2) involves the same parties. NY R USDCTND Order 12(G)(3). Presumptively, and subject to the power of a Judge to determine otherwise pursuant to NY R USDCTND Order 12(G)(5), civil cases shall not be deemed to be "related" unless both cases are still pending before the Court. NY R USDCTND Order 12(G)(4).

   a.  *New filings.* If an attorney or filing party indicates on the Civil Cover Sheet that a case is related to an earlier filed case, the Clerk shall instruct the filing party to file a notice of related cases. The allegedly related cases will be submitted by the Clerk to the Judge to whom the earliest filed case is assigned, who shall advise the Clerk whether such cases are related. NY R USDCTND Order 12(G)(1).

   b.  *Judicial determination that civil cases are "related."* Except for the cases described in the final sentence of NY R USDCTND Order 12(G)(6), all civil cases shall be randomly assigned when they are filed. Other than the cases described in the final sentence of NY R USDCTND Order 12(G)(6), civil cases shall not be deemed to be "related" for purposes of this guideline at the instance of any litigant or attorney unless and until there has been a determination by a Judge of this Court that the standard of NY R USDCTND Order 12(G)(2) is met. NY R USDCTND Order 12(G)(5).

      i.  *Notice of related filing.* Any party may apply for such a determination by filing with the Clerk a notice of related filing, which should include an explanation as to why the standard of NY R USDCTND Order 12(G)(2) is met. A form for this purpose is available on the Court's website. A copy of the notice shall be served on all other parties who have appeared. Such an application must be made after the date when at least a majority of the defendants have been served with the complaint. Before making such an application, the applicant must confer in good faith with all other parties in an effort to reach an agreement on whether or not the case is "related". After such an application is made, any other party may serve and file within seven (7) calendar days a letter of no more than two (2) pages supporting or opposing the application. The application to have the case assigned to another Judge shall be presented to the Judge with the earliest filed case for decision on whether the action(s) should be reassigned as related cases. The Judge with the earliest filed case may then enter an order in the case at bar, either deeming the case to be related and directing the Clerk to reassign the action, or denying the application for reassignment. Any disputes concerning the assignment of related cases will be referred to the Chief Judge for resolution. NY R USDCTND Order 12(G)(5).

   c.  For more information on related cases, refer to NY R USDCTND Order 12(G).

13.  *Alternative dispute resolution (ADR).* It is the mission of this court to do everything it can to help parties resolve their disputes as fairly, quickly, and efficiently as possible. NY R USDCTND Order 25(VIII).

   a.  *Arbitration.* NY R USDCTND L.R. 83.7 governs the consensual arbitration program for referral of civil actions to court-annexed arbitration. It may remain in effect until further order of the Court. Its purpose is to establish a less formal procedure for the just, efficient and economical resolution of disputes, while preserving the right to a full trial on demand. NY R USDCTND L.R. 83.7-1.

      i.  *Actions subject to arbitration.* The Clerk shall notify the parties in all civil cases, except as the Local Rules of Practice for the United States District Court for the Northern District of New York otherwise direct, that they may consent to non-binding arbitration under NY R US-DCTND L.R. 83.7. The notice shall be furnished to the parties at pretrial/scheduling conferences or shall be included with pretrial conference notices and instructions. Consent to arbitration under NY R USDCTND L.R. 83.7 shall be discussed at the pretrial/scheduling conference. No party or attorney shall be prejudiced for refusing to participate in arbitration. The Court shall allow the referral of any civil action pending before it to the arbitration process if the parties consent. The plaintiff shall be responsible for securing the execution of a consent form by the parties and for filing the form with the Clerk within fourteen (14) days after the parties receive the form. The parties shall freely and knowingly enter into the consent. NY R USDCTND L.R. 83.7-2.

    ii.   *Referral to arbitration.* The Clerk shall refer every action subject to NY R USDCTND L.R. 83.7 to arbitration in accordance with the procedures under NY R USDCTND L.R. 83.7 twenty-one (21) days after the filing of the last responsive pleading or within twenty-one (21) days of the filing of a stipulated consent order referring the action to arbitration, whichever event occurs last, except as otherwise provided. If any party notices a motion to dismiss under the provisions of FRCP 12(a) and/or FRCP 12(b), or a motion to join necessary parties pursuant to the Federal Rules of Civil Procedure prior to the expiration of the twenty-one (21) day period, the assigned judge shall hear the motion and further proceedings under NY R USDCTND L.R. 83.7 shall be deferred pending decision on the motion. If the Court does not dismiss the action on the motion, the Court shall refer the action to arbitration twenty-one (21) days after the filing of the decision. NY R USDCTND L.R. 83.7-3(a). Motions for summary judgment pursuant to FRCP 56 shall be filed and served within twenty-one (21) days following the close of discovery. The filing of a FRCP 56 motion shall defer further proceedings under NY R USDCTND L.R. 83.7 pending decision on the motion. NY R USDCTND L.R. 83.7-3(a).

        ●   *Relief from referral.* Any party shall request relief from the operation of NY R USDCTND L.R. 83.7 by filing with the Court a motion for the relief within twenty-one (21) days after entry of the initial stipulated consent order which refers the case for arbitration. The assigned judge shall, sua sponte, exempt an action from the application of NY R USDCTND L.R. 83.7 where the objectives of arbitration would not be realized because (1) the case involves complex or novel legal issues, (2) legal issues predominate over factual issues, or (3) for other good cause. NY R USDCTND L.R. 83.7-3(c).

    iii.   For more information on arbitration, refer to NY R USDCTND L.R. 83.7.

  b.  *Mediation.* The purpose of NY R USDCTND L.R. 83.11 is to provide a supplementary procedure to the Court's existing alternative dispute resolution procedures. NY R USDCTND L.R. 83.11 provides for an earlier resolution of civil disputes resulting in savings of time and cost to litigants and the Court without sacrificing the quality of justice rendered or the right of litigants to a full trial on all issues not resolved through mediation. NY R USDCTND L.R. 83.11-1(a). Mediation is a process by which an impartial person, the mediator, facilitates communication between disputing parties to promote understanding, reconciliation and settlement. The mediator is an advocate for settlement and uses the mediation process to help the parties fully explore any potential area of agreement. The mediator does not serve as a judge or arbitrator and has no authority to render any decision on any disputed issue or to force a settlement. The parties themselves are responsible for negotiating any resolution(s) to their dispute. NY R USDCTND L.R. 83.11-1(b).

    i.   *Actions subject to mediation.* The Court may refer any civil action (or any portion thereof) to mediation under NY R USDCTND L.R. 83.11: (1) by order of referral; or (2) on the motion of any party; or (3) by consent of the parties. NY R USDCTND L.R. 83.11-3(a).

        ●   *Withdrawal from mediation.* The parties may withdraw from mediation any civil action or claim that the Court refers to mediation pursuant to NY R USDCTND L.R. 83.11-3 by application to the assigned judge at least ten (10) days prior to the scheduled mediation session. NY R USDCTND L.R. 83.11-3(b).

    ii.   *Mandatory mediation program.* The United States District Court for the Northern District of New York has adopted this Mandatory Mediation Plan. The paid Mediation Program is designed to provide quicker, less expensive and potentially more satisfying alternatives to continuing litigation, without impairing the quality of justice or the right to trial. NY R USDCTND Order 47(1)(1.2)(A). This Mandatory Mediation Plan applies to civil actions pending as well as newly filed actions, except as otherwise indicated in NY R USDCTND Order

47. The Local Rules for voluntary mediation will apply only to Pro Se Cases that proceed through the Assisted Mediation Program. NY R USDCTND Order 47(1)(1.2)(B).

- *Referral into the pilot mandatory mediation program for new cases.* All civil cases shall be referred automatically into the Mandatory Mediation Program. Notice of the Mandatory Mediation requirements will be provided to all parties immediately upon the filing of a complaint and answer or a notice of removal. ADR intervention will be scheduled at the conference held pursuant to NY R USDCTND L.R. 16.1. NY R USDCTND Order 47(2)(2.1)(A). For a list of categories of actions exempted from automatic referral, refer to NY R USDCTND Order 47(2)(2.1)(A).

- *Referral into the pilot mandatory mediation program for pending cases.* The assigned Judge or Magistrate Judge on any pending civil case may, sua sponte or with status conference, issue an order referring the case into the Mandatory Mediation Program. The order shall specify a date on which the ADR intervention is to be completed. NY R USDCTND Order 47(2)(2.1)(B).

- *Referral into the pilot mandatory mediation program by stipulation.* A case may be referred into the Mandatory Mediation Program by stipulation of all parties. Stipulations shall be filed and shall designate the time frame within which the ADR process will be completed. Stipulations are presumed acceptable unless the assigned Judge or Magistrate Judge determines that the interests of justice are not served. NY R USDCTND Order 47(2)(2.1)(C).

- *Relief from referral.* Motions to opt out of the program will be addressed by the assigned Magistrate Judge at the FRCP 16 conference. NY R USDCTND Order 47(2)(2.2)(A). Opting Out Motions shall be granted only for "good cause" shown. Inconvenience, travel costs, attorney fees or other costs shall not constitute "good cause." A party seeking relief from the Mandatory Mediation Program must set forth the reasons why Mandatory Mediation has no reasonable chance of being productive. NY R USDCTND Order 47(2)(2.2)(B). The assigned Magistrate Judge may, sua sponte, exempt any case from the Court's Mandatory Mediation Program. NY R USDCTND Order 47(2)(2.2)(C).

iii. *Assisted mediation program.* The Court may assign specially trained pro bono Special Mediation Counsel to assist pro se civilian litigants with preparing for and participating in mediation. The Assisted Mediation Program is open to civilian pro se parties to actions in the Northern District of New York. The assigned judge or magistrate judge determines if the case would benefit from mediation and would also benefit from the assignment of Special Mediation Counsel to assist the pro se party with the mediation process. NY R USDCTND L.R. 83.8(a). Appointment of Special Mediation Counsel is in no way guaranteed, even if the action is referred to the court-annexed mediation program. Appointment is at the sole discretion of the presiding judge. NY R USDCTND L.R. 83.8(a).

- *Referral to assisted mediation program.* If the court determines that referral to the Assisted Mediation Program is appropriate, the Court shall enter an order of reference to the Assisted Mediation Program. NY R USDCTND L.R. 83.8(b).

iv. For more information on mediation, refer to NY R USDCTND L.R. 83.11 and NY R USDCTND Order 47.

c. *Early neutral evaluation (ENE).* Early neutral evaluation (ENE) is a process in which parties obtain from an experienced neutral (an "evaluator") a nonbinding, reasoned, oral evaluation of the merits of the case. The first step in the ENE process involves the Court appointing an evaluator who has expertise in the area of law in the case. After the parties exchange essential information and position statements early in the pretrial period (usually within one hundred fifty (150) to two hundred (200) days after a complaint has been filed), the evaluator convenes an ENE session that typically lasts about two hours. At the ENE meeting, each side briefly presents the factual and legal basis of its position. The evaluator may ask questions of the parties and help them identify the main issues in dispute and the areas of agreement. The evaluator may also help the parties explore options for settlement. If settlement does not occur, the evaluator then offers an opinion as to the settlement value of the case, including the likelihood of liability and the likely range of damages. With the benefit of this assessment, the parties are again encouraged to discuss settlement, with or without the evaluator's assistance. The parties may also explore ways to narrow the issues in dispute, exchange information about the case or otherwise prepare efficiently for trial. NY R USDCTND L.R. 83.12-1.

    i.   *Actions subject to early neutral evaluation.* The Court may refer any civil action (or any portion thereof) to ENE under NY R USDCTND L.R. 83.12: (1) by order of referral; (2) on the motion of any party; or (3) by consent of the parties. NY R USDCTND L.R. 83.12-3(a).

        •   *Withdrawal from the ENE process.* The parties may withdraw any civil action or claim that the Court has referred to the ENE Process pursuant to NY R USDCTND L.R. 83.12-3 by application to the assigned judge at least ten (10) days before the scheduled evaluation session. NY R USDCTND L.R. 83.12-3(b).

    ii.  For more information on early neutral evaluation (ENE), refer to NY R USDCTND L.R. 83.12.

14.  *Settlement procedures.* On notice to the Court or the Clerk that the parties have settled an action, and upon confirmation of the settlement by all parties, the Court may issue a judgment dismissing the action by reason of settlement. The Court shall issue the order without prejudice to the parties' right to secure reinstatement of the case within thirty (30) days after the date of judgment by making a showing that the settlement was not, in fact, consummated. NY R USDCTND L.R. 68.2(a). If the Court decides not to follow the procedures set forth in NY R USDCTND L.R. 68.2(a), the parties shall file within thirty (30) days of the notification to the Court, unless otherwise directed by written order, such notices, stipulations and/or motions as are necessary to terminate the action. If the required documents are not filed within the thirty (30) day period, the Clerk shall place the action on the dismissal calendar. NY R USDCTND L.R. 68.2(b).

15.  *Sanctions and penalties for noncompliance.* Failure of an attorney or of a party to comply with any provision of the Local Rules of Practice for the United States District Court for the Northern District of New York, General Orders of this District, Orders of the Court, or the Federal Rules of Civil Procedure shall be a ground for imposition of sanctions. NY R USDCTND L.R. 1.1(d).

16.  *Individual judge practices.* Refer to the Miscellaneous section of this document for information on individual judge practices on general requirements for documents.

## D.  Documents

  1.  *Documents for moving party*

    a.  *Required documents*

      i.   *Notice of motion and motion.* In the Notice of Motion, the moving party is required to set forth the date that the court conference with the Magistrate Judge was held regarding the issues being presented in the motion. Failure to include this information in the Notice of Motion may result in the Court rejecting the motion papers. NY R USDCTND L.R. 7.1(b)(2). Refer to the General Requirements section of this document for information on the notice of motion and motion.

        •   *Order to show cause.* A proceeding to adjudicate a person in civil contempt of court, including a case provided for in FRCP 37(b), shall be commenced by the service of a notice of motion or order to show cause. NY R USDCTND L.R. 83.5(a). If an order to show cause is sought, the order may, on necessity shown, embody a direction to the United States Marshal to arrest and hold the alleged contemnor on bail in an amount fixed by the order, conditioned upon appearance at the hearing and further conditioned upon the alleged contemnor's amenability to all orders of the Court for surrender. NY R USDCTND L.R. 83.5(a). Refer to the General Requirements section of this document for information on bringing a motion by order to show cause.

      ii.  *Certificate of compliance.* A motion for sanctions for failing to answer or respond must include a certification that the movant has in good faith conferred or attempted to confer with the party failing to act in an effort to obtain the answer or response without court action. FRCP 37(d)(1)(B).

      iii.  *Memorandum of law.* Except as otherwise provided in NY R USDCTND L.R. 7.1(a), all motions. . .require a memorandum of law. NY R USDCTND L.R. 7.1(a). Refer to the Format section of this document for the formatting requirements for memoranda of law.

iv. *Supporting affidavit.* Except as otherwise provided in NY R USDCTND L.R. 7.1(a), all motions. . .require a. . .supporting affidavit. NY R USDCTND L.R. 7.1(a). An affidavit must not contain legal arguments but must contain factual and procedural background that is relevant to the motion the affidavit supports. NY R USDCTND L.R. 7.1(a)(2).

v. *Certificate of service.* Except as otherwise provided in NY R USDCTND L.R. 7.1(a), all motions. . .require. . .proof of service on all the parties. See NY R USDCTND L.R. 5.1(a). NY R USDCTND L.R. 7.1(a). FRCP 5(d) requires that the person making service under FRCP 5 certify that service has been effected. FRCP 5(Advisory Committee Notes). Having such information on file may be useful for many purposes, including proof of service if an issue arises concerning the effectiveness of the service. FRCP 5(Advisory Committee Notes). The party or its designee shall declare, by affidavit or certification, that it has provided all other parties in the action with all documents it has filed with the Court. NY R USDCTND L.R. 5.1(a).

- Attorneys and pro se parties who are not Filing or Receiving Users must be served with a paper copy of any electronically filed pleading or other document. NY R USDCTND CM/ECF(5)(5.2). Such paper service must be documented by electronically filing a certificate of service. NY R USDCTND CM/ECF(5)(5.2).

b. *Supplemental documents*

i. *Supporting evidence.* When a motion relies on facts outside the record, the court may hear the matter on affidavits or may hear it wholly or partly on oral testimony or on depositions. FRCP 43(c).

- *Discovery materials.* A party shall accompany any motion that it files pursuant to FRCP 37 with the discovery materials to which the motion relates if the parties have not previously filed those materials with the Court. NY R USDCTND L.R. 7.1(d)(8); NY R USDCTND L.R. 26.2; NY R USDCTND CM/ECF(2)(2.1)(4).

- *Supporting affidavit for contempt proceedings.* The affidavit on which the notice of motion or order to show cause is based shall set out with particularity the misconduct complained of, the claim, if any, for resulting damages, and evidence as to the amount of damages that is available to the moving party. A reasonable attorney's fee, necessitated by the contempt proceeding, may be included as an item of damages. NY R USDCTND L.R. 83.5(a).

ii. *Notice of constitutional question.* A party that files a pleading, written motion, or other paper drawing into question the constitutionality of a federal or state statute must promptly:

- *File notice.* File a notice of constitutional question stating the question and identifying the paper that raises it, if: (1) a federal statute is questioned and the parties do not include the United States, one of its agencies, or one of its officers or employees in an official capacity; or (2) a state statute is questioned and the parties do not include the state, one of its agencies, or one of its officers or employees in an official capacity; and

- *Serve notice.* Serve the notice and paper on the Attorney General of the United States if a federal statute is questioned—or on the state attorney general if a state statute is questioned—either by certified or registered mail or by sending it to an electronic address designated by the attorney general for this purpose. FRCP 5.1(a).

- *No forfeiture.* A party's failure to file and serve the notice, or the court's failure to certify, does not forfeit a constitutional claim or defense that is otherwise timely asserted. FRCP 5.1(d).

iii. *Copies of authorities.* When serving a pro se litigant with a memorandum of law or any other paper which contains citations to authorities that are unpublished or published exclusively on electronic databases, counsel shall include a hard copy of those authorities. Although copies of authorities published only on electronic databases are not required to be filed, copies shall be provided upon request to opposing counsel who lack access to electronic databases. NY R USDCTND L.R. 7.1(a)(1).

iv. *Proposed order.* A document that is submitted in .pdf format cannot be modified; therefore, a proposed order or stipulation must be in a word processing format. The chambers of the assigned judge may request that a proposed order and/or a stipulation be e-mailed to the courtroom deputy for the presiding judge in either WordPerfect or Microsoft Word format. Please attach your proposed order and/or stipulation to an Internet e-mail sent to the appropriate e-mail address listed in NY R USDCTND CM/ECF(8)(8.2). NY R USDCTND CM/ECF(8)(8.2).

v. *Cover letter authorizing e-mail or facsimile filing.* Neither the Court nor the Clerk's Office will accept for filing any facsimile or e-mail transmission without prior authorization from the Court. The party using facsimile or e-mail transmissions to file its papers must accompany any such documents with a cover letter stating that the Court authorized such transmissions and the date on which the Court provided that authorization. Violations of NY R USDCTND L.R. 5.5 subject the offending party to the Court's full disciplinary powers. NY R USDCTND L.R. 5.5.

vi. *Affidavit attesting to failed attempts to file electronically.* If the Court's CM/ECF site experiences a technical failure, a Filing User may submit documents to the Court that day in an alternate manner provided that the documents are accompanied by the Filing User's affidavit stating that the Filing User attempted to file electronically at least two times in one (1) hour increments after 10:00 a.m. that day. The following methods are acceptable alternate means for filing documents in case of a technical failure: (1) via electronic mail in a PDF attachment sent to the e-mail address for technical failures; or (2) in person, by bringing the document to the Clerk's Office on paper accompanied by a CD/ROM that contains the document in .pdf format. NY R USDCTND CM/ECF(10)(10.1).

- A Filing User who cannot file documents electronically because of a problem on the Filing User's system must file the documents' conventionally along with an affidavit explaining the reason for not filing the documents electronically. NY R USDCTND CM/ECF(10)(10.2).

vii. *Notice of conventional filing.* If the Clerk's Office grants permission to conventionally file the document, the Filing User shall electronically file a notice of conventional filing for the documents. More information regarding this process can be obtained from the Court's web page. NY R USDCTND CM/ECF(4)(4.5).

viii. *CD/ROM with PDF of document(s).* If the Court grants permission to file a document traditionally, the attorney must submit the documents for filing to the Clerk's Office on CD/ROM in .pdf or pdf.A format. NY R USDCTND CM/ECF(2).

ix. *English translation.* The Court conducts its reviews and deliberations in English. Unless otherwise directed by the Court, any document that a party transmits to the Court (including one in the record on appeal) that is in a language other than English must be accompanied by an English translation that the translator has certified as true and accurate, pursuant to 28 U.S.C.A. § 1746. NY R USDCTND L.R. 10.1(e). For more information, refer to NY R USDCTND L.R. 10.1(e).

x. *Courtesy copies.* The Court may require that courtesy copies of electronically filed documents be submitted for its review and may amend these Administrative Procedures (NY R USDCTND CM/ECF) at any time without prior notice. NY R USDCTND CM/ECF(2).

xi. *Copies for three-judge court.* On the convening of a three-judge court, the parties shall make three (3) copies of all non-electronically filed pleadings, motion papers, and memoranda of law available to the Clerk for distribution. NY R USDCTND L.R. 9.1.

2. *Documents for opposing party*

a. *Required documents*

i. *Opposition.* Refer to the General Requirements section of this document for information on the opposing papers.

ii. *Memorandum of law.* Except as otherwise provided in NY R USDCTND L.R. 7.1(a), all. . .opposition to motions require a memorandum of law. NY R USDCTND L.R. 7.1(a).

- *Cross-motion brief.* If a party makes a cross-motion, it must join its cross motion brief with its opposition brief, and this combined brief may not exceed twenty-five (25) pages in length, exclusive of exhibits. A separate brief in opposition to the original motion is not permissible. NY R USDCTND L.R. 7.1(c).

- Refer to the Format section of this document for the formatting requirements for memoranda of law.

iii. *Supporting affidavit.* Except as otherwise provided in NY R USDCTND L.R. 7.1(a), all. . .opposition to motions require a. . .supporting affidavit. NY R USDCTND L.R. 7.1(a). An affidavit must not contain legal arguments but must contain factual and procedural background that is relevant to the motion the affidavit supports. NY R USDCTND L.R. 7.1(a)(2).

iv. *Certificate of service.* Except as otherwise provided in NY R USDCTND L.R. 7.1(a), all. . .opposition to motions require. . .proof of service on all the parties. See NY R USDCTND L.R. 5.1(a). NY R USDCTND L.R. 7.1(a). FRCP 5(d) requires that the person making service under FRCP 5 certify that service has been effected. FRCP 5(Advisory Committee Notes). Having such information on file may be useful for many purposes, including proof of service if an issue arises concerning the effectiveness of the service. FRCP 5(Advisory Committee Notes). The party or its designee shall declare, by affidavit or certification, that it has provided all other parties in the action with all documents it has filed with the Court. NY R USDCTND L.R. 5.1(a).

- Attorneys and pro se parties who are not Filing or Receiving Users must be served with a paper copy of any electronically filed pleading or other document. NY R USDCTND CM/ECF(5)(5.2). Such paper service must be documented by electronically filing a certificate of service. NY R USDCTND CM/ECF(5)(5.2).

b. *Supplemental documents*

i. *Supporting evidence.* When a motion relies on facts outside the record, the court may hear the matter on affidavits or may hear it wholly or partly on oral testimony or on depositions. FRCP 43(c).

ii. *Notice of constitutional question.* A party that files a pleading, written motion, or other paper drawing into question the constitutionality of a federal or state statute must promptly:

- *File notice.* File a notice of constitutional question stating the question and identifying the paper that raises it, if: (1) a federal statute is questioned and the parties do not include the United States, one of its agencies, or one of its officers or employees in an official capacity; or (2) a state statute is questioned and the parties do not include the state, one of its agencies, or one of its officers or employees in an official capacity; and

- *Serve notice.* Serve the notice and paper on the Attorney General of the United States if a federal statute is questioned—or on the state attorney general if a state statute is questioned—either by certified or registered mail or by sending it to an electronic address designated by the attorney general for this purpose. FRCP 5.1(a).

- *No forfeiture.* A party's failure to file and serve the notice, or the court's failure to certify, does not forfeit a constitutional claim or defense that is otherwise timely asserted. FRCP 5.1(d).

iii. *Cross-motion.* A party may file and serve a cross-motion (meaning a competing request for relief or order similar to that requested by another party against the cross-moving party) at the time it files and serves its opposition papers to the original motion, i.e., not less than SEVENTEEN (17) DAYS prior to the return date of the motion. NY R USDCTND L.R. 7.1(c).

iv. *Demand for jury trial.* When by law the alleged contemnor is entitled to a trial by jury, the contemnor shall make a written demand on or before the return day or adjourned day of the application; otherwise the Court will deem that the alleged contemnor has waived a trial by jury. NY R USDCTND L.R. 83.5(b).

v. *Copies of authorities.* When serving a pro se litigant with a memorandum of law or any other paper which contains citations to authorities that are unpublished or published exclusively on electronic databases, counsel shall include a hard copy of those authorities. Although copies of authorities published only on electronic databases are not required to be filed, copies shall be provided upon request to opposing counsel who lack access to electronic databases. NY R USDCTND L.R. 7.1(a)(1).

vi. *Cover letter authorizing e-mail or facsimile filing.* Neither the Court nor the Clerk's Office will accept for filing any facsimile or e-mail transmission without prior authorization from the Court. The party using facsimile or e-mail transmissions to file its papers must accompany any such documents with a cover letter stating that the Court authorized such transmissions and the date on which the Court provided that authorization. Violations of NY R USDCTND L.R. 5.5 subject the offending party to the Court's full disciplinary powers. NY R USDCTND L.R. 5.5.

vii. *Affidavit attesting to failed attempts to file electronically.* If the Court's CM/ECF site experiences a technical failure, a Filing User may submit documents to the Court that day in an alternate manner provided that the documents are accompanied by the Filing User's affidavit stating that the Filing User attempted to file electronically at least two times in one (1) hour increments after 10:00 a.m. that day. The following methods are acceptable alternate means for filing documents in case of a technical failure: (1) via electronic mail in a PDF attachment sent to the e-mail address for technical failures; or (2) in person, by bringing the document to the Clerk's Office on paper accompanied by a CD/ROM that contains the document in .pdf format. NY R USDCTND CM/ECF(10)(10.1).

  - A Filing User who cannot file documents electronically because of a problem on the Filing User's system must file the documents' conventionally along with an affidavit explaining the reason for not filing the documents electronically. NY R USDCTND CM/ECF(10)(10.2).

viii. *Notice of conventional filing.* If the Clerk's Office grants permission to conventionally file the document, the Filing User shall electronically file a notice of conventional filing for the documents. More information regarding this process can be obtained from the Court's web page. NY R USDCTND CM/ECF(4)(4.5).

ix. *CD/ROM with PDF of document(s).* If the Court grants permission to file a document traditionally, the attorney must submit the documents for filing to the Clerk's Office on CD/ROM in .pdf or pdf.A format. NY R USDCTND CM/ECF(2).

x. *English translation.* The Court conducts its reviews and deliberations in English. Unless otherwise directed by the Court, any document that a party transmits to the Court (including one in the record on appeal) that is in a language other than English must be accompanied by an English translation that the translator has certified as true and accurate, pursuant to 28 U.S.C.A. § 1746. NY R USDCTND L.R. 10.1(e). For more information, refer to NY R USDCTND L.R. 10.1(e).

xi. *Courtesy copies.* The Court may require that courtesy copies of electronically filed documents be submitted for its review and may amend these Administrative Procedures (NY R USDCTND CM/ECF) at any time without prior notice. NY R USDCTND CM/ECF(2).

xii. *Copies for three-judge court.* On the convening of a three-judge court, the parties shall make three (3) copies of all non-electronically filed pleadings, motion papers, and memoranda of law available to the Clerk for distribution. NY R USDCTND L.R. 9.1.

3. *Individual judge practices.* Refer to the Miscellaneous section of this document for information on individual judge practices on required documents.

## E. Format

1. *Form of documents.* The rules governing captions and other matters of form in pleadings apply to motions and other papers. FRCP 7(b)(2). All pleadings and other papers shall be served and filed in accordance

with the Federal Rules of Civil Procedure and shall be in the form prescribed by NY R USDCTND L.R. 10.1. NY R USDCTND L.R. 5.1(a).

a. *Form, generally.* All pleadings, motions, and other documents that a party presents for filing, whether in paper form or in electronic form, shall meet the following requirements:

    i. *Font size.* All text, whether in the body of the document or in footnotes, must be a minimum of twelve (12) point type. NY R USDCTND L.R. 10.1(a)(1).

    ii. *Margins.* All documents must have one (1) inch margins on all four sides of the page. NY R USDCTND L.R. 10.1(a)(2).

    iii. *Spacing.* All text in the body of the document must be double-spaced. NY R USDCTND L.R. 10.1(a)(3).

        • The text in block quotations and footnotes may be single-spaced. NY R USDCTND L.R. 10.1(a)(4).

    iv. *Page numbering.* Pages must be consecutively numbered. NY R USDCTND L.R. 10.1(a)(7).

    v. *Circumventing formatting limitations*

        • Extensive footnotes must not be used to circumvent page limitations. NY R USDCTND L.R. 10.1(a)(5).

        • Compacted or other compressed printing features must not be used. NY R USDCTND L.R. 10.1(a)(6).

b. *Additional requirements for paper filing.* Additional requirements for all pleadings, motions, and other documents that a party presents for filing in paper form:

    i. *Paper size.* All documents must be on eight and one-half by eleven (8-1/2 x 11) inch white paper of good quality. NY R USDCTND L.R. 10.1(b)(1).

    ii. *Text.* All text must be plainly and legibly written, typewritten, printed or reproduced without erasures or interlineations materially defacing them. NY R USDCTND L.R. 10.1(b)(2).

    iii. *Ink.* All documents must be in black or blue ink. NY R USDCTND L.R. 10.1(b)(3).

    iv. *Binding.* Pages of all documents must be stapled (or in some other way fastened) together. NY R USDCTND L.R. 10.1(b)(4).

    v. *Single-sided paper.* All documents must be single-sided. NY R USDCTND L.R. 10.1(b)(5).

    vi. *Electronic submission.* The Court, at its discretion, may require the electronic submission of any document in a WordPerfect-compatible format. NY R USDCTND L.R. 10.1(b)(6).

    vii. *Rejection of document.* The Court may reject documents that do not comply with the above-listed requirements. NY R USDCTND L.R. 10.1(b).

c. *Caption; Names of parties.* Every pleading must have a caption with the court's name, a title, a file number, and a FRCP 7(a) designation. The title of the complaint must name all the parties; the title of other pleadings, after naming the first party on each side, may refer generally to other parties. FRCP 10(a). Each document must contain a caption for the specific case to which it pertains. The caption must include the title of the Court, the title of the action, the civil action number of the case, the initials of the assigned judge(s), and the name or nature of the paper in sufficient detail for identification. If a litigant has more than one action pending in this Court, any and all papers filed in a case must contain and pertain to one civil action number, unless the civil actions have been consolidated by the Court. Any motion or other papers purporting to relate to more than one action will not be accepted for filing and may be stricken by the Court. NY R USDCTND L.R. 10.1(c)(1) shall not apply, as noted in NY R USDCTND L.R. 10.1(c), to notices of change of address filed by attorneys of record and pro se litigants. The parties must separately caption affidavits and declarations and must not physically attach them to the Notice of Motion or Memorandum of Law. NY R USDCTND L.R. 10.1(c)(1).

d. *Paragraphs; Separate statements.* A party must state its claims or defenses in numbered paragraphs, each limited as far as practicable to a single set of circumstances. A later pleading may refer by

number to a paragraph in an earlier pleading. If doing so would promote clarity, each claim founded on a separate transaction or occurrence—and each defense other than a denial—must be stated in a separate count or defense. FRCP 10(b).

e. *Adoption by reference; Exhibits.* A statement in a pleading may be adopted by reference elsewhere in the same pleading or in any other pleading or motion. A copy of a written instrument that is an exhibit to a pleading is a part of the pleading for all purposes. FRCP 10(c).

f. *Citation of local rules.* These are the Local Rules of Practice for the United States District Court for the Northern District of New York. They shall be cited as "L.R. ___." NY R USDCTND L.R. 1.1(a).

g. *Acceptance by the clerk.* The clerk must not refuse to file a paper solely because it is not in the form prescribed by the Federal Rules of Civil Procedure or by a local rule or practice. FRCP 5(d)(4).

2. *Form of electronic documents.* All pleadings, motions, and other documents that a party presents for filing, whether in paper form or in electronic form, shall meet the requirements in NY R USDCTND L.R. 10.1(a). NY R USDCTND L.R. 10.1(a). Refer above for more information.

a. *Attachments and exhibits.* A Filing User must submit in electronic form all documents referenced as exhibits or attachments in accordance with the Court's CM/ECF Users Manual unless the Court otherwise orders. A Filing User shall submit as exhibits or attachments only those excerpts of the referenced documents that are directly germane to the matter under the Court's consideration. Excerpted material must be clearly and prominently identified as such. Filing Users who file excerpts of documents as exhibits or attachments under these Administrative Procedures (NY R USDCTND CM/ECF) do so without prejudice to their right to timely file additional excerpts or the complete document. Responding parties may also timely file the complete document or additional excerpts that they believe are directly germane to the matter under the Court's consideration. NY R USDCTND CM/ECF(4)(4.4).

   i. All attachments must be described in sufficient detail so the Court and opposing counsel can easily identify and distinguish the filed attachments. Vague or general descriptions are insufficient (i.e., "Exhibit 1"). Rather, each attachment shall have a descriptive title identifying, with specificity, the document that is being filed (i.e., "Exhibit 12 Mulligan County Fire Investigation Report.") Failure to adequately describe attachments may result in the document being rejected by the Court. NY R USDCTND CM/ECF(4)(4.4).

b. *Large documents.* For information on the electronic filing of large documents, please consult the Court's CM/ECF Users Manual, which is available on the Court's web page. NY R USDCTND CM/ECF(4)(4.5).

   i. A party who believes a document is too lengthy to electronically image, i.e., "scan," may contact the Clerk's Office for permission to file that document conventionally. If the Clerk's Office grants permission to conventionally file the document, the Filing User shall electronically file a notice of conventional filing for the documents. More information regarding this process can be obtained from the Court's web page. Exhibits submitted conventionally shall be served on other parties as if they were not subject to these Administrative Procedures (NY R USDCTND CM/ECF). For a list of hints and tips for scanning large documents, please consult the Court's web page. NY R USDCTND CM/ECF(4)(4.5).

c. *Legibility.* It shall be the Filing User's responsibility to verify the legibility of scanned documents before filing them electronically with the Court. NY R USDCTND CM/ECF(4)(4.6).

d. *Color documents.* Since documents scanned in color or containing a graphic take much longer to upload, Filing Users are encouraged to configure their scanners to scan documents at 300 dpi and preferably in black and white rather than in color. NY R USDCTND CM/ECF(4)(4.7).

e. *Items not in .PDF format.* Parties wishing to file items not amenable to .pdf format (i.e. CD's, DVD's), shall file such items conventionally with the Clerk's Office. The Filing User shall electronically file a notice of conventional filing indicating that these items have been submitted to the clerk and shall serve copies of these items on other parties as if they were not subject to these Administrative Procedures (NY R USDCTND CM/ECF). These item(s) will be maintained by the Clerk's Office until the case is disposed, at which time they will be returned to the filing party for retention consistent with NY R USDCTND CM/ECF(4)(4.9). NY R USDCTND CM/ECF(4)(4.8).

3. *Form of memoranda of law*

   a. *Length limitation.* No party shall file or serve a memorandum of law that exceeds twenty-five (25) pages in length, unless that party obtains leave of the judge hearing the motion prior to filing. NY R USDCTND L.R. 7.1(a)(1).

   b. *Table of contents.* All memoranda of law shall contain a table of contents. NY R USDCTND L.R. 7.1(a)(1).

4. *Signing disclosures and discovery requests, responses, and objections.* FRCP 11 does not apply to disclosures and discovery requests, responses, objections, and motions under FRCP 26 through FRCP 37. FRCP 11(d).

   a. *Signature required.* Every disclosure under FRCP 26(a)(1) or FRCP 26(a)(3) and every discovery request, response, or objection must be signed by at least one attorney of record in the attorney's own name—or by the party personally, if unrepresented—and must state the signer's address, e-mail address, and telephone number. FRCP 26(g)(1). Each document must identify the person filing the document. This identification must include an original signature of the attorney or pro se litigant; the typewritten name of that person; the address of a pro se litigant; and the bar roll number, office address, telephone number, e-mail address and fax number of the attorney. Telephone numbers of non-prisoner pro se parties may be provided voluntarily or upon request of the Court. See General Order #22 (NY R USDCTND CM/ECF) for signature requirements. NY R USDCTND L.R. 10.1(c)(2).

      i. *Electronic signatures.* Documents filed under an attorney's login and password shall constitute that attorney's signature for purposes of the Local Rules of Practice for the United States District Court for the Northern District of New York and Federal Rules of Civil Procedure, including but not limited to FRCP 11. A pleading or other document requiring an attorney's signature shall be signed in the following manner, whether filed electronically or submitted on disk or CD/ROM to the Clerk's Office: "s/ (attorney name)." The correct format for an attorney signature is found in NY R USDCTND CM/ECF(6)(6.1). NY R USDCTND CM/ECF(6)(6.1).

         • *Non-attorney signature.* If an original document requires the signature of a non-attorney, the Filing User may scan the original document containing the original signature(s), then electronically file it on the System. Alternatively, the Filing User may convert the document into .pdf text format and submit the document using "s/" for the signature of the non-attorney. NY R USDCTND CM/ECF(6)(6.2).

         • *Multiple signatures.* A document requiring signatures of more than one party must be filed electronically either by (1) submitting a scanned document containing all necessary signatures; (2) representing the consent of the other parties on the document; or (3) in any other manner that the Court approves. NY R USDCTND CM/ECF(6)(6.3).

   b. *Effect of signature.* By signing, an attorney or party certifies that to the best of the person's knowledge, information, and belief formed after a reasonable inquiry:

      i. With respect to a disclosure, it is complete and correct as of the time it is made; and

      ii. With respect to a discovery request, response, or objection, it is:

         • Consistent with the Federal Rules of Civil Procedure and warranted by existing law or by a nonfrivolous argument for extending, modifying, or reversing existing law, or for establishing new law;

         • Not interposed for any improper purpose, such as to harass, cause unnecessary delay, or needlessly increase the cost of litigation; and

         • Neither unreasonable nor unduly burdensome or expensive, considering the needs of the case, prior discovery in the case, the amount in controversy, and the importance of the issues at stake in the action. FRCP 26(g)(1).

   c. *Failure to sign.* Other parties have no duty to act on an unsigned disclosure, request, response, or objection until it is signed, and the court must strike it unless a signature is promptly supplied after the omission is called to the attorney's or party's attention. FRCP 26(g)(2).

d.  *Sanction for improper certification.* Refer to the General Requirements section of this document for information on the sanction for improper certification.

5.  *Privacy protection for filings made with the court*

a.  *Redacted filings.* Unless the court orders otherwise, in an electronic or paper filing with the court that contains an individual's Social Security number, taxpayer-identification number, or birth date, the name of an individual known to be a minor, or a financial-account number, a party or nonparty making the filing may include only:

i.  The last four (4) digits of the Social Security number and taxpayer-identification number;

ii.  The year of the individual's birth;

iii.  The minor's initials; and

iv.  The last four (4) digits of the financial-account number. FRCP 5.2(a); NY R USDCTND L.R. 8.1; NY R USDCTND CM/ECF(11)(11.2).

v.  If a home address must be used, use only the City and State. NY R USDCTND L.R. 8.1; NY R USDCTND CM/ECF(11)(11.2).

vi.  If the victim of a sexual assault must be referenced, redact the name to 'Victim.' NY R USDCTND CM/ECF(11)(11.2); NY R USDCTND L.R. 8.1.

vii.  In addition, caution shall be exercised when filing documents that contain the following:

- Personal identifying number, such as a driver's license number;
- Medical records, treatment and diagnosis;
- Employment history;
- Individual financial information; and
- Proprietary or trade secret information. NY R USDCTND L.R. 8.1; NY R USDCTND CM/ECF(11)(11.2).

b.  *Exemptions from the redaction requirement.* The redaction requirement does not apply to the following:

i.  A financial-account number that identifies the property allegedly subject to forfeiture in a forfeiture proceeding;

ii.  The record of an administrative or agency proceeding;

iii.  The official record of a state-court proceeding;

iv.  The record of a court or tribunal, if that record was not subject to the redaction requirement when originally filed;

v.  A filing covered by FRCP 5.2(c) or FRCP 5.2(d); and

vi.  A pro se filing in an action brought under 28 U.S.C.A. § 2241, 28 U.S.C.A. § 2254, or 28 U.S.C.A. § 2255. FRCP 5.2(b).

vii.  Transcripts of the administrative record in social security proceedings are exempt from this requirement. State court records and other documents filed in habeas corpus proceedings are exempt from this requirement except for proceedings that involve victims of sex crimes. In habeas corpus cases involving sex crimes, the parties must redact the record and supporting papers, or may move to seal, if appropriate. NY R USDCTND L.R. 8.1.

c.  *Limitations on remote access to electronic files; Social Security appeals and immigration cases.* Unless the court orders otherwise, in an action for benefits under the Social Security Act, and in an action or proceeding relating to an order of removal, to relief from removal, or to immigration benefits or detention, access to an electronic file is authorized as follows:

i.  The parties and their attorneys may have remote electronic access to any part of the case file, including the administrative record;

      ii.   Any other person may have electronic access to the full record at the courthouse, but may have remote electronic access only to:

- The docket maintained by the court; and

- An opinion, order, judgment, or other disposition of the court, but not any other part of the case file or the administrative record. FRCP 5.2(c).

   d.  *Filings made under seal.* The court may order that a filing be made under seal without redaction. The court may later unseal the filing or order the person who made the filing to file a redacted version for the public record. FRCP 5.2(d); NY R USDCTND L.R. 8.1. For information on sealed matters, refer to NY R USDCTND L.R. 83.13 and NY R USDCTND CM/ECF(12).

   e.  *Protective orders.* For good cause, the court may by order in a case:

      i.   Require redaction of additional information; or

      ii.   Limit or prohibit a nonparty's remote electronic access to a document filed with the court. FRCP 5.2(e).

   f.  *Option for additional unredacted filing under seal.* A person making a redacted filing may also file an unredacted copy under seal. The court must retain the unredacted copy as part of the record. FRCP 5.2(f); NY R USDCTND L.R. 8.1; NY R USDCTND CM/ECF(11)(11.3).

   g.  *Option for filing a reference list.* A filing that contains redacted information may be filed together with a reference list that identifies each item of redacted information and specifies an appropriate identifier that uniquely corresponds to each item listed. The list must be filed under seal and may be amended as of right. Any reference in the case to a listed identifier will be construed to refer to the corresponding item of information. FRCP 5.2(g); NY R USDCTND L.R. 8.1; NY R USDCTND CM/ECF(11)(11.3).

   h.  *Responsibility for redaction.* Counsel is strongly urged to discuss this issue with all their clients so that they can make an informed decision about the inclusion of certain information. The responsibility for redacting these personal identifiers rests solely with counsel and the parties. The Clerk will not review each filing for compliance with NY R USDCTND L.R. 8.1. Counsel and the parties are cautioned that failure to redact these personal identifiers may subject them to the Court's full disciplinary power. NY R USDCTND L.R. 8.1; NY R USDCTND CM/ECF(11)(11.3).

   i.  *Waiver of protection of identifiers.* A person waives the protection of FRCP 5.2(a) as to the person's own information by filing it without redaction and not under seal. FRCP 5.2(h).

6.  *Individual judge practices.* Refer to the Miscellaneous section of this document for information on individual judge practices on formatting documents.

## F.  Filing and Service Requirements

1.  *Filing requirements.* Any paper after the complaint that is required to be served—together with a certificate of service—must be filed within a reasonable time after service. FRCP 5(d)(1).

   a.  *How filing is made; In general.* A paper is filed by delivering it:

      i.   To the clerk; or

      ii.   To a judge who agrees to accept it for filing, and who must then note the filing date on the paper and promptly send it to the clerk. FRCP 5(d)(2).

   b.  *Electronic filing*

      i.   *Authorization of electronic filing program.* A court may, by local rule, allow papers to be filed, signed, or verified by electronic means that are consistent with any technical standards established by the Judicial Conference of the United States. A local rule may require electronic filing only if reasonable exceptions are allowed. A paper filed electronically in compliance with a local rule is a written paper for purposes of the Federal Rules of Civil Procedure. FRCP 5(d)(3).

- All cases filed in this Court may be assigned to the Electronic Case Files System ("ECF") in accordance with the Procedural Order on Electronic Case Filing (General Order #22

(NY R USDCTND CM/ECF)), the provisions of which are incorporated herein by reference, and which the Court may amend from time to time. Copies of General Order #22 (NY R USDCTND CM/ECF) are available at the Clerk's office or at the Court's webpage. NY R USDCTND L.R. 5.1.1; NY R USDCTND Order 25(XII).

- The Court may deviate from these Administrative Procedures (NY R USDCTND CM/ECF) in specific cases, without prior notice, if deemed appropriate in the exercise of discretion, considering the need for the just, speedy, and inexpensive determination of matters pending before the Court. NY R USDCTND CM/ECF(2).

ii. *Scope of electronic filing.* After January 1, 2004, all documents that attorneys admitted to practice in the Northern District of New York submit for filing shall be filed electronically using the System or shall be scanned and uploaded to the System, no matter when a case was originally filed, unless these Administrative Procedures (NY R USDCTND CM/ECF) otherwise permit or unless the assigned judge otherwise authorizes. An attorney who is not a Filing User by January 1, 2004, must show good cause to the assigned judge to file and serve pleadings and other papers in the traditional manner. NY R USDCTND CM/ECF(2).

iii. *Exceptions and/or waivers from mandatory electronic filing.* The following types of cases and/or documents are not required to be filed electronically:

- If you are seeking to have your complaint filed under seal, please file your complaint and proposed sealing order traditionally at the Clerk's Office. NY R USDCTND CM/ECF(2)(2.1)(1).

- Any document that a party proceeding pro se files. (See NY R USDCTND CM/ECF(12)(12.1) for procedural details). NY R USDCTND CM/ECF(2)(2.1)(2). A non-prisoner who is a party to a civil action and who is not represented by an attorney may file a motion to obtain an Electronic Case Filing (ECF) login and password on a form prescribed by the Clerk's Office. The Pro Se CM/ECF Registration Form shall be submitted with the motion. If during the course of the action an attorney appears on behalf of the pro se party, the Clerk's Office shall terminate the pro se party's registration based upon the attorney's appearance. NY R USDCTND CM/ECF(12)(12.1). Absent permission to file electronically, pro se filers shall file paper originals of all complaints, pleadings, motions, affidavits, briefs, and other documents which must be signed or which require either verification or an unsworn declaration under any rule or statute. The Clerk's Office will scan these original documents into an electronic file in the System but will also maintain a paper file. NY R USDCTND CM/ECF(12)(12.1). A pro se party may also seek permission to receive immediate notice of all public documents filed in their cases. Notices of Electronic Filing (NEF) and attached documents would be transmitted to a non-prisoner pro se party who selects this option. Note: The pro se party would continue to file their documents with the Clerk's Office in paper form. NY R USDCTND CM/ECF(12)(12.1).

- Sealed documents, sealed cases, documents for in camera review, documents lodged with the Court, ex parte documents, confidential agreements, Qui Tam actions and Grand Jury material and warrants must be filed traditionally. (See NY R USDCTND CM/ECF(12)(12.2) for further information the filing of the above-referenced documents). NY R USDCTND CM/ECF(2)(2.1)(3).

- Discovery: In accordance with NY R USDCTND L.R. 26.2, parties shall not file discovery, provided, however, that discovery material to be used at trial or in support of any motion, including a motion to compel or for summary judgment, shall be filed electronically with the Court prior to the trial or with the motion. Any motion pursuant to FRCP 37 shall be accompanied by the electronically filed discovery materials to which the motion relates if those materials have not previously been filed with the Court. NY R USDCTND CM/ECF(2)(2.1)(4).

- Transport Orders: All orders requesting that an incarcerated individual be transported that a judicial officer of the Northern District of New York signs shall be filed traditionally.

These Orders will not be filed with the case or uploaded to the docket but rather will be processed in accordance with the procedures that the Clerk of Court promulgates. NY R USDCTND CM/ECF(2)(2.1)(5).

iv. *Filing defined.* Electronic transmission of a document to the System in accordance with these Administrative Procedures, together with the transmission of a Notice of Electronic Filing from the Court, constitutes filing of the document for all purposes of the Federal Rules of Civil Procedure and the Local Rules of Practice for the United States District Court for the Northern District of New York and constitutes entry of the document on the docket that the Clerk's Office keeps under FRCP 58 and FRCP 79. E-mailing a document to the Clerk's Office or to the assigned judge shall not constitute "filing" of the document. NY R USDCTND CM/ECF(4)(4.1).

v. *Filing fees.* Any fee required for filing a pleading or paper in this Court is payable to the Clerk of the Court. The Court will not maintain electronic billing or debit accounts for attorneys or law firms. Effective January 1, 2007, payment for filing fees will be mandatory through CM/ECF's Internet Credit Card Payment site--a secure Treasury Site. The Filing User will be prompted to enter either Bank Account Debit (ACH) or credit card information while filing the initial pleading. Any document that requires a filing fee (e.g., Notice of Appeal, Motion for Pro Hac Vice Admission) may also be paid through the federal electronic payment website. NY R USDCTND CM/ECF(7).

vi. For more information on electronic filing, refer to NY R USDCTND CM/ECF.

c. *E-mail or facsimile filing.* Neither the Court nor the Clerk's Office will accept for filing any facsimile or e-mail transmission without prior authorization from the Court. The party using facsimile or e-mail transmissions to file its papers must accompany any such documents with a cover letter stating that the Court authorized such transmissions and the date on which the Court provided that authorization. Violations of NY R USDCTND L.R. 5.5 subject the offending party to the Court's full disciplinary powers. NY R USDCTND L.R. 5.5.

2. *Service requirements*

a. *Service; When required*

i. *In general.* Unless the Federal Rules of Civil Procedure provide otherwise, each of the following papers must be served on every party:

- An order stating that service is required;
- A pleading filed after the original complaint, unless the court orders otherwise under FRCP 5(c) because there are numerous defendants;
- A discovery paper required to be served on a party, unless the court orders otherwise;
- A written motion, except one that may be heard ex parte; and
- A written notice, appearance, demand, or offer of judgment, or any similar paper. FRCP 5(a)(1).

ii. *If a party fails to appear.* No service is required on a party who is in default for failing to appear. But a pleading that asserts a new claim for relief against such a party must be served on that party under FRCP 4. FRCP 5(a)(2).

iii. *Seizing property.* If an action is begun by seizing property and no person is or need be named as a defendant, any service required before the filing of an appearance, answer, or claim must be made on the person who had custody or possession of the property when it was seized. FRCP 5(a)(3).

b. *Service; How made*

i. *Serving an attorney.* If a party is represented by an attorney, service under FRCP 5 must be made on the attorney unless the court orders service on the party. FRCP 5(b)(1).

ii. *Service in general.* A paper is served under FRCP 5 by:

- Handing it to the person;

- Leaving it: (1) at the person's office with a clerk or other person in charge or, if no one is in charge, in a conspicuous place in the office; or (2) if the person has no office or the office is closed, at the person's dwelling or usual place of abode with someone of suitable age and discretion who resides there;

- Mailing it to the person's last known address—in which event service is complete upon mailing;

- Leaving it with the court clerk if the person has no known address;

- Sending it by electronic means if the person consented in writing—in which event service is complete upon transmission, but is not effective if the serving party learns that it did not reach the person to be served; or

- Delivering it by any other means that the person consented to in writing—in which event service is complete when the person making service delivers it to the agency designated to make delivery. FRCP 5(b)(2).

   iii. *Service of electronically-filed documents.* Service is complete provided all parties receive a Notice of Electronic Filing (NEF), which is sent automatically by email from the Court (see the NEF for a list of who did/did not receive notice electronically). Transmission of the NEF constitutes service upon all Filing and Receiving Users who are listed as recipients of notice by electronic mail. It remains the responsibility of Filing and Receiving Users to maintain current contact information with the court and to regularly review the docket sheet of the case. NY R USDCTND CM/ECF(5)(5.2).

- *Non-filing or receiving users.* Attorneys and pro se parties who are not Filing or Receiving Users must be served with a paper copy of any electronically filed pleading or other document. Service of such paper copy must be made according to the Federal Rules of Civil Procedure and the Local Rules of Practice for the United States District Court for the Northern District of New York. Such paper service must be documented by electronically filing a certificate of service. NY R USDCTND CM/ECF(5)(5.2). A party who is not a Filing User of the System is entitled to a paper copy of any electronically-filed pleading, document, or order. The Filing User must therefore provide the non-Filing User with the pleading or document according to the Federal Rules of Civil Procedure. NY R US-DCTND CM/ECF(5)(5.3).

   iv. *Using court facilities.* If a local rule so authorizes, a party may use the court's transmission facilities to make service under FRCP 5(b)(2)(E). FRCP 5(b)(3).

  c. *Serving numerous defendants*

   i. *In general.* If an action involves an unusually large number of defendants, the court may, on motion or on its own, order that:

- Defendants' pleadings and replies to them need not be served on other defendants;

- Any crossclaim, counterclaim, avoidance, or affirmative defense in those pleadings and replies to them will be treated as denied or avoided by all other parties; and

- Filing any such pleading and serving it on the plaintiff constitutes notice of the pleading to all parties. FRCP 5(c)(1).

   ii. *Notifying parties.* A copy of every such order must be served on the parties as the court directs. FRCP 5(c)(2).

3. *Service in contempt proceedings.* Where the alleged contemnor has appeared in the action by an attorney, the notice of motion or order to show cause and the papers on which it is based shall be served on the contemnor's attorney; otherwise service shall be made personally in the manner provided by the Federal Rules of Civil Procedure for the service of summons. NY R USDCTND L.R. 83.5(a). Refer to the United States District Court for the Northern District of New York Complaint document for information on service in accordance with FRCP 4.

4. *Individual judge practices.* Refer to the Miscellaneous section of this document for information on individual judge practices on filing and serving documents.

## G. Hearings

1. *Hearings, generally*

   a. *Motion days.* Listings of the regularly scheduled motion days for all judges shall be available at each Clerk's office and are available on the Court's webpage. The Clerk shall provide notice of the regular motion days for all judges to the parties at the time an action is commenced. NY R USDCTND L.R. 78.1.

   b. *Return date.* Unless the Court directs otherwise, the moving party shall make its motion returnable at the next regularly scheduled motion date at least thirty-one (31) days from the date the moving party files and serves its motion. The moving party shall select a return date in accordance with the procedures set forth in NY R USDCTND L.R. 7.1(b). If the return date the moving party selects is not the next regularly scheduled motion date, or if the moving party selects no return date, the Clerk will set the proper return date and notify the parties. NY R USDCTND L.R. 7.1.

      i. Information regarding motion dates and times is specified on the case assignment form that the Court provides to the parties at the commencement of the litigation or the parties may obtain this form from the Clerk's office or at the Court's webpage. NY R USDCTND L.R. 7.1.

      ii. The Court hereby directs the Clerk to set a proper return date in motions that pro se litigants submit for filing that do not specify a return date or fail to allow for sufficient time pursuant to NY R USDCTND L.R. 7.1. Generally, the return date that the Clerk selects should not exceed thirty (30) days from the date of filing. Furthermore, the Clerk shall forward a copy of the revised or corrected notice of motion to the parties. NY R USDCTND L.R. 7.1.

   c. *Oral argument.* Due process does not require that oral argument be permitted on a motion and, except as otherwise provided by local rule, the district court has discretion to determine whether it will decide the motion on the papers or hear argument by counsel (and perhaps receive evidence). FPP § 1190; F.D.I.C. v. Deglau, 207 F.3d 153 (3d Cir. 2000).

      i. The parties shall appear for oral argument on all motions that they make returnable before a district court judge, except motions for reconsideration, on the scheduled return date of the motion. A motion may be disposed of without oral argument as described in NY R USDCTND Order 25, on consideration of a request of any party, or otherwise at the discretion of the presiding judge. Thus, the parties should be prepared to have their motion papers serve as the sole method of argument on the motion. NY R USDCTND L.R. 7.1(h).

      ii. The parties shall not appear for oral argument on motions that they make returnable before a Magistrate Judge on the scheduled return date of the motion unless the Magistrate Judge sua sponte directs or grants the request of any party for oral argument. NY R USDCTND L.R. 7.1(h).

   d. *Providing a regular schedule for oral hearings.* A court may establish regular times and places for oral hearings on motions. FRCP 78(a).

   e. *Providing for submission on briefs.* By rule or order, the court may provide for submitting and determining motions on briefs, without oral hearings. FRCP 78(b).

2. *Contempt proceedings.* If the alleged contemnor puts in issue the alleged misconduct or the resulting damages, the alleged contemnor shall, on demand, be entitled to have oral evidence taken either before the Court or before a master whom the Court appoints. When by law the alleged contemnor is entitled to a trial by jury, the contemnor shall make a written demand on or before the return day or adjourned day of the application; otherwise the Court will deem that the alleged contemnor has waived a trial by jury. NY R USDCTND L.R. 83.5(b).

3. *Individual judge practices.* Refer to the Miscellaneous section of this document for information on individual judge practices on hearings.

## H. Forms

1. **Federal Motion for Discovery Sanctions Forms**

   a. Motion for contempt. 3B FEDFORMS § 3721.

   b. Motion for sanctions for failure to appear at deposition. 3B FEDFORMS § 3722.

c. Motion that facts be taken as established for failure to answer questions upon deposition. 3B FEDFORMS § 3723.

d. Motion for order refusing to allow disobedient party to support or oppose designated claims or defenses. 3B FEDFORMS § 3724.

e. Motion for default judgment against defendant for failure to comply with order for production of documents. 3B FEDFORMS § 3725.

f. Motion for award of expenses incurred to prove matter opponent failed to admit under FRCP 36. 3B FEDFORMS § 3726.

g. Motion to strike answer or dismiss action for failure to comply with order requiring answer to interrogatories. 3B FEDFORMS § 3729.

h. Motion to dismiss for failure to comply with previous order requiring answer to interrogatories to party. 3B FEDFORMS § 3732.

i. Motion; For order that facts be taken to be established, and/or prohibiting certain claims, defenses, or evidence in opposition thereto. FEDPROF § 23:595.

j. Affidavit; By attorney; In support of motion for order that facts be taken to be established, etc; Failure to produce documents for inspection. FEDPROF § 23:596.

k. Affidavit; By attorney; In support of motion for order that facts be taken to be established, etc; Failure to obey order to answer questions. FEDPROF § 23:597.

l. Motion; For order striking pleadings, and for default judgment or dismissal of action. FEDPROF § 23:599.

m. Affidavit; By attorney; In support of motion for default judgment for defendant's failure to obey discovery order. FEDPROF § 23:600.

n. Motion; By defendant; For dismissal of action and other sanctions; For failure to comply with orders to complete deposition. FEDPROF § 23:601.

o. Motion; By defendant; For dismissal of action or other sanctions; For failure and refusal to comply with order to produce documents. FEDPROF § 23:602.

p. Motion; By defendant; For dismissal with prejudice; Failure to answer interrogatories as ordered. FEDPROF § 23:603.

q. Motion; For order staying further proceedings until adverse party obeys order compelling discovery. FEDPROF § 23:604.

r. Affidavit; By attorney; Opposing motion for order striking pleading and directing entry of default judgment; Good-faith attempt to obey discovery order; Production of documents illegal under foreign law. FEDPROF § 23:605.

s. Motion; For sanctions for failure to comply with examination order. FEDPROF § 23:610.

t. Motion; For order finding person in contempt of court; Refusal, after order, to answer question. FEDPROF § 23:612.

u. Affidavit; By attorney; In support of motion for order finding party in contempt. FEDPROF § 23:613.

v. Affidavit; By plaintiff; In support of motion for order holding defendant in contempt of court; Defendant disobeyed order for production of documents. FEDPROF § 23:614.

w. Motion; For order compelling opposing party to pay expenses incurred in proving facts such party refused to admit. FEDPROF § 23:616.

x. Motion; For sanctions; Failure to attend own deposition, serve answers to interrogatories, or respond to request for inspection. FEDPROF § 23:618.

y. Motion; For order staying proceedings until required response to discovery request is made. FEDPROF § 23:619.

z. Affidavit; By attorney; In support of motion for sanctions; Failure to attend own deposition, serve answers to interrogatories, or respond to request for inspection. FEDPROF § 23:620.

## I. Applicable Rules

1. *Federal rules*

   a. Counsel's liability for excessive costs. 28 U.S.C.A. § 1927.

   b. Serving and filing pleadings and other papers. FRCP 5.

   c. Constitutional challenge to a statute; Notice, certification, and intervention. FRCP 5.1.

   d. Privacy protection for filings made with the court. FRCP 5.2.

   e. Computing and extending time; Time for motion papers. FRCP 6.

   f. Pleadings allowed; Form of motions and other papers. FRCP 7.

   g. Form of pleadings. FRCP 10.

   h. Signing pleadings, motions, and other papers; Representations to the court; Sanctions. FRCP 11.

   i. Duty to disclose; General provisions governing discovery. FRCP 26.

   j. Failure to make disclosures or to cooperate in discovery; Sanctions. FRCP 37.

   k. Taking testimony. FRCP 43.

   l. Hearing motions; Submission on briefs. FRCP 78.

2. *Local rules*

   a. Scope of the rules. NY R USDCTND L.R. 1.1.

   b. Complex and multi-district litigation. NY R USDCTND L.R. 3.3.

   c. Service and filing of papers. NY R USDCTND L.R. 5.1.

   d. Filing by facsimile or e-mail. NY R USDCTND L.R. 5.5.

   e. Motion practice. NY R USDCTND L.R. 7.1.

   f. Personal privacy protection. NY R USDCTND L.R. 8.1.

   g. Request for three-judge court. NY R USDCTND L.R. 9.1.

   h. Form of papers. NY R USDCTND L.R. 10.1.

   i. Filing discovery. NY R USDCTND L.R. 26.2.

   j. Production of expert witness information. NY R USDCTND L.R. 26.3.

   k. Settlement procedures. NY R USDCTND L.R. 68.2.

   l. Orders. NY R USDCTND L.R. 77.2.

   m. Motion days. NY R USDCTND L.R. 78.1.

   n. Appearance and withdrawal of attorney. NY R USDCTND L.R. 83.2.

   o. Contempt. NY R USDCTND L.R. 83.5.

   p. Arbitration. NY R USDCTND L.R. 83.7-1; NY R USDCTND L.R. 83.7-2; NY R USDCTND L.R. 83.7-3.

   q. Assisted mediation program. NY R USDCTND L.R. 83.8.

   r. Mediation. NY R USDCTND L.R. 83.11-1; NY R USDCTND L.R. 83.11-3.

   s. Early neutral evaluation. NY R USDCTND L.R. 83.12-1; NY R USDCTND L.R. 83.12-3.

   t. Administrative procedures for electronic case filing. NY R USDCTND CM/ECF.

   u. Case assignment plan for the Northern District of New York. [NY R USDCTND Order 12, as amended by NY ORDER 16-4201, effective March 24, 2015].

   v. Directing the expedited service of the summons and complaint and further directing the completion of FRCP 16 stipulation for the timely progression of civil actions. [NY R USDCTND Order 25, as amended by NY ORDER 16-4187, effective June 23, 2016].

   w. Mandatory mediation program. NY R USDCTND Order 47.

**J. Miscellaneous**

**NOTE: Individual judges' rules may apply. For available judge-level information, refer to:**

DISTRICT JUDGE MAE A. D'AGOSTINO: [NY R USDCTND D'Agostino-Rules and Practices, as added by NY ORDER 16-4200, effective April 4, 2016].

DISTRICT JUDGE THOMAS J. McAVOY: NY R USDCTND McAvoy-Order.

## Motions, Oppositions and Replies
## Motion for Preliminary Injunction

### Document Last Updated September 2016

**A. Checklist**

(I) ❏ Matters to be considered by moving party

    (a) ❏ Required documents

        (1) ❏ Notice of motion and motion

        (2) ❏ Memorandum of law

        (3) ❏ Supporting affidavit

        (4) ❏ Security

        (5) ❏ Certificate of service

    (b) ❏ Supplemental documents

        (1) ❏ Supporting evidence

        (2) ❏ Pleadings

        (3) ❏ Notice of constitutional question

        (4) ❏ Nongovernmental corporate disclosure statement

        (5) ❏ Copies of authorities

        (6) ❏ Proposed order

        (7) ❏ Cover letter authorizing e-mail or facsimile filing

        (8) ❏ Affidavit attesting to failed attempts to file electronically

        (9) ❏ Notice of conventional filing

        (10) ❏ CD/ROM with PDF of document(s)

        (11) ❏ English translation

        (12) ❏ Courtesy copies

        (13) ❏ Copies for three-judge court

    (c) ❏ Timing

        (1) ❏ Unless the court orders otherwise, the moving party must file all motion papers with the court and serve them upon the other parties not less than thirty-one (31) days prior to the return date of the motion

        (2) ❏ A written motion and notice of the hearing must be served at least fourteen (14) days before the time specified for the hearing, with the following exceptions: (i) when the motion may be heard ex parte; (ii) when the Federal Rules of Civil Procedure set a different time; or (iii) when a court order—which a party may, for good cause, apply for ex parte—sets a different time

        (3) ❏ Any affidavit supporting a motion must be served with the motion

(II) ❑ Matters to be considered by opposing party

    (a) ❑ Required documents

        (1) ❑ Opposition

        (2) ❑ Memorandum of law

        (3) ❑ Supporting affidavit

        (4) ❑ Certificate of service

    (b) ❑ Supplemental documents

        (1) ❑ Supporting evidence

        (2) ❑ Pleadings

        (3) ❑ Notice of constitutional question

        (4) ❑ Nongovernmental corporate disclosure statement

        (5) ❑ Cross-motion

        (6) ❑ Copies of authorities

        (7) ❑ Cover letter authorizing e-mail or facsimile filing

        (8) ❑ Affidavit attesting to failed attempts to file electronically

        (9) ❑ Notice of conventional filing

        (10) ❑ CD/ROM with PDF of document(s)

        (11) ❑ English translation

        (12) ❑ Courtesy copies

        (13) ❑ Copies for three-judge court

    (c) ❑ Timing

        (1) ❑ The party opposing the motion must file its opposition papers with the court and serve them upon the other parties not less than seventeen (17) days prior to the return date of the motion

        (2) ❑ Except as FRCP 59(c) provides otherwise, any opposing affidavit must be served at least seven (7) days before the hearing, unless the court permits service at another time

        (3) ❑ A party may file and serve a cross-motion (meaning a competing request for relief or order similar to that requested by another party against the cross-moving party) at the time it files and serves its opposition papers to the original motion, i.e., not less than seventeen (17) days prior to the return date of the motion

## B. Timing

1. *Motion for preliminary injunction.* FRCP 65 is silent about when notice must be given. FPP § 2949.

2. *Timing of motions, generally.* Unless the Court orders otherwise, the moving party must file all motion papers with the Court and serve them upon the other parties not less than THIRTY-ONE (31) DAYS prior to the return date of the motion. NY R USDCTND L.R. 7.1(b)(2).

    a. *Motion and notice of hearing.* A written motion and notice of the hearing must be served at least fourteen (14) days before the time specified for the hearing, with the following exceptions:

        i. When the motion may be heard ex parte;

        ii. When the Federal Rules of Civil Procedure set a different time; or

        iii. When a court order—which a party may, for good cause, apply for ex parte—sets a different time. FRCP 6(c)(1).

    b. *Supporting affidavit.* Any affidavit supporting a motion must be served with the motion. FRCP 6(c)(2).

3. *Timing of opposing papers.* The party opposing the motion must file its Opposition papers with the Court

and serve them upon the other parties not less than SEVENTEEN (17) DAYS prior to the return date of the motion. NY R USDCTND L.R. 7.1(b)(2).

a. *Opposing affidavit.* Except as FRCP 59(c) provides otherwise, any opposing affidavit must be served at least seven (7) days before the hearing, unless the court permits service at another time. FRCP 6(c)(2).

b. *Cross-motion.* A party may file and serve a cross-motion (meaning a competing request for relief or order similar to that requested by another party against the cross-moving party) at the time it files and serves its opposition papers to the original motion, i.e., not less than SEVENTEEN (17) DAYS prior to the return date of the motion. NY R USDCTND L.R. 7.1(c).

4. *Timing of reply papers.* Where the respondent files an answering affidavit setting up a new matter, the moving party ordinarily is allowed a reasonable time to file a reply affidavit since failure to deny the new matter by affidavit may operate as an admission of its truth. AMJUR MOTIONS § 25.

a. *Reply papers.* Reply papers and adjournments are not permitted without the Court's prior permission. Permission to file a reply does not exist simply because CM/ECF generates a deadline for a reply on a nondispositive motion. NY R USDCTND L.R. 7.1(b)(2).

b. *Opposition to cross-motion.* The original moving party must file its reply/opposition papers with the Court and serve them on the other parties not less than ELEVEN (11) DAYS prior to the return date of the original motion. NY R USDCTND L.R. 7.1(c).

5. *Computation of time*

a. *Computing time.* FRCP 6 applies in computing any time period specified in the Federal Rules of Civil Procedure, in any local rule or court order, or in any statute that does not specify a method of computing time. FRCP 6(a).

   i. *Period stated in days or a longer unit.* When the period is stated in days or a longer unit of time:

- Exclude the day of the event that triggers the period;
- Count every day, including intermediate Saturdays, Sundays, and legal holidays; and
- Include the last day of the period, but if the last day is a Saturday, Sunday, or legal holiday, the period continues to run until the end of the next day that is not a Saturday, Sunday, or legal holiday. FRCP 6(a)(1).

   ii. *Period stated in hours.* When the period is stated in hours:

- Begin counting immediately on the occurrence of the event that triggers the period;
- Count every hour, including hours during intermediate Saturdays, Sundays, and legal holidays; and
- If the period would end on a Saturday, Sunday, or legal holiday, the period continues to run until the same time on the next day that is not a Saturday, Sunday, or legal holiday. FRCP 6(a)(2).

   iii. *Inaccessibility of the clerk's office.* Unless the court orders otherwise, if the clerk's office is inaccessible:

- On the last day for filing under FRCP 6(a)(1), then the time for filing is extended to the first accessible day that is not a Saturday, Sunday, or legal holiday; or
- During the last hour for filing under FRCP 6(a)(2), then the time for filing is extended to the same time on the first accessible day that is not a Saturday, Sunday, or legal holiday. FRCP 6(a)(3).

   iv. *"Last day" defined.* Unless a different time is set by a statute, local rule, or court order, the last day ends:

- For electronic filing, at midnight in the court's time zone; and
- For filing by other means, when the clerk's office is scheduled to close. FRCP 6(a)(4).

   v. *"Next day" defined.* The "next day" is determined by continuing to count forward when the period is measured after an event and backward when measured before an event. FRCP 6(a)(5).

vi. *"Legal holiday" defined.* "Legal holiday" means:

- The day set aside by statute for observing New Year's Day, Martin Luther King Jr.'s Birthday, Washington's Birthday, Memorial Day, Independence Day, Labor Day, Columbus Day, Veterans' Day, Thanksgiving Day, or Christmas Day;

- Any day declared a holiday by the President or Congress; and

- For periods that are measured after an event, any other day declared a holiday by the state where the district court is located. FRCP 6(a)(6).

b. *Computation of electronic filing deadlines.* A document will be deemed timely filed if electronically filed prior to midnight Eastern Time. However, if the time of day is of the essence, the assigned judge may order that the document be filed by a time certain. NY R USDCTND CM/ECF(4)(4.3).

    i. *Technical failures.* A Filing User, whose filing is untimely as the result of a technical failure of the Court's CM/ECF site, may seek appropriate relief from the Court. However, Filing Users are cautioned that, in some circumstances, the Court lacks the authority to grant an extension of time to file (e.g., FRCP 6(b) of the Federal Rules of Civil Procedure). NY R USDCTND CM/ECF(10)(10.1).

- *Technical failure of the filing user's system.* Problems with the Filing User's system, such as phone line problems, problems with the Filing User's Internet Service Provider ("ISP"), or hardware or software problems, will not constitute a technical failure under these Administrative Procedures nor excuse an untimely filing. A Filing User who cannot file documents electronically because of a problem on the Filing User's system must file the documents' conventionally along with an affidavit explaining the reason for not filing the documents electronically. NY R USDCTND CM/ECF(10)(10.2).

c. *Extending time*

    i. *In general.* When an act may or must be done within a specified time, the court may, for good cause, extend the time:

- With or without motion or notice if the court acts, or if a request is made, before the original time or its extension expires; or

- On motion made after the time has expired if the party failed to act because of excusable neglect. FRCP 6(b)(1).

    ii. *Exceptions.* A court must not extend the time to act under FRCP 50(b), FRCP 50(d), FRCP 52(b), FRCP 59(b), FRCP 59(d), FRCP 59(e), and FRCP 60(b). FRCP 6(b)(2).

    iii. Refer to the United States District Court for the Northern District of New York KeyRules Motion for Continuance/Extension of Time document for more information on extending time.

d. *Additional time after certain kinds of service.* When a party may or must act within a specified time after service and service is made under FRCP 5(b)(2)(C), FRCP 5(b)(2)(D), FRCP 5(b)(2)(E), or FRCP 5(b)(2)(F), three (3) days are added after the period would otherwise expire under FRCP 6(a). FRCP 6(d).

    i. In accordance with FRCP 6(e), service by electronic means is treated the same as service by mail for purposes of adding three (3) days to the prescribed period to respond. NY R USDCTND CM/ECF(5)(5.4). [Editor's note: the reference to FRCP 6(e) is likely meant to be a reference to FRCP 6(d)].

6. *Individual judge practices.* Refer to the Miscellaneous section of this document for information on individual judge practices on timing of documents.

## C. General Requirements

1. *Court conference for non-dispositive motions.* Prior to making any non-dispositive motion before the assigned Magistrate Judge, the parties must make good faith efforts among themselves to resolve or reduce all differences relating to the non-dispositive issue. If, after conferring, the parties are unable to arrive at a mutually satisfactory resolution, the party seeking relief must then request a court conference with the assigned Magistrate Judge. NY R USDCTND L.R. 7.1(b)(2). A court conference is a prerequisite

to filing a non-dispositive motion before the assigned Magistrate Judge. NY R USDCTND L.R. 7.1(b)(2). In addition, no non-dispositive or discovery motions should be presented to the Court unless authorized by the Magistrate Judge after communication with the Magistrate Judge's chambers. NY R USDCTND Order 25(IX)(A). Actions which involve an incarcerated, pro se party are not subject to the requirement that a court conference be held prior to filing a non-dispositive motion. NY R USDCTND L.R. 7.1(b)(2).

2. *Motions, generally*

   a. *Requirements.* A request for a court order must be made by motion. The motion must:

      i. Be in writing unless made during a hearing or trial;

      ii. State with particularity the grounds for seeking the order; and

      iii. State the relief sought. FRCP 7(b)(1).

      iv. When a moving party makes a motion based upon a rule or statute, the moving party must specify in its moving papers the rule or statute upon which it bases its motion. NY R USDCTND L.R. 7.1(a)(1).

   b. *Notice of motion.* A party interested in resisting the relief sought by a motion has a right to notice thereof, and an opportunity to be heard. AMJUR MOTIONS § 12.

      i. In addition to statutory or court rule provisions requiring notice of a motion—the purpose of such a notice requirement having been said to be to prevent a party from being prejudicially surprised by a motion—principles of natural justice dictate that an adverse party generally must be given notice that a motion will be presented to the court. AMJUR MOTIONS § 12.

      ii. "Notice," in this regard, means reasonable notice, including a meaningful opportunity to prepare and to defend against allegations of a motion. AMJUR MOTIONS § 12.

   c. *Writing requirement.* The writing requirement is intended to insure that the adverse parties are informed and have a record of both the motion's pendency and the grounds on which the movant seeks an order. FPP § 1191; Feldberg v. Quechee Lakes Corp., 463 F.3d 195 (2d Cir. 2006).

      i. It is sufficient "if the motion is stated in a written notice of the hearing of the motion." FPP § 1191.

   d. *Particularity requirement.* The particularity requirement insures that the opposing parties will have notice of their opponent's contentions. FEDPROC § 62:364; Goodman v. 1973 26 Foot Trojan Vessel, Arkansas Registration No. AR1439SN, 859 F.2d 71, 12 Fed.R.Serv.3d 645 (8th Cir. 1988). That requirement ensures that notice of the basis for the motion is provided to the court and to the opposing party so as to avoid prejudice, provide the opponent with a meaningful opportunity to respond, and provide the court with enough information to process the motion correctly. FEDPROC § 62:364; Andreas v. Volkswagen of America, Inc., 336 F.3d 789, 56 Fed.R.Serv.3d 6 (8th Cir. 2003).

      i. Reasonable specification of the grounds for a motion is sufficient. However, where a movant fails to state even one ground for granting the motion in question, the movant has failed to meet the minimal standard of "reasonable specification." FEDPROC § 62:364; Martinez v. Trainor, 556 F.2d 818, 23 Fed.R.Serv.2d 403 (7th Cir. 1977).

      ii. The court may excuse the failure to comply with the particularity requirement if it is inadvertent, and where no prejudice is shown by the opposing party. FEDPROC § 62:364.

   e. *Order to show cause.* All motions that a party brings by Order to Show Cause shall conform to the requirements set forth in NY R USDCTND L.R. 7.1(a)(1) and NY R USDCTND L.R. 7.1(a)(2). Immediately after filing an Order to Show Cause, the moving party must telephone the Chambers of the presiding judicial officer and inform Chambers staff that it has filed an Order to Show Cause. Parties may obtain the telephone numbers for all Chambers from the Clerk's office or at the Court's webpage. The Court shall determine the briefing schedule and return date applicable to motions brought by Order to Show Cause. NY R USDCTND L.R. 7.1(e).

      i. In addition to the requirements set forth in NY R USDCTND L.R. 7.1(a)(1) and NY R USDCTND L.R. 7.1(a)(2), a motion brought by Order to Show Cause must include an affidavit clearly and specifically showing good and sufficient cause why the standard Notice of Motion procedure cannot be used. The moving party must give reasonable advance notice of the application for an Order to Show Cause to the other parties, except in those circumstances where the movant can demonstrate, in a detailed and specific affidavit, good cause and substantial prejudice that would result from the requirement of reasonable notice. NY R USDCTND L.R. 7.1(e).

    ii.   An Order to Show Cause must contain a space for the assigned judge to set forth:

- The deadline for filing and serving supporting papers,
- The deadline for filing and serving opposing papers, and
- The date and time for the hearing. NY R USDCTND L.R. 7.1(e).

3.  *Motion for preliminary injunction.* The appropriate procedure for requesting a preliminary injunction is by motion, although it also commonly is requested by an order to show cause. FPP § 2949; James Luterbach Constr. Co. v. Adamkus, 781 F.2d 599, 603 (7th Cir. 1986); Studebaker Corp. v. Gittlin, 360 F.2d 692 (2d. Cir. 1966).

   a.  *Preliminary injunction.* An interim grant of specific relief is a preliminary injunction that may be issued only on notice to the adverse party. FEDPROC § 47:53; Westar Energy, Inc. v. Lake, 552 F.3d 1215 (10th Cir. 2009). Defined broadly, a preliminary injunction is an injunction that is issued to protect plaintiff from irreparable injury and to preserve the court's power to render a meaningful decision after a trial on the merits. FPP § 2947; Evans v. Buchanan, 555 F.2d 373, 387 (3d Cir. 1977).

     i.  *Disfavored injunctions.* There are three types of preliminary injunctions that are disfavored:

- Those that afford the moving party substantially all the relief it might recover after a full trial on the merits;
- Those that disturb the status quo; and
- Those that are mandatory as opposed to prohibitory. FEDPROC § 47:55; Prairie Band of Potawatomi Indians v. Pierce, 253 F.3d 1234, 50 Fed.R.Serv.3d 244 (10th Cir. 2001).

   b.  *Notice.* The court may issue a preliminary injunction only on notice to the adverse party. FRCP 65(a)(1). Although FRCP 65(a)(1) does not define what constitutes proper notice, it has been held that providing a copy of the motion and a specification of the time and place of the hearing are adequate. FPP § 2949.

   c.  *Security.* The court may issue a preliminary injunction or a temporary restraining order only if the movant gives security in an amount that the court considers proper to pay the costs and damages sustained by any party found to have been wrongfully enjoined or restrained. The United States, its officers, and its agencies are not required to give security. FRCP 65(c).

     i.  *Proceedings against a surety.* Whenever the Federal Rules of Civil Procedure (including the Supplemental Rules for Admiralty or Maritime Claims and Asset Forfeiture Actions) require or allow a party to give security, and security is given through a bond or other undertaking with one or more sureties, each surety submits to the court's jurisdiction and irrevocably appoints the court clerk as its agent for receiving service of any papers that affect its liability on the bond or undertaking. The surety's liability may be enforced on motion without an independent action. The motion and any notice that the court orders may be served on the court clerk, who must promptly mail a copy of each to every surety whose address is known. FRCP 65.1.

     ii.  For more information on sureties, refer to NY R USDCTND L.R. 65.1.1.

   d.  *Preliminary injunction versus temporary restraining order.* Care should be taken to distinguish preliminary injunctions under FRCP 65(a) from temporary restraining orders under FRCP 65(b). FPP § 2947.

     i.  *Notice and duration.* [Temporary restraining orders] may be issued ex parte without an adversary hearing in order to prevent an immediate, irreparable injury and are of limited duration—they typically remain in effect for a maximum of twenty-eight (28) days. On the other hand, FRCP 65(a)(1) requires that notice be given to the opposing party before a preliminary injunction may be issued. FPP § 2947. Furthermore, a preliminary injunction normally lasts until the completion of the trial on the merits, unless it is dissolved earlier by court order or the consent of the parties. FPP § 2947. Therefore, its duration varies and is controlled by the nature of the situation in which it is utilized. FPP § 2947; Fundicao Tupy S.A. v. U.S., 841 F.2d 1101, 1103 (Fed.Cir. 1988).

   ii.   *Hearing.* Some type of a hearing also implicitly is required by FRCP 65(a)(2), which was added in 1966 and provides either for the consolidation of the trial on the merits with the preliminary injunction hearing or the inclusion in the trial record of any evidence received at the FRCP 65(a) hearing. FPP § 2947.

e.   *Grounds for granting or denying a preliminary injunction.* The policies that bear on the propriety of granting a preliminary injunction rarely are discussed directly in the cases. Instead they are taken into account by the court considering a number of factors that have been found useful in deciding whether to grant or deny preliminary injunctions in particular cases. A formulation that has become popular in all kinds of cases, although it originally was devised in connection with stays of administrative orders, is that the four most important factors are: (1) the significance of the threat of irreparable harm to plaintiff if the injunction is not granted; (2) the state of the balance between this harm and the injury that granting the injunction would inflict on defendant; (3) the probability that plaintiff will succeed on the merits; and (4) the public interest. FPP § 2948; Pottgen v. Missouri State High School Activities Ass'n, 40 F.3d 926 (8th Cir. 1994).

   i.   *Irreparable harm.* Perhaps the single most important prerequisite for the issuance of a preliminary injunction is a demonstration that if it is not granted the applicant is likely to suffer irreparable harm before a decision on the merits can be rendered. FPP § 2948.1. Only when the threatened harm would impair the court's ability to grant an effective remedy is there really a need for preliminary relief. FPP § 2948.1.

- There must be a likelihood that irreparable harm will occur. Speculative injury is not sufficient; there must be more than an unfounded fear on the part of the applicant. FPP § 2948.1.

- Thus, a preliminary injunction will not be issued simply to prevent the possibility of some remote future injury. A presently existing actual threat must be shown. However, the injury need not have been inflicted when application is made or be certain to occur; a strong threat of irreparable injury before trial is an adequate basis. FPP § 2948.1.

   ii.   *Balancing hardship to parties.* The second factor bearing on the court's exercise of its discretion as to whether to grant preliminary relief involves an evaluation of the severity of the impact on defendant should the temporary injunction be granted and the hardship that would occur to plaintiff if the injunction should be denied. Two factors that frequently are considered when balancing the hardship on the respective parties of the grant or denial of relief are whether a preliminary injunction would give plaintiff all or most of the relief to which plaintiff would be entitled if successful at trial and whether mandatory relief is being sought. FPP § 2948.2.

   iii.   *Likelihood of prevailing on the merits.* The third factor that enters into the preliminary injunction calculus is the likelihood that plaintiff will prevail on the merits. This is relevant because the need for the court to act is, at least in part, a function of the validity of the applicant's claim. The courts use a bewildering variety of formulations of the need for showing some likelihood of success—the most common being that plaintiff must demonstrate a reasonable probability of success. But the verbal differences do not seem to reflect substantive disagreement. All courts agree that plaintiff must present a prima facie case but need not show a certainty of winning. FPP § 2948.3.

   iv.   *Public interest.* The final major factor bearing on the court's discretion to issue or deny a preliminary injunction is the public interest. Focusing on this factor is another way of inquiring whether there are policy considerations that bear on whether the order should issue. Thus, when granting preliminary relief, courts frequently emphasize that the public interest will be furthered by the injunction. Conversely, preliminary relief will be denied if the court finds that the public interest would be injured were an injunction to be issued. If the court finds there is no public interest supporting preliminary relief, that conclusion also supports denial of any injunction, even if the public interest would not be harmed by one. FPP § 2948.4. Consequently, an evaluation of the public interest should be given considerable weight in determining whether a motion for a preliminary injunction should be granted. FPP § 2948.4; Yakus v. U.S., 321 U.S. 414, 64 S.Ct. 660, 88 L.Ed. 834 (1944).

f. *Contents and scope of every injunction and restraining order*

    i. *Contents.* Every order granting an injunction and every restraining order must:

- State the reasons why it issued;

- State its terms specifically; and

- Describe in reasonable detail—and not by referring to the complaint or other document— the act or acts restrained or required. FRCP 65(d)(1).

    ii. *Persons bound.* The order binds only the following who receive actual notice of it by personal service or otherwise:

- The parties;

- The parties' officers, agents, servants, employees, and attorneys; and

- Other persons who are in active concert or participation with anyone described in FRCP 65(d)(2)(A) or FRCP 65(d)(2)(B). FRCP 65(d)(2).

g. *Other laws not modified.* FRCP 65 does not modify the following:

    i. Any federal statute relating to temporary restraining orders or preliminary injunctions in actions affecting employer and employee;

    ii. 28 U.S.C.A. § 2361, which relates to preliminary injunctions in actions of interpleader or in the nature of interpleader; or

    iii. 28 U.S.C.A. § 2284, which relates to actions that must be heard and decided by a three-judge district court. FRCP 65(e).

h. *Copyright impoundment.* FRCP 65 applies to copyright-impoundment proceedings. FRCP 65(f).

4. *Opposing papers.* The Federal Rules of Civil Procedure do not require any formal answer, return, or reply to a motion, except where the Federal Rules of Civil Procedure or local rules may require affidavits, memoranda, or other papers to be filed in opposition to a motion. Such papers are simply to apprise the court of such opposition and the grounds of that opposition. FEDPROC § 62:359.

a. *Effect of failure to respond to motion.* Although in the absence of statutory provision or court rule, a motion ordinarily does not require a written answer, when a party files a motion and the opposing party fails to respond, the court may construe such failure to respond as nonopposition to the motion or an admission that the motion was meritorious, may take the facts alleged in the motion as true—the rule in some jurisdictions being that the failure to respond to a fact set forth in a motion is deemed an admission—and may grant the motion if the relief requested appears to be justified. AMJUR MOTIONS § 28.

b. *Assent or no opposition not determinative.* However, a motion will not be granted automatically simply because an "assent" or a notation of "no opposition" has been filed; federal judges frequently deny motions that have been assented to when it is thought that justice so dictates. FPP § 1190.

c. *Responsive pleading inappropriate as response to motion.* An attempt to answer or oppose a motion with a responsive pleading usually is not appropriate. FPP § 1190.

5. *Reply papers.* Reply papers and adjournments are not permitted without the Court's prior permission. Permission to file a reply does not exist simply because CM/ECF generates a deadline for a reply on a nondispositive motion. NY R USDCTND L.R. 7.1(b)(2). A moving party may be required or permitted to prepare papers in addition to his original motion papers. AMJUR MOTIONS § 25. Papers answering or replying to opposing papers may be appropriate, in the interests of justice, where it appears there is a substantial reason for allowing a reply. Thus, a court may accept reply papers where a party demonstrates that the papers to which it seeks to file a reply raise new issues that are material to the disposition of the

question before the court, or where the court determines, sua sponte, that it wishes further briefing of an issue raised in those papers and orders the submission of additional papers. FEDPROC § 62:360.

a. *Function of reply papers.* The function of a reply affidavit is to answer the arguments made in opposition to the position taken by the movant and not to permit the movant to introduce new arguments in support of the motion. AMJUR MOTIONS § 25.

b. *Issues raised for the first time in a reply document.* However, the view has been followed in some jurisdictions, that as a matter of judicial economy, where there is no prejudice and where the issues could be raised simply by filing a motion to dismiss, the trial court has discretion to consider arguments raised for the first time in a reply memorandum, and that a trial court may grant a motion to strike issues raised for the first time in a reply memorandum. AMJUR MOTIONS § 26.

c. *Opposition to cross-motion.* The original moving party may reply in further support of the original motion and in opposition to the cross-motion with a reply/opposition brief that does not exceed twenty-five (25) pages in length, exclusive of exhibits. NY R USDCTND L.R. 7.1(c).

6. *Surreply in support of cross-motion.* The cross-moving party may not reply in further support of its cross-motion without the Court's prior permission. NY R USDCTND L.R. 7.1(c).

7. *Submission of proposed order by prevailing party.* If the assigned judge instructs the prevailing party to do so, the prevailing party shall submit a proposed order which the opposing party has approved and which contains the endorsement of the opposing party: "Approved as to form." NY R USDCTND L.R. 77.2(b). In civil actions where the Court has directed a party to submit an order or judgment, that party shall file all such orders or judgments in duplicate, and the Clerk's entry of such duplicate in the proper record book shall be deemed in compliance with FRCP 79(b). Such party shall also furnish the Clerk with a sufficient number of additional copies for each party to the action, which the Clerk shall mail with notice of entry in accordance with FRCP 77(d). NY R USDCTND L.R. 5.1(b).

a. *Disagreement as to form of proposed order.* When the parties are unable to agree as to the form of the proposed order, the prevailing party shall, on seven (7) days notice to all other parties, submit a proposed order and a written explanation for the form of that order. The Court may award costs and attorney's fees against a party whose unreasonable conduct the Court deemed to have required the bringing of the motion. The provisions of NY R USDCTND L.R. 7.1 shall not apply to such motion, and the Court shall not hear oral argument. NY R USDCTND L.R. 77.2(b).

b. For more information on orders, refer to NY R USDCTND L.R. 77.2.

8. *Sanctions for vexatious or frivolous motions or failure to comply with* NY R USDCTND L.R. 7.1. A party who presents vexatious or frivolous motion papers or fails to comply with NY R USDCTND L.R. 7.1 is subject to discipline as the Court deems appropriate, including sanctions and the imposition of costs and attorney's fees to the opposing party. NY R USDCTND L.R. 7.1(i).

9. *Complex and multi-district litigation.* If the assigned judge determines, in his or her discretion, that the case is of such a complex nature that it cannot reasonably be trial ready within eighteen (18) months from the date the complaint is filed, the assigned judge may design and issue a particularized case management order that will move the case to trial as quickly as the complexity of the case allows. NY R USDCTND L.R. 3.3(a). The parties shall promptly notify the Court in writing if any action commenced is appropriate for multi-district litigation. NY R USDCTND L.R. 3.3(b).

10. *Appearances.* An attorney appearing for a party in a civil case shall promptly file with the Clerk a written notice of appearance; however, an attorney does not need to file a notice of appearance if the attorney who would be filing the notice of appearance is the same individual who has signed the complaint, notice of removal, pre-answer motion, or answer. NY R USDCTND L.R. 83.2(a). For more information, refer to NY R USDCTND L.R. 83.2.

11. *Related cases.* A civil case is "related" to another civil case for purposes of this guideline when, because of the similarity of facts and legal issues or because the cases arise from the same transactions or events, a substantial saving of judicial resources is likely to result from assigning the cases to the same Judge and Magistrate Judge. NY R USDCTND Order 12(G)(2). A civil case shall not be deemed related to another civil case merely because the civil case: (1) involves similar legal issues, or (2) involves the same parties. NY R USDCTND Order 12(G)(3). Presumptively, and subject to the power of a Judge to determine

otherwise pursuant to NY R USDCTND Order 12(G)(5), civil cases shall not be deemed to be "related" unless both cases are still pending before the Court. NY R USDCTND Order 12(G)(4).

a. *New filings.* If an attorney or filing party indicates on the Civil Cover Sheet that a case is related to an earlier filed case, the Clerk shall instruct the filing party to file a notice of related cases. The allegedly related cases will be submitted by the Clerk to the Judge to whom the earliest filed case is assigned, who shall advise the Clerk whether such cases are related. NY R USDCTND Order 12(G)(1).

b. *Judicial determination that civil cases are "related."* Except for the cases described in the final sentence of NY R USDCTND Order 12(G)(6), all civil cases shall be randomly assigned when they are filed. Other than the cases described in the final sentence of NY R USDCTND Order 12(G)(6), civil cases shall not be deemed to be "related" for purposes of this guideline at the instance of any litigant or attorney unless and until there has been a determination by a Judge of this Court that the standard of NY R USDCTND Order 12(G)(2) is met. NY R USDCTND Order 12(G)(5).

   i. *Notice of related filing.* Any party may apply for such a determination by filing with the Clerk a notice of related filing, which should include an explanation as to why the standard of NY R USDCTND Order 12(G)(2) is met. A form for this purpose is available on the Court's website. A copy of the notice shall be served on all other parties who have appeared. Such an application must be made after the date when at least a majority of the defendants have been served with the complaint. Before making such an application, the applicant must confer in good faith with all other parties in an effort to reach an agreement on whether or not the case is "related". After such an application is made, any other party may serve and file within seven (7) calendar days a letter of no more than two (2) pages supporting or opposing the application. The application to have the case assigned to another Judge shall be presented to the Judge with the earliest filed case for decision on whether the action(s) should be reassigned as related cases. The Judge with the earliest filed case may then enter an order in the case at bar, either deeming the case to be related and directing the Clerk to reassign the action, or denying the application for reassignment. Any disputes concerning the assignment of related cases will be referred to the Chief Judge for resolution. NY R USDCTND Order 12(G)(5).

c. For more information on related cases, refer to NY R USDCTND Order 12(G).

12. *Alternative dispute resolution (ADR).* It is the mission of this court to do everything it can to help parties resolve their disputes as fairly, quickly, and efficiently as possible. NY R USDCTND Order 25(VIII).

a. *Arbitration.* NY R USDCTND L.R. 83.7 governs the consensual arbitration program for referral of civil actions to court-annexed arbitration. It may remain in effect until further order of the Court. Its purpose is to establish a less formal procedure for the just, efficient and economical resolution of disputes, while preserving the right to a full trial on demand. NY R USDCTND L.R. 83.7-1.

   i. *Actions subject to arbitration.* The Clerk shall notify the parties in all civil cases, except as the Local Rules of Practice for the United States District Court for the Northern District of New York otherwise direct, that they may consent to non-binding arbitration under NY R US-DCTND L.R. 83.7. The notice shall be furnished to the parties at pretrial/scheduling conferences or shall be included with pretrial conference notices and instructions. Consent to arbitration under NY R USDCTND L.R. 83.7 shall be discussed at the pretrial/scheduling conference. No party or attorney shall be prejudiced for refusing to participate in arbitration. The Court shall allow the referral of any civil action pending before it to the arbitration process if the parties consent. The plaintiff shall be responsible for securing the execution of a consent form by the parties and for filing the form with the Clerk within fourteen (14) days after the parties receive the form. The parties shall freely and knowingly enter into the consent. NY R USDCTND L.R. 83.7-2.

   ii. *Referral to arbitration.* The Clerk shall refer every action subject to NY R USDCTND L.R. 83.7 to arbitration in accordance with the procedures under NY R USDCTND L.R. 83.7 twenty-one (21) days after the filing of the last responsive pleading or within twenty-one (21) days of the filing of a stipulated consent order referring the action to arbitration, whichever event occurs last, except as otherwise provided. If any party notices a motion to dismiss under the provisions of FRCP 12(a) and/or FRCP 12(b), or a motion to join necessary parties pursuant to the Federal Rules of Civil Procedure prior to the expiration of the twenty-one (21) day period, the assigned judge shall hear the motion and further proceedings under NY R USDCTND L.R. 83.7 shall be deferred pending decision on the motion. If the Court does not dismiss the action on the motion, the Court shall refer the action to arbitration twenty-one (21) days after the filing of the decision. NY R USDCTND L.R. 83.7-3(a). Motions for summary judgment pursuant to FRCP 56 shall be filed and served within twenty-one (21) days following the close of discovery. The filing of a FRCP 56 motion shall defer further proceedings under NY R USDCTND L.R. 83.7 pending decision on the motion. NY R USDCTND L.R. 83.7-3(a).

- *Relief from referral.* Any party shall request relief from the operation of NY R USDCTND L.R. 83.7 by filing with the Court a motion for the relief within twenty-one (21) days after entry of the initial stipulated consent order which refers the case for arbitration. The assigned judge shall, sua sponte, exempt an action from the application of NY R USDCTND L.R. 83.7 where the objectives of arbitration would not be realized because (1) the case involves complex or novel legal issues, (2) legal issues predominate over factual issues, or (3) for other good cause. NY R USDCTND L.R. 83.7-3(c).

iii. For more information on arbitration, refer to NY R USDCTND L.R. 83.7.

b. *Mediation.* The purpose of NY R USDCTND L.R. 83.11 is to provide a supplementary procedure to the Court's existing alternative dispute resolution procedures. NY R USDCTND L.R. 83.11 provides for an earlier resolution of civil disputes resulting in savings of time and cost to litigants and the Court without sacrificing the quality of justice rendered or the right of litigants to a full trial on all issues not resolved through mediation. NY R USDCTND L.R. 83.11-1(a). Mediation is a process by which an impartial person, the mediator, facilitates communication between disputing parties to promote understanding, reconciliation and settlement. The mediator is an advocate for settlement and uses the mediation process to help the parties fully explore any potential area of agreement. The mediator does not serve as a judge or arbitrator and has no authority to render any decision on any disputed issue or to force a settlement. The parties themselves are responsible for negotiating any resolution(s) to their dispute. NY R USDCTND L.R. 83.11-1(b).

i. *Actions subject to mediation.* The Court may refer any civil action (or any portion thereof) to mediation under NY R USDCTND L.R. 83.11: (1) by order of referral; or (2) on the motion of any party; or (3) by consent of the parties. NY R USDCTND L.R. 83.11-3(a).

- *Withdrawal from mediation.* The parties may withdraw from mediation any civil action or claim that the Court refers to mediation pursuant to NY R USDCTND L.R. 83.11-3 by application to the assigned judge at least ten (10) days prior to the scheduled mediation session. NY R USDCTND L.R. 83.11-3(b).

ii. *Mandatory mediation program.* The United States District Court for the Northern District of New York has adopted this Mandatory Mediation Plan. The paid Mediation Program is designed to provide quicker, less expensive and potentially more satisfying alternatives to continuing litigation, without impairing the quality of justice or the right to trial. NY R USDCTND Order 47(1)(1.2)(A). This Mandatory Mediation Plan applies to civil actions pending as well as newly filed actions, except as otherwise indicated in NY R USDCTND Order 47. The Local Rules for voluntary mediation will apply only to Pro Se Cases that proceed through the Assisted Mediation Program. NY R USDCTND Order 47(1)(1.2)(B).

- *Referral into the pilot mandatory mediation program for new cases.* All civil cases shall be referred automatically into the Mandatory Mediation Program. Notice of the Mandatory Mediation requirements will be provided to all parties immediately upon the filing of a complaint and answer or a notice of removal. ADR intervention will be scheduled at the conference held pursuant to NY R USDCTND L.R. 16.1. NY R USDCTND Order 47(2)(2.1)(A). For a list of categories of actions exempted from automatic referral, refer to NY R USDCTND Order 47(2)(2.1)(A).

- *Referral into the pilot mandatory mediation program for pending cases.* The assigned Judge or Magistrate Judge on any pending civil case may, sua sponte or with status conference, issue an order referring the case into the Mandatory Mediation Program. The order shall specify a date on which the ADR intervention is to be completed. NY R USDCTND Order 47(2)(2.1)(B).

- *Referral into the pilot mandatory mediation program by stipulation.* A case may be referred into the Mandatory Mediation Program by stipulation of all parties. Stipulations shall be filed and shall designate the time frame within which the ADR process will be completed. Stipulations are presumed acceptable unless the assigned Judge or Magistrate Judge determines that the interests of justice are not served. NY R USDCTND Order 47(2)(2.1)(C).

- *Relief from referral.* Motions to opt out of the program will be addressed by the assigned Magistrate Judge at the FRCP 16 conference. NY R USDCTND Order 47(2)(2.2)(A). Opting Out Motions shall be granted only for "good cause" shown. Inconvenience, travel costs, attorney fees or other costs shall not constitute "good cause." A party seeking relief from the Mandatory Mediation Program must set forth the reasons why Mandatory Mediation has no reasonable chance of being productive. NY R USDCTND Order 47(2)(2.2)(B). The assigned Magistrate Judge may, sua sponte, exempt any case from the Court's Mandatory Mediation Program. NY R USDCTND Order 47(2)(2.2)(C).

iii. *Assisted mediation program.* The Court may assign specially trained pro bono Special Mediation Counsel to assist pro se civilian litigants with preparing for and participating in mediation. The Assisted Mediation Program is open to civilian pro se parties to actions in the Northern District of New York. The assigned judge or magistrate judge determines if the case would benefit from mediation and would also benefit from the assignment of Special Mediation Counsel to assist the pro se party with the mediation process. NY R USDCTND L.R. 83.8(a). Appointment of Special Mediation Counsel is in no way guaranteed, even if the action is referred to the court-annexed mediation program. Appointment is at the sole discretion of the presiding judge. NY R USDCTND L.R. 83.8(a).

- *Referral to assisted mediation program.* If the court determines that referral to the Assisted Mediation Program is appropriate, the Court shall enter an order of reference to the Assisted Mediation Program. NY R USDCTND L.R. 83.8(b).

iv. For more information on mediation, refer to NY R USDCTND L.R. 83.11 and NY R USDCTND Order 47.

c. *Early neutral evaluation (ENE).* Early neutral evaluation (ENE) is a process in which parties obtain from an experienced neutral (an "evaluator") a nonbinding, reasoned, oral evaluation of the merits of the case. The first step in the ENE process involves the Court appointing an evaluator who has expertise in the area of law in the case. After the parties exchange essential information and position statements early in the pretrial period (usually within one hundred fifty (150) to two hundred (200) days after a complaint has been filed), the evaluator convenes an ENE session that typically lasts about two hours. At the ENE meeting, each side briefly presents the factual and legal basis of its position. The evaluator may ask questions of the parties and help them identify the main issues in dispute and the areas of agreement. The evaluator may also help the parties explore options for settlement. If settlement does not occur, the evaluator then offers an opinion as to the settlement value of the case, including the likelihood of liability and the likely range of damages. With the benefit of this assessment, the parties are again encouraged to discuss settlement, with or without the evaluator's assistance. The parties may also explore ways to narrow the issues in dispute, exchange information about the case or otherwise prepare efficiently for trial. NY R USDCTND L.R. 83.12-1.

i. *Actions subject to early neutral evaluation.* The Court may refer any civil action (or any portion thereof) to ENE under NY R USDCTND L.R. 83.12: (1) by order of referral; (2) on the motion of any party; or (3) by consent of the parties. NY R USDCTND L.R. 83.12-3(a).

- *Withdrawal from the ENE process.* The parties may withdraw any civil action or claim that the Court has referred to the ENE Process pursuant to NY R USDCTND L.R. 83.12-3 by application to the assigned judge at least ten (10) days before the scheduled evaluation session. NY R USDCTND L.R. 83.12-3(b).

    ii.   For more information on early neutral evaluation (ENE), refer to NY R USDCTND L.R. 83.12.

13.   *Settlement procedures.* On notice to the Court or the Clerk that the parties have settled an action, and upon confirmation of the settlement by all parties, the Court may issue a judgment dismissing the action by reason of settlement. The Court shall issue the order without prejudice to the parties' right to secure reinstatement of the case within thirty (30) days after the date of judgment by making a showing that the settlement was not, in fact, consummated. NY R USDCTND L.R. 68.2(a). If the Court decides not to follow the procedures set forth in NY R USDCTND L.R. 68.2(a), the parties shall file within thirty (30) days of the notification to the Court, unless otherwise directed by written order, such notices, stipulations and/or motions as are necessary to terminate the action. If the required documents are not filed within the thirty (30) day period, the Clerk shall place the action on the dismissal calendar. NY R USDCTND L.R. 68.2(b).

14.   *Sanctions and penalties for noncompliance.* Failure of an attorney or of a party to comply with any provision of the Local Rules of Practice for the United States District Court for the Northern District of New York, General Orders of this District, Orders of the Court, or the Federal Rules of Civil Procedure shall be a ground for imposition of sanctions. NY R USDCTND L.R. 1.1(d).

15.   *Individual judge practices.* Refer to the Miscellaneous section of this document for information on individual judge practices on general requirements for documents.

## D. Documents

1.   *Documents for moving party*

   a.   *Required documents*

      i.   *Notice of motion and motion.* In the Notice of Motion, the moving party is required to set forth the date that the court conference with the Magistrate Judge was held regarding the issues being presented in the motion. Failure to include this information in the Notice of Motion may result in the Court rejecting the motion papers. NY R USDCTND L.R. 7.1(b)(2). Refer to the General Requirements section of this document for information on the notice of motion and motion.

         •  *Order to show cause.* Refer to the General Requirements section of this document for information on bringing a motion by order to show cause.

      ii.   *Memorandum of law.* Except as otherwise provided in NY R USDCTND L.R. 7.1(a), all motions. . .require a memorandum of law. NY R USDCTND L.R. 7.1(a). Refer to the Format section of this document for the formatting requirements for memoranda of law.

     iii.   *Supporting affidavit.* Except as otherwise provided in NY R USDCTND L.R. 7.1(a), all motions. . .require a. . .supporting affidavit. NY R USDCTND L.R. 7.1(a). An affidavit must not contain legal arguments but must contain factual and procedural background that is relevant to the motion the affidavit supports. NY R USDCTND L.R. 7.1(a)(2).

     iv.   *Security.* Refer to the General Requirements section of this document for information on the security required.

      v.   *Certificate of service.* Except as otherwise provided in NY R USDCTND L.R. 7.1(a), all motions. . .require. . .proof of service on all the parties. See NY R USDCTND L.R. 5.1(a). NY R USDCTND L.R. 7.1(a). FRCP 5(d) requires that the person making service under FRCP 5 certify that service has been effected. FRCP 5(Advisory Committee Notes). Having such information on file may be useful for many purposes, including proof of service if an issue arises concerning the effectiveness of the service. FRCP 5(Advisory Committee Notes). The party or its designee shall declare, by affidavit or certification, that it has provided all other parties in the action with all documents it has filed with the Court. NY R USDCTND L.R. 5.1(a).

         •  Attorneys and pro se parties who are not Filing or Receiving Users must be served with a paper copy of any electronically filed pleading or other document. NY R USDCTND CM/ECF(5)(5.2). Such paper service must be documented by electronically filing a certificate of service. NY R USDCTND CM/ECF(5)(5.2).

   b.   *Supplemental documents*

      i.   *Supporting evidence.* When a motion relies on facts outside the record, the court may hear the

matter on affidavits or may hear it wholly or partly on oral testimony or on depositions. FRCP 43(c). Evidence that goes beyond the unverified allegations of the pleadings and motion papers must be presented to support or oppose a motion for a preliminary injunction. FPP § 2949.

- *Affidavits.* Affidavits are appropriate on a preliminary injunction motion and typically will be offered by both parties. FPP § 2949. All affidavits should state the facts supporting the litigant's position clearly and specifically. Preliminary injunctions frequently are denied if the affidavits are too vague or conclusory to demonstrate a clear right to relief under FRCP 65. FPP § 2949.

ii. *Pleadings.* Pleadings may be considered if they have been verified. FPP § 2949; K-2 Ski Co. v. Head Ski Co., 467 F.2d 1087 (9th Cir. 1972).

iii. *Notice of constitutional question.* A party that files a pleading, written motion, or other paper drawing into question the constitutionality of a federal or state statute must promptly:

- *File notice.* File a notice of constitutional question stating the question and identifying the paper that raises it, if: (1) a federal statute is questioned and the parties do not include the United States, one of its agencies, or one of its officers or employees in an official capacity; or (2) a state statute is questioned and the parties do not include the state, one of its agencies, or one of its officers or employees in an official capacity; and

- *Serve notice.* Serve the notice and paper on the Attorney General of the United States if a federal statute is questioned—or on the state attorney general if a state statute is questioned—either by certified or registered mail or by sending it to an electronic address designated by the attorney general for this purpose. FRCP 5.1(a).

- *No forfeiture.* A party's failure to file and serve the notice, or the court's failure to certify, does not forfeit a constitutional claim or defense that is otherwise timely asserted. FRCP 5.1(d).

iv. *Nongovernmental corporate disclosure statement*

- *Contents.* A nongovernmental corporate party must file two (2) copies of a disclosure statement that: (1) identifies any parent corporation and any publicly held corporation owning ten percent (10%) or more of its stock; or (2) states that there is no such corporation. FRCP 7.1(a).

- *Time to file; Supplemental filing.* A party must: (1) file the disclosure statement with its first appearance, pleading, petition, motion, response, or other request addressed to the court; and (2) promptly file a supplemental statement if any required information changes. FRCP 7.1(b).

v. *Copies of authorities.* When serving a pro se litigant with a memorandum of law or any other paper which contains citations to authorities that are unpublished or published exclusively on electronic databases, counsel shall include a hard copy of those authorities. Although copies of authorities published only on electronic databases are not required to be filed, copies shall be provided upon request to opposing counsel who lack access to electronic databases. NY R USDCTND L.R. 7.1(a)(1).

vi. *Proposed order.* A document that is submitted in .pdf format cannot be modified; therefore, a proposed order or stipulation must be in a word processing format. The chambers of the assigned judge may request that a proposed order and/or a stipulation be e-mailed to the courtroom deputy for the presiding judge in either WordPerfect or Microsoft Word format. Please attach your proposed order and/or stipulation to an Internet e-mail sent to the appropriate e-mail address listed in NY R USDCTND CM/ECF(8)(8.2). NY R USDCTND CM/ECF(8)(8.2).

vii. *Cover letter authorizing e-mail or facsimile filing.* Neither the Court nor the Clerk's Office will accept for filing any facsimile or e-mail transmission without prior authorization from the Court. The party using facsimile or e-mail transmissions to file its papers must accompany any such documents with a cover letter stating that the Court authorized such transmissions and the date on which the Court provided that authorization. Violations of NY R USDCTND L.R. 5.5 subject the offending party to the Court's full disciplinary powers. NY R USDCTND L.R. 5.5.

viii. *Affidavit attesting to failed attempts to file electronically.* If the Court's CM/ECF site experiences a technical failure, a Filing User may submit documents to the Court that day in an alternate manner provided that the documents are accompanied by the Filing User's affidavit stating that the Filing User attempted to file electronically at least two times in one (1) hour increments after 10:00 a.m. that day. The following methods are acceptable alternate means for filing documents in case of a technical failure: (1) via electronic mail in a PDF attachment sent to the e-mail address for technical failures; or (2) in person, by bringing the document to the Clerk's Office on paper accompanied by a CD/ROM that contains the document in .pdf format. NY R USDCTND CM/ECF(10)(10.1).

- A Filing User who cannot file documents electronically because of a problem on the Filing User's system must file the documents' conventionally along with an affidavit explaining the reason for not filing the documents electronically. NY R USDCTND CM/ECF(10)(10.2).

ix. *Notice of conventional filing.* If the Clerk's Office grants permission to conventionally file the document, the Filing User shall electronically file a notice of conventional filing for the documents. More information regarding this process can be obtained from the Court's web page. NY R USDCTND CM/ECF(4)(4.5).

x. *CD/ROM with PDF of document(s).* If the Court grants permission to file a document traditionally, the attorney must submit the documents for filing to the Clerk's Office on CD/ROM in .pdf or pdf.A format. NY R USDCTND CM/ECF(2).

xi. *English translation.* The Court conducts its reviews and deliberations in English. Unless otherwise directed by the Court, any document that a party transmits to the Court (including one in the record on appeal) that is in a language other than English must be accompanied by an English translation that the translator has certified as true and accurate, pursuant to 28 U.S.C.A. § 1746. NY R USDCTND L.R. 10.1(e). For more information, refer to NY R USDCTND L.R. 10.1(e).

xii. *Courtesy copies.* The Court may require that courtesy copies of electronically filed documents be submitted for its review and may amend these Administrative Procedures (NY R USDCTND CM/ECF) at any time without prior notice. NY R USDCTND CM/ECF(2).

xiii. *Copies for three-judge court.* On the convening of a three-judge court, the parties shall make three (3) copies of all non-electronically filed pleadings, motion papers, and memoranda of law available to the Clerk for distribution. NY R USDCTND L.R. 9.1.

2. *Documents for opposing party*

   a. *Required documents*

      i. *Opposition.* Refer to the General Requirements section of this document for information on the opposing papers.

      ii. *Memorandum of law.* Except as otherwise provided in NY R USDCTND L.R. 7.1(a), all. . .opposition to motions require a memorandum of law. NY R USDCTND L.R. 7.1(a).

         - *Cross-motion brief.* If a party makes a cross-motion, it must join its cross motion brief with its opposition brief, and this combined brief may not exceed twenty-five (25) pages in length, exclusive of exhibits. A separate brief in opposition to the original motion is not permissible. NY R USDCTND L.R. 7.1(c).

         - Refer to the Format section of this document for the formatting requirements for memoranda of law.

      iii. *Supporting affidavit.* Except as otherwise provided in NY R USDCTND L.R. 7.1(a), all. . .opposition to motions require a. . .supporting affidavit. NY R USDCTND L.R. 7.1(a). An affidavit must not contain legal arguments but must contain factual and procedural background that is relevant to the motion the affidavit supports. NY R USDCTND L.R. 7.1(a)(2).

      iv. *Certificate of service.* Except as otherwise provided in NY R USDCTND L.R. 7.1(a), all. . .opposition to motions require. . .proof of service on all the parties. See NY R US-DCTND L.R. 5.1(a). NY R USDCTND L.R. 7.1(a). FRCP 5(d) requires that the person making service under FRCP 5 certify that service has been effected. FRCP 5(Advisory Committee Notes). Having such information on file may be useful for many purposes, including proof of service if an issue arises concerning the effectiveness of the service. FRCP 5(Advisory Committee Notes). The party or its designee shall declare, by affidavit or certification, that it has provided all other parties in the action with all documents it has filed with the Court. NY R USDCTND L.R. 5.1(a).

- Attorneys and pro se parties who are not Filing or Receiving Users must be served with a paper copy of any electronically filed pleading or other document. NY R USDCTND CM/ECF(5)(5.2). Such paper service must be documented by electronically filing a certificate of service. NY R USDCTND CM/ECF(5)(5.2).

b. *Supplemental documents*

   i. *Supporting evidence.* When a motion relies on facts outside the record, the court may hear the matter on affidavits or may hear it wholly or partly on oral testimony or on depositions. FRCP 43(c). Evidence that goes beyond the unverified allegations of the pleadings and motion papers must be presented to support or oppose a motion for a preliminary injunction. FPP § 2949.

      - *Affidavits.* Affidavits are appropriate on a preliminary injunction motion and typically will be offered by both parties. FPP § 2949. All affidavits should state the facts supporting the litigant's position clearly and specifically. Preliminary injunctions frequently are denied if the affidavits are too vague or conclusory to demonstrate a clear right to relief under FRCP 65. FPP § 2949.

   ii. *Pleadings.* Pleadings may be considered if they have been verified. FPP § 2949; K-2 Ski Co. v. Head Ski Co., 467 F.2d 1087 (9th Cir. 1972).

   iii. *Notice of constitutional question.* A party that files a pleading, written motion, or other paper drawing into question the constitutionality of a federal or state statute must promptly:

      - *File notice.* File a notice of constitutional question stating the question and identifying the paper that raises it, if: (1) a federal statute is questioned and the parties do not include the United States, one of its agencies, or one of its officers or employees in an official capacity; or (2) a state statute is questioned and the parties do not include the state, one of its agencies, or one of its officers or employees in an official capacity; and

      - *Serve notice.* Serve the notice and paper on the Attorney General of the United States if a federal statute is questioned—or on the state attorney general if a state statute is questioned—either by certified or registered mail or by sending it to an electronic address designated by the attorney general for this purpose. FRCP 5.1(a).

      - *No forfeiture.* A party's failure to file and serve the notice, or the court's failure to certify, does not forfeit a constitutional claim or defense that is otherwise timely asserted. FRCP 5.1(d).

   iv. *Nongovernmental corporate disclosure statement*

      - *Contents.* A nongovernmental corporate party must file two (2) copies of a disclosure statement that: (1) identifies any parent corporation and any publicly held corporation owning ten percent (10%) or more of its stock; or (2) states that there is no such corporation. FRCP 7.1(a).

      - *Time to file; Supplemental filing.* A party must: (1) file the disclosure statement with its first appearance, pleading, petition, motion, response, or other request addressed to the court; and (2) promptly file a supplemental statement if any required information changes. FRCP 7.1(b).

   v. *Cross-motion.* A party may file and serve a cross-motion (meaning a competing request for relief or order similar to that requested by another party against the cross-moving party) at the time it files and serves its opposition papers to the original motion, i.e., not less than SEVENTEEN (17) DAYS prior to the return date of the motion. NY R USDCTND L.R. 7.1(c).

vi. *Copies of authorities.* When serving a pro se litigant with a memorandum of law or any other paper which contains citations to authorities that are unpublished or published exclusively on electronic databases, counsel shall include a hard copy of those authorities. Although copies of authorities published only on electronic databases are not required to be filed, copies shall be provided upon request to opposing counsel who lack access to electronic databases. NY R USDCTND L.R. 7.1(a)(1).

vii. *Cover letter authorizing e-mail or facsimile filing.* Neither the Court nor the Clerk's Office will accept for filing any facsimile or e-mail transmission without prior authorization from the Court. The party using facsimile or e-mail transmissions to file its papers must accompany any such documents with a cover letter stating that the Court authorized such transmissions and the date on which the Court provided that authorization. Violations of NY R USDCTND L.R. 5.5 subject the offending party to the Court's full disciplinary powers. NY R USDCTND L.R. 5.5.

viii. *Affidavit attesting to failed attempts to file electronically.* If the Court's CM/ECF site experiences a technical failure, a Filing User may submit documents to the Court that day in an alternate manner provided that the documents are accompanied by the Filing User's affidavit stating that the Filing User attempted to file electronically at least two times in one (1) hour increments after 10:00 a.m. that day. The following methods are acceptable alternate means for filing documents in case of a technical failure: (1) via electronic mail in a PDF attachment sent to the e-mail address for technical failures; or (2) in person, by bringing the document to the Clerk's Office on paper accompanied by a CD/ROM that contains the document in .pdf format. NY R USDCTND CM/ECF(10)(10.1).

- A Filing User who cannot file documents electronically because of a problem on the Filing User's system must file the documents' conventionally along with an affidavit explaining the reason for not filing the documents electronically. NY R USDCTND CM/ECF(10)(10.2).

ix. *Notice of conventional filing.* If the Clerk's Office grants permission to conventionally file the document, the Filing User shall electronically file a notice of conventional filing for the documents. More information regarding this process can be obtained from the Court's web page. NY R USDCTND CM/ECF(4)(4.5).

x. *CD/ROM with PDF of document(s).* If the Court grants permission to file a document traditionally, the attorney must submit the documents for filing to the Clerk's Office on CD/ROM in .pdf or pdf.A format. NY R USDCTND CM/ECF(2).

xi. *English translation.* The Court conducts its reviews and deliberations in English. Unless otherwise directed by the Court, any document that a party transmits to the Court (including one in the record on appeal) that is in a language other than English must be accompanied by an English translation that the translator has certified as true and accurate, pursuant to 28 U.S.C.A. § 1746. NY R USDCTND L.R. 10.1(e). For more information, refer to NY R USDCTND L.R. 10.1(e).

xii. *Courtesy copies.* The Court may require that courtesy copies of electronically filed documents be submitted for its review and may amend these Administrative Procedures (NY R USDCTND CM/ECF) at any time without prior notice. NY R USDCTND CM/ECF(2).

xiii. *Copies for three-judge court.* On the convening of a three-judge court, the parties shall make three (3) copies of all non-electronically filed pleadings, motion papers, and memoranda of law available to the Clerk for distribution. NY R USDCTND L.R. 9.1.

3. *Individual judge practices.* Refer to the Miscellaneous section of this document for information on individual judge practices on required documents.

# E. Format

1. *Form of documents.* The rules governing captions and other matters of form in pleadings apply to motions and other papers. FRCP 7(b)(2). All pleadings and other papers shall be served and filed in accordance

with the Federal Rules of Civil Procedure and shall be in the form prescribed by NY R USDCTND L.R. 10.1. NY R USDCTND L.R. 5.1(a).

a. *Form, generally.* All pleadings, motions, and other documents that a party presents for filing, whether in paper form or in electronic form, shall meet the following requirements:

   i. *Font size.* All text, whether in the body of the document or in footnotes, must be a minimum of twelve (12) point type. NY R USDCTND L.R. 10.1(a)(1).

   ii. *Margins.* All documents must have one (1) inch margins on all four sides of the page. NY R USDCTND L.R. 10.1(a)(2).

   iii. *Spacing.* All text in the body of the document must be double-spaced. NY R USDCTND L.R. 10.1(a)(3).

   - The text in block quotations and footnotes may be single-spaced. NY R USDCTND L.R. 10.1(a)(4).

   iv. *Page numbering.* Pages must be consecutively numbered. NY R USDCTND L.R. 10.1(a)(7).

   v. *Circumventing formatting limitations*

   - Extensive footnotes must not be used to circumvent page limitations. NY R USDCTND L.R. 10.1(a)(5).

   - Compacted or other compressed printing features must not be used. NY R USDCTND L.R. 10.1(a)(6).

b. *Additional requirements for paper filing.* Additional requirements for all pleadings, motions, and other documents that a party presents for filing in paper form:

   i. *Paper size.* All documents must be on eight and one-half by eleven (8-1/2 x 11) inch white paper of good quality. NY R USDCTND L.R. 10.1(b)(1).

   ii. *Text.* All text must be plainly and legibly written, typewritten, printed or reproduced without erasures or interlineations materially defacing them. NY R USDCTND L.R. 10.1(b)(2).

   iii. *Ink.* All documents must be in black or blue ink. NY R USDCTND L.R. 10.1(b)(3).

   iv. *Binding.* Pages of all documents must be stapled (or in some other way fastened) together. NY R USDCTND L.R. 10.1(b)(4).

   v. *Single-sided paper.* All documents must be single-sided. NY R USDCTND L.R. 10.1(b)(5).

   vi. *Electronic submission.* The Court, at its discretion, may require the electronic submission of any document in a WordPerfect-compatible format. NY R USDCTND L.R. 10.1(b)(6).

   vii. *Rejection of document.* The Court may reject documents that do not comply with the above-listed requirements. NY R USDCTND L.R. 10.1(b).

c. *Caption; Names of parties.* Every pleading must have a caption with the court's name, a title, a file number, and a FRCP 7(a) designation. The title of the complaint must name all the parties; the title of other pleadings, after naming the first party on each side, may refer generally to other parties. FRCP 10(a). Each document must contain a caption for the specific case to which it pertains. The caption must include the title of the Court, the title of the action, the civil action number of the case, the initials of the assigned judge(s), and the name or nature of the paper in sufficient detail for identification. If a litigant has more than one action pending in this Court, any and all papers filed in a case must contain and pertain to one civil action number, unless the civil actions have been consolidated by the Court. Any motion or other papers purporting to relate to more than one action will not be accepted for filing and may be stricken by the Court. NY R USDCTND L.R. 10.1(c)(1) shall not apply, as noted in NY R USDCTND L.R. 10.1(c), to notices of change of address filed by attorneys of record and pro se litigants. The parties must separately caption affidavits and declarations and must not physically attach them to the Notice of Motion or Memorandum of Law. NY R USDCTND L.R. 10.1(c)(1).

d. *Paragraphs; Separate statements.* A party must state its claims or defenses in numbered paragraphs, each limited as far as practicable to a single set of circumstances. A later pleading may refer by

number to a paragraph in an earlier pleading. If doing so would promote clarity, each claim founded on a separate transaction or occurrence—and each defense other than a denial—must be stated in a separate count or defense. FRCP 10(b).

e. *Adoption by reference; Exhibits.* A statement in a pleading may be adopted by reference elsewhere in the same pleading or in any other pleading or motion. A copy of a written instrument that is an exhibit to a pleading is a part of the pleading for all purposes. FRCP 10(c).

f. *Citation of local rules.* These are the Local Rules of Practice for the United States District Court for the Northern District of New York. They shall be cited as "L.R. ___." NY R USDCTND L.R. 1.1(a).

g. *Acceptance by the clerk.* The clerk must not refuse to file a paper solely because it is not in the form prescribed by the Federal Rules of Civil Procedure or by a local rule or practice. FRCP 5(d)(4).

2. *Form of electronic documents.* All pleadings, motions, and other documents that a party presents for filing, whether in paper form or in electronic form, shall meet the requirements in NY R USDCTND L.R. 10.1(a). NY R USDCTND L.R. 10.1(a). Refer above for more information.

a. *Attachments and exhibits.* A Filing User must submit in electronic form all documents referenced as exhibits or attachments in accordance with the Court's CM/ECF Users Manual unless the Court otherwise orders. A Filing User shall submit as exhibits or attachments only those excerpts of the referenced documents that are directly germane to the matter under the Court's consideration. Excerpted material must be clearly and prominently identified as such. Filing Users who file excerpts of documents as exhibits or attachments under these Administrative Procedures (NY R USDCTND CM/ECF) do so without prejudice to their right to timely file additional excerpts or the complete document. Responding parties may also timely file the complete document or additional excerpts that they believe are directly germane to the matter under the Court's consideration. NY R USDCTND CM/ECF(4)(4.4).

   i. All attachments must be described in sufficient detail so the Court and opposing counsel can easily identify and distinguish the filed attachments. Vague or general descriptions are insufficient (i.e., "Exhibit 1"). Rather, each attachment shall have a descriptive title identifying, with specificity, the document that is being filed (i.e., "Exhibit 12 Mulligan County Fire Investigation Report.") Failure to adequately describe attachments may result in the document being rejected by the Court. NY R USDCTND CM/ECF(4)(4.4).

b. *Large documents.* For information on the electronic filing of large documents, please consult the Court's CM/ECF Users Manual, which is available on the Court's web page. NY R USDCTND CM/ECF(4)(4.5).

   i. A party who believes a document is too lengthy to electronically image, i.e., "scan," may contact the Clerk's Office for permission to file that document conventionally. If the Clerk's Office grants permission to conventionally file the document, the Filing User shall electronically file a notice of conventional filing for the documents. More information regarding this process can be obtained from the Court's web page. Exhibits submitted conventionally shall be served on other parties as if they were not subject to these Administrative Procedures (NY R USDCTND CM/ECF). For a list of hints and tips for scanning large documents, please consult the Court's web page. NY R USDCTND CM/ECF(4)(4.5).

c. *Legibility.* It shall be the Filing User's responsibility to verify the legibility of scanned documents before filing them electronically with the Court. NY R USDCTND CM/ECF(4)(4.6).

d. *Color documents.* Since documents scanned in color or containing a graphic take much longer to upload, Filing Users are encouraged to configure their scanners to scan documents at 300 dpi and preferably in black and white rather than in color. NY R USDCTND CM/ECF(4)(4.7).

e. *Items not in .PDF format.* Parties wishing to file items not amenable to .pdf format (i.e. CD's, DVD's), shall file such items conventionally with the Clerk's Office. The Filing User shall electronically file a notice of conventional filing indicating that these items have been submitted to the clerk and shall serve copies of these items on other parties as if they were not subject to these Administrative Procedures (NY R USDCTND CM/ECF). These item(s) will be maintained by the Clerk's Office until the case is disposed, at which time they will be returned to the filing party for retention consistent with NY R USDCTND CM/ECF(4)(4.9). NY R USDCTND CM/ECF(4)(4.8).

3.  *Form of memoranda of law*

    a.  *Length limitation.* No party shall file or serve a memorandum of law that exceeds twenty-five (25) pages in length, unless that party obtains leave of the judge hearing the motion prior to filing. NY R USDCTND L.R. 7.1(a)(1).

    b.  *Table of contents.* All memoranda of law shall contain a table of contents. NY R USDCTND L.R. 7.1(a)(1).

4.  *Signing of pleadings, motions and other papers*

    a.  *Signature.* Every pleading, written motion, and other paper must be signed by at least one attorney of record in the attorney's name—or by a party personally if the party is unrepresented. The paper must state the signer's address, e-mail address, and telephone number. FRCP 11(a). Each document must identify the person filing the document. This identification must include an original signature of the attorney or pro se litigant; the typewritten name of that person; the address of a pro se litigant; and the bar roll number, office address, telephone number, e-mail address and fax number of the attorney. Telephone numbers of non-prisoner pro se parties may be provided voluntarily or upon request of the Court. See General Order #22 (NY R USDCTND CM/ECF) for signature requirements. NY R USDCTND L.R. 10.1(c)(2).

        i.  *Electronic signatures.* Documents filed under an attorney's login and password shall constitute that attorney's signature for purposes of the Local Rules of Practice for the United States District Court for the Northern District of New York and Federal Rules of Civil Procedure, including but not limited to FRCP 11. A pleading or other document requiring an attorney's signature shall be signed in the following manner, whether filed electronically or submitted on disk or CD/ROM to the Clerk's Office: "s/ (attorney name)." The correct format for an attorney signature is found in NY R USDCTND CM/ECF(6)(6.1). NY R USDCTND CM/ECF(6)(6.1).

            • *Non-attorney signature.* If an original document requires the signature of a non-attorney, the Filing User may scan the original document containing the original signature(s), then electronically file it on the System. Alternatively, the Filing User may convert the document into .pdf text format and submit the document using "s/" for the signature of the non-attorney. NY R USDCTND CM/ECF(6)(6.2).

            • *Multiple signatures.* A document requiring signatures of more than one party must be filed electronically either by (1) submitting a scanned document containing all necessary signatures; (2) representing the consent of the other parties on the document; or (3) in any other manner that the Court approves. NY R USDCTND CM/ECF(6)(6.3).

        ii.  *No verification or accompanying affidavit required for pleadings.* Unless a rule or statute specifically states otherwise, a pleading need not be verified or accompanied by an affidavit. FRCP 11(a).

        iii.  *Unsigned papers.* The court must strike an unsigned paper unless the omission is promptly corrected after being called to the attorney's or party's attention. FRCP 11(a).

    b.  *Representations to the court.* By presenting to the court a pleading, written motion, or other paper—whether by signing, filing, submitting, or later advocating it—an attorney or unrepresented party certifies that to the best of the person's knowledge, information, and belief, formed after an inquiry reasonable under the circumstances:

        i.  It is not being presented for any improper purpose, such as to harass, cause unnecessary delay, or needlessly increase the cost of litigation;

        ii.  The claims, defenses, and other legal contentions are warranted by existing law or by a nonfrivolous argument for extending, modifying, or reversing existing law or for establishing new law;

        iii.  The factual contentions have evidentiary support or, if specifically so identified, will likely have evidentiary support after a reasonable opportunity for further investigation or discovery; and

        iv.  The denials of factual contentions are warranted on the evidence or, if specifically so identified, are reasonably based on belief or a lack of information. FRCP 11(b).

   c.  *Sanctions.* If, after notice and a reasonable opportunity to respond, the court determines that FRCP 11(b) has been violated, the court may impose an appropriate sanction on any attorney, law firm, or party that violated FRCP 11(b) or is responsible for the violation. FRCP 11(c)(1). Refer to the United States District Court for the Northern District of New York KeyRules Motion for Sanctions document for more information.

5.  *Privacy protection for filings made with the court*

   a.  *Redacted filings.* Unless the court orders otherwise, in an electronic or paper filing with the court that contains an individual's Social Security number, taxpayer-identification number, or birth date, the name of an individual known to be a minor, or a financial-account number, a party or nonparty making the filing may include only:

      i.  The last four (4) digits of the Social Security number and taxpayer-identification number;

      ii.  The year of the individual's birth;

     iii.  The minor's initials; and

     iv.  The last four (4) digits of the financial-account number. FRCP 5.2(a); NY R USDCTND L.R. 8.1; NY R USDCTND CM/ECF(11)(11.2).

      v.  If a home address must be used, use only the City and State. NY R USDCTND L.R. 8.1; NY R USDCTND CM/ECF(11)(11.2).

     vi.  If the victim of a sexual assault must be referenced, redact the name to 'Victim.' NY R USDCTND CM/ECF(11)(11.2); NY R USDCTND L.R. 8.1.

    vii.  In addition, caution shall be exercised when filing documents that contain the following:

        •  Personal identifying number, such as a driver's license number;

        •  Medical records, treatment and diagnosis;

        •  Employment history;

        •  Individual financial information; and

        •  Proprietary or trade secret information. NY R USDCTND L.R. 8.1; NY R USDCTND CM/ECF(11)(11.2).

   b.  *Exemptions from the redaction requirement.* The redaction requirement does not apply to the following:

      i.  A financial-account number that identifies the property allegedly subject to forfeiture in a forfeiture proceeding;

      ii.  The record of an administrative or agency proceeding;

     iii.  The official record of a state-court proceeding;

     iv.  The record of a court or tribunal, if that record was not subject to the redaction requirement when originally filed;

      v.  A filing covered by FRCP 5.2(c) or FRCP 5.2(d); and

     vi.  A pro se filing in an action brought under 28 U.S.C.A. § 2241, 28 U.S.C.A. § 2254, or 28 U.S.C.A. § 2255. FRCP 5.2(b).

    vii.  Transcripts of the administrative record in social security proceedings are exempt from this requirement. State court records and other documents filed in habeas corpus proceedings are exempt from this requirement except for proceedings that involve victims of sex crimes. In habeas corpus cases involving sex crimes, the parties must redact the record and supporting papers, or may move to seal, if appropriate. NY R USDCTND L.R. 8.1.

   c.  *Limitations on remote access to electronic files; Social Security appeals and immigration cases.* Unless the court orders otherwise, in an action for benefits under the Social Security Act, and in an action or proceeding relating to an order of removal, to relief from removal, or to immigration benefits or detention, access to an electronic file is authorized as follows:

      i.  The parties and their attorneys may have remote electronic access to any part of the case file, including the administrative record;

      ii.   Any other person may have electronic access to the full record at the courthouse, but may have remote electronic access only to:

- The docket maintained by the court; and

- An opinion, order, judgment, or other disposition of the court, but not any other part of the case file or the administrative record. FRCP 5.2(c).

    d.   *Filings made under seal.* The court may order that a filing be made under seal without redaction. The court may later unseal the filing or order the person who made the filing to file a redacted version for the public record. FRCP 5.2(d); NY R USDCTND L.R. 8.1. For information on sealed matters, refer to NY R USDCTND L.R. 83.13 and NY R USDCTND CM/ECF(12).

    e.   *Protective orders.* For good cause, the court may by order in a case:

      i.   Require redaction of additional information; or

      ii.   Limit or prohibit a nonparty's remote electronic access to a document filed with the court. FRCP 5.2(e).

    f.   *Option for additional unredacted filing under seal.* A person making a redacted filing may also file an unredacted copy under seal. The court must retain the unredacted copy as part of the record. FRCP 5.2(f); NY R USDCTND L.R. 8.1; NY R USDCTND CM/ECF(11)(11.3).

    g.   *Option for filing a reference list.* A filing that contains redacted information may be filed together with a reference list that identifies each item of redacted information and specifies an appropriate identifier that uniquely corresponds to each item listed. The list must be filed under seal and may be amended as of right. Any reference in the case to a listed identifier will be construed to refer to the corresponding item of information. FRCP 5.2(g); NY R USDCTND L.R. 8.1; NY R USDCTND CM/ECF(11)(11.3).

    h.   *Responsibility for redaction.* Counsel is strongly urged to discuss this issue with all their clients so that they can make an informed decision about the inclusion of certain information. The responsibility for redacting these personal identifiers rests solely with counsel and the parties. The Clerk will not review each filing for compliance with NY R USDCTND L.R. 8.1. Counsel and the parties are cautioned that failure to redact these personal identifiers may subject them to the Court's full disciplinary power. NY R USDCTND L.R. 8.1; NY R USDCTND CM/ECF(11)(11.3).

    i.   *Waiver of protection of identifiers.* A person waives the protection of FRCP 5.2(a) as to the person's own information by filing it without redaction and not under seal. FRCP 5.2(h).

  6.  *Individual judge practices.* Refer to the Miscellaneous section of this document for information on individual judge practices on formatting documents.

## F. Filing and Service Requirements

  1.  *Filing requirements.* Any paper after the complaint that is required to be served—together with a certificate of service—must be filed within a reasonable time after service. FRCP 5(d)(1).

    a.   *How filing is made; In general.* A paper is filed by delivering it:

      i.   To the clerk; or

      ii.   To a judge who agrees to accept it for filing, and who must then note the filing date on the paper and promptly send it to the clerk. FRCP 5(d)(2).

    b.   *Electronic filing*

      i.   *Authorization of electronic filing program.* A court may, by local rule, allow papers to be filed, signed, or verified by electronic means that are consistent with any technical standards established by the Judicial Conference of the United States. A local rule may require electronic filing only if reasonable exceptions are allowed. A paper filed electronically in compliance with a local rule is a written paper for purposes of the Federal Rules of Civil Procedure. FRCP 5(d)(3).

- All cases filed in this Court may be assigned to the Electronic Case Files System ("ECF") in accordance with the Procedural Order on Electronic Case Filing (General Order #22

(NY R USDCTND CM/ECF)), the provisions of which are incorporated herein by reference, and which the Court may amend from time to time. Copies of General Order #22 (NY R USDCTND CM/ECF) are available at the Clerk's office or at the Court's webpage. NY R USDCTND L.R. 5.1.1; NY R USDCTND Order 25(XII).

- The Court may deviate from these Administrative Procedures (NY R USDCTND CM/ECF) in specific cases, without prior notice, if deemed appropriate in the exercise of discretion, considering the need for the just, speedy, and inexpensive determination of matters pending before the Court. NY R USDCTND CM/ECF(2).

ii. *Scope of electronic filing.* After January 1, 2004, all documents that attorneys admitted to practice in the Northern District of New York submit for filing shall be filed electronically using the System or shall be scanned and uploaded to the System, no matter when a case was originally filed, unless these Administrative Procedures (NY R USDCTND CM/ECF) otherwise permit or unless the assigned judge otherwise authorizes. An attorney who is not a Filing User by January 1, 2004, must show good cause to the assigned judge to file and serve pleadings and other papers in the traditional manner. NY R USDCTND CM/ECF(2).

iii. *Exceptions and/or waivers from mandatory electronic filing.* The following types of cases and/or documents are not required to be filed electronically:

- If you are seeking to have your complaint filed under seal, please file your complaint and proposed sealing order traditionally at the Clerk's Office. NY R USDCTND CM/ECF(2)(2.1)(1).

- Any document that a party proceeding pro se files. (See NY R USDCTND CM/ECF(12)(12.1) for procedural details). NY R USDCTND CM/ECF(2)(2.1)(2). A non-prisoner who is a party to a civil action and who is not represented by an attorney may file a motion to obtain an Electronic Case Filing (ECF) login and password on a form prescribed by the Clerk's Office. The Pro Se CM/ECF Registration Form shall be submitted with the motion. If during the course of the action an attorney appears on behalf of the pro se party, the Clerk's Office shall terminate the pro se party's registration based upon the attorney's appearance. NY R USDCTND CM/ECF(12)(12.1). Absent permission to file electronically, pro se filers shall file paper originals of all complaints, pleadings, motions, affidavits, briefs, and other documents which must be signed or which require either verification or an unsworn declaration under any rule or statute. The Clerk's Office will scan these original documents into an electronic file in the System but will also maintain a paper file. NY R USDCTND CM/ECF(12)(12.1). A pro se party may also seek permission to receive immediate notice of all public documents filed in their cases. Notices of Electronic Filing (NEF) and attached documents would be transmitted to a non-prisoner pro se party who selects this option. Note: The pro se party would continue to file their documents with the Clerk's Office in paper form. NY R USDCTND CM/ECF(12)(12.1).

- Sealed documents, sealed cases, documents for in camera review, documents lodged with the Court, ex parte documents, confidential agreements, Qui Tam actions and Grand Jury material and warrants must be filed traditionally. (See NY R USDCTND CM/ECF(12)(12.2) for further information the filing of the above-referenced documents). NY R USDCTND CM/ECF(2)(2.1)(3).

- Discovery: In accordance with NY R USDCTND L.R. 26.2, parties shall not file discovery, provided, however, that discovery material to be used at trial or in support of any motion, including a motion to compel or for summary judgment, shall be filed electronically with the Court prior to the trial or with the motion. Any motion pursuant to FRCP 37 shall be accompanied by the electronically filed discovery materials to which the motion relates if those materials have not previously been filed with the Court. NY R USDCTND CM/ECF(2)(2.1)(4).

- Transport Orders: All orders requesting that an incarcerated individual be transported that a judicial officer of the Northern District of New York signs shall be filed traditionally.

These Orders will not be filed with the case or uploaded to the docket but rather will be processed in accordance with the procedures that the Clerk of Court promulgates. NY R USDCTND CM/ECF(2)(2.1)(5).

iv. *Filing defined.* Electronic transmission of a document to the System in accordance with these Administrative Procedures, together with the transmission of a Notice of Electronic Filing from the Court, constitutes filing of the document for all purposes of the Federal Rules of Civil Procedure and the Local Rules of Practice for the United States District Court for the Northern District of New York and constitutes entry of the document on the docket that the Clerk's Office keeps under FRCP 58 and FRCP 79. E-mailing a document to the Clerk's Office or to the assigned judge shall not constitute "filing" of the document. NY R USDCTND CM/ECF(4)(4.1).

v. *Filing fees.* Any fee required for filing a pleading or paper in this Court is payable to the Clerk of the Court. The Court will not maintain electronic billing or debit accounts for attorneys or law firms. Effective January 1, 2007, payment for filing fees will be mandatory through CM/ECF's Internet Credit Card Payment site--a secure Treasury Site. The Filing User will be prompted to enter either Bank Account Debit (ACH) or credit card information while filing the initial pleading. Any document that requires a filing fee (e.g., Notice of Appeal, Motion for Pro Hac Vice Admission) may also be paid through the federal electronic payment website. NY R USDCTND CM/ECF(7).

vi. For more information on electronic filing, refer to NY R USDCTND CM/ECF.

c. *E-mail or facsimile filing.* Neither the Court nor the Clerk's Office will accept for filing any facsimile or e-mail transmission without prior authorization from the Court. The party using facsimile or e-mail transmissions to file its papers must accompany any such documents with a cover letter stating that the Court authorized such transmissions and the date on which the Court provided that authorization. Violations of NY R USDCTND L.R. 5.5 subject the offending party to the Court's full disciplinary powers. NY R USDCTND L.R. 5.5.

2. *Service requirements*

a. *Service; When required*

i. *In general.* Unless the Federal Rules of Civil Procedure provide otherwise, each of the following papers must be served on every party:

- An order stating that service is required;

- A pleading filed after the original complaint, unless the court orders otherwise under FRCP 5(c) because there are numerous defendants;

- A discovery paper required to be served on a party, unless the court orders otherwise;

- A written motion, except one that may be heard ex parte; and

- A written notice, appearance, demand, or offer of judgment, or any similar paper. FRCP 5(a)(1).

ii. *If a party fails to appear.* No service is required on a party who is in default for failing to appear. But a pleading that asserts a new claim for relief against such a party must be served on that party under FRCP 4. FRCP 5(a)(2).

iii. *Seizing property.* If an action is begun by seizing property and no person is or need be named as a defendant, any service required before the filing of an appearance, answer, or claim must be made on the person who had custody or possession of the property when it was seized. FRCP 5(a)(3).

b. *Service; How made*

i. *Serving an attorney.* If a party is represented by an attorney, service under FRCP 5 must be made on the attorney unless the court orders service on the party. FRCP 5(b)(1).

ii. *Service in general.* A paper is served under FRCP 5 by:

- Handing it to the person;

- Leaving it: (1) at the person's office with a clerk or other person in charge or, if no one is in charge, in a conspicuous place in the office; or (2) if the person has no office or the office is closed, at the person's dwelling or usual place of abode with someone of suitable age and discretion who resides there;

- Mailing it to the person's last known address—in which event service is complete upon mailing;

- Leaving it with the court clerk if the person has no known address;

- Sending it by electronic means if the person consented in writing—in which event service is complete upon transmission, but is not effective if the serving party learns that it did not reach the person to be served; or

- Delivering it by any other means that the person consented to in writing—in which event service is complete when the person making service delivers it to the agency designated to make delivery. FRCP 5(b)(2).

iii. *Service of electronically-filed documents.* Service is complete provided all parties receive a Notice of Electronic Filing (NEF), which is sent automatically by email from the Court (see the NEF for a list of who did/did not receive notice electronically). Transmission of the NEF constitutes service upon all Filing and Receiving Users who are listed as recipients of notice by electronic mail. It remains the responsibility of Filing and Receiving Users to maintain current contact information with the court and to regularly review the docket sheet of the case. NY R USDCTND CM/ECF(5)(5.2).

- *Non-filing or receiving users.* Attorneys and pro se parties who are not Filing or Receiving Users must be served with a paper copy of any electronically filed pleading or other document. Service of such paper copy must be made according to the Federal Rules of Civil Procedure and the Local Rules of Practice for the United States District Court for the Northern District of New York. Such paper service must be documented by electronically filing a certificate of service. NY R USDCTND CM/ECF(5)(5.2). A party who is not a Filing User of the System is entitled to a paper copy of any electronically-filed pleading, document, or order. The Filing User must therefore provide the non-Filing User with the pleading or document according to the Federal Rules of Civil Procedure. NY R US-DCTND CM/ECF(5)(5.3).

iv. *Using court facilities.* If a local rule so authorizes, a party may use the court's transmission facilities to make service under FRCP 5(b)(2)(E). FRCP 5(b)(3).

c. *Serving numerous defendants*

i. *In general.* If an action involves an unusually large number of defendants, the court may, on motion or on its own, order that:

- Defendants' pleadings and replies to them need not be served on other defendants;

- Any crossclaim, counterclaim, avoidance, or affirmative defense in those pleadings and replies to them will be treated as denied or avoided by all other parties; and

- Filing any such pleading and serving it on the plaintiff constitutes notice of the pleading to all parties. FRCP 5(c)(1).

ii. *Notifying parties.* A copy of every such order must be served on the parties as the court directs. FRCP 5(c)(2).

3. *Individual judge practices.* Refer to the Miscellaneous section of this document for information on individual judge practices on filing and serving documents.

## G. Hearings

1. *Hearings, generally*

a. *Motion days.* Listings of the regularly scheduled motion days for all judges shall be available at each Clerk's office and are available on the Court's webpage. The Clerk shall provide notice of the regular motion days for all judges to the parties at the time an action is commenced. NY R USDCTND L.R. 78.1.

b. *Return date.* Unless the Court directs otherwise, the moving party shall make its motion returnable at the next regularly scheduled motion date at least thirty-one (31) days from the date the moving party files and serves its motion. The moving party shall select a return date in accordance with the procedures set forth in NY R USDCTND L.R. 7.1(b). If the return date the moving party selects is not the next regularly scheduled motion date, or if the moving party selects no return date, the Clerk will set the proper return date and notify the parties. NY R USDCTND L.R. 7.1.

    i. Information regarding motion dates and times is specified on the case assignment form that the Court provides to the parties at the commencement of the litigation or the parties may obtain this form from the Clerk's office or at the Court's webpage. NY R USDCTND L.R. 7.1.

    ii. The Court hereby directs the Clerk to set a proper return date in motions that pro se litigants submit for filing that do not specify a return date or fail to allow for sufficient time pursuant to NY R USDCTND L.R. 7.1. Generally, the return date that the Clerk selects should not exceed thirty (30) days from the date of filing. Furthermore, the Clerk shall forward a copy of the revised or corrected notice of motion to the parties. NY R USDCTND L.R. 7.1.

c. *Oral argument.* Due process does not require that oral argument be permitted on a motion and, except as otherwise provided by local rule, the district court has discretion to determine whether it will decide the motion on the papers or hear argument by counsel (and perhaps receive evidence). FPP § 1190; F.D.I.C. v. Deglau, 207 F.3d 153 (3d Cir. 2000).

    i. The parties shall appear for oral argument on all motions that they make returnable before a district court judge, except motions for reconsideration, on the scheduled return date of the motion. A motion may be disposed of without oral argument as described in NY R USDCTND Order 25, on consideration of a request of any party, or otherwise at the discretion of the presiding judge. Thus, the parties should be prepared to have their motion papers serve as the sole method of argument on the motion. NY R USDCTND L.R. 7.1(h).

    ii. The parties shall not appear for oral argument on motions that they make returnable before a Magistrate Judge on the scheduled return date of the motion unless the Magistrate Judge sua sponte directs or grants the request of any party for oral argument. NY R USDCTND L.R. 7.1(h).

d. *Providing a regular schedule for oral hearings.* A court may establish regular times and places for oral hearings on motions. FRCP 78(a).

e. *Providing for submission on briefs.* By rule or order, the court may provide for submitting and determining motions on briefs, without oral hearings. FRCP 78(b).

2. *Hearing on motion for preliminary injunction*

    a. *Consolidating the hearing with the trial on the merits.* Before or after beginning the hearing on a motion for a preliminary injunction, the court may advance the trial on the merits and consolidate it with the hearing. Even when consolidation is not ordered, evidence that is received on the motion and that would be admissible at trial becomes part of the trial record and need not be repeated at trial. But the court must preserve any party's right to a jury trial. FRCP 65(a)(2).

    b. *Expediting the hearing after temporary restraining order is issued without notice.* If the order is issued without notice, the motion for a preliminary injunction must be set for hearing at the earliest possible time, taking precedence over all other matters except hearings on older matters of the same character. At the hearing, the party who obtained the order must proceed with the motion; if the party does not, the court must dissolve the order. FRCP 65(b)(3).

3. *Individual judge practices.* Refer to the Miscellaneous section of this document for information on individual judge practices on hearings.

## H. Forms

### 1. Federal Motion for Preliminary Injunction Forms

    a. Declaration; In support of motion for preliminary injunction. AMJUR PP INJUNCTION § 38.

    b. Memorandum of points and authorities; In support of motion for preliminary injunction. AMJUR PP INJUNCTION § 39.

c. Notice; Motion for preliminary injunction. AMJUR PP INJUNCTION § 40.

d. Motion; For preliminary injunction. AMJUR PP INJUNCTION § 41.

e. Motion; For preliminary injunction; On pleadings and other papers without evidentiary hearing or oral argument. AMJUR PP INJUNCTION § 43.

f. Affidavit; In support of motion for preliminary injunction. AMJUR PP INJUNCTION § 52.

g. Motion for preliminary injunction. 4A FEDFORMS § 5284.

h. Motion enjoining use of information acquired from employment with plaintiff. 4A FEDFORMS § 5287.

i. Motion enjoining interference with public access. 4A FEDFORMS § 5288.

j. Motion enjoining collection of tax assessment. 4A FEDFORMS § 5289.

k. Motion enjoining conducting election or certifying representative. 4A FEDFORMS § 5290.

l. Motion enjoining preventing plaintiff's acting as teacher. 4A FEDFORMS § 5291.

m. Motion enjoining interference with plaintiff's enforcement of judgment in related case. 4A FED-FORMS § 5292.

n. Motion for preliminary injunction in patent infringement action. 4A FEDFORMS § 5293.

o. Motion for preliminary injunction on basis of prayer of complaint and for setting hearing on motion. 4A FEDFORMS § 5294.

p. Notice of motion. 4A FEDFORMS § 5308.

q. Notice of motion and motion. 4A FEDFORMS § 5310.

r. Bond; To obtain preliminary injunction. FEDPROF § 1:701.

s. Opposition; To motion; General form. FEDPROF § 1:750.

t. Brief; Supporting or opposing motion. FEDPROF § 1:752.

u. Motion for temporary restraining order and preliminary injunction. GOLDLTGFMS § 13A:6.

v. Motion for preliminary injunction. GOLDLTGFMS § 13A:18.

w. Motion for preliminary injunction; Based upon pleadings and other papers without evidentiary hearing or oral argument. GOLDLTGFMS § 13A:19.

x. Motion for preliminary injunction; Supporting affidavit. GOLDLTGFMS § 13A:20.

y. Bond. GOLDLTGFMS § 19:2.

z. Bond; In support of injunction. GOLDLTGFMS § 19:3.

## I. Applicable Rules

1. *Federal rules*

   a. Serving and filing pleadings and other papers. FRCP 5.

   b. Constitutional challenge to a statute; Notice, certification, and intervention. FRCP 5.1.

   c. Privacy protection for filings made with the court. FRCP 5.2.

   d. Computing and extending time; Time for motion papers. FRCP 6.

   e. Pleadings allowed; Form of motions and other papers. FRCP 7.

   f. Disclosure statement. FRCP 7.1.

   g. Form of pleadings. FRCP 10.

   h. Signing pleadings, motions, and other papers; Representations to the court; Sanctions. FRCP 11.

   i. Taking testimony. FRCP 43.

   j. Injunctions and restraining orders. FRCP 65.

   k. Proceedings against a surety. FRCP 65.1.

l. Hearing motions; Submission on briefs. FRCP 78.

2. *Local rules*

 a. Scope of the rules. NY R USDCTND L.R. 1.1.

 b. Complex and multi-district litigation. NY R USDCTND L.R. 3.3.

 c. Service and filing of papers. NY R USDCTND L.R. 5.1.

 d. Filing by facsimile or e-mail. NY R USDCTND L.R. 5.5.

 e. Motion practice. NY R USDCTND L.R. 7.1.

 f. Personal privacy protection. NY R USDCTND L.R. 8.1.

 g. Request for three-judge court. NY R USDCTND L.R. 9.1.

 h. Form of papers. NY R USDCTND L.R. 10.1.

 i. Settlement procedures. NY R USDCTND L.R. 68.2.

 j. Orders. NY R USDCTND L.R. 77.2.

 k. Motion days. NY R USDCTND L.R. 78.1.

 l. Appearance and withdrawal of attorney. NY R USDCTND L.R. 83.2.

 m. Arbitration. NY R USDCTND L.R. 83.7-1; NY R USDCTND L.R. 83.7-2; NY R USDCTND L.R. 83.7-3.

 n. Assisted mediation program. NY R USDCTND L.R. 83.8.

 o. Mediation. NY R USDCTND L.R. 83.11-1; NY R USDCTND L.R. 83.11-3.

 p. Early neutral evaluation. NY R USDCTND L.R. 83.12-1; NY R USDCTND L.R. 83.12-3.

 q. Administrative procedures for electronic case filing. NY R USDCTND CM/ECF.

 r. Case assignment plan for the Northern District of New York. [NY R USDCTND Order 12, as amended by NY ORDER 16-4201, effective March 24, 2015].

 s. Directing the expedited service of the summons and complaint and further directing the completion of FRCP 16 stipulation for the timely progression of civil actions. [NY R USDCTND Order 25, as amended by NY ORDER 16-4187, effective June 23, 2016].

 t. Mandatory mediation program. NY R USDCTND Order 47.

**J. Miscellaneous**

**NOTE: Individual judges' rules may apply. For available judge-level information, refer to:**

DISTRICT JUDGE MAE A. D'AGOSTINO: [NY R USDCTND D'Agostino-Rules and Practices, as added by NY ORDER 16-4200, effective April 4, 2016].

DISTRICT JUDGE THOMAS J. McAVOY: NY R USDCTND McAvoy-Order.

# Motions, Oppositions and Replies
# Motion to Dismiss for Failure to State a Claim

**Document Last Updated September 2016**

**A. Checklist**

 (I) ☐ Matters to be considered by moving party

 (a) ☐ Required documents

 (1) ☐ Notice of motion and motion

 (2) ☐ Memorandum of law

 (3) ☐ Certificate of service

    (b)  ❑ Supplemental documents

        (1)  ❑ Pleading

        (2)  ❑ Notice of constitutional question

        (3)  ❑ Nongovernmental corporate disclosure statement

        (4)  ❑ Copies of authorities

        (5)  ❑ Proposed order

        (6)  ❑ Cover letter authorizing e-mail or facsimile filing

        (7)  ❑ Affidavit attesting to failed attempts to file electronically

        (8)  ❑ Notice of conventional filing

        (9)  ❑ CD/ROM with PDF of document(s)

      (10)  ❑ English translation

      (11)  ❑ Courtesy copies

      (12)  ❑ Copies for three-judge court

    (c)  ❑ Timing

        (1)  ❑ Failure to state a claim upon which relief can be granted may be raised in any pleading allowed or ordered under FRCP 7(a); every defense to a claim for relief in any pleading must be asserted in the responsive pleading if one is required

        (2)  ❑ A motion asserting any of the defenses in FRCP 12(b) must be made before pleading if a responsive pleading is allowed

        (3)  ❑ Failure to state a claim upon which relief can be granted may be raised by a motion under FRCP 12(c); after the pleadings are closed—but early enough not to delay trial—a party may move for judgment on the pleadings

        (4)  ❑ Failure to state a claim upon which relief can be granted may be raised at trial; if a pleading sets out a claim for relief that does not require a responsive pleading, an opposing party may assert at trial any defense to that claim

        (5)  ❑ The moving party must file all motion papers with the court and serve them upon the other parties not less than thirty-one (31) days prior to the return date of the motion

        (6)  ❑ A written motion and notice of the hearing must be served at least fourteen (14) days before the time specified for the hearing, with the following exceptions: (i) when the motion may be heard ex parte; (ii) when the Federal Rules of Civil Procedure set a different time; or (iii) when a court order—which a party may, for good cause, apply for ex parte—sets a different time

        (7)  ❑ Any affidavit supporting a motion must be served with the motion

(II)  ❑ Matters to be considered by opposing party

    (a)  ❑ Required documents

        (1)  ❑ Opposition

        (2)  ❑ Memorandum of law

        (3)  ❑ Certificate of service

    (b)  ❑ Supplemental documents

        (1)  ❑ Pleading

        (2)  ❑ Notice of constitutional question

        (3)  ❑ Cross-motion

        (4)  ❑ Copies of authorities

        (5)  ❑ Cover letter authorizing e-mail or facsimile filing

(6) ❑ Affidavit attesting to failed attempts to file electronically

(7) ❑ Notice of conventional filing

(8) ❑ CD/ROM with PDF of document(s)

(9) ❑ English translation

(10) ❑ Courtesy copies

(11) ❑ Copies for three-judge court

(c) ❑ Timing

    (1) ❑ The party opposing the motion must file its opposition papers with the court and serve them upon the other parties not less than seventeen (17) days prior to the return date of the motion

    (2) ❑ Except as FRCP 59(c) provides otherwise, any opposing affidavit must be served at least seven (7) days before the hearing, unless the court permits service at another time

    (3) ❑ A party may file and serve a cross-motion (meaning a competing request for relief or order similar to that requested by another party against the cross-moving party) at the time it files and serves its opposition papers to the original motion, i.e., not less than seventeen (17) days prior to the return date of the motion

## B. Timing

1. *Motion to dismiss for failure to state a claim*

    a. *In a pleading under FRCP 7(a).* Failure to state a claim upon which relief can be granted may be raised in any pleading allowed or ordered under FRCP 7(a). FRCP 12(h)(2)(A).

        i. *In a responsive pleading.* Every defense to a claim for relief in any pleading must be asserted in the responsive pleading if one is required. FRCP 12(b).

    b. *By motion.* A motion asserting any of the defenses in FRCP 12(b) must be made before pleading if a responsive pleading is allowed. FRCP 12(b). Although FRCP 12(b) encourages the responsive pleader to file a motion to dismiss before filing the answer, nothing in FRCP 12 prohibits the filing of a motion to dismiss with the answer. An untimely motion to dismiss may be considered if the defense asserted in the motion was previously raised in the responsive pleading. FEDPROC § 62:427.

    c. *By motion under FRCP 12(c).* Failure to state a claim upon which relief can be granted may be raised by a motion under FRCP 12(c). FRCP 12(h)(2)(B). After the pleadings are closed—but early enough not to delay trial—a party may move for judgment on the pleadings. FRCP 12(c).

    d. *At trial.* Failure to state a claim upon which relief can be granted may be raised at trial. FRCP 12(h)(2)(C). If a pleading sets out a claim for relief that does not require a responsive pleading, an opposing party may assert at trial any defense to that claim. FRCP 12(b).

2. *Timing of motions, generally.* The moving party must file all motion papers with the Court and serve them upon the other parties not less than THIRTY-ONE (31) DAYS prior to the return date of the motion. NY R USDCTND L.R. 7.1(b)(1).

    a. *Motion and notice of hearing.* A written motion and notice of the hearing must be served at least fourteen (14) days before the time specified for the hearing, with the following exceptions:

        i. When the motion may be heard ex parte;

        ii. When the Federal Rules of Civil Procedure set a different time; or

        iii. When a court order—which a party may, for good cause, apply for ex parte—sets a different time. FRCP 6(c)(1).

    b. *Supporting affidavit.* Any affidavit supporting a motion must be served with the motion. FRCP 6(c)(2).

3. *Timing of opposing papers.* The party opposing the motion must file its opposition papers with the Court and serve them upon the other parties not less than SEVENTEEN (17) DAYS prior to the return date of the motion. NY R USDCTND L.R. 7.1(b)(1).

    a. *Opposing affidavit.* Except as FRCP 59(c) provides otherwise, any opposing affidavit must be served

at least seven (7) days before the hearing, unless the court permits service at another time. FRCP 6(c)(2).

b. *Cross-motion.* A party may file and serve a cross-motion (meaning a competing request for relief or order similar to that requested by another party against the cross-moving party) at the time it files and serves its opposition papers to the original motion, i.e., not less than SEVENTEEN (17) DAYS prior to the return date of the motion. NY R USDCTND L.R. 7.1(c).

4. *Timing of reply papers.* Where the respondent files an answering affidavit setting up a new matter, the moving party ordinarily is allowed a reasonable time to file a reply affidavit since failure to deny the new matter by affidavit may operate as an admission of its truth. AMJUR MOTIONS § 25.

a. *Reply papers.* The moving party must file its reply papers, which may not exceed (10) pages with the Court and serve them upon the other parties not less than ELEVEN (11) DAYS prior to the return date of the motion. NY R USDCTND L.R. 7.1(b)(1).

b. *Opposition to cross-motion.* The original moving party must file its reply/opposition papers with the Court and serve them on the other parties not less than ELEVEN (11) DAYS prior to the return date of the original motion. NY R USDCTND L.R. 7.1(c).

5. *Effect of a FRCP 12 motion on the time to serve a responsive pleading.* Unless the court sets a different time, serving a motion under FRCP 12 alters the periods in FRCP 12(a) as follows:

a. If the court denies the motion or postpones its disposition until trial, the responsive pleading must be served within fourteen (14) days after notice of the court's action; or

b. If the court grants a motion for a more definite statement, the responsive pleading must be served within fourteen (14) days after the more definite statement is served. FRCP 12(a)(4).

6. *Computation of time*

a. *Computing time.* FRCP 6 applies in computing any time period specified in the Federal Rules of Civil Procedure, in any local rule or court order, or in any statute that does not specify a method of computing time. FRCP 6(a).

i. *Period stated in days or a longer unit.* When the period is stated in days or a longer unit of time:

- Exclude the day of the event that triggers the period;

- Count every day, including intermediate Saturdays, Sundays, and legal holidays; and

- Include the last day of the period, but if the last day is a Saturday, Sunday, or legal holiday, the period continues to run until the end of the next day that is not a Saturday, Sunday, or legal holiday. FRCP 6(a)(1).

ii. *Period stated in hours.* When the period is stated in hours:

- Begin counting immediately on the occurrence of the event that triggers the period;

- Count every hour, including hours during intermediate Saturdays, Sundays, and legal holidays; and

- If the period would end on a Saturday, Sunday, or legal holiday, the period continues to run until the same time on the next day that is not a Saturday, Sunday, or legal holiday. FRCP 6(a)(2).

iii. *Inaccessibility of the clerk's office.* Unless the court orders otherwise, if the clerk's office is inaccessible:

- On the last day for filing under FRCP 6(a)(1), then the time for filing is extended to the first accessible day that is not a Saturday, Sunday, or legal holiday; or

- During the last hour for filing under FRCP 6(a)(2), then the time for filing is extended to the same time on the first accessible day that is not a Saturday, Sunday, or legal holiday. FRCP 6(a)(3).

iv. *"Last day" defined.* Unless a different time is set by a statute, local rule, or court order, the last day ends:

- For electronic filing, at midnight in the court's time zone; and

- For filing by other means, when the clerk's office is scheduled to close. FRCP 6(a)(4).

v. *"Next day" defined.* The "next day" is determined by continuing to count forward when the period is measured after an event and backward when measured before an event. FRCP 6(a)(5).

vi. *"Legal holiday" defined.* "Legal holiday" means:

- The day set aside by statute for observing New Year's Day, Martin Luther King Jr.'s Birthday, Washington's Birthday, Memorial Day, Independence Day, Labor Day, Columbus Day, Veterans' Day, Thanksgiving Day, or Christmas Day;

- Any day declared a holiday by the President or Congress; and

- For periods that are measured after an event, any other day declared a holiday by the state where the district court is located. FRCP 6(a)(6).

b. *Computation of electronic filing deadlines.* A document will be deemed timely filed if electronically filed prior to midnight Eastern Time. However, if the time of day is of the essence, the assigned judge may order that the document be filed by a time certain. NY R USDCTND CM/ECF(4)(4.3).

i. *Technical failures.* A Filing User, whose filing is untimely as the result of a technical failure of the Court's CM/ECF site, may seek appropriate relief from the Court. However, Filing Users are cautioned that, in some circumstances, the Court lacks the authority to grant an extension of time to file (e.g., FRCP 6(b) of the Federal Rules of Civil Procedure). NY R USDCTND CM/ECF(10)(10.1).

- *Technical failure of the filing user's system.* Problems with the Filing User's system, such as phone line problems, problems with the Filing User's Internet Service Provider ("ISP"), or hardware or software problems, will not constitute a technical failure under these Administrative Procedures nor excuse an untimely filing. A Filing User who cannot file documents electronically because of a problem on the Filing User's system must file the documents' conventionally along with an affidavit explaining the reason for not filing the documents electronically. NY R USDCTND CM/ECF(10)(10.2).

c. *Extending time*

i. *In general.* When an act may or must be done within a specified time, the court may, for good cause, extend the time:

- With or without motion or notice if the court acts, or if a request is made, before the original time or its extension expires; or

- On motion made after the time has expired if the party failed to act because of excusable neglect. FRCP 6(b)(1).

ii. *Exceptions.* A court must not extend the time to act under FRCP 50(b), FRCP 50(d), FRCP 52(b), FRCP 59(b), FRCP 59(d), FRCP 59(e), and FRCP 60(b). FRCP 6(b)(2).

iii. Refer to the United States District Court for the Northern District of New York KeyRules Motion for Continuance/Extension of Time document for more information on extending time.

d. *Additional time after certain kinds of service.* When a party may or must act within a specified time after service and service is made under FRCP 5(b)(2)(C), FRCP 5(b)(2)(D), FRCP 5(b)(2)(E), or FRCP 5(b)(2)(F), three (3) days are added after the period would otherwise expire under FRCP 6(a). FRCP 6(d).

i. In accordance with FRCP 6(e), service by electronic means is treated the same as service by mail for purposes of adding three (3) days to the prescribed period to respond. NY R USDCTND CM/ECF(5)(5.4). [Editor's note: the reference to FRCP 6(e) is likely meant to be a reference to FRCP 6(d)].

7. *Individual judge practices.* Refer to the Miscellaneous section of this document for information on individual judge practices on timing of documents.

## C.  General Requirements

1.  *Motions, generally*

    a.  *Requirements.* A request for a court order must be made by motion. The motion must:

        i.  Be in writing unless made during a hearing or trial;

        ii.  State with particularity the grounds for seeking the order; and

        iii.  State the relief sought. FRCP 7(b)(1).

        iv.  When a moving party makes a motion based upon a rule or statute, the moving party must specify in its moving papers the rule or statute upon which it bases its motion. NY R USDCTND L.R. 7.1(a)(1).

    b.  *Notice of motion.* A party interested in resisting the relief sought by a motion has a right to notice thereof, and an opportunity to be heard. AMJUR MOTIONS § 12.

        i.  In addition to statutory or court rule provisions requiring notice of a motion—the purpose of such a notice requirement having been said to be to prevent a party from being prejudicially surprised by a motion—principles of natural justice dictate that an adverse party generally must be given notice that a motion will be presented to the court. AMJUR MOTIONS § 12.

        ii.  "Notice," in this regard, means reasonable notice, including a meaningful opportunity to prepare and to defend against allegations of a motion. AMJUR MOTIONS § 12.

    c.  *Writing requirement.* The writing requirement is intended to insure that the adverse parties are informed and have a record of both the motion's pendency and the grounds on which the movant seeks an order. FPP § 1191; Feldberg v. Quechee Lakes Corp., 463 F.3d 195 (2d Cir. 2006).

        i.  It is sufficient "if the motion is stated in a written notice of the hearing of the motion." FPP § 1191.

    d.  *Particularity requirement.* The particularity requirement insures that the opposing parties will have notice of their opponent's contentions. FEDPROC § 62:364; Goodman v. 1973 26 Foot Trojan Vessel, Arkansas Registration No. AR1439SN, 859 F.2d 71, 12 Fed.R.Serv.3d 645 (8th Cir. 1988). That requirement ensures that notice of the basis for the motion is provided to the court and to the opposing party so as to avoid prejudice, provide the opponent with a meaningful opportunity to respond, and provide the court with enough information to process the motion correctly. FEDPROC § 62:364; Andreas v. Volkswagen of America, Inc., 336 F.3d 789, 56 Fed.R.Serv.3d 6 (8th Cir. 2003).

        i.  Reasonable specification of the grounds for a motion is sufficient. However, where a movant fails to state even one ground for granting the motion in question, the movant has failed to meet the minimal standard of "reasonable specification." FEDPROC § 62:364; Martinez v. Trainor, 556 F.2d 818, 23 Fed.R.Serv.2d 403 (7th Cir. 1977).

        ii.  The court may excuse the failure to comply with the particularity requirement if it is inadvertent, and where no prejudice is shown by the opposing party. FEDPROC § 62:364.

    e.  *Order to show cause.* All motions that a party brings by Order to Show Cause shall conform to the requirements set forth in NY R USDCTND L.R. 7.1(a)(1) and NY R USDCTND L.R. 7.1(a)(2). Immediately after filing an Order to Show Cause, the moving party must telephone the Chambers of the presiding judicial officer and inform Chambers staff that it has filed an Order to Show Cause. Parties may obtain the telephone numbers for all Chambers from the Clerk's office or at the Court's webpage. The Court shall determine the briefing schedule and return date applicable to motions brought by Order to Show Cause. NY R USDCTND L.R. 7.1(e).

        i.  In addition to the requirements set forth in NY R USDCTND L.R. 7.1(a)(1) and NY R USDCTND L.R. 7.1(a)(2), a motion brought by Order to Show Cause must include an affidavit clearly and specifically showing good and sufficient cause why the standard Notice of Motion procedure cannot be used. The moving party must give reasonable advance notice of the application for an Order to Show Cause to the other parties, except in those circumstances where the movant can demonstrate, in a detailed and specific affidavit, good cause and substantial prejudice that would result from the requirement of reasonable notice. NY R USDCTND L.R. 7.1(e).

      ii.    An Order to Show Cause must contain a space for the assigned judge to set forth:

- The deadline for filing and serving supporting papers,
- The deadline for filing and serving opposing papers, and
- The date and time for the hearing. NY R USDCTND L.R. 7.1(e).

2. *Motion to dismiss for failure to state a claim.* A party may assert the defense of failure to state a claim upon which relief can be granted by motion. FRCP 12(b)(6). The motion under FRCP 12(b)(6) is available to test a claim for relief in any pleading, whether it be in the plaintiff's original complaint, a defendant's counterclaim, a defendant's cross-claim or counterclaim thereto, or a third-party claim or any other FRCP 14 claim. Most commonly, of course, a FRCP 12(b)(6) motion is directed against the plaintiff's complaint. FPP § 1356.

    a.    *Applicable standard.* The FRCP 12(b)(6) motion is used to test the sufficiency of the complaint. FEDPROC § 62:461; Petruska v. Gannon University, 462 F.3d 294, 212 Ed.Law.Rep. 598 (3d Cir. 2006). In this regard, the applicable standard is stated in FRCP 8(a)(2), which requires that a pleading setting forth a claim for relief contain a short and plain statement of the claim showing that the pleader is entitled to relief. Thus, a complaint must set forth sufficient information to suggest that there is some recognized legal theory upon which relief can be granted. FEDPROC § 62:461. Only when the plaintiff's complaint fails to meet this liberal pleading standard is it subject to dismissal under FRCP 12(b)(6). FPP § 1356.

      i.    In order to withstand a motion to dismiss filed under FRCP 12(b)(6) in response to claims understood to raise a high risk of abusive litigation, addressed by FRCP 9(b), a plaintiff must state factual allegations with greater particularity than that required by FRCP 8. FEDPROC § 62:470; Bell Atlantic Corp. v. Twombly, 550 U.S. 544, 127 S.Ct. 1955, 167 L.Ed.2d 929, 68 Fed.R.Serv.3d 661 (2007).

      ii.    FRCP 12(b)(6) motions are looked on with disfavor by the courts, and are granted sparingly and with care. FEDPROC § 62:464. Even if it is doubtful that the plaintiff would ultimately prevail, if the plaintiff colorably states facts which, if proven, would entitle him or her to relief, a motion to dismiss for failure to state a claim should not be granted. FEDPROC § 62:464.

    b.    *Construction of allegations of complaint (or other pleading).* In considering a FRCP 12(b)(6) motion to dismiss, the complaint is liberally construed and is viewed in the light most favorable to the plaintiff. FEDPROC § 62:467; Bell Atlantic Corp. v. Twombly, 550 U.S. 544, 127 S.Ct. 1955, 167 L.Ed.2d 929, 68 Fed.R.Serv.3d 661 (2007).

      i.    On a motion to dismiss, a federal court presumes that general allegations embrace those specific facts that are necessary to support the claim. FEDPROC § 62:467; Steel Co. v. Citizens for a Better Environment, 523 U.S. 83, 118 S.Ct. 1003, 140 L.Ed.2d 210 (1998).

      ii.    In addition, the well-pleaded allegations of fact contained in the complaint and every inference fairly deducible therefrom are accepted as true for purposes of the motion, including facts alleged on information and belief. FEDPROC § 62:467; Bell Atlantic Corp. v. Twombly, 550 U.S. 544, 127 S.Ct. 1955, 167 L.Ed.2d 929, 68 Fed.R.Serv.3d 661 (2007); Tellabs, Inc. v. Makor Issues & Rights, Ltd., 551 U.S. 308, 127 S.Ct. 2499, 168 L.Ed.2d 179 (2007).

      iii.    However, the court will not accept as true the plaintiff's bare statements of opinions, conclusory allegations, and unwarranted inferences of fact. FEDPROC § 62:467; Leopoldo Fontanillas, Inc. v. Luis Ayala Colon Sucesores, Inc., 283 F.Supp.2d 579 (D.P.R. 2003); Hopkins v. Women's Div., General Bd. of Global Ministries, 238 F.Supp.2d 174 (D.D.C. 2002). Nor will the court accept as true facts which are legally impossible, facts which the court can take judicial notice of as being other than as alleged by the plaintiff, or facts which by the record or by a document attached to the complaint appear to be unfounded. FEDPROC § 62:467; Cohen v. U.S., 129 F.2d 733 (8th Cir. 1942); Henthorn v. Department of Navy, 29 F.3d 682, 29 Fed.R.Serv.3d 1007 (D.C. Cir. 1994).

    c.    *Affirmative defenses.* With some exception, it is generally agreed that affirmative defenses can be raised by a FRCP 12(b)(6) motion to dismiss. FEDPROC § 62:471; McCready v. eBay, Inc., 453 F.3d 882 (7th Cir. 2006). However, in order for these defenses to be raised on a FRCP 12(b)(6) motion to dismiss, the complaint must clearly show on its face that the affirmative defense is applicable and bars the action. FEDPROC § 62:471; In re Colonial Mortgage Bankers Corp., 324 F.3d 12 (1st Cir. 2003). Thus, FRCP 12(b)(6) motions may be used to raise the affirmative defenses of: (1) statute of limitations; (2) statute of frauds; (3) res judicata; (4) collateral estoppel; (5) release; (6) waiver; (7) estoppel; (8) sovereign immunity; (9) illegality; and (10) contributory negligence. FEDPROC § 62:471.

    d. *Joining motions*

        i. *Right to join.* A motion under FRCP 12 may be joined with any other motion allowed by FRCP 12. FRCP 12(g)(1).

        ii. *Limitation on further motions.* Except as provided in FRCP 12(h)(2) or FRCP 12(h)(3), a party that makes a motion under FRCP 12 must not make another motion under FRCP 12 raising a defense or objection that was available to the party but omitted from its earlier motion. FRCP 12(g)(2).

    e. *Waiving and preserving certain defenses.* No defense or objection is waived by joining it with one or more other defenses or objections in a responsive pleading or in a motion. FRCP 12(b).

        i. *When some are waived.* A party waives any defense listed in FRCP 12(b)(2) through FRCP 12(b)(5) by:

- Omitting it from a motion in the circumstances described in FRCP 12(g)(2); or

- Failing to either: (1) make it by motion under FRCP 12; or (2) include it in a responsive pleading or in an amendment allowed by FRCP 15(a)(1) as a matter of course. FRCP 12(h)(1).

        ii. *When to raise others.* Failure to state a claim upon which relief can be granted, to join a person required by FRCP 19(b), or to state a legal defense to a claim may be raised:

- In any pleading allowed or ordered under FRCP 7(a);

- By a motion under FRCP 12(c); or

- At trial. FRCP 12(h)(2).

        iii. *Lack of subject matter jurisdiction.* If the court determines at any time that it lacks subject-matter jurisdiction, the court must dismiss the action. FRCP 12(h)(3).

3. *Opposing papers.* The Federal Rules of Civil Procedure do not require any formal answer, return, or reply to a motion, except where the Federal Rules of Civil Procedure or local rules may require affidavits, memoranda, or other papers to be filed in opposition to a motion. Such papers are simply to apprise the court of such opposition and the grounds of that opposition. FEDPROC § 62:359.

    a. *Effect of failure to respond to motion.* Although in the absence of statutory provision or court rule, a motion ordinarily does not require a written answer, when a party files a motion and the opposing party fails to respond, the court may construe such failure to respond as nonopposition to the motion or an admission that the motion was meritorious, may take the facts alleged in the motion as true—the rule in some jurisdictions being that the failure to respond to a fact set forth in a motion is deemed an admission—and may grant the motion if the relief requested appears to be justified. AMJUR MOTIONS § 28.

    b. *Assent or no opposition not determinative.* However, a motion will not be granted automatically simply because an "assent" or a notation of "no opposition" has been filed; federal judges frequently deny motions that have been assented to when it is thought that justice so dictates. FPP § 1190.

    c. *Responsive pleading inappropriate as response to motion.* An attempt to answer or oppose a motion with a responsive pleading usually is not appropriate. FPP § 1190.

4. *Reply papers.* A moving party may be required or permitted to prepare papers in addition to his original motion papers. AMJUR MOTIONS § 25. Papers answering or replying to opposing papers may be appropriate, in the interests of justice, where it appears there is a substantial reason for allowing a reply. Thus, a court may accept reply papers where a party demonstrates that the papers to which it seeks to file a reply raise new issues that are material to the disposition of the question before the court, or where the

court determines, sua sponte, that it wishes further briefing of an issue raised in those papers and orders the submission of additional papers. FEDPROC § 62:360.

    a.   *Function of reply papers.* The function of a reply affidavit is to answer the arguments made in opposition to the position taken by the movant and not to permit the movant to introduce new arguments in support of the motion. AMJUR MOTIONS § 25.

    b.   *Issues raised for the first time in a reply document.* However, the view has been followed in some jurisdictions, that as a matter of judicial economy, where there is no prejudice and where the issues could be raised simply by filing a motion to dismiss, the trial court has discretion to consider arguments raised for the first time in a reply memorandum, and that a trial court may grant a motion to strike issues raised for the first time in a reply memorandum. AMJUR MOTIONS § 26.

    c.   *Opposition to cross-motion.* The original moving party may reply in further support of the original motion and in opposition to the cross-motion with a reply/opposition brief that does not exceed twenty-five (25) pages in length, exclusive of exhibits. NY R USDCTND L.R. 7.1(c).

5.   *Surreply.* A surreply is not permitted. NY R USDCTND L.R. 7.1(b)(1).

    a.   *Surreply in support of cross-motion.* The cross-moving party may not reply in further support of its cross-motion without the Court's prior permission. NY R USDCTND L.R. 7.1(c).

6.   *Submission of proposed order by prevailing party.* If the assigned judge instructs the prevailing party to do so, the prevailing party shall submit a proposed order which the opposing party has approved and which contains the endorsement of the opposing party: "Approved as to form." NY R USDCTND L.R. 77.2(b). In civil actions where the Court has directed a party to submit an order or judgment, that party shall file all such orders or judgments in duplicate, and the Clerk's entry of such duplicate in the proper record book shall be deemed in compliance with FRCP 79(b). Such party shall also furnish the Clerk with a sufficient number of additional copies for each party to the action, which the Clerk shall mail with notice of entry in accordance with FRCP 77(d). NY R USDCTND L.R. 5.1(b).

    a.   *Disagreement as to form of proposed order.* When the parties are unable to agree as to the form of the proposed order, the prevailing party shall, on seven (7) days notice to all other parties, submit a proposed order and a written explanation for the form of that order. The Court may award costs and attorney's fees against a party whose unreasonable conduct the Court deemed to have required the bringing of the motion. The provisions of NY R USDCTND L.R. 7.1 shall not apply to such motion, and the Court shall not hear oral argument. NY R USDCTND L.R. 77.2(b).

    b.   For more information on orders, refer to NY R USDCTND L.R. 77.2.

7.   *Sanctions for vexatious or frivolous motions or failure to comply with* NY R USDCTND L.R. 7.1. A party who presents vexatious or frivolous motion papers or fails to comply with NY R USDCTND L.R. 7.1 is subject to discipline as the Court deems appropriate, including sanctions and the imposition of costs and attorney's fees to the opposing party. NY R USDCTND L.R. 7.1(i).

8.   *Complex and multi-district litigation.* If the assigned judge determines, in his or her discretion, that the case is of such a complex nature that it cannot reasonably be trial ready within eighteen (18) months from the date the complaint is filed, the assigned judge may design and issue a particularized case management order that will move the case to trial as quickly as the complexity of the case allows. NY R USDCTND L.R. 3.3(a). The parties shall promptly notify the Court in writing if any action commenced is appropriate for multi-district litigation. NY R USDCTND L.R. 3.3(b).

9.   *Appearances.* An attorney appearing for a party in a civil case shall promptly file with the Clerk a written notice of appearance; however, an attorney does not need to file a notice of appearance if the attorney who would be filing the notice of appearance is the same individual who has signed the complaint, notice of removal, pre-answer motion, or answer. NY R USDCTND L.R. 83.2(a). For more information, refer to NY R USDCTND L.R. 83.2.

10.   *Related cases.* A civil case is "related" to another civil case for purposes of this guideline when, because of the similarity of facts and legal issues or because the cases arise from the same transactions or events, a substantial saving of judicial resources is likely to result from assigning the cases to the same Judge and Magistrate Judge. NY R USDCTND Order 12(G)(2). A civil case shall not be deemed related to another civil case merely because the civil case: (1) involves similar legal issues, or (2) involves the same parties.

NY R USDCTND Order 12(G)(3). Presumptively, and subject to the power of a Judge to determine otherwise pursuant to NY R USDCTND Order 12(G)(5), civil cases shall not be deemed to be "related" unless both cases are still pending before the Court. NY R USDCTND Order 12(G)(4).

a. *New filings.* If an attorney or filing party indicates on the Civil Cover Sheet that a case is related to an earlier filed case, the Clerk shall instruct the filing party to file a notice of related cases. The allegedly related cases will be submitted by the Clerk to the Judge to whom the earliest filed case is assigned, who shall advise the Clerk whether such cases are related. NY R USDCTND Order 12(G)(1).

b. *Judicial determination that civil cases are "related."* Except for the cases described in the final sentence of NY R USDCTND Order 12(G)(6), all civil cases shall be randomly assigned when they are filed. Other than the cases described in the final sentence of NY R USDCTND Order 12(G)(6), civil cases shall not be deemed to be "related" for purposes of this guideline at the instance of any litigant or attorney unless and until there has been a determination by a Judge of this Court that the standard of NY R USDCTND Order 12(G)(2) is met. NY R USDCTND Order 12(G)(5).

  i. *Notice of related filing.* Any party may apply for such a determination by filing with the Clerk a notice of related filing, which should include an explanation as to why the standard of NY R USDCTND Order 12(G)(2) is met. A form for this purpose is available on the Court's website. A copy of the notice shall be served on all other parties who have appeared. Such an application must be made after the date when at least a majority of the defendants have been served with the complaint. Before making such an application, the applicant must confer in good faith with all other parties in an effort to reach an agreement on whether or not the case is "related". After such an application is made, any other party may serve and file within seven (7) calendar days a letter of no more than two (2) pages supporting or opposing the application. The application to have the case assigned to another Judge shall be presented to the Judge with the earliest filed case for decision on whether the action(s) should be reassigned as related cases. The Judge with the earliest filed case may then enter an order in the case at bar, either deeming the case to be related and directing the Clerk to reassign the action, or denying the application for reassignment. Any disputes concerning the assignment of related cases will be referred to the Chief Judge for resolution. NY R USDCTND Order 12(G)(5).

c. For more information on related cases, refer to NY R USDCTND Order 12(G).

11. *Alternative dispute resolution (ADR).* It is the mission of this court to do everything it can to help parties resolve their disputes as fairly, quickly, and efficiently as possible. NY R USDCTND Order 25(VIII).

a. *Arbitration.* NY R USDCTND L.R. 83.7 governs the consensual arbitration program for referral of civil actions to court-annexed arbitration. It may remain in effect until further order of the Court. Its purpose is to establish a less formal procedure for the just, efficient and economical resolution of disputes, while preserving the right to a full trial on demand. NY R USDCTND L.R. 83.7-1.

  i. *Actions subject to arbitration.* The Clerk shall notify the parties in all civil cases, except as the Local Rules of Practice for the United States District Court for the Northern District of New York otherwise direct, that they may consent to non-binding arbitration under NY R US-DCTND L.R. 83.7. The notice shall be furnished to the parties at pretrial/scheduling conferences or shall be included with pretrial conference notices and instructions. Consent to arbitration under NY R USDCTND L.R. 83.7 shall be discussed at the pretrial/scheduling conference. No party or attorney shall be prejudiced for refusing to participate in arbitration. The Court shall allow the referral of any civil action pending before it to the arbitration process if the parties consent. The plaintiff shall be responsible for securing the execution of a consent form by the parties and for filing the form with the Clerk within fourteen (14) days after the parties receive the form. The parties shall freely and knowingly enter into the consent. NY R USDCTND L.R. 83.7-2.

  ii. *Referral to arbitration.* The Clerk shall refer every action subject to NY R USDCTND L.R. 83.7 to arbitration in accordance with the procedures under NY R USDCTND L.R. 83.7 twenty-one (21) days after the filing of the last responsive pleading or within twenty-one (21) days of the filing of a stipulated consent order referring the action to arbitration, whichever event occurs last, except as otherwise provided. If any party notices a motion to dismiss under the provisions of FRCP 12(a) and/or FRCP 12(b), or a motion to join necessary parties pursuant to the Federal Rules of Civil Procedure prior to the expiration of the twenty-one (21) day period, the assigned judge shall hear the motion and further proceedings under NY R USDCTND L.R. 83.7 shall be deferred pending decision on the motion. If the Court does not dismiss the action on the motion, the Court shall refer the action to arbitration twenty-one (21) days after the filing of the decision. NY R USDCTND L.R. 83.7-3(a). Motions for summary judgment pursuant to FRCP 56 shall be filed and served within twenty-one (21) days following the close of discovery. The filing of a FRCP 56 motion shall defer further proceedings under NY R USDCTND L.R. 83.7 pending decision on the motion. NY R USDCTND L.R. 83.7-3(a).

- *Relief from referral.* Any party shall request relief from the operation of NY R USDCTND L.R. 83.7 by filing with the Court a motion for the relief within twenty-one (21) days after entry of the initial stipulated consent order which refers the case for arbitration. The assigned judge shall, sua sponte, exempt an action from the application of NY R USDCTND L.R. 83.7 where the objectives of arbitration would not be realized because (1) the case involves complex or novel legal issues, (2) legal issues predominate over factual issues, or (3) for other good cause. NY R USDCTND L.R. 83.7-3(c).

iii. For more information on arbitration, refer to NY R USDCTND L.R. 83.7.

b. *Mediation.* The purpose of NY R USDCTND L.R. 83.11 is to provide a supplementary procedure to the Court's existing alternative dispute resolution procedures. NY R USDCTND L.R. 83.11 provides for an earlier resolution of civil disputes resulting in savings of time and cost to litigants and the Court without sacrificing the quality of justice rendered or the right of litigants to a full trial on all issues not resolved through mediation. NY R USDCTND L.R. 83.11-1(a). Mediation is a process by which an impartial person, the mediator, facilitates communication between disputing parties to promote understanding, reconciliation and settlement. The mediator is an advocate for settlement and uses the mediation process to help the parties fully explore any potential area of agreement. The mediator does not serve as a judge or arbitrator and has no authority to render any decision on any disputed issue or to force a settlement. The parties themselves are responsible for negotiating any resolution(s) to their dispute. NY R USDCTND L.R. 83.11-1(b).

i. *Actions subject to mediation.* The Court may refer any civil action (or any portion thereof) to mediation under NY R USDCTND L.R. 83.11: (1) by order of referral; or (2) on the motion of any party; or (3) by consent of the parties. NY R USDCTND L.R. 83.11-3(a).

- *Withdrawal from mediation.* The parties may withdraw from mediation any civil action or claim that the Court refers to mediation pursuant to NY R USDCTND L.R. 83.11-3 by application to the assigned judge at least ten (10) days prior to the scheduled mediation session. NY R USDCTND L.R. 83.11-3(b).

ii. *Mandatory mediation program.* The United States District Court for the Northern District of New York has adopted this Mandatory Mediation Plan. The paid Mediation Program is designed to provide quicker, less expensive and potentially more satisfying alternatives to continuing litigation, without impairing the quality of justice or the right to trial. NY R USDCTND Order 47(1)(1.2)(A). This Mandatory Mediation Plan applies to civil actions pending as well as newly filed actions, except as otherwise indicated in NY R USDCTND Order 47. The Local Rules for voluntary mediation will apply only to Pro Se Cases that proceed through the Assisted Mediation Program. NY R USDCTND Order 47(1)(1.2)(B).

- *Referral into the pilot mandatory mediation program for new cases.* All civil cases shall be referred automatically into the Mandatory Mediation Program. Notice of the Mandatory Mediation requirements will be provided to all parties immediately upon the filing of a complaint and answer or a notice of removal. ADR intervention will be scheduled at the conference held pursuant to NY R USDCTND L.R. 16.1. NY R USDCTND Order 47(2)(2.1)(A). For a list of categories of actions exempted from automatic referral, refer to NY R USDCTND Order 47(2)(2.1)(A).

- *Referral into the pilot mandatory mediation program for pending cases.* The assigned

Judge or Magistrate Judge on any pending civil case may, sua sponte or with status conference, issue an order referring the case into the Mandatory Mediation Program. The order shall specify a date on which the ADR intervention is to be completed. NY R USDCTND Order 47(2)(2.1)(B).

- *Referral into the pilot mandatory mediation program by stipulation.* A case may be referred into the Mandatory Mediation Program by stipulation of all parties. Stipulations shall be filed and shall designate the time frame within which the ADR process will be completed. Stipulations are presumed acceptable unless the assigned Judge or Magistrate Judge determines that the interests of justice are not served. NY R USDCTND Order 47(2)(2.1)(C).

- *Relief from referral.* Motions to opt out of the program will be addressed by the assigned Magistrate Judge at the FRCP 16 conference. NY R USDCTND Order 47(2)(2.2)(A). Opting Out Motions shall be granted only for "good cause" shown. Inconvenience, travel costs, attorney fees or other costs shall not constitute "good cause." A party seeking relief from the Mandatory Mediation Program must set forth the reasons why Mandatory Mediation has no reasonable chance of being productive. NY R USDCTND Order 47(2)(2.2)(B). The assigned Magistrate Judge may, sua sponte, exempt any case from the Court's Mandatory Mediation Program. NY R USDCTND Order 47(2)(2.2)(C).

iii. *Assisted mediation program.* The Court may assign specially trained pro bono Special Mediation Counsel to assist pro se civilian litigants with preparing for and participating in mediation. The Assisted Mediation Program is open to civilian pro se parties to actions in the Northern District of New York. The assigned judge or magistrate judge determines if the case would benefit from mediation and would also benefit from the assignment of Special Mediation Counsel to assist the pro se party with the mediation process. NY R USDCTND L.R. 83.8(a). Appointment of Special Mediation Counsel is in no way guaranteed, even if the action is referred to the court-annexed mediation program. Appointment is at the sole discretion of the presiding judge. NY R USDCTND L.R. 83.8(a).

- *Referral to assisted mediation program.* If the court determines that referral to the Assisted Mediation Program is appropriate, the Court shall enter an order of reference to the Assisted Mediation Program. NY R USDCTND L.R. 83.8(b).

iv. For more information on mediation, refer to NY R USDCTND L.R. 83.11 and NY R USDCTND Order 47.

c. *Early neutral evaluation (ENE).* Early neutral evaluation (ENE) is a process in which parties obtain from an experienced neutral (an "evaluator") a nonbinding, reasoned, oral evaluation of the merits of the case. The first step in the ENE process involves the Court appointing an evaluator who has expertise in the area of law in the case. After the parties exchange essential information and position statements early in the pretrial period (usually within one hundred fifty (150) to two hundred (200) days after a complaint has been filed), the evaluator convenes an ENE session that typically lasts about two hours. At the ENE meeting, each side briefly presents the factual and legal basis of its position. The evaluator may ask questions of the parties and help them identify the main issues in dispute and the areas of agreement. The evaluator may also help the parties explore options for settlement. If settlement does not occur, the evaluator then offers an opinion as to the settlement value of the case, including the likelihood of liability and the likely range of damages. With the benefit of this assessment, the parties are again encouraged to discuss settlement, with or without the evaluator's assistance. The parties may also explore ways to narrow the issues in dispute, exchange information about the case or otherwise prepare efficiently for trial. NY R USDCTND L.R. 83.12-1.

i. *Actions subject to early neutral evaluation.* The Court may refer any civil action (or any portion thereof) to ENE under NY R USDCTND L.R. 83.12: (1) by order of referral; (2) on the motion of any party; or (3) by consent of the parties. NY R USDCTND L.R. 83.12-3(a).

- *Withdrawal from the ENE process.* The parties may withdraw any civil action or claim that the Court has referred to the ENE Process pursuant to NY R USDCTND L.R. 83.12-3 by application to the assigned judge at least ten (10) days before the scheduled evaluation session. NY R USDCTND L.R. 83.12-3(b).

    ii.   For more information on early neutral evaluation (ENE), refer to NY R USDCTND L.R. 83.12.

12.   *Settlement procedures.* On notice to the Court or the Clerk that the parties have settled an action, and upon confirmation of the settlement by all parties, the Court may issue a judgment dismissing the action by reason of settlement. The Court shall issue the order without prejudice to the parties' right to secure reinstatement of the case within thirty (30) days after the date of judgment by making a showing that the settlement was not, in fact, consummated. NY R USDCTND L.R. 68.2(a). If the Court decides not to follow the procedures set forth in NY R USDCTND L.R. 68.2(a), the parties shall file within thirty (30) days of the notification to the Court, unless otherwise directed by written order, such notices, stipulations and/or motions as are necessary to terminate the action. If the required documents are not filed within the thirty (30) day period, the Clerk shall place the action on the dismissal calendar. NY R USDCTND L.R. 68.2(b).

13.   *Sanctions and penalties for noncompliance.* Failure of an attorney or of a party to comply with any provision of the Local Rules of Practice for the United States District Court for the Northern District of New York, General Orders of this District, Orders of the Court, or the Federal Rules of Civil Procedure shall be a ground for imposition of sanctions. NY R USDCTND L.R. 1.1(d).

14.   *Individual judge practices.* Refer to the Miscellaneous section of this document for information on individual judge practices on general requirements for documents.

## D. Documents

1.   *Documents for moving party*

    a.   *Required documents*

       i.   *Notice of motion and motion.* The Notice of Motion must state the return date that the moving party has selected. NY R USDCTND L.R. 7.1(b)(1). Refer to the General Requirements section of this document for information on the notice of motion and motion.

          • *Order to show cause.* Refer to the General Requirements section of this document for information on bringing a motion by order to show cause.

      ii.   *Memorandum of law.* Except as otherwise provided in NY R USDCTND L.R. 7.1(a), all motions. . .require a memorandum of law. NY R USDCTND L.R. 7.1(a). Refer to the Format section of this document for the formatting requirements for memoranda of law.

      iii.   *Certificate of service.* Except as otherwise provided in NY R USDCTND L.R. 7.1(a), all motions. . .require. . .proof of service on all the parties. See NY R USDCTND L.R. 5.1(a). NY R USDCTND L.R. 7.1(a). FRCP 5(d) requires that the person making service under FRCP 5 certify that service has been effected. FRCP 5(Advisory Committee Notes). Having such information on file may be useful for many purposes, including proof of service if an issue arises concerning the effectiveness of the service. FRCP 5(Advisory Committee Notes). The party or its designee shall declare, by affidavit or certification, that it has provided all other parties in the action with all documents it has filed with the Court. NY R USDCTND L.R. 5.1(a).

          • Attorneys and pro se parties who are not Filing or Receiving Users must be served with a paper copy of any electronically filed pleading or other document. NY R USDCTND CM/ECF(5)(5.2). Such paper service must be documented by electronically filing a certificate of service. NY R USDCTND CM/ECF(5)(5.2).

    b.   *Supplemental documents*

       i.   *Pleading.* As a general rule, the court may only consider the pleading which is attacked by a FRCP 12(b)(6) motion in determining its sufficiency. FEDPROC § 62:466; Armengau v. Cline, 7 Fed.Appx. 336 (6th Cir. 2001). The plaintiff is not entitled to discovery to obtain information relevant to the motion, and the court is not permitted to look at matters outside the record. FEDPROC § 62:466; Cooperativa de Ahorro y Credito Aguada v. Kidder, Peabody & Co., 993 F.2d 269, 37 Fed.R.Evid.Serv. 904, 25 Fed.R.Serv.3d 982 (1st Cir. 1993).

          • *Motion treated as one for summary judgment.* If, on a motion under FRCP 12(b)(6) or FRCP 12(c), matters outside the pleadings are presented to and not excluded by the court, the motion must be treated as one for summary judgment under FRCP 56. All parties must be given a reasonable opportunity to present all the material that is pertinent to the motion. FRCP 12(d).

- *Documents attached to pleadings.* However, the court may consider documents which are attached to or submitted with the complaint, as well as legal arguments presented in memorandums or briefs and arguments of counsel. FEDPROC § 62:466; Tellabs, Inc. v. Makor Issues & Rights, Ltd., 551 U.S. 308, 127 S.Ct. 2499, 168 L.Ed.2d 179 (2007); E.E.O.C. v. Ohio Edison Co., 7 F.3d 541 (6th Cir. 1993). Documents that the defendant attaches to the motion to dismiss are considered part of the pleadings if they are referred to in the plaintiff's complaint and are central to the claim, and as such may be considered by the court. FEDPROC § 62:466; Hoffman-Pugh v. Ramsey, 312 F.3d 1222 (11th Cir. 2002).

ii. *Notice of constitutional question.* A party that files a pleading, written motion, or other paper drawing into question the constitutionality of a federal or state statute must promptly:

- *File notice.* File a notice of constitutional question stating the question and identifying the paper that raises it, if: (1) a federal statute is questioned and the parties do not include the United States, one of its agencies, or one of its officers or employees in an official capacity; or (2) a state statute is questioned and the parties do not include the state, one of its agencies, or one of its officers or employees in an official capacity; and

- *Serve notice.* Serve the notice and paper on the Attorney General of the United States if a federal statute is questioned—or on the state attorney general if a state statute is questioned—either by certified or registered mail or by sending it to an electronic address designated by the attorney general for this purpose. FRCP 5.1(a).

- *No forfeiture.* A party's failure to file and serve the notice, or the court's failure to certify, does not forfeit a constitutional claim or defense that is otherwise timely asserted. FRCP 5.1(d).

iii. *Nongovernmental corporate disclosure statement*

- *Contents.* A nongovernmental corporate party must file two (2) copies of a disclosure statement that: (1) identifies any parent corporation and any publicly held corporation owning ten percent (10%) or more of its stock; or (2) states that there is no such corporation. FRCP 7.1(a).

- *Time to file; Supplemental filing.* A party must: (1) file the disclosure statement with its first appearance, pleading, petition, motion, response, or other request addressed to the court; and (2) promptly file a supplemental statement if any required information changes. FRCP 7.1(b).

iv. *Copies of authorities.* When serving a pro se litigant with a memorandum of law or any other paper which contains citations to authorities that are unpublished or published exclusively on electronic databases, counsel shall include a hard copy of those authorities. Although copies of authorities published only on electronic databases are not required to be filed, copies shall be provided upon request to opposing counsel who lack access to electronic databases. NY R USDCTND L.R. 7.1(a)(1).

v. *Proposed order.* A document that is submitted in .pdf format cannot be modified; therefore, a proposed order or stipulation must be in a word processing format. The chambers of the assigned judge may request that a proposed order and/or a stipulation be e-mailed to the courtroom deputy for the presiding judge in either WordPerfect or Microsoft Word format. Please attach your proposed order and/or stipulation to an Internet e-mail sent to the appropriate e-mail address listed in NY R USDCTND CM/ECF(8)(8.2). NY R USDCTND CM/ECF(8)(8.2).

vi. *Cover letter authorizing e-mail or facsimile filing.* Neither the Court nor the Clerk's Office will accept for filing any facsimile or e-mail transmission without prior authorization from the Court. The party using facsimile or e-mail transmissions to file its papers must accompany any such documents with a cover letter stating that the Court authorized such transmissions and the date on which the Court provided that authorization. Violations of NY R USDCTND L.R. 5.5 subject the offending party to the Court's full disciplinary powers. NY R USDCTND L.R. 5.5.

vii. *Affidavit attesting to failed attempts to file electronically.* If the Court's CM/ECF site experiences a technical failure, a Filing User may submit documents to the Court that day in an alternate manner provided that the documents are accompanied by the Filing User's affidavit stating that the Filing User attempted to file electronically at least two times in one (1) hour increments after 10:00 a.m. that day. The following methods are acceptable alternate means for filing documents in case of a technical failure: (1) via electronic mail in a PDF attachment sent to the e-mail address for technical failures; or (2) in person, by bringing the document to the Clerk's Office on paper accompanied by a CD/ROM that contains the document in .pdf format. NY R USDCTND CM/ECF(10)(10.1).

- A Filing User who cannot file documents electronically because of a problem on the Filing User's system must file the documents' conventionally along with an affidavit explaining the reason for not filing the documents electronically. NY R USDCTND CM/ECF(10)(10.2).

viii. *Notice of conventional filing.* If the Clerk's Office grants permission to conventionally file the document, the Filing User shall electronically file a notice of conventional filing for the documents. More information regarding this process can be obtained from the Court's web page. NY R USDCTND CM/ECF(4)(4.5).

ix. *CD/ROM with PDF of document(s).* If the Court grants permission to file a document traditionally, the attorney must submit the documents for filing to the Clerk's Office on CD/ROM in .pdf or pdf.A format. NY R USDCTND CM/ECF(2).

x. *English translation.* The Court conducts its reviews and deliberations in English. Unless otherwise directed by the Court, any document that a party transmits to the Court (including one in the record on appeal) that is in a language other than English must be accompanied by an English translation that the translator has certified as true and accurate, pursuant to 28 U.S.C.A. § 1746. NY R USDCTND L.R. 10.1(e). For more information, refer to NY R USDCTND L.R. 10.1(e).

xi. *Courtesy copies.* The Court may require that courtesy copies of electronically filed documents be submitted for its review and may amend these Administrative Procedures (NY R USDCTND CM/ECF) at any time without prior notice. NY R USDCTND CM/ECF(2).

- The parties need not provide a courtesy copy of their motion papers to the assigned judge unless the assigned judge requests a copy. NY R USDCTND L.R. 7.1(b)(1).

xii. *Copies for three-judge court.* On the convening of a three-judge court, the parties shall make three (3) copies of all non-electronically filed pleadings, motion papers, and memoranda of law available to the Clerk for distribution. NY R USDCTND L.R. 9.1.

2. *Documents for opposing party*

  a. *Required documents*

   i. *Opposition.* Refer to the General Requirements section of this document for information on the opposing papers.

   ii. *Memorandum of law.* Except as otherwise provided in NY R USDCTND L.R. 7.1(a), all. . .opposition to motions require a memorandum of law. NY R USDCTND L.R. 7.1(a).

   - *Cross-motion brief.* If a party makes a cross-motion, it must join its cross motion brief with its opposition brief, and this combined brief may not exceed twenty-five (25) pages in length, exclusive of exhibits. A separate brief in opposition to the original motion is not permissible. NY R USDCTND L.R. 7.1(c).

   - Refer to the Format section of this document for the formatting requirements for memoranda of law.

   iii. *Certificate of service.* Except as otherwise provided in NY R USDCTND L.R. 7.1(a), all. . .opposition to motions require. . .proof of service on all the parties. See NY R US-

DCTND L.R. 5.1(a). NY R USDCTND L.R. 7.1(a). FRCP 5(d) requires that the person making service under FRCP 5 certify that service has been effected. FRCP 5(Advisory Committee Notes). Having such information on file may be useful for many purposes, including proof of service if an issue arises concerning the effectiveness of the service. FRCP 5(Advisory Committee Notes). The party or its designee shall declare, by affidavit or certification, that it has provided all other parties in the action with all documents it has filed with the Court. NY R USDCTND L.R. 5.1(a).

- Attorneys and pro se parties who are not Filing or Receiving Users must be served with a paper copy of any electronically filed pleading or other document. NY R USDCTND CM/ECF(5)(5.2). Such paper service must be documented by electronically filing a certificate of service. NY R USDCTND CM/ECF(5)(5.2).

b. *Supplemental documents*

   i. *Pleading.* As a general rule, the court may only consider the pleading which is attacked by a FRCP 12(b)(6) motion in determining its sufficiency. FEDPROC § 62:466; Armengau v. Cline, 7 Fed.Appx. 336 (6th Cir. 2001). The plaintiff is not entitled to discovery to obtain information relevant to the motion, and the court is not permitted to look at matters outside the record. FEDPROC § 62:466; Cooperativa de Ahorro y Credito Aguada v. Kidder, Peabody & Co., 993 F.2d 269, 37 Fed.R.Evid.Serv. 904, 25 Fed.R.Serv.3d 982 (1st Cir. 1993).

      - *Motion treated as one for summary judgment.* If, on a motion under FRCP 12(b)(6) or FRCP 12(c), matters outside the pleadings are presented to and not excluded by the court, the motion must be treated as one for summary judgment under FRCP 56. All parties must be given a reasonable opportunity to present all the material that is pertinent to the motion. FRCP 12(d).

      - *Documents attached to pleadings.* However, the court may consider documents which are attached to or submitted with the complaint, as well as legal arguments presented in memorandums or briefs and arguments of counsel. FEDPROC § 62:466; Tellabs, Inc. v. Makor Issues & Rights, Ltd., 551 U.S. 308, 127 S.Ct. 2499, 168 L.Ed.2d 179 (2007); E.E.O.C. v. Ohio Edison Co., 7 F.3d 541 (6th Cir. 1993). Documents that the defendant attaches to the motion to dismiss are considered part of the pleadings if they are referred to in the plaintiff's complaint and are central to the claim, and as such may be considered by the court. FEDPROC § 62:466; Hoffman-Pugh v. Ramsey, 312 F.3d 1222 (11th Cir. 2002).

   ii. *Notice of constitutional question.* A party that files a pleading, written motion, or other paper drawing into question the constitutionality of a federal or state statute must promptly:

      - *File notice.* File a notice of constitutional question stating the question and identifying the paper that raises it, if: (1) a federal statute is questioned and the parties do not include the United States, one of its agencies, or one of its officers or employees in an official capacity; or (2) a state statute is questioned and the parties do not include the state, one of its agencies, or one of its officers or employees in an official capacity; and

      - *Serve notice.* Serve the notice and paper on the Attorney General of the United States if a federal statute is questioned—or on the state attorney general if a state statute is questioned—either by certified or registered mail or by sending it to an electronic address designated by the attorney general for this purpose. FRCP 5.1(a).

      - *No forfeiture.* A party's failure to file and serve the notice, or the court's failure to certify, does not forfeit a constitutional claim or defense that is otherwise timely asserted. FRCP 5.1(d).

   iii. *Cross-motion.* A party may file and serve a cross-motion (meaning a competing request for relief or order similar to that requested by another party against the cross-moving party) at the time it files and serves its opposition papers to the original motion, i.e., not less than SEVENTEEN (17) DAYS prior to the return date of the motion. NY R USDCTND L.R. 7.1(c).

   iv. *Copies of authorities.* When serving a pro se litigant with a memorandum of law or any other paper which contains citations to authorities that are unpublished or published exclusively on electronic databases, counsel shall include a hard copy of those authorities. Although copies of authorities published only on electronic databases are not required to be filed, copies shall be provided upon request to opposing counsel who lack access to electronic databases. NY R USDCTND L.R. 7.1(a)(1).

v. *Cover letter authorizing e-mail or facsimile filing.* Neither the Court nor the Clerk's Office will accept for filing any facsimile or e-mail transmission without prior authorization from the Court. The party using facsimile or e-mail transmissions to file its papers must accompany any such documents with a cover letter stating that the Court authorized such transmissions and the date on which the Court provided that authorization. Violations of NY R USDCTND L.R. 5.5 subject the offending party to the Court's full disciplinary powers. NY R USDCTND L.R. 5.5.

vi. *Affidavit attesting to failed attempts to file electronically.* If the Court's CM/ECF site experiences a technical failure, a Filing User may submit documents to the Court that day in an alternate manner provided that the documents are accompanied by the Filing User's affidavit stating that the Filing User attempted to file electronically at least two times in one (1) hour increments after 10:00 a.m. that day. The following methods are acceptable alternate means for filing documents in case of a technical failure: (1) via electronic mail in a PDF attachment sent to the e-mail address for technical failures; or (2) in person, by bringing the document to the Clerk's Office on paper accompanied by a CD/ROM that contains the document in .pdf format. NY R USDCTND CM/ECF(10)(10.1).

- A Filing User who cannot file documents electronically because of a problem on the Filing User's system must file the documents' conventionally along with an affidavit explaining the reason for not filing the documents electronically. NY R USDCTND CM/ECF(10)(10.2).

vii. *Notice of conventional filing.* If the Clerk's Office grants permission to conventionally file the document, the Filing User shall electronically file a notice of conventional filing for the documents. More information regarding this process can be obtained from the Court's web page. NY R USDCTND CM/ECF(4)(4.5).

viii. *CD/ROM with PDF of document(s).* If the Court grants permission to file a document traditionally, the attorney must submit the documents for filing to the Clerk's Office on CD/ROM in .pdf or pdf.A format. NY R USDCTND CM/ECF(2).

ix. *English translation.* The Court conducts its reviews and deliberations in English. Unless otherwise directed by the Court, any document that a party transmits to the Court (including one in the record on appeal) that is in a language other than English must be accompanied by an English translation that the translator has certified as true and accurate, pursuant to 28 U.S.C.A. § 1746. NY R USDCTND L.R. 10.1(e). For more information, refer to NY R USDCTND L.R. 10.1(e).

x. *Courtesy copies.* The Court may require that courtesy copies of electronically filed documents be submitted for its review and may amend these Administrative Procedures (NY R USDCTND CM/ECF) at any time without prior notice. NY R USDCTND CM/ECF(2).

- The parties need not provide a courtesy copy of their motion papers to the assigned judge unless the assigned judge requests a copy. NY R USDCTND L.R. 7.1(b)(1).

xi. *Copies for three-judge court.* On the convening of a three-judge court, the parties shall make three (3) copies of all non-electronically filed pleadings, motion papers, and memoranda of law available to the Clerk for distribution. NY R USDCTND L.R. 9.1.

3. *Individual judge practices.* Refer to the Miscellaneous section of this document for information on individual judge practices on required documents.

## E. Format

1. *Form of documents.* The rules governing captions and other matters of form in pleadings apply to motions and other papers. FRCP 7(b)(2). All pleadings and other papers shall be served and filed in accordance

with the Federal Rules of Civil Procedure and shall be in the form prescribed by NY R USDCTND L.R. 10.1. NY R USDCTND L.R. 5.1(a).

a. *Form, generally.* All pleadings, motions, and other documents that a party presents for filing, whether in paper form or in electronic form, shall meet the following requirements:

   i. *Font size.* All text, whether in the body of the document or in footnotes, must be a minimum of twelve (12) point type. NY R USDCTND L.R. 10.1(a)(1).

   ii. *Margins.* All documents must have one (1) inch margins on all four sides of the page. NY R USDCTND L.R. 10.1(a)(2).

   iii. *Spacing.* All text in the body of the document must be double-spaced. NY R USDCTND L.R. 10.1(a)(3).

      • The text in block quotations and footnotes may be single-spaced. NY R USDCTND L.R. 10.1(a)(4).

   iv. *Page numbering.* Pages must be consecutively numbered. NY R USDCTND L.R. 10.1(a)(7).

   v. *Circumventing formatting limitations*

      • Extensive footnotes must not be used to circumvent page limitations. NY R USDCTND L.R. 10.1(a)(5).

      • Compacted or other compressed printing features must not be used. NY R USDCTND L.R. 10.1(a)(6).

b. *Additional requirements for paper filing.* Additional requirements for all pleadings, motions, and other documents that a party presents for filing in paper form:

   i. *Paper size.* All documents must be on eight and one-half by eleven (8-1/2 x 11) inch white paper of good quality. NY R USDCTND L.R. 10.1(b)(1).

   ii. *Text.* All text must be plainly and legibly written, typewritten, printed or reproduced without erasures or interlineations materially defacing them. NY R USDCTND L.R. 10.1(b)(2).

   iii. *Ink.* All documents must be in black or blue ink. NY R USDCTND L.R. 10.1(b)(3).

   iv. *Binding.* Pages of all documents must be stapled (or in some other way fastened) together. NY R USDCTND L.R. 10.1(b)(4).

   v. *Single-sided paper.* All documents must be single-sided. NY R USDCTND L.R. 10.1(b)(5).

   vi. *Electronic submission.* The Court, at its discretion, may require the electronic submission of any document in a WordPerfect-compatible format. NY R USDCTND L.R. 10.1(b)(6).

   vii. *Rejection of document.* The Court may reject documents that do not comply with the above-listed requirements. NY R USDCTND L.R. 10.1(b).

c. *Caption; Names of parties.* Every pleading must have a caption with the court's name, a title, a file number, and a FRCP 7(a) designation. The title of the complaint must name all the parties; the title of other pleadings, after naming the first party on each side, may refer generally to other parties. FRCP 10(a). Each document must contain a caption for the specific case to which it pertains. The caption must include the title of the Court, the title of the action, the civil action number of the case, the initials of the assigned judge(s), and the name or nature of the paper in sufficient detail for identification. If a litigant has more than one action pending in this Court, any and all papers filed in a case must contain and pertain to one civil action number, unless the civil actions have been consolidated by the Court. Any motion or other papers purporting to relate to more than one action will not be accepted for filing and may be stricken by the Court. NY R USDCTND L.R. 10.1(c)(1) shall not apply, as noted in NY R USDCTND L.R. 10.1(c), to notices of change of address filed by attorneys of record and pro se litigants. The parties must separately caption affidavits and declarations and must not physically attach them to the Notice of Motion or Memorandum of Law. NY R USDCTND L.R. 10.1(c)(1).

d. *Paragraphs; Separate statements.* A party must state its claims or defenses in numbered paragraphs, each limited as far as practicable to a single set of circumstances. A later pleading may refer by

number to a paragraph in an earlier pleading. If doing so would promote clarity, each claim founded on a separate transaction or occurrence—and each defense other than a denial—must be stated in a separate count or defense. FRCP 10(b).

e. *Adoption by reference; Exhibits.* A statement in a pleading may be adopted by reference elsewhere in the same pleading or in any other pleading or motion. A copy of a written instrument that is an exhibit to a pleading is a part of the pleading for all purposes. FRCP 10(c).

f. *Citation of local rules.* These are the Local Rules of Practice for the United States District Court for the Northern District of New York. They shall be cited as "L.R. ___." NY R USDCTND L.R. 1.1(a).

g. *Acceptance by the clerk.* The clerk must not refuse to file a paper solely because it is not in the form prescribed by the Federal Rules of Civil Procedure or by a local rule or practice. FRCP 5(d)(4).

2. *Form of electronic documents.* All pleadings, motions, and other documents that a party presents for filing, whether in paper form or in electronic form, shall meet the requirements in NY R USDCTND L.R. 10.1(a). NY R USDCTND L.R. 10.1(a). Refer above for more information.

a. *Attachments and exhibits.* A Filing User must submit in electronic form all documents referenced as exhibits or attachments in accordance with the Court's CM/ECF Users Manual unless the Court otherwise orders. A Filing User shall submit as exhibits or attachments only those excerpts of the referenced documents that are directly germane to the matter under the Court's consideration. Excerpted material must be clearly and prominently identified as such. Filing Users who file excerpts of documents as exhibits or attachments under these Administrative Procedures (NY R USDCTND CM/ECF) do so without prejudice to their right to timely file additional excerpts or the complete document. Responding parties may also timely file the complete document or additional excerpts that they believe are directly germane to the matter under the Court's consideration. NY R USDCTND CM/ECF(4)(4.4).

   i. All attachments must be described in sufficient detail so the Court and opposing counsel can easily identify and distinguish the filed attachments. Vague or general descriptions are insufficient (i.e., "Exhibit 1"). Rather, each attachment shall have a descriptive title identifying, with specificity, the document that is being filed (i.e., "Exhibit 12 Mulligan County Fire Investigation Report.") Failure to adequately describe attachments may result in the document being rejected by the Court. NY R USDCTND CM/ECF(4)(4.4).

b. *Large documents.* For information on the electronic filing of large documents, please consult the Court's CM/ECF Users Manual, which is available on the Court's web page. NY R USDCTND CM/ECF(4)(4.5).

   i. A party who believes a document is too lengthy to electronically image, i.e., "scan," may contact the Clerk's Office for permission to file that document conventionally. If the Clerk's Office grants permission to conventionally file the document, the Filing User shall electronically file a notice of conventional filing for the documents. More information regarding this process can be obtained from the Court's web page. Exhibits submitted conventionally shall be served on other parties as if they were not subject to these Administrative Procedures (NY R USDCTND CM/ECF). For a list of hints and tips for scanning large documents, please consult the Court's web page. NY R USDCTND CM/ECF(4)(4.5).

c. *Legibility.* It shall be the Filing User's responsibility to verify the legibility of scanned documents before filing them electronically with the Court. NY R USDCTND CM/ECF(4)(4.6).

d. *Color documents.* Since documents scanned in color or containing a graphic take much longer to upload, Filing Users are encouraged to configure their scanners to scan documents at 300 dpi and preferably in black and white rather than in color. NY R USDCTND CM/ECF(4)(4.7).

e. *Items not in .PDF format.* Parties wishing to file items not amenable to .pdf format (i.e. CD's, DVD's), shall file such items conventionally with the Clerk's Office. The Filing User shall electronically file a notice of conventional filing indicating that these items have been submitted to the clerk and shall serve copies of these items on other parties as if they were not subject to these Administrative Procedures (NY R USDCTND CM/ECF). These item(s) will be maintained by the Clerk's Office until the case is disposed, at which time they will be returned to the filing party for retention consistent with NY R USDCTND CM/ECF(4)(4.9). NY R USDCTND CM/ECF(4)(4.8).

3. *Form of memoranda of law*

    a. *Length limitation.* No party shall file or serve a memorandum of law that exceeds twenty-five (25) pages in length, unless that party obtains leave of the judge hearing the motion prior to filing. NY R USDCTND L.R. 7.1(a)(1).

    b. *Table of contents.* All memoranda of law shall contain a table of contents. NY R USDCTND L.R. 7.1(a)(1).

4. *Signing of pleadings, motions and other papers*

    a. *Signature.* Every pleading, written motion, and other paper must be signed by at least one attorney of record in the attorney's name—or by a party personally if the party is unrepresented. The paper must state the signer's address, e-mail address, and telephone number. FRCP 11(a). Each document must identify the person filing the document. This identification must include an original signature of the attorney or pro se litigant; the typewritten name of that person; the address of a pro se litigant; and the bar roll number, office address, telephone number, e-mail address and fax number of the attorney. Telephone numbers of non-prisoner pro se parties may be provided voluntarily or upon request of the Court. See General Order #22 (NY R USDCTND CM/ECF) for signature requirements. NY R USDCTND L.R. 10.1(c)(2).

        i. *Electronic signatures.* Documents filed under an attorney's login and password shall constitute that attorney's signature for purposes of the Local Rules of Practice for the United States District Court for the Northern District of New York and Federal Rules of Civil Procedure, including but not limited to FRCP 11. A pleading or other document requiring an attorney's signature shall be signed in the following manner, whether filed electronically or submitted on disk or CD/ROM to the Clerk's Office: "s/ (attorney name)." The correct format for an attorney signature is found in NY R USDCTND CM/ECF(6)(6.1). NY R USDCTND CM/ECF(6)(6.1).

           • *Non-attorney signature.* If an original document requires the signature of a non-attorney, the Filing User may scan the original document containing the original signature(s), then electronically file it on the System. Alternatively, the Filing User may convert the document into .pdf text format and submit the document using "s/" for the signature of the non-attorney. NY R USDCTND CM/ECF(6)(6.2).

           • *Multiple signatures.* A document requiring signatures of more than one party must be filed electronically either by (1) submitting a scanned document containing all necessary signatures; (2) representing the consent of the other parties on the document; or (3) in any other manner that the Court approves. NY R USDCTND CM/ECF(6)(6.3).

        ii. *No verification or accompanying affidavit required for pleadings.* Unless a rule or statute specifically states otherwise, a pleading need not be verified or accompanied by an affidavit. FRCP 11(a).

        iii. *Unsigned papers.* The court must strike an unsigned paper unless the omission is promptly corrected after being called to the attorney's or party's attention. FRCP 11(a).

    b. *Representations to the court.* By presenting to the court a pleading, written motion, or other paper—whether by signing, filing, submitting, or later advocating it—an attorney or unrepresented party certifies that to the best of the person's knowledge, information, and belief, formed after an inquiry reasonable under the circumstances:

        i. It is not being presented for any improper purpose, such as to harass, cause unnecessary delay, or needlessly increase the cost of litigation;

        ii. The claims, defenses, and other legal contentions are warranted by existing law or by a nonfrivolous argument for extending, modifying, or reversing existing law or for establishing new law;

        iii. The factual contentions have evidentiary support or, if specifically so identified, will likely have evidentiary support after a reasonable opportunity for further investigation or discovery; and

        iv. The denials of factual contentions are warranted on the evidence or, if specifically so identified, are reasonably based on belief or a lack of information. FRCP 11(b).

   c. *Sanctions.* If, after notice and a reasonable opportunity to respond, the court determines that FRCP 11(b) has been violated, the court may impose an appropriate sanction on any attorney, law firm, or party that violated FRCP 11(b) or is responsible for the violation. FRCP 11(c)(1). Refer to the United States District Court for the Northern District of New York KeyRules Motion for Sanctions document for more information.

5. *Privacy protection for filings made with the court*

   a. *Redacted filings.* Unless the court orders otherwise, in an electronic or paper filing with the court that contains an individual's Social Security number, taxpayer-identification number, or birth date, the name of an individual known to be a minor, or a financial-account number, a party or nonparty making the filing may include only:

     i. The last four (4) digits of the Social Security number and taxpayer-identification number;

     ii. The year of the individual's birth;

     iii. The minor's initials; and

     iv. The last four (4) digits of the financial-account number. FRCP 5.2(a); NY R USDCTND L.R. 8.1; NY R USDCTND CM/ECF(11)(11.2).

     v. If a home address must be used, use only the City and State. NY R USDCTND L.R. 8.1; NY R USDCTND CM/ECF(11)(11.2).

     vi. If the victim of a sexual assault must be referenced, redact the name to 'Victim.' NY R USDCTND CM/ECF(11)(11.2); NY R USDCTND L.R. 8.1.

     vii. In addition, caution shall be exercised when filing documents that contain the following:

- Personal identifying number, such as a driver's license number;
- Medical records, treatment and diagnosis;
- Employment history;
- Individual financial information; and
- Proprietary or trade secret information. NY R USDCTND L.R. 8.1; NY R USDCTND CM/ECF(11)(11.2).

   b. *Exemptions from the redaction requirement.* The redaction requirement does not apply to the following:

     i. A financial-account number that identifies the property allegedly subject to forfeiture in a forfeiture proceeding;

     ii. The record of an administrative or agency proceeding;

     iii. The official record of a state-court proceeding;

     iv. The record of a court or tribunal, if that record was not subject to the redaction requirement when originally filed;

     v. A filing covered by FRCP 5.2(c) or FRCP 5.2(d); and

     vi. A pro se filing in an action brought under 28 U.S.C.A. § 2241, 28 U.S.C.A. § 2254, or 28 U.S.C.A. § 2255. FRCP 5.2(b).

     vii. Transcripts of the administrative record in social security proceedings are exempt from this requirement. State court records and other documents filed in habeas corpus proceedings are exempt from this requirement except for proceedings that involve victims of sex crimes. In habeas corpus cases involving sex crimes, the parties must redact the record and supporting papers, or may move to seal, if appropriate. NY R USDCTND L.R. 8.1.

   c. *Limitations on remote access to electronic files; Social Security appeals and immigration cases.* Unless the court orders otherwise, in an action for benefits under the Social Security Act, and in an action or proceeding relating to an order of removal, to relief from removal, or to immigration benefits or detention, access to an electronic file is authorized as follows:

     i. The parties and their attorneys may have remote electronic access to any part of the case file, including the administrative record;

    ii.   Any other person may have electronic access to the full record at the courthouse, but may have remote electronic access only to:

- The docket maintained by the court; and

- An opinion, order, judgment, or other disposition of the court, but not any other part of the case file or the administrative record. FRCP 5.2(c).

    d.   *Filings made under seal.* The court may order that a filing be made under seal without redaction. The court may later unseal the filing or order the person who made the filing to file a redacted version for the public record. FRCP 5.2(d); NY R USDCTND L.R. 8.1. For information on sealed matters, refer to NY R USDCTND L.R. 83.13 and NY R USDCTND CM/ECF(12).

    e.   *Protective orders.* For good cause, the court may by order in a case:

      i.   Require redaction of additional information; or

      ii.   Limit or prohibit a nonparty's remote electronic access to a document filed with the court. FRCP 5.2(e).

    f.   *Option for additional unredacted filing under seal.* A person making a redacted filing may also file an unredacted copy under seal. The court must retain the unredacted copy as part of the record. FRCP 5.2(f); NY R USDCTND L.R. 8.1; NY R USDCTND CM/ECF(11)(11.3).

    g.   *Option for filing a reference list.* A filing that contains redacted information may be filed together with a reference list that identifies each item of redacted information and specifies an appropriate identifier that uniquely corresponds to each item listed. The list must be filed under seal and may be amended as of right. Any reference in the case to a listed identifier will be construed to refer to the corresponding item of information. FRCP 5.2(g); NY R USDCTND L.R. 8.1; NY R USDCTND CM/ECF(11)(11.3).

    h.   *Responsibility for redaction.* Counsel is strongly urged to discuss this issue with all their clients so that they can make an informed decision about the inclusion of certain information. The responsibility for redacting these personal identifiers rests solely with counsel and the parties. The Clerk will not review each filing for compliance with NY R USDCTND L.R. 8.1. Counsel and the parties are cautioned that failure to redact these personal identifiers may subject them to the Court's full disciplinary power. NY R USDCTND L.R. 8.1; NY R USDCTND CM/ECF(11)(11.3).

    i.   *Waiver of protection of identifiers.* A person waives the protection of FRCP 5.2(a) as to the person's own information by filing it without redaction and not under seal. FRCP 5.2(h).

  6.  *Individual judge practices.* Refer to the Miscellaneous section of this document for information on individual judge practices on formatting documents.

## F. Filing and Service Requirements

  1.  *Filing requirements.* Any paper after the complaint that is required to be served—together with a certificate of service—must be filed within a reasonable time after service. FRCP 5(d)(1). Parties shall file all original motion papers, including memoranda of law and supporting affidavits, if any, in accordance with the Administrative Procedures for Electronic Case Filing (General Order #22 (NY R USDCTND CM/ECF)) and/or the case assignment form provided to the parties at the commencement of the litigation. NY R USDCTND L.R. 7.1(b)(1).

    a.   *How filing is made; In general.* A paper is filed by delivering it:

      i.   To the clerk; or

      ii.   To a judge who agrees to accept it for filing, and who must then note the filing date on the paper and promptly send it to the clerk. FRCP 5(d)(2).

    b.   *Electronic filing*

      i.   *Authorization of electronic filing program.* A court may, by local rule, allow papers to be filed, signed, or verified by electronic means that are consistent with any technical standards established by the Judicial Conference of the United States. A local rule may require electronic filing only if reasonable exceptions are allowed. A paper filed electronically in compliance with a local rule is a written paper for purposes of the Federal Rules of Civil Procedure. FRCP 5(d)(3).

- All cases filed in this Court may be assigned to the Electronic Case Files System ("ECF") in accordance with the Procedural Order on Electronic Case Filing (General Order #22 (NY R USDCTND CM/ECF)), the provisions of which are incorporated herein by reference, and which the Court may amend from time to time. Copies of General Order #22 (NY R USDCTND CM/ECF) are available at the Clerk's office or at the Court's webpage. NY R USDCTND L.R. 5.1.1; NY R USDCTND Order 25(XII).

- The Court may deviate from these Administrative Procedures (NY R USDCTND CM/ECF) in specific cases, without prior notice, if deemed appropriate in the exercise of discretion, considering the need for the just, speedy, and inexpensive determination of matters pending before the Court. NY R USDCTND CM/ECF(2).

ii. *Scope of electronic filing.* After January 1, 2004, all documents that attorneys admitted to practice in the Northern District of New York submit for filing shall be filed electronically using the System or shall be scanned and uploaded to the System, no matter when a case was originally filed, unless these Administrative Procedures (NY R USDCTND CM/ECF) otherwise permit or unless the assigned judge otherwise authorizes. An attorney who is not a Filing User by January 1, 2004, must show good cause to the assigned judge to file and serve pleadings and other papers in the traditional manner. NY R USDCTND CM/ECF(2).

iii. *Exceptions and/or waivers from mandatory electronic filing.* The following types of cases and/or documents are not required to be filed electronically:

- If you are seeking to have your complaint filed under seal, please file your complaint and proposed sealing order traditionally at the Clerk's Office. NY R USDCTND CM/ECF(2)(2.1)(1).

- Any document that a party proceeding pro se files. (See NY R USDCTND CM/ECF(12)(12.1) for procedural details). NY R USDCTND CM/ECF(2)(2.1)(2). A non-prisoner who is a party to a civil action and who is not represented by an attorney may file a motion to obtain an Electronic Case Filing (ECF) login and password on a form prescribed by the Clerk's Office. The Pro Se CM/ECF Registration Form shall be submitted with the motion. If during the course of the action an attorney appears on behalf of the pro se party, the Clerk's Office shall terminate the pro se party's registration based upon the attorney's appearance. NY R USDCTND CM/ECF(12)(12.1). Absent permission to file electronically, pro se filers shall file paper originals of all complaints, pleadings, motions, affidavits, briefs, and other documents which must be signed or which require either verification or an unsworn declaration under any rule or statute. The Clerk's Office will scan these original documents into an electronic file in the System but will also maintain a paper file. NY R USDCTND CM/ECF(12)(12.1). A pro se party may also seek permission to receive immediate notice of all public documents filed in their cases. Notices of Electronic Filing (NEF) and attached documents would be transmitted to a non-prisoner pro se party who selects this option. Note: The pro se party would continue to file their documents with the Clerk's Office in paper form. NY R USDCTND CM/ECF(12)(12.1).

- Sealed documents, sealed cases, documents for in camera review, documents lodged with the Court, ex parte documents, confidential agreements, Qui Tam actions and Grand Jury material and warrants must be filed traditionally. (See NY R USDCTND CM/ECF(12)(12.2) for further information the filing of the above-referenced documents). NY R USDCTND CM/ECF(2)(2.1)(3).

- Discovery: In accordance with NY R USDCTND L.R. 26.2, parties shall not file discovery, provided, however, that discovery material to be used at trial or in support of any motion, including a motion to compel or for summary judgment, shall be filed electronically with the Court prior to the trial or with the motion. Any motion pursuant to FRCP 37 shall be accompanied by the electronically filed discovery materials to which the motion relates if those materials have not previously been filed with the Court. NY R USDCTND CM/ECF(2)(2.1)(4).

- Transport Orders: All orders requesting that an incarcerated individual be transported that a judicial officer of the Northern District of New York signs shall be filed traditionally. These Orders will not be filed with the case or uploaded to the docket but rather will be processed in accordance with the procedures that the Clerk of Court promulgates. NY R USDCTND CM/ECF(2)(2.1)(5).

iv. *Filing defined.* Electronic transmission of a document to the System in accordance with these Administrative Procedures, together with the transmission of a Notice of Electronic Filing from the Court, constitutes filing of the document for all purposes of the Federal Rules of Civil Procedure and the Local Rules of Practice for the United States District Court for the Northern District of New York and constitutes entry of the document on the docket that the Clerk's Office keeps under FRCP 58 and FRCP 79. E-mailing a document to the Clerk's Office or to the assigned judge shall not constitute "filing" of the document. NY R USDCTND CM/ECF(4)(4.1).

v. *Filing fees.* Any fee required for filing a pleading or paper in this Court is payable to the Clerk of the Court. The Court will not maintain electronic billing or debit accounts for attorneys or law firms. Effective January 1, 2007, payment for filing fees will be mandatory through CM/ECF's Internet Credit Card Payment site--a secure Treasury Site. The Filing User will be prompted to enter either Bank Account Debit (ACH) or credit card information while filing the initial pleading. Any document that requires a filing fee (e.g., Notice of Appeal, Motion for Pro Hac Vice Admission) may also be paid through the federal electronic payment website. NY R USDCTND CM/ECF(7).

vi. For more information on electronic filing, refer to NY R USDCTND CM/ECF.

c. *E-mail or facsimile filing.* Neither the Court nor the Clerk's Office will accept for filing any facsimile or e-mail transmission without prior authorization from the Court. The party using facsimile or e-mail transmissions to file its papers must accompany any such documents with a cover letter stating that the Court authorized such transmissions and the date on which the Court provided that authorization. Violations of NY R USDCTND L.R. 5.5 subject the offending party to the Court's full disciplinary powers. NY R USDCTND L.R. 5.5.

2. *Service requirements*

a. *Service; When required*

i. *In general.* Unless the Federal Rules of Civil Procedure provide otherwise, each of the following papers must be served on every party:

- An order stating that service is required;
- A pleading filed after the original complaint, unless the court orders otherwise under FRCP 5(c) because there are numerous defendants;
- A discovery paper required to be served on a party, unless the court orders otherwise;
- A written motion, except one that may be heard ex parte; and
- A written notice, appearance, demand, or offer of judgment, or any similar paper. FRCP 5(a)(1).

ii. *If a party fails to appear.* No service is required on a party who is in default for failing to appear. But a pleading that asserts a new claim for relief against such a party must be served on that party under FRCP 4. FRCP 5(a)(2).

iii. *Seizing property.* If an action is begun by seizing property and no person is or need be named as a defendant, any service required before the filing of an appearance, answer, or claim must be made on the person who had custody or possession of the property when it was seized. FRCP 5(a)(3).

b. *Service; How made*

    i. *Serving an attorney.* If a party is represented by an attorney, service under FRCP 5 must be made on the attorney unless the court orders service on the party. FRCP 5(b)(1).

    ii. *Service in general.* A paper is served under FRCP 5 by:

- Handing it to the person;

- Leaving it: (1) at the person's office with a clerk or other person in charge or, if no one is in charge, in a conspicuous place in the office; or (2) if the person has no office or the office is closed, at the person's dwelling or usual place of abode with someone of suitable age and discretion who resides there;

- Mailing it to the person's last known address—in which event service is complete upon mailing;

- Leaving it with the court clerk if the person has no known address;

- Sending it by electronic means if the person consented in writing—in which event service is complete upon transmission, but is not effective if the serving party learns that it did not reach the person to be served; or

- Delivering it by any other means that the person consented to in writing—in which event service is complete when the person making service delivers it to the agency designated to make delivery. FRCP 5(b)(2).

    iii. *Service of electronically-filed documents.* Service is complete provided all parties receive a Notice of Electronic Filing (NEF), which is sent automatically by email from the Court (see the NEF for a list of who did/did not receive notice electronically). Transmission of the NEF constitutes service upon all Filing and Receiving Users who are listed as recipients of notice by electronic mail. It remains the responsibility of Filing and Receiving Users to maintain current contact information with the court and to regularly review the docket sheet of the case. NY R USDCTND CM/ECF(5)(5.2).

- *Non-filing or receiving users.* Attorneys and pro se parties who are not Filing or Receiving Users must be served with a paper copy of any electronically filed pleading or other document. Service of such paper copy must be made according to the Federal Rules of Civil Procedure and the Local Rules of Practice for the United States District Court for the Northern District of New York. Such paper service must be documented by electronically filing a certificate of service. NY R USDCTND CM/ECF(5)(5.2). A party who is not a Filing User of the System is entitled to a paper copy of any electronically-filed pleading, document, or order. The Filing User must therefore provide the non-Filing User with the pleading or document according to the Federal Rules of Civil Procedure. NY R US-DCTND CM/ECF(5)(5.3).

    iv. *Using court facilities.* If a local rule so authorizes, a party may use the court's transmission facilities to make service under FRCP 5(b)(2)(E). FRCP 5(b)(3).

c. *Serving numerous defendants*

    i. *In general.* If an action involves an unusually large number of defendants, the court may, on motion or on its own, order that:

- Defendants' pleadings and replies to them need not be served on other defendants;

- Any crossclaim, counterclaim, avoidance, or affirmative defense in those pleadings and replies to them will be treated as denied or avoided by all other parties; and

- Filing any such pleading and serving it on the plaintiff constitutes notice of the pleading to all parties. FRCP 5(c)(1).

    ii. *Notifying parties.* A copy of every such order must be served on the parties as the court directs. FRCP 5(c)(2).

3. *Individual judge practices.* Refer to the Miscellaneous section of this document for information on individual judge practices on filing and serving documents.

## G. Hearings

1. *Hearings, generally*

   a. *Motion days.* Listings of the regularly scheduled motion days for all judges shall be available at each Clerk's office and are available on the Court's webpage. The Clerk shall provide notice of the regular motion days for all judges to the parties at the time an action is commenced. NY R USDCTND L.R. 78.1.

   b. *Return date.* Unless the Court directs otherwise, the moving party shall make its motion returnable at the next regularly scheduled motion date at least thirty-one (31) days from the date the moving party files and serves its motion. The moving party shall select a return date in accordance with the procedures set forth in NY R USDCTND L.R. 7.1(b). If the return date the moving party selects is not the next regularly scheduled motion date, or if the moving party selects no return date, the Clerk will set the proper return date and notify the parties. NY R USDCTND L.R. 7.1.

      i. Information regarding motion dates and times is specified on the case assignment form that the Court provides to the parties at the commencement of the litigation or the parties may obtain this form from the Clerk's office or at the Court's webpage. NY R USDCTND L.R. 7.1.

      ii. The Court hereby directs the Clerk to set a proper return date in motions that pro se litigants submit for filing that do not specify a return date or fail to allow for sufficient time pursuant to NY R USDCTND L.R. 7.1. Generally, the return date that the Clerk selects should not exceed thirty (30) days from the date of filing. Furthermore, the Clerk shall forward a copy of the revised or corrected notice of motion to the parties. NY R USDCTND L.R. 7.1.

   c. *Oral argument.* Due process does not require that oral argument be permitted on a motion and, except as otherwise provided by local rule, the district court has discretion to determine whether it will decide the motion on the papers or hear argument by counsel (and perhaps receive evidence). FPP § 1190; F.D.I.C. v. Deglau, 207 F.3d 153 (3d Cir. 2000).

      i. The parties shall appear for oral argument on all motions that they make returnable before a district court judge, except motions for reconsideration, on the scheduled return date of the motion. A motion may be disposed of without oral argument as described in NY R USDCTND Order 25, on consideration of a request of any party, or otherwise at the discretion of the presiding judge. Thus, the parties should be prepared to have their motion papers serve as the sole method of argument on the motion. NY R USDCTND L.R. 7.1(h).

      ii. The parties shall not appear for oral argument on motions that they make returnable before a Magistrate Judge on the scheduled return date of the motion unless the Magistrate Judge sua sponte directs or grants the request of any party for oral argument. NY R USDCTND L.R. 7.1(h).

   d. *Providing a regular schedule for oral hearings.* A court may establish regular times and places for oral hearings on motions. FRCP 78(a).

   e. *Providing for submission on briefs.* By rule or order, the court may provide for submitting and determining motions on briefs, without oral hearings. FRCP 78(b).

2. *Adjournments of dispositive motions.* After the moving party files and serves its motion papers requesting dispositive relief, but before the time that the opposing party must file and serve its opposing papers, the parties may agree to an adjournment of the return date for the motion. However, any such adjournment may not be for more than THIRTY-ONE (31) DAYS from the return date that the moving party selected. In addition, the parties may agree to new dates for the filing and service of opposition and reply papers. However, the parties must file all papers with the Court and serve them upon the other parties not less than ELEVEN (11) DAYS prior to the newly selected return date of the motion. If the parties agree to such an adjournment, they must file a letter with the Court stating the following: (1) that they have agreed to an adjournment of the return date for the motion, (2) the new return date, (3) the date on which the opposing party must file and serve its opposition papers, and (4) the date on which the moving party must file and serve its reply papers. The parties may not agree to any further adjournment. NY R USDCTND L.R. 7.1(j).

   a. *Procedure when only one party seeks an adjournment.* If one of the parties seeks an adjournment of not more than THIRTY-ONE (31) DAYS from the return date that the moving party selected, but the other parties will not agree to such an adjournment, the party seeking the adjournment must file a letter request with the Court and serve the same upon the other parties, stating the following: (1) that the parties cannot agree to an adjournment, (2) the reason that the party is seeking the adjournment, and (3) the suggested return date for the motion. Within three days of receiving this letter request, the parties who have not agreed to an adjournment may file a letter with the Court and serve the same upon the other parties, setting forth the reasons that they do not agree to the requested adjournment. The Court will then take the request under advisement and, as soon as practicable, will enter an order granting or denying the request and, if granting the request, will set forth new dates for the filing and serving of opposition and reply papers. NY R USDCTND L.R. 7.1(j).

b. *Procedure when adjournment is more than thirty-one (31) days from the return date.* If any party seeks an adjournment of the return date that is more than THIRTY-ONE DAYS from the return date that the moving party selected, that party must file a letter request with the Court stating the following: (1) why the party needs a longer adjournment and (2) a suggested return date for the motion. The Court will grant such an adjournment only upon a showing of exceptional circumstances. In the alternative or if the Court denies the request for an adjournment, the moving party may withdraw its motion without prejudice to refile at a later date. The moving party must refile its motion within the time frame set in the Uniform Pretrial Scheduling Order unless either the assigned District Judge or the assigned Magistrate Judge has granted an extension of the motion-filing deadline. NY R USDCTND L.R. 7.1(j).

3. *Hearing on FRCP 12 defenses before trial.* If a party so moves, any defense listed in FRCP 12(b)(1) through FRCP 12(b)(7)—whether made in a pleading or by motion—and a motion under FRCP 12(c) must be heard and decided before trial unless the court orders a deferral until trial. FRCP 12(i).

4. *Individual judge practices.* Refer to the Miscellaneous section of this document for information on individual judge practices on hearings.

## H. Forms

### 1. Federal Motion to Dismiss for Failure to State a Claim Forms

a. Notice in federal court; Motion for involuntary dismissal of action without prejudice; Complaint fails to state a claim on which relief can be granted. AMJUR PP DISMISSAL § 109.

b. Motion; To dismiss; Failure to state a claim on which relief can be granted or facts sufficient to constitute cause of action. AMJUR PP LIMITATION § 100.

c. Motion to dismiss; For failure to state a claim, improper service of process, improper venue, and want of jurisdiction. AMJUR PP MOTIONS § 42.

d. Failure to state a claim upon which relief can be granted. 2C FEDFORMS § 11:80.

e. Failure to state a claim upon which relief can be granted; Long version. 2C FEDFORMS § 11:81.

f. Failure to state a claim upon which relief can be granted; Dismissal of certain allegations. 2C FEDFORMS § 11:82.

g. Failure to state a claim upon which relief can be granted; With supporting reasons. 2C FEDFORMS § 11:83.

h. Failure to state a claim upon which relief can be granted; With supporting reasons; Plaintiff not the real party in interest. 2C FEDFORMS § 11:85.

i. Failure to state a claim upon which relief can be granted; With supporting reasons; Failure to show implied contract. 2C FEDFORMS § 11:86.

j. Failure to state a claim upon which relief can be granted; With supporting reasons; Issue not arbitrable. 2C FEDFORMS § 11:87.

k. Failure to state a claim upon which relief can be granted; With supporting affidavits. 2C FED-FORMS § 11:88.

l. Failure to state a claim upon which relief can be granted; In alternative for summary judgment. 2C FEDFORMS § 11:89.

m.  Motion; To dismiss; Failure to state sufficient claim; By one of several defendants. FEDPROF § 1:923.

n.  Motion to dismiss; Failure to state sufficient claim; By third-party defendant. FEDPROF § 1:924.

o.  Motion to dismiss; Failure to state sufficient claim after successive attempts. FEDPROF § 1:925.

p.  Motion to dismiss; By individual defendants. FEDPROF § 1:926.

q.  Motion to dismiss; By state agency. FEDPROF § 1:927.

r.  Motion to dismiss counterclaim. FEDPROF § 1:931.

s.  Allegation; In motion to dismiss; Res judicata. FEDPROF § 1:933.

t.  Allegation; In motion to dismiss; Statute of limitations. FEDPROF § 1:935.

u.  Allegation; In motion to dismiss; Strict liability claim barred by statute. FEDPROF § 1:936.

v.  Allegation; In motion to dismiss; By United States; Absence of consent to suit. FEDPROF § 1:938.

w.  Reply; To motion to dismiss for failure to state sufficient claim. FEDPROF § 1:939.

x.  Motion to dismiss counterclaim. GOLDLTGFMS § 13:10.

y.  Motion to dismiss complaint; General form. GOLDLTGFMS § 20:24.

z.  Affidavit in support of motion to dismiss complaint. GOLDLTGFMS § 20:32.

## I. Applicable Rules

1. *Federal rules*

   a.  Serving and filing pleadings and other papers. FRCP 5.

   b.  Constitutional challenge to a statute; Notice, certification, and intervention. FRCP 5.1.

   c.  Privacy protection for filings made with the court. FRCP 5.2.

   d.  Computing and extending time; Time for motion papers. FRCP 6.

   e.  Pleadings allowed; Form of motions and other papers. FRCP 7.

   f.  Disclosure statement. FRCP 7.1.

   g.  Form of pleadings. FRCP 10.

   h.  Signing pleadings, motions, and other papers; Representations to the court; Sanctions. FRCP 11.

   i.  Defenses and objections; When and how presented; Motion for judgment on the pleadings; Consolidating motions; Waiving defenses; Pretrial hearing. FRCP 12.

   j.  Hearing motions; Submission on briefs. FRCP 78.

2. *Local rules*

   a.  Scope of the rules. NY R USDCTND L.R. 1.1.

   b.  Complex and multi-district litigation. NY R USDCTND L.R. 3.3.

   c.  Service and filing of papers. NY R USDCTND L.R. 5.1.

   d.  Filing by facsimile or e-mail. NY R USDCTND L.R. 5.5.

   e.  Personal privacy protection. NY R USDCTND L.R. 8.1.

   f.  Motion practice. NY R USDCTND L.R. 7.1.

   g.  Request for three-judge court. NY R USDCTND L.R. 9.1.

   h.  Form of papers. NY R USDCTND L.R. 10.1.

   i.  Settlement procedures. NY R USDCTND L.R. 68.2.

   j.  Orders. NY R USDCTND L.R. 77.2.

   k.  Motion days. NY R USDCTND L.R. 78.1.

   l.  Appearance and withdrawal of attorney. NY R USDCTND L.R. 83.2.

m. Arbitration. NY R USDCTND L.R. 83.7-1; NY R USDCTND L.R. 83.7-2; NY R USDCTND L.R. 83.7-3.

n. Assisted mediation program. NY R USDCTND L.R. 83.8.

o. Mediation. NY R USDCTND L.R. 83.11-1; NY R USDCTND L.R. 83.11-3.

p. Early neutral evaluation. NY R USDCTND L.R. 83.12-1; NY R USDCTND L.R. 83.12-3.

q. Administrative procedures for electronic case filing. NY R USDCTND CM/ECF.

r. Case assignment plan for the Northern District of New York. [NY R USDCTND Order 12, as amended by NY ORDER 16-4201, effective March 24, 2015].

s. Directing the expedited service of the summons and complaint and further directing the completion of FRCP 16 stipulation for the timely progression of civil actions. [NY R USDCTND Order 25, as amended by NY ORDER 16-4187, effective June 23, 2016].

t. Mandatory mediation program. NY R USDCTND Order 47.

## J. Miscellaneous

**NOTE: Individual judges' rules may apply. For available judge-level information, refer to:**

DISTRICT JUDGE MAE A. D'AGOSTINO: [NY R USDCTND D'Agostino-Rules and Practices, as added by NY ORDER 16-4200, effective April 4, 2016].

DISTRICT JUDGE THOMAS J. McAVOY: NY R USDCTND McAvoy-Order.

# Motions, Oppositions and Replies
# Motion to Dismiss for Lack of Subject Matter Jurisdiction

## Document Last Updated September 2016

## A. Checklist

(I)  ❑ Matters to be considered by moving party

   (a)  ❑ Required documents

      (1)  ❑ Notice of motion and motion

      (2)  ❑ Memorandum of law

      (3)  ❑ Supporting affidavit

      (4)  ❑ Certificate of service

   (b)  ❑ Supplemental documents

      (1)  ❑ Supporting evidence

      (2)  ❑ Notice of constitutional question

      (3)  ❑ Nongovernmental corporate disclosure statement

      (4)  ❑ Copies of authorities

      (5)  ❑ Proposed order

      (6)  ❑ Cover letter authorizing e-mail or facsimile filing

      (7)  ❑ Affidavit attesting to failed attempts to file electronically

      (8)  ❑ Notice of conventional filing

      (9)  ❑ CD/ROM with PDF of document(s)

     (10)  ❑ English translation

     (11)  ❑ Courtesy copies

     (12)  ❑ Copies for three-judge court

(c) ❑ Timing

    (1) ❑ The defense of lack of subject matter jurisdiction can be raised at any time

    (2) ❑ Every defense to a claim for relief in any pleading must be asserted in the responsive pleading if one is required

    (3) ❑ A motion asserting any of the defenses in FRCP 12(b) must be made before pleading if a responsive pleading is allowed

    (4) ❑ If a pleading sets out a claim for relief that does not require a responsive pleading, an opposing party may assert at trial any defense to that claim

    (5) ❑ The moving party must file all motion papers with the court and serve them upon the other parties not less than thirty-one (31) days prior to the return date of the motion

    (6) ❑ A written motion and notice of the hearing must be served at least fourteen (14) days before the time specified for the hearing, with the following exceptions: (i) when the motion may be heard ex parte; (ii) when the Federal Rules of Civil Procedure set a different time; or (iii) when a court order—which a party may, for good cause, apply for ex parte—sets a different time

    (7) ❑ Any affidavit supporting a motion must be served with the motion

(II) ❑ Matters to be considered by opposing party

  (a) ❑ Required documents

    (1) ❑ Opposition

    (2) ❑ Memorandum of law

    (3) ❑ Supporting affidavit

    (4) ❑ Certificate of service

  (b) ❑ Supplemental documents

    (1) ❑ Supporting evidence

    (2) ❑ Notice of constitutional question

    (3) ❑ Cross-motion

    (4) ❑ Copies of authorities

    (5) ❑ Cover letter authorizing e-mail or facsimile filing

    (6) ❑ Affidavit attesting to failed attempts to file electronically

    (7) ❑ Notice of conventional filing

    (8) ❑ CD/ROM with PDF of document(s)

    (9) ❑ English translation

    (10) ❑ Courtesy copies

    (11) ❑ Copies for three-judge court

  (c) ❑ Timing

    (1) ❑ The party opposing the motion must file its opposition papers with the court and serve them upon the other parties not less than seventeen (17) days prior to the return date of the motion

    (2) ❑ Except as FRCP 59(c) provides otherwise, any opposing affidavit must be served at least seven (7) days before the hearing, unless the court permits service at another time

    (3) ❑ A party may file and serve a cross-motion (meaning a competing request for relief or order similar to that requested by another party against the cross-moving party) at the time it files and serves its opposition papers to the original motion, i.e., not less than seventeen (17) days prior to the return date of the motion

## B. Timing

1. *Motion to dismiss for lack of subject matter jurisdiction.* [The defense of lack of subject matter jurisdiction] can be raised at any time. FEDPROC § 62:434.

   a. *In a responsive pleading.* Every defense to a claim for relief in any pleading must be asserted in the responsive pleading if one is required. FRCP 12(b).

   b. *By motion.* A motion asserting any of the defenses in FRCP 12(b) must be made before pleading if a responsive pleading is allowed. FRCP 12(b). Although FRCP 12(b) encourages the responsive pleader to file a motion to dismiss before filing the answer, nothing in FRCP 12 prohibits the filing of a motion to dismiss with the answer. An untimely motion to dismiss may be considered if the defense asserted in the motion was previously raised in the responsive pleading. FEDPROC § 62:427.

   c. *At trial.* If a pleading sets out a claim for relief that does not require a responsive pleading, an opposing party may assert at trial any defense to that claim. FRCP 12(b).

2. *Timing of motions, generally.* The moving party must file all motion papers with the Court and serve them upon the other parties not less than THIRTY-ONE (31) DAYS prior to the return date of the motion. NY R USDCTND L.R. 7.1(b)(1).

   a. *Motion and notice of hearing.* A written motion and notice of the hearing must be served at least fourteen (14) days before the time specified for the hearing, with the following exceptions:

      i. When the motion may be heard ex parte;

      ii. When the Federal Rules of Civil Procedure set a different time; or

      iii. When a court order—which a party may, for good cause, apply for ex parte—sets a different time. FRCP 6(c)(1).

   b. *Supporting affidavit.* Any affidavit supporting a motion must be served with the motion. FRCP 6(c)(2).

3. *Timing of opposing papers.* The party opposing the motion must file its opposition papers with the Court and serve them upon the other parties not less than SEVENTEEN (17) DAYS prior to the return date of the motion. NY R USDCTND L.R. 7.1(b)(1).

   a. *Opposing affidavit.* Except as FRCP 59(c) provides otherwise, any opposing affidavit must be served at least seven (7) days before the hearing, unless the court permits service at another time. FRCP 6(c)(2).

   b. *Cross-motion.* A party may file and serve a cross-motion (meaning a competing request for relief or order similar to that requested by another party against the cross-moving party) at the time it files and serves its opposition papers to the original motion, i.e., not less than SEVENTEEN (17) DAYS prior to the return date of the motion. NY R USDCTND L.R. 7.1(c).

4. *Timing of reply papers.* Where the respondent files an answering affidavit setting up a new matter, the moving party ordinarily is allowed a reasonable time to file a reply affidavit since failure to deny the new matter by affidavit may operate as an admission of its truth. AMJUR MOTIONS § 25.

   a. *Reply papers.* The moving party must file its reply papers, which may not exceed (10) pages with the Court and serve them upon the other parties not less than ELEVEN (11) DAYS prior to the return date of the motion. NY R USDCTND L.R. 7.1(b)(1).

   b. *Opposition to cross-motion.* The original moving party must file its reply/opposition papers with the Court and serve them on the other parties not less than ELEVEN (11) DAYS prior to the return date of the original motion. NY R USDCTND L.R. 7.1(c).

5. *Effect of a FRCP 12 motion on the time to serve a responsive pleading.* Unless the court sets a different time, serving a motion under FRCP 12 alters the periods in FRCP 12(a) as follows:

   a. If the court denies the motion or postpones its disposition until trial, the responsive pleading must be served within fourteen (14) days after notice of the court's action; or

   b. If the court grants a motion for a more definite statement, the responsive pleading must be served within fourteen (14) days after the more definite statement is served. FRCP 12(a)(4).

6.  *Computation of time*

   a.  *Computing time.* FRCP 6 applies in computing any time period specified in the Federal Rules of Civil Procedure, in any local rule or court order, or in any statute that does not specify a method of computing time. FRCP 6(a).

      i.  *Period stated in days or a longer unit.* When the period is stated in days or a longer unit of time:

         - Exclude the day of the event that triggers the period;
         - Count every day, including intermediate Saturdays, Sundays, and legal holidays; and
         - Include the last day of the period, but if the last day is a Saturday, Sunday, or legal holiday, the period continues to run until the end of the next day that is not a Saturday, Sunday, or legal holiday. FRCP 6(a)(1).

      ii.  *Period stated in hours.* When the period is stated in hours:

         - Begin counting immediately on the occurrence of the event that triggers the period;
         - Count every hour, including hours during intermediate Saturdays, Sundays, and legal holidays; and
         - If the period would end on a Saturday, Sunday, or legal holiday, the period continues to run until the same time on the next day that is not a Saturday, Sunday, or legal holiday. FRCP 6(a)(2).

      iii.  *Inaccessibility of the clerk's office.* Unless the court orders otherwise, if the clerk's office is inaccessible:

         - On the last day for filing under FRCP 6(a)(1), then the time for filing is extended to the first accessible day that is not a Saturday, Sunday, or legal holiday; or
         - During the last hour for filing under FRCP 6(a)(2), then the time for filing is extended to the same time on the first accessible day that is not a Saturday, Sunday, or legal holiday. FRCP 6(a)(3).

      iv.  *"Last day" defined.* Unless a different time is set by a statute, local rule, or court order, the last day ends:

         - For electronic filing, at midnight in the court's time zone; and
         - For filing by other means, when the clerk's office is scheduled to close. FRCP 6(a)(4).

      v.  *"Next day" defined.* The "next day" is determined by continuing to count forward when the period is measured after an event and backward when measured before an event. FRCP 6(a)(5).

      vi.  *"Legal holiday" defined.* "Legal holiday" means:

         - The day set aside by statute for observing New Year's Day, Martin Luther King Jr.'s Birthday, Washington's Birthday, Memorial Day, Independence Day, Labor Day, Columbus Day, Veterans' Day, Thanksgiving Day, or Christmas Day;
         - Any day declared a holiday by the President or Congress; and
         - For periods that are measured after an event, any other day declared a holiday by the state where the district court is located. FRCP 6(a)(6).

   b.  *Computation of electronic filing deadlines.* A document will be deemed timely filed if electronically filed prior to midnight Eastern Time. However, if the time of day is of the essence, the assigned judge may order that the document be filed by a time certain. NY R USDCTND CM/ECF(4)(4.3).

      i.  *Technical failures.* A Filing User, whose filing is untimely as the result of a technical failure of the Court's CM/ECF site, may seek appropriate relief from the Court. However, Filing Users are cautioned that, in some circumstances, the Court lacks the authority to grant an extension of time to file (e.g., FRCP 6(b) of the Federal Rules of Civil Procedure). NY R USDCTND CM/ECF(10)(10.1).

         - *Technical failure of the filing user's system.* Problems with the Filing User's system, such as phone line problems, problems with the Filing User's Internet Service Provider ("ISP"), or hardware or software problems, will not constitute a technical failure under these Administrative Procedures nor excuse an untimely filing. A Filing User who cannot file documents electronically because of a problem on the Filing User's system must file the documents' conventionally along with an affidavit explaining the reason for not filing the documents electronically. NY R USDCTND CM/ECF(10)(10.2).

 c. *Extending time*

  i. *In general.* When an act may or must be done within a specified time, the court may, for good cause, extend the time:

- With or without motion or notice if the court acts, or if a request is made, before the original time or its extension expires; or

- On motion made after the time has expired if the party failed to act because of excusable neglect. FRCP 6(b)(1).

  ii. *Exceptions.* A court must not extend the time to act under FRCP 50(b), FRCP 50(d), FRCP 52(b), FRCP 59(b), FRCP 59(d), FRCP 59(e), and FRCP 60(b). FRCP 6(b)(2).

  iii. Refer to the United States District Court for the Northern District of New York KeyRules Motion for Continuance/Extension of Time document for more information on extending time.

 d. *Additional time after certain kinds of service.* When a party may or must act within a specified time after service and service is made under FRCP 5(b)(2)(C), FRCP 5(b)(2)(D), FRCP 5(b)(2)(E), or FRCP 5(b)(2)(F), three (3) days are added after the period would otherwise expire under FRCP 6(a). FRCP 6(d).

  i. In accordance with FRCP 6(e), service by electronic means is treated the same as service by mail for purposes of adding three (3) days to the prescribed period to respond. NY R USDCTND CM/ECF(5)(5.4). [Editor's note: the reference to FRCP 6(e) is likely meant to be a reference to FRCP 6(d)].

7. *Individual judge practices.* Refer to the Miscellaneous section of this document for information on individual judge practices on timing of documents.

## C. General Requirements

1. *Motions, generally*

 a. *Requirements.* A request for a court order must be made by motion. The motion must:

  i. Be in writing unless made during a hearing or trial;

  ii. State with particularity the grounds for seeking the order; and

  iii. State the relief sought. FRCP 7(b)(1).

  iv. When a moving party makes a motion based upon a rule or statute, the moving party must specify in its moving papers the rule or statute upon which it bases its motion. NY R USDCTND L.R. 7.1(a)(1).

 b. *Notice of motion.* A party interested in resisting the relief sought by a motion has a right to notice thereof, and an opportunity to be heard. AMJUR MOTIONS § 12.

  i. In addition to statutory or court rule provisions requiring notice of a motion—the purpose of such a notice requirement having been said to be to prevent a party from being prejudicially surprised by a motion—principles of natural justice dictate that an adverse party generally must be given notice that a motion will be presented to the court. AMJUR MOTIONS § 12.

  ii. "Notice," in this regard, means reasonable notice, including a meaningful opportunity to prepare and to defend against allegations of a motion. AMJUR MOTIONS § 12.

 c. *Writing requirement.* The writing requirement is intended to insure that the adverse parties are informed and have a record of both the motion's pendency and the grounds on which the movant seeks an order. FPP § 1191; Feldberg v. Quechee Lakes Corp., 463 F.3d 195 (2d Cir. 2006).

  i. It is sufficient "if the motion is stated in a written notice of the hearing of the motion." FPP § 1191.

d. *Particularity requirement.* The particularity requirement insures that the opposing parties will have notice of their opponent's contentions. FEDPROC § 62:364; Goodman v. 1973 26 Foot Trojan Vessel, Arkansas Registration No. AR1439SN, 859 F.2d 71, 12 Fed.R.Serv.3d 645 (8th Cir. 1988). That requirement ensures that notice of the basis for the motion is provided to the court and to the opposing party so as to avoid prejudice, provide the opponent with a meaningful opportunity to respond, and provide the court with enough information to process the motion correctly. FEDPROC § 62:364; Andreas v. Volkswagen of America, Inc., 336 F.3d 789, 56 Fed.R.Serv.3d 6 (8th Cir. 2003).

   i. Reasonable specification of the grounds for a motion is sufficient. However, where a movant fails to state even one ground for granting the motion in question, the movant has failed to meet the minimal standard of "reasonable specification." FEDPROC § 62:364; Martinez v. Trainor, 556 F.2d 818, 23 Fed.R.Serv.2d 403 (7th Cir. 1977).

   ii. The court may excuse the failure to comply with the particularity requirement if it is inadvertent, and where no prejudice is shown by the opposing party. FEDPROC § 62:364.

e. *Order to show cause.* All motions that a party brings by Order to Show Cause shall conform to the requirements set forth in NY R USDCTND L.R. 7.1(a)(1) and NY R USDCTND L.R. 7.1(a)(2). Immediately after filing an Order to Show Cause, the moving party must telephone the Chambers of the presiding judicial officer and inform Chambers staff that it has filed an Order to Show Cause. Parties may obtain the telephone numbers for all Chambers from the Clerk's office or at the Court's webpage. The Court shall determine the briefing schedule and return date applicable to motions brought by Order to Show Cause. NY R USDCTND L.R. 7.1(e).

   i. In addition to the requirements set forth in NY R USDCTND L.R. 7.1(a)(1) and NY R USDCTND L.R. 7.1(a)(2), a motion brought by Order to Show Cause must include an affidavit clearly and specifically showing good and sufficient cause why the standard Notice of Motion procedure cannot be used. The moving party must give reasonable advance notice of the application for an Order to Show Cause to the other parties, except in those circumstances where the movant can demonstrate, in a detailed and specific affidavit, good cause and substantial prejudice that would result from the requirement of reasonable notice. NY R USDCTND L.R. 7.1(e).

   ii. An Order to Show Cause must contain a space for the assigned judge to set forth:

   - The deadline for filing and serving supporting papers,
   - The deadline for filing and serving opposing papers, and
   - The date and time for the hearing. NY R USDCTND L.R. 7.1(e).

2. *Motion to dismiss for lack of subject matter jurisdiction.* A party may assert the defense of lack of subject-matter jurisdiction by motion. FRCP 12(b)(1). The objection presented by a motion under FRCP 12(b)(1) challenging the court's subject matter jurisdiction is that the district judge has no authority or competence to hear and decide the case before it. A FRCP 12(b)(1) motion most typically is employed when the movant believes that the claim asserted by the plaintiff does not involve a federal question, and there is no diversity of citizenship between the parties or, in a diversity of citizenship case, the amount in controversy does not exceed the required jurisdictional amount. FPP § 1350.

   a. *Subject matter jurisdiction.* It always must be remembered that the federal courts are courts of limited jurisdiction and only can adjudicate those cases that fall within Article III of the Constitution (see U.S.C.A. Const. Art. III § 1, et seq.) and a congressional authorization enacted thereunder. FPP § 1350.

      i. *Federal question.* The district courts shall have original jurisdiction of all civil actions arising under the Constitution, laws, or treaties of the United States. 28 U.S.C.A. § 1331.

      ii. *Diversity of citizenship; Amount in controversy.* The district courts shall have original jurisdiction of all civil actions where the matter in controversy exceeds the sum or value of seventy-five thousand dollars ($75,000), exclusive of interest and costs, and is between:

      - Citizens of different States;
      - Citizens of a State and citizens or subjects of a foreign state, except that the district courts

shall not have original jurisdiction under 28 U.S.C.A. § 1332 of an action between citizens of a State and citizens or subjects of a foreign state who are lawfully admitted for permanent residence in the United States and are domiciled in the same State;

- Citizens of different States and in which citizens or subjects of a foreign state are additional parties; and

- A foreign state, defined in 28 U.S.C.A. § 1603(a), as plaintiff and citizens of a State or of different States. 28 U.S.C.A. § 1332(a).

b. *Types of FRCP 12(b)(1) motions.* There are two separate types of FRCP 12(b)(1) motions to dismiss for lack of subject matter jurisdiction: the "facial attack" and the "factual attack." FEDPROC § 62:440.

   i. *Facial attack.* The facial attack is addressed to the sufficiency of the allegations of the complaint itself. FEDPROC § 62:440; Stalley ex rel. U.S. v. Orlando Regional Healthcare System, Inc., 524 F.3d 1229 (11th Cir. 2008). On such a motion, the court is merely required to determine whether the plaintiff has sufficiently alleged a basis of subject matter jurisdiction, and the factual allegations of the complaint are taken as true. FEDPROC § 62:440; U.S. ex rel. Atkinson v. PA. Shipbuilding Co., 473 F.3d 506 (3d Cir. 2007).

   ii. *Factual attack.* The "factual attack," on the other hand, challenges the existence of subject matter jurisdiction in fact, irrespective of the pleadings, and matters outside the pleadings, such as testimony and affidavits, may be considered by the court. FEDPROC § 62:440; Kligman v. I.R.S., 272 Fed.Appx. 166 (3d Cir. 2008); Paper, Allied-Industrial, Chemical and Energy Workers Intern. Union v. Continental Carbon Co., 428 F.3d 1285 (10th Cir. 2005). The trial court in such a situation is free to weigh the evidence and satisfy itself as to the existence of its power to hear the case; therefore, no presumptive truthfulness attaches to the plaintiff's factual allegations. FEDPROC § 62:440; Land v. Dollar, 330 U.S. 731, 67 S.Ct. 1009, 91 L.Ed. 1209 (1947).

c. *Burden.* With the limited exception of the question whether the amount in controversy requirement in diversity of citizenship cases has been satisfied, the extensive case law on the subject makes clear that the burden of proof on a FRCP 12(b)(1) motion is on the party asserting that subject matter jurisdiction exists, which, of course, typically is the plaintiff. FPP § 1350; Thomson v. Gaskill, 315 U.S. 442, 62 S.Ct. 673, 86 L.Ed. 951 (1942). A plaintiff meets the burden of establishing subject matter jurisdiction at the pleading stage by pleading sufficient allegations to show the proper basis for the court to assert subject matter jurisdiction over the action. 2 FEDFORMS § 7:6.

   i. *Federal question.* If subject matter jurisdiction is based on the existence of a federal question, the pleader must show that he or she has alleged a claim for relief arising under federal law and that the claim is not frivolous. FPP § 1350; Baker v. Carr, 369 U.S. 186, 82 S.Ct. 691, 7 L.Ed.2d 663 (1962).

   ii. *Diversity of citizenship.* If jurisdiction is based on diversity of citizenship, on the other hand, the pleader must show that real and complete diversity exists between all of the plaintiffs and all of the defendants, and also that the assertion that the claim exceeds the requisite jurisdictional amount in controversy is made in good faith. FPP § 1350; City of Indianapolis v. Chase Nat. Bank, 314 U.S. 63, 62 S.Ct. 15, 86 L.Ed. 47 (1941). Satisfying this last requirement is a relatively simple task, however, because the claim is deemed to be made in good faith so long as it is not clear to a legal certainty that the claimant could not recover a judgment exceeding the statutorily mandated jurisdictional amount, a matter on which the party challenging the district court's jurisdiction has the burden. FPP § 1350.

d. *Joining motions.* When the motion is based on more than one ground, the cases are legion stating that the district court should consider the FRCP 12(b)(1) challenge first because if it must dismiss the complaint for lack of subject matter jurisdiction, the accompanying defenses and objections become moot and do not need to be determined by the judge. FPP § 1350; Steel Co. v. Citizens for a Better Environment, 523 U.S. 83, 118 S.Ct. 1003, 140 L.Ed.2d 210 (1998). However, there are a number of decisions in which the court has decided one or more defenses in addition to the subject matter jurisdiction question or simply assumed the existence of jurisdiction and gone on to decide another matter. FPP § 1350.

  i. *Right to join.* A motion under FRCP 12 may be joined with any other motion allowed by FRCP 12. FRCP 12(g)(1).

  ii. *Limitation on further motions.* Except as provided in FRCP 12(h)(2) or FRCP 12(h)(3), a party that makes a motion under FRCP 12 must not make another motion under FRCP 12 raising a defense or objection that was available to the party but omitted from its earlier motion. FRCP 12(g)(2).

e. *Waiving and preserving certain defenses.* No defense or objection is waived by joining it with one or more other defenses or objections in a responsive pleading or in a motion. FRCP 12(b).

  i. *Waiver by consent.* The defendant may waive the right to obtain a dismissal prior to trial either by express consent to be sued in a certain district or by some conduct that will be construed as implying consent. FPP § 1352.

  ii. *When some are waived.* A party waives any defense listed in FRCP 12(b)(2) through FRCP 12(b)(5) by:

   • Omitting it from a motion in the circumstances described in FRCP 12(g)(2); or

   • Failing to either: (1) make it by motion under FRCP 12; or (2) include it in a responsive pleading or in an amendment allowed by FRCP 15(a)(1) as a matter of course. FRCP 12(h)(1).

  iii. *When to raise others.* Failure to state a claim upon which relief can be granted, to join a person required by FRCP 19(b), or to state a legal defense to a claim may be raised:

   • In any pleading allowed or ordered under FRCP 7(a);

   • By a motion under FRCP 12(c); or

   • At trial. FRCP 12(h)(2).

  iv. *Lack of subject matter jurisdiction.* If the court determines at any time that it lacks subject-matter jurisdiction, the court must dismiss the action. FRCP 12(h)(3).

3. *Opposing papers.* The Federal Rules of Civil Procedure do not require any formal answer, return, or reply to a motion, except where the Federal Rules of Civil Procedure or local rules may require affidavits, memoranda, or other papers to be filed in opposition to a motion. Such papers are simply to apprise the court of such opposition and the grounds of that opposition. FEDPROC § 62:359.

a. *Effect of failure to respond to motion.* Although in the absence of statutory provision or court rule, a motion ordinarily does not require a written answer, when a party files a motion and the opposing party fails to respond, the court may construe such failure to respond as nonopposition to the motion or an admission that the motion was meritorious, may take the facts alleged in the motion as true—the rule in some jurisdictions being that the failure to respond to a fact set forth in a motion is deemed an admission—and may grant the motion if the relief requested appears to be justified. AMJUR MOTIONS § 28.

b. *Assent or no opposition not determinative.* However, a motion will not be granted automatically simply because an "assent" or a notation of "no opposition" has been filed; federal judges frequently deny motions that have been assented to when it is thought that justice so dictates. FPP § 1190.

c. *Responsive pleading inappropriate as response to motion.* An attempt to answer or oppose a motion with a responsive pleading usually is not appropriate. FPP § 1190.

4. *Reply papers.* A moving party may be required or permitted to prepare papers in addition to his original motion papers. AMJUR MOTIONS § 25. Papers answering or replying to opposing papers may be appropriate, in the interests of justice, where it appears there is a substantial reason for allowing a reply. Thus, a court may accept reply papers where a party demonstrates that the papers to which it seeks to file a reply raise new issues that are material to the disposition of the question before the court, or where the court determines, sua sponte, that it wishes further briefing of an issue raised in those papers and orders the submission of additional papers. FEDPROC § 62:360.

a. *Function of reply papers.* The function of a reply affidavit is to answer the arguments made in opposition to the position taken by the movant and not to permit the movant to introduce new arguments in support of the motion. AMJUR MOTIONS § 25.

    b.   *Issues raised for the first time in a reply document.* However, the view has been followed in some jurisdictions, that as a matter of judicial economy, where there is no prejudice and where the issues could be raised simply by filing a motion to dismiss, the trial court has discretion to consider arguments raised for the first time in a reply memorandum, and that a trial court may grant a motion to strike issues raised for the first time in a reply memorandum. AMJUR MOTIONS § 26.

    c.   *Opposition to cross-motion.* The original moving party may reply in further support of the original motion and in opposition to the cross-motion with a reply/opposition brief that does not exceed twenty-five (25) pages in length, exclusive of exhibits. NY R USDCTND L.R. 7.1(c).

5.   *Surreply.* A surreply is not permitted. NY R USDCTND L.R. 7.1(b)(1).

    a.   *Surreply in support of cross-motion.* The cross-moving party may not reply in further support of its cross-motion without the Court's prior permission. NY R USDCTND L.R. 7.1(c).

6.   *Submission of proposed order by prevailing party.* If the assigned judge instructs the prevailing party to do so, the prevailing party shall submit a proposed order which the opposing party has approved and which contains the endorsement of the opposing party: "Approved as to form." NY R USDCTND L.R. 77.2(b). In civil actions where the Court has directed a party to submit an order or judgment, that party shall file all such orders or judgments in duplicate, and the Clerk's entry of such duplicate in the proper record book shall be deemed in compliance with FRCP 79(b). Such party shall also furnish the Clerk with a sufficient number of additional copies for each party to the action, which the Clerk shall mail with notice of entry in accordance with FRCP 77(d). NY R USDCTND L.R. 5.1(b).

    a.   *Disagreement as to form of proposed order.* When the parties are unable to agree as to the form of the proposed order, the prevailing party shall, on seven (7) days notice to all other parties, submit a proposed order and a written explanation for the form of that order. The Court may award costs and attorney's fees against a party whose unreasonable conduct the Court deemed to have required the bringing of the motion. The provisions of NY R USDCTND L.R. 7.1 shall not apply to such motion, and the Court shall not hear oral argument. NY R USDCTND L.R. 77.2(b).

    b.   For more information on orders, refer to NY R USDCTND L.R. 77.2.

7.   *Sanctions for vexatious or frivolous motions or failure to comply with* NY R USDCTND L.R. 7.1. A party who presents vexatious or frivolous motion papers or fails to comply with NY R USDCTND L.R. 7.1 is subject to discipline as the Court deems appropriate, including sanctions and the imposition of costs and attorney's fees to the opposing party. NY R USDCTND L.R. 7.1(i).

8.   *Complex and multi-district litigation.* If the assigned judge determines, in his or her discretion, that the case is of such a complex nature that it cannot reasonably be trial ready within eighteen (18) months from the date the complaint is filed, the assigned judge may design and issue a particularized case management order that will move the case to trial as quickly as the complexity of the case allows. NY R USDCTND L.R. 3.3(a). The parties shall promptly notify the Court in writing if any action commenced is appropriate for multi-district litigation. NY R USDCTND L.R. 3.3(b).

9.   *Appearances.* An attorney appearing for a party in a civil case shall promptly file with the Clerk a written notice of appearance; however, an attorney does not need to file a notice of appearance if the attorney who would be filing the notice of appearance is the same individual who has signed the complaint, notice of removal, pre-answer motion, or answer. NY R USDCTND L.R. 83.2(a). For more information, refer to NY R USDCTND L.R. 83.2.

10.   *Related cases.* A civil case is "related" to another civil case for purposes of this guideline when, because of the similarity of facts and legal issues or because the cases arise from the same transactions or events, a substantial saving of judicial resources is likely to result from assigning the cases to the same Judge and Magistrate Judge. NY R USDCTND Order 12(G)(2). A civil case shall not be deemed related to another civil case merely because the civil case: (1) involves similar legal issues, or (2) involves the same parties. NY R USDCTND Order 12(G)(3). Presumptively, and subject to the power of a Judge to determine otherwise pursuant to NY R USDCTND Order 12(G)(5), civil cases shall not be deemed to be "related" unless both cases are still pending before the Court. NY R USDCTND Order 12(G)(4).

    a.   *New filings.* If an attorney or filing party indicates on the Civil Cover Sheet that a case is related to an earlier filed case, the Clerk shall instruct the filing party to file a notice of related cases. The allegedly related cases will be submitted by the Clerk to the Judge to whom the earliest filed case is assigned, who shall advise the Clerk whether such cases are related. NY R USDCTND Order 12(G)(1).

b. *Judicial determination that civil cases are "related."* Except for the cases described in the final sentence of NY R USDCTND Order 12(G)(6), all civil cases shall be randomly assigned when they are filed. Other than the cases described in the final sentence of NY R USDCTND Order 12(G)(6), civil cases shall not be deemed to be "related" for purposes of this guideline at the instance of any litigant or attorney unless and until there has been a determination by a Judge of this Court that the standard of NY R USDCTND Order 12(G)(2) is met. NY R USDCTND Order 12(G)(5).

   i. *Notice of related filing.* Any party may apply for such a determination by filing with the Clerk a notice of related filing, which should include an explanation as to why the standard of NY R USDCTND Order 12(G)(2) is met. A form for this purpose is available on the Court's website. A copy of the notice shall be served on all other parties who have appeared. Such an application must be made after the date when at least a majority of the defendants have been served with the complaint. Before making such an application, the applicant must confer in good faith with all other parties in an effort to reach an agreement on whether or not the case is "related". After such an application is made, any other party may serve and file within seven (7) calendar days a letter of no more than two (2) pages supporting or opposing the application. The application to have the case assigned to another Judge shall be presented to the Judge with the earliest filed case for decision on whether the action(s) should be reassigned as related cases. The Judge with the earliest filed case may then enter an order in the case at bar, either deeming the case to be related and directing the Clerk to reassign the action, or denying the application for reassignment. Any disputes concerning the assignment of related cases will be referred to the Chief Judge for resolution. NY R USDCTND Order 12(G)(5).

c. For more information on related cases, refer to NY R USDCTND Order 12(G).

11. *Alternative dispute resolution (ADR).* It is the mission of this court to do everything it can to help parties resolve their disputes as fairly, quickly, and efficiently as possible. NY R USDCTND Order 25(VIII).

a. *Arbitration.* NY R USDCTND L.R. 83.7 governs the consensual arbitration program for referral of civil actions to court-annexed arbitration. It may remain in effect until further order of the Court. Its purpose is to establish a less formal procedure for the just, efficient and economical resolution of disputes, while preserving the right to a full trial on demand. NY R USDCTND L.R. 83.7-1.

   i. *Actions subject to arbitration.* The Clerk shall notify the parties in all civil cases, except as the Local Rules of Practice for the United States District Court for the Northern District of New York otherwise direct, that they may consent to non-binding arbitration under NY R US-DCTND L.R. 83.7. The notice shall be furnished to the parties at pretrial/scheduling conferences or shall be included with pretrial conference notices and instructions. Consent to arbitration under NY R USDCTND L.R. 83.7 shall be discussed at the pretrial/scheduling conference. No party or attorney shall be prejudiced for refusing to participate in arbitration. The Court shall allow the referral of any civil action pending before it to the arbitration process if the parties consent. The plaintiff shall be responsible for securing the execution of a consent form by the parties and for filing the form with the Clerk within fourteen (14) days after the parties receive the form. The parties shall freely and knowingly enter into the consent. NY R USDCTND L.R. 83.7-2.

   ii. *Referral to arbitration.* The Clerk shall refer every action subject to NY R USDCTND L.R. 83.7 to arbitration in accordance with the procedures under NY R USDCTND L.R. 83.7 twenty-one (21) days after the filing of the last responsive pleading or within twenty-one (21) days of the filing of a stipulated consent order referring the action to arbitration, whichever event occurs last, except as otherwise provided. If any party notices a motion to dismiss under the provisions of FRCP 12(a) and/or FRCP 12(b), or a motion to join necessary parties pursuant to the Federal Rules of Civil Procedure prior to the expiration of the twenty-one (21) day period, the assigned judge shall hear the motion and further proceedings under NY R USDCTND L.R. 83.7 shall be deferred pending decision on the motion. If the Court does not dismiss the action on the motion, the Court shall refer the action to arbitration twenty-one (21) days after the filing of the decision. NY R USDCTND L.R. 83.7-3(a). Motions for summary judgment pursuant to FRCP 56 shall be filed and served within twenty-one (21) days following the close of discovery. The filing of a FRCP 56 motion shall defer further proceedings under NY R USDCTND L.R. 83.7 pending decision on the motion. NY R USDCTND L.R. 83.7-3(a).

- *Relief from referral.* Any party shall request relief from the operation of NY R USDCTND L.R. 83.7 by filing with the Court a motion for the relief within twenty-one (21) days after entry of the initial stipulated consent order which refers the case for arbitration. The assigned judge shall, sua sponte, exempt an action from the application of NY R USDCTND L.R. 83.7 where the objectives of arbitration would not be realized because (1) the case involves complex or novel legal issues, (2) legal issues predominate over factual issues, or (3) for other good cause. NY R USDCTND L.R. 83.7-3(c).

iii. For more information on arbitration, refer to NY R USDCTND L.R. 83.7.

b. *Mediation.* The purpose of NY R USDCTND L.R. 83.11 is to provide a supplementary procedure to the Court's existing alternative dispute resolution procedures. NY R USDCTND L.R. 83.11 provides for an earlier resolution of civil disputes resulting in savings of time and cost to litigants and the Court without sacrificing the quality of justice rendered or the right of litigants to a full trial on all issues not resolved through mediation. NY R USDCTND L.R. 83.11-1(a). Mediation is a process by which an impartial person, the mediator, facilitates communication between disputing parties to promote understanding, reconciliation and settlement. The mediator is an advocate for settlement and uses the mediation process to help the parties fully explore any potential area of agreement. The mediator does not serve as a judge or arbitrator and has no authority to render any decision on any disputed issue or to force a settlement. The parties themselves are responsible for negotiating any resolution(s) to their dispute. NY R USDCTND L.R. 83.11-1(b).

i. *Actions subject to mediation.* The Court may refer any civil action (or any portion thereof) to mediation under NY R USDCTND L.R. 83.11: (1) by order of referral; or (2) on the motion of any party; or (3) by consent of the parties. NY R USDCTND L.R. 83.11-3(a).

- *Withdrawal from mediation.* The parties may withdraw from mediation any civil action or claim that the Court refers to mediation pursuant to NY R USDCTND L.R. 83.11-3 by application to the assigned judge at least ten (10) days prior to the scheduled mediation session. NY R USDCTND L.R. 83.11-3(b).

ii. *Mandatory mediation program.* The United States District Court for the Northern District of New York has adopted this Mandatory Mediation Plan. The paid Mediation Program is designed to provide quicker, less expensive and potentially more satisfying alternatives to continuing litigation, without impairing the quality of justice or the right to trial. NY R USDCTND Order 47(1)(1.2)(A). This Mandatory Mediation Plan applies to civil actions pending as well as newly filed actions, except as otherwise indicated in NY R USDCTND Order 47. The Local Rules for voluntary mediation will apply only to Pro Se Cases that proceed through the Assisted Mediation Program. NY R USDCTND Order 47(1)(1.2)(B).

- *Referral into the pilot mandatory mediation program for new cases.* All civil cases shall be referred automatically into the Mandatory Mediation Program. Notice of the Mandatory Mediation requirements will be provided to all parties immediately upon the filing of a complaint and answer or a notice of removal. ADR intervention will be scheduled at the conference held pursuant to NY R USDCTND L.R. 16.1. NY R USDCTND Order 47(2)(2.1)(A). For a list of categories of actions exempted from automatic referral, refer to NY R USDCTND Order 47(2)(2.1)(A).

- *Referral into the pilot mandatory mediation program for pending cases.* The assigned Judge or Magistrate Judge on any pending civil case may, sua sponte or with status conference, issue an order referring the case into the Mandatory Mediation Program. The order shall specify a date on which the ADR intervention is to be completed. NY R USDCTND Order 47(2)(2.1)(B).

- *Referral into the pilot mandatory mediation program by stipulation.* A case may be referred into the Mandatory Mediation Program by stipulation of all parties. Stipulations shall be filed and shall designate the time frame within which the ADR process will be completed. Stipulations are presumed acceptable unless the assigned Judge or Magistrate Judge determines that the interests of justice are not served. NY R USDCTND Order 47(2)(2.1)(C).

- *Relief from referral.* Motions to opt out of the program will be addressed by the assigned Magistrate Judge at the FRCP 16 conference. NY R USDCTND Order 47(2)(2.2)(A). Opting Out Motions shall be granted only for "good cause" shown. Inconvenience, travel costs, attorney fees or other costs shall not constitute "good cause." A party seeking relief from the Mandatory Mediation Program must set forth the reasons why Mandatory Mediation has no reasonable chance of being productive. NY R USDCTND Order 47(2)(2.2)(B). The assigned Magistrate Judge may, sua sponte, exempt any case from the Court's Mandatory Mediation Program. NY R USDCTND Order 47(2)(2.2)(C).

iii. *Assisted mediation program.* The Court may assign specially trained pro bono Special Mediation Counsel to assist pro se civilian litigants with preparing for and participating in mediation. The Assisted Mediation Program is open to civilian pro se parties to actions in the Northern District of New York. The assigned judge or magistrate judge determines if the case would benefit from mediation and would also benefit from the assignment of Special Mediation Counsel to assist the pro se party with the mediation process. NY R USDCTND L.R. 83.8(a). Appointment of Special Mediation Counsel is in no way guaranteed, even if the action is referred to the court-annexed mediation program. Appointment is at the sole discretion of the presiding judge. NY R USDCTND L.R. 83.8(a).

- *Referral to assisted mediation program.* If the court determines that referral to the Assisted Mediation Program is appropriate, the Court shall enter an order of reference to the Assisted Mediation Program. NY R USDCTND L.R. 83.8(b).

iv. For more information on mediation, refer to NY R USDCTND L.R. 83.11 and NY R USDCTND Order 47.

c. *Early neutral evaluation (ENE).* Early neutral evaluation (ENE) is a process in which parties obtain from an experienced neutral (an "evaluator") a nonbinding, reasoned, oral evaluation of the merits of the case. The first step in the ENE process involves the Court appointing an evaluator who has expertise in the area of law in the case. After the parties exchange essential information and position statements early in the pretrial period (usually within one hundred fifty (150) to two hundred (200) days after a complaint has been filed), the evaluator convenes an ENE session that typically lasts about two hours. At the ENE meeting, each side briefly presents the factual and legal basis of its position. The evaluator may ask questions of the parties and help them identify the main issues in dispute and the areas of agreement. The evaluator may also help the parties explore options for settlement. If settlement does not occur, the evaluator then offers an opinion as to the settlement value of the case, including the likelihood of liability and the likely range of damages. With the benefit of this assessment, the parties are again encouraged to discuss settlement, with or without the evaluator's assistance. The parties may also explore ways to narrow the issues in dispute, exchange information about the case or otherwise prepare efficiently for trial. NY R USDCTND L.R. 83.12-1.

i. *Actions subject to early neutral evaluation.* The Court may refer any civil action (or any portion thereof) to ENE under NY R USDCTND L.R. 83.12: (1) by order of referral; (2) on the motion of any party; or (3) by consent of the parties. NY R USDCTND L.R. 83.12-3(a).

- *Withdrawal from the ENE process.* The parties may withdraw any civil action or claim that the Court has referred to the ENE Process pursuant to NY R USDCTND L.R. 83.12-3 by application to the assigned judge at least ten (10) days before the scheduled evaluation session. NY R USDCTND L.R. 83.12-3(b).

ii. For more information on early neutral evaluation (ENE), refer to NY R USDCTND L.R. 83.12.

12. *Settlement procedures.* On notice to the Court or the Clerk that the parties have settled an action, and upon confirmation of the settlement by all parties, the Court may issue a judgment dismissing the action by reason of settlement. The Court shall issue the order without prejudice to the parties' right to secure

reinstatement of the case within thirty (30) days after the date of judgment by making a showing that the settlement was not, in fact, consummated. NY R USDCTND L.R. 68.2(a). If the Court decides not to follow the procedures set forth in NY R USDCTND L.R. 68.2(a), the parties shall file within thirty (30) days of the notification to the Court, unless otherwise directed by written order, such notices, stipulations and/or motions as are necessary to terminate the action. If the required documents are not filed within the thirty (30) day period, the Clerk shall place the action on the dismissal calendar. NY R USDCTND L.R. 68.2(b).

13. *Sanctions and penalties for noncompliance.* Failure of an attorney or of a party to comply with any provision of the Local Rules of Practice for the United States District Court for the Northern District of New York, General Orders of this District, Orders of the Court, or the Federal Rules of Civil Procedure shall be a ground for imposition of sanctions. NY R USDCTND L.R. 1.1(d).

14. *Individual judge practices.* Refer to the Miscellaneous section of this document for information on individual judge practices on general requirements for documents.

## D. Documents

1. *Documents for moving party*

   a. *Required documents*

      i. *Notice of motion and motion.* The Notice of Motion must state the return date that the moving party has selected. NY R USDCTND L.R. 7.1(b)(1). Refer to the General Requirements section of this document for information on the notice of motion and motion.

         • *Order to show cause.* Refer to the General Requirements section of this document for information on bringing a motion by order to show cause.

      ii. *Memorandum of law.* Except as otherwise provided in NY R USDCTND L.R. 7.1(a), all motions. . .require a memorandum of law. NY R USDCTND L.R. 7.1(a). Refer to the Format section of this document for the formatting requirements for memoranda of law.

      iii. *Supporting affidavit.* Except as otherwise provided in NY R USDCTND L.R. 7.1(a), all motions. . .require a. . .supporting affidavit. NY R USDCTND L.R. 7.1(a). An affidavit must not contain legal arguments but must contain factual and procedural background that is relevant to the motion the affidavit supports. NY R USDCTND L.R. 7.1(a)(2).

      iv. *Certificate of service.* Except as otherwise provided in NY R USDCTND L.R. 7.1(a), all motions. . .require. . .proof of service on all the parties. See NY R USDCTND L.R. 5.1(a). NY R USDCTND L.R. 7.1(a). FRCP 5(d) requires that the person making service under FRCP 5 certify that service has been effected. FRCP 5(Advisory Committee Notes). Having such information on file may be useful for many purposes, including proof of service if an issue arises concerning the effectiveness of the service. FRCP 5(Advisory Committee Notes). The party or its designee shall declare, by affidavit or certification, that it has provided all other parties in the action with all documents it has filed with the Court. NY R USDCTND L.R. 5.1(a).

         • Attorneys and pro se parties who are not Filing or Receiving Users must be served with a paper copy of any electronically filed pleading or other document. NY R USDCTND CM/ECF(5)(5.2). Such paper service must be documented by electronically filing a certificate of service. NY R USDCTND CM/ECF(5)(5.2).

   b. *Supplemental documents*

      i. *Supporting evidence.* When a motion relies on facts outside the record, the court may hear the matter on affidavits or may hear it wholly or partly on oral testimony or on depositions. FRCP 43(c).

      ii. *Notice of constitutional question.* A party that files a pleading, written motion, or other paper drawing into question the constitutionality of a federal or state statute must promptly:

         • *File notice.* File a notice of constitutional question stating the question and identifying the paper that raises it, if: (1) a federal statute is questioned and the parties do not include the United States, one of its agencies, or one of its officers or employees in an official capacity;

or (2) a state statute is questioned and the parties do not include the state, one of its agencies, or one of its officers or employees in an official capacity; and

- *Serve notice.* Serve the notice and paper on the Attorney General of the United States if a federal statute is questioned—or on the state attorney general if a state statute is questioned—either by certified or registered mail or by sending it to an electronic address designated by the attorney general for this purpose. FRCP 5.1(a).

- *No forfeiture.* A party's failure to file and serve the notice, or the court's failure to certify, does not forfeit a constitutional claim or defense that is otherwise timely asserted. FRCP 5.1(d).

iii. *Nongovernmental corporate disclosure statement*

- *Contents.* A nongovernmental corporate party must file two (2) copies of a disclosure statement that: (1) identifies any parent corporation and any publicly held corporation owning ten percent (10%) or more of its stock; or (2) states that there is no such corporation. FRCP 7.1(a).

- *Time to file; Supplemental filing.* A party must: (1) file the disclosure statement with its first appearance, pleading, petition, motion, response, or other request addressed to the court; and (2) promptly file a supplemental statement if any required information changes. FRCP 7.1(b).

iv. *Copies of authorities.* When serving a pro se litigant with a memorandum of law or any other paper which contains citations to authorities that are unpublished or published exclusively on electronic databases, counsel shall include a hard copy of those authorities. Although copies of authorities published only on electronic databases are not required to be filed, copies shall be provided upon request to opposing counsel who lack access to electronic databases. NY R USDCTND L.R. 7.1(a)(1).

v. *Proposed order.* A document that is submitted in .pdf format cannot be modified; therefore, a proposed order or stipulation must be in a word processing format. The chambers of the assigned judge may request that a proposed order and/or a stipulation be e-mailed to the courtroom deputy for the presiding judge in either WordPerfect or Microsoft Word format. Please attach your proposed order and/or stipulation to an Internet e-mail sent to the appropriate e-mail address listed in NY R USDCTND CM/ECF(8)(8.2). NY R USDCTND CM/ECF(8)(8.2).

vi. *Cover letter authorizing e-mail or facsimile filing.* Neither the Court nor the Clerk's Office will accept for filing any facsimile or e-mail transmission without prior authorization from the Court. The party using facsimile or e-mail transmissions to file its papers must accompany any such documents with a cover letter stating that the Court authorized such transmissions and the date on which the Court provided that authorization. Violations of NY R USDCTND L.R. 5.5 subject the offending party to the Court's full disciplinary powers. NY R USDCTND L.R. 5.5.

vii. *Affidavit attesting to failed attempts to file electronically.* If the Court's CM/ECF site experiences a technical failure, a Filing User may submit documents to the Court that day in an alternate manner provided that the documents are accompanied by the Filing User's affidavit stating that the Filing User attempted to file electronically at least two times in one (1) hour increments after 10:00 a.m. that day. The following methods are acceptable alternate means for filing documents in case of a technical failure: (1) via electronic mail in a PDF attachment sent to the e-mail address for technical failures; or (2) in person, by bringing the document to the Clerk's Office on paper accompanied by a CD/ROM that contains the document in .pdf format. NY R USDCTND CM/ECF(10)(10.1).

- A Filing User who cannot file documents electronically because of a problem on the Filing User's system must file the documents' conventionally along with an affidavit explaining the reason for not filing the documents electronically. NY R USDCTND CM/ECF(10)(10.2).

viii. *Notice of conventional filing.* If the Clerk's Office grants permission to conventionally file the

document, the Filing User shall electronically file a notice of conventional filing for the documents. More information regarding this process can be obtained from the Court's web page. NY R USDCTND CM/ECF(4)(4.5).

ix.  *CD/ROM with PDF of document(s).* If the Court grants permission to file a document traditionally, the attorney must submit the documents for filing to the Clerk's Office on CD/ROM in .pdf or pdf.A format. NY R USDCTND CM/ECF(2).

x.  *English translation.* The Court conducts its reviews and deliberations in English. Unless otherwise directed by the Court, any document that a party transmits to the Court (including one in the record on appeal) that is in a language other than English must be accompanied by an English translation that the translator has certified as true and accurate, pursuant to 28 U.S.C.A. § 1746. NY R USDCTND L.R. 10.1(e). For more information, refer to NY R USDCTND L.R. 10.1(e).

xi.  *Courtesy copies.* The Court may require that courtesy copies of electronically filed documents be submitted for its review and may amend these Administrative Procedures (NY R USDCTND CM/ECF) at any time without prior notice. NY R USDCTND CM/ECF(2).

- The parties need not provide a courtesy copy of their motion papers to the assigned judge unless the assigned judge requests a copy. NY R USDCTND L.R. 7.1(b)(1).

xii.  *Copies for three-judge court.* On the convening of a three-judge court, the parties shall make three (3) copies of all non-electronically filed pleadings, motion papers, and memoranda of law available to the Clerk for distribution. NY R USDCTND L.R. 9.1.

2.  *Documents for opposing party*

a.  *Required documents*

i.  *Opposition.* Refer to the General Requirements section of this document for information on the opposing papers.

ii.  *Memorandum of law.* Except as otherwise provided in NY R USDCTND L.R. 7.1(a), all. . .opposition to motions require a memorandum of law. NY R USDCTND L.R. 7.1(a).

- *Cross-motion brief.* If a party makes a cross-motion, it must join its cross motion brief with its opposition brief, and this combined brief may not exceed twenty-five (25) pages in length, exclusive of exhibits. A separate brief in opposition to the original motion is not permissible. NY R USDCTND L.R. 7.1(c).

- Refer to the Format section of this document for the formatting requirements for memoranda of law.

iii.  *Supporting affidavit.* Except as otherwise provided in NY R USDCTND L.R. 7.1(a), all. . .opposition to motions require a. . .supporting affidavit. NY R USDCTND L.R. 7.1(a). An affidavit must not contain legal arguments but must contain factual and procedural background that is relevant to the motion the affidavit supports. NY R USDCTND L.R. 7.1(a)(2).

iv.  *Certificate of service.* Except as otherwise provided in NY R USDCTND L.R. 7.1(a), all. . .opposition to motions require. . .proof of service on all the parties. See NY R USDCTND L.R. 5.1(a). NY R USDCTND L.R. 7.1(a). FRCP 5(d) requires that the person making service under FRCP 5 certify that service has been effected. FRCP 5(Advisory Committee Notes). Having such information on file may be useful for many purposes, including proof of service if an issue arises concerning the effectiveness of the service. FRCP 5(Advisory Committee Notes). The party or its designee shall declare, by affidavit or certification, that it has provided all other parties in the action with all documents it has filed with the Court. NY R USDCTND L.R. 5.1(a).

- Attorneys and pro se parties who are not Filing or Receiving Users must be served with a paper copy of any electronically filed pleading or other document. NY R USDCTND CM/ECF(5)(5.2). Such paper service must be documented by electronically filing a certificate of service. NY R USDCTND CM/ECF(5)(5.2).

b. *Supplemental documents*

    i. *Supporting evidence.* When a motion relies on facts outside the record, the court may hear the matter on affidavits or may hear it wholly or partly on oral testimony or on depositions. FRCP 43(c).

    ii. *Notice of constitutional question.* A party that files a pleading, written motion, or other paper drawing into question the constitutionality of a federal or state statute must promptly:

- *File notice.* File a notice of constitutional question stating the question and identifying the paper that raises it, if: (1) a federal statute is questioned and the parties do not include the United States, one of its agencies, or one of its officers or employees in an official capacity; or (2) a state statute is questioned and the parties do not include the state, one of its agencies, or one of its officers or employees in an official capacity; and

- *Serve notice.* Serve the notice and paper on the Attorney General of the United States if a federal statute is questioned—or on the state attorney general if a state statute is questioned—either by certified or registered mail or by sending it to an electronic address designated by the attorney general for this purpose. FRCP 5.1(a).

- *No forfeiture.* A party's failure to file and serve the notice, or the court's failure to certify, does not forfeit a constitutional claim or defense that is otherwise timely asserted. FRCP 5.1(d).

    iii. *Cross-motion.* A party may file and serve a cross-motion (meaning a competing request for relief or order similar to that requested by another party against the cross-moving party) at the time it files and serves its opposition papers to the original motion, i.e., not less than SEVENTEEN (17) DAYS prior to the return date of the motion. NY R USDCTND L.R. 7.1(c).

    iv. *Copies of authorities.* When serving a pro se litigant with a memorandum of law or any other paper which contains citations to authorities that are unpublished or published exclusively on electronic databases, counsel shall include a hard copy of those authorities. Although copies of authorities published only on electronic databases are not required to be filed, copies shall be provided upon request to opposing counsel who lack access to electronic databases. NY R USDCTND L.R. 7.1(a)(1).

    v. *Cover letter authorizing e-mail or facsimile filing.* Neither the Court nor the Clerk's Office will accept for filing any facsimile or e-mail transmission without prior authorization from the Court. The party using facsimile or e-mail transmissions to file its papers must accompany any such documents with a cover letter stating that the Court authorized such transmissions and the date on which the Court provided that authorization. Violations of NY R USDCTND L.R. 5.5 subject the offending party to the Court's full disciplinary powers. NY R USDCTND L.R. 5.5.

    vi. *Affidavit attesting to failed attempts to file electronically.* If the Court's CM/ECF site experiences a technical failure, a Filing User may submit documents to the Court that day in an alternate manner provided that the documents are accompanied by the Filing User's affidavit stating that the Filing User attempted to file electronically at least two times in one (1) hour increments after 10:00 a.m. that day. The following methods are acceptable alternate means for filing documents in case of a technical failure: (1) via electronic mail in a PDF attachment sent to the e-mail address for technical failures; or (2) in person, by bringing the document to the Clerk's Office on paper accompanied by a CD/ROM that contains the document in .pdf format. NY R USDCTND CM/ECF(10)(10.1).

- A Filing User who cannot file documents electronically because of a problem on the Filing User's system must file the documents' conventionally along with an affidavit explaining the reason for not filing the documents electronically. NY R USDCTND CM/ECF(10)(10.2).

    vii. *Notice of conventional filing.* If the Clerk's Office grants permission to conventionally file the document, the Filing User shall electronically file a notice of conventional filing for the documents. More information regarding this process can be obtained from the Court's web page. NY R USDCTND CM/ECF(4)(4.5).

viii. *CD/ROM with PDF of document(s).* If the Court grants permission to file a document traditionally, the attorney must submit the documents for filing to the Clerk's Office on CD/ROM in .pdf or pdf.A format. NY R USDCTND CM/ECF(2).

ix. *English translation.* The Court conducts its reviews and deliberations in English. Unless otherwise directed by the Court, any document that a party transmits to the Court (including one in the record on appeal) that is in a language other than English must be accompanied by an English translation that the translator has certified as true and accurate, pursuant to 28 U.S.C.A. § 1746. NY R USDCTND L.R. 10.1(e). For more information, refer to NY R USDCTND L.R. 10.1(e).

x. *Courtesy copies.* The Court may require that courtesy copies of electronically filed documents be submitted for its review and may amend these Administrative Procedures (NY R USDCTND CM/ECF) at any time without prior notice. NY R USDCTND CM/ECF(2).

- The parties need not provide a courtesy copy of their motion papers to the assigned judge unless the assigned judge requests a copy. NY R USDCTND L.R. 7.1(b)(1).

xi. *Copies for three-judge court.* On the convening of a three-judge court, the parties shall make three (3) copies of all non-electronically filed pleadings, motion papers, and memoranda of law available to the Clerk for distribution. NY R USDCTND L.R. 9.1.

3. *Individual judge practices.* Refer to the Miscellaneous section of this document for information on individual judge practices on required documents.

## E. Format

1. *Form of documents.* The rules governing captions and other matters of form in pleadings apply to motions and other papers. FRCP 7(b)(2). All pleadings and other papers shall be served and filed in accordance with the Federal Rules of Civil Procedure and shall be in the form prescribed by NY R USDCTND L.R. 10.1. NY R USDCTND L.R. 5.1(a).

   a. *Form, generally.* All pleadings, motions, and other documents that a party presents for filing, whether in paper form or in electronic form, shall meet the following requirements:

      i. *Font size.* All text, whether in the body of the document or in footnotes, must be a minimum of twelve (12) point type. NY R USDCTND L.R. 10.1(a)(1).

      ii. *Margins.* All documents must have one (1) inch margins on all four sides of the page. NY R USDCTND L.R. 10.1(a)(2).

      iii. *Spacing.* All text in the body of the document must be double-spaced. NY R USDCTND L.R. 10.1(a)(3).

      - The text in block quotations and footnotes may be single-spaced. NY R USDCTND L.R. 10.1(a)(4).

      iv. *Page numbering.* Pages must be consecutively numbered. NY R USDCTND L.R. 10.1(a)(7).

      v. *Circumventing formatting limitations*

      - Extensive footnotes must not be used to circumvent page limitations. NY R USDCTND L.R. 10.1(a)(5).

      - Compacted or other compressed printing features must not be used. NY R USDCTND L.R. 10.1(a)(6).

   b. *Additional requirements for paper filing.* Additional requirements for all pleadings, motions, and other documents that a party presents for filing in paper form:

      i. *Paper size.* All documents must be on eight and one-half by eleven (8-1/2 x 11) inch white paper of good quality. NY R USDCTND L.R. 10.1(b)(1).

      ii. *Text.* All text must be plainly and legibly written, typewritten, printed or reproduced without erasures or interlineations materially defacing them. NY R USDCTND L.R. 10.1(b)(2).

      iii. *Ink.* All documents must be in black or blue ink. NY R USDCTND L.R. 10.1(b)(3).

      iv. *Binding.* Pages of all documents must be stapled (or in some other way fastened) together. NY R USDCTND L.R. 10.1(b)(4).

     v.   *Single-sided paper.* All documents must be single-sided. NY R USDCTND L.R. 10.1(b)(5).

    vi.   *Electronic submission.* The Court, at its discretion, may require the electronic submission of any document in a WordPerfect-compatible format. NY R USDCTND L.R. 10.1(b)(6).

   vii.   *Rejection of document.* The Court may reject documents that do not comply with the above-listed requirements. NY R USDCTND L.R. 10.1(b).

  c.   *Caption; Names of parties.* Every pleading must have a caption with the court's name, a title, a file number, and a FRCP 7(a) designation. The title of the complaint must name all the parties; the title of other pleadings, after naming the first party on each side, may refer generally to other parties. FRCP 10(a). Each document must contain a caption for the specific case to which it pertains. The caption must include the title of the Court, the title of the action, the civil action number of the case, the initials of the assigned judge(s), and the name or nature of the paper in sufficient detail for identification. If a litigant has more than one action pending in this Court, any and all papers filed in a case must contain and pertain to one civil action number, unless the civil actions have been consolidated by the Court. Any motion or other papers purporting to relate to more than one action will not be accepted for filing and may be stricken by the Court. NY R USDCTND L.R. 10.1(c)(1) shall not apply, as noted in NY R USDCTND L.R. 10.1(c), to notices of change of address filed by attorneys of record and pro se litigants. The parties must separately caption affidavits and declarations and must not physically attach them to the Notice of Motion or Memorandum of Law. NY R USDCTND L.R. 10.1(c)(1).

  d.   *Paragraphs; Separate statements.* A party must state its claims or defenses in numbered paragraphs, each limited as far as practicable to a single set of circumstances. A later pleading may refer by number to a paragraph in an earlier pleading. If doing so would promote clarity, each claim founded on a separate transaction or occurrence—and each defense other than a denial—must be stated in a separate count or defense. FRCP 10(b).

  e.   *Adoption by reference; Exhibits.* A statement in a pleading may be adopted by reference elsewhere in the same pleading or in any other pleading or motion. A copy of a written instrument that is an exhibit to a pleading is a part of the pleading for all purposes. FRCP 10(c).

  f.   *Citation of local rules.* These are the Local Rules of Practice for the United States District Court for the Northern District of New York. They shall be cited as "L.R. ___." NY R USDCTND L.R. 1.1(a).

  g.   *Acceptance by the clerk.* The clerk must not refuse to file a paper solely because it is not in the form prescribed by the Federal Rules of Civil Procedure or by a local rule or practice. FRCP 5(d)(4).

2.   *Form of electronic documents.* All pleadings, motions, and other documents that a party presents for filing, whether in paper form or in electronic form, shall meet the requirements in NY R USDCTND L.R. 10.1(a). NY R USDCTND L.R. 10.1(a). Refer above for more information.

  a.   *Attachments and exhibits.* A Filing User must submit in electronic form all documents referenced as exhibits or attachments in accordance with the Court's CM/ECF Users Manual unless the Court otherwise orders. A Filing User shall submit as exhibits or attachments only those excerpts of the referenced documents that are directly germane to the matter under the Court's consideration. Excerpted material must be clearly and prominently identified as such. Filing Users who file excerpts of documents as exhibits or attachments under these Administrative Procedures (NY R USDCTND CM/ECF) do so without prejudice to their right to timely file additional excerpts or the complete document. Responding parties may also timely file the complete document or additional excerpts that they believe are directly germane to the matter under the Court's consideration. NY R USDCTND CM/ECF(4)(4.4).

     i.   All attachments must be described in sufficient detail so the Court and opposing counsel can easily identify and distinguish the filed attachments. Vague or general descriptions are insufficient (i.e., "Exhibit 1"). Rather, each attachment shall have a descriptive title identifying, with specificity, the document that is being filed (i.e., "Exhibit 12 Mulligan County Fire Investigation Report.") Failure to adequately describe attachments may result in the document being rejected by the Court. NY R USDCTND CM/ECF(4)(4.4).

  b.   *Large documents.* For information on the electronic filing of large documents, please consult the

Court's CM/ECF Users Manual, which is available on the Court's web page. NY R USDCTND CM/ECF(4)(4.5).

    i.   A party who believes a document is too lengthy to electronically image, i.e., "scan," may contact the Clerk's Office for permission to file that document conventionally. If the Clerk's Office grants permission to conventionally file the document, the Filing User shall electronically file a notice of conventional filing for the documents. More information regarding this process can be obtained from the Court's web page. Exhibits submitted conventionally shall be served on other parties as if they were not subject to these Administrative Procedures (NY R USDCTND CM/ECF). For a list of hints and tips for scanning large documents, please consult the Court's web page. NY R USDCTND CM/ECF(4)(4.5).

  c.   *Legibility.* It shall be the Filing User's responsibility to verify the legibility of scanned documents before filing them electronically with the Court. NY R USDCTND CM/ECF(4)(4.6).

  d.   *Color documents.* Since documents scanned in color or containing a graphic take much longer to upload, Filing Users are encouraged to configure their scanners to scan documents at 300 dpi and preferably in black and white rather than in color. NY R USDCTND CM/ECF(4)(4.7).

  e.   *Items not in .PDF format.* Parties wishing to file items not amenable to .pdf format (i.e. CD's, DVD's), shall file such items conventionally with the Clerk's Office. The Filing User shall electronically file a notice of conventional filing indicating that these items have been submitted to the clerk and shall serve copies of these items on other parties as if they were not subject to these Administrative Procedures (NY R USDCTND CM/ECF). These item(s) will be maintained by the Clerk's Office until the case is disposed, at which time they will be returned to the filing party for retention consistent with NY R USDCTND CM/ECF(4)(4.9). NY R USDCTND CM/ECF(4)(4.8).

3.  *Form of memoranda of law*

  a.   *Length limitation.* No party shall file or serve a memorandum of law that exceeds twenty-five (25) pages in length, unless that party obtains leave of the judge hearing the motion prior to filing. NY R USDCTND L.R. 7.1(a)(1).

  b.   *Table of contents.* All memoranda of law shall contain a table of contents. NY R USDCTND L.R. 7.1(a)(1).

4.  *Signing of pleadings, motions and other papers*

  a.   *Signature.* Every pleading, written motion, and other paper must be signed by at least one attorney of record in the attorney's name—or by a party personally if the party is unrepresented. The paper must state the signer's address, e-mail address, and telephone number. FRCP 11(a). Each document must identify the person filing the document. This identification must include an original signature of the attorney or pro se litigant; the typewritten name of that person; the address of a pro se litigant; and the bar roll number, office address, telephone number, e-mail address and fax number of the attorney. Telephone numbers of non-prisoner pro se parties may be provided voluntarily or upon request of the Court. See General Order #22 (NY R USDCTND CM/ECF) for signature requirements. NY R USDCTND L.R. 10.1(c)(2).

    i.   *Electronic signatures.* Documents filed under an attorney's login and password shall constitute that attorney's signature for purposes of the Local Rules of Practice for the United States District Court for the Northern District of New York and Federal Rules of Civil Procedure, including but not limited to FRCP 11. A pleading or other document requiring an attorney's signature shall be signed in the following manner, whether filed electronically or submitted on disk or CD/ROM to the Clerk's Office: "s/ (attorney name)." The correct format for an attorney signature is found in NY R USDCTND CM/ECF(6)(6.1). NY R USDCTND CM/ECF(6)(6.1).

       •  *Non-attorney signature.* If an original document requires the signature of a non-attorney, the Filing User may scan the original document containing the original signature(s), then electronically file it on the System. Alternatively, the Filing User may convert the document into .pdf text format and submit the document using "s/" for the signature of the non-attorney. NY R USDCTND CM/ECF(6)(6.2).

       •  *Multiple signatures.* A document requiring signatures of more than one party must be filed electronically either by (1) submitting a scanned document containing all necessary signatures; (2) representing the consent of the other parties on the document; or (3) in any other manner that the Court approves. NY R USDCTND CM/ECF(6)(6.3).

ii. *No verification or accompanying affidavit required for pleadings.* Unless a rule or statute specifically states otherwise, a pleading need not be verified or accompanied by an affidavit. FRCP 11(a).

iii. *Unsigned papers.* The court must strike an unsigned paper unless the omission is promptly corrected after being called to the attorney's or party's attention. FRCP 11(a).

b. *Representations to the court.* By presenting to the court a pleading, written motion, or other paper—whether by signing, filing, submitting, or later advocating it—an attorney or unrepresented party certifies that to the best of the person's knowledge, information, and belief, formed after an inquiry reasonable under the circumstances:

i. It is not being presented for any improper purpose, such as to harass, cause unnecessary delay, or needlessly increase the cost of litigation;

ii. The claims, defenses, and other legal contentions are warranted by existing law or by a nonfrivolous argument for extending, modifying, or reversing existing law or for establishing new law;

iii. The factual contentions have evidentiary support or, if specifically so identified, will likely have evidentiary support after a reasonable opportunity for further investigation or discovery; and

iv. The denials of factual contentions are warranted on the evidence or, if specifically so identified, are reasonably based on belief or a lack of information. FRCP 11(b).

c. *Sanctions.* If, after notice and a reasonable opportunity to respond, the court determines that FRCP 11(b) has been violated, the court may impose an appropriate sanction on any attorney, law firm, or party that violated FRCP 11(b) or is responsible for the violation. FRCP 11(c)(1). Refer to the United States District Court for the Northern District of New York KeyRules Motion for Sanctions document for more information.

5. *Privacy protection for filings made with the court*

a. *Redacted filings.* Unless the court orders otherwise, in an electronic or paper filing with the court that contains an individual's Social Security number, taxpayer-identification number, or birth date, the name of an individual known to be a minor, or a financial-account number, a party or nonparty making the filing may include only:

i. The last four (4) digits of the Social Security number and taxpayer-identification number;

ii. The year of the individual's birth;

iii. The minor's initials; and

iv. The last four (4) digits of the financial-account number. FRCP 5.2(a); NY R USDCTND L.R. 8.1; NY R USDCTND CM/ECF(11)(11.2).

v. If a home address must be used, use only the City and State. NY R USDCTND L.R. 8.1; NY R USDCTND CM/ECF(11)(11.2).

vi. If the victim of a sexual assault must be referenced, redact the name to 'Victim.' NY R USDCTND CM/ECF(11)(11.2); NY R USDCTND L.R. 8.1.

vii. In addition, caution shall be exercised when filing documents that contain the following:

- Personal identifying number, such as a driver's license number;
- Medical records, treatment and diagnosis;
- Employment history;
- Individual financial information; and
- Proprietary or trade secret information. NY R USDCTND L.R. 8.1; NY R USDCTND CM/ECF(11)(11.2).

b. *Exemptions from the redaction requirement.* The redaction requirement does not apply to the following:

   i. A financial-account number that identifies the property allegedly subject to forfeiture in a forfeiture proceeding;

   ii. The record of an administrative or agency proceeding;

   iii. The official record of a state-court proceeding;

   iv. The record of a court or tribunal, if that record was not subject to the redaction requirement when originally filed;

   v. A filing covered by FRCP 5.2(c) or FRCP 5.2(d); and

   vi. A pro se filing in an action brought under 28 U.S.C.A. § 2241, 28 U.S.C.A. § 2254, or 28 U.S.C.A. § 2255. FRCP 5.2(b).

   vii. Transcripts of the administrative record in social security proceedings are exempt from this requirement. State court records and other documents filed in habeas corpus proceedings are exempt from this requirement except for proceedings that involve victims of sex crimes. In habeas corpus cases involving sex crimes, the parties must redact the record and supporting papers, or may move to seal, if appropriate. NY R USDCTND L.R. 8.1.

c. *Limitations on remote access to electronic files; Social Security appeals and immigration cases.* Unless the court orders otherwise, in an action for benefits under the Social Security Act, and in an action or proceeding relating to an order of removal, to relief from removal, or to immigration benefits or detention, access to an electronic file is authorized as follows:

   i. The parties and their attorneys may have remote electronic access to any part of the case file, including the administrative record;

   ii. Any other person may have electronic access to the full record at the courthouse, but may have remote electronic access only to:

     • The docket maintained by the court; and

     • An opinion, order, judgment, or other disposition of the court, but not any other part of the case file or the administrative record. FRCP 5.2(c).

d. *Filings made under seal.* The court may order that a filing be made under seal without redaction. The court may later unseal the filing or order the person who made the filing to file a redacted version for the public record. FRCP 5.2(d); NY R USDCTND L.R. 8.1. For information on sealed matters, refer to NY R USDCTND L.R. 83.13 and NY R USDCTND CM/ECF(12).

e. *Protective orders.* For good cause, the court may by order in a case:

   i. Require redaction of additional information; or

   ii. Limit or prohibit a nonparty's remote electronic access to a document filed with the court. FRCP 5.2(e).

f. *Option for additional unredacted filing under seal.* A person making a redacted filing may also file an unredacted copy under seal. The court must retain the unredacted copy as part of the record. FRCP 5.2(f); NY R USDCTND L.R. 8.1; NY R USDCTND CM/ECF(11)(11.3).

g. *Option for filing a reference list.* A filing that contains redacted information may be filed together with a reference list that identifies each item of redacted information and specifies an appropriate identifier that uniquely corresponds to each item listed. The list must be filed under seal and may be amended as of right. Any reference in the case to a listed identifier will be construed to refer to the corresponding item of information. FRCP 5.2(g); NY R USDCTND L.R. 8.1; NY R USDCTND CM/ECF(11)(11.3).

h. *Responsibility for redaction.* Counsel is strongly urged to discuss this issue with all their clients so that they can make an informed decision about the inclusion of certain information. The responsibility for redacting these personal identifiers rests solely with counsel and the parties. The Clerk will not review each filing for compliance with NY R USDCTND L.R. 8.1. Counsel and the parties are cautioned that failure to redact these personal identifiers may subject them to the Court's full disciplinary power. NY R USDCTND L.R. 8.1; NY R USDCTND CM/ECF(11)(11.3).

    i. *Waiver of protection of identifiers.* A person waives the protection of FRCP 5.2(a) as to the person's own information by filing it without redaction and not under seal. FRCP 5.2(h).

6. *Individual judge practices.* Refer to the Miscellaneous section of this document for information on individual judge practices on formatting documents.

## F. Filing and Service Requirements

1. *Filing requirements.* Any paper after the complaint that is required to be served—together with a certificate of service—must be filed within a reasonable time after service. FRCP 5(d)(1). Parties shall file all original motion papers, including memoranda of law and supporting affidavits, if any, in accordance with the Administrative Procedures for Electronic Case Filing (General Order #22 (NY R USDCTND CM/ECF)) and/or the case assignment form provided to the parties at the commencement of the litigation. NY R USDCTND L.R. 7.1(b)(1).

    a. *How filing is made; In general.* A paper is filed by delivering it:

        i. To the clerk; or

        ii. To a judge who agrees to accept it for filing, and who must then note the filing date on the paper and promptly send it to the clerk. FRCP 5(d)(2).

    b. *Electronic filing*

        i. *Authorization of electronic filing program.* A court may, by local rule, allow papers to be filed, signed, or verified by electronic means that are consistent with any technical standards established by the Judicial Conference of the United States. A local rule may require electronic filing only if reasonable exceptions are allowed. A paper filed electronically in compliance with a local rule is a written paper for purposes of the Federal Rules of Civil Procedure. FRCP 5(d)(3).

- All cases filed in this Court may be assigned to the Electronic Case Files System ("ECF") in accordance with the Procedural Order on Electronic Case Filing (General Order #22 (NY R USDCTND CM/ECF)), the provisions of which are incorporated herein by reference, and which the Court may amend from time to time. Copies of General Order #22 (NY R USDCTND CM/ECF) are available at the Clerk's office or at the Court's webpage. NY R USDCTND L.R. 5.1.1; NY R USDCTND Order 25(XII).

- The Court may deviate from these Administrative Procedures (NY R USDCTND CM/ECF) in specific cases, without prior notice, if deemed appropriate in the exercise of discretion, considering the need for the just, speedy, and inexpensive determination of matters pending before the Court. NY R USDCTND CM/ECF(2).

        ii. *Scope of electronic filing.* After January 1, 2004, all documents that attorneys admitted to practice in the Northern District of New York submit for filing shall be filed electronically using the System or shall be scanned and uploaded to the System, no matter when a case was originally filed, unless these Administrative Procedures (NY R USDCTND CM/ECF) otherwise permit or unless the assigned judge otherwise authorizes. An attorney who is not a Filing User by January 1, 2004, must show good cause to the assigned judge to file and serve pleadings and other papers in the traditional manner. NY R USDCTND CM/ECF(2).

        iii. *Exceptions and/or waivers from mandatory electronic filing.* The following types of cases and/or documents are not required to be filed electronically:

- If you are seeking to have your complaint filed under seal, please file your complaint and proposed sealing order traditionally at the Clerk's Office. NY R USDCTND CM/ECF(2)(2.1)(1).

- Any document that a party proceeding pro se files. (See NY R USDCTND CM/ECF(12)(12.1) for procedural details). NY R USDCTND CM/ECF(2)(2.1)(2). A non-prisoner who is a party to a civil action and who is not represented by an attorney may file a motion to obtain an Electronic Case Filing (ECF) login and password on a form prescribed by the Clerk's Office. The Pro Se CM/ECF Registration Form shall be submitted with the motion. If during the course of the action an attorney appears on behalf of the pro se party, the Clerk's Office shall terminate the pro se party's registration based upon the attorney's appearance. NY R USDCTND CM/ECF(12)(12.1). Absent permission to file electronically, pro se filers shall file paper originals of all complaints, pleadings, motions, affidavits, briefs, and other documents which must be signed or which require either verification or an unsworn declaration under any rule or statute. The Clerk's Office will scan these original documents into an electronic file in the System but will also maintain a paper file. NY R USDCTND CM/ECF(12)(12.1). A pro se party may also seek permission to receive immediate notice of all public documents filed in their cases. Notices of Electronic Filing (NEF) and attached documents would be transmitted to a non-prisoner pro se party who selects this option. Note: The pro se party would continue to file their documents with the Clerk's Office in paper form. NY R USDCTND CM/ECF(12)(12.1).

- Sealed documents, sealed cases, documents for in camera review, documents lodged with the Court, ex parte documents, confidential agreements, Qui Tam actions and Grand Jury material and warrants must be filed traditionally. (See NY R USDCTND CM/ECF(12)(12.2) for further information the filing of the above-referenced documents). NY R USDCTND CM/ECF(2)(2.1)(3).

- Discovery: In accordance with NY R USDCTND L.R. 26.2, parties shall not file discovery, provided, however, that discovery material to be used at trial or in support of any motion, including a motion to compel or for summary judgment, shall be filed electronically with the Court prior to the trial or with the motion. Any motion pursuant to FRCP 37 shall be accompanied by the electronically filed discovery materials to which the motion relates if those materials have not previously been filed with the Court. NY R USDCTND CM/ECF(2)(2.1)(4).

- Transport Orders: All orders requesting that an incarcerated individual be transported that a judicial officer of the Northern District of New York signs shall be filed traditionally. These Orders will not be filed with the case or uploaded to the docket but rather will be processed in accordance with the procedures that the Clerk of Court promulgates. NY R USDCTND CM/ECF(2)(2.1)(5).

iv. *Filing defined.* Electronic transmission of a document to the System in accordance with these Administrative Procedures, together with the transmission of a Notice of Electronic Filing from the Court, constitutes filing of the document for all purposes of the Federal Rules of Civil Procedure and the Local Rules of Practice for the United States District Court for the Northern District of New York and constitutes entry of the document on the docket that the Clerk's Office keeps under FRCP 58 and FRCP 79. E-mailing a document to the Clerk's Office or to the assigned judge shall not constitute "filing" of the document. NY R USDCTND CM/ECF(4)(4.1).

v. *Filing fees.* Any fee required for filing a pleading or paper in this Court is payable to the Clerk of the Court. The Court will not maintain electronic billing or debit accounts for attorneys or law firms. Effective January 1, 2007, payment for filing fees will be mandatory through CM/ECF's Internet Credit Card Payment site--a secure Treasury Site. The Filing User will be prompted to enter either Bank Account Debit (ACH) or credit card information while filing the initial pleading. Any document that requires a filing fee (e.g., Notice of Appeal, Motion for Pro Hac Vice Admission) may also be paid through the federal electronic payment website. NY R USDCTND CM/ECF(7).

vi. For more information on electronic filing, refer to NY R USDCTND CM/ECF.

c. *E-mail or facsimile filing.* Neither the Court nor the Clerk's Office will accept for filing any facsimile or e-mail transmission without prior authorization from the Court. The party using facsimile or e-mail transmissions to file its papers must accompany any such documents with a cover letter stating that the Court authorized such transmissions and the date on which the Court provided that authorization. Violations of NY R USDCTND L.R. 5.5 subject the offending party to the Court's full disciplinary powers. NY R USDCTND L.R. 5.5.

2. *Service requirements*

   a. *Service; When required*

      i. *In general.* Unless the Federal Rules of Civil Procedure provide otherwise, each of the following papers must be served on every party:

      - An order stating that service is required;

      - A pleading filed after the original complaint, unless the court orders otherwise under FRCP 5(c) because there are numerous defendants;

      - A discovery paper required to be served on a party, unless the court orders otherwise;

      - A written motion, except one that may be heard ex parte; and

      - A written notice, appearance, demand, or offer of judgment, or any similar paper. FRCP 5(a)(1).

      ii. *If a party fails to appear.* No service is required on a party who is in default for failing to appear. But a pleading that asserts a new claim for relief against such a party must be served on that party under FRCP 4. FRCP 5(a)(2).

      iii. *Seizing property.* If an action is begun by seizing property and no person is or need be named as a defendant, any service required before the filing of an appearance, answer, or claim must be made on the person who had custody or possession of the property when it was seized. FRCP 5(a)(3).

   b. *Service; How made*

      i. *Serving an attorney.* If a party is represented by an attorney, service under FRCP 5 must be made on the attorney unless the court orders service on the party. FRCP 5(b)(1).

      ii. *Service in general.* A paper is served under FRCP 5 by:

      - Handing it to the person;

      - Leaving it: (1) at the person's office with a clerk or other person in charge or, if no one is in charge, in a conspicuous place in the office; or (2) if the person has no office or the office is closed, at the person's dwelling or usual place of abode with someone of suitable age and discretion who resides there;

      - Mailing it to the person's last known address—in which event service is complete upon mailing;

      - Leaving it with the court clerk if the person has no known address;

      - Sending it by electronic means if the person consented in writing—in which event service is complete upon transmission, but is not effective if the serving party learns that it did not reach the person to be served; or

      - Delivering it by any other means that the person consented to in writing—in which event service is complete when the person making service delivers it to the agency designated to make delivery. FRCP 5(b)(2).

      iii. *Service of electronically-filed documents.* Service is complete provided all parties receive a Notice of Electronic Filing (NEF), which is sent automatically by email from the Court (see the NEF for a list of who did/did not receive notice electronically). Transmission of the NEF constitutes service upon all Filing and Receiving Users who are listed as recipients of notice by electronic mail. It remains the responsibility of Filing and Receiving Users to maintain current contact information with the court and to regularly review the docket sheet of the case. NY R USDCTND CM/ECF(5)(5.2).

      - *Non-filing or receiving users.* Attorneys and pro se parties who are not Filing or Receiving Users must be served with a paper copy of any electronically filed pleading or other document. Service of such paper copy must be made according to the Federal Rules of Civil Procedure and the Local Rules of Practice for the United States District Court for the Northern District of New York. Such paper service must be documented by electronically filing a certificate of service. NY R USDCTND CM/ECF(5)(5.2). A party who is not a Filing User of the System is entitled to a paper copy of any electronically-filed pleading, document, or order. The Filing User must therefore provide the non-Filing User with the pleading or document according to the Federal Rules of Civil Procedure. NY R US-DCTND CM/ECF(5)(5.3).

    iv. *Using court facilities.* If a local rule so authorizes, a party may use the court's transmission facilities to make service under FRCP 5(b)(2)(E). FRCP 5(b)(3).

  c. *Serving numerous defendants*

    i. *In general.* If an action involves an unusually large number of defendants, the court may, on motion or on its own, order that:

- Defendants' pleadings and replies to them need not be served on other defendants;
- Any crossclaim, counterclaim, avoidance, or affirmative defense in those pleadings and replies to them will be treated as denied or avoided by all other parties; and
- Filing any such pleading and serving it on the plaintiff constitutes notice of the pleading to all parties. FRCP 5(c)(1).

    ii. *Notifying parties.* A copy of every such order must be served on the parties as the court directs. FRCP 5(c)(2).

3. *Individual judge practices.* Refer to the Miscellaneous section of this document for information on individual judge practices on filing and serving documents.

## G. Hearings

1. *Hearings, generally*

  a. *Motion days.* Listings of the regularly scheduled motion days for all judges shall be available at each Clerk's office and are available on the Court's webpage. The Clerk shall provide notice of the regular motion days for all judges to the parties at the time an action is commenced. NY R USDCTND L.R. 78.1.

  b. *Return date.* Unless the Court directs otherwise, the moving party shall make its motion returnable at the next regularly scheduled motion date at least thirty-one (31) days from the date the moving party files and serves its motion. The moving party shall select a return date in accordance with the procedures set forth in NY R USDCTND L.R. 7.1(b). If the return date the moving party selects is not the next regularly scheduled motion date, or if the moving party selects no return date, the Clerk will set the proper return date and notify the parties. NY R USDCTND L.R. 7.1.

    i. Information regarding motion dates and times is specified on the case assignment form that the Court provides to the parties at the commencement of the litigation or the parties may obtain this form from the Clerk's office or at the Court's webpage. NY R USDCTND L.R. 7.1.

    ii. The Court hereby directs the Clerk to set a proper return date in motions that pro se litigants submit for filing that do not specify a return date or fail to allow for sufficient time pursuant to NY R USDCTND L.R. 7.1. Generally, the return date that the Clerk selects should not exceed thirty (30) days from the date of filing. Furthermore, the Clerk shall forward a copy of the revised or corrected notice of motion to the parties. NY R USDCTND L.R. 7.1.

  c. *Oral argument.* Due process does not require that oral argument be permitted on a motion and, except as otherwise provided by local rule, the district court has discretion to determine whether it will decide the motion on the papers or hear argument by counsel (and perhaps receive evidence). FPP § 1190; F.D.I.C. v. Deglau, 207 F.3d 153 (3d Cir. 2000).

    i. The parties shall appear for oral argument on all motions that they make returnable before a district court judge, except motions for reconsideration, on the scheduled return date of the motion. A motion may be disposed of without oral argument as described in NY R USDCTND Order 25, on consideration of a request of any party, or otherwise at the discretion of the presiding judge. Thus, the parties should be prepared to have their motion papers serve as the sole method of argument on the motion. NY R USDCTND L.R. 7.1(h).

ii. The parties shall not appear for oral argument on motions that they make returnable before a Magistrate Judge on the scheduled return date of the motion unless the Magistrate Judge sua sponte directs or grants the request of any party for oral argument. NY R USDCTND L.R. 7.1(h).

d. *Providing a regular schedule for oral hearings.* A court may establish regular times and places for oral hearings on motions. FRCP 78(a).

e. *Providing for submission on briefs.* By rule or order, the court may provide for submitting and determining motions on briefs, without oral hearings. FRCP 78(b).

2. *Adjournments of dispositive motions.* After the moving party files and serves its motion papers requesting dispositive relief, but before the time that the opposing party must file and serve its opposing papers, the parties may agree to an adjournment of the return date for the motion. However, any such adjournment may not be for more than THIRTY-ONE (31) DAYS from the return date that the moving party selected. In addition, the parties may agree to new dates for the filing and service of opposition and reply papers. However, the parties must file all papers with the Court and serve them upon the other parties not less than ELEVEN (11) DAYS prior to the newly selected return date of the motion. If the parties agree to such an adjournment, they must file a letter with the Court stating the following: (1) that they have agreed to an adjournment of the return date for the motion, (2) the new return date, (3) the date on which the opposing party must file and serve its opposition papers, and (4) the date on which the moving party must file and serve its reply papers. The parties may not agree to any further adjournment. NY R USDCTND L.R. 7.1(j).

a. *Procedure when only one party seeks an adjournment.* If one of the parties seeks an adjournment of not more than THIRTY-ONE (31) DAYS from the return date that the moving party selected, but the other parties will not agree to such an adjournment, the party seeking the adjournment must file a letter request with the Court and serve the same upon the other parties, stating the following: (1) that the parties cannot agree to an adjournment, (2) the reason that the party is seeking the adjournment, and (3) the suggested return date for the motion. Within three days of receiving this letter request, the parties who have not agreed to an adjournment may file a letter with the Court and serve the same upon the other parties, setting forth the reasons that they do not agree to the requested adjournment. The Court will then take the request under advisement and, as soon as practicable, will enter an order granting or denying the request and, if granting the request, will set forth new dates for the filing and serving of opposition and reply papers. NY R USDCTND L.R. 7.1(j).

b. *Procedure when adjournment is more than thirty-one (31) days from the return date.* If any party seeks an adjournment of the return date that is more than THIRTY-ONE DAYS from the return date that the moving party selected, that party must file a letter request with the Court stating the following: (1) why the party needs a longer adjournment and (2) a suggested return date for the motion. The Court will grant such an adjournment only upon a showing of exceptional circumstances. In the alternative or if the Court denies the request for an adjournment, the moving party may withdraw its motion without prejudice to refile at a later date. The moving party must refile its motion within the time frame set in the Uniform Pretrial Scheduling Order unless either the assigned District Judge or the assigned Magistrate Judge has granted an extension of the motion-filing deadline. NY R USDCTND L.R. 7.1(j).

3. *Hearing on FRCP 12 defenses before trial.* If a party so moves, any defense listed in FRCP 12(b)(1) through FRCP 12(b)(7)—whether made in a pleading or by motion—and a motion under FRCP 12(c) must be heard and decided before trial unless the court orders a deferral until trial. FRCP 12(i).

4. *Hearing on motion to dismiss for lack of subject matter jurisdiction.* It may be error for a court to dismiss a case on the defendant's motion to dismiss for lack of subject matter jurisdiction without first holding a hearing, as FRCP 12(b)(1) requires a preliminary hearing or hearing at trial to determine any disputed facts upon which the motion or opposition to it is predicated. FEDPROC § 62:435.

5. *Individual judge practices.* Refer to the Miscellaneous section of this document for information on individual judge practices on hearings.

## H. Forms

## 1. Federal Motion to Dismiss for Lack of Subject Matter Jurisdiction Forms

a. Motion to dismiss for lack of subject-matter jurisdiction. 2C FEDFORMS § 11:35.

b.  Motion to dismiss for lack of subject-matter jurisdiction; Want of diversity of citizenship because requisite diversity not alleged. 2C FEDFORMS § 11:37.

c.  Motion to dismiss for lack of subject-matter jurisdiction; Want of diversity on a factual basis and because requisite diversity not alleged. 2C FEDFORMS § 11:38.

d.  Motion to dismiss for lack of subject-matter jurisdiction; Want of diversity of citizenship because state of incorporation and principal place of business of defendant not as alleged. 2C FEDFORMS § 11:39.

e.  Motion to dismiss for lack of subject-matter jurisdiction; Want of diversity of citizenship because principal place of business of defendant not as alleged. 2C FEDFORMS § 11:40.

f.  Motion to dismiss for lack of subject-matter jurisdiction; Failure to comply with procedural requirements. 2C FEDFORMS § 11:41.

g.  Motion to dismiss for lack of subject-matter jurisdiction; Want of diversity upon realignment of parties according to interest. 2C FEDFORMS § 11:42.

h.  Motion to dismiss for lack of subject-matter jurisdiction; Want of federal question. 2C FEDFORMS § 11:43.

i.  Motion to dismiss for lack of subject-matter jurisdiction; Unsubstantial federal question. 2C FEDFORMS § 11:44.

j.  Motion to dismiss for lack of subject-matter jurisdiction; Want of amount in controversy. 2C FEDFORMS § 11:45.

k.  Motion to dismiss for lack of subject-matter jurisdiction; Want of amount in controversy; Insurance policy limits do not exceed required jurisdictional amount. 2C FEDFORMS § 11:46.

l.  Motion to dismiss for lack of subject-matter jurisdiction; Want of amount in controversy; Claim for damages in excess of jurisdictional amount not made in good faith. 2C FEDFORMS § 11:47.

m.  Motion to dismiss for lack of subject-matter jurisdiction; Want of amount in controversy; Made after judgment. 2C FEDFORMS § 11:48.

n.  Motion to dismiss for lack of subject-matter jurisdiction; Want of consent by the United States to be sued. 2C FEDFORMS § 11:49.

o.  Motion to dismiss for lack of subject-matter jurisdiction; Want of consent by United States to be sued; United States indispensable party. 2C FEDFORMS § 11:50.

p.  Affidavit; In opposition to motion to dismiss for lack of diversity; Assignment of claim to plaintiff bona fide. FEDPROF § 1:894.

q.  Motion; To dismiss; Plaintiff and defendant citizens of same state when action filed. FEDPROF § 1:888.

r.  Motion to dismiss; Assignment to nonresident for purpose of invoking federal jurisdiction sham and ineffective to confer jurisdiction. FEDPROF § 1:889.

s.  Motion to dismiss; For lack of diversity in third-party complaint. FEDPROF § 1:890.

t.  Affidavit; In support of motion to dismiss for want of diversity of citizenship; Plaintiff and defendant citizens of same state on date action filed. FEDPROF § 1:892.

u.  Motion; To dismiss; Insufficiency of amount in controversy. FEDPROF § 1:897.

v.  Motion to dismiss; Bad faith in claiming jurisdictional amount. FEDPROF § 1:898.

w.  Motion; To dismiss; Lack of jurisdiction over subject matter, generally. FEDPROF § 1:903.

x.  Motion to dismiss; Absence of federal question. FEDPROF § 1:904.

y.  Motion to dismiss; Absence of federal question; Failure to exhaust state remedies. FEDPROF § 1:905.

z.  Affidavit; In opposition to motion to dismiss for absence of jurisdiction over subject matter. FEDPROF § 1:906.

## I. Applicable Rules

1. *Federal rules*

   a. Federal question. 28 U.S.C.A. § 1331.

   b. Diversity of citizenship; Amount in controversy; Costs. 28 U.S.C.A. § 1332.

   c. Serving and filing pleadings and other papers. FRCP 5.

   d. Constitutional challenge to a statute; Notice, certification, and intervention. FRCP 5.1.

   e. Privacy protection for filings made with the court. FRCP 5.2.

   f. Computing and extending time; Time for motion papers. FRCP 6.

   g. Pleadings allowed; Form of motions and other papers. FRCP 7.

   h. Disclosure statement. FRCP 7.1.

   i. Form of pleadings. FRCP 10.

   j. Signing pleadings, motions, and other papers; Representations to the court; Sanctions. FRCP 11.

   k. Defenses and objections; When and how presented; Motion for judgment on the pleadings; Consolidating motions; Waiving defenses; Pretrial hearing. FRCP 12.

   l. Taking testimony. FRCP 43.

   m. Hearing motions; Submission on briefs. FRCP 78.

2. *Local rules*

   a. Scope of the rules. NY R USDCTND L.R. 1.1.

   b. Complex and multi-district litigation. NY R USDCTND L.R. 3.3.

   c. Service and filing of papers. NY R USDCTND L.R. 5.1.

   d. Filing by facsimile or e-mail. NY R USDCTND L.R. 5.5.

   e. Motion practice. NY R USDCTND L.R. 7.1.

   f. Personal privacy protection. NY R USDCTND L.R. 8.1.

   g. Request for three-judge court. NY R USDCTND L.R. 9.1.

   h. Form of papers. NY R USDCTND L.R. 10.1.

   i. Orders. NY R USDCTND L.R. 77.2.

   j. Motion days. NY R USDCTND L.R. 78.1.

   k. Settlement procedures. NY R USDCTND L.R. 68.2.

   l. Appearance and withdrawal of attorney. NY R USDCTND L.R. 83.2.

   m. Arbitration. NY R USDCTND L.R. 83.7-1; NY R USDCTND L.R. 83.7-2; NY R USDCTND L.R. 83.7-3.

   n. Assisted mediation program. NY R USDCTND L.R. 83.8.

   o. Mediation. NY R USDCTND L.R. 83.11-1; NY R USDCTND L.R. 83.11-3.

   p. Early neutral evaluation. NY R USDCTND L.R. 83.12-1; NY R USDCTND L.R. 83.12-3.

   q. Administrative procedures for electronic case filing. NY R USDCTND CM/ECF.

   r. Case assignment plan for the Northern District of New York. [NY R USDCTND Order 12, as amended by NY ORDER 16-4201, effective March 24, 2015].

   s. Directing the expedited service of the summons and complaint and further directing the completion of FRCP 16 stipulation for the timely progression of civil actions. [NY R USDCTND Order 25, as amended by NY ORDER 16-4187, effective June 23, 2016].

   t. Mandatory mediation program. NY R USDCTND Order 47.

**J. Miscellaneous**

**NOTE: Individual judges' rules may apply. For available judge-level information, refer to:**

DISTRICT JUDGE MAE A. D'AGOSTINO: [NY R USDCTND D'Agostino-Rules and Practices, as added by NY ORDER 16-4200, effective April 4, 2016].

DISTRICT JUDGE THOMAS J. McAVOY: NY R USDCTND McAvoy-Order.

# Motions, Oppositions and Replies
## Motion to Dismiss for Lack of Personal Jurisdiction

### Document Last Updated September 2016

## A. Checklist

(I) ❏ Matters to be considered by moving party

   (a) ❏ Required documents

     (1) ❏ Notice of motion and motion

     (2) ❏ Memorandum of law

     (3) ❏ Supporting affidavit

     (4) ❏ Certificate of service

   (b) ❏ Supplemental documents

     (1) ❏ Supporting evidence

     (2) ❏ Notice of constitutional question

     (3) ❏ Nongovernmental corporate disclosure statement

     (4) ❏ Copies of authorities

     (5) ❏ Proposed order

     (6) ❏ Cover letter authorizing e-mail or facsimile filing

     (7) ❏ Affidavit attesting to failed attempts to file electronically

     (8) ❏ Notice of conventional filing

     (9) ❏ CD/ROM with PDF of document(s)

     (10) ❏ English translation

     (11) ❏ Courtesy copies

     (12) ❏ Copies for three-judge court

   (c) ❏ Timing

     (1) ❏ Every defense to a claim for relief in any pleading must be asserted in the responsive pleading if one is required

     (2) ❏ A motion asserting any of the defenses in FRCP 12(b) must be made before pleading if a responsive pleading is allowed

     (3) ❏ If a pleading sets out a claim for relief that does not require a responsive pleading, an opposing party may assert at trial any defense to that claim

     (4) ❏ The moving party must file all motion papers with the court and serve them upon the other parties not less than thirty-one (31) days prior to the return date of the motion

     (5) ❏ A written motion and notice of the hearing must be served at least fourteen (14) days before the time specified for the hearing, with the following exceptions: (i) when the motion may be heard ex parte; (ii) when the Federal Rules of Civil Procedure set a different time; or (iii) when a court order—which a party may, for good cause, apply for ex parte—sets a different time

(6) ❑ Any affidavit supporting a motion must be served with the motion

(II) ❑ Matters to be considered by opposing party

    (a) ❑ Required documents

        (1) ❑ Opposition

        (2) ❑ Memorandum of law

        (3) ❑ Supporting affidavit

        (4) ❑ Certificate of service

    (b) ❑ Supplemental documents

        (1) ❑ Supporting evidence

        (2) ❑ Notice of constitutional question

        (3) ❑ Cross-motion

        (4) ❑ Copies of authorities

        (5) ❑ Cover letter authorizing e-mail or facsimile filing

        (6) ❑ Affidavit attesting to failed attempts to file electronically

        (7) ❑ Notice of conventional filing

        (8) ❑ CD/ROM with PDF of document(s)

        (9) ❑ English translation

        (10) ❑ Courtesy copies

        (11) ❑ Copies for three-judge court

    (c) ❑ Timing

        (1) ❑ The party opposing the motion must file its opposition papers with the court and serve them upon the other parties not less than seventeen (17) days prior to the return date of the motion

        (2) ❑ Except as FRCP 59(c) provides otherwise, any opposing affidavit must be served at least seven (7) days before the hearing, unless the court permits service at another time.

        (3) ❑ A party may file and serve a cross-motion (meaning a competing request for relief or order similar to that requested by another party against the cross-moving party) at the time it files and serves its opposition papers to the original motion, i.e., not less than seventeen (17) days prior to the return date of the motion

## B. Timing

1. *Motion to dismiss for lack of personal jurisdiction*

    a. *In a responsive pleading.* Every defense to a claim for relief in any pleading must be asserted in the responsive pleading if one is required. FRCP 12(b).

    b. *By motion.* A motion asserting any of the defenses in FRCP 12(b) must be made before pleading if a responsive pleading is allowed. FRCP 12(b). Although FRCP 12(b) encourages the responsive pleader to file a motion to dismiss before filing the answer, nothing in FRCP 12 prohibits the filing of a motion to dismiss with the answer. An untimely motion to dismiss may be considered if the defense asserted in the motion was previously raised in the responsive pleading. FEDPROC § 62:427.

    c. *At trial.* If a pleading sets out a claim for relief that does not require a responsive pleading, an opposing party may assert at trial any defense to that claim. FRCP 12(b).

2. *Timing of motions, generally.* The moving party must file all motion papers with the Court and serve them

upon the other parties not less than THIRTY-ONE (31) DAYS prior to the return date of the motion. NY R USDCTND L.R. 7.1(b)(1).

    a. *Motion and notice of hearing.* A written motion and notice of the hearing must be served at least fourteen (14) days before the time specified for the hearing, with the following exceptions:

        i. When the motion may be heard ex parte;

        ii. When the Federal Rules of Civil Procedure set a different time; or

        iii. When a court order—which a party may, for good cause, apply for ex parte—sets a different time. FRCP 6(c)(1).

    b. *Supporting affidavit.* Any affidavit supporting a motion must be served with the motion. FRCP 6(c)(2).

3. *Timing of opposing papers.* The party opposing the motion must file its opposition papers with the Court and serve them upon the other parties not less than SEVENTEEN (17) DAYS prior to the return date of the motion. NY R USDCTND L.R. 7.1(b)(1).

    a. *Opposing affidavit.* Except as FRCP 59(c) provides otherwise, any opposing affidavit must be served at least seven (7) days before the hearing, unless the court permits service at another time. FRCP 6(c)(2).

    b. *Cross-motion.* A party may file and serve a cross-motion (meaning a competing request for relief or order similar to that requested by another party against the cross-moving party) at the time it files and serves its opposition papers to the original motion, i.e., not less than SEVENTEEN (17) DAYS prior to the return date of the motion. NY R USDCTND L.R. 7.1(c).

4. *Timing of reply papers.* Where the respondent files an answering affidavit setting up a new matter, the moving party ordinarily is allowed a reasonable time to file a reply affidavit since failure to deny the new matter by affidavit may operate as an admission of its truth. AMJUR MOTIONS § 25.

    a. *Reply papers.* The moving party must file its reply papers, which may not exceed (10) pages with the Court and serve them upon the other parties not less than ELEVEN (11) DAYS prior to the return date of the motion. NY R USDCTND L.R. 7.1(b)(1).

    b. *Opposition to cross-motion.* The original moving party must file its reply/opposition papers with the Court and serve them on the other parties not less than ELEVEN (11) DAYS prior to the return date of the original motion. NY R USDCTND L.R. 7.1(c).

5. *Effect of a FRCP 12 motion on the time to serve a responsive pleading.* Unless the court sets a different time, serving a motion under FRCP 12 alters the periods in FRCP 12(a) as follows:

    a. If the court denies the motion or postpones its disposition until trial, the responsive pleading must be served within fourteen (14) days after notice of the court's action; or

    b. If the court grants a motion for a more definite statement, the responsive pleading must be served within fourteen (14) days after the more definite statement is served. FRCP 12(a)(4).

6. *Computation of time*

    a. *Computing time.* FRCP 6 applies in computing any time period specified in the Federal Rules of Civil Procedure, in any local rule or court order, or in any statute that does not specify a method of computing time. FRCP 6(a).

        i. *Period stated in days or a longer unit.* When the period is stated in days or a longer unit of time:

            • Exclude the day of the event that triggers the period;

            • Count every day, including intermediate Saturdays, Sundays, and legal holidays; and

            • Include the last day of the period, but if the last day is a Saturday, Sunday, or legal holiday, the period continues to run until the end of the next day that is not a Saturday, Sunday, or legal holiday. FRCP 6(a)(1).

        ii. *Period stated in hours.* When the period is stated in hours:

            • Begin counting immediately on the occurrence of the event that triggers the period;

- Count every hour, including hours during intermediate Saturdays, Sundays, and legal holidays; and

- If the period would end on a Saturday, Sunday, or legal holiday, the period continues to run until the same time on the next day that is not a Saturday, Sunday, or legal holiday. FRCP 6(a)(2).

   iii. *Inaccessibility of the clerk's office.* Unless the court orders otherwise, if the clerk's office is inaccessible:

- On the last day for filing under FRCP 6(a)(1), then the time for filing is extended to the first accessible day that is not a Saturday, Sunday, or legal holiday; or

- During the last hour for filing under FRCP 6(a)(2), then the time for filing is extended to the same time on the first accessible day that is not a Saturday, Sunday, or legal holiday. FRCP 6(a)(3).

   iv. *"Last day" defined.* Unless a different time is set by a statute, local rule, or court order, the last day ends:

- For electronic filing, at midnight in the court's time zone; and

- For filing by other means, when the clerk's office is scheduled to close. FRCP 6(a)(4).

   v. *"Next day" defined.* The "next day" is determined by continuing to count forward when the period is measured after an event and backward when measured before an event. FRCP 6(a)(5).

   vi. *"Legal holiday" defined.* "Legal holiday" means:

- The day set aside by statute for observing New Year's Day, Martin Luther King Jr.'s Birthday, Washington's Birthday, Memorial Day, Independence Day, Labor Day, Columbus Day, Veterans' Day, Thanksgiving Day, or Christmas Day;

- Any day declared a holiday by the President or Congress; and

- For periods that are measured after an event, any other day declared a holiday by the state where the district court is located. FRCP 6(a)(6).

b. *Computation of electronic filing deadlines.* A document will be deemed timely filed if electronically filed prior to midnight Eastern Time. However, if the time of day is of the essence, the assigned judge may order that the document be filed by a time certain. NY R USDCTND CM/ECF(4)(4.3).

   i. *Technical failures.* A Filing User, whose filing is untimely as the result of a technical failure of the Court's CM/ECF site, may seek appropriate relief from the Court. However, Filing Users are cautioned that, in some circumstances, the Court lacks the authority to grant an extension of time to file (e.g., FRCP 6(b) of the Federal Rules of Civil Procedure). NY R USDCTND CM/ECF(10)(10.1).

- *Technical failure of the filing user's system.* Problems with the Filing User's system, such as phone line problems, problems with the Filing User's Internet Service Provider ("ISP"), or hardware or software problems, will not constitute a technical failure under these Administrative Procedures nor excuse an untimely filing. A Filing User who cannot file documents electronically because of a problem on the Filing User's system must file the documents' conventionally along with an affidavit explaining the reason for not filing the documents electronically. NY R USDCTND CM/ECF(10)(10.2).

c. *Extending time*

   i. *In general.* When an act may or must be done within a specified time, the court may, for good cause, extend the time:

- With or without motion or notice if the court acts, or if a request is made, before the original time or its extension expires; or

- On motion made after the time has expired if the party failed to act because of excusable neglect. FRCP 6(b)(1).

   ii. *Exceptions.* A court must not extend the time to act under FRCP 50(b), FRCP 50(d), FRCP 52(b), FRCP 59(b), FRCP 59(d), FRCP 59(e), and FRCP 60(b). FRCP 6(b)(2).

     iii.   Refer to the United States District Court for the Northern District of New York KeyRules Motion for Continuance/Extension of Time document for more information on extending time.

  d.  *Additional time after certain kinds of service.* When a party may or must act within a specified time after service and service is made under FRCP 5(b)(2)(C), FRCP 5(b)(2)(D), FRCP 5(b)(2)(E), or FRCP 5(b)(2)(F), three (3) days are added after the period would otherwise expire under FRCP 6(a). FRCP 6(d).

     i.   In accordance with FRCP 6(e), service by electronic means is treated the same as service by mail for purposes of adding three (3) days to the prescribed period to respond. NY R USDCTND CM/ECF(5)(5.4). [Editor's note: the reference to FRCP 6(e) is likely meant to be a reference to FRCP 6(d)].

7.  *Individual judge practices.* Refer to the Miscellaneous section of this document for information on individual judge practices on timing of documents.

## C.  General Requirements

1.  *Motions, generally*

  a.  *Requirements.* A request for a court order must be made by motion. The motion must:

     i.   Be in writing unless made during a hearing or trial;

     ii.  State with particularity the grounds for seeking the order; and

     iii.  State the relief sought. FRCP 7(b)(1).

     iv.  When a moving party makes a motion based upon a rule or statute, the moving party must specify in its moving papers the rule or statute upon which it bases its motion. NY R USDCTND L.R. 7.1(a)(1).

  b.  *Notice of motion.* A party interested in resisting the relief sought by a motion has a right to notice thereof, and an opportunity to be heard. AMJUR MOTIONS § 12.

     i.   In addition to statutory or court rule provisions requiring notice of a motion—the purpose of such a notice requirement having been said to be to prevent a party from being prejudicially surprised by a motion—principles of natural justice dictate that an adverse party generally must be given notice that a motion will be presented to the court. AMJUR MOTIONS § 12.

     ii.  "Notice," in this regard, means reasonable notice, including a meaningful opportunity to prepare and to defend against allegations of a motion. AMJUR MOTIONS § 12.

  c.  *Writing requirement.* The writing requirement is intended to insure that the adverse parties are informed and have a record of both the motion's pendency and the grounds on which the movant seeks an order. FPP § 1191; Feldberg v. Quechee Lakes Corp., 463 F.3d 195 (2d Cir. 2006).

     i.   It is sufficient "if the motion is stated in a written notice of the hearing of the motion." FPP § 1191.

  d.  *Particularity requirement.* The particularity requirement insures that the opposing parties will have notice of their opponent's contentions. FEDPROC § 62:364; Goodman v. 1973 26 Foot Trojan Vessel, Arkansas Registration No. AR1439SN, 859 F.2d 71, 12 Fed.R.Serv.3d 645 (8th Cir. 1988). That requirement ensures that notice of the basis for the motion is provided to the court and to the opposing party so as to avoid prejudice, provide the opponent with a meaningful opportunity to respond, and provide the court with enough information to process the motion correctly. FEDPROC § 62:364; Andreas v. Volkswagen of America, Inc., 336 F.3d 789, 56 Fed.R.Serv.3d 6 (8th Cir. 2003).

     i.   Reasonable specification of the grounds for a motion is sufficient. However, where a movant fails to state even one ground for granting the motion in question, the movant has failed to meet the minimal standard of "reasonable specification." FEDPROC § 62:364; Martinez v. Trainor, 556 F.2d 818, 23 Fed.R.Serv.2d 403 (7th Cir. 1977).

     ii.  The court may excuse the failure to comply with the particularity requirement if it is inadvertent, and where no prejudice is shown by the opposing party. FEDPROC § 62:364.

  e.  *Order to show cause.* All motions that a party brings by Order to Show Cause shall conform to the requirements set forth in NY R USDCTND L.R. 7.1(a)(1) and NY R USDCTND L.R. 7.1(a)(2). Immediately after filing an Order to Show Cause, the moving party must telephone the Chambers of the presiding judicial officer and inform Chambers staff that it has filed an Order to Show Cause. Parties may obtain the telephone numbers for all Chambers from the Clerk's office or at the Court's webpage. The Court shall determine the briefing schedule and return date applicable to motions brought by Order to Show Cause. NY R USDCTND L.R. 7.1(e).

    i. In addition to the requirements set forth in NY R USDCTND L.R. 7.1(a)(1) and NY R USDCTND L.R. 7.1(a)(2), a motion brought by Order to Show Cause must include an affidavit clearly and specifically showing good and sufficient cause why the standard Notice of Motion procedure cannot be used. The moving party must give reasonable advance notice of the application for an Order to Show Cause to the other parties, except in those circumstances where the movant can demonstrate, in a detailed and specific affidavit, good cause and substantial prejudice that would result from the requirement of reasonable notice. NY R USDCTND L.R. 7.1(e).

    ii. An Order to Show Cause must contain a space for the assigned judge to set forth:

- The deadline for filing and serving supporting papers,
- The deadline for filing and serving opposing papers, and
- The date and time for the hearing. NY R USDCTND L.R. 7.1(e).

2. *Motion to dismiss for lack of personal jurisdiction.* A party may assert the defense of lack of subject-matter jurisdiction by motion. FRCP 12(b)(2). The most common use of the FRCP 12(b)(2) motion is to challenge the use of a state long-arm statute in a diversity action. FEDPROC § 62:445; Best Van Lines, Inc. v. Walker, 490 F.3d 239 (2d Cir. 2007). A dismissal pursuant to FRCP 12(b)(2) is proper where it appears that the assertion of jurisdiction over the defendant offends traditional notions of fair play and substantial justice—that is, where neither the defendant nor the controversy has a substantial enough connection with the forum state to make the exercise of jurisdiction reasonable. FEDPROC § 62:445; Neogen Corp. v. Neo Gen Screening, Inc., 282 F.3d 883, 2002 Fed.App. 0080P (6th Cir. 2002).

    a. *Personal jurisdiction, generally*

        i. *Due process limitations.* Due process requires that a court obtain jurisdiction over a defendant before it may adjudicate that defendant's personal rights. FEDPROC § 65:1; Omni Capital Intern., Ltd. v. Rudolf Wolff & Co., Ltd., 484 U.S. 97, 108 S.Ct. 404, 98 L.Ed.2d 415, 9 Fed.R.Serv.3d 691 (1987).

- Originally it was believed that a judgment in personam could only be entered against a defendant found and served within a state, but the increased flow of commerce between the states and the disuse of the writ of capias ad respondendum, which directed the sheriff to secure the defendant's appearance by taking him into custody, in civil cases led to the liberalization of the concept of personal jurisdiction over nonresidents, and the flexible "minimum contacts" test is now followed. FEDPROC § 65:1.

- Now the rule is that no binding judgment may be rendered against an individual or corporate defendant unless the defendant has sufficient contacts, ties, or relations with the jurisdiction. FEDPROC § 65:1; Burger King Corp. v. Rudzewicz, 471 U.S. 462, 105 S.Ct. 2174, 85 L.Ed.2d 528 (1985); International Shoe Co. v. State of Wash., Office of Unemployment Compensation and Placement, 326 U.S. 310, 66 S.Ct. 154, 90 L.Ed. 95, 161 A.L.R. 1057 (1945).

- Moreover, even if the defendant has sufficient contacts with the forum state to satisfy due process, a court nevertheless does not obtain personal jurisdiction over the defendant unless the defendant has notice sufficient to satisfy due process, and, if such notice requires service of a summons, that there is authorization for the type and manner of service used. FEDPROC § 65:1; Omni Capital Intern., Ltd. v. Rudolf Wolff & Co., Ltd., 484 U.S. 97, 108 S.Ct. 404, 98 L.Ed.2d 415, 9 Fed.R.Serv.3d 691 (1987).

- Personal jurisdiction is a prerequisite to the maintenance of an action, and must exist even though subject matter jurisdiction and venue are proper. FEDPROC § 65:1; Bookout v. Beck, 354 F.2d 823 (9th Cir. 1965).

- Personal jurisdiction over a nonresident defendant is appropriate under the due process clause only where the defendant has sufficient minimum contacts with the forum state that are more than random, fortuitous, or attenuated, such that summoning the defendant would not offend traditional notions of fair play and substantial justice. FEDPROC § 65:1; Pecoraro v. Sky Ranch for Boys, Inc., 340 F.3d 558 (8th Cir. 2003).

   ii. *Methods of obtaining jurisdiction over an individual.* There are four basic methods of obtaining jurisdiction over an individual:

- Personal service within the jurisdiction. FEDPROC § 65:22.

- Service on a domiciliary of the forum state who is temporarily outside the jurisdiction, on the theory that the authority of a state over one of its citizens is not terminated by the mere fact of his absence. FEDPROC § 65:22; Milliken v. Meyer, 311 U.S. 457, 61 S.Ct. 339, 85 L.Ed. 278, 132 A.L.R. 1357 (1940).

- Service on a nonresident who has sufficient contacts with the forum state, since the test of International Shoe is applicable to individuals. FEDPROC § 65:22; Kulko v. Superior Court of California In and For City and County of San Francisco, 436 U.S. 84, 98 S.Ct. 1690, 56 L.Ed.2d 132 (1978).

- Service on an agent who has been expressly appointed or appointed by operation of law, such as under a nonresident motorist statute. FEDPROC § 65:22; National Equipment Rental, Limited v. Szukhent, 375 U.S. 311, 84 S.Ct. 411, 11 L.Ed.2d 354, 7 Fed.R.Serv.2d 23 (1964).

   iii. *Territorial limits of effective service*

- *In general.* Serving a summons or filing a waiver of service establishes personal jurisdiction over a defendant: (1) who is subject to the jurisdiction of a court of general jurisdiction in the state where the district court is located; (2) who is a party joined under FRCP 14 or FRCP 19 and is served within a judicial district of the United States and not more than one hundred (100) miles from where the summons was issued; or (3) when authorized by a federal statute. FRCP 4(k)(1).

- *Federal claim outside state-court jurisdiction.* For a claim that arises under federal law, serving a summons or filing a waiver of service establishes personal jurisdiction over a defendant if: (1) the defendant is not subject to jurisdiction in any state's courts of general jurisdiction; and (2) exercising jurisdiction is consistent with the United States Constitution and laws. FRCP 4(k)(2).

b. *Motion based on lack of in rem or quasi-in-rem jurisdiction.* Although FRCP 12(b)(2) only refers to "jurisdiction over the person," the provision presumably is sufficiently elastic to embrace a defense or objection that the district court lacks in rem or quasi-in-rem jurisdiction, admittedly a subject that rarely arises in contemporary practice. FPP § 1351.

c. *Motion based on insufficient process or insufficient service of process.* FRCP 12(b)(2) motions to dismiss are frequently based on the failure to serve the defendant with process or a defective service of process, on the theory that if the defendant was not properly served with process, the court lacks personal jurisdiction over the defendant. FEDPROC § 62:446; Prokopiou v. Long Island R. Co., 2007 WL 1098696 (S.D.N.Y. 2007).

d. *Independent ground for dismissal.* Lack of overall reasonableness in the assertion of personal jurisdiction constitutes an independent ground for dismissal under FRCP 12(b)(2). FEDPROC § 62:448; Federal Ins. Co. v. Lake Shore Inc., 886 F.2d 654 (4th Cir. 1989).

e. *Burden.* On the motion, the plaintiff bears the burden to establish the court's jurisdiction, which normally is not a heavy one, although the standard of proof may vary depending on the procedure used by the court in making its determination and whether the defendant is successful in rebutting the plaintiff's initial showing. Moreover, the Supreme Court has intimated that in the case of a challenge to the constitutional fairness and reasonableness of the chosen forum, the burden is on the defendant. FPP § 1351; Burger King Corp. v. Rudzewicz, 471 U.S. 462, 105 S.Ct. 2174, 85 L.Ed.2d 528 (1985).

   i. The most common formulation found in the judicial opinions is that the plaintiff bears the ultimate burden of demonstrating that the court's personal jurisdiction over the defendant exists by a preponderance of the evidence, but needs only make a prima facie showing when the district judge restricts her review of the FRCP 12(b)(2) motion solely to affidavits and other written evidence. FPP § 1351; Mullins v. TestAmerica, Inc., 564 F.3d 386 (5th Cir. 2009).

ii.   In addition, for purposes of such a review, federal courts will, as they do on other motions under FRCP 12(b), take as true the allegations of the nonmoving party with regard to the jurisdictional issues and resolve all factual disputes in his or her favor. FPP § 1351.

f.   *Motion denied.* A party who has unsuccessfully raised an objection under FRCP 12(b)(2) may proceed to trial on the merits without waiving the ability to renew the objection to the court's jurisdiction. FPP § 1351.

g.   *Joining motions.* As a general rule, when the court is confronted by a motion raising a combination of FRCP 12(b) defenses, it will pass on the jurisdictional issues before considering whether a claim was stated by the complaint. FPP § 1351.

   i.   *Right to join.* A motion under FRCP 12 may be joined with any other motion allowed by FRCP 12. FRCP 12(g)(1).

   ii.   *Limitation on further motions.* Except as provided in FRCP 12(h)(2) or FRCP 12(h)(3), a party that makes a motion under FRCP 12 must not make another motion under FRCP 12 raising a defense or objection that was available to the party but omitted from its earlier motion. FRCP 12(g)(2).

h.   *Waiving and preserving certain defenses.* No defense or objection is waived by joining it with one or more other defenses or objections in a responsive pleading or in a motion. FRCP 12(b).

   i.   *Waiver by consent or stipulation.* A valid consent or a stipulation that the court has jurisdiction prevents the successful assertion of a FRCP 12(b)(2) defense. FPP § 1351.

   ii.   *Waiver by filing permissive counterclaim.* A defendant may be deemed to have waived an objection to personal jurisdiction if he or she files a permissive counterclaim under FRCP 13(b). FPP § 1351.

   iii.   *When some are waived.* A party waives any defense listed in FRCP 12(b)(2) through FRCP 12(b)(5) by:

   - Omitting it from a motion in the circumstances described in FRCP 12(g)(2); or

   - Failing to either: (1) make it by motion under FRCP 12; or (2) include it in a responsive pleading or in an amendment allowed by FRCP 15(a)(1) as a matter of course. FRCP 12(h)(1).

   iv.   *When to raise others.* Failure to state a claim upon which relief can be granted, to join a person required by FRCP 19(b), or to state a legal defense to a claim may be raised:

   - In any pleading allowed or ordered under FRCP 7(a);

   - By a motion under FRCP 12(c); or

   - At trial. FRCP 12(h)(2).

   v.   *Lack of subject matter jurisdiction.* If the court determines at any time that it lacks subject-matter jurisdiction, the court must dismiss the action. FRCP 12(h)(3).

3.   *Opposing papers.* The Federal Rules of Civil Procedure do not require any formal answer, return, or reply to a motion, except where the Federal Rules of Civil Procedure or local rules may require affidavits, memoranda, or other papers to be filed in opposition to a motion. Such papers are simply to apprise the court of such opposition and the grounds of that opposition. FEDPROC § 62:359.

a.   *Effect of failure to respond to motion.* Although in the absence of statutory provision or court rule, a motion ordinarily does not require a written answer, when a party files a motion and the opposing party fails to respond, the court may construe such failure to respond as nonopposition to the motion or an admission that the motion was meritorious, may take the facts alleged in the motion as true—the rule in some jurisdictions being that the failure to respond to a fact set forth in a motion is deemed an admission—and may grant the motion if the relief requested appears to be justified. AMJUR MOTIONS § 28.

b. *Assent or no opposition not determinative.* However, a motion will not be granted automatically simply because an "assent" or a notation of "no opposition" has been filed; federal judges frequently deny motions that have been assented to when it is thought that justice so dictates. FPP § 1190.

c. *Responsive pleading inappropriate as response to motion.* An attempt to answer or oppose a motion with a responsive pleading usually is not appropriate. FPP § 1190.

4. *Reply papers.* A moving party may be required or permitted to prepare papers in addition to his original motion papers. AMJUR MOTIONS § 25. Papers answering or replying to opposing papers may be appropriate, in the interests of justice, where it appears there is a substantial reason for allowing a reply. Thus, a court may accept reply papers where a party demonstrates that the papers to which it seeks to file a reply raise new issues that are material to the disposition of the question before the court, or where the court determines, sua sponte, that it wishes further briefing of an issue raised in those papers and orders the submission of additional papers. FEDPROC § 62:360.

a. *Function of reply papers.* The function of a reply affidavit is to answer the arguments made in opposition to the position taken by the movant and not to permit the movant to introduce new arguments in support of the motion. AMJUR MOTIONS § 25.

b. *Issues raised for the first time in a reply document.* However, the view has been followed in some jurisdictions, that as a matter of judicial economy, where there is no prejudice and where the issues could be raised simply by filing a motion to dismiss, the trial court has discretion to consider arguments raised for the first time in a reply memorandum, and that a trial court may grant a motion to strike issues raised for the first time in a reply memorandum. AMJUR MOTIONS § 26.

c. *Opposition to cross-motion.* The original moving party may reply in further support of the original motion and in opposition to the cross-motion with a reply/opposition brief that does not exceed twenty-five (25) pages in length, exclusive of exhibits. NY R USDCTND L.R. 7.1(c).

5. *Surreply.* A surreply is not permitted. NY R USDCTND L.R. 7.1(b)(1).

a. *Surreply in support of cross-motion.* The cross-moving party may not reply in further support of its cross-motion without the Court's prior permission. NY R USDCTND L.R. 7.1(c).

6. *Submission of proposed order by prevailing party.* If the assigned judge instructs the prevailing party to do so, the prevailing party shall submit a proposed order which the opposing party has approved and which contains the endorsement of the opposing party: "Approved as to form." NY R USDCTND L.R. 77.2(b). In civil actions where the Court has directed a party to submit an order or judgment, that party shall file all such orders or judgments in duplicate, and the Clerk's entry of such duplicate in the proper record book shall be deemed in compliance with FRCP 79(b). Such party shall also furnish the Clerk with a sufficient number of additional copies for each party to the action, which the Clerk shall mail with notice of entry in accordance with FRCP 77(d). NY R USDCTND L.R. 5.1(b).

a. *Disagreement as to form of proposed order.* When the parties are unable to agree as to the form of the proposed order, the prevailing party shall, on seven (7) days notice to all other parties, submit a proposed order and a written explanation for the form of that order. The Court may award costs and attorney's fees against a party whose unreasonable conduct the Court deemed to have required the bringing of the motion. The provisions of NY R USDCTND L.R. 7.1 shall not apply to such motion, and the Court shall not hear oral argument. NY R USDCTND L.R. 77.2(b).

b. For more information on orders, refer to NY R USDCTND L.R. 77.2.

7. *Sanctions for vexatious or frivolous motions or failure to comply with* NY R USDCTND L.R. 7.1. A party who presents vexatious or frivolous motion papers or fails to comply with NY R USDCTND L.R. 7.1 is subject to discipline as the Court deems appropriate, including sanctions and the imposition of costs and attorney's fees to the opposing party. NY R USDCTND L.R. 7.1(i).

8. *Complex and multi-district litigation.* If the assigned judge determines, in his or her discretion, that the case is of such a complex nature that it cannot reasonably be trial ready within eighteen (18) months from the date the complaint is filed, the assigned judge may design and issue a particularized case management order that will move the case to trial as quickly as the complexity of the case allows. NY R USDCTND L.R. 3.3(a). The parties shall promptly notify the Court in writing if any action commenced is appropriate for multi-district litigation. NY R USDCTND L.R. 3.3(b).

9.  *Appearances.* An attorney appearing for a party in a civil case shall promptly file with the Clerk a written notice of appearance; however, an attorney does not need to file a notice of appearance if the attorney who would be filing the notice of appearance is the same individual who has signed the complaint, notice of removal, pre-answer motion, or answer. NY R USDCTND L.R. 83.2(a). For more information, refer to NY R USDCTND L.R. 83.2.

10. *Related cases.* A civil case is "related" to another civil case for purposes of this guideline when, because of the similarity of facts and legal issues or because the cases arise from the same transactions or events, a substantial saving of judicial resources is likely to result from assigning the cases to the same Judge and Magistrate Judge. NY R USDCTND Order 12(G)(2). A civil case shall not be deemed related to another civil case merely because the civil case: (1) involves similar legal issues, or (2) involves the same parties. NY R USDCTND Order 12(G)(3). Presumptively, and subject to the power of a Judge to determine otherwise pursuant to NY R USDCTND Order 12(G)(5), civil cases shall not be deemed to be "related" unless both cases are still pending before the Court. NY R USDCTND Order 12(G)(4).

    a.  *New filings.* If an attorney or filing party indicates on the Civil Cover Sheet that a case is related to an earlier filed case, the Clerk shall instruct the filing party to file a notice of related cases. The allegedly related cases will be submitted by the Clerk to the Judge to whom the earliest filed case is assigned, who shall advise the Clerk whether such cases are related. NY R USDCTND Order 12(G)(1).

    b.  *Judicial determination that civil cases are "related."* Except for the cases described in the final sentence of NY R USDCTND Order 12(G)(6), all civil cases shall be randomly assigned when they are filed. Other than the cases described in the final sentence of NY R USDCTND Order 12(G)(6), civil cases shall not be deemed to be "related" for purposes of this guideline at the instance of any litigant or attorney unless and until there has been a determination by a Judge of this Court that the standard of NY R USDCTND Order 12(G)(2) is met. NY R USDCTND Order 12(G)(5).

        i.  *Notice of related filing.* Any party may apply for such a determination by filing with the Clerk a notice of related filing, which should include an explanation as to why the standard of NY R USDCTND Order 12(G)(2) is met. A form for this purpose is available on the Court's website. A copy of the notice shall be served on all other parties who have appeared. Such an application must be made after the date when at least a majority of the defendants have been served with the complaint. Before making such an application, the applicant must confer in good faith with all other parties in an effort to reach an agreement on whether or not the case is "related". After such an application is made, any other party may serve and file within seven (7) calendar days a letter of no more than two (2) pages supporting or opposing the application. The application to have the case assigned to another Judge shall be presented to the Judge with the earliest filed case for decision on whether the action(s) should be reassigned as related cases. The Judge with the earliest filed case may then enter an order in the case at bar, either deeming the case to be related and directing the Clerk to reassign the action, or denying the application for reassignment. Any disputes concerning the assignment of related cases will be referred to the Chief Judge for resolution. NY R USDCTND Order 12(G)(5).

    c.  For more information on related cases, refer to NY R USDCTND Order 12(G).

11. *Alternative dispute resolution (ADR).* It is the mission of this court to do everything it can to help parties resolve their disputes as fairly, quickly, and efficiently as possible. NY R USDCTND Order 25(VIII).

    a.  *Arbitration.* NY R USDCTND L.R. 83.7 governs the consensual arbitration program for referral of civil actions to court-annexed arbitration. It may remain in effect until further order of the Court. Its purpose is to establish a less formal procedure for the just, efficient and economical resolution of disputes, while preserving the right to a full trial on demand. NY R USDCTND L.R. 83.7-1.

        i.  *Actions subject to arbitration.* The Clerk shall notify the parties in all civil cases, except as the Local Rules of Practice for the United States District Court for the Northern District of New York otherwise direct, that they may consent to non-binding arbitration under NY R US-DCTND L.R. 83.7. The notice shall be furnished to the parties at pretrial/scheduling conferences or shall be included with pretrial conference notices and instructions. Consent to arbitration under NY R USDCTND L.R. 83.7 shall be discussed at the pretrial/scheduling conference. No party or attorney shall be prejudiced for refusing to participate in arbitration. The Court shall allow the referral of any civil action pending before it to the arbitration process if the parties consent. The plaintiff shall be responsible for securing the execution of a consent form by the parties and for filing the form with the Clerk within fourteen (14) days after the parties receive the form. The parties shall freely and knowingly enter into the consent. NY R USDCTND L.R. 83.7-2.

ii. *Referral to arbitration.* The Clerk shall refer every action subject to NY R USDCTND L.R. 83.7 to arbitration in accordance with the procedures under NY R USDCTND L.R. 83.7 twenty-one (21) days after the filing of the last responsive pleading or within twenty-one (21) days of the filing of a stipulated consent order referring the action to arbitration, whichever event occurs last, except as otherwise provided. If any party notices a motion to dismiss under the provisions of FRCP 12(a) and/or FRCP 12(b), or a motion to join necessary parties pursuant to the Federal Rules of Civil Procedure prior to the expiration of the twenty-one (21) day period, the assigned judge shall hear the motion and further proceedings under NY R USDCTND L.R. 83.7 shall be deferred pending decision on the motion. If the Court does not dismiss the action on the motion, the Court shall refer the action to arbitration twenty-one (21) days after the filing of the decision. NY R USDCTND L.R. 83.7-3(a). Motions for summary judgment pursuant to FRCP 56 shall be filed and served within twenty-one (21) days following the close of discovery. The filing of a FRCP 56 motion shall defer further proceedings under NY R USDCTND L.R. 83.7 pending decision on the motion. NY R USDCTND L.R. 83.7-3(a).

- *Relief from referral.* Any party shall request relief from the operation of NY R USDCTND L.R. 83.7 by filing with the Court a motion for the relief within twenty-one (21) days after entry of the initial stipulated consent order which refers the case for arbitration. The assigned judge shall, sua sponte, exempt an action from the application of NY R USDCTND L.R. 83.7 where the objectives of arbitration would not be realized because (1) the case involves complex or novel legal issues, (2) legal issues predominate over factual issues, or (3) for other good cause. NY R USDCTND L.R. 83.7-3(c).

iii. For more information on arbitration, refer to NY R USDCTND L.R. 83.7.

b. *Mediation.* The purpose of NY R USDCTND L.R. 83.11 is to provide a supplementary procedure to the Court's existing alternative dispute resolution procedures. NY R USDCTND L.R. 83.11 provides for an earlier resolution of civil disputes resulting in savings of time and cost to litigants and the Court without sacrificing the quality of justice rendered or the right of litigants to a full trial on all issues not resolved through mediation. NY R USDCTND L.R. 83.11-1(a). Mediation is a process by which an impartial person, the mediator, facilitates communication between disputing parties to promote understanding, reconciliation and settlement. The mediator is an advocate for settlement and uses the mediation process to help the parties fully explore any potential area of agreement. The mediator does not serve as a judge or arbitrator and has no authority to render any decision on any disputed issue or to force a settlement. The parties themselves are responsible for negotiating any resolution(s) to their dispute. NY R USDCTND L.R. 83.11-1(b).

i. *Actions subject to mediation.* The Court may refer any civil action (or any portion thereof) to mediation under NY R USDCTND L.R. 83.11: (1) by order of referral; or (2) on the motion of any party; or (3) by consent of the parties. NY R USDCTND L.R. 83.11-3(a).

- *Withdrawal from mediation.* The parties may withdraw from mediation any civil action or claim that the Court refers to mediation pursuant to NY R USDCTND L.R. 83.11-3 by application to the assigned judge at least ten (10) days prior to the scheduled mediation session. NY R USDCTND L.R. 83.11-3(b).

ii. *Mandatory mediation program.* The United States District Court for the Northern District of New York has adopted this Mandatory Mediation Plan. The paid Mediation Program is designed to provide quicker, less expensive and potentially more satisfying alternatives to continuing litigation, without impairing the quality of justice or the right to trial. NY R USDCTND Order 47(1)(1.2)(A). This Mandatory Mediation Plan applies to civil actions pending as well as newly filed actions, except as otherwise indicated in NY R USDCTND Order

47. The Local Rules for voluntary mediation will apply only to Pro Se Cases that proceed through the Assisted Mediation Program. NY R USDCTND Order 47(1)(1.2)(B).

- *Referral into the pilot mandatory mediation program for new cases.* All civil cases shall be referred automatically into the Mandatory Mediation Program. Notice of the Mandatory Mediation requirements will be provided to all parties immediately upon the filing of a complaint and answer or a notice of removal. ADR intervention will be scheduled at the conference held pursuant to NY R USDCTND L.R. 16.1. NY R USDCTND Order 47(2)(2.1)(A). For a list of categories of actions exempted from automatic referral, refer to NY R USDCTND Order 47(2)(2.1)(A).

- *Referral into the pilot mandatory mediation program for pending cases.* The assigned Judge or Magistrate Judge on any pending civil case may, sua sponte or with status conference, issue an order referring the case into the Mandatory Mediation Program. The order shall specify a date on which the ADR intervention is to be completed. NY R USDCTND Order 47(2)(2.1)(B).

- *Referral into the pilot mandatory mediation program by stipulation.* A case may be referred into the Mandatory Mediation Program by stipulation of all parties. Stipulations shall be filed and shall designate the time frame within which the ADR process will be completed. Stipulations are presumed acceptable unless the assigned Judge or Magistrate Judge determines that the interests of justice are not served. NY R USDCTND Order 47(2)(2.1)(C).

- *Relief from referral.* Motions to opt out of the program will be addressed by the assigned Magistrate Judge at the FRCP 16 conference. NY R USDCTND Order 47(2)(2.2)(A). Opting Out Motions shall be granted only for "good cause" shown. Inconvenience, travel costs, attorney fees or other costs shall not constitute "good cause." A party seeking relief from the Mandatory Mediation Program must set forth the reasons why Mandatory Mediation has no reasonable chance of being productive. NY R USDCTND Order 47(2)(2.2)(B). The assigned Magistrate Judge may, sua sponte, exempt any case from the Court's Mandatory Mediation Program. NY R USDCTND Order 47(2)(2.2)(C).

iii. *Assisted mediation program.* The Court may assign specially trained pro bono Special Mediation Counsel to assist pro se civilian litigants with preparing for and participating in mediation. The Assisted Mediation Program is open to civilian pro se parties to actions in the Northern District of New York. The assigned judge or magistrate judge determines if the case would benefit from mediation and would also benefit from the assignment of Special Mediation Counsel to assist the pro se party with the mediation process. NY R USDCTND L.R. 83.8(a). Appointment of Special Mediation Counsel is in no way guaranteed, even if the action is referred to the court-annexed mediation program. Appointment is at the sole discretion of the presiding judge. NY R USDCTND L.R. 83.8(a).

- *Referral to assisted mediation program.* If the court determines that referral to the Assisted Mediation Program is appropriate, the Court shall enter an order of reference to the Assisted Mediation Program. NY R USDCTND L.R. 83.8(b).

iv. For more information on mediation, refer to NY R USDCTND L.R. 83.11 and NY R USDCTND Order 47.

c. *Early neutral evaluation (ENE).* Early neutral evaluation (ENE) is a process in which parties obtain from an experienced neutral (an "evaluator") a nonbinding, reasoned, oral evaluation of the merits of the case. The first step in the ENE process involves the Court appointing an evaluator who has expertise in the area of law in the case. After the parties exchange essential information and position statements early in the pretrial period (usually within one hundred fifty (150) to two hundred (200) days after a complaint has been filed), the evaluator convenes an ENE session that typically lasts about two hours. At the ENE meeting, each side briefly presents the factual and legal basis of its position. The evaluator may ask questions of the parties and help them identify the main issues in dispute and the areas of agreement. The evaluator may also help the parties explore options for settlement. If settlement does not occur, the evaluator then offers an opinion as to the settlement value of the case, including the likelihood of liability and the likely range of damages. With the benefit of this assessment, the parties are again encouraged to discuss settlement, with or without the evaluator's assistance. The parties may also explore ways to narrow the issues in dispute, exchange information about the case or otherwise prepare efficiently for trial. NY R USDCTND L.R. 83.12-1.

   i. *Actions subject to early neutral evaluation.* The Court may refer any civil action (or any portion thereof) to ENE under NY R USDCTND L.R. 83.12: (1) by order of referral; (2) on the motion of any party; or (3) by consent of the parties. NY R USDCTND L.R. 83.12-3(a).

      ● *Withdrawal from the ENE process.* The parties may withdraw any civil action or claim that the Court has referred to the ENE Process pursuant to NY R USDCTND L.R. 83.12-3 by application to the assigned judge at least ten (10) days before the scheduled evaluation session. NY R USDCTND L.R. 83.12-3(b).

   ii. For more information on early neutral evaluation (ENE), refer to NY R USDCTND L.R. 83.12.

12. *Settlement procedures.* On notice to the Court or the Clerk that the parties have settled an action, and upon confirmation of the settlement by all parties, the Court may issue a judgment dismissing the action by reason of settlement. The Court shall issue the order without prejudice to the parties' right to secure reinstatement of the case within thirty (30) days after the date of judgment by making a showing that the settlement was not, in fact, consummated. NY R USDCTND L.R. 68.2(a). If the Court decides not to follow the procedures set forth in NY R USDCTND L.R. 68.2(a), the parties shall file within thirty (30) days of the notification to the Court, unless otherwise directed by written order, such notices, stipulations and/or motions as are necessary to terminate the action. If the required documents are not filed within the thirty (30) day period, the Clerk shall place the action on the dismissal calendar. NY R USDCTND L.R. 68.2(b).

13. *Sanctions and penalties for noncompliance.* Failure of an attorney or of a party to comply with any provision of the Local Rules of Practice for the United States District Court for the Northern District of New York, General Orders of this District, Orders of the Court, or the Federal Rules of Civil Procedure shall be a ground for imposition of sanctions. NY R USDCTND L.R. 1.1(d).

14. *Individual judge practices.* Refer to the Miscellaneous section of this document for information on individual judge practices on general requirements for documents.

## D. Documents

  1. *Documents for moving party*

    a. *Required documents*

      i. *Notice of motion and motion.* The Notice of Motion must state the return date that the moving party has selected. NY R USDCTND L.R. 7.1(b)(1). Refer to the General Requirements section of this document for information on the notice of motion and motion.

         ● *Order to show cause.* Refer to the General Requirements section of this document for information on bringing a motion by order to show cause.

      ii. *Memorandum of law.* Except as otherwise provided in NY R USDCTND L.R. 7.1(a), all motions. . .require a memorandum of law. NY R USDCTND L.R. 7.1(a). Refer to the Format section of this document for the formatting requirements for memoranda of law.

      iii. *Supporting affidavit.* Except as otherwise provided in NY R USDCTND L.R. 7.1(a), all motions. . .require a. . .supporting affidavit. NY R USDCTND L.R. 7.1(a). An affidavit must not contain legal arguments but must contain factual and procedural background that is relevant to the motion the affidavit supports. NY R USDCTND L.R. 7.1(a)(2).

      iv. *Certificate of service.* Except as otherwise provided in NY R USDCTND L.R. 7.1(a), all motions. . .require. . .proof of service on all the parties. See NY R USDCTND L.R. 5.1(a). NY R USDCTND L.R. 7.1(a). FRCP 5(d) requires that the person making service under FRCP 5 certify that service has been effected. FRCP 5(Advisory Committee Notes). Having such information on file may be useful for many purposes, including proof of service if an issue arises concerning the effectiveness of the service. FRCP 5(Advisory Committee Notes). The party or its designee shall declare, by affidavit or certification, that it has provided all other parties in the action with all documents it has filed with the Court. NY R USDCTND L.R. 5.1(a).

- Attorneys and pro se parties who are not Filing or Receiving Users must be served with a paper copy of any electronically filed pleading or other document. NY R USDCTND CM/ECF(5)(5.2). Such paper service must be documented by electronically filing a certificate of service. NY R USDCTND CM/ECF(5)(5.2).

b. *Supplemental documents*

    i. *Supporting evidence.* When a motion relies on facts outside the record, the court may hear the matter on affidavits or may hear it wholly or partly on oral testimony or on depositions. FRCP 43(c).

    ii. *Notice of constitutional question.* A party that files a pleading, written motion, or other paper drawing into question the constitutionality of a federal or state statute must promptly:

- *File notice.* File a notice of constitutional question stating the question and identifying the paper that raises it, if: (1) a federal statute is questioned and the parties do not include the United States, one of its agencies, or one of its officers or employees in an official capacity; or (2) a state statute is questioned and the parties do not include the state, one of its agencies, or one of its officers or employees in an official capacity; and

- *Serve notice.* Serve the notice and paper on the Attorney General of the United States if a federal statute is questioned—or on the state attorney general if a state statute is questioned—either by certified or registered mail or by sending it to an electronic address designated by the attorney general for this purpose. FRCP 5.1(a).

- *No forfeiture.* A party's failure to file and serve the notice, or the court's failure to certify, does not forfeit a constitutional claim or defense that is otherwise timely asserted. FRCP 5.1(d).

    iii. *Nongovernmental corporate disclosure statement*

- *Contents.* A nongovernmental corporate party must file two (2) copies of a disclosure statement that: (1) identifies any parent corporation and any publicly held corporation owning ten percent (10%) or more of its stock; or (2) states that there is no such corporation. FRCP 7.1(a).

- *Time to file; Supplemental filing.* A party must: (1) file the disclosure statement with its first appearance, pleading, petition, motion, response, or other request addressed to the court; and (2) promptly file a supplemental statement if any required information changes. FRCP 7.1(b).

    iv. *Copies of authorities.* When serving a pro se litigant with a memorandum of law or any other paper which contains citations to authorities that are unpublished or published exclusively on electronic databases, counsel shall include a hard copy of those authorities. Although copies of authorities published only on electronic databases are not required to be filed, copies shall be provided upon request to opposing counsel who lack access to electronic databases. NY R USDCTND L.R. 7.1(a)(1).

    v. *Proposed order.* A document that is submitted in .pdf format cannot be modified; therefore, a proposed order or stipulation must be in a word processing format. The chambers of the assigned judge may request that a proposed order and/or a stipulation be e-mailed to the courtroom deputy for the presiding judge in either WordPerfect or Microsoft Word format. Please attach your proposed order and/or stipulation to an Internet e-mail sent to the appropriate e-mail address listed in NY R USDCTND CM/ECF(8)(8.2). NY R USDCTND CM/ECF(8)(8.2).

    vi. *Cover letter authorizing e-mail or facsimile filing.* Neither the Court nor the Clerk's Office will accept for filing any facsimile or e-mail transmission without prior authorization from the Court. The party using facsimile or e-mail transmissions to file its papers must accompany any such documents with a cover letter stating that the Court authorized such transmissions and the date on which the Court provided that authorization. Violations of NY R USDCTND L.R. 5.5 subject the offending party to the Court's full disciplinary powers. NY R USDCTND L.R. 5.5.

vii. *Affidavit attesting to failed attempts to file electronically.* If the Court's CM/ECF site experiences a technical failure, a Filing User may submit documents to the Court that day in an alternate manner provided that the documents are accompanied by the Filing User's affidavit stating that the Filing User attempted to file electronically at least two times in one (1) hour increments after 10:00 a.m. that day. The following methods are acceptable alternate means for filing documents in case of a technical failure: (1) via electronic mail in a PDF attachment sent to the e-mail address for technical failures; or (2) in person, by bringing the document to the Clerk's Office on paper accompanied by a CD/ROM that contains the document in .pdf format. NY R USDCTND CM/ECF(10)(10.1).

- A Filing User who cannot file documents electronically because of a problem on the Filing User's system must file the documents' conventionally along with an affidavit explaining the reason for not filing the documents electronically. NY R USDCTND CM/ECF(10)(10.2).

viii. *Notice of conventional filing.* If the Clerk's Office grants permission to conventionally file the document, the Filing User shall electronically file a notice of conventional filing for the documents. More information regarding this process can be obtained from the Court's web page. NY R USDCTND CM/ECF(4)(4.5).

ix. *CD/ROM with PDF of document(s).* If the Court grants permission to file a document traditionally, the attorney must submit the documents for filing to the Clerk's Office on CD/ROM in .pdf or pdf.A format. NY R USDCTND CM/ECF(2).

x. *English translation.* The Court conducts its reviews and deliberations in English. Unless otherwise directed by the Court, any document that a party transmits to the Court (including one in the record on appeal) that is in a language other than English must be accompanied by an English translation that the translator has certified as true and accurate, pursuant to 28 U.S.C.A. § 1746. NY R USDCTND L.R. 10.1(e). For more information, refer to NY R USDCTND L.R. 10.1(e).

xi. *Courtesy copies.* The Court may require that courtesy copies of electronically filed documents be submitted for its review and may amend these Administrative Procedures (NY R USDCTND CM/ECF) at any time without prior notice. NY R USDCTND CM/ECF(2).

- The parties need not provide a courtesy copy of their motion papers to the assigned judge unless the assigned judge requests a copy. NY R USDCTND L.R. 7.1(b)(1).

xii. *Copies for three-judge court.* On the convening of a three-judge court, the parties shall make three (3) copies of all non-electronically filed pleadings, motion papers, and memoranda of law available to the Clerk for distribution. NY R USDCTND L.R. 9.1.

2. *Documents for opposing party*

   a. *Required documents*

      i. *Opposition.* Refer to the General Requirements section of this document for information on the opposing papers.

      ii. *Memorandum of law.* Except as otherwise provided in NY R USDCTND L.R. 7.1(a), all. . .opposition to motions require a memorandum of law. NY R USDCTND L.R. 7.1(a).

      - *Cross-motion brief.* If a party makes a cross-motion, it must join its cross motion brief with its opposition brief, and this combined brief may not exceed twenty-five (25) pages in length, exclusive of exhibits. A separate brief in opposition to the original motion is not permissible. NY R USDCTND L.R. 7.1(c).

      - Refer to the Format section of this document for the formatting requirements for memoranda of law.

      iii. *Supporting affidavit.* Except as otherwise provided in NY R USDCTND L.R. 7.1(a), all. . .opposition to motions require a. . .supporting affidavit. NY R USDCTND L.R. 7.1(a).

An affidavit must not contain legal arguments but must contain factual and procedural background that is relevant to the motion the affidavit supports. NY R USDCTND L.R. 7.1(a)(2).

iv. *Certificate of service.* Except as otherwise provided in NY R USDCTND L.R. 7.1(a), all. . .opposition to motions require. . .proof of service on all the parties. See NY R US-DCTND L.R. 5.1(a). NY R USDCTND L.R. 7.1(a). FRCP 5(d) requires that the person making service under FRCP 5 certify that service has been effected. FRCP 5(Advisory Committee Notes). Having such information on file may be useful for many purposes, including proof of service if an issue arises concerning the effectiveness of the service. FRCP 5(Advisory Committee Notes). The party or its designee shall declare, by affidavit or certification, that it has provided all other parties in the action with all documents it has filed with the Court. NY R USDCTND L.R. 5.1(a).

- Attorneys and pro se parties who are not Filing or Receiving Users must be served with a paper copy of any electronically filed pleading or other document. NY R USDCTND CM/ECF(5)(5.2). Such paper service must be documented by electronically filing a certificate of service. NY R USDCTND CM/ECF(5)(5.2).

b. *Supplemental documents*

i. *Supporting evidence.* When a motion relies on facts outside the record, the court may hear the matter on affidavits or may hear it wholly or partly on oral testimony or on depositions. FRCP 43(c).

ii. *Notice of constitutional question.* A party that files a pleading, written motion, or other paper drawing into question the constitutionality of a federal or state statute must promptly:

- *File notice.* File a notice of constitutional question stating the question and identifying the paper that raises it, if: (1) a federal statute is questioned and the parties do not include the United States, one of its agencies, or one of its officers or employees in an official capacity; or (2) a state statute is questioned and the parties do not include the state, one of its agencies, or one of its officers or employees in an official capacity; and

- *Serve notice.* Serve the notice and paper on the Attorney General of the United States if a federal statute is questioned—or on the state attorney general if a state statute is questioned—either by certified or registered mail or by sending it to an electronic address designated by the attorney general for this purpose. FRCP 5.1(a).

- *No forfeiture.* A party's failure to file and serve the notice, or the court's failure to certify, does not forfeit a constitutional claim or defense that is otherwise timely asserted. FRCP 5.1(d).

iii. *Cross-motion.* A party may file and serve a cross-motion (meaning a competing request for relief or order similar to that requested by another party against the cross-moving party) at the time it files and serves its opposition papers to the original motion, i.e., not less than SEVENTEEN (17) DAYS prior to the return date of the motion. NY R USDCTND L.R. 7.1(c).

iv. *Copies of authorities.* When serving a pro se litigant with a memorandum of law or any other paper which contains citations to authorities that are unpublished or published exclusively on electronic databases, counsel shall include a hard copy of those authorities. Although copies of authorities published only on electronic databases are not required to be filed, copies shall be provided upon request to opposing counsel who lack access to electronic databases. NY R USDCTND L.R. 7.1(a)(1).

v. *Cover letter authorizing e-mail or facsimile filing.* Neither the Court nor the Clerk's Office will accept for filing any facsimile or e-mail transmission without prior authorization from the Court. The party using facsimile or e-mail transmissions to file its papers must accompany any such documents with a cover letter stating that the Court authorized such transmissions and the date on which the Court provided that authorization. Violations of NY R USDCTND L.R. 5.5 subject the offending party to the Court's full disciplinary powers. NY R USDCTND L.R. 5.5.

vi. *Affidavit attesting to failed attempts to file electronically.* If the Court's CM/ECF site experiences a technical failure, a Filing User may submit documents to the Court that day in an alternate manner provided that the documents are accompanied by the Filing User's affidavit stating that the Filing User attempted to file electronically at least two times in one (1) hour increments after 10:00 a.m. that day. The following methods are acceptable alternate means for filing documents in case of a technical failure: (1) via electronic mail in a PDF attachment sent to the e-mail address for technical failures; or (2) in person, by bringing the document to the Clerk's Office on paper accompanied by a CD/ROM that contains the document in .pdf format. NY R USDCTND CM/ECF(10)(10.1).

- A Filing User who cannot file documents electronically because of a problem on the Filing User's system must file the documents' conventionally along with an affidavit explaining the reason for not filing the documents electronically. NY R USDCTND CM/ECF(10)(10.2).

vii. *Notice of conventional filing.* If the Clerk's Office grants permission to conventionally file the document, the Filing User shall electronically file a notice of conventional filing for the documents. More information regarding this process can be obtained from the Court's web page. NY R USDCTND CM/ECF(4)(4.5).

viii. *CD/ROM with PDF of document(s).* If the Court grants permission to file a document traditionally, the attorney must submit the documents for filing to the Clerk's Office on CD/ROM in .pdf or pdf.A format. NY R USDCTND CM/ECF(2).

ix. *English translation.* The Court conducts its reviews and deliberations in English. Unless otherwise directed by the Court, any document that a party transmits to the Court (including one in the record on appeal) that is in a language other than English must be accompanied by an English translation that the translator has certified as true and accurate, pursuant to 28 U.S.C.A. § 1746. NY R USDCTND L.R. 10.1(e). For more information, refer to NY R USDCTND L.R. 10.1(e).

x. *Courtesy copies.* The Court may require that courtesy copies of electronically filed documents be submitted for its review and may amend these Administrative Procedures (NY R USDCTND CM/ECF) at any time without prior notice. NY R USDCTND CM/ECF(2).

- The parties need not provide a courtesy copy of their motion papers to the assigned judge unless the assigned judge requests a copy. NY R USDCTND L.R. 7.1(b)(1).

xi. *Copies for three-judge court.* On the convening of a three-judge court, the parties shall make three (3) copies of all non-electronically filed pleadings, motion papers, and memoranda of law available to the Clerk for distribution. NY R USDCTND L.R. 9.1.

3. *Individual judge practices.* Refer to the Miscellaneous section of this document for information on individual judge practices on required documents.

## E. Format

1. *Form of documents.* The rules governing captions and other matters of form in pleadings apply to motions and other papers. FRCP 7(b)(2). All pleadings and other papers shall be served and filed in accordance with the Federal Rules of Civil Procedure and shall be in the form prescribed by NY R USDCTND L.R. 10.1. NY R USDCTND L.R. 5.1(a).

a. *Form, generally.* All pleadings, motions, and other documents that a party presents for filing, whether in paper form or in electronic form, shall meet the following requirements:

i. *Font size.* All text, whether in the body of the document or in footnotes, must be a minimum of twelve (12) point type. NY R USDCTND L.R. 10.1(a)(1).

ii. *Margins.* All documents must have one (1) inch margins on all four sides of the page. NY R USDCTND L.R. 10.1(a)(2).

iii. *Spacing.* All text in the body of the document must be double-spaced. NY R USDCTND L.R. 10.1(a)(3).

- The text in block quotations and footnotes may be single-spaced. NY R USDCTND L.R. 10.1(a)(4).

      iv.   *Page numbering.* Pages must be consecutively numbered. NY R USDCTND L.R. 10.1(a)(7).

      v.   *Circumventing formatting limitations*

- Extensive footnotes must not be used to circumvent page limitations. NY R USDCTND L.R. 10.1(a)(5).

- Compacted or other compressed printing features must not be used. NY R USDCTND L.R. 10.1(a)(6).

  b.  *Additional requirements for paper filing.* Additional requirements for all pleadings, motions, and other documents that a party presents for filing in paper form:

      i.   *Paper size.* All documents must be on eight and one-half by eleven (8-1/2 x 11) inch white paper of good quality. NY R USDCTND L.R. 10.1(b)(1).

      ii.   *Text.* All text must be plainly and legibly written, typewritten, printed or reproduced without erasures or interlineations materially defacing them. NY R USDCTND L.R. 10.1(b)(2).

      iii.  *Ink.* All documents must be in black or blue ink. NY R USDCTND L.R. 10.1(b)(3).

      iv.   *Binding.* Pages of all documents must be stapled (or in some other way fastened) together. NY R USDCTND L.R. 10.1(b)(4).

      v.   *Single-sided paper.* All documents must be single-sided. NY R USDCTND L.R. 10.1(b)(5).

      vi.   *Electronic submission.* The Court, at its discretion, may require the electronic submission of any document in a WordPerfect-compatible format. NY R USDCTND L.R. 10.1(b)(6).

      vii.  *Rejection of document.* The Court may reject documents that do not comply with the above-listed requirements. NY R USDCTND L.R. 10.1(b).

  c.  *Caption; Names of parties.* Every pleading must have a caption with the court's name, a title, a file number, and a FRCP 7(a) designation. The title of the complaint must name all the parties; the title of other pleadings, after naming the first party on each side, may refer generally to other parties. FRCP 10(a). Each document must contain a caption for the specific case to which it pertains. The caption must include the title of the Court, the title of the action, the civil action number of the case, the initials of the assigned judge(s), and the name or nature of the paper in sufficient detail for identification. If a litigant has more than one action pending in this Court, any and all papers filed in a case must contain and pertain to one civil action number, unless the civil actions have been consolidated by the Court. Any motion or other papers purporting to relate to more than one action will not be accepted for filing and may be stricken by the Court. NY R USDCTND L.R. 10.1(c)(1) shall not apply, as noted in NY R USDCTND L.R. 10.1(c), to notices of change of address filed by attorneys of record and pro se litigants. The parties must separately caption affidavits and declarations and must not physically attach them to the Notice of Motion or Memorandum of Law. NY R USDCTND L.R. 10.1(c)(1).

  d.  *Paragraphs; Separate statements.* A party must state its claims or defenses in numbered paragraphs, each limited as far as practicable to a single set of circumstances. A later pleading may refer by number to a paragraph in an earlier pleading. If doing so would promote clarity, each claim founded on a separate transaction or occurrence—and each defense other than a denial—must be stated in a separate count or defense. FRCP 10(b).

  e.  *Adoption by reference; Exhibits.* A statement in a pleading may be adopted by reference elsewhere in the same pleading or in any other pleading or motion. A copy of a written instrument that is an exhibit to a pleading is a part of the pleading for all purposes. FRCP 10(c).

  f.  *Citation of local rules.* These are the Local Rules of Practice for the United States District Court for the Northern District of New York. They shall be cited as "L.R. ___." NY R USDCTND L.R. 1.1(a).

  g.  *Acceptance by the clerk.* The clerk must not refuse to file a paper solely because it is not in the form prescribed by the Federal Rules of Civil Procedure or by a local rule or practice. FRCP 5(d)(4).

2.  *Form of electronic documents.* All pleadings, motions, and other documents that a party presents for filing, whether in paper form or in electronic form, shall meet the requirements in NY R USDCTND L.R. 10.1(a). NY R USDCTND L.R. 10.1(a). Refer above for more information.

  a.  *Attachments and exhibits.* A Filing User must submit in electronic form all documents referenced as

exhibits or attachments in accordance with the Court's CM/ECF Users Manual unless the Court otherwise orders. A Filing User shall submit as exhibits or attachments only those excerpts of the referenced documents that are directly germane to the matter under the Court's consideration. Excerpted material must be clearly and prominently identified as such. Filing Users who file excerpts of documents as exhibits or attachments under these Administrative Procedures (NY R USDCTND CM/ECF) do so without prejudice to their right to timely file additional excerpts or the complete document. Responding parties may also timely file the complete document or additional excerpts that they believe are directly germane to the matter under the Court's consideration. NY R USDCTND CM/ECF(4)(4.4).

    i.    All attachments must be described in sufficient detail so the Court and opposing counsel can easily identify and distinguish the filed attachments. Vague or general descriptions are insufficient (i.e., "Exhibit 1"). Rather, each attachment shall have a descriptive title identifying, with specificity, the document that is being filed (i.e., "Exhibit 12 Mulligan County Fire Investigation Report.") Failure to adequately describe attachments may result in the document being rejected by the Court. NY R USDCTND CM/ECF(4)(4.4).

b.    *Large documents.* For information on the electronic filing of large documents, please consult the Court's CM/ECF Users Manual, which is available on the Court's web page. NY R USDCTND CM/ECF(4)(4.5).

    i.    A party who believes a document is too lengthy to electronically image, i.e., "scan," may contact the Clerk's Office for permission to file that document conventionally. If the Clerk's Office grants permission to conventionally file the document, the Filing User shall electronically file a notice of conventional filing for the documents. More information regarding this process can be obtained from the Court's web page. Exhibits submitted conventionally shall be served on other parties as if they were not subject to these Administrative Procedures (NY R USDCTND CM/ECF). For a list of hints and tips for scanning large documents, please consult the Court's web page. NY R USDCTND CM/ECF(4)(4.5).

c.    *Legibility.* It shall be the Filing User's responsibility to verify the legibility of scanned documents before filing them electronically with the Court. NY R USDCTND CM/ECF(4)(4.6).

d.    *Color documents.* Since documents scanned in color or containing a graphic take much longer to upload, Filing Users are encouraged to configure their scanners to scan documents at 300 dpi and preferably in black and white rather than in color. NY R USDCTND CM/ECF(4)(4.7).

e.    *Items not in .PDF format.* Parties wishing to file items not amenable to .pdf format (i.e. CD's, DVD's), shall file such items conventionally with the Clerk's Office. The Filing User shall electronically file a notice of conventional filing indicating that these items have been submitted to the clerk and shall serve copies of these items on other parties as if they were not subject to these Administrative Procedures (NY R USDCTND CM/ECF). These item(s) will be maintained by the Clerk's Office until the case is disposed, at which time they will be returned to the filing party for retention consistent with NY R USDCTND CM/ECF(4)(4.9). NY R USDCTND CM/ECF(4)(4.8).

3.    *Form of memoranda of law*

    a.    *Length limitation.* No party shall file or serve a memorandum of law that exceeds twenty-five (25) pages in length, unless that party obtains leave of the judge hearing the motion prior to filing. NY R USDCTND L.R. 7.1(a)(1).

    b.    *Table of contents.* All memoranda of law shall contain a table of contents. NY R USDCTND L.R. 7.1(a)(1).

4.    *Signing of pleadings, motions and other papers*

    a.    *Signature.* Every pleading, written motion, and other paper must be signed by at least one attorney of record in the attorney's name—or by a party personally if the party is unrepresented. The paper must state the signer's address, e-mail address, and telephone number. FRCP 11(a). Each document must identify the person filing the document. This identification must include an original signature of the attorney or pro se litigant; the typewritten name of that person; the address of a pro se litigant; and the bar roll number, office address, telephone number, e-mail address and fax number of the attorney. Telephone numbers of non-prisoner pro se parties may be provided voluntarily or upon request of the Court. See General Order #22 (NY R USDCTND CM/ECF) for signature requirements. NY R USDCTND L.R. 10.1(c)(2).

    i.   *Electronic signatures.* Documents filed under an attorney's login and password shall constitute that attorney's signature for purposes of the Local Rules of Practice for the United States District Court for the Northern District of New York and Federal Rules of Civil Procedure, including but not limited to FRCP 11. A pleading or other document requiring an attorney's signature shall be signed in the following manner, whether filed electronically or submitted on disk or CD/ROM to the Clerk's Office: "s/ (attorney name)." The correct format for an attorney signature is found in NY R USDCTND CM/ECF(6)(6.1). NY R USDCTND CM/ECF(6)(6.1).

-    *Non-attorney signature.* If an original document requires the signature of a non-attorney, the Filing User may scan the original document containing the original signature(s), then electronically file it on the System. Alternatively, the Filing User may convert the document into .pdf text format and submit the document using "s/" for the signature of the non-attorney. NY R USDCTND CM/ECF(6)(6.2).

-    *Multiple signatures.* A document requiring signatures of more than one party must be filed electronically either by (1) submitting a scanned document containing all necessary signatures; (2) representing the consent of the other parties on the document; or (3) in any other manner that the Court approves. NY R USDCTND CM/ECF(6)(6.3).

    ii.   *No verification or accompanying affidavit required for pleadings.* Unless a rule or statute specifically states otherwise, a pleading need not be verified or accompanied by an affidavit. FRCP 11(a).

    iii.   *Unsigned papers.* The court must strike an unsigned paper unless the omission is promptly corrected after being called to the attorney's or party's attention. FRCP 11(a).

b.   *Representations to the court.* By presenting to the court a pleading, written motion, or other paper—whether by signing, filing, submitting, or later advocating it—an attorney or unrepresented party certifies that to the best of the person's knowledge, information, and belief, formed after an inquiry reasonable under the circumstances:

    i.   It is not being presented for any improper purpose, such as to harass, cause unnecessary delay, or needlessly increase the cost of litigation;

    ii.   The claims, defenses, and other legal contentions are warranted by existing law or by a nonfrivolous argument for extending, modifying, or reversing existing law or for establishing new law;

    iii.   The factual contentions have evidentiary support or, if specifically so identified, will likely have evidentiary support after a reasonable opportunity for further investigation or discovery; and

    iv.   The denials of factual contentions are warranted on the evidence or, if specifically so identified, are reasonably based on belief or a lack of information. FRCP 11(b).

c.   *Sanctions.* If, after notice and a reasonable opportunity to respond, the court determines that FRCP 11(b) has been violated, the court may impose an appropriate sanction on any attorney, law firm, or party that violated FRCP 11(b) or is responsible for the violation. FRCP 11(c)(1). Refer to the United States District Court for the Northern District of New York KeyRules Motion for Sanctions document for more information.

5.   *Privacy protection for filings made with the court*

a.   *Redacted filings.* Unless the court orders otherwise, in an electronic or paper filing with the court that contains an individual's Social Security number, taxpayer-identification number, or birth date, the name of an individual known to be a minor, or a financial-account number, a party or nonparty making the filing may include only:

    i.   The last four (4) digits of the Social Security number and taxpayer-identification number;

    ii.   The year of the individual's birth;

    iii.   The minor's initials; and

iv.  The last four (4) digits of the financial-account number. FRCP 5.2(a); NY R USDCTND L.R. 8.1; NY R USDCTND CM/ECF(11)(11.2).

v.  If a home address must be used, use only the City and State. NY R USDCTND L.R. 8.1; NY R USDCTND CM/ECF(11)(11.2).

vi.  If the victim of a sexual assault must be referenced, redact the name to 'Victim.' NY R USDCTND CM/ECF(11)(11.2); NY R USDCTND L.R. 8.1.

vii.  In addition, caution shall be exercised when filing documents that contain the following:

- Personal identifying number, such as a driver's license number;

- Medical records, treatment and diagnosis;

- Employment history;

- Individual financial information; and

- Proprietary or trade secret information. NY R USDCTND L.R. 8.1; NY R USDCTND CM/ECF(11)(11.2).

b. *Exemptions from the redaction requirement.* The redaction requirement does not apply to the following:

i.  A financial-account number that identifies the property allegedly subject to forfeiture in a forfeiture proceeding;

ii.  The record of an administrative or agency proceeding;

iii.  The official record of a state-court proceeding;

iv.  The record of a court or tribunal, if that record was not subject to the redaction requirement when originally filed;

v.  A filing covered by FRCP 5.2(c) or FRCP 5.2(d); and

vi.  A pro se filing in an action brought under 28 U.S.C.A. § 2241, 28 U.S.C.A. § 2254, or 28 U.S.C.A. § 2255. FRCP 5.2(b).

vii.  Transcripts of the administrative record in social security proceedings are exempt from this requirement. State court records and other documents filed in habeas corpus proceedings are exempt from this requirement except for proceedings that involve victims of sex crimes. In habeas corpus cases involving sex crimes, the parties must redact the record and supporting papers, or may move to seal, if appropriate. NY R USDCTND L.R. 8.1.

c. *Limitations on remote access to electronic files; Social Security appeals and immigration cases.* Unless the court orders otherwise, in an action for benefits under the Social Security Act, and in an action or proceeding relating to an order of removal, to relief from removal, or to immigration benefits or detention, access to an electronic file is authorized as follows:

i.  The parties and their attorneys may have remote electronic access to any part of the case file, including the administrative record;

ii.  Any other person may have electronic access to the full record at the courthouse, but may have remote electronic access only to:

- The docket maintained by the court; and

- An opinion, order, judgment, or other disposition of the court, but not any other part of the case file or the administrative record. FRCP 5.2(c).

d. *Filings made under seal.* The court may order that a filing be made under seal without redaction. The court may later unseal the filing or order the person who made the filing to file a redacted version for the public record. FRCP 5.2(d); NY R USDCTND L.R. 8.1. For information on sealed matters, refer to NY R USDCTND L.R. 83.13 and NY R USDCTND CM/ECF(12).

e. *Protective orders.* For good cause, the court may by order in a case:

i.  Require redaction of additional information; or

    ii.    Limit or prohibit a nonparty's remote electronic access to a document filed with the court. FRCP 5.2(e).

  f.  *Option for additional unredacted filing under seal.* A person making a redacted filing may also file an unredacted copy under seal. The court must retain the unredacted copy as part of the record. FRCP 5.2(f); NY R USDCTND L.R. 8.1; NY R USDCTND CM/ECF(11)(11.3).

  g.  *Option for filing a reference list.* A filing that contains redacted information may be filed together with a reference list that identifies each item of redacted information and specifies an appropriate identifier that uniquely corresponds to each item listed. The list must be filed under seal and may be amended as of right. Any reference in the case to a listed identifier will be construed to refer to the corresponding item of information. FRCP 5.2(g); NY R USDCTND L.R. 8.1; NY R USDCTND CM/ECF(11)(11.3).

  h.  *Responsibility for redaction.* Counsel is strongly urged to discuss this issue with all their clients so that they can make an informed decision about the inclusion of certain information. The responsibility for redacting these personal identifiers rests solely with counsel and the parties. The Clerk will not review each filing for compliance with NY R USDCTND L.R. 8.1. Counsel and the parties are cautioned that failure to redact these personal identifiers may subject them to the Court's full disciplinary power. NY R USDCTND L.R. 8.1; NY R USDCTND CM/ECF(11)(11.3).

  i.  *Waiver of protection of identifiers.* A person waives the protection of FRCP 5.2(a) as to the person's own information by filing it without redaction and not under seal. FRCP 5.2(h).

  6.  *Individual judge practices.* Refer to the Miscellaneous section of this document for information on individual judge practices on formatting documents.

## F.  Filing and Service Requirements

  1.  *Filing requirements.* Any paper after the complaint that is required to be served—together with a certificate of service—must be filed within a reasonable time after service. FRCP 5(d)(1). Parties shall file all original motion papers, including memoranda of law and supporting affidavits, if any, in accordance with the Administrative Procedures for Electronic Case Filing (General Order #22 (NY R USDCTND CM/ECF)) and/or the case assignment form provided to the parties at the commencement of the litigation. NY R USDCTND L.R. 7.1(b)(1).

  a.  *How filing is made; In general.* A paper is filed by delivering it:

    i.    To the clerk; or

    ii.    To a judge who agrees to accept it for filing, and who must then note the filing date on the paper and promptly send it to the clerk. FRCP 5(d)(2).

  b.  *Electronic filing*

    i.    *Authorization of electronic filing program.* A court may, by local rule, allow papers to be filed, signed, or verified by electronic means that are consistent with any technical standards established by the Judicial Conference of the United States. A local rule may require electronic filing only if reasonable exceptions are allowed. A paper filed electronically in compliance with a local rule is a written paper for purposes of the Federal Rules of Civil Procedure. FRCP 5(d)(3).

      •  All cases filed in this Court may be assigned to the Electronic Case Files System ("ECF") in accordance with the Procedural Order on Electronic Case Filing (General Order #22 (NY R USDCTND CM/ECF)), the provisions of which are incorporated herein by reference, and which the Court may amend from time to time. Copies of General Order #22 (NY R USDCTND CM/ECF) are available at the Clerk's office or at the Court's webpage. NY R USDCTND L.R. 5.1.1; NY R USDCTND Order 25(XII).

      •  The Court may deviate from these Administrative Procedures (NY R USDCTND CM/ECF) in specific cases, without prior notice, if deemed appropriate in the exercise of discretion, considering the need for the just, speedy, and inexpensive determination of matters pending before the Court. NY R USDCTND CM/ECF(2).

    ii.    *Scope of electronic filing.* After January 1, 2004, all documents that attorneys admitted to practice in the Northern District of New York submit for filing shall be filed electronically using the System or shall be scanned and uploaded to the System, no matter when a case was originally filed, unless these Administrative Procedures (NY R USDCTND CM/ECF) otherwise permit or unless the assigned judge otherwise authorizes. An attorney who is not a Filing User by January 1, 2004, must show good cause to the assigned judge to file and serve pleadings and other papers in the traditional manner. NY R USDCTND CM/ECF(2).

iii. *Exceptions and/or waivers from mandatory electronic filing.* The following types of cases and/or documents are not required to be filed electronically:

- If you are seeking to have your complaint filed under seal, please file your complaint and proposed sealing order traditionally at the Clerk's Office. NY R USDCTND CM/ECF(2)(2.1)(1).

- Any document that a party proceeding pro se files. (See NY R USDCTND CM/ECF(12)(12.1) for procedural details). NY R USDCTND CM/ECF(2)(2.1)(2). A non-prisoner who is a party to a civil action and who is not represented by an attorney may file a motion to obtain an Electronic Case Filing (ECF) login and password on a form prescribed by the Clerk's Office. The Pro Se CM/ECF Registration Form shall be submitted with the motion. If during the course of the action an attorney appears on behalf of the pro se party, the Clerk's Office shall terminate the pro se party's registration based upon the attorney's appearance. NY R USDCTND CM/ECF(12)(12.1). Absent permission to file electronically, pro se filers shall file paper originals of all complaints, pleadings, motions, affidavits, briefs, and other documents which must be signed or which require either verification or an unsworn declaration under any rule or statute. The Clerk's Office will scan these original documents into an electronic file in the System but will also maintain a paper file. NY R USDCTND CM/ECF(12)(12.1). A pro se party may also seek permission to receive immediate notice of all public documents filed in their cases. Notices of Electronic Filing (NEF) and attached documents would be transmitted to a non-prisoner pro se party who selects this option. Note: The pro se party would continue to file their documents with the Clerk's Office in paper form. NY R USDCTND CM/ECF(12)(12.1).

- Sealed documents, sealed cases, documents for in camera review, documents lodged with the Court, ex parte documents, confidential agreements, Qui Tam actions and Grand Jury material and warrants must be filed traditionally. (See NY R USDCTND CM/ECF(12)(12.2) for further information the filing of the above-referenced documents). NY R USDCTND CM/ECF(2)(2.1)(3).

- Discovery: In accordance with NY R USDCTND L.R. 26.2, parties shall not file discovery, provided, however, that discovery material to be used at trial or in support of any motion, including a motion to compel or for summary judgment, shall be filed electronically with the Court prior to the trial or with the motion. Any motion pursuant to FRCP 37 shall be accompanied by the electronically filed discovery materials to which the motion relates if those materials have not previously been filed with the Court. NY R USDCTND CM/ECF(2)(2.1)(4).

- Transport Orders: All orders requesting that an incarcerated individual be transported that a judicial officer of the Northern District of New York signs shall be filed traditionally. These Orders will not be filed with the case or uploaded to the docket but rather will be processed in accordance with the procedures that the Clerk of Court promulgates. NY R USDCTND CM/ECF(2)(2.1)(5).

iv. *Filing defined.* Electronic transmission of a document to the System in accordance with these Administrative Procedures, together with the transmission of a Notice of Electronic Filing from the Court, constitutes filing of the document for all purposes of the Federal Rules of Civil Procedure and the Local Rules of Practice for the United States District Court for the Northern District of New York and constitutes entry of the document on the docket that the Clerk's Office keeps under FRCP 58 and FRCP 79. E-mailing a document to the Clerk's Office or to the assigned judge shall not constitute "filing" of the document. NY R USDCTND CM/ECF(4)(4.1).

    v.  *Filing fees.* Any fee required for filing a pleading or paper in this Court is payable to the Clerk of the Court. The Court will not maintain electronic billing or debit accounts for attorneys or law firms. Effective January 1, 2007, payment for filing fees will be mandatory through CM/ECF's Internet Credit Card Payment site--a secure Treasury Site. The Filing User will be prompted to enter either Bank Account Debit (ACH) or credit card information while filing the initial pleading. Any document that requires a filing fee (e.g., Notice of Appeal, Motion for Pro Hac Vice Admission) may also be paid through the federal electronic payment website. NY R USDCTND CM/ECF(7).

    vi.  For more information on electronic filing, refer to NY R USDCTND CM/ECF.

  c.  *E-mail or facsimile filing.* Neither the Court nor the Clerk's Office will accept for filing any facsimile or e-mail transmission without prior authorization from the Court. The party using facsimile or e-mail transmissions to file its papers must accompany any such documents with a cover letter stating that the Court authorized such transmissions and the date on which the Court provided that authorization. Violations of NY R USDCTND L.R. 5.5 subject the offending party to the Court's full disciplinary powers. NY R USDCTND L.R. 5.5.

2.  *Service requirements*

  a.  *Service; When required*

    i.  *In general.* Unless the Federal Rules of Civil Procedure provide otherwise, each of the following papers must be served on every party:

- An order stating that service is required;

- A pleading filed after the original complaint, unless the court orders otherwise under FRCP 5(c) because there are numerous defendants;

- A discovery paper required to be served on a party, unless the court orders otherwise;

- A written motion, except one that may be heard ex parte; and

- A written notice, appearance, demand, or offer of judgment, or any similar paper. FRCP 5(a)(1).

    ii.  *If a party fails to appear.* No service is required on a party who is in default for failing to appear. But a pleading that asserts a new claim for relief against such a party must be served on that party under FRCP 4. FRCP 5(a)(2).

    iii.  *Seizing property.* If an action is begun by seizing property and no person is or need be named as a defendant, any service required before the filing of an appearance, answer, or claim must be made on the person who had custody or possession of the property when it was seized. FRCP 5(a)(3).

  b.  *Service; How made*

    i.  *Serving an attorney.* If a party is represented by an attorney, service under FRCP 5 must be made on the attorney unless the court orders service on the party. FRCP 5(b)(1).

    ii.  *Service in general.* A paper is served under FRCP 5 by:

- Handing it to the person;

- Leaving it: (1) at the person's office with a clerk or other person in charge or, if no one is in charge, in a conspicuous place in the office; or (2) if the person has no office or the office is closed, at the person's dwelling or usual place of abode with someone of suitable age and discretion who resides there;

- Mailing it to the person's last known address—in which event service is complete upon mailing;

- Leaving it with the court clerk if the person has no known address;

- Sending it by electronic means if the person consented in writing—in which event service is complete upon transmission, but is not effective if the serving party learns that it did not reach the person to be served; or

- Delivering it by any other means that the person consented to in writing—in which event service is complete when the person making service delivers it to the agency designated to make delivery. FRCP 5(b)(2).

    iii. *Service of electronically-filed documents.* Service is complete provided all parties receive a Notice of Electronic Filing (NEF), which is sent automatically by email from the Court (see the NEF for a list of who did/did not receive notice electronically). Transmission of the NEF constitutes service upon all Filing and Receiving Users who are listed as recipients of notice by electronic mail. It remains the responsibility of Filing and Receiving Users to maintain current contact information with the court and to regularly review the docket sheet of the case. NY R USDCTND CM/ECF(5)(5.2).

- *Non-filing or receiving users.* Attorneys and pro se parties who are not Filing or Receiving Users must be served with a paper copy of any electronically filed pleading or other document. Service of such paper copy must be made according to the Federal Rules of Civil Procedure and the Local Rules of Practice for the United States District Court for the Northern District of New York. Such paper service must be documented by electronically filing a certificate of service. NY R USDCTND CM/ECF(5)(5.2). A party who is not a Filing User of the System is entitled to a paper copy of any electronically-filed pleading, document, or order. The Filing User must therefore provide the non-Filing User with the pleading or document according to the Federal Rules of Civil Procedure. NY R US-DCTND CM/ECF(5)(5.3).

    iv. *Using court facilities.* If a local rule so authorizes, a party may use the court's transmission facilities to make service under FRCP 5(b)(2)(E). FRCP 5(b)(3).

  c. *Serving numerous defendants*

    i. *In general.* If an action involves an unusually large number of defendants, the court may, on motion or on its own, order that:

- Defendants' pleadings and replies to them need not be served on other defendants;

- Any crossclaim, counterclaim, avoidance, or affirmative defense in those pleadings and replies to them will be treated as denied or avoided by all other parties; and

- Filing any such pleading and serving it on the plaintiff constitutes notice of the pleading to all parties. FRCP 5(c)(1).

    ii. *Notifying parties.* A copy of every such order must be served on the parties as the court directs. FRCP 5(c)(2).

3. *Individual judge practices.* Refer to the Miscellaneous section of this document for information on individual judge practices on filing and serving documents.

## G. Hearings

1. *Hearings, generally*

  a. *Motion days.* Listings of the regularly scheduled motion days for all judges shall be available at each Clerk's office and are available on the Court's webpage. The Clerk shall provide notice of the regular motion days for all judges to the parties at the time an action is commenced. NY R USDCTND L.R. 78.1.

  b. *Return date.* Unless the Court directs otherwise, the moving party shall make its motion returnable at the next regularly scheduled motion date at least thirty-one (31) days from the date the moving party files and serves its motion. The moving party shall select a return date in accordance with the procedures set forth in NY R USDCTND L.R. 7.1(b). If the return date the moving party selects is not the next regularly scheduled motion date, or if the moving party selects no return date, the Clerk will set the proper return date and notify the parties. NY R USDCTND L.R. 7.1.

    i. Information regarding motion dates and times is specified on the case assignment form that the Court provides to the parties at the commencement of the litigation or the parties may obtain this form from the Clerk's office or at the Court's webpage. NY R USDCTND L.R. 7.1.

    ii. The Court hereby directs the Clerk to set a proper return date in motions that pro se litigants submit for filing that do not specify a return date or fail to allow for sufficient time pursuant to NY R USDCTND L.R. 7.1. Generally, the return date that the Clerk selects should not exceed thirty (30) days from the date of filing. Furthermore, the Clerk shall forward a copy of the revised or corrected notice of motion to the parties. NY R USDCTND L.R. 7.1.

c.  *Oral argument.* Due process does not require that oral argument be permitted on a motion and, except as otherwise provided by local rule, the district court has discretion to determine whether it will decide the motion on the papers or hear argument by counsel (and perhaps receive evidence). FPP § 1190; F.D.I.C. v. Deglau, 207 F.3d 153 (3d Cir. 2000).

    i.  The parties shall appear for oral argument on all motions that they make returnable before a district court judge, except motions for reconsideration, on the scheduled return date of the motion. A motion may be disposed of without oral argument as described in NY R USDCTND Order 25, on consideration of a request of any party, or otherwise at the discretion of the presiding judge. Thus, the parties should be prepared to have their motion papers serve as the sole method of argument on the motion. NY R USDCTND L.R. 7.1(h).

    ii.  The parties shall not appear for oral argument on motions that they make returnable before a Magistrate Judge on the scheduled return date of the motion unless the Magistrate Judge sua sponte directs or grants the request of any party for oral argument. NY R USDCTND L.R. 7.1(h).

d.  *Providing a regular schedule for oral hearings.* A court may establish regular times and places for oral hearings on motions. FRCP 78(a).

e.  *Providing for submission on briefs.* By rule or order, the court may provide for submitting and determining motions on briefs, without oral hearings. FRCP 78(b).

2.  *Adjournments of dispositive motions.* After the moving party files and serves its motion papers requesting dispositive relief, but before the time that the opposing party must file and serve its opposing papers, the parties may agree to an adjournment of the return date for the motion. However, any such adjournment may not be for more than THIRTY-ONE (31) DAYS from the return date that the moving party selected. In addition, the parties may agree to new dates for the filing and service of opposition and reply papers. However, the parties must file all papers with the Court and serve them upon the other parties not less than ELEVEN (11) DAYS prior to the newly selected return date of the motion. If the parties agree to such an adjournment, they must file a letter with the Court stating the following: (1) that they have agreed to an adjournment of the return date for the motion, (2) the new return date, (3) the date on which the opposing party must file and serve its opposition papers, and (4) the date on which the moving party must file and serve its reply papers. The parties may not agree to any further adjournment. NY R USDCTND L.R. 7.1(j).

a.  *Procedure when only one party seeks an adjournment.* If one of the parties seeks an adjournment of not more than THIRTY-ONE (31) DAYS from the return date that the moving party selected, but the other parties will not agree to such an adjournment, the party seeking the adjournment must file a letter request with the Court and serve the same upon the other parties, stating the following: (1) that the parties cannot agree to an adjournment, (2) the reason that the party is seeking the adjournment, and (3) the suggested return date for the motion. Within three days of receiving this letter request, the parties who have not agreed to an adjournment may file a letter with the Court and serve the same upon the other parties, setting forth the reasons that they do not agree to the requested adjournment. The Court will then take the request under advisement and, as soon as practicable, will enter an order granting or denying the request and, if granting the request, will set forth new dates for the filing and serving of opposition and reply papers. NY R USDCTND L.R. 7.1(j).

b.  *Procedure when adjournment is more than thirty-one (31) days from the return date.* If any party seeks an adjournment of the return date that is more than THIRTY-ONE DAYS from the return date that the moving party selected, that party must file a letter request with the Court stating the following: (1) why the party needs a longer adjournment and (2) a suggested return date for the motion. The Court will grant such an adjournment only upon a showing of exceptional circumstances. In the alternative or if the Court denies the request for an adjournment, the moving party may withdraw its motion without prejudice to refile at a later date. The moving party must refile its motion within the time frame set in the Uniform Pretrial Scheduling Order unless either the assigned District Judge or the assigned Magistrate Judge has granted an extension of the motion-filing deadline. NY R USDCTND L.R. 7.1(j).

3. *Hearing on FRCP 12 defenses before trial.* If a party so moves, any defense listed in FRCP 12(b)(1) through FRCP 12(b)(7)—whether made in a pleading or by motion—and a motion under FRCP 12(c) must be heard and decided before trial unless the court orders a deferral until trial. FRCP 12(i).

4. *Individual judge practices.* Refer to the Miscellaneous section of this document for information on individual judge practices on hearings.

## H. Forms

### 1. Federal Motion to Dismiss for Lack of Personal Jurisdiction Forms

a. Motion and notice; To dismiss; Defendant not present within state where district court is located. AMJUR PP FEDPRAC § 488.

b. Motion and notice; To dismiss; Lack of jurisdiction over person. AMJUR PP FEDPRAC § 489.

c. Motion and notice; To dismiss; Lack of jurisdiction over person; Ineffective service of process on foreign state. AMJUR PP FEDPRAC § 490.

d. Motion and notice; To dismiss; Lack of jurisdiction over person; Consul not agent of country represented for purpose of receiving service of process. AMJUR PP FEDPRAC § 491.

e. Motion and notice; To dismiss; Lack of jurisdiction over corporate defendant. AMJUR PP FEDPRAC § 492.

f. Motion and notice; To dismiss; International organization immune from suit. AMJUR PP FEDPRAC § 493.

g. Motion and notice; To dismiss; Officer or employee of international organization acting within official capacity; Immune from suit. AMJUR PP FEDPRAC § 494.

h. Motion and notice; To dismiss; Family member of member of foreign mission immune from suit. AMJUR PP FEDPRAC § 495.

i. Motion and notice; To dismiss complaint or, in alternative, to quash service of summons; Lack of jurisdiction over corporate defendant. AMJUR PP FEDPRAC § 496.

j. Motion to dismiss; Lack of personal jurisdiction; No minimum contacts. AMJUR PP FEDPRAC § 497.

k. Affidavit; Of Consul General; In support of motion to dismiss; Consular immunity and lack of authority to act as agent for service of process. AMJUR PP FEDPRAC § 498.

l. Motion to dismiss for lack of personal jurisdiction; Corporate defendant. 2C FEDFORMS § 11:52.

m. Motion to dismiss for lack of personal jurisdiction; By corporate defendant; With citation. 2C FEDFORMS § 11:53.

n. Motion to dismiss for lack of personal jurisdiction; By a foreign corporation. 2C FEDFORMS § 11:54.

o. Motion to dismiss for lack of personal jurisdiction; For insufficiency of service. 2C FEDFORMS § 11:55.

p. Motion to dismiss for lack of personal jurisdiction; Insufficiency of process and insufficiency of service of process. 2C FEDFORMS § 11:56.

q. Motion; To dismiss; Lack of jurisdiction over person of defendant. FEDPROF § 1:910.

r. Opposition; To motion; General form. FEDPROF § 1:750.

s. Affidavit; Supporting or opposing motion. FEDPROF § 1:751.

t. Brief; Supporting or opposing motion. FEDPROF § 1:752.

u. Statement of points and authorities; Opposing motion. FEDPROF § 1:753.

v. Motion to dismiss; Lack of jurisdiction over person of defendant; Short form. FEDPROF § 1:911.

w.  Motion to dismiss; Lack of jurisdiction over person of defendant; Accident in foreign country and defendants have no contacts with forum state. FEDPROF § 1:911.50.

x.  Motion to dismiss; Lack of jurisdiction over corporate defendant. FEDPROF § 1:912.

y.  Motion; To dismiss complaint or, in the alternative, to quash service of summons; Lack of jurisdiction over corporate defendant. FEDPROF § 1:913.

z.  Motion to dismiss complaint; General form. GOLDLTGFMS § 20:24.

# I. Applicable Rules

1. *Federal rules*

   a.  Summons. FRCP 4.

   b.  Serving and filing pleadings and other papers. FRCP 5.

   c.  Constitutional challenge to a statute; Notice, certification, and intervention. FRCP 5.1.

   d.  Privacy protection for filings made with the court. FRCP 5.2.

   e.  Computing and extending time; Time for motion papers. FRCP 6.

   f.  Pleadings allowed; Form of motions and other papers. FRCP 7.

   g.  Disclosure statement. FRCP 7.1.

   h.  Form of pleadings. FRCP 10.

   i.  Signing pleadings, motions, and other papers; Representations to the court; Sanctions. FRCP 11.

   j.  Defenses and objections; When and how presented; Motion for judgment on the pleadings; Consolidating motions; Waiving defenses; Pretrial hearing. FRCP 12.

   k.  Taking testimony. FRCP 43.

   l.  Hearing motions; Submission on briefs. FRCP 78.

2. *Local rules*

   a.  Scope of the rules. NY R USDCTND L.R. 1.1.

   b.  Complex and multi-district litigation. NY R USDCTND L.R. 3.3.

   c.  Service and filing of papers. NY R USDCTND L.R. 5.1.

   d.  Filing by facsimile or e-mail. NY R USDCTND L.R. 5.5.

   e.  Motion practice. NY R USDCTND L.R. 7.1.

   f.  Personal privacy protection. NY R USDCTND L.R. 8.1.

   g.  Request for three-judge court. NY R USDCTND L.R. 9.1.

   h.  Form of papers. NY R USDCTND L.R. 10.1.

   i.  Settlement procedures. NY R USDCTND L.R. 68.2.

   j.  Orders. NY R USDCTND L.R. 77.2.

   k.  Motion days. NY R USDCTND L.R. 78.1.

   l.  Appearance and withdrawal of attorney. NY R USDCTND L.R. 83.2.

   m.  Arbitration. NY R USDCTND L.R. 83.7-1; NY R USDCTND L.R. 83.7-2; NY R USDCTND L.R. 83.7-3.

   n.  Assisted mediation program. NY R USDCTND L.R. 83.8.

   o.  Mediation. NY R USDCTND L.R. 83.11-1; NY R USDCTND L.R. 83.11-3.

   p.  Early neutral evaluation. NY R USDCTND L.R. 83.12-1; NY R USDCTND L.R. 83.12-3.

   q.  Administrative procedures for electronic case filing. NY R USDCTND CM/ECF.

   r.  Case assignment plan for the Northern District of New York. [NY R USDCTND Order 12, as amended by NY ORDER 16-4201, effective March 24, 2015].

s.   Directing the expedited service of the summons and complaint and further directing the completion of FRCP 16 stipulation for the timely progression of civil actions. [NY R USDCTND Order 25, as amended by NY ORDER 16-4187, effective June 23, 2016].

t.   Mandatory mediation program. NY R USDCTND Order 47.

**J.  Miscellaneous**

**NOTE: Individual judges' rules may apply. For available judge-level information, refer to:**

DISTRICT JUDGE MAE A. D'AGOSTINO: [NY R USDCTND D'Agostino-Rules and Practices, as added by NY ORDER 16-4200, effective April 4, 2016].

DISTRICT JUDGE THOMAS J. McAVOY: NY R USDCTND McAvoy-Order.

## Motions, Oppositions and Replies
## Motion for Judgment on the Pleadings

### Document Last Updated September 2016

**A.  Checklist**

(I)   ❑  Matters to be considered by moving party

    (a)   ❑  Required documents

        (1)   ❑  Notice of motion and motion

        (2)   ❑  Memorandum of law

        (3)   ❑  Certificate of service

    (b)   ❑  Supplemental documents

        (1)   ❑  Pleadings

        (2)   ❑  Notice of constitutional question

        (3)   ❑  Nongovernmental corporate disclosure statement

        (4)   ❑  Copies of authorities

        (5)   ❑  Proposed order

        (6)   ❑  Cover letter authorizing e-mail or facsimile filing

        (7)   ❑  Affidavit attesting to failed attempts to file electronically

        (8)   ❑  Notice of conventional filing

        (9)   ❑  CD/ROM with PDF of document(s)

      (10)   ❑  English translation

      (11)   ❑  Courtesy copies

      (12)   ❑  Copies for three-judge court

    (c)   ❑  Timing

        (1)   ❑  After the pleadings are closed—but early enough not to delay trial—a party may move for judgment on the pleadings

        (2)   ❑  The moving party must file all motion papers with the court and serve them upon the other parties not less than thirty-one (31) days prior to the return date of the motion

        (3)   ❑  A written motion and notice of the hearing must be served at least fourteen (14) days before the time specified for the hearing, with the following exceptions: (i) when the motion may be heard ex parte; (ii) when the Federal Rules of Civil Procedure set a different time; or (iii) when a court order—which a party may, for good cause, apply for ex parte—sets a different time

        (4)   ❑  Any affidavit supporting a motion must be served with the motion

(II) ❑ Matters to be considered by opposing party

    (a) ❑ Required documents

        (1) ❑ Opposition

        (2) ❑ Memorandum of law

        (3) ❑ Certificate of service

    (b) ❑ Supplemental documents

        (1) ❑ Pleadings

        (2) ❑ Notice of constitutional question

        (3) ❑ Cross-motion

        (4) ❑ Copies of authorities

        (5) ❑ Cover letter authorizing e-mail or facsimile filing

        (6) ❑ Affidavit attesting to failed attempts to file electronically

        (7) ❑ Notice of conventional filing

        (8) ❑ CD/ROM with PDF of document(s)

        (9) ❑ English translation

      (10) ❑ Courtesy copies

      (11) ❑ Copies for three-judge court

    (c) ❑ Timing

        (1) ❑ The party opposing the motion must file its opposition papers with the court and serve them upon the other parties not less than seventeen (17) days prior to the return date of the motion

        (2) ❑ Except as FRCP 59(c) provides otherwise, any opposing affidavit must be served at least seven (7) days before the hearing, unless the court permits service at another time

        (3) ❑ A party may file and serve a cross-motion (meaning a competing request for relief or order similar to that requested by another party against the cross-moving party) at the time it files and serves its opposition papers to the original motion, i.e., not less than seventeen (17) days prior to the return date of the motion

## B. Timing

1. *Motion for judgment on the pleadings.* After the pleadings are closed—but early enough not to delay trial—a party may move for judgment on the pleadings. FRCP 12(c).

    a. *When pleadings are closed.* FRCP 7(a) provides that the pleadings are closed upon the filing of a complaint and an answer (absent a court-ordered reply), unless a counterclaim, cross-claim, or third-party claim is interposed, in which event the filing of a reply to a counterclaim, cross-claim answer, or third-party answer normally will mark the close of the pleadings. FPP § 1367.

    b. *Timeliness and delay.* Ordinarily, a motion for judgment on the pleadings should be made promptly after the close of the pleadings. Generally, however, a FRCP 12(c) motion is considered timely if it is made early enough not to delay trial or cause prejudice to the non-movant. FPP § 1367.

2. *Timing of motions, generally.* The moving party must file all motion papers with the Court and serve them upon the other parties not less than THIRTY-ONE (31) DAYS prior to the return date of the motion. NY R USDCTND L.R. 7.1(b)(1).

    a. *Motion and notice of hearing.* A written motion and notice of the hearing must be served at least fourteen (14) days before the time specified for the hearing, with the following exceptions:

        i. When the motion may be heard ex parte;

        ii. When the Federal Rules of Civil Procedure set a different time; or

        iii. When a court order—which a party may, for good cause, apply for ex parte—sets a different time. FRCP 6(c)(1).

b.  *Supporting affidavit.* Any affidavit supporting a motion must be served with the motion. FRCP 6(c)(2).

3.  *Timing of opposing papers.* The party opposing the motion must file its opposition papers with the Court and serve them upon the other parties not less than SEVENTEEN (17) DAYS prior to the return date of the motion. NY R USDCTND L.R. 7.1(b)(1).

    a.  *Opposing affidavit.* Except as FRCP 59(c) provides otherwise, any opposing affidavit must be served at least seven (7) days before the hearing, unless the court permits service at another time. FRCP 6(c)(2).

    b.  *Cross-motion.* A party may file and serve a cross-motion (meaning a competing request for relief or order similar to that requested by another party against the cross-moving party) at the time it files and serves its opposition papers to the original motion, i.e., not less than SEVENTEEN (17) DAYS prior to the return date of the motion. NY R USDCTND L.R. 7.1(c).

4.  *Timing of reply papers.* Where the respondent files an answering affidavit setting up a new matter, the moving party ordinarily is allowed a reasonable time to file a reply affidavit since failure to deny the new matter by affidavit may operate as an admission of its truth. AMJUR MOTIONS § 25.

    a.  *Reply papers.* The moving party must file its reply papers, which may not exceed (10) pages with the Court and serve them upon the other parties not less than ELEVEN (11) DAYS prior to the return date of the motion. NY R USDCTND L.R. 7.1(b)(1).

    b.  *Opposition to cross-motion.* The original moving party must file its reply/opposition papers with the Court and serve them on the other parties not less than ELEVEN (11) DAYS prior to the return date of the original motion. NY R USDCTND L.R. 7.1(c).

5.  *Effect of a FRCP 12 motion on the time to serve a responsive pleading.* Unless the court sets a different time, serving a motion under FRCP 12 alters the periods in FRCP 12(a) as follows:

    a.  If the court denies the motion or postpones its disposition until trial, the responsive pleading must be served within fourteen (14) days after notice of the court's action; or

    b.  If the court grants a motion for a more definite statement, the responsive pleading must be served within fourteen (14) days after the more definite statement is served. FRCP 12(a)(4).

6.  *Computation of time*

    a.  *Computing time.* FRCP 6 applies in computing any time period specified in the Federal Rules of Civil Procedure, in any local rule or court order, or in any statute that does not specify a method of computing time. FRCP 6(a).

        i.  *Period stated in days or a longer unit.* When the period is stated in days or a longer unit of time:

            •  Exclude the day of the event that triggers the period;

            •  Count every day, including intermediate Saturdays, Sundays, and legal holidays; and

            •  Include the last day of the period, but if the last day is a Saturday, Sunday, or legal holiday, the period continues to run until the end of the next day that is not a Saturday, Sunday, or legal holiday. FRCP 6(a)(1).

        ii. *Period stated in hours.* When the period is stated in hours:

            •  Begin counting immediately on the occurrence of the event that triggers the period;

            •  Count every hour, including hours during intermediate Saturdays, Sundays, and legal holidays; and

            •  If the period would end on a Saturday, Sunday, or legal holiday, the period continues to run until the same time on the next day that is not a Saturday, Sunday, or legal holiday. FRCP 6(a)(2).

        iii. *Inaccessibility of the clerk's office.* Unless the court orders otherwise, if the clerk's office is inaccessible:

            •  On the last day for filing under FRCP 6(a)(1), then the time for filing is extended to the first accessible day that is not a Saturday, Sunday, or legal holiday; or

- During the last hour for filing under FRCP 6(a)(2), then the time for filing is extended to the same time on the first accessible day that is not a Saturday, Sunday, or legal holiday. FRCP 6(a)(3).

iv. *"Last day" defined.* Unless a different time is set by a statute, local rule, or court order, the last day ends:

- For electronic filing, at midnight in the court's time zone; and
- For filing by other means, when the clerk's office is scheduled to close. FRCP 6(a)(4).

v. *"Next day" defined.* The "next day" is determined by continuing to count forward when the period is measured after an event and backward when measured before an event. FRCP 6(a)(5).

vi. *"Legal holiday" defined.* "Legal holiday" means:

- The day set aside by statute for observing New Year's Day, Martin Luther King Jr.'s Birthday, Washington's Birthday, Memorial Day, Independence Day, Labor Day, Columbus Day, Veterans' Day, Thanksgiving Day, or Christmas Day;
- Any day declared a holiday by the President or Congress; and
- For periods that are measured after an event, any other day declared a holiday by the state where the district court is located. FRCP 6(a)(6).

b. *Computation of electronic filing deadlines.* A document will be deemed timely filed if electronically filed prior to midnight Eastern Time. However, if the time of day is of the essence, the assigned judge may order that the document be filed by a time certain. NY R USDCTND CM/ECF(4)(4.3).

i. *Technical failures.* A Filing User, whose filing is untimely as the result of a technical failure of the Court's CM/ECF site, may seek appropriate relief from the Court. However, Filing Users are cautioned that, in some circumstances, the Court lacks the authority to grant an extension of time to file (e.g., FRCP 6(b) of the Federal Rules of Civil Procedure). NY R USDCTND CM/ECF(10)(10.1).

- *Technical failure of the filing user's system.* Problems with the Filing User's system, such as phone line problems, problems with the Filing User's Internet Service Provider ("ISP"), or hardware or software problems, will not constitute a technical failure under these Administrative Procedures nor excuse an untimely filing. A Filing User who cannot file documents electronically because of a problem on the Filing User's system must file the documents' conventionally along with an affidavit explaining the reason for not filing the documents electronically. NY R USDCTND CM/ECF(10)(10.2).

c. *Extending time*

i. *In general.* When an act may or must be done within a specified time, the court may, for good cause, extend the time:

- With or without motion or notice if the court acts, or if a request is made, before the original time or its extension expires; or
- On motion made after the time has expired if the party failed to act because of excusable neglect. FRCP 6(b)(1).

ii. *Exceptions.* A court must not extend the time to act under FRCP 50(b), FRCP 50(d), FRCP 52(b), FRCP 59(b), FRCP 59(d), FRCP 59(e), and FRCP 60(b). FRCP 6(b)(2).

iii. Refer to the United States District Court for the Northern District of New York KeyRules Motion for Continuance/Extension of Time document for more information on extending time.

d. *Additional time after certain kinds of service.* When a party may or must act within a specified time after service and service is made under FRCP 5(b)(2)(C), FRCP 5(b)(2)(D), FRCP 5(b)(2)(E), or FRCP 5(b)(2)(F), three (3) days are added after the period would otherwise expire under FRCP 6(a). FRCP 6(d).

i. In accordance with FRCP 6(e), service by electronic means is treated the same as service by mail for purposes of adding three (3) days to the prescribed period to respond. NY R

USDCTND CM/ECF(5)(5.4). [Editor's note: the reference to FRCP 6(e) is likely meant to be a reference to FRCP 6(d)].

7. *Individual judge practices.* Refer to the Miscellaneous section of this document for information on individual judge practices on timing of documents.

## C. General Requirements

1. *Motions, generally*

   a. *Requirements.* A request for a court order must be made by motion. The motion must:

      i. Be in writing unless made during a hearing or trial;

      ii. State with particularity the grounds for seeking the order; and

      iii. State the relief sought. FRCP 7(b)(1).

      iv. When a moving party makes a motion based upon a rule or statute, the moving party must specify in its moving papers the rule or statute upon which it bases its motion. NY R USDCTND L.R. 7.1(a)(1).

   b. *Notice of motion.* A party interested in resisting the relief sought by a motion has a right to notice thereof, and an opportunity to be heard. AMJUR MOTIONS § 12.

      i. In addition to statutory or court rule provisions requiring notice of a motion—the purpose of such a notice requirement having been said to be to prevent a party from being prejudicially surprised by a motion—principles of natural justice dictate that an adverse party generally must be given notice that a motion will be presented to the court. AMJUR MOTIONS § 12.

      ii. "Notice," in this regard, means reasonable notice, including a meaningful opportunity to prepare and to defend against allegations of a motion. AMJUR MOTIONS § 12.

   c. *Writing requirement.* The writing requirement is intended to insure that the adverse parties are informed and have a record of both the motion's pendency and the grounds on which the movant seeks an order. FPP § 1191; Feldberg v. Quechee Lakes Corp., 463 F.3d 195 (2d Cir. 2006).

      i. It is sufficient "if the motion is stated in a written notice of the hearing of the motion." FPP § 1191.

   d. *Particularity requirement.* The particularity requirement insures that the opposing parties will have notice of their opponent's contentions. FEDPROC § 62:364; Goodman v. 1973 26 Foot Trojan Vessel, Arkansas Registration No. AR1439SN, 859 F.2d 71, 12 Fed.R.Serv.3d 645 (8th Cir. 1988). That requirement ensures that notice of the basis for the motion is provided to the court and to the opposing party so as to avoid prejudice, provide the opponent with a meaningful opportunity to respond, and provide the court with enough information to process the motion correctly. FEDPROC § 62:364; Andreas v. Volkswagen of America, Inc., 336 F.3d 789, 56 Fed.R.Serv.3d 6 (8th Cir. 2003).

      i. Reasonable specification of the grounds for a motion is sufficient. However, where a movant fails to state even one ground for granting the motion in question, the movant has failed to meet the minimal standard of "reasonable specification." FEDPROC § 62:364; Martinez v. Trainor, 556 F.2d 818, 23 Fed.R.Serv.2d 403 (7th Cir. 1977).

      ii. The court may excuse the failure to comply with the particularity requirement if it is inadvertent, and where no prejudice is shown by the opposing party. FEDPROC § 62:364.

   e. *Order to show cause.* All motions that a party brings by Order to Show Cause shall conform to the requirements set forth in NY R USDCTND L.R. 7.1(a)(1) and NY R USDCTND L.R. 7.1(a)(2). Immediately after filing an Order to Show Cause, the moving party must telephone the Chambers of the presiding judicial officer and inform Chambers staff that it has filed an Order to Show Cause. Parties may obtain the telephone numbers for all Chambers from the Clerk's office or at the Court's webpage. The Court shall determine the briefing schedule and return date applicable to motions brought by Order to Show Cause. NY R USDCTND L.R. 7.1(e).

      i. In addition to the requirements set forth in NY R USDCTND L.R. 7.1(a)(1) and NY R USDCTND L.R. 7.1(a)(2), a motion brought by Order to Show Cause must include an affidavit clearly and specifically showing good and sufficient cause why the standard Notice of Motion procedure cannot be used. The moving party must give reasonable advance notice of the application for an Order to Show Cause to the other parties, except in those circumstances where the movant can demonstrate, in a detailed and specific affidavit, good cause and substantial prejudice that would result from the requirement of reasonable notice. NY R USDCTND L.R. 7.1(e).

   ii.  An Order to Show Cause must contain a space for the assigned judge to set forth:

- The deadline for filing and serving supporting papers,
- The deadline for filing and serving opposing papers, and
- The date and time for the hearing. NY R USDCTND L.R. 7.1(e).

2.  *Motion for judgment on the pleadings.* After the pleadings are closed—but early enough not to delay trial—a party may move for judgment on the pleadings. FRCP 12(c).

   a.  *Relationship to other motions*

     i.  *Common law demurrer.* The motion for judgment on the pleadings under FRCP 12(c) has its historical roots in common law practice, which permitted either party, at any point in the proceeding, to demur to his opponent's pleading and secure a dismissal or final judgment on the basis of the pleadings. FPP § 1367.

- The common law demurrer could be used to search the record and raise procedural defects, or it could be employed to resolve the substantive merits of the controversy as disclosed on the face of the pleadings. FPP § 1367.

- In contrast to the common law practice, the FRCP 12(c) judgment on the pleadings procedure primarily is addressed to the latter function of disposing of cases on the basis of the underlying substantive merits of the parties' claims and defenses as they are revealed in the formal pleadings. FPP § 1367. The purpose of FRCP 12(c) is to save time and expense in cases where the ultimate issues of fact are not in dispute, and to prevent the piecemeal process of judicial determination which prevailed under the old common-law practice. FEDPROC § 62:566.

    ii.  *Motions to dismiss.* While FRCP 12(b) motions to dismiss and FRCP 12(c) motions for judgment on the pleadings are to some extent merely interchangeable weapons in a party's arsenal of pretrial challenges, there are differences in the scope and effect of the two motions. A FRCP 12(b) motion to dismiss is directed solely toward the defects of the plaintiff's claim for relief, without concern for the merits of the controversy, while a FRCP 12(c) motion for judgment on the pleadings at least theoretically requires some scrutiny of the merits of the controversy. FEDPROC § 62:568.

    iii.  *Motion to strike.* The FRCP 12(c) motion also should be contrasted with the motion to strike under FRCP 12(f). The latter motion permits either party to strike redundant, immaterial, impertinent, or scandalous matter from an adversary's pleading and may be used to challenge the sufficiency of defenses asserted by that adversary. The motion serves as a pruning device to eliminate objectionable matter from an opponent's pleadings and, unlike the FRCP 12(c) procedure, it is not directed at gaining a final judgment on the merits, although a FRCP 12(f) motion that succeeds in eliminating the defenses to the action may have that purpose and, in some cases, may have that effect. FPP § 1369.

- If a plaintiff seeks to dispute the legal sufficiency of fewer than all of the defenses raised in the defendant's pleading, he should proceed under FRCP 12(f) rather than under FRCP 12(c) because the latter leads to the entry of a judgment. FPP § 1369.

    iv.  *Motion for summary judgment.* In most circumstances a party will find it preferable to proceed under FRCP 56 rather than FRCP 12(c) for a variety of reasons. For example, the summary judgment procedure is available when the defendant fails to file an answer, whereas technically no relief would be available under FRCP 12(c) because the pleadings have not been closed. If a party believes that it will be necessary to introduce evidence outside the formal pleadings in order to demonstrate that no material issue of fact exists and he is clearly entitled to judgment, it is advisable to proceed directly under FRCP 56 rather than taking the circuitous route through FRCP 12(c). Moreover, the FRCP 12(c) path may present certain risks because the court, in its discretion, may refuse to permit the introduction of matters beyond the pleadings and insist on treating the motion as one under FRCP 12(c) or apply the general motion time period set out in FRCP 6(d), rather than the special time provision in FRCP 56. FPP § 1369.

b. *Bringing a FRCP 12(c) motion.* As numerous judicial opinions make clear, a FRCP 12(c) motion is designed to provide a means of disposing of cases when the material facts are not in dispute between the parties and a judgment on the merits can be achieved by focusing on the content of the competing pleadings, exhibits thereto, matters incorporated by reference in the pleadings, whatever is central or integral to the claim for relief or defense, and any facts of which the district court will take judicial notice. FPP § 1367; DiCarlo v. St. Mary Hosp., 530 F.3d 255 (3d Cir. 2008); Buddy Bean Lumber Co. v. Axis Surplus Ins. Co., 715 F.3d 695, 697 (8th Cir. 2013).

    i. The motion for a judgment on the pleadings only has utility when all material allegations of fact are admitted or not controverted in the pleadings and only questions of law remain to be decided by the district court. FPP § 1367; Stafford v. Jewelers Mut. Ins. Co., 554 Fed. Appx. 360, 370 (6th Cir. 2014).

c. *Partial judgment on the pleadings.* Although not provided for by FRCP 12(c), a party may properly move for partial judgment on the pleadings to further the policy goal of efficient resolution of actions when there are no material facts in dispute. This conclusion has been said to be buttressed by FRCP 56(a), which provides that a party may move for summary judgment "on all or part of the claim." FEDPROC § 62:571.

d. *Granting of a motion for judgment on the pleadings.* The federal courts have followed a fairly restrictive standard in ruling on motions for judgment on the pleadings. FPP § 1368. A motion for judgment on the pleadings is a motion for judgment on the merits, and should only be granted if no material issue of fact remains to be resolved and the movant establishes entitlement to judgment as a matter of law. FEDPROC § 62:569; Great Plains Trust Co. v. Morgan Stanley Dean Witter & Co., 313 F.3d 305 (5th Cir. 2002); Sikirica v. Nationwide Ins. Co., 416 F.3d 214 (3d Cir. 2005). A motion for a judgment on the pleadings must be sustained where the undisputed facts appearing in the pleadings, supplemented by any facts of which the court will take judicial notice, show that no relief can be granted. Judgment on the pleadings is not appropriate where the answer raises issues of fact which, if proved, would defeat recovery. FEDPROC § 62:569.

    i. A motion for judgment on the pleadings admits, for purposes of the motion, the truth of all well-pleaded facts in the pleadings of the opposing party, together with all fair inferences to be drawn therefrom, even where the defendant asserts, in the FRCP 12(c) motion, a FRCP 12(b)(6) defense of failure to state a claim upon which relief can be granted. FEDPROC § 62:570; In re World Trade Center Disaster Site Litigation, 521 F.3d 169 (2d Cir. 2008); Massachusetts Nurses Ass'n v. North Adams Regional Hosp., 467 F.3d 27 (1st Cir. 2006). However, all allegations of the moving party which have been denied are taken as false. FEDPROC § 62:570; Volvo Const. Equipment North America, Inc. v. CLM Equipment Company, Inc., 386 F.3d 581 (4th Cir. 2004). In considering a motion for judgment on the pleadings, the trial court is thus required to view the facts presented in the pleadings and inferences to be drawn therefrom in the light most favorable to the nonmoving party. In this fashion the courts hope to insure that the rights of the nonmoving party are decided as fully and fairly on a FRCP 12(c) motion as if there had been a trial. FEDPROC § 62:570.

    ii. On a motion for judgment on the pleadings, the court may consider facts upon the basis of judicial notice. FEDPROC § 62:570; R.G. Financial Corp. v. Vergara-Nunez, 446 F.3d 178 (1st Cir. 2006). However, a motion for judgment on the pleadings does not admit conclusions of law or unwarranted factual inferences. FEDPROC § 62:570; JPMorgan Chase Bank, N.A. v. Winget, 510 F.3d 577 (6th Cir. 2007).

e. *Joining motions*

    i. *Right to join.* A motion under FRCP 12 may be joined with any other motion allowed by FRCP 12. FRCP 12(g)(1).

    ii.   *Limitation on further motions.* Except as provided in FRCP 12(h)(2) or FRCP 12(h)(3), a party that makes a motion under FRCP 12 must not make another motion under FRCP 12 raising a defense or objection that was available to the party but omitted from its earlier motion. FRCP 12(g)(2).

  f.  *Waiving and preserving certain defenses*

    i.   *When some are waived.* A party waives any defense listed in FRCP 12(b)(2) through FRCP 12(b)(5) by:

- Omitting it from a motion in the circumstances described in FRCP 12(g)(2); or

- Failing to either: (1) make it by motion under FRCP 12; or (2) include it in a responsive pleading or in an amendment allowed by FRCP 15(a)(1) as a matter of course. FRCP 12(h)(1).

    ii.  *When to raise others.* Failure to state a claim upon which relief can be granted, to join a person required by FRCP 19(b), or to state a legal defense to a claim may be raised:

- In any pleading allowed or ordered under FRCP 7(a);

- By a motion under FRCP 12(c); or

- At trial. FRCP 12(h)(2).

    iii.  *Lack of subject matter jurisdiction.* If the court determines at any time that it lacks subject-matter jurisdiction, the court must dismiss the action. FRCP 12(h)(3).

3.  *Opposing papers.* The Federal Rules of Civil Procedure do not require any formal answer, return, or reply to a motion, except where the Federal Rules of Civil Procedure or local rules may require affidavits, memoranda, or other papers to be filed in opposition to a motion. Such papers are simply to apprise the court of such opposition and the grounds of that opposition. FEDPROC § 62:359.

  a.  *Effect of failure to respond to motion.* Although in the absence of statutory provision or court rule, a motion ordinarily does not require a written answer, when a party files a motion and the opposing party fails to respond, the court may construe such failure to respond as nonopposition to the motion or an admission that the motion was meritorious, may take the facts alleged in the motion as true—the rule in some jurisdictions being that the failure to respond to a fact set forth in a motion is deemed an admission—and may grant the motion if the relief requested appears to be justified. AMJUR MOTIONS § 28.

  b.  *Assent or no opposition not determinative.* However, a motion will not be granted automatically simply because an "assent" or a notation of "no opposition" has been filed; federal judges frequently deny motions that have been assented to when it is thought that justice so dictates. FPP § 1190.

  c.  *Responsive pleading inappropriate as response to motion.* An attempt to answer or oppose a motion with a responsive pleading usually is not appropriate. FPP § 1190.

4.  *Reply papers.* A moving party may be required or permitted to prepare papers in addition to his original motion papers. AMJUR MOTIONS § 25. Papers answering or replying to opposing papers may be appropriate, in the interests of justice, where it appears there is a substantial reason for allowing a reply. Thus, a court may accept reply papers where a party demonstrates that the papers to which it seeks to file a reply raise new issues that are material to the disposition of the question before the court, or where the court determines, sua sponte, that it wishes further briefing of an issue raised in those papers and orders the submission of additional papers. FEDPROC § 62:360.

  a.  *Function of reply papers.* The function of a reply affidavit is to answer the arguments made in opposition to the position taken by the movant and not to permit the movant to introduce new arguments in support of the motion. AMJUR MOTIONS § 25.

  b.  *Issues raised for the first time in a reply document.* However, the view has been followed in some jurisdictions, that as a matter of judicial economy, where there is no prejudice and where the issues could be raised simply by filing a motion to dismiss, the trial court has discretion to consider arguments raised for the first time in a reply memorandum, and that a trial court may grant a motion to strike issues raised for the first time in a reply memorandum. AMJUR MOTIONS § 26.

c. *Opposition to cross-motion.* The original moving party may reply in further support of the original motion and in opposition to the cross-motion with a reply/opposition brief that does not exceed twenty-five (25) pages in length, exclusive of exhibits. NY R USDCTND L.R. 7.1(c).

5. *Surreply.* A surreply is not permitted. NY R USDCTND L.R. 7.1(b)(1).

a. *Surreply in support of cross-motion.* The cross-moving party may not reply in further support of its cross-motion without the Court's prior permission. NY R USDCTND L.R. 7.1(c).

6. *Submission of proposed order by prevailing party.* If the assigned judge instructs the prevailing party to do so, the prevailing party shall submit a proposed order which the opposing party has approved and which contains the endorsement of the opposing party: "Approved as to form." NY R USDCTND L.R. 77.2(b). In civil actions where the Court has directed a party to submit an order or judgment, that party shall file all such orders or judgments in duplicate, and the Clerk's entry of such duplicate in the proper record book shall be deemed in compliance with FRCP 79(b). Such party shall also furnish the Clerk with a sufficient number of additional copies for each party to the action, which the Clerk shall mail with notice of entry in accordance with FRCP 77(d). NY R USDCTND L.R. 5.1(b).

a. *Disagreement as to form of proposed order.* When the parties are unable to agree as to the form of the proposed order, the prevailing party shall, on seven (7) days notice to all other parties, submit a proposed order and a written explanation for the form of that order. The Court may award costs and attorney's fees against a party whose unreasonable conduct the Court deemed to have required the bringing of the motion. The provisions of NY R USDCTND L.R. 7.1 shall not apply to such motion, and the Court shall not hear oral argument. NY R USDCTND L.R. 77.2(b).

b. For more information on orders, refer to NY R USDCTND L.R. 77.2.

7. *Sanctions for vexatious or frivolous motions or failure to comply with* NY R USDCTND L.R. 7.1. A party who presents vexatious or frivolous motion papers or fails to comply with NY R USDCTND L.R. 7.1 is subject to discipline as the Court deems appropriate, including sanctions and the imposition of costs and attorney's fees to the opposing party. NY R USDCTND L.R. 7.1(i).

8. *Complex and multi-district litigation.* If the assigned judge determines, in his or her discretion, that the case is of such a complex nature that it cannot reasonably be trial ready within eighteen (18) months from the date the complaint is filed, the assigned judge may design and issue a particularized case management order that will move the case to trial as quickly as the complexity of the case allows. NY R USDCTND L.R. 3.3(a). The parties shall promptly notify the Court in writing if any action commenced is appropriate for multi-district litigation. NY R USDCTND L.R. 3.3(b).

9. *Appearances.* An attorney appearing for a party in a civil case shall promptly file with the Clerk a written notice of appearance; however, an attorney does not need to file a notice of appearance if the attorney who would be filing the notice of appearance is the same individual who has signed the complaint, notice of removal, pre-answer motion, or answer. NY R USDCTND L.R. 83.2(a). For more information, refer to NY R USDCTND L.R. 83.2.

10. *Related cases.* A civil case is "related" to another civil case for purposes of this guideline when, because of the similarity of facts and legal issues or because the cases arise from the same transactions or events, a substantial saving of judicial resources is likely to result from assigning the cases to the same Judge and Magistrate Judge. NY R USDCTND Order 12(G)(2). A civil case shall not be deemed related to another civil case merely because the civil case: (1) involves similar legal issues, or (2) involves the same parties. NY R USDCTND Order 12(G)(3). Presumptively, and subject to the power of a Judge to determine otherwise pursuant to NY R USDCTND Order 12(G)(5), civil cases shall not be deemed to be "related" unless both cases are still pending before the Court. NY R USDCTND Order 12(G)(4).

a. *New filings.* If an attorney or filing party indicates on the Civil Cover Sheet that a case is related to an earlier filed case, the Clerk shall instruct the filing party to file a notice of related cases. The allegedly related cases will be submitted by the Clerk to the Judge to whom the earliest filed case is assigned, who shall advise the Clerk whether such cases are related. NY R USDCTND Order 12(G)(1).

b. *Judicial determination that civil cases are "related."* Except for the cases described in the final sentence of NY R USDCTND Order 12(G)(6), all civil cases shall be randomly assigned when they are filed. Other than the cases described in the final sentence of NY R USDCTND Order 12(G)(6), civil cases shall not be deemed to be "related" for purposes of this guideline at the instance of any litigant or attorney unless and until there has been a determination by a Judge of this Court that the standard of NY R USDCTND Order 12(G)(2) is met. NY R USDCTND Order 12(G)(5).

    i. *Notice of related filing.* Any party may apply for such a determination by filing with the Clerk a notice of related filing, which should include an explanation as to why the standard of NY R USDCTND Order 12(G)(2) is met. A form for this purpose is available on the Court's website. A copy of the notice shall be served on all other parties who have appeared. Such an application must be made after the date when at least a majority of the defendants have been served with the complaint. Before making such an application, the applicant must confer in good faith with all other parties in an effort to reach an agreement on whether or not the case is "related". After such an application is made, any other party may serve and file within seven (7) calendar days a letter of no more than two (2) pages supporting or opposing the application. The application to have the case assigned to another Judge shall be presented to the Judge with the earliest filed case for decision on whether the action(s) should be reassigned as related cases. The Judge with the earliest filed case may then enter an order in the case at bar, either deeming the case to be related and directing the Clerk to reassign the action, or denying the application for reassignment. Any disputes concerning the assignment of related cases will be referred to the Chief Judge for resolution. NY R USDCTND Order 12(G)(5).

  c. For more information on related cases, refer to NY R USDCTND Order 12(G).

11. *Alternative dispute resolution (ADR).* It is the mission of this court to do everything it can to help parties resolve their disputes as fairly, quickly, and efficiently as possible. NY R USDCTND Order 25(VIII).

  a. *Arbitration.* NY R USDCTND L.R. 83.7 governs the consensual arbitration program for referral of civil actions to court-annexed arbitration. It may remain in effect until further order of the Court. Its purpose is to establish a less formal procedure for the just, efficient and economical resolution of disputes, while preserving the right to a full trial on demand. NY R USDCTND L.R. 83.7-1.

    i. *Actions subject to arbitration.* The Clerk shall notify the parties in all civil cases, except as the Local Rules of Practice for the United States District Court for the Northern District of New York otherwise direct, that they may consent to non-binding arbitration under NY R US-DCTND L.R. 83.7. The notice shall be furnished to the parties at pretrial/scheduling conferences or shall be included with pretrial conference notices and instructions. Consent to arbitration under NY R USDCTND L.R. 83.7 shall be discussed at the pretrial/scheduling conference. No party or attorney shall be prejudiced for refusing to participate in arbitration. The Court shall allow the referral of any civil action pending before it to the arbitration process if the parties consent. The plaintiff shall be responsible for securing the execution of a consent form by the parties and for filing the form with the Clerk within fourteen (14) days after the parties receive the form. The parties shall freely and knowingly enter into the consent. NY R USDCTND L.R. 83.7-2.

    ii. *Referral to arbitration.* The Clerk shall refer every action subject to NY R USDCTND L.R. 83.7 to arbitration in accordance with the procedures under NY R USDCTND L.R. 83.7 twenty-one (21) days after the filing of the last responsive pleading or within twenty-one (21) days of the filing of a stipulated consent order referring the action to arbitration, whichever event occurs last, except as otherwise provided. If any party notices a motion to dismiss under the provisions of FRCP 12(a) and/or FRCP 12(b), or a motion to join necessary parties pursuant to the Federal Rules of Civil Procedure prior to the expiration of the twenty-one (21) day period, the assigned judge shall hear the motion and further proceedings under NY R USDCTND L.R. 83.7 shall be deferred pending decision on the motion. If the Court does not dismiss the action on the motion, the Court shall refer the action to arbitration twenty-one (21) days after the filing of the decision. NY R USDCTND L.R. 83.7-3(a). Motions for summary judgment pursuant to FRCP 56 shall be filed and served within twenty-one (21) days following the close of discovery. The filing of a FRCP 56 motion shall defer further proceedings under NY R USDCTND L.R. 83.7 pending decision on the motion. NY R USDCTND L.R. 83.7-3(a).

    • *Relief from referral.* Any party shall request relief from the operation of NY R USDCTND

L.R. 83.7 by filing with the Court a motion for the relief within twenty-one (21) days after entry of the initial stipulated consent order which refers the case for arbitration. The assigned judge shall, sua sponte, exempt an action from the application of NY R USDCTND L.R. 83.7 where the objectives of arbitration would not be realized because (1) the case involves complex or novel legal issues, (2) legal issues predominate over factual issues, or (3) for other good cause. NY R USDCTND L.R. 83.7-3(c).

iii. For more information on arbitration, refer to NY R USDCTND L.R. 83.7.

b. *Mediation.* The purpose of NY R USDCTND L.R. 83.11 is to provide a supplementary procedure to the Court's existing alternative dispute resolution procedures. NY R USDCTND L.R. 83.11 provides for an earlier resolution of civil disputes resulting in savings of time and cost to litigants and the Court without sacrificing the quality of justice rendered or the right of litigants to a full trial on all issues not resolved through mediation. NY R USDCTND L.R. 83.11-1(a). Mediation is a process by which an impartial person, the mediator, facilitates communication between disputing parties to promote understanding, reconciliation and settlement. The mediator is an advocate for settlement and uses the mediation process to help the parties fully explore any potential area of agreement. The mediator does not serve as a judge or arbitrator and has no authority to render any decision on any disputed issue or to force a settlement. The parties themselves are responsible for negotiating any resolution(s) to their dispute. NY R USDCTND L.R. 83.11-1(b).

   i. *Actions subject to mediation.* The Court may refer any civil action (or any portion thereof) to mediation under NY R USDCTND L.R. 83.11: (1) by order of referral; or (2) on the motion of any party; or (3) by consent of the parties. NY R USDCTND L.R. 83.11-3(a).

   - *Withdrawal from mediation.* The parties may withdraw from mediation any civil action or claim that the Court refers to mediation pursuant to NY R USDCTND L.R. 83.11-3 by application to the assigned judge at least ten (10) days prior to the scheduled mediation session. NY R USDCTND L.R. 83.11-3(b).

   ii. *Mandatory mediation program.* The United States District Court for the Northern District of New York has adopted this Mandatory Mediation Plan. The paid Mediation Program is designed to provide quicker, less expensive and potentially more satisfying alternatives to continuing litigation, without impairing the quality of justice or the right to trial. NY R USDCTND Order 47(1)(1.2)(A). This Mandatory Mediation Plan applies to civil actions pending as well as newly filed actions, except as otherwise indicated in NY R USDCTND Order 47. The Local Rules for voluntary mediation will apply only to Pro Se Cases that proceed through the Assisted Mediation Program. NY R USDCTND Order 47(1)(1.2)(B).

   - *Referral into the pilot mandatory mediation program for new cases.* All civil cases shall be referred automatically into the Mandatory Mediation Program. Notice of the Mandatory Mediation requirements will be provided to all parties immediately upon the filing of a complaint and answer or a notice of removal. ADR intervention will be scheduled at the conference held pursuant to NY R USDCTND L.R. 16.1. NY R USDCTND Order 47(2)(2.1)(A). For a list of categories of actions exempted from automatic referral, refer to NY R USDCTND Order 47(2)(2.1)(A).

   - *Referral into the pilot mandatory mediation program for pending cases.* The assigned Judge or Magistrate Judge on any pending civil case may, sua sponte or with status conference, issue an order referring the case into the Mandatory Mediation Program. The order shall specify a date on which the ADR intervention is to be completed. NY R USDCTND Order 47(2)(2.1)(B).

   - *Referral into the pilot mandatory mediation program by stipulation.* A case may be referred into the Mandatory Mediation Program by stipulation of all parties. Stipulations shall be filed and shall designate the time frame within which the ADR process will be completed. Stipulations are presumed acceptable unless the assigned Judge or Magistrate Judge determines that the interests of justice are not served. NY R USDCTND Order 47(2)(2.1)(C).

   - *Relief from referral.* Motions to opt out of the program will be addressed by the assigned

Magistrate Judge at the FRCP 16 conference. NY R USDCTND Order 47(2)(2.2)(A). Opting Out Motions shall be granted only for "good cause" shown. Inconvenience, travel costs, attorney fees or other costs shall not constitute "good cause." A party seeking relief from the Mandatory Mediation Program must set forth the reasons why Mandatory Mediation has no reasonable chance of being productive. NY R USDCTND Order 47(2)(2.2)(B). The assigned Magistrate Judge may, sua sponte, exempt any case from the Court's Mandatory Mediation Program. NY R USDCTND Order 47(2)(2.2)(C).

iii. *Assisted mediation program.* The Court may assign specially trained pro bono Special Mediation Counsel to assist pro se civilian litigants with preparing for and participating in mediation. The Assisted Mediation Program is open to civilian pro se parties to actions in the Northern District of New York. The assigned judge or magistrate judge determines if the case would benefit from mediation and would also benefit from the assignment of Special Mediation Counsel to assist the pro se party with the mediation process. NY R USDCTND L.R. 83.8(a). Appointment of Special Mediation Counsel is in no way guaranteed, even if the action is referred to the court-annexed mediation program. Appointment is at the sole discretion of the presiding judge. NY R USDCTND L.R. 83.8(a).

- *Referral to assisted mediation program.* If the court determines that referral to the Assisted Mediation Program is appropriate, the Court shall enter an order of reference to the Assisted Mediation Program. NY R USDCTND L.R. 83.8(b).

iv. For more information on mediation, refer to NY R USDCTND L.R. 83.11 and NY R USDCTND Order 47.

c. *Early neutral evaluation (ENE).* Early neutral evaluation (ENE) is a process in which parties obtain from an experienced neutral (an "evaluator") a nonbinding, reasoned, oral evaluation of the merits of the case. The first step in the ENE process involves the Court appointing an evaluator who has expertise in the area of law in the case. After the parties exchange essential information and position statements early in the pretrial period (usually within one hundred fifty (150) to two hundred (200) days after a complaint has been filed), the evaluator convenes an ENE session that typically lasts about two hours. At the ENE meeting, each side briefly presents the factual and legal basis of its position. The evaluator may ask questions of the parties and help them identify the main issues in dispute and the areas of agreement. The evaluator may also help the parties explore options for settlement. If settlement does not occur, the evaluator then offers an opinion as to the settlement value of the case, including the likelihood of liability and the likely range of damages. With the benefit of this assessment, the parties are again encouraged to discuss settlement, with or without the evaluator's assistance. The parties may also explore ways to narrow the issues in dispute, exchange information about the case or otherwise prepare efficiently for trial. NY R USDCTND L.R. 83.12-1.

i. *Actions subject to early neutral evaluation.* The Court may refer any civil action (or any portion thereof) to ENE under NY R USDCTND L.R. 83.12: (1) by order of referral; (2) on the motion of any party; or (3) by consent of the parties. NY R USDCTND L.R. 83.12-3(a).

- *Withdrawal from the ENE process.* The parties may withdraw any civil action or claim that the Court has referred to the ENE Process pursuant to NY R USDCTND L.R. 83.12-3 by application to the assigned judge at least ten (10) days before the scheduled evaluation session. NY R USDCTND L.R. 83.12-3(b).

ii. For more information on early neutral evaluation (ENE), refer to NY R USDCTND L.R. 83.12.

12. *Settlement procedures.* On notice to the Court or the Clerk that the parties have settled an action, and upon confirmation of the settlement by all parties, the Court may issue a judgment dismissing the action by reason of settlement. The Court shall issue the order without prejudice to the parties' right to secure reinstatement of the case within thirty (30) days after the date of judgment by making a showing that the settlement was not, in fact, consummated. NY R USDCTND L.R. 68.2(a). If the Court decides not to follow the procedures set forth in NY R USDCTND L.R. 68.2(a), the parties shall file within thirty (30) days of the notification to the Court, unless otherwise directed by written order, such notices, stipulations and/or motions as are necessary to terminate the action. If the required documents are not filed within the thirty (30) day period, the Clerk shall place the action on the dismissal calendar. NY R USDCTND L.R. 68.2(b).

13. *Sanctions and penalties for noncompliance.* Failure of an attorney or of a party to comply with any provision of the Local Rules of Practice for the United States District Court for the Northern District of New York, General Orders of this District, Orders of the Court, or the Federal Rules of Civil Procedure shall be a ground for imposition of sanctions. NY R USDCTND L.R. 1.1(d).

14. *Individual judge practices.* Refer to the Miscellaneous section of this document for information on individual judge practices on general requirements for documents.

## D. Documents

1. *Documents for moving party*

   a. *Required documents*

      i. *Notice of motion and motion.* The Notice of Motion must state the return date that the moving party has selected. NY R USDCTND L.R. 7.1(b)(1). Refer to the General Requirements section of this document for information on the notice of motion and motion.

         • *Order to show cause.* Refer to the General Requirements section of this document for information on bringing a motion by order to show cause.

      ii. *Memorandum of law.* Except as otherwise provided in NY R USDCTND L.R. 7.1(a), all motions. . .require a memorandum of law. NY R USDCTND L.R. 7.1(a). Refer to the Format section of this document for the formatting requirements for memoranda of law.

      iii. *Certificate of service.* Except as otherwise provided in NY R USDCTND L.R. 7.1(a), all motions. . .require. . .proof of service on all the parties. See NY R USDCTND L.R. 5.1(a). NY R USDCTND L.R. 7.1(a). FRCP 5(d) requires that the person making service under FRCP 5 certify that service has been effected. FRCP 5(Advisory Committee Notes). Having such information on file may be useful for many purposes, including proof of service if an issue arises concerning the effectiveness of the service. FRCP 5(Advisory Committee Notes). The party or its designee shall declare, by affidavit or certification, that it has provided all other parties in the action with all documents it has filed with the Court. NY R USDCTND L.R. 5.1(a).

         • Attorneys and pro se parties who are not Filing or Receiving Users must be served with a paper copy of any electronically filed pleading or other document. NY R USDCTND CM/ECF(5)(5.2). Such paper service must be documented by electronically filing a certificate of service. NY R USDCTND CM/ECF(5)(5.2).

   b. *Supplemental documents*

      i. *Pleadings.* In considering a motion for judgment on the pleadings, the trial court is. . .required to view the facts presented in the pleadings and inferences to be drawn therefrom in the light most favorable to the nonmoving party. FEDPROC § 62:570.

         • *Motion treated as one for summary judgment.* If, on a motion under FRCP 12(b)(6) or FRCP 12(c), matters outside the pleadings are presented to and not excluded by the court, the motion must be treated as one for summary judgment under FRCP 56. All parties must be given a reasonable opportunity to present all the material that is pertinent to the motion. FRCP 12(d).

      ii. *Notice of constitutional question.* A party that files a pleading, written motion, or other paper drawing into question the constitutionality of a federal or state statute must promptly:

         • *File notice.* File a notice of constitutional question stating the question and identifying the paper that raises it, if: (1) a federal statute is questioned and the parties do not include the United States, one of its agencies, or one of its officers or employees in an official capacity; or (2) a state statute is questioned and the parties do not include the state, one of its agencies, or one of its officers or employees in an official capacity; and

         • *Serve notice.* Serve the notice and paper on the Attorney General of the United States if a federal statute is questioned—or on the state attorney general if a state statute is questioned—either by certified or registered mail or by sending it to an electronic address designated by the attorney general for this purpose. FRCP 5.1(a).

- *No forfeiture.* A party's failure to file and serve the notice, or the court's failure to certify, does not forfeit a constitutional claim or defense that is otherwise timely asserted. FRCP 5.1(d).

iii. *Nongovernmental corporate disclosure statement*

- *Contents.* A nongovernmental corporate party must file two (2) copies of a disclosure statement that: (1) identifies any parent corporation and any publicly held corporation owning ten percent (10%) or more of its stock; or (2) states that there is no such corporation. FRCP 7.1(a).

- *Time to file; Supplemental filing.* A party must: (1) file the disclosure statement with its first appearance, pleading, petition, motion, response, or other request addressed to the court; and (2) promptly file a supplemental statement if any required information changes. FRCP 7.1(b).

iv. *Copies of authorities.* When serving a pro se litigant with a memorandum of law or any other paper which contains citations to authorities that are unpublished or published exclusively on electronic databases, counsel shall include a hard copy of those authorities. Although copies of authorities published only on electronic databases are not required to be filed, copies shall be provided upon request to opposing counsel who lack access to electronic databases. NY R USDCTND L.R. 7.1(a)(1).

v. *Proposed order.* A document that is submitted in .pdf format cannot be modified; therefore, a proposed order or stipulation must be in a word processing format. The chambers of the assigned judge may request that a proposed order and/or a stipulation be e-mailed to the courtroom deputy for the presiding judge in either WordPerfect or Microsoft Word format. Please attach your proposed order and/or stipulation to an Internet e-mail sent to the appropriate e-mail address listed in NY R USDCTND CM/ECF(8)(8.2). NY R USDCTND CM/ECF(8)(8.2).

vi. *Cover letter authorizing e-mail or facsimile filing.* Neither the Court nor the Clerk's Office will accept for filing any facsimile or e-mail transmission without prior authorization from the Court. The party using facsimile or e-mail transmissions to file its papers must accompany any such documents with a cover letter stating that the Court authorized such transmissions and the date on which the Court provided that authorization. Violations of NY R USDCTND L.R. 5.5 subject the offending party to the Court's full disciplinary powers. NY R USDCTND L.R. 5.5.

vii. *Affidavit attesting to failed attempts to file electronically.* If the Court's CM/ECF site experiences a technical failure, a Filing User may submit documents to the Court that day in an alternate manner provided that the documents are accompanied by the Filing User's affidavit stating that the Filing User attempted to file electronically at least two times in one (1) hour increments after 10:00 a.m. that day. The following methods are acceptable alternate means for filing documents in case of a technical failure: (1) via electronic mail in a PDF attachment sent to the e-mail address for technical failures; or (2) in person, by bringing the document to the Clerk's Office on paper accompanied by a CD/ROM that contains the document in .pdf format. NY R USDCTND CM/ECF(10)(10.1).

- A Filing User who cannot file documents electronically because of a problem on the Filing User's system must file the documents' conventionally along with an affidavit explaining the reason for not filing the documents electronically. NY R USDCTND CM/ECF(10)(10.2).

viii. *Notice of conventional filing.* If the Clerk's Office grants permission to conventionally file the document, the Filing User shall electronically file a notice of conventional filing for the documents. More information regarding this process can be obtained from the Court's web page. NY R USDCTND CM/ECF(4)(4.5).

ix. *CD/ROM with PDF of document(s).* If the Court grants permission to file a document traditionally, the attorney must submit the documents for filing to the Clerk's Office on CD/ROM in .pdf or pdf.A format. NY R USDCTND CM/ECF(2).

x. *English translation.* The Court conducts its reviews and deliberations in English. Unless otherwise directed by the Court, any document that a party transmits to the Court (including one in the record on appeal) that is in a language other than English must be accompanied by an English translation that the translator has certified as true and accurate, pursuant to 28 U.S.C.A. § 1746. NY R USDCTND L.R. 10.1(e). For more information, refer to NY R USDCTND L.R. 10.1(e).

xi. *Courtesy copies.* The Court may require that courtesy copies of electronically filed documents be submitted for its review and may amend these Administrative Procedures (NY R USDCTND CM/ECF) at any time without prior notice. NY R USDCTND CM/ECF(2).

- The parties need not provide a courtesy copy of their motion papers to the assigned judge unless the assigned judge requests a copy. NY R USDCTND L.R. 7.1(b)(1).

xii. *Copies for three-judge court.* On the convening of a three-judge court, the parties shall make three (3) copies of all non-electronically filed pleadings, motion papers, and memoranda of law available to the Clerk for distribution. NY R USDCTND L.R. 9.1.

2. *Documents for opposing party*

a. *Required documents*

i. *Opposition.* Refer to the General Requirements section of this document for information on the opposing papers.

ii. *Memorandum of law.* Except as otherwise provided in NY R USDCTND L.R. 7.1(a), all. . .opposition to motions require a memorandum of law. NY R USDCTND L.R. 7.1(a).

- *Cross-motion brief.* If a party makes a cross-motion, it must join its cross motion brief with its opposition brief, and this combined brief may not exceed twenty-five (25) pages in length, exclusive of exhibits. A separate brief in opposition to the original motion is not permissible. NY R USDCTND L.R. 7.1(c).

- Refer to the Format section of this document for the formatting requirements for memoranda of law.

iii. *Certificate of service.* Except as otherwise provided in NY R USDCTND L.R. 7.1(a), all. . .opposition to motions require. . .proof of service on all the parties. See NY R USDCTND L.R. 5.1(a). NY R USDCTND L.R. 7.1(a). FRCP 5(d) requires that the person making service under FRCP 5 certify that service has been effected. FRCP 5(Advisory Committee Notes). Having such information on file may be useful for many purposes, including proof of service if an issue arises concerning the effectiveness of the service. FRCP 5(Advisory Committee Notes). The party or its designee shall declare, by affidavit or certification, that it has provided all other parties in the action with all documents it has filed with the Court. NY R USDCTND L.R. 5.1(a).

- Attorneys and pro se parties who are not Filing or Receiving Users must be served with a paper copy of any electronically filed pleading or other document. NY R USDCTND CM/ECF(5)(5.2). Such paper service must be documented by electronically filing a certificate of service. NY R USDCTND CM/ECF(5)(5.2).

b. *Supplemental documents*

i. *Pleadings.* In considering a motion for judgment on the pleadings, the trial court is. . .required to view the facts presented in the pleadings and inferences to be drawn therefrom in the light most favorable to the nonmoving party. FEDPROC § 62:570.

- *Motion treated as one for summary judgment.* If, on a motion under FRCP 12(b)(6) or FRCP 12(c), matters outside the pleadings are presented to and not excluded by the court, the motion must be treated as one for summary judgment under FRCP 56. All parties must be given a reasonable opportunity to present all the material that is pertinent to the motion. FRCP 12(d).

ii. *Notice of constitutional question.* A party that files a pleading, written motion, or other paper drawing into question the constitutionality of a federal or state statute must promptly:

- *File notice.* File a notice of constitutional question stating the question and identifying the

paper that raises it, if: (1) a federal statute is questioned and the parties do not include the United States, one of its agencies, or one of its officers or employees in an official capacity; or (2) a state statute is questioned and the parties do not include the state, one of its agencies, or one of its officers or employees in an official capacity; and

- *Serve notice.* Serve the notice and paper on the Attorney General of the United States if a federal statute is questioned—or on the state attorney general if a state statute is questioned—either by certified or registered mail or by sending it to an electronic address designated by the attorney general for this purpose. FRCP 5.1(a).

- *No forfeiture.* A party's failure to file and serve the notice, or the court's failure to certify, does not forfeit a constitutional claim or defense that is otherwise timely asserted. FRCP 5.1(d).

iii. *Cross-motion.* A party may file and serve a cross-motion (meaning a competing request for relief or order similar to that requested by another party against the cross-moving party) at the time it files and serves its opposition papers to the original motion, i.e., not less than SEVENTEEN (17) DAYS prior to the return date of the motion. NY R USDCTND L.R. 7.1(c).

iv. *Copies of authorities.* When serving a pro se litigant with a memorandum of law or any other paper which contains citations to authorities that are unpublished or published exclusively on electronic databases, counsel shall include a hard copy of those authorities. Although copies of authorities published only on electronic databases are not required to be filed, copies shall be provided upon request to opposing counsel who lack access to electronic databases. NY R USDCTND L.R. 7.1(a)(1).

v. *Cover letter authorizing e-mail or facsimile filing.* Neither the Court nor the Clerk's Office will accept for filing any facsimile or e-mail transmission without prior authorization from the Court. The party using facsimile or e-mail transmissions to file its papers must accompany any such documents with a cover letter stating that the Court authorized such transmissions and the date on which the Court provided that authorization. Violations of NY R USDCTND L.R. 5.5 subject the offending party to the Court's full disciplinary powers. NY R USDCTND L.R. 5.5.

vi. *Affidavit attesting to failed attempts to file electronically.* If the Court's CM/ECF site experiences a technical failure, a Filing User may submit documents to the Court that day in an alternate manner provided that the documents are accompanied by the Filing User's affidavit stating that the Filing User attempted to file electronically at least two times in one (1) hour increments after 10:00 a.m. that day. The following methods are acceptable alternate means for filing documents in case of a technical failure: (1) via electronic mail in a PDF attachment sent to the e-mail address for technical failures; or (2) in person, by bringing the document to the Clerk's Office on paper accompanied by a CD/ROM that contains the document in .pdf format. NY R USDCTND CM/ECF(10)(10.1).

- A Filing User who cannot file documents electronically because of a problem on the Filing User's system must file the documents' conventionally along with an affidavit explaining the reason for not filing the documents electronically. NY R USDCTND CM/ECF(10)(10.2).

vii. *Notice of conventional filing.* If the Clerk's Office grants permission to conventionally file the document, the Filing User shall electronically file a notice of conventional filing for the documents. More information regarding this process can be obtained from the Court's web page. NY R USDCTND CM/ECF(4)(4.5).

viii. *CD/ROM with PDF of document(s).* If the Court grants permission to file a document traditionally, the attorney must submit the documents for filing to the Clerk's Office on CD/ROM in .pdf or pdf.A format. NY R USDCTND CM/ECF(2).

ix. *English translation.* The Court conducts its reviews and deliberations in English. Unless otherwise directed by the Court, any document that a party transmits to the Court (including one in the record on appeal) that is in a language other than English must be accompanied by an English translation that the translator has certified as true and accurate, pursuant to 28 U.S.C.A.

§ 1746. NY R USDCTND L.R. 10.1(e). For more information, refer to NY R USDCTND L.R. 10.1(e).

    x.   *Courtesy copies.* The Court may require that courtesy copies of electronically filed documents be submitted for its review and may amend these Administrative Procedures (NY R USDCTND CM/ECF) at any time without prior notice. NY R USDCTND CM/ECF(2).

- The parties need not provide a courtesy copy of their motion papers to the assigned judge unless the assigned judge requests a copy. NY R USDCTND L.R. 7.1(b)(1).

    xi.   *Copies for three-judge court.* On the convening of a three-judge court, the parties shall make three (3) copies of all non-electronically filed pleadings, motion papers, and memoranda of law available to the Clerk for distribution. NY R USDCTND L.R. 9.1.

3.   *Individual judge practices.* Refer to the Miscellaneous section of this document for information on individual judge practices on required documents.

## E. Format

1.   *Form of documents.* The rules governing captions and other matters of form in pleadings apply to motions and other papers. FRCP 7(b)(2). All pleadings and other papers shall be served and filed in accordance with the Federal Rules of Civil Procedure and shall be in the form prescribed by NY R USDCTND L.R. 10.1. NY R USDCTND L.R. 5.1(a).

    a.   *Form, generally.* All pleadings, motions, and other documents that a party presents for filing, whether in paper form or in electronic form, shall meet the following requirements:

        i.   *Font size.* All text, whether in the body of the document or in footnotes, must be a minimum of twelve (12) point type. NY R USDCTND L.R. 10.1(a)(1).

        ii.   *Margins.* All documents must have one (1) inch margins on all four sides of the page. NY R USDCTND L.R. 10.1(a)(2).

        iii.   *Spacing.* All text in the body of the document must be double-spaced. NY R USDCTND L.R. 10.1(a)(3).

- The text in block quotations and footnotes may be single-spaced. NY R USDCTND L.R. 10.1(a)(4).

        iv.   *Page numbering.* Pages must be consecutively numbered. NY R USDCTND L.R. 10.1(a)(7).

        v.   *Circumventing formatting limitations*

- Extensive footnotes must not be used to circumvent page limitations. NY R USDCTND L.R. 10.1(a)(5).
- Compacted or other compressed printing features must not be used. NY R USDCTND L.R. 10.1(a)(6).

    b.   *Additional requirements for paper filing.* Additional requirements for all pleadings, motions, and other documents that a party presents for filing in paper form:

        i.   *Paper size.* All documents must be on eight and one-half by eleven (8-1/2 x 11) inch white paper of good quality. NY R USDCTND L.R. 10.1(b)(1).

        ii.   *Text.* All text must be plainly and legibly written, typewritten, printed or reproduced without erasures or interlineations materially defacing them. NY R USDCTND L.R. 10.1(b)(2).

        iii.   *Ink.* All documents must be in black or blue ink. NY R USDCTND L.R. 10.1(b)(3).

        iv.   *Binding.* Pages of all documents must be stapled (or in some other way fastened) together. NY R USDCTND L.R. 10.1(b)(4).

        v.   *Single-sided paper.* All documents must be single-sided. NY R USDCTND L.R. 10.1(b)(5).

        vi.   *Electronic submission.* The Court, at its discretion, may require the electronic submission of any document in a WordPerfect-compatible format. NY R USDCTND L.R. 10.1(b)(6).

        vii.   *Rejection of document.* The Court may reject documents that do not comply with the above-listed requirements. NY R USDCTND L.R. 10.1(b).

c. *Caption; Names of parties.* Every pleading must have a caption with the court's name, a title, a file number, and a FRCP 7(a) designation. The title of the complaint must name all the parties; the title of other pleadings, after naming the first party on each side, may refer generally to other parties. FRCP 10(a). Each document must contain a caption for the specific case to which it pertains. The caption must include the title of the Court, the title of the action, the civil action number of the case, the initials of the assigned judge(s), and the name or nature of the paper in sufficient detail for identification. If a litigant has more than one action pending in this Court, any and all papers filed in a case must contain and pertain to one civil action number, unless the civil actions have been consolidated by the Court. Any motion or other papers purporting to relate to more than one action will not be accepted for filing and may be stricken by the Court. NY R USDCTND L.R. 10.1(c)(1) shall not apply, as noted in NY R USDCTND L.R. 10.1(c), to notices of change of address filed by attorneys of record and pro se litigants. The parties must separately caption affidavits and declarations and must not physically attach them to the Notice of Motion or Memorandum of Law. NY R USDCTND L.R. 10.1(c)(1).

d. *Paragraphs; Separate statements.* A party must state its claims or defenses in numbered paragraphs, each limited as far as practicable to a single set of circumstances. A later pleading may refer by number to a paragraph in an earlier pleading. If doing so would promote clarity, each claim founded on a separate transaction or occurrence—and each defense other than a denial—must be stated in a separate count or defense. FRCP 10(b).

e. *Adoption by reference; Exhibits.* A statement in a pleading may be adopted by reference elsewhere in the same pleading or in any other pleading or motion. A copy of a written instrument that is an exhibit to a pleading is a part of the pleading for all purposes. FRCP 10(c).

f. *Citation of local rules.* These are the Local Rules of Practice for the United States District Court for the Northern District of New York. They shall be cited as "L.R. ___." NY R USDCTND L.R. 1.1(a).

g. *Acceptance by the clerk.* The clerk must not refuse to file a paper solely because it is not in the form prescribed by the Federal Rules of Civil Procedure or by a local rule or practice. FRCP 5(d)(4).

2. *Form of electronic documents.* All pleadings, motions, and other documents that a party presents for filing, whether in paper form or in electronic form, shall meet the requirements in NY R USDCTND L.R. 10.1(a). NY R USDCTND L.R. 10.1(a). Refer above for more information.

a. *Attachments and exhibits.* A Filing User must submit in electronic form all documents referenced as exhibits or attachments in accordance with the Court's CM/ECF Users Manual unless the Court otherwise orders. A Filing User shall submit as exhibits or attachments only those excerpts of the referenced documents that are directly germane to the matter under the Court's consideration. Excerpted material must be clearly and prominently identified as such. Filing Users who file excerpts of documents as exhibits or attachments under these Administrative Procedures (NY R USDCTND CM/ECF) do so without prejudice to their right to timely file additional excerpts or the complete document. Responding parties may also timely file the complete document or additional excerpts that they believe are directly germane to the matter under the Court's consideration. NY R USDCTND CM/ECF(4)(4.4).

    i. All attachments must be described in sufficient detail so the Court and opposing counsel can easily identify and distinguish the filed attachments. Vague or general descriptions are insufficient (i.e., "Exhibit 1"). Rather, each attachment shall have a descriptive title identifying, with specificity, the document that is being filed (i.e., "Exhibit 12 Mulligan County Fire Investigation Report.") Failure to adequately describe attachments may result in the document being rejected by the Court. NY R USDCTND CM/ECF(4)(4.4).

b. *Large documents.* For information on the electronic filing of large documents, please consult the Court's CM/ECF Users Manual, which is available on the Court's web page. NY R USDCTND CM/ECF(4)(4.5).

    i. A party who believes a document is too lengthy to electronically image, i.e., "scan," may contact the Clerk's Office for permission to file that document conventionally. If the Clerk's Office grants permission to conventionally file the document, the Filing User shall electronically file a notice of conventional filing for the documents. More information regarding this process can be obtained from the Court's web page. Exhibits submitted conventionally shall be served on other parties as if they were not subject to these Administrative Procedures (NY R USDCTND CM/ECF). For a list of hints and tips for scanning large documents, please consult the Court's web page. NY R USDCTND CM/ECF(4)(4.5).

c. *Legibility.* It shall be the Filing User's responsibility to verify the legibility of scanned documents before filing them electronically with the Court. NY R USDCTND CM/ECF(4)(4.6).

d. *Color documents.* Since documents scanned in color or containing a graphic take much longer to upload, Filing Users are encouraged to configure their scanners to scan documents at 300 dpi and preferably in black and white rather than in color. NY R USDCTND CM/ECF(4)(4.7).

e. *Items not in .PDF format.* Parties wishing to file items not amenable to .pdf format (i.e. CD's, DVD's), shall file such items conventionally with the Clerk's Office. The Filing User shall electronically file a notice of conventional filing indicating that these items have been submitted to the clerk and shall serve copies of these items on other parties as if they were not subject to these Administrative Procedures (NY R USDCTND CM/ECF). These item(s) will be maintained by the Clerk's Office until the case is disposed, at which time they will be returned to the filing party for retention consistent with NY R USDCTND CM/ECF(4)(4.9). NY R USDCTND CM/ECF(4)(4.8).

3. *Form of memoranda of law*

a. *Length limitation.* No party shall file or serve a memorandum of law that exceeds twenty-five (25) pages in length, unless that party obtains leave of the judge hearing the motion prior to filing. NY R USDCTND L.R. 7.1(a)(1).

b. *Table of contents.* All memoranda of law shall contain a table of contents. NY R USDCTND L.R. 7.1(a)(1).

4. *Signing of pleadings, motions and other papers*

a. *Signature.* Every pleading, written motion, and other paper must be signed by at least one attorney of record in the attorney's name—or by a party personally if the party is unrepresented. The paper must state the signer's address, e-mail address, and telephone number. FRCP 11(a). Each document must identify the person filing the document. This identification must include an original signature of the attorney or pro se litigant; the typewritten name of that person; the address of a pro se litigant; and the bar roll number, office address, telephone number, e-mail address and fax number of the attorney. Telephone numbers of non-prisoner pro se parties may be provided voluntarily or upon request of the Court. See General Order #22 (NY R USDCTND CM/ECF) for signature requirements. NY R USDCTND L.R. 10.1(c)(2).

i. *Electronic signatures.* Documents filed under an attorney's login and password shall constitute that attorney's signature for purposes of the Local Rules of Practice for the United States District Court for the Northern District of New York and Federal Rules of Civil Procedure, including but not limited to FRCP 11. A pleading or other document requiring an attorney's signature shall be signed in the following manner, whether filed electronically or submitted on disk or CD/ROM to the Clerk's Office: "s/ (attorney name)." The correct format for an attorney signature is found in NY R USDCTND CM/ECF(6)(6.1). NY R USDCTND CM/ECF(6)(6.1).

- *Non-attorney signature.* If an original document requires the signature of a non-attorney, the Filing User may scan the original document containing the original signature(s), then electronically file it on the System. Alternatively, the Filing User may convert the document into .pdf text format and submit the document using "s/" for the signature of the non-attorney. NY R USDCTND CM/ECF(6)(6.2).

- *Multiple signatures.* A document requiring signatures of more than one party must be filed electronically either by (1) submitting a scanned document containing all necessary signatures; (2) representing the consent of the other parties on the document; or (3) in any other manner that the Court approves. NY R USDCTND CM/ECF(6)(6.3).

ii. *No verification or accompanying affidavit required for pleadings.* Unless a rule or statute specifically states otherwise, a pleading need not be verified or accompanied by an affidavit. FRCP 11(a).

      iii.   *Unsigned papers.* The court must strike an unsigned paper unless the omission is promptly corrected after being called to the attorney's or party's attention. FRCP 11(a).

  b.  *Representations to the court.* By presenting to the court a pleading, written motion, or other paper—whether by signing, filing, submitting, or later advocating it—an attorney or unrepresented party certifies that to the best of the person's knowledge, information, and belief, formed after an inquiry reasonable under the circumstances:

      i.   It is not being presented for any improper purpose, such as to harass, cause unnecessary delay, or needlessly increase the cost of litigation;

      ii.   The claims, defenses, and other legal contentions are warranted by existing law or by a nonfrivolous argument for extending, modifying, or reversing existing law or for establishing new law;

      iii.   The factual contentions have evidentiary support or, if specifically so identified, will likely have evidentiary support after a reasonable opportunity for further investigation or discovery; and

      iv.   The denials of factual contentions are warranted on the evidence or, if specifically so identified, are reasonably based on belief or a lack of information. FRCP 11(b).

  c.  *Sanctions.* If, after notice and a reasonable opportunity to respond, the court determines that FRCP 11(b) has been violated, the court may impose an appropriate sanction on any attorney, law firm, or party that violated FRCP 11(b) or is responsible for the violation. FRCP 11(c)(1). Refer to the United States District Court for the Northern District of New York KeyRules Motion for Sanctions document for more information.

5.  *Privacy protection for filings made with the court*

  a.  *Redacted filings.* Unless the court orders otherwise, in an electronic or paper filing with the court that contains an individual's Social Security number, taxpayer-identification number, or birth date, the name of an individual known to be a minor, or a financial-account number, a party or nonparty making the filing may include only:

      i.   The last four (4) digits of the Social Security number and taxpayer-identification number;

      ii.   The year of the individual's birth;

      iii.   The minor's initials; and

      iv.   The last four (4) digits of the financial-account number. FRCP 5.2(a); NY R USDCTND L.R. 8.1; NY R USDCTND CM/ECF(11)(11.2).

      v.   If a home address must be used, use only the City and State. NY R USDCTND L.R. 8.1; NY R USDCTND CM/ECF(11)(11.2).

      vi.   If the victim of a sexual assault must be referenced, redact the name to 'Victim.' NY R USDCTND CM/ECF(11)(11.2); NY R USDCTND L.R. 8.1.

      vii.   In addition, caution shall be exercised when filing documents that contain the following:

         •  Personal identifying number, such as a driver's license number;

         •  Medical records, treatment and diagnosis;

         •  Employment history;

         •  Individual financial information; and

         •  Proprietary or trade secret information. NY R USDCTND L.R. 8.1; NY R USDCTND CM/ECF(11)(11.2).

  b.  *Exemptions from the redaction requirement.* The redaction requirement does not apply to the following:

      i.   A financial-account number that identifies the property allegedly subject to forfeiture in a forfeiture proceeding;

      ii.   The record of an administrative or agency proceeding;

      iii.   The official record of a state-court proceeding;

    iv.   The record of a court or tribunal, if that record was not subject to the redaction requirement when originally filed;

    v.   A filing covered by FRCP 5.2(c) or FRCP 5.2(d); and

    vi.   A pro se filing in an action brought under 28 U.S.C.A. § 2241, 28 U.S.C.A. § 2254, or 28 U.S.C.A. § 2255. FRCP 5.2(b).

    vii.   Transcripts of the administrative record in social security proceedings are exempt from this requirement. State court records and other documents filed in habeas corpus proceedings are exempt from this requirement except for proceedings that involve victims of sex crimes. In habeas corpus cases involving sex crimes, the parties must redact the record and supporting papers, or may move to seal, if appropriate. NY R USDCTND L.R. 8.1.

  c.  *Limitations on remote access to electronic files; Social Security appeals and immigration cases.* Unless the court orders otherwise, in an action for benefits under the Social Security Act, and in an action or proceeding relating to an order of removal, to relief from removal, or to immigration benefits or detention, access to an electronic file is authorized as follows:

    i.   The parties and their attorneys may have remote electronic access to any part of the case file, including the administrative record;

    ii.   Any other person may have electronic access to the full record at the courthouse, but may have remote electronic access only to:

       • The docket maintained by the court; and

       • An opinion, order, judgment, or other disposition of the court, but not any other part of the case file or the administrative record. FRCP 5.2(c).

  d.  *Filings made under seal.* The court may order that a filing be made under seal without redaction. The court may later unseal the filing or order the person who made the filing to file a redacted version for the public record. FRCP 5.2(d); NY R USDCTND L.R. 8.1. For information on sealed matters, refer to NY R USDCTND L.R. 83.13 and NY R USDCTND CM/ECF(12).

  e.  *Protective orders.* For good cause, the court may by order in a case:

    i.   Require redaction of additional information; or

    ii.   Limit or prohibit a nonparty's remote electronic access to a document filed with the court. FRCP 5.2(e).

  f.  *Option for additional unredacted filing under seal.* A person making a redacted filing may also file an unredacted copy under seal. The court must retain the unredacted copy as part of the record. FRCP 5.2(f); NY R USDCTND L.R. 8.1; NY R USDCTND CM/ECF(11)(11.3).

  g.  *Option for filing a reference list.* A filing that contains redacted information may be filed together with a reference list that identifies each item of redacted information and specifies an appropriate identifier that uniquely corresponds to each item listed. The list must be filed under seal and may be amended as of right. Any reference in the case to a listed identifier will be construed to refer to the corresponding item of information. FRCP 5.2(g); NY R USDCTND L.R. 8.1; NY R USDCTND CM/ECF(11)(11.3).

  h.  *Responsibility for redaction.* Counsel is strongly urged to discuss this issue with all their clients so that they can make an informed decision about the inclusion of certain information. The responsibility for redacting these personal identifiers rests solely with counsel and the parties. The Clerk will not review each filing for compliance with NY R USDCTND L.R. 8.1. Counsel and the parties are cautioned that failure to redact these personal identifiers may subject them to the Court's full disciplinary power. NY R USDCTND L.R. 8.1; NY R USDCTND CM/ECF(11)(11.3).

  i.  *Waiver of protection of identifiers.* A person waives the protection of FRCP 5.2(a) as to the person's own information by filing it without redaction and not under seal. FRCP 5.2(h).

  6.  *Individual judge practices.* Refer to the Miscellaneous section of this document for information on individual judge practices on formatting documents.

## F.  Filing and Service Requirements

  1.  *Filing requirements.* Any paper after the complaint that is required to be served—together with a

certificate of service—must be filed within a reasonable time after service. FRCP 5(d)(1). Parties shall file all original motion papers, including memoranda of law and supporting affidavits, if any, in accordance with the Administrative Procedures for Electronic Case Filing (General Order #22 (NY R USDCTND CM/ECF)) and/or the case assignment form provided to the parties at the commencement of the litigation. NY R USDCTND L.R. 7.1(b)(1).

a. *How filing is made; In general.* A paper is filed by delivering it:

    i. To the clerk; or

    ii. To a judge who agrees to accept it for filing, and who must then note the filing date on the paper and promptly send it to the clerk. FRCP 5(d)(2).

b. *Electronic filing*

    i. *Authorization of electronic filing program.* A court may, by local rule, allow papers to be filed, signed, or verified by electronic means that are consistent with any technical standards established by the Judicial Conference of the United States. A local rule may require electronic filing only if reasonable exceptions are allowed. A paper filed electronically in compliance with a local rule is a written paper for purposes of the Federal Rules of Civil Procedure. FRCP 5(d)(3).

- All cases filed in this Court may be assigned to the Electronic Case Files System ("ECF") in accordance with the Procedural Order on Electronic Case Filing (General Order #22 (NY R USDCTND CM/ECF)), the provisions of which are incorporated herein by reference, and which the Court may amend from time to time. Copies of General Order #22 (NY R USDCTND CM/ECF) are available at the Clerk's office or at the Court's webpage. NY R USDCTND L.R. 5.1.1; NY R USDCTND Order 25(XII).

- The Court may deviate from these Administrative Procedures (NY R USDCTND CM/ECF) in specific cases, without prior notice, if deemed appropriate in the exercise of discretion, considering the need for the just, speedy, and inexpensive determination of matters pending before the Court. NY R USDCTND CM/ECF(2).

    ii. *Scope of electronic filing.* After January 1, 2004, all documents that attorneys admitted to practice in the Northern District of New York submit for filing shall be filed electronically using the System or shall be scanned and uploaded to the System, no matter when a case was originally filed, unless these Administrative Procedures (NY R USDCTND CM/ECF) otherwise permit or unless the assigned judge otherwise authorizes. An attorney who is not a Filing User by January 1, 2004, must show good cause to the assigned judge to file and serve pleadings and other papers in the traditional manner. NY R USDCTND CM/ECF(2).

    iii. *Exceptions and/or waivers from mandatory electronic filing.* The following types of cases and/or documents are not required to be filed electronically:

- If you are seeking to have your complaint filed under seal, please file your complaint and proposed sealing order traditionally at the Clerk's Office. NY R USDCTND CM/ECF(2)(2.1)(1).

- Any document that a party proceeding pro se files. (See NY R USDCTND CM/ECF(12)(12.1) for procedural details). NY R USDCTND CM/ECF(2)(2.1)(2). A non-prisoner who is a party to a civil action and who is not represented by an attorney may file a motion to obtain an Electronic Case Filing (ECF) login and password on a form prescribed by the Clerk's Office. The Pro Se CM/ECF Registration Form shall be submitted with the motion. If during the course of the action an attorney appears on behalf of the pro se party, the Clerk's Office shall terminate the pro se party's registration based upon the attorney's appearance. NY R USDCTND CM/ECF(12)(12.1). Absent permission to file electronically, pro se filers shall file paper originals of all complaints, pleadings, motions, affidavits, briefs, and other documents which must be signed or which require either verification or an unsworn declaration under any rule or statute. The Clerk's Office will scan these original documents into an electronic file in the System but will also maintain a paper file. NY R USDCTND CM/ECF(12)(12.1). A pro se party may also seek permission to receive immediate notice of all public documents filed in their cases. Notices of Electronic Filing (NEF) and attached documents would be transmitted to a non-prisoner pro se party who selects this option. Note: The pro se party would continue to file their documents with the Clerk's Office in paper form. NY R USDCTND CM/ECF(12)(12.1).

- Sealed documents, sealed cases, documents for in camera review, documents lodged with the Court, ex parte documents, confidential agreements, Qui Tam actions and Grand Jury material and warrants must be filed traditionally. (See NY R USDCTND CM/ECF(12)(12.2) for further information the filing of the above-referenced documents). NY R USDCTND CM/ECF(2)(2.1)(3).

- Discovery: In accordance with NY R USDCTND L.R. 26.2, parties shall not file discovery, provided, however, that discovery material to be used at trial or in support of any motion, including a motion to compel or for summary judgment, shall be filed electronically with the Court prior to the trial or with the motion. Any motion pursuant to FRCP 37 shall be accompanied by the electronically filed discovery materials to which the motion relates if those materials have not previously been filed with the Court. NY R USDCTND CM/ECF(2)(2.1)(4).

- Transport Orders: All orders requesting that an incarcerated individual be transported that a judicial officer of the Northern District of New York signs shall be filed traditionally. These Orders will not be filed with the case or uploaded to the docket but rather will be processed in accordance with the procedures that the Clerk of Court promulgates. NY R USDCTND CM/ECF(2)(2.1)(5).

iv. *Filing defined.* Electronic transmission of a document to the System in accordance with these Administrative Procedures, together with the transmission of a Notice of Electronic Filing from the Court, constitutes filing of the document for all purposes of the Federal Rules of Civil Procedure and the Local Rules of Practice for the United States District Court for the Northern District of New York and constitutes entry of the document on the docket that the Clerk's Office keeps under FRCP 58 and FRCP 79. E-mailing a document to the Clerk's Office or to the assigned judge shall not constitute "filing" of the document. NY R USDCTND CM/ECF(4)(4.1).

v. *Filing fees.* Any fee required for filing a pleading or paper in this Court is payable to the Clerk of the Court. The Court will not maintain electronic billing or debit accounts for attorneys or law firms. Effective January 1, 2007, payment for filing fees will be mandatory through CM/ECF's Internet Credit Card Payment site--a secure Treasury Site. The Filing User will be prompted to enter either Bank Account Debit (ACH) or credit card information while filing the initial pleading. Any document that requires a filing fee (e.g., Notice of Appeal, Motion for Pro Hac Vice Admission) may also be paid through the federal electronic payment website. NY R USDCTND CM/ECF(7).

vi. For more information on electronic filing, refer to NY R USDCTND CM/ECF.

c. *E-mail or facsimile filing.* Neither the Court nor the Clerk's Office will accept for filing any facsimile or e-mail transmission without prior authorization from the Court. The party using facsimile or e-mail transmissions to file its papers must accompany any such documents with a cover letter stating that the Court authorized such transmissions and the date on which the Court provided that authorization. Violations of NY R USDCTND L.R. 5.5 subject the offending party to the Court's full disciplinary powers. NY R USDCTND L.R. 5.5.

2. *Service requirements*

   a. *Service; When required*

      i. *In general.* Unless the Federal Rules of Civil Procedure provide otherwise, each of the following papers must be served on every party:

         - An order stating that service is required;

         - A pleading filed after the original complaint, unless the court orders otherwise under FRCP 5(c) because there are numerous defendants;

- A discovery paper required to be served on a party, unless the court orders otherwise;

- A written motion, except one that may be heard ex parte; and

- A written notice, appearance, demand, or offer of judgment, or any similar paper. FRCP 5(a)(1).

ii. *If a party fails to appear.* No service is required on a party who is in default for failing to appear. But a pleading that asserts a new claim for relief against such a party must be served on that party under FRCP 4. FRCP 5(a)(2).

iii. *Seizing property.* If an action is begun by seizing property and no person is or need be named as a defendant, any service required before the filing of an appearance, answer, or claim must be made on the person who had custody or possession of the property when it was seized. FRCP 5(a)(3).

b. *Service; How made*

i. *Serving an attorney.* If a party is represented by an attorney, service under FRCP 5 must be made on the attorney unless the court orders service on the party. FRCP 5(b)(1).

ii. *Service in general.* A paper is served under FRCP 5 by:

- Handing it to the person;

- Leaving it: (1) at the person's office with a clerk or other person in charge or, if no one is in charge, in a conspicuous place in the office; or (2) if the person has no office or the office is closed, at the person's dwelling or usual place of abode with someone of suitable age and discretion who resides there;

- Mailing it to the person's last known address—in which event service is complete upon mailing;

- Leaving it with the court clerk if the person has no known address;

- Sending it by electronic means if the person consented in writing—in which event service is complete upon transmission, but is not effective if the serving party learns that it did not reach the person to be served; or

- Delivering it by any other means that the person consented to in writing—in which event service is complete when the person making service delivers it to the agency designated to make delivery. FRCP 5(b)(2).

iii. *Service of electronically-filed documents.* Service is complete provided all parties receive a Notice of Electronic Filing (NEF), which is sent automatically by email from the Court (see the NEF for a list of who did/did not receive notice electronically). Transmission of the NEF constitutes service upon all Filing and Receiving Users who are listed as recipients of notice by electronic mail. It remains the responsibility of Filing and Receiving Users to maintain current contact information with the court and to regularly review the docket sheet of the case. NY R USDCTND CM/ECF(5)(5.2).

- *Non-filing or receiving users.* Attorneys and pro se parties who are not Filing or Receiving Users must be served with a paper copy of any electronically filed pleading or other document. Service of such paper copy must be made according to the Federal Rules of Civil Procedure and the Local Rules of Practice for the United States District Court for the Northern District of New York. Such paper service must be documented by electronically filing a certificate of service. NY R USDCTND CM/ECF(5)(5.2). A party who is not a Filing User of the System is entitled to a paper copy of any electronically-filed pleading, document, or order. The Filing User must therefore provide the non-Filing User with the pleading or document according to the Federal Rules of Civil Procedure. NY R US-DCTND CM/ECF(5)(5.3).

iv. *Using court facilities.* If a local rule so authorizes, a party may use the court's transmission facilities to make service under FRCP 5(b)(2)(E). FRCP 5(b)(3).

c. *Serving numerous defendants*

    i. *In general.* If an action involves an unusually large number of defendants, the court may, on motion or on its own, order that:

- Defendants' pleadings and replies to them need not be served on other defendants;

- Any crossclaim, counterclaim, avoidance, or affirmative defense in those pleadings and replies to them will be treated as denied or avoided by all other parties; and

- Filing any such pleading and serving it on the plaintiff constitutes notice of the pleading to all parties. FRCP 5(c)(1).

    ii. *Notifying parties.* A copy of every such order must be served on the parties as the court directs. FRCP 5(c)(2).

3. *Individual judge practices.* Refer to the Miscellaneous section of this document for information on individual judge practices on filing and serving documents.

## G. Hearings

1. *Hearings, generally*

  a. *Motion days.* Listings of the regularly scheduled motion days for all judges shall be available at each Clerk's office and are available on the Court's webpage. The Clerk shall provide notice of the regular motion days for all judges to the parties at the time an action is commenced. NY R USDCTND L.R. 78.1.

  b. *Return date.* Unless the Court directs otherwise, the moving party shall make its motion returnable at the next regularly scheduled motion date at least thirty-one (31) days from the date the moving party files and serves its motion. The moving party shall select a return date in accordance with the procedures set forth in NY R USDCTND L.R. 7.1(b). If the return date the moving party selects is not the next regularly scheduled motion date, or if the moving party selects no return date, the Clerk will set the proper return date and notify the parties. NY R USDCTND L.R. 7.1.

    i. Information regarding motion dates and times is specified on the case assignment form that the Court provides to the parties at the commencement of the litigation or the parties may obtain this form from the Clerk's office or at the Court's webpage. NY R USDCTND L.R. 7.1.

    ii. The Court hereby directs the Clerk to set a proper return date in motions that pro se litigants submit for filing that do not specify a return date or fail to allow for sufficient time pursuant to NY R USDCTND L.R. 7.1. Generally, the return date that the Clerk selects should not exceed thirty (30) days from the date of filing. Furthermore, the Clerk shall forward a copy of the revised or corrected notice of motion to the parties. NY R USDCTND L.R. 7.1.

  c. *Oral argument.* Due process does not require that oral argument be permitted on a motion and, except as otherwise provided by local rule, the district court has discretion to determine whether it will decide the motion on the papers or hear argument by counsel (and perhaps receive evidence). FPP § 1190; F.D.I.C. v. Deglau, 207 F.3d 153 (3d Cir. 2000).

    i. The parties shall appear for oral argument on all motions that they make returnable before a district court judge, except motions for reconsideration, on the scheduled return date of the motion. A motion may be disposed of without oral argument as described in NY R USDCTND Order 25, on consideration of a request of any party, or otherwise at the discretion of the presiding judge. Thus, the parties should be prepared to have their motion papers serve as the sole method of argument on the motion. NY R USDCTND L.R. 7.1(h).

    ii. The parties shall not appear for oral argument on motions that they make returnable before a Magistrate Judge on the scheduled return date of the motion unless the Magistrate Judge sua sponte directs or grants the request of any party for oral argument. NY R USDCTND L.R. 7.1(h).

  d. *Providing a regular schedule for oral hearings.* A court may establish regular times and places for oral hearings on motions. FRCP 78(a).

  e. *Providing for submission on briefs.* By rule or order, the court may provide for submitting and determining motions on briefs, without oral hearings. FRCP 78(b).

2. *Adjournments of dispositive motions.* After the moving party files and serves its motion papers requesting dispositive relief, but before the time that the opposing party must file and serve its opposing papers, the parties may agree to an adjournment of the return date for the motion. However, any such adjournment may not be for more than THIRTY-ONE (31) DAYS from the return date that the moving party selected. In addition, the parties may agree to new dates for the filing and service of opposition and reply papers. However, the parties must file all papers with the Court and serve them upon the other parties not less than ELEVEN (11) DAYS prior to the newly selected return date of the motion. If the parties agree to such an adjournment, they must file a letter with the Court stating the following: (1) that they have agreed to an adjournment of the return date for the motion, (2) the new return date, (3) the date on which the opposing party must file and serve its opposition papers, and (4) the date on which the moving party must file and serve its reply papers. The parties may not agree to any further adjournment. NY R USDCTND L.R. 7.1(j).

 a. *Procedure when only one party seeks an adjournment.* If one of the parties seeks an adjournment of not more than THIRTY-ONE (31) DAYS from the return date that the moving party selected, but the other parties will not agree to such an adjournment, the party seeking the adjournment must file a letter request with the Court and serve the same upon the other parties, stating the following: (1) that the parties cannot agree to an adjournment, (2) the reason that the party is seeking the adjournment, and (3) the suggested return date for the motion. Within three days of receiving this letter request, the parties who have not agreed to an adjournment may file a letter with the Court and serve the same upon the other parties, setting forth the reasons that they do not agree to the requested adjournment. The Court will then take the request under advisement and, as soon as practicable, will enter an order granting or denying the request and, if granting the request, will set forth new dates for the filing and serving of opposition and reply papers. NY R USDCTND L.R. 7.1(j).

 b. *Procedure when adjournment is more than thirty-one (31) days from the return date.* If any party seeks an adjournment of the return date that is more than THIRTY-ONE DAYS from the return date that the moving party selected, that party must file a letter request with the Court stating the following: (1) why the party needs a longer adjournment and (2) a suggested return date for the motion. The Court will grant such an adjournment only upon a showing of exceptional circumstances. In the alternative or if the Court denies the request for an adjournment, the moving party may withdraw its motion without prejudice to refile at a later date. The moving party must refile its motion within the time frame set in the Uniform Pretrial Scheduling Order unless either the assigned District Judge or the assigned Magistrate Judge has granted an extension of the motion-filing deadline. NY R USDCTND L.R. 7.1(j).

3. *Individual judge practices.* Refer to the Miscellaneous section of this document for information on individual judge practices on hearings.

## H. Forms

### 1. Federal Motion for Judgment on the Pleadings Forms

 a. Motion and notice; For judgment on pleadings. AMJUR PP FEDPRAC § 532.

 b. Countermotion and notice; For judgment on pleadings; By defendants. AMJUR PP FEDPRAC § 533.

 c. Order; For judgment on pleadings; In favor of plaintiff. AMJUR PP FEDPRAC § 534.

 d. Order; For judgment on pleadings; In favor of defendant. AMJUR PP FEDPRAC § 535.

 e. Motion for judgment on the pleadings. 2C FEDFORMS § 11:131.

 f. Motion for judgment on the pleadings; Alternate wording. 2C FEDFORMS § 11:132.

 g. Motion for judgment on the pleadings; Long version. 2C FEDFORMS § 11:133.

 h. Motion for judgment on the pleadings; Several grounds. 2C FEDFORMS § 11:134.

 i. Notice of motion and motion for judgment on the pleadings. 2C FEDFORMS § 11:135.

 j. Notice of motion for judgment on the pleadings (partial) or for partial summary judgment. 2C FEDFORMS § 11:136.

 k. Order granting judgment on the pleadings. 2C FEDFORMS § 11:137.

l.   Order granting judgment on the pleadings; Motion by plaintiff. 2C FEDFORMS § 11:138.

m.   Judgment on the pleadings. 2C FEDFORMS § 11:139.

n.   Motion; General form. FEDPROF § 1:746.

o.   Notice; Of motion; General form. FEDPROF § 1:747.

p.   Notice; Of motion; With costs of motion. FEDPROF § 1:748.

q.   Notice; Of motion; Containing motion. FEDPROF § 1:749.

r.   Opposition; To motion; General form. FEDPROF § 1:750.

s.   Affidavit; Supporting or opposing motion. FEDPROF § 1:751.

t.   Brief; Supporting or opposing motion. FEDPROF § 1:752.

u.   Statement of points and authorities; Opposing motion. FEDPROF § 1:753.

v.   Motion; For judgment on the pleadings. FEDPROF § 1:1295.

w.   Order; For judgment on the pleadings; In favor of plaintiff. FEDPROF § 1:1296.

x.   Order; For judgment on the pleadings; In favor of defendant. FEDPROF § 1:1297.

y.   Motion for judgment on pleadings; Plaintiff. GOLDLTGFMS § 20:38.

z.   Motion for judgment on pleadings; Defendant. GOLDLTGFMS § 20:39.

## I. Applicable Rules

### 1. *Federal rules*

a.   Serving and filing pleadings and other papers. FRCP 5.

b.   Constitutional challenge to a statute; Notice, certification, and intervention. FRCP 5.1.

c.   Privacy protection for filings made with the court. FRCP 5.2.

d.   Computing and extending time; Time for motion papers. FRCP 6.

e.   Pleadings allowed; Form of motions and other papers. FRCP 7.

f.   Disclosure statement. FRCP 7.1.

g.   Form of pleadings. FRCP 10.

h.   Signing pleadings, motions, and other papers; Representations to the court; Sanctions. FRCP 11.

i.   Defenses and objections; When and how presented; Motion for judgment on the pleadings; Consolidating motions; Waiving defenses; Pretrial hearing. FRCP 12.

j.   Hearing motions; Submission on briefs. FRCP 78.

### 2. *Local rules*

a.   Scope of the rules. NY R USDCTND L.R. 1.1.

b.   Complex and multi-district litigation. NY R USDCTND L.R. 3.3.

c.   Service and filing of papers. NY R USDCTND L.R. 5.1.

d.   Filing by facsimile or e-mail. NY R USDCTND L.R. 5.5.

e.   Motion practice. NY R USDCTND L.R. 7.1.

f.   Personal privacy protection. NY R USDCTND L.R. 8.1.

g.   Request for three-judge court. NY R USDCTND L.R. 9.1.

h.   Form of papers. NY R USDCTND L.R. 10.1.

i.   Settlement procedures. NY R USDCTND L.R. 68.2.

j.   Orders. NY R USDCTND L.R. 77.2.

k.   Motion days. NY R USDCTND L.R. 78.1.

l.   Appearance and withdrawal of attorney. NY R USDCTND L.R. 83.2.

m. Arbitration. NY R USDCTND L.R. 83.7-1; NY R USDCTND L.R. 83.7-2; NY R USDCTND L.R. 83.7-3.

n. Assisted mediation program. NY R USDCTND L.R. 83.8.

o. Mediation. NY R USDCTND L.R. 83.11-1; NY R USDCTND L.R. 83.11-3.

p. Early neutral evaluation. NY R USDCTND L.R. 83.12-1; NY R USDCTND L.R. 83.12-3.

q. Administrative procedures for electronic case filing. NY R USDCTND CM/ECF.

r. Case assignment plan for the Northern District of New York. [NY R USDCTND Order 12, as amended by NY ORDER 16-4201, effective March 24, 2015].

s. Directing the expedited service of the summons and complaint and further directing the completion of FRCP 16 stipulation for the timely progression of civil actions. [NY R USDCTND Order 25, as amended by NY ORDER 16-4187, effective June 23, 2016].

t. Mandatory mediation program. NY R USDCTND Order 47.

## J. Miscellaneous

**NOTE: Individual judges' rules may apply. For available judge-level information, refer to:**

DISTRICT JUDGE MAE A. D'AGOSTINO: [NY R USDCTND D'Agostino-Rules and Practices, as added by NY ORDER 16-4200, effective April 4, 2016].

DISTRICT JUDGE THOMAS J. McAVOY: NY R USDCTND McAvoy-Order.

# Requests, Notices and Applications
# Interrogatories

**Document Last Updated September 2016**

## A. Checklist

(I) ❏ Matters to be considered by requesting party

    (a) ❏ Required documents

        (1) ❏ Interrogatories

    (b) ❏ Supplemental documents

        (1) ❏ Certificate of service

    (c) ❏ Timing

        (1) ❏ A party may not seek discovery from any source before the parties have conferred as required by FRCP 26(f), except in a proceeding exempted from initial disclosure under FRCP 26(a)(1)(B), or when authorized by the Federal Rules of Civil Procedure, by stipulation, or by court order

(II) ❏ Matters to be considered by responding party

    (a) ❏ Required documents

        (1) ❏ Response to interrogatories

    (b) ❏ Supplemental documents

        (1) ❏ Certificate of service

    (c) ❏ Timing

        (1) ❏ The responding party must serve its answers and any objections within thirty (30) days after being served with the interrogatories

## B. Timing

1. *Interrogatories.* FRCP 33(a) contains no limit on when interrogatories may first be served. FPP § 2170. FRCP 33 is also silent on how late in a case interrogatories may be served. But FRCP 16(b)(3)(A) provides

that the scheduling order in the case "must limit the time to . . . complete discovery." Although the scheduling order requirement does not apply to cases exempted by local rule, ordinarily there should be a scheduling order that sets a discovery cutoff. FPP § 2170.

2. *Timing of discovery, generally.* A party may not seek discovery from any source before the parties have conferred as required by FRCP 26(f), except in a proceeding exempted from initial disclosure under FRCP 26(a)(1)(B), or when authorized by the Federal Rules of Civil Procedure, by stipulation, or by court order. FRCP 26(d)(1). FRCP 26(d), which prohibits discovery prior to a meeting and conference between the parties, and FRCP 26(f), which directs parties to meet and confer with each other relative to the nature and basis of claims and defenses to a lawsuit, shall not apply to any action in which a party is incarcerated. NY R USDCTND L.R. 26.4.

3. *Discovery cut-off.* The "discovery cut-off" is that date by which all responses to written discovery, including requests for admissions, shall be due according to the Federal Rules of Civil Procedure and by which all depositions shall be concluded. Counsel are advised to initiate discovery requests and notice depositions sufficiently in advance of the cut-off date to comply with NY R USDCTND L.R. 16.2. Discovery requests that call for responses or scheduled depositions after the discovery cut-off will not be enforceable except by order of the Court for good cause shown. Parties shall file and serve motions to compel discovery no later than fourteen (14) days after the discovery cut-off. See NY R USDCTND L.R. 7.1(d)(8). NY R USDCTND L.R. 16.2.

4. *Computation of time*

   a. *Computing time.* FRCP 6 applies in computing any time period specified in the Federal Rules of Civil Procedure, in any local rule or court order, or in any statute that does not specify a method of computing time. FRCP 6(a).

      i. *Period stated in days or a longer unit.* When the period is stated in days or a longer unit of time:

         • Exclude the day of the event that triggers the period;

         • Count every day, including intermediate Saturdays, Sundays, and legal holidays; and

         • Include the last day of the period, but if the last day is a Saturday, Sunday, or legal holiday, the period continues to run until the end of the next day that is not a Saturday, Sunday, or legal holiday. FRCP 6(a)(1).

      ii. *Period stated in hours.* When the period is stated in hours:

         • Begin counting immediately on the occurrence of the event that triggers the period;

         • Count every hour, including hours during intermediate Saturdays, Sundays, and legal holidays; and

         • If the period would end on a Saturday, Sunday, or legal holiday, the period continues to run until the same time on the next day that is not a Saturday, Sunday, or legal holiday. FRCP 6(a)(2).

      iii. *Inaccessibility of the clerk's office.* Unless the court orders otherwise, if the clerk's office is inaccessible:

         • On the last day for filing under FRCP 6(a)(1), then the time for filing is extended to the first accessible day that is not a Saturday, Sunday, or legal holiday; or

         • During the last hour for filing under FRCP 6(a)(2), then the time for filing is extended to the same time on the first accessible day that is not a Saturday, Sunday, or legal holiday. FRCP 6(a)(3).

      iv. *"Last day" defined.* Unless a different time is set by a statute, local rule, or court order, the last day ends:

         • For electronic filing, at midnight in the court's time zone; and

         • For filing by other means, when the clerk's office is scheduled to close. FRCP 6(a)(4).

      v. *"Next day" defined.* The "next day" is determined by continuing to count forward when the period is measured after an event and backward when measured before an event. FRCP 6(a)(5).

vi. *"Legal holiday" defined.* "Legal holiday" means:

- The day set aside by statute for observing New Year's Day, Martin Luther King Jr.'s Birthday, Washington's Birthday, Memorial Day, Independence Day, Labor Day, Columbus Day, Veterans' Day, Thanksgiving Day, or Christmas Day;

- Any day declared a holiday by the President or Congress; and

- For periods that are measured after an event, any other day declared a holiday by the state where the district court is located. FRCP 6(a)(6).

b. *Computation of electronic filing deadlines.* A document will be deemed timely filed if electronically filed prior to midnight Eastern Time. However, if the time of day is of the essence, the assigned judge may order that the document be filed by a time certain. NY R USDCTND CM/ECF(4)(4.3).

i. *Technical failures.* A Filing User, whose filing is untimely as the result of a technical failure of the Court's CM/ECF site, may seek appropriate relief from the Court. However, Filing Users are cautioned that, in some circumstances, the Court lacks the authority to grant an extension of time to file (e.g., FRCP 6(b) of the Federal Rules of Civil Procedure). NY R USDCTND CM/ECF(10)(10.1).

- *Technical failure of the filing user's system.* Problems with the Filing User's system, such as phone line problems, problems with the Filing User's Internet Service Provider ("ISP"), or hardware or software problems, will not constitute a technical failure under these Administrative Procedures nor excuse an untimely filing. A Filing User who cannot file documents electronically because of a problem on the Filing User's system must file the documents' conventionally along with an affidavit explaining the reason for not filing the documents electronically. NY R USDCTND CM/ECF(10)(10.2).

c. *Extending time*

i. *In general.* When an act may or must be done within a specified time, the court may, for good cause, extend the time:

- With or without motion or notice if the court acts, or if a request is made, before the original time or its extension expires; or

- On motion made after the time has expired if the party failed to act because of excusable neglect. FRCP 6(b)(1).

ii. *Exceptions.* A court must not extend the time to act under FRCP 50(b), FRCP 50(d), FRCP 52(b), FRCP 59(b), FRCP 59(d), FRCP 59(e), and FRCP 60(b). FRCP 6(b)(2).

iii. Refer to the United States District Court for the Northern District of New York KeyRules Motion for Continuance/Extension of Time document for more information on extending time.

d. *Additional time after certain kinds of service.* When a party may or must act within a specified time after service and service is made under FRCP 5(b)(2)(C), FRCP 5(b)(2)(D), FRCP 5(b)(2)(E), or FRCP 5(b)(2)(F), three (3) days are added after the period would otherwise expire under FRCP 6(a). FRCP 6(d).

i. In accordance with FRCP 6(e), service by electronic means is treated the same as service by mail for purposes of adding three (3) days to the prescribed period to respond. NY R USDCTND CM/ECF(5)(5.4). [Editor's note: the reference to FRCP 6(e) is likely meant to be a reference to FRCP 6(d)].

5. *Individual judge practices.* Refer to the Miscellaneous section of this document for information on individual judge practices on timing of documents.

## C. General Requirements

1. *General provisions governing discovery*

a. *Discovery scope and limits*

i. *Scope in general.* Unless otherwise limited by court order, the scope of discovery is as follows: Parties may obtain discovery regarding any nonprivileged matter that is relevant to any party's claim or defense and proportional to the needs of the case, considering the importance of the issues at stake in the action, the amount in controversy, the parties' relative access to relevant information, the parties' resources, the importance of the discovery in resolving the issues, and whether the burden or expense of the proposed discovery outweighs its likely benefit. Information within this scope of discovery need not be admissible in evidence to be discoverable. FRCP 26(b)(1).

ii. *Limitations on frequency and extent*

- *When permitted.* By order, the court may alter the limits in the Federal Rules of Civil Procedure on the number of depositions and interrogatories or on the length of depositions under FRCP 30. By order or local rule, the court may also limit the number of requests under FRCP 36. FRCP 26(b)(2)(A).

- *Specific limitations on electronically stored information.* A party need not provide discovery of electronically stored information from sources that the party identifies as not reasonably accessible because of undue burden or cost. On motion to compel discovery or for a protective order, the party from whom discovery is sought must show that the information is not reasonably accessible because of undue burden or cost. If that showing is made, the court may nonetheless order discovery from such sources if the requesting party shows good cause, considering the limitations of FRCP 26(b)(2)(C). The court may specify conditions for the discovery. FRCP 26(b)(2)(B).

- *When required.* On motion or on its own, the court must limit the frequency or extent of discovery otherwise allowed by the Federal Rules of Civil Procedure or by local rule if it determines that: (1) the discovery sought is unreasonably cumulative or duplicative, or can be obtained from some other source that is more convenient, less burdensome, or less expensive; (2) the party seeking discovery has had ample opportunity to obtain the information by discovery in the action; or (3) the proposed discovery is outside the scope permitted by FRCP 26(b)(1). FRCP 26(b)(2)(C).

iii. *Trial preparation; Materials*

- *Documents and tangible things.* Ordinarily, a party may not discover documents and tangible things that are prepared in anticipation of litigation or for trial by or for another party or its representative (including the other party's attorney, consultant, surety, indemnitor, insurer, or agent). But, subject to FRCP 26(b)(4), those materials may be discovered if: (1) they are otherwise discoverable under FRCP 26(b)(1); and (2) the party shows that it has substantial need for the materials to prepare its case and cannot, without undue hardship, obtain their substantial equivalent by other means. FRCP 26(b)(3)(A).

- *Protection against disclosure.* If the court orders discovery of those materials, it must protect against disclosure of the mental impressions, conclusions, opinions, or legal theories of a party's attorney or other representative concerning the litigation. FRCP 26(b)(3)(B).

- *Previous statement.* Any party or other person may, on request and without the required showing, obtain the person's own previous statement about the action or its subject matter. If the request is refused, the person may move for a court order, and FRCP 37(a)(5) applies to the award of expenses. A previous statement is either: (1) a written statement that the person has signed or otherwise adopted or approved; or (2) a contemporaneous stenographic, mechanical, electrical, or other recording—or a transcription of it—that recites substantially verbatim the person's oral statement. FRCP 26(b)(3)(C).

iv. *Trial preparation; Experts*

- *Deposition of an expert who may testify.* A party may depose any person who has been identified as an expert whose opinions may be presented at trial. If FRCP 26(a)(2)(B) requires a report from the expert, the deposition may be conducted only after the report is provided. FRCP 26(b)(4)(A).

- *Trial-preparation protection for draft reports or disclosures.* FRCP 26(b)(3)(A) and

FRCP 26(b)(3)(B) protect drafts of any report or disclosure required under FRCP 26(a)(2), regardless of the form in which the draft is recorded. FRCP 26(b)(4)(B).

- *Trial-preparation protection for communications between a party's attorney and expert witnesses.* FRCP 26(b)(3)(A) and FRCP 26(b)(3)(B) protect communications between the party's attorney and any witness required to provide a report under FRCP 26(a)(2)(B), regardless of the form of the communications, except to the extent that the communications: (1) relate to compensation for the expert's study or testimony; (2) identify facts or data that the party's attorney provided and that the expert considered in forming the opinions to be expressed; or (3) identify assumptions that the party's attorney provided and that the expert relied on in forming the opinions to be expressed. FRCP 26(b)(4)(C).

- *Expert employed only for trial preparation.* Ordinarily, a party may not, by interrogatories or deposition, discover facts known or opinions held by an expert who has been retained or specially employed by another party in anticipation of litigation or to prepare for trial and who is not expected to be called as a witness at trial. But a party may do so only: (1) as provided in FRCP 35(b); or (2) on showing exceptional circumstances under which it is impracticable for the party to obtain facts or opinions on the same subject by other means. FRCP 26(b)(4)(D).

- *Payment.* Unless manifest injustice would result, the court must require that the party seeking discovery: (1) pay the expert a reasonable fee for time spent in responding to discovery under FRCP 26(b)(4)(A) or FRCP 26(b)(4)(D); and (2) for discovery FRCP 26(b)(4)(D), also pay the other party a fair portion of the fees and expenses it reasonably incurred in obtaining the expert's facts and opinions. FRCP 26(b)(4)(E).

v. *Claiming privilege or protecting trial-preparation materials*

- *Information withheld.* When a party withholds information otherwise discoverable by claiming that the information is privileged or subject to protection as trial-preparation material, the party must: (1) expressly make the claim; and (2) describe the nature of the documents, communications, or tangible things not produced or disclosed—and do so in a manner that, without revealing information itself privileged or protected, will enable other parties to assess the claim. FRCP 26(b)(5)(A).

- *Information produced.* If information produced in discovery is subject to a claim of privilege or of protection as trial-preparation material, the party making the claim may notify any party that received the information of the claim and the basis for it. After being notified, a party must promptly return, sequester, or destroy the specified information and any copies it has; must not use or disclose the information until the claim is resolved; must take reasonable steps to retrieve the information if the party disclosed it before being notified; and may promptly present the information to the court under seal for a determination of the claim. The producing party must preserve the information until the claim is resolved. FRCP 26(b)(5)(B).

b. *Protective orders.* A party or any person from whom discovery is sought may move for a protective order in the court where the action is pending—or as an alternative on matters relating to a deposition, in the court for the district where the deposition will be taken. FRCP 26(c)(1). Refer to the United States District Court for the Northern District of New York KeyRules Motion for Protective Order document for more information.

c. *Sequence of discovery.* Unless the parties stipulate or the court orders otherwise for the parties' and witnesses' convenience and in the interests of justice: (1) methods of discovery may be used in any sequence; and (2) discovery by one party does not require any other party to delay its discovery. FRCP 26(d)(3).

2. *Interrogatories*

a. *Number.* Unless otherwise stipulated or ordered by the court, a party may serve on any other party no more than twenty-five (25) written interrogatories, including all discrete subparts. Leave to serve additional interrogatories may be granted to the extent consistent with FRCP 26(b)(1) and FRCP 26(b)(2). FRCP 33(a)(1).

    b.   *Scope.* An interrogatory may relate to any matter that may be inquired into under FRCP 26(b). An interrogatory is not objectionable merely because it asks for an opinion or contention that relates to fact or the application of law to fact, but the court may order that the interrogatory need not be answered until designated discovery is complete, or until a pretrial conference or some other time. FRCP 33(a)(2).

    c.   *Parties subject to interrogatories.* Depositions may be taken of any person but interrogatories are limited to parties to the litigation. FPP § 2171. Interrogatories may not be directed to the attorney for a party. They must be addressed to the party, who is then required to give all information known to it or its attorney. FPP § 2171; Hickman v. Taylor, 329 U.S. 495, 504, 67 S.Ct. 385, 390, 91 L.Ed. 451 (1947). For more information, refer to FPP § 2171.

    d.   *Form.* Ideally an interrogatory should be a single direct question phrased in a fashion that will inform the other party what is requested. In fact the courts have given parties considerable latitude in framing interrogatories. Rather general language has been permitted so long as the interrogatory gives the other party a reasonably clear indication of the information to be included in its answer. FPP § 2168.

        i.   *Use of definitions.* There is no prohibition against the use of definitions in interrogatories, and definitions may be helpful in clarifying the meaning of obscure terms or avoiding repetitions in a long set of interrogatories. FPP § 2168.

        ii.   *Use of standardized form interrogatories.* There have been mixed reactions to the use of standardized form interrogatories. They have been referred to opprobriously as "canned sets of interrogatories of the shotgun variety" and it has been said that their indiscriminate use is an "undesirable practice." FPP § 2168.

    e.   *Numbering.* The parties shall number each interrogatory or request sequentially, regardless of the number of sets of interrogatories or requests. NY R USDCTND L.R. 26.1.

    f.   *Motion to compel.* The party submitting the interrogatories must attempt to confer with the responding party in an effort to secure the information without court action and, if that fails, move for an order under FRCP 37(a) compelling answers. FPP § 2182. Refer to the United States District Court for the Northern District of New York KeyRules Motion to Compel Discovery document for more information.

3.   *Sanctions for failure to cooperate in discovery.* The court where the action is pending may, on motion, order sanctions if a party, after being properly served with interrogatories under FRCP 33 or a request for inspection under FRCP 34, fails to serve its answers, objections, or written response. FRCP 37(d)(1)(A)(ii). If a motion to compel is granted, the court must, after giving an opportunity to be heard, require the party or deponent whose conduct necessitated the motion, the party or attorney advising that conduct, or both to pay the movant's reasonable expenses incurred in making the motion, including attorney's fees. But the court must not order this payment if the opposing party's nondisclosure, response, or objection was substantially justified. FRCP 37(a)(5)(A)(ii). Refer to the United States District Court for the Northern District of New York KeyRules Motion for Discovery Sanctions document for more information.

4.   *Stipulations about discovery procedure.* Unless the court orders otherwise, the parties may stipulate that: (1) a deposition may be taken before any person, at any time or place, on any notice, and in the manner specified—in which event it may be used in the same way as any other deposition; and (2) other procedures governing or limiting discovery be modified—but a stipulation extending the time for any form of discovery must have court approval if it would interfere with the time set for completing discovery, for hearing a motion, or for trial. FRCP 29.

5.   *Complex and multi-district litigation.* If the assigned judge determines, in his or her discretion, that the case is of such a complex nature that it cannot reasonably be trial ready within eighteen (18) months from the date the complaint is filed, the assigned judge may design and issue a particularized case management order that will move the case to trial as quickly as the complexity of the case allows. NY R USDCTND L.R. 3.3(a). The parties shall promptly notify the Court in writing if any action commenced is appropriate for multi-district litigation. NY R USDCTND L.R. 3.3(b).

6.   *Appearances.* An attorney appearing for a party in a civil case shall promptly file with the Clerk a written

notice of appearance; however, an attorney does not need to file a notice of appearance if the attorney who would be filing the notice of appearance is the same individual who has signed the complaint, notice of removal, pre-answer motion, or answer. NY R USDCTND L.R. 83.2(a). For more information, refer to NY R USDCTND L.R. 83.2.

7. *Related cases.* A civil case is "related" to another civil case for purposes of this guideline when, because of the similarity of facts and legal issues or because the cases arise from the same transactions or events, a substantial saving of judicial resources is likely to result from assigning the cases to the same Judge and Magistrate Judge. NY R USDCTND Order 12(G)(2). A civil case shall not be deemed related to another civil case merely because the civil case: (1) involves similar legal issues, or (2) involves the same parties. NY R USDCTND Order 12(G)(3). Presumptively, and subject to the power of a Judge to determine otherwise pursuant to NY R USDCTND Order 12(G)(5), civil cases shall not be deemed to be "related" unless both cases are still pending before the Court. NY R USDCTND Order 12(G)(4).

   a. *New filings.* If an attorney or filing party indicates on the Civil Cover Sheet that a case is related to an earlier filed case, the Clerk shall instruct the filing party to file a notice of related cases. The allegedly related cases will be submitted by the Clerk to the Judge to whom the earliest filed case is assigned, who shall advise the Clerk whether such cases are related. NY R USDCTND Order 12(G)(1).

   b. *Judicial determination that civil cases are "related."* Except for the cases described in the final sentence of NY R USDCTND Order 12(G)(6), all civil cases shall be randomly assigned when they are filed. Other than the cases described in the final sentence of NY R USDCTND Order 12(G)(6), civil cases shall not be deemed to be "related" for purposes of this guideline at the instance of any litigant or attorney unless and until there has been a determination by a Judge of this Court that the standard of NY R USDCTND Order 12(G)(2) is met. NY R USDCTND Order 12(G)(5).

      i. *Notice of related filing.* Any party may apply for such a determination by filing with the Clerk a notice of related filing, which should include an explanation as to why the standard of NY R USDCTND Order 12(G)(2) is met. A form for this purpose is available on the Court's website. A copy of the notice shall be served on all other parties who have appeared. Such an application must be made after the date when at least a majority of the defendants have been served with the complaint. Before making such an application, the applicant must confer in good faith with all other parties in an effort to reach an agreement on whether or not the case is "related". After such an application is made, any other party may serve and file within seven (7) calendar days a letter of no more than two (2) pages supporting or opposing the application. The application to have the case assigned to another Judge shall be presented to the Judge with the earliest filed case for decision on whether the action(s) should be reassigned as related cases. The Judge with the earliest filed case may then enter an order in the case at bar, either deeming the case to be related and directing the Clerk to reassign the action, or denying the application for reassignment. Any disputes concerning the assignment of related cases will be referred to the Chief Judge for resolution. NY R USDCTND Order 12(G)(5).

   c. For more information on related cases, refer to NY R USDCTND Order 12(G).

8. *Alternative dispute resolution (ADR).* It is the mission of this court to do everything it can to help parties resolve their disputes as fairly, quickly, and efficiently as possible. NY R USDCTND Order 25(VIII).

   a. *Arbitration.* NY R USDCTND L.R. 83.7 governs the consensual arbitration program for referral of civil actions to court-annexed arbitration. It may remain in effect until further order of the Court. Its purpose is to establish a less formal procedure for the just, efficient and economical resolution of disputes, while preserving the right to a full trial on demand. NY R USDCTND L.R. 83.7-1.

      i. *Actions subject to arbitration.* The Clerk shall notify the parties in all civil cases, except as the Local Rules of Practice for the United States District Court for the Northern District of New York otherwise direct, that they may consent to non-binding arbitration under NY R US-DCTND L.R. 83.7. The notice shall be furnished to the parties at pretrial/scheduling confer- ences or shall be included with pretrial conference notices and instructions. Consent to arbitration under NY R USDCTND L.R. 83.7 shall be discussed at the pretrial/scheduling conference. No party or attorney shall be prejudiced for refusing to participate in arbitration.

The Court shall allow the referral of any civil action pending before it to the arbitration process if the parties consent. The plaintiff shall be responsible for securing the execution of a consent form by the parties and for filing the form with the Clerk within fourteen (14) days after the parties receive the form. The parties shall freely and knowingly enter into the consent. NY R USDCTND L.R. 83.7-2.

    ii.   *Referral to arbitration.* The Clerk shall refer every action subject to NY R USDCTND L.R. 83.7 to arbitration in accordance with the procedures under NY R USDCTND L.R. 83.7 twenty-one (21) days after the filing of the last responsive pleading or within twenty-one (21) days of the filing of a stipulated consent order referring the action to arbitration, whichever event occurs last, except as otherwise provided. If any party notices a motion to dismiss under the provisions of FRCP 12(a) and/or FRCP 12(b), or a motion to join necessary parties pursuant to the Federal Rules of Civil Procedure prior to the expiration of the twenty-one (21) day period, the assigned judge shall hear the motion and further proceedings under NY R USDCTND L.R. 83.7 shall be deferred pending decision on the motion. If the Court does not dismiss the action on the motion, the Court shall refer the action to arbitration twenty-one (21) days after the filing of the decision. NY R USDCTND L.R. 83.7-3(a). Motions for summary judgment pursuant to FRCP 56 shall be filed and served within twenty-one (21) days following the close of discovery. The filing of a FRCP 56 motion shall defer further proceedings under NY R USDCTND L.R. 83.7 pending decision on the motion. NY R USDCTND L.R. 83.7-3(a).

-    *Relief from referral.* Any party shall request relief from the operation of NY R USDCTND L.R. 83.7 by filing with the Court a motion for the relief within twenty-one (21) days after entry of the initial stipulated consent order which refers the case for arbitration. The assigned judge shall, sua sponte, exempt an action from the application of NY R USDCTND L.R. 83.7 where the objectives of arbitration would not be realized because (1) the case involves complex or novel legal issues, (2) legal issues predominate over factual issues, or (3) for other good cause. NY R USDCTND L.R. 83.7-3(c).

    iii.   For more information on arbitration, refer to NY R USDCTND L.R. 83.7.

  b.   *Mediation.* The purpose of NY R USDCTND L.R. 83.11 is to provide a supplementary procedure to the Court's existing alternative dispute resolution procedures. NY R USDCTND L.R. 83.11 provides for an earlier resolution of civil disputes resulting in savings of time and cost to litigants and the Court without sacrificing the quality of justice rendered or the right of litigants to a full trial on all issues not resolved through mediation. NY R USDCTND L.R. 83.11-1(a). Mediation is a process by which an impartial person, the mediator, facilitates communication between disputing parties to promote understanding, reconciliation and settlement. The mediator is an advocate for settlement and uses the mediation process to help the parties fully explore any potential area of agreement. The mediator does not serve as a judge or arbitrator and has no authority to render any decision on any disputed issue or to force a settlement. The parties themselves are responsible for negotiating any resolution(s) to their dispute. NY R USDCTND L.R. 83.11-1(b).

    i.   *Actions subject to mediation.* The Court may refer any civil action (or any portion thereof) to mediation under NY R USDCTND L.R. 83.11: (1) by order of referral; or (2) on the motion of any party; or (3) by consent of the parties. NY R USDCTND L.R. 83.11-3(a).

-    *Withdrawal from mediation.* The parties may withdraw from mediation any civil action or claim that the Court refers to mediation pursuant to NY R USDCTND L.R. 83.11-3 by application to the assigned judge at least ten (10) days prior to the scheduled mediation session. NY R USDCTND L.R. 83.11-3(b).

    ii.   *Mandatory mediation program.* The United States District Court for the Northern District of New York has adopted this Mandatory Mediation Plan. The paid Mediation Program is designed to provide quicker, less expensive and potentially more satisfying alternatives to continuing litigation, without impairing the quality of justice or the right to trial. NY R USDCTND Order 47(1)(1.2)(A). This Mandatory Mediation Plan applies to civil actions pending as well as newly filed actions, except as otherwise indicated in NY R USDCTND Order 47. The Local Rules for voluntary mediation will apply only to Pro Se Cases that proceed through the Assisted Mediation Program. NY R USDCTND Order 47(1)(1.2)(B).

-    *Referral into the pilot mandatory mediation program for new cases.* All civil cases shall be referred automatically into the Mandatory Mediation Program. Notice of the Mandatory Mediation requirements will be provided to all parties immediately upon the filing of a complaint and answer or a notice of removal. ADR intervention will be scheduled at the conference held pursuant to NY R USDCTND L.R. 16.1. NY R USDCTND Order 47(2)(2.1)(A). For a list of categories of actions exempted from automatic referral, refer to NY R USDCTND Order 47(2)(2.1)(A).

- *Referral into the pilot mandatory mediation program for pending cases.* The assigned Judge or Magistrate Judge on any pending civil case may, sua sponte or with status conference, issue an order referring the case into the Mandatory Mediation Program. The order shall specify a date on which the ADR intervention is to be completed. NY R USDCTND Order 47(2)(2.1)(B).

- *Referral into the pilot mandatory mediation program by stipulation.* A case may be referred into the Mandatory Mediation Program by stipulation of all parties. Stipulations shall be filed and shall designate the time frame within which the ADR process will be completed. Stipulations are presumed acceptable unless the assigned Judge or Magistrate Judge determines that the interests of justice are not served. NY R USDCTND Order 47(2)(2.1)(C).

- *Relief from referral.* Motions to opt out of the program will be addressed by the assigned Magistrate Judge at the FRCP 16 conference. NY R USDCTND Order 47(2)(2.2)(A). Opting Out Motions shall be granted only for "good cause" shown. Inconvenience, travel costs, attorney fees or other costs shall not constitute "good cause." A party seeking relief from the Mandatory Mediation Program must set forth the reasons why Mandatory Mediation has no reasonable chance of being productive. NY R USDCTND Order 47(2)(2.2)(B). The assigned Magistrate Judge may, sua sponte, exempt any case from the Court's Mandatory Mediation Program. NY R USDCTND Order 47(2)(2.2)(C).

iii. *Assisted mediation program.* The Court may assign specially trained pro bono Special Mediation Counsel to assist pro se civilian litigants with preparing for and participating in mediation. The Assisted Mediation Program is open to civilian pro se parties to actions in the Northern District of New York. The assigned judge or magistrate judge determines if the case would benefit from mediation and would also benefit from the assignment of Special Mediation Counsel to assist the pro se party with the mediation process. NY R USDCTND L.R. 83.8(a). Appointment of Special Mediation Counsel is in no way guaranteed, even if the action is referred to the court-annexed mediation program. Appointment is at the sole discretion of the presiding judge. NY R USDCTND L.R. 83.8(a).

- *Referral to assisted mediation program.* If the court determines that referral to the Assisted Mediation Program is appropriate, the Court shall enter an order of reference to the Assisted Mediation Program. NY R USDCTND L.R. 83.8(b).

iv. For more information on mediation, refer to NY R USDCTND L.R. 83.11 and NY R USDCTND Order 47.

c. *Early neutral evaluation (ENE).* Early neutral evaluation (ENE) is a process in which parties obtain from an experienced neutral (an "evaluator") a nonbinding, reasoned, oral evaluation of the merits of the case. The first step in the ENE process involves the Court appointing an evaluator who has expertise in the area of law in the case. After the parties exchange essential information and position statements early in the pretrial period (usually within one hundred fifty (150) to two hundred (200) days after a complaint has been filed), the evaluator convenes an ENE session that typically lasts about two hours. At the ENE meeting, each side briefly presents the factual and legal basis of its position. The evaluator may ask questions of the parties and help them identify the main issues in dispute and the areas of agreement. The evaluator may also help the parties explore options for settlement. If settlement does not occur, the evaluator then offers an opinion as to the settlement value of the case, including the likelihood of liability and the likely range of damages. With the benefit of this assessment, the parties are again encouraged to discuss settlement, with or without the evaluator's assistance. The parties may also explore ways to narrow the issues in dispute, exchange information about the case or otherwise prepare efficiently for trial. NY R USDCTND L.R. 83.12-1.

i. *Actions subject to early neutral evaluation.* The Court may refer any civil action (or any portion thereof) to ENE under NY R USDCTND L.R. 83.12: (1) by order of referral; (2) on the motion of any party; or (3) by consent of the parties. NY R USDCTND L.R. 83.12-3(a).

- *Withdrawal from the ENE process.* The parties may withdraw any civil action or claim that the Court has referred to the ENE Process pursuant to NY R USDCTND L.R. 83.12-3 by application to the assigned judge at least ten (10) days before the scheduled evaluation session. NY R USDCTND L.R. 83.12-3(b).

ii. For more information on early neutral evaluation (ENE), refer to NY R USDCTND L.R. 83.12.

9. *Settlement procedures.* On notice to the Court or the Clerk that the parties have settled an action, and upon confirmation of the settlement by all parties, the Court may issue a judgment dismissing the action by reason of settlement. The Court shall issue the order without prejudice to the parties' right to secure reinstatement of the case within thirty (30) days after the date of judgment by making a showing that the settlement was not, in fact, consummated. NY R USDCTND L.R. 68.2(a). If the Court decides not to follow the procedures set forth in NY R USDCTND L.R. 68.2(a), the parties shall file within thirty (30) days of the notification to the Court, unless otherwise directed by written order, such notices, stipulations and/or motions as are necessary to terminate the action. If the required documents are not filed within the thirty (30) day period, the Clerk shall place the action on the dismissal calendar. NY R USDCTND L.R. 68.2(b).

10. *Sanctions and penalties for noncompliance.* Failure of an attorney or of a party to comply with any provision of the Local Rules of Practice for the United States District Court for the Northern District of New York, General Orders of this District, Orders of the Court, or the Federal Rules of Civil Procedure shall be a ground for imposition of sanctions. NY R USDCTND L.R. 1.1(d).

11. *Individual judge practices.* Refer to the Miscellaneous section of this document for information on individual judge practices on general requirements for documents.

## D. Documents

1. *Required documents*

   a. *Interrogatories.* Refer to the General Requirements section of this document for information on interrogatories.

2. *Supplemental documents*

   a. *Certificate of service.* FRCP 5(d) requires that the person making service under FRCP 5 certify that service has been effected. FRCP 5(Advisory Committee Notes). Having such information on file may be useful for many purposes, including proof of service if an issue arises concerning the effectiveness of the service. FRCP 5(Advisory Committee Notes).

3. *Individual judge practices.* Refer to the Miscellaneous section of this document for information on individual judge practices on required documents.

## E. Format

1. *Form of documents.* The rules governing captions and other matters of form in pleadings apply to motions and other papers. FRCP 7(b)(2). All pleadings and other papers shall be served and filed in accordance with the Federal Rules of Civil Procedure and shall be in the form prescribed by NY R USDCTND L.R. 10.1. NY R USDCTND L.R. 5.1(a).

   a. *Form, generally.* All pleadings, motions, and other documents that a party presents for filing, whether in paper form or in electronic form, shall meet the following requirements:

      i. *Font size.* All text, whether in the body of the document or in footnotes, must be a minimum of twelve (12) point type. NY R USDCTND L.R. 10.1(a)(1).

      ii. *Margins.* All documents must have one (1) inch margins on all four sides of the page. NY R USDCTND L.R. 10.1(a)(2).

      iii. *Spacing.* All text in the body of the document must be double-spaced. NY R USDCTND L.R. 10.1(a)(3).

         - The text in block quotations and footnotes may be single-spaced. NY R USDCTND L.R. 10.1(a)(4).

    iv.  *Page numbering.* Pages must be consecutively numbered. NY R USDCTND L.R. 10.1(a)(7).

    v.  *Circumventing formatting limitations*

- Extensive footnotes must not be used to circumvent page limitations. NY R USDCTND L.R. 10.1(a)(5).

- Compacted or other compressed printing features must not be used. NY R USDCTND L.R. 10.1(a)(6).

b.  *Additional requirements for paper filing.* Additional requirements for all pleadings, motions, and other documents that a party presents for filing in paper form:

    i.  *Paper size.* All documents must be on eight and one-half by eleven (8-1/2 x 11) inch white paper of good quality. NY R USDCTND L.R. 10.1(b)(1).

    ii.  *Text.* All text must be plainly and legibly written, typewritten, printed or reproduced without erasures or interlineations materially defacing them. NY R USDCTND L.R. 10.1(b)(2).

    iii.  *Ink.* All documents must be in black or blue ink. NY R USDCTND L.R. 10.1(b)(3).

    iv.  *Binding.* Pages of all documents must be stapled (or in some other way fastened) together. NY R USDCTND L.R. 10.1(b)(4).

    v.  *Single-sided paper.* All documents must be single-sided. NY R USDCTND L.R. 10.1(b)(5).

    vi.  *Electronic submission.* The Court, at its discretion, may require the electronic submission of any document in a WordPerfect-compatible format. NY R USDCTND L.R. 10.1(b)(6).

    vii.  *Rejection of document.* The Court may reject documents that do not comply with the above-listed requirements. NY R USDCTND L.R. 10.1(b).

c.  *Caption; Names of parties.* Every pleading must have a caption with the court's name, a title, a file number, and a FRCP 7(a) designation. The title of the complaint must name all the parties; the title of other pleadings, after naming the first party on each side, may refer generally to other parties. FRCP 10(a). Each document must contain a caption for the specific case to which it pertains. The caption must include the title of the Court, the title of the action, the civil action number of the case, the initials of the assigned judge(s), and the name or nature of the paper in sufficient detail for identification. If a litigant has more than one action pending in this Court, any and all papers filed in a case must contain and pertain to one civil action number, unless the civil actions have been consolidated by the Court. Any motion or other papers purporting to relate to more than one action will not be accepted for filing and may be stricken by the Court. NY R USDCTND L.R. 10.1(c)(1) shall not apply, as noted in NY R USDCTND L.R. 10.1(c), to notices of change of address filed by attorneys of record and pro se litigants. The parties must separately caption affidavits and declarations and must not physically attach them to the Notice of Motion or Memorandum of Law. NY R USDCTND L.R. 10.1(c)(1).

d.  *Paragraphs; Separate statements.* A party must state its claims or defenses in numbered paragraphs, each limited as far as practicable to a single set of circumstances. A later pleading may refer by number to a paragraph in an earlier pleading. If doing so would promote clarity, each claim founded on a separate transaction or occurrence—and each defense other than a denial—must be stated in a separate count or defense. FRCP 10(b).

e.  *Adoption by reference; Exhibits.* A statement in a pleading may be adopted by reference elsewhere in the same pleading or in any other pleading or motion. A copy of a written instrument that is an exhibit to a pleading is a part of the pleading for all purposes. FRCP 10(c).

f.  *Citation of local rules.* These are the Local Rules of Practice for the United States District Court for the Northern District of New York. They shall be cited as "L.R. ___." NY R USDCTND L.R. 1.1(a).

g.  *Acceptance by the clerk.* The clerk must not refuse to file a paper solely because it is not in the form prescribed by the Federal Rules of Civil Procedure or by a local rule or practice. FRCP 5(d)(4).

2.  *Form of electronic documents.* All pleadings, motions, and other documents that a party presents for filing, whether in paper form or in electronic form, shall meet the requirements in NY R USDCTND L.R. 10.1(a). NY R USDCTND L.R. 10.1(a). Refer above for more information.

  a.  *Attachments and exhibits.* A Filing User must submit in electronic form all documents referenced as

exhibits or attachments in accordance with the Court's CM/ECF Users Manual unless the Court otherwise orders. A Filing User shall submit as exhibits or attachments only those excerpts of the referenced documents that are directly germane to the matter under the Court's consideration. Excerpted material must be clearly and prominently identified as such. Filing Users who file excerpts of documents as exhibits or attachments under these Administrative Procedures (NY R USDCTND CM/ECF) do so without prejudice to their right to timely file additional excerpts or the complete document. Responding parties may also timely file the complete document or additional excerpts that they believe are directly germane to the matter under the Court's consideration. NY R USDCTND CM/ECF(4)(4.4).

    i.    All attachments must be described in sufficient detail so the Court and opposing counsel can easily identify and distinguish the filed attachments. Vague or general descriptions are insufficient (i.e., "Exhibit 1"). Rather, each attachment shall have a descriptive title identifying, with specificity, the document that is being filed (i.e., "Exhibit 12 Mulligan County Fire Investigation Report.") Failure to adequately describe attachments may result in the document being rejected by the Court. NY R USDCTND CM/ECF(4)(4.4).

  b.   *Large documents.* For information on the electronic filing of large documents, please consult the Court's CM/ECF Users Manual, which is available on the Court's web page. NY R USDCTND CM/ECF(4)(4.5).

    i.    A party who believes a document is too lengthy to electronically image, i.e., "scan," may contact the Clerk's Office for permission to file that document conventionally. If the Clerk's Office grants permission to conventionally file the document, the Filing User shall electronically file a notice of conventional filing for the documents. More information regarding this process can be obtained from the Court's web page. Exhibits submitted conventionally shall be served on other parties as if they were not subject to these Administrative Procedures (NY R USDCTND CM/ECF). For a list of hints and tips for scanning large documents, please consult the Court's web page. NY R USDCTND CM/ECF(4)(4.5).

  c.   *Legibility.* It shall be the Filing User's responsibility to verify the legibility of scanned documents before filing them electronically with the Court. NY R USDCTND CM/ECF(4)(4.6).

  d.   *Color documents.* Since documents scanned in color or containing a graphic take much longer to upload, Filing Users are encouraged to configure their scanners to scan documents at 300 dpi and preferably in black and white rather than in color. NY R USDCTND CM/ECF(4)(4.7).

  e.   *Items not in .PDF format.* Parties wishing to file items not amenable to .pdf format (i.e. CD's, DVD's), shall file such items conventionally with the Clerk's Office. The Filing User shall electronically file a notice of conventional filing indicating that these items have been submitted to the clerk and shall serve copies of these items on other parties as if they were not subject to these Administrative Procedures (NY R USDCTND CM/ECF). These item(s) will be maintained by the Clerk's Office until the case is disposed, at which time they will be returned to the filing party for retention consistent with NY R USDCTND CM/ECF(4)(4.9). NY R USDCTND CM/ECF(4)(4.8).

3.  *Signing disclosures and discovery requests, responses, and objections.* FRCP 11 does not apply to disclosures and discovery requests, responses, objections, and motions under FRCP 26 through FRCP 37. FRCP 11(d).

  a.   *Signature required.* Every disclosure under FRCP 26(a)(1) or FRCP 26(a)(3) and every discovery request, response, or objection must be signed by at least one attorney of record in the attorney's own name—or by the party personally, if unrepresented—and must state the signer's address, e-mail address, and telephone number. FRCP 26(g)(1). Each document must identify the person filing the document. This identification must include an original signature of the attorney or pro se litigant; the typewritten name of that person; the address of a pro se litigant; and the bar roll number, office address, telephone number, e-mail address and fax number of the attorney. Telephone numbers of non-prisoner pro se parties may be provided voluntarily or upon request of the Court. See General Order #22 (NY R USDCTND CM/ECF) for signature requirements. NY R USDCTND L.R. 10.1(c)(2).

    i.   *Electronic signatures.* Documents filed under an attorney's login and password shall constitute

that attorney's signature for purposes of the Local Rules of Practice for the United States District Court for the Northern District of New York and Federal Rules of Civil Procedure, including but not limited to FRCP 11. A pleading or other document requiring an attorney's signature shall be signed in the following manner, whether filed electronically or submitted on disk or CD/ROM to the Clerk's Office: "s/ (attorney name)." The correct format for an attorney signature is found in NY R USDCTND CM/ECF(6)(6.1). NY R USDCTND CM/ECF(6)(6.1).

- *Non-attorney signature.* If an original document requires the signature of a non-attorney, the Filing User may scan the original document containing the original signature(s), then electronically file it on the System. Alternatively, the Filing User may convert the document into .pdf text format and submit the document using "s/" for the signature of the non-attorney. NY R USDCTND CM/ECF(6)(6.2).

- *Multiple signatures.* A document requiring signatures of more than one party must be filed electronically either by (1) submitting a scanned document containing all necessary signatures; (2) representing the consent of the other parties on the document; or (3) in any other manner that the Court approves. NY R USDCTND CM/ECF(6)(6.3).

b. *Effect of signature.* By signing, an attorney or party certifies that to the best of the person's knowledge, information, and belief formed after a reasonable inquiry:

  i. With respect to a disclosure, it is complete and correct as of the time it is made; and

  ii. With respect to a discovery request, response, or objection, it is:

  - Consistent with the Federal Rules of Civil Procedure and warranted by existing law or by a nonfrivolous argument for extending, modifying, or reversing existing law, or for establishing new law;

  - Not interposed for any improper purpose, such as to harass, cause unnecessary delay, or needlessly increase the cost of litigation; and

  - Neither unreasonable nor unduly burdensome or expensive, considering the needs of the case, prior discovery in the case, the amount in controversy, and the importance of the issues at stake in the action. FRCP 26(g)(1).

c. *Failure to sign.* Other parties have no duty to act on an unsigned disclosure, request, response, or objection until it is signed, and the court must strike it unless a signature is promptly supplied after the omission is called to the attorney's or party's attention. FRCP 26(g)(2).

d. *Sanction for improper certification.* If a certification violates FRCP 26(g) without substantial justification, the court, on motion or on its own, must impose an appropriate sanction on the signer, the party on whose behalf the signer was acting, or both. The sanction may include an order to pay the reasonable expenses, including attorney's fees, caused by the violation. FRCP 26(g)(3). Refer to the United States District Court for the Northern District of New York KeyRules Motion for Discovery Sanctions document for more information.

4. *Privacy protection for filings made with the court*

a. *Redacted filings.* Unless the court orders otherwise, in an electronic or paper filing with the court that contains an individual's Social Security number, taxpayer-identification number, or birth date, the name of an individual known to be a minor, or a financial-account number, a party or nonparty making the filing may include only:

  i. The last four (4) digits of the Social Security number and taxpayer-identification number;

  ii. The year of the individual's birth;

  iii. The minor's initials; and

  iv. The last four (4) digits of the financial-account number. FRCP 5.2(a); NY R USDCTND L.R. 8.1; NY R USDCTND CM/ECF(11)(11.2).

  v. If a home address must be used, use only the City and State. NY R USDCTND L.R. 8.1; NY R USDCTND CM/ECF(11)(11.2).

  vi. If the victim of a sexual assault must be referenced, redact the name to 'Victim.' NY R USDCTND CM/ECF(11)(11.2); NY R USDCTND L.R. 8.1.

    vii.   In addition, caution shall be exercised when filing documents that contain the following:

- Personal identifying number, such as a driver's license number;
- Medical records, treatment and diagnosis;
- Employment history;
- Individual financial information; and
- Proprietary or trade secret information. NY R USDCTND L.R. 8.1; NY R USDCTND CM/ECF(11)(11.2).

b.  *Exemptions from the redaction requirement.* The redaction requirement does not apply to the following:

    i.   A financial-account number that identifies the property allegedly subject to forfeiture in a forfeiture proceeding;

    ii.   The record of an administrative or agency proceeding;

    iii.   The official record of a state-court proceeding;

    iv.   The record of a court or tribunal, if that record was not subject to the redaction requirement when originally filed;

    v.   A filing covered by FRCP 5.2(c) or FRCP 5.2(d); and

    vi.   A pro se filing in an action brought under 28 U.S.C.A. § 2241, 28 U.S.C.A. § 2254, or 28 U.S.C.A. § 2255. FRCP 5.2(b).

    vii.   Transcripts of the administrative record in social security proceedings are exempt from this requirement. State court records and other documents filed in habeas corpus proceedings are exempt from this requirement except for proceedings that involve victims of sex crimes. In habeas corpus cases involving sex crimes, the parties must redact the record and supporting papers, or may move to seal, if appropriate. NY R USDCTND L.R. 8.1.

c.  *Limitations on remote access to electronic files; Social Security appeals and immigration cases.* Unless the court orders otherwise, in an action for benefits under the Social Security Act, and in an action or proceeding relating to an order of removal, to relief from removal, or to immigration benefits or detention, access to an electronic file is authorized as follows:

    i.   The parties and their attorneys may have remote electronic access to any part of the case file, including the administrative record;

    ii.   Any other person may have electronic access to the full record at the courthouse, but may have remote electronic access only to:

- The docket maintained by the court; and
- An opinion, order, judgment, or other disposition of the court, but not any other part of the case file or the administrative record. FRCP 5.2(c).

d.  *Filings made under seal.* The court may order that a filing be made under seal without redaction. The court may later unseal the filing or order the person who made the filing to file a redacted version for the public record. FRCP 5.2(d); NY R USDCTND L.R. 8.1. For information on sealed matters, refer to NY R USDCTND L.R. 83.13 and NY R USDCTND CM/ECF(12).

e.  *Protective orders.* For good cause, the court may by order in a case:

    i.   Require redaction of additional information; or

    ii.   Limit or prohibit a nonparty's remote electronic access to a document filed with the court. FRCP 5.2(e).

f.  *Option for additional unredacted filing under seal.* A person making a redacted filing may also file an unredacted copy under seal. The court must retain the unredacted copy as part of the record. FRCP 5.2(f); NY R USDCTND L.R. 8.1; NY R USDCTND CM/ECF(11)(11.3).

g.  *Option for filing a reference list.* A filing that contains redacted information may be filed together

with a reference list that identifies each item of redacted information and specifies an appropriate identifier that uniquely corresponds to each item listed. The list must be filed under seal and may be amended as of right. Any reference in the case to a listed identifier will be construed to refer to the corresponding item of information. FRCP 5.2(g); NY R USDCTND L.R. 8.1; NY R USDCTND CM/ECF(11)(11.3).

h. *Responsibility for redaction.* Counsel is strongly urged to discuss this issue with all their clients so that they can make an informed decision about the inclusion of certain information. The responsibility for redacting these personal identifiers rests solely with counsel and the parties. The Clerk will not review each filing for compliance with NY R USDCTND L.R. 8.1. Counsel and the parties are cautioned that failure to redact these personal identifiers may subject them to the Court's full disciplinary power. NY R USDCTND L.R. 8.1; NY R USDCTND CM/ECF(11)(11.3).

i. *Waiver of protection of identifiers.* A person waives the protection of FRCP 5.2(a) as to the person's own information by filing it without redaction and not under seal. FRCP 5.2(h).

5. *Individual judge practices.* Refer to the Miscellaneous section of this document for information on individual judge practices on formatting documents.

## F. Filing and Service Requirements

1. *Filing requirements.* Any paper after the complaint that is required to be served—together with a certificate of service—must be filed within a reasonable time after service. But disclosures under FRCP 26(a)(1) or FRCP 26(a)(2) and the following discovery requests and responses must not be filed until they are used in the proceeding or the court orders filing: depositions, interrogatories, requests for documents or tangible things or to permit entry onto land, and requests for admission. FRCP 5(d)(1). Refer to the United States District Court for the Northern District of New York KeyRules pleading and motion documents for information on filing with the court.

   a. *Filing discovery.* Parties are directed not to file discovery material unless it is being filed in accordance with NY R USDCTND L.R. 26.2. NY R USDCTND Order 25(IX)(B). Parties shall not file notices to take depositions, transcripts of depositions, interrogatories, requests for documents, requests for admissions, disclosures, and answers and responses to these notices and requests unless the Court orders otherwise; provided, however, that a party shall file any discovery material that it expects to use at trial or to support any motion, including a motion to compel or for summary judgment prior to the trial or motion return date. NY R USDCTND L.R. 26.2; NY R USDCTND CM/ECF(2)(2.1)(4).

2. *Service requirements*

   a. *Service; When required*

      i. *In general.* Unless the Federal Rules of Civil Procedure provide otherwise, each of the following papers must be served on every party:

         • An order stating that service is required;

         • A pleading filed after the original complaint, unless the court orders otherwise under FRCP 5(c) because there are numerous defendants;

         • A discovery paper required to be served on a party, unless the court orders otherwise;

         • A written motion, except one that may be heard ex parte; and

         • A written notice, appearance, demand, or offer of judgment, or any similar paper. FRCP 5(a)(1).

      ii. *If a party fails to appear.* No service is required on a party who is in default for failing to appear. But a pleading that asserts a new claim for relief against such a party must be served on that party under FRCP 4. FRCP 5(a)(2).

      iii. *Seizing property.* If an action is begun by seizing property and no person is or need be named as a defendant, any service required before the filing of an appearance, answer, or claim must be made on the person who had custody or possession of the property when it was seized. FRCP 5(a)(3).

b. *Service; How made*

i. *Serving an attorney.* If a party is represented by an attorney, service under FRCP 5 must be made on the attorney unless the court orders service on the party. FRCP 5(b)(1).

ii. *Service in general.* A paper is served under FRCP 5 by:

- Handing it to the person;

- Leaving it: (1) at the person's office with a clerk or other person in charge or, if no one is in charge, in a conspicuous place in the office; or (2) if the person has no office or the office is closed, at the person's dwelling or usual place of abode with someone of suitable age and discretion who resides there;

- Mailing it to the person's last known address—in which event service is complete upon mailing;

- Leaving it with the court clerk if the person has no known address;

- Sending it by electronic means if the person consented in writing—in which event service is complete upon transmission, but is not effective if the serving party learns that it did not reach the person to be served; or

- Delivering it by any other means that the person consented to in writing—in which event service is complete when the person making service delivers it to the agency designated to make delivery. FRCP 5(b)(2).

iii. *Service of electronically-filed documents.* Service is complete provided all parties receive a Notice of Electronic Filing (NEF), which is sent automatically by email from the Court (see the NEF for a list of who did/did not receive notice electronically). Transmission of the NEF constitutes service upon all Filing and Receiving Users who are listed as recipients of notice by electronic mail. It remains the responsibility of Filing and Receiving Users to maintain current contact information with the court and to regularly review the docket sheet of the case. NY R USDCTND CM/ECF(5)(5.2).

- *Non-filing or receiving users.* Attorneys and pro se parties who are not Filing or Receiving Users must be served with a paper copy of any electronically filed pleading or other document. Service of such paper copy must be made according to the Federal Rules of Civil Procedure and the Local Rules of Practice for the United States District Court for the Northern District of New York. Such paper service must be documented by electronically filing a certificate of service. NY R USDCTND CM/ECF(5)(5.2). A party who is not a Filing User of the System is entitled to a paper copy of any electronically-filed pleading, document, or order. The Filing User must therefore provide the non-Filing User with the pleading or document according to the Federal Rules of Civil Procedure. NY R US-DCTND CM/ECF(5)(5.3).

iv. *Using court facilities.* If a local rule so authorizes, a party may use the court's transmission facilities to make service under FRCP 5(b)(2)(E). FRCP 5(b)(3).

c. *Serving numerous defendants*

i. *In general.* If an action involves an unusually large number of defendants, the court may, on motion or on its own, order that:

- Defendants' pleadings and replies to them need not be served on other defendants;

- Any crossclaim, counterclaim, avoidance, or affirmative defense in those pleadings and replies to them will be treated as denied or avoided by all other parties; and

- Filing any such pleading and serving it on the plaintiff constitutes notice of the pleading to all parties. FRCP 5(c)(1).

ii. *Notifying parties.* A copy of every such order must be served on the parties as the court directs. FRCP 5(c)(2).

3. *Individual judge practices.* Refer to the Miscellaneous section of this document for information on individual judge practices on filing and serving documents.

## G. Hearings

1. There is no hearing contemplated in the federal statutes or rules for interrogatories.

## H. Forms

### 1. Federal Interrogatories Forms

a. Introductory statement; Interrogatories to individual. AMJUR PP DEPOSITION § 405.

b. Introductory statement; Interrogatories to corporation. AMJUR PP DEPOSITION § 406.

c. Interrogatories. 3A FEDFORMS § 3488.

d. Interrogatories; Another form. 3A FEDFORMS § 3489.

e. Interrogatories by plaintiff; To corporation. 3A FEDFORMS § 3490.

f. Interrogatories by plaintiff; Complete set. 3A FEDFORMS § 3491.

g. Interrogatories by plaintiff; Requesting identification of documents and production under FRCP 34. 3A FEDFORMS § 3492.

h. Interrogatories by plaintiff; With definition of terms used and instructions for answering. 3A FEDFORMS § 3493.

i. Interrogatories by plaintiff; Employment discrimination case. 3A FEDFORMS § 3494.

j. Interrogatories by defendant. 3A FEDFORMS § 3495.

k. Interrogatories by defendant; Complete set. 3A FEDFORMS § 3496.

l. Interrogatories by defendant; Complete set; Another form. 3A FEDFORMS § 3497.

m. Interrogatories by defendant; Complete set; Another form. 3A FEDFORMS § 3498.

n. Interrogatories by defendant; Complete set; Another form. 3A FEDFORMS § 3499.

o. Interrogatories by defendant; Follow-up interrogatories to plaintiff after lapse of time since first set of interrogatories or deposition. 3A FEDFORMS § 3500.

p. Certificate of service of interrogatories. 3A FEDFORMS § 3501.

q. Interrogatories; Outline form. FEDPROF § 23:335.

r. Interrogatories; To defendant; Trademark action. FEDPROF § 23:347.

s. Interrogatories; With request for documents; To defendant; Collection of royalties. FEDPROF § 23:348.

t. Interrogatories; To defendant; Copyright infringement. FEDPROF § 23:350.

u. Interrogatories; To plaintiff; Products liability. FEDPROF § 23:352.

v. Interrogatories; To plaintiff; Personal injury. FEDPROF § 23:353.

w. Interrogatories; To defendant; Premises liability. FEDPROF § 23:356.

x. Interrogatories; To defendant; Medical malpractice. FEDPROF § 23:357.

y. General forms; Standard interrogatories. GOLDLTGFMS § 26:25.

z. General forms; Civil cases. GOLDLTGFMS § 26:26.

## I. Applicable Rules

1. *Federal rules*

a. Serving and filing pleadings and other papers. FRCP 5.

b. Privacy protection for filings made with the court. FRCP 5.2.

c. Computing and extending time; Time for motion papers. FRCP 6.

d. Pleadings allowed; Form of motions and other papers. FRCP 7.

e. Form of pleadings. FRCP 10.

f. Signing pleadings, motions, and other papers; Representations to the court; Sanctions. FRCP 11.

    g.   Duty to disclose; General provisions governing discovery. FRCP 26.

    h.   Stipulations about discovery procedure. FRCP 29.

    i.   Interrogatories to parties. FRCP 33.

    j.   Failure to make disclosures or to cooperate in discovery; Sanctions. FRCP 37.

2. *Local rules*

    a.   Scope of the rules. NY R USDCTND L.R. 1.1.

    b.   Complex and multi-district litigation. NY R USDCTND L.R. 3.3.

    c.   Service and filing of papers. NY R USDCTND L.R. 5.1.

    d.   Personal privacy protection. NY R USDCTND L.R. 8.1.

    e.   Form of papers. NY R USDCTND L.R. 10.1.

    f.   Discovery cut-off. NY R USDCTND L.R. 16.2.

    g.   Form of certain discovery documents. NY R USDCTND L.R. 26.1.

    h.   Filing discovery. NY R USDCTND L.R. 26.2.

    i.   Timing of discovery. NY R USDCTND L.R. 26.4.

    j.   Settlement procedures. NY R USDCTND L.R. 68.2.

    k.   Appearance and withdrawal of attorney. NY R USDCTND L.R. 83.2.

    l.   Arbitration. NY R USDCTND L.R. 83.7-1; NY R USDCTND L.R. 83.7-2; NY R USDCTND L.R. 83.7-3.

    m.   Assisted mediation program. NY R USDCTND L.R. 83.8.

    n.   Mediation. NY R USDCTND L.R. 83.11-1; NY R USDCTND L.R. 83.11-3.

    o.   Early neutral evaluation. NY R USDCTND L.R. 83.12-1; NY R USDCTND L.R. 83.12-3.

    p.   Administrative procedures for electronic case filing. NY R USDCTND CM/ECF.

    q.   Case assignment plan for the Northern District of New York. [NY R USDCTND Order 12, as amended by NY ORDER 16-4201, effective March 24, 2015].

    r.   Directing the expedited service of the summons and complaint and further directing the completion of FRCP 16 stipulation for the timely progression of civil actions. [NY R USDCTND Order 25, as amended by NY ORDER 16-4187, effective June 23, 2016].

    s.   Mandatory mediation program. NY R USDCTND Order 47.

**J. Miscellaneous**

**NOTE: Individual judges' rules may apply. For available judge-level information, refer to:**

DISTRICT JUDGE MAE A. D'AGOSTINO: [NY R USDCTND D'Agostino-Rules and Practices, as added by NY ORDER 16-4200, effective April 4, 2016].

DISTRICT JUDGE THOMAS J. McAVOY: NY R USDCTND McAvoy-Order.

## Requests, Notices and Applications
## Request for Production of Documents

**Document Last Updated September 2016**

**A. Checklist**

   (I)   ❑ Matters to be considered by requesting party

      (a)   ❑ Required documents

         (1)   ❑ Request for production of documents

     (b)  ❑  Supplemental documents

        (1)  ❑  Subpoena

        (2)  ❑  Certificate of service

     (c)  ❑  Timing

        (1)  ❑  A party may not seek discovery from any source before the parties have conferred as required by FRCP 26(f), except in a proceeding exempted from initial disclosure under FRCP 26(a)(1)(B), or when authorized by the Federal Rules of Civil Procedure, by stipulation, or by court order

        (2)  ❑  More than twenty-one (21) days after the summons and complaint are served on a party, a request under FRCP 34 may be delivered: (1) to that party by any other party, and (2) by that party to any plaintiff or to any other party that has been served

 (II)  ❑  Matters to be considered by responding party

     (a)  ❑  Required documents

        (1)  ❑  Response to request for production of documents

     (b)  ❑  Supplemental documents

        (1)  ❑  Certificate of service

     (c)  ❑  Timing

        (1)  ❑  The party to whom the request is directed must respond in writing within thirty (30) days after being served or—if the request was delivered under FRCP 26(d)(2)—within thirty (30) days after the parties' first FRCP 26(f) conference

## B. Timing

1. *Request for production of documents.* Without leave of court or written stipulation, a request may not be served before the time specified in FRCP 26(d). FEDPROC § 26:632. Of course, discovery under FRCP 34 should ordinarily precede the trial. FEDPROC § 26:632.

   a.  *Early FRCP 34 requests*

      i.  *Time to deliver.* More than twenty-one (21) days after the summons and complaint are served on a party, a request under FRCP 34 may be delivered:

         ●  To that party by any other party, and

         ●  By that party to any plaintiff or to any other party that has been served. FRCP 26(d)(2)(A).

     ii.  *When considered served.* The request is considered to have been served at the first FRCP 26(f) conference. FRCP 26(d)(2)(B).

2. *Timing of discovery, generally.* A party may not seek discovery from any source before the parties have conferred as required by FRCP 26(f), except in a proceeding exempted from initial disclosure under FRCP 26(a)(1)(B), or when authorized by the Federal Rules of Civil Procedure, by stipulation, or by court order. FRCP 26(d)(1). FRCP 26(d), which prohibits discovery prior to a meeting and conference between the parties, and FRCP 26(f), which directs parties to meet and confer with each other relative to the nature and basis of claims and defenses to a lawsuit, shall not apply to any action in which a party is incarcerated. NY R USDCTND L.R. 26.4.

3. *Discovery cut-off.* The "discovery cut-off" is that date by which all responses to written discovery, including requests for admissions, shall be due according to the Federal Rules of Civil Procedure and by which all depositions shall be concluded. Counsel are advised to initiate discovery requests and notice depositions sufficiently in advance of the cut-off date to comply with NY R USDCTND L.R. 16.2. Discovery requests that call for responses or scheduled depositions after the discovery cut-off will not be enforceable except by order of the Court for good cause shown. Parties shall file and serve motions to compel discovery no later than fourteen (14) days after the discovery cut-off. See NY R USDCTND L.R. 7.1(d)(8). NY R USDCTND L.R. 16.2.

4. *Computation of time*

   a.  *Computing time.* FRCP 6 applies in computing any time period specified in the Federal Rules of Civil

Procedure, in any local rule or court order, or in any statute that does not specify a method of computing time. FRCP 6(a).

  i.  *Period stated in days or a longer unit.* When the period is stated in days or a longer unit of time:

   • Exclude the day of the event that triggers the period;

   • Count every day, including intermediate Saturdays, Sundays, and legal holidays; and

   • Include the last day of the period, but if the last day is a Saturday, Sunday, or legal holiday, the period continues to run until the end of the next day that is not a Saturday, Sunday, or legal holiday. FRCP 6(a)(1).

  ii.  *Period stated in hours.* When the period is stated in hours:

   • Begin counting immediately on the occurrence of the event that triggers the period;

   • Count every hour, including hours during intermediate Saturdays, Sundays, and legal holidays; and

   • If the period would end on a Saturday, Sunday, or legal holiday, the period continues to run until the same time on the next day that is not a Saturday, Sunday, or legal holiday. FRCP 6(a)(2).

  iii.  *Inaccessibility of the clerk's office.* Unless the court orders otherwise, if the clerk's office is inaccessible:

   • On the last day for filing under FRCP 6(a)(1), then the time for filing is extended to the first accessible day that is not a Saturday, Sunday, or legal holiday; or

   • During the last hour for filing under FRCP 6(a)(2), then the time for filing is extended to the same time on the first accessible day that is not a Saturday, Sunday, or legal holiday. FRCP 6(a)(3).

  iv.  *"Last day" defined.* Unless a different time is set by a statute, local rule, or court order, the last day ends:

   • For electronic filing, at midnight in the court's time zone; and

   • For filing by other means, when the clerk's office is scheduled to close. FRCP 6(a)(4).

  v.  *"Next day" defined.* The "next day" is determined by continuing to count forward when the period is measured after an event and backward when measured before an event. FRCP 6(a)(5).

  vi.  *"Legal holiday" defined.* "Legal holiday" means:

   • The day set aside by statute for observing New Year's Day, Martin Luther King Jr.'s Birthday, Washington's Birthday, Memorial Day, Independence Day, Labor Day, Columbus Day, Veterans' Day, Thanksgiving Day, or Christmas Day;

   • Any day declared a holiday by the President or Congress; and

   • For periods that are measured after an event, any other day declared a holiday by the state where the district court is located. FRCP 6(a)(6).

 b.  *Computation of electronic filing deadlines.* A document will be deemed timely filed if electronically filed prior to midnight Eastern Time. However, if the time of day is of the essence, the assigned judge may order that the document be filed by a time certain. NY R USDCTND CM/ECF(4)(4.3).

  i.  *Technical failures.* A Filing User, whose filing is untimely as the result of a technical failure of the Court's CM/ECF site, may seek appropriate relief from the Court. However, Filing Users are cautioned that, in some circumstances, the Court lacks the authority to grant an extension of time to file (e.g., FRCP 6(b) of the Federal Rules of Civil Procedure). NY R USDCTND CM/ECF(10)(10.1).

   • *Technical failure of the filing user's system.* Problems with the Filing User's system, such as phone line problems, problems with the Filing User's Internet Service Provider ("ISP"), or hardware or software problems, will not constitute a technical failure under these Administrative Procedures nor excuse an untimely filing. A Filing User who cannot file

documents electronically because of a problem on the Filing User's system must file the documents' conventionally along with an affidavit explaining the reason for not filing the documents electronically. NY R USDCTND CM/ECF(10)(10.2).

c. *Extending time*

   i. *In general.* When an act may or must be done within a specified time, the court may, for good cause, extend the time:

   - With or without motion or notice if the court acts, or if a request is made, before the original time or its extension expires; or

   - On motion made after the time has expired if the party failed to act because of excusable neglect. FRCP 6(b)(1).

   ii. *Exceptions.* A court must not extend the time to act under FRCP 50(b), FRCP 50(d), FRCP 52(b), FRCP 59(b), FRCP 59(d), FRCP 59(e), and FRCP 60(b). FRCP 6(b)(2).

   iii. Refer to the United States District Court for the Northern District of New York KeyRules Motion for Continuance/Extension of Time document for more information on extending time.

d. *Additional time after certain kinds of service.* When a party may or must act within a specified time after service and service is made under FRCP 5(b)(2)(C), FRCP 5(b)(2)(D), FRCP 5(b)(2)(E), or FRCP 5(b)(2)(F), three (3) days are added after the period would otherwise expire under FRCP 6(a). FRCP 6(d).

   i. In accordance with FRCP 6(e), service by electronic means is treated the same as service by mail for purposes of adding three (3) days to the prescribed period to respond. NY R USDCTND CM/ECF(5)(5.4). [Editor's note: the reference to FRCP 6(e) is likely meant to be a reference to FRCP 6(d)].

5. *Individual judge practices.* Refer to the Miscellaneous section of this document for information on individual judge practices on timing of documents.

## C. General Requirements

1. *General provisions governing discovery*

   a. *Discovery scope and limits*

      i. *Scope in general.* Unless otherwise limited by court order, the scope of discovery is as follows: Parties may obtain discovery regarding any nonprivileged matter that is relevant to any party's claim or defense and proportional to the needs of the case, considering the importance of the issues at stake in the action, the amount in controversy, the parties' relative access to relevant information, the parties' resources, the importance of the discovery in resolving the issues, and whether the burden or expense of the proposed discovery outweighs its likely benefit. Information within this scope of discovery need not be admissible in evidence to be discoverable. FRCP 26(b)(1).

      ii. *Limitations on frequency and extent*

      - *When permitted.* By order, the court may alter the limits in the Federal Rules of Civil Procedure on the number of depositions and interrogatories or on the length of depositions under FRCP 30. By order or local rule, the court may also limit the number of requests under FRCP 36. FRCP 26(b)(2)(A).

      - *Specific limitations on electronically stored information.* A party need not provide discovery of electronically stored information from sources that the party identifies as not reasonably accessible because of undue burden or cost. On motion to compel discovery or for a protective order, the party from whom discovery is sought must show that the information is not reasonably accessible because of undue burden or cost. If that showing is made, the court may nonetheless order discovery from such sources if the requesting party shows good cause, considering the limitations of FRCP 26(b)(2)(C). The court may specify conditions for the discovery. FRCP 26(b)(2)(B).

      - *When required.* On motion or on its own, the court must limit the frequency or extent of

discovery otherwise allowed by the Federal Rules of Civil Procedure or by local rule if it determines that: (1) the discovery sought is unreasonably cumulative or duplicative, or can be obtained from some other source that is more convenient, less burdensome, or less expensive; (2) the party seeking discovery has had ample opportunity to obtain the information by discovery in the action; or (3) the proposed discovery is outside the scope permitted by FRCP 26(b)(1). FRCP 26(b)(2)(C).

iii. *Trial preparation; Materials*

- *Documents and tangible things.* Ordinarily, a party may not discover documents and tangible things that are prepared in anticipation of litigation or for trial by or for another party or its representative (including the other party's attorney, consultant, surety, indemnitor, insurer, or agent). But, subject to FRCP 26(b)(4), those materials may be discovered if: (1) they are otherwise discoverable under FRCP 26(b)(1); and (2) the party shows that it has substantial need for the materials to prepare its case and cannot, without undue hardship, obtain their substantial equivalent by other means. FRCP 26(b)(3)(A).

- *Protection against disclosure.* If the court orders discovery of those materials, it must protect against disclosure of the mental impressions, conclusions, opinions, or legal theories of a party's attorney or other representative concerning the litigation. FRCP 26(b)(3)(B).

- *Previous statement.* Any party or other person may, on request and without the required showing, obtain the person's own previous statement about the action or its subject matter. If the request is refused, the person may move for a court order, and FRCP 37(a)(5) applies to the award of expenses. A previous statement is either: (1) a written statement that the person has signed or otherwise adopted or approved; or (2) a contemporaneous stenographic, mechanical, electrical, or other recording—or a transcription of it—that recites substantially verbatim the person's oral statement. FRCP 26(b)(3)(C).

iv. *Trial preparation; Experts*

- *Deposition of an expert who may testify.* A party may depose any person who has been identified as an expert whose opinions may be presented at trial. If FRCP 26(a)(2)(B) requires a report from the expert, the deposition may be conducted only after the report is provided. FRCP 26(b)(4)(A).

- *Trial-preparation protection for draft reports or disclosures.* FRCP 26(b)(3)(A) and FRCP 26(b)(3)(B) protect drafts of any report or disclosure required under FRCP 26(a)(2), regardless of the form in which the draft is recorded. FRCP 26(b)(4)(B).

- *Trial-preparation protection for communications between a party's attorney and expert witnesses.* FRCP 26(b)(3)(A) and FRCP 26(b)(3)(B) protect communications between the party's attorney and any witness required to provide a report under FRCP 26(a)(2)(B), regardless of the form of the communications, except to the extent that the communications: (1) relate to compensation for the expert's study or testimony; (2) identify facts or data that the party's attorney provided and that the expert considered in forming the opinions to be expressed; or (3) identify assumptions that the party's attorney provided and that the expert relied on in forming the opinions to be expressed. FRCP 26(b)(4)(C).

- *Expert employed only for trial preparation.* Ordinarily, a party may not, by interrogatories or deposition, discover facts known or opinions held by an expert who has been retained or specially employed by another party in anticipation of litigation or to prepare for trial and who is not expected to be called as a witness at trial. But a party may do so only: (1) as provided in FRCP 35(b); or (2) on showing exceptional circumstances under which it is impracticable for the party to obtain facts or opinions on the same subject by other means. FRCP 26(b)(4)(D).

- *Payment.* Unless manifest injustice would result, the court must require that the party seeking discovery: (1) pay the expert a reasonable fee for time spent in responding to discovery under FRCP 26(b)(4)(A) or FRCP 26(b)(4)(D); and (2) for discovery FRCP

26(b)(4)(D), also pay the other party a fair portion of the fees and expenses it reasonably incurred in obtaining the expert's facts and opinions. FRCP 26(b)(4)(E).

    v. *Claiming privilege or protecting trial-preparation materials*

- *Information withheld.* When a party withholds information otherwise discoverable by claiming that the information is privileged or subject to protection as trial-preparation material, the party must: (1) expressly make the claim; and (2) describe the nature of the documents, communications, or tangible things not produced or disclosed—and do so in a manner that, without revealing information itself privileged or protected, will enable other parties to assess the claim. FRCP 26(b)(5)(A).

- *Information produced.* If information produced in discovery is subject to a claim of privilege or of protection as trial-preparation material, the party making the claim may notify any party that received the information of the claim and the basis for it. After being notified, a party must promptly return, sequester, or destroy the specified information and any copies it has; must not use or disclose the information until the claim is resolved; must take reasonable steps to retrieve the information if the party disclosed it before being notified; and may promptly present the information to the court under seal for a determination of the claim. The producing party must preserve the information until the claim is resolved. FRCP 26(b)(5)(B).

  b. *Protective orders.* A party or any person from whom discovery is sought may move for a protective order in the court where the action is pending—or as an alternative on matters relating to a deposition, in the court for the district where the deposition will be taken. FRCP 26(c)(1). Refer to the United States District Court for the Northern District of New York KeyRules Motion for Protective Order document for more information.

  c. *Sequence of discovery.* Unless the parties stipulate or the court orders otherwise for the parties' and witnesses' convenience and in the interests of justice: (1) methods of discovery may be used in any sequence; and (2) discovery by one party does not require any other party to delay its discovery. FRCP 26(d)(3).

2. *Request for production of documents*

  a. *In general.* A party may serve on any other party a request within the scope of FRCP 26(b):

    i. To produce and permit the requesting party or its representative to inspect, copy, test, or sample the following items in the responding party's possession, custody, or control:

- Any designated documents or electronically stored information—including writings, drawings, graphs, charts, photographs, sound recordings, images, and other data or data compilations—stored in any medium from which information can be obtained either directly or, if necessary, after translation by the responding party into a reasonably usable form; or

- Any designated tangible things; or

    ii. To permit entry onto designated land or other property possessed or controlled by the responding party, so that the requesting party may inspect, measure, survey, photograph, test, or sample the property or any designated object or operation on it. FRCP 34(a).

  b. *Contents of the request.* The request: (1) must describe with reasonable particularity each item or category of items to be inspected; (2) must specify a reasonable time, place, and manner for the inspection and for performing the related acts; and (3) may specify the form or forms in which electronically stored information is to be produced. FRCP 34(b)(1).

    i. *Description of items.* Although the phrase "reasonable particularity" eludes precise definition and depends on the facts and circumstances in each case, at least two tests have been suggested:

- The first test is whether the request places a party on "reasonable notice" of what is called for and what is not so that a reasonable person would know what documents or things are called for. FEDPROC § 26:634.

- The second is whether the request gives a court enough information to enable it to rule intelligently on objections. FEDPROC § 26:634.

c. *Numbering.* The parties shall number each interrogatory or request sequentially, regardless of the number of sets of interrogatories or requests. NY R USDCTND L.R. 26.1.

d. *Signature.* Though FRCP 34 does not say so, it is sufficient if the request is signed by the attorney for the party seeking discovery. FPP § 2212. Refer to the Format section of this document for more information on signing of discovery papers.

e. *Other authority on production and inspection*

   i. *Freedom of Information Act.* Although the Freedom of Information Act (FOIA) is fundamentally designed to inform the public about agency action, and not to benefit private litigants, Congress has not acted upon proposals to forbid or limit the use of the FOIA for discovery purposes. FEDPROC § 26:605; National Presto Industries, Inc., 218 Ct.Cl. 696, 1978 WL 8475 (1978). However, a FOIA request may not be used to supplement civil discovery under FRCP 34, as in the case where information is privileged and therefore outside the scope of civil discovery. FEDPROC § 26:605; U.S. v. Weber Aircraft Corp., 465 U.S. 792, 104 S.Ct. 1488, 79 L.Ed.2d 814 (1984).

   ii. *Hague Convention.* Under the Hague Convention, a party seeking evidence abroad must obtain and send a letter of request to the central authority of the country in which the evidence is sought, requesting service of the request on the desired person or entity; if the request complies with the Convention, the central authority will then obtain the desired evidence. FEDPROC § 26:606. [Editor's note: the Hague Convention can be found at T.I.A.S. No. 6638 and is also available in the appendix to FRCP 4].

f. *Motion to compel.* If a party who has been requested to permit discovery under FRCP 34 makes no response to the request, or if its response objects to all or part of the requested discovery, or if it otherwise fails to permit discovery as requested, the party who submitted the request, if it still wishes the discovery that has been refused, may move under FRCP 37(a) for an order compelling inspection in accordance with the request. FPP § 2214. Refer to the United States District Court for the Northern District of New York KeyRules Motion to Compel Discovery document for more information.

3. *Sanctions for failure to cooperate in discovery.* The court where the action is pending may, on motion, order sanctions if a party, after being properly served with interrogatories under FRCP 33 or a request for inspection under FRCP 34, fails to serve its answers, objections, or written response. FRCP 37(d)(1)(A)(ii). If a motion to compel is granted, the court must, after giving an opportunity to be heard, require the party or deponent whose conduct necessitated the motion, the party or attorney advising that conduct, or both to pay the movant's reasonable expenses incurred in making the motion, including attorney's fees. But the court must not order this payment if the opposing party's nondisclosure, response, or objection was substantially justified. FRCP 37(a)(5)(A)(ii). Refer to the United States District Court for the Northern District of New York KeyRules Motion for Discovery Sanctions document for more information.

4. *Stipulations about discovery procedure.* Unless the court orders otherwise, the parties may stipulate that: (1) a deposition may be taken before any person, at any time or place, on any notice, and in the manner specified—in which event it may be used in the same way as any other deposition; and (2) other procedures governing or limiting discovery be modified—but a stipulation extending the time for any form of discovery must have court approval if it would interfere with the time set for completing discovery, for hearing a motion, or for trial. FRCP 29.

5. *Complex and multi-district litigation.* If the assigned judge determines, in his or her discretion, that the case is of such a complex nature that it cannot reasonably be trial ready within eighteen (18) months from the date the complaint is filed, the assigned judge may design and issue a particularized case management order that will move the case to trial as quickly as the complexity of the case allows. NY R USDCTND L.R. 3.3(a). The parties shall promptly notify the Court in writing if any action commenced is appropriate for multi-district litigation. NY R USDCTND L.R. 3.3(b).

6. *Appearances.* An attorney appearing for a party in a civil case shall promptly file with the Clerk a written notice of appearance; however, an attorney does not need to file a notice of appearance if the attorney who would be filing the notice of appearance is the same individual who has signed the complaint, notice of removal, pre-answer motion, or answer. NY R USDCTND L.R. 83.2(a). For more information, refer to NY R USDCTND L.R. 83.2.

7. *Related cases.* A civil case is "related" to another civil case for purposes of this guideline when, because of the similarity of facts and legal issues or because the cases arise from the same transactions or events, a substantial saving of judicial resources is likely to result from assigning the cases to the same Judge and Magistrate Judge. NY R USDCTND Order 12(G)(2). A civil case shall not be deemed related to another civil case merely because the civil case: (1) involves similar legal issues, or (2) involves the same parties. NY R USDCTND Order 12(G)(3). Presumptively, and subject to the power of a Judge to determine otherwise pursuant to NY R USDCTND Order 12(G)(5), civil cases shall not be deemed to be "related" unless both cases are still pending before the Court. NY R USDCTND Order 12(G)(4).

   a. *New filings.* If an attorney or filing party indicates on the Civil Cover Sheet that a case is related to an earlier filed case, the Clerk shall instruct the filing party to file a notice of related cases. The allegedly related cases will be submitted by the Clerk to the Judge to whom the earliest filed case is assigned, who shall advise the Clerk whether such cases are related. NY R USDCTND Order 12(G)(1).

   b. *Judicial determination that civil cases are "related."* Except for the cases described in the final sentence of NY R USDCTND Order 12(G)(6), all civil cases shall be randomly assigned when they are filed. Other than the cases described in the final sentence of NY R USDCTND Order 12(G)(6), civil cases shall not be deemed to be "related" for purposes of this guideline at the instance of any litigant or attorney unless and until there has been a determination by a Judge of this Court that the standard of NY R USDCTND Order 12(G)(2) is met. NY R USDCTND Order 12(G)(5).

      i. *Notice of related filing.* Any party may apply for such a determination by filing with the Clerk a notice of related filing, which should include an explanation as to why the standard of NY R USDCTND Order 12(G)(2) is met. A form for this purpose is available on the Court's website. A copy of the notice shall be served on all other parties who have appeared. Such an application must be made after the date when at least a majority of the defendants have been served with the complaint. Before making such an application, the applicant must confer in good faith with all other parties in an effort to reach an agreement on whether or not the case is "related". After such an application is made, any other party may serve and file within seven (7) calendar days a letter of no more than two (2) pages supporting or opposing the application. The application to have the case assigned to another Judge shall be presented to the Judge with the earliest filed case for decision on whether the action(s) should be reassigned as related cases. The Judge with the earliest filed case may then enter an order in the case at bar, either deeming the case to be related and directing the Clerk to reassign the action, or denying the application for reassignment. Any disputes concerning the assignment of related cases will be referred to the Chief Judge for resolution. NY R USDCTND Order 12(G)(5).

   c. For more information on related cases, refer to NY R USDCTND Order 12(G).

8. *Alternative dispute resolution (ADR).* It is the mission of this court to do everything it can to help parties resolve their disputes as fairly, quickly, and efficiently as possible. NY R USDCTND Order 25(VIII).

   a. *Arbitration.* NY R USDCTND L.R. 83.7 governs the consensual arbitration program for referral of civil actions to court-annexed arbitration. It may remain in effect until further order of the Court. Its purpose is to establish a less formal procedure for the just, efficient and economical resolution of disputes, while preserving the right to a full trial on demand. NY R USDCTND L.R. 83.7-1.

      i. *Actions subject to arbitration.* The Clerk shall notify the parties in all civil cases, except as the Local Rules of Practice for the United States District Court for the Northern District of New York otherwise direct, that they may consent to non-binding arbitration under NY R US-DCTND L.R. 83.7. The notice shall be furnished to the parties at pretrial/scheduling confer-ences or shall be included with pretrial conference notices and instructions. Consent to arbitration under NY R USDCTND L.R. 83.7 shall be discussed at the pretrial/scheduling conference. No party or attorney shall be prejudiced for refusing to participate in arbitration. The Court shall allow the referral of any civil action pending before it to the arbitration process if the parties consent. The plaintiff shall be responsible for securing the execution of a consent form by the parties and for filing the form with the Clerk within fourteen (14) days after the parties receive the form. The parties shall freely and knowingly enter into the consent. NY R USDCTND L.R. 83.7-2.

ii. *Referral to arbitration.* The Clerk shall refer every action subject to NY R USDCTND L.R. 83.7 to arbitration in accordance with the procedures under NY R USDCTND L.R. 83.7 twenty-one (21) days after the filing of the last responsive pleading or within twenty-one (21) days of the filing of a stipulated consent order referring the action to arbitration, whichever event occurs last, except as otherwise provided. If any party notices a motion to dismiss under the provisions of FRCP 12(a) and/or FRCP 12(b), or a motion to join necessary parties pursuant to the Federal Rules of Civil Procedure prior to the expiration of the twenty-one (21) day period, the assigned judge shall hear the motion and further proceedings under NY R USDCTND L.R. 83.7 shall be deferred pending decision on the motion. If the Court does not dismiss the action on the motion, the Court shall refer the action to arbitration twenty-one (21) days after the filing of the decision. NY R USDCTND L.R. 83.7-3(a). Motions for summary judgment pursuant to FRCP 56 shall be filed and served within twenty-one (21) days following the close of discovery. The filing of a FRCP 56 motion shall defer further proceedings under NY R USDCTND L.R. 83.7 pending decision on the motion. NY R USDCTND L.R. 83.7-3(a).

- *Relief from referral.* Any party shall request relief from the operation of NY R USDCTND L.R. 83.7 by filing with the Court a motion for the relief within twenty-one (21) days after entry of the initial stipulated consent order which refers the case for arbitration. The assigned judge shall, sua sponte, exempt an action from the application of NY R USDCTND L.R. 83.7 where the objectives of arbitration would not be realized because (1) the case involves complex or novel legal issues, (2) legal issues predominate over factual issues, or (3) for other good cause. NY R USDCTND L.R. 83.7-3(c).

iii. For more information on arbitration, refer to NY R USDCTND L.R. 83.7.

b. *Mediation.* The purpose of NY R USDCTND L.R. 83.11 is to provide a supplementary procedure to the Court's existing alternative dispute resolution procedures. NY R USDCTND L.R. 83.11 provides for an earlier resolution of civil disputes resulting in savings of time and cost to litigants and the Court without sacrificing the quality of justice rendered or the right of litigants to a full trial on all issues not resolved through mediation. NY R USDCTND L.R. 83.11-1(a). Mediation is a process by which an impartial person, the mediator, facilitates communication between disputing parties to promote understanding, reconciliation and settlement. The mediator is an advocate for settlement and uses the mediation process to help the parties fully explore any potential area of agreement. The mediator does not serve as a judge or arbitrator and has no authority to render any decision on any disputed issue or to force a settlement. The parties themselves are responsible for negotiating any resolution(s) to their dispute. NY R USDCTND L.R. 83.11-1(b).

i. *Actions subject to mediation.* The Court may refer any civil action (or any portion thereof) to mediation under NY R USDCTND L.R. 83.11: (1) by order of referral; or (2) on the motion of any party; or (3) by consent of the parties. NY R USDCTND L.R. 83.11-3(a).

- *Withdrawal from mediation.* The parties may withdraw from mediation any civil action or claim that the Court refers to mediation pursuant to NY R USDCTND L.R. 83.11-3 by application to the assigned judge at least ten (10) days prior to the scheduled mediation session. NY R USDCTND L.R. 83.11-3(b).

ii. *Mandatory mediation program.* The United States District Court for the Northern District of New York has adopted this Mandatory Mediation Plan. The paid Mediation Program is designed to provide quicker, less expensive and potentially more satisfying alternatives to continuing litigation, without impairing the quality of justice or the right to trial. NY R USDCTND Order 47(1)(1.2)(A). This Mandatory Mediation Plan applies to civil actions pending as well as newly filed actions, except as otherwise indicated in NY R USDCTND Order 47. The Local Rules for voluntary mediation will apply only to Pro Se Cases that proceed through the Assisted Mediation Program. NY R USDCTND Order 47(1)(1.2)(B).

- *Referral into the pilot mandatory mediation program for new cases.* All civil cases shall be referred automatically into the Mandatory Mediation Program. Notice of the Mandatory Mediation requirements will be provided to all parties immediately upon the filing of a complaint and answer or a notice of removal. ADR intervention will be scheduled at the conference held pursuant to NY R USDCTND L.R. 16.1. NY R USDCTND Order

47(2)(2.1)(A). For a list of categories of actions exempted from automatic referral, refer to NY R USDCTND Order 47(2)(2.1)(A).

- *Referral into the pilot mandatory mediation program for pending cases.* The assigned Judge or Magistrate Judge on any pending civil case may, sua sponte or with status conference, issue an order referring the case into the Mandatory Mediation Program. The order shall specify a date on which the ADR intervention is to be completed. NY R USDCTND Order 47(2)(2.1)(B).

- *Referral into the pilot mandatory mediation program by stipulation.* A case may be referred into the Mandatory Mediation Program by stipulation of all parties. Stipulations shall be filed and shall designate the time frame within which the ADR process will be completed. Stipulations are presumed acceptable unless the assigned Judge or Magistrate Judge determines that the interests of justice are not served. NY R USDCTND Order 47(2)(2.1)(C).

- *Relief from referral.* Motions to opt out of the program will be addressed by the assigned Magistrate Judge at the FRCP 16 conference. NY R USDCTND Order 47(2)(2.2)(A). Opting Out Motions shall be granted only for "good cause" shown. Inconvenience, travel costs, attorney fees or other costs shall not constitute "good cause." A party seeking relief from the Mandatory Mediation Program must set forth the reasons why Mandatory Mediation has no reasonable chance of being productive. NY R USDCTND Order 47(2)(2.2)(B). The assigned Magistrate Judge may, sua sponte, exempt any case from the Court's Mandatory Mediation Program. NY R USDCTND Order 47(2)(2.2)(C).

iii. *Assisted mediation program.* The Court may assign specially trained pro bono Special Mediation Counsel to assist pro se civilian litigants with preparing for and participating in mediation. The Assisted Mediation Program is open to civilian pro se parties to actions in the Northern District of New York. The assigned judge or magistrate judge determines if the case would benefit from mediation and would also benefit from the assignment of Special Mediation Counsel to assist the pro se party with the mediation process. NY R USDCTND L.R. 83.8(a). Appointment of Special Mediation Counsel is in no way guaranteed, even if the action is referred to the court-annexed mediation program. Appointment is at the sole discretion of the presiding judge. NY R USDCTND L.R. 83.8(a).

- *Referral to assisted mediation program.* If the court determines that referral to the Assisted Mediation Program is appropriate, the Court shall enter an order of reference to the Assisted Mediation Program. NY R USDCTND L.R. 83.8(b).

iv. For more information on mediation, refer to NY R USDCTND L.R. 83.11 and NY R USDCTND Order 47.

c. *Early neutral evaluation (ENE).* Early neutral evaluation (ENE) is a process in which parties obtain from an experienced neutral (an "evaluator") a nonbinding, reasoned, oral evaluation of the merits of the case. The first step in the ENE process involves the Court appointing an evaluator who has expertise in the area of law in the case. After the parties exchange essential information and position statements early in the pretrial period (usually within one hundred fifty (150) to two hundred (200) days after a complaint has been filed), the evaluator convenes an ENE session that typically lasts about two hours. At the ENE meeting, each side briefly presents the factual and legal basis of its position. The evaluator may ask questions of the parties and help them identify the main issues in dispute and the areas of agreement. The evaluator may also help the parties explore options for settlement. If settlement does not occur, the evaluator then offers an opinion as to the settlement value of the case, including the likelihood of liability and the likely range of damages. With the benefit of this assessment, the parties are again encouraged to discuss settlement, with or without the evaluator's assistance. The parties may also explore ways to narrow the issues in dispute, exchange information about the case or otherwise prepare efficiently for trial. NY R USDCTND L.R. 83.12-1.

i. *Actions subject to early neutral evaluation.* The Court may refer any civil action (or any portion thereof) to ENE under NY R USDCTND L.R. 83.12: (1) by order of referral; (2) on the motion of any party; or (3) by consent of the parties. NY R USDCTND L.R. 83.12-3(a).

- *Withdrawal from the ENE process.* The parties may withdraw any civil action or claim that the Court has referred to the ENE Process pursuant to NY R USDCTND L.R. 83.12-3 by application to the assigned judge at least ten (10) days before the scheduled evaluation session. NY R USDCTND L.R. 83.12-3(b).

ii. For more information on early neutral evaluation (ENE), refer to NY R USDCTND L.R. 83.12.

9. *Settlement procedures.* On notice to the Court or the Clerk that the parties have settled an action, and upon confirmation of the settlement by all parties, the Court may issue a judgment dismissing the action by reason of settlement. The Court shall issue the order without prejudice to the parties' right to secure reinstatement of the case within thirty (30) days after the date of judgment by making a showing that the settlement was not, in fact, consummated. NY R USDCTND L.R. 68.2(a). If the Court decides not to follow the procedures set forth in NY R USDCTND L.R. 68.2(a), the parties shall file within thirty (30) days of the notification to the Court, unless otherwise directed by written order, such notices, stipulations and/or motions as are necessary to terminate the action. If the required documents are not filed within the thirty (30) day period, the Clerk shall place the action on the dismissal calendar. NY R USDCTND L.R. 68.2(b).

10. *Sanctions and penalties for noncompliance.* Failure of an attorney or of a party to comply with any provision of the Local Rules of Practice for the United States District Court for the Northern District of New York, General Orders of this District, Orders of the Court, or the Federal Rules of Civil Procedure shall be a ground for imposition of sanctions. NY R USDCTND L.R. 1.1(d).

11. *Individual judge practices.* Refer to the Miscellaneous section of this document for information on individual judge practices on general requirements for documents.

## D. Documents

1. *Required documents*

   a. *Request for production of documents.* Refer to the General Requirements section of this document for information on the request for production of documents.

2. *Supplemental documents*

   a. *Subpoena.* As provided in FRCP 45, a nonparty may be compelled to produce documents and tangible things or to permit an inspection. FRCP 34(c). For information on the form and contents of the subpoena, refer to FRCP 45.

   b. *Certificate of service.* FRCP 5(d) requires that the person making service under FRCP 5 certify that service has been effected. FRCP 5(Advisory Committee Notes). Having such information on file may be useful for many purposes, including proof of service if an issue arises concerning the effectiveness of the service. FRCP 5(Advisory Committee Notes).

3. *Individual judge practices.* Refer to the Miscellaneous section of this document for information on individual judge practices on required documents.

## E. Format

1. *Form of documents.* The rules governing captions and other matters of form in pleadings apply to motions and other papers. FRCP 7(b)(2). All pleadings and other papers shall be served and filed in accordance with the Federal Rules of Civil Procedure and shall be in the form prescribed by NY R USDCTND L.R. 10.1. NY R USDCTND L.R. 5.1(a).

   a. *Form, generally.* All pleadings, motions, and other documents that a party presents for filing, whether in paper form or in electronic form, shall meet the following requirements:

      i. *Font size.* All text, whether in the body of the document or in footnotes, must be a minimum of twelve (12) point type. NY R USDCTND L.R. 10.1(a)(1).

      ii. *Margins.* All documents must have one (1) inch margins on all four sides of the page. NY R USDCTND L.R. 10.1(a)(2).

      iii. *Spacing.* All text in the body of the document must be double-spaced. NY R USDCTND L.R. 10.1(a)(3).

         • The text in block quotations and footnotes may be single-spaced. NY R USDCTND L.R. 10.1(a)(4).

     iv.  *Page numbering.* Pages must be consecutively numbered. NY R USDCTND L.R. 10.1(a)(7).

     v.  *Circumventing formatting limitations*

- Extensive footnotes must not be used to circumvent page limitations. NY R USDCTND L.R. 10.1(a)(5).

- Compacted or other compressed printing features must not be used. NY R USDCTND L.R. 10.1(a)(6).

  b.  *Additional requirements for paper filing.* Additional requirements for all pleadings, motions, and other documents that a party presents for filing in paper form:

     i.  *Paper size.* All documents must be on eight and one-half by eleven (8-1/2 x 11) inch white paper of good quality. NY R USDCTND L.R. 10.1(b)(1).

     ii.  *Text.* All text must be plainly and legibly written, typewritten, printed or reproduced without erasures or interlineations materially defacing them. NY R USDCTND L.R. 10.1(b)(2).

     iii.  *Ink.* All documents must be in black or blue ink. NY R USDCTND L.R. 10.1(b)(3).

     iv.  *Binding.* Pages of all documents must be stapled (or in some other way fastened) together. NY R USDCTND L.R. 10.1(b)(4).

     v.  *Single-sided paper.* All documents must be single-sided. NY R USDCTND L.R. 10.1(b)(5).

     vi.  *Electronic submission.* The Court, at its discretion, may require the electronic submission of any document in a WordPerfect-compatible format. NY R USDCTND L.R. 10.1(b)(6).

     vii.  *Rejection of document.* The Court may reject documents that do not comply with the above-listed requirements. NY R USDCTND L.R. 10.1(b).

  c.  *Caption; Names of parties.* Every pleading must have a caption with the court's name, a title, a file number, and a FRCP 7(a) designation. The title of the complaint must name all the parties; the title of other pleadings, after naming the first party on each side, may refer generally to other parties. FRCP 10(a). Each document must contain a caption for the specific case to which it pertains. The caption must include the title of the Court, the title of the action, the civil action number of the case, the initials of the assigned judge(s), and the name or nature of the paper in sufficient detail for identification. If a litigant has more than one action pending in this Court, any and all papers filed in a case must contain and pertain to one civil action number, unless the civil actions have been consolidated by the Court. Any motion or other papers purporting to relate to more than one action will not be accepted for filing and may be stricken by the Court. NY R USDCTND L.R. 10.1(c)(1) shall not apply, as noted in NY R USDCTND L.R. 10.1(c), to notices of change of address filed by attorneys of record and pro se litigants. The parties must separately caption affidavits and declarations and must not physically attach them to the Notice of Motion or Memorandum of Law. NY R USDCTND L.R. 10.1(c)(1).

  d.  *Paragraphs; Separate statements.* A party must state its claims or defenses in numbered paragraphs, each limited as far as practicable to a single set of circumstances. A later pleading may refer by number to a paragraph in an earlier pleading. If doing so would promote clarity, each claim founded on a separate transaction or occurrence—and each defense other than a denial—must be stated in a separate count or defense. FRCP 10(b).

  e.  *Adoption by reference; Exhibits.* A statement in a pleading may be adopted by reference elsewhere in the same pleading or in any other pleading or motion. A copy of a written instrument that is an exhibit to a pleading is a part of the pleading for all purposes. FRCP 10(c).

  f.  *Citation of local rules.* These are the Local Rules of Practice for the United States District Court for the Northern District of New York. They shall be cited as "L.R. ___." NY R USDCTND L.R. 1.1(a).

  g.  *Acceptance by the clerk.* The clerk must not refuse to file a paper solely because it is not in the form prescribed by the Federal Rules of Civil Procedure or by a local rule or practice. FRCP 5(d)(4).

2.  *Form of electronic documents.* All pleadings, motions, and other documents that a party presents for filing, whether in paper form or in electronic form, shall meet the requirements in NY R USDCTND L.R. 10.1(a). NY R USDCTND L.R. 10.1(a). Refer above for more information.

  a.  *Attachments and exhibits.* A Filing User must submit in electronic form all documents referenced as

exhibits or attachments in accordance with the Court's CM/ECF Users Manual unless the Court otherwise orders. A Filing User shall submit as exhibits or attachments only those excerpts of the referenced documents that are directly germane to the matter under the Court's consideration. Excerpted material must be clearly and prominently identified as such. Filing Users who file excerpts of documents as exhibits or attachments under these Administrative Procedures (NY R USDCTND CM/ECF) do so without prejudice to their right to timely file additional excerpts or the complete document. Responding parties may also timely file the complete document or additional excerpts that they believe are directly germane to the matter under the Court's consideration. NY R USDCTND CM/ECF(4)(4.4).

    i. All attachments must be described in sufficient detail so the Court and opposing counsel can easily identify and distinguish the filed attachments. Vague or general descriptions are insufficient (i.e., "Exhibit 1"). Rather, each attachment shall have a descriptive title identifying, with specificity, the document that is being filed (i.e., "Exhibit 12 Mulligan County Fire Investigation Report.") Failure to adequately describe attachments may result in the document being rejected by the Court. NY R USDCTND CM/ECF(4)(4.4).

    b. *Large documents.* For information on the electronic filing of large documents, please consult the Court's CM/ECF Users Manual, which is available on the Court's web page. NY R USDCTND CM/ECF(4)(4.5).

        i. A party who believes a document is too lengthy to electronically image, i.e., "scan," may contact the Clerk's Office for permission to file that document conventionally. If the Clerk's Office grants permission to conventionally file the document, the Filing User shall electronically file a notice of conventional filing for the documents. More information regarding this process can be obtained from the Court's web page. Exhibits submitted conventionally shall be served on other parties as if they were not subject to these Administrative Procedures (NY R USDCTND CM/ECF). For a list of hints and tips for scanning large documents, please consult the Court's web page. NY R USDCTND CM/ECF(4)(4.5).

    c. *Legibility.* It shall be the Filing User's responsibility to verify the legibility of scanned documents before filing them electronically with the Court. NY R USDCTND CM/ECF(4)(4.6).

    d. *Color documents.* Since documents scanned in color or containing a graphic take much longer to upload, Filing Users are encouraged to configure their scanners to scan documents at 300 dpi and preferably in black and white rather than in color. NY R USDCTND CM/ECF(4)(4.7).

    e. *Items not in .PDF format.* Parties wishing to file items not amenable to .pdf format (i.e. CD's, DVD's), shall file such items conventionally with the Clerk's Office. The Filing User shall electronically file a notice of conventional filing indicating that these items have been submitted to the clerk and shall serve copies of these items on other parties as if they were not subject to these Administrative Procedures (NY R USDCTND CM/ECF). These item(s) will be maintained by the Clerk's Office until the case is disposed, at which time they will be returned to the filing party for retention consistent with NY R USDCTND CM/ECF(4)(4.9). NY R USDCTND CM/ECF(4)(4.8).

3. *Signing disclosures and discovery requests, responses, and objections.* FRCP 11 does not apply to disclosures and discovery requests, responses, objections, and motions under FRCP 26 through FRCP 37. FRCP 11(d).

    a. *Signature required.* Every disclosure under FRCP 26(a)(1) or FRCP 26(a)(3) and every discovery request, response, or objection must be signed by at least one attorney of record in the attorney's own name—or by the party personally, if unrepresented—and must state the signer's address, e-mail address, and telephone number. FRCP 26(g)(1). Each document must identify the person filing the document. This identification must include an original signature of the attorney or pro se litigant; the typewritten name of that person; the address of a pro se litigant; and the bar roll number, office address, telephone number, e-mail address and fax number of the attorney. Telephone numbers of non-prisoner pro se parties may be provided voluntarily or upon request of the Court. See General Order #22 (NY R USDCTND CM/ECF) for signature requirements. NY R USDCTND L.R. 10.1(c)(2).

        i. *Electronic signatures.* Documents filed under an attorney's login and password shall constitute

that attorney's signature for purposes of the Local Rules of Practice for the United States District Court for the Northern District of New York and Federal Rules of Civil Procedure, including but not limited to FRCP 11. A pleading or other document requiring an attorney's signature shall be signed in the following manner, whether filed electronically or submitted on disk or CD/ROM to the Clerk's Office: "s/ (attorney name)." The correct format for an attorney signature is found in NY R USDCTND CM/ECF(6)(6.1). NY R USDCTND CM/ECF(6)(6.1).

- *Non-attorney signature.* If an original document requires the signature of a non-attorney, the Filing User may scan the original document containing the original signature(s), then electronically file it on the System. Alternatively, the Filing User may convert the document into .pdf text format and submit the document using "s/" for the signature of the non-attorney. NY R USDCTND CM/ECF(6)(6.2).

- *Multiple signatures.* A document requiring signatures of more than one party must be filed electronically either by (1) submitting a scanned document containing all necessary signatures; (2) representing the consent of the other parties on the document; or (3) in any other manner that the Court approves. NY R USDCTND CM/ECF(6)(6.3).

    b. *Effect of signature.* By signing, an attorney or party certifies that to the best of the person's knowledge, information, and belief formed after a reasonable inquiry:

      i. With respect to a disclosure, it is complete and correct as of the time it is made; and

      ii. With respect to a discovery request, response, or objection, it is:

- Consistent with the Federal Rules of Civil Procedure and warranted by existing law or by a nonfrivolous argument for extending, modifying, or reversing existing law, or for establishing new law;

- Not interposed for any improper purpose, such as to harass, cause unnecessary delay, or needlessly increase the cost of litigation; and

- Neither unreasonable nor unduly burdensome or expensive, considering the needs of the case, prior discovery in the case, the amount in controversy, and the importance of the issues at stake in the action. FRCP 26(g)(1).

    c. *Failure to sign.* Other parties have no duty to act on an unsigned disclosure, request, response, or objection until it is signed, and the court must strike it unless a signature is promptly supplied after the omission is called to the attorney's or party's attention. FRCP 26(g)(2).

    d. *Sanction for improper certification.* If a certification violates FRCP 26(g) without substantial justification, the court, on motion or on its own, must impose an appropriate sanction on the signer, the party on whose behalf the signer was acting, or both. The sanction may include an order to pay the reasonable expenses, including attorney's fees, caused by the violation. FRCP 26(g)(3). Refer to the United States District Court for the Northern District of New York KeyRules Motion for Discovery Sanctions document for more information.

4. *Privacy protection for filings made with the court*

    a. *Redacted filings.* Unless the court orders otherwise, in an electronic or paper filing with the court that contains an individual's Social Security number, taxpayer-identification number, or birth date, the name of an individual known to be a minor, or a financial-account number, a party or nonparty making the filing may include only:

      i. The last four (4) digits of the Social Security number and taxpayer-identification number;

      ii. The year of the individual's birth;

      iii. The minor's initials; and

      iv. The last four (4) digits of the financial-account number. FRCP 5.2(a); NY R USDCTND L.R. 8.1; NY R USDCTND CM/ECF(11)(11.2).

      v. If a home address must be used, use only the City and State. NY R USDCTND L.R. 8.1; NY R USDCTND CM/ECF(11)(11.2).

      vi. If the victim of a sexual assault must be referenced, redact the name to 'Victim.' NY R USDCTND CM/ECF(11)(11.2); NY R USDCTND L.R. 8.1.

vii. In addition, caution shall be exercised when filing documents that contain the following:

- Personal identifying number, such as a driver's license number;

- Medical records, treatment and diagnosis;

- Employment history;

- Individual financial information; and

- Proprietary or trade secret information. NY R USDCTND L.R. 8.1; NY R USDCTND CM/ECF(11)(11.2).

b. *Exemptions from the redaction requirement.* The redaction requirement does not apply to the following:

i. A financial-account number that identifies the property allegedly subject to forfeiture in a forfeiture proceeding;

ii. The record of an administrative or agency proceeding;

iii. The official record of a state-court proceeding;

iv. The record of a court or tribunal, if that record was not subject to the redaction requirement when originally filed;

v. A filing covered by FRCP 5.2(c) or FRCP 5.2(d); and

vi. A pro se filing in an action brought under 28 U.S.C.A. § 2241, 28 U.S.C.A. § 2254, or 28 U.S.C.A. § 2255. FRCP 5.2(b).

vii. Transcripts of the administrative record in social security proceedings are exempt from this requirement. State court records and other documents filed in habeas corpus proceedings are exempt from this requirement except for proceedings that involve victims of sex crimes. In habeas corpus cases involving sex crimes, the parties must redact the record and supporting papers, or may move to seal, if appropriate. NY R USDCTND L.R. 8.1.

c. *Limitations on remote access to electronic files; Social Security appeals and immigration cases.* Unless the court orders otherwise, in an action for benefits under the Social Security Act, and in an action or proceeding relating to an order of removal, to relief from removal, or to immigration benefits or detention, access to an electronic file is authorized as follows:

i. The parties and their attorneys may have remote electronic access to any part of the case file, including the administrative record;

ii. Any other person may have electronic access to the full record at the courthouse, but may have remote electronic access only to:

- The docket maintained by the court; and

- An opinion, order, judgment, or other disposition of the court, but not any other part of the case file or the administrative record. FRCP 5.2(c).

d. *Filings made under seal.* The court may order that a filing be made under seal without redaction. The court may later unseal the filing or order the person who made the filing to file a redacted version for the public record. FRCP 5.2(d); NY R USDCTND L.R. 8.1. For information on sealed matters, refer to NY R USDCTND L.R. 83.13 and NY R USDCTND CM/ECF(12).

e. *Protective orders.* For good cause, the court may by order in a case:

i. Require redaction of additional information; or

ii. Limit or prohibit a nonparty's remote electronic access to a document filed with the court. FRCP 5.2(e).

f. *Option for additional unredacted filing under seal.* A person making a redacted filing may also file an unredacted copy under seal. The court must retain the unredacted copy as part of the record. FRCP 5.2(f); NY R USDCTND L.R. 8.1; NY R USDCTND CM/ECF(11)(11.3).

g. *Option for filing a reference list.* A filing that contains redacted information may be filed together

with a reference list that identifies each item of redacted information and specifies an appropriate identifier that uniquely corresponds to each item listed. The list must be filed under seal and may be amended as of right. Any reference in the case to a listed identifier will be construed to refer to the corresponding item of information. FRCP 5.2(g); NY R USDCTND L.R. 8.1; NY R USDCTND CM/ECF(11)(11.3).

h. *Responsibility for redaction.* Counsel is strongly urged to discuss this issue with all their clients so that they can make an informed decision about the inclusion of certain information. The responsibility for redacting these personal identifiers rests solely with counsel and the parties. The Clerk will not review each filing for compliance with NY R USDCTND L.R. 8.1. Counsel and the parties are cautioned that failure to redact these personal identifiers may subject them to the Court's full disciplinary power. NY R USDCTND L.R. 8.1; NY R USDCTND CM/ECF(11)(11.3).

i. *Waiver of protection of identifiers.* A person waives the protection of FRCP 5.2(a) as to the person's own information by filing it without redaction and not under seal. FRCP 5.2(h).

5. *Individual judge practices.* Refer to the Miscellaneous section of this document for information on individual judge practices on formatting documents.

## F. Filing and Service Requirements

1. *Filing requirements.* Any paper after the complaint that is required to be served—together with a certificate of service—must be filed within a reasonable time after service. But disclosures under FRCP 26(a)(1) or FRCP 26(a)(2) and the following discovery requests and responses must not be filed until they are used in the proceeding or the court orders filing: depositions, interrogatories, requests for documents or tangible things or to permit entry onto land, and requests for admission. FRCP 5(d)(1). Refer to the United States District Court for the Northern District of New York KeyRules pleading and motion documents for information on filing with the court.

a. *Filing discovery.* Parties are directed not to file discovery material unless it is being filed in accordance with NY R USDCTND L.R. 26.2. NY R USDCTND Order 25(IX)(B). Parties shall not file notices to take depositions, transcripts of depositions, interrogatories, requests for documents, requests for admissions, disclosures, and answers and responses to these notices and requests unless the Court orders otherwise; provided, however, that a party shall file any discovery material that it expects to use at trial or to support any motion, including a motion to compel or for summary judgment prior to the trial or motion return date. NY R USDCTND L.R. 26.2; NY R USDCTND CM/ECF(2)(2.1)(4).

2. *Service requirements*

a. *Service; When required*

i. *In general.* Unless the Federal Rules of Civil Procedure provide otherwise, each of the following papers must be served on every party:

- An order stating that service is required;
- A pleading filed after the original complaint, unless the court orders otherwise under FRCP 5(c) because there are numerous defendants;
- A discovery paper required to be served on a party, unless the court orders otherwise;
- A written motion, except one that may be heard ex parte; and
- A written notice, appearance, demand, or offer of judgment, or any similar paper. FRCP 5(a)(1).

ii. *If a party fails to appear.* No service is required on a party who is in default for failing to appear. But a pleading that asserts a new claim for relief against such a party must be served on that party under FRCP 4. FRCP 5(a)(2).

iii. *Seizing property.* If an action is begun by seizing property and no person is or need be named as a defendant, any service required before the filing of an appearance, answer, or claim must be made on the person who had custody or possession of the property when it was seized. FRCP 5(a)(3).

b. *Service; How made*

    i.   *Serving an attorney.* If a party is represented by an attorney, service under FRCP 5 must be made on the attorney unless the court orders service on the party. FRCP 5(b)(1).

    ii.   *Service in general.* A paper is served under FRCP 5 by:

- Handing it to the person;

- Leaving it: (1) at the person's office with a clerk or other person in charge or, if no one is in charge, in a conspicuous place in the office; or (2) if the person has no office or the office is closed, at the person's dwelling or usual place of abode with someone of suitable age and discretion who resides there;

- Mailing it to the person's last known address—in which event service is complete upon mailing;

- Leaving it with the court clerk if the person has no known address;

- Sending it by electronic means if the person consented in writing—in which event service is complete upon transmission, but is not effective if the serving party learns that it did not reach the person to be served; or

- Delivering it by any other means that the person consented to in writing—in which event service is complete when the person making service delivers it to the agency designated to make delivery. FRCP 5(b)(2).

    iii.   *Service of electronically-filed documents.* Service is complete provided all parties receive a Notice of Electronic Filing (NEF), which is sent automatically by email from the Court (see the NEF for a list of who did/did not receive notice electronically). Transmission of the NEF constitutes service upon all Filing and Receiving Users who are listed as recipients of notice by electronic mail. It remains the responsibility of Filing and Receiving Users to maintain current contact information with the court and to regularly review the docket sheet of the case. NY R USDCTND CM/ECF(5)(5.2).

- *Non-filing or receiving users.* Attorneys and pro se parties who are not Filing or Receiving Users must be served with a paper copy of any electronically filed pleading or other document. Service of such paper copy must be made according to the Federal Rules of Civil Procedure and the Local Rules of Practice for the United States District Court for the Northern District of New York. Such paper service must be documented by electronically filing a certificate of service. NY R USDCTND CM/ECF(5)(5.2). A party who is not a Filing User of the System is entitled to a paper copy of any electronically-filed pleading, document, or order. The Filing User must therefore provide the non-Filing User with the pleading or document according to the Federal Rules of Civil Procedure. NY R US-DCTND CM/ECF(5)(5.3).

    iv.   *Using court facilities.* If a local rule so authorizes, a party may use the court's transmission facilities to make service under FRCP 5(b)(2)(E). FRCP 5(b)(3).

c. *Serving numerous defendants*

    i.   *In general.* If an action involves an unusually large number of defendants, the court may, on motion or on its own, order that:

- Defendants' pleadings and replies to them need not be served on other defendants;

- Any crossclaim, counterclaim, avoidance, or affirmative defense in those pleadings and replies to them will be treated as denied or avoided by all other parties; and

- Filing any such pleading and serving it on the plaintiff constitutes notice of the pleading to all parties. FRCP 5(c)(1).

    ii.   *Notifying parties.* A copy of every such order must be served on the parties as the court directs. FRCP 5(c)(2).

3. *Individual judge practices.* Refer to the Miscellaneous section of this document for information on individual judge practices on filing and serving documents.

## G. Hearings

1. There is no hearing contemplated in the federal statutes or rules for requests for production of documents.

## H. Forms

### 1. Federal Request for Production of Documents Forms

a. Request; Production of documents for inspection and copying. AMJUR PP DEPOSITION § 498.

b. Request for production, inspection and copying of documents, and inspection and photographing of things and real property. 3A FEDFORMS § 3556.

c. Request for production of documents; Business records. 3A FEDFORMS § 3557.

d. Request for production of documents; Patent case. 3A FEDFORMS § 3558.

e. Request for production of documents; Government records and regulations. 3A FEDFORMS § 3559.

f. Request for production of documents; Government personnel files, memoranda, minutes of meetings, and statistics. 3A FEDFORMS § 3560.

g. Request for production of documents; Documents to be identified in physically separate but accompanying interrogatories under FRCP 33. 3A FEDFORMS § 3561.

h. Request for production of documents; Employment discrimination. 3A FEDFORMS § 3562.

i. Letter requesting production of files. 3A FEDFORMS § 3563.

j. Request; Production of documents, records, and objects, under FRCP 34. FEDPROF § 23:394.

k. Request; Production of documents for inspection and copying. FEDPROF § 23:395.

l. Request; Production of documents for inspection and copying; Business records. FEDPROF § 23:396.

m. Request; Production of objects for inspection and sampling. FEDPROF § 23:397.

n. Request; Production of documents for inspection and copying; Government records and files. FEDPROF § 23:398.

o. Request; Production of documents and things; Patent proceeding. FEDPROF § 23:399.

p. Request; Production of documents and things; Trademark action. FEDPROF § 23:400.

q. Request; Production of documents; Trademark action; Likelihood of confusion. FEDPROF § 23:401.

r. Request; Production of documents; Automobile negligence. FEDPROF § 23:402.

s. Request; Production of documents; Premises liability. FEDPROF § 23:403.

t. Request; Production of documents for inspection and copying; Wrongful death due to forklift accident. FEDPROF § 23:404.

u. Request; Production of documents; Products liability. FEDPROF § 23:405.

v. Request; Production of documents; Collection of tariff. FEDPROF § 23:406.

w. Request; Production of medical records. FEDPROF § 23:407.

x. Request; Production of employment records. FEDPROF § 23:408.

y. Request; Production of education records. FEDPROF § 23:409.

z. Request; Production of decedent's records. FEDPROF § 23:410.

## I. Applicable Rules

1. *Federal rules*

a. Serving and filing pleadings and other papers. FRCP 5.

b. Privacy protection for filings made with the court. FRCP 5.2.

c. Computing and extending time; Time for motion papers. FRCP 6.

    d.    Pleadings allowed; Form of motions and other papers. FRCP 7.

    e.    Form of pleadings. FRCP 10.

    f.    Signing pleadings, motions, and other papers; Representations to the court; Sanctions. FRCP 11.

    g.    Duty to disclose; General provisions governing discovery. FRCP 26.

    h.    Stipulations about discovery procedure. FRCP 29.

    i.    Producing documents, electronically stored information, and tangible things, or entering onto land, for inspection and other purposes. FRCP 34.

    j.    Failure to make disclosures or to cooperate in discovery; Sanctions. FRCP 37.

2.   *Local rules*

    a.    Scope of the rules. NY R USDCTND L.R. 1.1.

    b.    Complex and multi-district litigation. NY R USDCTND L.R. 3.3.

    c.    Service and filing of papers. NY R USDCTND L.R. 5.1.

    d.    Personal privacy protection. NY R USDCTND L.R. 8.1.

    e.    Form of papers. NY R USDCTND L.R. 10.1.

    f.    Discovery cut-off. NY R USDCTND L.R. 16.2.

    g.    Form of certain discovery documents. NY R USDCTND L.R. 26.1.

    h.    Filing discovery. NY R USDCTND L.R. 26.2.

    i.    Timing of discovery. NY R USDCTND L.R. 26.4.

    j.    Settlement procedures. NY R USDCTND L.R. 68.2.

    k.    Appearance and withdrawal of attorney. NY R USDCTND L.R. 83.2.

    l.    Arbitration. NY R USDCTND L.R. 83.7-1; NY R USDCTND L.R. 83.7-2; NY R USDCTND L.R. 83.7-3.

    m.    Assisted mediation program. NY R USDCTND L.R. 83.8.

    n.    Mediation. NY R USDCTND L.R. 83.11-1; NY R USDCTND L.R. 83.11-3.

    o.    Early neutral evaluation. NY R USDCTND L.R. 83.12-1; NY R USDCTND L.R. 83.12-3.

    p.    Administrative procedures for electronic case filing. NY R USDCTND CM/ECF.

    q.    Case assignment plan for the Northern District of New York. [NY R USDCTND Order 12, as amended by NY ORDER 16-4201, effective March 24, 2015].

    r.    Directing the expedited service of the summons and complaint and further directing the completion of FRCP 16 stipulation for the timely progression of civil actions. [NY R USDCTND Order 25, as amended by NY ORDER 16-4187, effective June 23, 2016].

    s.    Mandatory mediation program. NY R USDCTND Order 47.

## J.  Miscellaneous

**NOTE: Individual judges' rules may apply. For available judge-level information, refer to:**

DISTRICT JUDGE MAE A. D'AGOSTINO: [NY R USDCTND D'Agostino-Rules and Practices, as added by NY ORDER 16-4200, effective April 4, 2016].

DISTRICT JUDGE THOMAS J. McAVOY: NY R USDCTND McAvoy-Order.

# Requests, Notices and Applications
# Request for Admissions

## Document Last Updated September 2016

### A. Checklist

(I) ❏ Matters to be considered by requesting party

    (a) ❏ Required documents

        (1) ❏ Request for admissions

    (b) ❏ Supplemental documents

        (1) ❏ Document(s)

        (2) ❏ Certificate of service

    (c) ❏ Timing

        (1) ❏ A party may not seek discovery from any source before the parties have conferred as required by FRCP 26(f), except in a proceeding exempted from initial disclosure under FRCP 26(a)(1)(B), or when authorized by the Federal Rules of Civil Procedure, by stipulation, or by court order

(II) ❏ Matters to be considered by responding party

    (a) ❏ Required documents

        (1) ❏ Response to request for admissions

    (b) ❏ Supplemental documents

        (1) ❏ Certificate of service

    (c) ❏ Timing

        (1) ❏ A matter is admitted unless, within thirty (30) days after being served, the party to whom the request is directed serves on the requesting party a written answer or objection addressed to the matter and signed by the party or its attorney

### B. Timing

1. *Request for admissions.* Without leave of court or written stipulation, requests for admission may not be served before the time specified in FRCP 26(d). FEDPROC § 26:706.

2. *Timing of discovery, generally.* A party may not seek discovery from any source before the parties have conferred as required by FRCP 26(f), except in a proceeding exempted from initial disclosure under FRCP 26(a)(1)(B), or when authorized by the Federal Rules of Civil Procedure, by stipulation, or by court order. FRCP 26(d)(1). FRCP 26(d), which prohibits discovery prior to a meeting and conference between the parties, and FRCP 26(f), which directs parties to meet and confer with each other relative to the nature and basis of claims and defenses to a lawsuit, shall not apply to any action in which a party is incarcerated. NY R USDCTND L.R. 26.4.

3. *Discovery cut-off.* The "discovery cut-off" is that date by which all responses to written discovery, including requests for admissions, shall be due according to the Federal Rules of Civil Procedure and by which all depositions shall be concluded. Counsel are advised to initiate discovery requests and notice depositions sufficiently in advance of the cut-off date to comply with NY R USDCTND L.R. 16.2. Discovery requests that call for responses or scheduled depositions after the discovery cut-off will not be enforceable except by order of the Court for good cause shown. Parties shall file and serve motions to compel discovery no later than fourteen (14) days after the discovery cut-off. See NY R USDCTND L.R. 7.1(d)(8). NY R USDCTND L.R. 16.2.

4. *Computation of time*

    a. *Computing time.* FRCP 6 applies in computing any time period specified in the Federal Rules of Civil

Procedure, in any local rule or court order, or in any statute that does not specify a method of computing time. FRCP 6(a).

    i.   *Period stated in days or a longer unit.* When the period is stated in days or a longer unit of time:

- Exclude the day of the event that triggers the period;

- Count every day, including intermediate Saturdays, Sundays, and legal holidays; and

- Include the last day of the period, but if the last day is a Saturday, Sunday, or legal holiday, the period continues to run until the end of the next day that is not a Saturday, Sunday, or legal holiday. FRCP 6(a)(1).

    ii.   *Period stated in hours.* When the period is stated in hours:

- Begin counting immediately on the occurrence of the event that triggers the period;

- Count every hour, including hours during intermediate Saturdays, Sundays, and legal holidays; and

- If the period would end on a Saturday, Sunday, or legal holiday, the period continues to run until the same time on the next day that is not a Saturday, Sunday, or legal holiday. FRCP 6(a)(2).

    iii.   *Inaccessibility of the clerk's office.* Unless the court orders otherwise, if the clerk's office is inaccessible:

- On the last day for filing under FRCP 6(a)(1), then the time for filing is extended to the first accessible day that is not a Saturday, Sunday, or legal holiday; or

- During the last hour for filing under FRCP 6(a)(2), then the time for filing is extended to the same time on the first accessible day that is not a Saturday, Sunday, or legal holiday. FRCP 6(a)(3).

    iv.   *"Last day" defined.* Unless a different time is set by a statute, local rule, or court order, the last day ends:

- For electronic filing, at midnight in the court's time zone; and

- For filing by other means, when the clerk's office is scheduled to close. FRCP 6(a)(4).

    v.   *"Next day" defined.* The "next day" is determined by continuing to count forward when the period is measured after an event and backward when measured before an event. FRCP 6(a)(5).

    vi.   *"Legal holiday" defined.* "Legal holiday" means:

- The day set aside by statute for observing New Year's Day, Martin Luther King Jr.'s Birthday, Washington's Birthday, Memorial Day, Independence Day, Labor Day, Columbus Day, Veterans' Day, Thanksgiving Day, or Christmas Day;

- Any day declared a holiday by the President or Congress; and

- For periods that are measured after an event, any other day declared a holiday by the state where the district court is located. FRCP 6(a)(6).

b.   *Computation of electronic filing deadlines.* A document will be deemed timely filed if electronically filed prior to midnight Eastern Time. However, if the time of day is of the essence, the assigned judge may order that the document be filed by a time certain. NY R USDCTND CM/ECF(4)(4.3).

    i.   *Technical failures.* A Filing User, whose filing is untimely as the result of a technical failure of the Court's CM/ECF site, may seek appropriate relief from the Court. However, Filing Users are cautioned that, in some circumstances, the Court lacks the authority to grant an extension of time to file (e.g., FRCP 6(b) of the Federal Rules of Civil Procedure). NY R USDCTND CM/ECF(10)(10.1).

- *Technical failure of the filing user's system.* Problems with the Filing User's system, such as phone line problems, problems with the Filing User's Internet Service Provider ("ISP"), or hardware or software problems, will not constitute a technical failure under these Administrative Procedures nor excuse an untimely filing. A Filing User who cannot file

documents electronically because of a problem on the Filing User's system must file the documents' conventionally along with an affidavit explaining the reason for not filing the documents electronically. NY R USDCTND CM/ECF(10)(10.2).

c. *Extending time*

    i. *In general.* When an act may or must be done within a specified time, the court may, for good cause, extend the time:

- With or without motion or notice if the court acts, or if a request is made, before the original time or its extension expires; or

- On motion made after the time has expired if the party failed to act because of excusable neglect. FRCP 6(b)(1).

    ii. *Exceptions.* A court must not extend the time to act under FRCP 50(b), FRCP 50(d), FRCP 52(b), FRCP 59(b), FRCP 59(d), FRCP 59(e), and FRCP 60(b). FRCP 6(b)(2).

    iii. Refer to the United States District Court for the Northern District of New York KeyRules Motion for Continuance/Extension of Time document for more information on extending time.

d. *Additional time after certain kinds of service.* When a party may or must act within a specified time after service and service is made under FRCP 5(b)(2)(C), FRCP 5(b)(2)(D), FRCP 5(b)(2)(E), or FRCP 5(b)(2)(F), three (3) days are added after the period would otherwise expire under FRCP 6(a). FRCP 6(d).

    i. In accordance with FRCP 6(e), service by electronic means is treated the same as service by mail for purposes of adding three (3) days to the prescribed period to respond. NY R USDCTND CM/ECF(5)(5.4). [Editor's note: the reference to FRCP 6(e) is likely meant to be a reference to FRCP 6(d)].

5. *Individual judge practices.* Refer to the Miscellaneous section of this document for information on individual judge practices on timing of documents.

## C. General Requirements

1. *General provisions governing discovery*

  a. *Discovery scope and limits*

    i. *Scope in general.* Unless otherwise limited by court order, the scope of discovery is as follows: Parties may obtain discovery regarding any nonprivileged matter that is relevant to any party's claim or defense and proportional to the needs of the case, considering the importance of the issues at stake in the action, the amount in controversy, the parties' relative access to relevant information, the parties' resources, the importance of the discovery in resolving the issues, and whether the burden or expense of the proposed discovery outweighs its likely benefit. Information within this scope of discovery need not be admissible in evidence to be discoverable. FRCP 26(b)(1).

    ii. *Limitations on frequency and extent*

- *When permitted.* By order, the court may alter the limits in the Federal Rules of Civil Procedure on the number of depositions and interrogatories or on the length of depositions under FRCP 30. By order or local rule, the court may also limit the number of requests under FRCP 36. FRCP 26(b)(2)(A).

- *Specific limitations on electronically stored information.* A party need not provide discovery of electronically stored information from sources that the party identifies as not reasonably accessible because of undue burden or cost. On motion to compel discovery or for a protective order, the party from whom discovery is sought must show that the information is not reasonably accessible because of undue burden or cost. If that showing is made, the court may nonetheless order discovery from such sources if the requesting party shows good cause, considering the limitations of FRCP 26(b)(2)(C). The court may specify conditions for the discovery. FRCP 26(b)(2)(B).

- *When required.* On motion or on its own, the court must limit the frequency or extent of

discovery otherwise allowed by the Federal Rules of Civil Procedure or by local rule if it determines that: (1) the discovery sought is unreasonably cumulative or duplicative, or can be obtained from some other source that is more convenient, less burdensome, or less expensive; (2) the party seeking discovery has had ample opportunity to obtain the information by discovery in the action; or (3) the proposed discovery is outside the scope permitted by FRCP 26(b)(1). FRCP 26(b)(2)(C).

iii. *Trial preparation; Materials*

- *Documents and tangible things.* Ordinarily, a party may not discover documents and tangible things that are prepared in anticipation of litigation or for trial by or for another party or its representative (including the other party's attorney, consultant, surety, indemnitor, insurer, or agent). But, subject to FRCP 26(b)(4), those materials may be discovered if: (1) they are otherwise discoverable under FRCP 26(b)(1); and (2) the party shows that it has substantial need for the materials to prepare its case and cannot, without undue hardship, obtain their substantial equivalent by other means. FRCP 26(b)(3)(A).

- *Protection against disclosure.* If the court orders discovery of those materials, it must protect against disclosure of the mental impressions, conclusions, opinions, or legal theories of a party's attorney or other representative concerning the litigation. FRCP 26(b)(3)(B).

- *Previous statement.* Any party or other person may, on request and without the required showing, obtain the person's own previous statement about the action or its subject matter. If the request is refused, the person may move for a court order, and FRCP 37(a)(5) applies to the award of expenses. A previous statement is either: (1) a written statement that the person has signed or otherwise adopted or approved; or (2) a contemporaneous stenographic, mechanical, electrical, or other recording—or a transcription of it—that recites substantially verbatim the person's oral statement. FRCP 26(b)(3)(C).

iv. *Trial preparation; Experts*

- *Deposition of an expert who may testify.* A party may depose any person who has been identified as an expert whose opinions may be presented at trial. If FRCP 26(a)(2)(B) requires a report from the expert, the deposition may be conducted only after the report is provided. FRCP 26(b)(4)(A).

- *Trial-preparation protection for draft reports or disclosures.* FRCP 26(b)(3)(A) and FRCP 26(b)(3)(B) protect drafts of any report or disclosure required under FRCP 26(a)(2), regardless of the form in which the draft is recorded. FRCP 26(b)(4)(B).

- *Trial-preparation protection for communications between a party's attorney and expert witnesses.* FRCP 26(b)(3)(A) and FRCP 26(b)(3)(B) protect communications between the party's attorney and any witness required to provide a report under FRCP 26(a)(2)(B), regardless of the form of the communications, except to the extent that the communications: (1) relate to compensation for the expert's study or testimony; (2) identify facts or data that the party's attorney provided and that the expert considered in forming the opinions to be expressed; or (3) identify assumptions that the party's attorney provided and that the expert relied on in forming the opinions to be expressed. FRCP 26(b)(4)(C).

- *Expert employed only for trial preparation.* Ordinarily, a party may not, by interrogatories or deposition, discover facts known or opinions held by an expert who has been retained or specially employed by another party in anticipation of litigation or to prepare for trial and who is not expected to be called as a witness at trial. But a party may do so only: (1) as provided in FRCP 35(b); or (2) on showing exceptional circumstances under which it is impracticable for the party to obtain facts or opinions on the same subject by other means. FRCP 26(b)(4)(D).

- *Payment.* Unless manifest injustice would result, the court must require that the party seeking discovery: (1) pay the expert a reasonable fee for time spent in responding to discovery under FRCP 26(b)(4)(A) or FRCP 26(b)(4)(D); and (2) for discovery FRCP

26(b)(4)(D), also pay the other party a fair portion of the fees and expenses it reasonably incurred in obtaining the expert's facts and opinions. FRCP 26(b)(4)(E).

    v.   *Claiming privilege or protecting trial-preparation materials*

- *Information withheld.* When a party withholds information otherwise discoverable by claiming that the information is privileged or subject to protection as trial-preparation material, the party must: (1) expressly make the claim; and (2) describe the nature of the documents, communications, or tangible things not produced or disclosed—and do so in a manner that, without revealing information itself privileged or protected, will enable other parties to assess the claim. FRCP 26(b)(5)(A).

- *Information produced.* If information produced in discovery is subject to a claim of privilege or of protection as trial-preparation material, the party making the claim may notify any party that received the information of the claim and the basis for it. After being notified, a party must promptly return, sequester, or destroy the specified information and any copies it has; must not use or disclose the information until the claim is resolved; must take reasonable steps to retrieve the information if the party disclosed it before being notified; and may promptly present the information to the court under seal for a determination of the claim. The producing party must preserve the information until the claim is resolved. FRCP 26(b)(5)(B).

   b.   *Protective orders.* A party or any person from whom discovery is sought may move for a protective order in the court where the action is pending—or as an alternative on matters relating to a deposition, in the court for the district where the deposition will be taken. FRCP 26(c)(1). Refer to the United States District Court for the Northern District of New York KeyRules Motion for Protective Order document for more information.

   c.   *Sequence of discovery.* Unless the parties stipulate or the court orders otherwise for the parties' and witnesses' convenience and in the interests of justice: (1) methods of discovery may be used in any sequence; and (2) discovery by one party does not require any other party to delay its discovery. FRCP 26(d)(3).

2.   *Request for admissions*

   a.   *Scope.* A party may serve on any other party a written request to admit, for purposes of the pending action only, the truth of any matters within the scope of FRCP 26(b)(1) relating to: (1) facts, the application of law to fact, or opinions about either; and (2) the genuineness of any described documents. FRCP 36(a)(1).

     i.   A party may serve a request for admission even though the party has the burden of proving the matters asserted therein because FRCP 36 permits requests for admission to address claims of the party seeking discovery, and generally, the party asserting a claim bears the burden of proof thereon. FEDPROC § 26:715.

   b.   *Number.* FRCP 36 does not limit a party to a single request, or set of requests, for admissions. But FRCP 26(b)(2)(A) authorizes courts to limit the number of requests by order or local rule. In addition, the court has power to protect a party from harassment by repeated requests for admissions, but will not bar such repeated requests when the circumstances of the case justify them. Even a second request about the same fact or the genuineness of the same document is permissible if circumstances warrant a renewed request. FPP § 2258.

   c.   *Form.* Each matter must be separately stated. FRCP 36(a)(2). The party called upon to respond should not be required to go through a document and assume the responsibility of determining what facts it is being requested to admit. FPP § 2258. Each request for an admission should be phrased simply and directly so that it can be admitted or denied without explanation. FPP § 2258; United Coal Cos. v. Powell Const. Co., 839 F.2d 958, 968 (3d Cir. 1988).

     i.   A request for an admission need not state the source of information about the matter for which the request is made. FPP § 2258.

   d.   *Numbering.* The parties shall number each interrogatory or request sequentially, regardless of the number of sets of interrogatories or requests. NY R USDCTND L.R. 26.1.

e. *Effect of an admission; Withdrawing or amending it.* A matter admitted under FRCP 36 is conclusively established unless the court, on motion, permits the admission to be withdrawn or amended. Subject to FRCP 16(e), the court may permit withdrawal or amendment if it would promote the presentation of the merits of the action and if the court is not persuaded that it would prejudice the requesting party in maintaining or defending the action on the merits. An admission under FRCP 36 is not an admission for any other purpose and cannot be used against the party in any other proceeding. FRCP 36(b).

f. *Motion to compel.* The motion to compel discovery provided by FRCP 37(a) does not apply to a failure to respond to a request for admissions. The automatic admission from a failure to respond is a sufficient remedy for the party who made the request. If, however, a request is objected to, or the requesting party thinks that a response to a request is insufficient, it may move under FRCP 36(a)(6) to determine the sufficiency of the answers or objections. FPP § 2265.

g. *Motion regarding the sufficiency of an answer or objection.* The requesting party may move to determine the sufficiency of an answer or objection. Unless the court finds an objection justified, it must order that an answer be served. On finding that an answer does not comply with FRCP 36, the court may order either that the matter is admitted or that an amended answer be served. The court may defer its final decision until a pretrial conference or a specified time before trial. FRCP 37(a)(5) applies to an award of expenses. FRCP 36(a)(6). Refer to the United States District Court for the Northern District of New York KeyRules Motion for Discovery Sanctions document for more information on sanctions.

3. *Sanctions for failure to cooperate in discovery.* The pattern of sanctions for FRCP 36 is somewhat different from that for the other discovery rules. The most important sanctions are two:

   a. A failure to respond to a request is deemed an admission of the matter to which the request is directed; and

   b. A party who, without good reason, refuses to admit a matter will be required to pay the costs incurred in proving that matter. FPP § 2265. If a party fails to admit what is requested under FRCP 36 and if the requesting party later proves a document to be genuine or the matter true, the requesting party may move that the party who failed to admit pay the reasonable expenses, including attorney's fees, incurred in making that proof. The court must so order unless:

      i. The request was held objectionable under FRCP 36(a);

      ii. The admission sought was of no substantial importance;

      iii. The party failing to admit had a reasonable ground to believe that it might prevail on the matter; or

      iv. There was other good reason for the failure to admit. FRCP 37(c)(2).

   c. Refer to the United States District Court for the Northern District of New York KeyRules Motion for Discovery Sanctions document for more information on sanctions.

4. *Stipulations about discovery procedure.* Unless the court orders otherwise, the parties may stipulate that: (1) a deposition may be taken before any person, at any time or place, on any notice, and in the manner specified—in which event it may be used in the same way as any other deposition; and (2) other procedures governing or limiting discovery be modified—but a stipulation extending the time for any form of discovery must have court approval if it would interfere with the time set for completing discovery, for hearing a motion, or for trial. FRCP 29.

5. *Complex and multi-district litigation.* If the assigned judge determines, in his or her discretion, that the case is of such a complex nature that it cannot reasonably be trial ready within eighteen (18) months from the date the complaint is filed, the assigned judge may design and issue a particularized case management order that will move the case to trial as quickly as the complexity of the case allows. NY R USDCTND L.R. 3.3(a). The parties shall promptly notify the Court in writing if any action commenced is appropriate for multi-district litigation. NY R USDCTND L.R. 3.3(b).

6. *Appearances.* An attorney appearing for a party in a civil case shall promptly file with the Clerk a written notice of appearance; however, an attorney does not need to file a notice of appearance if the attorney who

would be filing the notice of appearance is the same individual who has signed the complaint, notice of removal, pre-answer motion, or answer. NY R USDCTND L.R. 83.2(a). For more information, refer to NY R USDCTND L.R. 83.2.

7. *Related cases.* A civil case is "related" to another civil case for purposes of this guideline when, because of the similarity of facts and legal issues or because the cases arise from the same transactions or events, a substantial saving of judicial resources is likely to result from assigning the cases to the same Judge and Magistrate Judge. NY R USDCTND Order 12(G)(2). A civil case shall not be deemed related to another civil case merely because the civil case: (1) involves similar legal issues, or (2) involves the same parties. NY R USDCTND Order 12(G)(3). Presumptively, and subject to the power of a Judge to determine otherwise pursuant to NY R USDCTND Order 12(G)(5), civil cases shall not be deemed to be "related" unless both cases are still pending before the Court. NY R USDCTND Order 12(G)(4).

   a. *New filings.* If an attorney or filing party indicates on the Civil Cover Sheet that a case is related to an earlier filed case, the Clerk shall instruct the filing party to file a notice of related cases. The allegedly related cases will be submitted by the Clerk to the Judge to whom the earliest filed case is assigned, who shall advise the Clerk whether such cases are related. NY R USDCTND Order 12(G)(1).

   b. *Judicial determination that civil cases are "related."* Except for the cases described in the final sentence of NY R USDCTND Order 12(G)(6), all civil cases shall be randomly assigned when they are filed. Other than the cases described in the final sentence of NY R USDCTND Order 12(G)(6), civil cases shall not be deemed to be "related" for purposes of this guideline at the instance of any litigant or attorney unless and until there has been a determination by a Judge of this Court that the standard of NY R USDCTND Order 12(G)(2) is met. NY R USDCTND Order 12(G)(5).

      i. *Notice of related filing.* Any party may apply for such a determination by filing with the Clerk a notice of related filing, which should include an explanation as to why the standard of NY R USDCTND Order 12(G)(2) is met. A form for this purpose is available on the Court's website. A copy of the notice shall be served on all other parties who have appeared. Such an application must be made after the date when at least a majority of the defendants have been served with the complaint. Before making such an application, the applicant must confer in good faith with all other parties in an effort to reach an agreement on whether or not the case is "related". After such an application is made, any other party may serve and file within seven (7) calendar days a letter of no more than two (2) pages supporting or opposing the application. The application to have the case assigned to another Judge shall be presented to the Judge with the earliest filed case for decision on whether the action(s) should be reassigned as related cases. The Judge with the earliest filed case may then enter an order in the case at bar, either deeming the case to be related and directing the Clerk to reassign the action, or denying the application for reassignment. Any disputes concerning the assignment of related cases will be referred to the Chief Judge for resolution. NY R USDCTND Order 12(G)(5).

   c. For more information on related cases, refer to NY R USDCTND Order 12(G).

8. *Alternative dispute resolution (ADR).* It is the mission of this court to do everything it can to help parties resolve their disputes as fairly, quickly, and efficiently as possible. NY R USDCTND Order 25(VIII).

   a. *Arbitration.* NY R USDCTND L.R. 83.7 governs the consensual arbitration program for referral of civil actions to court-annexed arbitration. It may remain in effect until further order of the Court. Its purpose is to establish a less formal procedure for the just, efficient and economical resolution of disputes, while preserving the right to a full trial on demand. NY R USDCTND L.R. 83.7-1.

      i. *Actions subject to arbitration.* The Clerk shall notify the parties in all civil cases, except as the Local Rules of Practice for the United States District Court for the Northern District of New York otherwise direct, that they may consent to non-binding arbitration under NY R US-DCTND L.R. 83.7. The notice shall be furnished to the parties at pretrial/scheduling confer-ences or shall be included with pretrial conference notices and instructions. Consent to arbitration under NY R USDCTND L.R. 83.7 shall be discussed at the pretrial/scheduling conference. No party or attorney shall be prejudiced for refusing to participate in arbitration. The Court shall allow the referral of any civil action pending before it to the arbitration process if the parties consent. The plaintiff shall be responsible for securing the execution of a consent form by the parties and for filing the form with the Clerk within fourteen (14) days after the parties receive the form. The parties shall freely and knowingly enter into the consent. NY R USDCTND L.R. 83.7-2.

    ii.   *Referral to arbitration.* The Clerk shall refer every action subject to NY R USDCTND L.R. 83.7 to arbitration in accordance with the procedures under NY R USDCTND L.R. 83.7 twenty-one (21) days after the filing of the last responsive pleading or within twenty-one (21) days of the filing of a stipulated consent order referring the action to arbitration, whichever event occurs last, except as otherwise provided. If any party notices a motion to dismiss under the provisions of FRCP 12(a) and/or FRCP 12(b), or a motion to join necessary parties pursuant to the Federal Rules of Civil Procedure prior to the expiration of the twenty-one (21) day period, the assigned judge shall hear the motion and further proceedings under NY R USDCTND L.R. 83.7 shall be deferred pending decision on the motion. If the Court does not dismiss the action on the motion, the Court shall refer the action to arbitration twenty-one (21) days after the filing of the decision. NY R USDCTND L.R. 83.7-3(a). Motions for summary judgment pursuant to FRCP 56 shall be filed and served within twenty-one (21) days following the close of discovery. The filing of a FRCP 56 motion shall defer further proceedings under NY R USDCTND L.R. 83.7 pending decision on the motion. NY R USDCTND L.R. 83.7-3(a).

- *Relief from referral.* Any party shall request relief from the operation of NY R USDCTND L.R. 83.7 by filing with the Court a motion for the relief within twenty-one (21) days after entry of the initial stipulated consent order which refers the case for arbitration. The assigned judge shall, sua sponte, exempt an action from the application of NY R USDCTND L.R. 83.7 where the objectives of arbitration would not be realized because (1) the case involves complex or novel legal issues, (2) legal issues predominate over factual issues, or (3) for other good cause. NY R USDCTND L.R. 83.7-3(c).

    iii.   For more information on arbitration, refer to NY R USDCTND L.R. 83.7.

b.   *Mediation.* The purpose of NY R USDCTND L.R. 83.11 is to provide a supplementary procedure to the Court's existing alternative dispute resolution procedures. NY R USDCTND L.R. 83.11 provides for an earlier resolution of civil disputes resulting in savings of time and cost to litigants and the Court without sacrificing the quality of justice rendered or the right of litigants to a full trial on all issues not resolved through mediation. NY R USDCTND L.R. 83.11-1(a). Mediation is a process by which an impartial person, the mediator, facilitates communication between disputing parties to promote understanding, reconciliation and settlement. The mediator is an advocate for settlement and uses the mediation process to help the parties fully explore any potential area of agreement. The mediator does not serve as a judge or arbitrator and has no authority to render any decision on any disputed issue or to force a settlement. The parties themselves are responsible for negotiating any resolution(s) to their dispute. NY R USDCTND L.R. 83.11-1(b).

    i.   *Actions subject to mediation.* The Court may refer any civil action (or any portion thereof) to mediation under NY R USDCTND L.R. 83.11: (1) by order of referral; or (2) on the motion of any party; or (3) by consent of the parties. NY R USDCTND L.R. 83.11-3(a).

- *Withdrawal from mediation.* The parties may withdraw from mediation any civil action or claim that the Court refers to mediation pursuant to NY R USDCTND L.R. 83.11-3 by application to the assigned judge at least ten (10) days prior to the scheduled mediation session. NY R USDCTND L.R. 83.11-3(b).

    ii.   *Mandatory mediation program.* The United States District Court for the Northern District of New York has adopted this Mandatory Mediation Plan. The paid Mediation Program is designed to provide quicker, less expensive and potentially more satisfying alternatives to continuing litigation, without impairing the quality of justice or the right to trial. NY R USDCTND Order 47(1)(1.2)(A). This Mandatory Mediation Plan applies to civil actions pending as well as newly filed actions, except as otherwise indicated in NY R USDCTND Order 47. The Local Rules for voluntary mediation will apply only to Pro Se Cases that proceed through the Assisted Mediation Program. NY R USDCTND Order 47(1)(1.2)(B).

- *Referral into the pilot mandatory mediation program for new cases.* All civil cases shall be referred automatically into the Mandatory Mediation Program. Notice of the Mandatory Mediation requirements will be provided to all parties immediately upon the filing of a complaint and answer or a notice of removal. ADR intervention will be scheduled at the conference held pursuant to NY R USDCTND L.R. 16.1. NY R USDCTND Order 47(2)(2.1)(A). For a list of categories of actions exempted from automatic referral, refer to NY R USDCTND Order 47(2)(2.1)(A).

- *Referral into the pilot mandatory mediation program for pending cases.* The assigned Judge or Magistrate Judge on any pending civil case may, sua sponte or with status conference, issue an order referring the case into the Mandatory Mediation Program. The order shall specify a date on which the ADR intervention is to be completed. NY R USDCTND Order 47(2)(2.1)(B).

- *Referral into the pilot mandatory mediation program by stipulation.* A case may be referred into the Mandatory Mediation Program by stipulation of all parties. Stipulations shall be filed and shall designate the time frame within which the ADR process will be completed. Stipulations are presumed acceptable unless the assigned Judge or Magistrate Judge determines that the interests of justice are not served. NY R USDCTND Order 47(2)(2.1)(C).

- *Relief from referral.* Motions to opt out of the program will be addressed by the assigned Magistrate Judge at the FRCP 16 conference. NY R USDCTND Order 47(2)(2.2)(A). Opting Out Motions shall be granted only for "good cause" shown. Inconvenience, travel costs, attorney fees or other costs shall not constitute "good cause." A party seeking relief from the Mandatory Mediation Program must set forth the reasons why Mandatory Mediation has no reasonable chance of being productive. NY R USDCTND Order 47(2)(2.2)(B). The assigned Magistrate Judge may, sua sponte, exempt any case from the Court's Mandatory Mediation Program. NY R USDCTND Order 47(2)(2.2)(C).

iii. *Assisted mediation program.* The Court may assign specially trained pro bono Special Mediation Counsel to assist pro se civilian litigants with preparing for and participating in mediation. The Assisted Mediation Program is open to civilian pro se parties to actions in the Northern District of New York. The assigned judge or magistrate judge determines if the case would benefit from mediation and would also benefit from the assignment of Special Mediation Counsel to assist the pro se party with the mediation process. NY R USDCTND L.R. 83.8(a). Appointment of Special Mediation Counsel is in no way guaranteed, even if the action is referred to the court-annexed mediation program. Appointment is at the sole discretion of the presiding judge. NY R USDCTND L.R. 83.8(a).

- *Referral to assisted mediation program.* If the court determines that referral to the Assisted Mediation Program is appropriate, the Court shall enter an order of reference to the Assisted Mediation Program. NY R USDCTND L.R. 83.8(b).

iv. For more information on mediation, refer to NY R USDCTND L.R. 83.11 and NY R USDCTND Order 47.

c. *Early neutral evaluation (ENE).* Early neutral evaluation (ENE) is a process in which parties obtain from an experienced neutral (an "evaluator") a nonbinding, reasoned, oral evaluation of the merits of the case. The first step in the ENE process involves the Court appointing an evaluator who has expertise in the area of law in the case. After the parties exchange essential information and position statements early in the pretrial period (usually within one hundred fifty (150) to two hundred (200) days after a complaint has been filed), the evaluator convenes an ENE session that typically lasts about two hours. At the ENE meeting, each side briefly presents the factual and legal basis of its position. The evaluator may ask questions of the parties and help them identify the main issues in dispute and the areas of agreement. The evaluator may also help the parties explore options for settlement. If settlement does not occur, the evaluator then offers an opinion as to the settlement value of the case, including the likelihood of liability and the likely range of damages. With the benefit of this assessment, the parties are again encouraged to discuss settlement, with or without the evaluator's assistance. The parties may also explore ways to narrow the issues in dispute, exchange information about the case or otherwise prepare efficiently for trial. NY R USDCTND L.R. 83.12-1.

i. *Actions subject to early neutral evaluation.* The Court may refer any civil action (or any portion thereof) to ENE under NY R USDCTND L.R. 83.12: (1) by order of referral; (2) on the motion of any party; or (3) by consent of the parties. NY R USDCTND L.R. 83.12-3(a).

- *Withdrawal from the ENE process.* The parties may withdraw any civil action or claim that the Court has referred to the ENE Process pursuant to NY R USDCTND L.R. 83.12-3 by application to the assigned judge at least ten (10) days before the scheduled evaluation session. NY R USDCTND L.R. 83.12-3(b).

ii. For more information on early neutral evaluation (ENE), refer to NY R USDCTND L.R. 83.12.

9. *Settlement procedures.* On notice to the Court or the Clerk that the parties have settled an action, and upon confirmation of the settlement by all parties, the Court may issue a judgment dismissing the action by reason of settlement. The Court shall issue the order without prejudice to the parties' right to secure reinstatement of the case within thirty (30) days after the date of judgment by making a showing that the settlement was not, in fact, consummated. NY R USDCTND L.R. 68.2(a). If the Court decides not to follow the procedures set forth in NY R USDCTND L.R. 68.2(a), the parties shall file within thirty (30) days of the notification to the Court, unless otherwise directed by written order, such notices, stipulations and/or motions as are necessary to terminate the action. If the required documents are not filed within the thirty (30) day period, the Clerk shall place the action on the dismissal calendar. NY R USDCTND L.R. 68.2(b).

10. *Sanctions and penalties for noncompliance.* Failure of an attorney or of a party to comply with any provision of the Local Rules of Practice for the United States District Court for the Northern District of New York, General Orders of this District, Orders of the Court, or the Federal Rules of Civil Procedure shall be a ground for imposition of sanctions. NY R USDCTND L.R. 1.1(d).

11. *Individual judge practices.* Refer to the Miscellaneous section of this document for information on individual judge practices on general requirements for documents.

## D. Documents

1. *Required documents*

   a. *Request for admissions.* Refer to the General Requirements section of this document for information on the request for admissions.

2. *Supplemental documents*

   a. *Document(s).* A request to admit the genuineness of a document must be accompanied by a copy of the document unless it is, or has been, otherwise furnished or made available for inspection and copying. FRCP 36(a)(2).

   b. *Certificate of service.* FRCP 5(d) requires that the person making service under FRCP 5 certify that service has been effected. FRCP 5(Advisory Committee Notes). Having such information on file may be useful for many purposes, including proof of service if an issue arises concerning the effectiveness of the service. FRCP 5(Advisory Committee Notes).

3. *Individual judge practices.* Refer to the Miscellaneous section of this document for information on individual judge practices on required documents.

## E. Format

1. *Form of documents.* The rules governing captions and other matters of form in pleadings apply to motions and other papers. FRCP 7(b)(2). All pleadings and other papers shall be served and filed in accordance with the Federal Rules of Civil Procedure and shall be in the form prescribed by NY R USDCTND L.R. 10.1. NY R USDCTND L.R. 5.1(a).

   a. *Form, generally.* All pleadings, motions, and other documents that a party presents for filing, whether in paper form or in electronic form, shall meet the following requirements:

   i. *Font size.* All text, whether in the body of the document or in footnotes, must be a minimum of twelve (12) point type. NY R USDCTND L.R. 10.1(a)(1).

   ii. *Margins.* All documents must have one (1) inch margins on all four sides of the page. NY R USDCTND L.R. 10.1(a)(2).

    iii.   *Spacing.* All text in the body of the document must be double-spaced. NY R USDCTND L.R. 10.1(a)(3).

- The text in block quotations and footnotes may be single-spaced. NY R USDCTND L.R. 10.1(a)(4).

    iv.   *Page numbering.* Pages must be consecutively numbered. NY R USDCTND L.R. 10.1(a)(7).

    v.   *Circumventing formatting limitations*

- Extensive footnotes must not be used to circumvent page limitations. NY R USDCTND L.R. 10.1(a)(5).

- Compacted or other compressed printing features must not be used. NY R USDCTND L.R. 10.1(a)(6).

b.   *Additional requirements for paper filing.* Additional requirements for all pleadings, motions, and other documents that a party presents for filing in paper form:

    i.   *Paper size.* All documents must be on eight and one-half by eleven (8-1/2 x 11) inch white paper of good quality. NY R USDCTND L.R. 10.1(b)(1).

    ii.   *Text.* All text must be plainly and legibly written, typewritten, printed or reproduced without erasures or interlineations materially defacing them. NY R USDCTND L.R. 10.1(b)(2).

    iii.   *Ink.* All documents must be in black or blue ink. NY R USDCTND L.R. 10.1(b)(3).

    iv.   *Binding.* Pages of all documents must be stapled (or in some other way fastened) together. NY R USDCTND L.R. 10.1(b)(4).

    v.   *Single-sided paper.* All documents must be single-sided. NY R USDCTND L.R. 10.1(b)(5).

    vi.   *Electronic submission.* The Court, at its discretion, may require the electronic submission of any document in a WordPerfect-compatible format. NY R USDCTND L.R. 10.1(b)(6).

    vii.   *Rejection of document.* The Court may reject documents that do not comply with the above-listed requirements. NY R USDCTND L.R. 10.1(b).

c.   *Caption; Names of parties.* Every pleading must have a caption with the court's name, a title, a file number, and a FRCP 7(a) designation. The title of the complaint must name all the parties; the title of other pleadings, after naming the first party on each side, may refer generally to other parties. FRCP 10(a). Each document must contain a caption for the specific case to which it pertains. The caption must include the title of the Court, the title of the action, the civil action number of the case, the initials of the assigned judge(s), and the name or nature of the paper in sufficient detail for identification. If a litigant has more than one action pending in this Court, any and all papers filed in a case must contain and pertain to one civil action number, unless the civil actions have been consolidated by the Court. Any motion or other papers purporting to relate to more than one action will not be accepted for filing and may be stricken by the Court. NY R USDCTND L.R. 10.1(c)(1) shall not apply, as noted in NY R USDCTND L.R. 10.1(c), to notices of change of address filed by attorneys of record and pro se litigants. The parties must separately caption affidavits and declarations and must not physically attach them to the Notice of Motion or Memorandum of Law. NY R USDCTND L.R. 10.1(c)(1).

d.   *Paragraphs; Separate statements.* A party must state its claims or defenses in numbered paragraphs, each limited as far as practicable to a single set of circumstances. A later pleading may refer by number to a paragraph in an earlier pleading. If doing so would promote clarity, each claim founded on a separate transaction or occurrence—and each defense other than a denial—must be stated in a separate count or defense. FRCP 10(b).

e.   *Adoption by reference; Exhibits.* A statement in a pleading may be adopted by reference elsewhere in the same pleading or in any other pleading or motion. A copy of a written instrument that is an exhibit to a pleading is a part of the pleading for all purposes. FRCP 10(c).

f.   *Citation of local rules.* These are the Local Rules of Practice for the United States District Court for the Northern District of New York. They shall be cited as "L.R. ___." NY R USDCTND L.R. 1.1(a).

g.   *Acceptance by the clerk.* The clerk must not refuse to file a paper solely because it is not in the form prescribed by the Federal Rules of Civil Procedure or by a local rule or practice. FRCP 5(d)(4).

2. *Form of electronic documents.* All pleadings, motions, and other documents that a party presents for filing, whether in paper form or in electronic form, shall meet the requirements in NY R USDCTND L.R. 10.1(a). NY R USDCTND L.R. 10.1(a). Refer above for more information.

    a. *Attachments and exhibits.* A Filing User must submit in electronic form all documents referenced as exhibits or attachments in accordance with the Court's CM/ECF Users Manual unless the Court otherwise orders. A Filing User shall submit as exhibits or attachments only those excerpts of the referenced documents that are directly germane to the matter under the Court's consideration. Excerpted material must be clearly and prominently identified as such. Filing Users who file excerpts of documents as exhibits or attachments under these Administrative Procedures (NY R USDCTND CM/ECF) do so without prejudice to their right to timely file additional excerpts or the complete document. Responding parties may also timely file the complete document or additional excerpts that they believe are directly germane to the matter under the Court's consideration. NY R USDCTND CM/ECF(4)(4.4).

        i. All attachments must be described in sufficient detail so the Court and opposing counsel can easily identify and distinguish the filed attachments. Vague or general descriptions are insufficient (i.e., "Exhibit 1"). Rather, each attachment shall have a descriptive title identifying, with specificity, the document that is being filed (i.e., "Exhibit 12 Mulligan County Fire Investigation Report.") Failure to adequately describe attachments may result in the document being rejected by the Court. NY R USDCTND CM/ECF(4)(4.4).

    b. *Large documents.* For information on the electronic filing of large documents, please consult the Court's CM/ECF Users Manual, which is available on the Court's web page. NY R USDCTND CM/ECF(4)(4.5).

        i. A party who believes a document is too lengthy to electronically image, i.e., "scan," may contact the Clerk's Office for permission to file that document conventionally. If the Clerk's Office grants permission to conventionally file the document, the Filing User shall electronically file a notice of conventional filing for the documents. More information regarding this process can be obtained from the Court's web page. Exhibits submitted conventionally shall be served on other parties as if they were not subject to these Administrative Procedures (NY R USDCTND CM/ECF). For a list of hints and tips for scanning large documents, please consult the Court's web page. NY R USDCTND CM/ECF(4)(4.5).

    c. *Legibility.* It shall be the Filing User's responsibility to verify the legibility of scanned documents before filing them electronically with the Court. NY R USDCTND CM/ECF(4)(4.6).

    d. *Color documents.* Since documents scanned in color or containing a graphic take much longer to upload, Filing Users are encouraged to configure their scanners to scan documents at 300 dpi and preferably in black and white rather than in color. NY R USDCTND CM/ECF(4)(4.7).

    e. *Items not in .PDF format.* Parties wishing to file items not amenable to .pdf format (i.e. CD's, DVD's), shall file such items conventionally with the Clerk's Office. The Filing User shall electronically file a notice of conventional filing indicating that these items have been submitted to the clerk and shall serve copies of these items on other parties as if they were not subject to these Administrative Procedures (NY R USDCTND CM/ECF). These item(s) will be maintained by the Clerk's Office until the case is disposed, at which time they will be returned to the filing party for retention consistent with NY R USDCTND CM/ECF(4)(4.9). NY R USDCTND CM/ECF(4)(4.8).

3. *Signing disclosures and discovery requests, responses, and objections.* FRCP 11 does not apply to disclosures and discovery requests, responses, objections, and motions under FRCP 26 through FRCP 37. FRCP 11(d).

    a. *Signature required.* Every disclosure under FRCP 26(a)(1) or FRCP 26(a)(3) and every discovery request, response, or objection must be signed by at least one attorney of record in the attorney's own name—or by the party personally, if unrepresented—and must state the signer's address, e-mail address, and telephone number. FRCP 26(g)(1). Each document must identify the person filing the document. This identification must include an original signature of the attorney or pro se litigant; the typewritten name of that person; the address of a pro se litigant; and the bar roll number, office address, telephone number, e-mail address and fax number of the attorney. Telephone numbers of non-prisoner pro se parties may be provided voluntarily or upon request of the Court. See General Order #22 (NY R USDCTND CM/ECF) for signature requirements. NY R USDCTND L.R. 10.1(c)(2).

    i.   *Electronic signatures.* Documents filed under an attorney's login and password shall constitute that attorney's signature for purposes of the Local Rules of Practice for the United States District Court for the Northern District of New York and Federal Rules of Civil Procedure, including but not limited to FRCP 11. A pleading or other document requiring an attorney's signature shall be signed in the following manner, whether filed electronically or submitted on disk or CD/ROM to the Clerk's Office: "s/ (attorney name)." The correct format for an attorney signature is found in NY R USDCTND CM/ECF(6)(6.1). NY R USDCTND CM/ECF(6)(6.1).

- *Non-attorney signature.* If an original document requires the signature of a non-attorney, the Filing User may scan the original document containing the original signature(s), then electronically file it on the System. Alternatively, the Filing User may convert the document into .pdf text format and submit the document using "s/" for the signature of the non-attorney. NY R USDCTND CM/ECF(6)(6.2).

- *Multiple signatures.* A document requiring signatures of more than one party must be filed electronically either by (1) submitting a scanned document containing all necessary signatures; (2) representing the consent of the other parties on the document; or (3) in any other manner that the Court approves. NY R USDCTND CM/ECF(6)(6.3).

  b.  *Effect of signature.* By signing, an attorney or party certifies that to the best of the person's knowledge, information, and belief formed after a reasonable inquiry:

    i.   With respect to a disclosure, it is complete and correct as of the time it is made; and

    ii.  With respect to a discovery request, response, or objection, it is:

- Consistent with the Federal Rules of Civil Procedure and warranted by existing law or by a nonfrivolous argument for extending, modifying, or reversing existing law, or for establishing new law;

- Not interposed for any improper purpose, such as to harass, cause unnecessary delay, or needlessly increase the cost of litigation; and

- Neither unreasonable nor unduly burdensome or expensive, considering the needs of the case, prior discovery in the case, the amount in controversy, and the importance of the issues at stake in the action. FRCP 26(g)(1).

  c.  *Failure to sign.* Other parties have no duty to act on an unsigned disclosure, request, response, or objection until it is signed, and the court must strike it unless a signature is promptly supplied after the omission is called to the attorney's or party's attention. FRCP 26(g)(2).

  d.  *Sanction for improper certification.* If a certification violates FRCP 26(g) without substantial justification, the court, on motion or on its own, must impose an appropriate sanction on the signer, the party on whose behalf the signer was acting, or both. The sanction may include an order to pay the reasonable expenses, including attorney's fees, caused by the violation. FRCP 26(g)(3). Refer to the United States District Court for the Northern District of New York KeyRules Motion for Discovery Sanctions document for more information.

4.  *Privacy protection for filings made with the court*

  a.  *Redacted filings.* Unless the court orders otherwise, in an electronic or paper filing with the court that contains an individual's Social Security number, taxpayer-identification number, or birth date, the name of an individual known to be a minor, or a financial-account number, a party or nonparty making the filing may include only:

    i.   The last four (4) digits of the Social Security number and taxpayer-identification number;

    ii.  The year of the individual's birth;

    iii. The minor's initials; and

    iv.  The last four (4) digits of the financial-account number. FRCP 5.2(a); NY R USDCTND L.R. 8.1; NY R USDCTND CM/ECF(11)(11.2).

    v.   If a home address must be used, use only the City and State. NY R USDCTND L.R. 8.1; NY R USDCTND CM/ECF(11)(11.2).

    vi.   If the victim of a sexual assault must be referenced, redact the name to 'Victim.' NY R USDCTND CM/ECF(11)(11.2); NY R USDCTND L.R. 8.1.

    vii.   In addition, caution shall be exercised when filing documents that contain the following:

- Personal identifying number, such as a driver's license number;
- Medical records, treatment and diagnosis;
- Employment history;
- Individual financial information; and
- Proprietary or trade secret information. NY R USDCTND L.R. 8.1; NY R USDCTND CM/ECF(11)(11.2).

b.   *Exemptions from the redaction requirement.* The redaction requirement does not apply to the following:

    i.   A financial-account number that identifies the property allegedly subject to forfeiture in a forfeiture proceeding;

    ii.   The record of an administrative or agency proceeding;

    iii.   The official record of a state-court proceeding;

    iv.   The record of a court or tribunal, if that record was not subject to the redaction requirement when originally filed;

    v.   A filing covered by FRCP 5.2(c) or FRCP 5.2(d); and

    vi.   A pro se filing in an action brought under 28 U.S.C.A. § 2241, 28 U.S.C.A. § 2254, or 28 U.S.C.A. § 2255. FRCP 5.2(b).

    vii.   Transcripts of the administrative record in social security proceedings are exempt from this requirement. State court records and other documents filed in habeas corpus proceedings are exempt from this requirement except for proceedings that involve victims of sex crimes. In habeas corpus cases involving sex crimes, the parties must redact the record and supporting papers, or may move to seal, if appropriate. NY R USDCTND L.R. 8.1.

c.   *Limitations on remote access to electronic files; Social Security appeals and immigration cases.* Unless the court orders otherwise, in an action for benefits under the Social Security Act, and in an action or proceeding relating to an order of removal, to relief from removal, or to immigration benefits or detention, access to an electronic file is authorized as follows:

    i.   The parties and their attorneys may have remote electronic access to any part of the case file, including the administrative record;

    ii.   Any other person may have electronic access to the full record at the courthouse, but may have remote electronic access only to:

- The docket maintained by the court; and
- An opinion, order, judgment, or other disposition of the court, but not any other part of the case file or the administrative record. FRCP 5.2(c).

d.   *Filings made under seal.* The court may order that a filing be made under seal without redaction. The court may later unseal the filing or order the person who made the filing to file a redacted version for the public record. FRCP 5.2(d); NY R USDCTND L.R. 8.1. For information on sealed matters, refer to NY R USDCTND L.R. 83.13 and NY R USDCTND CM/ECF(12).

e.   *Protective orders.* For good cause, the court may by order in a case:

    i.   Require redaction of additional information; or

    ii.   Limit or prohibit a nonparty's remote electronic access to a document filed with the court. FRCP 5.2(e).

f. *Option for additional unredacted filing under seal.* A person making a redacted filing may also file an unredacted copy under seal. The court must retain the unredacted copy as part of the record. FRCP 5.2(f); NY R USDCTND L.R. 8.1; NY R USDCTND CM/ECF(11)(11.3).

g. *Option for filing a reference list.* A filing that contains redacted information may be filed together with a reference list that identifies each item of redacted information and specifies an appropriate identifier that uniquely corresponds to each item listed. The list must be filed under seal and may be amended as of right. Any reference in the case to a listed identifier will be construed to refer to the corresponding item of information. FRCP 5.2(g); NY R USDCTND L.R. 8.1; NY R USDCTND CM/ECF(11)(11.3).

h. *Responsibility for redaction.* Counsel is strongly urged to discuss this issue with all their clients so that they can make an informed decision about the inclusion of certain information. The responsibility for redacting these personal identifiers rests solely with counsel and the parties. The Clerk will not review each filing for compliance with NY R USDCTND L.R. 8.1. Counsel and the parties are cautioned that failure to redact these personal identifiers may subject them to the Court's full disciplinary power. NY R USDCTND L.R. 8.1; NY R USDCTND CM/ECF(11)(11.3).

i. *Waiver of protection of identifiers.* A person waives the protection of FRCP 5.2(a) as to the person's own information by filing it without redaction and not under seal. FRCP 5.2(h).

5. *Individual judge practices.* Refer to the Miscellaneous section of this document for information on individual judge practices on formatting documents.

## F. Filing and Service Requirements

1. *Filing requirements.* Any paper after the complaint that is required to be served—together with a certificate of service—must be filed within a reasonable time after service. But disclosures under FRCP 26(a)(1) or FRCP 26(a)(2) and the following discovery requests and responses must not be filed until they are used in the proceeding or the court orders filing: depositions, interrogatories, requests for documents or tangible things or to permit entry onto land, and requests for admission. FRCP 5(d)(1). Refer to the United States District Court for the Northern District of New York KeyRules pleading and motion documents for information on filing with the court.

    a. *Filing discovery.* Parties are directed not to file discovery material unless it is being filed in accordance with NY R USDCTND L.R. 26.2. NY R USDCTND Order 25(IX)(B). Parties shall not file notices to take depositions, transcripts of depositions, interrogatories, requests for documents, requests for admissions, disclosures, and answers and responses to these notices and requests unless the Court orders otherwise; provided, however, that a party shall file any discovery material that it expects to use at trial or to support any motion, including a motion to compel or for summary judgment prior to the trial or motion return date. NY R USDCTND L.R. 26.2; NY R USDCTND CM/ECF(2)(2.1)(4).

2. *Service requirements.* [A request for an admission] must be served on the party from whom the admission is requested and, unless the court has otherwise ordered, a copy of the request must be served on every other party. FPP § 2258.

    a. *Service; When required*

        i. *In general.* Unless the Federal Rules of Civil Procedure provide otherwise, each of the following papers must be served on every party:

           - An order stating that service is required;

           - A pleading filed after the original complaint, unless the court orders otherwise under FRCP 5(c) because there are numerous defendants;

           - A discovery paper required to be served on a party, unless the court orders otherwise;

           - A written motion, except one that may be heard ex parte; and

           - A written notice, appearance, demand, or offer of judgment, or any similar paper. FRCP 5(a)(1).

        ii. *If a party fails to appear.* No service is required on a party who is in default for failing to appear.

But a pleading that asserts a new claim for relief against such a party must be served on that party under FRCP 4. FRCP 5(a)(2).

iii. *Seizing property.* If an action is begun by seizing property and no person is or need be named as a defendant, any service required before the filing of an appearance, answer, or claim must be made on the person who had custody or possession of the property when it was seized. FRCP 5(a)(3).

b. *Service; How made*

i. *Serving an attorney.* If a party is represented by an attorney, service under FRCP 5 must be made on the attorney unless the court orders service on the party. FRCP 5(b)(1).

ii. *Service in general.* A paper is served under FRCP 5 by:

- Handing it to the person;

- Leaving it: (1) at the person's office with a clerk or other person in charge or, if no one is in charge, in a conspicuous place in the office; or (2) if the person has no office or the office is closed, at the person's dwelling or usual place of abode with someone of suitable age and discretion who resides there;

- Mailing it to the person's last known address—in which event service is complete upon mailing;

- Leaving it with the court clerk if the person has no known address;

- Sending it by electronic means if the person consented in writing—in which event service is complete upon transmission, but is not effective if the serving party learns that it did not reach the person to be served; or

- Delivering it by any other means that the person consented to in writing—in which event service is complete when the person making service delivers it to the agency designated to make delivery. FRCP 5(b)(2).

iii. *Service of electronically-filed documents.* Service is complete provided all parties receive a Notice of Electronic Filing (NEF), which is sent automatically by email from the Court (see the NEF for a list of who did/did not receive notice electronically). Transmission of the NEF constitutes service upon all Filing and Receiving Users who are listed as recipients of notice by electronic mail. It remains the responsibility of Filing and Receiving Users to maintain current contact information with the court and to regularly review the docket sheet of the case. NY R USDCTND CM/ECF(5)(5.2).

- *Non-filing or receiving users.* Attorneys and pro se parties who are not Filing or Receiving Users must be served with a paper copy of any electronically filed pleading or other document. Service of such paper copy must be made according to the Federal Rules of Civil Procedure and the Local Rules of Practice for the United States District Court for the Northern District of New York. Such paper service must be documented by electronically filing a certificate of service. NY R USDCTND CM/ECF(5)(5.2). A party who is not a Filing User of the System is entitled to a paper copy of any electronically-filed pleading, document, or order. The Filing User must therefore provide the non-Filing User with the pleading or document according to the Federal Rules of Civil Procedure. NY R US-DCTND CM/ECF(5)(5.3).

iv. *Using court facilities.* If a local rule so authorizes, a party may use the court's transmission facilities to make service under FRCP 5(b)(2)(E). FRCP 5(b)(3).

c. *Serving numerous defendants*

i. *In general.* If an action involves an unusually large number of defendants, the court may, on motion or on its own, order that:

- Defendants' pleadings and replies to them need not be served on other defendants;

- Any crossclaim, counterclaim, avoidance, or affirmative defense in those pleadings and replies to them will be treated as denied or avoided by all other parties; and

- Filing any such pleading and serving it on the plaintiff constitutes notice of the pleading to all parties. FRCP 5(c)(1).

   ii. *Notifying parties.* A copy of every such order must be served on the parties as the court directs. FRCP 5(c)(2).

3. *Individual judge practices.* Refer to the Miscellaneous section of this document for information on individual judge practices on filing and serving documents.

## G. Hearings

1. There is no hearing contemplated in the federal statutes or rules for requests for admissions.

## H. Forms

### 1. Federal Request for Admissions Forms

   a. Request; For admission of facts and genuineness of documents. AMJUR PP DEPOSITION § 674.

   b. Plaintiff's request for admission. 3B FEDFORMS § 3650.

   c. Plaintiff's request for admission; Another form. 3B FEDFORMS § 3651.

   d. Plaintiff's request for admission; Statements in documents. 3B FEDFORMS § 3652.

   e. Plaintiff's request for admission; Statements in documents; Another form. 3B FEDFORMS § 3653.

   f. Plaintiff's request for admission; Specific facts. 3B FEDFORMS § 3654.

   g. Plaintiff's request for admission; Specific facts; Another form. 3B FEDFORMS § 3655.

   h. Plaintiff's request for admission; Specific documents and facts. 3B FEDFORMS § 3656.

   i. Plaintiff's request for admission; Specific documents and facts; Another form. 3B FEDFORMS § 3657.

   j. Plaintiff's request for admission; True copies, filing and operational effect of government documents. 3B FEDFORMS § 3658.

   k. Plaintiff's request for additional admission. 3B FEDFORMS § 3659.

   l. Defendant's request for admission of genuineness; Specific document. 3B FEDFORMS § 3660.

   m. Defendant's request for admission of genuineness; Specific document; Another form. 3B FED-FORMS § 3661.

   n. Defendant's request for admission of genuineness; Specific document; Another form. 3B FED-FORMS § 3662.

   o. Defendant's request for admission; Truth of statement. 3B FEDFORMS § 3663.

   p. Request for admissions under FRCP 36. FEDPROF § 23:535.

   q. Request for admissions; General form. FEDPROF § 23:536.

   r. Request for admissions; Action to collect royalties. FEDPROF § 23:537.

   s. Request for admissions; Trademark action. FEDPROF § 23:538.

   t. Request for admissions; Automobile negligence action. FEDPROF § 23:539.

   u. Request for admissions; Motor vehicle action. FEDPROF § 23:540.

   v. Request for admissions; Premises liability action. FEDPROF § 23:541.

   w. Request for admissions; Products liability action. FEDPROF § 23:542.

   x. Request for admissions; Medical malpractice action. FEDPROF § 23:543.

   y. Request for admissions; Genuineness of documents. FEDPROF § 23:544.

   z. Request for admissions; Wrongful death due to forklift accident. FEDPROF § 23:545.

## I. Applicable Rules

1. *Federal rules*

   a. Serving and filing pleadings and other papers. FRCP 5.

b. Privacy protection for filings made with the court. FRCP 5.2.

c. Computing and extending time; Time for motion papers. FRCP 6.

d. Pleadings allowed; Form of motions and other papers. FRCP 7.

e. Form of pleadings. FRCP 10.

f. Signing pleadings, motions, and other papers; Representations to the court; Sanctions. FRCP 11.

g. Duty to disclose; General provisions governing discovery. FRCP 26.

h. Stipulations about discovery procedure. FRCP 29.

i. Requests for admission. FRCP 36.

j. Failure to make disclosures or to cooperate in discovery; Sanctions. FRCP 37.

2. *Local rules*

a. Scope of the rules. NY R USDCTND L.R. 1.1.

b. Complex and multi-district litigation. NY R USDCTND L.R. 3.3.

c. Service and filing of papers. NY R USDCTND L.R. 5.1.

d. Personal privacy protection. NY R USDCTND L.R. 8.1.

e. Form of papers. NY R USDCTND L.R. 10.1.

f. Discovery cut-off. NY R USDCTND L.R. 16.2.

g. Form of certain discovery documents. NY R USDCTND L.R. 26.1.

h. Filing discovery. NY R USDCTND L.R. 26.2.

i. Timing of discovery. NY R USDCTND L.R. 26.4.

j. Settlement procedures. NY R USDCTND L.R. 68.2.

k. Appearance and withdrawal of attorney. NY R USDCTND L.R. 83.2.

l. Arbitration. NY R USDCTND L.R. 83.7-1; NY R USDCTND L.R. 83.7-2; NY R USDCTND L.R. 83.7-3.

m. Assisted mediation program. NY R USDCTND L.R. 83.8.

n. Mediation. NY R USDCTND L.R. 83.11-1; NY R USDCTND L.R. 83.11-3.

o. Early neutral evaluation. NY R USDCTND L.R. 83.12-1; NY R USDCTND L.R. 83.12-3.

p. Administrative procedures for electronic case filing. NY R USDCTND CM/ECF.

q. Case assignment plan for the Northern District of New York. [NY R USDCTND Order 12, as amended by NY ORDER 16-4201, effective March 24, 2015].

r. Directing the expedited service of the summons and complaint and further directing the completion of FRCP 16 stipulation for the timely progression of civil actions. [NY R USDCTND Order 25, as amended by NY ORDER 16-4187, effective June 23, 2016].

s. Mandatory mediation program. NY R USDCTND Order 47.

## J. Miscellaneous

**NOTE: Individual judges' rules may apply. For available judge-level information, refer to:**

DISTRICT JUDGE MAE A. D'AGOSTINO: [NY R USDCTND D'Agostino-Rules and Practices, as added by NY ORDER 16-4200, effective April 4, 2016].

DISTRICT JUDGE THOMAS J. McAVOY: NY R USDCTND McAvoy-Order.

# Requests, Notices and Applications
# Notice of Deposition

## Document Last Updated September 2016

**A. Checklist**

(I) ❏ Matters to be considered by deposing party for depositions by oral examination

    (a) ❏ Required documents

        (1) ❏ Notice of deposition

    (b) ❏ Supplemental documents

        (1) ❏ Subpoena

        (2) ❏ Subpoena duces tecum

        (3) ❏ Request for production of documents

        (4) ❏ Certificate of service

    (c) ❏ Timing

        (1) ❏ A party may, by oral questions, depose any person, including a party, without leave of court except as provided in FRCP 30(a)(2)

        (2) ❏ A party must obtain leave of court, and the court must grant leave to the extent consistent with FRCP 26(b)(1) and FRCP 26(b)(2):

            (i) ❏ If the parties have not stipulated to the deposition and: (1) the deposition would result in more than ten (10) depositions being taken under FRCP 30 or FRCP 31 by the plaintiffs, or by the defendants, or by the third-party defendants; (2) the deponent has already been deposed in the case; or (3) the party seeks to take the deposition before the time specified in FRCP 26(d), unless the party certifies in the notice, with supporting facts, that the deponent is expected to leave the United States and be unavailable for examination in this country after that time; or

            (ii) ❏ If the deponent is confined in prison

        (3) ❏ A party who wants to depose a person by oral questions must give reasonable written notice to every other party

(II) ❏ Matters to be considered by deposing party for depositions by written questions

    (a) ❏ Required documents

        (1) ❏ Notice of deposition

        (2) ❏ Written questions

    (b) ❏ Supplemental documents

        (1) ❏ Subpoena

        (2) ❏ Certificate of service

    (c) ❏ Timing

        (1) ❏ A party may, by written questions, depose any person, including a party, without leave of court except as provided in FRCP 31(a)(2)

        (2) ❏ A party must obtain leave of court, and the court must grant leave to the extent consistent with FRCP 26(b)(1) and FRCP 26(b)(2):

            (i) ❏ If the parties have not stipulated to the deposition and: (1) the deposition would result in more than ten (10) depositions being taken under FRCP 31 or FRCP 30 by the plaintiffs, or by the defendants, or by the third-party defendants; (2) the deponent has already been deposed in the case; or (3) the party seeks to take a deposition before the time specified in FRCP 26(d); or

       (ii)   ❑  If the deponent is confined in prison

   (3)   ❑  A party who wants to depose a person by written questions must serve them on every other party, with a notice

## B. Timing

1. *Depositions by oral examination*

   a.  *Without leave.* A party may, by oral questions, depose any person, including a party, without leave of court except as provided in FRCP 30(a)(2). FRCP 30(a)(1).

   b.  *With leave.* A party must obtain leave of court, and the court must grant leave to the extent consistent with FRCP 26(b)(1) and FRCP 26(b)(2):

      i.  If the parties have not stipulated to the deposition and: (1) the deposition would result in more than ten (10) depositions being taken under FRCP 30 or FRCP 31 by the plaintiffs, or by the defendants, or by the third-party defendants; (2) the deponent has already been deposed in the case; or (3) the party seeks to take the deposition before the time specified in FRCP 26(d), unless the party certifies in the notice, with supporting facts, that the deponent is expected to leave the United States and be unavailable for examination in this country after that time; or

      ii.  If the deponent is confined in prison. FRCP 30(a)(2).

   c.  *Notice of deposition.* A party who wants to depose a person by oral questions must give reasonable written notice to every other party. FRCP 30(b)(1).

2. *Depositions by written questions*

   a.  *Without leave.* A party may, by written questions, depose any person, including a party, without leave of court except as provided in FRCP 31(a)(2). FRCP 31(a)(1).

   b.  *With leave.* A party must obtain leave of court, and the court must grant leave to the extent consistent with FRCP 26(b)(1) and FRCP 26(b)(2):

      i.  If the parties have not stipulated to the deposition and: (1) the deposition would result in more than ten (10) depositions being taken under FRCP 31 or FRCP 30 by the plaintiffs, or by the defendants, or by the third-party defendants; (2) the deponent has already been deposed in the case; or (3) the party seeks to take a deposition before the time specified in FRCP 26(d); or

      ii.  If the deponent is confined in prison. FRCP 31(a)(2).

   c.  *Notice of deposition with written questions.* A party who wants to depose a person by written questions must serve them on every other party, with a notice. FRCP 31(a)(3). Refer to the General Requirements section of this document for the contents of the notice.

   d.  *Questions from other parties.* Any questions to the deponent from other parties must be served on all parties as follows:

      i.  *Cross-questions.* Cross-questions, within fourteen (14) days after being served with the notice and direct questions;

      ii.  *Redirect questions.* Redirect questions, within seven (7) days after being served with cross-questions; and

      iii.  *Recross-questions.* Recross-questions, within seven (7) days after being served with redirect questions. FRCP 31(a)(5).

      iv.  *Modification of timing requirements.* The court may, for good cause, extend or shorten these times. FRCP 31(a)(5).

3. *Timing of discovery, generally.* A party may not seek discovery from any source before the parties have conferred as required by FRCP 26(f), except in a proceeding exempted from initial disclosure under FRCP 26(a)(1)(B), or when authorized by the Federal Rules of Civil Procedure, by stipulation, or by court order. FRCP 26(d)(1). FRCP 26(d), which prohibits discovery prior to a meeting and conference between the parties, and FRCP 26(f), which directs parties to meet and confer with each other relative to the nature and basis of claims and defenses to a lawsuit, shall not apply to any action in which a party is incarcerated. NY R USDCTND L.R. 26.4.

4. *Discovery cut-off.* The "discovery cut-off" is that date by which all responses to written discovery, including requests for admissions, shall be due according to the Federal Rules of Civil Procedure and by which all depositions shall be concluded. Counsel are advised to initiate discovery requests and notice depositions sufficiently in advance of the cut-off date to comply with NY R USDCTND L.R. 16.2. Discovery requests that call for responses or scheduled depositions after the discovery cut-off will not be enforceable except by order of the Court for good cause shown. Parties shall file and serve motions to compel discovery no later than fourteen (14) days after the discovery cut-off. See NY R USDCTND L.R. 7.1(d)(8). NY R USDCTND L.R. 16.2.

5. *Computation of time*

   a. *Computing time.* FRCP 6 applies in computing any time period specified in the Federal Rules of Civil Procedure, in any local rule or court order, or in any statute that does not specify a method of computing time. FRCP 6(a).

      i. *Period stated in days or a longer unit.* When the period is stated in days or a longer unit of time:
         - Exclude the day of the event that triggers the period;
         - Count every day, including intermediate Saturdays, Sundays, and legal holidays; and
         - Include the last day of the period, but if the last day is a Saturday, Sunday, or legal holiday, the period continues to run until the end of the next day that is not a Saturday, Sunday, or legal holiday. FRCP 6(a)(1).

      ii. *Period stated in hours.* When the period is stated in hours:
         - Begin counting immediately on the occurrence of the event that triggers the period;
         - Count every hour, including hours during intermediate Saturdays, Sundays, and legal holidays; and
         - If the period would end on a Saturday, Sunday, or legal holiday, the period continues to run until the same time on the next day that is not a Saturday, Sunday, or legal holiday. FRCP 6(a)(2).

      iii. *Inaccessibility of the clerk's office.* Unless the court orders otherwise, if the clerk's office is inaccessible:
         - On the last day for filing under FRCP 6(a)(1), then the time for filing is extended to the first accessible day that is not a Saturday, Sunday, or legal holiday; or
         - During the last hour for filing under FRCP 6(a)(2), then the time for filing is extended to the same time on the first accessible day that is not a Saturday, Sunday, or legal holiday. FRCP 6(a)(3).

      iv. *"Last day" defined.* Unless a different time is set by a statute, local rule, or court order, the last day ends:
         - For electronic filing, at midnight in the court's time zone; and
         - For filing by other means, when the clerk's office is scheduled to close. FRCP 6(a)(4).

      v. *"Next day" defined.* The "next day" is determined by continuing to count forward when the period is measured after an event and backward when measured before an event. FRCP 6(a)(5).

      vi. *"Legal holiday" defined.* "Legal holiday" means:
         - The day set aside by statute for observing New Year's Day, Martin Luther King Jr.'s Birthday, Washington's Birthday, Memorial Day, Independence Day, Labor Day, Columbus Day, Veterans' Day, Thanksgiving Day, or Christmas Day;
         - Any day declared a holiday by the President or Congress; and
         - For periods that are measured after an event, any other day declared a holiday by the state where the district court is located. FRCP 6(a)(6).

   b. *Computation of electronic filing deadlines.* A document will be deemed timely filed if electronically filed prior to midnight Eastern Time. However, if the time of day is of the essence, the assigned judge may order that the document be filed by a time certain. NY R USDCTND CM/ECF(4)(4.3).

    i.   *Technical failures.* A Filing User, whose filing is untimely as the result of a technical failure of the Court's CM/ECF site, may seek appropriate relief from the Court. However, Filing Users are cautioned that, in some circumstances, the Court lacks the authority to grant an extension of time to file (e.g., FRCP 6(b) of the Federal Rules of Civil Procedure). NY R USDCTND CM/ECF(10)(10.1).

-    *Technical failure of the filing user's system.* Problems with the Filing User's system, such as phone line problems, problems with the Filing User's Internet Service Provider ("ISP"), or hardware or software problems, will not constitute a technical failure under these Administrative Procedures nor excuse an untimely filing. A Filing User who cannot file documents electronically because of a problem on the Filing User's system must file the documents' conventionally along with an affidavit explaining the reason for not filing the documents electronically. NY R USDCTND CM/ECF(10)(10.2).

  c.  *Extending time*

    i.   *In general.* When an act may or must be done within a specified time, the court may, for good cause, extend the time:

-    With or without motion or notice if the court acts, or if a request is made, before the original time or its extension expires; or

-    On motion made after the time has expired if the party failed to act because of excusable neglect. FRCP 6(b)(1).

    ii.  *Exceptions.* A court must not extend the time to act under FRCP 50(b), FRCP 50(d), FRCP 52(b), FRCP 59(b), FRCP 59(d), FRCP 59(e), and FRCP 60(b). FRCP 6(b)(2).

    iii.  Refer to the United States District Court for the Northern District of New York KeyRules Motion for Continuance/Extension of Time document for more information on extending time.

  d.  *Additional time after certain kinds of service.* When a party may or must act within a specified time after service and service is made under FRCP 5(b)(2)(C), FRCP 5(b)(2)(D), FRCP 5(b)(2)(E), or FRCP 5(b)(2)(F), three (3) days are added after the period would otherwise expire under FRCP 6(a). FRCP 6(d).

    i.   In accordance with FRCP 6(e), service by electronic means is treated the same as service by mail for purposes of adding three (3) days to the prescribed period to respond. NY R USDCTND CM/ECF(5)(5.4). [Editor's note: the reference to FRCP 6(e) is likely meant to be a reference to FRCP 6(d)].

6.  *Individual judge practices.* Refer to the Miscellaneous section of this document for information on individual judge practices on timing of documents.

## C. General Requirements

1.  *General provisions governing discovery*

  a.  *Discovery scope and limits*

    i.   *Scope in general.* Unless otherwise limited by court order, the scope of discovery is as follows: Parties may obtain discovery regarding any nonprivileged matter that is relevant to any party's claim or defense and proportional to the needs of the case, considering the importance of the issues at stake in the action, the amount in controversy, the parties' relative access to relevant information, the parties' resources, the importance of the discovery in resolving the issues, and whether the burden or expense of the proposed discovery outweighs its likely benefit. Information within this scope of discovery need not be admissible in evidence to be discoverable. FRCP 26(b)(1).

    ii.  *Limitations on frequency and extent*

-    *When permitted.* By order, the court may alter the limits in the Federal Rules of Civil Procedure on the number of depositions and interrogatories or on the length of depositions under FRCP 30. By order or local rule, the court may also limit the number of requests under FRCP 36. FRCP 26(b)(2)(A).

- *Specific limitations on electronically stored information.* A party need not provide discovery of electronically stored information from sources that the party identifies as not reasonably accessible because of undue burden or cost. On motion to compel discovery or for a protective order, the party from whom discovery is sought must show that the information is not reasonably accessible because of undue burden or cost. If that showing is made, the court may nonetheless order discovery from such sources if the requesting party shows good cause, considering the limitations of FRCP 26(b)(2)(C). The court may specify conditions for the discovery. FRCP 26(b)(2)(B).

- *When required.* On motion or on its own, the court must limit the frequency or extent of discovery otherwise allowed by the Federal Rules of Civil Procedure or by local rule if it determines that: (1) the discovery sought is unreasonably cumulative or duplicative, or can be obtained from some other source that is more convenient, less burdensome, or less expensive; (2) the party seeking discovery has had ample opportunity to obtain the information by discovery in the action; or (3) the proposed discovery is outside the scope permitted by FRCP 26(b)(1). FRCP 26(b)(2)(C).

iii. *Trial preparation; Materials*

- *Documents and tangible things.* Ordinarily, a party may not discover documents and tangible things that are prepared in anticipation of litigation or for trial by or for another party or its representative (including the other party's attorney, consultant, surety, indemnitor, insurer, or agent). But, subject to FRCP 26(b)(4), those materials may be discovered if: (1) they are otherwise discoverable under FRCP 26(b)(1); and (2) the party shows that it has substantial need for the materials to prepare its case and cannot, without undue hardship, obtain their substantial equivalent by other means. FRCP 26(b)(3)(A).

- *Protection against disclosure.* If the court orders discovery of those materials, it must protect against disclosure of the mental impressions, conclusions, opinions, or legal theories of a party's attorney or other representative concerning the litigation. FRCP 26(b)(3)(B).

- *Previous statement.* Any party or other person may, on request and without the required showing, obtain the person's own previous statement about the action or its subject matter. If the request is refused, the person may move for a court order, and FRCP 37(a)(5) applies to the award of expenses. A previous statement is either: (1) a written statement that the person has signed or otherwise adopted or approved; or (2) a contemporaneous stenographic, mechanical, electrical, or other recording—or a transcription of it—that recites substantially verbatim the person's oral statement. FRCP 26(b)(3)(C).

iv. *Trial preparation; Experts*

- *Deposition of an expert who may testify.* A party may depose any person who has been identified as an expert whose opinions may be presented at trial. If FRCP 26(a)(2)(B) requires a report from the expert, the deposition may be conducted only after the report is provided. FRCP 26(b)(4)(A).

- *Trial-preparation protection for draft reports or disclosures.* FRCP 26(b)(3)(A) and FRCP 26(b)(3)(B) protect drafts of any report or disclosure required under FRCP 26(a)(2), regardless of the form in which the draft is recorded. FRCP 26(b)(4)(B).

- *Trial-preparation protection for communications between a party's attorney and expert witnesses.* FRCP 26(b)(3)(A) and FRCP 26(b)(3)(B) protect communications between the party's attorney and any witness required to provide a report under FRCP 26(a)(2)(B), regardless of the form of the communications, except to the extent that the communications: (1) relate to compensation for the expert's study or testimony; (2) identify facts or data that the party's attorney provided and that the expert considered in forming the opinions to be expressed; or (3) identify assumptions that the party's attorney provided and that the expert relied on in forming the opinions to be expressed. FRCP 26(b)(4)(C).

- *Expert employed only for trial preparation.* Ordinarily, a party may not, by interrogatories or deposition, discover facts known or opinions held by an expert who has been retained or specially employed by another party in anticipation of litigation or to prepare for trial and who is not expected to be called as a witness at trial. But a party may do so only: (1) as provided in FRCP 35(b); or (2) on showing exceptional circumstances under which it is impracticable for the party to obtain facts or opinions on the same subject by other means. FRCP 26(b)(4)(D).

- *Payment.* Unless manifest injustice would result, the court must require that the party seeking discovery: (1) pay the expert a reasonable fee for time spent in responding to discovery under FRCP 26(b)(4)(A) or FRCP 26(b)(4)(D); and (2) for discovery FRCP 26(b)(4)(D), also pay the other party a fair portion of the fees and expenses it reasonably incurred in obtaining the expert's facts and opinions. FRCP 26(b)(4)(E).

  v. *Claiming privilege or protecting trial-preparation materials*

  - *Information withheld.* When a party withholds information otherwise discoverable by claiming that the information is privileged or subject to protection as trial-preparation material, the party must: (1) expressly make the claim; and (2) describe the nature of the documents, communications, or tangible things not produced or disclosed—and do so in a manner that, without revealing information itself privileged or protected, will enable other parties to assess the claim. FRCP 26(b)(5)(A).

  - *Information produced.* If information produced in discovery is subject to a claim of privilege or of protection as trial-preparation material, the party making the claim may notify any party that received the information of the claim and the basis for it. After being notified, a party must promptly return, sequester, or destroy the specified information and any copies it has; must not use or disclose the information until the claim is resolved; must take reasonable steps to retrieve the information if the party disclosed it before being notified; and may promptly present the information to the court under seal for a determination of the claim. The producing party must preserve the information until the claim is resolved. FRCP 26(b)(5)(B).

b. *Protective orders.* A party or any person from whom discovery is sought may move for a protective order in the court where the action is pending—or as an alternative on matters relating to a deposition, in the court for the district where the deposition will be taken. FRCP 26(c)(1). Refer to the United States District Court for the Northern District of New York KeyRules Motion for Protective Order document for more information.

c. *Sequence of discovery.* Unless the parties stipulate or the court orders otherwise for the parties' and witnesses' convenience and in the interests of justice: (1) methods of discovery may be used in any sequence; and (2) discovery by one party does not require any other party to delay its discovery. FRCP 26(d)(3).

2. *Persons before whom depositions may be taken*

a. *Within the United States.* Within the United States or a territory or insular possession subject to United States jurisdiction, a deposition must be taken before: (1) an officer authorized to administer oaths either by federal law or by the law in the place of examination; or (2) a person appointed by the court where the action is pending to administer oaths and take testimony. FRCP 28(a)(1).

  i. *Definition of "officer".* The term "officer" in FRCP 30, FRCP 31, and FRCP 32 includes a person appointed by the court under FRCP 28 or designated by the parties under FRCP 29(a). FRCP 28(a)(2).

b. *In a foreign country.* A deposition may be taken in a foreign country: (1) under an applicable treaty or convention; (2) under a letter of request, whether or not captioned a "letter rogatory"; (3) on notice, before a person authorized to administer oaths either by federal law or by the law in the place of examination; or (4) before a person commissioned by the court to administer any necessary oath and take testimony. FRCP 28(b)(1).

  i. *Issuing a letter of request or a commission.* A letter of request, a commission, or both may be issued: (1) on appropriate terms after an application and notice of it; and (2) without a showing that taking the deposition in another manner is impracticable or inconvenient. FRCP 28(b)(2).

ii.   *Form of a request, notice, or commission.* When a letter of request or any other device is used according to a treaty or convention, it must be captioned in the form prescribed by that treaty or convention. A letter of request may be addressed "To the Appropriate Authority in [name of country]." A deposition notice or a commission must designate by name or descriptive title the person before whom the deposition is to be taken. FRCP 28(b)(3).

iii.   *Letter of request; Admitting evidence.* Evidence obtained in response to a letter of request need not be excluded merely because it is not a verbatim transcript, because the testimony was not taken under oath, or because of any similar departure from the requirements for depositions taken within the United States. FRCP 28(b)(4).

c.   *Commission to take testimony.* Except as the law otherwise provides, in all actions or proceedings where the taking of depositions of witnesses or of parties is authorized, the procedure for obtaining and using the depositions shall comply with the Federal Rules of Civil Procedure. The party seeking the deposition shall furnish the officer to whom the commission is issued with a copy of the Federal Rules of Civil Procedure pertaining to discovery. NY R USDCTND L.R. 83.9(a).

d.   *Disqualification.* A deposition must not be taken before a person who is any party's relative, employee, or attorney; who is related to or employed by any party's attorney; or who is financially interested in the action. FRCP 28(c).

3.   *Depositions by oral examination*

a.   *Notice of the deposition.* A party who wants to depose a person by oral questions must give reasonable written notice to every other party. The notice must state the time and place of the deposition and, if known, the deponent's name and address. If the name is unknown, the notice must provide a general description sufficient to identify the person or the particular class or group to which the person belongs. FRCP 30(b)(1).

i.   *Notice or subpoena directed to an organization.* In its notice or subpoena, a party may name as the deponent a public or private corporation, a partnership, an association, a governmental agency, or other entity and must describe with reasonable particularity the matters for examination. The named organization must then designate one or more officers, directors, or managing agents, or designate other persons who consent to testify on its behalf; and it may set out the matters on which each person designated will testify. A subpoena must advise a nonparty organization of its duty to make this designation. The persons designated must testify about information known or reasonably available to the organization. FRCP 30(b)(6) does not preclude a deposition by any other procedure allowed by the Federal Rules of Civil Procedure. FRCP 30(b)(6).

b.   *Method of recording*

i.   *Method stated in the notice.* The party who notices the deposition must state in the notice the method for recording the testimony. Unless the court orders otherwise, testimony may be recorded by audio, audiovisual, or stenographic means. The noticing party bears the recording costs. Any party may arrange to transcribe a deposition. FRCP 30(b)(3)(A).

ii.   *Additional method.* With prior notice to the deponent and other parties, any party may designate another method for recording the testimony in addition to that specified in the original notice. That party bears the expense of the additional record or transcript unless the court orders otherwise. FRCP 30(b)(3)(B).

c.   *By remote means.* The parties may stipulate—or the court may on motion order—that a deposition be taken by telephone or other remote means. For the purpose of FRCP 30 and FRCP 28(a), FRCP 37(a)(2), and FRCP 37(b)(1), the deposition takes place where the deponent answers the questions. FRCP 30(b)(4).

d.   *Officer's duties*

i.   *Before the deposition.* Unless the parties stipulate otherwise, a deposition must be conducted before an officer appointed or designated under FRCP 28. The officer must begin the deposition with an on-the-record statement that includes: (1) the officer's name and business address; (2) the date, time, and place of the deposition; (3) the deponent's name; (4) the officer's administration of the oath or affirmation to the deponent; and (5) the identity of all persons present. FRCP 30(b)(5)(A).

ii. *Conducting the deposition; Avoiding distortion.* If the deposition is recorded non-stenographically, the officer must repeat the items in FRCP 30(b)(5)(A)(i) through FRCP 30(b)(5)(A)(iii) at the beginning of each unit of the recording medium. The deponent's and attorneys' appearance or demeanor must not be distorted through recording techniques. FRCP 30(b)(5)(B).

iii. *After the deposition.* At the end of a deposition, the officer must state on the record that the deposition is complete and must set out any stipulations made by the attorneys about custody of the transcript or recording and of the exhibits, or about any other pertinent matters. FRCP 30(b)(5)(C).

e. *Examination and cross-examination.* The examination and cross-examination of a deponent proceed as they would at trial under the Federal Rules of Evidence, except FRE 103 and FRE 615. FRCP 30(c)(1).

  i. *Record of the examination.* After putting the deponent under oath or affirmation, the officer must record the testimony by the method designated under FRCP 30(b)(3)(A). The testimony must be recorded by the officer personally or by a person acting in the presence and under the direction of the officer. FRCP 30(c)(1).

  ii. *Objections.* An objection at the time of the examination—whether to evidence, to a party's conduct, to the officer's qualifications, to the manner of taking the deposition, or to any other aspect of the deposition—must be noted on the record, but the examination still proceeds; the testimony is taken subject to any objection. An objection must be stated concisely in a nonargumentative and nonsuggestive manner. A person may instruct a deponent not to answer only when necessary to preserve a privilege, to enforce a limitation ordered by the court, or to present a motion under FRCP 30(d)(3). FRCP 30(c)(2).

  iii. *Participating through written questions.* Instead of participating in the oral examination, a party may serve written questions in a sealed envelope on the party noticing the deposition, who must deliver them to the officer. The officer must ask the deponent those questions and record the answers verbatim. FRCP 30(c)(3).

f. *Duration.* Unless otherwise stipulated or ordered by the court, a deposition is limited to one (1) day of seven (7) hours. The court must allow additional time consistent with FRCP 26(b)(1) and FRCP 26(b)(2) if needed to fairly examine the deponent or if the deponent, another person, or any other circumstance impedes or delays the examination. FRCP 30(d)(1).

g. *Sanction.* The court may impose an appropriate sanction—including the reasonable expenses and attorney's fees incurred by any party—on a person who impedes, delays, or frustrates the fair examination of the deponent. FRCP 30(d)(2). Refer to the United States District Court for the Northern District of New York KeyRules Motion for Discovery Sanctions document for more information on sanctions.

h. *Motion to terminate or limit.* At any time during a deposition, the deponent or a party may move to terminate or limit it on the ground that it is being conducted in bad faith or in a manner that unreasonably annoys, embarrasses, or oppresses the deponent or party. The motion may be filed in the court where the action is pending or the deposition is being taken. If the objecting deponent or party so demands, the deposition must be suspended for the time necessary to obtain an order. FRCP 30(d)(3)(A).

  i. *Order.* The court may order that the deposition be terminated or may limit its scope and manner as provided in FRCP 26(c). If terminated, the deposition may be resumed only by order of the court where the action is pending. FRCP 30(d)(3)(B).

  ii. *Award of expenses.* FRCP 37(a)(5) applies to the award of expenses. FRCP 30(d)(3)(C). Refer to the United States District Court for the Northern District of New York KeyRules Motion for Discovery Sanctions document for more information on sanctions.

i. *Review by the witness; Statement of changes.* On request by the deponent or a party before the deposition is completed, the deponent must be allowed thirty (30) days after being notified by the officer that the transcript or recording is available in which: (1) to review the transcript or recording; and (2) if there are changes in form or substance, to sign a statement listing the changes and the reasons for making them. FRCP 30(e)(1).

    i. *Changes indicated in the officer's certificate.* The officer must note in the certificate prescribed by FRCP 30(f)(1) whether a review was requested and, if so, must attach any changes the deponent makes during the thirty (30) day period. FRCP 30(e)(2).

j. *Certification and delivery.* The officer must certify in writing that the witness was duly sworn and that the deposition accurately records the witness's testimony. The certificate must accompany the record of the deposition. Unless the court orders otherwise, the officer must seal the deposition in an envelope or package bearing the title of the action and marked "Deposition of [witness's name]" and must promptly send it to the attorney who arranged for the transcript or recording. The attorney must store it under conditions that will protect it against loss, destruction, tampering, or deterioration. FRCP 30(f)(1).

k. *Documents and tangible things.* Documents and tangible things produced for inspection during a deposition must, on a party's request, be marked for identification and attached to the deposition. Any party may inspect and copy them. But if the person who produced them wants to keep the originals, the person may: (1) offer copies to be marked, attached to the deposition, and then used as originals—after giving all parties a fair opportunity to verify the copies by comparing them with the originals; or (2) give all parties a fair opportunity to inspect and copy the originals after they are marked—in which event the originals may be used as if attached to the deposition. FRCP 30(f)(2)(A).

    i. *Order regarding the originals.* Any party may move for an order that the originals be attached to the deposition pending final disposition of the case. FRCP 30(f)(2)(B).

l. *Copies of the transcript or recording.* Unless otherwise stipulated or ordered by the court, the officer must retain the stenographic notes of a deposition taken stenographically or a copy of the recording of a deposition taken by another method. When paid reasonable charges, the officer must furnish a copy of the transcript or recording to any party or the deponent. FRCP 30(f)(3).

m. *Failure to attend a deposition or serve a subpoena; Expenses.* A party who, expecting a deposition to be taken, attends in person or by an attorney may recover reasonable expenses for attending, including attorney's fees, if the noticing party failed to: (1) attend and proceed with the deposition; or (2) serve a subpoena on a nonparty deponent, who consequently did not attend. FRCP 30(g). Refer to the United States District Court for the Northern District of New York KeyRules Motion for Discovery Sanctions document for more information on sanctions.

4. *Depositions by written questions*

    a. *Notice of deposition.* A party who wants to depose a person by written questions must serve them on every other party, with a notice stating, if known, the deponent's name and address. If the name is unknown, the notice must provide a general description sufficient to identify the person or the particular class or group to which the person belongs. The notice must also state the name or descriptive title and the address of the officer before whom the deposition will be taken. FRCP 31(a)(3).

    b. *Questions directed to an organization.* A public or private corporation, a partnership, an association, or a governmental agency may be deposed by written questions in accordance with FRCP 30(b)(6). FRCP 31(a)(4).

    c. *Delivery to the officer; Officer's duties.* The party who noticed the deposition must deliver to the officer a copy of all the questions served and of the notice. The officer must promptly proceed in the manner provided in FRCP 30(c), FRCP 30(e), and FRCP 30(f) to:

        i. Take the deponent's testimony in response to the questions;

    ii.   Prepare and certify the deposition; and

    iii.   Send it to the party, attaching a copy of the questions and of the notice. FRCP 31(b).

  d.  *Notice of completion.* The party who noticed the deposition must notify all other parties when it is completed. FRCP 31(c)(1).

5.  *Depositions to perpetuate testimony.* For information on depositions to perpetuate testimony, refer to FRCP 27.

6.  *Stipulations about discovery procedure.* Unless the court orders otherwise, the parties may stipulate that: (1) a deposition may be taken before any person, at any time or place, on any notice, and in the manner specified—in which event it may be used in the same way as any other deposition; and (2) other procedures governing or limiting discovery be modified—but a stipulation extending the time for any form of discovery must have court approval if it would interfere with the time set for completing discovery, for hearing a motion, or for trial. FRCP 29.

7.  *Complex and multi-district litigation.* If the assigned judge determines, in his or her discretion, that the case is of such a complex nature that it cannot reasonably be trial ready within eighteen (18) months from the date the complaint is filed, the assigned judge may design and issue a particularized case management order that will move the case to trial as quickly as the complexity of the case allows. NY R USDCTND L.R. 3.3(a). The parties shall promptly notify the Court in writing if any action commenced is appropriate for multi-district litigation. NY R USDCTND L.R. 3.3(b).

8.  *Appearances.* An attorney appearing for a party in a civil case shall promptly file with the Clerk a written notice of appearance; however, an attorney does not need to file a notice of appearance if the attorney who would be filing the notice of appearance is the same individual who has signed the complaint, notice of removal, pre-answer motion, or answer. NY R USDCTND L.R. 83.2(a). For more information, refer to NY R USDCTND L.R. 83.2.

9.  *Related cases.* A civil case is "related" to another civil case for purposes of this guideline when, because of the similarity of facts and legal issues or because the cases arise from the same transactions or events, a substantial saving of judicial resources is likely to result from assigning the cases to the same Judge and Magistrate Judge. NY R USDCTND Order 12(G)(2). A civil case shall not be deemed related to another civil case merely because the civil case: (1) involves similar legal issues, or (2) involves the same parties. NY R USDCTND Order 12(G)(3). Presumptively, and subject to the power of a Judge to determine otherwise pursuant to NY R USDCTND Order 12(G)(5), civil cases shall not be deemed to be "related" unless both cases are still pending before the Court. NY R USDCTND Order 12(G)(4).

  a.  *New filings.* If an attorney or filing party indicates on the Civil Cover Sheet that a case is related to an earlier filed case, the Clerk shall instruct the filing party to file a notice of related cases. The allegedly related cases will be submitted by the Clerk to the Judge to whom the earliest filed case is assigned, who shall advise the Clerk whether such cases are related. NY R USDCTND Order 12(G)(1).

  b.  *Judicial determination that civil cases are "related."* Except for the cases described in the final sentence of NY R USDCTND Order 12(G)(6), all civil cases shall be randomly assigned when they are filed. Other than the cases described in the final sentence of NY R USDCTND Order 12(G)(6), civil cases shall not be deemed to be "related" for purposes of this guideline at the instance of any litigant or attorney unless and until there has been a determination by a Judge of this Court that the standard of NY R USDCTND Order 12(G)(2) is met. NY R USDCTND Order 12(G)(5).

    i.  *Notice of related filing.* Any party may apply for such a determination by filing with the Clerk a notice of related filing, which should include an explanation as to why the standard of NY R USDCTND Order 12(G)(2) is met. A form for this purpose is available on the Court's website. A copy of the notice shall be served on all other parties who have appeared. Such an application must be made after the date when at least a majority of the defendants have been served with the complaint. Before making such an application, the applicant must confer in good faith with all other parties in an effort to reach an agreement on whether or not the case is "related". After such an application is made, any other party may serve and file within seven (7) calendar days a letter of no more than two (2) pages supporting or opposing the application. The application to have the case assigned to another Judge shall be presented to the Judge with the earliest filed case for decision on whether the action(s) should be reassigned as related cases. The Judge with the earliest filed case may then enter an order in the case at bar, either deeming the case to be related and directing the Clerk to reassign the action, or denying the application for reassignment. Any disputes concerning the assignment of related cases will be referred to the Chief Judge for resolution. NY R USDCTND Order 12(G)(5).

   c. For more information on related cases, refer to NY R USDCTND Order 12(G).

10. *Alternative dispute resolution (ADR).* It is the mission of this court to do everything it can to help parties resolve their disputes as fairly, quickly, and efficiently as possible. NY R USDCTND Order 25(VIII).

   a. *Arbitration.* NY R USDCTND L.R. 83.7 governs the consensual arbitration program for referral of civil actions to court-annexed arbitration. It may remain in effect until further order of the Court. Its purpose is to establish a less formal procedure for the just, efficient and economical resolution of disputes, while preserving the right to a full trial on demand. NY R USDCTND L.R. 83.7-1.

      i. *Actions subject to arbitration.* The Clerk shall notify the parties in all civil cases, except as the Local Rules of Practice for the United States District Court for the Northern District of New York otherwise direct, that they may consent to non-binding arbitration under NY R US-DCTND L.R. 83.7. The notice shall be furnished to the parties at pretrial/scheduling conferences or shall be included with pretrial conference notices and instructions. Consent to arbitration under NY R USDCTND L.R. 83.7 shall be discussed at the pretrial/scheduling conference. No party or attorney shall be prejudiced for refusing to participate in arbitration. The Court shall allow the referral of any civil action pending before it to the arbitration process if the parties consent. The plaintiff shall be responsible for securing the execution of a consent form by the parties and for filing the form with the Clerk within fourteen (14) days after the parties receive the form. The parties shall freely and knowingly enter into the consent. NY R USDCTND L.R. 83.7-2.

      ii. *Referral to arbitration.* The Clerk shall refer every action subject to NY R USDCTND L.R. 83.7 to arbitration in accordance with the procedures under NY R USDCTND L.R. 83.7 twenty-one (21) days after the filing of the last responsive pleading or within twenty-one (21) days of the filing of a stipulated consent order referring the action to arbitration, whichever event occurs last, except as otherwise provided. If any party notices a motion to dismiss under the provisions of FRCP 12(a) and/or FRCP 12(b), or a motion to join necessary parties pursuant to the Federal Rules of Civil Procedure prior to the expiration of the twenty-one (21) day period, the assigned judge shall hear the motion and further proceedings under NY R USDCTND L.R. 83.7 shall be deferred pending decision on the motion. If the Court does not dismiss the action on the motion, the Court shall refer the action to arbitration twenty-one (21) days after the filing of the decision. NY R USDCTND L.R. 83.7-3(a). Motions for summary judgment pursuant to FRCP 56 shall be filed and served within twenty-one (21) days following the close of discovery. The filing of a FRCP 56 motion shall defer further proceedings under NY R USDCTND L.R. 83.7 pending decision on the motion. NY R USDCTND L.R. 83.7-3(a).

        &bull; *Relief from referral.* Any party shall request relief from the operation of NY R USDCTND L.R. 83.7 by filing with the Court a motion for the relief within twenty-one (21) days after entry of the initial stipulated consent order which refers the case for arbitration. The assigned judge shall, sua sponte, exempt an action from the application of NY R USDCTND L.R. 83.7 where the objectives of arbitration would not be realized because (1) the case involves complex or novel legal issues, (2) legal issues predominate over factual issues, or (3) for other good cause. NY R USDCTND L.R. 83.7-3(c).

      iii. For more information on arbitration, refer to NY R USDCTND L.R. 83.7.

   b. *Mediation.* The purpose of NY R USDCTND L.R. 83.11 is to provide a supplementary procedure to the Court's existing alternative dispute resolution procedures. NY R USDCTND L.R. 83.11 provides for an earlier resolution of civil disputes resulting in savings of time and cost to litigants and the Court without sacrificing the quality of justice rendered or the right of litigants to a full trial on all issues not resolved through mediation. NY R USDCTND L.R. 83.11-1(a). Mediation is a process by which an impartial person, the mediator, facilitates communication between disputing parties to promote understanding, reconciliation and settlement. The mediator is an advocate for settlement and uses the mediation process to help the parties fully explore any potential area of agreement. The mediator does not serve as a judge or arbitrator and has no authority to render any decision on any disputed issue or to force a settlement. The parties themselves are responsible for negotiating any resolution(s) to their dispute. NY R USDCTND L.R. 83.11-1(b).

i. *Actions subject to mediation.* The Court may refer any civil action (or any portion thereof) to mediation under NY R USDCTND L.R. 83.11: (1) by order of referral; or (2) on the motion of any party; or (3) by consent of the parties. NY R USDCTND L.R. 83.11-3(a).

- *Withdrawal from mediation.* The parties may withdraw from mediation any civil action or claim that the Court refers to mediation pursuant to NY R USDCTND L.R. 83.11-3 by application to the assigned judge at least ten (10) days prior to the scheduled mediation session. NY R USDCTND L.R. 83.11-3(b).

ii. *Mandatory mediation program.* The United States District Court for the Northern District of New York has adopted this Mandatory Mediation Plan. The paid Mediation Program is designed to provide quicker, less expensive and potentially more satisfying alternatives to continuing litigation, without impairing the quality of justice or the right to trial. NY R USDCTND Order 47(1)(1.2)(A). This Mandatory Mediation Plan applies to civil actions pending as well as newly filed actions, except as otherwise indicated in NY R USDCTND Order 47. The Local Rules for voluntary mediation will apply only to Pro Se Cases that proceed through the Assisted Mediation Program. NY R USDCTND Order 47(1)(1.2)(B).

- *Referral into the pilot mandatory mediation program for new cases.* All civil cases shall be referred automatically into the Mandatory Mediation Program. Notice of the Mandatory Mediation requirements will be provided to all parties immediately upon the filing of a complaint and answer or a notice of removal. ADR intervention will be scheduled at the conference held pursuant to NY R USDCTND L.R. 16.1. NY R USDCTND Order 47(2)(2.1)(A). For a list of categories of actions exempted from automatic referral, refer to NY R USDCTND Order 47(2)(2.1)(A).

- *Referral into the pilot mandatory mediation program for pending cases.* The assigned Judge or Magistrate Judge on any pending civil case may, sua sponte or with status conference, issue an order referring the case into the Mandatory Mediation Program. The order shall specify a date on which the ADR intervention is to be completed. NY R USDCTND Order 47(2)(2.1)(B).

- *Referral into the pilot mandatory mediation program by stipulation.* A case may be referred into the Mandatory Mediation Program by stipulation of all parties. Stipulations shall be filed and shall designate the time frame within which the ADR process will be completed. Stipulations are presumed acceptable unless the assigned Judge or Magistrate Judge determines that the interests of justice are not served. NY R USDCTND Order 47(2)(2.1)(C).

- *Relief from referral.* Motions to opt out of the program will be addressed by the assigned Magistrate Judge at the FRCP 16 conference. NY R USDCTND Order 47(2)(2.2)(A). Opting Out Motions shall be granted only for "good cause" shown. Inconvenience, travel costs, attorney fees or other costs shall not constitute "good cause." A party seeking relief from the Mandatory Mediation Program must set forth the reasons why Mandatory Mediation has no reasonable chance of being productive. NY R USDCTND Order 47(2)(2.2)(B). The assigned Magistrate Judge may, sua sponte, exempt any case from the Court's Mandatory Mediation Program. NY R USDCTND Order 47(2)(2.2)(C).

iii. *Assisted mediation program.* The Court may assign specially trained pro bono Special Mediation Counsel to assist pro se civilian litigants with preparing for and participating in mediation. The Assisted Mediation Program is open to civilian pro se parties to actions in the Northern District of New York. The assigned judge or magistrate judge determines if the case would benefit from mediation and would also benefit from the assignment of Special Mediation

Counsel to assist the pro se party with the mediation process. NY R USDCTND L.R. 83.8(a). Appointment of Special Mediation Counsel is in no way guaranteed, even if the action is referred to the court-annexed mediation program. Appointment is at the sole discretion of the presiding judge. NY R USDCTND L.R. 83.8(a).

- *Referral to assisted mediation program.* If the court determines that referral to the Assisted Mediation Program is appropriate, the Court shall enter an order of reference to the Assisted Mediation Program. NY R USDCTND L.R. 83.8(b).

iv. For more information on mediation, refer to NY R USDCTND L.R. 83.11 and NY R USDCTND Order 47.

c. *Early neutral evaluation (ENE).* Early neutral evaluation (ENE) is a process in which parties obtain from an experienced neutral (an "evaluator") a nonbinding, reasoned, oral evaluation of the merits of the case. The first step in the ENE process involves the Court appointing an evaluator who has expertise in the area of law in the case. After the parties exchange essential information and position statements early in the pretrial period (usually within one hundred fifty (150) to two hundred (200) days after a complaint has been filed), the evaluator convenes an ENE session that typically lasts about two hours. At the ENE meeting, each side briefly presents the factual and legal basis of its position. The evaluator may ask questions of the parties and help them identify the main issues in dispute and the areas of agreement. The evaluator may also help the parties explore options for settlement. If settlement does not occur, the evaluator then offers an opinion as to the settlement value of the case, including the likelihood of liability and the likely range of damages. With the benefit of this assessment, the parties are again encouraged to discuss settlement, with or without the evaluator's assistance. The parties may also explore ways to narrow the issues in dispute, exchange information about the case or otherwise prepare efficiently for trial. NY R USDCTND L.R. 83.12-1.

i. *Actions subject to early neutral evaluation.* The Court may refer any civil action (or any portion thereof) to ENE under NY R USDCTND L.R. 83.12: (1) by order of referral; (2) on the motion of any party; or (3) by consent of the parties. NY R USDCTND L.R. 83.12-3(a).

- *Withdrawal from the ENE process.* The parties may withdraw any civil action or claim that the Court has referred to the ENE Process pursuant to NY R USDCTND L.R. 83.12-3 by application to the assigned judge at least ten (10) days before the scheduled evaluation session. NY R USDCTND L.R. 83.12-3(b).

ii. For more information on early neutral evaluation (ENE), refer to NY R USDCTND L.R. 83.12.

11. *Settlement procedures.* On notice to the Court or the Clerk that the parties have settled an action, and upon confirmation of the settlement by all parties, the Court may issue a judgment dismissing the action by reason of settlement. The Court shall issue the order without prejudice to the parties' right to secure reinstatement of the case within thirty (30) days after the date of judgment by making a showing that the settlement was not, in fact, consummated. NY R USDCTND L.R. 68.2(a). If the Court decides not to follow the procedures set forth in NY R USDCTND L.R. 68.2(a), the parties shall file within thirty (30) days of the notification to the Court, unless otherwise directed by written order, such notices, stipulations and/or motions as are necessary to terminate the action. If the required documents are not filed within the thirty (30) day period, the Clerk shall place the action on the dismissal calendar. NY R USDCTND L.R. 68.2(b).

12. *Sanctions and penalties for noncompliance.* Failure of an attorney or of a party to comply with any provision of the Local Rules of Practice for the United States District Court for the Northern District of New York, General Orders of this District, Orders of the Court, or the Federal Rules of Civil Procedure shall be a ground for imposition of sanctions. NY R USDCTND L.R. 1.1(d).

13. *Individual judge practices.* Refer to the Miscellaneous section of this document for information on individual judge practices on general requirements for documents.

## D. Documents

1. *Depositions by oral examination*

a. *Required documents*

i. *Notice of deposition.* Refer to the General Requirements section of this document for the form and contents of the notice of deposition.

b. *Supplemental documents*

    i. *Subpoena.* The deponent's attendance may be compelled by subpoena under FRCP 45. FRCP 30(a)(1). For more information on subpoenas, refer to FRCP 45.

    ii. *Subpoena duces tecum.* If a subpoena duces tecum is to be served on the deponent, the materials designated for production, as set out in the subpoena, must be listed in the notice or in an attachment. FRCP 30(b)(2). For more information on subpoenas duces tecum, refer to FRCP 45.

    iii. *Request for production of documents.* The notice to a party deponent may be accompanied by a request under FRCP 34 to produce documents and tangible things at the deposition. FRCP 30(b)(2). Refer to the United States District Court for the Northern District of New York KeyRules Request for Production of Documents document for more information.

    iv. *Certificate of service.* FRCP 5(d) requires that the person making service under FRCP 5 certify that service has been effected. FRCP 5(Advisory Committee Notes). Having such information on file may be useful for many purposes, including proof of service if an issue arises concerning the effectiveness of the service. FRCP 5(Advisory Committee Notes).

2. *Depositions by written questions*

a. *Required documents*

    i. *Notice of deposition.* Refer to the General Requirements section of this document for the form and contents of the notice of deposition.

    ii. *Written questions.* A party who wants to depose a person by written questions must serve them on every other party, with a notice. FRCP 31(a)(3).

b. *Supplemental documents*

    i. *Subpoena.* The deponent's attendance may be compelled by subpoena under FRCP 45. FRCP 31(a)(1). For more information on subpoenas, refer to FRCP 45.

    ii. *Certificate of service.* FRCP 5(d) requires that the person making service under FRCP 5 certify that service has been effected. FRCP 5(Advisory Committee Notes). Having such information on file may be useful for many purposes, including proof of service if an issue arises concerning the effectiveness of the service. FRCP 5(Advisory Committee Notes).

3. *Individual judge practices.* Refer to the Miscellaneous section of this document for information on individual judge practices on required documents.

## E. Format

1. *Form of documents.* The rules governing captions and other matters of form in pleadings apply to motions and other papers. FRCP 7(b)(2). All pleadings and other papers shall be served and filed in accordance with the Federal Rules of Civil Procedure and shall be in the form prescribed by NY R USDCTND L.R. 10.1. NY R USDCTND L.R. 5.1(a).

a. *Form, generally.* All pleadings, motions, and other documents that a party presents for filing, whether in paper form or in electronic form, shall meet the following requirements:

    i. *Font size.* All text, whether in the body of the document or in footnotes, must be a minimum of twelve (12) point type. NY R USDCTND L.R. 10.1(a)(1).

    ii. *Margins.* All documents must have one (1) inch margins on all four sides of the page. NY R USDCTND L.R. 10.1(a)(2).

    iii. *Spacing.* All text in the body of the document must be double-spaced. NY R USDCTND L.R. 10.1(a)(3).

        • The text in block quotations and footnotes may be single-spaced. NY R USDCTND L.R. 10.1(a)(4).

    iv. *Page numbering.* Pages must be consecutively numbered. NY R USDCTND L.R. 10.1(a)(7).

    v. *Circumventing formatting limitations*

- Extensive footnotes must not be used to circumvent page limitations. NY R USDCTND L.R. 10.1(a)(5).
- Compacted or other compressed printing features must not be used. NY R USDCTND L.R. 10.1(a)(6).

b. *Additional requirements for paper filing.* Additional requirements for all pleadings, motions, and other documents that a party presents for filing in paper form:

    i. *Paper size.* All documents must be on eight and one-half by eleven (8-1/2 x 11) inch white paper of good quality. NY R USDCTND L.R. 10.1(b)(1).

    ii. *Text.* All text must be plainly and legibly written, typewritten, printed or reproduced without erasures or interlineations materially defacing them. NY R USDCTND L.R. 10.1(b)(2).

    iii. *Ink.* All documents must be in black or blue ink. NY R USDCTND L.R. 10.1(b)(3).

    iv. *Binding.* Pages of all documents must be stapled (or in some other way fastened) together. NY R USDCTND L.R. 10.1(b)(4).

    v. *Single-sided paper.* All documents must be single-sided. NY R USDCTND L.R. 10.1(b)(5).

    vi. *Electronic submission.* The Court, at its discretion, may require the electronic submission of any document in a WordPerfect-compatible format. NY R USDCTND L.R. 10.1(b)(6).

    vii. *Rejection of document.* The Court may reject documents that do not comply with the above-listed requirements. NY R USDCTND L.R. 10.1(b).

c. *Caption; Names of parties.* Every pleading must have a caption with the court's name, a title, a file number, and a FRCP 7(a) designation. The title of the complaint must name all the parties; the title of other pleadings, after naming the first party on each side, may refer generally to other parties. FRCP 10(a). Each document must contain a caption for the specific case to which it pertains. The caption must include the title of the Court, the title of the action, the civil action number of the case, the initials of the assigned judge(s), and the name or nature of the paper in sufficient detail for identification. If a litigant has more than one action pending in this Court, any and all papers filed in a case must contain and pertain to one civil action number, unless the civil actions have been consolidated by the Court. Any motion or other papers purporting to relate to more than one action will not be accepted for filing and may be stricken by the Court. NY R USDCTND L.R. 10.1(c)(1) shall not apply, as noted in NY R USDCTND L.R. 10.1(c), to notices of change of address filed by attorneys of record and pro se litigants. The parties must separately caption affidavits and declarations and must not physically attach them to the Notice of Motion or Memorandum of Law. NY R USDCTND L.R. 10.1(c)(1).

d. *Paragraphs; Separate statements.* A party must state its claims or defenses in numbered paragraphs, each limited as far as practicable to a single set of circumstances. A later pleading may refer by number to a paragraph in an earlier pleading. If doing so would promote clarity, each claim founded on a separate transaction or occurrence—and each defense other than a denial—must be stated in a separate count or defense. FRCP 10(b).

e. *Adoption by reference; Exhibits.* A statement in a pleading may be adopted by reference elsewhere in the same pleading or in any other pleading or motion. A copy of a written instrument that is an exhibit to a pleading is a part of the pleading for all purposes. FRCP 10(c).

f. *Citation of local rules.* These are the Local Rules of Practice for the United States District Court for the Northern District of New York. They shall be cited as "L.R. ___." NY R USDCTND L.R. 1.1(a).

g. *Acceptance by the clerk.* The clerk must not refuse to file a paper solely because it is not in the form prescribed by the Federal Rules of Civil Procedure or by a local rule or practice. FRCP 5(d)(4).

2. *Form of electronic documents.* All pleadings, motions, and other documents that a party presents for filing, whether in paper form or in electronic form, shall meet the requirements in NY R USDCTND L.R. 10.1(a). NY R USDCTND L.R. 10.1(a). Refer above for more information.

a. *Attachments and exhibits.* A Filing User must submit in electronic form all documents referenced as

exhibits or attachments in accordance with the Court's CM/ECF Users Manual unless the Court otherwise orders. A Filing User shall submit as exhibits or attachments only those excerpts of the referenced documents that are directly germane to the matter under the Court's consideration. Excerpted material must be clearly and prominently identified as such. Filing Users who file excerpts of documents as exhibits or attachments under these Administrative Procedures (NY R USDCTND CM/ECF) do so without prejudice to their right to timely file additional excerpts or the complete document. Responding parties may also timely file the complete document or additional excerpts that they believe are directly germane to the matter under the Court's consideration. NY R USDCTND CM/ECF(4)(4.4).

    i. All attachments must be described in sufficient detail so the Court and opposing counsel can easily identify and distinguish the filed attachments. Vague or general descriptions are insufficient (i.e., "Exhibit 1"). Rather, each attachment shall have a descriptive title identifying, with specificity, the document that is being filed (i.e., "Exhibit 12 Mulligan County Fire Investigation Report.") Failure to adequately describe attachments may result in the document being rejected by the Court. NY R USDCTND CM/ECF(4)(4.4).

b. *Large documents.* For information on the electronic filing of large documents, please consult the Court's CM/ECF Users Manual, which is available on the Court's web page. NY R USDCTND CM/ECF(4)(4.5).

    i. A party who believes a document is too lengthy to electronically image, i.e., "scan," may contact the Clerk's Office for permission to file that document conventionally. If the Clerk's Office grants permission to conventionally file the document, the Filing User shall electronically file a notice of conventional filing for the documents. More information regarding this process can be obtained from the Court's web page. Exhibits submitted conventionally shall be served on other parties as if they were not subject to these Administrative Procedures (NY R USDCTND CM/ECF). For a list of hints and tips for scanning large documents, please consult the Court's web page. NY R USDCTND CM/ECF(4)(4.5).

c. *Legibility.* It shall be the Filing User's responsibility to verify the legibility of scanned documents before filing them electronically with the Court. NY R USDCTND CM/ECF(4)(4.6).

d. *Color documents.* Since documents scanned in color or containing a graphic take much longer to upload, Filing Users are encouraged to configure their scanners to scan documents at 300 dpi and preferably in black and white rather than in color. NY R USDCTND CM/ECF(4)(4.7).

e. *Items not in .PDF format.* Parties wishing to file items not amenable to .pdf format (i.e. CD's, DVD's), shall file such items conventionally with the Clerk's Office. The Filing User shall electronically file a notice of conventional filing indicating that these items have been submitted to the clerk and shall serve copies of these items on other parties as if they were not subject to these Administrative Procedures (NY R USDCTND CM/ECF). These item(s) will be maintained by the Clerk's Office until the case is disposed, at which time they will be returned to the filing party for retention consistent with NY R USDCTND CM/ECF(4)(4.9). NY R USDCTND CM/ECF(4)(4.8).

3. *Signing disclosures and discovery requests, responses, and objections.* FRCP 11 does not apply to disclosures and discovery requests, responses, objections, and motions under FRCP 26 through FRCP 37. FRCP 11(d).

a. *Signature required.* Every disclosure under FRCP 26(a)(1) or FRCP 26(a)(3) and every discovery request, response, or objection must be signed by at least one attorney of record in the attorney's own name—or by the party personally, if unrepresented—and must state the signer's address, e-mail address, and telephone number. FRCP 26(g)(1). Each document must identify the person filing the document. This identification must include an original signature of the attorney or pro se litigant; the typewritten name of that person; the address of a pro se litigant; and the bar roll number, office address, telephone number, e-mail address and fax number of the attorney. Telephone numbers of non-prisoner pro se parties may be provided voluntarily or upon request of the Court. See General Order #22 (NY R USDCTND CM/ECF) for signature requirements. NY R USDCTND L.R. 10.1(c)(2).

    i. *Electronic signatures.* Documents filed under an attorney's login and password shall constitute

that attorney's signature for purposes of the Local Rules of Practice for the United States District Court for the Northern District of New York and Federal Rules of Civil Procedure, including but not limited to FRCP 11. A pleading or other document requiring an attorney's signature shall be signed in the following manner, whether filed electronically or submitted on disk or CD/ROM to the Clerk's Office: "s/ (attorney name)." The correct format for an attorney signature is found in NY R USDCTND CM/ECF(6)(6.1). NY R USDCTND CM/ECF(6)(6.1).

- *Non-attorney signature.* If an original document requires the signature of a non-attorney, the Filing User may scan the original document containing the original signature(s), then electronically file it on the System. Alternatively, the Filing User may convert the document into .pdf text format and submit the document using "s/" for the signature of the non-attorney. NY R USDCTND CM/ECF(6)(6.2).

- *Multiple signatures.* A document requiring signatures of more than one party must be filed electronically either by (1) submitting a scanned document containing all necessary signatures; (2) representing the consent of the other parties on the document; or (3) in any other manner that the Court approves. NY R USDCTND CM/ECF(6)(6.3).

b. *Effect of signature.* By signing, an attorney or party certifies that to the best of the person's knowledge, information, and belief formed after a reasonable inquiry:

   i. With respect to a disclosure, it is complete and correct as of the time it is made; and

   ii. With respect to a discovery request, response, or objection, it is:

   - Consistent with the Federal Rules of Civil Procedure and warranted by existing law or by a nonfrivolous argument for extending, modifying, or reversing existing law, or for establishing new law;

   - Not interposed for any improper purpose, such as to harass, cause unnecessary delay, or needlessly increase the cost of litigation; and

   - Neither unreasonable nor unduly burdensome or expensive, considering the needs of the case, prior discovery in the case, the amount in controversy, and the importance of the issues at stake in the action. FRCP 26(g)(1).

c. *Failure to sign.* Other parties have no duty to act on an unsigned disclosure, request, response, or objection until it is signed, and the court must strike it unless a signature is promptly supplied after the omission is called to the attorney's or party's attention. FRCP 26(g)(2).

d. *Sanction for improper certification.* If a certification violates FRCP 26(g) without substantial justification, the court, on motion or on its own, must impose an appropriate sanction on the signer, the party on whose behalf the signer was acting, or both. The sanction may include an order to pay the reasonable expenses, including attorney's fees, caused by the violation. FRCP 26(g)(3). Refer to the United States District Court for the Northern District of New York KeyRules Motion for Discovery Sanctions document for more information.

4. *Privacy protection for filings made with the court*

a. *Redacted filings.* Unless the court orders otherwise, in an electronic or paper filing with the court that contains an individual's Social Security number, taxpayer-identification number, or birth date, the name of an individual known to be a minor, or a financial-account number, a party or nonparty making the filing may include only:

   i. The last four (4) digits of the Social Security number and taxpayer-identification number;

   ii. The year of the individual's birth;

   iii. The minor's initials; and

   iv. The last four (4) digits of the financial-account number. FRCP 5.2(a); NY R USDCTND L.R. 8.1; NY R USDCTND CM/ECF(11)(11.2).

   v. If a home address must be used, use only the City and State. NY R USDCTND L.R. 8.1; NY R USDCTND CM/ECF(11)(11.2).

   vi. If the victim of a sexual assault must be referenced, redact the name to 'Victim.' NY R USDCTND CM/ECF(11)(11.2); NY R USDCTND L.R. 8.1.

     vii.   In addition, caution shall be exercised when filing documents that contain the following:

- Personal identifying number, such as a driver's license number;
- Medical records, treatment and diagnosis;
- Employment history;
- Individual financial information; and
- Proprietary or trade secret information. NY R USDCTND L.R. 8.1; NY R USDCTND CM/ECF(11)(11.2).

  b.   *Exemptions from the redaction requirement.* The redaction requirement does not apply to the following:

     i.   A financial-account number that identifies the property allegedly subject to forfeiture in a forfeiture proceeding;

     ii.   The record of an administrative or agency proceeding;

     iii.   The official record of a state-court proceeding;

     iv.   The record of a court or tribunal, if that record was not subject to the redaction requirement when originally filed;

     v.   A filing covered by FRCP 5.2(c) or FRCP 5.2(d); and

     vi.   A pro se filing in an action brought under 28 U.S.C.A. § 2241, 28 U.S.C.A. § 2254, or 28 U.S.C.A. § 2255. FRCP 5.2(b).

     vii.   Transcripts of the administrative record in social security proceedings are exempt from this requirement. State court records and other documents filed in habeas corpus proceedings are exempt from this requirement except for proceedings that involve victims of sex crimes. In habeas corpus cases involving sex crimes, the parties must redact the record and supporting papers, or may move to seal, if appropriate. NY R USDCTND L.R. 8.1.

  c.   *Limitations on remote access to electronic files; Social Security appeals and immigration cases.* Unless the court orders otherwise, in an action for benefits under the Social Security Act, and in an action or proceeding relating to an order of removal, to relief from removal, or to immigration benefits or detention, access to an electronic file is authorized as follows:

     i.   The parties and their attorneys may have remote electronic access to any part of the case file, including the administrative record;

     ii.   Any other person may have electronic access to the full record at the courthouse, but may have remote electronic access only to:

- The docket maintained by the court; and
- An opinion, order, judgment, or other disposition of the court, but not any other part of the case file or the administrative record. FRCP 5.2(c).

  d.   *Filings made under seal.* The court may order that a filing be made under seal without redaction. The court may later unseal the filing or order the person who made the filing to file a redacted version for the public record. FRCP 5.2(d); NY R USDCTND L.R. 8.1. For information on sealed matters, refer to NY R USDCTND L.R. 83.13 and NY R USDCTND CM/ECF(12).

  e.   *Protective orders.* For good cause, the court may by order in a case:

     i.   Require redaction of additional information; or

     ii.   Limit or prohibit a nonparty's remote electronic access to a document filed with the court. FRCP 5.2(e).

  f.   *Option for additional unredacted filing under seal.* A person making a redacted filing may also file an unredacted copy under seal. The court must retain the unredacted copy as part of the record. FRCP 5.2(f); NY R USDCTND L.R. 8.1; NY R USDCTND CM/ECF(11)(11.3).

  g.   *Option for filing a reference list.* A filing that contains redacted information may be filed together

with a reference list that identifies each item of redacted information and specifies an appropriate identifier that uniquely corresponds to each item listed. The list must be filed under seal and may be amended as of right. Any reference in the case to a listed identifier will be construed to refer to the corresponding item of information. FRCP 5.2(g); NY R USDCTND L.R. 8.1; NY R USDCTND CM/ECF(11)(11.3).

h. *Responsibility for redaction.* Counsel is strongly urged to discuss this issue with all their clients so that they can make an informed decision about the inclusion of certain information. The responsibility for redacting these personal identifiers rests solely with counsel and the parties. The Clerk will not review each filing for compliance with NY R USDCTND L.R. 8.1. Counsel and the parties are cautioned that failure to redact these personal identifiers may subject them to the Court's full disciplinary power. NY R USDCTND L.R. 8.1; NY R USDCTND CM/ECF(11)(11.3).

i. *Waiver of protection of identifiers.* A person waives the protection of FRCP 5.2(a) as to the person's own information by filing it without redaction and not under seal. FRCP 5.2(h).

5. *Individual judge practices.* Refer to the Miscellaneous section of this document for information on individual judge practices on formatting documents.

## F. Filing and Service Requirements

1. *Filing requirements.* Any paper after the complaint that is required to be served—together with a certificate of service—must be filed within a reasonable time after service. But disclosures under FRCP 26(a)(1) or FRCP 26(a)(2) and the following discovery requests and responses must not be filed until they are used in the proceeding or the court orders filing: depositions, interrogatories, requests for documents or tangible things or to permit entry onto land, and requests for admission. FRCP 5(d)(1). Refer to the United States District Court for the Northern District of New York KeyRules pleading and motion documents for information on filing with the court.

   a. *Filing discovery.* Parties are directed not to file discovery material unless it is being filed in accordance with NY R USDCTND L.R. 26.2. NY R USDCTND Order 25(IX)(B). Parties shall not file notices to take depositions, transcripts of depositions, interrogatories, requests for documents, requests for admissions, disclosures, and answers and responses to these notices and requests unless the Court orders otherwise; provided, however, that a party shall file any discovery material that it expects to use at trial or to support any motion, including a motion to compel or for summary judgment prior to the trial or motion return date. NY R USDCTND L.R. 26.2; NY R USDCTND CM/ECF(2)(2.1)(4).

      i. Unless the Court orders otherwise pursuant to FRCP 5(d) and FRCP 26(c), transcripts of depositions when received and filed by the Clerk, shall then be opened by the Clerk who shall affix the filing stamp to the cover page of the transcripts. NY R USDCTND L.R. 30.1.

      ii. Upon receipt of a deposition, the Clerk, unless otherwise ordered, shall open and file it promptly. NY R USDCTND L.R. 83.9(b).

   b. *Notice of filing*

      i. *Depositions by oral examination.* A party who files the deposition must promptly notify all other parties of the filing. FRCP 30(f)(4).

      ii. *Depositions by written questions.* A party who files the deposition must promptly notify all other parties of the filing. FRCP 31(c)(2).

2. *Service requirements*

   a. *Service; When required*

      i. *In general.* Unless the Federal Rules of Civil Procedure provide otherwise, each of the following papers must be served on every party:

         • An order stating that service is required;

         • A pleading filed after the original complaint, unless the court orders otherwise under FRCP 5(c) because there are numerous defendants;

         • A discovery paper required to be served on a party, unless the court orders otherwise;

- A written motion, except one that may be heard ex parte; and

- A written notice, appearance, demand, or offer of judgment, or any similar paper. FRCP 5(a)(1).

ii. *If a party fails to appear.* No service is required on a party who is in default for failing to appear. But a pleading that asserts a new claim for relief against such a party must be served on that party under FRCP 4. FRCP 5(a)(2).

iii. *Seizing property.* If an action is begun by seizing property and no person is or need be named as a defendant, any service required before the filing of an appearance, answer, or claim must be made on the person who had custody or possession of the property when it was seized. FRCP 5(a)(3).

b. *Service; How made*

i. *Serving an attorney.* If a party is represented by an attorney, service under FRCP 5 must be made on the attorney unless the court orders service on the party. FRCP 5(b)(1).

ii. *Service in general.* A paper is served under FRCP 5 by:

- Handing it to the person;

- Leaving it: (1) at the person's office with a clerk or other person in charge or, if no one is in charge, in a conspicuous place in the office; or (2) if the person has no office or the office is closed, at the person's dwelling or usual place of abode with someone of suitable age and discretion who resides there;

- Mailing it to the person's last known address—in which event service is complete upon mailing;

- Leaving it with the court clerk if the person has no known address;

- Sending it by electronic means if the person consented in writing—in which event service is complete upon transmission, but is not effective if the serving party learns that it did not reach the person to be served; or

- Delivering it by any other means that the person consented to in writing—in which event service is complete when the person making service delivers it to the agency designated to make delivery. FRCP 5(b)(2).

iii. *Service of electronically-filed documents.* Service is complete provided all parties receive a Notice of Electronic Filing (NEF), which is sent automatically by email from the Court (see the NEF for a list of who did/did not receive notice electronically). Transmission of the NEF constitutes service upon all Filing and Receiving Users who are listed as recipients of notice by electronic mail. It remains the responsibility of Filing and Receiving Users to maintain current contact information with the court and to regularly review the docket sheet of the case. NY R USDCTND CM/ECF(5)(5.2).

- *Non-filing or receiving users.* Attorneys and pro se parties who are not Filing or Receiving Users must be served with a paper copy of any electronically filed pleading or other document. Service of such paper copy must be made according to the Federal Rules of Civil Procedure and the Local Rules of Practice for the United States District Court for the Northern District of New York. Such paper service must be documented by electronically filing a certificate of service. NY R USDCTND CM/ECF(5)(5.2). A party who is not a Filing User of the System is entitled to a paper copy of any electronically-filed pleading, document, or order. The Filing User must therefore provide the non-Filing User with the pleading or document according to the Federal Rules of Civil Procedure. NY R US-DCTND CM/ECF(5)(5.3).

iv. *Using court facilities.* If a local rule so authorizes, a party may use the court's transmission facilities to make service under FRCP 5(b)(2)(E). FRCP 5(b)(3).

    c. *Serving numerous defendants*

       i. *In general.* If an action involves an unusually large number of defendants, the court may, on motion or on its own, order that:

- Defendants' pleadings and replies to them need not be served on other defendants;
- Any crossclaim, counterclaim, avoidance, or affirmative defense in those pleadings and replies to them will be treated as denied or avoided by all other parties; and
- Filing any such pleading and serving it on the plaintiff constitutes notice of the pleading to all parties. FRCP 5(c)(1).

      ii. *Notifying parties.* A copy of every such order must be served on the parties as the court directs. FRCP 5(c)(2).

3. *Individual judge practices.* Refer to the Miscellaneous section of this document for information on individual judge practices on filing and serving documents.

## G. Hearings

1. There is no hearing contemplated in the federal statutes or rules for the notice of deposition.

## H. Forms

### 1. Federal Notice of Deposition Forms

    a. Notice to take deposition to perpetuate testimony. 3A FEDFORMS § 3339.

    b. Notice of taking of deposition to perpetuate testimony pending appeal. 3A FEDFORMS § 3345.

    c. Notice of taking deposition upon oral examination. 3A FEDFORMS § 3422.

    d. Notice of taking deposition upon oral examination; Party. 3A FEDFORMS § 3423.

    e. Notice of taking deposition upon oral examination; Naming and describing person not a party. 3A FEDFORMS § 3424.

    f. Notice of taking deposition upon oral examination; Describing deponents whose names are unknown. 3A FEDFORMS § 3425.

    g. Notice of taking deposition upon oral examination; Pursuant to order granting leave to take deposition. 3A FEDFORMS § 3426.

    h. Notice of taking of deposition of party with notice to produce documents. 3A FEDFORMS § 3427.

    i. Notice of taking of deposition of witness; Including designation of materials in related subpoena duces tecum. 3A FEDFORMS § 3428.

    j. Notice of taking of deposition of witness; Including reference to materials designated in attached subpoena. 3A FEDFORMS § 3429.

    k. Notice of taking deposition upon written questions served with notice. 3A FEDFORMS § 3449.

    l. Questions to be attached to notice or served with it. 3A FEDFORMS § 3450.

    m. Notice of return and filing of deposition taken upon written questions. 3A FEDFORMS § 3456.

    n. Notice; Taking of deposition on oral examination. FEDPROF § 23:136.

    o. Notice; Taking of deposition on oral examination; Patent proceedings. FEDPROF § 23:137.

    p. Notice; Taking of deposition on oral examination; Corporate officer. FEDPROF § 23:138.

    q. Notice; Taking of deposition on oral examination; Corporate officers to be designated by corporation. FEDPROF § 23:139.

    r. Notice; Taking of deposition on written questions. FEDPROF § 23:140.

    s. Notice; Taking of deposition on oral examination or on written questions; Pursuant to court order. FEDPROF § 23:141.

    t. Notice; In connection with deposition on written questions; Of cross, redirect, or recross questions. FEDPROF § 23:142.

u. Attachment to notice; Taking of deposition on written questions; Questions to be propounded. FEDPROF § 23:143.

v. Attachment to notice; Cross, redirect, or recross questions to be propounded. FEDPROF § 23:144.

w. Notice; To party taking deposition; Written questions submitted in lieu of participation in oral examination. FEDPROF § 23:145.

x. Notice of taking deposition; Expert witness; Request for production of supporting documents. FEDPROF § 23:151.

y. Subpoena; To testify at taking of deposition and to produce documents or things. FEDPROF § 23:152.

z. Provision in subpoena; Advice to nonparty organization of its duty to designate witness. FEDPROF § 23:155.

## I. Applicable Rules

1. *Federal rules*

   a. Serving and filing pleadings and other papers. FRCP 5.

   b. Privacy protection for filings made with the court. FRCP 5.2.

   c. Computing and extending time; Time for motion papers. FRCP 6.

   d. Pleadings allowed; Form of motions and other papers. FRCP 7.

   e. Form of pleadings. FRCP 10.

   f. Signing pleadings, motions, and other papers; Representations to the court; Sanctions. FRCP 11.

   g. Duty to disclose; General provisions governing discovery. FRCP 26.

   h. Persons before whom depositions may be taken. FRCP 28.

   i. Stipulations about discovery procedure. FRCP 29.

   j. Depositions by oral examination. FRCP 30.

   k. Depositions by written questions. FRCP 31.

   l. Failure to make disclosures or to cooperate in discovery; Sanctions. FRCP 37.

2. *Local rules*

   a. Scope of the rules. NY R USDCTND L.R. 1.1.

   b. Complex and multi-district litigation. NY R USDCTND L.R. 3.3.

   c. Service and filing of papers. NY R USDCTND L.R. 5.1.

   d. Personal privacy protection. NY R USDCTND L.R. 8.1.

   e. Form of papers. NY R USDCTND L.R. 10.1.

   f. Discovery cut-off. NY R USDCTND L.R. 16.2.

   g. Filing discovery. NY R USDCTND L.R. 26.2.

   h. Depositions. NY R USDCTND L.R. 30.1.

   i. Settlement procedures. NY R USDCTND L.R. 68.2.

   j. Appearance and withdrawal of attorney. NY R USDCTND L.R. 83.2.

   k. Arbitration. NY R USDCTND L.R. 83.7-1; NY R USDCTND L.R. 83.7-2; NY R USDCTND L.R. 83.7-3.

   l. Assisted mediation program. NY R USDCTND L.R. 83.8.

   m. Commission to take testimony. NY R USDCTND L.R. 83.9.

   n. Mediation. NY R USDCTND L.R. 83.11-1; NY R USDCTND L.R. 83.11-3.

   o. Early neutral evaluation. NY R USDCTND L.R. 83.12-1; NY R USDCTND L.R. 83.12-3.

p. Administrative procedures for electronic case filing. NY R USDCTND CM/ECF.

q. Case assignment plan for the Northern District of New York. [NY R USDCTND Order 12, as amended by NY ORDER 16-4201, effective March 24, 2015].

r. Directing the expedited service of the summons and complaint and further directing the completion of FRCP 16 stipulation for the timely progression of civil actions. [NY R USDCTND Order 25, as amended by NY ORDER 16-4187, effective June 23, 2016].

s. Mandatory mediation program. NY R USDCTND Order 47.

## J. Miscellaneous

**NOTE: Individual judges' rules may apply. For available judge-level information, refer to:**

DISTRICT JUDGE MAE A. D'AGOSTINO: [NY R USDCTND D'Agostino-Rules and Practices, as added by NY ORDER 16-4200, effective April 4, 2016].

DISTRICT JUDGE THOMAS J. McAVOY: NY R USDCTND McAvoy-Order.

# Requests, Notices and Applications
# Application for Temporary Restraining Order

### Document Last Updated September 2016

## A. Checklist

(I) ❑ Matters to be considered by party applying (with notice)

    (a) ❑ Required documents

        (1) ❑ Notice of motion and motion

        (2) ❑ Memorandum of law

        (3) ❑ Supporting affidavit

        (4) ❑ Security

        (5) ❑ Certificate of service

    (b) ❑ Supplemental documents

        (1) ❑ Supporting evidence

        (2) ❑ Notice of constitutional question

        (3) ❑ Nongovernmental corporate disclosure statement

        (4) ❑ Copies of authorities

        (5) ❑ Proposed order

        (6) ❑ Cover letter authorizing e-mail or facsimile filing

        (7) ❑ Affidavit attesting to failed attempts to file electronically

        (8) ❑ Notice of conventional filing

        (9) ❑ CD/ROM with PDF of document(s)

        (10) ❑ English translation

        (11) ❑ Courtesy copies

        (12) ❑ Copies for three-judge court

    (c) ❑ Timing

        (1) ❑ Unless the court orders otherwise, the moving party must file all motion papers with the court and serve them upon the other parties not less than thirty-one (31) days prior to the return date of the motion

        (2) ❑ A written motion and notice of the hearing must be served at least fourteen (14) days before

the time specified for the hearing, with the following exceptions: (i) when the motion may be heard ex parte; (ii) when the Federal Rules of Civil Procedure set a different time; or (iii) when a court order—which a party may, for good cause, apply for ex parte—sets a different time

    (3)  ❑  Any affidavit supporting a motion must be served with the motion

(II)  ❑  Matters to be considered by party applying (without notice, or "ex parte")

    (a)  ❑  Required documents

        (1)  ❑  Motion

        (2)  ❑  Memorandum of law

        (3)  ❑  Supporting affidavit

        (4)  ❑  Affidavit or verified complaint

        (5)  ❑  Certificate of attorney

        (6)  ❑  Security

    (b)  ❑  Supplemental documents

        (1)  ❑  Supporting evidence

        (2)  ❑  Notice of constitutional question

        (3)  ❑  Nongovernmental corporate disclosure statement

        (4)  ❑  Copies of authorities

        (5)  ❑  Proposed order

        (6)  ❑  Cover letter authorizing e-mail or facsimile filing

        (7)  ❑  Affidavit attesting to failed attempts to file electronically

        (8)  ❑  Notice of conventional filing

        (9)  ❑  CD/ROM with PDF of document(s)

        (10)  ❑  English translation

        (11)  ❑  Courtesy copies

        (12)  ❑  Copies for three-judge court

    (c)  ❑  Timing

        (1)  ❑  There are no specific timing requirements for applying for a temporary restraining order without notice

        (2)  ❑  Any affidavit supporting a motion must be served with the motion

## B. Timing

1. *Application for temporary restraining order*

   a.  *With notice.* There are no specific timing requirements for applying for a temporary restraining order with notice.

   b.  *Without notice, or "ex parte."* There are no specific timing requirements for applying for a temporary restraining order without notice, or "ex parte."

2. *Motion to dissolve or modify.* On two (2) days' notice to the party who obtained the order without notice—or on shorter notice set by the court—the adverse party may appear and move to dissolve or modify the order. The court must then hear and decide the motion as promptly as justice requires. FRCP 65(b)(4).

3. *Timing of motions, generally.* Unless the Court orders otherwise, the moving party must file all motion

papers with the Court and serve them upon the other parties not less than THIRTY-ONE (31) DAYS prior to the return date of the motion. NY R USDCTND L.R. 7.1(b)(2).

a. *Motion and notice of hearing.* A written motion and notice of the hearing must be served at least fourteen (14) days before the time specified for the hearing, with the following exceptions:

    i. When the motion may be heard ex parte;

    ii. When the Federal Rules of Civil Procedure set a different time; or

    iii. When a court order—which a party may, for good cause, apply for ex parte—sets a different time. FRCP 6(c)(1).

b. *Supporting affidavit.* Any affidavit supporting a motion must be served with the motion. FRCP 6(c)(2).

4. *Computation of time*

a. *Computing time.* FRCP 6 applies in computing any time period specified in the Federal Rules of Civil Procedure, in any local rule or court order, or in any statute that does not specify a method of computing time. FRCP 6(a).

    i. *Period stated in days or a longer unit.* When the period is stated in days or a longer unit of time:

- Exclude the day of the event that triggers the period;

- Count every day, including intermediate Saturdays, Sundays, and legal holidays; and

- Include the last day of the period, but if the last day is a Saturday, Sunday, or legal holiday, the period continues to run until the end of the next day that is not a Saturday, Sunday, or legal holiday. FRCP 6(a)(1).

    ii. *Period stated in hours.* When the period is stated in hours:

- Begin counting immediately on the occurrence of the event that triggers the period;

- Count every hour, including hours during intermediate Saturdays, Sundays, and legal holidays; and

- If the period would end on a Saturday, Sunday, or legal holiday, the period continues to run until the same time on the next day that is not a Saturday, Sunday, or legal holiday. FRCP 6(a)(2).

    iii. *Inaccessibility of the clerk's office.* Unless the court orders otherwise, if the clerk's office is inaccessible:

- On the last day for filing under FRCP 6(a)(1), then the time for filing is extended to the first accessible day that is not a Saturday, Sunday, or legal holiday; or

- During the last hour for filing under FRCP 6(a)(2), then the time for filing is extended to the same time on the first accessible day that is not a Saturday, Sunday, or legal holiday. FRCP 6(a)(3).

    iv. *"Last day" defined.* Unless a different time is set by a statute, local rule, or court order, the last day ends:

- For electronic filing, at midnight in the court's time zone; and

- For filing by other means, when the clerk's office is scheduled to close. FRCP 6(a)(4).

    v. *"Next day" defined.* The "next day" is determined by continuing to count forward when the period is measured after an event and backward when measured before an event. FRCP 6(a)(5).

    vi. *"Legal holiday" defined.* "Legal holiday" means:

- The day set aside by statute for observing New Year's Day, Martin Luther King Jr.'s Birthday, Washington's Birthday, Memorial Day, Independence Day, Labor Day, Columbus Day, Veterans' Day, Thanksgiving Day, or Christmas Day;

- Any day declared a holiday by the President or Congress; and

- For periods that are measured after an event, any other day declared a holiday by the state where the district court is located. FRCP 6(a)(6).

b. *Computation of electronic filing deadlines.* A document will be deemed timely filed if electronically filed prior to midnight Eastern Time. However, if the time of day is of the essence, the assigned judge may order that the document be filed by a time certain. NY R USDCTND CM/ECF(4)(4.3).

    i. *Technical failures.* A Filing User, whose filing is untimely as the result of a technical failure of the Court's CM/ECF site, may seek appropriate relief from the Court. However, Filing Users are cautioned that, in some circumstances, the Court lacks the authority to grant an extension of time to file (e.g., FRCP 6(b) of the Federal Rules of Civil Procedure). NY R USDCTND CM/ECF(10)(10.1).

       • *Technical failure of the filing user's system.* Problems with the Filing User's system, such as phone line problems, problems with the Filing User's Internet Service Provider ("ISP"), or hardware or software problems, will not constitute a technical failure under these Administrative Procedures nor excuse an untimely filing. A Filing User who cannot file documents electronically because of a problem on the Filing User's system must file the documents' conventionally along with an affidavit explaining the reason for not filing the documents electronically. NY R USDCTND CM/ECF(10)(10.2).

c. *Extending time*

    i. *In general.* When an act may or must be done within a specified time, the court may, for good cause, extend the time:

       • With or without motion or notice if the court acts, or if a request is made, before the original time or its extension expires; or

       • On motion made after the time has expired if the party failed to act because of excusable neglect. FRCP 6(b)(1).

    ii. *Exceptions.* A court must not extend the time to act under FRCP 50(b), FRCP 50(d), FRCP 52(b), FRCP 59(b), FRCP 59(d), FRCP 59(e), and FRCP 60(b). FRCP 6(b)(2).

    iii. Refer to the United States District Court for the Northern District of New York KeyRules Motion for Continuance/Extension of Time document for more information on extending time.

d. *Additional time after certain kinds of service.* When a party may or must act within a specified time after service and service is made under FRCP 5(b)(2)(C), FRCP 5(b)(2)(D), FRCP 5(b)(2)(E), or FRCP 5(b)(2)(F), three (3) days are added after the period would otherwise expire under FRCP 6(a). FRCP 6(d).

    i. In accordance with FRCP 6(e), service by electronic means is treated the same as service by mail for purposes of adding three (3) days to the prescribed period to respond. NY R USDCTND CM/ECF(5)(5.4). [Editor's note: the reference to FRCP 6(e) is likely meant to be a reference to FRCP 6(d)].

5. *Individual judge practices.* Refer to the Miscellaneous section of this document for information on individual judge practices on timing of documents.

## C. General Requirements

1. *Court conference for non-dispositive motions.* Prior to making any non-dispositive motion before the assigned Magistrate Judge, the parties must make good faith efforts among themselves to resolve or reduce all differences relating to the non-dispositive issue. If, after conferring, the parties are unable to arrive at a mutually satisfactory resolution, the party seeking relief must then request a court conference with the assigned Magistrate Judge. NY R USDCTND L.R. 7.1(b)(2). A court conference is a prerequisite to filing a non-dispositive motion before the assigned Magistrate Judge. NY R USDCTND L.R. 7.1(b)(2). In addition, no non-dispositive or discovery motions should be presented to the Court unless authorized by the Magistrate Judge after communication with the Magistrate Judge's chambers. NY R USDCTND Order 25(IX)(A). Actions which involve an incarcerated, pro se party are not subject to the requirement that a court conference be held prior to filing a non-dispositive motion. NY R USDCTND L.R. 7.1(b)(2).

2. *Motions, generally*

a. *Requirements.* A request for a court order must be made by motion. The motion must:

    i. Be in writing unless made during a hearing or trial;

ii. State with particularity the grounds for seeking the order; and

iii. State the relief sought. FRCP 7(b)(1).

iv. When a moving party makes a motion based upon a rule or statute, the moving party must specify in its moving papers the rule or statute upon which it bases its motion. NY R USDCTND L.R. 7.1(a)(1).

b. *Notice of motion.* A party interested in resisting the relief sought by a motion has a right to notice thereof, and an opportunity to be heard. AMJUR MOTIONS § 12.

i. In addition to statutory or court rule provisions requiring notice of a motion—the purpose of such a notice requirement having been said to be to prevent a party from being prejudicially surprised by a motion—principles of natural justice dictate that an adverse party generally must be given notice that a motion will be presented to the court. AMJUR MOTIONS § 12.

ii. "Notice," in this regard, means reasonable notice, including a meaningful opportunity to prepare and to defend against allegations of a motion. AMJUR MOTIONS § 12.

c. *Writing requirement.* The writing requirement is intended to insure that the adverse parties are informed and have a record of both the motion's pendency and the grounds on which the movant seeks an order. FPP § 1191; Feldberg v. Quechee Lakes Corp., 463 F.3d 195 (2d Cir. 2006).

i. It is sufficient "if the motion is stated in a written notice of the hearing of the motion." FPP § 1191.

d. *Particularity requirement.* The particularity requirement insures that the opposing parties will have notice of their opponent's contentions. FEDPROC § 62:364; Goodman v. 1973 26 Foot Trojan Vessel, Arkansas Registration No. AR1439SN, 859 F.2d 71, 12 Fed.R.Serv.3d 645 (8th Cir. 1988). That requirement ensures that notice of the basis for the motion is provided to the court and to the opposing party so as to avoid prejudice, provide the opponent with a meaningful opportunity to respond, and provide the court with enough information to process the motion correctly. FEDPROC § 62:364; Andreas v. Volkswagen of America, Inc., 336 F.3d 789, 56 Fed.R.Serv.3d 6 (8th Cir. 2003).

i. Reasonable specification of the grounds for a motion is sufficient. However, where a movant fails to state even one ground for granting the motion in question, the movant has failed to meet the minimal standard of "reasonable specification." FEDPROC § 62:364; Martinez v. Trainor, 556 F.2d 818, 23 Fed.R.Serv.2d 403 (7th Cir. 1977).

ii. The court may excuse the failure to comply with the particularity requirement if it is inadvertent, and where no prejudice is shown by the opposing party. FEDPROC § 62:364.

e. *Order to show cause.* All motions that a party brings by Order to Show Cause shall conform to the requirements set forth in NY R USDCTND L.R. 7.1(a)(1) and NY R USDCTND L.R. 7.1(a)(2). Immediately after filing an Order to Show Cause, the moving party must telephone the Chambers of the presiding judicial officer and inform Chambers staff that it has filed an Order to Show Cause. Parties may obtain the telephone numbers for all Chambers from the Clerk's office or at the Court's webpage. The Court shall determine the briefing schedule and return date applicable to motions brought by Order to Show Cause. NY R USDCTND L.R. 7.1(e).

i. In addition to the requirements set forth in NY R USDCTND L.R. 7.1(a)(1) and NY R USDCTND L.R. 7.1(a)(2), a motion brought by Order to Show Cause must include an affidavit clearly and specifically showing good and sufficient cause why the standard Notice of Motion procedure cannot be used. The moving party must give reasonable advance notice of the application for an Order to Show Cause to the other parties, except in those circumstances where the movant can demonstrate, in a detailed and specific affidavit, good cause and substantial prejudice that would result from the requirement of reasonable notice. NY R USDCTND L.R. 7.1(e).

ii. An Order to Show Cause must contain a space for the assigned judge to set forth:

• The deadline for filing and serving supporting papers,

• The deadline for filing and serving opposing papers, and

• The date and time for the hearing. NY R USDCTND L.R. 7.1(e).

3. *Application for temporary restraining order.* Applicants for injunctive relief occasionally are faced with the possibility that irreparable injury will occur before the hearing for a preliminary injunction required by FRCP 65(a) can be held. In that event a temporary restraining order may be available under FRCP 65(b). FPP § 2951. The order is designed to preserve the status quo until there is an opportunity to hold a hearing on the application for a preliminary injunction and may be issued with or without notice to the adverse party. FPP § 2951; Granny Goose Foods, Inc. v. Brotherhood of Teamsters & Auto Truck Drivers Local No. 70 of Alameda County, 415 U.S. 423, 94 S.Ct. 1113, 39 L.Ed.2d 435 (1974).

    a. *Issuing with notice.* When the opposing party actually receives notice of the application for a restraining order, the procedure that is followed does not differ functionally from that on an application for a preliminary injunction and the proceeding is not subject to any special requirements. FPP § 2951; Dilworth v. Riner, 343 F.2d 226 (5th Cir. 1965).

        i. *Duration.* By its terms FRCP 65(b) only governs restraining orders issued without notice or a hearing. But. . .it has been argued that its provisions, at least with regard to the duration of a restraining order, apply even to an order granted when notice has been given to the adverse party but there has been no hearing. FPP § 2951.

    b. *Issuing without notice*

        i. *When available.* The court may issue a temporary restraining order without written or oral notice to the adverse party or its attorney only if:

- Specific facts in an affidavit or a verified complaint clearly show that immediate and irreparable injury, loss, or damage will result to the movant before the adverse party can be heard in opposition; and

- The movant's attorney certifies in writing any efforts made to give notice and the reasons why it should not be required. FRCP 65(b)(1).

        ii. *Contents.* Every temporary restraining order issued without notice must state the date and hour it was issued; describe the injury and state why it is irreparable; state why the order was issued without notice; and be promptly filed in the clerk's office and entered in the record. FRCP 65(b)(2).

        iii. *Expiration.* The order expires at the time after entry—not to exceed fourteen (14) days—that the court sets, unless before that time the court, for good cause, extends it for a like period or the adverse party consents to a longer extension. The reasons for an extension must be entered in the record. FRCP 65(b)(2).

    c. *Temporary restraining order versus preliminary injunction.* A temporary restraining order differs from a preliminary injunction, the core reasons being that a temporary restraining order is of limited duration and it may issue without notice to the opposing party before the adverse party can be heard in opposition. FEDPROC § 47:80.

    d. *Factors considered.* As in the case of an application for a preliminary injunction, four factors must be considered in determining whether a temporary restraining order is to be granted, which are whether the moving party has established: (1) a substantial likelihood of success on the merits; (2) that irreparable injury will be suffered if the relief is not granted; (3) that the threatened injury outweighs the harm the relief would inflict on the nonmoving party; and (4) that entry of the relief would serve the public interest. FEDPROC § 47:84; Schiavo ex rel. Schindler v. Schiavo, 403 F.3d 1223 (11th Cir. 2005).

        i. Plaintiffs are not required to prevail on each of these factors, rather, the factors must be viewed as a continuum, with more of one factor compensating for less of another. In each case, however, all of the factors must be considered to determine whether on balance they weigh toward granting relief. FEDPROC § 47:84.

        ii. In the context of a temporary restraining order, it is particularly important for the moving party to demonstrate a substantial likelihood of success on the merits, because otherwise, there would be no justification for the court's intrusion into the ordinary processes of administration and judicial review. FEDPROC § 47:84.

        iii. Refer to the United States District Court for the Northern District of New York KeyRules

Motion for Preliminary Injunction document for more information on the factors considered in moving for a preliminary injunction.

e. *Burden.* As with a preliminary injunction, the burden is on the moving party to establish that relief is appropriate. FEDPROC § 47:84.

f. *Security.* The court may issue a preliminary injunction or a temporary restraining order only if the movant gives security in an amount that the court considers proper to pay the costs and damages sustained by any party found to have been wrongfully enjoined or restrained. The United States, its officers, and its agencies are not required to give security. FRCP 65(c).

    i. *Proceedings against a surety.* Whenever the Federal Rules of Civil Procedure (including the Supplemental Rules for Admiralty or Maritime Claims and Asset Forfeiture Actions) require or allow a party to give security, and security is given through a bond or other undertaking with one or more sureties, each surety submits to the court's jurisdiction and irrevocably appoints the court clerk as its agent for receiving service of any papers that affect its liability on the bond or undertaking. The surety's liability may be enforced on motion without an independent action. The motion and any notice that the court orders may be served on the court clerk, who must promptly mail a copy of each to every surety whose address is known. FRCP 65.1.

    ii. For more information on sureties, refer to NY R USDCTND L.R. 65.1.1.

g. *Contents and scope of every injunction and restraining order*

    i. *Contents.* Every order granting an injunction and every restraining order must:

- State the reasons why it issued;
- State its terms specifically; and
- Describe in reasonable detail—and not by referring to the complaint or other document—the act or acts restrained or required. FRCP 65(d)(1).

    ii. *Persons bound.* The order binds only the following who receive actual notice of it by personal service or otherwise:

- The parties;
- The parties' officers, agents, servants, employees, and attorneys; and
- Other persons who are in active concert or participation with anyone described in FRCP 65(d)(2)(A) or FRCP 65(d)(2)(B). FRCP 65(d)(2).

h. *Other laws not modified.* FRCP 65 does not modify the following:

    i. Any federal statute relating to temporary restraining orders or preliminary injunctions in actions affecting employer and employee;

    ii. 28 U.S.C.A. § 2361, which relates to preliminary injunctions in actions of interpleader or in the nature of interpleader; or

    iii. 28 U.S.C.A. § 2284, which relates to actions that must be heard and decided by a three-judge district court. FRCP 65(e).

i. *Copyright impoundment.* FRCP 65 applies to copyright-impoundment proceedings. FRCP 65(f).

4. *Submission of proposed order by prevailing party.* If the assigned judge instructs the prevailing party to do so, the prevailing party shall submit a proposed order which the opposing party has approved and which contains the endorsement of the opposing party: "Approved as to form." NY R USDCTND L.R. 77.2(b). In civil actions where the Court has directed a party to submit an order or judgment, that party shall file all such orders or judgments in duplicate, and the Clerk's entry of such duplicate in the proper record book shall be deemed in compliance with FRCP 79(b). Such party shall also furnish the Clerk with a sufficient number of additional copies for each party to the action, which the Clerk shall mail with notice of entry in accordance with FRCP 77(d). NY R USDCTND L.R. 5.1(b).

a. *Disagreement as to form of proposed order.* When the parties are unable to agree as to the form of the proposed order, the prevailing party shall, on seven (7) days notice to all other parties, submit a proposed order and a written explanation for the form of that order. The Court may award costs and attorney's fees against a party whose unreasonable conduct the Court deemed to have required the bringing of the motion. The provisions of NY R USDCTND L.R. 7.1 shall not apply to such motion, and the Court shall not hear oral argument. NY R USDCTND L.R. 77.2(b).

b. For more information on orders, refer to NY R USDCTND L.R. 77.2.

5. *Sanctions for vexatious or frivolous motions or failure to comply with* NY R USDCTND L.R. 7.1. A party who presents vexatious or frivolous motion papers or fails to comply with NY R USDCTND L.R. 7.1 is subject to discipline as the Court deems appropriate, including sanctions and the imposition of costs and attorney's fees to the opposing party. NY R USDCTND L.R. 7.1(i).

6. *Complex and multi-district litigation.* If the assigned judge determines, in his or her discretion, that the case is of such a complex nature that it cannot reasonably be trial ready within eighteen (18) months from the date the complaint is filed, the assigned judge may design and issue a particularized case management order that will move the case to trial as quickly as the complexity of the case allows. NY R USDCTND L.R. 3.3(a). The parties shall promptly notify the Court in writing if any action commenced is appropriate for multi-district litigation. NY R USDCTND L.R. 3.3(b).

7. *Appearances.* An attorney appearing for a party in a civil case shall promptly file with the Clerk a written notice of appearance; however, an attorney does not need to file a notice of appearance if the attorney who would be filing the notice of appearance is the same individual who has signed the complaint, notice of removal, pre-answer motion, or answer. NY R USDCTND L.R. 83.2(a). For more information, refer to NY R USDCTND L.R. 83.2.

8. *Related cases.* A civil case is "related" to another civil case for purposes of this guideline when, because of the similarity of facts and legal issues or because the cases arise from the same transactions or events, a substantial saving of judicial resources is likely to result from assigning the cases to the same Judge and Magistrate Judge. NY R USDCTND Order 12(G)(2). A civil case shall not be deemed related to another civil case merely because the civil case: (1) involves similar legal issues, or (2) involves the same parties. NY R USDCTND Order 12(G)(3). Presumptively, and subject to the power of a Judge to determine otherwise pursuant to NY R USDCTND Order 12(G)(5), civil cases shall not be deemed to be "related" unless both cases are still pending before the Court. NY R USDCTND Order 12(G)(4).

a. *New filings.* If an attorney or filing party indicates on the Civil Cover Sheet that a case is related to an earlier filed case, the Clerk shall instruct the filing party to file a notice of related cases. The allegedly related cases will be submitted by the Clerk to the Judge to whom the earliest filed case is assigned, who shall advise the Clerk whether such cases are related. NY R USDCTND Order 12(G)(1).

b. *Judicial determination that civil cases are "related."* Except for the cases described in the final sentence of NY R USDCTND Order 12(G)(6), all civil cases shall be randomly assigned when they are filed. Other than the cases described in the final sentence of NY R USDCTND Order 12(G)(6), civil cases shall not be deemed to be "related" for purposes of this guideline at the instance of any litigant or attorney unless and until there has been a determination by a Judge of this Court that the standard of NY R USDCTND Order 12(G)(2) is met. NY R USDCTND Order 12(G)(5).

i. *Notice of related filing.* Any party may apply for such a determination by filing with the Clerk a notice of related filing, which should include an explanation as to why the standard of NY R USDCTND Order 12(G)(2) is met. A form for this purpose is available on the Court's website. A copy of the notice shall be served on all other parties who have appeared. Such an application must be made after the date when at least a majority of the defendants have been served with the complaint. Before making such an application, the applicant must confer in good faith with all other parties in an effort to reach an agreement on whether or not the case is "related". After such an application is made, any other party may serve and file within seven (7) calendar days a letter of no more than two (2) pages supporting or opposing the application. The application to have the case assigned to another Judge shall be presented to the Judge with the earliest filed case for decision on whether the action(s) should be reassigned as related cases. The Judge with the earliest filed case may then enter an order in the case at bar, either deeming the case to be related and directing the Clerk to reassign the action, or denying the application for reassignment. Any disputes concerning the assignment of related cases will be referred to the Chief Judge for resolution. NY R USDCTND Order 12(G)(5).

c. For more information on related cases, refer to NY R USDCTND Order 12(G).

9. *Alternative dispute resolution (ADR).* It is the mission of this court to do everything it can to help parties resolve their disputes as fairly, quickly, and efficiently as possible. NY R USDCTND Order 25(VIII).

a. *Arbitration.* NY R USDCTND L.R. 83.7 governs the consensual arbitration program for referral of civil actions to court-annexed arbitration. It may remain in effect until further order of the Court. Its purpose is to establish a less formal procedure for the just, efficient and economical resolution of disputes, while preserving the right to a full trial on demand. NY R USDCTND L.R. 83.7-1.

   i. *Actions subject to arbitration.* The Clerk shall notify the parties in all civil cases, except as the Local Rules of Practice for the United States District Court for the Northern District of New York otherwise direct, that they may consent to non-binding arbitration under NY R US-DCTND L.R. 83.7. The notice shall be furnished to the parties at pretrial/scheduling conferences or shall be included with pretrial conference notices and instructions. Consent to arbitration under NY R USDCTND L.R. 83.7 shall be discussed at the pretrial/scheduling conference. No party or attorney shall be prejudiced for refusing to participate in arbitration. The Court shall allow the referral of any civil action pending before it to the arbitration process if the parties consent. The plaintiff shall be responsible for securing the execution of a consent form by the parties and for filing the form with the Clerk within fourteen (14) days after the parties receive the form. The parties shall freely and knowingly enter into the consent. NY R USDCTND L.R. 83.7-2.

   ii. *Referral to arbitration.* The Clerk shall refer every action subject to NY R USDCTND L.R. 83.7 to arbitration in accordance with the procedures under NY R USDCTND L.R. 83.7 twenty-one (21) days after the filing of the last responsive pleading or within twenty-one (21) days of the filing of a stipulated consent order referring the action to arbitration, whichever event occurs last, except as otherwise provided. If any party notices a motion to dismiss under the provisions of FRCP 12(a) and/or FRCP 12(b), or a motion to join necessary parties pursuant to the Federal Rules of Civil Procedure prior to the expiration of the twenty-one (21) day period, the assigned judge shall hear the motion and further proceedings under NY R USDCTND L.R. 83.7 shall be deferred pending decision on the motion. If the Court does not dismiss the action on the motion, the Court shall refer the action to arbitration twenty-one (21) days after the filing of the decision. NY R USDCTND L.R. 83.7-3(a). Motions for summary judgment pursuant to FRCP 56 shall be filed and served within twenty-one (21) days following the close of discovery. The filing of a FRCP 56 motion shall defer further proceedings under NY R USDCTND L.R. 83.7 pending decision on the motion. NY R USDCTND L.R. 83.7-3(a).

      - *Relief from referral.* Any party shall request relief from the operation of NY R USDCTND L.R. 83.7 by filing with the Court a motion for the relief within twenty-one (21) days after entry of the initial stipulated consent order which refers the case for arbitration. The assigned judge shall, sua sponte, exempt an action from the application of NY R USDCTND L.R. 83.7 where the objectives of arbitration would not be realized because (1) the case involves complex or novel legal issues, (2) legal issues predominate over factual issues, or (3) for other good cause. NY R USDCTND L.R. 83.7-3(c).

   iii. For more information on arbitration, refer to NY R USDCTND L.R. 83.7.

b. *Mediation.* The purpose of NY R USDCTND L.R. 83.11 is to provide a supplementary procedure to the Court's existing alternative dispute resolution procedures. NY R USDCTND L.R. 83.11 provides for an earlier resolution of civil disputes resulting in savings of time and cost to litigants and the Court without sacrificing the quality of justice rendered or the right of litigants to a full trial on all issues not resolved through mediation. NY R USDCTND L.R. 83.11-1(a). Mediation is a process by which an impartial person, the mediator, facilitates communication between disputing parties to promote understanding, reconciliation and settlement. The mediator is an advocate for settlement and uses the mediation process to help the parties fully explore any potential area of agreement. The mediator does not serve as a judge or arbitrator and has no authority to render any decision on any disputed issue or to force a settlement. The parties themselves are responsible for negotiating any resolution(s) to their dispute. NY R USDCTND L.R. 83.11-1(b).

   i. *Actions subject to mediation.* The Court may refer any civil action (or any portion thereof) to mediation under NY R USDCTND L.R. 83.11: (1) by order of referral; or (2) on the motion of any party; or (3) by consent of the parties. NY R USDCTND L.R. 83.11-3(a).

- *Withdrawal from mediation.* The parties may withdraw from mediation any civil action or claim that the Court refers to mediation pursuant to NY R USDCTND L.R. 83.11-3 by application to the assigned judge at least ten (10) days prior to the scheduled mediation session. NY R USDCTND L.R. 83.11-3(b).

ii. *Mandatory mediation program.* The United States District Court for the Northern District of New York has adopted this Mandatory Mediation Plan. The paid Mediation Program is designed to provide quicker, less expensive and potentially more satisfying alternatives to continuing litigation, without impairing the quality of justice or the right to trial. NY R USDCTND Order 47(1)(1.2)(A). This Mandatory Mediation Plan applies to civil actions pending as well as newly filed actions, except as otherwise indicated in NY R USDCTND Order 47. The Local Rules for voluntary mediation will apply only to Pro Se Cases that proceed through the Assisted Mediation Program. NY R USDCTND Order 47(1)(1.2)(B).

- *Referral into the pilot mandatory mediation program for new cases.* All civil cases shall be referred automatically into the Mandatory Mediation Program. Notice of the Mandatory Mediation requirements will be provided to all parties immediately upon the filing of a complaint and answer or a notice of removal. ADR intervention will be scheduled at the conference held pursuant to NY R USDCTND L.R. 16.1. NY R USDCTND Order 47(2)(2.1)(A). For a list of categories of actions exempted from automatic referral, refer to NY R USDCTND Order 47(2)(2.1)(A).

- *Referral into the pilot mandatory mediation program for pending cases.* The assigned Judge or Magistrate Judge on any pending civil case may, sua sponte or with status conference, issue an order referring the case into the Mandatory Mediation Program. The order shall specify a date on which the ADR intervention is to be completed. NY R USDCTND Order 47(2)(2.1)(B).

- *Referral into the pilot mandatory mediation program by stipulation.* A case may be referred into the Mandatory Mediation Program by stipulation of all parties. Stipulations shall be filed and shall designate the time frame within which the ADR process will be completed. Stipulations are presumed acceptable unless the assigned Judge or Magistrate Judge determines that the interests of justice are not served. NY R USDCTND Order 47(2)(2.1)(C).

- *Relief from referral.* Motions to opt out of the program will be addressed by the assigned Magistrate Judge at the FRCP 16 conference. NY R USDCTND Order 47(2)(2.2)(A). Opting Out Motions shall be granted only for "good cause" shown. Inconvenience, travel costs, attorney fees or other costs shall not constitute "good cause." A party seeking relief from the Mandatory Mediation Program must set forth the reasons why Mandatory Mediation has no reasonable chance of being productive. NY R USDCTND Order 47(2)(2.2)(B). The assigned Magistrate Judge may, sua sponte, exempt any case from the Court's Mandatory Mediation Program. NY R USDCTND Order 47(2)(2.2)(C).

iii. *Assisted mediation program.* The Court may assign specially trained pro bono Special Mediation Counsel to assist pro se civilian litigants with preparing for and participating in mediation. The Assisted Mediation Program is open to civilian pro se parties to actions in the Northern District of New York. The assigned judge or magistrate judge determines if the case would benefit from mediation and would also benefit from the assignment of Special Mediation Counsel to assist the pro se party with the mediation process. NY R USDCTND L.R. 83.8(a). Appointment of Special Mediation Counsel is in no way guaranteed, even if the action is referred to the court-annexed mediation program. Appointment is at the sole discretion of the presiding judge. NY R USDCTND L.R. 83.8(a).

- *Referral to assisted mediation program.* If the court determines that referral to the Assisted Mediation Program is appropriate, the Court shall enter an order of reference to the Assisted Mediation Program. NY R USDCTND L.R. 83.8(b).

iv. For more information on mediation, refer to NY R USDCTND L.R. 83.11 and NY R USDCTND Order 47.

c. *Early neutral evaluation (ENE).* Early neutral evaluation (ENE) is a process in which parties obtain from an experienced neutral (an "evaluator") a nonbinding, reasoned, oral evaluation of the merits of the case. The first step in the ENE process involves the Court appointing an evaluator who has expertise in the area of law in the case. After the parties exchange essential information and position statements early in the pretrial period (usually within one hundred fifty (150) to two hundred (200) days after a complaint has been filed), the evaluator convenes an ENE session that typically lasts about two hours. At the ENE meeting, each side briefly presents the factual and legal basis of its position. The evaluator may ask questions of the parties and help them identify the main issues in dispute and the areas of agreement. The evaluator may also help the parties explore options for settlement. If settlement does not occur, the evaluator then offers an opinion as to the settlement value of the case, including the likelihood of liability and the likely range of damages. With the benefit of this assessment, the parties are again encouraged to discuss settlement, with or without the evaluator's assistance. The parties may also explore ways to narrow the issues in dispute, exchange information about the case or otherwise prepare efficiently for trial. NY R USDCTND L.R. 83.12-1.

   i. *Actions subject to early neutral evaluation.* The Court may refer any civil action (or any portion thereof) to ENE under NY R USDCTND L.R. 83.12: (1) by order of referral; (2) on the motion of any party; or (3) by consent of the parties. NY R USDCTND L.R. 83.12-3(a).

   - *Withdrawal from the ENE process.* The parties may withdraw any civil action or claim that the Court has referred to the ENE Process pursuant to NY R USDCTND L.R. 83.12-3 by application to the assigned judge at least ten (10) days before the scheduled evaluation session. NY R USDCTND L.R. 83.12-3(b).

   ii. For more information on early neutral evaluation (ENE), refer to NY R USDCTND L.R. 83.12.

10. *Settlement procedures.* On notice to the Court or the Clerk that the parties have settled an action, and upon confirmation of the settlement by all parties, the Court may issue a judgment dismissing the action by reason of settlement. The Court shall issue the order without prejudice to the parties' right to secure reinstatement of the case within thirty (30) days after the date of judgment by making a showing that the settlement was not, in fact, consummated. NY R USDCTND L.R. 68.2(a). If the Court decides not to follow the procedures set forth in NY R USDCTND L.R. 68.2(a), the parties shall file within thirty (30) days of the notification to the Court, unless otherwise directed by written order, such notices, stipulations and/or motions as are necessary to terminate the action. If the required documents are not filed within the thirty (30) day period, the Clerk shall place the action on the dismissal calendar. NY R USDCTND L.R. 68.2(b).

11. *Sanctions and penalties for noncompliance.* Failure of an attorney or of a party to comply with any provision of the Local Rules of Practice for the United States District Court for the Northern District of New York, General Orders of this District, Orders of the Court, or the Federal Rules of Civil Procedure shall be a ground for imposition of sanctions. NY R USDCTND L.R. 1.1(d).

12. *Individual judge practices.* Refer to the Miscellaneous section of this document for information on individual judge practices on general requirements for documents.

# D. Documents

1. *Application for temporary restraining order (with notice)*

   a. *Required documents*

      i. *Notice of motion and motion.* A party may seek a temporary restraining order by Notice of Motion or Order to Show Cause, as appropriate. NY R USDCTND L.R. 7.1(f). NY R USDCTND L.R. 7.1(b)(2) governs motions for injunctive relief, other than those brought by Order to Show Cause. NY R USDCTND L.R. 7.1(e) governs motions brought by Order to Show Cause. NY R USDCTND L.R. 7.1(f). In the Notice of Motion, the moving party is required to set forth the date that the court conference with the Magistrate Judge was held regarding the issues being presented in the motion. Failure to include this information in the Notice of Motion may result in the Court rejecting the motion papers. NY R USDCTND L.R.

7.1(b)(2). Refer to the General Requirements section of this document for information on the notice of motion and motion.

- *Order to show cause.* Refer to the General Requirements section of this document for information on bringing a motion by order to show cause.

ii. *Memorandum of law.* Except as otherwise provided in NY R USDCTND L.R. 7.1(a), all motions. . .require a memorandum of law. NY R USDCTND L.R. 7.1(a). Refer to the Format section of this document for the formatting requirements for memoranda of law.

iii. *Supporting affidavit.* Except as otherwise provided in NY R USDCTND L.R. 7.1(a), all motions. . .require a. . .supporting affidavit. NY R USDCTND L.R. 7.1(a). An affidavit must not contain legal arguments but must contain factual and procedural background that is relevant to the motion the affidavit supports. NY R USDCTND L.R. 7.1(a)(2).

iv. *Security.* Refer to the General Requirements section of this document for information on the security required.

v. *Certificate of service.* Except as otherwise provided in NY R USDCTND L.R. 7.1(a), all motions. . .require. . .proof of service on all the parties. See NY R USDCTND L.R. 5.1(a). NY R USDCTND L.R. 7.1(a). FRCP 5(d) requires that the person making service under FRCP 5 certify that service has been effected. FRCP 5(Advisory Committee Notes). Having such information on file may be useful for many purposes, including proof of service if an issue arises concerning the effectiveness of the service. FRCP 5(Advisory Committee Notes). The party or its designee shall declare, by affidavit or certification, that it has provided all other parties in the action with all documents it has filed with the Court. NY R USDCTND L.R. 5.1(a).

- Attorneys and pro se parties who are not Filing or Receiving Users must be served with a paper copy of any electronically filed pleading or other document. NY R USDCTND CM/ECF(5)(5.2). Such paper service must be documented by electronically filing a certificate of service. NY R USDCTND CM/ECF(5)(5.2).

b. *Supplemental documents*

i. *Supporting evidence.* When a motion relies on facts outside the record, the court may hear the matter on affidavits or may hear it wholly or partly on oral testimony or on depositions. FRCP 43(c).

ii. *Notice of constitutional question.* A party that files a pleading, written motion, or other paper drawing into question the constitutionality of a federal or state statute must promptly:

- *File notice.* File a notice of constitutional question stating the question and identifying the paper that raises it, if: (1) a federal statute is questioned and the parties do not include the United States, one of its agencies, or one of its officers or employees in an official capacity; or (2) a state statute is questioned and the parties do not include the state, one of its agencies, or one of its officers or employees in an official capacity; and

- *Serve notice.* Serve the notice and paper on the Attorney General of the United States if a federal statute is questioned—or on the state attorney general if a state statute is questioned—either by certified or registered mail or by sending it to an electronic address designated by the attorney general for this purpose. FRCP 5.1(a).

- *No forfeiture.* A party's failure to file and serve the notice, or the court's failure to certify, does not forfeit a constitutional claim or defense that is otherwise timely asserted. FRCP 5.1(d).

iii. *Nongovernmental corporate disclosure statement*

- *Contents.* A nongovernmental corporate party must file two (2) copies of a disclosure statement that: (1) identifies any parent corporation and any publicly held corporation owning ten percent (10%) or more of its stock; or (2) states that there is no such corporation. FRCP 7.1(a).

- *Time to file; Supplemental filing.* A party must: (1) file the disclosure statement with its first appearance, pleading, petition, motion, response, or other request addressed to the court; and (2) promptly file a supplemental statement if any required information changes. FRCP 7.1(b).

iv. *Copies of authorities.* When serving a pro se litigant with a memorandum of law or any other paper which contains citations to authorities that are unpublished or published exclusively on electronic databases, counsel shall include a hard copy of those authorities. Although copies of authorities published only on electronic databases are not required to be filed, copies shall be provided upon request to opposing counsel who lack access to electronic databases. NY R USDCTND L.R. 7.1(a)(1).

v. *Proposed order.* A document that is submitted in .pdf format cannot be modified; therefore, a proposed order or stipulation must be in a word processing format. The chambers of the assigned judge may request that a proposed order and/or a stipulation be e-mailed to the courtroom deputy for the presiding judge in either WordPerfect or Microsoft Word format. Please attach your proposed order and/or stipulation to an Internet e-mail sent to the appropriate e-mail address listed in NY R USDCTND CM/ECF(8)(8.2). NY R USDCTND CM/ECF(8)(8.2).

vi. *Cover letter authorizing e-mail or facsimile filing.* Neither the Court nor the Clerk's Office will accept for filing any facsimile or e-mail transmission without prior authorization from the Court. The party using facsimile or e-mail transmissions to file its papers must accompany any such documents with a cover letter stating that the Court authorized such transmissions and the date on which the Court provided that authorization. Violations of NY R USDCTND L.R. 5.5 subject the offending party to the Court's full disciplinary powers. NY R USDCTND L.R. 5.5.

vii. *Affidavit attesting to failed attempts to file electronically.* If the Court's CM/ECF site experiences a technical failure, a Filing User may submit documents to the Court that day in an alternate manner provided that the documents are accompanied by the Filing User's affidavit stating that the Filing User attempted to file electronically at least two times in one (1) hour increments after 10:00 a.m. that day. The following methods are acceptable alternate means for filing documents in case of a technical failure: (1) via electronic mail in a PDF attachment sent to the e-mail address for technical failures; or (2) in person, by bringing the document to the Clerk's Office on paper accompanied by a CD/ROM that contains the document in .pdf format. NY R USDCTND CM/ECF(10)(10.1).

- A Filing User who cannot file documents electronically because of a problem on the Filing User's system must file the documents' conventionally along with an affidavit explaining the reason for not filing the documents electronically. NY R USDCTND CM/ECF(10)(10.2).

viii. *Notice of conventional filing.* If the Clerk's Office grants permission to conventionally file the document, the Filing User shall electronically file a notice of conventional filing for the documents. More information regarding this process can be obtained from the Court's web page. NY R USDCTND CM/ECF(4)(4.5).

ix. *CD/ROM with PDF of document(s).* If the Court grants permission to file a document traditionally, the attorney must submit the documents for filing to the Clerk's Office on CD/ROM in .pdf or pdf.A format. NY R USDCTND CM/ECF(2).

x. *English translation.* The Court conducts its reviews and deliberations in English. Unless otherwise directed by the Court, any document that a party transmits to the Court (including one in the record on appeal) that is in a language other than English must be accompanied by an English translation that the translator has certified as true and accurate, pursuant to 28 U.S.C.A. § 1746. NY R USDCTND L.R. 10.1(e). For more information, refer to NY R USDCTND L.R. 10.1(e).

xi. *Courtesy copies.* The Court may require that courtesy copies of electronically filed documents be submitted for its review and may amend these Administrative Procedures (NY R USDCTND CM/ECF) at any time without prior notice. NY R USDCTND CM/ECF(2).

xii. *Copies for three-judge court.* On the convening of a three-judge court, the parties shall make three (3) copies of all non-electronically filed pleadings, motion papers, and memoranda of law available to the Clerk for distribution. NY R USDCTND L.R. 9.1.

2. *Application for temporary restraining order (without notice, or "ex parte")*

   a. *Required documents*

      i. *Motion.* A party may seek a temporary restraining order by Notice of Motion or Order to Show Cause, as appropriate. NY R USDCTND L.R. 7.1(f). NY R USDCTND L.R. 7.1(b)(2) governs motions for injunctive relief, other than those brought by Order to Show Cause. NY R USDCTND L.R. 7.1(e) governs motions brought by Order to Show Cause. NY R USDCTND L.R. 7.1(f). Refer to the General Requirements section of this document for information on the motion.

        • *Order to show cause.* Refer to the General Requirements section of this document for information on bringing a motion by order to show cause.

      ii. *Memorandum of law.* Except as otherwise provided in NY R USDCTND L.R. 7.1(a), all motions. . .require a memorandum of law. NY R USDCTND L.R. 7.1(a). Refer to the Format section of this document for the formatting requirements for memoranda of law.

      iii. *Supporting affidavit.* Except as otherwise provided in NY R USDCTND L.R. 7.1(a), all motions. . .require a. . .supporting affidavit. NY R USDCTND L.R. 7.1(a). An affidavit must not contain legal arguments but must contain factual and procedural background that is relevant to the motion the affidavit supports. NY R USDCTND L.R. 7.1(a)(2).

      iv. *Affidavit or verified complaint.* The applicant for an ex parte restraining order must present to the court, in an affidavit or a verified complaint, facts that clearly show irreparable injury. FPP § 2952.

      v. *Certificate of attorney.* The applicant's attorney must certify in writing any efforts made to give notice and the reasons why it should not be required. FEDPROC § 47:81.

      vi. *Security.* Refer to the General Requirements section of this document for information on the security required.

   b. *Supplemental documents*

      i. *Supporting evidence.* When a motion relies on facts outside the record, the court may hear the matter on affidavits or may hear it wholly or partly on oral testimony or on depositions. FRCP 43(c).

      ii. *Notice of constitutional question.* A party that files a pleading, written motion, or other paper drawing into question the constitutionality of a federal or state statute must promptly:

        • *File notice.* File a notice of constitutional question stating the question and identifying the paper that raises it, if: (1) a federal statute is questioned and the parties do not include the United States, one of its agencies, or one of its officers or employees in an official capacity; or (2) a state statute is questioned and the parties do not include the state, one of its agencies, or one of its officers or employees in an official capacity; and

        • *Serve notice.* Serve the notice and paper on the Attorney General of the United States if a federal statute is questioned—or on the state attorney general if a state statute is questioned—either by certified or registered mail or by sending it to an electronic address designated by the attorney general for this purpose. FRCP 5.1(a).

        • *No forfeiture.* A party's failure to file and serve the notice, or the court's failure to certify, does not forfeit a constitutional claim or defense that is otherwise timely asserted. FRCP 5.1(d).

      iii. *Nongovernmental corporate disclosure statement*

        • *Contents.* A nongovernmental corporate party must file two (2) copies of a disclosure statement that: (1) identifies any parent corporation and any publicly held corporation owning ten percent (10%) or more of its stock; or (2) states that there is no such corporation. FRCP 7.1(a).

- *Time to file; Supplemental filing.* A party must: (1) file the disclosure statement with its first appearance, pleading, petition, motion, response, or other request addressed to the court; and (2) promptly file a supplemental statement if any required information changes. FRCP 7.1(b).

iv. *Copies of authorities.* When serving a pro se litigant with a memorandum of law or any other paper which contains citations to authorities that are unpublished or published exclusively on electronic databases, counsel shall include a hard copy of those authorities. Although copies of authorities published only on electronic databases are not required to be filed, copies shall be provided upon request to opposing counsel who lack access to electronic databases. NY R USDCTND L.R. 7.1(a)(1).

v. *Proposed order.* A document that is submitted in .pdf format cannot be modified; therefore, a proposed order or stipulation must be in a word processing format. The chambers of the assigned judge may request that a proposed order and/or a stipulation be e-mailed to the courtroom deputy for the presiding judge in either WordPerfect or Microsoft Word format. Please attach your proposed order and/or stipulation to an Internet e-mail sent to the appropriate e-mail address listed in NY R USDCTND CM/ECF(8)(8.2). NY R USDCTND CM/ECF(8)(8.2).

vi. *Cover letter authorizing e-mail or facsimile filing.* Neither the Court nor the Clerk's Office will accept for filing any facsimile or e-mail transmission without prior authorization from the Court. The party using facsimile or e-mail transmissions to file its papers must accompany any such documents with a cover letter stating that the Court authorized such transmissions and the date on which the Court provided that authorization. Violations of NY R USDCTND L.R. 5.5 subject the offending party to the Court's full disciplinary powers. NY R USDCTND L.R. 5.5.

vii. *Affidavit attesting to failed attempts to file electronically.* If the Court's CM/ECF site experiences a technical failure, a Filing User may submit documents to the Court that day in an alternate manner provided that the documents are accompanied by the Filing User's affidavit stating that the Filing User attempted to file electronically at least two times in one (1) hour increments after 10:00 a.m. that day. The following methods are acceptable alternate means for filing documents in case of a technical failure: (1) via electronic mail in a PDF attachment sent to the e-mail address for technical failures; or (2) in person, by bringing the document to the Clerk's Office on paper accompanied by a CD/ROM that contains the document in .pdf format. NY R USDCTND CM/ECF(10)(10.1).

- A Filing User who cannot file documents electronically because of a problem on the Filing User's system must file the documents' conventionally along with an affidavit explaining the reason for not filing the documents electronically. NY R USDCTND CM/ECF(10)(10.2).

viii. *Notice of conventional filing.* If the Clerk's Office grants permission to conventionally file the document, the Filing User shall electronically file a notice of conventional filing for the documents. More information regarding this process can be obtained from the Court's web page. NY R USDCTND CM/ECF(4)(4.5).

ix. *CD/ROM with PDF of document(s).* If the Court grants permission to file a document traditionally, the attorney must submit the documents for filing to the Clerk's Office on CD/ROM in .pdf or pdf.A format. NY R USDCTND CM/ECF(2).

x. *English translation.* The Court conducts its reviews and deliberations in English. Unless otherwise directed by the Court, any document that a party transmits to the Court (including one in the record on appeal) that is in a language other than English must be accompanied by an English translation that the translator has certified as true and accurate, pursuant to 28 U.S.C.A. § 1746. NY R USDCTND L.R. 10.1(e). For more information, refer to NY R USDCTND L.R. 10.1(e).

xi. *Courtesy copies.* The Court may require that courtesy copies of electronically filed documents be submitted for its review and may amend these Administrative Procedures (NY R USDCTND CM/ECF) at any time without prior notice. NY R USDCTND CM/ECF(2).

      xii.   *Copies for three-judge court.* On the convening of a three-judge court, the parties shall make three (3) copies of all non-electronically filed pleadings, motion papers, and memoranda of law available to the Clerk for distribution. NY R USDCTND L.R. 9.1.

3.   *Individual judge practices.* Refer to the Miscellaneous section of this document for information on individual judge practices on required documents.

## E. Format

1.   *Form of documents.* The rules governing captions and other matters of form in pleadings apply to motions and other papers. FRCP 7(b)(2). All pleadings and other papers shall be served and filed in accordance with the Federal Rules of Civil Procedure and shall be in the form prescribed by NY R USDCTND L.R. 10.1. NY R USDCTND L.R. 5.1(a).

    a.   *Form, generally.* All pleadings, motions, and other documents that a party presents for filing, whether in paper form or in electronic form, shall meet the following requirements:

       i.   *Font size.* All text, whether in the body of the document or in footnotes, must be a minimum of twelve (12) point type. NY R USDCTND L.R. 10.1(a)(1).

      ii.   *Margins.* All documents must have one (1) inch margins on all four sides of the page. NY R USDCTND L.R. 10.1(a)(2).

    iii.   *Spacing.* All text in the body of the document must be double-spaced. NY R USDCTND L.R. 10.1(a)(3).

          • The text in block quotations and footnotes may be single-spaced. NY R USDCTND L.R. 10.1(a)(4).

     iv.   *Page numbering.* Pages must be consecutively numbered. NY R USDCTND L.R. 10.1(a)(7).

      v.   *Circumventing formatting limitations*

          • Extensive footnotes must not be used to circumvent page limitations. NY R USDCTND L.R. 10.1(a)(5).

          • Compacted or other compressed printing features must not be used. NY R USDCTND L.R. 10.1(a)(6).

    b.   *Additional requirements for paper filing.* Additional requirements for all pleadings, motions, and other documents that a party presents for filing in paper form:

       i.   *Paper size.* All documents must be on eight and one-half by eleven (8-1/2 x 11) inch white paper of good quality. NY R USDCTND L.R. 10.1(b)(1).

      ii.   *Text.* All text must be plainly and legibly written, typewritten, printed or reproduced without erasures or interlineations materially defacing them. NY R USDCTND L.R. 10.1(b)(2).

    iii.   *Ink.* All documents must be in black or blue ink. NY R USDCTND L.R. 10.1(b)(3).

     iv.   *Binding.* Pages of all documents must be stapled (or in some other way fastened) together. NY R USDCTND L.R. 10.1(b)(4).

      v.   *Single-sided paper.* All documents must be single-sided. NY R USDCTND L.R. 10.1(b)(5).

     vi.   *Electronic submission.* The Court, at its discretion, may require the electronic submission of any document in a WordPerfect-compatible format. NY R USDCTND L.R. 10.1(b)(6).

    vii.   *Rejection of document.* The Court may reject documents that do not comply with the above-listed requirements. NY R USDCTND L.R. 10.1(b).

    c.   *Caption; Names of parties.* Every pleading must have a caption with the court's name, a title, a file number, and a FRCP 7(a) designation. The title of the complaint must name all the parties; the title of other pleadings, after naming the first party on each side, may refer generally to other parties. FRCP 10(a). Each document must contain a caption for the specific case to which it pertains. The caption must include the title of the Court, the title of the action, the civil action number of the case, the initials of the assigned judge(s), and the name or nature of the paper in sufficient detail for identification. If a litigant has more than one action pending in this Court, any and all papers filed in a case must contain and pertain to one civil action number, unless the civil actions have been consolidated by the Court. Any motion or other papers purporting to relate to more than one action will not be accepted for filing and may be stricken by the Court. NY R USDCTND L.R. 10.1(c)(1) shall not apply, as noted in NY R USDCTND L.R. 10.1(c), to notices of change of address filed by attorneys of record and pro se litigants. The parties must separately caption affidavits and declarations and must not physically attach them to the Notice of Motion or Memorandum of Law. NY R USDCTND L.R. 10.1(c)(1).

d.  *Paragraphs; Separate statements.* A party must state its claims or defenses in numbered paragraphs, each limited as far as practicable to a single set of circumstances. A later pleading may refer by number to a paragraph in an earlier pleading. If doing so would promote clarity, each claim founded on a separate transaction or occurrence—and each defense other than a denial—must be stated in a separate count or defense. FRCP 10(b).

e.  *Adoption by reference; Exhibits.* A statement in a pleading may be adopted by reference elsewhere in the same pleading or in any other pleading or motion. A copy of a written instrument that is an exhibit to a pleading is a part of the pleading for all purposes. FRCP 10(c).

f.  *Citation of local rules.* These are the Local Rules of Practice for the United States District Court for the Northern District of New York. They shall be cited as "L.R. ___." NY R USDCTND L.R. 1.1(a).

g.  *Acceptance by the clerk.* The clerk must not refuse to file a paper solely because it is not in the form prescribed by the Federal Rules of Civil Procedure or by a local rule or practice. FRCP 5(d)(4).

2.  *Form of electronic documents.* All pleadings, motions, and other documents that a party presents for filing, whether in paper form or in electronic form, shall meet the requirements in NY R USDCTND L.R. 10.1(a). NY R USDCTND L.R. 10.1(a). Refer above for more information.

a.  *Attachments and exhibits.* A Filing User must submit in electronic form all documents referenced as exhibits or attachments in accordance with the Court's CM/ECF Users Manual unless the Court otherwise orders. A Filing User shall submit as exhibits or attachments only those excerpts of the referenced documents that are directly germane to the matter under the Court's consideration. Excerpted material must be clearly and prominently identified as such. Filing Users who file excerpts of documents as exhibits or attachments under these Administrative Procedures (NY R USDCTND CM/ECF) do so without prejudice to their right to timely file additional excerpts or the complete document. Responding parties may also timely file the complete document or additional excerpts that they believe are directly germane to the matter under the Court's consideration. NY R USDCTND CM/ECF(4)(4.4).

i.  All attachments must be described in sufficient detail so the Court and opposing counsel can easily identify and distinguish the filed attachments. Vague or general descriptions are insufficient (i.e., "Exhibit 1"). Rather, each attachment shall have a descriptive title identifying, with specificity, the document that is being filed (i.e., "Exhibit 12 Mulligan County Fire Investigation Report.") Failure to adequately describe attachments may result in the document being rejected by the Court. NY R USDCTND CM/ECF(4)(4.4).

b.  *Large documents.* For information on the electronic filing of large documents, please consult the Court's CM/ECF Users Manual, which is available on the Court's web page. NY R USDCTND CM/ECF(4)(4.5).

i.  A party who believes a document is too lengthy to electronically image, i.e., "scan," may contact the Clerk's Office for permission to file that document conventionally. If the Clerk's Office grants permission to conventionally file the document, the Filing User shall electronically file a notice of conventional filing for the documents. More information regarding this process can be obtained from the Court's web page. Exhibits submitted conventionally shall be served on other parties as if they were not subject to these Administrative Procedures (NY R USDCTND CM/ECF). For a list of hints and tips for scanning large documents, please consult the Court's web page. NY R USDCTND CM/ECF(4)(4.5).

c.  *Legibility.* It shall be the Filing User's responsibility to verify the legibility of scanned documents before filing them electronically with the Court. NY R USDCTND CM/ECF(4)(4.6).

d. *Color documents.* Since documents scanned in color or containing a graphic take much longer to upload, Filing Users are encouraged to configure their scanners to scan documents at 300 dpi and preferably in black and white rather than in color. NY R USDCTND CM/ECF(4)(4.7).

e. *Items not in .PDF format.* Parties wishing to file items not amenable to .pdf format (i.e. CD's, DVD's), shall file such items conventionally with the Clerk's Office. The Filing User shall electronically file a notice of conventional filing indicating that these items have been submitted to the clerk and shall serve copies of these items on other parties as if they were not subject to these Administrative Procedures (NY R USDCTND CM/ECF). These item(s) will be maintained by the Clerk's Office until the case is disposed, at which time they will be returned to the filing party for retention consistent with NY R USDCTND CM/ECF(4)(4.9). NY R USDCTND CM/ECF(4)(4.8).

3. *Form of memoranda of law*

a. *Length limitation.* No party shall file or serve a memorandum of law that exceeds twenty-five (25) pages in length, unless that party obtains leave of the judge hearing the motion prior to filing. NY R USDCTND L.R. 7.1(a)(1).

b. *Table of contents.* All memoranda of law shall contain a table of contents. NY R USDCTND L.R. 7.1(a)(1).

4. *Signing of pleadings, motions and other papers*

a. *Signature.* Every pleading, written motion, and other paper must be signed by at least one attorney of record in the attorney's name—or by a party personally if the party is unrepresented. The paper must state the signer's address, e-mail address, and telephone number. FRCP 11(a). Each document must identify the person filing the document. This identification must include an original signature of the attorney or pro se litigant; the typewritten name of that person; the address of a pro se litigant; and the bar roll number, office address, telephone number, e-mail address and fax number of the attorney. Telephone numbers of non-prisoner pro se parties may be provided voluntarily or upon request of the Court. See General Order #22 (NY R USDCTND CM/ECF) for signature requirements. NY R USDCTND L.R. 10.1(c)(2).

   i. *Electronic signatures.* Documents filed under an attorney's login and password shall constitute that attorney's signature for purposes of the Local Rules of Practice for the United States District Court for the Northern District of New York and Federal Rules of Civil Procedure, including but not limited to FRCP 11. A pleading or other document requiring an attorney's signature shall be signed in the following manner, whether filed electronically or submitted on disk or CD/ROM to the Clerk's Office: "s/ (attorney name)." The correct format for an attorney signature is found in NY R USDCTND CM/ECF(6)(6.1). NY R USDCTND CM/ECF(6)(6.1).

      • *Non-attorney signature.* If an original document requires the signature of a non-attorney, the Filing User may scan the original document containing the original signature(s), then electronically file it on the System. Alternatively, the Filing User may convert the document into .pdf text format and submit the document using "s/" for the signature of the non-attorney. NY R USDCTND CM/ECF(6)(6.2).

      • *Multiple signatures.* A document requiring signatures of more than one party must be filed electronically either by (1) submitting a scanned document containing all necessary signatures; (2) representing the consent of the other parties on the document; or (3) in any other manner that the Court approves. NY R USDCTND CM/ECF(6)(6.3).

   ii. *No verification or accompanying affidavit required for pleadings.* Unless a rule or statute specifically states otherwise, a pleading need not be verified or accompanied by an affidavit. FRCP 11(a).

   iii. *Unsigned papers.* The court must strike an unsigned paper unless the omission is promptly corrected after being called to the attorney's or party's attention. FRCP 11(a).

b. *Representations to the court.* By presenting to the court a pleading, written motion, or other paper—whether by signing, filing, submitting, or later advocating it—an attorney or unrepresented party certifies that to the best of the person's knowledge, information, and belief, formed after an inquiry reasonable under the circumstances:

    i.   It is not being presented for any improper purpose, such as to harass, cause unnecessary delay, or needlessly increase the cost of litigation;

    ii.  The claims, defenses, and other legal contentions are warranted by existing law or by a nonfrivolous argument for extending, modifying, or reversing existing law or for establishing new law;

    iii. The factual contentions have evidentiary support or, if specifically so identified, will likely have evidentiary support after a reasonable opportunity for further investigation or discovery; and

    iv. The denials of factual contentions are warranted on the evidence or, if specifically so identified, are reasonably based on belief or a lack of information. FRCP 11(b).

  c.  *Sanctions.* If, after notice and a reasonable opportunity to respond, the court determines that FRCP 11(b) has been violated, the court may impose an appropriate sanction on any attorney, law firm, or party that violated FRCP 11(b) or is responsible for the violation. FRCP 11(c)(1). Refer to the United States District Court for the Northern District of New York KeyRules Motion for Sanctions document for more information.

5.  *Privacy protection for filings made with the court*

  a.  *Redacted filings.* Unless the court orders otherwise, in an electronic or paper filing with the court that contains an individual's Social Security number, taxpayer-identification number, or birth date, the name of an individual known to be a minor, or a financial-account number, a party or nonparty making the filing may include only:

    i.   The last four (4) digits of the Social Security number and taxpayer-identification number;

    ii.  The year of the individual's birth;

    iii. The minor's initials; and

    iv. The last four (4) digits of the financial-account number. FRCP 5.2(a); NY R USDCTND L.R. 8.1; NY R USDCTND CM/ECF(11)(11.2).

    v.   If a home address must be used, use only the City and State. NY R USDCTND L.R. 8.1; NY R USDCTND CM/ECF(11)(11.2).

    vi.  If the victim of a sexual assault must be referenced, redact the name to 'Victim.' NY R USDCTND CM/ECF(11)(11.2); NY R USDCTND L.R. 8.1.

    vii. In addition, caution shall be exercised when filing documents that contain the following:

- Personal identifying number, such as a driver's license number;
- Medical records, treatment and diagnosis;
- Employment history;
- Individual financial information; and
- Proprietary or trade secret information. NY R USDCTND L.R. 8.1; NY R USDCTND CM/ECF(11)(11.2).

  b.  *Exemptions from the redaction requirement.* The redaction requirement does not apply to the following:

    i.   A financial-account number that identifies the property allegedly subject to forfeiture in a forfeiture proceeding;

    ii.  The record of an administrative or agency proceeding;

    iii. The official record of a state-court proceeding;

    iv. The record of a court or tribunal, if that record was not subject to the redaction requirement when originally filed;

    v.   A filing covered by FRCP 5.2(c) or FRCP 5.2(d); and

vi. A pro se filing in an action brought under 28 U.S.C.A. § 2241, 28 U.S.C.A. § 2254, or 28 U.S.C.A. § 2255. FRCP 5.2(b).

vii. Transcripts of the administrative record in social security proceedings are exempt from this requirement. State court records and other documents filed in habeas corpus proceedings are exempt from this requirement except for proceedings that involve victims of sex crimes. In habeas corpus cases involving sex crimes, the parties must redact the record and supporting papers, or may move to seal, if appropriate. NY R USDCTND L.R. 8.1.

c. *Limitations on remote access to electronic files; Social Security appeals and immigration cases.* Unless the court orders otherwise, in an action for benefits under the Social Security Act, and in an action or proceeding relating to an order of removal, to relief from removal, or to immigration benefits or detention, access to an electronic file is authorized as follows:

i. The parties and their attorneys may have remote electronic access to any part of the case file, including the administrative record;

ii. Any other person may have electronic access to the full record at the courthouse, but may have remote electronic access only to:

- The docket maintained by the court; and
- An opinion, order, judgment, or other disposition of the court, but not any other part of the case file or the administrative record. FRCP 5.2(c).

d. *Filings made under seal.* The court may order that a filing be made under seal without redaction. The court may later unseal the filing or order the person who made the filing to file a redacted version for the public record. FRCP 5.2(d); NY R USDCTND L.R. 8.1. For information on sealed matters, refer to NY R USDCTND L.R. 83.13 and NY R USDCTND CM/ECF(12).

e. *Protective orders.* For good cause, the court may by order in a case:

i. Require redaction of additional information; or

ii. Limit or prohibit a nonparty's remote electronic access to a document filed with the court. FRCP 5.2(e).

f. *Option for additional unredacted filing under seal.* A person making a redacted filing may also file an unredacted copy under seal. The court must retain the unredacted copy as part of the record. FRCP 5.2(f); NY R USDCTND L.R. 8.1; NY R USDCTND CM/ECF(11)(11.3).

g. *Option for filing a reference list.* A filing that contains redacted information may be filed together with a reference list that identifies each item of redacted information and specifies an appropriate identifier that uniquely corresponds to each item listed. The list must be filed under seal and may be amended as of right. Any reference in the case to a listed identifier will be construed to refer to the corresponding item of information. FRCP 5.2(g); NY R USDCTND L.R. 8.1; NY R USDCTND CM/ECF(11)(11.3).

h. *Responsibility for redaction.* Counsel is strongly urged to discuss this issue with all their clients so that they can make an informed decision about the inclusion of certain information. The responsibility for redacting these personal identifiers rests solely with counsel and the parties. The Clerk will not review each filing for compliance with NY R USDCTND L.R. 8.1. Counsel and the parties are cautioned that failure to redact these personal identifiers may subject them to the Court's full disciplinary power. NY R USDCTND L.R. 8.1; NY R USDCTND CM/ECF(11)(11.3).

i. *Waiver of protection of identifiers.* A person waives the protection of FRCP 5.2(a) as to the person's own information by filing it without redaction and not under seal. FRCP 5.2(h).

6. *Individual judge practices.* Refer to the Miscellaneous section of this document for information on individual judge practices on formatting documents.

## F. Filing and Service Requirements

1. *Filing requirements.* Any paper after the complaint that is required to be served—together with a certificate of service—must be filed within a reasonable time after service. FRCP 5(d)(1). Filing

procedures and requirements for supporting documents are the same as set forth in NY R USDCTND L.R. 7.1 for other motions. NY R USDCTND L.R. 7.1(f).

a. *How filing is made; In general.* A paper is filed by delivering it:

    i. To the clerk; or

    ii. To a judge who agrees to accept it for filing, and who must then note the filing date on the paper and promptly send it to the clerk. FRCP 5(d)(2).

b. *Electronic filing*

    i. *Authorization of electronic filing program.* A court may, by local rule, allow papers to be filed, signed, or verified by electronic means that are consistent with any technical standards established by the Judicial Conference of the United States. A local rule may require electronic filing only if reasonable exceptions are allowed. A paper filed electronically in compliance with a local rule is a written paper for purposes of the Federal Rules of Civil Procedure. FRCP 5(d)(3).

      • All cases filed in this Court may be assigned to the Electronic Case Files System ("ECF") in accordance with the Procedural Order on Electronic Case Filing (General Order #22 (NY R USDCTND CM/ECF)), the provisions of which are incorporated herein by reference, and which the Court may amend from time to time. Copies of General Order #22 (NY R USDCTND CM/ECF) are available at the Clerk's office or at the Court's webpage. NY R USDCTND L.R. 5.1.1; NY R USDCTND Order 25(XII).

      • The Court may deviate from these Administrative Procedures (NY R USDCTND CM/ECF) in specific cases, without prior notice, if deemed appropriate in the exercise of discretion, considering the need for the just, speedy, and inexpensive determination of matters pending before the Court. NY R USDCTND CM/ECF(2).

    ii. *Scope of electronic filing.* After January 1, 2004, all documents that attorneys admitted to practice in the Northern District of New York submit for filing shall be filed electronically using the System or shall be scanned and uploaded to the System, no matter when a case was originally filed, unless these Administrative Procedures (NY R USDCTND CM/ECF) otherwise permit or unless the assigned judge otherwise authorizes. An attorney who is not a Filing User by January 1, 2004, must show good cause to the assigned judge to file and serve pleadings and other papers in the traditional manner. NY R USDCTND CM/ECF(2).

    iii. *Exceptions and/or waivers from mandatory electronic filing.* The following types of cases and/or documents are not required to be filed electronically:

      • If you are seeking to have your complaint filed under seal, please file your complaint and proposed sealing order traditionally at the Clerk's Office. NY R USDCTND CM/ECF(2)(2.1)(1).

      • Any document that a party proceeding pro se files. (See NY R USDCTND CM/ECF(12)(12.1) for procedural details). NY R USDCTND CM/ECF(2)(2.1)(2). A non-prisoner who is a party to a civil action and who is not represented by an attorney may file a motion to obtain an Electronic Case Filing (ECF) login and password on a form prescribed by the Clerk's Office. The Pro Se CM/ECF Registration Form shall be submitted with the motion. If during the course of the action an attorney appears on behalf of the pro se party, the Clerk's Office shall terminate the pro se party's registration based upon the attorney's appearance. NY R USDCTND CM/ECF(12)(12.1). Absent permission to file electronically, pro se filers shall file paper originals of all complaints, pleadings, motions, affidavits, briefs, and other documents which must be signed or which require either verification or an unsworn declaration under any rule or statute. The Clerk's Office will scan these original documents into an electronic file in the System but will also maintain a paper file. NY R USDCTND CM/ECF(12)(12.1). A pro se party may also seek permission to receive immediate notice of all public documents filed in their cases. Notices of Electronic Filing (NEF) and attached documents would be transmitted to a non-prisoner pro se party who selects this option. Note: The pro se party would continue to file their documents with the Clerk's Office in paper form. NY R USDCTND CM/ECF(12)(12.1).

- Sealed documents, sealed cases, documents for in camera review, documents lodged with the Court, ex parte documents, confidential agreements, Qui Tam actions and Grand Jury material and warrants must be filed traditionally. (See NY R USDCTND CM/ECF(12)(12.2) for further information the filing of the above-referenced documents). NY R USDCTND CM/ECF(2)(2.1)(3).

- Discovery: In accordance with NY R USDCTND L.R. 26.2, parties shall not file discovery, provided, however, that discovery material to be used at trial or in support of any motion, including a motion to compel or for summary judgment, shall be filed electronically with the Court prior to the trial or with the motion. Any motion pursuant to FRCP 37 shall be accompanied by the electronically filed discovery materials to which the motion relates if those materials have not previously been filed with the Court. NY R USDCTND CM/ECF(2)(2.1)(4).

- Transport Orders: All orders requesting that an incarcerated individual be transported that a judicial officer of the Northern District of New York signs shall be filed traditionally. These Orders will not be filed with the case or uploaded to the docket but rather will be processed in accordance with the procedures that the Clerk of Court promulgates. NY R USDCTND CM/ECF(2)(2.1)(5).

iv. *Filing defined.* Electronic transmission of a document to the System in accordance with these Administrative Procedures, together with the transmission of a Notice of Electronic Filing from the Court, constitutes filing of the document for all purposes of the Federal Rules of Civil Procedure and the Local Rules of Practice for the United States District Court for the Northern District of New York and constitutes entry of the document on the docket that the Clerk's Office keeps under FRCP 58 and FRCP 79. E-mailing a document to the Clerk's Office or to the assigned judge shall not constitute "filing" of the document. NY R USDCTND CM/ECF(4)(4.1).

v. *Filing fees.* Any fee required for filing a pleading or paper in this Court is payable to the Clerk of the Court. The Court will not maintain electronic billing or debit accounts for attorneys or law firms. Effective January 1, 2007, payment for filing fees will be mandatory through CM/ECF's Internet Credit Card Payment site--a secure Treasury Site. The Filing User will be prompted to enter either Bank Account Debit (ACH) or credit card information while filing the initial pleading. Any document that requires a filing fee (e.g., Notice of Appeal, Motion for Pro Hac Vice Admission) may also be paid through the federal electronic payment website. NY R USDCTND CM/ECF(7).

vi. For more information on electronic filing, refer to NY R USDCTND CM/ECF.

c. *E-mail or facsimile filing.* Neither the Court nor the Clerk's Office will accept for filing any facsimile or e-mail transmission without prior authorization from the Court. The party using facsimile or e-mail transmissions to file its papers must accompany any such documents with a cover letter stating that the Court authorized such transmissions and the date on which the Court provided that authorization. Violations of NY R USDCTND L.R. 5.5 subject the offending party to the Court's full disciplinary powers. NY R USDCTND L.R. 5.5.

2. *Service requirements.* The moving party must serve any application for a temporary restraining order on all other parties unless FRCP 65 otherwise permits. NY R USDCTND L.R. 7.1(f).

a. *Service; When required*

i. *In general.* Unless the Federal Rules of Civil Procedure provide otherwise, each of the following papers must be served on every party:

- An order stating that service is required;

- A pleading filed after the original complaint, unless the court orders otherwise under FRCP 5(c) because there are numerous defendants;

- A discovery paper required to be served on a party, unless the court orders otherwise;

- A written motion, except one that may be heard ex parte; and

- A written notice, appearance, demand, or offer of judgment, or any similar paper. FRCP 5(a)(1).

ii. *If a party fails to appear.* No service is required on a party who is in default for failing to appear. But a pleading that asserts a new claim for relief against such a party must be served on that party under FRCP 4. FRCP 5(a)(2).

iii. *Seizing property.* If an action is begun by seizing property and no person is or need be named as a defendant, any service required before the filing of an appearance, answer, or claim must be made on the person who had custody or possession of the property when it was seized. FRCP 5(a)(3).

b. *Service; How made*

   i. *Serving an attorney.* If a party is represented by an attorney, service under FRCP 5 must be made on the attorney unless the court orders service on the party. FRCP 5(b)(1).

   ii. *Service in general.* A paper is served under FRCP 5 by:

   - Handing it to the person;

   - Leaving it: (1) at the person's office with a clerk or other person in charge or, if no one is in charge, in a conspicuous place in the office; or (2) if the person has no office or the office is closed, at the person's dwelling or usual place of abode with someone of suitable age and discretion who resides there;

   - Mailing it to the person's last known address—in which event service is complete upon mailing;

   - Leaving it with the court clerk if the person has no known address;

   - Sending it by electronic means if the person consented in writing—in which event service is complete upon transmission, but is not effective if the serving party learns that it did not reach the person to be served; or

   - Delivering it by any other means that the person consented to in writing—in which event service is complete when the person making service delivers it to the agency designated to make delivery. FRCP 5(b)(2).

   iii. *Service of electronically-filed documents.* Service is complete provided all parties receive a Notice of Electronic Filing (NEF), which is sent automatically by email from the Court (see the NEF for a list of who did/did not receive notice electronically). Transmission of the NEF constitutes service upon all Filing and Receiving Users who are listed as recipients of notice by electronic mail. It remains the responsibility of Filing and Receiving Users to maintain current contact information with the court and to regularly review the docket sheet of the case. NY R USDCTND CM/ECF(5)(5.2).

   - *Non-filing or receiving users.* Attorneys and pro se parties who are not Filing or Receiving Users must be served with a paper copy of any electronically filed pleading or other document. Service of such paper copy must be made according to the Federal Rules of Civil Procedure and the Local Rules of Practice for the United States District Court for the Northern District of New York. Such paper service must be documented by electronically filing a certificate of service. NY R USDCTND CM/ECF(5)(5.2). A party who is not a Filing User of the System is entitled to a paper copy of any electronically-filed pleading, document, or order. The Filing User must therefore provide the non-Filing User with the pleading or document according to the Federal Rules of Civil Procedure. NY R US-DCTND CM/ECF(5)(5.3).

   iv. *Using court facilities.* If a local rule so authorizes, a party may use the court's transmission facilities to make service under FRCP 5(b)(2)(E). FRCP 5(b)(3).

c. *Serving numerous defendants*

    i. *In general.* If an action involves an unusually large number of defendants, the court may, on motion or on its own, order that:

- Defendants' pleadings and replies to them need not be served on other defendants;

- Any crossclaim, counterclaim, avoidance, or affirmative defense in those pleadings and replies to them will be treated as denied or avoided by all other parties; and

- Filing any such pleading and serving it on the plaintiff constitutes notice of the pleading to all parties. FRCP 5(c)(1).

    ii. *Notifying parties.* A copy of every such order must be served on the parties as the court directs. FRCP 5(c)(2).

3. *Individual judge practices.* Refer to the Miscellaneous section of this document for information on individual judge practices on filing and serving documents.

# G. Hearings

1. *Hearings, generally*

a. *Motion days.* Listings of the regularly scheduled motion days for all judges shall be available at each Clerk's office and are available on the Court's webpage. The Clerk shall provide notice of the regular motion days for all judges to the parties at the time an action is commenced. NY R USDCTND L.R. 78.1.

b. *Return date.* Unless the Court directs otherwise, the moving party shall make its motion returnable at the next regularly scheduled motion date at least thirty-one (31) days from the date the moving party files and serves its motion. The moving party shall select a return date in accordance with the procedures set forth in NY R USDCTND L.R. 7.1(b). If the return date the moving party selects is not the next regularly scheduled motion date, or if the moving party selects no return date, the Clerk will set the proper return date and notify the parties. NY R USDCTND L.R. 7.1.

    i. Information regarding motion dates and times is specified on the case assignment form that the Court provides to the parties at the commencement of the litigation or the parties may obtain this form from the Clerk's office or at the Court's webpage. NY R USDCTND L.R. 7.1.

    ii. The Court hereby directs the Clerk to set a proper return date in motions that pro se litigants submit for filing that do not specify a return date or fail to allow for sufficient time pursuant to NY R USDCTND L.R. 7.1. Generally, the return date that the Clerk selects should not exceed thirty (30) days from the date of filing. Furthermore, the Clerk shall forward a copy of the revised or corrected notice of motion to the parties. NY R USDCTND L.R. 7.1.

c. *Oral argument.* Due process does not require that oral argument be permitted on a motion and, except as otherwise provided by local rule, the district court has discretion to determine whether it will decide the motion on the papers or hear argument by counsel (and perhaps receive evidence). FPP § 1190; F.D.I.C. v. Deglau, 207 F.3d 153 (3d Cir. 2000).

    i. The parties shall appear for oral argument on all motions that they make returnable before a district court judge, except motions for reconsideration, on the scheduled return date of the motion. A motion may be disposed of without oral argument as described in NY R USDCTND Order 25, on consideration of a request of any party, or otherwise at the discretion of the presiding judge. Thus, the parties should be prepared to have their motion papers serve as the sole method of argument on the motion. NY R USDCTND L.R. 7.1(h).

    ii. The parties shall not appear for oral argument on motions that they make returnable before a Magistrate Judge on the scheduled return date of the motion unless the Magistrate Judge sua sponte directs or grants the request of any party for oral argument. NY R USDCTND L.R. 7.1(h).

d. *Providing a regular schedule for oral hearings.* A court may establish regular times and places for oral hearings on motions. FRCP 78(a).

e. *Providing for submission on briefs.* By rule or order, the court may provide for submitting and determining motions on briefs, without oral hearings. FRCP 78(b).

2. *Hearing on motion for preliminary injunction after temporary restraining order is issued without notice*

    a. *Expediting the preliminary injunction hearing.* If the order is issued without notice, the motion for a preliminary injunction must be set for hearing at the earliest possible time, taking precedence over all other matters except hearings on older matters of the same character. At the hearing, the party who obtained the order must proceed with the motion; if the party does not, the court must dissolve the order. FRCP 65(b)(3). Refer to the United States District Court for the Northern District of New York KeyRules Motion for Preliminary Injunction document for more information on the hearing on the motion for preliminary injunction.

3. *Individual judge practices.* Refer to the Miscellaneous section of this document for information on individual judge practices on hearings.

## H. Forms

### 1. Federal Application for Temporary Restraining Order Forms

    a. Ex parte motion; For temporary restraining order and order to show cause; Interference with property rights. AMJUR PP INJUNCTION § 42.

    b. Affidavit; In support of ex parte motion for temporary restraining order. AMJUR PP INJUNCTION § 48.

    c. Certificate of attorney; In support of ex parte motion for temporary restraining order. AMJUR PP INJUNCTION § 50.

    d. Affidavit; In support of ex parte motion for temporary restraining order; Interference with property rights. AMJUR PP INJUNCTION § 51.

    e. Motion. 4A FEDFORMS § 5344.

    f. Motion; Another form. 4A FEDFORMS § 5345.

    g. Motion; Another form. 4A FEDFORMS § 5346.

    h. Motion without notice. 4A FEDFORMS § 5347.

    i. Motion without notice; Another form. 4A FEDFORMS § 5348.

    j. Motion without notice; Another form. 4A FEDFORMS § 5349.

    k. Motion without notice; Another form. 4A FEDFORMS § 5350.

    l. Motion without notice; Another form. 4A FEDFORMS § 5351.

    m. Motion without notice; Another form. 4A FEDFORMS § 5352.

    n. Certificate of attorney's efforts to give notice. 4A FEDFORMS § 5353.

    o. Certificate of attorney's efforts to give notice; Another form. 4A FEDFORMS § 5354.

    p. Certificate of attorney's efforts to give notice; Another form. 4A FEDFORMS § 5355.

    q. Certificate of attorney's efforts to give notice; Another form. 4A FEDFORMS § 5356.

    r. Motion requesting expedited hearing. 4A FEDFORMS § 5357.

    s. Motion seeking temporary restraining order. 4A FEDFORMS § 5359.

    t. Motion to dissolve or modify temporary restraining order. 4A FEDFORMS § 5361.

    u. Motion for temporary restraining order and preliminary injunction. GOLDLTGFMS § 13A:6.

    v. Motion for temporary restraining order; General form. GOLDLTGFMS § 13A:11.

    w. Motion for temporary restraining order; Ex parte application. GOLDLTGFMS § 13A:12.

    x. Motion for temporary restraining order; Ex parte application; Supporting affidavit by party. GOLDLTGFMS § 13A:13.

    y. Motion for temporary restraining order; Ex parte application; Supporting affidavit by party; Copyright infringement. GOLDLTGFMS § 13A:14.

    z. Motion for temporary restraining order; Ex parte application; Certificate by counsel. GOLDLTGFMS § 13A:15.

## I. Applicable Rules

1. *Federal rules*

   a. Serving and filing pleadings and other papers. FRCP 5.

   b. Constitutional challenge to a statute; Notice, certification, and intervention. FRCP 5.1.

   c. Privacy protection for filings made with the court. FRCP 5.2.

   d. Computing and extending time; Time for motion papers. FRCP 6.

   e. Pleadings allowed; Form of motions and other papers. FRCP 7.

   f. Disclosure statement. FRCP 7.1.

   g. Form of pleadings. FRCP 10.

   h. Signing pleadings, motions, and other papers; Representations to the court; Sanctions. FRCP 11.

   i. Taking testimony. FRCP 43.

   j. Injunctions and restraining orders. FRCP 65.

   k. Proceedings against a surety. FRCP 65.1.

   l. Hearing motions; Submission on briefs. FRCP 78.

2. *Local rules*

   a. Scope of the rules. NY R USDCTND L.R. 1.1.

   b. Complex and multi-district litigation. NY R USDCTND L.R. 3.3.

   c. Service and filing of papers. NY R USDCTND L.R. 5.1.

   d. Filing by facsimile or e-mail. NY R USDCTND L.R. 5.5.

   e. Motion practice. NY R USDCTND L.R. 7.1.

   f. Personal privacy protection. NY R USDCTND L.R. 8.1.

   g. Request for three-judge court. NY R USDCTND L.R. 9.1.

   h. Form of papers. NY R USDCTND L.R. 10.1.

   i. Settlement procedures. NY R USDCTND L.R. 68.2.

   j. Orders. NY R USDCTND L.R. 77.2.

   k. Motion days. NY R USDCTND L.R. 78.1.

   l. Appearance and withdrawal of attorney. NY R USDCTND L.R. 83.2.

   m. Arbitration. NY R USDCTND L.R. 83.7-1; NY R USDCTND L.R. 83.7-2; NY R USDCTND L.R. 83.7-3.

   n. Assisted mediation program. NY R USDCTND L.R. 83.8.

   o. Mediation. NY R USDCTND L.R. 83.11-1; NY R USDCTND L.R. 83.11-3.

   p. Early neutral evaluation. NY R USDCTND L.R. 83.12-1; NY R USDCTND L.R. 83.12-3.

   q. Administrative procedures for electronic case filing. NY R USDCTND CM/ECF.

   r. Case assignment plan for the Northern District of New York. [NY R USDCTND Order 12, as amended by NY ORDER 16-4201, effective March 24, 2015].

   s. Directing the expedited service of the summons and complaint and further directing the completion of FRCP 16 stipulation for the timely progression of civil actions. [NY R USDCTND Order 25, as amended by NY ORDER 16-4187, effective June 23, 2016].

   t. Mandatory mediation program. NY R USDCTND Order 47.

## J. Miscellaneous

**NOTE: Individual judges' rules may apply. For available judge-level information, refer to:**

DISTRICT JUDGE MAE A. D'AGOSTINO: [NY R USDCTND D'Agostino-Rules and Practices, as added by NY ORDER 16-4200, effective April 4, 2016].

DISTRICT JUDGE THOMAS J. McAVOY: NY R USDCTND McAvoy-Order.

# Requests, Notices and Applications
# Pretrial Conferences, Scheduling, Management

### Document Last Updated September 2016

**A. Checklist**

(I) ❑ Matters to be considered by parties for the pretrial conference

   (a) ❑ Documents to consider

      (1) ❑ Pretrial memorandum or statement

      (2) ❑ Cover letter authorizing e-mail or facsimile filing

      (3) ❑ Affidavit attesting to failed attempts to file electronically

      (4) ❑ Notice of conventional filing

      (5) ❑ CD/ROM with PDF of document(s)

      (6) ❑ English translation

      (7) ❑ Courtesy copies

      (8) ❑ Copies for three-judge court

   (b) ❑ Timing

      (1) ❑ The court determines at what stage in the action to hold a pretrial conference

(II) ❑ Matters to be considered by parties for the scheduling conference

   (a) ❑ Required documents

      (1) ❑ Case management plan

   (b) ❑ Supplemental documents

      (1) ❑ Request for scheduling conference

      (2) ❑ Cover letter authorizing e-mail or facsimile filing

      (3) ❑ Affidavit attesting to failed attempts to file electronically

      (4) ❑ Notice of conventional filing

      (5) ❑ CD/ROM with PDF of document(s)

      (6) ❑ English translation

      (7) ❑ Courtesy copies

      (8) ❑ Copies for three-judge court

   (c) ❑ Timing

      (1) ❑ If a scheduling conference is called, it is important to recognize that, unlike the ordinary pretrial conference, the scheduling conference occurs before the substantive issues have been defined and is directed toward organizing the processing of the action by setting deadlines for the completion of the various pretrial phases

      (2) ❑ Except in actions exempted under NY R USDCTND Order 25(II), or when otherwise ordered by the court, the parties shall, as soon as practicable, but no later than twenty-one (21) days before the FRCP 16 conference, confer to jointly address each item contained in the attached case management plan packet found in NY R USDCTND Order 25

      (3) ❑ The completed [case management] plan is to be filed with the clerk not later than seven (7) days prior to the conference date

(III) ❑ Matters to be considered by parties for the discovery planning conference

    (a) ❑ Required documents

        (1) ❑ Written report outlining proposed discovery plan

    (b) ❑ Supplemental documents

        (1) ❑ Cover letter authorizing e-mail or facsimile filing

        (2) ❑ Affidavit attesting to failed attempts to file electronically

        (3) ❑ Notice of conventional filing

        (4) ❑ CD/ROM with PDF of document(s)

        (5) ❑ English translation

        (6) ❑ Courtesy copies

        (7) ❑ Copies for three-judge court

    (c) ❑ Timing

        (1) ❑ Except in a proceeding exempted from initial disclosure under FRCP 26(a)(1)(B) or when the court orders otherwise, the parties must confer as soon as practicable—and in any event at least twenty-one (21) days before a scheduling conference is to be held or a scheduling order is due under FRCP 16(b)

        (2) ❑ Within fourteen (14) days after the conference, the attorneys of record are responsible for submitting a written report outlining the plan

## B. Timing

1. *Pretrial conferences, generally.* The court determines at what stage in the action to hold a pretrial conference. When only one conference is involved, the most favored practice seems to be to wait until after the case has been prepared for trial. FPP § 1524. Although there rarely will be any need to hold a conference in a relatively simple case until after the preliminary motions have been disposed of, the only inherently logical limitation on the court's discretion as to when to hold a conference is that it should not be held before all the necessary and indispensable parties are served. FPP § 1524.

2. *Scheduling conference.* If a scheduling conference is called, it is important to recognize that, unlike the ordinary pretrial conference, the scheduling conference occurs before the substantive issues have been defined and is directed toward organizing the processing of the action by setting deadlines for the completion of the various pretrial phases. FPP § 1522.1.

    a. *Case management conference.* Except in actions exempted under NY R USDCTND Order 25(II), or when otherwise ordered by the court, the parties shall, as soon as practicable, but no later than twenty-one (21) days before the FRCP 16 conference, confer to jointly address each item contained in the attached Case Management Plan packet found in NY R USDCTND Order 25. NY R USDCTND Order 25(XI).

    b. *Case management plan.* The completed [case management] plan is to be filed with the clerk not later than seven (7) days prior to the conference date. NY R USDCTND Order 25(XI).

3. *Discovery planning conference.* Except in a proceeding exempted from initial disclosure under FRCP 26(a)(1)(B) or when the court orders otherwise, the parties must confer as soon as practicable—and in any event at least twenty-one (21) days before a scheduling conference is to be held or a scheduling order is due under FRCP 16(b). FRCP 26(f)(1).

    a. *Submission of written report outlining proposed discovery plan.* The attorneys of record and all unrepresented parties that have appeared in the case are jointly responsible for arranging the conference, for attempting in good faith to agree on the proposed discovery plan, and for submitting to the court within fourteen (14) days after the conference a written report outlining the plan. FRCP 26(f)(2). The parties shall file their jointly-proposed plan, or if they cannot reach consensus, each party shall file its own proposed plan with the Clerk at least fourteen (14) business days prior to the scheduled pretrial conference. NY R USDCTND L.R. 16.1(c).

    b. *Expedited schedule.* If necessary to comply with its expedited schedule for FRCP 16(b) conferences, a court may by local rule: (1) require the parties' conference to occur less than twenty-one (21) days before the scheduling conference is held or a scheduling order is due under FRCP 16(b); and (2) require the written report outlining the discovery plan to be filed less than fourteen (14) days after the parties' conference, or excuse the parties from submitting a written report and permit them to report orally on their discovery plan at the FRCP 16(b) conference. FRCP 26(f)(4).

4. *Computation of time*

    a. *Computing time.* FRCP 6 applies in computing any time period specified in the Federal Rules of Civil Procedure, in any local rule or court order, or in any statute that does not specify a method of computing time. FRCP 6(a).

        i. *Period stated in days or a longer unit.* When the period is stated in days or a longer unit of time:

- Exclude the day of the event that triggers the period;
- Count every day, including intermediate Saturdays, Sundays, and legal holidays; and
- Include the last day of the period, but if the last day is a Saturday, Sunday, or legal holiday, the period continues to run until the end of the next day that is not a Saturday, Sunday, or legal holiday. FRCP 6(a)(1).

        ii. *Period stated in hours.* When the period is stated in hours:

- Begin counting immediately on the occurrence of the event that triggers the period;
- Count every hour, including hours during intermediate Saturdays, Sundays, and legal holidays; and
- If the period would end on a Saturday, Sunday, or legal holiday, the period continues to run until the same time on the next day that is not a Saturday, Sunday, or legal holiday. FRCP 6(a)(2).

        iii. *Inaccessibility of the clerk's office.* Unless the court orders otherwise, if the clerk's office is inaccessible:

- On the last day for filing under FRCP 6(a)(1), then the time for filing is extended to the first accessible day that is not a Saturday, Sunday, or legal holiday; or
- During the last hour for filing under FRCP 6(a)(2), then the time for filing is extended to the same time on the first accessible day that is not a Saturday, Sunday, or legal holiday. FRCP 6(a)(3).

        iv. *"Last day" defined.* Unless a different time is set by a statute, local rule, or court order, the last day ends:

- For electronic filing, at midnight in the court's time zone; and
- For filing by other means, when the clerk's office is scheduled to close. FRCP 6(a)(4).

        v. *"Next day" defined.* The "next day" is determined by continuing to count forward when the period is measured after an event and backward when measured before an event. FRCP 6(a)(5).

        vi. *"Legal holiday" defined.* "Legal holiday" means:

- The day set aside by statute for observing New Year's Day, Martin Luther King Jr.'s Birthday, Washington's Birthday, Memorial Day, Independence Day, Labor Day, Columbus Day, Veterans' Day, Thanksgiving Day, or Christmas Day;
- Any day declared a holiday by the President or Congress; and
- For periods that are measured after an event, any other day declared a holiday by the state where the district court is located. FRCP 6(a)(6).

    b. *Computation of electronic filing deadlines.* A document will be deemed timely filed if electronically filed prior to midnight Eastern Time. However, if the time of day is of the essence, the assigned judge may order that the document be filed by a time certain. NY R USDCTND CM/ECF(4)(4.3).

        i. *Technical failures.* A Filing User, whose filing is untimely as the result of a technical failure of the Court's CM/ECF site, may seek appropriate relief from the Court. However, Filing Users are cautioned that, in some circumstances, the Court lacks the authority to grant an extension of time to file (e.g., FRCP 6(b) of the Federal Rules of Civil Procedure). NY R USDCTND CM/ECF(10)(10.1).

- *Technical failure of the filing user's system.* Problems with the Filing User's system, such as phone line problems, problems with the Filing User's Internet Service Provider ("ISP"), or hardware or software problems, will not constitute a technical failure under these Administrative Procedures nor excuse an untimely filing. A Filing User who cannot file documents electronically because of a problem on the Filing User's system must file the documents' conventionally along with an affidavit explaining the reason for not filing the documents electronically. NY R USDCTND CM/ECF(10)(10.2).

c. *Extending time*

   i. *In general.* When an act may or must be done within a specified time, the court may, for good cause, extend the time:

- With or without motion or notice if the court acts, or if a request is made, before the original time or its extension expires; or

- On motion made after the time has expired if the party failed to act because of excusable neglect. FRCP 6(b)(1).

   ii. *Exceptions.* A court must not extend the time to act under FRCP 50(b), FRCP 50(d), FRCP 52(b), FRCP 59(b), FRCP 59(d), FRCP 59(e), and FRCP 60(b). FRCP 6(b)(2).

   iii. Refer to the United States District Court for the Northern District of New York KeyRules Motion for Continuance/Extension of Time document for more information on extending time.

d. *Additional time after certain kinds of service.* When a party may or must act within a specified time after service and service is made under FRCP 5(b)(2)(C), FRCP 5(b)(2)(D), FRCP 5(b)(2)(E), or FRCP 5(b)(2)(F), three (3) days are added after the period would otherwise expire under FRCP 6(a). FRCP 6(d).

   i. In accordance with FRCP 6(e), service by electronic means is treated the same as service by mail for purposes of adding three (3) days to the prescribed period to respond. NY R USDCTND CM/ECF(5)(5.4). [Editor's note: the reference to FRCP 6(e) is likely meant to be a reference to FRCP 6(d)].

5. *Individual judge practices.* Refer to the Miscellaneous section of this document for information on individual judge practices on timing of documents.

## C. General Requirements

1. *Pretrial conferences, generally.* This Court has found that the interests of justice are most effectively served by adopting a systematic, differential case management system that tailors the level of individualized and case- specific management to such criteria as case complexity, time required to prepare a case for trial, and availability of judicial and other resources. NY R USDCTND L.R. 16.1.

a. *Purposes of a pretrial conference.* FRCP 16 provides an important mechanism for carrying out one of the basic policies of the Federal Rules of Civil Procedure—the determination of disputes on their merits rather than on the basis of procedural niceties or tactical advantage. FPP § 1522. In any action, the court may order the attorneys and any unrepresented parties to appear for one or more pretrial conferences for such purposes as:

   i. Expediting disposition of the action;

   ii. Establishing early and continuing control so that the case will not be protracted because of lack of management;

   iii. Discouraging wasteful pretrial activities;

   iv. Improving the quality of the trial through more thorough preparation; and

   v. Facilitating settlement. FRCP 16(a).

b. *When appropriate.* FRCP 16 specifically provides that the court "may order the attorneys and any unrepresented parties to appear for one or more pretrial conferences." This language makes it clear that the utilization of the pretrial conference procedure lies within the discretion of the district court both as a matter of general policy and in terms of whether and when the rule should be invoked in a particular case. FPP § 1523; Mizwicki v. Helwig, 196 F.3d 828 (7th Cir. 1999). There is no requirement that any pretrial conferences be held or not held in certain types of actions. FPP § 1523.

    i.   Except for cases excluded under NY R USDCTND Order 25(II), an initial pretrial conference shall be scheduled in accordance with the time set forth in FRCP 16. The Clerk shall set the date of this conference upon the filing of the complaint. The purpose of this conference will be to prepare and adopt a case-specific management plan which will be memorialized in a case management order. See NY R USDCTND L.R. 16.1(d). NY R USDCTND L.R. 16.1(c).

c.   *Attendance at a pretrial conference.* A represented party must authorize at least one of its attorneys to make stipulations and admissions about all matters that can reasonably be anticipated for discussion at a pretrial conference. If appropriate, the court may require that a party or its representative be present or reasonably available by other means to consider possible settlement. FRCP 16(c)(1).

d.   *Matters for consideration at a pretrial conference.* At any pretrial conference, the court may consider and take appropriate action on the following matters:

    i.   Formulating and simplifying the issues, and eliminating frivolous claims or defenses;

    ii.   Amending the pleadings if necessary or desirable;

    iii.   Obtaining admissions and stipulations about facts and documents to avoid unnecessary proof, and ruling in advance on the admissibility of evidence;

    iv.   Avoiding unnecessary proof and cumulative evidence, and limiting the use of testimony under FRE 702;

    v.   Determining the appropriateness and timing of summary adjudication under FRCP 56;

    vi.   Controlling and scheduling discovery, including orders affecting disclosures and discovery under FRCP 26 and FRCP 29 through FRCP 37;

    vii.   Identifying witnesses and documents, scheduling the filing and exchange of any pretrial briefs, and setting dates for further conferences and for trial;

    viii.   Referring matters to a magistrate judge or a master;

    ix.   Settling the case and using special procedures to assist in resolving the dispute when authorized by statute or local rule;

    x.   Determining the form and content of the pretrial order;

    xi.   Disposing of pending motions;

    xii.   Adopting special procedures for managing potentially difficult or protracted actions that may involve complex issues, multiple parties, difficult legal questions, or unusual proof problems;

    xiii.   Ordering a separate trial under FRCP 42(b) of a claim, counterclaim, crossclaim, third-party claim, or particular issue;

    xiv.   Ordering the presentation of evidence early in the trial on a manageable issue that might, on the evidence, be the basis for a judgment as a matter of law under FRCP 50(a) or a judgment on partial findings under FRCP 52(c);

    xv.   Establishing a reasonable limit on the time allowed to present evidence; and

    xvi.   Facilitating in other ways the just, speedy, and inexpensive disposition of the action. FRCP 16(c)(2).

    xvii.   At the initial pretrial conference, the Court shall consider, and the parties shall be prepared to discuss, the following:

        •   Deadlines for joinder of parties, amendment of pleadings, completion of discovery, and filing of dispositive motions;

- Trial date;
- Requests for jury trial;
- Subject matter and personal jurisdiction;
- Factual and legal bases for claims and defenses;
- Factual and legal issues in dispute;
- Factual and legal issues upon which the parties can agree or which they can narrow through motion practice and which will expedite resolution of the dispute;
- Specific relief requested, including method for computing damages;
- Intended discovery and proposed methods to limit and/or decrease time and expense thereof;
- Suitability of case for voluntary arbitration;
- Measures for reducing length of trial;
- Related cases pending before this or other U.S. District Courts;
- Procedures for certifying class actions, if appropriate;
- Settlement prospects; and
- If the case is in the ADR track, choice of ADR method and estimated time for completion of ADR. NY R USDCTND L.R. 16.1(d).

e. *Pretrial orders.* After any conference under FRCP 16, the court should issue an order reciting the action taken. This order controls the course of the action unless the court modifies it. FRCP 16(d).

    i. *Uniform pretrial scheduling order.* Upon completion of the initial pretrial conference, the presiding judge may issue a Uniform Pretrial Scheduling Order setting forth deadlines for joinder of parties, amendment of pleadings, production of expert reports, completion of discovery, and filing of motions; a trial ready date; the requirements for all trial submissions; and if an ADR track case, the ADR method to be used and the deadline for completion of ADR. NY R USDCTND L.R. 16.1(e).

- *Submission of pretrial papers.* The parties shall file all pretrial submissions in accordance with the requirements of the Uniform Pretrial Scheduling Order unless the Court orders otherwise. NY R USDCTND L.R. 39.2.

f. *Sanctions.* On motion or on its own, the court may issue any just orders, including those authorized by FRCP 37(b)(2)(A)(ii) through FRCP 37(b)(2)(A)(vii), if a party or its attorney: (1) fails to appear at a scheduling or other pretrial conference; (2) is substantially unprepared to participate—or does not participate in good faith—in the conference; or (3) fails to obey a scheduling or other pretrial order. FRCP 16(f)(1). The Court shall strictly enforce any deadlines that it establishes in any case management order, and the Court shall not modify these, even upon stipulation of the parties, except upon a showing of good cause. NY R USDCTND L.R. 16.1(f).

    i. *Imposing fees and costs.* Instead of or in addition to any other sanction, the court must order the party, its attorney, or both to pay the reasonable expenses—including attorney's fees—incurred because of any noncompliance with FRCP 16, unless the noncompliance was substantially justified or other circumstances make an award of expenses unjust. FRCP 16(f)(2).

2. *Scheduling conference.* A scheduling conference may be requested by the judge or by the parties, but it is not mandatory. FPP § 1522.1.

    a. *Case management conference.* Except in actions exempted under NY R USDCTND Order 25(II), or when otherwise ordered by the court, the parties shall, as soon as practicable, but no later than twenty-one (21) days before the FRCP 16 conference, confer to jointly address each item contained in the attached Case Management Plan packet found in NY R USDCTND Order 25. The completed plan is to be filed with the clerk not later than seven (7) days prior to the conference date. The NOTICE setting the date, time, and location for the initial FRCP 16 conference with the court is included as part of this filing order. Mandatory disclosures under FRCP 26(a) shall be exchanged at least seven (7) days prior to the conference date, unless the parties have obtained prior approval from the assigned Magistrate Judge to extend that deadline. The Civil Justice Reform Act Plan of this court requires the court to set "early, firm" trial dates, such that the trial is scheduled to occur within eighteen (18) months after the filing of the complaint, unless a judicial officer certifies that (1) the demands of the case and its complexity make such a trial date incompatible with serving the ends of justice; or (2) the trial cannot reasonably be held within such time because of the complexity of the case or the number or complexity of pending criminal cases. NY R USDCTND Order 25(XI).

b. *Scheduling order.* Except in categories of actions exempted by local rule, the district judge—or a magistrate judge when authorized by local rule—must issue a scheduling order: (1) after receiving the parties' report under FRCP 26(f); or (2) after consulting with the parties' attorneys and any unrepresented parties at a scheduling conference. FRCP 16(b)(1).

   i. *Required contents of the order.* The scheduling order must limit the time to join other parties, amend the pleadings, complete discovery, and file motions. FRCP 16(b)(3)(A).

   ii. *Permitted contents of the order.* The scheduling order may:

   - Modify the timing of disclosures under FRCP 26(a) and FRCP 26(e)(1);

   - Modify the extent of discovery;

   - Provide for disclosure, discovery, or preservation of electronically stored information;

   - Include any agreements the parties reach for asserting claims of privilege or of protection as trial-preparation material after information is produced, including agreements reached under FRE 502;

   - Direct that before moving for an order relating to discovery, the movant must request a conference with the court;

   - Set dates for pretrial conferences and for trial; and

   - Include other appropriate matters. FRCP 16(b)(3)(B).

c. *Time to issue.* The judge must issue the scheduling order as soon as practicable, but unless the judge finds good cause for delay, the judge must issue it within the earlier of ninety (90) days after any defendant has been served with the complaint or sixty (60) days after any defendant has appeared. FRCP 16(b)(2).

d. *Modifying a schedule.* A schedule may be modified only for good cause and with the judge's consent. FRCP 16(b)(4).

3. *Final pretrial conference.* The court may hold a final pretrial conference to formulate a trial plan, including a plan to facilitate the admission of evidence. FRCP 16(e).

   a. *Timing and attendance.* The conference must be held as close to the start of trial as is reasonable, and must be attended by at least one attorney who will conduct the trial for each party and by any unrepresented party. FRCP 16(e).

   b. *Modification of final pretrial order.* The court may modify the order issued after a final pretrial conference only to prevent manifest injustice. FRCP 16(e).

4. *Discovery planning conference*

   a. *Conference content.* In conferring, the parties must consider the nature and basis of their claims and defenses and the possibilities for promptly settling or resolving the case; make or arrange for the disclosures required by FRCP 26(a)(1); discuss any issues about preserving discoverable information; and develop a proposed discovery plan. FRCP 26(f)(2).

   i. In order to facilitate the adoption of such a [case management] plan, prior to the scheduled conference, counsel for all parties shall confer among themselves as FRCP 26(f) requires and shall use the Civil Case Management Plan form contained in the NY R USDCTND Order 25 filing packet. NY R USDCTND L.R. 16.1(c).

   b. *Parties' responsibilities.* The attorneys of record and all unrepresented parties that have appeared in the case are jointly responsible for arranging the conference, for attempting in good faith to agree on the proposed discovery plan, and for submitting to the court within fourteen (14) days after the conference a written report outlining the plan. The court may order the parties or attorneys to attend the conference in person. FRCP 26(f)(2). The parties shall file their jointly-proposed plan, or if they cannot reach consensus, each party shall file its own proposed plan with the Clerk at least fourteen (14) business days prior to the scheduled pretrial conference. NY R USDCTND L.R. 16.1(c).

    i.    FRCP 26(d), which prohibits discovery prior to a meeting and conference between the parties, and FRCP 26(f), which directs parties to meet and confer with each other relative to the nature and basis of claims and defenses to a lawsuit, shall not apply to any action in which a party is incarcerated. NY R USDCTND L.R. 26.4.

  c.  *Discovery plan.* A discovery plan must state the parties' views and proposals on:

    i.    What changes should be made in the timing, form, or requirement for disclosures under FRCP 26(a), including a statement of when initial disclosures were made or will be made;

    ii.   The subjects on which discovery may be needed, when discovery should be completed, and whether discovery should be conducted in phases or be limited to or focused on particular issues;

    iii.  Any issues about disclosure, discovery, or preservation of electronically stored information, including the form or forms in which it should be produced;

    iv.  Any issues about claims of privilege or of protection as trial-preparation materials, including—if the parties agree on a procedure to assert these claims after production—whether to ask the court to include their agreement in an order under FRE 502;

    v.   What changes should be made in the limitations on discovery imposed under the Federal Rules of Civil Procedure or by local rule, and what other limitations should be imposed; and

    vi.  Any other orders that the court should issue under FRCP 26(c) or under FRCP 16(b) and FRCP 26(c). FRCP 26(f)(3).

5.  *Settlement conference.* The parties are advised that the court will honor a request for a settlement conference at any stage of the proceeding. A representative of the parties with the authority to bind the parties must be present with counsel or available by telephone at any settlement conference. NY R USDCTND Order 25(VIII)(A).

6.  *Complex and multi-district litigation.* If the assigned judge determines, in his or her discretion, that the case is of such a complex nature that it cannot reasonably be trial ready within eighteen (18) months from the date the complaint is filed, the assigned judge may design and issue a particularized case management order that will move the case to trial as quickly as the complexity of the case allows. NY R USDCTND L.R. 3.3(a). The parties shall promptly notify the Court in writing if any action commenced is appropriate for multi-district litigation. NY R USDCTND L.R. 3.3(b).

7.  *Appearances.* An attorney appearing for a party in a civil case shall promptly file with the Clerk a written notice of appearance; however, an attorney does not need to file a notice of appearance if the attorney who would be filing the notice of appearance is the same individual who has signed the complaint, notice of removal, pre-answer motion, or answer. NY R USDCTND L.R. 83.2(a). For more information, refer to NY R USDCTND L.R. 83.2.

8.  *Related cases.* A civil case is "related" to another civil case for purposes of this guideline when, because of the similarity of facts and legal issues or because the cases arise from the same transactions or events, a substantial saving of judicial resources is likely to result from assigning the cases to the same Judge and Magistrate Judge. NY R USDCTND Order 12(G)(2). A civil case shall not be deemed related to another civil case merely because the civil case: (1) involves similar legal issues, or (2) involves the same parties. NY R USDCTND Order 12(G)(3). Presumptively, and subject to the power of a Judge to determine otherwise pursuant to NY R USDCTND Order 12(G)(5), civil cases shall not be deemed to be "related" unless both cases are still pending before the Court. NY R USDCTND Order 12(G)(4).

  a.  *New filings.* If an attorney or filing party indicates on the Civil Cover Sheet that a case is related to an earlier filed case, the Clerk shall instruct the filing party to file a notice of related cases. The allegedly related cases will be submitted by the Clerk to the Judge to whom the earliest filed case is assigned, who shall advise the Clerk whether such cases are related. NY R USDCTND Order 12(G)(1).

b. *Judicial determination that civil cases are "related."* Except for the cases described in the final sentence of NY R USDCTND Order 12(G)(6), all civil cases shall be randomly assigned when they are filed. Other than the cases described in the final sentence of NY R USDCTND Order 12(G)(6), civil cases shall not be deemed to be "related" for purposes of this guideline at the instance of any litigant or attorney unless and until there has been a determination by a Judge of this Court that the standard of NY R USDCTND Order 12(G)(2) is met. NY R USDCTND Order 12(G)(5).

    i. *Notice of related filing.* Any party may apply for such a determination by filing with the Clerk a notice of related filing, which should include an explanation as to why the standard of NY R USDCTND Order 12(G)(2) is met. A form for this purpose is available on the Court's website. A copy of the notice shall be served on all other parties who have appeared. Such an application must be made after the date when at least a majority of the defendants have been served with the complaint. Before making such an application, the applicant must confer in good faith with all other parties in an effort to reach an agreement on whether or not the case is "related". After such an application is made, any other party may serve and file within seven (7) calendar days a letter of no more than two (2) pages supporting or opposing the application. The application to have the case assigned to another Judge shall be presented to the Judge with the earliest filed case for decision on whether the action(s) should be reassigned as related cases. The Judge with the earliest filed case may then enter an order in the case at bar, either deeming the case to be related and directing the Clerk to reassign the action, or denying the application for reassignment. Any disputes concerning the assignment of related cases will be referred to the Chief Judge for resolution. NY R USDCTND Order 12(G)(5).

c. For more information on related cases, refer to NY R USDCTND Order 12(G).

9. *Alternative dispute resolution (ADR).* It is the mission of this court to do everything it can to help parties resolve their disputes as fairly, quickly, and efficiently as possible. NY R USDCTND Order 25(VIII).

a. *Arbitration.* NY R USDCTND L.R. 83.7 governs the consensual arbitration program for referral of civil actions to court-annexed arbitration. It may remain in effect until further order of the Court. Its purpose is to establish a less formal procedure for the just, efficient and economical resolution of disputes, while preserving the right to a full trial on demand. NY R USDCTND L.R. 83.7-1.

    i. *Actions subject to arbitration.* The Clerk shall notify the parties in all civil cases, except as the Local Rules of Practice for the United States District Court for the Northern District of New York otherwise direct, that they may consent to non-binding arbitration under NY R US-DCTND L.R. 83.7. The notice shall be furnished to the parties at pretrial/scheduling conferences or shall be included with pretrial conference notices and instructions. Consent to arbitration under NY R USDCTND L.R. 83.7 shall be discussed at the pretrial/scheduling conference. No party or attorney shall be prejudiced for refusing to participate in arbitration. The Court shall allow the referral of any civil action pending before it to the arbitration process if the parties consent. The plaintiff shall be responsible for securing the execution of a consent form by the parties and for filing the form with the Clerk within fourteen (14) days after the parties receive the form. The parties shall freely and knowingly enter into the consent. NY R USDCTND L.R. 83.7-2.

    ii. *Referral to arbitration.* The Clerk shall refer every action subject to NY R USDCTND L.R. 83.7 to arbitration in accordance with the procedures under NY R USDCTND L.R. 83.7 twenty-one (21) days after the filing of the last responsive pleading or within twenty-one (21) days of the filing of a stipulated consent order referring the action to arbitration, whichever event occurs last, except as otherwise provided. If any party notices a motion to dismiss under the provisions of FRCP 12(a) and/or FRCP 12(b), or a motion to join necessary parties pursuant to the Federal Rules of Civil Procedure prior to the expiration of the twenty-one (21) day period, the assigned judge shall hear the motion and further proceedings under NY R USDCTND L.R. 83.7 shall be deferred pending decision on the motion. If the Court does not dismiss the action on the motion, the Court shall refer the action to arbitration twenty-one (21) days after the filing of the decision. NY R USDCTND L.R. 83.7-3(a). Motions for summary judgment pursuant to

FRCP 56 shall be filed and served within twenty-one (21) days following the close of discovery. The filing of a FRCP 56 motion shall defer further proceedings under NY R USDCTND L.R. 83.7 pending decision on the motion. NY R USDCTND L.R. 83.7-3(a).

- *Relief from referral.* Any party shall request relief from the operation of NY R USDCTND L.R. 83.7 by filing with the Court a motion for the relief within twenty-one (21) days after entry of the initial stipulated consent order which refers the case for arbitration. The assigned judge shall, sua sponte, exempt an action from the application of NY R USDCTND L.R. 83.7 where the objectives of arbitration would not be realized because (1) the case involves complex or novel legal issues, (2) legal issues predominate over factual issues, or (3) for other good cause. NY R USDCTND L.R. 83.7-3(c).

iii. For more information on arbitration, refer to NY R USDCTND L.R. 83.7.

b. *Mediation.* The purpose of NY R USDCTND L.R. 83.11 is to provide a supplementary procedure to the Court's existing alternative dispute resolution procedures. NY R USDCTND L.R. 83.11 provides for an earlier resolution of civil disputes resulting in savings of time and cost to litigants and the Court without sacrificing the quality of justice rendered or the right of litigants to a full trial on all issues not resolved through mediation. NY R USDCTND L.R. 83.11-1(a). Mediation is a process by which an impartial person, the mediator, facilitates communication between disputing parties to promote understanding, reconciliation and settlement. The mediator is an advocate for settlement and uses the mediation process to help the parties fully explore any potential area of agreement. The mediator does not serve as a judge or arbitrator and has no authority to render any decision on any disputed issue or to force a settlement. The parties themselves are responsible for negotiating any resolution(s) to their dispute. NY R USDCTND L.R. 83.11-1(b).

i. *Actions subject to mediation.* The Court may refer any civil action (or any portion thereof) to mediation under NY R USDCTND L.R. 83.11: (1) by order of referral; or (2) on the motion of any party; or (3) by consent of the parties. NY R USDCTND L.R. 83.11-3(a).

- *Withdrawal from mediation.* The parties may withdraw from mediation any civil action or claim that the Court refers to mediation pursuant to NY R USDCTND L.R. 83.11-3 by application to the assigned judge at least ten (10) days prior to the scheduled mediation session. NY R USDCTND L.R. 83.11-3(b).

ii. *Mandatory mediation program.* The United States District Court for the Northern District of New York has adopted this Mandatory Mediation Plan. The paid Mediation Program is designed to provide quicker, less expensive and potentially more satisfying alternatives to continuing litigation, without impairing the quality of justice or the right to trial. NY R USDCTND Order 47(1)(1.2)(A). This Mandatory Mediation Plan applies to civil actions pending as well as newly filed actions, except as otherwise indicated in NY R USDCTND Order 47. The Local Rules for voluntary mediation will apply only to Pro Se Cases that proceed through the Assisted Mediation Program. NY R USDCTND Order 47(1)(1.2)(B).

- *Referral into the pilot mandatory mediation program for new cases.* All civil cases shall be referred automatically into the Mandatory Mediation Program. Notice of the Mandatory Mediation requirements will be provided to all parties immediately upon the filing of a complaint and answer or a notice of removal. ADR intervention will be scheduled at the conference held pursuant to NY R USDCTND L.R. 16.1. NY R USDCTND Order 47(2)(2.1)(A). For a list of categories of actions exempted from automatic referral, refer to NY R USDCTND Order 47(2)(2.1)(A).

- *Referral into the pilot mandatory mediation program for pending cases.* The assigned Judge or Magistrate Judge on any pending civil case may, sua sponte or with status conference, issue an order referring the case into the Mandatory Mediation Program. The order shall specify a date on which the ADR intervention is to be completed. NY R USDCTND Order 47(2)(2.1)(B).

- *Referral into the pilot mandatory mediation program by stipulation.* A case may be referred into the Mandatory Mediation Program by stipulation of all parties. Stipulations shall be filed and shall designate the time frame within which the ADR process will be completed. Stipulations are presumed acceptable unless the assigned Judge or Magistrate Judge determines that the interests of justice are not served. NY R USDCTND Order 47(2)(2.1)(C).

- *Relief from referral.* Motions to opt out of the program will be addressed by the assigned Magistrate Judge at the FRCP 16 conference. NY R USDCTND Order 47(2)(2.2)(A). Opting Out Motions shall be granted only for "good cause" shown. Inconvenience, travel costs, attorney fees or other costs shall not constitute "good cause." A party seeking relief from the Mandatory Mediation Program must set forth the reasons why Mandatory Mediation has no reasonable chance of being productive. NY R USDCTND Order 47(2)(2.2)(B). The assigned Magistrate Judge may, sua sponte, exempt any case from the Court's Mandatory Mediation Program. NY R USDCTND Order 47(2)(2.2)(C).

iii. *Assisted mediation program.* The Court may assign specially trained pro bono Special Mediation Counsel to assist pro se civilian litigants with preparing for and participating in mediation. The Assisted Mediation Program is open to civilian pro se parties to actions in the Northern District of New York. The assigned judge or magistrate judge determines if the case would benefit from mediation and would also benefit from the assignment of Special Mediation Counsel to assist the pro se party with the mediation process. NY R USDCTND L.R. 83.8(a). Appointment of Special Mediation Counsel is in no way guaranteed, even if the action is referred to the court-annexed mediation program. Appointment is at the sole discretion of the presiding judge. NY R USDCTND L.R. 83.8(a).

- *Referral to assisted mediation program.* If the court determines that referral to the Assisted Mediation Program is appropriate, the Court shall enter an order of reference to the Assisted Mediation Program. NY R USDCTND L.R. 83.8(b).

iv. For more information on mediation, refer to NY R USDCTND L.R. 83.11 and NY R USDCTND Order 47.

c. *Early neutral evaluation (ENE).* Early neutral evaluation (ENE) is a process in which parties obtain from an experienced neutral (an "evaluator") a nonbinding, reasoned, oral evaluation of the merits of the case. The first step in the ENE process involves the Court appointing an evaluator who has expertise in the area of law in the case. After the parties exchange essential information and position statements early in the pretrial period (usually within one hundred fifty (150) to two hundred (200) days after a complaint has been filed), the evaluator convenes an ENE session that typically lasts about two hours. At the ENE meeting, each side briefly presents the factual and legal basis of its position. The evaluator may ask questions of the parties and help them identify the main issues in dispute and the areas of agreement. The evaluator may also help the parties explore options for settlement. If settlement does not occur, the evaluator then offers an opinion as to the settlement value of the case, including the likelihood of liability and the likely range of damages. With the benefit of this assessment, the parties are again encouraged to discuss settlement, with or without the evaluator's assistance. The parties may also explore ways to narrow the issues in dispute, exchange information about the case or otherwise prepare efficiently for trial. NY R USDCTND L.R. 83.12-1.

i. *Actions subject to early neutral evaluation.* The Court may refer any civil action (or any portion thereof) to ENE under NY R USDCTND L.R. 83.12: (1) by order of referral; (2) on the motion of any party; or (3) by consent of the parties. NY R USDCTND L.R. 83.12-3(a).

- *Withdrawal from the ENE process.* The parties may withdraw any civil action or claim that the Court has referred to the ENE Process pursuant to NY R USDCTND L.R. 83.12-3 by application to the assigned judge at least ten (10) days before the scheduled evaluation session. NY R USDCTND L.R. 83.12-3(b).

ii. For more information on early neutral evaluation (ENE), refer to NY R USDCTND L.R. 83.12.

10. *Settlement procedures.* On notice to the Court or the Clerk that the parties have settled an action, and upon confirmation of the settlement by all parties, the Court may issue a judgment dismissing the action by reason of settlement. The Court shall issue the order without prejudice to the parties' right to secure reinstatement of the case within thirty (30) days after the date of judgment by making a showing that the settlement was not, in fact, consummated. NY R USDCTND L.R. 68.2(a). If the Court decides not to

follow the procedures set forth in NY R USDCTND L.R. 68.2(a), the parties shall file within thirty (30) days of the notification to the Court, unless otherwise directed by written order, such notices, stipulations and/or motions as are necessary to terminate the action. If the required documents are not filed within the thirty (30) day period, the Clerk shall place the action on the dismissal calendar. NY R USDCTND L.R. 68.2(b).

11. *Sanctions and penalties for noncompliance.* Failure of an attorney or of a party to comply with any provision of the Local Rules of Practice for the United States District Court for the Northern District of New York, General Orders of this District, Orders of the Court, or the Federal Rules of Civil Procedure shall be a ground for imposition of sanctions. NY R USDCTND L.R. 1.1(d).

12. *Individual judge practices.* Refer to the Miscellaneous section of this document for information on individual judge practices on general requirements for documents.

## D. Documents

1. *Pretrial conference*

   a. *Documents to consider*

      i. *Pretrial memorandum or statement.* Even though it is not specifically mentioned in FRCP 16, most courts require the attorney for each side to file a pretrial memorandum or statement prior to the conference, which, if adopted by the court, may be binding at trial. FPP § 1524. The purpose of the memorandum is to reveal the lawyer's theory of the case and the issues counsel believes are in contention in order to aid the court in determining what matters should be considered at the conference itself. FPP § 1524; Manbeck v. Ostrowski, 384 F.2d 970 (D.C. Cir. 1967).

      ii. *Cover letter authorizing e-mail or facsimile filing.* Neither the Court nor the Clerk's Office will accept for filing any facsimile or e-mail transmission without prior authorization from the Court. The party using facsimile or e-mail transmissions to file its papers must accompany any such documents with a cover letter stating that the Court authorized such transmissions and the date on which the Court provided that authorization. Violations of NY R USDCTND L.R. 5.5 subject the offending party to the Court's full disciplinary powers. NY R USDCTND L.R. 5.5.

      iii. *Affidavit attesting to failed attempts to file electronically.* If the Court's CM/ECF site experiences a technical failure, a Filing User may submit documents to the Court that day in an alternate manner provided that the documents are accompanied by the Filing User's affidavit stating that the Filing User attempted to file electronically at least two times in one (1) hour increments after 10:00 a.m. that day. The following methods are acceptable alternate means for filing documents in case of a technical failure: (1) via electronic mail in a PDF attachment sent to the e-mail address for technical failures; or (2) in person, by bringing the document to the Clerk's Office on paper accompanied by a CD/ROM that contains the document in .pdf format. NY R USDCTND CM/ECF(10)(10.1).

         - A Filing User who cannot file documents electronically because of a problem on the Filing User's system must file the documents' conventionally along with an affidavit explaining the reason for not filing the documents electronically. NY R USDCTND CM/ECF(10)(10.2).

      iv. *Notice of conventional filing.* If the Clerk's Office grants permission to conventionally file the document, the Filing User shall electronically file a notice of conventional filing for the documents. More information regarding this process can be obtained from the Court's web page. NY R USDCTND CM/ECF(4)(4.5).

      v. *CD/ROM with PDF of document(s).* If the Court grants permission to file a document traditionally, the attorney must submit the documents for filing to the Clerk's Office on CD/ROM in .pdf or pdf.A format. NY R USDCTND CM/ECF(2).

      vi. *English translation.* The Court conducts its reviews and deliberations in English. Unless otherwise directed by the Court, any document that a party transmits to the Court (including one in the record on appeal) that is in a language other than English must be accompanied by an English translation that the translator has certified as true and accurate, pursuant to 28 U.S.C.A.

§ 1746. NY R USDCTND L.R. 10.1(e). For more information, refer to NY R USDCTND L.R. 10.1(e).

    vii. *Courtesy copies.* The Court may require that courtesy copies of electronically filed documents be submitted for its review and may amend these Administrative Procedures (NY R USDCTND CM/ECF) at any time without prior notice. NY R USDCTND CM/ECF(2).

    viii. *Copies for three-judge court.* On the convening of a three-judge court, the parties shall make three (3) copies of all non-electronically filed pleadings, motion papers, and memoranda of law available to the Clerk for distribution. NY R USDCTND L.R. 9.1.

2. *Scheduling conference*

  a. *Required documents*

    i. *Case management plan.* The completed [case management] plan is to be filed with the clerk not later than seven (7) days prior to the conference date. NY R USDCTND Order 25(XI).

  b. *Supplemental documents*

    i. *Request for scheduling conference.* A scheduling conference may be requested by the judge or by the parties, but it is not mandatory. FPP § 1522.1.

    ii. *Cover letter authorizing e-mail or facsimile filing.* Neither the Court nor the Clerk's Office will accept for filing any facsimile or e-mail transmission without prior authorization from the Court. The party using facsimile or e-mail transmissions to file its papers must accompany any such documents with a cover letter stating that the Court authorized such transmissions and the date on which the Court provided that authorization. Violations of NY R USDCTND L.R. 5.5 subject the offending party to the Court's full disciplinary powers. NY R USDCTND L.R. 5.5.

    iii. *Affidavit attesting to failed attempts to file electronically.* If the Court's CM/ECF site experiences a technical failure, a Filing User may submit documents to the Court that day in an alternate manner provided that the documents are accompanied by the Filing User's affidavit stating that the Filing User attempted to file electronically at least two times in one (1) hour increments after 10:00 a.m. that day. The following methods are acceptable alternate means for filing documents in case of a technical failure: (1) via electronic mail in a PDF attachment sent to the e-mail address for technical failures; or (2) in person, by bringing the document to the Clerk's Office on paper accompanied by a CD/ROM that contains the document in .pdf format. NY R USDCTND CM/ECF(10)(10.1).

      • A Filing User who cannot file documents electronically because of a problem on the Filing User's system must file the documents' conventionally along with an affidavit explaining the reason for not filing the documents electronically. NY R USDCTND CM/ECF(10)(10.2).

    iv. *Notice of conventional filing.* If the Clerk's Office grants permission to conventionally file the document, the Filing User shall electronically file a notice of conventional filing for the documents. More information regarding this process can be obtained from the Court's web page. NY R USDCTND CM/ECF(4)(4.5).

    v. *CD/ROM with PDF of document(s).* If the Court grants permission to file a document traditionally, the attorney must submit the documents for filing to the Clerk's Office on CD/ROM in .pdf or pdf.A format. NY R USDCTND CM/ECF(2).

    vi. *English translation.* The Court conducts its reviews and deliberations in English. Unless otherwise directed by the Court, any document that a party transmits to the Court (including one in the record on appeal) that is in a language other than English must be accompanied by an English translation that the translator has certified as true and accurate, pursuant to 28 U.S.C.A. § 1746. NY R USDCTND L.R. 10.1(e). For more information, refer to NY R USDCTND L.R. 10.1(e).

    vii. *Courtesy copies.* The Court may require that courtesy copies of electronically filed documents be submitted for its review and may amend these Administrative Procedures (NY R USDCTND CM/ECF) at any time without prior notice. NY R USDCTND CM/ECF(2).

viii. *Copies for three-judge court.* On the convening of a three-judge court, the parties shall make three (3) copies of all non-electronically filed pleadings, motion papers, and memoranda of law available to the Clerk for distribution. NY R USDCTND L.R. 9.1.

3. *Discovery planning conference*

   a. *Required documents*

      i. *Written report outlining proposed discovery plan.* Refer to the General Requirements section of this document for information on the parties' responsibilities for submitting a written report outlining the proposed discovery plan.

   b. *Supplemental documents*

      i. *Cover letter authorizing e-mail or facsimile filing.* Neither the Court nor the Clerk's Office will accept for filing any facsimile or e-mail transmission without prior authorization from the Court. The party using facsimile or e-mail transmissions to file its papers must accompany any such documents with a cover letter stating that the Court authorized such transmissions and the date on which the Court provided that authorization. Violations of NY R USDCTND L.R. 5.5 subject the offending party to the Court's full disciplinary powers. NY R USDCTND L.R. 5.5.

      ii. *Affidavit attesting to failed attempts to file electronically.* If the Court's CM/ECF site experiences a technical failure, a Filing User may submit documents to the Court that day in an alternate manner provided that the documents are accompanied by the Filing User's affidavit stating that the Filing User attempted to file electronically at least two times in one (1) hour increments after 10:00 a.m. that day. The following methods are acceptable alternate means for filing documents in case of a technical failure: (1) via electronic mail in a PDF attachment sent to the e-mail address for technical failures; or (2) in person, by bringing the document to the Clerk's Office on paper accompanied by a CD/ROM that contains the document in .pdf format. NY R USDCTND CM/ECF(10)(10.1).

         • A Filing User who cannot file documents electronically because of a problem on the Filing User's system must file the documents' conventionally along with an affidavit explaining the reason for not filing the documents electronically. NY R USDCTND CM/ECF(10)(10.2).

      iii. *Notice of conventional filing.* If the Clerk's Office grants permission to conventionally file the document, the Filing User shall electronically file a notice of conventional filing for the documents. More information regarding this process can be obtained from the Court's web page. NY R USDCTND CM/ECF(4)(4.5).

      iv. *CD/ROM with PDF of document(s).* If the Court grants permission to file a document traditionally, the attorney must submit the documents for filing to the Clerk's Office on CD/ROM in .pdf or pdf.A format. NY R USDCTND CM/ECF(2).

      v. *English translation.* The Court conducts its reviews and deliberations in English. Unless otherwise directed by the Court, any document that a party transmits to the Court (including one in the record on appeal) that is in a language other than English must be accompanied by an English translation that the translator has certified as true and accurate, pursuant to 28 U.S.C.A. § 1746. NY R USDCTND L.R. 10.1(e). For more information, refer to NY R USDCTND L.R. 10.1(e).

      vi. *Courtesy copies.* The Court may require that courtesy copies of electronically filed documents be submitted for its review and may amend these Administrative Procedures (NY R USDCTND CM/ECF) at any time without prior notice. NY R USDCTND CM/ECF(2).

      vii. *Copies for three-judge court.* On the convening of a three-judge court, the parties shall make three (3) copies of all non-electronically filed pleadings, motion papers, and memoranda of law available to the Clerk for distribution. NY R USDCTND L.R. 9.1.

4. *Individual judge practices.* Refer to the Miscellaneous section of this document for information on individual judge practices on required documents.

# E. Format

1. *Form of documents.* The rules governing captions and other matters of form in pleadings apply to motions

and other papers. FRCP 7(b)(2). All pleadings and other papers shall be served and filed in accordance with the Federal Rules of Civil Procedure and shall be in the form prescribed by NY R USDCTND L.R. 10.1. NY R USDCTND L.R. 5.1(a).

a. *Form, generally.* All pleadings, motions, and other documents that a party presents for filing, whether in paper form or in electronic form, shall meet the following requirements:

   i. *Font size.* All text, whether in the body of the document or in footnotes, must be a minimum of twelve (12) point type. NY R USDCTND L.R. 10.1(a)(1).

   ii. *Margins.* All documents must have one (1) inch margins on all four sides of the page. NY R USDCTND L.R. 10.1(a)(2).

   iii. *Spacing.* All text in the body of the document must be double-spaced. NY R USDCTND L.R. 10.1(a)(3).

   - The text in block quotations and footnotes may be single-spaced. NY R USDCTND L.R. 10.1(a)(4).

   iv. *Page numbering.* Pages must be consecutively numbered. NY R USDCTND L.R. 10.1(a)(7).

   v. *Circumventing formatting limitations*

   - Extensive footnotes must not be used to circumvent page limitations. NY R USDCTND L.R. 10.1(a)(5).

   - Compacted or other compressed printing features must not be used. NY R USDCTND L.R. 10.1(a)(6).

b. *Additional requirements for paper filing.* Additional requirements for all pleadings, motions, and other documents that a party presents for filing in paper form:

   i. *Paper size.* All documents must be on eight and one-half by eleven (8-1/2 x 11) inch white paper of good quality. NY R USDCTND L.R. 10.1(b)(1).

   ii. *Text.* All text must be plainly and legibly written, typewritten, printed or reproduced without erasures or interlineations materially defacing them. NY R USDCTND L.R. 10.1(b)(2).

   iii. *Ink.* All documents must be in black or blue ink. NY R USDCTND L.R. 10.1(b)(3).

   iv. *Binding.* Pages of all documents must be stapled (or in some other way fastened) together. NY R USDCTND L.R. 10.1(b)(4).

   v. *Single-sided paper.* All documents must be single-sided. NY R USDCTND L.R. 10.1(b)(5).

   vi. *Electronic submission.* The Court, at its discretion, may require the electronic submission of any document in a WordPerfect-compatible format. NY R USDCTND L.R. 10.1(b)(6).

   vii. *Rejection of document.* The Court may reject documents that do not comply with the above-listed requirements. NY R USDCTND L.R. 10.1(b).

c. *Caption; Names of parties.* Every pleading must have a caption with the court's name, a title, a file number, and a FRCP 7(a) designation. The title of the complaint must name all the parties; the title of other pleadings, after naming the first party on each side, may refer generally to other parties. FRCP 10(a). Each document must contain a caption for the specific case to which it pertains. The caption must include the title of the Court, the title of the action, the civil action number of the case, the initials of the assigned judge(s), and the name or nature of the paper in sufficient detail for identification. If a litigant has more than one action pending in this Court, any and all papers filed in a case must contain and pertain to one civil action number, unless the civil actions have been consolidated by the Court. Any motion or other papers purporting to relate to more than one action will not be accepted for filing and may be stricken by the Court. NY R USDCTND L.R. 10.1(c)(1) shall not apply, as noted in NY R USDCTND L.R. 10.1(c), to notices of change of address filed by attorneys of record and pro se litigants. The parties must separately caption affidavits and declarations and must not physically attach them to the Notice of Motion or Memorandum of Law. NY R USDCTND L.R. 10.1(c)(1).

d. *Paragraphs; Separate statements.* A party must state its claims or defenses in numbered paragraphs, each limited as far as practicable to a single set of circumstances. A later pleading may refer by number to a paragraph in an earlier pleading. If doing so would promote clarity, each claim founded on a separate transaction or occurrence—and each defense other than a denial—must be stated in a separate count or defense. FRCP 10(b).

e. *Adoption by reference; Exhibits.* A statement in a pleading may be adopted by reference elsewhere in the same pleading or in any other pleading or motion. A copy of a written instrument that is an exhibit to a pleading is a part of the pleading for all purposes. FRCP 10(c).

f. *Citation of local rules.* These are the Local Rules of Practice for the United States District Court for the Northern District of New York. They shall be cited as "L.R. ___." NY R USDCTND L.R. 1.1(a).

g. *Acceptance by the clerk.* The clerk must not refuse to file a paper solely because it is not in the form prescribed by the Federal Rules of Civil Procedure or by a local rule or practice. FRCP 5(d)(4).

2. *Form of electronic documents.* All pleadings, motions, and other documents that a party presents for filing, whether in paper form or in electronic form, shall meet the requirements in NY R USDCTND L.R. 10.1(a). NY R USDCTND L.R. 10.1(a). Refer above for more information.

a. *Attachments and exhibits.* A Filing User must submit in electronic form all documents referenced as exhibits or attachments in accordance with the Court's CM/ECF Users Manual unless the Court otherwise orders. A Filing User shall submit as exhibits or attachments only those excerpts of the referenced documents that are directly germane to the matter under the Court's consideration. Excerpted material must be clearly and prominently identified as such. Filing Users who file excerpts of documents as exhibits or attachments under these Administrative Procedures (NY R USDCTND CM/ECF) do so without prejudice to their right to timely file additional excerpts or the complete document. Responding parties may also timely file the complete document or additional excerpts that they believe are directly germane to the matter under the Court's consideration. NY R USDCTND CM/ECF(4)(4.4).

 i. All attachments must be described in sufficient detail so the Court and opposing counsel can easily identify and distinguish the filed attachments. Vague or general descriptions are insufficient (i.e., "Exhibit 1"). Rather, each attachment shall have a descriptive title identifying, with specificity, the document that is being filed (i.e., "Exhibit 12 Mulligan County Fire Investigation Report.") Failure to adequately describe attachments may result in the document being rejected by the Court. NY R USDCTND CM/ECF(4)(4.4).

b. *Large documents.* For information on the electronic filing of large documents, please consult the Court's CM/ECF Users Manual, which is available on the Court's web page. NY R USDCTND CM/ECF(4)(4.5).

 i. A party who believes a document is too lengthy to electronically image, i.e., "scan," may contact the Clerk's Office for permission to file that document conventionally. If the Clerk's Office grants permission to conventionally file the document, the Filing User shall electronically file a notice of conventional filing for the documents. More information regarding this process can be obtained from the Court's web page. Exhibits submitted conventionally shall be served on other parties as if they were not subject to these Administrative Procedures (NY R USDCTND CM/ECF). For a list of hints and tips for scanning large documents, please consult the Court's web page. NY R USDCTND CM/ECF(4)(4.5).

c. *Legibility.* It shall be the Filing User's responsibility to verify the legibility of scanned documents before filing them electronically with the Court. NY R USDCTND CM/ECF(4)(4.6).

d. *Color documents.* Since documents scanned in color or containing a graphic take much longer to upload, Filing Users are encouraged to configure their scanners to scan documents at 300 dpi and preferably in black and white rather than in color. NY R USDCTND CM/ECF(4)(4.7).

e. *Items not in .PDF format.* Parties wishing to file items not amenable to .pdf format (i.e. CD's, DVD's), shall file such items conventionally with the Clerk's Office. The Filing User shall electronically file a notice of conventional filing indicating that these items have been submitted to the clerk and shall serve copies of these items on other parties as if they were not subject to these Administrative Procedures (NY R USDCTND CM/ECF). These item(s) will be maintained by the

Clerk's Office until the case is disposed, at which time they will be returned to the filing party for retention consistent with NY R USDCTND CM/ECF(4)(4.9). NY R USDCTND CM/ECF(4)(4.8).

3. *Signing of pleadings, motions and other papers*

a. *Signature.* Every pleading, written motion, and other paper must be signed by at least one attorney of record in the attorney's name—or by a party personally if the party is unrepresented. The paper must state the signer's address, e-mail address, and telephone number. FRCP 11(a). Each document must identify the person filing the document. This identification must include an original signature of the attorney or pro se litigant; the typewritten name of that person; the address of a pro se litigant; and the bar roll number, office address, telephone number, e-mail address and fax number of the attorney. Telephone numbers of non-prisoner pro se parties may be provided voluntarily or upon request of the Court. See General Order #22 (NY R USDCTND CM/ECF) for signature requirements. NY R USDCTND L.R. 10.1(c)(2).

   i. *Electronic signatures.* Documents filed under an attorney's login and password shall constitute that attorney's signature for purposes of the Local Rules of Practice for the United States District Court for the Northern District of New York and Federal Rules of Civil Procedure, including but not limited to FRCP 11. A pleading or other document requiring an attorney's signature shall be signed in the following manner, whether filed electronically or submitted on disk or CD/ROM to the Clerk's Office: "s/ (attorney name)." The correct format for an attorney signature is found in NY R USDCTND CM/ECF(6)(6.1). NY R USDCTND CM/ECF(6)(6.1).

      - *Non-attorney signature.* If an original document requires the signature of a non-attorney, the Filing User may scan the original document containing the original signature(s), then electronically file it on the System. Alternatively, the Filing User may convert the document into .pdf text format and submit the document using "s/" for the signature of the non-attorney. NY R USDCTND CM/ECF(6)(6.2).

      - *Multiple signatures.* A document requiring signatures of more than one party must be filed electronically either by (1) submitting a scanned document containing all necessary signatures; (2) representing the consent of the other parties on the document; or (3) in any other manner that the Court approves. NY R USDCTND CM/ECF(6)(6.3).

   ii. *No verification or accompanying affidavit required for pleadings.* Unless a rule or statute specifically states otherwise, a pleading need not be verified or accompanied by an affidavit. FRCP 11(a).

   iii. *Unsigned papers.* The court must strike an unsigned paper unless the omission is promptly corrected after being called to the attorney's or party's attention. FRCP 11(a).

b. *Representations to the court.* By presenting to the court a pleading, written motion, or other paper—whether by signing, filing, submitting, or later advocating it—an attorney or unrepresented party certifies that to the best of the person's knowledge, information, and belief, formed after an inquiry reasonable under the circumstances:

   i. It is not being presented for any improper purpose, such as to harass, cause unnecessary delay, or needlessly increase the cost of litigation;

   ii. The claims, defenses, and other legal contentions are warranted by existing law or by a nonfrivolous argument for extending, modifying, or reversing existing law or for establishing new law;

   iii. The factual contentions have evidentiary support or, if specifically so identified, will likely have evidentiary support after a reasonable opportunity for further investigation or discovery; and

   iv. The denials of factual contentions are warranted on the evidence or, if specifically so identified, are reasonably based on belief or a lack of information. FRCP 11(b).

c. *Sanctions.* If, after notice and a reasonable opportunity to respond, the court determines that FRCP 11(b) has been violated, the court may impose an appropriate sanction on any attorney, law firm, or party that violated FRCP 11(b) or is responsible for the violation. FRCP 11(c)(1). Refer to the United States District Court for the Northern District of New York KeyRules Motion for Sanctions document for more information.

4. *Privacy protection for filings made with the court*

a. *Redacted filings.* Unless the court orders otherwise, in an electronic or paper filing with the court that contains an individual's Social Security number, taxpayer-identification number, or birth date, the name of an individual known to be a minor, or a financial-account number, a party or nonparty making the filing may include only:

   i. The last four (4) digits of the Social Security number and taxpayer-identification number;

   ii. The year of the individual's birth;

   iii. The minor's initials; and

   iv. The last four (4) digits of the financial-account number. FRCP 5.2(a); NY R USDCTND L.R. 8.1; NY R USDCTND CM/ECF(11)(11.2).

   v. If a home address must be used, use only the City and State. NY R USDCTND L.R. 8.1; NY R USDCTND CM/ECF(11)(11.2).

   vi. If the victim of a sexual assault must be referenced, redact the name to 'Victim.' NY R USDCTND CM/ECF(11)(11.2); NY R USDCTND L.R. 8.1.

   vii. In addition, caution shall be exercised when filing documents that contain the following:

   • Personal identifying number, such as a driver's license number;

   • Medical records, treatment and diagnosis;

   • Employment history;

   • Individual financial information; and

   • Proprietary or trade secret information. NY R USDCTND L.R. 8.1; NY R USDCTND CM/ECF(11)(11.2).

b. *Exemptions from the redaction requirement.* The redaction requirement does not apply to the following:

   i. A financial-account number that identifies the property allegedly subject to forfeiture in a forfeiture proceeding;

   ii. The record of an administrative or agency proceeding;

   iii. The official record of a state-court proceeding;

   iv. The record of a court or tribunal, if that record was not subject to the redaction requirement when originally filed;

   v. A filing covered by FRCP 5.2(c) or FRCP 5.2(d); and

   vi. A pro se filing in an action brought under 28 U.S.C.A. § 2241, 28 U.S.C.A. § 2254, or 28 U.S.C.A. § 2255. FRCP 5.2(b).

   vii. Transcripts of the administrative record in social security proceedings are exempt from this requirement. State court records and other documents filed in habeas corpus proceedings are exempt from this requirement except for proceedings that involve victims of sex crimes. In habeas corpus cases involving sex crimes, the parties must redact the record and supporting papers, or may move to seal, if appropriate. NY R USDCTND L.R. 8.1.

c. *Limitations on remote access to electronic files; Social Security appeals and immigration cases.* Unless the court orders otherwise, in an action for benefits under the Social Security Act, and in an action or proceeding relating to an order of removal, to relief from removal, or to immigration benefits or detention, access to an electronic file is authorized as follows:

   i. The parties and their attorneys may have remote electronic access to any part of the case file, including the administrative record;

   ii. Any other person may have electronic access to the full record at the courthouse, but may have remote electronic access only to:

   • The docket maintained by the court; and

- An opinion, order, judgment, or other disposition of the court, but not any other part of the case file or the administrative record. FRCP 5.2(c).

d. *Filings made under seal.* The court may order that a filing be made under seal without redaction. The court may later unseal the filing or order the person who made the filing to file a redacted version for the public record. FRCP 5.2(d); NY R USDCTND L.R. 8.1. For information on sealed matters, refer to NY R USDCTND L.R. 83.13 and NY R USDCTND CM/ECF(12).

e. *Protective orders.* For good cause, the court may by order in a case:

   i. Require redaction of additional information; or

   ii. Limit or prohibit a nonparty's remote electronic access to a document filed with the court. FRCP 5.2(e).

f. *Option for additional unredacted filing under seal.* A person making a redacted filing may also file an unredacted copy under seal. The court must retain the unredacted copy as part of the record. FRCP 5.2(f); NY R USDCTND L.R. 8.1; NY R USDCTND CM/ECF(11)(11.3).

g. *Option for filing a reference list.* A filing that contains redacted information may be filed together with a reference list that identifies each item of redacted information and specifies an appropriate identifier that uniquely corresponds to each item listed. The list must be filed under seal and may be amended as of right. Any reference in the case to a listed identifier will be construed to refer to the corresponding item of information. FRCP 5.2(g); NY R USDCTND L.R. 8.1; NY R USDCTND CM/ECF(11)(11.3).

h. *Responsibility for redaction.* Counsel is strongly urged to discuss this issue with all their clients so that they can make an informed decision about the inclusion of certain information. The responsibility for redacting these personal identifiers rests solely with counsel and the parties. The Clerk will not review each filing for compliance with NY R USDCTND L.R. 8.1. Counsel and the parties are cautioned that failure to redact these personal identifiers may subject them to the Court's full disciplinary power. NY R USDCTND L.R. 8.1; NY R USDCTND CM/ECF(11)(11.3).

i. *Waiver of protection of identifiers.* A person waives the protection of FRCP 5.2(a) as to the person's own information by filing it without redaction and not under seal. FRCP 5.2(h).

5. *Individual judge practices.* Refer to the Miscellaneous section of this document for information on individual judge practices on formatting documents.

## F. Filing and Service Requirements

1. *Filing requirements.* Any paper after the complaint that is required to be served—together with a certificate of service—must be filed within a reasonable time after service. FRCP 5(d)(1). All pretrial and settlement conference statements shall be provided to the Clerk but not filed. These documents are not for public view. Forms for preparation of pretrial and settlement conference statements are available from the Clerk's office or at the Court's webpage. NY R USDCTND L.R. 5.7.

   a. *How filing is made; In general.* A paper is filed by delivering it:

      i. To the clerk; or

      ii. To a judge who agrees to accept it for filing, and who must then note the filing date on the paper and promptly send it to the clerk. FRCP 5(d)(2).

   b. *Electronic filing*

      i. *Authorization of electronic filing program.* A court may, by local rule, allow papers to be filed, signed, or verified by electronic means that are consistent with any technical standards established by the Judicial Conference of the United States. A local rule may require electronic filing only if reasonable exceptions are allowed. A paper filed electronically in compliance with a local rule is a written paper for purposes of the Federal Rules of Civil Procedure. FRCP 5(d)(3).

         - All cases filed in this Court may be assigned to the Electronic Case Files System ("ECF") in accordance with the Procedural Order on Electronic Case Filing (General Order #22 (NY R USDCTND CM/ECF)), the provisions of which are incorporated herein by reference, and which the Court may amend from time to time. Copies of General Order #22 (NY R USDCTND CM/ECF) are available at the Clerk's office or at the Court's webpage. NY R USDCTND L.R. 5.1.1; NY R USDCTND Order 25(XII).

- The Court may deviate from these Administrative Procedures (NY R USDCTND CM/ECF) in specific cases, without prior notice, if deemed appropriate in the exercise of discretion, considering the need for the just, speedy, and inexpensive determination of matters pending before the Court. NY R USDCTND CM/ECF(2).

ii. *Scope of electronic filing.* After January 1, 2004, all documents that attorneys admitted to practice in the Northern District of New York submit for filing shall be filed electronically using the System or shall be scanned and uploaded to the System, no matter when a case was originally filed, unless these Administrative Procedures (NY R USDCTND CM/ECF) otherwise permit or unless the assigned judge otherwise authorizes. An attorney who is not a Filing User by January 1, 2004, must show good cause to the assigned judge to file and serve pleadings and other papers in the traditional manner. NY R USDCTND CM/ECF(2).

iii. *Exceptions and/or waivers from mandatory electronic filing.* The following types of cases and/or documents are not required to be filed electronically:

- If you are seeking to have your complaint filed under seal, please file your complaint and proposed sealing order traditionally at the Clerk's Office. NY R USDCTND CM/ECF(2)(2.1)(1).

- Any document that a party proceeding pro se files. (See NY R USDCTND CM/ECF(12)(12.1) for procedural details). NY R USDCTND CM/ECF(2)(2.1)(2). A non-prisoner who is a party to a civil action and who is not represented by an attorney may file a motion to obtain an Electronic Case Filing (ECF) login and password on a form prescribed by the Clerk's Office. The Pro Se CM/ECF Registration Form shall be submitted with the motion. If during the course of the action an attorney appears on behalf of the pro se party, the Clerk's Office shall terminate the pro se party's registration based upon the attorney's appearance. NY R USDCTND CM/ECF(12)(12.1). Absent permission to file electronically, pro se filers shall file paper originals of all complaints, pleadings, motions, affidavits, briefs, and other documents which must be signed or which require either verification or an unsworn declaration under any rule or statute. The Clerk's Office will scan these original documents into an electronic file in the System but will also maintain a paper file. NY R USDCTND CM/ECF(12)(12.1). A pro se party may also seek permission to receive immediate notice of all public documents filed in their cases. Notices of Electronic Filing (NEF) and attached documents would be transmitted to a non-prisoner pro se party who selects this option. Note: The pro se party would continue to file their documents with the Clerk's Office in paper form. NY R USDCTND CM/ECF(12)(12.1).

- Sealed documents, sealed cases, documents for in camera review, documents lodged with the Court, ex parte documents, confidential agreements, Qui Tam actions and Grand Jury material and warrants must be filed traditionally. (See NY R USDCTND CM/ECF(12)(12.2) for further information the filing of the above-referenced documents). NY R USDCTND CM/ECF(2)(2.1)(3).

- Discovery: In accordance with NY R USDCTND L.R. 26.2, parties shall not file discovery, provided, however, that discovery material to be used at trial or in support of any motion, including a motion to compel or for summary judgment, shall be filed electronically with the Court prior to the trial or with the motion. Any motion pursuant to FRCP 37 shall be accompanied by the electronically filed discovery materials to which the motion relates if those materials have not previously been filed with the Court. NY R USDCTND CM/ECF(2)(2.1)(4).

- Transport Orders: All orders requesting that an incarcerated individual be transported that a judicial officer of the Northern District of New York signs shall be filed traditionally. These Orders will not be filed with the case or uploaded to the docket but rather will be processed in accordance with the procedures that the Clerk of Court promulgates. NY R USDCTND CM/ECF(2)(2.1)(5).

iv. *Filing defined.* Electronic transmission of a document to the System in accordance with these Administrative Procedures, together with the transmission of a Notice of Electronic Filing from the Court, constitutes filing of the document for all purposes of the Federal Rules of Civil Procedure and the Local Rules of Practice for the United States District Court for the Northern District of New York and constitutes entry of the document on the docket that the Clerk's Office keeps under FRCP 58 and FRCP 79. E-mailing a document to the Clerk's Office or to the assigned judge shall not constitute "filing" of the document. NY R USDCTND CM/ECF(4)(4.1).

v. *Filing fees.* Any fee required for filing a pleading or paper in this Court is payable to the Clerk of the Court. The Court will not maintain electronic billing or debit accounts for attorneys or law firms. Effective January 1, 2007, payment for filing fees will be mandatory through CM/ECF's Internet Credit Card Payment site--a secure Treasury Site. The Filing User will be prompted to enter either Bank Account Debit (ACH) or credit card information while filing the initial pleading. Any document that requires a filing fee (e.g., Notice of Appeal, Motion for Pro Hac Vice Admission) may also be paid through the federal electronic payment website. NY R USDCTND CM/ECF(7).

vi. For more information on electronic filing, refer to NY R USDCTND CM/ECF.

c. *E-mail or facsimile filing.* Neither the Court nor the Clerk's Office will accept for filing any facsimile or e-mail transmission without prior authorization from the Court. The party using facsimile or e-mail transmissions to file its papers must accompany any such documents with a cover letter stating that the Court authorized such transmissions and the date on which the Court provided that authorization. Violations of NY R USDCTND L.R. 5.5 subject the offending party to the Court's full disciplinary powers. NY R USDCTND L.R. 5.5.

2. *Service requirements*

a. *Service; When required*

i. *In general.* Unless the Federal Rules of Civil Procedure provide otherwise, each of the following papers must be served on every party:

- An order stating that service is required;
- A pleading filed after the original complaint, unless the court orders otherwise under FRCP 5(c) because there are numerous defendants;
- A discovery paper required to be served on a party, unless the court orders otherwise;
- A written motion, except one that may be heard ex parte; and
- A written notice, appearance, demand, or offer of judgment, or any similar paper. FRCP 5(a)(1).

ii. *If a party fails to appear.* No service is required on a party who is in default for failing to appear. But a pleading that asserts a new claim for relief against such a party must be served on that party under FRCP 4. FRCP 5(a)(2).

iii. *Seizing property.* If an action is begun by seizing property and no person is or need be named as a defendant, any service required before the filing of an appearance, answer, or claim must be made on the person who had custody or possession of the property when it was seized. FRCP 5(a)(3).

b. *Service; How made*

i. *Serving an attorney.* If a party is represented by an attorney, service under FRCP 5 must be made on the attorney unless the court orders service on the party. FRCP 5(b)(1).

ii. *Service in general.* A paper is served under FRCP 5 by:

- Handing it to the person;
- Leaving it: (1) at the person's office with a clerk or other person in charge or, if no one is

in charge, in a conspicuous place in the office; or (2) if the person has no office or the office is closed, at the person's dwelling or usual place of abode with someone of suitable age and discretion who resides there;

- Mailing it to the person's last known address—in which event service is complete upon mailing;

- Leaving it with the court clerk if the person has no known address;

- Sending it by electronic means if the person consented in writing—in which event service is complete upon transmission, but is not effective if the serving party learns that it did not reach the person to be served; or

- Delivering it by any other means that the person consented to in writing—in which event service is complete when the person making service delivers it to the agency designated to make delivery. FRCP 5(b)(2).

    iii. *Service of electronically-filed documents.* Service is complete provided all parties receive a Notice of Electronic Filing (NEF), which is sent automatically by email from the Court (see the NEF for a list of who did/did not receive notice electronically). Transmission of the NEF constitutes service upon all Filing and Receiving Users who are listed as recipients of notice by electronic mail. It remains the responsibility of Filing and Receiving Users to maintain current contact information with the court and to regularly review the docket sheet of the case. NY R USDCTND CM/ECF(5)(5.2).

- *Non-filing or receiving users.* Attorneys and pro se parties who are not Filing or Receiving Users must be served with a paper copy of any electronically filed pleading or other document. Service of such paper copy must be made according to the Federal Rules of Civil Procedure and the Local Rules of Practice for the United States District Court for the Northern District of New York. Such paper service must be documented by electronically filing a certificate of service. NY R USDCTND CM/ECF(5)(5.2). A party who is not a Filing User of the System is entitled to a paper copy of any electronically-filed pleading, document, or order. The Filing User must therefore provide the non-Filing User with the pleading or document according to the Federal Rules of Civil Procedure. NY R US-DCTND CM/ECF(5)(5.3).

    iv. *Using court facilities.* If a local rule so authorizes, a party may use the court's transmission facilities to make service under FRCP 5(b)(2)(E). FRCP 5(b)(3).

  c. *Serving numerous defendants*

    i. *In general.* If an action involves an unusually large number of defendants, the court may, on motion or on its own, order that:

- Defendants' pleadings and replies to them need not be served on other defendants;

- Any crossclaim, counterclaim, avoidance, or affirmative defense in those pleadings and replies to them will be treated as denied or avoided by all other parties; and

- Filing any such pleading and serving it on the plaintiff constitutes notice of the pleading to all parties. FRCP 5(c)(1).

    ii. *Notifying parties.* A copy of every such order must be served on the parties as the court directs. FRCP 5(c)(2).

3. *Individual judge practices.* Refer to the Miscellaneous section of this document for information on individual judge practices on filing and serving documents.

## G. Hearings

1. Refer to the General Requirements section of this document for information on pretrial conferences, scheduling conferences, and discovery planning conferences.

## H. Forms

### 1. Federal Pretrial Conferences, Scheduling, Management Forms

  a. Plaintiff's informal summary of status of case to judge prior to pretrial conference in complex case. 2C FEDFORMS § 2807.

b.   Joint pretrial report. 2C FEDFORMS § 2807.10.

c.   Joint statement of undisputed facts. 2C FEDFORMS § 2807.20.

d.   Joint statement of disputed facts. 2C FEDFORMS § 2807.30.

e.   Joint report of counsel prior to pretrial conference. 2C FEDFORMS § 2807.40.

f.   Plaintiff's pretrial conference statement; Insurance case. 2C FEDFORMS § 2807.50.

g.   Defendant's pretrial conference statement; Insurance case. 2C FEDFORMS § 2807.60.

h.   Plaintiff's list of exhibits to be offered at trial. 2C FEDFORMS § 2811.

i.   Defendant's list of prospective witnesses. 2C FEDFORMS § 2811.10.

j.   Designation of witnesses whom plaintiff intends to call at trial pursuant to pretrial conference oral stipulation. 2C FEDFORMS § 2811.20.

k.   Defendant's list of prospective exhibits. 2C FEDFORMS § 2811.40.

l.   Report of parties' planning meeting. 3A FEDFORMS § 3314.

m.   Report of parties' discovery conference; Another form. 3A FEDFORMS § 3315.

n.   Report of parties' discovery conference; Another form. 3A FEDFORMS § 3316.

o.   Joint scheduling report. 3A FEDFORMS § 3316.5.

p.   Stipulation and order regarding discovery conference discussions. 3A FEDFORMS § 3316.6.

q.   Pretrial statement; By plaintiff; Automobile collision involving corporate defendant. FEDPROF § 1:658.

r.   Pretrial statement; By defendant; Automobile collision. FEDPROF § 1:659.

s.   Pretrial statement; By parties jointly; Automobile collision. FEDPROF § 1:660.

t.   Pretrial statement; Provision; Waiver of abandoned claims or defenses. FEDPROF § 1:661.

u.   Status report. GOLDLTGFMS § 34:2.

v.   Preliminary pretrial checklist. GOLDLTGFMS § 34:3.

w.   Pretrial memorandum. GOLDLTGFMS § 34:4.

x.   Pretrial memorandum; Short form. GOLDLTGFMS § 34:5.

y.   Pretrial memorandum; Civil action. GOLDLTGFMS § 34:6.

z.   Pretrial memorandum; Worker's compensation case. GOLDLTGFMS § 34:7.

**2.   Forms for the Northern District of New York**

a.   Civil case management plan. NY R USDCTND Order 25(Civil Case Management Plan).

# I.  Applicable Rules

1.  *Federal rules*

a.   Serving and filing pleadings and other papers. FRCP 5.

b.   Privacy protection for filings made with the court. FRCP 5.2.

c.   Computing and extending time; Time for motion papers. FRCP 6.

d.   Pleadings allowed; Form of motions and other papers. FRCP 7.

e.   Form of pleadings. FRCP 10.

f.   Signing pleadings, motions, and other papers; Representations to the court; Sanctions. FRCP 11.

g.   Pretrial conferences; Scheduling; Management. FRCP 16.

h.   Duty to disclose; General provisions governing discovery. FRCP 26.

2.  *Local rules*

a.   Scope of the rules. NY R USDCTND L.R. 1.1.

b. Complex and multi-district litigation. NY R USDCTND L.R. 3.3.

c. Service and filing of papers. NY R USDCTND L.R. 5.1.

d. Filing by facsimile or e-mail. NY R USDCTND L.R. 5.5.

e. Documents to be provided to the clerk. NY R USDCTND L.R. 5.7.

f. Personal privacy protection. NY R USDCTND L.R. 8.1.

g. Request for three-judge court. NY R USDCTND L.R. 9.1.

h. Form of papers. NY R USDCTND L.R. 10.1.

i. Civil case management. NY R USDCTND L.R. 16.1.

j. Timing of discovery. NY R USDCTND L.R. 26.4.

k. Submission of pretrial papers. NY R USDCTND L.R. 39.2.

l. Settlement procedures. NY R USDCTND L.R. 68.2.

m. Appearance and withdrawal of attorney. NY R USDCTND L.R. 83.2.

n. Arbitration. NY R USDCTND L.R. 83.7-1; NY R USDCTND L.R. 83.7-2; NY R USDCTND L.R. 83.7-3.

o. Assisted mediation program. NY R USDCTND L.R. 83.8.

p. Mediation. NY R USDCTND L.R. 83.11-1; NY R USDCTND L.R. 83.11-3.

q. Early neutral evaluation. NY R USDCTND L.R. 83.12-1; NY R USDCTND L.R. 83.12-3.

r. Administrative procedures for electronic case filing. NY R USDCTND CM/ECF.

s. Case assignment plan for the Northern District of New York. [NY R USDCTND Order 12, as amended by NY ORDER 16-4201, effective March 24, 2015].

t. Directing the expedited service of the summons and complaint and further directing the completion of FRCP 16 stipulation for the timely progression of civil actions. [NY R USDCTND Order 25, as amended by NY ORDER 16-4187, effective June 23, 2016].

u. Mandatory mediation program. NY R USDCTND Order 47.

## J. Miscellaneous

**NOTE: Individual judges' rules may apply. For available judge-level information, refer to:**

DISTRICT JUDGE MAE A. D'AGOSTINO: [NY R USDCTND D'Agostino-Rules and Practices, as added by NY ORDER 16-4200, effective April 4, 2016].

DISTRICT JUDGE THOMAS J. McAVOY: NY R USDCTND McAvoy-Order.

# WESTERN DISTRICT OF NEW YORK

## Pleadings
## Complaint

**Document Last Updated September 2016**

**A. Checklist**

- (I)  ❑ Matters to be considered by plaintiff
  - (a)  ❑ Required documents
    - (1)  ❑ Civil cover sheet
    - (2)  ❑ Complaint
    - (3)  ❑ Summons
    - (4)  ❑ Filing fee
    - (5)  ❑ Affidavit proving service
  - (b)  ❑ Supplemental documents
    - (1)  ❑ Notice and request for waiver of service
    - (2)  ❑ Notice of constitutional question
    - (3)  ❑ Notice of issue concerning foreign law
    - (4)  ❑ Nongovernmental corporate disclosure statement
    - (5)  ❑ RICO case statement
    - (6)  ❑ Disk or CD with PDF of complaint
    - (7)  ❑ Paper copy for date-stamping with self-addressed envelope
    - (8)  ❑ Courtesy copies
  - (c)  ❑ Timing
    - (1)  ❑ A civil action is commenced by filing a complaint with the court
    - (2)  ❑ If a defendant is not served within ninety (90) days after the complaint is filed, the court—on motion or on its own after notice to the plaintiff—must dismiss the action without prejudice against that defendant or order that service be made within a specified time
- (II)  ❑ Matters to be considered by defendant
  - (a)  ❑ Required documents
    - (1)  ❑ Answer
    - (2)  ❑ Certificate of service
  - (b)  ❑ Supplemental documents
    - (1)  ❑ Waiver of the service of summons
    - (2)  ❑ Notice of constitutional question
    - (3)  ❑ Notice of issue concerning foreign law
    - (4)  ❑ Nongovernmental corporate disclosure statement
    - (5)  ❑ RICO case statement
    - (6)  ❑ Paper copy for date-stamping with self-addressed envelope
    - (7)  ❑ Courtesy copies

    (c) ❏ Timing

        (1) ❏ A defendant must serve an answer:

            (i) ❏ Within twenty-one (21) days after being served with the summons and complaint; or

            (ii) ❏ If it has timely waived service under FRCP 4(d), within sixty (60) days after the request for a waiver was sent, or within ninety (90) days after it was sent to the defendant outside any judicial district of the United States

        (2) ❏ The United States, a United States agency, or a United States officer or employee sued only in an official capacity must serve an answer to a complaint, counterclaim, or crossclaim within sixty (60) days after service on the United States attorney

        (3) ❏ A United States officer or employee sued in an individual capacity for an act or omission occurring in connection with duties performed on the United States' behalf must serve an answer to a complaint, counterclaim, or crossclaim within sixty (60) days after service on the officer or employee or service on the United States attorney, whichever is later

        (4) ❏ Unless the court sets a different time, serving a motion under FRCP 12 alters these periods as follows:

            (i) ❏ If the court denies the motion or postpones its disposition until trial, the responsive pleading must be served within fourteen (14) days after notice of the court's action; or

            (ii) ❏ If the court grants a motion for a more definite statement, the responsive pleading must be served within fourteen (14) days after the more definite statement is served

        (5) ❏ Defendant is given a reasonable time of at least thirty (30) days after a waiver of service request is sent—or at least sixty (60) days if sent to defendant outside any judicial district of the United States—to return the waiver

## B. Timing

1. *Commencing an action.* A civil action is commenced by filing a complaint with the court. FRCP 3.

    a. *Statute of limitations.* An action will be barred if it is not commenced within the period set forth in the applicable statute of limitations. Under the Federal Rules of Civil Procedure (FRCP), an action is commenced by filing a complaint with the court. Thus, in a suit on a right created by federal law, filing a complaint suffices to satisfy the statute of limitations. FEDPROF § 61:2.

        i. *Federal question cases.* Absent a specific statutory provision for tolling the statute of limitations, in federal question cases, the filing of the complaint will toll the statute, even if not all filing fees have been paid, although some courts have added the requirement of reasonable diligence in effecting service. FEDPROF § 61:2.

        ii. *Diversity cases.* In diversity actions the matter is less clear. In the landmark Ragan case, the Supreme Court held in construing FRCP 3 that if, under local law, an action is not commenced until the defendant has been served, the statute is not tolled until service has been accomplished. FEDPROF § 61:2; Ragan v. Merchants Transfer & Warehouse Co., 337 U.S. 530, 69 S.Ct. 1233, 93 L.Ed. 1520 (1949). However, in a subsequent case, the Supreme Court distinguished Ragan in holding that the provision of FRCP 4 governing methods of service prevails over a conflicting state rule requiring personal service. FEDPROF § 61:2; Hanna v. Plumer, 380 U.S. 460, 85 S.Ct. 1136, 14 L.Ed.2d 8 (1965). The court reaffirmed Ragan and held that (1) a state law mandating actual service of a summons to toll the statute of limitations must be followed in a diversity case, and (2) FRCP 3 only governs other timing requirements in the federal rules. FEDPROF § 61:2; Walker v. Armco Steel Corp., 446 U.S. 740, 100 S.Ct. 1978, 64 L.Ed.2d 659 (1980).

2. *Service of summons and complaint.* If a defendant is not served within ninety (90) days after the complaint is filed, the court—on motion or on its own after notice to the plaintiff—must dismiss the action without prejudice against that defendant or order that service be made within a specified time. But if the plaintiff shows good cause for the failure, the court must extend the time for service for an appropriate period. FRCP 4(m) does not apply to service in a foreign country under FRCP 4(f) or FRCP 4(j)(1) or to service of a notice under FRCP 71.1(d)(3)(A). FRCP 4(m).

3. *Computation of time*

   a. *Computing time.* FRCP 6 applies in computing any time period specified in the Federal Rules of Civil Procedure, in any local rule or court order, or in any statute that does not specify a method of computing time. FRCP 6(a).

      i. *Period stated in days or a longer unit.* When the period is stated in days or a longer unit of time:

         • Exclude the day of the event that triggers the period;

         • Count every day, including intermediate Saturdays, Sundays, and legal holidays; and

         • Include the last day of the period, but if the last day is a Saturday, Sunday, or legal holiday, the period continues to run until the end of the next day that is not a Saturday, Sunday, or legal holiday. FRCP 6(a)(1).

      ii. *Period stated in hours.* When the period is stated in hours:

         • Begin counting immediately on the occurrence of the event that triggers the period;

         • Count every hour, including hours during intermediate Saturdays, Sundays, and legal holidays; and

         • If the period would end on a Saturday, Sunday, or legal holiday, the period continues to run until the same time on the next day that is not a Saturday, Sunday, or legal holiday. FRCP 6(a)(2).

      iii. *Inaccessibility of the clerk's office.* Unless the court orders otherwise, if the clerk's office is inaccessible:

         • On the last day for filing under FRCP 6(a)(1), then the time for filing is extended to the first accessible day that is not a Saturday, Sunday, or legal holiday; or

         • During the last hour for filing under FRCP 6(a)(2), then the time for filing is extended to the same time on the first accessible day that is not a Saturday, Sunday, or legal holiday. FRCP 6(a)(3).

      iv. *"Last day" defined.* Unless a different time is set by a statute, local rule, or court order, the last day ends:

         • For electronic filing, at midnight in the court's time zone; and

         • For filing by other means, when the clerk's office is scheduled to close. FRCP 6(a)(4).

      v. *"Next day" defined.* The "next day" is determined by continuing to count forward when the period is measured after an event and backward when measured before an event. FRCP 6(a)(5).

      vi. *"Legal holiday" defined.* "Legal holiday" means:

         • The day set aside by statute for observing New Year's Day, Martin Luther King Jr.'s Birthday, Washington's Birthday, Memorial Day, Independence Day, Labor Day, Columbus Day, Veterans' Day, Thanksgiving Day, or Christmas Day;

         • Any day declared a holiday by the President or Congress; and

         • For periods that are measured after an event, any other day declared a holiday by the state where the district court is located. FRCP 6(a)(6).

   b. *Computation of electronic filing deadlines.* A document will be deemed timely filed if filed prior to midnight Eastern Time, unless otherwise ordered by the Court. A document will be considered untimely if filed thereafter. When a Court order requires that a document be filed on a weekend or holiday, the document may be filed by close of business the next business day without further application to the Court. NY R USDCTWD ECF Procedures(2)(e)(i). A document filed electronically is deemed filed on the date and time stated on the Notice of Electronic Filing. NY R USDCTWD ECF Procedures(2)(e)(ii).

      i. *System availability.* Although parties may file documents electronically twenty-four (24) hours a day, registered users are strongly encouraged to file all documents during normal working hours of the Clerk's Office (8:30 a.m. to 5:00 p.m. Eastern Time). NY R USDCTWD ECF Procedures(2)(t)(i).

    ii.   *Technical failures.* A Filing User whose filing is made untimely as a result of a technical failure must seek appropriate relief from the Court. NY R USDCTWD ECF Procedures(2)(u)(i).

  c.  *Extending time*

    i.   *In general.* When an act may or must be done within a specified time, the court may, for good cause, extend the time:

- With or without motion or notice if the court acts, or if a request is made, before the original time or its extension expires; or

- On motion made after the time has expired if the party failed to act because of excusable neglect. FRCP 6(b)(1).

    ii.  *Exceptions.* A court must not extend the time to act under FRCP 50(b), FRCP 50(d), FRCP 52(b), FRCP 59(b), FRCP 59(d), FRCP 59(e), and FRCP 60(b). FRCP 6(b)(2).

   iii.  Refer to the United States District Court for the Western District of New York KeyRules Motion for Continuance/Extension of Time document for more information on extending time.

4.  *Individual judge practices.* Refer to the Miscellaneous section of this document for information on individual judge practices on timing of documents.

## C. General Requirements

1.  *Pleading, generally*

  a.  *Pleadings allowed.* Only these pleadings are allowed: (1) a complaint; (2) an answer to a complaint; (3) an answer to a counterclaim designated as a counterclaim; (4) an answer to a crossclaim; (5) a third-party complaint; (6) an answer to a third-party complaint; and (7) if the court orders one, a reply to an answer. FRCP 7(a).

  b.  *Pleading to be concise and direct.* Each allegation must be simple, concise, and direct. No technical form is required. FRCP 8(d)(1).

  c.  *Alternative statements of a claim or defense.* A party may set out two or more statements of a claim or defense alternatively or hypothetically, either in a single count or defense or in separate ones. If a party makes alternative statements, the pleading is sufficient if any one of them is sufficient. FRCP 8(d)(2).

  d.  *Inconsistent claims or defenses.* A party may state as many separate claims or defenses as it has, regardless of consistency. FRCP 8(d)(3).

  e.  *Construing pleadings.* Pleadings must be construed so as to do justice. FRCP 8(e).

2.  *Pleading special matters*

  a.  *Capacity or authority to sue; Legal existence*

    i.   *In general.* Except when required to show that the court has jurisdiction, a pleading need not allege:

- A party's capacity to sue or be sued;

- A party's authority to sue or be sued in a representative capacity; or

- The legal existence of an organized association of persons that is made a party. FRCP 9(a)(1).

    ii.  *Raising those issues.* To raise any of those issues, a party must do so by a specific denial, which must state any supporting facts that are peculiarly within the party's knowledge. FRCP 9(a)(2).

  b.  *Fraud or mistake; Conditions of mind.* In alleging fraud or mistake, a party must state with particularity the circumstances constituting fraud or mistake. Malice, intent, knowledge, and other conditions of a person's mind may be alleged generally. FRCP 9(b).

  c.  *Conditions precedent.* In pleading conditions precedent, it suffices to allege generally that all conditions precedent have occurred or been performed. But when denying that a condition precedent has occurred or been performed, a party must do so with particularity. FRCP 9(c).

  d.  *Official document or act.* In pleading an official document or official act, it suffices to allege that the document was legally issued or the act legally done. FRCP 9(d).

e. *Judgment.* In pleading a judgment or decision of a domestic or foreign court, a judicial or quasi-judicial tribunal, or a board or officer, it suffices to plead the judgment or decision without showing jurisdiction to render it. FRCP 9(e).

f. *Time and place.* An allegation of time or place is material when testing the sufficiency of a pleading. FRCP 9(f).

g. *Special damages.* If an item of special damage is claimed, it must be specifically stated. FRCP 9(g).

h. *Admiralty or maritime claim*

   i. *How designated.* If a claim for relief is within the admiralty or maritime jurisdiction and also within the court's subject-matter jurisdiction on some other ground, the pleading may designate the claim as an admiralty or maritime claim for purposes of FRCP 14(c), FRCP 38(e), and FRCP 82 and the Supplemental Rules for Admiralty or Maritime Claims and Asset Forfeiture Actions. A claim cognizable only in the admiralty or maritime jurisdiction is an admiralty or maritime claim for those purposes, whether or not so designated. FRCP 9(h)(1).

   ii. *Designation for appeal.* A case that includes an admiralty or maritime claim within FRCP 9(h) is an admiralty case within 28 U.S.C.A. § 1292(a)(3). FRCP 9(h)(2).

3. *Complaint.* A pleading that states a claim for relief must contain: (1) a short and plain statement of the grounds for the court's jurisdiction, unless the court already has jurisdiction and the claim needs no new jurisdictional support; (2) a short and plain statement of the claim showing that the pleader is entitled to relief; and (3) a demand for the relief sought, which may include relief in the alternative or different types of relief. FRCP 8(a).

a. *Statement of jurisdiction.* Federal courts are courts of limited jurisdiction, and it is presumed that they are without jurisdiction unless the contrary affirmatively appears. FEDPROC § 62:38; Kirkland Masonry, Inc. v. C.I.R., 614 F.2d 532 (5th Cir. 1980). Therefore, in order for a complaint to comply with the requirement that it contain a short and plain statement of the grounds upon which the court's jurisdiction depends, the jurisdictional basis must be alleged affirmatively and distinctly on the face of the complaint. FEDPROC § 62:38; Spain v. U.S. Through Atomic Nuclear Regulatory Commission Through U.S. Atomic Safety and Licensing Bd., 397 F.Supp. 15 (M.D.La. 1975).

   i. Although it has been said that the jurisdictional statement requirement contemplates reference to a federal statute, a sufficient jurisdictional statement is not made by simply citing a federal statute without alleging facts which bring the plaintiff within the purview of the statute. FEDPROC § 62:38; Atkins v. School Bd. of Halifax County, 379 F.Supp. 1060 (W.D.Va. 1974); Sims v. Mercy Hospital of Monroe, 451 F.2d 171 (6th Cir. 1971).

   ii. Improper venue is an affirmative defense, and a complaint need not include allegations showing venue to be proper. FEDPROC § 62:38; Ripperger v. A.C. Allyn & Co., 113 F.2d 332 (2d Cir. 1940).

b. *Statement of claim*

   i. *Notice pleading.* Because the only function left exclusively to the pleadings by the Federal Rules of Civil Procedure is that of giving notice, federal courts frequently have said that the Federal Rules of Civil Procedure have adopted a system of "notice pleading." FPP § 1202; Swierkiewicz v. Sorema N.A., 534 U.S. 506, 122 S.Ct. 992, 152 L.Ed.2d 1 (2002). To comply with the requirement that a complaint contain a short and plain statement of the claim, a pleading must give the opposing party fair notice of the nature of a claim and of the basis or grounds for it, so that the defendant will at least be notified as to which of its actions gave rise to the claim upon which the complaint is based. FEDPROC § 62:45.

     • *Plausibility standard.* Bell Atlantic Corporation v. Twombly and Ashcroft v. Iqbal have paved the way for a heightened "plausibility" pleading standard that requires plaintiffs to provide greater factual development in their complaints in order to survive a FRCP 12(b)(6) motion to dismiss. FPP § 1202; Bell Atlantic Corp. v. Twombly, 550 U.S. 544, 127 S.Ct. 1955, 167 L.Ed.2d 929, 68 Fed.R.Serv.3d 661 (2007); Ashcroft v. Iqbal, 556 U.S. 662, 129 S.Ct. 1937, 173 L.Ed.2d 868 (2009). In discussing what appears to be the new plausibility standard, the Court [in Bell Atlantic Corp. v. Twombly] stated: "While a complaint attacked by a FRCP 12(b)(6) motion to dismiss does not need detailed factual allegations. . .a plaintiff's obligation to provide the 'grounds' of his 'entitle[ment] to relief' requires more than labels and conclusions, and a formulaic recitation of the elements of a cause of action will not do. . .Factual allegations must be enough to raise a right to relief above the speculative level." FPP § 1216; Bell Atlantic Corp. v. Twombly, 550 U.S. 544, 127 S.Ct. 1955, 167 L.Ed.2d 929, 68 Fed.R.Serv.3d 661 (2007).

    ii. *Facts and evidence.* The complaint need only state enough facts to raise a reasonable expectation that discovery will reveal evidence of the necessary elements. FEDPROC § 62:52; Phillips v. County of Allegheny, 515 F.3d 224 (3d Cir. 2008). A complaint is not intended to formulate issues or fully summarize the facts involved. FEDPROC § 62:52; Hill v. MCI WorldCom Communications, Inc., 141 F.Supp.2d 1205 (S.D.Iowa 2001). Under notice pleading, the full development of the facts and the narrowing of contested issues are accomplished through discovery and other pretrial procedures. FEDPROC § 62:52.

    iii. *Particularity.* The claim should be particularized sufficiently for the defendant to prepare an adequate defense, file a responsive pleading, determine whether the defense of res judicata is appropriate, and commence discovery, and should insure that the court is sufficiently informed to determine the issue presented and to decide whether the complaint states a claim upon which relief can be had. FEDPROC § 62:45; Kelly v. Schmidberger, 806 F.2d 44, 6 Fed.R.Serv.3d 798 (2d Cir. 1986); Frank v. Mracek, 58 F.R.D. 365 (M.D.Ala. 1973); Barlow v. Pep Boys, Inc., 625 F.Supp. 130 (E.D.Pa. 1985); Philadelphia Dressed Beef Co. v. Wilson & Co., 19 F.R.D. 198 (E.D.Pa. 1956); Luckett v. Cohen, 145 F.Supp. 155 (S.D.N.Y. 1956).

c. *Class action allegations.* After stating the jurisdictional grounds for the claims, the complaint or other pleading shall set forth, under the heading "Class Action Allegations":

    i. The portion(s) of FRCP 23 under which it is claimed the action is properly maintained as a class action; and

    ii. Allegations thought to justify the claim, including, but not limited to:

- The size (or approximate size) and definition of the class;
- The basis on which the party or parties claim to adequately represent the class;
- The alleged questions of law and fact claimed to be common to the class; and
- In actions claimed to be maintainable under FRCP 23(b)(3), allegations thought to support the findings required by FRCP 23(b)(3). NY R USDCTWD Civ Rule 23(b).

    iii. For more information on class actions, refer to NY R USDCTWD Civ Rule 23.

d. *Demand for relief sought.* FRCP 8(a)(3) does not require a party to frame the demand for judgment according to a prescribed form or set of particular words; any concise statement identifying the remedies and the parties against whom relief is sought will be sufficient. FPP § 1255; Chandler v. McKee Foods Corp., 2009 WL 210858 (W.D.Va. 2009). Moreover, the pleader need only make one demand for relief regardless of the number of claims that are asserted. FPP § 1255; Liberty Mut. Ins. Co. v. Wetzel, 424 U.S. 737, 96 S.Ct. 1202, 47 L.Ed.2d 435 (1976).

    i. Relief must be requested as to each defendant. FEDPROC § 62:58; RKO-Stanley Warner Theatres, Inc. v. Mellon Nat. Bank & Trust Co., 436 F.2d 1297 (3d Cir. 1970).

4. *Joinder*

a. *Joinder of claims.* A party asserting a claim, counterclaim, crossclaim, or third-party claim may join, as independent or alternative claims, as many claims as it has against an opposing party. FRCP 18(a).

    i. *Joinder of contingent claims.* A party may join two claims even though one of them is contingent on the disposition of the other; but the court may grant relief only in accordance with the parties' relative substantive rights. In particular, a plaintiff may state a claim for money and a claim to set aside a conveyance that is fraudulent as to that plaintiff, without first obtaining a judgment for the money. FRCP 18(b).

b. *Joinder of parties; Required*

    i. *Persons required to be joined if feasible; Required party.* A person who is subject to service of process and whose joinder will not deprive the court of subject-matter jurisdiction must be joined as a party if:

- In that person's absence, the court cannot accord complete relief among existing parties; or

- That person claims an interest relating to the subject of the action and is so situated that disposing of the action in the person's absence may: (1) as a practical matter impair or impede the person's ability to protect the interest; or (2) leave an existing party subject to a substantial risk of incurring double, multiple, or otherwise inconsistent obligations because of the interest. FRCP 19(a)(1).

    ii.  *Joinder of parties by court order.* If a person has not been joined as required, the court must order that the person be made a party. A person who refuses to join as a plaintiff may be made either a defendant or, in a proper case, an involuntary plaintiff. FRCP 19(a)(2).

    iii.  *Venue.* If a joined party objects to venue and the joinder would make venue improper, the court must dismiss that party. FRCP 19(a)(3).

    iv.  *When joinder of parties is not feasible.* If a person who is required to be joined if feasible cannot be joined, the court must determine whether, in equity and good conscience, the action should proceed among the existing parties or should be dismissed. FRCP 19(b). For a list of the factors for the court to consider in determining whether joinder of parties is feasible, refer to FRCP 19(b)(1) through FRCP 19(b)(4).

    v.  *Pleading the reasons for nonjoinder.* When asserting a claim for relief, a party must state:

- The name, if known, of any person who is required to be joined if feasible but is not joined; and

- The reasons for not joining that person. FRCP 19(c).

    vi.  *Exception for class actions.* FRCP 19 is subject to FRCP 23. FRCP 19(d). For information on class actions, refer to FRCP 23.

  c.  *Joinder of parties; Permissible*

    i.  *Persons who may join or be joined*

- *Plaintiffs.* Persons may join in one action as plaintiffs if: (1) they assert any right to relief jointly, severally, or in the alternative with respect to or arising out of the same transaction, occurrence, or series of transactions or occurrences; and (2) any question of law or fact common to all plaintiffs will arise in the action. FRCP 20(a)(1).

- *Defendants.* Persons—as well as a vessel, cargo, or other property subject to admiralty process in rem—may be joined in one action as defendants if: (1) any right to relief is asserted against them jointly, severally, or in the alternative with respect to or arising out of the same transaction, occurrence, or series of transactions or occurrences; and (2) any question of law or fact common to all defendants will arise in the action. FRCP 20(a)(2).

- *Extent of relief.* Neither a plaintiff nor a defendant need be interested in obtaining or defending against all the relief demanded. The court may grant judgment to one or more plaintiffs according to their rights, and against one or more defendants according to their liabilities. FRCP 20(a)(3).

    ii.  *Protective measures.* The court may issue orders—including an order for separate trials—to protect a party against embarrassment, delay, expense, or other prejudice that arises from including a person against whom the party asserts no claim and who asserts no claim against the party. FRCP 20(b).

  d.  *Misjoinder and nonjoinder of parties.* Misjoinder of parties is not a ground for dismissing an action. On motion or on its own, the court may at any time, on just terms, add or drop a party. The court may also sever any claim against a party. FRCP 21.

5.  *Right to a jury trial; Demand*

  a.  *Right preserved.* The right of trial by jury as declared by U.S.C.A. Const. Amend. VII, or as provided by a federal statute, is preserved to the parties inviolate. FRCP 38(a).

b. *Demand.* On any issue triable of right by a jury, a party may demand a jury trial by:

    i. Serving the other parties with a written demand—which may be included in a pleading—no later than fourteen (14) days after the last pleading directed to the issue is served; and

    ii. Filing the demand in accordance with FRCP 5(d). FRCP 38(b).

c. *Specifying issues.* In its demand, a party may specify the issues that it wishes to have tried by a jury; otherwise, it is considered to have demanded a jury trial on all the issues so triable. If the party has demanded a jury trial on only some issues, any other party may—within fourteen (14) days after being served with the demand or within a shorter time ordered by the court—serve a demand for a jury trial on any other or all factual issues triable by jury. FRCP 38(c).

d. *Waiver; Withdrawal.* A party waives a jury trial unless its demand is properly served and filed. A proper demand may be withdrawn only if the parties consent. FRCP 38(d).

e. *Admiralty and maritime claims.* The rules in FRCP 38 do not create a right to a jury trial on issues in a claim that is an admiralty or maritime claim under FRCP 9(h). FRCP 38(e).

6. *Notice of appearance.* No notice of appearance is required of an attorney whose name and address appear at the end of a complaint, notice of removal, pre-answer motion, or answer. In all other circumstances, an attorney appearing for a party in a civil case shall promptly file a written notice of appearance. NY R USDCTWD Civ Rule 83.2(b). For more information on appearances and withdrawals, refer to NY R USDCTWD Civ Rule 83.2.

7. *Related cases.* Each attorney appearing in a civil case has a continuing duty to promptly notify the Clerk of Court when the attorney has reason to believe that said case is related to some other pending civil or criminal action(s) such that their assignment to the same Judge would avoid unnecessary duplication of judicial effort. As soon as the attorney becomes aware of such a relationship, the attorney shall notify the Clerk of Court by letter of the relevant facts, and the Clerk of Court will transmit that notification to the Judges to whom the cases have been assigned. NY R USDCTWD Civ Rule 5.1(e).

8. *Alternative dispute resolution (ADR).* This Court has adopted an Alternative Dispute Resolution Plan ("ADR"), as implemented by Standing Order (NY R USDCTWD ADR Plan), under which certain civil cases are referred automatically to ADR upon filing. NY R USDCTWD Civ Rule 16(a). The United States District Court for the Western District of New York (the "Court") adopted the ADR Plan on January 1, 2006 (the "Effective Date"), to make available to civil litigants court-administered ADR interventions and processes designed to provide quicker, less expensive and potentially more satisfying alternatives to continuing litigation, without impairing the quality of justice or the right to trial. NY R USDCTWD ADR Plan(1)(1.2)(A).

a. *Scope.* This ADR Plan (NY R USDCTWD ADR Plan) applies to civil actions pending or commenced on and after the Effective Date, except as otherwise indicated in NY R USDCTWD ADR Plan. The ADR Plan supplements the Local Rules of Civil Procedure for the United States District Court for the Western District of New York, which shall remain in full effect for all cases. NY R USDCTWD ADR Plan(1)(1.2)(B).

b. *Referral to ADR*

    i. *New cases.* All civil cases filed on and after the Effective Date of the ADR Plan shall be referred automatically for ADR. NY R USDCTWD ADR Plan(2)(2.1)(A). Notice of the ADR requirements will be provided to all parties immediately upon the filing of a complaint and answer or a notice of removal; NY R USDCTWD ADR Plan(2)(2.1)(A); NY R USDCTWD Civ Rule 16(a). ADR intervention will be scheduled at the conference held pursuant to Local Rule of Civil Procedure 16.1. NY R USDCTWD ADR Plan(2)(2.1)(A). [Editor's note: the reference to Local Rule of Civil Procedure 16.1 is likely meant to be a reference to NY R USDCTWD Civ Rule 16(b)].

- Litigants in cases not referred automatically to ADR must consider possible agreement to the use of an ADR process. NY R USDCTWD Civ Rule 16(a).

- For a list of exemptions from automatic referral, refer to NY R USDCTWD ADR Plan(2)(2.1)(A).

ii. *Pending cases.* The assigned Judge on any pending civil case may, sua sponte or with status conference, issue an order referring the case for ADR. NY R USDCTWD ADR Plan(2)(2.1)(B); NY R USDCTWD Civ Rule 16(a). The order shall specify a date on which the ADR intervention is to be completed. NY R USDCTWD ADR Plan(2)(2.1)(B).

iii. *Stipulation.* A case may be referred for ADR by stipulation of all parties. Stipulations shall be filed and shall designate the specific ADR intervention the parties have selected, the time frame within which the ADR process will be completed and the selected Neutral. Stipulations are presumed acceptable unless the assigned Judge determines that the interests of justice are not served. NY R USDCTWD ADR Plan(2)(2.1)(C).

iv. *Relief from ADR referral*

- *Opting out motions.* Any party may file, with the assigned Judge for that case, a motion to opt out of, or for relief from, ADR. NY R USDCTWD ADR Plan(2)(2.2)(A).

- *Motion.* Opting Out Motions must be made within fourteen (14) days from (1) the date of the first discovery conference under Local Rule 16.1 in new cases, or (2) the date of a sua sponte ADR Referral Order in pending cases. NY R USDCTWD ADR Plan(2)(2.2)(B). [Editor's note: the reference to Local Rule 16.1 is likely meant to be a reference to NY R USDCTWD Civ Rule 16(b)].

- *Criteria.* Opting Out Motions shall be granted only for "good cause" shown. Inconvenience, travel costs, attorney fees or other costs shall not constitute "good cause." A party seeking relief from ADR must set forth the reasons why ADR has no reasonable chance of being productive. NY R USDCTWD ADR Plan(2)(2.2)(C).

- *Judicial initiative.* The assigned Judge may, sua sponte, exempt any case from the Court's ADR Plan. NY R USDCTWD ADR Plan(2)(2.2)(D).

c. *ADR interventions*

i. *Options.* It is expected that cases referred for ADR will proceed to Mediation. However, the following options are also available upon the stipulation of all parties:

- Neutral Evaluation;
- Mini Summary Trial;
- Arbitration (Binding and Non-Binding);
- Case Valuation; and
- Settlement Week, when scheduled by the Court. NY R USDCTWD ADR Plan(4)(4.1)(A).

ii. *Timing.* Timing is specific to the intervention and process chosen, as set forth in the corresponding sections in NY R USDCTWD ADR Plan. NY R USDCTWD ADR Plan(4)(4.1)(B).

iii. *Scheduling.* The referral of a case to ADR does not delay or defer other dates established in the Scheduling Order and has no effect on the scheduled progress of the case toward trial. NY R USDCTWD ADR Plan(4)(4.1)(C).

d. *Selecting an ADR intervention*

i. *New cases.* Prior to the Local Rule 16.1 scheduling conference, counsel and any unrepresented parties shall confer about ADR as part of their discussion of "the possibilities for a prompt settlement or resolution of the case" pursuant to FRCP 26(f). Unless the parties agree to a different intervention, it is presumed that they will participate in mediation. [Editor's note: the reference to Local Rule 16.1 is likely meant to be a reference to NY R USDCTWD Civ Rule 16(b)].

ii. *Pending cases.* In pending cases, all sua sponte referrals will be to mediation. Should the parties agree that a different ADR intervention is more appropriate to their case, they may submit a stipulation designating the specific ADR intervention selected, the time frame within which the ADR process will be completed and the identity of the Neutral. Stipulations must be filed within fourteen (14) days from the date of the ADR Referral Order and are presumed acceptable unless the assigned Judge determines that the interests of justice are not served. NY R USDCTWD ADR Plan(4)(4.2)(B).

e.  For more information on alternative dispute resolution (ADR), refer to NY R USDCTWD ADR Plan.

9.  *Sanctions.* Failure of counsel for any party, or a party proceeding pro se, to appear before the Court at a conference, to complete the necessary preparations, or to be prepared to proceed to trial at the set time may be considered an abandonment of the case or a failure to prosecute or defend diligently. An appropriate order for sanctions may be entered against the defaulting party with respect to either a specific issue or the entire case. NY R USDCTWD Civ Rule 11(a). For more information, refer to NY R USDCTWD Civ Rule 11.

10. *Pro se actions.* For information on the requirements in pro se actions, refer to NY R USDCTWD Civ Rule 5.2.

11. *Individual judge practices.* Refer to the Miscellaneous section of this document for information on individual judge practices on general requirements for documents.

## D. Documents

1.  *Required documents*

    a.  *Civil cover sheet.* A completed civil cover sheet on a form available on the Court's website or from the Clerk's Office, shall be submitted with every complaint, notice of removal, or other document initiating a civil action. This requirement is solely for administrative purposes, and matters appearing on the civil cover sheet have no legal effect in the action. NY R USDCTWD Civ Rule 3. A civil cover sheet is submitted with each civil complaint filed in the district court. Copies of the cover sheet may be obtained from the Clerk of Court. 2 FEDFORMS § 3:29(Comment).

    b.  *Complaint.* Refer to the General Requirements section of this document for the form and contents of the complaint.

    c.  *Summons.* A summons must be served with a copy of the complaint. FRCP 4(c)(1). The filer should complete the summons prior to uploading it as an attachment to the opening document. NY R USDCTWD ECF Procedures(2)(c)(ii). A summons must:

        i.   Name the court and the parties;

        ii.  Be directed to the defendant;

        iii. State the name and address of the plaintiff's attorney or—if unrepresented—of the plaintiff;

        iv.  State the time within which the defendant must appear and defend;

        v.   Notify the defendant that a failure to appear and defend will result in a default judgment against the defendant for the relief demanded in the complaint;

        vi.  Be signed by the clerk; and

        vii. Bear the court's seal. FRCP 4(a)(1).

    d.  *Filing fee.* The clerk of each district court shall require the parties instituting any civil action, suit or proceeding in such court, whether by original process, removal or otherwise, to pay a filing fee. 28 U.S.C.A. § 1914(a). Each district court by rule or standing order may require advance payment of fees. 28 U.S.C.A. § 1914(c). A party commencing an action or removing an action from a state court must pay to the Clerk of Court the statutory filing fee, found in the District Court Schedule of Fees available on the Court's website before the case will be docketed and process issued. Indigent litigants should refer to NY R USDCTWD Civ Rule 5.2(c) for information on obtaining relief from this requirement. NY R USDCTWD Civ Rule 5.1(b). The Clerk of Court is not required to render any service for which a fee is prescribed by statute or by the Judicial Conference of the United States unless the fee for that service is paid in advance. NY R USDCTWD Civ Rule 5.4. Filing fees for civil cases opened on line are made using a credit card during the opening process. NY R USDCTWD ECF Procedures(2)(c)(i). For information on filing fees and the District Court Miscellaneous Fee Schedule, refer to 28 U.S.C.A. § 1914.

    e.  *Affidavit proving service.* Unless service is waived, proof of service must be made to the court. Except for service by a United States marshal or deputy marshal, proof must be by the server's affidavit. FRCP 4(l)(1). Proof of service shall be filed with the Clerk of Court. NY R USDCTWD Civ Rule 4. Refer to the Filing and Service Requirements section of this document for more information.

2. *Supplemental documents*

a. *Notice and request for waiver of service.* An individual, corporation, or association that is subject to service under FRCP 4(e), FRCP 4(f), or FRCP 4(h) has a duty to avoid unnecessary expenses of serving the summons. The plaintiff may notify such a defendant that an action has been commenced and request that the defendant waive service of a summons. The notice and request must:

   i. Be in writing and be addressed:

      • To the individual defendant; or

      • For a defendant subject to service under FRCP 4(h), to an officer, a managing or general agent, or any other agent authorized by appointment or by law to receive service of process;

   ii. Name the court where the complaint was filed;

   iii. Be accompanied by a copy of the complaint, two (2) copies of a waiver form appended to FRCP 4, and a prepaid means for returning the form;

   iv. Inform the defendant, using the form appended to FRCP 4, of the consequences of waiving and not waiving service;

   v. State the date when the request is sent;

   vi. Give the defendant a reasonable time of at least thirty (30) days after the request was sent—or at least sixty (60) days if sent to the defendant outside any judicial district of the United States—to return the waiver; and

   vii. Be sent by first-class mail or other reliable means. FRCP 4(d)(1).

b. *Notice of constitutional question.* A party that files a pleading, written motion, or other paper drawing into question the constitutionality of a federal or state statute must promptly:

   i. *File notice.* File a notice of constitutional question stating the question and identifying the paper that raises it, if:

      • A federal statute is questioned and the parties do not include the United States, one of its agencies, or one of its officers or employees in an official capacity; or

      • A state statute is questioned and the parties do not include the state, one of its agencies, or one of its officers or employees in an official capacity; and

   ii. *Serve notice.* Serve the notice and paper on the Attorney General of the United States if a federal statute is questioned—or on the state attorney general if a state statute is questioned—either by certified or registered mail or by sending it to an electronic address designated by the attorney general for this purpose. FRCP 5.1(a).

   iii. *No forfeiture.* A party's failure to file and serve the notice, or the court's failure to certify, does not forfeit a constitutional claim or defense that is otherwise timely asserted. FRCP 5.1(d).

c. *Notice of issue concerning foreign law.* A party who intends to raise an issue about a foreign country's law must give notice by a pleading or other writing. In determining foreign law, the court may consider any relevant material or source, including testimony, whether or not submitted by a party or admissible under the Federal Rules of Evidence. The court's determination must be treated as a ruling on a question of law. FRCP 44.1.

d. *Nongovernmental corporate disclosure statement*

   i. *Contents.* A nongovernmental corporate party must file two (2) copies of a disclosure statement that:

      • Identifies any parent corporation and any publicly held corporation owning ten percent (10%) or more of its stock; or

      • States that there is no such corporation. FRCP 7.1(a).

   ii. *Time to file; Supplemental filing.* A party must:

      • File the disclosure statement with its first appearance, pleading, petition, motion, response, or other request addressed to the court; and

- Promptly file a supplemental statement if any required information changes. FRCP 7.1(b).

e. *RICO case statement.* Any party asserting a claim, cross-claim, or counterclaim under the Racketeer Influenced & Corrupt Organizations Act ("RICO"), 18 U.S.C.A. § 1961 et seq., shall file and serve a "RICO Case Statement" under separate cover. This statement shall be filed contemporaneously with the papers first asserting the party's RICO claim, cross-claim or counterclaim, unless the Court grants an extension of time for filing. A party's failure to file a RICO Case Statement may result in dismissal of the party's RICO claim, cross-claim, or counterclaim. The RICO Case Statement must include those facts upon which the party is relying and which were obtained as a result of the reasonable inquiry required by FRCP 11. NY R USDCTWD Civ Rule 9. For more information, refer to NY R USDCTWD Civ Rule 9.

f. *Disk or CD with PDF of complaint.* In addition, when a case is opened in the traditional manner, registered attorneys shall provide the initiating document, in electronic format on a disk or CD, in PDF format, with signatures in accordance with NY R USDCTWD ECF Procedures(2)(g). NY R USDCTWD ECF Procedures(2)(c)(i).

g. *Paper copy for date-stamping with self-addressed envelope.* Parties requesting date-stamped copies of filed documents must provide a paper copy for date-stamping, and a self-addressed, adequately-sized envelope with proper postage affixed. NY R USDCTWD Civ Rule 5.1(d).

h. *Courtesy copies.* Courtesy copies of certain documents may be required. Filers should refer to the "Judge Preferences" published on the Court's website. NY R USDCTWD ECF Procedures(2)(a)(iii).

3. *Individual judge practices.* Refer to the Miscellaneous section of this document for information on individual judge practices on required documents.

# E.  Format

1. *Form of documents*

   a. *Form, generally.* All pleadings, motions, and other papers that a party presents for filing, whether in paper form or in electronic form, shall meet the following requirements:

      i. *Font size.* All text and footnotes shall be in a font size of at least twelve (12) point type. NY R USDCTWD Civ Rule 10(a)(1).

      ii. *Spacing.* All text in the body of the document must be double-spaced, except that text in block quotations and footnotes may be single-spaced. NY R USDCTWD Civ Rule 10(a)(2).

      - Extensive footnotes and block quotes may not be used to circumvent page limitations. NY R USDCTWD Civ Rule 10(a)(3).

      iii. *Margins.* Documents must have one (1) inch margins on all four sides. NY R USDCTWD Civ Rule 10(a)(4).

      iv. *Page numbering.* Pages must be consecutively numbered. NY R USDCTWD Civ Rule 10(a)(5).

   b. *Additional requirements for paper filing.* Documents presented for filing in paper form shall meet the following additional requirements:

      i. *Paper.* Documents must be on durable white eight and one-half by eleven (8-1/2 x 11) inch paper of good quality. NY R USDCTWD Civ Rule 10(b)(1).

      - All documents must be single-sided. NY R USDCTWD Civ Rule 10(b)(5).

      ii. *Text.* All text must be plainly and legibly written, typewritten, printed or reproduced. NY R USDCTWD Civ Rule 10(b)(2).

      iii. *Ink.* Documents must be in black or blue ink. NY R USDCTWD Civ Rule 10(b)(3).

      iv. *Binding.* The pages of each document must be stapled or in some other way fastened together. NY R USDCTWD Civ Rule 10(b)(4).

   c. *Caption; Names of parties.* Every pleading must have a caption with the court's name, a title, a file number, and a FRCP 7(a) designation. The title of the complaint must name all the parties; the title of other pleadings, after naming the first party on each side, may refer generally to other parties. FRCP 10(a).

    i.   *Class action.* Any pleading purporting to commence a class action shall include the term "Class Action" next to its caption. NY R USDCTWD Civ Rule 23(a). For more information on class actions, refer to NY R USDCTWD Civ Rule 23.

d.  *Paragraphs; Separate statements.* A party must state its claims or defenses in numbered paragraphs, each limited as far as practicable to a single set of circumstances. A later pleading may refer by number to a paragraph in an earlier pleading. If doing so would promote clarity, each claim founded on a separate transaction or occurrence—and each defense other than a denial—must be stated in a separate count or defense. FRCP 10(b).

e.  *Adoption by reference; Exhibits.* A statement in a pleading may be adopted by reference elsewhere in the same pleading or in any other pleading or motion. A copy of a written instrument that is an exhibit to a pleading is a part of the pleading for all purposes. FRCP 10(c).

f.  *Citation of local rules.* The Local Rules of Civil Procedure for the United States District Court for the Western District of New York shall be cited as "L.R.Civ.P." NY R USDCTWD Civ Rule 1.1.

g.  *Acceptance by the clerk.* The clerk must not refuse to file a paper solely because it is not in the form prescribed by the Federal Rules of Civil Procedure or by a local rule or practice. FRCP 5(d)(4). The Court may reject documents that do not comply with the requirements in NY R USDCTWD Civ Rule 10. NY R USDCTWD Civ Rule 10.

2.  *Form of electronic documents.* All pleadings, motions, and other papers that a party presents for filing, whether in paper form or in electronic form, shall meet the requirements in NY R USDCTWD Civ Rule 10(a). NY R USDCTWD Civ Rule 10(a). Refer above for more information.

a.  *Conversion to PDF.* A document created with a word processor, or a paper document, must be converted to Portable Document Format to be electronically filed with the court. NY R USDCTWD ECF Procedures(2)(a)(v).

    i.   Documents which exist only in paper form may be scanned into a portable document format (PDF) for electronic filing. NY R USDCTWD ECF Procedures(2)(a)(v). Before filing a scanned document with the court, a Filing User must verify its legibility. NY R USDCTWD ECF Procedures(2)(a)(iv).

    ii.  Electronic documents must be converted to .PDF from a word processing program and must be text searchable. Do not print, scan and .PDF your document when it has been created in a word processing program. Additional information on working with PDFs is located in NY R USDCTWD ECF Procedures(4b). NY R USDCTWD ECF Procedures(2)(a)(v).

b.  *Hyperlinks.* Pursuant to the policy set forth by the Judicial Conference in October 2005, a hyperlink contained in a filing is no more than a convenient mechanism for accessing material cited in a document. A hyperlink reference is extraneous to any filed document and is not part of the Court's record. NY R USDCTWD ECF Procedures(2)(a)(vi).

    i.   In order to preserve the integrity of the Court record, users wishing to insert hyperlinks in Court filings shall continue to use the conventional method for the cited authority, in addition to the hyperlink. NY R USDCTWD ECF Procedures(2)(a)(vi).

    ii.  The Court accepts no responsibility for, and does not endorse any product, organization, and content at any hyperlinked site, or at any site to which that site may be linked. The Court accepts no responsibility for the availability or functionality of any hyperlink. NY R USDCTWD ECF Procedures(2)(a)(vi).

c.  *Attachments and exhibits*

    i.   Attachments and exhibits larger than five megabytes (5 MB) shall be filed electronically in separate five megabyte (5 MB) segments. NY R USDCTWD ECF Procedures(2)(d)(i).

    ii.  Filing Users must submit in electronic form all documents referenced as exhibits or attachments, except as otherwise provided in NY R USDCTWD ECF Procedures. A Filing User must submit as exhibits or attachments only those excerpts of the referenced documents that are directly germane to the matter under consideration by the court. Excerpted material must be clearly and prominently identified as such. Filing Users who file excerpts of documents as exhibits or attachments under NY R USDCTWD ECF Procedures(2)(d)(ii) do so without prejudice to their right to timely file additional excerpts or the complete document. Responding parties may timely file additional excerpts or the complete document that they believe are directly germane. The Court may require parties to file additional excerpts or the complete document. A Filing User must request leave of the Court to file a document exhibit or attachment in non-electronic form. NY R USDCTWD ECF Procedures(2)(d)(ii).

    iii. Exhibits offered or admitted at trial will not be filed electronically or conventionally unless so ordered by the Court. NY R USDCTWD ECF Procedures(2)(d)(iii).

    iv. Exhibits such as videotapes and tape recordings shall be filed in the conventional manner with the Clerk of Court, and a Notice of Manual Filing shall be electronically filed by the party. Manually filed exhibits must have the case number and case name securely fastened or marked on the item. NY R USDCTWD ECF Procedures(2)(d)(iii).

    v. Continuation of exhibit entries (for exhibits that are too large to attach to a main document) must be filed and entered on the same day that the main document was filed. NY R USDCTWD ECF Procedures(2)(d)(iv).

d. *Color documents.* Documents in color or containing graphics take much longer to upload. Filing users are encouraged to configure their scanners to scan documents at 200 dpi and preferably in black and white rather than color. NY R USDCTWD ECF Procedures(2)(d)(v).

e. *Large documents.* Due to the length of time it takes to download large files, documents larger than five megabytes (5 MB) (approximately one hundred (100) pages of a .pdf scanned document) must be filed electronically in separate five megabyte (5 MB) segments. A party who believes a document is too lengthy to electronically image (i.e. scan), may contact the Court Room Deputy for the assigned judge and request permission to file that document conventionally. If granted permission to file the document conventionally, the Filing User shall electronically file a "notice of manual filing" for that item. Exhibits submitted to the Court conventionally shall be served on other parties conventionally. NY R USDCTWD ECF Procedures(2)(d)(vi).

3. *Signing of pleadings, motions and other papers*

a. *Signature.* Every pleading, written motion, and other paper must be signed by at least one attorney of record in the attorney's name—or by a party personally if the party is unrepresented. The paper must state the signer's address, e-mail address, and telephone number. FRCP 11(a). Documents presented for paper filing must contain an original signature. NY R USDCTWD Civ Rule 10(b)(6).

    i. *Electronic signatures*

       • *Non-attorney signature.* If the original document requires the signature of a non-attorney, the filing party shall obtain the signature of the non-attorney on the document. NY R USDCTWD ECF Procedures(2)(g)(i). The filing party or attorney then shall file the document electronically indicating the signatory's name in the form "s/(name)." NY R USDCTWD ECF Procedures(2)(g)(i)(1). A non-filing signatory or party who disputes the authenticity of an electronically filed document or the authenticity of the signature on that document must file an objection to the document within ten (10) days of receiving the Notice of Electronic Filing. NY R USDCTWD ECF Procedures(2)(g)(i)(2).

       • *Registered user signature.* The username and password required to file documents on the Electronic Filing System serve as the Filing User's signature on all electronic documents filed with this Court. The also serve as a signature for the purposes of FRCP 11, the Federal Rules of Civil Procedure, the Local Rules of Civil Procedure for the United States District Court for the Western District of New York, and any other purpose for which a signature is required in connection with proceedings before this Court. A pleading requiring a Registered User's signature must include a signature block in the format found in NY R USDCTWD ECF Procedures(2)(g)(iii). NY R USDCTWD ECF Procedures(2)(g)(iii). Any party challenging the authenticity of an electronically filed document or the attorney's signature on that document must file an objection to the document within ten (10) days of receiving the Notice of Electronic Filing. NY R USDCTWD ECF Procedures(2)(g)(iii)(1).

- *Multiple signatures.* The following procedure applies when a stipulation or other document requires two or more signatures: The filing party shall initially confirm that the document is acceptable to all persons required to sign the document and shall obtain the signatures of all parties on the document. NY R USDCTWD ECF Procedures(2)(g)(iv)(1). The filing party or attorney then shall file the document electronically indicating the signatories, e.g., "s/Jane Doe," "s/John Smith," etc. NY R USDCTWD ECF Procedures(2)(g)(iv)(2). A non-filing signatory or party who disputes the authenticity of an electronically filed document containing multiple signatures or the authenticity of the signatures themselves must file an objection to the document within ten (10) days of receiving the Notice of Electronic Filing. NY R USDCTWD ECF Procedures(2)(g)(iv)(3).

   ii. *No verification or accompanying affidavit required for pleadings.* Unless a rule or statute specifically states otherwise, a pleading need not be verified or accompanied by an affidavit. FRCP 11(a).

   iii. *Unsigned papers.* The court must strike an unsigned paper unless the omission is promptly corrected after being called to the attorney's or party's attention. FRCP 11(a).

b. *Representations to the court.* By presenting to the court a pleading, written motion, or other paper—whether by signing, filing, submitting, or later advocating it—an attorney or unrepresented party certifies that to the best of the person's knowledge, information, and belief, formed after an inquiry reasonable under the circumstances:

   i. It is not being presented for any improper purpose, such as to harass, cause unnecessary delay, or needlessly increase the cost of litigation;

   ii. The claims, defenses, and other legal contentions are warranted by existing law or by a nonfrivolous argument for extending, modifying, or reversing existing law or for establishing new law;

   iii. The factual contentions have evidentiary support or, if specifically so identified, will likely have evidentiary support after a reasonable opportunity for further investigation or discovery; and

   iv. The denials of factual contentions are warranted on the evidence or, if specifically so identified, are reasonably based on belief or a lack of information. FRCP 11(b).

c. *Sanctions.* If, after notice and a reasonable opportunity to respond, the court determines that FRCP 11(b) has been violated, the court may impose an appropriate sanction on any attorney, law firm, or party that violated FRCP 11(b) or is responsible for the violation. FRCP 11(c)(1). Refer to the United States District Court for the Western District of New York KeyRules Motion for Sanctions document for more information.

4. *Privacy protection for filings made with the court.* In all filings, parties shall comply with FRCP 5.2. NY R USDCTWD ECF Procedures(2)(m)(i).

a. *Redacted filings.* Unless the court orders otherwise, in an electronic or paper filing with the court that contains an individual's Social Security number, taxpayer-identification number, or birth date, the name of an individual known to be a minor, or a financial-account number, a party or nonparty making the filing may include only:

   i. The last four (4) digits of the Social Security number and taxpayer-identification number;

   ii. The year of the individual's birth;

   iii. The minor's initials; and

   iv. The last four (4) digits of the financial-account number. FRCP 5.2(a).

b. *Exemptions from the redaction requirement.* The redaction requirement does not apply to the following:

  i. A financial-account number that identifies the property allegedly subject to forfeiture in a forfeiture proceeding;

  ii. The record of an administrative or agency proceeding;

  iii. The official record of a state-court proceeding;

  iv. The record of a court or tribunal, if that record was not subject to the redaction requirement when originally filed;

  v. A filing covered by FRCP 5.2(c) or FRCP 5.2(d); and

  vi. A pro se filing in an action brought under 28 U.S.C.A. § 2241, 28 U.S.C.A. § 2254, or 28 U.S.C.A. § 2255. FRCP 5.2(b).

c. *Limitations on remote access to electronic files; Social Security appeals and immigration cases.* Unless the court orders otherwise, in an action for benefits under the Social Security Act, and in an action or proceeding relating to an order of removal, to relief from removal, or to immigration benefits or detention, access to an electronic file is authorized as follows:

  i. The parties and their attorneys may have remote electronic access to any part of the case file, including the administrative record;

  ii. Any other person may have electronic access to the full record at the courthouse, but may have remote electronic access only to:

  • The docket maintained by the court; and

  • An opinion, order, judgment, or other disposition of the court, but not any other part of the case file or the administrative record. FRCP 5.2(c).

d. *Filings made under seal.* The court may order that a filing be made under seal without redaction. The court may later unseal the filing or order the person who made the filing to file a redacted version for the public record. FRCP 5.2(d). For more information on sealing documents, refer to NY R USDCTWD Civ Rule 5.3, NY R USDCTWD ECF Procedures(2)(o)(i)(1), NY R USDCTWD ECF Procedures(2)(o)(i)(2), and NY R USDCTWD ECF Procedures(2)(o)(i)(3).

e. *Protective orders.* For good cause, the court may by order in a case:

  i. Require redaction of additional information; or

  ii. Limit or prohibit a nonparty's remote electronic access to a document filed with the court. FRCP 5.2(e).

f. *Option for additional unredacted filing under seal.* A person making a redacted filing may also file an unredacted copy under seal. The court must retain the unredacted copy as part of the record. FRCP 5.2(f).

g. *Option for filing a reference list.* A filing that contains redacted information may be filed together with a reference list that identifies each item of redacted information and specifies an appropriate identifier that uniquely corresponds to each item listed. The list must be filed under seal and may be amended as of right. Any reference in the case to a listed identifier will be construed to refer to the corresponding item of information. FRCP 5.2(g).

h. *Waiver of protection of identifiers.* A person waives the protection of FRCP 5.2(a) as to the person's own information by filing it without redaction and not under seal. FRCP 5.2(h).

5. *Individual judge practices.* Refer to the Miscellaneous section of this document for information on individual judge practices on formatting documents.

## F. Filing and Service Requirements

1. *Filing requirements.* A civil action is commenced by filing a complaint with the court. FRCP 3. The first step in a civil action in a United States district court is the filing of the complaint with the clerk or the judge. FPP § 1052. Filing a complaint requires nothing more than delivery of the document to a court

officer authorized to receive it. FPP § 1052; Central States, Southeast & Southwest Areas Pension Fund v. Paramount Liquor Co., 34 F.Supp.2d 1092 (N.D.Ill. 1999). Proof of service shall be filed with the Clerk of Court. NY R USDCTWD Civ Rule 4. All pleadings and other papers shall be filed and served in accordance with the Federal Rules of Civil Procedure and the CM/ECF Administrative Procedures Guide (NY R USDCTWD ECF Procedures). NY R USDCTWD Civ Rule 5.1(a). For information on filing of miscellaneous cases and irregular documents, refer to NY R USDCTWD Civ Rule 5.6.

a. *Opening a civil case.* Registered attorneys must open most civil complaints, notice of removals and petitions for habeas corpus on line (exemptions from NY R USDCTWD ECF Procedures(2)(c)(i) are located NY R USDCTWD ECF Procedures(2)(a)(i). NY R USDCTWD ECF Procedures(2)(c)(i). When opening a civil case on line, the civil cover sheet, summons (if applicable) and marshal forms (if applicable) must be attached to the initiating document as individual attachments. NY R USDCTWD ECF Procedures(2)(c)(ii). For information on conventional opening of certain types of cases, refer to NY R USDCTWD ECF Procedures(2)(n).

b. *Case assignment.* Upon filing, civil cases are assigned to a Judge in either Buffalo (typically, cases arising in Allegany, Cattaraugus, Chautauqua, Erie, Genesee, Niagara, Orleans and Wyoming counties), or Rochester (typically, cases arising in Chemung, Livingston, Monroe, Ontario, Schuyler, Seneca, Steuben, Wayne and Yates counties). The Court may transfer cases within the District, sua sponte. Parties requesting transfer of a case from Buffalo to Rochester, or vice versa, shall file a written motion requesting such relief, returnable before the Judge to whom the case is originally assigned. NY R USDCTWD Civ Rule 5.1(c).

c. *Pro se incarcerated litigants.* Individuals who are incarcerated and are filing their legal documents pro se may benefit from a special "mailbox rule," which fixes the time of commencement of an action at the point when the complaint enters the prison mail system, rather than when it reaches the court clerk. FPP § 1052; Houston v. Lack, 487 U.S. 266, 276, 108 S.Ct. 2379, 2385, 101 L.Ed.2d 245 (1988).

d. *Electronic filing*

  i. *Authorization of electronic filing program.* A court may, by local rule, allow papers to be filed, signed, or verified by electronic means that are consistent with any technical standards established by the Judicial Conference of the United States. A local rule may require electronic filing only if reasonable exceptions are allowed. A paper filed electronically in compliance with a local rule is a written paper for purposes of the Federal Rules of Civil Procedure. FRCP 5(d)(3).

    • All civil cases filed in this Court are assigned to the Electronic Case Filing System ("ECF"). The procedures for electronic filing and any exceptions to the electronic filing requirements are set forth in the CM/ECF Administrative Procedures Guide (NY R USDCTWD ECF Procedures) which is available on the Court's website. NY R USDCTWD Civ Rule 5.1(a).

  ii. *Scope of electronic filing.* The U.S. District Court for the Western District of New York requires attorneys in civil and criminal cases to file documents with the Court electronically over the Internet using its Case Management/Electronic Case Filing (CM/ECF) system. NY R USDCTWD ECF Procedures. Beginning January 1, 2004, all civil and criminal cases currently pending and newly filed, except as expressly noted herein, were assigned to the Electronic Case Filing System ("System"). Except as expressly provided and in exceptional circumstances preventing a Filing User from filing electronically, all petitions, motions, memoranda of law, or other pleadings and documents required to be filed with the Court in connection with a case assigned to the System must be electronically filed. NY R USDCTWD ECF Procedures(1)(a).

    • *Mandatory electronic filing.* All documents on civil, criminal, miscellaneous civil, miscellaneous criminal and new civil case openings, except sealed documents, sealed cases, opening of a criminal case, opening of a miscellaneous case and as expressly provided for in these procedures (NY R USDCTWD ECF Procedures), shall be electronically filed on the system. NY R USDCTWD ECF Procedures(2)(a)(i). NY R USDCTWD Civ Rule 29

    • *Stipulations.* Pursuant to NY R USDCTWD Civ Rule 29, all stipulations (whether the stipulation is final or when it requires a judge's signature) shall be filed electronically. NY R USDCTWD ECF Procedures(2)(p)(i).

- *Letters.* The electronic filing of letters is generally prohibited unless granted permission by an assigned judge. Letters to the Court must be submitted conventionally. NY R US-DCTWD ECF Procedures(2)(q)(i).

- *Exceptions.* The Court requires attorneys to file documents electronically, absent a showing of good cause, unless otherwise excused by the procedures set forth below or by Order of the Court. NY R USDCTWD ECF Procedures.

iii. *Conventional filing of documents.* The procedures in NY R USDCTWD ECF Procedures(2)(o) govern documents filed conventionally. The Court, upon application, may also authorize conventional filing of other documents otherwise subject to the procedures in NY R US-DCTWD ECF Procedures(2)(o). NY R USDCTWD ECF Procedures(2)(o)(i).

- *Documents filed under seal.* Unredacted documents filed with the Court pursuant to the privacy provisions of FRCP 5.2 shall be submitted in a sealing envelope with the information in NY R USDCTWD ECF Procedures(2)(o)(i)(1) on the envelope. NY R USDCTWD ECF Procedures(2)(o)(i)(1). If the document is larger than five (5) pages, a disk should be provided to the Clerks Office which contains the document in a .pdf format. NY R USDCTWD ECF Procedures(2)(o)(i)(1). For more information on documents filed under seal, refer to NY R USDCTWD ECF Procedures(2)(o)(i)(1), NY R USDCTWD ECF Procedures(2)(o)(i)(2), and NY R USDCTWD ECF Procedures(2)(o)(i)(3).

- *Magistrate judge consents.* Pursuant to FRCP 73(b), parties' filing consents to jurisdiction by United States Magistrate Judge will continue to be treated as non-public documents until all parties have consented. Therefore, parties must submit conventionally (in paper form) and not electronically file their consent forms so that the consent is not a public document. If all parties consent to the jurisdiction of a Magistrate Judge, the Clerk will scan all consent forms which will then become a public document. NY R USDCTWD ECF Procedures(2)(o)(i)(3).

- *Pro se filers.* Pro Se filers shall file paper originals of all initiating documents, pleadings, motions, affidavits, briefs and other documents which must be signed or which require either verification or an unsworn declaration under any rule or statute. The Clerk's Office will scan these original documents into an electronic file in the System. A certificate of service is required for all documents a pro se litigant files with the court. If a Pro Se filer is granted permission to register to electronically file documents, they shall comply with the guidelines contained in this document (NY R USDCTWD ECF Procedures). NY R USDCTWD ECF Procedures(2)(o)(i)(4).

- *Social Security cases.* Absent a showing of good cause, and except as provided in Section o(i)(4) above, all documents, notices and orders in Social Security reviews will be filed and noticed electronically, except as noted in NY R USDCTWD ECF Procedures(2)(o)(i)(6). For more information, refer to NY R USDCTWD ECF Procedures(2)(o)(i)(6).

- For more information on conventional filing of documents, refer to NY R USDCTWD ECF Procedures(2)(o)(i).

iv. *Consequences of electronic filing.* Electronic transmission of a document to the System consistent with these procedures (NY R USDCTWD ECF Procedures), whether accomplished by the Filing User or a Court User, together with the transmission of a Notice of Electronic Filing from the Court, constitutes filing of a document for all purposes of the Federal Rules of Civil Procedure and the Local Rules of Civil Procedure for the United States District Court for the Western District of New York, and constitutes entry of the document on the docket kept by the Clerk under FRCP 58 and FRCP 79. A document shall not be considered filed for purposes of the Federal Rules of Civil until the filing party receives a System generated Notice of Electronic Filing. NY R USDCTWD ECF Procedures(2)(a)(i).

- E-mailing a document to the Clerk's Office or to the assigned judge shall not constitute "filing" of such document. NY R USDCTWD ECF Procedures(2)(a)(i)(1).

     v.   *Filing fees.* Any fee required for filing of a pleading or paper in District Court is payable to the Clerk of Court by check or money order. In addition, when opening a civil case on line, filing a notice of appeal on line or applying to appear pro hac vice on line, the fees shall be paid on line by registered users through the federal electronic payment website. Users will be directed to the federal electronic payment website while entering their transaction and should have a credit card available. When opening a civil case and applying to proceed in forma pauperis or when the United States of America opens a case, the payment screen can by bypassed to complete the transaction. Additional information on making electronic payments can be located on the court's website. NY R USDCTWD ECF Procedures(2)(h)(i).

2. *Issuance of summons.* On or after filing the complaint, the plaintiff may present a summons to the clerk for signature and seal. If the summons is properly completed, the clerk must sign, seal, and issue it to the plaintiff for service on the defendant. A summons—or a copy of a summons that is addressed to multiple defendants—must be issued for each defendant to be served. FRCP 4(b).

    a.   *Electronic issuance.* Summons will be issued electronically and returned to the registered attorney through an entry in the System. NY R USDCTWD ECF Procedures(2)(c)(ii).

    b.   *Amendments.* The court may permit a summons to be amended. FRCP 4(a)(2).

3. *Service requirements.* A summons must be served with a copy of the complaint. The plaintiff is responsible for having the summons and complaint served within the time allowed by FRCP 4(m) and must furnish the necessary copies to the person who makes service. FRCP 4(c)(1). All pleadings and other papers shall be filed and served in accordance with the Federal Rules of Civil Procedure and the CM/ECF Administrative Procedures Guide (NY R USDCTWD ECF Procedures). NY R USDCTWD Civ Rule 5.1(a).

    a.   *By whom served.* Any person who is at least 18 years old and not a party may serve a summons and complaint. FRCP 4(c)(2).

       i.   *By a marshal or someone specially appointed.* At the plaintiff's request, the court may order that service be made by a United States marshal or deputy marshal or by a person specially appointed by the court. The court must so order if the plaintiff is authorized to proceed in forma pauperis under 28 U.S.C.A. § 1915 or as a seaman under 28 U.S.C.A. § 1916. FRCP 4(c)(3).

          •   In conformity with FRCP 4(c), in all civil actions filed in this Court, service shall be made other than by the United States Marshal Service, except for the following circumstances: (1) service of process on behalf of the United States; (2) service of process on behalf of litigants proceeding pro se who are authorized to proceed in forma pauperis pursuant to 28 U.S.C.A. § 1915; (3) service of process on behalf of litigants authorized to proceed as seamen under 28 U.S.C.A. § 1916; (4) service of writs of seizure, attachment, forfeiture, or execution; or (5) service of process pursuant to a specific order of this Court. NY R USDCTWD Civ Rule 4.

    b.   *Serving an individual within a judicial district of the United States.* Unless federal law provides otherwise, an individual—other than a minor, an incompetent person, or a person whose waiver has been filed—may be served in a judicial district of the United States by:

       i.   Following state law for serving a summons in an action brought in courts of general jurisdiction in the state where the district court is located or where service is made; or

       ii.   Doing any of the following:

          •   Delivering a copy of the summons and of the complaint to the individual personally;

          •   Leaving a copy of each at the individual's dwelling or usual place of abode with someone of suitable age and discretion who resides there; or

          •   Delivering a copy of each to an agent authorized by appointment or by law to receive service of process. FRCP 4(e).

    c.   *Serving an individual in a foreign country.* Unless federal law provides otherwise, an individual—other than a minor, an incompetent person, or a person whose waiver has been filed—may be served at a place not within any judicial district of the United States:

       i.   By any internationally agreed means of service that is reasonably calculated to give notice, such as those authorized by the Hague Convention on the Service Abroad of Judicial and Extrajudicial Documents;

ii.  If there is no internationally agreed means, or if an international agreement allows but does not specify other means, by a method that is reasonably calculated to give notice:

- As prescribed by the foreign country's law for service in that country in an action in its courts of general jurisdiction;

- As the foreign authority directs in response to a letter rogatory or letter of request; or

- Unless prohibited by the foreign country's law, by: (1) delivering a copy of the summons and of the complaint to the individual personally; or (2) using any form of mail that the clerk addresses and sends to the individual and that requires a signed receipt; or

- By other means not prohibited by international agreement, as the court orders. FRCP 4(f).

d.  *Serving a minor or an incompetent person.* A minor or an incompetent person in a judicial district of the United States must be served by following state law for serving a summons or like process on such a defendant in an action brought in the courts of general jurisdiction of the state where service is made. A minor or an incompetent person who is not within any judicial district of the United States must be served in the manner prescribed by FRCP 4(f)(2)(A), FRCP 4(f)(2)(B), or FRCP 4(f)(3). FRCP 4(g).

e.  *Serving a corporation, partnership, or association.* Unless federal law provides otherwise or the defendant's waiver has been filed, a domestic or foreign corporation, or a partnership or other unincorporated association that is subject to suit under a common name, must be served:

i.  In a judicial district of the United States:

- In the manner prescribed by FRCP 4(e)(1) for serving an individual; or

- By delivering a copy of the summons and of the complaint to an officer, a managing or general agent, or any other agent authorized by appointment or by law to receive service of process and—if the agent is one authorized by statute and the statute so requires—by also mailing a copy of each to the defendant; or

ii.  At a place not within any judicial district of the United States, in any manner prescribed by FRCP 4(f) for serving an individual, except personal delivery under FRCP 4(f)(2)(C)(i). FRCP 4(h).

f.  *Serving the United States and its agencies, corporations, officers, or employees*

i.  *United States.* To serve the United States, a party must:

- Deliver a copy of the summons and of the complaint to the United States attorney for the district where the action is brought—or to an assistant United States attorney or clerical employee whom the United States attorney designates in a writing filed with the court clerk—or send a copy of each by registered or certified mail to the civil-process clerk at the United States attorney's office;

- Send a copy of each by registered or certified mail to the Attorney General of the United States at Washington, D.C.; and

- If the action challenges an order of a nonparty agency or officer of the United States, send a copy of each by registered or certified mail to the agency or officer. FRCP 4(i)(1).

ii.  *Agency; Corporation; Officer or employee sued in an official capacity.* To serve a United States agency or corporation, or a United States officer or employee sued only in an official capacity, a party must serve the United States and also send a copy of the summons and of the complaint by registered or certified mail to the agency, corporation, officer, or employee. FRCP 4(i)(2).

iii.  *Officer or employee sued individually.* To serve a United States officer or employee sued in an individual capacity for an act or omission occurring in connection with duties performed on the United States' behalf (whether or not the officer or employee is also sued in an official capacity), a party must serve the United States and also serve the officer or employee under FRCP 4(e), FRCP 4(f), or FRCP 4(g). FRCP 4(i)(3).

iv. *Extending time.* The court must allow a party a reasonable time to cure its failure to:

- Serve a person required to be served under FRCP 4(i)(2), if the party has served either the United States attorney or the Attorney General of the United States; or

- Serve the United States under FRCP 4(i)(3), if the party has served the United States officer or employee. FRCP 4(i)(4).

g. *Serving a foreign, state, or local government*

i. *Foreign state.* A foreign state or its political subdivision, agency, or instrumentality must be served in accordance with 28 U.S.C.A. § 1608. FRCP 4(j)(1).

ii. *State or local government.* A state, a municipal corporation, or any other state-created governmental organization that is subject to suit must be served by:

- Delivering a copy of the summons and of the complaint to its chief executive officer; or

- Serving a copy of each in the manner prescribed by that state's law for serving a summons or like process on such a defendant. FRCP 4(j)(2).

h. *Territorial limits of effective service*

i. *In general.* Serving a summons or filing a waiver of service establishes personal jurisdiction over a defendant:

- Who is subject to the jurisdiction of a court of general jurisdiction in the state where the district court is located;

- Who is a party joined under FRCP 14 or FRCP 19 and is served within a judicial district of the United States and not more than one hundred (100) miles from where the summons was issued; or

- When authorized by a federal statute. FRCP 4(k)(1).

ii. *Federal claim outside state-court jurisdiction.* For a claim that arises under federal law, serving a summons or filing a waiver of service establishes personal jurisdiction over a defendant if:

- The defendant is not subject to jurisdiction in any state's courts of general jurisdiction; and

- Exercising jurisdiction is consistent with the United States Constitution and laws. FRCP 4(k)(2).

i. *Asserting jurisdiction over property or assets*

i. *Federal law.* The court may assert jurisdiction over property if authorized by a federal statute. Notice to claimants of the property must be given as provided in the statute or by serving a summons under FRCP 4. FRCP 4(n)(1).

ii. *State law.* On a showing that personal jurisdiction over a defendant cannot be obtained in the district where the action is brought by reasonable efforts to serve a summons under FRCP 4, the court may assert jurisdiction over the defendant's assets found in the district. Jurisdiction is acquired by seizing the assets under the circumstances and in the manner provided by state law in that district. FRCP 4(n)(2).

j. *Proving service*

i. *Affidavit required.* Unless service is waived, proof of service must be made to the court. Except for service by a United States marshal or deputy marshal, proof must be by the server's affidavit. FRCP 4(l)(1).

ii. *Service outside the United States.* Service not within any judicial district of the United States must be proved as follows:

- If made under FRCP 4(f)(1), as provided in the applicable treaty or convention; or

- If made under FRCP 4(f)(2) or FRCP 4(f)(3), by a receipt signed by the addressee, or by other evidence satisfying the court that the summons and complaint were delivered to the addressee. FRCP 4(l)(2).

iii. *Validity of service; Amending proof.* Failure to prove service does not affect the validity of service. The court may permit proof of service to be amended. FRCP 4(l)(3).

iv. *Results of filing a waiver of service.* When the plaintiff files a waiver, proof of service is not required and FRCP 4 applies as if a summons and complaint had been served at the time of filing the waiver. FRCP 4(d)(4).

k. *Service of other process.* For information on service of other process, refer to FRCP 4.1.

4. *Pro se actions.* For information on the requirements in pro se actions, refer to NY R USDCTWD Civ Rule 5.2.

5. *Individual judge practices.* Refer to the Miscellaneous section of this document for information on individual judge practices on filing and serving documents.

## G. Hearings

1. There is no hearing contemplated in the federal statutes or rules for the complaint and summons.

## H. Forms

### 1. Official Federal Complaint and Summons Forms

a. Rule 4 notice of a lawsuit and request to waive service of summons. FRCP 4.

### 2. Federal Complaint and Summons Forms

a. Summons. 2 FEDFORMS § 3:23.

b. Summons; With proof of service. 2 FEDFORMS § 3:24.

c. Summons; Suit against officers of the United States. 2 FEDFORMS § 3:26.

d. Request for summons. 2 FEDFORMS § 3:27.

e. Civil cover sheet. 2 FEDFORMS § 3:29.

f. Motion for appointment of person to serve process. 2 FEDFORMS § 3:30.

g. Motion for appointment of United States marshal to serve process. 2 FEDFORMS § 3:34.

h. Notice of lawsuit and request for waiver of service of summons and waiver of summons. 2 FEDFORMS § 3:36.

i. Motion for payment of costs of personal service. 2 FEDFORMS § 3:37.

j. Affidavit of personal service; Delivery to individual. 2 FEDFORMS § 3:54.

k. Declaration of service; Delivery to individual. 2 FEDFORMS § 3:55.

l. Declaration of service; Delivery at usual place of abode or residence. 2 FEDFORMS § 3:56.

m. Declaration of service; Service on corporation; Delivery to officer. 2 FEDFORMS § 3:57.

n. Declaration of service; Service on United States. 2 FEDFORMS § 3:69.

o. Declaration of service; Service on officer of United States. 2 FEDFORMS § 3:71.

p. Complaint. 2 FEDFORMS § 7:14.

q. Introductory clause; Single claim stated. 2 FEDFORMS § 7:16.

r. Introductory clause; Several claims stated in separate counts. 2 FEDFORMS § 7:18.

s. Allegations on information and belief. 2 FEDFORMS § 7:19.

t. General prayer for relief. 2 FEDFORMS § 7:21.

u. Disparate treatment; Sex discrimination; Sexual harassment and constructive discharge. 2A FEDFORMS § 7:143.

v. Against manufacturer for negligent design and manufacture. 2B FEDFORMS § 7:426.

w. Complaint; Single count. FEDPROF § 1:68.

x. Complaint; Multiple counts; With same jurisdictional basis. FEDPROF § 1:69.

y. Complaint; Multiple counts; With different jurisdictional basis for each. FEDPROF § 1:70.

z. Civil cover sheet; General form. FEDPROF § 1:144.

## I. Applicable Rules

1. *Federal rules*

   a. District court; Filing and miscellaneous fees; Rules of court. 28 U.S.C.A. § 1914.

   b. Commencing an action. FRCP 3.

   c. Summons. FRCP 4.

   d. Serving and filing pleadings and other papers. FRCP 5.

   e. Constitutional challenge to a statute; Notice, certification, and intervention. FRCP 5.1.

   f. Privacy protection for filings made with the court. FRCP 5.2.

   g. Computing and extending time; Time for motion papers. FRCP 6.

   h. Pleadings allowed; Form of motions and other papers. FRCP 7.

   i. Disclosure statement. FRCP 7.1.

   j. General rules of pleading. FRCP 8.

   k. Pleading special matters. FRCP 9.

   l. Form of pleadings. FRCP 10.

   m. Signing pleadings, motions, and other papers; Representations to the court; Sanctions. FRCP 11.

   n. Joinder of claims. FRCP 18.

   o. Required joinder of parties. FRCP 19.

   p. Permissive joinder of parties. FRCP 20.

   q. Misjoinder and nonjoinder of parties. FRCP 21.

   r. Right to a jury trial; Demand. FRCP 38.

   s. Determining foreign law. FRCP 44.1.

2. *Local rules*

   a. Title. NY R USDCTWD Civ Rule 1.1.

   b. Civil cover sheet. NY R USDCTWD Civ Rule 3.

   c. Summons. NY R USDCTWD Civ Rule 4.

   d. Filing and serving papers. NY R USDCTWD Civ Rule 5.1.

   e. Payment of fees in advance. NY R USDCTWD Civ Rule 5.4.

   f. Requirement to file a RICO case statement. NY R USDCTWD Civ Rule 9.

   g. Form of papers. NY R USDCTWD Civ Rule 10.

   h. Sanctions. NY R USDCTWD Civ Rule 11.

   i. Alternative dispute resolution and pretrial conferences. NY R USDCTWD Civ Rule 16.

   j. Class actions. NY R USDCTWD Civ Rule 23.

   k. Attorneys of record; Appearance and withdrawal. NY R USDCTWD Civ Rule 83.2.

   l. Administrative procedures guide for electronic filing. NY R USDCTWD ECF Procedures.

   m. Alternative dispute resolution plan. NY R USDCTWD ADR Plan.

## J. Miscellaneous

**NOTE: Individual judges' rules may apply. For available judge-level information, refer to:**

DISTRICT JUDGE RICHARD J. ARCARA: NY R USDCTWD Arcara-Procedures.

DISTRICT JUDGE FRANK P. GERACI, JR.: NY R USDCTWD Geraci-Procedures.

DISTRICT JUDGE DAVID G. LARIMER: NY R USDCTWD Larimer-Procedures.

DISTRICT JUDGE CHARLES J. SIRAGUSA: NY R USDCTWD Siragusa-Procedures.

DISTRICT JUDGE WILLIAM M. SKRETNY: NY R USDCTWD Skretny--Procedures.

DISTRICT JUDGE MICHAEL A. TELESCA: NY R USDCTWD Telesca-Procedures.

DISTRICT JUDGE LAWRENCE J. VILARDO: NY R USDCTWD Vilardo-Procedures.

DISTRICT JUDGE ELIZABETH A. WOLFORD: NY R USDCTWD Wolford-Procedures.

MAGISTRATE JUDGE JONATHAN W. FELDMAN: NY R USDCTWD Feldman-Procedures.

MAGISTRATE JUDGE LESLIE G. FOSCHIO: NY R USDCTWD Foschio-Procedures; NY R USDCTWD Foschio-Depositions.

MAGISTRATE JUDGE JEREMIAH J. McCARTHY: NY R USDCTWD McCarthy-Procedures.

MAGISTRATE JUDGE MARIAN W. PAYSON: NY R USDCTWD Payson-Procedures.

MAGISTRATE JUDGE MICHAEL J. ROEMER: NY R USDCTWD Roemer-Procedures.

MAGISTRATE JUDGE H. KENNETH SCHROEDER, JR.: NY R USDCTWD Schroeder-Proc.

MAGISTRATE JUDGE HUGH B. SCOTT: NY R USDCTWD Scott-Procedures.

# Pleadings
# Answer

## Document Last Updated September 2016

A. **Checklist**

(I)  ❏ Matters to be considered by plaintiff

    (a)  ❏ Required documents

        (1)  ❏ Civil cover sheet

        (2)  ❏ Complaint

        (3)  ❏ Summons

        (4)  ❏ Filing fee

        (5)  ❏ Affidavit proving service

    (b)  ❏ Supplemental documents

        (1)  ❏ Notice and request for waiver of service

        (2)  ❏ Notice of constitutional question

        (3)  ❏ Notice of issue concerning foreign law

        (4)  ❏ Nongovernmental corporate disclosure statement

        (5)  ❏ RICO case statement

        (6)  ❏ Disk or CD with PDF of complaint

        (7)  ❏ Paper copy for date-stamping with self-addressed envelope

        (8)  ❏ Courtesy copies

    (c)  ❏ Timing

        (1)  ❏ A civil action is commenced by filing a complaint with the court

        (2)  ❏ If a defendant is not served within ninety (90) days after the complaint is filed, the court—on motion or on its own after notice to the plaintiff—must dismiss the action without prejudice against that defendant or order that service be made within a specified time

(II)  ❏ Matters to be considered by defendant

    (a)  ❏ Required documents

        (1)  ❏ Answer

(2) ❑ Certificate of service

(b) ❑ Supplemental documents

(1) ❑ Waiver of the service of summons

(2) ❑ Notice of constitutional question

(3) ❑ Notice of issue concerning foreign law

(4) ❑ Nongovernmental corporate disclosure statement

(5) ❑ RICO case statement

(6) ❑ Paper copy for date-stamping with self-addressed envelope

(7) ❑ Courtesy copies

(c) ❑ Timing

(1) ❑ A defendant must serve an answer:

(i) ❑ Within twenty-one (21) days after being served with the summons and complaint; or

(ii) ❑ If it has timely waived service under FRCP 4(d), within sixty (60) days after the request for a waiver was sent, or within ninety (90) days after it was sent to the defendant outside any judicial district of the United States

(2) ❑ The United States, a United States agency, or a United States officer or employee sued only in an official capacity must serve an answer to a complaint, counterclaim, or crossclaim within sixty (60) days after service on the United States attorney

(3) ❑ A United States officer or employee sued in an individual capacity for an act or omission occurring in connection with duties performed on the United States' behalf must serve an answer to a complaint, counterclaim, or crossclaim within sixty (60) days after service on the officer or employee or service on the United States attorney, whichever is later

(4) ❑ Unless the court sets a different time, serving a motion under FRCP 12 alters these periods as follows:

(i) ❑ If the court denies the motion or postpones its disposition until trial, the responsive pleading must be served within fourteen (14) days after notice of the court's action; or

(ii) ❑ If the court grants a motion for a more definite statement, the responsive pleading must be served within fourteen (14) days after the more definite statement is served

(5) ❑ Defendant is given a reasonable time of at least thirty (30) days after a waiver of service request is sent—or at least sixty (60) days if sent to defendant outside any judicial district of the United States—to return the waiver

## B. Timing

1. *Answer.* Unless another time is specified by FRCP 12 or a federal statute. . .a defendant must serve an answer: (1) within twenty-one (21) days after being served with the summons and complaint; or (2) if it has timely waived service under FRCP 4(d), within sixty (60) days after the request for a waiver was sent, or within ninety (90) days after it was sent to the defendant outside any judicial district of the United States. FRCP 12(a)(1)(A).

   a. *Time to serve other responsive pleadings.* Unless another time is specified by FRCP 12 or a federal statute, the time for serving a responsive pleading is as follows:

      i. *Answer to counterclaim or crossclaim.* A party must serve an answer to a counterclaim or crossclaim within twenty-one (21) days after being served with the pleading that states the counterclaim or crossclaim. FRCP 12(a)(1)(B).

      ii. *Reply to an answer.* A party must serve a reply to an answer within twenty-one (21) days after being served with an order to reply, unless the order specifies a different time. FRCP 12(a)(1)(C).

   b. *United States and its agencies, officers, or employees sued in an official capacity.* The United States, a United States agency, or a United States officer or employee sued only in an official capacity must serve an answer to a complaint, counterclaim, or crossclaim within sixty (60) days after service on the United States attorney. FRCP 12(a)(2).

c. *United States officers or employees sued in an individual capacity.* A United States officer or employee sued in an individual capacity for an act or omission occurring in connection with duties performed on the United States' behalf must serve an answer to a complaint, counterclaim, or crossclaim within sixty (60) days after service on the officer or employee or service on the United States attorney, whichever is later. FRCP 12(a)(3).

d. *Effect of a FRCP 12 motion on the time to serve a responsive pleading.* Unless the court sets a different time, serving a motion under FRCP 12 alters the periods in FRCP 12(a) as follows:

    i. If the court denies the motion or postpones its disposition until trial, the responsive pleading must be served within fourteen (14) days after notice of the court's action; or

    ii. If the court grants a motion for a more definite statement, the responsive pleading must be served within fourteen (14) days after the more definite statement is served. FRCP 12(a)(4).

2. *Waiver of service.* The notice and request for waiver must give the defendant a reasonable time of at least thirty (30) days after the request was sent—or at least sixty (60) days if sent to defendant outside any judicial district of the United States—to return the waiver. FRCP 4(d)(1)(F).

a. *Time to answer after a waiver.* A defendant who, before being served with process, timely returns a waiver need not serve an answer to the complaint until sixty (60) days after the request was sent—or until ninety (90) days after it was sent to the defendant outside any judicial district of the United States. FRCP 4(d)(3).

3. *Computation of time*

a. *Computing time.* FRCP 6 applies in computing any time period specified in the Federal Rules of Civil Procedure, in any local rule or court order, or in any statute that does not specify a method of computing time. FRCP 6(a).

    i. *Period stated in days or a longer unit.* When the period is stated in days or a longer unit of time:

- Exclude the day of the event that triggers the period;

- Count every day, including intermediate Saturdays, Sundays, and legal holidays; and

- Include the last day of the period, but if the last day is a Saturday, Sunday, or legal holiday, the period continues to run until the end of the next day that is not a Saturday, Sunday, or legal holiday. FRCP 6(a)(1).

    ii. *Period stated in hours.* When the period is stated in hours:

- Begin counting immediately on the occurrence of the event that triggers the period;

- Count every hour, including hours during intermediate Saturdays, Sundays, and legal holidays; and

- If the period would end on a Saturday, Sunday, or legal holiday, the period continues to run until the same time on the next day that is not a Saturday, Sunday, or legal holiday. FRCP 6(a)(2).

    iii. *Inaccessibility of the clerk's office.* Unless the court orders otherwise, if the clerk's office is inaccessible:

- On the last day for filing under FRCP 6(a)(1), then the time for filing is extended to the first accessible day that is not a Saturday, Sunday, or legal holiday; or

- During the last hour for filing under FRCP 6(a)(2), then the time for filing is extended to the same time on the first accessible day that is not a Saturday, Sunday, or legal holiday. FRCP 6(a)(3).

    iv. *"Last day" defined.* Unless a different time is set by a statute, local rule, or court order, the last day ends:

- For electronic filing, at midnight in the court's time zone; and

- For filing by other means, when the clerk's office is scheduled to close. FRCP 6(a)(4).

v. *"Next day" defined.* The "next day" is determined by continuing to count forward when the period is measured after an event and backward when measured before an event. FRCP 6(a)(5).

vi. *"Legal holiday" defined.* "Legal holiday" means:

- The day set aside by statute for observing New Year's Day, Martin Luther King Jr.'s Birthday, Washington's Birthday, Memorial Day, Independence Day, Labor Day, Columbus Day, Veterans' Day, Thanksgiving Day, or Christmas Day;

- Any day declared a holiday by the President or Congress; and

- For periods that are measured after an event, any other day declared a holiday by the state where the district court is located. FRCP 6(a)(6).

b. *Computation of electronic filing deadlines.* A document will be deemed timely filed if filed prior to midnight Eastern Time, unless otherwise ordered by the Court. A document will be considered untimely if filed thereafter. When a Court order requires that a document be filed on a weekend or holiday, the document may be filed by close of business the next business day without further application to the Court. NY R USDCTWD ECF Procedures(2)(e)(i). A document filed electronically is deemed filed on the date and time stated on the Notice of Electronic Filing. NY R USDCTWD ECF Procedures(2)(e)(ii).

i. *System availability.* Although parties may file documents electronically twenty-four (24) hours a day, registered users are strongly encouraged to file all documents during normal working hours of the Clerk's Office (8:30 a.m. to 5:00 p.m. Eastern Time). NY R USDCTWD ECF Procedures(2)(t)(i).

ii. *Technical failures.* A Filing User whose filing is made untimely as a result of a technical failure must seek appropriate relief from the Court. NY R USDCTWD ECF Procedures(2)(u)(i).

c. *Extending time*

i. *In general.* When an act may or must be done within a specified time, the court may, for good cause, extend the time:

- With or without motion or notice if the court acts, or if a request is made, before the original time or its extension expires; or

- On motion made after the time has expired if the party failed to act because of excusable neglect. FRCP 6(b)(1).

ii. *Exceptions.* A court must not extend the time to act under FRCP 50(b), FRCP 50(d), FRCP 52(b), FRCP 59(b), FRCP 59(d), FRCP 59(e), and FRCP 60(b). FRCP 6(b)(2).

iii. Refer to the United States District Court for the Western District of New York KeyRules Motion for Continuance/Extension of Time document for more information on extending time.

d. *Additional time after certain kinds of service.* When a party may or must act within a specified time after service and service is made under FRCP 5(b)(2)(C), FRCP 5(b)(2)(D), FRCP 5(b)(2)(E), or FRCP 5(b)(2)(F), three (3) days are added after the period would otherwise expire under FRCP 6(a). FRCP 6(d).

i. *Service by overnight delivery.* Where a period of time prescribed by either the Federal Rules of Civil Procedure or the Local Rules of Civil Procedure for the United States District Court for the Western District of New York is measured from the service of a paper and service is by overnight delivery, one (1) business day shall be added to the prescribed period. NY R USDCTWD Civ Rule 5.1(g).

4. *Individual judge practices.* Refer to the Miscellaneous section of this document for information on individual judge practices on timing of documents.

## C. General Requirements

1. *Pleading, generally*

a. *Pleadings allowed.* Only these pleadings are allowed: (1) a complaint; (2) an answer to a complaint;

(3) an answer to a counterclaim designated as a counterclaim; (4) an answer to a crossclaim; (5) a third-party complaint; (6) an answer to a third-party complaint; and (7) if the court orders one, a reply to an answer. FRCP 7(a).

b. *Pleading to be concise and direct.* Each allegation must be simple, concise, and direct. No technical form is required. FRCP 8(d)(1).

c. *Alternative statements of a claim or defense.* A party may set out two or more statements of a claim or defense alternatively or hypothetically, either in a single count or defense or in separate ones. If a party makes alternative statements, the pleading is sufficient if any one of them is sufficient. FRCP 8(d)(2).

d. *Inconsistent claims or defenses.* A party may state as many separate claims or defenses as it has, regardless of consistency. FRCP 8(d)(3).

e. *Construing pleadings.* Pleadings must be construed so as to do justice. FRCP 8(e).

2. *Pleading special matters*

  a. *Capacity or authority to sue; Legal existence*

   i. *In general.* Except when required to show that the court has jurisdiction, a pleading need not allege:

      • A party's capacity to sue or be sued;

      • A party's authority to sue or be sued in a representative capacity; or

      • The legal existence of an organized association of persons that is made a party. FRCP 9(a)(1).

   ii. *Raising those issues.* To raise any of those issues, a party must do so by a specific denial, which must state any supporting facts that are peculiarly within the party's knowledge. FRCP 9(a)(2).

  b. *Fraud or mistake; Conditions of mind.* In alleging fraud or mistake, a party must state with particularity the circumstances constituting fraud or mistake. Malice, intent, knowledge, and other conditions of a person's mind may be alleged generally. FRCP 9(b).

  c. *Conditions precedent.* In pleading conditions precedent, it suffices to allege generally that all conditions precedent have occurred or been performed. But when denying that a condition precedent has occurred or been performed, a party must do so with particularity. FRCP 9(c).

  d. *Official document or act.* In pleading an official document or official act, it suffices to allege that the document was legally issued or the act legally done. FRCP 9(d).

  e. *Judgment.* In pleading a judgment or decision of a domestic or foreign court, a judicial or quasi-judicial tribunal, or a board or officer, it suffices to plead the judgment or decision without showing jurisdiction to render it. FRCP 9(e).

  f. *Time and place.* An allegation of time or place is material when testing the sufficiency of a pleading. FRCP 9(f).

  g. *Special damages.* If an item of special damage is claimed, it must be specifically stated. FRCP 9(g).

  h. *Admiralty or maritime claim*

   i. *How designated.* If a claim for relief is within the admiralty or maritime jurisdiction and also within the court's subject-matter jurisdiction on some other ground, the pleading may designate the claim as an admiralty or maritime claim for purposes of FRCP 14(c), FRCP 38(e), and FRCP 82 and the Supplemental Rules for Admiralty or Maritime Claims and Asset Forfeiture Actions. A claim cognizable only in the admiralty or maritime jurisdiction is an admiralty or maritime claim for those purposes, whether or not so designated. FRCP 9(h)(1).

   ii. *Designation for appeal.* A case that includes an admiralty or maritime claim within FRCP 9(h) is an admiralty case within 28 U.S.C.A. § 1292(a)(3). FRCP 9(h)(2).

3. *Answer*

  a. *Defenses; Admissions and denials*

   i. *In general.* In responding to a pleading, a party must: (1) state in short and plain terms its defenses to each claim asserted against it; and (2) admit or deny the allegations asserted against it by an opposing party. FRCP 8(b)(1).

- The purpose of an answer is to formulate issues by means of defenses addressed to the allegations of the complaint, and to give the plaintiff notice of the defenses he or she will be called upon to meet. FEDPROC § 62:70; Lopez v. U.S. Fidelity & Guaranty Co., 15 Alaska 633, 18 F.R.D. 59 (1955); Moriarty v. Curran, 18 F.R.D. 461 (S.D.N.Y. 1956).

- An answer is adequate where it accomplishes these purposes, even if it contains general and specific denials and at the same time asserts additional facts by way of justification or explanation, and even if it sets forth conclusions of law. FEDPROC § 62:70; Johnston v. Jones, 178 F.2d 481 (3d Cir. 1949); Burke v. Mesta Mach. Co., 5 F.R.D. 134 (W.D.Pa. 1946).

ii. *Denials; Responding to the substance.* A denial must fairly respond to the substance of the allegation. FRCP 8(b)(2).

iii. *General and specific denials.* A party that intends in good faith to deny all the allegations of a pleading—including the jurisdictional grounds—may do so by a general denial. A party that does not intend to deny all the allegations must either specifically deny designated allegations or generally deny all except those specifically admitted. FRCP 8(b)(3).

iv. *Denying part of an allegation.* A party that intends in good faith to deny only part of an allegation must admit the part that is true and deny the rest. FRCP 8(b)(4).

v. *Lacking knowledge or information.* A party that lacks knowledge or information sufficient to form a belief about the truth of an allegation must so state, and the statement has the effect of a denial. FRCP 8(b)(5).

- An answer merely stating that the defendant lacks knowledge to form a belief as to the plaintiff's allegations, and making no statement as to his or her lack of information, has been held to be insufficient, the court suggesting that the phrase might be used in an attempt to mask the defendant's inability to make a good-faith denial of the allegations. FEDPROC § 62:73; Gilbert v. Johnston, 127 F.R.D. 145 (N.D.Ill. 1989).

vi. *Effect of failing to deny.* An allegation—other than one relating to the amount of damages—is admitted if a responsive pleading is required and the allegation is not denied. If a responsive pleading is not required, an allegation is considered denied or avoided. FRCP 8(b)(6).

b. *Affirmative defenses.* In responding to a pleading, a party must affirmatively state any avoidance or affirmative defense, including: (1) accord and satisfaction; (2) arbitration and award; (3) assumption of risk; (4) contributory negligence; (5) duress; (6) estoppel; (7) failure of consideration; (8) fraud; (9) illegality; (10) injury by fellow servant; (11) laches; (12) license; (13) payment; (14) release; (15) res judicata; (16) statute of frauds; (17) statute of limitations; and (18) waiver. FRCP 8(c)(1).

i. *Mistaken designation.* If a party mistakenly designates a defense as a counterclaim, or a counterclaim as a defense, the court must, if justice requires, treat the pleading as though it were correctly designated, and may impose terms for doing so. FRCP 8(c)(2).

c. *How to present defenses.* Every defense to a claim for relief in any pleading must be asserted in the responsive pleading if one is required. But a party may assert the following defenses by motion: (1) lack of subject-matter jurisdiction; (2) lack of personal jurisdiction; (3) improper venue; (4) insufficient process; (5) insufficient service of process; (6) failure to state a claim upon which relief can be granted; and (7) failure to join a party under FRCP 19. FRCP 12(b).

i. A motion asserting any of these defenses must be made before pleading if a responsive pleading is allowed. If a pleading sets out a claim for relief that does not require a responsive pleading, an opposing party may assert at trial any defense to that claim. FRCP 12(b).

ii. Refer to the United States District Court for the Western District of New York KeyRules Motion to Dismiss for Lack of Subject Matter Jurisdiction, Motion to Dismiss for Lack of Personal Jurisdiction, Motion to Dismiss for Improper Venue, and Motion to Dismiss for Failure to State a Claim documents for more information on motions under FRCP 12(b)(1), FRCP 12(b)(2), FRCP 12(b)(3), and FRCP 12(b)(6).

d. *Waiving and preserving certain defenses.* No defense or objection is waived by joining it with one or more other defenses or objections in a responsive pleading or in a motion. FRCP 12(b).

    i. *When some are waived.* A party waives any defense listed in FRCP 12(b)(2) through FRCP 12(b)(5) by:

- Omitting it from a motion in the circumstances described in FRCP 12(g)(2); or

- Failing to either: (1) make it by motion under FRCP 12; or (2) include it in a responsive pleading or in an amendment allowed by FRCP 15(a)(1) as a matter of course. FRCP 12(h)(1).

    ii. *When to raise others.* Failure to state a claim upon which relief can be granted, to join a person required by FRCP 19(b), or to state a legal defense to a claim may be raised:

- In any pleading allowed or ordered under FRCP 7(a);

- By a motion under FRCP 12(c); or

- At trial. FRCP 12(h)(2).

    iii. *Lack of subject matter jurisdiction.* If the court determines at any time that it lacks subject-matter jurisdiction, the court must dismiss the action. FRCP 12(h)(3).

4. *Counterclaim and crossclaim*

  a. *Compulsory counterclaim*

    i. *In general.* A pleading must state as a counterclaim any claim that—at the time of its service—the pleader has against an opposing party if the claim:

- Arises out of the transaction or occurrence that is the subject matter of the opposing party's claim; and

- Does not require adding another party over whom the court cannot acquire jurisdiction. FRCP 13(a)(1).

    ii. *Exceptions.* The pleader need not state the claim if:

- When the action was commenced, the claim was the subject of another pending action; or

- The opposing party sued on its claim by attachment or other process that did not establish personal jurisdiction over the pleader on that claim, and the pleader does not assert any counterclaim under FRCP 13. FRCP 13(a)(2).

  b. *Permissive counterclaim.* A pleading may state as a counterclaim against an opposing party any claim that is not compulsory. FRCP 13(b).

  c. *Relief sought in a counterclaim.* A counterclaim need not diminish or defeat the recovery sought by the opposing party. It may request relief that exceeds in amount or differs in kind from the relief sought by the opposing party. FRCP 13(c).

  d. *Counterclaim against the United States.* The Federal Rules of Civil Procedure do not expand the right to assert a counterclaim—or to claim a credit—against the United States or a United States officer or agency. FRCP 13(d).

  e. *Counterclaim maturing or acquired after pleading.* The court may permit a party to file a supplemental pleading asserting a counterclaim that matured or was acquired by the party after serving an earlier pleading. FRCP 13(e).

  f. *Crossclaim against a coparty.* A pleading may state as a crossclaim any claim by one party against a coparty if the claim arises out of the transaction or occurrence that is the subject matter of the original action or of a counterclaim, or if the claim relates to any property that is the subject matter of the original action. The crossclaim may include a claim that the coparty is or may be liable to the cross-claimant for all or part of a claim asserted in the action against the cross-claimant. FRCP 13(g).

  g. *Joining additional parties.* FRCP 19 and FRCP 20 govern the addition of a person as a party to a counterclaim or crossclaim. FRCP 13(h).

  h. *Separate trials; Separate judgments.* If the court orders separate trials under FRCP 42(b), it may enter judgment on a counterclaim or crossclaim under FRCP 54(b) when it has jurisdiction to do so, even if the opposing party's claims have been dismissed or otherwise resolved. FRCP 13(i).

5. *Third-party practice*

    a. *Timing of the summons and complaint.* A defending party may, as third-party plaintiff, serve a summons and complaint on a nonparty who is or may be liable to it for all or part of the claim against it. But the third-party plaintiff must, by motion, obtain the court's leave if it files the third-party complaint more than fourteen (14) days after serving its original answer. FRCP 14(a)(1).

    b. *Third-party defendant's claims and defenses.* The person served with the summons and third-party complaint—the "third-party defendant":

        i. Must assert any defense against the third-party plaintiff's claim under FRCP 12;

        ii. Must assert any counterclaim against the third-party plaintiff under FRCP 13(a), and may assert any counterclaim against the third-party plaintiff under FRCP 13(b) or any crossclaim against another third-party defendant under FRCP 13(g);

        iii. May assert against the plaintiff any defense that the third-party plaintiff has to the plaintiff's claim; and

        iv. May also assert against the plaintiff any claim arising out of the transaction or occurrence that is the subject matter of the plaintiff's claim against the third-party plaintiff. FRCP 14(a)(2).

    c. For more information on third-party practice, refer to FRCP 14.

6. *Right to a jury trial; Demand*

    a. *Right preserved.* The right of trial by jury as declared by U.S.C.A. Const. Amend. VII, or as provided by a federal statute, is preserved to the parties inviolate. FRCP 38(a).

    b. *Demand.* On any issue triable of right by a jury, a party may demand a jury trial by:

        i. Serving the other parties with a written demand—which may be included in a pleading—no later than fourteen (14) days after the last pleading directed to the issue is served; and

        ii. Filing the demand in accordance with FRCP 5(d). FRCP 38(b).

    c. *Specifying issues.* In its demand, a party may specify the issues that it wishes to have tried by a jury; otherwise, it is considered to have demanded a jury trial on all the issues so triable. If the party has demanded a jury trial on only some issues, any other party may—within fourteen (14) days after being served with the demand or within a shorter time ordered by the court—serve a demand for a jury trial on any other or all factual issues triable by jury. FRCP 38(c).

    d. *Waiver; Withdrawal.* A party waives a jury trial unless its demand is properly served and filed. A proper demand may be withdrawn only if the parties consent. FRCP 38(d).

    e. *Admiralty and maritime claims.* The rules in FRCP 38 do not create a right to a jury trial on issues in a claim that is an admiralty or maritime claim under FRCP 9(h). FRCP 38(e).

7. *Notice of appearance.* No notice of appearance is required of an attorney whose name and address appear at the end of a complaint, notice of removal, pre-answer motion, or answer. In all other circumstances, an attorney appearing for a party in a civil case shall promptly file a written notice of appearance. NY R USDCTWD Civ Rule 83.2(b). For more information on appearances and withdrawals, refer to NY R USDCTWD Civ Rule 83.2.

8. *Related cases.* Each attorney appearing in a civil case has a continuing duty to promptly notify the Clerk of Court when the attorney has reason to believe that said case is related to some other pending civil or criminal action(s) such that their assignment to the same Judge would avoid unnecessary duplication of judicial effort. As soon as the attorney becomes aware of such a relationship, the attorney shall notify the Clerk of Court by letter of the relevant facts, and the Clerk of Court will transmit that notification to the Judges to whom the cases have been assigned. NY R USDCTWD Civ Rule 5.1(e).

9. *Alternative dispute resolution (ADR).* This Court has adopted an Alternative Dispute Resolution Plan ("ADR"), as implemented by Standing Order (NY R USDCTWD ADR Plan), under which certain civil cases are referred automatically to ADR upon filing. NY R USDCTWD Civ Rule 16(a). The United States

District Court for the Western District of New York (the "Court") adopted the ADR Plan on January 1, 2006 (the "Effective Date"), to make available to civil litigants court-administered ADR interventions and processes designed to provide quicker, less expensive and potentially more satisfying alternatives to continuing litigation, without impairing the quality of justice or the right to trial. NY R USDCTWD ADR Plan(1)(1.2)(A).

a.  *Scope.* This ADR Plan (NY R USDCTWD ADR Plan) applies to civil actions pending or commenced on and after the Effective Date, except as otherwise indicated in NY R USDCTWD ADR Plan. The ADR Plan supplements the Local Rules of Civil Procedure for the United States District Court for the Western District of New York, which shall remain in full effect for all cases. NY R USDCTWD ADR Plan(1)(1.2)(B).

b.  *Referral to ADR*

 i.  *New cases.* All civil cases filed on and after the Effective Date of the ADR Plan shall be referred automatically for ADR. NY R USDCTWD ADR Plan(2)(2.1)(A). Notice of the ADR requirements will be provided to all parties immediately upon the filing of a complaint and answer or a notice of removal; NY R USDCTWD ADR Plan(2)(2.1)(A); NY R USDCTWD Civ Rule 16(a). ADR intervention will be scheduled at the conference held pursuant to Local Rule of Civil Procedure 16.1. NY R USDCTWD ADR Plan(2)(2.1)(A). [Editor's note: the reference to Local Rule of Civil Procedure 16.1 is likely meant to be a reference to NY R USDCTWD Civ Rule 16(b)].

  - Litigants in cases not referred automatically to ADR must consider possible agreement to the use of an ADR process. NY R USDCTWD Civ Rule 16(a).

  - For a list of exemptions from automatic referral, refer to NY R USDCTWD ADR Plan(2)(2.1)(A).

 ii.  *Pending cases.* The assigned Judge on any pending civil case may, sua sponte or with status conference, issue an order referring the case for ADR. NY R USDCTWD ADR Plan(2)(2.1)(B); NY R USDCTWD Civ Rule 16(a). The order shall specify a date on which the ADR intervention is to be completed. NY R USDCTWD ADR Plan(2)(2.1)(B).

 iii.  *Stipulation.* A case may be referred for ADR by stipulation of all parties. Stipulations shall be filed and shall designate the specific ADR intervention the parties have selected, the time frame within which the ADR process will be completed and the selected Neutral. Stipulations are presumed acceptable unless the assigned Judge determines that the interests of justice are not served. NY R USDCTWD ADR Plan(2)(2.1)(C).

 iv.  *Relief from ADR referral*

  - *Opting out motions.* Any party may file, with the assigned Judge for that case, a motion to opt out of, or for relief from, ADR. NY R USDCTWD ADR Plan(2)(2.2)(A).

  - *Motion.* Opting Out Motions must be made within fourteen (14) days from (1) the date of the first discovery conference under Local Rule 16.1 in new cases, or (2) the date of a sua sponte ADR Referral Order in pending cases. NY R USDCTWD ADR Plan(2)(2.2)(B). [Editor's note: the reference to Local Rule 16.1 is likely meant to be a reference to NY R USDCTWD Civ Rule 16(b)].

  - *Criteria.* Opting Out Motions shall be granted only for "good cause" shown. Inconvenience, travel costs, attorney fees or other costs shall not constitute "good cause." A party seeking relief from ADR must set forth the reasons why ADR has no reasonable chance of being productive. NY R USDCTWD ADR Plan(2)(2.2)(C).

  - *Judicial initiative.* The assigned Judge may, sua sponte, exempt any case from the Court's ADR Plan. NY R USDCTWD ADR Plan(2)(2.2)(D).

c.  *ADR interventions*

 i.  *Options.* It is expected that cases referred for ADR will proceed to Mediation. However, the following options are also available upon the stipulation of all parties:

  - Neutral Evaluation;

- Mini Summary Trial;
- Arbitration (Binding and Non-Binding);
- Case Valuation; and
- Settlement Week, when scheduled by the Court. NY R USDCTWD ADR Plan(4)(4.1)(A).

    ii. *Timing.* Timing is specific to the intervention and process chosen, as set forth in the corresponding sections in NY R USDCTWD ADR Plan. NY R USDCTWD ADR Plan(4)(4.1)(B).

    iii. *Scheduling.* The referral of a case to ADR does not delay or defer other dates established in the Scheduling Order and has no effect on the scheduled progress of the case toward trial. NY R USDCTWD ADR Plan(4)(4.1)(C).

  d. *Selecting an ADR intervention*

    i. *New cases.* Prior to the Local Rule 16.1 scheduling conference, counsel and any unrepresented parties shall confer about ADR as part of their discussion of "the possibilities for a prompt settlement or resolution of the case" pursuant to FRCP 26(f). Unless the parties agree to a different intervention, it is presumed that they will participate in mediation. [Editor's note: the reference to Local Rule 16.1 is likely meant to be a reference to NY R USDCTWD Civ Rule 16(b)].

    ii. *Pending cases.* In pending cases, all sua sponte referrals will be to mediation. Should the parties agree that a different ADR intervention is more appropriate to their case, they may submit a stipulation designating the specific ADR intervention selected, the time frame within which the ADR process will be completed and the identity of the Neutral. Stipulations must be filed within fourteen (14) days from the date of the ADR Referral Order and are presumed acceptable unless the assigned Judge determines that the interests of justice are not served. NY R USDCTWD ADR Plan(4)(4.2)(B).

  e. For more information on alternative dispute resolution (ADR), refer to NY R USDCTWD ADR Plan.

10. *Sanctions.* Failure of counsel for any party, or a party proceeding pro se, to appear before the Court at a conference, to complete the necessary preparations, or to be prepared to proceed to trial at the set time may be considered an abandonment of the case or a failure to prosecute or defend diligently. An appropriate order for sanctions may be entered against the defaulting party with respect to either a specific issue or the entire case. NY R USDCTWD Civ Rule 11(a). For more information, refer to NY R USDCTWD Civ Rule 11.

11. *Pro se actions.* For information on the requirements in pro se actions, refer to NY R USDCTWD Civ Rule 5.2.

12. *Individual judge practices.* Refer to the Miscellaneous section of this document for information on individual judge practices on general requirements for documents.

## D. Documents

1. *Required documents*

  a. *Answer.* Refer to the General Requirements section of this document for information on the form and contents of the answer.

  b. *Certificate of service.* FRCP 5(d) requires that the person making service under FRCP 5 certify that service has been effected. FRCP 5(Advisory Committee Notes). Having such information on file may be useful for many purposes, including proof of service if an issue arises concerning the effectiveness of the service. FRCP 5(Advisory Committee Notes). The Notice of Electronic Filing effectuates service for all registered users and no certificate of service is required when all filers on an action are Registered Users. The following exemptions require a certificate of service to be filed:

    i. When a document is manually filed, a certificate of service must be filed stating the manner in which service or notice was accomplished on each party so entitled. NY R USDCTWD ECF Procedures(2)(f)(iv).

    ii. When a pro se filer (who isn't authorized to electronically file documents) is a party, a certificate of service must be filed stating the manner in which service or notice was accomplished on the pro se party. The Notice of Electronic Filing effectuates service for the Registered Users in this situation and it is not necessary to note service on those parties. A non-registered pro se filer is required to file certificates of service on all documents they file. NY R USDCTWD ECF Procedures(2)(f)(iv).

   iii.   If an attorney is exempt from electronic service, a certificate of service must be filed stating the manner in which service or notice was accomplished on the exempt attorney. The Notice of Electronic Filing effectuates service for the Registered Users in this situation and it is not necessary to note service on those parties. NY R USDCTWD ECF Procedures(2)(f)(iv).

2.   *Supplemental documents*

   a.   *Waiver of the service of summons.* An individual, corporation, or association that is subject to service under FRCP 4(e), FRCP 4(f), or FRCP 4(h) has a duty to avoid unnecessary expenses of serving the summons. FRCP 4(d)(1). Waiving service of a summons does not waive any objection to personal jurisdiction or to venue. FRCP 4(d)(5). If a defendant located within the United States fails, without good cause, to sign and return a waiver requested by a plaintiff located within the United States, the court must impose on the defendant:

      i.   The expenses later incurred in making service; and

     ii.   The reasonable expenses, including attorney's fees, of any motion required to collect those service expenses. FRCP 4(d)(2).

   b.   *Notice of constitutional question.* A party that files a pleading, written motion, or other paper drawing into question the constitutionality of a federal or state statute must promptly:

      i.   *File notice.* File a notice of constitutional question stating the question and identifying the paper that raises it, if:

- A federal statute is questioned and the parties do not include the United States, one of its agencies, or one of its officers or employees in an official capacity; or

- A state statute is questioned and the parties do not include the state, one of its agencies, or one of its officers or employees in an official capacity; and

     ii.   *Serve notice.* Serve the notice and paper on the Attorney General of the United States if a federal statute is questioned—or on the state attorney general if a state statute is questioned—either by certified or registered mail or by sending it to an electronic address designated by the attorney general for this purpose. FRCP 5.1(a).

    iii.   *No forfeiture.* A party's failure to file and serve the notice, or the court's failure to certify, does not forfeit a constitutional claim or defense that is otherwise timely asserted. FRCP 5.1(d).

   c.   *Notice of issue concerning foreign law.* A party who intends to raise an issue about a foreign country's law must give notice by a pleading or other writing. In determining foreign law, the court may consider any relevant material or source, including testimony, whether or not submitted by a party or admissible under the Federal Rules of Evidence. The court's determination must be treated as a ruling on a question of law. FRCP 44.1.

   d.   *Nongovernmental corporate disclosure statement*

      i.   *Contents.* A nongovernmental corporate party must file two (2) copies of a disclosure statement that:

- Identifies any parent corporation and any publicly held corporation owning ten percent (10%) or more of its stock; or

- States that there is no such corporation. FRCP 7.1(a).

     ii.   *Time to file; Supplemental filing.* A party must:

- File the disclosure statement with its first appearance, pleading, petition, motion, response, or other request addressed to the court; and

- Promptly file a supplemental statement if any required information changes. FRCP 7.1(b).

e. *RICO case statement.* Any party asserting a claim, cross-claim, or counterclaim under the Racketeer Influenced & Corrupt Organizations Act ("RICO"), 18 U.S.C.A. § 1961 et seq., shall file and serve a "RICO Case Statement" under separate cover. This statement shall be filed contemporaneously with the papers first asserting the party's RICO claim, cross-claim or counterclaim, unless the Court grants an extension of time for filing. A party's failure to file a RICO Case Statement may result in dismissal of the party's RICO claim, cross-claim, or counterclaim. The RICO Case Statement must include those facts upon which the party is relying and which were obtained as a result of the reasonable inquiry required by FRCP 11. NY R USDCTWD Civ Rule 9. For more information, refer to NY R USDCTWD Civ Rule 9.

f. *Paper copy for date-stamping with self-addressed envelope.* Parties requesting date-stamped copies of filed documents must provide a paper copy for date-stamping, and a self-addressed, adequately-sized envelope with proper postage affixed. NY R USDCTWD Civ Rule 5.1(d).

g. *Courtesy copies.* Courtesy copies of certain documents may be required. Filers should refer to the "Judge Preferences" published on the Court's website. NY R USDCTWD ECF Procedures(2)(a)(iii).

3. *Individual judge practices.* Refer to the Miscellaneous section of this document for information on individual judge practices on required documents.

## E. Format

1. *Form of documents*

   a. *Form, generally.* All pleadings, motions, and other papers that a party presents for filing, whether in paper form or in electronic form, shall meet the following requirements:

      i. *Font size.* All text and footnotes shall be in a font size of at least twelve (12) point type. NY R USDCTWD Civ Rule 10(a)(1).

      ii. *Spacing.* All text in the body of the document must be double-spaced, except that text in block quotations and footnotes may be single-spaced. NY R USDCTWD Civ Rule 10(a)(2).

      - Extensive footnotes and block quotes may not be used to circumvent page limitations. NY R USDCTWD Civ Rule 10(a)(3).

      iii. *Margins.* Documents must have one (1) inch margins on all four sides. NY R USDCTWD Civ Rule 10(a)(4).

      iv. *Page numbering.* Pages must be consecutively numbered. NY R USDCTWD Civ Rule 10(a)(5).

   b. *Additional requirements for paper filing.* Documents presented for filing in paper form shall meet the following additional requirements:

      i. *Paper.* Documents must be on durable white eight and one-half by eleven (8-1/2 x 11) inch paper of good quality. NY R USDCTWD Civ Rule 10(b)(1).

      - All documents must be single-sided. NY R USDCTWD Civ Rule 10(b)(5).

      ii. *Text.* All text must be plainly and legibly written, typewritten, printed or reproduced. NY R USDCTWD Civ Rule 10(b)(2).

      iii. *Ink.* Documents must be in black or blue ink. NY R USDCTWD Civ Rule 10(b)(3).

      iv. *Binding.* The pages of each document must be stapled or in some other way fastened together. NY R USDCTWD Civ Rule 10(b)(4).

   c. *Caption; Names of parties.* Every pleading must have a caption with the court's name, a title, a file number, and a FRCP 7(a) designation. The title of the complaint must name all the parties; the title of other pleadings, after naming the first party on each side, may refer generally to other parties. FRCP 10(a).

      i. *Class action.* Any pleading purporting to commence a class action shall include the term "Class Action" next to its caption. NY R USDCTWD Civ Rule 23(a). For more information on class actions, refer to NY R USDCTWD Civ Rule 23.

d. *Paragraphs; Separate statements.* A party must state its claims or defenses in numbered paragraphs, each limited as far as practicable to a single set of circumstances. A later pleading may refer by number to a paragraph in an earlier pleading. If doing so would promote clarity, each claim founded on a separate transaction or occurrence—and each defense other than a denial—must be stated in a separate count or defense. FRCP 10(b).

e. *Adoption by reference; Exhibits.* A statement in a pleading may be adopted by reference elsewhere in the same pleading or in any other pleading or motion. A copy of a written instrument that is an exhibit to a pleading is a part of the pleading for all purposes. FRCP 10(c).

f. *Citation of local rules.* The Local Rules of Civil Procedure for the United States District Court for the Western District of New York shall be cited as "L.R.Civ.P." NY R USDCTWD Civ Rule 1.1.

g. *Acceptance by the clerk.* The clerk must not refuse to file a paper solely because it is not in the form prescribed by the Federal Rules of Civil Procedure or by a local rule or practice. FRCP 5(d)(4). The Court may reject documents that do not comply with the requirements in NY R USDCTWD Civ Rule 10. NY R USDCTWD Civ Rule 10.

2. *Form of electronic documents.* All pleadings, motions, and other papers that a party presents for filing, whether in paper form or in electronic form, shall meet the requirements in NY R USDCTWD Civ Rule 10(a). NY R USDCTWD Civ Rule 10(a). Refer above for more information.

a. *Conversion to PDF.* A document created with a word processor, or a paper document, must be converted to Portable Document Format to be electronically filed with the court. NY R USDCTWD ECF Procedures(2)(a)(v).

   i. Documents which exist only in paper form may be scanned into a portable document format (PDF) for electronic filing. NY R USDCTWD ECF Procedures(2)(a)(v). Before filing a scanned document with the court, a Filing User must verify its legibility. NY R USDCTWD ECF Procedures(2)(a)(iv).

   ii. Electronic documents must be converted to .PDF from a word processing program and must be text searchable. Do not print, scan and .PDF your document when it has been created in a word processing program. Additional information on working with PDFs is located in NY R USDCTWD ECF Procedures(4b). NY R USDCTWD ECF Procedures(2)(a)(v).

b. *Hyperlinks.* Pursuant to the policy set forth by the Judicial Conference in October 2005, a hyperlink contained in a filing is no more than a convenient mechanism for accessing material cited in a document. A hyperlink reference is extraneous to any filed document and is not part of the Court's record. NY R USDCTWD ECF Procedures(2)(a)(vi).

   i. In order to preserve the integrity of the Court record, users wishing to insert hyperlinks in Court filings shall continue to use the conventional method for the cited authority, in addition to the hyperlink. NY R USDCTWD ECF Procedures(2)(a)(vi).

   ii. The Court accepts no responsibility for, and does not endorse any product, organization, and content at any hyperlinked site, or at any site to which that site may be linked. The Court accepts no responsibility for the availability or functionality of any hyperlink. NY R USDCTWD ECF Procedures(2)(a)(vi).

c. *Attachments and exhibits*

   i. Attachments and exhibits larger than five megabytes (5 MB) shall be filed electronically in separate five megabyte (5 MB) segments. NY R USDCTWD ECF Procedures(2)(d)(i).

   ii. Filing Users must submit in electronic form all documents referenced as exhibits or attachments, except as otherwise provided in NY R USDCTWD ECF Procedures. A Filing User must submit as exhibits or attachments only those excerpts of the referenced documents that are directly germane to the matter under consideration by the court. Excerpted material must be clearly and prominently identified as such. Filing Users who file excerpts of documents as exhibits or attachments under NY R USDCTWD ECF Procedures(2)(d)(ii) do so without prejudice to their right to timely file additional excerpts or the complete document. Responding parties may timely file additional excerpts or the complete document that they believe are directly germane. The Court may require parties to file additional excerpts or the complete document. A Filing User must request leave of the Court to file a document exhibit or attachment in non-electronic form. NY R USDCTWD ECF Procedures(2)(d)(ii).

iii. Exhibits offered or admitted at trial will not be filed electronically or conventionally unless so ordered by the Court. NY R USDCTWD ECF Procedures(2)(d)(iii).

iv. Exhibits such as videotapes and tape recordings shall be filed in the conventional manner with the Clerk of Court, and a Notice of Manual Filing shall be electronically filed by the party. Manually filed exhibits must have the case number and case name securely fastened or marked on the item. NY R USDCTWD ECF Procedures(2)(d)(iii).

v. Continuation of exhibit entries (for exhibits that are too large to attach to a main document) must be filed and entered on the same day that the main document was filed. NY R USDCTWD ECF Procedures(2)(d)(iv).

d. *Color documents.* Documents in color or containing graphics take much longer to upload. Filing users are encouraged to configure their scanners to scan documents at 200 dpi and preferably in black and white rather than color. NY R USDCTWD ECF Procedures(2)(d)(v).

e. *Large documents.* Due to the length of time it takes to download large files, documents larger than five megabytes (5 MB) (approximately one hundred (100) pages of a .pdf scanned document) must be filed electronically in separate five megabyte (5 MB) segments. A party who believes a document is too lengthy to electronically image (i.e. scan), may contact the Court Room Deputy for the assigned judge and request permission to file that document conventionally. If granted permission to file the document conventionally, the Filing User shall electronically file a "notice of manual filing" for that item. Exhibits submitted to the Court conventionally shall be served on other parties conventionally. NY R USDCTWD ECF Procedures(2)(d)(vi).

3. *Signing of pleadings, motions and other papers*

a. *Signature.* Every pleading, written motion, and other paper must be signed by at least one attorney of record in the attorney's name—or by a party personally if the party is unrepresented. The paper must state the signer's address, e-mail address, and telephone number. FRCP 11(a). Documents presented for paper filing must contain an original signature. NY R USDCTWD Civ Rule 10(b)(6).

i. *Electronic signatures*

• *Non-attorney signature.* If the original document requires the signature of a non-attorney, the filing party shall obtain the signature of the non-attorney on the document. NY R USDCTWD ECF Procedures(2)(g)(i). The filing party or attorney then shall file the document electronically indicating the signatory's name in the form "s/(name)." NY R USDCTWD ECF Procedures(2)(g)(i)(1). A non-filing signatory or party who disputes the authenticity of an electronically filed document or the authenticity of the signature on that document must file an objection to the document within ten (10) days of receiving the Notice of Electronic Filing. NY R USDCTWD ECF Procedures(2)(g)(i)(2).

• *Registered user signature.* The username and password required to file documents on the Electronic Filing System serve as the Filing User's signature on all electronic documents filed with this Court. The also serve as a signature for the purposes of FRCP 11, the Federal Rules of Civil Procedure, the Local Rules of Civil Procedure for the United States District Court for the Western District of New York, and any other purpose for which a signature is required in connection with proceedings before this Court. A pleading requiring a Registered User's signature must include a signature block in the format found in NY R USDCTWD ECF Procedures(2)(g)(iii). NY R USDCTWD ECF Procedures(2)(g)(iii). Any party challenging the authenticity of an electronically filed document or the attorney's signature on that document must file an objection to the document within ten (10) days of receiving the Notice of Electronic Filing. NY R USDCTWD ECF Procedures(2)(g)(iii)(1).

• *Multiple signatures.* The following procedure applies when a stipulation or other document requires two or more signatures: The filing party shall initially confirm that the document is acceptable to all persons required to sign the document and shall obtain the signatures of all parties on the document. NY R USDCTWD ECF Procedures(2)(g)(iv)(1). The filing party or attorney then shall file the document electronically indicating the signatories, e.g., "s/Jane Doe," "s/John Smith," etc. NY R USDCTWD ECF Procedures(2)(g)(iv)(2). A non-filing signatory or party who disputes the authenticity of an electronically filed document containing multiple signatures or the authenticity of the signatures themselves must file an objection to the document within ten (10) days of receiving the Notice of Electronic Filing. NY R USDCTWD ECF Procedures(2)(g)(iv)(3).

    ii. *No verification or accompanying affidavit required for pleadings.* Unless a rule or statute specifically states otherwise, a pleading need not be verified or accompanied by an affidavit. FRCP 11(a).

    iii. *Unsigned papers.* The court must strike an unsigned paper unless the omission is promptly corrected after being called to the attorney's or party's attention. FRCP 11(a).

  b. *Representations to the court.* By presenting to the court a pleading, written motion, or other paper—whether by signing, filing, submitting, or later advocating it—an attorney or unrepresented party certifies that to the best of the person's knowledge, information, and belief, formed after an inquiry reasonable under the circumstances:

    i. It is not being presented for any improper purpose, such as to harass, cause unnecessary delay, or needlessly increase the cost of litigation;

    ii. The claims, defenses, and other legal contentions are warranted by existing law or by a nonfrivolous argument for extending, modifying, or reversing existing law or for establishing new law;

    iii. The factual contentions have evidentiary support or, if specifically so identified, will likely have evidentiary support after a reasonable opportunity for further investigation or discovery; and

    iv. The denials of factual contentions are warranted on the evidence or, if specifically so identified, are reasonably based on belief or a lack of information. FRCP 11(b).

  c. *Sanctions.* If, after notice and a reasonable opportunity to respond, the court determines that FRCP 11(b) has been violated, the court may impose an appropriate sanction on any attorney, law firm, or party that violated FRCP 11(b) or is responsible for the violation. FRCP 11(c)(1). Refer to the United States District Court for the Western District of New York KeyRules Motion for Sanctions document for more information.

4. *Privacy protection for filings made with the court.* In all filings, parties shall comply with FRCP 5.2. NY R USDCTWD ECF Procedures(2)(m)(i).

  a. *Redacted filings.* Unless the court orders otherwise, in an electronic or paper filing with the court that contains an individual's Social Security number, taxpayer-identification number, or birth date, the name of an individual known to be a minor, or a financial-account number, a party or nonparty making the filing may include only:

    i. The last four (4) digits of the Social Security number and taxpayer-identification number;

    ii. The year of the individual's birth;

    iii. The minor's initials; and

    iv. The last four (4) digits of the financial-account number. FRCP 5.2(a).

  b. *Exemptions from the redaction requirement.* The redaction requirement does not apply to the following:

    i. A financial-account number that identifies the property allegedly subject to forfeiture in a forfeiture proceeding;

    ii. The record of an administrative or agency proceeding;

    iii. The official record of a state-court proceeding;

    iv. The record of a court or tribunal, if that record was not subject to the redaction requirement when originally filed;

v.   A filing covered by FRCP 5.2(c) or FRCP 5.2(d); and

vi.  A pro se filing in an action brought under 28 U.S.C.A. § 2241, 28 U.S.C.A. § 2254, or 28 U.S.C.A. § 2255. FRCP 5.2(b).

c.  *Limitations on remote access to electronic files; Social Security appeals and immigration cases.* Unless the court orders otherwise, in an action for benefits under the Social Security Act, and in an action or proceeding relating to an order of removal, to relief from removal, or to immigration benefits or detention, access to an electronic file is authorized as follows:

i.   The parties and their attorneys may have remote electronic access to any part of the case file, including the administrative record;

ii.  Any other person may have electronic access to the full record at the courthouse, but may have remote electronic access only to:

- The docket maintained by the court; and

- An opinion, order, judgment, or other disposition of the court, but not any other part of the case file or the administrative record. FRCP 5.2(c).

d.  *Filings made under seal.* The court may order that a filing be made under seal without redaction. The court may later unseal the filing or order the person who made the filing to file a redacted version for the public record. FRCP 5.2(d). For more information on sealing documents, refer to NY R USDCTWD Civ Rule 5.3, NY R USDCTWD ECF Procedures(2)(o)(i)(1), NY R USDCTWD ECF Procedures(2)(o)(i)(2), and NY R USDCTWD ECF Procedures(2)(o)(i)(3).

e.  *Protective orders.* For good cause, the court may by order in a case:

i.   Require redaction of additional information; or

ii.  Limit or prohibit a nonparty's remote electronic access to a document filed with the court. FRCP 5.2(e).

f.  *Option for additional unredacted filing under seal.* A person making a redacted filing may also file an unredacted copy under seal. The court must retain the unredacted copy as part of the record. FRCP 5.2(f).

g.  *Option for filing a reference list.* A filing that contains redacted information may be filed together with a reference list that identifies each item of redacted information and specifies an appropriate identifier that uniquely corresponds to each item listed. The list must be filed under seal and may be amended as of right. Any reference in the case to a listed identifier will be construed to refer to the corresponding item of information. FRCP 5.2(g).

h.  *Waiver of protection of identifiers.* A person waives the protection of FRCP 5.2(a) as to the person's own information by filing it without redaction and not under seal. FRCP 5.2(h).

5.  *Individual judge practices.* Refer to the Miscellaneous section of this document for information on individual judge practices on formatting documents.

## F.  Filing and Service Requirements

1.  *Filing requirements.* Any paper after the complaint that is required to be served—together with a certificate of service—must be filed within a reasonable time after service. FRCP 5(d)(1). All pleadings and other papers shall be filed and served in accordance with the Federal Rules of Civil Procedure and the CM/ECF Administrative Procedures Guide (NY R USDCTWD ECF Procedures). NY R USDCTWD Civ Rule 5.1(a). For information on filing of miscellaneous cases and irregular documents, refer to NY R USDCTWD Civ Rule 5.6.

a.  *How filing is made; In general.* A paper is filed by delivering it:

i.   To the clerk; or

ii.  To a judge who agrees to accept it for filing, and who must then note the filing date on the paper and promptly send it to the clerk. FRCP 5(d)(2).

b.  *Electronic filing*

i.   *Authorization of electronic filing program.* A court may, by local rule, allow papers to be filed, signed, or verified by electronic means that are consistent with any technical standards established by the Judicial Conference of the United States. A local rule may require electronic filing only if reasonable exceptions are allowed. A paper filed electronically in compliance with a local rule is a written paper for purposes of the Federal Rules of Civil Procedure. FRCP 5(d)(3).

- All civil cases filed in this Court are assigned to the Electronic Case Filing System ("ECF"). The procedures for electronic filing and any exceptions to the electronic filing requirements are set forth in the CM/ECF Administrative Procedures Guide (NY R USDCTWD ECF Procedures) which is available on the Court's website. NY R US-DCTWD Civ Rule 5.1(a).

ii. *Scope of electronic filing.* The U.S. District Court for the Western District of New York requires attorneys in civil and criminal cases to file documents with the Court electronically over the Internet using its Case Management/Electronic Case Filing (CM/ECF) system. NY R US-DCTWD ECF Procedures. Beginning January 1, 2004, all civil and criminal cases currently pending and newly filed, except as expressly noted herein, were assigned to the Electronic Case Filing System ("System"). Except as expressly provided and in exceptional circumstances preventing a Filing User from filing electronically, all petitions, motions, memoranda of law, or other pleadings and documents required to be filed with the Court in connection with a case assigned to the System must be electronically filed. NY R USDCTWD ECF Procedures(1)(a).

- *Mandatory electronic filing.* All documents on civil, criminal, miscellaneous civil, miscellaneous criminal and new civil case openings, except sealed documents, sealed cases, opening of a criminal case, opening of a miscellaneous case and as expressly provided for in these procedures (NY R USDCTWD ECF Procedures), shall be electronically filed on the system. NY R USDCTWD ECF Procedures(2)(a)(i). NY R USDCTWD Civ Rule 29

- *Stipulations.* Pursuant to NY R USDCTWD Civ Rule 29, all stipulations (whether the stipulation is final or when it requires a judge's signature) shall be filed electronically. NY R USDCTWD ECF Procedures(2)(p)(i).

- *Letters.* The electronic filing of letters is generally prohibited unless granted permission by an assigned judge. Letters to the Court must be submitted conventionally. NY R US-DCTWD ECF Procedures(2)(q)(i).

- *Exceptions.* The Court requires attorneys to file documents electronically, absent a showing of good cause, unless otherwise excused by the procedures set forth below or by Order of the Court. NY R USDCTWD ECF Procedures.

iii. *Conventional filing of documents.* The procedures in NY R USDCTWD ECF Procedures(2)(o) govern documents filed conventionally. The Court, upon application, may also authorize conventional filing of other documents otherwise subject to the procedures in NY R US-DCTWD ECF Procedures(2)(o). NY R USDCTWD ECF Procedures(2)(o)(i).

- *Documents filed under seal.* Unredacted documents filed with the Court pursuant to the privacy provisions of FRCP 5.2 shall be submitted in a sealing envelope with the information in NY R USDCTWD ECF Procedures(2)(o)(i)(1) on the envelope. NY R USDCTWD ECF Procedures(2)(o)(i)(1). If the document is larger than five (5) pages, a disk should be provided to the Clerks Office which contains the document in a .pdf format. NY R USDCTWD ECF Procedures(2)(o)(i)(1). For more information on documents filed under seal, refer to NY R USDCTWD ECF Procedures(2)(o)(i)(1), NY R USDCTWD ECF Procedures(2)(o)(i)(2), and NY R USDCTWD ECF Procedures(2)(o)(i)(3).

- *Magistrate judge consents.* Pursuant to FRCP 73(b), parties' filing consents to jurisdiction by United States Magistrate Judge will continue to be treated as non-public documents until all parties have consented. Therefore, parties must submit conventionally (in paper form) and not electronically file their consent forms so that the consent is not a public document. If all parties consent to the jurisdiction of a Magistrate Judge, the Clerk will scan all consent forms which will then become a public document. NY R USDCTWD ECF Procedures(2)(o)(i)(3).

- *Pro se filers.* Pro Se filers shall file paper originals of all initiating documents, pleadings, motions, affidavits, briefs and other documents which must be signed or which require either verification or an unsworn declaration under any rule or statute. The Clerk's Office will scan these original documents into an electronic file in the System. A certificate of service is required for all documents a pro se litigant files with the court. If a Pro Se filer is granted permission to register to electronically file documents, they shall comply with the guidelines contained in this document (NY R USDCTWD ECF Procedures). NY R USDCTWD ECF Procedures(2)(o)(i)(4).

- *Social Security cases.* Absent a showing of good cause, and except as provided in Section o(i)(4) above, all documents, notices and orders in Social Security reviews will be filed and noticed electronically, except as noted in NY R USDCTWD ECF Procedures(2)(o)(i)(6). For more information, refer to NY R USDCTWD ECF Procedures(2)(o)(i)(6).

- For more information on conventional filing of documents, refer to NY R USDCTWD ECF Procedures(2)(o)(i).

iv. *Consequences of electronic filing.* Electronic transmission of a document to the System consistent with these procedures (NY R USDCTWD ECF Procedures), whether accomplished by the Filing User or a Court User, together with the transmission of a Notice of Electronic Filing from the Court, constitutes filing of a document for all purposes of the Federal Rules of Civil Procedure and the Local Rules of Civil Procedure for the United States District Court for the Western District of New York, and constitutes entry of the document on the docket kept by the Clerk under FRCP 58 and FRCP 79. A document shall not be considered filed for purposes of the Federal Rules of Civil until the filing party receives a System generated Notice of Electronic Filing. NY R USDCTWD ECF Procedures(2)(a)(i).

- E-mailing a document to the Clerk's Office or to the assigned judge shall not constitute "filing" of such document. NY R USDCTWD ECF Procedures(2)(a)(i)(1).

v. *Filing fees.* Any fee required for filing of a pleading or paper in District Court is payable to the Clerk of Court by check or money order. In addition, when opening a civil case on line, filing a notice of appeal on line or applying to appear pro hac vice on line, the fees shall be paid on line by registered users through the federal electronic payment website. Users will be directed to the federal electronic payment website while entering their transaction and should have a credit card available. When opening a civil case and applying to proceed in forma pauperis or when the United States of America opens a case, the payment screen can by bypassed to complete the transaction. Additional information on making electronic payments can be located on the court's website. NY R USDCTWD ECF Procedures(2)(h)(i).

2. *Service requirements.* All pleadings and other papers shall be filed and served in accordance with the Federal Rules of Civil Procedure and the CM/ECF Administrative Procedures Guide (NY R USDCTWD ECF Procedures). NY R USDCTWD Civ Rule 5.1(a).

  a. *Service; When required*

  i. *In general.* Unless the Federal Rules of Civil Procedure provide otherwise, each of the following papers must be served on every party:

  - An order stating that service is required;

  - A pleading filed after the original complaint, unless the court orders otherwise under FRCP 5(c) because there are numerous defendants;

  - A discovery paper required to be served on a party, unless the court orders otherwise;

  - A written motion, except one that may be heard ex parte; and

  - A written notice, appearance, demand, or offer of judgment, or any similar paper. FRCP 5(a)(1).

  ii. *If a party fails to appear.* No service is required on a party who is in default for failing to appear. But a pleading that asserts a new claim for relief against such a party must be served on that party under FRCP 4. FRCP 5(a)(2).

iii.   *Seizing property.* If an action is begun by seizing property and no person is or need be named as a defendant, any service required before the filing of an appearance, answer, or claim must be made on the person who had custody or possession of the property when it was seized. FRCP 5(a)(3).

b.   *Service; How made*

i.   *Serving an attorney.* If a party is represented by an attorney, service under FRCP 5 must be made on the attorney unless the court orders service on the party. FRCP 5(b)(1).

ii.   *Service in general.* A paper is served under FRCP 5 by:

   • Handing it to the person;

   • Leaving it: (1) at the person's office with a clerk or other person in charge or, if no one is in charge, in a conspicuous place in the office; or (2) if the person has no office or the office is closed, at the person's dwelling or usual place of abode with someone of suitable age and discretion who resides there;

   • Mailing it to the person's last known address—in which event service is complete upon mailing;

   • Leaving it with the court clerk if the person has no known address;

   • Sending it by electronic means if the person consented in writing—in which event service is complete upon transmission, but is not effective if the serving party learns that it did not reach the person to be served; or

   • Delivering it by any other means that the person consented to in writing—in which event service is complete when the person making service delivers it to the agency designated to make delivery. FRCP 5(b)(2).

iii.   *Service by overnight delivery.* All papers, other than a subpoena or a summons and complaint, may be served on counsel of record by overnight delivery service at the address designated by the attorney for that purpose, or if none is designated, at the attorney's last known address. Service by overnight delivery shall be complete upon deposit of the paper(s), enclosed in a properly addressed wrapper, into the custody of the overnight delivery service, prior to the latest time designated by the service for overnight delivery. NY R USDCTWD Civ Rule 5.1(g). "Overnight delivery service" means any delivery service which regularly accepts items for overnight delivery to any address within the Court's jurisdiction. NY R USDCTWD Civ Rule 5.1(g).

iv.   *Service of documents by electronic means*

   • *Service on registered users.* Registered Users consent to the electronic service of all documents, and must make available an electronic mail address for service during the registration process. Upon the filing of a document by a party, a Notice of Electronic Filing, with a hyperlink to the filed document, will be automatically generated by the electronic filing system and sent via electronic mail to the e-mail addresses of all parties participating in the electronic filing system in the case. Electronic service of the Notice of Electronic Filing constitutes service of the filed document for all purposes of the Federal Rules of Civil Procedure and the Local Rules of Civil Procedure for the United States District Court for the Western District of New York. NY R USDCTWD ECF Procedures(2)(f)(i). The Notice of Electronic Filing effectuates service for all registered users and no certificate of service is required when all filers on an action are Registered Users. NY R USDCTWD ECF Procedures(2)(f)(iv).

   • *Time limit for opening hyperlink.* The hyperlink to filed documents contained in the Notice of Electronic Filing must be opened within fifteen (15) days from the date the document was filed to provide registered users access to the document. The hyperlink expires after fifteen (15) days and users will be unable to access documents for free after that time. Filing Users are encouraged to check their e-mail frequently for notice of filed documents. NY R USDCTWD ECF Procedures(2)(f)(ii).

- *Service on exempted attorneys or pro se litigants who do not have permission to file electronically.* Attorneys granted an exemption from electronically filing documents in the System and pro se litigants who have not been granted permission to electronically file documents are entitled to a paper copy of any electronically filed pleading, document or order. The filing party must therefore provide the non-registered party with the pleading, document or order according to the Federal Rules of Civil Procedure. NY R USDCTWD ECF Procedures(2)(f)(iii).

- *E-mailing or faxing documents.* E-mailing or faxing a pleading or document to any party shall not constitute service of the pleading or document. NY R USDCTWD ECF Procedures(2)(f)(v).

v. *Using court facilities.* If a local rule so authorizes, a party may use the court's transmission facilities to make service under FRCP 5(b)(2)(E). FRCP 5(b)(3).

c. *Serving numerous defendants*

i. *In general.* If an action involves an unusually large number of defendants, the court may, on motion or on its own, order that:

- Defendants' pleadings and replies to them need not be served on other defendants;

- Any crossclaim, counterclaim, avoidance, or affirmative defense in those pleadings and replies to them will be treated as denied or avoided by all other parties; and

- Filing any such pleading and serving it on the plaintiff constitutes notice of the pleading to all parties. FRCP 5(c)(1).

ii. *Notifying parties.* A copy of every such order must be served on the parties as the court directs. FRCP 5(c)(2).

3. *Pro se actions.* For information on the requirements in pro se actions, refer to NY R USDCTWD Civ Rule 5.2.

4. *Individual judge practices.* Refer to the Miscellaneous section of this document for information on individual judge practices on filing and serving documents.

## G. Hearings

1. *Hearing on FRCP 12 defenses before trial.* If a party so moves, any defense listed in FRCP 12(b)(1) through FRCP 12(b)(7)—whether made in a pleading or by motion—and a motion under FRCP 12(c) must be heard and decided before trial unless the court orders a deferral until trial. FRCP 12(i).

2. *Individual judge practices.* Refer to the Miscellaneous section of this document for information on individual judge practices on hearings.

## H. Forms

### 1. Official Federal Answer Forms

a. Rule 4 waiver of the service of summons. FRCP 4.

### 2. Federal Answer Forms

a. Generally. 2B FEDFORMS § 8:10.

b. Introduction to separate defenses. 2B FEDFORMS § 8:11.

c. Presenting defenses. 2B FEDFORMS § 8:12.

d. With counterclaim for interpleader. 2B FEDFORMS § 8:13.

e. Denials and admissions. 2B FEDFORMS § 8:14.

f. Denials, admissions and affirmative defenses. 2B FEDFORMS § 8:15.

g. Separate answer of two defendants; Duty of fair representation. 2B FEDFORMS § 8:16.

h. Separate answer of third defendant. 2B FEDFORMS § 8:17.

i. Reciting paragraphs and subparagraphs of complaint; Account malpractice. 2B FEDFORMS § 8:18.

j. One of multiple defendants. 2B FEDFORMS § 8:21.

1385

    k.   Answer to complaint for employment discrimination. 2B FEDFORMS § 8:22.

    l.   Denial of particular averment. 2B FEDFORMS § 8:24.

    m.  Admission of particular averment. 2B FEDFORMS § 8:25.

    n.   Denial of all averments of paragraph. 2B FEDFORMS § 8:26.

    o.   Admission of all averments of paragraph. 2B FEDFORMS § 8:27.

    p.   Denial in part and admission in part of paragraph. 2B FEDFORMS § 8:28.

    q.   General denial. 2B FEDFORMS § 8:29.

    r.   Qualified general denial. 2B FEDFORMS § 8:30.

    s.   Denial of knowledge or information sufficient to form a belief. 2B FEDFORMS § 8:31.

    t.   Denial of jurisdictional allegations; Jurisdictional amount. 2B FEDFORMS § 8:32.

    u.   Denial of jurisdictional allegations; Federal question. 2B FEDFORMS § 8:34.

    v.   Denial of jurisdictional allegations; Diversity of citizenship. 2B FEDFORMS § 8:37.

    w.  Contributory negligence. 2B FEDFORMS § 8:58.

    x.   Fraud. 2B FEDFORMS § 8:74.

    y.   Mistake. 2B FEDFORMS § 8:85.

    z.   Statute of limitations. 2B FEDFORMS § 8:103.

**3.  Forms for the Western District of New York**

    a.   Certificate of service. NY R USDCTWD ECF Procedures(4a).

# I.  Applicable Rules

1.  *Federal rules*

    a.   Summons. FRCP 4.

    b.   Serving and filing pleadings and other papers. FRCP 5.

    c.   Constitutional challenge to a statute; Notice, certification, and intervention. FRCP 5.1.

    d.   Privacy protection for filings made with the court. FRCP 5.2.

    e.   Computing and extending time; Time for motion papers. FRCP 6.

    f.   Pleadings allowed; Form of motions and other papers. FRCP 7.

    g.   Disclosure statement. FRCP 7.1.

    h.   General rules of pleading. FRCP 8.

    i.   Pleading special matters. FRCP 9.

    j.   Form of pleadings. FRCP 10.

    k.   Signing pleadings, motions, and other papers; Representations to the court; Sanctions. FRCP 11.

    l.   Defenses and objections; When and how presented; Motion for judgment on the pleadings; Consolidating motions; Waiving defenses; Pretrial hearing. FRCP 12.

    m.  Counterclaim and crossclaim. FRCP 13.

    n.   Third-party practice. FRCP 14.

    o.   Right to a jury trial; Demand. FRCP 38.

    p.   Determining foreign law. FRCP 44.1.

2.  *Local rules*

    a.   Title. NY R USDCTWD Civ Rule 1.1.

    b.   Filing and serving papers. NY R USDCTWD Civ Rule 5.1.

    c.   Requirement to file a RICO case statement. NY R USDCTWD Civ Rule 9.

    d.   Form of papers. NY R USDCTWD Civ Rule 10.

    e.   Sanctions. NY R USDCTWD Civ Rule 11.

    f.   Alternative dispute resolution and pretrial conferences. NY R USDCTWD Civ Rule 16.

    g.   Class actions. NY R USDCTWD Civ Rule 23.

    h.   Attorneys of record; Appearance and withdrawal. NY R USDCTWD Civ Rule 83.2.

    i.   Administrative procedures guide for electronic filing. NY R USDCTWD ECF Procedures.

    j.   Alternative dispute resolution plan. NY R USDCTWD ADR Plan.

**J.  Miscellaneous**

**NOTE: Individual judges' rules may apply. For available judge-level information, refer to:**

DISTRICT JUDGE RICHARD J. ARCARA: NY R USDCTWD Arcara-Procedures.

DISTRICT JUDGE FRANK P. GERACI, JR.: NY R USDCTWD Geraci-Procedures.

DISTRICT JUDGE DAVID G. LARIMER: NY R USDCTWD Larimer-Procedures.

DISTRICT JUDGE CHARLES J. SIRAGUSA: NY R USDCTWD Siragusa-Procedures.

DISTRICT JUDGE WILLIAM M. SKRETNY: NY R USDCTWD Skretny--Procedures.

DISTRICT JUDGE MICHAEL A. TELESCA: NY R USDCTWD Telesca-Procedures.

DISTRICT JUDGE LAWRENCE J. VILARDO: NY R USDCTWD Vilardo-Procedures.

DISTRICT JUDGE ELIZABETH A. WOLFORD: NY R USDCTWD Wolford-Procedures.

MAGISTRATE JUDGE JONATHAN W. FELDMAN: NY R USDCTWD Feldman-Procedures.

MAGISTRATE JUDGE LESLIE G. FOSCHIO: NY R USDCTWD Foschio-Procedures; NY R USDCTWD Foschio-Depositions.

MAGISTRATE JUDGE JEREMIAH J. McCARTHY: NY R USDCTWD McCarthy-Procedures.

MAGISTRATE JUDGE MARIAN W. PAYSON: NY R USDCTWD Payson-Procedures.

MAGISTRATE JUDGE MICHAEL J. ROEMER: NY R USDCTWD Roemer-Procedures.

MAGISTRATE JUDGE H. KENNETH SCHROEDER, JR.: NY R USDCTWD Schroeder-Proc.

MAGISTRATE JUDGE HUGH B. SCOTT: NY R USDCTWD Scott-Procedures.

# Pleadings
# Amended Pleading

### Document Last Updated September 2016

**A.  Checklist**

    (I)  ❑ Matters to be considered by plaintiff or defendant

        (a)  ❑ Required documents

            (1)  ❑ Amended pleading

            (2)  ❑ Certificate of service

        (b)  ❑ Supplemental documents

            (1)  ❑ Notice of constitutional question

            (2)  ❑ Notice of issue concerning foreign law

            (3)  ❑ RICO case statement

            (4)  ❑ Paper copy for date-stamping with self-addressed envelope

            (5)  ❑ Courtesy copies

   (c) ❑ Timing

      (1) ❑ A party may amend its pleading once as a matter of course within:

         (i) ❑ Twenty-one (21) days after serving it, or

         (ii) ❑ If the pleading is one to which a responsive pleading is required, twenty-one (21) days after service of a responsive pleading or twenty-one (21) days after service of a motion under FRCP 12(b), FRCP 12(e), or FRCP 12(f), whichever is earlier

## B. Timing

1. *Amended pleading*

   a. *Amending as a matter of course.* A party may amend its pleading once as a matter of course within:

      i. Twenty-one (21) days after serving it, or

      ii. If the pleading is one to which a responsive pleading is required, twenty-one (21) days after service of a responsive pleading or twenty-one (21) days after service of a motion under FRCP 12(b), FRCP 12(e), or FRCP 12(f), whichever is earlier. FRCP 15(a)(1).

   b. *Extension of time.* If the time for serving the responsive pleading is extended by a motion for enlargement of time under FRCP 6(b), or by a stipulation, the period for amending as of right also may be enlarged. FPP § 1480.

   c. *Other amendments.* In all other cases, a party may amend its pleading only with the opposing party's written consent or the court's leave. The court should freely give leave when justice so requires. FRCP 15(a)(2). Refer to the United States District Court for the Western District of New York KeyRules Motion for Leave to Amend document for more information.

2. *Time to respond to an amended pleading.* Unless the court orders otherwise, any required response to an amended pleading must be made within the time remaining to respond to the original pleading or within fourteen (14) days after service of the amended pleading, whichever is later. FRCP 15(a)(3).

3. *Computation of time*

   a. *Computing time.* FRCP 6 applies in computing any time period specified in the Federal Rules of Civil Procedure, in any local rule or court order, or in any statute that does not specify a method of computing time. FRCP 6(a).

      i. *Period stated in days or a longer unit.* When the period is stated in days or a longer unit of time:

         • Exclude the day of the event that triggers the period;

         • Count every day, including intermediate Saturdays, Sundays, and legal holidays; and

         • Include the last day of the period, but if the last day is a Saturday, Sunday, or legal holiday, the period continues to run until the end of the next day that is not a Saturday, Sunday, or legal holiday. FRCP 6(a)(1).

      ii. *Period stated in hours.* When the period is stated in hours:

         • Begin counting immediately on the occurrence of the event that triggers the period;

         • Count every hour, including hours during intermediate Saturdays, Sundays, and legal holidays; and

         • If the period would end on a Saturday, Sunday, or legal holiday, the period continues to run until the same time on the next day that is not a Saturday, Sunday, or legal holiday. FRCP 6(a)(2).

      iii. *Inaccessibility of the clerk's office.* Unless the court orders otherwise, if the clerk's office is inaccessible:

         • On the last day for filing under FRCP 6(a)(1), then the time for filing is extended to the first accessible day that is not a Saturday, Sunday, or legal holiday; or

         • During the last hour for filing under FRCP 6(a)(2), then the time for filing is extended to the same time on the first accessible day that is not a Saturday, Sunday, or legal holiday. FRCP 6(a)(3).

iv. *"Last day" defined.* Unless a different time is set by a statute, local rule, or court order, the last day ends:

- For electronic filing, at midnight in the court's time zone; and
- For filing by other means, when the clerk's office is scheduled to close. FRCP 6(a)(4).

v. *"Next day" defined.* The "next day" is determined by continuing to count forward when the period is measured after an event and backward when measured before an event. FRCP 6(a)(5).

vi. *"Legal holiday" defined.* "Legal holiday" means:

- The day set aside by statute for observing New Year's Day, Martin Luther King Jr.'s Birthday, Washington's Birthday, Memorial Day, Independence Day, Labor Day, Columbus Day, Veterans' Day, Thanksgiving Day, or Christmas Day;
- Any day declared a holiday by the President or Congress; and
- For periods that are measured after an event, any other day declared a holiday by the state where the district court is located. FRCP 6(a)(6).

b. *Computation of electronic filing deadlines.* A document will be deemed timely filed if filed prior to midnight Eastern Time, unless otherwise ordered by the Court. A document will be considered untimely if filed thereafter. When a Court order requires that a document be filed on a weekend or holiday, the document may be filed by close of business the next business day without further application to the Court. NY R USDCTWD ECF Procedures(2)(e)(i). A document filed electronically is deemed filed on the date and time stated on the Notice of Electronic Filing. NY R USDCTWD ECF Procedures(2)(e)(ii).

i. *System availability.* Although parties may file documents electronically twenty-four (24) hours a day, registered users are strongly encouraged to file all documents during normal working hours of the Clerk's Office (8:30 a.m. to 5:00 p.m. Eastern Time). NY R USDCTWD ECF Procedures(2)(t)(i).

ii. *Technical failures.* A Filing User whose filing is made untimely as a result of a technical failure must seek appropriate relief from the Court. NY R USDCTWD ECF Procedures(2)(u)(i).

c. *Extending time*

i. *In general.* When an act may or must be done within a specified time, the court may, for good cause, extend the time:

- With or without motion or notice if the court acts, or if a request is made, before the original time or its extension expires; or
- On motion made after the time has expired if the party failed to act because of excusable neglect. FRCP 6(b)(1).

ii. *Exceptions.* A court must not extend the time to act under FRCP 50(b), FRCP 50(d), FRCP 52(b), FRCP 59(b), FRCP 59(d), FRCP 59(e), and FRCP 60(b). FRCP 6(b)(2).

iii. Refer to the United States District Court for the Western District of New York KeyRules Motion for Continuance/Extension of Time document for more information on extending time.

d. *Additional time after certain kinds of service.* When a party may or must act within a specified time after service and service is made under FRCP 5(b)(2)(C), FRCP 5(b)(2)(D), FRCP 5(b)(2)(E), or FRCP 5(b)(2)(F), three (3) days are added after the period would otherwise expire under FRCP 6(a). FRCP 6(d).

i. *Service by overnight delivery.* Where a period of time prescribed by either the Federal Rules of Civil Procedure or the Local Rules of Civil Procedure for the United States District Court for the Western District of New York is measured from the service of a paper and service is by overnight delivery, one (1) business day shall be added to the prescribed period. NY R USDCTWD Civ Rule 5.1(g).

4. *Individual judge practices.* Refer to the Miscellaneous section of this document for information on individual judge practices on timing of documents.

## C. General Requirements

1. *Pleading, generally*

   a. *Pleadings allowed.* Only these pleadings are allowed: (1) a complaint; (2) an answer to a complaint; (3) an answer to a counterclaim designated as a counterclaim; (4) an answer to a crossclaim; (5) a third-party complaint; (6) an answer to a third-party complaint; and (7) if the court orders one, a reply to an answer. FRCP 7(a).

   b. *Pleading to be concise and direct.* Each allegation must be simple, concise, and direct. No technical form is required. FRCP 8(d)(1).

   c. *Alternative statements of a claim or defense.* A party may set out two or more statements of a claim or defense alternatively or hypothetically, either in a single count or defense or in separate ones. If a party makes alternative statements, the pleading is sufficient if any one of them is sufficient. FRCP 8(d)(2).

   d. *Inconsistent claims or defenses.* A party may state as many separate claims or defenses as it has, regardless of consistency. FRCP 8(d)(3).

   e. *Construing pleadings.* Pleadings must be construed so as to do justice. FRCP 8(e).

2. *Pleading special matters*

   a. *Capacity or authority to sue; Legal existence*

      i. *In general.* Except when required to show that the court has jurisdiction, a pleading need not allege:

      - A party's capacity to sue or be sued;
      - A party's authority to sue or be sued in a representative capacity; or
      - The legal existence of an organized association of persons that is made a party. FRCP 9(a)(1).

      ii. *Raising those issues.* To raise any of those issues, a party must do so by a specific denial, which must state any supporting facts that are peculiarly within the party's knowledge. FRCP 9(a)(2).

   b. *Fraud or mistake; Conditions of mind.* In alleging fraud or mistake, a party must state with particularity the circumstances constituting fraud or mistake. Malice, intent, knowledge, and other conditions of a person's mind may be alleged generally. FRCP 9(b).

   c. *Conditions precedent.* In pleading conditions precedent, it suffices to allege generally that all conditions precedent have occurred or been performed. But when denying that a condition precedent has occurred or been performed, a party must do so with particularity. FRCP 9(c).

   d. *Official document or act.* In pleading an official document or official act, it suffices to allege that the document was legally issued or the act legally done. FRCP 9(d).

   e. *Judgment.* In pleading a judgment or decision of a domestic or foreign court, a judicial or quasi-judicial tribunal, or a board or officer, it suffices to plead the judgment or decision without showing jurisdiction to render it. FRCP 9(e).

   f. *Time and place.* An allegation of time or place is material when testing the sufficiency of a pleading. FRCP 9(f).

   g. *Special damages.* If an item of special damage is claimed, it must be specifically stated. FRCP 9(g).

   h. *Admiralty or maritime claim*

      i. *How designated.* If a claim for relief is within the admiralty or maritime jurisdiction and also within the court's subject-matter jurisdiction on some other ground, the pleading may designate the claim as an admiralty or maritime claim for purposes of FRCP 14(c), FRCP 38(e), and FRCP 82 and the Supplemental Rules for Admiralty or Maritime Claims and Asset Forfeiture Actions. A claim cognizable only in the admiralty or maritime jurisdiction is an admiralty or maritime claim for those purposes, whether or not so designated. FRCP 9(h)(1).

      ii. *Designation for appeal.* A case that includes an admiralty or maritime claim within FRCP 9(h) is an admiralty case within 28 U.S.C.A. § 1292(a)(3). FRCP 9(h)(2).

3. *Amended pleading*

   a. *Amendments before trial.* The function of FRCP 15(a), which provides generally for the amendment of pleadings, is to enable a party to assert matters that were overlooked or were unknown at the time the party interposed the original complaint or answer. FPP § 1473; Smiga v. Dean Witter Reynolds, Inc., 766 F.2d 698, 703 (2d Cir. 1985).

      i. *Matters contained in amended pleading under FRCP 15(a).* Although FRCP 15(a) does not expressly state that an amendment must contain only matters that occurred within a particular time period, FRCP 15(d) provides that any "transaction, occurrence, or event that happened after the date of the pleading" should be set forth in a supplemental pleading. FPP § 1473. Thus, impliedly, an amended pleading, whether prepared with or without leave of court, only should relate to matters that have taken place prior to the date of the earlier pleading. FPP § 1473; Ford Motor Co. v. U.S., 19 C.I.T. 946, 896 F.Supp. 1224, 1230 (1995).

      ii. *Amending as a matter of course.* The right to amend as of course is not restricted to any particular litigant or pleading. FPP § 1480. It is a right conferred on all of the parties to an action and thus extends to persons who were not original parties to the litigation, but are brought into the action by way of counterclaim, crossclaim, third-party claim, or defensive interpleader. FPP § 1480; Johnson v. Walsh, 65 F.Supp. 157 (W.D.Mo. 1946).

         • *Amending a complaint with multiple defendants.* When a number of defendants are involved in an action, some of whom have answered and some of whom have filed no responsive pleading, the plaintiff can amend as a matter of course as to those defendants who have not answered. FEDPROC § 62:267; Pallant v. Sinatra, 7 F.R.D. 293 (S.D.N.Y. 1945). A plaintiff may not file an amended complaint as of right against those defendants who have not yet answered, if he or she has amended the complaint once already as a matter of course. FEDPROC § 62:267; Glaros v. Perse, 628 F.2d 679 (1st Cir. 1980).

      iii. *Amending with leave of court.* Refer to the United States District Court for the Western District of New York KeyRules Motion for Leave to Amend document for information on amending the pleadings with leave of court.

      iv. *Types of amendments permitted under FRCP 15(a)*

         • *Cure a defective pleading.* Perhaps the most common use of FRCP 15(a) is by a party seeking to amend in order to cure a defective pleading. FPP § 1474.

         • *Correct insufficiently stated claims or defenses.* A more common use of FRCP 15(a) amendments is to correct insufficiently stated claims or defenses. Typically, amendments of this character involve either adding a necessary allegation in order to state a claim for relief or correcting a misnomer of a party to the action. FPP § 1474.

         • *Change nature or theory of claim or capacity of party.* Courts also have allowed a party to amend in order to change the nature or theory of the party's claim or the capacity in which the party is bringing the action. FPP § 1474.

         • *State additional claims or defenses or drop claims or defenses.* Plaintiffs and defendants also have been permitted to amend their pleadings to state additional claims, to assert additional defenses, or to drop claims or defenses. FPP § 1474; Weinberger v. Retail Credit Co., 498 F.2d 552, 554, n.4 (4th Cir. 1974).

         • *Increase amount of damages or elect a different remedy.* A FRCP 15(a) amendment also is appropriate for increasing the amount of damages sought, or for electing a different remedy than the one originally requested. FPP § 1474; McFadden v. Sanchez, 710 F.2d 907 (2d Cir. 1983).

         • *Add, substitute, or drop parties.* Finally, a party may make a FRCP 15(a) amendment to add, substitute, or drop parties to the action. FPP § 1474.

   b. *Amendments during and after trial*

      i. *Based on an objection at trial.* If, at trial, a party objects that evidence is not within the issues raised in the pleadings, the court may permit the pleadings to be amended. The court should freely permit an amendment when doing so will aid in presenting the merits and the objecting party fails to satisfy the court that the evidence would prejudice that party's action or defense on the merits. The court may grant a continuance to enable the objecting party to meet the evidence. FRCP 15(b)(1).

    ii.   *For issues tried by consent.* When an issue not raised by the pleadings is tried by the parties' express or implied consent, it must be treated in all respects as if raised in the pleadings. A party may move—at any time, even after judgment—to amend the pleadings to conform them to the evidence and to raise an unpleaded issue. But failure to amend does not affect the result of the trial of that issue. FRCP 15(b)(2).

    iii.  Refer to the United States District Court for the Western District of New York KeyRules Motion for Leave to Amend document for more information on moving to amend the pleadings.

  c.  *Relation back of amendments*

    i.   *When an amendment relates back.* An amendment to a pleading relates back to the date of the original pleading when:

- The law that provides the applicable statute of limitations allows relation back;

- The amendment asserts a claim or defense that arose out of the conduct, transaction, or occurrence set out—or attempted to be set out—in the original pleading; or

- The amendment changes the party or the naming of the party against whom a claim is asserted, if FRCP 15(c)(1)(B) is satisfied and if, within the period provided by FRCP 4(m) for serving the summons and complaint, the party to be brought in by amendment: (1) received such notice of the action that it will not be prejudiced in defending on the merits; and (2) knew or should have known that the action would have been brought against it, but for a mistake concerning the proper party's identity. FRCP 15(c)(1).

    ii.   *Notice to the United States.* When the United States or a United States officer or agency is added as a defendant by amendment, the notice requirements of FRCP 15(c)(1)(C)(i) and FRCP 15(c)(1)(C)(ii) are satisfied if, during the stated period, process was delivered or mailed to the United States attorney or the United States attorney's designee, to the Attorney General of the United States, or to the officer or agency. FRCP 15(c)(2).

  d.  *Effect of an amended pleading.* A pleading that has been amended under FRCP 15(a) supersedes the pleading it modifies and remains in effect throughout the action unless it subsequently is modified. FPP § 1476. Once an amended pleading is interposed, the original pleading no longer performs any function in the case and any subsequent motion made by an opposing party should be directed at the amended pleading. FPP § 1476; Ferdik v. Bonzelet, 963 F.2d 1258, 1262 (9th Cir. 1992); Davis v. TXO Production Corp., 929 F.2d 1515, 1517 (10th Cir. 1991).

4.  *Amended complaint.* Refer to the United States District Court for the Western District of New York KeyRules Complaint document for the requirements specific to the amended complaint.

5.  *Amended answer.* Refer to the United States District Court for the Western District of New York KeyRules Answer document for the requirements specific to the amended answer.

6.  *Right to a jury trial; Demand*

  a.  *Right preserved.* The right of trial by jury as declared by U.S.C.A. Const. Amend. VII, or as provided by a federal statute, is preserved to the parties inviolate. FRCP 38(a).

  b.  *Demand.* On any issue triable of right by a jury, a party may demand a jury trial by:

    i.   Serving the other parties with a written demand—which may be included in a pleading—no later than fourteen (14) days after the last pleading directed to the issue is served; and

    ii.   Filing the demand in accordance with FRCP 5(d). FRCP 38(b).

  c.  *Specifying issues.* In its demand, a party may specify the issues that it wishes to have tried by a jury; otherwise, it is considered to have demanded a jury trial on all the issues so triable. If the party has demanded a jury trial on only some issues, any other party may—within fourteen (14) days after being served with the demand or within a shorter time ordered by the court—serve a demand for a jury trial on any other or all factual issues triable by jury. FRCP 38(c).

d. *Waiver; Withdrawal.* A party waives a jury trial unless its demand is properly served and filed. A proper demand may be withdrawn only if the parties consent. FRCP 38(d).

e. *Admiralty and maritime claims.* The rules in FRCP 38 do not create a right to a jury trial on issues in a claim that is an admiralty or maritime claim under FRCP 9(h). FRCP 38(e).

7. *Notice of appearance.* No notice of appearance is required of an attorney whose name and address appear at the end of a complaint, notice of removal, pre-answer motion, or answer. In all other circumstances, an attorney appearing for a party in a civil case shall promptly file a written notice of appearance. NY R USDCTWD Civ Rule 83.2(b). For more information on appearances and withdrawals, refer to NY R USDCTWD Civ Rule 83.2.

8. *Related cases.* Each attorney appearing in a civil case has a continuing duty to promptly notify the Clerk of Court when the attorney has reason to believe that said case is related to some other pending civil or criminal action(s) such that their assignment to the same Judge would avoid unnecessary duplication of judicial effort. As soon as the attorney becomes aware of such a relationship, the attorney shall notify the Clerk of Court by letter of the relevant facts, and the Clerk of Court will transmit that notification to the Judges to whom the cases have been assigned. NY R USDCTWD Civ Rule 5.1(e).

9. *Alternative dispute resolution (ADR).* This Court has adopted an Alternative Dispute Resolution Plan ("ADR"), as implemented by Standing Order (NY R USDCTWD ADR Plan), under which certain civil cases are referred automatically to ADR upon filing. NY R USDCTWD Civ Rule 16(a). The United States District Court for the Western District of New York (the "Court") adopted the ADR Plan on January 1, 2006 (the "Effective Date"), to make available to civil litigants court-administered ADR interventions and processes designed to provide quicker, less expensive and potentially more satisfying alternatives to continuing litigation, without impairing the quality of justice or the right to trial. NY R USDCTWD ADR Plan(1)(1.2)(A).

a. *Scope.* This ADR Plan (NY R USDCTWD ADR Plan) applies to civil actions pending or commenced on and after the Effective Date, except as otherwise indicated in NY R USDCTWD ADR Plan. The ADR Plan supplements the Local Rules of Civil Procedure for the United States District Court for the Western District of New York, which shall remain in full effect for all cases. NY R USDCTWD ADR Plan(1)(1.2)(B).

b. *Referral to ADR*

i. *New cases.* All civil cases filed on and after the Effective Date of the ADR Plan shall be referred automatically for ADR. NY R USDCTWD ADR Plan(2)(2.1)(A). Notice of the ADR requirements will be provided to all parties immediately upon the filing of a complaint and answer or a notice of removal; NY R USDCTWD ADR Plan(2)(2.1)(A); NY R USDCTWD Civ Rule 16(a). ADR intervention will be scheduled at the conference held pursuant to Local Rule of Civil Procedure 16.1. NY R USDCTWD ADR Plan(2)(2.1)(A). [Editor's note: the reference to Local Rule of Civil Procedure 16.1 is likely meant to be a reference to NY R USDCTWD Civ Rule 16(b)].

- Litigants in cases not referred automatically to ADR must consider possible agreement to the use of an ADR process. NY R USDCTWD Civ Rule 16(a).

- For a list of exemptions from automatic referral, refer to NY R USDCTWD ADR Plan(2)(2.1)(A).

ii. *Pending cases.* The assigned Judge on any pending civil case may, sua sponte or with status conference, issue an order referring the case for ADR. NY R USDCTWD ADR Plan(2)(2.1)(B); NY R USDCTWD Civ Rule 16(a). The order shall specify a date on which the ADR intervention is to be completed. NY R USDCTWD ADR Plan(2)(2.1)(B).

iii. *Stipulation.* A case may be referred for ADR by stipulation of all parties. Stipulations shall be filed and shall designate the specific ADR intervention the parties have selected, the time frame within which the ADR process will be completed and the selected Neutral. Stipulations are presumed acceptable unless the assigned Judge determines that the interests of justice are not served. NY R USDCTWD ADR Plan(2)(2.1)(C).

iv. *Relief from ADR referral*

- *Opting out motions.* Any party may file, with the assigned Judge for that case, a motion to opt out of, or for relief from, ADR. NY R USDCTWD ADR Plan(2)(2.2)(A).

- *Motion.* Opting Out Motions must be made within fourteen (14) days from (1) the date of the first discovery conference under Local Rule 16.1 in new cases, or (2) the date of a sua sponte ADR Referral Order in pending cases. NY R USDCTWD ADR Plan(2)(2.2)(B). [Editor's note: the reference to Local Rule 16.1 is likely meant to be a reference to NY R USDCTWD Civ Rule 16(b)].

- *Criteria.* Opting Out Motions shall be granted only for "good cause" shown. Inconvenience, travel costs, attorney fees or other costs shall not constitute "good cause." A party seeking relief from ADR must set forth the reasons why ADR has no reasonable chance of being productive. NY R USDCTWD ADR Plan(2)(2.2)(C).

- *Judicial initiative.* The assigned Judge may, sua sponte, exempt any case from the Court's ADR Plan. NY R USDCTWD ADR Plan(2)(2.2)(D).

c. *ADR interventions*

i. *Options.* It is expected that cases referred for ADR will proceed to Mediation. However, the following options are also available upon the stipulation of all parties:

- Neutral Evaluation;

- Mini Summary Trial;

- Arbitration (Binding and Non-Binding);

- Case Valuation; and

- Settlement Week, when scheduled by the Court. NY R USDCTWD ADR Plan(4)(4.1)(A).

ii. *Timing.* Timing is specific to the intervention and process chosen, as set forth in the corresponding sections in NY R USDCTWD ADR Plan. NY R USDCTWD ADR Plan(4)(4.1)(B).

iii. *Scheduling.* The referral of a case to ADR does not delay or defer other dates established in the Scheduling Order and has no effect on the scheduled progress of the case toward trial. NY R USDCTWD ADR Plan(4)(4.1)(C).

d. *Selecting an ADR intervention*

i. *New cases.* Prior to the Local Rule 16.1 scheduling conference, counsel and any unrepresented parties shall confer about ADR as part of their discussion of "the possibilities for a prompt settlement or resolution of the case" pursuant to FRCP 26(f). Unless the parties agree to a different intervention, it is presumed that they will participate in mediation. [Editor's note: the reference to Local Rule 16.1 is likely meant to be a reference to NY R USDCTWD Civ Rule 16(b)].

ii. *Pending cases.* In pending cases, all sua sponte referrals will be to mediation. Should the parties agree that a different ADR intervention is more appropriate to their case, they may submit a stipulation designating the specific ADR intervention selected, the time frame within which the ADR process will be completed and the identity of the Neutral. Stipulations must be filed within fourteen (14) days from the date of the ADR Referral Order and are presumed acceptable unless the assigned Judge determines that the interests of justice are not served. NY R USDCTWD ADR Plan(4)(4.2)(B).

e. For more information on alternative dispute resolution (ADR), refer to NY R USDCTWD ADR Plan.

10. *Sanctions.* Failure of counsel for any party, or a party proceeding pro se, to appear before the Court at a conference, to complete the necessary preparations, or to be prepared to proceed to trial at the set time may be considered an abandonment of the case or a failure to prosecute or defend diligently. An appropriate order for sanctions may be entered against the defaulting party with respect to either a specific issue or the entire case. NY R USDCTWD Civ Rule 11(a). For more information, refer to NY R USDCTWD Civ Rule 11.

11. *Pro se actions.* For information on the requirements in pro se actions, refer to NY R USDCTWD Civ Rule 5.2.

12. *Individual judge practices.* Refer to the Miscellaneous section of this document for information on individual judge practices on general requirements for documents.

## D. Documents

1. *Required documents*

    a. *Amended pleading.* Refer to the General Requirements section of this document for the form and contents of the amended pleading.

    b. *Certificate of service.* FRCP 5(d) requires that the person making service under FRCP 5 certify that service has been effected. FRCP 5(Advisory Committee Notes). Having such information on file may be useful for many purposes, including proof of service if an issue arises concerning the effectiveness of the service. FRCP 5(Advisory Committee Notes). The Notice of Electronic Filing effectuates service for all registered users and no certificate of service is required when all filers on an action are Registered Users. The following exemptions require a certificate of service to be filed:

        i. When a document is manually filed, a certificate of service must be filed stating the manner in which service or notice was accomplished on each party so entitled. NY R USDCTWD ECF Procedures(2)(f)(iv).

        ii. When a pro se filer (who isn't authorized to electronically file documents) is a party, a certificate of service must be filed stating the manner in which service or notice was accomplished on the pro se party. The Notice of Electronic Filing effectuates service for the Registered Users in this situation and it is not necessary to note service on those parties. A non-registered pro se filer is required to file certificates of service on all documents they file. NY R USDCTWD ECF Procedures(2)(f)(iv).

        iii. If an attorney is exempt from electronic service, a certificate of service must be filed stating the manner in which service or notice was accomplished on the exempt attorney. The Notice of Electronic Filing effectuates service for the Registered Users in this situation and it is not necessary to note service on those parties. NY R USDCTWD ECF Procedures(2)(f)(iv).

2. *Supplemental documents*

    a. *Notice of constitutional question.* A party that files a pleading, written motion, or other paper drawing into question the constitutionality of a federal or state statute must promptly:

        i. *File notice.* File a notice of constitutional question stating the question and identifying the paper that raises it, if:

        - A federal statute is questioned and the parties do not include the United States, one of its agencies, or one of its officers or employees in an official capacity; or

        - A state statute is questioned and the parties do not include the state, one of its agencies, or one of its officers or employees in an official capacity; and

        ii. *Serve notice.* Serve the notice and paper on the Attorney General of the United States if a federal statute is questioned—or on the state attorney general if a state statute is questioned—either by certified or registered mail or by sending it to an electronic address designated by the attorney general for this purpose. FRCP 5.1(a).

        iii. *No forfeiture.* A party's failure to file and serve the notice, or the court's failure to certify, does not forfeit a constitutional claim or defense that is otherwise timely asserted. FRCP 5.1(d).

    b. *Notice of issue concerning foreign law.* A party who intends to raise an issue about a foreign country's law must give notice by a pleading or other writing. In determining foreign law, the court may consider any relevant material or source, including testimony, whether or not submitted by a party or admissible under the Federal Rules of Evidence. The court's determination must be treated as a ruling on a question of law. FRCP 44.1.

    c. *RICO case statement.* Any party asserting a claim, cross-claim, or counterclaim under the Racketeer Influenced & Corrupt Organizations Act ("RICO"), 18 U.S.C.A. § 1961 et seq., shall file and serve a "RICO Case Statement" under separate cover. This statement shall be filed contemporaneously with the papers first asserting the party's RICO claim, cross-claim or counterclaim, unless the Court grants an extension of time for filing. A party's failure to file a RICO Case Statement may result in dismissal of the party's RICO claim, cross-claim, or counterclaim. The RICO Case Statement must include those facts upon which the party is relying and which were obtained as a result of the reasonable inquiry required by FRCP 11. NY R USDCTWD Civ Rule 9. For more information, refer to NY R USDCTWD Civ Rule 9.

    d. *Paper copy for date-stamping with self-addressed envelope.* Parties requesting date-stamped copies of filed documents must provide a paper copy for date-stamping, and a self-addressed, adequately-sized envelope with proper postage affixed. NY R USDCTWD Civ Rule 5.1(d).

    e. *Courtesy copies.* Courtesy copies of certain documents may be required. Filers should refer to the "Judge Preferences" published on the Court's website. NY R USDCTWD ECF Procedures(2)(a)(iii).

3. *Documents required for an amended complaint adding a new claim for relief or new party.* Refer to the United States District Court for the Western District of New York KeyRules Complaint document for the documents for an amended complaint adding a new claim for relief or being filed and served against a new party.

4. *Individual judge practices.* Refer to the Miscellaneous section of this document for information on individual judge practices on required documents.

## E. Format

1. *Form of documents*

    a. *Form, generally.* All pleadings, motions, and other papers that a party presents for filing, whether in paper form or in electronic form, shall meet the following requirements:

        i. *Font size.* All text and footnotes shall be in a font size of at least twelve (12) point type. NY R USDCTWD Civ Rule 10(a)(1).

        ii. *Spacing.* All text in the body of the document must be double-spaced, except that text in block quotations and footnotes may be single-spaced. NY R USDCTWD Civ Rule 10(a)(2).

           • Extensive footnotes and block quotes may not be used to circumvent page limitations. NY R USDCTWD Civ Rule 10(a)(3).

        iii. *Margins.* Documents must have one (1) inch margins on all four sides. NY R USDCTWD Civ Rule 10(a)(4).

        iv. *Page numbering.* Pages must be consecutively numbered. NY R USDCTWD Civ Rule 10(a)(5).

    b. *Additional requirements for paper filing.* Documents presented for filing in paper form shall meet the following additional requirements:

        i. *Paper.* Documents must be on durable white eight and one-half by eleven (8-1/2 x 11) inch paper of good quality. NY R USDCTWD Civ Rule 10(b)(1).

           • All documents must be single-sided. NY R USDCTWD Civ Rule 10(b)(5).

        ii. *Text.* All text must be plainly and legibly written, typewritten, printed or reproduced. NY R USDCTWD Civ Rule 10(b)(2).

        iii. *Ink.* Documents must be in black or blue ink. NY R USDCTWD Civ Rule 10(b)(3).

        iv. *Binding.* The pages of each document must be stapled or in some other way fastened together. NY R USDCTWD Civ Rule 10(b)(4).

    c. *Caption; Names of parties.* Every pleading must have a caption with the court's name, a title, a file number, and a FRCP 7(a) designation. The title of the complaint must name all the parties; the title of other pleadings, after naming the first party on each side, may refer generally to other parties. FRCP 10(a).

        i. *Class action.* Any pleading purporting to commence a class action shall include the term "Class

Action" next to its caption. NY R USDCTWD Civ Rule 23(a). For more information on class actions, refer to NY R USDCTWD Civ Rule 23.

d. *Paragraphs; Separate statements.* A party must state its claims or defenses in numbered paragraphs, each limited as far as practicable to a single set of circumstances. A later pleading may refer by number to a paragraph in an earlier pleading. If doing so would promote clarity, each claim founded on a separate transaction or occurrence—and each defense other than a denial—must be stated in a separate count or defense. FRCP 10(b).

e. *Adoption by reference; Exhibits.* A statement in a pleading may be adopted by reference elsewhere in the same pleading or in any other pleading or motion. A copy of a written instrument that is an exhibit to a pleading is a part of the pleading for all purposes. FRCP 10(c).

f. *Citation of local rules.* The Local Rules of Civil Procedure for the United States District Court for the Western District of New York shall be cited as "L.R.Civ.P." NY R USDCTWD Civ Rule 1.1.

g. *Acceptance by the clerk.* The clerk must not refuse to file a paper solely because it is not in the form prescribed by the Federal Rules of Civil Procedure or by a local rule or practice. FRCP 5(d)(4). The Court may reject documents that do not comply with the requirements in NY R USDCTWD Civ Rule 10. NY R USDCTWD Civ Rule 10.

2. *Form of electronic documents.* All pleadings, motions, and other papers that a party presents for filing, whether in paper form or in electronic form, shall meet the requirements in NY R USDCTWD Civ Rule 10(a). NY R USDCTWD Civ Rule 10(a). Refer above for more information.

   a. *Conversion to PDF.* A document created with a word processor, or a paper document, must be converted to Portable Document Format to be electronically filed with the court. NY R USDCTWD ECF Procedures(2)(a)(v).

      i. Documents which exist only in paper form may be scanned into a portable document format (PDF) for electronic filing. NY R USDCTWD ECF Procedures(2)(a)(v). Before filing a scanned document with the court, a Filing User must verify its legibility. NY R USDCTWD ECF Procedures(2)(a)(iv).

      ii. Electronic documents must be converted to .PDF from a word processing program and must be text searchable. Do not print, scan and .PDF your document when it has been created in a word processing program. Additional information on working with PDFs is located in NY R USDCTWD ECF Procedures(4b). NY R USDCTWD ECF Procedures(2)(a)(v).

   b. *Hyperlinks.* Pursuant to the policy set forth by the Judicial Conference in October 2005, a hyperlink contained in a filing is no more than a convenient mechanism for accessing material cited in a document. A hyperlink reference is extraneous to any filed document and is not part of the Court's record. NY R USDCTWD ECF Procedures(2)(a)(vi).

      i. In order to preserve the integrity of the Court record, users wishing to insert hyperlinks in Court filings shall continue to use the conventional method for the cited authority, in addition to the hyperlink. NY R USDCTWD ECF Procedures(2)(a)(vi).

      ii. The Court accepts no responsibility for, and does not endorse any product, organization, and content at any hyperlinked site, or at any site to which that site may be linked. The Court accepts no responsibility for the availability or functionality of any hyperlink. NY R USDCTWD ECF Procedures(2)(a)(vi).

   c. *Attachments and exhibits*

      i. Attachments and exhibits larger than five megabytes (5 MB) shall be filed electronically in separate five megabyte (5 MB) segments. NY R USDCTWD ECF Procedures(2)(d)(i).

      ii. Filing Users must submit in electronic form all documents referenced as exhibits or attachments, except as otherwise provided in NY R USDCTWD ECF Procedures. A Filing User must submit as exhibits or attachments only those excerpts of the referenced documents that are directly germane to the matter under consideration by the court. Excerpted material must be clearly and prominently identified as such. Filing Users who file excerpts of documents as exhibits or attachments under NY R USDCTWD ECF Procedures(2)(d)(ii) do so without prejudice to their right to timely file additional excerpts or the complete document. Responding parties may timely file additional excerpts or the complete document that they believe are directly germane. The Court may require parties to file additional excerpts or the complete document. A Filing User must request leave of the Court to file a document exhibit or attachment in non-electronic form. NY R USDCTWD ECF Procedures(2)(d)(ii).

    iii. Exhibits offered or admitted at trial will not be filed electronically or conventionally unless so ordered by the Court. NY R USDCTWD ECF Procedures(2)(d)(iii).

    iv. Exhibits such as videotapes and tape recordings shall be filed in the conventional manner with the Clerk of Court, and a Notice of Manual Filing shall be electronically filed by the party. Manually filed exhibits must have the case number and case name securely fastened or marked on the item. NY R USDCTWD ECF Procedures(2)(d)(iii).

    v. Continuation of exhibit entries (for exhibits that are too large to attach to a main document) must be filed and entered on the same day that the main document was filed. NY R USDCTWD ECF Procedures(2)(d)(iv).

d. *Color documents.* Documents in color or containing graphics take much longer to upload. Filing users are encouraged to configure their scanners to scan documents at 200 dpi and preferably in black and white rather than color. NY R USDCTWD ECF Procedures(2)(d)(v).

e. *Large documents.* Due to the length of time it takes to download large files, documents larger than five megabytes (5 MB) (approximately one hundred (100) pages of a .pdf scanned document) must be filed electronically in separate five megabyte (5 MB) segments. A party who believes a document is too lengthy to electronically image (i.e. scan), may contact the Court Room Deputy for the assigned judge and request permission to file that document conventionally. If granted permission to file the document conventionally, the Filing User shall electronically file a "notice of manual filing" for that item. Exhibits submitted to the Court conventionally shall be served on other parties conventionally. NY R USDCTWD ECF Procedures(2)(d)(vi).

3. *Signing of pleadings, motions and other papers*

a. *Signature.* Every pleading, written motion, and other paper must be signed by at least one attorney of record in the attorney's name—or by a party personally if the party is unrepresented. The paper must state the signer's address, e-mail address, and telephone number. FRCP 11(a). Documents presented for paper filing must contain an original signature. NY R USDCTWD Civ Rule 10(b)(6).

    i. *Electronic signatures*

- *Non-attorney signature.* If the original document requires the signature of a non-attorney, the filing party shall obtain the signature of the non-attorney on the document. NY R USDCTWD ECF Procedures(2)(g)(i). The filing party or attorney then shall file the document electronically indicating the signatory's name in the form "s/(name)." NY R USDCTWD ECF Procedures(2)(g)(i)(1). A non-filing signatory or party who disputes the authenticity of an electronically filed document or the authenticity of the signature on that document must file an objection to the document within ten (10) days of receiving the Notice of Electronic Filing. NY R USDCTWD ECF Procedures(2)(g)(i)(2).

- *Registered user signature.* The username and password required to file documents on the Electronic Filing System serve as the Filing User's signature on all electronic documents filed with this Court. The also serve as a signature for the purposes of FRCP 11, the Federal Rules of Civil Procedure, the Local Rules of Civil Procedure for the United States District Court for the Western District of New York, and any other purpose for which a signature is required in connection with proceedings before this Court. A pleading requiring a Registered User's signature must include a signature block in the format found in NY R USDCTWD ECF Procedures(2)(g)(iii). NY R USDCTWD ECF Procedures(2)(g)(iii). Any party challenging the authenticity of an electronically filed document or the attorney's signature on that document must file an objection to the document within ten (10) days of receiving the Notice of Electronic Filing. NY R USDCTWD ECF Procedures(2)(g)(iii)(1).

- *Multiple signatures.* The following procedure applies when a stipulation or other document requires two or more signatures: The filing party shall initially confirm that the document is acceptable to all persons required to sign the document and shall obtain the signatures of all parties on the document. NY R USDCTWD ECF Procedures(2)(g)(iv)(1). The filing party or attorney then shall file the document electronically indicating the signatories, e.g., "s/Jane Doe," "s/John Smith," etc. NY R USDCTWD ECF Procedures(2)(g)(iv)(2). A non-filing signatory or party who disputes the authenticity of an electronically filed document containing multiple signatures or the authenticity of the signatures themselves must file an objection to the document within ten (10) days of receiving the Notice of Electronic Filing. NY R USDCTWD ECF Procedures(2)(g)(iv)(3).

    ii. *No verification or accompanying affidavit required for pleadings.* Unless a rule or statute specifically states otherwise, a pleading need not be verified or accompanied by an affidavit. FRCP 11(a).

    iii. *Unsigned papers.* The court must strike an unsigned paper unless the omission is promptly corrected after being called to the attorney's or party's attention. FRCP 11(a).

b. *Representations to the court.* By presenting to the court a pleading, written motion, or other paper—whether by signing, filing, submitting, or later advocating it—an attorney or unrepresented party certifies that to the best of the person's knowledge, information, and belief, formed after an inquiry reasonable under the circumstances:

    i. It is not being presented for any improper purpose, such as to harass, cause unnecessary delay, or needlessly increase the cost of litigation;

    ii. The claims, defenses, and other legal contentions are warranted by existing law or by a nonfrivolous argument for extending, modifying, or reversing existing law or for establishing new law;

    iii. The factual contentions have evidentiary support or, if specifically so identified, will likely have evidentiary support after a reasonable opportunity for further investigation or discovery; and

    iv. The denials of factual contentions are warranted on the evidence or, if specifically so identified, are reasonably based on belief or a lack of information. FRCP 11(b).

c. *Sanctions.* If, after notice and a reasonable opportunity to respond, the court determines that FRCP 11(b) has been violated, the court may impose an appropriate sanction on any attorney, law firm, or party that violated FRCP 11(b) or is responsible for the violation. FRCP 11(c)(1). Refer to the United States District Court for the Western District of New York KeyRules Motion for Sanctions document for more information.

4. *Privacy protection for filings made with the court.* In all filings, parties shall comply with FRCP 5.2. NY R USDCTWD ECF Procedures(2)(m)(i).

a. *Redacted filings.* Unless the court orders otherwise, in an electronic or paper filing with the court that contains an individual's Social Security number, taxpayer-identification number, or birth date, the name of an individual known to be a minor, or a financial-account number, a party or nonparty making the filing may include only:

    i. The last four (4) digits of the Social Security number and taxpayer-identification number;

    ii. The year of the individual's birth;

    iii. The minor's initials; and

    iv. The last four (4) digits of the financial-account number. FRCP 5.2(a).

b. *Exemptions from the redaction requirement.* The redaction requirement does not apply to the following:

    i. A financial-account number that identifies the property allegedly subject to forfeiture in a forfeiture proceeding;

    ii. The record of an administrative or agency proceeding;

     iii.   The official record of a state-court proceeding;

     iv.   The record of a court or tribunal, if that record was not subject to the redaction requirement when originally filed;

     v.   A filing covered by FRCP 5.2(c) or FRCP 5.2(d); and

     vi.   A pro se filing in an action brought under 28 U.S.C.A. § 2241, 28 U.S.C.A. § 2254, or 28 U.S.C.A. § 2255. FRCP 5.2(b).

  c.  *Limitations on remote access to electronic files; Social Security appeals and immigration cases.* Unless the court orders otherwise, in an action for benefits under the Social Security Act, and in an action or proceeding relating to an order of removal, to relief from removal, or to immigration benefits or detention, access to an electronic file is authorized as follows:

     i.   The parties and their attorneys may have remote electronic access to any part of the case file, including the administrative record;

     ii.   Any other person may have electronic access to the full record at the courthouse, but may have remote electronic access only to:

- The docket maintained by the court; and

- An opinion, order, judgment, or other disposition of the court, but not any other part of the case file or the administrative record. FRCP 5.2(c).

  d.  *Filings made under seal.* The court may order that a filing be made under seal without redaction. The court may later unseal the filing or order the person who made the filing to file a redacted version for the public record. FRCP 5.2(d). For more information on sealing documents, refer to NY R USDCTWD Civ Rule 5.3, NY R USDCTWD ECF Procedures(2)(o)(i)(1), NY R USDCTWD ECF Procedures(2)(o)(i)(2), and NY R USDCTWD ECF Procedures(2)(o)(i)(3).

  e.  *Protective orders.* For good cause, the court may by order in a case:

     i.   Require redaction of additional information; or

     ii.   Limit or prohibit a nonparty's remote electronic access to a document filed with the court. FRCP 5.2(e).

  f.  *Option for additional unredacted filing under seal.* A person making a redacted filing may also file an unredacted copy under seal. The court must retain the unredacted copy as part of the record. FRCP 5.2(f).

  g.  *Option for filing a reference list.* A filing that contains redacted information may be filed together with a reference list that identifies each item of redacted information and specifies an appropriate identifier that uniquely corresponds to each item listed. The list must be filed under seal and may be amended as of right. Any reference in the case to a listed identifier will be construed to refer to the corresponding item of information. FRCP 5.2(g).

  h.  *Waiver of protection of identifiers.* A person waives the protection of FRCP 5.2(a) as to the person's own information by filing it without redaction and not under seal. FRCP 5.2(h).

5.  *Individual judge practices.* Refer to the Miscellaneous section of this document for information on individual judge practices on formatting documents.

## F. Filing and Service Requirements

1.  *Filing requirements.* Any paper after the complaint that is required to be served—together with a certificate of service—must be filed within a reasonable time after service. FRCP 5(d)(1). All pleadings and other papers shall be filed and served in accordance with the Federal Rules of Civil Procedure and the CM/ECF Administrative Procedures Guide (NY R USDCTWD ECF Procedures). NY R USDCTWD Civ Rule 5.1(a). For information on filing of miscellaneous cases and irregular documents, refer to NY R USDCTWD Civ Rule 5.6.

  a.  *How filing is made; In general.* A paper is filed by delivering it:

     i.   To the clerk; or

     ii.   To a judge who agrees to accept it for filing, and who must then note the filing date on the paper and promptly send it to the clerk. FRCP 5(d)(2).

b. *Electronic filing*

    i. *Authorization of electronic filing program.* A court may, by local rule, allow papers to be filed, signed, or verified by electronic means that are consistent with any technical standards established by the Judicial Conference of the United States. A local rule may require electronic filing only if reasonable exceptions are allowed. A paper filed electronically in compliance with a local rule is a written paper for purposes of the Federal Rules of Civil Procedure. FRCP 5(d)(3).

- All civil cases filed in this Court are assigned to the Electronic Case Filing System ("ECF"). The procedures for electronic filing and any exceptions to the electronic filing requirements are set forth in the CM/ECF Administrative Procedures Guide (NY R USDCTWD ECF Procedures) which is available on the Court's website. NY R US-DCTWD Civ Rule 5.1(a).

    ii. *Scope of electronic filing.* The U.S. District Court for the Western District of New York requires attorneys in civil and criminal cases to file documents with the Court electronically over the Internet using its Case Management/Electronic Case Filing (CM/ECF) system. NY R US-DCTWD ECF Procedures. Beginning January 1, 2004, all civil and criminal cases currently pending and newly filed, except as expressly noted herein, were assigned to the Electronic Case Filing System ("System"). Except as expressly provided and in exceptional circumstances preventing a Filing User from filing electronically, all petitions, motions, memoranda of law, or other pleadings and documents required to be filed with the Court in connection with a case assigned to the System must be electronically filed. NY R USDCTWD ECF Procedures(1)(a).

- *Mandatory electronic filing.* All documents on civil, criminal, miscellaneous civil, miscellaneous criminal and new civil case openings, except sealed documents, sealed cases, opening of a criminal case, opening of a miscellaneous case and as expressly provided for in these procedures (NY R USDCTWD ECF Procedures), shall be electronically filed on the system. NY R USDCTWD ECF Procedures(2)(a)(i). NY R USDCTWD Civ Rule 29

- *Stipulations.* Pursuant to NY R USDCTWD Civ Rule 29, all stipulations (whether the stipulation is final or when it requires a judge's signature) shall be filed electronically. NY R USDCTWD ECF Procedures(2)(p)(i).

- *Letters.* The electronic filing of letters is generally prohibited unless granted permission by an assigned judge. Letters to the Court must be submitted conventionally. NY R US-DCTWD ECF Procedures(2)(q)(i).

- *Exceptions.* The Court requires attorneys to file documents electronically, absent a showing of good cause, unless otherwise excused by the procedures set forth below or by Order of the Court. NY R USDCTWD ECF Procedures.

    iii. *Conventional filing of documents.* The procedures in NY R USDCTWD ECF Procedures(2)(o) govern documents filed conventionally. The Court, upon application, may also authorize conventional filing of other documents otherwise subject to the procedures in NY R US-DCTWD ECF Procedures(2)(o). NY R USDCTWD ECF Procedures(2)(o)(i).

- *Documents filed under seal.* Unredacted documents filed with the Court pursuant to the privacy provisions of FRCP 5.2 shall be submitted in a sealing envelope with the information in NY R USDCTWD ECF Procedures(2)(o)(i)(1) on the envelope. NY R USDCTWD ECF Procedures(2)(o)(i)(1). If the document is larger than five (5) pages, a disk should be provided to the Clerks Office which contains the document in a .pdf format. NY R USDCTWD ECF Procedures(2)(o)(i)(1). For more information on documents filed under seal, refer to NY R USDCTWD ECF Procedures(2)(o)(i)(1), NY R USDCTWD ECF Procedures(2)(o)(i)(2), and NY R USDCTWD ECF Procedures(2)(o)(i)(3).

- *Magistrate judge consents.* Pursuant to FRCP 73(b), parties' filing consents to jurisdiction by United States Magistrate Judge will continue to be treated as non-public documents until all parties have consented. Therefore, parties must submit conventionally (in paper form) and not electronically file their consent forms so that the consent is not a public

WESTERN DISTRICT OF NEW YORK

document. If all parties consent to the jurisdiction of a Magistrate Judge, the Clerk will scan all consent forms which will then become a public document. NY R USDCTWD ECF Procedures(2)(o)(i)(3).

- *Pro se filers.* Pro Se filers shall file paper originals of all initiating documents, pleadings, motions, affidavits, briefs and other documents which must be signed or which require either verification or an unsworn declaration under any rule or statute. The Clerk's Office will scan these original documents into an electronic file in the System. A certificate of service is required for all documents a pro se litigant files with the court. If a Pro Se filer is granted permission to register to electronically file documents, they shall comply with the guidelines contained in this document (NY R USDCTWD ECF Procedures). NY R USDCTWD ECF Procedures(2)(o)(i)(4).

- *Social Security cases.* Absent a showing of good cause, and except as provided in Section o(i)(4) above, all documents, notices and orders in Social Security reviews will be filed and noticed electronically, except as noted in NY R USDCTWD ECF Procedures(2)(o)(i)(6). For more information, refer to NY R USDCTWD ECF Procedures(2)(o)(i)(6).

- For more information on conventional filing of documents, refer to NY R USDCTWD ECF Procedures(2)(o)(i).

iv. *Consequences of electronic filing.* Electronic transmission of a document to the System consistent with these procedures (NY R USDCTWD ECF Procedures), whether accomplished by the Filing User or a Court User, together with the transmission of a Notice of Electronic Filing from the Court, constitutes filing of a document for all purposes of the Federal Rules of Civil Procedure and the Local Rules of Civil Procedure for the United States District Court for the Western District of New York, and constitutes entry of the document on the docket kept by the Clerk under FRCP 58 and FRCP 79. A document shall not be considered filed for purposes of the Federal Rules of Civil until the filing party receives a System generated Notice of Electronic Filing. NY R USDCTWD ECF Procedures(2)(a)(i).

- E-mailing a document to the Clerk's Office or to the assigned judge shall not constitute "filing" of such document. NY R USDCTWD ECF Procedures(2)(a)(i)(1).

v. *Filing fees.* Any fee required for filing of a pleading or paper in District Court is payable to the Clerk of Court by check or money order. In addition, when opening a civil case on line, filing a notice of appeal on line or applying to appear pro hac vice on line, the fees shall be paid on line by registered users through the federal electronic payment website. Users will be directed to the federal electronic payment website while entering their transaction and should have a credit card available. When opening a civil case and applying to proceed in forma pauperis or when the United States of America opens a case, the payment screen can by bypassed to complete the transaction. Additional information on making electronic payments can be located on the court's website. NY R USDCTWD ECF Procedures(2)(h)(i).

2. *Service requirements.* All pleadings and other papers shall be filed and served in accordance with the Federal Rules of Civil Procedure and the CM/ECF Administrative Procedures Guide (NY R USDCTWD ECF Procedures). NY R USDCTWD Civ Rule 5.1(a).

a. *Service; When required*

i. *In general.* Unless the Federal Rules of Civil Procedure provide otherwise, each of the following papers must be served on every party:

- An order stating that service is required;
- A pleading filed after the original complaint, unless the court orders otherwise under FRCP 5(c) because there are numerous defendants;
- A discovery paper required to be served on a party, unless the court orders otherwise;
- A written motion, except one that may be heard ex parte; and
- A written notice, appearance, demand, or offer of judgment, or any similar paper. FRCP 5(a)(1).

ii. *If a party fails to appear.* No service is required on a party who is in default for failing to appear. But a pleading that asserts a new claim for relief against such a party must be served on that party under FRCP 4. FRCP 5(a)(2).

iii. *Seizing property.* If an action is begun by seizing property and no person is or need be named as a defendant, any service required before the filing of an appearance, answer, or claim must be made on the person who had custody or possession of the property when it was seized. FRCP 5(a)(3).

b. *Service; How made*

  i. *Serving an attorney.* If a party is represented by an attorney, service under FRCP 5 must be made on the attorney unless the court orders service on the party. FRCP 5(b)(1).

  ii. *Service in general.* A paper is served under FRCP 5 by:

- Handing it to the person;
- Leaving it: (1) at the person's office with a clerk or other person in charge or, if no one is in charge, in a conspicuous place in the office; or (2) if the person has no office or the office is closed, at the person's dwelling or usual place of abode with someone of suitable age and discretion who resides there;
- Mailing it to the person's last known address—in which event service is complete upon mailing;
- Leaving it with the court clerk if the person has no known address;
- Sending it by electronic means if the person consented in writing—in which event service is complete upon transmission, but is not effective if the serving party learns that it did not reach the person to be served; or
- Delivering it by any other means that the person consented to in writing—in which event service is complete when the person making service delivers it to the agency designated to make delivery. FRCP 5(b)(2).

  iii. *Service by overnight delivery.* All papers, other than a subpoena or a summons and complaint, may be served on counsel of record by overnight delivery service at the address designated by the attorney for that purpose, or if none is designated, at the attorney's last known address. Service by overnight delivery shall be complete upon deposit of the paper(s), enclosed in a properly addressed wrapper, into the custody of the overnight delivery service, prior to the latest time designated by the service for overnight delivery. NY R USDCTWD Civ Rule 5.1(g). "Overnight delivery service" means any delivery service which regularly accepts items for overnight delivery to any address within the Court's jurisdiction. NY R USDCTWD Civ Rule 5.1(g).

  iv. *Service of documents by electronic means*

- *Service on registered users.* Registered Users consent to the electronic service of all documents, and must make available an electronic mail address for service during the registration process. Upon the filing of a document by a party, a Notice of Electronic Filing, with a hyperlink to the filed document, will be automatically generated by the electronic filing system and sent via electronic mail to the e-mail addresses of all parties participating in the electronic filing system in the case. Electronic service of the Notice of Electronic Filing constitutes service of the filed document for all purposes of the Federal Rules of Civil Procedure and the Local Rules of Civil Procedure for the United States District Court for the Western District of New York. NY R USDCTWD ECF Procedures(2)(f)(i). The Notice of Electronic Filing effectuates service for all registered users and no certificate of service is required when all filers on an action are Registered Users. NY R USDCTWD ECF Procedures(2)(f)(iv).
- *Time limit for opening hyperlink.* The hyperlink to filed documents contained in the Notice of Electronic Filing must be opened within fifteen (15) days from the date the document was filed to provide registered users access to the document. The hyperlink expires after

fifteen (15) days and users will be unable to access documents for free after that time. Filing Users are encouraged to check their e-mail frequently for notice of filed documents. NY R USDCTWD ECF Procedures(2)(f)(ii).

- *Service on exempted attorneys or pro se litigants who do not have permission to file electronically.* Attorneys granted an exemption from electronically filing documents in the System and pro se litigants who have not been granted permission to electronically file documents are entitled to a paper copy of any electronically filed pleading, document or order. The filing party must therefore provide the non-registered party with the pleading, document or order according to the Federal Rules of Civil Procedure. NY R USDCTWD ECF Procedures(2)(f)(iii).

- *E-mailing or faxing documents.* E-mailing or faxing a pleading or document to any party shall not constitute service of the pleading or document. NY R USDCTWD ECF Procedures(2)(f)(v).

    v. *Using court facilities.* If a local rule so authorizes, a party may use the court's transmission facilities to make service under FRCP 5(b)(2)(E). FRCP 5(b)(3).

  c. *Serving numerous defendants*

    i. *In general.* If an action involves an unusually large number of defendants, the court may, on motion or on its own, order that:

- Defendants' pleadings and replies to them need not be served on other defendants;

- Any crossclaim, counterclaim, avoidance, or affirmative defense in those pleadings and replies to them will be treated as denied or avoided by all other parties; and

- Filing any such pleading and serving it on the plaintiff constitutes notice of the pleading to all parties. FRCP 5(c)(1).

    ii. *Notifying parties.* A copy of every such order must be served on the parties as the court directs. FRCP 5(c)(2).

3. *Service requirements of an amended complaint asserting new or additional claims for relief.* The service of amended pleadings is generally governed by FRCP 5. Thus, except for an amended pleading against a defaulting party that does not assert new or additional claims for relief, an amended pleading must be served in accordance with FRCP 5. FEDPROC § 62:263; International Controls Corp. v. Vesco, 556 F.2d 665, 23 Fed.R.Serv.2d 923 (2d Cir. 1977). However, while FRCP 5 permits service of an amended complaint on counsel, where the amended complaint contains an entirely different cause of action that could not have been properly served originally by the method used in serving the original complaint, the amended complaint must be served in accordance with the terms of FRCP 4. FEDPROC § 62:263; Lasch v. Antkies, 161 F.Supp. 851 (E.D.Pa. 1958). Refer to the United States District Court for the Western District of New York KeyRules Complaint document for more information on serving the amended complaint in accordance with FRCP 4.

4. *Pro se actions.* For information on the requirements in pro se actions, refer to NY R USDCTWD Civ Rule 5.2.

5. *Individual judge practices.* Refer to the Miscellaneous section of this document for information on individual judge practices on filing and serving documents.

## G. Hearings

1. *Hearings, generally.* Generally, there is no hearing contemplated in the federal statutes or rules for the amended pleading.

  a. *Amended answer; Hearing on FRCP 12 defenses before trial.* If a party so moves, any defense listed in FRCP 12(b)(1) through FRCP 12(b)(7)—whether made in a pleading or by motion—and a motion under FRCP 12(c) must be heard and decided before trial unless the court orders a deferral until trial. FRCP 12(i).

2. *Individual judge practices.* Refer to the Miscellaneous section of this document for information on individual judge practices on hearings.

## H. Forms

### 1. Federal Amended Pleading Forms

a. Notice; Of filing amended pleading as of course. AMJUR PP FEDPRAC § 153.

b. Amendment; Of pleading as of course. AMJUR PP FEDPRAC § 154.

c. Civil cover sheet. 2 FEDFORMS § 3:29.

d. Notice of lawsuit and request for waiver of service of summons and waiver of summons. 2 FEDFORMS § 3:36.

e. Complaint. 2 FEDFORMS § 7:14.

f. Generally. 2B FEDFORMS § 8:10.

g. Presenting defenses; Official form. 2B FEDFORMS § 8:12.

h. Denials, admissions and affirmative defenses. 2B FEDFORMS § 8:15.

i. Denial of particular averment. 2B FEDFORMS § 8:24.

j. Admission of particular averment. 2B FEDFORMS § 8:25.

k. Denial of all averments of paragraph. 2B FEDFORMS § 8:26.

l. Admission of all averments of paragraph. 2B FEDFORMS § 8:27.

m. Denial in part and admission in part of paragraph. 2B FEDFORMS § 8:28.

n. Notice of amended complaint. 2C FEDFORMS § 14:10.

o. Amendment to complaint. 2C FEDFORMS § 14:47.

p. Amendment to complaint; Short version. 2C FEDFORMS § 14:48.

q. Amendment to complaint; As of course. 2C FEDFORMS § 14:49.

r. Complaint; Single count. FEDPROF § 1:68.

s. Complaint; Multiple counts; With same jurisdictional basis. FEDPROF § 1:69.

t. Amendment of pleading; As matter of course. FEDPROF § 1:220.

u. Notice of filing amended pleading; Where amendment is matter of course. FEDPROF § 1:221.

v. Amendment of pleading; Particular clauses. FEDPROF § 1:224.

w. Amendment of pleading; Clause; Change in title of action. FEDPROF § 1:225.

x. Amendment of pleading; Clause; To show amount in controversy. FEDPROF § 1:227.

y. Amendment of pleading; Clause; To show diversity of citizenship. FEDPROF § 1:228.

z. Amendment of pleading; Clause; Prayer for relief. FEDPROF § 1:229.

### 2. Forms for the Western District of New York

a. Certificate of service. NY R USDCTWD ECF Procedures(4a).

## I. Applicable Rules

### 1. *Federal rules*

a. Serving and filing pleadings and other papers. FRCP 5.

b. Constitutional challenge to a statute; Notice, certification, and intervention. FRCP 5.1.

c. Privacy protection for filings made with the court. FRCP 5.2.

d. Computing and extending time; Time for motion papers. FRCP 6.

e. Pleadings allowed; Form of motions and other papers. FRCP 7.

f. General rules of pleading. FRCP 8.

g. Pleading special matters. FRCP 9.

h. Form of pleadings. FRCP 10.

    i.    Signing pleadings, motions, and other papers; Representations to the court; Sanctions. FRCP 11.

    j.    Defenses and objections; When and how presented; Motion for judgment on the pleadings; Consolidating motions; Waiving defenses; Pretrial hearing. FRCP 12.

    k.    Amended and supplemental pleadings. FRCP 15.

    l.    Right to a jury trial; Demand. FRCP 38.

    m.    Determining foreign law. FRCP 44.1.

2.   *Local rules*

    a.    Title. NY R USDCTWD Civ Rule 1.1.

    b.    Filing and serving papers. NY R USDCTWD Civ Rule 5.1.

    c.    Requirement to file a RICO case statement. NY R USDCTWD Civ Rule 9.

    d.    Form of papers. NY R USDCTWD Civ Rule 10.

    e.    Sanctions. NY R USDCTWD Civ Rule 11.

    f.    Alternative dispute resolution and pretrial conferences. NY R USDCTWD Civ Rule 16.

    g.    Class actions. NY R USDCTWD Civ Rule 23.

    h.    Attorneys of record; Appearance and withdrawal. NY R USDCTWD Civ Rule 83.2.

    i.    Administrative procedures guide for electronic filing. NY R USDCTWD ECF Procedures.

    j.    Alternative dispute resolution plan. NY R USDCTWD ADR Plan.

## J.  Miscellaneous

**NOTE: Individual judges' rules may apply. For available judge-level information, refer to:**

DISTRICT JUDGE RICHARD J. ARCARA: NY R USDCTWD Arcara-Procedures.

DISTRICT JUDGE FRANK P. GERACI, JR.: NY R USDCTWD Geraci-Procedures.

DISTRICT JUDGE DAVID G. LARIMER: NY R USDCTWD Larimer-Procedures.

DISTRICT JUDGE CHARLES J. SIRAGUSA: NY R USDCTWD Siragusa-Procedures.

DISTRICT JUDGE WILLIAM M. SKRETNY: NY R USDCTWD Skretny--Procedures.

DISTRICT JUDGE MICHAEL A. TELESCA: NY R USDCTWD Telesca-Procedures.

DISTRICT JUDGE LAWRENCE J. VILARDO: NY R USDCTWD Vilardo-Procedures.

DISTRICT JUDGE ELIZABETH A. WOLFORD: NY R USDCTWD Wolford-Procedures.

MAGISTRATE JUDGE JONATHAN W. FELDMAN: NY R USDCTWD Feldman-Procedures.

MAGISTRATE JUDGE LESLIE G. FOSCHIO: NY R USDCTWD Foschio-Procedures; NY R USDCTWD Foschio-Depositions.

MAGISTRATE JUDGE JEREMIAH J. McCARTHY: NY R USDCTWD McCarthy-Procedures.

MAGISTRATE JUDGE MARIAN W. PAYSON: NY R USDCTWD Payson-Procedures.

MAGISTRATE JUDGE MICHAEL J. ROEMER: NY R USDCTWD Roemer-Procedures.

MAGISTRATE JUDGE H. KENNETH SCHROEDER, JR.: NY R USDCTWD Schroeder-Proc.

MAGISTRATE JUDGE HUGH B. SCOTT: NY R USDCTWD Scott-Procedures.

# Motions, Oppositions and Replies
## Motion to Strike

### Document Last Updated September 2016

**A. Checklist**

(I)  ❑ Matters to be considered by moving party

    (a)  ❑ Required documents

        (1)  ❑ Notice of motion and motion

        (2)  ❑ Memorandum of law

        (3)  ❑ Certificate of service

    (b)  ❑ Supplemental documents

        (1)  ❑ Deposition

        (2)  ❑ Notice of constitutional question

        (3)  ❑ Nongovernmental corporate disclosure statement

        (4)  ❑ Copies of authorities

        (5)  ❑ Proposed order

        (6)  ❑ Paper copy for date-stamping with self-addressed envelope

        (7)  ❑ Courtesy copies

    (c)  ❑ Timing

        (1)  ❑ The court may act on motion made by a party either before responding to the pleading or, if a response is not allowed, within twenty-one (21) days after being served with the pleading

        (2)  ❑ A written motion and notice of the hearing must be served at least fourteen (14) days before the time specified for the hearing, with the following exceptions: (i) when the motion may be heard ex parte; (ii) when the Federal Rules of Civil Procedure set a different time; or (iii) when a court order—which a party may, for good cause, apply for ex parte—sets a different time

        (3)  ❑ Any affidavit supporting a motion must be served with the motion

(II)  ❑ Matters to be considered by opposing party

    (a)  ❑ Required documents

        (1)  ❑ Opposition

        (2)  ❑ Answering memorandum

        (3)  ❑ Certificate of service

    (b)  ❑ Supplemental documents

        (1)  ❑ Deposition

        (2)  ❑ Notice of constitutional question

        (3)  ❑ Copies of authorities

        (4)  ❑ Paper copy for date-stamping with self-addressed envelope

        (5)  ❑ Courtesy copies

    (c)  ❑ Timing

        (1)  ❑ After a motion is filed, the court may issue an order setting deadlines for filing and service of opposing papers; if the court does not set deadlines by order, the opposing party shall have fourteen (14) days after service of the motion to file and serve responding papers

        (2)  ❑ Except as FRCP 59(c) provides otherwise, any opposing affidavit must be served at least seven (7) days before the hearing, unless the court permits service at another time

## B. Timing

1. *Motion to strike.* The court may act on motion made by a party either before responding to the pleading or, if a response is not allowed, within twenty-one (21) days after being served with the pleading. FRCP 12(f)(2).

2. *Timing of motions, generally*

    a. *Motion and notice of hearing.* A written motion and notice of the hearing must be served at least fourteen (14) days before the time specified for the hearing, with the following exceptions:

        i. When the motion may be heard ex parte;

        ii. When the Federal Rules of Civil Procedure set a different time; or

        iii. When a court order—which a party may, for good cause, apply for ex parte—sets a different time. FRCP 6(c)(1).

    b. *Supporting affidavit.* Any affidavit supporting a motion must be served with the motion. FRCP 6(c)(2).

3. *Timing of opposing papers.* After a motion is filed, the Court may issue an order setting deadlines for filing and service of opposing papers. NY R USDCTWD Civ Rule 7(b)(1). If the Court does not set deadlines by order, the following schedule shall apply: the opposing party shall have fourteen (14) days after service of the motion to file and serve responding papers. NY R USDCTWD Civ Rule 7(b)(2)(B).

    a. *Opposing affidavit.* Except as FRCP 59(c) provides otherwise, any opposing affidavit must be served at least seven (7) days before the hearing, unless the court permits service at another time. FRCP 6(c)(2).

4. *Timing of reply papers.* Where the respondent files an answering affidavit setting up a new matter, the moving party ordinarily is allowed a reasonable time to file a reply affidavit since failure to deny the new matter by affidavit may operate as an admission of its truth. AMJUR MOTIONS § 25.

    a. *Reply papers.* After a motion is filed, the Court may issue an order setting deadlines. . .for filing and service of reply papers if the moving party has stated an intent to reply. NY R USDCTWD Civ Rule 7(b)(1). If the Court does not set deadlines by order, the following schedule shall apply: the moving party shall have seven (7) days after service of the responding papers to file and serve reply papers. NY R USDCTWD Civ Rule 7(b)(2)(B).

    b. *Reply memorandum.* The moving party may file a reply memorandum, but is not required to do so. NY R USDCTWD Civ Rule 7(a)(2)(A).

5. *Motion for an expedited hearing.* A party seeking to shorten the schedule prescribed in NY R USDCTWD Civ Rule 7(b) must make a separate motion for an expedited hearing, setting forth the reasons why an expedited hearing is required. NY R USDCTWD Civ Rule 7(d)(1). For more information, refer to NY R USDCTWD Civ Rule 7(d)(1).

6. *Effect of a FRCP 12 motion on the time to serve a responsive pleading.* Unless the court sets a different time, serving a motion under FRCP 12 alters the periods in FRCP 12(a) as follows:

    a. If the court denies the motion or postpones its disposition until trial, the responsive pleading must be served within fourteen (14) days after notice of the court's action; or

    b. If the court grants a motion for a more definite statement, the responsive pleading must be served within fourteen (14) days after the more definite statement is served. FRCP 12(a)(4).

7. *Computation of time*

    a. *Computing time.* FRCP 6 applies in computing any time period specified in the Federal Rules of Civil Procedure, in any local rule or court order, or in any statute that does not specify a method of computing time. FRCP 6(a).

        i. *Period stated in days or a longer unit.* When the period is stated in days or a longer unit of time:

            • Exclude the day of the event that triggers the period;

            • Count every day, including intermediate Saturdays, Sundays, and legal holidays; and

1408

- Include the last day of the period, but if the last day is a Saturday, Sunday, or legal holiday, the period continues to run until the end of the next day that is not a Saturday, Sunday, or legal holiday. FRCP 6(a)(1).

ii. *Period stated in hours.* When the period is stated in hours:

- Begin counting immediately on the occurrence of the event that triggers the period;

- Count every hour, including hours during intermediate Saturdays, Sundays, and legal holidays; and

- If the period would end on a Saturday, Sunday, or legal holiday, the period continues to run until the same time on the next day that is not a Saturday, Sunday, or legal holiday. FRCP 6(a)(2).

iii. *Inaccessibility of the clerk's office.* Unless the court orders otherwise, if the clerk's office is inaccessible:

- On the last day for filing under FRCP 6(a)(1), then the time for filing is extended to the first accessible day that is not a Saturday, Sunday, or legal holiday; or

- During the last hour for filing under FRCP 6(a)(2), then the time for filing is extended to the same time on the first accessible day that is not a Saturday, Sunday, or legal holiday. FRCP 6(a)(3).

iv. *"Last day" defined.* Unless a different time is set by a statute, local rule, or court order, the last day ends:

- For electronic filing, at midnight in the court's time zone; and

- For filing by other means, when the clerk's office is scheduled to close. FRCP 6(a)(4).

v. *"Next day" defined.* The "next day" is determined by continuing to count forward when the period is measured after an event and backward when measured before an event. FRCP 6(a)(5).

vi. *"Legal holiday" defined.* "Legal holiday" means:

- The day set aside by statute for observing New Year's Day, Martin Luther King Jr.'s Birthday, Washington's Birthday, Memorial Day, Independence Day, Labor Day, Columbus Day, Veterans' Day, Thanksgiving Day, or Christmas Day;

- Any day declared a holiday by the President or Congress; and

- For periods that are measured after an event, any other day declared a holiday by the state where the district court is located. FRCP 6(a)(6).

b. *Computation of electronic filing deadlines.* A document will be deemed timely filed if filed prior to midnight Eastern Time, unless otherwise ordered by the Court. A document will be considered untimely if filed thereafter. When a Court order requires that a document be filed on a weekend or holiday, the document may be filed by close of business the next business day without further application to the Court. NY R USDCTWD ECF Procedures(2)(e)(i). A document filed electronically is deemed filed on the date and time stated on the Notice of Electronic Filing. NY R USDCTWD ECF Procedures(2)(e)(ii).

i. *System availability.* Although parties may file documents electronically twenty-four (24) hours a day, registered users are strongly encouraged to file all documents during normal working hours of the Clerk's Office (8:30 a.m. to 5:00 p.m. Eastern Time). NY R USDCTWD ECF Procedures(2)(t)(i).

ii. *Technical failures.* A Filing User whose filing is made untimely as a result of a technical failure must seek appropriate relief from the Court. NY R USDCTWD ECF Procedures(2)(u)(i).

c. *Extending time*

i. *In general.* When an act may or must be done within a specified time, the court may, for good cause, extend the time:

- With or without motion or notice if the court acts, or if a request is made, before the original time or its extension expires; or

- On motion made after the time has expired if the party failed to act because of excusable neglect. FRCP 6(b)(1).

    ii. *Exceptions.* A court must not extend the time to act under FRCP 50(b), FRCP 50(d), FRCP 52(b), FRCP 59(b), FRCP 59(d), FRCP 59(e), and FRCP 60(b). FRCP 6(b)(2).

    iii. Refer to the United States District Court for the Western District of New York KeyRules Motion for Continuance/Extension of Time document for more information on extending time.

  d. *Additional time after certain kinds of service.* When a party may or must act within a specified time after service and service is made under FRCP 5(b)(2)(C), FRCP 5(b)(2)(D), FRCP 5(b)(2)(E), or FRCP 5(b)(2)(F), three (3) days are added after the period would otherwise expire under FRCP 6(a). FRCP 6(d).

    i. *Service by overnight delivery.* Where a period of time prescribed by either the Federal Rules of Civil Procedure or the Local Rules of Civil Procedure for the United States District Court for the Western District of New York is measured from the service of a paper and service is by overnight delivery, one (1) business day shall be added to the prescribed period. NY R USDCTWD Civ Rule 5.1(g).

8. *Individual judge practices.* Refer to the Miscellaneous section of this document for information on individual judge practices on timing of documents.

## C. General Requirements

1. *Motions, generally*

  a. *Requirements.* A request for a court order must be made by motion. The motion must:

    i. Be in writing unless made during a hearing or trial;

    ii. State with particularity the grounds for seeking the order; and

    iii. State the relief sought. FRCP 7(b)(1).

  b. *Notice of motion.* A party interested in resisting the relief sought by a motion has a right to notice thereof, and an opportunity to be heard. AMJUR MOTIONS § 12.

    i. In addition to statutory or court rule provisions requiring notice of a motion—the purpose of such a notice requirement having been said to be to prevent a party from being prejudicially surprised by a motion—principles of natural justice dictate that an adverse party generally must be given notice that a motion will be presented to the court. AMJUR MOTIONS § 12.

    ii. "Notice," in this regard, means reasonable notice, including a meaningful opportunity to prepare and to defend against allegations of a motion. AMJUR MOTIONS § 12.

  c. *Writing requirement.* The writing requirement is intended to insure that the adverse parties are informed and have a record of both the motion's pendency and the grounds on which the movant seeks an order. FPP § 1191; Feldberg v. Quechee Lakes Corp., 463 F.3d 195 (2d Cir. 2006).

    i. It is sufficient "if the motion is stated in a written notice of the hearing of the motion." FPP § 1191.

  d. *Particularity requirement.* The particularity requirement insures that the opposing parties will have notice of their opponent's contentions. FEDPROC § 62:364; Goodman v. 1973 26 Foot Trojan Vessel, Arkansas Registration No. AR1439SN, 859 F.2d 71, 12 Fed.R.Serv.3d 645 (8th Cir. 1988). That requirement ensures that notice of the basis for the motion is provided to the court and to the opposing party so as to avoid prejudice, provide the opponent with a meaningful opportunity to respond, and provide the court with enough information to process the motion correctly. FEDPROC § 62:364; Andreas v. Volkswagen of America, Inc., 336 F.3d 789, 56 Fed.R.Serv.3d 6 (8th Cir. 2003).

    i. Reasonable specification of the grounds for a motion is sufficient. However, where a movant fails to state even one ground for granting the motion in question, the movant has failed to meet the minimal standard of "reasonable specification." FEDPROC § 62:364; Martinez v. Trainor, 556 F.2d 818, 23 Fed.R.Serv.2d 403 (7th Cir. 1977).

    ii. The court may excuse the failure to comply with the particularity requirement if it is inadvertent, and where no prejudice is shown by the opposing party. FEDPROC § 62:364.

2. *Motion to strike.* The court may strike from a pleading an insufficient defense or any redundant, immaterial, impertinent, or scandalous matter. The court may act: (1) on its own; or (2) on motion made by a party either before responding to the pleading or, if a response is not allowed, within twenty-one (21) days after being served with the pleading. FRCP 12(f). FRCP 12(f) also is designed to reinforce the requirement in FRCP 8(e) that pleadings be simple, concise, and direct. However, as the cases make clear, it is neither an authorized nor a proper way to procure the dismissal of all or a part of a complaint, or a counterclaim, or to strike an opponent's affidavits. FPP § 1380.

    a. *Practice on a motion to strike.* All well-pleaded facts are taken as admitted on a motion to strike but conclusions of law or conclusions drawn from the facts do not have to be treated in that fashion by the district judge. FPP § 1380. Both because striking a portion of a pleading is a drastic remedy and because it often is sought by the movant simply as a dilatory or harassing tactic, numerous judicial decisions make it clear that motions under FRCP 12(f) are viewed with disfavor by the federal courts and are infrequently granted. FPP § 1380.

    b. *Striking an insufficient defense.* Only if a defense is insufficient as a matter of law will it be stricken. If a defense cannot succeed under any set of circumstances alleged, the defense may be deemed insufficient as a matter of law. In other words, a defense may be stricken if, on the face of the pleadings, it is patently frivolous, or if it is clearly invalid as a matter of law. FEDPROC § 62:412.

        i. A defense will be stricken if it could not possibly prevent recovery by the plaintiff on its claim. FEDPROC § 62:413. In addition, a defense may be stricken if:

- The defense requires separate statements;
- The defense has been previously advanced and rejected; or
- The defense cannot be waived. FEDPROC § 62:413.

    c. *Striking immaterial or impertinent matter.* Immaterial or impertinent matter will be stricken from a pleading if it is clear that it can have no possible bearing upon the subject matter of the litigation, and that its inclusion will prejudice the movant. If there is any doubt as to whether under any contingency the matter may raise an issue, the motion should be denied. FEDPROC § 62:415.

        i. "Immaterial matter," for purposes of FRCP 12(f), is matter which has no essential or important relationship to the claim for relief or the defenses being pleaded. FEDPROC § 62:414. A statement of unnecessary particulars in connection with and descriptive of that which is material may be stricken as immaterial matter. FEDPROC § 62:416.

        ii. "Impertinent matter," for purposes of FRCP 12(f), consists of statements that do not pertain, and are not necessary, to the issues in question. FEDPROC § 62:414.

    d. *Striking redundant matter.* "Redundant matter," for purposes of FRCP 12(f), consists of allegations that constitute a needless repetition of other averments or which are wholly foreign to the issue to be decided. However, even if allegations are redundant, they need not be stricken if their presence in the pleading cannot prejudice the moving party. FEDPROC § 62:417.

        i. Merely duplicative remedies do not necessarily make claims "redundant," within the meaning of FRCP 12(f), if the claims otherwise require proof of different elements, but a claim that merely recasts the same elements under the guise of a different theory may be stricken as redundant. FEDPROC § 62:417.

    e. *Striking scandalous matter.* A matter is deemed scandalous, for purposes of FRCP 12(f), when it improperly casts a derogatory light on someone, usually a party to the action. Scandalous matter also consists of any unnecessary allegation which reflects cruelly upon the moral character of an individual, or states anything in repulsive language which detracts from the dignity of the court. To be scandalous, degrading charges must be irrelevant, or, if relevant, must go into in unnecessary detail. FEDPROC § 62:418.

        i. Allegations may be stricken as scandalous if the matter bears no possible relation to the controversy or may cause the objecting party prejudice. FEDPROC § 62:418.

        ii. But there are several limitations on the court's willingness to strike scandalous allegations. For example, it is not enough that the matter offends the sensibilities of the objecting party or the person who is the subject of the statements in the pleading, if the challenged allegations describe acts or events that are relevant to the action. FPP § 1382.

f. *Striking sham or false matter.* FRCP 12(f) does not authorize a motion to strike part or all of a pleading on the ground that it is sham, and the grounds for a motion to strike similarly do not include falsity of the matter alleged. FEDPROC § 62:419; PAE Government Services, Inc. v. MPRI, Inc., 514 F.3d 856 (9th Cir. 2007). However, it has been said that a court will strike a pleading according to FRCP 12(f) when it appears beyond peradventure that it is a sham and false and that its allegations are devoid of factual basis. FEDPROC § 62:419.

g. *Striking conclusions of law.* Unwarranted conclusions of law may be stricken from a pleading pursuant to FRCP 12(f), but ordinarily an allegation is not subject to being stricken merely because it is a conclusion of law. To the contrary, the Federal Rules of Civil Procedure do not condemn conclusions of law, but rather encourage them as at times the clearest and simplest way of stating a claim for relief. Conclusions of law must be unwarranted enough to justify a motion to strike, such as when a plaintiff states causes of action under a federal statute which provides no explicit private right of action. FEDPROC § 62:420.

h. *Striking other particular matter.* Under FRCP 12(f), which permits a court to order stricken from any pleading any redundant, immaterial, impertinent, or scandalous matter, courts have the authority to strike a prayer for relief seeking damages that are not recoverable as a matter of law. A motion to strike may be used to remove an excessive or unauthorized claim for damages. Furthermore, a motion to strike a demand for punitive damages under FRCP 12(f) may be proper if such damages are clearly not collectible, such as in an ordinary breach of contract action. However, there are other ways to raise this issue, and in a particular case, one of these other methods may be more appropriate, such as a motion to dismiss for failure to state a claim pursuant to FRCP 12(b)(6). FEDPROC § 62:421.

i. *Form.* On a motion to strike portions of a pleading, the movant must indicate what paragraphs are being challenged in order to fulfill the particularity requirement; the movant cannot merely state the conclusion that the allegations are too indefinite and insufficient to state a claim or defense. FPP § 1192.

j. *Joining motions*

  i. *Right to join.* A motion under FRCP 12 may be joined with any other motion allowed by FRCP 12. FRCP 12(g)(1).

  ii. *Limitation on further motions.* Except as provided in FRCP 12(h)(2) or FRCP 12(h)(3), a party that makes a motion under FRCP 12 must not make another motion under FRCP 12 raising a defense or objection that was available to the party but omitted from its earlier motion. FRCP 12(g)(2).

3. *Opposing papers.* The Federal Rules of Civil Procedure do not require any formal answer, return, or reply to a motion, except where the Federal Rules of Civil Procedure or local rules may require affidavits, memoranda, or other papers to be filed in opposition to a motion. Such papers are simply to apprise the court of such opposition and the grounds of that opposition. FEDPROC § 62:359.

a. *Effect of failure to respond to motion.* Although in the absence of statutory provision or court rule, a motion ordinarily does not require a written answer, when a party files a motion and the opposing party fails to respond, the court may construe such failure to respond as nonopposition to the motion or an admission that the motion was meritorious, may take the facts alleged in the motion as true—the rule in some jurisdictions being that the failure to respond to a fact set forth in a motion is deemed an admission—and may grant the motion if the relief requested appears to be justified. AMJUR MOTIONS § 28.

b. *Assent or no opposition not determinative.* However, a motion will not be granted automatically simply because an "assent" or a notation of "no opposition" has been filed; federal judges frequently deny motions that have been assented to when it is thought that justice so dictates. FPP § 1190.

c. *Responsive pleading inappropriate as response to motion.* An attempt to answer or oppose a motion with a responsive pleading usually is not appropriate. FPP § 1190.

4. *Reply papers.* A moving party may be required or permitted to prepare papers in addition to his original motion papers. AMJUR MOTIONS § 25. Papers answering or replying to opposing papers may be appropriate, in the interests of justice, where it appears there is a substantial reason for allowing a reply. Thus, a court may accept reply papers where a party demonstrates that the papers to which it seeks to file a reply raise new issues that are material to the disposition of the question before the court, or where the court determines, sua sponte, that it wishes further briefing of an issue raised in those papers and orders the submission of additional papers. FEDPROC § 62:360.

   a. *Function of reply papers.* The function of a reply affidavit is to answer the arguments made in opposition to the position taken by the movant and not to permit the movant to introduce new arguments in support of the motion. AMJUR MOTIONS § 25.

   b. *Issues raised for the first time in a reply document.* However, the view has been followed in some jurisdictions, that as a matter of judicial economy, where there is no prejudice and where the issues could be raised simply by filing a motion to dismiss, the trial court has discretion to consider arguments raised for the first time in a reply memorandum, and that a trial court may grant a motion to strike issues raised for the first time in a reply memorandum. AMJUR MOTIONS § 26.

5. *Sur-reply.* Absent permission of the Judge hearing the motion, sur-reply papers are not permitted. NY R USDCTWD Civ Rule 7(a)(6).

6. *Motion to settle an order.* When counsel are unable to agree on the form of a proposed order, the prevailing party may move, upon seven (7) days notice to all parties, to settle the order. The Court may award costs and attorney's fees against an attorney if it determines that the attorney's unreasonable conduct necessitated bringing the motion. NY R USDCTWD Civ Rule 7(d)(2).

7. *Notice of appearance.* No notice of appearance is required of an attorney whose name and address appear at the end of a complaint, notice of removal, pre-answer motion, or answer. In all other circumstances, an attorney appearing for a party in a civil case shall promptly file a written notice of appearance. NY R USDCTWD Civ Rule 83.2(b). For more information on appearances and withdrawals, refer to NY R USDCTWD Civ Rule 83.2.

8. *Related cases.* Each attorney appearing in a civil case has a continuing duty to promptly notify the Clerk of Court when the attorney has reason to believe that said case is related to some other pending civil or criminal action(s) such that their assignment to the same Judge would avoid unnecessary duplication of judicial effort. As soon as the attorney becomes aware of such a relationship, the attorney shall notify the Clerk of Court by letter of the relevant facts, and the Clerk of Court will transmit that notification to the Judges to whom the cases have been assigned. NY R USDCTWD Civ Rule 5.1(e).

9. *Alternative dispute resolution (ADR).* This Court has adopted an Alternative Dispute Resolution Plan ("ADR"), as implemented by Standing Order (NY R USDCTWD ADR Plan), under which certain civil cases are referred automatically to ADR upon filing. NY R USDCTWD Civ Rule 16(a). The United States District Court for the Western District of New York (the "Court") adopted the ADR Plan on January 1, 2006 (the "Effective Date"), to make available to civil litigants court-administered ADR interventions and processes designed to provide quicker, less expensive and potentially more satisfying alternatives to continuing litigation, without impairing the quality of justice or the right to trial. NY R USDCTWD ADR Plan(1)(1.2)(A).

   a. *Scope.* This ADR Plan (NY R USDCTWD ADR Plan) applies to civil actions pending or commenced on and after the Effective Date, except as otherwise indicated in NY R USDCTWD ADR Plan. The ADR Plan supplements the Local Rules of Civil Procedure for the United States District Court for the Western District of New York, which shall remain in full effect for all cases. NY R USDCTWD ADR Plan(1)(1.2)(B).

   b. *Referral to ADR*

      i. *New cases.* All civil cases filed on and after the Effective Date of the ADR Plan shall be referred automatically for ADR. NY R USDCTWD ADR Plan(2)(2.1)(A). Notice of the ADR requirements will be provided to all parties immediately upon the filing of a complaint and answer or a notice of removal; NY R USDCTWD ADR Plan(2)(2.1)(A); NY R USDCTWD Civ Rule 16(a). ADR intervention will be scheduled at the conference held pursuant to Local Rule of

Civil Procedure 16.1. NY R USDCTWD ADR Plan(2)(2.1)(A). [Editor's note: the reference to Local Rule of Civil Procedure 16.1 is likely meant to be a reference to NY R USDCTWD Civ Rule 16(b)].

- Litigants in cases not referred automatically to ADR must consider possible agreement to the use of an ADR process. NY R USDCTWD Civ Rule 16(a).

- For a list of exemptions from automatic referral, refer to NY R USDCTWD ADR Plan(2)(2.1)(A).

ii. *Pending cases.* The assigned Judge on any pending civil case may, sua sponte or with status conference, issue an order referring the case for ADR. NY R USDCTWD ADR Plan(2)(2.1)(B); NY R USDCTWD Civ Rule 16(a). The order shall specify a date on which the ADR intervention is to be completed. NY R USDCTWD ADR Plan(2)(2.1)(B).

iii. *Stipulation.* A case may be referred for ADR by stipulation of all parties. Stipulations shall be filed and shall designate the specific ADR intervention the parties have selected, the time frame within which the ADR process will be completed and the selected Neutral. Stipulations are presumed acceptable unless the assigned Judge determines that the interests of justice are not served. NY R USDCTWD ADR Plan(2)(2.1)(C).

iv. *Relief from ADR referral*

- *Opting out motions.* Any party may file, with the assigned Judge for that case, a motion to opt out of, or for relief from, ADR. NY R USDCTWD ADR Plan(2)(2.2)(A).

- *Motion.* Opting Out Motions must be made within fourteen (14) days from (1) the date of the first discovery conference under Local Rule 16.1 in new cases, or (2) the date of a sua sponte ADR Referral Order in pending cases. NY R USDCTWD ADR Plan(2)(2.2)(B). [Editor's note: the reference to Local Rule 16.1 is likely meant to be a reference to NY R USDCTWD Civ Rule 16(b)].

- *Criteria.* Opting Out Motions shall be granted only for "good cause" shown. Inconvenience, travel costs, attorney fees or other costs shall not constitute "good cause." A party seeking relief from ADR must set forth the reasons why ADR has no reasonable chance of being productive. NY R USDCTWD ADR Plan(2)(2.2)(C).

- *Judicial initiative.* The assigned Judge may, sua sponte, exempt any case from the Court's ADR Plan. NY R USDCTWD ADR Plan(2)(2.2)(D).

c. *ADR interventions*

i. *Options.* It is expected that cases referred for ADR will proceed to Mediation. However, the following options are also available upon the stipulation of all parties:

- Neutral Evaluation;

- Mini Summary Trial;

- Arbitration (Binding and Non-Binding);

- Case Valuation; and

- Settlement Week, when scheduled by the Court. NY R USDCTWD ADR Plan(4)(4.1)(A).

ii. *Timing.* Timing is specific to the intervention and process chosen, as set forth in the corresponding sections in NY R USDCTWD ADR Plan. NY R USDCTWD ADR Plan(4)(4.1)(B).

iii. *Scheduling.* The referral of a case to ADR does not delay or defer other dates established in the Scheduling Order and has no effect on the scheduled progress of the case toward trial. NY R USDCTWD ADR Plan(4)(4.1)(C).

d. *Selecting an ADR intervention*

i. *New cases.* Prior to the Local Rule 16.1 scheduling conference, counsel and any unrepresented parties shall confer about ADR as part of their discussion of "the possibilities for a prompt settlement or resolution of the case" pursuant to FRCP 26(f). Unless the parties agree to a different intervention, it is presumed that they will participate in mediation. [Editor's note: the reference to Local Rule 16.1 is likely meant to be a reference to NY R USDCTWD Civ Rule 16(b)].

    ii.   *Pending cases.* In pending cases, all sua sponte referrals will be to mediation. Should the parties agree that a different ADR intervention is more appropriate to their case, they may submit a stipulation designating the specific ADR intervention selected, the time frame within which the ADR process will be completed and the identity of the Neutral. Stipulations must be filed within fourteen (14) days from the date of the ADR Referral Order and are presumed acceptable unless the assigned Judge determines that the interests of justice are not served. NY R USDCTWD ADR Plan(4)(4.2)(B).

    e.   For more information on alternative dispute resolution (ADR), refer to NY R USDCTWD ADR Plan.

10.   *Sanctions.* Failure of counsel for any party, or a party proceeding pro se, to appear before the Court at a conference, to complete the necessary preparations, or to be prepared to proceed to trial at the set time may be considered an abandonment of the case or a failure to prosecute or defend diligently. An appropriate order for sanctions may be entered against the defaulting party with respect to either a specific issue or the entire case. NY R USDCTWD Civ Rule 11(a). For more information, refer to NY R USDCTWD Civ Rule 11.

11.   *Pro se actions.* For information on the requirements in pro se actions, refer to NY R USDCTWD Civ Rule 5.2.

12.   *Individual judge practices.* Refer to the Miscellaneous section of this document for information on individual judge practices on general requirements for documents.

## D.  Documents

  1.   *Documents for moving party*

    a.   *Required documents*

      i.   *Notice of motion and motion.* A notice of motion is required for all motions, and must state: the relief sought, the grounds for the request, the papers submitted in support, and the return date for the motion, if known. A moving party who intends to file and serve reply papers must so state in the notice of motion. NY R USDCTWD Civ Rule 7(a)(1). Refer to the General Requirements section of this document for information on the notice of motion and motion.

     ii.   *Memorandum of law.* Absent leave of Court or as otherwise specified, upon any motion filed pursuant to FRCP 12, FRCP 56 or FRCP 65(a), the moving party shall file and serve a memorandum of law. Failure to comply with this requirement may constitute grounds for resolving the motion against the non-complying party. NY R USDCTWD Civ Rule 7(a)(2)(A). Refer to the Format section of this document for the formatting requirements for memoranda of law.

    iii.   *Certificate of service.* FRCP 5(d) requires that the person making service under FRCP 5 certify that service has been effected. FRCP 5(Advisory Committee Notes). Having such information on file may be useful for many purposes, including proof of service if an issue arises concerning the effectiveness of the service. FRCP 5(Advisory Committee Notes). The Notice of Electronic Filing effectuates service for all registered users and no certificate of service is required when all filers on an action are Registered Users. The following exemptions require a certificate of service to be filed:

       •  When a document is manually filed, a certificate of service must be filed stating the manner in which service or notice was accomplished on each party so entitled. NY R USDCTWD ECF Procedures(2)(f)(iv).

       •  When a pro se filer (who isn't authorized to electronically file documents) is a party, a certificate of service must be filed stating the manner in which service or notice was accomplished on the pro se party. The Notice of Electronic Filing effectuates service for the Registered Users in this situation and it is not necessary to note service on those parties. A non-registered pro se filer is required to file certificates of service on all documents they file. NY R USDCTWD ECF Procedures(2)(f)(iv).

- If an attorney is exempt from electronic service, a certificate of service must be filed stating the manner in which service or notice was accomplished on the exempt attorney. The Notice of Electronic Filing effectuates service for the Registered Users in this situation and it is not necessary to note service on those parties. NY R USDCTWD ECF Procedures(2)(f)(iv).

b. *Supplemental documents.* Matter outside the pleadings normally is not considered on a FRCP 12(f) motion; for example, affidavits in support of or in opposition to the motion typically may not be used. FPP § 1380.

    i. *Deposition.* Notwithstanding the general rule that matters outside the pleadings should ordinarily not be considered in passing upon a motion to strike under FRCP 12(f), a court may consider a deposition in deciding a FRCP 12(f) motion if the attorneys for both the plaintiff and the defendant, in their respective briefs, refer to the deposition and to the testimony contained therein. FEDPROC § 62:407. A party seeking or opposing any relief under the Federal Rules of Civil Procedure shall file only the portion(s) of a deposition, interrogatory, request for documents, request for admission, or other supporting material that is pertinent to the application. NY R USDCTWD Civ Rule 7(a)(4).

    ii. *Notice of constitutional question.* A party that files a pleading, written motion, or other paper drawing into question the constitutionality of a federal or state statute must promptly:

- *File notice.* File a notice of constitutional question stating the question and identifying the paper that raises it, if: (1) a federal statute is questioned and the parties do not include the United States, one of its agencies, or one of its officers or employees in an official capacity; or (2) a state statute is questioned and the parties do not include the state, one of its agencies, or one of its officers or employees in an official capacity; and

- *Serve notice.* Serve the notice and paper on the Attorney General of the United States if a federal statute is questioned—or on the state attorney general if a state statute is questioned—either by certified or registered mail or by sending it to an electronic address designated by the attorney general for this purpose. FRCP 5.1(a).

- *No forfeiture.* A party's failure to file and serve the notice, or the court's failure to certify, does not forfeit a constitutional claim or defense that is otherwise timely asserted. FRCP 5.1(d).

    iii. *Nongovernmental corporate disclosure statement*

- *Contents.* A nongovernmental corporate party must file two (2) copies of a disclosure statement that: (1) identifies any parent corporation and any publicly held corporation owning ten percent (10%) or more of its stock; or (2) states that there is no such corporation. FRCP 7.1(a).

- *Time to file; Supplemental filing.* A party must: (1) file the disclosure statement with its first appearance, pleading, petition, motion, response, or other request addressed to the court; and (2) promptly file a supplemental statement if any required information changes. FRCP 7.1(b).

    iv. *Copies of authorities.* In cases involving a pro se litigant, counsel shall, when serving a memorandum of law (or other submissions to the Court), provide the pro se litigant (but not other counsel or the Court) with printed copies of decisions cited therein that are unreported or reported exclusively on computerized databases. NY R USDCTWD Civ Rule 7(a)(8).

    v. *Proposed order.* All proposed orders must be submitted in a format compatible with WordPerfect or Microsoft Word format, which is a "Save As" option in most word processing software. Judges will not accept proposed orders in PDF format. NY R USDCTWD ECF Procedures(2)(j)(ii). Proposed orders should be attached to an Internet e-mail sent to the e-mail address of the assigned judge. NY R USDCTWD ECF Procedures(2)(j)(i). For the list of email addresses for the judges, refer to NY R USDCTWD ECF Procedures(2)(j)(i).

    vi. *Paper copy for date-stamping with self-addressed envelope.* Parties requesting date-stamped copies of filed documents must provide a paper copy for date-stamping, and a self-addressed, adequately-sized envelope with proper postage affixed. NY R USDCTWD Civ Rule 5.1(d).

vii. *Courtesy copies.* The Court may, in its discretion, request courtesy copies on any other motion. NY R USDCTWD Civ Rule 7(a)(7). Courtesy copies of certain documents may be required. Filers should refer to the "Judge Preferences" published on the Court's website. NY R USDCTWD ECF Procedures(2)(a)(iii).

2. *Documents for opposing party*

   a. *Required documents*

      i. *Opposition.* Refer to the General Requirements section of this document for information on the opposing papers.

      ii. *Answering memorandum.* Absent leave of Court or as otherwise specified, upon any motion filed pursuant to FRCP 12, FRCP 56 or FRCP 65(a). . .the opposing party shall file and serve an answering memorandum. Failure to comply with this requirement may constitute grounds for resolving the motion against the non-complying party. NY R USDCTWD Civ Rule 7(a)(2)(A). Refer to the Format section of this document for the formatting requirements for memoranda of law.

      iii. *Certificate of service.* FRCP 5(d) requires that the person making service under FRCP 5 certify that service has been effected. FRCP 5(Advisory Committee Notes). Having such information on file may be useful for many purposes, including proof of service if an issue arises concerning the effectiveness of the service. FRCP 5(Advisory Committee Notes). The Notice of Electronic Filing effectuates service for all registered users and no certificate of service is required when all filers on an action are Registered Users. The following exemptions require a certificate of service to be filed:

         • When a document is manually filed, a certificate of service must be filed stating the manner in which service or notice was accomplished on each party so entitled. NY R USDCTWD ECF Procedures(2)(f)(iv).

         • When a pro se filer (who isn't authorized to electronically file documents) is a party, a certificate of service must be filed stating the manner in which service or notice was accomplished on the pro se party. The Notice of Electronic Filing effectuates service for the Registered Users in this situation and it is not necessary to note service on those parties. A non-registered pro se filer is required to file certificates of service on all documents they file. NY R USDCTWD ECF Procedures(2)(f)(iv).

         • If an attorney is exempt from electronic service, a certificate of service must be filed stating the manner in which service or notice was accomplished on the exempt attorney. The Notice of Electronic Filing effectuates service for the Registered Users in this situation and it is not necessary to note service on those parties. NY R USDCTWD ECF Procedures(2)(f)(iv).

   b. *Supplemental documents.* Matter outside the pleadings normally is not considered on a FRCP 12(f) motion; for example, affidavits in support of or in opposition to the motion typically may not be used. FPP § 1380.

      i. *Deposition.* Notwithstanding the general rule that matters outside the pleadings should ordinarily not be considered in passing upon a motion to strike under FRCP 12(f), a court may consider a deposition in deciding a FRCP 12(f) motion if the attorneys for both the plaintiff and the defendant, in their respective briefs, refer to the deposition and to the testimony contained therein. FEDPROC § 62:407. A party seeking or opposing any relief under the Federal Rules of Civil Procedure shall file only the portion(s) of a deposition, interrogatory, request for documents, request for admission, or other supporting material that is pertinent to the application. NY R USDCTWD Civ Rule 7(a)(4).

      ii. *Notice of constitutional question.* A party that files a pleading, written motion, or other paper drawing into question the constitutionality of a federal or state statute must promptly:

         • *File notice.* File a notice of constitutional question stating the question and identifying the paper that raises it, if: (1) a federal statute is questioned and the parties do not include the United States, one of its agencies, or one of its officers or employees in an official capacity;

or (2) a state statute is questioned and the parties do not include the state, one of its agencies, or one of its officers or employees in an official capacity; and

- *Serve notice.* Serve the notice and paper on the Attorney General of the United States if a federal statute is questioned—or on the state attorney general if a state statute is questioned—either by certified or registered mail or by sending it to an electronic address designated by the attorney general for this purpose. FRCP 5.1(a).

- *No forfeiture.* A party's failure to file and serve the notice, or the court's failure to certify, does not forfeit a constitutional claim or defense that is otherwise timely asserted. FRCP 5.1(d).

iii. *Copies of authorities.* In cases involving a pro se litigant, counsel shall, when serving a memorandum of law (or other submissions to the Court), provide the pro se litigant (but not other counsel or the Court) with printed copies of decisions cited therein that are unreported or reported exclusively on computerized databases. NY R USDCTWD Civ Rule 7(a)(8).

iv. *Paper copy for date-stamping with self-addressed envelope.* Parties requesting date-stamped copies of filed documents must provide a paper copy for date-stamping, and a self-addressed, adequately-sized envelope with proper postage affixed. NY R USDCTWD Civ Rule 5.1(d).

v. *Courtesy copies.* Courtesy copies of certain documents may be required. Filers should refer to the "Judge Preferences" published on the Court's website. NY R USDCTWD ECF Procedures(2)(a)(iii).

3. *Individual judge practices.* Refer to the Miscellaneous section of this document for information on individual judge practices on required documents.

## E. Format

1. *Form of documents.* The rules governing captions and other matters of form in pleadings apply to motions and other papers. FRCP 7(b)(2).

   a. *Form, generally.* All pleadings, motions, and other papers that a party presents for filing, whether in paper form or in electronic form, shall meet the following requirements:

      i. *Font size.* All text and footnotes shall be in a font size of at least twelve (12) point type. NY R USDCTWD Civ Rule 10(a)(1).

      ii. *Spacing.* All text in the body of the document must be double-spaced, except that text in block quotations and footnotes may be single-spaced. NY R USDCTWD Civ Rule 10(a)(2).

         - Extensive footnotes and block quotes may not be used to circumvent page limitations. NY R USDCTWD Civ Rule 10(a)(3).

      iii. *Margins.* Documents must have one (1) inch margins on all four sides. NY R USDCTWD Civ Rule 10(a)(4).

      iv. *Page numbering.* Pages must be consecutively numbered. NY R USDCTWD Civ Rule 10(a)(5).

   b. *Additional requirements for paper filing.* Documents presented for filing in paper form shall meet the following additional requirements:

      i. *Paper.* Documents must be on durable white eight and one-half by eleven (8-1/2 x 11) inch paper of good quality. NY R USDCTWD Civ Rule 10(b)(1).

         - All documents must be single-sided. NY R USDCTWD Civ Rule 10(b)(5).

      ii. *Text.* All text must be plainly and legibly written, typewritten, printed or reproduced. NY R USDCTWD Civ Rule 10(b)(2).

      iii. *Ink.* Documents must be in black or blue ink. NY R USDCTWD Civ Rule 10(b)(3).

      iv. *Binding.* The pages of each document must be stapled or in some other way fastened together. NY R USDCTWD Civ Rule 10(b)(4).

   c. *Caption; Names of parties.* Every pleading must have a caption with the court's name, a title, a file

number, and a FRCP 7(a) designation. The title of the complaint must name all the parties; the title of other pleadings, after naming the first party on each side, may refer generally to other parties. FRCP 10(a).

d. *Paragraphs; Separate statements.* A party must state its claims or defenses in numbered paragraphs, each limited as far as practicable to a single set of circumstances. A later pleading may refer by number to a paragraph in an earlier pleading. If doing so would promote clarity, each claim founded on a separate transaction or occurrence—and each defense other than a denial—must be stated in a separate count or defense. FRCP 10(b).

e. *Adoption by reference; Exhibits.* A statement in a pleading may be adopted by reference elsewhere in the same pleading or in any other pleading or motion. A copy of a written instrument that is an exhibit to a pleading is a part of the pleading for all purposes. FRCP 10(c).

f. *Citation of local rules.* The Local Rules of Civil Procedure for the United States District Court for the Western District of New York shall be cited as "L.R.Civ.P." NY R USDCTWD Civ Rule 1.1.

g. *Acceptance by the clerk.* The clerk must not refuse to file a paper solely because it is not in the form prescribed by the Federal Rules of Civil Procedure or by a local rule or practice. FRCP 5(d)(4). The Court may reject documents that do not comply with the requirements in NY R USDCTWD Civ Rule 10. NY R USDCTWD Civ Rule 10.

2. *Form of electronic documents.* All pleadings, motions, and other papers that a party presents for filing, whether in paper form or in electronic form, shall meet the requirements in NY R USDCTWD Civ Rule 10(a). NY R USDCTWD Civ Rule 10(a). Refer above for more information.

a. *Conversion to PDF.* A document created with a word processor, or a paper document, must be converted to Portable Document Format to be electronically filed with the court. NY R USDCTWD ECF Procedures(2)(a)(v).

i. Documents which exist only in paper form may be scanned into a portable document format (PDF) for electronic filing. NY R USDCTWD ECF Procedures(2)(a)(v). Before filing a scanned document with the court, a Filing User must verify its legibility. NY R USDCTWD ECF Procedures(2)(a)(iv).

ii. Electronic documents must be converted to .PDF from a word processing program and must be text searchable. Do not print, scan and .PDF your document when it has been created in a word processing program. Additional information on working with PDFs is located in NY R USDCTWD ECF Procedures(4b). NY R USDCTWD ECF Procedures(2)(a)(v).

b. *Hyperlinks.* Pursuant to the policy set forth by the Judicial Conference in October 2005, a hyperlink contained in a filing is no more than a convenient mechanism for accessing material cited in a document. A hyperlink reference is extraneous to any filed document and is not part of the Court's record. NY R USDCTWD ECF Procedures(2)(a)(vi).

i. In order to preserve the integrity of the Court record, users wishing to insert hyperlinks in Court filings shall continue to use the conventional method for the cited authority, in addition to the hyperlink. NY R USDCTWD ECF Procedures(2)(a)(vi).

ii. The Court accepts no responsibility for, and does not endorse any product, organization, and content at any hyperlinked site, or at any site to which that site may be linked. The Court accepts no responsibility for the availability or functionality of any hyperlink. NY R USDCTWD ECF Procedures(2)(a)(vi).

c. *Attachments and exhibits*

i. Attachments and exhibits larger than five megabytes (5 MB) shall be filed electronically in separate five megabyte (5 MB) segments. NY R USDCTWD ECF Procedures(2)(d)(i).

ii. Filing Users must submit in electronic form all documents referenced as exhibits or attachments, except as otherwise provided in NY R USDCTWD ECF Procedures. A Filing User must submit as exhibits or attachments only those excerpts of the referenced documents that are directly germane to the matter under consideration by the court. Excerpted material must be clearly and prominently identified as such. Filing Users who file excerpts of documents as exhibits or attachments under NY R USDCTWD ECF Procedures(2)(d)(ii) do so without prejudice to their right to timely file additional excerpts or the complete document. Responding parties may timely file additional excerpts or the complete document that they believe are directly germane. The Court may require parties to file additional excerpts or the complete document. A Filing User must request leave of the Court to file a document exhibit or attachment in non-electronic form. NY R USDCTWD ECF Procedures(2)(d)(ii).

iii. Exhibits offered or admitted at trial will not be filed electronically or conventionally unless so ordered by the Court. NY R USDCTWD ECF Procedures(2)(d)(iii).

iv. Exhibits such as videotapes and tape recordings shall be filed in the conventional manner with the Clerk of Court, and a Notice of Manual Filing shall be electronically filed by the party. Manually filed exhibits must have the case number and case name securely fastened or marked on the item. NY R USDCTWD ECF Procedures(2)(d)(iii).

v. Continuation of exhibit entries (for exhibits that are too large to attach to a main document) must be filed and entered on the same day that the main document was filed. NY R USDCTWD ECF Procedures(2)(d)(iv).

d. *Color documents.* Documents in color or containing graphics take much longer to upload. Filing users are encouraged to configure their scanners to scan documents at 200 dpi and preferably in black and white rather than color. NY R USDCTWD ECF Procedures(2)(d)(v).

e. *Large documents.* Due to the length of time it takes to download large files, documents larger than five megabytes (5 MB) (approximately one hundred (100) pages of a .pdf scanned document) must be filed electronically in separate five megabyte (5 MB) segments. A party who believes a document is too lengthy to electronically image (i.e. scan), may contact the Court Room Deputy for the assigned judge and request permission to file that document conventionally. If granted permission to file the document conventionally, the Filing User shall electronically file a "notice of manual filing" for that item. Exhibits submitted to the Court conventionally shall be served on other parties conventionally. NY R USDCTWD ECF Procedures(2)(d)(vi).

3. *Form of memoranda of law.* Memoranda in support of or in opposition to any motion shall not exceed twenty-five (25) pages in length, and reply memoranda shall not exceed ten (10) pages in length. A party seeking to exceed the page limit must make application by letter to the Judge hearing the motion, with copies to all counsel, at least seven (7) days before the date on which the memorandum must be filed. NY R USDCTWD Civ Rule 7(a)(2)(C).

4. *Signing of pleadings, motions and other papers*

a. *Signature.* Every pleading, written motion, and other paper must be signed by at least one attorney of record in the attorney's name—or by a party personally if the party is unrepresented. The paper must state the signer's address, e-mail address, and telephone number. FRCP 11(a). Documents presented for paper filing must contain an original signature. NY R USDCTWD Civ Rule 10(b)(6).

   i. *Electronic signatures*

   - *Non-attorney signature.* If the original document requires the signature of a non-attorney, the filing party shall obtain the signature of the non-attorney on the document. NY R USDCTWD ECF Procedures(2)(g)(i). The filing party or attorney then shall file the document electronically indicating the signatory's name in the form "s/(name)." NY R USDCTWD ECF Procedures(2)(g)(i)(1). A non-filing signatory or party who disputes the authenticity of an electronically filed document or the authenticity of the signature on that document must file an objection to the document within ten (10) days of receiving the Notice of Electronic Filing. NY R USDCTWD ECF Procedures(2)(g)(i)(2).

   - *Registered user signature.* The username and password required to file documents on the Electronic Filing System serve as the Filing User's signature on all electronic documents filed with this Court. The also serve as a signature for the purposes of FRCP 11, the Federal Rules of Civil Procedure, the Local Rules of Civil Procedure for the United States District Court for the Western District of New York, and any other purpose for which a signature is required in connection with proceedings before this Court. A pleading requiring a

Registered User's signature must include a signature block in the format found in NY R USDCTWD ECF Procedures(2)(g)(iii). NY R USDCTWD ECF Procedures(2)(g)(iii). Any party challenging the authenticity of an electronically filed document or the attorney's signature on that document must file an objection to the document within ten (10) days of receiving the Notice of Electronic Filing. NY R USDCTWD ECF Procedures(2)(g)(iii)(1).

- *Multiple signatures.* The following procedure applies when a stipulation or other document requires two or more signatures: The filing party shall initially confirm that the document is acceptable to all persons required to sign the document and shall obtain the signatures of all parties on the document. NY R USDCTWD ECF Procedures(2)(g)(iv)(1). The filing party or attorney then shall file the document electronically indicating the signatories, e.g., "s/Jane Doe," "s/John Smith," etc. NY R USDCTWD ECF Procedures(2)(g)(iv)(2). A non-filing signatory or party who disputes the authenticity of an electronically filed document containing multiple signatures or the authenticity of the signatures themselves must file an objection to the document within ten (10) days of receiving the Notice of Electronic Filing. NY R USDCTWD ECF Procedures(2)(g)(iv)(3).

   ii. *No verification or accompanying affidavit required for pleadings.* Unless a rule or statute specifically states otherwise, a pleading need not be verified or accompanied by an affidavit. FRCP 11(a).

   iii. *Unsigned papers.* The court must strike an unsigned paper unless the omission is promptly corrected after being called to the attorney's or party's attention. FRCP 11(a).

b. *Representations to the court.* By presenting to the court a pleading, written motion, or other paper—whether by signing, filing, submitting, or later advocating it—an attorney or unrepresented party certifies that to the best of the person's knowledge, information, and belief, formed after an inquiry reasonable under the circumstances:

   i. It is not being presented for any improper purpose, such as to harass, cause unnecessary delay, or needlessly increase the cost of litigation;

   ii. The claims, defenses, and other legal contentions are warranted by existing law or by a nonfrivolous argument for extending, modifying, or reversing existing law or for establishing new law;

   iii. The factual contentions have evidentiary support or, if specifically so identified, will likely have evidentiary support after a reasonable opportunity for further investigation or discovery; and

   iv. The denials of factual contentions are warranted on the evidence or, if specifically so identified, are reasonably based on belief or a lack of information. FRCP 11(b).

c. *Sanctions.* If, after notice and a reasonable opportunity to respond, the court determines that FRCP 11(b) has been violated, the court may impose an appropriate sanction on any attorney, law firm, or party that violated FRCP 11(b) or is responsible for the violation. FRCP 11(c)(1). Refer to the United States District Court for the Western District of New York KeyRules Motion for Sanctions document for more information.

5. *Privacy protection for filings made with the court.* In all filings, parties shall comply with FRCP 5.2. NY R USDCTWD ECF Procedures(2)(m)(i).

a. *Redacted filings.* Unless the court orders otherwise, in an electronic or paper filing with the court that contains an individual's Social Security number, taxpayer-identification number, or birth date, the name of an individual known to be a minor, or a financial-account number, a party or nonparty making the filing may include only:

   i. The last four (4) digits of the Social Security number and taxpayer-identification number;

   ii. The year of the individual's birth;

   iii. The minor's initials; and

   iv. The last four (4) digits of the financial-account number. FRCP 5.2(a).

b. *Exemptions from the redaction requirement.* The redaction requirement does not apply to the following:

    i.   A financial-account number that identifies the property allegedly subject to forfeiture in a forfeiture proceeding;

    ii.  The record of an administrative or agency proceeding;

    iii. The official record of a state-court proceeding;

    iv. The record of a court or tribunal, if that record was not subject to the redaction requirement when originally filed;

    v.  A filing covered by FRCP 5.2(c) or FRCP 5.2(d); and

    vi. A pro se filing in an action brought under 28 U.S.C.A. § 2241, 28 U.S.C.A. § 2254, or 28 U.S.C.A. § 2255. FRCP 5.2(b).

c. *Limitations on remote access to electronic files; Social Security appeals and immigration cases.* Unless the court orders otherwise, in an action for benefits under the Social Security Act, and in an action or proceeding relating to an order of removal, to relief from removal, or to immigration benefits or detention, access to an electronic file is authorized as follows:

    i.   The parties and their attorneys may have remote electronic access to any part of the case file, including the administrative record;

    ii.  Any other person may have electronic access to the full record at the courthouse, but may have remote electronic access only to:

        • The docket maintained by the court; and

        • An opinion, order, judgment, or other disposition of the court, but not any other part of the case file or the administrative record. FRCP 5.2(c).

d. *Filings made under seal.* The court may order that a filing be made under seal without redaction. The court may later unseal the filing or order the person who made the filing to file a redacted version for the public record. FRCP 5.2(d). For more information on sealing documents, refer to NY R USDCTWD Civ Rule 5.3, NY R USDCTWD ECF Procedures(2)(o)(i)(1), NY R USDCTWD ECF Procedures(2)(o)(i)(2), and NY R USDCTWD ECF Procedures(2)(o)(i)(3).

e. *Protective orders.* For good cause, the court may by order in a case:

    i.   Require redaction of additional information; or

    ii.  Limit or prohibit a nonparty's remote electronic access to a document filed with the court. FRCP 5.2(e).

f. *Option for additional unredacted filing under seal.* A person making a redacted filing may also file an unredacted copy under seal. The court must retain the unredacted copy as part of the record. FRCP 5.2(f).

g. *Option for filing a reference list.* A filing that contains redacted information may be filed together with a reference list that identifies each item of redacted information and specifies an appropriate identifier that uniquely corresponds to each item listed. The list must be filed under seal and may be amended as of right. Any reference in the case to a listed identifier will be construed to refer to the corresponding item of information. FRCP 5.2(g).

h. *Waiver of protection of identifiers.* A person waives the protection of FRCP 5.2(a) as to the person's own information by filing it without redaction and not under seal. FRCP 5.2(h).

6. *Individual judge practices.* Refer to the Miscellaneous section of this document for information on individual judge practices on formatting documents.

## F.  Filing and Service Requirements

1. *Filing requirements.* Any paper after the complaint that is required to be served—together with a certificate of service—must be filed within a reasonable time after service. FRCP 5(d)(1). All pleadings and other papers shall be filed and served in accordance with the Federal Rules of Civil Procedure and the

CM/ECF Administrative Procedures Guide (NY R USDCTWD ECF Procedures). NY R USDCTWD Civ Rule 5.1(a). For information on filing of miscellaneous cases and irregular documents, refer to NY R USDCTWD Civ Rule 5.6.

a. *How filing is made; In general.* A paper is filed by delivering it:

    i. To the clerk; or

    ii. To a judge who agrees to accept it for filing, and who must then note the filing date on the paper and promptly send it to the clerk. FRCP 5(d)(2).

b. *Electronic filing*

    i. *Authorization of electronic filing program.* A court may, by local rule, allow papers to be filed, signed, or verified by electronic means that are consistent with any technical standards established by the Judicial Conference of the United States. A local rule may require electronic filing only if reasonable exceptions are allowed. A paper filed electronically in compliance with a local rule is a written paper for purposes of the Federal Rules of Civil Procedure. FRCP 5(d)(3).

- All civil cases filed in this Court are assigned to the Electronic Case Filing System ("ECF"). The procedures for electronic filing and any exceptions to the electronic filing requirements are set forth in the CM/ECF Administrative Procedures Guide (NY R USDCTWD ECF Procedures) which is available on the Court's website. NY R USDCTWD Civ Rule 5.1(a).

    ii. *Scope of electronic filing.* The U.S. District Court for the Western District of New York requires attorneys in civil and criminal cases to file documents with the Court electronically over the Internet using its Case Management/Electronic Case Filing (CM/ECF) system. NY R USDCTWD ECF Procedures. Beginning January 1, 2004, all civil and criminal cases currently pending and newly filed, except as expressly noted herein, were assigned to the Electronic Case Filing System ("System"). Except as expressly provided and in exceptional circumstances preventing a Filing User from filing electronically, all petitions, motions, memoranda of law, or other pleadings and documents required to be filed with the Court in connection with a case assigned to the System must be electronically filed. NY R USDCTWD ECF Procedures(1)(a).

- *Mandatory electronic filing.* All documents on civil, criminal, miscellaneous civil, miscellaneous criminal and new civil case openings, except sealed documents, sealed cases, opening of a criminal case, opening of a miscellaneous case and as expressly provided for in these procedures (NY R USDCTWD ECF Procedures), shall be electronically filed on the system. NY R USDCTWD ECF Procedures(2)(a)(i). NY R USDCTWD Civ Rule 29

- *Stipulations.* Pursuant to NY R USDCTWD Civ Rule 29, all stipulations (whether the stipulation is final or when it requires a judge's signature) shall be filed electronically. NY R USDCTWD ECF Procedures(2)(p)(i).

- *Letters.* The electronic filing of letters is generally prohibited unless granted permission by an assigned judge. Letters to the Court must be submitted conventionally. NY R USDCTWD ECF Procedures(2)(q)(i).

- *Exceptions.* The Court requires attorneys to file documents electronically, absent a showing of good cause, unless otherwise excused by the procedures set forth below or by Order of the Court. NY R USDCTWD ECF Procedures.

    iii. *Conventional filing of documents.* The procedures in NY R USDCTWD ECF Procedures(2)(o) govern documents filed conventionally. The Court, upon application, may also authorize conventional filing of other documents otherwise subject to the procedures in NY R USDCTWD ECF Procedures(2)(o). NY R USDCTWD ECF Procedures(2)(o)(i).

- *Documents filed under seal.* Unredacted documents filed with the Court pursuant to the privacy provisions of FRCP 5.2 shall be submitted in a sealing envelope with the information in NY R USDCTWD ECF Procedures(2)(o)(i)(1) on the envelope. NY R USDCTWD ECF Procedures(2)(o)(i)(1). If the document is larger than five (5) pages, a

disk should be provided to the Clerks Office which contains the document in a .pdf format. NY R USDCTWD ECF Procedures(2)(o)(i)(1). For more information on documents filed under seal, refer to NY R USDCTWD ECF Procedures(2)(o)(i)(1), NY R USDCTWD ECF Procedures(2)(o)(i)(2), and NY R USDCTWD ECF Procedures(2)(o)(i)(3).

- *Magistrate judge consents.* Pursuant to FRCP 73(b), parties' filing consents to jurisdiction by United States Magistrate Judge will continue to be treated as non-public documents until all parties have consented. Therefore, parties must submit conventionally (in paper form) and not electronically file their consent forms so that the consent is not a public document. If all parties consent to the jurisdiction of a Magistrate Judge, the Clerk will scan all consent forms which will then become a public document. NY R USDCTWD ECF Procedures(2)(o)(i)(3).

- *Pro se filers.* Pro Se filers shall file paper originals of all initiating documents, pleadings, motions, affidavits, briefs and other documents which must be signed or which require either verification or an unsworn declaration under any rule or statute. The Clerk's Office will scan these original documents into an electronic file in the System. A certificate of service is required for all documents a pro se litigant files with the court. If a Pro Se filer is granted permission to register to electronically file documents, they shall comply with the guidelines contained in this document (NY R USDCTWD ECF Procedures). NY R USDCTWD ECF Procedures(2)(o)(i)(4).

- *Social Security cases.* Absent a showing of good cause, and except as provided in Section o(i)(4) above, all documents, notices and orders in Social Security reviews will be filed and noticed electronically, except as noted in NY R USDCTWD ECF Procedures(2)(o)(i)(6). For more information, refer to NY R USDCTWD ECF Procedures(2)(o)(i)(6).

- For more information on conventional filing of documents, refer to NY R USDCTWD ECF Procedures(2)(o)(i).

iv. *Consequences of electronic filing.* Electronic transmission of a document to the System consistent with these procedures (NY R USDCTWD ECF Procedures), whether accomplished by the Filing User or a Court User, together with the transmission of a Notice of Electronic Filing from the Court, constitutes filing of a document for all purposes of the Federal Rules of Civil Procedure and the Local Rules of Civil Procedure for the United States District Court for the Western District of New York, and constitutes entry of the document on the docket kept by the Clerk under FRCP 58 and FRCP 79. A document shall not be considered filed for purposes of the Federal Rules of Civil until the filing party receives a System generated Notice of Electronic Filing. NY R USDCTWD ECF Procedures(2)(a)(i).

- E-mailing a document to the Clerk's Office or to the assigned judge shall not constitute "filing" of such document. NY R USDCTWD ECF Procedures(2)(a)(i)(1).

v. *Filing fees.* Any fee required for filing of a pleading or paper in District Court is payable to the Clerk of Court by check or money order. In addition, when opening a civil case on line, filing a notice of appeal on line or applying to appear pro hac vice on line, the fees shall be paid on line by registered users through the federal electronic payment website. Users will be directed to the federal electronic payment website while entering their transaction and should have a credit card available. When opening a civil case and applying to proceed in forma pauperis or when the United States of America opens a case, the payment screen can by bypassed to complete the transaction. Additional information on making electronic payments can be located on the court's website. NY R USDCTWD ECF Procedures(2)(h)(i).

2. *Service requirements.* All pleadings and other papers shall be filed and served in accordance with the Federal Rules of Civil Procedure and the CM/ECF Administrative Procedures Guide (NY R USDCTWD ECF Procedures). NY R USDCTWD Civ Rule 5.1(a).

a. *Service; When required*

i. *In general.* Unless the Federal Rules of Civil Procedure provide otherwise, each of the following papers must be served on every party:

- An order stating that service is required;

- A pleading filed after the original complaint, unless the court orders otherwise under FRCP 5(c) because there are numerous defendants;

- A discovery paper required to be served on a party, unless the court orders otherwise;

- A written motion, except one that may be heard ex parte; and

- A written notice, appearance, demand, or offer of judgment, or any similar paper. FRCP 5(a)(1).

ii. *If a party fails to appear.* No service is required on a party who is in default for failing to appear. But a pleading that asserts a new claim for relief against such a party must be served on that party under FRCP 4. FRCP 5(a)(2).

iii. *Seizing property.* If an action is begun by seizing property and no person is or need be named as a defendant, any service required before the filing of an appearance, answer, or claim must be made on the person who had custody or possession of the property when it was seized. FRCP 5(a)(3).

b. *Service; How made*

i. *Serving an attorney.* If a party is represented by an attorney, service under FRCP 5 must be made on the attorney unless the court orders service on the party. FRCP 5(b)(1).

ii. *Service in general.* A paper is served under FRCP 5 by:

- Handing it to the person;

- Leaving it: (1) at the person's office with a clerk or other person in charge or, if no one is in charge, in a conspicuous place in the office; or (2) if the person has no office or the office is closed, at the person's dwelling or usual place of abode with someone of suitable age and discretion who resides there;

- Mailing it to the person's last known address—in which event service is complete upon mailing;

- Leaving it with the court clerk if the person has no known address;

- Sending it by electronic means if the person consented in writing—in which event service is complete upon transmission, but is not effective if the serving party learns that it did not reach the person to be served; or

- Delivering it by any other means that the person consented to in writing—in which event service is complete when the person making service delivers it to the agency designated to make delivery. FRCP 5(b)(2).

iii. *Service by overnight delivery.* All papers, other than a subpoena or a summons and complaint, may be served on counsel of record by overnight delivery service at the address designated by the attorney for that purpose, or if none is designated, at the attorney's last known address. Service by overnight delivery shall be complete upon deposit of the paper(s), enclosed in a properly addressed wrapper, into the custody of the overnight delivery service, prior to the latest time designated by the service for overnight delivery. NY R USDCTWD Civ Rule 5.1(g). "Overnight delivery service" means any delivery service which regularly accepts items for overnight delivery to any address within the Court's jurisdiction. NY R USDCTWD Civ Rule 5.1(g).

iv. *Service of documents by electronic means*

- *Service on registered users.* Registered Users consent to the electronic service of all documents, and must make available an electronic mail address for service during the registration process. Upon the filing of a document by a party, a Notice of Electronic Filing, with a hyperlink to the filed document, will be automatically generated by the electronic filing system and sent via electronic mail to the e-mail addresses of all parties participating in the electronic filing system in the case. Electronic service of the Notice of Electronic Filing constitutes service of the filed document for all purposes of the Federal Rules of Civil Procedure and the Local Rules of Civil Procedure for the United States

District Court for the Western District of New York. NY R USDCTWD ECF Procedures(2)(f)(i). The Notice of Electronic Filing effectuates service for all registered users and no certificate of service is required when all filers on an action are Registered Users. NY R USDCTWD ECF Procedures(2)(f)(iv).

- *Time limit for opening hyperlink.* The hyperlink to filed documents contained in the Notice of Electronic Filing must be opened within fifteen (15) days from the date the document was filed to provide registered users access to the document. The hyperlink expires after fifteen (15) days and users will be unable to access documents for free after that time. Filing Users are encouraged to check their e-mail frequently for notice of filed documents. NY R USDCTWD ECF Procedures(2)(f)(ii).

- *Service on exempted attorneys or pro se litigants who do not have permission to file electronically.* Attorneys granted an exemption from electronically filing documents in the System and pro se litigants who have not been granted permission to electronically file documents are entitled to a paper copy of any electronically filed pleading, document or order. The filing party must therefore provide the non-registered party with the pleading, document or order according to the Federal Rules of Civil Procedure. NY R USDCTWD ECF Procedures(2)(f)(iii).

- *E-mailing or faxing documents.* E-mailing or faxing a pleading or document to any party shall not constitute service of the pleading or document. NY R USDCTWD ECF Procedures(2)(f)(v).

    v. *Using court facilities.* If a local rule so authorizes, a party may use the court's transmission facilities to make service under FRCP 5(b)(2)(E). FRCP 5(b)(3).

  c. *Serving numerous defendants*

    i. *In general.* If an action involves an unusually large number of defendants, the court may, on motion or on its own, order that:

- Defendants' pleadings and replies to them need not be served on other defendants;

- Any crossclaim, counterclaim, avoidance, or affirmative defense in those pleadings and replies to them will be treated as denied or avoided by all other parties; and

- Filing any such pleading and serving it on the plaintiff constitutes notice of the pleading to all parties. FRCP 5(c)(1).

    ii. *Notifying parties.* A copy of every such order must be served on the parties as the court directs. FRCP 5(c)(2).

3. *Pro se actions.* For information on the requirements in pro se actions, refer to NY R USDCTWD Civ Rule 5.2.

4. *Individual judge practices.* Refer to the Miscellaneous section of this document for information on individual judge practices on filing and serving documents.

## G. Hearings

1. *Hearings, generally*

  a. *Oral argument.* Due process does not require that oral argument be permitted on a motion and, except as otherwise provided by local rule, the district court has discretion to determine whether it will decide the motion on the papers or hear argument by counsel (and perhaps receive evidence). FPP § 1190; F.D.I.C. v. Deglau, 207 F.3d 153 (3d Cir. 2000).

    i. The parties shall appear for oral argument on all motions they make returnable before a Judge on the scheduled return date for the motion. In its discretion, the Court may notify the parties that oral argument shall not be heard on any given motion. Thus, the parties should be prepared to have their motion papers serve as the sole method of argument. NY R USDCTWD Civ Rule 7(c).

  b. *Providing a regular schedule for oral hearings.* A court may establish regular times and places for oral hearings on motions. FRCP 78(a).

c. *Providing for submission on briefs.* By rule or order, the court may provide for submitting and determining motions on briefs, without oral hearings. FRCP 78(b).

2. *Individual judge practices.* Refer to the Miscellaneous section of this document for information on individual judge practices on hearings.

## H. Forms

### 1. Federal Motion to Strike Forms

a. Motion; By plaintiff; To strike insufficient defense from answer. AMJUR PP FEDPRAC § 441.

b. Motion; To strike redundant, immaterial, impertinent, or scandalous matter from pleading. AMJUR PP FEDPRAC § 442.

c. Motion; To strike portions of complaint. AMJUR PP FEDPRAC § 444.

d. Motion to strike insufficient affirmative defenses. 2C FEDFORMS § 11:151.

e. Motion to strike insufficient defense in answer; Stating particular reason. 2C FEDFORMS § 11:153.

f. Notice of motion and motion to strike insufficient affirmative defense. 2C FEDFORMS § 11:155.

g. Motion to strike impertinence and scandal. 2C FEDFORMS § 11:157.

h. Motion to strike impertinence and immateriality. 2C FEDFORMS § 11:158.

i. Motion to strike redundancy and scandal. 2C FEDFORMS § 11:159.

j. Motion to strike immaterial defense. 2C FEDFORMS § 11:160.

k. Motion to strike for immateriality. 2C FEDFORMS § 11:161.

l. Motion to strike counterclaim for lack of evidence. 2C FEDFORMS § 11:162.

m. Opposition; To motion; General form. FEDPROF § 1:750.

n. Affidavit; Supporting or opposing motion. FEDPROF § 1:751.

o. Brief; Supporting or opposing motion. FEDPROF § 1:752.

p. Statement of points and authorities; Opposing motion. FEDPROF § 1:753.

q. Motion; To strike material outside statute of limitations. FEDPROF § 1:773.

r. Opposition to motion; Material not contained in pleading. FEDPROF § 1:774.

s. General form. GOLDLTGFMS § 20:8.

t. General form; Federal form. GOLDLTGFMS § 20:10.

u. Notice and motion to strike immaterial, redundant or scandalous matter. GOLDLTGFMS § 20:13.

v. Motion to strike complaint and dismiss action as to one defendant. GOLDLTGFMS § 20:14.

w. Defendant's motion to strike. GOLDLTGFMS § 20:16.

x. Defendant's motion to strike; Plaintiff's response. GOLDLTGFMS § 20:17.

y. Motion to strike answer. GOLDLTGFMS § 20:19.

z. Objections to motion to strike. GOLDLTGFMS § 20:20.

### 2. Forms for the Western District of New York

a. Certificate of service. NY R USDCTWD ECF Procedures(4a).

## I. Applicable Rules

### 1. *Federal rules*

a. Serving and filing pleadings and other papers. FRCP 5.

b. Constitutional challenge to a statute; Notice, certification, and intervention. FRCP 5.1.

c. Privacy protection for filings made with the court. FRCP 5.2.

d. Computing and extending time; Time for motion papers. FRCP 6.

e. Pleadings allowed; Form of motions and other papers. FRCP 7.

    f.   Disclosure statement. FRCP 7.1.

    g.   Form of pleadings. FRCP 10.

    h.   Signing pleadings, motions, and other papers; Representations to the court; Sanctions. FRCP 11.

    i.   Defenses and objections; When and how presented; Motion for judgment on the pleadings; Consolidating motions; Waiving defenses; Pretrial hearing. FRCP 12.

    j.   Hearing motions; Submission on briefs. FRCP 78.

2.  *Local rules*

    a.   Title. NY R USDCTWD Civ Rule 1.1.

    b.   Filing and serving papers. NY R USDCTWD Civ Rule 5.1.

    c.   Motion practice. NY R USDCTWD Civ Rule 7.

    d.   Form of papers. NY R USDCTWD Civ Rule 10.

    e.   Sanctions. NY R USDCTWD Civ Rule 11.

    f.   Alternative dispute resolution and pretrial conferences. NY R USDCTWD Civ Rule 16.

    g.   Attorneys of record; Appearance and withdrawal. NY R USDCTWD Civ Rule 83.2.

    h.   Administrative procedures guide for electronic filing. NY R USDCTWD ECF Procedures.

    i.   Alternative dispute resolution plan. NY R USDCTWD ADR Plan.

## J.  Miscellaneous

**NOTE: Individual judges' rules may apply. For available judge-level information, refer to:**

DISTRICT JUDGE RICHARD J. ARCARA: NY R USDCTWD Arcara-Procedures.

DISTRICT JUDGE FRANK P. GERACI, JR.: NY R USDCTWD Geraci-Procedures.

DISTRICT JUDGE DAVID G. LARIMER: NY R USDCTWD Larimer-Procedures.

DISTRICT JUDGE CHARLES J. SIRAGUSA: NY R USDCTWD Siragusa-Procedures.

DISTRICT JUDGE WILLIAM M. SKRETNY: NY R USDCTWD Skretny--Procedures.

DISTRICT JUDGE MICHAEL A. TELESCA: NY R USDCTWD Telesca-Procedures.

DISTRICT JUDGE LAWRENCE J. VILARDO: NY R USDCTWD Vilardo-Procedures.

DISTRICT JUDGE ELIZABETH A. WOLFORD: NY R USDCTWD Wolford-Procedures.

MAGISTRATE JUDGE JONATHAN W. FELDMAN: NY R USDCTWD Feldman-Procedures.

MAGISTRATE JUDGE LESLIE G. FOSCHIO: NY R USDCTWD Foschio-Procedures; NY R USDCTWD Foschio-Depositions.

MAGISTRATE JUDGE JEREMIAH J. McCARTHY: NY R USDCTWD McCarthy-Procedures.

MAGISTRATE JUDGE MARIAN W. PAYSON: NY R USDCTWD Payson-Procedures.

MAGISTRATE JUDGE MICHAEL J. ROEMER: NY R USDCTWD Roemer-Procedures.

MAGISTRATE JUDGE H. KENNETH SCHROEDER, JR.: NY R USDCTWD Schroeder-Proc.

MAGISTRATE JUDGE HUGH B. SCOTT: NY R USDCTWD Scott-Procedures.

# Motions, Oppositions and Replies
## Motion for Leave to Amend

### Document Last Updated September 2016

## A. Checklist

- (I) ❑ Matters to be considered by moving party
  - (a) ❑ Required documents
    - (1) ❑ Notice of motion and motion
    - (2) ❑ Supporting affidavit
    - (3) ❑ Proposed amended pleading
    - (4) ❑ Certificate of service
  - (b) ❑ Supplemental documents
    - (1) ❑ Memorandum of law
    - (2) ❑ Supporting evidence
    - (3) ❑ Notice of constitutional question
    - (4) ❑ Copies of authorities
    - (5) ❑ Proposed order
    - (6) ❑ Paper copy for date-stamping with self-addressed envelope
    - (7) ❑ Courtesy copies
  - (c) ❑ Timing
    - (1) ❑ Unlike amendments as of course, amendments under FRCP 15(a)(2) may be made at any stage of the litigation
    - (2) ❑ A party may move—at any time, even after judgment—to amend the pleadings to conform them to the evidence and to raise an unpleaded issue
    - (3) ❑ A written motion and notice of the hearing must be served at least fourteen (14) days before the time specified for the hearing, with the following exceptions: (i) when the motion may be heard ex parte; (ii) when the Federal Rules of Civil Procedure set a different time; or (iii) when a court order—which a party may, for good cause, apply for ex parte—sets a different time
    - (4) ❑ Any affidavit supporting a motion must be served with the motion
- (II) ❑ Matters to be considered by opposing party
  - (a) ❑ Required documents
    - (1) ❑ Opposition
    - (2) ❑ Supporting affidavit
    - (3) ❑ Certificate of service
  - (b) ❑ Supplemental documents
    - (1) ❑ Supporting evidence
    - (2) ❑ Notice of constitutional question
    - (3) ❑ Copies of authorities
    - (4) ❑ Paper copy for date-stamping with self-addressed envelope
    - (5) ❑ Courtesy copies
  - (c) ❑ Timing
    - (1) ❑ After a motion is filed, the court may issue an order setting deadlines for filing and service

of opposing papers; if the court does not set deadlines by order, the opposing party shall have fourteen (14) days after service of the motion to file and serve responding papers

(2) ❑ Except as FRCP 59(c) provides otherwise, any opposing affidavit must be served at least seven (7) days before the hearing, unless the court permits service at another time

## B. Timing

1. *Motion for leave to amend.* Unlike amendments as of course, amendments under FRCP 15(a)(2) may be made at any stage of the litigation. FPP § 1484.

   a. *Amendments to conform to the evidence.* A party may move—at any time, even after judgment—to amend the pleadings to conform them to the evidence and to raise an unpleaded issue. FRCP 15(b)(2).

   b. *Time to respond to an amended pleading.* Unless the court orders otherwise, any required response to an amended pleading must be made within the time remaining to respond to the original pleading or within fourteen (14) days after service of the amended pleading, whichever is later. FRCP 15(a)(3).

2. *Timing of motions, generally*

   a. *Motion and notice of hearing.* A written motion and notice of the hearing must be served at least fourteen (14) days before the time specified for the hearing, with the following exceptions:

      i. When the motion may be heard ex parte;

      ii. When the Federal Rules of Civil Procedure set a different time; or

      iii. When a court order—which a party may, for good cause, apply for ex parte—sets a different time. FRCP 6(c)(1).

   b. *Supporting affidavit.* Any affidavit supporting a motion must be served with the motion. FRCP 6(c)(2).

3. *Timing of opposing papers.* After a motion is filed, the Court may issue an order setting deadlines for filing and service of opposing papers. NY R USDCTWD Civ Rule 7(b)(1). If the Court does not set deadlines by order, the following schedule shall apply: the opposing party shall have fourteen (14) days after service of the motion to file and serve responding papers. NY R USDCTWD Civ Rule 7(b)(2)(B).

   a. *Opposing affidavit.* Except as FRCP 59(c) provides otherwise, any opposing affidavit must be served at least seven (7) days before the hearing, unless the court permits service at another time. FRCP 6(c)(2).

4. *Timing of reply papers.* Where the respondent files an answering affidavit setting up a new matter, the moving party ordinarily is allowed a reasonable time to file a reply affidavit since failure to deny the new matter by affidavit may operate as an admission of its truth. AMJUR MOTIONS § 25.

   a. *Reply papers.* After a motion is filed, the Court may issue an order setting deadlines. . .for filing and service of reply papers if the moving party has stated an intent to reply. NY R USDCTWD Civ Rule 7(b)(1). If the Court does not set deadlines by order, the following schedule shall apply: the moving party shall have seven (7) days after service of the responding papers to file and serve reply papers. NY R USDCTWD Civ Rule 7(b)(2)(B).

5. *Motion for an expedited hearing.* A party seeking to shorten the schedule prescribed in NY R USDCTWD Civ Rule 7(b) must make a separate motion for an expedited hearing, setting forth the reasons why an expedited hearing is required. NY R USDCTWD Civ Rule 7(d)(1). For more information, refer to NY R USDCTWD Civ Rule 7(d)(1).

6. *Computation of time*

   a. *Computing time.* FRCP 6 applies in computing any time period specified in the Federal Rules of Civil Procedure, in any local rule or court order, or in any statute that does not specify a method of computing time. FRCP 6(a).

      i. *Period stated in days or a longer unit.* When the period is stated in days or a longer unit of time:

         • Exclude the day of the event that triggers the period;

1430

- Count every day, including intermediate Saturdays, Sundays, and legal holidays; and

- Include the last day of the period, but if the last day is a Saturday, Sunday, or legal holiday, the period continues to run until the end of the next day that is not a Saturday, Sunday, or legal holiday. FRCP 6(a)(1).

ii. *Period stated in hours.* When the period is stated in hours:

- Begin counting immediately on the occurrence of the event that triggers the period;

- Count every hour, including hours during intermediate Saturdays, Sundays, and legal holidays; and

- If the period would end on a Saturday, Sunday, or legal holiday, the period continues to run until the same time on the next day that is not a Saturday, Sunday, or legal holiday. FRCP 6(a)(2).

iii. *Inaccessibility of the clerk's office.* Unless the court orders otherwise, if the clerk's office is inaccessible:

- On the last day for filing under FRCP 6(a)(1), then the time for filing is extended to the first accessible day that is not a Saturday, Sunday, or legal holiday; or

- During the last hour for filing under FRCP 6(a)(2), then the time for filing is extended to the same time on the first accessible day that is not a Saturday, Sunday, or legal holiday. FRCP 6(a)(3).

iv. *"Last day" defined.* Unless a different time is set by a statute, local rule, or court order, the last day ends:

- For electronic filing, at midnight in the court's time zone; and

- For filing by other means, when the clerk's office is scheduled to close. FRCP 6(a)(4).

v. *"Next day" defined.* The "next day" is determined by continuing to count forward when the period is measured after an event and backward when measured before an event. FRCP 6(a)(5).

vi. *"Legal holiday" defined.* "Legal holiday" means:

- The day set aside by statute for observing New Year's Day, Martin Luther King Jr.'s Birthday, Washington's Birthday, Memorial Day, Independence Day, Labor Day, Columbus Day, Veterans' Day, Thanksgiving Day, or Christmas Day;

- Any day declared a holiday by the President or Congress; and

- For periods that are measured after an event, any other day declared a holiday by the state where the district court is located. FRCP 6(a)(6).

b. *Computation of electronic filing deadlines.* A document will be deemed timely filed if filed prior to midnight Eastern Time, unless otherwise ordered by the Court. A document will be considered untimely if filed thereafter. When a Court order requires that a document be filed on a weekend or holiday, the document may be filed by close of business the next business day without further application to the Court. NY R USDCTWD ECF Procedures(2)(e)(i). A document filed electronically is deemed filed on the date and time stated on the Notice of Electronic Filing. NY R USDCTWD ECF Procedures(2)(e)(ii).

i. *System availability.* Although parties may file documents electronically twenty-four (24) hours a day, registered users are strongly encouraged to file all documents during normal working hours of the Clerk's Office (8:30 a.m. to 5:00 p.m. Eastern Time). NY R USDCTWD ECF Procedures(2)(t)(i).

ii. *Technical failures.* A Filing User whose filing is made untimely as a result of a technical failure must seek appropriate relief from the Court. NY R USDCTWD ECF Procedures(2)(u)(i).

c. *Extending time*

    i. *In general.* When an act may or must be done within a specified time, the court may, for good cause, extend the time:

- With or without motion or notice if the court acts, or if a request is made, before the original time or its extension expires; or

- On motion made after the time has expired if the party failed to act because of excusable neglect. FRCP 6(b)(1).

    ii. *Exceptions.* A court must not extend the time to act under FRCP 50(b), FRCP 50(d), FRCP 52(b), FRCP 59(b), FRCP 59(d), FRCP 59(e), and FRCP 60(b). FRCP 6(b)(2).

    iii. Refer to the United States District Court for the Western District of New York KeyRules Motion for Continuance/Extension of Time document for more information on extending time.

d. *Additional time after certain kinds of service.* When a party may or must act within a specified time after service and service is made under FRCP 5(b)(2)(C), FRCP 5(b)(2)(D), FRCP 5(b)(2)(E), or FRCP 5(b)(2)(F), three (3) days are added after the period would otherwise expire under FRCP 6(a). FRCP 6(d).

    i. *Service by overnight delivery.* Where a period of time prescribed by either the Federal Rules of Civil Procedure or the Local Rules of Civil Procedure for the United States District Court for the Western District of New York is measured from the service of a paper and service is by overnight delivery, one (1) business day shall be added to the prescribed period. NY R USDCTWD Civ Rule 5.1(g).

7. *Individual judge practices.* Refer to the Miscellaneous section of this document for information on individual judge practices on timing of documents.

## C. General Requirements

1. *Motions, generally*

a. *Requirements.* A request for a court order must be made by motion. The motion must:

    i. Be in writing unless made during a hearing or trial;

    ii. State with particularity the grounds for seeking the order; and

    iii. State the relief sought. FRCP 7(b)(1).

b. *Notice of motion.* A party interested in resisting the relief sought by a motion has a right to notice thereof, and an opportunity to be heard. AMJUR MOTIONS § 12.

    i. In addition to statutory or court rule provisions requiring notice of a motion—the purpose of such a notice requirement having been said to be to prevent a party from being prejudicially surprised by a motion—principles of natural justice dictate that an adverse party generally must be given notice that a motion will be presented to the court. AMJUR MOTIONS § 12.

    ii. "Notice," in this regard, means reasonable notice, including a meaningful opportunity to prepare and to defend against allegations of a motion. AMJUR MOTIONS § 12.

c. *Writing requirement.* The writing requirement is intended to insure that the adverse parties are informed and have a record of both the motion's pendency and the grounds on which the movant seeks an order. FPP § 1191; Feldberg v. Quechee Lakes Corp., 463 F.3d 195 (2d Cir. 2006).

    i. It is sufficient "if the motion is stated in a written notice of the hearing of the motion." FPP § 1191.

d. *Particularity requirement.* The particularity requirement insures that the opposing parties will have notice of their opponent's contentions. FEDPROC § 62:364; Goodman v. 1973 26 Foot Trojan Vessel, Arkansas Registration No. AR1439SN, 859 F.2d 71, 12 Fed.R.Serv.3d 645 (8th Cir. 1988). That requirement ensures that notice of the basis for the motion is provided to the court and to the opposing party so as to avoid prejudice, provide the opponent with a meaningful opportunity to respond, and provide the court with enough information to process the motion correctly. FEDPROC § 62:364; Andreas v. Volkswagen of America, Inc., 336 F.3d 789, 56 Fed.R.Serv.3d 6 (8th Cir. 2003).

    i. Reasonable specification of the grounds for a motion is sufficient. However, where a movant fails to state even one ground for granting the motion in question, the movant has failed to meet the minimal standard of "reasonable specification." FEDPROC § 62:364; Martinez v. Trainor, 556 F.2d 818, 23 Fed.R.Serv.2d 403 (7th Cir. 1977).

 ii. The court may excuse the failure to comply with the particularity requirement if it is inadvertent, and where no prejudice is shown by the opposing party. FEDPROC § 62:364.

2. *Motion for leave to amend.* FRCP 15(a)(2) provides that after a party has amended a pleading once as of course or the time for amendments of that type has expired, a party may amend only by obtaining leave of the court or if the adverse party consents to it. FPP § 1484; In re Cessna Distributorship Antitrust Litigation, 532 F.2d 64 (8th Cir. 1976). FRCP 15(a) does not set forth any specific procedure for obtaining leave to amend. Typically, it is sought by a motion addressed to the court's discretion. FPP § 1485.

 a. *Pleadings to be amended.* As in the case of amendments as of course under FRCP 15(a)(1), any of the pleadings enumerated in FRCP 7(a) may be amended with the court's leave and FRCP 15 does not restrict the purposes for which an amendment may be made or its character. FPP § 1484.

 b. *Prerequisites for leave to amend.* The only prerequisites are that the district court have jurisdiction over the case and an appeal must not be pending. FPP § 1484. If these two conditions are met, the court will proceed to examine the effect and the timing of the proposed amendments to determine whether they would prejudice the rights of any of the other parties to the suit. FPP § 1484; Nilsen v. City of Moss Point, Miss., 674 F.2d 379, 388 (5th Cir. 1982).

 c. *When leave or consent is not obtained.* In general, if an amendment that cannot be made as of right is served without obtaining the court's leave or the opposing party's consent, it is without legal effect and any new matter it contains will not be considered unless the amendment is resubmitted for the court's approval. Some courts have held, however, that an untimely amended pleading served without judicial permission may be considered as properly introduced when leave to amend would have been granted had it been sought and when it does not appear that any of the parties will be prejudiced by allowing the change. FPP § 1484.

 d. *Form.* A motion to amend under FRCP 15(a), as is true of motions generally, is subject to the requirements of FRCP 7(b), and must set forth with particularity the relief or order requested and the grounds supporting the application. In order to satisfy these prerequisites a copy of the amendment should be submitted with the motion so that the court and the adverse party know the precise nature of the pleading changes being proposed. FPP § 1485.

 e. *Oral motion for leave to amend.* Courts have held that an oral request to amend a pleading that is made before the court in the presence of opposing party's counsel may be sufficient if the adverse party is put on notice of the nature and purpose of the request and is given the same opportunity to present objections to the proposed amendment as would have occurred if a formal motion had been made. FPP § 1485.

 f. *Conditions imposed on leave to amend.* While FRCP 15(a) does not specifically authorize the district court to impose conditions on its granting of leave to amend, it is well settled that the court may impose such conditions to avoid or minimize any prejudice to the opposing party. FEDPROC § 62:276. Conditions frequently are imposed because the amending party knew of the facts sought to be asserted in the amendment but failed to assert such facts until later, to the prejudice of the opposing party. Conversely, the court may decline to impose conditions where the amendment was asserted with relative promptness. FEDPROC § 62:276.

 i. The moving party's refusal to comply with the conditions imposed by the court normally will result in a denial of the right to amend. FPP § 1486.

 g. *When leave to amend may be granted.* If the underlying facts or circumstances relied upon by a plaintiff may be a proper subject of relief, he ought to be afforded an opportunity to test his claim on the merits. In the absence of any apparent or declared reason—such as undue delay, bad faith or dilatory motive on the part of the movant, repeated failure to cure deficiencies by amendments previously allowed, undue prejudice to the opposing party by virtue of allowance of the amendment, futility of amendment, etc.—the leave sought should, as the rules require, be "freely given." FPP § 1487; Foman v. Davis, 371 U.S. 178, 182, 83 S.Ct. 227, 230, 9 L.Ed.2d 222 (1962).

3.  *Amendments, generally*

    a.  *Amendments before trial.* The function of FRCP 15(a), which provides generally for the amendment of pleadings, is to enable a party to assert matters that were overlooked or were unknown at the time the party interposed the original complaint or answer. FPP § 1473; Smiga v. Dean Witter Reynolds, Inc., 766 F.2d 698, 703 (2d Cir. 1985).

        i.   *Matters contained in amended pleading under FRCP 15(a).* Although FRCP 15(a) does not expressly state that an amendment must contain only matters that occurred within a particular time period, FRCP 15(d) provides that any "transaction, occurrence, or event that happened after the date of the pleading" should be set forth in a supplemental pleading. FPP § 1473. Thus, impliedly, an amended pleading, whether prepared with or without leave of court, only should relate to matters that have taken place prior to the date of the earlier pleading. FPP § 1473; Ford Motor Co. v. U.S., 19 C.I.T. 946, 896 F.Supp. 1224, 1230 (1995).

        ii.  *Amending as a matter of course.* A party may amend its pleading once as a matter of course within: (1) twenty-one (21) days after serving it, or if the pleading is one to which a responsive pleading is required, twenty-one (21) days after service of a responsive pleading or twenty-one (21) days after service of a motion under FRCP 12(b), FRCP 12(e), or FRCP 12(f), whichever is earlier. FRCP 15(a)(1). Refer to the United States District Court for the Western District of New York KeyRules Amended Pleading document for more information on amending as a matter of course.

        iii. *Other amendments.* In all other cases, a party may amend its pleading only with the opposing party's written consent or the court's leave. The court should freely give leave when justice so requires. FRCP 15(a)(2).

        iv.  *Types of amendments permitted under FRCP 15(a)*

             •   *Cure a defective pleading.* Perhaps the most common use of FRCP 15(a) is by a party seeking to amend in order to cure a defective pleading. FPP § 1474.

             •   *Correct insufficiently stated claims or defenses.* A more common use of FRCP 15(a) amendments is to correct insufficiently stated claims or defenses. Typically, amendments of this character involve either adding a necessary allegation in order to state a claim for relief or correcting a misnomer of a party to the action. FPP § 1474.

             •   *Change nature or theory of claim or capacity of party.* Courts also have allowed a party to amend in order to change the nature or theory of the party's claim or the capacity in which the party is bringing the action. FPP § 1474.

             •   *State additional claims or defenses or drop claims or defenses.* Plaintiffs and defendants also have been permitted to amend their pleadings to state additional claims, to assert additional defenses, or to drop claims or defenses. FPP § 1474; Weinberger v. Retail Credit Co., 498 F.2d 552, 554, n.4 (4th Cir. 1974).

             •   *Increase amount of damages or elect a different remedy.* A FRCP 15(a) amendment also is appropriate for increasing the amount of damages sought, or for electing a different remedy than the one originally requested. FPP § 1474; McFadden v. Sanchez, 710 F.2d 907 (2d Cir. 1983).

             •   *Add, substitute, or drop parties.* Finally, a party may make a FRCP 15(a) amendment to add, substitute, or drop parties to the action. FPP § 1474.

    b.  *Amendments during and after trial*

        i.   *Based on an objection at trial.* If, at trial, a party objects that evidence is not within the issues raised in the pleadings, the court may permit the pleadings to be amended. The court should freely permit an amendment when doing so will aid in presenting the merits and the objecting party fails to satisfy the court that the evidence would prejudice that party's action or defense on the merits. The court may grant a continuance to enable the objecting party to meet the evidence. FRCP 15(b)(1).

        ii.  *For issues tried by consent.* When an issue not raised by the pleadings is tried by the parties' express or implied consent, it must be treated in all respects as if raised in the pleadings. A party may move—at any time, even after judgment—to amend the pleadings to conform them to the evidence and to raise an unpleaded issue. But failure to amend does not affect the result of the trial of that issue. FRCP 15(b)(2).

c. *Relation back of amendments*

    i. *When an amendment relates back.* An amendment to a pleading relates back to the date of the original pleading when:

- The law that provides the applicable statute of limitations allows relation back;

- The amendment asserts a claim or defense that arose out of the conduct, transaction, or occurrence set out—or attempted to be set out—in the original pleading; or

- The amendment changes the party or the naming of the party against whom a claim is asserted, if FRCP 15(c)(1)(B) is satisfied and if, within the period provided by FRCP 4(m) for serving the summons and complaint, the party to be brought in by amendment: (1) received such notice of the action that it will not be prejudiced in defending on the merits; and (2) knew or should have known that the action would have been brought against it, but for a mistake concerning the proper party's identity. FRCP 15(c)(1).

    ii. *Notice to the United States.* When the United States or a United States officer or agency is added as a defendant by amendment, the notice requirements of FRCP 15(c)(1)(C)(i) and FRCP 15(c)(1)(C)(ii) are satisfied if, during the stated period, process was delivered or mailed to the United States attorney or the United States attorney's designee, to the Attorney General of the United States, or to the officer or agency. FRCP 15(c)(2).

d. *Effect of an amended pleading.* A pleading that has been amended under FRCP 15(a) supersedes the pleading it modifies and remains in effect throughout the action unless it subsequently is modified. FPP § 1476. Once an amended pleading is interposed, the original pleading no longer performs any function in the case and any subsequent motion made by an opposing party should be directed at the amended pleading. FPP § 1476; Ferdik v. Bonzelet, 963 F.2d 1258, 1262 (9th Cir. 1992); Davis v. TXO Production Corp., 929 F.2d 1515, 1517 (10th Cir. 1991).

4. *Opposing papers.* The Federal Rules of Civil Procedure do not require any formal answer, return, or reply to a motion, except where the Federal Rules of Civil Procedure or local rules may require affidavits, memoranda, or other papers to be filed in opposition to a motion. Such papers are simply to apprise the court of such opposition and the grounds of that opposition. FEDPROC § 62:359.

a. *Effect of failure to respond to motion.* Although in the absence of statutory provision or court rule, a motion ordinarily does not require a written answer, when a party files a motion and the opposing party fails to respond, the court may construe such failure to respond as nonopposition to the motion or an admission that the motion was meritorious, may take the facts alleged in the motion as true—the rule in some jurisdictions being that the failure to respond to a fact set forth in a motion is deemed an admission—and may grant the motion if the relief requested appears to be justified. AMJUR MOTIONS § 28.

b. *Assent or no opposition not determinative.* However, a motion will not be granted automatically simply because an "assent" or a notation of "no opposition" has been filed; federal judges frequently deny motions that have been assented to when it is thought that justice so dictates. FPP § 1190.

c. *Responsive pleading inappropriate as response to motion.* An attempt to answer or oppose a motion with a responsive pleading usually is not appropriate. FPP § 1190.

5. *Sur-reply.* Absent permission of the Judge hearing the motion, sur-reply papers are not permitted. NY R USDCTWD Civ Rule 7(a)(6).

6. *Motion to settle an order.* When counsel are unable to agree on the form of a proposed order, the prevailing party may move, upon seven (7) days notice to all parties, to settle the order. The Court may award costs and attorney's fees against an attorney if it determines that the attorney's unreasonable conduct necessitated bringing the motion. NY R USDCTWD Civ Rule 7(d)(2).

7. *Reply papers.* A moving party may be required or permitted to prepare papers in addition to his original

motion papers. AMJUR MOTIONS § 25. Papers answering or replying to opposing papers may be appropriate, in the interests of justice, where it appears there is a substantial reason for allowing a reply. Thus, a court may accept reply papers where a party demonstrates that the papers to which it seeks to file a reply raise new issues that are material to the disposition of the question before the court, or where the court determines, sua sponte, that it wishes further briefing of an issue raised in those papers and orders the submission of additional papers. FEDPROC § 62:360.

a. *Function of reply papers.* The function of a reply affidavit is to answer the arguments made in opposition to the position taken by the movant and not to permit the movant to introduce new arguments in support of the motion. AMJUR MOTIONS § 25.

b. *Issues raised for the first time in a reply document.* However, the view has been followed in some jurisdictions, that as a matter of judicial economy, where there is no prejudice and where the issues could be raised simply by filing a motion to dismiss, the trial court has discretion to consider arguments raised for the first time in a reply memorandum, and that a trial court may grant a motion to strike issues raised for the first time in a reply memorandum. AMJUR MOTIONS § 26.

8. *Notice of appearance.* No notice of appearance is required of an attorney whose name and address appear at the end of a complaint, notice of removal, pre-answer motion, or answer. In all other circumstances, an attorney appearing for a party in a civil case shall promptly file a written notice of appearance. NY R USDCTWD Civ Rule 83.2(b). For more information on appearances and withdrawals, refer to NY R USDCTWD Civ Rule 83.2.

9. *Related cases.* Each attorney appearing in a civil case has a continuing duty to promptly notify the Clerk of Court when the attorney has reason to believe that said case is related to some other pending civil or criminal action(s) such that their assignment to the same Judge would avoid unnecessary duplication of judicial effort. As soon as the attorney becomes aware of such a relationship, the attorney shall notify the Clerk of Court by letter of the relevant facts, and the Clerk of Court will transmit that notification to the Judges to whom the cases have been assigned. NY R USDCTWD Civ Rule 5.1(e).

10. *Alternative dispute resolution (ADR).* This Court has adopted an Alternative Dispute Resolution Plan ("ADR"), as implemented by Standing Order (NY R USDCTWD ADR Plan), under which certain civil cases are referred automatically to ADR upon filing. NY R USDCTWD Civ Rule 16(a). The United States District Court for the Western District of New York (the "Court") adopted the ADR Plan on January 1, 2006 (the "Effective Date"), to make available to civil litigants court-administered ADR interventions and processes designed to provide quicker, less expensive and potentially more satisfying alternatives to continuing litigation, without impairing the quality of justice or the right to trial. NY R USDCTWD ADR Plan(1)(1.2)(A).

a. *Scope.* This ADR Plan (NY R USDCTWD ADR Plan) applies to civil actions pending or commenced on and after the Effective Date, except as otherwise indicated in NY R USDCTWD ADR Plan. The ADR Plan supplements the Local Rules of Civil Procedure for the United States District Court for the Western District of New York, which shall remain in full effect for all cases. NY R USDCTWD ADR Plan(1)(1.2)(B).

b. *Referral to ADR*

   i. *New cases.* All civil cases filed on and after the Effective Date of the ADR Plan shall be referred automatically for ADR. NY R USDCTWD ADR Plan(2)(2.1)(A). Notice of the ADR requirements will be provided to all parties immediately upon the filing of a complaint and answer or a notice of removal; NY R USDCTWD ADR Plan(2)(2.1)(A); NY R USDCTWD Civ Rule 16(a). ADR intervention will be scheduled at the conference held pursuant to Local Rule of Civil Procedure 16.1. NY R USDCTWD ADR Plan(2)(2.1)(A). [Editor's note: the reference to Local Rule of Civil Procedure 16.1 is likely meant to be a reference to NY R USDCTWD Civ Rule 16(b)].

   • Litigants in cases not referred automatically to ADR must consider possible agreement to the use of an ADR process. NY R USDCTWD Civ Rule 16(a).

   • For a list of exemptions from automatic referral, refer to NY R USDCTWD ADR Plan(2)(2.1)(A).

ii. *Pending cases.* The assigned Judge on any pending civil case may, sua sponte or with status conference, issue an order referring the case for ADR. NY R USDCTWD ADR Plan(2)(2.1)(B); NY R USDCTWD Civ Rule 16(a). The order shall specify a date on which the ADR intervention is to be completed. NY R USDCTWD ADR Plan(2)(2.1)(B).

iii. *Stipulation.* A case may be referred for ADR by stipulation of all parties. Stipulations shall be filed and shall designate the specific ADR intervention the parties have selected, the time frame within which the ADR process will be completed and the selected Neutral. Stipulations are presumed acceptable unless the assigned Judge determines that the interests of justice are not served. NY R USDCTWD ADR Plan(2)(2.1)(C).

iv. *Relief from ADR referral*

- *Opting out motions.* Any party may file, with the assigned Judge for that case, a motion to opt out of, or for relief from, ADR. NY R USDCTWD ADR Plan(2)(2.2)(A).

- *Motion.* Opting Out Motions must be made within fourteen (14) days from (1) the date of the first discovery conference under Local Rule 16.1 in new cases, or (2) the date of a sua sponte ADR Referral Order in pending cases. NY R USDCTWD ADR Plan(2)(2.2)(B). [Editor's note: the reference to Local Rule 16.1 is likely meant to be a reference to NY R USDCTWD Civ Rule 16(b)].

- *Criteria.* Opting Out Motions shall be granted only for "good cause" shown. Inconvenience, travel costs, attorney fees or other costs shall not constitute "good cause." A party seeking relief from ADR must set forth the reasons why ADR has no reasonable chance of being productive. NY R USDCTWD ADR Plan(2)(2.2)(C).

- *Judicial initiative.* The assigned Judge may, sua sponte, exempt any case from the Court's ADR Plan. NY R USDCTWD ADR Plan(2)(2.2)(D).

c. *ADR interventions*

i. *Options.* It is expected that cases referred for ADR will proceed to Mediation. However, the following options are also available upon the stipulation of all parties:

- Neutral Evaluation;

- Mini Summary Trial;

- Arbitration (Binding and Non-Binding);

- Case Valuation; and

- Settlement Week, when scheduled by the Court. NY R USDCTWD ADR Plan(4)(4.1)(A).

ii. *Timing.* Timing is specific to the intervention and process chosen, as set forth in the corresponding sections in NY R USDCTWD ADR Plan. NY R USDCTWD ADR Plan(4)(4.1)(B).

iii. *Scheduling.* The referral of a case to ADR does not delay or defer other dates established in the Scheduling Order and has no effect on the scheduled progress of the case toward trial. NY R USDCTWD ADR Plan(4)(4.1)(C).

d. *Selecting an ADR intervention*

i. *New cases.* Prior to the Local Rule 16.1 scheduling conference, counsel and any unrepresented parties shall confer about ADR as part of their discussion of "the possibilities for a prompt settlement or resolution of the case" pursuant to FRCP 26(f). Unless the parties agree to a different intervention, it is presumed that they will participate in mediation. [Editor's note: the reference to Local Rule 16.1 is likely meant to be a reference to NY R USDCTWD Civ Rule 16(b)].

ii. *Pending cases.* In pending cases, all sua sponte referrals will be to mediation. Should the parties agree that a different ADR intervention is more appropriate to their case, they may submit a stipulation designating the specific ADR intervention selected, the time frame within which the ADR process will be completed and the identity of the Neutral. Stipulations must be filed within fourteen (14) days from the date of the ADR Referral Order and are presumed acceptable unless the assigned Judge determines that the interests of justice are not served. NY R USDCTWD ADR Plan(4)(4.2)(B).

    e.   For more information on alternative dispute resolution (ADR), refer to NY R USDCTWD ADR Plan.

11.  *Sanctions.* Failure of counsel for any party, or a party proceeding pro se, to appear before the Court at a conference, to complete the necessary preparations, or to be prepared to proceed to trial at the set time may be considered an abandonment of the case or a failure to prosecute or defend diligently. An appropriate order for sanctions may be entered against the defaulting party with respect to either a specific issue or the entire case. NY R USDCTWD Civ Rule 11(a). For more information, refer to NY R USDCTWD Civ Rule 11.

12.  *Pro se actions.* For information on the requirements in pro se actions, refer to NY R USDCTWD Civ Rule 5.2.

13.  *Individual judge practices.* Refer to the Miscellaneous section of this document for information on individual judge practices on general requirements for documents.

## D.  Documents

  1.  *Documents for moving party*

    a.  *Required documents*

      i.  *Notice of motion and motion.* A notice of motion is required for all motions, and must state: the relief sought, the grounds for the request, the papers submitted in support, and the return date for the motion, if known. A moving party who intends to file and serve reply papers must so state in the notice of motion. NY R USDCTWD Civ Rule 7(a)(1). Refer to the General Requirements section of this document for information on the notice of motion and motion.

      ii.  *Supporting affidavit.* An affidavit must not contain legal arguments, but must contain factual and procedural background relevant to the motion it supports. Except for motions brought under FRCP 12(b)(1) (lack of subject matter jurisdiction), FRCP 12(b)(6) (failure to state a claim), FRCP 12(c) (judgment on the pleadings), and FRCP 12(f) (to strike), motions and opposition to motions shall be supported by at least one (1) affidavit and by such other evidence (i.e., deposition testimony, interrogatory answers, admissions, and documents) as appropriate to resolve the particular motion. Failure to comply with this requirement may constitute grounds for resolving the motion against the non-complying party. NY R USDCTWD Civ Rule 7(a)(3).

      iii.  *Proposed amended pleading.* A movant seeking to amend or supplement a pleading must attach an unsigned copy of the proposed amended pleading as an exhibit to the motion. The proposed amended pleading must be a complete pleading superseding the original pleading in all respects. No portion of the prior pleading shall be incorporated into the proposed amended pleading by reference. NY R USDCTWD Civ Rule 15(a). In order to satisfy the prerequisites of FRCP 7(b), a copy of the amendment should be submitted with the motion so that the court and the adverse party know the precise nature of the pleading changes being proposed. FPP § 1485. The amending party should submit a copy of the proposed amendment at least by the date of the hearing on the motion for leave to amend. FEDPROC § 62:274; Grombach v. Oerlikon Tool & Arms Corp. of America, 276 F.2d 155 (4th Cir. 1960).

         •  If the document to be filed requires leave of court, such as an amended complaint or a document to be filed out of time, the proposed document shall be attached as an exhibit to the motion (please refer to NY R USDCTWD Civ Rule 15 on submitting red-lined versions of amended pleadings). NY R USDCTWD ECF Procedures(2)(a)(ii).

         •  Unless the movant is proceeding pro se, the amendment(s) or supplement(s) to the original pleading shall be identified in the proposed pleading through the use of a word processing "redline" function or other similar markings that are visible in both electronic and paper format. NY R USDCTWD Civ Rule 15(b).

         •  The documents accompanying the motion for leave to amend may be an appropriate substitute for a formally proposed amendment, if the documents sufficiently indicate the gist of the amendment. FEDPROC § 62:274.

         •  If the motion is granted, the attorney must file the document electronically with the Court as a separate document. NY R USDCTWD ECF Procedures(2)(a)(ii). The granting of the motion does not constitute the filing of the amended pleading. Unless the order granting leave to amend or supplement contains a different deadline, the moving party must file and serve the amended pleading upon the existing parties within fourteen (14) days of entry of the order granting the motion. Service upon any new parties must be completed in accordance with FRCP 4(m). If the moving party is proceeding pro se, the Clerk of Court will file the amended pleading upon granting of the motion. NY R USDCTWD Civ Rule 15(c).

iv. *Certificate of service.* FRCP 5(d) requires that the person making service under FRCP 5 certify that service has been effected. FRCP 5(Advisory Committee Notes). Having such information on file may be useful for many purposes, including proof of service if an issue arises concerning the effectiveness of the service. FRCP 5(Advisory Committee Notes). The Notice of Electronic Filing effectuates service for all registered users and no certificate of service is required when all filers on an action are Registered Users. The following exemptions require a certificate of service to be filed:

- When a document is manually filed, a certificate of service must be filed stating the manner in which service or notice was accomplished on each party so entitled. NY R USDCTWD ECF Procedures(2)(f)(iv).

- When a pro se filer (who isn't authorized to electronically file documents) is a party, a certificate of service must be filed stating the manner in which service or notice was accomplished on the pro se party. The Notice of Electronic Filing effectuates service for the Registered Users in this situation and it is not necessary to note service on those parties. A non-registered pro se filer is required to file certificates of service on all documents they file. NY R USDCTWD ECF Procedures(2)(f)(iv).

- If an attorney is exempt from electronic service, a certificate of service must be filed stating the manner in which service or notice was accomplished on the exempt attorney. The Notice of Electronic Filing effectuates service for the Registered Users in this situation and it is not necessary to note service on those parties. NY R USDCTWD ECF Procedures(2)(f)(iv).

b. *Supplemental documents*

i. *Memorandum of law.* Nothing in the Local Rules of Civil Procedure for the United States District Court for the Western District of New York precludes a moving party from filing a memorandum in support of a motion made other than pursuant to FRCP 12, FRCP 56 or FRCP 65(a). The Court, in its discretion, may require written memoranda on such other motions. NY R USDCTWD Civ Rule 7(a)(2)(B). Refer to the Format section of this document for the formatting requirements for memoranda of law.

ii. *Supporting evidence.* When a motion relies on facts outside the record, the court may hear the matter on affidavits or may hear it wholly or partly on oral testimony or on depositions. FRCP 43(c). A party seeking or opposing any relief under the Federal Rules of Civil Procedure shall file only the portion(s) of a deposition, interrogatory, request for documents, request for admission, or other supporting material that is pertinent to the application. NY R USDCTWD Civ Rule 7(a)(4).

iii. *Notice of constitutional question.* A party that files a pleading, written motion, or other paper drawing into question the constitutionality of a federal or state statute must promptly:

- *File notice.* File a notice of constitutional question stating the question and identifying the paper that raises it, if: (1) a federal statute is questioned and the parties do not include the United States, one of its agencies, or one of its officers or employees in an official capacity; or (2) a state statute is questioned and the parties do not include the state, one of its agencies, or one of its officers or employees in an official capacity; and

- *Serve notice.* Serve the notice and paper on the Attorney General of the United States if a federal statute is questioned—or on the state attorney general if a state statute is

questioned—either by certified or registered mail or by sending it to an electronic address designated by the attorney general for this purpose. FRCP 5.1(a).

- *No forfeiture.* A party's failure to file and serve the notice, or the court's failure to certify, does not forfeit a constitutional claim or defense that is otherwise timely asserted. FRCP 5.1(d).

iv. *Copies of authorities.* In cases involving a pro se litigant, counsel shall, when serving a memorandum of law (or other submissions to the Court), provide the pro se litigant (but not other counsel or the Court) with printed copies of decisions cited therein that are unreported or reported exclusively on computerized databases. NY R USDCTWD Civ Rule 7(a)(8).

v. *Proposed order.* All proposed orders must be submitted in a format compatible with WordPerfect or Microsoft Word format, which is a "Save As" option in most word processing software. Judges will not accept proposed orders in PDF format. NY R USDCTWD ECF Procedures(2)(j)(ii). Proposed orders should be attached to an Internet e-mail sent to the e-mail address of the assigned judge. NY R USDCTWD ECF Procedures(2)(j)(i). For the list of email addresses for the judges, refer to NY R USDCTWD ECF Procedures(2)(j)(i).

vi. *Paper copy for date-stamping with self-addressed envelope.* Parties requesting date-stamped copies of filed documents must provide a paper copy for date-stamping, and a self-addressed, adequately-sized envelope with proper postage affixed. NY R USDCTWD Civ Rule 5.1(d).

vii. *Courtesy copies.* The Court may, in its discretion, request courtesy copies on any other motion. NY R USDCTWD Civ Rule 7(a)(7). Courtesy copies of certain documents may be required. Filers should refer to the "Judge Preferences" published on the Court's website. NY R USDCTWD ECF Procedures(2)(a)(iii).

2. *Documents for opposing party*

a. *Required documents*

i. *Opposition.* Refer to the General Requirements section of this document for information on the opposing papers.

ii. *Supporting affidavit.* An affidavit must not contain legal arguments, but must contain factual and procedural background relevant to the motion it supports. Except for motions brought under FRCP 12(b)(1) (lack of subject matter jurisdiction), FRCP 12(b)(6) (failure to state a claim), FRCP 12(c) (judgment on the pleadings), and FRCP 12(f) (to strike), motions and opposition to motions shall be supported by at least one (1) affidavit and by such other evidence (i.e., deposition testimony, interrogatory answers, admissions, and documents) as appropriate to resolve the particular motion. Failure to comply with this requirement may constitute grounds for resolving the motion against the non-complying party. NY R USDCTWD Civ Rule 7(a)(3).

iii. *Certificate of service.* FRCP 5(d) requires that the person making service under FRCP 5 certify that service has been effected. FRCP 5(Advisory Committee Notes). Having such information on file may be useful for many purposes, including proof of service if an issue arises concerning the effectiveness of the service. FRCP 5(Advisory Committee Notes). The Notice of Electronic Filing effectuates service for all registered users and no certificate of service is required when all filers on an action are Registered Users. The following exemptions require a certificate of service to be filed:

- When a document is manually filed, a certificate of service must be filed stating the manner in which service or notice was accomplished on each party so entitled. NY R USDCTWD ECF Procedures(2)(f)(iv).

- When a pro se filer (who isn't authorized to electronically file documents) is a party, a certificate of service must be filed stating the manner in which service or notice was accomplished on the pro se party. The Notice of Electronic Filing effectuates service for the Registered Users in this situation and it is not necessary to note service on those parties. A non-registered pro se filer is required to file certificates of service on all documents they file. NY R USDCTWD ECF Procedures(2)(f)(iv).

- If an attorney is exempt from electronic service, a certificate of service must be filed stating the manner in which service or notice was accomplished on the exempt attorney. The Notice of Electronic Filing effectuates service for the Registered Users in this situation and it is not necessary to note service on those parties. NY R USDCTWD ECF Procedures(2)(f)(iv).

b. *Supplemental documents*

    i. *Supporting evidence.* When a motion relies on facts outside the record, the court may hear the matter on affidavits or may hear it wholly or partly on oral testimony or on depositions. FRCP 43(c). A party seeking or opposing any relief under the Federal Rules of Civil Procedure shall file only the portion(s) of a deposition, interrogatory, request for documents, request for admission, or other supporting material that is pertinent to the application. NY R USDCTWD Civ Rule 7(a)(4).

    ii. *Notice of constitutional question.* A party that files a pleading, written motion, or other paper drawing into question the constitutionality of a federal or state statute must promptly:

- *File notice.* File a notice of constitutional question stating the question and identifying the paper that raises it, if: (1) a federal statute is questioned and the parties do not include the United States, one of its agencies, or one of its officers or employees in an official capacity; or (2) a state statute is questioned and the parties do not include the state, one of its agencies, or one of its officers or employees in an official capacity; and

- *Serve notice.* Serve the notice and paper on the Attorney General of the United States if a federal statute is questioned—or on the state attorney general if a state statute is questioned—either by certified or registered mail or by sending it to an electronic address designated by the attorney general for this purpose. FRCP 5.1(a).

- *No forfeiture.* A party's failure to file and serve the notice, or the court's failure to certify, does not forfeit a constitutional claim or defense that is otherwise timely asserted. FRCP 5.1(d).

    iii. *Copies of authorities.* In cases involving a pro se litigant, counsel shall, when serving a memorandum of law (or other submissions to the Court), provide the pro se litigant (but not other counsel or the Court) with printed copies of decisions cited therein that are unreported or reported exclusively on computerized databases. NY R USDCTWD Civ Rule 7(a)(8).

    iv. *Paper copy for date-stamping with self-addressed envelope.* Parties requesting date-stamped copies of filed documents must provide a paper copy for date-stamping, and a self-addressed, adequately-sized envelope with proper postage affixed. NY R USDCTWD Civ Rule 5.1(d).

    v. *Courtesy copies.* Courtesy copies of certain documents may be required. Filers should refer to the "Judge Preferences" published on the Court's website. NY R USDCTWD ECF Procedures(2)(a)(iii).

3. *Individual judge practices.* Refer to the Miscellaneous section of this document for information on individual judge practices on required documents.

## E. Format

1. *Form of documents.* The rules governing captions and other matters of form in pleadings apply to motions and other papers. FRCP 7(b)(2).

a. *Form, generally.* All pleadings, motions, and other papers that a party presents for filing, whether in paper form or in electronic form, shall meet the following requirements:

    i. *Font size.* All text and footnotes shall be in a font size of at least twelve (12) point type. NY R USDCTWD Civ Rule 10(a)(1).

    ii. *Spacing.* All text in the body of the document must be double-spaced, except that text in block quotations and footnotes may be single-spaced. NY R USDCTWD Civ Rule 10(a)(2).

- Extensive footnotes and block quotes may not be used to circumvent page limitations. NY R USDCTWD Civ Rule 10(a)(3).

    iii.  *Margins.* Documents must have one (1) inch margins on all four sides. NY R USDCTWD Civ Rule 10(a)(4).

    iv.  *Page numbering.* Pages must be consecutively numbered. NY R USDCTWD Civ Rule 10(a)(5).

  b.  *Additional requirements for paper filing.* Documents presented for filing in paper form shall meet the following additional requirements:

    i.  *Paper.* Documents must be on durable white eight and one-half by eleven (8-1/2 x 11) inch paper of good quality. NY R USDCTWD Civ Rule 10(b)(1).

      • All documents must be single-sided. NY R USDCTWD Civ Rule 10(b)(5).

    ii.  *Text.* All text must be plainly and legibly written, typewritten, printed or reproduced. NY R USDCTWD Civ Rule 10(b)(2).

    iii.  *Ink.* Documents must be in black or blue ink. NY R USDCTWD Civ Rule 10(b)(3).

    iv.  *Binding.* The pages of each document must be stapled or in some other way fastened together. NY R USDCTWD Civ Rule 10(b)(4).

  c.  *Caption; Names of parties.* Every pleading must have a caption with the court's name, a title, a file number, and a FRCP 7(a) designation. The title of the complaint must name all the parties; the title of other pleadings, after naming the first party on each side, may refer generally to other parties. FRCP 10(a).

  d.  *Paragraphs; Separate statements.* A party must state its claims or defenses in numbered paragraphs, each limited as far as practicable to a single set of circumstances. A later pleading may refer by number to a paragraph in an earlier pleading. If doing so would promote clarity, each claim founded on a separate transaction or occurrence—and each defense other than a denial—must be stated in a separate count or defense. FRCP 10(b).

  e.  *Adoption by reference; Exhibits.* A statement in a pleading may be adopted by reference elsewhere in the same pleading or in any other pleading or motion. A copy of a written instrument that is an exhibit to a pleading is a part of the pleading for all purposes. FRCP 10(c).

  f.  *Citation of local rules.* The Local Rules of Civil Procedure for the United States District Court for the Western District of New York shall be cited as "L.R.Civ.P." NY R USDCTWD Civ Rule 1.1.

  g.  *Acceptance by the clerk.* The clerk must not refuse to file a paper solely because it is not in the form prescribed by the Federal Rules of Civil Procedure or by a local rule or practice. FRCP 5(d)(4). The Court may reject documents that do not comply with the requirements in NY R USDCTWD Civ Rule 10. NY R USDCTWD Civ Rule 10.

2.  *Form of electronic documents.* All pleadings, motions, and other papers that a party presents for filing, whether in paper form or in electronic form, shall meet the requirements in NY R USDCTWD Civ Rule 10(a). NY R USDCTWD Civ Rule 10(a). Refer above for more information.

  a.  *Conversion to PDF.* A document created with a word processor, or a paper document, must be converted to Portable Document Format to be electronically filed with the court. NY R USDCTWD ECF Procedures(2)(a)(v).

    i.  Documents which exist only in paper form may be scanned into a portable document format (PDF) for electronic filing. NY R USDCTWD ECF Procedures(2)(a)(v). Before filing a scanned document with the court, a Filing User must verify its legibility. NY R USDCTWD ECF Procedures(2)(a)(iv).

    ii.  Electronic documents must be converted to .PDF from a word processing program and must be text searchable. Do not print, scan and .PDF your document when it has been created in a word processing program. Additional information on working with PDFs is located in NY R USDCTWD ECF Procedures(4b). NY R USDCTWD ECF Procedures(2)(a)(v).

  b.  *Hyperlinks.* Pursuant to the policy set forth by the Judicial Conference in October 2005, a hyperlink contained in a filing is no more than a convenient mechanism for accessing material cited in a document. A hyperlink reference is extraneous to any filed document and is not part of the Court's record. NY R USDCTWD ECF Procedures(2)(a)(vi).

    i.   In order to preserve the integrity of the Court record, users wishing to insert hyperlinks in Court filings shall continue to use the conventional method for the cited authority, in addition to the hyperlink. NY R USDCTWD ECF Procedures(2)(a)(vi).

    ii.   The Court accepts no responsibility for, and does not endorse any product, organization, and content at any hyperlinked site, or at any site to which that site may be linked. The Court accepts no responsibility for the availability or functionality of any hyperlink. NY R USDCTWD ECF Procedures(2)(a)(vi).

  c.  *Attachments and exhibits*

    i.   Attachments and exhibits larger than five megabytes (5 MB) shall be filed electronically in separate five megabyte (5 MB) segments. NY R USDCTWD ECF Procedures(2)(d)(i).

    ii.   Filing Users must submit in electronic form all documents referenced as exhibits or attachments, except as otherwise provided in NY R USDCTWD ECF Procedures. A Filing User must submit as exhibits or attachments only those excerpts of the referenced documents that are directly germane to the matter under consideration by the court. Excerpted material must be clearly and prominently identified as such. Filing Users who file excerpts of documents as exhibits or attachments under NY R USDCTWD ECF Procedures(2)(d)(ii) do so without prejudice to their right to timely file additional excerpts or the complete document. Responding parties may timely file additional excerpts or the complete document that they believe are directly germane. The Court may require parties to file additional excerpts or the complete document. A Filing User must request leave of the Court to file a document exhibit or attachment in non-electronic form. NY R USDCTWD ECF Procedures(2)(d)(ii).

    iii.   Exhibits offered or admitted at trial will not be filed electronically or conventionally unless so ordered by the Court. NY R USDCTWD ECF Procedures(2)(d)(iii).

    iv.   Exhibits such as videotapes and tape recordings shall be filed in the conventional manner with the Clerk of Court, and a Notice of Manual Filing shall be electronically filed by the party. Manually filed exhibits must have the case number and case name securely fastened or marked on the item. NY R USDCTWD ECF Procedures(2)(d)(iii).

    v.   Continuation of exhibit entries (for exhibits that are too large to attach to a main document) must be filed and entered on the same day that the main document was filed. NY R USDCTWD ECF Procedures(2)(d)(iv).

  d.  *Color documents.* Documents in color or containing graphics take much longer to upload. Filing users are encouraged to configure their scanners to scan documents at 200 dpi and preferably in black and white rather than color. NY R USDCTWD ECF Procedures(2)(d)(v).

  e.  *Large documents.* Due to the length of time it takes to download large files, documents larger than five megabytes (5 MB) (approximately one hundred (100) pages of a .pdf scanned document) must be filed electronically in separate five megabyte (5 MB) segments. A party who believes a document is too lengthy to electronically image (i.e. scan), may contact the Court Room Deputy for the assigned judge and request permission to file that document conventionally. If granted permission to file the document conventionally, the Filing User shall electronically file a "notice of manual filing" for that item. Exhibits submitted to the Court conventionally shall be served on other parties conventionally. NY R USDCTWD ECF Procedures(2)(d)(vi).

3.  *Form of memoranda of law.* Memoranda in support of or in opposition to any motion shall not exceed twenty-five (25) pages in length, and reply memoranda shall not exceed ten (10) pages in length. A party seeking to exceed the page limit must make application by letter to the Judge hearing the motion, with copies to all counsel, at least seven (7) days before the date on which the memorandum must be filed. NY R USDCTWD Civ Rule 7(a)(2)(C).

4.  *Signing of pleadings, motions and other papers*

  a.  *Signature.* Every pleading, written motion, and other paper must be signed by at least one attorney of record in the attorney's name—or by a party personally if the party is unrepresented. The paper must state the signer's address, e-mail address, and telephone number. FRCP 11(a). Documents presented for paper filing must contain an original signature. NY R USDCTWD Civ Rule 10(b)(6).

i. *Electronic signatures*

- *Non-attorney signature.* If the original document requires the signature of a non-attorney, the filing party shall obtain the signature of the non-attorney on the document. NY R USDCTWD ECF Procedures(2)(g)(i). The filing party or attorney then shall file the document electronically indicating the signatory's name in the form "s/(name)." NY R USDCTWD ECF Procedures(2)(g)(i)(1). A non-filing signatory or party who disputes the authenticity of an electronically filed document or the authenticity of the signature on that document must file an objection to the document within ten (10) days of receiving the Notice of Electronic Filing. NY R USDCTWD ECF Procedures(2)(g)(i)(2).

- *Registered user signature.* The username and password required to file documents on the Electronic Filing System serve as the Filing User's signature on all electronic documents filed with this Court. The also serve as a signature for the purposes of FRCP 11, the Federal Rules of Civil Procedure, the Local Rules of Civil Procedure for the United States District Court for the Western District of New York, and any other purpose for which a signature is required in connection with proceedings before this Court. A pleading requiring a Registered User's signature must include a signature block in the format found in NY R USDCTWD ECF Procedures(2)(g)(iii). NY R USDCTWD ECF Procedures(2)(g)(iii). Any party challenging the authenticity of an electronically filed document or the attorney's signature on that document must file an objection to the document within ten (10) days of receiving the Notice of Electronic Filing. NY R USDCTWD ECF Procedures(2)(g)(iii)(1).

- *Multiple signatures.* The following procedure applies when a stipulation or other document requires two or more signatures: The filing party shall initially confirm that the document is acceptable to all persons required to sign the document and shall obtain the signatures of all parties on the document. NY R USDCTWD ECF Procedures(2)(g)(iv)(1). The filing party or attorney then shall file the document electronically indicating the signatories, e.g., "s/Jane Doe," "s/John Smith," etc. NY R USDCTWD ECF Procedures(2)(g)(iv)(2). A non-filing signatory or party who disputes the authenticity of an electronically filed document containing multiple signatures or the authenticity of the signatures themselves must file an objection to the document within ten (10) days of receiving the Notice of Electronic Filing. NY R USDCTWD ECF Procedures(2)(g)(iv)(3).

ii. *No verification or accompanying affidavit required for pleadings.* Unless a rule or statute specifically states otherwise, a pleading need not be verified or accompanied by an affidavit. FRCP 11(a).

iii. *Unsigned papers.* The court must strike an unsigned paper unless the omission is promptly corrected after being called to the attorney's or party's attention. FRCP 11(a).

b. *Representations to the court.* By presenting to the court a pleading, written motion, or other paper—whether by signing, filing, submitting, or later advocating it—an attorney or unrepresented party certifies that to the best of the person's knowledge, information, and belief, formed after an inquiry reasonable under the circumstances:

i. It is not being presented for any improper purpose, such as to harass, cause unnecessary delay, or needlessly increase the cost of litigation;

ii. The claims, defenses, and other legal contentions are warranted by existing law or by a nonfrivolous argument for extending, modifying, or reversing existing law or for establishing new law;

iii. The factual contentions have evidentiary support or, if specifically so identified, will likely have evidentiary support after a reasonable opportunity for further investigation or discovery; and

    iv.   The denials of factual contentions are warranted on the evidence or, if specifically so identified, are reasonably based on belief or a lack of information. FRCP 11(b).

  c.  *Sanctions.* If, after notice and a reasonable opportunity to respond, the court determines that FRCP 11(b) has been violated, the court may impose an appropriate sanction on any attorney, law firm, or party that violated FRCP 11(b) or is responsible for the violation. FRCP 11(c)(1). Refer to the United States District Court for the Western District of New York KeyRules Motion for Sanctions document for more information.

5.  *Privacy protection for filings made with the court.* In all filings, parties shall comply with FRCP 5.2. NY R USDCTWD ECF Procedures(2)(m)(i).

  a.  *Redacted filings.* Unless the court orders otherwise, in an electronic or paper filing with the court that contains an individual's Social Security number, taxpayer-identification number, or birth date, the name of an individual known to be a minor, or a financial-account number, a party or nonparty making the filing may include only:

    i.   The last four (4) digits of the Social Security number and taxpayer-identification number;

    ii.  The year of the individual's birth;

    iii.  The minor's initials; and

    iv.  The last four (4) digits of the financial-account number. FRCP 5.2(a).

  b.  *Exemptions from the redaction requirement.* The redaction requirement does not apply to the following:

    i.   A financial-account number that identifies the property allegedly subject to forfeiture in a forfeiture proceeding;

    ii.  The record of an administrative or agency proceeding;

    iii.  The official record of a state-court proceeding;

    iv.  The record of a court or tribunal, if that record was not subject to the redaction requirement when originally filed;

    v.   A filing covered by FRCP 5.2(c) or FRCP 5.2(d); and

    vi.  A pro se filing in an action brought under 28 U.S.C.A. § 2241, 28 U.S.C.A. § 2254, or 28 U.S.C.A. § 2255. FRCP 5.2(b).

  c.  *Limitations on remote access to electronic files; Social Security appeals and immigration cases.* Unless the court orders otherwise, in an action for benefits under the Social Security Act, and in an action or proceeding relating to an order of removal, to relief from removal, or to immigration benefits or detention, access to an electronic file is authorized as follows:

    i.   The parties and their attorneys may have remote electronic access to any part of the case file, including the administrative record;

    ii.  Any other person may have electronic access to the full record at the courthouse, but may have remote electronic access only to:

      • The docket maintained by the court; and

      • An opinion, order, judgment, or other disposition of the court, but not any other part of the case file or the administrative record. FRCP 5.2(c).

  d.  *Filings made under seal.* The court may order that a filing be made under seal without redaction. The court may later unseal the filing or order the person who made the filing to file a redacted version for the public record. FRCP 5.2(d). For more information on sealing documents, refer to NY R USDCTWD Civ Rule 5.3, NY R USDCTWD ECF Procedures(2)(o)(i)(1), NY R USDCTWD ECF Procedures(2)(o)(i)(2), and NY R USDCTWD ECF Procedures(2)(o)(i)(3).

  e.  *Protective orders.* For good cause, the court may by order in a case:

    i.   Require redaction of additional information; or

    ii.  Limit or prohibit a nonparty's remote electronic access to a document filed with the court. FRCP 5.2(e).

f.  *Option for additional unredacted filing under seal.* A person making a redacted filing may also file an unredacted copy under seal. The court must retain the unredacted copy as part of the record. FRCP 5.2(f).

g.  *Option for filing a reference list.* A filing that contains redacted information may be filed together with a reference list that identifies each item of redacted information and specifies an appropriate identifier that uniquely corresponds to each item listed. The list must be filed under seal and may be amended as of right. Any reference in the case to a listed identifier will be construed to refer to the corresponding item of information. FRCP 5.2(g).

h.  *Waiver of protection of identifiers.* A person waives the protection of FRCP 5.2(a) as to the person's own information by filing it without redaction and not under seal. FRCP 5.2(h).

6.  *Individual judge practices.* Refer to the Miscellaneous section of this document for information on individual judge practices on formatting documents.

## F. Filing and Service Requirements

1.  *Filing requirements.* Any paper after the complaint that is required to be served—together with a certificate of service—must be filed within a reasonable time after service. FRCP 5(d)(1). All pleadings and other papers shall be filed and served in accordance with the Federal Rules of Civil Procedure and the CM/ECF Administrative Procedures Guide (NY R USDCTWD ECF Procedures). NY R USDCTWD Civ Rule 5.1(a). For information on filing of miscellaneous cases and irregular documents, refer to NY R USDCTWD Civ Rule 5.6.

    a.  *How filing is made; In general.* A paper is filed by delivering it:

        i.   To the clerk; or

        ii.  To a judge who agrees to accept it for filing, and who must then note the filing date on the paper and promptly send it to the clerk. FRCP 5(d)(2).

    b.  *Electronic filing*

        i.   *Authorization of electronic filing program.* A court may, by local rule, allow papers to be filed, signed, or verified by electronic means that are consistent with any technical standards established by the Judicial Conference of the United States. A local rule may require electronic filing only if reasonable exceptions are allowed. A paper filed electronically in compliance with a local rule is a written paper for purposes of the Federal Rules of Civil Procedure. FRCP 5(d)(3).

            •   All civil cases filed in this Court are assigned to the Electronic Case Filing System ("ECF"). The procedures for electronic filing and any exceptions to the electronic filing requirements are set forth in the CM/ECF Administrative Procedures Guide (NY R USDCTWD ECF Procedures) which is available on the Court's website. NY R US-DCTWD Civ Rule 5.1(a).

        ii.  *Scope of electronic filing.* The U.S. District Court for the Western District of New York requires attorneys in civil and criminal cases to file documents with the Court electronically over the Internet using its Case Management/Electronic Case Filing (CM/ECF) system. NY R US-DCTWD ECF Procedures. Beginning January 1, 2004, all civil and criminal cases currently pending and newly filed, except as expressly noted herein, were assigned to the Electronic Case Filing System ("System"). Except as expressly provided and in exceptional circumstances preventing a Filing User from filing electronically, all petitions, motions, memoranda of law, or other pleadings and documents required to be filed with the Court in connection with a case assigned to the System must be electronically filed. NY R USDCTWD ECF Procedures(1)(a).

            •   *Mandatory electronic filing.* All documents on civil, criminal, miscellaneous civil, miscellaneous criminal and new civil case openings, except sealed documents, sealed cases, opening of a criminal case, opening of a miscellaneous case and as expressly provided for in these procedures (NY R USDCTWD ECF Procedures), shall be electronically filed on the system. NY R USDCTWD ECF Procedures(2)(a)(i). NY R USDCTWD Civ Rule 29

            •   *Stipulations.* Pursuant to NY R USDCTWD Civ Rule 29, all stipulations (whether the stipulation is final or when it requires a judge's signature) shall be filed electronically. NY R USDCTWD ECF Procedures(2)(p)(i).

- *Letters.* The electronic filing of letters is generally prohibited unless granted permission by an assigned judge. Letters to the Court must be submitted conventionally. NY R US-DCTWD ECF Procedures(2)(q)(i).

- *Exceptions.* The Court requires attorneys to file documents electronically, absent a showing of good cause, unless otherwise excused by the procedures set forth below or by Order of the Court. NY R USDCTWD ECF Procedures.

iii.  *Conventional filing of documents.* The procedures in NY R USDCTWD ECF Procedures(2)(o) govern documents filed conventionally. The Court, upon application, may also authorize conventional filing of other documents otherwise subject to the procedures in NY R US-DCTWD ECF Procedures(2)(o). NY R USDCTWD ECF Procedures(2)(o)(i).

- *Documents filed under seal.* Unredacted documents filed with the Court pursuant to the privacy provisions of FRCP 5.2 shall be submitted in a sealing envelope with the information in NY R USDCTWD ECF Procedures(2)(o)(i)(1) on the envelope. NY R USDCTWD ECF Procedures(2)(o)(i)(1). If the document is larger than five (5) pages, a disk should be provided to the Clerks Office which contains the document in a .pdf format. NY R USDCTWD ECF Procedures(2)(o)(i)(1). For more information on documents filed under seal, refer to NY R USDCTWD ECF Procedures(2)(o)(i)(1), NY R USDCTWD ECF Procedures(2)(o)(i)(2), and NY R USDCTWD ECF Procedures(2)(o)(i)(3).

- *Magistrate judge consents.* Pursuant to FRCP 73(b), parties' filing consents to jurisdiction by United States Magistrate Judge will continue to be treated as non-public documents until all parties have consented. Therefore, parties must submit conventionally (in paper form) and not electronically file their consent forms so that the consent is not a public document. If all parties consent to the jurisdiction of a Magistrate Judge, the Clerk will scan all consent forms which will then become a public document. NY R USDCTWD ECF Procedures(2)(o)(i)(3).

- *Pro se filers.* Pro Se filers shall file paper originals of all initiating documents, pleadings, motions, affidavits, briefs and other documents which must be signed or which require either verification or an unsworn declaration under any rule or statute. The Clerk's Office will scan these original documents into an electronic file in the System. A certificate of service is required for all documents a pro se litigant files with the court. If a Pro Se filer is granted permission to register to electronically file documents, they shall comply with the guidelines contained in this document (NY R USDCTWD ECF Procedures). NY R USDCTWD ECF Procedures(2)(o)(i)(4).

- *Social Security cases.* Absent a showing of good cause, and except as provided in Section o(i)(4) above, all documents, notices and orders in Social Security reviews will be filed and noticed electronically, except as noted in NY R USDCTWD ECF Procedures(2)(o)(i)(6). For more information, refer to NY R USDCTWD ECF Procedures(2)(o)(i)(6).

- For more information on conventional filing of documents, refer to NY R USDCTWD ECF Procedures(2)(o)(i).

iv.  *Consequences of electronic filing.* Electronic transmission of a document to the System consistent with these procedures (NY R USDCTWD ECF Procedures), whether accomplished by the Filing User or a Court User, together with the transmission of a Notice of Electronic Filing from the Court, constitutes filing of a document for all purposes of the Federal Rules of Civil Procedure and the Local Rules of Civil Procedure for the United States District Court for the Western District of New York, and constitutes entry of the document on the docket kept by the Clerk under FRCP 58 and FRCP 79. A document shall not be considered filed for purposes of the Federal Rules of Civil until the filing party receives a System generated Notice of Electronic Filing. NY R USDCTWD ECF Procedures(2)(a)(i).

- E-mailing a document to the Clerk's Office or to the assigned judge shall not constitute "filing" of such document. NY R USDCTWD ECF Procedures(2)(a)(i)(1).

v. *Filing fees.* Any fee required for filing of a pleading or paper in District Court is payable to the Clerk of Court by check or money order. In addition, when opening a civil case on line, filing a notice of appeal on line or applying to appear pro hac vice on line, the fees shall be paid on line by registered users through the federal electronic payment website. Users will be directed to the federal electronic payment website while entering their transaction and should have a credit card available. When opening a civil case and applying to proceed in forma pauperis or when the United States of America opens a case, the payment screen can by bypassed to complete the transaction. Additional information on making electronic payments can be located on the court's website. NY R USDCTWD ECF Procedures(2)(h)(i).

2. *Service requirements.* All pleadings and other papers shall be filed and served in accordance with the Federal Rules of Civil Procedure and the CM/ECF Administrative Procedures Guide (NY R USDCTWD ECF Procedures). NY R USDCTWD Civ Rule 5.1(a).

a. *Service; When required*

i. *In general.* Unless the Federal Rules of Civil Procedure provide otherwise, each of the following papers must be served on every party:

- An order stating that service is required;

- A pleading filed after the original complaint, unless the court orders otherwise under FRCP 5(c) because there are numerous defendants;

- A discovery paper required to be served on a party, unless the court orders otherwise;

- A written motion, except one that may be heard ex parte; and

- A written notice, appearance, demand, or offer of judgment, or any similar paper. FRCP 5(a)(1).

ii. *If a party fails to appear.* No service is required on a party who is in default for failing to appear. But a pleading that asserts a new claim for relief against such a party must be served on that party under FRCP 4. FRCP 5(a)(2).

iii. *Seizing property.* If an action is begun by seizing property and no person is or need be named as a defendant, any service required before the filing of an appearance, answer, or claim must be made on the person who had custody or possession of the property when it was seized. FRCP 5(a)(3).

b. *Service; How made*

i. *Serving an attorney.* If a party is represented by an attorney, service under FRCP 5 must be made on the attorney unless the court orders service on the party. FRCP 5(b)(1).

ii. *Service in general.* A paper is served under FRCP 5 by:

- Handing it to the person;

- Leaving it: (1) at the person's office with a clerk or other person in charge or, if no one is in charge, in a conspicuous place in the office; or (2) if the person has no office or the office is closed, at the person's dwelling or usual place of abode with someone of suitable age and discretion who resides there;

- Mailing it to the person's last known address—in which event service is complete upon mailing;

- Leaving it with the court clerk if the person has no known address;

- Sending it by electronic means if the person consented in writing—in which event service is complete upon transmission, but is not effective if the serving party learns that it did not reach the person to be served; or

- Delivering it by any other means that the person consented to in writing—in which event service is complete when the person making service delivers it to the agency designated to make delivery. FRCP 5(b)(2).

iii. *Service by overnight delivery.* All papers, other than a subpoena or a summons and complaint, may be served on counsel of record by overnight delivery service at the address designated by the attorney for that purpose, or if none is designated, at the attorney's last known address. Service by overnight delivery shall be complete upon deposit of the paper(s), enclosed in a properly addressed wrapper, into the custody of the overnight delivery service, prior to the latest time designated by the service for overnight delivery. NY R USDCTWD Civ Rule 5.1(g). "Overnight delivery service" means any delivery service which regularly accepts items for overnight delivery to any address within the Court's jurisdiction. NY R USDCTWD Civ Rule 5.1(g).

    iv. *Service of documents by electronic means*

- *Service on registered users.* Registered Users consent to the electronic service of all documents, and must make available an electronic mail address for service during the registration process. Upon the filing of a document by a party, a Notice of Electronic Filing, with a hyperlink to the filed document, will be automatically generated by the electronic filing system and sent via electronic mail to the e-mail addresses of all parties participating in the electronic filing system in the case. Electronic service of the Notice of Electronic Filing constitutes service of the filed document for all purposes of the Federal Rules of Civil Procedure and the Local Rules of Civil Procedure for the United States District Court for the Western District of New York. NY R USDCTWD ECF Procedures(2)(f)(i). The Notice of Electronic Filing effectuates service for all registered users and no certificate of service is required when all filers on an action are Registered Users. NY R USDCTWD ECF Procedures(2)(f)(iv).

- *Time limit for opening hyperlink.* The hyperlink to filed documents contained in the Notice of Electronic Filing must be opened within fifteen (15) days from the date the document was filed to provide registered users access to the document. The hyperlink expires after fifteen (15) days and users will be unable to access documents for free after that time. Filing Users are encouraged to check their e-mail frequently for notice of filed documents. NY R USDCTWD ECF Procedures(2)(f)(ii).

- *Service on exempted attorneys or pro se litigants who do not have permission to file electronically.* Attorneys granted an exemption from electronically filing documents in the System and pro se litigants who have not been granted permission to electronically file documents are entitled to a paper copy of any electronically filed pleading, document or order. The filing party must therefore provide the non-registered party with the pleading, document or order according to the Federal Rules of Civil Procedure. NY R USDCTWD ECF Procedures(2)(f)(iii).

- *E-mailing or faxing documents.* E-mailing or faxing a pleading or document to any party shall not constitute service of the pleading or document. NY R USDCTWD ECF Procedures(2)(f)(v).

    v. *Using court facilities.* If a local rule so authorizes, a party may use the court's transmission facilities to make service under FRCP 5(b)(2)(E). FRCP 5(b)(3).

  c. *Serving numerous defendants*

    i. *In general.* If an action involves an unusually large number of defendants, the court may, on motion or on its own, order that:

- Defendants' pleadings and replies to them need not be served on other defendants;

- Any crossclaim, counterclaim, avoidance, or affirmative defense in those pleadings and replies to them will be treated as denied or avoided by all other parties; and

- Filing any such pleading and serving it on the plaintiff constitutes notice of the pleading to all parties. FRCP 5(c)(1).

    ii. *Notifying parties.* A copy of every such order must be served on the parties as the court directs. FRCP 5(c)(2).

3. *Pro se actions.* For information on the requirements in pro se actions, refer to NY R USDCTWD Civ Rule 5.2.

4.  *Individual judge practices.* Refer to the Miscellaneous section of this document for information on individual judge practices on filing and serving documents.

## G. Hearings

1.  *Hearings, generally*

    a.  *Oral argument.* Due process does not require that oral argument be permitted on a motion and, except as otherwise provided by local rule, the district court has discretion to determine whether it will decide the motion on the papers or hear argument by counsel (and perhaps receive evidence). FPP § 1190; F.D.I.C. v. Deglau, 207 F.3d 153 (3d Cir. 2000).

        i.  The parties shall appear for oral argument on all motions they make returnable before a Judge on the scheduled return date for the motion. In its discretion, the Court may notify the parties that oral argument shall not be heard on any given motion. Thus, the parties should be prepared to have their motion papers serve as the sole method of argument. NY R USDCTWD Civ Rule 7(c).

    b.  *Providing a regular schedule for oral hearings.* A court may establish regular times and places for oral hearings on motions. FRCP 78(a).

    c.  *Providing for submission on briefs.* By rule or order, the court may provide for submitting and determining motions on briefs, without oral hearings. FRCP 78(b).

2.  *Individual judge practices.* Refer to the Miscellaneous section of this document for information on individual judge practices on hearings.

## H. Forms

1.  **Federal Motion for Leave to Amend Forms**

    a.  Leave to amend complaint; Attaching copy of amendment. 2C FEDFORMS § 14:18.

    b.  Leave to amend complaint; Inserting amendment. 2C FEDFORMS § 14:19.

    c.  Leave to amend complaint; Interlineation. 2C FEDFORMS § 14:20.

    d.  Leave to amend complaint; Responding to motion to dismiss complaint. 2C FEDFORMS § 14:21.

    e.  Leave to amend complaint; Close to trial. 2C FEDFORMS § 14:22.

    f.  Leave to amend complaint; Adding new count. 2C FEDFORMS § 14:24.

    g.  Leave to amend complaint; Asserting lack of knowledge of facts at time of original complaint. 2C FEDFORMS § 14:25.

    h.  Leave to amend complaint; Seeking fourth amendment. 2C FEDFORMS § 14:26.

    i.  Leave to amend complaint; Substituting plaintiff and dropping defendant. 2C FEDFORMS § 14:27.

    j.  Leave to amend answer. 2C FEDFORMS § 14:30.

    k.  Leave to amend answer; With leave endorsed. 2C FEDFORMS § 14:31.

    l.  Leave to amend answer; Correcting errors, deleting and interlining. 2C FEDFORMS § 14:32.

    m.  Leave to amend answer; Adding paragraph. 2C FEDFORMS § 14:33.

    n.  Leave to amend answer; Adding defense. 2C FEDFORMS § 14:34.

    o.  Leave to amend answer; During trial. 2C FEDFORMS § 14:35.

    p.  Defendant's response to motion for leave to amend complaint a fourth time. 2C FEDFORMS § 14:36.

    q.  Motion and notice; For leave to file amended pleading. FEDPROF § 1:222.

    r.  Motion; To amend pleading to conform to findings of master. FEDPROF § 1:223.

    s.  Affidavit; In support of motion for amendment of pleading. FEDPROF § 1:230.

    t.  Opposition; To motion; General form. FEDPROF § 1:750.

    u.  Affidavit; Supporting or opposing motion. FEDPROF § 1:751.

v. Brief; Supporting or opposing motion. FEDPROF § 1:752.

w. Statement of points and authorities; Opposing motion. FEDPROF § 1:753.

x. Motion for leave to amend pleading. GOLDLTGFMS § 14:3.

y. Motion to file second amended complaint on ground of newly discovered evidence. GOLDLTGFMS § 14:20.

z. Motion for leave to file amended answer. GOLDLTGFMS § 14:22.

2. **Forms for the Western District of New York**

a. Certificate of service. NY R USDCTWD ECF Procedures(4a).

## I. Applicable Rules

1. *Federal rules*

a. Serving and filing pleadings and other papers. FRCP 5.

b. Constitutional challenge to a statute; Notice, certification, and intervention. FRCP 5.1.

c. Privacy protection for filings made with the court. FRCP 5.2.

d. Computing and extending time; Time for motion papers. FRCP 6.

e. Pleadings allowed; Form of motions and other papers. FRCP 7.

f. Form of pleadings. FRCP 10.

g. Signing pleadings, motions, and other papers; Representations to the court; Sanctions. FRCP 11.

h. Amended and supplemental pleadings. FRCP 15.

i. Taking testimony. FRCP 43.

j. Hearing motions; Submission on briefs. FRCP 78.

2. *Local rules*

a. Title. NY R USDCTWD Civ Rule 1.1.

b. Filing and serving papers. NY R USDCTWD Civ Rule 5.1.

c. Motion practice. NY R USDCTWD Civ Rule 7.

d. Form of papers. NY R USDCTWD Civ Rule 10.

e. Sanctions. NY R USDCTWD Civ Rule 11.

f. Amending pleadings. NY R USDCTWD Civ Rule 15.

g. Alternative dispute resolution and pretrial conferences. NY R USDCTWD Civ Rule 16.

h. Attorneys of record; Appearance and withdrawal. NY R USDCTWD Civ Rule 83.2.

i. Administrative procedures guide for electronic filing. NY R USDCTWD ECF Procedures.

j. Alternative dispute resolution plan. NY R USDCTWD ADR Plan.

## J. Miscellaneous

**NOTE: Individual judges' rules may apply. For available judge-level information, refer to:**

DISTRICT JUDGE RICHARD J. ARCARA: NY R USDCTWD Arcara-Procedures.

DISTRICT JUDGE FRANK P. GERACI, JR.: NY R USDCTWD Geraci-Procedures.

DISTRICT JUDGE DAVID G. LARIMER: NY R USDCTWD Larimer-Procedures.

DISTRICT JUDGE CHARLES J. SIRAGUSA: NY R USDCTWD Siragusa-Procedures.

DISTRICT JUDGE WILLIAM M. SKRETNY: NY R USDCTWD Skretny--Procedures.

DISTRICT JUDGE MICHAEL A. TELESCA: NY R USDCTWD Telesca-Procedures.

DISTRICT JUDGE LAWRENCE J. VILARDO: NY R USDCTWD Vilardo-Procedures.

DISTRICT JUDGE ELIZABETH A. WOLFORD: NY R USDCTWD Wolford-Procedures.

MAGISTRATE JUDGE JONATHAN W. FELDMAN: NY R USDCTWD Feldman-Procedures.

MAGISTRATE JUDGE LESLIE G. FOSCHIO: NY R USDCTWD Foschio-Procedures; NY R USDCTWD Foschio-Depositions.

MAGISTRATE JUDGE JEREMIAH J. McCARTHY: NY R USDCTWD McCarthy-Procedures.

MAGISTRATE JUDGE MARIAN W. PAYSON: NY R USDCTWD Payson-Procedures.

MAGISTRATE JUDGE MICHAEL J. ROEMER: NY R USDCTWD Roemer-Procedures.

MAGISTRATE JUDGE H. KENNETH SCHROEDER, JR.: NY R USDCTWD Schroeder-Proc.

MAGISTRATE JUDGE HUGH B. SCOTT: NY R USDCTWD Scott-Procedures.

# Motions, Oppositions and Replies
## Motion for Continuance/Extension of Time

### Document Last Updated September 2016

A. **Checklist**

(I) ❑ Matters to be considered by moving party

    (a) ❑ Required documents

        (1) ❑ Notice of motion and motion

        (2) ❑ Supporting affidavit

        (3) ❑ Certificate of service

    (b) ❑ Supplemental documents

        (1) ❑ Memorandum of law

        (2) ❑ Supporting evidence

        (3) ❑ Notice of constitutional question

        (4) ❑ Nongovernmental corporate disclosure statement

        (5) ❑ Copies of authorities

        (6) ❑ Proposed order

        (7) ❑ Paper copy for date-stamping with self-addressed envelope

        (8) ❑ Courtesy copies

    (c) ❑ Timing

        (1) ❑ Continuance: there are no specific timing requirements for moving for a continuance

        (2) ❑ Extension of time: when an act may or must be done within a specified time, the court may, for good cause, extend the time:

            (i) ❑ With or without motion or notice if the court acts, or if a request is made, before the original time or its extension expires; or

            (ii) ❑ On motion made after the time has expired if the party failed to act because of excusable neglect

        (3) ❑ A written motion and notice of the hearing must be served at least fourteen (14) days before the time specified for the hearing, with the following exceptions: (i) when the motion may be heard ex parte; (ii) when the Federal Rules of Civil Procedure set a different time; or (iii) when a court order—which a party may, for good cause, apply for ex parte—sets a different time

        (4) ❑ Any affidavit supporting a motion must be served with the motion

(II) ❏ Matters to be considered by opposing party

    (a) ❏ Required documents

        (1) ❏ Opposition

        (2) ❏ Supporting affidavit

        (3) ❏ Certificate of service

    (b) ❏ Supplemental documents

        (1) ❏ Supporting evidence

        (2) ❏ Notice of constitutional question

        (3) ❏ Copies of authorities

        (4) ❏ Paper copy for date-stamping with self-addressed envelope

        (5) ❏ Courtesy copies

    (c) ❏ Timing

        (1) ❏ After a motion is filed, the court may issue an order setting deadlines for filing and service of opposing papers; if the court does not set deadlines by order, the opposing party shall have fourteen (14) days after service of the motion to file and serve responding papers

        (2) ❏ Except as FRCP 59(c) provides otherwise, any opposing affidavit must be served at least seven (7) days before the hearing, unless the court permits service at another time

## B. Timing

1. *Motion for continuance/extension of time*

    a. *Continuance.* There are no specific timing requirements for moving for a continuance.

    b. *Extension of time.* When an act may or must be done within a specified time, the court may, for good cause, extend the time:

        i. With or without motion or notice if the court acts, or if a request is made, before the original time or its extension expires; or

        ii. On motion made after the time has expired if the party failed to act because of excusable neglect. FRCP 6(b)(1).

2. *Timing of motions, generally*

    a. *Motion and notice of hearing.* A written motion and notice of the hearing must be served at least fourteen (14) days before the time specified for the hearing, with the following exceptions:

        i. When the motion may be heard ex parte;

        ii. When the Federal Rules of Civil Procedure set a different time; or

        iii. When a court order—which a party may, for good cause, apply for ex parte—sets a different time. FRCP 6(c)(1).

    b. *Supporting affidavit.* Any affidavit supporting a motion must be served with the motion. FRCP 6(c)(2).

3. *Timing of opposing papers.* After a motion is filed, the Court may issue an order setting deadlines for filing and service of opposing papers. NY R USDCTWD Civ Rule 7(b)(1). If the Court does not set deadlines by order, the following schedule shall apply: the opposing party shall have fourteen (14) days after service of the motion to file and serve responding papers. NY R USDCTWD Civ Rule 7(b)(2)(B).

    a. *Opposing affidavit.* Except as FRCP 59(c) provides otherwise, any opposing affidavit must be served at least seven (7) days before the hearing, unless the court permits service at another time. FRCP 6(c)(2).

4. *Timing of reply papers.* Where the respondent files an answering affidavit setting up a new matter, the moving party ordinarily is allowed a reasonable time to file a reply affidavit since failure to deny the new matter by affidavit may operate as an admission of its truth. AMJUR MOTIONS § 25.

    a. *Reply papers.* After a motion is filed, the Court may issue an order setting deadlines. . .for filing and service of reply papers if the moving party has stated an intent to reply. NY R USDCTWD Civ Rule 7(b)(1). If the Court does not set deadlines by order, the following schedule shall apply: the moving party shall have seven (7) days after service of the responding papers to file and serve reply papers. NY R USDCTWD Civ Rule 7(b)(2)(B).

5. *Motion for an expedited hearing.* A party seeking to shorten the schedule prescribed in NY R USDCTWD Civ Rule 7(b) must make a separate motion for an expedited hearing, setting forth the reasons why an expedited hearing is required. NY R USDCTWD Civ Rule 7(d)(1). For more information, refer to NY R USDCTWD Civ Rule 7(d)(1).

6. *Computation of time*

   a. *Computing time.* FRCP 6 applies in computing any time period specified in the Federal Rules of Civil Procedure, in any local rule or court order, or in any statute that does not specify a method of computing time. FRCP 6(a).

      i. *Period stated in days or a longer unit.* When the period is stated in days or a longer unit of time:
         - Exclude the day of the event that triggers the period;
         - Count every day, including intermediate Saturdays, Sundays, and legal holidays; and
         - Include the last day of the period, but if the last day is a Saturday, Sunday, or legal holiday, the period continues to run until the end of the next day that is not a Saturday, Sunday, or legal holiday. FRCP 6(a)(1).

      ii. *Period stated in hours.* When the period is stated in hours:
         - Begin counting immediately on the occurrence of the event that triggers the period;
         - Count every hour, including hours during intermediate Saturdays, Sundays, and legal holidays; and
         - If the period would end on a Saturday, Sunday, or legal holiday, the period continues to run until the same time on the next day that is not a Saturday, Sunday, or legal holiday. FRCP 6(a)(2).

      iii. *Inaccessibility of the clerk's office.* Unless the court orders otherwise, if the clerk's office is inaccessible:
         - On the last day for filing under FRCP 6(a)(1), then the time for filing is extended to the first accessible day that is not a Saturday, Sunday, or legal holiday; or
         - During the last hour for filing under FRCP 6(a)(2), then the time for filing is extended to the same time on the first accessible day that is not a Saturday, Sunday, or legal holiday. FRCP 6(a)(3).

      iv. *"Last day" defined.* Unless a different time is set by a statute, local rule, or court order, the last day ends:
         - For electronic filing, at midnight in the court's time zone; and
         - For filing by other means, when the clerk's office is scheduled to close. FRCP 6(a)(4).

      v. *"Next day" defined.* The "next day" is determined by continuing to count forward when the period is measured after an event and backward when measured before an event. FRCP 6(a)(5).

      vi. *"Legal holiday" defined.* "Legal holiday" means:
         - The day set aside by statute for observing New Year's Day, Martin Luther King Jr.'s Birthday, Washington's Birthday, Memorial Day, Independence Day, Labor Day, Columbus Day, Veterans' Day, Thanksgiving Day, or Christmas Day;
         - Any day declared a holiday by the President or Congress; and
         - For periods that are measured after an event, any other day declared a holiday by the state where the district court is located. FRCP 6(a)(6).

   b. *Computation of electronic filing deadlines.* A document will be deemed timely filed if filed prior to midnight Eastern Time, unless otherwise ordered by the Court. A document will be considered untimely if filed thereafter. When a Court order requires that a document be filed on a weekend or holiday, the document may be filed by close of business the next business day without further application to the Court. NY R USDCTWD ECF Procedures(2)(e)(i). A document filed electronically is deemed filed on the date and time stated on the Notice of Electronic Filing. NY R USDCTWD ECF Procedures(2)(e)(ii).

    i.   *System availability.* Although parties may file documents electronically twenty-four (24) hours a day, registered users are strongly encouraged to file all documents during normal working hours of the Clerk's Office (8:30 a.m. to 5:00 p.m. Eastern Time). NY R USDCTWD ECF Procedures(2)(t)(i).

    ii.  *Technical failures.* A Filing User whose filing is made untimely as a result of a technical failure must seek appropriate relief from the Court. NY R USDCTWD ECF Procedures(2)(u)(i).

  c.  *Extending time.* Refer to the General Requirements section of this document for information on extending time.

  d.  *Additional time after certain kinds of service.* When a party may or must act within a specified time after service and service is made under FRCP 5(b)(2)(C), FRCP 5(b)(2)(D), FRCP 5(b)(2)(E), or FRCP 5(b)(2)(F), three (3) days are added after the period would otherwise expire under FRCP 6(a). FRCP 6(d).

    i.   *Service by overnight delivery.* Where a period of time prescribed by either the Federal Rules of Civil Procedure or the Local Rules of Civil Procedure for the United States District Court for the Western District of New York is measured from the service of a paper and service is by overnight delivery, one (1) business day shall be added to the prescribed period. NY R USDCTWD Civ Rule 5.1(g).

7.  *Individual judge practices.* Refer to the Miscellaneous section of this document for information on individual judge practices on timing of documents.

## C.  General Requirements

1.  *Motions, generally*

  a.  *Requirements.* A request for a court order must be made by motion. The motion must:

    i.   Be in writing unless made during a hearing or trial;

    ii.  State with particularity the grounds for seeking the order; and

    iii. State the relief sought. FRCP 7(b)(1).

  b.  *Notice of motion.* A party interested in resisting the relief sought by a motion has a right to notice thereof, and an opportunity to be heard. AMJUR MOTIONS § 12.

    i.   In addition to statutory or court rule provisions requiring notice of a motion—the purpose of such a notice requirement having been said to be to prevent a party from being prejudicially surprised by a motion—principles of natural justice dictate that an adverse party generally must be given notice that a motion will be presented to the court. AMJUR MOTIONS § 12.

    ii.  "Notice," in this regard, means reasonable notice, including a meaningful opportunity to prepare and to defend against allegations of a motion. AMJUR MOTIONS § 12.

  c.  *Writing requirement.* The writing requirement is intended to insure that the adverse parties are informed and have a record of both the motion's pendency and the grounds on which the movant seeks an order. FPP § 1191; Feldberg v. Quechee Lakes Corp., 463 F.3d 195 (2d Cir. 2006).

    i.   It is sufficient "if the motion is stated in a written notice of the hearing of the motion." FPP § 1191.

  d.  *Particularity requirement.* The particularity requirement insures that the opposing parties will have notice of their opponent's contentions. FEDPROC § 62:364; Goodman v. 1973 26 Foot Trojan Vessel, Arkansas Registration No. AR1439SN, 859 F.2d 71, 12 Fed.R.Serv.3d 645 (8th Cir. 1988). That requirement ensures that notice of the basis for the motion is provided to the court and to the opposing party so as to avoid prejudice, provide the opponent with a meaningful opportunity to respond, and provide the court with enough information to process the motion correctly. FEDPROC § 62:364; Andreas v. Volkswagen of America, Inc., 336 F.3d 789, 56 Fed.R.Serv.3d 6 (8th Cir. 2003).

    i.    Reasonable specification of the grounds for a motion is sufficient. However, where a movant fails to state even one ground for granting the motion in question, the movant has failed to meet the minimal standard of "reasonable specification." FEDPROC § 62:364; Martinez v. Trainor, 556 F.2d 818, 23 Fed.R.Serv.2d 403 (7th Cir. 1977).

    ii.    The court may excuse the failure to comply with the particularity requirement if it is inadvertent, and where no prejudice is shown by the opposing party. FEDPROC § 62:364.

2.   *Motion for continuance/extension of time*

    a.   *Continuance.* Absent a controlling statute, the grant or denial of a continuance rests in the discretion of the trial judge to whom application is made, taking into consideration not only the facts of the particular case but also all of the demands on counsel's time and the court's. FEDPROC § 77:28; Star Financial Services, Inc. v. AASTAR Mortg. Corp., 89 F.3d 5 (1st Cir. 1996); Streber v. Hunter, 221 F.3d 701, 55 Fed.R.Evid.Serv. 376 (5th Cir. 2000). The grounds upon which a continuance is sought may include the following:

    i.    Unpreparedness of a party. FEDPROC § 77:29; U.S. v. 110 Bars of Silver, 3 Crucibles of Silver, 11 Bags of Silver Coins, 508 F.2d 799 (5th Cir. 1975).

    ii.    Absence of a party. FEDPROC § 77:29. Since it is generally recognized that a party to a civil action ordinarily has a right to attend the trial, an illness severe enough to prevent a party from appearing in court is always a legitimate ground for asking for a continuance. FEDPROC § 77:30; Davis v. Operation Amigo, Inc., 378 F.2d 101 (10th Cir. 1967). However, the failure of the moving party to produce any competent medical evidence of the reasons and necessities for the party's unavailability will result in the denial of the continuance. FEDPROC § 77:30; Weisman v. Alleco, Inc., 925 F.2d 77 (4th Cir. 1991). Some courts, moreover, require a showing that the party has some particular contribution to make to the trial as a material witness or otherwise before granting a continuance due to the party's illness. FEDPROC § 77:30; Johnston v. Harris County Flood Control Dist., 869 F.2d 1565 (5th Cir. 1989).

    iii.    Absence of counsel. FEDPROC § 77:29. The courts have shown greater leniency when the illness of counsel is the ground for the continuance, especially where the case presents complex issues. FEDPROC § 77:31; Smith-Weik Machinery Corp. v. Murdock Mach. & Engineering Co., 423 F.2d 842 (5th Cir. 1970). However, many courts do not favor the granting of a continuance where counsel is unavailable due to a claimed engagement elsewhere or where it is not clear that counsel's illness was genuine. FEDPROC § 77:31; Community Nat. Life Ins. Co. v. Parker Square Sav. & Loan Ass'n, 406 F.2d 603 (10th Cir. 1969); Williams v. Johanns, 518 F.Supp.2d 205 (D.D.C. 2007).

    iv.    Absence of a witness or evidence. FEDPROC § 77:29. The moving party must show. . .that the witness's testimony would be competent and material and that there are no other witnesses who can establish the same facts. FEDPROC § 77:32; Krodel v. Houghtaling, 468 F.2d 887 (4th Cir. 1972); Vitarelle v. Long Island R. Co., 415 F.2d 302 (2d Cir. 1969).

    v.    Surprise and prejudice. FEDPROC § 77:29. The action complained of should not be one which could have been anticipated by due diligence or of which the movant had actual notice. FEDPROC § 77:33; Communications Maintenance, Inc. v. Motorola, Inc., 761 F.2d 1202, 2 Fed.R.Serv.3d 126 (7th Cir. 1985). Surprise and prejudice are often claimed as a result of the court allowing the other party to amend its pleadings under FRCP 15(b). FEDPROC § 77:29.

    vi.    In determining whether to grant a continuance, the court will consider a variety of factors, including:

        • Good faith on the part of the moving party;

        • Due diligence of the moving party;

        • The likelihood that the need prompting the request for a continuance will be met if the continuance is granted;

- Inconvenience to the court and the nonmoving party, including the witnesses, if the continuance is granted;

- Possible harm to the moving party if the continuance is denied;

- Prior delays in the proceedings;

- The court's prior refusal to grant the opposing party a continuance;

- Judicial economy. FEDPROC § 77:29; Amarin Plastics, Inc. v. Maryland Cup Corp., 946 F.2d 147, 34 Fed.R.Evid.Serv. 528 (1st Cir. 1991); Lewis v. Rawson, 564 F.3d 569 (2d Cir. 2009); U.S. v. 2.61 Acres of Land, More or Less, Situated in Mariposa County, State of Cal., 791 F.2d 666 (9th Cir. 1985); In re Homestore.com, Inc. Securities Litigation, 347 F.Supp.2d 814 (C.D.Cal. 2004).

b. *Extension of time.* When an act may or must be done within a specified time, the court may, for good cause, extend the time:

    i. *Before original time or its extension expires.* With or without motion or notice if the court acts, or if a request is made, before the original time or its extension expires. FRCP 6(b)(1)(A).

- An application for the enlargement of time under FRCP 6(b)(1)(A) normally will be granted in the absence of bad faith on the part of the party seeking relief or prejudice to the adverse party. FPP § 1165.

- Neither a formal motion for enlargement nor notice to the adverse party is expressly required by FRCP 6(b). FPP § 1165.

    ii. *After the time has expired.* On motion made after the time has expired if the party failed to act because of excusable neglect. FRCP 6(b)(1)(B).

- *Excusable neglect.* Excusable neglect is intended and has proven to be quite elastic in its application. In essence it is an equitable concept that must take account of all relevant circumstances of the party's failure to act within the required time. FPP § 1165.

- *Burden.* The burden is on the movant to establish that the failure to act in a timely manner was the result of excusable neglect. FEDPROC § 77:5. Common sense indicates that among the most important factors are the possibility of prejudice to the other parties, the length of the applicant's delay and its impact on the proceeding, the reason for the delay and whether it was within the control of the movant, and whether the movant has acted in good faith. FPP § 1165; Kettle Range Conservation Group v. U.S. Forest Service, 8 Fed.Appx. 729 (9th Cir. 2001).

- *Motion required.* No relief may be granted under FRCP 6(b)(1)(B) after the expiration of the specified period, even though the failure to act may have been the result of excusable neglect, if no motion is made by the party who failed to act. FEDPROC § 77:3.

    iii. *Exceptions.* A court must not extend the time to act under FRCP 50(b), FRCP 50(d), FRCP 52(b), FRCP 59(b), FRCP 59(d), FRCP 59(e), and FRCP 60(b). FRCP 6(b)(2). FRCP 6(b) does not require the district courts to extend a time period where the extension would contravene a local court rule and does not apply to periods of time that are definitely fixed by statute. FEDPROC § 77:4; Truncale v. Universal Pictures Co., 82 F.Supp. 576 (S.D.N.Y. 1949); Lusk v. Lyon Metal Products, 9 F.R.D. 250 (W.D.Mo. 1949).

3. *Opposing papers.* The Federal Rules of Civil Procedure do not require any formal answer, return, or reply to a motion, except where the Federal Rules of Civil Procedure or local rules may require affidavits, memoranda, or other papers to be filed in opposition to a motion. Such papers are simply to apprise the court of such opposition and the grounds of that opposition. FEDPROC § 62:359.

a. *Effect of failure to respond to motion.* Although in the absence of statutory provision or court rule, a motion ordinarily does not require a written answer, when a party files a motion and the opposing party fails to respond, the court may construe such failure to respond as nonopposition to the motion or an admission that the motion was meritorious, may take the facts alleged in the motion as true—the rule in some jurisdictions being that the failure to respond to a fact set forth in a motion is deemed an admission—and may grant the motion if the relief requested appears to be justified. AMJUR MOTIONS § 28.

b. *Assent or no opposition not determinative.* However, a motion will not be granted automatically simply because an "assent" or a notation of "no opposition" has been filed; federal judges frequently deny motions that have been assented to when it is thought that justice so dictates. FPP § 1190.

c. *Responsive pleading inappropriate as response to motion.* An attempt to answer or oppose a motion with a responsive pleading usually is not appropriate. FPP § 1190.

4. *Reply papers.* A moving party may be required or permitted to prepare papers in addition to his original motion papers. AMJUR MOTIONS § 25. Papers answering or replying to opposing papers may be appropriate, in the interests of justice, where it appears there is a substantial reason for allowing a reply. Thus, a court may accept reply papers where a party demonstrates that the papers to which it seeks to file a reply raise new issues that are material to the disposition of the question before the court, or where the court determines, sua sponte, that it wishes further briefing of an issue raised in those papers and orders the submission of additional papers. FEDPROC § 62:360.

   a. *Function of reply papers.* The function of a reply affidavit is to answer the arguments made in opposition to the position taken by the movant and not to permit the movant to introduce new arguments in support of the motion. AMJUR MOTIONS § 25.

   b. *Issues raised for the first time in a reply document.* However, the view has been followed in some jurisdictions, that as a matter of judicial economy, where there is no prejudice and where the issues could be raised simply by filing a motion to dismiss, the trial court has discretion to consider arguments raised for the first time in a reply memorandum, and that a trial court may grant a motion to strike issues raised for the first time in a reply memorandum. AMJUR MOTIONS § 26.

5. *Sur-reply.* Absent permission of the Judge hearing the motion, sur-reply papers are not permitted. NY R USDCTWD Civ Rule 7(a)(6).

6. *Motion to settle an order.* When counsel are unable to agree on the form of a proposed order, the prevailing party may move, upon seven (7) days notice to all parties, to settle the order. The Court may award costs and attorney's fees against an attorney if it determines that the attorney's unreasonable conduct necessitated bringing the motion. NY R USDCTWD Civ Rule 7(d)(2).

7. *Notice of appearance.* No notice of appearance is required of an attorney whose name and address appear at the end of a complaint, notice of removal, pre-answer motion, or answer. In all other circumstances, an attorney appearing for a party in a civil case shall promptly file a written notice of appearance. NY R USDCTWD Civ Rule 83.2(b). For more information on appearances and withdrawals, refer to NY R USDCTWD Civ Rule 83.2.

8. *Related cases.* Each attorney appearing in a civil case has a continuing duty to promptly notify the Clerk of Court when the attorney has reason to believe that said case is related to some other pending civil or criminal action(s) such that their assignment to the same Judge would avoid unnecessary duplication of judicial effort. As soon as the attorney becomes aware of such a relationship, the attorney shall notify the Clerk of Court by letter of the relevant facts, and the Clerk of Court will transmit that notification to the Judges to whom the cases have been assigned. NY R USDCTWD Civ Rule 5.1(e).

9. *Alternative dispute resolution (ADR).* This Court has adopted an Alternative Dispute Resolution Plan ("ADR"), as implemented by Standing Order (NY R USDCTWD ADR Plan), under which certain civil cases are referred automatically to ADR upon filing. NY R USDCTWD Civ Rule 16(a). The United States District Court for the Western District of New York (the "Court") adopted the ADR Plan on January 1, 2006 (the "Effective Date"), to make available to civil litigants court-administered ADR interventions and processes designed to provide quicker, less expensive and potentially more satisfying alternatives to continuing litigation, without impairing the quality of justice or the right to trial. NY R USDCTWD ADR Plan(1)(1.2)(A).

   a. *Scope.* This ADR Plan (NY R USDCTWD ADR Plan) applies to civil actions pending or commenced on and after the Effective Date, except as otherwise indicated in NY R USDCTWD ADR Plan. The ADR Plan supplements the Local Rules of Civil Procedure for the United States District Court for the Western District of New York, which shall remain in full effect for all cases. NY R USDCTWD ADR Plan(1)(1.2)(B).

   b. *Referral to ADR*

      i. *New cases.* All civil cases filed on and after the Effective Date of the ADR Plan shall be referred automatically for ADR. NY R USDCTWD ADR Plan(2)(2.1)(A). Notice of the ADR require-ments will be provided to all parties immediately upon the filing of a complaint and answer or a notice of removal; NY R USDCTWD ADR Plan(2)(2.1)(A); NY R USDCTWD Civ Rule 16(a). ADR intervention will be scheduled at the conference held pursuant to Local Rule of Civil Procedure 16.1. NY R USDCTWD ADR Plan(2)(2.1)(A). [Editor's note: the reference to Local Rule of Civil Procedure 16.1 is likely meant to be a reference to NY R USDCTWD Civ Rule 16(b)].

- Litigants in cases not referred automatically to ADR must consider possible agreement to the use of an ADR process. NY R USDCTWD Civ Rule 16(a).

- For a list of exemptions from automatic referral, refer to NY R USDCTWD ADR Plan(2)(2.1)(A).

ii. *Pending cases.* The assigned Judge on any pending civil case may, sua sponte or with status conference, issue an order referring the case for ADR. NY R USDCTWD ADR Plan(2)(2.1)(B); NY R USDCTWD Civ Rule 16(a). The order shall specify a date on which the ADR intervention is to be completed. NY R USDCTWD ADR Plan(2)(2.1)(B).

iii. *Stipulation.* A case may be referred for ADR by stipulation of all parties. Stipulations shall be filed and shall designate the specific ADR intervention the parties have selected, the time frame within which the ADR process will be completed and the selected Neutral. Stipulations are presumed acceptable unless the assigned Judge determines that the interests of justice are not served. NY R USDCTWD ADR Plan(2)(2.1)(C).

iv. *Relief from ADR referral*

- *Opting out motions.* Any party may file, with the assigned Judge for that case, a motion to opt out of, or for relief from, ADR. NY R USDCTWD ADR Plan(2)(2.2)(A).

- *Motion.* Opting Out Motions must be made within fourteen (14) days from (1) the date of the first discovery conference under Local Rule 16.1 in new cases, or (2) the date of a sua sponte ADR Referral Order in pending cases. NY R USDCTWD ADR Plan(2)(2.2)(B). [Editor's note: the reference to Local Rule 16.1 is likely meant to be a reference to NY R USDCTWD Civ Rule 16(b)].

- *Criteria.* Opting Out Motions shall be granted only for "good cause" shown. Inconve-nience, travel costs, attorney fees or other costs shall not constitute "good cause." A party seeking relief from ADR must set forth the reasons why ADR has no reasonable chance of being productive. NY R USDCTWD ADR Plan(2)(2.2)(C).

- *Judicial initiative.* The assigned Judge may, sua sponte, exempt any case from the Court's ADR Plan. NY R USDCTWD ADR Plan(2)(2.2)(D).

c. *ADR interventions*

i. *Options.* It is expected that cases referred for ADR will proceed to Mediation. However, the following options are also available upon the stipulation of all parties:

- Neutral Evaluation;

- Mini Summary Trial;

- Arbitration (Binding and Non-Binding);

- Case Valuation; and

- Settlement Week, when scheduled by the Court. NY R USDCTWD ADR Plan(4)(4.1)(A).

ii. *Timing.* Timing is specific to the intervention and process chosen, as set forth in the correspond-ing sections in NY R USDCTWD ADR Plan. NY R USDCTWD ADR Plan(4)(4.1)(B).

iii. *Scheduling.* The referral of a case to ADR does not delay or defer other dates established in the Scheduling Order and has no effect on the scheduled progress of the case toward trial. NY R USDCTWD ADR Plan(4)(4.1)(C).

d. *Selecting an ADR intervention*

i. *New cases.* Prior to the Local Rule 16.1 scheduling conference, counsel and any unrepresented parties shall confer about ADR as part of their discussion of "the possibilities for a prompt settlement or resolution of the case" pursuant to FRCP 26(f). Unless the parties agree to a different intervention, it is presumed that they will participate in mediation. [Editor's note: the reference to Local Rule 16.1 is likely meant to be a reference to NY R USDCTWD Civ Rule 16(b)].

    ii.   *Pending cases.* In pending cases, all sua sponte referrals will be to mediation. Should the parties agree that a different ADR intervention is more appropriate to their case, they may submit a stipulation designating the specific ADR intervention selected, the time frame within which the ADR process will be completed and the identity of the Neutral. Stipulations must be filed within fourteen (14) days from the date of the ADR Referral Order and are presumed acceptable unless the assigned Judge determines that the interests of justice are not served. NY R USDCTWD ADR Plan(4)(4.2)(B).

  e.  For more information on alternative dispute resolution (ADR), refer to NY R USDCTWD ADR Plan.

10.  *Sanctions.* Failure of counsel for any party, or a party proceeding pro se, to appear before the Court at a conference, to complete the necessary preparations, or to be prepared to proceed to trial at the set time may be considered an abandonment of the case or a failure to prosecute or defend diligently. An appropriate order for sanctions may be entered against the defaulting party with respect to either a specific issue or the entire case. NY R USDCTWD Civ Rule 11(a). For more information, refer to NY R USDCTWD Civ Rule 11.

11.  *Pro se actions.* For information on the requirements in pro se actions, refer to NY R USDCTWD Civ Rule 5.2.

12.  *Individual judge practices.* Refer to the Miscellaneous section of this document for information on individual judge practices on general requirements for documents.

## D. Documents

1.  *Documents for moving party*

  a.  *Required documents*

    i.   *Notice of motion and motion.* A notice of motion is required for all motions, and must state: the relief sought, the grounds for the request, the papers submitted in support, and the return date for the motion, if known. A moving party who intends to file and serve reply papers must so state in the notice of motion. NY R USDCTWD Civ Rule 7(a)(1). Refer to the General Requirements section of this document for information on the notice of motion and motion.

    ii.  *Supporting affidavit.* An affidavit must not contain legal arguments, but must contain factual and procedural background relevant to the motion it supports. Except for motions brought under FRCP 12(b)(1) (lack of subject matter jurisdiction), FRCP 12(b)(6) (failure to state a claim), FRCP 12(c) (judgment on the pleadings), and FRCP 12(f) (to strike), motions and opposition to motions shall be supported by at least one (1) affidavit and by such other evidence (i.e., deposition testimony, interrogatory answers, admissions, and documents) as appropriate to resolve the particular motion. Failure to comply with this requirement may constitute grounds for resolving the motion against the non-complying party. NY R USDCTWD Civ Rule 7(a)(3).

    iii.  *Certificate of service.* FRCP 5(d) requires that the person making service under FRCP 5 certify that service has been effected. FRCP 5(Advisory Committee Notes). Having such information on file may be useful for many purposes, including proof of service if an issue arises concerning the effectiveness of the service. FRCP 5(Advisory Committee Notes). The Notice of Electronic Filing effectuates service for all registered users and no certificate of service is required when all filers on an action are Registered Users. The following exemptions require a certificate of service to be filed:

       •  When a document is manually filed, a certificate of service must be filed stating the manner in which service or notice was accomplished on each party so entitled. NY R USDCTWD ECF Procedures(2)(f)(iv).

- When a pro se filer (who isn't authorized to electronically file documents) is a party, a certificate of service must be filed stating the manner in which service or notice was accomplished on the pro se party. The Notice of Electronic Filing effectuates service for the Registered Users in this situation and it is not necessary to note service on those parties. A non-registered pro se filer is required to file certificates of service on all documents they file. NY R USDCTWD ECF Procedures(2)(f)(iv).

- If an attorney is exempt from electronic service, a certificate of service must be filed stating the manner in which service or notice was accomplished on the exempt attorney. The Notice of Electronic Filing effectuates service for the Registered Users in this situation and it is not necessary to note service on those parties. NY R USDCTWD ECF Procedures(2)(f)(iv).

b. *Supplemental documents*

    i. *Memorandum of law.* Nothing in the Local Rules of Civil Procedure for the United States District Court for the Western District of New York precludes a moving party from filing a memorandum in support of a motion made other than pursuant to FRCP 12, FRCP 56 or FRCP 65(a). The Court, in its discretion, may require written memoranda on such other motions. NY R USDCTWD Civ Rule 7(a)(2)(B). Refer to the Format section of this document for the formatting requirements for memoranda of law.

    ii. *Supporting evidence.* When a motion relies on facts outside the record, the court may hear the matter on affidavits or may hear it wholly or partly on oral testimony or on depositions. FRCP 43(c). A party seeking or opposing any relief under the Federal Rules of Civil Procedure shall file only the portion(s) of a deposition, interrogatory, request for documents, request for admission, or other supporting material that is pertinent to the application. NY R USDCTWD Civ Rule 7(a)(4).

    iii. *Notice of constitutional question.* A party that files a pleading, written motion, or other paper drawing into question the constitutionality of a federal or state statute must promptly:

- *File notice.* File a notice of constitutional question stating the question and identifying the paper that raises it, if: (1) a federal statute is questioned and the parties do not include the United States, one of its agencies, or one of its officers or employees in an official capacity; or (2) a state statute is questioned and the parties do not include the state, one of its agencies, or one of its officers or employees in an official capacity; and

- *Serve notice.* Serve the notice and paper on the Attorney General of the United States if a federal statute is questioned—or on the state attorney general if a state statute is questioned—either by certified or registered mail or by sending it to an electronic address designated by the attorney general for this purpose. FRCP 5.1(a).

- *No forfeiture.* A party's failure to file and serve the notice, or the court's failure to certify, does not forfeit a constitutional claim or defense that is otherwise timely asserted. FRCP 5.1(d).

    iv. *Nongovernmental corporate disclosure statement*

- *Contents.* A nongovernmental corporate party must file two (2) copies of a disclosure statement that: (1) identifies any parent corporation and any publicly held corporation owning ten percent (10%) or more of its stock; or (2) states that there is no such corporation. FRCP 7.1(a).

- *Time to file; Supplemental filing.* A party must: (1) file the disclosure statement with its first appearance, pleading, petition, motion, response, or other request addressed to the court; and (2) promptly file a supplemental statement if any required information changes. FRCP 7.1(b).

    v. *Copies of authorities.* In cases involving a pro se litigant, counsel shall, when serving a memorandum of law (or other submissions to the Court), provide the pro se litigant (but not other counsel or the Court) with printed copies of decisions cited therein that are unreported or reported exclusively on computerized databases. NY R USDCTWD Civ Rule 7(a)(8).

vi. *Proposed order.* All proposed orders must be submitted in a format compatible with WordPerfect or Microsoft Word format, which is a "Save As" option in most word processing software. Judges will not accept proposed orders in PDF format. NY R USDCTWD ECF Procedures(2)(j)(ii). Proposed orders should be attached to an Internet e-mail sent to the e-mail address of the assigned judge. NY R USDCTWD ECF Procedures(2)(j)(i). For the list of email addresses for the judges, refer to NY R USDCTWD ECF Procedures(2)(j)(i).

vii. *Paper copy for date-stamping with self-addressed envelope.* Parties requesting date-stamped copies of filed documents must provide a paper copy for date-stamping, and a self-addressed, adequately-sized envelope with proper postage affixed. NY R USDCTWD Civ Rule 5.1(d).

viii. *Courtesy copies.* The Court may, in its discretion, request courtesy copies on any other motion. NY R USDCTWD Civ Rule 7(a)(7). Courtesy copies of certain documents may be required. Filers should refer to the "Judge Preferences" published on the Court's website. NY R USDCTWD ECF Procedures(2)(a)(iii).

2. *Documents for opposing party*

  a. *Required documents*

    i. *Opposition.* Refer to the General Requirements section of this document for information on the opposing papers.

    ii. *Supporting affidavit.* An affidavit must not contain legal arguments, but must contain factual and procedural background relevant to the motion it supports. Except for motions brought under FRCP 12(b)(1) (lack of subject matter jurisdiction), FRCP 12(b)(6) (failure to state a claim), FRCP 12(c) (judgment on the pleadings), and FRCP 12(f) (to strike), motions and opposition to motions shall be supported by at least one (1) affidavit and by such other evidence (i.e., deposition testimony, interrogatory answers, admissions, and documents) as appropriate to resolve the particular motion. Failure to comply with this requirement may constitute grounds for resolving the motion against the non-complying party. NY R USDCTWD Civ Rule 7(a)(3).

    iii. *Certificate of service.* FRCP 5(d) requires that the person making service under FRCP 5 certify that service has been effected. FRCP 5(Advisory Committee Notes). Having such information on file may be useful for many purposes, including proof of service if an issue arises concerning the effectiveness of the service. FRCP 5(Advisory Committee Notes). The Notice of Electronic Filing effectuates service for all registered users and no certificate of service is required when all filers on an action are Registered Users. The following exemptions require a certificate of service to be filed:

- When a document is manually filed, a certificate of service must be filed stating the manner in which service or notice was accomplished on each party so entitled. NY R USDCTWD ECF Procedures(2)(f)(iv).

- When a pro se filer (who isn't authorized to electronically file documents) is a party, a certificate of service must be filed stating the manner in which service or notice was accomplished on the pro se party. The Notice of Electronic Filing effectuates service for the Registered Users in this situation and it is not necessary to note service on those parties. A non-registered pro se filer is required to file certificates of service on all documents they file. NY R USDCTWD ECF Procedures(2)(f)(iv).

- If an attorney is exempt from electronic service, a certificate of service must be filed stating the manner in which service or notice was accomplished on the exempt attorney. The Notice of Electronic Filing effectuates service for the Registered Users in this situation and it is not necessary to note service on those parties. NY R USDCTWD ECF Procedures(2)(f)(iv).

  b. *Supplemental documents*

    i. *Supporting evidence.* When a motion relies on facts outside the record, the court may hear the matter on affidavits or may hear it wholly or partly on oral testimony or on depositions. FRCP 43(c). A party seeking or opposing any relief under the Federal Rules of Civil Procedure shall file only the portion(s) of a deposition, interrogatory, request for documents, request for admission, or other supporting material that is pertinent to the application. NY R USDCTWD Civ Rule 7(a)(4).

ii. *Notice of constitutional question.* A party that files a pleading, written motion, or other paper drawing into question the constitutionality of a federal or state statute must promptly:

- *File notice.* File a notice of constitutional question stating the question and identifying the paper that raises it, if: (1) a federal statute is questioned and the parties do not include the United States, one of its agencies, or one of its officers or employees in an official capacity; or (2) a state statute is questioned and the parties do not include the state, one of its agencies, or one of its officers or employees in an official capacity; and

- *Serve notice.* Serve the notice and paper on the Attorney General of the United States if a federal statute is questioned—or on the state attorney general if a state statute is questioned—either by certified or registered mail or by sending it to an electronic address designated by the attorney general for this purpose. FRCP 5.1(a).

- *No forfeiture.* A party's failure to file and serve the notice, or the court's failure to certify, does not forfeit a constitutional claim or defense that is otherwise timely asserted. FRCP 5.1(d).

iii. *Copies of authorities.* In cases involving a pro se litigant, counsel shall, when serving a memorandum of law (or other submissions to the Court), provide the pro se litigant (but not other counsel or the Court) with printed copies of decisions cited therein that are unreported or reported exclusively on computerized databases. NY R USDCTWD Civ Rule 7(a)(8).

iv. *Paper copy for date-stamping with self-addressed envelope.* Parties requesting date-stamped copies of filed documents must provide a paper copy for date-stamping, and a self-addressed, adequately-sized envelope with proper postage affixed. NY R USDCTWD Civ Rule 5.1(d).

v. *Courtesy copies.* Courtesy copies of certain documents may be required. Filers should refer to the "Judge Preferences" published on the Court's website. NY R USDCTWD ECF Procedures(2)(a)(iii).

3. *Individual judge practices.* Refer to the Miscellaneous section of this document for information on individual judge practices on required documents.

## E. Format

1. *Form of documents.* The rules governing captions and other matters of form in pleadings apply to motions and other papers. FRCP 7(b)(2).

   a. *Form, generally.* All pleadings, motions, and other papers that a party presents for filing, whether in paper form or in electronic form, shall meet the following requirements:

   i. *Font size.* All text and footnotes shall be in a font size of at least twelve (12) point type. NY R USDCTWD Civ Rule 10(a)(1).

   ii. *Spacing.* All text in the body of the document must be double-spaced, except that text in block quotations and footnotes may be single-spaced. NY R USDCTWD Civ Rule 10(a)(2).

   - Extensive footnotes and block quotes may not be used to circumvent page limitations. NY R USDCTWD Civ Rule 10(a)(3).

   iii. *Margins.* Documents must have one (1) inch margins on all four sides. NY R USDCTWD Civ Rule 10(a)(4).

   iv. *Page numbering.* Pages must be consecutively numbered. NY R USDCTWD Civ Rule 10(a)(5).

   b. *Additional requirements for paper filing.* Documents presented for filing in paper form shall meet the following additional requirements:

   i. *Paper.* Documents must be on durable white eight and one-half by eleven (8-1/2 x 11) inch paper of good quality. NY R USDCTWD Civ Rule 10(b)(1).

   - All documents must be single-sided. NY R USDCTWD Civ Rule 10(b)(5).

    ii.   *Text.* All text must be plainly and legibly written, typewritten, printed or reproduced. NY R USDCTWD Civ Rule 10(b)(2).

    iii.  *Ink.* Documents must be in black or blue ink. NY R USDCTWD Civ Rule 10(b)(3).

    iv.  *Binding.* The pages of each document must be stapled or in some other way fastened together. NY R USDCTWD Civ Rule 10(b)(4).

c.  *Caption; Names of parties.* Every pleading must have a caption with the court's name, a title, a file number, and a FRCP 7(a) designation. The title of the complaint must name all the parties; the title of other pleadings, after naming the first party on each side, may refer generally to other parties. FRCP 10(a).

d.  *Paragraphs; Separate statements.* A party must state its claims or defenses in numbered paragraphs, each limited as far as practicable to a single set of circumstances. A later pleading may refer by number to a paragraph in an earlier pleading. If doing so would promote clarity, each claim founded on a separate transaction or occurrence—and each defense other than a denial—must be stated in a separate count or defense. FRCP 10(b).

e.  *Adoption by reference; Exhibits.* A statement in a pleading may be adopted by reference elsewhere in the same pleading or in any other pleading or motion. A copy of a written instrument that is an exhibit to a pleading is a part of the pleading for all purposes. FRCP 10(c).

f.  *Citation of local rules.* The Local Rules of Civil Procedure for the United States District Court for the Western District of New York shall be cited as "L.R.Civ.P." NY R USDCTWD Civ Rule 1.1.

g.  *Acceptance by the clerk.* The clerk must not refuse to file a paper solely because it is not in the form prescribed by the Federal Rules of Civil Procedure or by a local rule or practice. FRCP 5(d)(4). The Court may reject documents that do not comply with the requirements in NY R USDCTWD Civ Rule 10. NY R USDCTWD Civ Rule 10.

2.  *Form of electronic documents.* All pleadings, motions, and other papers that a party presents for filing, whether in paper form or in electronic form, shall meet the requirements in NY R USDCTWD Civ Rule 10(a). NY R USDCTWD Civ Rule 10(a). Refer above for more information.

a.  *Conversion to PDF.* A document created with a word processor, or a paper document, must be converted to Portable Document Format to be electronically filed with the court. NY R USDCTWD ECF Procedures(2)(a)(v).

    i.   Documents which exist only in paper form may be scanned into a portable document format (PDF) for electronic filing. NY R USDCTWD ECF Procedures(2)(a)(v). Before filing a scanned document with the court, a Filing User must verify its legibility. NY R USDCTWD ECF Procedures(2)(a)(iv).

    ii.  Electronic documents must be converted to .PDF from a word processing program and must be text searchable. Do not print, scan and .PDF your document when it has been created in a word processing program. Additional information on working with PDFs is located in NY R USDCTWD ECF Procedures(4b). NY R USDCTWD ECF Procedures(2)(a)(v).

b.  *Hyperlinks.* Pursuant to the policy set forth by the Judicial Conference in October 2005, a hyperlink contained in a filing is no more than a convenient mechanism for accessing material cited in a document. A hyperlink reference is extraneous to any filed document and is not part of the Court's record. NY R USDCTWD ECF Procedures(2)(a)(vi).

    i.   In order to preserve the integrity of the Court record, users wishing to insert hyperlinks in Court filings shall continue to use the conventional method for the cited authority, in addition to the hyperlink. NY R USDCTWD ECF Procedures(2)(a)(vi).

    ii.  The Court accepts no responsibility for, and does not endorse any product, organization, and content at any hyperlinked site, or at any site to which that site may be linked. The Court accepts no responsibility for the availability or functionality of any hyperlink. NY R USDCTWD ECF Procedures(2)(a)(vi).

c.  *Attachments and exhibits*

    i.   Attachments and exhibits larger than five megabytes (5 MB) shall be filed electronically in separate five megabyte (5 MB) segments. NY R USDCTWD ECF Procedures(2)(d)(i).

    ii.  Filing Users must submit in electronic form all documents referenced as exhibits or attachments, except as otherwise provided in NY R USDCTWD ECF Procedures. A Filing User must submit as exhibits or attachments only those excerpts of the referenced documents that are directly germane to the matter under consideration by the court. Excerpted material must be clearly and prominently identified as such. Filing Users who file excerpts of documents as exhibits or attachments under NY R USDCTWD ECF Procedures(2)(d)(ii) do so without prejudice to their right to timely file additional excerpts or the complete document. Responding parties may timely file additional excerpts or the complete document that they believe are directly germane. The Court may require parties to file additional excerpts or the complete document. A Filing User must request leave of the Court to file a document exhibit or attachment in non-electronic form. NY R USDCTWD ECF Procedures(2)(d)(ii).

    iii.  Exhibits offered or admitted at trial will not be filed electronically or conventionally unless so ordered by the Court. NY R USDCTWD ECF Procedures(2)(d)(iii).

    iv.  Exhibits such as videotapes and tape recordings shall be filed in the conventional manner with the Clerk of Court, and a Notice of Manual Filing shall be electronically filed by the party. Manually filed exhibits must have the case number and case name securely fastened or marked on the item. NY R USDCTWD ECF Procedures(2)(d)(iii).

    v.  Continuation of exhibit entries (for exhibits that are too large to attach to a main document) must be filed and entered on the same day that the main document was filed. NY R USDCTWD ECF Procedures(2)(d)(iv).

  d.  *Color documents.* Documents in color or containing graphics take much longer to upload. Filing users are encouraged to configure their scanners to scan documents at 200 dpi and preferably in black and white rather than color. NY R USDCTWD ECF Procedures(2)(d)(v).

  e.  *Large documents.* Due to the length of time it takes to download large files, documents larger than five megabytes (5 MB) (approximately one hundred (100) pages of a .pdf scanned document) must be filed electronically in separate five megabyte (5 MB) segments. A party who believes a document is too lengthy to electronically image (i.e. scan), may contact the Court Room Deputy for the assigned judge and request permission to file that document conventionally. If granted permission to file the document conventionally, the Filing User shall electronically file a "notice of manual filing" for that item. Exhibits submitted to the Court conventionally shall be served on other parties conventionally. NY R USDCTWD ECF Procedures(2)(d)(vi).

3.  *Form of memoranda of law.* Memoranda in support of or in opposition to any motion shall not exceed twenty-five (25) pages in length, and reply memoranda shall not exceed ten (10) pages in length. A party seeking to exceed the page limit must make application by letter to the Judge hearing the motion, with copies to all counsel, at least seven (7) days before the date on which the memorandum must be filed. NY R USDCTWD Civ Rule 7(a)(2)(C).

4.  *Signing of pleadings, motions and other papers*

  a.  *Signature.* Every pleading, written motion, and other paper must be signed by at least one attorney of record in the attorney's name—or by a party personally if the party is unrepresented. The paper must state the signer's address, e-mail address, and telephone number. FRCP 11(a). Documents presented for paper filing must contain an original signature. NY R USDCTWD Civ Rule 10(b)(6).

    i.  *Electronic signatures*

      •  *Non-attorney signature.* If the original document requires the signature of a non-attorney, the filing party shall obtain the signature of the non-attorney on the document. NY R USDCTWD ECF Procedures(2)(g)(i). The filing party or attorney then shall file the document electronically indicating the signatory's name in the form "s/(name)." NY R USDCTWD ECF Procedures(2)(g)(i)(1). A non-filing signatory or party who disputes the authenticity of an electronically filed document or the authenticity of the signature on that document must file an objection to the document within ten (10) days of receiving the Notice of Electronic Filing. NY R USDCTWD ECF Procedures(2)(g)(i)(2).

      •  *Registered user signature.* The username and password required to file documents on the

Electronic Filing System serve as the Filing User's signature on all electronic documents filed with this Court. The also serve as a signature for the purposes of FRCP 11, the Federal Rules of Civil Procedure, the Local Rules of Civil Procedure for the United States District Court for the Western District of New York, and any other purpose for which a signature is required in connection with proceedings before this Court. A pleading requiring a Registered User's signature must include a signature block in the format found in NY R USDCTWD ECF Procedures(2)(g)(iii). NY R USDCTWD ECF Procedures(2)(g)(iii). Any party challenging the authenticity of an electronically filed document or the attorney's signature on that document must file an objection to the document within ten (10) days of receiving the Notice of Electronic Filing. NY R USDCTWD ECF Procedures(2)(g)(iii)(1).

- *Multiple signatures.* The following procedure applies when a stipulation or other document requires two or more signatures: The filing party shall initially confirm that the document is acceptable to all persons required to sign the document and shall obtain the signatures of all parties on the document. NY R USDCTWD ECF Procedures(2)(g)(iv)(1). The filing party or attorney then shall file the document electronically indicating the signatories, e.g., "s/Jane Doe," "s/John Smith," etc. NY R USDCTWD ECF Procedures(2)(g)(iv)(2). A non-filing signatory or party who disputes the authenticity of an electronically filed document containing multiple signatures or the authenticity of the signatures themselves must file an objection to the document within ten (10) days of receiving the Notice of Electronic Filing. NY R USDCTWD ECF Procedures(2)(g)(iv)(3).

ii. *No verification or accompanying affidavit required for pleadings.* Unless a rule or statute specifically states otherwise, a pleading need not be verified or accompanied by an affidavit. FRCP 11(a).

iii. *Unsigned papers.* The court must strike an unsigned paper unless the omission is promptly corrected after being called to the attorney's or party's attention. FRCP 11(a).

b. *Representations to the court.* By presenting to the court a pleading, written motion, or other paper—whether by signing, filing, submitting, or later advocating it—an attorney or unrepresented party certifies that to the best of the person's knowledge, information, and belief, formed after an inquiry reasonable under the circumstances:

i. It is not being presented for any improper purpose, such as to harass, cause unnecessary delay, or needlessly increase the cost of litigation;

ii. The claims, defenses, and other legal contentions are warranted by existing law or by a nonfrivolous argument for extending, modifying, or reversing existing law or for establishing new law;

iii. The factual contentions have evidentiary support or, if specifically so identified, will likely have evidentiary support after a reasonable opportunity for further investigation or discovery; and

iv. The denials of factual contentions are warranted on the evidence or, if specifically so identified, are reasonably based on belief or a lack of information. FRCP 11(b).

c. *Sanctions.* If, after notice and a reasonable opportunity to respond, the court determines that FRCP 11(b) has been violated, the court may impose an appropriate sanction on any attorney, law firm, or party that violated FRCP 11(b) or is responsible for the violation. FRCP 11(c)(1). Refer to the United States District Court for the Western District of New York KeyRules Motion for Sanctions document for more information.

5. *Privacy protection for filings made with the court.* In all filings, parties shall comply with FRCP 5.2. NY R USDCTWD ECF Procedures(2)(m)(i).

a. *Redacted filings.* Unless the court orders otherwise, in an electronic or paper filing with the court that contains an individual's Social Security number, taxpayer-identification number, or birth date, the name of an individual known to be a minor, or a financial-account number, a party or nonparty making the filing may include only:

i. The last four (4) digits of the Social Security number and taxpayer-identification number;

    ii.   The year of the individual's birth;

    iii.  The minor's initials; and

    iv.  The last four (4) digits of the financial-account number. FRCP 5.2(a).

  b.  *Exemptions from the redaction requirement.* The redaction requirement does not apply to the following:

    i.   A financial-account number that identifies the property allegedly subject to forfeiture in a forfeiture proceeding;

    ii.  The record of an administrative or agency proceeding;

    iii.  The official record of a state-court proceeding;

    iv.  The record of a court or tribunal, if that record was not subject to the redaction requirement when originally filed;

    v.   A filing covered by FRCP 5.2(c) or FRCP 5.2(d); and

    vi.  A pro se filing in an action brought under 28 U.S.C.A. § 2241, 28 U.S.C.A. § 2254, or 28 U.S.C.A. § 2255. FRCP 5.2(b).

  c.  *Limitations on remote access to electronic files; Social Security appeals and immigration cases.* Unless the court orders otherwise, in an action for benefits under the Social Security Act, and in an action or proceeding relating to an order of removal, to relief from removal, or to immigration benefits or detention, access to an electronic file is authorized as follows:

    i.   The parties and their attorneys may have remote electronic access to any part of the case file, including the administrative record;

    ii.  Any other person may have electronic access to the full record at the courthouse, but may have remote electronic access only to:

       • The docket maintained by the court; and

       • An opinion, order, judgment, or other disposition of the court, but not any other part of the case file or the administrative record. FRCP 5.2(c).

  d.  *Filings made under seal.* The court may order that a filing be made under seal without redaction. The court may later unseal the filing or order the person who made the filing to file a redacted version for the public record. FRCP 5.2(d). For more information on sealing documents, refer to NY R USDCTWD Civ Rule 5.3, NY R USDCTWD ECF Procedures(2)(o)(i)(1), NY R USDCTWD ECF Procedures(2)(o)(i)(2), and NY R USDCTWD ECF Procedures(2)(o)(i)(3).

  e.  *Protective orders.* For good cause, the court may by order in a case:

    i.   Require redaction of additional information; or

    ii.  Limit or prohibit a nonparty's remote electronic access to a document filed with the court. FRCP 5.2(e).

  f.  *Option for additional unredacted filing under seal.* A person making a redacted filing may also file an unredacted copy under seal. The court must retain the unredacted copy as part of the record. FRCP 5.2(f).

  g.  *Option for filing a reference list.* A filing that contains redacted information may be filed together with a reference list that identifies each item of redacted information and specifies an appropriate identifier that uniquely corresponds to each item listed. The list must be filed under seal and may be amended as of right. Any reference in the case to a listed identifier will be construed to refer to the corresponding item of information. FRCP 5.2(g).

  h.  *Waiver of protection of identifiers.* A person waives the protection of FRCP 5.2(a) as to the person's own information by filing it without redaction and not under seal. FRCP 5.2(h).

6.  *Individual judge practices.* Refer to the Miscellaneous section of this document for information on individual judge practices on formatting documents.

## F. Filing and Service Requirements

1.  *Filing requirements.* Any paper after the complaint that is required to be served—together with a

certificate of service—must be filed within a reasonable time after service. FRCP 5(d)(1). All pleadings and other papers shall be filed and served in accordance with the Federal Rules of Civil Procedure and the CM/ECF Administrative Procedures Guide (NY R USDCTWD ECF Procedures). NY R USDCTWD Civ Rule 5.1(a). For information on filing of miscellaneous cases and irregular documents, refer to NY R USDCTWD Civ Rule 5.6.

a. *How filing is made; In general.* A paper is filed by delivering it:

   i.  To the clerk; or

   ii. To a judge who agrees to accept it for filing, and who must then note the filing date on the paper and promptly send it to the clerk. FRCP 5(d)(2).

b. *Electronic filing*

   i.  *Authorization of electronic filing program.* A court may, by local rule, allow papers to be filed, signed, or verified by electronic means that are consistent with any technical standards established by the Judicial Conference of the United States. A local rule may require electronic filing only if reasonable exceptions are allowed. A paper filed electronically in compliance with a local rule is a written paper for purposes of the Federal Rules of Civil Procedure. FRCP 5(d)(3).

   - All civil cases filed in this Court are assigned to the Electronic Case Filing System ("ECF"). The procedures for electronic filing and any exceptions to the electronic filing requirements are set forth in the CM/ECF Administrative Procedures Guide (NY R USDCTWD ECF Procedures) which is available on the Court's website. NY R US-DCTWD Civ Rule 5.1(a).

   ii. *Scope of electronic filing.* The U.S. District Court for the Western District of New York requires attorneys in civil and criminal cases to file documents with the Court electronically over the Internet using its Case Management/Electronic Case Filing (CM/ECF) system. NY R US-DCTWD ECF Procedures. Beginning January 1, 2004, all civil and criminal cases currently pending and newly filed, except as expressly noted herein, were assigned to the Electronic Case Filing System ("System"). Except as expressly provided and in exceptional circumstances preventing a Filing User from filing electronically, all petitions, motions, memoranda of law, or other pleadings and documents required to be filed with the Court in connection with a case assigned to the System must be electronically filed. NY R USDCTWD ECF Procedures(1)(a).

   - *Mandatory electronic filing.* All documents on civil, criminal, miscellaneous civil, miscellaneous criminal and new civil case openings, except sealed documents, sealed cases, opening of a criminal case, opening of a miscellaneous case and as expressly provided for in these procedures (NY R USDCTWD ECF Procedures), shall be electronically filed on the system. NY R USDCTWD ECF Procedures(2)(a)(i). NY R USDCTWD Civ Rule 29

   - *Stipulations.* Pursuant to NY R USDCTWD Civ Rule 29, all stipulations (whether the stipulation is final or when it requires a judge's signature) shall be filed electronically. NY R USDCTWD ECF Procedures(2)(p)(i).

   - *Letters.* The electronic filing of letters is generally prohibited unless granted permission by an assigned judge. Letters to the Court must be submitted conventionally. NY R US-DCTWD ECF Procedures(2)(q)(i).

   - *Exceptions.* The Court requires attorneys to file documents electronically, absent a showing of good cause, unless otherwise excused by the procedures set forth below or by Order of the Court. NY R USDCTWD ECF Procedures.

   iii. *Conventional filing of documents.* The procedures in NY R USDCTWD ECF Procedures(2)(o) govern documents filed conventionally. The Court, upon application, may also authorize conventional filing of other documents otherwise subject to the procedures in NY R US-DCTWD ECF Procedures(2)(o). NY R USDCTWD ECF Procedures(2)(o)(i).

   - *Documents filed under seal.* Unredacted documents filed with the Court pursuant to the privacy provisions of FRCP 5.2 shall be submitted in a sealing envelope with the

information in NY R USDCTWD ECF Procedures(2)(o)(i)(1) on the envelope. NY R USDCTWD ECF Procedures(2)(o)(i)(1). If the document is larger than five (5) pages, a disk should be provided to the Clerks Office which contains the document in a .pdf format. NY R USDCTWD ECF Procedures(2)(o)(i)(1). For more information on documents filed under seal, refer to NY R USDCTWD ECF Procedures(2)(o)(i)(1), NY R USDCTWD ECF Procedures(2)(o)(i)(2), and NY R USDCTWD ECF Procedures(2)(o)(i)(3).

- *Magistrate judge consents.* Pursuant to FRCP 73(b), parties' filing consents to jurisdiction by United States Magistrate Judge will continue to be treated as non-public documents until all parties have consented. Therefore, parties must submit conventionally (in paper form) and not electronically file their consent forms so that the consent is not a public document. If all parties consent to the jurisdiction of a Magistrate Judge, the Clerk will scan all consent forms which will then become a public document. NY R USDCTWD ECF Procedures(2)(o)(i)(3).

- *Pro se filers.* Pro Se filers shall file paper originals of all initiating documents, pleadings, motions, affidavits, briefs and other documents which must be signed or which require either verification or an unsworn declaration under any rule or statute. The Clerk's Office will scan these original documents into an electronic file in the System. A certificate of service is required for all documents a pro se litigant files with the court. If a Pro Se filer is granted permission to register to electronically file documents, they shall comply with the guidelines contained in this document (NY R USDCTWD ECF Procedures). NY R USDCTWD ECF Procedures(2)(o)(i)(4).

- *Social Security cases.* Absent a showing of good cause, and except as provided in Section o(i)(4) above, all documents, notices and orders in Social Security reviews will be filed and noticed electronically, except as noted in NY R USDCTWD ECF Procedures(2)(o)(i)(6). For more information, refer to NY R USDCTWD ECF Procedures(2)(o)(i)(6).

- For more information on conventional filing of documents, refer to NY R USDCTWD ECF Procedures(2)(o)(i).

iv. *Consequences of electronic filing.* Electronic transmission of a document to the System consistent with these procedures (NY R USDCTWD ECF Procedures), whether accomplished by the Filing User or a Court User, together with the transmission of a Notice of Electronic Filing from the Court, constitutes filing of a document for all purposes of the Federal Rules of Civil Procedure and the Local Rules of Civil Procedure for the United States District Court for the Western District of New York, and constitutes entry of the document on the docket kept by the Clerk under FRCP 58 and FRCP 79. A document shall not be considered filed for purposes of the Federal Rules of Civil until the filing party receives a System generated Notice of Electronic Filing. NY R USDCTWD ECF Procedures(2)(a)(i).

- E-mailing a document to the Clerk's Office or to the assigned judge shall not constitute "filing" of such document. NY R USDCTWD ECF Procedures(2)(a)(i)(1).

v. *Filing fees.* Any fee required for filing of a pleading or paper in District Court is payable to the Clerk of Court by check or money order. In addition, when opening a civil case on line, filing a notice of appeal on line or applying to appear pro hac vice on line, the fees shall be paid on line by registered users through the federal electronic payment website. Users will be directed to the federal electronic payment website while entering their transaction and should have a credit card available. When opening a civil case and applying to proceed in forma pauperis or when the United States of America opens a case, the payment screen can by bypassed to complete the transaction. Additional information on making electronic payments can be located on the court's website. NY R USDCTWD ECF Procedures(2)(h)(i).

2. *Service requirements.* All pleadings and other papers shall be filed and served in accordance with the

Federal Rules of Civil Procedure and the CM/ECF Administrative Procedures Guide (NY R USDCTWD ECF Procedures). NY R USDCTWD Civ Rule 5.1(a).

a. *Service; When required*

   i. *In general.* Unless the Federal Rules of Civil Procedure provide otherwise, each of the following papers must be served on every party:

- An order stating that service is required;
- A pleading filed after the original complaint, unless the court orders otherwise under FRCP 5(c) because there are numerous defendants;
- A discovery paper required to be served on a party, unless the court orders otherwise;
- A written motion, except one that may be heard ex parte; and
- A written notice, appearance, demand, or offer of judgment, or any similar paper. FRCP 5(a)(1).

   ii. *If a party fails to appear.* No service is required on a party who is in default for failing to appear. But a pleading that asserts a new claim for relief against such a party must be served on that party under FRCP 4. FRCP 5(a)(2).

   iii. *Seizing property.* If an action is begun by seizing property and no person is or need be named as a defendant, any service required before the filing of an appearance, answer, or claim must be made on the person who had custody or possession of the property when it was seized. FRCP 5(a)(3).

b. *Service; How made*

   i. *Serving an attorney.* If a party is represented by an attorney, service under FRCP 5 must be made on the attorney unless the court orders service on the party. FRCP 5(b)(1).

   ii. *Service in general.* A paper is served under FRCP 5 by:

- Handing it to the person;
- Leaving it: (1) at the person's office with a clerk or other person in charge or, if no one is in charge, in a conspicuous place in the office; or (2) if the person has no office or the office is closed, at the person's dwelling or usual place of abode with someone of suitable age and discretion who resides there;
- Mailing it to the person's last known address—in which event service is complete upon mailing;
- Leaving it with the court clerk if the person has no known address;
- Sending it by electronic means if the person consented in writing—in which event service is complete upon transmission, but is not effective if the serving party learns that it did not reach the person to be served; or
- Delivering it by any other means that the person consented to in writing—in which event service is complete when the person making service delivers it to the agency designated to make delivery. FRCP 5(b)(2).

   iii. *Service by overnight delivery.* All papers, other than a subpoena or a summons and complaint, may be served on counsel of record by overnight delivery service at the address designated by the attorney for that purpose, or if none is designated, at the attorney's last known address. Service by overnight delivery shall be complete upon deposit of the paper(s), enclosed in a properly addressed wrapper, into the custody of the overnight delivery service, prior to the latest time designated by the service for overnight delivery. NY R USDCTWD Civ Rule 5.1(g). "Overnight delivery service" means any delivery service which regularly accepts items for overnight delivery to any address within the Court's jurisdiction. NY R USDCTWD Civ Rule 5.1(g).

   iv. *Service of documents by electronic means*

- *Service on registered users.* Registered Users consent to the electronic service of all

documents, and must make available an electronic mail address for service during the registration process. Upon the filing of a document by a party, a Notice of Electronic Filing, with a hyperlink to the filed document, will be automatically generated by the electronic filing system and sent via electronic mail to the e-mail addresses of all parties participating in the electronic filing system in the case. Electronic service of the Notice of Electronic Filing constitutes service of the filed document for all purposes of the Federal Rules of Civil Procedure and the Local Rules of Civil Procedure for the United States District Court for the Western District of New York. NY R USDCTWD ECF Procedures(2)(f)(i). The Notice of Electronic Filing effectuates service for all registered users and no certificate of service is required when all filers on an action are Registered Users. NY R USDCTWD ECF Procedures(2)(f)(iv).

- *Time limit for opening hyperlink.* The hyperlink to filed documents contained in the Notice of Electronic Filing must be opened within fifteen (15) days from the date the document was filed to provide registered users access to the document. The hyperlink expires after fifteen (15) days and users will be unable to access documents for free after that time. Filing Users are encouraged to check their e-mail frequently for notice of filed documents. NY R USDCTWD ECF Procedures(2)(f)(ii).

- *Service on exempted attorneys or pro se litigants who do not have permission to file electronically.* Attorneys granted an exemption from electronically filing documents in the System and pro se litigants who have not been granted permission to electronically file documents are entitled to a paper copy of any electronically filed pleading, document or order. The filing party must therefore provide the non-registered party with the pleading, document or order according to the Federal Rules of Civil Procedure. NY R USDCTWD ECF Procedures(2)(f)(iii).

- *E-mailing or faxing documents.* E-mailing or faxing a pleading or document to any party shall not constitute service of the pleading or document. NY R USDCTWD ECF Procedures(2)(f)(v).

    v. *Using court facilities.* If a local rule so authorizes, a party may use the court's transmission facilities to make service under FRCP 5(b)(2)(E). FRCP 5(b)(3).

  c. *Serving numerous defendants*

    i. *In general.* If an action involves an unusually large number of defendants, the court may, on motion or on its own, order that:

- Defendants' pleadings and replies to them need not be served on other defendants;

- Any crossclaim, counterclaim, avoidance, or affirmative defense in those pleadings and replies to them will be treated as denied or avoided by all other parties; and

- Filing any such pleading and serving it on the plaintiff constitutes notice of the pleading to all parties. FRCP 5(c)(1).

    ii. *Notifying parties.* A copy of every such order must be served on the parties as the court directs. FRCP 5(c)(2).

3. *Pro se actions.* For information on the requirements in pro se actions, refer to NY R USDCTWD Civ Rule 5.2.

4. *Individual judge practices.* Refer to the Miscellaneous section of this document for information on individual judge practices on filing and serving documents.

## G. Hearings

1. *Hearings, generally*

  a. *Oral argument.* Due process does not require that oral argument be permitted on a motion and, except as otherwise provided by local rule, the district court has discretion to determine whether it will decide the motion on the papers or hear argument by counsel (and perhaps receive evidence). FPP § 1190; F.D.I.C. v. Deglau, 207 F.3d 153 (3d Cir. 2000).

    i. The parties shall appear for oral argument on all motions they make returnable before a Judge

on the scheduled return date for the motion. In its discretion, the Court may notify the parties that oral argument shall not be heard on any given motion. Thus, the parties should be prepared to have their motion papers serve as the sole method of argument. NY R USDCTWD Civ Rule 7(c).

b. *Providing a regular schedule for oral hearings.* A court may establish regular times and places for oral hearings on motions. FRCP 78(a).

c. *Providing for submission on briefs.* By rule or order, the court may provide for submitting and determining motions on briefs, without oral hearings. FRCP 78(b).

2. *Individual judge practices.* Refer to the Miscellaneous section of this document for information on individual judge practices on hearings.

## H. Forms

### 1. Federal Motion for Continuance/Extension of Time Forms

a. Opposition in federal district court; To motion for continuance; On ground of additional time required to prepare for trial; No excusable neglect shown. AMJUR PP CONTIN § 79.

b. Affidavit in opposition to motion for continuance; By plaintiff's attorney; Lack of due diligence in discovery of documents. AMJUR PP CONTIN § 80.

c. Affidavit in opposition to motion for continuance; By plaintiff's attorney; Defendant's absent witness previously absent; Lack of due diligence in compelling attendance of witness. AMJUR PP CONTIN § 81.

d. Affidavit in opposition to motion for continuance; By plaintiff; Admission that absent witness of defendant would testify according to affidavit. AMJUR PP CONTIN § 83.

e. Affidavit in opposition to defendant's motion for continuance; By plaintiff's counsel; Testimony of absent witness merely cumulative. AMJUR PP CONTIN § 85.

f. Motion for enlargement of time. 2 FEDFORMS § 5:11.

g. Motion for enlargement of time; By plaintiff. 2 FEDFORMS § 5:12.

h. Motion for enlargement of time; To answer motion. 2 FEDFORMS § 5:14.

i. Motion for continuance. 2 FEDFORMS § 5:36.

j. Motion for continuance; Reciting supporting facts; New allegations in amended answer. 2 FEDFORMS § 5:37.

k. Motion for continuance; Reciting supporting facts; Absence of witness. 2 FEDFORMS § 5:38.

l. Motion for continuance; Reciting supporting facts; Absence of witness; Witness outside the country. 2 FEDFORMS § 5:39.

m. Motion for continuance or in the alternative for change of venue; Hostility against defendant. 2 FEDFORMS § 5:40.

n. Notice; Of motion; Containing motion. FEDPROF § 1:749.

o. Brief; Supporting or opposing motion. FEDPROF § 1:752.

p. Opposition to motion; For continuance; No excusable neglect. FEDPROF § 1:808.

q. Affidavit; Opposing motion for continuance; Offer to stipulate to testimony of unavailable witness. FEDPROF § 1:813.

r. Reply to motion for extension of time. GOLDLTGFMS § 10:40.

s. Motions; Extension of time to file jury demand. GOLDLTGFMS § 12:6.

t. Motion for extension of time. GOLDLTGFMS § 25:37.

u. Motion for extension of time to answer. GOLDLTGFMS § 26:13.

v. Motion to extend time for serving answers. GOLDLTGFMS § 26:14.

w. Motion for continuance. GOLDLTGFMS § 43:2.

    x.   Motion for continuance; Lawyer unavailable. GOLDLTGFMS § 43:3.

    y.   Motion for continuance; Witness unavailable. GOLDLTGFMS § 43:4.

    z.   Motion for continuance; Party in military service. GOLDLTGFMS § 43:6.

  **2.  Forms for the Western District of New York**

    a.   Certificate of service. NY R USDCTWD ECF Procedures(4a).

# I.  Applicable Rules

  1.  *Federal rules*

    a.   Serving and filing pleadings and other papers. FRCP 5.

    b.   Constitutional challenge to a statute; Notice, certification, and intervention. FRCP 5.1.

    c.   Privacy protection for filings made with the court. FRCP 5.2.

    d.   Computing and extending time; Time for motion papers. FRCP 6.

    e.   Pleadings allowed; Form of motions and other papers. FRCP 7.

    f.   Disclosure statement. FRCP 7.1.

    g.   Form of pleadings. FRCP 10.

    h.   Signing pleadings, motions, and other papers; Representations to the court; Sanctions. FRCP 11.

    i.   Taking testimony. FRCP 43.

    j.   Hearing motions; Submission on briefs. FRCP 78.

  2.  *Local rules*

    a.   Title. NY R USDCTWD Civ Rule 1.1.

    b.   Filing and serving papers. NY R USDCTWD Civ Rule 5.1.

    c.   Motion practice. NY R USDCTWD Civ Rule 7.

    d.   Form of papers. NY R USDCTWD Civ Rule 10.

    e.   Sanctions. NY R USDCTWD Civ Rule 11.

    f.   Alternative dispute resolution and pretrial conferences. NY R USDCTWD Civ Rule 16.

    g.   Attorneys of record; Appearance and withdrawal. NY R USDCTWD Civ Rule 83.2.

    h.   Administrative procedures guide for electronic filing. NY R USDCTWD ECF Procedures.

    i.   Alternative dispute resolution plan. NY R USDCTWD ADR Plan.

# J.  Miscellaneous

**NOTE: Individual judges' rules may apply. For available judge-level information, refer to:**

DISTRICT JUDGE RICHARD J. ARCARA: NY R USDCTWD Arcara-Procedures.

DISTRICT JUDGE FRANK P. GERACI, JR.: NY R USDCTWD Geraci-Procedures.

DISTRICT JUDGE DAVID G. LARIMER: NY R USDCTWD Larimer-Procedures.

DISTRICT JUDGE CHARLES J. SIRAGUSA: NY R USDCTWD Siragusa-Procedures.

DISTRICT JUDGE WILLIAM M. SKRETNY: NY R USDCTWD Skretny--Procedures.

DISTRICT JUDGE MICHAEL A. TELESCA: NY R USDCTWD Telesca-Procedures.

DISTRICT JUDGE LAWRENCE J. VILARDO: NY R USDCTWD Vilardo-Procedures.

DISTRICT JUDGE ELIZABETH A. WOLFORD: NY R USDCTWD Wolford-Procedures.

MAGISTRATE JUDGE JONATHAN W. FELDMAN: NY R USDCTWD Feldman-Procedures.

MAGISTRATE JUDGE LESLIE G. FOSCHIO: NY R USDCTWD Foschio-Procedures; NY R USDCTWD Foschio-Depositions.

MAGISTRATE JUDGE JEREMIAH J. McCARTHY: NY R USDCTWD McCarthy-Procedures.

MAGISTRATE JUDGE MARIAN W. PAYSON: NY R USDCTWD Payson-Procedures.

MAGISTRATE JUDGE MICHAEL J. ROEMER: NY R USDCTWD Roemer-Procedures.

MAGISTRATE JUDGE H. KENNETH SCHROEDER, JR.: NY R USDCTWD Schroeder-Proc.

MAGISTRATE JUDGE HUGH B. SCOTT: NY R USDCTWD Scott-Procedures.

# Motions, Oppositions and Replies
# Motion for Summary Judgment

**Document Last Updated September 2016**

## A. Checklist

(I) ❑ Matters to be considered by moving party

   (a) ❑ Required documents

      (1) ❑ Notice of motion and motion

      (2) ❑ Statement of material facts

      (3) ❑ Memorandum of law

      (4) ❑ Supporting affidavit

      (5) ❑ Certificate of service

   (b) ❑ Supplemental documents

      (1) ❑ Supporting evidence

      (2) ❑ Notice of constitutional question

      (3) ❑ Nongovernmental corporate disclosure statement

      (4) ❑ Notice to pro se litigant

      (5) ❑ Copies of authorities

      (6) ❑ Proposed order

      (7) ❑ Paper copy for date-stamping with self-addressed envelope

      (8) ❑ Courtesy copies

   (c) ❑ Timing

      (1) ❑ Unless a different time is set by local rule or the court orders otherwise, a party may file a motion for summary judgment at any time until thirty (30) days after the close of all discovery

      (2) ❑ A written motion and notice of the hearing must be served at least fourteen (14) days before the time specified for the hearing, with the following exceptions: (i) when the motion may be heard ex parte; (ii) when the Federal Rules of Civil Procedure set a different time; or (iii) when a court order—which a party may, for good cause, apply for ex parte—sets a different time

      (3) ❑ Any affidavit supporting a motion must be served with the motion

(II) ❑ Matters to be considered by opposing party

   (a) ❑ Required documents

      (1) ❑ Opposition

      (2) ❑ Opposing statement of material facts

      (3) ❑ Answering memorandum

      (4) ❑ Supporting affidavit

      (5) ❑ Certificate of service

    (b) ❑ Supplemental documents

        (1) ❑ Supporting evidence

        (2) ❑ Notice of constitutional question

        (3) ❑ Cross-motion

        (4) ❑ Copies of authorities

        (5) ❑ Paper copy for date-stamping with self-addressed envelope

        (6) ❑ Courtesy copies

    (c) ❑ Timing

        (1) ❑ After a motion is filed, the court may issue an order setting deadlines for filing and service of opposing papers; if the court does not set deadlines by order, the opposing party shall have twenty-eight (28) days after service of the motion to file and serve responding papers

        (2) ❑ Except as FRCP 59(c) provides otherwise, any opposing affidavit must be served at least seven (7) days before the hearing, unless the court permits service at another time

## B. Timing

1. *Motion for summary judgment.* Unless a different time is set by local rule or the court orders otherwise, a party may file a motion for summary judgment at any time until thirty (30) days after the close of all discovery. FRCP 56(b).

2. *Timing of motions, generally*

    a. *Motion and notice of hearing.* A written motion and notice of the hearing must be served at least fourteen (14) days before the time specified for the hearing, with the following exceptions:

        i. When the motion may be heard ex parte;

        ii. When the Federal Rules of Civil Procedure set a different time; or

        iii. When a court order—which a party may, for good cause, apply for ex parte—sets a different time. FRCP 6(c)(1).

    b. *Supporting affidavit.* Any affidavit supporting a motion must be served with the motion. FRCP 6(c)(2).

3. *Timing of opposing papers.* After a motion is filed, the Court may issue an order setting deadlines for filing and service of opposing papers. NY R USDCTWD Civ Rule 7(b)(1). If the Court does not set deadlines by order, the following schedule shall apply: the opposing party shall have twenty-eight (28) days after service of the motion to file and serve responding papers. NY R USDCTWD Civ Rule 7(b)(2)(A).

    a. *Opposing affidavit.* Except as FRCP 59(c) provides otherwise, any opposing affidavit must be served at least seven (7) days before the hearing, unless the court permits service at another time. FRCP 6(c)(2).

    b. *Opposition to cross-motion.* If the party opposing the original motion files a cross-motion, the moving party shall have twenty-eight (28) days after service of the cross-motion to file and serve responding papers in opposition to the cross-motion, and the party filing the cross-motion shall have fourteen (14) days after service of the responding papers to file and serve reply papers in support of the cross-motion. NY R USDCTWD Civ Rule 7(b)(2)(A).

4. *Timing of reply papers.* Where the respondent files an answering affidavit setting up a new matter, the moving party ordinarily is allowed a reasonable time to file a reply affidavit since failure to deny the new matter by affidavit may operate as an admission of its truth. AMJUR MOTIONS § 25.

    a. *Reply papers.* After a motion is filed, the Court may issue an order setting deadlines. . .for filing and service of reply papers if the moving party has stated an intent to reply. NY R USDCTWD Civ Rule 7(b)(1). If the Court does not set deadlines by order, the following schedule shall apply: the moving party shall have fourteen (14) days after service of the responding papers to file and serve reply papers. NY R USDCTWD Civ Rule 7(b)(2)(A).

    b. *Reply memorandum.* The moving party may file a reply memorandum, but is not required to do so. NY R USDCTWD Civ Rule 7(a)(2)(A).

   c. *Reply in support of cross-motion.* If the party opposing the original motion files a cross-motion. . .the party filing the cross-motion shall have fourteen (14) days after service of the responding papers to file and serve reply papers in support of the cross-motion. NY R USDCTWD Civ Rule 7(b)(2)(A).

5. *Motion for an expedited hearing.* A party seeking to shorten the schedule prescribed in NY R USDCTWD Civ Rule 7(b) must make a separate motion for an expedited hearing, setting forth the reasons why an expedited hearing is required. NY R USDCTWD Civ Rule 7(d)(1). For more information, refer to NY R USDCTWD Civ Rule 7(d)(1).

6. *Computation of time*

   a. *Computing time.* FRCP 6 applies in computing any time period specified in the Federal Rules of Civil Procedure, in any local rule or court order, or in any statute that does not specify a method of computing time. FRCP 6(a).

     i. *Period stated in days or a longer unit.* When the period is stated in days or a longer unit of time:

- Exclude the day of the event that triggers the period;
- Count every day, including intermediate Saturdays, Sundays, and legal holidays; and
- Include the last day of the period, but if the last day is a Saturday, Sunday, or legal holiday, the period continues to run until the end of the next day that is not a Saturday, Sunday, or legal holiday. FRCP 6(a)(1).

     ii. *Period stated in hours.* When the period is stated in hours:

- Begin counting immediately on the occurrence of the event that triggers the period;
- Count every hour, including hours during intermediate Saturdays, Sundays, and legal holidays; and
- If the period would end on a Saturday, Sunday, or legal holiday, the period continues to run until the same time on the next day that is not a Saturday, Sunday, or legal holiday. FRCP 6(a)(2).

     iii. *Inaccessibility of the clerk's office.* Unless the court orders otherwise, if the clerk's office is inaccessible:

- On the last day for filing under FRCP 6(a)(1), then the time for filing is extended to the first accessible day that is not a Saturday, Sunday, or legal holiday; or
- During the last hour for filing under FRCP 6(a)(2), then the time for filing is extended to the same time on the first accessible day that is not a Saturday, Sunday, or legal holiday. FRCP 6(a)(3).

     iv. *"Last day" defined.* Unless a different time is set by a statute, local rule, or court order, the last day ends:

- For electronic filing, at midnight in the court's time zone; and
- For filing by other means, when the clerk's office is scheduled to close. FRCP 6(a)(4).

     v. *"Next day" defined.* The "next day" is determined by continuing to count forward when the period is measured after an event and backward when measured before an event. FRCP 6(a)(5).

     vi. *"Legal holiday" defined.* "Legal holiday" means:

- The day set aside by statute for observing New Year's Day, Martin Luther King Jr.'s Birthday, Washington's Birthday, Memorial Day, Independence Day, Labor Day, Columbus Day, Veterans' Day, Thanksgiving Day, or Christmas Day;
- Any day declared a holiday by the President or Congress; and
- For periods that are measured after an event, any other day declared a holiday by the state where the district court is located. FRCP 6(a)(6).

   b. *Computation of electronic filing deadlines.* A document will be deemed timely filed if filed prior to midnight Eastern Time, unless otherwise ordered by the Court. A document will be considered untimely if filed thereafter. When a Court order requires that a document be filed on a weekend or holiday, the document may be filed by close of business the next business day without further application to the Court. NY R USDCTWD ECF Procedures(2)(e)(i). A document filed electronically is deemed filed on the date and time stated on the Notice of Electronic Filing. NY R USDCTWD ECF Procedures(2)(e)(ii).

    i. *System availability.* Although parties may file documents electronically twenty-four (24) hours a day, registered users are strongly encouraged to file all documents during normal working hours of the Clerk's Office (8:30 a.m. to 5:00 p.m. Eastern Time). NY R USDCTWD ECF Procedures(2)(t)(i).

    ii. *Technical failures.* A Filing User whose filing is made untimely as a result of a technical failure must seek appropriate relief from the Court. NY R USDCTWD ECF Procedures(2)(u)(i).

c. *Extending time*

    i. *In general.* When an act may or must be done within a specified time, the court may, for good cause, extend the time:

- With or without motion or notice if the court acts, or if a request is made, before the original time or its extension expires; or

- On motion made after the time has expired if the party failed to act because of excusable neglect. FRCP 6(b)(1).

    ii. *Exceptions.* A court must not extend the time to act under FRCP 50(b), FRCP 50(d), FRCP 52(b), FRCP 59(b), FRCP 59(d), FRCP 59(e), and FRCP 60(b). FRCP 6(b)(2).

    iii. Refer to the United States District Court for the Western District of New York KeyRules Motion for Continuance/Extension of Time document for more information on extending time.

d. *Additional time after certain kinds of service.* When a party may or must act within a specified time after service and service is made under FRCP 5(b)(2)(C), FRCP 5(b)(2)(D), FRCP 5(b)(2)(E), or FRCP 5(b)(2)(F), three (3) days are added after the period would otherwise expire under FRCP 6(a). FRCP 6(d).

    i. *Service by overnight delivery.* Where a period of time prescribed by either the Federal Rules of Civil Procedure or the Local Rules of Civil Procedure for the United States District Court for the Western District of New York is measured from the service of a paper and service is by overnight delivery, one (1) business day shall be added to the prescribed period. NY R USDCTWD Civ Rule 5.1(g).

7. *Individual judge practices.* Refer to the Miscellaneous section of this document for information on individual judge practices on timing of documents.

## C. General Requirements

1. *Motions, generally*

a. *Requirements.* A request for a court order must be made by motion. The motion must:

    i. Be in writing unless made during a hearing or trial;

    ii. State with particularity the grounds for seeking the order; and

    iii. State the relief sought. FRCP 7(b)(1).

b. *Notice of motion.* A party interested in resisting the relief sought by a motion has a right to notice thereof, and an opportunity to be heard. AMJUR MOTIONS § 12.

    i. In addition to statutory or court rule provisions requiring notice of a motion—the purpose of such a notice requirement having been said to be to prevent a party from being prejudicially surprised by a motion—principles of natural justice dictate that an adverse party generally must be given notice that a motion will be presented to the court. AMJUR MOTIONS § 12.

    ii. "Notice," in this regard, means reasonable notice, including a meaningful opportunity to prepare and to defend against allegations of a motion. AMJUR MOTIONS § 12.

c. *Writing requirement.* The writing requirement is intended to insure that the adverse parties are

informed and have a record of both the motion's pendency and the grounds on which the movant seeks an order. FPP § 1191; Feldberg v. Quechee Lakes Corp., 463 F.3d 195 (2d Cir. 2006).

    i.   It is sufficient "if the motion is stated in a written notice of the hearing of the motion." FPP § 1191.

    d.  *Particularity requirement.* The particularity requirement insures that the opposing parties will have notice of their opponent's contentions. FEDPROC § 62:364; Goodman v. 1973 26 Foot Trojan Vessel, Arkansas Registration No. AR1439SN, 859 F.2d 71, 12 Fed.R.Serv.3d 645 (8th Cir. 1988). That requirement ensures that notice of the basis for the motion is provided to the court and to the opposing party so as to avoid prejudice, provide the opponent with a meaningful opportunity to respond, and provide the court with enough information to process the motion correctly. FEDPROC § 62:364; Andreas v. Volkswagen of America, Inc., 336 F.3d 789, 56 Fed.R.Serv.3d 6 (8th Cir. 2003).

        i.   Reasonable specification of the grounds for a motion is sufficient. However, where a movant fails to state even one ground for granting the motion in question, the movant has failed to meet the minimal standard of "reasonable specification." FEDPROC § 62:364; Martinez v. Trainor, 556 F.2d 818, 23 Fed.R.Serv.2d 403 (7th Cir. 1977).

        ii.   The court may excuse the failure to comply with the particularity requirement if it is inadvertent, and where no prejudice is shown by the opposing party. FEDPROC § 62:364.

2.  *Motion for summary judgment.* A party may move for summary judgment, identifying each claim or defense—or the part of each claim or defense—on which summary judgment is sought. The court shall grant summary judgment if the movant shows that there is no genuine dispute as to any material fact and the movant is entitled to judgment as a matter of law. The court should state on the record the reasons for granting or denying the motion. FRCP 56(a).

    a.  *Burden of proof and presumptions*

        i.   *Movant's burden.* It is well-settled that the party moving for summary judgment has the burden of demonstrating that the FRCP 56(c) test—"no genuine issue as to any material fact"—is satisfied and that the movant is entitled to judgment as a matter of law. FPP § 2727; Adickes v. S. H. Kress & Co., 398 U.S. 144, 157, 90 S.Ct. 1598, 1608, 26 L.Ed.2d 142 (1970).

           •   The movant is held to a stringent standard. FPP § 2727. Before summary judgment will be granted it must be clear what the truth is and any doubt as to the existence of a genuine issue of material fact will be resolved against the movant. FPP § 2727; Poller v. Columbia Broadcasting Sys., Inc., 368 U.S. 464, 82 S.Ct. 486, 7 L.Ed.2d 458 (1962); Adickes v. S. H. Kress & Co., 398 U.S. 144, 90 S.Ct. 1598, 26 L.Ed.2d 142 (1970).

           •   Because the burden is on the movant, the evidence presented to the court always is construed in favor of the party opposing the motion and the opponent is given the benefit of all favorable inferences that can be drawn from it. FPP § 2727; Scott v. Harris, 550 U.S. 372, 127 S.Ct. 1769, 167 L.Ed.2d 686 (2007).

           •   Finally, facts asserted by the party opposing the motion, if supported by affidavits or other evidentiary material, are regarded as true. FPP § 2727; McLaughlin v. Liu, 849 F.2d 1205, 1208 (9th Cir. 1988).

        ii.   *Opponent's burden.* If the movant makes out a prima facie case that would entitle him to a judgment as a matter of law if uncontroverted at trial, summary judgment will be granted unless the opposing party offers some competent evidence that could be presented at trial showing that there is a genuine issue as to a material fact. FPP § 2727; First Nat. Bank of Arizona v. Cities Serv. Co., 391 U.S. 253, 289, 88 S.Ct. 1575, 1593, 20 L.Ed.2d 569 (1968). In this way the burden of producing evidence is shifted to the party opposing the motion. FPP § 2727; Celotex Corp. v. Catrett, 477 U.S. 317, 331, 106 S.Ct. 2548, 2557, 91 L.Ed.2d 265 (1986).

           •   The burden on the nonmoving party is not a heavy one; the nonmoving party simply is required to show specific facts, as opposed to general allegations, that present a genuine issue worthy of trial. FPP § 2727; Lujan v. Defenders of Wildlife, 504 U.S. 555, 112 S.Ct. 2130, 119 L.Ed.2d 351 (1992).

           •   The nonmoving party has two options once the moving party has met its burden of production of evidence demonstrating the absence of a genuine issue of material fact: either come forward with countervailing evidence showing that a genuine issue does exist, or submit an affidavit under FRCP 56(f) demonstrating that more time or further discovery are necessary to enable it to oppose the summary judgment motion. FEDPROC § 62:589.

b. *Failing to properly support or address a fact.* If a party fails to properly support an assertion of fact or fails to properly address another party's assertion of fact as required by FRCP 56(c), the court may:

    i. Give an opportunity to properly support or address the fact;

    ii. Consider the fact undisputed for purposes of the motion;

    iii. Grant summary judgment if the motion and supporting materials—including the facts considered undisputed—show that the movant is entitled to it; or

    iv. Issue any other appropriate order. FRCP 56(e).

c. *Judgment independent of the motion.* After giving notice and a reasonable time to respond, the court may:

    i. Grant summary judgment for a nonmovant;

    ii. Grant the motion on grounds not raised by a party; or

    iii. Consider summary judgment on its own after identifying for the parties material facts that may not be genuinely in dispute. FRCP 56(f).

d. *Failing to grant all the requested relief.* If the court does not grant all the relief requested by the motion, it may enter an order stating any material fact—including an item of damages or other relief—that is not genuinely in dispute and treating the fact as established in the case. FRCP 56(g).

e. *Affidavit or declaration submitted in bad faith.* If satisfied that an affidavit or declaration under FRCP 56 is submitted in bad faith or solely for delay, the court—after notice and a reasonable time to respond—may order the submitting party to pay the other party the reasonable expenses, including attorney's fees, it incurred as a result. An offending party or attorney may also be held in contempt or subjected to other appropriate sanctions. FRCP 56(h).

f. *Conversion of motions under FRCP 12(b)(6) and FRCP 12(c).* If, on a motion under FRCP 12(b)(6) or FRCP 12(c), matters outside the pleadings are presented to and not excluded by the court, the motion must be treated as one for summary judgment under FRCP 56. FRCP 12(d).

3. *Opposing papers*

a. *Opposing papers, generally.* The Federal Rules of Civil Procedure do not require any formal answer, return, or reply to a motion, except where the Federal Rules of Civil Procedure or local rules may require affidavits, memoranda, or other papers to be filed in opposition to a motion. Such papers are simply to apprise the court of such opposition and the grounds of that opposition. FEDPROC § 62:359.

    i. *Effect of failure to respond to motion.* Although in the absence of statutory provision or court rule, a motion ordinarily does not require a written answer, when a party files a motion and the opposing party fails to respond, the court may construe such failure to respond as nonopposition to the motion or an admission that the motion was meritorious, may take the facts alleged in the motion as true—the rule in some jurisdictions being that the failure to respond to a fact set forth in a motion is deemed an admission—and may grant the motion if the relief requested appears to be justified. AMJUR MOTIONS § 28.

    ii. *Assent or no opposition not determinative.* However, a motion will not be granted automatically simply because an "assent" or a notation of "no opposition" has been filed; federal judges frequently deny motions that have been assented to when it is thought that justice so dictates. FPP § 1190.

    iii. *Responsive pleading inappropriate as response to motion.* An attempt to answer or oppose a motion with a responsive pleading usually is not appropriate. FPP § 1190.

b. *Opposition to motion for summary judgment.* The party opposing summary judgment does not have a duty to present evidence in opposition to a motion under FRCP 56 in all circumstances. FPP § 2727; Jaroma v. Massey, 873 F.2d 17 (1st Cir. 1989).

  i. *When facts are unavailable to the nonmovant.* If a nonmovant shows by affidavit or declaration that, for specified reasons, it cannot present facts essential to justify its opposition, the court may:

  - Defer considering the motion or deny it;

  - Allow time to obtain affidavits or declarations or to take discovery; or

  - Issue any other appropriate order. FRCP 56(d).

4. *Reply papers.* A moving party may be required or permitted to prepare papers in addition to his original motion papers. AMJUR MOTIONS § 25. Papers answering or replying to opposing papers may be appropriate, in the interests of justice, where it appears there is a substantial reason for allowing a reply. Thus, a court may accept reply papers where a party demonstrates that the papers to which it seeks to file a reply raise new issues that are material to the disposition of the question before the court, or where the court determines, sua sponte, that it wishes further briefing of an issue raised in those papers and orders the submission of additional papers. FEDPROC § 62:360.

  a. *Function of reply papers.* The function of a reply affidavit is to answer the arguments made in opposition to the position taken by the movant and not to permit the movant to introduce new arguments in support of the motion. AMJUR MOTIONS § 25.

  b. *Issues raised for the first time in a reply document.* However, the view has been followed in some jurisdictions, that as a matter of judicial economy, where there is no prejudice and where the issues could be raised simply by filing a motion to dismiss, the trial court has discretion to consider arguments raised for the first time in a reply memorandum, and that a trial court may grant a motion to strike issues raised for the first time in a reply memorandum. AMJUR MOTIONS § 26.

5. *Sur-reply.* Absent permission of the Judge hearing the motion, sur-reply papers are not permitted. NY R USDCTWD Civ Rule 7(a)(6).

6. *Motion to settle an order.* When counsel are unable to agree on the form of a proposed order, the prevailing party may move, upon seven (7) days notice to all parties, to settle the order. The Court may award costs and attorney's fees against an attorney if it determines that the attorney's unreasonable conduct necessitated bringing the motion. NY R USDCTWD Civ Rule 7(d)(2).

7. *Notice of appearance.* No notice of appearance is required of an attorney whose name and address appear at the end of a complaint, notice of removal, pre-answer motion, or answer. In all other circumstances, an attorney appearing for a party in a civil case shall promptly file a written notice of appearance. NY R USDCTWD Civ Rule 83.2(b). For more information on appearances and withdrawals, refer to NY R USDCTWD Civ Rule 83.2.

8. *Related cases.* Each attorney appearing in a civil case has a continuing duty to promptly notify the Clerk of Court when the attorney has reason to believe that said case is related to some other pending civil or criminal action(s) such that their assignment to the same Judge would avoid unnecessary duplication of judicial effort. As soon as the attorney becomes aware of such a relationship, the attorney shall notify the Clerk of Court by letter of the relevant facts, and the Clerk of Court will transmit that notification to the Judges to whom the cases have been assigned. NY R USDCTWD Civ Rule 5.1(e).

9. *Alternative dispute resolution (ADR).* This Court has adopted an Alternative Dispute Resolution Plan ("ADR"), as implemented by Standing Order (NY R USDCTWD ADR Plan), under which certain civil cases are referred automatically to ADR upon filing. NY R USDCTWD Civ Rule 16(a). The United States District Court for the Western District of New York (the "Court") adopted the ADR Plan on January 1, 2006 (the "Effective Date"), to make available to civil litigants court-administered ADR interventions and processes designed to provide quicker, less expensive and potentially more satisfying alternatives to continuing litigation, without impairing the quality of justice or the right to trial. NY R USDCTWD ADR Plan(1)(1.2)(A).

  a. *Scope.* This ADR Plan (NY R USDCTWD ADR Plan) applies to civil actions pending or commenced on and after the Effective Date, except as otherwise indicated in NY R USDCTWD ADR

Plan. The ADR Plan supplements the Local Rules of Civil Procedure for the United States District Court for the Western District of New York, which shall remain in full effect for all cases. NY R USDCTWD ADR Plan(1)(1.2)(B).

b. *Referral to ADR*

   i. *New cases.* All civil cases filed on and after the Effective Date of the ADR Plan shall be referred automatically for ADR. NY R USDCTWD ADR Plan(2)(2.1)(A). Notice of the ADR requirements will be provided to all parties immediately upon the filing of a complaint and answer or a notice of removal; NY R USDCTWD ADR Plan(2)(2.1)(A); NY R USDCTWD Civ Rule 16(a). ADR intervention will be scheduled at the conference held pursuant to Local Rule of Civil Procedure 16.1. NY R USDCTWD ADR Plan(2)(2.1)(A). [Editor's note: the reference to Local Rule of Civil Procedure 16.1 is likely meant to be a reference to NY R USDCTWD Civ Rule 16(b)].

   • Litigants in cases not referred automatically to ADR must consider possible agreement to the use of an ADR process. NY R USDCTWD Civ Rule 16(a).

   • For a list of exemptions from automatic referral, refer to NY R USDCTWD ADR Plan(2)(2.1)(A).

   ii. *Pending cases.* The assigned Judge on any pending civil case may, sua sponte or with status conference, issue an order referring the case for ADR. NY R USDCTWD ADR Plan(2)(2.1)(B); NY R USDCTWD Civ Rule 16(a). The order shall specify a date on which the ADR intervention is to be completed. NY R USDCTWD ADR Plan(2)(2.1)(B).

   iii. *Stipulation.* A case may be referred for ADR by stipulation of all parties. Stipulations shall be filed and shall designate the specific ADR intervention the parties have selected, the time frame within which the ADR process will be completed and the selected Neutral. Stipulations are presumed acceptable unless the assigned Judge determines that the interests of justice are not served. NY R USDCTWD ADR Plan(2)(2.1)(C).

   iv. *Relief from ADR referral*

   • *Opting out motions.* Any party may file, with the assigned Judge for that case, a motion to opt out of, or for relief from, ADR. NY R USDCTWD ADR Plan(2)(2.2)(A).

   • *Motion.* Opting Out Motions must be made within fourteen (14) days from (1) the date of the first discovery conference under Local Rule 16.1 in new cases, or (2) the date of a sua sponte ADR Referral Order in pending cases. NY R USDCTWD ADR Plan(2)(2.2)(B). [Editor's note: the reference to Local Rule 16.1 is likely meant to be a reference to NY R USDCTWD Civ Rule 16(b)].

   • *Criteria.* Opting Out Motions shall be granted only for "good cause" shown. Inconvenience, travel costs, attorney fees or other costs shall not constitute "good cause." A party seeking relief from ADR must set forth the reasons why ADR has no reasonable chance of being productive. NY R USDCTWD ADR Plan(2)(2.2)(C).

   • *Judicial initiative.* The assigned Judge may, sua sponte, exempt any case from the Court's ADR Plan. NY R USDCTWD ADR Plan(2)(2.2)(D).

c. *ADR interventions*

   i. *Options.* It is expected that cases referred for ADR will proceed to Mediation. However, the following options are also available upon the stipulation of all parties:

   • Neutral Evaluation;

   • Mini Summary Trial;

   • Arbitration (Binding and Non-Binding);

   • Case Valuation; and

   • Settlement Week, when scheduled by the Court. NY R USDCTWD ADR Plan(4)(4.1)(A).

   ii. *Timing.* Timing is specific to the intervention and process chosen, as set forth in the corresponding sections in NY R USDCTWD ADR Plan. NY R USDCTWD ADR Plan(4)(4.1)(B).

      iii.   *Scheduling.* The referral of a case to ADR does not delay or defer other dates established in the Scheduling Order and has no effect on the scheduled progress of the case toward trial. NY R USDCTWD ADR Plan(4)(4.1)(C).

  d.  *Selecting an ADR intervention*

      i.   *New cases.* Prior to the Local Rule 16.1 scheduling conference, counsel and any unrepresented parties shall confer about ADR as part of their discussion of "the possibilities for a prompt settlement or resolution of the case" pursuant to FRCP 26(f). Unless the parties agree to a different intervention, it is presumed that they will participate in mediation. [Editor's note: the reference to Local Rule 16.1 is likely meant to be a reference to NY R USDCTWD Civ Rule 16(b)].

      ii.  *Pending cases.* In pending cases, all sua sponte referrals will be to mediation. Should the parties agree that a different ADR intervention is more appropriate to their case, they may submit a stipulation designating the specific ADR intervention selected, the time frame within which the ADR process will be completed and the identity of the Neutral. Stipulations must be filed within fourteen (14) days from the date of the ADR Referral Order and are presumed acceptable unless the assigned Judge determines that the interests of justice are not served. NY R USDCTWD ADR Plan(4)(4.2)(B).

  e.  For more information on alternative dispute resolution (ADR), refer to NY R USDCTWD ADR Plan.

10.  *Sanctions.* Failure of counsel for any party, or a party proceeding pro se, to appear before the Court at a conference, to complete the necessary preparations, or to be prepared to proceed to trial at the set time may be considered an abandonment of the case or a failure to prosecute or defend diligently. An appropriate order for sanctions may be entered against the defaulting party with respect to either a specific issue or the entire case. NY R USDCTWD Civ Rule 11(a). For more information, refer to NY R USDCTWD Civ Rule 11.

11.  *Pro se actions.* For information on the requirements in pro se actions, refer to NY R USDCTWD Civ Rule 5.2.

12.  *Individual judge practices.* Refer to the Miscellaneous section of this document for information on individual judge practices on general requirements for documents.

## D.  Documents

  1.  *Documents for moving party*

    a.  *Required documents*

      i.   *Notice of motion and motion.* A notice of motion is required for all motions, and must state: the relief sought, the grounds for the request, the papers submitted in support, and the return date for the motion, if known. A moving party who intends to file and serve reply papers must so state in the notice of motion. NY R USDCTWD Civ Rule 7(a)(1). Refer to the General Requirements section of this document for information on the notice of motion and motion.

      ii.  *Statement of material facts.* Upon any motion for summary judgment pursuant to FRCP 56, there shall be annexed to the notice of motion a separate, short, and concise statement, in numbered paragraphs, of the material facts as to which the moving party contends there is no genuine issue to be tried. Each such statement must be followed by citation to admissible evidence as required by FRCP 56(c)(1)(A). Citations shall identify with specificity the relevant page and paragraph or line number of the evidence cited. Failure to submit such a statement may constitute grounds for denial of the motion. NY R USDCTWD Civ Rule 56(a)(1).

        •  *Appendix.* All cited evidence, such as affidavits, relevant deposition testimony, responses to discovery requests, or other documents, that has not otherwise been filed in conjunction with the motion shall be filed as an appendix to the statement of facts prescribed by NY R USDCTWD Civ Rule 56(a)(1) or NY R USDCTWD Civ Rule 56(a)(2), supra, in conformity with FRCP 56(c)(1)(A), and denominated "Plaintiff's/Defendant's Appendix to Local Rule 56 Statement of Material Facts." NY R USDCTWD Civ Rule 56(a)(3).

iii. *Memorandum of law.* Absent leave of Court or as otherwise specified, upon any motion filed pursuant to FRCP 12, FRCP 56 or FRCP 65(a), the moving party shall file and serve a memorandum of law. Failure to comply with this requirement may constitute grounds for resolving the motion against the non-complying party. NY R USDCTWD Civ Rule 7(a)(2)(A). Refer to the Format section of this document for the formatting requirements for memoranda of law.

iv. *Supporting affidavit.* An affidavit must not contain legal arguments, but must contain factual and procedural background relevant to the motion it supports. Except for motions brought under FRCP 12(b)(1) (lack of subject matter jurisdiction), FRCP 12(b)(6) (failure to state a claim), FRCP 12(c) (judgment on the pleadings), and FRCP 12(f) (to strike), motions and opposition to motions shall be supported by at least one (1) affidavit and by such other evidence (i.e., deposition testimony, interrogatory answers, admissions, and documents) as appropriate to resolve the particular motion. Failure to comply with this requirement may constitute grounds for resolving the motion against the non-complying party. NY R USDCTWD Civ Rule 7(a)(3).

v. *Certificate of service.* FRCP 5(d) requires that the person making service under FRCP 5 certify that service has been effected. FRCP 5(Advisory Committee Notes). Having such information on file may be useful for many purposes, including proof of service if an issue arises concerning the effectiveness of the service. FRCP 5(Advisory Committee Notes). The Notice of Electronic Filing effectuates service for all registered users and no certificate of service is required when all filers on an action are Registered Users. The following exemptions require a certificate of service to be filed:

- When a document is manually filed, a certificate of service must be filed stating the manner in which service or notice was accomplished on each party so entitled. NY R USDCTWD ECF Procedures(2)(f)(iv).

- When a pro se filer (who isn't authorized to electronically file documents) is a party, a certificate of service must be filed stating the manner in which service or notice was accomplished on the pro se party. The Notice of Electronic Filing effectuates service for the Registered Users in this situation and it is not necessary to note service on those parties. A non-registered pro se filer is required to file certificates of service on all documents they file. NY R USDCTWD ECF Procedures(2)(f)(iv).

- If an attorney is exempt from electronic service, a certificate of service must be filed stating the manner in which service or notice was accomplished on the exempt attorney. The Notice of Electronic Filing effectuates service for the Registered Users in this situation and it is not necessary to note service on those parties. NY R USDCTWD ECF Procedures(2)(f)(iv).

b. *Supplemental documents*

i. *Supporting evidence.* When a motion relies on facts outside the record, the court may hear the matter on affidavits or may hear it wholly or partly on oral testimony or on depositions. FRCP 43(c). A party seeking or opposing any relief under the Federal Rules of Civil Procedure shall file only the portion(s) of a deposition, interrogatory, request for documents, request for admission, or other supporting material that is pertinent to the application. NY R USDCTWD Civ Rule 7(a)(4).

- *Supporting factual positions.* A party asserting that a fact cannot be or is genuinely disputed must support the assertion by: (1) citing to particular parts of materials in the record, including depositions, documents, electronically stored information, affidavits or declarations, stipulations (including those made for purposes of the motion only), admissions, interrogatory answers, or other materials; or (2) showing that the materials cited do not establish the absence or presence of a genuine dispute, or that an adverse party cannot produce admissible evidence to support the fact. FRCP 56(c)(1).

- *Objection that a fact is not supported by admissible evidence.* A party may object that the material cited to support or dispute a fact cannot be presented in a form that would be admissible in evidence. FRCP 56(c)(2).

- *Materials not cited.* The court need consider only the cited materials, but it may consider other materials in the record. FRCP 56(c)(3).

- *Affidavits or declarations.* An affidavit or declaration used to support or oppose a motion must be made on personal knowledge, set out facts that would be admissible in evidence, and show that the affiant or declarant is competent to testify on the matters stated. FRCP 56(c)(4).

ii. *Notice of constitutional question.* A party that files a pleading, written motion, or other paper drawing into question the constitutionality of a federal or state statute must promptly:

- *File notice.* File a notice of constitutional question stating the question and identifying the paper that raises it, if: (1) a federal statute is questioned and the parties do not include the United States, one of its agencies, or one of its officers or employees in an official capacity; or (2) a state statute is questioned and the parties do not include the state, one of its agencies, or one of its officers or employees in an official capacity; and

- *Serve notice.* Serve the notice and paper on the Attorney General of the United States if a federal statute is questioned—or on the state attorney general if a state statute is questioned—either by certified or registered mail or by sending it to an electronic address designated by the attorney general for this purpose. FRCP 5.1(a).

- *No forfeiture.* A party's failure to file and serve the notice, or the court's failure to certify, does not forfeit a constitutional claim or defense that is otherwise timely asserted. FRCP 5.1(d).

iii. *Nongovernmental corporate disclosure statement*

- *Contents.* A nongovernmental corporate party must file two (2) copies of a disclosure statement that: (1) identifies any parent corporation and any publicly held corporation owning ten percent (10%) or more of its stock; or (2) states that there is no such corporation. FRCP 7.1(a).

- *Time to file; Supplemental filing.* A party must: (1) file the disclosure statement with its first appearance, pleading, petition, motion, response, or other request addressed to the court; and (2) promptly file a supplemental statement if any required information changes. FRCP 7.1(b).

iv. *Notice to pro se litigant.* Any party moving for summary judgment against a pro se litigant shall file and serve with the motion papers a "Notice to Pro Se Litigant Regarding Rule 56 Motion For Summary Judgment" in the form provided by the Court. Failure to file and serve the form notice shall result in denial of the motion, without prejudice to proper renewal. Where the pro se party is not the plaintiff, the movant shall amend the form notice as necessary to reflect that fact. NY R USDCTWD Civ Rule 56(b).

v. *Copies of authorities.* In cases involving a pro se litigant, counsel shall, when serving a memorandum of law (or other submissions to the Court), provide the pro se litigant (but not other counsel or the Court) with printed copies of decisions cited therein that are unreported or reported exclusively on computerized databases. NY R USDCTWD Civ Rule 7(a)(8).

vi. *Proposed order.* All proposed orders must be submitted in a format compatible with WordPerfect or Microsoft Word format, which is a "Save As" option in most word processing software. Judges will not accept proposed orders in PDF format. NY R USDCTWD ECF Procedures(2)(j)(ii). Proposed orders should be attached to an Internet e-mail sent to the e-mail address of the assigned judge. NY R USDCTWD ECF Procedures(2)(j)(i). For the list of email addresses for the judges, refer to NY R USDCTWD ECF Procedures(2)(j)(i).

vii. *Paper copy for date-stamping with self-addressed envelope.* Parties requesting date-stamped copies of filed documents must provide a paper copy for date-stamping, and a self-addressed, adequately-sized envelope with proper postage affixed. NY R USDCTWD Civ Rule 5.1(d).

viii. *Courtesy copies.* The Court may, in its discretion, request courtesy copies on any other motion. NY R USDCTWD Civ Rule 7(a)(7). Courtesy copies of certain documents may be required.

Filers should refer to the "Judge Preferences" published on the Court's website. NY R USDCTWD ECF Procedures(2)(a)(iii).

2. *Documents for opposing party*

  a. *Required documents*

  i. *Opposition.* Refer to the General Requirements section of this document for information on the opposing papers.

  ii. *Opposing statement of material facts.* The papers opposing a motion for summary judgment shall include a response to each numbered paragraph in the moving party's statement, in correspondingly numbered paragraphs and, if necessary, additional paragraphs containing a short and concise statement of additional material facts as to which it is contended there exists a genuine issue to be tried. Each numbered paragraph in the moving party's statement of material facts may be deemed admitted for purposes of the motion unless it is specifically controverted by a correspondingly numbered paragraph in the opposing statement. NY R USDCTWD Civ Rule 56(a)(2).

  - *Appendix.* All cited evidence, such as affidavits, relevant deposition testimony, responses to discovery requests, or other documents, that has not otherwise been filed in conjunction with the motion shall be filed as an appendix to the statement of facts prescribed by NY R USDCTWD Civ Rule 56(a)(1) or NY R USDCTWD Civ Rule 56(a)(2), supra, in conformity with FRCP 56(c)(1)(A), and denominated "Plaintiff's/Defendant's Appendix to Local Rule 56 Statement of Material Facts." NY R USDCTWD Civ Rule 56(a)(3).

  iii. *Answering memorandum.* Absent leave of Court or as otherwise specified, upon any motion filed pursuant to FRCP 12, FRCP 56 or FRCP 65(a). . .the opposing party shall file and serve an answering memorandum. Failure to comply with this requirement may constitute grounds for resolving the motion against the non-complying party. NY R USDCTWD Civ Rule 7(a)(2)(A). Refer to the Format section of this document for the formatting requirements for memoranda of law.

  iv. *Supporting affidavit.* An affidavit must not contain legal arguments, but must contain factual and procedural background relevant to the motion it supports. Except for motions brought under FRCP 12(b)(1) (lack of subject matter jurisdiction), FRCP 12(b)(6) (failure to state a claim), FRCP 12(c) (judgment on the pleadings), and FRCP 12(f) (to strike), motions and opposition to motions shall be supported by at least one (1) affidavit and by such other evidence (i.e., deposition testimony, interrogatory answers, admissions, and documents) as appropriate to resolve the particular motion. Failure to comply with this requirement may constitute grounds for resolving the motion against the non-complying party. NY R USDCTWD Civ Rule 7(a)(3).

  v. *Certificate of service.* FRCP 5(d) requires that the person making service under FRCP 5 certify that service has been effected. FRCP 5(Advisory Committee Notes). Having such information on file may be useful for many purposes, including proof of service if an issue arises concerning the effectiveness of the service. FRCP 5(Advisory Committee Notes). The Notice of Electronic Filing effectuates service for all registered users and no certificate of service is required when all filers on an action are Registered Users. The following exemptions require a certificate of service to be filed:

  - When a document is manually filed, a certificate of service must be filed stating the manner in which service or notice was accomplished on each party so entitled. NY R USDCTWD ECF Procedures(2)(f)(iv).

  - When a pro se filer (who isn't authorized to electronically file documents) is a party, a certificate of service must be filed stating the manner in which service or notice was accomplished on the pro se party. The Notice of Electronic Filing effectuates service for the Registered Users in this situation and it is not necessary to note service on those parties. A non-registered pro se filer is required to file certificates of service on all documents they file. NY R USDCTWD ECF Procedures(2)(f)(iv).

- If an attorney is exempt from electronic service, a certificate of service must be filed stating the manner in which service or notice was accomplished on the exempt attorney. The Notice of Electronic Filing effectuates service for the Registered Users in this situation and it is not necessary to note service on those parties. NY R USDCTWD ECF Procedures(2)(f)(iv).

b. *Supplemental documents*

   i. *Supporting evidence.* When a motion relies on facts outside the record, the court may hear the matter on affidavits or may hear it wholly or partly on oral testimony or on depositions. FRCP 43(c). A party seeking or opposing any relief under the Federal Rules of Civil Procedure shall file only the portion(s) of a deposition, interrogatory, request for documents, request for admission, or other supporting material that is pertinent to the application. NY R USDCTWD Civ Rule 7(a)(4).

   - *Supporting factual positions.* A party asserting that a fact cannot be or is genuinely disputed must support the assertion by: (1) citing to particular parts of materials in the record, including depositions, documents, electronically stored information, affidavits or declarations, stipulations (including those made for purposes of the motion only), admissions, interrogatory answers, or other materials; or (2) showing that the materials cited do not establish the absence or presence of a genuine dispute, or that an adverse party cannot produce admissible evidence to support the fact. FRCP 56(c)(1).

   - *Objection that a fact is not supported by admissible evidence.* A party may object that the material cited to support or dispute a fact cannot be presented in a form that would be admissible in evidence. FRCP 56(c)(2).

   - *Materials not cited.* The court need consider only the cited materials, but it may consider other materials in the record. FRCP 56(c)(3).

   - *Affidavits or declarations.* An affidavit or declaration used to support or oppose a motion must be made on personal knowledge, set out facts that would be admissible in evidence, and show that the affiant or declarant is competent to testify on the matters stated. FRCP 56(c)(4).

   ii. *Notice of constitutional question.* A party that files a pleading, written motion, or other paper drawing into question the constitutionality of a federal or state statute must promptly:

   - *File notice.* File a notice of constitutional question stating the question and identifying the paper that raises it, if: (1) a federal statute is questioned and the parties do not include the United States, one of its agencies, or one of its officers or employees in an official capacity; or (2) a state statute is questioned and the parties do not include the state, one of its agencies, or one of its officers or employees in an official capacity; and

   - *Serve notice.* Serve the notice and paper on the Attorney General of the United States if a federal statute is questioned—or on the state attorney general if a state statute is questioned—either by certified or registered mail or by sending it to an electronic address designated by the attorney general for this purpose. FRCP 5.1(a).

   - *No forfeiture.* A party's failure to file and serve the notice, or the court's failure to certify, does not forfeit a constitutional claim or defense that is otherwise timely asserted. FRCP 5.1(d).

   iii. *Cross-motion.* Refer to the Timing section of this document for information on the cross-motion, opposition to the cross-motion, and reply in support of the cross-motion.

   iv. *Copies of authorities.* In cases involving a pro se litigant, counsel shall, when serving a memorandum of law (or other submissions to the Court), provide the pro se litigant (but not other counsel or the Court) with printed copies of decisions cited therein that are unreported or reported exclusively on computerized databases. NY R USDCTWD Civ Rule 7(a)(8).

   v. *Paper copy for date-stamping with self-addressed envelope.* Parties requesting date-stamped copies of filed documents must provide a paper copy for date-stamping, and a self-addressed, adequately-sized envelope with proper postage affixed. NY R USDCTWD Civ Rule 5.1(d).

      vi.   *Courtesy copies.* Courtesy copies of certain documents may be required. Filers should refer to the "Judge Preferences" published on the Court's website. NY R USDCTWD ECF Procedures(2)(a)(iii).

3.  *Individual judge practices.* Refer to the Miscellaneous section of this document for information on individual judge practices on required documents.

## E. Format

1.  *Form of documents.* The rules governing captions and other matters of form in pleadings apply to motions and other papers. FRCP 7(b)(2).

    a.  *Form, generally.* All pleadings, motions, and other papers that a party presents for filing, whether in paper form or in electronic form, shall meet the following requirements:

       i.  *Font size.* All text and footnotes shall be in a font size of at least twelve (12) point type. NY R USDCTWD Civ Rule 10(a)(1).

      ii.  *Spacing.* All text in the body of the document must be double-spaced, except that text in block quotations and footnotes may be single-spaced. NY R USDCTWD Civ Rule 10(a)(2).

- Extensive footnotes and block quotes may not be used to circumvent page limitations. NY R USDCTWD Civ Rule 10(a)(3).

     iii.  *Margins.* Documents must have one (1) inch margins on all four sides. NY R USDCTWD Civ Rule 10(a)(4).

     iv.  *Page numbering.* Pages must be consecutively numbered. NY R USDCTWD Civ Rule 10(a)(5).

    b.  *Additional requirements for paper filing.* Documents presented for filing in paper form shall meet the following additional requirements:

       i.  *Paper.* Documents must be on durable white eight and one-half by eleven (8-1/2 x 11) inch paper of good quality. NY R USDCTWD Civ Rule 10(b)(1).

- All documents must be single-sided. NY R USDCTWD Civ Rule 10(b)(5).

      ii.  *Text.* All text must be plainly and legibly written, typewritten, printed or reproduced. NY R USDCTWD Civ Rule 10(b)(2).

     iii.  *Ink.* Documents must be in black or blue ink. NY R USDCTWD Civ Rule 10(b)(3).

     iv.  *Binding.* The pages of each document must be stapled or in some other way fastened together. NY R USDCTWD Civ Rule 10(b)(4).

    c.  *Caption; Names of parties.* Every pleading must have a caption with the court's name, a title, a file number, and a FRCP 7(a) designation. The title of the complaint must name all the parties; the title of other pleadings, after naming the first party on each side, may refer generally to other parties. FRCP 10(a).

    d.  *Paragraphs; Separate statements.* A party must state its claims or defenses in numbered paragraphs, each limited as far as practicable to a single set of circumstances. A later pleading may refer by number to a paragraph in an earlier pleading. If doing so would promote clarity, each claim founded on a separate transaction or occurrence—and each defense other than a denial—must be stated in a separate count or defense. FRCP 10(b).

    e.  *Adoption by reference; Exhibits.* A statement in a pleading may be adopted by reference elsewhere in the same pleading or in any other pleading or motion. A copy of a written instrument that is an exhibit to a pleading is a part of the pleading for all purposes. FRCP 10(c).

    f.  *Citation of local rules.* The Local Rules of Civil Procedure for the United States District Court for the Western District of New York shall be cited as "L.R.Civ.P." NY R USDCTWD Civ Rule 1.1.

    g.  *Acceptance by the clerk.* The clerk must not refuse to file a paper solely because it is not in the form prescribed by the Federal Rules of Civil Procedure or by a local rule or practice. FRCP 5(d)(4). The Court may reject documents that do not comply with the requirements in NY R USDCTWD Civ Rule 10. NY R USDCTWD Civ Rule 10.

2. *Form of electronic documents.* All pleadings, motions, and other papers that a party presents for filing, whether in paper form or in electronic form, shall meet the requirements in NY R USDCTWD Civ Rule 10(a). NY R USDCTWD Civ Rule 10(a). Refer above for more information.

    a. *Conversion to PDF.* A document created with a word processor, or a paper document, must be converted to Portable Document Format to be electronically filed with the court. NY R USDCTWD ECF Procedures(2)(a)(v).

        i. Documents which exist only in paper form may be scanned into a portable document format (PDF) for electronic filing. NY R USDCTWD ECF Procedures(2)(a)(v). Before filing a scanned document with the court, a Filing User must verify its legibility. NY R USDCTWD ECF Procedures(2)(a)(iv).

        ii. Electronic documents must be converted to .PDF from a word processing program and must be text searchable. Do not print, scan and .PDF your document when it has been created in a word processing program. Additional information on working with PDFs is located in NY R USDCTWD ECF Procedures(4b). NY R USDCTWD ECF Procedures(2)(a)(v).

    b. *Hyperlinks.* Pursuant to the policy set forth by the Judicial Conference in October 2005, a hyperlink contained in a filing is no more than a convenient mechanism for accessing material cited in a document. A hyperlink reference is extraneous to any filed document and is not part of the Court's record. NY R USDCTWD ECF Procedures(2)(a)(vi).

        i. In order to preserve the integrity of the Court record, users wishing to insert hyperlinks in Court filings shall continue to use the conventional method for the cited authority, in addition to the hyperlink. NY R USDCTWD ECF Procedures(2)(a)(vi).

        ii. The Court accepts no responsibility for, and does not endorse any product, organization, and content at any hyperlinked site, or at any site to which that site may be linked. The Court accepts no responsibility for the availability or functionality of any hyperlink. NY R USDCTWD ECF Procedures(2)(a)(vi).

    c. *Attachments and exhibits*

        i. Attachments and exhibits larger than five megabytes (5 MB) shall be filed electronically in separate five megabyte (5 MB) segments. NY R USDCTWD ECF Procedures(2)(d)(i).

        ii. Filing Users must submit in electronic form all documents referenced as exhibits or attachments, except as otherwise provided in NY R USDCTWD ECF Procedures. A Filing User must submit as exhibits or attachments only those excerpts of the referenced documents that are directly germane to the matter under consideration by the court. Excerpted material must be clearly and prominently identified as such. Filing Users who file excerpts of documents as exhibits or attachments under NY R USDCTWD ECF Procedures(2)(d)(ii) do so without prejudice to their right to timely file additional excerpts or the complete document. Responding parties may timely file additional excerpts or the complete document that they believe are directly germane. The Court may require parties to file additional excerpts or the complete document. A Filing User must request leave of the Court to file a document exhibit or attachment in non-electronic form. NY R USDCTWD ECF Procedures(2)(d)(ii).

        iii. Exhibits offered or admitted at trial will not be filed electronically or conventionally unless so ordered by the Court. NY R USDCTWD ECF Procedures(2)(d)(iii).

        iv. Exhibits such as videotapes and tape recordings shall be filed in the conventional manner with the Clerk of Court, and a Notice of Manual Filing shall be electronically filed by the party. Manually filed exhibits must have the case number and case name securely fastened or marked on the item. NY R USDCTWD ECF Procedures(2)(d)(iii).

        v. Continuation of exhibit entries (for exhibits that are too large to attach to a main document) must be filed and entered on the same day that the main document was filed. NY R USDCTWD ECF Procedures(2)(d)(iv).

    d. *Color documents.* Documents in color or containing graphics take much longer to upload. Filing users are encouraged to configure their scanners to scan documents at 200 dpi and preferably in black and white rather than color. NY R USDCTWD ECF Procedures(2)(d)(v).

e. *Large documents.* Due to the length of time it takes to download large files, documents larger than five megabytes (5 MB) (approximately one hundred (100) pages of a .pdf scanned document) must be filed electronically in separate five megabyte (5 MB) segments. A party who believes a document is too lengthy to electronically image (i.e. scan), may contact the Court Room Deputy for the assigned judge and request permission to file that document conventionally. If granted permission to file the document conventionally, the Filing User shall electronically file a "notice of manual filing" for that item. Exhibits submitted to the Court conventionally shall be served on other parties conventionally. NY R USDCTWD ECF Procedures(2)(d)(vi).

3. *Form of memoranda of law.* Memoranda in support of or in opposition to any motion shall not exceed twenty-five (25) pages in length, and reply memoranda shall not exceed ten (10) pages in length. A party seeking to exceed the page limit must make application by letter to the Judge hearing the motion, with copies to all counsel, at least seven (7) days before the date on which the memorandum must be filed. NY R USDCTWD Civ Rule 7(a)(2)(C).

4. *Signing of pleadings, motions and other papers*

a. *Signature.* Every pleading, written motion, and other paper must be signed by at least one attorney of record in the attorney's name—or by a party personally if the party is unrepresented. The paper must state the signer's address, e-mail address, and telephone number. FRCP 11(a). Documents presented for paper filing must contain an original signature. NY R USDCTWD Civ Rule 10(b)(6).

  i. *Electronic signatures*

  - *Non-attorney signature.* If the original document requires the signature of a non-attorney, the filing party shall obtain the signature of the non-attorney on the document. NY R USDCTWD ECF Procedures(2)(g)(i). The filing party or attorney then shall file the document electronically indicating the signatory's name in the form "s/(name)." NY R USDCTWD ECF Procedures(2)(g)(i)(1). A non-filing signatory or party who disputes the authenticity of an electronically filed document or the authenticity of the signature on that document must file an objection to the document within ten (10) days of receiving the Notice of Electronic Filing. NY R USDCTWD ECF Procedures(2)(g)(i)(2).

  - *Registered user signature.* The username and password required to file documents on the Electronic Filing System serve as the Filing User's signature on all electronic documents filed with this Court. The also serve as a signature for the purposes of FRCP 11, the Federal Rules of Civil Procedure, the Local Rules of Civil Procedure for the United States District Court for the Western District of New York, and any other purpose for which a signature is required in connection with proceedings before this Court. A pleading requiring a Registered User's signature must include a signature block in the format found in NY R USDCTWD ECF Procedures(2)(g)(iii). NY R USDCTWD ECF Procedures(2)(g)(iii). Any party challenging the authenticity of an electronically filed document or the attorney's signature on that document must file an objection to the document within ten (10) days of receiving the Notice of Electronic Filing. NY R USDCTWD ECF Procedures(2)(g)(iii)(1).

  - *Multiple signatures.* The following procedure applies when a stipulation or other document requires two or more signatures: The filing party shall initially confirm that the document is acceptable to all persons required to sign the document and shall obtain the signatures of all parties on the document. NY R USDCTWD ECF Procedures(2)(g)(iv)(1). The filing party or attorney then shall file the document electronically indicating the signatories, e.g., "s/Jane Doe," "s/John Smith," etc. NY R USDCTWD ECF Procedures(2)(g)(iv)(2). A non-filing signatory or party who disputes the authenticity of an electronically filed document containing multiple signatures or the authenticity of the signatures themselves must file an objection to the document within ten (10) days of receiving the Notice of Electronic Filing. NY R USDCTWD ECF Procedures(2)(g)(iv)(3).

  ii. *No verification or accompanying affidavit required for pleadings.* Unless a rule or statute specifically states otherwise, a pleading need not be verified or accompanied by an affidavit. FRCP 11(a).

    iii.  *Unsigned papers.* The court must strike an unsigned paper unless the omission is promptly corrected after being called to the attorney's or party's attention. FRCP 11(a).

  b.  *Representations to the court.* By presenting to the court a pleading, written motion, or other paper—whether by signing, filing, submitting, or later advocating it—an attorney or unrepresented party certifies that to the best of the person's knowledge, information, and belief, formed after an inquiry reasonable under the circumstances:

    i.  It is not being presented for any improper purpose, such as to harass, cause unnecessary delay, or needlessly increase the cost of litigation;

    ii.  The claims, defenses, and other legal contentions are warranted by existing law or by a nonfrivolous argument for extending, modifying, or reversing existing law or for establishing new law;

    iii.  The factual contentions have evidentiary support or, if specifically so identified, will likely have evidentiary support after a reasonable opportunity for further investigation or discovery; and

    iv.  The denials of factual contentions are warranted on the evidence or, if specifically so identified, are reasonably based on belief or a lack of information. FRCP 11(b).

  c.  *Sanctions.* If, after notice and a reasonable opportunity to respond, the court determines that FRCP 11(b) has been violated, the court may impose an appropriate sanction on any attorney, law firm, or party that violated FRCP 11(b) or is responsible for the violation. FRCP 11(c)(1). Refer to the United States District Court for the Western District of New York KeyRules Motion for Sanctions document for more information.

5.  *Privacy protection for filings made with the court.* In all filings, parties shall comply with FRCP 5.2. NY R USDCTWD ECF Procedures(2)(m)(i).

  a.  *Redacted filings.* Unless the court orders otherwise, in an electronic or paper filing with the court that contains an individual's Social Security number, taxpayer-identification number, or birth date, the name of an individual known to be a minor, or a financial-account number, a party or nonparty making the filing may include only:

    i.  The last four (4) digits of the Social Security number and taxpayer-identification number;

    ii.  The year of the individual's birth;

    iii.  The minor's initials; and

    iv.  The last four (4) digits of the financial-account number. FRCP 5.2(a).

  b.  *Exemptions from the redaction requirement.* The redaction requirement does not apply to the following:

    i.  A financial-account number that identifies the property allegedly subject to forfeiture in a forfeiture proceeding;

    ii.  The record of an administrative or agency proceeding;

    iii.  The official record of a state-court proceeding;

    iv.  The record of a court or tribunal, if that record was not subject to the redaction requirement when originally filed;

    v.  A filing covered by FRCP 5.2(c) or FRCP 5.2(d); and

    vi.  A pro se filing in an action brought under 28 U.S.C.A. § 2241, 28 U.S.C.A. § 2254, or 28 U.S.C.A. § 2255. FRCP 5.2(b).

  c.  *Limitations on remote access to electronic files; Social Security appeals and immigration cases.* Unless the court orders otherwise, in an action for benefits under the Social Security Act, and in an action or proceeding relating to an order of removal, to relief from removal, or to immigration benefits or detention, access to an electronic file is authorized as follows:

    i.  The parties and their attorneys may have remote electronic access to any part of the case file, including the administrative record;

    ii.   Any other person may have electronic access to the full record at the courthouse, but may have remote electronic access only to:

- The docket maintained by the court; and

- An opinion, order, judgment, or other disposition of the court, but not any other part of the case file or the administrative record. FRCP 5.2(c).

  d.  *Filings made under seal.* The court may order that a filing be made under seal without redaction. The court may later unseal the filing or order the person who made the filing to file a redacted version for the public record. FRCP 5.2(d). For more information on sealing documents, refer to NY R USDCTWD Civ Rule 5.3, NY R USDCTWD ECF Procedures(2)(o)(i)(1), NY R USDCTWD ECF Procedures(2)(o)(i)(2), and NY R USDCTWD ECF Procedures(2)(o)(i)(3).

  e.  *Protective orders.* For good cause, the court may by order in a case:

    i.   Require redaction of additional information; or

    ii.   Limit or prohibit a nonparty's remote electronic access to a document filed with the court. FRCP 5.2(e).

  f.  *Option for additional unredacted filing under seal.* A person making a redacted filing may also file an unredacted copy under seal. The court must retain the unredacted copy as part of the record. FRCP 5.2(f).

  g.  *Option for filing a reference list.* A filing that contains redacted information may be filed together with a reference list that identifies each item of redacted information and specifies an appropriate identifier that uniquely corresponds to each item listed. The list must be filed under seal and may be amended as of right. Any reference in the case to a listed identifier will be construed to refer to the corresponding item of information. FRCP 5.2(g).

  h.  *Waiver of protection of identifiers.* A person waives the protection of FRCP 5.2(a) as to the person's own information by filing it without redaction and not under seal. FRCP 5.2(h).

6.  *Individual judge practices.* Refer to the Miscellaneous section of this document for information on individual judge practices on formatting documents.

## F. Filing and Service Requirements

1.  *Filing requirements.* Any paper after the complaint that is required to be served—together with a certificate of service—must be filed within a reasonable time after service. FRCP 5(d)(1). All pleadings and other papers shall be filed and served in accordance with the Federal Rules of Civil Procedure and the CM/ECF Administrative Procedures Guide (NY R USDCTWD ECF Procedures). NY R USDCTWD Civ Rule 5.1(a). For information on filing of miscellaneous cases and irregular documents, refer to NY R USDCTWD Civ Rule 5.6.

  a.  *How filing is made; In general.* A paper is filed by delivering it:

    i.   To the clerk; or

    ii.   To a judge who agrees to accept it for filing, and who must then note the filing date on the paper and promptly send it to the clerk. FRCP 5(d)(2).

  b.  *Electronic filing*

    i.   *Authorization of electronic filing program.* A court may, by local rule, allow papers to be filed, signed, or verified by electronic means that are consistent with any technical standards established by the Judicial Conference of the United States. A local rule may require electronic filing only if reasonable exceptions are allowed. A paper filed electronically in compliance with a local rule is a written paper for purposes of the Federal Rules of Civil Procedure. FRCP 5(d)(3).

- All civil cases filed in this Court are assigned to the Electronic Case Filing System ("ECF"). The procedures for electronic filing and any exceptions to the electronic filing requirements are set forth in the CM/ECF Administrative Procedures Guide (NY R USDCTWD ECF Procedures) which is available on the Court's website. NY R US-DCTWD Civ Rule 5.1(a).

ii. *Scope of electronic filing.* The U.S. District Court for the Western District of New York requires attorneys in civil and criminal cases to file documents with the Court electronically over the Internet using its Case Management/Electronic Case Filing (CM/ECF) system. NY R US-DCTWD ECF Procedures. Beginning January 1, 2004, all civil and criminal cases currently pending and newly filed, except as expressly noted herein, were assigned to the Electronic Case Filing System ("System"). Except as expressly provided and in exceptional circumstances preventing a Filing User from filing electronically, all petitions, motions, memoranda of law, or other pleadings and documents required to be filed with the Court in connection with a case assigned to the System must be electronically filed. NY R USDCTWD ECF Procedures(1)(a).

- *Mandatory electronic filing.* All documents on civil, criminal, miscellaneous civil, miscellaneous criminal and new civil case openings, except sealed documents, sealed cases, opening of a criminal case, opening of a miscellaneous case and as expressly provided for in these procedures (NY R USDCTWD ECF Procedures), shall be electronically filed on the system. NY R USDCTWD ECF Procedures(2)(a)(i). NY R USDCTWD Civ Rule 29

- *Stipulations.* Pursuant to NY R USDCTWD Civ Rule 29, all stipulations (whether the stipulation is final or when it requires a judge's signature) shall be filed electronically. NY R USDCTWD ECF Procedures(2)(p)(i).

- *Letters.* The electronic filing of letters is generally prohibited unless granted permission by an assigned judge. Letters to the Court must be submitted conventionally. NY R US-DCTWD ECF Procedures(2)(q)(i).

- *Exceptions.* The Court requires attorneys to file documents electronically, absent a showing of good cause, unless otherwise excused by the procedures set forth below or by Order of the Court. NY R USDCTWD ECF Procedures.

iii. *Conventional filing of documents.* The procedures in NY R USDCTWD ECF Procedures(2)(o) govern documents filed conventionally. The Court, upon application, may also authorize conventional filing of other documents otherwise subject to the procedures in NY R US-DCTWD ECF Procedures(2)(o). NY R USDCTWD ECF Procedures(2)(o)(i).

- *Documents filed under seal.* Unredacted documents filed with the Court pursuant to the privacy provisions of FRCP 5.2 shall be submitted in a sealing envelope with the information in NY R USDCTWD ECF Procedures(2)(o)(i)(1) on the envelope. NY R USDCTWD ECF Procedures(2)(o)(i)(1). If the document is larger than five (5) pages, a disk should be provided to the Clerks Office which contains the document in a .pdf format. NY R USDCTWD ECF Procedures(2)(o)(i)(1). For more information on documents filed under seal, refer to NY R USDCTWD ECF Procedures(2)(o)(i)(1), NY R USDCTWD ECF Procedures(2)(o)(i)(2), and NY R USDCTWD ECF Procedures(2)(o)(i)(3).

- *Magistrate judge consents.* Pursuant to FRCP 73(b), parties' filing consents to jurisdiction by United States Magistrate Judge will continue to be treated as non-public documents until all parties have consented. Therefore, parties must submit conventionally (in paper form) and not electronically file their consent forms so that the consent is not a public document. If all parties consent to the jurisdiction of a Magistrate Judge, the Clerk will scan all consent forms which will then become a public document. NY R USDCTWD ECF Procedures(2)(o)(i)(3).

- *Pro se filers.* Pro Se filers shall file paper originals of all initiating documents, pleadings, motions, affidavits, briefs and other documents which must be signed or which require either verification or an unsworn declaration under any rule or statute. The Clerk's Office will scan these original documents into an electronic file in the System. A certificate of service is required for all documents a pro se litigant files with the court. If a Pro Se filer is granted permission to register to electronically file documents, they shall comply with the guidelines contained in this document (NY R USDCTWD ECF Procedures). NY R USDCTWD ECF Procedures(2)(o)(i)(4).

- *Social Security cases.* Absent a showing of good cause, and except as provided in Section o(i)(4) above, all documents, notices and orders in Social Security reviews will be filed and noticed electronically, except as noted in NY R USDCTWD ECF Procedures(2)(o)(i)(6). For more information, refer to NY R USDCTWD ECF Procedures(2)(o)(i)(6).

- For more information on conventional filing of documents, refer to NY R USDCTWD ECF Procedures(2)(o)(i).

iv. *Consequences of electronic filing.* Electronic transmission of a document to the System consistent with these procedures (NY R USDCTWD ECF Procedures), whether accomplished by the Filing User or a Court User, together with the transmission of a Notice of Electronic Filing from the Court, constitutes filing of a document for all purposes of the Federal Rules of Civil Procedure and the Local Rules of Civil Procedure for the United States District Court for the Western District of New York, and constitutes entry of the document on the docket kept by the Clerk under FRCP 58 and FRCP 79. A document shall not be considered filed for purposes of the Federal Rules of Civil until the filing party receives a System generated Notice of Electronic Filing. NY R USDCTWD ECF Procedures(2)(a)(i).

- E-mailing a document to the Clerk's Office or to the assigned judge shall not constitute "filing" of such document. NY R USDCTWD ECF Procedures(2)(a)(i)(1).

v. *Filing fees.* Any fee required for filing of a pleading or paper in District Court is payable to the Clerk of Court by check or money order. In addition, when opening a civil case on line, filing a notice of appeal on line or applying to appear pro hac vice on line, the fees shall be paid on line by registered users through the federal electronic payment website. Users will be directed to the federal electronic payment website while entering their transaction and should have a credit card available. When opening a civil case and applying to proceed in forma pauperis or when the United States of America opens a case, the payment screen can by bypassed to complete the transaction. Additional information on making electronic payments can be located on the court's website. NY R USDCTWD ECF Procedures(2)(h)(i).

2. *Service requirements.* All pleadings and other papers shall be filed and served in accordance with the Federal Rules of Civil Procedure and the CM/ECF Administrative Procedures Guide (NY R USDCTWD ECF Procedures). NY R USDCTWD Civ Rule 5.1(a).

   a. *Service; When required*

      i. *In general.* Unless the Federal Rules of Civil Procedure provide otherwise, each of the following papers must be served on every party:

         - An order stating that service is required;
         - A pleading filed after the original complaint, unless the court orders otherwise under FRCP 5(c) because there are numerous defendants;
         - A discovery paper required to be served on a party, unless the court orders otherwise;
         - A written motion, except one that may be heard ex parte; and
         - A written notice, appearance, demand, or offer of judgment, or any similar paper. FRCP 5(a)(1).

      ii. *If a party fails to appear.* No service is required on a party who is in default for failing to appear. But a pleading that asserts a new claim for relief against such a party must be served on that party under FRCP 4. FRCP 5(a)(2).

      iii. *Seizing property.* If an action is begun by seizing property and no person is or need be named as a defendant, any service required before the filing of an appearance, answer, or claim must be made on the person who had custody or possession of the property when it was seized. FRCP 5(a)(3).

   b. *Service; How made*

      i. *Serving an attorney.* If a party is represented by an attorney, service under FRCP 5 must be made on the attorney unless the court orders service on the party. FRCP 5(b)(1).

      ii. *Service in general.* A paper is served under FRCP 5 by:

         - Handing it to the person;

1493

- Leaving it: (1) at the person's office with a clerk or other person in charge or, if no one is in charge, in a conspicuous place in the office; or (2) if the person has no office or the office is closed, at the person's dwelling or usual place of abode with someone of suitable age and discretion who resides there;

- Mailing it to the person's last known address—in which event service is complete upon mailing;

- Leaving it with the court clerk if the person has no known address;

- Sending it by electronic means if the person consented in writing—in which event service is complete upon transmission, but is not effective if the serving party learns that it did not reach the person to be served; or

- Delivering it by any other means that the person consented to in writing—in which event service is complete when the person making service delivers it to the agency designated to make delivery. FRCP 5(b)(2).

iii. *Service by overnight delivery.* All papers, other than a subpoena or a summons and complaint, may be served on counsel of record by overnight delivery service at the address designated by the attorney for that purpose, or if none is designated, at the attorney's last known address. Service by overnight delivery shall be complete upon deposit of the paper(s), enclosed in a properly addressed wrapper, into the custody of the overnight delivery service, prior to the latest time designated by the service for overnight delivery. NY R USDCTWD Civ Rule 5.1(g). "Overnight delivery service" means any delivery service which regularly accepts items for overnight delivery to any address within the Court's jurisdiction. NY R USDCTWD Civ Rule 5.1(g).

iv. *Service of documents by electronic means*

- *Service on registered users.* Registered Users consent to the electronic service of all documents, and must make available an electronic mail address for service during the registration process. Upon the filing of a document by a party, a Notice of Electronic Filing, with a hyperlink to the filed document, will be automatically generated by the electronic filing system and sent via electronic mail to the e-mail addresses of all parties participating in the electronic filing system in the case. Electronic service of the Notice of Electronic Filing constitutes service of the filed document for all purposes of the Federal Rules of Civil Procedure and the Local Rules of Civil Procedure for the United States District Court for the Western District of New York. NY R USDCTWD ECF Procedures(2)(f)(i). The Notice of Electronic Filing effectuates service for all registered users and no certificate of service is required when all filers on an action are Registered Users. NY R USDCTWD ECF Procedures(2)(f)(iv).

- *Time limit for opening hyperlink.* The hyperlink to filed documents contained in the Notice of Electronic Filing must be opened within fifteen (15) days from the date the document was filed to provide registered users access to the document. The hyperlink expires after fifteen (15) days and users will be unable to access documents for free after that time. Filing Users are encouraged to check their e-mail frequently for notice of filed documents. NY R USDCTWD ECF Procedures(2)(f)(ii).

- *Service on exempted attorneys or pro se litigants who do not have permission to file electronically.* Attorneys granted an exemption from electronically filing documents in the System and pro se litigants who have not been granted permission to electronically file documents are entitled to a paper copy of any electronically filed pleading, document or order. The filing party must therefore provide the non-registered party with the pleading, document or order according to the Federal Rules of Civil Procedure. NY R USDCTWD ECF Procedures(2)(f)(iii).

- *E-mailing or faxing documents.* E-mailing or faxing a pleading or document to any party shall not constitute service of the pleading or document. NY R USDCTWD ECF Procedures(2)(f)(v).

    v.   *Using court facilities.* If a local rule so authorizes, a party may use the court's transmission facilities to make service under FRCP 5(b)(2)(E). FRCP 5(b)(3).

   c.  *Serving numerous defendants*

     i.  *In general.* If an action involves an unusually large number of defendants, the court may, on motion or on its own, order that:

- Defendants' pleadings and replies to them need not be served on other defendants;

- Any crossclaim, counterclaim, avoidance, or affirmative defense in those pleadings and replies to them will be treated as denied or avoided by all other parties; and

- Filing any such pleading and serving it on the plaintiff constitutes notice of the pleading to all parties. FRCP 5(c)(1).

     ii.  *Notifying parties.* A copy of every such order must be served on the parties as the court directs. FRCP 5(c)(2).

3.  *Pro se actions.* For information on the requirements in pro se actions, refer to NY R USDCTWD Civ Rule 5.2.

4.  *Individual judge practices.* Refer to the Miscellaneous section of this document for information on individual judge practices on filing and serving documents.

## G. Hearings

1.  *Hearings, generally*

   a.  *Oral argument.* Due process does not require that oral argument be permitted on a motion and, except as otherwise provided by local rule, the district court has discretion to determine whether it will decide the motion on the papers or hear argument by counsel (and perhaps receive evidence). FPP § 1190; F.D.I.C. v. Deglau, 207 F.3d 153 (3d Cir. 2000).

     i.  The parties shall appear for oral argument on all motions they make returnable before a Judge on the scheduled return date for the motion. In its discretion, the Court may notify the parties that oral argument shall not be heard on any given motion. Thus, the parties should be prepared to have their motion papers serve as the sole method of argument. NY R USDCTWD Civ Rule 7(c).

   b.  *Providing a regular schedule for oral hearings.* A court may establish regular times and places for oral hearings on motions. FRCP 78(a).

   c.  *Providing for submission on briefs.* By rule or order, the court may provide for submitting and determining motions on briefs, without oral hearings. FRCP 78(b).

2.  *Hearing on motion for summary judgment.* Even though FRCP 56(c) makes reference to a hearing on the motion for summary judgment, FRCP 56 confers no right to an oral hearing on the summary judgment motion, nor is a hearing required by due process considerations. FEDPROC § 62:673; Forjan v. Leprino Foods, Inc., 209 Fed.Appx. 8, 2006 WL 3623496 (2d Cir. 2006).

   a.  *Oral argument.* Oral argument on a motion for summary judgment may be considered ordinarily appropriate, so that as a general rule, a district court should grant a request for oral argument on all but frivolous summary judgment motions, or a nonmovant's request for oral argument must be granted unless summary judgment is also denied, according to some courts. FEDPROC § 62:674; Season-All Industries, Inc. v. Turkiye Sise Ve Cam Fabrikalari, A. S., 425 F.2d 34 (3d Cir. 1970); Houston v. Bryan, 725 F.2d 516 (9th Cir. 1984); Fernhoff v. Tahoe Regional Planning Agency, 803 F.2d 979 (9th Cir. 1986).

     i.  Oral argument on a summary judgment motion may be deemed waived where the opposing party does not request it. FEDPROC § 62:674; McCormack v. Citibank, N.A., 100 F.3d 532, 30 UCC Rep.Serv.2d 1175 (8th Cir. 1996).

3.  *Individual judge practices.* Refer to the Miscellaneous section of this document for information on individual judge practices on hearings.

**H. Forms**

**1. Federal Motion for Summary Judgment Forms**

    a.  Answer; To plaintiff's motion for summary judgment. AMJUR PP SUMMARY § 56.

    b.  Affidavit opposing defendant's motion for summary judgment; By plaintiff. AMJUR PP SUMMARY § 64.

    c.  Affidavit opposing motion for summary judgment; By party; Dispute as to issues of fact. AMJUR PP SUMMARY § 73.

    d.  Affidavit opposing motion for summary judgment; By party; Inability to present facts. AMJUR PP SUMMARY § 74.

    e.  Affidavit opposing motion for summary judgment; By party; Good defense to part of claim. AMJUR PP SUMMARY § 77.

    f.  Statement of disputed and undisputed material facts; In opposition to motion for summary judgment. AMJUR PP SUMMARY § 89.

    g.  Motion and notice of motion for summary judgment. 4 FEDFORMS § 4708.

    h.  Motion for summary judgment by plaintiff. 4 FEDFORMS § 4709.

    i.  Motion for summary judgment by defendant. 4 FEDFORMS § 4713.

    j.  Motion for summary judgment by defendant; Claims of plaintiff and counterclaims of defendant. 4 FEDFORMS § 4717.

    k.  Motion for summary judgment by defendant; Interpleader against another claimant. 4 FEDFORMS § 4718.

    l.  Motion for summary judgment by defendant; Failure of plaintiff to produce evidence. 4 FEDFORMS § 4719.

    m.  Motion for summary judgment by defendant; Statute of limitations. 4 FEDFORMS § 4720.

    n.  Notice of motion for summary judgment. 4 FEDFORMS § 4744.

    o.  Affidavit in support of motion for summary judgment. 4 FEDFORMS § 4773.

    p.  Movant's contention there are no genuine issues of material facts. 4 FEDFORMS § 4776.

    q.  Opposition to statement of uncontested material facts. 4 FEDFORMS § 4777.

    r.  Response to movant's contention there are no genuine issues with respect to listed material facts. 4 FEDFORMS § 4778.

    s.  Motion; For summary judgment; By claimant. FEDPROF § 1:1298.

    t.  Motion; For summary judgment; By defending party. FEDPROF § 1:1302.

    u.  Motion; By plaintiff; For partial summary judgment. FEDPROF § 1:1305.

    v.  Notice of cross motion; For summary judgment; By defending party. FEDPROF § 1:1306.

    w.  Statement of material facts; In support of summary judgment motion. FEDPROF § 1:1311.

    x.  Statement in support of defendant's summary judgment motion; By codefendant. FEDPROF § 1:1312.

    y.  Affidavit; Opposing claimant's motion for summary judgment; Witnesses unavailable. FEDPROF § 1:1316.

    z.  Affidavit; Opposing part of claim. FEDPROF § 1:1317.

**2. Forms for the Western District of New York**

    a.  Certificate of service. NY R USDCTWD ECF Procedures(4a).

**I. Applicable Rules**

1. *Federal rules*

    a.  Serving and filing pleadings and other papers. FRCP 5.

   b. Constitutional challenge to a statute; Notice, certification, and intervention. FRCP 5.1.

   c. Privacy protection for filings made with the court. FRCP 5.2.

   d. Computing and extending time; Time for motion papers. FRCP 6.

   e. Pleadings allowed; Form of motions and other papers. FRCP 7.

   f. Disclosure statement. FRCP 7.1.

   g. Form of pleadings. FRCP 10.

   h. Signing pleadings, motions, and other papers; Representations to the court; Sanctions. FRCP 11.

   i. Defenses and objections; When and how presented; Motion for judgment on the pleadings; Consolidating motions; Waiving defenses; Pretrial hearing. FRCP 12.

   j. Taking testimony. FRCP 43.

   k. Summary judgment. FRCP 56.

   l. Hearing motions; Submission on briefs. FRCP 78.

2. *Local rules*

   a. Title. NY R USDCTWD Civ Rule 1.1.

   b. Filing and serving papers. NY R USDCTWD Civ Rule 5.1.

   c. Motion practice. NY R USDCTWD Civ Rule 7.

   d. Form of papers. NY R USDCTWD Civ Rule 10.

   e. Sanctions. NY R USDCTWD Civ Rule 11.

   f. Alternative dispute resolution and pretrial conferences. NY R USDCTWD Civ Rule 16.

   g. Motions for summary judgment. NY R USDCTWD Civ Rule 56.

   h. Attorneys of record; Appearance and withdrawal. NY R USDCTWD Civ Rule 83.2.

   i. Administrative procedures guide for electronic filing. NY R USDCTWD ECF Procedures.

   j. Alternative dispute resolution plan. NY R USDCTWD ADR Plan.

## J. Miscellaneous

**NOTE: Individual judges' rules may apply. For available judge-level information, refer to:**

DISTRICT JUDGE RICHARD J. ARCARA: NY R USDCTWD Arcara-Procedures.

DISTRICT JUDGE FRANK P. GERACI, JR.: NY R USDCTWD Geraci-Procedures.

DISTRICT JUDGE DAVID G. LARIMER: NY R USDCTWD Larimer-Procedures.

DISTRICT JUDGE CHARLES J. SIRAGUSA: NY R USDCTWD Siragusa-Procedures.

DISTRICT JUDGE WILLIAM M. SKRETNY: NY R USDCTWD Skretny--Procedures.

DISTRICT JUDGE MICHAEL A. TELESCA: NY R USDCTWD Telesca-Procedures.

DISTRICT JUDGE LAWRENCE J. VILARDO: NY R USDCTWD Vilardo-Procedures.

DISTRICT JUDGE ELIZABETH A. WOLFORD: NY R USDCTWD Wolford-Procedures.

MAGISTRATE JUDGE JONATHAN W. FELDMAN: NY R USDCTWD Feldman-Procedures.

MAGISTRATE JUDGE LESLIE G. FOSCHIO: NY R USDCTWD Foschio-Procedures; NY R USDCTWD Foschio-Depositions.

MAGISTRATE JUDGE JEREMIAH J. McCARTHY: NY R USDCTWD McCarthy-Procedures.

MAGISTRATE JUDGE MARIAN W. PAYSON: NY R USDCTWD Payson-Procedures.

MAGISTRATE JUDGE MICHAEL J. ROEMER: NY R USDCTWD Roemer-Procedures.

MAGISTRATE JUDGE H. KENNETH SCHROEDER, JR.: NY R USDCTWD Schroeder-Proc.

MAGISTRATE JUDGE HUGH B. SCOTT: NY R USDCTWD Scott-Procedures.

# Motions, Oppositions and Replies
# Motion to Compel Discovery

### Document Last Updated September 2016

## A. Checklist

(I) ❑ Matters to be considered by moving party

    (a) ❑ Required documents

        (1) ❑ Notice of motion and motion

        (2) ❑ Affidavit of efforts to resolve discovery dispute

        (3) ❑ Supporting affidavit

        (4) ❑ Certificate of service

    (b) ❑ Supplemental documents

        (1) ❑ Memorandum of law

        (2) ❑ Supporting evidence

        (3) ❑ Notice of constitutional question

        (4) ❑ Copies of authorities

        (5) ❑ Proposed order

        (6) ❑ Paper copy for date-stamping with self-addressed envelope

        (7) ❑ Courtesy copies

    (c) ❑ Timing

        (1) ❑ A motion must simply be submitted within a reasonable time; however, a motion to compel discovery filed under FRCP 37(a) is premature if it is filed before any request for discovery is made

        (2) ❑ A written motion and notice of the hearing must be served at least fourteen (14) days before the time specified for the hearing, with the following exceptions: (i) when the motion may be heard ex parte; (ii) when the Federal Rules of Civil Procedure set a different time; or (iii) when a court order—which a party may, for good cause, apply for ex parte—sets a different time

        (3) ❑ Any affidavit supporting a motion must be served with the motion

(II) ❑ Matters to be considered by opposing party

    (a) ❑ Required documents

        (1) ❑ Opposition

        (2) ❑ Supporting affidavit

        (3) ❑ Certificate of service

    (b) ❑ Supplemental documents

        (1) ❑ Supporting evidence

        (2) ❑ Notice of constitutional question

        (3) ❑ Copies of authorities

        (4) ❑ Paper copy for date-stamping with self-addressed envelope

        (5) ❑ Courtesy copies

    (c) ❑ Timing

        (1) ❑ After a motion is filed, the court may issue an order setting deadlines for filing and service of opposing papers; if the court does not set deadlines by order, the opposing party shall have fourteen (14) days after service of the motion to file and serve responding papers

(2) ❑ Except as FRCP 59(c) provides otherwise, any opposing affidavit must be served at least seven (7) days before the hearing, unless the court permits service at another time

## B. Timing

1. *Motion to compel discovery.* There is no specific time limit for a motion to compel discovery under FRCP 37(a); rather, a motion must simply be submitted within a reasonable time. FEDPROC § 26:779. However, a motion to compel discovery filed under FRCP 37(a) is premature if it is filed before any request for discovery is made. FEDPROC § 26:779; Bermudez v. Duenas, 936 F.2d 1064, 19 Fed.R.Serv.3d 1443 (9th Cir. 1991).

2. *Timing of motions, generally*

   a. *Motion and notice of hearing.* A written motion and notice of the hearing must be served at least fourteen (14) days before the time specified for the hearing, with the following exceptions:

      i. When the motion may be heard ex parte;

      ii. When the Federal Rules of Civil Procedure set a different time; or

      iii. When a court order—which a party may, for good cause, apply for ex parte—sets a different time. FRCP 6(c)(1).

   b. *Supporting affidavit.* Any affidavit supporting a motion must be served with the motion. FRCP 6(c)(2).

3. *Timing of opposing papers.* After a motion is filed, the Court may issue an order setting deadlines for filing and service of opposing papers. NY R USDCTWD Civ Rule 7(b)(1). If the Court does not set deadlines by order, the following schedule shall apply: the opposing party shall have fourteen (14) days after service of the motion to file and serve responding papers. NY R USDCTWD Civ Rule 7(b)(2)(B).

   a. *Opposing affidavit.* Except as FRCP 59(c) provides otherwise, any opposing affidavit must be served at least seven (7) days before the hearing, unless the court permits service at another time. FRCP 6(c)(2).

4. *Timing of reply papers.* Where the respondent files an answering affidavit setting up a new matter, the moving party ordinarily is allowed a reasonable time to file a reply affidavit since failure to deny the new matter by affidavit may operate as an admission of its truth. AMJUR MOTIONS § 25.

   a. *Reply papers.* After a motion is filed, the Court may issue an order setting deadlines. . .for filing and service of reply papers if the moving party has stated an intent to reply. NY R USDCTWD Civ Rule 7(b)(1). If the Court does not set deadlines by order, the following schedule shall apply: the moving party shall have seven (7) days after service of the responding papers to file and serve reply papers. NY R USDCTWD Civ Rule 7(b)(2)(B).

5. *Motion for an expedited hearing.* A party seeking to shorten the schedule prescribed in NY R USDCTWD Civ Rule 7(b) must make a separate motion for an expedited hearing, setting forth the reasons why an expedited hearing is required. NY R USDCTWD Civ Rule 7(d)(1). For more information, refer to NY R USDCTWD Civ Rule 7(d)(1).

6. *Computation of time*

   a. *Computing time.* FRCP 6 applies in computing any time period specified in the Federal Rules of Civil Procedure, in any local rule or court order, or in any statute that does not specify a method of computing time. FRCP 6(a).

      i. *Period stated in days or a longer unit.* When the period is stated in days or a longer unit of time:

         • Exclude the day of the event that triggers the period;

         • Count every day, including intermediate Saturdays, Sundays, and legal holidays; and

         • Include the last day of the period, but if the last day is a Saturday, Sunday, or legal holiday, the period continues to run until the end of the next day that is not a Saturday, Sunday, or legal holiday. FRCP 6(a)(1).

      ii. *Period stated in hours.* When the period is stated in hours:

         • Begin counting immediately on the occurrence of the event that triggers the period;

- Count every hour, including hours during intermediate Saturdays, Sundays, and legal holidays; and

- If the period would end on a Saturday, Sunday, or legal holiday, the period continues to run until the same time on the next day that is not a Saturday, Sunday, or legal holiday. FRCP 6(a)(2).

   iii. *Inaccessibility of the clerk's office.* Unless the court orders otherwise, if the clerk's office is inaccessible:

- On the last day for filing under FRCP 6(a)(1), then the time for filing is extended to the first accessible day that is not a Saturday, Sunday, or legal holiday; or

- During the last hour for filing under FRCP 6(a)(2), then the time for filing is extended to the same time on the first accessible day that is not a Saturday, Sunday, or legal holiday. FRCP 6(a)(3).

   iv. *"Last day" defined.* Unless a different time is set by a statute, local rule, or court order, the last day ends:

- For electronic filing, at midnight in the court's time zone; and

- For filing by other means, when the clerk's office is scheduled to close. FRCP 6(a)(4).

   v. *"Next day" defined.* The "next day" is determined by continuing to count forward when the period is measured after an event and backward when measured before an event. FRCP 6(a)(5).

   vi. *"Legal holiday" defined.* "Legal holiday" means:

- The day set aside by statute for observing New Year's Day, Martin Luther King Jr.'s Birthday, Washington's Birthday, Memorial Day, Independence Day, Labor Day, Columbus Day, Veterans' Day, Thanksgiving Day, or Christmas Day;

- Any day declared a holiday by the President or Congress; and

- For periods that are measured after an event, any other day declared a holiday by the state where the district court is located. FRCP 6(a)(6).

b. *Computation of electronic filing deadlines.* A document will be deemed timely filed if filed prior to midnight Eastern Time, unless otherwise ordered by the Court. A document will be considered untimely if filed thereafter. When a Court order requires that a document be filed on a weekend or holiday, the document may be filed by close of business the next business day without further application to the Court. NY R USDCTWD ECF Procedures(2)(e)(i). A document filed electronically is deemed filed on the date and time stated on the Notice of Electronic Filing. NY R USDCTWD ECF Procedures(2)(e)(ii).

   i. *System availability.* Although parties may file documents electronically twenty-four (24) hours a day, registered users are strongly encouraged to file all documents during normal working hours of the Clerk's Office (8:30 a.m. to 5:00 p.m. Eastern Time). NY R USDCTWD ECF Procedures(2)(t)(i).

   ii. *Technical failures.* A Filing User whose filing is made untimely as a result of a technical failure must seek appropriate relief from the Court. NY R USDCTWD ECF Procedures(2)(u)(i).

c. *Extending time*

   i. *In general.* When an act may or must be done within a specified time, the court may, for good cause, extend the time:

- With or without motion or notice if the court acts, or if a request is made, before the original time or its extension expires; or

- On motion made after the time has expired if the party failed to act because of excusable neglect. FRCP 6(b)(1).

   ii. *Exceptions.* A court must not extend the time to act under FRCP 50(b), FRCP 50(d), FRCP 52(b), FRCP 59(b), FRCP 59(d), FRCP 59(e), and FRCP 60(b). FRCP 6(b)(2).

   iii. Refer to the United States District Court for the Western District of New York KeyRules Motion for Continuance/Extension of Time document for more information on extending time.

    d. *Additional time after certain kinds of service.* When a party may or must act within a specified time after service and service is made under FRCP 5(b)(2)(C), FRCP 5(b)(2)(D), FRCP 5(b)(2)(E), or FRCP 5(b)(2)(F), three (3) days are added after the period would otherwise expire under FRCP 6(a). FRCP 6(d).

        i. *Service by overnight delivery.* Where a period of time prescribed by either the Federal Rules of Civil Procedure or the Local Rules of Civil Procedure for the United States District Court for the Western District of New York is measured from the service of a paper and service is by overnight delivery, one (1) business day shall be added to the prescribed period. NY R USDCTWD Civ Rule 5.1(g).

7. *Individual judge practices.* Refer to the Miscellaneous section of this document for information on individual judge practices on timing of documents.

## C. General Requirements

1. *Motions, generally*

    a. *Requirements.* A request for a court order must be made by motion. The motion must:

        i. Be in writing unless made during a hearing or trial;

        ii. State with particularity the grounds for seeking the order; and

        iii. State the relief sought. FRCP 7(b)(1).

    b. *Notice of motion.* A party interested in resisting the relief sought by a motion has a right to notice thereof, and an opportunity to be heard. AMJUR MOTIONS § 12.

        i. In addition to statutory or court rule provisions requiring notice of a motion—the purpose of such a notice requirement having been said to be to prevent a party from being prejudicially surprised by a motion—principles of natural justice dictate that an adverse party generally must be given notice that a motion will be presented to the court. AMJUR MOTIONS § 12.

        ii. "Notice," in this regard, means reasonable notice, including a meaningful opportunity to prepare and to defend against allegations of a motion. AMJUR MOTIONS § 12.

    c. *Writing requirement.* The writing requirement is intended to insure that the adverse parties are informed and have a record of both the motion's pendency and the grounds on which the movant seeks an order. FPP § 1191; Feldberg v. Quechee Lakes Corp., 463 F.3d 195 (2d Cir. 2006).

        i. It is sufficient "if the motion is stated in a written notice of the hearing of the motion." FPP § 1191.

    d. *Particularity requirement.* The particularity requirement insures that the opposing parties will have notice of their opponent's contentions. FEDPROC § 62:364; Goodman v. 1973 26 Foot Trojan Vessel, Arkansas Registration No. AR1439SN, 859 F.2d 71, 12 Fed.R.Serv.3d 645 (8th Cir. 1988). That requirement ensures that notice of the basis for the motion is provided to the court and to the opposing party so as to avoid prejudice, provide the opponent with a meaningful opportunity to respond, and provide the court with enough information to process the motion correctly. FEDPROC § 62:364; Andreas v. Volkswagen of America, Inc., 336 F.3d 789, 56 Fed.R.Serv.3d 6 (8th Cir. 2003).

        i. Reasonable specification of the grounds for a motion is sufficient. However, where a movant fails to state even one ground for granting the motion in question, the movant has failed to meet the minimal standard of "reasonable specification." FEDPROC § 62:364; Martinez v. Trainor, 556 F.2d 818, 23 Fed.R.Serv.2d 403 (7th Cir. 1977).

        ii. The court may excuse the failure to comply with the particularity requirement if it is inadvertent, and where no prejudice is shown by the opposing party. FEDPROC § 62:364.

2. *Motion to compel discovery.* On notice to other parties and all affected persons, a party may move for an order compelling disclosure or discovery. FRCP 37(a)(1). A party must request the specific documents in issue from the opposing party before filing a motion to compel the production of documents. FEDPROC § 26:778.

    a. *Appropriate court.* A motion for an order to a party must be made in the court where the action is pending. A motion for an order to a nonparty must be made in the court where the discovery is or will be taken. FRCP 37(a)(2).

b. *Specific motions*

    i. *To compel disclosure.* If a party fails to make a disclosure required by FRCP 26(a), any other party may move to compel disclosure and for appropriate sanctions. FRCP 37(a)(3)(A). Refer to the United States District Court for the Western District of New York KeyRules Motion for Discovery Sanctions document for more information on sanctions.

    ii. *To compel a discovery response.* A party seeking discovery may move for an order compelling an answer, designation, production, or inspection. This motion may be made if:

- A deponent fails to answer a question asked under FRCP 30 or FRCP 31;

- A corporation or other entity fails to make a designation under FRCP 30(b)(6) or FRCP 31(a)(4);

- A party fails to answer an interrogatory submitted under FRCP 33; or

- A party fails to produce documents or fails to respond that inspection will be permitted—or fails to permit inspection—as requested under FRCP 34. FRCP 37(a)(3)(B).

    iii. *Related to a deposition.* When taking an oral deposition, the party asking a question may complete or adjourn the examination before moving for an order. FRCP 37(a)(3)(C).

    iv. *Evasive or incomplete disclosure, answer, or response.* For purposes of FRCP 37(a), an evasive or incomplete disclosure, answer, or response must be treated as a failure to disclose, answer, or respond. FRCP 37(a)(4).

c. *Payment of expenses; Protective orders*

    i. *If the motion is granted (or disclosure or discovery is provided after filing).* If the motion is granted—or if the disclosure or requested discovery is provided after the motion was filed—the court must, after giving an opportunity to be heard, require the party or deponent whose conduct necessitated the motion, the party or attorney advising that conduct, or both to pay the movant's reasonable expenses incurred in making the motion, including attorney's fees. But the court must not order this payment if:

- The movant filed the motion before attempting in good faith to obtain the disclosure or discovery without court action;

- The opposing party's nondisclosure, response, or objection was substantially justified; or

- Other circumstances make an award of expenses unjust. FRCP 37(a)(5)(A).

    ii. *If the motion is denied.* If the motion is denied, the court may issue any protective order authorized under FRCP 26(c) and must, after giving an opportunity to be heard, require the movant, the attorney filing the motion, or both to pay the party or deponent who opposed the motion its reasonable expenses incurred in opposing the motion, including attorney's fees. But the court must not order this payment if the motion was substantially justified or other circumstances make an award of expenses unjust. FRCP 37(a)(5)(B).

    iii. *If the motion is granted in part and denied in part.* If the motion is granted in part and denied in part, the court may issue any protective order authorized under FRCP 26(c) and may, after giving an opportunity to be heard, apportion the reasonable expenses for the motion. FRCP 37(a)(5)(C).

3. *Opposing papers.* The Federal Rules of Civil Procedure do not require any formal answer, return, or reply to a motion, except where the Federal Rules of Civil Procedure or local rules may require affidavits, memoranda, or other papers to be filed in opposition to a motion. Such papers are simply to apprise the court of such opposition and the grounds of that opposition. FEDPROC § 62:359.

a. *Effect of failure to respond to motion.* Although in the absence of statutory provision or court rule, a motion ordinarily does not require a written answer, when a party files a motion and the opposing party fails to respond, the court may construe such failure to respond as nonopposition to the motion or an admission that the motion was meritorious, may take the facts alleged in the motion as true—the rule in some jurisdictions being that the failure to respond to a fact set forth in a motion is deemed an admission—and may grant the motion if the relief requested appears to be justified. AMJUR MOTIONS § 28.

b. *Assent or no opposition not determinative.* However, a motion will not be granted automatically simply because an "assent" or a notation of "no opposition" has been filed; federal judges frequently deny motions that have been assented to when it is thought that justice so dictates. FPP § 1190.

c. *Responsive pleading inappropriate as response to motion.* An attempt to answer or oppose a motion with a responsive pleading usually is not appropriate. FPP § 1190.

4. *Reply papers.* A moving party may be required or permitted to prepare papers in addition to his original motion papers. AMJUR MOTIONS § 25. Papers answering or replying to opposing papers may be appropriate, in the interests of justice, where it appears there is a substantial reason for allowing a reply. Thus, a court may accept reply papers where a party demonstrates that the papers to which it seeks to file a reply raise new issues that are material to the disposition of the question before the court, or where the court determines, sua sponte, that it wishes further briefing of an issue raised in those papers and orders the submission of additional papers. FEDPROC § 62:360.

a. *Function of reply papers.* The function of a reply affidavit is to answer the arguments made in opposition to the position taken by the movant and not to permit the movant to introduce new arguments in support of the motion. AMJUR MOTIONS § 25.

b. *Issues raised for the first time in a reply document.* However, the view has been followed in some jurisdictions, that as a matter of judicial economy, where there is no prejudice and where the issues could be raised simply by filing a motion to dismiss, the trial court has discretion to consider arguments raised for the first time in a reply memorandum, and that a trial court may grant a motion to strike issues raised for the first time in a reply memorandum. AMJUR MOTIONS § 26.

5. *Sur-reply.* Absent permission of the Judge hearing the motion, sur-reply papers are not permitted. NY R USDCTWD Civ Rule 7(a)(6).

6. *Motion to settle an order.* When counsel are unable to agree on the form of a proposed order, the prevailing party may move, upon seven (7) days notice to all parties, to settle the order. The Court may award costs and attorney's fees against an attorney if it determines that the attorney's unreasonable conduct necessitated bringing the motion. NY R USDCTWD Civ Rule 7(d)(2).

7. *Notice of appearance.* No notice of appearance is required of an attorney whose name and address appear at the end of a complaint, notice of removal, pre-answer motion, or answer. In all other circumstances, an attorney appearing for a party in a civil case shall promptly file a written notice of appearance. NY R USDCTWD Civ Rule 83.2(b). For more information on appearances and withdrawals, refer to NY R USDCTWD Civ Rule 83.2.

8. *Related cases.* Each attorney appearing in a civil case has a continuing duty to promptly notify the Clerk of Court when the attorney has reason to believe that said case is related to some other pending civil or criminal action(s) such that their assignment to the same Judge would avoid unnecessary duplication of judicial effort. As soon as the attorney becomes aware of such a relationship, the attorney shall notify the Clerk of Court by letter of the relevant facts, and the Clerk of Court will transmit that notification to the Judges to whom the cases have been assigned. NY R USDCTWD Civ Rule 5.1(e).

9. *Alternative dispute resolution (ADR).* This Court has adopted an Alternative Dispute Resolution Plan ("ADR"), as implemented by Standing Order (NY R USDCTWD ADR Plan), under which certain civil cases are referred automatically to ADR upon filing. NY R USDCTWD Civ Rule 16(a). The United States District Court for the Western District of New York (the "Court") adopted the ADR Plan on January 1, 2006 (the "Effective Date"), to make available to civil litigants court-administered ADR interventions and processes designed to provide quicker, less expensive and potentially more satisfying alternatives to continuing litigation, without impairing the quality of justice or the right to trial. NY R USDCTWD ADR Plan(1)(1.2)(A).

a. *Scope.* This ADR Plan (NY R USDCTWD ADR Plan) applies to civil actions pending or commenced on and after the Effective Date, except as otherwise indicated in NY R USDCTWD ADR Plan. The ADR Plan supplements the Local Rules of Civil Procedure for the United States District Court for the Western District of New York, which shall remain in full effect for all cases. NY R USDCTWD ADR Plan(1)(1.2)(B).

b. *Referral to ADR*

    i. *New cases.* All civil cases filed on and after the Effective Date of the ADR Plan shall be referred automatically for ADR. NY R USDCTWD ADR Plan(2)(2.1)(A). Notice of the ADR requirements will be provided to all parties immediately upon the filing of a complaint and answer or a notice of removal; NY R USDCTWD ADR Plan(2)(2.1)(A); NY R USDCTWD Civ Rule 16(a). ADR intervention will be scheduled at the conference held pursuant to Local Rule of Civil Procedure 16.1. NY R USDCTWD ADR Plan(2)(2.1)(A). [Editor's note: the reference to Local Rule of Civil Procedure 16.1 is likely meant to be a reference to NY R USDCTWD Civ Rule 16(b)].

- Litigants in cases not referred automatically to ADR must consider possible agreement to the use of an ADR process. NY R USDCTWD Civ Rule 16(a).

- For a list of exemptions from automatic referral, refer to NY R USDCTWD ADR Plan(2)(2.1)(A).

    ii. *Pending cases.* The assigned Judge on any pending civil case may, sua sponte or with status conference, issue an order referring the case for ADR. NY R USDCTWD ADR Plan(2)(2.1)(B); NY R USDCTWD Civ Rule 16(a). The order shall specify a date on which the ADR intervention is to be completed. NY R USDCTWD ADR Plan(2)(2.1)(B).

    iii. *Stipulation.* A case may be referred for ADR by stipulation of all parties. Stipulations shall be filed and shall designate the specific ADR intervention the parties have selected, the time frame within which the ADR process will be completed and the selected Neutral. Stipulations are presumed acceptable unless the assigned Judge determines that the interests of justice are not served. NY R USDCTWD ADR Plan(2)(2.1)(C).

    iv. *Relief from ADR referral*

- *Opting out motions.* Any party may file, with the assigned Judge for that case, a motion to opt out of, or for relief from, ADR. NY R USDCTWD ADR Plan(2)(2.2)(A).

- *Motion.* Opting Out Motions must be made within fourteen (14) days from (1) the date of the first discovery conference under Local Rule 16.1 in new cases, or (2) the date of a sua sponte ADR Referral Order in pending cases. NY R USDCTWD ADR Plan(2)(2.2)(B). [Editor's note: the reference to Local Rule 16.1 is likely meant to be a reference to NY R USDCTWD Civ Rule 16(b)].

- *Criteria.* Opting Out Motions shall be granted only for "good cause" shown. Inconvenience, travel costs, attorney fees or other costs shall not constitute "good cause." A party seeking relief from ADR must set forth the reasons why ADR has no reasonable chance of being productive. NY R USDCTWD ADR Plan(2)(2.2)(C).

- *Judicial initiative.* The assigned Judge may, sua sponte, exempt any case from the Court's ADR Plan. NY R USDCTWD ADR Plan(2)(2.2)(D).

c. *ADR interventions*

    i. *Options.* It is expected that cases referred for ADR will proceed to Mediation. However, the following options are also available upon the stipulation of all parties:

- Neutral Evaluation;

- Mini Summary Trial;

- Arbitration (Binding and Non-Binding);

- Case Valuation; and

- Settlement Week, when scheduled by the Court. NY R USDCTWD ADR Plan(4)(4.1)(A).

    ii. *Timing.* Timing is specific to the intervention and process chosen, as set forth in the corresponding sections in NY R USDCTWD ADR Plan. NY R USDCTWD ADR Plan(4)(4.1)(B).

    iii. *Scheduling.* The referral of a case to ADR does not delay or defer other dates established in the Scheduling Order and has no effect on the scheduled progress of the case toward trial. NY R USDCTWD ADR Plan(4)(4.1)(C).

    d.  *Selecting an ADR intervention*

        i.  *New cases.* Prior to the Local Rule 16.1 scheduling conference, counsel and any unrepresented parties shall confer about ADR as part of their discussion of "the possibilities for a prompt settlement or resolution of the case" pursuant to FRCP 26(f). Unless the parties agree to a different intervention, it is presumed that they will participate in mediation. [Editor's note: the reference to Local Rule 16.1 is likely meant to be a reference to NY R USDCTWD Civ Rule 16(b)].

       ii.  *Pending cases.* In pending cases, all sua sponte referrals will be to mediation. Should the parties agree that a different ADR intervention is more appropriate to their case, they may submit a stipulation designating the specific ADR intervention selected, the time frame within which the ADR process will be completed and the identity of the Neutral. Stipulations must be filed within fourteen (14) days from the date of the ADR Referral Order and are presumed acceptable unless the assigned Judge determines that the interests of justice are not served. NY R USDCTWD ADR Plan(4)(4.2)(B).

    e.  For more information on alternative dispute resolution (ADR), refer to NY R USDCTWD ADR Plan.

10.  *Sanctions.* Failure of counsel for any party, or a party proceeding pro se, to appear before the Court at a conference, to complete the necessary preparations, or to be prepared to proceed to trial at the set time may be considered an abandonment of the case or a failure to prosecute or defend diligently. An appropriate order for sanctions may be entered against the defaulting party with respect to either a specific issue or the entire case. NY R USDCTWD Civ Rule 11(a). For more information, refer to NY R USDCTWD Civ Rule 11.

11.  *Pro se actions.* For information on the requirements in pro se actions, refer to NY R USDCTWD Civ Rule 5.2.

12.  *Individual judge practices.* Refer to the Miscellaneous section of this document for information on individual judge practices on general requirements for documents.

## D. Documents

  1.  *Documents for moving party*

    a.  *Required documents*

        i.  *Notice of motion and motion.* A notice of motion is required for all motions, and must state: the relief sought, the grounds for the request, the papers submitted in support, and the return date for the motion, if known. A moving party who intends to file and serve reply papers must so state in the notice of motion. NY R USDCTWD Civ Rule 7(a)(1). Refer to the General Requirements section of this document for information on the notice of motion and motion.

       ii.  *Affidavit of efforts to resolve discovery dispute.* No motion for discovery and/or production of documents under FRCP 37 shall be heard unless accompanied by an affidavit showing that sincere attempts to resolve the discovery dispute have been made. Such affidavit shall detail the times and places of the parties' meetings or discussions concerning the discovery dispute and the names of all parties participating therein, and all related correspondence must be attached. NY R USDCTWD Civ Rule 7(d)(4). The motion must include a certification that the movant has in good faith conferred or attempted to confer with the person or party failing to make disclosure or discovery in an effort to obtain it without court action. FRCP 37(a)(1).

      iii.  *Supporting affidavit.* An affidavit must not contain legal arguments, but must contain factual and procedural background relevant to the motion it supports. Except for motions brought under FRCP 12(b)(1) (lack of subject matter jurisdiction), FRCP 12(b)(6) (failure to state a claim), FRCP 12(c) (judgment on the pleadings), and FRCP 12(f) (to strike), motions and opposition to motions shall be supported by at least one (1) affidavit and by such other evidence (i.e., deposition testimony, interrogatory answers, admissions, and documents) as appropriate to resolve the particular motion. Failure to comply with this requirement may constitute grounds for resolving the motion against the non-complying party. NY R USDCTWD Civ Rule 7(a)(3).

iv. *Certificate of service.* FRCP 5(d) requires that the person making service under FRCP 5 certify that service has been effected. FRCP 5(Advisory Committee Notes). Having such information on file may be useful for many purposes, including proof of service if an issue arises concerning the effectiveness of the service. FRCP 5(Advisory Committee Notes). The Notice of Electronic Filing effectuates service for all registered users and no certificate of service is required when all filers on an action are Registered Users. The following exemptions require a certificate of service to be filed:

- When a document is manually filed, a certificate of service must be filed stating the manner in which service or notice was accomplished on each party so entitled. NY R USDCTWD ECF Procedures(2)(f)(iv).

- When a pro se filer (who isn't authorized to electronically file documents) is a party, a certificate of service must be filed stating the manner in which service or notice was accomplished on the pro se party. The Notice of Electronic Filing effectuates service for the Registered Users in this situation and it is not necessary to note service on those parties. A non-registered pro se filer is required to file certificates of service on all documents they file. NY R USDCTWD ECF Procedures(2)(f)(iv).

- If an attorney is exempt from electronic service, a certificate of service must be filed stating the manner in which service or notice was accomplished on the exempt attorney. The Notice of Electronic Filing effectuates service for the Registered Users in this situation and it is not necessary to note service on those parties. NY R USDCTWD ECF Procedures(2)(f)(iv).

b. *Supplemental documents*

i. *Memorandum of law.* Nothing in the Local Rules of Civil Procedure for the United States District Court for the Western District of New York precludes a moving party from filing a memorandum in support of a motion made other than pursuant to FRCP 12, FRCP 56 or FRCP 65(a). The Court, in its discretion, may require written memoranda on such other motions. NY R USDCTWD Civ Rule 7(a)(2)(B). Refer to the Format section of this document for the formatting requirements for memoranda of law.

ii. *Supporting evidence.* When a motion relies on facts outside the record, the court may hear the matter on affidavits or may hear it wholly or partly on oral testimony or on depositions. FRCP 43(c). A party seeking or opposing any relief under the Federal Rules of Civil Procedure shall file only the portion(s) of a deposition, interrogatory, request for documents, request for admission, or other supporting material that is pertinent to the application. NY R USDCTWD Civ Rule 7(a)(4).

iii. *Notice of constitutional question.* A party that files a pleading, written motion, or other paper drawing into question the constitutionality of a federal or state statute must promptly:

- *File notice.* File a notice of constitutional question stating the question and identifying the paper that raises it, if: (1) a federal statute is questioned and the parties do not include the United States, one of its agencies, or one of its officers or employees in an official capacity; or (2) a state statute is questioned and the parties do not include the state, one of its agencies, or one of its officers or employees in an official capacity; and

- *Serve notice.* Serve the notice and paper on the Attorney General of the United States if a federal statute is questioned—or on the state attorney general if a state statute is questioned—either by certified or registered mail or by sending it to an electronic address designated by the attorney general for this purpose. FRCP 5.1(a).

- *No forfeiture.* A party's failure to file and serve the notice, or the court's failure to certify, does not forfeit a constitutional claim or defense that is otherwise timely asserted. FRCP 5.1(d).

iv. *Copies of authorities.* In cases involving a pro se litigant, counsel shall, when serving a memorandum of law (or other submissions to the Court), provide the pro se litigant (but not other counsel or the Court) with printed copies of decisions cited therein that are unreported or reported exclusively on computerized databases. NY R USDCTWD Civ Rule 7(a)(8).

v. *Proposed order.* All proposed orders must be submitted in a format compatible with WordPerfect or Microsoft Word format, which is a "Save As" option in most word processing software. Judges will not accept proposed orders in PDF format. NY R USDCTWD ECF Procedures(2)(j)(ii). Proposed orders should be attached to an Internet e-mail sent to the e-mail address of the assigned judge. NY R USDCTWD ECF Procedures(2)(j)(i). For the list of email addresses for the judges, refer to NY R USDCTWD ECF Procedures(2)(j)(i).

vi. *Paper copy for date-stamping with self-addressed envelope.* Parties requesting date-stamped copies of filed documents must provide a paper copy for date-stamping, and a self-addressed, adequately-sized envelope with proper postage affixed. NY R USDCTWD Civ Rule 5.1(d).

vii. *Courtesy copies.* The Court may, in its discretion, request courtesy copies on any other motion. NY R USDCTWD Civ Rule 7(a)(7). Courtesy copies of certain documents may be required. Filers should refer to the "Judge Preferences" published on the Court's website. NY R USDCTWD ECF Procedures(2)(a)(iii).

2. *Documents for opposing party*

  a. *Required documents*

    i. *Opposition.* Refer to the General Requirements section of this document for information on the opposing papers.

    ii. *Supporting affidavit.* An affidavit must not contain legal arguments, but must contain factual and procedural background relevant to the motion it supports. Except for motions brought under FRCP 12(b)(1) (lack of subject matter jurisdiction), FRCP 12(b)(6) (failure to state a claim), FRCP 12(c) (judgment on the pleadings), and FRCP 12(f) (to strike), motions and opposition to motions shall be supported by at least one (1) affidavit and by such other evidence (i.e., deposition testimony, interrogatory answers, admissions, and documents) as appropriate to resolve the particular motion. Failure to comply with this requirement may constitute grounds for resolving the motion against the non-complying party. NY R USDCTWD Civ Rule 7(a)(3).

    iii. *Certificate of service.* FRCP 5(d) requires that the person making service under FRCP 5 certify that service has been effected. FRCP 5(Advisory Committee Notes). Having such information on file may be useful for many purposes, including proof of service if an issue arises concerning the effectiveness of the service. FRCP 5(Advisory Committee Notes). The Notice of Electronic Filing effectuates service for all registered users and no certificate of service is required when all filers on an action are Registered Users. The following exemptions require a certificate of service to be filed:

      • When a document is manually filed, a certificate of service must be filed stating the manner in which service or notice was accomplished on each party so entitled. NY R USDCTWD ECF Procedures(2)(f)(iv).

      • When a pro se filer (who isn't authorized to electronically file documents) is a party, a certificate of service must be filed stating the manner in which service or notice was accomplished on the pro se party. The Notice of Electronic Filing effectuates service for the Registered Users in this situation and it is not necessary to note service on those parties. A non-registered pro se filer is required to file certificates of service on all documents they file. NY R USDCTWD ECF Procedures(2)(f)(iv).

      • If an attorney is exempt from electronic service, a certificate of service must be filed stating the manner in which service or notice was accomplished on the exempt attorney. The Notice of Electronic Filing effectuates service for the Registered Users in this situation and it is not necessary to note service on those parties. NY R USDCTWD ECF Procedures(2)(f)(iv).

  b. *Supplemental documents*

    i. *Supporting evidence.* When a motion relies on facts outside the record, the court may hear the matter on affidavits or may hear it wholly or partly on oral testimony or on depositions. FRCP 43(c). A party seeking or opposing any relief under the Federal Rules of Civil Procedure shall file only the portion(s) of a deposition, interrogatory, request for documents, request for admission, or other supporting material that is pertinent to the application. NY R USDCTWD Civ Rule 7(a)(4).

ii. *Notice of constitutional question.* A party that files a pleading, written motion, or other paper drawing into question the constitutionality of a federal or state statute must promptly:

- *File notice.* File a notice of constitutional question stating the question and identifying the paper that raises it, if: (1) a federal statute is questioned and the parties do not include the United States, one of its agencies, or one of its officers or employees in an official capacity; or (2) a state statute is questioned and the parties do not include the state, one of its agencies, or one of its officers or employees in an official capacity; and

- *Serve notice.* Serve the notice and paper on the Attorney General of the United States if a federal statute is questioned—or on the state attorney general if a state statute is questioned—either by certified or registered mail or by sending it to an electronic address designated by the attorney general for this purpose. FRCP 5.1(a).

- *No forfeiture.* A party's failure to file and serve the notice, or the court's failure to certify, does not forfeit a constitutional claim or defense that is otherwise timely asserted. FRCP 5.1(d).

iii. *Copies of authorities.* In cases involving a pro se litigant, counsel shall, when serving a memorandum of law (or other submissions to the Court), provide the pro se litigant (but not other counsel or the Court) with printed copies of decisions cited therein that are unreported or reported exclusively on computerized databases. NY R USDCTWD Civ Rule 7(a)(8).

iv. *Paper copy for date-stamping with self-addressed envelope.* Parties requesting date-stamped copies of filed documents must provide a paper copy for date-stamping, and a self-addressed, adequately-sized envelope with proper postage affixed. NY R USDCTWD Civ Rule 5.1(d).

v. *Courtesy copies.* Courtesy copies of certain documents may be required. Filers should refer to the "Judge Preferences" published on the Court's website. NY R USDCTWD ECF Procedures(2)(a)(iii).

3. *Individual judge practices.* Refer to the Miscellaneous section of this document for information on individual judge practices on required documents.

## E. Format

1. *Form of documents.* The rules governing captions and other matters of form in pleadings apply to motions and other papers. FRCP 7(b)(2).

a. *Form, generally.* All pleadings, motions, and other papers that a party presents for filing, whether in paper form or in electronic form, shall meet the following requirements:

i. *Font size.* All text and footnotes shall be in a font size of at least twelve (12) point type. NY R USDCTWD Civ Rule 10(a)(1).

ii. *Spacing.* All text in the body of the document must be double-spaced, except that text in block quotations and footnotes may be single-spaced. NY R USDCTWD Civ Rule 10(a)(2).

- Extensive footnotes and block quotes may not be used to circumvent page limitations. NY R USDCTWD Civ Rule 10(a)(3).

iii. *Margins.* Documents must have one (1) inch margins on all four sides. NY R USDCTWD Civ Rule 10(a)(4).

iv. *Page numbering.* Pages must be consecutively numbered. NY R USDCTWD Civ Rule 10(a)(5).

b. *Additional requirements for paper filing.* Documents presented for filing in paper form shall meet the following additional requirements:

i. *Paper.* Documents must be on durable white eight and one-half by eleven (8-1/2 x 11) inch paper of good quality. NY R USDCTWD Civ Rule 10(b)(1).

- All documents must be single-sided. NY R USDCTWD Civ Rule 10(b)(5).

    ii.   *Text.* All text must be plainly and legibly written, typewritten, printed or reproduced. NY R USDCTWD Civ Rule 10(b)(2).

    iii.   *Ink.* Documents must be in black or blue ink. NY R USDCTWD Civ Rule 10(b)(3).

    iv.   *Binding.* The pages of each document must be stapled or in some other way fastened together. NY R USDCTWD Civ Rule 10(b)(4).

  c.  *Caption; Names of parties.* Every pleading must have a caption with the court's name, a title, a file number, and a FRCP 7(a) designation. The title of the complaint must name all the parties; the title of other pleadings, after naming the first party on each side, may refer generally to other parties. FRCP 10(a).

  d.  *Paragraphs; Separate statements.* A party must state its claims or defenses in numbered paragraphs, each limited as far as practicable to a single set of circumstances. A later pleading may refer by number to a paragraph in an earlier pleading. If doing so would promote clarity, each claim founded on a separate transaction or occurrence—and each defense other than a denial—must be stated in a separate count or defense. FRCP 10(b).

  e.  *Adoption by reference; Exhibits.* A statement in a pleading may be adopted by reference elsewhere in the same pleading or in any other pleading or motion. A copy of a written instrument that is an exhibit to a pleading is a part of the pleading for all purposes. FRCP 10(c).

  f.  *Citation of local rules.* The Local Rules of Civil Procedure for the United States District Court for the Western District of New York shall be cited as "L.R.Civ.P." NY R USDCTWD Civ Rule 1.1.

  g.  *Acceptance by the clerk.* The clerk must not refuse to file a paper solely because it is not in the form prescribed by the Federal Rules of Civil Procedure or by a local rule or practice. FRCP 5(d)(4). The Court may reject documents that do not comply with the requirements in NY R USDCTWD Civ Rule 10. NY R USDCTWD Civ Rule 10.

2.  *Form of electronic documents.* All pleadings, motions, and other papers that a party presents for filing, whether in paper form or in electronic form, shall meet the requirements in NY R USDCTWD Civ Rule 10(a). NY R USDCTWD Civ Rule 10(a). Refer above for more information.

  a.  *Conversion to PDF.* A document created with a word processor, or a paper document, must be converted to Portable Document Format to be electronically filed with the court. NY R USDCTWD ECF Procedures(2)(a)(v).

    i.   Documents which exist only in paper form may be scanned into a portable document format (PDF) for electronic filing. NY R USDCTWD ECF Procedures(2)(a)(v). Before filing a scanned document with the court, a Filing User must verify its legibility. NY R USDCTWD ECF Procedures(2)(a)(iv).

    ii.   Electronic documents must be converted to .PDF from a word processing program and must be text searchable. Do not print, scan and .PDF your document when it has been created in a word processing program. Additional information on working with PDFs is located in NY R USDCTWD ECF Procedures(4b). NY R USDCTWD ECF Procedures(2)(a)(v).

  b.  *Hyperlinks.* Pursuant to the policy set forth by the Judicial Conference in October 2005, a hyperlink contained in a filing is no more than a convenient mechanism for accessing material cited in a document. A hyperlink reference is extraneous to any filed document and is not part of the Court's record. NY R USDCTWD ECF Procedures(2)(a)(vi).

    i.   In order to preserve the integrity of the Court record, users wishing to insert hyperlinks in Court filings shall continue to use the conventional method for the cited authority, in addition to the hyperlink. NY R USDCTWD ECF Procedures(2)(a)(vi).

    ii.   The Court accepts no responsibility for, and does not endorse any product, organization, and content at any hyperlinked site, or at any site to which that site may be linked. The Court accepts no responsibility for the availability or functionality of any hyperlink. NY R USDCTWD ECF Procedures(2)(a)(vi).

  c.  *Attachments and exhibits*

    i.   Attachments and exhibits larger than five megabytes (5 MB) shall be filed electronically in separate five megabyte (5 MB) segments. NY R USDCTWD ECF Procedures(2)(d)(i).

ii.  Filing Users must submit in electronic form all documents referenced as exhibits or attachments, except as otherwise provided in NY R USDCTWD ECF Procedures. A Filing User must submit as exhibits or attachments only those excerpts of the referenced documents that are directly germane to the matter under consideration by the court. Excerpted material must be clearly and prominently identified as such. Filing Users who file excerpts of documents as exhibits or attachments under NY R USDCTWD ECF Procedures(2)(d)(ii) do so without prejudice to their right to timely file additional excerpts or the complete document. Responding parties may timely file additional excerpts or the complete document that they believe are directly germane. The Court may require parties to file additional excerpts or the complete document. A Filing User must request leave of the Court to file a document exhibit or attachment in non-electronic form. NY R USDCTWD ECF Procedures(2)(d)(ii).

iii.  Exhibits offered or admitted at trial will not be filed electronically or conventionally unless so ordered by the Court. NY R USDCTWD ECF Procedures(2)(d)(iii).

iv.  Exhibits such as videotapes and tape recordings shall be filed in the conventional manner with the Clerk of Court, and a Notice of Manual Filing shall be electronically filed by the party. Manually filed exhibits must have the case number and case name securely fastened or marked on the item. NY R USDCTWD ECF Procedures(2)(d)(iii).

v.  Continuation of exhibit entries (for exhibits that are too large to attach to a main document) must be filed and entered on the same day that the main document was filed. NY R USDCTWD ECF Procedures(2)(d)(iv).

d.  *Color documents.* Documents in color or containing graphics take much longer to upload. Filing users are encouraged to configure their scanners to scan documents at 200 dpi and preferably in black and white rather than color. NY R USDCTWD ECF Procedures(2)(d)(v).

e.  *Large documents.* Due to the length of time it takes to download large files, documents larger than five megabytes (5 MB) (approximately one hundred (100) pages of a .pdf scanned document) must be filed electronically in separate five megabyte (5 MB) segments. A party who believes a document is too lengthy to electronically image (i.e. scan), may contact the Court Room Deputy for the assigned judge and request permission to file that document conventionally. If granted permission to file the document conventionally, the Filing User shall electronically file a "notice of manual filing" for that item. Exhibits submitted to the Court conventionally shall be served on other parties conventionally. NY R USDCTWD ECF Procedures(2)(d)(vi).

3.  *Form of memoranda of law.* Memoranda in support of or in opposition to any motion shall not exceed twenty-five (25) pages in length, and reply memoranda shall not exceed ten (10) pages in length. A party seeking to exceed the page limit must make application by letter to the Judge hearing the motion, with copies to all counsel, at least seven (7) days before the date on which the memorandum must be filed. NY R USDCTWD Civ Rule 7(a)(2)(C).

4.  *Signing disclosures and discovery requests, responses, and objections.* FRCP 11 does not apply to disclosures and discovery requests, responses, objections, and motions under FRCP 26 through FRCP 37. FRCP 11(d).

a.  *Signature required.* Every disclosure under FRCP 26(a)(1) or FRCP 26(a)(3) and every discovery request, response, or objection must be signed by at least one attorney of record in the attorney's own name—or by the party personally, if unrepresented—and must state the signer's address, e-mail address, and telephone number. FRCP 26(g)(1). Documents presented for paper filing must contain an original signature. NY R USDCTWD Civ Rule 10(b)(6).

i.  *Electronic signatures*

•  *Non-attorney signature.* If the original document requires the signature of a non-attorney, the filing party shall obtain the signature of the non-attorney on the document. NY R USDCTWD ECF Procedures(2)(g)(i). The filing party or attorney then shall file the document electronically indicating the signatory's name in the form "s/(name)." NY R USDCTWD ECF Procedures(2)(g)(i)(1). A non-filing signatory or party who disputes the authenticity of an electronically filed document or the authenticity of the signature on that document must file an objection to the document within ten (10) days of receiving the Notice of Electronic Filing. NY R USDCTWD ECF Procedures(2)(g)(i)(2).

- *Registered user signature.* The username and password required to file documents on the Electronic Filing System serve as the Filing User's signature on all electronic documents filed with this Court. The also serve as a signature for the purposes of FRCP 11, the Federal Rules of Civil Procedure, the Local Rules of Civil Procedure for the United States District Court for the Western District of New York, and any other purpose for which a signature is required in connection with proceedings before this Court. A pleading requiring a Registered User's signature must include a signature block in the format found in NY R USDCTWD ECF Procedures(2)(g)(iii). NY R USDCTWD ECF Procedures(2)(g)(iii). Any party challenging the authenticity of an electronically filed document or the attorney's signature on that document must file an objection to the document within ten (10) days of receiving the Notice of Electronic Filing. NY R USDCTWD ECF Procedures(2)(g)(iii)(1).

- *Multiple signatures.* The following procedure applies when a stipulation or other document requires two or more signatures: The filing party shall initially confirm that the document is acceptable to all persons required to sign the document and shall obtain the signatures of all parties on the document. NY R USDCTWD ECF Procedures(2)(g)(iv)(1). The filing party or attorney then shall file the document electronically indicating the signatories, e.g., "s/Jane Doe," "s/John Smith," etc. NY R USDCTWD ECF Procedures(2)(g)(iv)(2). A non-filing signatory or party who disputes the authenticity of an electronically filed document containing multiple signatures or the authenticity of the signatures themselves must file an objection to the document within ten (10) days of receiving the Notice of Electronic Filing. NY R USDCTWD ECF Procedures(2)(g)(iv)(3).

b. *Effect of signature.* By signing, an attorney or party certifies that to the best of the person's knowledge, information, and belief formed after a reasonable inquiry:

   i.  With respect to a disclosure, it is complete and correct as of the time it is made; and

   ii. With respect to a discovery request, response, or objection, it is:

   - Consistent with the Federal Rules of Civil Procedure and warranted by existing law or by a nonfrivolous argument for extending, modifying, or reversing existing law, or for establishing new law;

   - Not interposed for any improper purpose, such as to harass, cause unnecessary delay, or needlessly increase the cost of litigation; and

   - Neither unreasonable nor unduly burdensome or expensive, considering the needs of the case, prior discovery in the case, the amount in controversy, and the importance of the issues at stake in the action. FRCP 26(g)(1).

c. *Failure to sign.* Other parties have no duty to act on an unsigned disclosure, request, response, or objection until it is signed, and the court must strike it unless a signature is promptly supplied after the omission is called to the attorney's or party's attention. FRCP 26(g)(2).

d. *Sanction for improper certification.* If a certification violates FRCP 26(g) without substantial justification, the court, on motion or on its own, must impose an appropriate sanction on the signer, the party on whose behalf the signer was acting, or both. The sanction may include an order to pay the reasonable expenses, including attorney's fees, caused by the violation. FRCP 26(g)(3). Refer to the United States District Court for the Western District of New York KeyRules Motion for Discovery Sanctions document for more information.

5. *Privacy protection for filings made with the court.* In all filings, parties shall comply with FRCP 5.2. NY R USDCTWD ECF Procedures(2)(m)(i).

   a. *Redacted filings.* Unless the court orders otherwise, in an electronic or paper filing with the court that contains an individual's Social Security number, taxpayer-identification number, or birth date, the

name of an individual known to be a minor, or a financial-account number, a party or nonparty making the filing may include only:

    i.    The last four (4) digits of the Social Security number and taxpayer-identification number;

    ii.    The year of the individual's birth;

    iii.    The minor's initials; and

    iv.    The last four (4) digits of the financial-account number. FRCP 5.2(a).

b.    *Exemptions from the redaction requirement.* The redaction requirement does not apply to the following:

    i.    A financial-account number that identifies the property allegedly subject to forfeiture in a forfeiture proceeding;

    ii.    The record of an administrative or agency proceeding;

    iii.    The official record of a state-court proceeding;

    iv.    The record of a court or tribunal, if that record was not subject to the redaction requirement when originally filed;

    v.    A filing covered by FRCP 5.2(c) or FRCP 5.2(d); and

    vi.    A pro se filing in an action brought under 28 U.S.C.A. § 2241, 28 U.S.C.A. § 2254, or 28 U.S.C.A. § 2255. FRCP 5.2(b).

c.    *Limitations on remote access to electronic files; Social Security appeals and immigration cases.* Unless the court orders otherwise, in an action for benefits under the Social Security Act, and in an action or proceeding relating to an order of removal, to relief from removal, or to immigration benefits or detention, access to an electronic file is authorized as follows:

    i.    The parties and their attorneys may have remote electronic access to any part of the case file, including the administrative record;

    ii.    Any other person may have electronic access to the full record at the courthouse, but may have remote electronic access only to:

        • The docket maintained by the court; and

        • An opinion, order, judgment, or other disposition of the court, but not any other part of the case file or the administrative record. FRCP 5.2(c).

d.    *Filings made under seal.* The court may order that a filing be made under seal without redaction. The court may later unseal the filing or order the person who made the filing to file a redacted version for the public record. FRCP 5.2(d). For more information on sealing documents, refer to NY R USDCTWD Civ Rule 5.3, NY R USDCTWD ECF Procedures(2)(o)(i)(1), NY R USDCTWD ECF Procedures(2)(o)(i)(2), and NY R USDCTWD ECF Procedures(2)(o)(i)(3).

e.    *Protective orders.* For good cause, the court may by order in a case:

    i.    Require redaction of additional information; or

    ii.    Limit or prohibit a nonparty's remote electronic access to a document filed with the court. FRCP 5.2(e).

f.    *Option for additional unredacted filing under seal.* A person making a redacted filing may also file an unredacted copy under seal. The court must retain the unredacted copy as part of the record. FRCP 5.2(f).

g.    *Option for filing a reference list.* A filing that contains redacted information may be filed together with a reference list that identifies each item of redacted information and specifies an appropriate identifier that uniquely corresponds to each item listed. The list must be filed under seal and may be amended as of right. Any reference in the case to a listed identifier will be construed to refer to the corresponding item of information. FRCP 5.2(g).

h.    *Waiver of protection of identifiers.* A person waives the protection of FRCP 5.2(a) as to the person's own information by filing it without redaction and not under seal. FRCP 5.2(h).

6. *Individual judge practices.* Refer to the Miscellaneous section of this document for information on individual judge practices on formatting documents.

## F. Filing and Service Requirements

1. *Filing requirements.* Any paper after the complaint that is required to be served—together with a certificate of service—must be filed within a reasonable time after service. FRCP 5(d)(1). All pleadings and other papers shall be filed and served in accordance with the Federal Rules of Civil Procedure and the CM/ECF Administrative Procedures Guide (NY R USDCTWD ECF Procedures). NY R USDCTWD Civ Rule 5.1(a). For information on filing of miscellaneous cases and irregular documents, refer to NY R USDCTWD Civ Rule 5.6.

   a. *How filing is made; In general.* A paper is filed by delivering it:

      i. To the clerk; or

      ii. To a judge who agrees to accept it for filing, and who must then note the filing date on the paper and promptly send it to the clerk. FRCP 5(d)(2).

   b. *Electronic filing*

      i. *Authorization of electronic filing program.* A court may, by local rule, allow papers to be filed, signed, or verified by electronic means that are consistent with any technical standards established by the Judicial Conference of the United States. A local rule may require electronic filing only if reasonable exceptions are allowed. A paper filed electronically in compliance with a local rule is a written paper for purposes of the Federal Rules of Civil Procedure. FRCP 5(d)(3).

         • All civil cases filed in this Court are assigned to the Electronic Case Filing System ("ECF"). The procedures for electronic filing and any exceptions to the electronic filing requirements are set forth in the CM/ECF Administrative Procedures Guide (NY R USDCTWD ECF Procedures) which is available on the Court's website. NY R USDCTWD Civ Rule 5.1(a).

      ii. *Scope of electronic filing.* The U.S. District Court for the Western District of New York requires attorneys in civil and criminal cases to file documents with the Court electronically over the Internet using its Case Management/Electronic Case Filing (CM/ECF) system. NY R USDCTWD ECF Procedures. Beginning January 1, 2004, all civil and criminal cases currently pending and newly filed, except as expressly noted herein, were assigned to the Electronic Case Filing System ("System"). Except as expressly provided and in exceptional circumstances preventing a Filing User from filing electronically, all petitions, motions, memoranda of law, or other pleadings and documents required to be filed with the Court in connection with a case assigned to the System must be electronically filed. NY R USDCTWD ECF Procedures(1)(a).

         • *Mandatory electronic filing.* All documents on civil, criminal, miscellaneous civil, miscellaneous criminal and new civil case openings, except sealed documents, sealed cases, opening of a criminal case, opening of a miscellaneous case and as expressly provided for in these procedures (NY R USDCTWD ECF Procedures), shall be electronically filed on the system. NY R USDCTWD ECF Procedures(2)(a)(i). NY R USDCTWD Civ Rule 29

         • *Stipulations.* Pursuant to NY R USDCTWD Civ Rule 29, all stipulations (whether the stipulation is final or when it requires a judge's signature) shall be filed electronically. NY R USDCTWD ECF Procedures(2)(p)(i).

         • *Letters.* The electronic filing of letters is generally prohibited unless granted permission by an assigned judge. Letters to the Court must be submitted conventionally. NY R USDCTWD ECF Procedures(2)(q)(i).

         • *Exceptions.* The Court requires attorneys to file documents electronically, absent a showing of good cause, unless otherwise excused by the procedures set forth below or by Order of the Court. NY R USDCTWD ECF Procedures.

      iii. *Conventional filing of documents.* The procedures in NY R USDCTWD ECF Procedures(2)(o) govern documents filed conventionally. The Court, upon application, may also authorize conventional filing of other documents otherwise subject to the procedures in NY R US-DCTWD ECF Procedures(2)(o). NY R USDCTWD ECF Procedures(2)(o)(i).

- *Documents filed under seal.* Unredacted documents filed with the Court pursuant to the privacy provisions of FRCP 5.2 shall be submitted in a sealing envelope with the information in NY R USDCTWD ECF Procedures(2)(o)(i)(1) on the envelope. NY R USDCTWD ECF Procedures(2)(o)(i)(1). If the document is larger than five (5) pages, a disk should be provided to the Clerks Office which contains the document in a .pdf format. NY R USDCTWD ECF Procedures(2)(o)(i)(1). For more information on documents filed under seal, refer to NY R USDCTWD ECF Procedures(2)(o)(i)(1), NY R USDCTWD ECF Procedures(2)(o)(i)(2), and NY R USDCTWD ECF Procedures(2)(o)(i)(3).

- *Magistrate judge consents.* Pursuant to FRCP 73(b), parties' filing consents to jurisdiction by United States Magistrate Judge will continue to be treated as non-public documents until all parties have consented. Therefore, parties must submit conventionally (in paper form) and not electronically file their consent forms so that the consent is not a public document. If all parties consent to the jurisdiction of a Magistrate Judge, the Clerk will scan all consent forms which will then become a public document. NY R USDCTWD ECF Procedures(2)(o)(i)(3).

- *Pro se filers.* Pro Se filers shall file paper originals of all initiating documents, pleadings, motions, affidavits, briefs and other documents which must be signed or which require either verification or an unsworn declaration under any rule or statute. The Clerk's Office will scan these original documents into an electronic file in the System. A certificate of service is required for all documents a pro se litigant files with the court. If a Pro Se filer is granted permission to register to electronically file documents, they shall comply with the guidelines contained in this document (NY R USDCTWD ECF Procedures). NY R USDCTWD ECF Procedures(2)(o)(i)(4).

- *Social Security cases.* Absent a showing of good cause, and except as provided in Section o(i)(4) above, all documents, notices and orders in Social Security reviews will be filed and noticed electronically, except as noted in NY R USDCTWD ECF Procedures(2)(o)(i)(6). For more information, refer to NY R USDCTWD ECF Procedures(2)(o)(i)(6).

- For more information on conventional filing of documents, refer to NY R USDCTWD ECF Procedures(2)(o)(i).

iv. *Consequences of electronic filing.* Electronic transmission of a document to the System consistent with these procedures (NY R USDCTWD ECF Procedures), whether accomplished by the Filing User or a Court User, together with the transmission of a Notice of Electronic Filing from the Court, constitutes filing of a document for all purposes of the Federal Rules of Civil Procedure and the Local Rules of Civil Procedure for the United States District Court for the Western District of New York, and constitutes entry of the document on the docket kept by the Clerk under FRCP 58 and FRCP 79. A document shall not be considered filed for purposes of the Federal Rules of Civil until the filing party receives a System generated Notice of Electronic Filing. NY R USDCTWD ECF Procedures(2)(a)(i).

- E-mailing a document to the Clerk's Office or to the assigned judge shall not constitute "filing" of such document. NY R USDCTWD ECF Procedures(2)(a)(i)(1).

v. *Filing fees.* Any fee required for filing of a pleading or paper in District Court is payable to the Clerk of Court by check or money order. In addition, when opening a civil case on line, filing a notice of appeal on line or applying to appear pro hac vice on line, the fees shall be paid on line by registered users through the federal electronic payment website. Users will be directed to the federal electronic payment website while entering their transaction and should have a credit card available. When opening a civil case and applying to proceed in forma pauperis or when the United States of America opens a case, the payment screen can by bypassed to complete the transaction. Additional information on making electronic payments can be located on the court's website. NY R USDCTWD ECF Procedures(2)(h)(i).

2. *Service requirements.* All pleadings and other papers shall be filed and served in accordance with the Federal Rules of Civil Procedure and the CM/ECF Administrative Procedures Guide (NY R USDCTWD ECF Procedures). NY R USDCTWD Civ Rule 5.1(a).

   a. *Service; When required*

      i. *In general.* Unless the Federal Rules of Civil Procedure provide otherwise, each of the following papers must be served on every party:

- An order stating that service is required;
- A pleading filed after the original complaint, unless the court orders otherwise under FRCP 5(c) because there are numerous defendants;
- A discovery paper required to be served on a party, unless the court orders otherwise;
- A written motion, except one that may be heard ex parte; and
- A written notice, appearance, demand, or offer of judgment, or any similar paper. FRCP 5(a)(1).

      ii. *If a party fails to appear.* No service is required on a party who is in default for failing to appear. But a pleading that asserts a new claim for relief against such a party must be served on that party under FRCP 4. FRCP 5(a)(2).

      iii. *Seizing property.* If an action is begun by seizing property and no person is or need be named as a defendant, any service required before the filing of an appearance, answer, or claim must be made on the person who had custody or possession of the property when it was seized. FRCP 5(a)(3).

   b. *Service; How made*

      i. *Serving an attorney.* If a party is represented by an attorney, service under FRCP 5 must be made on the attorney unless the court orders service on the party. FRCP 5(b)(1).

      ii. *Service in general.* A paper is served under FRCP 5 by:

- Handing it to the person;
- Leaving it: (1) at the person's office with a clerk or other person in charge or, if no one is in charge, in a conspicuous place in the office; or (2) if the person has no office or the office is closed, at the person's dwelling or usual place of abode with someone of suitable age and discretion who resides there;
- Mailing it to the person's last known address—in which event service is complete upon mailing;
- Leaving it with the court clerk if the person has no known address;
- Sending it by electronic means if the person consented in writing—in which event service is complete upon transmission, but is not effective if the serving party learns that it did not reach the person to be served; or
- Delivering it by any other means that the person consented to in writing—in which event service is complete when the person making service delivers it to the agency designated to make delivery. FRCP 5(b)(2).

      iii. *Service by overnight delivery.* All papers, other than a subpoena or a summons and complaint, may be served on counsel of record by overnight delivery service at the address designated by the attorney for that purpose, or if none is designated, at the attorney's last known address. Service by overnight delivery shall be complete upon deposit of the paper(s), enclosed in a properly addressed wrapper, into the custody of the overnight delivery service, prior to the latest time designated by the service for overnight delivery. NY R USDCTWD Civ Rule 5.1(g). "Overnight delivery service" means any delivery service which regularly accepts items for overnight delivery to any address within the Court's jurisdiction. NY R USDCTWD Civ Rule 5.1(g).

      iv. *Service of documents by electronic means*

- *Service on registered users.* Registered Users consent to the electronic service of all

documents, and must make available an electronic mail address for service during the registration process. Upon the filing of a document by a party, a Notice of Electronic Filing, with a hyperlink to the filed document, will be automatically generated by the electronic filing system and sent via electronic mail to the e-mail addresses of all parties participating in the electronic filing system in the case. Electronic service of the Notice of Electronic Filing constitutes service of the filed document for all purposes of the Federal Rules of Civil Procedure and the Local Rules of Civil Procedure for the United States District Court for the Western District of New York. NY R USDCTWD ECF Procedures(2)(f)(i). The Notice of Electronic Filing effectuates service for all registered users and no certificate of service is required when all filers on an action are Registered Users. NY R USDCTWD ECF Procedures(2)(f)(iv).

- *Time limit for opening hyperlink.* The hyperlink to filed documents contained in the Notice of Electronic Filing must be opened within fifteen (15) days from the date the document was filed to provide registered users access to the document. The hyperlink expires after fifteen (15) days and users will be unable to access documents for free after that time. Filing Users are encouraged to check their e-mail frequently for notice of filed documents. NY R USDCTWD ECF Procedures(2)(f)(ii).

- *Service on exempted attorneys or pro se litigants who do not have permission to file electronically.* Attorneys granted an exemption from electronically filing documents in the System and pro se litigants who have not been granted permission to electronically file documents are entitled to a paper copy of any electronically filed pleading, document or order. The filing party must therefore provide the non-registered party with the pleading, document or order according to the Federal Rules of Civil Procedure. NY R USDCTWD ECF Procedures(2)(f)(iii).

- *E-mailing or faxing documents.* E-mailing or faxing a pleading or document to any party shall not constitute service of the pleading or document. NY R USDCTWD ECF Procedures(2)(f)(v).

    v. *Using court facilities.* If a local rule so authorizes, a party may use the court's transmission facilities to make service under FRCP 5(b)(2)(E). FRCP 5(b)(3).

  c. *Serving numerous defendants*

    i. *In general.* If an action involves an unusually large number of defendants, the court may, on motion or on its own, order that:

- Defendants' pleadings and replies to them need not be served on other defendants;

- Any crossclaim, counterclaim, avoidance, or affirmative defense in those pleadings and replies to them will be treated as denied or avoided by all other parties; and

- Filing any such pleading and serving it on the plaintiff constitutes notice of the pleading to all parties. FRCP 5(c)(1).

    ii. *Notifying parties.* A copy of every such order must be served on the parties as the court directs. FRCP 5(c)(2).

3. *Pro se actions.* For information on the requirements in pro se actions, refer to NY R USDCTWD Civ Rule 5.2.

4. *Individual judge practices.* Refer to the Miscellaneous section of this document for information on individual judge practices on filing and serving documents.

## G. Hearings

1. *Hearings, generally*

  a. *Oral argument.* Due process does not require that oral argument be permitted on a motion and, except as otherwise provided by local rule, the district court has discretion to determine whether it will decide the motion on the papers or hear argument by counsel (and perhaps receive evidence). FPP § 1190; F.D.I.C. v. Deglau, 207 F.3d 153 (3d Cir. 2000).

    i. The parties shall appear for oral argument on all motions they make returnable before a Judge

on the scheduled return date for the motion. In its discretion, the Court may notify the parties that oral argument shall not be heard on any given motion. Thus, the parties should be prepared to have their motion papers serve as the sole method of argument. NY R USDCTWD Civ Rule 7(c).

b. *Providing a regular schedule for oral hearings.* A court may establish regular times and places for oral hearings on motions. FRCP 78(a).

c. *Providing for submission on briefs.* By rule or order, the court may provide for submitting and determining motions on briefs, without oral hearings. FRCP 78(b).

2. *Individual judge practices.* Refer to the Miscellaneous section of this document for information on individual judge practices on hearings.

## H. Forms

### 1. Federal Motion to Compel Discovery Forms

a. Notice of motion; To compel required disclosure of names and addresses of witnesses and persons having knowledge of the claims involved; Civil proceeding. AMJUR PP DEPOSITION § 6.

b. Motion; To compel required disclosure of names and addresses of witnesses and persons having knowledge of the claims involved. AMJUR PP DEPOSITION § 7.

c. Motion; To compel answer to interrogatories; Complete failure to answer. AMJUR PP DEPOSITION § 403.

d. Affidavit; In opposition of motion to compel psychiatric or physical examinations; By attorney. AMJUR PP DEPOSITION § 645.

e. Motion; To compel further responses to interrogatories; Various grounds. AMJUR PP DEPOSITION § 713.

f. Affidavit; In support of motion to compel answers to interrogatories and to impose sanctions. AMJUR PP DEPOSITION § 715.

g. Opposition; To motion to compel electronic discovery; Federal class action. AMJUR PP DEPOSITION § 721.

h. Notice of motion; For order to compel compliance with request to permit entry on real property for inspection. AMJUR PP DEPOSITION § 733.

i. Motion; To compel production of documents; After rejected request; Request for sanctions. AMJUR PP DEPOSITION § 734.

j. Affidavit; In support of motion to compel production of documents; By attorney. AMJUR PP DEPOSITION § 736.

k. Motion; To compel doctor's production of medical records for trial. AMJUR PP DEPOSITION § 744.

l. Notice of motion to compel party to answer deposition questions. 3B FEDFORMS § 3695.

m. Motion to compel deposition, request for sanctions and request for expedited hearing. 3B FEDFORMS § 3698.

n. Motion to compel answer to interrogatories. 3B FEDFORMS § 3699.

o. Affidavit in support of motion. 3B FEDFORMS § 3702.

p. Objection to motion for order requiring witness to answer oral questions on deposition. 3B FEDFORMS § 3705.

q. Motion; To compel answers to outstanding discovery requests. FEDPROF § 23:43.

r. Motion; To compel required disclosure of names and addresses of witnesses and persons having knowledge of the claims involved. FEDPROF § 23:44.

s. Motion; To compel answer to questions asked on oral or written examination. FEDPROF § 23:207.

t. Motion; To compel further answers to questions asked on oral or written examination and to award expenses of motion. FEDPROF § 23:208.

u.   Motion; To compel party to produce witness at deposition. FEDPROF § 23:209.

v.   Affidavit; By opposing attorney; In opposition to motion to compel answers asked at deposition; Answers tend to incriminate. FEDPROF § 23:212.

w.   Motion; To compel answer to interrogatories; Complete failure to answer. FEDPROF § 23:375.

x.   Motion; To compel further responses to interrogatories; Various grounds. FEDPROF § 23:376.

y.   Motion to compel discovery. GOLDLTGFMS § 21:2.

**2.   Forms for the Western District of New York**

a.   Certificate of service. NY R USDCTWD ECF Procedures(4a).

# I.  Applicable Rules

1.   *Federal rules*

a.   Serving and filing pleadings and other papers. FRCP 5.

b.   Constitutional challenge to a statute; Notice, certification, and intervention. FRCP 5.1.

c.   Privacy protection for filings made with the court. FRCP 5.2.

d.   Computing and extending time; Time for motion papers. FRCP 6.

e.   Pleadings allowed; Form of motions and other papers. FRCP 7.

f.   Form of pleadings. FRCP 10.

g.   Signing pleadings, motions, and other papers; Representations to the court; Sanctions. FRCP 11.

h.   Duty to disclose; General provisions governing discovery. FRCP 26.

i.   Failure to make disclosures or to cooperate in discovery; Sanctions. FRCP 37.

j.   Taking testimony. FRCP 43.

k.   Hearing motions; Submission on briefs. FRCP 78.

2.   *Local rules*

a.   Title. NY R USDCTWD Civ Rule 1.1.

b.   Filing and serving papers. NY R USDCTWD Civ Rule 5.1.

c.   Motion practice. NY R USDCTWD Civ Rule 7.

d.   Form of papers. NY R USDCTWD Civ Rule 10.

e.   Sanctions. NY R USDCTWD Civ Rule 11.

f.   Alternative dispute resolution and pretrial conferences. NY R USDCTWD Civ Rule 16.

g.   Attorneys of record; Appearance and withdrawal. NY R USDCTWD Civ Rule 83.2.

h.   Administrative procedures guide for electronic filing. NY R USDCTWD ECF Procedures.

i.   Alternative dispute resolution plan. NY R USDCTWD ADR Plan.

# J.  Miscellaneous

**NOTE: Individual judges' rules may apply. For available judge-level information, refer to:**

DISTRICT JUDGE RICHARD J. ARCARA: NY R USDCTWD Arcara-Procedures.

DISTRICT JUDGE FRANK P. GERACI, JR.: NY R USDCTWD Geraci-Procedures.

DISTRICT JUDGE DAVID G. LARIMER: NY R USDCTWD Larimer-Procedures.

DISTRICT JUDGE CHARLES J. SIRAGUSA: NY R USDCTWD Siragusa-Procedures.

DISTRICT JUDGE WILLIAM M. SKRETNY: NY R USDCTWD Skretny--Procedures.

DISTRICT JUDGE MICHAEL A. TELESCA: NY R USDCTWD Telesca-Procedures.

DISTRICT JUDGE LAWRENCE J. VILARDO: NY R USDCTWD Vilardo-Procedures.

DISTRICT JUDGE ELIZABETH A. WOLFORD: NY R USDCTWD Wolford-Procedures.

MAGISTRATE JUDGE JONATHAN W. FELDMAN: NY R USDCTWD Feldman-Procedures.

MAGISTRATE JUDGE LESLIE G. FOSCHIO: NY R USDCTWD Foschio-Procedures; NY R USDCTWD Foschio-Depositions.

MAGISTRATE JUDGE JEREMIAH J. McCARTHY: NY R USDCTWD McCarthy-Procedures.

MAGISTRATE JUDGE MARIAN W. PAYSON: NY R USDCTWD Payson-Procedures.

MAGISTRATE JUDGE MICHAEL J. ROEMER: NY R USDCTWD Roemer-Procedures.

MAGISTRATE JUDGE H. KENNETH SCHROEDER, JR.: NY R USDCTWD Schroeder-Proc.

MAGISTRATE JUDGE HUGH B. SCOTT: NY R USDCTWD Scott-Procedures.

# Motions, Oppositions and Replies
# Motion for Discovery Sanctions

### Document Last Updated September 2016

## A. Checklist

(I) ❑ Matters to be considered by moving party

   (a) ❑ Required documents

      (1) ❑ Notice of motion and motion

      (2) ❑ Affidavit of efforts to resolve discovery dispute

      (3) ❑ Supporting affidavit

      (4) ❑ Certificate of service

   (b) ❑ Supplemental documents

      (1) ❑ Memorandum of law

      (2) ❑ Supporting evidence

      (3) ❑ Notice of constitutional question

      (4) ❑ Copies of authorities

      (5) ❑ Proposed order

      (6) ❑ Paper copy for date-stamping with self-addressed envelope

      (7) ❑ Courtesy copies

   (c) ❑ Timing

      (1) ❑ A written motion and notice of the hearing must be served at least fourteen (14) days before the time specified for the hearing, with the following exceptions: (i) when the motion may be heard ex parte; (ii) when the Federal Rules of Civil Procedure set a different time; or (iii) when a court order—which a party may, for good cause, apply for ex parte—sets a different time

      (2) ❑ Any affidavit supporting a motion must be served with the motion

(II) ❑ Matters to be considered by opposing party

   (a) ❑ Required documents

      (1) ❑ Opposition

      (2) ❑ Supporting affidavit

      (3) ❑ Certificate of service

   (b) ❑ Supplemental documents

      (1) ❑ Supporting evidence

      (2) ❑ Notice of constitutional question

    (3)  ❑  Demand for jury trial

    (4)  ❑  Copies of authorities

    (5)  ❑  Paper copy for date-stamping with self-addressed envelope

    (6)  ❑  Courtesy copies

  (c)  ❑  Timing

    (1)  ❑  After a motion is filed, the court may issue an order setting deadlines for filing and service of opposing papers; if the court does not set deadlines by order, the opposing party shall have fourteen (14) days after service of the motion to file and serve responding papers

    (2)  ❑  Except as FRCP 59(c) provides otherwise, any opposing affidavit must be served at least seven (7) days before the hearing, unless the court permits service at another time

## B. Timing

1. *Motion for discovery sanctions.* There are no specific timing requirements for moving for discovery sanctions.

2. *Timing of motions, generally*

  a. *Motion and notice of hearing.* A written motion and notice of the hearing must be served at least fourteen (14) days before the time specified for the hearing, with the following exceptions:

    i. When the motion may be heard ex parte;

    ii. When the Federal Rules of Civil Procedure set a different time; or

    iii. When a court order—which a party may, for good cause, apply for ex parte—sets a different time. FRCP 6(c)(1).

  b. *Supporting affidavit.* Any affidavit supporting a motion must be served with the motion. FRCP 6(c)(2).

3. *Timing of opposing papers.* After a motion is filed, the Court may issue an order setting deadlines for filing and service of opposing papers. NY R USDCTWD Civ Rule 7(b)(1). If the Court does not set deadlines by order, the following schedule shall apply: the opposing party shall have fourteen (14) days after service of the motion to file and serve responding papers. NY R USDCTWD Civ Rule 7(b)(2)(B).

  a. *Opposing affidavit.* Except as FRCP 59(c) provides otherwise, any opposing affidavit must be served at least seven (7) days before the hearing, unless the court permits service at another time. FRCP 6(c)(2).

4. *Timing of reply papers.* Where the respondent files an answering affidavit setting up a new matter, the moving party ordinarily is allowed a reasonable time to file a reply affidavit since failure to deny the new matter by affidavit may operate as an admission of its truth. AMJUR MOTIONS § 25.

  a. *Reply papers.* After a motion is filed, the Court may issue an order setting deadlines. . .for filing and service of reply papers if the moving party has stated an intent to reply. NY R USDCTWD Civ Rule 7(b)(1). If the Court does not set deadlines by order, the following schedule shall apply: the moving party shall have seven (7) days after service of the responding papers to file and serve reply papers. NY R USDCTWD Civ Rule 7(b)(2)(B).

5. *Motion for an expedited hearing.* A party seeking to shorten the schedule prescribed in NY R USDCTWD Civ Rule 7(b) must make a separate motion for an expedited hearing, setting forth the reasons why an expedited hearing is required. NY R USDCTWD Civ Rule 7(d)(1). For more information, refer to NY R USDCTWD Civ Rule 7(d)(1).

6. *Computation of time*

  a. *Computing time.* FRCP 6 applies in computing any time period specified in the Federal Rules of Civil Procedure, in any local rule or court order, or in any statute that does not specify a method of computing time. FRCP 6(a).

    i. *Period stated in days or a longer unit.* When the period is stated in days or a longer unit of time:

      • Exclude the day of the event that triggers the period;

- Count every day, including intermediate Saturdays, Sundays, and legal holidays; and

- Include the last day of the period, but if the last day is a Saturday, Sunday, or legal holiday, the period continues to run until the end of the next day that is not a Saturday, Sunday, or legal holiday. FRCP 6(a)(1).

ii. *Period stated in hours.* When the period is stated in hours:

- Begin counting immediately on the occurrence of the event that triggers the period;

- Count every hour, including hours during intermediate Saturdays, Sundays, and legal holidays; and

- If the period would end on a Saturday, Sunday, or legal holiday, the period continues to run until the same time on the next day that is not a Saturday, Sunday, or legal holiday. FRCP 6(a)(2).

iii. *Inaccessibility of the clerk's office.* Unless the court orders otherwise, if the clerk's office is inaccessible:

- On the last day for filing under FRCP 6(a)(1), then the time for filing is extended to the first accessible day that is not a Saturday, Sunday, or legal holiday; or

- During the last hour for filing under FRCP 6(a)(2), then the time for filing is extended to the same time on the first accessible day that is not a Saturday, Sunday, or legal holiday. FRCP 6(a)(3).

iv. *"Last day" defined.* Unless a different time is set by a statute, local rule, or court order, the last day ends:

- For electronic filing, at midnight in the court's time zone; and

- For filing by other means, when the clerk's office is scheduled to close. FRCP 6(a)(4).

v. *"Next day" defined.* The "next day" is determined by continuing to count forward when the period is measured after an event and backward when measured before an event. FRCP 6(a)(5).

vi. *"Legal holiday" defined.* "Legal holiday" means:

- The day set aside by statute for observing New Year's Day, Martin Luther King Jr.'s Birthday, Washington's Birthday, Memorial Day, Independence Day, Labor Day, Columbus Day, Veterans' Day, Thanksgiving Day, or Christmas Day;

- Any day declared a holiday by the President or Congress; and

- For periods that are measured after an event, any other day declared a holiday by the state where the district court is located. FRCP 6(a)(6).

b. *Computation of electronic filing deadlines.* A document will be deemed timely filed if filed prior to midnight Eastern Time, unless otherwise ordered by the Court. A document will be considered untimely if filed thereafter. When a Court order requires that a document be filed on a weekend or holiday, the document may be filed by close of business the next business day without further application to the Court. NY R USDCTWD ECF Procedures(2)(e)(i). A document filed electronically is deemed filed on the date and time stated on the Notice of Electronic Filing. NY R USDCTWD ECF Procedures(2)(e)(ii).

i. *System availability.* Although parties may file documents electronically twenty-four (24) hours a day, registered users are strongly encouraged to file all documents during normal working hours of the Clerk's Office (8:30 a.m. to 5:00 p.m. Eastern Time). NY R USDCTWD ECF Procedures(2)(t)(i).

ii. *Technical failures.* A Filing User whose filing is made untimely as a result of a technical failure must seek appropriate relief from the Court. NY R USDCTWD ECF Procedures(2)(u)(i).

c. *Extending time*

   i. *In general.* When an act may or must be done within a specified time, the court may, for good cause, extend the time:

   - With or without motion or notice if the court acts, or if a request is made, before the original time or its extension expires; or

   - On motion made after the time has expired if the party failed to act because of excusable neglect. FRCP 6(b)(1).

   ii. *Exceptions.* A court must not extend the time to act under FRCP 50(b), FRCP 50(d), FRCP 52(b), FRCP 59(b), FRCP 59(d), FRCP 59(e), and FRCP 60(b). FRCP 6(b)(2).

   iii. Refer to the United States District Court for the Western District of New York KeyRules Motion for Continuance/Extension of Time document for more information on extending time.

d. *Additional time after certain kinds of service.* When a party may or must act within a specified time after service and service is made under FRCP 5(b)(2)(C), FRCP 5(b)(2)(D), FRCP 5(b)(2)(E), or FRCP 5(b)(2)(F), three (3) days are added after the period would otherwise expire under FRCP 6(a). FRCP 6(d).

   i. *Service by overnight delivery.* Where a period of time prescribed by either the Federal Rules of Civil Procedure or the Local Rules of Civil Procedure for the United States District Court for the Western District of New York is measured from the service of a paper and service is by overnight delivery, one (1) business day shall be added to the prescribed period. NY R USDCTWD Civ Rule 5.1(g).

7. *Individual judge practices.* Refer to the Miscellaneous section of this document for information on individual judge practices on timing of documents.

## C. General Requirements

1. *Motions, generally*

   a. *Requirements.* A request for a court order must be made by motion. The motion must:

      i. Be in writing unless made during a hearing or trial;

      ii. State with particularity the grounds for seeking the order; and

      iii. State the relief sought. FRCP 7(b)(1).

   b. *Notice of motion.* A party interested in resisting the relief sought by a motion has a right to notice thereof, and an opportunity to be heard. AMJUR MOTIONS § 12.

      i. In addition to statutory or court rule provisions requiring notice of a motion—the purpose of such a notice requirement having been said to be to prevent a party from being prejudicially surprised by a motion—principles of natural justice dictate that an adverse party generally must be given notice that a motion will be presented to the court. AMJUR MOTIONS § 12.

      ii. "Notice," in this regard, means reasonable notice, including a meaningful opportunity to prepare and to defend against allegations of a motion. AMJUR MOTIONS § 12.

   c. *Writing requirement.* The writing requirement is intended to insure that the adverse parties are informed and have a record of both the motion's pendency and the grounds on which the movant seeks an order. FPP § 1191; Feldberg v. Quechee Lakes Corp., 463 F.3d 195 (2d Cir. 2006).

      i. It is sufficient "if the motion is stated in a written notice of the hearing of the motion." FPP § 1191.

   d. *Particularity requirement.* The particularity requirement insures that the opposing parties will have notice of their opponent's contentions. FEDPROC § 62:364; Goodman v. 1973 26 Foot Trojan Vessel, Arkansas Registration No. AR1439SN, 859 F.2d 71, 12 Fed.R.Serv.3d 645 (8th Cir. 1988). That requirement ensures that notice of the basis for the motion is provided to the court and to the opposing party so as to avoid prejudice, provide the opponent with a meaningful opportunity to respond, and provide the court with enough information to process the motion correctly. FEDPROC § 62:364; Andreas v. Volkswagen of America, Inc., 336 F.3d 789, 56 Fed.R.Serv.3d 6 (8th Cir. 2003).

      i. Reasonable specification of the grounds for a motion is sufficient. However, where a movant fails to state even one ground for granting the motion in question, the movant has failed to meet the minimal standard of "reasonable specification." FEDPROC § 62:364; Martinez v. Trainor, 556 F.2d 818, 23 Fed.R.Serv.2d 403 (7th Cir. 1977).

    ii.   The court may excuse the failure to comply with the particularity requirement if it is inadvertent, and where no prejudice is shown by the opposing party. FEDPROC § 62:364.

2.   *Motion for discovery sanctions*

    a.   *Sanctions, generally.* FRCP 37 is flexible. The court is directed to make such orders as are "just" and is not limited in any case of disregard of the discovery rules or court orders under them to a stereotyped response. The sanctions enumerated in FRCP 37 are not exclusive and arbitrary but flexible, selective, and plural. The district court may, within reason, use as many and as varied sanctions as are necessary to hold the scales of justice even. FPP § 2284.

        i.   There is one fixed limitation that should be noted. A party may not be imprisoned or otherwise punished for contempt of court for failure to submit to a physical or mental examination, or for failure to produce a person in his or her custody or under his or her control for such an examination. FPP § 2284; Sibbach v. Wilson & Co., 312 U.S. 1, 312 U.S. 655, 61 S.Ct. 422, 85 L.Ed. 479 (1941).

        ii.   Although FRCP 37 is very broad, and the courts have considerable discretion in imposing sanctions as authorized by FRCP 37, there are constitutional limits, stemming from the Due Process Clause of U.S.C.A. Const. Amend. V and U.S.C.A. Const. Amend. XIV, on the imposition of sanctions. There are two principal facets of the due process issues:

            ●   First, the court must ask whether there is a sufficient relationship between the discovery and the merits sought to be foreclosed by the sanction to legitimate depriving a party of the opportunity to litigate the merits. FPP § 2283.

            ●   Second, before imposing a serious merits sanction the court should determine whether the party guilty of a failure to provide discovery was unable to comply with the discovery. FPP § 2283.

    b.   *Sanction for improper certification.* If a certification violates FRCP 26(g) without substantial justification, the court, on motion or on its own, must impose an appropriate sanction on the signer, the party on whose behalf the signer was acting, or both. The sanction may include an order to pay the reasonable expenses, including attorney's fees, caused by the violation. FRCP 26(g)(3).

    c.   *Motion to compel discovery; Payment of expenses; Protective orders*

        i.   *If the motion is granted (or disclosure or discovery is provided after filing).* If the motion is granted—or if the disclosure or requested discovery is provided after the motion was filed—the court must, after giving an opportunity to be heard, require the party or deponent whose conduct necessitated the motion, the party or attorney advising that conduct, or both to pay the movant's reasonable expenses incurred in making the motion, including attorney's fees. But the court must not order this payment if:

            ●   The movant filed the motion before attempting in good faith to obtain the disclosure or discovery without court action;

            ●   The opposing party's nondisclosure, response, or objection was substantially justified; or

            ●   Other circumstances make an award of expenses unjust. FRCP 37(a)(5)(A).

        ii.   *If the motion is denied.* If the motion is denied, the court may issue any protective order authorized under FRCP 26(c) and must, after giving an opportunity to be heard, require the movant, the attorney filing the motion, or both to pay the party or deponent who opposed the motion its reasonable expenses incurred in opposing the motion, including attorney's fees. But the court must not order this payment if the motion was substantially justified or other circumstances make an award of expenses unjust. FRCP 37(a)(5)(B).

        iii.   *If the motion is granted in part and denied in part.* If the motion is granted in part and denied in part, the court may issue any protective order authorized under FRCP 26(c) and may, after giving an opportunity to be heard, apportion the reasonable expenses for the motion. FRCP 37(a)(5)(C).

d. *Failure to comply with a court order*

i. *Sanctions in the district where the deposition is taken.* If the court where the discovery is taken orders a deponent to be sworn or to answer a question and the deponent fails to obey, the failure may be treated as contempt of court. If a deposition-related motion is transferred to the court where the action is pending, and that court orders a deponent to be sworn or to answer a question and the deponent fails to obey, the failure may be treated as contempt of either the court where the discovery is taken or the court where the action is pending. FRCP 37(b)(1).

ii. *Sanctions in the district where the action is pending; For not obeying a discovery order.* If a party or a party's officer, director, or managing agent—or a witness designated under FRCP 30(b)(6) or FRCP 31(a)(4)—fails to obey an order to provide or permit discovery, including an order under FRCP 26(f), FRCP 35, or FRCP 37(a), the court where the action is pending may issue further just orders. They may include the following:

- Directing that the matters embraced in the order or other designated facts be taken as established for purposes of the action, as the prevailing party claims;

- Prohibiting the disobedient party from supporting or opposing designated claims or defenses, or from introducing designated matters in evidence;

- Striking pleadings in whole or in part;

- Staying further proceedings until the order is obeyed;

- Dismissing the action or proceeding in whole or in part;

- Rendering a default judgment against the disobedient party; or

- Treating as contempt of court the failure to obey any order except an order to submit to a physical or mental examination. FRCP 37(b)(2)(A).

iii. *Sanctions in the district where the action is pending; For not producing a person for examination.* If a party fails to comply with an order under FRCP 35(a) requiring it to produce another person for examination, the court may issue any of the orders listed in FRCP 37(b)(2)(A)(i) through FRCP 37(b)(2)(A)(vi), unless the disobedient party shows that it cannot produce the other person. FRCP 37(b)(2)(B).

iv. *Sanctions in the district where the action is pending; Payment of expenses.* Instead of or in addition to the orders in FRCP 37(b)(2)(A) and FRCP 37(b)(2)(B), the court must order the disobedient party, the attorney advising that party, or both to pay the reasonable expenses, including attorney's fees, caused by the failure, unless the failure was substantially justified or other circumstances make an award of expenses unjust. FRCP 37(b)(2)(C).

v. *Contempt.* A proceeding to adjudicate a person in civil contempt of court, including a case provided for in FRCP 37(b)(1) and FRCP 37(b)(2)(A), shall be commenced by the service of a notice of motion or order to show cause. NY R USDCTWD Civ Rule 83.4(a).

- *Alleged contemnor found guilty.* In the event the alleged contemnor is found to be in contempt of court, an order shall be made and entered: (1) reciting or referring to the verdict or findings of fact upon which the adjudication is based; (2) setting forth the amount of the damages to which the complainant is entitled; (3) fixing the fine, if any, imposed by the Court, which fine shall include the damages found, and naming the person to whom such fine shall be payable; (4) stating any other conditions, the performance of which will operate to purge the contempt; and (5) directing the arrest of the contemnor by the United States Marshal, and their confinement until the performance of the condition fixed in the order and the payment of the fine, or until the contemnor be otherwise discharged pursuant to law. The order shall specify the place of confinement. No party shall be required to pay or to advance to the Marshal any expenses for the upkeep of the prisoner. Upon such an order, no person shall be detained in prison by reason of the nonpayment of the fine for a period exceeding six (6) months. A certified copy of the order committing the contemnor shall be sufficient warrant to the Marshal for the arrest and confinement. The aggrieved party shall also have the same remedies against the property of the contemnor as if the order awarding the fine were a final judgment. NY R USDCTWD Civ Rule 83.4(c).

- *Alleged contemnor found not guilty.* In the event the alleged contemnor shall be found not guilty of the charges made against them, they shall be discharged from the proceeding and, in the discretion of the Court, may have judgment against the complainant for their costs and disbursements and a reasonable counsel fee. NY R USDCTWD Civ Rule 83.4(d).

e. *Failure to disclose, to supplement an earlier response, or to admit*

   i. *Failure to disclose or supplement.* If a party fails to provide information or identify a witness as required by FRCP 26(a) or FRCP 26(e), the party is not allowed to use that information or witness to supply evidence on a motion, at a hearing, or at a trial, unless the failure was substantially justified or is harmless. In addition to or instead of this sanction, the court, on motion and after giving an opportunity to be heard:

- May order payment of the reasonable expenses, including attorney's fees, caused by the failure;

- May inform the jury of the party's failure; and

- May impose other appropriate sanctions, including any of the orders listed in FRCP 37(b)(2)(A)(i) through FRCP 37(b)(2)(A)(vi). FRCP 37(c)(1).

   ii. *Failure to admit.* If a party fails to admit what is requested under FRCP 36 and if the requesting party later proves a document to be genuine or the matter true, the requesting party may move that the party who failed to admit pay the reasonable expenses, including attorney's fees, incurred in making that proof. The court must so order unless:

- The request was held objectionable under FRCP 36(a);

- The admission sought was of no substantial importance;

- The party failing to admit had a reasonable ground to believe that it might prevail on the matter; or

- There was other good reason for the failure to admit. FRCP 37(c)(2).

f. *Party's failure to attend its own deposition, serve answers to interrogatories, or respond to a request for inspection*

   i. *Motion; Grounds for sanctions.* The court where the action is pending may, on motion, order sanctions if:

- A party or a party's officer, director, or managing agent—or a person designated under FRCP 30(b)(6) or FRCP 31(a)(4)—fails, after being served with proper notice, to appear for that person's deposition; or

- A party, after being properly served with interrogatories under FRCP 33 or a request for inspection under FRCP 34, fails to serve its answers, objections, or written response. FRCP 37(d)(1)(A).

   ii. *Unacceptable excuse for failing to act.* A failure described in FRCP 37(d)(1)(A) is not excused on the ground that the discovery sought was objectionable, unless the party failing to act has a pending motion for a protective order under FRCP 26(c). FRCP 37(d)(2).

   iii. *Types of sanctions.* Sanctions may include any of the orders listed in FRCP 37(b)(2)(A)(i) through FRCP 37(b)(2)(A)(vi). Instead of or in addition to these sanctions, the court must require the party failing to act, the attorney advising that party, or both to pay the reasonable expenses, including attorney's fees, caused by the failure, unless the failure was substantially justified or other circumstances make an award of expenses unjust. FRCP 37(d)(3).

g. *Failure to provide electronically stored information.* If electronically stored information that should have been preserved in the anticipation or conduct of litigation is lost because a party failed to take reasonable steps to preserve it, and it cannot be restored or replaced through additional discovery, the court:

   i. Upon finding prejudice to another party from loss of the information, may order measures no greater than necessary to cure the prejudice; or

ii. Only upon finding that the party acted with the intent to deprive another party of the information's use in the litigation may: (1) presume that the lost information was unfavorable to the party; (2) instruct the jury that it may or must presume the information was unfavorable to the party; or (3) dismiss the action or enter a default judgment. FRCP 37(e).

h. *Failure to participate in framing a discovery plan.* If a party or its attorney fails to participate in good faith in developing and submitting a proposed discovery plan as required by FRCP 26(f), the court may, after giving an opportunity to be heard, require that party or attorney to pay to any other party the reasonable expenses, including attorney's fees, caused by the failure. FRCP 37(f).

i. *Counsel's liability for excessive costs.* 28 U.S.C.A. § 1927 is a basis for sanctioning attorney misconduct in discovery proceedings. DISCPROFED § 22:3. Any attorney or other person admitted to conduct cases in any court of the United States or any Territory thereof who so multiplies the proceedings in any case unreasonably and vexatiously may be required by the court to satisfy personally the excess costs, expenses, and attorneys' fees reasonably incurred because of such conduct. 28 U.S.C.A. § 1927.

3. *Opposing papers.* The Federal Rules of Civil Procedure do not require any formal answer, return, or reply to a motion, except where the Federal Rules of Civil Procedure or local rules may require affidavits, memoranda, or other papers to be filed in opposition to a motion. Such papers are simply to apprise the court of such opposition and the grounds of that opposition. FEDPROC § 62:359.

a. *Effect of failure to respond to motion.* Although in the absence of statutory provision or court rule, a motion ordinarily does not require a written answer, when a party files a motion and the opposing party fails to respond, the court may construe such failure to respond as nonopposition to the motion or an admission that the motion was meritorious, may take the facts alleged in the motion as true—the rule in some jurisdictions being that the failure to respond to a fact set forth in a motion is deemed an admission—and may grant the motion if the relief requested appears to be justified. AMJUR MOTIONS § 28.

b. *Assent or no opposition not determinative.* However, a motion will not be granted automatically simply because an "assent" or a notation of "no opposition" has been filed; federal judges frequently deny motions that have been assented to when it is thought that justice so dictates. FPP § 1190.

c. *Responsive pleading inappropriate as response to motion.* An attempt to answer or oppose a motion with a responsive pleading usually is not appropriate. FPP § 1190.

4. *Reply papers.* A moving party may be required or permitted to prepare papers in addition to his original motion papers. AMJUR MOTIONS § 25. Papers answering or replying to opposing papers may be appropriate, in the interests of justice, where it appears there is a substantial reason for allowing a reply. Thus, a court may accept reply papers where a party demonstrates that the papers to which it seeks to file a reply raise new issues that are material to the disposition of the question before the court, or where the court determines, sua sponte, that it wishes further briefing of an issue raised in those papers and orders the submission of additional papers. FEDPROC § 62:360.

a. *Function of reply papers.* The function of a reply affidavit is to answer the arguments made in opposition to the position taken by the movant and not to permit the movant to introduce new arguments in support of the motion. AMJUR MOTIONS § 25.

b. *Issues raised for the first time in a reply document.* However, the view has been followed in some jurisdictions, that as a matter of judicial economy, where there is no prejudice and where the issues could be raised simply by filing a motion to dismiss, the trial court has discretion to consider arguments raised for the first time in a reply memorandum, and that a trial court may grant a motion to strike issues raised for the first time in a reply memorandum. AMJUR MOTIONS § 26.

5. *Sur-reply.* Absent permission of the Judge hearing the motion, sur-reply papers are not permitted. NY R USDCTWD Civ Rule 7(a)(6).

6. *Motion to settle an order.* When counsel are unable to agree on the form of a proposed order, the prevailing party may move, upon seven (7) days notice to all parties, to settle the order. The Court may award costs and attorney's fees against an attorney if it determines that the attorney's unreasonable conduct necessitated bringing the motion. NY R USDCTWD Civ Rule 7(d)(2).

7. *Notice of appearance.* No notice of appearance is required of an attorney whose name and address appear at the end of a complaint, notice of removal, pre-answer motion, or answer. In all other circumstances, an attorney appearing for a party in a civil case shall promptly file a written notice of appearance. NY R USDCTWD Civ Rule 83.2(b). For more information on appearances and withdrawals, refer to NY R USDCTWD Civ Rule 83.2.

8. *Related cases.* Each attorney appearing in a civil case has a continuing duty to promptly notify the Clerk of Court when the attorney has reason to believe that said case is related to some other pending civil or criminal action(s) such that their assignment to the same Judge would avoid unnecessary duplication of judicial effort. As soon as the attorney becomes aware of such a relationship, the attorney shall notify the Clerk of Court by letter of the relevant facts, and the Clerk of Court will transmit that notification to the Judges to whom the cases have been assigned. NY R USDCTWD Civ Rule 5.1(e).

9. *Alternative dispute resolution (ADR).* This Court has adopted an Alternative Dispute Resolution Plan ("ADR"), as implemented by Standing Order (NY R USDCTWD ADR Plan), under which certain civil cases are referred automatically to ADR upon filing. NY R USDCTWD Civ Rule 16(a). The United States District Court for the Western District of New York (the "Court") adopted the ADR Plan on January 1, 2006 (the "Effective Date"), to make available to civil litigants court-administered ADR interventions and processes designed to provide quicker, less expensive and potentially more satisfying alternatives to continuing litigation, without impairing the quality of justice or the right to trial. NY R USDCTWD ADR Plan(1)(1.2)(A).

   a. *Scope.* This ADR Plan (NY R USDCTWD ADR Plan) applies to civil actions pending or commenced on and after the Effective Date, except as otherwise indicated in NY R USDCTWD ADR Plan. The ADR Plan supplements the Local Rules of Civil Procedure for the United States District Court for the Western District of New York, which shall remain in full effect for all cases. NY R USDCTWD ADR Plan(1)(1.2)(B).

   b. *Referral to ADR*

      i. *New cases.* All civil cases filed on and after the Effective Date of the ADR Plan shall be referred automatically for ADR. NY R USDCTWD ADR Plan(2)(2.1)(A). Notice of the ADR requirements will be provided to all parties immediately upon the filing of a complaint and answer or a notice of removal; NY R USDCTWD ADR Plan(2)(2.1)(A); NY R USDCTWD Civ Rule 16(a). ADR intervention will be scheduled at the conference held pursuant to Local Rule of Civil Procedure 16.1. NY R USDCTWD ADR Plan(2)(2.1)(A). [Editor's note: the reference to Local Rule of Civil Procedure 16.1 is likely meant to be a reference to NY R USDCTWD Civ Rule 16(b)].

         • Litigants in cases not referred automatically to ADR must consider possible agreement to the use of an ADR process. NY R USDCTWD Civ Rule 16(a).

         • For a list of exemptions from automatic referral, refer to NY R USDCTWD ADR Plan(2)(2.1)(A).

      ii. *Pending cases.* The assigned Judge on any pending civil case may, sua sponte or with status conference, issue an order referring the case for ADR. NY R USDCTWD ADR Plan(2)(2.1)(B); NY R USDCTWD Civ Rule 16(a). The order shall specify a date on which the ADR intervention is to be completed. NY R USDCTWD ADR Plan(2)(2.1)(B).

      iii. *Stipulation.* A case may be referred for ADR by stipulation of all parties. Stipulations shall be filed and shall designate the specific ADR intervention the parties have selected, the time frame within which the ADR process will be completed and the selected Neutral. Stipulations are presumed acceptable unless the assigned Judge determines that the interests of justice are not served. NY R USDCTWD ADR Plan(2)(2.1)(C).

      iv. *Relief from ADR referral*

         • *Opting out motions.* Any party may file, with the assigned Judge for that case, a motion to opt out of, or for relief from, ADR. NY R USDCTWD ADR Plan(2)(2.2)(A).

         • *Motion.* Opting Out Motions must be made within fourteen (14) days from (1) the date of the first discovery conference under Local Rule 16.1 in new cases, or (2) the date of a sua sponte ADR Referral Order in pending cases. NY R USDCTWD ADR Plan(2)(2.2)(B). [Editor's note: the reference to Local Rule 16.1 is likely meant to be a reference to NY R USDCTWD Civ Rule 16(b)].

- *Criteria.* Opting Out Motions shall be granted only for "good cause" shown. Inconvenience, travel costs, attorney fees or other costs shall not constitute "good cause." A party seeking relief from ADR must set forth the reasons why ADR has no reasonable chance of being productive. NY R USDCTWD ADR Plan(2)(2.2)(C).

- *Judicial initiative.* The assigned Judge may, sua sponte, exempt any case from the Court's ADR Plan. NY R USDCTWD ADR Plan(2)(2.2)(D).

  c. *ADR interventions*

    i. *Options.* It is expected that cases referred for ADR will proceed to Mediation. However, the following options are also available upon the stipulation of all parties:

- Neutral Evaluation;
- Mini Summary Trial;
- Arbitration (Binding and Non-Binding);
- Case Valuation; and
- Settlement Week, when scheduled by the Court. NY R USDCTWD ADR Plan(4)(4.1)(A).

    ii. *Timing.* Timing is specific to the intervention and process chosen, as set forth in the corresponding sections in NY R USDCTWD ADR Plan. NY R USDCTWD ADR Plan(4)(4.1)(B).

    iii. *Scheduling.* The referral of a case to ADR does not delay or defer other dates established in the Scheduling Order and has no effect on the scheduled progress of the case toward trial. NY R USDCTWD ADR Plan(4)(4.1)(C).

  d. *Selecting an ADR intervention*

    i. *New cases.* Prior to the Local Rule 16.1 scheduling conference, counsel and any unrepresented parties shall confer about ADR as part of their discussion of "the possibilities for a prompt settlement or resolution of the case" pursuant to FRCP 26(f). Unless the parties agree to a different intervention, it is presumed that they will participate in mediation. [Editor's note: the reference to Local Rule 16.1 is likely meant to be a reference to NY R USDCTWD Civ Rule 16(b)].

    ii. *Pending cases.* In pending cases, all sua sponte referrals will be to mediation. Should the parties agree that a different ADR intervention is more appropriate to their case, they may submit a stipulation designating the specific ADR intervention selected, the time frame within which the ADR process will be completed and the identity of the Neutral. Stipulations must be filed within fourteen (14) days from the date of the ADR Referral Order and are presumed acceptable unless the assigned Judge determines that the interests of justice are not served. NY R USDCTWD ADR Plan(4)(4.2)(B).

  e. For more information on alternative dispute resolution (ADR), refer to NY R USDCTWD ADR Plan.

10. *Sanctions.* Failure of counsel for any party, or a party proceeding pro se, to appear before the Court at a conference, to complete the necessary preparations, or to be prepared to proceed to trial at the set time may be considered an abandonment of the case or a failure to prosecute or defend diligently. An appropriate order for sanctions may be entered against the defaulting party with respect to either a specific issue or the entire case. NY R USDCTWD Civ Rule 11(a). For more information, refer to NY R USDCTWD Civ Rule 11.

11. *Pro se actions.* For information on the requirements in pro se actions, refer to NY R USDCTWD Civ Rule 5.2.

12. *Individual judge practices.* Refer to the Miscellaneous section of this document for information on individual judge practices on general requirements for documents.

**D. Documents**

1. *Documents for moving party*

    a. *Required documents*

       i. *Notice of motion and motion.* A notice of motion is required for all motions, and must state: the relief sought, the grounds for the request, the papers submitted in support, and the return date for the motion, if known. A moving party who intends to file and serve reply papers must so state in the notice of motion. NY R USDCTWD Civ Rule 7(a)(1). Refer to the General Requirements section of this document for information on the notice of motion and motion.

          - *Order to show cause.* A proceeding to adjudicate a person in civil contempt of court, including a case provided for in FRCP 37(b)(1) and FRCP 37(b)(2)(A), shall be commenced by the service of a notice of motion or order to show cause. NY R USDCTWD Civ Rule 83.4(a). If an order to show cause is sought, such order may upon good cause shown embody a direction to the United States Marshal to arrest the alleged contemnor and hold him or her in bail in an amount fixed by the order, conditioned upon his or her appearance at the hearing and upon his or her holding himself or herself amenable thereafter to all orders of the Court for surrender. NY R USDCTWD Civ Rule 83.4(a).

       ii. *Affidavit of efforts to resolve discovery dispute.* No motion for discovery and/or production of documents under FRCP 37 shall be heard unless accompanied by an affidavit showing that sincere attempts to resolve the discovery dispute have been made. Such affidavit shall detail the times and places of the parties' meetings or discussions concerning the discovery dispute and the names of all parties participating therein, and all related correspondence must be attached. NY R USDCTWD Civ Rule 7(d)(4). A motion for sanctions for failing to answer or respond must include a certification that the movant has in good faith conferred or attempted to confer with the party failing to act in an effort to obtain the answer or response without court action. FRCP 37(d)(1)(B).

       iii. *Supporting affidavit.* An affidavit must not contain legal arguments, but must contain factual and procedural background relevant to the motion it supports. Except for motions brought under FRCP 12(b)(1) (lack of subject matter jurisdiction), FRCP 12(b)(6) (failure to state a claim), FRCP 12(c) (judgment on the pleadings), and FRCP 12(f) (to strike), motions and opposition to motions shall be supported by at least one (1) affidavit and by such other evidence (i.e., deposition testimony, interrogatory answers, admissions, and documents) as appropriate to resolve the particular motion. Failure to comply with this requirement may constitute grounds for resolving the motion against the non-complying party. NY R USDCTWD Civ Rule 7(a)(3).

       iv. *Certificate of service.* FRCP 5(d) requires that the person making service under FRCP 5 certify that service has been effected. FRCP 5(Advisory Committee Notes). Having such information on file may be useful for many purposes, including proof of service if an issue arises concerning the effectiveness of the service. FRCP 5(Advisory Committee Notes). The Notice of Electronic Filing effectuates service for all registered users and no certificate of service is required when all filers on an action are Registered Users. The following exemptions require a certificate of service to be filed:

          - When a document is manually filed, a certificate of service must be filed stating the manner in which service or notice was accomplished on each party so entitled. NY R USDCTWD ECF Procedures(2)(f)(iv).

          - When a pro se filer (who isn't authorized to electronically file documents) is a party, a certificate of service must be filed stating the manner in which service or notice was accomplished on the pro se party. The Notice of Electronic Filing effectuates service for the Registered Users in this situation and it is not necessary to note service on those parties. A non-registered pro se filer is required to file certificates of service on all documents they file. NY R USDCTWD ECF Procedures(2)(f)(iv).

          - If an attorney is exempt from electronic service, a certificate of service must be filed

1529

stating the manner in which service or notice was accomplished on the exempt attorney. The Notice of Electronic Filing effectuates service for the Registered Users in this situation and it is not necessary to note service on those parties. NY R USDCTWD ECF Procedures(2)(f)(iv).

b. *Supplemental documents*

    i. *Memorandum of law.* Nothing in the Local Rules of Civil Procedure for the United States District Court for the Western District of New York precludes a moving party from filing a memorandum in support of a motion made other than pursuant to FRCP 12, FRCP 56 or FRCP 65(a). The Court, in its discretion, may require written memoranda on such other motions. NY R USDCTWD Civ Rule 7(a)(2)(B). Refer to the Format section of this document for the formatting requirements for memoranda of law.

    ii. *Supporting evidence.* When a motion relies on facts outside the record, the court may hear the matter on affidavits or may hear it wholly or partly on oral testimony or on depositions. FRCP 43(c). A party seeking or opposing any relief under the Federal Rules of Civil Procedure shall file only the portion(s) of a deposition, interrogatory, request for documents, request for admission, or other supporting material that is pertinent to the application. NY R USDCTWD Civ Rule 7(a)(4).

- *Supporting affidavit for contempt proceedings.* The affidavit upon which such notice of motion or order to show cause is based shall set forth with particularity the misconduct complained of, the claim, if any, for damages occasioned thereby, and such evidence as to the amount of damages as may be available to the moving party. Reasonable attorney's fees necessitated by the contempt proceeding may be included as an item of damage. NY R USDCTWD Civ Rule 83.4(a).

    iii. *Notice of constitutional question.* A party that files a pleading, written motion, or other paper drawing into question the constitutionality of a federal or state statute must promptly:

- *File notice.* File a notice of constitutional question stating the question and identifying the paper that raises it, if: (1) a federal statute is questioned and the parties do not include the United States, one of its agencies, or one of its officers or employees in an official capacity; or (2) a state statute is questioned and the parties do not include the state, one of its agencies, or one of its officers or employees in an official capacity; and

- *Serve notice.* Serve the notice and paper on the Attorney General of the United States if a federal statute is questioned—or on the state attorney general if a state statute is questioned—either by certified or registered mail or by sending it to an electronic address designated by the attorney general for this purpose. FRCP 5.1(a).

- *No forfeiture.* A party's failure to file and serve the notice, or the court's failure to certify, does not forfeit a constitutional claim or defense that is otherwise timely asserted. FRCP 5.1(d).

    iv. *Copies of authorities.* In cases involving a pro se litigant, counsel shall, when serving a memorandum of law (or other submissions to the Court), provide the pro se litigant (but not other counsel or the Court) with printed copies of decisions cited therein that are unreported or reported exclusively on computerized databases. NY R USDCTWD Civ Rule 7(a)(8).

    v. *Proposed order.* All proposed orders must be submitted in a format compatible with WordPerfect or Microsoft Word format, which is a "Save As" option in most word processing software. Judges will not accept proposed orders in PDF format. NY R USDCTWD ECF Procedures(2)(j)(ii). Proposed orders should be attached to an Internet e-mail sent to the e-mail address of the assigned judge. NY R USDCTWD ECF Procedures(2)(j)(i). For the list of email addresses for the judges, refer to NY R USDCTWD ECF Procedures(2)(j)(i).

    vi. *Paper copy for date-stamping with self-addressed envelope.* Parties requesting date-stamped copies of filed documents must provide a paper copy for date-stamping, and a self-addressed, adequately-sized envelope with proper postage affixed. NY R USDCTWD Civ Rule 5.1(d).

    vii. *Courtesy copies.* The Court may, in its discretion, request courtesy copies on any other motion.

NY R USDCTWD Civ Rule 7(a)(7). Courtesy copies of certain documents may be required. Filers should refer to the "Judge Preferences" published on the Court's website. NY R USDCTWD ECF Procedures(2)(a)(iii).

2. *Documents for opposing party*

   a. *Required documents*

      i. *Opposition.* Refer to the General Requirements section of this document for information on the opposing papers.

      ii. *Supporting affidavit.* An affidavit must not contain legal arguments, but must contain factual and procedural background relevant to the motion it supports. Except for motions brought under FRCP 12(b)(1) (lack of subject matter jurisdiction), FRCP 12(b)(6) (failure to state a claim), FRCP 12(c) (judgment on the pleadings), and FRCP 12(f) (to strike), motions and opposition to motions shall be supported by at least one (1) affidavit and by such other evidence (i.e., deposition testimony, interrogatory answers, admissions, and documents) as appropriate to resolve the particular motion. Failure to comply with this requirement may constitute grounds for resolving the motion against the non-complying party. NY R USDCTWD Civ Rule 7(a)(3).

      iii. *Certificate of service.* FRCP 5(d) requires that the person making service under FRCP 5 certify that service has been effected. FRCP 5(Advisory Committee Notes). Having such information on file may be useful for many purposes, including proof of service if an issue arises concerning the effectiveness of the service. FRCP 5(Advisory Committee Notes). The Notice of Electronic Filing effectuates service for all registered users and no certificate of service is required when all filers on an action are Registered Users. The following exemptions require a certificate of service to be filed:

          • When a document is manually filed, a certificate of service must be filed stating the manner in which service or notice was accomplished on each party so entitled. NY R USDCTWD ECF Procedures(2)(f)(iv).

          • When a pro se filer (who isn't authorized to electronically file documents) is a party, a certificate of service must be filed stating the manner in which service or notice was accomplished on the pro se party. The Notice of Electronic Filing effectuates service for the Registered Users in this situation and it is not necessary to note service on those parties. A non-registered pro se filer is required to file certificates of service on all documents they file. NY R USDCTWD ECF Procedures(2)(f)(iv).

          • If an attorney is exempt from electronic service, a certificate of service must be filed stating the manner in which service or notice was accomplished on the exempt attorney. The Notice of Electronic Filing effectuates service for the Registered Users in this situation and it is not necessary to note service on those parties. NY R USDCTWD ECF Procedures(2)(f)(iv).

   b. *Supplemental documents*

      i. *Supporting evidence.* When a motion relies on facts outside the record, the court may hear the matter on affidavits or may hear it wholly or partly on oral testimony or on depositions. FRCP 43(c). A party seeking or opposing any relief under the Federal Rules of Civil Procedure shall file only the portion(s) of a deposition, interrogatory, request for documents, request for admission, or other supporting material that is pertinent to the application. NY R USDCTWD Civ Rule 7(a)(4).

      ii. *Notice of constitutional question.* A party that files a pleading, written motion, or other paper drawing into question the constitutionality of a federal or state statute must promptly:

          • *File notice.* File a notice of constitutional question stating the question and identifying the paper that raises it, if: (1) a federal statute is questioned and the parties do not include the United States, one of its agencies, or one of its officers or employees in an official capacity; or (2) a state statute is questioned and the parties do not include the state, one of its agencies, or one of its officers or employees in an official capacity; and

- *Serve notice.* Serve the notice and paper on the Attorney General of the United States if a federal statute is questioned—or on the state attorney general if a state statute is questioned—either by certified or registered mail or by sending it to an electronic address designated by the attorney general for this purpose. FRCP 5.1(a).

- *No forfeiture.* A party's failure to file and serve the notice, or the court's failure to certify, does not forfeit a constitutional claim or defense that is otherwise timely asserted. FRCP 5.1(d).

 iii. *Demand for jury trial.* When by law the alleged contemnor is entitled to a trial by jury, they shall make a written demand therefor on or before the return day or adjourned day of the application; otherwise, they will be deemed to have waived a trial by jury. NY R USDCTWD Civ Rule 83.4(b).

 iv. *Copies of authorities.* In cases involving a pro se litigant, counsel shall, when serving a memorandum of law (or other submissions to the Court), provide the pro se litigant (but not other counsel or the Court) with printed copies of decisions cited therein that are unreported or reported exclusively on computerized databases. NY R USDCTWD Civ Rule 7(a)(8).

 v. *Paper copy for date-stamping with self-addressed envelope.* Parties requesting date-stamped copies of filed documents must provide a paper copy for date-stamping, and a self-addressed, adequately-sized envelope with proper postage affixed. NY R USDCTWD Civ Rule 5.1(d).

 vi. *Courtesy copies.* Courtesy copies of certain documents may be required. Filers should refer to the "Judge Preferences" published on the Court's website. NY R USDCTWD ECF Procedures(2)(a)(iii).

3. *Individual judge practices.* Refer to the Miscellaneous section of this document for information on individual judge practices on required documents.

## E. Format

1. *Form of documents.* The rules governing captions and other matters of form in pleadings apply to motions and other papers. FRCP 7(b)(2).

 a. *Form, generally.* All pleadings, motions, and other papers that a party presents for filing, whether in paper form or in electronic form, shall meet the following requirements:

  i. *Font size.* All text and footnotes shall be in a font size of at least twelve (12) point type. NY R USDCTWD Civ Rule 10(a)(1).

  ii. *Spacing.* All text in the body of the document must be double-spaced, except that text in block quotations and footnotes may be single-spaced. NY R USDCTWD Civ Rule 10(a)(2).

- Extensive footnotes and block quotes may not be used to circumvent page limitations. NY R USDCTWD Civ Rule 10(a)(3).

  iii. *Margins.* Documents must have one (1) inch margins on all four sides. NY R USDCTWD Civ Rule 10(a)(4).

  iv. *Page numbering.* Pages must be consecutively numbered. NY R USDCTWD Civ Rule 10(a)(5).

 b. *Additional requirements for paper filing.* Documents presented for filing in paper form shall meet the following additional requirements:

  i. *Paper.* Documents must be on durable white eight and one-half by eleven (8-1/2 x 11) inch paper of good quality. NY R USDCTWD Civ Rule 10(b)(1).

- All documents must be single-sided. NY R USDCTWD Civ Rule 10(b)(5).

  ii. *Text.* All text must be plainly and legibly written, typewritten, printed or reproduced. NY R USDCTWD Civ Rule 10(b)(2).

  iii. *Ink.* Documents must be in black or blue ink. NY R USDCTWD Civ Rule 10(b)(3).

  iv. *Binding.* The pages of each document must be stapled or in some other way fastened together. NY R USDCTWD Civ Rule 10(b)(4).

c. *Caption; Names of parties.* Every pleading must have a caption with the court's name, a title, a file number, and a FRCP 7(a) designation. The title of the complaint must name all the parties; the title of other pleadings, after naming the first party on each side, may refer generally to other parties. FRCP 10(a).

d. *Paragraphs; Separate statements.* A party must state its claims or defenses in numbered paragraphs, each limited as far as practicable to a single set of circumstances. A later pleading may refer by number to a paragraph in an earlier pleading. If doing so would promote clarity, each claim founded on a separate transaction or occurrence—and each defense other than a denial—must be stated in a separate count or defense. FRCP 10(b).

e. *Adoption by reference; Exhibits.* A statement in a pleading may be adopted by reference elsewhere in the same pleading or in any other pleading or motion. A copy of a written instrument that is an exhibit to a pleading is a part of the pleading for all purposes. FRCP 10(c).

f. *Citation of local rules.* The Local Rules of Civil Procedure for the United States District Court for the Western District of New York shall be cited as "L.R.Civ.P." NY R USDCTWD Civ Rule 1.1.

g. *Acceptance by the clerk.* The clerk must not refuse to file a paper solely because it is not in the form prescribed by the Federal Rules of Civil Procedure or by a local rule or practice. FRCP 5(d)(4). The Court may reject documents that do not comply with the requirements in NY R USDCTWD Civ Rule 10. NY R USDCTWD Civ Rule 10.

2. *Form of electronic documents.* All pleadings, motions, and other papers that a party presents for filing, whether in paper form or in electronic form, shall meet the requirements in NY R USDCTWD Civ Rule 10(a). NY R USDCTWD Civ Rule 10(a). Refer above for more information.

a. *Conversion to PDF.* A document created with a word processor, or a paper document, must be converted to Portable Document Format to be electronically filed with the court. NY R USDCTWD ECF Procedures(2)(a)(v).

   i. Documents which exist only in paper form may be scanned into a portable document format (PDF) for electronic filing. NY R USDCTWD ECF Procedures(2)(a)(v). Before filing a scanned document with the court, a Filing User must verify its legibility. NY R USDCTWD ECF Procedures(2)(a)(iv).

   ii. Electronic documents must be converted to .PDF from a word processing program and must be text searchable. Do not print, scan and .PDF your document when it has been created in a word processing program. Additional information on working with PDFs is located in NY R USDCTWD ECF Procedures(4b). NY R USDCTWD ECF Procedures(2)(a)(v).

b. *Hyperlinks.* Pursuant to the policy set forth by the Judicial Conference in October 2005, a hyperlink contained in a filing is no more than a convenient mechanism for accessing material cited in a document. A hyperlink reference is extraneous to any filed document and is not part of the Court's record. NY R USDCTWD ECF Procedures(2)(a)(vi).

   i. In order to preserve the integrity of the Court record, users wishing to insert hyperlinks in Court filings shall continue to use the conventional method for the cited authority, in addition to the hyperlink. NY R USDCTWD ECF Procedures(2)(a)(vi).

   ii. The Court accepts no responsibility for, and does not endorse any product, organization, and content at any hyperlinked site, or at any site to which that site may be linked. The Court accepts no responsibility for the availability or functionality of any hyperlink. NY R USDCTWD ECF Procedures(2)(a)(vi).

c. *Attachments and exhibits*

   i. Attachments and exhibits larger than five megabytes (5 MB) shall be filed electronically in separate five megabyte (5 MB) segments. NY R USDCTWD ECF Procedures(2)(d)(i).

   ii. Filing Users must submit in electronic form all documents referenced as exhibits or attachments, except as otherwise provided in NY R USDCTWD ECF Procedures. A Filing User must submit as exhibits or attachments only those excerpts of the referenced documents that are directly germane to the matter under consideration by the court. Excerpted material must be clearly and prominently identified as such. Filing Users who file excerpts of documents as exhibits or attachments under NY R USDCTWD ECF Procedures(2)(d)(ii) do so without prejudice to their right to timely file additional excerpts or the complete document. Responding parties may timely file additional excerpts or the complete document that they believe are directly germane. The Court may require parties to file additional excerpts or the complete document. A Filing User must request leave of the Court to file a document exhibit or attachment in non-electronic form. NY R USDCTWD ECF Procedures(2)(d)(ii).

   iii.  Exhibits offered or admitted at trial will not be filed electronically or conventionally unless so ordered by the Court. NY R USDCTWD ECF Procedures(2)(d)(iii).

   iv.  Exhibits such as videotapes and tape recordings shall be filed in the conventional manner with the Clerk of Court, and a Notice of Manual Filing shall be electronically filed by the party. Manually filed exhibits must have the case number and case name securely fastened or marked on the item. NY R USDCTWD ECF Procedures(2)(d)(iii).

   v.  Continuation of exhibit entries (for exhibits that are too large to attach to a main document) must be filed and entered on the same day that the main document was filed. NY R USDCTWD ECF Procedures(2)(d)(iv).

  d.  *Color documents.* Documents in color or containing graphics take much longer to upload. Filing users are encouraged to configure their scanners to scan documents at 200 dpi and preferably in black and white rather than color. NY R USDCTWD ECF Procedures(2)(d)(v).

  e.  *Large documents.* Due to the length of time it takes to download large files, documents larger than five megabytes (5 MB) (approximately one hundred (100) pages of a .pdf scanned document) must be filed electronically in separate five megabyte (5 MB) segments. A party who believes a document is too lengthy to electronically image (i.e. scan), may contact the Court Room Deputy for the assigned judge and request permission to file that document conventionally. If granted permission to file the document conventionally, the Filing User shall electronically file a "notice of manual filing" for that item. Exhibits submitted to the Court conventionally shall be served on other parties conventionally. NY R USDCTWD ECF Procedures(2)(d)(vi).

3.  *Form of memoranda of law.* Memoranda in support of or in opposition to any motion shall not exceed twenty-five (25) pages in length, and reply memoranda shall not exceed ten (10) pages in length. A party seeking to exceed the page limit must make application by letter to the Judge hearing the motion, with copies to all counsel, at least seven (7) days before the date on which the memorandum must be filed. NY R USDCTWD Civ Rule 7(a)(2)(C).

4.  *Signing disclosures and discovery requests, responses, and objections.* FRCP 11 does not apply to disclosures and discovery requests, responses, objections, and motions under FRCP 26 through FRCP 37. FRCP 11(d).

  a.  *Signature required.* Every disclosure under FRCP 26(a)(1) or FRCP 26(a)(3) and every discovery request, response, or objection must be signed by at least one attorney of record in the attorney's own name—or by the party personally, if unrepresented—and must state the signer's address, e-mail address, and telephone number. FRCP 26(g)(1). Documents presented for paper filing must contain an original signature. NY R USDCTWD Civ Rule 10(b)(6).

    i.  *Electronic signatures*

      &bull;  *Non-attorney signature.* If the original document requires the signature of a non-attorney, the filing party shall obtain the signature of the non-attorney on the document. NY R USDCTWD ECF Procedures(2)(g)(i). The filing party or attorney then shall file the document electronically indicating the signatory's name in the form "s/(name)." NY R USDCTWD ECF Procedures(2)(g)(i)(1). A non-filing signatory or party who disputes the authenticity of an electronically filed document or the authenticity of the signature on that document must file an objection to the document within ten (10) days of receiving the Notice of Electronic Filing. NY R USDCTWD ECF Procedures(2)(g)(i)(2).

      &bull;  *Registered user signature.* The username and password required to file documents on the Electronic Filing System serve as the Filing User's signature on all electronic documents filed with this Court. The also serve as a signature for the purposes of FRCP 11, the Federal Rules of Civil Procedure, the Local Rules of Civil Procedure for the United States District Court for the Western District of New York, and any other purpose for which a signature is required in connection with proceedings before this Court. A pleading requiring a Registered User's signature must include a signature block in the format found in NY R USDCTWD ECF Procedures(2)(g)(iii). NY R USDCTWD ECF Procedures(2)(g)(iii). Any party challenging the authenticity of an electronically filed document or the attorney's signature on that document must file an objection to the document within ten (10) days of receiving the Notice of Electronic Filing. NY R USDCTWD ECF Procedures(2)(g)(iii)(1).

- *Multiple signatures.* The following procedure applies when a stipulation or other document requires two or more signatures: The filing party shall initially confirm that the document is acceptable to all persons required to sign the document and shall obtain the signatures of all parties on the document. NY R USDCTWD ECF Procedures(2)(g)(iv)(1). The filing party or attorney then shall file the document electronically indicating the signatories, e.g., "s/Jane Doe," "s/John Smith," etc. NY R USDCTWD ECF Procedures(2)(g)(iv)(2). A non-filing signatory or party who disputes the authenticity of an electronically filed document containing multiple signatures or the authenticity of the signatures themselves must file an objection to the document within ten (10) days of receiving the Notice of Electronic Filing. NY R USDCTWD ECF Procedures(2)(g)(iv)(3).

b. *Effect of signature.* By signing, an attorney or party certifies that to the best of the person's knowledge, information, and belief formed after a reasonable inquiry:

   i. With respect to a disclosure, it is complete and correct as of the time it is made; and

   ii. With respect to a discovery request, response, or objection, it is:

   - Consistent with the Federal Rules of Civil Procedure and warranted by existing law or by a nonfrivolous argument for extending, modifying, or reversing existing law, or for establishing new law;

   - Not interposed for any improper purpose, such as to harass, cause unnecessary delay, or needlessly increase the cost of litigation; and

   - Neither unreasonable nor unduly burdensome or expensive, considering the needs of the case, prior discovery in the case, the amount in controversy, and the importance of the issues at stake in the action. FRCP 26(g)(1).

c. *Failure to sign.* Other parties have no duty to act on an unsigned disclosure, request, response, or objection until it is signed, and the court must strike it unless a signature is promptly supplied after the omission is called to the attorney's or party's attention. FRCP 26(g)(2).

d. *Sanction for improper certification.* Refer to the General Requirements section of this document for information on the sanction for improper certification.

5. *Privacy protection for filings made with the court.* In all filings, parties shall comply with FRCP 5.2. NY R USDCTWD ECF Procedures(2)(m)(i).

a. *Redacted filings.* Unless the court orders otherwise, in an electronic or paper filing with the court that contains an individual's Social Security number, taxpayer-identification number, or birth date, the name of an individual known to be a minor, or a financial-account number, a party or nonparty making the filing may include only:

   i. The last four (4) digits of the Social Security number and taxpayer-identification number;

   ii. The year of the individual's birth;

   iii. The minor's initials; and

   iv. The last four (4) digits of the financial-account number. FRCP 5.2(a).

b. *Exemptions from the redaction requirement.* The redaction requirement does not apply to the following:

    i.   A financial-account number that identifies the property allegedly subject to forfeiture in a forfeiture proceeding;

    ii.  The record of an administrative or agency proceeding;

    iii. The official record of a state-court proceeding;

    iv.  The record of a court or tribunal, if that record was not subject to the redaction requirement when originally filed;

    v.   A filing covered by FRCP 5.2(c) or FRCP 5.2(d); and

    vi.  A pro se filing in an action brought under 28 U.S.C.A. § 2241, 28 U.S.C.A. § 2254, or 28 U.S.C.A. § 2255. FRCP 5.2(b).

c. *Limitations on remote access to electronic files; Social Security appeals and immigration cases.* Unless the court orders otherwise, in an action for benefits under the Social Security Act, and in an action or proceeding relating to an order of removal, to relief from removal, or to immigration benefits or detention, access to an electronic file is authorized as follows:

    i.   The parties and their attorneys may have remote electronic access to any part of the case file, including the administrative record;

    ii.  Any other person may have electronic access to the full record at the courthouse, but may have remote electronic access only to:

- The docket maintained by the court; and

- An opinion, order, judgment, or other disposition of the court, but not any other part of the case file or the administrative record. FRCP 5.2(c).

d. *Filings made under seal.* The court may order that a filing be made under seal without redaction. The court may later unseal the filing or order the person who made the filing to file a redacted version for the public record. FRCP 5.2(d). For more information on sealing documents, refer to NY R USDCTWD Civ Rule 5.3, NY R USDCTWD ECF Procedures(2)(o)(i)(1), NY R USDCTWD ECF Procedures(2)(o)(i)(2), and NY R USDCTWD ECF Procedures(2)(o)(i)(3).

e. *Protective orders.* For good cause, the court may by order in a case:

    i.   Require redaction of additional information; or

    ii.  Limit or prohibit a nonparty's remote electronic access to a document filed with the court. FRCP 5.2(e).

f. *Option for additional unredacted filing under seal.* A person making a redacted filing may also file an unredacted copy under seal. The court must retain the unredacted copy as part of the record. FRCP 5.2(f).

g. *Option for filing a reference list.* A filing that contains redacted information may be filed together with a reference list that identifies each item of redacted information and specifies an appropriate identifier that uniquely corresponds to each item listed. The list must be filed under seal and may be amended as of right. Any reference in the case to a listed identifier will be construed to refer to the corresponding item of information. FRCP 5.2(g).

h. *Waiver of protection of identifiers.* A person waives the protection of FRCP 5.2(a) as to the person's own information by filing it without redaction and not under seal. FRCP 5.2(h).

6. *Individual judge practices.* Refer to the Miscellaneous section of this document for information on individual judge practices on formatting documents.

## F. Filing and Service Requirements

1. *Filing requirements.* Any paper after the complaint that is required to be served—together with a certificate of service—must be filed within a reasonable time after service. FRCP 5(d)(1). All pleadings and other papers shall be filed and served in accordance with the Federal Rules of Civil Procedure and the

CM/ECF Administrative Procedures Guide (NY R USDCTWD ECF Procedures). NY R USDCTWD Civ Rule 5.1(a). For information on filing of miscellaneous cases and irregular documents, refer to NY R USDCTWD Civ Rule 5.6.

a. *How filing is made; In general.* A paper is filed by delivering it:

    i. To the clerk; or

    ii. To a judge who agrees to accept it for filing, and who must then note the filing date on the paper and promptly send it to the clerk. FRCP 5(d)(2).

b. *Electronic filing*

    i. *Authorization of electronic filing program.* A court may, by local rule, allow papers to be filed, signed, or verified by electronic means that are consistent with any technical standards established by the Judicial Conference of the United States. A local rule may require electronic filing only if reasonable exceptions are allowed. A paper filed electronically in compliance with a local rule is a written paper for purposes of the Federal Rules of Civil Procedure. FRCP 5(d)(3).

        • All civil cases filed in this Court are assigned to the Electronic Case Filing System ("ECF"). The procedures for electronic filing and any exceptions to the electronic filing requirements are set forth in the CM/ECF Administrative Procedures Guide (NY R USDCTWD ECF Procedures) which is available on the Court's website. NY R USDCTWD Civ Rule 5.1(a).

    ii. *Scope of electronic filing.* The U.S. District Court for the Western District of New York requires attorneys in civil and criminal cases to file documents with the Court electronically over the Internet using its Case Management/Electronic Case Filing (CM/ECF) system. NY R USDCTWD ECF Procedures. Beginning January 1, 2004, all civil and criminal cases currently pending and newly filed, except as expressly noted herein, were assigned to the Electronic Case Filing System ("System"). Except as expressly provided and in exceptional circumstances preventing a Filing User from filing electronically, all petitions, motions, memoranda of law, or other pleadings and documents required to be filed with the Court in connection with a case assigned to the System must be electronically filed. NY R USDCTWD ECF Procedures(1)(a).

        • *Mandatory electronic filing.* All documents on civil, criminal, miscellaneous civil, miscellaneous criminal and new civil case openings, except sealed documents, sealed cases, opening of a criminal case, opening of a miscellaneous case and as expressly provided for in these procedures (NY R USDCTWD ECF Procedures), shall be electronically filed on the system. NY R USDCTWD ECF Procedures(2)(a)(i). NY R USDCTWD Civ Rule 29

        • *Stipulations.* Pursuant to NY R USDCTWD Civ Rule 29, all stipulations (whether the stipulation is final or when it requires a judge's signature) shall be filed electronically. NY R USDCTWD ECF Procedures(2)(p)(i).

        • *Letters.* The electronic filing of letters is generally prohibited unless granted permission by an assigned judge. Letters to the Court must be submitted conventionally. NY R USDCTWD ECF Procedures(2)(q)(i).

        • *Exceptions.* The Court requires attorneys to file documents electronically, absent a showing of good cause, unless otherwise excused by the procedures set forth below or by Order of the Court. NY R USDCTWD ECF Procedures.

    iii. *Conventional filing of documents.* The procedures in NY R USDCTWD ECF Procedures(2)(o) govern documents filed conventionally. The Court, upon application, may also authorize conventional filing of other documents otherwise subject to the procedures in NY R USDCTWD ECF Procedures(2)(o). NY R USDCTWD ECF Procedures(2)(o)(i).

        • *Documents filed under seal.* Unredacted documents filed with the Court pursuant to the privacy provisions of FRCP 5.2 shall be submitted in a sealing envelope with the information in NY R USDCTWD ECF Procedures(2)(o)(i)(1) on the envelope. NY R USDCTWD ECF Procedures(2)(o)(i)(1). If the document is larger than five (5) pages, a

disk should be provided to the Clerks Office which contains the document in a .pdf format. NY R USDCTWD ECF Procedures(2)(o)(i)(1). For more information on documents filed under seal, refer to NY R USDCTWD ECF Procedures(2)(o)(i)(1), NY R USDCTWD ECF Procedures(2)(o)(i)(2), and NY R USDCTWD ECF Procedures(2)(o)(i)(3).

- *Magistrate judge consents.* Pursuant to FRCP 73(b), parties' filing consents to jurisdiction by United States Magistrate Judge will continue to be treated as non-public documents until all parties have consented. Therefore, parties must submit conventionally (in paper form) and not electronically file their consent forms so that the consent is not a public document. If all parties consent to the jurisdiction of a Magistrate Judge, the Clerk will scan all consent forms which will then become a public document. NY R USDCTWD ECF Procedures(2)(o)(i)(3).

- *Pro se filers.* Pro Se filers shall file paper originals of all initiating documents, pleadings, motions, affidavits, briefs and other documents which must be signed or which require either verification or an unsworn declaration under any rule or statute. The Clerk's Office will scan these original documents into an electronic file in the System. A certificate of service is required for all documents a pro se litigant files with the court. If a Pro Se filer is granted permission to register to electronically file documents, they shall comply with the guidelines contained in this document (NY R USDCTWD ECF Procedures). NY R USDCTWD ECF Procedures(2)(o)(i)(4).

- *Social Security cases.* Absent a showing of good cause, and except as provided in Section o(i)(4) above, all documents, notices and orders in Social Security reviews will be filed and noticed electronically, except as noted in NY R USDCTWD ECF Procedures(2)(o)(i)(6). For more information, refer to NY R USDCTWD ECF Procedures(2)(o)(i)(6).

- For more information on conventional filing of documents, refer to NY R USDCTWD ECF Procedures(2)(o)(i).

iv. *Consequences of electronic filing.* Electronic transmission of a document to the System consistent with these procedures (NY R USDCTWD ECF Procedures), whether accomplished by the Filing User or a Court User, together with the transmission of a Notice of Electronic Filing from the Court, constitutes filing of a document for all purposes of the Federal Rules of Civil Procedure and the Local Rules of Civil Procedure for the United States District Court for the Western District of New York, and constitutes entry of the document on the docket kept by the Clerk under FRCP 58 and FRCP 79. A document shall not be considered filed for purposes of the Federal Rules of Civil until the filing party receives a System generated Notice of Electronic Filing. NY R USDCTWD ECF Procedures(2)(a)(i).

- E-mailing a document to the Clerk's Office or to the assigned judge shall not constitute "filing" of such document. NY R USDCTWD ECF Procedures(2)(a)(i)(1).

v. *Filing fees.* Any fee required for filing of a pleading or paper in District Court is payable to the Clerk of Court by check or money order. In addition, when opening a civil case on line, filing a notice of appeal on line or applying to appear pro hac vice on line, the fees shall be paid on line by registered users through the federal electronic payment website. Users will be directed to the federal electronic payment website while entering their transaction and should have a credit card available. When opening a civil case and applying to proceed in forma pauperis or when the United States of America opens a case, the payment screen can by bypassed to complete the transaction. Additional information on making electronic payments can be located on the court's website. NY R USDCTWD ECF Procedures(2)(h)(i).

2. *Service requirements.* All pleadings and other papers shall be filed and served in accordance with the Federal Rules of Civil Procedure and the CM/ECF Administrative Procedures Guide (NY R USDCTWD ECF Procedures). NY R USDCTWD Civ Rule 5.1(a).

a. *Service; When required*

i. *In general.* Unless the Federal Rules of Civil Procedure provide otherwise, each of the following papers must be served on every party:

- An order stating that service is required;

- A pleading filed after the original complaint, unless the court orders otherwise under FRCP 5(c) because there are numerous defendants;

- A discovery paper required to be served on a party, unless the court orders otherwise;

- A written motion, except one that may be heard ex parte; and

- A written notice, appearance, demand, or offer of judgment, or any similar paper. FRCP 5(a)(1).

   ii. *If a party fails to appear.* No service is required on a party who is in default for failing to appear. But a pleading that asserts a new claim for relief against such a party must be served on that party under FRCP 4. FRCP 5(a)(2).

   iii. *Seizing property.* If an action is begun by seizing property and no person is or need be named as a defendant, any service required before the filing of an appearance, answer, or claim must be made on the person who had custody or possession of the property when it was seized. FRCP 5(a)(3).

b. *Service; How made*

   i. *Serving an attorney.* If a party is represented by an attorney, service under FRCP 5 must be made on the attorney unless the court orders service on the party. FRCP 5(b)(1).

   ii. *Service in general.* A paper is served under FRCP 5 by:

   - Handing it to the person;

   - Leaving it: (1) at the person's office with a clerk or other person in charge or, if no one is in charge, in a conspicuous place in the office; or (2) if the person has no office or the office is closed, at the person's dwelling or usual place of abode with someone of suitable age and discretion who resides there;

   - Mailing it to the person's last known address—in which event service is complete upon mailing;

   - Leaving it with the court clerk if the person has no known address;

   - Sending it by electronic means if the person consented in writing—in which event service is complete upon transmission, but is not effective if the serving party learns that it did not reach the person to be served; or

   - Delivering it by any other means that the person consented to in writing—in which event service is complete when the person making service delivers it to the agency designated to make delivery. FRCP 5(b)(2).

   iii. *Service by overnight delivery.* All papers, other than a subpoena or a summons and complaint, may be served on counsel of record by overnight delivery service at the address designated by the attorney for that purpose, or if none is designated, at the attorney's last known address. Service by overnight delivery shall be complete upon deposit of the paper(s), enclosed in a properly addressed wrapper, into the custody of the overnight delivery service, prior to the latest time designated by the service for overnight delivery. NY R USDCTWD Civ Rule 5.1(g). "Overnight delivery service" means any delivery service which regularly accepts items for overnight delivery to any address within the Court's jurisdiction. NY R USDCTWD Civ Rule 5.1(g).

   iv. *Service of documents by electronic means*

   - *Service on registered users.* Registered Users consent to the electronic service of all documents, and must make available an electronic mail address for service during the registration process. Upon the filing of a document by a party, a Notice of Electronic Filing, with a hyperlink to the filed document, will be automatically generated by the electronic filing system and sent via electronic mail to the e-mail addresses of all parties participating in the electronic filing system in the case. Electronic service of the Notice of Electronic Filing constitutes service of the filed document for all purposes of the Federal Rules of Civil Procedure and the Local Rules of Civil Procedure for the United States

District Court for the Western District of New York. NY R USDCTWD ECF Procedures(2)(f)(i). The Notice of Electronic Filing effectuates service for all registered users and no certificate of service is required when all filers on an action are Registered Users. NY R USDCTWD ECF Procedures(2)(f)(iv).

- *Time limit for opening hyperlink.* The hyperlink to filed documents contained in the Notice of Electronic Filing must be opened within fifteen (15) days from the date the document was filed to provide registered users access to the document. The hyperlink expires after fifteen (15) days and users will be unable to access documents for free after that time. Filing Users are encouraged to check their e-mail frequently for notice of filed documents. NY R USDCTWD ECF Procedures(2)(f)(ii).

- *Service on exempted attorneys or pro se litigants who do not have permission to file electronically.* Attorneys granted an exemption from electronically filing documents in the System and pro se litigants who have not been granted permission to electronically file documents are entitled to a paper copy of any electronically filed pleading, document or order. The filing party must therefore provide the non-registered party with the pleading, document or order according to the Federal Rules of Civil Procedure. NY R USDCTWD ECF Procedures(2)(f)(iii).

- *E-mailing or faxing documents.* E-mailing or faxing a pleading or document to any party shall not constitute service of the pleading or document. NY R USDCTWD ECF Procedures(2)(f)(v).

    v. *Using court facilities.* If a local rule so authorizes, a party may use the court's transmission facilities to make service under FRCP 5(b)(2)(E). FRCP 5(b)(3).

  c. *Serving numerous defendants*

    i. *In general.* If an action involves an unusually large number of defendants, the court may, on motion or on its own, order that:

- Defendants' pleadings and replies to them need not be served on other defendants;

- Any crossclaim, counterclaim, avoidance, or affirmative defense in those pleadings and replies to them will be treated as denied or avoided by all other parties; and

- Filing any such pleading and serving it on the plaintiff constitutes notice of the pleading to all parties. FRCP 5(c)(1).

    ii. *Notifying parties.* A copy of every such order must be served on the parties as the court directs. FRCP 5(c)(2).

3. *Service in contempt proceedings.* Where the alleged contemnor has appeared in the action by an attorney, the notice of motion or order to show cause and the papers upon which it is based may be served upon the attorney; otherwise, service shall be made personally, in the manner provided in FRCP 4 for the service of a summons. NY R USDCTWD Civ Rule 83.4(a). Refer to the United States District Court for the Northern District of New York Complaint document for information on service in accordance with FRCP 4.

4. *Pro se actions.* For information on the requirements in pro se actions, refer to NY R USDCTWD Civ Rule 5.2.

5. *Individual judge practices.* Refer to the Miscellaneous section of this document for information on individual judge practices on filing and serving documents.

## G. Hearings

1. *Hearings, generally*

  a. *Oral argument.* Due process does not require that oral argument be permitted on a motion and, except as otherwise provided by local rule, the district court has discretion to determine whether it will decide the motion on the papers or hear argument by counsel (and perhaps receive evidence). FPP § 1190; F.D.I.C. v. Deglau, 207 F.3d 153 (3d Cir. 2000).

    i. The parties shall appear for oral argument on all motions they make returnable before a Judge

on the scheduled return date for the motion. In its discretion, the Court may notify the parties that oral argument shall not be heard on any given motion. Thus, the parties should be prepared to have their motion papers serve as the sole method of argument. NY R USDCTWD Civ Rule 7(c).

   b. *Providing a regular schedule for oral hearings.* A court may establish regular times and places for oral hearings on motions. FRCP 78(a).

   c. *Providing for submission on briefs.* By rule or order, the court may provide for submitting and determining motions on briefs, without oral hearings. FRCP 78(b).

2. *Contempt proceedings.* If the alleged contemnor puts in issue the alleged misconduct or the damages thereby occasioned, they shall upon demand be entitled to have oral evidence taken on the issues, either before the Court or before a master appointed by the Court. When by law the alleged contemnor is entitled to a trial by jury, they shall make a written demand therefor on or before the return day or adjourned day of the application; otherwise, they will be deemed to have waived a trial by jury. NY R USDCTWD Civ Rule 83.4(b).

3. *Individual judge practices.* Refer to the Miscellaneous section of this document for information on individual judge practices on hearings.

## H. Forms

### 1. Federal Motion for Discovery Sanctions Forms

   a. Motion for contempt. 3B FEDFORMS § 3721.

   b. Motion for sanctions for failure to appear at deposition. 3B FEDFORMS § 3722.

   c. Motion that facts be taken as established for failure to answer questions upon deposition. 3B FEDFORMS § 3723.

   d. Motion for order refusing to allow disobedient party to support or oppose designated claims or defenses. 3B FEDFORMS § 3724.

   e. Motion for default judgment against defendant for failure to comply with order for production of documents. 3B FEDFORMS § 3725.

   f. Motion for award of expenses incurred to prove matter opponent failed to admit under FRCP 36. 3B FEDFORMS § 3726.

   g. Motion to strike answer or dismiss action for failure to comply with order requiring answer to interrogatories. 3B FEDFORMS § 3729.

   h. Motion to dismiss for failure to comply with previous order requiring answer to interrogatories to party. 3B FEDFORMS § 3732.

   i. Motion; For order that facts be taken to be established, and/or prohibiting certain claims, defenses, or evidence in opposition thereto. FEDPROF § 23:595.

   j. Affidavit; By attorney; In support of motion for order that facts be taken to be established, etc; Failure to produce documents for inspection. FEDPROF § 23:596.

   k. Affidavit; By attorney; In support of motion for order that facts be taken to be established, etc; Failure to obey order to answer questions. FEDPROF § 23:597.

   l. Motion; For order striking pleadings, and for default judgment or dismissal of action. FEDPROF § 23:599.

   m. Affidavit; By attorney; In support of motion for default judgment for defendant's failure to obey discovery order. FEDPROF § 23:600.

   n. Motion; By defendant; For dismissal of action and other sanctions; For failure to comply with orders to complete deposition. FEDPROF § 23:601.

   o. Motion; By defendant; For dismissal of action or other sanctions; For failure and refusal to comply with order to produce documents. FEDPROF § 23:602.

   p. Motion; By defendant; For dismissal with prejudice; Failure to answer interrogatories as ordered. FEDPROF § 23:603.

q.  Motion; For order staying further proceedings until adverse party obeys order compelling discovery. FEDPROF § 23:604.

r.  Affidavit; By attorney; Opposing motion for order striking pleading and directing entry of default judgment; Good-faith attempt to obey discovery order; Production of documents illegal under foreign law. FEDPROF § 23:605.

s.  Motion; For sanctions for failure to comply with examination order. FEDPROF § 23:610.

t.  Motion; For order finding person in contempt of court; Refusal, after order, to answer question. FEDPROF § 23:612.

u.  Affidavit; By attorney; In support of motion for order finding party in contempt. FEDPROF § 23:613.

v.  Affidavit; By plaintiff; In support of motion for order holding defendant in contempt of court; Defendant disobeyed order for production of documents. FEDPROF § 23:614.

w.  Motion; For order compelling opposing party to pay expenses incurred in proving facts such party refused to admit. FEDPROF § 23:616.

x.  Motion; For sanctions; Failure to attend own deposition, serve answers to interrogatories, or respond to request for inspection. FEDPROF § 23:618.

y.  Motion; For order staying proceedings until required response to discovery request is made. FEDPROF § 23:619.

z.  Affidavit; By attorney; In support of motion for sanctions; Failure to attend own deposition, serve answers to interrogatories, or respond to request for inspection. FEDPROF § 23:620.

2.  **Forms for the Western District of New York**

a.  Certificate of service. NY R USDCTWD ECF Procedures(4a).

# I. Applicable Rules

1.  *Federal rules*

a.  Counsel's liability for excessive costs. 28 U.S.C.A. § 1927.

b.  Serving and filing pleadings and other papers. FRCP 5.

c.  Constitutional challenge to a statute; Notice, certification, and intervention. FRCP 5.1.

d.  Privacy protection for filings made with the court. FRCP 5.2.

e.  Computing and extending time; Time for motion papers. FRCP 6.

f.  Pleadings allowed; Form of motions and other papers. FRCP 7.

g.  Form of pleadings. FRCP 10.

h.  Signing pleadings, motions, and other papers; Representations to the court; Sanctions. FRCP 11.

i.  Duty to disclose; General provisions governing discovery. FRCP 26.

j.  Failure to make disclosures or to cooperate in discovery; Sanctions. FRCP 37.

k.  Taking testimony. FRCP 43.

l.  Hearing motions; Submission on briefs. FRCP 78.

2.  *Local rules*

a.  Title. NY R USDCTWD Civ Rule 1.1.

b.  Filing and serving papers. NY R USDCTWD Civ Rule 5.1.

c.  Motion practice. NY R USDCTWD Civ Rule 7.

d.  Form of papers. NY R USDCTWD Civ Rule 10.

e.  Sanctions. NY R USDCTWD Civ Rule 11.

f.  Alternative dispute resolution and pretrial conferences. NY R USDCTWD Civ Rule 16.

g. Attorneys of record; Appearance and withdrawal. NY R USDCTWD Civ Rule 83.2.

h. Contempts. NY R USDCTWD Civ Rule 83.4.

i. Administrative procedures guide for electronic filing. NY R USDCTWD ECF Procedures.

j. Alternative dispute resolution plan. NY R USDCTWD ADR Plan.

**J. Miscellaneous**

**NOTE: Individual judges' rules may apply. For available judge-level information, refer to:**

DISTRICT JUDGE RICHARD J. ARCARA: NY R USDCTWD Arcara-Procedures.

DISTRICT JUDGE FRANK P. GERACI, JR.: NY R USDCTWD Geraci-Procedures.

DISTRICT JUDGE DAVID G. LARIMER: NY R USDCTWD Larimer-Procedures.

DISTRICT JUDGE CHARLES J. SIRAGUSA: NY R USDCTWD Siragusa-Procedures.

DISTRICT JUDGE WILLIAM M. SKRETNY: NY R USDCTWD Skretny--Procedures.

DISTRICT JUDGE MICHAEL A. TELESCA: NY R USDCTWD Telesca-Procedures.

DISTRICT JUDGE LAWRENCE J. VILARDO: NY R USDCTWD Vilardo-Procedures.

DISTRICT JUDGE ELIZABETH A. WOLFORD: NY R USDCTWD Wolford-Procedures.

MAGISTRATE JUDGE JONATHAN W. FELDMAN: NY R USDCTWD Feldman-Procedures.

MAGISTRATE JUDGE LESLIE G. FOSCHIO: NY R USDCTWD Foschio-Procedures; NY R USDCTWD Foschio-Depositions.

MAGISTRATE JUDGE JEREMIAH J. McCARTHY: NY R USDCTWD McCarthy-Procedures.

MAGISTRATE JUDGE MARIAN W. PAYSON: NY R USDCTWD Payson-Procedures.

MAGISTRATE JUDGE MICHAEL J. ROEMER: NY R USDCTWD Roemer-Procedures.

MAGISTRATE JUDGE H. KENNETH SCHROEDER, JR.: NY R USDCTWD Schroeder-Proc.

MAGISTRATE JUDGE HUGH B. SCOTT: NY R USDCTWD Scott-Procedures.

# Motions, Oppositions and Replies
# Motion for Preliminary Injunction

**Document Last Updated September 2016**

**A. Checklist**

(I) ❑ Matters to be considered by moving party

    (a) ❑ Required documents

        (1) ❑ Notice of motion and motion

        (2) ❑ Memorandum of law

        (3) ❑ Supporting affidavit

        (4) ❑ Complaint

        (5) ❑ List of witnesses and exhibits

        (6) ❑ Proposed order

        (7) ❑ Security

        (8) ❑ Certificate of service

    (b) ❑ Supplemental documents

        (1) ❑ Supporting evidence

        (2) ❑ Pleadings

        (3) ❑ Notice of constitutional question

     (4) ❑ Nongovernmental corporate disclosure statement

     (5) ❑ Motion for an expedited hearing

     (6) ❑ Copies of authorities

     (7) ❑ Paper copy for date-stamping with self-addressed envelope

     (8) ❑ Courtesy copies

  (c) ❑ Timing

     (1) ❑ A written motion and notice of the hearing must be served at least fourteen (14) days before the time specified for the hearing, with the following exceptions: (i) when the motion may be heard ex parte; (ii) when the Federal Rules of Civil Procedure set a different time; or (iii) when a court order—which a party may, for good cause, apply for ex parte—sets a different time

     (2) ❑ Any affidavit supporting a motion must be served with the motion

(II) ❑ Matters to be considered by opposing party

  (a) ❑ Required documents

     (1) ❑ Opposition

     (2) ❑ Answering memorandum

     (3) ❑ Supporting affidavit

     (4) ❑ Certificate of service

  (b) ❑ Supplemental documents

     (1) ❑ Supporting evidence

     (2) ❑ Pleadings

     (3) ❑ Notice of constitutional question

     (4) ❑ Nongovernmental corporate disclosure statement

     (5) ❑ Copies of authorities

     (6) ❑ Paper copy for date-stamping with self-addressed envelope

     (7) ❑ Courtesy copies

  (c) ❑ Timing

     (1) ❑ After a motion is filed, the court may issue an order setting deadlines for filing and service of opposing papers; if the court does not set deadlines by order, the opposing party shall have fourteen (14) days after service of the motion to file and serve responding papers

     (2) ❑ Except as FRCP 59(c) provides otherwise, any opposing affidavit must be served at least seven (7) days before the hearing, unless the court permits service at another time

## B. Timing

1. *Motion for preliminary injunction.* FRCP 65 is silent about when notice must be given. FPP § 2949.

2. *Timing of motions, generally*

  a. *Motion and notice of hearing.* A written motion and notice of the hearing must be served at least fourteen (14) days before the time specified for the hearing, with the following exceptions:

    i. When the motion may be heard ex parte;

    ii. When the Federal Rules of Civil Procedure set a different time; or

    iii. When a court order—which a party may, for good cause, apply for ex parte—sets a different time. FRCP 6(c)(1).

  b. *Supporting affidavit.* Any affidavit supporting a motion must be served with the motion. FRCP 6(c)(2).

3. *Timing of opposing papers.* After a motion is filed, the Court may issue an order setting deadlines for filing and service of opposing papers. NY R USDCTWD Civ Rule 7(b)(1). If the Court does not set deadlines by order, the following schedule shall apply: the opposing party shall have fourteen (14) days after service of the motion to file and serve responding papers. NY R USDCTWD Civ Rule 7(b)(2)(B).

   a. *Opposing affidavit.* Except as FRCP 59(c) provides otherwise, any opposing affidavit must be served at least seven (7) days before the hearing, unless the court permits service at another time. FRCP 6(c)(2).

4. *Timing of reply papers.* Where the respondent files an answering affidavit setting up a new matter, the moving party ordinarily is allowed a reasonable time to file a reply affidavit since failure to deny the new matter by affidavit may operate as an admission of its truth. AMJUR MOTIONS § 25.

   a. *Reply papers.* After a motion is filed, the Court may issue an order setting deadlines. . .for filing and service of reply papers if the moving party has stated an intent to reply. NY R USDCTWD Civ Rule 7(b)(1). If the Court does not set deadlines by order, the following schedule shall apply: the moving party shall have seven (7) days after service of the responding papers to file and serve reply papers. NY R USDCTWD Civ Rule 7(b)(2)(B).

   b. *Reply memorandum.* The moving party may file a reply memorandum, but is not required to do so. NY R USDCTWD Civ Rule 7(a)(2)(A).

5. *Motion for an expedited hearing.* A party seeking to shorten the schedule prescribed in NY R USDCTWD Civ Rule 7(b) must make a separate motion for an expedited hearing, setting forth the reasons why an expedited hearing is required. NY R USDCTWD Civ Rule 7(d)(1). For more information, refer to NY R USDCTWD Civ Rule 7(d)(1).

6. *Computation of time*

   a. *Computing time.* FRCP 6 applies in computing any time period specified in the Federal Rules of Civil Procedure, in any local rule or court order, or in any statute that does not specify a method of computing time. FRCP 6(a).

      i. *Period stated in days or a longer unit.* When the period is stated in days or a longer unit of time:

         - Exclude the day of the event that triggers the period;

         - Count every day, including intermediate Saturdays, Sundays, and legal holidays; and

         - Include the last day of the period, but if the last day is a Saturday, Sunday, or legal holiday, the period continues to run until the end of the next day that is not a Saturday, Sunday, or legal holiday. FRCP 6(a)(1).

      ii. *Period stated in hours.* When the period is stated in hours:

         - Begin counting immediately on the occurrence of the event that triggers the period;

         - Count every hour, including hours during intermediate Saturdays, Sundays, and legal holidays; and

         - If the period would end on a Saturday, Sunday, or legal holiday, the period continues to run until the same time on the next day that is not a Saturday, Sunday, or legal holiday. FRCP 6(a)(2).

      iii. *Inaccessibility of the clerk's office.* Unless the court orders otherwise, if the clerk's office is inaccessible:

         - On the last day for filing under FRCP 6(a)(1), then the time for filing is extended to the first accessible day that is not a Saturday, Sunday, or legal holiday; or

         - During the last hour for filing under FRCP 6(a)(2), then the time for filing is extended to the same time on the first accessible day that is not a Saturday, Sunday, or legal holiday. FRCP 6(a)(3).

      iv. *"Last day" defined.* Unless a different time is set by a statute, local rule, or court order, the last day ends:

         - For electronic filing, at midnight in the court's time zone; and

- For filing by other means, when the clerk's office is scheduled to close. FRCP 6(a)(4).

v. *"Next day" defined.* The "next day" is determined by continuing to count forward when the period is measured after an event and backward when measured before an event. FRCP 6(a)(5).

vi. *"Legal holiday" defined.* "Legal holiday" means:

- The day set aside by statute for observing New Year's Day, Martin Luther King Jr.'s Birthday, Washington's Birthday, Memorial Day, Independence Day, Labor Day, Columbus Day, Veterans' Day, Thanksgiving Day, or Christmas Day;

- Any day declared a holiday by the President or Congress; and

- For periods that are measured after an event, any other day declared a holiday by the state where the district court is located. FRCP 6(a)(6).

b. *Computation of electronic filing deadlines.* A document will be deemed timely filed if filed prior to midnight Eastern Time, unless otherwise ordered by the Court. A document will be considered untimely if filed thereafter. When a Court order requires that a document be filed on a weekend or holiday, the document may be filed by close of business the next business day without further application to the Court. NY R USDCTWD ECF Procedures(2)(e)(i). A document filed electronically is deemed filed on the date and time stated on the Notice of Electronic Filing. NY R USDCTWD ECF Procedures(2)(e)(ii).

i. *System availability.* Although parties may file documents electronically twenty-four (24) hours a day, registered users are strongly encouraged to file all documents during normal working hours of the Clerk's Office (8:30 a.m. to 5:00 p.m. Eastern Time). NY R USDCTWD ECF Procedures(2)(t)(i).

ii. *Technical failures.* A Filing User whose filing is made untimely as a result of a technical failure must seek appropriate relief from the Court. NY R USDCTWD ECF Procedures(2)(u)(i).

c. *Extending time*

i. *In general.* When an act may or must be done within a specified time, the court may, for good cause, extend the time:

- With or without motion or notice if the court acts, or if a request is made, before the original time or its extension expires; or

- On motion made after the time has expired if the party failed to act because of excusable neglect. FRCP 6(b)(1).

ii. *Exceptions.* A court must not extend the time to act under FRCP 50(b), FRCP 50(d), FRCP 52(b), FRCP 59(b), FRCP 59(d), FRCP 59(e), and FRCP 60(b). FRCP 6(b)(2).

iii. Refer to the United States District Court for the Western District of New York KeyRules Motion for Continuance/Extension of Time document for more information on extending time.

d. *Additional time after certain kinds of service.* When a party may or must act within a specified time after service and service is made under FRCP 5(b)(2)(C), FRCP 5(b)(2)(D), FRCP 5(b)(2)(E), or FRCP 5(b)(2)(F), three (3) days are added after the period would otherwise expire under FRCP 6(a). FRCP 6(d).

i. *Service by overnight delivery.* Where a period of time prescribed by either the Federal Rules of Civil Procedure or the Local Rules of Civil Procedure for the United States District Court for the Western District of New York is measured from the service of a paper and service is by overnight delivery, one (1) business day shall be added to the prescribed period. NY R USDCTWD Civ Rule 5.1(g).

7. *Individual judge practices.* Refer to the Miscellaneous section of this document for information on individual judge practices on timing of documents.

## C. General Requirements

1. *Motions, generally*

a. *Requirements.* A request for a court order must be made by motion. The motion must:

i. Be in writing unless made during a hearing or trial;

      ii.   State with particularity the grounds for seeking the order; and

      iii.  State the relief sought. FRCP 7(b)(1).

  b.  *Notice of motion.* A party interested in resisting the relief sought by a motion has a right to notice thereof, and an opportunity to be heard. AMJUR MOTIONS § 12.

      i.   In addition to statutory or court rule provisions requiring notice of a motion—the purpose of such a notice requirement having been said to be to prevent a party from being prejudicially surprised by a motion—principles of natural justice dictate that an adverse party generally must be given notice that a motion will be presented to the court. AMJUR MOTIONS § 12.

      ii.   "Notice," in this regard, means reasonable notice, including a meaningful opportunity to prepare and to defend against allegations of a motion. AMJUR MOTIONS § 12.

  c.  *Writing requirement.* The writing requirement is intended to insure that the adverse parties are informed and have a record of both the motion's pendency and the grounds on which the movant seeks an order. FPP § 1191; Feldberg v. Quechee Lakes Corp., 463 F.3d 195 (2d Cir. 2006).

      i.   It is sufficient "if the motion is stated in a written notice of the hearing of the motion." FPP § 1191.

  d.  *Particularity requirement.* The particularity requirement insures that the opposing parties will have notice of their opponent's contentions. FEDPROC § 62:364; Goodman v. 1973 26 Foot Trojan Vessel, Arkansas Registration No. AR1439SN, 859 F.2d 71, 12 Fed.R.Serv.3d 645 (8th Cir. 1988). That requirement ensures that notice of the basis for the motion is provided to the court and to the opposing party so as to avoid prejudice, provide the opponent with a meaningful opportunity to respond, and provide the court with enough information to process the motion correctly. FEDPROC § 62:364; Andreas v. Volkswagen of America, Inc., 336 F.3d 789, 56 Fed.R.Serv.3d 6 (8th Cir. 2003).

      i.   Reasonable specification of the grounds for a motion is sufficient. However, where a movant fails to state even one ground for granting the motion in question, the movant has failed to meet the minimal standard of "reasonable specification." FEDPROC § 62:364; Martinez v. Trainor, 556 F.2d 818, 23 Fed.R.Serv.2d 403 (7th Cir. 1977).

      ii.   The court may excuse the failure to comply with the particularity requirement if it is inadvertent, and where no prejudice is shown by the opposing party. FEDPROC § 62:364.

2.  *Motion for preliminary injunction.* The appropriate procedure for requesting a preliminary injunction is by motion, although it also commonly is requested by an order to show cause. FPP § 2949; James Luterbach Constr. Co. v. Adamkus, 781 F.2d 599, 603 (7th Cir. 1986); Studebaker Corp. v. Gittlin, 360 F.2d 692 (2d. Cir. 1966).

  a.  *Preliminary injunction.* An interim grant of specific relief is a preliminary injunction that may be issued only on notice to the adverse party. FEDPROC § 47:53; Westar Energy, Inc. v. Lake, 552 F.3d 1215 (10th Cir. 2009). Defined broadly, a preliminary injunction is an injunction that is issued to protect plaintiff from irreparable injury and to preserve the court's power to render a meaningful decision after a trial on the merits. FPP § 2947; Evans v. Buchanan, 555 F.2d 373, 387 (3d Cir. 1977).

      i.   *Disfavored injunctions.* There are three types of preliminary injunctions that are disfavored:

         •  Those that afford the moving party substantially all the relief it might recover after a full trial on the merits;

         •  Those that disturb the status quo; and

         •  Those that are mandatory as opposed to prohibitory. FEDPROC § 47:55; Prairie Band of Potawatomi Indians v. Pierce, 253 F.3d 1234, 50 Fed.R.Serv.3d 244 (10th Cir. 2001).

  b.  *Notice.* A preliminary injunction will only issue after notice and hearing, unless there is a waiver. NY R USDCTWD Civ Rule 65(a)(3). The court may issue a preliminary injunction only on notice to the adverse party. FRCP 65(a)(1). Although FRCP 65(a)(1) does not define what constitutes proper notice, it has been held that providing a copy of the motion and a specification of the time and place of the hearing are adequate. FPP § 2949.

  c.  *Security.* The parties shall be prepared to address the security requirements of FRCP 65(c) whenever applying for injunctive relief. NY R USDCTWD Civ Rule 65(c). The court may issue a preliminary injunction or a temporary restraining order only if the movant gives security in an amount that the court considers proper to pay the costs and damages sustained by any party found to have been wrongfully enjoined or restrained. The United States, its officers, and its agencies are not required to give security. FRCP 65(c).

    i. *Proceedings against a surety.* Whenever the Federal Rules of Civil Procedure (including the Supplemental Rules for Admiralty or Maritime Claims and Asset Forfeiture Actions) require or allow a party to give security, and security is given through a bond or other undertaking with one or more sureties, each surety submits to the court's jurisdiction and irrevocably appoints the court clerk as its agent for receiving service of any papers that affect its liability on the bond or undertaking. The surety's liability may be enforced on motion without an independent action. The motion and any notice that the court orders may be served on the court clerk, who must promptly mail a copy of each to every surety whose address is known. FRCP 65.1.

d. *Preliminary injunction versus temporary restraining order.* Care should be taken to distinguish preliminary injunctions under FRCP 65(a) from temporary restraining orders under FRCP 65(b). FPP § 2947.

    i. *Notice and duration.* [Temporary restraining orders] may be issued ex parte without an adversary hearing in order to prevent an immediate, irreparable injury and are of limited duration—they typically remain in effect for a maximum of twenty-eight (28) days. On the other hand, FRCP 65(a)(1) requires that notice be given to the opposing party before a preliminary injunction may be issued. FPP § 2947. Furthermore, a preliminary injunction normally lasts until the completion of the trial on the merits, unless it is dissolved earlier by court order or the consent of the parties. FPP § 2947. Therefore, its duration varies and is controlled by the nature of the situation in which it is utilized. FPP § 2947; Fundicao Tupy S.A. v. U.S., 841 F.2d 1101, 1103 (Fed.Cir. 1988).

    ii. *Hearing.* Some type of a hearing also implicitly is required by FRCP 65(a)(2), which was added in 1966 and provides either for the consolidation of the trial on the merits with the preliminary injunction hearing or the inclusion in the trial record of any evidence received at the FRCP 65(a) hearing. FPP § 2947.

e. *Grounds for granting or denying a preliminary injunction.* The policies that bear on the propriety of granting a preliminary injunction rarely are discussed directly in the cases. Instead they are taken into account by the court considering a number of factors that have been found useful in deciding whether to grant or deny preliminary injunctions in particular cases. A formulation that has become popular in all kinds of cases, although it originally was devised in connection with stays of administrative orders, is that the four most important factors are: (1) the significance of the threat of irreparable harm to plaintiff if the injunction is not granted; (2) the state of the balance between this harm and the injury that granting the injunction would inflict on defendant; (3) the probability that plaintiff will succeed on the merits; and (4) the public interest. FPP § 2948; Pottgen v. Missouri State High School Activities Ass'n, 40 F.3d 926 (8th Cir. 1994).

    i. *Irreparable harm.* Perhaps the single most important prerequisite for the issuance of a preliminary injunction is a demonstration that if it is not granted the applicant is likely to suffer irreparable harm before a decision on the merits can be rendered. FPP § 2948.1. Only when the threatened harm would impair the court's ability to grant an effective remedy is there really a need for preliminary relief. FPP § 2948.1.

        • There must be a likelihood that irreparable harm will occur. Speculative injury is not sufficient; there must be more than an unfounded fear on the part of the applicant. FPP § 2948.1.

        • Thus, a preliminary injunction will not be issued simply to prevent the possibility of some remote future injury. A presently existing actual threat must be shown. However, the injury need not have been inflicted when application is made or be certain to occur; a strong threat of irreparable injury before trial is an adequate basis. FPP § 2948.1.

    ii. *Balancing hardship to parties.* The second factor bearing on the court's exercise of its discretion as to whether to grant preliminary relief involves an evaluation of the severity of the impact on defendant should the temporary injunction be granted and the hardship that would occur to plaintiff if the injunction should be denied. Two factors that frequently are considered when balancing the hardship on the respective parties of the grant or denial of relief are whether a preliminary injunction would give plaintiff all or most of the relief to which plaintiff would be entitled if successful at trial and whether mandatory relief is being sought. FPP § 2948.2.

iii. *Likelihood of prevailing on the merits.* The third factor that enters into the preliminary injunction calculus is the likelihood that plaintiff will prevail on the merits. This is relevant because the need for the court to act is, at least in part, a function of the validity of the applicant's claim. The courts use a bewildering variety of formulations of the need for showing some likelihood of success—the most common being that plaintiff must demonstrate a reasonable probability of success. But the verbal differences do not seem to reflect substantive disagreement. All courts agree that plaintiff must present a prima facie case but need not show a certainty of winning. FPP § 2948.3.

iv. *Public interest.* The final major factor bearing on the court's discretion to issue or deny a preliminary injunction is the public interest. Focusing on this factor is another way of inquiring whether there are policy considerations that bear on whether the order should issue. Thus, when granting preliminary relief, courts frequently emphasize that the public interest will be furthered by the injunction. Conversely, preliminary relief will be denied if the court finds that the public interest would be injured were an injunction to be issued. If the court finds there is no public interest supporting preliminary relief, that conclusion also supports denial of any injunction, even if the public interest would not be harmed by one. FPP § 2948.4. Consequently, an evaluation of the public interest should be given considerable weight in determining whether a motion for a preliminary injunction should be granted. FPP § 2948.4; Yakus v. U.S., 321 U.S. 414, 64 S.Ct. 660, 88 L.Ed. 834 (1944).

f. *Contents and scope of every injunction and restraining order*

    i. *Contents.* Every order granting an injunction and every restraining order must:

- State the reasons why it issued;
- State its terms specifically; and
- Describe in reasonable detail—and not by referring to the complaint or other document—the act or acts restrained or required. FRCP 65(d)(1).

    ii. *Persons bound.* The order binds only the following who receive actual notice of it by personal service or otherwise:

- The parties;
- The parties' officers, agents, servants, employees, and attorneys; and
- Other persons who are in active concert or participation with anyone described in FRCP 65(d)(2)(A) or FRCP 65(d)(2)(B). FRCP 65(d)(2).

g. *Other laws not modified.* FRCP 65 does not modify the following:

    i. Any federal statute relating to temporary restraining orders or preliminary injunctions in actions affecting employer and employee;

    ii. 28 U.S.C.A. § 2361, which relates to preliminary injunctions in actions of interpleader or in the nature of interpleader; or

    iii. 28 U.S.C.A. § 2284, which relates to actions that must be heard and decided by a three-judge district court. FRCP 65(e).

h. *Copyright impoundment.* FRCP 65 applies to copyright-impoundment proceedings. FRCP 65(f).

3. *Opposing papers.* The Federal Rules of Civil Procedure do not require any formal answer, return, or reply to a motion, except where the Federal Rules of Civil Procedure or local rules may require affidavits, memoranda, or other papers to be filed in opposition to a motion. Such papers are simply to apprise the court of such opposition and the grounds of that opposition. FEDPROC § 62:359.

a. *Effect of failure to respond to motion.* Although in the absence of statutory provision or court rule, a motion ordinarily does not require a written answer, when a party files a motion and the opposing party fails to respond, the court may construe such failure to respond as nonopposition to the motion or an admission that the motion was meritorious, may take the facts alleged in the motion as true—the rule in some jurisdictions being that the failure to respond to a fact set forth in a motion is deemed an admission—and may grant the motion if the relief requested appears to be justified. AMJUR MOTIONS § 28.

b. *Assent or no opposition not determinative.* However, a motion will not be granted automatically simply because an "assent" or a notation of "no opposition" has been filed; federal judges frequently deny motions that have been assented to when it is thought that justice so dictates. FPP § 1190.

c. *Responsive pleading inappropriate as response to motion.* An attempt to answer or oppose a motion with a responsive pleading usually is not appropriate. FPP § 1190.

4. *Reply papers.* A moving party may be required or permitted to prepare papers in addition to his original motion papers. AMJUR MOTIONS § 25. Papers answering or replying to opposing papers may be appropriate, in the interests of justice, where it appears there is a substantial reason for allowing a reply. Thus, a court may accept reply papers where a party demonstrates that the papers to which it seeks to file a reply raise new issues that are material to the disposition of the question before the court, or where the court determines, sua sponte, that it wishes further briefing of an issue raised in those papers and orders the submission of additional papers. FEDPROC § 62:360.

a. *Function of reply papers.* The function of a reply affidavit is to answer the arguments made in opposition to the position taken by the movant and not to permit the movant to introduce new arguments in support of the motion. AMJUR MOTIONS § 25.

b. *Issues raised for the first time in a reply document.* However, the view has been followed in some jurisdictions, that as a matter of judicial economy, where there is no prejudice and where the issues could be raised simply by filing a motion to dismiss, the trial court has discretion to consider arguments raised for the first time in a reply memorandum, and that a trial court may grant a motion to strike issues raised for the first time in a reply memorandum. AMJUR MOTIONS § 26.

5. *Sur-reply.* Absent permission of the Judge hearing the motion, sur-reply papers are not permitted. NY R USDCTWD Civ Rule 7(a)(6).

6. *Motion to settle an order.* When counsel are unable to agree on the form of a proposed order, the prevailing party may move, upon seven (7) days notice to all parties, to settle the order. The Court may award costs and attorney's fees against an attorney if it determines that the attorney's unreasonable conduct necessitated bringing the motion. NY R USDCTWD Civ Rule 7(d)(2).

7. *Notice of appearance.* No notice of appearance is required of an attorney whose name and address appear at the end of a complaint, notice of removal, pre-answer motion, or answer. In all other circumstances, an attorney appearing for a party in a civil case shall promptly file a written notice of appearance. NY R USDCTWD Civ Rule 83.2(b). For more information on appearances and withdrawals, refer to NY R USDCTWD Civ Rule 83.2.

8. *Related cases.* Each attorney appearing in a civil case has a continuing duty to promptly notify the Clerk of Court when the attorney has reason to believe that said case is related to some other pending civil or criminal action(s) such that their assignment to the same Judge would avoid unnecessary duplication of judicial effort. As soon as the attorney becomes aware of such a relationship, the attorney shall notify the Clerk of Court by letter of the relevant facts, and the Clerk of Court will transmit that notification to the Judges to whom the cases have been assigned. NY R USDCTWD Civ Rule 5.1(e).

9. *Alternative dispute resolution (ADR).* This Court has adopted an Alternative Dispute Resolution Plan ("ADR"), as implemented by Standing Order (NY R USDCTWD ADR Plan), under which certain civil cases are referred automatically to ADR upon filing. NY R USDCTWD Civ Rule 16(a). The United States District Court for the Western District of New York (the "Court") adopted the ADR Plan on January 1, 2006 (the "Effective Date"), to make available to civil litigants court-administered ADR interventions and processes designed to provide quicker, less expensive and potentially more satisfying alternatives to continuing litigation, without impairing the quality of justice or the right to trial. NY R USDCTWD ADR Plan(1)(1.2)(A).

a. *Scope.* This ADR Plan (NY R USDCTWD ADR Plan) applies to civil actions pending or commenced on and after the Effective Date, except as otherwise indicated in NY R USDCTWD ADR Plan. The ADR Plan supplements the Local Rules of Civil Procedure for the United States District Court for the Western District of New York, which shall remain in full effect for all cases. NY R USDCTWD ADR Plan(1)(1.2)(B).

b. *Referral to ADR*

 i. *New cases.* All civil cases filed on and after the Effective Date of the ADR Plan shall be referred automatically for ADR. NY R USDCTWD ADR Plan(2)(2.1)(A). Notice of the ADR requirements will be provided to all parties immediately upon the filing of a complaint and answer or a notice of removal; NY R USDCTWD ADR Plan(2)(2.1)(A); NY R USDCTWD Civ Rule 16(a). ADR intervention will be scheduled at the conference held pursuant to Local Rule of Civil Procedure 16.1. NY R USDCTWD ADR Plan(2)(2.1)(A). [Editor's note: the reference to Local Rule of Civil Procedure 16.1 is likely meant to be a reference to NY R USDCTWD Civ Rule 16(b)].

 - Litigants in cases not referred automatically to ADR must consider possible agreement to the use of an ADR process. NY R USDCTWD Civ Rule 16(a).

 - For a list of exemptions from automatic referral, refer to NY R USDCTWD ADR Plan(2)(2.1)(A).

 ii. *Pending cases.* The assigned Judge on any pending civil case may, sua sponte or with status conference, issue an order referring the case for ADR. NY R USDCTWD ADR Plan(2)(2.1)(B); NY R USDCTWD Civ Rule 16(a). The order shall specify a date on which the ADR intervention is to be completed. NY R USDCTWD ADR Plan(2)(2.1)(B).

 iii. *Stipulation.* A case may be referred for ADR by stipulation of all parties. Stipulations shall be filed and shall designate the specific ADR intervention the parties have selected, the time frame within which the ADR process will be completed and the selected Neutral. Stipulations are presumed acceptable unless the assigned Judge determines that the interests of justice are not served. NY R USDCTWD ADR Plan(2)(2.1)(C).

 iv. *Relief from ADR referral*

 - *Opting out motions.* Any party may file, with the assigned Judge for that case, a motion to opt out of, or for relief from, ADR. NY R USDCTWD ADR Plan(2)(2.2)(A).

 - *Motion.* Opting Out Motions must be made within fourteen (14) days from (1) the date of the first discovery conference under Local Rule 16.1 in new cases, or (2) the date of a sua sponte ADR Referral Order in pending cases. NY R USDCTWD ADR Plan(2)(2.2)(B). [Editor's note: the reference to Local Rule 16.1 is likely meant to be a reference to NY R USDCTWD Civ Rule 16(b)].

 - *Criteria.* Opting Out Motions shall be granted only for "good cause" shown. Inconvenience, travel costs, attorney fees or other costs shall not constitute "good cause." A party seeking relief from ADR must set forth the reasons why ADR has no reasonable chance of being productive. NY R USDCTWD ADR Plan(2)(2.2)(C).

 - *Judicial initiative.* The assigned Judge may, sua sponte, exempt any case from the Court's ADR Plan. NY R USDCTWD ADR Plan(2)(2.2)(D).

c. *ADR interventions*

 i. *Options.* It is expected that cases referred for ADR will proceed to Mediation. However, the following options are also available upon the stipulation of all parties:

 - Neutral Evaluation;

 - Mini Summary Trial;

 - Arbitration (Binding and Non-Binding);

 - Case Valuation; and

 - Settlement Week, when scheduled by the Court. NY R USDCTWD ADR Plan(4)(4.1)(A).

 ii. *Timing.* Timing is specific to the intervention and process chosen, as set forth in the corresponding sections in NY R USDCTWD ADR Plan. NY R USDCTWD ADR Plan(4)(4.1)(B).

       iii.   *Scheduling.* The referral of a case to ADR does not delay or defer other dates established in the Scheduling Order and has no effect on the scheduled progress of the case toward trial. NY R USDCTWD ADR Plan(4)(4.1)(C).

    d.  *Selecting an ADR intervention*

       i.   *New cases.* Prior to the Local Rule 16.1 scheduling conference, counsel and any unrepresented parties shall confer about ADR as part of their discussion of "the possibilities for a prompt settlement or resolution of the case" pursuant to FRCP 26(f). Unless the parties agree to a different intervention, it is presumed that they will participate in mediation. [Editor's note: the reference to Local Rule 16.1 is likely meant to be a reference to NY R USDCTWD Civ Rule 16(b)].

       ii.  *Pending cases.* In pending cases, all sua sponte referrals will be to mediation. Should the parties agree that a different ADR intervention is more appropriate to their case, they may submit a stipulation designating the specific ADR intervention selected, the time frame within which the ADR process will be completed and the identity of the Neutral. Stipulations must be filed within fourteen (14) days from the date of the ADR Referral Order and are presumed acceptable unless the assigned Judge determines that the interests of justice are not served. NY R USDCTWD ADR Plan(4)(4.2)(B).

    e.  For more information on alternative dispute resolution (ADR), refer to NY R USDCTWD ADR Plan.

10.   *Sanctions.* Failure of counsel for any party, or a party proceeding pro se, to appear before the Court at a conference, to complete the necessary preparations, or to be prepared to proceed to trial at the set time may be considered an abandonment of the case or a failure to prosecute or defend diligently. An appropriate order for sanctions may be entered against the defaulting party with respect to either a specific issue or the entire case. NY R USDCTWD Civ Rule 11(a). For more information, refer to NY R USDCTWD Civ Rule 11.

11.   *Pro se actions.* For information on the requirements in pro se actions, refer to NY R USDCTWD Civ Rule 5.2.

12.   *Individual judge practices.* Refer to the Miscellaneous section of this document for information on individual judge practices on general requirements for documents.

## D.  Documents

  1.  *Documents for moving party*

    a.  *Required documents*

       i.   *Notice of motion and motion.* An application for a preliminary injunction shall include: the motion for a preliminary injunction. NY R USDCTWD Civ Rule 65(a)(2). A notice of motion is required for all motions, and must state: the relief sought, the grounds for the request, the papers submitted in support, and the return date for the motion, if known. A moving party who intends to file and serve reply papers must so state in the notice of motion. NY R USDCTWD Civ Rule 7(a)(1). Refer to the General Requirements section of this document for information on the notice of motion and motion.

       ii.  *Memorandum of law.* An application for a preliminary injunction shall include: a memorandum of law in support of the motion citing legal authority showing that the moving party is entitled to the relief requested. NY R USDCTWD Civ Rule 65(a)(3). Absent leave of Court or as otherwise specified, upon any motion filed pursuant to FRCP 12, FRCP 56 or FRCP 65(a), the moving party shall file and serve a memorandum of law. Failure to comply with this requirement may constitute grounds for resolving the motion against the non-complying party. NY R USDCTWD Civ Rule 7(a)(2)(A). Refer to the Format section of this document for the formatting requirements for memoranda of law.

       iii.  *Supporting affidavit.* An affidavit must not contain legal arguments, but must contain factual and procedural background relevant to the motion it supports. Except for motions brought under FRCP 12(b)(1) (lack of subject matter jurisdiction), FRCP 12(b)(6) (failure to state a claim), FRCP 12(c) (judgment on the pleadings), and FRCP 12(f) (to strike), motions and opposition to motions shall be supported by at least one (1) affidavit and by such other evidence (i.e., deposition testimony, interrogatory answers, admissions, and documents) as appropriate to resolve the particular motion. Failure to comply with this requirement may constitute grounds for resolving the motion against the non-complying party. NY R USDCTWD Civ Rule 7(a)(3).

iv. *Complaint.* An application for a preliminary injunction shall include: a copy of the complaint, if the case has been recently filed. NY R USDCTWD Civ Rule 65(a)(1).

v. *List of witnesses and exhibits.* An application for a preliminary injunction shall include: a list of witnesses and exhibits to be presented at the preliminary injunction hearing, and a brief summary of the anticipated testimony of such witnesses. NY R USDCTWD Civ Rule 65(a)(4).

vi. *Proposed order.* An application for a preliminary injunction shall include: a proposed order granting the injunctive relief. NY R USDCTWD Civ Rule 65(a)(5). All proposed orders must be submitted in a format compatible with WordPerfect or Microsoft Word format, which is a "Save As" option in most word processing software. Judges will not accept proposed orders in PDF format. NY R USDCTWD ECF Procedures(2)(j)(ii). Proposed orders should be attached to an Internet e-mail sent to the e-mail address of the assigned judge. NY R USDCTWD ECF Procedures(2)(j)(i). For the list of email addresses for the judges, refer to NY R USDCTWD ECF Procedures(2)(j)(i).

vii. *Security.* Refer to the General Requirements section of this document for information on the security required.

viii. *Certificate of service.* FRCP 5(d) requires that the person making service under FRCP 5 certify that service has been effected. FRCP 5(Advisory Committee Notes). Having such information on file may be useful for many purposes, including proof of service if an issue arises concerning the effectiveness of the service. FRCP 5(Advisory Committee Notes). The Notice of Electronic Filing effectuates service for all registered users and no certificate of service is required when all filers on an action are Registered Users. The following exemptions require a certificate of service to be filed:

- When a document is manually filed, a certificate of service must be filed stating the manner in which service or notice was accomplished on each party so entitled. NY R USDCTWD ECF Procedures(2)(f)(iv).

- When a pro se filer (who isn't authorized to electronically file documents) is a party, a certificate of service must be filed stating the manner in which service or notice was accomplished on the pro se party. The Notice of Electronic Filing effectuates service for the Registered Users in this situation and it is not necessary to note service on those parties. A non-registered pro se filer is required to file certificates of service on all documents they file. NY R USDCTWD ECF Procedures(2)(f)(iv).

- If an attorney is exempt from electronic service, a certificate of service must be filed stating the manner in which service or notice was accomplished on the exempt attorney. The Notice of Electronic Filing effectuates service for the Registered Users in this situation and it is not necessary to note service on those parties. NY R USDCTWD ECF Procedures(2)(f)(iv).

b. *Supplemental documents*

i. *Supporting evidence.* When a motion relies on facts outside the record, the court may hear the matter on affidavits or may hear it wholly or partly on oral testimony or on depositions. FRCP 43(c). Evidence that goes beyond the unverified allegations of the pleadings and motion papers must be presented to support or oppose a motion for a preliminary injunction. FPP § 2949. A party seeking or opposing any relief under the Federal Rules of Civil Procedure shall file only the portion(s) of a deposition, interrogatory, request for documents, request for admission, or other supporting material that is pertinent to the application. NY R USDCTWD Civ Rule 7(a)(4).

- *Affidavits.* Affidavits are appropriate on a preliminary injunction motion and typically will be offered by both parties. FPP § 2949. All affidavits should state the facts supporting the litigant's position clearly and specifically. Preliminary injunctions frequently are denied if the affidavits are too vague or conclusory to demonstrate a clear right to relief under FRCP 65. FPP § 2949.

ii. *Pleadings.* Pleadings may be considered if they have been verified. FPP § 2949; K-2 Ski Co. v. Head Ski Co., 467 F.2d 1087 (9th Cir. 1972).

iii. *Notice of constitutional question.* A party that files a pleading, written motion, or other paper drawing into question the constitutionality of a federal or state statute must promptly:

- *File notice.* File a notice of constitutional question stating the question and identifying the paper that raises it, if: (1) a federal statute is questioned and the parties do not include the United States, one of its agencies, or one of its officers or employees in an official capacity; or (2) a state statute is questioned and the parties do not include the state, one of its agencies, or one of its officers or employees in an official capacity; and

- *Serve notice.* Serve the notice and paper on the Attorney General of the United States if a federal statute is questioned—or on the state attorney general if a state statute is questioned—either by certified or registered mail or by sending it to an electronic address designated by the attorney general for this purpose. FRCP 5.1(a).

- *No forfeiture.* A party's failure to file and serve the notice, or the court's failure to certify, does not forfeit a constitutional claim or defense that is otherwise timely asserted. FRCP 5.1(d).

iv. *Nongovernmental corporate disclosure statement*

- *Contents.* A nongovernmental corporate party must file two (2) copies of a disclosure statement that: (1) identifies any parent corporation and any publicly held corporation owning ten percent (10%) or more of its stock; or (2) states that there is no such corporation. FRCP 7.1(a).

- *Time to file; Supplemental filing.* A party must: (1) file the disclosure statement with its first appearance, pleading, petition, motion, response, or other request addressed to the court; and (2) promptly file a supplemental statement if any required information changes. FRCP 7.1(b).

v. *Motion for an expedited hearing.* Additionally, if the moving party seeks to have the motion heard on an expedited basis, such party shall include a motion for an expedited hearing pursuant to NY R USDCTWD Civ Rule 7(d)(1). NY R USDCTWD Civ Rule 65(a).

vi. *Copies of authorities.* In cases involving a pro se litigant, counsel shall, when serving a memorandum of law (or other submissions to the Court), provide the pro se litigant (but not other counsel or the Court) with printed copies of decisions cited therein that are unreported or reported exclusively on computerized databases. NY R USDCTWD Civ Rule 7(a)(8).

vii. *Paper copy for date-stamping with self-addressed envelope.* Parties requesting date-stamped copies of filed documents must provide a paper copy for date-stamping, and a self-addressed, adequately-sized envelope with proper postage affixed. NY R USDCTWD Civ Rule 5.1(d).

viii. *Courtesy copies.* The Court may, in its discretion, request courtesy copies on any other motion. NY R USDCTWD Civ Rule 7(a)(7). Courtesy copies of certain documents may be required. Filers should refer to the "Judge Preferences" published on the Court's website. NY R USDCTWD ECF Procedures(2)(a)(iii).

2. *Documents for opposing party*

   a. *Required documents*

      i. *Opposition.* Refer to the General Requirements section of this document for information on the opposing papers.

      ii. *Answering memorandum.* Absent leave of Court or as otherwise specified, upon any motion filed pursuant to FRCP 12, FRCP 56 or FRCP 65(a). . .the opposing party shall file and serve an answering memorandum. Failure to comply with this requirement may constitute grounds for resolving the motion against the non-complying party. NY R USDCTWD Civ Rule 7(a)(2)(A). Refer to the Format section of this document for the formatting requirements for memoranda of law.

iii. *Supporting affidavit.* An affidavit must not contain legal arguments, but must contain factual and procedural background relevant to the motion it supports. Except for motions brought under FRCP 12(b)(1) (lack of subject matter jurisdiction), FRCP 12(b)(6) (failure to state a claim), FRCP 12(c) (judgment on the pleadings), and FRCP 12(f) (to strike), motions and opposition to motions shall be supported by at least one (1) affidavit and by such other evidence (i.e., deposition testimony, interrogatory answers, admissions, and documents) as appropriate to resolve the particular motion. Failure to comply with this requirement may constitute grounds for resolving the motion against the non-complying party. NY R USDCTWD Civ Rule 7(a)(3).

iv. *Certificate of service.* FRCP 5(d) requires that the person making service under FRCP 5 certify that service has been effected. FRCP 5(Advisory Committee Notes). Having such information on file may be useful for many purposes, including proof of service if an issue arises concerning the effectiveness of the service. FRCP 5(Advisory Committee Notes). The Notice of Electronic Filing effectuates service for all registered users and no certificate of service is required when all filers on an action are Registered Users. The following exemptions require a certificate of service to be filed:

- When a document is manually filed, a certificate of service must be filed stating the manner in which service or notice was accomplished on each party so entitled. NY R USDCTWD ECF Procedures(2)(f)(iv).

- When a pro se filer (who isn't authorized to electronically file documents) is a party, a certificate of service must be filed stating the manner in which service or notice was accomplished on the pro se party. The Notice of Electronic Filing effectuates service for the Registered Users in this situation and it is not necessary to note service on those parties. A non-registered pro se filer is required to file certificates of service on all documents they file. NY R USDCTWD ECF Procedures(2)(f)(iv).

- If an attorney is exempt from electronic service, a certificate of service must be filed stating the manner in which service or notice was accomplished on the exempt attorney. The Notice of Electronic Filing effectuates service for the Registered Users in this situation and it is not necessary to note service on those parties. NY R USDCTWD ECF Procedures(2)(f)(iv).

b. *Supplemental documents*

i. *Supporting evidence.* When a motion relies on facts outside the record, the court may hear the matter on affidavits or may hear it wholly or partly on oral testimony or on depositions. FRCP 43(c). Evidence that goes beyond the unverified allegations of the pleadings and motion papers must be presented to support or oppose a motion for a preliminary injunction. FPP § 2949. A party seeking or opposing any relief under the Federal Rules of Civil Procedure shall file only the portion(s) of a deposition, interrogatory, request for documents, request for admission, or other supporting material that is pertinent to the application. NY R USDCTWD Civ Rule 7(a)(4).

- *Affidavits.* Affidavits are appropriate on a preliminary injunction motion and typically will be offered by both parties. FPP § 2949. All affidavits should state the facts supporting the litigant's position clearly and specifically. Preliminary injunctions frequently are denied if the affidavits are too vague or conclusory to demonstrate a clear right to relief under FRCP 65. FPP § 2949.

ii. *Pleadings.* Pleadings may be considered if they have been verified. FPP § 2949; K-2 Ski Co. v. Head Ski Co., 467 F.2d 1087 (9th Cir. 1972).

iii. *Notice of constitutional question.* A party that files a pleading, written motion, or other paper drawing into question the constitutionality of a federal or state statute must promptly:

- *File notice.* File a notice of constitutional question stating the question and identifying the

paper that raises it, if: (1) a federal statute is questioned and the parties do not include the United States, one of its agencies, or one of its officers or employees in an official capacity; or (2) a state statute is questioned and the parties do not include the state, one of its agencies, or one of its officers or employees in an official capacity; and

- *Serve notice.* Serve the notice and paper on the Attorney General of the United States if a federal statute is questioned—or on the state attorney general if a state statute is questioned—either by certified or registered mail or by sending it to an electronic address designated by the attorney general for this purpose. FRCP 5.1(a).

- *No forfeiture.* A party's failure to file and serve the notice, or the court's failure to certify, does not forfeit a constitutional claim or defense that is otherwise timely asserted. FRCP 5.1(d).

iv. *Nongovernmental corporate disclosure statement*

- *Contents.* A nongovernmental corporate party must file two (2) copies of a disclosure statement that: (1) identifies any parent corporation and any publicly held corporation owning ten percent (10%) or more of its stock; or (2) states that there is no such corporation. FRCP 7.1(a).

- *Time to file; Supplemental filing.* A party must: (1) file the disclosure statement with its first appearance, pleading, petition, motion, response, or other request addressed to the court; and (2) promptly file a supplemental statement if any required information changes. FRCP 7.1(b).

v. *Copies of authorities.* In cases involving a pro se litigant, counsel shall, when serving a memorandum of law (or other submissions to the Court), provide the pro se litigant (but not other counsel or the Court) with printed copies of decisions cited therein that are unreported or reported exclusively on computerized databases. NY R USDCTWD Civ Rule 7(a)(8).

vi. *Paper copy for date-stamping with self-addressed envelope.* Parties requesting date-stamped copies of filed documents must provide a paper copy for date-stamping, and a self-addressed, adequately-sized envelope with proper postage affixed. NY R USDCTWD Civ Rule 5.1(d).

vii. *Courtesy copies.* Courtesy copies of certain documents may be required. Filers should refer to the "Judge Preferences" published on the Court's website. NY R USDCTWD ECF Procedures(2)(a)(iii).

3. *Individual judge practices.* Refer to the Miscellaneous section of this document for information on individual judge practices on required documents.

## E. Format

1. *Form of documents.* The rules governing captions and other matters of form in pleadings apply to motions and other papers. FRCP 7(b)(2).

a. *Form, generally.* All pleadings, motions, and other papers that a party presents for filing, whether in paper form or in electronic form, shall meet the following requirements:

i. *Font size.* All text and footnotes shall be in a font size of at least twelve (12) point type. NY R USDCTWD Civ Rule 10(a)(1).

ii. *Spacing.* All text in the body of the document must be double-spaced, except that text in block quotations and footnotes may be single-spaced. NY R USDCTWD Civ Rule 10(a)(2).

- Extensive footnotes and block quotes may not be used to circumvent page limitations. NY R USDCTWD Civ Rule 10(a)(3).

iii. *Margins.* Documents must have one (1) inch margins on all four sides. NY R USDCTWD Civ Rule 10(a)(4).

iv. *Page numbering.* Pages must be consecutively numbered. NY R USDCTWD Civ Rule 10(a)(5).

b. *Additional requirements for paper filing.* Documents presented for filing in paper form shall meet the following additional requirements:

    i. *Paper.* Documents must be on durable white eight and one-half by eleven (8-1/2 x 11) inch paper of good quality. NY R USDCTWD Civ Rule 10(b)(1).

      • All documents must be single-sided. NY R USDCTWD Civ Rule 10(b)(5).

    ii. *Text.* All text must be plainly and legibly written, typewritten, printed or reproduced. NY R USDCTWD Civ Rule 10(b)(2).

    iii. *Ink.* Documents must be in black or blue ink. NY R USDCTWD Civ Rule 10(b)(3).

    iv. *Binding.* The pages of each document must be stapled or in some other way fastened together. NY R USDCTWD Civ Rule 10(b)(4).

c. *Caption; Names of parties.* Every pleading must have a caption with the court's name, a title, a file number, and a FRCP 7(a) designation. The title of the complaint must name all the parties; the title of other pleadings, after naming the first party on each side, may refer generally to other parties. FRCP 10(a).

d. *Paragraphs; Separate statements.* A party must state its claims or defenses in numbered paragraphs, each limited as far as practicable to a single set of circumstances. A later pleading may refer by number to a paragraph in an earlier pleading. If doing so would promote clarity, each claim founded on a separate transaction or occurrence—and each defense other than a denial—must be stated in a separate count or defense. FRCP 10(b).

e. *Adoption by reference; Exhibits.* A statement in a pleading may be adopted by reference elsewhere in the same pleading or in any other pleading or motion. A copy of a written instrument that is an exhibit to a pleading is a part of the pleading for all purposes. FRCP 10(c).

f. *Citation of local rules.* The Local Rules of Civil Procedure for the United States District Court for the Western District of New York shall be cited as "L.R.Civ.P." NY R USDCTWD Civ Rule 1.1.

g. *Acceptance by the clerk.* The clerk must not refuse to file a paper solely because it is not in the form prescribed by the Federal Rules of Civil Procedure or by a local rule or practice. FRCP 5(d)(4). The Court may reject documents that do not comply with the requirements in NY R USDCTWD Civ Rule 10. NY R USDCTWD Civ Rule 10.

2. *Form of electronic documents.* All pleadings, motions, and other papers that a party presents for filing, whether in paper form or in electronic form, shall meet the requirements in NY R USDCTWD Civ Rule 10(a). NY R USDCTWD Civ Rule 10(a). Refer above for more information.

a. *Conversion to PDF.* A document created with a word processor, or a paper document, must be converted to Portable Document Format to be electronically filed with the court. NY R USDCTWD ECF Procedures(2)(a)(v).

    i. Documents which exist only in paper form may be scanned into a portable document format (PDF) for electronic filing. NY R USDCTWD ECF Procedures(2)(a)(v). Before filing a scanned document with the court, a Filing User must verify its legibility. NY R USDCTWD ECF Procedures(2)(a)(iv).

    ii. Electronic documents must be converted to .PDF from a word processing program and must be text searchable. Do not print, scan and .PDF your document when it has been created in a word processing program. Additional information on working with PDFs is located in NY R USDCTWD ECF Procedures(4b). NY R USDCTWD ECF Procedures(2)(a)(v).

b. *Hyperlinks.* Pursuant to the policy set forth by the Judicial Conference in October 2005, a hyperlink contained in a filing is no more than a convenient mechanism for accessing material cited in a document. A hyperlink reference is extraneous to any filed document and is not part of the Court's record. NY R USDCTWD ECF Procedures(2)(a)(vi).

    i. In order to preserve the integrity of the Court record, users wishing to insert hyperlinks in Court filings shall continue to use the conventional method for the cited authority, in addition to the hyperlink. NY R USDCTWD ECF Procedures(2)(a)(vi).

ii. The Court accepts no responsibility for, and does not endorse any product, organization, and content at any hyperlinked site, or at any site to which that site may be linked. The Court accepts no responsibility for the availability or functionality of any hyperlink. NY R USDCTWD ECF Procedures(2)(a)(vi).

c. *Attachments and exhibits*

   i. Attachments and exhibits larger than five megabytes (5 MB) shall be filed electronically in separate five megabyte (5 MB) segments. NY R USDCTWD ECF Procedures(2)(d)(i).

   ii. Filing Users must submit in electronic form all documents referenced as exhibits or attachments, except as otherwise provided in NY R USDCTWD ECF Procedures. A Filing User must submit as exhibits or attachments only those excerpts of the referenced documents that are directly germane to the matter under consideration by the court. Excerpted material must be clearly and prominently identified as such. Filing Users who file excerpts of documents as exhibits or attachments under NY R USDCTWD ECF Procedures(2)(d)(ii) do so without prejudice to their right to timely file additional excerpts or the complete document. Responding parties may timely file additional excerpts or the complete document that they believe are directly germane. The Court may require parties to file additional excerpts or the complete document. A Filing User must request leave of the Court to file a document exhibit or attachment in non-electronic form. NY R USDCTWD ECF Procedures(2)(d)(ii).

   iii. Exhibits offered or admitted at trial will not be filed electronically or conventionally unless so ordered by the Court. NY R USDCTWD ECF Procedures(2)(d)(iii).

   iv. Exhibits such as videotapes and tape recordings shall be filed in the conventional manner with the Clerk of Court, and a Notice of Manual Filing shall be electronically filed by the party. Manually filed exhibits must have the case number and case name securely fastened or marked on the item. NY R USDCTWD ECF Procedures(2)(d)(iii).

   v. Continuation of exhibit entries (for exhibits that are too large to attach to a main document) must be filed and entered on the same day that the main document was filed. NY R USDCTWD ECF Procedures(2)(d)(iv).

d. *Color documents.* Documents in color or containing graphics take much longer to upload. Filing users are encouraged to configure their scanners to scan documents at 200 dpi and preferably in black and white rather than color. NY R USDCTWD ECF Procedures(2)(d)(v).

e. *Large documents.* Due to the length of time it takes to download large files, documents larger than five megabytes (5 MB) (approximately one hundred (100) pages of a .pdf scanned document) must be filed electronically in separate five megabyte (5 MB) segments. A party who believes a document is too lengthy to electronically image (i.e. scan), may contact the Court Room Deputy for the assigned judge and request permission to file that document conventionally. If granted permission to file the document conventionally, the Filing User shall electronically file a "notice of manual filing" for that item. Exhibits submitted to the Court conventionally shall be served on other parties conventionally. NY R USDCTWD ECF Procedures(2)(d)(vi).

3. *Form of memoranda of law.* Memoranda in support of or in opposition to any motion shall not exceed twenty-five (25) pages in length, and reply memoranda shall not exceed ten (10) pages in length. A party seeking to exceed the page limit must make application by letter to the Judge hearing the motion, with copies to all counsel, at least seven (7) days before the date on which the memorandum must be filed. NY R USDCTWD Civ Rule 7(a)(2)(C).

4. *Signing of pleadings, motions and other papers*

a. *Signature.* Every pleading, written motion, and other paper must be signed by at least one attorney of record in the attorney's name—or by a party personally if the party is unrepresented. The paper must state the signer's address, e-mail address, and telephone number. FRCP 11(a). Documents presented for paper filing must contain an original signature. NY R USDCTWD Civ Rule 10(b)(6).

   i. *Electronic signatures*

      • *Non-attorney signature.* If the original document requires the signature of a non-attorney, the filing party shall obtain the signature of the non-attorney on the document. NY R USDCTWD ECF Procedures(2)(g)(i). The filing party or attorney then shall file the document electronically indicating the signatory's name in the form "s/(name)." NY R USDCTWD ECF Procedures(2)(g)(i)(1). A non-filing signatory or party who disputes the authenticity of an electronically filed document or the authenticity of the signature on that document must file an objection to the document within ten (10) days of receiving the Notice of Electronic Filing. NY R USDCTWD ECF Procedures(2)(g)(i)(2).

- *Registered user signature.* The username and password required to file documents on the Electronic Filing System serve as the Filing User's signature on all electronic documents filed with this Court. The also serve as a signature for the purposes of FRCP 11, the Federal Rules of Civil Procedure, the Local Rules of Civil Procedure for the United States District Court for the Western District of New York, and any other purpose for which a signature is required in connection with proceedings before this Court. A pleading requiring a Registered User's signature must include a signature block in the format found in NY R USDCTWD ECF Procedures(2)(g)(iii). NY R USDCTWD ECF Procedures(2)(g)(iii). Any party challenging the authenticity of an electronically filed document or the attorney's signature on that document must file an objection to the document within ten (10) days of receiving the Notice of Electronic Filing. NY R USDCTWD ECF Procedures(2)(g)(iii)(1).

- *Multiple signatures.* The following procedure applies when a stipulation or other document requires two or more signatures: The filing party shall initially confirm that the document is acceptable to all persons required to sign the document and shall obtain the signatures of all parties on the document. NY R USDCTWD ECF Procedures(2)(g)(iv)(1). The filing party or attorney then shall file the document electronically indicating the signatories, e.g., "s/Jane Doe," "s/John Smith," etc. NY R USDCTWD ECF Procedures(2)(g)(iv)(2). A non-filing signatory or party who disputes the authenticity of an electronically filed document containing multiple signatures or the authenticity of the signatures themselves must file an objection to the document within ten (10) days of receiving the Notice of Electronic Filing. NY R USDCTWD ECF Procedures(2)(g)(iv)(3).

ii. *No verification or accompanying affidavit required for pleadings.* Unless a rule or statute specifically states otherwise, a pleading need not be verified or accompanied by an affidavit. FRCP 11(a).

iii. *Unsigned papers.* The court must strike an unsigned paper unless the omission is promptly corrected after being called to the attorney's or party's attention. FRCP 11(a).

b. *Representations to the court.* By presenting to the court a pleading, written motion, or other paper—whether by signing, filing, submitting, or later advocating it—an attorney or unrepresented party certifies that to the best of the person's knowledge, information, and belief, formed after an inquiry reasonable under the circumstances:

i. It is not being presented for any improper purpose, such as to harass, cause unnecessary delay, or needlessly increase the cost of litigation;

ii. The claims, defenses, and other legal contentions are warranted by existing law or by a nonfrivolous argument for extending, modifying, or reversing existing law or for establishing new law;

iii. The factual contentions have evidentiary support or, if specifically so identified, will likely have evidentiary support after a reasonable opportunity for further investigation or discovery; and

iv. The denials of factual contentions are warranted on the evidence or, if specifically so identified, are reasonably based on belief or a lack of information. FRCP 11(b).

c. *Sanctions.* If, after notice and a reasonable opportunity to respond, the court determines that FRCP 11(b) has been violated, the court may impose an appropriate sanction on any attorney, law firm, or party that violated FRCP 11(b) or is responsible for the violation. FRCP 11(c)(1). Refer to the United

States District Court for the Western District of New York KeyRules Motion for Sanctions document for more information.

5.  *Privacy protection for filings made with the court.* In all filings, parties shall comply with FRCP 5.2. NY R USDCTWD ECF Procedures(2)(m)(i).

    a.  *Redacted filings.* Unless the court orders otherwise, in an electronic or paper filing with the court that contains an individual's Social Security number, taxpayer-identification number, or birth date, the name of an individual known to be a minor, or a financial-account number, a party or nonparty making the filing may include only:

        i.  The last four (4) digits of the Social Security number and taxpayer-identification number;

        ii.  The year of the individual's birth;

        iii.  The minor's initials; and

        iv.  The last four (4) digits of the financial-account number. FRCP 5.2(a).

    b.  *Exemptions from the redaction requirement.* The redaction requirement does not apply to the following:

        i.  A financial-account number that identifies the property allegedly subject to forfeiture in a forfeiture proceeding;

        ii.  The record of an administrative or agency proceeding;

        iii.  The official record of a state-court proceeding;

        iv.  The record of a court or tribunal, if that record was not subject to the redaction requirement when originally filed;

        v.  A filing covered by FRCP 5.2(c) or FRCP 5.2(d); and

        vi.  A pro se filing in an action brought under 28 U.S.C.A. § 2241, 28 U.S.C.A. § 2254, or 28 U.S.C.A. § 2255. FRCP 5.2(b).

    c.  *Limitations on remote access to electronic files; Social Security appeals and immigration cases.* Unless the court orders otherwise, in an action for benefits under the Social Security Act, and in an action or proceeding relating to an order of removal, to relief from removal, or to immigration benefits or detention, access to an electronic file is authorized as follows:

        i.  The parties and their attorneys may have remote electronic access to any part of the case file, including the administrative record;

        ii.  Any other person may have electronic access to the full record at the courthouse, but may have remote electronic access only to:

            •  The docket maintained by the court; and

            •  An opinion, order, judgment, or other disposition of the court, but not any other part of the case file or the administrative record. FRCP 5.2(c).

    d.  *Filings made under seal.* The court may order that a filing be made under seal without redaction. The court may later unseal the filing or order the person who made the filing to file a redacted version for the public record. FRCP 5.2(d). For more information on sealing documents, refer to NY R USDCTWD Civ Rule 5.3, NY R USDCTWD ECF Procedures(2)(o)(i)(1), NY R USDCTWD ECF Procedures(2)(o)(i)(2), and NY R USDCTWD ECF Procedures(2)(o)(i)(3).

    e.  *Protective orders.* For good cause, the court may by order in a case:

        i.  Require redaction of additional information; or

        ii.  Limit or prohibit a nonparty's remote electronic access to a document filed with the court. FRCP 5.2(e).

    f.  *Option for additional unredacted filing under seal.* A person making a redacted filing may also file an unredacted copy under seal. The court must retain the unredacted copy as part of the record. FRCP 5.2(f).

    g.  *Option for filing a reference list.* A filing that contains redacted information may be filed together

with a reference list that identifies each item of redacted information and specifies an appropriate identifier that uniquely corresponds to each item listed. The list must be filed under seal and may be amended as of right. Any reference in the case to a listed identifier will be construed to refer to the corresponding item of information. FRCP 5.2(g).

h. *Waiver of protection of identifiers.* A person waives the protection of FRCP 5.2(a) as to the person's own information by filing it without redaction and not under seal. FRCP 5.2(h).

6. *Individual judge practices.* Refer to the Miscellaneous section of this document for information on individual judge practices on formatting documents.

## F. Filing and Service Requirements

1. *Filing requirements.* Any paper after the complaint that is required to be served—together with a certificate of service—must be filed within a reasonable time after service. FRCP 5(d)(1). All pleadings and other papers shall be filed and served in accordance with the Federal Rules of Civil Procedure and the CM/ECF Administrative Procedures Guide (NY R USDCTWD ECF Procedures). NY R USDCTWD Civ Rule 5.1(a). For information on filing of miscellaneous cases and irregular documents, refer to NY R USDCTWD Civ Rule 5.6.

   a. *How filing is made; In general.* A paper is filed by delivering it:

      i. To the clerk; or

      ii. To a judge who agrees to accept it for filing, and who must then note the filing date on the paper and promptly send it to the clerk. FRCP 5(d)(2).

   b. *Electronic filing*

      i. *Authorization of electronic filing program.* A court may, by local rule, allow papers to be filed, signed, or verified by electronic means that are consistent with any technical standards established by the Judicial Conference of the United States. A local rule may require electronic filing only if reasonable exceptions are allowed. A paper filed electronically in compliance with a local rule is a written paper for purposes of the Federal Rules of Civil Procedure. FRCP 5(d)(3).

         - All civil cases filed in this Court are assigned to the Electronic Case Filing System ("ECF"). The procedures for electronic filing and any exceptions to the electronic filing requirements are set forth in the CM/ECF Administrative Procedures Guide (NY R USDCTWD ECF Procedures) which is available on the Court's website. NY R US-DCTWD Civ Rule 5.1(a).

      ii. *Scope of electronic filing.* The U.S. District Court for the Western District of New York requires attorneys in civil and criminal cases to file documents with the Court electronically over the Internet using its Case Management/Electronic Case Filing (CM/ECF) system. NY R US-DCTWD ECF Procedures. Beginning January 1, 2004, all civil and criminal cases currently pending and newly filed, except as expressly noted herein, were assigned to the Electronic Case Filing System ("System"). Except as expressly provided and in exceptional circumstances preventing a Filing User from filing electronically, all petitions, motions, memoranda of law, or other pleadings and documents required to be filed with the Court in connection with a case assigned to the System must be electronically filed. NY R USDCTWD ECF Procedures(1)(a).

         - *Mandatory electronic filing.* All documents on civil, criminal, miscellaneous civil, miscellaneous criminal and new civil case openings, except sealed documents, sealed cases, opening of a criminal case, opening of a miscellaneous case and as expressly provided for in these procedures (NY R USDCTWD ECF Procedures), shall be electronically filed on the system. NY R USDCTWD ECF Procedures(2)(a)(i). NY R USDCTWD Civ Rule 29

         - *Stipulations.* Pursuant to NY R USDCTWD Civ Rule 29, all stipulations (whether the stipulation is final or when it requires a judge's signature) shall be filed electronically. NY R USDCTWD ECF Procedures(2)(p)(i).

         - *Letters.* The electronic filing of letters is generally prohibited unless granted permission by an assigned judge. Letters to the Court must be submitted conventionally. NY R US-DCTWD ECF Procedures(2)(q)(i).

- *Exceptions.* The Court requires attorneys to file documents electronically, absent a showing of good cause, unless otherwise excused by the procedures set forth below or by Order of the Court. NY R USDCTWD ECF Procedures.

iii. *Conventional filing of documents.* The procedures in NY R USDCTWD ECF Procedures(2)(o) govern documents filed conventionally. The Court, upon application, may also authorize conventional filing of other documents otherwise subject to the procedures in NY R USDCTWD ECF Procedures(2)(o). NY R USDCTWD ECF Procedures(2)(o)(i).

- *Documents filed under seal.* Unredacted documents filed with the Court pursuant to the privacy provisions of FRCP 5.2 shall be submitted in a sealing envelope with the information in NY R USDCTWD ECF Procedures(2)(o)(i)(1) on the envelope. NY R USDCTWD ECF Procedures(2)(o)(i)(1). If the document is larger than five (5) pages, a disk should be provided to the Clerks Office which contains the document in a .pdf format. NY R USDCTWD ECF Procedures(2)(o)(i)(1). For more information on documents filed under seal, refer to NY R USDCTWD ECF Procedures(2)(o)(i)(1), NY R USDCTWD ECF Procedures(2)(o)(i)(2), and NY R USDCTWD ECF Procedures(2)(o)(i)(3).

- *Magistrate judge consents.* Pursuant to FRCP 73(b), parties' filing consents to jurisdiction by United States Magistrate Judge will continue to be treated as non-public documents until all parties have consented. Therefore, parties must submit conventionally (in paper form) and not electronically file their consent forms so that the consent is not a public document. If all parties consent to the jurisdiction of a Magistrate Judge, the Clerk will scan all consent forms which will then become a public document. NY R USDCTWD ECF Procedures(2)(o)(i)(3).

- *Pro se filers.* Pro Se filers shall file paper originals of all initiating documents, pleadings, motions, affidavits, briefs and other documents which must be signed or which require either verification or an unsworn declaration under any rule or statute. The Clerk's Office will scan these original documents into an electronic file in the System. A certificate of service is required for all documents a pro se litigant files with the court. If a Pro Se filer is granted permission to register to electronically file documents, they shall comply with the guidelines contained in this document (NY R USDCTWD ECF Procedures). NY R USDCTWD ECF Procedures(2)(o)(i)(4).

- *Social Security cases.* Absent a showing of good cause, and except as provided in Section o(i)(4) above, all documents, notices and orders in Social Security reviews will be filed and noticed electronically, except as noted in NY R USDCTWD ECF Procedures(2)(o)(i)(6). For more information, refer to NY R USDCTWD ECF Procedures(2)(o)(i)(6).

- For more information on conventional filing of documents, refer to NY R USDCTWD ECF Procedures(2)(o)(i).

iv. *Consequences of electronic filing.* Electronic transmission of a document to the System consistent with these procedures (NY R USDCTWD ECF Procedures), whether accomplished by the Filing User or a Court User, together with the transmission of a Notice of Electronic Filing from the Court, constitutes filing of a document for all purposes of the Federal Rules of Civil Procedure and the Local Rules of Civil Procedure for the United States District Court for the Western District of New York, and constitutes entry of the document on the docket kept by the Clerk under FRCP 58 and FRCP 79. A document shall not be considered filed for purposes of the Federal Rules of Civil until the filing party receives a System generated Notice of Electronic Filing. NY R USDCTWD ECF Procedures(2)(a)(i).

- E-mailing a document to the Clerk's Office or to the assigned judge shall not constitute "filing" of such document. NY R USDCTWD ECF Procedures(2)(a)(i)(1).

v. *Filing fees.* Any fee required for filing of a pleading or paper in District Court is payable to the Clerk of Court by check or money order. In addition, when opening a civil case on line, filing a notice of appeal on line or applying to appear pro hac vice on line, the fees shall be paid on line by registered users through the federal electronic payment website. Users will be directed to the federal electronic payment website while entering their transaction and should have a credit card available. When opening a civil case and applying to proceed in forma pauperis or when the United States of America opens a case, the payment screen can by bypassed to complete the transaction. Additional information on making electronic payments can be located on the court's website. NY R USDCTWD ECF Procedures(2)(h)(i).

2. *Service requirements.* All pleadings and other papers shall be filed and served in accordance with the Federal Rules of Civil Procedure and the CM/ECF Administrative Procedures Guide (NY R USDCTWD ECF Procedures). NY R USDCTWD Civ Rule 5.1(a).

a. *Service; When required*

   i. *In general.* Unless the Federal Rules of Civil Procedure provide otherwise, each of the following papers must be served on every party:

- An order stating that service is required;
- A pleading filed after the original complaint, unless the court orders otherwise under FRCP 5(c) because there are numerous defendants;
- A discovery paper required to be served on a party, unless the court orders otherwise;
- A written motion, except one that may be heard ex parte; and
- A written notice, appearance, demand, or offer of judgment, or any similar paper. FRCP 5(a)(1).

   ii. *If a party fails to appear.* No service is required on a party who is in default for failing to appear. But a pleading that asserts a new claim for relief against such a party must be served on that party under FRCP 4. FRCP 5(a)(2).

   iii. *Seizing property.* If an action is begun by seizing property and no person is or need be named as a defendant, any service required before the filing of an appearance, answer, or claim must be made on the person who had custody or possession of the property when it was seized. FRCP 5(a)(3).

b. *Service; How made*

   i. *Serving an attorney.* If a party is represented by an attorney, service under FRCP 5 must be made on the attorney unless the court orders service on the party. FRCP 5(b)(1).

   ii. *Service in general.* A paper is served under FRCP 5 by:

- Handing it to the person;
- Leaving it: (1) at the person's office with a clerk or other person in charge or, if no one is in charge, in a conspicuous place in the office; or (2) if the person has no office or the office is closed, at the person's dwelling or usual place of abode with someone of suitable age and discretion who resides there;
- Mailing it to the person's last known address—in which event service is complete upon mailing;
- Leaving it with the court clerk if the person has no known address;
- Sending it by electronic means if the person consented in writing—in which event service is complete upon transmission, but is not effective if the serving party learns that it did not reach the person to be served; or
- Delivering it by any other means that the person consented to in writing—in which event service is complete when the person making service delivers it to the agency designated to make delivery. FRCP 5(b)(2).

   iii. *Service by overnight delivery.* All papers, other than a subpoena or a summons and complaint, may be served on counsel of record by overnight delivery service at the address designated by the attorney for that purpose, or if none is designated, at the attorney's last known address. Service by overnight delivery shall be complete upon deposit of the paper(s), enclosed in a properly addressed wrapper, into the custody of the overnight delivery service, prior to the latest time designated by the service for overnight delivery. NY R USDCTWD Civ Rule 5.1(g). "Overnight delivery service" means any delivery service which regularly accepts items for overnight delivery to any address within the Court's jurisdiction. NY R USDCTWD Civ Rule 5.1(g).

    iv. *Service of documents by electronic means*

- *Service on registered users.* Registered Users consent to the electronic service of all documents, and must make available an electronic mail address for service during the registration process. Upon the filing of a document by a party, a Notice of Electronic Filing, with a hyperlink to the filed document, will be automatically generated by the electronic filing system and sent via electronic mail to the e-mail addresses of all parties participating in the electronic filing system in the case. Electronic service of the Notice of Electronic Filing constitutes service of the filed document for all purposes of the Federal Rules of Civil Procedure and the Local Rules of Civil Procedure for the United States District Court for the Western District of New York. NY R USDCTWD ECF Procedures(2)(f)(i). The Notice of Electronic Filing effectuates service for all registered users and no certificate of service is required when all filers on an action are Registered Users. NY R USDCTWD ECF Procedures(2)(f)(iv).

- *Time limit for opening hyperlink.* The hyperlink to filed documents contained in the Notice of Electronic Filing must be opened within fifteen (15) days from the date the document was filed to provide registered users access to the document. The hyperlink expires after fifteen (15) days and users will be unable to access documents for free after that time. Filing Users are encouraged to check their e-mail frequently for notice of filed documents. NY R USDCTWD ECF Procedures(2)(f)(ii).

- *Service on exempted attorneys or pro se litigants who do not have permission to file electronically.* Attorneys granted an exemption from electronically filing documents in the System and pro se litigants who have not been granted permission to electronically file documents are entitled to a paper copy of any electronically filed pleading, document or order. The filing party must therefore provide the non-registered party with the pleading, document or order according to the Federal Rules of Civil Procedure. NY R USDCTWD ECF Procedures(2)(f)(iii).

- *E-mailing or faxing documents.* E-mailing or faxing a pleading or document to any party shall not constitute service of the pleading or document. NY R USDCTWD ECF Procedures(2)(f)(v).

    v. *Using court facilities.* If a local rule so authorizes, a party may use the court's transmission facilities to make service under FRCP 5(b)(2)(E). FRCP 5(b)(3).

  c. *Serving numerous defendants*

    i. *In general.* If an action involves an unusually large number of defendants, the court may, on motion or on its own, order that:

- Defendants' pleadings and replies to them need not be served on other defendants;

- Any crossclaim, counterclaim, avoidance, or affirmative defense in those pleadings and replies to them will be treated as denied or avoided by all other parties; and

- Filing any such pleading and serving it on the plaintiff constitutes notice of the pleading to all parties. FRCP 5(c)(1).

    ii. *Notifying parties.* A copy of every such order must be served on the parties as the court directs. FRCP 5(c)(2).

3. *Pro se actions.* For information on the requirements in pro se actions, refer to NY R USDCTWD Civ Rule 5.2.

4. *Individual judge practices.* Refer to the Miscellaneous section of this document for information on individual judge practices on filing and serving documents.

## G. Hearings

1. *Hearings, generally*

   a. *Oral argument.* Due process does not require that oral argument be permitted on a motion and, except as otherwise provided by local rule, the district court has discretion to determine whether it will decide the motion on the papers or hear argument by counsel (and perhaps receive evidence). FPP § 1190; F.D.I.C. v. Deglau, 207 F.3d 153 (3d Cir. 2000).

      i. The parties shall appear for oral argument on all motions they make returnable before a Judge on the scheduled return date for the motion. In its discretion, the Court may notify the parties that oral argument shall not be heard on any given motion. Thus, the parties should be prepared to have their motion papers serve as the sole method of argument. NY R USDCTWD Civ Rule 7(c).

   b. *Providing a regular schedule for oral hearings.* A court may establish regular times and places for oral hearings on motions. FRCP 78(a).

   c. *Providing for submission on briefs.* By rule or order, the court may provide for submitting and determining motions on briefs, without oral hearings. FRCP 78(b).

2. *Hearing on motion for preliminary injunction*

   a. *Consolidating the hearing with the trial on the merits.* Before or after beginning the hearing on a motion for a preliminary injunction, the court may advance the trial on the merits and consolidate it with the hearing. Even when consolidation is not ordered, evidence that is received on the motion and that would be admissible at trial becomes part of the trial record and need not be repeated at trial. But the court must preserve any party's right to a jury trial. FRCP 65(a)(2).

   b. *Expediting the hearing after temporary restraining order is issued without notice.* If the order is issued without notice, the motion for a preliminary injunction must be set for hearing at the earliest possible time, taking precedence over all other matters except hearings on older matters of the same character. At the hearing, the party who obtained the order must proceed with the motion; if the party does not, the court must dissolve the order. FRCP 65(b)(3).

3. *Individual judge practices.* Refer to the Miscellaneous section of this document for information on individual judge practices on hearings.

## H. Forms

### 1. Federal Motion for Preliminary Injunction Forms

   a. Declaration; In support of motion for preliminary injunction. AMJUR PP INJUNCTION § 38.

   b. Memorandum of points and authorities; In support of motion for preliminary injunction. AMJUR PP INJUNCTION § 39.

   c. Notice; Motion for preliminary injunction. AMJUR PP INJUNCTION § 40.

   d. Motion; For preliminary injunction. AMJUR PP INJUNCTION § 41.

   e. Motion; For preliminary injunction; On pleadings and other papers without evidentiary hearing or oral argument. AMJUR PP INJUNCTION § 43.

   f. Affidavit; In support of motion for preliminary injunction. AMJUR PP INJUNCTION § 52.

   g. Motion for preliminary injunction. 4A FEDFORMS § 5284.

   h. Motion enjoining use of information acquired from employment with plaintiff. 4A FEDFORMS § 5287.

   i. Motion enjoining interference with public access. 4A FEDFORMS § 5288.

   j. Motion enjoining collection of tax assessment. 4A FEDFORMS § 5289.

   k. Motion enjoining conducting election or certifying representative. 4A FEDFORMS § 5290.

   l. Motion enjoining preventing plaintiff's acting as teacher. 4A FEDFORMS § 5291.

   m. Motion enjoining interference with plaintiff's enforcement of judgment in related case. 4A FED-FORMS § 5292.

n. Motion for preliminary injunction in patent infringement action. 4A FEDFORMS § 5293.

o. Motion for preliminary injunction on basis of prayer of complaint and for setting hearing on motion. 4A FEDFORMS § 5294.

p. Notice of motion. 4A FEDFORMS § 5308.

q. Notice of motion and motion. 4A FEDFORMS § 5310.

r. Bond; To obtain preliminary injunction. FEDPROF § 1:701.

s. Opposition; To motion; General form. FEDPROF § 1:750.

t. Brief; Supporting or opposing motion. FEDPROF § 1:752.

u. Motion for temporary restraining order and preliminary injunction. GOLDLTGFMS § 13A:6.

v. Motion for preliminary injunction. GOLDLTGFMS § 13A:18.

w. Motion for preliminary injunction; Based upon pleadings and other papers without evidentiary hearing or oral argument. GOLDLTGFMS § 13A:19.

x. Motion for preliminary injunction; Supporting affidavit. GOLDLTGFMS § 13A:20.

y. Bond. GOLDLTGFMS § 19:2.

z. Bond; In support of injunction. GOLDLTGFMS § 19:3.

**2. Forms for the Western District of New York**

a. Certificate of service. NY R USDCTWD ECF Procedures(4a).

# I. Applicable Rules

1. *Federal rules*

a. Serving and filing pleadings and other papers. FRCP 5.

b. Constitutional challenge to a statute; Notice, certification, and intervention. FRCP 5.1.

c. Privacy protection for filings made with the court. FRCP 5.2.

d. Computing and extending time; Time for motion papers. FRCP 6.

e. Pleadings allowed; Form of motions and other papers. FRCP 7.

f. Disclosure statement. FRCP 7.1.

g. Form of pleadings. FRCP 10.

h. Signing pleadings, motions, and other papers; Representations to the court; Sanctions. FRCP 11.

i. Taking testimony. FRCP 43.

j. Injunctions and restraining orders. FRCP 65.

k. Proceedings against a surety. FRCP 65.1.

l. Hearing motions; Submission on briefs. FRCP 78.

2. *Local rules*

a. Title. NY R USDCTWD Civ Rule 1.1.

b. Filing and serving papers. NY R USDCTWD Civ Rule 5.1.

c. Motion practice. NY R USDCTWD Civ Rule 7.

d. Form of papers. NY R USDCTWD Civ Rule 10.

e. Sanctions. NY R USDCTWD Civ Rule 11.

f. Alternative dispute resolution and pretrial conferences. NY R USDCTWD Civ Rule 16.

g. Temporary restraining orders and preliminary injunctions. NY R USDCTWD Civ Rule 65.

h. Attorneys of record; Appearance and withdrawal. NY R USDCTWD Civ Rule 83.2.

i. Administrative procedures guide for electronic filing. NY R USDCTWD ECF Procedures.

    j.   Alternative dispute resolution plan. NY R USDCTWD ADR Plan.

**J. Miscellaneous**

**NOTE: Individual judges' rules may apply. For available judge-level information, refer to:**

DISTRICT JUDGE RICHARD J. ARCARA: NY R USDCTWD Arcara-Procedures.

DISTRICT JUDGE FRANK P. GERACI, JR.: NY R USDCTWD Geraci-Procedures.

DISTRICT JUDGE DAVID G. LARIMER: NY R USDCTWD Larimer-Procedures.

DISTRICT JUDGE CHARLES J. SIRAGUSA: NY R USDCTWD Siragusa-Procedures.

DISTRICT JUDGE WILLIAM M. SKRETNY: NY R USDCTWD Skretny--Procedures.

DISTRICT JUDGE MICHAEL A. TELESCA: NY R USDCTWD Telesca-Procedures.

DISTRICT JUDGE LAWRENCE J. VILARDO: NY R USDCTWD Vilardo-Procedures.

DISTRICT JUDGE ELIZABETH A. WOLFORD: NY R USDCTWD Wolford-Procedures.

MAGISTRATE JUDGE JONATHAN W. FELDMAN: NY R USDCTWD Feldman-Procedures.

MAGISTRATE JUDGE LESLIE G. FOSCHIO: NY R USDCTWD Foschio-Procedures; NY R USDCTWD Foschio-Depositions.

MAGISTRATE JUDGE JEREMIAH J. McCARTHY: NY R USDCTWD McCarthy-Procedures.

MAGISTRATE JUDGE MARIAN W. PAYSON: NY R USDCTWD Payson-Procedures.

MAGISTRATE JUDGE MICHAEL J. ROEMER: NY R USDCTWD Roemer-Procedures.

MAGISTRATE JUDGE H. KENNETH SCHROEDER, JR.: NY R USDCTWD Schroeder-Proc.

MAGISTRATE JUDGE HUGH B. SCOTT: NY R USDCTWD Scott-Procedures.

# Motions, Oppositions and Replies
# Motion to Dismiss for Failure to State a Claim

**Document Last Updated September 2016**

**A. Checklist**

  (I)  ❑  Matters to be considered by moving party

    (a)  ❑  Required documents

        (1)  ❑  Notice of motion and motion

        (2)  ❑  Memorandum of law

        (3)  ❑  Certificate of service

    (b)  ❑  Supplemental documents

        (1)  ❑  Pleading

        (2)  ❑  Notice of constitutional question

        (3)  ❑  Nongovernmental corporate disclosure statement

        (4)  ❑  Copies of authorities

        (5)  ❑  Proposed order

        (6)  ❑  Paper copy for date-stamping with self-addressed envelope

        (7)  ❑  Courtesy copies

    (c)  ❑  Timing

        (1)  ❑  Failure to state a claim upon which relief can be granted may be raised in any pleading allowed or ordered under FRCP 7(a); every defense to a claim for relief in any pleading must be asserted in the responsive pleading if one is required

    (2) ❑ A motion asserting any of the defenses in FRCP 12(b) must be made before pleading if a responsive pleading is allowed

    (3) ❑ Failure to state a claim upon which relief can be granted may be raised by a motion under FRCP 12(c); after the pleadings are closed—but early enough not to delay trial—a party may move for judgment on the pleadings

    (4) ❑ Failure to state a claim upon which relief can be granted may be raised at trial; if a pleading sets out a claim for relief that does not require a responsive pleading, an opposing party may assert at trial any defense to that claim

    (5) ❑ A written motion and notice of the hearing must be served at least fourteen (14) days before the time specified for the hearing, with the following exceptions: (i) when the motion may be heard ex parte; (ii) when the Federal Rules of Civil Procedure set a different time; or (iii) when a court order—which a party may, for good cause, apply for ex parte—sets a different time

    (6) ❑ Any affidavit supporting a motion must be served with the motion

(II) ❑ Matters to be considered by opposing party

    (a) ❑ Required documents

        (1) ❑ Opposition

        (2) ❑ Answering memorandum

        (3) ❑ Certificate of service

    (b) ❑ Supplemental documents

        (1) ❑ Pleading

        (2) ❑ Notice of constitutional question

        (3) ❑ Copies of authorities

        (4) ❑ Paper copy for date-stamping with self-addressed envelope

        (5) ❑ Courtesy copies

    (c) ❑ Timing

        (1) ❑ After a motion is filed, the court may issue an order setting deadlines for filing and service of opposing papers; if the court does not set deadlines by order, the opposing party shall have fourteen (14) days after service of the motion to file and serve responding papers

        (2) ❑ Except as FRCP 59(c) provides otherwise, any opposing affidavit must be served at least seven (7) days before the hearing, unless the court permits service at another time

## B. Timing

1. *Motion to dismiss for failure to state a claim*

    a. *In a pleading under FRCP 7(a).* Failure to state a claim upon which relief can be granted may be raised in any pleading allowed or ordered under FRCP 7(a). FRCP 12(h)(2)(A).

        i. *In a responsive pleading.* Every defense to a claim for relief in any pleading must be asserted in the responsive pleading if one is required. FRCP 12(b).

    b. *By motion.* A motion asserting any of the defenses in FRCP 12(b) must be made before pleading if a responsive pleading is allowed. FRCP 12(b). Although FRCP 12(b) encourages the responsive pleader to file a motion to dismiss before filing the answer, nothing in FRCP 12 prohibits the filing of a motion to dismiss with the answer. An untimely motion to dismiss may be considered if the defense asserted in the motion was previously raised in the responsive pleading. FEDPROC § 62:427.

    c. *By motion under FRCP 12(c).* Failure to state a claim upon which relief can be granted may be raised by a motion under FRCP 12(c). FRCP 12(h)(2)(B). After the pleadings are closed—but early enough not to delay trial—a party may move for judgment on the pleadings. FRCP 12(c).

    d.   *At trial.* Failure to state a claim upon which relief can be granted may be raised at trial. FRCP 12(h)(2)(C). If a pleading sets out a claim for relief that does not require a responsive pleading, an opposing party may assert at trial any defense to that claim. FRCP 12(b).

2.   *Timing of motions, generally*

    a.   *Motion and notice of hearing.* A written motion and notice of the hearing must be served at least fourteen (14) days before the time specified for the hearing, with the following exceptions:

        i.   When the motion may be heard ex parte;

        ii.   When the Federal Rules of Civil Procedure set a different time; or

        iii.   When a court order—which a party may, for good cause, apply for ex parte—sets a different time. FRCP 6(c)(1).

    b.   *Supporting affidavit.* Any affidavit supporting a motion must be served with the motion. FRCP 6(c)(2).

3.   *Timing of opposing papers.* After a motion is filed, the Court may issue an order setting deadlines for filing and service of opposing papers. NY R USDCTWD Civ Rule 7(b)(1). If the Court does not set deadlines by order, the following schedule shall apply: the opposing party shall have fourteen (14) days after service of the motion to file and serve responding papers. NY R USDCTWD Civ Rule 7(b)(2)(B).

    a.   *Opposing affidavit.* Except as FRCP 59(c) provides otherwise, any opposing affidavit must be served at least seven (7) days before the hearing, unless the court permits service at another time. FRCP 6(c)(2).

4.   *Timing of reply papers.* Where the respondent files an answering affidavit setting up a new matter, the moving party ordinarily is allowed a reasonable time to file a reply affidavit since failure to deny the new matter by affidavit may operate as an admission of its truth. AMJUR MOTIONS § 25.

    a.   *Reply papers.* After a motion is filed, the Court may issue an order setting deadlines. . .for filing and service of reply papers if the moving party has stated an intent to reply. NY R USDCTWD Civ Rule 7(b)(1). If the Court does not set deadlines by order, the following schedule shall apply: the moving party shall have seven (7) days after service of the responding papers to file and serve reply papers. NY R USDCTWD Civ Rule 7(b)(2)(B).

    b.   *Reply memorandum.* The moving party may file a reply memorandum, but is not required to do so. NY R USDCTWD Civ Rule 7(a)(2)(A).

5.   *Motion for an expedited hearing.* A party seeking to shorten the schedule prescribed in NY R USDCTWD Civ Rule 7(b) must make a separate motion for an expedited hearing, setting forth the reasons why an expedited hearing is required. NY R USDCTWD Civ Rule 7(d)(1). For more information, refer to NY R USDCTWD Civ Rule 7(d)(1).

6.   *Effect of a FRCP 12 motion on the time to serve a responsive pleading.* Unless the court sets a different time, serving a motion under FRCP 12 alters the periods in FRCP 12(a) as follows:

    a.   If the court denies the motion or postpones its disposition until trial, the responsive pleading must be served within fourteen (14) days after notice of the court's action; or

    b.   If the court grants a motion for a more definite statement, the responsive pleading must be served within fourteen (14) days after the more definite statement is served. FRCP 12(a)(4).

7.   *Computation of time*

    a.   *Computing time.* FRCP 6 applies in computing any time period specified in the Federal Rules of Civil Procedure, in any local rule or court order, or in any statute that does not specify a method of computing time. FRCP 6(a).

        i.   *Period stated in days or a longer unit.* When the period is stated in days or a longer unit of time:

          • Exclude the day of the event that triggers the period;

          • Count every day, including intermediate Saturdays, Sundays, and legal holidays; and

          • Include the last day of the period, but if the last day is a Saturday, Sunday, or legal holiday, the period continues to run until the end of the next day that is not a Saturday, Sunday, or legal holiday. FRCP 6(a)(1).

ii.  *Period stated in hours.* When the period is stated in hours:

- Begin counting immediately on the occurrence of the event that triggers the period;

- Count every hour, including hours during intermediate Saturdays, Sundays, and legal holidays; and

- If the period would end on a Saturday, Sunday, or legal holiday, the period continues to run until the same time on the next day that is not a Saturday, Sunday, or legal holiday. FRCP 6(a)(2).

iii.  *Inaccessibility of the clerk's office.* Unless the court orders otherwise, if the clerk's office is inaccessible:

- On the last day for filing under FRCP 6(a)(1), then the time for filing is extended to the first accessible day that is not a Saturday, Sunday, or legal holiday; or

- During the last hour for filing under FRCP 6(a)(2), then the time for filing is extended to the same time on the first accessible day that is not a Saturday, Sunday, or legal holiday. FRCP 6(a)(3).

iv.  *"Last day" defined.* Unless a different time is set by a statute, local rule, or court order, the last day ends:

- For electronic filing, at midnight in the court's time zone; and

- For filing by other means, when the clerk's office is scheduled to close. FRCP 6(a)(4).

v.  *"Next day" defined.* The "next day" is determined by continuing to count forward when the period is measured after an event and backward when measured before an event. FRCP 6(a)(5).

vi.  *"Legal holiday" defined.* "Legal holiday" means:

- The day set aside by statute for observing New Year's Day, Martin Luther King Jr.'s Birthday, Washington's Birthday, Memorial Day, Independence Day, Labor Day, Columbus Day, Veterans' Day, Thanksgiving Day, or Christmas Day;

- Any day declared a holiday by the President or Congress; and

- For periods that are measured after an event, any other day declared a holiday by the state where the district court is located. FRCP 6(a)(6).

b.  *Computation of electronic filing deadlines.* A document will be deemed timely filed if filed prior to midnight Eastern Time, unless otherwise ordered by the Court. A document will be considered untimely if filed thereafter. When a Court order requires that a document be filed on a weekend or holiday, the document may be filed by close of business the next business day without further application to the Court. NY R USDCTWD ECF Procedures(2)(e)(i). A document filed electronically is deemed filed on the date and time stated on the Notice of Electronic Filing. NY R USDCTWD ECF Procedures(2)(e)(ii).

i.  *System availability.* Although parties may file documents electronically twenty-four (24) hours a day, registered users are strongly encouraged to file all documents during normal working hours of the Clerk's Office (8:30 a.m. to 5:00 p.m. Eastern Time). NY R USDCTWD ECF Procedures(2)(t)(i).

ii.  *Technical failures.* A Filing User whose filing is made untimely as a result of a technical failure must seek appropriate relief from the Court. NY R USDCTWD ECF Procedures(2)(u)(i).

c.  *Extending time*

i.  *In general.* When an act may or must be done within a specified time, the court may, for good cause, extend the time:

- With or without motion or notice if the court acts, or if a request is made, before the original time or its extension expires; or

- On motion made after the time has expired if the party failed to act because of excusable neglect. FRCP 6(b)(1).

   ii. *Exceptions.* A court must not extend the time to act under FRCP 50(b), FRCP 50(d), FRCP 52(b), FRCP 59(b), FRCP 59(d), FRCP 59(e), and FRCP 60(b). FRCP 6(b)(2).

   iii. Refer to the United States District Court for the Western District of New York KeyRules Motion for Continuance/Extension of Time document for more information on extending time.

  d. *Additional time after certain kinds of service.* When a party may or must act within a specified time after service and service is made under FRCP 5(b)(2)(C), FRCP 5(b)(2)(D), FRCP 5(b)(2)(E), or FRCP 5(b)(2)(F), three (3) days are added after the period would otherwise expire under FRCP 6(a). FRCP 6(d).

   i. *Service by overnight delivery.* Where a period of time prescribed by either the Federal Rules of Civil Procedure or the Local Rules of Civil Procedure for the United States District Court for the Western District of New York is measured from the service of a paper and service is by overnight delivery, one (1) business day shall be added to the prescribed period. NY R USDCTWD Civ Rule 5.1(g).

8. *Individual judge practices.* Refer to the Miscellaneous section of this document for information on individual judge practices on timing of documents.

## C. General Requirements

1. *Motions, generally*

  a. *Requirements.* A request for a court order must be made by motion. The motion must:

   i. Be in writing unless made during a hearing or trial;

   ii. State with particularity the grounds for seeking the order; and

   iii. State the relief sought. FRCP 7(b)(1).

  b. *Notice of motion.* A party interested in resisting the relief sought by a motion has a right to notice thereof, and an opportunity to be heard. AMJUR MOTIONS § 12.

   i. In addition to statutory or court rule provisions requiring notice of a motion—the purpose of such a notice requirement having been said to be to prevent a party from being prejudicially surprised by a motion—principles of natural justice dictate that an adverse party generally must be given notice that a motion will be presented to the court. AMJUR MOTIONS § 12.

   ii. "Notice," in this regard, means reasonable notice, including a meaningful opportunity to prepare and to defend against allegations of a motion. AMJUR MOTIONS § 12.

  c. *Writing requirement.* The writing requirement is intended to insure that the adverse parties are informed and have a record of both the motion's pendency and the grounds on which the movant seeks an order. FPP § 1191; Feldberg v. Quechee Lakes Corp., 463 F.3d 195 (2d Cir. 2006).

   i. It is sufficient "if the motion is stated in a written notice of the hearing of the motion." FPP § 1191.

  d. *Particularity requirement.* The particularity requirement insures that the opposing parties will have notice of their opponent's contentions. FEDPROC § 62:364; Goodman v. 1973 26 Foot Trojan Vessel, Arkansas Registration No. AR1439SN, 859 F.2d 71, 12 Fed.R.Serv.3d 645 (8th Cir. 1988). That requirement ensures that notice of the basis for the motion is provided to the court and to the opposing party so as to avoid prejudice, provide the opponent with a meaningful opportunity to respond, and provide the court with enough information to process the motion correctly. FEDPROC § 62:364; Andreas v. Volkswagen of America, Inc., 336 F.3d 789, 56 Fed.R.Serv.3d 6 (8th Cir. 2003).

   i. Reasonable specification of the grounds for a motion is sufficient. However, where a movant fails to state even one ground for granting the motion in question, the movant has failed to meet the minimal standard of "reasonable specification." FEDPROC § 62:364; Martinez v. Trainor, 556 F.2d 818, 23 Fed.R.Serv.2d 403 (7th Cir. 1977).

   ii. The court may excuse the failure to comply with the particularity requirement if it is inadvertent, and where no prejudice is shown by the opposing party. FEDPROC § 62:364.

2. *Motion to dismiss for failure to state a claim.* A party may assert the defense of failure to state a claim upon which relief can be granted by motion. FRCP 12(b)(6). The motion under FRCP 12(b)(6) is available to test a claim for relief in any pleading, whether it be in the plaintiff's original complaint, a defendant's counterclaim, a defendant's cross-claim or counterclaim thereto, or a third-party claim or any other FRCP 14 claim. Most commonly, of course, a FRCP 12(b)(6) motion is directed against the plaintiff's complaint. FPP § 1356.

   a. *Applicable standard.* The FRCP 12(b)(6) motion is used to test the sufficiency of the complaint. FEDPROC § 62:461; Petruska v. Gannon University, 462 F.3d 294, 212 Ed.Law.Rep. 598 (3d Cir. 2006). In this regard, the applicable standard is stated in FRCP 8(a)(2), which requires that a pleading setting forth a claim for relief contain a short and plain statement of the claim showing that the pleader is entitled to relief. Thus, a complaint must set forth sufficient information to suggest that there is some recognized legal theory upon which relief can be granted. FEDPROC § 62:461. Only when the plaintiff's complaint fails to meet this liberal pleading standard is it subject to dismissal under FRCP 12(b)(6). FPP § 1356.

      i. In order to withstand a motion to dismiss filed under FRCP 12(b)(6) in response to claims understood to raise a high risk of abusive litigation, addressed by FRCP 9(b), a plaintiff must state factual allegations with greater particularity than that required by FRCP 8. FEDPROC § 62:470; Bell Atlantic Corp. v. Twombly, 550 U.S. 544, 127 S.Ct. 1955, 167 L.Ed.2d 929, 68 Fed.R.Serv.3d 661 (2007).

      ii. FRCP 12(b)(6) motions are looked on with disfavor by the courts, and are granted sparingly and with care. FEDPROC § 62:464. Even if it is doubtful that the plaintiff would ultimately prevail, if the plaintiff colorably states facts which, if proven, would entitle him or her to relief, a motion to dismiss for failure to state a claim should not be granted. FEDPROC § 62:464.

   b. *Construction of allegations of complaint (or other pleading).* In considering a FRCP 12(b)(6) motion to dismiss, the complaint is liberally construed and is viewed in the light most favorable to the plaintiff. FEDPROC § 62:467; Bell Atlantic Corp. v. Twombly, 550 U.S. 544, 127 S.Ct. 1955, 167 L.Ed.2d 929, 68 Fed.R.Serv.3d 661 (2007).

      i. On a motion to dismiss, a federal court presumes that general allegations embrace those specific facts that are necessary to support the claim. FEDPROC § 62:467; Steel Co. v. Citizens for a Better Environment, 523 U.S. 83, 118 S.Ct. 1003, 140 L.Ed.2d 210 (1998).

      ii. In addition, the well-pleaded allegations of fact contained in the complaint and every inference fairly deducible therefrom are accepted as true for purposes of the motion, including facts alleged on information and belief. FEDPROC § 62:467; Bell Atlantic Corp. v. Twombly, 550 U.S. 544, 127 S.Ct. 1955, 167 L.Ed.2d 929, 68 Fed.R.Serv.3d 661 (2007); Tellabs, Inc. v. Makor Issues & Rights, Ltd., 551 U.S. 308, 127 S.Ct. 2499, 168 L.Ed.2d 179 (2007).

      iii. However, the court will not accept as true the plaintiff's bare statements of opinions, conclusory allegations, and unwarranted inferences of fact. FEDPROC § 62:467; Leopoldo Fontanillas, Inc. v. Luis Ayala Colon Sucesores, Inc., 283 F.Supp.2d 579 (D.P.R. 2003); Hopkins v. Women's Div., General Bd. of Global Ministries, 238 F.Supp.2d 174 (D.D.C. 2002). Nor will the court accept as true facts which are legally impossible, facts which the court can take judicial notice of as being other than as alleged by the plaintiff, or facts which by the record or by a document attached to the complaint appear to be unfounded. FEDPROC § 62:467; Cohen v. U.S., 129 F.2d 733 (8th Cir. 1942); Henthorn v. Department of Navy, 29 F.3d 682, 29 Fed.R.Serv.3d 1007 (D.C. Cir. 1994).

   c. *Affirmative defenses.* With some exception, it is generally agreed that affirmative defenses can be raised by a FRCP 12(b)(6) motion to dismiss. FEDPROC § 62:471; McCready v. eBay, Inc., 453 F.3d 882 (7th Cir. 2006). However, in order for these defenses to be raised on a FRCP 12(b)(6) motion to dismiss, the complaint must clearly show on its face that the affirmative defense is applicable and bars the action. FEDPROC § 62:471; In re Colonial Mortgage Bankers Corp., 324 F.3d 12 (1st Cir. 2003). Thus, FRCP 12(b)(6) motions may be used to raise the affirmative defenses of: (1) statute of limitations; (2) statute of frauds; (3) res judicata; (4) collateral estoppel; (5) release; (6) waiver; (7) estoppel; (8) sovereign immunity; (9) illegality; and (10) contributory negligence. FEDPROC § 62:471.

   d. *Joining motions*

      i. *Right to join.* A motion under FRCP 12 may be joined with any other motion allowed by FRCP 12. FRCP 12(g)(1).

      ii. *Limitation on further motions.* Except as provided in FRCP 12(h)(2) or FRCP 12(h)(3), a party that makes a motion under FRCP 12 must not make another motion under FRCP 12 raising a defense or objection that was available to the party but omitted from its earlier motion. FRCP 12(g)(2).

   e. *Waiving and preserving certain defenses.* No defense or objection is waived by joining it with one or more other defenses or objections in a responsive pleading or in a motion. FRCP 12(b).

      i. *When some are waived.* A party waives any defense listed in FRCP 12(b)(2) through FRCP 12(b)(5) by:

         • Omitting it from a motion in the circumstances described in FRCP 12(g)(2); or

         • Failing to either: (1) make it by motion under FRCP 12; or (2) include it in a responsive pleading or in an amendment allowed by FRCP 15(a)(1) as a matter of course. FRCP 12(h)(1).

      ii. *When to raise others.* Failure to state a claim upon which relief can be granted, to join a person required by FRCP 19(b), or to state a legal defense to a claim may be raised:

         • In any pleading allowed or ordered under FRCP 7(a);

         • By a motion under FRCP 12(c); or

         • At trial. FRCP 12(h)(2).

      iii. *Lack of subject matter jurisdiction.* If the court determines at any time that it lacks subject-matter jurisdiction, the court must dismiss the action. FRCP 12(h)(3).

3. *Opposing papers.* The Federal Rules of Civil Procedure do not require any formal answer, return, or reply to a motion, except where the Federal Rules of Civil Procedure or local rules may require affidavits, memoranda, or other papers to be filed in opposition to a motion. Such papers are simply to apprise the court of such opposition and the grounds of that opposition. FEDPROC § 62:359.

   a. *Effect of failure to respond to motion.* Although in the absence of statutory provision or court rule, a motion ordinarily does not require a written answer, when a party files a motion and the opposing party fails to respond, the court may construe such failure to respond as nonopposition to the motion or an admission that the motion was meritorious, may take the facts alleged in the motion as true—the rule in some jurisdictions being that the failure to respond to a fact set forth in a motion is deemed an admission—and may grant the motion if the relief requested appears to be justified. AMJUR MOTIONS § 28.

   b. *Assent or no opposition not determinative.* However, a motion will not be granted automatically simply because an "assent" or a notation of "no opposition" has been filed; federal judges frequently deny motions that have been assented to when it is thought that justice so dictates. FPP § 1190.

   c. *Responsive pleading inappropriate as response to motion.* An attempt to answer or oppose a motion with a responsive pleading usually is not appropriate. FPP § 1190.

4. *Reply papers.* A moving party may be required or permitted to prepare papers in addition to his original motion papers. AMJUR MOTIONS § 25. Papers answering or replying to opposing papers may be appropriate, in the interests of justice, where it appears there is a substantial reason for allowing a reply. Thus, a court may accept reply papers where a party demonstrates that the papers to which it seeks to file a reply raise new issues that are material to the disposition of the question before the court, or where the court determines, sua sponte, that it wishes further briefing of an issue raised in those papers and orders the submission of additional papers. FEDPROC § 62:360.

   a. *Function of reply papers.* The function of a reply affidavit is to answer the arguments made in opposition to the position taken by the movant and not to permit the movant to introduce new arguments in support of the motion. AMJUR MOTIONS § 25.

   b. *Issues raised for the first time in a reply document.* However, the view has been followed in some jurisdictions, that as a matter of judicial economy, where there is no prejudice and where the issues could be raised simply by filing a motion to dismiss, the trial court has discretion to consider arguments raised for the first time in a reply memorandum, and that a trial court may grant a motion to strike issues raised for the first time in a reply memorandum. AMJUR MOTIONS § 26.

5. *Sur-reply.* Absent permission of the Judge hearing the motion, sur-reply papers are not permitted. NY R USDCTWD Civ Rule 7(a)(6).

6. *Motion to settle an order.* When counsel are unable to agree on the form of a proposed order, the prevailing party may move, upon seven (7) days notice to all parties, to settle the order. The Court may award costs and attorney's fees against an attorney if it determines that the attorney's unreasonable conduct necessitated bringing the motion. NY R USDCTWD Civ Rule 7(d)(2).

7. *Notice of appearance.* No notice of appearance is required of an attorney whose name and address appear at the end of a complaint, notice of removal, pre-answer motion, or answer. In all other circumstances, an attorney appearing for a party in a civil case shall promptly file a written notice of appearance. NY R USDCTWD Civ Rule 83.2(b). For more information on appearances and withdrawals, refer to NY R USDCTWD Civ Rule 83.2.

8. *Related cases.* Each attorney appearing in a civil case has a continuing duty to promptly notify the Clerk of Court when the attorney has reason to believe that said case is related to some other pending civil or criminal action(s) such that their assignment to the same Judge would avoid unnecessary duplication of judicial effort. As soon as the attorney becomes aware of such a relationship, the attorney shall notify the Clerk of Court by letter of the relevant facts, and the Clerk of Court will transmit that notification to the Judges to whom the cases have been assigned. NY R USDCTWD Civ Rule 5.1(e).

9. *Alternative dispute resolution (ADR).* This Court has adopted an Alternative Dispute Resolution Plan ("ADR"), as implemented by Standing Order (NY R USDCTWD ADR Plan), under which certain civil cases are referred automatically to ADR upon filing. NY R USDCTWD Civ Rule 16(a). The United States District Court for the Western District of New York (the "Court") adopted the ADR Plan on January 1, 2006 (the "Effective Date"), to make available to civil litigants court-administered ADR interventions and processes designed to provide quicker, less expensive and potentially more satisfying alternatives to continuing litigation, without impairing the quality of justice or the right to trial. NY R USDCTWD ADR Plan(1)(1.2)(A).

   a. *Scope.* This ADR Plan (NY R USDCTWD ADR Plan) applies to civil actions pending or commenced on and after the Effective Date, except as otherwise indicated in NY R USDCTWD ADR Plan. The ADR Plan supplements the Local Rules of Civil Procedure for the United States District Court for the Western District of New York, which shall remain in full effect for all cases. NY R USDCTWD ADR Plan(1)(1.2)(B).

   b. *Referral to ADR*

      i. *New cases.* All civil cases filed on and after the Effective Date of the ADR Plan shall be referred automatically for ADR. NY R USDCTWD ADR Plan(2)(2.1)(A). Notice of the ADR requirements will be provided to all parties immediately upon the filing of a complaint and answer or a notice of removal; NY R USDCTWD ADR Plan(2)(2.1)(A); NY R USDCTWD Civ Rule 16(a). ADR intervention will be scheduled at the conference held pursuant to Local Rule of Civil Procedure 16.1. NY R USDCTWD ADR Plan(2)(2.1)(A). [Editor's note: the reference to Local Rule of Civil Procedure 16.1 is likely meant to be a reference to NY R USDCTWD Civ Rule 16(b)].

         • Litigants in cases not referred automatically to ADR must consider possible agreement to the use of an ADR process. NY R USDCTWD Civ Rule 16(a).

         • For a list of exemptions from automatic referral, refer to NY R USDCTWD ADR Plan(2)(2.1)(A).

      ii. *Pending cases.* The assigned Judge on any pending civil case may, sua sponte or with status conference, issue an order referring the case for ADR. NY R USDCTWD ADR Plan(2)(2.1)(B); NY R USDCTWD Civ Rule 16(a). The order shall specify a date on which the ADR intervention is to be completed. NY R USDCTWD ADR Plan(2)(2.1)(B).

iii. *Stipulation.* A case may be referred for ADR by stipulation of all parties. Stipulations shall be filed and shall designate the specific ADR intervention the parties have selected, the time frame within which the ADR process will be completed and the selected Neutral. Stipulations are presumed acceptable unless the assigned Judge determines that the interests of justice are not served. NY R USDCTWD ADR Plan(2)(2.1)(C).

iv. *Relief from ADR referral*

- *Opting out motions.* Any party may file, with the assigned Judge for that case, a motion to opt out of, or for relief from, ADR. NY R USDCTWD ADR Plan(2)(2.2)(A).

- *Motion.* Opting Out Motions must be made within fourteen (14) days from (1) the date of the first discovery conference under Local Rule 16.1 in new cases, or (2) the date of a sua sponte ADR Referral Order in pending cases. NY R USDCTWD ADR Plan(2)(2.2)(B). [Editor's note: the reference to Local Rule 16.1 is likely meant to be a reference to NY R USDCTWD Civ Rule 16(b)].

- *Criteria.* Opting Out Motions shall be granted only for "good cause" shown. Inconvenience, travel costs, attorney fees or other costs shall not constitute "good cause." A party seeking relief from ADR must set forth the reasons why ADR has no reasonable chance of being productive. NY R USDCTWD ADR Plan(2)(2.2)(C).

- *Judicial initiative.* The assigned Judge may, sua sponte, exempt any case from the Court's ADR Plan. NY R USDCTWD ADR Plan(2)(2.2)(D).

c. *ADR interventions*

i. *Options.* It is expected that cases referred for ADR will proceed to Mediation. However, the following options are also available upon the stipulation of all parties:

- Neutral Evaluation;
- Mini Summary Trial;
- Arbitration (Binding and Non-Binding);
- Case Valuation; and
- Settlement Week, when scheduled by the Court. NY R USDCTWD ADR Plan(4)(4.1)(A).

ii. *Timing.* Timing is specific to the intervention and process chosen, as set forth in the corresponding sections in NY R USDCTWD ADR Plan. NY R USDCTWD ADR Plan(4)(4.1)(B).

iii. *Scheduling.* The referral of a case to ADR does not delay or defer other dates established in the Scheduling Order and has no effect on the scheduled progress of the case toward trial. NY R USDCTWD ADR Plan(4)(4.1)(C).

d. *Selecting an ADR intervention*

i. *New cases.* Prior to the Local Rule 16.1 scheduling conference, counsel and any unrepresented parties shall confer about ADR as part of their discussion of "the possibilities for a prompt settlement or resolution of the case" pursuant to FRCP 26(f). Unless the parties agree to a different intervention, it is presumed that they will participate in mediation. [Editor's note: the reference to Local Rule 16.1 is likely meant to be a reference to NY R USDCTWD Civ Rule 16(b)].

ii. *Pending cases.* In pending cases, all sua sponte referrals will be to mediation. Should the parties agree that a different ADR intervention is more appropriate to their case, they may submit a stipulation designating the specific ADR intervention selected, the time frame within which the ADR process will be completed and the identity of the Neutral. Stipulations must be filed within fourteen (14) days from the date of the ADR Referral Order and are presumed acceptable unless the assigned Judge determines that the interests of justice are not served. NY R USDCTWD ADR Plan(4)(4.2)(B).

e. For more information on alternative dispute resolution (ADR), refer to NY R USDCTWD ADR Plan.

10. *Sanctions.* Failure of counsel for any party, or a party proceeding pro se, to appear before the Court at a

conference, to complete the necessary preparations, or to be prepared to proceed to trial at the set time may be considered an abandonment of the case or a failure to prosecute or defend diligently. An appropriate order for sanctions may be entered against the defaulting party with respect to either a specific issue or the entire case. NY R USDCTWD Civ Rule 11(a). For more information, refer to NY R USDCTWD Civ Rule 11.

11. *Pro se actions.* For information on the requirements in pro se actions, refer to NY R USDCTWD Civ Rule 5.2.

12. *Individual judge practices.* Refer to the Miscellaneous section of this document for information on individual judge practices on general requirements for documents.

## D. Documents

1. *Documents for moving party*

   a. *Required documents*

      i. *Notice of motion and motion.* A notice of motion is required for all motions, and must state: the relief sought, the grounds for the request, the papers submitted in support, and the return date for the motion, if known. A moving party who intends to file and serve reply papers must so state in the notice of motion. NY R USDCTWD Civ Rule 7(a)(1). Refer to the General Requirements section of this document for information on the notice of motion and motion.

      ii. *Memorandum of law.* Absent leave of Court or as otherwise specified, upon any motion filed pursuant to FRCP 12, FRCP 56 or FRCP 65(a), the moving party shall file and serve a memorandum of law. Failure to comply with this requirement may constitute grounds for resolving the motion against the non-complying party. NY R USDCTWD Civ Rule 7(a)(2)(A). Refer to the Format section of this document for the formatting requirements for memoranda of law.

      iii. *Certificate of service.* FRCP 5(d) requires that the person making service under FRCP 5 certify that service has been effected. FRCP 5(Advisory Committee Notes). Having such information on file may be useful for many purposes, including proof of service if an issue arises concerning the effectiveness of the service. FRCP 5(Advisory Committee Notes). The Notice of Electronic Filing effectuates service for all registered users and no certificate of service is required when all filers on an action are Registered Users. The following exemptions require a certificate of service to be filed:

         • When a document is manually filed, a certificate of service must be filed stating the manner in which service or notice was accomplished on each party so entitled. NY R USDCTWD ECF Procedures(2)(f)(iv).

         • When a pro se filer (who isn't authorized to electronically file documents) is a party, a certificate of service must be filed stating the manner in which service or notice was accomplished on the pro se party. The Notice of Electronic Filing effectuates service for the Registered Users in this situation and it is not necessary to note service on those parties. A non-registered pro se filer is required to file certificates of service on all documents they file. NY R USDCTWD ECF Procedures(2)(f)(iv).

         • If an attorney is exempt from electronic service, a certificate of service must be filed stating the manner in which service or notice was accomplished on the exempt attorney. The Notice of Electronic Filing effectuates service for the Registered Users in this situation and it is not necessary to note service on those parties. NY R USDCTWD ECF Procedures(2)(f)(iv).

   b. *Supplemental documents*

      i. *Pleading.* As a general rule, the court may only consider the pleading which is attacked by a FRCP 12(b)(6) motion in determining its sufficiency. FEDPROC § 62:466; Armengau v. Cline, 7 Fed.Appx. 336 (6th Cir. 2001). The plaintiff is not entitled to discovery to obtain information relevant to the motion, and the court is not permitted to look at matters outside the record.

FEDPROC § 62:466; Cooperativa de Ahorro y Credito Aguada v. Kidder, Peabody & Co., 993 F.2d 269, 37 Fed.R.Evid.Serv. 904, 25 Fed.R.Serv.3d 982 (1st Cir. 1993).

- *Motion treated as one for summary judgment.* If, on a motion under FRCP 12(b)(6) or FRCP 12(c), matters outside the pleadings are presented to and not excluded by the court, the motion must be treated as one for summary judgment under FRCP 56. All parties must be given a reasonable opportunity to present all the material that is pertinent to the motion. FRCP 12(d).

- *Documents attached to pleadings.* However, the court may consider documents which are attached to or submitted with the complaint, as well as legal arguments presented in memorandums or briefs and arguments of counsel. FEDPROC § 62:466; Tellabs, Inc. v. Makor Issues & Rights, Ltd., 551 U.S. 308, 127 S.Ct. 2499, 168 L.Ed.2d 179 (2007); E.E.O.C. v. Ohio Edison Co., 7 F.3d 541 (6th Cir. 1993). Documents that the defendant attaches to the motion to dismiss are considered part of the pleadings if they are referred to in the plaintiff's complaint and are central to the claim, and as such may be considered by the court. FEDPROC § 62:466; Hoffman-Pugh v. Ramsey, 312 F.3d 1222 (11th Cir. 2002).

ii. *Notice of constitutional question.* A party that files a pleading, written motion, or other paper drawing into question the constitutionality of a federal or state statute must promptly:

- *File notice.* File a notice of constitutional question stating the question and identifying the paper that raises it, if: (1) a federal statute is questioned and the parties do not include the United States, one of its agencies, or one of its officers or employees in an official capacity; or (2) a state statute is questioned and the parties do not include the state, one of its agencies, or one of its officers or employees in an official capacity; and

- *Serve notice.* Serve the notice and paper on the Attorney General of the United States if a federal statute is questioned—or on the state attorney general if a state statute is questioned—either by certified or registered mail or by sending it to an electronic address designated by the attorney general for this purpose. FRCP 5.1(a).

- *No forfeiture.* A party's failure to file and serve the notice, or the court's failure to certify, does not forfeit a constitutional claim or defense that is otherwise timely asserted. FRCP 5.1(d).

iii. *Nongovernmental corporate disclosure statement*

- *Contents.* A nongovernmental corporate party must file two (2) copies of a disclosure statement that: (1) identifies any parent corporation and any publicly held corporation owning ten percent (10%) or more of its stock; or (2) states that there is no such corporation. FRCP 7.1(a).

- *Time to file; Supplemental filing.* A party must: (1) file the disclosure statement with its first appearance, pleading, petition, motion, response, or other request addressed to the court; and (2) promptly file a supplemental statement if any required information changes. FRCP 7.1(b).

iv. *Copies of authorities.* In cases involving a pro se litigant, counsel shall, when serving a memorandum of law (or other submissions to the Court), provide the pro se litigant (but not other counsel or the Court) with printed copies of decisions cited therein that are unreported or reported exclusively on computerized databases. NY R USDCTWD Civ Rule 7(a)(8).

v. *Proposed order.* All proposed orders must be submitted in a format compatible with WordPerfect or Microsoft Word format, which is a "Save As" option in most word processing software. Judges will not accept proposed orders in PDF format. NY R USDCTWD ECF Procedures(2)(j)(ii). Proposed orders should be attached to an Internet e-mail sent to the e-mail address of the assigned judge. NY R USDCTWD ECF Procedures(2)(j)(i). For the list of email addresses for the judges, refer to NY R USDCTWD ECF Procedures(2)(j)(i).

vi. *Paper copy for date-stamping with self-addressed envelope.* Parties requesting date-stamped copies of filed documents must provide a paper copy for date-stamping, and a self-addressed, adequately-sized envelope with proper postage affixed. NY R USDCTWD Civ Rule 5.1(d).

vii. *Courtesy copies.* The Court may, in its discretion, request courtesy copies on any other motion. NY R USDCTWD Civ Rule 7(a)(7). Courtesy copies of certain documents may be required. Filers should refer to the "Judge Preferences" published on the Court's website. NY R USDCTWD ECF Procedures(2)(a)(iii).

2. *Documents for opposing party*

   a. *Required documents*

      i. *Opposition.* Refer to the General Requirements section of this document for information on the opposing papers.

      ii. *Answering memorandum.* Absent leave of Court or as otherwise specified, upon any motion filed pursuant to FRCP 12, FRCP 56 or FRCP 65(a). . .the opposing party shall file and serve an answering memorandum. Failure to comply with this requirement may constitute grounds for resolving the motion against the non-complying party. NY R USDCTWD Civ Rule 7(a)(2)(A). Refer to the Format section of this document for the formatting requirements for memoranda of law.

      iii. *Certificate of service.* FRCP 5(d) requires that the person making service under FRCP 5 certify that service has been effected. FRCP 5(Advisory Committee Notes). Having such information on file may be useful for many purposes, including proof of service if an issue arises concerning the effectiveness of the service. FRCP 5(Advisory Committee Notes). The Notice of Electronic Filing effectuates service for all registered users and no certificate of service is required when all filers on an action are Registered Users. The following exemptions require a certificate of service to be filed:

         • When a document is manually filed, a certificate of service must be filed stating the manner in which service or notice was accomplished on each party so entitled. NY R USDCTWD ECF Procedures(2)(f)(iv).

         • When a pro se filer (who isn't authorized to electronically file documents) is a party, a certificate of service must be filed stating the manner in which service or notice was accomplished on the pro se party. The Notice of Electronic Filing effectuates service for the Registered Users in this situation and it is not necessary to note service on those parties. A non-registered pro se filer is required to file certificates of service on all documents they file. NY R USDCTWD ECF Procedures(2)(f)(iv).

         • If an attorney is exempt from electronic service, a certificate of service must be filed stating the manner in which service or notice was accomplished on the exempt attorney. The Notice of Electronic Filing effectuates service for the Registered Users in this situation and it is not necessary to note service on those parties. NY R USDCTWD ECF Procedures(2)(f)(iv).

   b. *Supplemental documents*

      i. *Pleading.* As a general rule, the court may only consider the pleading which is attacked by a FRCP 12(b)(6) motion in determining its sufficiency. FEDPROC § 62:466; Armengau v. Cline, 7 Fed.Appx. 336 (6th Cir. 2001). The plaintiff is not entitled to discovery to obtain information relevant to the motion, and the court is not permitted to look at matters outside the record. FEDPROC § 62:466; Cooperativa de Ahorro y Credito Aguada v. Kidder, Peabody & Co., 993 F.2d 269, 37 Fed.R.Evid.Serv. 904, 25 Fed.R.Serv.3d 982 (1st Cir. 1993).

         • *Motion treated as one for summary judgment.* If, on a motion under FRCP 12(b)(6) or FRCP 12(c), matters outside the pleadings are presented to and not excluded by the court, the motion must be treated as one for summary judgment under FRCP 56. All parties must be given a reasonable opportunity to present all the material that is pertinent to the motion. FRCP 12(d).

         • *Documents attached to pleadings.* However, the court may consider documents which are attached to or submitted with the complaint, as well as legal arguments presented in memorandums or briefs and arguments of counsel. FEDPROC § 62:466; Tellabs, Inc. v. Makor Issues & Rights, Ltd., 551 U.S. 308, 127 S.Ct. 2499, 168 L.Ed.2d 179 (2007);

E.E.O.C. v. Ohio Edison Co., 7 F.3d 541 (6th Cir. 1993). Documents that the defendant attaches to the motion to dismiss are considered part of the pleadings if they are referred to in the plaintiff's complaint and are central to the claim, and as such may be considered by the court. FEDPROC § 62:466; Hoffman-Pugh v. Ramsey, 312 F.3d 1222 (11th Cir. 2002).

    ii. *Notice of constitutional question.* A party that files a pleading, written motion, or other paper drawing into question the constitutionality of a federal or state statute must promptly:

- *File notice.* File a notice of constitutional question stating the question and identifying the paper that raises it, if: (1) a federal statute is questioned and the parties do not include the United States, one of its agencies, or one of its officers or employees in an official capacity; or (2) a state statute is questioned and the parties do not include the state, one of its agencies, or one of its officers or employees in an official capacity; and

- *Serve notice.* Serve the notice and paper on the Attorney General of the United States if a federal statute is questioned—or on the state attorney general if a state statute is questioned—either by certified or registered mail or by sending it to an electronic address designated by the attorney general for this purpose. FRCP 5.1(a).

- *No forfeiture.* A party's failure to file and serve the notice, or the court's failure to certify, does not forfeit a constitutional claim or defense that is otherwise timely asserted. FRCP 5.1(d).

    iii. *Copies of authorities.* In cases involving a pro se litigant, counsel shall, when serving a memorandum of law (or other submissions to the Court), provide the pro se litigant (but not other counsel or the Court) with printed copies of decisions cited therein that are unreported or reported exclusively on computerized databases. NY R USDCTWD Civ Rule 7(a)(8).

    iv. *Paper copy for date-stamping with self-addressed envelope.* Parties requesting date-stamped copies of filed documents must provide a paper copy for date-stamping, and a self-addressed, adequately-sized envelope with proper postage affixed. NY R USDCTWD Civ Rule 5.1(d).

    v. *Courtesy copies.* Courtesy copies of certain documents may be required. Filers should refer to the "Judge Preferences" published on the Court's website. NY R USDCTWD ECF Procedures(2)(a)(iii).

3. *Individual judge practices.* Refer to the Miscellaneous section of this document for information on individual judge practices on required documents.

# E. Format

1. *Form of documents.* The rules governing captions and other matters of form in pleadings apply to motions and other papers. FRCP 7(b)(2).

    a. *Form, generally.* All pleadings, motions, and other papers that a party presents for filing, whether in paper form or in electronic form, shall meet the following requirements:

       i. *Font size.* All text and footnotes shall be in a font size of at least twelve (12) point type. NY R USDCTWD Civ Rule 10(a)(1).

       ii. *Spacing.* All text in the body of the document must be double-spaced, except that text in block quotations and footnotes may be single-spaced. NY R USDCTWD Civ Rule 10(a)(2).

- Extensive footnotes and block quotes may not be used to circumvent page limitations. NY R USDCTWD Civ Rule 10(a)(3).

       iii. *Margins.* Documents must have one (1) inch margins on all four sides. NY R USDCTWD Civ Rule 10(a)(4).

       iv. *Page numbering.* Pages must be consecutively numbered. NY R USDCTWD Civ Rule 10(a)(5).

    b. *Additional requirements for paper filing.* Documents presented for filing in paper form shall meet the following additional requirements:

       i. *Paper.* Documents must be on durable white eight and one-half by eleven (8-1/2 x 11) inch paper of good quality. NY R USDCTWD Civ Rule 10(b)(1).

- All documents must be single-sided. NY R USDCTWD Civ Rule 10(b)(5).

    ii.  *Text.* All text must be plainly and legibly written, typewritten, printed or reproduced. NY R USDCTWD Civ Rule 10(b)(2).

    iii.  *Ink.* Documents must be in black or blue ink. NY R USDCTWD Civ Rule 10(b)(3).

    iv.  *Binding.* The pages of each document must be stapled or in some other way fastened together. NY R USDCTWD Civ Rule 10(b)(4).

c.  *Caption; Names of parties.* Every pleading must have a caption with the court's name, a title, a file number, and a FRCP 7(a) designation. The title of the complaint must name all the parties; the title of other pleadings, after naming the first party on each side, may refer generally to other parties. FRCP 10(a).

d.  *Paragraphs; Separate statements.* A party must state its claims or defenses in numbered paragraphs, each limited as far as practicable to a single set of circumstances. A later pleading may refer by number to a paragraph in an earlier pleading. If doing so would promote clarity, each claim founded on a separate transaction or occurrence—and each defense other than a denial—must be stated in a separate count or defense. FRCP 10(b).

e.  *Adoption by reference; Exhibits.* A statement in a pleading may be adopted by reference elsewhere in the same pleading or in any other pleading or motion. A copy of a written instrument that is an exhibit to a pleading is a part of the pleading for all purposes. FRCP 10(c).

f.  *Citation of local rules.* The Local Rules of Civil Procedure for the United States District Court for the Western District of New York shall be cited as "L.R.Civ.P." NY R USDCTWD Civ Rule 1.1.

g.  *Acceptance by the clerk.* The clerk must not refuse to file a paper solely because it is not in the form prescribed by the Federal Rules of Civil Procedure or by a local rule or practice. FRCP 5(d)(4). The Court may reject documents that do not comply with the requirements in NY R USDCTWD Civ Rule 10. NY R USDCTWD Civ Rule 10.

2.  *Form of electronic documents.* All pleadings, motions, and other papers that a party presents for filing, whether in paper form or in electronic form, shall meet the requirements in NY R USDCTWD Civ Rule 10(a). NY R USDCTWD Civ Rule 10(a). Refer above for more information.

a.  *Conversion to PDF.* A document created with a word processor, or a paper document, must be converted to Portable Document Format to be electronically filed with the court. NY R USDCTWD ECF Procedures(2)(a)(v).

    i.  Documents which exist only in paper form may be scanned into a portable document format (PDF) for electronic filing. NY R USDCTWD ECF Procedures(2)(a)(v). Before filing a scanned document with the court, a Filing User must verify its legibility. NY R USDCTWD ECF Procedures(2)(a)(iv).

    ii.  Electronic documents must be converted to .PDF from a word processing program and must be text searchable. Do not print, scan and .PDF your document when it has been created in a word processing program. Additional information on working with PDFs is located in NY R USDCTWD ECF Procedures(4b). NY R USDCTWD ECF Procedures(2)(a)(v).

b.  *Hyperlinks.* Pursuant to the policy set forth by the Judicial Conference in October 2005, a hyperlink contained in a filing is no more than a convenient mechanism for accessing material cited in a document. A hyperlink reference is extraneous to any filed document and is not part of the Court's record. NY R USDCTWD ECF Procedures(2)(a)(vi).

    i.  In order to preserve the integrity of the Court record, users wishing to insert hyperlinks in Court filings shall continue to use the conventional method for the cited authority, in addition to the hyperlink. NY R USDCTWD ECF Procedures(2)(a)(vi).

    ii.  The Court accepts no responsibility for, and does not endorse any product, organization, and content at any hyperlinked site, or at any site to which that site may be linked. The Court accepts no responsibility for the availability or functionality of any hyperlink. NY R USDCTWD ECF Procedures(2)(a)(vi).

c.  *Attachments and exhibits*

    i.  Attachments and exhibits larger than five megabytes (5 MB) shall be filed electronically in separate five megabyte (5 MB) segments. NY R USDCTWD ECF Procedures(2)(d)(i).

ii. Filing Users must submit in electronic form all documents referenced as exhibits or attachments, except as otherwise provided in NY R USDCTWD ECF Procedures. A Filing User must submit as exhibits or attachments only those excerpts of the referenced documents that are directly germane to the matter under consideration by the court. Excerpted material must be clearly and prominently identified as such. Filing Users who file excerpts of documents as exhibits or attachments under NY R USDCTWD ECF Procedures(2)(d)(ii) do so without prejudice to their right to timely file additional excerpts or the complete document. Responding parties may timely file additional excerpts or the complete document that they believe are directly germane. The Court may require parties to file additional excerpts or the complete document. A Filing User must request leave of the Court to file a document exhibit or attachment in non-electronic form. NY R USDCTWD ECF Procedures(2)(d)(ii).

iii. Exhibits offered or admitted at trial will not be filed electronically or conventionally unless so ordered by the Court. NY R USDCTWD ECF Procedures(2)(d)(iii).

iv. Exhibits such as videotapes and tape recordings shall be filed in the conventional manner with the Clerk of Court, and a Notice of Manual Filing shall be electronically filed by the party. Manually filed exhibits must have the case number and case name securely fastened or marked on the item. NY R USDCTWD ECF Procedures(2)(d)(iii).

v. Continuation of exhibit entries (for exhibits that are too large to attach to a main document) must be filed and entered on the same day that the main document was filed. NY R USDCTWD ECF Procedures(2)(d)(iv).

d. *Color documents.* Documents in color or containing graphics take much longer to upload. Filing users are encouraged to configure their scanners to scan documents at 200 dpi and preferably in black and white rather than color. NY R USDCTWD ECF Procedures(2)(d)(v).

e. *Large documents.* Due to the length of time it takes to download large files, documents larger than five megabytes (5 MB) (approximately one hundred (100) pages of a .pdf scanned document) must be filed electronically in separate five megabyte (5 MB) segments. A party who believes a document is too lengthy to electronically image (i.e. scan), may contact the Court Room Deputy for the assigned judge and request permission to file that document conventionally. If granted permission to file the document conventionally, the Filing User shall electronically file a "notice of manual filing" for that item. Exhibits submitted to the Court conventionally shall be served on other parties conventionally. NY R USDCTWD ECF Procedures(2)(d)(vi).

3. *Form of memoranda of law.* Memoranda in support of or in opposition to any motion shall not exceed twenty-five (25) pages in length, and reply memoranda shall not exceed ten (10) pages in length. A party seeking to exceed the page limit must make application by letter to the Judge hearing the motion, with copies to all counsel, at least seven (7) days before the date on which the memorandum must be filed. NY R USDCTWD Civ Rule 7(a)(2)(C).

4. *Signing of pleadings, motions and other papers*

a. *Signature.* Every pleading, written motion, and other paper must be signed by at least one attorney of record in the attorney's name—or by a party personally if the party is unrepresented. The paper must state the signer's address, e-mail address, and telephone number. FRCP 11(a). Documents presented for paper filing must contain an original signature. NY R USDCTWD Civ Rule 10(b)(6).

i. *Electronic signatures*

- *Non-attorney signature.* If the original document requires the signature of a non-attorney, the filing party shall obtain the signature of the non-attorney on the document. NY R USDCTWD ECF Procedures(2)(g)(i). The filing party or attorney then shall file the document electronically indicating the signatory's name in the form "s/(name)." NY R USDCTWD ECF Procedures(2)(g)(i)(1). A non-filing signatory or party who disputes the authenticity of an electronically filed document or the authenticity of the signature on that document must file an objection to the document within ten (10) days of receiving the Notice of Electronic Filing. NY R USDCTWD ECF Procedures(2)(g)(i)(2).

- *Registered user signature.* The username and password required to file documents on the

Electronic Filing System serve as the Filing User's signature on all electronic documents filed with this Court. The also serve as a signature for the purposes of FRCP 11, the Federal Rules of Civil Procedure, the Local Rules of Civil Procedure for the United States District Court for the Western District of New York, and any other purpose for which a signature is required in connection with proceedings before this Court. A pleading requiring a Registered User's signature must include a signature block in the format found in NY R USDCTWD ECF Procedures(2)(g)(iii). NY R USDCTWD ECF Procedures(2)(g)(iii). Any party challenging the authenticity of an electronically filed document or the attorney's signature on that document must file an objection to the document within ten (10) days of receiving the Notice of Electronic Filing. NY R USDCTWD ECF Procedures(2)(g)(iii)(1).

- *Multiple signatures.* The following procedure applies when a stipulation or other document requires two or more signatures: The filing party shall initially confirm that the document is acceptable to all persons required to sign the document and shall obtain the signatures of all parties on the document. NY R USDCTWD ECF Procedures(2)(g)(iv)(1). The filing party or attorney then shall file the document electronically indicating the signatories, e.g., "s/Jane Doe," "s/John Smith," etc. NY R USDCTWD ECF Procedures(2)(g)(iv)(2). A non-filing signatory or party who disputes the authenticity of an electronically filed document containing multiple signatures or the authenticity of the signatures themselves must file an objection to the document within ten (10) days of receiving the Notice of Electronic Filing. NY R USDCTWD ECF Procedures(2)(g)(iv)(3).

    ii. *No verification or accompanying affidavit required for pleadings.* Unless a rule or statute specifically states otherwise, a pleading need not be verified or accompanied by an affidavit. FRCP 11(a).

    iii. *Unsigned papers.* The court must strike an unsigned paper unless the omission is promptly corrected after being called to the attorney's or party's attention. FRCP 11(a).

b. *Representations to the court.* By presenting to the court a pleading, written motion, or other paper—whether by signing, filing, submitting, or later advocating it—an attorney or unrepresented party certifies that to the best of the person's knowledge, information, and belief, formed after an inquiry reasonable under the circumstances:

    i. It is not being presented for any improper purpose, such as to harass, cause unnecessary delay, or needlessly increase the cost of litigation;

    ii. The claims, defenses, and other legal contentions are warranted by existing law or by a nonfrivolous argument for extending, modifying, or reversing existing law or for establishing new law;

    iii. The factual contentions have evidentiary support or, if specifically so identified, will likely have evidentiary support after a reasonable opportunity for further investigation or discovery; and

    iv. The denials of factual contentions are warranted on the evidence or, if specifically so identified, are reasonably based on belief or a lack of information. FRCP 11(b).

c. *Sanctions.* If, after notice and a reasonable opportunity to respond, the court determines that FRCP 11(b) has been violated, the court may impose an appropriate sanction on any attorney, law firm, or party that violated FRCP 11(b) or is responsible for the violation. FRCP 11(c)(1). Refer to the United States District Court for the Western District of New York KeyRules Motion for Sanctions document for more information.

5. *Privacy protection for filings made with the court.* In all filings, parties shall comply with FRCP 5.2. NY R USDCTWD ECF Procedures(2)(m)(i).

a. *Redacted filings.* Unless the court orders otherwise, in an electronic or paper filing with the court that contains an individual's Social Security number, taxpayer-identification number, or birth date, the name of an individual known to be a minor, or a financial-account number, a party or nonparty making the filing may include only:

    i. The last four (4) digits of the Social Security number and taxpayer-identification number;

      ii.   The year of the individual's birth;

     iii.   The minor's initials; and

     iv.   The last four (4) digits of the financial-account number. FRCP 5.2(a).

  b.  *Exemptions from the redaction requirement.* The redaction requirement does not apply to the following:

      i.   A financial-account number that identifies the property allegedly subject to forfeiture in a forfeiture proceeding;

      ii.   The record of an administrative or agency proceeding;

     iii.   The official record of a state-court proceeding;

     iv.   The record of a court or tribunal, if that record was not subject to the redaction requirement when originally filed;

      v.   A filing covered by FRCP 5.2(c) or FRCP 5.2(d); and

     vi.   A pro se filing in an action brought under 28 U.S.C.A. § 2241, 28 U.S.C.A. § 2254, or 28 U.S.C.A. § 2255. FRCP 5.2(b).

  c.  *Limitations on remote access to electronic files; Social Security appeals and immigration cases.* Unless the court orders otherwise, in an action for benefits under the Social Security Act, and in an action or proceeding relating to an order of removal, to relief from removal, or to immigration benefits or detention, access to an electronic file is authorized as follows:

      i.   The parties and their attorneys may have remote electronic access to any part of the case file, including the administrative record;

      ii.   Any other person may have electronic access to the full record at the courthouse, but may have remote electronic access only to:

        • The docket maintained by the court; and

        • An opinion, order, judgment, or other disposition of the court, but not any other part of the case file or the administrative record. FRCP 5.2(c).

  d.  *Filings made under seal.* The court may order that a filing be made under seal without redaction. The court may later unseal the filing or order the person who made the filing to file a redacted version for the public record. FRCP 5.2(d). For more information on sealing documents, refer to NY R USDCTWD Civ Rule 5.3, NY R USDCTWD ECF Procedures(2)(o)(i)(1), NY R USDCTWD ECF Procedures(2)(o)(i)(2), and NY R USDCTWD ECF Procedures(2)(o)(i)(3).

  e.  *Protective orders.* For good cause, the court may by order in a case:

      i.   Require redaction of additional information; or

      ii.   Limit or prohibit a nonparty's remote electronic access to a document filed with the court. FRCP 5.2(e).

  f.  *Option for additional unredacted filing under seal.* A person making a redacted filing may also file an unredacted copy under seal. The court must retain the unredacted copy as part of the record. FRCP 5.2(f).

  g.  *Option for filing a reference list.* A filing that contains redacted information may be filed together with a reference list that identifies each item of redacted information and specifies an appropriate identifier that uniquely corresponds to each item listed. The list must be filed under seal and may be amended as of right. Any reference in the case to a listed identifier will be construed to refer to the corresponding item of information. FRCP 5.2(g).

  h.  *Waiver of protection of identifiers.* A person waives the protection of FRCP 5.2(a) as to the person's own information by filing it without redaction and not under seal. FRCP 5.2(h).

6.  *Individual judge practices.* Refer to the Miscellaneous section of this document for information on individual judge practices on formatting documents.

## F.  Filing and Service Requirements

1.  *Filing requirements.* Any paper after the complaint that is required to be served—together with a

certificate of service—must be filed within a reasonable time after service. FRCP 5(d)(1). All pleadings and other papers shall be filed and served in accordance with the Federal Rules of Civil Procedure and the CM/ECF Administrative Procedures Guide (NY R USDCTWD ECF Procedures). NY R USDCTWD Civ Rule 5.1(a). For information on filing of miscellaneous cases and irregular documents, refer to NY R USDCTWD Civ Rule 5.6.

a. *How filing is made; In general.* A paper is filed by delivering it:

   i. To the clerk; or

   ii. To a judge who agrees to accept it for filing, and who must then note the filing date on the paper and promptly send it to the clerk. FRCP 5(d)(2).

b. *Electronic filing*

   i. *Authorization of electronic filing program.* A court may, by local rule, allow papers to be filed, signed, or verified by electronic means that are consistent with any technical standards established by the Judicial Conference of the United States. A local rule may require electronic filing only if reasonable exceptions are allowed. A paper filed electronically in compliance with a local rule is a written paper for purposes of the Federal Rules of Civil Procedure. FRCP 5(d)(3).

   - All civil cases filed in this Court are assigned to the Electronic Case Filing System ("ECF"). The procedures for electronic filing and any exceptions to the electronic filing requirements are set forth in the CM/ECF Administrative Procedures Guide (NY R USDCTWD ECF Procedures) which is available on the Court's website. NY R US-DCTWD Civ Rule 5.1(a).

   ii. *Scope of electronic filing.* The U.S. District Court for the Western District of New York requires attorneys in civil and criminal cases to file documents with the Court electronically over the Internet using its Case Management/Electronic Case Filing (CM/ECF) system. NY R US-DCTWD ECF Procedures. Beginning January 1, 2004, all civil and criminal cases currently pending and newly filed, except as expressly noted herein, were assigned to the Electronic Case Filing System ("System"). Except as expressly provided and in exceptional circumstances preventing a Filing User from filing electronically, all petitions, motions, memoranda of law, or other pleadings and documents required to be filed with the Court in connection with a case assigned to the System must be electronically filed. NY R USDCTWD ECF Procedures(1)(a).

   - *Mandatory electronic filing.* All documents on civil, criminal, miscellaneous civil, miscellaneous criminal and new civil case openings, except sealed documents, sealed cases, opening of a criminal case, opening of a miscellaneous case and as expressly provided for in these procedures (NY R USDCTWD ECF Procedures), shall be electronically filed on the system. NY R USDCTWD ECF Procedures(2)(a)(i). NY R USDCTWD Civ Rule 29

   - *Stipulations.* Pursuant to NY R USDCTWD Civ Rule 29, all stipulations (whether the stipulation is final or when it requires a judge's signature) shall be filed electronically. NY R USDCTWD ECF Procedures(2)(p)(i).

   - *Letters.* The electronic filing of letters is generally prohibited unless granted permission by an assigned judge. Letters to the Court must be submitted conventionally. NY R US-DCTWD ECF Procedures(2)(q)(i).

   - *Exceptions.* The Court requires attorneys to file documents electronically, absent a showing of good cause, unless otherwise excused by the procedures set forth below or by Order of the Court. NY R USDCTWD ECF Procedures.

   iii. *Conventional filing of documents.* The procedures in NY R USDCTWD ECF Procedures(2)(o) govern documents filed conventionally. The Court, upon application, may also authorize conventional filing of other documents otherwise subject to the procedures in NY R US-DCTWD ECF Procedures(2)(o). NY R USDCTWD ECF Procedures(2)(o)(i).

   - *Documents filed under seal.* Unredacted documents filed with the Court pursuant to the privacy provisions of FRCP 5.2 shall be submitted in a sealing envelope with the

information in NY R USDCTWD ECF Procedures(2)(o)(i)(1) on the envelope. NY R USDCTWD ECF Procedures(2)(o)(i)(1). If the document is larger than five (5) pages, a disk should be provided to the Clerks Office which contains the document in a .pdf format. NY R USDCTWD ECF Procedures(2)(o)(i)(1). For more information on documents filed under seal, refer to NY R USDCTWD ECF Procedures(2)(o)(i)(1), NY R USDCTWD ECF Procedures(2)(o)(i)(2), and NY R USDCTWD ECF Procedures(2)(o)(i)(3).

- *Magistrate judge consents.* Pursuant to FRCP 73(b), parties' filing consents to jurisdiction by United States Magistrate Judge will continue to be treated as non-public documents until all parties have consented. Therefore, parties must submit conventionally (in paper form) and not electronically file their consent forms so that the consent is not a public document. If all parties consent to the jurisdiction of a Magistrate Judge, the Clerk will scan all consent forms which will then become a public document. NY R USDCTWD ECF Procedures(2)(o)(i)(3).

- *Pro se filers.* Pro Se filers shall file paper originals of all initiating documents, pleadings, motions, affidavits, briefs and other documents which must be signed or which require either verification or an unsworn declaration under any rule or statute. The Clerk's Office will scan these original documents into an electronic file in the System. A certificate of service is required for all documents a pro se litigant files with the court. If a Pro Se filer is granted permission to register to electronically file documents, they shall comply with the guidelines contained in this document (NY R USDCTWD ECF Procedures). NY R USDCTWD ECF Procedures(2)(o)(i)(4).

- *Social Security cases.* Absent a showing of good cause, and except as provided in Section o(i)(4) above, all documents, notices and orders in Social Security reviews will be filed and noticed electronically, except as noted in NY R USDCTWD ECF Procedures(2)(o)(i)(6). For more information, refer to NY R USDCTWD ECF Procedures(2)(o)(i)(6).

- For more information on conventional filing of documents, refer to NY R USDCTWD ECF Procedures(2)(o)(i).

iv. *Consequences of electronic filing.* Electronic transmission of a document to the System consistent with these procedures (NY R USDCTWD ECF Procedures), whether accomplished by the Filing User or a Court User, together with the transmission of a Notice of Electronic Filing from the Court, constitutes filing of a document for all purposes of the Federal Rules of Civil Procedure and the Local Rules of Civil Procedure for the United States District Court for the Western District of New York, and constitutes entry of the document on the docket kept by the Clerk under FRCP 58 and FRCP 79. A document shall not be considered filed for purposes of the Federal Rules of Civil until the filing party receives a System generated Notice of Electronic Filing. NY R USDCTWD ECF Procedures(2)(a)(i).

- E-mailing a document to the Clerk's Office or to the assigned judge shall not constitute "filing" of such document. NY R USDCTWD ECF Procedures(2)(a)(i)(1).

v. *Filing fees.* Any fee required for filing of a pleading or paper in District Court is payable to the Clerk of Court by check or money order. In addition, when opening a civil case on line, filing a notice of appeal on line or applying to appear pro hac vice on line, the fees shall be paid on line by registered users through the federal electronic payment website. Users will be directed to the federal electronic payment website while entering their transaction and should have a credit card available. When opening a civil case and applying to proceed in forma pauperis or when the United States of America opens a case, the payment screen can by bypassed to complete the transaction. Additional information on making electronic payments can be located on the court's website. NY R USDCTWD ECF Procedures(2)(h)(i).

2. *Service requirements.* All pleadings and other papers shall be filed and served in accordance with the

Federal Rules of Civil Procedure and the CM/ECF Administrative Procedures Guide (NY R USDCTWD ECF Procedures). NY R USDCTWD Civ Rule 5.1(a).

a. *Service; When required*

    i. *In general.* Unless the Federal Rules of Civil Procedure provide otherwise, each of the following papers must be served on every party:

- An order stating that service is required;

- A pleading filed after the original complaint, unless the court orders otherwise under FRCP 5(c) because there are numerous defendants;

- A discovery paper required to be served on a party, unless the court orders otherwise;

- A written motion, except one that may be heard ex parte; and

- A written notice, appearance, demand, or offer of judgment, or any similar paper. FRCP 5(a)(1).

    ii. *If a party fails to appear.* No service is required on a party who is in default for failing to appear. But a pleading that asserts a new claim for relief against such a party must be served on that party under FRCP 4. FRCP 5(a)(2).

    iii. *Seizing property.* If an action is begun by seizing property and no person is or need be named as a defendant, any service required before the filing of an appearance, answer, or claim must be made on the person who had custody or possession of the property when it was seized. FRCP 5(a)(3).

b. *Service; How made*

    i. *Serving an attorney.* If a party is represented by an attorney, service under FRCP 5 must be made on the attorney unless the court orders service on the party. FRCP 5(b)(1).

    ii. *Service in general.* A paper is served under FRCP 5 by:

- Handing it to the person;

- Leaving it: (1) at the person's office with a clerk or other person in charge or, if no one is in charge, in a conspicuous place in the office; or (2) if the person has no office or the office is closed, at the person's dwelling or usual place of abode with someone of suitable age and discretion who resides there;

- Mailing it to the person's last known address—in which event service is complete upon mailing;

- Leaving it with the court clerk if the person has no known address;

- Sending it by electronic means if the person consented in writing—in which event service is complete upon transmission, but is not effective if the serving party learns that it did not reach the person to be served; or

- Delivering it by any other means that the person consented to in writing—in which event service is complete when the person making service delivers it to the agency designated to make delivery. FRCP 5(b)(2).

    iii. *Service by overnight delivery.* All papers, other than a subpoena or a summons and complaint, may be served on counsel of record by overnight delivery service at the address designated by the attorney for that purpose, or if none is designated, at the attorney's last known address. Service by overnight delivery shall be complete upon deposit of the paper(s), enclosed in a properly addressed wrapper, into the custody of the overnight delivery service, prior to the latest time designated by the service for overnight delivery. NY R USDCTWD Civ Rule 5.1(g). "Overnight delivery service" means any delivery service which regularly accepts items for overnight delivery to any address within the Court's jurisdiction. NY R USDCTWD Civ Rule 5.1(g).

    iv. *Service of documents by electronic means*

- *Service on registered users.* Registered Users consent to the electronic service of all

documents, and must make available an electronic mail address for service during the registration process. Upon the filing of a document by a party, a Notice of Electronic Filing, with a hyperlink to the filed document, will be automatically generated by the electronic filing system and sent via electronic mail to the e-mail addresses of all parties participating in the electronic filing system in the case. Electronic service of the Notice of Electronic Filing constitutes service of the filed document for all purposes of the Federal Rules of Civil Procedure and the Local Rules of Civil Procedure for the United States District Court for the Western District of New York. NY R USDCTWD ECF Procedures(2)(f)(i). The Notice of Electronic Filing effectuates service for all registered users and no certificate of service is required when all filers on an action are Registered Users. NY R USDCTWD ECF Procedures(2)(f)(iv).

- *Time limit for opening hyperlink.* The hyperlink to filed documents contained in the Notice of Electronic Filing must be opened within fifteen (15) days from the date the document was filed to provide registered users access to the document. The hyperlink expires after fifteen (15) days and users will be unable to access documents for free after that time. Filing Users are encouraged to check their e-mail frequently for notice of filed documents. NY R USDCTWD ECF Procedures(2)(f)(ii).

- *Service on exempted attorneys or pro se litigants who do not have permission to file electronically.* Attorneys granted an exemption from electronically filing documents in the System and pro se litigants who have not been granted permission to electronically file documents are entitled to a paper copy of any electronically filed pleading, document or order. The filing party must therefore provide the non-registered party with the pleading, document or order according to the Federal Rules of Civil Procedure. NY R USDCTWD ECF Procedures(2)(f)(iii).

- *E-mailing or faxing documents.* E-mailing or faxing a pleading or document to any party shall not constitute service of the pleading or document. NY R USDCTWD ECF Procedures(2)(f)(v).

    v.  *Using court facilities.* If a local rule so authorizes, a party may use the court's transmission facilities to make service under FRCP 5(b)(2)(E). FRCP 5(b)(3).

  c.  *Serving numerous defendants*

    i.  *In general.* If an action involves an unusually large number of defendants, the court may, on motion or on its own, order that:

- Defendants' pleadings and replies to them need not be served on other defendants;

- Any crossclaim, counterclaim, avoidance, or affirmative defense in those pleadings and replies to them will be treated as denied or avoided by all other parties; and

- Filing any such pleading and serving it on the plaintiff constitutes notice of the pleading to all parties. FRCP 5(c)(1).

    ii.  *Notifying parties.* A copy of every such order must be served on the parties as the court directs. FRCP 5(c)(2).

3.  *Pro se actions.* For information on the requirements in pro se actions, refer to NY R USDCTWD Civ Rule 5.2.

4.  *Individual judge practices.* Refer to the Miscellaneous section of this document for information on individual judge practices on filing and serving documents.

## G. Hearings

1.  *Hearings, generally*

  a.  *Oral argument.* Due process does not require that oral argument be permitted on a motion and, except as otherwise provided by local rule, the district court has discretion to determine whether it will decide the motion on the papers or hear argument by counsel (and perhaps receive evidence). FPP § 1190; F.D.I.C. v. Deglau, 207 F.3d 153 (3d Cir. 2000).

    i.  The parties shall appear for oral argument on all motions they make returnable before a Judge

on the scheduled return date for the motion. In its discretion, the Court may notify the parties that oral argument shall not be heard on any given motion. Thus, the parties should be prepared to have their motion papers serve as the sole method of argument. NY R USDCTWD Civ Rule 7(c).

    b. *Providing a regular schedule for oral hearings.* A court may establish regular times and places for oral hearings on motions. FRCP 78(a).

    c. *Providing for submission on briefs.* By rule or order, the court may provide for submitting and determining motions on briefs, without oral hearings. FRCP 78(b).

2. *Hearing on FRCP 12 defenses before trial.* If a party so moves, any defense listed in FRCP 12(b)(1) through FRCP 12(b)(7)—whether made in a pleading or by motion—and a motion under FRCP 12(c) must be heard and decided before trial unless the court orders a deferral until trial. FRCP 12(i).

3. *Individual judge practices.* Refer to the Miscellaneous section of this document for information on individual judge practices on hearings.

## H. Forms

### 1. Federal Motion to Dismiss for Failure to State a Claim Forms

    a. Notice in federal court; Motion for involuntary dismissal of action without prejudice; Complaint fails to state a claim on which relief can be granted. AMJUR PP DISMISSAL § 109.

    b. Motion; To dismiss; Failure to state a claim on which relief can be granted or facts sufficient to constitute cause of action. AMJUR PP LIMITATION § 100.

    c. Motion to dismiss; For failure to state a claim, improper service of process, improper venue, and want of jurisdiction. AMJUR PP MOTIONS § 42.

    d. Failure to state a claim upon which relief can be granted. 2C FEDFORMS § 11:80.

    e. Failure to state a claim upon which relief can be granted; Long version. 2C FEDFORMS § 11:81.

    f. Failure to state a claim upon which relief can be granted; Dismissal of certain allegations. 2C FEDFORMS § 11:82.

    g. Failure to state a claim upon which relief can be granted; With supporting reasons. 2C FEDFORMS § 11:83.

    h. Failure to state a claim upon which relief can be granted; With supporting reasons; Plaintiff not the real party in interest. 2C FEDFORMS § 11:85.

    i. Failure to state a claim upon which relief can be granted; With supporting reasons; Failure to show implied contract. 2C FEDFORMS § 11:86.

    j. Failure to state a claim upon which relief can be granted; With supporting reasons; Issue not arbitrable. 2C FEDFORMS § 11:87.

    k. Failure to state a claim upon which relief can be granted; With supporting affidavits. 2C FEDFORMS § 11:88.

    l. Failure to state a claim upon which relief can be granted; In alternative for summary judgment. 2C FEDFORMS § 11:89.

    m. Motion; To dismiss; Failure to state sufficient claim; By one of several defendants. FEDPROF § 1:923.

    n. Motion to dismiss; Failure to state sufficient claim; By third-party defendant. FEDPROF § 1:924.

    o. Motion to dismiss; Failure to state sufficient claim after successive attempts. FEDPROF § 1:925.

    p. Motion to dismiss; By individual defendants. FEDPROF § 1:926.

    q. Motion to dismiss; By state agency. FEDPROF § 1:927.

    r. Motion to dismiss counterclaim. FEDPROF § 1:931.

    s. Allegation; In motion to dismiss; Res judicata. FEDPROF § 1:933.

    t. Allegation; In motion to dismiss; Statute of limitations. FEDPROF § 1:935.

u. Allegation; In motion to dismiss; Strict liability claim barred by statute. FEDPROF § 1:936.

v. Allegation; In motion to dismiss; By United States; Absence of consent to suit. FEDPROF § 1:938.

w. Reply; To motion to dismiss for failure to state sufficient claim. FEDPROF § 1:939.

x. Motion to dismiss counterclaim. GOLDLTGFMS § 13:10.

y. Motion to dismiss complaint; General form. GOLDLTGFMS § 20:24.

z. Affidavit in support of motion to dismiss complaint. GOLDLTGFMS § 20:32.

**2. Forms for the Western District of New York**

a. Certificate of service. NY R USDCTWD ECF Procedures(4a).

# I. Applicable Rules

1. *Federal rules*

a. Serving and filing pleadings and other papers. FRCP 5.

b. Constitutional challenge to a statute; Notice, certification, and intervention. FRCP 5.1.

c. Privacy protection for filings made with the court. FRCP 5.2.

d. Computing and extending time; Time for motion papers. FRCP 6.

e. Pleadings allowed; Form of motions and other papers. FRCP 7.

f. Disclosure statement. FRCP 7.1.

g. Form of pleadings. FRCP 10.

h. Signing pleadings, motions, and other papers; Representations to the court; Sanctions. FRCP 11.

i. Defenses and objections; When and how presented; Motion for judgment on the pleadings; Consolidating motions; Waiving defenses; Pretrial hearing. FRCP 12.

j. Hearing motions; Submission on briefs. FRCP 78.

2. *Local rules*

a. Title. NY R USDCTWD Civ Rule 1.1.

b. Filing and serving papers. NY R USDCTWD Civ Rule 5.1.

c. Motion practice. NY R USDCTWD Civ Rule 7.

d. Form of papers. NY R USDCTWD Civ Rule 10.

e. Sanctions. NY R USDCTWD Civ Rule 11.

f. Alternative dispute resolution and pretrial conferences. NY R USDCTWD Civ Rule 16.

g. Attorneys of record; Appearance and withdrawal. NY R USDCTWD Civ Rule 83.2.

h. Administrative procedures guide for electronic filing. NY R USDCTWD ECF Procedures.

i. Alternative dispute resolution plan. NY R USDCTWD ADR Plan.

# J. Miscellaneous

**NOTE: Individual judges' rules may apply. For available judge-level information, refer to:**

DISTRICT JUDGE RICHARD J. ARCARA: NY R USDCTWD Arcara-Procedures.

DISTRICT JUDGE FRANK P. GERACI, JR.: NY R USDCTWD Geraci-Procedures.

DISTRICT JUDGE DAVID G. LARIMER: NY R USDCTWD Larimer-Procedures.

DISTRICT JUDGE CHARLES J. SIRAGUSA: NY R USDCTWD Siragusa-Procedures.

DISTRICT JUDGE WILLIAM M. SKRETNY: NY R USDCTWD Skretny--Procedures.

DISTRICT JUDGE MICHAEL A. TELESCA: NY R USDCTWD Telesca-Procedures.

DISTRICT JUDGE LAWRENCE J. VILARDO: NY R USDCTWD Vilardo-Procedures.

DISTRICT JUDGE ELIZABETH A. WOLFORD: NY R USDCTWD Wolford-Procedures.

MAGISTRATE JUDGE JONATHAN W. FELDMAN: NY R USDCTWD Feldman-Procedures.

MAGISTRATE JUDGE LESLIE G. FOSCHIO: NY R USDCTWD Foschio-Procedures; NY R USDCTWD Foschio-Depositions.

MAGISTRATE JUDGE JEREMIAH J. McCARTHY: NY R USDCTWD McCarthy-Procedures.

MAGISTRATE JUDGE MARIAN W. PAYSON: NY R USDCTWD Payson-Procedures.

MAGISTRATE JUDGE MICHAEL J. ROEMER: NY R USDCTWD Roemer-Procedures.

MAGISTRATE JUDGE H. KENNETH SCHROEDER, JR.: NY R USDCTWD Schroeder-Proc.

MAGISTRATE JUDGE HUGH B. SCOTT: NY R USDCTWD Scott-Procedures.

## Motions, Oppositions and Replies
## Motion to Dismiss for Lack of Subject Matter Jurisdiction

### Document Last Updated September 2016

A. **Checklist**
 (I) ❑ Matters to be considered by moving party
  (a) ❑ Required documents
   (1) ❑ Notice of motion and motion
   (2) ❑ Memorandum of law
   (3) ❑ Certificate of service
  (b) ❑ Supplemental documents
   (1) ❑ Supporting evidence
   (2) ❑ Notice of constitutional question
   (3) ❑ Nongovernmental corporate disclosure statement
   (4) ❑ Copies of authorities
   (5) ❑ Proposed order
   (6) ❑ Paper copy for date-stamping with self-addressed envelope
   (7) ❑ Courtesy copies
  (c) ❑ Timing
   (1) ❑ The defense of lack of subject matter jurisdiction can be raised at any time
   (2) ❑ Every defense to a claim for relief in any pleading must be asserted in the responsive pleading if one is required
   (3) ❑ A motion asserting any of the defenses in FRCP 12(b) must be made before pleading if a responsive pleading is allowed
   (4) ❑ If a pleading sets out a claim for relief that does not require a responsive pleading, an opposing party may assert at trial any defense to that claim
   (5) ❑ A written motion and notice of the hearing must be served at least fourteen (14) days before the time specified for the hearing, with the following exceptions: (i) when the motion may be heard ex parte; (ii) when the Federal Rules of Civil Procedure set a different time; or (iii) when a court order—which a party may, for good cause, apply for ex parte—sets a different time
   (6) ❑ Any affidavit supporting a motion must be served with the motion
 (II) ❑ Matters to be considered by opposing party
  (a) ❑ Required documents
   (1) ❑ Opposition

      (2)   ❑   Answering memorandum

      (3)   ❑   Certificate of service

   (b)   ❑   Supplemental documents

      (1)   ❑   Supporting evidence

      (2)   ❑   Notice of constitutional question

      (3)   ❑   Copies of authorities

      (4)   ❑   Paper copy for date-stamping with self-addressed envelope

      (5)   ❑   Courtesy copies

   (c)   ❑   Timing

      (1)   ❑   After a motion is filed, the court may issue an order setting deadlines for filing and service of opposing papers; if the court does not set deadlines by order, the opposing party shall have fourteen (14) days after service of the motion to file and serve responding papers

      (2)   ❑   Except as FRCP 59(c) provides otherwise, any opposing affidavit must be served at least seven (7) days before the hearing, unless the court permits service at another time

## B. Timing

1. *Motion to dismiss for lack of subject matter jurisdiction.* [The defense of lack of subject matter jurisdiction] can be raised at any time. FEDPROC § 62:434.

   a. *In a responsive pleading.* Every defense to a claim for relief in any pleading must be asserted in the responsive pleading if one is required. FRCP 12(b).

   b. *By motion.* A motion asserting any of the defenses in FRCP 12(b) must be made before pleading if a responsive pleading is allowed. FRCP 12(b). Although FRCP 12(b) encourages the responsive pleader to file a motion to dismiss before filing the answer, nothing in FRCP 12 prohibits the filing of a motion to dismiss with the answer. An untimely motion to dismiss may be considered if the defense asserted in the motion was previously raised in the responsive pleading. FEDPROC § 62:427.

   c. *At trial.* If a pleading sets out a claim for relief that does not require a responsive pleading, an opposing party may assert at trial any defense to that claim. FRCP 12(b).

2. *Timing of motions, generally*

   a. *Motion and notice of hearing.* A written motion and notice of the hearing must be served at least fourteen (14) days before the time specified for the hearing, with the following exceptions:

      i.   When the motion may be heard ex parte;

      ii.   When the Federal Rules of Civil Procedure set a different time; or

      iii.   When a court order—which a party may, for good cause, apply for ex parte—sets a different time. FRCP 6(c)(1).

   b. *Supporting affidavit.* Any affidavit supporting a motion must be served with the motion. FRCP 6(c)(2).

3. *Timing of opposing papers.* After a motion is filed, the Court may issue an order setting deadlines for filing and service of opposing papers. NY R USDCTWD Civ Rule 7(b)(1). If the Court does not set deadlines by order, the following schedule shall apply: the opposing party shall have fourteen (14) days after service of the motion to file and serve responding papers. NY R USDCTWD Civ Rule 7(b)(2)(B).

   a. *Opposing affidavit.* Except as FRCP 59(c) provides otherwise, any opposing affidavit must be served at least seven (7) days before the hearing, unless the court permits service at another time. FRCP 6(c)(2).

4. *Timing of reply papers.* Where the respondent files an answering affidavit setting up a new matter, the moving party ordinarily is allowed a reasonable time to file a reply affidavit since failure to deny the new matter by affidavit may operate as an admission of its truth. AMJUR MOTIONS § 25.

   a. *Reply papers.* After a motion is filed, the Court may issue an order setting deadlines. . .for filing and service of reply papers if the moving party has stated an intent to reply. NY R USDCTWD Civ Rule 7(b)(1). If the Court does not set deadlines by order, the following schedule shall apply: the moving party shall have seven (7) days after service of the responding papers to file and serve reply papers. NY R USDCTWD Civ Rule 7(b)(2)(B).

b. *Reply memorandum.* The moving party may file a reply memorandum, but is not required to do so. NY R USDCTWD Civ Rule 7(a)(2)(A).

5. *Motion for an expedited hearing.* A party seeking to shorten the schedule prescribed in NY R USDCTWD Civ Rule 7(b) must make a separate motion for an expedited hearing, setting forth the reasons why an expedited hearing is required. NY R USDCTWD Civ Rule 7(d)(1). For more information, refer to NY R USDCTWD Civ Rule 7(d)(1).

6. *Effect of a FRCP 12 motion on the time to serve a responsive pleading.* Unless the court sets a different time, serving a motion under FRCP 12 alters the periods in FRCP 12(a) as follows:

a. If the court denies the motion or postpones its disposition until trial, the responsive pleading must be served within fourteen (14) days after notice of the court's action; or

b. If the court grants a motion for a more definite statement, the responsive pleading must be served within fourteen (14) days after the more definite statement is served. FRCP 12(a)(4).

7. *Computation of time*

a. *Computing time.* FRCP 6 applies in computing any time period specified in the Federal Rules of Civil Procedure, in any local rule or court order, or in any statute that does not specify a method of computing time. FRCP 6(a).

i. *Period stated in days or a longer unit.* When the period is stated in days or a longer unit of time:
- Exclude the day of the event that triggers the period;
- Count every day, including intermediate Saturdays, Sundays, and legal holidays; and
- Include the last day of the period, but if the last day is a Saturday, Sunday, or legal holiday, the period continues to run until the end of the next day that is not a Saturday, Sunday, or legal holiday. FRCP 6(a)(1).

ii. *Period stated in hours.* When the period is stated in hours:
- Begin counting immediately on the occurrence of the event that triggers the period;
- Count every hour, including hours during intermediate Saturdays, Sundays, and legal holidays; and
- If the period would end on a Saturday, Sunday, or legal holiday, the period continues to run until the same time on the next day that is not a Saturday, Sunday, or legal holiday. FRCP 6(a)(2).

iii. *Inaccessibility of the clerk's office.* Unless the court orders otherwise, if the clerk's office is inaccessible:
- On the last day for filing under FRCP 6(a)(1), then the time for filing is extended to the first accessible day that is not a Saturday, Sunday, or legal holiday; or
- During the last hour for filing under FRCP 6(a)(2), then the time for filing is extended to the same time on the first accessible day that is not a Saturday, Sunday, or legal holiday. FRCP 6(a)(3).

iv. *"Last day" defined.* Unless a different time is set by a statute, local rule, or court order, the last day ends:
- For electronic filing, at midnight in the court's time zone; and
- For filing by other means, when the clerk's office is scheduled to close. FRCP 6(a)(4).

v. *"Next day" defined.* The "next day" is determined by continuing to count forward when the period is measured after an event and backward when measured before an event. FRCP 6(a)(5).

vi. *"Legal holiday" defined.* "Legal holiday" means:
- The day set aside by statute for observing New Year's Day, Martin Luther King Jr.'s

Birthday, Washington's Birthday, Memorial Day, Independence Day, Labor Day, Columbus Day, Veterans' Day, Thanksgiving Day, or Christmas Day;

- Any day declared a holiday by the President or Congress; and

- For periods that are measured after an event, any other day declared a holiday by the state where the district court is located. FRCP 6(a)(6).

b. *Computation of electronic filing deadlines.* A document will be deemed timely filed if filed prior to midnight Eastern Time, unless otherwise ordered by the Court. A document will be considered untimely if filed thereafter. When a Court order requires that a document be filed on a weekend or holiday, the document may be filed by close of business the next business day without further application to the Court. NY R USDCTWD ECF Procedures(2)(e)(i). A document filed electronically is deemed filed on the date and time stated on the Notice of Electronic Filing. NY R USDCTWD ECF Procedures(2)(e)(ii).

   i. *System availability.* Although parties may file documents electronically twenty-four (24) hours a day, registered users are strongly encouraged to file all documents during normal working hours of the Clerk's Office (8:30 a.m. to 5:00 p.m. Eastern Time). NY R USDCTWD ECF Procedures(2)(t)(i).

   ii. *Technical failures.* A Filing User whose filing is made untimely as a result of a technical failure must seek appropriate relief from the Court. NY R USDCTWD ECF Procedures(2)(u)(i).

c. *Extending time*

   i. *In general.* When an act may or must be done within a specified time, the court may, for good cause, extend the time:

   - With or without motion or notice if the court acts, or if a request is made, before the original time or its extension expires; or

   - On motion made after the time has expired if the party failed to act because of excusable neglect. FRCP 6(b)(1).

   ii. *Exceptions.* A court must not extend the time to act under FRCP 50(b), FRCP 50(d), FRCP 52(b), FRCP 59(b), FRCP 59(d), FRCP 59(e), and FRCP 60(b). FRCP 6(b)(2).

   iii. Refer to the United States District Court for the Western District of New York KeyRules Motion for Continuance/Extension of Time document for more information on extending time.

d. *Additional time after certain kinds of service.* When a party may or must act within a specified time after service and service is made under FRCP 5(b)(2)(C), FRCP 5(b)(2)(D), FRCP 5(b)(2)(E), or FRCP 5(b)(2)(F), three (3) days are added after the period would otherwise expire under FRCP 6(a). FRCP 6(d).

   i. *Service by overnight delivery.* Where a period of time prescribed by either the Federal Rules of Civil Procedure or the Local Rules of Civil Procedure for the United States District Court for the Western District of New York is measured from the service of a paper and service is by overnight delivery, one (1) business day shall be added to the prescribed period. NY R USDCTWD Civ Rule 5.1(g).

8. *Individual judge practices.* Refer to the Miscellaneous section of this document for information on individual judge practices on timing of documents.

## C. General Requirements

1. *Motions, generally*

   a. *Requirements.* A request for a court order must be made by motion. The motion must:

      i. Be in writing unless made during a hearing or trial;

      ii. State with particularity the grounds for seeking the order; and

      iii. State the relief sought. FRCP 7(b)(1).

b. *Notice of motion.* A party interested in resisting the relief sought by a motion has a right to notice thereof, and an opportunity to be heard. AMJUR MOTIONS § 12.

    i. In addition to statutory or court rule provisions requiring notice of a motion—the purpose of such a notice requirement having been said to be to prevent a party from being prejudicially surprised by a motion—principles of natural justice dictate that an adverse party generally must be given notice that a motion will be presented to the court. AMJUR MOTIONS § 12.

    ii. "Notice," in this regard, means reasonable notice, including a meaningful opportunity to prepare and to defend against allegations of a motion. AMJUR MOTIONS § 12.

c. *Writing requirement.* The writing requirement is intended to insure that the adverse parties are informed and have a record of both the motion's pendency and the grounds on which the movant seeks an order. FPP § 1191; Feldberg v. Quechee Lakes Corp., 463 F.3d 195 (2d Cir. 2006).

    i. It is sufficient "if the motion is stated in a written notice of the hearing of the motion." FPP § 1191.

d. *Particularity requirement.* The particularity requirement insures that the opposing parties will have notice of their opponent's contentions. FEDPROC § 62:364; Goodman v. 1973 26 Foot Trojan Vessel, Arkansas Registration No. AR1439SN, 859 F.2d 71, 12 Fed.R.Serv.3d 645 (8th Cir. 1988). That requirement ensures that notice of the basis for the motion is provided to the court and to the opposing party so as to avoid prejudice, provide the opponent with a meaningful opportunity to respond, and provide the court with enough information to process the motion correctly. FEDPROC § 62:364; Andreas v. Volkswagen of America, Inc., 336 F.3d 789, 56 Fed.R.Serv.3d 6 (8th Cir. 2003).

    i. Reasonable specification of the grounds for a motion is sufficient. However, where a movant fails to state even one ground for granting the motion in question, the movant has failed to meet the minimal standard of "reasonable specification." FEDPROC § 62:364; Martinez v. Trainor, 556 F.2d 818, 23 Fed.R.Serv.2d 403 (7th Cir. 1977).

    ii. The court may excuse the failure to comply with the particularity requirement if it is inadvertent, and where no prejudice is shown by the opposing party. FEDPROC § 62:364.

2. *Motion to dismiss for lack of subject matter jurisdiction.* A party may assert the defense of lack of subject-matter jurisdiction by motion. FRCP 12(b)(1). The objection presented by a motion under FRCP 12(b)(1) challenging the court's subject matter jurisdiction is that the district judge has no authority or competence to hear and decide the case before it. A FRCP 12(b)(1) motion most typically is employed when the movant believes that the claim asserted by the plaintiff does not involve a federal question, and there is no diversity of citizenship between the parties or, in a diversity of citizenship case, the amount in controversy does not exceed the required jurisdictional amount. FPP § 1350.

a. *Subject matter jurisdiction.* It always must be remembered that the federal courts are courts of limited jurisdiction and only can adjudicate those cases that fall within Article III of the Constitution (see U.S.C.A. Const. Art. III § 1, et seq.) and a congressional authorization enacted thereunder. FPP § 1350.

    i. *Federal question.* The district courts shall have original jurisdiction of all civil actions arising under the Constitution, laws, or treaties of the United States. 28 U.S.C.A. § 1331.

    ii. *Diversity of citizenship; Amount in controversy.* The district courts shall have original jurisdiction of all civil actions where the matter in controversy exceeds the sum or value of seventy-five thousand dollars ($75,000), exclusive of interest and costs, and is between:

- Citizens of different States;

- Citizens of a State and citizens or subjects of a foreign state, except that the district courts shall not have original jurisdiction under 28 U.S.C.A. § 1332 of an action between citizens of a State and citizens or subjects of a foreign state who are lawfully admitted for permanent residence in the United States and are domiciled in the same State;

- Citizens of different States and in which citizens or subjects of a foreign state are additional parties; and

- A foreign state, defined in 28 U.S.C.A. § 1603(a), as plaintiff and citizens of a State or of different States. 28 U.S.C.A. § 1332(a).

b. *Types of FRCP 12(b)(1) motions.* There are two separate types of FRCP 12(b)(1) motions to dismiss for lack of subject matter jurisdiction: the "facial attack" and the "factual attack." FEDPROC § 62:440.

    i. *Facial attack.* The facial attack is addressed to the sufficiency of the allegations of the complaint itself. FEDPROC § 62:440; Stalley ex rel. U.S. v. Orlando Regional Healthcare System, Inc., 524 F.3d 1229 (11th Cir. 2008). On such a motion, the court is merely required to determine whether the plaintiff has sufficiently alleged a basis of subject matter jurisdiction, and the factual allegations of the complaint are taken as true. FEDPROC § 62:440; U.S. ex rel. Atkinson v. PA. Shipbuilding Co., 473 F.3d 506 (3d Cir. 2007).

    ii. *Factual attack.* The "factual attack," on the other hand, challenges the existence of subject matter jurisdiction in fact, irrespective of the pleadings, and matters outside the pleadings, such as testimony and affidavits, may be considered by the court. FEDPROC § 62:440; Kligman v. I.R.S., 272 Fed.Appx. 166 (3d Cir. 2008); Paper, Allied-Industrial, Chemical and Energy Workers Intern. Union v. Continental Carbon Co., 428 F.3d 1285 (10th Cir. 2005). The trial court in such a situation is free to weigh the evidence and satisfy itself as to the existence of its power to hear the case; therefore, no presumptive truthfulness attaches to the plaintiff's factual allegations. FEDPROC § 62:440; Land v. Dollar, 330 U.S. 731, 67 S.Ct. 1009, 91 L.Ed. 1209 (1947).

c. *Burden.* With the limited exception of the question whether the amount in controversy requirement in diversity of citizenship cases has been satisfied, the extensive case law on the subject makes clear that the burden of proof on a FRCP 12(b)(1) motion is on the party asserting that subject matter jurisdiction exists, which, of course, typically is the plaintiff. FPP § 1350; Thomson v. Gaskill, 315 U.S. 442, 62 S.Ct. 673, 86 L.Ed. 951 (1942). A plaintiff meets the burden of establishing subject matter jurisdiction at the pleading stage by pleading sufficient allegations to show the proper basis for the court to assert subject matter jurisdiction over the action. 2 FEDFORMS § 7:6.

    i. *Federal question.* If subject matter jurisdiction is based on the existence of a federal question, the pleader must show that he or she has alleged a claim for relief arising under federal law and that the claim is not frivolous. FPP § 1350; Baker v. Carr, 369 U.S. 186, 82 S.Ct. 691, 7 L.Ed.2d 663 (1962).

    ii. *Diversity of citizenship.* If jurisdiction is based on diversity of citizenship, on the other hand, the pleader must show that real and complete diversity exists between all of the plaintiffs and all of the defendants, and also that the assertion that the claim exceeds the requisite jurisdictional amount in controversy is made in good faith. FPP § 1350; City of Indianapolis v. Chase Nat. Bank, 314 U.S. 63, 62 S.Ct. 15, 86 L.Ed. 47 (1941). Satisfying this last requirement is a relatively simple task, however, because the claim is deemed to be made in good faith so long as it is not clear to a legal certainty that the claimant could not recover a judgment exceeding the statutorily mandated jurisdictional amount, a matter on which the party challenging the district court's jurisdiction has the burden. FPP § 1350.

d. *Joining motions.* When the motion is based on more than one ground, the cases are legion stating that the district court should consider the FRCP 12(b)(1) challenge first because if it must dismiss the complaint for lack of subject matter jurisdiction, the accompanying defenses and objections become moot and do not need to be determined by the judge. FPP § 1350; Steel Co. v. Citizens for a Better Environment, 523 U.S. 83, 118 S.Ct. 1003, 140 L.Ed.2d 210 (1998). However, there are a number of decisions in which the court has decided one or more defenses in addition to the subject matter jurisdiction question or simply assumed the existence of jurisdiction and gone on to decide another matter. FPP § 1350.

    i. *Right to join.* A motion under FRCP 12 may be joined with any other motion allowed by FRCP 12. FRCP 12(g)(1).

    ii. *Limitation on further motions.* Except as provided in FRCP 12(h)(2) or FRCP 12(h)(3), a party that makes a motion under FRCP 12 must not make another motion under FRCP 12 raising a defense or objection that was available to the party but omitted from its earlier motion. FRCP 12(g)(2).

e. *Waiving and preserving certain defenses.* No defense or objection is waived by joining it with one or more other defenses or objections in a responsive pleading or in a motion. FRCP 12(b).

    i. *Waiver by consent.* The defendant may waive the right to obtain a dismissal prior to trial either by express consent to be sued in a certain district or by some conduct that will be construed as implying consent. FPP § 1352.

    ii. *When some are waived.* A party waives any defense listed in FRCP 12(b)(2) through FRCP 12(b)(5) by:

- Omitting it from a motion in the circumstances described in FRCP 12(g)(2); or

- Failing to either: (1) make it by motion under FRCP 12; or (2) include it in a responsive pleading or in an amendment allowed by FRCP 15(a)(1) as a matter of course. FRCP 12(h)(1).

    iii. *When to raise others.* Failure to state a claim upon which relief can be granted, to join a person required by FRCP 19(b), or to state a legal defense to a claim may be raised:

- In any pleading allowed or ordered under FRCP 7(a);

- By a motion under FRCP 12(c); or

- At trial. FRCP 12(h)(2).

    iv. *Lack of subject matter jurisdiction.* If the court determines at any time that it lacks subject-matter jurisdiction, the court must dismiss the action. FRCP 12(h)(3).

3. *Opposing papers.* The Federal Rules of Civil Procedure do not require any formal answer, return, or reply to a motion, except where the Federal Rules of Civil Procedure or local rules may require affidavits, memoranda, or other papers to be filed in opposition to a motion. Such papers are simply to apprise the court of such opposition and the grounds of that opposition. FEDPROC § 62:359.

    a. *Effect of failure to respond to motion.* Although in the absence of statutory provision or court rule, a motion ordinarily does not require a written answer, when a party files a motion and the opposing party fails to respond, the court may construe such failure to respond as nonopposition to the motion or an admission that the motion was meritorious, may take the facts alleged in the motion as true—the rule in some jurisdictions being that the failure to respond to a fact set forth in a motion is deemed an admission—and may grant the motion if the relief requested appears to be justified. AMJUR MOTIONS § 28.

    b. *Assent or no opposition not determinative.* However, a motion will not be granted automatically simply because an "assent" or a notation of "no opposition" has been filed; federal judges frequently deny motions that have been assented to when it is thought that justice so dictates. FPP § 1190.

    c. *Responsive pleading inappropriate as response to motion.* An attempt to answer or oppose a motion with a responsive pleading usually is not appropriate. FPP § 1190.

4. *Reply papers.* A moving party may be required or permitted to prepare papers in addition to his original motion papers. AMJUR MOTIONS § 25. Papers answering or replying to opposing papers may be appropriate, in the interests of justice, where it appears there is a substantial reason for allowing a reply. Thus, a court may accept reply papers where a party demonstrates that the papers to which it seeks to file a reply raise new issues that are material to the disposition of the question before the court, or where the court determines, sua sponte, that it wishes further briefing of an issue raised in those papers and orders the submission of additional papers. FEDPROC § 62:360.

    a. *Function of reply papers.* The function of a reply affidavit is to answer the arguments made in opposition to the position taken by the movant and not to permit the movant to introduce new arguments in support of the motion. AMJUR MOTIONS § 25.

    b. *Issues raised for the first time in a reply document.* However, the view has been followed in some jurisdictions, that as a matter of judicial economy, where there is no prejudice and where the issues could be raised simply by filing a motion to dismiss, the trial court has discretion to consider arguments raised for the first time in a reply memorandum, and that a trial court may grant a motion to strike issues raised for the first time in a reply memorandum. AMJUR MOTIONS § 26.

5. *Sur-reply.* Absent permission of the Judge hearing the motion, sur-reply papers are not permitted. NY R USDCTWD Civ Rule 7(a)(6).

6. *Motion to settle an order.* When counsel are unable to agree on the form of a proposed order, the prevailing party may move, upon seven (7) days notice to all parties, to settle the order. The Court may award costs and attorney's fees against an attorney if it determines that the attorney's unreasonable conduct necessitated bringing the motion. NY R USDCTWD Civ Rule 7(d)(2).

7. *Notice of appearance.* No notice of appearance is required of an attorney whose name and address appear at the end of a complaint, notice of removal, pre-answer motion, or answer. In all other circumstances, an attorney appearing for a party in a civil case shall promptly file a written notice of appearance. NY R USDCTWD Civ Rule 83.2(b). For more information on appearances and withdrawals, refer to NY R USDCTWD Civ Rule 83.2.

8. *Related cases.* Each attorney appearing in a civil case has a continuing duty to promptly notify the Clerk of Court when the attorney has reason to believe that said case is related to some other pending civil or criminal action(s) such that their assignment to the same Judge would avoid unnecessary duplication of judicial effort. As soon as the attorney becomes aware of such a relationship, the attorney shall notify the Clerk of Court by letter of the relevant facts, and the Clerk of Court will transmit that notification to the Judges to whom the cases have been assigned. NY R USDCTWD Civ Rule 5.1(e).

9. *Alternative dispute resolution (ADR).* This Court has adopted an Alternative Dispute Resolution Plan ("ADR"), as implemented by Standing Order (NY R USDCTWD ADR Plan), under which certain civil cases are referred automatically to ADR upon filing. NY R USDCTWD Civ Rule 16(a). The United States District Court for the Western District of New York (the "Court") adopted the ADR Plan on January 1, 2006 (the "Effective Date"), to make available to civil litigants court-administered ADR interventions and processes designed to provide quicker, less expensive and potentially more satisfying alternatives to continuing litigation, without impairing the quality of justice or the right to trial. NY R USDCTWD ADR Plan(1)(1.2)(A).

a. *Scope.* This ADR Plan (NY R USDCTWD ADR Plan) applies to civil actions pending or commenced on and after the Effective Date, except as otherwise indicated in NY R USDCTWD ADR Plan. The ADR Plan supplements the Local Rules of Civil Procedure for the United States District Court for the Western District of New York, which shall remain in full effect for all cases. NY R USDCTWD ADR Plan(1)(1.2)(B).

b. *Referral to ADR*

i. *New cases.* All civil cases filed on and after the Effective Date of the ADR Plan shall be referred automatically for ADR. NY R USDCTWD ADR Plan(2)(2.1)(A). Notice of the ADR requirements will be provided to all parties immediately upon the filing of a complaint and answer or a notice of removal; NY R USDCTWD ADR Plan(2)(2.1)(A); NY R USDCTWD Civ Rule 16(a). ADR intervention will be scheduled at the conference held pursuant to Local Rule of Civil Procedure 16.1. NY R USDCTWD ADR Plan(2)(2.1)(A). [Editor's note: the reference to Local Rule of Civil Procedure 16.1 is likely meant to be a reference to NY R USDCTWD Civ Rule 16(b)].

- Litigants in cases not referred automatically to ADR must consider possible agreement to the use of an ADR process. NY R USDCTWD Civ Rule 16(a).

- For a list of exemptions from automatic referral, refer to NY R USDCTWD ADR Plan(2)(2.1)(A).

ii. *Pending cases.* The assigned Judge on any pending civil case may, sua sponte or with status conference, issue an order referring the case for ADR. NY R USDCTWD ADR Plan(2)(2.1)(B); NY R USDCTWD Civ Rule 16(a). The order shall specify a date on which the ADR intervention is to be completed. NY R USDCTWD ADR Plan(2)(2.1)(B).

iii. *Stipulation.* A case may be referred for ADR by stipulation of all parties. Stipulations shall be filed and shall designate the specific ADR intervention the parties have selected, the time frame within which the ADR process will be completed and the selected Neutral. Stipulations are presumed acceptable unless the assigned Judge determines that the interests of justice are not served. NY R USDCTWD ADR Plan(2)(2.1)(C).

iv. *Relief from ADR referral*

- *Opting out motions.* Any party may file, with the assigned Judge for that case, a motion to opt out of, or for relief from, ADR. NY R USDCTWD ADR Plan(2)(2.2)(A).

- *Motion.* Opting Out Motions must be made within fourteen (14) days from (1) the date of the first discovery conference under Local Rule 16.1 in new cases, or (2) the date of a sua sponte ADR Referral Order in pending cases. NY R USDCTWD ADR Plan(2)(2.2)(B). [Editor's note: the reference to Local Rule 16.1 is likely meant to be a reference to NY R USDCTWD Civ Rule 16(b)].

- *Criteria.* Opting Out Motions shall be granted only for "good cause" shown. Inconvenience, travel costs, attorney fees or other costs shall not constitute "good cause." A party seeking relief from ADR must set forth the reasons why ADR has no reasonable chance of being productive. NY R USDCTWD ADR Plan(2)(2.2)(C).

- *Judicial initiative.* The assigned Judge may, sua sponte, exempt any case from the Court's ADR Plan. NY R USDCTWD ADR Plan(2)(2.2)(D).

c. *ADR interventions*

i. *Options.* It is expected that cases referred for ADR will proceed to Mediation. However, the following options are also available upon the stipulation of all parties:

- Neutral Evaluation;

- Mini Summary Trial;

- Arbitration (Binding and Non-Binding);

- Case Valuation; and

- Settlement Week, when scheduled by the Court. NY R USDCTWD ADR Plan(4)(4.1)(A).

ii. *Timing.* Timing is specific to the intervention and process chosen, as set forth in the corresponding sections in NY R USDCTWD ADR Plan. NY R USDCTWD ADR Plan(4)(4.1)(B).

iii. *Scheduling.* The referral of a case to ADR does not delay or defer other dates established in the Scheduling Order and has no effect on the scheduled progress of the case toward trial. NY R USDCTWD ADR Plan(4)(4.1)(C).

d. *Selecting an ADR intervention*

i. *New cases.* Prior to the Local Rule 16.1 scheduling conference, counsel and any unrepresented parties shall confer about ADR as part of their discussion of "the possibilities for a prompt settlement or resolution of the case" pursuant to FRCP 26(f). Unless the parties agree to a different intervention, it is presumed that they will participate in mediation. [Editor's note: the reference to Local Rule 16.1 is likely meant to be a reference to NY R USDCTWD Civ Rule 16(b)].

ii. *Pending cases.* In pending cases, all sua sponte referrals will be to mediation. Should the parties agree that a different ADR intervention is more appropriate to their case, they may submit a stipulation designating the specific ADR intervention selected, the time frame within which the ADR process will be completed and the identity of the Neutral. Stipulations must be filed within fourteen (14) days from the date of the ADR Referral Order and are presumed acceptable unless the assigned Judge determines that the interests of justice are not served. NY R USDCTWD ADR Plan(4)(4.2)(B).

e. For more information on alternative dispute resolution (ADR), refer to NY R USDCTWD ADR Plan.

10. *Sanctions.* Failure of counsel for any party, or a party proceeding pro se, to appear before the Court at a conference, to complete the necessary preparations, or to be prepared to proceed to trial at the set time may be considered an abandonment of the case or a failure to prosecute or defend diligently. An appropriate order for sanctions may be entered against the defaulting party with respect to either a specific issue or the entire case. NY R USDCTWD Civ Rule 11(a). For more information, refer to NY R USDCTWD Civ Rule 11.

11. *Pro se actions.* For information on the requirements in pro se actions, refer to NY R USDCTWD Civ Rule 5.2.

12. *Individual judge practices.* Refer to the Miscellaneous section of this document for information on individual judge practices on general requirements for documents.

## D. Documents

1. *Documents for moving party*

   a. *Required documents*

      i. *Notice of motion and motion.* A notice of motion is required for all motions, and must state: the relief sought, the grounds for the request, the papers submitted in support, and the return date for the motion, if known. A moving party who intends to file and serve reply papers must so state in the notice of motion. NY R USDCTWD Civ Rule 7(a)(1). Refer to the General Requirements section of this document for information on the notice of motion and motion.

      ii. *Memorandum of law.* Absent leave of Court or as otherwise specified, upon any motion filed pursuant to FRCP 12, FRCP 56 or FRCP 65(a), the moving party shall file and serve a memorandum of law. Failure to comply with this requirement may constitute grounds for resolving the motion against the non-complying party. NY R USDCTWD Civ Rule 7(a)(2)(A). Refer to the Format section of this document for the formatting requirements for memoranda of law.

      iii. *Certificate of service.* FRCP 5(d) requires that the person making service under FRCP 5 certify that service has been effected. FRCP 5(Advisory Committee Notes). Having such information on file may be useful for many purposes, including proof of service if an issue arises concerning the effectiveness of the service. FRCP 5(Advisory Committee Notes). The Notice of Electronic Filing effectuates service for all registered users and no certificate of service is required when all filers on an action are Registered Users. The following exemptions require a certificate of service to be filed:

         • When a document is manually filed, a certificate of service must be filed stating the manner in which service or notice was accomplished on each party so entitled. NY R USDCTWD ECF Procedures(2)(f)(iv).

         • When a pro se filer (who isn't authorized to electronically file documents) is a party, a certificate of service must be filed stating the manner in which service or notice was accomplished on the pro se party. The Notice of Electronic Filing effectuates service for the Registered Users in this situation and it is not necessary to note service on those parties. A non-registered pro se filer is required to file certificates of service on all documents they file. NY R USDCTWD ECF Procedures(2)(f)(iv).

         • If an attorney is exempt from electronic service, a certificate of service must be filed stating the manner in which service or notice was accomplished on the exempt attorney. The Notice of Electronic Filing effectuates service for the Registered Users in this situation and it is not necessary to note service on those parties. NY R USDCTWD ECF Procedures(2)(f)(iv).

   b. *Supplemental documents*

      i. *Supporting evidence.* When a motion relies on facts outside the record, the court may hear the matter on affidavits or may hear it wholly or partly on oral testimony or on depositions. FRCP 43(c). A party seeking or opposing any relief under the Federal Rules of Civil Procedure shall file only the portion(s) of a deposition, interrogatory, request for documents, request for admission, or other supporting material that is pertinent to the application. NY R USDCTWD Civ Rule 7(a)(4).

      ii. *Notice of constitutional question.* A party that files a pleading, written motion, or other paper drawing into question the constitutionality of a federal or state statute must promptly:

         • *File notice.* File a notice of constitutional question stating the question and identifying the paper that raises it, if: (1) a federal statute is questioned and the parties do not include the

United States, one of its agencies, or one of its officers or employees in an official capacity; or (2) a state statute is questioned and the parties do not include the state, one of its agencies, or one of its officers or employees in an official capacity; and

- *Serve notice.* Serve the notice and paper on the Attorney General of the United States if a federal statute is questioned—or on the state attorney general if a state statute is questioned—either by certified or registered mail or by sending it to an electronic address designated by the attorney general for this purpose. FRCP 5.1(a).

- *No forfeiture.* A party's failure to file and serve the notice, or the court's failure to certify, does not forfeit a constitutional claim or defense that is otherwise timely asserted. FRCP 5.1(d).

iii. *Nongovernmental corporate disclosure statement*

- *Contents.* A nongovernmental corporate party must file two (2) copies of a disclosure statement that: (1) identifies any parent corporation and any publicly held corporation owning ten percent (10%) or more of its stock; or (2) states that there is no such corporation. FRCP 7.1(a).

- *Time to file; Supplemental filing.* A party must: (1) file the disclosure statement with its first appearance, pleading, petition, motion, response, or other request addressed to the court; and (2) promptly file a supplemental statement if any required information changes. FRCP 7.1(b).

iv. *Copies of authorities.* In cases involving a pro se litigant, counsel shall, when serving a memorandum of law (or other submissions to the Court), provide the pro se litigant (but not other counsel or the Court) with printed copies of decisions cited therein that are unreported or reported exclusively on computerized databases. NY R USDCTWD Civ Rule 7(a)(8).

v. *Proposed order.* All proposed orders must be submitted in a format compatible with WordPerfect or Microsoft Word format, which is a "Save As" option in most word processing software. Judges will not accept proposed orders in PDF format. NY R USDCTWD ECF Procedures(2)(j)(ii). Proposed orders should be attached to an Internet e-mail sent to the e-mail address of the assigned judge. NY R USDCTWD ECF Procedures(2)(j)(i). For the list of email addresses for the judges, refer to NY R USDCTWD ECF Procedures(2)(j)(i).

vi. *Paper copy for date-stamping with self-addressed envelope.* Parties requesting date-stamped copies of filed documents must provide a paper copy for date-stamping, and a self-addressed, adequately-sized envelope with proper postage affixed. NY R USDCTWD Civ Rule 5.1(d).

vii. *Courtesy copies.* The Court may, in its discretion, request courtesy copies on any other motion. NY R USDCTWD Civ Rule 7(a)(7). Courtesy copies of certain documents may be required. Filers should refer to the "Judge Preferences" published on the Court's website. NY R USDCTWD ECF Procedures(2)(a)(iii).

2. *Documents for opposing party*

a. *Required documents*

i. *Opposition.* Refer to the General Requirements section of this document for information on the opposing papers.

ii. *Answering memorandum.* Absent leave of Court or as otherwise specified, upon any motion filed pursuant to FRCP 12, FRCP 56 or FRCP 65(a). . .the opposing party shall file and serve an answering memorandum. Failure to comply with this requirement may constitute grounds for resolving the motion against the non-complying party. NY R USDCTWD Civ Rule 7(a)(2)(A). Refer to the Format section of this document for the formatting requirements for memoranda of law.

iii. *Certificate of service.* FRCP 5(d) requires that the person making service under FRCP 5 certify that service has been effected. FRCP 5(Advisory Committee Notes). Having such information on file may be useful for many purposes, including proof of service if an issue arises concerning the effectiveness of the service. FRCP 5(Advisory Committee Notes). The Notice of Electronic

Filing effectuates service for all registered users and no certificate of service is required when all filers on an action are Registered Users. The following exemptions require a certificate of service to be filed:

- When a document is manually filed, a certificate of service must be filed stating the manner in which service or notice was accomplished on each party so entitled. NY R USDCTWD ECF Procedures(2)(f)(iv).

- When a pro se filer (who isn't authorized to electronically file documents) is a party, a certificate of service must be filed stating the manner in which service or notice was accomplished on the pro se party. The Notice of Electronic Filing effectuates service for the Registered Users in this situation and it is not necessary to note service on those parties. A non-registered pro se filer is required to file certificates of service on all documents they file. NY R USDCTWD ECF Procedures(2)(f)(iv).

- If an attorney is exempt from electronic service, a certificate of service must be filed stating the manner in which service or notice was accomplished on the exempt attorney. The Notice of Electronic Filing effectuates service for the Registered Users in this situation and it is not necessary to note service on those parties. NY R USDCTWD ECF Procedures(2)(f)(iv).

b. *Supplemental documents*

i. *Supporting evidence.* When a motion relies on facts outside the record, the court may hear the matter on affidavits or may hear it wholly or partly on oral testimony or on depositions. FRCP 43(c). A party seeking or opposing any relief under the Federal Rules of Civil Procedure shall file only the portion(s) of a deposition, interrogatory, request for documents, request for admission, or other supporting material that is pertinent to the application. NY R USDCTWD Civ Rule 7(a)(4).

ii. *Notice of constitutional question.* A party that files a pleading, written motion, or other paper drawing into question the constitutionality of a federal or state statute must promptly:

- *File notice.* File a notice of constitutional question stating the question and identifying the paper that raises it, if: (1) a federal statute is questioned and the parties do not include the United States, one of its agencies, or one of its officers or employees in an official capacity; or (2) a state statute is questioned and the parties do not include the state, one of its agencies, or one of its officers or employees in an official capacity; and

- *Serve notice.* Serve the notice and paper on the Attorney General of the United States if a federal statute is questioned—or on the state attorney general if a state statute is questioned—either by certified or registered mail or by sending it to an electronic address designated by the attorney general for this purpose. FRCP 5.1(a).

- *No forfeiture.* A party's failure to file and serve the notice, or the court's failure to certify, does not forfeit a constitutional claim or defense that is otherwise timely asserted. FRCP 5.1(d).

iii. *Copies of authorities.* In cases involving a pro se litigant, counsel shall, when serving a memorandum of law (or other submissions to the Court), provide the pro se litigant (but not other counsel or the Court) with printed copies of decisions cited therein that are unreported or reported exclusively on computerized databases. NY R USDCTWD Civ Rule 7(a)(8).

iv. *Paper copy for date-stamping with self-addressed envelope.* Parties requesting date-stamped copies of filed documents must provide a paper copy for date-stamping, and a self-addressed, adequately-sized envelope with proper postage affixed. NY R USDCTWD Civ Rule 5.1(d).

v. *Courtesy copies.* Courtesy copies of certain documents may be required. Filers should refer to the "Judge Preferences" published on the Court's website. NY R USDCTWD ECF Procedures(2)(a)(iii).

3. *Individual judge practices.* Refer to the Miscellaneous section of this document for information on individual judge practices on required documents.

WESTERN DISTRICT OF NEW YORK

## E. Format

1. *Form of documents.* The rules governing captions and other matters of form in pleadings apply to motions and other papers. FRCP 7(b)(2).

    a. *Form, generally.* All pleadings, motions, and other papers that a party presents for filing, whether in paper form or in electronic form, shall meet the following requirements:

        i. *Font size.* All text and footnotes shall be in a font size of at least twelve (12) point type. NY R USDCTWD Civ Rule 10(a)(1).

        ii. *Spacing.* All text in the body of the document must be double-spaced, except that text in block quotations and footnotes may be single-spaced. NY R USDCTWD Civ Rule 10(a)(2).

        • Extensive footnotes and block quotes may not be used to circumvent page limitations. NY R USDCTWD Civ Rule 10(a)(3).

        iii. *Margins.* Documents must have one (1) inch margins on all four sides. NY R USDCTWD Civ Rule 10(a)(4).

        iv. *Page numbering.* Pages must be consecutively numbered. NY R USDCTWD Civ Rule 10(a)(5).

    b. *Additional requirements for paper filing.* Documents presented for filing in paper form shall meet the following additional requirements:

        i. *Paper.* Documents must be on durable white eight and one-half by eleven (8-1/2 x 11) inch paper of good quality. NY R USDCTWD Civ Rule 10(b)(1).

        • All documents must be single-sided. NY R USDCTWD Civ Rule 10(b)(5).

        ii. *Text.* All text must be plainly and legibly written, typewritten, printed or reproduced. NY R USDCTWD Civ Rule 10(b)(2).

        iii. *Ink.* Documents must be in black or blue ink. NY R USDCTWD Civ Rule 10(b)(3).

        iv. *Binding.* The pages of each document must be stapled or in some other way fastened together. NY R USDCTWD Civ Rule 10(b)(4).

    c. *Caption; Names of parties.* Every pleading must have a caption with the court's name, a title, a file number, and a FRCP 7(a) designation. The title of the complaint must name all the parties; the title of other pleadings, after naming the first party on each side, may refer generally to other parties. FRCP 10(a).

    d. *Paragraphs; Separate statements.* A party must state its claims or defenses in numbered paragraphs, each limited as far as practicable to a single set of circumstances. A later pleading may refer by number to a paragraph in an earlier pleading. If doing so would promote clarity, each claim founded on a separate transaction or occurrence—and each defense other than a denial—must be stated in a separate count or defense. FRCP 10(b).

    e. *Adoption by reference; Exhibits.* A statement in a pleading may be adopted by reference elsewhere in the same pleading or in any other pleading or motion. A copy of a written instrument that is an exhibit to a pleading is a part of the pleading for all purposes. FRCP 10(c).

    f. *Citation of local rules.* The Local Rules of Civil Procedure for the United States District Court for the Western District of New York shall be cited as "L.R.Civ.P." NY R USDCTWD Civ Rule 1.1.

    g. *Acceptance by the clerk.* The clerk must not refuse to file a paper solely because it is not in the form prescribed by the Federal Rules of Civil Procedure or by a local rule or practice. FRCP 5(d)(4). The Court may reject documents that do not comply with the requirements in NY R USDCTWD Civ Rule 10. NY R USDCTWD Civ Rule 10.

2. *Form of electronic documents.* All pleadings, motions, and other papers that a party presents for filing, whether in paper form or in electronic form, shall meet the requirements in NY R USDCTWD Civ Rule 10(a). NY R USDCTWD Civ Rule 10(a). Refer above for more information.

    a. *Conversion to PDF.* A document created with a word processor, or a paper document, must be converted to Portable Document Format to be electronically filed with the court. NY R USDCTWD ECF Procedures(2)(a)(v).

    i.    Documents which exist only in paper form may be scanned into a portable document format (PDF) for electronic filing. NY R USDCTWD ECF Procedures(2)(a)(v). Before filing a scanned document with the court, a Filing User must verify its legibility. NY R USDCTWD ECF Procedures(2)(a)(iv).

    ii.    Electronic documents must be converted to .PDF from a word processing program and must be text searchable. Do not print, scan and .PDF your document when it has been created in a word processing program. Additional information on working with PDFs is located in NY R USDCTWD ECF Procedures(4b). NY R USDCTWD ECF Procedures(2)(a)(v).

  b.  *Hyperlinks.* Pursuant to the policy set forth by the Judicial Conference in October 2005, a hyperlink contained in a filing is no more than a convenient mechanism for accessing material cited in a document. A hyperlink reference is extraneous to any filed document and is not part of the Court's record. NY R USDCTWD ECF Procedures(2)(a)(vi).

    i.    In order to preserve the integrity of the Court record, users wishing to insert hyperlinks in Court filings shall continue to use the conventional method for the cited authority, in addition to the hyperlink. NY R USDCTWD ECF Procedures(2)(a)(vi).

    ii.    The Court accepts no responsibility for, and does not endorse any product, organization, and content at any hyperlinked site, or at any site to which that site may be linked. The Court accepts no responsibility for the availability or functionality of any hyperlink. NY R USDCTWD ECF Procedures(2)(a)(vi).

  c.  *Attachments and exhibits*

    i.    Attachments and exhibits larger than five megabytes (5 MB) shall be filed electronically in separate five megabyte (5 MB) segments. NY R USDCTWD ECF Procedures(2)(d)(i).

    ii.    Filing Users must submit in electronic form all documents referenced as exhibits or attachments, except as otherwise provided in NY R USDCTWD ECF Procedures. A Filing User must submit as exhibits or attachments only those excerpts of the referenced documents that are directly germane to the matter under consideration by the court. Excerpted material must be clearly and prominently identified as such. Filing Users who file excerpts of documents as exhibits or attachments under NY R USDCTWD ECF Procedures(2)(d)(ii) do so without prejudice to their right to timely file additional excerpts or the complete document. Responding parties may timely file additional excerpts or the complete document that they believe are directly germane. The Court may require parties to file additional excerpts or the complete document. A Filing User must request leave of the Court to file a document exhibit or attachment in non-electronic form. NY R USDCTWD ECF Procedures(2)(d)(ii).

    iii.    Exhibits offered or admitted at trial will not be filed electronically or conventionally unless so ordered by the Court. NY R USDCTWD ECF Procedures(2)(d)(iii).

    iv.    Exhibits such as videotapes and tape recordings shall be filed in the conventional manner with the Clerk of Court, and a Notice of Manual Filing shall be electronically filed by the party. Manually filed exhibits must have the case number and case name securely fastened or marked on the item. NY R USDCTWD ECF Procedures(2)(d)(iii).

    v.    Continuation of exhibit entries (for exhibits that are too large to attach to a main document) must be filed and entered on the same day that the main document was filed. NY R USDCTWD ECF Procedures(2)(d)(iv).

  d.  *Color documents.* Documents in color or containing graphics take much longer to upload. Filing users are encouraged to configure their scanners to scan documents at 200 dpi and preferably in black and white rather than color. NY R USDCTWD ECF Procedures(2)(d)(v).

  e.  *Large documents.* Due to the length of time it takes to download large files, documents larger than five megabytes (5 MB) (approximately one hundred (100) pages of a .pdf scanned document) must be filed electronically in separate five megabyte (5 MB) segments. A party who believes a document is too lengthy to electronically image (i.e. scan), may contact the Court Room Deputy for the assigned judge and request permission to file that document conventionally. If granted permission to file the document conventionally, the Filing User shall electronically file a "notice of manual filing" for that item. Exhibits submitted to the Court conventionally shall be served on other parties conventionally. NY R USDCTWD ECF Procedures(2)(d)(vi).

3. *Form of memoranda of law.* Memoranda in support of or in opposition to any motion shall not exceed twenty-five (25) pages in length, and reply memoranda shall not exceed ten (10) pages in length. A party seeking to exceed the page limit must make application by letter to the Judge hearing the motion, with copies to all counsel, at least seven (7) days before the date on which the memorandum must be filed. NY R USDCTWD Civ Rule 7(a)(2)(C).

4. *Signing of pleadings, motions and other papers*

  a. *Signature.* Every pleading, written motion, and other paper must be signed by at least one attorney of record in the attorney's name—or by a party personally if the party is unrepresented. The paper must state the signer's address, e-mail address, and telephone number. FRCP 11(a). Documents presented for paper filing must contain an original signature. NY R USDCTWD Civ Rule 10(b)(6).

    i. *Electronic signatures*

      • *Non-attorney signature.* If the original document requires the signature of a non-attorney, the filing party shall obtain the signature of the non-attorney on the document. NY R USDCTWD ECF Procedures(2)(g)(i). The filing party or attorney then shall file the document electronically indicating the signatory's name in the form "s/(name)." NY R USDCTWD ECF Procedures(2)(g)(i)(1). A non-filing signatory or party who disputes the authenticity of an electronically filed document or the authenticity of the signature on that document must file an objection to the document within ten (10) days of receiving the Notice of Electronic Filing. NY R USDCTWD ECF Procedures(2)(g)(i)(2).

      • *Registered user signature.* The username and password required to file documents on the Electronic Filing System serve as the Filing User's signature on all electronic documents filed with this Court. The also serve as a signature for the purposes of FRCP 11, the Federal Rules of Civil Procedure, the Local Rules of Civil Procedure for the United States District Court for the Western District of New York, and any other purpose for which a signature is required in connection with proceedings before this Court. A pleading requiring a Registered User's signature must include a signature block in the format found in NY R USDCTWD ECF Procedures(2)(g)(iii). NY R USDCTWD ECF Procedures(2)(g)(iii). Any party challenging the authenticity of an electronically filed document or the attorney's signature on that document must file an objection to the document within ten (10) days of receiving the Notice of Electronic Filing. NY R USDCTWD ECF Procedures(2)(g)(iii)(1).

      • *Multiple signatures.* The following procedure applies when a stipulation or other document requires two or more signatures: The filing party shall initially confirm that the document is acceptable to all persons required to sign the document and shall obtain the signatures of all parties on the document. NY R USDCTWD ECF Procedures(2)(g)(iv)(1). The filing party or attorney then shall file the document electronically indicating the signatories, e.g., "s/Jane Doe," "s/John Smith," etc. NY R USDCTWD ECF Procedures(2)(g)(iv)(2). A non-filing signatory or party who disputes the authenticity of an electronically filed document containing multiple signatures or the authenticity of the signatures themselves must file an objection to the document within ten (10) days of receiving the Notice of Electronic Filing. NY R USDCTWD ECF Procedures(2)(g)(iv)(3).

    ii. *No verification or accompanying affidavit required for pleadings.* Unless a rule or statute specifically states otherwise, a pleading need not be verified or accompanied by an affidavit. FRCP 11(a).

    iii. *Unsigned papers.* The court must strike an unsigned paper unless the omission is promptly corrected after being called to the attorney's or party's attention. FRCP 11(a).

b. *Representations to the court.* By presenting to the court a pleading, written motion, or other paper—whether by signing, filing, submitting, or later advocating it—an attorney or unrepresented party certifies that to the best of the person's knowledge, information, and belief, formed after an inquiry reasonable under the circumstances:

    i. It is not being presented for any improper purpose, such as to harass, cause unnecessary delay, or needlessly increase the cost of litigation;

    ii. The claims, defenses, and other legal contentions are warranted by existing law or by a nonfrivolous argument for extending, modifying, or reversing existing law or for establishing new law;

    iii. The factual contentions have evidentiary support or, if specifically so identified, will likely have evidentiary support after a reasonable opportunity for further investigation or discovery; and

    iv. The denials of factual contentions are warranted on the evidence or, if specifically so identified, are reasonably based on belief or a lack of information. FRCP 11(b).

c. *Sanctions.* If, after notice and a reasonable opportunity to respond, the court determines that FRCP 11(b) has been violated, the court may impose an appropriate sanction on any attorney, law firm, or party that violated FRCP 11(b) or is responsible for the violation. FRCP 11(c)(1). Refer to the United States District Court for the Western District of New York KeyRules Motion for Sanctions document for more information.

5. *Privacy protection for filings made with the court.* In all filings, parties shall comply with FRCP 5.2. NY R USDCTWD ECF Procedures(2)(m)(i).

a. *Redacted filings.* Unless the court orders otherwise, in an electronic or paper filing with the court that contains an individual's Social Security number, taxpayer-identification number, or birth date, the name of an individual known to be a minor, or a financial-account number, a party or nonparty making the filing may include only:

    i. The last four (4) digits of the Social Security number and taxpayer-identification number;

    ii. The year of the individual's birth;

    iii. The minor's initials; and

    iv. The last four (4) digits of the financial-account number. FRCP 5.2(a).

b. *Exemptions from the redaction requirement.* The redaction requirement does not apply to the following:

    i. A financial-account number that identifies the property allegedly subject to forfeiture in a forfeiture proceeding;

    ii. The record of an administrative or agency proceeding;

    iii. The official record of a state-court proceeding;

    iv. The record of a court or tribunal, if that record was not subject to the redaction requirement when originally filed;

    v. A filing covered by FRCP 5.2(c) or FRCP 5.2(d); and

    vi. A pro se filing in an action brought under 28 U.S.C.A. § 2241, 28 U.S.C.A. § 2254, or 28 U.S.C.A. § 2255. FRCP 5.2(b).

c. *Limitations on remote access to electronic files; Social Security appeals and immigration cases.* Unless the court orders otherwise, in an action for benefits under the Social Security Act, and in an action or proceeding relating to an order of removal, to relief from removal, or to immigration benefits or detention, access to an electronic file is authorized as follows:

    i. The parties and their attorneys may have remote electronic access to any part of the case file, including the administrative record;

    ii. Any other person may have electronic access to the full record at the courthouse, but may have remote electronic access only to:

        • The docket maintained by the court; and

- An opinion, order, judgment, or other disposition of the court, but not any other part of the case file or the administrative record. FRCP 5.2(c).

d.  *Filings made under seal.* The court may order that a filing be made under seal without redaction. The court may later unseal the filing or order the person who made the filing to file a redacted version for the public record. FRCP 5.2(d). For more information on sealing documents, refer to NY R USDCTWD Civ Rule 5.3, NY R USDCTWD ECF Procedures(2)(o)(i)(1), NY R USDCTWD ECF Procedures(2)(o)(i)(2), and NY R USDCTWD ECF Procedures(2)(o)(i)(3).

e.  *Protective orders.* For good cause, the court may by order in a case:

    i.  Require redaction of additional information; or

    ii. Limit or prohibit a nonparty's remote electronic access to a document filed with the court. FRCP 5.2(e).

f.  *Option for additional unredacted filing under seal.* A person making a redacted filing may also file an unredacted copy under seal. The court must retain the unredacted copy as part of the record. FRCP 5.2(f).

g.  *Option for filing a reference list.* A filing that contains redacted information may be filed together with a reference list that identifies each item of redacted information and specifies an appropriate identifier that uniquely corresponds to each item listed. The list must be filed under seal and may be amended as of right. Any reference in the case to a listed identifier will be construed to refer to the corresponding item of information. FRCP 5.2(g).

h.  *Waiver of protection of identifiers.* A person waives the protection of FRCP 5.2(a) as to the person's own information by filing it without redaction and not under seal. FRCP 5.2(h).

6.  *Individual judge practices.* Refer to the Miscellaneous section of this document for information on individual judge practices on formatting documents.

## F. Filing and Service Requirements

1.  *Filing requirements.* Any paper after the complaint that is required to be served—together with a certificate of service—must be filed within a reasonable time after service. FRCP 5(d)(1). All pleadings and other papers shall be filed and served in accordance with the Federal Rules of Civil Procedure and the CM/ECF Administrative Procedures Guide (NY R USDCTWD ECF Procedures). NY R USDCTWD Civ Rule 5.1(a). For information on filing of miscellaneous cases and irregular documents, refer to NY R USDCTWD Civ Rule 5.6.

    a.  *How filing is made; In general.* A paper is filed by delivering it:

        i.  To the clerk; or

        ii. To a judge who agrees to accept it for filing, and who must then note the filing date on the paper and promptly send it to the clerk. FRCP 5(d)(2).

    b.  *Electronic filing*

        i.  *Authorization of electronic filing program.* A court may, by local rule, allow papers to be filed, signed, or verified by electronic means that are consistent with any technical standards established by the Judicial Conference of the United States. A local rule may require electronic filing only if reasonable exceptions are allowed. A paper filed electronically in compliance with a local rule is a written paper for purposes of the Federal Rules of Civil Procedure. FRCP 5(d)(3).

            - All civil cases filed in this Court are assigned to the Electronic Case Filing System ("ECF"). The procedures for electronic filing and any exceptions to the electronic filing requirements are set forth in the CM/ECF Administrative Procedures Guide (NY R USDCTWD ECF Procedures) which is available on the Court's website. NY R US-DCTWD Civ Rule 5.1(a).

        ii. *Scope of electronic filing.* The U.S. District Court for the Western District of New York requires attorneys in civil and criminal cases to file documents with the Court electronically over the Internet using its Case Management/Electronic Case Filing (CM/ECF) system. NY R US-

DCTWD ECF Procedures. Beginning January 1, 2004, all civil and criminal cases currently pending and newly filed, except as expressly noted herein, were assigned to the Electronic Case Filing System ("System"). Except as expressly provided and in exceptional circumstances preventing a Filing User from filing electronically, all petitions, motions, memoranda of law, or other pleadings and documents required to be filed with the Court in connection with a case assigned to the System must be electronically filed. NY R USDCTWD ECF Procedures(1)(a).

- *Mandatory electronic filing.* All documents on civil, criminal, miscellaneous civil, miscellaneous criminal and new civil case openings, except sealed documents, sealed cases, opening of a criminal case, opening of a miscellaneous case and as expressly provided for in these procedures (NY R USDCTWD ECF Procedures), shall be electronically filed on the system. NY R USDCTWD ECF Procedures(2)(a)(i). NY R USDCTWD Civ Rule 29

- *Stipulations.* Pursuant to NY R USDCTWD Civ Rule 29, all stipulations (whether the stipulation is final or when it requires a judge's signature) shall be filed electronically. NY R USDCTWD ECF Procedures(2)(p)(i).

- *Letters.* The electronic filing of letters is generally prohibited unless granted permission by an assigned judge. Letters to the Court must be submitted conventionally. NY R USDCTWD ECF Procedures(2)(q)(i).

- *Exceptions.* The Court requires attorneys to file documents electronically, absent a showing of good cause, unless otherwise excused by the procedures set forth below or by Order of the Court. NY R USDCTWD ECF Procedures.

iii. *Conventional filing of documents.* The procedures in NY R USDCTWD ECF Procedures(2)(o) govern documents filed conventionally. The Court, upon application, may also authorize conventional filing of other documents otherwise subject to the procedures in NY R USDCTWD ECF Procedures(2)(o). NY R USDCTWD ECF Procedures(2)(o)(i).

- *Documents filed under seal.* Unredacted documents filed with the Court pursuant to the privacy provisions of FRCP 5.2 shall be submitted in a sealing envelope with the information in NY R USDCTWD ECF Procedures(2)(o)(i)(1) on the envelope. NY R USDCTWD ECF Procedures(2)(o)(i)(1). If the document is larger than five (5) pages, a disk should be provided to the Clerks Office which contains the document in a .pdf format. NY R USDCTWD ECF Procedures(2)(o)(i)(1). For more information on documents filed under seal, refer to NY R USDCTWD ECF Procedures(2)(o)(i)(1), NY R USDCTWD ECF Procedures(2)(o)(i)(2), and NY R USDCTWD ECF Procedures(2)(o)(i)(3).

- *Magistrate judge consents.* Pursuant to FRCP 73(b), parties' filing consents to jurisdiction by United States Magistrate Judge will continue to be treated as non-public documents until all parties have consented. Therefore, parties must submit conventionally (in paper form) and not electronically file their consent forms so that the consent is not a public document. If all parties consent to the jurisdiction of a Magistrate Judge, the Clerk will scan all consent forms which will then become a public document. NY R USDCTWD ECF Procedures(2)(o)(i)(3).

- *Pro se filers.* Pro Se filers shall file paper originals of all initiating documents, pleadings, motions, affidavits, briefs and other documents which must be signed or which require either verification or an unsworn declaration under any rule or statute. The Clerk's Office will scan these original documents into an electronic file in the System. A certificate of service is required for all documents a pro se litigant files with the court. If a Pro Se filer is granted permission to register to electronically file documents, they shall comply with the guidelines contained in this document (NY R USDCTWD ECF Procedures). NY R USDCTWD ECF Procedures(2)(o)(i)(4).

- *Social Security cases.* Absent a showing of good cause, and except as provided in Section o(i)(4) above, all documents, notices and orders in Social Security reviews will be filed and noticed electronically, except as noted in NY R USDCTWD ECF Procedures(2)(o)(i)(6). For more information, refer to NY R USDCTWD ECF Procedures(2)(o)(i)(6).

- For more information on conventional filing of documents, refer to NY R USDCTWD ECF Procedures(2)(o)(i).

    iv. *Consequences of electronic filing.* Electronic transmission of a document to the System consistent with these procedures (NY R USDCTWD ECF Procedures), whether accomplished by the Filing User or a Court User, together with the transmission of a Notice of Electronic Filing from the Court, constitutes filing of a document for all purposes of the Federal Rules of Civil Procedure and the Local Rules of Civil Procedure for the United States District Court for the Western District of New York, and constitutes entry of the document on the docket kept by the Clerk under FRCP 58 and FRCP 79. A document shall not be considered filed for purposes of the Federal Rules of Civil until the filing party receives a System generated Notice of Electronic Filing. NY R USDCTWD ECF Procedures(2)(a)(i).

- E-mailing a document to the Clerk's Office or to the assigned judge shall not constitute "filing" of such document. NY R USDCTWD ECF Procedures(2)(a)(i)(1).

    v. *Filing fees.* Any fee required for filing of a pleading or paper in District Court is payable to the Clerk of Court by check or money order. In addition, when opening a civil case on line, filing a notice of appeal on line or applying to appear pro hac vice on line, the fees shall be paid on line by registered users through the federal electronic payment website. Users will be directed to the federal electronic payment website while entering their transaction and should have a credit card available. When opening a civil case and applying to proceed in forma pauperis or when the United States of America opens a case, the payment screen can by bypassed to complete the transaction. Additional information on making electronic payments can be located on the court's website. NY R USDCTWD ECF Procedures(2)(h)(i).

2. *Service requirements.* All pleadings and other papers shall be filed and served in accordance with the Federal Rules of Civil Procedure and the CM/ECF Administrative Procedures Guide (NY R USDCTWD ECF Procedures). NY R USDCTWD Civ Rule 5.1(a).

  a. *Service; When required*

    i. *In general.* Unless the Federal Rules of Civil Procedure provide otherwise, each of the following papers must be served on every party:

- An order stating that service is required;

- A pleading filed after the original complaint, unless the court orders otherwise under FRCP 5(c) because there are numerous defendants;

- A discovery paper required to be served on a party, unless the court orders otherwise;

- A written motion, except one that may be heard ex parte; and

- A written notice, appearance, demand, or offer of judgment, or any similar paper. FRCP 5(a)(1).

    ii. *If a party fails to appear.* No service is required on a party who is in default for failing to appear. But a pleading that asserts a new claim for relief against such a party must be served on that party under FRCP 4. FRCP 5(a)(2).

    iii. *Seizing property.* If an action is begun by seizing property and no person is or need be named as a defendant, any service required before the filing of an appearance, answer, or claim must be made on the person who had custody or possession of the property when it was seized. FRCP 5(a)(3).

  b. *Service; How made*

    i. *Serving an attorney.* If a party is represented by an attorney, service under FRCP 5 must be made on the attorney unless the court orders service on the party. FRCP 5(b)(1).

    ii. *Service in general.* A paper is served under FRCP 5 by:

- Handing it to the person;

- Leaving it: (1) at the person's office with a clerk or other person in charge or, if no one is in charge, in a conspicuous place in the office; or (2) if the person has no office or the office is closed, at the person's dwelling or usual place of abode with someone of suitable age and discretion who resides there;

- Mailing it to the person's last known address—in which event service is complete upon mailing;

- Leaving it with the court clerk if the person has no known address;

- Sending it by electronic means if the person consented in writing—in which event service is complete upon transmission, but is not effective if the serving party learns that it did not reach the person to be served; or

- Delivering it by any other means that the person consented to in writing—in which event service is complete when the person making service delivers it to the agency designated to make delivery. FRCP 5(b)(2).

iii. *Service by overnight delivery.* All papers, other than a subpoena or a summons and complaint, may be served on counsel of record by overnight delivery service at the address designated by the attorney for that purpose, or if none is designated, at the attorney's last known address. Service by overnight delivery shall be complete upon deposit of the paper(s), enclosed in a properly addressed wrapper, into the custody of the overnight delivery service, prior to the latest time designated by the service for overnight delivery. NY R USDCTWD Civ Rule 5.1(g). "Overnight delivery service" means any delivery service which regularly accepts items for overnight delivery to any address within the Court's jurisdiction. NY R USDCTWD Civ Rule 5.1(g).

iv. *Service of documents by electronic means*

- *Service on registered users.* Registered Users consent to the electronic service of all documents, and must make available an electronic mail address for service during the registration process. Upon the filing of a document by a party, a Notice of Electronic Filing, with a hyperlink to the filed document, will be automatically generated by the electronic filing system and sent via electronic mail to the e-mail addresses of all parties participating in the electronic filing system in the case. Electronic service of the Notice of Electronic Filing constitutes service of the filed document for all purposes of the Federal Rules of Civil Procedure and the Local Rules of Civil Procedure for the United States District Court for the Western District of New York. NY R USDCTWD ECF Procedures(2)(f)(i). The Notice of Electronic Filing effectuates service for all registered users and no certificate of service is required when all filers on an action are Registered Users. NY R USDCTWD ECF Procedures(2)(f)(iv).

- *Time limit for opening hyperlink.* The hyperlink to filed documents contained in the Notice of Electronic Filing must be opened within fifteen (15) days from the date the document was filed to provide registered users access to the document. The hyperlink expires after fifteen (15) days and users will be unable to access documents for free after that time. Filing Users are encouraged to check their e-mail frequently for notice of filed documents. NY R USDCTWD ECF Procedures(2)(f)(ii).

- *Service on exempted attorneys or pro se litigants who do not have permission to file electronically.* Attorneys granted an exemption from electronically filing documents in the System and pro se litigants who have not been granted permission to electronically file documents are entitled to a paper copy of any electronically filed pleading, document or order. The filing party must therefore provide the non-registered party with the pleading, document or order according to the Federal Rules of Civil Procedure. NY R USDCTWD ECF Procedures(2)(f)(iii).

- *E-mailing or faxing documents.* E-mailing or faxing a pleading or document to any party shall not constitute service of the pleading or document. NY R USDCTWD ECF Procedures(2)(f)(v).

v. *Using court facilities.* If a local rule so authorizes, a party may use the court's transmission facilities to make service under FRCP 5(b)(2)(E). FRCP 5(b)(3).

c. *Serving numerous defendants*

  i. *In general.* If an action involves an unusually large number of defendants, the court may, on motion or on its own, order that:

  - Defendants' pleadings and replies to them need not be served on other defendants;

  - Any crossclaim, counterclaim, avoidance, or affirmative defense in those pleadings and replies to them will be treated as denied or avoided by all other parties; and

  - Filing any such pleading and serving it on the plaintiff constitutes notice of the pleading to all parties. FRCP 5(c)(1).

  ii. *Notifying parties.* A copy of every such order must be served on the parties as the court directs. FRCP 5(c)(2).

3. *Pro se actions.* For information on the requirements in pro se actions, refer to NY R USDCTWD Civ Rule 5.2.

4. *Individual judge practices.* Refer to the Miscellaneous section of this document for information on individual judge practices on filing and serving documents.

## G. Hearings

1. *Hearings, generally*

  a. *Oral argument.* Due process does not require that oral argument be permitted on a motion and, except as otherwise provided by local rule, the district court has discretion to determine whether it will decide the motion on the papers or hear argument by counsel (and perhaps receive evidence). FPP § 1190; F.D.I.C. v. Deglau, 207 F.3d 153 (3d Cir. 2000).

  i. The parties shall appear for oral argument on all motions they make returnable before a Judge on the scheduled return date for the motion. In its discretion, the Court may notify the parties that oral argument shall not be heard on any given motion. Thus, the parties should be prepared to have their motion papers serve as the sole method of argument. NY R USDCTWD Civ Rule 7(c).

  b. *Providing a regular schedule for oral hearings.* A court may establish regular times and places for oral hearings on motions. FRCP 78(a).

  c. *Providing for submission on briefs.* By rule or order, the court may provide for submitting and determining motions on briefs, without oral hearings. FRCP 78(b).

2. *Hearing on FRCP 12 defenses before trial.* If a party so moves, any defense listed in FRCP 12(b)(1) through FRCP 12(b)(7)—whether made in a pleading or by motion—and a motion under FRCP 12(c) must be heard and decided before trial unless the court orders a deferral until trial. FRCP 12(i).

3. *Hearing on motion to dismiss for lack of subject matter jurisdiction.* It may be error for a court to dismiss a case on the defendant's motion to dismiss for lack of subject matter jurisdiction without first holding a hearing, as FRCP 12(b)(1) requires a preliminary hearing or hearing at trial to determine any disputed facts upon which the motion or opposition to it is predicated. FEDPROC § 62:435.

4. *Individual judge practices.* Refer to the Miscellaneous section of this document for information on individual judge practices on hearings.

## H. Forms

### 1. Federal Motion to Dismiss for Lack of Subject Matter Jurisdiction Forms

  a. Motion to dismiss for lack of subject-matter jurisdiction. 2C FEDFORMS § 11:35.

  b. Motion to dismiss for lack of subject-matter jurisdiction; Want of diversity of citizenship because requisite diversity not alleged. 2C FEDFORMS § 11:37.

  c. Motion to dismiss for lack of subject-matter jurisdiction; Want of diversity on a factual basis and because requisite diversity not alleged. 2C FEDFORMS § 11:38.

  d. Motion to dismiss for lack of subject-matter jurisdiction; Want of diversity of citizenship because state of incorporation and principal place of business of defendant not as alleged. 2C FEDFORMS § 11:39.

e.  Motion to dismiss for lack of subject-matter jurisdiction; Want of diversity of citizenship because principal place of business of defendant not as alleged. 2C FEDFORMS § 11:40.

f.  Motion to dismiss for lack of subject-matter jurisdiction; Failure to comply with procedural requirements. 2C FEDFORMS § 11:41.

g.  Motion to dismiss for lack of subject-matter jurisdiction; Want of diversity upon realignment of parties according to interest. 2C FEDFORMS § 11:42.

h.  Motion to dismiss for lack of subject-matter jurisdiction; Want of federal question. 2C FEDFORMS § 11:43.

i.  Motion to dismiss for lack of subject-matter jurisdiction; Unsubstantial federal question. 2C FEDFORMS § 11:44.

j.  Motion to dismiss for lack of subject-matter jurisdiction; Want of amount in controversy. 2C FEDFORMS § 11:45.

k.  Motion to dismiss for lack of subject-matter jurisdiction; Want of amount in controversy; Insurance policy limits do not exceed required jurisdictional amount. 2C FEDFORMS § 11:46.

l.  Motion to dismiss for lack of subject-matter jurisdiction; Want of amount in controversy; Claim for damages in excess of jurisdictional amount not made in good faith. 2C FEDFORMS § 11:47.

m.  Motion to dismiss for lack of subject-matter jurisdiction; Want of amount in controversy; Made after judgment. 2C FEDFORMS § 11:48.

n.  Motion to dismiss for lack of subject-matter jurisdiction; Want of consent by the United States to be sued. 2C FEDFORMS § 11:49.

o.  Motion to dismiss for lack of subject-matter jurisdiction; Want of consent by United States to be sued; United States indispensable party. 2C FEDFORMS § 11:50.

p.  Affidavit; In opposition to motion to dismiss for lack of diversity; Assignment of claim to plaintiff bona fide. FEDPROF § 1:894.

q.  Motion; To dismiss; Plaintiff and defendant citizens of same state when action filed. FEDPROF § 1:888.

r.  Motion to dismiss; Assignment to nonresident for purpose of invoking federal jurisdiction sham and ineffective to confer jurisdiction. FEDPROF § 1:889.

s.  Motion to dismiss; For lack of diversity in third-party complaint. FEDPROF § 1:890.

t.  Affidavit; In support of motion to dismiss for want of diversity of citizenship; Plaintiff and defendant citizens of same state on date action filed. FEDPROF § 1:892.

u.  Motion; To dismiss; Insufficiency of amount in controversy. FEDPROF § 1:897.

v.  Motion to dismiss; Bad faith in claiming jurisdictional amount. FEDPROF § 1:898.

w.  Motion; To dismiss; Lack of jurisdiction over subject matter, generally. FEDPROF § 1:903.

x.  Motion to dismiss; Absence of federal question. FEDPROF § 1:904.

y.  Motion to dismiss; Absence of federal question; Failure to exhaust state remedies. FEDPROF § 1:905.

z.  Affidavit; In opposition to motion to dismiss for absence of jurisdiction over subject matter. FEDPROF § 1:906.

2.  **Forms for the Western District of New York**

   a.  Certificate of service. NY R USDCTWD ECF Procedures(4a).

# I.  Applicable Rules

1.  *Federal rules*

   a.  Federal question. 28 U.S.C.A. § 1331.

   b.  Diversity of citizenship; Amount in controversy; Costs. 28 U.S.C.A. § 1332.

    c.   Serving and filing pleadings and other papers. FRCP 5.

    d.   Constitutional challenge to a statute; Notice, certification, and intervention. FRCP 5.1.

    e.   Privacy protection for filings made with the court. FRCP 5.2.

    f.   Computing and extending time; Time for motion papers. FRCP 6.

    g.   Pleadings allowed; Form of motions and other papers. FRCP 7.

    h.   Disclosure statement. FRCP 7.1.

    i.   Form of pleadings. FRCP 10.

    j.   Signing pleadings, motions, and other papers; Representations to the court; Sanctions. FRCP 11.

    k.   Defenses and objections; When and how presented; Motion for judgment on the pleadings; Consolidating motions; Waiving defenses; Pretrial hearing. FRCP 12.

    l.   Taking testimony. FRCP 43.

    m.   Hearing motions; Submission on briefs. FRCP 78.

  2.  *Local rules*

    a.   Title. NY R USDCTWD Civ Rule 1.1.

    b.   Filing and serving papers. NY R USDCTWD Civ Rule 5.1.

    c.   Motion practice. NY R USDCTWD Civ Rule 7.

    d.   Form of papers. NY R USDCTWD Civ Rule 10.

    e.   Sanctions. NY R USDCTWD Civ Rule 11.

    f.   Alternative dispute resolution and pretrial conferences. NY R USDCTWD Civ Rule 16.

    g.   Attorneys of record; Appearance and withdrawal. NY R USDCTWD Civ Rule 83.2.

    h.   Administrative procedures guide for electronic filing. NY R USDCTWD ECF Procedures.

    i.   Alternative dispute resolution plan. NY R USDCTWD ADR Plan.

**J.  Miscellaneous**

**NOTE: Individual judges' rules may apply. For available judge-level information, refer to:**

DISTRICT JUDGE RICHARD J. ARCARA: NY R USDCTWD Arcara-Procedures.

DISTRICT JUDGE FRANK P. GERACI, JR.: NY R USDCTWD Geraci-Procedures.

DISTRICT JUDGE DAVID G. LARIMER: NY R USDCTWD Larimer-Procedures.

DISTRICT JUDGE CHARLES J. SIRAGUSA: NY R USDCTWD Siragusa-Procedures.

DISTRICT JUDGE WILLIAM M. SKRETNY: NY R USDCTWD Skretny--Procedures.

DISTRICT JUDGE MICHAEL A. TELESCA: NY R USDCTWD Telesca-Procedures.

DISTRICT JUDGE LAWRENCE J. VILARDO: NY R USDCTWD Vilardo-Procedures.

DISTRICT JUDGE ELIZABETH A. WOLFORD: NY R USDCTWD Wolford-Procedures.

MAGISTRATE JUDGE JONATHAN W. FELDMAN: NY R USDCTWD Feldman-Procedures.

MAGISTRATE JUDGE LESLIE G. FOSCHIO: NY R USDCTWD Foschio-Procedures; NY R USDCTWD Foschio-Depositions.

MAGISTRATE JUDGE JEREMIAH J. McCARTHY: NY R USDCTWD McCarthy-Procedures.

MAGISTRATE JUDGE MARIAN W. PAYSON: NY R USDCTWD Payson-Procedures.

MAGISTRATE JUDGE MICHAEL J. ROEMER: NY R USDCTWD Roemer-Procedures.

MAGISTRATE JUDGE H. KENNETH SCHROEDER, JR.: NY R USDCTWD Schroeder-Proc.

MAGISTRATE JUDGE HUGH B. SCOTT: NY R USDCTWD Scott-Procedures.

# Motions, Oppositions and Replies
# Motion to Dismiss for Lack of Personal Jurisdiction

### Document Last Updated September 2016

## A. Checklist

(I) ❑ Matters to be considered by moving party

    (a) ❑ Required documents

        (1) ❑ Notice of motion and motion

        (2) ❑ Memorandum of law

        (3) ❑ Supporting affidavit

        (4) ❑ Certificate of service

    (b) ❑ Supplemental documents

        (1) ❑ Supporting evidence

        (2) ❑ Notice of constitutional question

        (3) ❑ Nongovernmental corporate disclosure statement

        (4) ❑ Copies of authorities

        (5) ❑ Proposed order

        (6) ❑ Paper copy for date-stamping with self-addressed envelope

        (7) ❑ Courtesy copies

    (c) ❑ Timing

        (1) ❑ Every defense to a claim for relief in any pleading must be asserted in the responsive pleading if one is required

        (2) ❑ A motion asserting any of the defenses in FRCP 12(b) must be made before pleading if a responsive pleading is allowed

        (3) ❑ If a pleading sets out a claim for relief that does not require a responsive pleading, an opposing party may assert at trial any defense to that claim

        (4) ❑ A written motion and notice of the hearing must be served at least fourteen (14) days before the time specified for the hearing, with the following exceptions: (i) when the motion may be heard ex parte; (ii) when the Federal Rules of Civil Procedure set a different time; or (iii) when a court order—which a party may, for good cause, apply for ex parte—sets a different time

        (5) ❑ Any affidavit supporting a motion must be served with the motion

(II) ❑ Matters to be considered by opposing party

    (a) ❑ Required documents

        (1) ❑ Opposition

        (2) ❑ Answering memorandum

        (3) ❑ Supporting affidavit

        (4) ❑ Certificate of service

    (b) ❑ Supplemental documents

        (1) ❑ Supporting evidence

        (2) ❑ Notice of constitutional question

        (3) ❑ Copies of authorities

        (4) ❑ Paper copy for date-stamping with self-addressed envelope

      (5)  ❏ Courtesy copies

  (c)  ❏ Timing

      (1)  ❏ After a motion is filed, the court may issue an order setting deadlines for filing and service of opposing papers; if the court does not set deadlines by order, the opposing party shall have fourteen (14) days after service of the motion to file and serve responding papers

      (2)  ❏ Except as FRCP 59(c) provides otherwise, any opposing affidavit must be served at least seven (7) days before the hearing, unless the court permits service at another time

## B. Timing

1. *Motion to dismiss for lack of personal jurisdiction*

   a. *In a responsive pleading.* Every defense to a claim for relief in any pleading must be asserted in the responsive pleading if one is required. FRCP 12(b).

   b. *By motion.* A motion asserting any of the defenses in FRCP 12(b) must be made before pleading if a responsive pleading is allowed. FRCP 12(b). Although FRCP 12(b) encourages the responsive pleader to file a motion to dismiss before filing the answer, nothing in FRCP 12 prohibits the filing of a motion to dismiss with the answer. An untimely motion to dismiss may be considered if the defense asserted in the motion was previously raised in the responsive pleading. FEDPROC § 62:427.

   c. *At trial.* If a pleading sets out a claim for relief that does not require a responsive pleading, an opposing party may assert at trial any defense to that claim. FRCP 12(b).

2. *Timing of motions, generally*

   a. *Motion and notice of hearing.* A written motion and notice of the hearing must be served at least fourteen (14) days before the time specified for the hearing, with the following exceptions:

      i. When the motion may be heard ex parte;

      ii. When the Federal Rules of Civil Procedure set a different time; or

      iii. When a court order—which a party may, for good cause, apply for ex parte—sets a different time. FRCP 6(c)(1).

   b. *Supporting affidavit.* Any affidavit supporting a motion must be served with the motion. FRCP 6(c)(2).

3. *Timing of opposing papers.* After a motion is filed, the Court may issue an order setting deadlines for filing and service of opposing papers. NY R USDCTWD Civ Rule 7(b)(1). If the Court does not set deadlines by order, the following schedule shall apply: the opposing party shall have fourteen (14) days after service of the motion to file and serve responding papers. NY R USDCTWD Civ Rule 7(b)(2)(B).

   a. *Opposing affidavit.* Except as FRCP 59(c) provides otherwise, any opposing affidavit must be served at least seven (7) days before the hearing, unless the court permits service at another time. FRCP 6(c)(2).

4. *Timing of reply papers.* Where the respondent files an answering affidavit setting up a new matter, the moving party ordinarily is allowed a reasonable time to file a reply affidavit since failure to deny the new matter by affidavit may operate as an admission of its truth. AMJUR MOTIONS § 25.

   a. *Reply papers.* After a motion is filed, the Court may issue an order setting deadlines. . .for filing and service of reply papers if the moving party has stated an intent to reply. NY R USDCTWD Civ Rule 7(b)(1). If the Court does not set deadlines by order, the following schedule shall apply: the moving party shall have seven (7) days after service of the responding papers to file and serve reply papers. NY R USDCTWD Civ Rule 7(b)(2)(B).

   b. *Reply memorandum.* The moving party may file a reply memorandum, but is not required to do so. NY R USDCTWD Civ Rule 7(a)(2)(A).

5. *Motion for an expedited hearing.* A party seeking to shorten the schedule prescribed in NY R USDCTWD Civ Rule 7(b) must make a separate motion for an expedited hearing, setting forth the reasons why an expedited hearing is required. NY R USDCTWD Civ Rule 7(d)(1). For more information, refer to NY R USDCTWD Civ Rule 7(d)(1).

6. *Effect of a FRCP 12 motion on the time to serve a responsive pleading.* Unless the court sets a different time, serving a motion under FRCP 12 alters the periods in FRCP 12(a) as follows:

   a. If the court denies the motion or postpones its disposition until trial, the responsive pleading must be served within fourteen (14) days after notice of the court's action; or

   b. If the court grants a motion for a more definite statement, the responsive pleading must be served within fourteen (14) days after the more definite statement is served. FRCP 12(a)(4).

7. *Computation of time*

   a. *Computing time.* FRCP 6 applies in computing any time period specified in the Federal Rules of Civil Procedure, in any local rule or court order, or in any statute that does not specify a method of computing time. FRCP 6(a).

      i. *Period stated in days or a longer unit.* When the period is stated in days or a longer unit of time:
         - Exclude the day of the event that triggers the period;
         - Count every day, including intermediate Saturdays, Sundays, and legal holidays; and
         - Include the last day of the period, but if the last day is a Saturday, Sunday, or legal holiday, the period continues to run until the end of the next day that is not a Saturday, Sunday, or legal holiday. FRCP 6(a)(1).

      ii. *Period stated in hours.* When the period is stated in hours:
         - Begin counting immediately on the occurrence of the event that triggers the period;
         - Count every hour, including hours during intermediate Saturdays, Sundays, and legal holidays; and
         - If the period would end on a Saturday, Sunday, or legal holiday, the period continues to run until the same time on the next day that is not a Saturday, Sunday, or legal holiday. FRCP 6(a)(2).

      iii. *Inaccessibility of the clerk's office.* Unless the court orders otherwise, if the clerk's office is inaccessible:
         - On the last day for filing under FRCP 6(a)(1), then the time for filing is extended to the first accessible day that is not a Saturday, Sunday, or legal holiday; or
         - During the last hour for filing under FRCP 6(a)(2), then the time for filing is extended to the same time on the first accessible day that is not a Saturday, Sunday, or legal holiday. FRCP 6(a)(3).

      iv. *"Last day" defined.* Unless a different time is set by a statute, local rule, or court order, the last day ends:
         - For electronic filing, at midnight in the court's time zone; and
         - For filing by other means, when the clerk's office is scheduled to close. FRCP 6(a)(4).

      v. *"Next day" defined.* The "next day" is determined by continuing to count forward when the period is measured after an event and backward when measured before an event. FRCP 6(a)(5).

      vi. *"Legal holiday" defined.* "Legal holiday" means:
         - The day set aside by statute for observing New Year's Day, Martin Luther King Jr.'s Birthday, Washington's Birthday, Memorial Day, Independence Day, Labor Day, Columbus Day, Veterans' Day, Thanksgiving Day, or Christmas Day;
         - Any day declared a holiday by the President or Congress; and
         - For periods that are measured after an event, any other day declared a holiday by the state where the district court is located. FRCP 6(a)(6).

   b. *Computation of electronic filing deadlines.* A document will be deemed timely filed if filed prior to midnight Eastern Time, unless otherwise ordered by the Court. A document will be considered untimely if filed thereafter. When a Court order requires that a document be filed on a weekend or holiday, the document may be filed by close of business the next business day without further application to the Court. NY R USDCTWD ECF Procedures(2)(e)(i). A document filed electronically is deemed filed on the date and time stated on the Notice of Electronic Filing. NY R USDCTWD ECF Procedures(2)(e)(ii).

    i. *System availability.* Although parties may file documents electronically twenty-four (24) hours a day, registered users are strongly encouraged to file all documents during normal working hours of the Clerk's Office (8:30 a.m. to 5:00 p.m. Eastern Time). NY R USDCTWD ECF Procedures(2)(t)(i).

    ii. *Technical failures.* A Filing User whose filing is made untimely as a result of a technical failure must seek appropriate relief from the Court. NY R USDCTWD ECF Procedures(2)(u)(i).

  c. *Extending time*

    i. *In general.* When an act may or must be done within a specified time, the court may, for good cause, extend the time:

- With or without motion or notice if the court acts, or if a request is made, before the original time or its extension expires; or

- On motion made after the time has expired if the party failed to act because of excusable neglect. FRCP 6(b)(1).

    ii. *Exceptions.* A court must not extend the time to act under FRCP 50(b), FRCP 50(d), FRCP 52(b), FRCP 59(b), FRCP 59(d), FRCP 59(e), and FRCP 60(b). FRCP 6(b)(2).

    iii. Refer to the United States District Court for the Western District of New York KeyRules Motion for Continuance/Extension of Time document for more information on extending time.

  d. *Additional time after certain kinds of service.* When a party may or must act within a specified time after service and service is made under FRCP 5(b)(2)(C), FRCP 5(b)(2)(D), FRCP 5(b)(2)(E), or FRCP 5(b)(2)(F), three (3) days are added after the period would otherwise expire under FRCP 6(a). FRCP 6(d).

    i. *Service by overnight delivery.* Where a period of time prescribed by either the Federal Rules of Civil Procedure or the Local Rules of Civil Procedure for the United States District Court for the Western District of New York is measured from the service of a paper and service is by overnight delivery, one (1) business day shall be added to the prescribed period. NY R USDCTWD Civ Rule 5.1(g).

8. *Individual judge practices.* Refer to the Miscellaneous section of this document for information on individual judge practices on timing of documents.

## C. General Requirements

1. *Motions, generally*

  a. *Requirements.* A request for a court order must be made by motion. The motion must:

    i. Be in writing unless made during a hearing or trial;

    ii. State with particularity the grounds for seeking the order; and

    iii. State the relief sought. FRCP 7(b)(1).

  b. *Notice of motion.* A party interested in resisting the relief sought by a motion has a right to notice thereof, and an opportunity to be heard. AMJUR MOTIONS § 12.

    i. In addition to statutory or court rule provisions requiring notice of a motion—the purpose of such a notice requirement having been said to be to prevent a party from being prejudicially surprised by a motion—principles of natural justice dictate that an adverse party generally must be given notice that a motion will be presented to the court. AMJUR MOTIONS § 12.

    ii. "Notice," in this regard, means reasonable notice, including a meaningful opportunity to prepare and to defend against allegations of a motion. AMJUR MOTIONS § 12.

  c. *Writing requirement.* The writing requirement is intended to insure that the adverse parties are

informed and have a record of both the motion's pendency and the grounds on which the movant seeks an order. FPP § 1191; Feldberg v. Quechee Lakes Corp., 463 F.3d 195 (2d Cir. 2006).

    i.   It is sufficient "if the motion is stated in a written notice of the hearing of the motion." FPP § 1191.

  d.  *Particularity requirement.* The particularity requirement insures that the opposing parties will have notice of their opponent's contentions. FEDPROC § 62:364; Goodman v. 1973 26 Foot Trojan Vessel, Arkansas Registration No. AR1439SN, 859 F.2d 71, 12 Fed.R.Serv.3d 645 (8th Cir. 1988). That requirement ensures that notice of the basis for the motion is provided to the court and to the opposing party so as to avoid prejudice, provide the opponent with a meaningful opportunity to respond, and provide the court with enough information to process the motion correctly. FEDPROC § 62:364; Andreas v. Volkswagen of America, Inc., 336 F.3d 789, 56 Fed.R.Serv.3d 6 (8th Cir. 2003).

    i.   Reasonable specification of the grounds for a motion is sufficient. However, where a movant fails to state even one ground for granting the motion in question, the movant has failed to meet the minimal standard of "reasonable specification." FEDPROC § 62:364; Martinez v. Trainor, 556 F.2d 818, 23 Fed.R.Serv.2d 403 (7th Cir. 1977).

    ii.  The court may excuse the failure to comply with the particularity requirement if it is inadvertent, and where no prejudice is shown by the opposing party. FEDPROC § 62:364.

2.  *Motion to dismiss for lack of personal jurisdiction.* A party may assert the defense of lack of subject-matter jurisdiction by motion. FRCP 12(b)(2). The most common use of the FRCP 12(b)(2) motion is to challenge the use of a state long-arm statute in a diversity action. FEDPROC § 62:445; Best Van Lines, Inc. v. Walker, 490 F.3d 239 (2d Cir. 2007). A dismissal pursuant to FRCP 12(b)(2) is proper where it appears that the assertion of jurisdiction over the defendant offends traditional notions of fair play and substantial justice—that is, where neither the defendant nor the controversy has a substantial enough connection with the forum state to make the exercise of jurisdiction reasonable. FEDPROC § 62:445; Neogen Corp. v. Neo Gen Screening, Inc., 282 F.3d 883, 2002 Fed.App. 0080P (6th Cir. 2002).

  a.  *Personal jurisdiction, generally*

    i.   *Due process limitations.* Due process requires that a court obtain jurisdiction over a defendant before it may adjudicate that defendant's personal rights. FEDPROC § 65:1; Omni Capital Intern., Ltd. v. Rudolf Wolff & Co., Ltd., 484 U.S. 97, 108 S.Ct. 404, 98 L.Ed.2d 415, 9 Fed.R.Serv.3d 691 (1987).

      • Originally it was believed that a judgment in personam could only be entered against a defendant found and served within a state, but the increased flow of commerce between the states and the disuse of the writ of capias ad respondendum, which directed the sheriff to secure the defendant's appearance by taking him into custody, in civil cases led to the liberalization of the concept of personal jurisdiction over nonresidents, and the flexible "minimum contacts" test is now followed. FEDPROC § 65:1.

      • Now the rule is that no binding judgment may be rendered against an individual or corporate defendant unless the defendant has sufficient contacts, ties, or relations with the jurisdiction. FEDPROC § 65:1; Burger King Corp. v. Rudzewicz, 471 U.S. 462, 105 S.Ct. 2174, 85 L.Ed.2d 528 (1985); International Shoe Co. v. State of Wash., Office of Unemployment Compensation and Placement, 326 U.S. 310, 66 S.Ct. 154, 90 L.Ed. 95, 161 A.L.R. 1057 (1945).

      • Moreover, even if the defendant has sufficient contacts with the forum state to satisfy due process, a court nevertheless does not obtain personal jurisdiction over the defendant unless the defendant has notice sufficient to satisfy due process, and, if such notice requires service of a summons, that there is authorization for the type and manner of service used. FEDPROC § 65:1; Omni Capital Intern., Ltd. v. Rudolf Wolff & Co., Ltd., 484 U.S. 97, 108 S.Ct. 404, 98 L.Ed.2d 415, 9 Fed.R.Serv.3d 691 (1987).

      • Personal jurisdiction is a prerequisite to the maintenance of an action, and must exist even though subject matter jurisdiction and venue are proper. FEDPROC § 65:1; Bookout v. Beck, 354 F.2d 823 (9th Cir. 1965).

- Personal jurisdiction over a nonresident defendant is appropriate under the due process clause only where the defendant has sufficient minimum contacts with the forum state that are more than random, fortuitous, or attenuated, such that summoning the defendant would not offend traditional notions of fair play and substantial justice. FEDPROC § 65:1; Pecoraro v. Sky Ranch for Boys, Inc., 340 F.3d 558 (8th Cir. 2003).

ii. *Methods of obtaining jurisdiction over an individual.* There are four basic methods of obtaining jurisdiction over an individual:

- Personal service within the jurisdiction. FEDPROC § 65:22.

- Service on a domiciliary of the forum state who is temporarily outside the jurisdiction, on the theory that the authority of a state over one of its citizens is not terminated by the mere fact of his absence. FEDPROC § 65:22; Milliken v. Meyer, 311 U.S. 457, 61 S.Ct. 339, 85 L.Ed. 278, 132 A.L.R. 1357 (1940).

- Service on a nonresident who has sufficient contacts with the forum state, since the test of International Shoe is applicable to individuals. FEDPROC § 65:22; Kulko v. Superior Court of California In and For City and County of San Francisco, 436 U.S. 84, 98 S.Ct. 1690, 56 L.Ed.2d 132 (1978).

- Service on an agent who has been expressly appointed or appointed by operation of law, such as under a nonresident motorist statute. FEDPROC § 65:22; National Equipment Rental, Limited v. Szukhent, 375 U.S. 311, 84 S.Ct. 411, 11 L.Ed.2d 354, 7 Fed.R.Serv.2d 23 (1964).

iii. *Territorial limits of effective service*

- *In general.* Serving a summons or filing a waiver of service establishes personal jurisdiction over a defendant: (1) who is subject to the jurisdiction of a court of general jurisdiction in the state where the district court is located; (2) who is a party joined under FRCP 14 or FRCP 19 and is served within a judicial district of the United States and not more than one hundred (100) miles from where the summons was issued; or (3) when authorized by a federal statute. FRCP 4(k)(1).

- *Federal claim outside state-court jurisdiction.* For a claim that arises under federal law, serving a summons or filing a waiver of service establishes personal jurisdiction over a defendant if: (1) the defendant is not subject to jurisdiction in any state's courts of general jurisdiction; and (2) exercising jurisdiction is consistent with the United States Constitution and laws. FRCP 4(k)(2).

b. *Motion based on lack of in rem or quasi-in-rem jurisdiction.* Although FRCP 12(b)(2) only refers to "jurisdiction over the person," the provision presumably is sufficiently elastic to embrace a defense or objection that the district court lacks in rem or quasi-in-rem jurisdiction, admittedly a subject that rarely arises in contemporary practice. FPP § 1351.

c. *Motion based on insufficient process or insufficient service of process.* FRCP 12(b)(2) motions to dismiss are frequently based on the failure to serve the defendant with process or a defective service of process, on the theory that if the defendant was not properly served with process, the court lacks personal jurisdiction over the defendant. FEDPROC § 62:446; Prokopiou v. Long Island R. Co., 2007 WL 1098696 (S.D.N.Y. 2007).

d. *Independent ground for dismissal.* Lack of overall reasonableness in the assertion of personal jurisdiction constitutes an independent ground for dismissal under FRCP 12(b)(2). FEDPROC § 62:448; Federal Ins. Co. v. Lake Shore Inc., 886 F.2d 654 (4th Cir. 1989).

e. *Burden.* On the motion, the plaintiff bears the burden to establish the court's jurisdiction, which normally is not a heavy one, although the standard of proof may vary depending on the procedure used by the court in making its determination and whether the defendant is successful in rebutting the plaintiff's initial showing. Moreover, the Supreme Court has intimated that in the case of a challenge to the constitutional fairness and reasonableness of the chosen forum, the burden is on the defendant. FPP § 1351; Burger King Corp. v. Rudzewicz, 471 U.S. 462, 105 S.Ct. 2174, 85 L.Ed.2d 528 (1985).

i. The most common formulation found in the judicial opinions is that the plaintiff bears the ultimate burden of demonstrating that the court's personal jurisdiction over the defendant exists by a preponderance of the evidence, but needs only make a prima facie showing when the district judge restricts her review of the FRCP 12(b)(2) motion solely to affidavits and other written evidence. FPP § 1351; Mullins v. TestAmerica, Inc., 564 F.3d 386 (5th Cir. 2009).

    ii. In addition, for purposes of such a review, federal courts will, as they do on other motions under FRCP 12(b), take as true the allegations of the nonmoving party with regard to the jurisdictional issues and resolve all factual disputes in his or her favor. FPP § 1351.

f. *Motion denied.* A party who has unsuccessfully raised an objection under FRCP 12(b)(2) may proceed to trial on the merits without waiving the ability to renew the objection to the court's jurisdiction. FPP § 1351.

g. *Joining motions.* As a general rule, when the court is confronted by a motion raising a combination of FRCP 12(b) defenses, it will pass on the jurisdictional issues before considering whether a claim was stated by the complaint. FPP § 1351.

    i. *Right to join.* A motion under FRCP 12 may be joined with any other motion allowed by FRCP 12. FRCP 12(g)(1).

    ii. *Limitation on further motions.* Except as provided in FRCP 12(h)(2) or FRCP 12(h)(3), a party that makes a motion under FRCP 12 must not make another motion under FRCP 12 raising a defense or objection that was available to the party but omitted from its earlier motion. FRCP 12(g)(2).

h. *Waiving and preserving certain defenses.* No defense or objection is waived by joining it with one or more other defenses or objections in a responsive pleading or in a motion. FRCP 12(b).

    i. *Waiver by consent or stipulation.* A valid consent or a stipulation that the court has jurisdiction prevents the successful assertion of a FRCP 12(b)(2) defense. FPP § 1351.

    ii. *Waiver by filing permissive counterclaim.* A defendant may be deemed to have waived an objection to personal jurisdiction if he or she files a permissive counterclaim under FRCP 13(b). FPP § 1351.

    iii. *When some are waived.* A party waives any defense listed in FRCP 12(b)(2) through FRCP 12(b)(5) by:

- Omitting it from a motion in the circumstances described in FRCP 12(g)(2); or
- Failing to either: (1) make it by motion under FRCP 12; or (2) include it in a responsive pleading or in an amendment allowed by FRCP 15(a)(1) as a matter of course. FRCP 12(h)(1).

    iv. *When to raise others.* Failure to state a claim upon which relief can be granted, to join a person required by FRCP 19(b), or to state a legal defense to a claim may be raised:

- In any pleading allowed or ordered under FRCP 7(a);
- By a motion under FRCP 12(c); or
- At trial. FRCP 12(h)(2).

    v. *Lack of subject matter jurisdiction.* If the court determines at any time that it lacks subject-matter jurisdiction, the court must dismiss the action. FRCP 12(h)(3).

3. *Opposing papers.* The Federal Rules of Civil Procedure do not require any formal answer, return, or reply to a motion, except where the Federal Rules of Civil Procedure or local rules may require affidavits, memoranda, or other papers to be filed in opposition to a motion. Such papers are simply to apprise the court of such opposition and the grounds of that opposition. FEDPROC § 62:359.

a. *Effect of failure to respond to motion.* Although in the absence of statutory provision or court rule, a motion ordinarily does not require a written answer, when a party files a motion and the opposing party fails to respond, the court may construe such failure to respond as nonopposition to the motion or an admission that the motion was meritorious, may take the facts alleged in the motion as true—the rule in some jurisdictions being that the failure to respond to a fact set forth in a motion is deemed an admission—and may grant the motion if the relief requested appears to be justified. AMJUR MOTIONS § 28.

b. *Assent or no opposition not determinative.* However, a motion will not be granted automatically simply because an "assent" or a notation of "no opposition" has been filed; federal judges frequently deny motions that have been assented to when it is thought that justice so dictates. FPP § 1190.

c. *Responsive pleading inappropriate as response to motion.* An attempt to answer or oppose a motion with a responsive pleading usually is not appropriate. FPP § 1190.

4. *Reply papers.* A moving party may be required or permitted to prepare papers in addition to his original motion papers. AMJUR MOTIONS § 25. Papers answering or replying to opposing papers may be appropriate, in the interests of justice, where it appears there is a substantial reason for allowing a reply. Thus, a court may accept reply papers where a party demonstrates that the papers to which it seeks to file a reply raise new issues that are material to the disposition of the question before the court, or where the court determines, sua sponte, that it wishes further briefing of an issue raised in those papers and orders the submission of additional papers. FEDPROC § 62:360.

a. *Function of reply papers.* The function of a reply affidavit is to answer the arguments made in opposition to the position taken by the movant and not to permit the movant to introduce new arguments in support of the motion. AMJUR MOTIONS § 25.

b. *Issues raised for the first time in a reply document.* However, the view has been followed in some jurisdictions, that as a matter of judicial economy, where there is no prejudice and where the issues could be raised simply by filing a motion to dismiss, the trial court has discretion to consider arguments raised for the first time in a reply memorandum, and that a trial court may grant a motion to strike issues raised for the first time in a reply memorandum. AMJUR MOTIONS § 26.

5. *Sur-reply.* Absent permission of the Judge hearing the motion, sur-reply papers are not permitted. NY R USDCTWD Civ Rule 7(a)(6).

6. *Motion to settle an order.* When counsel are unable to agree on the form of a proposed order, the prevailing party may move, upon seven (7) days notice to all parties, to settle the order. The Court may award costs and attorney's fees against an attorney if it determines that the attorney's unreasonable conduct necessitated bringing the motion. NY R USDCTWD Civ Rule 7(d)(2).

7. *Notice of appearance.* No notice of appearance is required of an attorney whose name and address appear at the end of a complaint, notice of removal, pre-answer motion, or answer. In all other circumstances, an attorney appearing for a party in a civil case shall promptly file a written notice of appearance. NY R USDCTWD Civ Rule 83.2(b). For more information on appearances and withdrawals, refer to NY R USDCTWD Civ Rule 83.2.

8. *Related cases.* Each attorney appearing in a civil case has a continuing duty to promptly notify the Clerk of Court when the attorney has reason to believe that said case is related to some other pending civil or criminal action(s) such that their assignment to the same Judge would avoid unnecessary duplication of judicial effort. As soon as the attorney becomes aware of such a relationship, the attorney shall notify the Clerk of Court by letter of the relevant facts, and the Clerk of Court will transmit that notification to the Judges to whom the cases have been assigned. NY R USDCTWD Civ Rule 5.1(e).

9. *Alternative dispute resolution (ADR).* This Court has adopted an Alternative Dispute Resolution Plan ("ADR"), as implemented by Standing Order (NY R USDCTWD ADR Plan), under which certain civil cases are referred automatically to ADR upon filing. NY R USDCTWD Civ Rule 16(a). The United States District Court for the Western District of New York (the "Court") adopted the ADR Plan on January 1, 2006 (the "Effective Date"), to make available to civil litigants court-administered ADR interventions and processes designed to provide quicker, less expensive and potentially more satisfying alternatives to continuing litigation, without impairing the quality of justice or the right to trial. NY R USDCTWD ADR Plan(1)(1.2)(A).

a. *Scope.* This ADR Plan (NY R USDCTWD ADR Plan) applies to civil actions pending or commenced on and after the Effective Date, except as otherwise indicated in NY R USDCTWD ADR Plan. The ADR Plan supplements the Local Rules of Civil Procedure for the United States District Court for the Western District of New York, which shall remain in full effect for all cases. NY R USDCTWD ADR Plan(1)(1.2)(B).

b. *Referral to ADR*

i. *New cases.* All civil cases filed on and after the Effective Date of the ADR Plan shall be referred

automatically for ADR. NY R USDCTWD ADR Plan(2)(2.1)(A). Notice of the ADR requirements will be provided to all parties immediately upon the filing of a complaint and answer or
a notice of removal; NY R USDCTWD ADR Plan(2)(2.1)(A); NY R USDCTWD Civ Rule
16(a). ADR intervention will be scheduled at the conference held pursuant to Local Rule of
Civil Procedure 16.1. NY R USDCTWD ADR Plan(2)(2.1)(A). [Editor's note: the reference to
Local Rule of Civil Procedure 16.1 is likely meant to be a reference to NY R USDCTWD Civ
Rule 16(b)].

- Litigants in cases not referred automatically to ADR must consider possible agreement to
  the use of an ADR process. NY R USDCTWD Civ Rule 16(a).

- For a list of exemptions from automatic referral, refer to NY R USDCTWD ADR
  Plan(2)(2.1)(A).

ii. *Pending cases.* The assigned Judge on any pending civil case may, sua sponte or with status
conference, issue an order referring the case for ADR. NY R USDCTWD ADR Plan(2)(2.1)(B);
NY R USDCTWD Civ Rule 16(a). The order shall specify a date on which the ADR
intervention is to be completed. NY R USDCTWD ADR Plan(2)(2.1)(B).

iii. *Stipulation.* A case may be referred for ADR by stipulation of all parties. Stipulations shall be
filed and shall designate the specific ADR intervention the parties have selected, the time frame
within which the ADR process will be completed and the selected Neutral. Stipulations are
presumed acceptable unless the assigned Judge determines that the interests of justice are not
served. NY R USDCTWD ADR Plan(2)(2.1)(C).

iv. *Relief from ADR referral*

- *Opting out motions.* Any party may file, with the assigned Judge for that case, a motion to
  opt out of, or for relief from, ADR. NY R USDCTWD ADR Plan(2)(2.2)(A).

- *Motion.* Opting Out Motions must be made within fourteen (14) days from (1) the date of
  the first discovery conference under Local Rule 16.1 in new cases, or (2) the date of a sua
  sponte ADR Referral Order in pending cases. NY R USDCTWD ADR Plan(2)(2.2)(B).
  [Editor's note: the reference to Local Rule 16.1 is likely meant to be a reference to NY R
  USDCTWD Civ Rule 16(b)].

- *Criteria.* Opting Out Motions shall be granted only for "good cause" shown. Inconvenience, travel costs, attorney fees or other costs shall not constitute "good cause." A party
  seeking relief from ADR must set forth the reasons why ADR has no reasonable chance of
  being productive. NY R USDCTWD ADR Plan(2)(2.2)(C).

- *Judicial initiative.* The assigned Judge may, sua sponte, exempt any case from the Court's
  ADR Plan. NY R USDCTWD ADR Plan(2)(2.2)(D).

c. *ADR interventions*

i. *Options.* It is expected that cases referred for ADR will proceed to Mediation. However, the
following options are also available upon the stipulation of all parties:

- Neutral Evaluation;

- Mini Summary Trial;

- Arbitration (Binding and Non-Binding);

- Case Valuation; and

- Settlement Week, when scheduled by the Court. NY R USDCTWD ADR Plan(4)(4.1)(A).

ii. *Timing.* Timing is specific to the intervention and process chosen, as set forth in the corresponding sections in NY R USDCTWD ADR Plan. NY R USDCTWD ADR Plan(4)(4.1)(B).

iii. *Scheduling.* The referral of a case to ADR does not delay or defer other dates established in the
Scheduling Order and has no effect on the scheduled progress of the case toward trial. NY R
USDCTWD ADR Plan(4)(4.1)(C).

d. *Selecting an ADR intervention*

i. *New cases.* Prior to the Local Rule 16.1 scheduling conference, counsel and any unrepresented parties shall confer about ADR as part of their discussion of "the possibilities for a prompt settlement or resolution of the case" pursuant to FRCP 26(f). Unless the parties agree to a different intervention, it is presumed that they will participate in mediation. [Editor's note: the reference to Local Rule 16.1 is likely meant to be a reference to NY R USDCTWD Civ Rule 16(b)].

    ii.  *Pending cases.* In pending cases, all sua sponte referrals will be to mediation. Should the parties agree that a different ADR intervention is more appropriate to their case, they may submit a stipulation designating the specific ADR intervention selected, the time frame within which the ADR process will be completed and the identity of the Neutral. Stipulations must be filed within fourteen (14) days from the date of the ADR Referral Order and are presumed acceptable unless the assigned Judge determines that the interests of justice are not served. NY R USDCTWD ADR Plan(4)(4.2)(B).

  e.  For more information on alternative dispute resolution (ADR), refer to NY R USDCTWD ADR Plan.

10.  *Sanctions.* Failure of counsel for any party, or a party proceeding pro se, to appear before the Court at a conference, to complete the necessary preparations, or to be prepared to proceed to trial at the set time may be considered an abandonment of the case or a failure to prosecute or defend diligently. An appropriate order for sanctions may be entered against the defaulting party with respect to either a specific issue or the entire case. NY R USDCTWD Civ Rule 11(a). For more information, refer to NY R USDCTWD Civ Rule 11.

11.  *Pro se actions.* For information on the requirements in pro se actions, refer to NY R USDCTWD Civ Rule 5.2.

12.  *Individual judge practices.* Refer to the Miscellaneous section of this document for information on individual judge practices on general requirements for documents.

## D. Documents

1.  *Documents for moving party*

  a.  *Required documents*

    i.  *Notice of motion and motion.* A notice of motion is required for all motions, and must state: the relief sought, the grounds for the request, the papers submitted in support, and the return date for the motion, if known. A moving party who intends to file and serve reply papers must so state in the notice of motion. NY R USDCTWD Civ Rule 7(a)(1). Refer to the General Requirements section of this document for information on the notice of motion and motion.

    ii.  *Memorandum of law.* Absent leave of Court or as otherwise specified, upon any motion filed pursuant to FRCP 12, FRCP 56 or FRCP 65(a), the moving party shall file and serve a memorandum of law. Failure to comply with this requirement may constitute grounds for resolving the motion against the non-complying party. NY R USDCTWD Civ Rule 7(a)(2)(A). Refer to the Format section of this document for the formatting requirements for memoranda of law.

    iii.  *Supporting affidavit.* An affidavit must not contain legal arguments, but must contain factual and procedural background relevant to the motion it supports. Except for motions brought under FRCP 12(b)(1) (lack of subject matter jurisdiction), FRCP 12(b)(6) (failure to state a claim), FRCP 12(c) (judgment on the pleadings), and FRCP 12(f) (to strike), motions and opposition to motions shall be supported by at least one (1) affidavit and by such other evidence (i.e., deposition testimony, interrogatory answers, admissions, and documents) as appropriate to resolve the particular motion. Failure to comply with this requirement may constitute grounds for resolving the motion against the non-complying party. NY R USDCTWD Civ Rule 7(a)(3).

    iv.  *Certificate of service.* FRCP 5(d) requires that the person making service under FRCP 5 certify that service has been effected. FRCP 5(Advisory Committee Notes). Having such information on file may be useful for many purposes, including proof of service if an issue arises concerning the effectiveness of the service. FRCP 5(Advisory Committee Notes). The Notice of Electronic

Filing effectuates service for all registered users and no certificate of service is required when all filers on an action are Registered Users. The following exemptions require a certificate of service to be filed:

- When a document is manually filed, a certificate of service must be filed stating the manner in which service or notice was accomplished on each party so entitled. NY R USDCTWD ECF Procedures(2)(f)(iv).

- When a pro se filer (who isn't authorized to electronically file documents) is a party, a certificate of service must be filed stating the manner in which service or notice was accomplished on the pro se party. The Notice of Electronic Filing effectuates service for the Registered Users in this situation and it is not necessary to note service on those parties. A non-registered pro se filer is required to file certificates of service on all documents they file. NY R USDCTWD ECF Procedures(2)(f)(iv).

- If an attorney is exempt from electronic service, a certificate of service must be filed stating the manner in which service or notice was accomplished on the exempt attorney. The Notice of Electronic Filing effectuates service for the Registered Users in this situation and it is not necessary to note service on those parties. NY R USDCTWD ECF Procedures(2)(f)(iv).

b. *Supplemental documents*

   i. *Supporting evidence.* When a motion relies on facts outside the record, the court may hear the matter on affidavits or may hear it wholly or partly on oral testimony or on depositions. FRCP 43(c). A party seeking or opposing any relief under the Federal Rules of Civil Procedure shall file only the portion(s) of a deposition, interrogatory, request for documents, request for admission, or other supporting material that is pertinent to the application. NY R USDCTWD Civ Rule 7(a)(4).

   ii. *Notice of constitutional question.* A party that files a pleading, written motion, or other paper drawing into question the constitutionality of a federal or state statute must promptly:

- *File notice.* File a notice of constitutional question stating the question and identifying the paper that raises it, if: (1) a federal statute is questioned and the parties do not include the United States, one of its agencies, or one of its officers or employees in an official capacity; or (2) a state statute is questioned and the parties do not include the state, one of its agencies, or one of its officers or employees in an official capacity; and

- *Serve notice.* Serve the notice and paper on the Attorney General of the United States if a federal statute is questioned—or on the state attorney general if a state statute is questioned—either by certified or registered mail or by sending it to an electronic address designated by the attorney general for this purpose. FRCP 5.1(a).

- *No forfeiture.* A party's failure to file and serve the notice, or the court's failure to certify, does not forfeit a constitutional claim or defense that is otherwise timely asserted. FRCP 5.1(d).

   iii. *Nongovernmental corporate disclosure statement*

- *Contents.* A nongovernmental corporate party must file two (2) copies of a disclosure statement that: (1) identifies any parent corporation and any publicly held corporation owning ten percent (10%) or more of its stock; or (2) states that there is no such corporation. FRCP 7.1(a).

- *Time to file; Supplemental filing.* A party must: (1) file the disclosure statement with its first appearance, pleading, petition, motion, response, or other request addressed to the court; and (2) promptly file a supplemental statement if any required information changes. FRCP 7.1(b).

   iv. *Copies of authorities.* In cases involving a pro se litigant, counsel shall, when serving a memorandum of law (or other submissions to the Court), provide the pro se litigant (but not other counsel or the Court) with printed copies of decisions cited therein that are unreported or reported exclusively on computerized databases. NY R USDCTWD Civ Rule 7(a)(8).

    v.   *Proposed order.* All proposed orders must be submitted in a format compatible with WordPerfect or Microsoft Word format, which is a "Save As" option in most word processing software. Judges will not accept proposed orders in PDF format. NY R USDCTWD ECF Procedures(2)(j)(ii). Proposed orders should be attached to an Internet e-mail sent to the e-mail address of the assigned judge. NY R USDCTWD ECF Procedures(2)(j)(i). For the list of email addresses for the judges, refer to NY R USDCTWD ECF Procedures(2)(j)(i).

    vi.   *Paper copy for date-stamping with self-addressed envelope.* Parties requesting date-stamped copies of filed documents must provide a paper copy for date-stamping, and a self-addressed, adequately-sized envelope with proper postage affixed. NY R USDCTWD Civ Rule 5.1(d).

    vii.   *Courtesy copies.* The Court may, in its discretion, request courtesy copies on any other motion. NY R USDCTWD Civ Rule 7(a)(7). Courtesy copies of certain documents may be required. Filers should refer to the "Judge Preferences" published on the Court's website. NY R USDCTWD ECF Procedures(2)(a)(iii).

2. *Documents for opposing party*

  a.  *Required documents*

    i.   *Opposition.* Refer to the General Requirements section of this document for information on the opposing papers.

    ii.   *Answering memorandum.* Absent leave of Court or as otherwise specified, upon any motion filed pursuant to FRCP 12, FRCP 56 or FRCP 65(a). . .the opposing party shall file and serve an answering memorandum. Failure to comply with this requirement may constitute grounds for resolving the motion against the non-complying party. NY R USDCTWD Civ Rule 7(a)(2)(A). Refer to the Format section of this document for the formatting requirements for memoranda of law.

    iii.   *Supporting affidavit.* An affidavit must not contain legal arguments, but must contain factual and procedural background relevant to the motion it supports. Except for motions brought under FRCP 12(b)(1) (lack of subject matter jurisdiction), FRCP 12(b)(6) (failure to state a claim), FRCP 12(c) (judgment on the pleadings), and FRCP 12(f) (to strike), motions and opposition to motions shall be supported by at least one (1) affidavit and by such other evidence (i.e., deposition testimony, interrogatory answers, admissions, and documents) as appropriate to resolve the particular motion. Failure to comply with this requirement may constitute grounds for resolving the motion against the non-complying party. NY R USDCTWD Civ Rule 7(a)(3).

    iv.   *Certificate of service.* FRCP 5(d) requires that the person making service under FRCP 5 certify that service has been effected. FRCP 5(Advisory Committee Notes). Having such information on file may be useful for many purposes, including proof of service if an issue arises concerning the effectiveness of the service. FRCP 5(Advisory Committee Notes). The Notice of Electronic Filing effectuates service for all registered users and no certificate of service is required when all filers on an action are Registered Users. The following exemptions require a certificate of service to be filed:

- When a document is manually filed, a certificate of service must be filed stating the manner in which service or notice was accomplished on each party so entitled. NY R USDCTWD ECF Procedures(2)(f)(iv).

- When a pro se filer (who isn't authorized to electronically file documents) is a party, a certificate of service must be filed stating the manner in which service or notice was accomplished on the pro se party. The Notice of Electronic Filing effectuates service for the Registered Users in this situation and it is not necessary to note service on those parties. A non-registered pro se filer is required to file certificates of service on all documents they file. NY R USDCTWD ECF Procedures(2)(f)(iv).

- If an attorney is exempt from electronic service, a certificate of service must be filed stating the manner in which service or notice was accomplished on the exempt attorney. The Notice of Electronic Filing effectuates service for the Registered Users in this situation and it is not necessary to note service on those parties. NY R USDCTWD ECF Procedures(2)(f)(iv).

b. *Supplemental documents*

   i. *Supporting evidence.* When a motion relies on facts outside the record, the court may hear the matter on affidavits or may hear it wholly or partly on oral testimony or on depositions. FRCP 43(c). A party seeking or opposing any relief under the Federal Rules of Civil Procedure shall file only the portion(s) of a deposition, interrogatory, request for documents, request for admission, or other supporting material that is pertinent to the application. NY R USDCTWD Civ Rule 7(a)(4).

   ii. *Notice of constitutional question.* A party that files a pleading, written motion, or other paper drawing into question the constitutionality of a federal or state statute must promptly:

- *File notice.* File a notice of constitutional question stating the question and identifying the paper that raises it, if: (1) a federal statute is questioned and the parties do not include the United States, one of its agencies, or one of its officers or employees in an official capacity; or (2) a state statute is questioned and the parties do not include the state, one of its agencies, or one of its officers or employees in an official capacity; and

- *Serve notice.* Serve the notice and paper on the Attorney General of the United States if a federal statute is questioned—or on the state attorney general if a state statute is questioned—either by certified or registered mail or by sending it to an electronic address designated by the attorney general for this purpose. FRCP 5.1(a).

- *No forfeiture.* A party's failure to file and serve the notice, or the court's failure to certify, does not forfeit a constitutional claim or defense that is otherwise timely asserted. FRCP 5.1(d).

   iii. *Copies of authorities.* In cases involving a pro se litigant, counsel shall, when serving a memorandum of law (or other submissions to the Court), provide the pro se litigant (but not other counsel or the Court) with printed copies of decisions cited therein that are unreported or reported exclusively on computerized databases. NY R USDCTWD Civ Rule 7(a)(8).

   iv. *Paper copy for date-stamping with self-addressed envelope.* Parties requesting date-stamped copies of filed documents must provide a paper copy for date-stamping, and a self-addressed, adequately-sized envelope with proper postage affixed. NY R USDCTWD Civ Rule 5.1(d).

   v. *Courtesy copies.* Courtesy copies of certain documents may be required. Filers should refer to the "Judge Preferences" published on the Court's website. NY R USDCTWD ECF Procedures(2)(a)(iii).

3. *Individual judge practices.* Refer to the Miscellaneous section of this document for information on individual judge practices on required documents.

# E. Format

1. *Form of documents.* The rules governing captions and other matters of form in pleadings apply to motions and other papers. FRCP 7(b)(2).

a. *Form, generally.* All pleadings, motions, and other papers that a party presents for filing, whether in paper form or in electronic form, shall meet the following requirements:

   i. *Font size.* All text and footnotes shall be in a font size of at least twelve (12) point type. NY R USDCTWD Civ Rule 10(a)(1).

   ii. *Spacing.* All text in the body of the document must be double-spaced, except that text in block quotations and footnotes may be single-spaced. NY R USDCTWD Civ Rule 10(a)(2).

- Extensive footnotes and block quotes may not be used to circumvent page limitations. NY R USDCTWD Civ Rule 10(a)(3).

   iii. *Margins.* Documents must have one (1) inch margins on all four sides. NY R USDCTWD Civ Rule 10(a)(4).

   iv. *Page numbering.* Pages must be consecutively numbered. NY R USDCTWD Civ Rule 10(a)(5).

b. *Additional requirements for paper filing.* Documents presented for filing in paper form shall meet the following additional requirements:

    i. *Paper.* Documents must be on durable white eight and one-half by eleven (8-1/2 x 11) inch paper of good quality. NY R USDCTWD Civ Rule 10(b)(1).

       • All documents must be single-sided. NY R USDCTWD Civ Rule 10(b)(5).

    ii. *Text.* All text must be plainly and legibly written, typewritten, printed or reproduced. NY R USDCTWD Civ Rule 10(b)(2).

    iii. *Ink.* Documents must be in black or blue ink. NY R USDCTWD Civ Rule 10(b)(3).

    iv. *Binding.* The pages of each document must be stapled or in some other way fastened together. NY R USDCTWD Civ Rule 10(b)(4).

c. *Caption; Names of parties.* Every pleading must have a caption with the court's name, a title, a file number, and a FRCP 7(a) designation. The title of the complaint must name all the parties; the title of other pleadings, after naming the first party on each side, may refer generally to other parties. FRCP 10(a).

d. *Paragraphs; Separate statements.* A party must state its claims or defenses in numbered paragraphs, each limited as far as practicable to a single set of circumstances. A later pleading may refer by number to a paragraph in an earlier pleading. If doing so would promote clarity, each claim founded on a separate transaction or occurrence—and each defense other than a denial—must be stated in a separate count or defense. FRCP 10(b).

e. *Adoption by reference; Exhibits.* A statement in a pleading may be adopted by reference elsewhere in the same pleading or in any other pleading or motion. A copy of a written instrument that is an exhibit to a pleading is a part of the pleading for all purposes. FRCP 10(c).

f. *Citation of local rules.* The Local Rules of Civil Procedure for the United States District Court for the Western District of New York shall be cited as "L.R.Civ.P." NY R USDCTWD Civ Rule 1.1.

g. *Acceptance by the clerk.* The clerk must not refuse to file a paper solely because it is not in the form prescribed by the Federal Rules of Civil Procedure or by a local rule or practice. FRCP 5(d)(4). The Court may reject documents that do not comply with the requirements in NY R USDCTWD Civ Rule 10. NY R USDCTWD Civ Rule 10.

2. *Form of electronic documents.* All pleadings, motions, and other papers that a party presents for filing, whether in paper form or in electronic form, shall meet the requirements in NY R USDCTWD Civ Rule 10(a). NY R USDCTWD Civ Rule 10(a). Refer above for more information.

a. *Conversion to PDF.* A document created with a word processor, or a paper document, must be converted to Portable Document Format to be electronically filed with the court. NY R USDCTWD ECF Procedures(2)(a)(v).

    i. Documents which exist only in paper form may be scanned into a portable document format (PDF) for electronic filing. NY R USDCTWD ECF Procedures(2)(a)(v). Before filing a scanned document with the court, a Filing User must verify its legibility. NY R USDCTWD ECF Procedures(2)(a)(iv).

    ii. Electronic documents must be converted to .PDF from a word processing program and must be text searchable. Do not print, scan and .PDF your document when it has been created in a word processing program. Additional information on working with PDFs is located in NY R USDCTWD ECF Procedures(4b). NY R USDCTWD ECF Procedures(2)(a)(v).

b. *Hyperlinks.* Pursuant to the policy set forth by the Judicial Conference in October 2005, a hyperlink contained in a filing is no more than a convenient mechanism for accessing material cited in a document. A hyperlink reference is extraneous to any filed document and is not part of the Court's record. NY R USDCTWD ECF Procedures(2)(a)(vi).

    i. In order to preserve the integrity of the Court record, users wishing to insert hyperlinks in Court filings shall continue to use the conventional method for the cited authority, in addition to the hyperlink. NY R USDCTWD ECF Procedures(2)(a)(vi).

ii. The Court accepts no responsibility for, and does not endorse any product, organization, and content at any hyperlinked site, or at any site to which that site may be linked. The Court accepts no responsibility for the availability or functionality of any hyperlink. NY R USDCTWD ECF Procedures(2)(a)(vi).

c. *Attachments and exhibits*

i. Attachments and exhibits larger than five megabytes (5 MB) shall be filed electronically in separate five megabyte (5 MB) segments. NY R USDCTWD ECF Procedures(2)(d)(i).

ii. Filing Users must submit in electronic form all documents referenced as exhibits or attachments, except as otherwise provided in NY R USDCTWD ECF Procedures. A Filing User must submit as exhibits or attachments only those excerpts of the referenced documents that are directly germane to the matter under consideration by the court. Excerpted material must be clearly and prominently identified as such. Filing Users who file excerpts of documents as exhibits or attachments under NY R USDCTWD ECF Procedures(2)(d)(ii) do so without prejudice to their right to timely file additional excerpts or the complete document. Responding parties may timely file additional excerpts or the complete document that they believe are directly germane. The Court may require parties to file additional excerpts or the complete document. A Filing User must request leave of the Court to file a document exhibit or attachment in non-electronic form. NY R USDCTWD ECF Procedures(2)(d)(ii).

iii. Exhibits offered or admitted at trial will not be filed electronically or conventionally unless so ordered by the Court. NY R USDCTWD ECF Procedures(2)(d)(iii).

iv. Exhibits such as videotapes and tape recordings shall be filed in the conventional manner with the Clerk of Court, and a Notice of Manual Filing shall be electronically filed by the party. Manually filed exhibits must have the case number and case name securely fastened or marked on the item. NY R USDCTWD ECF Procedures(2)(d)(iii).

v. Continuation of exhibit entries (for exhibits that are too large to attach to a main document) must be filed and entered on the same day that the main document was filed. NY R USDCTWD ECF Procedures(2)(d)(iv).

d. *Color documents.* Documents in color or containing graphics take much longer to upload. Filing users are encouraged to configure their scanners to scan documents at 200 dpi and preferably in black and white rather than color. NY R USDCTWD ECF Procedures(2)(d)(v).

e. *Large documents.* Due to the length of time it takes to download large files, documents larger than five megabytes (5 MB) (approximately one hundred (100) pages of a .pdf scanned document) must be filed electronically in separate five megabyte (5 MB) segments. A party who believes a document is too lengthy to electronically image (i.e. scan), may contact the Court Room Deputy for the assigned judge and request permission to file that document conventionally. If granted permission to file the document conventionally, the Filing User shall electronically file a "notice of manual filing" for that item. Exhibits submitted to the Court conventionally shall be served on other parties conventionally. NY R USDCTWD ECF Procedures(2)(d)(vi).

3. *Form of memoranda of law.* Memoranda in support of or in opposition to any motion shall not exceed twenty-five (25) pages in length, and reply memoranda shall not exceed ten (10) pages in length. A party seeking to exceed the page limit must make application by letter to the Judge hearing the motion, with copies to all counsel, at least seven (7) days before the date on which the memorandum must be filed. NY R USDCTWD Civ Rule 7(a)(2)(C).

4. *Signing of pleadings, motions and other papers*

a. *Signature.* Every pleading, written motion, and other paper must be signed by at least one attorney of record in the attorney's name—or by a party personally if the party is unrepresented. The paper must state the signer's address, e-mail address, and telephone number. FRCP 11(a). Documents presented for paper filing must contain an original signature. NY R USDCTWD Civ Rule 10(b)(6).

i. *Electronic signatures*

• *Non-attorney signature.* If the original document requires the signature of a non-attorney, the filing party shall obtain the signature of the non-attorney on the document. NY R USDCTWD ECF Procedures(2)(g)(i). The filing party or attorney then shall file the document electronically indicating the signatory's name in the form "s/(name)." NY R USDCTWD ECF Procedures(2)(g)(i)(1). A non-filing signatory or party who disputes the authenticity of an electronically filed document or the authenticity of the signature on that document must file an objection to the document within ten (10) days of receiving the Notice of Electronic Filing. NY R USDCTWD ECF Procedures(2)(g)(i)(2).

- *Registered user signature.* The username and password required to file documents on the Electronic Filing System serve as the Filing User's signature on all electronic documents filed with this Court. The also serve as a signature for the purposes of FRCP 11, the Federal Rules of Civil Procedure, the Local Rules of Civil Procedure for the United States District Court for the Western District of New York, and any other purpose for which a signature is required in connection with proceedings before this Court. A pleading requiring a Registered User's signature must include a signature block in the format found in NY R USDCTWD ECF Procedures(2)(g)(iii). NY R USDCTWD ECF Procedures(2)(g)(iii). Any party challenging the authenticity of an electronically filed document or the attorney's signature on that document must file an objection to the document within ten (10) days of receiving the Notice of Electronic Filing. NY R USDCTWD ECF Procedures(2)(g)(iii)(1).

- *Multiple signatures.* The following procedure applies when a stipulation or other document requires two or more signatures: The filing party shall initially confirm that the document is acceptable to all persons required to sign the document and shall obtain the signatures of all parties on the document. NY R USDCTWD ECF Procedures(2)(g)(iv)(1). The filing party or attorney then shall file the document electronically indicating the signatories, e.g., "s/Jane Doe," "s/John Smith," etc. NY R USDCTWD ECF Procedures(2)(g)(iv)(2). A non-filing signatory or party who disputes the authenticity of an electronically filed document containing multiple signatures or the authenticity of the signatures themselves must file an objection to the document within ten (10) days of receiving the Notice of Electronic Filing. NY R USDCTWD ECF Procedures(2)(g)(iv)(3).

ii. *No verification or accompanying affidavit required for pleadings.* Unless a rule or statute specifically states otherwise, a pleading need not be verified or accompanied by an affidavit. FRCP 11(a).

iii. *Unsigned papers.* The court must strike an unsigned paper unless the omission is promptly corrected after being called to the attorney's or party's attention. FRCP 11(a).

b. *Representations to the court.* By presenting to the court a pleading, written motion, or other paper—whether by signing, filing, submitting, or later advocating it—an attorney or unrepresented party certifies that to the best of the person's knowledge, information, and belief, formed after an inquiry reasonable under the circumstances:

i. It is not being presented for any improper purpose, such as to harass, cause unnecessary delay, or needlessly increase the cost of litigation;

ii. The claims, defenses, and other legal contentions are warranted by existing law or by a nonfrivolous argument for extending, modifying, or reversing existing law or for establishing new law;

iii. The factual contentions have evidentiary support or, if specifically so identified, will likely have evidentiary support after a reasonable opportunity for further investigation or discovery; and

iv. The denials of factual contentions are warranted on the evidence or, if specifically so identified, are reasonably based on belief or a lack of information. FRCP 11(b).

c. *Sanctions.* If, after notice and a reasonable opportunity to respond, the court determines that FRCP 11(b) has been violated, the court may impose an appropriate sanction on any attorney, law firm, or party that violated FRCP 11(b) or is responsible for the violation. FRCP 11(c)(1). Refer to the United

States District Court for the Western District of New York KeyRules Motion for Sanctions document for more information.

5. *Privacy protection for filings made with the court.* In all filings, parties shall comply with FRCP 5.2. NY R USDCTWD ECF Procedures(2)(m)(i).

    a. *Redacted filings.* Unless the court orders otherwise, in an electronic or paper filing with the court that contains an individual's Social Security number, taxpayer-identification number, or birth date, the name of an individual known to be a minor, or a financial-account number, a party or nonparty making the filing may include only:

        i. The last four (4) digits of the Social Security number and taxpayer-identification number;

        ii. The year of the individual's birth;

        iii. The minor's initials; and

        iv. The last four (4) digits of the financial-account number. FRCP 5.2(a).

    b. *Exemptions from the redaction requirement.* The redaction requirement does not apply to the following:

        i. A financial-account number that identifies the property allegedly subject to forfeiture in a forfeiture proceeding;

        ii. The record of an administrative or agency proceeding;

        iii. The official record of a state-court proceeding;

        iv. The record of a court or tribunal, if that record was not subject to the redaction requirement when originally filed;

        v. A filing covered by FRCP 5.2(c) or FRCP 5.2(d); and

        vi. A pro se filing in an action brought under 28 U.S.C.A. § 2241, 28 U.S.C.A. § 2254, or 28 U.S.C.A. § 2255. FRCP 5.2(b).

    c. *Limitations on remote access to electronic files; Social Security appeals and immigration cases.* Unless the court orders otherwise, in an action for benefits under the Social Security Act, and in an action or proceeding relating to an order of removal, to relief from removal, or to immigration benefits or detention, access to an electronic file is authorized as follows:

        i. The parties and their attorneys may have remote electronic access to any part of the case file, including the administrative record;

        ii. Any other person may have electronic access to the full record at the courthouse, but may have remote electronic access only to:

            • The docket maintained by the court; and

            • An opinion, order, judgment, or other disposition of the court, but not any other part of the case file or the administrative record. FRCP 5.2(c).

    d. *Filings made under seal.* The court may order that a filing be made under seal without redaction. The court may later unseal the filing or order the person who made the filing to file a redacted version for the public record. FRCP 5.2(d). For more information on sealing documents, refer to NY R USDCTWD Civ Rule 5.3, NY R USDCTWD ECF Procedures(2)(o)(i)(1), NY R USDCTWD ECF Procedures(2)(o)(i)(2), and NY R USDCTWD ECF Procedures(2)(o)(i)(3).

    e. *Protective orders.* For good cause, the court may by order in a case:

        i. Require redaction of additional information; or

        ii. Limit or prohibit a nonparty's remote electronic access to a document filed with the court. FRCP 5.2(e).

    f. *Option for additional unredacted filing under seal.* A person making a redacted filing may also file an unredacted copy under seal. The court must retain the unredacted copy as part of the record. FRCP 5.2(f).

    g. *Option for filing a reference list.* A filing that contains redacted information may be filed together

1629

with a reference list that identifies each item of redacted information and specifies an appropriate identifier that uniquely corresponds to each item listed. The list must be filed under seal and may be amended as of right. Any reference in the case to a listed identifier will be construed to refer to the corresponding item of information. FRCP 5.2(g).

    h.   *Waiver of protection of identifiers.* A person waives the protection of FRCP 5.2(a) as to the person's own information by filing it without redaction and not under seal. FRCP 5.2(h).

6.   *Individual judge practices.* Refer to the Miscellaneous section of this document for information on individual judge practices on formatting documents.

## F. Filing and Service Requirements

1.   *Filing requirements.* Any paper after the complaint that is required to be served—together with a certificate of service—must be filed within a reasonable time after service. FRCP 5(d)(1). All pleadings and other papers shall be filed and served in accordance with the Federal Rules of Civil Procedure and the CM/ECF Administrative Procedures Guide (NY R USDCTWD ECF Procedures). NY R USDCTWD Civ Rule 5.1(a). For information on filing of miscellaneous cases and irregular documents, refer to NY R USDCTWD Civ Rule 5.6.

    a.   *How filing is made; In general.* A paper is filed by delivering it:

        i.   To the clerk; or

        ii.   To a judge who agrees to accept it for filing, and who must then note the filing date on the paper and promptly send it to the clerk. FRCP 5(d)(2).

    b.   *Electronic filing*

        i.   *Authorization of electronic filing program.* A court may, by local rule, allow papers to be filed, signed, or verified by electronic means that are consistent with any technical standards established by the Judicial Conference of the United States. A local rule may require electronic filing only if reasonable exceptions are allowed. A paper filed electronically in compliance with a local rule is a written paper for purposes of the Federal Rules of Civil Procedure. FRCP 5(d)(3).

- All civil cases filed in this Court are assigned to the Electronic Case Filing System ("ECF"). The procedures for electronic filing and any exceptions to the electronic filing requirements are set forth in the CM/ECF Administrative Procedures Guide (NY R USDCTWD ECF Procedures) which is available on the Court's website. NY R US-DCTWD Civ Rule 5.1(a).

        ii.   *Scope of electronic filing.* The U.S. District Court for the Western District of New York requires attorneys in civil and criminal cases to file documents with the Court electronically over the Internet using its Case Management/Electronic Case Filing (CM/ECF) system. NY R US-DCTWD ECF Procedures. Beginning January 1, 2004, all civil and criminal cases currently pending and newly filed, except as expressly noted herein, were assigned to the Electronic Case Filing System ("System"). Except as expressly provided and in exceptional circumstances preventing a Filing User from filing electronically, all petitions, motions, memoranda of law, or other pleadings and documents required to be filed with the Court in connection with a case assigned to the System must be electronically filed. NY R USDCTWD ECF Procedures(1)(a).

- *Mandatory electronic filing.* All documents on civil, criminal, miscellaneous civil, miscellaneous criminal and new civil case openings, except sealed documents, sealed cases, opening of a criminal case, opening of a miscellaneous case and as expressly provided for in these procedures (NY R USDCTWD ECF Procedures), shall be electronically filed on the system. NY R USDCTWD ECF Procedures(2)(a)(i). NY R USDCTWD Civ Rule 29

- *Stipulations.* Pursuant to NY R USDCTWD Civ Rule 29, all stipulations (whether the stipulation is final or when it requires a judge's signature) shall be filed electronically. NY R USDCTWD ECF Procedures(2)(p)(i).

- *Letters.* The electronic filing of letters is generally prohibited unless granted permission by an assigned judge. Letters to the Court must be submitted conventionally. NY R US-DCTWD ECF Procedures(2)(q)(i).

- *Exceptions.* The Court requires attorneys to file documents electronically, absent a showing of good cause, unless otherwise excused by the procedures set forth below or by Order of the Court. NY R USDCTWD ECF Procedures.

iii. *Conventional filing of documents.* The procedures in NY R USDCTWD ECF Procedures(2)(o) govern documents filed conventionally. The Court, upon application, may also authorize conventional filing of other documents otherwise subject to the procedures in NY R US-DCTWD ECF Procedures(2)(o). NY R USDCTWD ECF Procedures(2)(o)(i).

- *Documents filed under seal.* Unredacted documents filed with the Court pursuant to the privacy provisions of FRCP 5.2 shall be submitted in a sealing envelope with the information in NY R USDCTWD ECF Procedures(2)(o)(i)(1) on the envelope. NY R USDCTWD ECF Procedures(2)(o)(i)(1). If the document is larger than five (5) pages, a disk should be provided to the Clerks Office which contains the document in a .pdf format. NY R USDCTWD ECF Procedures(2)(o)(i)(1). For more information on documents filed under seal, refer to NY R USDCTWD ECF Procedures(2)(o)(i)(1), NY R USDCTWD ECF Procedures(2)(o)(i)(2), and NY R USDCTWD ECF Procedures(2)(o)(i)(3).

- *Magistrate judge consents.* Pursuant to FRCP 73(b), parties' filing consents to jurisdiction by United States Magistrate Judge will continue to be treated as non-public documents until all parties have consented. Therefore, parties must submit conventionally (in paper form) and not electronically file their consent forms so that the consent is not a public document. If all parties consent to the jurisdiction of a Magistrate Judge, the Clerk will scan all consent forms which will then become a public document. NY R USDCTWD ECF Procedures(2)(o)(i)(3).

- *Pro se filers.* Pro Se filers shall file paper originals of all initiating documents, pleadings, motions, affidavits, briefs and other documents which must be signed or which require either verification or an unsworn declaration under any rule or statute. The Clerk's Office will scan these original documents into an electronic file in the System. A certificate of service is required for all documents a pro se litigant files with the court. If a Pro Se filer is granted permission to register to electronically file documents, they shall comply with the guidelines contained in this document (NY R USDCTWD ECF Procedures). NY R USDCTWD ECF Procedures(2)(o)(i)(4).

- *Social Security cases.* Absent a showing of good cause, and except as provided in Section o(i)(4) above, all documents, notices and orders in Social Security reviews will be filed and noticed electronically, except as noted in NY R USDCTWD ECF Procedures(2)(o)(i)(6). For more information, refer to NY R USDCTWD ECF Procedures(2)(o)(i)(6).

- For more information on conventional filing of documents, refer to NY R USDCTWD ECF Procedures(2)(o)(i).

iv. *Consequences of electronic filing.* Electronic transmission of a document to the System consistent with these procedures (NY R USDCTWD ECF Procedures), whether accomplished by the Filing User or a Court User, together with the transmission of a Notice of Electronic Filing from the Court, constitutes filing of a document for all purposes of the Federal Rules of Civil Procedure and the Local Rules of Civil Procedure for the United States District Court for the Western District of New York, and constitutes entry of the document on the docket kept by the Clerk under FRCP 58 and FRCP 79. A document shall not be considered filed for purposes of the Federal Rules of Civil until the filing party receives a System generated Notice of Electronic Filing. NY R USDCTWD ECF Procedures(2)(a)(i).

- E-mailing a document to the Clerk's Office or to the assigned judge shall not constitute "filing" of such document. NY R USDCTWD ECF Procedures(2)(a)(i)(1).

v. *Filing fees.* Any fee required for filing of a pleading or paper in District Court is payable to the Clerk of Court by check or money order. In addition, when opening a civil case on line, filing a notice of appeal on line or applying to appear pro hac vice on line, the fees shall be paid on line by registered users through the federal electronic payment website. Users will be directed to the federal electronic payment website while entering their transaction and should have a credit card available. When opening a civil case and applying to proceed in forma pauperis or when the United States of America opens a case, the payment screen can by bypassed to complete the transaction. Additional information on making electronic payments can be located on the court's website. NY R USDCTWD ECF Procedures(2)(h)(i).

2. *Service requirements.* All pleadings and other papers shall be filed and served in accordance with the Federal Rules of Civil Procedure and the CM/ECF Administrative Procedures Guide (NY R USDCTWD ECF Procedures). NY R USDCTWD Civ Rule 5.1(a).

  a. *Service; When required*

    i. *In general.* Unless the Federal Rules of Civil Procedure provide otherwise, each of the following papers must be served on every party:

      - An order stating that service is required;

      - A pleading filed after the original complaint, unless the court orders otherwise under FRCP 5(c) because there are numerous defendants;

      - A discovery paper required to be served on a party, unless the court orders otherwise;

      - A written motion, except one that may be heard ex parte; and

      - A written notice, appearance, demand, or offer of judgment, or any similar paper. FRCP 5(a)(1).

    ii. *If a party fails to appear.* No service is required on a party who is in default for failing to appear. But a pleading that asserts a new claim for relief against such a party must be served on that party under FRCP 4. FRCP 5(a)(2).

    iii. *Seizing property.* If an action is begun by seizing property and no person is or need be named as a defendant, any service required before the filing of an appearance, answer, or claim must be made on the person who had custody or possession of the property when it was seized. FRCP 5(a)(3).

  b. *Service; How made*

    i. *Serving an attorney.* If a party is represented by an attorney, service under FRCP 5 must be made on the attorney unless the court orders service on the party. FRCP 5(b)(1).

    ii. *Service in general.* A paper is served under FRCP 5 by:

      - Handing it to the person;

      - Leaving it: (1) at the person's office with a clerk or other person in charge or, if no one is in charge, in a conspicuous place in the office; or (2) if the person has no office or the office is closed, at the person's dwelling or usual place of abode with someone of suitable age and discretion who resides there;

      - Mailing it to the person's last known address—in which event service is complete upon mailing;

      - Leaving it with the court clerk if the person has no known address;

      - Sending it by electronic means if the person consented in writing—in which event service is complete upon transmission, but is not effective if the serving party learns that it did not reach the person to be served; or

      - Delivering it by any other means that the person consented to in writing—in which event service is complete when the person making service delivers it to the agency designated to make delivery. FRCP 5(b)(2).

    iii. *Service by overnight delivery.* All papers, other than a subpoena or a summons and complaint, may be served on counsel of record by overnight delivery service at the address designated by the attorney for that purpose, or if none is designated, at the attorney's last known address. Service by overnight delivery shall be complete upon deposit of the paper(s), enclosed in a properly addressed wrapper, into the custody of the overnight delivery service, prior to the latest time designated by the service for overnight delivery. NY R USDCTWD Civ Rule 5.1(g). "Overnight delivery service" means any delivery service which regularly accepts items for overnight delivery to any address within the Court's jurisdiction. NY R USDCTWD Civ Rule 5.1(g).

    iv. *Service of documents by electronic means*

- *Service on registered users.* Registered Users consent to the electronic service of all documents, and must make available an electronic mail address for service during the registration process. Upon the filing of a document by a party, a Notice of Electronic Filing, with a hyperlink to the filed document, will be automatically generated by the electronic filing system and sent via electronic mail to the e-mail addresses of all parties participating in the electronic filing system in the case. Electronic service of the Notice of Electronic Filing constitutes service of the filed document for all purposes of the Federal Rules of Civil Procedure and the Local Rules of Civil Procedure for the United States District Court for the Western District of New York. NY R USDCTWD ECF Procedures(2)(f)(i). The Notice of Electronic Filing effectuates service for all registered users and no certificate of service is required when all filers on an action are Registered Users. NY R USDCTWD ECF Procedures(2)(f)(iv).

- *Time limit for opening hyperlink.* The hyperlink to filed documents contained in the Notice of Electronic Filing must be opened within fifteen (15) days from the date the document was filed to provide registered users access to the document. The hyperlink expires after fifteen (15) days and users will be unable to access documents for free after that time. Filing Users are encouraged to check their e-mail frequently for notice of filed documents. NY R USDCTWD ECF Procedures(2)(f)(ii).

- *Service on exempted attorneys or pro se litigants who do not have permission to file electronically.* Attorneys granted an exemption from electronically filing documents in the System and pro se litigants who have not been granted permission to electronically file documents are entitled to a paper copy of any electronically filed pleading, document or order. The filing party must therefore provide the non-registered party with the pleading, document or order according to the Federal Rules of Civil Procedure. NY R USDCTWD ECF Procedures(2)(f)(iii).

- *E-mailing or faxing documents.* E-mailing or faxing a pleading or document to any party shall not constitute service of the pleading or document. NY R USDCTWD ECF Procedures(2)(f)(v).

    v. *Using court facilities.* If a local rule so authorizes, a party may use the court's transmission facilities to make service under FRCP 5(b)(2)(E). FRCP 5(b)(3).

  c. *Serving numerous defendants*

    i. *In general.* If an action involves an unusually large number of defendants, the court may, on motion or on its own, order that:

- Defendants' pleadings and replies to them need not be served on other defendants;

- Any crossclaim, counterclaim, avoidance, or affirmative defense in those pleadings and replies to them will be treated as denied or avoided by all other parties; and

- Filing any such pleading and serving it on the plaintiff constitutes notice of the pleading to all parties. FRCP 5(c)(1).

    ii. *Notifying parties.* A copy of every such order must be served on the parties as the court directs. FRCP 5(c)(2).

3. *Pro se actions.* For information on the requirements in pro se actions, refer to NY R USDCTWD Civ Rule 5.2.

4. *Individual judge practices.* Refer to the Miscellaneous section of this document for information on individual judge practices on filing and serving documents.

## G. Hearings

1. *Hearings, generally*

 a. *Oral argument.* Due process does not require that oral argument be permitted on a motion and, except as otherwise provided by local rule, the district court has discretion to determine whether it will decide the motion on the papers or hear argument by counsel (and perhaps receive evidence). FPP § 1190; F.D.I.C. v. Deglau, 207 F.3d 153 (3d Cir. 2000).

  i. The parties shall appear for oral argument on all motions they make returnable before a Judge on the scheduled return date for the motion. In its discretion, the Court may notify the parties that oral argument shall not be heard on any given motion. Thus, the parties should be prepared to have their motion papers serve as the sole method of argument. NY R USDCTWD Civ Rule 7(c).

 b. *Providing a regular schedule for oral hearings.* A court may establish regular times and places for oral hearings on motions. FRCP 78(a).

 c. *Providing for submission on briefs.* By rule or order, the court may provide for submitting and determining motions on briefs, without oral hearings. FRCP 78(b).

2. *Hearing on FRCP 12 defenses before trial.* If a party so moves, any defense listed in FRCP 12(b)(1) through FRCP 12(b)(7)—whether made in a pleading or by motion—and a motion under FRCP 12(c) must be heard and decided before trial unless the court orders a deferral until trial. FRCP 12(i).

3. *Individual judge practices.* Refer to the Miscellaneous section of this document for information on individual judge practices on hearings.

## H. Forms

### 1. Federal Motion to Dismiss for Lack of Personal Jurisdiction Forms

 a. Motion and notice; To dismiss; Defendant not present within state where district court is located. AMJUR PP FEDPRAC § 488.

 b. Motion and notice; To dismiss; Lack of jurisdiction over person. AMJUR PP FEDPRAC § 489.

 c. Motion and notice; To dismiss; Lack of jurisdiction over person; Ineffective service of process on foreign state. AMJUR PP FEDPRAC § 490.

 d. Motion and notice; To dismiss; Lack of jurisdiction over person; Consul not agent of country represented for purpose of receiving service of process. AMJUR PP FEDPRAC § 491.

 e. Motion and notice; To dismiss; Lack of jurisdiction over corporate defendant. AMJUR PP FEDPRAC § 492.

 f. Motion and notice; To dismiss; International organization immune from suit. AMJUR PP FEDPRAC § 493.

 g. Motion and notice; To dismiss; Officer or employee of international organization acting within official capacity; Immune from suit. AMJUR PP FEDPRAC § 494.

 h. Motion and notice; To dismiss; Family member of member of foreign mission immune from suit. AMJUR PP FEDPRAC § 495.

 i. Motion and notice; To dismiss complaint or, in alternative, to quash service of summons; Lack of jurisdiction over corporate defendant. AMJUR PP FEDPRAC § 496.

 j. Motion to dismiss; Lack of personal jurisdiction; No minimum contacts. AMJUR PP FEDPRAC § 497.

 k. Affidavit; Of Consul General; In support of motion to dismiss; Consular immunity and lack of authority to act as agent for service of process. AMJUR PP FEDPRAC § 498.

 l. Motion to dismiss for lack of personal jurisdiction; Corporate defendant. 2C FEDFORMS § 11:52.

 m. Motion to dismiss for lack of personal jurisdiction; By corporate defendant; With citation. 2C FEDFORMS § 11:53.

 n. Motion to dismiss for lack of personal jurisdiction; By a foreign corporation. 2C FEDFORMS § 11:54.

o. Motion to dismiss for lack of personal jurisdiction; For insufficiency of service. 2C FEDFORMS § 11:55.

p. Motion to dismiss for lack of personal jurisdiction; Insufficiency of process and insufficiency of service of process. 2C FEDFORMS § 11:56.

q. Motion; To dismiss; Lack of jurisdiction over person of defendant. FEDPROF § 1:910.

r. Opposition; To motion; General form. FEDPROF § 1:750.

s. Affidavit; Supporting or opposing motion. FEDPROF § 1:751.

t. Brief; Supporting or opposing motion. FEDPROF § 1:752.

u. Statement of points and authorities; Opposing motion. FEDPROF § 1:753.

v. Motion to dismiss; Lack of jurisdiction over person of defendant; Short form. FEDPROF § 1:911.

w. Motion to dismiss; Lack of jurisdiction over person of defendant; Accident in foreign country and defendants have no contacts with forum state. FEDPROF § 1:911.50.

x. Motion to dismiss; Lack of jurisdiction over corporate defendant. FEDPROF § 1:912.

y. Motion; To dismiss complaint or, in the alternative, to quash service of summons; Lack of jurisdiction over corporate defendant. FEDPROF § 1:913.

z. Motion to dismiss complaint; General form. GOLDLTGFMS § 20:24.

**2. Forms for the Western District of New York**

a. Certificate of service. NY R USDCTWD ECF Procedures(4a).

# I. Applicable Rules

1. *Federal rules*

a. Summons. FRCP 4.

b. Serving and filing pleadings and other papers. FRCP 5.

c. Constitutional challenge to a statute; Notice, certification, and intervention. FRCP 5.1.

d. Privacy protection for filings made with the court. FRCP 5.2.

e. Computing and extending time; Time for motion papers. FRCP 6.

f. Pleadings allowed; Form of motions and other papers. FRCP 7.

g. Disclosure statement. FRCP 7.1.

h. Form of pleadings. FRCP 10.

i. Signing pleadings, motions, and other papers; Representations to the court; Sanctions. FRCP 11.

j. Defenses and objections; When and how presented; Motion for judgment on the pleadings; Consolidating motions; Waiving defenses; Pretrial hearing. FRCP 12.

k. Taking testimony. FRCP 43.

l. Hearing motions; Submission on briefs. FRCP 78.

2. *Local rules*

a. Title. NY R USDCTWD Civ Rule 1.1.

b. Filing and serving papers. NY R USDCTWD Civ Rule 5.1.

c. Motion practice. NY R USDCTWD Civ Rule 7.

d. Form of papers. NY R USDCTWD Civ Rule 10.

e. Sanctions. NY R USDCTWD Civ Rule 11.

f. Alternative dispute resolution and pretrial conferences. NY R USDCTWD Civ Rule 16.

g. Attorneys of record; Appearance and withdrawal. NY R USDCTWD Civ Rule 83.2.

h. Administrative procedures guide for electronic filing. NY R USDCTWD ECF Procedures.

i. Alternative dispute resolution plan. NY R USDCTWD ADR Plan.

**J. Miscellaneous**

**NOTE: Individual judges' rules may apply. For available judge-level information, refer to:**

DISTRICT JUDGE RICHARD J. ARCARA: NY R USDCTWD Arcara-Procedures.

DISTRICT JUDGE FRANK P. GERACI, JR.: NY R USDCTWD Geraci-Procedures.

DISTRICT JUDGE DAVID G. LARIMER: NY R USDCTWD Larimer-Procedures.

DISTRICT JUDGE CHARLES J. SIRAGUSA: NY R USDCTWD Siragusa-Procedures.

DISTRICT JUDGE WILLIAM M. SKRETNY: NY R USDCTWD Skretny--Procedures.

DISTRICT JUDGE MICHAEL A. TELESCA: NY R USDCTWD Telesca-Procedures.

DISTRICT JUDGE LAWRENCE J. VILARDO: NY R USDCTWD Vilardo-Procedures.

DISTRICT JUDGE ELIZABETH A. WOLFORD: NY R USDCTWD Wolford-Procedures.

MAGISTRATE JUDGE JONATHAN W. FELDMAN: NY R USDCTWD Feldman-Procedures.

MAGISTRATE JUDGE LESLIE G. FOSCHIO: NY R USDCTWD Foschio-Procedures; NY R USDCTWD Foschio-Depositions.

MAGISTRATE JUDGE JEREMIAH J. McCARTHY: NY R USDCTWD McCarthy-Procedures.

MAGISTRATE JUDGE MARIAN W. PAYSON: NY R USDCTWD Payson-Procedures.

MAGISTRATE JUDGE MICHAEL J. ROEMER: NY R USDCTWD Roemer-Procedures.

MAGISTRATE JUDGE H. KENNETH SCHROEDER, JR.: NY R USDCTWD Schroeder-Proc.

MAGISTRATE JUDGE HUGH B. SCOTT: NY R USDCTWD Scott-Procedures.

# Motions, Oppositions and Replies
## Motion for Judgment on the Pleadings

**Document Last Updated September 2016**

**A. Checklist**

(I) ❑ Matters to be considered by moving party

    (a) ❑ Required documents

        (1) ❑ Notice of motion and motion

        (2) ❑ Memorandum of law

        (3) ❑ Certificate of service

    (b) ❑ Supplemental documents

        (1) ❑ Pleadings

        (2) ❑ Notice of constitutional question

        (3) ❑ Nongovernmental corporate disclosure statement

        (4) ❑ Copies of authorities

        (5) ❑ Proposed order

        (6) ❑ Paper copy for date-stamping with self-addressed envelope

        (7) ❑ Courtesy copies

    (c) ❑ Timing

        (1) ❑ After the pleadings are closed—but early enough not to delay trial—a party may move for judgment on the pleadings

        (2) ❑ A written motion and notice of the hearing must be served at least fourteen (14) days before

the time specified for the hearing, with the following exceptions: (i) when the motion may be heard ex parte; (ii) when the Federal Rules of Civil Procedure set a different time; or (iii) when a court order—which a party may, for good cause, apply for ex parte—sets a different time

    (3)  ❑ Any affidavit supporting a motion must be served with the motion

(II)  ❑ Matters to be considered by opposing party

  (a)  ❑ Required documents

    (1)  ❑ Opposition

    (2)  ❑ Answering memorandum

    (3)  ❑ Certificate of service

  (b)  ❑ Supplemental documents

    (1)  ❑ Pleadings

    (2)  ❑ Notice of constitutional question

    (3)  ❑ Copies of authorities

    (4)  ❑ Paper copy for date-stamping with self-addressed envelope

    (5)  ❑ Courtesy copies

  (c)  ❑ Timing

    (1)  ❑ After a motion is filed, the court may issue an order setting deadlines for filing and service of opposing papers; if the court does not set deadlines by order, the opposing party shall have fourteen (14) days after service of the motion to file and serve responding papers

    (2)  ❑ Except as FRCP 59(c) provides otherwise, any opposing affidavit must be served at least seven (7) days before the hearing, unless the court permits service at another time

## B.  Timing

1.  *Motion for judgment on the pleadings.* After the pleadings are closed—but early enough not to delay trial—a party may move for judgment on the pleadings. FRCP 12(c).

  a.  *When pleadings are closed.* FRCP 7(a) provides that the pleadings are closed upon the filing of a complaint and an answer (absent a court-ordered reply), unless a counterclaim, cross-claim, or third-party claim is interposed, in which event the filing of a reply to a counterclaim, cross-claim answer, or third-party answer normally will mark the close of the pleadings. FPP § 1367.

  b.  *Timeliness and delay.* Ordinarily, a motion for judgment on the pleadings should be made promptly after the close of the pleadings. Generally, however, a FRCP 12(c) motion is considered timely if it is made early enough not to delay trial or cause prejudice to the non-movant. FPP § 1367.

2.  *Timing of motions, generally*

  a.  *Motion and notice of hearing.* A written motion and notice of the hearing must be served at least fourteen (14) days before the time specified for the hearing, with the following exceptions:

    i.  When the motion may be heard ex parte;

    ii.  When the Federal Rules of Civil Procedure set a different time; or

    iii.  When a court order—which a party may, for good cause, apply for ex parte—sets a different time. FRCP 6(c)(1).

  b.  *Supporting affidavit.* Any affidavit supporting a motion must be served with the motion. FRCP 6(c)(2).

3.  *Timing of opposing papers.* After a motion is filed, the Court may issue an order setting deadlines for filing and service of opposing papers. NY R USDCTWD Civ Rule 7(b)(1). If the Court does not set deadlines by order, the following schedule shall apply: the opposing party shall have fourteen (14) days after service of the motion to file and serve responding papers. NY R USDCTWD Civ Rule 7(b)(2)(B).

  a.  *Opposing affidavit.* Except as FRCP 59(c) provides otherwise, any opposing affidavit must be served

at least seven (7) days before the hearing, unless the court permits service at another time. FRCP 6(c)(2).

4. *Timing of reply papers.* Where the respondent files an answering affidavit setting up a new matter, the moving party ordinarily is allowed a reasonable time to file a reply affidavit since failure to deny the new matter by affidavit may operate as an admission of its truth. AMJUR MOTIONS § 25.

   a. *Reply papers.* After a motion is filed, the Court may issue an order setting deadlines. . .for filing and service of reply papers if the moving party has stated an intent to reply. NY R USDCTWD Civ Rule 7(b)(1). If the Court does not set deadlines by order, the following schedule shall apply: the moving party shall have seven (7) days after service of the responding papers to file and serve reply papers. NY R USDCTWD Civ Rule 7(b)(2)(B).

   b. *Reply memorandum.* The moving party may file a reply memorandum, but is not required to do so. NY R USDCTWD Civ Rule 7(a)(2)(A).

5. *Motion for an expedited hearing.* A party seeking to shorten the schedule prescribed in NY R USDCTWD Civ Rule 7(b) must make a separate motion for an expedited hearing, setting forth the reasons why an expedited hearing is required. NY R USDCTWD Civ Rule 7(d)(1). For more information, refer to NY R USDCTWD Civ Rule 7(d)(1).

6. *Effect of a FRCP 12 motion on the time to serve a responsive pleading.* Unless the court sets a different time, serving a motion under FRCP 12 alters the periods in FRCP 12(a) as follows:

   a. If the court denies the motion or postpones its disposition until trial, the responsive pleading must be served within fourteen (14) days after notice of the court's action; or

   b. If the court grants a motion for a more definite statement, the responsive pleading must be served within fourteen (14) days after the more definite statement is served. FRCP 12(a)(4).

7. *Computation of time*

   a. *Computing time.* FRCP 6 applies in computing any time period specified in the Federal Rules of Civil Procedure, in any local rule or court order, or in any statute that does not specify a method of computing time. FRCP 6(a).

      i. *Period stated in days or a longer unit.* When the period is stated in days or a longer unit of time:

         • Exclude the day of the event that triggers the period;

         • Count every day, including intermediate Saturdays, Sundays, and legal holidays; and

         • Include the last day of the period, but if the last day is a Saturday, Sunday, or legal holiday, the period continues to run until the end of the next day that is not a Saturday, Sunday, or legal holiday. FRCP 6(a)(1).

      ii. *Period stated in hours.* When the period is stated in hours:

         • Begin counting immediately on the occurrence of the event that triggers the period;

         • Count every hour, including hours during intermediate Saturdays, Sundays, and legal holidays; and

         • If the period would end on a Saturday, Sunday, or legal holiday, the period continues to run until the same time on the next day that is not a Saturday, Sunday, or legal holiday. FRCP 6(a)(2).

      iii. *Inaccessibility of the clerk's office.* Unless the court orders otherwise, if the clerk's office is inaccessible:

         • On the last day for filing under FRCP 6(a)(1), then the time for filing is extended to the first accessible day that is not a Saturday, Sunday, or legal holiday; or

         • During the last hour for filing under FRCP 6(a)(2), then the time for filing is extended to the same time on the first accessible day that is not a Saturday, Sunday, or legal holiday. FRCP 6(a)(3).

iv. *"Last day" defined.* Unless a different time is set by a statute, local rule, or court order, the last day ends:

- For electronic filing, at midnight in the court's time zone; and

- For filing by other means, when the clerk's office is scheduled to close. FRCP 6(a)(4).

v. *"Next day" defined.* The "next day" is determined by continuing to count forward when the period is measured after an event and backward when measured before an event. FRCP 6(a)(5).

vi. *"Legal holiday" defined.* "Legal holiday" means:

- The day set aside by statute for observing New Year's Day, Martin Luther King Jr.'s Birthday, Washington's Birthday, Memorial Day, Independence Day, Labor Day, Columbus Day, Veterans' Day, Thanksgiving Day, or Christmas Day;

- Any day declared a holiday by the President or Congress; and

- For periods that are measured after an event, any other day declared a holiday by the state where the district court is located. FRCP 6(a)(6).

b. *Computation of electronic filing deadlines.* A document will be deemed timely filed if filed prior to midnight Eastern Time, unless otherwise ordered by the Court. A document will be considered untimely if filed thereafter. When a Court order requires that a document be filed on a weekend or holiday, the document may be filed by close of business the next business day without further application to the Court. NY R USDCTWD ECF Procedures(2)(e)(i). A document filed electronically is deemed filed on the date and time stated on the Notice of Electronic Filing. NY R USDCTWD ECF Procedures(2)(e)(ii).

i. *System availability.* Although parties may file documents electronically twenty-four (24) hours a day, registered users are strongly encouraged to file all documents during normal working hours of the Clerk's Office (8:30 a.m. to 5:00 p.m. Eastern Time). NY R USDCTWD ECF Procedures(2)(t)(i).

ii. *Technical failures.* A Filing User whose filing is made untimely as a result of a technical failure must seek appropriate relief from the Court. NY R USDCTWD ECF Procedures(2)(u)(i).

c. *Extending time*

i. *In general.* When an act may or must be done within a specified time, the court may, for good cause, extend the time:

- With or without motion or notice if the court acts, or if a request is made, before the original time or its extension expires; or

- On motion made after the time has expired if the party failed to act because of excusable neglect. FRCP 6(b)(1).

ii. *Exceptions.* A court must not extend the time to act under FRCP 50(b), FRCP 50(d), FRCP 52(b), FRCP 59(b), FRCP 59(d), FRCP 59(e), and FRCP 60(b). FRCP 6(b)(2).

iii. Refer to the United States District Court for the Western District of New York KeyRules Motion for Continuance/Extension of Time document for more information on extending time.

d. *Additional time after certain kinds of service.* When a party may or must act within a specified time after service and service is made under FRCP 5(b)(2)(C), FRCP 5(b)(2)(D), FRCP 5(b)(2)(E), or FRCP 5(b)(2)(F), three (3) days are added after the period would otherwise expire under FRCP 6(a). FRCP 6(d).

i. *Service by overnight delivery.* Where a period of time prescribed by either the Federal Rules of Civil Procedure or the Local Rules of Civil Procedure for the United States District Court for the Western District of New York is measured from the service of a paper and service is by overnight delivery, one (1) business day shall be added to the prescribed period. NY R USDCTWD Civ Rule 5.1(g).

8. *Individual judge practices.* Refer to the Miscellaneous section of this document for information on individual judge practices on timing of documents.

## C. General Requirements

1. *Motions, generally*

   a. *Requirements.* A request for a court order must be made by motion. The motion must:

      i. Be in writing unless made during a hearing or trial;

      ii. State with particularity the grounds for seeking the order; and

      iii. State the relief sought. FRCP 7(b)(1).

   b. *Notice of motion.* A party interested in resisting the relief sought by a motion has a right to notice thereof, and an opportunity to be heard. AMJUR MOTIONS § 12.

      i. In addition to statutory or court rule provisions requiring notice of a motion—the purpose of such a notice requirement having been said to be to prevent a party from being prejudicially surprised by a motion—principles of natural justice dictate that an adverse party generally must be given notice that a motion will be presented to the court. AMJUR MOTIONS § 12.

      ii. "Notice," in this regard, means reasonable notice, including a meaningful opportunity to prepare and to defend against allegations of a motion. AMJUR MOTIONS § 12.

   c. *Writing requirement.* The writing requirement is intended to insure that the adverse parties are informed and have a record of both the motion's pendency and the grounds on which the movant seeks an order. FPP § 1191; Feldberg v. Quechee Lakes Corp., 463 F.3d 195 (2d Cir. 2006).

      i. It is sufficient "if the motion is stated in a written notice of the hearing of the motion." FPP § 1191.

   d. *Particularity requirement.* The particularity requirement insures that the opposing parties will have notice of their opponent's contentions. FEDPROC § 62:364; Goodman v. 1973 26 Foot Trojan Vessel, Arkansas Registration No. AR1439SN, 859 F.2d 71, 12 Fed.R.Serv.3d 645 (8th Cir. 1988). That requirement ensures that notice of the basis for the motion is provided to the court and to the opposing party so as to avoid prejudice, provide the opponent with a meaningful opportunity to respond, and provide the court with enough information to process the motion correctly. FEDPROC § 62:364; Andreas v. Volkswagen of America, Inc., 336 F.3d 789, 56 Fed.R.Serv.3d 6 (8th Cir. 2003).

      i. Reasonable specification of the grounds for a motion is sufficient. However, where a movant fails to state even one ground for granting the motion in question, the movant has failed to meet the minimal standard of "reasonable specification." FEDPROC § 62:364; Martinez v. Trainor, 556 F.2d 818, 23 Fed.R.Serv.2d 403 (7th Cir. 1977).

      ii. The court may excuse the failure to comply with the particularity requirement if it is inadvertent, and where no prejudice is shown by the opposing party. FEDPROC § 62:364.

2. *Motion for judgment on the pleadings.* After the pleadings are closed—but early enough not to delay trial—a party may move for judgment on the pleadings. FRCP 12(c).

   a. *Relationship to other motions*

      i. *Common law demurrer.* The motion for judgment on the pleadings under FRCP 12(c) has its historical roots in common law practice, which permitted either party, at any point in the proceeding, to demur to his opponent's pleading and secure a dismissal or final judgment on the basis of the pleadings. FPP § 1367.

         • The common law demurrer could be used to search the record and raise procedural defects, or it could be employed to resolve the substantive merits of the controversy as disclosed on the face of the pleadings. FPP § 1367.

         • In contrast to the common law practice, the FRCP 12(c) judgment on the pleadings procedure primarily is addressed to the latter function of disposing of cases on the basis of the underlying substantive merits of the parties' claims and defenses as they are revealed in the formal pleadings. FPP § 1367. The purpose of FRCP 12(c) is to save time and expense in cases where the ultimate issues of fact are not in dispute, and to prevent the piecemeal process of judicial determination which prevailed under the old common-law practice. FEDPROC § 62:566.

ii.  *Motions to dismiss.* While FRCP 12(b) motions to dismiss and FRCP 12(c) motions for judgment on the pleadings are to some extent merely interchangeable weapons in a party's arsenal of pretrial challenges, there are differences in the scope and effect of the two motions. A FRCP 12(b) motion to dismiss is directed solely toward the defects of the plaintiff's claim for relief, without concern for the merits of the controversy, while a FRCP 12(c) motion for judgment on the pleadings at least theoretically requires some scrutiny of the merits of the controversy. FEDPROC § 62:568.

iii.  *Motion to strike.* The FRCP 12(c) motion also should be contrasted with the motion to strike under FRCP 12(f). The latter motion permits either party to strike redundant, immaterial, impertinent, or scandalous matter from an adversary's pleading and may be used to challenge the sufficiency of defenses asserted by that adversary. The motion serves as a pruning device to eliminate objectionable matter from an opponent's pleadings and, unlike the FRCP 12(c) procedure, it is not directed at gaining a final judgment on the merits, although a FRCP 12(f) motion that succeeds in eliminating the defenses to the action may have that purpose and, in some cases, may have that effect. FPP § 1369.

- If a plaintiff seeks to dispute the legal sufficiency of fewer than all of the defenses raised in the defendant's pleading, he should proceed under FRCP 12(f) rather than under FRCP 12(c) because the latter leads to the entry of a judgment. FPP § 1369.

iv.  *Motion for summary judgment.* In most circumstances a party will find it preferable to proceed under FRCP 56 rather than FRCP 12(c) for a variety of reasons. For example, the summary judgment procedure is available when the defendant fails to file an answer, whereas technically no relief would be available under FRCP 12(c) because the pleadings have not been closed. If a party believes that it will be necessary to introduce evidence outside the formal pleadings in order to demonstrate that no material issue of fact exists and he is clearly entitled to judgment, it is advisable to proceed directly under FRCP 56 rather than taking the circuitous route through FRCP 12(c). Moreover, the FRCP 12(c) path may present certain risks because the court, in its discretion, may refuse to permit the introduction of matters beyond the pleadings and insist on treating the motion as one under FRCP 12(c) or apply the general motion time period set out in FRCP 6(d), rather than the special time provision in FRCP 56. FPP § 1369.

b.  *Bringing a FRCP 12(c) motion.* As numerous judicial opinions make clear, a FRCP 12(c) motion is designed to provide a means of disposing of cases when the material facts are not in dispute between the parties and a judgment on the merits can be achieved by focusing on the content of the competing pleadings, exhibits thereto, matters incorporated by reference in the pleadings, whatever is central or integral to the claim for relief or defense, and any facts of which the district court will take judicial notice. FPP § 1367; DiCarlo v. St. Mary Hosp., 530 F.3d 255 (3d Cir. 2008); Buddy Bean Lumber Co. v. Axis Surplus Ins. Co., 715 F.3d 695, 697 (8th Cir. 2013).

i.  The motion for a judgment on the pleadings only has utility when all material allegations of fact are admitted or not controverted in the pleadings and only questions of law remain to be decided by the district court. FPP § 1367; Stafford v. Jewelers Mut. Ins. Co., 554 Fed. Appx. 360, 370 (6th Cir. 2014).

c.  *Partial judgment on the pleadings.* Although not provided for by FRCP 12(c), a party may properly move for partial judgment on the pleadings to further the policy goal of efficient resolution of actions when there are no material facts in dispute. This conclusion has been said to be buttressed by FRCP 56(a), which provides that a party may move for summary judgment "on all or part of the claim." FEDPROC § 62:571.

d.  *Granting of a motion for judgment on the pleadings.* The federal courts have followed a fairly restrictive standard in ruling on motions for judgment on the pleadings. FPP § 1368. A motion for judgment on the pleadings is a motion for judgment on the merits, and should only be granted if no material issue of fact remains to be resolved and the movant establishes entitlement to judgment as a matter of law. FEDPROC § 62:569; Great Plains Trust Co. v. Morgan Stanley Dean Witter & Co., 313 F.3d 305 (5th Cir. 2002); Sikirica v. Nationwide Ins. Co., 416 F.3d 214 (3d Cir. 2005). A motion for a judgment on the pleadings must be sustained where the undisputed facts appearing in the pleadings, supplemented by any facts of which the court will take judicial notice, show that no relief can be granted. Judgment on the pleadings is not appropriate where the answer raises issues of fact which, if proved, would defeat recovery. FEDPROC § 62:569.

    i.  A motion for judgment on the pleadings admits, for purposes of the motion, the truth of all well-pleaded facts in the pleadings of the opposing party, together with all fair inferences to be drawn therefrom, even where the defendant asserts, in the FRCP 12(c) motion, a FRCP 12(b)(6) defense of failure to state a claim upon which relief can be granted. FEDPROC § 62:570; In re World Trade Center Disaster Site Litigation, 521 F.3d 169 (2d Cir. 2008); Massachusetts Nurses Ass'n v. North Adams Regional Hosp., 467 F.3d 27 (1st Cir. 2006). However, all allegations of the moving party which have been denied are taken as false. FEDPROC § 62:570; Volvo Const. Equipment North America, Inc. v. CLM Equipment Company, Inc., 386 F.3d 581 (4th Cir. 2004). In considering a motion for judgment on the pleadings, the trial court is thus required to view the facts presented in the pleadings and inferences to be drawn therefrom in the light most favorable to the nonmoving party. In this fashion the courts hope to insure that the rights of the nonmoving party are decided as fully and fairly on a FRCP 12(c) motion as if there had been a trial. FEDPROC § 62:570.

    ii.  On a motion for judgment on the pleadings, the court may consider facts upon the basis of judicial notice. FEDPROC § 62:570; R.G. Financial Corp. v. Vergara-Nunez, 446 F.3d 178 (1st Cir. 2006). However, a motion for judgment on the pleadings does not admit conclusions of law or unwarranted factual inferences. FEDPROC § 62:570; JPMorgan Chase Bank, N.A. v. Winget, 510 F.3d 577 (6th Cir. 2007).

e.  *Joining motions*

    i.  *Right to join.* A motion under FRCP 12 may be joined with any other motion allowed by FRCP 12. FRCP 12(g)(1).

    ii.  *Limitation on further motions.* Except as provided in FRCP 12(h)(2) or FRCP 12(h)(3), a party that makes a motion under FRCP 12 must not make another motion under FRCP 12 raising a defense or objection that was available to the party but omitted from its earlier motion. FRCP 12(g)(2).

f.  *Waiving and preserving certain defenses*

    i.  *When some are waived.* A party waives any defense listed in FRCP 12(b)(2) through FRCP 12(b)(5) by:

- Omitting it from a motion in the circumstances described in FRCP 12(g)(2); or
- Failing to either: (1) make it by motion under FRCP 12; or (2) include it in a responsive pleading or in an amendment allowed by FRCP 15(a)(1) as a matter of course. FRCP 12(h)(1).

    ii.  *When to raise others.* Failure to state a claim upon which relief can be granted, to join a person required by FRCP 19(b), or to state a legal defense to a claim may be raised:

- In any pleading allowed or ordered under FRCP 7(a);
- By a motion under FRCP 12(c); or
- At trial. FRCP 12(h)(2).

    iii.  *Lack of subject matter jurisdiction.* If the court determines at any time that it lacks subject-matter jurisdiction, the court must dismiss the action. FRCP 12(h)(3).

3.  *Opposing papers.* The Federal Rules of Civil Procedure do not require any formal answer, return, or reply to a motion, except where the Federal Rules of Civil Procedure or local rules may require affidavits, memoranda, or other papers to be filed in opposition to a motion. Such papers are simply to apprise the court of such opposition and the grounds of that opposition. FEDPROC § 62:359.

a.  *Effect of failure to respond to motion.* Although in the absence of statutory provision or court rule, a motion ordinarily does not require a written answer, when a party files a motion and the opposing party fails to respond, the court may construe such failure to respond as nonopposition to the motion or an admission that the motion was meritorious, may take the facts alleged in the motion as true—the rule in some jurisdictions being that the failure to respond to a fact set forth in a motion is deemed an admission—and may grant the motion if the relief requested appears to be justified. AMJUR MOTIONS § 28.

b.  *Assent or no opposition not determinative.* However, a motion will not be granted automatically simply because an "assent" or a notation of "no opposition" has been filed; federal judges frequently deny motions that have been assented to when it is thought that justice so dictates. FPP § 1190.

c.  *Responsive pleading inappropriate as response to motion.* An attempt to answer or oppose a motion with a responsive pleading usually is not appropriate. FPP § 1190.

4.  *Reply papers.* A moving party may be required or permitted to prepare papers in addition to his original motion papers. AMJUR MOTIONS § 25. Papers answering or replying to opposing papers may be appropriate, in the interests of justice, where it appears there is a substantial reason for allowing a reply. Thus, a court may accept reply papers where a party demonstrates that the papers to which it seeks to file a reply raise new issues that are material to the disposition of the question before the court, or where the court determines, sua sponte, that it wishes further briefing of an issue raised in those papers and orders the submission of additional papers. FEDPROC § 62:360.

a.  *Function of reply papers.* The function of a reply affidavit is to answer the arguments made in opposition to the position taken by the movant and not to permit the movant to introduce new arguments in support of the motion. AMJUR MOTIONS § 25.

b.  *Issues raised for the first time in a reply document.* However, the view has been followed in some jurisdictions, that as a matter of judicial economy, where there is no prejudice and where the issues could be raised simply by filing a motion to dismiss, the trial court has discretion to consider arguments raised for the first time in a reply memorandum, and that a trial court may grant a motion to strike issues raised for the first time in a reply memorandum. AMJUR MOTIONS § 26.

5.  *Sur-reply.* Absent permission of the Judge hearing the motion, sur-reply papers are not permitted. NY R USDCTWD Civ Rule 7(a)(6).

6.  *Motion to settle an order.* When counsel are unable to agree on the form of a proposed order, the prevailing party may move, upon seven (7) days notice to all parties, to settle the order. The Court may award costs and attorney's fees against an attorney if it determines that the attorney's unreasonable conduct necessitated bringing the motion. NY R USDCTWD Civ Rule 7(d)(2).

7.  *Notice of appearance.* No notice of appearance is required of an attorney whose name and address appear at the end of a complaint, notice of removal, pre-answer motion, or answer. In all other circumstances, an attorney appearing for a party in a civil case shall promptly file a written notice of appearance. NY R USDCTWD Civ Rule 83.2(b). For more information on appearances and withdrawals, refer to NY R USDCTWD Civ Rule 83.2.

8.  *Related cases.* Each attorney appearing in a civil case has a continuing duty to promptly notify the Clerk of Court when the attorney has reason to believe that said case is related to some other pending civil or criminal action(s) such that their assignment to the same Judge would avoid unnecessary duplication of judicial effort. As soon as the attorney becomes aware of such a relationship, the attorney shall notify the Clerk of Court by letter of the relevant facts, and the Clerk of Court will transmit that notification to the Judges to whom the cases have been assigned. NY R USDCTWD Civ Rule 5.1(e).

9.  *Alternative dispute resolution (ADR).* This Court has adopted an Alternative Dispute Resolution Plan ("ADR"), as implemented by Standing Order (NY R USDCTWD ADR Plan), under which certain civil cases are referred automatically to ADR upon filing. NY R USDCTWD Civ Rule 16(a). The United States District Court for the Western District of New York (the "Court") adopted the ADR Plan on January 1, 2006 (the "Effective Date"), to make available to civil litigants court-administered ADR interventions and processes designed to provide quicker, less expensive and potentially more satisfying alternatives to continuing litigation, without impairing the quality of justice or the right to trial. NY R USDCTWD ADR Plan(1)(1.2)(A).

a.  *Scope.* This ADR Plan (NY R USDCTWD ADR Plan) applies to civil actions pending or commenced on and after the Effective Date, except as otherwise indicated in NY R USDCTWD ADR Plan. The ADR Plan supplements the Local Rules of Civil Procedure for the United States District

Court for the Western District of New York, which shall remain in full effect for all cases. NY R USDCTWD ADR Plan(1)(1.2)(B).

b. *Referral to ADR*

    i. *New cases.* All civil cases filed on and after the Effective Date of the ADR Plan shall be referred automatically for ADR. NY R USDCTWD ADR Plan(2)(2.1)(A). Notice of the ADR requirements will be provided to all parties immediately upon the filing of a complaint and answer or a notice of removal; NY R USDCTWD ADR Plan(2)(2.1)(A); NY R USDCTWD Civ Rule 16(a). ADR intervention will be scheduled at the conference held pursuant to Local Rule of Civil Procedure 16.1. NY R USDCTWD ADR Plan(2)(2.1)(A). [Editor's note: the reference to Local Rule of Civil Procedure 16.1 is likely meant to be a reference to NY R USDCTWD Civ Rule 16(b)].

- Litigants in cases not referred automatically to ADR must consider possible agreement to the use of an ADR process. NY R USDCTWD Civ Rule 16(a).
- For a list of exemptions from automatic referral, refer to NY R USDCTWD ADR Plan(2)(2.1)(A).

    ii. *Pending cases.* The assigned Judge on any pending civil case may, sua sponte or with status conference, issue an order referring the case for ADR. NY R USDCTWD ADR Plan(2)(2.1)(B); NY R USDCTWD Civ Rule 16(a). The order shall specify a date on which the ADR intervention is to be completed. NY R USDCTWD ADR Plan(2)(2.1)(B).

    iii. *Stipulation.* A case may be referred for ADR by stipulation of all parties. Stipulations shall be filed and shall designate the specific ADR intervention the parties have selected, the time frame within which the ADR process will be completed and the selected Neutral. Stipulations are presumed acceptable unless the assigned Judge determines that the interests of justice are not served. NY R USDCTWD ADR Plan(2)(2.1)(C).

    iv. *Relief from ADR referral*

- *Opting out motions.* Any party may file, with the assigned Judge for that case, a motion to opt out of, or for relief from, ADR. NY R USDCTWD ADR Plan(2)(2.2)(A).
- *Motion.* Opting Out Motions must be made within fourteen (14) days from (1) the date of the first discovery conference under Local Rule 16.1 in new cases, or (2) the date of a sua sponte ADR Referral Order in pending cases. NY R USDCTWD ADR Plan(2)(2.2)(B). [Editor's note: the reference to Local Rule 16.1 is likely meant to be a reference to NY R USDCTWD Civ Rule 16(b)].
- *Criteria.* Opting Out Motions shall be granted only for "good cause" shown. Inconvenience, travel costs, attorney fees or other costs shall not constitute "good cause." A party seeking relief from ADR must set forth the reasons why ADR has no reasonable chance of being productive. NY R USDCTWD ADR Plan(2)(2.2)(C).
- *Judicial initiative.* The assigned Judge may, sua sponte, exempt any case from the Court's ADR Plan. NY R USDCTWD ADR Plan(2)(2.2)(D).

c. *ADR interventions*

    i. *Options.* It is expected that cases referred for ADR will proceed to Mediation. However, the following options are also available upon the stipulation of all parties:

- Neutral Evaluation;
- Mini Summary Trial;
- Arbitration (Binding and Non-Binding);
- Case Valuation; and
- Settlement Week, when scheduled by the Court. NY R USDCTWD ADR Plan(4)(4.1)(A).

    ii. *Timing.* Timing is specific to the intervention and process chosen, as set forth in the corresponding sections in NY R USDCTWD ADR Plan. NY R USDCTWD ADR Plan(4)(4.1)(B).

iii. *Scheduling.* The referral of a case to ADR does not delay or defer other dates established in the Scheduling Order and has no effect on the scheduled progress of the case toward trial. NY R USDCTWD ADR Plan(4)(4.1)(C).

d. *Selecting an ADR intervention*

i. *New cases.* Prior to the Local Rule 16.1 scheduling conference, counsel and any unrepresented parties shall confer about ADR as part of their discussion of "the possibilities for a prompt settlement or resolution of the case" pursuant to FRCP 26(f). Unless the parties agree to a different intervention, it is presumed that they will participate in mediation. [Editor's note: the reference to Local Rule 16.1 is likely meant to be a reference to NY R USDCTWD Civ Rule 16(b)].

ii. *Pending cases.* In pending cases, all sua sponte referrals will be to mediation. Should the parties agree that a different ADR intervention is more appropriate to their case, they may submit a stipulation designating the specific ADR intervention selected, the time frame within which the ADR process will be completed and the identity of the Neutral. Stipulations must be filed within fourteen (14) days from the date of the ADR Referral Order and are presumed acceptable unless the assigned Judge determines that the interests of justice are not served. NY R USDCTWD ADR Plan(4)(4.2)(B).

e. For more information on alternative dispute resolution (ADR), refer to NY R USDCTWD ADR Plan.

10. *Sanctions.* Failure of counsel for any party, or a party proceeding pro se, to appear before the Court at a conference, to complete the necessary preparations, or to be prepared to proceed to trial at the set time may be considered an abandonment of the case or a failure to prosecute or defend diligently. An appropriate order for sanctions may be entered against the defaulting party with respect to either a specific issue or the entire case. NY R USDCTWD Civ Rule 11(a). For more information, refer to NY R USDCTWD Civ Rule 11.

11. *Pro se actions.* For information on the requirements in pro se actions, refer to NY R USDCTWD Civ Rule 5.2.

12. *Individual judge practices.* Refer to the Miscellaneous section of this document for information on individual judge practices on general requirements for documents.

# D. Documents

1. *Documents for moving party*

a. *Required documents*

i. *Notice of motion and motion.* A notice of motion is required for all motions, and must state: the relief sought, the grounds for the request, the papers submitted in support, and the return date for the motion, if known. A moving party who intends to file and serve reply papers must so state in the notice of motion. NY R USDCTWD Civ Rule 7(a)(1). Refer to the General Requirements section of this document for information on the notice of motion and motion.

ii. *Memorandum of law.* Absent leave of Court or as otherwise specified, upon any motion filed pursuant to FRCP 12, FRCP 56 or FRCP 65(a), the moving party shall file and serve a memorandum of law. Failure to comply with this requirement may constitute grounds for resolving the motion against the non-complying party. NY R USDCTWD Civ Rule 7(a)(2)(A). Refer to the Format section of this document for the formatting requirements for memoranda of law.

iii. *Certificate of service.* FRCP 5(d) requires that the person making service under FRCP 5 certify that service has been effected. FRCP 5(Advisory Committee Notes). Having such information on file may be useful for many purposes, including proof of service if an issue arises concerning the effectiveness of the service. FRCP 5(Advisory Committee Notes). The Notice of Electronic Filing effectuates service for all registered users and no certificate of service is required when all filers on an action are Registered Users. The following exemptions require a certificate of service to be filed:

- When a document is manually filed, a certificate of service must be filed stating the manner in which service or notice was accomplished on each party so entitled. NY R USDCTWD ECF Procedures(2)(f)(iv).

- When a pro se filer (who isn't authorized to electronically file documents) is a party, a certificate of service must be filed stating the manner in which service or notice was accomplished on the pro se party. The Notice of Electronic Filing effectuates service for the Registered Users in this situation and it is not necessary to note service on those parties. A non-registered pro se filer is required to file certificates of service on all documents they file. NY R USDCTWD ECF Procedures(2)(f)(iv).

- If an attorney is exempt from electronic service, a certificate of service must be filed stating the manner in which service or notice was accomplished on the exempt attorney. The Notice of Electronic Filing effectuates service for the Registered Users in this situation and it is not necessary to note service on those parties. NY R USDCTWD ECF Procedures(2)(f)(iv).

b. *Supplemental documents*

    i. *Pleadings.* In considering a motion for judgment on the pleadings, the trial court is. . .required to view the facts presented in the pleadings and inferences to be drawn therefrom in the light most favorable to the nonmoving party. FEDPROC § 62:570.

- *Motion treated as one for summary judgment.* If, on a motion under FRCP 12(b)(6) or FRCP 12(c), matters outside the pleadings are presented to and not excluded by the court, the motion must be treated as one for summary judgment under FRCP 56. All parties must be given a reasonable opportunity to present all the material that is pertinent to the motion. FRCP 12(d).

    ii. *Notice of constitutional question.* A party that files a pleading, written motion, or other paper drawing into question the constitutionality of a federal or state statute must promptly:

- *File notice.* File a notice of constitutional question stating the question and identifying the paper that raises it, if: (1) a federal statute is questioned and the parties do not include the United States, one of its agencies, or one of its officers or employees in an official capacity; or (2) a state statute is questioned and the parties do not include the state, one of its agencies, or one of its officers or employees in an official capacity; and

- *Serve notice.* Serve the notice and paper on the Attorney General of the United States if a federal statute is questioned—or on the state attorney general if a state statute is questioned—either by certified or registered mail or by sending it to an electronic address designated by the attorney general for this purpose. FRCP 5.1(a).

- *No forfeiture.* A party's failure to file and serve the notice, or the court's failure to certify, does not forfeit a constitutional claim or defense that is otherwise timely asserted. FRCP 5.1(d).

    iii. *Nongovernmental corporate disclosure statement*

- *Contents.* A nongovernmental corporate party must file two (2) copies of a disclosure statement that: (1) identifies any parent corporation and any publicly held corporation owning ten percent (10%) or more of its stock; or (2) states that there is no such corporation. FRCP 7.1(a).

- *Time to file; Supplemental filing.* A party must: (1) file the disclosure statement with its first appearance, pleading, petition, motion, response, or other request addressed to the court; and (2) promptly file a supplemental statement if any required information changes. FRCP 7.1(b).

    iv. *Copies of authorities.* In cases involving a pro se litigant, counsel shall, when serving a memorandum of law (or other submissions to the Court), provide the pro se litigant (but not other counsel or the Court) with printed copies of decisions cited therein that are unreported or reported exclusively on computerized databases. NY R USDCTWD Civ Rule 7(a)(8).

    v. *Proposed order.* All proposed orders must be submitted in a format compatible with WordPerfect or Microsoft Word format, which is a "Save As" option in most word processing software. Judges will not accept proposed orders in PDF format. NY R USDCTWD ECF Procedures(2)(j)(ii). Proposed orders should be attached to an Internet e-mail sent to the e-mail address of the assigned judge. NY R USDCTWD ECF Procedures(2)(j)(i). For the list of email addresses for the judges, refer to NY R USDCTWD ECF Procedures(2)(j)(i).

vi. *Paper copy for date-stamping with self-addressed envelope.* Parties requesting date-stamped copies of filed documents must provide a paper copy for date-stamping, and a self-addressed, adequately-sized envelope with proper postage affixed. NY R USDCTWD Civ Rule 5.1(d).

vii. *Courtesy copies.* The Court may, in its discretion, request courtesy copies on any other motion. NY R USDCTWD Civ Rule 7(a)(7). Courtesy copies of certain documents may be required. Filers should refer to the "Judge Preferences" published on the Court's website. NY R USDCTWD ECF Procedures(2)(a)(iii).

2. *Documents for opposing party*

   a. *Required documents*

      i. *Opposition.* Refer to the General Requirements section of this document for information on the opposing papers.

      ii. *Answering memorandum.* Absent leave of Court or as otherwise specified, upon any motion filed pursuant to FRCP 12, FRCP 56 or FRCP 65(a). . .the opposing party shall file and serve an answering memorandum. Failure to comply with this requirement may constitute grounds for resolving the motion against the non-complying party. NY R USDCTWD Civ Rule 7(a)(2)(A). Refer to the Format section of this document for the formatting requirements for memoranda of law.

      iii. *Certificate of service.* FRCP 5(d) requires that the person making service under FRCP 5 certify that service has been effected. FRCP 5(Advisory Committee Notes). Having such information on file may be useful for many purposes, including proof of service if an issue arises concerning the effectiveness of the service. FRCP 5(Advisory Committee Notes). The Notice of Electronic Filing effectuates service for all registered users and no certificate of service is required when all filers on an action are Registered Users. The following exemptions require a certificate of service to be filed:

         • When a document is manually filed, a certificate of service must be filed stating the manner in which service or notice was accomplished on each party so entitled. NY R USDCTWD ECF Procedures(2)(f)(iv).

         • When a pro se filer (who isn't authorized to electronically file documents) is a party, a certificate of service must be filed stating the manner in which service or notice was accomplished on the pro se party. The Notice of Electronic Filing effectuates service for the Registered Users in this situation and it is not necessary to note service on those parties. A non-registered pro se filer is required to file certificates of service on all documents they file. NY R USDCTWD ECF Procedures(2)(f)(iv).

         • If an attorney is exempt from electronic service, a certificate of service must be filed stating the manner in which service or notice was accomplished on the exempt attorney. The Notice of Electronic Filing effectuates service for the Registered Users in this situation and it is not necessary to note service on those parties. NY R USDCTWD ECF Procedures(2)(f)(iv).

   b. *Supplemental documents*

      i. *Pleadings.* In considering a motion for judgment on the pleadings, the trial court is. . .required to view the facts presented in the pleadings and inferences to be drawn therefrom in the light most favorable to the nonmoving party. FEDPROC § 62:570.

         • *Motion treated as one for summary judgment.* If, on a motion under FRCP 12(b)(6) or FRCP 12(c), matters outside the pleadings are presented to and not excluded by the court, the motion must be treated as one for summary judgment under FRCP 56. All parties must be given a reasonable opportunity to present all the material that is pertinent to the motion. FRCP 12(d).

ii. *Notice of constitutional question.* A party that files a pleading, written motion, or other paper drawing into question the constitutionality of a federal or state statute must promptly:

- *File notice.* File a notice of constitutional question stating the question and identifying the paper that raises it, if: (1) a federal statute is questioned and the parties do not include the United States, one of its agencies, or one of its officers or employees in an official capacity; or (2) a state statute is questioned and the parties do not include the state, one of its agencies, or one of its officers or employees in an official capacity; and

- *Serve notice.* Serve the notice and paper on the Attorney General of the United States if a federal statute is questioned—or on the state attorney general if a state statute is questioned—either by certified or registered mail or by sending it to an electronic address designated by the attorney general for this purpose. FRCP 5.1(a).

- *No forfeiture.* A party's failure to file and serve the notice, or the court's failure to certify, does not forfeit a constitutional claim or defense that is otherwise timely asserted. FRCP 5.1(d).

iii. *Copies of authorities.* In cases involving a pro se litigant, counsel shall, when serving a memorandum of law (or other submissions to the Court), provide the pro se litigant (but not other counsel or the Court) with printed copies of decisions cited therein that are unreported or reported exclusively on computerized databases. NY R USDCTWD Civ Rule 7(a)(8).

iv. *Paper copy for date-stamping with self-addressed envelope.* Parties requesting date-stamped copies of filed documents must provide a paper copy for date-stamping, and a self-addressed, adequately-sized envelope with proper postage affixed. NY R USDCTWD Civ Rule 5.1(d).

v. *Courtesy copies.* Courtesy copies of certain documents may be required. Filers should refer to the "Judge Preferences" published on the Court's website. NY R USDCTWD ECF Procedures(2)(a)(iii).

3. *Individual judge practices.* Refer to the Miscellaneous section of this document for information on individual judge practices on required documents.

## E. Format

1. *Form of documents.* The rules governing captions and other matters of form in pleadings apply to motions and other papers. FRCP 7(b)(2).

a. *Form, generally.* All pleadings, motions, and other papers that a party presents for filing, whether in paper form or in electronic form, shall meet the following requirements:

i. *Font size.* All text and footnotes shall be in a font size of at least twelve (12) point type. NY R USDCTWD Civ Rule 10(a)(1).

ii. *Spacing.* All text in the body of the document must be double-spaced, except that text in block quotations and footnotes may be single-spaced. NY R USDCTWD Civ Rule 10(a)(2).

- Extensive footnotes and block quotes may not be used to circumvent page limitations. NY R USDCTWD Civ Rule 10(a)(3).

iii. *Margins.* Documents must have one (1) inch margins on all four sides. NY R USDCTWD Civ Rule 10(a)(4).

iv. *Page numbering.* Pages must be consecutively numbered. NY R USDCTWD Civ Rule 10(a)(5).

b. *Additional requirements for paper filing.* Documents presented for filing in paper form shall meet the following additional requirements:

i. *Paper.* Documents must be on durable white eight and one-half by eleven (8-1/2 x 11) inch paper of good quality. NY R USDCTWD Civ Rule 10(b)(1).

- All documents must be single-sided. NY R USDCTWD Civ Rule 10(b)(5).

    ii.    *Text.* All text must be plainly and legibly written, typewritten, printed or reproduced. NY R USDCTWD Civ Rule 10(b)(2).

    iii.    *Ink.* Documents must be in black or blue ink. NY R USDCTWD Civ Rule 10(b)(3).

    iv.    *Binding.* The pages of each document must be stapled or in some other way fastened together. NY R USDCTWD Civ Rule 10(b)(4).

c.    *Caption; Names of parties.* Every pleading must have a caption with the court's name, a title, a file number, and a FRCP 7(a) designation. The title of the complaint must name all the parties; the title of other pleadings, after naming the first party on each side, may refer generally to other parties. FRCP 10(a).

d.    *Paragraphs; Separate statements.* A party must state its claims or defenses in numbered paragraphs, each limited as far as practicable to a single set of circumstances. A later pleading may refer by number to a paragraph in an earlier pleading. If doing so would promote clarity, each claim founded on a separate transaction or occurrence—and each defense other than a denial—must be stated in a separate count or defense. FRCP 10(b).

e.    *Adoption by reference; Exhibits.* A statement in a pleading may be adopted by reference elsewhere in the same pleading or in any other pleading or motion. A copy of a written instrument that is an exhibit to a pleading is a part of the pleading for all purposes. FRCP 10(c).

f.    *Citation of local rules.* The Local Rules of Civil Procedure for the United States District Court for the Western District of New York shall be cited as "L.R.Civ.P." NY R USDCTWD Civ Rule 1.1.

g.    *Acceptance by the clerk.* The clerk must not refuse to file a paper solely because it is not in the form prescribed by the Federal Rules of Civil Procedure or by a local rule or practice. FRCP 5(d)(4). The Court may reject documents that do not comply with the requirements in NY R USDCTWD Civ Rule 10. NY R USDCTWD Civ Rule 10.

2.    *Form of electronic documents.* All pleadings, motions, and other papers that a party presents for filing, whether in paper form or in electronic form, shall meet the requirements in NY R USDCTWD Civ Rule 10(a). NY R USDCTWD Civ Rule 10(a). Refer above for more information.

    a.    *Conversion to PDF.* A document created with a word processor, or a paper document, must be converted to Portable Document Format to be electronically filed with the court. NY R USDCTWD ECF Procedures(2)(a)(v).

        i.    Documents which exist only in paper form may be scanned into a portable document format (PDF) for electronic filing. NY R USDCTWD ECF Procedures(2)(a)(v). Before filing a scanned document with the court, a Filing User must verify its legibility. NY R USDCTWD ECF Procedures(2)(a)(iv).

        ii.    Electronic documents must be converted to .PDF from a word processing program and must be text searchable. Do not print, scan and .PDF your document when it has been created in a word processing program. Additional information on working with PDFs is located in NY R USDCTWD ECF Procedures(4b). NY R USDCTWD ECF Procedures(2)(a)(v).

    b.    *Hyperlinks.* Pursuant to the policy set forth by the Judicial Conference in October 2005, a hyperlink contained in a filing is no more than a convenient mechanism for accessing material cited in a document. A hyperlink reference is extraneous to any filed document and is not part of the Court's record. NY R USDCTWD ECF Procedures(2)(a)(vi).

        i.    In order to preserve the integrity of the Court record, users wishing to insert hyperlinks in Court filings shall continue to use the conventional method for the cited authority, in addition to the hyperlink. NY R USDCTWD ECF Procedures(2)(a)(vi).

        ii.    The Court accepts no responsibility for, and does not endorse any product, organization, and content at any hyperlinked site, or at any site to which that site may be linked. The Court accepts no responsibility for the availability or functionality of any hyperlink. NY R USDCTWD ECF Procedures(2)(a)(vi).

    c.    *Attachments and exhibits*

        i.    Attachments and exhibits larger than five megabytes (5 MB) shall be filed electronically in separate five megabyte (5 MB) segments. NY R USDCTWD ECF Procedures(2)(d)(i).

    ii.  Filing Users must submit in electronic form all documents referenced as exhibits or attachments, except as otherwise provided in NY R USDCTWD ECF Procedures. A Filing User must submit as exhibits or attachments only those excerpts of the referenced documents that are directly germane to the matter under consideration by the court. Excerpted material must be clearly and prominently identified as such. Filing Users who file excerpts of documents as exhibits or attachments under NY R USDCTWD ECF Procedures(2)(d)(ii) do so without prejudice to their right to timely file additional excerpts or the complete document. Responding parties may timely file additional excerpts or the complete document that they believe are directly germane. The Court may require parties to file additional excerpts or the complete document. A Filing User must request leave of the Court to file a document exhibit or attachment in non-electronic form. NY R USDCTWD ECF Procedures(2)(d)(ii).

    iii.  Exhibits offered or admitted at trial will not be filed electronically or conventionally unless so ordered by the Court. NY R USDCTWD ECF Procedures(2)(d)(iii).

    iv.  Exhibits such as videotapes and tape recordings shall be filed in the conventional manner with the Clerk of Court, and a Notice of Manual Filing shall be electronically filed by the party. Manually filed exhibits must have the case number and case name securely fastened or marked on the item. NY R USDCTWD ECF Procedures(2)(d)(iii).

    v.  Continuation of exhibit entries (for exhibits that are too large to attach to a main document) must be filed and entered on the same day that the main document was filed. NY R USDCTWD ECF Procedures(2)(d)(iv).

  d.  *Color documents.* Documents in color or containing graphics take much longer to upload. Filing users are encouraged to configure their scanners to scan documents at 200 dpi and preferably in black and white rather than color. NY R USDCTWD ECF Procedures(2)(d)(v).

  e.  *Large documents.* Due to the length of time it takes to download large files, documents larger than five megabytes (5 MB) (approximately one hundred (100) pages of a .pdf scanned document) must be filed electronically in separate five megabyte (5 MB) segments. A party who believes a document is too lengthy to electronically image (i.e. scan), may contact the Court Room Deputy for the assigned judge and request permission to file that document conventionally. If granted permission to file the document conventionally, the Filing User shall electronically file a "notice of manual filing" for that item. Exhibits submitted to the Court conventionally shall be served on other parties conventionally. NY R USDCTWD ECF Procedures(2)(d)(vi).

3.  *Form of memoranda of law.* Memoranda in support of or in opposition to any motion shall not exceed twenty-five (25) pages in length, and reply memoranda shall not exceed ten (10) pages in length. A party seeking to exceed the page limit must make application by letter to the Judge hearing the motion, with copies to all counsel, at least seven (7) days before the date on which the memorandum must be filed. NY R USDCTWD Civ Rule 7(a)(2)(C).

4.  *Signing of pleadings, motions and other papers*

  a.  *Signature.* Every pleading, written motion, and other paper must be signed by at least one attorney of record in the attorney's name—or by a party personally if the party is unrepresented. The paper must state the signer's address, e-mail address, and telephone number. FRCP 11(a). Documents presented for paper filing must contain an original signature. NY R USDCTWD Civ Rule 10(b)(6).

    i.  *Electronic signatures*

      •  *Non-attorney signature.* If the original document requires the signature of a non-attorney, the filing party shall obtain the signature of the non-attorney on the document. NY R USDCTWD ECF Procedures(2)(g)(i). The filing party or attorney then shall file the document electronically indicating the signatory's name in the form "s/(name)." NY R USDCTWD ECF Procedures(2)(g)(i)(1). A non-filing signatory or party who disputes the authenticity of an electronically filed document or the authenticity of the signature on that document must file an objection to the document within ten (10) days of receiving the Notice of Electronic Filing. NY R USDCTWD ECF Procedures(2)(g)(i)(2).

      •  *Registered user signature.* The username and password required to file documents on the

Electronic Filing System serve as the Filing User's signature on all electronic documents filed with this Court. The also serve as a signature for the purposes of FRCP 11, the Federal Rules of Civil Procedure, the Local Rules of Civil Procedure for the United States District Court for the Western District of New York, and any other purpose for which a signature is required in connection with proceedings before this Court. A pleading requiring a Registered User's signature must include a signature block in the format found in NY R USDCTWD ECF Procedures(2)(g)(iii). NY R USDCTWD ECF Procedures(2)(g)(iii). Any party challenging the authenticity of an electronically filed document or the attorney's signature on that document must file an objection to the document within ten (10) days of receiving the Notice of Electronic Filing. NY R USDCTWD ECF Procedures(2)(g)(iii)(1).

- *Multiple signatures.* The following procedure applies when a stipulation or other document requires two or more signatures: The filing party shall initially confirm that the document is acceptable to all persons required to sign the document and shall obtain the signatures of all parties on the document. NY R USDCTWD ECF Procedures(2)(g)(iv)(1). The filing party or attorney then shall file the document electronically indicating the signatories, e.g., "s/Jane Doe," "s/John Smith," etc. NY R USDCTWD ECF Procedures(2)(g)(iv)(2). A non-filing signatory or party who disputes the authenticity of an electronically filed document containing multiple signatures or the authenticity of the signatures themselves must file an objection to the document within ten (10) days of receiving the Notice of Electronic Filing. NY R USDCTWD ECF Procedures(2)(g)(iv)(3).

  ii. *No verification or accompanying affidavit required for pleadings.* Unless a rule or statute specifically states otherwise, a pleading need not be verified or accompanied by an affidavit. FRCP 11(a).

  iii. *Unsigned papers.* The court must strike an unsigned paper unless the omission is promptly corrected after being called to the attorney's or party's attention. FRCP 11(a).

b. *Representations to the court.* By presenting to the court a pleading, written motion, or other paper—whether by signing, filing, submitting, or later advocating it—an attorney or unrepresented party certifies that to the best of the person's knowledge, information, and belief, formed after an inquiry reasonable under the circumstances:

  i. It is not being presented for any improper purpose, such as to harass, cause unnecessary delay, or needlessly increase the cost of litigation;

  ii. The claims, defenses, and other legal contentions are warranted by existing law or by a nonfrivolous argument for extending, modifying, or reversing existing law or for establishing new law;

  iii. The factual contentions have evidentiary support or, if specifically so identified, will likely have evidentiary support after a reasonable opportunity for further investigation or discovery; and

  iv. The denials of factual contentions are warranted on the evidence or, if specifically so identified, are reasonably based on belief or a lack of information. FRCP 11(b).

c. *Sanctions.* If, after notice and a reasonable opportunity to respond, the court determines that FRCP 11(b) has been violated, the court may impose an appropriate sanction on any attorney, law firm, or party that violated FRCP 11(b) or is responsible for the violation. FRCP 11(c)(1). Refer to the United States District Court for the Western District of New York KeyRules Motion for Sanctions document for more information.

5. *Privacy protection for filings made with the court.* In all filings, parties shall comply with FRCP 5.2. NY R USDCTWD ECF Procedures(2)(m)(i).

   a. *Redacted filings.* Unless the court orders otherwise, in an electronic or paper filing with the court that contains an individual's Social Security number, taxpayer-identification number, or birth date, the name of an individual known to be a minor, or a financial-account number, a party or nonparty making the filing may include only:

      i. The last four (4) digits of the Social Security number and taxpayer-identification number;

    ii.   The year of the individual's birth;

    iii.  The minor's initials; and

    iv.  The last four (4) digits of the financial-account number. FRCP 5.2(a).

b.  *Exemptions from the redaction requirement.* The redaction requirement does not apply to the following:

    i.    A financial-account number that identifies the property allegedly subject to forfeiture in a forfeiture proceeding;

    ii.   The record of an administrative or agency proceeding;

    iii.  The official record of a state-court proceeding;

    iv.  The record of a court or tribunal, if that record was not subject to the redaction requirement when originally filed;

    v.   A filing covered by FRCP 5.2(c) or FRCP 5.2(d); and

    vi.  A pro se filing in an action brought under 28 U.S.C.A. § 2241, 28 U.S.C.A. § 2254, or 28 U.S.C.A. § 2255. FRCP 5.2(b).

c.  *Limitations on remote access to electronic files; Social Security appeals and immigration cases.* Unless the court orders otherwise, in an action for benefits under the Social Security Act, and in an action or proceeding relating to an order of removal, to relief from removal, or to immigration benefits or detention, access to an electronic file is authorized as follows:

    i.    The parties and their attorneys may have remote electronic access to any part of the case file, including the administrative record;

    ii.   Any other person may have electronic access to the full record at the courthouse, but may have remote electronic access only to:

        • The docket maintained by the court; and

        • An opinion, order, judgment, or other disposition of the court, but not any other part of the case file or the administrative record. FRCP 5.2(c).

d.  *Filings made under seal.* The court may order that a filing be made under seal without redaction. The court may later unseal the filing or order the person who made the filing to file a redacted version for the public record. FRCP 5.2(d). For more information on sealing documents, refer to NY R USDCTWD Civ Rule 5.3, NY R USDCTWD ECF Procedures(2)(o)(i)(1), NY R USDCTWD ECF Procedures(2)(o)(i)(2), and NY R USDCTWD ECF Procedures(2)(o)(i)(3).

e.  *Protective orders.* For good cause, the court may by order in a case:

    i.    Require redaction of additional information; or

    ii.   Limit or prohibit a nonparty's remote electronic access to a document filed with the court. FRCP 5.2(e).

f.  *Option for additional unredacted filing under seal.* A person making a redacted filing may also file an unredacted copy under seal. The court must retain the unredacted copy as part of the record. FRCP 5.2(f).

g.  *Option for filing a reference list.* A filing that contains redacted information may be filed together with a reference list that identifies each item of redacted information and specifies an appropriate identifier that uniquely corresponds to each item listed. The list must be filed under seal and may be amended as of right. Any reference in the case to a listed identifier will be construed to refer to the corresponding item of information. FRCP 5.2(g).

h.  *Waiver of protection of identifiers.* A person waives the protection of FRCP 5.2(a) as to the person's own information by filing it without redaction and not under seal. FRCP 5.2(h).

6.  *Individual judge practices.* Refer to the Miscellaneous section of this document for information on individual judge practices on formatting documents.

## F.  Filing and Service Requirements

1.  *Filing requirements.* Any paper after the complaint that is required to be served—together with a

certificate of service—must be filed within a reasonable time after service. FRCP 5(d)(1). All pleadings and other papers shall be filed and served in accordance with the Federal Rules of Civil Procedure and the CM/ECF Administrative Procedures Guide (NY R USDCTWD ECF Procedures). NY R USDCTWD Civ Rule 5.1(a). For information on filing of miscellaneous cases and irregular documents, refer to NY R USDCTWD Civ Rule 5.6.

a. *How filing is made; In general.* A paper is filed by delivering it:

   i. To the clerk; or

   ii. To a judge who agrees to accept it for filing, and who must then note the filing date on the paper and promptly send it to the clerk. FRCP 5(d)(2).

b. *Electronic filing*

   i. *Authorization of electronic filing program.* A court may, by local rule, allow papers to be filed, signed, or verified by electronic means that are consistent with any technical standards established by the Judicial Conference of the United States. A local rule may require electronic filing only if reasonable exceptions are allowed. A paper filed electronically in compliance with a local rule is a written paper for purposes of the Federal Rules of Civil Procedure. FRCP 5(d)(3).

- All civil cases filed in this Court are assigned to the Electronic Case Filing System ("ECF"). The procedures for electronic filing and any exceptions to the electronic filing requirements are set forth in the CM/ECF Administrative Procedures Guide (NY R USDCTWD ECF Procedures) which is available on the Court's website. NY R US-DCTWD Civ Rule 5.1(a).

   ii. *Scope of electronic filing.* The U.S. District Court for the Western District of New York requires attorneys in civil and criminal cases to file documents with the Court electronically over the Internet using its Case Management/Electronic Case Filing (CM/ECF) system. NY R US-DCTWD ECF Procedures. Beginning January 1, 2004, all civil and criminal cases currently pending and newly filed, except as expressly noted herein, were assigned to the Electronic Case Filing System ("System"). Except as expressly provided and in exceptional circumstances preventing a Filing User from filing electronically, all petitions, motions, memoranda of law, or other pleadings and documents required to be filed with the Court in connection with a case assigned to the System must be electronically filed. NY R USDCTWD ECF Procedures(1)(a).

- *Mandatory electronic filing.* All documents on civil, criminal, miscellaneous civil, miscellaneous criminal and new civil case openings, except sealed documents, sealed cases, opening of a criminal case, opening of a miscellaneous case and as expressly provided for in these procedures (NY R USDCTWD ECF Procedures), shall be electronically filed on the system. NY R USDCTWD ECF Procedures(2)(a)(i). NY R USDCTWD Civ Rule 29

- *Stipulations.* Pursuant to NY R USDCTWD Civ Rule 29, all stipulations (whether the stipulation is final or when it requires a judge's signature) shall be filed electronically. NY R USDCTWD ECF Procedures(2)(p)(i).

- *Letters.* The electronic filing of letters is generally prohibited unless granted permission by an assigned judge. Letters to the Court must be submitted conventionally. NY R US-DCTWD ECF Procedures(2)(q)(i).

- *Exceptions.* The Court requires attorneys to file documents electronically, absent a showing of good cause, unless otherwise excused by the procedures set forth below or by Order of the Court. NY R USDCTWD ECF Procedures.

   iii. *Conventional filing of documents.* The procedures in NY R USDCTWD ECF Procedures(2)(o) govern documents filed conventionally. The Court, upon application, may also authorize conventional filing of other documents otherwise subject to the procedures in NY R US-DCTWD ECF Procedures(2)(o). NY R USDCTWD ECF Procedures(2)(o)(i).

- *Documents filed under seal.* Unredacted documents filed with the Court pursuant to the privacy provisions of FRCP 5.2 shall be submitted in a sealing envelope with the

information in NY R USDCTWD ECF Procedures(2)(o)(i)(1) on the envelope. NY R USDCTWD ECF Procedures(2)(o)(i)(1). If the document is larger than five (5) pages, a disk should be provided to the Clerks Office which contains the document in a .pdf format. NY R USDCTWD ECF Procedures(2)(o)(i)(1). For more information on documents filed under seal, refer to NY R USDCTWD ECF Procedures(2)(o)(i)(1), NY R USDCTWD ECF Procedures(2)(o)(i)(2), and NY R USDCTWD ECF Procedures(2)(o)(i)(3).

- *Magistrate judge consents.* Pursuant to FRCP 73(b), parties' filing consents to jurisdiction by United States Magistrate Judge will continue to be treated as non-public documents until all parties have consented. Therefore, parties must submit conventionally (in paper form) and not electronically file their consent forms so that the consent is not a public document. If all parties consent to the jurisdiction of a Magistrate Judge, the Clerk will scan all consent forms which will then become a public document. NY R USDCTWD ECF Procedures(2)(o)(i)(3).

- *Pro se filers.* Pro Se filers shall file paper originals of all initiating documents, pleadings, motions, affidavits, briefs and other documents which must be signed or which require either verification or an unsworn declaration under any rule or statute. The Clerk's Office will scan these original documents into an electronic file in the System. A certificate of service is required for all documents a pro se litigant files with the court. If a Pro Se filer is granted permission to register to electronically file documents, they shall comply with the guidelines contained in this document (NY R USDCTWD ECF Procedures). NY R USDCTWD ECF Procedures(2)(o)(i)(4).

- *Social Security cases.* Absent a showing of good cause, and except as provided in Section o(i)(4) above, all documents, notices and orders in Social Security reviews will be filed and noticed electronically, except as noted in NY R USDCTWD ECF Procedures(2)(o)(i)(6). For more information, refer to NY R USDCTWD ECF Procedures(2)(o)(i)(6).

- For more information on conventional filing of documents, refer to NY R USDCTWD ECF Procedures(2)(o)(i).

iv. *Consequences of electronic filing.* Electronic transmission of a document to the System consistent with these procedures (NY R USDCTWD ECF Procedures), whether accomplished by the Filing User or a Court User, together with the transmission of a Notice of Electronic Filing from the Court, constitutes filing of a document for all purposes of the Federal Rules of Civil Procedure and the Local Rules of Civil Procedure for the United States District Court for the Western District of New York, and constitutes entry of the document on the docket kept by the Clerk under FRCP 58 and FRCP 79. A document shall not be considered filed for purposes of the Federal Rules of Civil until the filing party receives a System generated Notice of Electronic Filing. NY R USDCTWD ECF Procedures(2)(a)(i).

- E-mailing a document to the Clerk's Office or to the assigned judge shall not constitute "filing" of such document. NY R USDCTWD ECF Procedures(2)(a)(i)(1).

v. *Filing fees.* Any fee required for filing of a pleading or paper in District Court is payable to the Clerk of Court by check or money order. In addition, when opening a civil case on line, filing a notice of appeal on line or applying to appear pro hac vice on line, the fees shall be paid on line by registered users through the federal electronic payment website. Users will be directed to the federal electronic payment website while entering their transaction and should have a credit card available. When opening a civil case and applying to proceed in forma pauperis or when the United States of America opens a case, the payment screen can by bypassed to complete the transaction. Additional information on making electronic payments can be located on the court's website. NY R USDCTWD ECF Procedures(2)(h)(i).

2. *Service requirements.* All pleadings and other papers shall be filed and served in accordance with the

Federal Rules of Civil Procedure and the CM/ECF Administrative Procedures Guide (NY R USDCTWD ECF Procedures). NY R USDCTWD Civ Rule 5.1(a).

a. *Service; When required*

    i. *In general.* Unless the Federal Rules of Civil Procedure provide otherwise, each of the following papers must be served on every party:

- An order stating that service is required;

- A pleading filed after the original complaint, unless the court orders otherwise under FRCP 5(c) because there are numerous defendants;

- A discovery paper required to be served on a party, unless the court orders otherwise;

- A written motion, except one that may be heard ex parte; and

- A written notice, appearance, demand, or offer of judgment, or any similar paper. FRCP 5(a)(1).

    ii. *If a party fails to appear.* No service is required on a party who is in default for failing to appear. But a pleading that asserts a new claim for relief against such a party must be served on that party under FRCP 4. FRCP 5(a)(2).

    iii. *Seizing property.* If an action is begun by seizing property and no person is or need be named as a defendant, any service required before the filing of an appearance, answer, or claim must be made on the person who had custody or possession of the property when it was seized. FRCP 5(a)(3).

b. *Service; How made*

    i. *Serving an attorney.* If a party is represented by an attorney, service under FRCP 5 must be made on the attorney unless the court orders service on the party. FRCP 5(b)(1).

    ii. *Service in general.* A paper is served under FRCP 5 by:

- Handing it to the person;

- Leaving it: (1) at the person's office with a clerk or other person in charge or, if no one is in charge, in a conspicuous place in the office; or (2) if the person has no office or the office is closed, at the person's dwelling or usual place of abode with someone of suitable age and discretion who resides there;

- Mailing it to the person's last known address—in which event service is complete upon mailing;

- Leaving it with the court clerk if the person has no known address;

- Sending it by electronic means if the person consented in writing—in which event service is complete upon transmission, but is not effective if the serving party learns that it did not reach the person to be served; or

- Delivering it by any other means that the person consented to in writing—in which event service is complete when the person making service delivers it to the agency designated to make delivery. FRCP 5(b)(2).

    iii. *Service by overnight delivery.* All papers, other than a subpoena or a summons and complaint, may be served on counsel of record by overnight delivery service at the address designated by the attorney for that purpose, or if none is designated, at the attorney's last known address. Service by overnight delivery shall be complete upon deposit of the paper(s), enclosed in a properly addressed wrapper, into the custody of the overnight delivery service, prior to the latest time designated by the service for overnight delivery. NY R USDCTWD Civ Rule 5.1(g). "Overnight delivery service" means any delivery service which regularly accepts items for overnight delivery to any address within the Court's jurisdiction. NY R USDCTWD Civ Rule 5.1(g).

    iv. *Service of documents by electronic means*

- *Service on registered users.* Registered Users consent to the electronic service of all

documents, and must make available an electronic mail address for service during the registration process. Upon the filing of a document by a party, a Notice of Electronic Filing, with a hyperlink to the filed document, will be automatically generated by the electronic filing system and sent via electronic mail to the e-mail addresses of all parties participating in the electronic filing system in the case. Electronic service of the Notice of Electronic Filing constitutes service of the filed document for all purposes of the Federal Rules of Civil Procedure and the Local Rules of Civil Procedure for the United States District Court for the Western District of New York. NY R USDCTWD ECF Procedures(2)(f)(i). The Notice of Electronic Filing effectuates service for all registered users and no certificate of service is required when all filers on an action are Registered Users. NY R USDCTWD ECF Procedures(2)(f)(iv).

- *Time limit for opening hyperlink.* The hyperlink to filed documents contained in the Notice of Electronic Filing must be opened within fifteen (15) days from the date the document was filed to provide registered users access to the document. The hyperlink expires after fifteen (15) days and users will be unable to access documents for free after that time. Filing Users are encouraged to check their e-mail frequently for notice of filed documents. NY R USDCTWD ECF Procedures(2)(f)(ii).

- *Service on exempted attorneys or pro se litigants who do not have permission to file electronically.* Attorneys granted an exemption from electronically filing documents in the System and pro se litigants who have not been granted permission to electronically file documents are entitled to a paper copy of any electronically filed pleading, document or order. The filing party must therefore provide the non-registered party with the pleading, document or order according to the Federal Rules of Civil Procedure. NY R USDCTWD ECF Procedures(2)(f)(iii).

- *E-mailing or faxing documents.* E-mailing or faxing a pleading or document to any party shall not constitute service of the pleading or document. NY R USDCTWD ECF Procedures(2)(f)(v).

    v.  *Using court facilities.* If a local rule so authorizes, a party may use the court's transmission facilities to make service under FRCP 5(b)(2)(E). FRCP 5(b)(3).

  c.  *Serving numerous defendants*

    i.  *In general.* If an action involves an unusually large number of defendants, the court may, on motion or on its own, order that:

- Defendants' pleadings and replies to them need not be served on other defendants;

- Any crossclaim, counterclaim, avoidance, or affirmative defense in those pleadings and replies to them will be treated as denied or avoided by all other parties; and

- Filing any such pleading and serving it on the plaintiff constitutes notice of the pleading to all parties. FRCP 5(c)(1).

    ii.  *Notifying parties.* A copy of every such order must be served on the parties as the court directs. FRCP 5(c)(2).

3.  *Pro se actions.* For information on the requirements in pro se actions, refer to NY R USDCTWD Civ Rule 5.2.

4.  *Individual judge practices.* Refer to the Miscellaneous section of this document for information on individual judge practices on filing and serving documents.

## G. Hearings

1.  *Hearings, generally*

  a.  *Oral argument.* Due process does not require that oral argument be permitted on a motion and, except as otherwise provided by local rule, the district court has discretion to determine whether it will decide the motion on the papers or hear argument by counsel (and perhaps receive evidence). FPP § 1190; F.D.I.C. v. Deglau, 207 F.3d 153 (3d Cir. 2000).

    i.  The parties shall appear for oral argument on all motions they make returnable before a Judge

on the scheduled return date for the motion. In its discretion, the Court may notify the parties that oral argument shall not be heard on any given motion. Thus, the parties should be prepared to have their motion papers serve as the sole method of argument. NY R USDCTWD Civ Rule 7(c).

b. *Providing a regular schedule for oral hearings.* A court may establish regular times and places for oral hearings on motions. FRCP 78(a).

c. *Providing for submission on briefs.* By rule or order, the court may provide for submitting and determining motions on briefs, without oral hearings. FRCP 78(b).

2. *Individual judge practices.* Refer to the Miscellaneous section of this document for information on individual judge practices on hearings.

## H. Forms

### 1. Federal Motion for Judgment on the Pleadings Forms

a. Motion and notice; For judgment on pleadings. AMJUR PP FEDPRAC § 532.

b. Countermotion and notice; For judgment on pleadings; By defendants. AMJUR PP FEDPRAC § 533.

c. Order; For judgment on pleadings; In favor of plaintiff. AMJUR PP FEDPRAC § 534.

d. Order; For judgment on pleadings; In favor of defendant. AMJUR PP FEDPRAC § 535.

e. Motion for judgment on the pleadings. 2C FEDFORMS § 11:131.

f. Motion for judgment on the pleadings; Alternate wording. 2C FEDFORMS § 11:132.

g. Motion for judgment on the pleadings; Long version. 2C FEDFORMS § 11:133.

h. Motion for judgment on the pleadings; Several grounds. 2C FEDFORMS § 11:134.

i. Notice of motion and motion for judgment on the pleadings. 2C FEDFORMS § 11:135.

j. Notice of motion for judgment on the pleadings (partial) or for partial summary judgment. 2C FEDFORMS § 11:136.

k. Order granting judgment on the pleadings. 2C FEDFORMS § 11:137.

l. Order granting judgment on the pleadings; Motion by plaintiff. 2C FEDFORMS § 11:138.

m. Judgment on the pleadings. 2C FEDFORMS § 11:139.

n. Motion; General form. FEDPROF § 1:746.

o. Notice; Of motion; General form. FEDPROF § 1:747.

p. Notice; Of motion; With costs of motion. FEDPROF § 1:748.

q. Notice; Of motion; Containing motion. FEDPROF § 1:749.

r. Opposition; To motion; General form. FEDPROF § 1:750.

s. Affidavit; Supporting or opposing motion. FEDPROF § 1:751.

t. Brief; Supporting or opposing motion. FEDPROF § 1:752.

u. Statement of points and authorities; Opposing motion. FEDPROF § 1:753.

v. Motion; For judgment on the pleadings. FEDPROF § 1:1295.

w. Order; For judgment on the pleadings; In favor of plaintiff. FEDPROF § 1:1296.

x. Order; For judgment on the pleadings; In favor of defendant. FEDPROF § 1:1297.

y. Motion for judgment on pleadings; Plaintiff. GOLDLTGFMS § 20:38.

z. Motion for judgment on pleadings; Defendant. GOLDLTGFMS § 20:39.

### 2. Forms for the Western District of New York

a. Certificate of service. NY R USDCTWD ECF Procedures(4a).

## I. Applicable Rules

1. *Federal rules*

    a. Serving and filing pleadings and other papers. FRCP 5.

    b. Constitutional challenge to a statute; Notice, certification, and intervention. FRCP 5.1.

    c. Privacy protection for filings made with the court. FRCP 5.2.

    d. Computing and extending time; Time for motion papers. FRCP 6.

    e. Pleadings allowed; Form of motions and other papers. FRCP 7.

    f. Disclosure statement. FRCP 7.1.

    g. Form of pleadings. FRCP 10.

    h. Signing pleadings, motions, and other papers; Representations to the court; Sanctions. FRCP 11.

    i. Defenses and objections; When and how presented; Motion for judgment on the pleadings; Consolidating motions; Waiving defenses; Pretrial hearing. FRCP 12.

    j. Hearing motions; Submission on briefs. FRCP 78.

2. *Local rules*

    a. Title. NY R USDCTWD Civ Rule 1.1.

    b. Filing and serving papers. NY R USDCTWD Civ Rule 5.1.

    c. Motion practice. NY R USDCTWD Civ Rule 7.

    d. Form of papers. NY R USDCTWD Civ Rule 10.

    e. Sanctions. NY R USDCTWD Civ Rule 11.

    f. Alternative dispute resolution and pretrial conferences. NY R USDCTWD Civ Rule 16.

    g. Attorneys of record; Appearance and withdrawal. NY R USDCTWD Civ Rule 83.2.

    h. Administrative procedures guide for electronic filing. NY R USDCTWD ECF Procedures.

    i. Alternative dispute resolution plan. NY R USDCTWD ADR Plan.

## J. Miscellaneous

**NOTE: Individual judges' rules may apply. For available judge-level information, refer to:**

DISTRICT JUDGE RICHARD J. ARCARA: NY R USDCTWD Arcara-Procedures.

DISTRICT JUDGE FRANK P. GERACI, JR.: NY R USDCTWD Geraci-Procedures.

DISTRICT JUDGE DAVID G. LARIMER: NY R USDCTWD Larimer-Procedures.

DISTRICT JUDGE CHARLES J. SIRAGUSA: NY R USDCTWD Siragusa-Procedures.

DISTRICT JUDGE WILLIAM M. SKRETNY: NY R USDCTWD Skretny--Procedures.

DISTRICT JUDGE MICHAEL A. TELESCA: NY R USDCTWD Telesca-Procedures.

DISTRICT JUDGE LAWRENCE J. VILARDO: NY R USDCTWD Vilardo-Procedures.

DISTRICT JUDGE ELIZABETH A. WOLFORD: NY R USDCTWD Wolford-Procedures.

MAGISTRATE JUDGE JONATHAN W. FELDMAN: NY R USDCTWD Feldman-Procedures.

MAGISTRATE JUDGE LESLIE G. FOSCHIO: NY R USDCTWD Foschio-Procedures; NY R USDCTWD Foschio-Depositions.

MAGISTRATE JUDGE JEREMIAH J. McCARTHY: NY R USDCTWD McCarthy-Procedures.

MAGISTRATE JUDGE MARIAN W. PAYSON: NY R USDCTWD Payson-Procedures.

MAGISTRATE JUDGE MICHAEL J. ROEMER: NY R USDCTWD Roemer-Procedures.

MAGISTRATE JUDGE H. KENNETH SCHROEDER, JR.: NY R USDCTWD Schroeder-Proc.

MAGISTRATE JUDGE HUGH B. SCOTT: NY R USDCTWD Scott-Procedures.

# Requests, Notices and Applications
# Interrogatories

## Document Last Updated September 2016

### A. Checklist

(I) ❑ Matters to be considered by requesting party

    (a) ❑ Required documents

        (1) ❑ Interrogatories

        (2) ❑ Electronic courtesy copy

    (b) ❑ Supplemental documents

        (1) ❑ Certificate of service

    (c) ❑ Timing

        (1) ❑ A party may not seek discovery from any source before the parties have conferred as required by FRCP 26(f), except in a proceeding exempted from initial disclosure under FRCP 26(a)(1)(B), or when authorized by the Federal Rules of Civil Procedure, by stipulation, or by court order

(II) ❑ Matters to be considered by responding party

    (a) ❑ Required documents

        (1) ❑ Response to interrogatories

    (b) ❑ Supplemental documents

        (1) ❑ Certificate of service

    (c) ❑ Timing

        (1) ❑ The responding party must serve its answers and any objections within thirty (30) days after being served with the interrogatories

### B. Timing

1. *Interrogatories.* FRCP 33(a) contains no limit on when interrogatories may first be served. FPP § 2170. FRCP 33 is also silent on how late in a case interrogatories may be served. But FRCP 16(b)(3)(A) provides that the scheduling order in the case "must limit the time to . . . complete discovery." Although the scheduling order requirement does not apply to cases exempted by local rule, ordinarily there should be a scheduling order that sets a discovery cutoff. FPP § 2170.

2. *Timing of discovery, generally.* A party may not seek discovery from any source before the parties have conferred as required by FRCP 26(f), except in a proceeding exempted from initial disclosure under FRCP 26(a)(1)(B), or when authorized by the Federal Rules of Civil Procedure, by stipulation, or by court order. FRCP 26(d)(1).

3. *Computation of time*

    a. *Computing time.* FRCP 6 applies in computing any time period specified in the Federal Rules of Civil Procedure, in any local rule or court order, or in any statute that does not specify a method of computing time. FRCP 6(a).

        i. *Period stated in days or a longer unit.* When the period is stated in days or a longer unit of time:

            • Exclude the day of the event that triggers the period;

            • Count every day, including intermediate Saturdays, Sundays, and legal holidays; and

            • Include the last day of the period, but if the last day is a Saturday, Sunday, or legal holiday, the period continues to run until the end of the next day that is not a Saturday, Sunday, or legal holiday. FRCP 6(a)(1).

        ii. *Period stated in hours.* When the period is stated in hours:

            • Begin counting immediately on the occurrence of the event that triggers the period;

- Count every hour, including hours during intermediate Saturdays, Sundays, and legal holidays; and

- If the period would end on a Saturday, Sunday, or legal holiday, the period continues to run until the same time on the next day that is not a Saturday, Sunday, or legal holiday. FRCP 6(a)(2).

iii. *Inaccessibility of the clerk's office.* Unless the court orders otherwise, if the clerk's office is inaccessible:

- On the last day for filing under FRCP 6(a)(1), then the time for filing is extended to the first accessible day that is not a Saturday, Sunday, or legal holiday; or

- During the last hour for filing under FRCP 6(a)(2), then the time for filing is extended to the same time on the first accessible day that is not a Saturday, Sunday, or legal holiday. FRCP 6(a)(3).

iv. *"Last day" defined.* Unless a different time is set by a statute, local rule, or court order, the last day ends:

- For electronic filing, at midnight in the court's time zone; and

- For filing by other means, when the clerk's office is scheduled to close. FRCP 6(a)(4).

v. *"Next day" defined.* The "next day" is determined by continuing to count forward when the period is measured after an event and backward when measured before an event. FRCP 6(a)(5).

vi. *"Legal holiday" defined.* "Legal holiday" means:

- The day set aside by statute for observing New Year's Day, Martin Luther King Jr.'s Birthday, Washington's Birthday, Memorial Day, Independence Day, Labor Day, Columbus Day, Veterans' Day, Thanksgiving Day, or Christmas Day;

- Any day declared a holiday by the President or Congress; and

- For periods that are measured after an event, any other day declared a holiday by the state where the district court is located. FRCP 6(a)(6).

b. *Computation of electronic filing deadlines.* A document will be deemed timely filed if filed prior to midnight Eastern Time, unless otherwise ordered by the Court. A document will be considered untimely if filed thereafter. When a Court order requires that a document be filed on a weekend or holiday, the document may be filed by close of business the next business day without further application to the Court. NY R USDCTWD ECF Procedures(2)(e)(i). A document filed electronically is deemed filed on the date and time stated on the Notice of Electronic Filing. NY R USDCTWD ECF Procedures(2)(e)(ii).

i. *System availability.* Although parties may file documents electronically twenty-four (24) hours a day, registered users are strongly encouraged to file all documents during normal working hours of the Clerk's Office (8:30 a.m. to 5:00 p.m. Eastern Time). NY R USDCTWD ECF Procedures(2)(t)(i).

ii. *Technical failures.* A Filing User whose filing is made untimely as a result of a technical failure must seek appropriate relief from the Court. NY R USDCTWD ECF Procedures(2)(u)(i).

c. *Extending time*

i. *In general.* When an act may or must be done within a specified time, the court may, for good cause, extend the time:

- With or without motion or notice if the court acts, or if a request is made, before the original time or its extension expires; or

- On motion made after the time has expired if the party failed to act because of excusable neglect. FRCP 6(b)(1).

ii. *Exceptions.* A court must not extend the time to act under FRCP 50(b), FRCP 50(d), FRCP 52(b), FRCP 59(b), FRCP 59(d), FRCP 59(e), and FRCP 60(b). FRCP 6(b)(2).

iii. Refer to the United States District Court for the Western District of New York KeyRules Motion for Continuance/Extension of Time document for more information on extending time.

    d. *Additional time after certain kinds of service.* When a party may or must act within a specified time after service and service is made under FRCP 5(b)(2)(C), FRCP 5(b)(2)(D), FRCP 5(b)(2)(E), or FRCP 5(b)(2)(F), three (3) days are added after the period would otherwise expire under FRCP 6(a). FRCP 6(d).

        i. *Service by overnight delivery.* Where a period of time prescribed by either the Federal Rules of Civil Procedure or the Local Rules of Civil Procedure for the United States District Court for the Western District of New York is measured from the service of a paper and service is by overnight delivery, one (1) business day shall be added to the prescribed period. NY R USDCTWD Civ Rule 5.1(g).

4. *Individual judge practices.* Refer to the Miscellaneous section of this document for information on individual judge practices on timing of documents.

## C. General Requirements

1. *General provisions governing discovery*

    a. *Discovery scope and limits*

        i. *Scope in general.* Unless otherwise limited by court order, the scope of discovery is as follows: Parties may obtain discovery regarding any nonprivileged matter that is relevant to any party's claim or defense and proportional to the needs of the case, considering the importance of the issues at stake in the action, the amount in controversy, the parties' relative access to relevant information, the parties' resources, the importance of the discovery in resolving the issues, and whether the burden or expense of the proposed discovery outweighs its likely benefit. Information within this scope of discovery need not be admissible in evidence to be discoverable. FRCP 26(b)(1).

        ii. *Limitations on frequency and extent*

           • *When permitted.* By order, the court may alter the limits in the Federal Rules of Civil Procedure on the number of depositions and interrogatories or on the length of depositions under FRCP 30. By order or local rule, the court may also limit the number of requests under FRCP 36. FRCP 26(b)(2)(A).

           • *Specific limitations on electronically stored information.* A party need not provide discovery of electronically stored information from sources that the party identifies as not reasonably accessible because of undue burden or cost. On motion to compel discovery or for a protective order, the party from whom discovery is sought must show that the information is not reasonably accessible because of undue burden or cost. If that showing is made, the court may nonetheless order discovery from such sources if the requesting party shows good cause, considering the limitations of FRCP 26(b)(2)(C). The court may specify conditions for the discovery. FRCP 26(b)(2)(B).

           • *When required.* On motion or on its own, the court must limit the frequency or extent of discovery otherwise allowed by the Federal Rules of Civil Procedure or by local rule if it determines that: (1) the discovery sought is unreasonably cumulative or duplicative, or can be obtained from some other source that is more convenient, less burdensome, or less expensive; (2) the party seeking discovery has had ample opportunity to obtain the information by discovery in the action; or (3) the proposed discovery is outside the scope permitted by FRCP 26(b)(1). FRCP 26(b)(2)(C).

        iii. *Trial preparation; Materials*

           • *Documents and tangible things.* Ordinarily, a party may not discover documents and tangible things that are prepared in anticipation of litigation or for trial by or for another party or its representative (including the other party's attorney, consultant, surety, indemnitor, insurer, or agent). But, subject to FRCP 26(b)(4), those materials may be discovered if: (1) they are otherwise discoverable under FRCP 26(b)(1); and (2) the party shows that it has substantial need for the materials to prepare its case and cannot, without undue hardship, obtain their substantial equivalent by other means. FRCP 26(b)(3)(A).

           • *Protection against disclosure.* If the court orders discovery of those materials, it must protect against disclosure of the mental impressions, conclusions, opinions, or legal theories of a party's attorney or other representative concerning the litigation. FRCP 26(b)(3)(B).

- *Previous statement.* Any party or other person may, on request and without the required showing, obtain the person's own previous statement about the action or its subject matter. If the request is refused, the person may move for a court order, and FRCP 37(a)(5) applies to the award of expenses. A previous statement is either: (1) a written statement that the person has signed or otherwise adopted or approved; or (2) a contemporaneous steno-graphic, mechanical, electrical, or other recording—or a transcription of it—that recites substantially verbatim the person's oral statement. FRCP 26(b)(3)(C).

iv. *Trial preparation; Experts*

- *Deposition of an expert who may testify.* A party may depose any person who has been identified as an expert whose opinions may be presented at trial. If FRCP 26(a)(2)(B) requires a report from the expert, the deposition may be conducted only after the report is provided. FRCP 26(b)(4)(A).

- *Trial-preparation protection for draft reports or disclosures.* FRCP 26(b)(3)(A) and FRCP 26(b)(3)(B) protect drafts of any report or disclosure required under FRCP 26(a)(2), regardless of the form in which the draft is recorded. FRCP 26(b)(4)(B).

- *Trial-preparation protection for communications between a party's attorney and expert witnesses.* FRCP 26(b)(3)(A) and FRCP 26(b)(3)(B) protect communications between the party's attorney and any witness required to provide a report under FRCP 26(a)(2)(B), regardless of the form of the communications, except to the extent that the communica-tions: (1) relate to compensation for the expert's study or testimony; (2) identify facts or data that the party's attorney provided and that the expert considered in forming the opinions to be expressed; or (3) identify assumptions that the party's attorney provided and that the expert relied on in forming the opinions to be expressed. FRCP 26(b)(4)(C).

- *Expert employed only for trial preparation.* Ordinarily, a party may not, by interrogatories or deposition, discover facts known or opinions held by an expert who has been retained or specially employed by another party in anticipation of litigation or to prepare for trial and who is not expected to be called as a witness at trial. But a party may do so only: (1) as provided in FRCP 35(b); or (2) on showing exceptional circumstances under which it is impracticable for the party to obtain facts or opinions on the same subject by other means. FRCP 26(b)(4)(D).

- *Payment.* Unless manifest injustice would result, the court must require that the party seeking discovery: (1) pay the expert a reasonable fee for time spent in responding to discovery under FRCP 26(b)(4)(A) or FRCP 26(b)(4)(D); and (2) for discovery FRCP 26(b)(4)(D), also pay the other party a fair portion of the fees and expenses it reasonably incurred in obtaining the expert's facts and opinions. FRCP 26(b)(4)(E).

v. *Claiming privilege or protecting trial-preparation materials*

- *Information withheld.* When a party withholds information otherwise discoverable by claiming that the information is privileged or subject to protection as trial-preparation material, the party must: (1) expressly make the claim; and (2) describe the nature of the documents, communications, or tangible things not produced or disclosed—and do so in a manner that, without revealing information itself privileged or protected, will enable other parties to assess the claim. FRCP 26(b)(5)(A). Where a party asserts a claim of privilege in objecting to any means of discovery or disclosure, and withholds otherwise responsive information based on that assertion: (1) the party asserting the privilege shall identify the nature of the privilege (including work product) being claimed and, if the privilege is governed by state law, indicate the state's privilege rule being invoked; and (2) shall provide the following information, unless to divulge such information would cause disclosure of the allegedly privileged information: (i) for documents: (a) the type of document, i.e., letter or memorandum; (b) the general subject matter of the document; (c) the date of the document; and (d) such other information as is sufficient to identify the document for a subpoena duces tecum, including, where appropriate, the author of the document, the addressees of the document, and any other recipients shown in the document, and, where not apparent, the relationship of the author, addressees, and recipients to each other; (ii) for oral communications: (a) the names of the person making the communication and the person(s) present while the communication was made and, where not apparent, the relationship of the person making the communication to the person(s) present; (b) the date and place of communication; and (c) its general subject matter. NY R USDCTWD Civ Rule 26(d)(1).

- *Information produced.* If information produced in discovery is subject to a claim of privilege or of protection as trial-preparation material, the party making the claim may notify any party that received the information of the claim and the basis for it. After being notified, a party must promptly return, sequester, or destroy the specified information and any copies it has; must not use or disclose the information until the claim is resolved; must take reasonable steps to retrieve the information if the party disclosed it before being notified; and may promptly present the information to the court under seal for a determination of the claim. The producing party must preserve the information until the claim is resolved. FRCP 26(b)(5)(B). Where the claim of privilege is asserted in response to discovery or disclosure other than at a deposition, the information set forth in NY R USDCTWD Civ Rule 26(d)(1) shall be furnished in writing when the party responds to such discovery or disclosure, unless otherwise ordered by the Court. NY R USDCTWD Civ Rule 26(d)(2). Where the claim of privilege is asserted during a deposition, the information set forth in NY R USDCTWD Civ Rule 26(d)(1) shall be furnished: (1) at the deposition, to the extent it is readily available from the witness being deposed or otherwise, and (2) to the extent it not readily available, in writing within fourteen (14) days after the privilege is asserted, unless otherwise ordered by the Court. NY R USDCTWD Civ Rule 26(d)(3).

b. *Protective orders.* A party or any person from whom discovery is sought may move for a protective order in the court where the action is pending—or as an alternative on matters relating to a deposition, in the court for the district where the deposition will be taken. FRCP 26(c)(1). Refer to the United States District Court for the Western District of New York KeyRules Motion for Protective Order document for more information.

c. *Sequence of discovery.* Unless the parties stipulate or the court orders otherwise for the parties' and witnesses' convenience and in the interests of justice: (1) methods of discovery may be used in any sequence; and (2) discovery by one party does not require any other party to delay its discovery. FRCP 26(d)(3).

d. *Uniform definitions for all discovery requests.* The full text of the definitions and rules of construction set forth in NY R USDCTWD Civ Rule 26(c)(3) and NY R USDCTWD Civ Rule 26(c)(4) is deemed incorporated by reference into all discovery requests. No discovery request shall use broader definitions or rules of construction than those set forth in NY R USDCTWD Civ Rule 26(c)(3) and NY R USDCTWD Civ Rule 26(c)(4). NY R USDCTWD Civ Rule 26(c) shall not preclude (1) the definition of other terms specific to the particular litigation, (2) the use of abbreviations, or (3) a more narrow definition of a term defined in NY R USDCTWD Civ Rule 26(c)(3). NY R USDCTWD Civ Rule 26(c)(1). NY R USDCTWD Civ Rule 26(c) is not intended to broaden or narrow the scope of discovery permitted by the Federal Rules of Civil Procedure. NY R USDCTWD Civ Rule 26(c)(2).

i. *Definitions.* The following definitions apply to all discovery requests:

- *Communication.* The term "communication" means the transmittal of information (in the form of facts, ideas, inquiries or otherwise). NY R USDCTWD Civ Rule 26(c)(3)(A).

- *Document.* The term "document" is defined to be synonymous in meaning and equal in scope to the usage of this term in FRCP 34(a), including, without limitation, electronic or computerized data compilations. A draft or non-identical copy is a separate document within the meaning of this term. NY R USDCTWD Civ Rule 26(c)(3)(B).

- *Identify (with respect to persons).* When referring to a person, "to identify" means to give, to the extent known, the person's full name, present or last known address, and when referring to a natural person, the present or last known place of employment. Once a person has been identified in accordance with NY R USDCTWD Civ Rule 26(c)(3)(C), only the person's name need be listed in response to subsequent discovery requesting the identification of that person. NY R USDCTWD Civ Rule 26(c)(3)(C).

- *Identify (with respect to documents).* When referring to documents, "to identify" means to give, to the extent known, the (1) type of document; (2) general subject matter; (3) date of the document; and (4) author(s), addressee(s), and recipients(s). NY R USDCTWD Civ Rule 26(c)(3)(D).

- *Parties.* The terms "plaintiff" and "defendant," as well as a party's full or abbreviated name or a pronoun referring to a party, mean the party and, where applicable, its officers, directors, employees, partners, corporate parent, subsidiaries, or affiliates. This definition is not intended to impose a discovery obligation on any person who is not a party to the litigation. NY R USDCTWD Civ Rule 26(c)(3)(E).

- *Person.* The term "person" is defined as any natural person or any business, legal or governmental entity, or association. NY R USDCTWD Civ Rule 26(c)(3)(F).

- *Concerning.* The term "concerning" means relating to, referring to, describing, evidencing or constituting. NY R USDCTWD Civ Rule 26(c)(3)(G).

ii. *Rules of construction.* The following rules of construction apply to all discovery requests:

- *All/each.* The terms "all" and "each" shall be construed as all and each. NY R USDCTWD Civ Rule 26(c)(4)(A).

- *And/or.* The connectives "and" and "or" shall be construed either disjunctively or conjunctively as necessary to bring within the scope of the discovery request all responses that might otherwise be construed to be outside of its scope. NY R USDCTWD Civ Rule 26(c)(4)(B).

- *Number.* The use of the singular form of any word includes the plural and vice versa. NY R USDCTWD Civ Rule 26(c)(4)(C).

e. *Electronically stored information (ESI).* Discovery of relevant electronically stored information shall proceed as follows:

i. *Searches and production of ESI.* After receiving requests for document production, the parties shall search their documents, including ESI other than ESI that has been identified as not reasonably accessible, and produce relevant responsive ESI in accordance with FRCP 26(b)(2). NY R USDCTWD Civ Rule 26(e)(1).

ii. *Non-accessible ESI.* Searches and production of ESI identified as not reasonably accessible shall not be required to be conducted until the initial disclosure of reasonably accessible ESI has been completed. Requests for information expected to be found in ESI that is not reasonably accessible must be narrowly focused with some basis in fact supporting the request, and good cause must be provided. The party seeking such discovery may be required to pay all or a portion of the costs of search, retrieval, review, and production of the information, upon application to the Court. NY R USDCTWD Civ Rule 26(e)(2).

iii. *Search methodology.* If a party intends to employ an electronic search to locate relevant ESI, the parties shall discuss and attempt to reach agreement as to the method of searching, and the words, terms, and phrases to be searched and any restrictions as to scope and method which might affect their ability to conduct a complete electronic search of the ESI. The parties shall also attempt to reach agreement as to the timing and conditions of any additional searches which may become necessary in the normal course of discovery. To minimize undue expense, the parties may consider limiting the scope of the electronic search (i.e., time frames, fields, document types). NY R USDCTWD Civ Rule 26(e)(3).

iv. *Metadata.* Except as otherwise provided, metadata, especially substantive metadata, need not be routinely produced, except upon agreement of the requesting and producing litigants, or upon a showing of good cause in a motion filed by the requesting party. NY R USDCTWD Civ Rule 26(e)(4).

v. *Format.* If the parties have not agreed or cannot agree to the format for document production, ESI shall be produced to the requesting party as image files (i.e. PDF or TIFF). When the image file is produced, the producing party must preserve the integrity of the electronic document's contents, i.e., the original formatting of the document, its metadata and, where applicable, its revision history. After initial production in image file format is complete, a party must demonstrate particularized need for production of ESI in its native format. NY R USDCTWD Civ Rule 26(e)(5).

vi. *Costs.* Generally, the costs of discovery, other than the costs associated with ESI that is not reasonably accessible, shall be borne by each party. However, the Court will apportion the costs of discovery or presentation of ESI, including discovery of ESI that is not reasonably accessible, upon a showing of good cause, or unequal burdens, or unreasonable request. NY R USDCTWD Civ Rule 26(e)(6).

f. *Cooperation among counsel in the discovery context.* See the Civility Principles of the United States District Court for the Western District of New York which can be found on the Court's website. NY R USDCTWD Civ Rule 26(g).

2. *Interrogatories*

a. *Number.* Unless otherwise stipulated or ordered by the court, a party may serve on any other party no more than twenty-five (25) written interrogatories, including all discrete subparts. Leave to serve additional interrogatories may be granted to the extent consistent with FRCP 26(b)(1) and FRCP 26(b)(2). FRCP 33(a)(1).

b. *Scope.* An interrogatory may relate to any matter that may be inquired into under FRCP 26(b). An interrogatory is not objectionable merely because it asks for an opinion or contention that relates to fact or the application of law to fact, but the court may order that the interrogatory need not be answered until designated discovery is complete, or until a pretrial conference or some other time. FRCP 33(a)(2).

c. *Parties subject to interrogatories.* Depositions may be taken of any person but interrogatories are limited to parties to the litigation. FPP § 2171. Interrogatories may not be directed to the attorney for a party. They must be addressed to the party, who is then required to give all information known to it or its attorney. FPP § 2171; Hickman v. Taylor, 329 U.S. 495, 504, 67 S.Ct. 385, 390, 91 L.Ed. 451 (1947). For more information, refer to FPP § 2171.

d. *Form.* Ideally an interrogatory should be a single direct question phrased in a fashion that will inform the other party what is requested. In fact the courts have given parties considerable latitude in framing interrogatories. Rather general language has been permitted so long as the interrogatory gives the other party a reasonably clear indication of the information to be included in its answer. FPP § 2168.

i. *Use of definitions.* There is no prohibition against the use of definitions in interrogatories, and definitions may be helpful in clarifying the meaning of obscure terms or avoiding repetitions in a long set of interrogatories. FPP § 2168.

ii. *Use of standardized form interrogatories.* There have been mixed reactions to the use of standardized form interrogatories. They have been referred to opprobriously as "canned sets of interrogatories of the shotgun variety" and it has been said that their indiscriminate use is an "undesirable practice." FPP § 2168.

e. *Numbering.* The parties shall sequentially number each interrogatory or discovery request. NY R USDCTWD Civ Rule 26(b).

f. *Motion to compel.* The party submitting the interrogatories must attempt to confer with the responding party in an effort to secure the information without court action and, if that fails, move for an order under FRCP 37(a) compelling answers. FPP § 2182. Refer to the United States District Court for the Western District of New York KeyRules Motion to Compel Discovery document for more information.

3. *Sanctions for failure to cooperate in discovery.* The court where the action is pending may, on motion, order sanctions if a party, after being properly served with interrogatories under FRCP 33 or a request for inspection under FRCP 34, fails to serve its answers, objections, or written response. FRCP 37(d)(1)(A)(ii). If a motion to compel is granted, the court must, after giving an opportunity to be heard, require the party or deponent whose conduct necessitated the motion, the party or attorney advising that conduct, or both to pay the movant's reasonable expenses incurred in making the motion, including attorney's fees. But the court must not order this payment if the opposing party's nondisclosure, response, or objection was substantially justified. FRCP 37(a)(5)(A)(ii). Refer to the United States District Court for the Western District of New York KeyRules Motion for Discovery Sanctions document for more information.

4. *Stipulations about discovery procedure.* Unless the court orders otherwise, the parties may stipulate that: (1) a deposition may be taken before any person, at any time or place, on any notice, and in the manner specified—in which event it may be used in the same way as any other deposition; and (2) other procedures governing or limiting discovery be modified—but a stipulation extending the time for any form of discovery must have court approval if it would interfere with the time set for completing discovery, for hearing a motion, or for trial. FRCP 29. All stipulations, except stipulations made in open court and recorded by the court reporter, shall be in writing and signed by each attorney and/or pro se litigant. The parties shall determine who will be responsible for filing, and a copy of the stipulation, with signatures conformed (e.g., "s/Jane Doe," "s/John Smith"), shall be filed electronically. The Court will act on the filed stipulation, as necessary and appropriate. NY R USDCTWD Civ Rule 29.

5. *Notice of appearance.* No notice of appearance is required of an attorney whose name and address appear at the end of a complaint, notice of removal, pre-answer motion, or answer. In all other circumstances, an attorney appearing for a party in a civil case shall promptly file a written notice of appearance. NY R USDCTWD Civ Rule 83.2(b). For more information on appearances and withdrawals, refer to NY R USDCTWD Civ Rule 83.2.

6. *Related cases.* Each attorney appearing in a civil case has a continuing duty to promptly notify the Clerk of Court when the attorney has reason to believe that said case is related to some other pending civil or criminal action(s) such that their assignment to the same Judge would avoid unnecessary duplication of judicial effort. As soon as the attorney becomes aware of such a relationship, the attorney shall notify the Clerk of Court by letter of the relevant facts, and the Clerk of Court will transmit that notification to the Judges to whom the cases have been assigned. NY R USDCTWD Civ Rule 5.1(e).

7. *Alternative dispute resolution (ADR).* This Court has adopted an Alternative Dispute Resolution Plan ("ADR"), as implemented by Standing Order (NY R USDCTWD ADR Plan), under which certain civil cases are referred automatically to ADR upon filing. NY R USDCTWD Civ Rule 16(a). The United States District Court for the Western District of New York (the "Court") adopted the ADR Plan on January 1, 2006 (the "Effective Date"), to make available to civil litigants court-administered ADR interventions and processes designed to provide quicker, less expensive and potentially more satisfying alternatives to continuing litigation, without impairing the quality of justice or the right to trial. NY R USDCTWD ADR Plan(1)(1.2)(A).

   a. *Scope.* This ADR Plan (NY R USDCTWD ADR Plan) applies to civil actions pending or commenced on and after the Effective Date, except as otherwise indicated in NY R USDCTWD ADR Plan. The ADR Plan supplements the Local Rules of Civil Procedure for the United States District Court for the Western District of New York, which shall remain in full effect for all cases. NY R USDCTWD ADR Plan(1)(1.2)(B).

   b. *Referral to ADR*

      i. *New cases.* All civil cases filed on and after the Effective Date of the ADR Plan shall be referred automatically for ADR. NY R USDCTWD ADR Plan(2)(2.1)(A). Notice of the ADR requirements will be provided to all parties immediately upon the filing of a complaint and answer or a notice of removal; NY R USDCTWD ADR Plan(2)(2.1)(A); NY R USDCTWD Civ Rule 16(a). ADR intervention will be scheduled at the conference held pursuant to Local Rule of Civil Procedure 16.1. NY R USDCTWD ADR Plan(2)(2.1)(A). [Editor's note: the reference to

Local Rule of Civil Procedure 16.1 is likely meant to be a reference to NY R USDCTWD Civ Rule 16(b)].

- Litigants in cases not referred automatically to ADR must consider possible agreement to the use of an ADR process. NY R USDCTWD Civ Rule 16(a).

- For a list of exemptions from automatic referral, refer to NY R USDCTWD ADR Plan(2)(2.1)(A).

ii. *Pending cases.* The assigned Judge on any pending civil case may, sua sponte or with status conference, issue an order referring the case for ADR. NY R USDCTWD ADR Plan(2)(2.1)(B); NY R USDCTWD Civ Rule 16(a). The order shall specify a date on which the ADR intervention is to be completed. NY R USDCTWD ADR Plan(2)(2.1)(B).

iii. *Stipulation.* A case may be referred for ADR by stipulation of all parties. Stipulations shall be filed and shall designate the specific ADR intervention the parties have selected, the time frame within which the ADR process will be completed and the selected Neutral. Stipulations are presumed acceptable unless the assigned Judge determines that the interests of justice are not served. NY R USDCTWD ADR Plan(2)(2.1)(C).

iv. *Relief from ADR referral*

- *Opting out motions.* Any party may file, with the assigned Judge for that case, a motion to opt out of, or for relief from, ADR. NY R USDCTWD ADR Plan(2)(2.2)(A).

- *Motion.* Opting Out Motions must be made within fourteen (14) days from (1) the date of the first discovery conference under Local Rule 16.1 in new cases, or (2) the date of a sua sponte ADR Referral Order in pending cases. NY R USDCTWD ADR Plan(2)(2.2)(B). [Editor's note: the reference to Local Rule 16.1 is likely meant to be a reference to NY R USDCTWD Civ Rule 16(b)].

- *Criteria.* Opting Out Motions shall be granted only for "good cause" shown. Inconvenience, travel costs, attorney fees or other costs shall not constitute "good cause." A party seeking relief from ADR must set forth the reasons why ADR has no reasonable chance of being productive. NY R USDCTWD ADR Plan(2)(2.2)(C).

- *Judicial initiative.* The assigned Judge may, sua sponte, exempt any case from the Court's ADR Plan. NY R USDCTWD ADR Plan(2)(2.2)(D).

c. *ADR interventions*

i. *Options.* It is expected that cases referred for ADR will proceed to Mediation. However, the following options are also available upon the stipulation of all parties:

- Neutral Evaluation;

- Mini Summary Trial;

- Arbitration (Binding and Non-Binding);

- Case Valuation; and

- Settlement Week, when scheduled by the Court. NY R USDCTWD ADR Plan(4)(4.1)(A).

ii. *Timing.* Timing is specific to the intervention and process chosen, as set forth in the corresponding sections in NY R USDCTWD ADR Plan. NY R USDCTWD ADR Plan(4)(4.1)(B).

iii. *Scheduling.* The referral of a case to ADR does not delay or defer other dates established in the Scheduling Order and has no effect on the scheduled progress of the case toward trial. NY R USDCTWD ADR Plan(4)(4.1)(C).

d. *Selecting an ADR intervention*

i. *New cases.* Prior to the Local Rule 16.1 scheduling conference, counsel and any unrepresented parties shall confer about ADR as part of their discussion of "the possibilities for a prompt settlement or resolution of the case" pursuant to FRCP 26(f). Unless the parties agree to a different intervention, it is presumed that they will participate in mediation. [Editor's note: the reference to Local Rule 16.1 is likely meant to be a reference to NY R USDCTWD Civ Rule 16(b)].

ii. *Pending cases.* In pending cases, all sua sponte referrals will be to mediation. Should the parties agree that a different ADR intervention is more appropriate to their case, they may submit a stipulation designating the specific ADR intervention selected, the time frame within which the ADR process will be completed and the identity of the Neutral. Stipulations must be filed within fourteen (14) days from the date of the ADR Referral Order and are presumed acceptable unless the assigned Judge determines that the interests of justice are not served. NY R USDCTWD ADR Plan(4)(4.2)(B).

e. For more information on alternative dispute resolution (ADR), refer to NY R USDCTWD ADR Plan.

8. *Sanctions.* Failure of counsel for any party, or a party proceeding pro se, to appear before the Court at a conference, to complete the necessary preparations, or to be prepared to proceed to trial at the set time may be considered an abandonment of the case or a failure to prosecute or defend diligently. An appropriate order for sanctions may be entered against the defaulting party with respect to either a specific issue or the entire case. NY R USDCTWD Civ Rule 11(a). For more information, refer to NY R USDCTWD Civ Rule 11.

9. *Pro se actions.* For information on the requirements in pro se actions, refer to NY R USDCTWD Civ Rule 5.2.

10. *Individual judge practices.* Refer to the Miscellaneous section of this document for information on individual judge practices on general requirements for documents.

## D. Documents

1. *Required documents*

a. *Interrogatories.* Refer to the General Requirements section of this document for information on interrogatories.

b. *Electronic courtesy copy.* In addition to service pursuant to FRCP 5, the party to whom interrogatories or discovery requests are directed shall, whenever practicable, be supplied with an electronic courtesy copy of the served document in a word processing format. NY R USDCTWD Civ Rule 26(b).

2. *Supplemental documents*

a. *Certificate of service.* FRCP 5(d) requires that the person making service under FRCP 5 certify that service has been effected. FRCP 5(Advisory Committee Notes). Having such information on file may be useful for many purposes, including proof of service if an issue arises concerning the effectiveness of the service. FRCP 5(Advisory Committee Notes).

3. *Individual judge practices.* Refer to the Miscellaneous section of this document for information on individual judge practices on required documents.

## E. Format

1. *Form of documents.* The rules governing captions and other matters of form in pleadings apply to motions and other papers. FRCP 7(b)(2).

a. *Form, generally.* All pleadings, motions, and other papers that a party presents for filing, whether in paper form or in electronic form, shall meet the following requirements:

i. *Font size.* All text and footnotes shall be in a font size of at least twelve (12) point type. NY R USDCTWD Civ Rule 10(a)(1).

ii. *Spacing.* All text in the body of the document must be double-spaced, except that text in block quotations and footnotes may be single-spaced. NY R USDCTWD Civ Rule 10(a)(2).

- Extensive footnotes and block quotes may not be used to circumvent page limitations. NY R USDCTWD Civ Rule 10(a)(3).

iii. *Margins.* Documents must have one (1) inch margins on all four sides. NY R USDCTWD Civ Rule 10(a)(4).

iv. *Page numbering.* Pages must be consecutively numbered. NY R USDCTWD Civ Rule 10(a)(5).

b. *Additional requirements for paper filing.* Documents presented for filing in paper form shall meet the following additional requirements:

    i. *Paper.* Documents must be on durable white eight and one-half by eleven (8-1/2 x 11) inch paper of good quality. NY R USDCTWD Civ Rule 10(b)(1).

        • All documents must be single-sided. NY R USDCTWD Civ Rule 10(b)(5).

    ii. *Text.* All text must be plainly and legibly written, typewritten, printed or reproduced. NY R USDCTWD Civ Rule 10(b)(2).

    iii. *Ink.* Documents must be in black or blue ink. NY R USDCTWD Civ Rule 10(b)(3).

    iv. *Binding.* The pages of each document must be stapled or in some other way fastened together. NY R USDCTWD Civ Rule 10(b)(4).

c. *Caption; Names of parties.* Every pleading must have a caption with the court's name, a title, a file number, and a FRCP 7(a) designation. The title of the complaint must name all the parties; the title of other pleadings, after naming the first party on each side, may refer generally to other parties. FRCP 10(a).

d. *Paragraphs; Separate statements.* A party must state its claims or defenses in numbered paragraphs, each limited as far as practicable to a single set of circumstances. A later pleading may refer by number to a paragraph in an earlier pleading. If doing so would promote clarity, each claim founded on a separate transaction or occurrence—and each defense other than a denial—must be stated in a separate count or defense. FRCP 10(b).

e. *Adoption by reference; Exhibits.* A statement in a pleading may be adopted by reference elsewhere in the same pleading or in any other pleading or motion. A copy of a written instrument that is an exhibit to a pleading is a part of the pleading for all purposes. FRCP 10(c).

f. *Citation of local rules.* The Local Rules of Civil Procedure for the United States District Court for the Western District of New York shall be cited as "L.R.Civ.P." NY R USDCTWD Civ Rule 1.1.

g. *Acceptance by the clerk.* The clerk must not refuse to file a paper solely because it is not in the form prescribed by the Federal Rules of Civil Procedure or by a local rule or practice. FRCP 5(d)(4). The Court may reject documents that do not comply with the requirements in NY R USDCTWD Civ Rule 10. NY R USDCTWD Civ Rule 10.

2. *Form of electronic documents.* All pleadings, motions, and other papers that a party presents for filing, whether in paper form or in electronic form, shall meet the requirements in NY R USDCTWD Civ Rule 10(a). NY R USDCTWD Civ Rule 10(a). Refer above for more information.

a. *Conversion to PDF.* A document created with a word processor, or a paper document, must be converted to Portable Document Format to be electronically filed with the court. NY R USDCTWD ECF Procedures(2)(a)(v).

    i. Documents which exist only in paper form may be scanned into a portable document format (PDF) for electronic filing. NY R USDCTWD ECF Procedures(2)(a)(v). Before filing a scanned document with the court, a Filing User must verify its legibility. NY R USDCTWD ECF Procedures(2)(a)(iv).

    ii. Electronic documents must be converted to .PDF from a word processing program and must be text searchable. Do not print, scan and .PDF your document when it has been created in a word processing program. Additional information on working with PDFs is located in NY R USDCTWD ECF Procedures(4b). NY R USDCTWD ECF Procedures(2)(a)(v).

b. *Hyperlinks.* Pursuant to the policy set forth by the Judicial Conference in October 2005, a hyperlink contained in a filing is no more than a convenient mechanism for accessing material cited in a document. A hyperlink reference is extraneous to any filed document and is not part of the Court's record. NY R USDCTWD ECF Procedures(2)(a)(vi).

    i. In order to preserve the integrity of the Court record, users wishing to insert hyperlinks in Court filings shall continue to use the conventional method for the cited authority, in addition to the hyperlink. NY R USDCTWD ECF Procedures(2)(a)(vi).

      ii.   The Court accepts no responsibility for, and does not endorse any product, organization, and content at any hyperlinked site, or at any site to which that site may be linked. The Court accepts no responsibility for the availability or functionality of any hyperlink. NY R USDCTWD ECF Procedures(2)(a)(vi).

    c.  *Attachments and exhibits*

      i.   Attachments and exhibits larger than five megabytes (5 MB) shall be filed electronically in separate five megabyte (5 MB) segments. NY R USDCTWD ECF Procedures(2)(d)(i).

      ii.   Filing Users must submit in electronic form all documents referenced as exhibits or attachments, except as otherwise provided in NY R USDCTWD ECF Procedures. A Filing User must submit as exhibits or attachments only those excerpts of the referenced documents that are directly germane to the matter under consideration by the court. Excerpted material must be clearly and prominently identified as such. Filing Users who file excerpts of documents as exhibits or attachments under NY R USDCTWD ECF Procedures(2)(d)(ii) do so without prejudice to their right to timely file additional excerpts or the complete document. Responding parties may timely file additional excerpts or the complete document that they believe are directly germane. The Court may require parties to file additional excerpts or the complete document. A Filing User must request leave of the Court to file a document exhibit or attachment in non-electronic form. NY R USDCTWD ECF Procedures(2)(d)(ii).

      iii.   Exhibits offered or admitted at trial will not be filed electronically or conventionally unless so ordered by the Court. NY R USDCTWD ECF Procedures(2)(d)(iii).

      iv.   Exhibits such as videotapes and tape recordings shall be filed in the conventional manner with the Clerk of Court, and a Notice of Manual Filing shall be electronically filed by the party. Manually filed exhibits must have the case number and case name securely fastened or marked on the item. NY R USDCTWD ECF Procedures(2)(d)(iii).

      v.   Continuation of exhibit entries (for exhibits that are too large to attach to a main document) must be filed and entered on the same day that the main document was filed. NY R USDCTWD ECF Procedures(2)(d)(iv).

    d.  *Color documents.* Documents in color or containing graphics take much longer to upload. Filing users are encouraged to configure their scanners to scan documents at 200 dpi and preferably in black and white rather than color. NY R USDCTWD ECF Procedures(2)(d)(v).

    e.  *Large documents.* Due to the length of time it takes to download large files, documents larger than five megabytes (5 MB) (approximately one hundred (100) pages of a .pdf scanned document) must be filed electronically in separate five megabyte (5 MB) segments. A party who believes a document is too lengthy to electronically image (i.e. scan), may contact the Court Room Deputy for the assigned judge and request permission to file that document conventionally. If granted permission to file the document conventionally, the Filing User shall electronically file a "notice of manual filing" for that item. Exhibits submitted to the Court conventionally shall be served on other parties conventionally. NY R USDCTWD ECF Procedures(2)(d)(vi).

3.  *Signing disclosures and discovery requests, responses, and objections.* FRCP 11 does not apply to disclosures and discovery requests, responses, objections, and motions under FRCP 26 through FRCP 37. FRCP 11(d).

    a.  *Signature required.* Every disclosure under FRCP 26(a)(1) or FRCP 26(a)(3) and every discovery request, response, or objection must be signed by at least one attorney of record in the attorney's own name—or by the party personally, if unrepresented—and must state the signer's address, e-mail address, and telephone number. FRCP 26(g)(1). Documents presented for paper filing must contain an original signature. NY R USDCTWD Civ Rule 10(b)(6).

      i.  *Electronic signatures*

        •  *Non-attorney signature.* If the original document requires the signature of a non-attorney, the filing party shall obtain the signature of the non-attorney on the document. NY R USDCTWD ECF Procedures(2)(g)(i). The filing party or attorney then shall file the document electronically indicating the signatory's name in the form "s/(name)." NY R

USDCTWD ECF Procedures(2)(g)(i)(1). A non-filing signatory or party who disputes the authenticity of an electronically filed document or the authenticity of the signature on that document must file an objection to the document within ten (10) days of receiving the Notice of Electronic Filing. NY R USDCTWD ECF Procedures(2)(g)(i)(2).

- *Registered user signature.* The username and password required to file documents on the Electronic Filing System serve as the Filing User's signature on all electronic documents filed with this Court. The also serve as a signature for the purposes of FRCP 11, the Federal Rules of Civil Procedure, the Local Rules of Civil Procedure for the United States District Court for the Western District of New York, and any other purpose for which a signature is required in connection with proceedings before this Court. A pleading requiring a Registered User's signature must include a signature block in the format found in NY R USDCTWD ECF Procedures(2)(g)(iii). NY R USDCTWD ECF Procedures(2)(g)(iii). Any party challenging the authenticity of an electronically filed document or the attorney's signature on that document must file an objection to the document within ten (10) days of receiving the Notice of Electronic Filing. NY R USDCTWD ECF Procedures(2)(g)(iii)(1).

- *Multiple signatures.* The following procedure applies when a stipulation or other document requires two or more signatures: The filing party shall initially confirm that the document is acceptable to all persons required to sign the document and shall obtain the signatures of all parties on the document. NY R USDCTWD ECF Procedures(2)(g)(iv)(1). The filing party or attorney then shall file the document electronically indicating the signatories, e.g., "s/Jane Doe," "s/John Smith," etc. NY R USDCTWD ECF Procedures(2)(g)(iv)(2). A non-filing signatory or party who disputes the authenticity of an electronically filed document containing multiple signatures or the authenticity of the signatures themselves must file an objection to the document within ten (10) days of receiving the Notice of Electronic Filing. NY R USDCTWD ECF Procedures(2)(g)(iv)(3).

b. *Effect of signature.* By signing, an attorney or party certifies that to the best of the person's knowledge, information, and belief formed after a reasonable inquiry:

   i. With respect to a disclosure, it is complete and correct as of the time it is made; and

   ii. With respect to a discovery request, response, or objection, it is:

   - Consistent with the Federal Rules of Civil Procedure and warranted by existing law or by a nonfrivolous argument for extending, modifying, or reversing existing law, or for establishing new law;

   - Not interposed for any improper purpose, such as to harass, cause unnecessary delay, or needlessly increase the cost of litigation; and

   - Neither unreasonable nor unduly burdensome or expensive, considering the needs of the case, prior discovery in the case, the amount in controversy, and the importance of the issues at stake in the action. FRCP 26(g)(1).

c. *Failure to sign.* Other parties have no duty to act on an unsigned disclosure, request, response, or objection until it is signed, and the court must strike it unless a signature is promptly supplied after the omission is called to the attorney's or party's attention. FRCP 26(g)(2).

d. *Sanction for improper certification.* If a certification violates FRCP 26(g) without substantial justification, the court, on motion or on its own, must impose an appropriate sanction on the signer, the party on whose behalf the signer was acting, or both. The sanction may include an order to pay the reasonable expenses, including attorney's fees, caused by the violation. FRCP 26(g)(3). Refer to the United States District Court for the Western District of New York KeyRules Motion for Discovery Sanctions document for more information.

4. *Privacy protection for filings made with the court.* In all filings, parties shall comply with FRCP 5.2. NY R USDCTWD ECF Procedures(2)(m)(i).

   a. *Redacted filings.* Unless the court orders otherwise, in an electronic or paper filing with the court that

contains an individual's Social Security number, taxpayer-identification number, or birth date, the name of an individual known to be a minor, or a financial-account number, a party or nonparty making the filing may include only:

    i.   The last four (4) digits of the Social Security number and taxpayer-identification number;

    ii.   The year of the individual's birth;

    iii.   The minor's initials; and

    iv.   The last four (4) digits of the financial-account number. FRCP 5.2(a).

b.  *Exemptions from the redaction requirement.* The redaction requirement does not apply to the following:

    i.   A financial-account number that identifies the property allegedly subject to forfeiture in a forfeiture proceeding;

    ii.   The record of an administrative or agency proceeding;

    iii.   The official record of a state-court proceeding;

    iv.   The record of a court or tribunal, if that record was not subject to the redaction requirement when originally filed;

    v.   A filing covered by FRCP 5.2(c) or FRCP 5.2(d); and

    vi.   A pro se filing in an action brought under 28 U.S.C.A. § 2241, 28 U.S.C.A. § 2254, or 28 U.S.C.A. § 2255. FRCP 5.2(b).

c.  *Limitations on remote access to electronic files; Social Security appeals and immigration cases.* Unless the court orders otherwise, in an action for benefits under the Social Security Act, and in an action or proceeding relating to an order of removal, to relief from removal, or to immigration benefits or detention, access to an electronic file is authorized as follows:

    i.   The parties and their attorneys may have remote electronic access to any part of the case file, including the administrative record;

    ii.   Any other person may have electronic access to the full record at the courthouse, but may have remote electronic access only to:

        •   The docket maintained by the court; and

        •   An opinion, order, judgment, or other disposition of the court, but not any other part of the case file or the administrative record. FRCP 5.2(c).

d.  *Filings made under seal.* The court may order that a filing be made under seal without redaction. The court may later unseal the filing or order the person who made the filing to file a redacted version for the public record. FRCP 5.2(d). For more information on sealing documents, refer to NY R USDCTWD Civ Rule 5.3, NY R USDCTWD ECF Procedures(2)(o)(i)(1), NY R USDCTWD ECF Procedures(2)(o)(i)(2), and NY R USDCTWD ECF Procedures(2)(o)(i)(3).

e.  *Protective orders.* For good cause, the court may by order in a case:

    i.   Require redaction of additional information; or

    ii.   Limit or prohibit a nonparty's remote electronic access to a document filed with the court. FRCP 5.2(e).

f.  *Option for additional unredacted filing under seal.* A person making a redacted filing may also file an unredacted copy under seal. The court must retain the unredacted copy as part of the record. FRCP 5.2(f).

g.  *Option for filing a reference list.* A filing that contains redacted information may be filed together with a reference list that identifies each item of redacted information and specifies an appropriate identifier that uniquely corresponds to each item listed. The list must be filed under seal and may be amended as of right. Any reference in the case to a listed identifier will be construed to refer to the corresponding item of information. FRCP 5.2(g).

h.  *Waiver of protection of identifiers.* A person waives the protection of FRCP 5.2(a) as to the person's own information by filing it without redaction and not under seal. FRCP 5.2(h).

5. *Individual judge practices.* Refer to the Miscellaneous section of this document for information on individual judge practices on formatting documents.

## F. Filing and Service Requirements

1. *Filing requirements.* Any paper after the complaint that is required to be served—together with a certificate of service—must be filed within a reasonable time after service. But disclosures under FRCP 26(a)(1) or FRCP 26(a)(2) and the following discovery requests and responses must not be filed until they are used in the proceeding or the court orders filing: depositions, interrogatories, requests for documents or tangible things or to permit entry onto land, and requests for admission. FRCP 5(d)(1). Parties shall comply with FRCP 5(d)(1), except that in cases involving a pro se litigant, all discovery materials must be filed with the Court pursuant to NY R USDCTWD Civ Rule 5.2(f). NY R USDCTWD Civ Rule 26(f). Refer to the United States District Court for the Western District of New York KeyRules pleading and motion documents for information on filing with the court.

2. *Service requirements.* All pleadings and other papers shall be filed and served in accordance with the Federal Rules of Civil Procedure and the CM/ECF Administrative Procedures Guide. NY R USDCTWD Civ Rule 5.1(a).

   a. *Service; When required*

      i. *In general.* Unless the Federal Rules of Civil Procedure provide otherwise, each of the following papers must be served on every party:

         - An order stating that service is required;

         - A pleading filed after the original complaint, unless the court orders otherwise under FRCP 5(c) because there are numerous defendants;

         - A discovery paper required to be served on a party, unless the court orders otherwise;

         - A written motion, except one that may be heard ex parte; and

         - A written notice, appearance, demand, or offer of judgment, or any similar paper. FRCP 5(a)(1).

      ii. *If a party fails to appear.* No service is required on a party who is in default for failing to appear. But a pleading that asserts a new claim for relief against such a party must be served on that party under FRCP 4. FRCP 5(a)(2).

      iii. *Seizing property.* If an action is begun by seizing property and no person is or need be named as a defendant, any service required before the filing of an appearance, answer, or claim must be made on the person who had custody or possession of the property when it was seized. FRCP 5(a)(3).

   b. *Service; How made*

      i. *Serving an attorney.* If a party is represented by an attorney, service under FRCP 5 must be made on the attorney unless the court orders service on the party. FRCP 5(b)(1).

      ii. *Service in general.* A paper is served under FRCP 5 by:

         - Handing it to the person;

         - Leaving it: (1) at the person's office with a clerk or other person in charge or, if no one is in charge, in a conspicuous place in the office; or (2) if the person has no office or the office is closed, at the person's dwelling or usual place of abode with someone of suitable age and discretion who resides there;

         - Mailing it to the person's last known address—in which event service is complete upon mailing;

         - Leaving it with the court clerk if the person has no known address;

         - Sending it by electronic means if the person consented in writing—in which event service is complete upon transmission, but is not effective if the serving party learns that it did not reach the person to be served; or

         - Delivering it by any other means that the person consented to in writing—in which event service is complete when the person making service delivers it to the agency designated to make delivery. FRCP 5(b)(2).

iii. *Service by overnight delivery.* All papers, other than a subpoena or a summons and complaint, may be served on counsel of record by overnight delivery service at the address designated by the attorney for that purpose, or if none is designated, at the attorney's last known address. Service by overnight delivery shall be complete upon deposit of the paper(s), enclosed in a properly addressed wrapper, into the custody of the overnight delivery service, prior to the latest time designated by the service for overnight delivery. NY R USDCTWD Civ Rule 5.1(g). "Overnight delivery service" means any delivery service which regularly accepts items for overnight delivery to any address within the Court's jurisdiction. NY R USDCTWD Civ Rule 5.1(g).

iv. *Service of documents by electronic means*

- *Service on registered users.* Registered Users consent to the electronic service of all documents, and must make available an electronic mail address for service during the registration process. Upon the filing of a document by a party, a Notice of Electronic Filing, with a hyperlink to the filed document, will be automatically generated by the electronic filing system and sent via electronic mail to the e-mail addresses of all parties participating in the electronic filing system in the case. Electronic service of the Notice of Electronic Filing constitutes service of the filed document for all purposes of the Federal Rules of Civil Procedure and the Local Rules of Civil Procedure for the United States District Court for the Western District of New York. NY R USDCTWD ECF Procedures(2)(f)(i). The Notice of Electronic Filing effectuates service for all registered users and no certificate of service is required when all filers on an action are Registered Users. NY R USDCTWD ECF Procedures(2)(f)(iv).

- *Time limit for opening hyperlink.* The hyperlink to filed documents contained in the Notice of Electronic Filing must be opened within fifteen (15) days from the date the document was filed to provide registered users access to the document. The hyperlink expires after fifteen (15) days and users will be unable to access documents for free after that time. Filing Users are encouraged to check their e-mail frequently for notice of filed documents. NY R USDCTWD ECF Procedures(2)(f)(ii).

- *Service on exempted attorneys or pro se litigants who do not have permission to file electronically.* Attorneys granted an exemption from electronically filing documents in the System and pro se litigants who have not been granted permission to electronically file documents are entitled to a paper copy of any electronically filed pleading, document or order. The filing party must therefore provide the non-registered party with the pleading, document or order according to the Federal Rules of Civil Procedure. NY R USDCTWD ECF Procedures(2)(f)(iii).

- *E-mailing or faxing documents.* E-mailing or faxing a pleading or document to any party shall not constitute service of the pleading or document. NY R USDCTWD ECF Procedures(2)(f)(v).

v. *Using court facilities.* If a local rule so authorizes, a party may use the court's transmission facilities to make service under FRCP 5(b)(2)(E). FRCP 5(b)(3).

c. *Serving numerous defendants*

i. *In general.* If an action involves an unusually large number of defendants, the court may, on motion or on its own, order that:

- Defendants' pleadings and replies to them need not be served on other defendants;

- Any crossclaim, counterclaim, avoidance, or affirmative defense in those pleadings and replies to them will be treated as denied or avoided by all other parties; and

- Filing any such pleading and serving it on the plaintiff constitutes notice of the pleading to all parties. FRCP 5(c)(1).

ii. *Notifying parties.* A copy of every such order must be served on the parties as the court directs. FRCP 5(c)(2).

3. *Pro se actions.* For information on the requirements in pro se actions, refer to NY R USDCTWD Civ Rule 5.2.

4. *Individual judge practices.* Refer to the Miscellaneous section of this document for information on individual judge practices on filing and serving documents.

## G. Hearings

1. There is no hearing contemplated in the federal statutes or rules for interrogatories.

## H. Forms

### 1. Federal Interrogatories Forms

a. Introductory statement; Interrogatories to individual. AMJUR PP DEPOSITION § 405.

b. Introductory statement; Interrogatories to corporation. AMJUR PP DEPOSITION § 406.

c. Interrogatories. 3A FEDFORMS § 3488.

d. Interrogatories; Another form. 3A FEDFORMS § 3489.

e. Interrogatories by plaintiff; To corporation. 3A FEDFORMS § 3490.

f. Interrogatories by plaintiff; Complete set. 3A FEDFORMS § 3491.

g. Interrogatories by plaintiff; Requesting identification of documents and production under FRCP 34. 3A FEDFORMS § 3492.

h. Interrogatories by plaintiff; With definition of terms used and instructions for answering. 3A FEDFORMS § 3493.

i. Interrogatories by plaintiff; Employment discrimination case. 3A FEDFORMS § 3494.

j. Interrogatories by defendant. 3A FEDFORMS § 3495.

k. Interrogatories by defendant; Complete set. 3A FEDFORMS § 3496.

l. Interrogatories by defendant; Complete set; Another form. 3A FEDFORMS § 3497.

m. Interrogatories by defendant; Complete set; Another form. 3A FEDFORMS § 3498.

n. Interrogatories by defendant; Complete set; Another form. 3A FEDFORMS § 3499.

o. Interrogatories by defendant; Follow-up interrogatories to plaintiff after lapse of time since first set of interrogatories or deposition. 3A FEDFORMS § 3500.

p. Certificate of service of interrogatories. 3A FEDFORMS § 3501.

q. Interrogatories; Outline form. FEDPROF § 23:335.

r. Interrogatories; To defendant; Trademark action. FEDPROF § 23:347.

s. Interrogatories; With request for documents; To defendant; Collection of royalties. FEDPROF § 23:348.

t. Interrogatories; To defendant; Copyright infringement. FEDPROF § 23:350.

u. Interrogatories; To plaintiff; Products liability. FEDPROF § 23:352.

v. Interrogatories; To plaintiff; Personal injury. FEDPROF § 23:353.

w. Interrogatories; To defendant; Premises liability. FEDPROF § 23:356.

x. Interrogatories; To defendant; Medical malpractice. FEDPROF § 23:357.

y. General forms; Standard interrogatories. GOLDLTGFMS § 26:25.

z. General forms; Civil cases. GOLDLTGFMS § 26:26.

### 2. Forms for the Western District of New York

a. Certificate of service. NY R USDCTWD ECF Procedures(4a).

## I. Applicable Rules

1. *Federal rules*

a. Serving and filing pleadings and other papers. FRCP 5.

  b. Privacy protection for filings made with the court. FRCP 5.2.

  c. Computing and extending time; Time for motion papers. FRCP 6.

  d. Pleadings allowed; Form of motions and other papers. FRCP 7.

  e. Form of pleadings. FRCP 10.

  f. Signing pleadings, motions, and other papers; Representations to the court; Sanctions. FRCP 11.

  g. Duty to disclose; General provisions governing discovery. FRCP 26.

  h. Stipulations about discovery procedure. FRCP 29.

  i. Interrogatories to parties. FRCP 33.

  j. Failure to make disclosures or to cooperate in discovery; Sanctions. FRCP 37.

 2. *Local rules*

  a. Title. NY R USDCTWD Civ Rule 1.1.

  b. Filing and serving papers. NY R USDCTWD Civ Rule 5.1.

  c. Form of papers. NY R USDCTWD Civ Rule 10.

  d. Sanctions. NY R USDCTWD Civ Rule 11.

  e. Alternative dispute resolution and pretrial conferences. NY R USDCTWD Civ Rule 16.

  f. General rules governing discovery. NY R USDCTWD Civ Rule 26.

  g. Stipulations. NY R USDCTWD Civ Rule 29.

  h. Attorneys of record; Appearance and withdrawal. NY R USDCTWD Civ Rule 83.2.

  i. Administrative procedures guide for electronic filing. NY R USDCTWD ECF Procedures.

  j. Alternative dispute resolution plan. NY R USDCTWD ADR Plan.

## J. Miscellaneous

**NOTE: Individual judges' rules may apply. For available judge-level information, refer to:**

DISTRICT JUDGE RICHARD J. ARCARA: NY R USDCTWD Arcara-Procedures.

DISTRICT JUDGE FRANK P. GERACI, JR.: NY R USDCTWD Geraci-Procedures.

DISTRICT JUDGE DAVID G. LARIMER: NY R USDCTWD Larimer-Procedures.

DISTRICT JUDGE CHARLES J. SIRAGUSA: NY R USDCTWD Siragusa-Procedures.

DISTRICT JUDGE WILLIAM M. SKRETNY: NY R USDCTWD Skretny--Procedures.

DISTRICT JUDGE MICHAEL A. TELESCA: NY R USDCTWD Telesca-Procedures.

DISTRICT JUDGE LAWRENCE J. VILARDO: NY R USDCTWD Vilardo-Procedures.

DISTRICT JUDGE ELIZABETH A. WOLFORD: NY R USDCTWD Wolford-Procedures.

MAGISTRATE JUDGE JONATHAN W. FELDMAN: NY R USDCTWD Feldman-Procedures.

MAGISTRATE JUDGE LESLIE G. FOSCHIO: NY R USDCTWD Foschio-Procedures; NY R USDCTWD Foschio-Depositions.

MAGISTRATE JUDGE JEREMIAH J. McCARTHY: NY R USDCTWD McCarthy-Procedures.

MAGISTRATE JUDGE MARIAN W. PAYSON: NY R USDCTWD Payson-Procedures.

MAGISTRATE JUDGE MICHAEL J. ROEMER: NY R USDCTWD Roemer-Procedures.

MAGISTRATE JUDGE H. KENNETH SCHROEDER, JR.: NY R USDCTWD Schroeder-Proc.

MAGISTRATE JUDGE HUGH B. SCOTT: NY R USDCTWD Scott-Procedures.

# Requests, Notices and Applications
# Request for Production of Documents

### Document Last Updated September 2016

## A. Checklist

(I)  ❑ Matters to be considered by requesting party

    (a)  ❑ Required documents

        (1)  ❑ Request for production of documents

        (2)  ❑ Electronic courtesy copy

    (b)  ❑ Supplemental documents

        (1)  ❑ Subpoena

        (2)  ❑ Certificate of service

    (c)  ❑ Timing

        (1)  ❑ A party may not seek discovery from any source before the parties have conferred as required by FRCP 26(f), except in a proceeding exempted from initial disclosure under FRCP 26(a)(1)(B), or when authorized by the Federal Rules of Civil Procedure, by stipulation, or by court order

        (2)  ❑ More than twenty-one (21) days after the summons and complaint are served on a party, a request under FRCP 34 may be delivered: (1) to that party by any other party, and (2) by that party to any plaintiff or to any other party that has been served

(II)  ❑ Matters to be considered by responding party

    (a)  ❑ Required documents

        (1)  ❑ Response to request for production of documents

    (b)  ❑ Supplemental documents

        (1)  ❑ Certificate of service

    (c)  ❑ Timing

        (1)  ❑ The party to whom the request is directed must respond in writing within thirty (30) days after being served or—if the request was delivered under FRCP 26(d)(2)—within thirty (30) days after the parties' first FRCP 26(f) conference

## B. Timing

1. *Request for production of documents.* Without leave of court or written stipulation, a request may not be served before the time specified in FRCP 26(d). FEDPROC § 26:632. Of course, discovery under FRCP 34 should ordinarily precede the trial. FEDPROC § 26:632.

    a. *Early FRCP 34 requests*

        i. *Time to deliver.* More than twenty-one (21) days after the summons and complaint are served on a party, a request under FRCP 34 may be delivered:

           • To that party by any other party, and

           • By that party to any plaintiff or to any other party that has been served. FRCP 26(d)(2)(A).

        ii. *When considered served.* The request is considered to have been served at the first FRCP 26(f) conference. FRCP 26(d)(2)(B).

2. *Timing of discovery, generally.* A party may not seek discovery from any source before the parties have conferred as required by FRCP 26(f), except in a proceeding exempted from initial disclosure under FRCP 26(a)(1)(B), or when authorized by the Federal Rules of Civil Procedure, by stipulation, or by court order. FRCP 26(d)(1).

3. *Computation of time*

    a. *Computing time.* FRCP 6 applies in computing any time period specified in the Federal Rules of Civil Procedure, in any local rule or court order, or in any statute that does not specify a method of computing time. FRCP 6(a).

        i. *Period stated in days or a longer unit.* When the period is stated in days or a longer unit of time:

- Exclude the day of the event that triggers the period;
- Count every day, including intermediate Saturdays, Sundays, and legal holidays; and
- Include the last day of the period, but if the last day is a Saturday, Sunday, or legal holiday, the period continues to run until the end of the next day that is not a Saturday, Sunday, or legal holiday. FRCP 6(a)(1).

        ii. *Period stated in hours.* When the period is stated in hours:

- Begin counting immediately on the occurrence of the event that triggers the period;
- Count every hour, including hours during intermediate Saturdays, Sundays, and legal holidays; and
- If the period would end on a Saturday, Sunday, or legal holiday, the period continues to run until the same time on the next day that is not a Saturday, Sunday, or legal holiday. FRCP 6(a)(2).

        iii. *Inaccessibility of the clerk's office.* Unless the court orders otherwise, if the clerk's office is inaccessible:

- On the last day for filing under FRCP 6(a)(1), then the time for filing is extended to the first accessible day that is not a Saturday, Sunday, or legal holiday; or
- During the last hour for filing under FRCP 6(a)(2), then the time for filing is extended to the same time on the first accessible day that is not a Saturday, Sunday, or legal holiday. FRCP 6(a)(3).

        iv. *"Last day" defined.* Unless a different time is set by a statute, local rule, or court order, the last day ends:

- For electronic filing, at midnight in the court's time zone; and
- For filing by other means, when the clerk's office is scheduled to close. FRCP 6(a)(4).

        v. *"Next day" defined.* The "next day" is determined by continuing to count forward when the period is measured after an event and backward when measured before an event. FRCP 6(a)(5).

        vi. *"Legal holiday" defined.* "Legal holiday" means:

- The day set aside by statute for observing New Year's Day, Martin Luther King Jr.'s Birthday, Washington's Birthday, Memorial Day, Independence Day, Labor Day, Columbus Day, Veterans' Day, Thanksgiving Day, or Christmas Day;
- Any day declared a holiday by the President or Congress; and
- For periods that are measured after an event, any other day declared a holiday by the state where the district court is located. FRCP 6(a)(6).

    b. *Computation of electronic filing deadlines.* A document will be deemed timely filed if filed prior to midnight Eastern Time, unless otherwise ordered by the Court. A document will be considered untimely if filed thereafter. When a Court order requires that a document be filed on a weekend or holiday, the document may be filed by close of business the next business day without further application to the Court. NY R USDCTWD ECF Procedures(2)(e)(i). A document filed electronically is deemed filed on the date and time stated on the Notice of Electronic Filing. NY R USDCTWD ECF Procedures(2)(e)(ii).

        i. *System availability.* Although parties may file documents electronically twenty-four (24) hours a day, registered users are strongly encouraged to file all documents during normal working hours of the Clerk's Office (8:30 a.m. to 5:00 p.m. Eastern Time). NY R USDCTWD ECF Procedures(2)(t)(i).

    ii. *Technical failures.* A Filing User whose filing is made untimely as a result of a technical failure must seek appropriate relief from the Court. NY R USDCTWD ECF Procedures(2)(u)(i).

  c. *Extending time*

    i. *In general.* When an act may or must be done within a specified time, the court may, for good cause, extend the time:

- With or without motion or notice if the court acts, or if a request is made, before the original time or its extension expires; or

- On motion made after the time has expired if the party failed to act because of excusable neglect. FRCP 6(b)(1).

    ii. *Exceptions.* A court must not extend the time to act under FRCP 50(b), FRCP 50(d), FRCP 52(b), FRCP 59(b), FRCP 59(d), FRCP 59(e), and FRCP 60(b). FRCP 6(b)(2).

    iii. Refer to the United States District Court for the Western District of New York KeyRules Motion for Continuance/Extension of Time document for more information on extending time.

  d. *Additional time after certain kinds of service.* When a party may or must act within a specified time after service and service is made under FRCP 5(b)(2)(C), FRCP 5(b)(2)(D), FRCP 5(b)(2)(E), or FRCP 5(b)(2)(F), three (3) days are added after the period would otherwise expire under FRCP 6(a). FRCP 6(d).

    i. *Service by overnight delivery.* Where a period of time prescribed by either the Federal Rules of Civil Procedure or the Local Rules of Civil Procedure for the United States District Court for the Western District of New York is measured from the service of a paper and service is by overnight delivery, one (1) business day shall be added to the prescribed period. NY R USDCTWD Civ Rule 5.1(g).

4. *Individual judge practices.* Refer to the Miscellaneous section of this document for information on individual judge practices on timing of documents.

## C. General Requirements

1. *General provisions governing discovery*

  a. *Discovery scope and limits*

    i. *Scope in general.* Unless otherwise limited by court order, the scope of discovery is as follows: Parties may obtain discovery regarding any nonprivileged matter that is relevant to any party's claim or defense and proportional to the needs of the case, considering the importance of the issues at stake in the action, the amount in controversy, the parties' relative access to relevant information, the parties' resources, the importance of the discovery in resolving the issues, and whether the burden or expense of the proposed discovery outweighs its likely benefit. Information within this scope of discovery need not be admissible in evidence to be discoverable. FRCP 26(b)(1).

    ii. *Limitations on frequency and extent*

- *When permitted.* By order, the court may alter the limits in the Federal Rules of Civil Procedure on the number of depositions and interrogatories or on the length of depositions under FRCP 30. By order or local rule, the court may also limit the number of requests under FRCP 36. FRCP 26(b)(2)(A).

- *Specific limitations on electronically stored information.* A party need not provide discovery of electronically stored information from sources that the party identifies as not reasonably accessible because of undue burden or cost. On motion to compel discovery or for a protective order, the party from whom discovery is sought must show that the information is not reasonably accessible because of undue burden or cost. If that showing is made, the court may nonetheless order discovery from such sources if the requesting party shows good cause, considering the limitations of FRCP 26(b)(2)(C). The court may specify conditions for the discovery. FRCP 26(b)(2)(B).

- *When required.* On motion or on its own, the court must limit the frequency or extent of

discovery otherwise allowed by the Federal Rules of Civil Procedure or by local rule if it determines that: (1) the discovery sought is unreasonably cumulative or duplicative, or can be obtained from some other source that is more convenient, less burdensome, or less expensive; (2) the party seeking discovery has had ample opportunity to obtain the information by discovery in the action; or (3) the proposed discovery is outside the scope permitted by FRCP 26(b)(1). FRCP 26(b)(2)(C).

iii. *Trial preparation; Materials*

- *Documents and tangible things.* Ordinarily, a party may not discover documents and tangible things that are prepared in anticipation of litigation or for trial by or for another party or its representative (including the other party's attorney, consultant, surety, indemnitor, insurer, or agent). But, subject to FRCP 26(b)(4), those materials may be discovered if: (1) they are otherwise discoverable under FRCP 26(b)(1); and (2) the party shows that it has substantial need for the materials to prepare its case and cannot, without undue hardship, obtain their substantial equivalent by other means. FRCP 26(b)(3)(A).

- *Protection against disclosure.* If the court orders discovery of those materials, it must protect against disclosure of the mental impressions, conclusions, opinions, or legal theories of a party's attorney or other representative concerning the litigation. FRCP 26(b)(3)(B).

- *Previous statement.* Any party or other person may, on request and without the required showing, obtain the person's own previous statement about the action or its subject matter. If the request is refused, the person may move for a court order, and FRCP 37(a)(5) applies to the award of expenses. A previous statement is either: (1) a written statement that the person has signed or otherwise adopted or approved; or (2) a contemporaneous stenographic, mechanical, electrical, or other recording—or a transcription of it—that recites substantially verbatim the person's oral statement. FRCP 26(b)(3)(C).

iv. *Trial preparation; Experts*

- *Deposition of an expert who may testify.* A party may depose any person who has been identified as an expert whose opinions may be presented at trial. If FRCP 26(a)(2)(B) requires a report from the expert, the deposition may be conducted only after the report is provided. FRCP 26(b)(4)(A).

- *Trial-preparation protection for draft reports or disclosures.* FRCP 26(b)(3)(A) and FRCP 26(b)(3)(B) protect drafts of any report or disclosure required under FRCP 26(a)(2), regardless of the form in which the draft is recorded. FRCP 26(b)(4)(B).

- *Trial-preparation protection for communications between a party's attorney and expert witnesses.* FRCP 26(b)(3)(A) and FRCP 26(b)(3)(B) protect communications between the party's attorney and any witness required to provide a report under FRCP 26(a)(2)(B), regardless of the form of the communications, except to the extent that the communications: (1) relate to compensation for the expert's study or testimony; (2) identify facts or data that the party's attorney provided and that the expert considered in forming the opinions to be expressed; or (3) identify assumptions that the party's attorney provided and that the expert relied on in forming the opinions to be expressed. FRCP 26(b)(4)(C).

- *Expert employed only for trial preparation.* Ordinarily, a party may not, by interrogatories or deposition, discover facts known or opinions held by an expert who has been retained or specially employed by another party in anticipation of litigation or to prepare for trial and who is not expected to be called as a witness at trial. But a party may do so only: (1) as provided in FRCP 35(b); or (2) on showing exceptional circumstances under which it is impracticable for the party to obtain facts or opinions on the same subject by other means. FRCP 26(b)(4)(D).

- *Payment.* Unless manifest injustice would result, the court must require that the party seeking discovery: (1) pay the expert a reasonable fee for time spent in responding to discovery under FRCP 26(b)(4)(A) or FRCP 26(b)(4)(D); and (2) for discovery FRCP

26(b)(4)(D), also pay the other party a fair portion of the fees and expenses it reasonably incurred in obtaining the expert's facts and opinions. FRCP 26(b)(4)(E).

    v. *Claiming privilege or protecting trial-preparation materials*

- *Information withheld.* When a party withholds information otherwise discoverable by claiming that the information is privileged or subject to protection as trial-preparation material, the party must: (1) expressly make the claim; and (2) describe the nature of the documents, communications, or tangible things not produced or disclosed—and do so in a manner that, without revealing information itself privileged or protected, will enable other parties to assess the claim. FRCP 26(b)(5)(A). Where a party asserts a claim of privilege in objecting to any means of discovery or disclosure, and withholds otherwise responsive information based on that assertion: (1) the party asserting the privilege shall identify the nature of the privilege (including work product) being claimed and, if the privilege is governed by state law, indicate the state's privilege rule being invoked; and (2) shall provide the following information, unless to divulge such information would cause disclosure of the allegedly privileged information: (i) for documents: (a) the type of document, i.e., letter or memorandum; (b) the general subject matter of the document; (c) the date of the document; and (d) such other information as is sufficient to identify the document for a subpoena duces tecum, including, where appropriate, the author of the document, the addressees of the document, and any other recipients shown in the document, and, where not apparent, the relationship of the author, addressees, and recipients to each other; (ii) for oral communications: (a) the names of the person making the communication and the person(s) present while the communication was made and, where not apparent, the relationship of the person making the communication to the person(s) present; (b) the date and place of communication; and (c) its general subject matter. NY R USDCTWD Civ Rule 26(d)(1).

- *Information produced.* If information produced in discovery is subject to a claim of privilege or of protection as trial-preparation material, the party making the claim may notify any party that received the information of the claim and the basis for it. After being notified, a party must promptly return, sequester, or destroy the specified information and any copies it has; must not use or disclose the information until the claim is resolved; must take reasonable steps to retrieve the information if the party disclosed it before being notified; and may promptly present the information to the court under seal for a determination of the claim. The producing party must preserve the information until the claim is resolved. FRCP 26(b)(5)(B). Where the claim of privilege is asserted in response to discovery or disclosure other than at a deposition, the information set forth in NY R USDCTWD Civ Rule 26(d)(1) shall be furnished in writing when the party responds to such discovery or disclosure, unless otherwise ordered by the Court. NY R USDCTWD Civ Rule 26(d)(2). Where the claim of privilege is asserted during a deposition, the information set forth in NY R USDCTWD Civ Rule 26(d)(1) shall be furnished: (1) at the deposition, to the extent it is readily available from the witness being deposed or otherwise, and (2) to the extent it not readily available, in writing within fourteen (14) days after the privilege is asserted, unless otherwise ordered by the Court. NY R USDCTWD Civ Rule 26(d)(3).

b. *Protective orders.* A party or any person from whom discovery is sought may move for a protective order in the court where the action is pending—or as an alternative on matters relating to a deposition, in the court for the district where the deposition will be taken. FRCP 26(c)(1). Refer to the United States District Court for the Western District of New York KeyRules Motion for Protective Order document for more information.

c. *Sequence of discovery.* Unless the parties stipulate or the court orders otherwise for the parties' and witnesses' convenience and in the interests of justice: (1) methods of discovery may be used in any sequence; and (2) discovery by one party does not require any other party to delay its discovery. FRCP 26(d)(3).

d. *Uniform definitions for all discovery requests.* The full text of the definitions and rules of construction set forth in NY R USDCTWD Civ Rule 26(c)(3) and NY R USDCTWD Civ Rule 26(c)(4) is deemed incorporated by reference into all discovery requests. No discovery request shall use broader definitions or rules of construction than those set forth in NY R USDCTWD Civ Rule 26(c)(3) and NY R USDCTWD Civ Rule 26(c)(4). NY R USDCTWD Civ Rule 26(c) shall not preclude (1) the definition of other terms specific to the particular litigation, (2) the use of abbreviations, or (3) a more narrow definition of a term defined in NY R USDCTWD Civ Rule 26(c)(3). NY R USDCTWD Civ Rule 26(c)(1). NY R USDCTWD Civ Rule 26(c) is not intended to broaden or narrow the scope of discovery permitted by the Federal Rules of Civil Procedure. NY R USDCTWD Civ Rule 26(c)(2).

i. *Definitions.* The following definitions apply to all discovery requests:

- *Communication.* The term "communication" means the transmittal of information (in the form of facts, ideas, inquiries or otherwise). NY R USDCTWD Civ Rule 26(c)(3)(A).

- *Document.* The term "document" is defined to be synonymous in meaning and equal in scope to the usage of this term in FRCP 34(a), including, without limitation, electronic or computerized data compilations. A draft or non-identical copy is a separate document within the meaning of this term. NY R USDCTWD Civ Rule 26(c)(3)(B).

- *Identify (with respect to persons).* When referring to a person, "to identify" means to give, to the extent known, the person's full name, present or last known address, and when referring to a natural person, the present or last known place of employment. Once a person has been identified in accordance with NY R USDCTWD Civ Rule 26(c)(3)(C), only the person's name need be listed in response to subsequent discovery requesting the identification of that person. NY R USDCTWD Civ Rule 26(c)(3)(C).

- *Identify (with respect to documents).* When referring to documents, "to identify" means to give, to the extent known, the (1) type of document; (2) general subject matter; (3) date of the document; and (4) author(s), addressee(s), and recipients(s). NY R USDCTWD Civ Rule 26(c)(3)(D).

- *Parties.* The terms "plaintiff" and "defendant," as well as a party's full or abbreviated name or a pronoun referring to a party, mean the party and, where applicable, its officers, directors, employees, partners, corporate parent, subsidiaries, or affiliates. This definition is not intended to impose a discovery obligation on any person who is not a party to the litigation. NY R USDCTWD Civ Rule 26(c)(3)(E).

- *Person.* The term "person" is defined as any natural person or any business, legal or governmental entity, or association. NY R USDCTWD Civ Rule 26(c)(3)(F).

- *Concerning.* The term "concerning" means relating to, referring to, describing, evidencing or constituting. NY R USDCTWD Civ Rule 26(c)(3)(G).

ii. *Rules of construction.* The following rules of construction apply to all discovery requests:

- *All/each.* The terms "all" and "each" shall be construed as all and each. NY R USDCTWD Civ Rule 26(c)(4)(A).

- *And/or.* The connectives "and" and "or" shall be construed either disjunctively or conjunctively as necessary to bring within the scope of the discovery request all responses that might otherwise be construed to be outside of its scope. NY R USDCTWD Civ Rule 26(c)(4)(B).

- *Number.* The use of the singular form of any word includes the plural and vice versa. NY R USDCTWD Civ Rule 26(c)(4)(C).

e. *Electronically stored information (ESI).* Discovery of relevant electronically stored information shall proceed as follows:

i. *Searches and production of ESI.* After receiving requests for document production, the parties shall search their documents, including ESI other than ESI that has been identified as not reasonably accessible, and produce relevant responsive ESI in accordance with FRCP 26(b)(2). NY R USDCTWD Civ Rule 26(e)(1).

ii. *Non-accessible ESI.* Searches and production of ESI identified as not reasonably accessible shall not be required to be conducted until the initial disclosure of reasonably accessible ESI has been completed. Requests for information expected to be found in ESI that is not reasonably accessible must be narrowly focused with some basis in fact supporting the request, and good cause must be provided. The party seeking such discovery may be required to pay all or a portion of the costs of search, retrieval, review, and production of the information, upon application to the Court. NY R USDCTWD Civ Rule 26(e)(2).

iii.  *Search methodology.* If a party intends to employ an electronic search to locate relevant ESI, the parties shall discuss and attempt to reach agreement as to the method of searching, and the words, terms, and phrases to be searched and any restrictions as to scope and method which might affect their ability to conduct a complete electronic search of the ESI. The parties shall also attempt to reach agreement as to the timing and conditions of any additional searches which may become necessary in the normal course of discovery. To minimize undue expense, the parties may consider limiting the scope of the electronic search (i.e., time frames, fields, document types). NY R USDCTWD Civ Rule 26(e)(3).

iv.  *Metadata.* Except as otherwise provided, metadata, especially substantive metadata, need not be routinely produced, except upon agreement of the requesting and producing litigants, or upon a showing of good cause in a motion filed by the requesting party. NY R USDCTWD Civ Rule 26(e)(4).

v.  *Format.* If the parties have not agreed or cannot agree to the format for document production, ESI shall be produced to the requesting party as image files (i.e. PDF or TIFF). When the image file is produced, the producing party must preserve the integrity of the electronic document's contents, i.e., the original formatting of the document, its metadata and, where applicable, its revision history. After initial production in image file format is complete, a party must demonstrate particularized need for production of ESI in its native format. NY R USDCTWD Civ Rule 26(e)(5).

vi.  *Costs.* Generally, the costs of discovery, other than the costs associated with ESI that is not reasonably accessible, shall be borne by each party. However, the Court will apportion the costs of discovery or presentation of ESI, including discovery of ESI that is not reasonably accessible, upon a showing of good cause, or unequal burdens, or unreasonable request. NY R USDCTWD Civ Rule 26(e)(6).

f.  *Cooperation among counsel in the discovery context.* See the Civility Principles of the United States District Court for the Western District of New York which can be found on the Court's website. NY R USDCTWD Civ Rule 26(g).

2.  *Request for production of documents*

a.  *In general.* A party may serve on any other party a request within the scope of FRCP 26(b):

i.  To produce and permit the requesting party or its representative to inspect, copy, test, or sample the following items in the responding party's possession, custody, or control:

- Any designated documents or electronically stored information—including writings, drawings, graphs, charts, photographs, sound recordings, images, and other data or data compilations—stored in any medium from which information can be obtained either directly or, if necessary, after translation by the responding party into a reasonably usable form; or

- Any designated tangible things; or

ii.  To permit entry onto designated land or other property possessed or controlled by the responding party, so that the requesting party may inspect, measure, survey, photograph, test, or sample the property or any designated object or operation on it. FRCP 34(a).

b.  *Contents of the request.* The request: (1) must describe with reasonable particularity each item or category of items to be inspected; (2) must specify a reasonable time, place, and manner for the inspection and for performing the related acts; and (3) may specify the form or forms in which electronically stored information is to be produced. FRCP 34(b)(1).

    i. *Description of items.* Although the phrase "reasonable particularity" eludes precise definition and depends on the facts and circumstances in each case, at least two tests have been suggested:

- The first test is whether the request places a party on "reasonable notice" of what is called for and what is not so that a reasonable person would know what documents or things are called for. FEDPROC § 26:634.

- The second is whether the request gives a court enough information to enable it to rule intelligently on objections. FEDPROC § 26:634.

c. *Numbering.* The parties shall sequentially number each interrogatory or discovery request. NY R USDCTWD Civ Rule 26(b).

d. *Signature.* Though FRCP 34 does not say so, it is sufficient if the request is signed by the attorney for the party seeking discovery. FPP § 2212. Refer to the Format section of this document for more information on signing of discovery papers.

e. *Production of documents in connection with depositions.* Consistent with the requirements of FRCP 30 and FRCP 34, a party seeking production of documents of another party or witness in connection with a deposition shall schedule the deposition to allow for production of the documents at least seven (7) calendar days prior to the deposition. Upon receipt of the documents, the party noticing the deposition shall immediately inform counsel for all other noticed parties that the requested documents have been produced and shall make the documents available for their inspection and reproduction. If timely requested documents are not produced at least seven (7) days prior to the deposition, the party noticing the deposition may either adjourn the deposition until a minimum of seven (7) days after the documents are produced or, without waiving the right to access to the documents, proceed with the deposition on the originally scheduled date. NY R USDCTWD Civ Rule 30(b).

f. *Other authority on production and inspection*

    i. *Freedom of Information Act.* Although the Freedom of Information Act (FOIA) is fundamentally designed to inform the public about agency action, and not to benefit private litigants, Congress has not acted upon proposals to forbid or limit the use of the FOIA for discovery purposes. FEDPROC § 26:605; National Presto Industries, Inc., 218 Ct.Cl. 696, 1978 WL 8475 (1978). However, a FOIA request may not be used to supplement civil discovery under FRCP 34, as in the case where information is privileged and therefore outside the scope of civil discovery. FEDPROC § 26:605; U.S. v. Weber Aircraft Corp., 465 U.S. 792, 104 S.Ct. 1488, 79 L.Ed.2d 814 (1984).

    ii. *Hague Convention.* Under the Hague Convention, a party seeking evidence abroad must obtain and send a letter of request to the central authority of the country in which the evidence is sought, requesting service of the request on the desired person or entity; if the request complies with the Convention, the central authority will then obtain the desired evidence. FEDPROC § 26:606. [Editor's note: the Hague Convention can be found at T.I.A.S. No. 6638 and is also available in the appendix to FRCP 4].

g. *Motion to compel.* If a party who has been requested to permit discovery under FRCP 34 makes no response to the request, or if its response objects to all or part of the requested discovery, or if it otherwise fails to permit discovery as requested, the party who submitted the request, if it still wishes the discovery that has been refused, may move under FRCP 37(a) for an order compelling inspection in accordance with the request. FPP § 2214. Refer to the United States District Court for the Western District of New York KeyRules Motion to Compel Discovery document for more information.

3. *Sanctions for failure to cooperate in discovery.* The court where the action is pending may, on motion, order sanctions if a party, after being properly served with interrogatories under FRCP 33 or a request for inspection under FRCP 34, fails to serve its answers, objections, or written response. FRCP 37(d)(1)(A)(ii). If a motion to compel is granted, the court must, after giving an opportunity to be heard, require the party or deponent whose conduct necessitated the motion, the party or attorney advising that

conduct, or both to pay the movant's reasonable expenses incurred in making the motion, including attorney's fees. But the court must not order this payment if the opposing party's nondisclosure, response, or objection was substantially justified. FRCP 37(a)(5)(A)(ii). Refer to the United States District Court for the Western District of New York KeyRules Motion for Discovery Sanctions document for more information.

4. *Stipulations about discovery procedure.* Unless the court orders otherwise, the parties may stipulate that: (1) a deposition may be taken before any person, at any time or place, on any notice, and in the manner specified—in which event it may be used in the same way as any other deposition; and (2) other procedures governing or limiting discovery be modified—but a stipulation extending the time for any form of discovery must have court approval if it would interfere with the time set for completing discovery, for hearing a motion, or for trial. FRCP 29. All stipulations, except stipulations made in open court and recorded by the court reporter, shall be in writing and signed by each attorney and/or pro se litigant. The parties shall determine who will be responsible for filing, and a copy of the stipulation, with signatures conformed (e.g., "s/Jane Doe," "s/John Smith"), shall be filed electronically. The Court will act on the filed stipulation, as necessary and appropriate. NY R USDCTWD Civ Rule 29.

5. *Notice of appearance.* No notice of appearance is required of an attorney whose name and address appear at the end of a complaint, notice of removal, pre-answer motion, or answer. In all other circumstances, an attorney appearing for a party in a civil case shall promptly file a written notice of appearance. NY R USDCTWD Civ Rule 83.2(b). For more information on appearances and withdrawals, refer to NY R USDCTWD Civ Rule 83.2.

6. *Related cases.* Each attorney appearing in a civil case has a continuing duty to promptly notify the Clerk of Court when the attorney has reason to believe that said case is related to some other pending civil or criminal action(s) such that their assignment to the same Judge would avoid unnecessary duplication of judicial effort. As soon as the attorney becomes aware of such a relationship, the attorney shall notify the Clerk of Court by letter of the relevant facts, and the Clerk of Court will transmit that notification to the Judges to whom the cases have been assigned. NY R USDCTWD Civ Rule 5.1(e).

7. *Alternative dispute resolution (ADR).* This Court has adopted an Alternative Dispute Resolution Plan ("ADR"), as implemented by Standing Order (NY R USDCTWD ADR Plan), under which certain civil cases are referred automatically to ADR upon filing. NY R USDCTWD Civ Rule 16(a). The United States District Court for the Western District of New York (the "Court") adopted the ADR Plan on January 1, 2006 (the "Effective Date"), to make available to civil litigants court-administered ADR interventions and processes designed to provide quicker, less expensive and potentially more satisfying alternatives to continuing litigation, without impairing the quality of justice or the right to trial. NY R USDCTWD ADR Plan(1)(1.2)(A).

 a. *Scope.* This ADR Plan (NY R USDCTWD ADR Plan) applies to civil actions pending or commenced on and after the Effective Date, except as otherwise indicated in NY R USDCTWD ADR Plan. The ADR Plan supplements the Local Rules of Civil Procedure for the United States District Court for the Western District of New York, which shall remain in full effect for all cases. NY R USDCTWD ADR Plan(1)(1.2)(B).

 b. *Referral to ADR*

   i. *New cases.* All civil cases filed on and after the Effective Date of the ADR Plan shall be referred automatically for ADR. NY R USDCTWD ADR Plan(2)(2.1)(A). Notice of the ADR requirements will be provided to all parties immediately upon the filing of a complaint and answer or a notice of removal; NY R USDCTWD ADR Plan(2)(2.1)(A); NY R USDCTWD Civ Rule 16(a). ADR intervention will be scheduled at the conference held pursuant to Local Rule of Civil Procedure 16.1. NY R USDCTWD ADR Plan(2)(2.1)(A). [Editor's note: the reference to Local Rule of Civil Procedure 16.1 is likely meant to be a reference to NY R USDCTWD Civ Rule 16(b)].

   • Litigants in cases not referred automatically to ADR must consider possible agreement to the use of an ADR process. NY R USDCTWD Civ Rule 16(a).

   • For a list of exemptions from automatic referral, refer to NY R USDCTWD ADR Plan(2)(2.1)(A).

ii. *Pending cases.* The assigned Judge on any pending civil case may, sua sponte or with status conference, issue an order referring the case for ADR. NY R USDCTWD ADR Plan(2)(2.1)(B); NY R USDCTWD Civ Rule 16(a). The order shall specify a date on which the ADR intervention is to be completed. NY R USDCTWD ADR Plan(2)(2.1)(B).

iii. *Stipulation.* A case may be referred for ADR by stipulation of all parties. Stipulations shall be filed and shall designate the specific ADR intervention the parties have selected, the time frame within which the ADR process will be completed and the selected Neutral. Stipulations are presumed acceptable unless the assigned Judge determines that the interests of justice are not served. NY R USDCTWD ADR Plan(2)(2.1)(C).

iv. *Relief from ADR referral*

- *Opting out motions.* Any party may file, with the assigned Judge for that case, a motion to opt out of, or for relief from, ADR. NY R USDCTWD ADR Plan(2)(2.2)(A).

- *Motion.* Opting Out Motions must be made within fourteen (14) days from (1) the date of the first discovery conference under Local Rule 16.1 in new cases, or (2) the date of a sua sponte ADR Referral Order in pending cases. NY R USDCTWD ADR Plan(2)(2.2)(B). [Editor's note: the reference to Local Rule 16.1 is likely meant to be a reference to NY R USDCTWD Civ Rule 16(b)].

- *Criteria.* Opting Out Motions shall be granted only for "good cause" shown. Inconvenience, travel costs, attorney fees or other costs shall not constitute "good cause." A party seeking relief from ADR must set forth the reasons why ADR has no reasonable chance of being productive. NY R USDCTWD ADR Plan(2)(2.2)(C).

- *Judicial initiative.* The assigned Judge may, sua sponte, exempt any case from the Court's ADR Plan. NY R USDCTWD ADR Plan(2)(2.2)(D).

c. *ADR interventions*

i. *Options.* It is expected that cases referred for ADR will proceed to Mediation. However, the following options are also available upon the stipulation of all parties:

- Neutral Evaluation;
- Mini Summary Trial;
- Arbitration (Binding and Non-Binding);
- Case Valuation; and
- Settlement Week, when scheduled by the Court. NY R USDCTWD ADR Plan(4)(4.1)(A).

ii. *Timing.* Timing is specific to the intervention and process chosen, as set forth in the corresponding sections in NY R USDCTWD ADR Plan. NY R USDCTWD ADR Plan(4)(4.1)(B).

iii. *Scheduling.* The referral of a case to ADR does not delay or defer other dates established in the Scheduling Order and has no effect on the scheduled progress of the case toward trial. NY R USDCTWD ADR Plan(4)(4.1)(C).

d. *Selecting an ADR intervention*

i. *New cases.* Prior to the Local Rule 16.1 scheduling conference, counsel and any unrepresented parties shall confer about ADR as part of their discussion of "the possibilities for a prompt settlement or resolution of the case" pursuant to FRCP 26(f). Unless the parties agree to a different intervention, it is presumed that they will participate in mediation. [Editor's note: the reference to Local Rule 16.1 is likely meant to be a reference to NY R USDCTWD Civ Rule 16(b)].

ii. *Pending cases.* In pending cases, all sua sponte referrals will be to mediation. Should the parties agree that a different ADR intervention is more appropriate to their case, they may submit a stipulation designating the specific ADR intervention selected, the time frame within which the ADR process will be completed and the identity of the Neutral. Stipulations must be filed within fourteen (14) days from the date of the ADR Referral Order and are presumed acceptable unless the assigned Judge determines that the interests of justice are not served. NY R USDCTWD ADR Plan(4)(4.2)(B).

e. For more information on alternative dispute resolution (ADR), refer to NY R USDCTWD ADR Plan.

8. *Sanctions.* Failure of counsel for any party, or a party proceeding pro se, to appear before the Court at a conference, to complete the necessary preparations, or to be prepared to proceed to trial at the set time may be considered an abandonment of the case or a failure to prosecute or defend diligently. An appropriate order for sanctions may be entered against the defaulting party with respect to either a specific issue or the entire case. NY R USDCTWD Civ Rule 11(a). For more information, refer to NY R USDCTWD Civ Rule 11.

9. *Pro se actions.* For information on the requirements in pro se actions, refer to NY R USDCTWD Civ Rule 5.2.

10. *Individual judge practices.* Refer to the Miscellaneous section of this document for information on individual judge practices on general requirements for documents.

## D. Documents

1. *Required documents*

   a. *Request for production of documents.* Refer to the General Requirements section of this document for information on the request for production of documents.

   b. *Electronic courtesy copy.* In addition to service pursuant to FRCP 5, the party to whom interrogatories or discovery requests are directed shall, whenever practicable, be supplied with an electronic courtesy copy of the served document in a word processing format. NY R USDCTWD Civ Rule 26(b).

2. *Supplemental documents*

   a. *Subpoena.* As provided in FRCP 45, a nonparty may be compelled to produce documents and tangible things or to permit an inspection. FRCP 34(c). For information on the form and contents of the subpoena, refer to FRCP 45.

   b. *Certificate of service.* FRCP 5(d) requires that the person making service under FRCP 5 certify that service has been effected. FRCP 5(Advisory Committee Notes). Having such information on file may be useful for many purposes, including proof of service if an issue arises concerning the effectiveness of the service. FRCP 5(Advisory Committee Notes).

3. *Individual judge practices.* Refer to the Miscellaneous section of this document for information on individual judge practices on required documents.

## E. Format

1. *Form of documents.* The rules governing captions and other matters of form in pleadings apply to motions and other papers. FRCP 7(b)(2).

   a. *Form, generally.* All pleadings, motions, and other papers that a party presents for filing, whether in paper form or in electronic form, shall meet the following requirements:

      i. *Font size.* All text and footnotes shall be in a font size of at least twelve (12) point type. NY R USDCTWD Civ Rule 10(a)(1).

      ii. *Spacing.* All text in the body of the document must be double-spaced, except that text in block quotations and footnotes may be single-spaced. NY R USDCTWD Civ Rule 10(a)(2).

      - Extensive footnotes and block quotes may not be used to circumvent page limitations. NY R USDCTWD Civ Rule 10(a)(3).

      iii. *Margins.* Documents must have one (1) inch margins on all four sides. NY R USDCTWD Civ Rule 10(a)(4).

      iv. *Page numbering.* Pages must be consecutively numbered. NY R USDCTWD Civ Rule 10(a)(5).

b. *Additional requirements for paper filing.* Documents presented for filing in paper form shall meet the following additional requirements:

   i. *Paper.* Documents must be on durable white eight and one-half by eleven (8-1/2 x 11) inch paper of good quality. NY R USDCTWD Civ Rule 10(b)(1).

      - All documents must be single-sided. NY R USDCTWD Civ Rule 10(b)(5).

   ii. *Text.* All text must be plainly and legibly written, typewritten, printed or reproduced. NY R USDCTWD Civ Rule 10(b)(2).

   iii. *Ink.* Documents must be in black or blue ink. NY R USDCTWD Civ Rule 10(b)(3).

   iv. *Binding.* The pages of each document must be stapled or in some other way fastened together. NY R USDCTWD Civ Rule 10(b)(4).

c. *Caption; Names of parties.* Every pleading must have a caption with the court's name, a title, a file number, and a FRCP 7(a) designation. The title of the complaint must name all the parties; the title of other pleadings, after naming the first party on each side, may refer generally to other parties. FRCP 10(a).

d. *Paragraphs; Separate statements.* A party must state its claims or defenses in numbered paragraphs, each limited as far as practicable to a single set of circumstances. A later pleading may refer by number to a paragraph in an earlier pleading. If doing so would promote clarity, each claim founded on a separate transaction or occurrence—and each defense other than a denial—must be stated in a separate count or defense. FRCP 10(b).

e. *Adoption by reference; Exhibits.* A statement in a pleading may be adopted by reference elsewhere in the same pleading or in any other pleading or motion. A copy of a written instrument that is an exhibit to a pleading is a part of the pleading for all purposes. FRCP 10(c).

f. *Citation of local rules.* The Local Rules of Civil Procedure for the United States District Court for the Western District of New York shall be cited as "L.R.Civ.P." NY R USDCTWD Civ Rule 1.1.

g. *Acceptance by the clerk.* The clerk must not refuse to file a paper solely because it is not in the form prescribed by the Federal Rules of Civil Procedure or by a local rule or practice. FRCP 5(d)(4). The Court may reject documents that do not comply with the requirements in NY R USDCTWD Civ Rule 10. NY R USDCTWD Civ Rule 10.

2. *Form of electronic documents.* All pleadings, motions, and other papers that a party presents for filing, whether in paper form or in electronic form, shall meet the requirements in NY R USDCTWD Civ Rule 10(a). NY R USDCTWD Civ Rule 10(a). Refer above for more information.

   a. *Conversion to PDF.* A document created with a word processor, or a paper document, must be converted to Portable Document Format to be electronically filed with the court. NY R USDCTWD ECF Procedures(2)(a)(v).

      i. Documents which exist only in paper form may be scanned into a portable document format (PDF) for electronic filing. NY R USDCTWD ECF Procedures(2)(a)(v). Before filing a scanned document with the court, a Filing User must verify its legibility. NY R USDCTWD ECF Procedures(2)(a)(iv).

      ii. Electronic documents must be converted to .PDF from a word processing program and must be text searchable. Do not print, scan and .PDF your document when it has been created in a word processing program. Additional information on working with PDFs is located in NY R USDCTWD ECF Procedures(4b). NY R USDCTWD ECF Procedures(2)(a)(v).

   b. *Hyperlinks.* Pursuant to the policy set forth by the Judicial Conference in October 2005, a hyperlink contained in a filing is no more than a convenient mechanism for accessing material cited in a document. A hyperlink reference is extraneous to any filed document and is not part of the Court's record. NY R USDCTWD ECF Procedures(2)(a)(vi).

      i. In order to preserve the integrity of the Court record, users wishing to insert hyperlinks in Court filings shall continue to use the conventional method for the cited authority, in addition to the hyperlink. NY R USDCTWD ECF Procedures(2)(a)(vi).

    ii.   The Court accepts no responsibility for, and does not endorse any product, organization, and content at any hyperlinked site, or at any site to which that site may be linked. The Court accepts no responsibility for the availability or functionality of any hyperlink. NY R USDCTWD ECF Procedures(2)(a)(vi).

  c.  *Attachments and exhibits*

    i.   Attachments and exhibits larger than five megabytes (5 MB) shall be filed electronically in separate five megabyte (5 MB) segments. NY R USDCTWD ECF Procedures(2)(d)(i).

    ii.   Filing Users must submit in electronic form all documents referenced as exhibits or attachments, except as otherwise provided in NY R USDCTWD ECF Procedures. A Filing User must submit as exhibits or attachments only those excerpts of the referenced documents that are directly germane to the matter under consideration by the court. Excerpted material must be clearly and prominently identified as such. Filing Users who file excerpts of documents as exhibits or attachments under NY R USDCTWD ECF Procedures(2)(d)(ii) do so without prejudice to their right to timely file additional excerpts or the complete document. Responding parties may timely file additional excerpts or the complete document that they believe are directly germane. The Court may require parties to file additional excerpts or the complete document. A Filing User must request leave of the Court to file a document exhibit or attachment in non-electronic form. NY R USDCTWD ECF Procedures(2)(d)(ii).

    iii.   Exhibits offered or admitted at trial will not be filed electronically or conventionally unless so ordered by the Court. NY R USDCTWD ECF Procedures(2)(d)(iii).

    iv.   Exhibits such as videotapes and tape recordings shall be filed in the conventional manner with the Clerk of Court, and a Notice of Manual Filing shall be electronically filed by the party. Manually filed exhibits must have the case number and case name securely fastened or marked on the item. NY R USDCTWD ECF Procedures(2)(d)(iii).

    v.   Continuation of exhibit entries (for exhibits that are too large to attach to a main document) must be filed and entered on the same day that the main document was filed. NY R USDCTWD ECF Procedures(2)(d)(iv).

  d.  *Color documents.* Documents in color or containing graphics take much longer to upload. Filing users are encouraged to configure their scanners to scan documents at 200 dpi and preferably in black and white rather than color. NY R USDCTWD ECF Procedures(2)(d)(v).

  e.  *Large documents.* Due to the length of time it takes to download large files, documents larger than five megabytes (5 MB) (approximately one hundred (100) pages of a .pdf scanned document) must be filed electronically in separate five megabyte (5 MB) segments. A party who believes a document is too lengthy to electronically image (i.e. scan), may contact the Court Room Deputy for the assigned judge and request permission to file that document conventionally. If granted permission to file the document conventionally, the Filing User shall electronically file a "notice of manual filing" for that item. Exhibits submitted to the Court conventionally shall be served on other parties conventionally. NY R USDCTWD ECF Procedures(2)(d)(vi).

3.  *Signing disclosures and discovery requests, responses, and objections.* FRCP 11 does not apply to disclosures and discovery requests, responses, objections, and motions under FRCP 26 through FRCP 37. FRCP 11(d).

  a.  *Signature required.* Every disclosure under FRCP 26(a)(1) or FRCP 26(a)(3) and every discovery request, response, or objection must be signed by at least one attorney of record in the attorney's own name—or by the party personally, if unrepresented—and must state the signer's address, e-mail address, and telephone number. FRCP 26(g)(1). Documents presented for paper filing must contain an original signature. NY R USDCTWD Civ Rule 10(b)(6).

    i.   *Electronic signatures*

        •  *Non-attorney signature.* If the original document requires the signature of a non-attorney, the filing party shall obtain the signature of the non-attorney on the document. NY R USDCTWD ECF Procedures(2)(g)(i). The filing party or attorney then shall file the document electronically indicating the signatory's name in the form "s/(name)." NY R

USDCTWD ECF Procedures(2)(g)(i)(1). A non-filing signatory or party who disputes the authenticity of an electronically filed document or the authenticity of the signature on that document must file an objection to the document within ten (10) days of receiving the Notice of Electronic Filing. NY R USDCTWD ECF Procedures(2)(g)(i)(2).

- *Registered user signature.* The username and password required to file documents on the Electronic Filing System serve as the Filing User's signature on all electronic documents filed with this Court. The also serve as a signature for the purposes of FRCP 11, the Federal Rules of Civil Procedure, the Local Rules of Civil Procedure for the United States District Court for the Western District of New York, and any other purpose for which a signature is required in connection with proceedings before this Court. A pleading requiring a Registered User's signature must include a signature block in the format found in NY R USDCTWD ECF Procedures(2)(g)(iii). NY R USDCTWD ECF Procedures(2)(g)(iii). Any party challenging the authenticity of an electronically filed document or the attorney's signature on that document must file an objection to the document within ten (10) days of receiving the Notice of Electronic Filing. NY R USDCTWD ECF Procedures(2)(g)(iii)(1).

- *Multiple signatures.* The following procedure applies when a stipulation or other document requires two or more signatures: The filing party shall initially confirm that the document is acceptable to all persons required to sign the document and shall obtain the signatures of all parties on the document. NY R USDCTWD ECF Procedures(2)(g)(iv)(1). The filing party or attorney then shall file the document electronically indicating the signatories, e.g., "s/Jane Doe," "s/John Smith," etc. NY R USDCTWD ECF Procedures(2)(g)(iv)(2). A non-filing signatory or party who disputes the authenticity of an electronically filed document containing multiple signatures or the authenticity of the signatures themselves must file an objection to the document within ten (10) days of receiving the Notice of Electronic Filing. NY R USDCTWD ECF Procedures(2)(g)(iv)(3).

b. *Effect of signature.* By signing, an attorney or party certifies that to the best of the person's knowledge, information, and belief formed after a reasonable inquiry:

   i. With respect to a disclosure, it is complete and correct as of the time it is made; and

   ii. With respect to a discovery request, response, or objection, it is:

   - Consistent with the Federal Rules of Civil Procedure and warranted by existing law or by a nonfrivolous argument for extending, modifying, or reversing existing law, or for establishing new law;

   - Not interposed for any improper purpose, such as to harass, cause unnecessary delay, or needlessly increase the cost of litigation; and

   - Neither unreasonable nor unduly burdensome or expensive, considering the needs of the case, prior discovery in the case, the amount in controversy, and the importance of the issues at stake in the action. FRCP 26(g)(1).

c. *Failure to sign.* Other parties have no duty to act on an unsigned disclosure, request, response, or objection until it is signed, and the court must strike it unless a signature is promptly supplied after the omission is called to the attorney's or party's attention. FRCP 26(g)(2).

d. *Sanction for improper certification.* If a certification violates FRCP 26(g) without substantial justification, the court, on motion or on its own, must impose an appropriate sanction on the signer, the party on whose behalf the signer was acting, or both. The sanction may include an order to pay the reasonable expenses, including attorney's fees, caused by the violation. FRCP 26(g)(3). Refer to the United States District Court for the Western District of New York KeyRules Motion for Discovery Sanctions document for more information.

4. *Privacy protection for filings made with the court.* In all filings, parties shall comply with FRCP 5.2. NY R USDCTWD ECF Procedures(2)(m)(i).

   a. *Redacted filings.* Unless the court orders otherwise, in an electronic or paper filing with the court that

contains an individual's Social Security number, taxpayer-identification number, or birth date, the name of an individual known to be a minor, or a financial-account number, a party or nonparty making the filing may include only:

    i.   The last four (4) digits of the Social Security number and taxpayer-identification number;

    ii.   The year of the individual's birth;

    iii.   The minor's initials; and

    iv.   The last four (4) digits of the financial-account number. FRCP 5.2(a).

b.   *Exemptions from the redaction requirement.* The redaction requirement does not apply to the following:

    i.   A financial-account number that identifies the property allegedly subject to forfeiture in a forfeiture proceeding;

    ii.   The record of an administrative or agency proceeding;

    iii.   The official record of a state-court proceeding;

    iv.   The record of a court or tribunal, if that record was not subject to the redaction requirement when originally filed;

    v.   A filing covered by FRCP 5.2(c) or FRCP 5.2(d); and

    vi.   A pro se filing in an action brought under 28 U.S.C.A. § 2241, 28 U.S.C.A. § 2254, or 28 U.S.C.A. § 2255. FRCP 5.2(b).

c.   *Limitations on remote access to electronic files; Social Security appeals and immigration cases.* Unless the court orders otherwise, in an action for benefits under the Social Security Act, and in an action or proceeding relating to an order of removal, to relief from removal, or to immigration benefits or detention, access to an electronic file is authorized as follows:

    i.   The parties and their attorneys may have remote electronic access to any part of the case file, including the administrative record;

    ii.   Any other person may have electronic access to the full record at the courthouse, but may have remote electronic access only to:

        • The docket maintained by the court; and

        • An opinion, order, judgment, or other disposition of the court, but not any other part of the case file or the administrative record. FRCP 5.2(c).

d.   *Filings made under seal.* The court may order that a filing be made under seal without redaction. The court may later unseal the filing or order the person who made the filing to file a redacted version for the public record. FRCP 5.2(d). For more information on sealing documents, refer to NY R USDCTWD Civ Rule 5.3, NY R USDCTWD ECF Procedures(2)(o)(i)(1), NY R USDCTWD ECF Procedures(2)(o)(i)(2), and NY R USDCTWD ECF Procedures(2)(o)(i)(3).

e.   *Protective orders.* For good cause, the court may by order in a case:

    i.   Require redaction of additional information; or

    ii.   Limit or prohibit a nonparty's remote electronic access to a document filed with the court. FRCP 5.2(e).

f.   *Option for additional unredacted filing under seal.* A person making a redacted filing may also file an unredacted copy under seal. The court must retain the unredacted copy as part of the record. FRCP 5.2(f).

g.   *Option for filing a reference list.* A filing that contains redacted information may be filed together with a reference list that identifies each item of redacted information and specifies an appropriate identifier that uniquely corresponds to each item listed. The list must be filed under seal and may be amended as of right. Any reference in the case to a listed identifier will be construed to refer to the corresponding item of information. FRCP 5.2(g).

h.   *Waiver of protection of identifiers.* A person waives the protection of FRCP 5.2(a) as to the person's own information by filing it without redaction and not under seal. FRCP 5.2(h).

5. *Individual judge practices.* Refer to the Miscellaneous section of this document for information on individual judge practices on formatting documents.

## F. Filing and Service Requirements

1. *Filing requirements.* Any paper after the complaint that is required to be served—together with a certificate of service—must be filed within a reasonable time after service. But disclosures under FRCP 26(a)(1) or FRCP 26(a)(2) and the following discovery requests and responses must not be filed until they are used in the proceeding or the court orders filing: depositions, interrogatories, requests for documents or tangible things or to permit entry onto land, and requests for admission. FRCP 5(d)(1). Parties shall comply with FRCP 5(d)(1), except that in cases involving a pro se litigant, all discovery materials must be filed with the Court pursuant to NY R USDCTWD Civ Rule 5.2(f). NY R USDCTWD Civ Rule 26(f). Refer to the United States District Court for the Western District of New York KeyRules pleading and motion documents for information on filing with the court.

2. *Service requirements.* All pleadings and other papers shall be filed and served in accordance with the Federal Rules of Civil Procedure and the CM/ECF Administrative Procedures Guide. NY R USDCTWD Civ Rule 5.1(a).

   a. *Service; When required*

      i. *In general.* Unless the Federal Rules of Civil Procedure provide otherwise, each of the following papers must be served on every party:

         - An order stating that service is required;

         - A pleading filed after the original complaint, unless the court orders otherwise under FRCP 5(c) because there are numerous defendants;

         - A discovery paper required to be served on a party, unless the court orders otherwise;

         - A written motion, except one that may be heard ex parte; and

         - A written notice, appearance, demand, or offer of judgment, or any similar paper. FRCP 5(a)(1).

      ii. *If a party fails to appear.* No service is required on a party who is in default for failing to appear. But a pleading that asserts a new claim for relief against such a party must be served on that party under FRCP 4. FRCP 5(a)(2).

      iii. *Seizing property.* If an action is begun by seizing property and no person is or need be named as a defendant, any service required before the filing of an appearance, answer, or claim must be made on the person who had custody or possession of the property when it was seized. FRCP 5(a)(3).

   b. *Service; How made*

      i. *Serving an attorney.* If a party is represented by an attorney, service under FRCP 5 must be made on the attorney unless the court orders service on the party. FRCP 5(b)(1).

      ii. *Service in general.* A paper is served under FRCP 5 by:

         - Handing it to the person;

         - Leaving it: (1) at the person's office with a clerk or other person in charge or, if no one is in charge, in a conspicuous place in the office; or (2) if the person has no office or the office is closed, at the person's dwelling or usual place of abode with someone of suitable age and discretion who resides there;

         - Mailing it to the person's last known address—in which event service is complete upon mailing;

         - Leaving it with the court clerk if the person has no known address;

         - Sending it by electronic means if the person consented in writing—in which event service is complete upon transmission, but is not effective if the serving party learns that it did not reach the person to be served; or

         - Delivering it by any other means that the person consented to in writing—in which event service is complete when the person making service delivers it to the agency designated to make delivery. FRCP 5(b)(2).

iii. *Service by overnight delivery.* All papers, other than a subpoena or a summons and complaint, may be served on counsel of record by overnight delivery service at the address designated by the attorney for that purpose, or if none is designated, at the attorney's last known address. Service by overnight delivery shall be complete upon deposit of the paper(s), enclosed in a properly addressed wrapper, into the custody of the overnight delivery service, prior to the latest time designated by the service for overnight delivery. NY R USDCTWD Civ Rule 5.1(g). "Overnight delivery service" means any delivery service which regularly accepts items for overnight delivery to any address within the Court's jurisdiction. NY R USDCTWD Civ Rule 5.1(g).

iv. *Service of documents by electronic means*

- *Service on registered users.* Registered Users consent to the electronic service of all documents, and must make available an electronic mail address for service during the registration process. Upon the filing of a document by a party, a Notice of Electronic Filing, with a hyperlink to the filed document, will be automatically generated by the electronic filing system and sent via electronic mail to the e-mail addresses of all parties participating in the electronic filing system in the case. Electronic service of the Notice of Electronic Filing constitutes service of the filed document for all purposes of the Federal Rules of Civil Procedure and the Local Rules of Civil Procedure for the United States District Court for the Western District of New York. NY R USDCTWD ECF Procedures(2)(f)(i). The Notice of Electronic Filing effectuates service for all registered users and no certificate of service is required when all filers on an action are Registered Users. NY R USDCTWD ECF Procedures(2)(f)(iv).

- *Time limit for opening hyperlink.* The hyperlink to filed documents contained in the Notice of Electronic Filing must be opened within fifteen (15) days from the date the document was filed to provide registered users access to the document. The hyperlink expires after fifteen (15) days and users will be unable to access documents for free after that time. Filing Users are encouraged to check their e-mail frequently for notice of filed documents. NY R USDCTWD ECF Procedures(2)(f)(ii).

- *Service on exempted attorneys or pro se litigants who do not have permission to file electronically.* Attorneys granted an exemption from electronically filing documents in the System and pro se litigants who have not been granted permission to electronically file documents are entitled to a paper copy of any electronically filed pleading, document or order. The filing party must therefore provide the non-registered party with the pleading, document or order according to the Federal Rules of Civil Procedure. NY R USDCTWD ECF Procedures(2)(f)(iii).

- *E-mailing or faxing documents.* E-mailing or faxing a pleading or document to any party shall not constitute service of the pleading or document. NY R USDCTWD ECF Procedures(2)(f)(v).

v. *Using court facilities.* If a local rule so authorizes, a party may use the court's transmission facilities to make service under FRCP 5(b)(2)(E). FRCP 5(b)(3).

c. *Serving numerous defendants*

i. *In general.* If an action involves an unusually large number of defendants, the court may, on motion or on its own, order that:

- Defendants' pleadings and replies to them need not be served on other defendants;

- Any crossclaim, counterclaim, avoidance, or affirmative defense in those pleadings and replies to them will be treated as denied or avoided by all other parties; and

- Filing any such pleading and serving it on the plaintiff constitutes notice of the pleading to all parties. FRCP 5(c)(1).

ii. *Notifying parties.* A copy of every such order must be served on the parties as the court directs. FRCP 5(c)(2).

3. *Pro se actions.* For information on the requirements in pro se actions, refer to NY R USDCTWD Civ Rule 5.2.

4. *Individual judge practices.* Refer to the Miscellaneous section of this document for information on individual judge practices on filing and serving documents.

## G. Hearings

1. There is no hearing contemplated in the federal statutes or rules for requests for production of documents.

## H. Forms

### 1. Federal Request for Production of Documents Forms

a. Request; Production of documents for inspection and copying. AMJUR PP DEPOSITION § 498.

b. Request for production, inspection and copying of documents, and inspection and photographing of things and real property. 3A FEDFORMS § 3556.

c. Request for production of documents; Business records. 3A FEDFORMS § 3557.

d. Request for production of documents; Patent case. 3A FEDFORMS § 3558.

e. Request for production of documents; Government records and regulations. 3A FEDFORMS § 3559.

f. Request for production of documents; Government personnel files, memoranda, minutes of meetings, and statistics. 3A FEDFORMS § 3560.

g. Request for production of documents; Documents to be identified in physically separate but accompanying interrogatories under FRCP 33. 3A FEDFORMS § 3561.

h. Request for production of documents; Employment discrimination. 3A FEDFORMS § 3562.

i. Letter requesting production of files. 3A FEDFORMS § 3563.

j. Request; Production of documents, records, and objects, under FRCP 34. FEDPROF § 23:394.

k. Request; Production of documents for inspection and copying. FEDPROF § 23:395.

l. Request; Production of documents for inspection and copying; Business records. FEDPROF § 23:396.

m. Request; Production of objects for inspection and sampling. FEDPROF § 23:397.

n. Request; Production of documents for inspection and copying; Government records and files. FEDPROF § 23:398.

o. Request; Production of documents and things; Patent proceeding. FEDPROF § 23:399.

p. Request; Production of documents and things; Trademark action. FEDPROF § 23:400.

q. Request; Production of documents; Trademark action; Likelihood of confusion. FEDPROF § 23:401.

r. Request; Production of documents; Automobile negligence. FEDPROF § 23:402.

s. Request; Production of documents; Premises liability. FEDPROF § 23:403.

t. Request; Production of documents for inspection and copying; Wrongful death due to forklift accident. FEDPROF § 23:404.

u. Request; Production of documents; Products liability. FEDPROF § 23:405.

v. Request; Production of documents; Collection of tariff. FEDPROF § 23:406.

w. Request; Production of medical records. FEDPROF § 23:407.

x. Request; Production of employment records. FEDPROF § 23:408.

y. Request; Production of education records. FEDPROF § 23:409.

z. Request; Production of decedent's records. FEDPROF § 23:410.

### 2. Forms for the Western District of New York

a. Certificate of service. NY R USDCTWD ECF Procedures(4a).

# I. Applicable Rules

1. *Federal rules*

   a. Serving and filing pleadings and other papers. FRCP 5.

   b. Privacy protection for filings made with the court. FRCP 5.2.

   c. Computing and extending time; Time for motion papers. FRCP 6.

   d. Pleadings allowed; Form of motions and other papers. FRCP 7.

   e. Form of pleadings. FRCP 10.

   f. Signing pleadings, motions, and other papers; Representations to the court; Sanctions. FRCP 11.

   g. Duty to disclose; General provisions governing discovery. FRCP 26.

   h. Stipulations about discovery procedure. FRCP 29.

   i. Producing documents, electronically stored information, and tangible things, or entering onto land, for inspection and other purposes. FRCP 34.

   j. Failure to make disclosures or to cooperate in discovery; Sanctions. FRCP 37.

2. *Local rules*

   a. Title. NY R USDCTWD Civ Rule 1.1.

   b. Filing and serving papers. NY R USDCTWD Civ Rule 5.1.

   c. Form of papers. NY R USDCTWD Civ Rule 10.

   d. Sanctions. NY R USDCTWD Civ Rule 11.

   e. Alternative dispute resolution and pretrial conferences. NY R USDCTWD Civ Rule 16.

   f. General rules governing discovery. NY R USDCTWD Civ Rule 26.

   g. Stipulations. NY R USDCTWD Civ Rule 29.

   h. Depositions. NY R USDCTWD Civ Rule 30.

   i. Attorneys of record; Appearance and withdrawal. NY R USDCTWD Civ Rule 83.2.

   j. Administrative procedures guide for electronic filing. NY R USDCTWD ECF Procedures.

   k. Alternative dispute resolution plan. NY R USDCTWD ADR Plan.

# J. Miscellaneous

**NOTE: Individual judges' rules may apply. For available judge-level information, refer to:**

DISTRICT JUDGE RICHARD J. ARCARA: NY R USDCTWD Arcara-Procedures.

DISTRICT JUDGE FRANK P. GERACI, JR.: NY R USDCTWD Geraci-Procedures.

DISTRICT JUDGE DAVID G. LARIMER: NY R USDCTWD Larimer-Procedures.

DISTRICT JUDGE CHARLES J. SIRAGUSA: NY R USDCTWD Siragusa-Procedures.

DISTRICT JUDGE WILLIAM M. SKRETNY: NY R USDCTWD Skretny--Procedures.

DISTRICT JUDGE MICHAEL A. TELESCA: NY R USDCTWD Telesca-Procedures.

DISTRICT JUDGE LAWRENCE J. VILARDO: NY R USDCTWD Vilardo-Procedures.

DISTRICT JUDGE ELIZABETH A. WOLFORD: NY R USDCTWD Wolford-Procedures.

MAGISTRATE JUDGE JONATHAN W. FELDMAN: NY R USDCTWD Feldman-Procedures.

MAGISTRATE JUDGE LESLIE G. FOSCHIO: NY R USDCTWD Foschio-Procedures; NY R USDCTWD Foschio-Depositions.

MAGISTRATE JUDGE JEREMIAH J. McCARTHY: NY R USDCTWD McCarthy-Procedures.

MAGISTRATE JUDGE MARIAN W. PAYSON: NY R USDCTWD Payson-Procedures.

MAGISTRATE JUDGE MICHAEL J. ROEMER: NY R USDCTWD Roemer-Procedures.

MAGISTRATE JUDGE H. KENNETH SCHROEDER, JR.: NY R USDCTWD Schroeder-Proc.

MAGISTRATE JUDGE HUGH B. SCOTT: NY R USDCTWD Scott-Procedures.

# Requests, Notices and Applications
# Request for Admissions

## Document Last Updated September 2016

## A. Checklist

(I) ❑ Matters to be considered by requesting party

    (a) ❑ Required documents

        (1) ❑ Request for admissions

        (2) ❑ Electronic courtesy copy

    (b) ❑ Supplemental documents

        (1) ❑ Document(s)

        (2) ❑ Certificate of service

    (c) ❑ Timing

        (1) ❑ A party may not seek discovery from any source before the parties have conferred as required by FRCP 26(f), except in a proceeding exempted from initial disclosure under FRCP 26(a)(1)(B), or when authorized by the Federal Rules of Civil Procedure, by stipulation, or by court order

(II) ❑ Matters to be considered by responding party

    (a) ❑ Required documents

        (1) ❑ Response to request for admissions

    (b) ❑ Supplemental documents

        (1) ❑ Certificate of service

    (c) ❑ Timing

        (1) ❑ A matter is admitted unless, within thirty (30) days after being served, the party to whom the request is directed serves on the requesting party a written answer or objection addressed to the matter and signed by the party or its attorney

## B. Timing

1. *Request for admissions.* Without leave of court or written stipulation, requests for admission may not be served before the time specified in FRCP 26(d). FEDPROC § 26:706.

2. *Timing of discovery, generally.* A party may not seek discovery from any source before the parties have conferred as required by FRCP 26(f), except in a proceeding exempted from initial disclosure under FRCP 26(a)(1)(B), or when authorized by the Federal Rules of Civil Procedure, by stipulation, or by court order. FRCP 26(d)(1).

3. *Computation of time*

    a. *Computing time.* FRCP 6 applies in computing any time period specified in the Federal Rules of Civil Procedure, in any local rule or court order, or in any statute that does not specify a method of computing time. FRCP 6(a).

        i. *Period stated in days or a longer unit.* When the period is stated in days or a longer unit of time:

            • Exclude the day of the event that triggers the period;

            • Count every day, including intermediate Saturdays, Sundays, and legal holidays; and

            • Include the last day of the period, but if the last day is a Saturday, Sunday, or legal holiday, the period continues to run until the end of the next day that is not a Saturday, Sunday, or legal holiday. FRCP 6(a)(1).

ii. *Period stated in hours.* When the period is stated in hours:

- Begin counting immediately on the occurrence of the event that triggers the period;

- Count every hour, including hours during intermediate Saturdays, Sundays, and legal holidays; and

- If the period would end on a Saturday, Sunday, or legal holiday, the period continues to run until the same time on the next day that is not a Saturday, Sunday, or legal holiday. FRCP 6(a)(2).

iii. *Inaccessibility of the clerk's office.* Unless the court orders otherwise, if the clerk's office is inaccessible:

- On the last day for filing under FRCP 6(a)(1), then the time for filing is extended to the first accessible day that is not a Saturday, Sunday, or legal holiday; or

- During the last hour for filing under FRCP 6(a)(2), then the time for filing is extended to the same time on the first accessible day that is not a Saturday, Sunday, or legal holiday. FRCP 6(a)(3).

iv. *"Last day" defined.* Unless a different time is set by a statute, local rule, or court order, the last day ends:

- For electronic filing, at midnight in the court's time zone; and

- For filing by other means, when the clerk's office is scheduled to close. FRCP 6(a)(4).

v. *"Next day" defined.* The "next day" is determined by continuing to count forward when the period is measured after an event and backward when measured before an event. FRCP 6(a)(5).

vi. *"Legal holiday" defined.* "Legal holiday" means:

- The day set aside by statute for observing New Year's Day, Martin Luther King Jr.'s Birthday, Washington's Birthday, Memorial Day, Independence Day, Labor Day, Columbus Day, Veterans' Day, Thanksgiving Day, or Christmas Day;

- Any day declared a holiday by the President or Congress; and

- For periods that are measured after an event, any other day declared a holiday by the state where the district court is located. FRCP 6(a)(6).

b. *Computation of electronic filing deadlines.* A document will be deemed timely filed if filed prior to midnight Eastern Time, unless otherwise ordered by the Court. A document will be considered untimely if filed thereafter. When a Court order requires that a document be filed on a weekend or holiday, the document may be filed by close of business the next business day without further application to the Court. NY R USDCTWD ECF Procedures(2)(e)(i). A document filed electronically is deemed filed on the date and time stated on the Notice of Electronic Filing. NY R USDCTWD ECF Procedures(2)(e)(ii).

i. *System availability.* Although parties may file documents electronically twenty-four (24) hours a day, registered users are strongly encouraged to file all documents during normal working hours of the Clerk's Office (8:30 a.m. to 5:00 p.m. Eastern Time). NY R USDCTWD ECF Procedures(2)(t)(i).

ii. *Technical failures.* A Filing User whose filing is made untimely as a result of a technical failure must seek appropriate relief from the Court. NY R USDCTWD ECF Procedures(2)(u)(i).

c. *Extending time*

i. *In general.* When an act may or must be done within a specified time, the court may, for good cause, extend the time:

- With or without motion or notice if the court acts, or if a request is made, before the original time or its extension expires; or

- On motion made after the time has expired if the party failed to act because of excusable neglect. FRCP 6(b)(1).

   ii. *Exceptions.* A court must not extend the time to act under FRCP 50(b), FRCP 50(d), FRCP 52(b), FRCP 59(b), FRCP 59(d), FRCP 59(e), and FRCP 60(b). FRCP 6(b)(2).

   iii. Refer to the United States District Court for the Western District of New York KeyRules Motion for Continuance/Extension of Time document for more information on extending time.

   d. *Additional time after certain kinds of service.* When a party may or must act within a specified time after service and service is made under FRCP 5(b)(2)(C), FRCP 5(b)(2)(D), FRCP 5(b)(2)(E), or FRCP 5(b)(2)(F), three (3) days are added after the period would otherwise expire under FRCP 6(a). FRCP 6(d).

   i. *Service by overnight delivery.* Where a period of time prescribed by either the Federal Rules of Civil Procedure or the Local Rules of Civil Procedure for the United States District Court for the Western District of New York is measured from the service of a paper and service is by overnight delivery, one (1) business day shall be added to the prescribed period. NY R USDCTWD Civ Rule 5.1(g).

4. *Individual judge practices.* Refer to the Miscellaneous section of this document for information on individual judge practices on timing of documents.

## C. General Requirements

1. *General provisions governing discovery*

   a. *Discovery scope and limits*

   i. *Scope in general.* Unless otherwise limited by court order, the scope of discovery is as follows: Parties may obtain discovery regarding any nonprivileged matter that is relevant to any party's claim or defense and proportional to the needs of the case, considering the importance of the issues at stake in the action, the amount in controversy, the parties' relative access to relevant information, the parties' resources, the importance of the discovery in resolving the issues, and whether the burden or expense of the proposed discovery outweighs its likely benefit. Information within this scope of discovery need not be admissible in evidence to be discoverable. FRCP 26(b)(1).

   ii. *Limitations on frequency and extent*

   - *When permitted.* By order, the court may alter the limits in the Federal Rules of Civil Procedure on the number of depositions and interrogatories or on the length of depositions under FRCP 30. By order or local rule, the court may also limit the number of requests under FRCP 36. FRCP 26(b)(2)(A).

   - *Specific limitations on electronically stored information.* A party need not provide discovery of electronically stored information from sources that the party identifies as not reasonably accessible because of undue burden or cost. On motion to compel discovery or for a protective order, the party from whom discovery is sought must show that the information is not reasonably accessible because of undue burden or cost. If that showing is made, the court may nonetheless order discovery from such sources if the requesting party shows good cause, considering the limitations of FRCP 26(b)(2)(C). The court may specify conditions for the discovery. FRCP 26(b)(2)(B).

   - *When required.* On motion or on its own, the court must limit the frequency or extent of discovery otherwise allowed by the Federal Rules of Civil Procedure or by local rule if it determines that: (1) the discovery sought is unreasonably cumulative or duplicative, or can be obtained from some other source that is more convenient, less burdensome, or less expensive; (2) the party seeking discovery has had ample opportunity to obtain the information by discovery in the action; or (3) the proposed discovery is outside the scope permitted by FRCP 26(b)(1). FRCP 26(b)(2)(C).

   iii. *Trial preparation; Materials*

   - *Documents and tangible things.* Ordinarily, a party may not discover documents and tangible things that are prepared in anticipation of litigation or for trial by or for another party or its representative (including the other party's attorney, consultant, surety, indemnitor, insurer, or agent). But, subject to FRCP 26(b)(4), those materials may be discovered if: (1) they are otherwise discoverable under FRCP 26(b)(1); and (2) the party shows that it has substantial need for the materials to prepare its case and cannot, without undue hardship, obtain their substantial equivalent by other means. FRCP 26(b)(3)(A).

- *Protection against disclosure.* If the court orders discovery of those materials, it must protect against disclosure of the mental impressions, conclusions, opinions, or legal theories of a party's attorney or other representative concerning the litigation. FRCP 26(b)(3)(B).

- *Previous statement.* Any party or other person may, on request and without the required showing, obtain the person's own previous statement about the action or its subject matter. If the request is refused, the person may move for a court order, and FRCP 37(a)(5) applies to the award of expenses. A previous statement is either: (1) a written statement that the person has signed or otherwise adopted or approved; or (2) a contemporaneous stenographic, mechanical, electrical, or other recording—or a transcription of it—that recites substantially verbatim the person's oral statement. FRCP 26(b)(3)(C).

iv. *Trial preparation; Experts*

- *Deposition of an expert who may testify.* A party may depose any person who has been identified as an expert whose opinions may be presented at trial. If FRCP 26(a)(2)(B) requires a report from the expert, the deposition may be conducted only after the report is provided. FRCP 26(b)(4)(A).

- *Trial-preparation protection for draft reports or disclosures.* FRCP 26(b)(3)(A) and FRCP 26(b)(3)(B) protect drafts of any report or disclosure required under FRCP 26(a)(2), regardless of the form in which the draft is recorded. FRCP 26(b)(4)(B).

- *Trial-preparation protection for communications between a party's attorney and expert witnesses.* FRCP 26(b)(3)(A) and FRCP 26(b)(3)(B) protect communications between the party's attorney and any witness required to provide a report under FRCP 26(a)(2)(B), regardless of the form of the communications, except to the extent that the communications: (1) relate to compensation for the expert's study or testimony; (2) identify facts or data that the party's attorney provided and that the expert considered in forming the opinions to be expressed; or (3) identify assumptions that the party's attorney provided and that the expert relied on in forming the opinions to be expressed. FRCP 26(b)(4)(C).

- *Expert employed only for trial preparation.* Ordinarily, a party may not, by interrogatories or deposition, discover facts known or opinions held by an expert who has been retained or specially employed by another party in anticipation of litigation or to prepare for trial and who is not expected to be called as a witness at trial. But a party may do so only: (1) as provided in FRCP 35(b); or (2) on showing exceptional circumstances under which it is impracticable for the party to obtain facts or opinions on the same subject by other means. FRCP 26(b)(4)(D).

- *Payment.* Unless manifest injustice would result, the court must require that the party seeking discovery: (1) pay the expert a reasonable fee for time spent in responding to discovery under FRCP 26(b)(4)(A) or FRCP 26(b)(4)(D); and (2) for discovery FRCP 26(b)(4)(D), also pay the other party a fair portion of the fees and expenses it reasonably incurred in obtaining the expert's facts and opinions. FRCP 26(b)(4)(E).

v. *Claiming privilege or protecting trial-preparation materials*

- *Information withheld.* When a party withholds information otherwise discoverable by claiming that the information is privileged or subject to protection as trial-preparation material, the party must: (1) expressly make the claim; and (2) describe the nature of the documents, communications, or tangible things not produced or disclosed—and do so in a manner that, without revealing information itself privileged or protected, will enable other parties to assess the claim. FRCP 26(b)(5)(A). Where a party asserts a claim of privilege in objecting to any means of discovery or disclosure, and withholds otherwise responsive information based on that assertion: (1) the party asserting the privilege shall identify the nature of the privilege (including work product) being claimed and, if the privilege is governed by state law, indicate the state's privilege rule being invoked; and (2) shall provide the following information, unless to divulge such information would cause disclosure of the allegedly privileged information: (i) for documents: (a) the type of document, i.e., letter or memorandum; (b) the general subject matter of the document; (c) the date of the document; and (d) such other information as is sufficient to identify the document for a subpoena duces tecum, including, where appropriate, the author of the document, the addressees of the document, and any other recipients shown in the document, and, where not apparent, the relationship of the author, addressees, and recipients to each other; (ii) for oral communications: (a) the names of the person making the communication and the person(s) present while the communication was made and, where not apparent, the relationship of the person making the communication to the person(s) present; (b) the date and place of communication; and (c) its general subject matter. NY R USDCTWD Civ Rule 26(d)(1).

- *Information produced.* If information produced in discovery is subject to a claim of privilege or of protection as trial-preparation material, the party making the claim may notify any party that received the information of the claim and the basis for it. After being notified, a party must promptly return, sequester, or destroy the specified information and any copies it has; must not use or disclose the information until the claim is resolved; must take reasonable steps to retrieve the information if the party disclosed it before being notified; and may promptly present the information to the court under seal for a determination of the claim. The producing party must preserve the information until the claim is resolved. FRCP 26(b)(5)(B). Where the claim of privilege is asserted in response to discovery or disclosure other than at a deposition, the information set forth in NY R USDCTWD Civ Rule 26(d)(1) shall be furnished in writing when the party responds to such discovery or disclosure, unless otherwise ordered by the Court. NY R USDCTWD Civ Rule 26(d)(2). Where the claim of privilege is asserted during a deposition, the information set forth in NY R USDCTWD Civ Rule 26(d)(1) shall be furnished: (1) at the deposition, to the extent it is readily available from the witness being deposed or otherwise, and (2) to the extent it not readily available, in writing within fourteen (14) days after the privilege is asserted, unless otherwise ordered by the Court. NY R USDCTWD Civ Rule 26(d)(3).

b. *Protective orders.* A party or any person from whom discovery is sought may move for a protective order in the court where the action is pending—or as an alternative on matters relating to a deposition, in the court for the district where the deposition will be taken. FRCP 26(c)(1). Refer to the United States District Court for the Western District of New York KeyRules Motion for Protective Order document for more information.

c. *Sequence of discovery.* Unless the parties stipulate or the court orders otherwise for the parties' and witnesses' convenience and in the interests of justice: (1) methods of discovery may be used in any sequence; and (2) discovery by one party does not require any other party to delay its discovery. FRCP 26(d)(3).

d. *Uniform definitions for all discovery requests.* The full text of the definitions and rules of construction set forth in NY R USDCTWD Civ Rule 26(c)(3) and NY R USDCTWD Civ Rule 26(c)(4) is deemed incorporated by reference into all discovery requests. No discovery request shall use broader definitions or rules of construction than those set forth in NY R USDCTWD Civ Rule 26(c)(3) and NY R USDCTWD Civ Rule 26(c)(4). NY R USDCTWD Civ Rule 26(c) shall not preclude (1) the definition of other terms specific to the particular litigation, (2) the use of abbreviations, or (3) a more narrow definition of a term defined in NY R USDCTWD Civ Rule 26(c)(3). NY R USDCTWD Civ

Rule 26(c)(1). NY R USDCTWD Civ Rule 26(c) is not intended to broaden or narrow the scope of discovery permitted by the Federal Rules of Civil Procedure. NY R USDCTWD Civ Rule 26(c)(2).

i. *Definitions.* The following definitions apply to all discovery requests:

- *Communication.* The term "communication" means the transmittal of information (in the form of facts, ideas, inquiries or otherwise). NY R USDCTWD Civ Rule 26(c)(3)(A).

- *Document.* The term "document" is defined to be synonymous in meaning and equal in scope to the usage of this term in FRCP 34(a), including, without limitation, electronic or computerized data compilations. A draft or non-identical copy is a separate document within the meaning of this term. NY R USDCTWD Civ Rule 26(c)(3)(B).

- *Identify (with respect to persons).* When referring to a person, "to identify" means to give, to the extent known, the person's full name, present or last known address, and when referring to a natural person, the present or last known place of employment. Once a person has been identified in accordance with NY R USDCTWD Civ Rule 26(c)(3)(C), only the person's name need be listed in response to subsequent discovery requesting the identification of that person. NY R USDCTWD Civ Rule 26(c)(3)(C).

- *Identify (with respect to documents).* When referring to documents, "to identify" means to give, to the extent known, the (1) type of document; (2) general subject matter; (3) date of the document; and (4) author(s), addressee(s), and recipients(s). NY R USDCTWD Civ Rule 26(c)(3)(D).

- *Parties.* The terms "plaintiff" and "defendant," as well as a party's full or abbreviated name or a pronoun referring to a party, mean the party and, where applicable, its officers, directors, employees, partners, corporate parent, subsidiaries, or affiliates. This definition is not intended to impose a discovery obligation on any person who is not a party to the litigation. NY R USDCTWD Civ Rule 26(c)(3)(E).

- *Person.* The term "person" is defined as any natural person or any business, legal or governmental entity, or association. NY R USDCTWD Civ Rule 26(c)(3)(F).

- *Concerning.* The term "concerning" means relating to, referring to, describing, evidencing or constituting. NY R USDCTWD Civ Rule 26(c)(3)(G).

ii. *Rules of construction.* The following rules of construction apply to all discovery requests:

- *All/each.* The terms "all" and "each" shall be construed as all and each. NY R USDCTWD Civ Rule 26(c)(4)(A).

- *And/or.* The connectives "and" and "or" shall be construed either disjunctively or conjunctively as necessary to bring within the scope of the discovery request all responses that might otherwise be construed to be outside of its scope. NY R USDCTWD Civ Rule 26(c)(4)(B).

- *Number.* The use of the singular form of any word includes the plural and vice versa. NY R USDCTWD Civ Rule 26(c)(4)(C).

e. *Electronically stored information (ESI).* Discovery of relevant electronically stored information shall proceed as follows:

i. *Searches and production of ESI.* After receiving requests for document production, the parties shall search their documents, including ESI other than ESI that has been identified as not reasonably accessible, and produce relevant responsive ESI in accordance with FRCP 26(b)(2). NY R USDCTWD Civ Rule 26(e)(1).

ii. *Non-accessible ESI.* Searches and production of ESI identified as not reasonably accessible shall not be required to be conducted until the initial disclosure of reasonably accessible ESI has been completed. Requests for information expected to be found in ESI that is not reasonably accessible must be narrowly focused with some basis in fact supporting the request, and good cause must be provided. The party seeking such discovery may be required to pay all or a portion of the costs of search, retrieval, review, and production of the information, upon application to the Court. NY R USDCTWD Civ Rule 26(e)(2).

    iii.   *Search methodology.* If a party intends to employ an electronic search to locate relevant ESI, the parties shall discuss and attempt to reach agreement as to the method of searching, and the words, terms, and phrases to be searched and any restrictions as to scope and method which might affect their ability to conduct a complete electronic search of the ESI. The parties shall also attempt to reach agreement as to the timing and conditions of any additional searches which may become necessary in the normal course of discovery. To minimize undue expense, the parties may consider limiting the scope of the electronic search (i.e., time frames, fields, document types). NY R USDCTWD Civ Rule 26(e)(3).

    iv.   *Metadata.* Except as otherwise provided, metadata, especially substantive metadata, need not be routinely produced, except upon agreement of the requesting and producing litigants, or upon a showing of good cause in a motion filed by the requesting party. NY R USDCTWD Civ Rule 26(e)(4).

    v.   *Format.* If the parties have not agreed or cannot agree to the format for document production, ESI shall be produced to the requesting party as image files (i.e. PDF or TIFF). When the image file is produced, the producing party must preserve the integrity of the electronic document's contents, i.e., the original formatting of the document, its metadata and, where applicable, its revision history. After initial production in image file format is complete, a party must demonstrate particularized need for production of ESI in its native format. NY R USDCTWD Civ Rule 26(e)(5).

    vi.   *Costs.* Generally, the costs of discovery, other than the costs associated with ESI that is not reasonably accessible, shall be borne by each party. However, the Court will apportion the costs of discovery or presentation of ESI, including discovery of ESI that is not reasonably accessible, upon a showing of good cause, or unequal burdens, or unreasonable request. NY R USDCTWD Civ Rule 26(e)(6).

  f.  *Cooperation among counsel in the discovery context.* See the Civility Principles of the United States District Court for the Western District of New York which can be found on the Court's website. NY R USDCTWD Civ Rule 26(g).

2.  *Request for admissions*

  a.  *Scope.* A party may serve on any other party a written request to admit, for purposes of the pending action only, the truth of any matters within the scope of FRCP 26(b)(1) relating to: (1) facts, the application of law to fact, or opinions about either; and (2) the genuineness of any described documents. FRCP 36(a)(1).

    i.   A party may serve a request for admission even though the party has the burden of proving the matters asserted therein because FRCP 36 permits requests for admission to address claims of the party seeking discovery, and generally, the party asserting a claim bears the burden of proof thereon. FEDPROC § 26:715.

  b.  *Number.* FRCP 36 does not limit a party to a single request, or set of requests, for admissions. But FRCP 26(b)(2)(A) authorizes courts to limit the number of requests by order or local rule. In addition, the court has power to protect a party from harassment by repeated requests for admissions, but will not bar such repeated requests when the circumstances of the case justify them. Even a second request about the same fact or the genuineness of the same document is permissible if circumstances warrant a renewed request. FPP § 2258.

  c.  *Form.* Each matter must be separately stated. FRCP 36(a)(2). The party called upon to respond should not be required to go through a document and assume the responsibility of determining what facts it is being requested to admit. FPP § 2258. Each request for an admission should be phrased simply and directly so that it can be admitted or denied without explanation. FPP § 2258; United Coal Cos. v. Powell Const. Co., 839 F.2d 958, 968 (3d Cir. 1988).

    i.   A request for an admission need not state the source of information about the matter for which the request is made. FPP § 2258.

  d.  *Numbering.* The parties shall sequentially number each interrogatory or discovery request. NY R USDCTWD Civ Rule 26(b).

e. *Effect of an admission; Withdrawing or amending it.* A matter admitted under FRCP 36 is conclusively established unless the court, on motion, permits the admission to be withdrawn or amended. Subject to FRCP 16(e), the court may permit withdrawal or amendment if it would promote the presentation of the merits of the action and if the court is not persuaded that it would prejudice the requesting party in maintaining or defending the action on the merits. An admission under FRCP 36 is not an admission for any other purpose and cannot be used against the party in any other proceeding. FRCP 36(b).

f. *Motion to compel.* The motion to compel discovery provided by FRCP 37(a) does not apply to a failure to respond to a request for admissions. The automatic admission from a failure to respond is a sufficient remedy for the party who made the request. If, however, a request is objected to, or the requesting party thinks that a response to a request is insufficient, it may move under FRCP 36(a)(6) to determine the sufficiency of the answers or objections. FPP § 2265.

g. *Motion regarding the sufficiency of an answer or objection.* The requesting party may move to determine the sufficiency of an answer or objection. Unless the court finds an objection justified, it must order that an answer be served. On finding that an answer does not comply with FRCP 36, the court may order either that the matter is admitted or that an amended answer be served. The court may defer its final decision until a pretrial conference or a specified time before trial. FRCP 37(a)(5) applies to an award of expenses. FRCP 36(a)(6). Refer to the United States District Court for the Western District of New York KeyRules Motion for Discovery Sanctions document for more information on sanctions.

3. *Sanctions for failure to cooperate in discovery.* The pattern of sanctions for FRCP 36 is somewhat different from that for the other discovery rules. The most important sanctions are two:

   a. A failure to respond to a request is deemed an admission of the matter to which the request is directed; and

   b. A party who, without good reason, refuses to admit a matter will be required to pay the costs incurred in proving that matter. FPP § 2265. If a party fails to admit what is requested under FRCP 36 and if the requesting party later proves a document to be genuine or the matter true, the requesting party may move that the party who failed to admit pay the reasonable expenses, including attorney's fees, incurred in making that proof. The court must so order unless:

      i. The request was held objectionable under FRCP 36(a);

      ii. The admission sought was of no substantial importance;

      iii. The party failing to admit had a reasonable ground to believe that it might prevail on the matter; or

      iv. There was other good reason for the failure to admit. FRCP 37(c)(2).

   c. Refer to the United States District Court for the Western District of New York KeyRules Motion for Discovery Sanctions document for more information on sanctions.

4. *Stipulations about discovery procedure.* Unless the court orders otherwise, the parties may stipulate that: (1) a deposition may be taken before any person, at any time or place, on any notice, and in the manner specified—in which event it may be used in the same way as any other deposition; and (2) other procedures governing or limiting discovery be modified—but a stipulation extending the time for any form of discovery must have court approval if it would interfere with the time set for completing discovery, for hearing a motion, or for trial. FRCP 29. All stipulations, except stipulations made in open court and recorded by the court reporter, shall be in writing and signed by each attorney and/or pro se litigant. The parties shall determine who will be responsible for filing, and a copy of the stipulation, with signatures conformed (e.g., "s/Jane Doe," "s/John Smith"), shall be filed electronically. The Court will act on the filed stipulation, as necessary and appropriate. NY R USDCTWD Civ Rule 29.

5. *Notice of appearance.* No notice of appearance is required of an attorney whose name and address appear at the end of a complaint, notice of removal, pre-answer motion, or answer. In all other circumstances, an attorney appearing for a party in a civil case shall promptly file a written notice of appearance. NY R USDCTWD Civ Rule 83.2(b). For more information on appearances and withdrawals, refer to NY R USDCTWD Civ Rule 83.2.

6.  *Related cases.* Each attorney appearing in a civil case has a continuing duty to promptly notify the Clerk of Court when the attorney has reason to believe that said case is related to some other pending civil or criminal action(s) such that their assignment to the same Judge would avoid unnecessary duplication of judicial effort. As soon as the attorney becomes aware of such a relationship, the attorney shall notify the Clerk of Court by letter of the relevant facts, and the Clerk of Court will transmit that notification to the Judges to whom the cases have been assigned. NY R USDCTWD Civ Rule 5.1(e).

7.  *Alternative dispute resolution (ADR).* This Court has adopted an Alternative Dispute Resolution Plan ("ADR"), as implemented by Standing Order (NY R USDCTWD ADR Plan), under which certain civil cases are referred automatically to ADR upon filing. NY R USDCTWD Civ Rule 16(a). The United States District Court for the Western District of New York (the "Court") adopted the ADR Plan on January 1, 2006 (the "Effective Date"), to make available to civil litigants court-administered ADR interventions and processes designed to provide quicker, less expensive and potentially more satisfying alternatives to continuing litigation, without impairing the quality of justice or the right to trial. NY R USDCTWD ADR Plan(1)(1.2)(A).

    a.  *Scope.* This ADR Plan (NY R USDCTWD ADR Plan) applies to civil actions pending or commenced on and after the Effective Date, except as otherwise indicated in NY R USDCTWD ADR Plan. The ADR Plan supplements the Local Rules of Civil Procedure for the United States District Court for the Western District of New York, which shall remain in full effect for all cases. NY R USDCTWD ADR Plan(1)(1.2)(B).

    b.  *Referral to ADR*

        i.  *New cases.* All civil cases filed on and after the Effective Date of the ADR Plan shall be referred automatically for ADR. NY R USDCTWD ADR Plan(2)(2.1)(A). Notice of the ADR requirements will be provided to all parties immediately upon the filing of a complaint and answer or a notice of removal; NY R USDCTWD ADR Plan(2)(2.1)(A); NY R USDCTWD Civ Rule 16(a). ADR intervention will be scheduled at the conference held pursuant to Local Rule of Civil Procedure 16.1. NY R USDCTWD ADR Plan(2)(2.1)(A). [Editor's note: the reference to Local Rule of Civil Procedure 16.1 is likely meant to be a reference to NY R USDCTWD Civ Rule 16(b)].

            •   Litigants in cases not referred automatically to ADR must consider possible agreement to the use of an ADR process. NY R USDCTWD Civ Rule 16(a).

            •   For a list of exemptions from automatic referral, refer to NY R USDCTWD ADR Plan(2)(2.1)(A).

        ii. *Pending cases.* The assigned Judge on any pending civil case may, sua sponte or with status conference, issue an order referring the case for ADR. NY R USDCTWD ADR Plan(2)(2.1)(B); NY R USDCTWD Civ Rule 16(a). The order shall specify a date on which the ADR intervention is to be completed. NY R USDCTWD ADR Plan(2)(2.1)(B).

        iii. *Stipulation.* A case may be referred for ADR by stipulation of all parties. Stipulations shall be filed and shall designate the specific ADR intervention the parties have selected, the time frame within which the ADR process will be completed and the selected Neutral. Stipulations are presumed acceptable unless the assigned Judge determines that the interests of justice are not served. NY R USDCTWD ADR Plan(2)(2.1)(C).

        iv. *Relief from ADR referral*

            •   *Opting out motions.* Any party may file, with the assigned Judge for that case, a motion to opt out of, or for relief from, ADR. NY R USDCTWD ADR Plan(2)(2.2)(A).

            •   *Motion.* Opting Out Motions must be made within fourteen (14) days from (1) the date of the first discovery conference under Local Rule 16.1 in new cases, or (2) the date of a sua sponte ADR Referral Order in pending cases. NY R USDCTWD ADR Plan(2)(2.2)(B). [Editor's note: the reference to Local Rule 16.1 is likely meant to be a reference to NY R USDCTWD Civ Rule 16(b)].

            •   *Criteria.* Opting Out Motions shall be granted only for "good cause" shown. Inconvenience, travel costs, attorney fees or other costs shall not constitute "good cause." A party seeking relief from ADR must set forth the reasons why ADR has no reasonable chance of being productive. NY R USDCTWD ADR Plan(2)(2.2)(C).

- *Judicial initiative.* The assigned Judge may, sua sponte, exempt any case from the Court's ADR Plan. NY R USDCTWD ADR Plan(2)(2.2)(D).

c. *ADR interventions*

   i. *Options.* It is expected that cases referred for ADR will proceed to Mediation. However, the following options are also available upon the stipulation of all parties:

- Neutral Evaluation;
- Mini Summary Trial;
- Arbitration (Binding and Non-Binding);
- Case Valuation; and
- Settlement Week, when scheduled by the Court. NY R USDCTWD ADR Plan(4)(4.1)(A).

   ii. *Timing.* Timing is specific to the intervention and process chosen, as set forth in the corresponding sections in NY R USDCTWD ADR Plan. NY R USDCTWD ADR Plan(4)(4.1)(B).

   iii. *Scheduling.* The referral of a case to ADR does not delay or defer other dates established in the Scheduling Order and has no effect on the scheduled progress of the case toward trial. NY R USDCTWD ADR Plan(4)(4.1)(C).

d. *Selecting an ADR intervention*

   i. *New cases.* Prior to the Local Rule 16.1 scheduling conference, counsel and any unrepresented parties shall confer about ADR as part of their discussion of "the possibilities for a prompt settlement or resolution of the case" pursuant to FRCP 26(f). Unless the parties agree to a different intervention, it is presumed that they will participate in mediation. [Editor's note: the reference to Local Rule 16.1 is likely meant to be a reference to NY R USDCTWD Civ Rule 16(b)].

   ii. *Pending cases.* In pending cases, all sua sponte referrals will be to mediation. Should the parties agree that a different ADR intervention is more appropriate to their case, they may submit a stipulation designating the specific ADR intervention selected, the time frame within which the ADR process will be completed and the identity of the Neutral. Stipulations must be filed within fourteen (14) days from the date of the ADR Referral Order and are presumed acceptable unless the assigned Judge determines that the interests of justice are not served. NY R USDCTWD ADR Plan(4)(4.2)(B).

e. For more information on alternative dispute resolution (ADR), refer to NY R USDCTWD ADR Plan.

8. *Sanctions.* Failure of counsel for any party, or a party proceeding pro se, to appear before the Court at a conference, to complete the necessary preparations, or to be prepared to proceed to trial at the set time may be considered an abandonment of the case or a failure to prosecute or defend diligently. An appropriate order for sanctions may be entered against the defaulting party with respect to either a specific issue or the entire case. NY R USDCTWD Civ Rule 11(a). For more information, refer to NY R USDCTWD Civ Rule 11.

9. *Pro se actions.* For information on the requirements in pro se actions, refer to NY R USDCTWD Civ Rule 5.2.

10. *Individual judge practices.* Refer to the Miscellaneous section of this document for information on individual judge practices on general requirements for documents.

## D. Documents

1. *Required documents*

a. *Request for admissions.* Refer to the General Requirements section of this document for information on the request for admissions.

b. *Electronic courtesy copy.* In addition to service pursuant to FRCP 5, the party to whom interrogatories or discovery requests are directed shall, whenever practicable, be supplied with an electronic courtesy copy of the served document in a word processing format. NY R USDCTWD Civ Rule 26(b).

2. *Supplemental documents*

 a. *Document(s).* A request to admit the genuineness of a document must be accompanied by a copy of the document unless it is, or has been, otherwise furnished or made available for inspection and copying. FRCP 36(a)(2).

 b. *Certificate of service.* FRCP 5(d) requires that the person making service under FRCP 5 certify that service has been effected. FRCP 5(Advisory Committee Notes). Having such information on file may be useful for many purposes, including proof of service if an issue arises concerning the effectiveness of the service. FRCP 5(Advisory Committee Notes).

3. *Individual judge practices.* Refer to the Miscellaneous section of this document for information on individual judge practices on required documents.

## E. Format

1. *Form of documents.* The rules governing captions and other matters of form in pleadings apply to motions and other papers. FRCP 7(b)(2).

 a. *Form, generally.* All pleadings, motions, and other papers that a party presents for filing, whether in paper form or in electronic form, shall meet the following requirements:

 i. *Font size.* All text and footnotes shall be in a font size of at least twelve (12) point type. NY R USDCTWD Civ Rule 10(a)(1).

 ii. *Spacing.* All text in the body of the document must be double-spaced, except that text in block quotations and footnotes may be single-spaced. NY R USDCTWD Civ Rule 10(a)(2).

 • Extensive footnotes and block quotes may not be used to circumvent page limitations. NY R USDCTWD Civ Rule 10(a)(3).

 iii. *Margins.* Documents must have one (1) inch margins on all four sides. NY R USDCTWD Civ Rule 10(a)(4).

 iv. *Page numbering.* Pages must be consecutively numbered. NY R USDCTWD Civ Rule 10(a)(5).

 b. *Additional requirements for paper filing.* Documents presented for filing in paper form shall meet the following additional requirements:

 i. *Paper.* Documents must be on durable white eight and one-half by eleven (8-1/2 x 11) inch paper of good quality. NY R USDCTWD Civ Rule 10(b)(1).

 • All documents must be single-sided. NY R USDCTWD Civ Rule 10(b)(5).

 ii. *Text.* All text must be plainly and legibly written, typewritten, printed or reproduced. NY R USDCTWD Civ Rule 10(b)(2).

 iii. *Ink.* Documents must be in black or blue ink. NY R USDCTWD Civ Rule 10(b)(3).

 iv. *Binding.* The pages of each document must be stapled or in some other way fastened together. NY R USDCTWD Civ Rule 10(b)(4).

 c. *Caption; Names of parties.* Every pleading must have a caption with the court's name, a title, a file number, and a FRCP 7(a) designation. The title of the complaint must name all the parties; the title of other pleadings, after naming the first party on each side, may refer generally to other parties. FRCP 10(a).

 d. *Paragraphs; Separate statements.* A party must state its claims or defenses in numbered paragraphs, each limited as far as practicable to a single set of circumstances. A later pleading may refer by number to a paragraph in an earlier pleading. If doing so would promote clarity, each claim founded on a separate transaction or occurrence—and each defense other than a denial—must be stated in a separate count or defense. FRCP 10(b).

 e. *Adoption by reference; Exhibits.* A statement in a pleading may be adopted by reference elsewhere in the same pleading or in any other pleading or motion. A copy of a written instrument that is an exhibit to a pleading is a part of the pleading for all purposes. FRCP 10(c).

f. *Citation of local rules.* The Local Rules of Civil Procedure for the United States District Court for the Western District of New York shall be cited as "L.R.Civ.P." NY R USDCTWD Civ Rule 1.1.

g. *Acceptance by the clerk.* The clerk must not refuse to file a paper solely because it is not in the form prescribed by the Federal Rules of Civil Procedure or by a local rule or practice. FRCP 5(d)(4). The Court may reject documents that do not comply with the requirements in NY R USDCTWD Civ Rule 10. NY R USDCTWD Civ Rule 10.

2. *Form of electronic documents.* All pleadings, motions, and other papers that a party presents for filing, whether in paper form or in electronic form, shall meet the requirements in NY R USDCTWD Civ Rule 10(a). NY R USDCTWD Civ Rule 10(a). Refer above for more information.

   a. *Conversion to PDF.* A document created with a word processor, or a paper document, must be converted to Portable Document Format to be electronically filed with the court. NY R USDCTWD ECF Procedures(2)(a)(v).

      i. Documents which exist only in paper form may be scanned into a portable document format (PDF) for electronic filing. NY R USDCTWD ECF Procedures(2)(a)(v). Before filing a scanned document with the court, a Filing User must verify its legibility. NY R USDCTWD ECF Procedures(2)(a)(iv).

      ii. Electronic documents must be converted to .PDF from a word processing program and must be text searchable. Do not print, scan and .PDF your document when it has been created in a word processing program. Additional information on working with PDFs is located in NY R USDCTWD ECF Procedures(4b). NY R USDCTWD ECF Procedures(2)(a)(v).

   b. *Hyperlinks.* Pursuant to the policy set forth by the Judicial Conference in October 2005, a hyperlink contained in a filing is no more than a convenient mechanism for accessing material cited in a document. A hyperlink reference is extraneous to any filed document and is not part of the Court's record. NY R USDCTWD ECF Procedures(2)(a)(vi).

      i. In order to preserve the integrity of the Court record, users wishing to insert hyperlinks in Court filings shall continue to use the conventional method for the cited authority, in addition to the hyperlink. NY R USDCTWD ECF Procedures(2)(a)(vi).

      ii. The Court accepts no responsibility for, and does not endorse any product, organization, and content at any hyperlinked site, or at any site to which that site may be linked. The Court accepts no responsibility for the availability or functionality of any hyperlink. NY R USDCTWD ECF Procedures(2)(a)(vi).

   c. *Attachments and exhibits*

      i. Attachments and exhibits larger than five megabytes (5 MB) shall be filed electronically in separate five megabyte (5 MB) segments. NY R USDCTWD ECF Procedures(2)(d)(i).

      ii. Filing Users must submit in electronic form all documents referenced as exhibits or attachments, except as otherwise provided in NY R USDCTWD ECF Procedures. A Filing User must submit as exhibits or attachments only those excerpts of the referenced documents that are directly germane to the matter under consideration by the court. Excerpted material must be clearly and prominently identified as such. Filing Users who file excerpts of documents as exhibits or attachments under NY R USDCTWD ECF Procedures(2)(d)(ii) do so without prejudice to their right to timely file additional excerpts or the complete document. Responding parties may timely file additional excerpts or the complete document that they believe are directly germane. The Court may require parties to file additional excerpts or the complete document. A Filing User must request leave of the Court to file a document exhibit or attachment in non-electronic form. NY R USDCTWD ECF Procedures(2)(d)(ii).

      iii. Exhibits offered or admitted at trial will not be filed electronically or conventionally unless so ordered by the Court. NY R USDCTWD ECF Procedures(2)(d)(iii).

      iv. Exhibits such as videotapes and tape recordings shall be filed in the conventional manner with the Clerk of Court, and a Notice of Manual Filing shall be electronically filed by the party. Manually filed exhibits must have the case number and case name securely fastened or marked on the item. NY R USDCTWD ECF Procedures(2)(d)(iii).

    v.    Continuation of exhibit entries (for exhibits that are too large to attach to a main document) must be filed and entered on the same day that the main document was filed. NY R USDCTWD ECF Procedures(2)(d)(iv).

d.   *Color documents.* Documents in color or containing graphics take much longer to upload. Filing users are encouraged to configure their scanners to scan documents at 200 dpi and preferably in black and white rather than color. NY R USDCTWD ECF Procedures(2)(d)(v).

e.   *Large documents.* Due to the length of time it takes to download large files, documents larger than five megabytes (5 MB) (approximately one hundred (100) pages of a .pdf scanned document) must be filed electronically in separate five megabyte (5 MB) segments. A party who believes a document is too lengthy to electronically image (i.e. scan), may contact the Court Room Deputy for the assigned judge and request permission to file that document conventionally. If granted permission to file the document conventionally, the Filing User shall electronically file a "notice of manual filing" for that item. Exhibits submitted to the Court conventionally shall be served on other parties conventionally. NY R USDCTWD ECF Procedures(2)(d)(vi).

3.   *Signing disclosures and discovery requests, responses, and objections.* FRCP 11 does not apply to disclosures and discovery requests, responses, objections, and motions under FRCP 26 through FRCP 37. FRCP 11(d).

a.   *Signature required.* Every disclosure under FRCP 26(a)(1) or FRCP 26(a)(3) and every discovery request, response, or objection must be signed by at least one attorney of record in the attorney's own name—or by the party personally, if unrepresented—and must state the signer's address, e-mail address, and telephone number. FRCP 26(g)(1). Documents presented for paper filing must contain an original signature. NY R USDCTWD Civ Rule 10(b)(6).

    i.   *Electronic signatures*

- *Non-attorney signature.* If the original document requires the signature of a non-attorney, the filing party shall obtain the signature of the non-attorney on the document. NY R USDCTWD ECF Procedures(2)(g)(i). The filing party or attorney then shall file the document electronically indicating the signatory's name in the form "s/(name)." NY R USDCTWD ECF Procedures(2)(g)(i)(1). A non-filing signatory or party who disputes the authenticity of an electronically filed document or the authenticity of the signature on that document must file an objection to the document within ten (10) days of receiving the Notice of Electronic Filing. NY R USDCTWD ECF Procedures(2)(g)(i)(2).

- *Registered user signature.* The username and password required to file documents on the Electronic Filing System serve as the Filing User's signature on all electronic documents filed with this Court. The also serve as a signature for the purposes of FRCP 11, the Federal Rules of Civil Procedure, the Local Rules of Civil Procedure for the United States District Court for the Western District of New York, and any other purpose for which a signature is required in connection with proceedings before this Court. A pleading requiring a Registered User's signature must include a signature block in the format found in NY R USDCTWD ECF Procedures(2)(g)(iii). NY R USDCTWD ECF Procedures(2)(g)(iii). Any party challenging the authenticity of an electronically filed document or the attorney's signature on that document must file an objection to the document within ten (10) days of receiving the Notice of Electronic Filing. NY R USDCTWD ECF Procedures(2)(g)(iii)(1).

- *Multiple signatures.* The following procedure applies when a stipulation or other document requires two or more signatures: The filing party shall initially confirm that the document is acceptable to all persons required to sign the document and shall obtain the signatures of all parties on the document. NY R USDCTWD ECF Procedures(2)(g)(iv)(1). The filing party or attorney then shall file the document electronically indicating the signatories, e.g., "s/Jane Doe," "s/John Smith," etc. NY R USDCTWD ECF

Procedures(2)(g)(iv)(2). A non-filing signatory or party who disputes the authenticity of an electronically filed document containing multiple signatures or the authenticity of the signatures themselves must file an objection to the document within ten (10) days of receiving the Notice of Electronic Filing. NY R USDCTWD ECF Procedures(2)(g)(iv)(3).

   b. *Effect of signature.* By signing, an attorney or party certifies that to the best of the person's knowledge, information, and belief formed after a reasonable inquiry:

      i. With respect to a disclosure, it is complete and correct as of the time it is made; and

      ii. With respect to a discovery request, response, or objection, it is:

- Consistent with the Federal Rules of Civil Procedure and warranted by existing law or by a nonfrivolous argument for extending, modifying, or reversing existing law, or for establishing new law;

- Not interposed for any improper purpose, such as to harass, cause unnecessary delay, or needlessly increase the cost of litigation; and

- Neither unreasonable nor unduly burdensome or expensive, considering the needs of the case, prior discovery in the case, the amount in controversy, and the importance of the issues at stake in the action. FRCP 26(g)(1).

   c. *Failure to sign.* Other parties have no duty to act on an unsigned disclosure, request, response, or objection until it is signed, and the court must strike it unless a signature is promptly supplied after the omission is called to the attorney's or party's attention. FRCP 26(g)(2).

   d. *Sanction for improper certification.* If a certification violates FRCP 26(g) without substantial justification, the court, on motion or on its own, must impose an appropriate sanction on the signer, the party on whose behalf the signer was acting, or both. The sanction may include an order to pay the reasonable expenses, including attorney's fees, caused by the violation. FRCP 26(g)(3). Refer to the United States District Court for the Western District of New York KeyRules Motion for Discovery Sanctions document for more information.

4. *Privacy protection for filings made with the court.* In all filings, parties shall comply with FRCP 5.2. NY R USDCTWD ECF Procedures(2)(m)(i).

   a. *Redacted filings.* Unless the court orders otherwise, in an electronic or paper filing with the court that contains an individual's Social Security number, taxpayer-identification number, or birth date, the name of an individual known to be a minor, or a financial-account number, a party or nonparty making the filing may include only:

      i. The last four (4) digits of the Social Security number and taxpayer-identification number;

      ii. The year of the individual's birth;

      iii. The minor's initials; and

      iv. The last four (4) digits of the financial-account number. FRCP 5.2(a).

   b. *Exemptions from the redaction requirement.* The redaction requirement does not apply to the following:

      i. A financial-account number that identifies the property allegedly subject to forfeiture in a forfeiture proceeding;

      ii. The record of an administrative or agency proceeding;

      iii. The official record of a state-court proceeding;

      iv. The record of a court or tribunal, if that record was not subject to the redaction requirement when originally filed;

      v. A filing covered by FRCP 5.2(c) or FRCP 5.2(d); and

      vi. A pro se filing in an action brought under 28 U.S.C.A. § 2241, 28 U.S.C.A. § 2254, or 28 U.S.C.A. § 2255. FRCP 5.2(b).

    c.  *Limitations on remote access to electronic files; Social Security appeals and immigration cases.* Unless the court orders otherwise, in an action for benefits under the Social Security Act, and in an action or proceeding relating to an order of removal, to relief from removal, or to immigration benefits or detention, access to an electronic file is authorized as follows:

        i.  The parties and their attorneys may have remote electronic access to any part of the case file, including the administrative record;

        ii.  Any other person may have electronic access to the full record at the courthouse, but may have remote electronic access only to:

- The docket maintained by the court; and
- An opinion, order, judgment, or other disposition of the court, but not any other part of the case file or the administrative record. FRCP 5.2(c).

    d.  *Filings made under seal.* The court may order that a filing be made under seal without redaction. The court may later unseal the filing or order the person who made the filing to file a redacted version for the public record. FRCP 5.2(d). For more information on sealing documents, refer to NY R USDCTWD Civ Rule 5.3, NY R USDCTWD ECF Procedures(2)(o)(i)(1), NY R USDCTWD ECF Procedures(2)(o)(i)(2), and NY R USDCTWD ECF Procedures(2)(o)(i)(3).

    e.  *Protective orders.* For good cause, the court may by order in a case:

        i.  Require redaction of additional information; or

        ii.  Limit or prohibit a nonparty's remote electronic access to a document filed with the court. FRCP 5.2(e).

    f.  *Option for additional unredacted filing under seal.* A person making a redacted filing may also file an unredacted copy under seal. The court must retain the unredacted copy as part of the record. FRCP 5.2(f).

    g.  *Option for filing a reference list.* A filing that contains redacted information may be filed together with a reference list that identifies each item of redacted information and specifies an appropriate identifier that uniquely corresponds to each item listed. The list must be filed under seal and may be amended as of right. Any reference in the case to a listed identifier will be construed to refer to the corresponding item of information. FRCP 5.2(g).

    h.  *Waiver of protection of identifiers.* A person waives the protection of FRCP 5.2(a) as to the person's own information by filing it without redaction and not under seal. FRCP 5.2(h).

  5.  *Individual judge practices.* Refer to the Miscellaneous section of this document for information on individual judge practices on formatting documents.

## F.  Filing and Service Requirements

  1.  *Filing requirements.* Any paper after the complaint that is required to be served—together with a certificate of service—must be filed within a reasonable time after service. But disclosures under FRCP 26(a)(1) or FRCP 26(a)(2) and the following discovery requests and responses must not be filed until they are used in the proceeding or the court orders filing: depositions, interrogatories, requests for documents or tangible things or to permit entry onto land, and requests for admission. FRCP 5(d)(1). Parties shall comply with FRCP 5(d)(1), except that in cases involving a pro se litigant, all discovery materials must be filed with the Court pursuant to NY R USDCTWD Civ Rule 5.2(f). NY R USDCTWD Civ Rule 26(f). Refer to the United States District Court for the Western District of New York KeyRules pleading and motion documents for information on filing with the court.

  2.  *Service requirements.* [A request for an admission] must be served on the party from whom the admission is requested and, unless the court has otherwise ordered, a copy of the request must be served on every other party. FPP § 2258. All pleadings and other papers shall be filed and served in accordance with the

Federal Rules of Civil Procedure and the CM/ECF Administrative Procedures Guide. NY R USDCTWD Civ Rule 5.1(a).

a. *Service; When required*

    i. *In general.* Unless the Federal Rules of Civil Procedure provide otherwise, each of the following papers must be served on every party:

- An order stating that service is required;

- A pleading filed after the original complaint, unless the court orders otherwise under FRCP 5(c) because there are numerous defendants;

- A discovery paper required to be served on a party, unless the court orders otherwise;

- A written motion, except one that may be heard ex parte; and

- A written notice, appearance, demand, or offer of judgment, or any similar paper. FRCP 5(a)(1).

    ii. *If a party fails to appear.* No service is required on a party who is in default for failing to appear. But a pleading that asserts a new claim for relief against such a party must be served on that party under FRCP 4. FRCP 5(a)(2).

    iii. *Seizing property.* If an action is begun by seizing property and no person is or need be named as a defendant, any service required before the filing of an appearance, answer, or claim must be made on the person who had custody or possession of the property when it was seized. FRCP 5(a)(3).

b. *Service; How made*

    i. *Serving an attorney.* If a party is represented by an attorney, service under FRCP 5 must be made on the attorney unless the court orders service on the party. FRCP 5(b)(1).

    ii. *Service in general.* A paper is served under FRCP 5 by:

- Handing it to the person;

- Leaving it: (1) at the person's office with a clerk or other person in charge or, if no one is in charge, in a conspicuous place in the office; or (2) if the person has no office or the office is closed, at the person's dwelling or usual place of abode with someone of suitable age and discretion who resides there;

- Mailing it to the person's last known address—in which event service is complete upon mailing;

- Leaving it with the court clerk if the person has no known address;

- Sending it by electronic means if the person consented in writing—in which event service is complete upon transmission, but is not effective if the serving party learns that it did not reach the person to be served; or

- Delivering it by any other means that the person consented to in writing—in which event service is complete when the person making service delivers it to the agency designated to make delivery. FRCP 5(b)(2).

    iii. *Service by overnight delivery.* All papers, other than a subpoena or a summons and complaint, may be served on counsel of record by overnight delivery service at the address designated by the attorney for that purpose, or if none is designated, at the attorney's last known address. Service by overnight delivery shall be complete upon deposit of the paper(s), enclosed in a properly addressed wrapper, into the custody of the overnight delivery service, prior to the latest time designated by the service for overnight delivery. NY R USDCTWD Civ Rule 5.1(g). "Overnight delivery service" means any delivery service which regularly accepts items for overnight delivery to any address within the Court's jurisdiction. NY R USDCTWD Civ Rule 5.1(g).

    iv. *Service of documents by electronic means*

- *Service on registered users.* Registered Users consent to the electronic service of all

documents, and must make available an electronic mail address for service during the registration process. Upon the filing of a document by a party, a Notice of Electronic Filing, with a hyperlink to the filed document, will be automatically generated by the electronic filing system and sent via electronic mail to the e-mail addresses of all parties participating in the electronic filing system in the case. Electronic service of the Notice of Electronic Filing constitutes service of the filed document for all purposes of the Federal Rules of Civil Procedure and the Local Rules of Civil Procedure for the United States District Court for the Western District of New York. NY R USDCTWD ECF Procedures(2)(f)(i). The Notice of Electronic Filing effectuates service for all registered users and no certificate of service is required when all filers on an action are Registered Users. NY R USDCTWD ECF Procedures(2)(f)(iv).

- *Time limit for opening hyperlink.* The hyperlink to filed documents contained in the Notice of Electronic Filing must be opened within fifteen (15) days from the date the document was filed to provide registered users access to the document. The hyperlink expires after fifteen (15) days and users will be unable to access documents for free after that time. Filing Users are encouraged to check their e-mail frequently for notice of filed documents. NY R USDCTWD ECF Procedures(2)(f)(ii).

- *Service on exempted attorneys or pro se litigants who do not have permission to file electronically.* Attorneys granted an exemption from electronically filing documents in the System and pro se litigants who have not been granted permission to electronically file documents are entitled to a paper copy of any electronically filed pleading, document or order. The filing party must therefore provide the non-registered party with the pleading, document or order according to the Federal Rules of Civil Procedure. NY R USDCTWD ECF Procedures(2)(f)(iii).

- *E-mailing or faxing documents.* E-mailing or faxing a pleading or document to any party shall not constitute service of the pleading or document. NY R USDCTWD ECF Procedures(2)(f)(v).

   v. *Using court facilities.* If a local rule so authorizes, a party may use the court's transmission facilities to make service under FRCP 5(b)(2)(E). FRCP 5(b)(3).

  c. *Serving numerous defendants*

    i. *In general.* If an action involves an unusually large number of defendants, the court may, on motion or on its own, order that:

- Defendants' pleadings and replies to them need not be served on other defendants;

- Any crossclaim, counterclaim, avoidance, or affirmative defense in those pleadings and replies to them will be treated as denied or avoided by all other parties; and

- Filing any such pleading and serving it on the plaintiff constitutes notice of the pleading to all parties. FRCP 5(c)(1).

    ii. *Notifying parties.* A copy of every such order must be served on the parties as the court directs. FRCP 5(c)(2).

3. *Pro se actions.* For information on the requirements in pro se actions, refer to NY R USDCTWD Civ Rule 5.2.

4. *Individual judge practices.* Refer to the Miscellaneous section of this document for information on individual judge practices on filing and serving documents.

## G. Hearings

1. There is no hearing contemplated in the federal statutes or rules for requests for admissions.

## H. Forms

### 1. Federal Request for Admissions Forms

  a. Request; For admission of facts and genuineness of documents. AMJUR PP DEPOSITION § 674.

  b. Plaintiff's request for admission. 3B FEDFORMS § 3650.

c. Plaintiff's request for admission; Another form. 3B FEDFORMS § 3651.

d. Plaintiff's request for admission; Statements in documents. 3B FEDFORMS § 3652.

e. Plaintiff's request for admission; Statements in documents; Another form. 3B FEDFORMS § 3653.

f. Plaintiff's request for admission; Specific facts. 3B FEDFORMS § 3654.

g. Plaintiff's request for admission; Specific facts; Another form. 3B FEDFORMS § 3655.

h. Plaintiff's request for admission; Specific documents and facts. 3B FEDFORMS § 3656.

i. Plaintiff's request for admission; Specific documents and facts; Another form. 3B FEDFORMS § 3657.

j. Plaintiff's request for admission; True copies, filing and operational effect of government documents. 3B FEDFORMS § 3658.

k. Plaintiff's request for additional admission. 3B FEDFORMS § 3659.

l. Defendant's request for admission of genuineness; Specific document. 3B FEDFORMS § 3660.

m. Defendant's request for admission of genuineness; Specific document; Another form. 3B FED-FORMS § 3661.

n. Defendant's request for admission of genuineness; Specific document; Another form. 3B FED-FORMS § 3662.

o. Defendant's request for admission; Truth of statement. 3B FEDFORMS § 3663.

p. Request for admissions under FRCP 36. FEDPROF § 23:535.

q. Request for admissions; General form. FEDPROF § 23:536.

r. Request for admissions; Action to collect royalties. FEDPROF § 23:537.

s. Request for admissions; Trademark action. FEDPROF § 23:538.

t. Request for admissions; Automobile negligence action. FEDPROF § 23:539.

u. Request for admissions; Motor vehicle action. FEDPROF § 23:540.

v. Request for admissions; Premises liability action. FEDPROF § 23:541.

w. Request for admissions; Products liability action. FEDPROF § 23:542.

x. Request for admissions; Medical malpractice action. FEDPROF § 23:543.

y. Request for admissions; Genuineness of documents. FEDPROF § 23:544.

z. Request for admissions; Wrongful death due to forklift accident. FEDPROF § 23:545.

**2. Forms for the Western District of New York**

a. Certificate of service. NY R USDCTWD ECF Procedures(4a).

# I. Applicable Rules

1. *Federal rules*

a. Serving and filing pleadings and other papers. FRCP 5.

b. Privacy protection for filings made with the court. FRCP 5.2.

c. Computing and extending time; Time for motion papers. FRCP 6.

d. Pleadings allowed; Form of motions and other papers. FRCP 7.

e. Form of pleadings. FRCP 10.

f. Signing pleadings, motions, and other papers; Representations to the court; Sanctions. FRCP 11.

g. Duty to disclose; General provisions governing discovery. FRCP 26.

h. Stipulations about discovery procedure. FRCP 29.

i. Requests for admission. FRCP 36.

j. Failure to make disclosures or to cooperate in discovery; Sanctions. FRCP 37.

2. *Local rules*

    a.   Title. NY R USDCTWD Civ Rule 1.1.

    b.   Filing and serving papers. NY R USDCTWD Civ Rule 5.1.

    c.   Form of papers. NY R USDCTWD Civ Rule 10.

    d.   Sanctions. NY R USDCTWD Civ Rule 11.

    e.   Alternative dispute resolution and pretrial conferences. NY R USDCTWD Civ Rule 16.

    f.   General rules governing discovery. NY R USDCTWD Civ Rule 26.

    g.   Stipulations. NY R USDCTWD Civ Rule 29.

    h.   Attorneys of record; Appearance and withdrawal. NY R USDCTWD Civ Rule 83.2.

    i.   Administrative procedures guide for electronic filing. NY R USDCTWD ECF Procedures.

    j.   Alternative dispute resolution plan. NY R USDCTWD ADR Plan.

## J.  Miscellaneous

**NOTE: Individual judges' rules may apply. For available judge-level information, refer to:**

DISTRICT JUDGE RICHARD J. ARCARA: NY R USDCTWD Arcara-Procedures.

DISTRICT JUDGE FRANK P. GERACI, JR.: NY R USDCTWD Geraci-Procedures.

DISTRICT JUDGE DAVID G. LARIMER: NY R USDCTWD Larimer-Procedures.

DISTRICT JUDGE CHARLES J. SIRAGUSA: NY R USDCTWD Siragusa-Procedures.

DISTRICT JUDGE WILLIAM M. SKRETNY: NY R USDCTWD Skretny--Procedures.

DISTRICT JUDGE MICHAEL A. TELESCA: NY R USDCTWD Telesca-Procedures.

DISTRICT JUDGE LAWRENCE J. VILARDO: NY R USDCTWD Vilardo-Procedures.

DISTRICT JUDGE ELIZABETH A. WOLFORD: NY R USDCTWD Wolford-Procedures.

MAGISTRATE JUDGE JONATHAN W. FELDMAN: NY R USDCTWD Feldman-Procedures.

MAGISTRATE JUDGE LESLIE G. FOSCHIO: NY R USDCTWD Foschio-Procedures; NY R USDCTWD Foschio-Depositions.

MAGISTRATE JUDGE JEREMIAH J. McCARTHY: NY R USDCTWD McCarthy-Procedures.

MAGISTRATE JUDGE MARIAN W. PAYSON: NY R USDCTWD Payson-Procedures.

MAGISTRATE JUDGE MICHAEL J. ROEMER: NY R USDCTWD Roemer-Procedures.

MAGISTRATE JUDGE H. KENNETH SCHROEDER, JR.: NY R USDCTWD Schroeder-Proc.

MAGISTRATE JUDGE HUGH B. SCOTT: NY R USDCTWD Scott-Procedures.

# Requests, Notices and Applications
# Notice of Deposition

**Document Last Updated September 2016**

## A.  Checklist

    (I)  ❑  Matters to be considered by deposing party for depositions by oral examination

        (a)  ❑  Required documents

           (1)  ❑  Notice of deposition

        (b)  ❑  Supplemental documents

           (1)  ❑  Subpoena

           (2)  ❑  Subpoena duces tecum

           (3)  ❑  Request for production of documents

        (4)  ❑ Certificate of service

   (c)  ❑ Timing

        (1)  ❑ A party may, by oral questions, depose any person, including a party, without leave of court except as provided in FRCP 30(a)(2)

        (2)  ❑ A party must obtain leave of court, and the court must grant leave to the extent consistent with FRCP 26(b)(1) and FRCP 26(b)(2):

            (i)  ❑ If the parties have not stipulated to the deposition and: (1) the deposition would result in more than ten (10) depositions being taken under FRCP 30 or FRCP 31 by the plaintiffs, or by the defendants, or by the third-party defendants; (2) the deponent has already been deposed in the case; or (3) the party seeks to take the deposition before the time specified in FRCP 26(d), unless the party certifies in the notice, with supporting facts, that the deponent is expected to leave the United States and be unavailable for examination in this country after that time; or

           (ii)  ❑ If the deponent is confined in prison

        (3)  ❑ A party who wants to depose a person by oral questions must give reasonable written notice to every other party

            (i)  ❑ Absent agreement of the parties or court order, each notice to take the deposition of a party or other witness shall be served at least twenty-one (21) days prior to the date set for examination

(II)  ❑ Matters to be considered by deposing party for depositions by written questions

   (a)  ❑ Required documents

        (1)  ❑ Notice of deposition

        (2)  ❑ Written questions

   (b)  ❑ Supplemental documents

        (1)  ❑ Subpoena

        (2)  ❑ Certificate of service

   (c)  ❑ Timing

        (1)  ❑ A party may, by written questions, depose any person, including a party, without leave of court except as provided in FRCP 31(a)(2)

        (2)  ❑ A party must obtain leave of court, and the court must grant leave to the extent consistent with FRCP 26(b)(1) and FRCP 26(b)(2):

            (i)  ❑ If the parties have not stipulated to the deposition and: (1) the deposition would result in more than ten (10) depositions being taken under FRCP 31 or FRCP 30 by the plaintiffs, or by the defendants, or by the third-party defendants; (2) the deponent has already been deposed in the case; or (3) the party seeks to take a deposition before the time specified in FRCP 26(d); or

           (ii)  ❑ If the deponent is confined in prison

        (3)  ❑ A party who wants to depose a person by written questions must serve them on every other party, with a notice

## B. Timing

1.  *Depositions by oral examination*

    a.  *Without leave.* A party may, by oral questions, depose any person, including a party, without leave of court except as provided in FRCP 30(a)(2). FRCP 30(a)(1).

    b.  *With leave.* A party must obtain leave of court, and the court must grant leave to the extent consistent with FRCP 26(b)(1) and FRCP 26(b)(2):

        i.  If the parties have not stipulated to the deposition and: (1) the deposition would result in more than ten (10) depositions being taken under FRCP 30 or FRCP 31 by the plaintiffs, or by the defendants, or by the third-party defendants; (2) the deponent has already been deposed in the case; or (3) the party seeks to take the deposition before the time specified in FRCP 26(d), unless the party certifies in the notice, with supporting facts, that the deponent is expected to leave the United States and be unavailable for examination in this country after that time; or

    ii.   If the deponent is confined in prison. FRCP 30(a)(2).

  c.  *Notice of deposition.* A party who wants to depose a person by oral questions must give reasonable written notice to every other party. FRCP 30(b)(1).

    i.   Absent agreement of the parties or Court order, each notice to take the deposition of a party or other witness shall be served at least twenty-one (21) days prior to the date set for examination. NY R USDCTWD Civ Rule 30(a).

2.  *Depositions by written questions*

  a.  *Without leave.* A party may, by written questions, depose any person, including a party, without leave of court except as provided in FRCP 31(a)(2). FRCP 31(a)(1).

  b.  *With leave.* A party must obtain leave of court, and the court must grant leave to the extent consistent with FRCP 26(b)(1) and FRCP 26(b)(2):

    i.   If the parties have not stipulated to the deposition and: (1) the deposition would result in more than ten (10) depositions being taken under FRCP 31 or FRCP 30 by the plaintiffs, or by the defendants, or by the third-party defendants; (2) the deponent has already been deposed in the case; or (3) the party seeks to take a deposition before the time specified in FRCP 26(d); or

    ii.   If the deponent is confined in prison. FRCP 31(a)(2).

  c.  *Notice of deposition with written questions.* A party who wants to depose a person by written questions must serve them on every other party, with a notice. FRCP 31(a)(3). Refer to the General Requirements section of this document for the contents of the notice.

  d.  *Questions from other parties.* Any questions to the deponent from other parties must be served on all parties as follows:

    i.   *Cross-questions.* Cross-questions, within fourteen (14) days after being served with the notice and direct questions;

    ii.   *Redirect questions.* Redirect questions, within seven (7) days after being served with cross-questions; and

    iii.   *Recross-questions.* Recross-questions, within seven (7) days after being served with redirect questions. FRCP 31(a)(5).

    iv.   *Modification of timing requirements.* The court may, for good cause, extend or shorten these times. FRCP 31(a)(5).

3.  *Timing of discovery, generally.* A party may not seek discovery from any source before the parties have conferred as required by FRCP 26(f), except in a proceeding exempted from initial disclosure under FRCP 26(a)(1)(B), or when authorized by the Federal Rules of Civil Procedure, by stipulation, or by court order. FRCP 26(d)(1).

4.  *Computation of time*

  a.  *Computing time.* FRCP 6 applies in computing any time period specified in the Federal Rules of Civil Procedure, in any local rule or court order, or in any statute that does not specify a method of computing time. FRCP 6(a).

    i.   *Period stated in days or a longer unit.* When the period is stated in days or a longer unit of time:

- Exclude the day of the event that triggers the period;

- Count every day, including intermediate Saturdays, Sundays, and legal holidays; and

- Include the last day of the period, but if the last day is a Saturday, Sunday, or legal holiday, the period continues to run until the end of the next day that is not a Saturday, Sunday, or legal holiday. FRCP 6(a)(1).

ii. *Period stated in hours.* When the period is stated in hours:

- Begin counting immediately on the occurrence of the event that triggers the period;

- Count every hour, including hours during intermediate Saturdays, Sundays, and legal holidays; and

- If the period would end on a Saturday, Sunday, or legal holiday, the period continues to run until the same time on the next day that is not a Saturday, Sunday, or legal holiday. FRCP 6(a)(2).

iii. *Inaccessibility of the clerk's office.* Unless the court orders otherwise, if the clerk's office is inaccessible:

- On the last day for filing under FRCP 6(a)(1), then the time for filing is extended to the first accessible day that is not a Saturday, Sunday, or legal holiday; or

- During the last hour for filing under FRCP 6(a)(2), then the time for filing is extended to the same time on the first accessible day that is not a Saturday, Sunday, or legal holiday. FRCP 6(a)(3).

iv. *"Last day" defined.* Unless a different time is set by a statute, local rule, or court order, the last day ends:

- For electronic filing, at midnight in the court's time zone; and

- For filing by other means, when the clerk's office is scheduled to close. FRCP 6(a)(4).

v. *"Next day" defined.* The "next day" is determined by continuing to count forward when the period is measured after an event and backward when measured before an event. FRCP 6(a)(5).

vi. *"Legal holiday" defined.* "Legal holiday" means:

- The day set aside by statute for observing New Year's Day, Martin Luther King Jr.'s Birthday, Washington's Birthday, Memorial Day, Independence Day, Labor Day, Columbus Day, Veterans' Day, Thanksgiving Day, or Christmas Day;

- Any day declared a holiday by the President or Congress; and

- For periods that are measured after an event, any other day declared a holiday by the state where the district court is located. FRCP 6(a)(6).

b. *Computation of electronic filing deadlines.* A document will be deemed timely filed if filed prior to midnight Eastern Time, unless otherwise ordered by the Court. A document will be considered untimely if filed thereafter. When a Court order requires that a document be filed on a weekend or holiday, the document may be filed by close of business the next business day without further application to the Court. NY R USDCTWD ECF Procedures(2)(e)(i). A document filed electronically is deemed filed on the date and time stated on the Notice of Electronic Filing. NY R USDCTWD ECF Procedures(2)(e)(ii).

i. *System availability.* Although parties may file documents electronically twenty-four (24) hours a day, registered users are strongly encouraged to file all documents during normal working hours of the Clerk's Office (8:30 a.m. to 5:00 p.m. Eastern Time). NY R USDCTWD ECF Procedures(2)(t)(i).

ii. *Technical failures.* A Filing User whose filing is made untimely as a result of a technical failure must seek appropriate relief from the Court. NY R USDCTWD ECF Procedures(2)(u)(i).

c. *Extending time*

i. *In general.* When an act may or must be done within a specified time, the court may, for good cause, extend the time:

- With or without motion or notice if the court acts, or if a request is made, before the original time or its extension expires; or

- On motion made after the time has expired if the party failed to act because of excusable neglect. FRCP 6(b)(1).

ii. *Exceptions.* A court must not extend the time to act under FRCP 50(b), FRCP 50(d), FRCP 52(b), FRCP 59(b), FRCP 59(d), FRCP 59(e), and FRCP 60(b). FRCP 6(b)(2).

iii. Refer to the United States District Court for the Western District of New York KeyRules Motion for Continuance/Extension of Time document for more information on extending time.

d. *Additional time after certain kinds of service.* When a party may or must act within a specified time after service and service is made under FRCP 5(b)(2)(C), FRCP 5(b)(2)(D), FRCP 5(b)(2)(E), or FRCP 5(b)(2)(F), three (3) days are added after the period would otherwise expire under FRCP 6(a). FRCP 6(d).

   i. *Service by overnight delivery.* Where a period of time prescribed by either the Federal Rules of Civil Procedure or the Local Rules of Civil Procedure for the United States District Court for the Western District of New York is measured from the service of a paper and service is by overnight delivery, one (1) business day shall be added to the prescribed period. NY R USDCTWD Civ Rule 5.1(g).

5. *Individual judge practices.* Refer to the Miscellaneous section of this document for information on individual judge practices on timing of documents.

## C. General Requirements

1. *General provisions governing discovery*

   a. *Discovery scope and limits*

      i. *Scope in general.* Unless otherwise limited by court order, the scope of discovery is as follows: Parties may obtain discovery regarding any nonprivileged matter that is relevant to any party's claim or defense and proportional to the needs of the case, considering the importance of the issues at stake in the action, the amount in controversy, the parties' relative access to relevant information, the parties' resources, the importance of the discovery in resolving the issues, and whether the burden or expense of the proposed discovery outweighs its likely benefit. Information within this scope of discovery need not be admissible in evidence to be discoverable. FRCP 26(b)(1).

      ii. *Limitations on frequency and extent*

         • *When permitted.* By order, the court may alter the limits in the Federal Rules of Civil Procedure on the number of depositions and interrogatories or on the length of depositions under FRCP 30. By order or local rule, the court may also limit the number of requests under FRCP 36. FRCP 26(b)(2)(A).

         • *Specific limitations on electronically stored information.* A party need not provide discovery of electronically stored information from sources that the party identifies as not reasonably accessible because of undue burden or cost. On motion to compel discovery or for a protective order, the party from whom discovery is sought must show that the information is not reasonably accessible because of undue burden or cost. If that showing is made, the court may nonetheless order discovery from such sources if the requesting party shows good cause, considering the limitations of FRCP 26(b)(2)(C). The court may specify conditions for the discovery. FRCP 26(b)(2)(B).

         • *When required.* On motion or on its own, the court must limit the frequency or extent of discovery otherwise allowed by the Federal Rules of Civil Procedure or by local rule if it determines that: (1) the discovery sought is unreasonably cumulative or duplicative, or can be obtained from some other source that is more convenient, less burdensome, or less expensive; (2) the party seeking discovery has had ample opportunity to obtain the information by discovery in the action; or (3) the proposed discovery is outside the scope permitted by FRCP 26(b)(1). FRCP 26(b)(2)(C).

      iii. *Trial preparation; Materials*

         • *Documents and tangible things.* Ordinarily, a party may not discover documents and tangible things that are prepared in anticipation of litigation or for trial by or for another party or its representative (including the other party's attorney, consultant, surety, indemnitor, insurer, or agent). But, subject to FRCP 26(b)(4), those materials may be discovered if: (1) they are otherwise discoverable under FRCP 26(b)(1); and (2) the party shows that it has substantial need for the materials to prepare its case and cannot, without undue hardship, obtain their substantial equivalent by other means. FRCP 26(b)(3)(A).

- *Protection against disclosure.* If the court orders discovery of those materials, it must protect against disclosure of the mental impressions, conclusions, opinions, or legal theories of a party's attorney or other representative concerning the litigation. FRCP 26(b)(3)(B).

- *Previous statement.* Any party or other person may, on request and without the required showing, obtain the person's own previous statement about the action or its subject matter. If the request is refused, the person may move for a court order, and FRCP 37(a)(5) applies to the award of expenses. A previous statement is either: (1) a written statement that the person has signed or otherwise adopted or approved; or (2) a contemporaneous steno-graphic, mechanical, electrical, or other recording—or a transcription of it—that recites substantially verbatim the person's oral statement. FRCP 26(b)(3)(C).

iv. *Trial preparation; Experts*

- *Deposition of an expert who may testify.* A party may depose any person who has been identified as an expert whose opinions may be presented at trial. If FRCP 26(a)(2)(B) requires a report from the expert, the deposition may be conducted only after the report is provided. FRCP 26(b)(4)(A).

- *Trial-preparation protection for draft reports or disclosures.* FRCP 26(b)(3)(A) and FRCP 26(b)(3)(B) protect drafts of any report or disclosure required under FRCP 26(a)(2), regardless of the form in which the draft is recorded. FRCP 26(b)(4)(B).

- *Trial-preparation protection for communications between a party's attorney and expert witnesses.* FRCP 26(b)(3)(A) and FRCP 26(b)(3)(B) protect communications between the party's attorney and any witness required to provide a report under FRCP 26(a)(2)(B), regardless of the form of the communications, except to the extent that the communica-tions: (1) relate to compensation for the expert's study or testimony; (2) identify facts or data that the party's attorney provided and that the expert considered in forming the opinions to be expressed; or (3) identify assumptions that the party's attorney provided and that the expert relied on in forming the opinions to be expressed. FRCP 26(b)(4)(C).

- *Expert employed only for trial preparation.* Ordinarily, a party may not, by interrogatories or deposition, discover facts known or opinions held by an expert who has been retained or specially employed by another party in anticipation of litigation or to prepare for trial and who is not expected to be called as a witness at trial. But a party may do so only: (1) as provided in FRCP 35(b); or (2) on showing exceptional circumstances under which it is impracticable for the party to obtain facts or opinions on the same subject by other means. FRCP 26(b)(4)(D).

- *Payment.* Unless manifest injustice would result, the court must require that the party seeking discovery: (1) pay the expert a reasonable fee for time spent in responding to discovery under FRCP 26(b)(4)(A) or FRCP 26(b)(4)(D); and (2) for discovery FRCP 26(b)(4)(D), also pay the other party a fair portion of the fees and expenses it reasonably incurred in obtaining the expert's facts and opinions. FRCP 26(b)(4)(E).

v. *Claiming privilege or protecting trial-preparation materials*

- *Information withheld.* When a party withholds information otherwise discoverable by claiming that the information is privileged or subject to protection as trial-preparation material, the party must: (1) expressly make the claim; and (2) describe the nature of the documents, communications, or tangible things not produced or disclosed—and do so in a manner that, without revealing information itself privileged or protected, will enable other parties to assess the claim. FRCP 26(b)(5)(A). Where a party asserts a claim of privilege in objecting to any means of discovery or disclosure, and withholds otherwise responsive information based on that assertion: (1) the party asserting the privilege shall identify the nature of the privilege (including work product) being claimed and, if the privilege is governed by state law, indicate the state's privilege rule being invoked; and (2) shall provide the following information, unless to divulge such information would cause disclosure of the allegedly privileged information: (i) for documents: (a) the type of document, i.e., letter or memorandum; (b) the general subject matter of the document; (c) the date of the document; and (d) such other information as is sufficient to identify the document for a subpoena duces tecum, including, where appropriate, the author of the document, the addressees of the document, and any other recipients shown in the document, and, where not apparent, the relationship of the author, addressees, and recipients to each other; (ii) for oral communications: (a) the names of the person making the communication and the person(s) present while the communication was made and, where not apparent, the relationship of the person making the communication to the person(s) present; (b) the date and place of communication; and (c) its general subject matter. NY R USDCTWD Civ Rule 26(d)(1).

- *Information produced.* If information produced in discovery is subject to a claim of privilege or of protection as trial-preparation material, the party making the claim may notify any party that received the information of the claim and the basis for it. After being notified, a party must promptly return, sequester, or destroy the specified information and any copies it has; must not use or disclose the information until the claim is resolved; must take reasonable steps to retrieve the information if the party disclosed it before being notified; and may promptly present the information to the court under seal for a determination of the claim. The producing party must preserve the information until the claim is resolved. FRCP 26(b)(5)(B). Where the claim of privilege is asserted in response to discovery or disclosure other than at a deposition, the information set forth in NY R USDCTWD Civ Rule 26(d)(1) shall be furnished in writing when the party responds to such discovery or disclosure, unless otherwise ordered by the Court. NY R USDCTWD Civ Rule 26(d)(2). Where the claim of privilege is asserted during a deposition, the information set forth in NY R USDCTWD Civ Rule 26(d)(1) shall be furnished: (1) at the deposition, to the extent it is readily available from the witness being deposed or otherwise, and (2) to the extent it not readily available, in writing within fourteen (14) days after the privilege is asserted, unless otherwise ordered by the Court. NY R USDCTWD Civ Rule 26(d)(3).

b. *Protective orders.* A party or any person from whom discovery is sought may move for a protective order in the court where the action is pending—or as an alternative on matters relating to a deposition, in the court for the district where the deposition will be taken. FRCP 26(c)(1). Refer to the United States District Court for the Western District of New York KeyRules Motion for Protective Order document for more information.

c. *Sequence of discovery.* Unless the parties stipulate or the court orders otherwise for the parties' and witnesses' convenience and in the interests of justice: (1) methods of discovery may be used in any sequence; and (2) discovery by one party does not require any other party to delay its discovery. FRCP 26(d)(3).

d. *Uniform definitions for all discovery requests.* The full text of the definitions and rules of construction set forth in NY R USDCTWD Civ Rule 26(c)(3) and NY R USDCTWD Civ Rule 26(c)(4) is deemed incorporated by reference into all discovery requests. No discovery request shall use broader definitions or rules of construction than those set forth in NY R USDCTWD Civ Rule 26(c)(3) and NY R USDCTWD Civ Rule 26(c)(4). NY R USDCTWD Civ Rule 26(c) shall not preclude (1) the definition of other terms specific to the particular litigation, (2) the use of abbreviations, or (3) a more narrow definition of a term defined in NY R USDCTWD Civ Rule 26(c)(3). NY R USDCTWD Civ Rule 26(c)(1). NY R USDCTWD Civ Rule 26(c) is not intended to broaden or narrow the scope of discovery permitted by the Federal Rules of Civil Procedure. NY R USDCTWD Civ Rule 26(c)(2).

i. *Definitions.* The following definitions apply to all discovery requests:

- *Communication.* The term "communication" means the transmittal of information (in the form of facts, ideas, inquiries or otherwise). NY R USDCTWD Civ Rule 26(c)(3)(A).

- *Document.* The term "document" is defined to be synonymous in meaning and equal in scope to the usage of this term in FRCP 34(a), including, without limitation, electronic or computerized data compilations. A draft or non-identical copy is a separate document within the meaning of this term. NY R USDCTWD Civ Rule 26(c)(3)(B).

- *Identify (with respect to persons).* When referring to a person, "to identify" means to give, to the extent known, the person's full name, present or last known address, and when referring to a natural person, the present or last known place of employment. Once a person has been identified in accordance with NY R USDCTWD Civ Rule 26(c)(3)(C), only the person's name need be listed in response to subsequent discovery requesting the identification of that person. NY R USDCTWD Civ Rule 26(c)(3)(C).

- *Identify (with respect to documents).* When referring to documents, "to identify" means to give, to the extent known, the (1) type of document; (2) general subject matter; (3) date of the document; and (4) author(s), addressee(s), and recipients(s). NY R USDCTWD Civ Rule 26(c)(3)(D).

- *Parties.* The terms "plaintiff" and "defendant," as well as a party's full or abbreviated name or a pronoun referring to a party, mean the party and, where applicable, its officers, directors, employees, partners, corporate parent, subsidiaries, or affiliates. This definition is not intended to impose a discovery obligation on any person who is not a party to the litigation. NY R USDCTWD Civ Rule 26(c)(3)(E).

- *Person.* The term "person" is defined as any natural person or any business, legal or governmental entity, or association. NY R USDCTWD Civ Rule 26(c)(3)(F).

- *Concerning.* The term "concerning" means relating to, referring to, describing, evidencing or constituting. NY R USDCTWD Civ Rule 26(c)(3)(G).

ii. *Rules of construction.* The following rules of construction apply to all discovery requests:

- *All/each.* The terms "all" and "each" shall be construed as all and each. NY R USDCTWD Civ Rule 26(c)(4)(A).

- *And/or.* The connectives "and" and "or" shall be construed either disjunctively or conjunctively as necessary to bring within the scope of the discovery request all responses that might otherwise be construed to be outside of its scope. NY R USDCTWD Civ Rule 26(c)(4)(B).

- *Number.* The use of the singular form of any word includes the plural and vice versa. NY R USDCTWD Civ Rule 26(c)(4)(C).

e. *Electronically stored information (ESI).* Discovery of relevant electronically stored information shall proceed as follows:

i. *Searches and production of ESI.* After receiving requests for document production, the parties shall search their documents, including ESI other than ESI that has been identified as not reasonably accessible, and produce relevant responsive ESI in accordance with FRCP 26(b)(2). NY R USDCTWD Civ Rule 26(e)(1).

ii. *Non-accessible ESI.* Searches and production of ESI identified as not reasonably accessible shall not be required to be conducted until the initial disclosure of reasonably accessible ESI has been completed. Requests for information expected to be found in ESI that is not reasonably accessible must be narrowly focused with some basis in fact supporting the request, and good cause must be provided. The party seeking such discovery may be required to pay all or a portion of the costs of search, retrieval, review, and production of the information, upon application to the Court. NY R USDCTWD Civ Rule 26(e)(2).

iii. *Search methodology.* If a party intends to employ an electronic search to locate relevant ESI, the parties shall discuss and attempt to reach agreement as to the method of searching, and the words, terms, and phrases to be searched and any restrictions as to scope and method which might affect their ability to conduct a complete electronic search of the ESI. The parties shall also attempt to reach agreement as to the timing and conditions of any additional searches which may become necessary in the normal course of discovery. To minimize undue expense, the parties may consider limiting the scope of the electronic search (i.e., time frames, fields, document types). NY R USDCTWD Civ Rule 26(e)(3).

iv. *Metadata.* Except as otherwise provided, metadata, especially substantive metadata, need not be routinely produced, except upon agreement of the requesting and producing litigants, or upon a showing of good cause in a motion filed by the requesting party. NY R USDCTWD Civ Rule 26(e)(4).

v. *Format.* If the parties have not agreed or cannot agree to the format for document production, ESI shall be produced to the requesting party as image files (i.e. PDF or TIFF). When the image file is produced, the producing party must preserve the integrity of the electronic document's contents, i.e., the original formatting of the document, its metadata and, where applicable, its revision history. After initial production in image file format is complete, a party must demonstrate particularized need for production of ESI in its native format. NY R USDCTWD Civ Rule 26(e)(5).

vi. *Costs.* Generally, the costs of discovery, other than the costs associated with ESI that is not reasonably accessible, shall be borne by each party. However, the Court will apportion the costs of discovery or presentation of ESI, including discovery of ESI that is not reasonably accessible, upon a showing of good cause, or unequal burdens, or unreasonable request. NY R USDCTWD Civ Rule 26(e)(6).

f. *Cooperation among counsel in the discovery context.* See the Civility Principles of the United States District Court for the Western District of New York which can be found on the Court's website. NY R USDCTWD Civ Rule 26(g).

2. *Persons before whom depositions may be taken*

a. *Within the United States.* Within the United States or a territory or insular possession subject to United States jurisdiction, a deposition must be taken before: (1) an officer authorized to administer oaths either by federal law or by the law in the place of examination; or (2) a person appointed by the court where the action is pending to administer oaths and take testimony. FRCP 28(a)(1).

i. *Definition of "officer".* The term "officer" in FRCP 30, FRCP 31, and FRCP 32 includes a person appointed by the court under FRCP 28 or designated by the parties under FRCP 29(a). FRCP 28(a)(2).

b. *In a foreign country.* A deposition may be taken in a foreign country: (1) under an applicable treaty or convention; (2) under a letter of request, whether or not captioned a "letter rogatory"; (3) on notice, before a person authorized to administer oaths either by federal law or by the law in the place of examination; or (4) before a person commissioned by the court to administer any necessary oath and take testimony. FRCP 28(b)(1).

i. *Issuing a letter of request or a commission.* A letter of request, a commission, or both may be issued: (1) on appropriate terms after an application and notice of it; and (2) without a showing that taking the deposition in another manner is impracticable or inconvenient. FRCP 28(b)(2).

ii. *Form of a request, notice, or commission.* When a letter of request or any other device is used according to a treaty or convention, it must be captioned in the form prescribed by that treaty or convention. A letter of request may be addressed "To the Appropriate Authority in [name of country]." A deposition notice or a commission must designate by name or descriptive title the person before whom the deposition is to be taken. FRCP 28(b)(3).

iii. *Letter of request; Admitting evidence.* Evidence obtained in response to a letter of request need not be excluded merely because it is not a verbatim transcript, because the testimony was not taken under oath, or because of any similar departure from the requirements for depositions taken within the United States. FRCP 28(b)(4).

c. *Disqualification.* A deposition must not be taken before a person who is any party's relative, employee, or attorney; who is related to or employed by any party's attorney; or who is financially interested in the action. FRCP 28(c).

3. *Depositions by oral examination*

   a. *Scheduling depositions*

      i. *Production of documents in connection with depositions.* Consistent with the requirements of FRCP 30 and FRCP 34, a party seeking production of documents of another party or witness in connection with a deposition shall schedule the deposition to allow for production of the documents at least seven (7) calendar days prior to the deposition. Upon receipt of the documents, the party noticing the deposition shall immediately inform counsel for all other noticed parties that the requested documents have been produced and shall make the documents available for their inspection and reproduction. If timely requested documents are not produced at least seven (7) days prior to the deposition, the party noticing the deposition may either adjourn the deposition until a minimum of seven (7) days after the documents are produced or, without waiving the right to access to the documents, proceed with the deposition on the originally scheduled date. NY R USDCTWD Civ Rule 30(b).

   b. *Notice of the deposition.* A party who wants to depose a person by oral questions must give reasonable written notice to every other party. The notice must state the time and place of the deposition and, if known, the deponent's name and address. If the name is unknown, the notice must provide a general description sufficient to identify the person or the particular class or group to which the person belongs. FRCP 30(b)(1).

      i. *Notice or subpoena directed to an organization.* In its notice or subpoena, a party may name as the deponent a public or private corporation, a partnership, an association, a governmental agency, or other entity and must describe with reasonable particularity the matters for examination. The named organization must then designate one or more officers, directors, or managing agents, or designate other persons who consent to testify on its behalf; and it may set out the matters on which each person designated will testify. A subpoena must advise a nonparty organization of its duty to make this designation. The persons designated must testify about information known or reasonably available to the organization. FRCP 30(b)(6) does not preclude a deposition by any other procedure allowed by the Federal Rules of Civil Procedure. FRCP 30(b)(6).

   c. *Method of recording*

      i. *Method stated in the notice.* The party who notices the deposition must state in the notice the method for recording the testimony. Unless the court orders otherwise, testimony may be recorded by audio, audiovisual, or stenographic means. The noticing party bears the recording costs. Any party may arrange to transcribe a deposition. FRCP 30(b)(3)(A).

      ii. *Additional method.* With prior notice to the deponent and other parties, any party may designate another method for recording the testimony in addition to that specified in the original notice. That party bears the expense of the additional record or transcript unless the court orders otherwise. FRCP 30(b)(3)(B).

   d. *By remote means.* The parties may stipulate—or the court may on motion order—that a deposition be taken by telephone or other remote means. For the purpose of FRCP 30 and FRCP 28(a), FRCP 37(a)(2), and FRCP 37(b)(1), the deposition takes place where the deponent answers the questions. FRCP 30(b)(4).

   e. *Officer's duties*

      i. *Before the deposition.* Unless the parties stipulate otherwise, a deposition must be conducted before an officer appointed or designated under FRCP 28. The officer must begin the deposition with an on-the-record statement that includes: (1) the officer's name and business address; (2) the date, time, and place of the deposition; (3) the deponent's name; (4) the officer's administration of the oath or affirmation to the deponent; and (5) the identity of all persons present. FRCP 30(b)(5)(A).

      ii. *Conducting the deposition; Avoiding distortion.* If the deposition is recorded non-stenographically, the officer must repeat the items in FRCP 30(b)(5)(A)(i) through FRCP 30(b)(5)(A)(iii) at the beginning of each unit of the recording medium. The deponent's and attorneys' appearance or demeanor must not be distorted through recording techniques. FRCP 30(b)(5)(B).

    iii. *After the deposition.* At the end of a deposition, the officer must state on the record that the deposition is complete and must set out any stipulations made by the attorneys about custody of the transcript or recording and of the exhibits, or about any other pertinent matters. FRCP 30(b)(5)(C).

f. *Examination and cross-examination.* The examination and cross-examination of a deponent proceed as they would at trial under the Federal Rules of Evidence, except FRE 103 and FRE 615. FRCP 30(c)(1).

    i. *Record of the examination.* After putting the deponent under oath or affirmation, the officer must record the testimony by the method designated under FRCP 30(b)(3)(A). The testimony must be recorded by the officer personally or by a person acting in the presence and under the direction of the officer. FRCP 30(c)(1).

    ii. *Objections.* An objection at the time of the examination—whether to evidence, to a party's conduct, to the officer's qualifications, to the manner of taking the deposition, or to any other aspect of the deposition—must be noted on the record, but the examination still proceeds; the testimony is taken subject to any objection. An objection must be stated concisely in a nonargumentative and nonsuggestive manner. A person may instruct a deponent not to answer only when necessary to preserve a privilege, to enforce a limitation ordered by the court, or to present a motion under FRCP 30(d)(3). FRCP 30(c)(2).

    iii. *Participating through written questions.* Instead of participating in the oral examination, a party may serve written questions in a sealed envelope on the party noticing the deposition, who must deliver them to the officer. The officer must ask the deponent those questions and record the answers verbatim. FRCP 30(c)(3).

g. *Procedures for video depositions.* A Court order is required before taking a deposition by other than stenographic means (i.e., without the use of a stenographic record). However, a prior order is not required to record a deposition both on video and stenographically. In the latter circumstance, the following procedures apply:

    i. The deposition notice shall state that the deposition will be recorded both stenographically and on video. At the deposition, the camera operator shall be identified. An employee of the attorney who noticed the deposition may act as the camera operator. NY R USDCTWD Civ Rule 30(c)(1).

    ii. The camera shall be directed at the witness at all times showing a head and shoulders view, except that close-up views of exhibits are permitted where requested by the questioning attorney. NY R USDCTWD Civ Rule 30(c)(2).

    iii. Prior to trial, counsel for the party seeking to use the video deposition shall approach opposing counsel and attempt to resolve voluntarily all objections made at the deposition. NY R USDCTWD Civ Rule 30(c)(3).

    iv. The party seeking to use the video deposition at trial shall submit unresolved objections to the Court by way of a motion in limine. The motion may be made at any time after the deposition, but shall be made no later than seven (7) days before trial or any earlier deadline established by Court order. The objected-to portion(s) of the transcript shall be annexed to the motion papers. NY R USDCTWD Civ Rule 30(c)(4).

    v. In accordance with the Court's ruling on objections, the party seeking to use the video deposition shall notify opposing counsel of the transcript pages and line numbers the party plans to delete from the video. The party seeking to use the video shall then edit the video accordingly, and shall bear the expenses of editing. If the Court overrules an objection made during the deposition, the objection need not be deleted. If requested, the Court will give an instruction at the time the video is shown regarding objections heard on the video. NY R USDCTWD Civ Rule 30(c)(5).

    vi. At least three (3) days before showing the video, the party seeking to use the video deposition at trial shall deliver a copy of the edited video to opposing counsel. Opposing counsel may then object only if the edited version does not comply with the Court's ruling and counsels' agreement, or if the video's quality is such that it will be difficult for the jury to understand. Such objections, if any, must be made in writing and served at least twenty-four (24) hours before the video is to be shown. NY R USDCTWD Civ Rule 30(c)(6).

    vii.   The party seeking to use the video deposition should attempt to utilize a storage format compatible with the Court's display equipment. A party utilizing an incompatible format must provide the equipment necessary to display the video in Court. NY R USDCTWD Civ Rule 30(c)(7).

    viii.   See NY R USDCTWD Civ Rule 54(c) for prerequisites to the receipt of video expenses as a component of taxable costs. NY R USDCTWD Civ Rule 30(c)(8).

h.   *Duration.* Unless otherwise stipulated or ordered by the court, a deposition is limited to one (1) day of seven (7) hours. The court must allow additional time consistent with FRCP 26(b)(1) and FRCP 26(b)(2) if needed to fairly examine the deponent or if the deponent, another person, or any other circumstance impedes or delays the examination. FRCP 30(d)(1).

i.   *Sanction.* The court may impose an appropriate sanction—including the reasonable expenses and attorney's fees incurred by any party—on a person who impedes, delays, or frustrates the fair examination of the deponent. FRCP 30(d)(2). Refer to the United States District Court for the Western District of New York KeyRules Motion for Discovery Sanctions document for more information on sanctions.

j.   *Motion to terminate or limit.* At any time during a deposition, the deponent or a party may move to terminate or limit it on the ground that it is being conducted in bad faith or in a manner that unreasonably annoys, embarrasses, or oppresses the deponent or party. The motion may be filed in the court where the action is pending or the deposition is being taken. If the objecting deponent or party so demands, the deposition must be suspended for the time necessary to obtain an order. FRCP 30(d)(3)(A).

    i.   *Order.* The court may order that the deposition be terminated or may limit its scope and manner as provided in FRCP 26(c). If terminated, the deposition may be resumed only by order of the court where the action is pending. FRCP 30(d)(3)(B).

    ii.   *Award of expenses.* FRCP 37(a)(5) applies to the award of expenses. FRCP 30(d)(3)(C). Refer to the United States District Court for the Western District of New York KeyRules Motion for Discovery Sanctions document for more information on sanctions.

k.   *Review by the witness; Statement of changes.* On request by the deponent or a party before the deposition is completed, the deponent must be allowed thirty (30) days after being notified by the officer that the transcript or recording is available in which: (1) to review the transcript or recording; and (2) if there are changes in form or substance, to sign a statement listing the changes and the reasons for making them. FRCP 30(e)(1).

    i.   *Changes indicated in the officer's certificate.* The officer must note in the certificate prescribed by FRCP 30(f)(1) whether a review was requested and, if so, must attach any changes the deponent makes during the thirty (30) day period. FRCP 30(e)(2).

l.   *Certification and delivery.* The officer must certify in writing that the witness was duly sworn and that the deposition accurately records the witness's testimony. The certificate must accompany the record of the deposition. Unless the court orders otherwise, the officer must seal the deposition in an envelope or package bearing the title of the action and marked "Deposition of [witness's name]" and must promptly send it to the attorney who arranged for the transcript or recording. The attorney must store it under conditions that will protect it against loss, destruction, tampering, or deterioration. FRCP 30(f)(1).

m.   *Documents and tangible things.* Documents and tangible things produced for inspection during a deposition must, on a party's request, be marked for identification and attached to the deposition. Any party may inspect and copy them. But if the person who produced them wants to keep the originals, the person may: (1) offer copies to be marked, attached to the deposition, and then used as originals—after giving all parties a fair opportunity to verify the copies by comparing them with the originals; or (2) give all parties a fair opportunity to inspect and copy the originals after they are marked—in which event the originals may be used as if attached to the deposition. FRCP 30(f)(2)(A).

    i.   *Order regarding the originals.* Any party may move for an order that the originals be attached to the deposition pending final disposition of the case. FRCP 30(f)(2)(B).

n.  *Copies of the transcript or recording.* Unless otherwise stipulated or ordered by the court, the officer must retain the stenographic notes of a deposition taken stenographically or a copy of the recording of a deposition taken by another method. When paid reasonable charges, the officer must furnish a copy of the transcript or recording to any party or the deponent. FRCP 30(f)(3).

o.  *Failure to attend a deposition or serve a subpoena; Expenses.* A party who, expecting a deposition to be taken, attends in person or by an attorney may recover reasonable expenses for attending, including attorney's fees, if the noticing party failed to: (1) attend and proceed with the deposition; or (2) serve a subpoena on a nonparty deponent, who consequently did not attend. FRCP 30(g). Refer to the United States District Court for the Western District of New York KeyRules Motion for Discovery Sanctions document for more information on sanctions.

4.  *Depositions by written questions*

a.  *Notice of deposition.* A party who wants to depose a person by written questions must serve them on every other party, with a notice stating, if known, the deponent's name and address. If the name is unknown, the notice must provide a general description sufficient to identify the person or the particular class or group to which the person belongs. The notice must also state the name or descriptive title and the address of the officer before whom the deposition will be taken. FRCP 31(a)(3).

b.  *Questions directed to an organization.* A public or private corporation, a partnership, an association, or a governmental agency may be deposed by written questions in accordance with FRCP 30(b)(6). FRCP 31(a)(4).

c.  *Delivery to the officer; Officer's duties.* The party who noticed the deposition must deliver to the officer a copy of all the questions served and of the notice. The officer must promptly proceed in the manner provided in FRCP 30(c), FRCP 30(e), and FRCP 30(f) to:

    i.   Take the deponent's testimony in response to the questions;

    ii.  Prepare and certify the deposition; and

    iii. Send it to the party, attaching a copy of the questions and of the notice. FRCP 31(b).

d.  *Notice of completion.* The party who noticed the deposition must notify all other parties when it is completed. FRCP 31(c)(1).

5.  *Depositions to perpetuate testimony.* For information on depositions to perpetuate testimony, refer to FRCP 27.

6.  *Stipulations about discovery procedure.* Unless the court orders otherwise, the parties may stipulate that: (1) a deposition may be taken before any person, at any time or place, on any notice, and in the manner specified—in which event it may be used in the same way as any other deposition; and (2) other procedures governing or limiting discovery be modified—but a stipulation extending the time for any form of discovery must have court approval if it would interfere with the time set for completing discovery, for hearing a motion, or for trial. FRCP 29. All stipulations, except stipulations made in open court and recorded by the court reporter, shall be in writing and signed by each attorney and/or pro se litigant. The parties shall determine who will be responsible for filing, and a copy of the stipulation, with signatures conformed (e.g., "s/Jane Doe," "s/John Smith"), shall be filed electronically. The Court will act on the filed stipulation, as necessary and appropriate. NY R USDCTWD Civ Rule 29.

7.  *Notice of appearance.* No notice of appearance is required of an attorney whose name and address appear at the end of a complaint, notice of removal, pre-answer motion, or answer. In all other circumstances, an attorney appearing for a party in a civil case shall promptly file a written notice of appearance. NY R USDCTWD Civ Rule 83.2(b). For more information on appearances and withdrawals, refer to NY R USDCTWD Civ Rule 83.2.

S NOTICE OF DEPOSITION

8. *Related cases.* Each attorney appearing in a civil case has a continuing duty to promptly notify the Clerk of Court when the attorney has reason to believe that said case is related to some other pending civil or criminal action(s) such that their assignment to the same Judge would avoid unnecessary duplication of judicial effort. As soon as the attorney becomes aware of such a relationship, the attorney shall notify the Clerk of Court by letter of the relevant facts, and the Clerk of Court will transmit that notification to the Judges to whom the cases have been assigned. NY R USDCTWD Civ Rule 5.1(e).

9. *Alternative dispute resolution (ADR).* This Court has adopted an Alternative Dispute Resolution Plan ("ADR"), as implemented by Standing Order (NY R USDCTWD ADR Plan), under which certain civil cases are referred automatically to ADR upon filing. NY R USDCTWD Civ Rule 16(a). The United States District Court for the Western District of New York (the "Court") adopted the ADR Plan on January 1, 2006 (the "Effective Date"), to make available to civil litigants court-administered ADR interventions and processes designed to provide quicker, less expensive and potentially more satisfying alternatives to continuing litigation, without impairing the quality of justice or the right to trial. NY R USDCTWD ADR Plan(1)(1.2)(A).

   a. *Scope.* This ADR Plan (NY R USDCTWD ADR Plan) applies to civil actions pending or commenced on and after the Effective Date, except as otherwise indicated in NY R USDCTWD ADR Plan. The ADR Plan supplements the Local Rules of Civil Procedure for the United States District Court for the Western District of New York, which shall remain in full effect for all cases. NY R USDCTWD ADR Plan(1)(1.2)(B).

   b. *Referral to ADR*

      i. *New cases.* All civil cases filed on and after the Effective Date of the ADR Plan shall be referred automatically for ADR. NY R USDCTWD ADR Plan(2)(2.1)(A). Notice of the ADR requirements will be provided to all parties immediately upon the filing of a complaint and answer or a notice of removal; NY R USDCTWD ADR Plan(2)(2.1)(A); NY R USDCTWD Civ Rule 16(a). ADR intervention will be scheduled at the conference held pursuant to Local Rule of Civil Procedure 16.1. NY R USDCTWD ADR Plan(2)(2.1)(A). [Editor's note: the reference to Local Rule of Civil Procedure 16.1 is likely meant to be a reference to NY R USDCTWD Civ Rule 16(b)].

         • Litigants in cases not referred automatically to ADR must consider possible agreement to the use of an ADR process. NY R USDCTWD Civ Rule 16(a).

         • For a list of exemptions from automatic referral, refer to NY R USDCTWD ADR Plan(2)(2.1)(A).

      ii. *Pending cases.* The assigned Judge on any pending civil case may, sua sponte or with status conference, issue an order referring the case for ADR. NY R USDCTWD ADR Plan(2)(2.1)(B); NY R USDCTWD Civ Rule 16(a). The order shall specify a date on which the ADR intervention is to be completed. NY R USDCTWD ADR Plan(2)(2.1)(B).

      iii. *Stipulation.* A case may be referred for ADR by stipulation of all parties. Stipulations shall be filed and shall designate the specific ADR intervention the parties have selected, the time frame within which the ADR process will be completed and the selected Neutral. Stipulations are presumed acceptable unless the assigned Judge determines that the interests of justice are not served. NY R USDCTWD ADR Plan(2)(2.1)(C).

      iv. *Relief from ADR referral*

         • *Opting out motions.* Any party may file, with the assigned Judge for that case, a motion to opt out of, or for relief from, ADR. NY R USDCTWD ADR Plan(2)(2.2)(A).

         • *Motion.* Opting Out Motions must be made within fourteen (14) days from (1) the date of the first discovery conference under Local Rule 16.1 in new cases, or (2) the date of a sua sponte ADR Referral Order in pending cases. NY R USDCTWD ADR Plan(2)(2.2)(B). [Editor's note: the reference to Local Rule 16.1 is likely meant to be a reference to NY R USDCTWD Civ Rule 16(b)].

         • *Criteria.* Opting Out Motions shall be granted only for "good cause" shown. Inconvenience, travel costs, attorney fees or other costs shall not constitute "good cause." A party

1727

seeking relief from ADR must set forth the reasons why ADR has no reasonable chance of being productive. NY R USDCTWD ADR Plan(2)(2.2)(C).

- *Judicial initiative.* The assigned Judge may, sua sponte, exempt any case from the Court's ADR Plan. NY R USDCTWD ADR Plan(2)(2.2)(D).

c. *ADR interventions*

 i. *Options.* It is expected that cases referred for ADR will proceed to Mediation. However, the following options are also available upon the stipulation of all parties:

- Neutral Evaluation;
- Mini Summary Trial;
- Arbitration (Binding and Non-Binding);
- Case Valuation; and
- Settlement Week, when scheduled by the Court. NY R USDCTWD ADR Plan(4)(4.1)(A).

 ii. *Timing.* Timing is specific to the intervention and process chosen, as set forth in the corresponding sections in NY R USDCTWD ADR Plan. NY R USDCTWD ADR Plan(4)(4.1)(B).

 iii. *Scheduling.* The referral of a case to ADR does not delay or defer other dates established in the Scheduling Order and has no effect on the scheduled progress of the case toward trial. NY R USDCTWD ADR Plan(4)(4.1)(C).

d. *Selecting an ADR intervention*

 i. *New cases.* Prior to the Local Rule 16.1 scheduling conference, counsel and any unrepresented parties shall confer about ADR as part of their discussion of "the possibilities for a prompt settlement or resolution of the case" pursuant to FRCP 26(f). Unless the parties agree to a different intervention, it is presumed that they will participate in mediation. [Editor's note: the reference to Local Rule 16.1 is likely meant to be a reference to NY R USDCTWD Civ Rule 16(b)].

 ii. *Pending cases.* In pending cases, all sua sponte referrals will be to mediation. Should the parties agree that a different ADR intervention is more appropriate to their case, they may submit a stipulation designating the specific ADR intervention selected, the time frame within which the ADR process will be completed and the identity of the Neutral. Stipulations must be filed within fourteen (14) days from the date of the ADR Referral Order and are presumed acceptable unless the assigned Judge determines that the interests of justice are not served. NY R USDCTWD ADR Plan(4)(4.2)(B).

e. For more information on alternative dispute resolution (ADR), refer to NY R USDCTWD ADR Plan.

10. *Sanctions.* Failure of counsel for any party, or a party proceeding pro se, to appear before the Court at a conference, to complete the necessary preparations, or to be prepared to proceed to trial at the set time may be considered an abandonment of the case or a failure to prosecute or defend diligently. An appropriate order for sanctions may be entered against the defaulting party with respect to either a specific issue or the entire case. NY R USDCTWD Civ Rule 11(a). For more information, refer to NY R USDCTWD Civ Rule 11.

11. *Pro se actions.* For information on the requirements in pro se actions, refer to NY R USDCTWD Civ Rule 5.2.

12. *Individual judge practices.* Refer to the Miscellaneous section of this document for information on individual judge practices on general requirements for documents.

## D. Documents

1. *Depositions by oral examination*

 a. *Required documents*

  i. *Notice of deposition.* Refer to the General Requirements section of this document for the form and contents of the notice of deposition.

b. *Supplemental documents*

    i. *Subpoena.* The deponent's attendance may be compelled by subpoena under FRCP 45. FRCP 30(a)(1). For more information on subpoenas, refer to FRCP 45.

    ii. *Subpoena duces tecum.* If a subpoena duces tecum is to be served on the deponent, the materials designated for production, as set out in the subpoena, must be listed in the notice or in an attachment. FRCP 30(b)(2). For more information on subpoenas duces tecum, refer to FRCP 45.

    iii. *Request for production of documents.* The notice to a party deponent may be accompanied by a request under FRCP 34 to produce documents and tangible things at the deposition. FRCP 30(b)(2). Refer to the United States District Court for the Western District of New York KeyRules Request for Production of Documents document for more information.

    iv. *Certificate of service.* FRCP 5(d) requires that the person making service under FRCP 5 certify that service has been effected. FRCP 5(Advisory Committee Notes). Having such information on file may be useful for many purposes, including proof of service if an issue arises concerning the effectiveness of the service. FRCP 5(Advisory Committee Notes).

2. *Depositions by written questions*

a. *Required documents*

    i. *Notice of deposition.* Refer to the General Requirements section of this document for the form and contents of the notice of deposition.

    ii. *Written questions.* A party who wants to depose a person by written questions must serve them on every other party, with a notice. FRCP 31(a)(3).

b. *Supplemental documents*

    i. *Subpoena.* The deponent's attendance may be compelled by subpoena under FRCP 45. FRCP 31(a)(1). For more information on subpoenas, refer to FRCP 45.

    ii. *Certificate of service.* FRCP 5(d) requires that the person making service under FRCP 5 certify that service has been effected. FRCP 5(Advisory Committee Notes). Having such information on file may be useful for many purposes, including proof of service if an issue arises concerning the effectiveness of the service. FRCP 5(Advisory Committee Notes).

3. *Individual judge practices.* Refer to the Miscellaneous section of this document for information on individual judge practices on required documents.

# E. Format

1. *Form of documents.* The rules governing captions and other matters of form in pleadings apply to motions and other papers. FRCP 7(b)(2).

a. *Form, generally.* All pleadings, motions, and other papers that a party presents for filing, whether in paper form or in electronic form, shall meet the following requirements:

    i. *Font size.* All text and footnotes shall be in a font size of at least twelve (12) point type. NY R USDCTWD Civ Rule 10(a)(1).

    ii. *Spacing.* All text in the body of the document must be double-spaced, except that text in block quotations and footnotes may be single-spaced. NY R USDCTWD Civ Rule 10(a)(2).

        • Extensive footnotes and block quotes may not be used to circumvent page limitations. NY R USDCTWD Civ Rule 10(a)(3).

    iii. *Margins.* Documents must have one (1) inch margins on all four sides. NY R USDCTWD Civ Rule 10(a)(4).

    iv. *Page numbering.* Pages must be consecutively numbered. NY R USDCTWD Civ Rule 10(a)(5).

b.  *Additional requirements for paper filing.* Documents presented for filing in paper form shall meet the following additional requirements:

    i.  *Paper.* Documents must be on durable white eight and one-half by eleven (8-1/2 x 11) inch paper of good quality. NY R USDCTWD Civ Rule 10(b)(1).

       • All documents must be single-sided. NY R USDCTWD Civ Rule 10(b)(5).

    ii.  *Text.* All text must be plainly and legibly written, typewritten, printed or reproduced. NY R USDCTWD Civ Rule 10(b)(2).

    iii.  *Ink.* Documents must be in black or blue ink. NY R USDCTWD Civ Rule 10(b)(3).

    iv.  *Binding.* The pages of each document must be stapled or in some other way fastened together. NY R USDCTWD Civ Rule 10(b)(4).

c.  *Caption; Names of parties.* Every pleading must have a caption with the court's name, a title, a file number, and a FRCP 7(a) designation. The title of the complaint must name all the parties; the title of other pleadings, after naming the first party on each side, may refer generally to other parties. FRCP 10(a).

d.  *Paragraphs; Separate statements.* A party must state its claims or defenses in numbered paragraphs, each limited as far as practicable to a single set of circumstances. A later pleading may refer by number to a paragraph in an earlier pleading. If doing so would promote clarity, each claim founded on a separate transaction or occurrence—and each defense other than a denial—must be stated in a separate count or defense. FRCP 10(b).

e.  *Adoption by reference; Exhibits.* A statement in a pleading may be adopted by reference elsewhere in the same pleading or in any other pleading or motion. A copy of a written instrument that is an exhibit to a pleading is a part of the pleading for all purposes. FRCP 10(c).

f.  *Citation of local rules.* The Local Rules of Civil Procedure for the United States District Court for the Western District of New York shall be cited as "L.R.Civ.P." NY R USDCTWD Civ Rule 1.1.

g.  *Acceptance by the clerk.* The clerk must not refuse to file a paper solely because it is not in the form prescribed by the Federal Rules of Civil Procedure or by a local rule or practice. FRCP 5(d)(4). The Court may reject documents that do not comply with the requirements in NY R USDCTWD Civ Rule 10. NY R USDCTWD Civ Rule 10.

2.  *Form of electronic documents.* All pleadings, motions, and other papers that a party presents for filing, whether in paper form or in electronic form, shall meet the requirements in NY R USDCTWD Civ Rule 10(a). NY R USDCTWD Civ Rule 10(a). Refer above for more information.

a.  *Conversion to PDF.* A document created with a word processor, or a paper document, must be converted to Portable Document Format to be electronically filed with the court. NY R USDCTWD ECF Procedures(2)(a)(v).

    i.  Documents which exist only in paper form may be scanned into a portable document format (PDF) for electronic filing. NY R USDCTWD ECF Procedures(2)(a)(v). Before filing a scanned document with the court, a Filing User must verify its legibility. NY R USDCTWD ECF Procedures(2)(a)(iv).

    ii.  Electronic documents must be converted to .PDF from a word processing program and must be text searchable. Do not print, scan and .PDF your document when it has been created in a word processing program. Additional information on working with PDFs is located in NY R USDCTWD ECF Procedures(4b). NY R USDCTWD ECF Procedures(2)(a)(v).

b.  *Hyperlinks.* Pursuant to the policy set forth by the Judicial Conference in October 2005, a hyperlink contained in a filing is no more than a convenient mechanism for accessing material cited in a document. A hyperlink reference is extraneous to any filed document and is not part of the Court's record. NY R USDCTWD ECF Procedures(2)(a)(vi).

    i.  In order to preserve the integrity of the Court record, users wishing to insert hyperlinks in Court filings shall continue to use the conventional method for the cited authority, in addition to the hyperlink. NY R USDCTWD ECF Procedures(2)(a)(vi).

ii. The Court accepts no responsibility for, and does not endorse any product, organization, and content at any hyperlinked site, or at any site to which that site may be linked. The Court accepts no responsibility for the availability or functionality of any hyperlink. NY R USDCTWD ECF Procedures(2)(a)(vi).

c. *Attachments and exhibits*

i. Attachments and exhibits larger than five megabytes (5 MB) shall be filed electronically in separate five megabyte (5 MB) segments. NY R USDCTWD ECF Procedures(2)(d)(i).

ii. Filing Users must submit in electronic form all documents referenced as exhibits or attachments, except as otherwise provided in NY R USDCTWD ECF Procedures. A Filing User must submit as exhibits or attachments only those excerpts of the referenced documents that are directly germane to the matter under consideration by the court. Excerpted material must be clearly and prominently identified as such. Filing Users who file excerpts of documents as exhibits or attachments under NY R USDCTWD ECF Procedures(2)(d)(ii) do so without prejudice to their right to timely file additional excerpts or the complete document. Responding parties may timely file additional excerpts or the complete document that they believe are directly germane. The Court may require parties to file additional excerpts or the complete document. A Filing User must request leave of the Court to file a document exhibit or attachment in non-electronic form. NY R USDCTWD ECF Procedures(2)(d)(ii).

iii. Exhibits offered or admitted at trial will not be filed electronically or conventionally unless so ordered by the Court. NY R USDCTWD ECF Procedures(2)(d)(iii).

iv. Exhibits such as videotapes and tape recordings shall be filed in the conventional manner with the Clerk of Court, and a Notice of Manual Filing shall be electronically filed by the party. Manually filed exhibits must have the case number and case name securely fastened or marked on the item. NY R USDCTWD ECF Procedures(2)(d)(iii).

v. Continuation of exhibit entries (for exhibits that are too large to attach to a main document) must be filed and entered on the same day that the main document was filed. NY R USDCTWD ECF Procedures(2)(d)(iv).

d. *Color documents.* Documents in color or containing graphics take much longer to upload. Filing users are encouraged to configure their scanners to scan documents at 200 dpi and preferably in black and white rather than color. NY R USDCTWD ECF Procedures(2)(d)(v).

e. *Large documents.* Due to the length of time it takes to download large files, documents larger than five megabytes (5 MB) (approximately one hundred (100) pages of a .pdf scanned document) must be filed electronically in separate five megabyte (5 MB) segments. A party who believes a document is too lengthy to electronically image (i.e. scan), may contact the Court Room Deputy for the assigned judge and request permission to file that document conventionally. If granted permission to file the document conventionally, the Filing User shall electronically file a "notice of manual filing" for that item. Exhibits submitted to the Court conventionally shall be served on other parties conventionally. NY R USDCTWD ECF Procedures(2)(d)(vi).

3. *Signing disclosures and discovery requests, responses, and objections.* FRCP 11 does not apply to disclosures and discovery requests, responses, objections, and motions under FRCP 26 through FRCP 37. FRCP 11(d).

a. *Signature required.* Every disclosure under FRCP 26(a)(1) or FRCP 26(a)(3) and every discovery request, response, or objection must be signed by at least one attorney of record in the attorney's own name—or by the party personally, if unrepresented—and must state the signer's address, e-mail address, and telephone number. FRCP 26(g)(1): Documents presented for paper filing must contain an original signature. NY R USDCTWD Civ Rule 10(b)(6).

i. *Electronic signatures*

- *Non-attorney signature.* If the original document requires the signature of a non-attorney, the filing party shall obtain the signature of the non-attorney on the document. NY R USDCTWD ECF Procedures(2)(g)(i). The filing party or attorney then shall file the document electronically indicating the signatory's name in the form "s/(name)." NY R

USDCTWD ECF Procedures(2)(g)(i)(1). A non-filing signatory or party who disputes the authenticity of an electronically filed document or the authenticity of the signature on that document must file an objection to the document within ten (10) days of receiving the Notice of Electronic Filing. NY R USDCTWD ECF Procedures(2)(g)(i)(2).

- *Registered user signature.* The username and password required to file documents on the Electronic Filing System serve as the Filing User's signature on all electronic documents filed with this Court. The also serve as a signature for the purposes of FRCP 11, the Federal Rules of Civil Procedure, the Local Rules of Civil Procedure for the United States District Court for the Western District of New York, and any other purpose for which a signature is required in connection with proceedings before this Court. A pleading requiring a Registered User's signature must include a signature block in the format found in NY R USDCTWD ECF Procedures(2)(g)(iii). NY R USDCTWD ECF Procedures(2)(g)(iii). Any party challenging the authenticity of an electronically filed document or the attorney's signature on that document must file an objection to the document within ten (10) days of receiving the Notice of Electronic Filing. NY R USDCTWD ECF Procedures(2)(g)(iii)(1).

- *Multiple signatures.* The following procedure applies when a stipulation or other document requires two or more signatures: The filing party shall initially confirm that the document is acceptable to all persons required to sign the document and shall obtain the signatures of all parties on the document. NY R USDCTWD ECF Procedures(2)(g)(iv)(1). The filing party or attorney then shall file the document electronically indicating the signatories, e.g., "s/Jane Doe," "s/John Smith," etc. NY R USDCTWD ECF Procedures(2)(g)(iv)(2). A non-filing signatory or party who disputes the authenticity of an electronically filed document containing multiple signatures or the authenticity of the signatures themselves must file an objection to the document within ten (10) days of receiving the Notice of Electronic Filing. NY R USDCTWD ECF Procedures(2)(g)(iv)(3).

b. *Effect of signature.* By signing, an attorney or party certifies that to the best of the person's knowledge, information, and belief formed after a reasonable inquiry:

   i. With respect to a disclosure, it is complete and correct as of the time it is made; and

   ii. With respect to a discovery request, response, or objection, it is:

- Consistent with the Federal Rules of Civil Procedure and warranted by existing law or by a nonfrivolous argument for extending, modifying, or reversing existing law, or for establishing new law;

- Not interposed for any improper purpose, such as to harass, cause unnecessary delay, or needlessly increase the cost of litigation; and

- Neither unreasonable nor unduly burdensome or expensive, considering the needs of the case, prior discovery in the case, the amount in controversy, and the importance of the issues at stake in the action. FRCP 26(g)(1).

c. *Failure to sign.* Other parties have no duty to act on an unsigned disclosure, request, response, or objection until it is signed, and the court must strike it unless a signature is promptly supplied after the omission is called to the attorney's or party's attention. FRCP 26(g)(2).

d. *Sanction for improper certification.* If a certification violates FRCP 26(g) without substantial justification, the court, on motion or on its own, must impose an appropriate sanction on the signer, the party on whose behalf the signer was acting, or both. The sanction may include an order to pay the reasonable expenses, including attorney's fees, caused by the violation. FRCP 26(g)(3). Refer to the United States District Court for the Western District of New York KeyRules Motion for Discovery Sanctions document for more information.

4. *Privacy protection for filings made with the court.* In all filings, parties shall comply with FRCP 5.2. NY R USDCTWD ECF Procedures(2)(m)(i).

   a. *Redacted filings.* Unless the court orders otherwise, in an electronic or paper filing with the court that

contains an individual's Social Security number, taxpayer-identification number, or birth date, the name of an individual known to be a minor, or a financial-account number, a party or nonparty making the filing may include only:

 i. The last four (4) digits of the Social Security number and taxpayer-identification number;

 ii. The year of the individual's birth;

 iii. The minor's initials; and

 iv. The last four (4) digits of the financial-account number. FRCP 5.2(a).

b. *Exemptions from the redaction requirement.* The redaction requirement does not apply to the following:

 i. A financial-account number that identifies the property allegedly subject to forfeiture in a forfeiture proceeding;

 ii. The record of an administrative or agency proceeding;

 iii. The official record of a state-court proceeding;

 iv. The record of a court or tribunal, if that record was not subject to the redaction requirement when originally filed;

 v. A filing covered by FRCP 5.2(c) or FRCP 5.2(d); and

 vi. A pro se filing in an action brought under 28 U.S.C.A. § 2241, 28 U.S.C.A. § 2254, or 28 U.S.C.A. § 2255. FRCP 5.2(b).

c. *Limitations on remote access to electronic files; Social Security appeals and immigration cases.* Unless the court orders otherwise, in an action for benefits under the Social Security Act, and in an action or proceeding relating to an order of removal, to relief from removal, or to immigration benefits or detention, access to an electronic file is authorized as follows:

 i. The parties and their attorneys may have remote electronic access to any part of the case file, including the administrative record;

 ii. Any other person may have electronic access to the full record at the courthouse, but may have remote electronic access only to:

  • The docket maintained by the court; and

  • An opinion, order, judgment, or other disposition of the court, but not any other part of the case file or the administrative record. FRCP 5.2(c).

d. *Filings made under seal.* The court may order that a filing be made under seal without redaction. The court may later unseal the filing or order the person who made the filing to file a redacted version for the public record. FRCP 5.2(d). For more information on sealing documents, refer to NY R USDCTWD Civ Rule 5.3, NY R USDCTWD ECF Procedures(2)(o)(i)(1), NY R USDCTWD ECF Procedures(2)(o)(i)(2), and NY R USDCTWD ECF Procedures(2)(o)(i)(3).

e. *Protective orders.* For good cause, the court may by order in a case:

 i. Require redaction of additional information; or

 ii. Limit or prohibit a nonparty's remote electronic access to a document filed with the court. FRCP 5.2(e).

f. *Option for additional unredacted filing under seal.* A person making a redacted filing may also file an unredacted copy under seal. The court must retain the unredacted copy as part of the record. FRCP 5.2(f).

g. *Option for filing a reference list.* A filing that contains redacted information may be filed together with a reference list that identifies each item of redacted information and specifies an appropriate identifier that uniquely corresponds to each item listed. The list must be filed under seal and may be amended as of right. Any reference in the case to a listed identifier will be construed to refer to the corresponding item of information. FRCP 5.2(g).

h. *Waiver of protection of identifiers.* A person waives the protection of FRCP 5.2(a) as to the person's own information by filing it without redaction and not under seal. FRCP 5.2(h).

5. *Individual judge practices.* Refer to the Miscellaneous section of this document for information on individual judge practices on formatting documents.

## F. Filing and Service Requirements

1. *Filing requirements.* Any paper after the complaint that is required to be served—together with a certificate of service—must be filed within a reasonable time after service. But disclosures under FRCP 26(a)(1) or FRCP 26(a)(2) and the following discovery requests and responses must not be filed until they are used in the proceeding or the court orders filing: depositions, interrogatories, requests for documents or tangible things or to permit entry onto land, and requests for admission. FRCP 5(d)(1). Parties shall comply with FRCP 5(d)(1), except that in cases involving a pro se litigant, all discovery materials must be filed with the Court pursuant to NY R USDCTWD Civ Rule 5.2(f). NY R USDCTWD Civ Rule 26(f). Refer to the United States District Court for the Western District of New York KeyRules pleading and motion documents for information on filing with the court.

   a. *Notice of filing*

      i. *Depositions by oral examination.* A party who files the deposition must promptly notify all other parties of the filing. FRCP 30(f)(4).

      ii. *Depositions by written questions.* A party who files the deposition must promptly notify all other parties of the filing. FRCP 31(c)(2).

2. *Service requirements.* All pleadings and other papers shall be filed and served in accordance with the Federal Rules of Civil Procedure and the CM/ECF Administrative Procedures Guide. NY R USDCTWD Civ Rule 5.1(a).

   a. *Service; When required*

      i. *In general.* Unless the Federal Rules of Civil Procedure provide otherwise, each of the following papers must be served on every party:

         • An order stating that service is required;

         • A pleading filed after the original complaint, unless the court orders otherwise under FRCP 5(c) because there are numerous defendants;

         • A discovery paper required to be served on a party, unless the court orders otherwise;

         • A written motion, except one that may be heard ex parte; and

         • A written notice, appearance, demand, or offer of judgment, or any similar paper. FRCP 5(a)(1).

      ii. *If a party fails to appear.* No service is required on a party who is in default for failing to appear. But a pleading that asserts a new claim for relief against such a party must be served on that party under FRCP 4. FRCP 5(a)(2).

      iii. *Seizing property.* If an action is begun by seizing property and no person is or need be named as a defendant, any service required before the filing of an appearance, answer, or claim must be made on the person who had custody or possession of the property when it was seized. FRCP 5(a)(3).

   b. *Service; How made*

      i. *Serving an attorney.* If a party is represented by an attorney, service under FRCP 5 must be made on the attorney unless the court orders service on the party. FRCP 5(b)(1).

      ii. *Service in general.* A paper is served under FRCP 5 by:

         • Handing it to the person;

         • Leaving it: (1) at the person's office with a clerk or other person in charge or, if no one is in charge, in a conspicuous place in the office; or (2) if the person has no office or the office is closed, at the person's dwelling or usual place of abode with someone of suitable age and discretion who resides there;

         • Mailing it to the person's last known address—in which event service is complete upon mailing;

- Leaving it with the court clerk if the person has no known address;

- Sending it by electronic means if the person consented in writing—in which event service is complete upon transmission, but is not effective if the serving party learns that it did not reach the person to be served; or

- Delivering it by any other means that the person consented to in writing—in which event service is complete when the person making service delivers it to the agency designated to make delivery. FRCP 5(b)(2).

iii. *Service by overnight delivery.* All papers, other than a subpoena or a summons and complaint, may be served on counsel of record by overnight delivery service at the address designated by the attorney for that purpose, or if none is designated, at the attorney's last known address. Service by overnight delivery shall be complete upon deposit of the paper(s), enclosed in a properly addressed wrapper, into the custody of the overnight delivery service, prior to the latest time designated by the service for overnight delivery. NY R USDCTWD Civ Rule 5.1(g). "Overnight delivery service" means any delivery service which regularly accepts items for overnight delivery to any address within the Court's jurisdiction. NY R USDCTWD Civ Rule 5.1(g).

iv. *Service of documents by electronic means*

- *Service on registered users.* Registered Users consent to the electronic service of all documents, and must make available an electronic mail address for service during the registration process. Upon the filing of a document by a party, a Notice of Electronic Filing, with a hyperlink to the filed document, will be automatically generated by the electronic filing system and sent via electronic mail to the e-mail addresses of all parties participating in the electronic filing system in the case. Electronic service of the Notice of Electronic Filing constitutes service of the filed document for all purposes of the Federal Rules of Civil Procedure and the Local Rules of Civil Procedure for the United States District Court for the Western District of New York. NY R USDCTWD ECF Procedures(2)(f)(i). The Notice of Electronic Filing effectuates service for all registered users and no certificate of service is required when all filers on an action are Registered Users. NY R USDCTWD ECF Procedures(2)(f)(iv).

- *Time limit for opening hyperlink.* The hyperlink to filed documents contained in the Notice of Electronic Filing must be opened within fifteen (15) days from the date the document was filed to provide registered users access to the document. The hyperlink expires after fifteen (15) days and users will be unable to access documents for free after that time. Filing Users are encouraged to check their e-mail frequently for notice of filed documents. NY R USDCTWD ECF Procedures(2)(f)(ii).

- *Service on exempted attorneys or pro se litigants who do not have permission to file electronically.* Attorneys granted an exemption from electronically filing documents in the System and pro se litigants who have not been granted permission to electronically file documents are entitled to a paper copy of any electronically filed pleading, document or order. The filing party must therefore provide the non-registered party with the pleading, document or order according to the Federal Rules of Civil Procedure. NY R USDCTWD ECF Procedures(2)(f)(iii).

- *E-mailing or faxing documents.* E-mailing or faxing a pleading or document to any party shall not constitute service of the pleading or document. NY R USDCTWD ECF Procedures(2)(f)(v).

v. *Using court facilities.* If a local rule so authorizes, a party may use the court's transmission facilities to make service under FRCP 5(b)(2)(E). FRCP 5(b)(3).

c. *Serving numerous defendants*

i. *In general.* If an action involves an unusually large number of defendants, the court may, on motion or on its own, order that:

- Defendants' pleadings and replies to them need not be served on other defendants;

- Any crossclaim, counterclaim, avoidance, or affirmative defense in those pleadings and replies to them will be treated as denied or avoided by all other parties; and

- Filing any such pleading and serving it on the plaintiff constitutes notice of the pleading to all parties. FRCP 5(c)(1).

    ii.   *Notifying parties.* A copy of every such order must be served on the parties as the court directs. FRCP 5(c)(2).

3.   *Pro se actions.* For information on the requirements in pro se actions, refer to NY R USDCTWD Civ Rule 5.2.

4.   *Individual judge practices.* Refer to the Miscellaneous section of this document for information on individual judge practices on filing and serving documents.

## G.  Hearings

1.   There is no hearing contemplated in the federal statutes or rules for the notice of deposition.

## H.  Forms

### 1.  Federal Notice of Deposition Forms

    a.   Notice to take deposition to perpetuate testimony. 3A FEDFORMS § 3339.

    b.   Notice of taking of deposition to perpetuate testimony pending appeal. 3A FEDFORMS § 3345.

    c.   Notice of taking deposition upon oral examination. 3A FEDFORMS § 3422.

    d.   Notice of taking deposition upon oral examination; Party. 3A FEDFORMS § 3423.

    e.   Notice of taking deposition upon oral examination; Naming and describing person not a party. 3A FEDFORMS § 3424.

    f.   Notice of taking deposition upon oral examination; Describing deponents whose names are unknown. 3A FEDFORMS § 3425.

    g.   Notice of taking deposition upon oral examination; Pursuant to order granting leave to take deposition. 3A FEDFORMS § 3426.

    h.   Notice of taking of deposition of party with notice to produce documents. 3A FEDFORMS § 3427.

    i.   Notice of taking of deposition of witness; Including designation of materials in related subpoena duces tecum. 3A FEDFORMS § 3428.

    j.   Notice of taking deposition of witness; Including reference to materials designated in attached subpoena. 3A FEDFORMS § 3429.

    k.   Notice of taking deposition upon written questions served with notice. 3A FEDFORMS § 3449.

    l.   Questions to be attached to notice or served with it. 3A FEDFORMS § 3450.

    m.   Notice of return and filing of deposition taken upon written questions. 3A FEDFORMS § 3456.

    n.   Notice; Taking of deposition on oral examination. FEDPROF § 23:136.

    o.   Notice; Taking of deposition on oral examination; Patent proceedings. FEDPROF § 23:137.

    p.   Notice; Taking of deposition on oral examination; Corporate officer. FEDPROF § 23:138.

    q.   Notice; Taking of deposition on oral examination; Corporate officers to be designated by corporation. FEDPROF § 23:139.

    r.   Notice; Taking of deposition on written questions. FEDPROF § 23:140.

    s.   Notice; Taking of deposition on oral examination or on written questions; Pursuant to court order. FEDPROF § 23:141.

    t.   Notice; In connection with deposition on written questions; Of cross, redirect, or recross questions. FEDPROF § 23:142.

    u.   Attachment to notice; Taking of deposition on written questions; Questions to be propounded. FEDPROF § 23:143.

    v.   Attachment to notice; Cross, redirect, or recross questions to be propounded. FEDPROF § 23:144.

w.   Notice; To party taking deposition; Written questions submitted in lieu of participation in oral examination. FEDPROF § 23:145.

x.   Notice of taking deposition; Expert witness; Request for production of supporting documents. FEDPROF § 23:151.

y.   Subpoena; To testify at taking of deposition and to produce documents or things. FEDPROF § 23:152.

z.   Provision in subpoena; Advice to nonparty organization of its duty to designate witness. FEDPROF § 23:155.

**2.   Forms for the Western District of New York**

a.   Certificate of service. NY R USDCTWD ECF Procedures(4a).

# I.  Applicable Rules

1.   *Federal rules*

a.   Serving and filing pleadings and other papers. FRCP 5.

b.   Privacy protection for filings made with the court. FRCP 5.2.

c.   Computing and extending time; Time for motion papers. FRCP 6.

d.   Pleadings allowed; Form of motions and other papers. FRCP 7.

e.   Form of pleadings. FRCP 10.

f.   Signing pleadings, motions, and other papers; Representations to the court; Sanctions. FRCP 11.

g.   Duty to disclose; General provisions governing discovery. FRCP 26.

h.   Persons before whom depositions may be taken. FRCP 28.

i.   Stipulations about discovery procedure. FRCP 29.

j.   Depositions by oral examination. FRCP 30.

k.   Depositions by written questions. FRCP 31.

l.   Failure to make disclosures or to cooperate in discovery; Sanctions. FRCP 37.

2.   *Local rules*

a.   Title. NY R USDCTWD Civ Rule 1.1.

b.   Filing and serving papers. NY R USDCTWD Civ Rule 5.1.

c.   Form of papers. NY R USDCTWD Civ Rule 10.

d.   Sanctions. NY R USDCTWD Civ Rule 11.

e.   Alternative dispute resolution and pretrial conferences. NY R USDCTWD Civ Rule 16.

f.   General rules governing discovery. NY R USDCTWD Civ Rule 26.

g.   Stipulations. NY R USDCTWD Civ Rule 29.

h.   Depositions. NY R USDCTWD Civ Rule 30.

i.   Attorneys of record; Appearance and withdrawal. NY R USDCTWD Civ Rule 83.2.

j.   Administrative procedures guide for electronic filing. NY R USDCTWD ECF Procedures.

k.   Alternative dispute resolution plan. NY R USDCTWD ADR Plan.

# J.  Miscellaneous

**NOTE: Individual judges' rules may apply. For available judge-level information, refer to:**

DISTRICT JUDGE RICHARD J. ARCARA: NY R USDCTWD Arcara-Procedures.

DISTRICT JUDGE FRANK P. GERACI, JR.: NY R USDCTWD Geraci-Procedures.

DISTRICT JUDGE DAVID G. LARIMER: NY R USDCTWD Larimer-Procedures.

DISTRICT JUDGE CHARLES J. SIRAGUSA: NY R USDCTWD Siragusa-Procedures.

DISTRICT JUDGE WILLIAM M. SKRETNY: NY R USDCTWD Skretny--Procedures.

DISTRICT JUDGE MICHAEL A. TELESCA: NY R USDCTWD Telesca-Procedures.

DISTRICT JUDGE LAWRENCE J. VILARDO: NY R USDCTWD Vilardo-Procedures.

DISTRICT JUDGE ELIZABETH A. WOLFORD: NY R USDCTWD Wolford-Procedures.

MAGISTRATE JUDGE JONATHAN W. FELDMAN: NY R USDCTWD Feldman-Procedures.

MAGISTRATE JUDGE LESLIE G. FOSCHIO: NY R USDCTWD Foschio-Procedures; NY R USDCTWD Foschio-Depositions.

MAGISTRATE JUDGE JEREMIAH J. McCARTHY: NY R USDCTWD McCarthy-Procedures.

MAGISTRATE JUDGE MARIAN W. PAYSON: NY R USDCTWD Payson-Procedures.

MAGISTRATE JUDGE MICHAEL J. ROEMER: NY R USDCTWD Roemer-Procedures.

MAGISTRATE JUDGE H. KENNETH SCHROEDER, JR.: NY R USDCTWD Schroeder-Proc.

MAGISTRATE JUDGE HUGH B. SCOTT: NY R USDCTWD Scott-Procedures.

## Requests, Notices and Applications
## Application for Temporary Restraining Order

### Document Last Updated September 2016

**A. Checklist**

(I) ❑ Matters to be considered by party applying (with notice)

    (a) ❑ Required documents

        (1) ❑ Notice of motion and motion

        (2) ❑ Memorandum of law

        (3) ❑ Supporting affidavit

        (4) ❑ Complaint

        (5) ❑ Proposed order

        (6) ❑ Motion for an expedited hearing

        (7) ❑ Security

        (8) ❑ Certificate of service

    (b) ❑ Supplemental documents

        (1) ❑ Supporting evidence

        (2) ❑ Notice of constitutional question

        (3) ❑ Nongovernmental corporate disclosure statement

        (4) ❑ Copies of authorities

        (5) ❑ Paper copy for date-stamping with self-addressed envelope

        (6) ❑ Courtesy copies

    (c) ❑ Timing

        (1) ❑ A written motion and notice of the hearing must be served at least fourteen (14) days before the time specified for the hearing, with the following exceptions: (i) when the motion may be heard ex parte; (ii) when the Federal Rules of Civil Procedure set a different time; or (iii) when a court order—which a party may, for good cause, apply for ex parte—sets a different time

        (2) ❑ Any affidavit supporting a motion must be served with the motion

(II) ❑ Matters to be considered by party applying (without notice, or "ex parte")

    (a) ❑ Required documents

        (1) ❑ Motion

        (2) ❑ Memorandum of law

        (3) ❑ Supporting affidavit

        (4) ❑ Affidavit or verified complaint

        (5) ❑ Complaint

        (6) ❑ Proposed order

        · (7) ❑ Certificate of attorney

        (8) ❑ Security

    (b) ❑ Supplemental documents

        (1) ❑ Supporting evidence

        (2) ❑ Notice of constitutional question

        (3) ❑ Nongovernmental corporate disclosure statement

        (4) ❑ Copies of authorities

        (5) ❑ Paper copy for date-stamping with self-addressed envelope

        (6) ❑ Courtesy copies

    (c) ❑ Timing

        (1) ❑ There are no specific timing requirements for applying for a temporary restraining order without notice

        (2) ❑ Any affidavit supporting a motion must be served with the motion

## B. Timing

1. *Application for temporary restraining order*

    a. *With notice.* There are no specific timing requirements for applying for a temporary restraining order with notice.

    b. *Without notice, or "ex parte."* There are no specific timing requirements for applying for a temporary restraining order without notice, or "ex parte."

2. *Motion to dissolve or modify.* On two (2) days' notice to the party who obtained the order without notice—or on shorter notice set by the court—the adverse party may appear and move to dissolve or modify the order. The court must then hear and decide the motion as promptly as justice requires. FRCP 65(b)(4).

3. *Timing of motions, generally*

    a. *Motion and notice of hearing.* A written motion and notice of the hearing must be served at least fourteen (14) days before the time specified for the hearing, with the following exceptions:

        i. When the motion may be heard ex parte;

        ii. When the Federal Rules of Civil Procedure set a different time; or

        iii. When a court order—which a party may, for good cause, apply for ex parte—sets a different time. FRCP 6(c)(1).

    b. *Supporting affidavit.* Any affidavit supporting a motion must be served with the motion. FRCP 6(c)(2).

4. *Motion for an expedited hearing.* A party seeking to shorten the schedule prescribed in NY R USDCTWD Civ Rule 7(b) must make a separate motion for an expedited hearing, setting forth the reasons why an expedited hearing is required. NY R USDCTWD Civ Rule 7(d)(1). For more information, refer to NY R USDCTWD Civ Rule 7(d)(1).

5. *Computation of time*

   a. *Computing time.* FRCP 6 applies in computing any time period specified in the Federal Rules of Civil Procedure, in any local rule or court order, or in any statute that does not specify a method of computing time. FRCP 6(a).

      i. *Period stated in days or a longer unit.* When the period is stated in days or a longer unit of time:

         • Exclude the day of the event that triggers the period;

         • Count every day, including intermediate Saturdays, Sundays, and legal holidays; and

         • Include the last day of the period, but if the last day is a Saturday, Sunday, or legal holiday, the period continues to run until the end of the next day that is not a Saturday, Sunday, or legal holiday. FRCP 6(a)(1).

      ii. *Period stated in hours.* When the period is stated in hours:

         • Begin counting immediately on the occurrence of the event that triggers the period;

         • Count every hour, including hours during intermediate Saturdays, Sundays, and legal holidays; and

         • If the period would end on a Saturday, Sunday, or legal holiday, the period continues to run until the same time on the next day that is not a Saturday, Sunday, or legal holiday. FRCP 6(a)(2).

      iii. *Inaccessibility of the clerk's office.* Unless the court orders otherwise, if the clerk's office is inaccessible:

         • On the last day for filing under FRCP 6(a)(1), then the time for filing is extended to the first accessible day that is not a Saturday, Sunday, or legal holiday; or

         • During the last hour for filing under FRCP 6(a)(2), then the time for filing is extended to the same time on the first accessible day that is not a Saturday, Sunday, or legal holiday. FRCP 6(a)(3).

      iv. *"Last day" defined.* Unless a different time is set by a statute, local rule, or court order, the last day ends:

         • For electronic filing, at midnight in the court's time zone; and

         • For filing by other means, when the clerk's office is scheduled to close. FRCP 6(a)(4).

      v. *"Next day" defined.* The "next day" is determined by continuing to count forward when the period is measured after an event and backward when measured before an event. FRCP 6(a)(5).

      vi. *"Legal holiday" defined.* "Legal holiday" means:

         • The day set aside by statute for observing New Year's Day, Martin Luther King Jr.'s Birthday, Washington's Birthday, Memorial Day, Independence Day, Labor Day, Columbus Day, Veterans' Day, Thanksgiving Day, or Christmas Day;

         • Any day declared a holiday by the President or Congress; and

         • For periods that are measured after an event, any other day declared a holiday by the state where the district court is located. FRCP 6(a)(6).

   b. *Computation of electronic filing deadlines.* A document will be deemed timely filed if filed prior to midnight Eastern Time, unless otherwise ordered by the Court. A document will be considered untimely if filed thereafter. When a Court order requires that a document be filed on a weekend or holiday, the document may be filed by close of business the next business day without further application to the Court. NY R USDCTWD ECF Procedures(2)(e)(i). A document filed electronically is deemed filed on the date and time stated on the Notice of Electronic Filing. NY R USDCTWD ECF Procedures(2)(e)(ii).

      i. *System availability.* Although parties may file documents electronically twenty-four (24) hours a day, registered users are strongly encouraged to file all documents during normal working hours of the Clerk's Office (8:30 a.m. to 5:00 p.m. Eastern Time). NY R USDCTWD ECF Procedures(2)(t)(i).

      ii.   *Technical failures.* A Filing User whose filing is made untimely as a result of a technical failure must seek appropriate relief from the Court. NY R USDCTWD ECF Procedures(2)(u)(i).

  c.  *Extending time*

      i.   *In general.* When an act may or must be done within a specified time, the court may, for good cause, extend the time:

- With or without motion or notice if the court acts, or if a request is made, before the original time or its extension expires; or

- On motion made after the time has expired if the party failed to act because of excusable neglect. FRCP 6(b)(1).

      ii.   *Exceptions.* A court must not extend the time to act under FRCP 50(b), FRCP 50(d), FRCP 52(b), FRCP 59(b), FRCP 59(d), FRCP 59(e), and FRCP 60(b). FRCP 6(b)(2).

     iii.  Refer to the United States District Court for the Western District of New York KeyRules Motion for Continuance/Extension of Time document for more information on extending time.

  d.  *Additional time after certain kinds of service.* When a party may or must act within a specified time after service and service is made under FRCP 5(b)(2)(C), FRCP 5(b)(2)(D), FRCP 5(b)(2)(E), or FRCP 5(b)(2)(F), three (3) days are added after the period would otherwise expire under FRCP 6(a). FRCP 6(d).

      i.   *Service by overnight delivery.* Where a period of time prescribed by either the Federal Rules of Civil Procedure or the Local Rules of Civil Procedure for the United States District Court for the Western District of New York is measured from the service of a paper and service is by overnight delivery, one (1) business day shall be added to the prescribed period. NY R USDCTWD Civ Rule 5.1(g).

6.  *Individual judge practices.* Refer to the Miscellaneous section of this document for information on individual judge practices on timing of documents.

## C. General Requirements

1.  *Motions, generally*

  a.  *Requirements.* A request for a court order must be made by motion. The motion must:

      i.   Be in writing unless made during a hearing or trial;

      ii.   State with particularity the grounds for seeking the order; and

     iii.  State the relief sought. FRCP 7(b)(1).

  b.  *Notice of motion.* A party interested in resisting the relief sought by a motion has a right to notice thereof, and an opportunity to be heard. AMJUR MOTIONS § 12.

      i.   In addition to statutory or court rule provisions requiring notice of a motion—the purpose of such a notice requirement having been said to be to prevent a party from being prejudicially surprised by a motion—principles of natural justice dictate that an adverse party generally must be given notice that a motion will be presented to the court. AMJUR MOTIONS § 12.

      ii.   "Notice," in this regard, means reasonable notice, including a meaningful opportunity to prepare and to defend against allegations of a motion. AMJUR MOTIONS § 12.

  c.  *Writing requirement.* The writing requirement is intended to insure that the adverse parties are informed and have a record of both the motion's pendency and the grounds on which the movant seeks an order. FPP § 1191; Feldberg v. Quechee Lakes Corp., 463 F.3d 195 (2d Cir. 2006).

      i.   It is sufficient "if the motion is stated in a written notice of the hearing of the motion." FPP § 1191.

  d.  *Particularity requirement.* The particularity requirement insures that the opposing parties will have notice of their opponent's contentions. FEDPROC § 62:364; Goodman v. 1973 26 Foot Trojan Vessel, Arkansas Registration No. AR1439SN, 859 F.2d 71, 12 Fed.R.Serv.3d 645 (8th Cir. 1988). That requirement ensures that notice of the basis for the motion is provided to the court and to the opposing party so as to avoid prejudice, provide the opponent with a meaningful opportunity to respond, and provide the court with enough information to process the motion correctly. FEDPROC § 62:364; Andreas v. Volkswagen of America, Inc., 336 F.3d 789, 56 Fed.R.Serv.3d 6 (8th Cir. 2003).

  i.  Reasonable specification of the grounds for a motion is sufficient. However, where a movant fails to state even one ground for granting the motion in question, the movant has failed to meet the minimal standard of "reasonable specification." FEDPROC § 62:364; Martinez v. Trainor, 556 F.2d 818, 23 Fed.R.Serv.2d 403 (7th Cir. 1977).

  ii. The court may excuse the failure to comply with the particularity requirement if it is inadvertent, and where no prejudice is shown by the opposing party. FEDPROC § 62:364.

2. *Application for temporary restraining order.* Applicants for injunctive relief occasionally are faced with the possibility that irreparable injury will occur before the hearing for a preliminary injunction required by FRCP 65(a) can be held. In that event a temporary restraining order may be available under FRCP 65(b). FPP § 2951. The order is designed to preserve the status quo until there is an opportunity to hold a hearing on the application for a preliminary injunction and may be issued with or without notice to the adverse party. FPP § 2951; Granny Goose Foods, Inc. v. Brotherhood of Teamsters & Auto Truck Drivers Local No. 70 of Alameda County, 415 U.S. 423, 94 S.Ct. 1113, 39 L.Ed.2d 435 (1974).

  a. *Temporary restraining orders, generally.* An Order to Show Cause is not specifically authorized under the Federal Rules of Civil Procedure. Such relief is available upon motion for a TRO, pursuant to FRCP 65, and a motion for an expedited hearing, pursuant to NY R USDCTWD Civ Rule 7(d)(1). There are two types of TROs: an ex parte TRO and a TRO issued upon notice to the adverse party. An ex parte TRO is available only in extraordinary circumstances. In most cases, the Court will require both notice to the adverse party and an opportunity to be heard before granting a TRO. NY R USDCTWD Civ Rule 65(b).

  b. *Issuing with notice.* When the opposing party actually receives notice of the application for a restraining order, the procedure that is followed does not differ functionally from that on an application for a preliminary injunction and the proceeding is not subject to any special requirements. FPP § 2951; Dilworth v. Riner, 343 F.2d 226 (5th Cir. 1965).

    i. *Duration.* By its terms FRCP 65(b) only governs restraining orders issued without notice or a hearing. But. . .it has been argued that its provisions, at least with regard to the duration of a restraining order, apply even to an order granted when notice has been given to the adverse party but there has been no hearing. FPP § 2951.

  c. *Issuing without notice.* A party seeking an ex parte TRO must comply with the requirements of FRCP 65(b)(1) and FRCP 65(b)(2). Because an application for a TRO rarely will be granted ex parte, a party moving under NY R USDCTWD Civ Rule 65(b)(1) should be prepared to proceed pursuant to NY R USDCTWD Civ Rule 65(b)(2), in the event that the Court finds that an ex parte proceeding is unwarranted. NY R USDCTWD Civ Rule 65(b)(1).

    i. *When available.* The court may issue a temporary restraining order without written or oral notice to the adverse party or its attorney only if:

      • Specific facts in an affidavit or a verified complaint clearly show that immediate and irreparable injury, loss, or damage will result to the movant before the adverse party can be heard in opposition; and

      • The movant's attorney certifies in writing any efforts made to give notice and the reasons why it should not be required. FRCP 65(b)(1).

    ii. *Contents.* Every temporary restraining order issued without notice must state the date and hour it was issued; describe the injury and state why it is irreparable; state why the order was issued without notice; and be promptly filed in the clerk's office and entered in the record. FRCP 65(b)(2).

    iii. *Expiration.* The order expires at the time after entry—not to exceed fourteen (14) days—that the court sets, unless before that time the court, for good cause, extends it for a like period or the adverse party consents to a longer extension. The reasons for an extension must be entered in the record. FRCP 65(b)(2).

d. *Temporary restraining order versus preliminary injunction.* A temporary restraining order differs from a preliminary injunction, the core reasons being that a temporary restraining order is of limited duration and it may issue without notice to the opposing party before the adverse party can be heard in opposition. FEDPROC § 47:80.

e. *Factors considered.* As in the case of an application for a preliminary injunction, four factors must be considered in determining whether a temporary restraining order is to be granted, which are whether the moving party has established: (1) a substantial likelihood of success on the merits; (2) that irreparable injury will be suffered if the relief is not granted; (3) that the threatened injury outweighs the harm the relief would inflict on the nonmoving party; and (4) that entry of the relief would serve the public interest. FEDPROC § 47:84; Schiavo ex rel. Schindler v. Schiavo, 403 F.3d 1223 (11th Cir. 2005).

   i. Plaintiffs are not required to prevail on each of these factors, rather, the factors must be viewed as a continuum, with more of one factor compensating for less of another. In each case, however, all of the factors must be considered to determine whether on balance they weigh toward granting relief. FEDPROC § 47:84.

   ii. In the context of a temporary restraining order, it is particularly important for the moving party to demonstrate a substantial likelihood of success on the merits, because otherwise, there would be no justification for the court's intrusion into the ordinary processes of administration and judicial review. FEDPROC § 47:84.

   iii. Refer to the United States District Court for the Western District of New York KeyRules Motion for Preliminary Injunction document for more information on the factors considered in moving for a preliminary injunction.

f. *Burden.* As with a preliminary injunction, the burden is on the moving party to establish that relief is appropriate. FEDPROC § 47:84.

g. *Security.* The parties shall be prepared to address the security requirements of FRCP 65(c) whenever applying for injunctive relief. NY R USDCTWD Civ Rule 65(c). The court may issue a preliminary injunction or a temporary restraining order only if the movant gives security in an amount that the court considers proper to pay the costs and damages sustained by any party found to have been wrongfully enjoined or restrained. The United States, its officers, and its agencies are not required to give security. FRCP 65(c).

   i. *Proceedings against a surety.* Whenever the Federal Rules of Civil Procedure (including the Supplemental Rules for Admiralty or Maritime Claims and Asset Forfeiture Actions) require or allow a party to give security, and security is given through a bond or other undertaking with one or more sureties, each surety submits to the court's jurisdiction and irrevocably appoints the court clerk as its agent for receiving service of any papers that affect its liability on the bond or undertaking. The surety's liability may be enforced on motion without an independent action. The motion and any notice that the court orders may be served on the court clerk, who must promptly mail a copy of each to every surety whose address is known. FRCP 65.1.

h. *Contents and scope of every injunction and restraining order*

   i. *Contents.* Every order granting an injunction and every restraining order must:

   - State the reasons why it issued;
   - State its terms specifically; and
   - Describe in reasonable detail—and not by referring to the complaint or other document— the act or acts restrained or required. FRCP 65(d)(1).

   ii. *Persons bound.* The order binds only the following who receive actual notice of it by personal service or otherwise:

   - The parties;
   - The parties' officers, agents, servants, employees, and attorneys; and
   - Other persons who are in active concert or participation with anyone described in FRCP 65(d)(2)(A) or FRCP 65(d)(2)(B). FRCP 65(d)(2).

    i. *Other laws not modified.* FRCP 65 does not modify the following:

        i. Any federal statute relating to temporary restraining orders or preliminary injunctions in actions affecting employer and employee;

        ii. 28 U.S.C.A. § 2361, which relates to preliminary injunctions in actions of interpleader or in the nature of interpleader; or

        iii. 28 U.S.C.A. § 2284, which relates to actions that must be heard and decided by a three-judge district court. FRCP 65(e).

    j. *Copyright impoundment.* FRCP 65 applies to copyright-impoundment proceedings. FRCP 65(f).

3. *Motion to settle an order.* When counsel are unable to agree on the form of a proposed order, the prevailing party may move, upon seven (7) days notice to all parties, to settle the order. The Court may award costs and attorney's fees against an attorney if it determines that the attorney's unreasonable conduct necessitated bringing the motion. NY R USDCTWD Civ Rule 7(d)(2).

4. *Notice of appearance.* No notice of appearance is required of an attorney whose name and address appear at the end of a complaint, notice of removal, pre-answer motion, or answer. In all other circumstances, an attorney appearing for a party in a civil case shall promptly file a written notice of appearance. NY R USDCTWD Civ Rule 83.2(b). For more information on appearances and withdrawals, refer to NY R USDCTWD Civ Rule 83.2.

5. *Related cases.* Each attorney appearing in a civil case has a continuing duty to promptly notify the Clerk of Court when the attorney has reason to believe that said case is related to some other pending civil or criminal action(s) such that their assignment to the same Judge would avoid unnecessary duplication of judicial effort. As soon as the attorney becomes aware of such a relationship, the attorney shall notify the Clerk of Court by letter of the relevant facts, and the Clerk of Court will transmit that notification to the Judges to whom the cases have been assigned. NY R USDCTWD Civ Rule 5.1(e).

6. *Alternative dispute resolution (ADR).* This Court has adopted an Alternative Dispute Resolution Plan ("ADR"), as implemented by Standing Order (NY R USDCTWD ADR Plan), under which certain civil cases are referred automatically to ADR upon filing. NY R USDCTWD Civ Rule 16(a). The United States District Court for the Western District of New York (the "Court") adopted the ADR Plan on January 1, 2006 (the "Effective Date"), to make available to civil litigants court-administered ADR interventions and processes designed to provide quicker, less expensive and potentially more satisfying alternatives to continuing litigation, without impairing the quality of justice or the right to trial. NY R USDCTWD ADR Plan(1)(1.2)(A).

    a. *Scope.* This ADR Plan (NY R USDCTWD ADR Plan) applies to civil actions pending or commenced on and after the Effective Date, except as otherwise indicated in NY R USDCTWD ADR Plan. The ADR Plan supplements the Local Rules of Civil Procedure for the United States District Court for the Western District of New York, which shall remain in full effect for all cases. NY R USDCTWD ADR Plan(1)(1.2)(B).

    b. *Referral to ADR*

        i. *New cases.* All civil cases filed on and after the Effective Date of the ADR Plan shall be referred automatically for ADR. NY R USDCTWD ADR Plan(2)(2.1)(A). Notice of the ADR requirements will be provided to all parties immediately upon the filing of a complaint and answer or a notice of removal; NY R USDCTWD ADR Plan(2)(2.1)(A); NY R USDCTWD Civ Rule 16(a). ADR intervention will be scheduled at the conference held pursuant to Local Rule of Civil Procedure 16.1. NY R USDCTWD ADR Plan(2)(2.1)(A). [Editor's note: the reference to Local Rule of Civil Procedure 16.1 is likely meant to be a reference to NY R USDCTWD Civ Rule 16(b)].

          • Litigants in cases not referred automatically to ADR must consider possible agreement to the use of an ADR process. NY R USDCTWD Civ Rule 16(a).

          • For a list of exemptions from automatic referral, refer to NY R USDCTWD ADR Plan(2)(2.1)(A).

        ii. *Pending cases.* The assigned Judge on any pending civil case may, sua sponte or with status conference, issue an order referring the case for ADR. NY R USDCTWD ADR Plan(2)(2.1)(B); NY R USDCTWD Civ Rule 16(a). The order shall specify a date on which the ADR intervention is to be completed. NY R USDCTWD ADR Plan(2)(2.1)(B).

    iii.  *Stipulation.* A case may be referred for ADR by stipulation of all parties. Stipulations shall be filed and shall designate the specific ADR intervention the parties have selected, the time frame within which the ADR process will be completed and the selected Neutral. Stipulations are presumed acceptable unless the assigned Judge determines that the interests of justice are not served. NY R USDCTWD ADR Plan(2)(2.1)(C).

    iv.  *Relief from ADR referral*

- *Opting out motions.* Any party may file, with the assigned Judge for that case, a motion to opt out of, or for relief from, ADR. NY R USDCTWD ADR Plan(2)(2.2)(A).

- *Motion.* Opting Out Motions must be made within fourteen (14) days from (1) the date of the first discovery conference under Local Rule 16.1 in new cases, or (2) the date of a sua sponte ADR Referral Order in pending cases. NY R USDCTWD ADR Plan(2)(2.2)(B). [Editor's note: the reference to Local Rule 16.1 is likely meant to be a reference to NY R USDCTWD Civ Rule 16(b)].

- *Criteria.* Opting Out Motions shall be granted only for "good cause" shown. Inconvenience, travel costs, attorney fees or other costs shall not constitute "good cause." A party seeking relief from ADR must set forth the reasons why ADR has no reasonable chance of being productive. NY R USDCTWD ADR Plan(2)(2.2)(C).

- *Judicial initiative.* The assigned Judge may, sua sponte, exempt any case from the Court's ADR Plan. NY R USDCTWD ADR Plan(2)(2.2)(D).

**c.** *ADR interventions*

    i.  *Options.* It is expected that cases referred for ADR will proceed to Mediation. However, the following options are also available upon the stipulation of all parties:

- Neutral Evaluation;

- Mini Summary Trial;

- Arbitration (Binding and Non-Binding);

- Case Valuation; and

- Settlement Week, when scheduled by the Court. NY R USDCTWD ADR Plan(4)(4.1)(A).

    ii.  *Timing.* Timing is specific to the intervention and process chosen, as set forth in the corresponding sections in NY R USDCTWD ADR Plan. NY R USDCTWD ADR Plan(4)(4.1)(B).

    iii.  *Scheduling.* The referral of a case to ADR does not delay or defer other dates established in the Scheduling Order and has no effect on the scheduled progress of the case toward trial. NY R USDCTWD ADR Plan(4)(4.1)(C).

**d.** *Selecting an ADR intervention*

    i.  *New cases.* Prior to the Local Rule 16.1 scheduling conference, counsel and any unrepresented parties shall confer about ADR as part of their discussion of "the possibilities for a prompt settlement or resolution of the case" pursuant to FRCP 26(f). Unless the parties agree to a different intervention, it is presumed that they will participate in mediation. [Editor's note: the reference to Local Rule 16.1 is likely meant to be a reference to NY R USDCTWD Civ Rule 16(b)].

    ii.  *Pending cases.* In pending cases, all sua sponte referrals will be to mediation. Should the parties agree that a different ADR intervention is more appropriate to their case, they may submit a stipulation designating the specific ADR intervention selected, the time frame within which the ADR process will be completed and the identity of the Neutral. Stipulations must be filed within fourteen (14) days from the date of the ADR Referral Order and are presumed acceptable unless the assigned Judge determines that the interests of justice are not served. NY R USDCTWD ADR Plan(4)(4.2)(B).

e. For more information on alternative dispute resolution (ADR), refer to NY R USDCTWD ADR Plan.

7. *Sanctions.* Failure of counsel for any party, or a party proceeding pro se, to appear before the Court at a conference, to complete the necessary preparations, or to be prepared to proceed to trial at the set time may be considered an abandonment of the case or a failure to prosecute or defend diligently. An appropriate order for sanctions may be entered against the defaulting party with respect to either a specific issue or the entire case. NY R USDCTWD Civ Rule 11(a). For more information, refer to NY R USDCTWD Civ Rule 11.

8. *Pro se actions.* For information on the requirements in pro se actions, refer to NY R USDCTWD Civ Rule 5.2.

9. *Individual judge practices.* Refer to the Miscellaneous section of this document for information on individual judge practices on general requirements for documents.

## D. Documents

1. *Application for temporary restraining order (with notice)*

   a. *Required documents*

      i. *Notice of motion and motion.* An application for a TRO on notice shall include: the document required by NY R USDCTWD Civ Rule 65(b)(1)(B) (the motion for a TRO). NY R US-DCTWD Civ Rule 65(b)(2)(A). A notice of motion is required for all motions, and must state: the relief sought, the grounds for the request, the papers submitted in support, and the return date for the motion, if known. A moving party who intends to file and serve reply papers must so state in the notice of motion. NY R USDCTWD Civ Rule 7(a)(1). Refer to the General Requirements section of this document for information on the notice of motion and motion.

      ii. *Memorandum of law.* An application for a TRO on notice shall include: the document required by NY R USDCTWD Civ Rule 65(b)(1)(C) (a memorandum of law in support of the TRO, citing legal authority showing that the party is entitled to the relief requested). NY R US-DCTWD Civ Rule 65(b)(2)(A). Nothing in the Local Rules of Civil Procedure for the United States District Court for the Western District of New York precludes a moving party from filing a memorandum in support of a motion made other than pursuant to FRCP 12, FRCP 56 or FRCP 65(a). The Court, in its discretion, may require written memoranda on such other motions. NY R USDCTWD Civ Rule 7(a)(2)(B). Refer to the Format section of this document for the formatting requirements for memoranda of law.

      iii. *Supporting affidavit.* An affidavit must not contain legal arguments, but must contain factual and procedural background relevant to the motion it supports. Except for motions brought under FRCP 12(b)(1) (lack of subject matter jurisdiction), FRCP 12(b)(6) (failure to state a claim), FRCP 12(c) (judgment on the pleadings), and FRCP 12(f) (to strike), motions and opposition to motions shall be supported by at least one (1) affidavit and by such other evidence (i.e., deposition testimony, interrogatory answers, admissions, and documents) as appropriate to resolve the particular motion. Failure to comply with this requirement may constitute grounds for resolving the motion against the non-complying party. NY R USDCTWD Civ Rule 7(a)(3).

      iv. *Complaint.* An application for a TRO on notice shall include: the document required by NY R USDCTWD Civ Rule 65(b)(1)(A) (a copy of the complaint, if the case has been recently filed). NY R USDCTWD Civ Rule 65(b)(2)(A).

      v. *Proposed order.* An application for a TRO on notice shall include: the document required by NY R USDCTWD Civ Rule 65(b)(1)(D) (a proposed order granting the TRO, in accordance with FRCP 65(b)(2) and FRCP 65(d)(1)). NY R USDCTWD Civ Rule 65(b)(2)(A). All proposed orders must be submitted in a format compatible with WordPerfect or Microsoft Word format, which is a "Save As" option in most word processing software. Judges will not accept proposed orders in PDF format. NY R USDCTWD ECF Procedures(2)(j)(ii). Proposed orders should be attached to an Internet e-mail sent to the e-mail address of the assigned judge. NY R USDCTWD ECF Procedures(2)(j)(i). For the list of email addresses for the judges, refer to NY R USDCTWD ECF Procedures(2)(j)(i).

vi. *Motion for an expedited hearing.* An application for a TRO on notice shall include: a motion for an expedited hearing pursuant to NY R USDCTWD Civ Rule 7(d)(1). NY R USDCTWD Civ Rule 65(b)(2)(B).

vii. *Security.* Refer to the General Requirements section of this document for information on the security required.

viii. *Certificate of service.* FRCP 5(d) requires that the person making service under FRCP 5 certify that service has been effected. FRCP 5(Advisory Committee Notes). Having such information on file may be useful for many purposes, including proof of service if an issue arises concerning the effectiveness of the service. FRCP 5(Advisory Committee Notes). The Notice of Electronic Filing effectuates service for all registered users and no certificate of service is required when all filers on an action are Registered Users. The following exemptions require a certificate of service to be filed:

- When a document is manually filed, a certificate of service must be filed stating the manner in which service or notice was accomplished on each party so entitled. NY R USDCTWD ECF Procedures(2)(f)(iv).

- When a pro se filer (who isn't authorized to electronically file documents) is a party, a certificate of service must be filed stating the manner in which service or notice was accomplished on the pro se party. The Notice of Electronic Filing effectuates service for the Registered Users in this situation and it is not necessary to note service on those parties. A non-registered pro se filer is required to file certificates of service on all documents they file. NY R USDCTWD ECF Procedures(2)(f)(iv).

- If an attorney is exempt from electronic service, a certificate of service must be filed stating the manner in which service or notice was accomplished on the exempt attorney. The Notice of Electronic Filing effectuates service for the Registered Users in this situation and it is not necessary to note service on those parties. NY R USDCTWD ECF Procedures(2)(f)(iv).

b. *Supplemental documents*

i. *Supporting evidence.* When a motion relies on facts outside the record, the court may hear the matter on affidavits or may hear it wholly or partly on oral testimony or on depositions. FRCP 43(c). A party seeking or opposing any relief under the Federal Rules of Civil Procedure shall file only the portion(s) of a deposition, interrogatory, request for documents, request for admission, or other supporting material that is pertinent to the application. NY R USDCTWD Civ Rule 7(a)(4).

ii. *Notice of constitutional question.* A party that files a pleading, written motion, or other paper drawing into question the constitutionality of a federal or state statute must promptly:

- *File notice.* File a notice of constitutional question stating the question and identifying the paper that raises it, if: (1) a federal statute is questioned and the parties do not include the United States, one of its agencies, or one of its officers or employees in an official capacity; or (2) a state statute is questioned and the parties do not include the state, one of its agencies, or one of its officers or employees in an official capacity; and

- *Serve notice.* Serve the notice and paper on the Attorney General of the United States if a federal statute is questioned—or on the state attorney general if a state statute is questioned—either by certified or registered mail or by sending it to an electronic address designated by the attorney general for this purpose. FRCP 5.1(a).

- *No forfeiture.* A party's failure to file and serve the notice, or the court's failure to certify, does not forfeit a constitutional claim or defense that is otherwise timely asserted. FRCP 5.1(d).

iii. *Nongovernmental corporate disclosure statement*

- *Contents.* A nongovernmental corporate party must file two (2) copies of a disclosure statement that: (1) identifies any parent corporation and any publicly held corporation owning ten percent (10%) or more of its stock; or (2) states that there is no such corporation. FRCP 7.1(a).

- *Time to file; Supplemental filing.* A party must: (1) file the disclosure statement with its first appearance, pleading, petition, motion, response, or other request addressed to the court; and (2) promptly file a supplemental statement if any required information changes. FRCP 7.1(b).

iv. \*Copies of authorities.* In cases involving a pro se litigant, counsel shall, when serving a memorandum of law (or other submissions to the Court), provide the pro se litigant (but not other counsel or the Court) with printed copies of decisions cited therein that are unreported or reported exclusively on computerized databases. NY R USDCTWD Civ Rule 7(a)(8).

v. *Paper copy for date-stamping with self-addressed envelope.* Parties requesting date-stamped copies of filed documents must provide a paper copy for date-stamping, and a self-addressed, adequately-sized envelope with proper postage affixed. NY R USDCTWD Civ Rule 5.1(d).

vi. *Courtesy copies.* The Court may, in its discretion, request courtesy copies on any other motion. NY R USDCTWD Civ Rule 7(a)(7). Courtesy copies of certain documents may be required. Filers should refer to the "Judge Preferences" published on the Court's website. NY R USDCTWD ECF Procedures(2)(a)(iii). Immediately after filing a motion for an expedited hearing (NY R USDCTWD Civ Rule 7(d)(1)), or motion for a temporary restraining order (NY R USDCTWD Civ Rule 65(a)), the moving party must deliver a courtesy copy of the motion papers to the chambers of the assigned Judge. NY R USDCTWD Civ Rule 7(a)(7). [Editor's note: the reference to NY R USDCTWD Civ Rule 65(a) is likely meant to be a reference to NY R USDCTWD Civ Rule 65(b)].

- Immediately after filing the TRO application, counsel for the moving party shall personally deliver courtesy copies of the documents listed in NY R USDCTWD Civ Rule 65(b)(2) to chambers and await further instructions from the Court. In the event that the moving party is represented by out-of-town counsel who is unable to personally deliver courtesy copies, counsel shall contact chambers by telephone to request a waiver of this requirement. NY R USDCTWD Civ Rule 65(b)(2).

2. *Application for temporary restraining order (without notice, or "ex parte")*

   a. *Required documents*

      i. *Motion.* An application for an ex parte TRO also shall include: the motion for a TRO. NY R USDCTWD Civ Rule 65(b)(1)(B). Refer to the General Requirements section of this document for information on the motion.

      ii. *Memorandum of law.* An application for an ex parte TRO also shall include: a memorandum of law in support of the TRO, citing legal authority showing that the party is entitled to the relief requested. NY R USDCTWD Civ Rule 65(b)(1)(C). Nothing in the Local Rules of Civil Procedure for the United States District Court for the Western District of New York precludes a moving party from filing a memorandum in support of a motion made other than pursuant to FRCP 12, FRCP 56 or FRCP 65(a). The Court, in its discretion, may require written memoranda on such other motions. NY R USDCTWD Civ Rule 7(a)(2)(B). Refer to the Format section of this document for the formatting requirements for memoranda of law.

      iii. *Supporting affidavit.* An affidavit must not contain legal arguments, but must contain factual and procedural background relevant to the motion it supports. Except for motions brought under FRCP 12(b)(1) (lack of subject matter jurisdiction), FRCP 12(b)(6) (failure to state a claim), FRCP 12(c) (judgment on the pleadings), and FRCP 12(f) (to strike), motions and opposition to motions shall be supported by at least one (1) affidavit and by such other evidence (i.e., deposition testimony, interrogatory answers, admissions, and documents) as appropriate to resolve the particular motion. Failure to comply with this requirement may constitute grounds for resolving the motion against the non-complying party. NY R USDCTWD Civ Rule 7(a)(3).

      iv. *Affidavit or verified complaint.* The applicant for an ex parte restraining order must present to the court, in an affidavit or a verified complaint, facts that clearly show irreparable injury. FPP § 2952.

v. *Complaint.* An application for an ex parte TRO also shall include: a copy of the complaint, if the case has been recently filed. NY R USDCTWD Civ Rule 65(b)(1)(A).

vi. *Proposed order.* An application for an ex parte TRO also shall include: a proposed order granting the TRO, in accordance with FRCP 65(b)(2) and FRCP 65(d)(1). NY R USDCTWD Civ Rule 65(b)(1)(D). All proposed orders must be submitted in a format compatible with WordPerfect or Microsoft Word format, which is a "Save As" option in most word processing software. Judges will not accept proposed orders in PDF format. NY R USDCTWD ECF Procedures(2)(j)(ii). Proposed orders should be attached to an Internet e-mail sent to the e-mail address of the assigned judge. NY R USDCTWD ECF Procedures(2)(j)(i). For the list of email addresses for the judges, refer to NY R USDCTWD ECF Procedures(2)(j)(i).

vii. *Certificate of attorney.* The applicant's attorney must certify in writing any efforts made to give notice and the reasons why it should not be required. FEDPROC § 47:81.

viii. *Security.* Refer to the General Requirements section of this document for information on the security required.

b. *Supplemental documents*

i. *Supporting evidence.* When a motion relies on facts outside the record, the court may hear the matter on affidavits or may hear it wholly or partly on oral testimony or on depositions. FRCP 43(c). A party seeking or opposing any relief under the Federal Rules of Civil Procedure shall file only the portion(s) of a deposition, interrogatory, request for documents, request for admission, or other supporting material that is pertinent to the application. NY R USDCTWD Civ Rule 7(a)(4).

ii. *Notice of constitutional question.* A party that files a pleading, written motion, or other paper drawing into question the constitutionality of a federal or state statute must promptly:

- *File notice.* File a notice of constitutional question stating the question and identifying the paper that raises it, if: (1) a federal statute is questioned and the parties do not include the United States, one of its agencies, or one of its officers or employees in an official capacity; or (2) a state statute is questioned and the parties do not include the state, one of its agencies, or one of its officers or employees in an official capacity; and

- *Serve notice.* Serve the notice and paper on the Attorney General of the United States if a federal statute is questioned—or on the state attorney general if a state statute is questioned—either by certified or registered mail or by sending it to an electronic address designated by the attorney general for this purpose. FRCP 5.1(a).

- *No forfeiture.* A party's failure to file and serve the notice, or the court's failure to certify, does not forfeit a constitutional claim or defense that is otherwise timely asserted. FRCP 5.1(d).

iii. *Nongovernmental corporate disclosure statement*

- *Contents.* A nongovernmental corporate party must file two (2) copies of a disclosure statement that: (1) identifies any parent corporation and any publicly held corporation owning ten percent (10%) or more of its stock; or (2) states that there is no such corporation. FRCP 7.1(a).

- *Time to file; Supplemental filing.* A party must: (1) file the disclosure statement with its first appearance, pleading, petition, motion, response, or other request addressed to the court; and (2) promptly file a supplemental statement if any required information changes. FRCP 7.1(b).

iv. *Copies of authorities.* In cases involving a pro se litigant, counsel shall, when serving a memorandum of law (or other submissions to the Court), provide the pro se litigant (but not other counsel or the Court) with printed copies of decisions cited therein that are unreported or reported exclusively on computerized databases. NY R USDCTWD Civ Rule 7(a)(8).

v. *Paper copy for date-stamping with self-addressed envelope.* Parties requesting date-stamped copies of filed documents must provide a paper copy for date-stamping, and a self-addressed, adequately-sized envelope with proper postage affixed. NY R USDCTWD Civ Rule 5.1(d).

vi. *Courtesy copies.* The Court may, in its discretion, request courtesy copies on any other motion. NY R USDCTWD Civ Rule 7(a)(7). Courtesy copies of certain documents may be required. Filers should refer to the "Judge Preferences" published on the Court's website. NY R USDCTWD ECF Procedures(2)(a)(iii). Immediately after filing a motion for an expedited hearing (NY R USDCTWD Civ Rule 7(d)(1)), or motion for a temporary restraining order (NY R USDCTWD Civ Rule 65(a)), the moving party must deliver a courtesy copy of the motion papers to the chambers of the assigned Judge. NY R USDCTWD Civ Rule 7(a)(7). [Editor's note: the reference to NY R USDCTWD Civ Rule 65(a) is likely meant to be a reference to NY R USDCTWD Civ Rule 65(b)].

- Immediately after filing the TRO application, counsel for the moving party shall personally deliver courtesy copies of the documents listed in NY R USDCTWD Civ Rule 65(b)(2) to chambers and await further instructions from the Court. In the event that the moving party is represented by out-of-town counsel who is unable to personally deliver courtesy copies, counsel shall contact chambers by telephone to request a waiver of this requirement. NY R USDCTWD Civ Rule 65(b)(2).

3. *Individual judge practices.* Refer to the Miscellaneous section of this document for information on individual judge practices on required documents.

## E. Format

1. *Form of documents.* The rules governing captions and other matters of form in pleadings apply to motions and other papers. FRCP 7(b)(2).

a. *Form, generally.* All pleadings, motions, and other papers that a party presents for filing, whether in paper form or in electronic form, shall meet the following requirements:

i. *Font size.* All text and footnotes shall be in a font size of at least twelve (12) point type. NY R USDCTWD Civ Rule 10(a)(1).

ii. *Spacing.* All text in the body of the document must be double-spaced, except that text in block quotations and footnotes may be single-spaced. NY R USDCTWD Civ Rule 10(a)(2).

- Extensive footnotes and block quotes may not be used to circumvent page limitations. NY R USDCTWD Civ Rule 10(a)(3).

iii. *Margins.* Documents must have one (1) inch margins on all four sides. NY R USDCTWD Civ Rule 10(a)(4).

iv. *Page numbering.* Pages must be consecutively numbered. NY R USDCTWD Civ Rule 10(a)(5).

b. *Additional requirements for paper filing.* Documents presented for filing in paper form shall meet the following additional requirements:

i. *Paper.* Documents must be on durable white eight and one-half by eleven (8-1/2 x 11) inch paper of good quality. NY R USDCTWD Civ Rule 10(b)(1).

- All documents must be single-sided. NY R USDCTWD Civ Rule 10(b)(5).

ii. *Text.* All text must be plainly and legibly written, typewritten, printed or reproduced. NY R USDCTWD Civ Rule 10(b)(2).

iii. *Ink.* Documents must be in black or blue ink. NY R USDCTWD Civ Rule 10(b)(3).

iv. *Binding.* The pages of each document must be stapled or in some other way fastened together. NY R USDCTWD Civ Rule 10(b)(4).

c. *Caption; Names of parties.* Every pleading must have a caption with the court's name, a title, a file number, and a FRCP 7(a) designation. The title of the complaint must name all the parties; the title of other pleadings, after naming the first party on each side, may refer generally to other parties. FRCP 10(a).

d. *Paragraphs; Separate statements.* A party must state its claims or defenses in numbered paragraphs, each limited as far as practicable to a single set of circumstances. A later pleading may refer by number to a paragraph in an earlier pleading. If doing so would promote clarity, each claim founded on a separate transaction or occurrence—and each defense other than a denial—must be stated in a separate count or defense. FRCP 10(b).

e. *Adoption by reference; Exhibits.* A statement in a pleading may be adopted by reference elsewhere in the same pleading or in any other pleading or motion. A copy of a written instrument that is an exhibit to a pleading is a part of the pleading for all purposes. FRCP 10(c).

f. *Citation of local rules.* The Local Rules of Civil Procedure for the United States District Court for the Western District of New York shall be cited as "L.R.Civ.P." NY R USDCTWD Civ Rule 1.1.

g. *Acceptance by the clerk.* The clerk must not refuse to file a paper solely because it is not in the form prescribed by the Federal Rules of Civil Procedure or by a local rule or practice. FRCP 5(d)(4). The Court may reject documents that do not comply with the requirements in NY R USDCTWD Civ Rule 10. NY R USDCTWD Civ Rule 10.

2. *Form of electronic documents.* All pleadings, motions, and other papers that a party presents for filing, whether in paper form or in electronic form, shall meet the requirements in NY R USDCTWD Civ Rule 10(a). NY R USDCTWD Civ Rule 10(a). Refer above for more information.

a. *Conversion to PDF.* A document created with a word processor, or a paper document, must be converted to Portable Document Format to be electronically filed with the court. NY R USDCTWD ECF Procedures(2)(a)(v).

   i. Documents which exist only in paper form may be scanned into a portable document format (PDF) for electronic filing. NY R USDCTWD ECF Procedures(2)(a)(v). Before filing a scanned document with the court, a Filing User must verify its legibility. NY R USDCTWD ECF Procedures(2)(a)(iv).

   ii. Electronic documents must be converted to .PDF from a word processing program and must be text searchable. Do not print, scan and .PDF your document when it has been created in a word processing program. Additional information on working with PDFs is located in NY R USDCTWD ECF Procedures(4b). NY R USDCTWD ECF Procedures(2)(a)(v).

b. *Hyperlinks.* Pursuant to the policy set forth by the Judicial Conference in October 2005, a hyperlink contained in a filing is no more than a convenient mechanism for accessing material cited in a document. A hyperlink reference is extraneous to any filed document and is not part of the Court's record. NY R USDCTWD ECF Procedures(2)(a)(vi).

   i. In order to preserve the integrity of the Court record, users wishing to insert hyperlinks in Court filings shall continue to use the conventional method for the cited authority, in addition to the hyperlink. NY R USDCTWD ECF Procedures(2)(a)(vi).

   ii. The Court accepts no responsibility for, and does not endorse any product, organization, and content at any hyperlinked site, or at any site to which that site may be linked. The Court accepts no responsibility for the availability or functionality of any hyperlink. NY R USDCTWD ECF Procedures(2)(a)(vi).

c. *Attachments and exhibits*

   i. Attachments and exhibits larger than five megabytes (5 MB) shall be filed electronically in separate five megabyte (5 MB) segments. NY R USDCTWD ECF Procedures(2)(d)(i).

   ii. Filing Users must submit in electronic form all documents referenced as exhibits or attach-ments, except as otherwise provided in NY R USDCTWD ECF Procedures. A Filing User must submit as exhibits or attachments only those excerpts of the referenced documents that are directly germane to the matter under consideration by the court. Excerpted material must be clearly and prominently identified as such. Filing Users who file excerpts of documents as exhibits or attachments under NY R USDCTWD ECF Procedures(2)(d)(ii) do so without prejudice to their right to timely file additional excerpts or the complete document. Responding parties may timely file additional excerpts or the complete document that they believe are directly germane. The Court may require parties to file additional excerpts or the complete document. A Filing User must request leave of the Court to file a document exhibit or attachment in non-electronic form. NY R USDCTWD ECF Procedures(2)(d)(ii).

    iii. Exhibits offered or admitted at trial will not be filed electronically or conventionally unless so ordered by the Court. NY R USDCTWD ECF Procedures(2)(d)(iii).

    iv. Exhibits such as videotapes and tape recordings shall be filed in the conventional manner with the Clerk of Court, and a Notice of Manual Filing shall be electronically filed by the party. Manually filed exhibits must have the case number and case name securely fastened or marked on the item. NY R USDCTWD ECF Procedures(2)(d)(iii).

    v. Continuation of exhibit entries (for exhibits that are too large to attach to a main document) must be filed and entered on the same day that the main document was filed. NY R USDCTWD ECF Procedures(2)(d)(iv).

  d. *Color documents.* Documents in color or containing graphics take much longer to upload. Filing users are encouraged to configure their scanners to scan documents at 200 dpi and preferably in black and white rather than color. NY R USDCTWD ECF Procedures(2)(d)(v).

  e. *Large documents.* Due to the length of time it takes to download large files, documents larger than five megabytes (5 MB) (approximately one hundred (100) pages of a .pdf scanned document) must be filed electronically in separate five megabyte (5 MB) segments. A party who believes a document is too lengthy to electronically image (i.e. scan), may contact the Court Room Deputy for the assigned judge and request permission to file that document conventionally. If granted permission to file the document conventionally, the Filing User shall electronically file a "notice of manual filing" for that item. Exhibits submitted to the Court conventionally shall be served on other parties conventionally. NY R USDCTWD ECF Procedures(2)(d)(vi).

3. *Form of memoranda of law.* Memoranda in support of or in opposition to any motion shall not exceed twenty-five (25) pages in length, and reply memoranda shall not exceed ten (10) pages in length. A party seeking to exceed the page limit must make application by letter to the Judge hearing the motion, with copies to all counsel, at least seven (7) days before the date on which the memorandum must be filed. NY R USDCTWD Civ Rule 7(a)(2)(C).

4. *Signing of pleadings, motions and other papers*

  a. *Signature.* Every pleading, written motion, and other paper must be signed by at least one attorney of record in the attorney's name—or by a party personally if the party is unrepresented. The paper must state the signer's address, e-mail address, and telephone number. FRCP 11(a). Documents presented for paper filing must contain an original signature. NY R USDCTWD Civ Rule 10(b)(6).

    i. *Electronic signatures*

      • *Non-attorney signature.* If the original document requires the signature of a non-attorney, the filing party shall obtain the signature of the non-attorney on the document. NY R USDCTWD ECF Procedures(2)(g)(i). The filing party or attorney then shall file the document electronically indicating the signatory's name in the form "s/(name)." NY R USDCTWD ECF Procedures(2)(g)(i)(1). A non-filing signatory or party who disputes the authenticity of an electronically filed document or the authenticity of the signature on that document must file an objection to the document within ten (10) days of receiving the Notice of Electronic Filing. NY R USDCTWD ECF Procedures(2)(g)(i)(2).

      • *Registered user signature.* The username and password required to file documents on the Electronic Filing System serve as the Filing User's signature on all electronic documents filed with this Court. The also serve as a signature for the purposes of FRCP 11, the Federal Rules of Civil Procedure, the Local Rules of Civil Procedure for the United States District Court for the Western District of New York, and any other purpose for which a signature is required in connection with proceedings before this Court. A pleading requiring a Registered User's signature must include a signature block in the format found in NY R USDCTWD ECF Procedures(2)(g)(iii). NY R USDCTWD ECF Procedures(2)(g)(iii). Any party challenging the authenticity of an electronically filed document or the attorney's signature on that document must file an objection to the document within ten (10) days of receiving the Notice of Electronic Filing. NY R USDCTWD ECF Procedures(2)(g)(iii)(1).

- *Multiple signatures.* The following procedure applies when a stipulation or other document requires two or more signatures: The filing party shall initially confirm that the document is acceptable to all persons required to sign the document and shall obtain the signatures of all parties on the document. NY R USDCTWD ECF Procedures(2)(g)(iv)(1). The filing party or attorney then shall file the document electronically indicating the signatories, e.g., "s/Jane Doe," "s/John Smith," etc. NY R USDCTWD ECF Procedures(2)(g)(iv)(2). A non-filing signatory or party who disputes the authenticity of an electronically filed document containing multiple signatures or the authenticity of the signatures themselves must file an objection to the document within ten (10) days of receiving the Notice of Electronic Filing. NY R USDCTWD ECF Procedures(2)(g)(iv)(3).

    ii. *No verification or accompanying affidavit required for pleadings.* Unless a rule or statute specifically states otherwise, a pleading need not be verified or accompanied by an affidavit. FRCP 11(a).

    iii. *Unsigned papers.* The court must strike an unsigned paper unless the omission is promptly corrected after being called to the attorney's or party's attention. FRCP 11(a).

b. *Representations to the court.* By presenting to the court a pleading, written motion, or other paper—whether by signing, filing, submitting, or later advocating it—an attorney or unrepresented party certifies that to the best of the person's knowledge, information, and belief, formed after an inquiry reasonable under the circumstances:

    i. It is not being presented for any improper purpose, such as to harass, cause unnecessary delay, or needlessly increase the cost of litigation;

    ii. The claims, defenses, and other legal contentions are warranted by existing law or by a nonfrivolous argument for extending, modifying, or reversing existing law or for establishing new law;

    iii. The factual contentions have evidentiary support or, if specifically so identified, will likely have evidentiary support after a reasonable opportunity for further investigation or discovery; and

    iv. The denials of factual contentions are warranted on the evidence or, if specifically so identified, are reasonably based on belief or a lack of information. FRCP 11(b).

c. *Sanctions.* If, after notice and a reasonable opportunity to respond, the court determines that FRCP 11(b) has been violated, the court may impose an appropriate sanction on any attorney, law firm, or party that violated FRCP 11(b) or is responsible for the violation. FRCP 11(c)(1). Refer to the United States District Court for the Western District of New York KeyRules Motion for Sanctions document for more information.

5. *Privacy protection for filings made with the court.* In all filings, parties shall comply with FRCP 5.2. NY R USDCTWD ECF Procedures(2)(m)(i).

a. *Redacted filings.* Unless the court orders otherwise, in an electronic or paper filing with the court that contains an individual's Social Security number, taxpayer-identification number, or birth date, the name of an individual known to be a minor, or a financial-account number, a party or nonparty making the filing may include only:

    i. The last four (4) digits of the Social Security number and taxpayer-identification number;

    ii. The year of the individual's birth;

    iii. The minor's initials; and

    iv. The last four (4) digits of the financial-account number. FRCP 5.2(a).

b. *Exemptions from the redaction requirement.* The redaction requirement does not apply to the following:

    i. A financial-account number that identifies the property allegedly subject to forfeiture in a forfeiture proceeding;

    ii. The record of an administrative or agency proceeding;

    iii. The official record of a state-court proceeding;

    iv. The record of a court or tribunal, if that record was not subject to the redaction requirement when originally filed;

    v. A filing covered by FRCP 5.2(c) or FRCP 5.2(d); and

    vi. A pro se filing in an action brought under 28 U.S.C.A. § 2241, 28 U.S.C.A. § 2254, or 28 U.S.C.A. § 2255. FRCP 5.2(b).

c. *Limitations on remote access to electronic files; Social Security appeals and immigration cases.* Unless the court orders otherwise, in an action for benefits under the Social Security Act, and in an action or proceeding relating to an order of removal, to relief from removal, or to immigration benefits or detention, access to an electronic file is authorized as follows:

    i. The parties and their attorneys may have remote electronic access to any part of the case file, including the administrative record;

    ii. Any other person may have electronic access to the full record at the courthouse, but may have remote electronic access only to:

        • The docket maintained by the court; and

        • An opinion, order, judgment, or other disposition of the court, but not any other part of the case file or the administrative record. FRCP 5.2(c).

d. *Filings made under seal.* The court may order that a filing be made under seal without redaction. The court may later unseal the filing or order the person who made the filing to file a redacted version for the public record. FRCP 5.2(d). For more information on sealing documents, refer to NY R USDCTWD Civ Rule 5.3, NY R USDCTWD ECF Procedures(2)(o)(i)(1), NY R USDCTWD ECF Procedures(2)(o)(i)(2), and NY R USDCTWD ECF Procedures(2)(o)(i)(3).

e. *Protective orders.* For good cause, the court may by order in a case:

    i. Require redaction of additional information; or

    ii. Limit or prohibit a nonparty's remote electronic access to a document filed with the court. FRCP 5.2(e).

f. *Option for additional unredacted filing under seal.* A person making a redacted filing may also file an unredacted copy under seal. The court must retain the unredacted copy as part of the record. FRCP 5.2(f).

g. *Option for filing a reference list.* A filing that contains redacted information may be filed together with a reference list that identifies each item of redacted information and specifies an appropriate identifier that uniquely corresponds to each item listed. The list must be filed under seal and may be amended as of right. Any reference in the case to a listed identifier will be construed to refer to the corresponding item of information. FRCP 5.2(g).

h. *Waiver of protection of identifiers.* A person waives the protection of FRCP 5.2(a) as to the person's own information by filing it without redaction and not under seal. FRCP 5.2(h).

6. *Individual judge practices.* Refer to the Miscellaneous section of this document for information on individual judge practices on formatting documents.

## F. Filing and Service Requirements

1. *Filing requirements.* Any paper after the complaint that is required to be served—together with a certificate of service—must be filed within a reasonable time after service. FRCP 5(d)(1). All pleadings and other papers shall be filed and served in accordance with the Federal Rules of Civil Procedure and the

CM/ECF Administrative Procedures Guide (NY R USDCTWD ECF Procedures). NY R USDCTWD Civ Rule 5.1(a). For information on filing of miscellaneous cases and irregular documents, refer to NY R USDCTWD Civ Rule 5.6.

a. *How filing is made; In general.* A paper is filed by delivering it:

   i. To the clerk; or

   ii. To a judge who agrees to accept it for filing, and who must then note the filing date on the paper and promptly send it to the clerk. FRCP 5(d)(2).

b. *Electronic filing*

   i. *Authorization of electronic filing program.* A court may, by local rule, allow papers to be filed, signed, or verified by electronic means that are consistent with any technical standards established by the Judicial Conference of the United States. A local rule may require electronic filing only if reasonable exceptions are allowed. A paper filed electronically in compliance with a local rule is a written paper for purposes of the Federal Rules of Civil Procedure. FRCP 5(d)(3).

     • All civil cases filed in this Court are assigned to the Electronic Case Filing System ("ECF"). The procedures for electronic filing and any exceptions to the electronic filing requirements are set forth in the CM/ECF Administrative Procedures Guide (NY R USDCTWD ECF Procedures) which is available on the Court's website. NY R US-DCTWD Civ Rule 5.1(a).

   ii. *Scope of electronic filing.* The U.S. District Court for the Western District of New York requires attorneys in civil and criminal cases to file documents with the Court electronically over the Internet using its Case Management/Electronic Case Filing (CM/ECF) system. NY R US-DCTWD ECF Procedures. Beginning January 1, 2004, all civil and criminal cases currently pending and newly filed, except as expressly noted herein, were assigned to the Electronic Case Filing System ("System"). Except as expressly provided and in exceptional circumstances preventing a Filing User from filing electronically, all petitions, motions, memoranda of law, or other pleadings and documents required to be filed with the Court in connection with a case assigned to the System must be electronically filed. NY R USDCTWD ECF Procedures(1)(a).

     • *Mandatory electronic filing.* All documents on civil, criminal, miscellaneous civil, miscellaneous criminal and new civil case openings, except sealed documents, sealed cases, opening of a criminal case, opening of a miscellaneous case and as expressly provided for in these procedures (NY R USDCTWD ECF Procedures), shall be electronically filed on the system. NY R USDCTWD ECF Procedures(2)(a)(i). NY R USDCTWD Civ Rule 29

     • *Stipulations.* Pursuant to NY R USDCTWD Civ Rule 29, all stipulations (whether the stipulation is final or when it requires a judge's signature) shall be filed electronically. NY R USDCTWD ECF Procedures(2)(p)(i).

     • *Letters.* The electronic filing of letters is generally prohibited unless granted permission by an assigned judge. Letters to the Court must be submitted conventionally. NY R US-DCTWD ECF Procedures(2)(q)(i).

     • *Exceptions.* The Court requires attorneys to file documents electronically, absent a showing of good cause, unless otherwise excused by the procedures set forth below or by Order of the Court. NY R USDCTWD ECF Procedures.

   iii. *Conventional filing of documents.* The procedures in NY R USDCTWD ECF Procedures(2)(o) govern documents filed conventionally. The Court, upon application, may also authorize conventional filing of other documents otherwise subject to the procedures in NY R US-DCTWD ECF Procedures(2)(o). NY R USDCTWD ECF Procedures(2)(o)(i).

     • *Documents filed under seal.* Unredacted documents filed with the Court pursuant to the privacy provisions of FRCP 5.2 shall be submitted in a sealing envelope with the information in NY R USDCTWD ECF Procedures(2)(o)(i)(1) on the envelope. NY R USDCTWD ECF Procedures(2)(o)(i)(1). If the document is larger than five (5) pages, a

disk should be provided to the Clerks Office which contains the document in a .pdf format. NY R USDCTWD ECF Procedures(2)(o)(i)(1). For more information on documents filed under seal, refer to NY R USDCTWD ECF Procedures(2)(o)(i)(1), NY R USDCTWD ECF Procedures(2)(o)(i)(2), and NY R USDCTWD ECF Procedures(2)(o)(i)(3).

- *Magistrate judge consents.* Pursuant to FRCP 73(b), parties' filing consents to jurisdiction by United States Magistrate Judge will continue to be treated as non-public documents until all parties have consented. Therefore, parties must submit conventionally (in paper form) and not electronically file their consent forms so that the consent is not a public document. If all parties consent to the jurisdiction of a Magistrate Judge, the Clerk will scan all consent forms which will then become a public document. NY R USDCTWD ECF Procedures(2)(o)(i)(3).

- *Pro se filers.* Pro Se filers shall file paper originals of all initiating documents, pleadings, motions, affidavits, briefs and other documents which must be signed or which require either verification or an unsworn declaration under any rule or statute. The Clerk's Office will scan these original documents into an electronic file in the System. A certificate of service is required for all documents a pro se litigant files with the court. If a Pro Se filer is granted permission to register to electronically file documents, they shall comply with the guidelines contained in this document (NY R USDCTWD ECF Procedures). NY R USDCTWD ECF Procedures(2)(o)(i)(4).

- *Social Security cases.* Absent a showing of good cause, and except as provided in Section o(i)(4) above, all documents, notices and orders in Social Security reviews will be filed and noticed electronically, except as noted in NY R USDCTWD ECF Procedures(2)(o)(i)(6). For more information, refer to NY R USDCTWD ECF Procedures(2)(o)(i)(6).

- For more information on conventional filing of documents, refer to NY R USDCTWD ECF Procedures(2)(o)(i).

iv. *Consequences of electronic filing.* Electronic transmission of a document to the System consistent with these procedures (NY R USDCTWD ECF Procedures), whether accomplished by the Filing User or a Court User, together with the transmission of a Notice of Electronic Filing from the Court, constitutes filing of a document for all purposes of the Federal Rules of Civil Procedure and the Local Rules of Civil Procedure for the United States District Court for the Western District of New York, and constitutes entry of the document on the docket kept by the Clerk under FRCP 58 and FRCP 79. A document shall not be considered filed for purposes of the Federal Rules of Civil until the filing party receives a System generated Notice of Electronic Filing. NY R USDCTWD ECF Procedures(2)(a)(i).

- E-mailing a document to the Clerk's Office or to the assigned judge shall not constitute "filing" of such document. NY R USDCTWD ECF Procedures(2)(a)(i)(1).

v. *Filing fees.* Any fee required for filing of a pleading or paper in District Court is payable to the Clerk of Court by check or money order. In addition, when opening a civil case on line, filing a notice of appeal on line or applying to appear pro hac vice on line, the fees shall be paid on line by registered users through the federal electronic payment website. Users will be directed to the federal electronic payment website while entering their transaction and should have a credit card available. When opening a civil case and applying to proceed in forma pauperis or when the United States of America opens a case, the payment screen can by bypassed to complete the transaction. Additional information on making electronic payments can be located on the court's website. NY R USDCTWD ECF Procedures(2)(h)(i).

2. *Service requirements.* All pleadings and other papers shall be filed and served in accordance with the Federal Rules of Civil Procedure and the CM/ECF Administrative Procedures Guide (NY R USDCTWD ECF Procedures). NY R USDCTWD Civ Rule 5.1(a).

a. *Service; When required*

i. *In general.* Unless the Federal Rules of Civil Procedure provide otherwise, each of the following papers must be served on every party:

- An order stating that service is required;

- A pleading filed after the original complaint, unless the court orders otherwise under FRCP 5(c) because there are numerous defendants;

- A discovery paper required to be served on a party, unless the court orders otherwise;

- A written motion, except one that may be heard ex parte; and

- A written notice, appearance, demand, or offer of judgment, or any similar paper. FRCP 5(a)(1).

ii. *If a party fails to appear.* No service is required on a party who is in default for failing to appear. But a pleading that asserts a new claim for relief against such a party must be served on that party under FRCP 4. FRCP 5(a)(2).

iii. *Seizing property.* If an action is begun by seizing property and no person is or need be named as a defendant, any service required before the filing of an appearance, answer, or claim must be made on the person who had custody or possession of the property when it was seized. FRCP 5(a)(3).

b. *Service; How made*

i. *Serving an attorney.* If a party is represented by an attorney, service under FRCP 5 must be made on the attorney unless the court orders service on the party. FRCP 5(b)(1).

ii. *Service in general.* A paper is served under FRCP 5 by:

- Handing it to the person;

- Leaving it: (1) at the person's office with a clerk or other person in charge or, if no one is in charge, in a conspicuous place in the office; or (2) if the person has no office or the office is closed, at the person's dwelling or usual place of abode with someone of suitable age and discretion who resides there;

- Mailing it to the person's last known address—in which event service is complete upon mailing;

- Leaving it with the court clerk if the person has no known address;

- Sending it by electronic means if the person consented in writing—in which event service is complete upon transmission, but is not effective if the serving party learns that it did not reach the person to be served; or

- Delivering it by any other means that the person consented to in writing—in which event service is complete when the person making service delivers it to the agency designated to make delivery. FRCP 5(b)(2).

iii. *Service by overnight delivery.* All papers, other than a subpoena or a summons and complaint, may be served on counsel of record by overnight delivery service at the address designated by the attorney for that purpose, or if none is designated, at the attorney's last known address. Service by overnight delivery shall be complete upon deposit of the paper(s), enclosed in a properly addressed wrapper, into the custody of the overnight delivery service, prior to the latest time designated by the service for overnight delivery. NY R USDCTWD Civ Rule 5.1(g). "Overnight delivery service" means any delivery service which regularly accepts items for overnight delivery to any address within the Court's jurisdiction. NY R USDCTWD Civ Rule 5.1(g).

iv. *Service of documents by electronic means*

- *Service on registered users.* Registered Users consent to the electronic service of all documents, and must make available an electronic mail address for service during the registration process. Upon the filing of a document by a party, a Notice of Electronic Filing, with a hyperlink to the filed document, will be automatically generated by the electronic filing system and sent via electronic mail to the e-mail addresses of all parties participating in the electronic filing system in the case. Electronic service of the Notice of Electronic Filing constitutes service of the filed document for all purposes of the Federal Rules of Civil Procedure and the Local Rules of Civil Procedure for the United States

District Court for the Western District of New York. NY R USDCTWD ECF Procedures(2)(f)(i). The Notice of Electronic Filing effectuates service for all registered users and no certificate of service is required when all filers on an action are Registered Users. NY R USDCTWD ECF Procedures(2)(f)(iv).

- *Time limit for opening hyperlink.* The hyperlink to filed documents contained in the Notice of Electronic Filing must be opened within fifteen (15) days from the date the document was filed to provide registered users access to the document. The hyperlink expires after fifteen (15) days and users will be unable to access documents for free after that time. Filing Users are encouraged to check their e-mail frequently for notice of filed documents. NY R USDCTWD ECF Procedures(2)(f)(ii).

- *Service on exempted attorneys or pro se litigants who do not have permission to file electronically.* Attorneys granted an exemption from electronically filing documents in the System and pro se litigants who have not been granted permission to electronically file documents are entitled to a paper copy of any electronically filed pleading, document or order. The filing party must therefore provide the non-registered party with the pleading, document or order according to the Federal Rules of Civil Procedure. NY R USDCTWD ECF Procedures(2)(f)(iii).

- *E-mailing or faxing documents.* E-mailing or faxing a pleading or document to any party shall not constitute service of the pleading or document. NY R USDCTWD ECF Procedures(2)(f)(v).

    v. *Using court facilities.* If a local rule so authorizes, a party may use the court's transmission facilities to make service under FRCP 5(b)(2)(E). FRCP 5(b)(3).

  c. *Serving numerous defendants*

    i. *In general.* If an action involves an unusually large number of defendants, the court may, on motion or on its own, order that:

- Defendants' pleadings and replies to them need not be served on other defendants;

- Any crossclaim, counterclaim, avoidance, or affirmative defense in those pleadings and replies to them will be treated as denied or avoided by all other parties; and

- Filing any such pleading and serving it on the plaintiff constitutes notice of the pleading to all parties. FRCP 5(c)(1).

    ii. *Notifying parties.* A copy of every such order must be served on the parties as the court directs. FRCP 5(c)(2).

3. *Pro se actions.* For information on the requirements in pro se actions, refer to NY R USDCTWD Civ Rule 5.2.

4. *Individual judge practices.* Refer to the Miscellaneous section of this document for information on individual judge practices on filing and serving documents.

## G. Hearings

1. *Hearings, generally*

  a. *Oral argument.* Due process does not require that oral argument be permitted on a motion and, except as otherwise provided by local rule, the district court has discretion to determine whether it will decide the motion on the papers or hear argument by counsel (and perhaps receive evidence). FPP § 1190; F.D.I.C. v. Deglau, 207 F.3d 153 (3d Cir. 2000).

    i. The parties shall appear for oral argument on all motions they make returnable before a Judge on the scheduled return date for the motion. In its discretion, the Court may notify the parties that oral argument shall not be heard on any given motion. Thus, the parties should be prepared to have their motion papers serve as the sole method of argument. NY R USDCTWD Civ Rule 7(c).

  b. *Providing a regular schedule for oral hearings.* A court may establish regular times and places for oral hearings on motions. FRCP 78(a).

    c.   *Providing for submission on briefs.* By rule or order, the court may provide for submitting and determining motions on briefs, without oral hearings. FRCP 78(b).

  2.   *Hearing on motion for preliminary injunction after temporary restraining order is issued without notice*

    a.   *Expediting the preliminary injunction hearing.* If the order is issued without notice, the motion for a preliminary injunction must be set for hearing at the earliest possible time, taking precedence over all other matters except hearings on older matters of the same character. At the hearing, the party who obtained the order must proceed with the motion; if the party does not, the court must dissolve the order. FRCP 65(b)(3). Refer to the United States District Court for the Western District of New York KeyRules Motion for Preliminary Injunction document for more information on the hearing on the motion for preliminary injunction.

  3.   *Individual judge practices.* Refer to the Miscellaneous section of this document for information on individual judge practices on hearings.

## H.  Forms

### 1.  Federal Application for Temporary Restraining Order Forms

    a.   Ex parte motion; For temporary restraining order and order to show cause; Interference with property rights. AMJUR PP INJUNCTION § 42.

    b.   Affidavit; In support of ex parte motion for temporary restraining order. AMJUR PP INJUNCTION § 48.

    c.   Certificate of attorney; In support of ex parte motion for temporary restraining order. AMJUR PP INJUNCTION § 50.

    d.   Affidavit; In support of ex parte motion for temporary restraining order; Interference with property rights. AMJUR PP INJUNCTION § 51.

    e.   Motion. 4A FEDFORMS § 5344.

    f.   Motion; Another form. 4A FEDFORMS § 5345.

    g.   Motion; Another form. 4A FEDFORMS § 5346.

    h.   Motion without notice. 4A FEDFORMS § 5347.

    i.   Motion without notice; Another form. 4A FEDFORMS § 5348.

    j.   Motion without notice; Another form. 4A FEDFORMS § 5349.

    k.   Motion without notice; Another form. 4A FEDFORMS § 5350.

    l.   Motion without notice; Another form. 4A FEDFORMS § 5351.

    m.   Motion without notice; Another form. 4A FEDFORMS § 5352.

    n.   Certificate of attorney's efforts to give notice. 4A FEDFORMS § 5353.

    o.   Certificate of attorney's efforts to give notice; Another form. 4A FEDFORMS § 5354.

    p.   Certificate of attorney's efforts to give notice; Another form. 4A FEDFORMS § 5355.

    q.   Certificate of attorney's efforts to give notice; Another form. 4A FEDFORMS § 5356.

    r.   Motion requesting expedited hearing. 4A FEDFORMS § 5357.

    s.   Motion seeking temporary restraining order. 4A FEDFORMS § 5359.

    t.   Motion to dissolve or modify temporary restraining order. 4A FEDFORMS § 5361.

    u.   Motion for temporary restraining order and preliminary injunction. GOLDLTGFMS § 13A:6.

    v.   Motion for temporary restraining order; General form. GOLDLTGFMS § 13A:11.

    w.   Motion for temporary restraining order; Ex parte application. GOLDLTGFMS § 13A:12.

    x.   Motion for temporary restraining order; Ex parte application; Supporting affidavit by party. GOLDLTGFMS § 13A:13.

    y.   Motion for temporary restraining order; Ex parte application; Supporting affidavit by party; Copyright infringement. GOLDLTGFMS § 13A:14.

z. Motion for temporary restraining order; Ex parte application; Certificate by counsel. GOLDLTGFMS § 13A:15.

**2. Forms for the Western District of New York**

a. Certificate of service. NY R USDCTWD ECF Procedures(4a).

# I. Applicable Rules

1. *Federal rules*

a. Serving and filing pleadings and other papers. FRCP 5.

b. Constitutional challenge to a statute; Notice, certification, and intervention. FRCP 5.1.

c. Privacy protection for filings made with the court. FRCP 5.2.

d. Computing and extending time; Time for motion papers. FRCP 6.

e. Pleadings allowed; Form of motions and other papers. FRCP 7.

f. Disclosure statement. FRCP 7.1.

g. Form of pleadings. FRCP 10.

h. Signing pleadings, motions, and other papers; Representations to the court; Sanctions. FRCP 11.

i. Taking testimony. FRCP 43.

j. Injunctions and restraining orders. FRCP 65.

k. Proceedings against a surety. FRCP 65.1.

l. Hearing motions; Submission on briefs. FRCP 78.

2. *Local rules*

a. Title. NY R USDCTWD Civ Rule 1.1.

b. Filing and serving papers. NY R USDCTWD Civ Rule 5.1.

c. Motion practice. NY R USDCTWD Civ Rule 7.

d. Form of papers. NY R USDCTWD Civ Rule 10.

e. Sanctions. NY R USDCTWD Civ Rule 11.

f. Alternative dispute resolution and pretrial conferences. NY R USDCTWD Civ Rule 16.

g. Temporary restraining orders and preliminary injunctions. NY R USDCTWD Civ Rule 65.

h. Attorneys of record; Appearance and withdrawal. NY R USDCTWD Civ Rule 83.2.

i. Administrative procedures guide for electronic filing. NY R USDCTWD ECF Procedures.

j. Alternative dispute resolution plan. NY R USDCTWD ADR Plan.

# J. Miscellaneous

**NOTE: Individual judges' rules may apply. For available judge-level information, refer to:**

DISTRICT JUDGE RICHARD J. ARCARA: NY R USDCTWD Arcara-Procedures.

DISTRICT JUDGE FRANK P. GERACI, JR.: NY R USDCTWD Geraci-Procedures.

DISTRICT JUDGE DAVID G. LARIMER: NY R USDCTWD Larimer-Procedures.

DISTRICT JUDGE CHARLES J. SIRAGUSA: NY R USDCTWD Siragusa-Procedures.

DISTRICT JUDGE WILLIAM M. SKRETNY: NY R USDCTWD Skretny--Procedures.

DISTRICT JUDGE MICHAEL A. TELESCA: NY R USDCTWD Telesca-Procedures.

DISTRICT JUDGE LAWRENCE J. VILARDO: NY R USDCTWD Vilardo-Procedures.

DISTRICT JUDGE ELIZABETH A. WOLFORD: NY R USDCTWD Wolford-Procedures.

MAGISTRATE JUDGE JONATHAN W. FELDMAN: NY R USDCTWD Feldman-Procedures.

MAGISTRATE JUDGE LESLIE G. FOSCHIO: NY R USDCTWD Foschio-Procedures; NY R USDCTWD Foschio-Depositions.

MAGISTRATE JUDGE JEREMIAH J. McCARTHY: NY R USDCTWD McCarthy-Procedures.

MAGISTRATE JUDGE MARIAN W. PAYSON: NY R USDCTWD Payson-Procedures.

MAGISTRATE JUDGE MICHAEL J. ROEMER: NY R USDCTWD Roemer-Procedures.

MAGISTRATE JUDGE H. KENNETH SCHROEDER, JR.: NY R USDCTWD Schroeder-Proc.

MAGISTRATE JUDGE HUGH B. SCOTT: NY R USDCTWD Scott-Procedures.

# Requests, Notices and Applications
# Pretrial Conferences, Scheduling, Management

## Document Last Updated September 2016

A. **Checklist**

(I) ❑ Matters to be considered by parties for the pretrial conference

    (a) ❑ Documents to consider

        (1) ❑ Pretrial memorandum or statement

        (2) ❑ Paper copy for date-stamping with self-addressed envelope

        (3) ❑ Courtesy copies

    (b) ❑ Timing

        (1) ❑ The court determines at what stage in the action to hold a pretrial conference

(II) ❑ Matters to be considered by parties for the scheduling conference

    (a) ❑ Documents to consider

        (1) ❑ Request for scheduling conference

        (2) ❑ Paper copy for date-stamping with self-addressed envelope

        (3) ❑ Courtesy copies

    (b) ❑ Timing

        (1) ❑ If a scheduling conference is called, it is important to recognize that, unlike the ordinary pretrial conference, the scheduling conference occurs before the substantive issues have been defined and is directed toward organizing the processing of the action by setting deadlines for the completion of the various pretrial phases

(III) ❑ Matters to be considered by parties for the final pretrial conference

    (a) ❑ Required documents

        (1) ❑ Pretrial statement

        (2) ❑ Exhibits

    (b) ❑ Supplemental documents

        (1) ❑ Paper copy for date-stamping with self-addressed envelope

        (2) ❑ Courtesy copies

    (c) ❑ Timing

        (1) ❑ A final pretrial conference shall be held at the direction of the court within thirty (30) days of the trial date

        (2) ❑ No later than fourteen (14) days before the date of the final pretrial conference, or by such other date as may be set by court order, counsel for each party shall file and serve a pretrial statement

        (3) ❑ At the conference, counsel shall produce a copy of each exhibit for examination by opposing counsel and for notice of any objection to its admission in evidence

(IV) ❑ Matters to be considered by parties for the discovery planning conference

    (a) ❑ Required documents

        (1) ❑ Written report outlining proposed discovery plan

    (b) ❑ Supplemental documents

        (1) ❑ Paper copy for date-stamping with self-addressed envelope

        (2) ❑ Courtesy copies

    (c) ❑ Timing

        (1) ❑ Except in a proceeding exempted from initial disclosure under FRCP 26(a)(1)(B) or when the court orders otherwise, the parties must confer as soon as practicable—and in any event at least twenty-one (21) days before a scheduling conference is to be held or a scheduling order is due under FRCP 16(b)

        (2) ❑ Within fourteen (14) days after the conference, the attorneys of record are responsible for submitting a written report outlining the plan

(V) ❑ Matters to be considered by parties for the settlement conference

    (a) ❑ Required documents

        (1) ❑ Written settlement demand

        (2) ❑ Response to written settlement demand

    (b) ❑ Supplemental documents

        (1) ❑ Paper copy for date-stamping with self-addressed envelope

        (2) ❑ Courtesy copies

    (c) ❑ Timing

        (1) ❑ Unless a case will proceed to ADR, the court's scheduling order will include a date for a first judicial settlement conference

        (2) ❑ The plaintiff(s) shall provide the defendant(s) with a written settlement demand at least fourteen (14) days before the first settlement conference

        (3) ❑ The defendant(s) shall respond to the demand in writing at least seven (7) days before the conference, so that the parties and their attorneys have a meaningful opportunity to consider and discuss the settlement proposals

## B. Timing

1. *Pretrial conferences, generally.* The court determines at what stage in the action to hold a pretrial conference. When only one conference is involved, the most favored practice seems to be to wait until after the case has been prepared for trial. FPP § 1524. Although there rarely will be any need to hold a conference in a relatively simple case until after the preliminary motions have been disposed of, the only inherently logical limitation on the court's discretion as to when to hold a conference is that it should not be held before all the necessary and indispensable parties are served. FPP § 1524.

2. *Scheduling conference.* If a scheduling conference is called, it is important to recognize that, unlike the ordinary pretrial conference, the scheduling conference occurs before the substantive issues have been defined and is directed toward organizing the processing of the action by setting deadlines for the completion of the various pretrial phases. FPP § 1522.1.

3. *Final pretrial conference.* A final pretrial conference shall be held at the direction of the Court within thirty (30) days of the trial date. NY R USDCTWD Civ Rule 16(e)(1).

    a. *Pretrial statement.* No later than fourteen (14) days before the date of the final pretrial conference, or by such other date as may be set by Court order, counsel for each party shall file and serve a pretrial statement. NY R USDCTWD Civ Rule 16(e)(2).

    b. *Exhibits.* Prior to the final pre-trial conference, counsel shall meet to mark and list each exhibit contained in the pre-trial statements. At the conference, counsel shall produce a copy of each exhibit for examination by opposing counsel and for notice of any objection to its admission in evidence. NY R USDCTWD Civ Rule 16(e)(3).

4. *Discovery planning conference.* Except in a proceeding exempted from initial disclosure under FRCP 26(a)(1)(B) or when the court orders otherwise, the parties must confer as soon as practicable—and in any event at least twenty-one (21) days before a scheduling conference is to be held or a scheduling order is due under FRCP 16(b). FRCP 26(f)(1).

   a. *Submission of written report outlining proposed discovery plan.* The attorneys of record and all unrepresented parties that have appeared in the case are jointly responsible for arranging the conference, for attempting in good faith to agree on the proposed discovery plan, and for submitting to the court within fourteen (14) days after the conference a written report outlining the plan. FRCP 26(f)(2).

   b. *Expedited schedule.* If necessary to comply with its expedited schedule for FRCP 16(b) conferences, a court may by local rule: (1) require the parties' conference to occur less than twenty-one (21) days before the scheduling conference is held or a scheduling order is due under FRCP 16(b); and (2) require the written report outlining the discovery plan to be filed less than fourteen (14) days after the parties' conference, or excuse the parties from submitting a written report and permit them to report orally on their discovery plan at the FRCP 16(b) conference. FRCP 26(f)(4).

5. *Settlement conference.* Unless a case will proceed to ADR, the Court's scheduling order will include a date for a first judicial settlement conference. NY R USDCTWD Civ Rule 16(c)(1).

   a. *Written settlement demand.* The plaintiff(s) shall provide the defendant(s) with a written settlement demand at least fourteen (14) days before the first settlement conference. NY R USDCTWD Civ Rule 16(c)(2).

   b. *Response to written settlement demand.* The defendant(s) shall respond to the demand in writing at least seven (7) days before the conference, so that the parties and their attorneys have a meaningful opportunity to consider and discuss the settlement proposals. NY R USDCTWD Civ Rule 16(c)(2).

6. *Computation of time*

   a. *Computing time.* FRCP 6 applies in computing any time period specified in the Federal Rules of Civil Procedure, in any local rule or court order, or in any statute that does not specify a method of computing time. FRCP 6(a).

      i. *Period stated in days or a longer unit.* When the period is stated in days or a longer unit of time:

         • Exclude the day of the event that triggers the period;

         • Count every day, including intermediate Saturdays, Sundays, and legal holidays; and

         • Include the last day of the period, but if the last day is a Saturday, Sunday, or legal holiday, the period continues to run until the end of the next day that is not a Saturday, Sunday, or legal holiday. FRCP 6(a)(1).

      ii. *Period stated in hours.* When the period is stated in hours:

         • Begin counting immediately on the occurrence of the event that triggers the period;

         • Count every hour, including hours during intermediate Saturdays, Sundays, and legal holidays; and

         • If the period would end on a Saturday, Sunday, or legal holiday, the period continues to run until the same time on the next day that is not a Saturday, Sunday, or legal holiday. FRCP 6(a)(2).

      iii. *Inaccessibility of the clerk's office.* Unless the court orders otherwise, if the clerk's office is inaccessible:

         • On the last day for filing under FRCP 6(a)(1), then the time for filing is extended to the first accessible day that is not a Saturday, Sunday, or legal holiday; or

         • During the last hour for filing under FRCP 6(a)(2), then the time for filing is extended to the same time on the first accessible day that is not a Saturday, Sunday, or legal holiday. FRCP 6(a)(3).

    iv. *"Last day" defined.* Unless a different time is set by a statute, local rule, or court order, the last day ends:

- For electronic filing, at midnight in the court's time zone; and

- For filing by other means, when the clerk's office is scheduled to close. FRCP 6(a)(4).

    v. *"Next day" defined.* The "next day" is determined by continuing to count forward when the period is measured after an event and backward when measured before an event. FRCP 6(a)(5).

    vi. *"Legal holiday" defined.* "Legal holiday" means:

- The day set aside by statute for observing New Year's Day, Martin Luther King Jr.'s Birthday, Washington's Birthday, Memorial Day, Independence Day, Labor Day, Columbus Day, Veterans' Day, Thanksgiving Day, or Christmas Day;

- Any day declared a holiday by the President or Congress; and

- For periods that are measured after an event, any other day declared a holiday by the state where the district court is located. FRCP 6(a)(6).

  b. *Computation of electronic filing deadlines.* A document will be deemed timely filed if filed prior to midnight Eastern Time, unless otherwise ordered by the Court. A document will be considered untimely if filed thereafter. When a Court order requires that a document be filed on a weekend or holiday, the document may be filed by close of business the next business day without further application to the Court. NY R USDCTWD ECF Procedures(2)(e)(i). A document filed electronically is deemed filed on the date and time stated on the Notice of Electronic Filing. NY R USDCTWD ECF Procedures(2)(e)(ii).

    i. *System availability.* Although parties may file documents electronically twenty-four (24) hours a day, registered users are strongly encouraged to file all documents during normal working hours of the Clerk's Office (8:30 a.m. to 5:00 p.m. Eastern Time). NY R USDCTWD ECF Procedures(2)(t)(i).

    ii. *Technical failures.* A Filing User whose filing is made untimely as a result of a technical failure must seek appropriate relief from the Court. NY R USDCTWD ECF Procedures(2)(u)(i).

  c. *Extending time*

    i. *In general.* When an act may or must be done within a specified time, the court may, for good cause, extend the time:

- With or without motion or notice if the court acts, or if a request is made, before the original time or its extension expires; or

- On motion made after the time has expired if the party failed to act because of excusable neglect. FRCP 6(b)(1).

    ii. *Exceptions.* A court must not extend the time to act under FRCP 50(b), FRCP 50(d), FRCP 52(b), FRCP 59(b), FRCP 59(d), FRCP 59(e), and FRCP 60(b). FRCP 6(b)(2).

    iii. Refer to the United States District Court for the Western District of New York KeyRules Motion for Continuance/Extension of Time document for more information on extending time.

  d. *Additional time after certain kinds of service.* When a party may or must act within a specified time after service and service is made under FRCP 5(b)(2)(C), FRCP 5(b)(2)(D), FRCP 5(b)(2)(E), or FRCP 5(b)(2)(F), three (3) days are added after the period would otherwise expire under FRCP 6(a). FRCP 6(d).

    i. *Service by overnight delivery.* Where a period of time prescribed by either the Federal Rules of Civil Procedure or the Local Rules of Civil Procedure for the United States District Court for the Western District of New York is measured from the service of a paper and service is by overnight delivery, one (1) business day shall be added to the prescribed period. NY R USDCTWD Civ Rule 5.1(g).

7. *Individual judge practices.* Refer to the Miscellaneous section of this document for information on individual judge practices on timing of documents.

## C. General Requirements

1. *Pretrial conferences, generally*

   a. *Purposes of a pretrial conference.* FRCP 16 provides an important mechanism for carrying out one of the basic policies of the Federal Rules of Civil Procedure—the determination of disputes on their merits rather than on the basis of procedural niceties or tactical advantage. FPP § 1522. In any action, the court may order the attorneys and any unrepresented parties to appear for one or more pretrial conferences for such purposes as:

      i. Expediting disposition of the action;

      ii. Establishing early and continuing control so that the case will not be protracted because of lack of management;

      iii. Discouraging wasteful pretrial activities;

      iv. Improving the quality of the trial through more thorough preparation; and

      v. Facilitating settlement. FRCP 16(a).

   b. *When appropriate.* FRCP 16 specifically provides that the court "may order the attorneys and any unrepresented parties to appear for one or more pretrial conferences." This language makes it clear that the utilization of the pretrial conference procedure lies within the discretion of the district court both as a matter of general policy and in terms of whether and when the rule should be invoked in a particular case. FPP § 1523; Mizwicki v. Helwig, 196 F.3d 828 (7th Cir. 1999). There is no requirement that any pretrial conferences be held or not held in certain types of actions. FPP § 1523.

      i. The Court shall hold an initial pretrial conference in all cases except those exempted from initial disclosure requirements under FRCP 26(a)(1)(B). The purpose of this conference is to establish a case management plan. NY R USDCTWD Civ Rule 16(b)(1).

   c. *Attendance at a pretrial conference.* A represented party must authorize at least one of its attorneys to make stipulations and admissions about all matters that can reasonably be anticipated for discussion at a pretrial conference. If appropriate, the court may require that a party or its representative be present or reasonably available by other means to consider possible settlement. FRCP 16(c)(1).

      i. *Attorneys' binding authority.* Each party represented by an attorney shall be represented at each Court conference by an attorney who has the authority to bind that party regarding all matters previously identified by the Court for discussion at the conference and all reasonably related matters. NY R USDCTWD Civ Rule 16(f).

   d. *Matters for consideration at a pretrial conference.* At any pretrial conference, the court may consider and take appropriate action on the following matters:

      i. Formulating and simplifying the issues, and eliminating frivolous claims or defenses;

      ii. Amending the pleadings if necessary or desirable;

      iii. Obtaining admissions and stipulations about facts and documents to avoid unnecessary proof, and ruling in advance on the admissibility of evidence;

      iv. Avoiding unnecessary proof and cumulative evidence, and limiting the use of testimony under FRE 702;

      v. Determining the appropriateness and timing of summary adjudication under FRCP 56;

      vi. Controlling and scheduling discovery, including orders affecting disclosures and discovery under FRCP 26 and FRCP 29 through FRCP 37;

      vii. Identifying witnesses and documents, scheduling the filing and exchange of any pretrial briefs, and setting dates for further conferences and for trial;

      viii. Referring matters to a magistrate judge or a master;

      ix. Settling the case and using special procedures to assist in resolving the dispute when authorized by statute or local rule;

x.   Determining the form and content of the pretrial order;

xi.  Disposing of pending motions;

xii. Adopting special procedures for managing potentially difficult or protracted actions that may involve complex issues, multiple parties, difficult legal questions, or unusual proof problems;

xiii. Ordering a separate trial under FRCP 42(b) of a claim, counterclaim, crossclaim, third-party claim, or particular issue;

xiv. Ordering the presentation of evidence early in the trial on a manageable issue that might, on the evidence, be the basis for a judgment as a matter of law under FRCP 50(a) or a judgment on partial findings under FRCP 52(c);

xv.  Establishing a reasonable limit on the time allowed to present evidence; and

xvi. Facilitating in other ways the just, speedy, and inexpensive disposition of the action. FRCP 16(c)(2).

xvii. In addition to all of the matters in FRCP 16(c)(2), counsel and unrepresented parties shall be prepared to discuss meaningfully the following:

- If the case is referred automatically to ADR pursuant to the Court's Alternative Dispute Resolution Plan, selection of a neutral, and timing for ADR;

- If the case is not referred automatically to ADR, possible stipulation to the use of a confidential ADR process;

- Any problems currently known and reasonably anticipated to arise in connection with discovery of ESI;

- Proposed methods to limit and/or decrease the time and expense of discovery;

- The use of experts during discovery and at trial; and

- The willingness to consent to the Magistrate Judge conducting any or all proceedings in the case. NY R USDCTWD Civ Rule 16(b)(3).

e.  *Pretrial orders.* After any conference under FRCP 16, the court should issue an order reciting the action taken. This order controls the course of the action unless the court modifies it. FRCP 16(d).

f.  *Sanctions.* On motion or on its own, the court may issue any just orders, including those authorized by FRCP 37(b)(2)(A)(ii) through FRCP 37(b)(2)(A)(vii), if a party or its attorney: (1) fails to appear at a scheduling or other pretrial conference; (2) is substantially unprepared to participate—or does not participate in good faith—in the conference; or (3) fails to obey a scheduling or other pretrial order. FRCP 16(f)(1).

i.  *Imposing fees and costs.* Instead of or in addition to any other sanction, the court must order the party, its attorney, or both to pay the reasonable expenses—including attorney's fees—incurred because of any noncompliance with FRCP 16, unless the noncompliance was substantially justified or other circumstances make an award of expenses unjust. FRCP 16(f)(2).

2.  *Scheduling conference.* A scheduling conference may be requested by the judge or by the parties, but it is not mandatory. FPP § 1522.1.

a.  *Scheduling order.* Except in categories of actions exempted by local rule, the district judge—or a magistrate judge when authorized by local rule—must issue a scheduling order: (1) after receiving the parties' report under FRCP 26(f); or (2) after consulting with the parties' attorneys and any unrepresented parties at a scheduling conference. FRCP 16(b)(1).

i.  *Required contents of the order.* The scheduling order must limit the time to join other parties, amend the pleadings, complete discovery, and file motions. FRCP 16(b)(3)(A).

- The parties shall attempt to agree upon a Neutral and, at the scheduling conference, shall be prepared to report on the outcome of their ADR discussion pursuant to Local Rule 16.1(a)(3)(F). The initial Scheduling Order shall include a deadline for the completion of ADR. NY R USDCTWD ADR Plan(4)(4.2)(A). [Editor's note: the reference to Local Rule 16.1(a)(3)(F) is likely meant to be a reference to NY R USDCTWD Civ Rule 16(b)(3)(A)].

- After the initial pretrial conference, pursuant to FRCP 16(b), the Court shall issue an order providing: (1) deadlines for joinder of parties and amendment of pleadings; (2) a date for a first judicial settlement conference, or, if the case will proceed to ADR, deadlines for an initial ADR session and the conclusion of ADR; (3) a discovery cut-off date; (4) a deadline for filing dispositive motions; (5) deadlines for the disclosure of expert witnesses, if applicable; and (6) any other matter decided or agreed upon at the initial pretrial conference. NY R USDCTWD Civ Rule 16(b)(4).

ii. *Permitted contents of the order.* The scheduling order may:

- Modify the timing of disclosures under FRCP 26(a) and FRCP 26(e)(1);
- Modify the extent of discovery;
- Provide for disclosure, discovery, or preservation of electronically stored information;
- Include any agreements the parties reach for asserting claims of privilege or of protection as trial-preparation material after information is produced, including agreements reached under FRE 502;
- Direct that before moving for an order relating to discovery, the movant must request a conference with the court;
- Set dates for pretrial conferences and for trial; and
- Include other appropriate matters. FRCP 16(b)(3)(B).

b. *Time to issue.* The judge must issue the scheduling order as soon as practicable, but unless the judge finds good cause for delay, the judge must issue it within the earlier of ninety (90) days after any defendant has been served with the complaint or sixty (60) days after any defendant has appeared. FRCP 16(b)(2).

c. *Modifying a schedule.* A schedule may be modified only for good cause and with the judge's consent. FRCP 16(b)(4). A scheduling order cannot be modified except by Court order. NY R USDCTWD Civ Rule 16(b)(4).

3. *Final pretrial conference.* The court may hold a final pretrial conference to formulate a trial plan, including a plan to facilitate the admission of evidence. FRCP 16(e).

a. *Timing and attendance.* The conference must be held as close to the start of trial as is reasonable, and must be attended by at least one attorney who will conduct the trial for each party and by any unrepresented party. FRCP 16(e). A final pretrial conference shall be held at the direction of the Court within thirty (30) days of the trial date. NY R USDCTWD Civ Rule 16(e)(1).

b. *Content of conference.* Trial counsel shall be present at this conference and shall be prepared to discuss all aspects of the case and any matters which may narrow the issues and aid in its prompt disposition, including:

i. The possibility of settlement;

ii. Motions in limine;

iii. The resolution of any legal or factual issues raised in the pre-trial statement of any party (see NY R USDCTWD Civ Rule 16(e)(2));

iv. Stipulations (which shall be in writing); and

v. Any other matters that counsel or the Court deems appropriate. NY R USDCTWD Civ Rule 16(e)(1).

c. *Pretrial statement.* No later than fourteen (14) days before the date of the final pretrial conference, or by such other date as may be set by Court order, counsel for each party shall file and serve a pretrial statement which includes the following:

i. A detailed statement of contested and uncontested facts, and of the party's position regarding contested facts;

ii. A detailed statement of the issues of law involved and any unusual questions relative to the admissibility of evidence, together with supporting authority;

     iii.   Proposed jury instructions and verdict form, if any, which shall also be provided to chambers in Word format;

     iv.   The names and addresses of witnesses (other than rebuttal witnesses) expected to testify, together with a brief statement of their anticipated testimony;

     v.   A brief summary of the qualifications of all expert witnesses, and a concise statement of each expert's expected opinion testimony and the material upon which that testimony is expected to be based;

     vi.   A list of exhibits anticipated to be used at trial, except exhibits which may be used solely for impeachment or rebuttal;

     vii.   A list of any deposition testimony to be offered in evidence;

     viii.   An itemized statement of each element of special damages and other relief sought; and

     ix.   Such additional submissions as the Court directs. NY R USDCTWD Civ Rule 16(e)(2).

     x.   Counsel are encouraged to review the individual Rules of the assigned District Judge or Magistrate Judge for specific pretrial statement requirements. NY R USDCTWD Civ Rule 16(e)(2).

   d.  *Marking exhibits.* Prior to the final pre-trial conference, counsel shall meet to mark and list each exhibit contained in the pre-trial statements. At the conference, counsel shall produce a copy of each exhibit for examination by opposing counsel and for notice of any objection to its admission in evidence. NY R USDCTWD Civ Rule 16(e)(3).

   e.  *Post-conference order.* Following the final pretrial conference, a pretrial order may be entered as directed by the Court, and the case certified as ready for trial. NY R USDCTWD Civ Rule 16(e)(4).

   f.  *Modification of final pretrial order.* The court may modify the order issued after a final pretrial conference only to prevent manifest injustice. FRCP 16(e).

4.  *Discovery planning conference*

   a.  *Conference content.* In conferring, the parties must consider the nature and basis of their claims and defenses and the possibilities for promptly settling or resolving the case; make or arrange for the disclosures required by FRCP 26(a)(1); discuss any issues about preserving discoverable information; and develop a proposed discovery plan. FRCP 26(f)(2).

     i.   The parties shall confer about all of the matters contemplated by FRCP 26(f) and NY R USDCTWD Civ Rule 16(a)(3), unless the case is excepted from this requirement by NY R USDCTWD Civ Rule 16(a)(1). NY R USDCTWD Civ Rule 26(a).

     ii.   Prior to the Local Rule 16.1 scheduling conference, counsel and any unrepresented parties shall confer about ADR as part of their discussion of "the possibilities for a prompt settlement or resolution of the case" pursuant to FRCP 26(f). NY R USDCTWD ADR Plan(4)(4.2)(A). [Editor's note: the reference to Local Rule 16.1 is likely meant to be a reference to NY R USDCTWD Civ Rule 16(b)].

   b.  *Parties' responsibilities.* The attorneys of record and all unrepresented parties that have appeared in the case are jointly responsible for arranging the conference, for attempting in good faith to agree on the proposed discovery plan, and for submitting to the court within fourteen (14) days after the conference a written report outlining the plan. The court may order the parties or attorneys to attend the conference in person. FRCP 26(f)(2).

     i.   Prior to the initial pretrial conference, counsel for all parties and any pro se litigants shall confer as required by FRCP 26(f), and shall file with the Court a joint, written discovery plan consistent with FRCP 26(f). If they are unable to agree to a plan, each party shall file its own proposed plan. NY R USDCTWD Civ Rule 16(b)(2).

   c.  *Discovery plan.* A discovery plan must state the parties' views and proposals on:

     i.   What changes should be made in the timing, form, or requirement for disclosures under FRCP 26(a), including a statement of when initial disclosures were made or will be made;

     ii.   The subjects on which discovery may be needed, when discovery should be completed, and whether discovery should be conducted in phases or be limited to or focused on particular issues;

iii. Any issues about disclosure, discovery, or preservation of electronically stored information, including the form or forms in which it should be produced;

iv. Any issues about claims of privilege or of protection as trial-preparation materials, including—if the parties agree on a procedure to assert these claims after production—whether to ask the court to include their agreement in an order under FRE 502;

v. What changes should be made in the limitations on discovery imposed under the Federal Rules of Civil Procedure or by local rule, and what other limitations should be imposed; and

vi. Any other orders that the court should issue under FRCP 26(c) or under FRCP 16(b) and FRCP 26(c). FRCP 26(f)(3).

d. *Electronically stored information (ESI).* The Court expects the parties to cooperatively reach agreement on how to preserve and conduct discovery of electronically stored information ("ESI"). Prior to the FRCP 26(f) conference, counsel should become knowledgeable about their clients' information management systems and their operation, including how information is stored and retrieved. In addition, counsel should make a reasonable attempt to ascertain the contents of their client's ESI, including backup, archival, and legacy data (outdated formats or media) and ESI that may not be reasonably accessible. In particular, prior to or at the FRCP 26(f) conference, the parties should confer regarding the following matters:

i. *Preservation.* Counsel should attempt to agree on steps the parties will take to segregate and preserve ESI in order to avoid accusations of spoliation. NY R USDCTWD Civ Rule 16(b)(2)(A)(i).

ii. *E-mail information.* Counsel should attempt to agree on the scope of e-mail discovery and e-mail search protocol. NY R USDCTWD Civ Rule 16(b)(2)(A)(ii).

iii. *Back-up and archival data.* Counsel should attempt to agree on whether responsive back-up and archival data exists, the extent to which back-up and archival data is reasonably accessible, and who will bear the cost of obtaining such data. NY R USDCTWD Civ Rule 16(b)(2)(A)(iii).

iv. *Format and media.* Counsel should attempt to agree on the format and media to be used in the production of ESI, and whether production of some or all ESI in paper form is agreeable in lieu of production in electronic format. NY R USDCTWD Civ Rule 16(b)(2)(A)(iv).

v. *Reasonably accessible information and costs.* Counsel should attempt to determine if any responsive ESI is not reasonably accessible, i.e., is accessible only by incurring undue burdens or costs. NY R USDCTWD Civ Rule 16(b)(2)(A)(v).

e. *Privileged or trial preparation materials.* Counsel also should attempt to reach agreement regarding what will happen in the event privileged or trial preparation materials are inadvertently disclosed. NY R USDCTWD Civ Rule 16(b)(2)(B).

5. *Settlement conference*

a. *Applicable cases.* Unless a case will proceed to ADR, the Court's scheduling order will include a date for a first judicial settlement conference. NY R USDCTWD Civ Rule 16(c)(1).

b. *Party obligations.* The plaintiff(s) shall provide the defendant(s) with a written settlement demand at least fourteen (14) days before the first settlement conference, and the defendant(s) shall respond to the demand in writing at least seven (7) days before the conference, so that the parties and their attorneys have a meaningful opportunity to consider and discuss the settlement proposals. In cases involving insurance coverage, defense counsel also shall consult with the insurance carrier prior to the conference regarding its position. Judges may, at their discretion, require a preconference, written submission from each party. NY R USDCTWD Civ Rule 16(c)(2).

c. *Attendance.* At the settlement conference, the attorneys shall be present and shall be prepared to state their clients' respective positions to the Court. Judges may, at their discretion, require the attendance of parties, party representatives, insurance carriers, and others whose attendance they believe may facilitate settlement, either in person or by telephone. NY R USDCTWD Civ Rule 16(c)(3).

    d.   *Further settlement conferences.* If a settlement is not reached at the first conference, the Court may schedule additional settlement conferences from time to time, as appropriate. NY R USDCTWD Civ Rule 16(c)(4).

6.   *Additional pretrial conferences.* The Court may schedule additional pretrial conferences in its discretion, or at a party's request. Counsel and pro se litigants shall be prepared to provide a status update on discovery, motion practice, and the prospects for settlement. NY R USDCTWD Civ Rule 16(d).

7.   *Notice of appearance.* No notice of appearance is required of an attorney whose name and address appear at the end of a complaint, notice of removal, pre-answer motion, or answer. In all other circumstances, an attorney appearing for a party in a civil case shall promptly file a written notice of appearance. NY R USDCTWD Civ Rule 83.2(b). For more information on appearances and withdrawals, refer to NY R USDCTWD Civ Rule 83.2.

8.   *Related cases.* Each attorney appearing in a civil case has a continuing duty to promptly notify the Clerk of Court when the attorney has reason to believe that said case is related to some other pending civil or criminal action(s) such that their assignment to the same Judge would avoid unnecessary duplication of judicial effort. As soon as the attorney becomes aware of such a relationship, the attorney shall notify the Clerk of Court by letter of the relevant facts, and the Clerk of Court will transmit that notification to the Judges to whom the cases have been assigned. NY R USDCTWD Civ Rule 5.1(e).

9.   *Alternative dispute resolution (ADR).* This Court has adopted an Alternative Dispute Resolution Plan ("ADR"), as implemented by Standing Order (NY R USDCTWD ADR Plan), under which certain civil cases are referred automatically to ADR upon filing. NY R USDCTWD Civ Rule 16(a). The United States District Court for the Western District of New York (the "Court") adopted the ADR Plan on January 1, 2006 (the "Effective Date"), to make available to civil litigants court-administered ADR interventions and processes designed to provide quicker, less expensive and potentially more satisfying alternatives to continuing litigation, without impairing the quality of justice or the right to trial. NY R USDCTWD ADR Plan(1)(1.2)(A).

    a.   *Scope.* This ADR Plan (NY R USDCTWD ADR Plan) applies to civil actions pending or commenced on and after the Effective Date, except as otherwise indicated in NY R USDCTWD ADR Plan. The ADR Plan supplements the Local Rules of Civil Procedure for the United States District Court for the Western District of New York, which shall remain in full effect for all cases. NY R USDCTWD ADR Plan(1)(1.2)(B).

    b.   *Referral to ADR*

        i.   *New cases.* All civil cases filed on and after the Effective Date of the ADR Plan shall be referred automatically for ADR. NY R USDCTWD ADR Plan(2)(2.1)(A). Notice of the ADR requirements will be provided to all parties immediately upon the filing of a complaint and answer or a notice of removal; NY R USDCTWD ADR Plan(2)(2.1)(A); NY R USDCTWD Civ Rule 16(a). ADR intervention will be scheduled at the conference held pursuant to Local Rule of Civil Procedure 16.1. NY R USDCTWD ADR Plan(2)(2.1)(A). [Editor's note: the reference to Local Rule of Civil Procedure 16.1 is likely meant to be a reference to NY R USDCTWD Civ Rule 16(b)].

        •   Litigants in cases not referred automatically to ADR must consider possible agreement to the use of an ADR process. NY R USDCTWD Civ Rule 16(a).

        •   For a list of exemptions from automatic referral, refer to NY R USDCTWD ADR Plan(2)(2.1)(A).

        ii.   *Pending cases.* The assigned Judge on any pending civil case may, sua sponte or with status conference, issue an order referring the case for ADR. NY R USDCTWD ADR Plan(2)(2.1)(B); NY R USDCTWD Civ Rule 16(a). The order shall specify a date on which the ADR intervention is to be completed. NY R USDCTWD ADR Plan(2)(2.1)(B).

        iii.   *Stipulation.* A case may be referred for ADR by stipulation of all parties. Stipulations shall be filed and shall designate the specific ADR intervention the parties have selected, the time frame within which the ADR process will be completed and the selected Neutral. Stipulations are presumed acceptable unless the assigned Judge determines that the interests of justice are not served. NY R USDCTWD ADR Plan(2)(2.1)(C).

iv. *Relief from ADR referral*

- *Opting out motions.* Any party may file, with the assigned Judge for that case, a motion to opt out of, or for relief from, ADR. NY R USDCTWD ADR Plan(2)(2.2)(A).

- *Motion.* Opting Out Motions must be made within fourteen (14) days from (1) the date of the first discovery conference under Local Rule 16.1 in new cases, or (2) the date of a sua sponte ADR Referral Order in pending cases. NY R USDCTWD ADR Plan(2)(2.2)(B). [Editor's note: the reference to Local Rule 16.1 is likely meant to be a reference to NY R USDCTWD Civ Rule 16(b)].

- *Criteria.* Opting Out Motions shall be granted only for "good cause" shown. Inconvenience, travel costs, attorney fees or other costs shall not constitute "good cause." A party seeking relief from ADR must set forth the reasons why ADR has no reasonable chance of being productive. NY R USDCTWD ADR Plan(2)(2.2)(C).

- *Judicial initiative.* The assigned Judge may, sua sponte, exempt any case from the Court's ADR Plan. NY R USDCTWD ADR Plan(2)(2.2)(D).

c. *ADR interventions*

i. *Options.* It is expected that cases referred for ADR will proceed to Mediation. However, the following options are also available upon the stipulation of all parties:

- Neutral Evaluation;

- Mini Summary Trial;

- Arbitration (Binding and Non-Binding);

- Case Valuation; and

- Settlement Week, when scheduled by the Court. NY R USDCTWD ADR Plan(4)(4.1)(A).

ii. *Timing.* Timing is specific to the intervention and process chosen, as set forth in the corresponding sections in NY R USDCTWD ADR Plan. NY R USDCTWD ADR Plan(4)(4.1)(B).

iii. *Scheduling.* The referral of a case to ADR does not delay or defer other dates established in the Scheduling Order and has no effect on the scheduled progress of the case toward trial. NY R USDCTWD ADR Plan(4)(4.1)(C).

d. *Selecting an ADR intervention*

i. *New cases.* Prior to the Local Rule 16.1 scheduling conference, counsel and any unrepresented parties shall confer about ADR as part of their discussion of "the possibilities for a prompt settlement or resolution of the case" pursuant to FRCP 26(f). Unless the parties agree to a different intervention, it is presumed that they will participate in mediation. [Editor's note: the reference to Local Rule 16.1 is likely meant to be a reference to NY R USDCTWD Civ Rule 16(b)].

ii. *Pending cases.* In pending cases, all sua sponte referrals will be to mediation. Should the parties agree that a different ADR intervention is more appropriate to their case, they may submit a stipulation designating the specific ADR intervention selected, the time frame within which the ADR process will be completed and the identity of the Neutral. Stipulations must be filed within fourteen (14) days from the date of the ADR Referral Order and are presumed acceptable unless the assigned Judge determines that the interests of justice are not served. NY R USDCTWD ADR Plan(4)(4.2)(B).

e. For more information on alternative dispute resolution (ADR), refer to NY R USDCTWD ADR Plan.

10. *Sanctions.* Failure of counsel for any party, or a party proceeding pro se, to appear before the Court at a conference, to complete the necessary preparations, or to be prepared to proceed to trial at the set time may be considered an abandonment of the case or a failure to prosecute or defend diligently. An appropriate order for sanctions may be entered against the defaulting party with respect to either a specific issue or the entire case. NY R USDCTWD Civ Rule 11(a). For more information, refer to NY R USDCTWD Civ Rule 11.

11. *Pro se actions.* For information on the requirements in pro se actions, refer to NY R USDCTWD Civ Rule 5.2.

12. *Individual judge practices.* Refer to the Miscellaneous section of this document for information on individual judge practices on general requirements for documents.

## D. Documents

1. *Pretrial conference*

   a. *Documents to consider*

      i. *Pretrial memorandum or statement.* Even though it is not specifically mentioned in FRCP 16, most courts require the attorney for each side to file a pretrial memorandum or statement prior to the conference, which, if adopted by the court, may be binding at trial. FPP § 1524. The purpose of the memorandum is to reveal the lawyer's theory of the case and the issues counsel believes are in contention in order to aid the court in determining what matters should be considered at the conference itself. FPP § 1524; Manbeck v. Ostrowski, 384 F.2d 970 (D.C. Cir. 1967).

      ii. *Paper copy for date-stamping with self-addressed envelope.* Parties requesting date-stamped copies of filed documents must provide a paper copy for date-stamping, and a self-addressed, adequately-sized envelope with proper postage affixed. NY R USDCTWD Civ Rule 5.1(d).

      iii. *Courtesy copies.* Courtesy copies of certain documents may be required. Filers should refer to the "Judge Preferences" published on the Court's website. NY R USDCTWD ECF Procedures(2)(a)(iii).

2. *Scheduling conference*

   a. *Documents to consider*

      i. *Request for scheduling conference.* A scheduling conference may be requested by the judge or by the parties, but it is not mandatory. FPP § 1522.1.

      ii. *Paper copy for date-stamping with self-addressed envelope.* Parties requesting date-stamped copies of filed documents must provide a paper copy for date-stamping, and a self-addressed, adequately-sized envelope with proper postage affixed. NY R USDCTWD Civ Rule 5.1(d).

      iii. *Courtesy copies.* Courtesy copies of certain documents may be required. Filers should refer to the "Judge Preferences" published on the Court's website. NY R USDCTWD ECF Procedures(2)(a)(iii).

3. *Final pretrial conference*

   a. *Required documents*

      i. *Pretrial statement.* No later than fourteen (14) days before the date of the final pretrial conference, or by such other date as may be set by Court order, counsel for each party shall file and serve a pretrial statement. NY R USDCTWD Civ Rule 16(e)(2). Refer to the General Requirements section of this document for the contents of the pretrial statement.

      ii. *Exhibits.* Prior to the final pre-trial conference, counsel shall meet to mark and list each exhibit contained in the pre-trial statements. At the conference, counsel shall produce a copy of each exhibit for examination by opposing counsel and for notice of any objection to its admission in evidence. NY R USDCTWD Civ Rule 16(e)(3).

   b. *Supplemental documents*

      i. *Paper copy for date-stamping with self-addressed envelope.* Parties requesting date-stamped copies of filed documents must provide a paper copy for date-stamping, and a self-addressed, adequately-sized envelope with proper postage affixed. NY R USDCTWD Civ Rule 5.1(d).

      ii. *Courtesy copies.* Courtesy copies of certain documents may be required. Filers should refer to the "Judge Preferences" published on the Court's website. NY R USDCTWD ECF Procedures(2)(a)(iii).

4. *Discovery planning conference*

   a. *Required documents*

      i. *Written report outlining proposed discovery plan.* If they are unable to agree to a plan, each party shall file its own proposed plan. NY R USDCTWD Civ Rule 16(b)(2). Refer to the General Requirements section of this document for information on the parties' responsibilities for submitting a written report outlining the proposed discovery plan.

   b. *Supplemental documents*

      i. *Paper copy for date-stamping with self-addressed envelope.* Parties requesting date-stamped copies of filed documents must provide a paper copy for date-stamping, and a self-addressed, adequately-sized envelope with proper postage affixed. NY R USDCTWD Civ Rule 5.1(d).

      ii. *Courtesy copies.* Courtesy copies of certain documents may be required. Filers should refer to the "Judge Preferences" published on the Court's website. NY R USDCTWD ECF Procedures(2)(a)(iii).

5. *Settlement conference*

   a. *Required documents*

      i. *Written settlement demand.* The plaintiff(s) shall provide the defendant(s) with a written settlement demand at least fourteen (14) days before the first settlement conference. NY R USDCTWD Civ Rule 16(c)(2).

      ii. *Response to written settlement demand.* The defendant(s) shall respond to the demand in writing at least seven (7) days before the conference, so that the parties and their attorneys have a meaningful opportunity to consider and discuss the settlement proposals. NY R USDCTWD Civ Rule 16(c)(2).

   b. *Supplemental documents*

      i. *Paper copy for date-stamping with self-addressed envelope.* Parties requesting date-stamped copies of filed documents must provide a paper copy for date-stamping, and a self-addressed, adequately-sized envelope with proper postage affixed. NY R USDCTWD Civ Rule 5.1(d).

      ii. *Courtesy copies.* Courtesy copies of certain documents may be required. Filers should refer to the "Judge Preferences" published on the Court's website. NY R USDCTWD ECF Procedures(2)(a)(iii).

6. *Individual judge practices.* Refer to the Miscellaneous section of this document for information on individual judge practices on required documents.

## E. Format

1. *Form of documents.* The rules governing captions and other matters of form in pleadings apply to motions and other papers. FRCP 7(b)(2).

   a. *Form, generally.* All pleadings, motions, and other papers that a party presents for filing, whether in paper form or in electronic form, shall meet the following requirements:

      i. *Font size.* All text and footnotes shall be in a font size of at least twelve (12) point type. NY R USDCTWD Civ Rule 10(a)(1).

      ii. *Spacing.* All text in the body of the document must be double-spaced, except that text in block quotations and footnotes may be single-spaced. NY R USDCTWD Civ Rule 10(a)(2).

         • Extensive footnotes and block quotes may not be used to circumvent page limitations. NY R USDCTWD Civ Rule 10(a)(3).

      iii. *Margins.* Documents must have one (1) inch margins on all four sides. NY R USDCTWD Civ Rule 10(a)(4).

      iv. *Page numbering.* Pages must be consecutively numbered. NY R USDCTWD Civ Rule 10(a)(5).

    b. *Additional requirements for paper filing.* Documents presented for filing in paper form shall meet the following additional requirements:

        i. *Paper.* Documents must be on durable white eight and one-half by eleven (8-1/2 x 11) inch paper of good quality. NY R USDCTWD Civ Rule 10(b)(1).

           • All documents must be single-sided. NY R USDCTWD Civ Rule 10(b)(5).

        ii. *Text.* All text must be plainly and legibly written, typewritten, printed or reproduced. NY R USDCTWD Civ Rule 10(b)(2).

        iii. *Ink.* Documents must be in black or blue ink. NY R USDCTWD Civ Rule 10(b)(3).

        iv. *Binding.* The pages of each document must be stapled or in some other way fastened together. NY R USDCTWD Civ Rule 10(b)(4).

    c. *Caption; Names of parties.* Every pleading must have a caption with the court's name, a title, a file number, and a FRCP 7(a) designation. The title of the complaint must name all the parties; the title of other pleadings, after naming the first party on each side, may refer generally to other parties. FRCP 10(a).

    d. *Paragraphs; Separate statements.* A party must state its claims or defenses in numbered paragraphs, each limited as far as practicable to a single set of circumstances. A later pleading may refer by number to a paragraph in an earlier pleading. If doing so would promote clarity, each claim founded on a separate transaction or occurrence—and each defense other than a denial—must be stated in a separate count or defense. FRCP 10(b).

    e. *Adoption by reference; Exhibits.* A statement in a pleading may be adopted by reference elsewhere in the same pleading or in any other pleading or motion. A copy of a written instrument that is an exhibit to a pleading is a part of the pleading for all purposes. FRCP 10(c).

    f. *Citation of local rules.* The Local Rules of Civil Procedure for the United States District Court for the Western District of New York shall be cited as "L.R.Civ.P." NY R USDCTWD Civ Rule 1.1.

    g. *Acceptance by the clerk.* The clerk must not refuse to file a paper solely because it is not in the form prescribed by the Federal Rules of Civil Procedure or by a local rule or practice. FRCP 5(d)(4). The Court may reject documents that do not comply with the requirements in NY R USDCTWD Civ Rule 10. NY R USDCTWD Civ Rule 10.

2. *Form of electronic documents.* All pleadings, motions, and other papers that a party presents for filing, whether in paper form or in electronic form, shall meet the requirements in NY R USDCTWD Civ Rule 10(a). NY R USDCTWD Civ Rule 10(a). Refer above for more information.

    a. *Conversion to PDF.* A document created with a word processor, or a paper document, must be converted to Portable Document Format to be electronically filed with the court. NY R USDCTWD ECF Procedures(2)(a)(v).

        i. Documents which exist only in paper form may be scanned into a portable document format (PDF) for electronic filing. NY R USDCTWD ECF Procedures(2)(a)(v). Before filing a scanned document with the court, a Filing User must verify its legibility. NY R USDCTWD ECF Procedures(2)(a)(iv).

        ii. Electronic documents must be converted to .PDF from a word processing program and must be text searchable. Do not print, scan and .PDF your document when it has been created in a word processing program. Additional information on working with PDFs is located in NY R USDCTWD ECF Procedures(4b). NY R USDCTWD ECF Procedures(2)(a)(v).

    b. *Hyperlinks.* Pursuant to the policy set forth by the Judicial Conference in October 2005, a hyperlink contained in a filing is no more than a convenient mechanism for accessing material cited in a document. A hyperlink reference is extraneous to any filed document and is not part of the Court's record. NY R USDCTWD ECF Procedures(2)(a)(vi).

        i. In order to preserve the integrity of the Court record, users wishing to insert hyperlinks in Court filings shall continue to use the conventional method for the cited authority, in addition to the hyperlink. NY R USDCTWD ECF Procedures(2)(a)(vi).

    ii.  The Court accepts no responsibility for, and does not endorse any product, organization, and content at any hyperlinked site, or at any site to which that site may be linked. The Court accepts no responsibility for the availability or functionality of any hyperlink. NY R USDCTWD ECF Procedures(2)(a)(vi).

  c.  *Attachments and exhibits*

    i.  Attachments and exhibits larger than five megabytes (5 MB) shall be filed electronically in separate five megabyte (5 MB) segments. NY R USDCTWD ECF Procedures(2)(d)(i).

    ii.  Filing Users must submit in electronic form all documents referenced as exhibits or attachments, except as otherwise provided in NY R USDCTWD ECF Procedures. A Filing User must submit as exhibits or attachments only those excerpts of the referenced documents that are directly germane to the matter under consideration by the court. Excerpted material must be clearly and prominently identified as such. Filing Users who file excerpts of documents as exhibits or attachments under NY R USDCTWD ECF Procedures(2)(d)(ii) do so without prejudice to their right to timely file additional excerpts or the complete document. Responding parties may timely file additional excerpts or the complete document that they believe are directly germane. The Court may require parties to file additional excerpts or the complete document. A Filing User must request leave of the Court to file a document exhibit or attachment in non-electronic form. NY R USDCTWD ECF Procedures(2)(d)(ii).

    iii.  Exhibits offered or admitted at trial will not be filed electronically or conventionally unless so ordered by the Court. NY R USDCTWD ECF Procedures(2)(d)(iii).

    iv.  Exhibits such as videotapes and tape recordings shall be filed in the conventional manner with the Clerk of Court, and a Notice of Manual Filing shall be electronically filed by the party. Manually filed exhibits must have the case number and case name securely fastened or marked on the item. NY R USDCTWD ECF Procedures(2)(d)(iii).

    v.  Continuation of exhibit entries (for exhibits that are too large to attach to a main document) must be filed and entered on the same day that the main document was filed. NY R USDCTWD ECF Procedures(2)(d)(iv).

  d.  *Color documents.* Documents in color or containing graphics take much longer to upload. Filing users are encouraged to configure their scanners to scan documents at 200 dpi and preferably in black and white rather than color. NY R USDCTWD ECF Procedures(2)(d)(v).

  e.  *Large documents.* Due to the length of time it takes to download large files, documents larger than five megabytes (5 MB) (approximately one hundred (100) pages of a .pdf scanned document) must be filed electronically in separate five megabyte (5 MB) segments. A party who believes a document is too lengthy to electronically image (i.e. scan), may contact the Court Room Deputy for the assigned judge and request permission to file that document conventionally. If granted permission to file the document conventionally, the Filing User shall electronically file a "notice of manual filing" for that item. Exhibits submitted to the Court conventionally shall be served on other parties conventionally. NY R USDCTWD ECF Procedures(2)(d)(vi).

3.  *Signing of pleadings, motions and other papers*

  a.  *Signature.* Every pleading, written motion, and other paper must be signed by at least one attorney of record in the attorney's name—or by a party personally if the party is unrepresented. The paper must state the signer's address, e-mail address, and telephone number. FRCP 11(a). Documents presented for paper filing must contain an original signature. NY R USDCTWD Civ Rule 10(b)(6).

    i.  *Electronic signatures*

      •  *Non-attorney signature.* If the original document requires the signature of a non-attorney, the filing party shall obtain the signature of the non-attorney on the document. NY R USDCTWD ECF Procedures(2)(g)(i). The filing party or attorney then shall file the document electronically indicating the signatory's name in the form "s/(name)." NY R USDCTWD ECF Procedures(2)(g)(i)(1). A non-filing signatory or party who disputes the authenticity of an electronically filed document or the authenticity of the signature on that document must file an objection to the document within ten (10) days of receiving the Notice of Electronic Filing. NY R USDCTWD ECF Procedures(2)(g)(i)(2).

- *Registered user signature.* The username and password required to file documents on the Electronic Filing System serve as the Filing User's signature on all electronic documents filed with this Court. The also serve as a signature for the purposes of FRCP 11, the Federal Rules of Civil Procedure, the Local Rules of Civil Procedure for the United States District Court for the Western District of New York, and any other purpose for which a signature is required in connection with proceedings before this Court. A pleading requiring a Registered User's signature must include a signature block in the format found in NY R USDCTWD ECF Procedures(2)(g)(iii). NY R USDCTWD ECF Procedures(2)(g)(iii). Any party challenging the authenticity of an electronically filed document or the attorney's signature on that document must file an objection to the document within ten (10) days of receiving the Notice of Electronic Filing. NY R USDCTWD ECF Procedures(2)(g)(iii)(1).

- *Multiple signatures.* The following procedure applies when a stipulation or other document requires two or more signatures: The filing party shall initially confirm that the document is acceptable to all persons required to sign the document and shall obtain the signatures of all parties on the document. NY R USDCTWD ECF Procedures(2)(g)(iv)(1). The filing party or attorney then shall file the document electronically indicating the signatories, e.g., "s/Jane Doe," "s/John Smith," etc. NY R USDCTWD ECF Procedures(2)(g)(iv)(2). A non-filing signatory or party who disputes the authenticity of an electronically filed document containing multiple signatures or the authenticity of the signatures themselves must file an objection to the document within ten (10) days of receiving the Notice of Electronic Filing. NY R USDCTWD ECF Procedures(2)(g)(iv)(3).

  ii. *No verification or accompanying affidavit required for pleadings.* Unless a rule or statute specifically states otherwise, a pleading need not be verified or accompanied by an affidavit. FRCP 11(a).

  iii. *Unsigned papers.* The court must strike an unsigned paper unless the omission is promptly corrected after being called to the attorney's or party's attention. FRCP 11(a).

b. *Representations to the court.* By presenting to the court a pleading, written motion, or other paper—whether by signing, filing, submitting, or later advocating it—an attorney or unrepresented party certifies that to the best of the person's knowledge, information, and belief, formed after an inquiry reasonable under the circumstances:

  i. It is not being presented for any improper purpose, such as to harass, cause unnecessary delay, or needlessly increase the cost of litigation;

  ii. The claims, defenses, and other legal contentions are warranted by existing law or by a nonfrivolous argument for extending, modifying, or reversing existing law or for establishing new law;

  iii. The factual contentions have evidentiary support or, if specifically so identified, will likely have evidentiary support after a reasonable opportunity for further investigation or discovery; and

  iv. The denials of factual contentions are warranted on the evidence or, if specifically so identified, are reasonably based on belief or a lack of information. FRCP 11(b).

c. *Sanctions.* If, after notice and a reasonable opportunity to respond, the court determines that FRCP 11(b) has been violated, the court may impose an appropriate sanction on any attorney, law firm, or party that violated FRCP 11(b) or is responsible for the violation. FRCP 11(c)(1). Refer to the United States District Court for the Western District of New York KeyRules Motion for Sanctions document for more information.

4. *Privacy protection for filings made with the court.* In all filings, parties shall comply with FRCP 5.2. NY R USDCTWD ECF Procedures(2)(m)(i).

a. *Redacted filings.* Unless the court orders otherwise, in an electronic or paper filing with the court that contains an individual's Social Security number, taxpayer-identification number, or birth date, the

name of an individual known to be a minor, or a financial-account number, a party or nonparty making the filing may include only:

    i.    The last four (4) digits of the Social Security number and taxpayer-identification number;

    ii.   The year of the individual's birth;

    iii.  The minor's initials; and

    iv.  The last four (4) digits of the financial-account number. FRCP 5.2(a).

b.   *Exemptions from the redaction requirement.* The redaction requirement does not apply to the following:

    i.    A financial-account number that identifies the property allegedly subject to forfeiture in a forfeiture proceeding;

    ii.   The record of an administrative or agency proceeding;

    iii.  The official record of a state-court proceeding;

    iv.  The record of a court or tribunal, if that record was not subject to the redaction requirement when originally filed;

    v.   A filing covered by FRCP 5.2(c) or FRCP 5.2(d); and

    vi.  A pro se filing in an action brought under 28 U.S.C.A. § 2241, 28 U.S.C.A. § 2254, or 28 U.S.C.A. § 2255. FRCP 5.2(b).

c.   *Limitations on remote access to electronic files; Social Security appeals and immigration cases.* Unless the court orders otherwise, in an action for benefits under the Social Security Act, and in an action or proceeding relating to an order of removal, to relief from removal, or to immigration benefits or detention, access to an electronic file is authorized as follows:

    i.    The parties and their attorneys may have remote electronic access to any part of the case file, including the administrative record;

    ii.   Any other person may have electronic access to the full record at the courthouse, but may have remote electronic access only to:

        •  The docket maintained by the court; and

        •  An opinion, order, judgment, or other disposition of the court, but not any other part of the case file or the administrative record. FRCP 5.2(c).

d.   *Filings made under seal.* The court may order that a filing be made under seal without redaction. The court may later unseal the filing or order the person who made the filing to file a redacted version for the public record. FRCP 5.2(d). For more information on sealing documents, refer to NY R USDCTWD Civ Rule 5.3, NY R USDCTWD ECF Procedures(2)(o)(i)(1), NY R USDCTWD ECF Procedures(2)(o)(i)(2), and NY R USDCTWD ECF Procedures(2)(o)(i)(3).

e.   *Protective orders.* For good cause, the court may by order in a case:

    i.    Require redaction of additional information; or

    ii.   Limit or prohibit a nonparty's remote electronic access to a document filed with the court. FRCP 5.2(e).

f.   *Option for additional unredacted filing under seal.* A person making a redacted filing may also file an unredacted copy under seal. The court must retain the unredacted copy as part of the record. FRCP 5.2(f).

g.   *Option for filing a reference list.* A filing that contains redacted information may be filed together with a reference list that identifies each item of redacted information and specifies an appropriate identifier that uniquely corresponds to each item listed. The list must be filed under seal and may be amended as of right. Any reference in the case to a listed identifier will be construed to refer to the corresponding item of information. FRCP 5.2(g).

h.   *Waiver of protection of identifiers.* A person waives the protection of FRCP 5.2(a) as to the person's own information by filing it without redaction and not under seal. FRCP 5.2(h).

5. *Individual judge practices.* Refer to the Miscellaneous section of this document for information on individual judge practices on formatting documents.

## F. Filing and Service Requirements

1. *Filing requirements.* Any paper after the complaint that is required to be served—together with a certificate of service—must be filed within a reasonable time after service. FRCP 5(d)(1). All pleadings and other papers shall be filed and served in accordance with the Federal Rules of Civil Procedure and the CM/ECF Administrative Procedures Guide (NY R USDCTWD ECF Procedures). NY R USDCTWD Civ Rule 5.1(a). For information on filing of miscellaneous cases and irregular documents, refer to NY R USDCTWD Civ Rule 5.6.

   a. *How filing is made; In general.* A paper is filed by delivering it:

      i. To the clerk; or

      ii. To a judge who agrees to accept it for filing, and who must then note the filing date on the paper and promptly send it to the clerk. FRCP 5(d)(2).

   b. *Electronic filing*

      i. *Authorization of electronic filing program.* A court may, by local rule, allow papers to be filed, signed, or verified by electronic means that are consistent with any technical standards established by the Judicial Conference of the United States. A local rule may require electronic filing only if reasonable exceptions are allowed. A paper filed electronically in compliance with a local rule is a written paper for purposes of the Federal Rules of Civil Procedure. FRCP 5(d)(3).

         • All civil cases filed in this Court are assigned to the Electronic Case Filing System ("ECF"). The procedures for electronic filing and any exceptions to the electronic filing requirements are set forth in the CM/ECF Administrative Procedures Guide (NY R USDCTWD ECF Procedures) which is available on the Court's website. NY R US-DCTWD Civ Rule 5.1(a).

      ii. *Scope of electronic filing.* The U.S. District Court for the Western District of New York requires attorneys in civil and criminal cases to file documents with the Court electronically over the Internet using its Case Management/Electronic Case Filing (CM/ECF) system. NY R US-DCTWD ECF Procedures. Beginning January 1, 2004, all civil and criminal cases currently pending and newly filed, except as expressly noted herein, were assigned to the Electronic Case Filing System ("System"). Except as expressly provided and in exceptional circumstances preventing a Filing User from filing electronically, all petitions, motions, memoranda of law, or other pleadings and documents required to be filed with the Court in connection with a case assigned to the System must be electronically filed. NY R USDCTWD ECF Procedures(1)(a).

         • *Mandatory electronic filing.* All documents on civil, criminal, miscellaneous civil, miscellaneous criminal and new civil case openings, except sealed documents, sealed cases, opening of a criminal case, opening of a miscellaneous case and as expressly provided for in these procedures (NY R USDCTWD ECF Procedures), shall be electronically filed on the system. NY R USDCTWD ECF Procedures(2)(a)(i). NY R USDCTWD Civ Rule 29

         • *Stipulations.* Pursuant to NY R USDCTWD Civ Rule 29, all stipulations (whether the stipulation is final or when it requires a judge's signature) shall be filed electronically. NY R USDCTWD ECF Procedures(2)(p)(i).

         • *Letters.* The electronic filing of letters is generally prohibited unless granted permission by an assigned judge. Letters to the Court must be submitted conventionally. NY R US-DCTWD ECF Procedures(2)(q)(i).

         • *Exceptions.* The Court requires attorneys to file documents electronically, absent a showing of good cause, unless otherwise excused by the procedures set forth below or by Order of the Court. NY R USDCTWD ECF Procedures.

      iii. *Conventional filing of documents.* The procedures in NY R USDCTWD ECF Procedures(2)(o) govern documents filed conventionally. The Court, upon application, may also authorize conventional filing of other documents otherwise subject to the procedures in NY R US-DCTWD ECF Procedures(2)(o). NY R USDCTWD ECF Procedures(2)(o)(i).

- *Documents filed under seal.* Unredacted documents filed with the Court pursuant to the privacy provisions of FRCP 5.2 shall be submitted in a sealing envelope with the information in NY R USDCTWD ECF Procedures(2)(o)(i)(1) on the envelope. NY R USDCTWD ECF Procedures(2)(o)(i)(1). If the document is larger than five (5) pages, a disk should be provided to the Clerks Office which contains the document in a .pdf format. NY R USDCTWD ECF Procedures(2)(o)(i)(1). For more information on documents filed under seal, refer to NY R USDCTWD ECF Procedures(2)(o)(i)(1), NY R USDCTWD ECF Procedures(2)(o)(i)(2), and NY R USDCTWD ECF Procedures(2)(o)(i)(3).

- *Magistrate judge consents.* Pursuant to FRCP 73(b), parties' filing consents to jurisdiction by United States Magistrate Judge will continue to be treated as non-public documents until all parties have consented. Therefore, parties must submit conventionally (in paper form) and not electronically file their consent forms so that the consent is not a public document. If all parties consent to the jurisdiction of a Magistrate Judge, the Clerk will scan all consent forms which will then become a public document. NY R USDCTWD ECF Procedures(2)(o)(i)(3).

- *Pro se filers.* Pro Se filers shall file paper originals of all initiating documents, pleadings, motions, affidavits, briefs and other documents which must be signed or which require either verification or an unsworn declaration under any rule or statute. The Clerk's Office will scan these original documents into an electronic file in the System. A certificate of service is required for all documents a pro se litigant files with the court. If a Pro Se filer is granted permission to register to electronically file documents, they shall comply with the guidelines contained in this document (NY R USDCTWD ECF Procedures). NY R USDCTWD ECF Procedures(2)(o)(i)(4).

- *Social Security cases.* Absent a showing of good cause, and except as provided in Section o(i)(4) above, all documents, notices and orders in Social Security reviews will be filed and noticed electronically, except as noted in NY R USDCTWD ECF Procedures(2)(o)(i)(6). For more information, refer to NY R USDCTWD ECF Procedures(2)(o)(i)(6).

- For more information on conventional filing of documents, refer to NY R USDCTWD ECF Procedures(2)(o)(i).

iv. *Consequences of electronic filing.* Electronic transmission of a document to the System consistent with these procedures (NY R USDCTWD ECF Procedures), whether accomplished by the Filing User or a Court User, together with the transmission of a Notice of Electronic Filing from the Court, constitutes filing of a document for all purposes of the Federal Rules of Civil Procedure and the Local Rules of Civil Procedure for the United States District Court for the Western District of New York, and constitutes entry of the document on the docket kept by the Clerk under FRCP 58 and FRCP 79. A document shall not be considered filed for purposes of the Federal Rules of Civil until the filing party receives a System generated Notice of Electronic Filing. NY R USDCTWD ECF Procedures(2)(a)(i).

- E-mailing a document to the Clerk's Office or to the assigned judge shall not constitute "filing" of such document. NY R USDCTWD ECF Procedures(2)(a)(i)(1).

v. *Filing fees.* Any fee required for filing of a pleading or paper in District Court is payable to the Clerk of Court by check or money order. In addition, when opening a civil case on line, filing a notice of appeal on line or applying to appear pro hac vice on line, the fees shall be paid on line by registered users through the federal electronic payment website. Users will be directed to the federal electronic payment website while entering their transaction and should have a credit card available. When opening a civil case and applying to proceed in forma pauperis or when the United States of America opens a case, the payment screen can by bypassed to complete the transaction. Additional information on making electronic payments can be located on the court's website. NY R USDCTWD ECF Procedures(2)(h)(i).

2. *Service requirements.* All pleadings and other papers shall be filed and served in accordance with the Federal Rules of Civil Procedure and the CM/ECF Administrative Procedures Guide (NY R USDCTWD ECF Procedures). NY R USDCTWD Civ Rule 5.1(a).

   a. *Service; When required*

   i. *In general.* Unless the Federal Rules of Civil Procedure provide otherwise, each of the following papers must be served on every party:

   - An order stating that service is required;

   - A pleading filed after the original complaint, unless the court orders otherwise under FRCP 5(c) because there are numerous defendants;

   - A discovery paper required to be served on a party, unless the court orders otherwise;

   - A written motion, except one that may be heard ex parte; and

   - A written notice, appearance, demand, or offer of judgment, or any similar paper. FRCP 5(a)(1).

   ii. *If a party fails to appear.* No service is required on a party who is in default for failing to appear. But a pleading that asserts a new claim for relief against such a party must be served on that party under FRCP 4. FRCP 5(a)(2).

   iii. *Seizing property.* If an action is begun by seizing property and no person is or need be named as a defendant, any service required before the filing of an appearance, answer, or claim must be made on the person who had custody or possession of the property when it was seized. FRCP 5(a)(3).

   b. *Service; How made*

   i. *Serving an attorney.* If a party is represented by an attorney, service under FRCP 5 must be made on the attorney unless the court orders service on the party. FRCP 5(b)(1).

   ii. *Service in general.* A paper is served under FRCP 5 by:

   - Handing it to the person;

   - Leaving it: (1) at the person's office with a clerk or other person in charge or, if no one is in charge, in a conspicuous place in the office; or (2) if the person has no office or the office is closed, at the person's dwelling or usual place of abode with someone of suitable age and discretion who resides there;

   - Mailing it to the person's last known address—in which event service is complete upon mailing;

   - Leaving it with the court clerk if the person has no known address;

   - Sending it by electronic means if the person consented in writing—in which event service is complete upon transmission, but is not effective if the serving party learns that it did not reach the person to be served; or

   - Delivering it by any other means that the person consented to in writing—in which event service is complete when the person making service delivers it to the agency designated to make delivery. FRCP 5(b)(2).

   iii. *Service by overnight delivery.* All papers, other than a subpoena or a summons and complaint, may be served on counsel of record by overnight delivery service at the address designated by the attorney for that purpose, or if none is designated, at the attorney's last known address. Service by overnight delivery shall be complete upon deposit of the paper(s), enclosed in a properly addressed wrapper, into the custody of the overnight delivery service, prior to the latest time designated by the service for overnight delivery. NY R USDCTWD Civ Rule 5.1(g). "Overnight delivery service" means any delivery service which regularly accepts items for overnight delivery to any address within the Court's jurisdiction. NY R USDCTWD Civ Rule 5.1(g).

   iv. *Service of documents by electronic means*

   - *Service on registered users.* Registered Users consent to the electronic service of all

documents, and must make available an electronic mail address for service during the registration process. Upon the filing of a document by a party, a Notice of Electronic Filing, with a hyperlink to the filed document, will be automatically generated by the electronic filing system and sent via electronic mail to the e-mail addresses of all parties participating in the electronic filing system in the case. Electronic service of the Notice of Electronic Filing constitutes service of the filed document for all purposes of the Federal Rules of Civil Procedure and the Local Rules of Civil Procedure for the United States District Court for the Western District of New York. NY R USDCTWD ECF Procedures(2)(f)(i). The Notice of Electronic Filing effectuates service for all registered users and no certificate of service is required when all filers on an action are Registered Users. NY R USDCTWD ECF Procedures(2)(f)(iv).

- *Time limit for opening hyperlink.* The hyperlink to filed documents contained in the Notice of Electronic Filing must be opened within fifteen (15) days from the date the document was filed to provide registered users access to the document. The hyperlink expires after fifteen (15) days and users will be unable to access documents for free after that time. Filing Users are encouraged to check their e-mail frequently for notice of filed documents. NY R USDCTWD ECF Procedures(2)(f)(ii).

- *Service on exempted attorneys or pro se litigants who do not have permission to file electronically.* Attorneys granted an exemption from electronically filing documents in the System and pro se litigants who have not been granted permission to electronically file documents are entitled to a paper copy of any electronically filed pleading, document or order. The filing party must therefore provide the non-registered party with the pleading, document or order according to the Federal Rules of Civil Procedure. NY R USDCTWD ECF Procedures(2)(f)(iii).

- *E-mailing or faxing documents.* E-mailing or faxing a pleading or document to any party shall not constitute service of the pleading or document. NY R USDCTWD ECF Procedures(2)(f)(v).

v. *Using court facilities.* If a local rule so authorizes, a party may use the court's transmission facilities to make service under FRCP 5(b)(2)(E). FRCP 5(b)(3).

c. *Serving numerous defendants*

i. *In general.* If an action involves an unusually large number of defendants, the court may, on motion or on its own, order that:

- Defendants' pleadings and replies to them need not be served on other defendants;

- Any crossclaim, counterclaim, avoidance, or affirmative defense in those pleadings and replies to them will be treated as denied or avoided by all other parties; and

- Filing any such pleading and serving it on the plaintiff constitutes notice of the pleading to all parties. FRCP 5(c)(1).

ii. *Notifying parties.* A copy of every such order must be served on the parties as the court directs. FRCP 5(c)(2).

3. *Pro se actions.* For information on the requirements in pro se actions, refer to NY R USDCTWD Civ Rule 5.2.

4. *Individual judge practices.* Refer to the Miscellaneous section of this document for information on individual judge practices on filing and serving documents.

## G. Hearings

1. Refer to the General Requirements section of this document for information on pretrial conferences, scheduling conferences, and discovery planning conferences.

## H. Forms

### 1. Federal Pretrial Conferences, Scheduling, Management Forms

a. Plaintiff's informal summary of status of case to judge prior to pretrial conference in complex case. 2C FEDFORMS § 2807.

b.   Joint pretrial report. 2C FEDFORMS § 2807.10.

c.   Joint statement of undisputed facts. 2C FEDFORMS § 2807.20.

d.   Joint statement of disputed facts. 2C FEDFORMS § 2807.30.

e.   Joint report of counsel prior to pretrial conference. 2C FEDFORMS § 2807.40.

f.   Plaintiff's pretrial conference statement; Insurance case. 2C FEDFORMS § 2807.50.

g.   Defendant's pretrial conference statement; Insurance case. 2C FEDFORMS § 2807.60.

h.   Plaintiff's list of exhibits to be offered at trial. 2C FEDFORMS § 2811.

i.   Defendant's list of prospective witnesses. 2C FEDFORMS § 2811.10.

j.   Designation of witnesses whom plaintiff intends to call at trial pursuant to pretrial conference oral stipulation. 2C FEDFORMS § 2811.20.

k.   Defendant's list of prospective exhibits. 2C FEDFORMS § 2811.40.

l.   Report of parties' planning meeting. 3A FEDFORMS § 3314.

m.   Report of parties' discovery conference; Another form. 3A FEDFORMS § 3315.

n.   Report of parties' discovery conference; Another form. 3A FEDFORMS § 3316.

o.   Joint scheduling report. 3A FEDFORMS § 3316.5.

p.   Stipulation and order regarding discovery conference discussions. 3A FEDFORMS § 3316.6.

q.   Pretrial statement; By plaintiff; Automobile collision involving corporate defendant. FEDPROF § 1:658.

r.   Pretrial statement; By defendant; Automobile collision. FEDPROF § 1:659.

s.   Pretrial statement; By parties jointly; Automobile collision. FEDPROF § 1:660.

t.   Pretrial statement; Provision; Waiver of abandoned claims or defenses. FEDPROF § 1:661.

u.   Status report. GOLDLTGFMS § 34:2.

v.   Preliminary pretrial checklist. GOLDLTGFMS § 34:3.

w.   Pretrial memorandum. GOLDLTGFMS § 34:4.

x.   Pretrial memorandum; Short form. GOLDLTGFMS § 34:5.

y.   Pretrial memorandum; Civil action. GOLDLTGFMS § 34:6.

z.   Pretrial memorandum; Worker's compensation case. GOLDLTGFMS § 34:7.

**2.   Forms for the Western District of New York**

a.   Certificate of service. NY R USDCTWD ECF Procedures(4a).

# I. Applicable Rules

1.   *Federal rules*

a.   Serving and filing pleadings and other papers. FRCP 5.

b.   Privacy protection for filings made with the court. FRCP 5.2.

c.   Computing and extending time; Time for motion papers. FRCP 6.

d.   Pleadings allowed; Form of motions and other papers. FRCP 7.

e.   Form of pleadings. FRCP 10.

f.   Signing pleadings, motions, and other papers; Representations to the court; Sanctions. FRCP 11.

g.   Pretrial conferences; Scheduling; Management. FRCP 16.

h.   Duty to disclose; General provisions governing discovery. FRCP 26.

2.   *Local rules*

a.   Title. NY R USDCTWD Civ Rule 1.1.

b.  Filing and serving papers. NY R USDCTWD Civ Rule 5.1.

c.  Form of papers. NY R USDCTWD Civ Rule 10.

d.  Sanctions. NY R USDCTWD Civ Rule 11.

e.  Alternative dispute resolution and pretrial conferences. NY R USDCTWD Civ Rule 16.

f.  General rules governing discovery. NY R USDCTWD Civ Rule 26.

g.  Attorneys of record; Appearance and withdrawal. NY R USDCTWD Civ Rule 83.2.

h.  Administrative procedures guide for electronic filing. NY R USDCTWD ECF Procedures.

i.  Alternative dispute resolution plan. NY R USDCTWD ADR Plan.

## J.  Miscellaneous

**NOTE: Individual judges' rules may apply. For available judge-level information, refer to:**

DISTRICT JUDGE RICHARD J. ARCARA: NY R USDCTWD Arcara-Procedures.

DISTRICT JUDGE FRANK P. GERACI, JR.: NY R USDCTWD Geraci-Procedures.

DISTRICT JUDGE DAVID G. LARIMER: NY R USDCTWD Larimer-Procedures.

DISTRICT JUDGE CHARLES J. SIRAGUSA: NY R USDCTWD Siragusa-Procedures.

DISTRICT JUDGE WILLIAM M. SKRETNY: NY R USDCTWD Skretny--Procedures.

DISTRICT JUDGE MICHAEL A. TELESCA: NY R USDCTWD Telesca-Procedures.

DISTRICT JUDGE LAWRENCE J. VILARDO: NY R USDCTWD Vilardo-Procedures.

DISTRICT JUDGE ELIZABETH A. WOLFORD: NY R USDCTWD Wolford-Procedures.

MAGISTRATE JUDGE JONATHAN W. FELDMAN: NY R USDCTWD Feldman-Procedures.

MAGISTRATE JUDGE LESLIE G. FOSCHIO: NY R USDCTWD Foschio-Procedures; NY R USDCTWD Foschio-Depositions.

MAGISTRATE JUDGE JEREMIAH J. McCARTHY: NY R USDCTWD McCarthy-Procedures.

MAGISTRATE JUDGE MARIAN W. PAYSON: NY R USDCTWD Payson-Procedures.

MAGISTRATE JUDGE MICHAEL J. ROEMER: NY R USDCTWD Roemer-Procedures.

MAGISTRATE JUDGE H. KENNETH SCHROEDER, JR.: NY R USDCTWD Schroeder-Proc.

MAGISTRATE JUDGE HUGH B. SCOTT: NY R USDCTWD Scott-Procedures.

# Appendix - Related Court Documents

# Complaint

2016 WL 5335215 (S.D.N.Y.)

United States District Court, S.D. New York.

Kali KANONGATAA, Plaintiff,

v.

CBS BROADCASTING INC., CBS Radio Inc., CBS Interactive Inc., and Microsoft Corporation, Defendants.

No. 1:16-cv-07421.

September 22, 2016.

Complaint

**Westlaw Query>>**

To find more Complaint filings on Westlaw: access New York Trial Court Documents (from the Home page, click Trial Court Documents, then New York), click the Advanced Search link, select Complaint, and click Search. Use the Jurisdiction filter on the left to narrow results to Federal.

Richard P. Liebowitz, Liebowitz Law Firm, PLLC, 11 Sunrise Plaza, Suite 305, Valley Stream, NY 11580, Tel: (516) 233-1660, RL@LiebowitzLawFirm.com, for plaintiff Kali Kanongataa.

### JURY TRIAL DEMANDED

Plaintiff Kali Kanongataa ("Kali" or "Plaintiff") by and through his undersigned counsel, as and for his Complaint against Defendants CBS Broadcasting Inc., ("CBS") CBS Radio Inc., ("CBS Radio") and CBS Interactive Inc., ("CBS Interactive") and Microsoft Corporation ("Microsoft" and together with CBS, CBS Radio, and CBS Interactive "Defendants") hereby alleges as follows:

### NATURE OF THE ACTION

1. This is an action for copyright infringement under Section 501 of the Copyright Act. This action arises out of Defendants unauthorized reproduction and public display of Facebook's First Live Birth, owned and registered by Kali. Accordingly, Kali seeks injunctive and monetary relief under the Copyright Act of the United States, as amended, 17 U.S.C. § 101 *et seq.*

### JURISDICTION AND VENUE

2. This claim arises under the Copyright Act, 17 U.S.C. § 101 *et seq.*, and this Court has subject matter jurisdiction over this action pursuant to 28 U.S.C. §§ 1331 and 1338(a).

3. This Court has personal jurisdiction over Defendants because Defendants reside in and/or are transacting business in New York.

4. Venue is proper in this District pursuant to 28 U.S.C. § 1391(b).

### PARTIES

5. Kali is the owner of the Polynesian Cultural Exchange which is a non-profit organization that helps those of

COMPLAINT

Pacific Islander decent utilize their talents with leaders in creating avenues to educate, promote and advance cultural competency. Kali has a place of business at 1495 Silver Avenue, San Francisco, CA 94134.

6. Upon information and belief, CBS is a corporation duly organized and existing under the laws of the State of the New York, with a place of business at 51 West 52 Street, New York, New York 10019. Upon information and belief, CBS is registered with the New York Department of State, Division of Corporations to do business in the State of New York. At all times material hereto, CBS has operated and continued to operate a terrestrial television station in New York City under the call letters WCBS-TV, a terrestrial television station in Minneapolis, Minnesota under the call letters WCCO-TV, and a terrestrial television station in Stockton, California under the call letters KOVR.

7. Upon information and belief, CBS Radio is a corporation duly organized and existing under the laws of the State of Delaware with its principal place of business at 1271 Avenue of the Americas, New York, NY 10020. Upon information and belief, CBS Radio is registered with the New York Department State, Division of Corporation to do business in the State of New York. At all times material hereto, CBS Radio has operated and continues to operate the websites: http://minnesota.cbslocal.com/ ("Minnesota Website"), http://sacramento.cbslocal.com/ ("Sacramento Website"), http://morehits1037.cbslocal.com/ ("1037 Website"), http://965amp.cbslocal.com/ ("965 Website") (all together the "Websites").

8. Upon information and belief, CBS Interactive is a corporation duly organized and existing under the laws of the State of Delaware with its principal place of business at 28 East 28 Street, New York, New York 10016. Upon information and belief, CBS Interactive is registered with the New York Department State, Division of Corporation to do business in the State of New York. At all times material hereto, CBS Interactive has operated and continues to operate the website: www.CBSNews.com ("Interactive Website").

9. Upon information and belief, Microsoft is a corporation duly organized an existing under the laws of the State of Washington with its principal place of business at One Microsoft Way, Redmond, WA 98052. Upon information and belief, Microsoft is registered with the New York Department State, Division of Corporation to do business in the State of New York. At all times material hereto, Microsoft has operated and continues to operate the website: www.MSN.com. ("MSN Website").

## STATEMENT OF FACTS

### A. Background and Plaintiffs Ownership of the Video

10. On or about May 16, 2016, Kali videotaped his partner giving birth and broadcasted it on his Facebook page (the "Video").

11. Kali is the author of the Video and has at all times been the sole owner of all right, title and interest in and to the Video, including the copyright thereto.

12. The Video was registered with United States Copyright Office and was given Copyright Registration Number PA 1-995-583.

### B. Defendants Infringing Activities

13. **CBS-** Upon information and belief, during its evening telecast of CBS2 News in New York on or about May 17, 2016, CBS publically displayed the Video. Upon information and belief, CBS produced the telecast.

14. Upon information and belief, during its morning telecast of CBS4 News Minneapolis on or about May 18, 2016, CBS publically displayed the Video. Upon information and belief, CBS produced the telecast.

15. Upon information and belief, during its morning telecast of CBS13 News Sacramento on or about May 17, 2016, CBS publically displayed the Video. Upon information and belief CBS produced the telecast.

16. CBS did not license the Video from Plaintiff to use on CBS2, CBS4, or CBS13 nor did CBS have Plaintiffs permission or consent to publish the Video on CBS2, CBS4, or CBS13.

17. **CBS Radio-** Upon information and belief, on or about May 18, 2016, CBS Radio ran an article on its Minnesota Website, entitled *Viewers Weigh In On Live Birth On Facebook*. See (http://minnesota.cbslocal.com/video/category/local-community/3401712-viewers-weigh-in-on-live-birth-on-facebook/). The article prominently featured the Video.

18. Upon information and belief, on or about May 17, 2016, CBS Radio ran another article on its Sacramento

Website, entitled *Carmichael Woman Give Birth Live on Facebook, Doesn't Know Till Later.* See http://sacramento.cbslocal.com/2016/05/17/carmichael-woman-gives-birth-live-on-facebook/). The article prominently featured the Video.

19. Upon information and belief, on or about May 18, 2016, CBS Radio ran an article on its 1037 Website, entitled *VIDEO: Man Live Streams His Wife Giving Birth on Facebook!* See http://morehits1037.cbslocal.com/2016/05/18/video-man-live-streams-his-wife-giving-birth-on-facebook/. The article prominently featured the Video.

20. Upon information and belief, on or about May 20, 2016, CBS Radio ran an article on its 965 Website entitled *Dad Didn't Mean To Broadcast The Birth Of His Child To The Entire Internet.* See http://965amp.cbslocal.com/2016/05/20/watch-dad-didnt-mean-to-broadcast-the-birth-of-his-child-to-the-entire-internet/. The article prominently featured the Video.

21. CBS Radio did not license the Video from Plaintiff for use in its articles, nor did CBS Radio have Plaintiffs permission or consent to publish the Video on its Websites. A copy of the screen shots of the Video on the Websites and a copy of the Video on the Websites on a CD is attached hereto as Exhibit A.

22. **CBS Interactive-** Upon information and belief, on or about May 18, 2016, CBS Interactive ran an article on its Interactive Website entitled *Dad live streams wife giving birth on Facebook- doesn't tell her.* See http://www.cbsnews.com/news/dad-live-streams-wife-giving-birth-on-facebook-doesnt-tell-her-until-after/. The article prominently featured the Video and a screen shot of the Video.

23. CBS Interactive did not license the Video from Plaintiff for use in its article, nor did CBS Interactive have Plaintiffs permission or consent to publish the Video on its Interactive Website. A copy of the screen shots of the Video on the Interactive Website and a copy of the Video on the Websites on a CD is attached hereto as Exhibit B.

24. **Microsoft-** Upon information and belief, on or about May 18, 2016, CBS placed the CBS4 Video on the MSN Website. See https://www.msn.com/en-us/news/us/viewers-weigh-in-on-live-birth-on-facebook/vp-BBtcosD. The article prominently featured the Video.

25. Microsoft did not license the Video from Plaintiff for use in its article, nor did Microsoft have Plaintiffs permission or consent to publish the Video on its MSN Website. A copy of the screen shots of the Video on the MSN Website and a copy of the Video on the Websites on a CD is attached hereto as Exhibit C.

## FIRST CLAIM FOR RELIEF (COPYRIGHT INFRINGEMENT AGAINST DEFENDANTS)

### (17 U.S.C. §§ 106, 501)

26. Plaintiff incorporates by reference each and every allegation contained in Paragraphs 1-25 above.

27. Defendants infringed Plaintiffs copyright in the Video by reproducing and publicly displaying the the Video. Defendants are not, and have never been, licensed or otherwise authorized to reproduce, publically display, distribute and/or use the Video.

28. The acts of Defendants complained of herein constitute infringement of Plaintiff's copyright and exclusive rights under copyright in violation of Sections 106 and 501 of the Copyright Act, 17 U.S.C. §§ 106 and 501.

29. Upon information and belief, the foregoing acts of infringement by Defendants have been willful, intentional, and purposeful, in disregard of and indifference to Plaintiffs rights.

30. As a direct and proximate cause of the infringement by the Defendants of Plaintiffs copyright and exclusive rights under copyright, Plaintiff is entitled to damages and Defendants profits pursuant to 17 U.S.C. § 504(b) for the infringement.

31. Alternatively, Plaintiff is entitled to statutory damages up to $150,000 per work infringed for Defendants willful infringement of the Video, pursuant to 17 U.S.C. § 504(c).

32. Plaintiff further is entitled to his attorney's fees and full costs pursuant to 17 U.S.C. § 505.

33. Defendants conduct, described above, is causing, and unless enjoined and restrained by this Court, will continue to cause Plaintiff irreparable injury that cannot be fully compensated by or measured in money damages. Plaintiff has no adequate remedy at law. Pursuant to 17 U.S.C. § 502, Plaintiff is entitled to a permanent injunction prohibiting further infringement of Plaintiff's copyrights and exclusive rights under copyright.

COMPLAINT

## *PRAYER FOR RELIEF*

WHEREFORE, Plaintiff respectfully requests judgment as follows:

1. That Defendants be adjudged to have infringed upon Plaintiff's copyright in the Video in violation of 17 U.S.C §§ 106 and 501;

2. That Defendants, and their officers, directors, employees, agents, representatives, affiliates, subsidiaries, distributors, licensees and all persons or entities acting in concert or participation with Defendants, be enjoined from copying, reproducing, distributing, adapting, or publicly displaying Plaintiffs Video, pursuant to 17 U.S.C. § 502.

3. Plaintiff be awarded either: a) Plaintiffs actual damages and Defendant profits, gains or advantages of any kind attributable to Defendant infringement of Plaintiffs Video; or b) alternatively, statutory damages of up to $150,000 per copyrighted work infringed pursuant to 17 U.S.C. § 504;

4. That Defendants be required to account for all profits, income, receipts, or other benefits derived by Defendants as a result of its unlawful conduct;

5. That Plaintiff be awarded his costs, expenses and attorneys' fees pursuant to 17 U.S.C. § 505;

6. That Plaintiff be awarded pre-judgment interest; and

7. Such other and further relief as the Court may deem just and proper.

## *DEMAND FOR JURY TRIAL*

Plaintiff hereby demands a trial by jury on all issues so triable in accordance with Federal Rule of Civil Procedure 38(b).

Dated: Valley Stream, New York

September 22, 2016

LIEBOWITZ LAW FIRM, PLLC

By: */s/ Richard Liebowitz*

Richard P. Liebowitz

11 Sunrise Plaza, Suite 305

Valley Stream, NY 11580

Tel: (516) 233-1660

RL@LiebowitzLawFirm.com

*Attorneys for Plaintiff Kali Kanongataa*

# Answer

**2016 WL 824878 (E.D.N.Y.)**

United States District Court, E.D. New York.

Dana KAPRAT, individually, and Dana Kaprat as Guardian of S.K., Plaintiffs,

v.

CITY OF LONG BEACH, City of Long Beach Police Department, Long Beach Public Schools, Nassau Health Care Corporation d/b/a Nassau University Medical Center and The County of Nassau, Defendants.

No. 15-CV-7250 (LDW)(AKT).

January 13, 2016.

## Answer on Behalf of Defendant County of Nassau with Cross Claim

Carnell T. Foskey, County Attorney, Michael J. Barresi, Deputy County Attorney, One West Street, Mineola, New York 11501, (516) 571-3933, Via ECF: Massimo & Panetta, P.C., Nicholas J. Massimo, 200 Willis Avenue, Mineola, NY 11501.

The COUNTY OF NASSAU (hereinafter "County Defendant") by its attorney, Carnell T. Foskey, Nassau County Attorney, by Deputy County Attorney Michael J. Barresi, answer the Complaint as follows:

1. Deny the allegations set forth in paragraph "1" of the Complaint and respectfully refer all questions of law to the Court.

2. Deny the allegations in paragraph "2" of the Complaint.

3. Deny knowledge or information sufficient to form a belief as to the truth of the allegations contained in paragraph "3" of the Complaint.

4. Deny knowledge or information sufficient to form a belief as to the truth of the allegations contained in paragraph "4" of the Complaint.

5. Deny knowledge or information sufficient to form a belief as to the truth of the allegations contained in paragraph "5" of the Complaint.

6. Deny knowledge or information sufficient to form a belief as to the truth of the allegations contained in paragraph "6" of the Complaint.

7. Deny knowledge or information sufficient to form a belief as to the truth of the allegations contained in paragraph "7" of the Complaint.

8. Deny knowledge or information sufficient to form a belief as to the truth of the allegations contained in paragraph "8" of the Complaint.

9. Deny the allegations set forth in paragraph "9" of the Complaint.

ANSWER

10. Deny the allegations set forth in paragraph "10" of the Complaint and respectfully refer all questions of law to the Court.

11. Deny the allegations set forth in paragraph "11" of the Complaint.

12. Deny knowledge or information sufficient to form a belief as to the truth of the allegations contained in paragraph "12" of the Complaint, but respectfully refer all questions of law to the Court.

13. Deny knowledge or information sufficient to form a belief as to the truth of the allegations contained in paragraph "13" of the Complaint.

14. Deny knowledge or information sufficient to form a belief as to the truth of the allegations contained in paragraph "14" of the Complaint.

15. Deny knowledge or information sufficient to form a belief as to the truth of the allegations contained in paragraph "15" of the Complaint.

16. Deny knowledge or information sufficient to form a belief as to the truth of the allegations contained in paragraph "16" of the Complaint.

17. Deny knowledge or information sufficient to form a belief as to the truth of the allegations contained in paragraph "17" of the Complaint.

18. Admit the allegations in paragraph "18" of the Complaint.

19. Deny the allegations set forth in paragraph "19" of the Complaint, except aver, that a document purporting to be a Notice of Claim was received on February 17, 2015.

20. Deny knowledge or information sufficient to form a belief as to the truth of the allegations contained in paragraph "20" of the Complaint.

21. Deny the allegations set forth in paragraph "21" of the Complaint and respectfully refer all questions of law to the Court.

### ANSWER TO COUNT I

22. Answering paragraph "22" of the Complaint, Defendant repeats and reavers each and every response herein to paragraphs "1" through "21" of the Complaint as though fully set forth herein.

23. Deny the allegations set forth in paragraph "23" of the Complaint.

24. Deny knowledge or information sufficient to form a belief as to the truth of the allegations contained in paragraph "24" of the Complaint.

25. Deny the allegations set forth in paragraph "25" of the Complaint.

26. Deny the allegations set forth in paragraph "26" of the Complaint and respectfully refer all questions of law to the Court.

27. Deny knowledge or information sufficient to form a belief as to the truth of the allegations contained in paragraph "27" of the Complaint.

28. Deny the allegations set forth in paragraph "28" of the Complaint.

29. Deny the allegations set forth in paragraph "29" of the Complaint and respectfully refer all questions of law to the Court.

30. Deny knowledge or information sufficient to form a belief as to the truth of the allegations contained in paragraph "30" of the Complaint.

31. Deny the allegations set forth in paragraph "31" of the Complaint and respectfully refer all questions of law to the Court.

### ANSWER TO COUNT II

32. Answering paragraph "32" of the Complaint, Defendant repeats and reavers each and every response herein to paragraphs "1" through "31" of the Complaint as though fully set forth herein.

33. Deny the allegations set forth in paragraph "33" of the Complaint.

1789

34. Deny knowledge or information sufficient to form a belief as to the truth of the allegations contained in paragraph "34" of the Complaint.

35. Deny the allegations set forth in paragraph "35" of the Complaint.

36. Deny the allegations set forth in paragraph "36" of the Complaint and respectfully refer all questions of law to the Court.

37. Deny knowledge or information sufficient to form a belief as to the truth of the allegations contained in paragraph "37" of the Complaint.

38. Deny the allegations set forth in paragraph "38" of the Complaint.

39. Deny the allegations set forth in paragraph "39" of the Complaint and respectfully refer all questions of law to the Court.

40. Deny knowledge or information sufficient to form a belief as to the truth of the allegations contained in paragraph "40" of the Complaint.

41. Deny the allegations set forth in paragraph "41" of the Complaint and respectfully refer all questions of law to the Court.

## ANSWER TO COUNT III

42. Answering paragraph "42" of the Complaint, Defendant repeats and reavers each and every response herein to paragraphs "1" through "41" of the Complaint as though fully set forth herein.

43. Deny knowledge or information sufficient to form a belief as to the truth of the allegations contained in paragraph "43" of the Complaint.

44. Deny knowledge or information sufficient to form a belief as to the truth of the allegations contained in paragraph "44" of the Complaint.

45. Deny knowledge or information sufficient to form a belief as to the truth of the allegations contained in paragraph "45" of the Complaint.

46. Deny knowledge or information sufficient to form a belief as to the truth of the allegations contained in paragraph "46" of the Complaint and respectfully refer all questions of law to the Court.

## ANSWER TO COUNT IV

47. Answering paragraph "47" of the Complaint, Defendant repeats and reavers each and every response herein to paragraphs "1" through "46" of the Complaint as though fully set forth herein.

48. Deny knowledge or information sufficient to form a belief as to the truth of the allegations contained in paragraph "48" of the Complaint and respectfully refer all questions of law to the Court.

49. Deny knowledge or information sufficient to form a belief as to the truth of the allegations contained in paragraph "49" of the Complaint.

50. Deny knowledge or information sufficient to form a belief as to the truth of the allegations contained in paragraph "50" of the Complaint.

## ANSWER TO COUNT V

51. Answering paragraph "51" of the Complaint, Defendant repeats and reavers each and every response herein to paragraphs "1" through "50" of the Complaint as though fully set forth herein.

52. Deny knowledge or information sufficient to form a belief as to the truth of the allegations contained in paragraph "52" of the Complaint and respectfully refer all questions of law to the Court.

53. Deny knowledge or information sufficient to form a belief as to the truth of the allegations contained in paragraph "53" of the Complaint.

54. Deny knowledge or information sufficient to form a belief as to the truth of the allegations contained in paragraph "54" of the Complaint.

ANSWER

## ANSWER TO COUNT VI

55.  Answering paragraph "55" of the Complaint, Defendant repeats and reavers each and every response herein to paragraphs "1" through "54" of the Complaint as though fully set forth herein.

56.  Deny knowledge or information sufficient to form a belief as to the truth of the allegations contained in paragraph "56" of the Complaint and respectfully refer all questions of law to the Court.

57.  Deny knowledge or information sufficient to form a belief as to the truth of the allegations contained in paragraph "57" of the Complaint.

58.  Deny knowledge or information sufficient to form a belief as to the truth of the allegations contained in paragraph "58" of the Complaint.

## ANSWER TO COUNT VII

59.  Answering paragraph "59" of the Complaint, Defendant repeats and reavers each and every response herein to paragraphs "1" through "58" of the Complaint as though fully set forth herein.

60.  Deny the allegations set forth in paragraph "60" of the Complaint and respectfully refer all questions of law to the Court.

61.  Deny the allegations set forth in paragraph "61" of the Complaint and respectfully refer all questions of law to the Court.

## ANSWER TO COUNT VIII

62.  Answering paragraph "62" of the Complaint, Defendant repeats and reavers each and every response herein to paragraphs "1" through "61" of the Complaint as though fully set forth herein.

63.  Deny the allegations set forth in paragraph "63" of the Complaint.

64.  Deny knowledge or information sufficient to form a belief as to the truth of the allegations contained in paragraph "64" of the Complaint.

65.  Deny the allegations set forth in paragraph "65" of the Complaint.

66.  Deny the allegations set forth in paragraph "66" of the Complaint.

## ANSWER TO COUNT IX

67.  Answering paragraph "67" of the Complaint, Defendant repeats and reavers each and every response herein to paragraphs "1" through "66" of the Complaint as though fully set forth herein.

68.  Deny the allegations set forth in paragraph "68" of the Complaint.

69.  Deny knowledge or information sufficient to form a belief as to the truth of the allegations contained in paragraph "69" of the Complaint.

70.  Deny the allegations set forth in paragraph "70" of the Complaint.

71.  Deny the allegations set forth in paragraph "71" of the Complaint.

72.  Deny the allegations set forth in paragraph "72" of the Complaint.

## RESPONDING TO RELIEF REQUESTED IN PLAINTIFF'S AMENDED COMPLAINT

73.  County Defendants deny that Plaintiff is entitled to the relief requested in the paragraph designated "WHERE-FORE" following Paragraph "72" of the Complaint.

## AFFIRMATIVE DEFENSES

74.  Plaintiff has failed to state a cause of action against County Defendant upon which relief can be granted.

75.  Plaintiff has not complied with Section 50-e and/or 50-i and/or 50-h of the General Municipal Law of the State of New York.

76.  Plaintiff has failed to exhaust all administrative remedies.

77. Plaintiff lacks standing to bring this action.

78. Plaintiff has not complied with Section 52 of County Law of the State of New York.

79. Plaintiff has failed to mitigate his damages in this matter.

80. In taking the actions plaintiffs allege Defendants have taken, Plaintiffs assumed the risk of injury and that Defendants are not responsible in law or fact for Plaintiffs' injuries, if any.

81. That at all times herein mentioned and mentioned in the Complaint, the peace officers, and/or agents, servants or employees of the Defendant County of Nassau, having anything to do with the Plaintiffs were in the performance of their respective duties as peace officers, and/or agents, servants or employees of the Defendant County of Nassau; that all of the acts performed by said peace officers, and/or agents, servants or employees of the County of Nassau in connection with Plaintiffs were performed in good faith, without malice, and with reasonable and proper cause in the ordinary course of their duties as such peace officers, and/or agents, servants or employees of the Defendant County of Nassau, and as peace officers of the State of New York, and as required by them and each of them by reason of Plaintiff's conduct and Plaintiff's arrest and confinement.

82. Pursuant to the *Monell* doctrine, the County of Nassau cannot be held liable for the acts of its employees solely on the basis of *respondeat superior* in a 42 U.S.C. § 1983 action, and consequently the County cannot be liable for the acts or conduct of any individual defendant herein, as a matter of law.

83. The actions complained of were in full accord with the applicable law, regulations and/or NYS Department of Health protocols.

84. Plaintiff's constitutional and statutory rights have not been violated by the County Defendants herein.

85. The County of Nassau, its agencies, departments and/or employees at all applicable times herein enjoyed a full, partial or qualified immunity from civil suit.

86. The alleged acts or omissions of the County Defendants were not the proximate cause of any injuries or damages incurred by Plaintiff. Any injuries or damages incurred by Plaintiff were the result of his own actions, the actions of others and/or the superseding intervention of causes outside the control of the County Defendants.

87. Punitive damages may not be recovered against the County of Nassau as a matter of law.

88. Pursuant to the New York Civil Procedure Law and Rules ("CPLR") Section 1603, the Defendants assert the limitations contained in CPLR Sections 1601 and 1602 and all rights contained therein.

89. If the Plaintiffs sustained the damages as alleged in the Complaint, such damages were sustained through and by virtue of the negligent and/or wrongful conduct, acts or omissions of a third party, without any negligence, wrongdoing acts or omissions on the part of the Defendants contributing thereto.

90. If the Plaintiffs sustained the damages as alleged in the Complaint, such damages were sustained solely through and by virtue of the negligent and/or wrongful conduct of the Plaintiffs, without any negligence or wrongdoing on the part of the Defendants contributing thereto.

91. Should the Plaintiff recover damages as a result of a finding of liability in whole or in part as against Defendants, such recovery should be reduced and diminished in proportion to the degree of comparative negligence and/or wrongdoing of plaintiff in contributing to such damages.

## AS AND FOR A CROSS-CLAIM AGAINST THE CO-DEFENDANTS CITY OF LONG BEACH, CITY OF LONG BEACH POLICE DEPARTMENT, LONG BEACH PUBLIC SCHOOLS and NASSAU HEALTH CARE CORPORATION d/b/a NASSAU UNIVERSITY MEDICAL CENTER

92. If the Plaintiffs sustained the damages alleged in the Complaint through any action, omission, negligence, wrongdoing or illegality other than that of the Plaintiff, such damages were caused by and resulted from the act(s), omission(s), negligence wrongdoing and/or illegal conduct of the co-Defendants CITY OF LONG BEACH, CITY OF LONG BEACH POLICE DEPARTMENT, LONG BEACH PUBLIC SCHOOLS and NASSAU HEALTH CARE CORPORATION d/b/a NASSAU UNIVERSITY MEDICAL CENTER.

93. If the Plaintiff recovers a verdict against the Defendant County of Nassau for the damages alleged in the Complaint, such liability would have been caused by the act(s), omission(s), negligence wrongdoing and/or illegal conduct of the co-Defendants CITY OF LONG BEACH, CITY OF LONG BEACH POLICE DEPARTMENT, LONG BEACH PUBLIC SCHOOLS and NASSAU HEALTH CARE CORPORATION d/b/a NASSAU UNIVERSITY MEDICAL CENTER.

94. By reason of the foregoing, if any judgment is rendered in favor of the Plaintiff against the answering Defendant County of Nassau, then co-defendants, CITY OF LONG BEACH, CITY OF LONG BEACH POLICE DEPARTMENT, LONG BEACH PUBLIC SCHOOLS and NASSAU HEALTH CARE CORPORATION d/b/a NASSAU UNIVERSITY MEDICAL CENTER will be liable to the County of Nassau in whole or in part for said verdict and for the costs and expenses incurred by the Defendant County of Nassau in the defense of this action.

95. If Plaintiffs were caused to sustain damages at the time and place set forth in Plaintiffs' complaint through any carelessness, recklessness, and/or negligence other than the Plaintiffs' own, such damages were sustained in whole due to the primary and active carelessness, recklessness, and/or negligent acts or omissions, or commissions by co-defendants CITY OF LONG BEACH, CITY OF LONG BEACH POLICE DEPARTMENT, LONG BEACH PUBLIC SCHOOLS and NASSAU HEALTH CARE CORPORATION d/b/a NASSAU UNIVERSITY MEDICAL CENTER, its agents, servants, and/or employees with the negligence of the answering County Defendant, if any, being secondary, derivative, and by operation of law. Further, if Plaintiffs should recover judgment against the answering County Defendant, then the County Defendant is entitled to common law indemnification from and judgment over and against the co-defendants CITY OF LONG BEACH, CITY OF LONG BEACH POLICE DEPARTMENT, LONG BEACH PUBLIC SCHOOLS and NASSAU HEALTH CARE CORPORATION d/b/a NASSAU UNIVERSITY MEDICAL CENTER for all or any part of any verdict or judgment which the Plaintiff may recover in such amounts as the Court or jury may direct. By reason of the action, said answering County Defendant has been and will be put to costs and expenses, including attorney's fees.

**WHEREFORE,** Defendant County of Nassau demands judgment dismissing the Complaint herein as against them in its entirety and with prejudice, and/or if judgment is rendered against said Defendant, that the Defendant County of Nassau have judgment in a like amount against the co-defendants, CITY OF LONG BEACH, CITY OF LONG BEACH POLICE DEPARTMENT, LONG BEACH PUBLIC SCHOOLS and NASSAU HEALTH CARE CORPORATION d/b/a NASSAU UNIVERSITY MEDICAL CENTER, together with the costs and disbursements of this action.

Dated: Mineola, New York

January 12, 2016

**CARNELL T. FOSKEY**

**County Attorney**

By: *Michael J. Barresi*

Michael J. Barresi

Deputy County Attorney

One West Street

Mineola, New York 11501

(516) 571-3933

*Via ECF*:

MASSIMO & PANETTA, P.C.

Nicholas J. Massimo

200 Willis Avenue

Mineola, NY 11501

# Amended Pleading

2016 WL 3662472 (S.D.N.Y.)

United States District Court, S.D. New York.

S. DOE, Plaintiff,

v.

Kurt LUDWIGSEN, in his individual capacity, Kirsten Lambertson, in her individual capacity, Michael G. Scales, individually and as President of Nyack College, David C. Jennings, individually and as Executive Vice President of Nyack Collage, Keith Davie, individually and as Athletic Director for Nyack College, Amanda Aikens, individually and as Assistant Athletic Director for Nyack College, Taylor Brown, individually and as Assistant Softball Coach for Nyack College, Karen Davie, individually and as Director of Human Resources and Title Ix Coordinator for Nyack College, Nyack College, and Does 1-10, Defendants.

No. 15 CIV 7867 (CS).

June 16, 2016.

## Amended Answer to Second Amended Complaint

Michael K. Burke, Esq. (7554), Burke, Miele & Golden, LLP, 40 Matthews Street, Suite 209, Post Office Box 216, Goshen, New York 10924, (845) 294-4080, for defendant Ludwigsen.

Defendant Kurt Ludwigsen ("Defendant'), by his attorneys, Burke, Miele & Golden, LLP, as and for his Answer to the Second Amended Complaint, respectfully alleges as follows:

1. Denies the allegations stated or contained in Paragraphs "1," "2," "11," "22," "23," "33," "34," "35," "36," "37," "38," "39," "40," "41," "43," "57," "58," "59," "60," "61," "62," "63," "64," "72," "73," "74," "75," "76," "77," "78," "79," "80," "88," "89," "90," "91," "92," "93," "94," "95," "97," "98," "99," "101," "101," "105," "112," "113," "114," "115," "116," "117," "119," "120," and "122" of the Second Amended Complaint.

2. Denies the allegations stated or contained in Paragraph "3" of the Second Amended Complaint, except denies knowledge or information sufficient to form a belief about the truth or falsity of the allegations therein as to what information was publicly available.

3. Denies knowledge or information sufficient to form a belief about the truth or falsity of the allegations stated or contained in Paragraph "4" of the Fist Amended Complaint except denies that there was outrageous conduct by Defendant in connection with his female student athletes.

4. Neither admits nor denies the allegations stated or contained in Paragraph "5" of the Second Amended Complaint, as Plaintiff's characterization of her lawsuit requires no response. To the extent that this Court deems

a response necessary, Respondent denies each and every allegation stated or contained in Paragraph "5" of the Second Amended Complaint.

5. Denies the allegations stated or contained in Paragraph "6" of the Second Amended Complaint except admits that jurisdiction is conferred for a federal question under Title 28 U.S.C. § 1331 and that supplemental jurisdiction is conferred under Title 28 U.S.C. § 1367.

6. Denies the allegations stated or contained in Paragraph "7" of the Second Amended Complaint except admits that venue in general is provided under 28 U.S.C. § 1391(b).

7. Denies knowledge or information sufficient to form a belief about the truth or falsity of the allegations stated or contained in Paragraphs "8," "9," "12," "13," "31," "32," "42," "47," "48," "49," "52," "53," "54," "55," "56," "67," "68," "69," "70," "71," "83," "84," "85," "86," "87," "100," "103," "106," "107," "108," "109," 110," "111," and "121" of the Second Amended Complaint.

8. Denies the allegations stated or contained in Paragraph "10" of the Second Amended Complaint except admits that Defendant resided in Ridgewood. New Jersey while he was employed by Nyack College as Head Coach of the Nyack College women's softball team; that Defendant previously was employed by the University of Arizona's prestigious women's softball program on a coaching scholarship, under the leadership of coach Mike Candrea, who coached eight national champion softball teams and two Team USA Olympic women's softball teams; that during Defendant's tenure at the University of Arizona, the university's women's softball program won its first two national championships; that Defendant's employment at the University of Arizona ended when he graduated.

9. Denies knowledge or information sufficient to form a belief about the truth or falsity of the allegations stated or contained in Paragraphs "14," "15," "16," "17," and "18" of the Second Amended Complaint except denies that there was any misconduct by Defendant that others could have been present for and/or witnessed.

10. Denies the allegations stated or contained in Paragraph "19" of the Second Amended Complaint except admits that Defendant was Head Coach of the Nyack College women's softball team.

11. Admits the allegations stated or contained in Paragraph "20" of the Second Amended Complaint, except denies that Defendant hosted numerous mandatory social gatherings for team members and made frequent after-hours contact with team members via telephone, text messages and/or instant messaging, including but not limited to Facebook Chat.

12. Denies the allegations stated or contained in Paragraphs "21" of the Second Amended Complaint, including the allegations stated or contained in subparagraphs "a," "b," "c," and "d" of Paragraph "21."

13. Denies the allegations stated or contained in Paragraph "24" of the Second Amended Complaint including the allegations stated or contained in subparagraphs "a," "b," "c," "d," "e," "f," "g," and "h" of Paragraph "24," except admits that on or about November 14, 2014 the Softball Team went to New York City where they visited the Waldorf Astoria and a nearby museum and then to the Whiskey Cafe´ restaurant in Lyndhurst, New Jersey and that they were transported by Nyack College vans, and that in or about March 2015 the team stayed at a rented house for a tournament in Arizona.

14. Denies the allegations stated or contained in Paragraph "25" of the Second Amended Complaint, including the allegations stated or contained in subparagraphs "a," "b," "c," "d," "e," "f," "g," "h," "i," "j," "k," "l," and "m" of Paragraph "25."

15. Denies the allegations stated or contained in Paragraph "26" of the Second Amended Complaint, except denies knowledge or information sufficient to form a belief about the truth or falsity of the allegations that the Team members collectively confronted Mr. Davie and Mrs. Aikens to complain about Defendant.

16. Denies the allegations stated or contained in Paragraph "27" of the Second Amended Complaint as to Defendant and denies knowledge or information sufficient to form a belief about the truth or falsity of the remaining allegations stated or contained therein.

17. Denies the allegations stated or contained in Paragraph "28" of the Second Amended Complaint as to Defendant, including the allegations stated or contained in subparagraphs "a," "b," "c," "d," and "e" of Paragraph "28," and denies knowledge or information sufficient to form a belief about the truth or falsity of the remaining allegations stated or contained therein.

18. Denies knowledge or information sufficient to form a belief about the truth or falsity of the allegations stated or contained in Paragraph "29" of the Second Amended Complaint, except denies that Defendant was terminated and denies allegations of sexual harassment by Defendant.

19. As to Paragraphs "30," "44," "50," "65," "81," "96," "102," and "118" of the Second Amended Complaint, Defendant repeats and realleges each and every response previously and hereinafter set forth in response to the allegations stated or contained in the Paragraphs referenced in Paragraphs "30," "44," "50," "65," "81," "96," "102," and "118" of the Second Amended Complaint, as though set forth at length in this Paragraph "19."

20. Denies knowledge or information sufficient to form a belief about the truth or falsity of the remaining allegations stated or contained in Paragraph "45" of the Second Amended Complaint, except denies the allegations of sexual harassment by Defendant.

21. Denies knowledge or information sufficient to form a belief about the truth or falsity of the remaining allegations stated or contained in Paragraph "51," "66," and "82" of the Second Amended Complaint, except admits that Nyack College and Defendant were in an employer-employee relationship during the time Defendant was employed by Nyack College, from in or around June or July 2014 through on or about March 13, 2015 or March 14, 2015.

## AS AND FOR A FIRST AFFIRMATIVE DEFENSE

22. Plaintiff's sixth and eighth causes of action are time-barred under New York's one-year statute of limitations.

## AS AND FOR A SECOND AFFIRMATIVE DEFENSE

23. Plaintiff failed to state a cause of action upon which relief may be granted.

## AS AND FOR A THIRD AFFIRMATIVE DEFENSE

24. Plaintiff consented explicitly or implicitly to Defendant's conduct.

## AS AND FOR A FOURTH AFFIRMATIVE DEFENSE

25. The injuries, if any, alleged to have been sustained by Plaintiff were caused, in whole or in part, by the culpable conduct of Plaintiff.

## AS AND FOR A FIFTH AFFIRMATIVE DEFENSE

26. Defendant did not intend to harm Plaintiff in any way.

## AS AND FOR A SIXTH AFFIRMATIVE DEFENSE

27. Plaintiff's claim for punitive damages must be stricken for failure to state a claim upon which relief may be granted.

## AS AND FOR A SEVENTH AFFIRMATIVE DEFENSE

28. Plaintiff has failed to mitigate her damages.

## AS AND FOR AN EIGHTH AFFIRMATIVE DEFENSE

29. As to any damages allegedly suffered by Plaintiff, Defendant is entitled to a setoff, contribution, collateral sources and/or apportionment from Plaintiff and/or other individuals and/or entities.

## AS AND FOR A NINTH AFFIRMATIVE DEFENSE

30. As to any damages allegedly suffered by Plaintiff, Defendant is entitled to contribution and/or indemnification from the Codefendants.

## AS AND FOR A CROSSCLAIM AGAINST NYACK COLLEGE

31. Defendant repeats and realleges each and every allegation stated or contained in Paragraphs "1" through "30" above, with the same force and to the same effect as though set forth at length in this Paragraph "31."

32. If Plaintiff were caused to sustain damages at the time and place set forth in the plaintiffs' complaint through

1796

any fault other than Plaintiff's own fault, the damages were sustained due to the sole or primary fault of Codefendant Nyack College, its agents, servants, and/or employees, with the negligence if any on the part of this answering defendant being secondary and/or derivative only.

33. In the event judgment is recovered by Plaintiff, Codefendant Nyack College shall be liable to the answering Defendant for the full amount of the judgment or in an amount equal to the excess over and above this answering Defendant's equitable share of the judgment, as determined in accordance with the relative culpability of this answering Defendant and all Codefendants.

WHEREFORE, Defendant demands judgment as follows:

(i) Dismissing the complaint as to Defendant;

(ii) Against Codefendant Nyack College on its Crossclaim, the amount of any judgment which may be obtained herein by Plaintiff against Defendant, or in an amount equal to the excess over and above Defendant's equitable share of any such judgment; and

(iii) Costs, disbursements and fees, and such other and further relief as this Court deems just and proper.

Dated: June 16, 2016

Goshen, New York

*/s/ Michael K. Burke*

Michael K. Burke, Esq. (7554)

Burke, Miele & Golden, LLP

*Attorneys for Defendant Ludwigsen*

40 Matthews Street, Suite 209

Post Office Box 216

Goshen, New York 10924

(845) 294-4080

# Motion for Summary Judgment

2014 WL 8722608 (E.D.N.Y.)

United States District Court, E.D. New York.

GENERAL STAR INDEMNITY COMPANY, Plaintiff,

v.

DRIVEN SPORTS, INC., Defendant.

No. 14-cv-3579.

July 28, 2014.

**Westlaw Query>>**

To find more Motion for Summary Judgment filings on Westlaw: access New York Trial Court Documents (from the Home page, click Trial Court Documents, then New York), click the Advanced Search link, select Motion for Summary Judgment, and click Search. Use the Jurisdiction filter on the left to narrow results to Federal.

### Driven Sports, Inc.'s Notice of Motion and Motion for Partial Summary Judgment

The Killian Firm, P.C., Eugene Killian, Jr., Esq. [EK-9972], Ryan Milun, Esq. [RM-1062], 14 Wall Street, 20th Floor, New York, New York 10005, Telephone: (212) 618-1409, Facsimile: (212) 618-1705, ekillian@tkfpc.com, rmilun@tkfpc.com * * * and * * * 555 Route 1 South, Suite 430, Iselin, New Jersey 08830-3151, Telephone: (732) 912-2100, Facsimile: (732) 912-2101, Gauntlett & Associates, By: David A. Gauntlett, Esq. (pro hac vice), James A. Lowe, Esq. (pro hac vice), 18400 Von Karman, Suite 300, Irvine, California 92612, Telephone: (949) 553-1010, Facsimile: (949) 553-2050, info@gauntlettlaw.com, jal@gauntlettlaw.com, for defendant Driven Sports, Inc.

TO ALL PARTIES AND THEIR ATTORNEYS OF RECORD:

YOU ARE HEREBY NOTIFIED THAT on September 26, 2014 at 1:30 p.m. in Courtroom 920 of this court, located at 100 Federal Plaza, Central Islip, NY, Defendant Driven Sports, Inc. ("Driven") will move this court pursuant to Rule 56 of the Federal Rules of Civil Procedure for partial summary judgment in favor of Driven and against General Star Indemnity Company ("General Star") on the grounds that:

(1) General Star owes Driven a defense in the four actions styled *Nutrition Distribution, LLC v. Driven Sports*, No, 2:13-cv-6195 United States District Court, Central District of California; *Olvera v. Driven Sports, Inc.*, No. 3:13-cv-4830, United States District Court, Northern District of California; *Wagner v. Driven Sports, Inc.*, No. 3:13-cv-5239, United States District Court, Northern District of California; and *Stewart v. Driven Sports Inc.*, No. 1:13-cv-8789, United States District Court, Northern District of Illinois;

(2) The General Star insurance policy under which it owes a defense in the four cases is not self-liquidating;

(3) General Star has no right to recoup any defense expenses from Driven; and

(4) General Star owes Driven coverage fees for having to defend this lawsuit. Damages and establishment of attorneys' fees will be addressed later.

This Motion is based upon this Notice of Motion and Motion for Partial Summary Judgment, the accompanying Memorandum In Support Of Defendant Driven Sports, Inc.'s Motion For Partial Summary Judgment, The Statement Of Material Facts In Support Of Defendant Driven Sports, Inc.'s Motion For Partial Summary Judgment, the Declaration of Melissa Cahill, the Declaration of James Lowe, the Proposed Order, and the papers, records, and file in this action and such oral and documentary evidence as may be presented at the hearing on this Motion.

Respectfully submitted,

**THE KILLIAN FIRM, P.C.**

Eugene Killian, Jr., Esq. [EK-9972]

Ryan Milun, Esq. [RM-1062]

14 Wall Street, 20th Floor

New York, New York 10005

Telephone: (212) 618-1409

Facsimile: (212) 618-1705

ekillian@tkfpc.com

rmilun@tkfpc.com

* * * AND * * *

555 Route 1 South, Suite 430

Iselin, New Jersey 08830-3151

Telephone: (732) 912-2100

Facsimile: (732) 912-2101


**GAUNTLETT & ASSOCIATES**

By: /s/ David A. Gauntlett

David A. Gauntlett, Esq. (*pro hac vice*)

James A. Lowe, Esq. (*pro hac vice*)

18400 Von Karman, Suite 300

Irvine, California 92612

Telephone: (949) 553-1010

Facsimile: (949) 553-2050

info@gauntlettlaw.com

jal@gauntlettlaw.com


Attorneys for Defendant Driven Sports, Inc.

DATED: July 28, 2014

# Motion to Compel Discovery

2014 WL 3728747 (S.D.N.Y.)

United States District Court, S.D. New York.

THE GEORGE NELSON FOUNDATION, Plaintiff,

v.

MODERNICA, INC., Defendant.

No. 1:13-CV-03427-MMB.

July 15, 2014.

Plaintiff's Motion to Compel Discovery

**Westlaw Query>>**

To find more Motion to Compel Discovery filings on Westlaw: access New York Trial Court Documents (from the Home page, click Trial Court Documents, then New York), click the Advanced Search link, select Motion to Compel, and click Search. Use the Jurisdiction filter on the left to narrow results to Federal.

William J. Dorsey, Carolyn M. Passen, Katten Muchin Rosenman LLP, 525 West Monroe Street, Chicago, Illinois 60661-3693, Tel. (312) 902-5200, Jessica M. Garrett, Katten Muchin Rosenman LLP, 575 Madison Avenue, New York, NY 10022-2585, Tel: (212) 940-8800, Counsel for Plaintiff The George Nelson Foundation.

Plaintiff The George Nelson Foundation ("The Foundation") seeks an order compelling Defendant Modernica, Inc. ("Modernica") to produce documents and substantive responses to The Foundation's discovery requests regarding Modernica's sales and customer communications relevant to the instant dispute. In support of its motion, The Foundation states as follows:

## Background

1. George Nelson was a famous American industrial designer who created many iconic modern products offered and sold under the marks GEORGE NELSON or NELSON ("NELSON Marks"). These products include the George Nelson Marshmallow Sofa, Ball Clock, Bubble Lamps, Half Nelson Table Lamp, and Net Lights. The Foundation is Mr. Nelson's successor-in-interest and the current owner of the NELSON Marks.

2. The Foundation initiated this suit to stop Modernica from trading on the fame of Mr. Nelson and the NELSON Marks through the sale of unlicensed, unauthorized copies of Mr. Nelson's lighting designs and use of his name and marks. For instance, Modernica falsely holds itself out as the official and exclusive manufacturer of authentic GEORGE NELSON and NELSON lamps, even though it never sought or obtained a license from Mr. Nelson or his heirs to use the design or name. The infringement is willful and expressly intended to trade on the goodwill of the NELSON marks.

3. In discovery, The Foundation has asked for documents and other information regarding Modernica's alleged sales of infringing products. Among other things, this information is relevant to the period of Modernica's infringement, the extent and scope of that infringement, Modernica's defense that its use allegedly predates The Foundation's use, the profits generated by Modernica's sales of infringing products, and The Foundation's damage claims.

4. On August 27, 2013, The Foundation served Plaintiff's First Set of Requests for Production to Defendant ("The Foundation's First RFP") and Plaintiff's First Set of Interrogatories to Defendant ("The Foundation's First Interrogatories") (attached as Exhibits A and B, respectively). Modernica served responses to The Foundation's First Interrogatories and The Foundation's First RFP on September 30, 2013. It supplemented its responses to The

Foundation's First RFP on March 31, 2014, and The Foundation's First Interrogatories on July 3, 2014 (attached as Exhibits C and D, respectively).

5. On June 6, 2014, The Foundation served Plaintiff's Second Set of Requests for Production to Defendant ("The Foundation's Second RFP") and Plaintiff's Second Set of Interrogatories ("The Foundation's Second Interrogatories") (attached as Exhibits E and F, respectively). Modernica served its responses to both sets of discovery requests on July 3, 2014 (attached as Exhibits G and H, respectively).

6. In these requests, The Foundation sought sales-related documents and information related to Modernica's use of the NELSON Marks and sales. *See, e.g.*, Exhibit B, Interrogatory No. 7; Exhibit A, Request Nos. 21, 22, 32-34; Exhibit F, Interrogatory Nos. 10, 11, 12, 14; Exhibit E, Request Nos. 39, 40.

7. Other than a limited number of invoices from 1998 and 1999, Modernica has not produced a single sales document predating 2008 and has to date not produced any summary documents reflecting yearly sales.

8. In addition, Modernica has refused to produce documents or information regarding its communications with retailers about the lamps it markets under the NELSON Marks. The Foundation expects these documents will confirm that Modernica is falsely advising its customers that Modernica is "licensed" and "authorized" to sell lamps under the NELSON Marks, and that this misinformation is then passed on to consumers.

9. Modernica claims that it should not have to produce documents predating 2008 because it is outside the alleged six-year "limitations period." Modernica has offered no explanation for why no communications with its retailers have been produced.

### The Requested Documents and Written Responses Are Relevant to The Foundation's Claims and Modernica's Defenses

10. Under Rule 26(b)(1) of the Federal Rules of Civil Procedure, a party may "obtain discovery regarding any nonprivileged matter that is relevant to any party's claim or defense." Fed. R. Civ. P. 26(b)(1). This includes evidence that is ultimately deemed inadmissible at trial, as long as the discovery request "appears reasonably calculated to lead to the discovery of admissible evidence." *Id.*

11. A "court may order discovery of any matter relevant to the subject matter involved in the action." Fed. R. Civ. P. 26(b)(1). This encompasses "any matter that bears on, or that reasonably could lead to other matter that could bear on, any issue that is or may be in the case." *Oppenheimer Fund, Inc. v. Sanders*, 437 U.S. 340, 351 (1978). "It is well-settled within this Circuit that 'any possibility' that the sought-after information may be relevant to the subjectmatter of the action will satisfy Rule 26(b)(1)'s requirements." *Estee Lauder, Inc. v. The Fragrance Counter, Inc.*, 189 F.R.D. 269, 274 (S.D.N.Y. 1999) (denying request for protective order because information sought to be protected might be relevant to subject matter of the suit).

12. Here, the requested sales-related documents and substantive written responses, including for pre-2008 sales, directly bear on the issue of Modernica's infringing use of the NELSON Marks. Each sale of a product offered under the NELSON Marks is an act of willful infringement. Without documents and written responses that show Modernica's monthly sales of each product offered under the NELSON Marks and the source of those sales -- including for sales made before 2008 -- The Foundation cannot determine where Modernica is infringing its marks, the length of Modernica's infringement, or the frequency of Modernica's infringement. Thus, The Foundation is entitled to know which products were sold, when those sales occurred, and where those sales were made (e.g., from Modernica's showroom, Modernica's website, or by its retailers) for all sales of products offered under the NELSON Marks.

13. Further, in support of its affirmative defenses, Modernica alleged that it has continually and extensively used the NELSON Marks since 1998. (Answer, Affirmative Defenses ¶ 25.) It claims to have "priority of usage" with respect to these marks. (*Id.* at ¶ 28.) Discovery is broad to ensure that "civil trials are not conducted in the dark." *Estee Lauder, Inc.*, 189 F.R.D. at 274. However, without the requested sales information, The Foundation cannot learn of or test the bases for Modernica's defenses before trial. If The Foundation does not receive the requested sales information for all sales, The Foundation will be in the dark as to not only the degree of Modernica's infringing use of the NELSON Marks, but also the evidence that Modernica believes supports its defenses.

14. The requested sales information will also reveal the identity of Modernica's retailers and is reasonably calculated to lead to the discovery of confusion evidence and evidence of Modernica's intent. For instance, some retailers may have stopped doing business with Modernica after questioning the authenticity or quality of

Modernica's products. Changes in sales volume and patterns may also be tied to Modernica's more recent, brazen efforts to brand the lamps they are selling "George Nelson lamps." The scope and extent of Modernica's sales over the years may also be relevant to what injunctive relief is appropriate under the circumstances.

15. In addition, the requested sales information is relevant to The Foundation's damages from Modernica's intentional infringement. One of the remedies The Foundation seeks is an accounting of all profits derived by Modernica from its infringement. (*Id.* at Prayer for Relief ¶ 5.) This necessarily includes sales made before 2008, as Modernica claims it began selling the lamps under the NELSON Marks years earlier. (*See* Answer, Affirmative Defenses ¶ 25). Thus, the requested sales documents and written responses bear on the issue of damages in this case, meeting the standard set forth in Rule 26(b)(1). *See ABC Rug & Carpet Cleaning Service Inc. v. ABC Rug Cleaners, Inc.*, Case No. 08 Civ. 5737, 2009 WL 105503, at *5 (S.D.N.Y. Jan. 14, 2009) (directing defendants to produce documents relevant to the calculation of damages under the Lanham Act); McCarthy on Trademarks and Unfair Competition § 30:70 (4th ed.) (accounting period should be co-extensive with the period of infringement).

16. Modernica's objection to the requested pre-2008 sales documents and information on statute of limitations grounds is both insufficient and premature.[1] Modernica's objection addresses only The Foundation's damage claims, and not the myriad of other reasons why the requested sales information is discoverable. Furthermore, Modernica has not demonstrated that a statute of limitations would have any application in this case. *See Emmpresa Cubana del Tabaco v. Culbro Corp.*, 213 F. Supp. 2d 247, 278 (S.D.N.Y. 2002) ("six-year period does not run until plaintiffs discover or should have discovered the facts that create the cause of action"). Similarly, as the Court has noted, there are several issues of disputed fact that must be addressed before any limitation period could be applied. (*See* Memorandum re Motion to Dismiss at 30.) Consequently, the requested sales information is relevant to Modernica's laches defense, as Modernica alleges that its "open, continuous and extensive use" was known by The Foundation and its predecessors-in-interest. (*See* Answer, Affirmative Defenses ¶ 28.)

17. Communications between Modernica and its retailers regarding the promotion of products offered under the NELSON Marks are relevant to The Foundation's trademark infringement claim. The Foundation is entitled to know if Modernica is instructing retailers that its products are authentic and to market them accordingly, as this would exacerbate the potential for confusion in the marketplace and demonstrate the willfulness of Modernica's infringement. Similarly, the identities of the retail outlets receiving Modernica's communications are relevant to the likelihood of confusion analysis, including the proximity of the goods factor. Therefore, the requested communications are discoverable under Rule 26.

18. The Foundation is concerned that further delay in receiving the requested discovery will unfairly prejudice it. As the Court is aware, the deadline for The Foundation's expert report on its damages is September 30, 2014. Additionally, the depositions of the individuals at Modernica who likely have the most knowledge of "Defendant's income" are scheduled for August 4, 2014 and August 5, 2014. *See* Exhibit D, Response No. 7. Without the documents that Modernica refuses to produce, The Foundation may be precluded from obtaining the testimony it needs for its expert report.

19. Further, those same two individuals are the persons Modernica identified as having primary responsibility for the advertising and marketing strategy of the products offered under the NELSON Marks. *See* id., Response No. 5. It appears that they would be the most knowledgeable about Modernica's directions to retailers regarding how to portray these products to consumers. Without access to Modernica's communications before the depositions, The Foundation could miss its opportunity to fully explore Modernica's marketing strategy and the willfulness of Modernica's infringement with the individuals that have the most knowledge on these topics.

WHEREFORE, The Foundation respectfully requests that the Court order Modernica to produce documents and written responses to Foundation's discovery requests regarding Modernica's sales and customer communications, including: (1) documents and substantive written responses showing Modernica's monthly sales for each product and the source of those sales (e.g., showroom, website, retailer); (2) a summary chart showing Modernica's yearly sales of products offered under the NELSON Marks and the source of those sales; and (3) communications with retail outlets regarding the marketing of products offered under the NELSON Marks.

Dated: July 15, 2014

---

1. Moreover, it appears that Modernica has miscalculated the limitations period. The Complaint was filed on May 21, 2013. Under Modernica's limitations argument, it should have produced sales information for sales dating back to May 21, 2012.

MOTION TO COMPEL DISCOVERY

Respectfully submitted,

Counsel for Plaintiff The George Nelson Foundation

/s/ William J. Dorsey

William J. Dorsey

Carolyn M. Passen

Katten Muchin Rosenman LLP

525 West Monroe Street

Chicago, Illinois 60661-3693

Tel. (312) 902-5200

Jessica M. Garrett

Katten Muchin Rosenman LLP

575 Madison Avenue

New York, NY 10022-2585

Tel: (212) 940-8800

# Table of Laws and Rules

## UNITED STATES CONSTITUTION

## UNITED STATES CODE ANNOTATED

# FEDERAL RULES OF CIVIL PROCEDURE

## FEDERAL RULES OF CIVIL PROCEDURE—Continued

## FEDERAL RULES OF CIVIL PROCEDURE—Continued

## FEDERAL RULES OF CIVIL PROCEDURE—Continued

## FEDERAL RULES OF CIVIL PROCEDURE—Continued

## FEDERAL RULES OF CIVIL PROCEDURE—Continued

## FEDERAL RULES OF CIVIL PROCEDURE—Continued

## FEDERAL RULES OF CIVIL PROCEDURE—Continued

## FEDERAL RULES OF CIVIL PROCEDURE—Continued

## FEDERAL RULES OF CIVIL PROCEDURE—Continued

## FEDERAL RULES OF CIVIL PROCEDURE—Continued

## FEDERAL RULES OF CIVIL PROCEDURE—Continued

## FEDERAL RULES OF CIVIL PROCEDURE—Continued

## FEDERAL RULES OF CIVIL PROCEDURE—Continued

## FEDERAL RULES OF CIVIL PROCEDURE—Continued

## FEDERAL RULES OF CIVIL PROCEDURE—Continued

## FEDERAL RULES OF EVIDENCE

## LOCAL RULES OF THE U.S. DISTRICT COURT FOR THE SOUTHERN AND EASTERN DISTRICTS OF NEW YORK

# LOCAL RULES OF THE U.S. DISTRICT COURT FOR THE SOUTHERN AND EASTERN DISTRICTS OF NEW YORK—Continued

## LOCAL RULES OF THE U.S. DISTRICT COURT FOR THE NORTHERN DISTRICT OF NEW YORK—Continued

# LOCAL RULES OF THE U.S. DISTRICT COURT FOR THE NORTHERN DISTRICT OF NEW YORK—Continued

# LOCAL RULES OF THE U.S. DISTRICT COURT FOR THE WESTERN DISTRICT OF NEW YORK

## LOCAL RULES OF THE U.S. DISTRICT COURT FOR THE WESTERN DISTRICT OF NEW YORK—Continued

## NEW YORK COURT ORDERS

# Table of Cases